Film Reviews
1907-1980

A SIXTEEN-VOLUME SET,

Including an Index to Titles

Garland Publishing, Inc.
New York and London
1983

Contents

OF THE SIXTEEN-VOLUME SET

1. *1907–1920*

2. *1921–1925*

3. *1926–1929*

4. *1930–1933*

5. *1934–1937*

6. *1938–1942*

7. *1943–1948*

8. *1949–1953*

9. *1954–1958*

10. *1959–1963*

11. *1964–1967*

12. *1968–1970*

13. *1971–1974*

14. *1975–1977*

15. *1978–1980*

16. *Index to Titles*

Film Reviews
1959–1963

VOLUME TEN

Garland Publishing, Inc.
New York and London
1983

Library of Congress Cataloging in Publication Data
Main entry under title:

Variety film reviews.
  Includes index.

   1. Moving-pictures—Reviews.   I. Daily variety.
PN1995.V34   1982   791.43′75   82-15691
ISBN 0-8240-5200-5 (v. 1)
ISBN 0-8240-5209-9 (v. 10)

Manufactured in the United States of America

Printed on acid-free,
250-year-life paper

User's Guide

The reviews in this collection are published in chronological order, by the date on which the review appeared. The date of each issue appears at the top of the column where the reviews for that issue begin. The reviews continue through that column and all following columns until a new date appears at the top of the page. Where blank spaces occur at the end of a column, this indicates the end of that particular week's reviews. An index to film titles, giving date of review, is published as the last volume in this set.

1959

I, Mobster
(C'SCOPE)

Well-turned-out gangster film; good indications for better program market.

Hollywood, Dec. 27.

20th-Fox release of Edward L. Alperson-Roger and Gene Corman production. Stars Steve Cochran, Lita Milan; features Robert Strauss, Celia Lovsky, Lili St. Cyr, Grant Withers, John Brinkley, Yvette Vickers. Directed by Roger Corman. Screenplay, Steve Fisher; camera, Floyd Crosby; editor, William B. Murphy; music, Gerald Fried, Edward L. Alperson Jr. Previewed Dec. 26, '58. Running time, 80 MINS.

Joe Sante .... Steve Cochran
Teresa Porter .... Lita Milan
Black Frankie Udino .... Robert Strauss
Mrs. Sante .... Celia Lovsky
Lili St. Cyr .... Lili St. Cyr
Ernie Porter .... John Brinkley
The Blonde .... Yvette Vickers
Senator .... Robert Shayne
Joe Moran .... Grant Withers
District Attorney .... Frank Gerstle
Cherry-Nose .... Wally Cassell
Mr. Sante .... John Mylong

"I, Mobster" is a return to the long-absent gangster cycle. It's a well-turned-out melodrama with Steve Cochran in title role delivering a slick characterization of the rise and fall of a mobsman. Dual producership of Roger and Gene Corman is responsible for values which should pay off in the better program market, where a film of this type, given such a story and performances as offered here, usually is popular.

Steve Fisher screenplay utilizes the flashback technique, opening with Cochran, who heads the national crime syndicate, invoking the Fifth Amendment as he appears before the Senate Rackets Committee in Washington. Narrative dips back to his youth, when he collected horse race bets for a local hoodlum, Robert Strauss; then spans his whole career in crime as he becomes involved in dope traffic, later his hard-hitting entry into strike-breaking and "protection" of strike-breaking unions. He becomes the crime czar when he personally murders Grant Withers, Number One.

Under Roger Corman's know-how direction action unfolds smoothly and swiftly. Through very creditable performances, Corman manages to capture the gangster feeling and in addition to Cochran outstanding portrayals are contributed by Lita Milan, as his sweetheart; Strauss, socking over his henchman role after Cochran rises above him; and Celia Lovsky, as Cochran's sorely tried mother, in one of her finest characterizations to date. It is Strauss, the underling, who finally turns and kills Cochran so he can become top man.

Lili St. Cyr is in for a production number, the camera doing well by her bathrub routine. Jeri Southern warbles a song, "Give Me Love."

Technical credits are generally skillfully handled, topped by Floyd Crosby's photography and William B. Murphy's fast editing. Art direction by Daniel Haller is quality stuff, and music score by Gerald Fried and Edward L. Alperson Jr., lends atmospheric backing to action. *Whit.*

The Captain's Table
(BRITISH—EASTMANCOLOR)

Somewhat scrappy, but amusingly lighthearted comedy providing plentiful yocks and some choice supporting performances.

London, Jan. 6.

Rank release of Joseph Janni and Jack Lee production. Stars John Gregson, Peggy Cummins, Donald Sinden, Nadia Gray. Directed by Jack Lee. Screenplay, John Whiting, Bryan Forbes, Nicholas Phipps, from Richard Gordon's novel; camera, Christopher Challis; editor, Frederick Wilson; music, Frank Cordell. At Odeon, Leicester Square, London. Running time, 89 MINS.

Captain Ebbs .... John Gregson
Mrs. Judd .... Peggy Cummins
Shawe-Wilson .... Donald Sinden
Mrs. Porteous .... Nadia Gray
Major Broster .... Maurice Denham
Prittlewell .... Richard Wattis
Burtweed .... Reginald Beckwith
Bernie Floate .... Lionel Murton
Bill Coke .... Bill Kerr
Reddish .... Nicholas Phipps
Maude Pritchett .... Joan Sims
Canon Swingler .... Miles Malleson
Sir Angus .... John Le Mesurier
Farnshaw .... James Hayter
Gwenny Coke .... June Jago
Mrs. Lomax .... Nora Nicholson
Hole .... Harry Locke
Annette .... Rosalie Ashley

Based on a novel by Richard Gordon, whose previous "Doctor" novels have provided an excellent series of boxoffice hits, "The Captain's Table" has the same light-hearted touch, and should fare equally well at the b.o. Its stars are popular in Britain and there is ample opportunity for some standout supporting performances by British feature players. Acted as lightheartedly as it has been directed, this provides plenty of yocks even though the laughter situations are largely disconnected and usually extremely predictible.

John Gregson, after 2 years as skipper of cargo vessels, gets command of a luxury liner. He soon finds his error when he decides that passengers are only animated cargo. Having first got on the wrong side of his crew by brushing up on discipline, he soon finds the passengers and his social duties getting into his hair. However, by the end of the voyage he has picked up the tricks of the trade, and found romance with a young widow.

There are some neat gleams of wit in the screenplay, a chance of showing off some pulchritude in the ship's beauty contest and a fair number of amusing situations. But most of the fun comes from the stock characters usually to be found in shipboard comedies. There's the inevitable ship's vamp invading the captain's cabin, the very important passenger who knows the chairman of the shipping line, the chief officer with a weakness for girls, the over-efficient steward, the absent-minded cleric and the debonair, swindling purser.

Gregson gives a nicely balanced picture of bewilderment and frustration as the captain while Donald Sinden is a likeable philanderer. Peggy Cummins makes a sweet heroine as the widow who gets her man. Nadia Gray is a most attractive ship's vamp.

But it is the smaller-part players who have most of the fat in this amiable diversion. Reginald Beckworth, as the captain's steward, a model of efficiency and with a sharp line of dialog, gives one of the best supporting comedy performances of the year. Maurice Denham, a testy V.I.P.; Nicholas Phipps, a dilettante novelist; Richard Wattis, the purser, and Miles Malleson, the cleric, all enjoy some sparkling moments. There also is one tiny cameo by Joan Sims, as the ship's wallflower who turns out to be an heiress and is hooked by Sinden, which is delightful.

The shipboard setting is admirably photographed in color. Frederick Wilson's editing is as smooth as the spasmodic construction of the screenplay will allow. *Rich.*

Asa-Nisse I Kronans Klader
(Asa-Nisse In Military Uniform) (SWEDISH)

Stockholm.

Svensk Telfilm production and release. Features John Elfstrom, Arthur Bolen, Mona Geijer-Falkner, Brita Oberg, Ann-Marie Adamsson, Lennart Lindberg, Gustav Lovas, Bertil Boo, Gus Dahlstrom, Stellan Agerloo, Little Gerhard and His Rocking Men. Directed by Ragnar Frisk. Screenplay, Per-Lennart; camera, Harry Lindberg; music, Sven Runo. At Anglais, Stockholm. Running time, 87 MINS.

Asa-Nisse .... John Elfstrom
Klabbarparn .... Arthur Rolen
Kristin .... Mona Geijer-Falkner
Eulalia .... Brita Oberg
Ulla .... Ann-Marie Adamsson
Olle .... Sven Lindberg
Sjokvist, the merchant .... Gustav Lovas
Bertil Boo .... Himself
Gangster One .... Gus Dahlstrom
Gangster Two .... Stellan Agerloo
Colonel .... Sven Holmberg
Lieutenant .... Lennart Tollen

Every film-producing country in the world has its B films. This is Sweden's contribution to films of a quality that if they were exported, it would surprise the cinemagoers all over the world. Back in 1949, the No. 1 in the Asa-Nisse serial opened at the Anglais in Stockholm with about the same cast as above. Since then the serial has continued, and this is number nine in Asa-Nisse's adventures.

Asa-Nisse obviously is a profitable person for the producers. This stems from a series of short stories appearing in a weekly magazine. The principal character is a small village man of about 50 who is married to a woman used "to having the last word." His favorite sport is hunting, especially thief-hunting when in the mood. This brings him into small collisions with the law.

Someone realized that during all the many adventures in which he has been involved, he never was seen in military uniform. So in this, Asa-Nisse is in the army, a little too old for a soldier, but a soldier with the same difficulties found in most military farces. As always the film brings in a young couple (the girl is newcomer Ann-Marie Adamsson) and Sweden's No. 1 Rock-n-Roll King, Little Gerhard.

It is perhaps lucky for Sweden's reputation as film producing nation that none of the many films in this serial ever was shown outside Scandinavia. Made as low-budget productions, however, the serial has an unbelievable popularity among Swedish patrons.

If anything, the film at least stresses one or two things—the camerawork and music. The latter includes a couple of acceptable r-and-r numbers written by Little Gerhard. *Winq.*

Ansiktet
(The Face) (SWEDISH)

Stockholm, Dec. 30.

Svensk Filmindustri release. With Max von Sydow, Ingrid Thulin, Gunnar Bjornstrand, Naima Wifstrand, Bengt Ekerot, Bibi Andersson, Gertrud Fridh, Lars Ekborg, Toivo Pawlo, Erland Josephson, Ake Fridell, Sif Ruud, Oscar Ljung, Ulla Sjoblom, Axel Duberg, Birgitta Pettersson. Directed by Ingmar Bergman. Screenplay, Bergman; camera, Gunnar Fischer; music, Erik Nordgren. At Roda Kvarn, Stockholm. Running time 102 MINS.

Vogler .... Max von Sydow
Manda Aman .... Ingrid Thulin
Vergerus .... Gunnar Bjornstrand
Grandmother .... Naima Wifstrand
Spegel .... Bengt Ekerot
Sara .... Bibi Andersson
Ottilia .... Gertrud Fridh
Simson .... Lars Ekborg
Starbeck .... Toivo Pawlo
Egerman .... Erland Josephson
Tubal .... Ake Fridell
Sofia .... Sif Ruud
Antonsson .... Oscar Ljung
Henrietta .... Ulla Sjoblom
Rustan .... Axel Duberg
Sanna .... Birgitta Pettersson

In a world filled with mysticism, Ingmar Bergman manifests his artistic screen skill to excite, frighten, fascinate, entertain and seduce his audience. He strives for an impression of the whole and has a most watchful eye for details. Ponderings on love and death, the meaninglessness of life, and the insolvable problems of man form the basis of "The Face."

This feature dwells on the question of whether there are supernatural powers or not. Bergman comes to no conclusion, but shows that man is susceptible to the tricks of a magician. Fascinated by happenings for which there is no immediate explanation, man is seduced and made to believe.

The story is set in Stockholm during the 1840s and surrounds an unsuccessful magician, strikingly portrayed by Max von Sydow. He and his troupe are brought to the home of the police commissioner, who along with a doctor and a civil servant want to test his mystical powers. The magician's supernatural gifts are doubtful, but his presence results in numerous strange and unexpected happenings.

By setting his film more than 100 years in the past, Bergman avoids the problems of modern day realism. With death and fright always lurking in the background, he has created a mystical thriller that belongs among the better recent European films. When he has built up an overpowering tension he lets his audience relax in moments burlesque. However, time and time again he gets away from the main theme and thereby slows up the motion.

Without question "The Face" rates along with Bergman's outstanding recent releases, but it doesn't quite reach the heights and concentration he attained in "Wild Strawberries," "Close to Life," "Summer Interlude" or his astounding prologue to "The Naked Night."

The large cast is made up of a good many of Sweden's leading actors. A lasting impression is made by the magician's grandmother played by experienced actress Naima Wifstrand. Throughout, however, it can be said that Bergman displays his ability to get the most out of his actors as many of them give inspired performances. The photography by Gunnar Fischer, who has filmed a number of his movies, rates with the best anywhere.

Like many of Bergman's other pics, "The Face" is aimed at a rather exclusive film-minded audience.

1958 was a big year for Bergman as several of his pics were awarded prizes at festivals in Cannes, Berlin, Venice, Stratford, Canada, and Buenos Aires. They also received special attention at the Edinburgh festival. "The Seventh Seal" was rated the best foreign film of the year by Helsinki critics and "Wild Strawberries" was praised in London. *Sher.*

Der Pauker
(The Crammer) (GERMAN)

Berlin, Dec. 23.

Gloria release of Kurt Ulrich production. Stars Heinz Ruehmann; features Wera Frydtberg, Gert Froebe, Bruni Loebel, Peter Kraus, Ernst Reinhold, E. F. Fuerbringer, Hans Leibelt. Directed by Axel von Ambesser. Screenplay, Curth Flatow and Eckart Hachfeld; camera, Erich Claunigk; music, Karl von Feilitzsch. At Gloria Palast. Running time, 93 MINS.

Subjectwise, this Kurt Ulrich production may be compared to

"Blackboard Jungle" if only a lighter version of this Metro pic. Mainly concentrating on the personality of an amicable teacher, brilliantly portrayed by Heinz Ruehmann, it is a film that likely will be talked about. Pic contains a great deal of humor as well as the problem of the leather-jacket juveniles. This belongs in the category of above-average German pix for 1958. The Ruehmann name and good crix appraisal will make it a surefire boxoffice here. Foreign possibilities appear beyond the usual German postwar average.

Ruehmann is cast as a small-town teacher who gets an assignment in a big city where he faces the problem of handling a real tough class. At first, it looks like a hopeless job since this bunch of toughies is misled by a real hoodlum. Ultimately he manages them, partly helped by his own understanding that the modern bigtown youth needs a different kind of pedagogical treatment.

Ruehmann's portrayal of the teacher is masterful, and actually he nearly steals the show. His performance is an intelligent mixture of fine humor and warm-hearted acting. Another fine performance is turned in by Gert Froebe, his wrestler-friend, from whom he learns some judo tricks which eventually help him make an impression on his tough pupils.

The lineup of the latter is headed by Peter Kraus, pop German rock 'n' roller, whose acting job also is very satisfactory. Good support is given by Hans Leibelt, as a school director, and E. F. Fuerbringer, as senior inspector of schools. Romantic interest is only slight as provided by Wera Frydtberg, as Kraus' sister, and Bruni Loebel, Ruehmann's teacher colleague.

Script is well turned out being strongest in the sharp dialog. Axel von Ambesser's direction is smooth. The score and lensing measure up to a fine standard. This good German film is probably the best turned out by Berlin's Kurt Ulrich Productions this year.

Hans.

Buehne Frei Fuer Marika

(Stage Free For Marika)
(GERMAN-SONGS-COLOR)

Berlin, Dec. 23.

Europa release of Real production. Stars Marika Roekk and Johannes Heesters. Directed by Georg Jacoby. Screenplay, Helmuth M. Backhaus; camera (Eastmancolor), Willy Winterstein; music, Franz Grothe; editor, Klaus Dudenhoefer. At UFA Pavillon, Berlin. Running time, **93 MINS.**

Marika	Marika Roekk
Michael Norman	Johannes Heesters
Inge	Carla Hagen
Frank Flemming	Harald Juhnke
Brand	Rudolf Platte
Elvira	Susanne v. Almassy
Director Schuehlein	Kurt Grosskurth

Marika Roekk celebrated a much applauded comeback with Real's "At Green Cockatoo" some 10 months ago. The big success of "Cockatoo" let the Hamburg company waste no time and soon came along with another Roekk vehicle. Latter falls considerably short of "Cockatoo," primarily storywise, yet its financial outcome should be satisfactory, too. The domestically powerful Marika Roekk name should lure the masses.

One can't help but admire Miss Roekk. Already more than 40 years old, she's still the temperamentful dancer she used to be two decades ago. Without blushing, this ex-Hungarian whirlwind is still this country's No. 1 musical star. Aside from being a superlative dancer, she's a competent actress with a fine sense of humor and an appealing personality.

It's a pity that the script of this film is, with corny gags galore, so much on the banal if not silly side. Admittedly, story in this plays a secondary role. But a more intelligent script with some touches of charm (which this one lacks completely) could have made this pic much more enjoyable.

Miss Roekk portrays an ambitious manager who wants to become a celebrated revue star. Her aim is to prove to her divorced husband, a famous composer, that she doesn't need his popularity and can very well make a career of her own.

Johannes Heesters, with whom she has been filming for more than 20 years, enacts the composer. He too handles his role with fine results.

Georg Jacoby, Marika Roekk's director-husband, an experienced musical creator, made the most of this rather superficial script. Production dress is, as with "Cockatoo," quite lavish and beyond present German musical standards. Franz Grothe's songs are not bad. The Eastmancolor is an asset and actually, along with Marika Roekk's dance sequences the best about this.

Hans.

The Last Mile

Grim, tough "death row" meller with Mickey Rooney for marquee. Should do well with action crowd.

United Artists release of Max J. Rosenberg and Milton Subotsky production. Stars Mickey Rooney; features Clifford David, Harry Millard, John McCurry, Ford Rainey, Donald Barry, Alan Bunce, Frank Overton, Leon Janney, Clifton James, John Seven, Michael Constantine, John Vari, George Marcy, Milton Selzer, Frank Conroy. Directed by Howard W. Koch; screenplay, Milton Subotsky and Seton I. Miller; camera, Joseph Brun; music, Van Alexander; editors, Robert Brockman, Patricia Jaffe. Previewed in N.Y. at UA homeoffice Jan. 5, '59. Running time, **81 MINS.**

"Killer" John Mears	Mickey Rooney
Richard Walters	Clifford David
Fred Mayor	Harry Millard
Vince Jackson	John McCurry
"Red Kirby"	Ford Rainey
Tom D'Amoro	John Seven
Ed Werner	Michael Constantine
Jimmy Martin	John Vari
Pete Rodrigues	George Marcy
Drake	Donald Barry
Callahan	Leon Janney
Harris	Clifton James
Peddie	Milton Selzer
O'Flaherty	Frank Conroy
Warden	Alan Bunce

Since shock and horror in the supernatural have proved highly salable merchandise in past months, producers Max J. Rosenberg and Milton Subotsky dish it out in rich, full doses in this remake of the 1931 prison film, "The Last Mile." A throwback to the "prison break" cycle of pictures, this is a rough, tough-as-nails kind of production which gets off to an excruciatingly slow start, but picks up speed in the second half and ends up with enough mayhem to keep the action crowd happy.

Shot completely in New York, "Last Mile" is set in the "death row" cellblock of a large prison where nine men wait to be executed on the electric chair. With one or two exceptions, they're an oddly sympathetic lot compared with the sadistic and callous guards, and as they go through the agony of waiting for that last-minute reprieve, the criminals (their crimes never identified) begin to sound more and more like an amiable, scared bunch of guys who shouldn't really be behind bars.

Either by accident or by design, the first half of the film is virtually all talk and taken up with the grizzly, sickening details of a man's last walk to the chair. Director Howard W. Koch doesn't spare the realism, and since the acting is good, the overpowering sense of nearness of death comes through strongly. But then, with all the characters carefully established, "Killer" Mears—played by Mickey Rooney with the expected sneer and swagger—goes into action and all hell breaks loose.

If one accepts the theory that films like "The Last Mile" make for good entertainment, this picture certainly packs quite a wallop. Inevitably, the audience must identify with the men waiting for the hour of execution, and it's a fairly sickening sensation that produces both tension and terror. Once Rooney goes on his rampage and stages the "break," the zing of bullets comes almost as a relief in a picture that's almost monotonously downbeat.

Rooney, despite some over-acting, is convincing as the sadistic killer who knows he's beyond punishment. He completely dominates the second half of the picture, much as Clifford David and John Vari carry it during the first. Latter's "last walk" scene is touching and very well acted. David also turns in a most competent performance. So does Frank Overton as Father O'Connors whose dignity never falters, even in the face of the death.

In the smaller parts, character actors Harry Millard, John McCurry, Ford Rainey, John Seven, Michael Constantine and George Marcy come through with strongly-etched performances as the prisoners. Donald Barry has the required mean streak as Drake, the guard; Alan Bunce plays the warden and Leon Janney's smug air as deathrow warden melts when he's faced with death from Rooney's gun.

Koch's direction and Joseph Brun's lensing combine for strong realism in the bare set, where the sounds of the clanging doors are used to good advantage. They cook up plenty of excitement after the break is staged. Some of the scenes are raw and deliberately staged for "shock" value. Van Alexander's musical backgrounds, mostly jazz, create a good mood setting. Robert Brockman and Patricia Jaffe's editing is competent.

"Last Mile" obviously was aimed at a certain type of patron and situation, and it should hit the mark there. If, in its careful enumeration of "character" it's slightly old-fashioned in approach, the "killer" exploitation should provide UA with a very satisfactory grosser.

Hift.

Sleeping Beauty

(TECHNIRAMA 70-COLOR-SONGS)

Top-notch Disney cartoon job.

Buena Vista release of Walt Disney production. Associate producer, Erdman Penner; Supervising director, Clyde Geronimi; sequence director, Eric Larson, Wolfgang Reitherman, Les Clark; adaptation of the Charles Perrault version, by Penner; music adaptation by George Bruns from Tschaikowsky's "Sleeping Beauty Ballet"; songs, George Bruns, Erdman Penner, Tom Adair, Sammy Fain, Winston Hibler, Jack Lawrence, Ted Sears; editors, Roy M. Brewer Jr. and Donald Halliday. Previewed at the Carthay Circle Theatre, L.A., Jan. 15, '59. Running time, **75 MINS.**

Princess Aurora	Mary Costa
Prince Philip	Bill Shirley
Maleficent	Eleanor Audley
Flora	Verna Felton
Fauna	Barbara Jo Allen
Merry weather	Barbara Luddy
King Hubert	Bill Thompson
King Stefan	Taylor Holmes

Hollywood, Jan. 16.

Walt Disney apparently has another cartoon winner in "Sleeping Beauty." Despite the huge cost of it (reportedly $6,000,000), it is a fairly short (75 minute) film and the money will not show to the average patron. But with the Technicolor-Technirama picture set for a lavish campaign, the returns will be over a long haul. Also "Sleeping Beauty" may be as hardy a perennial as "Snow White."

The ingredients are familiar, only the mixture is somewhat different. There is a handsome prince and a lovely princess. There is a witch who supplies the horror and three good fairies who supply what humor there is. It is the usual Disney combination of Grand Guignol and Punch-and-Judy, with good triumphant.

"Sleeping Beauty," adapted by Erdman Penner from the Charles Perrault version of the fairy tale, is no surprise in its familiar outlines. It's the story of Princess Aurora, who is put under a spell at birth by the bad fairy, Maleficent. She is to prick her finger on a spinning wheel and die before she grows up. But the good fairies, Flora, Fauna and Merryweather, are able to amend the curse. The princess shall not die, but shall fall into a deep sleep. She will be awakened by her true love, Prince Philip (latter a character name likely to cause some confusion in the British Commonwealth).

Adults must suspend sophistication to enjoy such a story, but the effort is worth it. Production gives them every assistance. Children, even those reared on the red-meat diet of television, are likely to take to it without reservation. Usually, just when it seems to get too airy-fairy, Disney gives a shot of full-blown horror.

Mary Costa's rich and expressive voice for the title character gives substance and strength to it. It is a stronger voice than Disney ordinarily uses, and its choice was wise. The music is an adaptation by George Bruns of Tschaikowsky's "Sleeping Beauty Ballet," and it is music—where adapted for song—that requires something more than just a pleasant voice. One number in particular, which Miss Costa introduces, is called "One Upon A Dream," wih the delightful Tschaikowsky waltz for the melody, and is the best from the score and the most likely for popularity. Bill Shirley, as the prince, contributes some good vocal work. His cartoon character, incidentally, is considerably more masculine than these Disney heroes usually are, and Shirley's voice matches the visual concept.

Some of the best parts of the picture are those dealing with the

three good fairies, spoken and sung by Verna Felton, Barbara Jo Allen and Barbara Luddy.

The process being used here to show "Sleeping Beauty" is the biggest Disney has yet used. The picture was shot in Technirama and Technicolor, and then, when completed, printed for 70 m on special printer lenses developed for Disney by Panavision. It was shown here on the same screen used for Todd-AO and was free of distortion, clear and firm. It is suitable for adaptation to 35m CinemaScope and may eventually be shown some places in that process. The larger areas and their greater depth and height are well utilized to extend dazzle.

Disney gives credit to more than 70 contributors on "Sleeping Beauty" in the screen credits. Clyde Geronimi was supervising director, and Eric Larson, Wolfgang Reitherman and Les Clark, the sequence directors. It is an individual credit to all that they have combined to make the film seem all of a piece.

Show with "Sleeping Beauty" is one of Disney's nature featurettes, "Grand Canyon." It will be programmed with the feature on its road show. Set to Ferde Grofe's "Grand Canyon Suite," and shot in Technicolor and CinemaScope, the 28-minute film is a good color story of the great natural phenomenon. It has the customary Disney whimsy with animals and the accents of terror. There is no dialog or narration, and no humans in the picture. Its few incidents are visually explanatory. Although it does not conform to Grofe's program notes for his music, it is acceptable in its interpretation. The final sequence, literally an eagle's eye view of the Canyon at sunset, is splendid. Ernest A. Heiniger was chief photographer and Ray Fernstrom did the aerial camera work, while James Algar directed. *Powe.*

Escort West

Routine oater for duallers.

Hollywood, Jan. 16.

United Artists release of Robert E. Morrison-Nate H. Edwards production. Stars Victor Mature; costars Elaine Stewart and Faith Domergue. Directed by Francis D. Lyon. Screenplay, Leo Gordon and Fred Hartsook; from a story by Steven Hayes; camera, William Clothier; music, Henry Vars; editor, Otto Ludwig. Previewed at Goldwyn studio, Jan. 16, '59. Running time, **75 MINS.**

Ben Lassiter .... Victor Mature
Beth Drury .... Elaine Stewart
Martha Drury .... Faith Domergue
Abbey Lassiter .... Reba Waters
Jamison .... Noah Berry
Vogel .... Leo Gordon
Nelson .... Rex Ingram
Lieutenant Weeks .... John Hubbard
Travis .... Henry Carey Jr.
Wheeler .... Slim Pickens
Doyle .... Ray Barcroft
Captain Poole .... William Ching
Burch .... Ken Curtis
Mrs. Fenniman .... Claire Dubrey
Elwood .... Syd Saylor
Tago .... X. Brands
Indians . . Chuck Hayward, Charles Soldani

"Escort West" is a routine, low-budget western set in that familiar period following the end of the Civil War. The script does not offer much opportunity for action. What there is, director Francis D. Lyon makes the most of.

Victor Mature plays a former Confederate officer heading west with his young daughter, Reba Waters, when he gets tied up with Union troopers patrolling the area. He is involved in a series of skirmishes, sometimes with the Army and sometimes with the Modoc Indians.

There is a love interest between Mature and a woman of the Army party, Elaine Stewart. There is some conflict between Mature and Miss Stewart's sister, an embittered opponent of the Confederacy, Faith Domergue. There is some interest provided by Rex Ingram, as one of the Union soldiers. But the screenplay by Leo Gordon and Fred Hartsook, from a story by Steven Hayes, never makes much of these possibilities beyond some hackneyed and obvious sequences.

Robert E. Morrison and Nate H. Edwards produced. *Powe.*

The Cosmic Man

Dull science fictioner.

Hollywood, Jan. 16.

Allied Artists release of Robert A. Terry production. Stars Bruce Bennett, John Carradine, Angela Greene, Paul Langdon. Directed by Herbert Greene. Screenplay, Arthur C. Pierce; camera, John F. Warren; music, Paul Sawtell and Bert Shefter; editors, Richard C. Currier and Helene Turner. Previewed at the studio, Jan. 12, '59. Running time, 72 **MINS.**

Dr. Karl Sorenson .... Bruce Bennett
Cosmic Man .... John Carradine
Kathy Grant .... Angela Greene
Colonel Mathews .... Paul Langton
Ken Grant .... Scotty Morrow
Sergeant Gray .... Lyn Osborn
Dr. Richie .... Walter Maslow
General Knowland .... Robert Lytton

"The Cosmic Man" apparently was designed to be a thoughtful science-fiction thriller, but thought, in drama, is no substitute for action, and certainly not when the thoughts are as banal as they are in this one. Word of mouth is likely to be deadly.

John Carradine plays the title role, mostly in double-exposure, a wraith-like figure who has come to earth in a mysterious, ball-shaped object. Its arrival immediately sets off an argument between science and the military on what is to be done with it, this conflict being the chief claim to plot. The military wants to blow it up, a course science warns may also demolish considerable landscape. Carradine, meanwhile, is prowling about attempting to discover what

Aside from obvious comments about the necessity of international understanding, dangers in indiscriminate use of atomic energy, etc., the picture lacks the rudiments necessary for a picture of this class, i.e., some effects that would justify its classification as fiction or fantasy. Aside from Carradine's ghostly appearance and some shots of the circular vehicle from outer space, these are lacking.

The screenplay, by Arthur C. Pierce, fails to develop any recognizable characters and wastes considerable time on a diversionary interest, a handicapped child, that is particularly sticky. Besides Carradine, Bruce Bennett, Angela Greene, Paul Langton and Scotty Morrow are those chiefly involved.

Robert A. Terry produced and Herbert Greene directed. *Powe.*

City of Fear

Above - average exploitation dualler.

Hollywood, Jan. 16.

Columbia release of Leon Chooluck production. Stars Vince Edwards; costars John Archer, Steven Ritch, Patricia Blair. Directed by Irving Lerner. Screenplay, Steven Ritch and Robert Dillon; camera, Lucien Ballard; music, Jerry Goldsmith; editor, Robert Lawrence. Previewed at the studio, Jan. 8, '59. Running time, **75 MINS.**

Vince .... Vince Edwards
Richards .... John Archer
Wallace .... Steven Ritch
June .... Patricia Blair
Johnson .... Kelly Thordsen
Jensen .... Lyle Talbot
Jeanne .... Cathy Browne
Hallon .... Sherwood Price
Crown .... Joseph Mell

A detective story with an atomic twist, Columbia's "City of Fear" has exploitation values and will be a good half of a double-bill. Parts of it are good—above its class—and while parts are also not so good, it is never a dull picture and it is occasionally gripping. Leon Chooluck produced and Irving Lerner directed.

Vince Edwards plays an escaped convict in the Steven Ritch-Robert Dillon screenplay. He has taken from the prison medical center a metal cylinder he believes is full of heroin, worth millions if it is pure. What he doesn't know, but what the audience soon learns, is that the cylinder contains not heroin but Cobalt 60, said to be a highly radio-active substance. Reduced to essentials, the story becomes a chase and a race; a chase by police to catch Edwards, and a race to get him before he kills himself or anyone else by extensive exposure to his deadly container.

Sequences showing Edwards' frenzied efforts to dispose of the "heroin," his deepening illness as he hugs the container he believes contains a promise of easy living and instead spells sure death, and the assortment of crooks and grifters he deals with, these are excellent. They have reality and impact. Intercut with them are scenes of the city's authorities, faced with trying to track their criminal and handicapped by their reluctance to publish the urgent reasons for his early apprehension. These scenes are tiresome because they are largely repetitive ("We don't want to panic the people"). They slow down the narrative rather than accelerating it.

Vince Edwards gives a strong performance in the leading role, and Joseph Mell and Sherwood Price as two of his unsavory confederates are particularly interesting in support. Patricia Blair is nice as Edwards' girl, and Steven Ritch, John Archer, Kelly Thordsen and Lyle Talbot are capable in straight parts.

Jerry Goldsmith's musical score is a bright one, complementing Lucien Ballard's realistic camera work, and the slick editing of Robert Lawrence. Jack Solomon's sound on the exteriors is also in the proper naturalism of the whole picture. *Powe.*

Operation Amsterdam
(BRITISH)

Brisk, true-life war yarn providing plenty of excitement; effective stellar performances by Peter Finch, Tony Britton and Eva Bartok.

London, Jan. 12.

Rank (Maurice Cowan) production and release. Stars Peter Finch, Eva Bartok, Tony Britton. Directed by Michael McCarthy. Screenplay, Michael McCarthy and John Eldridge, from David E. Walker's book, "Adventure in Diamonds"; camera, Reginald Wyer; editor, Arthur Stevens; music, Philip Green. At Leicester Square Theatre, London. Running time, **104 MINS.**

Jan Smit .... Peter Finch
Anna .... Eva Bartok
Major Dillon .... Tony Britton
Walter Keyser .... Alexander Knox
Johan Smit .... Malcolm Keen
Dutch Lieutenant .... Tim Turner
Bowerman .... John Horsley
Willem .... Melvyn Hayes
Alex .... Christopher Rhodes

This is yet another of those incredible slices of wartime enterprise which makes an audience sit up and think; "Surely it couldn't have happened?" But it did. Of course, the story-line and atmosphere have been pepped up to give added dramatic and cinematic punch. But, fundamentally, the screenplay writers have taken only legitimate liberties with David E. Walker's book which, thinly disguised as fiction, revealed a closely-guarded and thrilling secret wartime mission. Taut dialog plus some first-class performances provide tension which rarely lets up and make this a more-than-useful b.o. prospect.

It happened in Holland in May, 1940, with the conquering Nazi troops advancing swiftly on Amsterdam. An English major and two Dutch civilians had the sticky task of proceeding from London to Amsterdam to bring back a fortune in diamonds to prevent them falling into enemy hands. They had just 14 hours to pull off this coup. Landing in Holland under gunfire from a British destroyer, they are in constant danger. Everybody around them is a potential fifth columnist, even the attractive young woman who drives them to Amsterdam and later reveals herself to be as brave a patriot as anybody in Holland.

Their remarkable 14 hours involved negotiations with the Dutch diamond merchants, some hair-raising skirmishes with Nazi soldiers, moments of agonizing suspense as they wondered whom they could trust, the blowing up of a bank vault and a car race against time to get back to the harbor, harassed throughout by strafing Nazi airplanes. The major also found time to arrange for the blowing up of an oil dump. If all this seemed to have been accomplished with unexpected aplomb it may well be that, as with many dangerous war missions, that was how it did happen.

Director Michael McCarthy has evoked a fascinating picture of a scared, torn city on the verge of disaster. He has created a sense of lonely desolation which makes for a highly dramatic background. The street battle following the blowing up of the vault also seems a bit far-fetched but leads up to a sock climax. And the scenes of refugees being strafed by planes cannot be faulted. Every now and again the director pulls off a brilliant little cameo. A stray dog in a deserted square, frightened by a speeding car. A few citizens at an outdoor cafe table sipping their drinks with sniping going on and the rumble of the advancing German army clearly audible. Some effective music by Philip Green also adds greatly to the tension.

Tony Britton, stiff-lipped and completely dedicated to his immediate task, forfeits some of the easy charm which has established him on the British screen, but he gives a strong, authoritative performance. Peter Finch, as the dashing Dutch civilian, and Alexander Knox, as the older, more sober diamond expert drawn into the adventure, remain credible characters even as the pic develops into a somewhat unbelievable melodrama. Eva Bartok gives what is probably her best performance as the Dutch girl who in a few dangerous hours grows up and proves herself a heroine. Among the many smaller roles there are noteworthy jobs from Malcolm Keen, as the diamond merchant who sways his colleagues into falling in with the British-Dutch plot, and from Christopher Rhodes, as a fearless saboteur.

"Operation Amsterdam" may have embellished the incredible yarn in the cause of screen thrills

but it remains a well-conceived and smoothly holding piece of film making. *Rich.*

Das Dreimaederlhaus
(House of the Three Girls)
(AUSTRIAN-COLOR)

Vienna, Jan. 13.
Sascha Film release of Aspa-Erina production. Stars Johanna Matz, Karlheinz Boehm; features Gustav Knuth, Magda Schneider, Richard Romanowsky, Rudolf Schock, Erich Kunz. Directed by Ernst Marischka. Screenplay, Ernst Marischka after the operetta of same title by Dr. A. M. Willner, Heinz Reichart and Heinrich Berte; camera (Agfacolor), Bruno Mondi; music, Franz Schubert. At Loewen Kino, Vienna. Running time, **92 MINS.**

Franz Schubert	Karlheinz Boehm
Christian Tschoell	Gustav Knuth
His wife	Magda Schneider
L. v. Beethoven	Ewald Balser
Hannerl	Johanna Matz
Heiderl	Helga Neuner
Hederl	Gerda Sigell
Diabelli	Richard Romanowsky
Franz von Schober	Rudolf Schock
Moritz von Schwind	Helmuth Lohner
Johann Mayrhofer	Erich Kunz
Leopold Kupelwieser	Albert Rueprecht
Operasinger Vogel	Eberhard Waechter
Frau Prametzberger	Else Rambausek
Franzl Seidl	Edith Elmay
Therese Pichler	Liselotte Bay
Kathi	Lotte Lang

This film starts out as a possible lucrative winner. Ernst Marischka directed and scripted this film version of the Franz Schubert operetta and did a good job as usual. It seems to have limited possibilities for arty spots.

Plot comes from a novel by Rudolf Hans Bartsch. Karlhein Boehm as Franz Schubert is too shy to propose to Johanna Matz, Hannerl of the pic. He dedicates a song, his friend sings the song, and the girl falls in love with the singer. Schubert remains a bachelor. This scene in the film is as it was in the operetta, the dramatic climax.

Miss Matz and Boehm are very good. Gustv Knuth and Magda Schneider have lots of opportunity to underscore the troubles of having three marriageable daughters. Richard Romanowsky, as the onetime famed music publisher, Diabelli, deserves special praise, so does Ewald Balser as Beethoven.

In other roles, Rudolf Schock and Helmuth Lohner are excellent. The two comediennes, Lotte Lang and Else Rambausek, handle the slang and keep the laughs coming.

Cameraman Bruno Mondi's work is generally proficient, original scenes being shown from Dreimaedrel Haus' opposite the University. In fact, all technical credits are good. *Maas.*

These Thousand Hills
(COLOR; C'SCOPE)

Big western with good names, should be comfortable b.o.

Hollywood, Jan. 16.
Twentieth-Fox release of David Weisbart production. Stars Don Murray, Richard Egan, Lee Remick, Patricia Owens, Stuart Whitman. Directed by Richard Fleischer. Screenplay, Alfred Hayes; from the novel by A. B. Guthrie Jr.; camera, Charles G. Clarke; music, Leigh Harline; editor, Hugh S. Fowler. Previewed at the studio, Jan. 16, '59. Running time, **96 MINS.**

Lat Evans	Don Murray
Jehu	Richard Egan
Callie	Lee Remick
Joyce	Patricia Owens
Tom Ping	Stuart Whitman
Conrad	Albert Dekker
Ram Butler	Harold J. Stone
Carmichael	Royal Dano
Jen	Jean Willes
Whitey	Douglas Fowley
Sally, the Cook	Fuzzy Knight
Godwin	Robert Adler
Miss Fran	Barbara Morrison
Gorham	Ned Wever
Happy	Ken Renard
McLean	Steve Darrell
Chenault	Tom Greenway
Little Runner	Frank Lavier
Brother Van	Nelson Leigh
Frenchy	Ben Wright
Strain	Jesse Kirkpatrick
Swede	John Epper

There are a passel of good young names in 20th-Fox's "These Thousand Hills," a class western with action, romance and a share of spectacle. The David Weisbart production, directed by Richard Fleischer, should have a broad base of acceptance among western fans, plus younger audiences of all tastes.

The film is based on A. B. Guthrie Jr.'s novel of the same name, third in his trilogy begun with his Pulitzer Prize-winning, "The Way West." Alfred Hayes' screenplay captures all the action and some of the deeper values in Guthrie's story, aided by an excellent cast.

The picture attempts to compress a great deal of action and perhaps too much meaning into conventional running time. Whether through story or film editing, the result has a tendency to be jerky in transition and occasionally shallow in motivation. The central theme is not entirely clear, either.

Don Murray plans a penniless young man on the make in the frontier Northwest. He teams with a buddy, Stuart Whitman, determined to get very rich very quick. His schemes with Whitman don't work out, and he is finally staked to the beginning of his wealth and respectability by one of the town's gambling hall hostesses, Lee Remick.

Murray seems to be in love with Miss Remick, but he marries Patricia Owens, niece of the town banker. He achieves money and position, but he loses contract with Whitman, who saved his life, and Miss Remick, who gave him the financial push he needed to start a new one. He is brought back to them in a tangle with Richard Egan, the town bad man, who kills Whitman in a vigilante hanging and beats up Miss Remick. The ending is not definite. Murray avenges Miss Remick's beating by a brawl with Egan and then goes home to his wife and family.

Murray's need for the substance of big money is well laid in, so his apparently callous attitude later towards his somewhat disreputable friends—Whitman and Miss Remick—is acceptable. The title, taken from the Bible, seems to indicate that greed and despoliation of nature incurs the wrath of heaven, and its justice. What's difficult to understand is who incurs the wrath and who gets the justice.

Despite these reservations, it is an interesting picture. The dialog is often very good. Hayes has paced his script so there are periodic explosions of action that contrast the passive portions. Two of these sequences, a bronc-busting scene and a fight between Egan and Murray, are superbly staged.

Murray's sincerity sustains his role even in portions where his motivation and meanings are not too clear (through no fault of his). Egan is interesting as a heavy, and Miss Remick gets considerable pathos out of her role as the good-hearted "hostess." Miss Owens manages dignity and charm as the good wife, and Stuart Whitman is particularly ingratiating as Murray's doomed comrade. Others who achieve individuality are Albert Dekker, Harold J. Stone, Royal Dano and Jean Willes. Good in smaller roles are Douglas Fowley, Fuzzy Knight, Robert Adler, Barbara Morrison, Ned Wever, Ken Renard and Nelson Leigh.

Charles G. Clarke's camerawork is good, and other behind-camera credits are equally impressive. There is a pretty title song by Ned Washington and Harry Warren, sung well by Randy Sparks. While its pop tune quality will undoubtedly make it a good exploitation item for the picture, its use in the picture itself seems to undermine the qualities of toughness and candor that otherwise are inherent. *Powe.*

The Hanging Tree
(COLOR)

Western with all stops out; lively, colorful; strong b.o. promised.

Hollywood, Jan. 23.
Warner Bros. release of Martin Jurow-Richard Shepherd production. Stars Gary Cooper, Maria Schell, Karl Malden; "introduces" Ben Piazza. Directed by Delmer Daves. Screenplay, Wendell Mayes and Halstead Welles; based on a story by Dorothy M. Johnson; camera, Ted McCord; music, Max Steiner; editor, Owen Marks. Previewed at the studio, Jan. 22, '59. Running time, **106 MINS.**

Doc Frail	Gary Cooper
Elizabeth	Maria Schell
Frenchie	Karl Malden
Rune	Ben Piazza
Grubb	George C. Scott
Flaunce	Karl Swenson
Mrs. Flaunce	Virginia Gregg
Society Red	John Dierkes
Wonder	King Donovan

Mystery, suspense, action and romance are the elements of "The Hanging Tree," a high-budget, high-class western that promises to be high-powered boxoffice. The Warner Bros. presentation is the initial film production for Martin Jurow and Richard Shepherd and it is an exceptionally promising bow. It represents an effort to serve both art and commerce, and while its success in the first category is not entirely consistent, it will be a strong entry in the second. Delmer Daves directed.

Wendell Mayes and Halstead Welles did the screenplay from a long short story by Dorothy M. Johnson, who is a kind of western writers' western writer. Miss Johnson's stories show the west as it was, not as it is nowadays often shown, with tinted romance or dubious Freudianism. Her west is a hard, cruel, lonely frontier, in which the humans were often stripped of the savagery of the country. In transmitting this kind of story to the screen, the dramatic solution is either to soften it or present it so skillfully that it is understood in human terms. Mayes and Welles have chosen the latter course, the harder and better way.

"The Hanging Tree" is a frank melodrama, but with touches of poetry and significance. At least when you have four leading characters named Frail, Rune, Grubb and Wonder, it is fair to assume significance. The story is told with some salty dialog and some frank situations, not, however, provocative, but tough and accurate to life.

In essence, the story follows western classic form. Gary Cooper is the mysterious stranger in "The Hanging Tree," a taciturn and quixotic man who drifts into a Montana gold-mining town. He quickly establishes himself as a man equally handy with a scalpel, a Colt and an inside straight, tender in his professional role as M.D., and a paradoxically tough man when dealing with gamblers and con men.

His first action is to rescue young Ben Piazza from a lynch-minded mob and make him his bond-servant on threat of exposure. His second is to take on the recovery of Maria Schell, a Swiss immigrant, who is ill and blinded from exposure. Stirring in these complicated relationships is the character of Karl Malden, an evil and lascivious gold prospector, who wants Piazza's life, Cooper's money and Miss Schell's body, more or less in that order.

When these and other elements get sufficiently brewed, the blowoff comes in the discovery of gold and the berserk efforts by the drunken miners to burn down the town and lynch Cooper. This scene, while wildly effective, is weak in

motivation, or seems so. There doesn't seem to be much reason for murdering Cooper except a vague resentment against him, that doesn't seem strong enough for such violent action. Still the scene plays.

There are fine performances from a good cast, but the main contribution comes from the director. Daves uses an exceptional number of camera set-ups. He, and his cameraman, Ted McCord, don't lose any chances to show the location backgrounds, but they also come in for plenty of revealing closeups. Since the picture is in what might be called modified wide-screen (1.85), the frame is suitable for both long and close shots. The natural splendor of the Washington location is thoroughly exploited in Technicolor, but Daves doesn't allow his characters to get lost in the forest or mountains. Daves uses one technique, of presenting his background scene and then letting his characters walk into it, that is intriguing. It is not, of course, new, but by his deliberate repetition of it, it achieves freshness and importance.

Cooper has one of his best roles. His mystery and tight-lipped refusal to discuss it perfectly suit his laconic style. Miss Schell was an inspired casting, giving her role unusual sensitivity and strength. Karl Malden, with an out-sized role of a leering and lewd sadist, gives it king-sized treatment. There is a trend (and it's a good one) to bolster romantic stories with strong character actors, i.e., Burl Ives, Lee Cobb, etc., and it spices the screen considerably.

Ben Piazza in his first bow, delivers a compelling performance. He is different from what had come to be considered a New York stage type, and his playing has a cleaner style. Another pic bow is that of George S. Scott, a saturnine fellow playing a burning zealot, and very interestingly. In more conventional characters and very well done, are Karl Swenson, Virginia Gregg, John Dierkes and King Donovan.

The picture ends on a note of inflammatory excitement, with Cooper rescued from the hanging tree when Miss Schell diverts his murderers with sacks of raw gold. The final scene, as the camera pans slowly away, is a stark frieze of the gallows tree, with Cooper, Miss Schell and Piazza grouped beneath it. It is a beautifully framed and striking tableau.

Title song by Mack David and Jerry Livingston, is repeated behind this scene as it is behind the titles. It is a good song, done in semi-folk song style. But it suffers by comparison with the realism of the scene on the screen, and the scene itself suffers in the same relation. Nobody would dispute the value in exploitation of a good title song, as this is. But there is no law that a title song has to be in the picture at all, and in the case of "The Hanging Tree," neither art nor commerce seem to be served by use of this song. Max Steiner's score, elsewhere in the picture, is helpful and unobtrusive.

In the technical sense, both editing by Owen Marks and sound by Stanley Jones are worth noting. Marks because he notably increases the pace and tension by the clean, sharp editing, and Jones by maintaining authenticity through preserving the natural sounds without loosing any dialog. *Powe.*

Paratroop Command

Good low-budgeter, war meller for exploitation.

Hollywood Jan. 23.

American International release of James H. Nicholson-Samuel Z. Arkoff production. Stars Richard Bakalyan, Ken Lynch, Jack Hogan and Jimmy Murphy. Produced by Stanley Shpetner. Directed by William Witney. Screenplay, Shpetner; camera, Gilbert Warrenton; music, Ronald Stein; editor, Robert Eisen. Previewed at Warner Theatre projection room, Jan. 19, '59. Running time, 77 MINS.

Charlie	Richard Bakalyan
Lieutenant	Ken Lynch
Ace	Jack Hogan
Sergeant	Jimmy Murphy
Pigpen	Jeffrey Morris
Cowboy	Jim Beck
Gina	Carolyn Hughes
Amy	Patricia Huston

"Paratroop Command," a war melodrama, is an unusually good film for a low budget production. Stanley Shpetner produced and William Witney directed the American-International picture, which is being paired with the same company's "Submarine Seahawk" for dualling. There are no names to speak of, but with this unit's usual exploitation, the pair will make a strong action twin-bill.

Richard Bakalyan plays a member of a paratroop unit who soon becomes an outcast when he inadvertently kills one of the group's members. His action creates tension within the squad that mounts as it sees action through North Africa, Sicily and finally in Italy. It complicates his own personality problems, too, until he is able to reach a solution at the end where he is killed in a gesture that resolves his life and the story.

Shpetner's story moves smoothly, managing to create individual characters and believable, interesting ones, not so easy in a film of action. Mercifully, he avoids the usual collection of types considered a "cross-section" of radical and regional America. He gets some natural and effective humor out of his story, humor that is not extraneous, but is inherent in his people, exposing characterization and advancing the story. The screenplay halts abruptly once in a too-long scene where Bakalyan explains his background, and it has a hard time getting back into motion but aside from this script plays well. Witney's direction exploits every bit of it.

Bakalyan seems miscast in the central role, but he approaches it sensitively, while Ken Lynch is strong as the unit's commanding officer. Jack Hogan, Jimmy Murphy, Jeffrey Morris and Jim Beck, all young players, are those others most important and they handle their assignments well. Carolyn Hughes and Patricia Huston are helpful in smaller roles.

Gilbert Warrenton's photography is notable. His utilization of two-and three-shots is unusual in these days of the wide, wide screen, and they have freshness and perception. Ronald Stein's music is an asset and other technical credits are good. *Powe.*

The Black Orchid
(VISTAVISION)

Warm story of Italian-Americans, with Sophia Loren and Anthony Quinn.

Hollywood, Jan. 22.

Paramount release of a Carlo Ponti-Marcello Girosi production. Stars Sophia Loren and Anthony Quinn; features Mark Richman; introduces Ina Balin. Directed by Martin Ritt. Screenplay, Joseph Stefano; camera, Robert Burks; editor, Howard Smith; music, Allessandro Cicognini. Previewed Jan. 19, '59. Running time, 94 MINS.

Rose Bianco	Sophia Loren
Frank Valente	Anthony Quinn
Noble	Mark Richman
Alma Gallo	Virginia Vincent
Henry Gallo	Frank Puglia
Ralph Bianco	Jimmy Baird
Guilia Gallo	Naomi Stevens
Mr. Harmon	Whit Bissell
Pirest	Robert Carricart
Joe	Joe Di Reda
Tony Bianco	Jack Washburn
Luisa	Majel Barrett
Paul	Scotti Vito
Consuello	Zolya Talma

"The Black Orchid" is a fine picture, substantially plotted and legitimately peopled, bearing a blend of conflict and warmth that has been potently filmed. Sophia Loren and Anthony Quinn, who star in the Carlo Ponti-Marcello Girosi production, will attract filmgoers, but Paramount also will have to bank on word-of-mouth to overcome a title that, for this story of Italian-Americans, is a misnomer.

"Orchid" is an original story and screenplay by Joseph Stefano, his first dramatic writing. There's a flavor of "Marty," a touch of "Wild Is the Wind" to season what primarily is an intelligent non-imitation, and with this work, Stefano gives more than promise of joining the rank of first-class screenwriters.

The story threads and changing emotions are securely locked in through Martin Ritt's honest direction. Without pushing, he tells an intricately drawn story with a smooth, authoritative hand. Many scenes—particularly the card-playing and proposal sequences—are masterful pieces of film, part of an expert whole.

As the widower who falls in love with the pretty widow, Quinn is excellent, uniting charm with strength and creating a role that will be thoroughly appealing and memorable to filmgoers of all genre. Miss Loren plays with notable feeling and turns in her most impressive acting job to date, while convincingly portraying the mother, the widow and the bride. Mark Richman tops the supporting cast and is a stand-out, as is Ina Balin in her first film role. Also tops are Virginia Vincent, young Jimmy Baird, Frank Puglia, Naomi Stevens, Joe Di Reda and Zolya Talma.

The black orchid literally is a white rose—Rose Bianco—who is the late widow of a man she helped turn to crime to satisfy her own desires. Played by Miss Loren, she mourns her husband and mourns what she has done when a widower (Quinn), with a daughter about to be married, comes along with a joyous manner and serious intentions. They fall in love, but complications exist in his daughter's not approving of "that gangster's wife." When the daughter locks herself in her bedroom for days at a time, Quinn fears she will lose her mind as did her mother. Miss Loren's son, on the other hand, is on a work farm for having stolen, is told he will be able to go home when his mother remarries and finally runs away with disappointment when he hears the marriage is off.

The film technically is excellent, Robert Burks' photography standing out adeptly in black-and-white VistaVision. Hal Pereira and Roland Anderson created authentic settings which were nicely decorated by Sam Comer and Robert Benton. Sound by Hugo Grensbach and Winston Loverett, costumes by Edith Head and tight editing by Howard Smith also are assets. The musical score by Allesandro Cicognini is an interesting one that aptly points up contrasts in the story. *Ron.*

Submarine Seahawk

So-so meller for exploitation.

Hollywood, Jan. 23.

American International release of James H. Nicholson-Samuel Z. Arkoff production. Stars John Bentley and Brett Halsey. Executive producer, Lou Rusoff; producer, Alex Gordon; director, Spencer C. Bennet; screenplay, Lou Rusoff and Owen Harris; camera, Gilbert Warrenton; music, Alexander Laszlo; editor, Ronald Sinclair. Preview at Warner Theatre projection room, Jan. 19, '59. Running time, 83 MINS.

Paul Turner	John Bentley
David Shore	Brett Halsey
Dean Stoker	Wayne Heffley
Andy Flowers	Steve Mitchell
Ellis	Henry McCann
Capt. Boardman	Frank Gerstle
Bill	Paul Maxwell
Ellen	Jan Brooks
Maisie	Mabel Rea

Producer Alex Gordon has taken some stock footage, some standing sets from more expensive productions, and adding some miniature work, has put together a story around these elements for "Submarine Seahawk." Except for some occasionally over-ripe dialog, and some misguided humor, the American-International production makes an absorbing adventure film. Paired with the same unit's "Paratroop Command," the dual booking should mean brisk business at the boxoffice.

Setting for the Lou Rusoff-Owen Harris screenplay is a submarine on Pacific patrol during World War II. John Bentley plays a naval officer who is an expert on Japan but short on command experience when he is made commander of the Submarine Seahawk. His crew soon gets restless when he insists on keeping strictly to reconnaissance, passing up some sure shots at Japanese ships. Eventually all hands see the wisdom of his actions when his plans lead to destruction of large elements of the Jap fleet.

"Submarine Seahawk" is most effective when it sticks to the tension-building sequences of the sub stalking the enemy, fully utilizing all visual and audible aspects of the special circumstances of the surroundings, i.e., the sonar and radar equipment, etc. It's been done before, but it's still engrossing. The production weakens when it gets ashore or when it explores some of the human relationships of the crew-members. An unstable Navy officer who attempts to take over the sub's command the first time his two superiors are absent from the bridge, is strongly incredible. Still Spencer Bennet's direction builds tension and interest to offset the less successful writing.

John Bentley is good as the misunderstood commander, and Brett Halsey interesting as the unstable young officer. Others who impress include Wayne Heffley, Steve Mitchell, Henry McCann, Frank Gerstle and Paul Maxwell.

Gilbert Warrenton's photography is good, and Ronald Sinclair's editing does an important job of welding together the stock, miniature and staged shots. Other technical credits are adequate. *Powe.*

Helden
(Heroes)
(GERMAN-COLOR)

Berlin, Jan. 20.

Bavaria release of H. R. Sokal and P. Goldbaum production. Stars O. W. Fischer and Liselotte Pulver; features Ellen Schwiers, Jan Hendriks, Ljuba Welitsch, Kurt Kasznar, Manfred Inger. Directed by Franz Peter Wirth. Screenplay, Johanna Sibelius and Eberhard Keindorff, adapted from "Arms and Man," comedy by G. B. Shaw; music, Franz Grothe; camera (Agfacolor), Klaus v. Rautenfeld; editor, Claus von Boro. Previewed at Zoo Palast, Berlin. Running time, **98 MINS.**

Bluntschli	O. W. Fischer
Raina	Liselotte Pulver
Louka	Ellen Schwiers
Sergius	Jan Hendrika
Katharina	Ljuba Welitsch
Petkoff	Kurt Kasznar
Nicola	Manfred Inger

"Heroes," a filmization of G. B. Shaw's comedy, "Arms and the Man" (1894), comes to the screen as nice, solid entertainment benefitting primarily from handsome settings and some sturdy acting performances. Although this parody about heroes, heroism and militarism is a departure from the usual cliche, there's nothing much special or exciting about it. Comedies of this type have it usually tough finding buyers on the local market, but the names of O. W. Fischer and Liselotte Pulver, two of Germany's top stars, will probably make this an exception. (Miss Pulver was starred in Universal's "A Time to Love and a Time to Die." Pic has some foreign chances and U.S. art circuit.

Despite the fact that the creators of this held closely to the original, the irony of the latter somehow got lost. One may put part of the blame on the players: They all tend to exaggerate so that the story itself nearly becomes secondary. Most of the players talk a bit too much. With not much action, "Heroes" occasionally borders on the dull.

It's Franz Peter Wirth's second directorial job of a feature film after his various vidpic successes. It is questionable whether he could have made more of this material.

One knows what's the score is after 10 minutes when Swiss-born Serbian artillery captain Bluntschli (O. W. Fischer) is on his flight hidden by the Bulgarian girl Raina (Liselotte Pulver) in the latter's sleeping room. She is engaged to a certain Bulgarian lieutenant (Jan Hendriks), the officer who put Fischer to flight.

Score by Franz Grothe is an asset. Same goes for the settings which, via solid Agfacolor, have often very impressive effects.

Hans.

Room at the Top
(BRITISH)

First-class emotional drama with standout direction. Uncompromising dialog and adult plot offer fine opportunity for impressive performances; big b.o. entry.

London, Jan. 20.

British Lion release of a Remus (John and James Woolf) production. Stars Simone Signoret, Laurence Harvey, Heather Sears. Directed by Jack Clayton. Screenplay, Neil Paterson, from novel by John Braine; editor, Ralph Kemplen; camera, Freddie Francis; music, Mario Nascimbene. At Plaza Theatre, London. Running time, **117 MINS.**

Joe Lampton	Laurence Harvey
Alice Aisgill	Simone Signoret
Susan Brown	Heather Sears
Mr. Brown	Donald Wolfit
Mrs. Brown	Ambrose Phillpotts
Charles Soames	Donald Houston
Mr. Hoylake	Raymond Huntley
Jack Wales	John Westbrook
George Aisgill	Allan Cuthbertson
June Samson	Mary Peach
Elspeth	Hermione Baddeley
Miss Breith	Thelma Ruby
Janet	Anne Leon
Joan	Wendy Craig
Miss Gilchrist	Avril Elgar
Aunt	Beatrice Varley
Gertrude	Miriam Karlin
Teddy	Richard Pasco
Mavis	April Olrich
Mayor	John Welsh
Mayoress	Everley Gregg
Priest	Basil Dignam
Man at Bar	Paul Whitsun-Jones
Girl at Window	Yvonne Buckingham
High Stepping Girl	Doreen Dawn

"Room at the Top," based on John Braine's best-selling novel, suddenly establishes Jack Clayton as a major British director. Some three years ago, he directed "Bespoke Overcoat," a Venice fest award-winning short feature. Since then he has concentrated on producing. Now, with his first important directorial chore, Clayton has made an indelible impression with an adult, human picture. Neil Paterson's literate, well-molded screenplay has been enhanced by subtle, intelligent direction and a batch of topnotch performances. The film should be a winner with all adult British audiences.

The occasionally raw dialog and frank approach to sex has earned it an "X" certificate which means that children under 16 may not see it. Even the localized North country accent is unlikely to mar U.S. appreciation of a film solid in story-line and emotional values.

Laurence Harvey takes a job as an accountant in the local government offices of a North Country town. He is an alert young man with a chip on his shoulder because of his humble background. He is partly determined to be true to himself, but even more eager to be on the make. He quickly finds that the small town is riddled with snobbishness. It is virtually controlled by a self-made millionaire and is dominated by those with money and power. Harvey is determined to break down this class-consciousness and sets his cap at the millionaire's daughter. At the same time he is irresistibly drawn to an unhappily married Frenchwoman with whom he has a violent affair.

In this relationship he finds genuine happiness and also an awareness of the necessity of clinging to his own ideals. But his mistress is driven to suicide when he marries the rich young girl after making her pregnant. So he "gets to the top" in social and business standing, but at the loss of his self-respect.

The Clayton touch produces some fine scenes. These include the young girl's first capitulation to Harvey, the manner in which the millionaire stresses his power over the young upstart, the love scenes between Harvey and Simone Signoret and their quarrel and parting. Above all, Clayton never loses the authentic "small town" atmosphere. The result is that he has directed a film which deals with real human beings. These are flesh and blood characters, with all the average frailties.

The director has been assisted with several fine performances. Harvey makes a credible figure of the young man, likeable despite his weaknesses, torn between love and ambition, and he brings strength and feeling to his love scenes with Simone Signoret. She gives, perhaps, the best performance in a capital all-round cast. She is all woman, combining tenderness and passion and she is pathetic in her loneliness when deserted. Heather Sears has less opportunity as the young girl.

In the string of rich supporting roles are Donald Wolfit's ruthless millionaire, the "best friend," breezily played by Donald Houston; a ripe cameo by Hermione Baddeley, as a blowsy music mistress, Alan Cuthbertson's playing of Mlle. Signoret's husband and a neat study of a snobbish woman by Ambrosine Phillpotts. But one of the strengths of this satisfying film is that even the tiniest part has been given to an artist of calibre.

Freddie Francis's lensing, Ralph Brinton's art work, Ralph Kemplin's editing and Mario Nascimbene's music all fit soundly into a worthwhile yarn. Only once does the film lag. That is towards the end when a piece of symbolism, tied up with Simone Signoret's death in a car smash, does not quite jell with the earthiness of the remainder of the film. *Rich.*

Christine
(FRENCH; COLOR)

Paris, Jan. 20.

Cinedis Films release of Speva-Play Art production. Stars Romy Schneider, Alain Delon; features Micheline Presle, Sophie Grimaldi, Jean-Claude Brialy, Fernand Ledoux, Jacques Duby. Directed by Pierre-Gaspard-Huit. Screenplay, Georges Neveux, Gaspard-Huit from play by Arthur Schnitzler; camera (Eastmancolor), Christian Matras; editor, L. Hautecoeur. At Colisee, Paris. Running time, **100 MINS.**

Christine	Romy Schneider
Franz	Alain Delon
Lena	Micheline Presle
Mizzie	Sophie Grimaldi
Weiring	Fernand Ledoux
Binder	Jacques Duby

Arthur Schnitzler's play served as the basis for one of the late Max Ophuls' pix, "Leibelei," which he made with Magda Schneider in Austria, back in 1932. Now it is remade as a French pic with Miss Schneider's daughter Romy. It seems mother was righter. Her version as seen in reissue is fresher than this one made as a French entry.

Lacking a feel for the times and the characters, this appears curiously old-fashioned. The bite of a decaying class system and society is absent. So this is about a young lieutenant in turn-of-century Vienna who loves a pure little singer. It ends in tragedy when he is killed in a duel over a married woman.

Color and technical aspects are all right but Alain Lelon's wooden thesping, as the lover, and Romy Schneider's playing as the girl do not give this the needed feeling to make the dramatic piece very effective. Lacklustre direction is also against this, and it remains mainly a Continental item with dubious possibilities for the U.S. *Mosk.*

Les Vignes Du Seigneur
(The Vines of the Lord)
(FRENCH)

Paris, Jan. 20.

Cocinor release of Fides-Cocinor-Regis production. Stars Fernandel; features Pierre Dux, Simone Valere, Beatrice Bretty. Directed by Jean Boyer. Screenplay, Serge Veber, Jean Manse, Boyer from play by R. De Flers and F. De Croisset; camera, Charles Suin; editor, Leonide Azav. At Balzac, Paris. Running time, **95 MINS.**

Henri	Fernandel
Hubert	Pierre Dux
Gisele	Simone Valere
Mother	Beatrice Bretty

Fernandel has a couple of drunk scenes in this which are fairly risible. But otherwise, this is a stagey item with little chance for America except possible dualer status on the Fernandel moniker.

He, Fernandel, comes back to stay with his best friend after years abroad. The latter, very rich, is keeping a woman the former once loved. Love begins to blossom but ends harmlessly when Fernandel's drunkenness has everything going awry.

Direction by Jean Boyer does not help this get over its talkiness. Technical aspects are only fair. Thus, this is another Fernandel item with only his name as a possible selling point abroad. Support is okay. *Mosk.*

The Journey
(COLOR)

Strong b.o. for this east-west story of the 1956 Hungarian revolt.

Hollywood, Jan. 30.

Metro release of Alby production. Stars Deborah Kerr, Yul Brynner; costars Richard Morley, E. G. Marshall; "introduces" Jason Robards Jr. Producerdirector, Anatole Litvak. Screenplay, George Tabori; camera, Jack Hildyard; music. Georges Auric; editor, Dorothy Spencer. Previewed at the studio, Jan. 28, '59. Running time, 122 MINS.

Lady Diana Ashmore	Deborah Kerr
Major Surov	Yul Brynner
Hugh Deverill	Robert Morley
Rhinelander	E. G. Marshall
Paul Kedes (Fleming)	Jason Robards Jr.
Czepege	Kurt Kasznar
Mr. Avron	David Kossoff
Madame Hafouli	Marie Daems
Mr. Hafouli	Gerald Oury
Borbala	Barbara Von Nady
Jacques Fabry	Maurice Sarfati
Mrs. Rhinelander	Anne Jackson
Rosso	Fred Roby
Anna	Anouk Aimee
Von Rachlitz	Siegfried Schurenberg
Gisela	Maria Urban
Mitsu	Jerry Fujikawa

"The Journey" is a powerful and provocative film. Its novel background is the abortive Hungarian revolt of 1956. Anatole Litvak, who produced and directed, apparently aimed at illuminating this event by the familiar technique of showing the rebellion's effect on an international group of characters. This aspect has not been fully realized, but strong and striking individual characterizations, and their interplay, nonetheless provide a compelling story. What's going to sell tickets to this Metro release—and sell a lot of them—is the romantic combination of Deborah Kerr and Yul Brynner.

"The Journey" described in George Tabori's screenplay is a relatively short one, geographically speaking. It leads from Budapest to the Austrian frontier, a distance of about 100 miles. A group of passengers, American, British, French, Israeli, etc., is trapped at the Budapest airport by the Hungarian uprising. The Red Army grounds the civilian planes, so this particular group has to take a bus to Vienna. They seem due to suffer no greater discomfort than substitution of surface travel for air, until they arrive at the last check point on the border, where the Russian commander is Yul Brynner.

He delays the party, ostensibly to verify their passports and exit permits. His reasons are not clear. One seems to be his purely whimsical desire for western company. Another is his suspicion—a correct one—that one member of the party, Jason Robards Jr., is not a harmless tourist, but one of the Hungarian rebel leaders.

The plot is a complex one, made more complicated by the fact that none of the characters on either side, Communist and non-Communist, is simple. When it eventually simmers down to, is a politicalsexual triangle, with Brynner jealous of Miss Kerr's attachment to Robards. The picture ends with Brynner sacrificing himself to allow Miss Kerr and Robards to escape after the other have been legally released.

The film seems to have started out being one thing and ended up another. A "Grand Hotel" technique, and the enfoldment of diverse nationalities, dimmed as the three principal characters emerged stronger and more vital. Litvak found he could tell his story almost entirely through Miss Kerr (the west) and Brynner (the east),

so the subsidiary characters and their subplots suffer.

This neglect is justified, however, chiefly by the projection of Brynner's characterization. He is capricious, sentimental, cruel, eager for love and suspicious of attention. He is bright as a precocious child and just as unsophisticated. He is not the type to defect, but he will never be completely comfortable again. Brynner does a fine job in projecting all this.

Miss Kerr has the difficult assignment of being in love with one man, Robards, and yet unwillingly attracted to another, Brynner, who is the opposite of all she admires and loves. She is brilliant and moving as a woman alone in an unbearable situation.

In the strong cast of players, Robert Morley stands out as a Blimpish British traveler; E. G. Marshall as a nice American (not caricatured, for once); Kurt Kasznar provides good contrast as the inn-keeper, and David Kossoff as an Israeli. Anne Jackson has one strong scene in which she turns in a glowing performance. Others worth noting include Anouk Aimee, Siegfried Schurenberg, Maria Urban and Barbara Von Nady.

Jason Robards Jr., in his film bow, is excellent. His gaunt and haunted face, his halting speech, at first do not make an impression, except visual. He, too, has but one real scene, but he uses it to raise the drama to passionate conviction.

Tabori's screenplay is an honest work, and his insight into his various nationalities is especially perceptive. The international cast helps, and so does the fine camera work by Jack Hildyard and the musical score by Georges Auric.
Powe.

Imitation of Life

Fine remake of 1934 film. Tears will be shed, but not by exhibs if Lana Turner-John Gavin starrer is properly promoted.

Hollywood, Jan. 7.

Universal release of a Ross Hunter production. Stars Lana Turner, John Gavin; co-stars Sandra Dee, Dan O'Herlihy, Susan Kohner, Robert Alda; with Juanita Moore, Mahalia Jackson. Directed by Douglas Sirk. Screenplay by Eleanore Griffin and Allan Scott, from the novel by Fannie Hurst; camera (Eastman Color), Russell Metty; editor, Milton Carruth; music, Frank Skinner. Previewed Jan. 7, '59. Running time, 125 MINS.

Lora Meredith	Lana Turner
Steve Archer	John Gavin
Susie (age 16)	Sandra Dee
David Edwards	Dan O'Herlihy
Sarah Jane (age 18)	Susan Kohner
Allen Loomis	Robert Alda
Annie Johnson	Juanita Moore
Herself	Mahalia Jackson
Sarah Jane (age 8)	Karen Dicker
Susie (age 6)	Terry Burnham
Young Man	John Vivyan
Photographer	Lee Goodman
Show Girl	Ann Robinson
Frankie	Troy Donahue
Receptionist	Sandra Gould
Burly Man	David Tomack
Minister	Joel Fluellen
Stage Manager	Jack Weston
Fat Man	Billy House
Teacher	Maida Severn
Romano	Than Wyenn
Fay	Peg Shirley

"Imitation of Life" crosses a succession of emotional bridges, hitting the heart with each step in one of the best Universal films of recent years. It's a film that will benefit from word-of-mouth, particularly of lipsticked mouth. A remake of Fannie Hurst's novel of the early 30's, it will need selling, and this time U has something to sell.

Lana Turner, looking in early scenes as she did 15 years ago, is

outstanding in the pivotal role played in Universal's 1934 version by Claudette Colbert. Scripters Eleanore Griffin and Allan Scott, whose screenplay is intelligent, basically honest and always moving, transplanted her from the original pancake-and-flour business to the American stage.

While this device lends more scope, it also results in the overdone busy actress-neglected daughter conflict, and thus the secondary plot of a fair-skinned Negress passing as white becomes the film's primary force. The relationship of the young colored girl and her mother—played memorably by Susan Kohner and Juanita Moore —is sometimes overpowering, while the relationship of Miss Turner and her daughter, Sandra Dee, comes to life only briefly when both are in love with same man, John Gavin. Threading its way through these relationships is the association of the two women, a most notable bit of story-telling.

The film is a fine achievement for producer Ross Hunter and director Douglas Sirk who made 125 minutes, lacing back and forth from one story to the other, play tightly and intensely.

Handling of the racial angle is strong, with both the girl, who wants to "pass," and the mother, who calls it a sin to pretend, presenting their cases admirably. In a stirring portrayal, Miss Kohner gives every indication of being one of the finest young actresses in films, and Miss Moore, as the mother, is a find in the Negro character actress field. Gavin admirably underplays, leaving the theatrics to the actress he loves, and with this role is on his way to the ranks of full-blooded screen heroes. Miss Dee is exuberant and rather forceful when he role demands it, turning in a spirited performance.

Miss Turner plays a character of changing moods, and her changes are remarkably effective, as she blends love and understanding, sincerity and ambition. The growth of maturity is reflected neatly in her distinguished portrayal.

In smaller roles, both Robert Alda, as an opportunist agent, and Dan O'Herlihy, as a playwright, are excellent, with top performances from Karen Dicker and Terry Burnham as the daughters at age eight and six. Mahalia Jackson makes a brief appearance, singing "Trouble of the World," in the final sequence.

Russell Metty's color photography is an important asset, as is art direction by Alexander Colitzen and Richard H. Riedel, set decoration by Russell A. Gausman and Julia Heron, sound by Leslie I. Carey and Joe Lapis and editing by Milton Carruth.

Frank Skinner's score is very good, with title song by Sammy Fain and Paul Francis Webster, sung over credits by Earl Grant, another bonus. *Ron.*

Compulsion
(C'SCOPE)

Tense, well-made drama based on the 1924 Leopold-Loeb murder case. Despite lack of names, it shapes as plenty strong b.o. entry.

20th-Fox release of Darryl F. Zanuck Productions presentation. Produced by Richard D. Zanuck. Stars Orson Welles, Diane Varsi, Dean Stockwell, Bradford Dillman; features E. G. Marshall, Martin Milner, Richard Anderson, Robert Simon, Edward Binns, Robert Burton, Wilton Graff, Louise Lorimer, Voltaire Perkins. Directed by Richard Fleischer; screenplay, Richard Murphy, from Meyer Levin novel

of same title; camera, William C. Mellor; music, Lionel Newman; editor, William Reynolds. Previewed at the 20th homeoffice in N.Y., Jan. 29, '59. Running time, 103 MINS.

Jonathan Wilk	Orson Welles
Ruth Evans	Diane Varsi
Judd Steiner	Dean Stockwell
Artie Straus	Bradford Dillman
Horn	E. G. Marshall
Sid	Martin Milner
Max	Richard Anderson
Lt. Johnson	Robert Simon
Tom Daly	Edward Binns
Mr. Straus	Robert Burton
Mr. Steiner	Wilton Graff
Mrs. Straus	Louise Lorimer
Padua	Gavin MacLeod
Benson	Terry Becker
Edgar Llewellyn	Russ Bender
Emma	Gerry Lock
Detective Davis	Harry Carter
Detective Brown	Simon Scott
Judge	Voltaire Perkins

"Compulsion," which made fascinating reading in Meyer Levin's novel, has been made into a compellingly frank and exciting film. Amounting almost to a literal case study of the notorious LeopoldLoeb murder of Bobby Franks, the Richard D. Zanuck production brings the two brilliant young sexdeviates to life with searching clarity, a superb sense for dramatic pacing and a certain bold honesty that culminates in the final, unabashed message against capital punishment.

Under Richard Fleischer's expert direction, with its overtones of the documentary, the picture—in blackand-white CinemaScope—achieves not only a good deal of tension as the police piece together the clues that finally net the arrogant culprits, but it provides a superb insight into the inter-relation of the two protagonists, here called Artie and Judd.

Both have highly neurotic, seething minds bent on destruction as twisted proof of their superiority. That the boys have a homosexual relationship is quite clear, though the subject is not overstressed. Both come from wealthy families that spoiled them.

These are the key roles in the film. They must carry the burden. As Artie Straus, the sneering, arrogant youth who can no longer distinguish between reality and his dreams, but who knows how to hide under the veneer of smooth politeness, Bradford Dillman turns in a superb performance. This mind is evil, and with the camera helping to establish his character by focussing on his face, his eyes and his mouth, the whole of Artie Straus gets to be translated to the screen.

Dillman so far has been seen in "A Certain Smile" and in "In Love and War." In "Compulsion" he emerges as an intelligent, convincing actor, a performer of major stature. Despite the distinct negative qualities. Artie has human dimension. Dillman rates tops after this.

Opposite him, as Judd Steiner, Dean Stockwell plays an impressionable, sensitive youth, caught up in the spell of his strong-willed companion. If not sympathy, at least he evokes pity. Stockwell's desperate scene with Diane Varsi, in which he almost rapes her and then breaks down, is acted with skill and is moving in its impact.

But it is the interplay between Artie and Judd, the sense of being partners in crime in the context of a larger and more intimate relationship, that gives the picture much of its fascination. Director Fleischer establishes it from the terrifying opening shot when the two try to run down a drunk on the road to their appearance in court, where lawyer Orson Welles pleads for their life in the same idiom that Clarence Darrow used to save

Nathan Leopold Jr. and Richard Loeb from the Illinois gallows.

Welles, delivering one of the longest monologes ever filmed, is admirable in his restraint. For once, no one will have trouble understanding him. The lines he speaks become part of the man himself, an almost classic oration against capital punishment. As the girl who understands more than she knows, and who reaches out for Stockwell, Miss Varsi seems at times awkward. It's not an easy part, and, still new to acting, she brings to it a tenseness that doesn't always register.

In smaller roles, Martin Milner is sympathetic as the student-reporter who helps break the case by finding Stockwell's glasses on the body of the murdered boy. E. G. Marshall is dryly efficient as the State's Attorney who cracks the case and who, in the end, is made to look almost guilty by Welles. Richard Anderson is natural as Judd's brother and Robert Simon brings a fine sense of humor to his portrayal of Lt. Johnson. Edward Binns is effective as Tom Daly, the reported. Louise Lorimer hits the right note as Artie's socialite mother.

Richard Murphy, who wrote the screenplay, did a gratifying job in sticking closely to the Levin book. The dialog is completely believable. William C. Mellor's photography is a big plus. His camera moves without any contrived angles, yet in a host of clever little shots catches the essence of the characters.

But in the final accounting it is still the direction and the performances that gvie the picture its electric quality. There are some lapses, to be sure. The two boys are explained, the viewer can understand them, but it is impossible to get involved. A revolting crime has been committed, but the very terror of it never fully penetrates. The film is artful in its technical detail, which extends to the performances, yet it is curiously artless and devoid of imagination when it comes to the expressions that are purely filmic and beyond the scope of dialog. There is about it an almost sober atmosphere, relieved somewhat by the expert and extraordinarily effective cutting of editor William Reynolds.

Lionel Newman wrote the music. "Compulsion" latches on to headlines of yesterday that still seem to intrigue the public of today. It's certainly a well-made picture with plenty of boxoffice allure that, as the younger Zanuck's maiden effort, gives one the right to expect even better things of him.

Hift.

Alaska Passage

Adventure pic for lower-half billing.

Hollywood, Jan. 27.

Twentieth-Fox release of an Associated Producers Inc. production. Stars Bill Williams, Nora Hayden, Lyn Thomas, Leslie Bradley. Produced by Bernard Glasser. Written and directed by Edward Bernds; camera (RegalScope), William Whitley; editor, Richard C. Meyer; music, Alex Alexander. Previewed in Beverly Hills, Jan. 7, '59. Running time, **71 MINS.**

Al	Bill Williams
Pete	Nick Dennis
Tina	Nora Hayden
Mason	Leslie Bradley
Janet	Lyn Thomas
Barney	Jess Kirkpatrick
Radabaugh	Fred Sherman
Hank	Raymond Hatton
Hubie	Tommy Cook
Claudette	Jorie Wyler
McCormick	Greg Martell
MacKilliop	Court Shepard
Anderson	Ralph Sanford

Although the first few feet of "Alaska Passage" give promise of a timely documentary look-see at our 49th state, the film takes a quick detour into a trucking yarn whose locale is inconsequential. It marks the debut for Associated Producers Inc., new indie releasing through 20th-Fox, and though it's probably one of the more routine and least ambitious productions on the company's slate, it remains a well-done lowbudgeter.

Scripted by Edward Bernds, "Passage" is the story of truckers who move their goods from a small town, Tanana Crossing, to a big town, Fairbanks. The roads aren't good, the mountains fall down and the whole show, run by friendly Bill Williams, is in the red. The silent partner (Leslie Bradley) invades the wilds to check on the operation, and his wife (Lyn Thomas), who once threw Williams over for a fortune, immediately lures her old beau.

There's a sexy doll, Nora Hayden, who eyes Williams and finally grabs him away from the cunning adulteress, and when the silent partner—"he's not so silent anymore"—threatens to leave his wife, she hauls out a pistol and gives him a couple of shots in the shoulder. She races, off, forces a trucker to transport her away from it all and finally ends up quite dead in a fiery crash.

Williams is fine, as is Miss Thomas, while Bradley is a bit too unnatural. Miss Hayden's talents aren't subtle. There are top supporting performances from Tommy Cook and Jorie Wyler, and Nick Dennis delightfully is responsible for the film's finest moments.

Writer-director Bernds managed to come up with some excitement, particularly in a truck chase sequence, and his direction holds his screenplay together. Producer Bernard Glasser added good production values for this low-budgeter, with William Whitley's photography of the chase most effective. Other credits are well handled—editing by Richard C. Meyer, art direction by John Mansbridge, sound by Frank Goodwin and musical score by Alex Alexander.

Ron.

The Trap
(COLOR)

Crime meller misfires. Despite top cast, spotty b.o. likely.

Hollywood, Jan. 30.

Paramount release of Parkwood-Heath coproduction. Stars Richard Widmark, Lee J. Cobb, Tina Louise and Earl Holliman. Produced by Norman Panama and Melvin Frank. Directed by Panama. Screenplay, Panama and Richard Alan Simmons; camera, Daniel L. Fapp; editor Everett Douglas. Previewed at Westwood Village Theatre, Jan. 6, '59. Running time, **82 MINS.**

Ralph Anderson	Richard Widmark
Victor Massonetti	Lee J. Cobb
Linda Anderson	Tina Louise
Tippy Anderson	Earl Holliman
Sheriff Anderson	Carl Benton Reid
Mr. Davis	Lorne Greene
Mellon	Peter Baldwin
1st Policeman	Chuck Wassil
Len Karger	Richard Shannon
Joey	Carl Milletaire

"The Trap" has strong marquee names and some handsome pictorial values, both geographical and physical. But it is a crime melodrama so over-wrought that it often falls into unintentional parody, and will have only spotty success. Melvin Frank and Norman Panama produced the independent coproduction (of their Parkwood and Richard Widmark's Heath units) for Paramount. The faults of the picture are most noticeable in writing and direction.

Widmark plays the son of a small town sheriff, Carl Benton Reid, who has expelled him some years before for a minor, youthful indiscretion. Widmark comes home as the mouthpiece of a crime boss, Lee J. Cobb, now on the lam. Cobb and his organization hoods have shut off the little desert community from all outside contact. An airplane is to touch down at its isolated field and take Cobb to another country.

Widmark is the willing tool of the syndicate until Cobb's henchmen kill Reid. Then Widmark turns and attempts to bring Cobb to justice. He is handicapped by his brother, Earl Holliman, who should be helping him, but is a lush and a weakling. Another complication is Holliman's luscious wife, Tina Louise, who was formerly Widmark's girl. Their reunion sparks the old flame, a fact that further confuses Holliman.

"The Trap" is not much different in mood and general plot from several other pictures. It would have justified this familiarity if its excellent cast had been allowed to give it importance or special interest. Unfortunately, the cast members have been ill-served by the writing and the direction. Even such reliable actors as Widmark and Cobb often look foolish with scowling interpretations and overripe dialog. Cobb has a couple good cynical lines and he delivers them with his usual authority. But too often he and Widmark appear unintentionally and fatally humorous in moments when menace is intended.

Tina Louise, after an auspicious picture bow in "God's Little Acre," does nothing to advance her career, and Earl Holliman makes little impression in a poorly conceived role. The supporting cast, Carl Benton Reid, Lorne Green, Peter Baldwin and Richard Shannon, come off best, perhaps because they are on least.

Panama directed the screenplay which he wrote with Richard Alan Simmons. The one solid asset of the picture is the Technicolor photography of the desert. These backgrounds, and the exterior scenes shot there, have interest and often some excitement. Daniel L. Fapp was cameraman, with Wallace Kelley on second unit camera, and Michael Moore as second unit director.

Powe.

Tokyo After Dark

Mild low-budget meller with exploitation possibilities.

Hollywood, Jan. 30.

Paramount release of a Nacirema Production. Stars Michi Kobi, Richard Long, Lawrence Dobkin, Paul Dubov, Teru Shimada. Producer-writers, Norman T. Herman and Marvin Segal. Directed by Herman. Camera, William Margulies; music, Alexander Courage; editor, Robert Lawrence. Previewed at the studio, Jan. 29, '59. Running time, **80 MINS.**

Sumi	Michi Kobi
Sgt. Douglas	Richard Long
Major Bradley	Lawrence Dobkin
Jesse Bronson	Paul Dubov
Sen-Sci	Teru Shimada
Store Proprietor	Robert Okazaki
Mr. Johnson	Carlyle Mitchell
Nakamura	Frank Kumagai
2nd GI	John Brinkley
Kojima	Edo Mito
1st GI	Lowell Brown
Toshio	Don Keigo Takeuchi
Sgt. Williams	Jerry Adler

The title of "Tokyo After Dark" will lend itself to lurid exploitation, and presumably this is what Paramount is counting on to sell this Nacirema production. The picture itself gets little emotional or dramatic value out of a basically interesting premise, that of a GI in Japan who accidentally kills a Japanese civilian. "Tokyo After Dark" will be sold on its advertising, not its production values.

Norman T. Herman and Marvin Segal, the producers, did the screenplay, and Herman directed, as well. They have taken their story from the headlines of a year or so ago. Richard Long is the American Army officer who is responsible for the death of a Japanese youth, when his pistol accidentally discharges. Japanese sentiment designates him an overbearing and heartless murderer and there is agitation for his trial by Japanese courts.

Actually, as the script makes clear, Long is not typical of the U.S. Occupation forces. He has made a sincere effort to understand Japan and its people, and is an admirer of its customs. He is engaged to a lovely Japanese entertainer, Michi Kobi, so his accusation as a murderer and the possibilities it raises, are interestingly complicated. But nothing much is done with any of these doorways that are intriguingly opened. They don't lead anywhere. What is substituted for action is a series of sequences in which the principals discuss what action might occur. The only motivation offered for Long's temporary decision to desert the Army, and escape Japanese judicial jurisdiction is his vague feeling that he will not get fair treatment. But it is not strong enough. The spectator knows this will not be carried through, hence suspense is lost and with it, interest. The ending is too clearly seen.

The film has a quiet authenticity, although it was shot here on standing sets and in L.A.'s "Little Tokyo." The Japanese feeling is delicately done and in good taste. The approach, indeed, is so correct, that the picture's failure is regrettable. But its virtues are passive and of no help to the film.

Miss Kobi is a lovely and capable actress, and Long is adequate, although barely so. Nobody else registers with any particular impression, the characters are too stock.

William Margulies' photography is good, and the music by Alexander Courage is particularly pleasant, including the highlighting of genuine Koto-playing that has interest in itself.

Powe.

Al Capone

Vivid recreation of the prohibition era folk-monster. Big production values, strong payoff.

Hollywood, Feb. 6.

Allied Artists release of John H. Burrows-Leonard J. Ackerman production. Stars Rod Steiger; costars Fay Spain, James Gregory, Martin Balsam; features Nehemiah Persoff, Murvyn Vye. Directed by Richard Wilson. Screenplay, Malvin Wald and Henry F. Greenberg; camera, Lucien Ballard; music, David Raksin; editor, Walter Hannemann. Previewed at the studio, Feb. 4, '59. Running time, **105 MINS.**

Al Capone .... Rod Steiger
Maureen .... Fay Spain
Schaefer .... James Gregory
Keely .... Martin Balsam
Johnny Torrio .... Nehemiah Persoff
Bugs Moran .... Murvyn Vye
Jim Colosimo .... Joe De Santis
Hymie Weiss .... Lewis Charles
O'Banion .... Robert Gist
Bones Corelli .... Sandy Kenyon
Mr. Brancato .... Raymond Bailey
Tony Genaro .... Al Ruscio
Joe Lorenzo .... Louis Quinn
Scalisi .... Ron Soble
Anselmo .... Steve Gravers
Ben Hoffman .... Ben Ari
Pete Flannery .... Peter Dane

A tough, ruthless and generally unsentimental account of the most notorious gangster of the prohibition-repeal era, Allied Artists' "Al Capone" is a contender for top boxoffice. It is also a very well-made picture, jarring at times in its devotion to the last bloody detail, but with importance and significance observed, though not stressed. John H. Burrows and Leonard J. Ackerman produced the realistic film and Richard Wilson has given it fine direction.

There isn't much "motivation" given for Capone in the Malvin Wald-Henry F. Greenberg screenplay at least not in the usual sense. There is nothing about an unhappy childhood or any other such handy device to explain his brutality and corruption. But the screenplay does supply reasons and they are more logical than the usual once-over lightly on the warped youth bit.

Without excusing Capone in any way, the screenplay does make clear that Capone was an effect of lax community and police morals rather than a cause of it. Capone, played by Rod Steiger, is shown as an amoral personality with a native genius for leadership and organization. He became rich and famous in a way that seemed to him dandy. Nobody was more genuinely surprised than Capone when the revulsion his acts caused finally overwhelmed him. Without attempting to be conspicuously significant, the film also makes clear that the tentacles Capone put into respectable business are still there today, controlled by other men outside the law and above it.

Some of those named in "Al Capone" are given pseudonyms, such as the reporter for the Chicago paper (Ja came a part of the Capone oufit and was murdered when he misguidedly changed sides. Others are called by correct name.

The story picks up when Steiger is brought to Chicago as a low-grade torpedo by a fellow countryman, Nehemiah Persoff, to act as bouncer in his gambling establishment. Capone begins his rise when he murders the local political boss, Joe DeSantis, and eventually takes over Persoff's territory, on the latter's retirement. He teams with Bugs Moran and Dion O'Banion, to divide Chicago into territories. Each gang is to respect the other's territory. Naturally this treaty is eventually dissolved in blood, and reaches its climax in the St. Valentine's Day Massacre. It was this event that finally convinced a great many people that the Capone mob and its associates were not just a group of especially frisky businessmen, and Federal Income Tax action put Capone away.

"Al Capone" contrives no happy moral. There is no claim that by Capone's imprisonment and his subsequent death from paresis, gangsterism and racketeering had been slowed down. To the contrary. Using a semi-documentary style, with occasional narration from an honest cop, James Gregory, it is made clear that this story of a generation ago has particular pertinancy today. Film's letdown at the end is the expected letdown after exceptionally tense melodrama.

Steiger gives perhaps the best performance of his film career, mostly free of obvious technique, getting inside the character both physically and emotionally. Fay Spain has a role, that of the romantic attachment of Capone's life, that is probably more distracting than helpful. But she plays well. Through no fault of hers, too many of her scenes seem to be pitched at a hysterical level, but Miss Spain at least demonstrates that she is not just another ingenue. James Gregory as the honest cop, Martin Balsam as the dishonest reporter and Persoff as Capone's mentor, give skillful performances. Others who register include Murvyn Vye, Joe DeSantis, Lewis Charles, Robert Gist, Sandy Kenyon and Raymond Bailey.

"Al Capone" is not a gangster "cheapie." There are obviously expensive things about its production. Richard Wilson's splendidly-paced direction, his care with development of his characters, and his attention to their personalities, is the greatest contributor to the film's success.

Lucien Ballard's camera work is superb, and it is enhanced by Walter Hannemann's editing. Other important assets are the David Raksin score, an unlikely but judicious combination of 20's jazz, operatic themes and straight mood music; and the imaginative are direction by Hilyard Brown. *Powe.*

The Remarkable Mr. Pennypacker (COLOR; C'SCOPE)

Disappointing version of legit farce. Mildly funny. Mild b.o.

Hollywood, Feb. 6.

Twentieth-Fox release of Charles Brackett production. Stars Clifton Webb, Dorothy McGuire, Charles Coburn. Director, Henry Levin; screenplay, Walter Reisch; based on the play by Liam O'Brien; camera, Milton Krasner; music, Leigh Harline; editor, William Mace. Previewed at the studio, Feb. 2, '59. Running time, **87 MINS.**

Pa Pennypacker .... Clifton Webb
Ma Pennypacker .... Dorothy McGuire
Grampa .... Charles Coburn
Kate Pennypacker .... Jill St. John
Wilbur Fielding .... Ron Ely
Horace Pennypacker III .... Ray Stricklyn
Henry Pennypacker .... David Nelson
Aunt Jane .... Dorothy Stickney
Rev. Dr. Fielding .... Larry Gates
Sheriff .... Richard Deacon
Laurie Pennypacker
Mary Jayne Saunders
Elizabeth Pennypacker ...... Mimi Gibson
Benny .... Donald Losby
David .... Chris Van Scoyk
Edward .... Jon Van Scoyk
Teddy .... Terry Rangno
Mrs. McNair .... Nora O'Mahoney
Miss Haskins .... Doro Merande
The Verger .... Harvey B. Dunn
The Fire Chief .... Ralph Sanford
Mary Pennypacker ...... Joan Freeman
Twins .... Donald, David Harrison
Nancy .... Pamela Baird
Ann .... Nancy Ann DeCarl
Babs .... Anna Marie Nanasi
Trudy .... Diane Mountford
Charlie .... Ray Ferrell

"The Remarkable Mr. Pennypacker" is an amiable film from the stage play, but amiable is about the strongest word that can be used. The Charles Brackett production for 20th-Fox doesn't add anything to the legit version and it loses most of the humor the original had. Starring Clifton Webb in this kind of film is obviously an effort to repeat the success of his "Belvedere" roles.

The basic premise of Liam O'Brien's play, screenplayed by Walter Reisch, is the heady effect of new ideas and progressive thinking on Webb, an impressionable sausage manufacturer in the 1890s. He is a proponent of Darwinism, single taxes, feminism and free-thinking. It is the last idea that gets him undone and supplies the plot for the picture.

Webb divides his business life between two plants of his company, with alternate months in Philadelphia and in Harrisburg. It soon develops he has created a homelife in each city, with eight children in one household and nine in the other. As Webb points out to his Harrisburg wife, Dorothy McGuire, she has no reason to be surprised when she learns of the second family, since it is merely a logical extension of ideas she knows he's espoused.

This is a basically amusing premise, especially since Webb's bland bigamy is set against the ornate background and rigid moral standards of Victorian America. Nothing, however, gets developed. The direction, by Henry Levin, doesn't set up the jokes, so when they appear they don't play. There are even times when an audience is likely to wonder whether or not it is supposed to laugh, and when an audience is in doubt, it doesn't. One fault seems to have been Levin's (or the screenwriter's) attempt to "humanize" the farcial characters. This cuts considerable ground out from under the comic premise. (*Actually the two family premise has drawn Catholic objection on the grounds, Taint funny, McGee—Ed.*).

Even such experts as Clifton Webb and Charles Coburn are defeated. Webb seems too casual and Coburn too broad. Dorothy McGuire manages credibility because her role is straight anyway, but others in the large and generally good cast—Jill St. John, Ray Stricklyn, David Nelson, Dorothy Stickney and a raft of attractive youngsters—are sunk.

Visually, the film is lovely, in CinemaScope and DeLuxe color. It is a lavish and nostalgic evocation of a placid and bountiful period. But again, it seems an error of too much weight for the fragile structure.

Lone Texan

Well-done low-budget western.

Hollywood, Jan. 29.

Twentieth-Fox release of a Regal Films production. Stars Willard Parker, Grant Williams, Audrey Dalton, Douglas Kennedy, June Blair. Produced by Jack Leewood. Directed by Paul Landres. Screenplay by James Landis and Jack Thomas, from novel by Landis; camera, Walter Strenge; editor, Robert Fritch; music, Paul Dunlap. Previewed Jan. 29, '59. Running time, **71 MINS.**

Clint Banister .... Willard Parker
Greg Banister .... Grant Williams
Susan Harvey .... Audrey Dalton
Phillip Harvey .... Douglas Kennedy
Florrie Stuart .... June Blair
Doc Jansen .... Dabbs Greer
Amy Todd .... Barbara Heller
Finch .... Rayford Barnes
Henry Biggs .... Tyler McVey
Riff .... Lee Farr
Ric .... Jimmy Murphy
Jesse .... Dick Monahan
Carpetbagger .... Robert Dix
Ben Hollis .... Gregg Barton
Trades .... L. Stanford Jolley
Gus Pringle .... Sid Melton
Nancy .... Shirle Haven
Jack Stone .... Hank Patterson
Charlie .... Frank Marlowe
Indians . . Boyd Stockman, Jerry Summers, Bill Coontz
Old Dan .... Tom London
Women Passengers ...... Elena DaVinci, Doe Swain

Regal Films makes a regal farewell with "Lone Texan," last of 42 low-budget features it has turned out for 20th-Fox in the past two years. Skillfully scripted by James Landis and Jack Thomas, it's a strikingly good film that will pep up more than one double-feature.

Producer Jack Leewood made good use of all his assets, casting well with Willard Parker, Grant Williams, Audrey Dalton, Douglas Kennedy and June Blair in the top roles. Paul Landres' direction moves the brother-versus-brother battle in taut fashion, ably mirroring the conflict in his other players.

Screenplayed from a novel by Landis, the lone Texan (Parker) returns from the Union forces at the end of the Civil War and is labled a "turncoat" by most of his friends. His younger brother (Williams) has taken over as sheriff and as judge, jury and executioner as well. He and his young hoodlum deputies terrorize the town, and Parker's return makes a showdown inevitable. When it finally comes, the off-beat finish has Williams reaching for a gun to shoot a deputy about to plug Parker in the back, and Parker, thinking his brother is drawing on him, shooting his brother first and accurately, thus restoring ye olde law and order.

Parker and Williams are excellent as the brothers, with Kennedy turning in a fine performance as a lawyer. Misses Dalton and Blair add beauty and a little excitement besides. Also tops are Dabbs Greer as the town doctor, Barbara Heller as a town prude, and Lee Farr, Rayford Barnes, Jimmy Murphy and Dick Monahan as the deputies.

Walter Strenge's lensing of a backlot western street is a plus, as is the work done by art director Edward Shiells, editor Robert Fritch, soundman Victor Appel and scorer Paul Dunlap. *Ron.*

The Young Captives

Another psycho killer but well-made low-budget suspense meller for good support on duallers.

Hollywood, Feb. 6.

Paramount release of Andrew J. Fenady production. Stars Steven Marlo, Luana Patten, Tom Selden. Directed by Irvin Kershner. Screenplay, Fenady; based on a story by Gordon Hunt and Al Burton; camera, Wallace Kelley; music, Richard Markowitz; editor, Terry Morse. Previewed at the studio, Jan. 29, '59. Running time, **66 MINS.**

Jamie Forbes .... Steven Marlo
Ann Howel .... Luana Patten
Benjie Whitney .... Tom Selden
Tony .... James Chandler
Norm Britt .... Ed Nelson
Dave .... Dan Sheridan
Blonde Woman .... Marjorie Stapp
Rusty Webster .... Miles Stephens
Gas Station Attendant .. Edward Schaaf
American Officer ...... William C. Shaw
Mexican Officer .... Carlo Fiore
Sheriff Parker . Lawrence J. Gelbmann
Roughneck (Oil Field) ...... Dan Blocker
Shorty .... Allen Kramer
Patrolman .... Phillip A. Mansour
Mrs. Howel .... Joan Granville
Other Woman .... Lenore Kingston
Mr. Kingston .... Raymond Guth
Waitress .... Carol Nelson

"The Young Captives" is a straight suspense melodrama that is well done in all departments for a low-budget feature. It has some attempts at pyschological insight into the central character, a mentally disturbed young man, but these explorations are not allowed to slow down the basic story. The Paramount presentation, produced by Andrew J. Fenady and directed by Irvin Kershner, is only the second feature this pair has made, but it shows a sure hand for films. "The Young Captives" will make a strong supporting feature on a double-bill with a more expensive production, or could be the stronger half of an all-exploitation dualler.

Steven Marlo plays the young man with the warped background who is picked up by eloping Luana Patten and Tom Selden. Marlo has already killed one man and is ready to kill again whenever he feels pressures developing that he cannot understand. There is, in the screenplay by Fenady, from a story by Gordon Hunt and Al Burton, a well-developed situation of double jeopardy. Miss Patten and Selden are attempting to elude possible police intervention to avert their marriage. Marlo convinces them that his accompanying them will confuse such investigators. Although the couple grows increasingly apprehensive about Marlo, they face the dilemma of which danger is more eminent, Marlo or the police.

Fenady's screenplay is accurate in its presentation of the psycho killer and interesting in this character's effect on his captives, the young lovers. Kershner's direction sets his characters early and well, remains true to them as the story develops, and correctly concentrates on action.

Performances are capable, particularly those by Marlo, Miss Patten and Selden. They manage to achieve some pathos and depth in their playing despite the accent on action. Others who register include James Chandler, Ed Nelson, Dan Sheridan, Marjorie Stapp and Miles Stephens, although some are called on for some rather extraneous philosophy that is dramatically unnecessary since it has already by implied in the straight action.

Wallace Kelley's camera work, mostly location exteriors, captures the documentary atmosphere without losing technical clarity, and Terry Morse's editing maintains pace. Richard Markowitz' score, particularly the use of progressive jazz, is good. *Powe.*

Forbidden Island
(COLOR)

Routine but with off-beat color and underwater photography.

Hollywood, Feb. 5.

Columbia release of a Charles B. Griffith production. Stars Jon Hall; features Nan Adams, John Farrow, Jonathan Haze, Greigh Phillips. Producer-director-writer, Charles B. Griffith; camera (Columbia Color), Gilbert Warrenton; underwater camera, Lamar Boren; editor, Jerome Thoms; sound, Ben Winkler; music, Alexander Laszlo. Previewed at the studio, Feb. 5, '59. Running time, **66 MINS.**

Dave Courtney	Jon Hall
Joanne	Nan Adams
Stuart Godfrey	John Farrow
Jack Mautner	Jonathan Haze
Dean Pike	Greigh Phillips
Fermin Fry	Dave "Howdy" Peters
Raul Estoril	Tookie Evans
Marty	Martin Denny
Cal Priest	Bob LaVarre
Mike	Bill Anderson
Abe	Abraham Kaluna

"Forbidden Island," because of its color, alluring locations and its fascination for skin divers, is an off-beat programmer that will fill the bills. A Charles B. Griffith production for Columbia, it will not be remembered for stirring performances or an unusual storyline, but there is something to be said for a macabre underwater tussle with a decaying skelton.

Griffith wrote, produced and directed this Jon Hall starrer which was filmed above the water in Hawaii and below the water off Florida. The transitions are invisible.

Hall leads a bevy of peacetime frogmen who are hired by John Farrow to dive for an emerald lost in a shipwreck. One of the divers finds a skelton with Farrow's belt still knotted around her bony neck, and Farrow louses up his aqualung to get him out of the way. He leads a second diver to think Hall killed the first diver for the emerald, and in an ensuing battle, the second diver accidentally kills himself with an underwater flare. Farrow tries to escape, popping off his six-shooter some nine or 10 times before it empties, and he finally kills himself when his jimmy-hook catches his own throat instead of his intended victim's.

There is, of course, a love interest—Nan Adams, a substantially endowed young lady—who, after being blackmailed into pretending to be Farrow's wife, is finally shot by him. To be sure, she ends up only wounded, and Hall gets the girl.

Joining Hall, Miss Adams and Farrow in the cast are Jonathan Haze and Greigh Phillips, who perform admirably.

Although several of the sequences were not properly matched in the review print, Gilbert Warrenton did an overall fine job of Columbia Color lensing, and Lamar Boren's underwater photography is outstanding. Editing by Jerome Thoms and sound by Ben Winkler are capably done.

One of the film's most notable assets is an interesting, sometimes exciting musical score by Alexander Laszlo, with a title song by Martin Denny. *Ron.*

Night of the Quarter Moon
(C-SCOPE)

Miscegenation-themed romance and courtroom melodrama starring Julie London and John Drew Barrymore. Exploitable but spotty returns indicated.

Hollywood, Feb. 5.

Metro release of Albert Zugsmith production. Stars Julie London, John Drew Barrymore, Anna Kashfi, Dean Jones, Agnes Moorehead, Nat "King" Cole. Directed by Hugo Haas. Screenplay, Frank Davis, Franklin Coen; camera, Ellis Carter; editor, Ben Lewis; music, Albert Glasser. Previewed Feb. 4, '59. Running time, **95 MINS.**

Ginny Nelson	Julie London
Roderic (Chuck) Nelson	John Drew Barrymore
Cy Robbin	Nat King Cole
Maria Robbin	Anna Kashfi
Lexington Nelson	Dean Jones
Cornelia Nelson	Agnes Moorehead
The Singer	Cathy Crosby
Hotel Manager	Ray Anthony
Sergeant Bragan	Jackie Coogan
The Neighbor	Charles Chaplin Jr.
The Headwaiter	Billy Daniels
Asa Tully	James Edwards
Captain O'Sullivan	Arthur Shields
Clinton Page	Edward Andrews
The Judge	Robert Warwick
The Hostess	Marguerite Belafonte
The Girl in the Woods	Bobi Byrnes

"Night of the Quarter Moon" is an attempt at controversy, fairly well premised but burdened with a trite story. Its miscegenation theme, particularly in light of past film excursions into this realm, is likely to militate against general acceptance. Despite certain exploitation values which manifest themselves, only spotty biz is indicated.

The Albert Zugsmith production touches on the love story of a wealthy young San Franciscan and a quadroon whom he meets and marries in Mexico. The social angle appears in the refusal of both the man's fashionable family and others to accept the one-quarter Negro bride, after her dark blood is revealed. Conflict arises when the mother in a spectacular court trial attempts to have the marriage annulled.

The Frank Davis-Franklin Coen screenplay leaves spectator with the feeling that in the windup, as the young couple departs the courtroom arm-in-arm, their problems instead of being ended are only just beginning.

Julie London and John Drew Barrymore handle the two principal roles well enough, despite certain uninspired direction by Hugo Haas who fails to give the courtroom sequences especially the punch they needed. Agnes Moorehead as the mother who high-handedly brings annulment proceedings despite her son's opposition delivers her usual competent performance, Dean Jones is okay as her other son, and Anna Kashfi and Nat "King" Cole are good as the beleaguered wife's cousin and uncle. Cole socks over one vocal number, "To Whom It May Concern."

Smoothest portrayal in cast is offered by James Edwards as the Negro lawyer defending the young wife. Veteran Robert Warwick is persuasive as the judge. Appearing in brief roles are Jackie Coogan, Ray Anthony, Billy Daniels, Charles Chaplin Jr., and Cathy Crosby makes her screen bow warbling "Blue Moon" in a nitery sequence.

Technical departments are satisfactorily handled, with Ellis Carter on camera; music, Albert Glasser; art direction, William A. Horning and Malcolm Brown; editing, Ben Lewis. *Whit.*

Up Periscope
(COLOR-WARNERSCOPE)

Romantis underseas meller. Good b.o.

Warner Bros. release of Aubrey Schenck production. Stars James Garner, Edmond O'Brien. Directed by Gordon Douglas. Screenplay, Richard Landau; based on a novel by Robb White; camera (Technicolor), Carl Guthrie; music, Ray Heindorf; editor, John F. Schreyer. Previewed at the studio, Jan. 27, '59. Running time, **111 MINS.**

Ken	James Garner
Stevenson	Edmond O'Brien
Sally	Andra Martin
Malone	Alan Hale
Carney	Carleton Carpenter
Mount	Frank Gifford
Doherty	William Leslie
Peck	Richard Bakalyan
Ash	Edward Byrnes
Floyd	Sean Garrison
York	Henry Kulky
Murphy	George Crise

A straight war adventure film, told straight and mostly true, "Up Periscope" has humor and action well-mixed to provide an interesting and entertaining feature. The top names do not appear to be very strong for a picture of this class (million plus), and the Warner Bros. presentation is a little long (almost two hours) for its likely bookings. But these are the only two possible major objections to Aubrey Schenck's production. "Up Periscope" should do very well.

Edmond O'Brien plays a submarine commander in Richard Landau's screenplay, a man who goes so completely by the book that he finally sends a letter to the Navy Board recommending himself for censure when he exceeds his instructions. Based on a novel by Robb White, the story has two plot complications, O'Brien's devotion to the letter of his command, and James Garner's exploits in a mission behind Japanese lines. The two come into conflict when O'Brien must decide whether to relax for once and allow a little leeway to insure getting Garner away from his sabotage errand on a Japanese-held Pacific island.

Some of this is slightly familiar, i.e., the crew's misunderstanding of O'Brien's martinet tactics, his refusal to tangle with the enemy, etc. But Gordon Douglas' direction of the Landau script has a fresh and lively feel. He plays the good humor for contrast and effect against the tenseness and excitement, and creates full characters than are usually realized in dramas of this sort. Douglas also achieves good tension in a long sequence near the end where Garner is virtually alone on the screen for around 15 minutes as he sneaks to the Japanese island and accomplishes his mission.

The production, in WarnerScope and Technicolor, is strong on its realistic scenes inside the submarine and in the frogman sequences where Garner goes underwater. It avoids most of the cliches of a submarine picture and seems to have lagged only in the interpolation of a flashback dream sequence that doesn't help much. The ending, where the sub returns victoriously to Pearl Harbor to find wives, sweethearts, etc., all standing on the pier cheering their men home seems a little unbelievable, considering it's wartime. This rosy romanticism also damages the straight action suspense and climax so well achieved previously. Despite these reservations, "Up Periscope" is a satisfying film, and with Warner Bros.' planned promotion campaign, should make good returns.

James Garner, a husky and good-looking young leading man, shows a nice flair for comedy that hasn't been too evident previously, and handles himself well in all situations. Edmond O'Brien, looking better than he has in some time, gives his role considerable depth and interest. Others in the case who make an impression are Alan Hale, Carleton Carpenter, Frank Gifford, William Leslie and Edward Byrnes.

Carl Guthrie's photography, in WarnerScope and Technicolor, is good and particularly interesting in the underwater sequences. John F. Schreyer's editing is first-rate. *Powe.*

The Lady Is a Square
(BRITISH)

Amiable, amusing romantic-comedy drama helped by Frankie Vaughan's songs.

London, Feb. 3.

Associated-British release of a Wilcox-Neagle (Herbert Wilcox) production. Stars Anna Neagle, Frankie Vaughan, Janette Scott. Directed by Herbert Wilcox. Screenplay, Harold Purcell and Pamela Bower; dialog, Nicholas Phipps; camera, Gordon Dines; editor, Basil Warren; music, Wally Stott. At Warner Theatre, London. Running time, **100 MINS.**

Frances Baring .... Anna Neagle
Johnny Burns .... Frankie Vaughan
Joanna Baring .... Janette Scott
Freddy .... Anthony Newley
Charles .... Wilfrid Hyde White
Greenslade .... Christopher Rhodes
Derek .... Kenneth Cope
Mrs. Eady .... Josephine Fitzgerald
Spolenski .... Harold Kaskett
Fergusson .... John Le Mesurier
Harry Shuttleworth .... Ted Lune

With "The Lady is a Square," Herbert Wilcox has whipped up a shrewd concoction of romance, comedy and music, with the pic having a foot in both camps—the "pop" and classical music fields. The names of the three stars, Anna Neagle, Frankie Vaughan and Janette Scott will insure British b.o. success. Though the yarn may be a bit slim for American consumption the growing popularity of Vaughan in the U. S. should help this pic.

Wilcox has mixed his ingredients with an eye on the two age groups but it is probable that the youngsters get the better of the deal. The yarn has Miss Neagle as the financially embarrassed widow of a concert impresario. Determined to launch a series of classical concerts under the baton of an international conductor, she is still up against the problem of finding the coin. Vaughan is a young pop singer who, falling for Miss Neagle's daughter (Janette Scott), poses as a piano tuner to get into the house. The ruse is soon discovered and, to help Miss Neagle out, he becomes her butler.

The widow's intolerance of popular music makes it difficult for the young couple to continue their flowering romance. However, after a series of misunderstandings, a Hit Parade disk made by Vaughan enables him to raise the cash to pay the conductor's fees and the widow's outstanding bills. When she discovers this, she suddenly decides that maybe pop music isn't so bad after all. It all finishes with her jiving like a teenager and proving that "the lady's not a square."

Once this fairly implausible yarn is accepted in the escapist spirit intended, there is quite a lot to amuse and entertain in "Square." Miss Neagle, as the widow who doesn't dig modern music, is the essence of well-bred culture while Vaughan continues to establish himself as one of the most vital, likeable personalities in British pix. He displays a neat comedy ability if not proving his ability as a dramatic actor. Janette Scott has little to do except moon over Vaughan but does this with charm.

A supporting performance which virtually steals the picture comes from Anthony Newley, an up-and-coming young actor who is making a habit of thefting scenes. He plays a song-plugger and manager to Vaughan with a wry humor and brashness. It is an exuberant, funny piece of work. Wilfrid Hyde White, suave and bland as ever as a financial adviser; Christopher Rhodes, cast as an impresario, and Harold Kaskett, as a voluble excitable German conductor, also help the film along. A new comedian, Ted Lune, is dragged in for one scene. Though he is funny enough, the scene seems out of place.

Musically, the film is alive throughout. The British National Youth Orch plays brilliantly both on its own and when accompanying Vaughan as he sings Handel's "Largo." Vaughan also has a couple of other numbers which he may well turn into hits. He also gives a new look to the Ray Noble oldie, "Love Is The Sweetest Thing." Scenes at the Royal Festival Hall, in a recording studio and in Tin Pan Alley are authentically put over with good lensing by Gordon Dines. A production highspot shows Vaughan doing his act at "The Talk of the Town," new theatre-restaurant in the West End.

Screenplay by Harold Purcell and Pamela Bower has a number of loose ends. For instance, there no real explanation of why the prejudiced Miss Neagle should turn up at this theatre-cafe, and thus discover Vaughan to be a singer. The dialog has some static patches. But, all in all, "The Lady Is A Square" contains enough of the ingredients of pop entertainment to get well into the boxoffice groove.   *Rich.*

The Mating Game
(C-SCOPE—COLOR)

Broad and racy romantic farce. Good names, good performances, good b.o.

Hollywood, Feb. 13.

Metro release of Philip Barry Jr. production. Stars Debbie Reynolds, Tony Randall. Paul Douglas; features Fred Clark, Una Merkel. Directed by George Marshall. Screenplay, William Roberts; based on the novel, "The Darling Buds of May," by H. E. Bates; camera (Metrocolor), Robert Bronner; music, Jeff Alexander; editor, John McSweeney Jr. Previewed at the Hollywood Paramount Theatre, Feb. 13, '59. Running time, 97 MINS.
Mariette Larkin .... Debbie Reynolds
Lorenzo Charlton .... Tony Randall
Pop Larkin .... Paul Douglas
Oliver Kelsey .... Fred Clark
Ma Larkin................. Una Merkel
Wendell Burnshaw ..... Philip Ober
Rev. Osgood .... Philip Coolidge
Bigelow .... Charles Lane
Chief Guthrie .... Trevor Bardette
Barney .... Bill Smith
DeGroot .... Addison Powell
Lee Larkin .... Rickey Murray
Grant Larkin .... Donald Losby
Victoria Larkin .... Cheryl Bailey
Susan Larkin .... Caryl Bailey

Figure a combination of "You Can't Take It With You" and elements of "Tobacco Road," and it is a pretty fair indication of what "The Mating Game" is about and how the jokes are played. This romantic farce from Metro is as broad as its CinemaScope projection and as racy as anything seen to date. It is a funny show, but by conventional reckoning it's not for the kiddies.

The production of Philip Barry Jr.—his film bow—is based on H. E. Bates' English novel, "The Darling Buds of May," which was a light, farcical tilt at the welfare state in Britain. Adapted for the screen by William Roberts, it becomes an American situation chiefly involving free enterprise versus the internal revenue department, or—in a modern treatment—the moonshiners versus the revenuers.

Basically the premise of "The Mating Game" is a stock one in American literature, and is probably universal. Despite its familiarity, there is lots of fun in it of a fairly simple-minded nature.

Tony Randall plays a tax agent assigned to investigate the Maryland farm family headed by Paul Douglas and Una Merkel. Douglas has never filed an income tax return or paid a tax. His case comes to the revenue department's attention when a rich neighbor informs on him in the hopes that he will be jailed or bankrupted and removed from the landscape.

Randall, whose neat black homburg covers a CPA-mind, discovers Douglas lives in an economic morass. Attempting to track down Douglas' system of finance, he discovers a typical transaction involves the trade of a ton of manure for a couple of hogs, with the hogs swapped for a refrigerator and the refrigerator traded for an electric organ. How much profit does all this represent? Douglas doesn't know. He gave the organ to the church.

Douglas gets Randall predictably drunk, and Randall is predictably smitten with one of the Douglas-Merkel offspring, hoydenish Debbie Reynolds. She is a toothsome child of nature who is taking care of the mating of the farm stock when she isn't wrestling in the hay with some of the livelier neighbor boys. Randall's apoplectic superior, Fred Clark, finally arrives to take over, after Randall has been suitably corrupted. Clark figures Douglas owes $50,000 in back taxes. But Randall then figures the government owes Douglas some $14,000,000 on a claim dating from the Civil War. Douglas has no use for money and agrees to forget the whole thing if the government will be equally forgiving about all past and future taxes.

Most of this is foreseeable farce, and much of it is done with allusions to sex, regarding both humans and animals, that will leave no doubt in any minds whatsoever, except the most unawakened. Most of it plays well due to George Marshall's expert direction and some of it—the cleanest portions—are pure hilarity.

Miss Reynolds, duplicating in a way the sort of role she had in "Tammy and the Bachelor," is very good. Randall, somewhat uncomfortable as a straight actor, is brilliant in his comedy scenes, particularly an athletic drunk sequence and its aftermath. Douglas is capable and Fred Clark reprises his now familiar bit as a sort of later-day Edgar Kennedy. Una Merkel gets her share of laughs and others who contribute include Philip Ober, Philip Coolidge and Charles Lane.

Robert Bronner's camera work keeps the photography bright and clean for the comedy, and prevents the CinemaScope screen from seeming unwieldy or heavy on the reaction jokes, the double-takers, etc. Jeff Alexander's sprightly music is a good score, aimed at highlighting the action. There is a title song by Charles Strouse and Lee Adams, sung by Miss Reynolds, that, for a change, fits the title and the film.   *Powe.*

Rio Bravo
(COLOR—SONGS

Topnotch western with names of John Wayne, Dean Martin and Ricky Nelson to run up slick grosses.

Hollywood, Feb. 11.

Warner Bros. release of Howard Hawks production. Stars John Wayne, Dean Martin, Ricky Nelson, Angie Dickinson, Walter Brennan, Ward Bond; features John Russell, Pedro Gonzales-Ganzales, Estelita Rodriguez, Claude Akins. Directed by Hawks. Screenplay, Jules Furthman, Leigh Brackett; from short story by B. H. McCampbell; camera (Technicolor), Russell Harlan; editor, Folmar Blangsted; music, Dimitri Tiomkin. Previewed Feb. 10, '59. Running time, 140 MINS.
John T. Chance........... John Wayne
Dude .... Dean Martin
Colorado .... Ricky Nelson
Feathers .... Angie Dickinson
Stumpy .... Walter Brennan
Pat Wheeler .... Ward Bond
Nathan Burdette .... John Russell
Carlos .... Pedro Gonzales
Consuela .... Estelita Rodriguez
Joe Burdette .... Claude Akins
Jake .... Malcolm Atterbury
Harold .... Harry Carey Jr.
Matt Harris .... Bob Steele

"Rio Bravo" is a big, brawling western with enough action and marquee voltage to assure hefty reception at the boxoffice. Casting of Dean Martin and Ricky Nelson with such vet range stalwarts as John Wayne and Walter Brennan is a smart showmanship move bound to pay off in an expanded market, and performances generally are superior to the average western. While somewhat long, interest is sustained and net effect is one of the better class oaters of the year.

Howard Hawks as producer-director turned out picture under his Armada Productions banner for Warner Bros. release, and gives distribution company some highly-seasoned Technicolor footage which may be handily exploited. Both Martin and Nelson, latter making his first feature appearance since a

couple of moppet parts years ago, play gunman roles, offbeat casting but coming off in slick fashion. They're in for a couple of songs, too, which may be a little out of character for the action but certain to attract and surefire ingredients. They pair up on "My Pony, My Rifle, and Me," cleffed by Dimitri Tiomkin and Paul Francis Webster, and Nelson is on with "Cindy." One of the true assets of picture is Tiomkin's unusual score, directed mainly at guitars, which helps set the mood and has a potent effect in punching over the action.

Script by Jules Furthman and Leigh Brackett, based on the B. H. McCampbell short story, gets off to one of the fastest slam-bang openings on record. Within 90 seconds Wayne, a fast-shooting sheriff, is clubbed, another man knocked out and a third man murdered. Plot thereafter revolves around Wayne's attempts to hold the murderer, brother of the most powerful rancher in the area, until the arrival some days hence of the U.S. marshal. He's up against the rancher utilizing gunman tactics to free the jailed killer.

Hawks makes handsome use of force in logically unravelling his hard-hitting narrative, creating suspense at times and occasionally inserting lighter moments to give variety to his unfoldment. Wayne delivers a faithful portrayal of the peace officer who must fight his battle with the aid of only two deputies. One of these is Martin, his ex-deputy who attempts to kick off a two-year drunk to help his friend, becoming his old fast-shooting self eventually but only after some pretty difficult times in throwing off the shakes. Role is one of thesp's most interesting. The other deputy is Brennan, a cantankerous old cripple assigned to guard the prisoner in the jail. Brennan makes of this character a comic masterpiece, one of his top performances.

Nelson, as a baby-faced two-gunman, is finely convincing as he throws in with Wayne in helping him fend off the rancher's efforts to seize the killer, and Ward Bond makes the most of his brief appearance as a friend of Wayne's, killed because of this friendship. In for distaff interest and with more legitimate footage than usual in a western is Angie Dickinson, a looker and one of the most interesting newcomers in many a day, fashioned into an important key character who delivers in every way. John Russell as the rancher, Pedro Gonzalez-Gonzalez the hotel Pedro Gonzalez-Gonzalez the hotel owner, and Claude Akins, the killer

Technical credits lend strong support, headed by Russell Harlan's color photography, editing by Folmar Blangsted and art direction by Leo K. Kuter. *Whit.*

The Angry Hills
(BRITISH)

Rather confused but entertaining war yarn, slickly directed and good performances by cast headed by Robert Mitchum; sound b.o. prospects.

London, Feb. 17.

Metro release of a Raymond Stross production. Stars Robert Mitchum, Stanley Baker, Elisabeth Mueller, Gia Scala. Directed by Robert Aldrich. Screenplay, A. I. Bezzerides, from Leon Uris's book; camera, Stephen Dade; editor, Peter Tanner; music, Richard Bennett. Previewed at Metro Private Theatre, London. Running time, **105 MINS.**

Mike Morrison .... Robert Mitchum
Lisa .... Elisabeth Mueller
Heisler .... Stanley Baker
Kleftheria .... Gia Scala
Stergiou .... Donald Wolfit
Andreas .... Kieron Moore
Tassos .... Theodore Bikel
Chesney .... Sebastian Cabot
Leonidas .... Peter Illing
Ray Tayllr .... Leslie Phillips
Colonel Oberg .... Marius Goring

The endless parade of war pix continues with "The Angry Hills," this one being set in Greece. It's a rather confused yarn but has the merit of good direction by Robert Aldrich and some very competent performances. "Hills" could be a useful b.o. bet in average houses. Producer Raymond Stross has shrewdly widened his marquee appeal by adding Italian Gia Scala and German Elisabeth Mueller to the cast already adorned by Robert Mitchum and Britain's popular Stanley Baker.

Mitchum plays an American war correspondent who is hunted by Gestapo chief Stanley Baker and fifth columnist Theadore Bikel when he arrives in Athens as Greece is about to fall to the Nazis. Baker and Bikel want Mitchum because he has a list of 16 Greek underground leaders which he is conveying to British intelligence in London.

He is helped by Gia Scala and also by Miss Mueller, both of whom fall in love with Mitchum. Eventually he manages to escape from Greece with Miss Mueller's two children, who Baker was using as a hostage.

Both Baker and Mitchum give very sound performances. Elisabeth Mueller brings a radiant charm to the part of the widow who nearly betrays Mitchum but eventually assists him. Donald Wolfit, Sebastian Cabot, Peter Illing, Marius Goring and Keiron Moore are among those who bring distinction to smaller roles.

A. I. Bezzerides' screenplay falters towards the end when the love complications arise but he tells the story briskly and well. Robert Aldrich's direction has been given some slick editing by Peter Tanner while Stephen Dade's lensing has made the utmost use of the Greek scenery. *Rich.*

Ride Lonesome
(COLOR—C'SCOPE)

High-grade oater.

Hollywood, Feb. 6.

Columbia release of Ranown Production. Star Randolph Scott; costars Karen Steele. Executive producer. Harry Joe Brown; producer-director, Budd Boetticher; screenplay, Burt Kennedy; camera, Charles Lawton Jr.; music, Heinz Roemheld; editor, Jerome Thoms. Previewed at the studio, Feb. 2, '59. Running time, **74 MINS.**

Ben Brigade .... Randolph Scott
Carrie Lane .... Karen Steele
Sam Boone .... Parnell Roberts
Billy John .... James Best
Frank .... Lee Van Cleef
Wid .... James Coburn
Charlie .... Dyke Johnson
Indian Chief .... Boyd Stockman

"Ride Lonesome" is another good western from the Ranown Production team of Randolph Scott and Harry Joe Brown. It is a medium budget film and above the general run. Budd Boetticher, who produced and directed, had a tough, honest screenplay by Burt Kennedy, and he has given it perception and tension.

The Columbia release has Randolph Scott as a bounty hunter whose interest in a young murderer, James Best, seems to be solely the money he will collect for his delivery. Along the way, he picks up a young widow, Karen Steele, and two feckless outlaws, Parnell Roberts and James Coburn. Soon Best's brother, Lee Van Cleef, is trailing them with his own band, intent on rescuing Best.

"Ride Lonesome" has several good plots and sub-plots going for it, creating a chase melodrama that is often a chase-within-a-chase. There is Scott's inscrutable reason for hunting men for their bounty. There is a conflict between him and Roberts and Coburn. This latter pair is tired of larking and want to settle down. If they, instead of Scott, can turn Best in, they will get an amnesty for their past misdeeds. The only one who can lose in all this is Best, who does, when he is turned in by Roberts and Coburn, after Scott settles an old score with Van Cleef.

Kennedy has used genuine speech of the frontier and some offhand, often rather grim humor, to give the screenplay additional interest where the pursuit portions necessarily lag. Boetticher and his cast handle it well, only occasionally overreaching in brief scenes where Miss Steele's sex seems stressed beyond reason.

Scott does a good job as the taciturn and misunderstood hero, but the two standouts are Best as the giggling killer and Roberts as the sardonic outlaw who wants to get away to a new start. They got good lines to work with and they give them and their characterizations full treatment. Miss Steele doesn't seem quite suited to her role, although she is pleasant. Lee Van Cleef, Dyke Johnson and Boyd Stockman do capably with smaller parts.

Charles Lawton Jr.'s photography, in Eastman color by Pathe and in CinemaScope, captures some stunning location shots, a combination of semi-desert and mountains, often in unusual natural lighting. Jerome Thoms' editing is first-rate. Some of Lawton's work is not helped by a musical score that is trite and the sound quality which is uneven. *Powe.*

Too Many Crooks
(BRITISH)

Dim-witted, minor crooks up to their ears in comedy trouble.

London, Feb. 10.

Rank (Mario Zampi) production and release. Stars Terry-Thomas, George Cole, Brenda De Banzie, Bernard Bresslaw. Directed by Mario Zampi. Screenplay, Michael Pertwee; camera, Stanley Pavey; editor, Mill Lewthwaite; music, Stanley Black. At Rank Private Theatre, London. Running time, **87 MINS.**

Billy Gordon .... Terry-Thomas
Fingers .... George Cole
Lucy .... Brenda De Banzie
Snowdrop .... Bernard Bresslaw
Sid .... Sidney James
Whisper .... Joe Melia
Charmaine .... Vera Day
Secretary .... Delphi Lawrence
Magistrate .... John Le Mesurier
Solicitor .... Sydney Tafler
Angela .... Rosalie Ashley
Tommy .... Nicholas Parsons
Girl Journalist ...... Vilma Ann Leslie
Gordon's Mother .... Edie Martin
Swarthy Man .... Tutte Lemkow
Inspector Jensen .... John Stuart
Fire Policeman .... Terry Scott

Mario Zampi's brisk comedy, "Too Many Crooks," has been artfully constructed in the search of yocks by Michael Pertwee, a skilled purveyor of the kind of plot, situation, characterization and dialog needed for this sort of unambitious, happy-go-lucky lark. Satire, slapstick and light comedy are mingled, sometimes uneasily. Much of the pic is irresistibly funny, but it occasionally lags.

"Crooks" will certainly satisfy most U.K. houses in search of laffs, since it features many favorite British performers. But the stellar lineup carries too few big guns to make it a certain click in the American market.

Pertwee has infused some neat twists into a basically amusing idea. A gang of four smalltime crooks, blunderingly led by their dim-wit chief, disastrously bungle some minor jobs. They set their sights higher. They plan to rob a shady tycoon who keeps his money in hard cash in his office, home and other hideouts.

When this fails, they plan to kidnap his daughter. Unfortunately, they land up, instead, with his wife. Their humiliation is that this seems a splendid idea to the tycoon, who refuses to pay any ransom, is unmoved by their threats to murder her and regards it as a great chance of continuing his shenanigans with his mistress. Equally humiliated is the wife, who determines to teach him a lesson.

This framework provides opportunities for a number of hilarious sequences. The "snatching" done by the gang posing as undertakers, with their victim drugged in a runaway hearse; a court scene; and attempts to rescue money from a blazing house.

Terry-Thomas, over-acting unmercifully, is the rich victim of the gang's attentions and his performance has some riotous moments. George Cole, Sidney James, Joe Melia and Bernard Bresslaw form the gang and contribute much to the fun. Unfortunately, all of these players are more acceptable in small doses, rather than in carrying a film on their own shoulders. James, who never fails to make impact, is the best of the quartet. Bresslaw, a tv character who has rocketed to the top, is a dim-witted ex-wrestler.

Vera Day, a trim "gangster's moll"; Brenda De Banzie as the wife who turns the tables on her erring husband; Delphi Lawrence, as a secretary; John Le Mesurier, as a bewildered magistrate; and Sydney Tafler, a too-smart attorney, all provide effective cameos. Stanley Pavey has lensed some London and location scenes very well. Mario Zampi's direction never lets up in his eager search for laughter. *Rich.*

First Man Into Space
(BRITISH)

Competent science-fantasy adventure film for duallers.

Hollywood, Feb. 6.

Metro release of Amalgamated production. Stars Marshall Thompson and Marla Landi. Produced by John Croydon and Charles Vetter Jr. Directed by Robert Day. Screenplay, John C. Cooper and Lance Z. Hargreaves; based on a story by Wyott Ordung; camera, Geoffrey Faithfull; music, Buxton Orr; editor, Peter Mayhew. Previewed at the studio, Jan. 29, '59. Running time, **77 MINS.**

Commander C. E.
Prescott .... Marshall Thompson
Tia Francesca .... Marla Landi
Lt. Dan Prescott .... Bill Edwards
Capt. Ben Richards ...... Robert Ayres
Wilson .... Bill Nagy
Dr. Paul von Essen .... Carl Jaffe
Mexican Consul .... Roger Delgado
State Dept. Official ...... John McLaren
Witney .... Richard Shaw
Clancy .... Bill Nick

A British production being released by Metro, "First Man Into Space" is a good entry in the exploitation class. It has excitement and some genuine horror. It is generally well-made and suffers only from a tendency to get cosmic in philosophy as well as geography.

The screenplay by John C. Cooper and Lance Z. Hargreaves, based on a story by Wyott Ordung,

is located in New Mexico, at a U.S. missile base. (An interesting technical point, since the picture was filmed entirely in Britain.) Marshall Thompson plays the U.S. officer in charge of the project, which is testing pilot-manned rockets. Thompson's brother, Bill Edwards, is the pilot on one of these space-bound vessels. Once launched, Edwards gets infected by thin air hysteria or derringdo and takes the ship beyond its scheduled altitude ceiling. When he returns to earth he is coated with some mysterious substance composed of meteor dust and has been changed into a blood-sucking monster. There is the usual pursuit and eventual capture of the zombie.

Since these films are stories of effect rather than character or plot, there is little point in evaluating the performances. The cast performs acceptably, and is generally successful in employing American accents. Despite the best efforts, an occasional clipped syllable slips through, but the verisimilitude is mostly maintained. Thompson, Marla Landi, Robert Ayres, Bill Edwards, Bill Nagy and Carl Jaffe are those chiefly involved, and handle their assignments capably.

John Croydon and Charles Vetter Jr. produced the film, and Robert Day directed. One unusual aspect is that it was shot in the old 1.66 frame.   *Powe.*

La Loi
(The Law)
(FRENCH—ITALIAN)
Paris, Feb. 10.
Corona release of Groupe Ves Quatre-Titanus production. Stars Gina Lollobrigida, Yves Montand; features Pierre Brasseur, Melina Mercouri, Marcello Mastroianni, Raf Mattioli, Paola Stoppa. Written and directed by Jules Dassin from the novel by Roger Vailland; dialog, Francoise Giroud; camera, Otello Martelli; editor, Roger Dwyre. At Colisee, Paris. Running time, **125 MINS.**
Marietta .... Gina Lollobrigida
Matteo .... Yves Montand
Cesare .... Pierre Brasseur
Lucrezia .... Melina Mercouri
Francesco .... Raf Mattioli
Tonio .... Paola Stoppa

Jules Dassin, Yank director, had a general hit in America with his "Rififi" and a prestige art success with his "He Who Must Die." Now, in his third foreign feature, he combines the dexterity and picaresque qualities of the former with the more ambitious qualities of the latter. The result is an uneven pic, yet with enough entertainment and exploitation facets to make this a possibility for U.S.

Dassin has adapted a French prizewinning novel and told a tale of a small Mediterranean town which serves as a crucible for a study of power. He details how people come to be in a position to dictate to others by either invested powers or those gotten from the weapons of desire, fear, knowhow etc.

Tale revolves around a desirable morsel, Gina Lollobrigida, who is coveted by (a) the local squire, (b) a gangster, (c) her brother-in-law and (d) others. She picks a visiting engineer to be her husband. In this is woven a fabric of passion and related doings plus a game called "The Law" in which one person can dictate to the others and say and do whatever he pleases.

Well mounted by Dassin and well acted by most of the actors. With the added name of Miss Lollobrigida, for U.S. familiarity though the Italian beauty plays her role too much in the breezy vein of "Bread, Love and Fantasy."

Melina Mercouri is more in tune as an aging woman whose liaison with a young boy leads to tragedy.

Yves Montand, Paolo Stoppa, Raf Mattioli and especially Pierre Brasseur are all assets as the rest of the players involved in this offbeat tale.   *Mosk.*

Some Like It Hot
(SONGS)

Hilarious farce-comedy marks return of Marilyn Monroe. Great entertainment and a winner with a zing.

United Artists release of Ashton Productions presenting a Mirisch Co picture, a Billy Wilder production. Stars Marilyn Monroe, Tony Curtis, Jack Lemmon; co-stars George Raft, Pat O'Brien, Joe E. Brown; features Nehemiah Persoff, Joan Shawlee, Billy Gray, George E. Stone, Dave Barry, Mike Mazurki, Henry Wilson. Directed by Wilder; screenplay, Wilder and I. A. L. Diamond; suggested by story by R. Thoeren and M. Logan; camera, Charles Lang; background score, Adolph Deutsch; songs supervised by Matty Malneck; editor, Arthur Schmidt. Previewed at Loew's Lexington Theatre, N.Y., Feb. 5, '59. Running time, **105 MINS.**
Sugar .... Marilyn Monroe
Joe .... Tony Curtis
Jerry .... Jack Lemmon
Spats .... George Raft
Mulligan .... Pat O'Brien
Osgood .... Joe E. Brown
Bonaparte .... Nehemiah Persoff
Sue .... Joan Shawlee
Poliakoff .... Billy Gray
Toothpick .... George E. Stone
Beinstock .... Dave Barry
Spats' Henchmen .... Mike Mazurki,
                          Harry Wilson
Dolores .... Beverly Wills
Nellie .... Barbara Drew
Paradise .... Edward G. Robinson Jr.

"Some Like It Hot," directed in masterly style by Billy Wilder, is probably the funniest picture of recent memory. It's a whacky, clever, farcical comedy that starts off like a firecracker and keeps on throwing off lively sparks till the very end.

Pictures like this, with a sense of humor that is as broad as it can be sophisticated, come along only infrequently. Add to this the attraction of Marilyn Monroe, returning to the screen after a two year absence in a part that's tailor-made for her particular talents, topnotch performances by Tony Curtis and Jack Lemmon, and the directorial brilliance of Wilder, and the concoction becomes irresistible.

Even so, the film has faults. It's too long, for one, being a small joke milked like a dairy; one or two scenes skirt the limits of good taste. But who'll care?

Story revolves around the age-old theme of men masquerading as women. Curtis and Lemmon escape from a Chicago nightclub that's being raided, witness the St. Valentine's Day massacre and "escape" into the anonymity of a girl band by dressing up as femme musicians. This leads to the obvious complications, particularly since Curtis meets Miss Monroe (ukulele player, vocalist and gin addict) and falls for her. Lemmon, in turn, is propositioned by an addle-brained millionaire.

While romance blossoms in Miami, gangsters led by George Raft come on the scene for a convention, and Curtis and Lemmon are recognized. Eventually, Raft & Co. are "rubbed" out. Curtis and Lemmon can then reveal their identity. On this plot skeleton, Wilder has put the flesh of farce. He has done this so deftly that the ridiculous somehow appears possible, and the shocking turns into laugher.

Picture opens with a hearse being chased by police. It's the 1920s. In the coffin repose dozens of bottles of bootleg gin. Bullets rip through hearse and the coffin starts spouting liquid. It's that sort of thing all the way through. Shot of Curtis and Lemmon walking down the station platform dressed as girls, swinging their hips with the anxious look of one who has yet to learn to walk on high heels, brings the house down.

Again, the scene on the train, where the "private" pullman berth party of Lemmon and Miss Monroe

in her nightie is invaded by guzzling dames, represents humor of Lubitsch proportions. And the alternating shots of Miss Monroe trying to "stimulate" Curtis on a couch, while Lemmon and Joe E. Brown live it up on the dance floor, rate as a classic sequence.

To coin a phrase, Marilyn has never looked better. Her performance as "Sugar," the fuzzy blonde who likes saxophone players "and men with glasses," has a deliciously naive quality. She's a comedienne with that combination of sex-appeal and timing that just can't be beat. If, at the time of filming, she was pregnant, and the tight dresses she's asked to wear just don't fit very well, never mind. This gal can take it, and so can the audience.

It's a tossup whether Curtis beats out Lemmon or whether it goes the other way 'round. Both are excellent. Curtis has the upper hand because he can change back and forth from his femme role to that of a fake "millionaire" who woos Miss Monroe. He employs a take-off on Cary Grant, which scores with a bang at first, but tends to lose its appeal as the picture progresses. It's obvious that Curtis enjoys the part of a comedian, and he makes the most of it.

Lemmon here draws a choice assignment. Some of the funniest bits fall to him, such as his announcement that he's "engaged" to Brown. There is about him the air of desperation of any man who might find himself in this kind of unreal predicament. The audience virtually explodes when, after being grabbed by Curtis in his bosomy disguise, Lemmon announces angrily: "I lost one of my chests!"

In the smaller parts, Raft hams it up as a caricature of himself in a "tough guy" gangster bit. Brown is very funny as Osgood, the smitten millionaire, who tries to lure Lemmon on his yacht. Pat O'Brien has a small role as a federal agent, and Nehemiah Persoff acts the role of "Little Bonaparte," who looks very much like Al Capone, and whose boys machinegun Raft and his toughs out of existence.

But, in the final accounting, this is still a director's picture and the Wilder "touch" is indelible, particularly since he collaborated with I. A. L. Diamond on the script. If the action is funny, the lines are there to match it. In fact, laughs often step on oneanother. Of course, in a two-hour picture, the pace is bound to slacken eventually, and it does. But the momentum of this madcap comedy is such that it keeps rolling along, a gay romp that knows just when to draw back before crossing the line to the vulgar.

Miss Monroe performs a couple of songs capably and in the style of the twenties. Charles Lang's photography, in black-and-white, is just fine and so is Adolph Deutsch's background score. Arthur Schmidt's editing makes for smooth continuity and, in several scenes, contributes importantly.

"Some Like It Hot" goes on the premise that a laugh is a laugh, regardless where you find it, and it knows that men dressed as women tickle the risibilities of male and female alike. Since much of it is also clever, the film should provide United Artists with one of its top grossers for the year.
           Hift.

The Shaggy Dog

Pleasant Disney comedy, attractive to family or youngster audiences. Fred MacMurray back to comedy.

Hollywood, Feb. 20.

Buena Vista release of Walt Disney production. Stars Fred MacMurray, Jean Hagen; features Tommy Kirk, Annette Funicello, Tim Considine, Kevin Corcoran. Directed by Charles Barton. Associate producer, Bill Walsh; screenplay, Bill Walsh and Lillie Hayward; suggested by Felix Salten's "The Hound of Florence"; camera, Edward Colman; music, Paul Smith; editor, James D. Ballas. Previewed at the studio, Feb. 20, '59. Running time, 101 MINS.

Mr. Daniels	Fred MacMurray
Mrs. Daniels	Jean Hagen
Wilby Daniels	Tommy Kirk
Allison D'Allessio	Annette Funicello
Buzz Miller	Tim Considine
Moochie Daniels	Kevin Corcoran
Prof. Aldous Plumcutt	Cecil Kellaway
Dr. Mikhail Andrassy	Alexander Scourby
Franceska Andrassy	Roberta Shore
Hanson	James Westerfield
Stefano	Jacques Aubuchon
Thurm	Strother Martin
Kelly	Forrest Lewis
E. P. Hackett	Ned Wever
Capt. Scanlon	Gordon Jones

"The Shaggy Dog" is said to be the first live action film by Walt Disney set in the present. True enough, but Disney, even dealing with a contemporary setting, is unlikely to be confined by conventional limitations of the world, so this farce fantasy bears the familiar Disney trademarks.

The film is about what's called "shape-shifting," and it doesn't refer to the foundation garment. According to the screenplay by Bill Walsh and Lillie Hayward, suggested by Felix Salten's "The Hound of Florence," there used to be a great deal of shifting of shapes, from man to beast and sometimes back.

There are a good many laughs on this simple premise and the script's exploitation of them. The only time the film falters badly is in its choice of a gimmick to get the boy-who-turns-into-a-dog turned back, for good and all, into a boy. According to the legend, it takes an act of heroism on the part of the shifting shape to be restored, finally. Walsh and Miss Hayward have introduced a nest of Soviet spies for him to operate on, and this seems to reach so far into left-ish field, it's silly.

Fred MacMurray plays the father of the two boys chiefly involved, Tommy Kirk and Kevin Corcoran. MacMurray himself is a mailman physically allergic to dogs (a premise that is introduced and then, as far as the mailman bit goes, is just dropped). Young Kirk accidentally transforms himself into a large, shaggy sheep dog when he comes into possession of a spell-casting ring once owned by the Borgias. The jokes are predictable, but often amusing until the spy ring crops up, when things tend to get out of hand.

Charles Barton's comedy direction is expert in almost every instance, although there is a tendency in some scenes to carry a joke just a beat past its payoff, producing a few fizzlers. Whether this is to be blamed on direction or editing, it's impossible to say. But a few of the scenes could be clipped sharper for more hilarious impact and faster transition.

It's a pleasure to see such a master of timing and emphasis as Fred MacMurray back in comedy again, even though he is somewhat limited in his material. Where he has a good line, he shows that he has few peers in this special field of comedy. Jean Hagen, as his wife, is pretty and pleasant in a more or less straight role, while the two boys, Kirk and Considine, handle their comedy nicely. Others who contribute ably include Tim Considine, Annette Funicello, Cecil Kellaway, Alexander Scourby, Roberta Shore, James Westerfield and Gordon Jones.   *Powe.*

Danger Within
(BRITISH)

Prisoner-of-war story, well-acted by a prominent British cast, which provides brisk, exciting entertainment.

London, Feb. 17.

British Lion release of a Colin Lesslie production. Stars Richard Todd, Richard Attenborough, Bernard Lee. Directed by Don Chaffey. Screenplay, Bryan Forbes and Frank Harvey, based on novel by Michael Gilbert; camera, Arthur Grant; editor, John Trumper; music, Francis Chagrin. At Hammer Theatre, London. Running time, 101 MINS.

Lt. Col. David Baird, M.C.	Richard Todd
Lt. Col. Huxley	Bernard Lee
Major Charles Marquand	Michael Wilding
Capt. "Buster" Phillips	Richard Attenborough
Capt. Rupert Callender	Dennis Price
Capt. Roger Byfold	Donald Houston
Capt. Tony Long	William Franklyn
Capt. Pat Foster	Vincent Ball
Capitano Benucci	Peter Arne
Capt. Alfred Piker	Peter Jones
Lt. Meynell	Ronnie Stevens
Lt. Coutoules	Cyril Shaps
Capt. "Tag" Burchnall	Harold Siddons
2nd Lt. Betts-Hanger	Ian Whittaker

"Danger Within" is a smooth, alert prisoner-of-war film which may have lost some impact by lagging a long time behind several other pix of similar setting. But it provides sound, tense entertainment. Its all-male cast carries useful marquee value which makes it worthwhile as a b.o. proposition despite a complete lack of romantic appeal.

Based on a novel by Michael Gilbert, this is a simple yarn of how the efforts of British officers to escape from an Italian p.o.w. camp are constantly thwarted by one of them who is an informer. He is discovered in time for a mass escape of the 400 prisoners on the day Italy capitulates and just before the camp is due to be taken over by the Germans.

Much of the interest in the film comes from the clash of Richard Todd, as a colonel passionately dedicated to the job of escaping, and Bernard Lee, senior British officer, who advocates patience but eventually organizes the breakout. But some interest is unnecessarily dissipated by the "spy" being revealed to the audience too early in the picture.

Director Don Chaffey and lenser Arthur Grant have combined to make an apparently authentic prison camp atmosphere. They are helped by a brisk script by Bryan Forbes and Frank Harvey.

Varied officer-types are skillfully portrayed by a fine cast. Lee gives a realistic performance as the senior officer aware of his responsibilities while Todd makes a useful foil as the impatient, disgruntled character who does not appreciate Lee's responsibilities.

There are, too, a number of other highly effective pieces of acting by Richard Attenborough, William Franklyn, Peter Arne, as the suave camp commandant; Donald Houston and Dennis Price, the last a delight as an actor-type who is more concerned with staging "Hamlet" than in escaping. Michael Wilding also makes a welcome appearance as a debonair officer who, with Peter Jones, gives a disarming appearance of ineffectuality. Both really are on the ball when it comes to outwitting their captors. "Danger" would have been a very routine screen adventure, but, manned throughout by actors who know their jobs, it is raised to a rather higher league.   *Rich.*

Gunmen From Laredo
(COLOR)

Routine oater for smaller markets.

Hollywood, Feb. 20.

Columbia Pictures release of Wallace MacDonald production. Features Robert Knapp, Jana Davi, Walter Coy, Paul Birch, Don C. Harvey, Clarence Straight, Jerry Marclay, Ron Hayes, Charles Horvath. Directed by MacDonald. Screenplay, Clark E. Reynolds; camera (Columbia Color), Irving Lippman; editor, Al Clark. Previewed Feb. 19, '59. Running time, 67 MINS.

Gil Reardon	Robert Knapp
Rosita	Jana Davi
Ben	Walter Coy
Matt Crawford	Paul Birch
Dave Marlow	Don C. Harvey
Frank Bass	Clarence Straight
Jordan Keefer	Jerry Barclay
Walt Keefer	Ron Hayes
Coloradas	Charles Horvath
Katy Reardon	Jean Moorhead
Delgados	X. Brands
Judge Parker	Henry Antrim

"Gunmen From Laredo" is a routine western, somewhat slow in takeoff but carrying enough later action to rate okay for the minor oater market. Color production is good but there are no cast names to brighten its prospects.

Wallace MacDonald handles dual chore of producer-director and manages a creditable job with the rambling Clark E. Reynolds screenplay. Plot deals with a revenge theme, a rancher escaping from a New Mexico territorial prison where he's been sent on false testimony, to return to Laredo to face the men who murdered his wife. Showdown climax on a Laredo street is slickly developed for a few exciting moments.

Robert Knapp heads cast as the rancher who has incurred the enmity of Walter Coy, a Laredo saloonkeeper responsible for his wife's violent death, and turns in a competent performance. Coy is a return to the old-fashioned heavy, but makes his work count. Jana Davi, as an Indian girl who helps Knapp across the desert back to Laredo after his prison break, lends color and Paul Birch handles himself well as a U.S. marshal, although it's doubtful if he would have permitted the escaped man his freedom after capturing him. Final sequences are reminiscent of "Stagecoach" in this respect. Balance of cast generally stack up satisfactorily.

Technical departments are headed by Irving Lippman's color photography.

Whit.

The Great St. Louis Bank Robbery

Inept programmer for smaller situations.

Hollywood, Feb. 20.

United Artists release of Charles Guggenheim production. Stars Steve McQueen, David Clarke, Graham Denton; features Molly McCarthy, James Dukas. Directed by Guggenheim; John Stix. Screenplay, Richard T. Heffron; camera, Victor Duncan; editor, Warren Adams; music, Bernardo Segall. Previewed Jan. 28, '59. Running time, 85 MINS.

George Fowler	Steve McQueen
Gino	David Clarke
John Egan	Graham Denton
Ann	Molly McCarthy
Willie	James Dukas

"The Great St. Louis Bank Robbery," based upon actual incident, is a low-budgetter lensed on the spot. A semi-documentary approach is adopted, but inept handling of events leading up to the holdup in closing reels will hold bookings to smaller program situations.

Where the Charles Guggenheim production misses particularly is in the endless detail showing the crooks prepping the crime, which results in long passages of tiresome footage. The four men involved—three professional criminals and one a local youth picked to drive the getaway car—dry-run every move until their actual entrance into the bank. Their careful planning, however, is tripped up by a teller sounding the alarm, and the police arrive before the gang can make its getaway for a blasting climax.

Bank heist is well played and Guggenheim and John Stix as co-directors sock over this action. Much of their earlier helming of the Richard T. Heffron screenplay, however, is over-leisurely, with the cast sometimes suffering. Steve McQueen as the youth and David Clark, Graham Denton and James Dukas in criminal roles manage to make parts fairly persuasive, and Molly McCarthy delivers well as McQueen's former girl-friend, killed by gang leader.

Technical credits are headed by Victor Duncan's realistic photography.   *Whit.*

Nudist Paradise
(BRITISH-COLOR)

Naive propaganda for the naturism movement, with trite story and dialog; obvious exploitation angles.

London, Feb. 12.

Orb International Ltd. release of a Nat Miller-Geoffrey Bernard (Frank Bevis) production. Stars Anita Love. Directed by Charles Saunders. Screenplay, Leslie Bell and Denise Kaye, from Bell's story; camera, Henry Hall; editor, Helen Wiggins. At Cinephone Theatre, London. Running time, 72 MINS.

Joan Stanton	Anita Love
Mike Malone	Carl Conway
Pat Beatty	Katy Cashfield
Jimmy Ross	Dennis Carnell
Interviewer	Celia Hewitt
Receptionist	Emma Young
Camp Warden	Walter Randall

There's nothing objectionable about "Nudist Paradise." It is just trite, and rather stupid. Filmed in Eastmancolor and "Nudiscope"—whatever that may mean —it is simply a piece of unwieldy propaganda for naturism, which will appeal only to sun-worshippers and the curious, but which has obvious angles of exploitation.

Filmed at a naturecamp near London and at Woburn Abbey, where, last year, a world of naturism convention was held, the flimsy story is merely an excuse for showing families relaxing sans clothing, and the human form not-always-so-divine. This quickly palls. A half a dozen professional performers appear in the leading roles and the others in the cast are the genuine article.

The pic concerns two young couples who spend their weekends at a nature camp and eventually marry. Of the two leading girls, Anita Love proves herself the better actress although Katy Cashfield's figure is more suited to disrobing. Carl Conway is a husky young man with a pleasant personality who looks as if he might have a future in he-man roles.

Apart from a Venus Contest in which a number of pretty young women strike various extraordinary poses such as The Bath of Psyche, Sports Girl, Streamline

Girl and so on, nothing very much happens. The four principals gradually fall in love in between swimming, badminton and exercising on a trampoline. The one vital piece of information which might have made this film worthwhile is not revealed. This is, where do nudists keep their cigarettes?

Helen Wiggins' editing is erratic and, in juxtaposition to some stilted dialog, occasionally raises unintended yocks. The main merit of "Nudist" is some very good lensing and excellent color.

Rich.

Primo Amore
(First Love)
(ITALIAN)

Rome, Feb. 17.

Cineriz release of a Cirac-Rizzoli Film production. Features Carla Gravina, Lorella De Luca, Raf Mattioli, Geronimo Meynier, Christine Kaufmann, Luciano Marin Paola Quattrini, Marcello Paolini, Niccolo Deguido, Catherine Boyle, Luciana Angiolillo, Mario Carotenuto. Directed by Mario Camerini. Story and screenplay by Age. Scarpelli, Scola, Benvenuti, DeBernardi, Camerini; music, Francesco Lavagnino; camera, Tonino delli Colli; editor, Giuliana Attenni. At Metropolitan, Rome. Running time, 97 MINS.

Betty .... Carla Gravina
Francesca .... Lorella de Luca
Giggi .... Geronimo Meynier
Piero .... Raf Mattioli
Silvia .... Christine Kaufman
Lello .... Marcello Paolini
Andreina .... Paola Quattrini
Signora Luciana .... Catherine Boyle

Able direction, a good script, and winning thesping by a large cast of young talent are neatly packaged in this pleasant and entertaining film. It is many notches above similar fare which has recently flooded the local market. Several foreign markets should find this an okay acquisition for lightweight general fare.

Intertwined tales of related and/or acquainted Roman youths basically illustrate the pic's title. The choice of refreshing new faces and dialog, which almost always permits audience identification add up to pleasurable screen time, especially with the young set. Parental problems and foibles, and their reflections on teenagers' upbringing, are touched upon. But generally the youngsters have their way and the accent is on lightness, comedy and some sentiment, with taste generally prevailing.

Thesping is unusually good throughout, denoting vet director Mario Camerini's able hand. Top credits go to Carla Gravina and Geronimo Meynier while Marcello Paolini stands out via an easygoing rendition of the "fat boy" role. Catherine Boyle provides grace and talent as a young mother who unconsciously makes her own daughter's boyfriend fall passionately in love with her. Among many other good performances, Christine Kaufman shows promise and good looks.

Technically, pic is a top-rate job in all sectors.

Hawk.

The Sound and the Fury
(C'SCOPE—COLOR)

Impressive, provocative Faulkner, sensitively presented with Yul Brynner, Joanne Woodward, Margaret Leighton spotlighted. Moving and commercial.

20th-Fox release of Jerry Wald production. Stars Yul Brynner and Joanne Woodward; features Ethel Waters, Stuart Whitman, Margaret Leighton, Francoise Rosay, Jack Warden, Albert Dekker. Directed by Martin Ritt. Screenplay, Irving Ravetch and Harriet Frank Jr., from the novel by William Faulkner; camera (De Luxe color), Charles G. Clarke; editor, Stuart Gilmore; music, Alex North. Previewed at 20th-Fox homeoffice, N.Y., Feb. 20, '59. Running time, 115 MINS.

Jason .... Yul Brynner
Quentin .... Joanne Woodward
Caddy .... Margaret Leighton
Charles Busch .... Stuart Whitman
Dilsey .... Ethel Waters
Ben Compson .... Jack Warden
Mrs. Compson .... Francoise Rosay
Howard .... John Beal
Earl .... Albert Dekker
Luster .... Stephen Perry
T.P. .... William Gunn
Job .... Roy Glenn

Considerable talents have gotten together to make "Sound and the Fury" a work of cinematic stature. It is a mature, provocative and sensitively-executed study of the decadent remnants of an erstwhile eminent family of a small southern town.

The characters of the William Faulkner allegorical novel may be looked upon alternately with revulsion and compassion. They are a lost generation whose heritage is only the family name. They represent skid-row morality. The audience is given to decide, and in the course of so doing is exposed to some picture-making that at times must be considered masterful. The honesty of the approach, the sustained interest and the high-level of the Jerry Wald production in every department doubtless will be appreciated.

Screenplay by Irving Ravetch and Harriet Frank Jr., the direction by Martin Ritt and the performances form the major part of an expert collaboration. The Faulkner touches of literary quality distinguishes tale from the brute-force depictions of southern (and other) elements suffering from malnutrition of the soul. What it says has meaning, perhaps elusive, but somehow there.

Very serious consideration of all the components is a requisite to conclusions about the total result in terms of boxoffice. And the various parts add up to an important whole. Opinions may vary, but no one is likely to go away mad. There ought to be an abundance of word-of-mouth, and resultantly an abundance of dollars.

The family name is Compson and it is significant that the nature of the relationships among members need to be parenthetically underlined by 20th-Fox in its press material for reviewers. For without this given explanation, mainly as pertaining to the role played by Yul Brynner, the who's who is bewildering until about midway through the picture. This is a disturbing flaw, one that cannot be overlooked.

The Compsons are two brothers, one a weak alcoholic and the other a mute idiot (John Beal and Jack Warden), and a sister (Margaret Leighton) who has a long history of promiscuity. Their father, before his own death and following the death of his wife, had taken on a second mate and a stepson. Yul Brynner. Latter in turn has taken on the Compson name and rules as master over a decrepit estate and his wretched second-hand relatives. Subject to his control also is Joanne Woodward, cast as Miss Leighton's youthful, illegitimate daughter. A Negro servant family, headed by Ethel Waters, completes the cast of residents.

This indeed is an offbeat lot, the Compsons. Miss Woodward gives firm conviction to the part of the girl who cries out desperately for the love and affection she can't find in her own home and, somewhat giddily, takes up with a crude mechanic (lecherous, bare-chested type) who's in town with a traveling carnival.

Miss Leighton is remarkably realistic as the washed-out hag who had abandoned her daughter at childbirth and now has returned for refuge from a world (of men) no longer holding out hands to her.

Beal as the gin hound and Warden as the helpless mute are fitting characters sketched into this family portrait; and their presence gives consistency to the study of ethical and mental degeneracy.

Brynner is every inch the household tyrant. He's a fierce domineering personality, bent on keeping the family together so that the name he has adopted will not lose all its social value. Brynner has subtlely shaded the character with maximum skill, eventually emerging from Miss Woodward's bitter and cold keeper to benefactor concerned with her integrity and, it's suggested, a more closer role in her future. Pygmalion or in-law uncle with an incestuous drive?

Wald's production provides a vivid recreation of the southern town; the settings are unusually effective in communicating atmosphere.

Ritt's direction is fine all the way. His staging reflects genuine feeling, his story points are made via strong suggestion rather than any crude, graphic illustration.

Miss Waters is splendid as the servant; Stuart Whitman completely convinces as the carny muscle man who actually is a coward; Albert Dekker, Francoise Rosay, Stephen Perry, William Gunn and Roy Glenn all contribute meaningful work. Perry, a Negro boy who takes care of Warden, turns in a particularly touching performance.

Alex North's music complements the screen action forcefully; the theme could well have a chance on its own. Charles G. Clarke's camera work (De Luxe color and CinemaScope) has gotten the feel of the Mississippi location and otherwise adds to the dramatic effectiveness. Stuart Gilmore's editing provides consistently even continuity and other technical credits are all top-notch.

Gene.

Tank Commandos

So-so dynamics but exploitable war meller coupled with same company's "Operation Dames."

Hollywood, Feb. 26.

American International Pictures release of a James H. Nicholson-Samuel Z. Arkoff production. Stars Robert Barron, Maggie Lawrence, Wally Campo; introduces Donato Faretta. Produced, directed and written by Burt Topper; camera, John Nicholaus Jr.; music, Ronald Stein; editor, Asa Clark. Previewed Feb. 23, '59. Running time, 79 MINS.

Lieutenant Blaine .... Robert Barron
Jean .... Maggie Lawrence
Lazzotti .... Wally Campo
Diano .... Donato Farretta
Shorty .... Leo V. Netranga
Todd .... Jack Sowards
Sands .... Anthony Rich
Capt. Praxton .... Larry Hudson
Italian Girl .... Maria Monay
Tessie .... Carmen D'Antonio
Cliffen .... David Addis
Taylor .... Russ Prescott
Italian Prisoner .... Freddy Roberto
Bartender .... Jerry Lear
German Prisoner .... Fred Gavlin
Streetwalker .... Joan Connors
G.I. Sgt. .... Larry Shuttleworth
G.I. .... Lee Redman
Nazi Sgt. .... Norberto Kermer

American International Pictures, theorizing that double-billing of similar genre is more potent than dualing a pair of opposites, has come up with a couple of war films, "Tank Commandos" and "Operation Dames" as its newest package. "Tank Commandos," written, produced and directed by Burt Topper, is the more animated of the two features, though it seldom builds enough energy to lift it above routine action fare. Still, there's enough to exploit in this package, and the low budgeters should return a profit from the exploitation market.

Artistically, the problem is Topper didn't or couldn't take the time to meet his potential. He has created a poignant scene or two, a sensuous one and a suspenseful one, but the vivid tone isn't consistent. He has, however, taken full advantage of the battle-destroyed Italian settings which are remarkably picturesque and interesting for a low-budget film.

The story tells nothing new—a demolition squad must destroy an underwater bridge that is giving German tanks free passage. The only person knowing the exact location of the bridge is an Italian boy who, with more exposure, could have given this film a more alluring point of view.

Action, though it's not always focused, is extensive in the James H. Nicholson-Samuel Z. Arkoff production, this, after all, is one of the prime demands made by audiences who have turned the exploitation field into a lucrative harvest.

Robert Barron, as the squad's leader, is perfectly hard as the lieutenant, soft as the friend in a fine performance, and Wally Campo is equally good as an Italian-American buffer between the G.I.s and the residents. Donato Farretta is excellent as the young boy, with good performances turned in by Maggie Lawrence, Leo V. Netranga, Jack Sowards, Anthony Rich, Larry Hudson and pretty Maria Monay.

John Nicholaus Jr.'s photography is exceptional for this field, with Dan Haller's art direction, Ronald Stein's music, Asa Clark's editing and Al Overton's sound all capable. It might be noted that, in the review print, Anthony Rich popped up big as life to join his comrades after dying at length in the previous scene.

Ron.

Never Steal Anything Small
(C'SCOPE—COLOR)

Labor racketeering on the waterfront spiced with music and comedy efforts. A peculiar hodgepodge with mild b.o. potential. Stars James Cagney and Shirley Jones.

Universal release of Aaron Rosenberg production. Stars James Cagney, Shirley Jones, Robert Smith and Cara Williams. Features Nehemiah Persoff, Royal Dano and Anthony Caruso. Directed by Charles Lederer. Story and screenplay, Lederer, based on the play, "Devil's Hornpipe," by Maxwell Anderson and Rouben Mamou-

lian. Camera (Eastman-C'Scope), Harold Lipstein; editor, Russell Schoengarth; music, Allie Wrubel; lyrics, Anderson. At Capitol Theatre, N.Y., Feb. 11, '59. Running time, **94 MINS.**

Jake MacIllaney .... James Cagney
Linda Cabot .... Shirley Jones
Dan Cabot .... Roger Smith
Finnipeg .... Cara Williams
Pinelli .... Nehemiah Persoff
Words Cannon .... Royal Dano
Lt. Tevis .... Anthony Caruso
Merritt .... Horace McMahon
Ginger .... Virginia Vincent
Sleep-Out Charlie ...... Jack Albertson
Lennie .... Robert J. Wilke
Hymie .... Herbie Faye
Ed .... Billy M. Greene
Ward .... John Duke
Osborne .... Jack Orrison
Doctor .... Roland Winters
Model .... Ingrid Goude
Fats Ranney ...... Sanford Seeger
Thomas .... Ed "Skipper" McNally
Deputy Warden ...... Gregg Barton

If you accept the theme of Universal's "Never Steal Anything Small," honesty is NOT the best policy, especially not in union politics on the New York waterfront. But no matter how much Charles Lederer's story and screenplay, based on an unproduced legit musical, "Devil's Hornpipe," by Maxwell Anderson and Rouben Mamoulian, attempts to make Jake MacIllaney, the waterfront labor boss portrayed by James Cagney, a charming, if unscrupulous, Robin Hood, the fact remains that MacIllaney is a crook and a hoodlum.

The taste in such a hero, a man who'll use any unprincipled method, even stealing another man's wife, to gain his own ends, is to be questioned. Film attempts to soften the reaction, by spicing the proceedings with musical interludes and attempting to present the mobsters as good-natured Damon Runyon characters, but these half-hearted efforts fail to justify the overall premise. Moreover, MacIllaney's feeble attempt to explain his motivations fall flat.

The result is a peculiar hodgepodge, being neither musical, comedy nor drama. It'll hardly satisfy the demands of present-day filmgoers and appears destined for a fast, unheralded playoff.

The character Cagney is called on to play is a breeze for the veteran performer, for he's done it so many times before. He's the tough hood who employs the bread and circus technique to win the rank-and-file longshoremen to his side. He, however, does not omit the necessary strong arm tactics when it meets his purpose. And, when the occasion arises, there's Cagney turning song-and-dance man.

Shirley Jones is a shade too saccharine as the young lawyer's wife who catches Cagney's eye. As the young lawyer, corrupted and framed by Cagney, Roger Smith gives a standard portrayal of an unpretentious Ivy Leaguer out of his league. And Cara Williams is the familiarly tough, heart-of-gold mobster's moll. Nehemiah Persoff covers well-worn territory in his depiction of the national boss of the longshoremen's union. Ditto the various sidekicks and rivals of the waterfront labor battle.

The musical interludes are mildly diverting. Best among these is Cagney's duet with Miss Williams—"I'm Sorry—I Want a Ferrari." Miss Jones comes off well in "I Haven't Got a Thing to Wear" and in a song-an-dance tv commercial, "It Takes Love to Make a Home." "Never Steal Anything Small" and "Helping Our Friends" feature Cagney and the crowd on the waterfront. The music was furnished by Allie Wrubel, with Anderson providing the lyrics.

The Aaron Rosenberg production, in Eastman color and CinemaScope, is slick from a technical standpoint, Lederer's direction is standard and adds little to the overall effect. Harold Lipstein's cinematography is excellent and catches some fine scenes of the Manhattan skyline. *Holl.*

Operation Dames

Paired with "Tank Commandos" in an exploitable package.

Hollywood, Feb. 26.

American International Pictures release of a Camera Eye Production. Stars Eve Meyer, Chuck Henderson, Don Devlin. Produced by Stanley Kallis. Directed by Louis Clyde Stoumen. Screenplay by Ed Lakso, from a story by Stanley Kallis; camera, Edward R. Martin; editor, Louis Clyde Stoumen; music, Richard Markowitz. Previewed Feb. 23, '59. Running time, **74 MINS.**

Lorry Evering .... Eve Meyer
Sgt. Valido .... Chuck Henderson
Tony .... Don Devlin
Hal .... Ed Craig
Roberta .... Cindy Girard
Marsha .... Barbara Skyler
Billy .... Chuck Van Haren
Dinny .... Andrew Munro
Benny .... Byron Morrow
Marge .... Alice Allyn
George .... Ed Lakso

"Operation Dames," being billed by American International Pictures with "Tank Commandos," has an interesting premise that doesn't come off. What does come off, however, is the apparel of one Eve Meyer, a voluptuous femme, seen fully only from the back, who lends a certain exploitable charm to this Camera Eye Production.

There's more operation than dames in this story of a USO troupe caught behind North Korean lines in the most recent skirmish. Subtleties of character give way to action, the result being a long march through enemy territory that somehow seems to have been filmed before.

Camera Eye Productions has made its name in the documentary field, winning an Oscar for "The True Story of the Civil War" two years ago. It might be wise for the talented group to take at least a semi-documentary approach to feature filmmaking rather than select a property that ranges so far afield.

Stanley Kallis produced and penned the story which Ed Lakso screenplayed. Director Louis Clyde Stoumen wasn't able to come up with consistently good performances, but some are notable. Miss Meyer is okay, not nearly so grand as her measurements. Chuck Henderson, as the group's leader through rough terrain, is excellent and a likely contender as a successful new face. Don Devlin and Andrew Munro are very good as a couple of soldiers, with Ed Craig equally fine and okay work from Cindy Girard, Barbara Skyler, Byron Morrow, Alice Allyn and Lakso.

Credits—from Edward R. Martin's camera to sound by John Mack, editing by Stoumen and art direction by Mervyn Barbert—are capably accomplished. Richard Markowitz's interesting musical score, expressive and heavy on percussion, is a top bonus. So is Lakso's catchy "Girls, Girls, Girls" sung over titles. *Ron.*

Les Cousins
(FRENCH)

Paris, Feb. 24.

Marceau release of AJYM Films production. With Jean-Claude Brialy, Gerard Blain, Juliette Mayniel, Claude Cerval, Michele Meritz. Written and directed by Claude Chabrol, with dialog by Paul Gegauff. Camera, Henri Decae; editor, Jacques Gaillard. Preemed in Paris. Running time, **110 MINS.**

Charles .... Gerard Blain
Paul .... Jean-Claude Brialy
Florence .... Juliette Mayniel
Clovis .... Claude Cerval
Genevieve .... Genevieve Cluny
Yvonne .... Michele Meritz

Tale of the country cousin trying to make it in the big city, and destroyed in the process, gets offbeat treatment from promising new and youthful director Claude Chabrol. It develops into a looksee at a certain restless youth. Pic possesses probable exploitation aspects for offshore spots on its frankness of theme.

The country cousin comes to stay with his worldly, decadent cousin. His attempts at love and exams fail while his indolent, debauched cousin gets all. It ends in an ironic bit as the visitor is killed by a gun thought to be empty.

Director Chabrol has gone in for a little too much symbolism. The characters sometimes remain murky and literary rather than real form. But a concisive progression, fine technical aspects, and a look at innocence destroyed by the profane keeps it absorbing despite the slightly pretentious treatment at times.

Its wild surprise parties, the lack of concession in showing morality destroyed by directionless living and some pungent love scenes make this a bit different from run-of-mill pix. *Mosk.*

Make Mine a Million
(BRITISH)

Unsophisticated skit on television with Arthur Askey and Sidney James running a pirate tv station and undermining the non-commercial national company; well-geared for family audience laughter.

London, Feb. 24.

British Lion release of a John Baxter production. Stars Arthur Askey, Sidney James. Directed by Lance Comfort. Screenplay, Peter Blackmore from story by Jack Francis; camera, Desmond Davis; editor, Peter Pitt. At Rialto Theatre, London. Running time, **82 MINS.**

Arthur Ashton .... Arthur Askey
Sid Gibson .... Sidney James
Martin Russell .... Dermot Walsh
Anxious Husband .... Kenneth Connor
Director-Gen. of National TV
Clive Morton
Chairman of Commercial TV
Martin Benson
Sally .... Sally Barnes
Director of Commercial TV
Lionel Murton
Mrs. Burgess .... Olga Lindo
Diana .... Leigh Madison
Jack .... Bernard Cribbins
Police Superintendent .... Bruce Seton
Sid's Bodyguard .... George Margo
Production Supervisor ...... Tom Gill
The Professor ...... David Nettheim
Assistant Director-General
Richard Caldicott
Ballet Dancer .... Gillian Lynne

Arthur Askey is a popular, genial comedian who has made huge impact on stage, tv and radio but whose film appearances have been conspicuously less successful. However, his latest entry, "Make Mine a Million," should ring the bell with unsophisticated audiences and will prove a useful dualer for U.K. houses.

The pic is a light-hearted skit on tele with some shrewd digs at the BBC, thinly disguised as the National Television Co. Askey is a humble makeup man in National tele studio who becomes mixed up with Sidney James, a fast-talking, seedy, unsuccessful peddler of a new detergent, which the public refuses to buy because it is not advertised on "the telly."

James persuades Askey to slip an advertisement for the detergent into one of the National programs and Askey is fired. The one commercial, however, makes the detergent a sweeping success. The problem is how they can keep up the good work. They hit on the idea of starting the first pirate tv station and manage to get pirate advertisements into such important outside broadcasts as Ascot races and the Edinburgh Festival. Askey finishes up as a public hero and finally gets his own program on the National Television.

This neat idea could have been treated satirically and, occasionally, satire does creep into the script. But mainly it goes all out for straightforward comedy effect. A good cast brings a cheerful, boisterous good humor to its job. Lance Comfort has directed briskly and Arthur Grant's lensing has helped the film to look a rather more expensively mounted proposition than it is.

Askey and James team up splendidly as the main burden of the entertainment falls on them. But there is some effective support from Olga Lindo, an understanding landlady; Clive Morton, as the pompous director-general of the National TV Co.; Tom Gill, as a mannered production supervisor; and Dermot Walsh, as an advertiser who cashes in on the Askey-James enterprise.

To boost the marquee value, a number of big names make fleeting guest appearances as themselves. These include Tommy Trinder, Evelyn Laye, Dickie Henderson, Raymond Glendinning, Dennis Lotis, Patricia Bredin and Sabrina. *Rich.*

Le Vent Se Leve
(The Wind Rises)
(FRENCH)

Paris, Feb. 24.

Terra release of Groupe De Quatre production. Stars Curd Jurgens; features Mylene Demongeot, Alain Saury, Daniel Sorano. Directed by Yves Ciampi. Screenplay, Jean-Charles Tacchella, H. F. Rey, J. L. Bost; camera, Armand Thirard; editor, G. Alepee. At Biarritz, Paris. Running time, **95 MINS.**

Eric .... Curd Jurgens
Catherine .... Mylene Demongeot
Michel .... Alain Saury
Friend .... Daniel Sorano

Lacklustre direction and acting put this tale of a middleaged man's affair with a young girl on a dubious basis. Lagging pacing does not help to imbue this with any feeling for the characters and their problems. The result is a pic with mainly home market possibilities.

Curd Jurgens decides to wreck a ship for the insurance coin at the instigation of his flighty young mistress. But he finally decides against it as both he and the girl come of age and realize they have moral duties to society. The aim is high but the execution is low. Jurgens' impassive acting and Mylene Demongeot's lack of ease, plus banal dialog, do not help give this the movement and direction it needs. Technical aspects are only fair. *Mosk.*

No Trees in the Street
(BRITISH)

Dramatic study of life in a London slum and the inhabitants' battle for survival against the environment; solid acting, writing and playing make this an acceptable b.o. entry despite lack of star names known in U.S.

London, March 3.

Associated British Pathe release of Associated British-Lee Thompson-Godwin-Willis production. Stars Sylvia Syms, Herbert Lom, Ronald Howard, Stanley Holloway. Directed by J. Lee-Thompson. Screenplay, Ted Willis; camera, Gilbert Taylor; editor, Richard Best; music, Laurie Johnson. At Studio One, London. Running time, 98 MINS.

Hetty	Sylvia Syms
Wilkie	Herbert Lom
Frank	Ronald Howard
Kipper	Stanley Holloway
Jess	Joan Miller
Tommy	Melvyn Hayes
Bill	Liam Redmond
Lova	Carole Lesley
Marge	Lana Morris
Mrs. Jacobson	Lilly Kann
Mrs. Jokel	Marianne Stone
Jackie	Edwin Richfield
Inspector	Campbell Singer
Superintendent	Lloyd Lamble
Kenny	David Hemmings
Reg	Richard Shaw
Mrs. Brown	Rita Webb
Street Orator	Fred Griffiths
Bookie's Clerk	Victor Brooks

Ted Willis is a writer with a sympathetic eye for problems of the middle and lower-classes. His beat is the suburbs and the less desirable and drab areas of big towns, rather than Mayfair. He brings a documentary touch to his screenplays and the formula has frequently paid off, notably with "Woman In a Dressing Gown." Now, again teamed up with director J. Lee-Thompson, his "No Trees In Street" plays out a seamy slice of life in a London slum 20 years ago.

Film is played on a violently strident note. Though Willis has the gift of evoking strong, dramatic situations and creating authentic atmosphere with his dialog, he has little to say that's new on the old-hat subject of the effect of environment on character. He hammers home the point that people are more important than places.

Combination of Lee-Thompson, Willis and some useful performances makes an interesting picture but much of its philosophy is contrived. Apart from its own worth, the previous success of "Dressing Gown" must make "No Trees" a worthwhile b.o. proposition. Obviously it's short on star names for the U.S.

The scene is a squalid slum, with kids playing in the dirty streets. A seedy, sinister air of poverty and despair hangs over the tenements. It's inhabitants are raucously, cunningly and bitterly engaged in a fight for survival. There is the constant clinging to the dream of escape before the decaying atmosphere of the district gets them down. But it is a faint dream

Thompson's nose for detail and Gilbert Taylor's lensing all help to create a slum atmosphere which is unbearably realistic and which, even in this Welfare State, still exists in many big towns and cities. The slim story line shows how the various larger-than-life characters face up to the challenge of The Street. The drab blowsy mother who has given up long ago. Her daughter, longing to get away from it with her young brother, but lacking the resources or the courage. The boy racketeer, who has made money by shady activities and now ruthlessly rules the Street.

While "No Trees" is probing the fumbling philosophies, ambitions and reactions of its trapped characters, it is holding entertainment. But it develops into the hackneyed situation of the young brother coming under the influence of the crook, shooting an old woman for a few dollars and forfeiting his life trying to escape from the police.

Sylvia Syms gives a moving performance as the gentle girl who is sick of her surroundings but refuses to marry the cheap racketeer just to escape. It is one of the best performances of an actress of sensibility and charm. Herbert Lom, as the opportunist who dominates the street, is sufficiently suave and unpleasant while Joan Miller, as the mother, only occasionally falls into the temptation of hamming an over-written role.

Stanley Holloway is a bookmaker's tout with the cheerful philosophy that the world's gone mad. Ronald Howard's decent young policeman, frustrated at not being able to help the inhabitants of the Street, is a thoughtful study. Melvyn Hayes plays the teenage youngster who gets into trouble. His is a sharp piece of acting.

"No Trees" is a not entirely satisfactory film. Some of the dialog is too glibly superficial and some of the situations too stock. But there is enough quality in writing, direction and acting to make it worth seeing. *Rich.*

Home Is the Hero
(IRISH)

Dublin, March 3.

British Lion release of Emmet Dalton production. Stars Arthur Kennedy. Directe by J. Fielder Cook. Screenplay by Henry Keating from Walter Macken play of same name. Running time, 80 MINS.

Paddo	Walter Macken
Daylia	Eileen Crowe
Willie	Arthur Kennedy
Josie	Joan O'Hara
Maura Green	Maire O'Donnell
Dovetail	Harry Brogan
Bid	Maire Keane
Trapper	Philip O'Flynn
Mr. Green	Patrick Layde
Mr. Shannon	Eddie Golden
Finegan	John Hoey
Manchester Monaghan	Michael Hennessy
First Pub Customer	Michael O'Briian
Second Pub Customer	Dermot Kelly
O'Connor	Geoffrey Golden

Walter Macken story of a rumpot strongman, Paddo, who kills a man and returns to his home after a five-year jail stretch, was staged at Abbey some years ago and later on Broadway. Piece has improved on translation to screen and provides a standout role for Arthur Kennedy, the only actor outside Abbey Theatre Company in the cast. It looks doubtful for the general market.

This concerns the unsettlement of family in Paddo's absence and readjustment while he is in jail. His return creates fresh problems of adjustment for Paddo himself, rejecting the goodwill of many old acquaintances who wanted to rebuild their one-time hero. Piece has a smooth quality and excellent direction with some first-rate performances.

Arthur Kennedy, as Willie, the son of Paddo, who finds a new life, turns in a performance which will hold audiences closely. His playing is subdued and sympathetic, building into romance with dead man's daughter despite his self-consciousness of a limp. The strength and decay of the family are warmly shown, and there are some first-class performances from the quiet friend, done by Philip O'Flynn, the daughter of Joan O'Hara, and Bid as done by Maire Keane. The tinker, Dovetail, portrayed by Harry Brogan is a clown role.

Director Fielder Cook has caught atmosphere of group, and the settings are effective. This seems to rate top billing as a piece which is Irish. *Mac.*

Stranger In My Arms
(C'SCOPE)

Mom's a snob. Sonny died a bum. Lukewarm soap rinse though names of Allyson, Chandler, Astor, Nagel may help.

Universal release of Ross Hunter production. Stars Jeff Chandler, June Allyson with Sandra Dee, Charles Coburn, Mary Astor, Peter Graves, Conrad Nagel and Hayden Rorke. Directed by Helmut Kautner. Screenplay, Peter Berneis, from the novel "And Ride a Tiger" by Robert Wilder; camera (C'Scope), William Daniels; editor, Frank Gross. At Odeon Theatre, N.Y., March 3, '59. Running time, 88 MINS.

Christina Beasley	June Allyson
Pike Yarnell	Jeff Chandler
Pat Beasley	Sandra Dee
Vance Beasley	Charles Coburn
Mrs. Beasley	Mary Astor
Donald Beasley	Peter Graves
Harley Beasley	Conrad Nagel
Marcus Beasley	Hayden Rorke
Bessie Logan	Reita Green
Colonel Bert Wayne	Bartlett Robinson
Congressman	Howard Wendell

Mumsy gets hers in this film version of Robert Wilder's novel, "And Ride a Tiger." A contrived yarn, the entry is another example of the so-called "woman's picture" long favored at Universal, per "Magnificent Obsession," the same novelist's "Written in the Wind," and others. The present batch of laundry bears a strong odor of soap.

Ross Hunter production, directed by Helmut Kautner, tries hard to give meaning to the story, but succeeds mostly in artificial heart-tugging overtones, complete with a hearts-and-flowers musical background.

Ever since Freudians removed the halo mother, she's a Capital B for plotting. "Stranger in My Arms" puts "smother" type through the ringer again with Mary Astor depicting a domineering social snob determined to obtain a posthumhumous Medal of Honor for her son. She is supported in this project by Charles Coburn, her arrogant father-in-law who attempts to bribe Jeff Chandler, an Air Force major, to testify that his grandson had died a hero's death.

Chandler, knowing that the family's pride-and-joy was actually a coward who committed suicide and who hated his mother, balks. Meanwhile, however, he becomes romantically attached to the dead man's widow, June Allyson, who has practically shut herself off from the outside world as the permanent guest of her husband's family. Conrad Nagel is seen as Miss Astor's weak, cowed husband who finally rebels when the chips are down. And there's Sandra Dee as the rebellious and effervescent teenage sister of the dead flyer.

Most of the action takes place around the sumptious southern old magnolia mansion of the Beasley family where Chandler has come to attend the dedication of a veteran's hospital named after the alleged hero. He's quick to catch on to the family's scheme, but has to go through some soul-searching of his own to free himself of his own guilt, for he had accidently provided the gun with which young Beasley killed himself.

The Peter Berneis screenplay fails to give the character of Pike Yarnell, the role played by Chandler, much dimension and the actor, as a result, goes through his paces rather woodenly. Miss Allyson, as the young widow, and Nagel, as the weak head of the household, are also handicapped in the scripting. Miss Astor, however, gets an opportunity to sink her teeth in a juicy part and she makes the best of it. Ditto Coburn as the money-can-buy-anything father-in-law. Miss Dee is a trifle too cute as the teenager.

Technical aspects, including William Daniels' photography, are fine. *Holl.*

Treichville
(FRENCH-COLOR)

Paris, March 3.

Pleiade Films production and release. Written, directed and lensed by Jean Rouch. Editor, Marie Yoyote. Preemed in Paris. Running time, 75 MINS.

This pic won the French film critic's award, Le Prix Delluc. It is an offbeat, documentary-type film in Agfacolor which traces the everyday lives and thoughts of two natives of Nigeria. The two have drifted into the burgeoning Ivory Coast town of Abidjah with its more slummy outskirts, Treichville.

Filmmaker Jean Rouch, who usually has made pix for museums, has done this one on his own. His definite filmic feeling had some of his earlier pix released theatrically, and this one is due for specialized distribution.

The film looks difficult for offshore placement. However, it has an unusual flair for revealing the lives of the natives between happy primitivism and the ties of Western civilization which they have not assimilated as yet.

Nothing much happens as the work, dreams, hopes and everyday movements of the heroes, who call themselves Eddie Constantine and Edward G. Robinson, are unveiled. But it adds up to an unusual entry for specialized slotting and for school and lecture use.

Producer Pierre Braunberger, now that the pic has won a prize, has decided to give the vehicle a more commercial title when it is released. It will be called "Moi, Un Noir" (I, A Negro). Its length makes this a possible good filler for a specialized program with another shorter feature. *Mosk.*

The Wild and the Innocent
(COLOR—C'SCOPE)

Another mild one from Universal. Will have to sell on names.

Hollywood, March 6.

Universal release of Sy Gomberg production. Stars Audie Murphy, Joanne Dru; costars Gilbert Roland, Jim Backus, Sandra Dee. Directed by Jack Sher. Screenplay, Gomberg and Sher; based on a story by Gomberg; camera, Harold Lipstein; music, Hans J. Salter; editor, George Gittens. Previewed at the Hawaii Theatre, March 4, '59. Running time, 84 MINS.

Yancy	Audie Murphy
Marcy	Joanne Dru
Paul	Gilbert Roland
Mr. Forbes	Jim Backus
Rosalie	Sandra Dee
Uncle Liji	George Mitchell
Chip	Peter Breck
Ben Stocker	Strother Martin
Ma Ransome	Wesley Marie Tackitt
Mrs. Forbes	Betty Harford
Pitchman	Mel Leonard
Kiri	Lillian Adams
Richie	Val Benedict
Henchmen	Jim Sheppard, Ed Stroll, John Qualls, Frank Wolff
Dancehall Girls	Rosemary Eliot Barbara Morris, Louise Glenn
Bouncer	Stephen Roberts
Townswoman	Tammy Windsor

"The Wild and The Innocent" was variously titled during its pro-

duction (first "The Wild Innocents" then "The Buckskin Kid and the Calico Gal") and there seems to have been a similar uncertainty about its intent and purpose. Despite an attractive cast and the benefits of color and CinemaScope, the Sy Gomberg production for Universal, directed by Jack Sher, "The Wild and The Innocent" contains neither elements of its present title and shapes up only as an "adequate" program picture.

The Gomberg-Sher screenplay, from a story by Gomberg, seems to be a pastoral farce set in the early west in its opening scenes. Audie Murphy is sent off by his beaver-trapping uncle, George Mitchell, to exchange two seasons' pelts for supplies. On his way to the nearest community—Murphy's first brush with civilization—he picks up urchin Sandra Dee, promising her folks to get her a city job.

Murphy is so naive he believes town boss Gilbert Roland when Roland tells him a good job for Miss Dee will be in the local dance hall. Murphy is equally backward in understanding Joanne Dru's status in town as an established member of the dance hall. This leads, via his early romance with Miss Dru, to his championing of her rights, and in his later realization that Miss Dee is the girl for him, in his rescue of her from the toils of the lecherous Roland.

Murphy is getting a little mature to be playing a gawky boy, and he hasn't the comedy lightness to kid a role such as this. Miss Dru, despite her top-billing, plays a subsidiary role, although adequately. Roland is his usual dashing self, and Jim Backus is amusing in a side-line character. Miss Dee, disguised in the early scenes by a fright wig and tattered rags, blossoms in later scenes, adding youth and freshness to the film. In the supporting cast, Strother Martin scores as her conniving father, Wesley Marie Tackit as the dance hall madam, and Betty Hardford as Backus' wife. *Powe.*

Le Fauve Est Lache
(The Beast Is Loose)
(FRENCH)

Paris, March 3.

Gaumont release of Cinephonic-Elan Films production. Stars Lino Ventura; features Estella Blain, Nadine Alari, Paul Frankeur, Philippe Mareuil, Jess Hahn. Directed by Maurice Labro. Screenplay, Jean Redon, Claude Sautet, Frederic Dard, Francois Chavane; camera, Pierre Petit; editor, Germaine Artus. At Balzac, Paris. Running time, **95 MINS.**

Paul .... Lino Ventura
Nadine .... Estella Blain
Pierrette .... Nadine Alari
Raymond .... Paul Frankeur
Regis .... Philippe Mareuil
American .... Jess Hahn
Colonel .... Alfred Adam

The second in a popular series, about a secret service man who is forced into his work by both his chief and the underworld, is following the first in popularity here. But only fair plotting, workmanship and handling make this of little offshore interest where foreign dualers are not standard.

Lino Ventura has the force and presence to keep the well shaped, but conventional plot moving and fairly credible. As a former secret service man with two children, a beautiful wife and a good business, he is forced back into the game by ruthless police tactics. He gets back some stolen plans after some hectic battles. *Mosk.*

The Bandit of Zhobe
(C'SCOPE)

A Far Eastern Indians in India add up to period action meller for programming.

Hollywod, March 6.

Columbia release of Warwick production. Stars Victor Mature, Anthony Newley, Anne Aubrey. Produced by Irving Allen and Albert Broccoli. Directed by John Gilling. Screenplay, John Gilling; based on a story by Richard Maibaum; camera (Eastman Color) Ted Moore, Cyril Knowles; music, Kenneth V. Jones; editor, Bert Rule. Previewed at the studio, March 5, '59. Running time, **80 MINS.**

Kasin Khan .... Victor Mature
Zenda .... Anne Aubrey
Stokes .... Anthony Newley
Major Crowley .... Norman Wooland
Captain Sounders .... Dermot Walsh
Azhad Khan .... Walter Gotell
Lieutenant Wylie .... Sean Kelly
Hatti .... Paul Stassino
Ahmed .... Laurence Taylor
Hussu .... Dennis Shaw
Zecco .... Murray Kash
Tamara .... Maya Koumani

Indians bite the dust with monotonous regularity in "The Bandit of Zhobe," a Warwick production with the elements of an old-fashioned American western. The difference is that in the case of this Columbia release, the Indians are Indians, from India.

British have a fertile field for outdoor action melodrama in Victorian India, but the approach here is so innocently "Beau Geste" that it cannot be taken seriously. Upper lips are so generally stiff as to suggest an epidemic of frostbite. "Zhobe" was made by much the same team as "Zarak" of a couple years ago, and will probably do the same kind of business as that feature.

Victor Mature plays the misunderstood Indian leader in the John Gilling screenplay, from a story by Richard Maibaum. His family is wiped out by another Indian chieftain, Walter Gotell, but since Gotell's men were disguised as British troopers, Mature swears a vendetta on the redcoats. Norman Wooland is the British commander who tries to capture Mature for his subsequent banditry and pillage, and Anne Aubrey is Wooland's idealistic daughter. Anthony Newland supplies a portrayal of a comic ranker, a comedy portrait whose ancestors can be found in the same tedious detail in any of Shakespeare's low clowns. The wrap-up involves a clarification of everyone's true position and general understanding and forgiveness.

"Zhobe" employs some massive scenes of considerable color in the battles between the British troops and their Indian opponents. Photography, by Ted Moore and Cyril Knowles in mostly good Eastman color, is lively and interesting. John Gilling's direction, however, doesn't take full advantage of the scenes, mostly because the spectator isn't involved in the contest. It just seems a melee, without any clearcut issues for which to root. The same fault is characteristic of the human conflicts. The characters are so stereotyped, so Kiplingesque, that little involvement is aroused.

Victor Mature seems to be getting a litle heavy to play the dashing juvenile, and his apparent decision to play his Indian leader as stoically as posible somewhat cuts down emotional appeal. Miss Aubrey is attractive but is hopelessly saddled with one of those characterizations of Victorian womanhood that seems today merely tiresome. Anthony Newley's comedy role is equally unimpressive. Others involved include Dermot Walsh, Sean Kelly, Paul Stassino and Laurence Taylor.

Irving Allen and Albert Broccoli produced, apparently with an eye to the American action market. If so, it should be noted that this market of recent years demands something more than chase and capture. The adult western, whether set in the U. S. Southwest or India's Northwest Frontier, has the accent these days on adult. *Powe.*

Nella Citta L'Inferno
(Hell in the City)
(ITALIAN)

Rome, March 3.

Cineriz release of a Riama (Giuseppe Amato) production. Stars Anna Magnani, Giulietta Masina; features Cristina Gajone, Angela Portaluri, Milly Monti, Myriam Bru, Marcella Rovena, Virginia Bennati, Miranda Campi, Gina Roveri. Directed by Renato Castellani. Screenplay, Suso Cecchi D'Amico, from novel, "Roma, Via delle Mantellate" by Isa Mari; camera, Leonida Barboni; editor, Jolanda Benvenuti; music, Roman Vlad. At Barberini, Rome. Running time, **110 MINS.**

Egle .... Anna Magnani
Lina .... Giulietta Masina
Marietta .... Cristina Gajoni

Hard-hitting prison drama with excellent performances including Anna Magnani at her best. While the pic in itself is good entertainment for all Italian audiences, export chances will best spotlight name values of the Anna Magnani-Giulietta Masina acting team for the quality film market.

While obviously a condemnation of some prison systems, and their tendency to foster, rather than cure crime, "L'Inferno" is more than that thanks to a moving and human story told through the main characters of Egle (Anna Magnani) and Lina (Giulietta Masina). Egle is the vet who corrupts first-timer Lina, in prison by mistake, into a wised-up attitude on life and crime. She overdoes her schooling, however, and when Lina returns to jail a seasoned and calloused pro, deprived of all her previous innocence and ingeniousness, it's Egle who is finally shocked to her senses at what she has done. Pic is dominated by Anna Magnani's personality and performance, probably her best to date which perforce pales such other excellent performances as that of Giulietta Masina and some others.

The Magnani role is made to order for her talents and temperament. The film would be worth seeing even for her performance alone. However, this is a good, well-constructed, strongly-worded and colorful item per se, in which the hand of Renato Castellani is noted. His direction rarely errs. And he has as usual obtained some fine performances from all concerned in this vastly populated pic. Suso Cecchi D'Amico's script is also a top contribution in delineating the character developments, sketching in backdrop performances of color and vitality, and in bringing Miss Mari's book to the screen with hard-hitting, realistic dialogue, much of which will unfortunately will be lost in translation or on foreign ears.

Except for soundtrack, which was poor on the print seen, technical credits reflect Castellani's care for detail in every sector, to which must be added Giuseppe Amato's expert personal production supervision. Lensing by Leonida Barboni is tops while the musical scoring by Roman Vlad appropriately suit moods and action. *Hawk.*

Froeken April
(Miss April)
(SWEDISH-EASTMANCOLOR)

Stockholm, March 3.

Europa Film production and release. Stars Gunnar Bjoernstrand, Lena Soederblom; features Jarl Kulle, Gaby Stenberg, Douglas Hage, Hjordis Pettersson, Meg Westergren, Lena Madsen, Sif Ruud, Birgitta Valberg, Per Oscarsson. Written and directed by Goeran Gentele. Camera, Karl-Erik Alberts; music, Harry Arnold. At Saga, Stockholm. Running time, **97 MINS.**

Marcus Arwidson .... Gunnar Bjoernstrand
"Miss April" .... Lena Soederblom
Oswald Berg .... Jarl Kulle
Vera .... Gaby Stenberg
Chorus Master .... Douglas Hage
Mrs. Berg .... Hjoerdis Pettersson
Anna .... Meg Westergren
Siri .... Lena Madsen
Opera Manager .... Olof Sandborg
Mrs. Nilsson .... Sif Ruud
Sverker Ek, pianist .... Per Oscarsson
Miss Holm, secretary .. Birgitta Valberg

It is April 1, spring is just arriving and the world is beginning to look more friendly. The mailman stands in front of two mail-boxes with a letter addressed to "Master of the House" and the street number. Nothing more. He can take a chance by putting the letter in one of the two boxes, and he does just that. And that's how the manager of a great bank a few minutes later is reading a passionate love letter from someone who calls herself Miss April. He is Gunnar Bjoernstrand, one of Sweden't top character players. Actually, the letter was sent by Lena Soederblom, a young girl in the Opera Ballet, and intended for the Opera's tenor, Jarl Kulle, with whom she is secretly in love.

Bjoernstrand, too old for such things as romance, can't forget the letter and when by some strange reason, he meets the girl who sent it, things start to happen. The bank manager happens to look for the girl at the Royal Opera, and he is forced to try to sing. Immediately he is "discovered." This starts a double life, being the distinguished bank manager at daytime and the promising new hope at the Opera at nights. The climax is reached during a gala performance at the opera with the bank manager singing the lead in Mozart's "Don Giovanni." This may have a chance in the world market since it has speed and singing.

Since neither Bjoernstrand nor Kulle are opera singers, their voices obviously were brilliantly dubbed in. An unusual scene has Bjoernstrand and Kulle, in their cabriolets driving into town, both singing the Toreador Aria from "Carmen." It is one of the films highlights.

Bjoernstrand, as the bank manager who falls in love with the ballet dancer and opera music, is a new high in his acting career. **The role Kulle's has as a big tenor-diva** is highly amusing. As the famous Oswald Berg, he portrays a really self-conscious singer and a Don Juan in both real life and on the stage. Gaby Stenberg, as the very jealous singer and his girl friend, is also standout.

Three newcomers in Swedish films, Lena Soederblom, Meg Westergren (has been in small parts before) and Lena Madsen show future promise.

Eastmancolor camerawork by Karl-Erik Alberts is outstanding as are the other technical credits. A waltz-melody, sung by Joy Ardon, sounds promising. *Winq.*

Faibles Femmes
(Weak Women)
(FRENCH—COLOR)

Paris, March 3.

Marceau release of Paul Graetz production. Stars Mylene Demongeot, Pascale Petit, Jacqueline Sassard, Alain

Lelon; features Pierre Mondy, Noel Roquever, Andre Lugue, Somone Renant. Directed by Michel Boisrond. Screenplay, Annette Wademant: camera (Eastmancolor), Robert Le Febvre; editor, Madeleine Gug. At Biarritz, Paris. Running time, **100 MINS.**

Sabine .... Mylene Demongeot
Agathe .... Pascale Petit
Helene .... Jacqueline Sassard
Julien .... Alain Delon
Edouard .... Noel Roquevert
Father .... Andre Luget
Marguerite .... Somone Renant
Andre .... Pierre Mondy

Peppy filmcomedy deals with a Don Juanesque young man. Three girls he is stringing along try to murder him. It all backfires, of course, but not before a flock of amusing episodes. Looks a good local bet, with strong entertainment and exploitation facets for foreign art houses. It is the kind of comedy with appeal that makes it a promising bet for general playoff. It seems worth dubbing for the Yank mart.

Director Michel Boisrond, who made the Brigitte Bardot starrer "Une Parisienne," has managed to skirt the cynical to make this a fluffy, amusing entry. Though it lacks the irony to give it a sophisticated sting, this has large amounts of Gallic insouciance and impertinence, plus a slick quality which Americans should appreciate.

Three teenage females, a newly married girl, her more flirtatious sidekick and a convent-bred friend, find that a handsome, reckless young man is courting all three though he is engaged. The scorned beauties all dream of killing him and concoct a plan which misfires but lands them in prison while the chastened Don Juan marries the convent-bread girl.

The young leads are all fresh and full of guile, being well aided by the oldsters. Though lightweight fare, it has enough froth and risibility, especially when the three girls have a fight with the boy, to make this interesting fare for some Yank spots. Technical credits are good as are the top production aspects by Paul Graetz.

Mylene Demongeot has the pouting charm necessary for the head instigator of the crime while Pascale Petit and Jacqueline Sassard are also eyefuls. Alain Delond has the looks, if not the smoothness in playing as yet, for the would-be victim role. *Mosk.*

Diary of Anne Frank
(C'SCOPE)

George Stevens' compassionate re-telling of the Anne Frank story makes for long, but profoundly moving film. Expertly produced, it shapes as top grosser.

Twentieth-Fox release of George Stevens production. Stars Millie Perkins, Joseph Schildkraut, Shelley Winters, Richard Beymer, Gusti Huber, Lou Jacobi, Ed Wynn. Directed by George Stevens. Screenplay, Frances Goodrich and Albert Hackett, based on their stage play, taken from "Anne Frank: Diary of a Young Girl"; camera, William C. Mellor and Jack Cardiff; music, Alfred Newman; editors, David Bretherton, Robert Swink, William Mace. Previewed in N.Y., March 16, '59. Running time, **170 MINS.**

Anne Frank .... Millie Perkins
Otto Frank .... Joseph Schildkraut
Mrs. Van Daan .... Shelley Winters
Peter Van Daan .... Richard Beymer
Mrs. Frank .... Gusti Huber
Mr. Van Daan .... Lou Jacobi
Margot Frank .... Diane Baker
Kraier .... Douglas Spencer
Miep .... Dody Heath
Mr. Dussel .... Ed Wynn

Few stories in our time have so caught the imagination and moved the emotions as has "The Diary of Anne Frank," first published in its original form, then made into a play by Frances Goodrich and Albert Hackett and now produced and directed as a fine motion picture by George Stevens. It is a heart-breaking story and yet also an uplifting one that speaks of the dignity of the human spirit, of hope and of decency, through the image of a young girl.

"The Diary of Anne Frank," photographed in black-and-white C'Scope, is a film of often extraordinary quality, not only because of the excellence of its acting, direction and the technical execution, but also because it manages, within the framework of a tense and tragic situation, to convey the beauty of a young and inquiring spirit that soars beyond the cramped confinement of the Frank family's hideout in Nazi-occupied Amsterdam.

Cinematographically, the picture is a major accomplishment. The camera moves in with the Franks, the Van Daans and Dussell, the dentist; it lives with them during those frightful months when a single wrong move could draw attention and bring the "Green Police," the Dutch Gestapo to the hideout; it tunes in on the frictions, the personal jealousies, the resentments generated by this long period of close living; it shares the group's little celebrations, the touching pathos of the present-giving ceremony at Hannukah time, the tender growth of love between Anne Frank and Peter Van Daan and that moment of final terror when the knock of the Gestapo men signals that the end has come.

And yet, with all its technical perfection, the inspired direction and the sensitivity with which many of the scenes are handled, "Diary" is simply too long. It runs very close to three hours, and is being shown with an intermission. Though the camera moves out, providing shots of the outside as it is seen from the hideout atop the spice factory, the length of the picture detracts from its impact.

Everything possible is being done to keep the action moving within its narrow, cluttered space, and a remarkable balance is achieved between stark terror and comedy relief, yet, there are moments, particularly right after the intermission, when the film lags and the dialog becomes forced. Unlike the play, the picture leaves too little to the imagination.

Because Stevens is a craftsman of such high order, a stickler for detail who nevertheless manages to create a great diversity of moods, "Diary" has—for the most part—a well-developed sense of authenticity about it. There is nothing "phoney" about the ingeniously contrived set, which corresponds exactly to the original in Amsterdam, which still exists today, having been turned into a museum. But, more important, the picture has to a large degree retained the spirit of the play, even though its final impact may not be quite as great.

Perhaps this is due to the fact that the picture, even more than the legiter, puts the accent on hope and faith, on the unquenchably youthful and buoyant spirit of Anne who so loved life that those around her were nourished and inspired by the strength of her belief in people and the better tomorrow. The film, with a great many moving touches, and some exquisitely humorous ones, portrays the flowering of a young girl into womanhood, the adult world seen through her eyes.

20th's pre-sell on "Diary" is tremendous, and its international appeal is unquestioned, yet the distributor may have to overcome some resistance on the grounds that this appears to be a "depressing" picture. Actually, the way it's been done, the film is almost inspirational and the action includes some delightful sequences.

Millie Perkins plays Anne. It is her first film role and, in Stevens' capable hands, she turns in a charming and captivating performance. She's devoid of mannerisms. Not beautiful, girl has an expressive face, dominated by large, dark eyes. Whether Miss Perkins, a model, is absolutely right for the part is open to question. It's certainly difficult to accept her as a 13-year old, which was Anne's age at the time the Franks went into hiding. She has the right, awkward, high-pitched voice for the role, which is important since a good deal of the time it is heard in narration. But the voice barely changes from beginning to end, and it's difficult to completely believe in the process of growing-up as portrayed by Miss Perkins. Though her outward behavior changes with the passage of time and the maturing of the emotions, that inner feeling of passing into adulthood is missing.

As Otto Frank, Joseph Schildkraut repeats his marvellous performance on the stage. There is dignity and wisdom in this man, a deep sadness too, and a love for Anne that makes the scene of his return to the hideout after the war a moment full of pain and compassion. Schildkraut, in his restrained way, is a tower of strength in a world gone mad. There is not a false note in his performance, only a kind of warm beauty and understanding that brings to the film some of its most poignant scenes.

As the Van Daan couple, Shelley Winters and Lou Jacobi come up with vivid characterizations that score on all levels. Miss Winters, emotional and frank, turns in an excellent performance, a simple woman with meager resources who can barely cope with the situation and who goes to pieces when her greedy husband wants to sell her fur coat. Jacob is nothing short of superb as the disgruntled, grabbing Van Daan, who misses his comforts and his food and who, in the end, turns thief to fill his stomach.

As young Peter Van Daan, Richard Beymer is touchingly sincere and perfectly matched with Miss Perkins, a boy who discovers in the girl the depth he has been seeking in himself. Gusti Huber is convincing as Mrs. Frank, worrying about her family and unable to comprehend the growing-up of Anne. Ed Wynn registers solidly as the dour Dussell, and he tosses off his many good lines in style.

Diane Baker's sensitive face is pleasing in the comparatively small role of Margot Frank. Douglas Spencer plays Kraler and Dody Heath plays Miep—the two Gentiles who risk their lives hiding out the little group of Jews.

But the key to the film is Stevens who has created here a picture of depth and frequently stunning, throat-catching impact. Perhaps because he tends to be his own editor, some scenes become too extended. Jack Cardiff's lensing is perfect and compassionate, catching every nuance. The Goodrich-Hackett script at no point cheapens the story for the sake of the photographic medium. It is still essentially based on the lines in Anne's diary, and the ending remains unchanged, with Anne's voice saying: "In spite of everything, I still believe that people are really good at heart" and Otto Frank closing her diary with the quiet comment, "She puts me to shame." It is probably one of the most moving curtain lines every written.

George Stevens Jr. directed the location sequences in Amsterdam. William C. Mellor was director of photography and Alfred Newman wrote the background music, which is on the saccharine side. David Bretherton, Robert Swink and William Mace are credited for the editing.

With the tremendous interest that exists in "The Diary of Anne Frank," the picture shapes as a potent earner for 20th. And here is a film for which the industry can take a prideful bow. *Hift.*

The Sad Horse
(C'SCOPE-COLOR)

Story of a boy and his dog, starring David Ladd and Chill Wills; good program entry.

Hollywood, March 11.

Twentieth-Fox release of Richard E. Lyons production. Stars David Ladd, Chill Wills, Rex Reason, Patrice Wymore; feaaures Gregg Palmer, Eve Brent. Directed by James B. Clark. Screenplay, Charles Hoffman; based on story by Zoe Akins; camera (DeLuxeColor), Karl Struss; editor, Richard C. Meyer; music, Paul Sawtell, Bert Shefter. Previewed March 10, '59. Running time, **78 MINS.**

Jackie .... David Ladd
Captain .... Chill Wills
Leslie .... Patrice Wymore
Bill .... Rex Reason
Bart .... Gregg Palmer
Sheila .... Eve Brent
Ben .... William Yip
Jonas .... Leslie Bradley
Sam .... David De Paul

The perennially-favorite boy-and-dog theme gets fresh exposure in this heartwarming film starring David Ladd and Chill Wills. Subject, backed by fine use of color, is interestingly developed through excellent performances and able production and pic emerges as a good entry for the program market.

The Zoe Akins original takes its title from an ailing racing champ, brought to Wills' horse ranch by its owner, Patrice Wymore, to recuperate from a state of depression caused by the disappearance of its dog-mascot. Arriving at the same

time is young Ladd, sent to spend the summer with his grandfather while his father reweds. With the 10-year-old youngster comes his dog. Drama of the Charles Hoffman screenplay twirls around the efforts of the nag's owner to get canine away from the boy as new mascot for her horse, which has regained its spirit because of the dog.

Plottage unravels legitimately under James B. Clark's understanding direction, action never becoming maudlin in dealing with the boy's problem of losing his dog. For melodramatic suspense there's the attack of a rattlesnake while the boy-dog combo is searching for supposed treasure in the hills, and a giant puma stalking the pair through the darkness of night. Production helming by Richard E. Lyons is expert.

Young Ladd, who scored so favorably previously in "Proud Rebel," repeats with a slick portrayal of a lad whose summer on the ranch endows him with maturity, and Wills turns in one of his customary sympathetic characters. Miss Wymore, semi-heavy in her role, acquits herself well and Rex Reason scores as her estranged husband, the pair brought back together by Wills. Gregg Palmer, Eve Brent and William Yip top supporting cast.

Color camera work by Karl Struss shows quality, Richard C. Meyer's editing is tight, music score by Paul Sawtell and Bert Shefter appropriate and art direction by Lyle R. Wheeler and John Mansbridge fits the backgrounds.
Whit.

Gidget
(COLOR; C'SCOPE; SONGS)

Summer comedy - romance; New young names for younger trade. "I Was a Normal Teen-Age American" is basic idea. Promising release though story thin.

Hollywood, March 13.
Columbia release of Lewis J. Rachmil production. Stars Sandra Dee, Cliff Robertson, James Darren, Arthur O'Connell. Directed by Paul Wendkos. Screenplay, Gabrielle Upton; based on the novel by Frederick Kohner; camera, Burnett Guffey; music, Morris Stoloff; editor, William A. Lyon. Previewed at the Stanley Warner Theatre, Beverly Hills, March 11, '59. Running time, **95 MINS.**

Francie	Sandra Dee
Kahoona	Cliff Robertson
Moondoggie	James Darren
Russell Lawrence	Arthur O'Connell
Dorothy Lawrence	Mary La Roche
Mary Lou	Jo Morrow
Stinky	Joby Baker
The Four Preps	Themselves
Lover Boy	Tom Laughlin
B.L.	Sue George
Hot Shot	Robert Ellis
Nan	Yvonne Craig
Patty	Patti Kane
Waikiki	Doug McClure
Lord Byron	Burt Metcalfe
Cop No. 1	Richard Newton
Cop No. 2	Ed Hinton

"Gidget" is a class teen-age comedy in which the kids are, for once, healthy and attractive young people instead of in some phase of juvenile depravity. Lewis J. Rachmil's production for Columbia, directed by Paul Wendkos, has a gaggle of attractive youngsters cavorting on the California beaches as the chief action, so for spring and summer playdates it has a certain timeliness. "Gidget" seems a natural for younger audiences.

Sandra Dee is the "gidget" of the title, being a young woman so slight in stature she is tagged with the nickname which is a contraction of girl and midget. Miss Dee is in that crucial period of growing

up where she doesn't like boys very much but is beginning to realize they are going to play a big part in her life.

Gabrielle Upton's screenplay, based on the book by Frederick Kohner, is played mostly out-of-doors on the ocean front west of Los Angeles that constitutes the play grounds and mating grounds for the young of the area. It makes for handsome backgrounds, and with the youngsters involved chiefly costumed in brief bathing suits, the foregrounds are bright, too.

The simple plot is a contemporary restatement of the "Student Prince" theme. The "surf bum," as surf board enthusiasts are termed, who Miss Dee falls in love with, James Darren, turns out to be the respectable son of a business acquaintance of her father. Young Darren, with summer's end, faces maturity, abandons plans to follow the sun and returns instead to college.

Miss Upton's screenplay is somewhat short on improvisation, in elaborating the slight story, so there is repetition in some scenes. Paul Wendkos' direction is ingenious in delineating the youthful characters, not so easy in presenting normal youngsters of no particular depth or variety. Direction could have been more fluid, however, particularly in the musical numbers. A greater number of camera set-ups would have defeated a certain static quality that occasionally crops up. But Burnett Guffey's sun-washed photography effectively captures the summer spirit and has some exciting shots of surfing.

Miss Dee makes a pert and pretty heroine, and Cliff Robertson, as the only adult of the beach group, is acceptable although the part isn't much for an actor of his stature. James Darren is especially effective as the young man torn between the carefree life and the problems of growing up. Darren, who becomes increasingly impressive as a character juvenile with each outing, also displays a pleasant singing voice in the film's best song, "The Next Best Thing To Love," by Stanley Styne and Fred Karger. Arthur O'Connell and Mary LaRoche are aimable as Miss Dee's Parents, and Jo Morrow, Joby Baker, Tom Laughlin, Sue George, Robert Ellis, Yvonne Craig, Patti Kane, Doug McClure and Burt Metcalfe make up the beach gang, and it's a pleasure to see much handsome young people.

Morris Stoloff's conducting of orchestrations by Arthur Morton and John Williams Jr. is helpful, utilizing the songs, including a nice title tune by Patti Washington and Fred Karger. Josh Westmoreland's sound is good, preserving the location feel without losing dialog. Eastman Color of the print shown for review was often unbalanced, but this will probably be corrected.
Powe.

Les Tripes au Soleil
(Guts In The Sun)
(FRENCH)

Paris, March 17.
Fernand Rivers release of Lodice-Zodiaque-Globe production. With Jacques Robert, Gregoire Aslan, Douta Seck, Millie Vitale, Toto Bissainthe, Roger Blin, Anne Carrere. Written and directed by Claude-Bernard Aubert. Dialog, Claude Accursi; camera, Jean Isnard; editor, Gabriel Rognier. Preemed in Paris. Running time, **105 MINS.**

Bob	Jacques Robert
Bessie	Toto Bissainthe
Stanley	Gregoire Aslan
Vance	Douta Seck
Prostie	Millie Vitale
Tourist	Anne Carrere
Guide	Roger Blin

Tale of racial tension takes place in a supposedly mythical, somnolent town which looks like a cross between a town in the American Southwest and one in Latin America. Also it's a cross between a satire and problem pic, and does not quite jell. This emerges mainly an exploitation item for local and foreign marts.

A guide shows some tourists around the town where a local harlot makes love before a window, the Negroes dance in the streets and the local bagnio operates for tourist pleasures. Tourists are driven off after sampling the townhall and examples of town justice, etc., done like revue sketches. Then the film settles down to show how a lynching is almost accomplished.

A local white man desires a lovely Negress and is beaten up by white bullies. It is blamed on the Negroes and trouble starts. But the boy manages to stop it and throws an artificial leg into the white faces. Pic goes on to show how the boy's and girl's fathers find water to bring prosperity to the town.

Production is technically well done. Acting is fair, but a strident jazz music score and the general talkiness make this a limited affair. Its main chances are on the notoriety it has garnered on its censorship ban here and its theme.
Mosk.

Alias Jesse James
(COLOR—V'VISION)

B.O. will rest entirely on Bob Hope appeal in this mild satire on the traditional oater.

Hollywood, March 13.
United Artists release of Hope Enterprises, Inc., production. Stars Bob Hope, Rhonda Fleming, Wendell Corey. Produced by Jack Hope. Directed by Norman McLeod. Screenplay, William Bowers and Daniel D. Beauchamp; based on a story by Robert St. Aubrey and Bert Lawrence; camera, Lionel Lindon; music, Joseph S. Lilley; editors, Marvin Coil and Jack Bachom. Previewed at the Picwood Theatre, March 9, '59. Running time, **92 MINS.**

Milford Farnsworth	Bob Hope
Cora Lee Collins	Rhonda Fleming
Jesse James	Wendell Corey
Frank James	Jim Davis
Indian Maiden	Gloria Talbot
Titus Queasley	Will Wright
"Ma" James	Mary Young

Bob Hope's latest cinema outing is a broad spoof of the traditional western, with the star as a cowardly, greenhorn insurance man who has, misguidedly, sold a life insurance policy to Jesse James. This is a fair enough premise for the kind of gags and situations that Hope can play off his left hand. Unfortunately, not enough script has been given him for even one finger of the left hand, and the result is an extremely mild comedy that will find fans only among the staunchest Hope adherents. United Artists is releasing.

William Bowers and Daniel D. Beauchamp did the screenplay, from a story by Robert St. Aubrey and Bert Lawrence. It gets off to a slow start with a semi-documentary approach that could be immediately cut; it slows the initial stride to a halting walk without any compensating humor. Hope is sent off to chase Jesse James when it's discovered a $100,000 policy he issued, covers the extremely poor risk of James' life.

Beneficiary of the policy is Jesse's girl, Rhonda Fleming, so Hope must look her up, which he

does; up and down. Wendell Corey, as Jesse James, gets the idea that he can substitute Hope for himself. Hope will then be killed, and Jesse will collect the principal along with Miss Fleming. When Hope tumbles he begins to fight back, eventually knocking off the whole James' gang with the surprise appearance (and aid) of every tv lawman in the west. The finale has surprise. bit appearances by James Arness, Ward Bond, Hugh O'Brian, Gail Davis, Gene Autrey, Hugh O'Brian, James Garner, etc., as his unexpected allies.

Some of the dialog is amusing, and director Norman McLeod has created some traditional film slapstick sequences. But often the lines don't play, and the gag setups and their playoffs miss, almost consistently in the early and middle portions of the picture, indicating the direction and timing are off. It's only in the last half hour or so of the film that it really gets going.

Hope does not show to particular advantage; he has been funnier in a five-minute, stand-up spot. But he's likeable as ever, and creates sympathy. Miss Fleming is only required to look stunning, an assignment she fills admirably. Wendell Corey, as the cold-eyed Jesse, plays it down the middle. Others chiefly involved are Jim Davis, Gloria Talbott, Will Wright and Mary Young, and they perform acceptably.

Jack Hope produced "Alias Jesse James," for Hope Enterprises.
Powe.

The 39 Steps
(BRITISH—COLOR)

Slick, exciting remake of John Buchan's "chase" yarn, with Kenneth More in good form as the hero; worthwhile b.o. prospect for all houses.

London, March 17.
Rank Film Distributors release of Betty Box-Ralph Thomas production. Stars Kenneth More, Taina Elg, Brenda de Banzie, Barry Jones. Directed by Ralph Thomas. Screenplay, Frank Harvey based on novel by John Buchan; camera, Ernest Steward; editor, Alfred Roome; music, Clifton Parker. At Odeon, Leicester Square, London. Running time, **93 MINS.**

Richard Hannay	Kenneth More
Fisher	Taina Elg
Nellie Lumsden	Brenda de Banzie
Professor Logan	Barry Jones
Lumsden	Reginald Beckwith
Nannie	Faith Brook
Brown	Michael Goodliffe
Mr. Memory	James Hayter
Kennedy	Duncan Lamont
McDougal	Jameson Clark
Sheriff	Andrew Cruikshank
Milkman	Leslie Dwyer
Mrs. McDougal	Betty Henderson
Miss Dobson	Joan Hickson
Perce	Sidney James
Mr. Pringle	Brian Oulton

It's been about 25 years since Alfred Hitchcock, taking considerable liberties with John Buchan's novel, "The 39 Steps," turned out a brisk, tense thriller. With a new generation of filmgoers on hand, it was a smart move on the part of Betty E. Box and Ralph Thomas to have another stab at a yarn that has all the ingredients for popular adventure, mystery, thrills and comedy. Though somewhat altered from Hitchcock's original, the main idea remains unchanged and the new version stands up very well. With Kenneth More and Taina Elg starring in the roles first played by the late Robert Donat and Madeleine Carroll, the pic should be a winner in most houses.

When a strange young woman is stabbed to death in his flat, More finds himself involved in a mysterious adventure involving espionage and murder. Before her death

the girl tells him that she is a secret agent and gives him all the clues she knows about a spy organization seeking to smuggle some important plans out of the country. All he knows is that the top man is somewhere in Scotland and that the tangle is tied up with strange words told him by the victim—"The 39 Steps."

Suspected of the murder of the girl, More has just 48 hours to pull off a stiff job, to find out the secret of the 39 Steps, expose the gang and so clear himself of the murder rap. With the police and members of the secret organization on his trail, More gets to Scotland and has some rather odd adventures before the trail leads back to London and a hefty climax in a London vaude house.

Film starts off brilliantly with tremendous tension and suitably sinister atmosphere. After awhile that mood wears off as the pic settles down to an exciting and often amusing chase yarn, set amid some easy-on-the-eye Scottish scenery. More's escape from a train and getaway over the Forth Bridge, a funny scene where he is mistaken for a lecturer and has to deliver a natural history lecture to a girls' school, the dilemma when he finds himself handcuffed to a pretty schoolmistress and has to drag her all through the Scottish moors on his quest (including a night spent in a small hotel) and the final sock climax are all high spots in a film which only occasionally lags.

More's performance is a likeable mixture of humor and toughness while Miss Elg is appealing as the pretty schoolmistress who is dragged into the adventure against her will. Then there are Barry Jones, as a sinister professor; Brenda de Banzie, as a fake spiritualist who, with her eccentric husband (Reginald Beckwith) helps More's getaway; James Hayter as a vaude "memory man" who is a tool of the gang; and Faith Brook, whose murder sparks off the drama, all pitch in splendidly in a well acted picture.

Ralph Thomas has kept the action moving and brought out the best in Frank Harvey's neatly constructed screenplay. Cameraman Ernest Steward has keept the atmosphere of the film well and at the same time taken full advantage of the pictorial opportunities provided by the Scottish moors. "39 Steps" should not disappoint those who remember the original with affection. For newcomers, it should click entertainingly. *Rich.*

The Little Savage

Unimportant pirate yarn strictly for the kids.

Hollywood, Mrach 11.

Twentieth-Fox release of Jack Leewood production. Stars Pedro Armendariz, Christiane Martel, Rodolfo Hoyos, Terry Rangno, Robert Palmer. Directed by Byron Haskin. Screenplay, Eric Norden; based on story by Frederick Marryat; camera, George Stahl Jr.; editor, Albert E. Valenzuela; music, Paul Lavista. Previewed March 10, '59. Running time, **73 MINS**

Captain Tiburon	Pedro Armendariz
Taursus	Rodolfo Hoyos
Frank (Boy)	Terry Rangno
Nanoa	Christiane Martel
Frank (Man)	Robert Palmer

This low-budgetter is strictly for the juve trade, there being little or no appeal for the adult patron. Filmed entirely in Mexico, its story lines the relationship between a pirate and a small boy on a deserted island, well enough handled for what it is but of questionable value in today's market. It will be lower-bracketed with "The Sad Horse."

The Jack Leewood production swings back into the 1700's on the Spanish Main for period, although it will be touch and go how acceptable some of the contrived dialog will be accepted by modern-day kids. Eric Norden screenplay gets underway after Pedro Armendariz, first mate on a pirate ship, is shot and left for dead by Rodolfo Hoyos, the captain, after they have buried two treasure chests on a Caribbean island.

He is found by Terry Rangno, only other occupant of the island and a survivor of a ship sunk by pirates some years before, and their life together is etched down through the years as they await rescue. When the captain returns for his loot, he is killed by his former mate, who in turn is killed in an exchange of shots. The boy, now grown to young manhood, sails away with the treasure and a girl whom he and the old pirate rescued from a war party of natives, who had brought the girl from another island as a sacrifice.

Armendariz portrays the pirate in flambuoyant and lusty style, and Terry Rangno as the boy, and Robert Palmer in same role after he gains maturity, are okay. Christiane Martel looks fetching in her brief appearance, and Hayos delivers a violent characterization in his few scenes. Direction by Byron Haskin fits the assignment.

Technical credits are competently handled, with George Stahl Jr., at the cameras; Albert E. Valenzuela, editor; Paul Lavista, music; John Mansbridge and Ramon Rodriguez, art direction. *Whit.*

Arson for Hire

Weak half of Allied Artists package with "The Giant Behemoth."

Hollywood, March 10.

Allied Artists release of a William F. Broidy Pictures Production. Stars Steve Brodie, Lyn Thomas. Directed by Thor Brooks. Screenplay, Tom Hubbard; camera, William Margulies; editor, Herbert R. Hoffman. Previewed at the studio March 10, '59. Running time, **67 MINS.**

John	Steve Brodie
Keely	Lyn Thomas
Pop	Frank Scannell
Foxy	Antony Carbone
Clete	John Merrick
Yarbo	Jason Johnson
Boswell	Robert Riordan
Marily	Wendy Wilde
Hollister	Walter Reed
Cindy	Lari Laine
Barney	Reed Howes
Jim	Lyn Osborn
Dink	Frank Richards
Hot Dog Vendor	Ben Frommer
Dispatcher	Lester Dorr
Nurse	Florence Useem
Ben	Tom Hubbard

"Arson For Hire" is a crime, no matter how you look at it. A cold story about a hot subject, it lends no support in its Allied Artists' packaging with "The Giant Behemoth," thus serving only to separate the monster's end from its beginning.

Producer William F. Broidy and his staff perhaps deserve credit for ferreting out some rather good holocaust footage and interpolating it skillfully into their storyline. It's when the firemen take off their red hats that the tale bogs down. Tom Hubbard's screenplay, while ridden with cliches, deserves better rendering than was given it by director Thor Brooks. The scenes are static, the characters often immobile, and the result is that badly needed action only infrequently is part of the picture, its wind-up being the most effective.

The story tells of a professional ring of arsonists, led by no less than the arson squad's second-in-command, which sets fire to the biggest buildings in town, then blackmails or bullies the owners into splitting the insurance money with them. Steve Brodie, as the squad's chief inspector, is believable, with okay support from Lyn Thomas, as one of the ring's victims, and scripter Hubbard does a fine job of acting as the heavy. From the supporting cast comes a bit of overacting from Antony Carbone, a bit of sex from Lari Laine, capable performances from Frank Scannell and Jason Johnson and a fine sincere portrayal from Wendy Wilde, as the daughter of the firesetter.

Film editor Herbert R. Hoffman did a good job of lacing William Margulies' photography with the newsreel-like fire shots, and other technical credits, including sound by Ralph Butler and art direction by George Troast, are adequate. *Ron.*

Mustang

Low-grade oater.

Hollywood, March 13.

United Artists release of Robert Arnell production. Directed by Peter Stephens; screenplay, Tom Gries; based on the book, "Capture of the Golden Stallion," by Rutherford Montgomery; camera, William C. Thompson; music, Raoul Kraushaar; editor, Mike Pozen. Previewed at Goldwyn studio, March 10, '59. Running time, **73 MINS.**

Gabe	Jack Beutel
Nancy	Madalyn Trahey
Lou	Steve Keyes

Practically everything that could be wrong with a motion picture afflicts "Mustang," produced in**dependently and then peddled to United Artists, which will release it. UA has a job on its hands, because this film is likely to be rejected even by audiences at the most rudimentary action level, and even as double-bill filler.**

The story line, in the screenplay by Tom Gries, has Jack Beutel as a rodeo star forced to earn a living as a cowhand, after he gambles away his prize earnings. He goes to work for Steve Keyes and his sister, Madalyn Trahey, ranch owners. The plot revolves around a wild stallion, which Keyes wants killed and which Beutel wants to save. The horse is disrupting Keyes' tame mares. All ends with Beutel, the horse and Miss Trahey a happy menage a trois.

The film, produced by Robert Arnell and directed by Peter Stephens, actually has an acceptable story line and some knowledgeable dialog about the contemporary west. However, its development is decidely amateur. It also has, for an outdoors film, some stunning bloopers, such as identifying an opossum as a raccoon, making casual reference to seeing moose in Oklahoma, where they haven't been since approximately the Pleistocene Age, and worst of all, calling the lead horse a mustang when he is plainly (and later so identified) as a purebred Palcmino.

The film seems to have been shot in 16m, then blown up and masked for 1.85 projection. The result is a consistently fuzzy and grainy print, with awkward compositions, heads cropped, etc. The sound seems to have been largely dubbed, editing is poor, shots don't match. It is padded with incongruous shots of wild life, some of which wouldn't be found within a hundred miles of each other, apparently inserted for no other reason than to stretch the thin dramatic sections. No contributions to this film can be credited, except, possibly, for persistence. *Powe.*

Carlton-Browne of the F.O.

(BRITISH)

Offbeat, satirical comedy on misadventures of a dim-witted Foreign Office diplomat; joke wears thin, but creates plenty of yocks.

London, March 10.

British Lion release of Boulting Bros. production. Stars Terry-Thomas, Peter Sellers, Luciana Paoluzzi. Directed by Jeffrey Dell, Roy Boulting. Screenplay, Jeffrey Dell, Roy Boulting; camera, Max Greene; editor, Anthony Harvey; music, John Addison. At Studio One, London. Running time, **87 MINS.**

Carlton-Browne	Terry-Thomas
Prime Minister	Peter Sellers
Princess Ilyena	Luciana Paoluzzi
Colonel Bellingham	Thorley Walters
Young King	Ian Bannon
British resident	Miles Malleson
Foreign Office minister	Raymond Huntley
Grand Duke	John Le Mesurier
Sir Arthur Carlton-Browne	Kynaston Reeves
Lady Carlton-Browne	Marie Lohr
Archipelagos	Marne Maitland
Hewitt	John Van Eyssen
Rodgers	Nicholas Parsons
Security Officer	Basil Dignam
Sir John Farthing	Ronald Adam
Signaller	Sam Kydd
Hotel receptionist	Michael Ward
Mother in newsreel	Irene Handl
Interviewer	John Glyn Jones
Commentator	Harry Locke
Admiral	James Dyrenforth

Celebrating their 21st year as a film producing team, John and Roy Boulting take another of their satirical, irreverent swings at British institutions. They did it to the army in "Private's Progress" and to the law via "Brothers In Law." The F.O. in the title of this current entry stands for Foreign Office and the film is a crazy peek at the indiscretions of foreign diplomacy. The film certainly will entertain most British audiences but may prove too private a joke for international consumption.

Much of the dialog is brilliantly witty. There are some excellent situations and some firstclass prods at dignity. But the comedy tends to get out of hand and, at times, develops merely into a series of not totally relevant sketches. The many plums in it guarantee a carefree evening, but the Boulting Brothers have done better than this. Part of the trouble stems from the fact that they have put their faith in two comedians who are far too associated with their own tele personalities to fit snugly into the general scheme of things. Terry-Thomas and Peter Sellers are often wildly funny but they cannot be accepted in the roles they are playing. Hence, the thin edge of satire is blunted.

The pic concerns the mishaps that happen to a Foreign Office junior official when an ex-colony of Britain's—Gailliardia—becomes news. Rich mineral deposits are indicated on the tiny island. Learning that other Great Powers are sniffing around the island, Carleton-Browne (Terry-Thomas) is dis**patched to sort things out. A series of incredible diplomatic blunders leads to a revolution and peace eventually is restored by a sheer, incredible accident. Here's a good idea which veers between satire, light comedy and utter farce. The result is funny, but of-**

ten unsatisfactory. A "show-of-strength" demonstration by the Gaillardians' puny military forces and a haywire Commando engagement in the revolution are both yock-rousing though the latter is too prolonged.

There are also some neat throwaway gags and a few choice moments but he is a comedian better enjoyed in smaller doses. Sellers plays the Gaillardian blackguard of a Prime Minister with relish. But, here again, the Sellers personality tends to throw the part off-balance.

Best of the major performances come from Raymond Huntley, as a pompous Foreign Office minister, and Ian Bannon, who, as the young king suddenly brought to the throne, brings a most engaging charm and humor to his role. Luciana Paoluzzi provides the glamor. Among the many supporting pieces of thesping which labor successfully to the film's benefit are those of Harry Locke as a local radio commentator; Miles Malleson, as the British resident, and Thorley Walters an inefficient Military Adviser.

The uneven trend of the directing may be because it was shared by Roy Boulting and Jeffrey Dell, who also wrote the screenplay. There are obvious moments when the couple's ideas clash. Max Greene's lensing is sound and atmosphere is polished and convincing. With this film, the dignity of the Foreign Office is often amusingly pricked but never fully punctured. It is the sad case of a film rarely living up to the promise of its initial moments. *Rich.*

The Giant Behemoth

Exploitable, well-done horror.

Hollywood, March 9.

Allied Artists release of a David Diamond production. Stars Gene Evans, Andre Morell, John Turner; features Leigh Madison, Jack MacGowran, Maurice Kaufman, Henry Vidon, Leonard Sachs. Directed by Eugene Lourie. Screenplay, Lourie, from a story by Robert Abel and Allen Adler; camera, Ken Hodges; special effects, Jack Rabin, Irving Block, Louis De Witt, Willis O'Brien, Pete Petterson; music, Ted Astley; editor, Lee Doig. Previewed at the studio March 9, '59. Running time, **79 MINS.**

Steven Karnes .... Gene Evans
Prof. Bickford .... Andre Morell
Ian Duncan .... John Turner
Jean MacDougall .... Leigh Madison
Dr. Sampson .... Jack MacGowran
Submarine Commdr... Maurice Kaufman
Thomas MacDougall ...... Henry Vidon
Interrupting Scientist....Leonard Sacks

"The Giant Behemoth" has been around before, terrorizing citizens and generally tearing urban and rural life to shreds. Still, his curious behavior commands attention, particularly when it's as alluringly horrifying as it is in this David Diamond production. An Allied Artists release being booked with "Arson For Hire," it should be exploitable, marketable and profitable.

Special effects were designed and created by the talented team of Jack Rabin, Irving Block and Louis De Witt plus Willis O'Brien and Pete Petterson. It's effective, but as is the case in so many monster films, the true terror is in the reaction of the people, the fear of the victims and the effect of the unseen monster rather than in the ugly sight of the creature itself. In this case it's due to skillful handling by producer Diamond and scripter-director Eugene Lourie. The Robert Abel-Allen Adler story is believable enough, moving quickly and never getting out of

hand. It tells of a prehistoric creature, revitalized by radiation from atomic blasts, which grows to gigantic proportions and sizzles its British victims to death.

Director Lourie has successfully piled one chill an another, a proposition that the cast goes along with. Gene Evans and Andre Morell, as the calm but fearful scientists, are fine, and equally good work comes from co-star John Turner and the remainder of the cast, Jack MacGowran, Maurice Kaufman, Henry Vidon and Leonard Sachs. A stand-out is Leigh Madison, a striking young woman who, in a small role as the daughter of a victim, proves entirely capable of acting as well as attracting.

Filmed in England, the benefits of seldom-scene settings are a decided bonus as effectively caught by photographer Ken Hodges. Sound by Sid Wiles, editing by Lee Doig and art direction by Harry White are completely professional, and Ted Astley's music builds the suspense appropriately. Make-up by Jimmy Evans rates a terrifying nod. *Ron.*

Carry on Nurse
(BRITISH)

Rollicking hospital farce that will raise the laughs with all but complete eggheads; predictable slapstick situations and dialog, but a surefire b.o. winner here.

London, March 10.

Anglo Amalgamated release of a Peter Rogers production. Stars Shirley Eaton, Kenneth Connor, Charles Hawtrey, Hattie Jacques, Terence Longdon, Bill Owen, Leslie Phillips, Joan Sims, Susan Stephen, Kenneth Williams, Wilfrid Hyde White. Directed by Gerald Thomas. Screenplay, Norman Hinds; camera, Reg Wyler; editor, John Shirley; music, Bruce Montgomery. At Studio One, London. Running time, 86 MINS.

Bernie Bishop .... Kenneth Connor
Oliver Reckitt .... Kenneth Williams
Hinton .... Charles Hawtrey
Ted York .... Terence Longdon
Percy Hickson .... Bill Owen
Jack Bell .... Leslie Phillips
Bert Able .... Cyril Chamberlain
Henry Bray .... Brian Oulton
Colonel .... Wilfrid Hyde White
Matron .... Hattie Jacques
Sister .... Joan Hickson
Dorothy Denton .... Shirley Eaton
Georgie Axwell .... Susan Stephen
Stella Dawson .... Joan Sims
Frances James .... Susan Beaumont
Helen Lloyd .... Ann Firbank
Nightie Nightingale .... Rosalind Knight
Rose Harper .... Marita Stanton
Mick .... Harry Locke
Miss Winn .... Leigh Madison
Stephens .... John Van Eyssen
Anaesthetist .... John Horsley
1st Ambulance Man ..... Anthony Sagar
1nd Ambulance Man ..... Fred Griffiths

Hard on the tremendous boxoffice click of "Carry On, Sergeant," a slapstick army farce which kept both audiences and exhibitors happy over here, comes a similar winner from the same stable. "Carry On, Nurse" is the second in what should be a golden series. It does for hospital what its predecessor did for military life. It likely will chalk up an equal or even bigger financial success. For this one has the added advantage of girls and glamor. Unlike most hospital pix, it ignores drama and scorns pathos. It is an unabashed assault on the patrons' funnybones.

The yocks come thick and fast. There is no concession to subtlety between them, director Gerald Thomas, scriptwriter Norman Hudis and a large cast have provided a fun-fest which is irresistible, even though the average patron will be able to see the gags, puns and situations coming up a mile away. The humor tends to be repe-

titious, flirting with sex and dealing with such typical hospital subjects as bedpans, enemas, preparing patients for operations and so on. Often risque, it is never offensive, being done with such high humor.

There is no story, as such. Hinds has merely dreamed up an anthology of hospital humor, involving a string of vaude situations and eccentric characters. Several of the performers who were in "Carry On, Sergeant" crop up again. Others are added, including a number of easy-on-the-eye girls.

The dialog is brisk. For instance, a nurse hisses to patient: "Shhssh, matron's round." Patient to nurse; "I don't care if she's triangular. I want to sleep." Oddly enough, this corny stuff fits into the pic. Situations are not much more original. Patient falls in love with his nurse. Clumsy nurse causes disaster in the hospital routine.

That the film gets over is considerably due to the actors. In a long cast which involves every type of nurse, a gorgon-like matron and a mixed bag of eccentric patients it is only possible to pick out Hattie Jacques, as the matron; Wilfrid Hyde White, as a suave patient; Ann Firbank, Shirley Eaton, Susan Stephen and Diana Beaumont as pretty, efficient nurses; Joan Sims, as the blunderer, and Kenneth Connor, a pugilist-patient with a broken hand. But Terence Longdon, Kenneth Williams, Charles Hawtrey, Michael Medwin, Bill Owen and Harry Locke are also among the long string of popular British players who enter into this romp as if it were a Christmas party.

Reginald Wyler's photography helps this film, which cost only about $200,000 to make. At the boxoffice, it certainly will be worth very much more. *Rich.*

The Naked Maja
(COLOR; T'RAMA)

Lavish costume meller with Anthony Franciosa and Ava Gardner. Long on camera values, short on characterization. Needs hard sell.

United Artists release of Titanus production. Stars Ava Gardner and Anthony Franciosa. Produced by Goffredo Lombardo. Directed by Henry Koster. Screenplay, Norman Corwin and Giorgio Prosperi; from a story by Oscar Saul and Talbot Jennings; camera (Technicolor), Giuseppe Rotunno; music, Angelo Lavagnino. Previewed at UA homeoffice, March 12, '59. Running time, 110 MINS.

Duchess of Alba.......... Ava Gardner
Francisco Goya ...... Anthony Franciosa
Manual Godoy .... Amedeo Nazzari
Carlos IV .... Gino Cervi
Maria Luisa .... Lea Padovani
Sanchez .... Massimo Serato
Juanito .... Carlo Rizzo
Bayeu .... Renzo Cesana
Pepa .... Ivana Kislinger
Anita .... Audrey MacDonald
Enrique .... Patrick Crean
Aranda .... Tonio Selwart
Dr. Peral .... Peter Meersman
Navarra .... Enzo Fiermonte
Maria de la Luz........ Yemiko Fullwood
Jose .... Carlo Giustini
Rojas, the Innkeeper......Erminio Spalla
The Inquisitor .... John Karlsen
French Ambassador .... Paul Muller
A Maja .... Renata Mauro
A Maja .... Pina Bottin
The Singer .... Amru Sani
The Ballerina .... Carmen Mora
Goya's Assistant .... Clayton Hall
The Priest .... Gustavo De Nardo
Count De Fuentes ..... Andre Estcherasi
Governess Assuncion .. Amina Pirani Maggi
Prince Ferdinando ..... Leonardo Botta
Princess of Portugal. Roberta Primavera
Maria Isabella .... Pamela Sharp
Don Antonio .... Alberto Plebani
Carlotta Joaquina ..... Nadia Balabin
Luigi of Perma .... Giuseppe Giardina
Maria Josefa .... Stella Vitelleschi

There are two people who rate a bonus in connection with "The Naked Maja." One is the fellow who decided to use that original and certainly provocative title for the film. The other is the man in the Post Office who decided to ban the Goya reproduction of "The Naked Maja" from the mails. Along with the unquestionable draw of Ava Gardner, these are the picture's main commercial assets.

Ostensibly, this is the story of the tempestuous love affair of the young Goya, played by Anthony Franciosa, with the Duchess of Alba, i.e. Miss Gardner. It unfolds against the background of Spain in the last stages of the 18th century when, according to the film at least, the Inquisition in Spain still burned people at the stake and revolution rumbled around the Royal Court.

Shot in Rome, the costumes are colorful, the backgrounds seem authentic and the dancing is fiery. "The Naked Maja" is often visually exciting and action, when it does occur, captures the interest. But for the most part this Titanus production just drags on, a maze of pompous dialog and muddled emotions that seldom ring true. Considering the talents that produced "The Naked Maja," this cries for explanation.

The main trouble perhaps is that nothing really happens, though Franciosa goes through various kinds of torture, ranging from his amorous frustrations and jealousies to trial by the Inquisition. The "Naked Maja," incidentally, figures very briefly in the picture itself, though there's little doubt that the controversy over the UA ad is going to sell tickets.

"Leisurely" is the word for the pace which director Henry Koster adopted. His camera lingers endlessly. His characters become stereotypes. In the end, what should have been an intensely moving farewell between Goya and the dying Duchess dissipates its impact

and becomes something closer to opera, a badly-acted last scene of "Boheme."

It's worth mentioning that Koster literally duplicated a scene from Eisenstein's "Potemkin," with soldiers herding a frantic group of men, women and children down a flight of stairs. The similarity is too striking to be overlooked.

With one or two exceptions, the performances are badly overdrawn. Miss Gardner, still very beautiful and attired in some stunning costumes, plays the adventurous Duchess with a combination of haughty dignity, defiance and trembling emotion which doesn't quite come off. She may be excused her final scenes as just badly directed. Franciosa tries hard, but his Goya, hot-eyed and confused, is given to a good deal of staring violence. There's little identification to be felt with this man, just a sense of pity as he falls apart in the yearning for his love.

As Manuel Godoy, the Spanish Prime Minister who schemes to let Napoleon's troops come in, Amedeo Nazzari is handsome and sinister. Gino Cervi infuses a sense of character into the weak person of Carlos IV. Lea Padovani plays the vengeful queen, and Carlo Rizzo stands up well as Goya's friend, Juanito.

There are individual scenes which are well done, and which suddenly open up glimpses of what this film—a coproduction involving UA, Metro and Titanus — could have been. Several of these moments are created by the camera of Giuseppe Rotunno, who knows how to capture the dank tenor of a dungeon and the sun-drenched drowziness of a warm summer afternoon. Several of the crowd scenes also are excitingly handled. The color is good, though many shots are dark.

Considering that it was Norman Corwin who, together with Giorgio Prosperi, wrote the dialog, the lines are more than disappointing. Angelo Francesco Lavagnino did the musical score which is easy on the ear and imaginatively catches the mood of the picture.

There are moments of grandeur in this film, such as the one when the king comes to inspect Goya's work in the church and finds street urchins looking down on him from the frescos. There is never a very clear explanation of what makes the unpredictable painter conform so utterly after having staged his artistic rebellion, nor does his work play much of a part in the story after that, being usurped by his emotional involvment with the Duchess who, in the end, dies of poisoning ordered by Godoy.

Goya deserved a better Hollywood epitaph.   *Hift.*

Juke Box Rhythm
(SONGS)

Nice musical for programmer.

Hollywood, March 20.
Columbia Pictures release of Sam Katzman production. Stars Jo Morrow, Jack Jones; costars Brian Donlevy; features George Jessel, Hans Conried, Karen Booth, Marjorie Reynolds, Frieda Inescort, Edgar Barrier, Fitz Feld, Earl Grant Trio, The Nitwits, Johnny Otis, The Treniers. Directed by Arthur Dreifuss. Screenplay, Mary C. McCall Jr., Earl Baldwin; story, Lou Morheim, camera, Fred Jackman; editor, Saul A. Goodkind. Previewed March 19, '59. Running time, 82 MINS.

Princess Ann .... Jo Morrow
Riff Manton .... Jack Jones
George Manton .... Brian Donlevy
George Jessel .... Himself
Brodine .... Hans Conried
Leslie Anders .... Karin Booth
Martha Manton .... Marjorie Reynolds
Aunt Margaret .... Frieda Inescort
Ambassador Truex .... Edgar Barrier
Ambrose .... Fritz Feld
Redhead .... Hortense Petra
Earl Grant Trio
The Nitwits
Johnny Otis
The Treniers .... Themselves

Sam Katzman continues his parade of pleasant little musicals for the program market with "Juke Box Rhythm," likely to pay off in fashion of past entries. Film is "contrived" but acceptable story line is backgrounded by an assortment of musical turns which should appeal to followers of the pop field. Name of George Jessel—in as guest star—may spark it exploitationwise in some situations.

Jo Morrow and Jack Jones, latter a Capitol recording artist and son of Allan Jones, topbill the cast, which also includes Brian Donlevy as co-star and Hans Conried, Karin Booth, Marjorie Reynolds, Frieda Inescort and Edgar Barrier in prominent support. Screenplay by Mary C. McCall Jr., and Earl Baldwin twirls around situation of a European princess and her aunt—Misses Morrow and Inescort — arriving in N.Y. to purchase the princess' coronation wardrobe, and efforts of a young singer, Jones, to swing the order to an unknown designer, Conried, a former junkman.

Musical numbers are inserted logically through party action and rehearsals for a Broadway revue produced by Donlevy, who plays Jones' errant father. Miss Morrow handles herself nicely with a singleton, "Let's Fall in Love," and Jones warbles three numbers, including the title tune, "The Freeze" and "Make Room for the Joy," all in good voice. The Earl Grant Trio, of Decca, is in for two, "I Feel It Right Here" and "Last Night"; The Treniers give out with "Get Out of the Car"; Johnny Otis combo does "Willie and the Hand Jive"; and The Nitwits, with Sid Millward and Wally Stewart, clown through a couple of instrumental numbers. Jessel sings "Spring Is the Time for Remembering."

Principals deliver well, Miss Morrow pretty and Jones displaying a likable personality. Donlevy is persuasive as theatrical producer, separated from Marjorie Reynolds, and who falls for Karin Booth, a wealthy beauty, and both femmes turn in brief but interesting portrayals. Conried is solid in his role, too, and Miss Inescort plays an autocratic aunt. Jessel plays himself.

Arthur Dreifuss' direction fits the mood and technical credits are well handled, including Fred Jackman's camera work, Saul A. Goodkind's editing, Paul Palmentola's art direction and choreography and musical numbers created by Hal Belfer.   *Whit.*

Green Mansions
(COLOR; C'SCOPE)

Disappointing filmization of the W. H. Hudson Novel. Spotty b.o.

Hollywood, March 13.
Metro release of Edmund Grainger production. Stars Audrey Hepburn and Anthony Perkins; costars Lee J. Cobb, Sessue Hayakawa, Henry Silva. Directed by Mel Ferrer. Screenplay, Dorothy Kingsley; based on the novel by W. H. Hudson; Camera, Joseph Ruttenberg; special music, Heitor Villa-Lobos; score, Bronislau Kaper; editor, Ferris Webster. Previewed at the studio, March 6, '59. Running time, 104 MINS.

Rima .... Audrey Hepburn
Abel .... Anthony Perkins
Nuflo .... Lee J. Cobb
Runi .... Sessue Hayakawa
Kua-Ko .... Henry Silva
Don Panta .... Nehemiah Persoff
Priest .... Michael Pate
Cla-Cla .... Estelle Hemsley

This is one of those screen versions that is likely to confuse those who haven't read the book and irritate those who have. While novelty is an important element of showmanship, and "Green Mansions" has this quality, it isn't enough and it isn't sustained to provide successful entertainment.

The Metro release, produced by Edmund Grainger and directed by Mel Ferrer, has two good young stars, Audrey Hepburn and Anthony Perkins, but it's unlikely they're strong enough to carry this film on their sole appeal. Although it has been made with an eye to class and artistic appeal, "Green Mansions" probably will get its heaviest response if billed as, a high-grade jungle film.

Filmization of W. H. Hudson's novel has been approached with reverence and taste but fantastic elements puzzle and annoy. Psuedo-poetic ending solves (and resolves) nothing.

Hudson wrote an allegory of eternal love in his story of Rima, the bird-girl, who is discovered in the Venezuelan jungles by the political refugee, Abel. In Dorothy Kingsley's screenplay, Rima, played by Audrey Hepburn, is a real girl, but one with unusual communion with the forest and its wild life. She is found by Abel, portrayed by Anthony Perkins, when he hides out with an Indian tribe after fleeing a political uprising in which his father had been killed.

Rumors of gold in the neighborhood stir Perkins' imagination because he needs money to avenge his father's assassination. He soon finds himself caught in a cross-fire of ambitions and emotions. The superstitious tribesmen, fired by Henry Silva, the chief's son, want to kill Miss Hepburn, whom they consider an evil spirit. While trying to protect her, Perkins is also at odds with Miss Hepburn's foster grandfather, Lee J. Cobb. Cobb knows where there's gold, and he's intent on protecting it from Perkins, and Miss Hepburn from Silva.

As in the book, the girl is finally destroyed by the Indians, who catch her at the top of a huge, hollow tree. They build a fire at its base and she is consumed by flames shooting up the flue-like trunk. The moral is that love, like one of the legendary flowers of the forest jungle, rises again no matter how often it seems obliterated.

Ferrer and his cameraman, Joseph Ruttenberg, had done some good location work in South America. It is skillfully utilized, by process and editing, with backlot work. But Ferrer has been less successful in getting his characters to come alive, or in getting his audience to care about them. Dreamy and dream-like they seem in the early stages of the film, and they never achieve reality for emotional tug on the spectator's mind or heart.

Miss Hepburn is pretty as the strange young woman, but with no particular depth. Perkins seems rather frail for his role, despite a trial by ordeal given him by Silva's tribe. Silva, on the other hand, gives an exciting performance, fatally damaging to Perkins, the hero, overshadowing him in their dramatic conflict. Cobb's role is not well realized and shows this good actor to no particular advantage. Another casualty is Sessue

Hayakawa, who seems uncompromisingly Oriental, even more so than he might otherwise, because the casting department has surrounded him with "natives" who genuinely resemble South American Indians. Nehemiah Persoff is another lost in a meaningless part.

Impressive credits were brought into "Green Mansions," including the Brazilian composer Heitor Villa-Lobos and the Illinois choreographer Katherine Dunham. There are several themes in the score for the picture (for which credit goes to Bronislau Kaper) that sound like Villa-Lobos, but the credits make it impossible to separately credit anyone. There is also a title song, by Kaper and Paul Francis Webster, that is rather incongruously introduced by Anthony Perkins, but it is a pretty tune and despite its awkward introduction, is a pleasant diversion. Miss Dunham's dance scene, on which considerable time was spent in the filming, is brushed off so abruptly as to leave little impression.   *Powe.*

Whirlpool
(BRITISH-COLOR)

Turgid drama with indifferent acting, flat dialog and uneven lensing; marquee names may make it a draw on the Continent, but it's not likely elsewhere.

London, March 17.
Rank production (George Petcher) and release. Stars Juliette Greco, O. W. Fischer. Directed by Lewis Allen. Screenplay, Lawrence P. Bachmann; camera, Geoffrey Unsworth; editor, Russell Lloyd; music, Ron Goodwin. At Gaumont, Haymarket, London. Running time, 95 MINS.

Lora .... Juliette Greco
Rolph .... O. W. Fischer
Georg .... Marius Goring
Dina .... Muriel Pavlow
Herman .... William Sylvester
Derek .... Richard Palmer
Mrs. Steen .... Lilly Kann
Braun .... Peter Illing
Wendel .... Geoffrey Bayldon
Riverman .... Victor Brooks
Pilot .... Arthur Howell
Stiebel .... Harold Kasket

Still wooing the profitable German market, the Rank Organization shrewdly signed up Germany's top actor, O. W. Fischer. For further international flavor in this pic co-starred him with Juliette Greco and added a Hollywood director, Lewis Allen. But even this combo of talent cannot save "Whirlpool" from emerging as a major disappointement, with flat performances, uninspired direction and stilted dialog and situations. Fischer's name may well bring in the patrons in Germany, but elsewhere it seems unlikely that this trite item will receive much of a welcome.

The yarn is set on the German River Rhine and its main advantage is that it offers some attractive views of the river and its surroundings. Indeed, the director and the cameraman tend to linger so lovingly over the scenery that plot and characterization gets lost. The story has Miss Greco as a waitress, tring to break away from her conman boy friend. When he knifes a man in her cafe and later shoots a cop she panics and makes a getaway on a tanker, skippered by Fischer. Bitter and cynical, Miss Greco rejects the friendly overtures of the skipper, his mate and the deckboy and also runs up against the jealousy of the mate's wife.

Determined not to lose the girl,

the criminal decides to smuggle on to the tanker and duck the cops. The police know that the waitress is on board and decide to leave her there as a decoy. This turgid story winds up with a scrap in the wheelhouse, the drowning of the crook and a fadeout when the girl is nabbed by the police but she promises to return to marry the river-captain when freed.

After a promisingly brisk start, the film becomes moribund and the characters mostly spend their time bickering and mouthing pseudo-philosophy about life and living. The uniformly mediocre performances certainly can be attributed in part to Lawrence Bachmann's screenplay, which is deadly dull and full of unexplained holes. Uninspired cutting also hurt. There are no production highlights. Even the promising gaiety of a German wine festival splutters out miserably with a few desultory shots of fireworks.

Miss Greco, who made an impact in her two previous pix, "Naked Earth" and "Roots of Heaven," gloomes her way through this one as if her heart is not in it. Fischer, a blond, stolid young man, rarely seen without his pipe, reveals little of the star quality which he apparently must possess to have reached his German pinnacle. Muriel Pavlow is ill-cast as the jealous wife and Marius Goring, in a jaunty way, and Richard Palmer, as an infatuated deckboy, emerge best out of the proceedings. William Sylvester does what he can with the badly written role of the crook, but he has a tough job.

When the camera is covering the river and banks, it produces some attractive results, but is less merciful to the thesps whose complexions are often the hue of ripe tomatoes. The black fringes around the artists on the traveling shots reveal technical flaws. More urgent direction and brisker editing might have helped out. But it looks suspiciously as if the screenplay itself got out of hand either before or during shooting. *Rich.*

Westbound
(WARNERCOLOR)

Action western for action houses.

Hollywood, March 17.
Warner Bros. release of a Henry Blanke production. Stars Randolph Scott, Virginia Mayo; also stars Karen Steele, Michael Dante. Directed by Budd Boetticher. Screenplay, Berne Giler, from story by Giler and Albert Shelby LeVino; camera, J. Peverell Marley; editor, Philip W. Anderson; music, David Buttolph. Previewed at the studio, March 17, '59. Running time, 72 MINS.
John Hayes .... Randolph Scott
Norma Putnam .... Virginia Mayo
Jeannie Miller .... Karen Steele
Rod Miller .... Michael Dante
Clay Putnam .... Andrew Duggan
Mace .... Michael Pate
Stubby .... Wally Brown
Russ .... John Day
Willis .... Walter Barnes

"Westbound" is bound for the bevy of action houses corralled these many years by its star, Randolph Scott, and the Warner Bros. picture, produced by Henry Blanke and directed by Budd Boetticher, should run considerably in the black for the Burbank filmmakers.

Finely mounted in WarnerColor and with a bouncy musical score by David Buttolph, "Westbound" combines the essential, if not uncommon, element of greed, jealousy and hate to come up with a more than passable story by Berne Giler and Albert Shelby Levine, with tight screenplay by Giler.

Boetticher's direction keeps the action at properly spaced peaks, thus bringing the chases, gun battles and ambushes right out where audiences can get lost in their excitement.

Scott stars as a Union cavalry officer takes over as a major-domo of the Overland Stage Lines to bring the gold from California to the North's coffers. He's based in a decidedly pro-Southern Colorado city where dwells Andrew Duggan, who just happens to be married to Virginia Mayo who just happens to be Scott's one-time love. Duggan is up to no good, trying hard to intercept the gold for the South, but he's not nearly as bad as his henchmen who seem to care more for themselves than the glory of the Confederacy. And, so, Duggan is killed saving Scott from his men, and, with his head in the dust, asks the hero to look after his widow. Scott promises he will and promptly sends the woman back East, then turns his fatherly eyes to a fetching young blonde widow, Karen Steele, who's been a whole lot more wholesome in the first place.

All concerned handle their roles well, Scott coming across strong, with Miss Steele and Michael Dante, her soldier-husband destined for death, turning in excellent performances. Michael Pate is fine as the heavy, with good work from Miss Mayo and Duggan as well as the supporting players, Wally Brown, John Day and Walter Barnes.

Photography by J. Peverell Marley, art direction by Howard Campbell, set decoration by Gene Redd, sound by Sam Goode and editing by Philip W. Anderson are all well done. *Ron.*

Thunder In the Sun
(COLOR)

Strictly for the action market. An unappetizing hash of old west cliches, with only stars Susan Hayward and Jeff Chandler for b.o. bait.

Hollywood, March 20.
Paramount release of Seven Arts-Carrollton Production. Stars Susan Hayward and Jeff Chandler. Produced by Clarence Greene. Director-writer, Russell Rouse; adaptation by Stewart Stern; camera (Technicolor), Stanley Cortez; music, Cyril Mockridge; editor, Chester Schaeffer. Previewed at the studio, March 18, '59. Running time, 81 MINS.
Gabrielle Dauphin .... Susan Hayward
Lon Bennett .... Jeff Chandler
Pepe Dauphin .... Jacques Bergerac
Louise Dauphin .... Blanche Yurka
Andre Dauphin .... Carl Esmond
Fernando Christophe .. Fortunio Bonanova
Edmond Duquette ...... Bertrand Castelli

The original story for "Thunder In the Sun" has some freshness and vitality, but the treatment it is given is so leaden and mundane that, except for a short portion near the end, it seems more suitable to the libretto for a Romberg operetta than a period western. Appeal will rest entirely on the stars, Susan Hayward and Jeff Chandler. Paramount is releasing the film, produced by Clarence Greene. Russell Rouse wrote and directed it.

Miss Hayward, with a Fifi D'Orsay accent, is one of a group of Basques attempting a cross-country trek of the United States in 1847. The party intends to take up wine-making in the valleys of California and is transporting its precious grapevines via covered wagon across the great plains. Jeff Chandler is hired as guide to the group and in contradiction to most accounts of such hard-bitten, but rigidly moral gents, immediately

begins to lay his calloused paws on Miss Hayward, wife of the party's leader, Carl Esmond.

He won't take "non" for an answer, although Miss Hayward keeps reminding him, somewhat unconvincingly, that she's already married. Finally, when Chandler catches her at one of those outdoor bathing scenes that apparently were staples of the Conestoga parties, Chandler again attacks her. Esmond starts to come to her rescue, is mistaken for an Indian by a nervous sentry and is shot dead. By Basque custom, Miss Hayward is then immediately betrothed to Esmond's younger brother, Jacques Bergerac. Such outlandish foreign customs cut no ice with Chandler, who continues puffing after Miss Hayward until, in the end, he gets her. Seldom has a "hero" been limned so unappetizingly.

It is a small point, but the Basques are represented as speaking French, although this singular race between the French and Spaniards is unique in speaking a language unrelated to any other in Europe. It was a further mistake to impose this inaccurate accent on Miss Hayward, particularly since the rest of the cast, except for Bergerac, uses any accent handy.

There are some good points of authentic historical accuracy. The custom of the mountaineering Basques of communicating by a fearful warbling scream, for instance, and their rugged fierceness. The latter is utilized in a really good sequence at the end, largely staged by second unit director Winston Jones. Indians threaten to ambush the party at a mountain pass. Since the Basques are as handy on a craggy peak as the Indians, the Europeans decide to ambush the aborigines, instead of following the customary script. What follows is a rolling, tumbling, bloody battle-scene that is genuinely different and exciting. It is over too soon, however, and the film ends with Chandler getting Miss Hayward, as clear-cut example of vice triumphant as the screen has ever attempted.

Miss Hayward, such a good actress, founders on the role as she does on the improbable accent. Her characterization, at least as it appears on film, consists largely of eye-flashing and bosom-heaving. Chandler's character is so unpleasant that he is neither sympathetic nor interesting. Bergerac comes off pretty well, and Blanche Yurka, as a Basque matriarch, shrewdly ignores the French accent altogether, and succeeds largely by force of personality in making an impression. Carl Esmond, Fortunio Bonanova and Bertrand Castelli are those most prominent in the supporting cast who appear to some advantage.

Stanley Cortes' camera work is capable, and other credits are acceptable. Cyril Mockridge's music contains some interesting orchestration, but the title song seems entirely out of key with the film, although what the title means is never explained, anyway. *Powe.*

Verboten

Well-done film with shocking Nazi footage. Lends itself to exploitation.

Hollywood, March 13.
J. Arthur Rank (via Ilya Lopert-UA) release of a Globe Enterprises-RKO Radio production. Stars James Best and Susan Cummings; introduces Tom Pittman. Written, produced and directed by Samuel Fuller; camera, Joseph Biroc; editor, Philip Cahn; music, Harry Sukman. Previewed March 13, '59. Running time, 86 MINS.
David .... James Best
Helga .... Susan Cummings
Bruno .... Tom Pittman
Capt. Harvey .... Paul Dubov
Franz .... Harold Daye
Helmuth .... Dick Kallman
Colonel .... Stuart Randall
Burgermeister .... Steven Geray
Frau Schiller .... Anna Hope
SS Officer .... Robert Boon
Erich .... Sasha Harden
Guenther .... Paul Busch
Sgt. Kellogg .... Neyle Morrow
Infantryman .... Joseph Turkel

The photographic record of Nazi atrocities which Samuel Fuller has incorporated in "Verboten" is timeless horror and piercing documentation of the low point in modern history. Grim authenticity gives this exploitability. J. Arthur Rank (since out of U.S. distribution) releases this Globe Enterprises Production, financed by RKO Radio, and, while it lacks star value, "Verboten" can be properly exploited to a profitable boxoffice.

Fuller wrote, produced and directed the film and has created an interesting picture of a German city in the first days of U.S. occupation following World War II. The adventures, emotions and deceits that befall its characters are strong enough and only their comparison to the most inhumanely vile acts ever to be exhibited commercially makes the storyline seem mild.

The initial scenes build a troubled romance between a warm G.I. (James Best) and a sympathetic German girl (Susan Cummings), with the latter part of the film being devoted to the thought-provoking resurgence of the Hitler youth into a "Werewolf" band—a kind of ersatz ratpack — which loots, kills, aids escaped war criminals and generally poses intolerable trouble to the American Military Government. Key to the band's destruction is the girl's 15-year-old brother, a member of the gang, who becomes disillusioned upon attending the Nuremberg War Criminal Trials and seeing the captured German film of Nazi horrors. "I didn't know," he sobs, and it's believable he didn't. He provides the military with information on the pack, and its death follows.

Fuller's production is excellent, having the look and feel of a film more costly than it likely was. His direction is good, often excellent, and his cast responds adeptly. Best is forceful in his determination to love in the days when it, as so many things, was forbidden. Miss Cummings is very good throughout, growing steadily with the film coming across expertly in the final sequences. The late Tom Pittman has introductory billing in the film, and, as the leader of the wild youth, showed fine style and sound talent. Also good are Paul Dubov as the commanding officer, Harold Daye as the boy, Sasha Harden as a young German, with Dick Kallman, as a hungry pack member, turning in an outstanding performance.

The film is put together with skill, lacing back and forth from Hollywood shots to German footage with finesse. Photographer Joseph Biroc and editor Philip Cahn rate special nods, with John Mansbridge's art direction topnotch and sound by Jean Speak and Bert Schoenfeld particularly good. Harry Sukman's musical score, while too heavy on Beethoven's Fifth, is adeptly written. As for the Sukman-Mack David title tune (sung by Paul Anka), it is a lilting love ballad that is completely out

of harmony with the scenes ot battle and death over which it is heard. *Ron.*

SOS Gletscherpilot
(SOS Glacier Pilot)
(SWISS)
Zurich, March 17.

Praesens-Film release of Unitas-Film (Oscar Dueby) production. Stars Annemarie Duringer, Robert Freitag, Leopold Biberti, Anna Marie Blanc, Hannes Schmidhauser, Hermann Geiger. Directed by Victor Vicas. Screenplay, Werner Wollenberger; camera, Emil Berna; editor, Hans Heinrich Egger; music, Hans Moeckel. At Scala Theatre, Zurich. Running time, **100 MINS.**

Monica	Annemarie Duringer
Gisler	Robert Freitag
Dr. Gruber	Leopold Biberti
Frau Gruber	Anne Marie Blanc
Charly	Hannes Schmidhauser
Glacier Pilot	Hermann Geiger
Rita	Anneliese Betschart
Perren	Robert Bichler
Baumann	Zarli Carigiet
Portmann	Ettore Cella
Roby	Helmut Foernbacher
Perren, Sr.	Fritz Gammenthaler
Puckle	Patrick Jordan
Garage Owner	Max Knapp
Kalbermatten	Erwin Kohlund

This latest Swiss feature, brought in at a (by Swiss standards) relatively high budget of $175,000, impresses as an honest attempt at a theme long overdue for local filming. It is a story about the often mortally dangerous rescue actions of lost or wounded mountaineers in the Swiss Alps by mountain guides and glacier pilots. Three months of shooting under hazardous circumstances on location, at altitudes of 11,000 to 14,000 feet, resulted in a visually exciting film whose stark realism in the mountain scenes make it a contender for presentation abroad, including the U.S. Of the cast members, Annemarie Duringer, under contract to 20th-Fox, is not unfamiliar to Yank audiences.

Participation of real-life Swiss glacier pilot Hermann Geiger, adds to the plausibility of the rescue sequences which make up most of the film's second half. Up to this point, screenplay developments are often sketchy and sometimes unconvincing. Film's forte, therefore, lies definitely in all semi-documentary passages of which there are many.

Plot involves the personal destinies of a group of people of various backgrounds, reunited in a perilous mountain tour, and their different reasons for participating in the undertaking. Drama sets in when they get stuck in the glaciers by accident, with some of them killed immediately and others dangerously injured. Immediate search parties over the glaciers and by air succeed in rescuing some of the victims, but not all of them.

French-U.S. director Victor Vicas, experienced in documentaries and feature pix, lead to his being chosen for this one, does a commendable job but cannot overcome the film's earlier script weaknesses. Camera work by Swiss vet cameraman Emil Berna is masterful and one of the brightest assets.

Cast is well chosen, although Miss Duringer and Robert Freitag, both satisfactory acting-wise, have been handed some especially trite dialog as the romantic interest. Anne Marie Blanc and Leopold Biberti as a married couple with the difference-in-ages problem, are convincing while Hannes Schmidhauser, usually cast in romantic leads, is excellent as a ruthless young leather-jacketeer. Among featured roles, Patrick Jordan, recruited from Britain, is standout as an English mountaineer finding death in the glaciers. Locally the pic is in Swiss-German, but Praesens also makes a German version available. *Mezo.*

L'Ile Du Bout Du Monde
(Island At the End of The World)
(FRENCH)
Paris, March 24.

Lux release of Riviera Films production. Stars Rossana Podesta, Magali Noel, Dawn Addams, Christian Marquand. Directed by Edmond Greville. Screenplay, Greville, L.-A. Pascal, Henri Crouzat from novel by Crouzat; camera, Jacques Lemare; editor, Jean Ravel. At Balzac, Paris. Running time, **105 MINS.**

Jane	Magali Noel
Victoria	Dawn Addams
Caterina	Rossono Podesta
Patrick	Christian Marquand

Film's plot has three comely femmes shipwrecked on a tropical isle during the last war along with one virile male. Their adventures, and sex involvements, gives this mainly exploitation pegs on some forthright love scenes and justifiable nudity.

However, this vehicle has a tendency to be literary. Too, it spills many aphorisms on life with three women and a man. He falls for all three femmes but ends with none because one dies in trying to reach another isle for help, the second is killed by the third, who turns out to be a homicidal maniac. She, in turn, commits suicide, allowing the man to be rescued alone.

Christian Marquand fares well as the male but Magali Noel overcharges her nympho role. However, she makes up for it with plenty of heavy breathing and unveiled charms. Rossana Podesta and Dawn Addams are effective as the other two women. Pic is only intermittently effective, with characterizations uneven and the sudden twists in the plot too much telegraphed.

But this film has a good technical mounting and probably is in store for good local biz, with obvious okay hypo possibilities for abroad. *Mosk.*

Fangelse
(Prison)
(SWEDISH)
Paris, March 17.

Teleclnez release of Terra Film production. With Doris Svedlund, Birger Malmsten, Eva Henning, Hasse Ekman, Stig Olin, Irma Christenson, Anders Henriksson. Written and directed by Ingmar Bergman. Camera, Goran Strindberg; editor, Lennart Wallen. At Studio Des Ursulines, Paris. Running time, **80 MINS.**

Brigitte	Doris Svedlund
Thomas	Birger Malmsten
Sophie	Eva Henning
Martin	Hasse Ekman
Peter	Stig Olin
Linnea	Irma Christenson
Professor	Anders Henriksson

This makes the 10th pic by Swedish writer-director Ingmar Bergman to get art house unveiling here this season. Bergman, however, is more than a fad but a definite, original film talent. But this film, an earlier one, is somewhat loaded with private symbolism and expressionistic bric-a-brac to be anything more than a limited, arty entry abroad.

The theme concerns a film director toying with the idea of doing a production with the theme of hell on earth. Then pic tells three stories, bound together with that of the director, concerning a group of people whose life is hell. Though adroitly interspersed and well notated, this lacks the breadth to make all the grim activity meaningful.

Bergman shows his versatility in the handling of actors, symbols and tensions. However, he misses out by turning this into a downbeat affair without the true revealing facets to make all this suffering and dreariness a comment on human problems. Technical credits are fine. *Mosk.*

April 1, 1959

Warlock
(COLOR; C'SCOPE)

Big western with top stars in class production. Strong b.o.

Hollywood, March 27.

Twentieth-Fox release of Edward Dmytryk production. Stars Richard Widmark, Henry Fonda, Anthony Quinn, Dorothy Malone, Dolores Michaels. Directed by Edward Dmytryk. Screenplay, Robert Alan Aurthur; based on the novel by Oakley Hall; camera, Joe MacDonald; music, Leigh Harline; editor, Jack W. Holmes. Previewed at the studio, March 27, '59. Running time, **122 MINS.**

Gannon	Richard Widmark
Blaisdell	Henry Fonda
Morgan	Anthony Quinn
Lily Dollar	Dorothy Malone
Jessie	Dolores Michaels
Judge Holloway	Wallace Ford
Abe McQuown	Tom Drake
Bacon	Richard Arlen
Curley	De Forest Kelley
Skinner	Regis Toomey
Richardson	Vaughn Taylor
Dr. Wagner	Don Beddoe
Petrix	Whit Bissell
Slavin	Bartlett Robinson
Shaw	J. Anthony Hughes
Calhoun	Donald Barry
Billy Gannon	Frank Gorshin
Mac Donald	Ian Mac Donald
Hutchinson	Stan Kamber

Many of the familiar elements of the western story, the frontier town cowed by unruly elements, the imported lawman with a killer's reputation, the citizens who finally assert themselves to gain control of their community, these are all part of "Warlock." But the 20th-Fox presentation, produced and directed by Edward Dmtryk, is an effort to take such a theme, familiar in its basic outline, and carry it beyond the ordinary conclusion and behind the usual facade. It is an "adult" western in depth, and given a class production, it should be a strong box-office attraction.

The title, "Warlock," refers to the name of the town where the action occurs, not to the fact that the word is defined as a male witch, although this may have some implication. Robert Alan Aurthur's screenplay, based on a novel by Oakley Hall, opens with a scene that is usually the end in many westerns, the gunman's walk. It is effective as an immediate means of setting the locale's lawless mood.

Richard Widmark is a member of the cowboy gang bossed by Tom Drake, but he early shows he is not happy with the barbarous pleasures of the group, which include sadistic teasing and wanton murder. When some of the town elders invite a gun-slinging marshal, Henry Fonda, to take over the town on his own terms, it is laid in that Widmark has a yen to desert his yahoo comrades and line up with law and order. Fonda takes over accompanied by his enigmatic companion, Anthony Quinn. Part of the deal is that Quinn and Fonda will run the local dance hall-gambling parlor; controlled vice.

Fonda cleans up the town, runs Drake's boys out, but then finds personal problems he must solve. Quinn wants to move on, to the "next town," as he and Fonda have always done. Fonda is in love with a girl of the town, Dolores Michaels. He is also aware that the west is changing (the time is 1881), and men of his breed may be running out of towns. There are other complications, such as Dorothy Malone, whom Quinn has loved hopelessly, and who realizes that Quinn is using Fonda as a human crutch for his physical handicap, a deformed foot, and the emo-

tional crippling it has inflicted on him.

Ending finds Widmark as the official deputy sheriff, forced to outlaw Fonda's effective, if vigilante-style, rule. Fonda frees himself of Quinn in a duel provoked by Quinn in which the latter is killed. Fonda then throws in his hand, represented by a pair of gold-plated Colts, and rides out of town. The plot, dealing as it does with very complicated people, is involved, but not puzzling.

Authur's characters and their dialog are fresh and picturesque. Widmark's portrayal is vital, although his early position as a member of the hell-raising gang is not entirely clear. Fonda is particularly fine. It may not be a romantic conception, but Fonda gives his role great validity. It embodies the qualities of mock-chivalric disillusion that seems to have characterized some of these members of the 19th Century "lost generation," rootless and eventually aimless as the frontier outgrew them. Quinn's brooding performance is menacing and purposely perplexing, given considerable breadth by this good actor's native intelligence.

Miss Malone is satisfactory as one of the girls in the story, winding up romantically with Widmark, and Miss Michaels is impressive as the other, although her character gets somewhat lost towards the end.

Dmytryk has taken the trouble to etch some memorable minor characters, important as they stress the divergent points of view in the town, and important to personalize the town's struggle for maturity. Wallace Ford, Tom Drake, Richard Arlen, DeForrest Kelley, Regis Toomey, Frank Gorshin and David Garcia are outstanding. Others in the large cast who contribute include Vaughn Taylor, Don Beddoe, Whit Bissell, Bartlett Robinson, J. Anthony Hughes, James Philbrook, Paul Comi, Joe Turkel and Donald Barry.

Joe MacDonald's camera catches some magnificent location backgrounds, thoughtfully composed, and is equally adept at the closer range work. Leigh Harline's music, in orchestrations by Edward B. Powell and conducted by Joseph Newman, is unobtrusive, but valuable. Art direction by Lyle R. Wheeler and Herman A. Blumenthal, with set decoration by Walter M. Scott and Stuart A. Reiss, is strongly alive to the period. Editing, by Jack W. Holmes is capable. Sound seems to be somewhat too slick. In some outdoor scenes, natural noises seems entirely wiped out, with dialog entirely too clear.

Powe.

The Hound of the Baskervilles
(BRITISH-COLOR)

Well-made remake of Sherlock Holmes yarn, with obvious marquee appeal in the title.

London, March 24.

United Artists release of a Hammer Film (Anthony Hinds) production. Stars Peter Cushing, Andre Morell, Christopher Lee. Directed by Terence Fisher. Screenplay, Peter Bryan; editor, James Needs; camera, Jack Asher. At Hammer Theatre, London. Running time, **88 MINS.**

Sherlock Holmes	Peter Cushing
Dr. Watson	Andre Morell
Sir Henry Baskerville	Christopher Lee
Cecile	Marla Landi
Sir Hugo Baskerville	David Oxley
Bishop Frankland	Miles Malleson
Dr. Mortimer	Francis De Wolff
Stapelton	Ewen Solon
Barrymore	John Le Mesurier
Perkins	Sam Kydd
Servant Girl	Judi Moyens
Mrs. Barrymore	Helen Goss
Servant	Dave Birks
Seldon	Michael Mulcaster

"The Hound Of The Baskervilles" is one of Conan Doyle's bestknown Sherlock Holmes yarns, but it still holds up in interest, and Hammer has done a good job with this latest remake of the meller. Relying less on star names than on title value for marquee appeal, "Baskervilles" should prove a useful booking at many popular houses. It's the first Sherlock Holmes pic in color which should be a handy selling point for United Artists.

For those unfamiliar with the yarn, it takes place in the desolate setting of Dartmoor. The famous private eye and his faithful stooge, Doctor Watson, are called in following the mysterious slaying of Sir Charles Baskerville. It's thought that his successor, Sir Henry, may meet the same fate. The action fringes on the Legend of the Baskervilles, which suggests that the family is cursed because of the crimes of an earlier Baskerville. A mad hound roaming the moor is the instrument of death.

Holmes and Watson go to Dartmoor to protect the new holder of the title and the ingenious sleuth, after some creepy adventures, unearths the criminal and winds up the mysterious legend in the nick of time.

Although every patron will have his own idea of Sherlock Holmes, it is difficult to fault the performance of Peter Cushing, who looks, talks and behaves in precisely the way approved by the Sherlock Holmes Society. Andre Morell is also a very good Watson—stolid, reliable and not as stupidly bovine as he is sometimes depicted. Christopher Lee has a fairly colorless role as the potential victim of the legendary hound, but he plays it competently.

Miles Malleson contributes most of the rare humor with one of his firstclass studies, as a bumbling bishop. Francis De Wolff and Ewen Solon as the "heavies" and John Le Mesurier and Helen Goss as the staff of Baskerville Hall also turn in sound performances. Marla Landi is the girl in the case. And she considerably overplays the one scene that gives her a chance to reveal her talent.

Peter Bryan's screenplay and dialog is custom-made for the Holmes and Watson characters and handles the suspense and dramatic high spots well. Terence Fisher's direction captures the eeriness of the atmosphere. Some of the settings are a shade stagey but Jack Asher's lensing also helps to build up the dank gloom of the Dartmoor area.

Rich.

Idle on Parade
(BRITISH-C'SCOPE)

Straightforward army farce, with good performances by Lionel Jeffries and Anthony Newley, which should raise the yocks in all popular houses.

London, March 24.

Columbia release of a Warwick (Harold Huth) production. Stars William Bendix, Anthony Newley, Anne Aubrey. Directed by John Gilling. Screenplay, John Antrobus, from novel by William Camp; camera, Ted Moore; editor, Bert Rule; music, Bill Shepherd. At Metropole, London. Running time, **88 MINS.**

Sgt. Lush	William Bendix
Jeep Jackson	Anthony Newley
Caroline	Anne Aubrey
Bertie	Lionel Jeffries
Herbie	Sidney James
Shorty	David Lodge
Rene	Dilys Laye
Commanding Officer	William Kendall
Joseph Jackson	Bernie Winters
Ron	Harry Fowler
Stage Manager	Norman Atkyns
Sgt. Herbrides	Percy Herbert
Iris	Jane Navello
Club Manager	Andre Charisse
Spinster	Rosamund Greenwood
Naafi Girls	Maurene Riscoe, Marigold Russell, Rosemary Davis
Jeremy	John Wood
Man in Cinema	Ian Wilson
Sergeant	Rupert Davies
Chucker-Out	Martin Boddey

The British Army once again provides the framework for a screen farce which is an unabashed anthology of army jokes and situations, suspended on a very slender story line. "Idle On Parade" has the good fortune of having a topical slant. It hinges on the incident of a rock-'n'-roll idol being called up for National Service. Press publicity on the cases of Elvis Presley and a British pop singer, Terry Dene, provides a useful gimmick for a pic which should be a fine laughter-raiser in all popular houses.

"Parade" is pure corn, a series of more-or-less unrelated situations and gags. But it gains in effect by a number of very funny farcical performances. Lionel Jeffries as a fussy, worried adjutant has a bigger role than usual in films, and carries it off with witty aplomb. Anthony Newley, as the hero, also continues to advance his claims as one of the most hilarious young actors in British films. They are supported by Sidney James, as the rock-'n'-roller's 10 percenter; William Bendix, as a loud-mouthed sergeant with a heart of gold; David Lodge, William Kendall and Bernie Winters.

Femme appeal is in the hands of Anne Aubrey as the commanding officer's daughter, who falls for Newley's singing, and Dilys Laye. Both young women handle their small chores satisfactorily. The film is pepped up with three or four beat songs handled well by Newley, which seem neither better nor worse than similar songs that have for [illegible] their way into the Hit Parade.

John Gilling's direction makes the most of a screenplay by John Antrobus which seems to have been the victim of some rather haphazard editing. "Parade" is an unambitious film which will garner enough yocks to keep the b.o. clicking merrily.

Rich.

Crime and Punishment, U.S.A.

Sometimes technically crude but interesting, often striking, U. S. replant of Dostoevski's classic. Good b.o.

Hollywood, March 27.

Allied Artists release of Sanders Associates Production. Stars Mary Murphy, Frank Silvera, Marian Seloes, John Harding; "introduces" George Hamilton. Produced by Terry Sanders. Directed by Denis Sanders. Associate producer, Jacqueline Donnet; screenplay, Walter Newman; based on the novel by Feodor Dostoevski; camera, Floyd Crosby; music, Herschel Burke Gilbert; editor Merrill G. White. Previewed at the Screen Directors Guild theatre, March 23, '59. running time, **96 MINS.**

Robert	George Hamilton
Sally	Mary Murphy
Porter	Frank Silvera
Debbie	Marian Seldes
Swanson	John Harding
Rafe	Wayne Heffley
Mrs. Cole	Toni Merrill
Samuels	Lew Brown
Doctor	Sid Clute
Hendicks	Ken Drake
Man in Coffee Shop	Jim Hyland
Desk Officer	Len Lesser

Allied Artists has taken a chance on more than one count with "Crime and Punishment, U.S.A.," a contemporary retelling of Dostoevski's classic. It is the first professional motion picture by Terry and Denis Sanders, former the producer and latter the director, and the story in previous film versions has not been a money success.

The present result, however, while it does not succeed completely, is an exciting and interesting film. It is good enough to stand the long playoff as an art film, and it could be sold profitably as an exploitation item. In neither case would it be unsatisfying to the customers.

Walter Newman's screenplay updates the story from 19th Century Czarist St. Petersburg, to present-day Santa Monica. Raskolnikov of the original is now Robert Cole, American law student. His nemisis, in the strict sense of that work, is now Lieutenant Porter of the Santa Monica police. George Hamilton, in a striking film bow, plays Cole, and Frank Silvera, gives a brilliant performance as the Inspector. The transition from past to present does not basically effect the underlying philosophy. What was called nihilism then seems now to translate as existentialism. In a word, beat.

Hamilton has murdered a pawnbroker, ostensibly because he is worried that his school tuition is driving his sister, Marian Seldes, to marry an older man for his money. Actually, his crime is motivated by his belief that he is one of the supermen; that he can commit crime and escape without penalty or remorse. A suspect has confessed, but Silvera, once he meets Hamilton, is not satisfied. Silvera's police instinct tells him Hamilton is the murderer. His police training tells him Hamilton will eventually claim the crime.

"Crime and Punishment, U.S.A.," is an akward, sometimes crude film, technically. Some of the scenes do not match. Some of the dialog in Newman's screenplay is stilted. The film, at points, has the effect of having been edited to a different continuity than it was shot for. The result is an occasional jerkiness that somewhat breaks the mood. But conceding these flaws, there is a vigor and an intelligence about the film that holds the spectator. While the conception of the picture may be quarreled with, there is no doubt that, granting the conception, the execution is stimulating and lively.

Hamilton, a good-looking young man, makes one of the most impressive film bows of any juvenile in several years. Silvera, a veteran character man, displays a virtuosity that is compelling. Mary Murphy, as the prostitute with whom Hamilton falls in love, is very effective. Miss Seldes, in a comparatively brief and undeveloped role, is most touching. Others who contribute ably include John Harding, Wayne Heffley, Toni Merrill, Lew Brown and Sid Clute.

Floyd Crosby's camera work is a notable asset, particularly in capturing the wonderfully weird Santa Monica architecture. Herschel Burke Gilbert's score combines jazz and some elegant classical themes for unusual contrast and impact. Mort Rabinowitz' production design, and Robert Tyler Lee's art direction, are perceptive in physically setting the background the Sanders sought. Phil Mitchell's sound is gritty with realism.

Powe.

Ich Werde Dich Auf Haenden Tragen
("I'll Carry You On My Hands")
(GERMAN-COLOR)

Berlin, March 24.

Constantin release of Arca (Gero Wecker) production. Stars Kristina Soederbaum, Hans Holt; features Hans Nielsen, Barbara Haller, Hilde Koerber, Guenter Pfitzmann. Directed by Veit Harlan, Screenplay, Harlan and Guido Fuerst, after "Viola Tricolor," novelette by Theodor Storm; camera (Afracolor), Gerhard Krueger; music, Werner Eisbrenner. At Adria, Berlin. Running time, 92 MINS.

Veit Harlan's latest opus, a modernized version of Theodor Storm's novelette, "Viola Tricolor," emerges as a remarkably old-fashioned pic. Overly conventional direction, acting and story devlopment, an overdose of sentiment along with the familiar tear-jerking elements make this an item strictly for home consumption.

Plot shows a widower who marries again and his eight-year old daughter who doesn't want to accept her new mother. Latter goes through the usual situations and complications and nearly dies when she gives birth to twins. This brings her embittered stepdaughter back to senses.

Acting is only so-so. Harlan's actress-wife, Swedish-born Kristina Soederbaum, enacts the young suffering stepmother with the kind of sentimentality that will probably please most of her fans. Hans Holt is her always gentleman-like husband. Hans Nielsen contributes a medico with much routine, while sympathetic Guenter Pfitzmann, as Holt's chauffeur, takes care of some comedy relief. A more polished performance is turned in by Hilde Koerber in the role of a nurse who opposes Miss Soederbaum.

Film was partly shot in Italy (Florence) and on the North Sea, giving it some nice outdoor shots although the Agfacolor often tends to be watery. Music plays an important factor in creating the mood . *Hans.*

Born Reckless
(SONGS)

Fast-paced rodeo yarn with songs and Mamie Van Doren to attract in program situations.

Hollywood, March 25.

Warner release of Aubrey Schenck production. Stars Mamie Van Doren; costars Jeff Richards, Arthur Hunnicutt, Carol Ohmart; features Tom Duggan, Tex Williams, Donald Barry, Nacko Galindo, Orlando Rodriguez, Johnny Olenn. Directed by Howard W. Koch. Screenplay, Richard Landau; story, Landau, Schenck; camera, Joseph F. Biroc; editor, John F. Schreyer; music, Buddy Bregman. Previewed March 24, '59. Running time, 79 MINS.
Jackie .... Mamie Van Doren
Kelly .... Jeff Richards
Cool Man .... Arthur Hunnicutt
Liz .... Carol Ohmart
Wilson .... Tom Duggan
Tex Williams .... Himself
Oakie .... Donald Barry
Papa Gomez .... Nacko Galindo
Manuel .... Orlando Rodriguez
Johnny Olenn and group .... Themselves

"Born Reckless" blends enough romance, rodeo action and bouncy song numbers to come off as very acceptable divertisement for the program trade. With name of Mamie Van Doren to serve as lure specially for the younger audiences, film may be exploited for good returns.

The Aubrey Schenck production, turned out with an eye to the lighter side, is packed with type of songs which pay off in pop response. Miss Van Doren, playing a rodeo rider hopelessly in love with another rodeo performer, Jeff Richards, socks over five numbers for good effect, and Tex Williams is in for a singleton, "Song of the Rodeo," by Buddy Bregman and Stanley Styne. Bregman cleffed four of femme star's quintet, including "Home Type Girl," "Separate the Men from the Boys," "A Little Longer" and title song. Her fifth is "Something to Dream About," by Charles Singelton and Larry Coleman. Also on the vocal side, Johnny Olenn warbles "You Lovable You" and title song, backed by his combo.

Script by Richard Landau, based on original by himself and Schenck, follows three rodeo artists—Miss Van Doren, Richards and old-timer Arthur Hunnicutt—as they trek from rodeo to rodeo, femme carrying a fiery torch but Richards hard to get. Liberally splashed in footage are the rodeo episodes, some exciting stock clips giving fast movement and used legitimately in the story line.

Miss Van Doren lends an enticing presence throughout pic, and is given some rather breathtaking (or holding) rodeo costumes which probably will bring whistles from the audience. Her singing is pleasant and she knows how to handle a song. Richards delivers a likable performance as the rider who wants to retire before he's too badly broken up by rigors of the rodeo, who insists upon being femme star's protector rather than her boy friend. Hunnicutt is in for one of his familiar characters, Carol Ohmart ably plays a rich divorcee on the make for Richards and Nacho Galindo heads a Mexican family who have taken Richards to their hearts.

Direction by Howard W. Koch is on the fast side and he gets good technical backing through Joseph F. Biroc's camera work, editing by John F. Schreyer and art direction by Jack T. Collis. *Whit.*

Guinguette
(FRENCH)

Paris, March 24.

Gaumont release of Franco London-Gibe production. Stars Zizi Jeanmaire, Jean-Claude Pascal, Paul Meurisse; features, Maria-Christina Gajoni, Raymond Bussieres, Maria Megey, Henri Vilbert. Directed by Jean Delannoy. Screenplay, Henri Jeanson, Dominique Daudre, Delannoy; camera, Pierre Montazel, editor, Henri Taverna. At Madeleine, Paris. Running time, 105 MINS.
Guinguette .... Zizi Jeanmaire
Marco .... Jean-Claude Pascal
Maryse .... Maria-Christina Gajoni
Vicomte .... Paul Meurisse
Julie .... Maria Megey
Chauffeur .... Raymond Bussieres
Client .... Henri Vilbert
Inspector .... Paul Descombies

Film is about an ex-prostie who finally gets her dream of a little bar and dancehall in the country. But a new love, gangsters and a perverse, teen-age girl almost ruin her new life. Mixture of themes makes this somewhat talky, but has zesty acting by Zizi Jeanmaire for an okay local entry with possible foreign playoffs.

Miss Jeanmaire is breezy, and delightful as the joy girl who gets taken in by love, but the film's multitude of side plots acts against her and keeps her out of touch with other complications. She has a rival in a 16-year-old girl who tries to get her man by vile means. Maria-Christina Gajoni is a sultry looker but emerges here as too much like Brigitte Bardot.

Pic is slickly mounted and technically fine with good performances. Pruning would help to keep attention on Miss Jeanmaire's role. *Mosk.*

The World, The Flesh and The Devil
(C'SCOPE)

Atomic wipeout, three-character drama. Well-made.

Hollywood, March 20.

Metro release of Sol C. Siegel-HarBel Production. Stars Harry Belafonte, Inger Stevens, Mel Ferrer. Produced by George Englund. Director-writer, Ranald MacDougall; screen story by Ferinand Reyher; suggested by a story by M. P. Shiel; camera, Harold J. Marzorati; music, Miklos Rozsa; editor, Harold F. Kress. Previewed at the studio, March 18, '59. Running time, 95 MINS.
Ralph Burton .... Harry Belafonte
Sarah Crandall .... Inger Stevens
Benson Thacker .... Mel Ferrer

"The World, The Flesh and The Devil" is a provocative three-character story dealing with some pertinant issues (racism, atomic destruction) in a frame of suspense melodrama. The Sol C. Siegel-Har-Bel production is a thoughtful, adult film, but it is also a superior exploitation picture. With Harry Belafonte top-starred, it should have appeal on several counts, and collectively do well. George Englund produced.

Ranald MacDougall, who directed his own screenplay (based on an ancient novel), has left a few holes in his story, but deliberately. This is not a science-fiction story where every odd point has to be entirely cleared up. It is a philosophical querying, a "what if?" tale. So the few still unraveled story threads at the film's conclusion, while possibly puzzling, are rather intriguing than annoying.

There is no relation between this film and any previous one of similar title.

Belafonte is a coal miner who fights his way out of a wrecked Pennsylvania shaft to find himself apparently alone in a devastated world. He takes off for New York and finds there the same situation. Through Civil Defense posters, and later by play-back of a radio station tape, it is learned that the desolation was caused by atomic warfare.

After about a third of the film, Inger Stevens turns up, spared because she was in a decompression chamber when the bombs burst. Near the ending, in the last half-hour or so, Mel Ferrer arrives in a small power boat from a fishing expedition. His survival is less adequately explained.

There is, first, the question of survival beyond the bomb. For this, there is full and interesting development of methods by which Belafonte restores a semblance of civilized amenities. This "Robinson Crusoe" approach, in the heart of Manhattan, is dramatically fruitful and often amusing.

With the arrival of Miss Stevens in Belafonte's world, there arises the obvious issue of survival beyond their immediate selves, via procreation. Ironically, since at the time they seem to be the only two persons alive in the world, racial purity raises its head. This issue is further complicated when Ferrer makes his appearance.

Although, overall the film is engrossing, it gets curiously less effective as additional survivors turn up. When Belafonte is entirely alone on the screen for the film's first one-third of the film, and virtually alone for the first half, the semi-documentary style keeps the film crisp and credible. Perhaps it is in the handling of the problems brought on by Miss Stevens' appearance and Ferrer's that the letdown comes.

It is not clear in the relationship between Belafonte and Miss Stevens whether they are kept apart by her prejudice of his unfounded fear that such an attitude might exist. Ferrer's character is unsatisfying. He seems to be a racist of sorts, but how virulent isn't entirely clarified. MacDougall is justified in leaving the future obscure, but the characters could have been more firm.

At the end, the three walk off hand-in-hand, knowing then that elsewhere others, too, survive. They are united, apparently, in a decision to begin life again although it isn't really settled about who gets whom. There is the suspicion, too, that life in the brave new world is likely to contain more than vestiges of the tired, old one.

MacDougall shot a great deal of the film in Manhattan, and the realism (and the pains taken to achieve it) pay off. CinemaScope's horizontal dimensions do not lend themselves particularly to skyscraper compositions, but cameraman Harold J. Marzorati takes full advantage of the empty, echoing streets and the peculiar spirit of a city deserted. New Yorkers might complain, however, that their geography is a little mixed up, but this is of small consequence. Photography is of great value in this film especially in the early portions, where Belafonte is alone, and Marzorati achieves some eerie effects.

Belafonte is very fine, contributing variety and pace often by the subtle play of his moods alone. Miss Stevens is appealing despite the somewhat diffused nature of her character. Ferrer is the least satisfactory, perhaps because of uncertainty about his role.

It's not easy to say some important things and say them in the framework of melodrama, but MacDougall's screenplay doesn't strike a false note. Miklos Rozsa's music is a very gentle counterpoint to the mood and action, and Franklin Milton's sound (and the lack of it) is another asset. *Powe.*

Count Your Blessings
(C'SCOPE-COLOR)

French versus English viewpoint on amour. Pleasantly presented but lacking in solid b.o. values. Names of Deborah Kerr, Maurice Chevalier and Rossano Brazzi should help.

Metro release of Karl Tunberg production. Stars Deborah Kerr, Maurice Chevalier and Rossano Brazzi. Directed by Jean Negulesco. Screenplay, Tunberg, based on Nancy Mitford's novel, "The Blessing"; camera (C'Scope-Metrocolor), Milton Krasner and George J. Folsey; editor, Harold F. Kress. Previewed in New York, March 26, '59. Running time, **102 MINS.**

Grace Allingham .... Deborah Kerr
Charles-Edouard de Valhubert . Rossano Brazzi
Duc de St. Cloud ...... Maurice Chevalier
Sigismond (Sigi) .... Martin Stephens
Sir Conrad Allingham ... Ronald Squire
Nanny .... Mona Washbourne
Albertine .... Patricia Medina
Hugh Palgrave .... Tom Helmore
Guide .... Steven Geray
John .... Lumsden Hare

"Count Your Blessings" adds up to a slight story, garnished by exquisite interior sets of millionaire households and colorful outdoor excursions of London, Paris and their environs. These garnishments may offer a vicarious thrill to the housewife confined to a three-room city apartment, but all production values and a wisp of a story do not make for sock boxoffice in today's highly competitive market. The names of Deborah Kerr, Maurice Chevalier and Rossano Brazzi may prove of some value in overcoming the negative aspects.

The Karl Tunberg screenplay, based on Nancy Mitford's piquant novel, "The Blessing," is dedicated to the idea that a Frenchman is something special when it comes to amour and sex. And the story further contends that an Englishwoman, accustomed to different moral values, must learn to accept her husband's extra-curricular activities as long as she is the number one femme on his list. It's questionable how many American women are willing to accept this premise. Say, to be sporting, 2%.

The story is leisurely in getting started. As a World War II aviator, Brazzi woos, weds and impregnates Miss Kerr and goes back to war after a three-day honeymoon. It is some nine years before Brazzi reappears, having taken off—much in the fashion of a modern Ulysses—to fight France's little wars at such places as Lebanon, Dienbenphu and Algeria. On reclaiming his patient wife and precious English-educated son, he moves his family to his ancestral home in Paris.

At this point, the problem of the other women begins, causing domestic spats and an eventual separation, extended by the machinations of nine-year-old Sigi who enjoys the individual attention he receives from both parents as he hops back and forth across the channel. Sigi's conscience, however, gets the best of him and fearing exposure and punishment runs away while visiting his father in Paris. The incident serves to reunite his parents.

Maurice Chevalier is cast in the familiar role of the kindly uncle who tries his best to present the French viewpoint to his nephew's wife. It's a non-singing role for Chevalier, but he carries it off with his usual aplomb. Miss Kerr, as the daughter of a member of Parliament, turns in a fine performance as the Englishwoman confronted with French moral values. Brazzi is suave and dashing as the roving-eye French millionaire. Martin Stephens, as their nine-year-old son, is excellent. Good performances are rendered by Tom Helmore, as a disappointed but steadfast suitor; Ronald Squire, as Miss Kerr's father; Mona Washbourne, as a grumpy governess, and Patrica Medina, as Brazzi's mistress.

Jean Negulesco guides his charges competetently, but he's handicapped by the slow-paced yarn. Cameramen Milton Krasner and George J. Folsey have etched eye-catching sights with their CinemaScope-Metrocolor camera as they range through lush homes and Paris and London streets.

Overall "Count Your Blessings" can be termed a pleasant entry, but it lacks the sock ingredients that spell success today. *Holl.*

Island of Lost Women

Routine tropical isle melodrama okay for program situations.

Hollywood, April 3.

Warner Bros. release of Albert J. Cohen production. Stars Jeff Richards, Venetia Stevenson, John Smith, Diane Jergens, June Blair; features Alan Napier. Directed by Frank W. Tuttle. Screenplay, Ray Buffum, based on story by Prescott Chaplain; camera, John Seitz; editor, Roland Gross; music, Raoul Kraushaar. Previewed April 1, '59. Running time, **66 MINS.**

Mark Bradley .... Jeff Richards
Venus .... Venetia Stevenson
Joe Walker .... John Smith
Urana .... Diane Jergens
Mercuria .... June Blair
Dr. Lujan .... Alan Napier
McBain .... Gaven Muir
Garland .... George Brand

"Island of Lost Women" carries the familiar theme of a plane forced down on a tropical isle, but has been well enough handled to provide okay entertainment for the program trade. Film's comparatively short length should enable handy packaging.

The Albert J. Cohen production for Alan Ladd's Jaguar indie outfit unfolds on the tiny uncharted island in the Pacific where Jeff Richards, an American radio commentator, and John Smith, his pilot, make an emergency landing en route to Australia. Only inhabitants are Alan Napier, a brilliant atomic scientist who has taken refuge there with his family, convinced the world is mad and bound for certain destruction, and his three daughters, who have never seen a man before. Contact with the outer world, however, has been maintained via radio and scientist's large library.

Conflict rises between scientist and the Americans after Napier learns Richards has discovered his identity and will report it when he leaves the island. To avoid this, Napier destroys the plane, leaving Americans stranded. The daughters try to help in the secret building of a raft, but before it is finished certain atomic experiments being conducted by scientist cause an explosion. The explosion is recorded in Australia, which leads to party's eventual rescue.

Direction by Frank W. Tuttle of Ray Buffum's screenplay is leisurely but to the point, and he gets satisfactory if standard performances from cast. Richards and Smith play their roles easily and Napier is good in a straight character (he's not the mad scientist as usually happens in this type of yarn). Femme trio is portrayed charmingly—and in brief attire—by Venetia Stevenson, Diane Jergens and June Blair.

Technical credits stack up well, including John Seitz' photography, Roland Gross' editing, Jack Collis' art direction and music score by Raoul Kraushaar. *Whit.*

Tiger Bay
(BRITISH)

Effective crime yarn with a standout performance by a new youngster, 12-year-old Hayley Mills; worthwhile booking for pop audiences.

London, March 31.

Rank release of a Julian Wintle-Leslie Parkyn production. Stars John Mills and Horst Buchholz. Directed by J. Lee Thompson. Screenplay, John Hawkesworth and Shelley Smith; camera, Eric Cross; editor, Sidney Hayers; music, Laurie Johnson. At Leicester Square Theatre, London. Running time, **105 MINS.**

Supt. Graham .... John Mills
Korchinsky .... Horst Buchholz
Gillie .... Hayley Mills
Anya .... Yvonne Mitchell
Mrs. Philips .... Megs Jenkins
Barclay .... Anthony Dawson
Det. Sergeant Harvey .... George Selway
Christine .... Shari
"Poloma" Captain .... George Pastell
"Poloma" 1st Officer .... Paul Stassino
Dr. Das .... Marne Maitland
P. C. Williams .... Meredith Edwards
Mrs. Williams .... Marianne Stone
Mrs. Parry .... Rachel Thomas
Choirmaster .... Kenneth Griffith
Inspector Bridges .... Christopher Rhodes

A disarming, snub-nosed youngster makes her debut in "Tiger Bay," and registers a sock impact. She is Hayley Hills, 12-year-old daughter of actor John Mills, star of the film. Young Miss Mills gives a lift to a pic which, anyway, stacks up as a lively piece of drama. It has been smoothly directed by J. Lee Thompson, is sharply cut and slickly lensed. The main snag is that, apart from John Mills, it has no names with marquee appeal.

This story concerns a Polish seaman who, returning from a voyage, finds that his mistress has moved in with another man. In a burst of anger he kills her. The slaying is witnessed by the child who also rescues the gun. She is a lonely youngster whose attachment for the killer seriously complicates the police investigations.

Apart from the child, who appears to have a great career ahead of her, there are a number of other sound performances. Mills is authoritative as the detective while Horst Buchholz, a German actor pulled in to boost Rank's wooing of the Teutonic market, brings charm to a role which could easily have been played by British actor. Yvonne Mitchell makes a brief but effective appearance as the murdered woman. Marne Maitland, Anthony Dawson, Megs Jenkins and Meredith Edwards also score in small, but well-written roles.

Lee Thompson and his cameraman, Eric Cross, capture the dockland area of Cardiff arrestingly. The screenplay by John Hawkesworth and Shelley Smith is taut and literate. "Tiger Bay" is no blockbuster but it is plausible and holding. Looks like a worthwhile booking. *Rich.*

La Femme et le Pantin
(The Woman and the Puppet)
(FRENCH; DYALISCOPE; COLOR)

Paris, March 29.

Pather release of Gray-Dear-Progefi-Pathe production. Stars Brigitte Bardot, Antonio Vilar; features Dario Moreno, Michel Roux, Jacques Mauclair, Lila Kedrova, Espanita Cortez, Jess Hahn. Directed by Julien Duvivier. Screenplay, Jean Aurenche, Albert Valentin from novel by Pierre Louys; dialog, Marcel Achard; camera (Eastmancolor), Roger Hubert; editor, Jacqueline Sadoul. At Berlitz, Paris. Running time, **100 MINS.**

Eva .... Brigitte Bardot
Don Mateo .... Antonio Vilar
Arababjian .... Dario Moreno
Albert .... Michel Roux
Marchand .... Jacques Mauclair
Maria .... Espanita Cortez
Sydney .... Jess Hahn
Berthier .... Daniel Ivernel

Another Brigitte Bardot opus which shapes as a good possibility for Yank playoff dates, with dubbing in order. United Artists has this for the U.S. via a production investment. B.B. is par in this vehicle because she does many of the same things that made her an American boxoffice bet in the first place.

She is a free-wheeling lass who roams the streets of Seville in Spain upsetting all the men. A rich man gets the bug and leaves his home, his wife and money to follow her with a ragged dance troupe. But she fights off his favors, while leading him on, until his public humiliation makes her feel they are equal. Then she finally takes him up to her place.

Pic has overtones of the Marlene Dietrich German pic, "The Blue Angel." Now, this yarn appears somewhat old-fashioned though brought up to date.

Yarn has B.B. as the daughter of a French collaborator. This explains here presence in Spain. Miss Bardot exudes that nubile, girl-woman quality and appears skimpily dressed, does a semi-nude dance, and displays her, by now familiar physical qualities. Her acting still leaves something to be

desired but she still can talk with her body which seems to suffice.

Director Julien Duvivier gets some good local color into this and tells the tale of passion competently. Done in a CinemaScope-like process, in good color, this will hinge on B.B.'s continued popularity in the U.S. It could not stand on its own very well without it, which calls for exploitation.

Mosk.

Bobosse
(FRENCH)

Paris, April 7.

Paramount release of Editions Cinegraphique Production. Stars Francois Perier, Micheline Presle; features Jacques Jouanneau, Armande Navarre, Jean Tissier, Jacques Dufilho. Directed by Etienne Perier. Screenplay, Sherban Sidery, Frederic Grendel, Perier from play by Andre Roussin; camera, Roger Fellous; editor, Robert Isnardon. At Mercury, Paris. Running time, 95 MINS.

Bobosse .... Francois Perier
Regine .... Micheline Presle
Anne-Marie .... Armande Navarre
Edgar .... Jacques Jouanneau
Uncle .... Jean Tissier
Minouche .... Elisabeth Manet

A popular play, with the pop actor who created the role originally, Francois Perier, this looks to be well received here. But it looms somewhat talky and lightweight for the foreign market.

Yarn reveals an actor back home one night with his fellow thesps discussing the play and insisting he is not like the character he portrays in real life. But, like the play, his wife has ankled and he gets drunk. In his intoxicated dream he gives out with a monolog to a judge and jury, all played by himself, explaining why he killed his wife. Next day he ruins the play, but there is a happy ending as his wife comes back.

Perier, the actor, sagely brings out the differences in his stage and real personalities. But Etienne Perier, the director and no kin, has been content to rely on the legiter and it shows up its stage sources too clearly. There are some comic scenes but the wordinessmakes this primarily for special slotting abroad. Technical credits are fine as is the remainder of the cast.

Mosk.

Die Trapp Familie in Amerika
(The Trapp Family in America) (GERMAN—SONGS—COLOR)

Berlin, March 31.

Gloria release of Divina production. Stars Ruth Leuwerik; features Hans Holt, Josef Meinrad, Wolfgang Wahl. Directed by Wolfgang Liebeneiner. Screenplay, Herbert Reinecker, based on memories by Baroness Maria von Trapp; camera (Eastmancolor), Werner Krein; music, Franz Grothe; sets, Robert Herlth and Gottfried Will. At Zoo Palast, Berlin. Running time, 105 MINS.

Baroness Maria von Trapp
.... Ruth Leuwerik
Baron Trapp .... Hans Holt
Dr. Wasner .... Josef Meinrad
Patrick .... Wolfgang Wahl
Mrs. Hammerfield .... Adrienne Gessner

This is the sequel to "Trapp Family," one of the biggest German post-war grossers. It falls considerably short of the original although this one cost much less. Put the blame on an overly sentimental and a superficially written story which stands in sharp contrast to the slick adaptation job of the first pic. Large part of the sequel was shot in the U.S. (mostly N. Y.) but remarkably little happens in this portion. The whole story could have been told in an hour instead of 105 minutes.

This sequel likely won't bring as much money as the original. Costs allegedly came up to more than $2,000,000 D-Marks (with a substantial percentage left in the U.S.), which is nearly too much for a German production. It's a family picture which, skilfully exploited, could be given some U.S. chances. Those who don't mind an overdose of sentiment may take a fancy to it.

First portion shows Ruth Leuwerik, former novice, being assigned to take care of the children of Baron von Trapp and eventually marrying the widower. The anti-Nazi family fled Austria when Hitler's "Anschluss" took place. Now in America, we see the Trapps trying to make an earnest living via their vocal group. They have it tough finding audiences and one disappointment follows the other. Very late they realize that it's their program that fails to click. So they go over to something more popular ("Tales of Viennese Woods" and so) and now they become successful.

Ruth Leuwerik, just decorated with the German Bambi award, is again the moving spirit of this film. She possesses the kind of charm that appeals to most audiences. Sensitive actress is definitely an ideal cast for her role of Baroness Trapp. Liebeneiner's direction is okay. Of better quality are pic's technical standards, particularly Werner Krien's Eastmancolor lensing. There are quite a number of both interesting and beautiful shots of U.S. localities.

Hans.

Le Grand Chef
(The Big Chief) (FRENCH)

Paris, April 7.

Gaumont release of Gibe-Franco London Film production. Stars Fernandel, Gino Cervi; features Papouf. Directed by Henri Verneuil. Screenplay, Henri Troyat, Jean Manse, Verneuil from short story by O. Henry; camera, Roger Hubert; editor, Borys Lewin. At Biarritz, Paris. Running time, 105 MINS.

Antoine .... Fernandel
Paolo .... Gino Cervi
Erick .... Papouf
Father .... Jean-Jacques Delbo
Mother .... Noelle Norman
Butler .... Georgres Chamarat

A French adaptation of O. Henry's short story about the two harassed kidnapers who become the victims of their hostage and have to pay his parents to get them to take him back, is one of the better recent Fernandel comedies.

Teamed here with Gino Cervi, with whom he made the popular "Don Camillo" series, this may have good chances locally and abroad on its general entertainment values and the Fernandel name.

Two car washers, to buy their own garage, decide to kidnap a rich man's son. The kid is spirited to their apartment when Fernandel dresses like an Indian which is the kid's favorite pastime. The kid then proceeds to make life a hell on wheels for the kidnapers.

Fernandel has some comic moments while Gino Cervi is the perfect foil as the main victim of the brat, expertly played by Papouf. Director Henri Verneuil has not quite gotten the right balance in the comedy moments. Technical credits are good. Despite some slow spots, this has enough yocks for general chances abroad.

Mosk.

Last Train From Gun Hill
(COLOR; V'VISION)

Superior western. Good b.o.

Hollywood, April 10.

Paramount release of Hal Wallis production (in association with Bryna Productions). Stars Kirk Douglas and Anthony Quinn; costars Carolyn Jones and Earl Holliman. Associate producer, Paul Nathan. Directed by John Sturges. Screenplay, James Poe; based on a story by Les Crutchfield; camera (Technicolor), Charles Lang Jr.; music, Dimitri Tiomkin; editor, Warren Low. Previewed at the studio, April 10, '59. Running time, 94 MINS.

Matt Morgan .... Kirk Douglas
Craig Belden .... Anthony Quinn
Linda .... Carolyn Jones
Rick Belden .... Earl Holliman
Beero .... Brad Dexter
Lee Smithers .... Brian Hutton
Catherine .... Ziva Rodann
Skag .... Bing Russell
Bartender .... Val Avery
Sheriff Bartlett .... Walter Sande

Hal Wallis' "Last Train From Gun Hill" is a top western. Although there are some psychological undertones, it is a film that plays for almost pure action. In addition to characters of dimension, there is suspense, romance and humor. With stars in a top-drawer production the prognosis is big draw at the boxoffice.

James Poe's screenplay can be summed up succinctly. Kirk Douglas' Indian wife is raped and killed by two young brutes, Earl Holliman and Brian Hutton. Douglas, marshal of the town of Pauley, finds a clue that leads him to the neighboring community of Gun Hill. He discovers his fugitive, Holliman, is the son of his old friend, Anthony Quinn. His problem, aside from the complexities of personal relationships with Quinn, is how to get Holliman away to justice on that "last train," with Quinn and his hired gunhands determined to thwart him.

Director John Sturges has taken Poe's screenplay and used it to employ the rule: get the characters in jeopardy in the first reel and keep them there until the last. This is accomplished by a lean storyline embellished only with enough invention and variety to maintain the suspense. Even Sturges' transition shots, such as ones of a vintage locomotive, double in value by contributing atmosphere and pace. Time, an important story element, is bridged without resorting to such devices as the moving clock-hand or conspicuous dissolves. In short, imagination and skill raise a simple story above its apparent level.

Sturges also uses his gifted cameraman, Charles Lang Jr., to the film's advantage. Poe's screenplay slips into a few cliches in dialog, but it is remarkable in that it avoids more. It is refreshing in its ability to shut up when action should take over, when a gesture or look completely conveys meaning and words would be irrelevant or redundant and weakening.

Lang has one technique, opening on a background with a medium shot and then pulling back to bring in the scene's central character that seems fresh and effective. Lang also employs an unusual number of very long shots in his sunbaked exteriors, with the human figures barely discernible black minatures on the raw, yellow landscape. None of this is consciously "arty," but acts as an imperceptible aid in heightening tension and involvement.

It helps considerably to have actors who are arrestng in their own right, able to concentrate attention as Douglas and Quinn do. They must be equally strong, and, to some degree, equally sympathetic. There is a casual parallel, in that Quinn is a widower and has raised his son alone (to be a rapist and murderer, as it turns out). Now Douglas, though the action of Quinn's son, faces the same rearing of a motherless son. Douglas and Quinn, by performances in depth, give the film the inevitability of tragedy.

Carolyn Jones delivers impressively, leaving no doubt that her earlier work in smaller roles was no accident, and she will be seen in increasingly more important parts from now on. Earl Holliman is most effective and sympathetic as the weakling son. Brian Hutton, heretofore handicapped by some Method mannerisms, shakes this limitation to create a realistic character of considerable perspective. A good supporting cast includes Brad Dexter, Ziva Rodann, Bing Russell, Val Avery and Walter Sande.

Dimitri Tiomkin's score is excitingly orchestrated, reverberating with tautness and passion. Warren Low's editing deserves a note. Done often in purposely short takes, it is never blurred or confusing, but always adept at conveying the elements of melodrama sought by the other contributors.

Powe.

Serious Charge
(BRITISH)

Well-made, impressive drama of scandal in a small town with a fine performance by Anthony Quayle. Lacks stellar names for U. S. but is a worthwhile entry.

London, April 7.

Eros release of a Mickey Delamar production. Stars Anthony Quayle, Sarah Churchill, Andrew Ray. Directed by Terence Young. Screenplay, Guy Elmes, Mickey Delamar; camera, George Perinal; editor, Reginald Beck; music, Leighton Lucas. Previewed at Studio One, London. Running time, 105 MINS.

Howard Phillips .... Anthony Quayle
Hester Peters .... Sarah Churchill
Larry Thompson .... Andrew Ray
Mrs. Phillips .... Irene Browne
Mr. Thompson .... Percy Herbert
Mr. Peters .... Noel Howlett
Police Sergeant .... Wensley Pithers
Mary Williams .... Leigh Madison
Probation Officer .... Judith Furse
Almshouse Matron .... Jean Cadell
Verger .... Wilfred Brambell
Mrs. Browning .... Olive Sloane
Fishmonger .... George Roderick
Curley Thompson .... Cliff Richard
Michelle .... Liliane Brousse

Producer Mickey Delamar and director Terence Young have done a smooth, conscientious job in transferring Philip King's play, "Serious Charge," to the screen. Its basic theme — alleged homosexuality—is a tricky one and of course has earned the pic an "X" certificate. But the guiding hands have resisted all temptation towards sensationalism. The result is a holding, thoughtful drama which will satisfy any intelligent audience, & could make a worthwhile U. S. entry despite its lack of stellar weight.

The screenplay, by Delmar and Guy Elmes, is a literate piece of craftsmanship with plenty of shafts of quiet humor. It sticks very faithfully to the play. The plausible and rather alarming situation takes

place in a small British town which is riddled with gossipmongers and the current problem of juve delinquency. A new vicar arrives. He's a young goodlooking bachelor, athletic, sincere, keen and he tries to grapple with the situation. He comes up against a vindictive teenager who leads a local gang of smalltime hoodlums. The kid frames the vicar by alleging a homo attack. An attractive, but frustrated young spinster who loves the vicar, unwittingly becomes the chief witness for the prosecution and the cleric is practically forced out of town as a result of the scandal.

Terence Young's direction is slick and he has obviously kept a keen eye on the editing. The atmosphere of the small town is well conveyed while the camerawork is lively and alert. Young also has the benefit of a first-rate cast. Anthony Quayle's well rounded portrayal of the vicar is sympathetic and gripping.

He convincingly stresses the strained inner feelings of a man who, unjustly accused of an abominable act, feels that his reactions to the filthy slander prove that he is not fitted for his calling. Sarah Churchill's role as the spinster is drab and not a highly rewarding one. However, she still has some good moments, particularly when she realizes how her action has compromised the man she loves. Andrew Ray, the despicable youngster who is the cause of all the trouble, gives a well-observed performance and is a typical, credible juve delinquent.

There are also some telling performances by those in lesser roles. Notably the wise, slyly humorous piece of work by Irene Browne, as Quayle's worldly mother; a moving cameo by Leigh Madison, as a girl whose death is caused by Ray, and by Percy Herbert, as Ray's wooden-headed father. The film also introduces Cliff Richard, an up-and-coming pop singer. As well as singing a trio of useful beat songs, the youngster shows up as a likeable personality as an actor. "Serious Charge," without being a world beater, is a pic that any indie producer can be quietly proud of having made. *Rich.*

Life in Emergency Ward 10
(BRITISH)

Pleasant hospital yarn based on successful tv series—story of the fight to save a small boy with a hole in his heart is topical and soundly done. Okay b.o. prospects.

Eros (Ted Lloyd) production and release. Stars Michael Craig, Wilfrid Hyde White and Dorothy Alison. Directed by Robert Day. Screenplay, Tessa Diamond, Hazel Adair; editor, Lito Carruthers; camera, Geoffrey Faithfull; music, Phillip Green. At Plaza, London. Running time 86 MINS.

Dr. Stephen Russell	Michael Craig
Prof. Bourne-Evans	Wilfrid Hyde White
Sister Janet Fraser	Dorothy Alison
Dr. Paddy O'Meara	Glyn Owen
Nurse Pat Roberts	Rosemary Miller
Dr. Dawson	Charles Tingwell
Dr. Forrester	Frederick Bartman
Mrs. Pryor	Joan Sims
Dr. Tom Hunter	Rupert Davies
Anne Hunter	Sheila Sweet
Mr. Phillips	David Lodge
Mrs. Phillips	Dorothy Gordon
David Phillips	Christopher Witty
Joe Cooney	Tony Quinn
Potter	Douglas Ives
Mr. Pryor	George Tovey
Nurse Vincent	Pauline Stroud
Nurse April Andrews	Christina Gregg

Hospital yarns have an irresistible fascination for filmmakers. Understandably, because drama, comedy and pathos can be neatly plotted against a background which offers audience participation. Either audiences are familiar with hospitals or, regrettably, may be at some time. "Life" is the latest British hospital pic and its somewhat cumbersome, documentary title is due to it being based on a highly successful commercial tv series called "Emergency Ward 10." It should prove more than useful as a booking in U.K.

There is nothing new about this film, but it is directed and acted with real enthusiasm. Though it has all the hospital cliches, there is a disarming sincerity about the pic. Main theme concerns a little boy with a hole in his heart. Although it's obvious that the operation will be a success in time for the fadeout, interest and some tension is held till the end. There is also the friction between a new surgeon, who arrives back from the U.S. with a modification of a heart-and-lung machine, and the man who thought he was going to get the job.

There was some romance between various members of the staff; a woman patient, due to have quadruplets, the oldest inhabitant among the patients who dies at the first use of the new man's invention, some mixed nurses and medicos, a neglected wife, the inevitable hospital party—all providing enough material to keep this film going nicely for its 86 minutes.

Screenplay, written by Tessa Diamond and Hazel Adair, who wrote the original tv skein, concentrates neither entirely on comedy nor mawkish pathos but seems to capture the average hospital atmosphere.

Some very good acting stints help. Michael Craig is the stalwart new surgeon whose belief in his new experiment sparks off much of the drama. Wilfrid Hyde White sails wittily and blandly through his role of chief surgeon. Dorothy Alison has an unrewarding part as the hospital sister who wins Craig's affections.

Among the hospital surgeons, Glyn Owen brings robust comedy to the role of the obstetrician, while Rupert Davies, Charles Tingwell and Frederick Bartman are the other varied surgeons. Sheila Sweet as a neglected wife; Rosemary Miller and Pauline Stroud, as a couple of understanding nurses, also contribute useful cameos. Some comedy touches are provided by Tony Quinn as the oldest inhabitant of the ward and by Joan Sims as the expectant mother of the quads. Touching moments come from Dorothy Gordon and David Lodge as the parents of the small boy, who himself is charmingly played by Christopher Witty.

The operation sequences are well directed by Robert Day, who had the benefit of close liaison with the Royal College of Surgeons. *Rich.*

Ist Mama Nicht Fabelhaft?
(Isn't Mama Fabulous?)
(GERMAN)

Berlin, April 7.

UFA release of UFA production. Stars Luise Ulrich; features Gunnar Moeller, Charles Brauer, Harold Martens, Paul Klinger, Fita Benhoff. Directed by Peter Beauvais. Screenplay, Barbara Noack and Ilse Lutz-Dupont; camera, Igor Oberberg; music, Nobert Schultze. At UFA Pavilion, Berlin. Running time, 95 MINS.

"Isn't Mama Fabulous?" is of special importance since it's first UFA-made feature film. (Before "Mama," the new UFA has only made vidpix via its own production setup or only financed theatrical pix. **The best that can be said about UFA's first venture on its own is that it's a nice, little film.** Some may wonder why it was not a more ambitious effort, but at least it isn't disappointing.

Screenplay by Barbara Noack and Ilse Lutz-Dupont centers around Luise Ulrich who contributes another of her mother roles which have won her a following here. Here she takes care of her three sons of whom the first one is suffering from marriage, the second from first love and the last and smallest one from boyhood troubles. Miss Ulrich manages all trials to everyone's satisfaction. Film mainly benefits from her fine acting as well as the polished dialog.

Peter Beauvais directed this smoothly. UFA, incidentally, took him under exclusive contract after this pic. *Hans.*

Watusi
(COLOR)

African adventure pic using old "King Solomon's Mines" footage. Exploitable.

Hollywodo, April 10.

Metro release of Al Zimbalist production. Stars George Montgomery, Taina Elg, David Farrar. Associate producer, Donald Zimbalist; director, Kurt Neumann; screenplay, James Clavell; based on "King Solomon's Mines" by H. Rider Haggard; camera (Technicolor), Harold E. Wellman; editor, William B. Gulick. Previewed at Academy Awards Theatre, April 8, '59. Running time, 85 MINS.

Harry Quartermain	George Montgomery
Erica Neuler	Taina Elg
Rick Cobb	David Farrar
Umbopa	Rex Ingram
Mohamet	Dan Seymour
Jim-Jim	Robert Goodwin
Amtaga	Anthony M. Davis
Gagool	Paul Thompson
Wilhelm Von Kentner	Harold Dyrenforth

Credits on "Watusi" say it is based on H. Rider Haggard's "King Solomon's Mines." More accurately, the new Metro production should be credited to the same studio's film of the Haggard novel. The Al Zimbalist production is frankly an effort to take advantage of some superior African location film lensed 10 years ago for the original feature. Photographically, the new film is a triumph of matching shots and authentic atmosphere. Dramatically it is as old-hat as H. Rider Haggard. Metro has a smart ad campaign on 'Watusi" that will give it initial draw, but a fast playoff is indicated.

James Clavell's screenplay sets the action in 1919. George Montgomery is the son of the original hero, returned to Africa to pursue the original quest, King Solomon's legendary mines. As his helper in penetrating the "forbidden country," Montgomery enlists an ald friend of his father, David Farrar. En route they pick up Taina Elg, daughter of a native-massacred missionary. They find the "mines,' which turn out to be not mines but caves packed with chests loaded with uncut gems. But after suffering extreme hardship and danger to possess the treasure, Montgomery and Miss Elg elect to remain in the Watusi country. Farrar departs with his well-gotten gains.

Clavell's story is poorly conceived. Aside from the standard hazards of crocidiles, snakes et al., the only plot centers around Montgomery's hatred of Germans. His mother was killed in a U-boat sinking in World War I. Miss Elg is German. This keeps them apart until tolerance breaks on all parties and it is decided that each man is an individual and must be so judged. This naive premise could have been credible if the dialog supported it, but it does not.

There is another flaw in the film. Original footage for "King Solomon's Mines" is excellently matched by camerman Harold E. Wellman and editor William E. Gulick. New exteriors are remarkable in duplicating the African veldt. But it was surely an error to use in "Watusi," two of the most famous sequences from the earlier the stampede scene and the Watusi dance scene. The stampede was one of the most widely (and deservedly) commented upon. In the dance scene, the lead dancer was practically a trademark of the 1950 production, instantly recognizable to anyone who saw that film or its ad campaign. Audiences might get the idea from recognition of these two scenes that they have seen the whole film before. There are other sequences, too, of less importance, but of disturbing reminiscence.

George Montgomery tries hard to fit himself into a role that is entirely alien to his background, but is not successful. Miss Elg's character is never defined beyond being a handy female to provide romantic interest. David Farrar is wasted in a meaningless role. Others involved are no more successful.

The late Kurt Neumann directed "Watusi," and Donald Zimbalist served as associate producer. *Powe.*

Riot in Juvenile Prison

Male delinquents and female dittoes go co-educational. Sensational angles.

Hollywood, April 14.

United Artists release of a Vogue Pictures production. Stars Jerome Thor, Marcia Henderson, Scott Marlowe, John Hoyt; co-stars Virginia Aldridge; features Dick Tyler, Dorothy Provine, Jack Grinnage, George Brenlin, Ann Doran, Richard Reeves, Al McGranary, Paul Jasmin. Produced by Robert E. Kent. Directed by Edward L. Cahn. Story and screenplay, Orville H. Hampton; camera, Maury Gertsman; music, Emil Newman; editor, Eddie Mann. Previewed at Goldwyn Studios, April 9, '59. Running time, 71 MINS.

Dr. Paul Furman	Jerome Thor
Grace Hartwell	Marcia Henderson
Eddie Bassett	Scott Marlowe
Colonel Walton	John Hoyt
Stu Killion	Dick Tyler
Kitty	Virginia Aldridge
Babe	Dorothy Provine
Dink	Jack Grinnage
Matches	George Brenlin
Bess Monahan	Ann Doran
Andy Quillan	Richard Reeves
Governor	Al McGranary
Bobby	Paul Jasmin

"Riot in Juvenile Prison," producer Robert E. Kent's Vogue Picture for United Artists, is a standard teen meller in which a coeducational reform school is the central idea. The attempted rape and the fights over girls make possible sensational campaign, but weaknesses in the screenplay will keep the film at the bottom half of double bills in most situations.

The use of a large number of youthful extras gives the film some size and the spacious private-school-type setting relieves the picture of prison pallor.

A social psychiatrist, Jerome Thor, takes over a boys' reformatory following a public scandal involving the death of two inmates under the brutal administration of the warden, John Hoyt.

The doctor's first action is to make the "prison" co-educational by bringing girls in from the distaff delinquency dorm. A matron, Marcia Henderson, objects to the merger on the ground that there are probably rapists among the male inmates. The warden objects on the ground that soft treatment is too good for the "young punks."

The objections seem vindicated when two troublemakers, Scott Marlowe and Dick Tyler, fight one another over two girls, Virginia Aldridge and Dorothy Provine, and when Tyler attempts rape upon Miss Aldridge. Public clamor at the new scandal causes power to revert to Hoyt.

Resentment at renewed brutality causes a riot which brings Jerome Thor back into the driver's seat and, presumably, his premise—that lovingkindness and science will accomplish more than brutality—is proved. It isn't, for the character changes needed to support the point never take place. It's the old "love of a good woman" which changes Marlowe, if indeed he has changed, and there is only the characters' word for it that changes have taken place in others.

A capable cast makes up for much of the screenplay's deficiency but they're often left hanging with impossible dialog. Director Edward L. Cahn handles what could have been questionable scenes with good taste. Maury Gertsman's camera work and Eddie Mann's editing are slickly professional and Emil Newman's music adds a punch. *Glen.*

Hey Boy, Hey Girl

Low-budget exploitationer for Louis Prima-Keely Smith fans.

(SONGS)

Hollywood, April 10.

Columbia release of Harry Romm production. Stars Louis Prima, Keely Smith, James Gregory. Directed by David Lowell Rich. Screenplay, Raphael Hayes, James West; camera, Ray Cory; editor, Al Clark. Previewed at the studio, April 2, '59. Running time, **83 MINS.**

Louis Prima .... Louis Prima
Dorothy Spencer .... Keely Smith
Father Burton .... James Gregory
Marty Moran .... Henry Slate
Buzz .... Kim Charney
Grace Dawson .... Barbara Heller
Shirley .... Asa Maynor
Sam Butera and The Witnesses

Considering the popularity of Louis Prima and Keely Smith in their recordings and personal apperances. Harry Romm's production of "Hey Boy, Hey Girl" should turn a neat profit on its probable cost. The Columbia release in which they're starred is an unpretentious item, but it will be attractive to Prima-Smith fans and an acceptable programming item in general.

The problem in these productions is to give non-acting personalities something to do between musical numbers. A hazard is that if too much is given them to do, they don't show up well. The screenplay by Raphael Hayes and James West makes a neat compromise. Prima plays himself and Miss Smith essays a relatively simple characterization and both are given plenty of opportunity to sing.

The story is simply but expertly contrived. Character is briefly established when Miss Smith, as a helper to her parish priest, James Gregory, approaches Prima to do a benefit for their church and boys' camp. Prima succumbs to the charity pitch and, in the ensuing developments, to Miss Smith. The first proves his good heart, the second his good sense. With a few laughs provided by the Hayes-West script, and some nice scenes, both musical and non-musical, the film exercises a pleasant feeling.

Director David Lowell Rich succeeds in getting at least two good dramatic scenes out of Miss Smith and Prima, and he handles the musical scenes with some freshness. James Gregory, as the priest, plays casually, keeping his more expert technique from overshadowing the less experienced (acting-wise) stars. Henry Slate and young Kim Charney also contribute, although Barbara Heller, a fine comedienne, is wastefully mishandled.

Prima and Miss Smith are competently backed in the musical sections by Sam Butera and the Witnesses. There is an infectious title tune that sounds like a hit, as well as performance of several standards associated with the singing stars. Ray Cory's camera work helps keep the musical portions lively, not always easy in these low-budget musicals. *Powe.*

Cafe Odeon

(SWISS)

Zurich, March 29.

Rex-Film release of Gloriafilm (Max Dora) production. Directed by Kurt Frueh. Screenplay, Frueh; camera, Georges C. Stilly; editor, Rene Martinet; music, Walter Baumgartner. Stars Emil Hegetschweiler, Margrit Winter; features Erwin Kohlund, Eva Langraf, Hans Gaugler, Blanche Aubry, Sylvia Frank, Ettore Cella, Max Werner Lenz. At Capitol Theatre, Zurich, March 28, '59. Running time, **90 MINS.**

Walter .... Emil Hegetschweiler
Leni .... Margrit Winter
Prof. Kartmann .... Erwin Kohlund
Mrs. Kartmann .... Eva Langraf
Feller .... Hans Gaugler
Blanche .... Blanche Aubry
Anni .... Sylvia Frank
Kovacs .... Ettore Cella
Herr Laeubli .... Max Werner Lenz
(In Swiss-German)

Latest Swiss entry is a departure from the usual type of local product depicting either peasant life or the man from the street. Filmed partly on location at Zurich's historical Cafe Odeon, onetime rendezvous of artistic and literary greats from all over Europe, this is the first Swiss attempt at a prostie theme within a typical big-city frame. Lack of marquee names for consumption abroad (though most players are familiar here) is compensated by obvious exploitation values, although maudlin aspects often found in pix dealing with streetwalkers have been avoided. Good performances and tight editing also help to make this a bet for U.S. offbeat bookings.

Plot concerns a girl from the provinces, whose husband is serving a jail term, coming to Zurich to stay with her sister, a prostie. Latter headquarters, as many of her trade, at the Cafe Odeon. The girl's attempt at making quick money by following her sister's example, fails when she falls in love with a married man. The Odeon's old headquarters straightens things out for her, and when her husband breaks jail to join her, they reconcile with a view to a better life when he has finally served his term.

Kurt Frueh, directing from his own original screenplay, has garnished the story with dramatic and human-interest incidents. Story is realistic and believable, with blunt, true-to-life dialog an important asset. The prostie scenes, though uncanny, are done with taste.

Performances are firstrate. Margrit Winter as the province girl offers a dimensional, sensitive and expressive portrayal. Emil Hegetschweiler as the headwaiter hoping the girl might share his old-age loneliness, is touching and remarkably unsentimental. Fine performances are also turned in by Hans Gaugler as the criminal husband, Blanche Aubry as a rundown prostie and newcomer Sylvia Frank as the girl's pleasure-seeking sister. Erwin Kohlund and Eva Langraf are satisfactory.

Camerawork, in black-and-white standard size, by Georges C. Stilly is above par, and incidental music by Walter Baumgartner, including several jazz themes, is unobtrusive. *Mezo.*

Der Schinderhannes

(GERMAN-COLOR)

Berlin, April 7.

Europa release of Real (Gyula Trebitsh) production. Stars Curt Juergens and Maria Schell; features Christian Wolff, Fritz Tillmann, Siegfried Lowitz, Til Kiwe, Bobby Todd, Walter Buschoff. Directed by Helmut Kaeutner. Screenplay, Georg Hurdalek, after a legit play by Carl Zuckmayer; camera (Eastmancolor), Heinz Pehlke; music, Bernard Eichhorn; editors, Klaus Dudenhoefer. At Marmorhaus, Berlin. Running time, **115 MINS.**

Schinderhannes .... Curt Juergens
Julchen .... Maria Schell
Carl von Cleve-Boost .... Christian Wolff
Hans Bast .... Fritz Tillman
Benzel .... Siegfried Lowitz
Gendarme Adam .... Til Kiwe
Siebert .... Bobby Todd
Leyendecker .... Joseph Offenbach
Iltis Jakob .... Walter Buschhoff
Welscher Jockel ...... Guenther Jerschke
Philipp .... Michael Burk

A cast of 83, headed by Curt Juergens and Maria Schell, 4,000 extras, the names of Helmut Kaeutner and Carl Zuckmayer and a big budget are this pic's exploitation values which, no doubt, will impress the local public and guarantee mass bookings here. Also, "Schinderhannes" looks to have better chances than most other German pix finished lately in the foreign market. On names and production dress, this Europa release is undeniably an extraordinary German film.

Films of this type do not seem to be Kaeutner's forte. The director doesn't seem quite at home doing this spectacular subject. Although there's quite a bit of action in this, pic comes often close to being dull.

Curt Juergens, who portrays Schinderhannes, the legendary German robber-chief who stood up against the bourgeoisie and Napoleon's occupation forces, has he-man quality. He's too much of a carpet-knight to make the role of a wild revolutionary believable. Maria Schell who enacts Julchen, his moll, has some impressive moments. But generally this is just another Maria Schell performance, with routine smiles and emotions. More believable are the supporting members such as Christian Wolff, as a young nobleman who turns against his class; Joseph Offenbach, in a particularly effective study of a shoemaker who sides with the rebels, and Paul Esser, a robust blacksmith, one of Juergen's pals.

Also the script by Georg Hurdalek (Zuckmayer took care of the dialog) has its flaws. Another weakness is the (Eastmancolor) photography. The color photography treats the players' faces not too kindly. *Hans.*

Policarpo

(Color)

(ITALO-FRANCO-SPANISH)

Titanus release of a Titanus-S. G. C.-Hispamex co-production. Stars Renato Rascel; features Peppino DeFilippo, Renato Salvatori, Carla Gravina, Luigi DeFilippo, Lidia Maresca, Romolo Valli. Directed by Mario Soldati. Screenplay, Age and Scarpelli. Camera (Eastmancolor), Giuseppe Rotunno. Previewed in Rome. Running time, **100 MINS.**

Policarpo .... Renato Rascel
Cesare Pancarano .... Peppino DeFilippo
Mario .... Renato Salvatori
Celeste .... Carla Gravina
Gege .... Luigi DeFilippo
Amelia .... Lidia Maresca

Charming and colorful period item (one of Italy's 52 entries at Cannes) which chronicles the various battles fought on a human as well as bureaucratic level by Policarpo, a lowly but conscientious scrivener in a government office, in order to win a minute pay raise. When Policarpo's daughter becomes the fiance of his boss' son, things begin looking up. But the youngsters soon turn to other leanings, and it's only by chance that Policarpo gets his raise anyway.

Renato Rascel, who played a similar role in "Il Capotto" some years ago, is here again at his measured best, giving the role warmth and just the right dose of eccentric innocence. He gets top support from Peppino DeFilippo, as the boss whose one desire is to find a noble strain of blood in his family tree; from Carla Gravina, as Policarpo's romantic daughter, from Luigi DeFilippo and Renato Salvatori, well chosen as her two suitors; and from a host of other fine thesps, including Romolo Valli, as a government official. There are also some amusing one-shot guest stints by top Italian actors.

Just as big a performer in this item, however, is the period setting and the nostalgic memories it revives. Director Mario Soldati obviously has made this part of his efforts a labor of love down to the last detail of setting, action, dialogue and other shading. It should go a long way, together with the film's other values, towards helping "Policarpo" to a healthy home-market gross. Elsewhere, some of the local nuances may be lost, but some markets should prove responsive on film's general values.

Vehicle is slow in getting started, and the story's pace often lags overly long. But the total effect is charming. Humor is ever-present, even in the dark moments, but never hilarious.

Cameraman Giuseppe Rotunno, obviously working closely with Soldati, has come up with some of the best color work seen here in ages, being perfectly suited to the period caught. Other technical credits, including costume and set design, are likewise first-rate. *Hawk.*

Les Motards

(The Motorcycle Cops)

(FRENCH)

Paris, April 17.

Lux release of Telefrance production. Stars Jean-Marc Thibault, Roger Pierre; features Francis Blanche, Veronique Zuber, Colette Doreal. Directed by Jean Laviron. Screenplay, Tibault, Pierre, Laviron; camera, Claude Matalou; editor, Denise Baby. At Triomphe, Paris. Running time, **90 MINS.**

Marc .... Jean-Marc Thibault
Roger .... Roger Pierre
Veronique .... Veronique Zuber
Ambassador .... Francis Blanche
Wanda .... Colette Doreal

Lightweight comedy entry has a couple of engaging young comics who give this a lot of yocks. This looks like a good local entry with possibilities for offshore dualer or video situations on its okay general entertainment qualities.

Story is the familiar one about a harassed motorcycle cop bothered by his silly future brother-in-law who also wants to be a cop. They manage to break up a spy

ring, after a flock of zany adventures.

Nothing is forced in this and it flows along agreeably with some well worked out gags and timing as well as tongue-in-cheek takeoffs on bureaucracy. Comic tandem of Jean-Marc Thibault and Roger Pierre looks to be heard from in the future. This slight but okay entry is technically well made having good pacing. *Mosk.*

Les Dragcurs
(The Girl Hunters)
(FRENCH)

Paris, April 14.

Fernand Rivers release of Lisbon Films production. Stars Jacques Charrier, Charles Aznavour; features Dany Robin, Dany Carrel, Estella Blain, Margit Saad, Anouk Aimee, Inge Schoener, Nicole Berger, Belinda Lee. Directed by Jean-Pierre Mocky. Screenplay, Mocky, Jean-Charles Pichon, Louis Sapin; camera, Edmond Sechan; editor, Armand Psenny. Preemed in Paris. Running time, 75 MINS.

Freddy	Jacques Charrier
Joseph	Charles Aznavour
Denise	Dany Robin
Dadou	Dany Carrel
Sylviane	Estella Blain
Jeanne	Anouk Aimee
Ingrid	Margit Saad
Monica	Inga Schoener
Francoise	Nicole Berger
Ghislaine	Belinda Lee

Made by a producer and director, both under 30, this emerges a looksee at the sex and morals of contemporary French youth told via a night of girl hunting by two young men. Both hope for that miracle of finding the ideal girl. Instead, they discover mostly a hopeless array of searching and disoriented women and girls.

The two young men go through a wide variety of experiences in one night with one lad finally meeting a girl he has some feeling for. The other goes off to loneliness or easy conquest.

Director Jean-Pierre Mocky has filled this with some fairly acute observation on pickups and Paris nightlife, with a wild party also thrown in. It is sometimes sketchy and one-track but has exploitation handles on its looksee of Paris at night.

Jacques Charrier and Charles Aznavour give body to the roles of the two searchers. The women remain facets of the female pysche. However, they are all lookers and dress up the pic. Technical credits and production values are fine, with on-the-spot lensing a help. This is an offbeater with possibilities for offshore specialized programs. *Mosk.*

It Happened to Jane

Most - funny farce loses steam towards the end, but should do good biz off its general success and good marquee names.

Hollywood, April 17.

Columbia release produced and directed by Richard Quine. Stars Doris Day, Jack Lemmon, Ernie Kovacs. Executive producer, Martin Melcher; screenplay, Norman Katkov; from a story by Katkov and Max Wilk; camera (Eastman Color by Pathe), Charles Lawton Jr.; music, George Duning; editor, Charles Nelson. Previewed at the Stanley Warner Beverly Hills Theatre, April 17, '59. Running time, **100 MINS.**

Jane Osgood	Doris Day
George Denham	Jack Lemmon
Harry Foster Malone	Ernie Kovacs
Larry Hall	Steve Forrest
Billy Osgood	Teddy Rooney
Uncle Otis	Russ Brown
Crawford Sloan	Walter Greaza
Homer Bean	Parker Fennelyl
Matilda Runyon	Mary Wickes
Wilbur Peterson	Philip Coolidge
Selwyn Harris	Casey Adams
Aaron Caldwell	John Cecil Holm
Betty Osgood	Gina Gillespie
Clarence Runyon	Dick Crockett
Porter	Napoleon Whiting

Up to a point, this is funny comedy. The point is reached about three-quarters of the way through when the film abruptly changes form and loses momentum never to regain it. The Columbia presentation has good stars in a generally fresh format, and it has enough laughs and romantic interest to insure good boxoffice response. It is not a completely satisfying film because it does not sustain to the end.

The story runs out of steam—much as the locomotive in the picture that is a central point—because Norman Katkov's screenplay is not clearly either farce or romantic comedy. It is farce through the major portion. About half an hour before the windup, Jack Lemmon delivers a ringing speech about good government. The sentiments are laudable, but it's the wrong place for them. The note of serious reality in what has been a framework of lunatic frenzy brings the proceedings to a schreeching halt and nothing that follows can play with the preceding abandon.

Katkov's story has its genesis in the eastern railroad battles of some years ago, and the eccentric financiers who occasionally got control of these ancient and debt-saddled carriers. Ernie Kovacs is such a money-man. He is a caricature of a capitalist out of the Stone Age of finance, who obviously loathes passengers and stockholders with equal enthusiasm. He tangles with Doris Day, a young widow trying to make a livelihood out of Maine lobster pots. One of her lobster deliveries has died en route due to the railroad's casual neglect. Determined to have justice, Miss Day sics her lawyer and longtime admirer, Jack Lemmon, on Kovacs and his legal legions. Although injustice for a time proliferates, simple, country, New England virtue in the end triumphs over city slickers and their cunning ways.

While played for pure farce, in which every development and strategem for laughs is permissible, Quine's direction gets a great deal of fun out of Katkov's good script. Kovacs' scenes, for instance, while they often have little to do with the central story idea—except in a general way displaying his character—are skits of considerable humor. Lemmon plays with a broad style that is effective, retaining just a remote connection with enough reality so that his romantic attachment to Miss Day is acceptable. Miss Day, a beguiling figure of outraged womanhood, doesn't lose her essential femininity in the glory of the cause. She is pugnacious but perceptibly female.

The serious flaw in "It Happened To Jane" is the long windup. It leaves the impression that the film is not as amusing as most of it really was. If some way could be found to seed up this portion, the damage caused by shifting gear from one form of comedy to another might be overcome. This might allow the picture to conclude in almost the same brainless, happy spirit in which most of it now plays.

As a handsome and likable menace, Steve Forrest does well and there are a raft of subsidiary characters, many of them New England types. Notably contributing are Parker Fennelly, Russ Brown, Mary Wickes, Philip Collidge and John Cecil Holm. Teddy Rooney and Gina Gillespie are pleasant as Miss Day's children, and Walter Greaza, Casey Adams and Dick Crockett round out the cast admirably.

There are sequences in New York where a number of tv stars appear and these names may have some added exploitation value. Miss Day sings two songs, a title tune by Joe Lubin and I. J. Roth, and "Be Prepared," by Fred Karger and Richard Quine. The latter is charmingly staged as a round, Miss Day assisted by Lemmon and some bright children.

Technically, the Eastman color print shown for review was dark and often fuzzy, while the sound had a hard and echoing quality. *Powe.*

This Earth Is Mine
(COLOR; C'SCOPE)

Fuzzy story handicaps star and production values on this heavy-handed opus.

Hollywood, April 17.

Universal release of Vintage Production. Stars Rock Hudson, Jean Simmons, Dorothy McGuire, Claude Rains. Produced by Casey Robinson and Claude Heilman. Directed by Henry King. Executive producer, Edward Muhl; screenplay, Casey Robinson; based on the novel, "The Cup and the Sword," by Alice Tisdale Hobart; camera (Technicolor), Winton Hoch and Russell Metty; music, Hugo Friedhofer; editor, Ted J. Kent. Previewed at the Screen Directors Guild Theatre, April 10, '59. Running time, **123 MINS.**

John Rambeau	Rock Hudson
Elizabeth Rambeau	Jean Simmons
Martha Fairon	Dorothy McGuire
Philippe Rambeau	Claude Rains
Francis Fairon	Kent Smith
Charlotte Rambeau	Anna Lee
Luigi	Ken Scott
Buz	Cindy Robbins
Mrs. Griffanti	Augusta Merighi
Andre Swann	Francis Bethencourt
Monica	Stacy Graham
Chu	Peter Chong
Maria	Geraldine Wall
Petucci	Alberto Morin
Mrs. Petucci	Penny Santon
Dietrick	Jack Mather
Yakowitz	Ben Astar
Judge Gruber	Daniel White
David	Lawrence Ung
Tim Rambeau	Ford Dunhill

This film seems to have almost every element needed for a dramatic and financial success, numbers of colorful characters, novel background and story, and marquee luminaries. However, it is almost completely lacking in dramatic cohesion. It is verbose and contradictory, and its complex plot relationships begin with confusion and end in tedium. Boxoffice success must rest on what "This Earth Is Mine" promises, not what it delivers.

Edward Muhl, was executive producer for the Universal release, which Henry King directed. Casey Robinson and Claude Heilman produced, and Robinson also did the screenplay from Alice Tisdale Hobart's novel, "The Cup and the Sword."

The setting of the film is the Napa Valley wine country in the waning years of Prohibition. Considering first the film's merits, the backgrounds are lush and bountiful. There are distinctive aspects of wine-making which are fruitfully explored for novelty and subsidiary interest. The performances, generally, are capable, and some are better than that.

The basic plot is a conflict between generations — the older, European-born vintners, headed by Claude Rains, with traditions of dedication to the craft, and the younger men, represented by Rock Hudson, who are interested in selling their crop to the highest bidders, even if it means their grapes will be made into bootleg liquor.

This is clear enough, and a theme of some value, given freshness via novelty of the background. But when the characters begin to move, when they get involved in background and supplementary plot threads, the film becomes digressive and finally annoyingly obfuscating. Introduction of anti-Semitic prejudice, and also similar feelings against the Italians, for instance, is brought in and then neither developed nor cleared up.

It is damaging to audience interest not to be sure what is the blood relationship between Hudson and Jean Simmons. They apparently are first cousins, a startling relationship, in view of their romance. The point is neither elucidated nor eliminated. Hudson's apparent backing of Klan-like raids on the grape-growers who oppose his ideas indicates there is coloration to his character not elsewhere indicated.

In another plot hinge, and an important one, Hudson is shown forcibly abducting a vineyard worker, Cindy Robbins, for obviously carnal purposes. Miss Robbins gets with child that she represents as Hudson's, and she is married off to Ken Scott. Then, in a surprise denouement, the audience is informed the child isn't Hudson's after all. This makes a farce of preceding scenes. It is an unfair device and a bad one.

Some of the scenes are pure bathos, such as the one where Hudson learns (or is supposed to learn; he has known all the time) that he is actually the son of his uncle, Kent Smith. What's lacking mostly in the script, and not supplemented in the direction, is an overall intelligence that would have appraised these complexities, discarded the irrelevant, and welded the remainder into a coherent story.

Hudson gives a sympathetic portrayal, but not a satisfying one, because his characterization is riddled by inconsistencies. Miss Simmons achieves involvement but little sympathy because her motivations are so sketchy and superficial. Claude Rains fares best. His role is not explored for any depth, but it has the merit of being easily recognizable and consistent. Miss McGuire verges on tragedy, but she is tripped by the sentimentality of the film's conception. Others in important roles—Kent Smith, Ken Scott, Anna Lee, Cindy Robbins—are competent.

As Scott's mother, Augusta Merighi is a standout. Her gusty realism suddenly creates a vivid human being in the midst of limp marionettes. Among others who register are Francis Bethencourt, Stacy Graham, Peter Chong and Geraldine Wall.

Technicolor photography by Winton Hoch and Russell Metty is accomplished, and Hugo Freidhofer's score at times is as tangy as the first pressing of the grape. There is a title song by Sammy Cahn and Jimmy Van Heusen that deserves better presentation than the bellowing behind the main titles it gets. *Powe.*

The Man In the Net

Unsuccessful whodunit. Star names only lure.

Hollywood, April 17.

United Artists release of Mirisch Co. production. Stars Alan Ladd; costars Carolyn Jones. Produced by Walter Mirisch. Directed by Michael Curtis. Screenplay, Reginald Rose; based on a book by Patrick Quentin; camera, John Seitz; music, Hans J. Salter; editor, Harold Lavelle. Previewed at the Hawaii Theatre, April 16, '59. Running time, 96 MINS.

John Hamilton	Alan Ladd
Linda Hamilton	Carolyn Jones
Vickie Carey	Diane Brewster
Brad Carey	John Lupton
Steve Ritter	Charles McGraw
Gordon Moreland	Tom Helmore
Roz Moreland	Betty Lou Holland
Mr. Carey	John Alexander
Captain Green	Edward Binns
Mrs. Carey	Kathryn Givney
Emily Jones	Barbara Beaird
Angel Jones	Susan Gordon
Timmie Moreland	Charles Herbert
Buck Ritter	Mike McGreevy
Leroy	Steven Perry
Alonzo	Alvin Childress
Charlie Raines	Douglas Evans
Mrs. Jones	Natalie Masterson
State Troopers	Pat Miller, Bill Cassidy

Genuine murder mysteries have been in short supply lately. "The Man In The Net" isn't good, or even competent. Instead of mystery, it creates muddle. What is intended as the perilous is more often ludicrous.

The Mirisch Co. production for United Artists has valued names, Alan Ladd and Carolyn Jones, but neither is particularly satisfactory. Miss Jones is handicapped by her role. Ladd elects to play his so stoically that he is likely to leave even his die-hard fans feeling balked. Reginald Rose's screenplay must be faulted on a number of counts, and Michael Curtiz' direction emphasizes rather than minimizes its deficiencies.

What the producer, Walter Mirisch, apparently saw in "The Man In The Net" was another potential "Laura." There are superficial similarities. Miss Jones, Ladd's enigmatic wife, disappears from the New England community where they have been living while Ladd is having a go at being a serious artist. Miss Jones wants him to go back to Madison Avenue. He won't. He wants to have his chance at art and he also believes his wife's mental problems have been aggravated by New York.

When she disappears, the audience is supposed to believe none of the neighbors suspects she was an alcoholic and a psychopath. The title refers to Ladd's being caught in a web (or net) of filmsy circumstances indicating he did away with his wife. The premise doesn't hold.

It is improbable that when Miss Jones arrives at a party, bruised and obviously the worse for wine, that her word would be unquestioningly accepted against Ladd's. It is dubious that a local constable would adopt a bullying, presumptive attitude about Ladd's guilt, and even less likely that a state trooper would. The notion that New Englanders would threaten Ladd with a necktie party even before Miss Jones' body is found, is incredible. On the last score, lynchings in New England are most uncommon. And, as anyone knows who has ever been exposed to a commuter community, it is more likely that the natives would sit in taciturn approval if the "outsiders" got to doing away with one another.

The most serious flaw, however, is in the identity of the true murderer. Mystery fiction has at least one rule that should not be violated. That is that while the criminal's trail can be well covered, the criminal himself should be plainly visible to the audience.

There is no point to belaboring the flaws. But Ladd's portrayal is far from sympathetic. An undergraduate student in psychology could tell him that his method of treating a disintegrating personality is blatantly wrong. Miss Jones achieves some moments of pathos but she seems at other times to be giving it the old-Bette-Davis, eyes, hands, hips and all. Children are misused for plot and character insight. The kids are good, particularly Barbara Beaird, Susan Gordon and Steven Perry. But they aren't given proper treatment either. And that sums up "The Man In The Net." *Powe.*

The Young Land
(COLOR)

Mild historical item in C. V. Whitney's Americana series. Little b.o. response indicated.

Hollywood, April 17.

Columbia release of C. V. Whitney production. Stars Pat Wayne, Yvonne Craig, Dennis Hopper, Dan O'Herlihy. Produced by Patrick Ford. Directed by Ted Tetzlaff. Screenplay, Norman Shannon Hall; based on a story by John Reese; camera (Technicolor), Winton C. Hoch and Henry Sharp; music, Dimitri Tiomkin; editor, Tom McAdoo. Previewed at the studio, April 9, '59. Running time, 92 MINS.

Jim Ellison	Pat Wayne
Elena de la Madrid	Yvonne Craig
Hatfield Carnes	Dennis Hopper
Judge Isham	Dan O'Herlihy
Roberto de la Madrid	Robert de la Madrid
Ben Stroud	Cliff Ketchum
Lee Hearn	Ken Curtis
Santiago	Pedro Gonzalez Gonzalez
Sully	Edward Sweeny
Vaquero	John Quijada
Comacho	Miguel Camacho
Court Clerk	Tom Tiner
Quiroga	Carlos Romero
Drifter	Edward Jaurequi

This film is another in C. V. Whitney's Americana series, in the current instance concerned with the early days in California. "The Young Land" has a basically interesting premise but it gets no development, and the result is superficial, repititious and awkwardly naive. Its boxoffice prospects are poor.

The film was made almost two years ago, originally for Buena Vista, and is now being released by Columbia. There are some nice young names connected with it, Patrick Ford and Patrick Wayne, for two, as producer and star respectively. But this is the best and only recommendation for it.

Actually the original story by John Reese has the ring of truth. It is concerned with the murder trial of an American, Dennis Hopper, who has killed a Mexican. The trial is important because the locale is California and the time 1848. U. S. justice is also on trial with new citizens of Mexican extraction or birth. A fair trial will demonstrate that their loyalty to their new government is justified.

Norman Shannon Hall's screenplay, however, does not enlarge on the theme. It wastes time with a tedious and gawky romance between young Wayne and Yvonne Craig, with courtroom recreation of action already depicted and repeated for no effect, with pointless fringe action, and with talk too often the inadequate substitute for action of any kind.

While Hall's screenplay is not inventive, Ted Tetzlaff's direction does not do much to enliven what there is. One aspect of this failure is the fact that not until almost the end of film is a single full close-up shown. Even with the paucity of action, real or implied, and wasteful dialog, pointless of any implication or interesting in itself, some greater interest might have been aroused through more skillful use of photography.

Wayne is an attractive youngster but he is not adequate to carry such a large load of a feature film. Miss Craig is similarly endowed, but equally inadequate. Dennis Hopper and Dan O'Herlihy manage to put some bite into their roles. The rest of the cast is beset with stock characterizations.

Dimitri Tiomkin's score is good, but it rather shows up the thinness of the film itself. There is a theme song, "Strange Are The Ways of Love," sung by Randy Sparks. It was released some time ago. *Powe.*

Horrors of the Black Museum

Potential horror click in C'Scope and color with good sales gimmick, "Hypnovista." But offensively gory for non-addicts.

Hollywood, April 16.

American International Pictures release of Herman Cohen production. Stars Michael Gough, Graham Curnow, June Cunningham; features Geoffrey Keen, Shirley Ann Field, Gerald Andersen, John Warwick, Beatrice Varley. Directed by Arthur Crabtree. Screenplay, Aben Kandel, Herman Cohen; camera, Desmond Dickinson; music, Gerard Schurmann, Ken Jones; editor, Geoffrey Muller. Previewed at Universal, April 13, '59. Running time, 94 MINS.

Edmond Bancroft	Michael Gough
Joan Berkley	June Cunningham
Rick	Graham Curnow
Angela	Shirley Ann Field
Superintendent Graham	Geoffrey Keen
Dr. Ballan	Gerald Andersen
Inspector Lodge	John Warwick
Aggie	Beatrice Varley
Commissioner Wayne	Austin Trevor
Peggy	Malou Pantera
Tom Rivers	Howard Greene
Gail	Dorinda Stevens
FunFair Barker	Stuart Saunders
Woman in Hall	Hilda Barry
Woman in Hall	Nora Gordon

For the market at which it is aimed, American International's "Horrors of the Black Museum" is potentially big, despite—or perhaps because of—the fact that it panders to base tastes. In lieu of star names, the picture has a handsome production and a built-in sales gimmick, "Hypnovista."

The film vends horror in its most nauseating form for the sake of slaking a thirst for gore. So long as this is commercially profitable, such pictures will be made but thoughtful tradesters wonder to what expedients producers will resort when the public is sated with the current extremes.

"Horrors," produced in London by Herman Cohen, is AIP's first CinemaScope-and-color release. Particular attention has been paid to making the Eastman color as vivid and balanced as possible. When this is used to bring out the warmth and richness of art director Wilfred Arnold's sumptuous sets, the result is gratifying. But when it is used to emphasize the gouts of blood in the murder scenes, it is disgusting. Scenes similar to the ones shown are less objectionable when done in black and white.

For example, the first scene is of a girl who dies from two spikes driven into her brain through her eyes. The spikes are in a pair of trick binoculars. Blood is shown coming from between her fingers as she holds her face and the instrument is shown on the floor covered with blood.

Fortunately, it never gets worse than this although: a girl is guillotined on her bed; an old woman is impaled on ice tongs; a doctor is slowly electrocuted then dissolved in a vat of acid and his skeleton hung up to dry and two others are bloodily stabbed with a kris. In these latter cases the horror is modified somewhat by skillful editing by Geoffrey Muller.

The screenplay is a rambling affair about a wealthy, crippled author, Michael Gough, who commits a chain of murders in modern London to obtain material for his crime books and newspaper articles. He has his boyish assistant, Graham Curnow, under a hypnotic drug which turns him into a kind of Mr. Hyde. The "Black Museum" is the author's laboratory. There is scant dramatic suspense past the mid-point of the film when the author's homicidal nature is exposed, except that the viewer is kept edgy wondering what new horror is in store.

Michale Gough ably and forcefully limns the author; Geoffrey Keen does his usually competent job as a Scotland Yard inspector; Beatrice Varley is just right as the old woman; June Cunningham displays an animal vitality which serves in lieu of thesping talent and the rest of the cast is satisfactory.

"Hypnovista," it develops, is a 13-minute prolog in which some unremarkable psychological phenomena are demonstrated in a fairly interesting fashion by hypnotist Emile Franchel. As with the rest of the production, the technical aspects of the prolog are expert. Franchel, while not attempting to hypnotise the audience, uses special effects such as a revolving red and black spiral and a calculatedly monotonous voice to heighten suggestibility in the viewer. It is effective.

The taste may be deplored, and certainly small children should be prevented from seeing the picture, but it will probably find a large audience among those who crave their bucket of blood while it's still hot. *Glen.*

Darby O'Gill and the Little People

Fine fun with Irish fantasy and horror. Good prospects.

Buena Vista release of Walt Disney production. Director, Robert Stevenson; screenplay, Lawrence Edward Watkin; suggested by H. T. Kavanagh's "Darby O'Gill" stories; camera, Winton C. Hoch; editor, Stanley Johnson; music, Oliver Wallace; orchestration, Clifford Vaughan; art direction, Carroll Clark; sound, Dean Thomas.

Cast: Stars Albert Sharpe, Janet Munro, Sean Connery, Jimmy O'Dea; with Kieron Moore, Estelle Winwood, Walter Fitzgerald; features Denis O'Dea, J. G. Devlin, Jack MacGowran, Farrell Pelly, Nora O'Mahony.

Previewed at the Academy Award Theatre, April 24, '59. Running time, 95 MINS.

People of all sizes will get a bang out of "Darby O'Gill and the Little People." What the cast can't do for a marquee, the "Walt Disney Presents" should, and the film will hold its own inside the theatre. It is rollicking Gaelic fantasy.

Lawrence E. Watkin's screenplay, suggested by H. T. Kavanagh's "Darby O'Gill" stories, never restricts itself to fantasy alone, although everything revolves around Albert Sharpe's (Darby) puckish escapades with the 21-inch-tall portion of Ireland's population. Along the way there's a good deal of heated, but healthy, romance, a bristling fist-fight, and a climactic dose of genuine horror that should bare a lot of moppet eyeballs and work a shiver or two up the spine of stoical mommies and daddies. Juves, teeners, adults and oldsters will find something to get excited about.

The story is knit together by Sharpe's running clash with Jimmy O'Dea, cast as the king of the leprechauns. After a slow start, things get rolling when Sharpe is booted down a deep hole and into the underground "court" of the little folk by a pookah (spirit horse) whose humorous silent double-takes throughout are droll.

Sharpe's visit to leprechaun headquarters offers the film's most scintillating moments. It is a sequence in which the meticulously painstaking production is most in evidence, from the gaily-bounding dance of the diminutive creatures (accomplished, it is understood, via trampolines) to the striking gold-shaded color photography to the remarkably life-like process-shot matching.

Eventually, Sharpe captures O'Dea when the latter's magic powers have vanished with the dawn, and promises him freedom for the price of three wishes. But the old man's hopes for riches and happiness go down the drain when his daughter (Janet Munro) becomes gravely ill. When the mystic "death coach" comes to carry her away, Sharpe makes use of his final wish to ride to his death in her place, but matters manage to wind up happily (and a bit anti-climactically, from a more sophisticated viewpoint) through the efforts of the leprechaun king.

Sharpe's performance is a gem. He benefits from the combination of being lovable, yet humanly frail and prone to greed and pride, as Watkin has penned the character, but embellishes the role with a refreshingly individual manner of expression that should endear him. Similar excellence is achieved by O'Dea as the dangerous, but rather good-natured king.

Miss Munro, a delight to behold, may be at the threshold of a glamorous career. It is evident that her healthy beauty and coy thespic approach will make her a particular favorite with the important teen audience. Sean Connery is artificial as her lover, and is the weakest link in Robert Stevenson's otherwise distinguished direction. Kieron Moore gets in a few solid licks as the lead heavy, and the balance of the cast, largely imported from England and Ireland, is spirited and competent.

A potential sore spot, however, is the language barrier of foreign speech inflections. It will give children considerable difficulty, and even adults will have to cock their ears to catch all the words, particularly those of Estelle Winwood.

Animation effects, by Joshua Meador, are terrifying, serving, as they do, for the wrapup horror scenes. Art director Carroll Clark's settings are authentically imaginative, and technical credits are generally proficient. Music by Oliver Wallace created a stimulating atmosphere throughout. There are a pair of tunes, penned by Watkin and Wallace, of which "Pretty Irish Girl" is the better. It's hummable enough to linger in the mind, and could go places.

Tube.

Young Philadelphians

Pulp mag view of life among the very rich. Exploitable elements.

Hollywood, April 24.

Warner Bros. production and release. Stars Paul Newman, Barbara Rush, Alexis Smith, Brian Keith, Diane Brewster, Billie Burke, John Williams. Directed by Vincent Sherman. Screenplay, James Gunn; based on Richard Powell's novel, "The Philadelphian"; camera, Harry Stradling Sr.; music, Ernest Gold; editor, William Ziegler. Previewed at the studio, April 15, '59. Running time, 136 MINS.

Tony Lawrence	Paul Newman
Joan Dickinson	Barbara Rush
Carol Wharton	Alexis Smith
Mike Flannagan	Brian Keith
Kate Judson	Diane Brewster
Mrs. J. A. Allen	Billie Burke
Gil Dickinson	John Williams
Chet Gwynn	Robert Vaughn
John M. Wharton	Otto Kruger
Louis Donetti	Paul Picerni
Morton Stearns	Robert Douglas
Dr. Shippen Stearns	Frank Conroy
William Lawrence	Adam West
Carter Henry	Fred Eisley
George Archibald	Richard Deacon
Mrs. Lawrence	Isobel Elsom

"The Young Philadelphians" cannot be taken seriously as social drama, which is what it aims to be, but as a pulp magazine view of life on the Main Line, it has its points as film entertainment. The Warner Bros. production could click as a kind of urban, upper-class "Peyton Place," although its treatment is ponderous and uneven. It has exploitable elements, bastardy, illicit sex, alcoholism and murder. Vincent Sherman directed. It's far too long in its present form.

James Gunn's screenplay, from Richard Powell's novel, "The Philadelphian," depicts the majority of Philadelphia's respected citizens as avaricious, effete or sadistic. The story conflict arises from a challenge to the established order by Paul Newman, possessor of a distinguished local name but actually the son of Irish upstarts.

Newman learns late in the film that his mother, Diane Brewster, fled her socialite husband on their wedding night when he couldn't consummate their marriage. She sought comfort with Brian Keith, a brogueу Irishman of her own class. Newman is the result.

His mother's genteel poverty propels Newman into an unprincipled drive for success. He drops his girl, Barbara Rush, when her father offers him a job in his law firm as a payoff. He does a fellow law student out of another job by palling around with a more successful lawyer's wife, Alexis Smith. There are other illustrations of his single-minded purpose. His regeneration is shown when he learns of his parentage but purposely imperils all he has gained through ruthlessness and chicanery to save a sick and friendless scion of the wealthy accused of murder.

Although overfamiliar, this kind of story would be permissible if it had a novel or special point of view. But a requisite of any genre drama is that its background and people be authentic. The approach of "The Young Philadelphians" to the rich is the same concept that believes kings wear their crowns at breakfast.

One scene, in which a butler testifies in court, still wearing his household livery, is naive and improbable. The subplot skulduggery of stolen inheritances, while conceivable, is not credible in its presentation.

Newman, ordinarily a very reliable actor, plays his role as though he had contractual obligations to discharge and found them distasteful. He is sporadically effective, but he cannot get the audience's heart into the proceedings when his own is not. Despite a silly role, Barbara Rush conveys a winning kind of hopeless desperation. Alexis Smith, in briefly, limns a character of pathos and some dimension in a few, deft strokes.

Brian Keith and Diane Brewster are throttled by foolish roles. Billie Burke brings things alive momentarily with one of her airy, expert readings, and Robert Vaughn gets vitality and even some reality into an overdrawn part. John Williams, Otto Kruger, Frank Conroy and Fred Eisley give able supporting characterizations.

There is no producer listed on "The Young Philadelphians," a custom Warners has followed from time to time, so it is hard to place the blame for the inaccurate overall conception. Within the limits of the script, Sherman's direction is competent.

Harry Stradling Sr.'s camera work is notable, particularly in the lighting that has become almost a trademark of his lensing. *Powe.*

Face of a Fugitive
(COLOR)

Technically slick but slow-paced western with Fred MacMurray.

Hollywood, April 17.

Columbia release of Morningside production. Stars Mred MacMurray; co-stars Lin McCarthy, Dorothy Green; features Alan Baxter, Myrna Fahey, James Coburn, Francis de Sales, Gina Gillespie, Ron Hayes, Paul Burns. Executive producer, Charles H. Schneer; producer, David Heilweil; directed by Paul Wendkos. Screenplay, David T. Chantler, Daniel B. Ullman; story, Peter Dawson; camera, Wilfrid M. Cline; editor, Jerome Thoms; music, Jerrald Goldsmith. Previewed at the studio, April 16, '59. Running time, 80 MINS.

Jim Larson, Ray Kincaid	Fred MacMurray
Mark Riley	Lin McCarthy
Ellen Bailey	Dorothy Green
Reed Williams	Alan Baxter
Janet	Myrna Fahey
Purdy	James Coburn
Allison	Francis De Sales
Alice Bailey	Gina Gillespie
Danny	Ron Hayes
Jake	Paul Burns
Burton	Buzz Henry
Haley	John Milford
Stockton	James Gavin
Stableman	Hal K. Dawson
Eakins	Stanley Farrar
Minister	Rankin Mansfield
Bartender	Harrison Lewis

Columbia's "Face of a Fugitive" is a fair program western which attempts to be offbeat and succeeds in being downbeat. Good production values and the name of Fred MacMurray, who's experiencing renewed good will because of his appearance in Disney's "Shaggy Dog," make it a suitable entry at the bottom half of double bills.

Flying Charles Schneer's Morningside banner and produced by David Heilwell, the Eastman color film has an interesting cast which, under Paul Wendkos' direction, extracts some above-par characterizations from the screenplay by David Chantler and Daniel Ullman. But the story on the one hand lacks sufficient action to greatly attract the thud-and-blunder addicts and on the other hand is not tightly enough written to sell as an "adult western."

Withal, there is a touching quality about MacMurray's portrayal of a bank robber who is rescued, against his will, by his younger brother, who dies in the process. Not a killer, he is accused of killing a deputy whom the brother shot during the rescue. Taking refuge in a town where he is not known, he falls in love with the acting sheriff's sister. The delay occasioned by his pausing to rescue from certain death the young sheriff, who reminds him of his brother, results in his capture. The only ray of hope offered is that the sheriff, who's also a lawyer, will defend him at trial. The premise unintentionally proven is that criminals, like cobblers, should stick to their chosen professions.

The difficulty with the script is that all this happens in the space of a single day, hardly enough time to develop among strangers the deep relationships the audience is expected to believe; i.e., MacMurray becomes the sheriff's best man at marriage and wins a love which, presumably, will have to endure several years in prison. Not adequately supported is the premise that being a prisoner is preferable to being a fugitive.

Alan Baxter and his henchmen, James Coburn, Buzz Henry and John Milford, develop an excellent feeling of tension heckling the young lawyer-sheriff. Lin McCarthy, and Dorothy Green is suitably warm as the sheriff's sister. Numerous scenes — horse trading with the local stableman, kidding the barber, applying for a job as a deputy to hunt himself — lend an air of homely believability to the film, but they take up too much time and the result is a slow pace. It's retrieved by an exciting chase through a ghost town during the film's final minutes.

Wilfrid Cline's photography, Robert Peterson's art direction and Jerome Thoms' editing are slick and the color is generally good. Fly-speck pickers may notice that the player piano, a good choice of sound effect for the fight scene, rises and lowers in pitch rather than tempo to indicate it's out of order—a giveaway that a recording was used—but generally the technical aspects are professional.

Despite script deficiencies, the dialog usually impresses as being sincere, which helps to make the film acceptable entertainment, but it will have to rely on a stronger companion feature to lure customers away from their tv sets.

Glen.

The Hangman

Program western. Not much action, but familiar faces.

Hollywood, April 24.

Paramount release of Frank Freeman Jr. production. Stars Robert Taylor, Tina Louise, Fess Parker, Jack Lord. Directed by Michael Curtiz. Screenplay, Dudley Nichols; from a story by Luke Short; camera, Loyal Griggs; music, Harry Sukman; editor, Terry Morse. Previewed at the studio, April 20, '59. Running time, 87 MINS.

Mackenzie Bovard	Robert Taylor
Selah	Tina Louise
Buck Weston	Fess Parker
Johnny Bishop	Jack Lord
Big Murph	Gene Evans
Al Cruse	Mickey Shaughnessy
Kitty	Shirley Harmer
Herb Loftus	James Westerfield

"The Hangman" is a fair western for programming. It is hard to believe the screenplay came from Dudley Nichols, it is so sparsely and barrenly plotted, and its characters so perfunctory. The Frank Freeman Jr. production for Paramount is Robert Taylor's first film since he ended his marathon contract at Metro.

Taylor plays "The Hangman," so-called because he is a deputy U. S. Marshal resolute in his duty of bringing in badmen for their due session at the end of a rope. His current assignment brings him in search of Jack Lord, and his duty conflicts with principle. Lord is living a new life, and his right to do it is supported by everyone including the local sheriff, Fess Parker. In the end Taylor allows Lord to make a getaway, being convinced he is tempering justice with common sense.

This kind of story, the lawman against the frontier community, is a staple of western folklore. It is a natural dramatic setup, fairly simple to establish and to make credible. There should be, however, suspense as to the outcome as the story unfolds, and this the director, Michael Curtiz, fails to create. There must also be a powerful reason behind the change of heart by Taylor, the lawman, and this Nichols' screenplay does not supply. The film also dips into the ridiculous with not one but two (count 'em) bathing scenes of the heroine, Tina Louise. Any story, no matter how taut its intention, can do with diversion. No man should object to a diversion as tempting as Miss Louise in the alltogether. But the scene of the western heroine relentlessly seeking cleanliness in the nearest pond has been done and overdone and deserves retirement.

One of Robert Taylor's chief assets has always been his quality of conviction. He contributes a great deal of this to his role, but it is a hollow figure, despite cursory attempts at providing reasons for his being a "hangman." Miss Louise is an acceptable romantic vis-a-vis for Taylor, but Miss Louise, endowed as she is with plentiful physical charms, has yet to get her pretty teeth into a characterization. Fess Parker is acceptable as the local lawman, and Jack Lord is wasted in a part of no discernible depth. Gene Evans, Mickey Shaughnessy and James Westerfield are capable in support, and Lucille Curtis creates a subsidiary character of some humor.

Powe.

Sapphire
(BRITISH—COLOR)

Sound murder drama which compromises uneasily on question of color discrimination. Persuasive performances by Nigel Patrick, Paul Massie, Michael Craig.

London, April 21.

Rank Organization release of a Michael Relph & Basil Dearden production. Stars Nigel Patrick, Yvonne Mitchell, Michael Craig, Paul Massie. Directed by Basil Dearden. Screenplay, Janet Green; camera, Harry Waxman; editor, John Guthridge; music, Philip Green. Previewed at Rank Film Distributors' private cinema. Running time, 92 MINS.

Hazard	Nigel Patrick
Mildred	Yvonne Mitchell
Learoyd	Michael Craig
David	Paul Massie
Mr. Harris	Bernard Miles
Mrs. Harris	Olga Lindo
Dr. Robbins	Earl Cameron
Paul Slade	Gordon Heath
Patsy	Jocelyn Britton
Johnny Fiddle	Harry Baird
Barman	Orlando Martins
Ferris	Rupert Davies
Sgt. Cook	Freda Bamford
Horace Big Cigar	Robert Adams
Sapphire	Yvonne Buckingham

"Sapphire" is a well-knit pic showing how the police patiently track down a murderer. Although it hasn't anything very sensational in the way of stellar lure for houses outside of England, it is a holding yarn, acted persuasively. But, though obviously inspired by last year's outbreak of color-bar riots in London and Nottingham, it ducks the issue, refusing to face boldly up to the problem. Thus the pic does not get its message over as effectively as it might. There is constant haggling over the problem and some snide remarks, but it eventually adds up merely to another whodunit.

Victim of a savage murder in a London open space is attractive music student Yvonne Buckingham (Sapphire). The girl is revealed as having a dual personality. As well as being a student, she is also a good-time girl with a love for the bright lights. She is pregnant after an affair with a young man with a brilliant career as architect awaiting him. She is also a "lily-skin," a colored girl who is able to pose as white and does so.

There are a number of people—some white, some Negro — who have a motive for killing Sapphire. Two or three Negro friends who are angry with her for dropping them when she gets her "white" fixation. The young man who has promised to marry her. The youth's father who sees her as an obstruction to the hopes of his son's career. Patiently, Scotland Yard pursues the various red herrings, sorting out the malice, the racial hatred, and finally tracking down the culprit.

Janet Green's screenplay is a neat, absorbing job but there seems evidence that the survey of the rankling color bar problem that exists in Britain has been watered down. Basil Dearden has directed with sincerity. Hence, a most convincing picture of certain aspects of London life and the work Scotland Yard is put over with the help of some smooth lensing by Harry Waxman.

Dearden has a very effective cast. Nigel Patrick is fine as a suave, polite but ruthlessly efficient cop. Michael Craig, his assistant, is equally good as a less tolerant man who, for some unexplained reason, loathes Colored people. Paul Massie, as the nervy boy-friend, who for most of the film is the chief suspect; Bernard Miles, his father; Olga Lindo, as his mother, and Yvonne Mitchell, giving one of her familiar performances as a taut, repressed wife, all contribute excellently to the thesping.

But perhaps the best performance of all is that of Earl Cameron as an intelligent, tolerant Negro doctor who is the brother of the slain girl. Cameron brings immense dignity to a small role. Most of the other colored characters, however, are too obviously caricatures, particularly Harry Baird, who is suspected of the murder and gives a short but dramatically exciting performance as a bewildered Negro man at bay.

Concessions to the boxoffice make "Sapphire" a near-miss. But, if it does and says little to explain the edgy existence of Colored people in Britain, it provides a reasonably absorbing screen murder and sleuth vehicle.

Rich.

Europa di Notte
(Europe by Night)
(ITALO-FRENCH-COLOR)

Rome, April 21.

Warner Bros. release of an Avers Film (Paris-Rome) production. Features Domenico Modugno, The Platters Henry Salvador, Carmen Sevilla, Channing Pollock, Robert Lamouret, The Rastellis, Colin Hicks and his band, La Nouvelle Eve with the Charley Ballet; the Crazy Horse Saloon with Dolly Bell, Lady Phu Qui Cho, Lilly Niagra, and Les Croq' Messieurs; El Corral de la Moreria with Alba, Sandoval, Quintero, Carmen Casaburrios, Maria Marques; Le Carousel de Paris with Cocinelle; Alaa Arnova; Princesse Badia; Roland Davell; Stanley Watson; The Three Monarchs; Eddie Gray; Chu Fu and May; The Condoras; Mac Ronay; Ukrainian Chorus and the Orlyk Ballet; Archie Savage Dancers. Directed by Alessandro Blasetti. Screenplay, Ennio de Concini, Gualtiero Jacopetti; camera, (Eastmancolor) Gabor Pogany; editor, Mario Serandrei; music, Carlo Savina. At Rivoli, Rome. Running time, 102 MINS.

This slickly packaged and ably blended pot-pourri of vaude and nitery entertainment should bring a healthy return from almost any market. It will doubtlessly start another filmic cycle in the genre. As its impact is almost entirely visual and/or musical, adaptation expenses for "foreign" versions should be minimum, thus forming another not indifferent advantage.

Tasteful mounting, amusing commentary, and extremely refined technical outfitting also distinguish this from other filmed items of its kind. Gabor Pogany's pro lensing and a fast-paced editing job by Mario Sarandrei are other plus factors. All tastes are catered to in choice of numbers, the blend being a true sampling of the best the international nitery-vaudeville-music field has to offer today.

Pic opens to show an ideal composite European city at night, made up of portions of Rome, Paris, Madrid, Berlin and London. It then moves on to the various numbers, skillfully knit via the spoken commentary, and with no lag in pace. Choice of numbers also, with very few exceptions, guarantees high entertainment and quality standard in this "ideal" variety package.

The top-lined Platters and Domenico Modugno, along with Henry Salvador, ably hold up the vocal side of the show. Another starred performer, Carmen Sevilla, is in for a skillfully executed Spanish dance number. Among the magicos, Channing Pollock and Stanley Watson (the former also shown in a fascinating slow-motion sequence) do their stints well. Mac Ronay contributes a grotesque and humorous note.

Humor per se in this film comes from the commentary, as well as from such numbers as Robert Lamouret, the Rastellis, or the male strip number from Paris' Crazy Horse Saloon. Last-named will also go a long way to please those who like exploitation fare, even in the toned-down Italo version which however undoubtedly gains in humor whot it may have lost in the way of total peeling by the Gallic boite's now famous vedettes.

Also easy on the eyes are the Nouvelle Eve line and its Charley Ballet, plus the Archie Savage Dancers, while Princesse Badia shakes a mean torso to good effect. Secret of film's success in this sector (and undoubtedly, much of film's b.o. at least locally can be attributed to the "forbidden fruit" types of entertainment rarely if ever seen in Italy) is that it's always handled with taste, even in potentially risque moments. Among other numbers to be mentioned are naturally the now-fabulous Cocinelle, here seen very much in the flesh; Colin Hicks and his rock-n-roll crew, the Condoras, the Ukrainian Chorus and the Orlyk Dance Group and many others.

Hawk.

Dorogoi Tsenoi
(At Risk of Life)
(RUSSIAN—COLOR)

Paris, April 21.

Mosfilm release of Dovzhenko Studios production. With Vera Donskoi, Yury Dedovich, Ivan Tverkokhleb, Olgo Petrova, Sergei Shishkov. Directed by Marc Donskoi. Screenplay, Irina Donskoi from novel by M. Kotsyubinsky; camera (Sovcolor), N. Topchy; editor, N. Resnik. At Cinemathecque Francaise, Paris. Running time, 95 MINS.

Solomyi	Vera Donskoi
Ostap	Yury Dedovich
Kotigoroshek	Ivan Tverkokhleb
Mariutsa	Olga Petrova
Radu	Sergei Shishkov

Colorful pic, with a fine mixture of adventure and poetics, might be a worthy one to add to the list of Soviet pic exports to the U.S. if the exchange is finally concluded. It is extremely well mounted and made, with sound entertainment and dramatic values.

This concerns a young couple who run off when the girl is forced into a marriage with a rich kulak in the 1830s. They join other roaming serfs and escape to Bessarabia. But here the boy is arrested by mistake, with a group of thieving gypsies who have given them refuge. The girl is killed in trying to save him from being deported.

It has some propaganda aspects in its theme that leaving one's country is like death, but the feeling for time, place and its tender love story, helped by expert thesping, mounting and direction, make this a fine piece of filmmaking on its own. Color is rich and well used. This emerges a beguiling film.

Les Quatre Cents Coups
(The Four Hundred Blows)
(FRENCH-DYALISCOPE)

Cannes, April 28.

Cocinor release of Carrosse production. Features Patrick Auffay, Robert Beauvais, Albert Remy, Claire Maurier, Guy Decomble. Written and directed by Francois Truffaut. Camera (Dyaliscope), Henri Decae; editor, Marie-Josephe Yoyotte. At Cannes Film Fest. Running time, 98 MINS.

Antoine	Patrick Auffay
Rene	Robert Beauvais
Father	Albert Remy

Mother ... Claire Maurier
Teacher ... Guy Decomble

Offbeat pic gets deep into the life of a 12-year-old boy, his disorientation with school and parents and his final commitment to, and escape from, an institution. It eschews conventional blames and emerges an engaging, moving film with good arty theatre chances abroad. For more limited general distrib its lack of names and sprawling style will hurt.

It recalls "The Little Fugitive" and shows influences of the late Jean Vigo's pix. But young director Francois Truffaut, for his first film, denotes a knack for human detail. The child's world is not overly dramatic but essentially brave in the calm ability to adapt to the usually unthinking adult world around him.

Boy has a mother who cheats on his weak father. One day he runs off when, to explain a truancy, he suddenly makes up a tale that his mother is dead. He steals something and is committed to an institution as his parents wash their hands of him. Pix ends with his escape and dash to freedom via the sea.

Moppets are well handled and adults properly one dimensional in this astute look at the child's world. Truffaut still lacks form and polish but emerges an important new director here.

Technical qualities are uneven but blend with the meandering but sensitive look at a child's world and revolt. It has the earmarks for a good video pic, too. It has both moppet and adult appeal. It is in Dyaliscope which is akin to C'Scope in screen size.

Mosk.

Delit de Fuite
(Hit and Run)
(FRENCH)

Paris, April 21.

Corona release of Groupe Des Quatre production. Stars Antonella Lualdi, Felix Marten; features Folco Lulli, Aime Clariond, Franco Interlenghi, Robert Berri. Directed by Bernard Borderie. Screenplay by Jean Aurel from novel by James Hadley-Chase; camera, Claude Renoir; editor, Christian Gaudin. At Paris, Paris. Running time, **110 MINS.**

Fred ... Felix Marten
Lucile ... Antonella Lualdi
Franco ... Folco Lulli
Rossi ... Franco Interlenghi
Aitken ... Aime Clariond
Hackett ... Robert Berri

Slick cops and robbers yarn gives its hand away too early to make much impact. It shapes a pattern like many Yank pix of this type but is not up to their calibre in execution, playing or pacing. Result is that this is mainly for local fare.

A journalist gets mixed up with the young wife of an old industrialist and is soon knee deep in murder, blackmail and love. All is straightened out after an overlong story. Playing is ordinary but a pruning could make this okay telefodder. It is another in a series of smooth, violent murder yarns. It is technically good.

Pork Chop Hill

Grim, unrelieved war picture with minimum heroics and maximum realism. With Gregory Peck in lead, actioner shapes as strong entry.

United Artists release of a Melville Production. Produced by Sy Bartlett. Stars Gregory Peck; features Harry Guardino, Rip Torn, George Peppard, James Edwards, Bob Steele, Woody Strode, George Shibata. Directed by Lewis Milestone. Screenplay, James H. Webb, based on a work by S. L. A. Marshall, U.S.A.R.; camera, Sam Leavitt; music composed and conducted by Leonard Roseman. Previewed at the UA homeoffice in N.Y., April 30, '59. Running time, **97 MINS.**

Lt. Clemons ... Gregory Peck
Forstman ... Harry Guardino
Lt. Russell ... Rip Torn
Fedderson ... George Peppard
Cpl. Jurgens ... James Edwards
Kern ... Bob Steele
Franklin ... Woody Strode
Lt. O'Hashi ... George Shibata
Sgt. Coleman ... Norman Fell
Velie ... Robert Blake
Bowen ... Biff Elliot
Davis ... Barry Atwater
S-2 Officer ... Michael Garth
Gen. Trudeau ... Ken Lynch
Sgt. Kreucheberg ... Paul Comi
McKinley ... Abel Fernandez
P. I. Officer ... Lou Gallo
Cpl. Payne ... Cliff Ketchum
Marshall ... Martin Landau
Lt. Cummings ... Bert Remson
Cpl. Kissell ... Kevin Hagen
MacFarland ... Dean Stanton
Lt. Cook ... Leonard Graves
Sgt. Kuzmick ... Syl. Lamont
Saxon ... Gavin McCloud
Lt. Waldorf ... John Alderman
Olds ... John McKee
Harrold ... Charles Aidman
Chalmers ... Chuck Hayward
Radio Operator ... Buzz Martin
Soldier Runner ... Robert Williams
Iron Man ... Bill Wellman Jr.
Chinese Broadcaster ... Viraj Amonsin
Lt. Attridge ... Barry Maguire

Hollywood has come a long way to be able to make war films such as "Pork Chop Hill." The pretense and the heroics have been stripped from this picture. What is left is a grim, utterly realistic story that drives home both the irony of war and the courage men can summon to die in a cause which they don't understand and for an objective which they know to be totally irrelevant.

There is little but war in this film, which Sy Bartlett produced with a view to simplicity and Lewis Milestone directed with a flair for the documentary. Yarn essentially doesn't deviate from its simple story line: King Company, commanded by Gregory Peck as Lt. Joe Clemons, is ordered to take Pork Chop Hill from the Chinese Reds and to hold it against attack. Though his unit suffers frightful casualties, it accomplishes its objective, and in the end is ordered down the mountain.

The time, of course, is the Korean war, and the irony of the situation is that (1.) armistice negotiations at Panmunjon are virtually concluded, and (2.) Pork Chop has absolutely no tactical importance. It must be taken simply because its loss means a loss of face on the part of the Americans in the eyes of the Communist negotiators. The U.S. command knows this, and so do the G.I.s, and yet the pitched battle is ordered and the pain and the killing go on, defying logic and reason.

There is virtually no relief in this film. The humor is kept within reason and fits in. The dialog lines avoid speechmaking. The language that comes through the loudest is the chatter of machine-guns and the noise of shells and handgrenades bursting. This is probably one of the most honest war films to be made, and it doesn't shrink from showing the American mistakes, such as the turning on of the lights during the initial attack, making the U.S. soldiers a perfect target.

Peck's performance as the company commander is completely believable. He comes through as a born leader, and yet it is quite clear that he has his moments of doubt and of uncertainty. This is no customary Hollywood hero and the picture gains immeasurably from the human factor with which Peck imbues the role of Lt. Clemons (who, incidentally, exists in real life).

Milestone and Webb have tried to break the unending image of dirt, noise and death with some human touches. One sees Woody Strode, a Negro, trying to desert under fire, and he eventually tries to kill Peck. It's amazing that Webb should have chosen a Negro to be featured in this incident. It could have been a white man, and the effect would have been the same. The producers of the picture surely are aware that the tendency to generalize where a Negro is involved is far greater, and more harmful.

The accent on the combat is such in this film that, besides Peck, the other men barely emerge as people. They look real, they sound real, but there's no chance to get to know them, though the picture makes it very clear that they all know that their objective is secondary at best. Harry Guardino, Rip Torn, George Peppard, George Shibata, James Edwards, Bob Steele and Strode all blend perfectly into the picture, giving valuable support.

Sam Leavitt's photography is little short of masterful. The scenes come alive through his camera until one can virtually taste the dust and smell the acrid smoke. As his camera pans over the battlefield, strewn with dead, one is reminded of another great war film directed by Milestone, "All Quiet on the Western Front."

"Pork Chop Hill" is an important reminder of the futility of war. It doesn't offer much action beyond the fighting itself, and the dying, and after a while the scenes seem to take on a certain sameness and the mind dulls to the impact of the bravery of the men who give their lives. As war pictures go, this one makes most of the rest look pale. It should get its just rewards at the box office. "Pork Chop Hill" is unique in its class.

Hift.

Horrors of Black Museum
(BRITISH—C'SCOPE—COLOR)

Unpleasant and ridiculous horror pic; likely will satisfy the more indulgent and lower tastes.

London, April 28.

Anglo Amalgamated (Jack Greenwood) production and release. Stars Michael Gough, June Cunningham. Directed by Arthur Crabtree. Screenplay, Aben Kandel, Herman Cohen; editor, Geoffrey Muller; camera, Desmond Dickinson; music, Gerard Schurmann. At Studio One, London. Running time, **80 MINS.**

Edmond Bancroft ... Michael Gough
Joan Berkeley ... June Cunningham
Rick ... Graham Curnow
Angela ... Shirley Ann Field
Superintendent Graham ... Geoffrey Keen
Dr. Ballan ... Gerald Andersen
Inspector Lodge ... John Warwick
Aggie ... Beatrice Varley
Commissioner Wayne ... Austin Trevor
Peggy ... Malou Pantera
Tom Rivers ... Howard Greene
Gail ... Dorinda Stevens
Funfair Barker ... Stuart Saunders

Sheer horror for horror's sake is usually the refuge of the unimaginative and rarely clicks. "Horrors of the Black Museum" is a case in point. The producers have relied on sensationalism without subtlety of characterization, situation or dialog. As a result, this rather distasteful item is likely to gather more misplaced laughs than shudders among discriminating audiences.

Yarn is hinged on a skein of hideous London murders. It is quickly obvious to everybody except Scotland Yard that they are the work of a deranged, crippled crime journalist and author, who runs a horror museum in the cellar of his house, based on the Black Museum of Scotland Yard. Once it is established who is responsible, there remains only the doubtful suspense of wondering who his victims will be (and these are readily telegraphed), the method of their dispatch and how soon a meandering Scotland Yard will catch up with the murderers.

The story and screenplay by Aben Kandel and Herman Cohen is as full of holes as a fishing net. The reason for the author's actions is never satisfactorily explained, any more than how he comes to have a young man as his assistant who shares in his crimes with a blind obedience. Among the tasty murders that the writer dreams up are a woman's jugular vein severed by ice-tongs, a girl guillotined in her bed, an electrocuted doctor being disposed of in an acid bath, a girl stabbed while with her murderer in a fairground "Tunnel of Love" and the juicy opening when a victim receives a pair of binoculars in an anonymous parcel. She clamps them to her eyes whereupon a couple of spikes penetrate her eyes and brain. Accompanied by artificial blood and curdling screams, these are all supposed to thrill, but don't.

There is little to commend in "Black Museum" except Desmond Dickinson's lensing, Michael Gough, as the murderer, sardonically ploughs through the screenplay while Geoffrey Keen makes as much of the cop as the role will allow. June Cunningham, Shirley Ann Field and Dorinda Stevens are three of the femme victims who meet their fate with appropriate hysteria. Arthur Crabtree's direction is plodding and even the climax falls lamentably flat.

The Nun's Story
(COLOR)

Unusual theme and story. Audrey Hepburn in habit. Needs selling, but worth the effort.

Hollywood, May 1.

Warner Bros. release of a Fred Zinnemann production. Stars Audrey Hepburn; costars Peter Finch, Edith Evans, Peggy Ashcroft, Dean Jagger. Producer by Henry Blanke. Directed by Fred Zinnemann. Screenplay, Robert Anderson; based on the book by Kathryn C. Hulme; camera (Technicolor), Franz Planer; music, Franz Waxman; editor, Walter Thompson. Previewed at the studio, April 21, '59. Running time, **149 MINS.**

Sister Luke ... Audrey Hepburn
Dr. Fortuati ... Peter Finch
Mother Emmanuel ... Dame Edith Evans
Mother Mathilde ... Dame Peggy Ashcroft
Dr. VanDerMal ... Dean Jagger
Sister Margharita ... Mildred Dunnock
Mother Christophe ... Beatrice Straight
Sister Williams ... Patricia Collinge
Sister Eleanor ... Rosalie Crutchley
Mother Marcella ... Ruth White
Mother Kathrine ... Barbara O'Neil
Sister Pauline ... Margaret Phillips
Simone ... Patricia Bosworth
Archangel ... Colleen Dewhurst
Chaplain ... Stephen Murray
Dr. Goovarts ... Lionel Jeffries
Father Vermeuhlen ... Niall MacGinnis

The theme of "The Nun's Story"

is the most tenuous of human conflicts to translate into dramatic terms. It is the story of a God-dedicated soul's striving to find its vocation. It is obviously a very different kind of production than motion pictures generally attempt. Warner Bros. has its work cut out in presenting this film, with its esoteric theme and this austere title, and persuading the public it is entertainment.

Despite some minor objections, it is entertainment. Fred Zinnemann's production is a soaring and luminous film. In it, Audrey Hepburn has her most demanding film role, and she gives her finest performance. Despite the seriousness of the underlying theme, "The Nun's Story" has the elements of absorbing drama, pathos, humor, and a gallery of memorable scenes and characters.

It is a long picture, and despite the necessity for careful preparation in the early scenes of the kind of life it is concerned with, some of the later scenes are drawn beyond their length. The ending, when it comes, seems abrupt and incomplete. Dramatically it is sound, and has been properly laid in. Esthetically it is too sharp a transition, perhaps because the struggle which proceeds it has been drawn to such lengths.

The struggle is that of a young Belgian woman, played by Audrey Hepburn, to be a successful member of an order of cloistered nuns. The Order (not specified) is as different from the ordinary "regular guy" motion picture conception of nuns as the Army is from the Boy Scouts. Its aim is total merging of self. One of the greatest faults its members can fall into is to "singularize" themselves. This, the lay world would characterize as "expressing" oneself. So it is, as the Mother Superior (splendidly played by Edith Evans) says, a life against nature.

It is a super-human life that Miss Hepburn is expected to create, on earth, among humans. Although the story is confined chiefly to three convents, in Belgium and the Congo, the struggle is fierce. Miss Hepburn, attempting to be something she is not, is burned fine in the process. In the end, when World War II strikes, and her father is killed by the Germans, she knows she is not a true nun, at least of this Order. She cannot feel Christ-like love, she cannot turn the other cheek to the Nazis. With her superior's consent, she leaves the convent.

Although the narrative reduces to fairly simple synopsis, it is a subtle and labyrinthine affair, and Robert Anderson's screenplay is exceptional in expressing the cerebral and spiritual conflict in vocal and pictorial terms. There is not a false note in it.

One of the consistent gratifications is the cast. In addition to Miss Evans, who might have been a Renaissance prelate, there is Peggy Ashcroft, another convent superior, but less the dignitary, more the anchorite. Mildred Dunnock is a gentle, maiden aunt of a nun; Patricia Collinge, a gossipy cousin. Beatrice Straight is the lovely, rather glamorous nun almost every convent has; Margaret Phillips, a dessicated spinster.

Peter Finch and Dean Jagger are the only males in the cast of any stature. Finch, as an intelligent, attractive agnostic, conveys a romantic attachment for Miss Hepburn, but in terms that can give no offense. Dagger, as Miss Hepburn's perturbed by loving father, contributes a valuable facet on the story.

Despite the seeming austerity of the story, Zinnemann has achieved a pictorial sweep and majesty. Franz Planer's Technicolor photography has a Gothic grace and muted splendor, the timelessness of the nuns' garb, their backgrounds, their lives, creating a rich and medieval pomp and pageantry.

Alexander Trauner's art direction is responsible for a good deal of this atmosphere, and so is Marjorie Best with her costumes. Franz Waxman's score is a great one, giving proper place to cathedral organs and Congo drums. Walter Thompson's editing, and Oliver S. Garretson's sound, are both fine. Color balance is notable. *Powe.*

Beyond This Place
(BRITISH)

Entertaining drama of a young man's fight to clear his father's name, with nice performances by Van Johnson and feature players; sound b.o. prospect.

London, April 28.

Renown release of a George Minter-Georgefield Production. Stars Van Johnson, Vera Miles, Emlyn Williams, Bernard Lee. Directed by Jack Cardiff. Screenplay, Kenneth Taylor, from novel by A. J. Cronin; editor, Ernest Walter; camera, Wilkie Cooper; music, Douglas Gamley. At Gaumont, Haymarket, London. Running time, **90 MINS.**

Paul Mathry .... Van Johnson
Lena Anderson .... Vera Miles
Enoch Oswald .... Emlyn Williams
Patrick Mathry .... Bernard Lee
Louise Burt .... Jean Kent
Chief Inspector Dale.....Moultrie Kelsall
McEvoy .... Leo McKern
Sir Matthew Sprott.......Ralph Truman
Prison Governor .... Geoffrey Keen
Swann .... Jameson Clark
Ella Mathry .... Rosalie Crutchley
Prusty .... Oliver Johnston
Lady Catherine Sprott .....Joyce Heron
Dunn .... Anthony Newlands
Paul Mathry (Aged 6)....Vincent Winter
Alderman Sharpe .... Henry Oscar
Magistrate .... John Glyn-Jones
Mrs. Hanley .... Hope Jackman
Det.-Sgt. Trevor.........Michael Collins
Roach .... Danny Green

A. J. Cronin's novel, "Beyond This Place," has been turned into a workmanlike, holding drama, though the tender, human love theme has been somewhat swamped by the stronger plot of a young man's efforts to prove his father innocent of murder. Soundly directed by Jack Cardiff, and with a competent list of British feature players in support of the two Yank stars, this is a useful booking for many popular houses.

A girl is strangled during a Liverpool air-raid and Irish docker Bernard Lee is found guilty of the crime. But because of flimsy evidence and a petition organized by a wealthy, religious ship tycoon, Lee escapes the noose and is flung into the cooler for life. Some 20 years later, his son (Van Johnson) returns from America, where he was evacuated with his mother, to learn that his dad did not die a hero's death, as he believed, but is languishing in jail, branded a murderer.

Playing a sentimental hunch rather than on any real evidence, Johnson is convinced that his father is no killer and sets out to prove it. He comes up against the local police and is frustrated by wire-pulling from local big shots who, for various reasons, don't want the case reopened. Nevertheless, with the help of a local newspaperman, Van Johnson succeeds in clearing his father's good name.

This straightforward plot is given a fair amount of bite by Cardiff's direction. Though the ending rather falls apart unconvincingly, Kenneth Taylor's screenplay moves doggedly and interestingly towards the payoff. Wilkie Cooper's lensing helps to capture the Liverpool atmosphere.

Although the roles could have been effectively played by British performers, Van Johnson is a tenacious and likeable hero while Vera Miles is adequate in a colorless role as a timid librarian. The relationship between these two is not developed too clearly and is relegated to a slight, routine love story.

Lee's two performances are in striking contrast. At the beginning he is the amiable, reckless young Irishman. At the end, he is the sullen, embittered ex-convict. Both performances are first-class. Jean Kent, as a night club floozy, and Emlyn Williams, suavely assured as the shipping magnate, both contribute key performances. One of the most significant roles is that of the newspaperman, played by Anthony Newlands. It is good to see, almost for the first time in recent memory, a newspaper office that looks like one and reporters who behave like newspapermen. **Among a long list of supporting roles Oliver Johnston, Jameson Clark, Moultrie Kelsall, Leo McKern and Ralph Truman do particularly useful jobs.**

"Beyond This Place" (a seemingly meaningless title) has certainly lost a great deal in condensation to the screen. Yet even some slow patches and the rather contrived ending does not detract from the pic's merit as entertainment. ***Rich.***

The Five Pennies
(SONGS—COLOR—V'VISION)

Kaye's best comedy in years though script peters out. Lotsa good promotion going for it. Good b.o.

Hollywood, May 1.

Paramount release of Dena Production. Stars Danny Kaye; costars Barbara Bel Geddes, Louis Armstrong, Harry Guardino, Bob Crosby, Bobby Troup. Produced by Jack Rose. Directed by Melville Shavelson. Screenplay, Rose and Shavelson; story by Robert Smith; suggested by the life of Loring "Red" Nichols; camera (Technicolor), Daniel L. Papp; music, Leith Stevens; songs, Sylvia Fine; editor, Frank P. Keller. Previewed at the Westwood Village Theatre, April 27, '59. Running time, **117 MINS.**

Loring "Red" Nichols ......Danny Kaye
Bobbie Meredith .....Barbara Bel Geddes
Louis Armstrong ...... Louis Armstrong
Wil Paradise .... Bob Crosby
Tony Valani .... Harry Guardion
Dorothy Nichols (6-8 years). Susan Gordon
Dorothy Nichols (13 years)..Tuesday Weld
Jimmy Dorsey .... Ray Anthony
Artie Schutt .... Bobby Troup
Dave Touch .... Shelley Manne
Glenn Miller .... Ray Daley
Tommye Eden .... Valerie Allen

"The Five Pennies" is a sentimental comedy with music, a biographical story based pretty firmly on the career of "Red" Nichols. Plot devices put in the film get a little creaky, and the later portions are somewhat lachrymose, but overall it is diverting entertainment. It is probably going to be Danny Kaye's most successful picture in years.

The weaknesses of the Paramount release would not be so obvious if the film were a careless, "And Then I Wrote (or Played) . . ." musical. The screenplay, by Jack Rose and Melville Shavelson, is astringent and humorous, often close to wit. Rose, who also produced, and Shavelson, who directed, have their own high standards to blame if the closing sequences seem mawkish.

Kaye plays "Red" Nichols in the Paramount release. Whether it's Kaye or Nichols he's actually portraying is a moot point, but a point likely to trouble only music historians. Whoever it is, it's a likable, interesting personality. His story follows a familiar route. Musician wants to play a new kind of music. Musical bigshots won't let him play it. Musician organizes his own group. New music is socko. It's all true, but the problem in these true stories is to make them interesting.

The production gets sparkle and vitality with comedy routines for Kaye that are funny in their own right. He has able sidemen, too, in both the film and musical sense. There is Louis Armstrong (playing himself), Ray Anthony (Jimmy Dorsey), Bobby Troup (Artie Schutt), Shelley Manne (Dave Touch), Ray Daley (Glenn Miller), and Bob Crosby as a prototype of the 20's pop bandleader, complete with the megaphone, the schmaltz voice and the limp beat. Shavelson and Rose know how to bring comedy naturally out of situation, and it plays.

It's true, too, that Nichols abandoned his career and that the renunciation was motivated by his daughter's polio. But story line here isn't used for character change or development, only plot change and development. It is awkward and uncomfortable.

On the more or less straight dramatic side, Barbara Bel Geddes is fresh and appealing as Kaye's wife. It is a part that would ordinarily have been cast with the conventional ingenue, and Miss Bel Geddes' quiet authority gives the role dignity and importance. Young Susan Gordon is a standout as Kaye's daughter in her early years, and Tuesday Weld is attractive as the same girl in her teens.

"The Five Pennies" has unusual technical credits for a musical, although "technical" is scarcely correct for some of the artistic contributions. Sylvia Fine, who served as associate to the producer, has written four new songs for Kaye, from a tender "Lullaby In Ragtime," to a pattering "Follow The Leader." The latter gives the classical composers another going over, reminiscent of the famed Kaye number in "Lady in The Dark." Leith Stevens has put these numbers in perspective with his film score, as well as including some of the standards from the 20's, and, by a muted trumpet or broken chord, done a dramatic scoring.

Daniel L. Papp's photography is clean and brilliant, matching the music and the mood. Hoyningen-Huene, the photographer, served as color coordinator, on the Technicolor film, and the color is notable. *Powe.*

Ask Any Girl
C'SCOPE-COLOR

Outstanding comedy performance of Shirley MacLaine makes this a hot b.o. entry. David Niven, Gig Young and a generally funny script contribute to over-all hilarity.

Metro release of Joe Pasternak production. Stars Shirley MacLaine, David Niven and Gig Young. Features Rod Taylor, Jim Backus, Claire Kelly, Elisabeth Frazer, Dody Heath, Read Morgan and Carmen Phillips. Directed by Charles Walters. Screenplay, George Wells, from the novel by Winifred Wolfe; camera, Robert Bronner; editor, John McSweeney Jr., music Jeff Alexander. Previewed at Loew's 72d St., N.Y. April 28, '57. Running time, **98 MINS.**

Miles Doughton .... David Niven
Meg Wheeler .... Shirley MacLaine
Evan Doughton .... Gig Young
Ross Taford .... Rod Taylor
Mr. Maxwell .... Jim Backus
Lisa .... Claire Kelly
Jeannie Boyden .... Elisabeth Frazer
Terri Richards .... Dody Heath
Bert .... Read Morgan
Refined Young Lady ... Carmen Phillips

There's no need to "Ask Any Girl." Shirley MacLaine is sufficient. The pert and effervescent actress, who gains increased stature as a performer and a personality with each new outing, again comes through with a performance that is a sheer delight, even topping her Academy Award nomination stint in "Some Came Running." Her brand of whackiness is contagious and her appeal is unique in that it commands attention among both sexes and all age groups. "Ask Any Girl" is worth seeing just to watch Miss MacLaine in action as a smalltown girl on the loose in the big city.

Moreover, the picture, which looms as a strong boxoffice contender, is endowed with additional satisfying ingredients. David Niven, fresh from his Academy Award as the unstable major in "Separate Tables," displays his versatility as he returns to comedy. He makes the perfect foil for Miss MacLaine in his depiction as her serious-minded boss. And Gig Young, as the perennial wolf, again (as in "Teacher's Pet") gives hefty evidence of being a superior delineator of a comedy role.

The trio is helped no end by the hep and mostly hilarious screenplay George Wells has fashioned from Winifred Wolfe's novel. A preview audience roared contentedly through the unfolding of the adventures of a girl who comes to New York not to seek fame and fortune but in search of a husband. The picture's premise is that any girl in similar circumstances has a hell of a time preserving her virginity before landing the legal ring on her left hand.

Miss MacLaine has a penchant for losing her clothes—not a la Brigitte Bardot, of course. On her arrival at Penn Station, her suitcase is stolen. Later an angry roommate locks her out of their apartment.

She changes jobs when bosses make passes. She is lured to a country house on false pretenses. A supposed aunt and uncle are not present. She staves off what men want most with ingenuity, a strong right, and plain fast running. But when she sets her sights on a husband, he's a dead pigeon.

As a secretary and interviewer in a motivational research agency, headed by the brother team of Niven and Young, Miss MacLaine supposedly has her eye on Young and convinces Niven to join her in employing modern marketing techniques to nail Young to the altar. Niven, formerly the all-business-and-no-play type, con-

fiscates his brother's little black book and, in the interest of research, samples the telephone numbers and addresses. The result is a composite femme that Miss MacLaine assumes and which results in eliciting a proposal from Young. The obvious switch, however, takes place and she ends up in Niven's arms.

The plot line occasionally bogs down but the overall effect, helped considerably by Charles Walters' fast-paced direction, is maintained by the comedy inherent in the individual scenes. There's the time, for example, when Miss MacLaine, as a house-to-house interviewer, is picked up in a raid of a toll-sex establishment. Or Miss MacLaine becoming acquainted with martinis for the first time, fending off ardent swains, coping with beatniks, and acting as the composite femme fatale. The picture lends itself to the introduction of a parade of pulchritude as represented by such lookers as Claire Kelly, Casey Rogers, Dody Heath, Carmen Philips and Myrna Hansen.

Top-drawer supporting performances are offered by Rod Taylor, as a subtle pursuer; Jim Backus, as a boss who gets ideas, and Elisabeth Fraser, as a chubby sympathetic friend.

Joe Pasternak has provided lush production values and Robert Bronner's CinemaScope-Metrocolor camera has finely captured various aspects of New York life. Other technical contributions are equally outstanding. *Holl.*

Hercules
(EASTMAN COLOR)

An inexpert "epic" relying on a pile-driver campaign which should help initial showings.

Warner release of Joseph E. Levine (Embassy Pictures) import. Produced by Federico Teti. Stars Steve Reeves, Sylva Koscina; features Fabrizio Mioni, Ivo Garrani, Arturo Dominici, Mimmo Palmara, Lidia Alfonsi, Gina Rovere. Directed by Pietro Francisci. Screenplay, Francisci, Ennio De Concini and Gaio Frattini, from story by Francisci; camera, Mario Bava; editor, Mario Serandrei; music, Enzo Masetti. Screened at WB homeoffice projection room May 7, '59. Running time, **107 MINS.**

Hercules .... Steve Reeves
Iole .... Sylva Koscina
Jason .... Fabrizio Mioni
Pelias .... Ivo Garrani
Eurysteus .... Arturo Dominici
Iphitus .... Mimmo Palmara
The Sybil .... Lidia Alfonsi
Amazon .... Gina Rovere
Ulysses .... Gabriel Antonini
Laertes .... Andrea Fantasia
Argos .... Aldo Fiorelli
Orpheus .... Gino Nattera
Esculapius .... G. P. Rosmino
Chiron .... Afro Poli
Antea .... Gianna Maria Canale

There's an important trade angle which, perhaps, rates Paragraph One attention in a trade analysis of "Hercules," the Italian-made production imported by Joseph E. Levine of Boston and Embassy Pictures. This centers on Levine's wisdom in blueprinting an ad-pub campaign which figures to cost several times over the expense for distribution rights. And to be accounted for, too, before he can recoup are the outlay for prints and WB's participation in the gross. One look at the picture, which lacks professional production know-how, makes it a certainty that Levine is taking a gamble in a manner interpreted widely as dynamic showmanship.

"Hercules" on it's own in the American market has not too much to recommend it. It has production size, to be sure, and a subject (mythology's great man of muscle)

that inspires interest. Clearly Levine and Warners, which is handling the release, have seen enough in these two items to have become interested.

Detracting from them in terms of Yank audience acceptance, for the most part, is a story line that lacks clear continuity. It's a sketchy affair in which Hercules and his 12 labors (imposed upon him because of Juno's animosity toward him) are unveiled only in part, and with not one seguing into the other evenly.

The strongboy of Mythology saves the princess from a runaway chariot, and conquers the famed Nemean lion. In pursuit of his assignment he also downs the Cretan Bull which was designed as his malefactor. Enter the story of Jason, and his search for the Golden Fleece, which will justify Jason's claim to the throne, and the tale of the Argonauts—a familiar matter for those who remember their high school Latin. The princess, whom Hercules has so bravely saved, and Hercules provide the romantic interests. The meller-dramatics further focus on an enchained Hercules belting down an army of would-be captors, Jason taking over his rightful throne and the evil King Pelias taking poison as a way out.

Backgrounds are good and photography in Eastman Color not bad at all. The abrupt change of scenes and story sequences are responsible for the major letdown. No help is a dubbing job that admirably is sometimes not apparent at all, and at other times glaringly out of sync.

Any attempt to judge individual performances or credits could easily run amiss because of the modest caliber of the overall work. Suffice to say that Steve Reeves looks the part of Hercules, Sylva Koscina makes an attractive princess, Fabrizio Mioni and Jason might have had a lot in common and Ivo Garrani is properly sinister as the bad monarch.

Music by Enzo Masetti is a lot of pounding business in keeping with the screen action's emphasis on strong derring-do. Technical credits are fair.

Non - discriminating audiences may accept "Hercules". It does have some robust action scenes. As for the sophisticates, well, how stop that word of mouth? *Gene.*

Shake Hands With The Devil

Name-stacked cast in story of 1921 Irish revolt. Fairish b.o.

Hollywood, May 8.

United Artists release of Pennebaker production. Stars James Cagney, Don Murray, Dana Wynter, Glynis Johns. Producer-director, Michael Anderson. Executive producers, George Glass and Walter Seltzer. Screenplay, Ivan Goff and Ben Roberts; based on the novel by Rearden Conner; camera, Erwin Hillier; music, William Alwyn; editor, Gordon Pilkington. Previewed at Goldwyn studio, May 5, '59. Running time, **104 MINS.**

Sean Lenihan .... James Cagney
Kerry O'Shea .... Don Murray
Jennifer Curtis .... Dana Wynter
Kitty Brady .... Glynis Johns
The General .... Michael Redgrave
Lady Fitzhugh .... Sybil Thorndike
Chris Noonan .... Cyril Cusack
Mary Madigan .... Marianne Benet
McGrath .... John Breslin
Cassidy .... Harry Brogan
Sergeant .... Robert Brown
The Judge .... Lewis Casson
Mike O'Callaghan .... John Cairney
Clancy .... Harry Corbett
Mrs. Madigan .... Eileen Crowe
Captain .... Allan Cuthbertson
Willie Cafferty .... Donal Donnelly
Tommy Connor .... Wilfred Downing
Eileen O'Leary .... Eithne Dunne
Doyle .... Paul Farrell
Terence O'Brien .... Richard Harris

Sgt. Jenkins .... William Hartnell
British General .... John LeMesurier
Michael O'Leary .... Niall MacGinnis
Donovan .... Patrick McAlinney
Paddy Nolan .... Ray McAnally
Sir Arnold Fielding .... Clive Morton
Liam O'Sullivan .... Noel Purcell
Captain .... Peter Reynolds
Col. Smithson .... Christopher Rhodes
Sergeant .... Ronald Walsh
Capt. Fleming .... Alan White

A strong and unusual story has been diluted in its telling. The double-ply, action-psychological theme suffers most from the interpolation of unnecessary elements, including some naive and some shabby sex.

The stars, James Cagney, Don Murray, Dana Wynter and Glynis Johns, fare least well in the Pennebaker production for United Artists. It was produced and directed by Michael Anderson, with George Glass and Walter Seltzer as executive producers. Thanks to an exceptional supporting cast, the picture has moments of quiet truth and beauty.

The theme is that those who "Shake Hands With The Devil" often find they have difficulty getting their hands back. Two such, in the Ivan Goff-Ben Roberts screenplay, from the novel by Rearden Conner, are Cagney and Murray. Against a background of the 1921 Irish Rebellion, Cagney is a professor of medicine at a Dublin university, and Murray, an American veteran of World War I, is his student. Cagney is also a "commandant" of the underground, and Murray's father, an Irish patriot, was killed while working with Cagney.

The problem, aside from action incidents pacing the story, is that of the intellectual idealist forced into the role of gun-toting—and using—revolutionary. Cagney has already embraced the part, and Murray reluctantly assumes it.

The film makes a try at penetrating this intriguing aspect of revolt, in showing that when compassionate intellectuals such as Cagney turn to terror, usually in what seems self-defense, they often become the most merciless and determined killers. For it is Cagney who wants to continue the terror when the leader of the Irish independence movement, Michael Redgrave, works out a treaty with the British that eventually leads to freedom.

As a straight narrative exploring these paradoxes, "Shake Hands With The Devil" could have been an important film. Instead, it seems to have decided to play it "safe" by injection of elements as synthetic as a Paddy brogue.

A nude bathing scene by Miss Johns is dubious considering the locale and the climate, and its use as motivation for Cagney is misleading. Romantic interest between Murray and Miss Wynter is not basically wrong, but it is allowed to assume improbable importance. Again, a scene of Miss Wynter in bed, apparently covered by nothing but a blanket, is out of key.

The principals, paced by Cagney, are interesting and sometimes moving. But they seem posed against the Irish background, rather than part of it. Perhaps because they are required to posture in situations not authentic, the supporting cast looms larger than it should.

Sybil Thorndike, for instance, as a titled Irish lady lending her name and fierce old heart to the

cause, is fine. Redgrave has dignity and strength in his few scenes. Cyril Cusack, Ray McAnally, Lewis Casson, Harry Brogan and Richard Harris, some in for only bits, have impact.

Erwin Hillier's camera work is good, creating a grim, gray Ireland that is a natural setting for the sanguine struggle. Tom Morahan's art direction is valuable, and, on the basis of this film, Ireland's new studios at Bray seem adequate to handle almost any production.

Powe.

Invisible Invaders

Dull science fiction. For juveniles.

United Artists release of a Premium Pictures Inc. presentation produced by Robert E. Kent. Co-stars John Agar, Jean Byron; features Philip Tonge, Robert Hutton, John Carradine. Directed by Edward L. Cahn. Written by Samuel Newman. Camera, Maury Gertsman; editor, Grant Whytock. Previewed N.Y., May 7, '59. Running time, **67 MINS.**

Major Bruce Jay .... John Agar
Phyllis Penner .... Jean Byron
Dr. John LaMont .... Robert Hutton
Dr. Adam Penner .... Philip Tonge
The Farmer .... Hal Torey
Dr. Karol Noymann......John Carradine
WAAF Secretary .... Eden Hartford
Cab Driver .... Jack Kenney
General Stone .... Paul Langton

Half of a UA "thriller" package is "Invisible Invaders," a science fictioner produced by Robert E. Kent. It offers little interest to adult audiences, but the Saturday matinee trade should find it interesting escapist fare.

Kent has assembled some good actors for this bargain basement chiller but they're largely wasted in the Samuel Newman script. Here we have invisible invaders from outer space who give the earth 24 hours to capitulate. Within a couple days more than half the globe has been laid waste.

Although the spacemen are literally breathing on their underground bunker, scientists Robert Hutton and Philip Tonge come up with a weapon that saves man and the world. Hutton and the late Tonge do as best they can under Edward L. Cahn's undistinguished direction.

John Agar is forthright as an Army major who battles the invaders while Jean Byron, as Tonge's daughter, provides the romantic interest. John Carradine is seen briefly as a scientist who loses his life in an atomic explosion. Stock characterizations are supplied by the balance of the cast.

Technical aspects of the picture reflect the low budget. Much of the footage is padded with newsreel shots of floods, fires and other disastrous scenes. This, however, has been expertly spliced by editor Grant Whytock. Maury Gartsman's fresh lensing is good. Al Overton's sound and art direction of William Glasgow are fairish.

Gilb.

Hoppla, Jetzt Kommt Eddie
(Hoppla, Now Comes Eddie) (GERMAN)

Berlin, May 5.

Gloria release of Kurt Ulrich production. Stars Eddie Constantine; features Maria Sebaldt, Guenther Lueders, Margit Saad, Peter Mosbacher, Bum Krueger, Directed by Werner Klinger. Screenplay, Curt J. Braun, with utilization of an idea by H. F. Koellner; camera, Erich Claunigk; music, Michael Jary; editor, Klaus Eckstein. At UFA Pavillon, Berlin. Running time, **92 MINS.**

Eddie Petersen ....Eddie Constantine
Maria Mattoni ....Maria Sebaldt
Fred Uhlman ....Guenther Lueders
Juanita Perez ....Margit Saad
Manuel Fanton ....Peter Mosbacher
Consul Almeida ....Bum Krueger

The first German Eddie Constantine film made under Constantine's four-year contract with Berlin's Kurt Ulrich Productions. Film makes an obvious attempt to follow the pattern of those French gangster parody pix which made the Constantine name so popular on the Continent.

Germans haven't exactly an easy hand when it comes to such type of films, not too much was expected. However, this pic comes through nicely. It hasn't the imagination of Constantine's better known French vehicles, it's true, but there is enough pace so that Eddie's numerous German fans will hardly see the difference. He's at his usual ease with uppercuts, tough guys, all types of femmes and whisky. Constantine easily doninates the film.

Constantine is a Hamburg seaman who has been hired to take care of a bunch of South American beauties of whom one, daughter of a Nobel Prize-winner, is of special importance. Her late father has made an invention which could replace the expensive gasoline in cars. An international gangster ring is after this invention and there are the usual fights, chases and complications until the whole matter is cleared up.

Werner Klinger's direction is okay. Background music has a real rhythm. Michael Jary has written a song, "Hoppla Eddie," lyrics by Bruno Balz, occasionally sung by Constantine, which is easy on the ear. Technical credits are good.

Hans.

Battle Flame

Routine war feature.

Hollywood, May 5.

Allied Artists production and release. Stars Scott Brady and Elaine Edwards; features Robert Blake, Wayne Heffley, Gordon Jones, Ken Miller, Arthur Walsh, Richard Harrison, Gary Kent, Peggy Moffitt, Jean Robbins, Richard Crane. Producer, Lester A. Sansom. Directed by R. G. Springsteen. Screenplay by Elwood Ullman, from a story by Sansom and Ullman; camera, Carl Guthrie; editor, William Austin; music, Marlin Skiles. Previewed April 28, '59. Running time, **78 MINS.**

1st Lt. Frank Davis..........Scott Brady
Mary .... Elaine Edwards
Corp. Pachecho .... Robert Blake
Teach .... Wayne Heffley
Sgt. McKelvey .... Gordon Jones
Orlando .... Ken Miller
Nawlins .... Arthur Walsh
2nd Lt. Wechsler.......Richard Harrison
Gilchrest .... Gary Kent
Nurse Fisher .... Peggy Moffitt
Nurse Claycomb .... Jean Robbins
Dr. Stoddard .... Richard Crane

"Battle Flame" sputters through wartime cliches as if lonely marines and lousy rations were fresh enough to arouse an audience's untouched sympathies. They're not and, while the Allied Artists production gains zest midway through its 78 minutes, a rambling start makes it just another programmer.

The half-way boost, which follows a run-of-the-mill war story interlaced with nondescript stock war footage, is powered by a plot development by which five American nurses are captured by the North Koreans. At this point the film finally sets a goal for itself—the freeing of the femmes—and the picture, under R. G. Springsteen's direction, begins to roll. Elwood Ullman screenplayed from a story he co-authored with producer Lester A. Sansom.

Scott Brady and Miss Edwards perform admirably, he as a marine lieutenant and she as one of the nurses. Brady has all the guts and strength his position demands and he appears genuine in his love for Miss Edwards who, in turn, ably depicts the conflict that weighs her love for the lieutenant and her engagement to Richard Crane, a navy surgeon.

Wayne Heffley, Gordon Jones, Ken Miller, Arthur Walsh, Richard Harrison and Gary Kent are fine as gyrenes, with Robert Blake a standout. Nurses Peggy Moffitt and Jean Robbins also are good.

Technically, the film was well photographed by Carl Guthrie, well edited by William Austin, with art direction by David Milton and sound by Ralph Butler and Anthony Carras capably handled.

Ron.

Archimede Le Clochard
(Archimede The Tramp) (FRENCH)

Paris, May 5.

Cinedis release of Filmsonor-Intermondia poduction. Stars Jean Gabin; features Darry Cowl, Bernard Blier, Carette, Dora Doll, Jacqueline Maillan. Directed by Gilles Grangier. Screenplay, Albert Valentin, Michel Audiard; camera, Louis Page; editor, Jacqueline Thiedot. At Balzac, Paris. Running time, **85 MINS.**

Archimede ....Jean Gabin
Tramp ....Darry Cowl
Felix ....Carette
Pinchon ....Bernard Blier
Lucette ....Dora Doll

Film is primarily a vehicle for Jean Gabin who plays a crusty old tramp. It delves into a series of his adventures making this sketchy, in spite of some good bits. It is also talky, slanting this primarily as a local bet. Foreign chances will lean mainly on the Gabin name.

Gabin wrecks a bar to spend winter in jail but is foiled by court leniency. He gets involved with a dog stealing tramp and has some run-ins with the rich. He spouts tramp philosophy but all this is too slim and held together only by Gabin's exuberant antics. It is technically good, with a nice supporting cast.

Mosk.

Douze Heures D'Horloge
(Twelve Hours By the Clock) (FRENCH—GERMAN)

Paris, May 5.

Fernand Rivers release of Estela-Transocean production. Stars Eva Bartok; features Hans Messemer, Lino Ventura, Laurent Terzieff, Ginette Pigeon. Gil Vidal, Guy Trejan. Directed by Geza Radvenyi. Screenplay, Boileau, Narcejac; camera, Henri Alekan; editor, Rene Le Henaff. At Biarritz, Paris. Running time, **105 MINS.**

Barbara .... Eva Bartok
Serge .... Hans Messemer
Albert .... Lino Ventura
Kopetski .... Laurent Terzieff
Lucette .... Ginette Pigeon
Maurice .... Guy Vidal
Policeman .... Guy Trejan

Familiar tale follows three escaped cons on the run. Attempt to join the wife of one with some getaway dough is foiled by love and some tragic twists. But this does not shape with enough originality to be anything but a programmer both here and abroad.

Acting is acceptable. Lino Ventura has the best bit as one of the cons saddled with an affectionate cop. Technical credits are par.

Mosk.

Gunfight at Dodge City
(COLOR; C'SCOPE)

Competent Joel McCrea program western; strong for its class.

Hollywood, May 1.

United Artists release of Mirisch Co. production. Stars Joel McCrea; costars Julie Adams, John McIntire, Nancy Gates. Produced by Walter M. Mirisch. Directed by Joseph M. Newman. Screenplay, Daniel B. Ullman and Martin M. Goldsmith; story, Daniel B. Ullman; camera, (DeLuxe Color) Carl Guthrie; music, Hans J. Salter; editor, Richard V. Heermance. Previewed at Goldwyn Studio, April 30, '59. Running time, **80 MINS.**

Bat .... Joel McCrea
Pauline .... Julie Adams
Doc ....John McIntire
Lily .... Nancy Gates
Dave .... Richard Anderson
Rev. Howard ....Jim Westerfield
Ben .... Walter Coy
Regan ....Don Haggerty
Billy .... Wright King
Ed ....Harry Lauter
Forbes ....Myron Healy
Purley ....Mauritz Hugo
Bartender ....Henry Kulkey

This is a competent western of the kind the Mirisches used to turn out for Allied Artists and are now releasing via United Artists. There's no pretention about "The Gunfight At Dodge City," but there's nothing disappointing about it either. It's frankly a program picture and it fills the bill.

Joseph M. Newman directed the Daniel B. Ullman-Martin M. Goldsmith screenplay, from a story by Ullman. It has Joel McCrea as Bat Masterson, at a point in his career where he takes over as the law in Dodge City under pressure of the love of a pure woman.

Neither works out very well, law or love, but McCrea holds the bullies and the toughs to a stand-off. He doesn't get the girl he thought he wanted, but he gets a girl and the wrap-up is satisfactory to all concerned except the bad guys.

McCrea can do this sort of thing with his left hand (leaving his right hand free for the gun), and he even has a few chances in "The Gunfight at Dodge City" to give a reminder that when he wants to be, and has the chance, he is one of the most accomplished light comedians around. Julie Adams is competent as the initial love interest to take McCrea's eye, and Nancy Gates is interesting as the girl who eventually gets him. John McIntire contributes a good character portrait, and Wright King, Walter Coy, Richard Anderson and Jim Westerfield are notable in support.

Newman's direction is first-rate handling of an action script, a script, incidentally, that is refreshingly free of the cliches of the western. Carl Guthrie's CinemaScope photography is also interesting, and the DeLuxe color is generally good, although a print shown for review had a tendency to be blue-ish in cast.

Powe.

The Four Skulls of Jonathan Drake

Weak horror meller for the duals; thin b.o. prospects.

United Artists release of a Vogue Pictures presentation produced by Robert E. Kent. Co-stard Eduard Franz, Valerie French, Grant Richards, Henry Daniell. Directed by Edward L. Cahn. Written by Orville H. Hampton. Camera, Maury Gertsman; editor, Edward Mann; music, Paul Dunlap. Previewed N.Y., May 7, '59. Running time, **70 MINS.**

Jonathan Drake .... Eduard Franz
Alison .... Valerie French
Dr. Zurich .... Henry Daniell
Lieut. Rowan .... Grant Richards
Kenneth Drake .... Paul Cavanaugh
Dr. Bradford .... Howard Wendell
Zutai .... Paul Wexler

Rogers .... Lumsden Hare
Leo Coulter .... Frank Gerstle

Replete with shrunken heads and boiling cauldrons, "The Four Skulls of Jonathan Drake" is an inept horror meller turned out by Robert E. Kent for United Artists release. It's packaged with the same producer's "Invisible Invaders," a science fiction entry.

Cast of both films is light on marquee values. But despite this deficiency and a pair of far-fetched stories, the package has some exploitable angles that could pay off in the juvenile market and with horror fans.

Black arts as practiced by the Jivaro Indians of the upper Amazon are tapped somewhat ineffectually by scripter Orville H. Hampton. It seems that Eduard Franz, descendant of an Amazon trader, has fallen heir to a curse decreed by the savages 180 years ago.

Curse calls for decapitation and shrinking of the victim's head. Franz narrowly misses this gruesome fate with the help of daughter Valerie French and detective Grant Richards. Latter eventually solves the case by exposing archaeologist Henry Daniell as the true culprit.

Performances are mechanical under Edward L. Cahn's wooden direction. Franz, however, manages to appear suitably frightened and Daniell is relatively menacing as the heavy. Richards is unconvincing as the copper while Miss French is on hand mostly as a decoration. Fair support is contributed by Howard Wendell and Paul Wexler, among others.

Film's meagre production values are attested to by its use of a station wagon to transport victims in lieu of the customary ambulance. Maury Gertsman's camerawork is par for the course as is Edward Mann's editing and other technical credits. The Paul Dunlap score frequently is more hair-raising than the shrunken heads. *Gilb.*

Tutti Innamorati
(Everyone's in Love)
(ITALIAN-FRENCH)

Rome, May 5.

Cineriz release of a Royal Film (Rome)-France Cinema (Paris) coproduction. Features Marcello Mastroianni, Jacqueline Sassard, Marisa Merlini, Gabriele Ferzetti, Memmo Carotenuto, Nando Bruno, Leopoldo Trieste, Ruggero Marchi, Franco di Trocchio. Directed by Giuseppe Orlandini. Screenplay, Guerra, Rossi, Prosperi, Festa Campanile, Franciosa; from an idea by Franciosa and Campanile. At Metropolitan, Rome. Running time, **100 MINS.**

Giovanni .... Marcello Mastrianni
Allegra .... Jacqueline Sassard
Jolanda .... Marisa Merlini
Arturo .... Gabriele Ferzetti
Ferruccio .... Nando Bruno
Libero .... Franco di Trocchio

Lightweight item with tight script and excellent dialogue cutting it several notches above the local norm. Winning performances are another plus factor. Several foreign markets even outside the lingual orbit should be interested.

It's one of those interwined story lines, with a good main plot concerned with a young widower who falls for a teenage schoolgirl—and vice-versa. He's tempted, she's game, but his conscience bothers him into feeling he's robbing the cradle. His son is another obstacle.

It all works out in the end, after some warm and charming moments as he rediscovers young love's beauty. Marcello Mastroianni and Jacqueline Sassard are very good as the couple while Gabriele Ferzetti and Marisa Merlini animate one of the subplots. Able characterizations are also turned in by Nando Bruno, Leopoldo Trieste, Ruggero Marchi, and Franco di Trocchio, who steals many scenes as Mastroianni's infant.

Giuseppe Orlandini directed his first picture with a light hand. Technical credits are all good. *Hawk.*

Cannes Festival

Sen Noci Svatojanske
(A Midsummer Night's Dream)
(CZECHO—COLOR—C'SCOPE)

Czech State Film production and release. Written, directed and animated by Jiri Trnka, after the play by William Shakespeare. Camera (Eastmancolor), Jiri Vojta; editor, Hana Walachova. At Cannes Film Fest. Running time, **80 MINS.**

Enchanting is the word for this puppet film which tells the story of Shakespeare's "A Midsummer Night's Dream." But its poetic mingling of the real and supernatural does have some repetitiveness and remains mainly an arty house item. There is some commentary to explain the characters but then they go their way visually.

Jiri Trnka has filled the C'Scope screen with uncannily animated puppets who give it all a dreamlike quality. Blending of color, the right music and the sly underlining this an unusual pic. However, it will need specialized handling abroad. *Mosk.*

Touha
(Desire)
(CZECHOSLAVAKIAN)

Cannes, May 12.

Czech State Film production and release. Features Jan Jakes, Vaclav Babka Jana Brejchova, Jiri Vala, Vera Tichankova and Vaclav Lohnisky. Directed by Vojetch Jasny. Screenplay, Jasny, Valdimir Valenta; camera, Jaroslav Kucera; editor, Jan Chaloupek. At Cannes Film Fest. Running time, **95 MINS.**

Joska .... Jan Jakes
Father .... Vaclav Babka
Lenka .... Jana Brejchova
Jan .... Jiri Vala
Angele .... Vera Tichankova
Michal .... Vaclav Lohnisky
Mother .... Anna Meliskova

This tender film deals with the phases of childhood, adolescence, middle age and old age via four sketches. It has touches of poetry and imagination, but its delicate, tenuous structure, and its dealing only with a sentimental phase of things, makes this only for special or art situations abroad. Individual handling might make this pay off.

A child gets his first feel of life with the arrival of a baby sister. A young girl is shown having her first short-lived love affair one summer. A hard headed peasant girl, over 30, fights against co-op farms in another sketch. A mother dies as her son's wife awaits a baby in the final sketch.

Knowing imagery from director Vojtech Jasny is well supported by sensitive performances and fine technical work. But with its Czech origin and subject matter this looks like a chancey if deserving entry for foreign marts. *Mosk.*

Sudba Czelovieka
(Destiny of a Man)
(RUSSIAN)

Cannes, May 12.

Mosfilm production and release. Stars Serge Bondartchouk; features Zinaida Kirienko, Pavlik Boriskine, Youri Averine. Directed by Bondartchouk. Screenplay, Youri Loukine, F. Chakhmagonova from story by Mikhail Cholokhov; camera, Vladimir Monarkhov; editor, B. Bassner. At Cannes Film Fest. Running time, **95 MINS.**

Sokolov .... Serge Bondartchouk
Irinia .... Zinaida Kirienko
Vanioucha .... Pavlik Boriskine
Muller .... Youri Averine

Though shown outside the Cannes Fest in a private theatre, this got plenty of press coverage. It was the official Soviet entry that the fest authorities asked the Russians to replace because of its lucid portrayal of Nazi atrocities during the last war. It is a well made, moving film with fairly good chances abroad.

It details how a Russian prisoner of war has only the thought of getting back alive to his family. After many adventures and privations he does find them but all are dead. He adopts a homeless boy to give him the necessary love and reason to go on living.

Serge Bondartchouk has served himself well as director except for some slow progression and overdone camera bravura. But it has an eyecatching style and depicts Nazi brutality. Pic scored in a recent Russo Film Week in France. *Mosk.*

Hiroshima Mon Amour
(Hiroshima My Love)
(FRENCH-JAPANESE)

Cannes, May 12.

Pathe release of Argos-Daiei production. With Emmanuele Riva, Eiji Okada, Stella Dassas, Pierre Barbaud, Bernard Fresson. Directed by Alain Resnais. Screenplay, Marguerite Duras; camera, Sacha Vierny, Takahashi Michio; editor, Henri Colpi. At Cannes Film Fest. Running time, **95 MINS.**

French Woman .... Emmanuele Rivas
Japanese Man .... Eiji Okada
Mother .... Stella Dassas
German Soldier .... Bernard Fresson

A "first" for its director, film can be classed as a noble try to make a statement on human love and the Atom Bomb (hardly a lovable thing) but it's too literary in conception and too cerebral in treatment; makes it chancy and specialized art item.

A woman and a man, in a lover's embrace, talk of Hiroshima. Horrors of the Bomb are evoked. Lovers are a French woman, in Japan working on a film calling for world peace, and a Japanese architect. Then follows their realization of the impossibility of their love since both are married.

Film then welds in her souvenirs of a first love during the war in France with a German soldier, his death, her breakdown and her reacceptance of life. The film plods.

Director Alain Resnais has directed with sombre feeling and tact. It makes a plea for love and world humanity but does it without finally making the love a real, palpable thing, and it remains a symbolical trauma tied up with Hiroshima and the occupation. *Mosk.*

Edes Anna
(Sweet Anna)
(HUNGARIAN)

Hunnia Film production and release. Stars Mari Torocsik; features Karoly Kovacs, Maria Mezey, Zsigmond Fulop. Directed by Zoltan Fabir. Screenplay, Peter Bacsi, Fabir from novel by Deszo Kosztolany; camera, Szecsenyi Ferenc; editor, Maria Szecsenyi. At Cannes Film Fest. Running time, **85 MINS.**

Anna .... Mari Torocsik
Monsieur .... Karoly Kovacs
Madame .... Maria Mezey
Nephew .... Zsigmond Fulop

A little, timid maid is driven to kill her employers in the Hungary of 1919 when maids were treated like slaves. Film is somewhat too didactic in making its villains completely black. But it is well told and expertly directed.

Mari Torocsik imbues the maid with a pulsating life and tenderness, under her drabness, to give her role dimension. Her seducer, the nephew of her employers, and her bosses all remain somewhat one-sided. The aborted Communist revolt of the time remains in the story's background.

Direction by Zoltan Fabir is knowing but too academic to miss the feel of life the pic needs. Technical credits are excellent. This emerges a worthy offbeater with chancey possibilities abroad. *Mosk.*

Die Halbzarte
(Eva)
(AUSTRIAN—COLOR)

Cosmopol Film production and release. Stars Romy Schneider; features, Carlos Thompson, Magda Schneider, Gertrud Jesserer, Alfred Costas. Directed by Rolf Thiele. Screenplay, Hans Jacoby, Fritz Rotter; camera, (Agfacolor), Klaus Von Rautenfeld; editor, Henny Bausch. At Cannes Film Fest. Running time, **92 MINS.**

Nicole .... Romy Schneider
Irving .... Carlos Thompson
Dassou .... Magda Schneider
Brigitie .... Gertrud Jesserer
Thomas .... Alfred Costas

Film tries to satirize the young girls who write sexy novels, but turns out heavyhanded and stilted. This is primarily a local bet with foreign chances restricted to foreign language markets.

A zany family pools its reserves to write a naughty play about an immoral youth. An American buyer demands the writer, who is the innocent if curious teenager of the house. A series of complications keep her pure till she marries her American. Directing is obvious, acting ordinary and any chances will depend on the exploitation of a timely, if badly done, theme. *Mosk.*

Sterne
(Stars)
(BULGARIAN-EAST GERMAN)

DEFA production and release. Features Sasha Kroucharska, Jurgen Frothripp, Erich Klein, Gueorgui Naoumov, Naytcho Petrov. Directed by Konrad Wolf. Screenplay, Angel Wagenstein, camera, Werner Bergmann; editor, Christa Wernicke. At Cannes Film Fest. Running time, **94 MINS**

Ruth .... Sasha Kroucharska
Walter .... Jurgen Frohripp
Kurt .... Erich Klein
Bay Petko .... Gueorgui Naoumov

A tale of a so-called "good German" during the last world war is spared the "rehabilitation" tag by achieving a universality in denouncing man's inhumanity to man. This is a story about a German soldier who falls in love with a Jewish girl which his outfit is deporting to a concentration camp and certain death.

This may be a somewhat familiar theme by now, and since Eastern pic, with its downbeat theme, it is chancey for Yank marts. But it is well made and has a sincerity and depth which could slant it for arty theatre or special situations.

Director Konrad Wolf has given this vehicle a good mounting but has let it lag somewhat via too much philosophical talk before ending it on a powerful note. Technical credits are excellent. *Mosk.*

Matomeno Heliovasilema
(Bloody Twilight)
(GREEK)

Lambrinos production and release. With Efi Oikonomou, Spyros Fokas, Kakia Analyti. Written and directed by Andreas

Lambrinos. Camera, Kostas Philippou; editor, Kostas Kapmissis. At Cannes Film Fest. Running time, **91 MINS.**

A Swedish girl goes to Greece looking for a reincarnation of the God Pan and finds it in a shepherd. However, it leads to tragedy when she is killed by her suitor and he in turn by the father of his jilted fiancee.

Execution of plot is amateurish. This emerges mainly an exploitation item on its heavy-breathing love scenes and nudity. But direction fails to give it the depth it needs for a tragic affair. Acting is only passable and technical credits below par. *Mosk.*

Zafra
(Sugar Harvest)
(ARGENTINIAN-ALEXSCOPE-COLOR)

Sono Film production and release. Features Graciela Borges, Alfredo Alcon, Enrique Fava, Atahualpa Yupanqui, Luis Castro. Directed by Lucas Demare. Screenplay, Sixto Pondal Rios; camera (Agfacolor), Antonio Morayo; editor, Jorge Garate. At Cannes Film Fest. Running time, **85 MINS.**

Damaina	Graciela Borges
Teodoro	Alfredo Alcon
Bruno	Enrique Fava
Galvan	Atahualpa Yupanqui
Fabian	Luis Castro

Pic is a familiar one about the revolt of some exploited Indians on a sugar cane plantation. But it is soberly executed even if having some color in the native dances and songs.

Thus shapes mainly for lingo spots in the U.S. Its adventuresome qualities and C'Scope-type screen and tinting could also slant this for dualers abroad. It is well acted and conventionally directed. *Mosk.*

Tang Fu Yu Sheng Nu
(The Sinner)
(CHINESE)

Hsing-Chou production and release. With Mu Hung, Li Ying. Directed by Tien Shen. Screenplay, Chung Lei, Wang Yun-Mei; Camera, Hung Ching-Yun; editor, Chou Lan-Ping. At Cannes Film Fest. Running time, **102 MINS.**

Clair De Lune	Mu Hung
Ling Chu	Li Ying

The first Chinese pic to enter an international film fest from Formosa, this shapes a fairly well-made yarn about a heroic woman during the Sino-Japanese war of 1895. She is branded a traitor by error when a wily brother-in-law blames her to save his own skin. But she is exonerated 50 years later.

This is somewhat slow and looks stilted for any chances in the U.S. except for in foreign language spots. However, it shows a budding film industry with a comprehension of technique, thesping and production filmically. *Mosk.*

Historie D'Un Poisson Rouge
(Story of a Goldfish)
(FRENCH-COLOR)

Requin release of J. Y. Cousteau production. Directed, photographed (Eastmancolor) and edited by Edmond Sechan. Screenplay, Roger Mauge; music, Henri Crolla, Andre Hodier. At Cannes Film Fest. Running time, **20 MINS.**

Color short is in the same vein as "The Red Balloon." It concerns a little boy, who owns a canary and who wins a goldfish. This is well photographed and has a beguiling quality though lacking the whimsy "Balloon." This could run as a fine short for art houses or general spots.

Cavortings of the animals to the jazz music of Henri Crolla and Andre Hodier are the highlights. Edmond Sechan's direction is knowing. *Mosk.*

Vlak Bez Vosnog Reda
(Train Without a Timetable)
(YUGOSLAVIAN-TOTALVISION)

Jadran production and release. With Stole Arandjelovic, Olivera Markovic, Ivica Pajer, Milan Milosevic. Directed by Veljko Bulajic. Screenplay, Slavko Kolar, Stepjan Ferovic, Ivo Braut, Ello Petri; camera, Krexo Grcevic; editor, Blazenka Jenci. At Cannes Film Fest. Running time, **120 MINS.**

Lovre	Stole Arandjelovic
Ika	Olivera Markovic
Nikolica	Ivica Pajer
Peso	Milan Milosevic

Film is somewhat reminiscent of "Grapes of Wrath," since it has the same human values. It deals with a group of peasants uprooted from their old sterile lands and their trip to new land given them by the state. It is long and somewhat conventional but is given sound thesping, story values and colorful aspects on the voyage.

As a Yugoslavian film, it still looks limited for foreign chances except for language spots. Firmness in progression might make it possible in some special spots of the U.S.

Various love stories unfold during the trip, with different characters reacting to the new life differently. Director Veljko Bulajic always has everything under control to keep this overlong pic moving. It has fine technical values. *Mosk.*

Lajwanti
(INDIAN)

Delux Films production and release. Stars Nargis; features Balraj Sahni, Baby Naaz, Prabhu Dayal, Radhakishen. Directed by Narenda Suri. Screenplay, Sachin Bhan; camera, M. Malhotra; editor, Pratap Dave. At Cannes Film Fest. Running time, **120 MINS.**

Kavita	Nargis
Nirmal	Balraj Sahni
Renu	Baby Naaz
Sunil	Prabhu Dayal
Uncle	Radhakishen

This is the type of Indian film mainly for home consumption and only for a few lingo spots abroad. It is an old fashioned meller about a husband who throws out his wife when he thinks she is cheating with an artist friend. Actually, she was only having a portrait made for him.

Ten years later, he tries to get her back, but there is the problem of winning over the daughter, now grown up. Songs and dances are dumped into this haphazardly. All this treacle and modernism is well done technically. But it is not of fest calibre or interest. *Mosk.*

Zamach
(The Attempt)
(POLISH)

Polski Film production and release. With Bozena Kurowska, Graznya Staniszewska, Zbigniew Cynkutis, Tadeusz Womnicki. Directed by Jerzy Passendorfer. Screenplay, Jerzy Stawinski; camera, Jerzy Lipman; editor, Czeslaw Raniszewski. At Cannes Film Fest. Running time, **85 MINS.**

Slick little film details an attack by a young resistance group on Nazi headquarters during the occupation in Poland. It emerges a well-paced actioner but sans any undue eclat or depth. Pic may do as possible actioner spotting abroad.

This moves along well and builds up suspense before and during the attack as well as in the ensuing escape. Direction is clean and functional. The actors all contribute to make it all creditable. Technical credits are fine. *Mosk.*

Rhapsodia Portuguesa
(Portugese Rhapsody)
(DOCUMENTARY-COLOR-TOTALVISION)

Cannes, May 5.

Sonora Film release and production. Directed by Jsao Mendes. Written by Antonio Ferro, Fernanda De Costro; camera (Eastmancolor), Mario Moreira; editor, Louis Barao. At Cannes Film Fest. Running time, **80 MINS.**

This amounts to a travelog on little-known Portugal. However, a lack of clear progression suggests drastic need of trimming. Edited down it could be a good program filler for possible foreign situations, for it has some well done moments on fishermen and their lot, bullfights, folk dances and holiday manifestations.

Color is okay and Totalvision gives it a sweep in spots. *Mosk.*

A Hole in the Head
(COLOR)

Good comedy-drama with Frank Sinatra, Edward G. Robinson, et al., skillfully assembled by producer-director Frank Capra. Undoubtedly a firm boxoffice product.

United Artists release of Frank Capra (Sincap Productions) production. Stars Frank Sinatra, Edward G. Robinson, Eleanor Parker, Carolyn Jones, Thelma Ritter, Keenan Wynn; features Joi Lansing, Connie Sawyer, Edie Hodges. Directed by Capra. Play and screenplay, Arnold Schulman; camera (Eastmancolor), William H. Daniels; editor, William Hornbeck; music, Nelson Riddle. Caught at UA homeoffice, N.Y., May 14, '59. Running time, **120 MINS.**

Tony Manetta	Frank Sinatra
Mario Manetta	Edward G. Robinson
Mrs. Rogers	Eleanor Parker
Shirl	Carolyn Jones
Sophie Manetta	Thelma Ritter
Jerry Marks	Keenan Wynn
Ally Manetta	Eddie Hodges
Dorine	Joi Lansing
Mendy	George DeWitt
Julius Manetta	Jimmy Komack
Fred	Dub Taylor
Miss Wexler	Connie Sawyer
Mr. Diamond	Benny Rubin
Sally	Ruby Dandridge
Hood No. 1	B. S. Pully
Alice	Joyce Nizzari
Master of Ceremonies	Pupi Campo

First an enthusiastically-received television show, then a modest Broadway legiter—and now a film entry that's bound to sell tickets. The reference is to Arnold Schulman's human comedy, "A Hole in the Head," which has been produced and directed by Frank Capra with obvious alertness to the comedy and dramatic values in Schulman's own screenplay and the ingratiating nature of most of the characters.

The Schulman story that focuses on an idle dreamer, whose devotion to the impractical, places his minor Miami Beach Hotel in jeopardy, has a flaw here and there, to be sure. Who could have faith in such an irresponsible citizen? But the part is given such a sincere portrayal, and the key figure in turn is surrounded by such believable characters, that credulity is subjected to only the slightest of strains.

The assortment of people are a colorful lot, and histrionically very well behaved under Capra's direction. Each is in his and her proper place—they all seem to rightfully belong in the show. They make for a winning, amusing combination in the story whose basics might not otherwise have been too easily accepted.

Net result is that Sincap Productions, taken from the Sinatra and Capra names, and distributor-financier United Artists have a finished commodity of wide appeal. The material for the marquee plus the know-about anent the Schulman property further bolster the money-making potential.

The story—a quick reprise being in order—has Sinatra, a widower with a young son—looking to his brother, Edward G. Robinson, rich New York merchant, for a financial assist. Robinson and his wife, Thelma Ritter, trek to the Florida resort, figure on taking custody of the boy, Eddie Hodges, and then come upon the scheme of mating Sinatra with a nice widow, fetchingly played by Eleanor Parker, as a means of endowing him with some sense of responsibility.

Sinatra, to repeat, works with conviction. Robinson, bewildered by the behavior of his brother and not savvy to the ways of the unconventional Miami, turns in a cleverly funny job in a subdued way.

Hodges, the carrot-topped boy and a newcomer, is an appealing

performer, drawing top sympathy as he shows unalterable devotion to his father. Miss Ritter is the understandable aunt all the way; Carolyn Jones is Sinatra's somewhat goofy girlfriend and provides laughs unerringly; Keenan Wynn looks authentic as a flashy gambler and other spots are well filled by Joi Lansing, Connie Sawyer, B. S. Pully, etc.

Capra has given the proceedings sufficient pace to avoid criticism about that 120-minute running time. Nelson Riddle's music is good background and William H. Daniels on camera and William Hormbeck as editor do highly professional work. The Miami atmosphere is caught with maximum effectiveness in Eastman color.
Gene.

Middle of the Night

Often moving filmization of the stage play, but overall diffuse and disappointing. Star names for draw.

Hollywood, May 15.

Columbia release of Sudan production. Stars Kim Novak, Fredric March. Produced in N.Y. by George Justin. Directed by Delbert Mann. Screenplay, Paddy Chayefsky; based on his own play; camera, Joseph Brun; music, George Bassman; editor, Carl Lerner. Previewed at the Screen Directors Guild Theatre, May 13, '59. Running time, **117 MINS.**

Betty Preisser	Kim Novak
Jerry Kingsley	Fredric March
Mrs. Preisser	Glenda Farrell
Lockman	Albert Dekker
Jack	Martin Balsam
Marilyn	Lee Grant
George	Lee Philips
Evelyn	Edith Meiser
Lillian	Joan Copeland
Widow	Betty Walker
Sherman	Lou Gilbert
Gould	Rudy Bond
Neighbor	Effie Afton
Alice	Jan Norris
Paul	David Ford
Elizabeth	Audrey Peters
Mrs. Lockman	Dora Weissman
Lockman's Son	Lee Richardson
Caroline	Anna Berger
Ellman	Alfred Leberfeld

Concessions to what is presumed to be popular taste, in casting and in story, have produced a halting, unsatisfactory film of Paddy Chayefsky's Broadway legit hit, "The Middle of the Night." Delbert Mann's direction of the Columbia release is often sensitive and understanding and some of the performances, notably Fredric March's, are fine. Despite these merits, film falters and fails of cumulative impact.

Chayefsky has changed his screenplay from previous versions to delete or at least make uncertain the fact that some of his characters are Jewish, some not. This was a story point in the play and a logical one. The strategy of its omission leaves a gaping hole of ambiguity.

Fredric March plays the widowed clothing manufacturer who falls in love with an employee, a divorcee 30 years his junior, Kim Novak. A lonely man who feels himself occupied in little but edging towards the grave, the affair rejuvenates and revitalizes him until the disparity in ages begins to attract convention's adverse notice. Censorship of their conduct, direct or implied, and the natural pull of opposite ages, separate them for a time.

It seems to be Chayefsky's contention that the only genuine love is that between a man and woman. All other forms are shown to be grasping, narrow and degrading. Miss Novak's mother, Glenda Farrell, resents that she has given her life to her children and now they intend to dispose of theirs as they please. March's spinster sister, Edith Meiser, sees herself crowded out by Miss Novak after having sacrificed her life to her family. Joan Copeland, March's daughter, despite a facade of pseudo-intellectualizing of modern psychology, does not want to share her father even though she sees it means his happiness to have Miss Novak. There are other examples of the blindness and self-centeredness of self-asserted "love" when threatened by displacement. By omitting any mitigating characteristics, except for a couple of men, Chayefsky here makes virtually his whole cast basically hateful.

The typically naturalistic Chayefsky dialog and situations at first arrest, like conversations unintentionally eavesdropped. But they eventually pall by their seeming unselectivity, their deliberate repetition, their only inadvertent revelation. Where revelation should be implicit in every line, in "Middle of the Night" it often seems haphazard, secondary to the author's devotion to accurate reproduction, journalistically, of genre speech.

March is appealing and sometimes broadly human, enhancing his lines with silences, reactions and movements, deftly emphasized by Mann's direction. Miss Novak's performance indicates that Mann has been somewhat successful in getting this enigmatic star to indicate some variety of feeling. But there is a static, shallow approach in the scripting that prevents Miss Novak from obtaining conviction except for her staunch admirers. Others may find Miss Novak hopelessly lost and inadequate in attempting to give even surface value to her role.

Joan Copeland is brilliant as the daughter, and Albert Dekker forlornly memorable as March's partner. Betty Walker (from the New York production) scores resoundingly in her one scene. Glenda Farrell, Martin Balsam, Lee Grant, Lee Philips and Edith Meiser are uniformly excellent.

Produced in Manhattan by George Justin, "The Middle of the Night" is distinguished by Joseph Brun's photography. George Bassman's score is also significant.
Powe.

King of the Wild Stallions
(COLOR; C'SCOPE)

Non-Freudian, well-done western.

Hollywood, May 15.

Allied Artists release of Ben Schwalb production. Stars George Montgomery, Diane Brewster, Edgar Buchanan. Directed by R. G. Springsteen. Screenplay, Ford Beebe; camera, Carl Guthrie; music, Marlin Skiles; editor, George White. Reviewed at the studio, May 11, '59. Running time, **76 MINS.**

Randy	George Montgomery
Martha	Diane Brewster
Idaho	Edgar Buchanan
Matt	Emile Meyer
Bucky	Jerry Hartleben
Orcutt	Byron Foulger
Doc	Denver Pyle
Woody	Dan Sheridan
Sheriff	Rory Mallinson

"King of the Wild Stallions" is one of a vanishing breed. It is an almost pure western of the once-standard type, no Freudian angles, no psychopaths to probe. Considering the simplicity of its plot, it is soundly constructed for maximum interest and will be a good addition to double-billing. Ben Schwalb's production for Allied Artists was directed by R. G. Springsteen.

Diane Brewster is a pretty widow woman in Ford Beebe's screenplay. Her problem is to hang on to her ranch lands in the face of shenanigans on the part of the local cattle baron, Emile Meyer, who wants to annex them. She needs $500 and when Meyer offers that sum for the capture of a wild stallion, the solution seems obvious. There is some complication because Miss Brewster's son, young Jerry Hartleben, wants to keep the horse once he catches him. George Montgomery, Miss Brewster's foreman and her suitor, solves all these problems for a satisfactory conclusion.

There is nice outdoor CinemaScope photography by Carl Guthrie in DeLuxe color, including some attractive shots of the wild herds. Some of the shots apparently were edited in, skillfully so, by George White.

Montgomery and Miss Brewster make a nice romantic team, and character man Edgar Buchanan contributes an interesting seriocomic portrait. Young Hartleben handles his assignment well, and others in the cast who stand out include Emile Meyer, Byron Foulger, Denver Pyle and Dan Sheridan.

Springsteen's direction is capable and Marlin Skiles' music is another asset.
Powe.

Speed Crazy

Substandard teen meller likely to produce hoots in wrong places.

Hollywood, May 15.

Allied Artists release of Viscount Production. Produced by Richard Bernstein. Stars Brett Halsey, Yvonne Lime, Charles Willcox; features Slick Slavin, Jacqueline Ravell, Baynes Barron, Regina Gleason, Keith Byron, Charlotte Fletcher, Jackie Joseph, Vic Marlo. Directed by William Hole Jr. Screenplay, Bernstein, George Waters; camera, Ernest Haller; music, Dick LaSalle; editor, Irving Berlin. Previewed at studio, May 13, '59. Running time, **75 MINS.**

Nick	Brett Halsey
Peggy	Yvonne Lime
Hap	Charles Willcox
Smiley	Slick Slavin
Gina	Jacqueline Ravell
Ace	Baynes Barron
Linda	Regina Gleason
Jim Brand	Keith Byron
Dee	Charlotte Fletcher
Laura	Jackie Joseph
Charlie Dale	Vic Marlo
Tommy	Robert Swan
Tolliver	Mark Sheeler
Leather Jacket No. 1	Troy Patterson
Ella	Lucita
Leather Jacket No. 2	Eddie Durkin

"Speed Crazy" is not up to a dualer's routine standard. It's of an hour and a quarter for undiscriminating teenage situations.

Richard Bernstein, who produced and co-scripted the film, provides some sports car road-race scenes, at least one moderately sexy love scene and a fight or two as grist but fate of film may be as butt of jokes, as is frequently teenagers wont when writing and acting are not believable.

The story concerns a drifter who murders an old man while robbing him. He flees in his souped-up MGA and becomes a mechanic in a small town where he makes himself unpopular with the young sports car set by winning races, bragging, fighting and making crude passes at other men's women. In the end, he dies in a crash while running away from the cops.

Brett Halsey limns the killer and Yvonne Lime and Charles Willcox portray a nice, bland couple who represent the good element in sports car racing. Slick Slavin sings some tunes and plays an unfunny comic relief.

Colorless dialog—and too much of it—by Bernstein and George Waters leaves little for the actors or director William Hole Jr. to work with, but they frequently botch what little there is. The plot wanders aimlessly toward a racing meet finish which might have salvaged the film, but the thrills never develop. Typical of the production is the fact that the heavy dies in a dated Studebaker rather than the logical, but more expensive, MGA.

Except for some sharp night photography by Ernest Haller at the film's onset, the technical aspects are merely routine and Dick LaSalle's scoring is notably uninspired.
Glen.

Der Tiger Von Eschnapur
(The Tiger of Eschnapur)
(GERMAN-COLOR)

Berlin, May 12.

Gloria release of CCC production. Stars Debra Paget, Paul Hubschmid, Claus Holm, Sabine Bethmann, Walther Reyer, Rene Deltgen. Directed by Fritz Lang. Screenplay, Warner Joerg Lueddecke, after a story by Thea von Harbou; camera (Eastmancolor), Richard Angst; music, Michel Michelet. At Zoo Palast, Berlin. Running time, **100 MINS.**

Seetha	Debra Paget
Harald Berger	Paul Hubschmid
Dr. Walter Rhode	Claus Holm
Irene Rhode	Sabine Bethmann
Chandra	Walther Reyer
Bharani	Luciana Paluzzi
Ramigani	Rene Deltgen
Padhu	Jochen Brockmann

The names of Fritz Lang and Debra Paget plus the huge budget made this pic an attention-getter here even long before its completion. It's the third version of a now nearly classical German film yarn written by Fritz Lang and the late Thea von Harbou (who later became Mrs. Lang) almost four decades ago.

While the first version made history and a second venture could at least be classified as an impressive adventure film, this third production comes to the screen as quite a disappointment. Apart from some eye-filling scenery, there's little of which this film can be proud.

A corny script, mediocre acting performances and old-fashioned direction make "Tiger" one of the most unfortunate German postwar productions. As per its suspense, it falls short of even third-rate Hollywood adventure vehicles. What's even worse, pic comes near to insulting India. It's the most gruesome closeup of the middle ages that's been presented here.

Much local attention was focused on Debra Paget, as one of the few Hollywoodites used in native pix. Aside from unconvincing acting, she delivers dance sequences that don't belong in an Indian temple. Paul Hubschmid (in Hollywood once Paul Christian) enacts a German architect assigned to build European-styled buildings here. Both fall in love and flee. *Hans.*

Sube Y Baja
UP AND DOWN
(MEXICAN-COLOR)

Mexio City, May 12.

Columbia release of a Posa Films, S.A. (Cantinflas) production. Stars Mario Moreno (Cantinflas); features Teresa Velazquez, Joaquin Garcia, Domingo Soler and Carlos Agosti. Directed by Miguel M. Delgado. Screenplay by Delgado from an original story by Jaime Salvador; camera (Eastmancolor), Alex Phillips; music, Raul Lavista. At the Roble Theatre, Mexico City. Running time, **105 MINS.**

This is the annual film comedy of Cantinflas. And, as in recent years, it is just so-so film fare. It is typical of the stereotyped pattern of his former productions, with comic relying on a dual-role

situation. Pic does not add stature to Cantinflas, but a dubious entry in world market except in lingo houses.

Curvaceous beauties falling for the comic as he plays the role of both rich man and poor one are part of the plot. In a football game he is the rah-rah hero who makes the touchdown. In a speedboat race, he is the victor. And always the gals are falling all over our individualistic hero as he ambles through a string of slapstick incidents.

It is the same theme and atmosphere of former films, with accent on slapstick, fast double talk mixed-up patter and double takes that endear Cantinflas as the screen symbol of the average man in the street with empty pockets.

With his eyes on the international scene, ever since his appearance in "Around World in 80 Days," Cantinflas has been turning out film potboilers for the Spanish language market. Cantinflas defends the unilateral pattern of his recent films, of which this is the latest, as "what the public wants." He is right to the extent that this picture preemed here three houses.

Miguel M. Delgado's direction is routine. The gags produce the required number of laughs for they are psychologically geared to a Mexican audience's reactions. Tere Velazquez is a beauteous adornment as the comic now insists on having voluptuous teenagers for his leading ladies. Technical work is competent. *Emil.*

Cannes Festival

Eroica
(POLISH)

Polski State Film release of Kadr production. With Tadeusz Womnicki, K. Rudzki, B. Polomska, E. Dziewonski, L. Niemczyk. Directed by Andrej Munk. Screenplay, Jerzy Stawinski; camera, Z. Wocjik; editor, A. Wocjik. At Cannes Film Fest. Running time, 90 MINS.

This is a broadside at futile heroism, a supposedly inborn Polish trait, via two sketches covering parts of the last war. It contains an excellent balance between humor and drama, and emerges a possible specialized offshore entry. But being Polish, it still remains limited for the U.S. market and very difficult for general runs.

In the first part a shrewd son, trying to preserve his skin, ultimately becomes a hero and finds a reason for fighting. It has witty progression and inventiveness. The second portion is more sombre in detailing a hopeless attempt at escape from a prison camp by a man who can no longer stand the confinement and idiocy of the professional soldiers trying to keep up military pretenses in prison.

Direction is adroit and a homogeneous acting troupe, with an intelligent script, make this an offbeat war film with arty possibilities. *Mosk.*

Otchi Dom
(Native House)
(RUSSIAN)

Mosfilm production and release. With V. Kouzneizova, L. Martchenko, N. Novlianski, V. Zoubkov. Directed by L. Koulidjanov. Screenplay, B. Metalnikov; camera, P. Kataiev; editor, L. Joutchkova. At Cannes Film Fest. Running time, 95 MINS.

Bucolic drama shapes mainly a local Russo bet. It has a feeling for characterization and is well directed but slow in progression with a theme that's not of much interest in the Western World.

An 18-year-old adopted girl finds out that her real mother is still alive. Pic details her readjustment and acceptance of kolkhouse life over her old city ways. Technical credits are fine and acting is fairly good. *Mosk.*

Araya
(VENEZUELAN— DOCUMENTARY)

Caroni Films production and release. Directed and conceived by Margot Benacerral. Commentary, Pierre Seghers (spoken by Laurent Terzieff); camera, Giuseppi Nisoli; editor, Pierre Jalluad. At Cannes Film Fest. Running time, 80 MINS.

Well conceived documentary shows the everyday lives of the salt workers and fishermen in an isolated, arid section of Venezuela. It is supposed to depict for the populace how progress is contemplated for them and is successful in this aim.

For commercial chances it is much more problematical. But it is well made and poetically carried out and could be a good lingo entry abroad with chances for arties if intelligently sheared.

It is a good possibility for specialized video shows. Director Margot Benacerrai shows a good feel for imagery, pacing and movement. *Mosk.*

Nazarin
(MEXICAN)

Barbachano Ponce production and release. Stars Francisco Rabal; features Marga Lopez, Rita Macedo, Ignacio Tarso, Jesus Fernandez. Directed by Luis Bunuel. Screenplay, Julio Alepjandro. Bunuel from novel by Benito Parez Galdos; camera, Gabriel Figueroa; editor, Edward Fitzgerald. At Cannes Film Fest. Running time, 95 MINS.
Nazarin .... Francisco Rabal
Beatriz .... Marga Lopez
Andara .... Rita Macedo
Sacrilegio .... Ignacio Tarso
Ujo .... Jesus Fernandez

A priest unfrocks himself and takes to the road to live on alms when he is implicated by the law for harboring a prostitute after she had killed another one. However, he is followed in his pilgrimage by the escaped prostitute and a woman who has been left by a lover. Film details their wanderings and attempts to help humanity and their constant rebuffs until the priest realizes one must love humanity first before one can be a human being or a priest.

Careful handling could make this pay off in the U.S. Film abounds in a profound feeling for man. There are grotesque scenes. One involves a dwarf who falls in love with the prostie. There are also scenes of a plague.

This is a difficult but rewarding pic. Thus it is mainly for special arty showing abroad or for lingo spots. Acting is excellent as are technical aspects. Director Luis Bunuel's mastery of his theme and subject make this an unusual offbeater. *Mosk.*

Male Dramaty
(Small Dramas)
(POLISH) (COLOR)

Polski Film production and release. Features Aleksander Kornel, Lech Rzegocki, Henryk Fogiel, Andrej Paprotny, Tadeusz Wisniewski. Written and directed by Janusz Nasfeter; camera (Agfacolor), Kazimierz Konrad, Karel Chodura; editor,

W. Tomaski. At Cannes Film Fest. Running time, 65 MINS.
Millionaire .... Aleksander Kornel
Noiraud .... Lech Rzegocki
Trapu .... Hanryk Fogiel
Maigriot .... Andrej Paprotny
Fcureuil .... Tadeuz Wisniewski

Well played and made moppet pic is strictly for the juveniles. It tells two tales involving little morals among a group of kids. It has insight into child behavior and is engagingly made, but its sentimental aspects peg this primarily for kiddie shows abroad. Ditto its length, episodes could be separated for good supporting short fare or video use.

Color, technical values and good child acting are well welded by the knowing direction of Janusz Nasfeter. *Mosk.*

Shirasagui
(The White Heron)
(JAPANESE) (COLOR)
(C'SCOPE)

Daiei production and release. Features Fujiko Yamamoto, Keizo Kawasaki, Shuji Sano, Hitomi Nozoe, Hideo Takamatsu. Directed by Teinosuka Kinugasa. Screenplay, Kinugasa from novel by Kyoka Izumi; camera (Agfacolor). Kimio Watanabe; editor, Ichiro Saito. At Cannes Film Fest. Running time, 102 MINS.
Oshino .... Fujiko Yamamoto
Junichi .... Keizo Kawasaki
Kumajiro .... Shuji Sano
Nanae .... Hitomi Nozoe
Yokichi .... Hideo Takamatsu

Exquisite tinter tells the tale of a girl who is forced to become a Geisha when her family is ruin in turn-of-the-century Japan. Her attempt to stay faithful to a young artist leads to her suicide. However, its slowness in unfoldment and its general story make this primarily for local consumption, with only certain special arty theatre at best in overseas market.

C'Scope and color are brilliantly utilized as are thesps. Direction gives this plenty of eye appeal which turns out a moving interpretation of the Japanese past when women where chattel. Technical values are tops. Direction is restrained and acting excellent. *Mosk.*

India
(FRENCH—DOCUMENTARY— COLOR)

Cannes, May 19.
UGC release of Amiene production. Written and directed by Roberto Rossellini. Camera (Geva-color), Aldo Tonti; editor, Cesare Cavagna. At Cannes Film Fest. Running time, 95 MINS.

Roberto Rossellini also brought back a full length documentary from his Indian trek. It emerges a fairly interesting look at this changing country as of today, with its progress but with its ties still deep in ritual and the past.

Rossellini has chosen to make the land the central aspect of the country. He depicts the cities as only melting pots. A group of sketches show the building of a dam, an affair between an elephant boy and an actress and two tales involving a tiger and a monkey.

Though uneven and haphazard at times, this is constantly interesting and might be an okay specialized entry abroad with good video and lecture use in view. Rossellini has shown a love and fondness for this country, and it seeps into his film. Lensing is uneven but tops in its good sections with color and asset. This also has the Rossellini name as a hypo asset. *Mosk.*

Orfeu Negro
(Negro Orpheus)
(FRENCH-COLOR)

Lux release of Sacha Gordine production. Stars Marpessa Dawn, Breno Mello; features Lourdes De Oliveira, Lea Garcia, Adhemar Silva. Directed by Marcel Camus. Screenplay, Jacques Viot, Camus based on play by Vinicius De Moraes; camera (Eastmancolor), Jean Bourgoin; editor, Andree Feix. At Cannes Film Fest. Running time, 100 MINS.
Orpheus .... Breno Mello
Eurydice .... Marpessa Dawn
Mira .... Lourdes De Oliveira
Serafina .... Lea Garcia
Death .... Adhemar Da Silva

With a background of the pulsating, colorful Rio carnival in Brazil, a reenactment of the Orpheus legend is executed in this vehicle. This time they are Negroes and there is a clever transposition of the tragedy to modern times. If it gets too demanding in following the legend, this still gives warmth and depth to the characters. It is beautifully dressed up in color to emerge a good possibility for some arty theatres abroad.

Eurydice (Marpessa Dawn) is a girl who comes to visit her cousin in the city in order to escape from a man trying to kill her after she turned him down. However, she is pursued by him (disguised as Death) in a carnival getup. She meets Orpheus, a streetcar conductor who is engaged to another girl. They fall in love but she is killed inadvertently by Orpheus.

The descent into Hades is smartly engineered at a revival meeting when her voice comes thorough from an old, possessed woman. He is joined with Miss Dawn when he is accidentally killed by his jilted fiancee.

This is the way the Orpheus tale is adroitly transposed, but pic is somewhat cerebral being mainly helped by the fresh playing of the cast especially Yank actress, Miss Dawn. She makes a sensitive, beauteous Eurydice whose doom is foreshadowed. Color is excellent and director Marcel Camus gives this movement. *Mosk.*

Woman Obsessed
(COLOR—C'SCOPE)

Teary meller with action for males, sentiment for females. Satisfactory b.o.

Hollywood, May 22.

Twentieth Fox production and release. Stars Susan Hayward, Stephen Boyd; co-stars Barbara Nichols. Producer-writer, Sydney Boehm. Directed by Henry Hathaway. Screenplay based on the novel by John Mantley; camera, William C. Mellor; music, Hugo Friedhofer; editor, Robert Simpson. Previewed at the studio, May 19, '59. Running time, **103 MINS.**

Mary Sharron .... Susan Hayward
Fred Carter .... Stephen Boyd
Mayme Radzevitch........Barbara Nichols
Robbie .... Dennis Holmes
Dr. Gibbs .... Theodore Bikel
Sgt. Le Moyne .... Ken Scott
Henri .... James Philbrook
Mrs. Gibbs .... Florence Mac Michael
Ian Campbell .... Jack Raine
Mrs. Campbell .... Mary Carroll
Officer Follette .... Fred Graham
Ticket Taker .... Mike Lally

In "Woman Obsessed," the hazards faced by the principals include, in fairly rapid success, forest fire, blizzard, cyclonic rains and near-drowning in quicksand. This in addition to assorted sluggings and a miscarriage.

Sydney Boehm's production for 20th-Fox is frankly a melodrama. Henry Hathaway's direction keeps the action coming, and plays against it with a steady strumming on sentiment that seems fairly certain to dissolve female audiences.

Susan Hayward portrays a young widow in Boehm's screenplay, which is based on a novel by John Mantley. It is set in contemporary northeastern Canada. Miss Hayward marries Stephen Boyd after he comes to help her on her farm when her husband is killed.

Boyd is an inarticulate roughneck whose personal background leads him to smacking Miss Hayward and her young son, Dennis Holmes, around. He means well, but he's a little too handy with the open palm and the crude psychology. The film ends with Miss Hayward understanding Boyd, and he her, and the child forgiving both.

The film is a throwback, in a way, to the days of motion picture drama when stories were told in bold strokes, filled in with vivid and dee-hued colors. Although it does not resemble "Imitation of Life" in any way, there is the same direct, simple approach. It is not thoughtful drama, but it is absorbing melodrama.

Hathaway's direction plunges the spectator directly into the heart of the excitement in the opening scenes. With only a few lines of dialog, the story is under way and running. Hathaway's handling of the forest fire scenes and other natural disasters, are especially adroit.

Miss Hayward, who seems to be the only actress around today whose eyes really blaze on occasion, has plenty of room to act in this kind of story and delivers convincingly. Boyd, although his role is something bewildering, does his most effective work to date. Young Dennis Holmes is a real charmer, and Hathaway has provided plenty of footage to show it. Others in the cast who contribute include Theodore Bikel, Ken Scott, Barbara Nichols, Florence MacMichael and Arthur Franz.

William C. Mellor's photography is good, and Hugo Friedhofer has provided a lusty score. *Powe.*

Gigantis

Mediocre Science Fantasy. Dim b.o.

Hollywood, May 22.

Warner Bros. release of Toho production. Produced by Tomoyuki Tanaka. Directed by Motoyoshi Odo. Screenplay, Takeo Murata and Sigeaki Hidaka; camera, Seiichi Endo; special photographic effects, Eliji Tsuburaya; special effects, Akira Watanabe, Hiroshi Mukoyama and Masso Shirota. American version: Producer, Paul Schreibman; director-film editor, Hugo Grimaldi. Previewed at the studio, May 21, '59. Running time, **78 MINS.**

Tsukioka .... Hiroshi Koizumi
Hedemi .... Setsuko Wakayama
Kobayashi .... Mindru Chiaki

"Gigantis," subtitled "The Fire Monster," is a Japanese-made film being released here by Warner Bros. It is an inept and tedious attempt at an exploitation film of the science fantasy variety. The Japanese have made some good ones of this type, but "Gigantis" is not one of them. It is likely to have rough sledding even in situations normally devoted to this brand of film.

The title refers to a pre-historic monster re-activated off the coasts of Japan by atomic blasts in the Pacific. Stirred from the deep sleep, he crashes out of the ocean to begin ravaging the Japanese city of Osaka. The film gives the impression that if he had been left alone instead of being deviled by man, he would have been perfectly happy. Of course that wouldn't have made much of a picture, but then as things turned out, it didn't anyway.

The Japanese miniature work is remarkably good. Scenes of the dinosaur-like animal crunching his way through houses, traffic and high-tension wires are interesting and exciting. But the film spends very little time with Gigantis, and spends more with the humans involved. Although the dubbing is adequate to an understanding of the action, the language is often ill-chosen, even granting the special intricacies of adapting dialog to fit lip movement. The use of the phrase "banana oil," as a term of derision, for instance, while arresting, does not have exactly the audience effect intended. *Powe.*

Serenade Einer Grossen Liebe
(Serenade of a Big Love)
(GERMAN—COLOR—SONGS)

Berlin, May 19.

Constantin release of Corona production Stars Mario Lanza and Johanna von Koczian; features Zsa Zsa Gabor, Kurt Kasznar, Hans Soehnker. Directed by Rudy Mate. Screenplay, Andrew Solt; camera (Technicolor), Aldo Tonti; music, Georgie Stoll; editors, Gene Ruggiero and Peter Zinner. At Zoo Palast, Berlin. Running time, **97 MINS.**

Tony Costa .... Mario Lanza
Christa Bruckner...Johanna von Koczian
Albert Bruckner .... Hans Soehnker
Gloria de Vadux .... Zsa Zsa Gabor
Ladislas Tabory .... Kurt Kasznar
Mathilde .... Annie Rosar
Dr. Bessart .... Walter Rilla

This is first German-language Mario Lanza film but won't be the last one since Berlin's CCC (Arthur Brauner) has him under contract for at least three pix. "Serenade," since it was produced by a German (Corona) outfit, is called a German film here.

However, it's also much of an American pic. Metro contributed the lion's share of the financial costs and also has (except the German language-areas and Benelux countries) world rights. It employed five U.S. key men: director Rudy Mate, screenwriter Andrew Solt, music director Georgie Stoll and the two chief cutters, Gene Ruggiero and Peter Zinner. Viewed here, it seems to have as much chance in the U.S. as some other Lanza vehicles.

In many respects, it's more of a German film. The most disappointing thing about "Serenade" is its story. It teems with sentimentality, banalities and old-fashioned situations. Admittedly, the story may not play too big a role in a Mario Lanza film, where one expects music in the first place, but oddly enough, the makers seem to have dedicated much to dramatic incidents.

Story centers around a celebrated U.S. singer (Lanza) who falls in love with a deaf girl. Love surmounts all difficulties and the girl eventually gets back her hearing.

Main value is Lanza's voice of which he makes substantial use. Lineup of songs includes "Come Prima," "Oh, Capri," "I Love You" (Grieg), "O Sole Mio," "Ritorna Vincitor," "La Donna e mobile," "Ave Maria," "Vesti La Giubba" and the laugh trio from "Cosi Fan Tutte."

The Technirama-Technicolor photography is quite good. There are some beautiful shots of Salzburg, Rome and Capri. Other technical standards are satisfying. *Hans.*

Marie-Octobre
(FRENCH)

Paris, May 19.

Pathe release of Orex-Abbey-S.F.-Doxa Films production. Stars Danielle Darrieux; features Serge Reggiani, Bernard Blier, Daniel Ivernel, Paul Guera, Paul Meurisse, Noel Roquevert, Lino Ventura. Directed by Julien Duvivier. Screenplay, Jacques Robert Henri Jeanson; camera, Robert Le Febvre; editor, Martha Poncin. At Marignan, Paris. Running time, **100 MINS.**

Marie .... Danielle Darrieux
Rogier .... Serge Reggiani
Simoneau .... Bernard Blier
Priest .... Paul Guers
Renaud .... Paul Meurisse
Van Dan .... Noel Roquevert

Nine men and a woman, 15 years after the war, who had been in the same underground setup, meet to unmask one of them who had betrayed their leader during the war. Pic keeps the unity of time, place and action and stakes all on dialogue, some suspense and characterization.

Obviously influenced by "12 Angry Men," this lacks feeling and sting of the other. It is slickly made but wanting in penetrating characterization. Its inferences and occupation talk make this primarily a local entry possibility with overseas chances limited on its prolonged talkiness except for some arty house situations.

Acting is good but characters are too one-dimensional to allow for accomplished execution. Direction is smart but without the needed warmth to build up the necessary suspense. Technical credits are good.

The Mysterians
(WIDESCREEN-COLOR)

Well-produced but loaded with science-fiction cliches. Will stand up under heavy exploitation, and b.o. could be good.

Metro release of a Toho Production. Produced by Tamoyuki Tanaka. Directed by Inoshiro Honda. Screenplay, Takeshi Kimura, from an original Jojiro Okami story adapted by Shigeru Kayama; camera, Hajime Koizumi; editor, Hiroichi Iwashita; music, Akaira Ifukube; special effects, Eiji Tsuburaya. Previewed at the Academy Theatre, May 15, '59. Running time, **87 MINS.**

Joji Atsumi .... Kenji Sahara
Etsuko Shiraishi .... Yumi Shirakawa
Hiroko .... Momoko Kochi
Ryoichi Shiraishi .... Akihiko Hirata
Dr. Adachi .... Takashi Shirmura
Commander Morita .... Susumu Fujita
Captain Seki .... Hisaya Ito
Commander Sugimoto......Yoshio Kosugi
Dr. Kawanami .... Fuyuki Murakami
General Hamamoto....Minosuke Yamada

As corny as it is furious, "The Mysterians" is red-blooded phantasmagoria—made in Japan and dedicated to those undiscerning enough to be taken in by its hokum. While Junior may be moved by the arrival of outer-space gremlins, big brother and all like him will laugh their heads off. Metro can take advantage of both and by soaking the Toho Production's special effects with its own special exploitation, the returns could be admirable.

"Mysterians" is in color and widescreen with production values comparable to those in high-budget American pictures. The special effects involving sliding land, quaking earth and melting mortars are realistically accomplished, proving the facility with which the Japanese filmmakers deal in miniatures. But, as has been the misfortune of more than one Hollywood science-fiction entry, the omnipresent robot monster is so outlandish, it draws more snickers than gasps.

Mysterians are superior beings from the planet Mysteroid which has been destroyed by nuclear warfare. The Buck Rogers atmosphere in which they land on Earth leads Japanese scientists to doubt their intentions, and though the intruders claim they want only a small parcel of land as a base for exploration (plus a few femmes to help procreate a normal generation), the Earthmen suspect more ambitious desires are in store. The Japanese set up an offense that would stagger a Juggernaut, but the Mysterians drill forward. At this point an American blurts, "Good news! Good news! The United States has developed a machine that will . . ." And, sure enough it does.

Metro lists triple credit for the creation of this plot—original story by Jojiro Okami, adaptation by Shigeru Kayama and screenplay by Takeshi Kimura. Dubbed into English by Peter Riethof and Carlos Montalban, it's understandable enough, but one might easily believe something was lost in translation. Tamoyuki Tanaka produced and Inoshiro Honda directed, with top work from special effects director Eiji Tsuburaya, cinematographer Hajime Koizumi and composer Akaira Ifukube.

The cast—from Kenji Sahara to Minosuke Yamada—isn't intended to sell many Yankee tickets. *Ron.*

Calypso
(ITALIAN—FRENCH)
(Color—Scope)

Rome, May 19.

Cineriz release of an Enalpa (Rome)-Filmsonor (Paris) co-production. Features Cy Grant, Sally Neal, Luise Bennett, Carlton Gumbs, Paul Savain, Didier Petrus and E. W. Minto. Directed by Franco Rossi, Golfiero Colonna, Leonardo Benvenuti. Camera (Eastmancolor-Totalscope), Pierludovico Pavoni. Music, A. F. Lavagnino. Editor, Mario Serandrei. At Galleria, Rome. Running time, **95 MINS.**

Peter .... Cy Grant
Resy .... Sally Neal
Martha .... Louise Bennet
Cicero .... Carlton Gumbs
Grandpa .... Paul Savain
Washington .... Didier Petrus
Rick .... W. E. Minto

Colorful locationer with principal appeal for lovers of the calypso rhythm as seen in its natural

habitat. This has some exploitation appeal which will help it to spotty export interest.

Thin story line is generally a pretext to frame various insular song and dance manifestations, which are film's main attraction, though there's an attempt at an offbeat miscegenation angle—mulatto family in film at one point seeks a white husband for a daughter in order to insure her social standing. Remainder of footage is replete with bouncy, often suggestive dances, cockfights, island traditions. as well as a healthy dosage of calypso music, well orchestrated by A. F. Lavagnino.

Cy Grant and Sally Neal a bit self-consciously play the leads while a host of colorful characters populate the background. Film has some fine location photography by P. L. Pavoni. The musical score made up of local tunes and the aforementioned orchestration by Lavagnino is a decided plus. Other credits okay. *Hawk.*

Ercole e la Regina di Lidia
(Hercules and Queen of Lydia)
(ITALO—FRENCH)
(Color—Scope)

Rome, May 19.
Lux Film release of a Lux-Galatea-Lux de France co-production. Stars Steve Reeves; features Sylvia Koscina, Sylvia Lopez, Primo Carnera, Patrizia della Rovere, Gabriele Antonini, Carlo D'Angelo, Sergio Fantoni, Mimmo Palmara. Directed by Pietro Francisci. Story and screenplay, Francisci and Ennio de Concini. Camera (Eastmancolor-Dyaliscope), Mario Bava. Music, Enzo Masetti. Editor, Mario Serandrei. At Adriano, Rome. Running time, 105 MINS.
Hercules .... Steve Reeves
Queen of Lydia .... Sylvia Lopez
Jole .... Sylvia Koscina
Ulysses .... Gabriele Antonini
Penelope .... Patricia della Rovere
Antheus .... Primo Carnera

Second item in the successful "Hercules" eries finds the same author-director team mixing similar ingredients to good effect, promising fine returns in the exploitation-spectacle niche. Export chances are equally good for dubbed versions in most countries.

Handsome and muscular Steve Reeves once more portrays the harried Hercules in his various mythological and fictional adventures, this time principally involving the beautiful but treacherous Queen of Lydia. She keeps him enslaved via repeated dose of a magic potion. Also features are a battle between Hercules and the giant Antheus, appropriately played by Primo Carnera, as well as some well-staged battles. dance, fights with leopards and a generous sprinkling of amorous interludes. These last-named, linked with lightweight garbing of most principals, make the pic highly exploitable.

Thesping all along the line is competent in the required broad manner. Costumes and sets are rich and colorful while lensing in studio or on locations takes full advantage of the spectacular ingredients at hand. *Hawk.*

La Cucaracha
(MEXICAN-COLOR)

Cannes, May 19.
Cimex release of Rodriguez production. Stars Maria Felix, Pedro Armendariz, Dolores Del Rio; features, Emilio Fernandez, Flor Silvestre, Antonio Aguilar. Directed by Ismael Rodriguez. Screenplay, Jose Prado, Ricardo Garibay, Jose Celis; camera (Eastmancolor), Gabriel Figueroa; editor, R. Lavista. At Cannes Film Fest. Running time, 89 MINS.
Refugio .... Maria Felix
Chabela .... Dolores Del Rio
Valentin .... Pedro Armendariz
Antonio .... Emilio Fernandez

The Mexican revolution backgrounds a tale of a manly peasant general torn between a hard femme warrior and a more sedate widow. He finally chooses the latter but leaves a child with the former before dying and leaving the two women trudging on in the revolution together.

Feeling for time and place is only fair. Characterization is conventional, with the thesping only adequate. It's slanted for only Spanish language spots in the U.S. It is a passable western in calibre. *Mosk.*

Don't Give Up The Ship

Mild Jerry Lewis comedy. Sporadically amusing. Fair b.o.

Hollywood, May 29.
Paramount release of Hal Wallis production. Stars Jerry Lewis. Directed by Norman Taurog. Screenplay, Herbert Baker, Edmund Beloin and Henry Garson; based on a story by Ellis Kadison; camera, Haskell Boggs; music, Walter Scharf; editor, Warren Low. Previewed at the Picwood Theatre, May 25, '59. Running time, 89 MINS.
John Paul Steckler .... Jerry Lewis
Ensign Benson .... Dina Merrill
Prudence .... Diana Spencer
Stan Wychinski......Mickey Shaughnessy
Admiral Bludde .... Robert Middleton
Congressman Mandeville .. Gale Gordon
Mrs. Trabert .... Mabel Albertson
Lieut. Comdr. Farber......Claude Akins

Jerry Lewis tries hard to get up a full head of comedy steam in "Don't Give Up the Ship," but the laughs are scanty and its boxoffice prospects mild. The Hal Wallis production for Paramount has too few situations to exploit for humor, and must work those it has very thin to get what fun there is out of the service farce.

Lewis has jettisoned some of the more frantic aspects of his technique for this film, and that gives it qualities that make it more pleasant than it might otherwise have been. He is a more likable, more human actor who gets laughs this time without the audience feeling the strain of the effort.

The screenplay by Herbert Baker, Edmund Beloin and Henry Garson is based on an intrinsically humorous story by Ellis Kadison. At the end of World War II, Lewis commanded a destroyer escort. The Navy has no record he ever turned it in. Like other service property, unless he can prove he delivered the ship to the proper authorities, he must pay for it. The film traces, through flashbacks, the career of the ship and of Lewis.

There are some funny scenes. such as an embarkation of the DE from Pearl Harbor with Lewis in command for the first time, issuing orders as he surreptitiously reads them from a book. But a honeymoon gag, with Lewis torn from his bride on their wedding night to face a naval inquiry, is overdone and the jokes pertaining to it flat and single-meaning. There simply isn't enough material in "Don't Give Up the Ship" to sustain the length, or enough good lines to enliven individual scenes.

Norman Taurog, who directed, has attempted to juice things up by incorporation of sight gags, some purely photographic tricks, and this helps. An underwater sequence starts promisingly when Lewis, equipped with aqualung and other subaqueous paraphernalia, dives into the water and keeps going straight down until his head gets stuck in the muddy bottom. But these promises do not pay off or are extended beyond their value.

Dina Merrill makes an exceedingly attractive Navy ensign who gets entangled with Lewis, and Diana Spencer does the best she can with a simpering role as Lewis' wife, "unkissed," as the saying goes. although the script makes clear this is not what's meant. Mickey Shaughnessy is haphazardly amusing as a dense Navy chief, and Robert Middleton is capable as a bemused admiral. Gale Gordon, Mabel Albertson and Claude Akins do well by what they have to work with.

Haskell Boggs' camera work is competent, and Walter Scharf's music is an asset. Michael Moore

---

gets credit as second unit director and Lamar Boren did the underwater photography. *Powe.*

Look Back in Anger

A good job technically and actor-wise. But this adult film is very downbeat though presold on play's transatlantic success; stars and author provide marquee value.

London, May 26.
Associated-British-Pathe release of a Woodfall (Gordon L. T. Scott) production. (Warner Bros. release in U.S.). Stars Richard Burton, Claire Bloom, Mary Ure; features Edith Evans, Gary Raymond. Directed by Tony Richardson. Screenplay, Nigel Kneale, from John Osborne's play; editor, Richard Best; camera, Oswald Morris; music supervised by John Addison. At Empire, London. Running time, 115 MINS.
Jimmy Porter .... Richard Burton
Helena Charles .... Claire Bloom
Alison Porter .... Mary Ure
Mrs. Tanner .... Edith Evans
Cliff Lewis .... Gary Raymond
Colonel Redfern .... Glen Byam Shaw
Mrs. Redforn......Phyllis Nielson-Terry
Hurst .... Donald Pleasence
Miss Drury .... Jane Eccles
Kapoor .... S. P. Kapoor
Doctor .... George Devine
Actor .... Walter Hudd
Girl A.S.M. .... Anne Dickins
Sally .... Bernice Swanson

Tony Richardson, who staged the play, "Look Back In Anger," which helped to hoist John Osborne into the bigtime, has now tackled the same subject as his first directorial chore. By adroit juxtaposition of studio sets and location he has effectively captured the moody atmosphere of a drab, rain-soaked provincial town. He has encouraged Oswald Morris's camera to move brilliantly and has used sound excitingly. Richardson's bow into film direction is a technical triumph, but somewhere along the line he has lost the heart and the throb that made the play an adventure. The film simultaneously impresses and depresses.

With an "X" certificate, which means that nobody under 16 may see it in Britain, there are still enough adults who will want to see it partly because of its presold publicity. Nigel Kneale's screenplay is a creditable job, with human if occasionally violent dialog. He brings in the market-place, jazz-club and seedy apartment atmosphere only hinted at in the play. But obviously somewhere along the line the film has lost its way. Jimmy Porter, the central character, is an angry young man but there are few indications of why he is angry or for what he is striving.

He emerges as a selfish, incredibly rude, almost psychopathic who hardly ever sparks off a mood that engenders pity or understanding. In the play, Porter (Richard Burton) was a rebel—but a mixed-up weakling of a rebel. In the film, as played by Burton, he is an arrogant young man who thinks the world owes him something but cannot make up his mind what it is—and certainly doesn't deserve the handout.

As a reminder, "Anger" concerns an ex-college student who runs a confectionery push-cart in a market, plays trumpet and goes out of his way to humiliate his wife and friends. His wife leaves him and he has an affair with her best friend. The girl leaves him and he snuggles up again with his wife after she has lost their baby. This thin theme is merely a peg for Osborne to vent his spleen about a number of conventions which

have served the world fairly well for a number of years.

Burton glowers sullenly, violently and well as Jimmy Porter and it is not his fault that the role gives him little opportunity for variety. Mary Ure (repeating her London & Broadway stage role) as the downtrodden, degraded young wife is first-class. Claire Bloom plays the "other woman" with a neat variation of bite and come-hitherness. Gary Raymond makes an instant impact as the cosy, kindly friend of the unhappy couple.

Donald Pleasence as a mean, mealy-mouthed market official, and S. P. Kapoor. as an Indian trader, both score. The distinguished actress, Edith Evans, appears as a Cockney woman and has one or two excellent moments.

Chris Barber's music helps the film no end, especially in the arresting under-title sequences. Trumpeter Pat Halcox does a fine job in dubbing Burton's horn sequences.

"Look Back In Anger" is an oddly aggravating film. It has some splendid touches but falls down often in important matters. But there is considerable evidence of adult brains getting together on an adult theme. It is just a pity that the theme is too much "Johnny-One-Note." *Rich.*

Parque De Madrid
(Retiro Park)
(ITALIAN—SPANISH—COLOR)
Madrid, May 26.
Selecciones Capitolio release of a P. C. Brio production. With Luisa Della Noce, Fernando Rey, Jose Luis Ozores, Vicky Lagos, Tony Leblanc, Juanjo Menendez, Maria Martin, Walter Chiari, Mary Santpere, Marisa de Leza and Gustavo Rojo. Directed by Cahen Salaberry. Written by Lucas, Gallardo, Del Castillo and Salvador. At Callao, Madrid. Running time, **100 MINS.**

Movement in this sketch-filled panorama of a day in Madrid's Retiro Park is almost limited to fades. "Parque" is strongly reminiscent of and pointedly inferior to Italy's "Villa Barghese," as it weaves coarse comedy and park bench soap opera behind a trail of sun-drenched types who read lines befitting the brittle-dialog.

Brightest sketch pairs affable Walter Chiari as a fortune-hunter with popular Catalan comedienne Mary Santpere. But it's no more than a vaude act. In the main, a talent-studded cast including Fernando Rey, Ozores, Tony Leblanc, Marisa de Leza and Gustavo Rojo are bench-bound in static talk. The Agfacolor looked good. *Werb.*

Here Come the Jets
(C'SCOPE)

Well-made programmer. Action meller will give strength to double-bills.

Hollywood, May 29.
Twentieth-Fox release of Associated Producers, Inc. production. Stars Steve Brodie, Lyn Thomas, Mark Dana, John Doucette; costars Jean Carson. Produced by Richard Einfeld. Directed by Gene Fowler Jr. Screenplay, Louis Vittes; camera, Karl Struss; music, Paul Dunlap; editor, Harry Gerstad. Previewed at Jack Wrather's screening room, May 28, '59. Running time, **72 MINS.**

Logan .... Steve Brodie
Joyce .... Lyn Thomas
Wallack .... Mark Dana
Randall .... John Doucette
Jean .... Jean Carson
Burton .... Carleton Young
Henley .... Joseph Turkel
B-Girl .... Gloria Moreland
Blonde .... Vikki Dougan
Bartender .... I. Stanford Jolley

"Here Come the Jets" is a budget film designed for second place on a double bill. The Richard Einfeld production for 20th-Fox is, nonetheless, a compact and interesting melodrama with a topical background, testing of jet airliners. While it is not designed to be a prime attraction, it will be a satisfaction to the customers.

Steve Brodie plays an alcoholic Korean War hero in Louis Vittes' screenplay. He is hauled out of the drunk tank and put to work as a test pilot by John Doucette, driving genius of an aircraft plant, who believes he can be rehabilitated. Brodie has some setbacks but he overcomes them in time to be in on testing of the big new jetliner that is Doucette's star creation.

Vittes' story is clean and his dialog is generally lean and sharp. Fowler has taken excellent advantage of technical aspects of jet construction and testing to have suspense and excitement arise naturally out of situation. One scene, in a "flight simulator," where Brodie cracks up (mentally) as he is unable to handle a plane in theoretical flight, is a good example of this. The scene is as gripping as if it were an actual plane in trouble. Fowler makes good use of Karl Struss's camera work, and Harry Gerstad's editing. Transitional shots have unusual value, and double-exposures and establishing shots help tell the story without superfluous wordage. Kay Norton did the good aerial photography, which is also adroitly utilized.

Brodie gives a performance of depth, without letting his character get out of hand. Doucette is interesting as a pleasantly humorous rugged individualist, and Jean Carson contributes an ingratiating comedy-romantic character. Lyn Thomas, Mark Dana, Carleton Young and Joseph Turkel are also good in important roles.

Paul Dunlap's musical score is inventive, and sound by Steve Bass is good. *Powe.*

The H-Man
(WIDESCREEN—COLOR)

Good story well made. Pic is exploitable.

Hollywood, June 2.
Columbia release of a Toho production. Produced by Tomoyuki Tanaka. Directed by Inoshiro Honda. Screenplay, Takeshi Kimura, from original story by Hideo Kaijo; special effects, Eiji Tsuburaya; camera (Eastmancolor), Hajime Koizumi; sound, Choshichiro Mikami and Masanobu Migami. Previewed at Columbia, May 28, '59. Running time, **79 MINS.**
Actors: Yumi Shirakawa, Kenji Sahara, Akihiko Hirata, Eitaro Ozawa, Koreya Senda, Bitzuru Sato.

"The H-Man" is a filmy green monster created from a slimy liquid that dissolves human beings as it oozes through Tokyo like jellied consomme. The Japanese Toho Production is well made and seemingly more thoughtful than the company's two other U.S. summer releases (Metro's "The Mysterians" and Warner Bros.' "Gigantis") and Columbia will be able to exploit good bookings with the widescreen, color production.

The story is reminiscent of last year's Paramount release, "The Blob," and while recollective science-fiction addicts may pooh-pooh the idea of an Oriental copy, they should be pleased indeed with the quality of the replica. It abounds in fewer special effects than either "Mysterians" or "Gigantis," but its one effect—namely, the disintegration of the human body—is skillfully and terrifyingly adept.

"H-Man" is as timely a Strontium 90 in describing how hydrogen bomb tests have reduced living things to a gelitanous mass which, in turn, can dissolve any other living tissue it touches. The liquid lives, and, to stay alive, seeks a repast mostly composed of the heroes, heroines and heavies of this picture. Once the authorities believe those who have seen the nuclear monster, it is a comparatively simple matter to do away with it via a manmade holocaust.

Yumi Shirakawa, as a delightful looking nightclub entertainer, is excellent, as are Kenji Sahara, as the chief detective, and Akihiko Hirata, as a scientist. The Takeshi Kimura screenplay (from an original story by Hideo Kaijo) is effective, and Inoshiro Honda's direction takes full advantage of the story, the special effect (directed by Eiji Tsuburaya) and the terror generated by both. Tomoyuki Tanaka produced, with the technically excellent production aided by Hajime Koizumi's cinematography, Takeo Kita's art direction, Masuru Sato's music and the sound by Choshichiro Mikami and Masanobu Migami.

Culturally, it is unfortunate the West has made such inroads in the Orient that a Japanese picture, such as this one, looks more like an American film with Japanese actors. *Ron.*

Teenagers From Outer Space

Unusual sci-fi programmer to be paired, in most situations, with "Gigantis."

Hollywood, June 2.
Warner Bros. release of a Tom Graeff production. Stars David Love, Dawn Anderson, Harvey B. Dunn, Bryan Grant, Tom Lockyear, King Moody, Helen Sage, Frederic Welch. Written, produced and directed by Tom Graeff. Previewed at Warner's, May 29, '59. Running time, **85 MINS.**

Derek .... David Love
Betty Morgan .... Dawn Anderson
Grandpa Morgan .... Harvey B. Dunn
Thor .... Bryan Grant
Joe Rogers .... Tom Lockyear
Captain .... King Moody
Miss Morse .... Helen Sage
Dr. Brandt .... Frederic Welch

"Teenagers From Outer Space" was written, produced and directed by Tom Graeff. He also photographed the film, edited it, supervised its sound and music, created its special effects, played one of its leading roles and released it through Warner Bros. The science-fiction melodrama, an off-beat dualer for WB packaging with "Gigantis," is oddly appealing.

Perhaps due in part to a lower than low budget, the film often is inescapably inept. Lighting is poor, interiors are pallid, the monster is pathetically makeshift. The film is impudently grandiose in its tone and is more likely to elecit shrieks of amusement than horror.

But the film also is carefully thought out, concocted of exploitable elements, yet different from its many predecessors. While Graeff may not have made a good picture, he has made an interesting one that every now and again smacks of brilliance. Several scenes—e.g., a sequence of youngsters peering wide-eyed at their first spaceman—are composed of an artistry that marks Graeff as a filmmaker to be heard from.

The story is of outer-space beings who have scoured the universe for a place to graze their gargons, crab-like animals that grow as big as houses in a single day and enjoy people more than alfalfa. The spacemen land on Earth, and one of them finds family life here a darn sight better than the automative society which raised him. He decides to convert and, in the end, is killed while saving Earth from the possibility of being overrun by the herds of man-eating creatures.

The cast carries out its assignment efficiently when allowed to be unpretentious. David Love is epecially affable as the good spacemen, and Bryan Grant and King Moody are appropriately nasty as the bad ones. Dawn Anderson is fine as the young love interest, and Harvey B. Dunn, as Grandpa, is sympathetically good. Sonia Torgeson, seen only briefly in a swimming pool sequence, should have stayed around a bit longer before being turned, as were so many, into a bare skeleton via Graeff's focusing disintegration ray gun. *Ron.*

The Horse Soldiers
(COLOR)

Spectacular telling of a Civil War story finds John Ford in top form. Teaming John Wayne and William Holden, plus action, adds up to a major moneymaker.

United Artists release of Mirisch Co. presentation of Mahin-Rackin production. Stars John Wayne, William Holden; features Constance Towers, Althea Gibson, Hoot Gibson, Anna Lee, Russell Simpson, Stan Jones, Carleton Young, Basil Ruysdael. Directed by John Ford. Script, John Lee Mahin and Martin Rackin, from novel by Harold Sinclair; camera (color by DeLuxe), William Clothier; music, David Buttolph; song, "I Left My Love" by Stan Jones. Previewed at Astor Theatre, N.Y., June 4, '59. Running time, **120 MINS**.

Colonel Marlowe	John Wayne
Major Kendall	William Holden
Hannah	Constance Towers
Lukey	Althea Gibson
Brown	Hoot Gibson
Mrs. Buford	Anna Lee
Sheriff	Russell Simpson
General U. S. Grant	Stan Jones
Colonel Miles	Carleton Young
Commandant	Basil Ruysdael

It's always been that way. Give John Ford a company of brawny men, let him train his cameras on the U.S. cavalry and provide a a script with plenty of action and he's off on the road to glory. In "The Horse Soldiers," which involves a little-known incident in the Civil War, all these elements are present and the picture consequently adds up to a whopping big, colorful spectacle in the "grand" tradition.

As for boxoffice, the names of John Wayne and William Holden alone provide the kind of draw that no exhibitor can quarrel with. So "The Horse Soldiers," with names, tried-and-true action and the Civil War background, is one of those pictures that just can't miss. There are "buts—."

With all of Ford's skill for staging battle scenes, and his superb eye for pictorial composition, the film is extremely uneven. Pictorially, it's probably one of the best Ford has ever done and there's one stunning scene after another. But these long shots of men on horses tend to become tedious and they considerably slow up the flow of the story.

Also, where Ford is a master in creating visual excitement, the dramatic scenes involving Wayne, Holden and newcomer Constance Towers don't come off with much conviction. For that matter, the whole script, written by John Lee Mahin and Martin Rackin, strains credulity, switching back and forth from grim war and suffering to broad humor and—in one instance —something resembling farce.

This is the story of Colonel Benjamin Grierson who, in April of 1863, was ordered by General Grant to take three cavalry regiments and ride 300 miles into the heart of the Confederacy to destroy the rail link between Newton Station and Vicksburg and thus choke off supplies from Southern-held Vicksburg. Grierson accomplished his objective, riding 600 miles in 16 days and bringing his troupe back into the Northern lines at Baton Rouge.

Woven into this is a romantic involvement between Wayne as the colonel and a Southern belle who learns of the planned route and whom he takes along on the entire expedition to keep her from conveying her knowledge to the Confederacy instead of shooting her as a spy. A subplot concerns the rivalry between Wayne and Holden, playing a dedicated Northern surgeon assigned to accompany Wayne on the mission.

The combination of Ford and Wayne has clicked so often before, it's no surprise that they're in the groove again this time 'round. Wayne is rugged as the colonel, feared and respected by his men who depend on his resourcefulness to bring them out alive. It's obviously the kind of John Wayne which the public appreciates. Holden has the role of the "intellectual" and the humanitarian and he plays it well, putting a great deal of sarcasm into his lines.

Miss Towers is blonde and attractive to the eye as the Southern belle. Since it's difficult to believe in her role, it's also hard to believe in her performance which is standard, but shows promise in one or two emotional scenes. It's one of the one-dimensional parts.

In small roles, Hoot Gibson recalls another era of filmmaking and tennis star Althea Gibson makes her screen debut as Miss Towers' servant and companion.

"The Horse Soldiers" understandably bends backwards to do justice to both sides. Wayne's men, while rough 'n' tough in battle, are a remarkably considerate lot and Wayne himself exhibits some almost super-human traits. North and South emerge heroically in the various encounters, and the point is underscored to an almost naive degree. In one scene, played strictly for laughs, Wayne's veterans beat a retreat before a group of very young Southern cadets rather than fire back on small fry.

It's probably asking too much to expect historical accuracy. This is the kind of Civil War as audiences imagine it—full of blazing action and romance. Thrown in are some brutal scenes of battlefield surgery, including an amputation. The sequence of Wayne's men destroying supplies and rolling stock at Newton Station and laying a trap for Southern reenforcements is Ford at his best.

William Clothier's photography is outstanding. Some of the scenes have the quality of paintings. The Deluxe color brings the whole thing vividly to life and Jack Solomon's sound is unusually good. David Buttolph has concocted a medley of Northern and Southern tunes which rate importantly, and Stan Jones' "I Left My Love" provides a catchy theme. As in all of the Ford films, the music has a fitting, masculine quality, being sung mostly by a male chorus.

"The Horse Soldiers" applies the Western formula to the Civil War theme. With John Ford at the helm, it becomes a high adventure drama that makes its robust pitch right to the broad audience for whom it is meant. *Hift.*

The Womaneater

Old-fashioned mad doctor meller with n.g. prospects.

Hollywood, June 5.

Columbia Pictures release of Guido Coen production. Stars George Coulouris, Vera Day; features Peter Wayn, Joyce Gregg, Joy Webster, Jimmy Vaughan. Directed by Charles Saunders. Original story-screenplay, Brandon Fleming; camera, Ernest Palmer; editor, Seymour Logie; music, Edwin Astley. Previewed June 4, '59. Running time, **70 MINS**.

Doctor Moran	George Coulouris
Lewis Carling	Robert Mackenzie
Doctor Patterson	Norman Claridge
Native Girl	Marpessa Dawn
Tanga	Jimmy Vaughan
Susan Curtis	Sara Leighton
Sergeant Bolton	Edward Higgings
Mrs. Santor	Joyce Gregg
Bristow	Harry Ross
Sally	Vera Day
Jack Venner	Peter Wayn
Fair Attendant	Alexander Field
Judy	Joy Webster
Man in Club	David Lawton
Lascar	John Tinn
Constable	Roger Avon

This British import is an old-fashioned meller which even in England could not rise above the indiscriminate program market. For American audiences it's unable to overcome an old-hat plot carelessly put together.

Title of the Guido Coen production takes its meaning from a South American plant, which natives call the Ju-Ju and idolize, which catches women in its flaring tentacles and consumes. George Coulouris, a half-mad British scientist, uses this tree and its human victims for the purpose of extracting a liquid supposed to bring back the dead. His experiments are conducted in a lab in his home after he brings back the tree from the tropical jungles. Victims are young femmes he lures to his lab.

Coulouris is called upon for over-acting by Charles Saunders, whose direction generally is static. Vera Day, his co-star, is pretty as an employee in his home but has little to do but be terrified. Peter Wayn, as her fiance who saves her from the lab; Joyce Gregg, a discarded housekeeper; and Edward Higgings, a police sergeant, are as good as the Brandon Fleming script will permit. *Whit.*

I Tartassati
(The Overtaxed)
(ITALIAN)

Rome, June 2.

CEI-INCOM release of a Maxima-Cei-Incom production. Stras Toto, Aldo Fabrizi; features Louis de Funes, Luciano Marin, Catha Caro, Anna Campori, Miranda Campa, Ciccio Barbi, Anna Maria Bottini. Directed by Steno. Screenplay, Metz, Gianviti, Maccari from story by Metz and Gianviti. Camera, Marco Scarpelli. Editor, Eraldo da Roma. Tradeshown in Rome.

Fast-paced and amusing topical comedy with winning performances by Toto and Aldo Fabrizi. Excellent chances on the home market, especially in respect to cost. Lightweight for export, but good for Italo areas abroad.

Pic deals with attempts by a rich storeowner, played by Toto, to avoid paying heavy taxes by convincing and/or bribing tax inspector Aldo Fabrizi to go easy on his double-check of the firm's accounts. Tax problems remain unsolved at the end (solution offered is to try to win tax-free football pool) but families are linked nevertheless when the taxer's daughter falls for shopkeeper's son.

Dialogue is topically fine. The combo of a top comic team makes for plenty of laughs. Technical credits are good. *Hawk.*

Say One for Me
(C'SCOPE—COLOR)

Musical has a Catholic priest bestowing his blessings on some Manhattan show biz characters. Doesn't come off well but Bing Crosby and Debbie Reynolds will help the initial sell.

Twentieth-Fox release of Frank Tashlin production. Stars Bing Crosby, Debbie Reynolds, Robert Wagner; features Ray Walston, Les Tremayne, Connie Gilchrist, Frank McHugh, Joe Besser, Alena Murray. Directed by Tashlin. Written by Robert O'Brien; songs, Sammy Cahn and James Van Heusen; dances staged by Alex Romero; camera (De Luxe Color), Leo Tover; music, Lionel Newman; editor, Hugh S. Fowler. At Paramount Theatre, N.Y., June 2, '59. Running time, **119 MINS**.

Father Conroy	Bing Crosby
Holly	Debbie Reynolds
Tony Vincent	Robert Wagner
Phil Stanley	Ray Walston
Harry LaMaise	Les Tremayne
Mary Manning	Connie Gilchrist
Jim Dugan	Frank McHugh
Joe Greb	Joe Besser
Sunny	Alena Murray
Chorine	Stella Stevens
Fay Flagg	Nina Shipman
Monsignor	Sebastian Cabot
June January	Judy Harriet
Lou Christy	Dick Whittinghill
Hotel Clerk	Robert Montgomery Jr.
Otto	Murray Alper
Capt. Bradford	Richard Collier
Rabbi Berman	David Leonard
Dr. Leventhal	Thomas B. Henry
Rev. Kendall	Wilkie de Martel
Pastor Johnson	Alexander Campbell
Detective Minelli	Bruce McFarlane

Basic idea in Robert O'Brien's story probably had potentialities. It's a "Going My Way" sort of affair with Bing Crosby again as the priest with his target shifted from juvenile roughnecks to show business delinquents. But something went wrong in the development; the entertainment values are short of impressive and the box-office will have to depend on Crosby and Debbie Reynolds as the marquee names.

Frank Tashlin's production divides its time between smalltime night club activity and the efforts of Father Conroy (Crosby) to keep the flock from straying. Latter conducts a midnight mass for entertainers and others in Manhattan (as does St. Malachy's on West 48th Street), and this provides the peg for such cracks as the clergyman having his own late show and "the padre is running an after-hours joint."

Tasteless and disturbing facet of "Say One for Me" is the type of entertainment these entertainers dish out. For example, the opening has Miss Reynolds rehearsing a number for a church benefit while Crosby and a nun look on approvingly. Garbed in a tight-fitting costume, Miss Reynolds goes through a torso-wriggling routine that would be more at home in a Minsky grind.

Yarn has Miss Reynolds crashing into show biz—leaving school to do so—as her father, an oldtime vaudevillian becomes ill. Crosby, at the request of the girl's father, undertakes to look after her.

Miss Reynolds auditions at a spot called the Black Garter and is accepted by Robert Wagner, producer-star of the show, and a first-class wolf. From this comes the obvious romantic ins and outs culminating in marriage.

Tashlin as the director works the musical items into the proceedings with smoothness but seems a little oldfashioned in emphasizing story situations. Camera's focusing on the figure of Christ on the cross is heavy-handed business; the spirituality angle could have been gotten across with more subtlety.

Songs by Sammy Cahn and James Van Heusen are not likely to be listed among their best credits although the title number is top quality—good lyrics, pleasant melody—and stands a chance on its own. "The Secret of Christmas," so far as the picture's story goes, is a sure click but actually is a modest offering that might get action at yule time.

Crosby turns in a curiously inhibited performance. He plays the role tight, not at all like the free-wheeling, liesurely-paced Crosby of yore, but the voice is still there. Miss Reynolds is a cutie, handles the dialog and emoting competently and is particularly agreeable when making with the song and dance.

Wagner, in an assignment quite similar to "Pal Joey," is a dis-

agreeable heel who'd double-cross a loved one for a choice booking. The character is not a completely plausible one but Wagner does pretty will by it.

Comedian Ray Walston contributes the highlights of "Say One for Me." He's supposed to be a former songwriter of importance but now on a continual binge. His is an affable personality and the performance as a drunk is frequently amusing.

Connie Gilchrist, as Crosby's housekeeper, also scores notably. Les Tremayne, Frank McHugh, Joe Besser and Alena Murray, among others, round out the cast in agreeable fashion.

Music, as supervised and conducted by Lionel Newman, has its ups and downs. Leo Tover's photography (De Luxe Color) is on the beam all the way. Editing might have been closer in certain spots.

Tashlin has dressed up "Say One for Me" with colorful and realistic settings, all well framed in CinemaScope. But the finished product is no "Going My Way." *Gene.*

Croquemitoufle
(FRENCH-SONGS)

Paris, June 2.

Cocinor release of Cocinex-Sedif-Noel Films production. Stars Gilbert Becaud; features Mireille Granelli, Michel Roux, Robert Manuel, Roger Carel, Michele Luccioni. Directed by Claude Barma. Screenplay, Jacques Emmanuel, Jean-Charles Tacchella; camera, Jacques Lemare; editor, Charles Bretoneiche; music, Becaud. At Biarritz, Paris. Running time, **90 MINS.**

Dernard	Gilbert Becaud
Katherine	Mireille Granelli
Michel	Michel Roux
Fred	Robert Manuel
Maurice	Roger Carel
Nina	Michele Luccioni

This fairly bright situation comedy is familiar but brought off with enough invention and zest to make for a good local playoff with foreign chances for dualers a possibility. But the pic lacks the weight and originality for arty theatres. A man hears his friend's wife has run off while he was out of town. Said man sets off to help. He has never seen the wife and plenty of complications ensue before he gets the girl who is not really the pal's wife. Claude Barma, in his first pic, shows a flair for comedics and is able to give enough depth to his conventional characters, aided by their breezy playing, to make this good entertainment.

Gilbert Becaud, a top singer here, supplies some catchy tunes and also displays a nice screen personality. Others are also good and technical credits are fine. *Mosk.*

Du Rififi Chez Les Femmes
(Rififi Among the Women) (FRENCH)

Paris, June 2.

Cinedis release of Dismage production. Stars Nadja Tiller, Robert Hossein; features Silvia Montfort, Roger Hanin, Pierre Blanchar, Francoise Rosay, Jean Gaven. Directed by Alex Joffe. Screenplay, Auguste Le Breton, Gabriel Arout, Joffe; camera, Pierre Montazel; editor, Leonide Azar. At Paris, Paris. Running time, **105 MINS.**

Vicky	Nadja Tiller
Marcel	Robert Hossein
Yoko	Silvia Montfort
Bug	Roger Hanin
Le Pirate	Pierre Blanchar
Berthe	Francoise Rosay
James	Jean Gaven

Film coasts on the name of its hit predecessor "Rififi," but has neither the feel nor original mounting to equal. It has some violence and the usual incisive detailing of a robbery to make this an okay gangster entry with possible exploitation chances abroad.

Here the plan is to rob the supposedly burglar-proof Bank of Belgium. It is done, but gangland feuds wipe out everybody for the usual "crime does not pay" tag. Director Alex Joffe has larded this with okay scuffles, erotics and suspense during the robbery, but it lacks the zest to make this more than a gangster opus with corresponding dualer chances offshore.

Acting is good but can do little with the sketchy characterizations. Technical credits are topnotch. *Mosk.*

Ce Corps Tant Desire
(This Desired Body) (FRENCH)

Paris, June 2.

Fernand Rivers release of SB-Chaillot production. Stars Belina Lee, Dany Carrel, Daniel Gelin, Maurice Ronet; features Jane Marken, Balpetre. Directed by Luis Saslavsky. Screenplay, Juliette Saint Giniez; camera, Pierre Petit; editor, Marinette Cadix. At Normandie, Paris. Running time, **105 MINS.**

Lina	Belinda Lee
Guillaume	Daniel Gelin
Henri	Maurice Ronet
Marinette	Dany Carrel
Father	Balpetre
Mother	Jane Marken

Pic is a sort of laborious version of "And God Created Woman" sans the snap and jolt of the latter. Result is a fairly plodding vehicle with some exploitation factors on its theme and sex scenes. Otherwise, its literary tone and unshaped characters limit this for stronger chances abroad.

Two half-brothers fall for a prostie. One marries her. The pic then denotes the frictions set up in the home until the girl realizes that one really loves her in spite of what she was. Film has a good production gloss but actors can not do much with their unclear roles. On-the-spot lensing in a little fishing village helps. *Mosk.*

Born to Be Loved

Low-budget double-biller, nice approach although not much else.

Hollywood, June 5.

Universal release produced, directed and written by Hugo Haas. Stars Carol Morris, Vera Vague, Hugo Haas; introduces Dick Kallman. Camera, Maury Gerstman; music, Franz Steininger; editor, Stefan Arnsten. Previewed at the studio, June 1, '59. Running time, **82 MINS.**

Dorothy	Carol Morris
Mrs. Hoffman	Vera Vague
Prof. Brauner	Hugo Haas
Eddie	Dick Kallman
Dame	Jacqueline Fontaine
Drunk's Wife	Billie Bird
Saxophone	Pat Goldin
Drunk	Robert C. Foulk
Woman	Mary Esther Denver
Mother	Margot Baker
Fred	Tony Jochim

Although "Born To Be Loved" isn't very well written or acted, it cannot be discounted entirely. Inexpensively made by Hugo Haas as an independent, Universal has now bought it for double-bill booking. Despite limitations, there's a certain charm about it, a refreshing change from the resolutely drab and determinedly downbeat.

Haas' screenplay, which he produced and directed, and in which he stars, has to do with romance. Carol (Miss Universe) Morris is a bespectacled seamstress who can't even make a dress to fit herself, judging by the sacks with which her prize-winning figure is masked throughout the film. Haas is a music teacher, her neighbor. He tries to lighten her life by promoting a romance between her and his pupil, Dick Kallman. She, in turn, lightens his life by promoting a romance for him with a wealthy widow, Vera Vague. All ends happily with a double wedding.

Haas' production has a naivete about it that reaches way back to the early days of films. For the locale of his central action, Haas has a gemuhtlich tenement such as hasn't been seen for years in films and probably longer in real life. The halls are always clogged with the residents, gossiping, haranguing, meddling. There is an artless approach to humans and their problems that goes back to some of the Viennese comedy-dramas done early in the century. Haas' point is that love does triumph, that it can exist in innocence and goodwill, and that it can be portrayed without dropping the shoulder straps.

This is a delicate dish for audiences weaned on stronger meat. And it is not very well done, in truth. Miss Morris is appealing, and her romantic vis-a-vis, Dick Hallman, has possibilities. Vera Vague comes on strongly. Her style is at variance with Haas' general aim, but it livens things considerably. Haas, as always when directing himself, tends to underplay.

"Born To Be Loved" is not a good picture from any standpoint except its approach. This is fresh despite its perennial use. It will be a welcome addition to double-billing, and it is one of the few low-budget films that can safely be used with all audiences. *Powe.*

The Angry Hills
(C'SCOPE)

Espionage-underground yarn. Confusing treatment indicates mild b.o.

Hollywood, June 5.

Metro release of Raymond Stross production. Stars Robert Mitchum; co-stars Stanley Baker, Elisabeth Mueller, Gia Scala. Directed by Robert Aldrich, Screenplay, A. I. Bezzerides; based on the book by Leon Uris; camera, Stephen Dade; music, Richard Bennett; editor, Peter Tanner. Previewed at the studio, May 29, '59. Running time, **105 MINS.**

Michael Morrison	Robert Mitchum
Lisa	Elisabeth Mueller
Konrad Heisler	Stanley Baker
Eleftheria	Gia Scala
Tassos	Theodore Bikel
Chesney	Sebastian Cabot
Leonidas	Peter Illing
Ray Taylor	Leslie Phillips
Dr. Stergiou	Donald Wolfit
Comdr. Oberg	Marius Goring
Maria	Jackie Lane
Andreas	Kieron Moore
Papa Panos	George Pastell
Bluey	Patrick Jordan
Kleopatra	Marita Constantiou
Tavern Proprietor	Stanley Van Beers
Papa Philibos	Alec Mango

What Robert Aldrich apparently was attempting, in story and in treatment, was the kind of espionage-intrigue film that the Europeans frequently do so well. That he does not succeed is due partly to script deficiencies and inadequacies, but also to the overall conception of the story. The Raymond Stross production for Metro has some fair names, but it is not likely to stir much interest.

A. I. Bezzerides did the screenplay from a novel by Leon Uris. The setting is Greece at the time it was overwhelmed by the German-Italian invasion of the Balkans. The plotting is extremely complicated and the characters are attempts at more than the usual two-dimensional seen in melodrama. Perhaps in book form there were subtleties that were made credible. In screenplay they seem to have been condensed or crystallized with results that are surprising and, in some cases, surely unintentional. One, for instance, is that the head of the Gestapo in Greece emerges as a likable, troubled thinker, in all a sympathetic character.

Robert Mitchum plays an American war correspondent trying to get out of Greece. Even for the conventional portrait of the cynical U. S. reporter, Mitchum seems to have few qualms. He agrees to take $20,000 to deliver the names of the Greek underground to British intelligence in London. A chase develops in which the pro-Nazis try to get the list and the anti-Nazis try to get Mitchum out of the country.

Although the screenplay is loose and untidy, Aldrich's direction has not done much to tighten it up. He takes good advantage of his Greek locations. His casting is good. But he sometimes sacrifices movement and story to the background. Scenes in a Greek convent, for instance, while atmospheric, are otherwise unrewarding, and atmosphere by that time should have been implicit.

Mitchum's character is never defined, or very pleasing. Gia Scala, as a peasant girl, does not achieve much interest because her role is not very interesting. Elisabeth Mueller is so vivid in her few scenes that she seems a likely bet for further work, particularly with today's international casting. Stanley Baker plays the Gestapo chief, a thoroughly agreeable fellow. Kieron Moore, Theodore Bikel, Donald Wolfit and Marius Goring are acceptable as conspirators on both sides, and Sebastian Cabot is a standout as another.

Stephen Dade's camera work seems to have been done largely at night, under adverse lighting conditions. Richard Bennett's music is often strikingly effective. *Powe.*

Oh! Que Mambo

Paris, June 2.

Boreal release of Peg production. Stars Dario Moreno; features Magali Noel, Alberto Sordi, Jean Poiret, Michel Serrault, Duvalles. Directed by John Berry. Screenplay, Rene Masson, Jean Aurel, Yvan Audouard; camera, Paul Cotteret; editor, Genevieve Vaury; music, Guy Magenta. At Triomphe, Paris. Running time, **85 MINS.**

Dario	Dario Moreno
Liliane	Magali Noel
Nando	Alberto Sordi
Detective	Jean Poiret
Inspector	Michel Serrault

This trifling pic was made for hefty pop singer Dario Moreno who acquits himself well as a bankteller who becomes a singer. But the simple treatment and familiar tale rank this mainly a bet for France.

Director John Berry has kept this moving and inserted some good comic shenanigans. However, this could not overcome the lacklustre material. Support and technical credits are average as is the music. *Mosk.*

John Paul Jones
(COLOR; TECHRIAMA)

Big, long, slow historical pic. B.O. fair.

Hollywood, June 12.

Warner Bros. release of Samuel Bronston production. Stars Robert Stack; co-stars Marisa Pavan, Charles Coburn, Erin O'Brien. Directed by John Farrow. Screenplay, Farrow and Jesse Lasky Jr.; camera (Technicolor), Michel Kelber; music, Max Steiner; editor, Eda Warren. Previewed at the studio, June 2, '59. Running time, **126 MINS.**

John Paul Jones .... Robert Stack
Aimee de Tellison .... Marisa Pavan
Benjamin Franklin ..... Charles Coburn
Dorothea Danders .... Erin O'Brien
Patrick Henry .... Macdonald Carey
Louis XVI .... Jean Pierre Aumont
Pearson .... Peter Cushing
Marie Antoinette .... Susana Canales
Russian Chamberlain ...... Jorge Riviere
Peter Wooley .... Tom Brannum
Gunner Lowrie .... Bruce Cabot
Sir William Young .... Basil Sydney
Duncan MacBean .... Archie Duncan

"John Paul Jones" has some spectacular sea action scenes and achieves some freshness in dealing with the Revolutionary War, a period seldom explored in motion pictures. But the Samuel Bronston production for Warner Bros. doesn't get much fire-power into its characters. They end, as they begin, as historical personages rather than human being.

Photographed in remarkably faithful Technicolor and Technirama, the film could be shortened drastically and tightened to give it better pace and emphasis. The strong portions would then show to better advantage and eliminate the drag of unnecessary plotting.

John Farrow's direction of such scenes as the battle of Jones' Bon Homme Richard with the British Serapis is fine, colorful and exciting. Perhaps because Jones himself was a man of action, the story gets stiff and awkward when it moves off the quarterdeck and into the drawing room.

The screenplay, by Farrow and Jesse Lasky Jr., attempts to give the story contemporary significance by opening and closing with shots of the present U. S. Navy, emphasizing the tradition Jones began almost single-handed. The interim picks up Jones as a Scottish boy who runs away to sea, becomes a sea captain, and winds up in the American colonies as they prepare for the War of Independence.

The Farrow-Lasky screenplay is interestingly enough plotted. There is irony in the fact that the young United States attempting to throw off British bureaucracy, gets ensnarled itself in the same kind of nepotism. Jones' struggles to be allowed to fight the British are genuine and interesting.

On the other hand, the historical figures tend to be stiff or unbelievable. Charles Coburn, as Benjamin Franklin, has a fussy charm, and Macdonald Carey, as Patrick Henry, is good. However, the treatment of Washington is stagey (shot entirely from his back), and the brief appearance of Bette Davis as Catherine the Great of Russia is the cliche portrait of that vigorous empress, a woman bordering on nymphomania.

Jones has two romances in the story, one with a high-born Virginian, Erin O'Brien, and another with a titled Frenchwoman of the bar sinister, Marisa Pavan. Neither is very convincing, and in both cases Jones is thwarted because of his plebeian background.

Robert Stack in the title role gives a robust portrayal. Miss Pavan is sweet but rather lifeless, while Jean Pierre Aumont, as Louis XVI, seems a stronger monarch than the usual portrait of that doomed king. Others who register include David Farrar, Peter Cushing, Tom Brannum, Bruce Cabot, Thomas Gomez, Mitchell Kowal and Eric Pohlmann. Two youngsters, John Charles Farrow and Patrick Villiers, do very well.

Michel Kelber's Technirama camera work is fine, and so is Max Steiner's score. *Powe.*

Tarzan's Greatest Adventure
(EASTMAN COLOR)

A knock-'em-down, drag-'em-out jungle yarn which Tarzan fans will eat up.

Hollywood, June 8.

Paramount release of a Sy Weintraub-Harvey Hayutin Production. Stars Gordon Scott, Anthony Quayle, Sara Shane. Produced by Sy Weintraub. Directed by John Guillermin. Screenplay by Bernie Giler and John Guillermin, from a story by Les Crutchfield; camera, Ted Scaife; music, Douglas Gamley; editor, Bert Rule. Previewed at the studio, June 8, '59. Running time, **90 MINS.**

Tarzan .... Gordon Scott
Slade .... Anthony Quayle
Angie .... Sara Shane
Kreiger .... Niall MacGinnis
O'Bannion .... Sean Connery
Dino .... Al Mulock
Toni .... Scilla Gabel

Tarzan, one of the Dark Continent's more celebrated natives, finally has stepped away from Hollywood's process screens to pound his chest amid authentic terrors in the heart of Africa. The authenticity pays off, and "Tarzan's Greatest Adventure," a Sy Weintraub-Harvey Hayutin Production for Paramount release, is wholesale violence. While the corn runs deep, so does the blood, making the film a hearty boxoffice prospect.

In 90 Eastman Color minutes death and trauma are the stars, and the supporting players are bullets, arrows, knives, hatchets, dynamite, neck-choking paraphernalia, crocodiles, lions, snakes, spiders, boulders, spikes, pits, quicksand and prickly cactus. It's a furious affair, with an exciting chase or two, and it's packed to the hilt with exploitable gore.

Tarzan, as played by Gordon Scott, is a modern he-man, still adorned in loincloth but more conversational than Edgar Rice Burroughs pictured him. It has even gotten to the point that the now-famous Tarzan posture and yell seem almost out of time and place. Scott puts little emotion into his greatest adventure, but he swings neatly from tree to tree, takes good care of a crocodile, even if it does appear dead from the start, deciphers with ease the sounds of his animal friends and, more than anything else, looks the part.

"Greatest Adventure" was screenplayed by Bernie Giler and director John Guillermin from a story by Les Crutchfield. The drama is subordinate to the danger, and the script makes no bones about giving Tarzan fans what Tarzan fans want. Guillermin's direction brings out occasionally interesting performances, but, for the most part, the screenplay's stereotypes remain so. His direction of the high action, however, results in some rather exciting footage.

Film's storyline has Tarzan and another white man as mortal enemies. The antagonist, as played by Anthony Quayle, is leading a five-member boat expedition to get rich in diamonds, and Tarzan, knowing of his bestial attitude, follows in hot pursuit. An approximately beautiful female, Sara Shane, drops out of the sky to tag along with Tarzan and turns out to be quite handy in helping the apeman through a bad time or two. And, whether by Tarzan's hand or their own, the five diamond seekers, including a blonde Italian beauty, are done in.

Quayle is excellent as the scar-faced villain, and Niall MacGinnis as a nearly blind diamond expert is equally fine. Sean Connery and Al Mulock, the two other male members of the expedition, are okay, and Scilla Gabel, looking like a miniature Sophia Loren, is easy to look at. Miss Shane, nearly as unemotional as Tarzan, does display a light touch and a luscious mood that adds a spark and a good deal of interest along the way.

Ted Scaife's color photography is first-rate, with an off-beat angle here and there. Art direction by Michael Stringer, editing by Bert Rule and music by Douglas Gamley are fine, and sound, recorded by Charles Knott and Bob Jones, is outstanding enough to be one of the "Greatest Adventure's" greatest additions. *Ron.*

The Heart of a Man
(BRITISH)

Frankie Vaughan provides some marquee appeal in this light yarn about a down-and-out sailor who becomes a disk star; set against a London background of night life and gambling.

London, June 9.

Rank release of an Anna Neagle production. Stars Frankie Vaughan, Anne Heywood, Tony Britton. Directed by Herbert Wilcox. Screenplay, Jack Trevor Story and Pamela Bower from story by Rex North; camera, Reginald Wyer; editor, Basil Warren; music, Wally Stott. At RFD Private Theatre, London. Running time, **92 MINS.**

Frankie .... Frankie Vaughan
Julie .... Anne Heywood
Tony .... Tony Britton
Bud .... Peter Sinclair
Sid .... Michael Medwin
Johnnie .... Anthony Newley
Razor .... Harry Fowler
Charlie .... George Rose
Oscar .... Harold Kasket
Cha Cha .... Vanda
As Themselves .... Leslie Mitchell,
Kent Walton, Hogan "Kid" Bassey

"The Heart of A Man" is Frankie Vaughan's fourth starring pic for Anna Neagle and his personality should guarantee a sturdy success in family houses in the U.K. and some U.S. spots. "Heart" is shrewdly designed to exploit his growing stature as a film star. But, wisely, Miss Neagle has not put all her eggs in the Vaughan basket. She has assembled a very sound cast around him. Result is an amiable romantic comedy, with three hep pop songs injected for good measure.

It's a London yarn with a background of the West End smart set, night life and show biz. The setting and the slightly bizarre characters have the ring of authenticity about them which is not surprising since the story-line is written by Rex North, widely read columnist, whose beat is largely the swagger joints of the world's capitals and the offbeat folk who haunt them. The racy dialog is the verbal coinage that is tossed around the West End saloons, niteries and theatres.

Though slim, North's story line is entertaining. Unfortunately the screenplay of Jack Trevor Story and Pamela Bower introduces no surprises; hence, the situations and reactions of the characters are predictable throughout. There are two or three irrelevant scenes (notably one on a race-track) which are apparently written into the film merely to drop a couple of gags. These criticisms apart, "Heart" stands up as an acceptable vehicle for Vaughan.

Vaughan is a down-and-out seaman who eventually becomes a top disk and tv singer. He is inspired by a chance meeting with an eccentric hobo on the Embankment and by his love for a night club singer whom he meets when he is a bouncer for a shady character running gambling parties on a ship in the Thames. The singing angle enables Vaughan to put over three songs which stand a good chance of clicking in the popularity parade . . . "The Heart Of A Man," "Sometime, Somewhere" and "Walking Tall." "Sometime Somewhere" is a particularly attractive ditty, marred in one instance by a dream dance sequence in which, accompanied by a celestial choir, Vaughan and Anne Heywood uneasily and gingerly dance on clouds that look rather like a white detergent. This scene is readily expendable.

Vaughan's virile personality, sense of humor and singing voice carry him easily through his role. Miss Heywood is a fittingly attractive heroine even though for much of the time she has merely to register admiration for her boy friend. She also sings one number with charm and poise.

The major acting contribution comes from Anthony Newley, who is wryly funny as an absent-minded, opportunistic 10-percenter. He garners yocks with accomplished ease. Tony Britton is a debonair and handsome crook who runs the gambling parties and clashes with Vaughan over Miss Heywood. Michael Medwin, Harry Fowler and George Rose also score as his henchmen. Harold Kasket is a superb amalgam of every West End night club owner while Peter Sinclair brings some homespun philosophy and a touch of pathos as the eccentric hobo.

Herbert Wilcox's direction is straighforward and polished while Reginald Wyer's photography is excellent. Those familiar with the slick world against which "The Heart Of A Man" is staged will get a lot of quiet amusement out of identifying the types pinpointed by the author. Those to whom the world of Mayfair is a closed book should also get fun out of a peep at a luxury and seemingly incredible strata of society which does, in fact, exist. *Rich.*

The Legend of Tom Dooley

Good, grim little enactment of the pop song. Teener draw especially good.

Hollywood, June 12.

Columbia release of Stan Shpetner production. Features Michael Landon, Jo Morrow, Jack Hogan, Richard Rust, Dee Pollock, Ken Lynch. Directed by Ted Post. Screenplay, Stan Shpetner; camera, Gilbert Warrenton; music, Ronald Stein; "Tom Dooley" sung by the Kingston Trio; editor, Robert S. Eisen. Previewed at the studio, June 11, '59. Running time, **79 MINS.**

Tom Dooley .... Michael Landon
Laura .... Jo Morrow
Charlie Grayson .... Jack Hogan
Country Boy .... Richard Rust
Abel .... Dee Pollock
Father .... Ken Lynch
Sheriff .... Howard Wright
Doc Henry .... Ralph Moody
Lieutenant .... John Cliff
Meg .... Cheerio Meredith
The Kid .... Gary Hunley
Preacher .... Anthony Jochim

Confederate Soldier	Jeff Marris
Frank	Jason Johnson
Bix	Joe Yrigoyen
Rand	Sandy Sanders
1st Old Maid	Juney Ellis
2nd Old Maid	Maudie Prickett

This film was obviously planned as an exploitation item to cash in on the popularity of the song, but it has turned out to be something else. It is, surprisingly, a tragedy in concept and execution. That it is a serious film, and a good one, should not be a deterrent, however. It will stand up very comfortably as a strong double-bill item with special appeal for younger fans.

Stan Shpetner's production and Ted Post's direction do not always live up to the high concept of the project. The film slips from time to time, and the way is made more slippery by lines from the heroine such as "I always wondered what it was that made a girl into a woman, now I know." These lapses, however, are minor, and they are only noticeable because the rest of the film sets a high standard.

The screenplay by Shpetner follows the theme of the song almost exactly. Three young Confederates, Michael Landon, Richard Rust and Dee Pollock, are behind-the-lines raiders. They discover after they have ambushed a Yankee stagecoach and killed two Union soldiers that the war is over. What's legal killing in wartime, is murder in peacetime, and if the boys are caught by the nearest authorities they will swing for their work. They must flee to the South, but first Dooley (Landon) wants to get his Northern girl, Jo Morrow. He gets through to her and they elope, but as in the song, the girl is accidentally killed and Landon is apprehended. The final scene shows him being led off —"Hang Down Your Head, Tom Dooley; Poor Boy, You're Gonna Die." And he does.

Shpetner and Post deserve a great deal of credit for their handling of the theme and the story. The young men are believable in the inevitable situation in which they become involved. There seems, without straining, a relation between these youths and the frustrated younger men of today.

Landon is particularly fine as the title character, and he gets good support from Richard Rust, another interesting young actor. Jo Morrow is capable as the girl involved, and other cast members who contribute include Jack Hogan, Dee Pollock, Ken Lynch, Ralph Moody, Cheerio Meredith and Gary Hunley.

Gilbert Warrenton's camera work, Ronald Stein's music, and Robert S. Eisen's film editing are all plus factors. *Powe.*

Son of Robin Hood
(CINEMASCOPE—COLOR)

Deserves top billing in action houses. Good production values; interesting story.

Hollywood, June 16.

Twentieth-Fox release of Argo Film Production. Stars David Hedison, June Laverick, David Farrar, Marius Goring. Produced and directed by George Sherman. Story and screenplay, George George and George Slavin; camera, Arthur Grant; editor, Alan Osbiston; music, Leighton Lucas. Previewed at the studio, June 16, '59. Running time, **81 MINS.**

Jamie	David Hedison
Deering	June Laverick
Des Roches	David Farrar
Chester	Marius Goring
Dorchester	Philip Friend
Sylvia	Delphi Lawrence
Alan Adale	George Colouris
Little John	George Woodbridge
Blunt	Humphrey Lestocq
Prioress	Noel Hood
Constance	Shelagh Fraser

A novel twist, insuring attention along Sherwood Forest's Cinema-Scope path, is that "Son of Robin Hood" is a girl. The color film, made in Britain for 20th-Fox, is a good compromise between desired spectacle and required budget, and, while the only name of note is Robin's, the pic should fare well in the action market.

Although the action isn't as dashing as it was in the Errol Flynn days, it's fast enough to hold the juvenile trade in a flurry of bows and arrows and swords. Producer-director George Sherman successfully has captured the period, putting it to good work in the George George-George Slavin screenplay.

David Hedison is a strong hero, intriguingly youthful yet sufficiently mature. He shows a good deal of promise which 20th should continue to develop.

"Son of Robin Hood," as have most of the Sherwood Forest yarns before it, sets out to save England from a beastly heel who has his eyes set on the throne. He comes bloody well close to being crowned, too, when the departed Robin Hood's followers pledge themselves to the coronation of the young prince. But green hats and bows notwithstanding, the followers need a new leader. To head their revival, they send for Deering Hood, the son Robin sired, but Deering turns out to be a daughter. She's brave, a whiz with an arrow and wholly capable of saving England, but the Sherwood advisors feel it's a man's job, pick Hedison for the job, and England is saved.

June Laverick, as Deering, has a lovely quality and adeptly puts it to work through her courage and well-meaning jealousies. David Farrar, as the villain, and Marius Goring, as the regent, are very good, with equally fine work from Philip Friend, Delphi Lawrence, George Colouris and George Woodbridge.

The George-Slavin screenplay, from their original story, is carefully laid out, giving full vent to rapid action, and Sherman's direction of both the intimate scenes and the fights is excellent. He is assisted in good measure by fine technical work from cinematographer Arthur Grant, art director Norman Arnold, film editor Alan Osbiston, soundman Don Weeks and composer Leighton Lucas. *Ron.*

Alive and Kicking
(BRITISH)

Pleasantly diverting comedy about three old ladies who run away from an old folks' home; good entertainment for family audiences, but lacking in U.S. marquee value.

London, June 23.

Associated-British Pathe release of a Victor Skutezky production. Stars Sybil Thorndike, Kathleen Harrison, Estelle Winwood, Stanley Holloway. Directed by Cyril Frankel. Screenplay by Denis Cannan, based on idea by William Dinner, William Morum; camera, Gilbert Taylor; editor, Bernard Gribble; music, Philip Green. Previewed at Studio One, London. Running time, **95 MINS.**

Dora	Sybil Thorndike
Rosie	Kathleen Harrison
Mabel	Estelle Winwood
MacDonagh	Stanley Holloway
Matron	Joyce Carey
Russian Captain	Eric Pohlmann
Birdwatcher	Colin Gordon
Solicitor	John Salew
Old Man	Liam Redmond
Old Woman	Marjorie Rhodes
The Lovers	Richard Harris, Olive McFarland
Postmistress	Anita Sharp Bolster
Postman	Paul Farrell
Policeman	Patrick McAlinney
Little Boy	Raymond Manthorpe
Villagers	Tony Quinn, Harry Hutchinson
Singers	Brendan O'Dowda, Joseph MacNally

"Alive and Kicking" is a pleasantly diverting comedy which makes up in good humor what it lacks in wit. It should be a click with most family audiences though lacking in marquee value for U.S. consumption.

It was inspired casting to bring together Sybil Thorndike, Estelle Winwood and Kathleen Harrison, whose combined ages total 214 years. They play devoted friends who, when they are about to be split up, run away from the Sunset Old Folks' Home. They evade a full-scale search by the police, army, air force and navy, reach the coast, escape in a speed boat and are picked up by a Russian trawler. Because of language difficulties they are nearly whisked off to Russia, but instead are put ashore on what turns out to be a remote, uncivilized Irish island.

There they meet a wealthy American who has bought three cottages for his retirement. He disappears, and believing he has been drowned, the old ladies decide to take over the cottages and pretend that they are his nieces. Also, that their uncle is too ill to be seen by the islanders. At first the simple villagers are suspicious of the women but eventually get to like them especially when they organize a knitting industry which brings prosperity to the island. Of course, the American turns up in time to save the old ladies from exposure, he adopts them as nieces, becomes a partner in the knitting business and everything winds up cosily.

Simplicity is the keynote of this engaging little film. The dialog and situations lack subtlety having to do largely with Irish whimsey. Such spectacles as the villagers getting loaded at a whisky party, Miss Thorndike clambering down a cliff to gather gulls' eggs and the Russian sailors becoming complicated in their efforts to talk with the old ladies are highlights. But though there is not a great deal of inventiveness in either writing or direction, the film is carried along cheerfully by the sheer exuberance of the cast, and particularly the four stars.

The Misses Thorndike, Winwood and Harrison, with their contrasting forms of humor, blend into a formidable trio while Stanley Holloway plays the American with appropriate breeziness. Eric Pohl-mann makes a brief but effective appearance as the Russian sea captain. Colin Gordon is also on hand with one of his amusing cameos as a bird-watcher. The Irish villagers are conventional types, outstanding being Liam Redmond and Marjorie Rhodes, Patrick McAlinney, a comic policeman; and Richard Harris and Olive McFarland, as a pair of young lovers.

The film was largely shot in a remote Scottish island with the result that the locale had an authentic "out-of-this-world" atmosphere. Gilbert Taylor's black and white lensing made the best of the scenery, though the film fairly shrieks for color. Philip Green has contributed a lively score and, with Michael Carr, has served up some pleasant Irish songs plus one zestful title song. Denis Cannan's screenplay starts off briskly but then settles down to an appropriate leisurely pace. "Alive" and Kicking" is a totally unambitious piece of work but it offers a full quota of yocks and smiles. *Rich.*

Diez Fusiles Esperan
(10 Ready Rifles)
(HISPANO-ITALIAN)

Madrid, June 16.

Dipenfa release of a Procusa-Chapalo coproduction with Domizana Internazionale of Rome. Stars Paco Rabal, Ettore Manni, Rosita Arena; features Berta Riaza, Memmo Carotenuto, Felix de Pomes, Milly Vitale. Directed by Saenz de Heredia. Screenplay by Carlos Blanco; camera, Francisco Sempere; art director, Ramiro Gomez; music, Tomas Garbizu and Francisco Escudero. At Palacio de la Prensa, Madrid. Running time, **95 MINS.**

One of history's strange wars, the Carlist fracas of the 1830's identified the enemy as a gentleman with opposing views. This distinction hindered the valiant attempt by director Saenz de Heredia and scripter Carlos Blanco to create war-torn emotions and characters.

Despite the many creditable film values in this yarn of a demoralized Carlist officer who deserts and later reneges on a promise to face an enemy firing squad in exchange for overnight freedom. the principal theme of the officer's reintegration with honor and a sense of duty (returning to face the rifles) goes astray. Recovered ideals spring from the final reel in a flurry of melodrama.

Paco Rabal, as an undermined Carlist, continues to reveal maturing screen talent. Italo Ettore Manni convinces as the idealist brother officer who uses fists with telling didactic effect on Rabal. Budget no doubt accounts for Milly Vitale's brief role though she would have added femme vitality to the lead role played by Mexico's Rosita Arenas. Berta Riaza, Memmo Carotenuto and Felix de Pomes offer effective support.

Saenz de Heredia's direction, Sampere's lensing and the authenticity of Navarran background give "Rifles" a sustained quality. Film will not draw salvos as the Spanish entry at Berlin Film Fest but with the stars' selling power should do biz in European sectors and Latin America. *Werb.*

Pier 5, Havana

Cuban timeliness boosts chances for routinely-plotted tale.

Hollywood, June 19.

United Artists release of Robert E. Kent production. Stars Cameron Mitchell; features Allison Hayes, Eduardo Noriega, Michael Granger, Logan Field, Nestor Paiva. Directed by Edward L. Cahn.

Screenplay, James B. Gordon; story,
Joseph Hoffman; camera, Maury Gerts-
man; editor, Grant Wyhtock. Previewed
June 18, '59. Running time, 68 MINS.

Steve Daggett .... Cameron Mitchell
Monica Gray .... Allison Hayes
Fernando Ricardo .... Eduardo Noriega
Lt. Garcia .... Michael Granger
Hank Miller .... Logan Field
Lopez .... Nestor Paiva
Schluss .... Otto Waldis
Sergeant .... Paul Fierro
1st Man .... Edward Foster
2nd Man .... Ken Terrell
Monica's Maid .... Donna Dale
General .... Vincent Padula
Capt. Emilio .... Fred Engelberg
Pablo .... Rick Vallin
Radio Operator .... Walter Kray
Burly Man .... Joe Yrigoyan

One of the first releases to take
advantage of the Cuban revolution
aftermath, "Pier 5, Havana" will
probably garner higher grosses in
program market via exploitation
than its routine plot merits. Uninspired handling keeps pace at a
monotone, but timeliness of subject matter will help its b.o.
chances.

Robert E. Kent production twirls
around Cameron Mitchell, an
American, arriving in Havana to
locate an old friend who has disappeared during revolution, and
landing squarely in the midst of a
plot by a group of Batistas to
overthrow the Castro government.
He gets assistance from the
Cuban police, and in climax is responsible for breakup of the plotters.

Direction by Edward L. Cahn
doesn't give much color to the
James B. Gordon screenplay, and
Mitchell emerges as a pretty
stodgy character. Allison Hayes, as
his former girl-friend now wed to
the missing man, lends distaff interest, and Michael Granger is
okay as the Havana police lieutenant who comes to Mitchell's aid.
Eduardo Noriega, leader of opposition group, and Logan Field, missing man whom plotters force to
convert stolen planes into bombers, are capable.

Technical departments, headed
by Maury Gertsman's excellent
photography, are well executed.
                              Whit.

Left, Right and Centre
(BRITISH)

**Brisk light-hearted comedy
about a by-election; excellent
work by Ian Carmichael &
Alastair Sim, making pica
surefire yock-raiser over here.**

London, June 23.
British Lion release of a Launder-Gilliat
production. Stars Ian Carmichael, Alastair
Sim; features Richard Wattis, Patricia
Bredin, Eric Barker. Directed by Sidney
Gilliat. Screenplay by Sidney Gilliat from
story by Gilliat and Val Valentine; cam-
era, Gerald Gibbs; editor, Geoffrey Foot;
music, Humphrey Searle. Previewed at
Studio One, London. Running time, 95
MINS.

Stella Stoker .... Patricia Bredin
Bert Glimmer .... Eric Barker
Bill Hemingway .... Jack Hedley
Alf Stoker .... Leslie Dwyer
Mr. Bray .... Russell Waters
Woman in Car .... Hattie Jacques
Robert Wilcot .... Ian Carmichael
Harding-Pratt .... Richard Wattis
Annabel .... Moyra Fraser
Pottle .... William Kendall
Egerton .... George Benson
Peterson .... Anthony Sharp
Grimsby-Armfield ...... Moultrie Kelsall
Lord Wilcot .... Alastair Sim
Hardy .... Gordon Harker
Dr. Rushall .... Frederick Leister
Mayor .... John Salew
Bastingdtoke .... Bill Shine
TV Interviewer .... Jeremy Hawke
Mrs. Maggs .... Irene Handl
TV Panel.... Eamonn Andrews, Gilbert
    Harding, Josephine Douglas,
                        Carole Carr

It may well be that "Left Right
and Centre" will prove too parochial for the U.S. and it probably
lacks star value for American

tastes. But in Britain, this light-
hearted skit on British politics
should prove a b.o. champ. It ripples along gaily, is short enough
for its slim joke not to become labored, has a sharp sense of fun,
quite a lot of wit and, in addition,
has a well-stacked and reliable cast
of pop British players to make the
most of the dialog and situations.

Sidney Gilliat and Val Valentine
have dreamed up a simple enough
idea, that of Cupid playing merry
havoc with a local bye-election.
Standing for the Conservatives is
Ian Carmichael, an amiable tv
panel-game celebrity who has been
put up by his uncle as a boost for
his very commercialized "stately
home." Carmichael's Socialist opponent is Patricia Bredin, pretty
daughter of a Billingsgate fish-
merchant.

The two fall for each other and
the film largely consists of the
frantic efforts of their respective
agents to throw a monkey-wrench
into the romance which is threatening to blow up the entire election
campaign.

Gilliat's screenplay and direction
never flag. He gets in some neat
digs at television, politics and the
present craze for turning aristocratic homes into peep-shows.
Among the particularly hilarious
sequences are a tour of the Stately
Home, a romantic mixup in a maze,
and a wordy match between the
two candidates at a public meeting.
Many of the gags and situations are
irrelevant, but they all add up to
a good-humored piece of nonsense.

The producers owe a great deal
to their cast, headed by Carmichael
and Alastair Sim. Carmichael, one
of Britain's best exponents of light,
charming throwaway comedy, is in
topnotch form as the lovesick Tory
while Sim is richly funny as the
opportunistic peer with a heart
shaped like a cash-register. Patricia Bredin is a comparative newcomer but a welcome fresh, attractive face.

Two heavy parts are filled by
Richard Wattis, as Carmichael's
political agent, and Eric Barker,
as his Socialist counterpart. Their
two styles of comedy blend admirably. Moyra Fraser, stage revue
artist, etches in a sharp and witty
portrayal of a dumb but shapely
model with a yen for Carmichael.
Anthony Sharp, George Benson,
Gordon Harker, Bill Shine and
Jack Hedley are among a long
string of other feature players who
contribute effectively to this bright
pic. Gerald Gibbs' lensing, John
Box's artwork and authentic locations all help towards a smooth
piece of work.   Rich.

The Man Who Could
Cheat Death
(COLOR)

**Well-made by rather mild hor-
ror item.**

Hollywood, June 19.
Paramount release of Hammer Production. Stars Anton Diffring, Hazel Court,
Christopher Lee. Produced by Michael
Carreras. Directed by Terence Fisher.
Screenplay, Jimmy Sangster; based on a
play by Barre Lyndon; camera (Technicolor), Jack Asher; music, Richard Bennett; editor, James Needs. Previewed at
the studio, June 16, '59. Running time,
83 MINS.

Georges .... Anton Diffring
Janine .... Hazel Court
Pierre .... Christopher Lee
Ludwig .... Arnold Marle
Margo .... Delphi Lawrence
Legris .... Francis De Wolf

It is apparent from the Hammer
production, "The Man Who Could

Cheat Death," that horror films are
nearing the end of their current
cycle. The Paramount release is
in good Technicolor, it is well-acted
and intelligently conceived. But
invention and imbellishment in
this field appear to have been exhausted. If it is to succeed, "The
Man Who Could Cheat Death" will
have to be heavily exploited.

Horror films are victims of their
own past success. Lavish with
monsters and laced with gore, what
first popped the eyeballs later only
droops the lids. As ever-greater
horror is required, there is less and
less that is horrible enough. "The
Man Who Could Cheat Death" is,
in a sense, hoist by its own bloody
scalpel. Aside from a few macabre
scenes, there is nothing that will
more than ripple the surface sensibilities of even the most impressionable.

Jimmy Sangster's screenplay has
Anton Diffring as the man of the
title. The time of the action is
1902. Diffring, who appears to be
a hale and hearty 35 years of age is
actually 104. He has kept inserting
in trim, he explains, by inserting
into his system the "uter parathy-
roid" gland of living victims. The
fate of the victims finally attracts
the attention of the police and
Diffring is halted in his experiment.

Hammer is the only production
unit concentrating on class horror
films. Like its past successes, "The
Man Who Could Cheat Death" has
nothing foolish about it. Sangster's
intelligent screenplay is directed
seriously and straight by Terence
Fisher. The cast responds with
alacrity. The trouble is as a
straight story it does not have
enough about it to keep it consistently or intermittently interesting. And there's not enough horror
to compensate.

The cast is good, headed by
Diffring, and supported by Hazel
Court as his unwitting fiancee, and
Christopher Lee, an unwilling
accomplice.
Richard Bennett's music has
novelty, particularly in setting the
mood behind the titles.   Powe.

Der Mann, Der Sich
Verkaufte
(The Man Who Sold Himself)
(GERMAN)

Berlin, June 16.
Europa release of Filmaufbau produc-
tion. Stars Hildegard Neff, Hansjoerg
Felmy, Antje Weissgerber, Kurt Ehrhardt,
Katharina Matz, Ernst Schroeder. Di-
rected by Josef von Baky. Screenplay,
Erich Kuby; camera, Friedl Behn-Grundl;
music, Georg Haertzschel. At Atelier am
Zoo, Berlin. Running time, 104 MINS.

An ambitious yarn, competently
directed by Josef von Baky, this
fails to convince because of a very
inadequate script. Film has a remarkably well chosen cast, headed
by Hildegard Neff, which is an
asset. However, commercial
chances appear rather problematical.

Story concerns an ambitious
young reporter of a scandal sheet
who lands a big scoop via writing
an article series about the "dark
past" of a newly rich and now reputable hotel owner. The series
kills the man.

Pic attempts to take sharp aim
at the new German society and
simultaneously at the scandal
press. But the attacks are so exaggerated the whole thing has a false
ring. Thanks to Baky's efficient
direction, there's still a certain
amount of suspense at the start

but he fails to save the pic from
getting dull later on.
Despite his good direction and a
homogenous cast plus fine technical credits, this one rates as a disappointing film on a basically interesting subject. Failure to exploit
all angles is blamed on the writer.
                              Hans.

Le Gendarme De
Champignol
(FRENCH)

Paris, June 22.
Cinedis release of Chronos Film production. Stars Jean Richard, Roger-Pierre;
features Veronique Zuber, Noel Roquevert, Alfred Adam, Nadine Basil. Directed
by Jean Bastia. Screenplay, Roger-Pierre;
camera, Maro Fassard; editor, Jacques
Desagneaux. At Balzac, Paris. Running
time, 95 MINS.

Claudius .... Jean Richard
Vittorio .... Roger-Pierre
Suzette .... Veronique Zuber
Raspec .... Noel Roquevert
Gregorio .... Alfred Adam
Suzette G. .... Nadine Basil

Bucolic comedy about a bumbling
policeman in a little town and an
outlaw he both befriends and
chases has some risible situations
and some adroit comic timing and
emoting by Jean Richard as the cop
and Roger-Pierre as the bandit.
But its sectional humor and accents
has this mainly a local bet with
only chancey possibilities in foreign marts.

Pic is conventional and familiar
but plays along brightly and looks
an okay entry here. Technical
credits are good and assorted
character actors lend nice support
to the principals.   Mosk.

Porgy and Bess
(MUSICAL-TECHNICOLOR-TODD-AO)

Gershwin's folk opera handsomely mounted by Samuel Goldwyn. A big picture.

Columbia release of Samuel Goldwyn production. Features Sidney Poitier, Dorothy Dandridge, Pearl Bailey, Sammy Davis Jr. Directed by Otto Preminger. Based on George Gershwin stage operetta derived from novel of DuBose and Dorothy Heyward. Libretto by DuBose Heyward; lyrics by Heyward and Ira Gershwin. Screenplay by N. Richard Nash. Camera (Technicolor & Todd AO), Leon Shamroy; choreography, Hermes Pan; sets, Oliver Smith; costumes, Irene Sharaff; art direction, Serge Krizman, Joseph Wright. Film editor, Daniel Mandell. Opened June 24, 1959, Warner Theatre, N.Y. Running time, 136 MINS.

Porgy	Sidney Poitier
Bess	Dorothy Dandridge
Sporting Life	Sammy Davis Jr.
Maria	Pearl Bailey
Crown	Brock Peters
Jake	Leslie Scott
Clara	Diahann Carroll
Serena	Ruth Attaway
Peter	Clarence Muse
Annie	Everdinne Wilson
Robbins	Joel Fluellen
Mingo	Earl Jackson
Nelson	Moses La Marr
Lily	Margaret Hairston
Jim	Ivan Dixon
Scipio	Antoine Durousseau
Strawberry	Helen Thigpen
Old Man	Vince Townsend Jr.
Undertaker	William Walker
Frazier	Roy Glenn
Coroner	Maurice Manson
Detective	Claude Akins

As screen entertainment, "Porgy and Bess" retains most of the virtues and some of the libretto traits of this folk opera. It is, of course, an American classic of its genre. Transferred to widescreen and Technicolor in a handsome, intelligent and often gripping production there are the boxoffice questions of (a) the drab story, (b) the opera form, (c) the known fact that all-Negro casts usually run a hard course.

Scaled to $3.75 as a hard ticket at the Warner Theatre, N. Y. the appeal lies in the George Gershwin music and the Samuel Goldwyn name. The film will take selling at these prices.

To recall the truism that "Porgy" is a classic is to suggest some of the built-in prestige values which Goldwyn purchased. The score has had, by now, one of the sustained, long-pull plugs of all time. The familiarity of the beloved music must mean much in momentum, want-to-see sentimental tug and pre-sell aspects. Against that is the unknown X of "Porgy" being an oft-told tale.

The work has exhibited durability. Also somewhat slow catch-on. A novel first in 1925 it became a play in 1927, running 217 performances for the Theatre Guild. The opera version of 1935, also for the Guild, eked out only 124 performances. It was not until the revival, after Gershwin's death, that "Porgy and Bess" came into its own. Since then the folk opera has been widely played around the world, and a hit in Soviet Russia, partly perhaps on its persecuted minority angles.

Suffice that the melodrama of a Charleston waterfront slum, which might otherwise have been forgotten, was elevated into a world favorite, folklorically and operatically, by the Gershwin genius, not overlooking the wonderful lyrics of Brother Ira and DuBose Heyward's book and strong lyrical assist.

Porgy, of course, is a cripple and a beggar, who gets about drawn in a goat cart. Sidney Poitier makes him thoroughly believable though when he opens his voice to sing it is not Poitier but Robert McPherrin. Bess, the incompletely regenerate floozie, is Dorothy Dandridge, but again the voice is another's—Adele Addison. (Neither voice gets screen credit).

The love affair of this oddly-assorted pair has considerable humanity though Miss Dandridge is perhaps too "refined" in type to be quite convincing as the split-skirt, heroin-sniffing tramp. Even so, their tortured but honest try for true love is plausible.

The story ends with Bess lured to New York, a woman of easy persuasion and fragile faith. Porgy then mounts his pathetic goat-cart to drive from South Carolina to Manhattan, in pursuit of her. There is a surviving "heart" quality in this "theatrical" curtain, which wowed 'em in 1927.

There are two villains. First the callous Crown, played with fine arrogance by Brooks Peters. The nasty-worm, Sporting Life, as interpreted by Sammy Davis Jr. seems unduly the vaudevillian and modern hipster—gaining a certain song-and-dance cleverness at some damage to the 1905 period piece quality.

Pearl Bailey is consistently likeable as Maria but has no chance to belt out any vocals. There are a number of the Gershwin "arias" entrusted to Diahann Carroll, Ruth Attaway, Earl Jackson and others. These tend to be sheerly delightful.

Otto Preminger has manipulated the characters in the Catfish Row (of Oliver Smith's design) to develop as much tension and pathos as the N. Richard Nash screenplay (fairly close to the original text) allows. The editing (Daniel Mandell) is tight. The necessities of providing a hard-ticket intermission does interrupt the picture at its maximum momentum and suspense point, with the murderous Crown re-seducing Bess in the tall grass.

If memory serves, many of the old slum life details of the stage production have been faded down, the hawkers' street-cries being notably less prominent. The racial stereotype dangers, more or less implicit in a story where ignorant and exploited denizens of a Dixie black ghetto are involved, have been sterilized in the present production. An exception, perhaps, is the use of the $1.50 "divorce" which Porgy buys for Bess from the outlandish Negro shyster. This scene is right out of the white Southern stock-in-trade of amused condescension and may be resented. In the main, the desperate poverty of Catfish Row is presented sympathetically. Especially compassionate is the saucer funeral for Robbins (Joel Fluellen) after he's killed by the brutal Crown. Both musically and humanely this highly folkloric sequence is one of Preminger's best.

In costuming the Negroes Irene Sharaff has followed a conscious policy. The garb shows them dirt-poor but never dirty. The same may be said of the scenery. So, too, the dialect respects basic dignity. The picnic parade does skirt the sort of high-strutting-in-"Darktown" which the late Octavus Roy Cohen used to write for the Satevepost. However, it is redeemed by Preminger directing to laugh with, not at, the picnickers.

During this cook-out on the Island Davis renders the sardonic, pastor-gibing "'Tain't Necessarily So" but does it three generations too smart. Hermes Pan's choreography is, with this exception, safely subordinated to the time, place and mood.

For ordinary audience purposes the handling of the music by conductor Andre Previn, including a three-minute overture before the story opens, will be deemed professional. Some liberties with the arrangements, in the de-operatizing direction, may irritate the loyal followers of Gershwin who notice such matters.

The production is subordinated to the telling of the tale, with the racial stereotype precautions beforementioned. Leon Shamroy's camera work stands forth. A few of the scenes are idyllic, the storm realistic, and the whole thing top-drawer photography.

The lip-sync work on Poitier and Miss Dandridge is not without flaw and a few other quibbles could be registered. No matter. For much of the way the melodramatics and the tunes are astutely blended for good effect and more than offset this.

Summing up, the two big come-on names here are Gershwin and Goldwyn. A classic has received the high-gloss treatment and should find plenty of admirers. There seems small reason to suppose that the South won't play "Porgy." It is almost entirely self-contained on Catfish Row though a white detective (pretty high-handed) and a white coroner (quite decent) show in the slum in the wake of the murders, one by and one of Crown.

Time alone can report whether the screening of the folk opera adds up to a selective-appeal or a universal-appeal feature. The end-result may fall between. *Land.*

La Bete a L'Affut
(Beast at Bay)
(FRENCH)

Paris, June 30.

Corona release of Trident-Hoche production. Stars Francoise Arnoul, Henri Vidal; features Michael Piccoli, Agnes Laury, Gaby Silvia, Madeleine Barbulee. Directed by Pierre Chenal. Screenplay, Michael Audiard, R.M. Arlaud, Georges Tabet. Andre from novel by Day Kenne; camera, Christian Matras; editor, Suzanne Rondeau. At Paris, Paris. Running time, 90 MINS.

Elizabeth	Francoise Arnoul
Daniel	Henri Vidal
Jacques	Michael Piccoli
Gilberte	Gaby Silvia
Agnes	Agnes Laury
Maria	Madeleine Barbulee

This yarn has been seen before. An escaped con breaks in on a pretty widow and she is soon in love with him. This adds a twist or two to the usual outcome but is sans the feel for character and motivation to make the film plausible. Hence, it emerges mainly a dualer item for offshore chances with exploitation aspects on some nudity by star Francoise Arnoul and some well done love scenes.

Film has some advantages from on-the-spot shooting in a small town and some okay acting and technical aspects. But this lacks the individuality and eclat to make this more than a routine filler both for local and foreign marts.

Mosk.

Anatomy of a Murder

Top-notch courtroom meller. Strong b.o.

Hollywood, June 26.

Columbia release of Carlyle Production produced and directed by Otto Preminger. Stars James Stewart, Lee Remick, Ben Gazzara, Arthur O'Connell, Eve Arden, Kathryn Grant. Screenplay, Wendell Mayes; based on the book by Robert Traver; camera, Sam Leavitt; music, Duke Ellington; editor, Louis R. Loeffler. Previewed at Stanley Warner Theatre, June 19, '59. Running time: 160 MINS.

Paul Biegler	James Stewart
Laura Manion	Lee Remick
Lt. Frederick Manion	Ben Gazzara
Parnell McCarthy	Arthur O'Connell
Maida	Eve Arden
Mary Pilant	Kathryn Grant
Judge Weaver	Joseph N. Welch
Mitch Lodwick	Brooks West
Claude Dancer	George C. Scott
Alphonse Paquette	Murray Hamilton
Dr. Smith	Orsen Bean
Dr. Harcourt	Alexander Campbell
Mr. Burke	Joseph Kearns
Mr. Lemon	Russ Brown
Dr. Dompierre	Howard McNear
Dr. Raschid	Ned Wever
Madigan	Jimmy Conlin
Sgt. Durgo	Ken Lynch
Duane Miller	Don Russ
Court Clerk	Lloyd Le Vasseur
Sheriff Battisfore	Royal Beal
Sulo	John Qualen
An army sergeant	James Waters
Pie-eye	Duke Ellington
Distinguished gentleman	Irving Kupcinet

Not since "Witness For the Prosecution" has there been a courtroom melodrama as beguiling, forceful and enthralling as Otto Preminger's "Anatomy of a Murder." Its mystery is adult, it is complex and confounding, and it is laced with humor and human touches. The Columbia release looks like one of the summer's strong boxoffice contenders.

Preminger got his film on the screen for preview only 21 days after the final shooting on Michigan location, certainly something of a record for a big budget motion picture. This dispatch, commendable as it is, may be one reason why "Anatomy" is over-long at its present length. It could be snipped without losing anything.

There are a few scenes that contain language certainly never before heard in an American film with the Code Seal. Such words as "contraceptive," "climax" (as in the s e x u a l act), "spermatogenisis," and others dealing with the legal technicalities of rape — a point at issue in the trial that is the film's focal point—are likely to be startling and distasteful to many customers. It would be too bad if this lively and absorbing film were to lose trade on points such as these. It seems to be realism for its own sake, rather than for the necessities of the story.

Wendell Mayes' screenplay otherwise, is a large reason for the film's general excellence. In swift, brief strokes it introduces a large number of diverse characters and sets them in motion. An Army lieutenant, Ben Gazzara, has killed a tavern operator whom he suspects of attempting to rape his wife, Lee Remick. James Stewart, former district attorney and now a privately-practicing attorney in a small Michigan city, is engaged for the defense.

Stewart succeeds in proving Gazzara was correct to shoot the usurper, or, at least, is innocent of the first degree murder with which he is charged. So a jury finds, and juries are more often right than not, as one character in the film notes.

Mayes' screenplay, taken from the book by the Michigan judge who uses the nom de plume, Robert Traver, differs in some respects from the novel. Partly through casting, the audience is in considerable doubt about the real innocence of Gazzara and Miss R e m i c k. This handsome young couple astray of the law are far from admirable. Utterly unmoral, they are pleasure-bent and pleasure-battered, as unpredictable as a pair of minks, which they resemble in more ways than one. It is never precisely clear that they are as innocent as Stewart must plead them and as the jury finds.

This does not seem to be the point. The victim of the shooting was not one of nature's gentlemen, either. A trio of unlovely people,

brought together for unlovely purposes, has produced no good end. But it is not to serve them that the law is maintained. The law's majesty is an end in itself, and this does seem to be the point.

Preminger purposely creates situations that flicker with uncertainty, that may be evaluated in different ways. Motives are mixed and dubious, and, therefore, sustain interest. Balancing the fascinating nastiness of the younger players, there is the warmth and intelligence of James Stewart and Arthur O'Connell. Although Stewart doesn't get a girl, in the conventional sense, there is some romantic interest stirred, and he has his best role in years as the sardonically humorous, thoughtful attorney. O'Connell, a bright, but booze-prone Irishman of great charm, is his ally. Although O'Connell's drinking may seem a weakness against the chilly intensity of the younger players, he has reserves of strength they don't know exist. Eve Arden shows that her technique has not been seriously maimed by her stock work in television, and Kathryn Grant gives a dignified and polished performance.

Joseph N. Welch, the Boston attorney, is tremendous as the trial judge. He seems at first to be trying too hard, but he settles down and fills the role completely as the film unwinds. George C. Scott, as the prosecution attorney, has the suave menace of a small-time Torquemada, and the legal and philosophical duel between him and Stewart is instructive to behold. Brooks West is a good comical local legal beagle, and the cast is studded with fine supporting roles. Highlights are contributed by Murray Hamilton, Orson Bean, Alexander Campbell, Howard Mc Near, Russ Brown and Ken Lynch. There is a brief appearance by Duke Ellington, who also did the nervous jazz score.

"Anatomy" was shot entirely on Michigan location. The dreary, but homey, atmosphere seeps into every frame of Sam Leavitt's black-and-white photography, enhancing the realism of the effort. Boris Leven's production design is an important factor in this effect, of course, and so is the sound by Jack Solomon, which does not strain out the natural sounds, but uses them. Editing by Louis R. Loeffler is top-notch. *Powe.*

Curse of the Undead

Lower-berth horror film.

Universal release of Joseph Gershenson production. Stars Eric Fleming, Michael Pate, Kathleen Crowley; with John Hoyt, Bruce Gordon, Edward Binns, Jimmy Murphy, Helen Kleeb, Jay Adler, Edwin Parker, John Truax, Frankie Van, Rush Williams. Directed by Edward Dein. Screenplay, Edward and Mildred Dein; camera, Ellis W. Carter; art direction, Alexander Golitzen, Robert Clatworthy; editor, George Gittens; music, Irving Gertz; sound, Leslie I. Carey, Joe Lapis. Previewed June 17, '59. Running time: **79 MINS.**

In "Curse of the Undead," writers Edward and Mildred Dein have come up with a sentimental vampire and a novel way to kill him. Also, instead of updating this business of "Draculeze" to embrace the space age, they have set their bloodthirsty fellow loose in the old west, producing a sort of "Dracula Meets the Californians" situation. Although the Dein's have created few other surprises in their screenplay, there is no reason to suspect that the popularity of the vampire character has diminished to the extent that this lower-berth picture is going to lose coin for Universal-International. On the contrary, "blood" money is probably as fashionable as ever.

While not exactly the living end in horror films, producer Joseph Gershenson, director Edward Dein, cameraman Ellis W. Carter, music masterminds Irving Gertz and Milton Rosen, and others assigned by U have utilized all the horror-pix tricks in the book to make "Curse" engrossing. Techniques used successfully in the past for other grisly films are adopted throughout, providing the film's best moments.

Basically, the story pits a teacher, Eric Fleming, against an undead vampire, Michael Pate, who, being no mere sucker, finds Kathleen Crowley's lips as attractive as her plasma. After a number of murders by Pate, preacher Fleming swings into action. Ignoring the more accepted "wooden stake" method of dispatching with Hollywood's breed of blood-letters, he imbeds a wooden cross in the head of a bullet and fires at the pesky fellow (an exceedingly slow gunman), who happily shrivels away into vampire heaven, providing a happy "curses foiled again" ending.

Fleming, who does an able job, will also help the film's boxoffice prospects through his current popularity as the star of tv's "Rawhide" series (good timing on U's part). Pate is an excellent choice for the "undead" character, particularly in the early sequences in which he is required only to stand around, looking sinister. Miss Crowley has understandable difficulty relaxing in the classic role of the monster's helplessly-entranced femme victim. John Hoyt, Bruce Gordon, Edward Binns and Jimmy Murphy do as well as can be expected in vital secondary roles. Helen Kleeb and Jay Adler are adequate in small parts.

Nerve-gnawing music and interesting photography, however, are easily the best ingredients in this uninspired production. *Tube.*

The Beat Generation
(CINEMASCOPE)

An exploitable, if ridiculous, picture of beatniks.

Hollywood, June 26.

Metro release of an Albert Zugsmith production. Stars Steve Cochran, Mamie Van Doren, Ray Danton, Fay Spain, Maggie Hayes, Jackie Coogan, Louis Armstrong. Directed by Charles Haas. Screenplay by Richard Matheson and Lewis Meltzer; camera, Walter H. Castle; editor, Ben Lewis; music, Albert Glasser. Previewed at the studio, June 26, '59. Running time: **95 MINS.**

Dave Culloran .... Steve Cochran
Georgia Altera .... Mamie Van Doren
Stan Hess .... Ray Danton
Francee Culloran .... Fay Spain
Louis Armstrong .... Louis Armstrong
Joyce Greenfield .... Maggie Hayes
Jake Baron .... Jackie Coogan
Art Jester .... Jim Mitchum
The Singer .... Cathy Crosby
Harry Altera .... Ray Anthony
The Singing Beatnik .... Dick Contino
Marie Baron .... Irish McCalla
The Poetess .... Vampira
Dr. Elcott .... Billy Daniels
The Wrestling Beatnik Maxie Rosenbloom
Lover Boy .... Charles Chaplin Jr.
The Beat Beatnik .... Grabowski

The beatniks of Albert Zugsmith's "The Beat Generation" are not angry young men, at all, but Freudian cases who impersonate statues and gaze moronically at Vampira reading a jingle on how to loathe one's parents. They constitute little more than atmosphere within the framework of an average cop-and-culprit yarn, but it's an atmosphere that's entertaining and off-beat enough to back up the exploitable title. Metro release can look forward to a way-out summer.

There's a man-size portion of sex in this production which is geared mainly to the wish-they-were market. Both its hero (Steve Cochran) and its villain (Ray Danton) are woman-haters, a point that's made none too subtly. Danton goes around raping young married women, playing a kind of cat-and-mouse game with Cochran, a police sergeant who chases him and hounds his female victims at the same time. The fire of the pursuit is fanned when the rapist attacks the policeman's wife. She subsequently finds she is pregnant, not knowing whether the baby is her husband's or the attacker's. Cochran finally catches his man, deep in the waters of the Pacific, and sees the error in his judgment of women through Danton's personality.

It's difficult to tell whether producer Zugsmith, director Charles Haas or screenwriters Richard Matheson and Lewis Meltzer are responsible for the way the beat generation is depicted. Even to the person who feels the beatnik is a pseudo-intellectual living in a fake Bohemia, this depiction is a ludicrous one. It come out more as satire than realism.

The screenplay often is obvious but just as often is exciting, and Matheson and Meltzer fuse the interesting locations and angles with skill. Haas' direction of the main conflict is sharp, making the chase an important one.

The cast is divided into two camps, the sane living in one and the so-called beatniks in the other. As the rapist, Danton plays a good maniac, but his characterization weakens when he's made to spout excessive coffee-house jargon. Cochran does well as the policeman, but he, too, is handicapped because the role, as written is developed only superficially, leaving his personality to be examined through another person's dialog.

Fay Spain, as the policeman's wife, is, by far, the film's outstanding component. Her portrayal of a woman grasping for her husband's love is expert, her honesty and perception a vital asset to the production. Mamie Van Doren looks her sexy self, plays her sexy self and is wholly believable. Maggie Hayes, as another victim, is excellent, with equally fine work from Jackie Coogan, as Cochran's sidekick. Jim Mitchum looks lost as a would-be rapist.

Louis Armstrong and his All-Stars add a brief, but notable, scene or two, and Zugsmith employed Cathy Crosby, Ray Anthony, Dick Contino, Irish McCalla, Vampira, Billy Daniels, Maxie Rosenbloom, Charles Chaplin Jr. and Grabowski as guestars. Miss Crosby looks lovely and sings that way; Rosenbloom plays a dumb wrestler; Chaplin is fine as "Lover Boy"; etc.

Walter H. Castle's photography is very good, with art direction by William A. Horning and Addison Hehr a bit more authentic than the people who inhabit it. Other assets include Ben Lewis' editing and a bevy of songs, some good and some not, by Albert Glasser and Lewis Meltzer and Tom Walton and Walter Kent. *Ron.*

Great Is My Country
(KINOPANORAMA - COLOR)

Soviet travelog in technically poor widescreen medium mixes scenery and politics. Curiosity item for summer 1959, but little more.

Presentation of the Ministry of Culture of the USSR playing at the Mayfair Theatre, N.Y., in conjunction with the Soviet Exhibition of Science, Technology and Culture at The Coliseum. Produced by the Moscow Popular Science Film Studio. Produced and directed by R. Karmen; co-director, Z. Feldman; camera (Sovcolor), S. Medynsky, V. Ryklin, G. Kholnyi; sound (stereophonic-nine channels), K. Bek-Nazarov; music, K. Molchanov, V. Knushevitsky; commentary, E. Dolmatovsky, R. Karmen. Previewed at the Mayfair Theatre, N.Y. June 29. Running time, **90 MINS.**

As part of their big exhibition at the Coliseum in New York City, the Soviets have opened "Great Is My Country" at the Mayfair Theatre, N.Y. The film, representing a wideangle swing around Russia, was photographed in the Soviets' own Kinopanorama process, which—in technical detail—resembles the American CineMiracle system. It is in Sovcolor and was recorded with nine-channel stereophonic sound.

Inasmuch as the Soviets have free access to the U.S., where they must have seen both Cinerama and CineMiracle, it is astonishing that they would risk their Kinopanorama process on Broadway. They may have been ahead with the sputniks. They're certainly behind when it comes to widescreen.

In theory, content and technique should be separable. Unfortunately, however, in this case they are not since one so intimately depends on the other. Because the technique (at least as seen at the Mayfair preview) is faulty and almost primitive, the otherwise impressive photography suffers and the whole thing is reduced to the level of a so-so travelog.

It's fair to assume that a view of Russia, idealized and slicked-up as it unquestionably is, will still be of interest to Americans who consider the Soviet Union as a land of mystery. It is doubly unfortunate, under these circumstances, that the Russians saw fit to tie politics into what otherwise might have been only an informative and scenic tour. The better part of the second half of "Great Is My Country" is taken up with scenes from the Sixth World Youth and Student Festival in Moscow. To the average American it will be a strange spectacle to watch, and those with long memories may recall echoes from another era, when similar sounds would emanate from the Congresses at Nuremberg.

There is something frightening about "organized spontaneity," the rythmic shouting, the gleaming faces and the tightly disciplined march-past. A group of bedraggled-looking Americans comes into the camera's range and is almost immediately followed by Japanese carrying aloft a banner saying: *"Never Again Hiroshima!"* There's nothing very subtle about such anti-Americanism nor is there anything subtle about the glorification of Lenin and Communism which is expressed both visually and in the narration. But, of course, we have Lincoln.

In short, the Soviets weren't content to turn out a travelog. They're presenting a propaganda picture. They're saying *"we've got a great country because we've got Communism."* This unquestionably appeals to them, but they can't expect most Americans to stand up and applaud.

Photographically, and ignoring for the moment the defects of Kinopanorama, "Great Is My Country" contains some very exciting and beautiful sequences. In a couple of spots the Soviet technicians are playing with the wide screen (60 ft. x 25 ft at the Mayfair) much as Cinerama did in its fledgling days. A plane lands and takes off with a camera strapped to its belly, a car rides on a winding highway and in traffic, the camera goes on a motorboat ride and down a river on a raft. There is a good sense of participation in this. There are views of Moscow and Leningrad and of the Black Sea, of rivers, dams and steel mills. The vastness of Sibera is caught and often the picture composition shows dramatic imagination. Sovcolor, for the most part, is excellent.

But the overall impact suffers from the inadequacy of the process. The film is being shown on CineMiracle equipment, i.e. via three locked projectors out of a single booth. The resultant three panels are divided by very prominent matchlines and the images don't always match. There is a great deal of distortion on both sides, the side panels have a tendency to jiggle and blur, and objects on the screen literally change direction as they reach one of the matchlines. Also, the color in the three panels (representing three separate strips of film) rarely matches so that a river will be blue on the left, almost black in the middle and a dirty gray on the right.

The much-vaunted nine-channel stereophonic sound (Cinerama uses seven channels) adds little to this show. In fact, the male commentator is difficult to understand, which isn't much of a loss since the narration borders on the inane.

Although the Kinopanorama process won the Grand Prize at the Brussels Fair, it remains a puzzle why the Soviets would present such a technically inferior product to Amerians whom they are trying to impress with the very opposite. "Great Is My Country" is hard on the eyes (particularly when the camera pans along a subject) and it tends to be static. The Russia it shows is often beautiful, though many will be struck by the contrast of beautiful highways and boulevards with virtually no cars in sight. It's a curiosity item because it was made in the Soviet Union. *Hift.*

Jack the Ripper
(BRITISH)

Competent variation on an old theme, with title and subject as marquee value, plus obvious exploitation angles.

London June 23.

Regal Films International release of a Mid-Century Film (Robert S. Baker-Monty Berman) production. Features Lee Patterson, Eddie Byrne, Betty McDowall, Ewen Solon. Directed and photographed by Baker and Berman. Screenplay, Jimmy Sangster, from original story by Peter Hammond and Colin Craig; music, Stanley Black; editor, Peter Benzencenet. At Studio One, London. Running time, **84 MINS.**

Sam Lowry .... Lee Patterson
Inspector O'Neill .... Eddie Byrne
Anne Ford .... Betty McDowall
Sir David Rogers .... Ewen Solon
Dr. Tranter ....John Le Mesurier
Clarke .... George Rose
Music Hall Manager ...... Philip Leaver
Kitty Knowles .... Barbara Burke
Helen .... Anne Sharpe
Simes .... Denis Shaw
Louis Benz .... Endre Muller
Nelly .... Esma Cannon
Blake .... George Woodbridge
Lord Sopwith .... Bill Shine
Drunken Woman ....Marianne Stone
Dr. Urquhart .... Garard Green
Assistant Commissioner ...... Jack Allen
Hazel .... Jane Taylor
Margaret .... Dorinda Stevens
Snakey .... Hal Osmond
Station Sergeant .... George Street
Mrs. Bolton .... Olwen Brooks

"Jack The Ripper" has no star names to sell it, but its title and theme have obvious exploitation value for right situations. Those patrons who revel in the morbid will be well satisfied by this modestly-made but holding little drama. Because its "X" certificate, children under 16 will be unable to see it in U.K. which makes it a chancey booking for family houses, but is a selling aid in other situations.

The film is based on the notorious series of crimes that rocked the East End of London at the turn of the century. A number of women, mainly streetwalkers, were foully murdered and mutilated, and the inflicted wounds suggested that the criminal was a skilled surgeon. Swiftly nicknamed "Jack The Ripper" by the terrorized East Enders, the criminal was never identified. It was generally thought that the crimes were revenge by a man who had himself suffered at the hands of a prostie.

This Peter Hammond - Colin Craig version of the yarn varies to some extent from the above layout. In their theory, the criminal is looking for a specific woman, his identity is revealed but he comes to a sticky end before the cops can arrest him, thus leading up to a grim climax.

Jimmy Sangster's screenplay keeps the audience guessing as to who the murderer is, and he cheats only slightly in laying his red herrings. An aura of suspense and fear is built up and the actual crimes are put over skilfully. Though the characters are often more like caricatures, a plausible picture of the fear-ridden East End of the period is shown.

The film relies on a solid cast of sound feature players many of whom obviously have greater opportunities than others. Eddie Byrne brings considerable force to his performance as the worried detective in charge of inquiries while Lee Patterson as a Yank dick sitting in on the case is a likeable hero.

John Le Mesurier and Ewen Solon play surgeons who have key roles in the mystery. Betty McDowall is the girl almoner who unwittingly helps to unmask the villain. There are also a number of effective cameos, notably Denis Shaw, as a trouble-raiser; George Rose, George Woodbridge, as an amorous aristocrat, and Jane Taylor and Anne Sharpe, as two of the Ripper's victims.

Stanley Black's music is fittingly eerie while the editing and camerawork are both sound. *Rich.*

The Big Fisherman
(COLOR; 70M)

Overlong Biblical epic, although handsomely done. Seems dubious for sophisticated areas, but may be strong elsewhere.

Hollywood, June 26.

Buena Vista release of Rowland V. Lee production. Stars Howard Keel, Susan Kohner, John Saxon, Martha Hyer, Herbert Lom. Directed by Frank Borzage. Screenplay, Howard Estabrook and Rowland V. Lee; based on Lloyd C. Douglas' novel; camera (Eastman color by Technicolor) Lee Garmes; music, Albert Hay Malotte; editor, Paul Weatherwax. Previewed at Fox Wilshire theatre, June 23, '59. Running time: **180 MINS**

Simon-Peter ....Howard Keel
Princess Fara..............Susan Kohner
Prince Voldi................. John Saxon
Herodias ....Martha Hyer
Herod-Antipas ....Herbert Lom
Prince Deran ....Ray Stricklyn
Princess Arnon.............Marian Seldes
Mag. David Ben-Zadok....Alex. Scourby
Hannah ....Beulah Bondi
John The Baptist............Jay Barney
Queen Rennah........Charlotte Fletcher
King Zendi ....Mark Dana
Andrew ....Rhodes Reason
Mencius ....Henry Brandon
John ....Brian Hutton
James .... Thomas Troupe
Ione ....Marianne Stewart
Lysias ....Jonathan Harris
Ilderan ....Leonard Mudie
The Begger .... James Griffith
Herod-Phillip ....Peter Adams
Deborah ....Jo Gilbert
Innkeeper ....Michael Mark
Arab Assassin............. Joe Di Reda
King Aretas .... Stuart Randall
Emperor Tiberius........Herbert Rudley
Lucius ....Phillip Pine
Scribe Spokesman.....Francis McDonald
Pharisee Spokesman......... Perry Ivins
Aged Pharisee ....Ralph Moody
Sadducee Spokesman.......Tony Jochim
Roman Captain..............Dan Turner

Rowland V. Lee's "The Big Fisherman" is a pious but plodding account of the conversion to Christianity of Simon-Peter, the apostle called "the fisher of men." Its treatment is reverent but so far from rousing that in its present three-hour running time it is far over-length. As a hard-ticket attraction, the Technicolor-Panavision 70m release from Buena Vista looks dubious for the big city playdates, although its low-brow, literal approach could make it big in general areas.

These biblical attractions can't be evaluated on quite the same level as ordinary film dramas. There is a semi-educational quality about them that excuses some stateliness of pace and stiffness of characterization. But the screenplay for "The Big Fisherman," by Lee and Howard Estabrook, and the direction by Frank Borzage, is overweight with these qualities, while lacking the compensations needed to relieve them.

From a popular point of view, of course, nobody ever touched C. B. DeMille on these films. One reason is that he never neglected what seem to be the two most important elements for their success, spectacle and sex. There is plenty of opportunity for both in "The Big Fisherman," and it is all the more curious, considering its big budget and leisurely production schedule, that both are almost absent. Although the climax of the film is the scene in Herod's palace where Salome served the head of John the Baptist to the tyrant, this scene, laid in a sumptuous and impressively lavish banquet hall, is done almost entirely by shadows and is swiftly over. Salome, in fact, is not only never shown, she is never mentioned.

Actually, although the title seems to make Simon-Peter the central character, the film is only incidentally about him. His part in the story is his influence on two young lovers, John Saxon as an Arab prince, and Susan Kohner, as the daughter of Herod by an Arab princess. Saxon wants to succeed his father as chieftan of an Arab tribe and Miss Kohner wants to kill her father for the unhappiness he has inflicted on her mother. They are both finally deflected from their purpose by meeting Simon-Peter, who has been converted from a life of violence to peace by his exposure to Jesus.

The screenplay is a mixed affair in which the often ringing scriptural passages are incongruously are uncomfortably spliced with mundane conversation couched in contemporary language. Miss Kohner and Saxon make a handsome young couple. Saxon, particularly, is dashing in a neat beard and moustache. But their problems seem trivial against the turbulent ferment that was the birth of the Christian era. Miss Kohner is a gifted young actress, but she does not establish the conviction that she has the grim vindictiveness to carry through the murder of her father.

Howard Keel is handsomely picturesque as Simon-Peter, and shows he can hold his own as a straight actor. It is not his fault that there is no suggestion of the doughty strength identified with the chief apostle. His name, of course, means "Peter, the Rock," but there is none of this feeling as the character is written.

Martha Hyer, as Herodias, manages to convey a sensuality that is welcome, and Herbert Lom, as Herod, creates a psychopathic figure of considerable interest. Ray Stricklyn plays an Arab prince whose frustrations lead him to intrigue against Miss Kohner and Saxon, and he does it well. Marian Seldes has intrinsic integrity and it carries across. Others who contribute capably include Alexander Scourby, Jay Barney, Charlotte Fletcher, Mark Dana, Rhodes Reason, Henry Brandon, Brian Hutton, Thomas Troupe and Marianne Stewart. Beulah Bondi, as Simon-Peter's mother, is genuinely moving in a standout performance.

Of interest from a technical point of view is that "The Big Fisherman" was filmed entirely in this country, reversing a trend of recent years. The "Palestine" that is the film's setting was shot entirely on locations in the San Fernando Valley and the California desert. It seems entirely authentic. One reason probably is Lee Garmes' camera work, done in fine Technicolor and a new Panavision 70m process. This process has fine definition and exceptional depth of focus, at times a three-dimensional feeling. Photographed in Eastman Color by Technicolor, the exteriors are skillfully composed and unfailingly effective, visually.

The technical portions of the film are excellent throughout. The production design by John De Cuir ranging from simple homes to lavish palaces, is evocative and useful. Costumes, by Renie, are a consistent pleasure to the eye. Paul Weatherwax, who did the editing, has done considerable to keep the production fluid. Sound, by Leslie I. Carey and Frank H. Wilkinson, is proficient. Julia Heron's set decoration is another asset. The musical score, by Albert Hay Malotte, is adequate, but it does not have the grandeur that might have been expected from this composer. Joseph Gershenson's conducting, from David Tampkin's orchestration, is first-rate. *Powe.*

Das Indische Grabmal
(The Indian Tomb)
(GERMAN—COLOR)

Berlin, June 23.

Gloria release of CCC (Artur Brauner) production. Stars Debra Paget and Paul Hubschmid. Directed by Fritz Lang. Screenplay, Werner Joerg Lueddecke, after story by Thea von Harbou. Camera (Eastmancolor), Richard Angst; music, Gerhard Becker. At Zoo Palast, Berlin. Running time, **101 MINS.**

Seetha .... Debra Paget
Harald Berger .... Paul Hubschmid
Chandra .... Walther Reyer
Dr. Walter Rhode .... Claus Holm
Irene Rhode .... Sabine Bethmann
Ramigani .... Rene Deltgen

This is the sequel to "Tiger of Eschnapur" and it's as mild as the first production. Again place the blame on the various flaws which made already "Tiger of Eschnapur" such an unfortunate item.

First portion ended with the flight of the German architect Paul Hubschmid and Seetha, the temple dancer (Debra Paget). Both are captured by the men of the jealous Maharajah Chandra (Walther Reyer). The audience sees another series of killings, cruelties, tortures and intrigues until the corny conclusion.

There's a certain plus about picture's exotic background, but that's about the only asset here. *Hans.*

Johansson-Patterson

United Artists Theatre release of Tele-Prompter pay-see production. Producer, E. J. Spiro; cameraman, Frank Zukor; narration, Chris Schenkel. Previewed in N.Y. June 29. Running time, 17 MINS

It's axiomatic that the value of fight films are dependant on the fight itself. Ingemar Johansson's sensational, unexpected, third round knockout victory over Floyd Patterson for the heavyweight championship has provided United Artists, which is distributing the films theatrically for TelePrompter, with perhaps the best fistic footage in a decade.

The films, excellently photographed and edited down to an action-packed 17 minutes, including slow motion reprises of each of the seven knockdowns, are a boxoffice natural and should chalk up hefty returns in worldwide showings. Chris Schenkel's narration has been wisely kept to a minimum. The action on the screen speaks potently for itself.

The first two rounds, in which the contestants resorted mainly to left jabs, are shown in their entirety. Then came the climatic third frame with Johansson unleashing the right hand which he had kept under wraps until fight time. The fury of the Swede's attack and the dazed anguish of Patterson can be seen dramatically.

E. J. Spiro produced for TelePrompter and Frank Zukor supervised the nine-man camera crew. UA will have 800 prints available, said to be a record for fight films. *Holl.*

North By Northwest
(COLOR; V'VISION)

Hitchcock and Cary Grant, Top stars for good b.o.

Hollywood, June 26.
Metro release produced and directed by Alfred Hitchcock. Stars Cary Grant, Eva Marie Saint, James Mason. Screenplay, Ernest Lehman; camera, (Technicolor) Robert Burks; music, Bernard Herrmann; editor, George Tomasini. Previewed at the Westwood Village Theatre, June 24, '59. Running time: 136 MINS.
Roger Thornhill .... Cary Grant
Eve Kendall .... Eva Marie Saint
Phillip Vandamm .... James Mason
Clara Thornhill ...... Jessie Royce Landis
Professor .... Leo G. Carroll
Lester Townsend .... Philip Ober
Handsome Woman .. Josephine Hutchinson
Leonard .... Martin Landau
Valerian .... Adam Williams
Victor Larrabee .... Edward Platt
Licht .... Robert Ellenstein
Auctioneer .... Les Tremayne
Dr. Cross .... Philip Coolidge
Chicago Policeman .... Patrick McVey
Capt. Junket .... Edward Binns
Chicago Policeman .... Ken Lynch

Metro's "North by Northwest" is the Alfred Hitchcock mixture as before—suspense, intrigue, comedy, humor. Seldom has the con-

coction been served up so delectably. It should be top b.o.

Second thoughts on the film will produce the feeling that there are loose ends and stray threads that are never quite bound up or followed through. But the form of the spy melodrama, especially when it is being none too gently spoofed, with counter-espionage and double-agenting rampant, is a loose one and license is permissible. Ernest Lehman has contributed a blithe and funny script.

"North By Northwest" creates for this country the glamorous background achieved so often and so well in Europe. Hitchcock uses actual locations, the Plaza in New York, the Ambassador East in Chicago, Grand Central Station, the 20th Century, Limited, United Nations headquarters in Manhattan, Mount Rushmore (S.D.) National Monument, the plains of Indiana. One scene, where the hero is ambushed by an airplane on the flat, sun-baked prairie, is a brilliant use of location. The scene would not have one-tenth its effect if done in a studio, no matter how skillfully contrived.

Cary Grant brings technique and charm to the central character. He is a Madison Avenue man-about-Manhattan, sleekly handsome, carelessly twice-divorced, debonair as a cigaret ad. The story gets underway when he's mistaken for a U.S. intelligence agent by a pack of foreign agents headed by James Mason. Actually the man he is mistaken for does not exist. The character has been created by U.S. Central Intelligence as a diversion so the foreign spies (never identified as to origin, but presumbaly Communist) will not spot the true U.S. agent in their midst. The complications are staggering but they play like an Olympic version of a three-legged race.

Grant's problem is to avoid getting knocked off by Mason's gang without tipping them that he is a classic case of the innocent bystander. The case is serious, but Hitchcock's macabre sense of humor and instinct for romantic byplay, for which Lehman's screenplay gives plenty of opportunity, never allows it to stay grim for too long. Suspense is deliberately broken for relief and then skillfully re-established. At times it seems Hitchcock is kidding his own penchant for the bizarre, but this sardonic attitude is so deftly handled it only enhances the thrills.

Hitchcock also displays again his ability to see qualities in an actress not hitherto shown. Eva Marie Saint has been effectively drab and convincingly sweet in previous roles, but she dives headfirst into Mata Hari in "North By Northwest" and shows she can be unexpectedly and thoroughly glamorous. She also manages the difficult impression of seeming basically innocent while explaining how she becomes Mason's mistress. Mason, in a rather stock role, is properly forbidding.

Jessie Royce Landis has a fluttery comedy role from which she extracts all possible laughter, and Leo G. Carroll is delightful as the head of a U.S. intelligence unit. Others in key roles are Philip Ober, Josephine Hutchinson, Martin Landau, Adam Williams and Edward Platt. Each creates individuality and excitement.

Sure to be widely-commented upon, among other scenes and lines in "North By Northwest," is a love scene between Miss Saint and Grant, as memorable as Hitchcock's famous love scene between Grant and Ingrid Bergman in "Notorious." The current scene takes

place in a train compartment, as the pair are en route to Chicago, and Grant's comment as he comes up for air—"beats flying"—may well enter the language.

Robert Burks' VistaVision-Technicolor photography, whether in the hot yellows of the prairie plain, or the soft greens of South Dakota forests, is lucid and imaginatively composed. It is the first Metro release in VistaVision, a process Hitchcock prefers. Robert Boyle's production design, abetted by art direction by William A. Horning and Merrill Pye, is fine in every detail. Set decoration, by Henry Grace and Frank McKelvey, is equally an asset.

Bernard Herrmann's score is a tingling one, particularly in the Mount Rushmore sequences, but light where mood requires. Editing by George Tomasini is slick and enhances the process work. Sound by Franklin Milton, who is especially adept at exterior realism, is first-rate. Herbert Coleman was associate producer. *Powe.*

The Killer Shrews

Second of Texas-made fantasies sold together. Production better than script.

Dallas, June 25.
McLendon Radio Pictures release of Hollywood Pictures Corp. production. Stars James Best, Ingrid Goude; features Baruch Lumet, Ken Curtis, Gordon McLendon. Executive producer, Gordon McLendon. Produced by Ken Curtis. Directed by Ray Kellogg. Story and screenplay by Jay Simms; camera, Wilfred Cline; production manager, Ben Chapman; music, Harry Bluestone, Emil Cadkin; editor, Aaron Steel. Premiered at Majestic Theatre, Dallas, June 25, '59. Running time, 69 MINS.
Thorne Sherman .... James Best
Ann Craigis .... Ingrid Goude
Dr. Craigis .... Baruch Lumet
Jerry Lacer .... Ken Curtis
Radford Baines ...... Gordon McLendon
Mario .... Alfredo DeSoto
Rook .... J. H. (Judge) Dupree

This is first of two feature-length productions shot in Texas during 1959 by McLendon Radio Pictures Corp. (teamed with "The Giant Gila Monster."

Gordon McLendon, young head of a six-station Texas radio group, also prexy of Tri-State Theatres, has been acting as he preaches in connection with his radio "network" hard-sell of regular Hollywood releases. Young McLendon believes "*If we can sell pictures, we can make pictures.*" (VARIETY, June 10, 1959.) This quickie originally budgeted at $300,000 was wrapped up in a fortnight's shooting at Lake Dallas studios at the local United Nations Studios for $123,000.

Light story, on the science-fiction side, concerns a river boat captain bringing supplies to a scientist's isolated island, where tiny Blarina shrews—through injections—have grown to wolf-size and escaped the laboratory. For survival they must eat three times their weight daily and prey on the human beings.

Able acting bits are contributed by James Best, as the river boat captain, and blonde Ingrid Goude. Supporting roles are capably handled by Ken Curtis, Baruch Lumet, Gordon McLendon (sic) and Judge Dupree.

As a "horror" film it's quite good under the economics involved and as a dual bill the b.o. prospects are okay. Good houses greeted "Shrews" and "Gila Monster" combo the first two days here.

Assets include excellent direction by Ray Kellogg, fine lighting and photography in the numerous outdoor shots. Special effects by Kellogg, especially in closeups of the "huge" shrews, are firstrate. *Bark.*

The Big Circus
(CINEMASCOPE-TECHNICOLOR)

Top production of Big Top story. Allied Artists has something to sell in the Irwin Allen pic, and b.o. should be strong.

Hollywood, June 30.

Allied Artists release of a Saratoga-Vic Mature Production. Stars Victor Mature, Red Buttons, Rhonda Fleming, Kathryn Grant, Vincent Price, Peter Lorre, David Nelson. Produced by Irwin Allen. Directed by Joseph M. Newman. Screenplay by Irwin Allen, Charles Bennett and Irving Wallace; camera, Winton Hoch; editor, Adrienne Fazan; music, Paul Sawtell and Bert Shefter. Previewed at Academy Theatre, June 22, '59. Running time, **108 MIN.**

Hank Whirling	Victor Mature
Randy Sherman	Red Buttons
Helen Harrison	Rhonda Fleming
Jeannie Whirling	Kathryn Grant
Hans Hagenfeld	Vincent Price
Skeeter	Peter Lorre
Tommy Gordon	David Nelson
Zach Colino	Gilbert Roland
Mama Colino	Adele Mara
Mr. Lomax	Howard McNear
Jonathan Nelson	Charles Watts
Himself	Steve Allen

Irwin Allen's "The Big Circus" is a rousingly lavish film, stocked with tinted elephants, snarling lions and three rings of handsome production. While at times it looks too much like Hollywood's view of the big top, rather than reality, it is shrewdly calculated to satisfy the peanut-and-sawdust yen of the millions to whom circus-going is a less frequently available diversion than in past generations. Allied Artists is giving "The Big Circus" the big push, and its chance at the boxoffice stands at a similarly grand level.

Victor Mature, Red Buttons and Rhonda Fleming top a good cast that is a substantial asset. Each member — also including Kathryn Grant, Vincent Price, Peter Lorre, David Nelson and Gilbert Roland — delivers a performance that is as complete as can reasonably be expected within the framework of spectacle. The adventure, drama and humor of "Circus" are put into precise, sometimes expert, perspective by director Joseph Newman who capitalizes on the big top atmosphere to create a film with extensive mass appeal. Producer Allen conceived the screen story, which has a tendency to become rather pedestrian through the use of such cliches as a circus fire, an escaped lion, a nasty saboteur and a misunderstood hero. Yet the screenplay, by Allen, Charles Bennett and Irving Wallace, is skillfully constructed to give the most dramatic moments free reign.

"The Big Circus" shows how "the biggest show on earth" stays out of the grave, surviving one setback after another. Mature is owner of the enterprise, and, to gain a needed bank loan, must make room for Red Buttons, a bank employee who watches dollars and cents as intently as a tow-headed youngster watches the man on the flying trapeze.

When unremitting rains practically ruin the show's chance for survival, the big toppers dream up a stunt that will put the star wire walker, Gilbert Roland, on a line spanning Niagara Falls. After many dramatic asides, Roland successfully walks above the rapids, insuring the circus' immortality and his own. (*This stunt has been performed by Blondin and others — but long ago.*)

The role of circus impresario Henry Jasper Whirling is the kind Victor Mature does best. He's strong, exhibiting an underlying softness, and he's sincere in achieving what he alone can achieve, in this case setting the wheels in motion to save his circus. Buttons is excellent, mild as the cold banker, strikingly human as a substitute clown and minute-man aerialist. Rhonda Fleming's beauty is an asset to "Circus," her portrayal of a femme flack an honest, highly skilled one.

Roland adeptly combines confidence and fear as the star attraction, creating a sharp characterization. Kathryn Grant is thoroughly appealing as Mature's sister, coming across sweet, yet strong and indicating her future abilities.

Vincent Price is perfect as the ringmaster, his voice bellowing through the big tent with precision and authority. Peter Lorre is tops as a clown, and in more than one scene he is more the circus performer than any of his cohorts. David Nelson, in an offbeat role, is very good, keeping his early character a mystery so his later actions won't be tipped off. Also good are Adele Mara, as a female aerialist, and Howard McNear and Charles Watts as bankmen.

Allen has billed his real-life specialty performers as "the world's greatest circus acts." The Flying Alexanders double well for the stars in the more difficult aerial maneuvers, and the other acts—Hugo Zacchini, the human cannonball; Dick Walker's lions; Gene Mendez, walking the wire for Roland; the Ronnie Lewis Trio; Jungleland elephants; Tex Carr's chimps; and Dick Berg's seals — are well integrated into the story and production.

If most of the creative forces of "The Big Circus" are bent toward the mass audience, the technical credits should excite the most artistic film devotee. Photographically, the picture is, or comes close to being, the finest CinemaScope film yet made. Its Technicolor hues are vivid, the color being a strong part of the production's feeling. And the technical quality of the shots themselves, photographed with warmth and excitement by Winton Hoch, are excellent, the Panavision lenses producing a clarity which should be noticeable even to the average viewer.

The music by Paul Sawtell and Bert Shefter is a potent asset, and the title tune, by Sammy Fain and Paul Francis Webster, is a lilting waltz that is a plus for the film. Albert D'Agosino's art direction is marvelous recreation and beauty unto itself, with Robert Priestley's set decoration an accomplished job.

Film editor Adrienne Fazan caught the excitement and put it into swift, flowing form. Sound by Conrad Kahn is excellent, increasing one's participation in the circus, as do the sound effects by Finn Ulback and Bert Schoenfeld. Costume designer Paul Zastupnevich created authentic big top apparel, and choreographer Barbette put the performers through proper paces. Despite one or two artificial looking angles in Roland's Niagara Falls crossing, the major portion of his feat is vividly created through optical effects.

In all, the elements are here for Allied Artists to exploit, and when "The Big Circus" comes rolling into town, the b.o. receipts should roll right along with it. *Ron.*

The Rabbit Trap

Simple story about Mr. Average rebelling against system that keeps him so. Ernest Borgnine stars. Average possibilities.

United Artists release of Canon Productions presentation. Stars Ernest Borgnine, David Brian; co-stars Bethel Leslie, Kevin Corcoran, June Blair; features Jeanette Nolan, Russell-Collins, Christopher Dark, Don Rickles. Produced by Harry Kleiner. Directed by Philip Leacock; script, J. P. Miller; camera, Irving Glassberg; music, Jack Marshall; editor, Ted Kent. Previewed in N.Y. June 26, '59. Running time, **72 MINS.**

Eddie Colt	Ernest Borgnine
Everett Spellman	David Brian
Abby Colt	Bethel Leslie
Duncan Colt	Kevin Corcoran
Judy	June Blair

and Jeanette Nolan, Russell Collins Christopher Dark, Don Rickles.

The symbolism in "The Rabbit Trap" may be somewhat strained, but there's little doubt that the public will get the point. This is one of these pictures that puts an average man into an average though potentially dramatic situation and then works it out so that the individual can triumph and the presumably identifying audience with him.

Since, at no point in the proceedings, is there any attempt to coat the issues with subtlety or the acting with finesse, the film states what it has to say very simply. Its basic theme is that there is a lack of communication between people when it comes to sensitivity concerning needs and feelings, and that the economic pressures on the little man today are such that fear and insecurity keep him in his — limited—place.

It's as if J. P. Miller, who wrote the script from his original television play, had decided to make these points and then to cover the moral skeleton with the barest dramatic clothes to provide the required entertainment values. The rabbit trap is a neat device, though an obvious one. It triggers the action, and at the same time provides the symbolism, for the man —like the rabbit in the trap—is caught in a situation which he must endure for the sake of his own and his family's security.

Thrown into this, for good measure and without much justification, is a bit about a girl who has an affair with her boss, who's a married man. It is made plain that such affairs tend to mix up girls and make them unhappy.

The trouble with "The Rabbit Trap" is that it deals in stereotypes rather than characters. There's Ernest Borgnine, a capable draftsman who can't get ahead in the construction outfit where he works and which is headed by the aggressive, insensitive David Brian. Borgnine is a devoted family man with a lovely wife (Bethel Leslie) and a cute youngster (Kevin Corcoran). They go off on their first vacation in several years, but Brian calls Borgnine back for a special job.

When Borgnine's boy realizes that they've forgotten the rabbit trap in the country, he insists they must go back to release any rabbit that might be caught. But Brian won't give Borgnine the day off and this sets in motion a chain of events that, finally, sees Borgnine walking out of the job, the "little man" who asserts his independence. Thrown in are lengthy scenes between Borgnine and Brian, the employee who struggles to retain his dignity and the bull-headed boss who can't understand why the life of a rabbit should be important.

Borgnine's performance has a kind of plodding quality, but it's not really convincing and it radiates very little warmth. Miss Leslie as his wife is very good and very aptly cast. In fact, her performance rates as one of the best things in the picture. Brian is okay and Corcoran portrays a rather sulky youngster. June Blair is pretty as the secretary.

Philip Leacock's direction does achieve a natural quality, and the scenes when the little boy runs away from home to free his rabbit are very well done. Irving Glassberg's photography is cued to the simplicity of the yarn. Jack Marshall's music and Ted Kent's editing are standard.

"Rabbit Trap" tackles a lot of important things—almost too many —but in its eagerness to make a point it overlooks the fact that there's nothing as deadly in a picture as the "obvious" pitch and the forced conclusion. *Hift.*

The Siege of Pinchgut
(BRITISH)

Suspenseful yarn of escaped prisoner holding out on an island. Brisk b.o. possibilities.

Berlin, July 7.

Associated British-Pathe release of a Michael Balcon-Ealing (L. C. Rudkin) production. Stars Aldo Ray and Heather Sears. Directed by Harry Watt. Screenplay, Inman Hunter, Lee Robinson, Watt and John Cleary; camera, Gordon Dines; music, Kennth V. Jones. At Zoo Palast, Berlin. Running time, **105 MINS.**

Matt Kirk	Aldo Ray
Johnny Kirk	Neil McCallum
Luke	Carlo Justini
Bert	Victor Maddern
Fulton	Gerry Duggan
Ann Fulton	Heather Sears
Her mother	Barbara Mullen

Ever since he filmed "The Overlanders" in Australia some years back, Harry Watt has returned at periodic intervals to search for stories to fit the background. This time the formula has been changed; he had the story in advance and instead of having the wide open spaces of the country as his canvas, the action is largely confined to a small fortress island inside the Sydney (Australia) harbor.

Within the first couple of minutes, even before the credit titles, an atmosphere of considerable tension is created, but suspense at that pace and standard is hard to maintain. Nevertheless, "Siege of Pinchgut" is a lively action pic with prospects of brisk b.o. returns. In the U.S., the star billing of Aldo Ray should help some.

Ray plays an escaped prisoner whose previous criminal record didn't help when he protested his innocence to judge and jury. Now all he wants is to clear his name and is prepared to surrender in return for a public assurance from the Attorney General of a new trial. Helped by his brother and two friends, he first makes his getaway in an ambulance, and later sets sail in a ketch. The boat breaks down and drifts towards the island of Pinchgut, in the harbor.

In a desperate bid to get his retrial, the escaped convict threatens to turn a four-inch naval gun on to a ship filled with explosives, which would blow up half the city. While the ship is being offloaded, the city is being evacuated. Meantime the police are taking pot shots

at the fugitives and only Ray and his brother are left before frogmen actually invade the island.

The siege of the island has its complement of suspense, but not to compare with original getaway scenes. The ambulance in which they're making the dash for freedom is stopped by the police after an accident, and to make sure it gets to the hospital without delay, the cop provides his own motorcycle escort. All that, however, before the titles.

Ray's virile and vigorous portrayal is right for the role. Victor Maddern turns in another fine part as one of his friends. Heather Sears, as the caretaker's daughter, gives a completely negative performance. The kid brother role is ably filled by Neil McCallum. Carlo Justini makes an acceptable showing as the fourth fugitive. Gerry Duggan and Barbara Mullen hit the right note of restrained fear as the girl's parents.

Berlin Festival

Und Das Am Montagmorgen
(And That on Monday Morning) (GERMAN)

Neue Film (Munich) release of H.R. Sokal-P. Goldbaum production for CCC-Arthur Brauner (Berlin). Stars O. W. Fischer, Ulla Jacobsson. Directed by Luigi Commencini. Screenplay, Peter Goldbaum and Franz Hoellering; camera, Karl Lob; editor, Walter Wischniewsky; music, Hans-Martin Majewski. At Congress Hall, Berlin. Running time, **88 MINS.**

Adapted from J. B. Priestley's "Mr. Kettle and Mrs. Moon," this Neue Film production should do well enough in its domestic market because of the b.o. strength of O. W. Fischer. But it's a slim prospect for the U.S. market. Production fails to capture the light touch which the frivolous plot demands, editing is erratic and the direction more painstaking than frothy.

Fischer plays a bank manager who, on a Monday morning, rebels against the monotony of his life, plays truant from work, and amuses himself by playing with toys and accompanying a radio concert with wind instruments. His costar, Ulla Jacobsson, is a woman analyst whom he has always admired from a distance. She's sent to help him out, and he seizes the opportunity to come to grips with her. Fischer gives an animated performance while Miss Jacobsson relies on spectacles to convince that she's a medico. Vera Tschechowa adds a provocative note with some revealing shots in a bathtub.
Myro.

Der Rest Ist Schweigen
(The Rest Is Silence) (GERMAN)
Berlin, July 7.

Europa release of a Real Film (Hamburg) production. Stars Hardy Kruger. Directed and scripted by Helmut Kautner. Camera, Igor Oberberg; editor, Claus Dudenhofer; music, Bernhard Eichhorn. At Zoo Palast, Berlin. Running time, **104 MINS.**

A modern version of "Hamlet," this German production looks a potentially big grosser in the domestic market here, for which it has stout marquee values. In the

attempt to parallel the original, however, the story is blatantly contrived. This might well make the going hard in overseas markets. It is an interesting example of film making by one of Germany's leading directors which doesn't quite make the grade.

The Prince of the story is a Harvard educated German youth who returns home to his mother and accuses his stepfather of murdering his father. The play sequence is done in the form of a modern ballet, there's a girl in the house to parallel Ophelia, and a burial scene featuring the gravediggers. Hardy Kruger gives a sincere and earnest performance in the lead while Peter Van Eyck, Ingrid Andree and Adelheid Seeck fill major parts adequately.

As a footnote, it's worth recording that this latter-day Hamlet features a plug for VARIETY. *Myro.*

La Caida
(Strange Guests) (ARGENTINIAN)
Berlin, July 7.

Argentine Sono Film production of a Leopoldo Torre Nilsson production. Stars Elsa Daniel. Directed by Leopoldo Torre Nilson. Camera, Alberto Echebehere; sets by Juan Jose Saavedra and Emilio Rodriguez Mentasti; music, Juan Carlo Paz. At Zoo Palast, Berlin. Running time, **85 MINS.**

Two contrasting styles are merged somewhat uneasily here, but there are many interesting aspects to this Argentinian festival entry. Leopoldo Torre Nillson is a stylish director. At his best in handling scenes featuring four children (brought up without any parental control), he's not entirely at home dealing with romantic angles. But even so, the pic may well have a limited art house success.

Elsa Daniel plays a university student who takes lodgings at the home of a bedridden woman, whose children run almost wild, but who occasionally display surprising moments of tenderness. Her romance with a lawyer goes cold when she refuses to leave what he describes as "that lunatic asylum." Miss Daniel is completely overshadowed by the four moppets who score a walkaway victory in the acting stakes. For the record their names are Carlos Lopez Monet, Hebe Marbec, Oscar Orlegui and Nora Singerman. *Myro.*

Lupi Nell'Abisso
(Wolves in the Depth) (ITALIAN)
Berlin, July 7.

A Sagittario Film (Rome) and Radius (Paris) release of an Italo Zingarelli production. Stars Massimo Girotti, Jean Marc-Bory, Horst Frank. Directed by Silvio Amadio. Screenplay, Gino de Santis, Carlo Romano, Silvio Amadio; camera, Luciano Trasatti; music, Bruno Canfora. At Zoo Palast, Berlin. Running time, **101 MINS.**

Reminiscent of the comparatively recent British pic, "Morning Departure," this Franco-Italian co-production (which is an invited Italian entry at the Berlin festival) is a holding yarn of a submarine crew in wartime, trapped at the bottom of the ocean. The escape hatch is damaged, and only one man will be able to get away.

The screenplay dramatically illustrates how the men react to this tense situation. As the moment of reckoning arrives, there are no heroes, but a bunch of nervous,

anxious and frightened men. Technically, the subject puts a strain on the resources of the director as the entire action takes place inside the wrecked submarine. Its main failing is that it does not wholly establish a grim claustrophobic atmosphere. Acting is fine all round, but tighter editing would help considerably, particularly for overseas markets. *Myro.*

Kakushitoride No Sanakumia
(Three Rascals in Hidden Fortress) (JAPANESE)
Berlin, July 7.

Toho (Tokyo) production and release. Stars Toshiro Mifune, Misa Uehara, Minori Chiaki, Kamatari Fujiwara. Directed by Akira Kurosawa. Screenplay, Ryuzo Kikushima, Hideo Kokuni, Shinobu Hashimoto, Akira Kurosawa; camera, Kazuo Yamazaki; music, Masaru Sato. At Zoo Palast, Berlin. Running time, **123 MINS.**

One of the best recent examples of Japanese film-making, this festival entry is distinguished by high grade direction. It also abounds in action, and is handsomely acted and produced. Pic is, however, somewhat overlong. Perhaps with a little discreet scissoring, it could make an offbeat proposition for arty houses.

Set in the middle ages, the yarn describes the misadventures of two soldiers on the ren from invading armies. When they're down on their luck, they find a bar of gold stashed away in the branch of a tree, part of the loot concealed by the runaway princess. From then on, the mood changes with subtle skill from outright brutality to downright good humor. The two vagrant soldiers are magnificently played by Minoru Chiaki and Kamatari Fujiwara. Remainder of the cast maintains the high acting standard. Technical credits are excellent. *Myro.*

Paradies und Feuerofen
(Paradise and Fire Oven) (GERMAN-COLOR)
Berlin, July 7.

Europa release of an IFAG production. Direction and commentary by Herbert Victor. Camera, Heinz Holscher; editor, Ludolf Grisebach; music, Bernhard Eichhorn. At Zoo Palast, Berlin. Running time, **84 MINS.**

A decade or two back, this would have been an impossible subject for a German producer, but this feature-length documentary of Israel has been handled with commendable sincerity and objectivity. Up to a point it is first-class, but it misses out by not focusing adequate attention on the explosive situation of a nation surrounded by hostile states. The title is partially misleading: the paradisical virtues are shown in some detail, but there is only the glimpse of a nation nearing boiling point.

The film has been handsomely photographed in Agfacolor, and the commentary, written and spoken by the director, is literate and honest. Pictorially, the feature breaks some new ground, particularly in showing a combined air and land operation in catching a gang of camel-borne Arab dope smugglers. Subject and source of origin could provide unusual exploitation angles in many markets. *Myro.*

The Rebel Set

Well-made crime suspense meller for exploitation or programming.

Hollywood, July 10.

Allied Artists release of E. and L. Production. Stars Gregg Palmer, Kathleen Crowley, Edward Platt, John Lupton. Produced by Earle Lyon. Directed by Gene Fowler Jr. Screenplay, Lou Vittes and Bernard Girard; music, Paul Dunlap; editor, William Austin. Previewed at the studio, July 9, '59. Running time, **72 MINS.**

John Mapes	Gregg Palmer
Jeanne Mapes	Kathleen Crowley
Mr. Tucker	Edward Platt
Ray Miller	John Lupton
Sidney Horner	Ned Glass
George Leland	Don Sullivan
Karen	Vikki Dougan
King Invader	I. Stanford Jolley
Lieut. Cassidy	Robert Shayne
Bali Dancer	Gloria Moreland
Rita Leland	Colette Lyons
Policeman	Joe Marsh

After an unpromising start, when "The Rebel Set" strikes an unconvincing attitude as a story on the beat generation, the film gets down to business as a straight crime suspense melodrama and from then on is reasonably taut and absorbing. Gene Fowler Jr. directed with competence for producer Earle Lyon. "The Rebel Set" will lend itself to exploitation or be a satisfactory program picture.

Plot of the screenplay by Lou Vittes and Bernard Girard is concerned mainly with the holdup of an armored truck carrying $1,000,-000 in cash. Edward Platt is the mastermind of the crime. His confederates are three young men, an unsuccessful actor, Gregg Palmer; an unpublished writer, John Lupton; and the ne'er-do-well son, Don Sullivan, of a fading film star. The holdup is a success but the getaway isn't. All are killed except Palmer, who escapes when he has a change of heart and wins leniency for his help to the police.

Fowler, who knows editing and the technical uses of film for dramatic purposes as well as any young director around, uses his knowledge well in building and maintaining suspense through inter-cutting and contrasting shots. Karl Struss' photography is realistic but bright. Paul Dunlap contributes one of his good scores, a considerable help. David Milton's art direction is inventive in locations and backgrounds that suggest the mid-western locale of most of the action.

The cast is capable. In addition to Palmer, Platt, Lupton and Sullivan, particularly notable are Kathleen Crowley, Ned Glass, Nikki Dougan and Collette Lyons. *Powe.*

Holiday for Lovers
(COLOR; C'SCOPE)

Good holiday fare. Romance, comedy, travel.

Hollywood, July 10.

Twentieth-Fox production and release. Stars Clifton Webb, Jane Wyman, Jill St. John, Carol Lynley, Paul Henreid, Gary Crosby. Produced by David Weisbart. Directed by Henry Levin. Screenplay, Luther Davis; based on the play by Ronald Alexander; camera (DeLuxe Color), Charles G. Clarke; music, Leigh Harline; title song, Sammy Cahn and James Van Heusen; editor, Stuart Gilmore. Previewed at Pantages Theatre, July 7, '59. Running time, **103 MINS.**

Robert Dean	Clifton Webb
Mary Dean	Jane Wyman
Meg Dean	Jill St. John
Betsy Dean	Carol Lynley
Eduardo Barroso	Paul Henreid
Paul Gattling	Gary Crosby
Carlos	Nico Minardos
Joe	Wally Brown
Connie	Henry Backus
Mrs. Murphy	Nora O'Mahoney
Staff Sergeant	Buck Class

Technical Sergeant	Al Austin
Jose Greco	Himself
Nestor Amaral Orchestra	

This is a 20th-Fox summertime package, not designed to tax the intellect but not very likely to ruffle it, either. It's a romantic farce travelog that plays smoothly with a good many solid laughs. There are drags in spots, the plotting is not always smooth, not all the situations play off. But David Weisbart's production has a good mixture of young players salted with veterans, and Henry Levin's direction keeps things lively.

The point of Luther Davis' screenplay, based on Ronald Alexander's Broadway play, is that daughter, not father, knows best. The point may be questioned by some older members of the audience, but with younger fans it will go down like cherry Coke.

Clifton Webb is a Boston psychiatrist confronted with two daughters, Jill St. John and Carol Lynley, who are simultaneously bursting the adolescent cocoon to fall in love. The plot requires Webb and the girls' mother, Jane Wyman, to trek through South America in frustrated chaperonage. All ends happily, in the contemporary American idiom, when dense parents capitulate to siblings' wishes.

The background of the film, chiefly Sao Paulo and Rio de Janeiro, gives a fine opportunity to show a good deal of spectacular South American landscape and skyscrapers. The long shots of Sao Paulo are particularly interesting. This city makes most North American architecture look parochial, and the freshness of this background gives a lift to the story.

Webb, with his customary acerbity, takes a line and pins it to the wall, often managing to make humor seem like wit. There is some tired dialog, too. Approximate sample: "Mother — Our daughter is studying under a famous South American architect." "Father — Please say with not under."

Miss Wyman has only a few opportunities for laughs but these she gets adroitly, otherwise being an attractively young and harried mother. Miss St. John is pretty, but seems confused by some of her dialog. Carol Lynley is a real film find, a cameo beauty who plays beat or sensitive and makes the transition with finesse. Paul Henreid handles his assignment suavely, and Gary Crosby is a strong comedy asset. Others who register include Nico Minardos, Wally Brown, Henry Backus, Nora O'Mahoney, Buck Class, Al Austin and Tom Hernandez. Gardner McKay, Life magazine's new candidate for Eros, is seen briefly in a crowd scene. Jose Greco, in for a specialty at the film's end, gives the production a sock next-to-closing.

Charles G. Clarke's CinemaScope photography in DeLuxe Color is generally fine, although the superimposed scenes of principals against Brazilian backgrounds are not convincing. Color balance is off and the process work is easily discernible. It would have enhanced the film to have gone all the way for locations. This is not Clarke's fault, of course, and his shots of Sao Paulo and Rio are stunning. Lima is inaccurately reproduced.

There's a catchy title tune by Sammy Cahn and James Van Heusen for further exploitation.

Powe.

The Alligator People
(C'SCOPE)

Good program horror film packaged with "Return of the Fly."

Hollywood, July 9.

Twentieth-Fox release of a Jack Leewood production. Stars Beverly Garland; co-stars Bruce Bennett, Lon Chaney, George Macready, Frieda Inescort, Richard Crane, Douglas Kennedy; with Vince Townsend Jr., Ruby Goodwin, Hal K. Dawson, Dudley Dickerson, John Merrick, Bill Bradley, Lee Warren, Boyd Stockman. Producer, Jack Leewood. Director, Roy Del Ruth. Screenplay, Orville H. Hampton, based on a story by Hampton and Charles O'Neal; camera, Karl Struss; editor, Harry Gerstad; music, Irving Gertz; art direction, Lyle R. Wheeler, John Mansbridge; sound, W. Donald Flick. Previewed at the studio, July 8, '59. Running time, 73 MINS.

Jane Marvin	Beverly Garland
Dr. Mark Sinclair	George Macready
Paul Webster	Richard Crane
Mannon	Lon Chaney
Mrs. Henry Hawthorne	Frieda Inescort
Toby	Vince Townsend Jr.
Lou Ann	Ruby Goodwin
Paula Double	Boyd Stockman
Nurse No. 1	John Merrick
Nurse No. 2	Lee Warren
Dr. Erik Lorimer	Bruce Bennett
Dr. Wayne McGregor	Doug Kennedy
Patient No. 6	Bill Bradley
Porter	Dudley Dickerson
Conductor	Hal K. Dawson

In "The Alligator People" producer Jack Leewood and director Roy Del Ruth have a good program horror film which 20th-Fox intends to package with "Return of the Fly." Dramatically the stronger of the two, "Alligator" should help the bill considerably and the two pix should do okay in their specialized market.

Orville H. Hampton's screenplay is logically developed and provides some good characterizations which actress Beverly Garland and actors Richard Crane and Lon Chaney make the most of.

The story is told in flashbacks. Two psychiatrists are questioning a nurse, portrayed by Miss Garland, who has been put under pentothal. She tells a story which she doesn't remember while conscious.

Her tale, perhaps imaginary, is that her husband (Richard Crane) abandoned her on their wedding night. After a year's search, she arrives at a mansion in Louisiana's bayou country. Near the mansion is a hideway clinic where a physician (George Macready) is trying to discover an antidote to a serum he had developed.

The serum, extracted from alligators, permits humans to regrow damaged body parts just as some reptiles do. An unforeseen aftereffect—the reason the husband so treated fled from his wife—is that the humans gradually acquire the physical characteristics of alligators.

The wife elects to stand by her horribly disfigured husband, but in his anxiety to return to normal he forces the conscious-stricken doctor to use an untried technique involving radioactive cobalt to cure him. The cure backfires and he is transformed into a real human alligator. In grief and terror he flees to the swamp and dies in quicksand while his hysterical wife watches helplessly. The cobalt machine explodes and destroyes the clinic, the doctor, the other "alligator" patients and the drunk, well played by Lon Chaney, who caused the hitch in the treatment.

The psychiatrists, assuming that the shock may have caused amnesia or that it was a delusion best left undisturbed. elect not to treat the nurse who is apparently happy except when under pentothal.

Hampton's script provides plausible explanations for the implausible and injects warmth and humor at points making the horror more horrible. Equipped with well motivated lines, Miss Garland turns in a fine performance. While Frieda Inescort overacts her well written mother role, the rest of the principal supporting cast does well.

The picture lags in the middle stretch—after the girl has arrived at the mansion but before she discovers her husband—which prevents the film from being exceptional, but it's more than good enough for the market at which it's aimed.

Karl Struss' photography, Arthur Cornell's sound effects and Harry Gerstad's editing are decided plusses and Lyle R. Wheeler and John Mansbridge's art direction is masterful, particularly when the budget is taken into consideration.

Glen.

Return of the Fly
(C'SCOPE)

Inept sequel to "The Fly." Quickie bookings may exploit the original's reputation.

Hollywood, July 9.

Twentieth-Fox release of Berhard Glasser production. Stars Vincent Price; co-stars Brett Halsey, David Frankham, John Sutton, Dan Seymour; features Danielle De Metz, Janine Grandel, Richard Flato; with Barry Bernard, Pat O'Hara, Jack Daly, Michael Mark, Gregg Martell, Francisco Villalobas, Joan Cotton. Directed by Edward L. Bernds. Screenplay by Bernds; camera, Brydon Baker; editor, Richard C. Meyer; music, Paul Sawtell, Bert Shefter. Previewed at studio, July 8, '59. Running time, 78 MINS.

Francois	Vincent Price
Philippe	Brett Halsey
Alan	David Frankham
Charas	John Sutton
Max Barthold	Dan Seymour
Cecile	Danielle De Metz
Mme. Bonnard	Janine Grandel
Dubois	Richard Flato

"Return of the Fly" was conceived and executed as a sequel to "The Fly" in order to cash in on the latter's reputation as a grosser. On the title alone, it should make back its relatively modest budget and may turn a small profit.

Word-of-mouth will injure the film's chances, however, because, with justice, it will be unfavorably compared with the first, which was a superior horror film.

The sequel's amateurishly contrived plot picks up at the death of the inventor's widow, who had been acquitted of murdering him. Vincent Price, the only actor carried over from the original, explains to the inventor's now-grown son, played by Brett Halsey, the plot of the other picture.

Halsey's mother, Price explains, had actually crushed his father in a high-pressure press at the man's request. The inventor had botched an experiment which resulted in his head and right arm being replaced with those of a fly. He chose suicide because the fly's instincts were beginning to rule him.

It's typical of writer-director Edward Bernds' script that this incredible and dreadful tale, told to the loving son himself on the day of his mother's funeral, should be made to seem almost banal for a lack of imaginative dialog and absence of appropriate tempo in the scene. What follows is one unmotivated episode after another, loosely tied to the theme that the son, in following in his father's footsteps, will come to the same bad end. An obnoxious reporter is featured in initial scenes but simply doesn't appear in later scenes, although he was clearly being set up for some horrible demise.

Suspense is attempted by making the son's assistant a traitor who is trying to steal the secret of the "matter transmitter." Horror is achieved when the assistant uses the device to scramble a policeman's corpse with a guinea pig and to scramble the inventor's scientist son with a fly.

Halsey, with a fly's head and limbs, kills the assistant and his confederate but these deeds are not depicted as the crimes they certainly are. Ultimately, Halsey is unscrambled and co-eds will be relieved to see his handsome face again; their dates will appreciate his girlfriend Danielle De Metz. John Sutton is wasted in the Herbert Marshall role. Dan Seymour does a good characterization of the slimy confederate and David Frankham does his best with the assistant role. Considering the script's limitations, the cast does fairly well.

The picture is technically slick and the special effects—for which no credit is given—are good. Except for the art director (Lyle Wheeler, who shares credit with John Mansbridge) the technical crew is different from the original. Paul Sawtell, who scored the original, assists Bert Shefter in scoring the sequel, adding a plus factor. But without the reputation of "The Fly" to trade on, this one would be a dud.

Glen.

The Giant Gila Monster

Texas-made science - fiction "horror" thriller; photography best bet. Trite story. Part of package.

Dallas, July 7.

McLendon Radio Pictures release of Hollywood Pictures Corp. production. Stars Don Sullivan, Lisa Simone; features Shug Fisher, Fred Graham, Ken Knox. Executive producer, Gordon McLendon. Produced by Ken Curtis. Directed by Ray Kellogg. Story and screenplay by Kellogg, Jay Sims; camera, Wilfred Cline; production manager, Ben Chapman; sound effects, Milton Citron, James Richard; music, Jack Marshall; editor, Aaron Stell. Premiered at Majestic Theatre, Dallas, June 25, '59. Running time, 74 MINS.

Chace Winstead	Don Sullivan
Lisa	Lisa Simone
Mr. Harris	Shug Fisher
Bob	Jerry Cortwright
Gay	Beverly Thurman
Gordy	Don Flourney
Chucky	Clarke Browne
Sherry	Pat Simmons
Rick	Pat Reeves
Whila	Anne Sonka
Sheriff	Fred Graham
Wheeler	Bob Thompson
Compton	Cecil Hunt
Steamroller Smith	Ken Knox
Liz Humphries	Yolanda Salas
Eb Humphries	Howard Ware
Agatha Humphries	Stormey Meadows

This second McLendon Radio Pictures feature (budgeted at $300,000, but under the wire at $138,000, tandems with the earlier (Jan., '59) feature, "The Killer Shrews," as a good double-bill. It got that treatment in a "world premiere" June 25 at the Interstate Circuit's flagship house, the Majestic, here, also at the Palace in Fort Worth and in 11 other Texas towns.

Story is mild, but as an "audience reaction" feature, "Gila Monster" has appeal for the science-fiction situations. Slick black-and-white photography, mostly outdoors, captures some fine North Texas scenery, to make this a worthwhile feature. Trick camera work has a Gila monster, giant sized, feeding its way through wooded areas, wrecking a train, breaking into a dance hall to panic a teenage "record hop."

Director Ray Kellogg's special effects rate the big nod against trite yarn about a sheriff who calls on the leader of a hot-rod gang to

help him find a missing couple — and then chances upon the giant reptile.

Don Sullivan is adequate as the male lead; he uses the appearance to exploit three of his own compositions. A dubious interpolation. His vocal assets don't match even his minor acting talents. Add that Lisa Simone, a beauty contest winner, is a dull leading lady. Ken Knox, a local deejay, gets off a slick stint, before posing as a KILT jock (that's the McLendon station in Houston, hence the plug) at the teenage hop.

Acting honors goes to veteran Fred Graham, who plays the diligent sheriff. *Bark.*

J'Irai Cracher Sur Vos Tombes

(I Will Go Spit On Your Graves) (FRENCH)

Paris, July 14.

Lux release of CTI-SIPRO production. Stars Christian Marquand, Antonella Lualdi; features, Renate Ewert, Paul Guers, Fernand Ledoux, Marina Petrowa, Daniel Cauchy. Directed by Michel Gast. Screenplay, Boris Vian, Jacques Decombe, adapted from Vian's novel; camera, Marc Fossart; editor, Eliane Bensdorp. At Biarritz, Paris, Running time, 95 MINS.,

Joe Grant .... Christian Marquand
Lisbeth .... Antonella Lualdi
Sylvia .... Renata Ewart
Sheila .... Marina Petrowa
Chandley .... Fernand Ledoux
Stan .... Paul Guers
Sonny .... Daniel Cauchy

After "The Respectful Prostitute" and "Guts In The Sun," the French are still making films on race problems in the U.S. It just does not work, particularly in this case where the problem is used as an exploitation gambit in an essentially sensational film.

Besides the difficulty in properly portraying the U.S., this drags in the long line of juve delinquent French pix which of late are trying to cast them in a Yank mold via black jackets, violence, tests of juve endurance. What is left is a film with some exploitation chances here and abroad on its nudity and love candor but sans much continuity and lacking characterization. This is strictly for bally hypo chances in the U.S.—nothing more.

A Negro who looks white sees his brother lynched in the south. He decides to go up north, and pass as a white man thereby ostensibly getting some sort of revenge on the whites. All the girls in a little town go for him but he can not bring himself to kill any. Finally he falls for a rich girl betrothed to a local hoodlum. It ends in death for the Negro as well as the girl who loves him.

Director Michel Gast rarely gets any feeling for the plight of the hero into this. The indecisive playing of Christian Marquand in this role does not help either. Technical credits are okay but the spurious set, supposedly an American town, is flimsy. A fair resemblance is ruined by the English papers on display, French telephones, and signs like "Cross The Street." This is too naive for Yank arties with only possible exploitation on its theme and love scenes.

Yank pix like "Paths of Glory" and "I Accuse" are not allowed to play here because they show the French army in a bad light. "Graves" is not objectionable on its plot so much as on the lacklustre way it is made and the exploiting of an important theme for strictly sensational reasons. French producers perhaps could treat more local problems of this type rather than dabbling in this sectional American problem. *Mosk.*

Operation Bullshine

(BRITISH-COLOR)

Pleasantly amusing Army comedy with gags and gal which raises plenty of laughter.

London, July 7.

Associated British-Pathe release of an Associated British Production. Stars Donald Sinden, Barbara Murray, Carole Lesley, Ronald Shiner, Naunton Wayne, Dora Bryan. Producer, Frank Godwin; director, Gilbert Gunn; screenplay, Anne Burnaby and Rupert Lang, camera, Gilbert Taylor; editor, E. B. Jarvis; music, Laurie Johnson. At Carlton, London, June 30 '59. Running time, 90 MINS.

Lieut. Gordon Brown .... Donald Sinden
Private Betty Brown .... Barbara Murray
Private Marge White .... Carole Lesley
Gunner Slocum .... Ronald Shiner
Major Pym .... Naunton Wayne
Private Cox .... Dora Bryan
Gunner Willie Ross .... John Cairney
Junior Commander Maddox .. Fabia Drake
Private Finch .... Joan Rice
Bombardier Palmer .... Daniel Massey
Gunner Perkins .... Peter Jones
Serg. Merrifield .... Barbara Hicks
Brigadier .... John Welsh
P. T. Instructress .... Judy Grinham
Orderly Serg. .... Cyril Chamberlain
Reporter .... Ambrosine Phillpotts
Subaltern Godfrey .... Naomi Chance
Serg. Cook .... Marianne Stone
Gunner Wilkinson .... Harry Landis
Gunner Pooley .... Brian Weske
German Airman .... George Mikell

By now, pretty well every branch of service life has been exploited as a picture, either dramatically or comically. It seems the well's not drained. With "Operation Bullshine," which originally had the more appealing title of "Girls In Arms," it's the turn of a mixed ack-ack gun site. It's an unashamed supplicant for yocks and garners them with ease.

Many of the usual cliches of this type of film crop up but it has the advantage of a basically amusing idea, an accomplished cast and a screenplay by Anne Burnaby and Rupert Lang which does attempt to keep to its theme and not become merely a string of disconnected gags and situations.

When a bunch of A.T.S. girls are posted to a Light Ack-Ack post the commanding officer rightly fears that the glamor will upset his men's morale. But his good-looking second-in-command (Donald Sinden) revels in the idea and soon gets the reputation of being a lady-kiler. He's doing particularly well with a blonde cutie who sets her sights firmly on him. All's well, till his wife is posted to the unit as a private. Since it's against Army Regulations for husband and wife to serve at the same unit they have to keep it a secret, which causes endless matrimonial mix-ups. The tangle is, of course, suitably sorted out in the required 90 minutes.

Sinden brings charm and a quiet humor to his role and Barbara Murray has both prettiness and attack, a useful combination. Naunton Wayne fusses and blusters amusingly as the commanding officer and Fabia Drake is a formidable dragon as boss of the A.T.S. unit. The blonde who causes Sinden all his grief is Carole Lesley, a cute miss who sails through this role with no trouble at all . Two certain insurances for laughs in this type of pic are Ronald Shiner and Dora Bryan and both score heavily. One of the biggest yocks is gained by Peter Jones as a private soldier with a specialty of double talk which adds to the confusion of lectures.

Daniel Massey, Joan Rice, Barbara Hicks, John Cairney and John Welsh are others on hand to help the fun moving, and glamor is represented by a dozen or so girls who take every opportunity to reveal underwear more suitable for the Folies Bergere than an Army unit. Gilbert Gunn's direction is brisk, especially in one hilarious sequence when the sudden, unexpected arrival of a Brigadier necessitates the sudden smartening-up of the camp causing Operation Bullshine to snap miraculously into effect. Gilbert Taylor's lensing is okay and the sets authentic.

"Operation Bullshine" is no comedy epic but it sets out to amuse and does so for a respectable portion of its running time. *Rich.*

Ferry to Hong Kong

(BRITISH-C'SCOPE-COLOR)

Hokum treatment of a romanticmeller. Overlong, but presenting some intriguing scenes of Hong Kong. Good stellar value, but routine b.o. prospects.

London, July 7.

Rank (George Maynard) production and release. Stars Curt Jurgens, Orson Welles, Sylvia Syms. Directed by Lewis Gilbert. Screenplay, Vernon Harris, Lewis Gilbert; camera, Otto Heller; editor, Peter Hunt; music, Ken Jones. At Rank Private Theatre, London. Running time: 113 MINS.

Mark Conrad .... Curt Jurgens
Captain Hart .... Orson Welles
Liz Ferrers .... Sylvia Syms
Miguel Henriques .... Jeremy Spenser
Joe Skinner .... Noel Purcell
Miss Carter .... Margaret Withers
Police Inspector .... John Wallace
Johnny Sing-Up .... Roy Chiao
Foo Soo .... Shelley Shen
Tommy Cheng .... Louis Seto
Yen .... Milton Reid
Portugese Major .... Ronald Decent
Archdeacon .... Don Carlos
Second Police Inspector .. Nick Kendall
First Guardian .... Kwan Shan Lam

The most fascinating aspect of this slice of meller-hokum is the way Orson Welles has clearly conned director Lewis Gilbert. Welles seems to have been allowed to write his own dialog and give his own interpretation of his role. He might just as well have taken over direction. The result is a piece of hammy over-acting which might have been fun for a few minutes. But, carried on for around two hours remorselessly, it becomes grotesque and, in the end a boring caricature.

The film is a slab of commercial cinema. Intriguing glimpses of Hong Kong locations, star value and some splendid storm-at-sea scenes will fascinate the average cinemagoer. But it doesn't look like the film that the bosses tried to turn out. Artistically, it's a mess. Financially, it may well prove a click.

Welles, with a magnificently phoney makeup and an irritating accent which veers from the "refeened" to the Cockney, is a phoney skipper who runs a ferryboat between Hong Kong and Macao, a five-hour trip.

Jurgens is a no-good bum who is exiled from his native Austria. Hong Kong tosses him out. Macao wants no part of him. So he spends most of the film travelling on the ferryboat to the annoyance of Skipper Welles. Welles hates him and tries to get rid of him. Jurgens is, for the first time, happy. He has a home. The clash between these two offbeat characters is emceed by Sylvia Syms, a schoolmistress, who falls for Jurgens and prods him into action. It winds up with him saving the ship when it becomes involved in a giant storm and a raid from some Chinese pirates.

Otto Heller's lensing and Lewis Gilbert's direction are at their best in the storm and hold-up scenes. The acting is as good as can be expected considering the dialog and leisurely yarn. Welles, as has been indicated, has had himself an actor's holiday. Jurgens wanders through the film with the air of a man whose heart isn't in it. Miss Syms, comely and charming, does wonders with a colorless role.

Best pieces of thesping come from Noel Purcell, as the ship's engineer, and Margaret Withers, as a busybody spinster. Jeremy Spenser, as a young ship's officer, doesn't stand a chance. Milton Reid as the chief of the Chinese pirates, brings brawn and some brain to an unbelievably written part, which must cause twinges of conscience for script-writers Lewis Gilbert and Vernon Harris.

Authentic peeks at Hong Kong will stimulate any patron into taking a ticket to that exciting city, if only for the nightlife. Some Chinese kids bring fun to the piece. Some 25 minutes, ruthlessly scrapped from "Ferry To Hong Kong," could have helped a pic which doesn't deserve to succeed but may well do so, despite its faults. *Rich.*

The Mummy

(COLOR)

Mild horror film well produced and with exploitation potential for intended market.

Hollywood, July 7.

Universal release of Michael Carreras production. Stars Peter Cushing, Christopher Lee, Yvonne Furneaux; features Eddie Byrne, Felix Aylmer, Raymond Huntley, George Pastell. Directed by Terence Fisher. Screenplay, Jimmy Sangster; camera (Technicolor), Jack Asher; production designer, Bernard Robinson; music, Frank Reizenstein; editors, James Needs, Alfred Cox. Previewed July 7, '59. Running time, 86 MINS.

John Banning .... Peter Cushing
Kharis .... Christopher Lee
Isobel .... Yvonne Furneaux
Ananka .... Yvonne Furneaux
Mulrooney .... Eddie Byrne
Stephen Banning .... Felix Aylmer
Joseph Whemple .... Raymond Huntley
Mehemet .... George Pastell
Coroner .... John Stuart
Pat .... Harold Goodwin
Mike .... Dennis Shaw

Producers of this British import twirl their narrative around the old Egyptian curse, that whoever desecrates the dead in their tombs shall die. Premise is fairly well developed while offering little of actual newness to plot, and via U's planned exploitation campaign pic should do okay in is particular market.

Lavishly produced by Michael Carreras, film's subject benefits sharply by use of Technicolor, which gives tone and quality to unfoldment. Yarn carries the type of action expected, and while chiller aspects aren't too pronounced they're sufficient for those who want to find them. Acting fits the requirements of script by Jimmy Sangster and Terence Fisher's direction makes good use of characters.

Plottage follows three English archaeologists who discover the 4,000-year-old tomb of Princess Ananka, high priestess in the court of the Egyptian god Karnak, and events befalling them when they return home. Menace is provided by the return to life of a high priest, buried alive as a guardian of the embalmed princess, who is brought to England by a mysterious Egyptian to avenge the desecration of the sacred tomb. He kills two of the scientists, but the third is saved by his wife resembling the ancient princess.

Peter Cushing delivers handily as the third archaeologist, and Yvonne Furneaux, seen briefly, lends distaff interest. Christopher Lee scores as the avenger, who seemingly cannot be destroyed by bullets or spears. Felix Aylmer and Raymond Huntley, the other two scientists; George Pastell, the Egyptian; and Eddie Byrne, a police inspector, handle their roles creditably.

Technical departments are excellently executed, including Jack Asher's camera work; Bernard Robinson's production designing, editing by Jack Needs and Alfred Cox, and music score by Frank Reizenstein. *Whit.*

Ten Seconds to Hell

Marquee lure of Jeff Chandler, Jack Palance and Martine Carol, plus exploitation values, should push this so-so meller into fair b.o. returns.

United Artists release of a Seven Arts-Hammer Production produced by Michael Carreras. Stars Jeff Chandler, Jack Palance, Martine Carol; features Virginia Baker, Wes Addy, Robert Cornthwaite. Directed by Robert Aldrich. Screenplay, Aldrich and Teddi Sherman, from the novel "The Phoenix" by Lawrence P. Bachmann: camera, Ernest Laszlo: editor, Harry Richardson: music, Kenneth V. Jones. Previewed N.Y., July 9, '59. Running time, **93 MINS**

Wirtz	Jeff Chandler
Koertner	Jack Palance
Margot	Martine Carol
Loeffler	Robert Cornthwaite
Tillig	Dave Willock
Sulke	Wes Addy
Globke	Jimmy Goodwin
Frau Bauer	Virginia Baker
Major Haven	Richard Wattis

Hazardous job of deactivating dud bombs after World War II appears sound material for a melodramatic and suspenseful film. But curiously "Ten Seconds to Hell" emerges as a downbeat picture that registers little audience impact. Names of Jeff Chandler, Jack Palance and Martine Carol, however, offer some b.o. insurance.

While the story has some negative aspects, nevertheless it contains some exploitable values. A campaign designed to take advantage of the latter, plus the star power, should help generate fair returns in the general market for this United Artists release.

Based on Lawrence P. Bachmann's novel, "The Phoenix," the Robert Aldrich-Teddi Sherman screenplay seldom draws sympathy for any of its characters. Of six former German soldiers who form a bomb disposal unit in Berlin at the war's end, three are quickly killed in performance of their duties. The audience knows little of their backgrounds, and is affected only impersonally by their deaths.

Palance, self-styled leader of the unit, is a man of courage and conviction. But he's a moody individual who appears to be continually wrestling with inner problems. Ruthless and egotistical is Chandler who has regard for no one except himself. Miss Carol, in an unglamorous role, runs a boarding house, where Palance and Chandler reside.

Instead of developing the characters more fully, the script chooses to train the cameras on one bomb deactivation after another. While this is a nerve-tingling operation, anything can be made dull through repetition. A pact made at the unit's inception under which half of each member's earnings will go to the survivor (s) at the end of three months also tends to make filmgoers sit back in their seats and wait for te inevitable.

Co-scripter Aldrich apparently keyed his direction around the story's grim and sombre qualities. The depressing atmosphere undeniably is there. There's little relief from it with exceptions of a few scenes where Chandler and Palance vie for Miss Carol's affections. A night club scene, which would have offered some contrast, wound up on the cutting room floor.

Performances are only fair. Neither Palance nor Chandler appears at ease in their respective assignments. Sexy Miss Carol, whose flair for romantic roles is celebrated, is largely wasted as the rooming house landlady. Virginia Baker has little to do as a telephone operator at the unit's "command post." Seen briefly before meeting death are unit members Robert Cornthwaite, Dave Willock, Wes Addy and Jimmy Goodwin. All have the proper fatalistic attitude.

With the film shot on location in Berlin, cameraman Ernest Laszlo has provided some realistic backgrounds. Kenneth V. Jones' score is effective but Harry Richardson's editing has some weak points. Physical values of this Seven Arts-Hammer Production are adequate for a film of this nature. *Gilb.*

Far Jag Lana Din Fru?
(Lend Me Your Wife)

Stockholm, July 7.

Sandrew Film production and release. Stars: Edvin Adolphson, Sven Lindberg, Bengt Brunskog, Elsa Prawitz, Features Annalisa Ericson, Nils Hallberg, Sif Ruud, Mona Malm, Lena Granhagen, Torsten Winge, Curt Lofgren, Ludde Juberg. Director: Arne Mattsson. Screenplay: Lars Widding & Eva Seeberg. Camera: Sven Nykvist. Editor: Lennart Wallen. Music: Jules Sylvain. At Royal, Stockholm. Running time: **104 MINS.**

Fredrik Fredrikson	Edvin Adolphson
Bertil Lund	Sven Lindberg
Thorbjorn	Bengt Brunskog
Ulla, his wife	Elsa Prawitz
Fanny, secretary	Annalisa Ericson
Kurre, salesman	Nils Hallberg
Kurre's wife	Sif Rund
Ingrid Fredriksson	Mona Malm
Stella	Lena Granhagen
The vicar	Torsten Winge
Bartender	Curt Lofgren
The Coachman	Ludde Juberg
Hansson	John Norrman

A job as vice-president is vacant at Everything-For-Baby-Company, but the man most qualified for it has one fault, he's a bachelor. His best friend (Bengt Brunskog), who happens to be married, decides to help him, first by a telephone call to the president of the company (Edvin Adolphson) when he spreads word that the bachelor is a married man. The president is very happy to find out and arranges a party for the employees, including their wives and husbands. The bachelor is now back in an even more difficult situation, but again his friend wants to help, suggesting him to bring along his wife, introducing her as his own.

What seems a fine solution naturally develops complications, when the president sends the couple on a business trip out of town, and, at the same time, the bachelor has happened to fall in love with the president's daughter (Mona Malm). The husband in the story has become jealous and carefully follows the couple on their trip.

Story is not new, and not particularly well made, but the film has some commercial appeal, at least in the European market. A handsome tune by Jules Sylvain sounds as having Hit-Parade-appeals if well exploited.

Sven Lindberg as the bachelor who pretends to be married to get the job he wants, is doing very good, well assisted by well - routined veteran Edvin Adolphson as the big boss of the wholesale - company. Elsa Prawitz as the pretended wife of Lindberg as well as real wife of jealous Bengt Brunskog has the very best part of the film.

Technical credits are okay. *Wing.*

Berlin Festival

Un Uomo Facile
(The Defeated Victor) (ITALIAN)

Berlin, July 14.

Serena Film (Rome) (Romano Dandi) production. Stars Maurizio Arena, Giovanna Ralli. Directed by Paolo Heusch. Screenplay, Fausto Tozzi; camera, Roberto Gerardi; music, Carlo Rustichelli, Piero Umiliani. At Zoo Palast, Berlin. Running time, **95 MINS.**

An interesting theme has been smoothly developed in this Berlin festival entry. The subject has a boxing background, and the central male characters are the champ who is beginning to slide from the peak, and the novice who is starting to climb.

Careers of the two men are viewed through the eyes of the women in their lives. The champ has married the novice's sister at the height of his career, and she has to suffer the subsequent humiliation and misery of poverty.

Although the development is somewhat uneasy, the overall effect yields a holding entertainment. The two femme roles are filled by lookers, and acting all round is okay. *Myro.*

Hadaka No Taiyo
(The Naked Sun) (JAPANESE—C'SCOPE)

Berlin, July 14.

Toei (Hiroshi Okawa) Motion Picture Co. (Tokyo) production and release. Stars Tatsuya Nakadai, Hitomi Nakahara. directed by Miyoji Ieki. Screenplay, Kazutoshi Himuro, Kaneto Shindo; camera, Giyu Miyajima; music, Yasushi Akutagawa. At Zoo Palast, Berlin. Running time, **85 MINS.**

A pleasant disarming tale of a young lover's tiff, "The Naked Sun" is a competently made pic which has basic entertainment ingredients, but no outstanding qualities to hypo it in Western markets.

The two principal characters in the story are a young couple who deny themselves the little luxuries so that they can save to get married, Then, impetuously, the boy lends all their savings to a friend, and the girl is furious. But she relents later when she learns the money was needed to help someone undergo surgery.

Both the stars play their respective roles with a measure of charm. Direction is smooth, and handled. CinemaScope lensing is fine. *Myro.*

Sagar Sangame
(The Holy Island) (INDIAN)

DeLuxe Film Distributoris (Calcutta) production and release. Stars Bharati Devi and Monju Adhikary. Directed by Debaki Kumar Bose. Camera, Bimal Mukherjee; screenplay, Premen Mitra and Bose; music, B. C. Boral. At Zoo Palast, Berlin. Running time, **90 MINS.**

A modest production, obviously intended primarily for local consumption, "The Holy Island" hardly merited a late night screening at an international film fest. It's a slow, tedious subject, naively acted and directed, with no chances whatsoever in Western markets.

This is a story of a childless widow, shipwrecked while en route to the Holy Island, who rescues a brat of a girl, and finds herself developing maternal instincts towards the child, against her better judgment. It's virtually a two-character yarn and is related in a pedestrian way, without warmth, without humor and without shading. Inadequate lighting robs the pic of its scenic values, too.
Myro.

Meus Amores No Rio
(Three Loves In Rio) (BRAZILIAN—COLOR)

Berlin, July 14.

Carlos Hugo Christensen production. Directed by Christensen. Camera (Agfacolor), Anibal Gonzales Paz; screenplay, Pedro Bloch. At Berlin Film Fest. **116 MINS.**

The Girl	Suzana Freyre
First Man	Fabio Cardoso
Second Man	Jardel Filho
Third Man	Domingo Alzugaray

As a feature film, this has little if any value. However, as a documentary about the Brazilian capital, it's an appealing item. Pic offers a number of excellent shots of the "world's most beautiful city." If properly cut to about 80 to 90 minutes, "Rio" stands a good commercial chance on the European market.

The story line that goes through the whole thing is harmless but occasionally very amusing. It concerns a young Argentinian girl, who has won a trip to Rio de Janeiro on a tele quiz. Three young men—a pilot, a playboy and a journalist—fall in love with her. With each of them, she experiences the excitement of this city. The Agfacolor camera exploits the latter substantially. *Hans.*

Flor de Mayo
(Tumult of Sentiments) (MEXICAN)

Berlin, July 14.

Cinematografica Latino Americana, Mexico (Alallo Rubio Jr.), production and release. Stars Jack Palance, Maria Felix, Pedro Armendariz and Juanito Musquiz. Directed by Roberto Gavaldon. Screenplay, Edwin Blum, Julien Silvera from a novel by Vicente Blasco Ibanez; camera, Gabriel Figueroa; music, Gustavo C. Carrion. At Congress Hall, Berlin. Running time, **100 MINS.**

Althoug it has Jack Palance as a name for the marquee, this Mexican film, which was the windup presentation for the Berlin Festival, is a sub-standard entry with mild entertainment values and limited commercial chances. It's naive, sentimental and unsophisticated to a degree.

Palance plays the heavy, the role of an American adventurer who returns to a Mexican fishing village and meets up again with the girl he once loved. She's married to a wealthy fisherman and her husband soon suspects—with justification—that the visitor is the father of the boy he believed to be his own child. Leisurely direction and indifferent scripting are matched by casual performances. Maria Felix plays the woman, Pedro Armandariz, the husband and Juanito Musquiz, the son. *Myro.*

Korkarlen
(Thy Soul Shall Bear Witness) (SWEDISH-AGASCOPE)

Berlin, July 7.

Svenska AB Nordisk Tonefilm (Stockholm) production and release. Stars

George Fant, Ulla Jacobsson. Directed by Arne Nattsson. Screenplay, Rune Lindstrom, from novel by Selma Lagerlof; camera, Max Wilen; music, Dag Wiren. At Zoo Palast, Berlin. Running time, 108 MINS.

A remake of a famous silent film, this Swedish production is arty-type pic with a somewhat involved and confusing story-line. Slow in development, it is nicely photographed and directed. Commercially, its prospects must be restricted, but it will have some appeal to ardent cinema patrons who respect and admire the current Swedish trends in film-making.

The plot is based on the old legend about the last person to die on New Year's eve. The victim is George Fant. Once he's dead, he looks back on a miserable past of suffering and drunkenness. It's largely an essay in despair and hope, but thanks to a fine cast is occasionally very moving. *Myro.*

Diez Fusiles Esperan
(Ten Rifles Wait)
(SPANISH)

Berlin, July 14.
Eduardo de la Fuente production. Directed by Jose Luis Saenz de Heredia. Camera, Francisco Sempere; screenplay, Carlos Blanco. At Berlin Film Fest. Running time, 100 MINS.
Jose .... Francisco Rabal
Miguel .... Ettore Manni
Teresa .... Rosita Arenas
Lucia .... Berta Riaza
Don Leopoldo .... Memmo Carotenuto
Mother .... Carola Fernan Gomez

This drama about love, honor and duty shapes mainly a local Spanish bet. It offers good acting, some suspense plus a number of nice dialog sequences. However, the theme and an overdose of pathos and passion makes this an item that's not of much interest outside of Spain.

A Spanish officer has been sentenced to death but is granted a leave before the execution. First, he intends to flee with his girl but later decides to remain a man of honor and choses death. Direction is somewhat slow. Technical credits are fair. *Hans.*

Sven Tuuava
(Sven Dufva, the Hero)
(FINNISH)

Berlin, July 7.
Oy Suomen Filmiteollisuus (Helsinki) production and release. Stars Veikko Sinisalo, Salme Karppinen. Directed by Edvin Laine. Screenplay, Vaino Ninna, from poem by J. L. Runeberg; camera, Osmo Harkimo and Olavi Tuomi; music, Heikki Aaltoila. At Zoo Palast, Berlin. Running time, 106 MINS.

The title character in this Finnish production is an historic figure of the Finnish-Russian war of some 150 years ago. He's a sort of good soldier Schwelk, but without the cunning and guile of the legendary Czech soldier.

The war scenes are capably handled, with an adequate amount of action. This is counterbalanced by a deft light touch, introducing a humorous note at the right moment. There's not much subtlety in the plot. However, the femme star (Salme Karppinen is an attractive, well-developed blonde with an easy thesping style. Her costar, Veikko Sinisalo, is an able actor and realistically suggests the simpleton soldier. *Myro.*

The Enchanted Mirror
(KINOPANORAMA—COLOR)

Imaginative documentary treatment of various aspects of Soviet life. Informative and entertaining, but technically still short of the mark.

Ministry of Culture of the USSR presentation of a Sovexport in release. Shown in conjunction with the Soviet Exhibition of Science, Technology and Culture at the Coliseum, N.Y. Produced at the Central Studio for Documentary Films, Moscow, with cartoon sequences photographed at Soyuzmultfilm Studio. Direction and script, L. Kristi and V. Komissarjevsky; camera (Sovcolor), V. Voronzov, I. Gutman, A. Koloshin, S. Medynsky; cartoon director, I. Aksenchuk; cartoon photography, A. Astafiev and N. Klimova; cartoon artists, L. Milchin, I. Shwarzman, A. Vinokurov, T. Sazonova. Appearing in the film are artists from the Peking Classical Theatre of the USSR, the Peking Classical Opera, the Dance Ensemble of the Platnitzky Chorus and the ensemble ARF. Previewed in N.Y., July 20, 1959. Running time, 90 MINS.

For their second Kinopanorama offering at the Mayfair Theatre, N.Y., supplementing the Soviet Cultural and Scientific Exhibition at the Coliseum, the Russians have chosen "The Enchanted Mirror," a lively, far-ranging and at times quite beautiful screen tour of the Soviet Union and its people. Technically, at the U.S. CineMiracle projection end, the picture suffers from severe defects, as did its predecessor, "Great Is My Country." Artistically, and from an entertainment point-of-view, it's a lot of fun and very well done.

It's as if the Russians, having limbered up with their first picture, and having lived down the "thrill" approach to the wide screen, had gotten down to work on putting their Kinopanorama process to best use. Much of the photography is impressive, and in a couple of sequences it's even stunning. It's obvious that no effort has been spared to do justice to a widescreen system which, inherently is capable of marvellous effects. Here, the determination to make a documentary with a human interest touch has paid off.

A good deal of Russia, and something also of Red China, can be gleaned from the film which has been cut into four separate segments and built into an intriguing cartoon frame that has symbolic overtones. If there is propaganda in this second picture it's either so obvious as to be valueless, or else it's so subtle that the vast majority of people won't even get it. Through it all comes the tremendous pride of the Soviets in their achievements in science and industry, and their well-developed sense of joint effort and success through Communism.

"The Enchanted Mirror" pulls together a great many facets of Soviet life though, as in "Great Is My Country," no individual ever really comes alive and identification is impossible. These people look good, they smile when they go to work and when they come from work, they love children and they're all very hard at work to build, construct and devote themselves to the arts. If they have private thoughts of their own, they don't share them with the camera.

Kinopanorama is projected on a very large screen from three synchronized projectors working out of the same booth. Nine-channel stereophonic sound is used and in spots very effectively, too. But Kinopanorama simply isn't very good. The matchlines are more pronounced than ever and one—separating the left panel from the center one—is so wide that a person

passing it on the screen appears to be going into one side of a door and coming out on the other. There's also considerable distortion as a result. Yet "Enchanted Mirror" has plenty to balance those imperfections.

The first part, "Snow Queen," starts with an indication of the Hans Christian Anderson fairy tale and then spreads out for a breathtaking view of the North Pole, a visit to a Soviet Scientific Station on an ice floe, a tour of the Siberian Taiga forest where bulldozers and tractors are at work clearing the bottom of the future Obsk Sea. The scene concludes with an exciting and very real ride in which a Russian "Troika" comes galloping towards the camera at full speed.

Part two is called "A Fairy Tale of Wondrous Transformations" and prominently features the superb Galina Olanova performing both the white and the black swan in "Swan Lake." Part three deals with Red China and offers some revealing glimpses of Chinese at work building the huge Shisanlinsk Reservoir. Since so little of Red China is seen in the States, the scenes take on unusual interest. There's also a bit of a performance by the Peking Classical Opera Co. Here, as in other scenes, the excellent Sovcolor process helps.

Picture winds up with a tour of the Brussels Fair of 1958 and a whirling and beautifully coordinated folk dance number. "Enchanted Mirror" is again Russia putting her best foot forward, but this time the tour is rich and varied and the pace is just right. Kinopanorama for the most part provides a very clear image with good depth and a strong sense of participation, with dizzying panning shots avoided. *Hift.*

The Scapegoat

The look-alike substitute plot makes off-and-on Alec Guinness mystery puzzler. Fair for his fans.

Hollywood, July 17.
Metro release of a Michael Balcon production. Stars Alec Guinness; features Nicole Maurey, Irene Worth, Pamela Brown; guest star, Bette Davis. Director-writer, Robert Hamer; screenplay based on Daphne DuMaurier's novel as adapted by Gore Vidal; camera, Paul Beeson; music, Bronislau Kaper; editor, Jack Harris. Previewed at the studio, July 16, '59. Running time, 92 MINS.
John Barratt,
Jacques De Gue .... Alec Guinness
The Countess .... Bette Davis
Bela .... Nicole Maurey
Francoise .... Irene Worth
Blanche .... Pamela Brown
Marie-Noel .... Annabel Bartlett
Gaston .... Geoffrey Keen
Dr. Aloin .... Noel Howlett
Aristide .... Peter Bull
Lacoste .... Leslie French
Inspector .... Alan Webb
Maid .... Maria Britneva
Barman .... Eddie Byrne
Gamekeeper .... Alexander Archdale
Customs Official .... Peter Sallis

Alec Guinness indulges his interest in portraying multiple characters in "The Scapegoat," an unusual mystery story with undertones of murder. Both characters played by Guinness look-alike, although their personalities are radically different. Impersonation, when one man is the identical image of another, and the effects it produces, provide the interesting story of Michael Balcon's production for Metro.

The filmization of Daphne DuMaurier's novel will be partially satisfying to Guinness fans, although the excellence of its production is subverted by an abrupt and unsatisfactory conclusion and

a screenplay that leaves too much unexplained.

Guinness plays a colorless English teacher of the French language on vacation in France. While there he is tricked into assuming the identity of a very colorful, decadent and amoral French count who is his physical twin. There is humor, suspense and mounting interest as he takes his place in his twin's setting — a la Anthony Hope's old "Prisoner of Zenda."

He discovers his mother is Bette Davis, the Dowager Countess, a morphine addict. His daughter, Annabel Bartlett, is a religious minded teenager, fascinated by the gorier martyrdoms; his sister, Pamela Brown, hates him so much she doesn't speak to him; his wife, Irene Worth, is psychopathic with fear (not without cause) that she is likely to be murdered, and his brother-in-law, Peter Bull, is a crafty boozer who is diverting the profits of the family business to himself. On the bright side, Guinness finds his alter ego has a lovely Italian mistress, Nicole Maurey, stashed away in a town adjacent to the family chateau.

The screenplay by Robert Hamer, from an adaptation by Gore Vidal from Miss DuMaurier's novel, displays these exotic characters with unflinching zeal. It does not, however, give much if any indication of how they got that way, or why. The ending is bad. Guinness has a gun duel with himself when the English teacher character decides he makes a better French count than the French count, and Hamer's method of showing which man won is strictly old-hat and a letdown.

The film would not be disappointing if it were not, as it is, so interesting and well-done in some individual portions. Guinness, again, seems unable to give less than a superior performance. Bette Davis, as the ravaged countess, gives a baroque and fascinating portrayal. It is possible to sympathize with both the wife, Miss Worth, and the mistress, Miss Maurey, so expert are their performances. Pamela Brown suffers from an insufficiently developed role, but is good within limits imposed on her. Others contributing, sometimes strikingly, are young Miss Bartlett, Geoffrey Keen, Bull and Leslie French.

Except for the final trick, Hamer's direction is discreet but pointed. The fault of the film is that either through too-stringent editing or too-loose writing, scenes of motivation and background, and some of development, have been omitted. This creates, for a mystery, too much unsatisfactory confusion.

French locations are useful and they have been captured with perception by cameraman Paul Beeson. *Powe.*

Desert Desperadoes

Desert caravan tries to make its way to Alexandria (Egypt) against the forces of King ..., with trouble along the way, entertainment-wise.

RKO release (via franchise dealers) of John Nasht production. Stars Ruth Roman; features Akim Tamiroff, Othelo Toso, Gianni Glori, Arnoldo Foa, Alan Furlan, Directed by Steve Sekely. Story and screenplay, Victor Stolloff and Robert Hill. Other credits unavailable. Previewed in N.Y. July 2, '59. Running time, 81 MINS.
The Woman .... Ruth Roman
The Merchant .... Akim Tamiroff
Verrus .... Othelo Toso
Fabius .... Gianni Glori
The Chaldean .... Arnoldo Foa

Rais .... Alan Furlan
Metullus .... Nino Marchetti

Listed by Principal Film Exchange, the New York franchise distributor, as an RKO picture presented by John Nasht, "Desert Desperadoes" is a meller of the old-fashioned cinema school set in Biblical times. The theatrical values are limited this modern day; the approach to picture making, as observed. from the uncertain print shown, goes back some years.

Project undertakes to combine what looks like routine action-on-the-sands stuff with a strong inference that the infant being carried on the desert safari could well be the Judean Saviour.

And interwined with this is the story of the rich merchant ,Akim Tamiroff) who makes passes at a sultry and gammy (Cleopatra-type) unkown-origin femme who is found stranded in the desert. Tamiroff is sponsor of the caravan, which has a group of Roman soldiers as convoy. The girl is Ruth Roman, not particularly appropriate as the siren who has both Tamiroff and at least one of the Romans in a flesh-and-blood tizzy.

Print shown indicates some cutting has been done and this impairs the organization of the story, sometimes to the point of disconcerting the onlooker.

Technical work on the feature, which was made in Italy and on location in Egypt, is of modest proportions. *Gene.*

A Private's Affair
(C'SCOPE-COLOR)

Screwball service comedy with an attractive young cast. Good entertainment and o.k. box-office prospects.

20th-Fox release of David Weisbart production. Stars Sal Mineo, Christine Carere, Barry Coe, Barbara Eden, Gary Crosby; features Jim Backus, Jessie Royce Landis, Rubert Burton, Alan Hewitt. Directed by Raoul Walsh; script, Winston Miller, based on story by Ray Livingston Murphy; camera (De Luxe color), Charles G. Clarke; songs, Jimmy McHugh, Jay Livingston and Ray Evans; music, Cyril J. Mockridge, conducted by Lionel Newman; editor, Dorothy Spencer. Previewed at the Paramount Theatre, N.Y., July 20, '59. Running time, 92 MINS.

Luigi .... Sal Mineo
Marie .... Christine Carere
Jerry .... Barry Coe
Katey .... Barbara Eden
Mike .... Gary Crosby
Louise .... Terry Moore
Jim Gordon .... Jim Backus
Elizabeth Chapman .. Jessie Royce Landis
Gen. Hargrave .... Robert Burton
Maj. Hanley .... Alan Hewitt
Macintosh .... Robert Denver
Sgt. Pickerell .... Tige Andrews
Capt. Hickman .... Ray Montgomery
Doctor Leyden .... Rudolph Anders
Magdalena .... Debbie Joyce
Young Rookie .. Robert Montgomery Jr.

Ever hear of a private marrying a lady Assistant Secretary of War at her request while he's snoring away under the influence of drugs, and all this to save a little Dutch girl who's father is dying and who otherwise would be shipped back to Holland? It's that kind of a plot that they've cooked up from a story by Ray Livingston Murphy and the result is a featherlight comedy that pretends to be little more than a good show for a hot summer night.

Since the customers aren't burdened with having to take any of this zany routine seriously, the young and attractive cast works away at it with an unconcerned gusto that's good for some hearty laughs and very funny situation comedy. A dash of romance and a

couple of nice song-and-dance routines are thrown in to fill the formula bill.

Almost from the very start, director Raoul Walsh aims for the yocks, and after that he doesn't care how he gets 'em, a necessity since it's a small joke milked to exhaustion and farce is a tough thing to maintain. Winston Miller has written some genuinely funny lines and they've put over with a good sense of timing that makes 'em explode like firecrackers.

Almost the best thing about "A Private's Affair" is its introduction of a bunch of new faces. Sal Mineo, Barry Coe and Gary Crosby play a trio of soldiers in basic training who win a chance to compete for their camp on a national tv show. That gives them a chance to do a couple of amusing routines, that should earn them a teenage following. The gals are played by Christine Carere, Barbara Eden and Terry Moore.

Mineo is good as a sort of modified beatnik type. Coe has an appealing personality and clearly is a comer. He's the fellow who, through a mixup, gets to marry Jessie Royce Landis, the Assistant Secretary of War. Crosby obviously has a good sense of humor and is given some of the best lines, but he misses in affecting his father's easy casualness. He should find a style of his own.

Miss Carere, playing a French miss, is charming in an undemanding role. Miss Eden, acting in her first theatrical film role, is a natural comedienne and easy on the eyes. Miss Moore has virtually nothing to do, but looks pretty. All of them have one thing in their favor — they're attractive and they're young, and that's a big asset today.

The talented team of Jimmy McHugh, Jay Livingston and Ray Evans has written three songs for the film, with "It's the Same Old Army" as the lead refrain. Mineo, Coe and Crosby create a smart routine for it early in the picture, singing it while on K.P. duty.

In the smaller roles, Jim Backus is his reliable self as the tv producer, Miss Landis somehow manages to infuse a sense of dignity into the part of the Secretary and Robert Burton is broadly comic as the general. Alan Hewitt skillfully handles the role of the camp psychiatrist.

Charles G. Clarke's lensing has quality and the DeLuxe color is all one could wish for. Dorothy Spencer's editing keeps everything rolling along just fine. This isn't the kind of picture that will win prizes, but it shapes as a very satisfactory grosser in a market that always seems to be able to stand another service comedy, be it even a slim one. *Hift.*

Llegaron Dos Hombres
(Two Men in Town)
(HISPANO-SWEDISH)

Madrid, July 14.
Paramount (Spain) release of a Molino-Terrafilm production. Stars Francisco Rabal, Ulla Jacobsson, Christian Marquand, Moulodji, Ana Esmeralda; features Fernando, Sancho, Felix Defauce, Roberto Camardiel. Directed by Arne Mattson and E. F. Ardavin from story by Volodja Semitjoy; adapted by Enrique Alarcon and Jose Lopez Rubio. Camera, Alfredo Fraile; music, Cristobal Halffter. At Roxy "B," Madrid. Running time. 91 MINS.

Spanish village is locale for the familiar theme of cornered criminals holding a stunned schoolmarm (Ulla Jacobsson) and her terrorized moppets as hostages. After a good suspense jump-off,

main action is played in town-square where Guardia Civil (Spain's feared rural police) and townsfolk assemble to parley with two homicidal lunatics (Marquand and Moulodji) for the urchins' lives.

From there in, it's mostly meller stuff bordering on farce. Police chief (Francisco Rabal) and lieutenants give an inept demonstration, the desperados stretch their tyranny to king-for-a-day limits and the villagers emerge as panic-stricken seeds. The non-pro kids are fine.

Tri-nation thespian talent labors hard but fails to cope with the fuzzy direction of a potential thriller. Spain's Ana Esmeralda alone reveals depth. Cristobal, Halffter, score and Alfredo Fraile's lensing surpass.

All Yank companies here are now releasing locally one Spanish film for every four imported. Which explains the Paramount trademark. *Werb.*

Pecheur D'Islande
(Island Fisherman)
(FRENCH-DY'SCOPE-COLOR)

Paris, July 14.
Imperia release of Iberia production. Stars Jean-Claude Pascal, Juliette Mayniel, Charles Vanel; features Michel Garland, Georges Poujouly, Joelle Bernard. Directed by Pierre Schoendoerfer. Screenplay, Andre Tabet. Schoendoerfer from novel by Pierre Loti; camera (Eastmancolor), Raoul Coutard; editor, B. Menapard. At Cameo, Paris. Running time, 90 MINS.

Yan ....Jean-Claude Pascal
Gaud ....Juliette Mayniel
Mevel ....Charles Vanel
Berger ....Michel Garland
Jenny ....Joelle Bernard
Moan ....Georges Poujouly

This pedestrian pic is about the young captain of an outdated fishing boat who ends up landing the boss' daughter after proving himself at sea. Film has some good production values in its exteriors but the old hat tale is not given enough feeling, depth or characterization to keep it from dragging along.

Actors can do little with their roles which are too routine. Fishing scenes have scope (via Dyaliscope) and the color and technical aspects are good. But this looks like largely local fare. *Mosk.*

Berlin Festival

Telesme Schekaste
(The Broken Talisman)
(IRAN—COLOR

Berlin, July 14.
Studio Pars-Film (Teheran) production. Directed by Syamak Yassami. Screenplay, Ibrahim Zamani; camera (Agfacolor), Mah'moud Koushan. At Berlin Film Fest. Running time, 91 MINS.

Iran, last year repped at the Berlin festival, came along with a fairly well made adventure yarn which obviously tries to follow the American western pattern. Subject and acting are somewhat on the naive side but there's a certain plus factor in the lensing. Not much for the world market.

Story revolves around a Khan who doesn't notice the intrigues around him. Then his nephew decides to track down the evil-doers. Despite technical and artistic deficiencies, this hints that the young film industry of Iran is progressing. *Hans.*

Tierra Magica
(Magic Country)
(VENEZUELA)

Berlin, July 14.
Elvi Films and Tiuana Films production. Directed by Vittorio Valentini, Massimo Dalla Mano. Screenplay, Mano, Elso and Vittorio Valentini; camera, Mano. At Berlin Film Fest. Running time, 92 MINS.

A spectacular documentary leading the viewer this way and that through Venezuela. Pic gives an impressive insight into this country and makes one familiar with the people living there. Apart from overly intensive mood music. Film deserves the compliment of being a good one in its class. Could be a good programmer for matinees. *Hans.*

Herren Og Hans Tjenere
(The Master and His Servants)
(NORWEGIAN)

Berlin, July 14.
Norsk Film A/S Oslo production. With Claes Gill and Wenche Voss. Directed by Arne Skouen. Screenplay, Axel Kielland and Arne Skouen; camera, Finn Bergan. At Berlin Film Fest. Running time, 84 MINS.

This film's central-figure is a bishop who's been accused of having libelled his theological rival via anonymous letters. Although he's innocent (his secretary wrote the letters) in a legal sense, he calls himself guilty as he's the spiritual initiator of the letters and thereby shows his Christian responsibility and attitude.

Execution of plot is interesting but suffers slightly from conventional direction. The producers deserve the compliment for having dedicated themselves to a daring subject which is an attack against the hypocrites who say God and mean business. *Hans.*

Dorp Aan De Rivier
(Village on the River)
(DUTCH)

Berlin, July 14.
Nationale Film Productie Maatschappij production. With Max Croiset, Mary Dresselhuys, Bernard Droog, Jan Teulings. Directed by Fous Rademakers. Screenplay, Hugo Claus, Rademakers; camera, Eduard van Dalsum. At Berlin Film Fest. Running time, 91 MINS.

This Dutch feature was one of the better films shown at the Berlin festival. It primarily benefits from outstanding direction (Fous Rademarkers) which is somewhat reminiscent of that of Swedish Ingmar Bergman, only not so hard-hitten. Pic should be a good bet for the arties.

It's the heart-warming tale of a country doctor who is both loved and feared. His friends are the little people, his opponents are the members of the village council, in particular the burgomaster. Latter succeeds in chasing him out of the village to which the medico had dedicated his entire life. Good acting and fine technical credits. *Hans.*

Poeten Og Lillemor
(The Poet and the Little Mother)
(DENMARK)

Berlin, July 14.
A/S Nordisk Films (Copenhagen) production. Stars Henning Moritzen and Helle Virkner; features Ove Sprogoe, Lis Lowert. Directed by Erik Balling. Screenplay, Balling; camera, Poul Pedersen. At Berlin Film Fest. Running time, 97 MINS.

Denmark often has come along with amusing comedies in recent years. This one doesn't quite reach the standard of some such pix but

it's still an enjoyable piece of entertainment. Mixture of wit and slapstick contains general appeal. This has found a German distrib already.

Story has to do with a young poet and his wife who have to struggle along with financial difficulties. Then they suddenly win 10,000 crowns but this also is gone in less than no time. *Hans.*

Blue Denim
(C'SCOPE)

Provocative drama about teenagers contemplating an abortion because of their inability to communicate with their parents. Excellent b.o. chances.

20th-Fox release of Charles Brackett production. Stars Carol Lynley, Brandon de Wilde, Macdonald Carey and Marsha Hunt. Features Warren Berliner, Buck Class, Nina Shipman and Vaughn Taylor. Directed by Philip Dunne. Screenplay, Dunne and Edith Sommer; based on the stage play by James Leo Herlihy and William Noble; camera (C'Scope), Leo Tover; editor, William Reynolds; music, Bernard Hermann. Previewed in N.Y., July 23, '59. Running time, **89 MINS.**

Janet Willard	Carol Lynley
Arthur Bartley	Brandon de Wilde
Major Malcom Bartley	Macdonald Carey
Jessie Bartley	Marsha Hunt
Ernie	Warren Berlinger
Axel Sorenson	Buck Class
Lillian Bartley	Nina Shipman
Professor Willard	Vaughn Taylor
Cherie	Roberta Shore
Aunt Bidda	Mary Young
Vice President	William Schallert
Hobie	Michael Gainey
Marion	Jenny Maxwell
Woman in car	Junie Ellis

"Blue Denim" is a provocative drama with strong appeal for teenagers and their parents. Since the Charles Brackett production has the ability to attract the blue denim set, rated as the most frequent film-goers, as well as a substantial number of adults who will be interested in the theme, the picture rates as a strong boxoffice contender.

Based on the Broadway stage play of the same name by James Leo Herlihy and William Noble, it recounts, often movingly and intelligently, the torments of a pair of high school lovers who are about to become unwed parents. The desperation of these babes in the basement—a 15-year-old girl and a 16-year-old boy—is further highlighted by their inability to communicate with their parents.

The youngsters depicted in the film are not juvenile delinquents. Both stem from fine, upstanding middle class families. The girl's father is a college professor determined to raise his only daughter to emulate his dead wife. The boy's father is a retired Army officer given to reciting platitudes about the value of service life and unable to forget his moments of past glory. His mother is preoccupied with the preparations for the upcoming wedding of her older (19) daughter.

The distance that exists between the parents and the children makes the former the last ones that the troubled teenagers would turn to in their moment of utmost despair. Consequently, the children seek their own solution and make arrangements for an abortion. They are aware of the consequences of such a move, but feeling neglected and alone, attempt to proceed with the plan of desperation.

It is only at the last moment that the parents discover the utter helplessness of their children and realize, for the first time, their failure to establish a rapport with the young members of their family.

Undoubtedly due to production code restrictions, the Edith Sommer and Philip Dunne screenplay has been considerably watered down. The picture is tied up neatly in a blue ribbon to conform with code standards. The word "abortion" is never mentioned although it is obvious what is taking place. Moreover, the ending deteriorates to cliche melodrama. A big, black limousine, complete with a Charles Adams-looking femme, shows up to take the girl to the abortion rendezvous. Then there is the last-minute automobile chase as the two parents speed through the night to save the girl in the nick of time from the clutches of the unethical physician. In the play, the abortion is completed and the girl survives and it is from this point that the education of the obtuse parents begins. The film has the girl going off to have her baby in another city and the boy—this time with support of his father—joining her on the train.

Despite the subject matter, stark dramatics are interspersed with comedy scenes. The boy and his sidekick meet in the basement to guzzle beer, smoke cigarets, play poker and otherwise act as "big shots." There are also sequences involving a high school dance and a basketball game.

Carol Lynley, 20th-Fox's new teenage hope, repeats her stage role with the same eclat and sensitivity. She gives evidence of realizing the plans that the film company has in store for her. As her young lover, Brandon de Wilde, successfully bridging the gap from his moppet roles in "Member of the Wedding" and "Shane," gives a moving performance as the confused 16-year old learning the realities of sex. Warren Berliner, also from the stage play, is fine as his wise-cracking buddy and confidante.

Good depictions are also rendered by Macdonald Carey, as the boy's father; Marsha Hunt, as his mother; Vaughn Taylor, as the girl's father; Nina Shipman, as the boy's sister, and Buck Class, as her fiance.

For the most part, Philip Dunne's direction captures the spirit of the theme. It is best in displaying the torments of the adolescents, but falls down when it resorts to melodrama. The film, in black and white, has been given topnotch production values. Technical aspects, including Bernard Hermann's music, Leo Tover's cinematography, and Lyle R. Wheeler and Leland Fuller's art direction, are all first-rate. *Holl.*

Cry Tough

Topnotch melodrama set in a N.Y. Puerto Rican quarter; strong entry for program market.

Hollywood, July 24.

United Artists release of Harry Kleiner production. Stars John Saxon, Linda Cristal; costars Joseph Calleia; features Harry Townes, Don Gordon, Perry Lopez, Frank Puglia, Joe de Santis, Arthur Batanides, Paul Clarke, Penny Santon, Barbara Luna. Directed by Paul Stanley. Screenplay, Kleiner, based on novel by Irving Shulman; camera, Philip Lathrop, Irving Glassberg; music, Laurindo Almeida; editor, Frederic Knudtson. Previewed July 23, '59. Running time, **84 MINS.**

Miguel Estrada	John Saxon
Sarita	Linda Cristal
Senor Estrada	Joseph Calleia
Alvears	Arthur Batanides
Emilio	Paul Clarke
Cortez	Joe De Santis
Incho	Don Gordon
Toro	Perry Lopez
Tina	Barbara Luna
Lavandero	Frank Puglia
Senora Estrada	Penny Santon
Carlos	Harry Townes

Producers of "Cry Tough" latch onto fresh territory to backdrop the action of this punchy melo about a Puerto Rican quarter of N.Y. Well-produced right down the line and studded with better-than-average performances for this type of film, subject matter despite certain downbeat features is given interesting development which will help its chances in the program market.

The Harry Kleiner production marks the first time that a film has dealt with problems of the second generation Puerto Ricans in Manhattan, where in a squalid Spanish Harlem—the barrio, as it's known—life is filled with violence and unrest. John Saxon takes on the role of a restless young man just released from a year in prison, determined now to go straight and break loose from his festering environment "the hard way," rather than return to the gang and easy money.

Kleiner, who also scripted from an Irving Shulman novel, builds his plot dramatically and with logic, sum total emerging a strong exposition on one of today's social problems while providing suitable entertainment. Saxon delivers powerfully in what is probably his outstanding performance to date, and in Linda Cristal, as one of the quarter's "hostesses" who would rather live with a man than be married, he has an engaging co-star. Joseph Calleia registers effectively as the father, unable to understand ambition and a desire to get away. In standout roles, Harry Townes is the gang leader who wants Saxon back; Don Gordon is a menacing figure with a vicious blade-tipped umbrella always at hand; Perry Lopez, another gangster, dies in a knife fight with Saxon; and Barbara Luna is the sister.

Paul Stanley's direction is sharp and rigorous and photography by Philip Lathrop and Irving Glassberg sets a fine mood, as does Frederic Knudtson's fast editing. Laurindo Almeida's musical score and Edward Carrere's art direction are atmospheric. *Whit.*

Have Rocket, Will Travel

Revived Three Stooges in a sci-fi comedy. Strictly for juve market.

Hollywood, July 28.

Columbia Pictures production and release. Stars The Three Stooges (Moe Howard, Larry Fine, Joe De Rita); with Jerome Cowan, Anna-Lisa, Bob Colbert. Producer, Harry Romm. Director, David Lowell Rich. Screenplay, Raphel Hayes; camera, Ray Cory; music, Mischa Bakaleinikoff; are director, John T. McCormack; title song, George Duning and Stanley Styne; editor, Danny B. Landres. Previewed at Iris Theatre, July 17, '59. Running time, **76 MINS.**

Moe	Moe Howard
Larry	Larry Fine
Curley Joe	Joe De Rita
J. P. Morse	Jerome Cowan
Dr. Ingrid Naarveg	Anna-Lisa
Dr. Ted Benson	Bob Colbert

Columbia is bringing out "Have Rocket, Will Travel" at a time when the Three Stooges are enjoying "rediscovery" and new popularity via television. Hence, whatever the picture's production shortcomings, it will probably do well in the summertime juvenile market.

It's a silly hash of sight gags and sound effects loosely organized around a funny enough theme: handymen Moe Howard, Larry Fine and Joe Di Rita (who replaced the late Curly Howard) accidently get trapped in a rocket programmed for Venus and become Earth's first representatives on that planet.

Producer Harry Romm has given the film a fairly handsome physical presentation for a picture of this type. The rocket props have a cinematically businesslike look

and footage shot at real rocket installations is used effectively as a realistic backdrop for the zany antics of the Stooges.

With the juvenile audience almost exclusively in mind, Romm and director David Lowell Rich concentrated on the usual Stooges routines, which have amused juveniles for more than 20 years, and on a large variety of very good special effects. While most adults will consider the films a crashing bore, there's entertainment in: a flame-throwing giant spider, a talking unicorn, an arm-waving thinking machine, a variety of space phenomena and a number of photographic stunts—shrinking the Stooges to fit in a bird cage, materializing objects in thin air and a chase through corridor of doors involving two sets of Stooges.

Space limitations prohibit explaining how all of these elements are worked into the plot, but it doesn't matter anyway since the story was not considered foremost. The time devoted to the romantic sub-plot, awkwardly written for Anna-Lisa and Bob Colbert, is wasted as were the talents of these attractive young people. A title song by George Duning and Stanley Styne also seems superfluous. Jerome Cowan does his usually professional job as the apoplectic boss.

In the opening scenes there is a monkey which promises some hilarious situations but these never transpire. Ray Corry's camera work is efficient. The editing, however, is choppy, particularly in the latter half. John T. McCormack's art direction is generally apt, but whoever selected the chaparral setting as the surface of Venus erred. It's a fairly safe bet that the audience for whom this production is designed will not seriously object to these defects. *Glen.*

Face of Fire

Ponderous New England-set, British-produced film carrying poor indications for American market.

Hollywood, July 7.

Allied Artists release of Albert Band-Louis Garfinkle production. Stars Cameron Mitchell, James Whitmore; costars Bettye Ackerman, Royal Dano, Mike Oscard, Robert Simon, Richard Erdman; features Howard Smith, Lois Maxwell, Jill Donahue. Directed by Band. Screenplay, Band; story Stephen Crane; camera-art director, Edward Vorkapich; editor, Ingemar Ejve; music, Erik Nordgren. Previewed July 1, '59. Running time, 79 MINS.

Ned Trescott	Cameron Mitchell
Monk Johnson	James Whitmore
Grace Trescott	Bettye Ackerman
Jake Winter	Royal Dano
Jimmie Trescott	Miko Oscard
The Judge	Robert Simon
Al Williams	Richard Erdman
Sheriff Nolan	Howard Smith
Ethel Winter	Lois Maxwell

This British import, lensed in Sweden with a partial Hollywood cast, is based on Stephen Crane's short story, "The Monster," carrying a New England background at turn of the century. Dull and ponderous, film is old-hat by today's standards and will probably have rough going.

Cameron Mitchell and James Whitmore delineate the two principal characters, a small-town physician and his handyman, latter beloved by hamlet's entire population. When the handyman's face is burned off in a fire which ravishes the doctor's home, during which he rescues his employer's young son, his frightful appearance causes panic and feelings of the town's-people change to the extent that they try to kill him. Yarn ends on an upbeat note.

Produced by Albert Band and Louis Garfinkle, from latter's screenplay, action is practically nil. Under Band's slow direction, cast suffers via unrealistic roles and performances are little more than walk-throughs, although acting itself is competent enough. Betty Ackerman portrays Mitchell's wife, Mike Oscard their son, Royal Dano leader of group out to destroy the faceless Whitmore, Richard Erdman a bum, Robert Simon a judge, in co-star roles.

Technical departments are capably handled, including Edward Vorkapich's camera work and art direction, and music by Erik Nordgren. *Whit.*

Locarno Fest

O Vecech Nadprirozonych

(About Supernatural Things)
(CZECHOSLAVAKIAN)

Locarno, July 21.

Czech State Film production and release. With Jan Pelikan, Milos Kopecky, Ladislav Pesek, Oldrich Novy, Irena Kacirkova, Jaroslav Marvan. Directed by Milos Markovec, Jiri Krejcik, Jaroslav Mach. Screenplay, Vladimir Bor, Frantisek Daneil from three stories by Karel Capek; camera, Jiri Safar, Vladimir Novotny, Josef Stecha; editor, Jan Kahout. At Locarno Film Fest. Running time, 100 MINS.

Old Man	Jan Pelikan
Kupr	Milos Kopecky
Knotek	Ladislav Pesek
Karas	Oldrich Novy
Marta	Irena Kacirkova
Hubner	Jaroslav Marvan

Sketch pic comes up with two out of three fairy tales which are successful in making the supernatural and the macabre quite risible. Third is somewhat talky. This type film is chancey at best Abroad and looms mainly for dualers or lingo situations.

One tale has a timid clerk who takes the blame for another's mistake. He suddenly sprouts a halo and some fine satiric jibes at bureaucracy and medicine follow. Then he tells off his boss, reveals he did not make the mistake and loses his halo. Second is about a man who accidentally hits a hearse and awakens a dead old man about to be buried. He is hounded to death by the old man, who has lost his pension, and the old man ends up tending his grave.

Foregoing two yarns have pace and bring off their whimsy well. Third is about a jealous husband whose young wife fools him via a mindreader. It is somewhat overdone. Acting is fine as are technical aspects. *Mosk.*

Unruhige Nacht

(All Night Through)
(WEST GERMAN)

Locarno, July 21.

Europa release of Carlton-Realfilm production. Stars Bernhard Wicki; features Ulla Jacobsson, Hansjorg Felmy, Ann Savo, Erik Schuman, Werner Hinz. Directed by Falk Harnack. Screenplay, Hurst Bud Juhn; camera, Friedl Behn-Grund; editor, Georg Jauss. At Locarno Film Fest. Running time, 100 MINS.

Pastor	Bernhard Wicki
Melanie	Ulla Jacobsson
Fedor	Hansjorg Felmy
Ljuba	Ann Savo
Ernst	Erik Schuman
Arnim	Werner Hinz

Sombre pic deals with "good" Germans during the last World War. A pastor discourses on the guilt of those who knew the war was wrong and did nothing about it. Warnings are given that similar states of mind may be springing up in Germany. But all this is wrapped up in a slow moving, sanctimonious film that makes its points only in talk—not in feeling. So this looms primarily a local item with slim chances abroad.

A protestant pastor is called in to minister last rites for a man who is to be shot for desertion during the last war. In looking over his papers the pastor finds that the man deserted to help a Russian girl he loved and really did no overt harm for he had never had love in his life before. The man gets some consolation from the pastor, and is shot.

Direction is somewhat stolid and fails to transfer the theme from words to visuals. Result is a plodding pic. Russian atmosphere is to obviously studio and lacks feeling and authenticity. Playing is heavy though Bernhard Wicki manages to give the pastor some depth. Practically complete low key lighting is in keeping with the downbeat theme and slow progression. Technical credits are good. *Mosk.*

Musik I Morker

(Music and Shadows)
(SWEDISH)

Locarno, July 21.

Terra Films production and release. With Mai Zetterling, Berger Malmsten. Written and directed by Ingmar Bergman. Camera, G. Strindberg; editor, Lennart Wallen. At Locarno Film Fest. Running time, 90 MINS.

Ingrid	Mai Zetterling
Bengt	Birger Malmsten

Ingmar Bergman has become a directorial name to be reckoned with among film buffs in most Western countries. His "Wild Strawberries" is clicking currently in N.Y. and he also got stateside attention for "Naked Night" "Seventh Seal" and "Smiles of a Summer Night." His old pix are now being released abroad as interest in his highly personalized pix continues.

This is an early one with melodramatic aspects but already attesting to his individual outlook and talents. Here a pianist loses his sight in a military training accident and finally finds a meaning in life through the love of a young housemaid. Set in the 1930's, this also brings in class issues. It is the fine insight into a blind man's world and his final adaptation that give this film its main values.

It is well acted and incisively directed by Bergman. But his insistence on some sentimentality makes this somewhat chancey for offshore placement except for arty spots on his name alone. This is technically excellent. *Mosk.*

Les Quatre Du Moana

(The Four of the Moana)
(FRENCH-DOCUMENTARY-COLOR)

Locarno, July 21.

Gaumont production and release. Lensed (Ansco), and interpreted by Bernard Gorsky, Pierre Pasquier, Roger Lesage, Serge Arnoux; editor, Raymond Lamy; commentary, Paul Guimard spoken by Gerard Oury. At Locarno Film Fest. Running time, 90 MINS.

The Moana is a small sailing ship that took four men around the world in three years. Pic details their adventures and underwater fishing, etc. This is simply made and well welded together and gives some arresting undersea footage.

But the pic is somewhat long and emerges primarily of dualer possibilities abroad or could be trimmed down for a good medium-length supporting feature. Color is good. A straightforward commentary has kept this always coherent. *Mosk.*

Kapitanskaia Dotschka

(The Captain's Daughter)
(RUSSIAN-SCOPE)

Locarno, July 21.

Mosfilm production and release. Stars Ia Arepina, Oleg Strijenov, Serguei Loukianov. Directed by Vladimir Kaplounovsky. Screenplay, N. Kovarski from story by Alexandre Pushkin; camera, E. Goulidov; editor, A. Antokoloski. At Locarno Film Fest. Running time, 100 MINS.

Grinev	Oleg Strijenov
Macha	Ia Arepina
Pougachev	Sergeui Loukianov
Chavrabine	V. Dorofeev

Russians have filmed the same Alexandre Pushkin short story that served as a basis for the Yank-Italian pic, "The Tempest" (Par). It has less production aspects but a clearer story line. It emerges a well-made, well-told tale with possible exploitation aspects abroad but limited by being preceded by "Tempest."

Here a young Czarist officer is sent off to a military outpost for gambling and drunkeness. He falls in love with the captain's daughter but has to fight a sinister officer also condemned to the outpost. All is brought to a head by the conquering arrival of a peasant who has a tartar and peasant following, by passing himself off as the real Czar.

Film abounds in solidly photographed sequences plus fine acting and narrative. It rarely shows big battles or the court figures of the time, and even has the peasant usurper begging forgiveness of the people before his execution. Pic is in a scope process, and has fine technical aspects. It is well directed to make this an absorbing Russo costumer. *Mosk.*

Pozegnania

(The Farewells)
(POLISH)

Locarno, July 21.

Polski State Film production and release. With Maria Wachowiak, Tadeusz Janczar, Gustaw Holoubek, Saturnin Zurawski. Directed by Wolkcieck Has. Screenplay, Stanislaw Dygat from story by St. Dygat; camera, Mieczyslaw Jahoda; editor, Zofia Dwornik. At Locarno Film Fest. Running time, 100 MINS.

Lidka	Maria Wachowiak
Paul	Tadeusz Janczar
Mirek	Gustaw Holoubek
Felix	Saturnin Zurawski

This film deals with upper class comportment in Poland just before the last war and during it. It sketches interclass relations and coming of age of an upper-class, meandering boy and a lower class girl who has married well. Its theme and rather melodramatic treatment make this a chancey item abroad except for some lingo or arty spots.

Pic is well mounted and displays a good feeling for the period and the disorientation of the upper classes. In keeping with the so-called new freedom in Poland, this tries to show both sides of the question, and leaves its hero a fairly sympathetic character. Acting is good and direction knowing if somewhat overdone in its nostalgia for early periods and its **black painting of most of the upper classes. It emerges a curio item at best. *Mosk.***

The Big Operator
(C'SCOPE)

Mickey Rooney playing a brutal, crooked labor boss in a hardhitting melo; stout returns indicated.

Hollywood, July 30.

Metro release of Red Doff production. Stars Mickey Rooney, Steve Cochran, Mamie Van Doren; costars Mel Torme, Ray Danton, Jim Backus; features Ray Anthony, Jackie Coogan, Charles Chaplin Jr., Jay North, Donald Barry, Lawrence Dobkin. Directed by Charles Haas. Screenplay, Robert Smith, Allen Rivkin, based on Cosmo mag story by Paul Gallico; camera, Walter H. Castle; music, Van Alexander; editor, Ben Lewis. Previewed July 29, '59. Running time, 90 MINS.

Little Joe Braun .... Mickey Rooney
Bill Gibson .... Steve Cochran
Mary Gibson .... Mamie Van Doren
Fred McAfee .... Mel Torme
Oscar Wetzel .... Ray Danton
Cliff Heldon .... Jim Backus
Slim Cayhurn .... Ray Anthony
Ed Brannell .... Jackie Coogan
Bill Tragg .... Charles Chaplin Jr.
Gina .... Vampira
Tony Webson .... Billy Daniels
Bert Carr .... Ben Gage
Timmy Gibson .... Jay North
Phil Cernak .... Lawrence Dobkin
Danny Sacanzi .... Leo Gordon
Det.-Sgt. .... Donald Barry
Alice .... Ziva Rodann
Raymond Bailey .... Joey Forman
Lou Green .... Grabowski
Picket Captain .... Vido Musso

"The Big Operator" is a walloping labor rackets melo with enough stamina to carry it through the general market to hefty grosses. Continuing Mickey Rooney's excursions into hardboiled characterization — previously exposed in "The Last Mile" and "Baby Face Nelson" — the Albert Zugsmith-Red Doff production packs highly topical exploitation potential.

Rooney plays a tough and vicious labor boss under investigation by a Senate Rackets Committee in the Robert Smith-Allen Rivkin screenplay, based on a Cosmo yarn by Paul Gallico. Taking refuge behind the Fifth Amendment, he makes a single slip when he denies knowing one of his henchmen. Bulk of the fast-paced story unfoldment is built around his trying to button up two union members whom he knows saw him with this goon.

Film, sparked by Charles Haas' sock direction, opens on a shocker note: a man is thrown into a cement mixer to keep him from testifying against Rooney, and continues on the same chord. Opposing Rooney is Steve Cochran, one of the twosome whom the boss is trying to muffle, a peace-loving family man responsible for Rooney's downfall after latter kidnaps Cochran's son as a hostage. Unreeling benefits by constantly mounting suspense, with no holds barred on labor racket tactics: Cochran's pal, Mel Torme, is set afire and badly burned, and Cochran himself undergoes brutal punishment.

Rooney comes through in realistic fashion, capturing the mood required for such a character, and Cochran makes his work count strongly as the aroused unionist. Mamie Van Doren, as Cochran's wife, lands excellent distaff interest, and Jay North is okay as their young sprout. Torme also socks over his role of one of the men Rooney is out to get, and Ray Danton is properly menacing as the goon whom Rooney refuses to acknowledge. In brief roles, Jim Backus, Jackie Coogan and Lawrence Dobkin stand out.

Film is given top backing in all technical departments, including Walter H. Castle's camera work, Ben Lewis' editing, Van Alexander's music score and direction, Hans Peters and Preston Ames' art direction. Film was produced by Zugsmith's company in association with Fryman Enterprises, in which Doff and Rooney are partnered.

Whit.

The Mouse That Roared
(BRITISH-COLOR)

Lively spoof with Peter Sellers playing three roles. This good-humored satire on world politics and diplomacy should provide ready business from most audiences.

London, July 28.

Columbia release of an Open Road (Walter Shenson) production Stars Peter Sellers, Jean Seberg, William Hartnell. Directed by Jack Arnold. Screenplay, Roger MacDougall, Stanley Mann, from novel by Leonard Wibberley; camera, John Wilcox; editor, Raymond Poulton; music, Edwin Astley. At Odeon, Marble Arch, London, July 13. Running time, 83 MINS.

Tully, Gloriana, Mountjoy ... Peter Sellers
Helen .... Jean Seberg
Kokintz .... David Kossoff
Will .... William Hartnell
Roger .... Timothy Bateson
Cobbley .... Monty Landis
Pedro .... Harold Kasket
Benter .... Leo McKern
BBC Announcer .... Colin Gordon
Snippet .... Macdonald Parke
U.S. Secretary of Defense ... Austin Willis
O'Hara .... George Margo
Mulligan .... Richard Gatehouse
Ticket Collector .... Jacques Cey
Cunard Captain .... Stuart Sanders
Cunard 2d Officer .... Ken Stanley
U. S. Policeman .... Bill Nagy
Telephone Operator .... Mavis Villiers
British Ambassador .... Charles Clay
French Ambassador .... Harry De Bray
Army Captain .... Bill Edwards

Screen satire can be as risky as a banana-skin on a sidewalk. There are a few occasions when "The Mouse That Roared" gets over-smart and then some of its witty sallies, gimmicks and gags may well go over the heads of the patrons. But on the whole it has kept its slight amusing idea bubbling happily in the realms of straightforward comedy. "Mouse" has, wisely, been geared to only 83 minutes, thus avoiding any flagging of pace. Here's a good-humored, witty pic which, with Peter Sellers as its star, should make a lively b.o. prospect throughout the U.K. U.S. audiences, if prepared to laugh both with and at themselves (as well as at other major and minor powers) will also find it deft, satisfying entertainment. It's a comedy in the old Ealing tradition.

The yarn concerns the Grand Duchy of Grand Fenwick, the world's smallest country, which relies for its existence on the export of a local wine to the U.S. Wren California bottles a cheaper, inferior imitation Grand Fenwick is on verge of going broke. So the Prime Minister hits on the wily scheme of going to war against America, on the grounds that the loser in any war is invariably on the receiving end of hefty financial handouts from the winners.

But the invasion of N.Y. by an army of 20 men with mail uniforms and bows and arrows goes awry. The "army" arrives when New York is deserted. Everybody's undercover for a giant air-raid drill. In the confusion Grand Fenwick's nit-wit field-marshal manages to capture America's new, powerful weapon, the Q-bomb, together with its inventor and his daughter, plus the military commander of N.Y. and several cops. Grand Fenwick has won the war. It now becomes the target of the attentions of all the big powers and America has to negotiate peace terms which mainly consist of taking the Californian wine off the market, and a million-dollar loan from the American Treasury.

Sellers plays three roles in the film and this is achieved mainly by skillful writing and editing and not by trick lensing. He is the Grand Duchess Gloriana, the Prime Minister and also the hapless field marshal who upsets the Prime Minister's plans. With versatility in voice and subtle characterization Sellers scores cheerfully in all three roles, with the Prime Minister probably being the best. While not necessary for one man to play all three roles, it is a standout gimmick which adds greatly to the fun.

Jean Seberg is pretty, but makes little impact, as the heroine. But there is useful work from William Hartnell, David Kossoff, as the scientist; Leo McKern, as Grand Fenwick's leader of the loyal opposition; and Macdonald Parke, as a pompous American general. Among the highlight scenes are the arrival of the token army in deserted N.Y. and the abduction of the hostages. The sight of the completely deserted city is an awesome one and owes considerably to Jack Arnold's direction, and remarkable artwork and lensing.

Other moments that supply plentiful yocks are the preparations in Grand Fenwick for welcoming the U.S. Army of Occupation, the voyage to America, with the Grand Fenwick army cheerfully taking potshots with arrows at the passing Queen Elizabeth (while Sellers is continuously seasick) and an hilarious chase scene with the Q-bomb liable to explode anytime.

Witty credit titles designed by Maurice Binder which set the film off on the right satirical note with a neat spoof on the Columbia trademark and in-the-mood music by Edwin Astley both help Walter Shenson's Open Road production no end.

Rich.

Asi Era Pancho Villa
(This Was Pancho Villa)
(MEXICAN—COLOR)

Mexico City, July 28.

A Rodrigues Productions release. Stars Pedro Armendariz, Carlos Lopez Moctezuma, Maria Elena Marques. Written and directed by Ismael Rodriques. At the Mariscala Theatre, Mexico City. Running time, 90 MINS.

This is yet another Pancho Villa film biog with this one tending to whitewash the Centaur of the North as a simple, noble man at heart although brusque and violent in his reactions.

Pedro Armendariz is at home in this one, but laurels really go to Carlos Lopez Moetezuma as his first lieutenant, Colonel Fierro. Maria Elenea Marques flickers weakly in female role. Strictly run-of-the-mill program fare, in color.

Emil.

The Tingler

Good gimmicks used well within horror framework.

Hollywood, July 23.

Columbia release of a William Castle production. Stars Vincent Price; with Judith Evelyn; also, Darryl Hickman, Patricia Cutts, Pamela Lincoln, Philip Coolidge. Producer-director, William Castle. Screenplay, Robb White; camera, Wilfrid M. Cline; editor, Chester W. Schaeffer; music, Von Dexter. Previewed at the Academy Theatre, July 23, '59. Running time, 80 MINS.

Dr. William Chapin .... Vincent Price
Mrs. Higgins .... Judith Evelyn
David Morris .... Darryl Hickman
Isabel Chapin .... Patricia Cutts
Lucy Stevens .... Pamela Lincoln
Ollie Higgins .... Philip Coolidge

"The Tingler" stamps producer William Castle as an imaginative, often ingenious showman. The film abounds in hokum, camouflaged as science, and it has been gimmicked to insure exploitation. Overall, it's a highly entertaining property. If sold, Columbia release might be one of the year's surprise grossers.

"Tingler" is Castle's third successive horror film and his first since moving his independent unit from Allied Artists to Columbia. Both in tricks and story, it's superior to either his first, "Macabre," or his second, "House on Haunted Hill."

The major gimmick, labeled "Percepto," is comprised of a series of war surplus vibrating motors, attached to the undersides of the theatre seats and set off at at the proper moment to send "tingling" sensations through the customers. Four test engagements will be used to determine how extensively "Percepto" will be spread throughout a theatre; i.e., how many seats will be wired to "get it." And Castle, in a tongue-in-cheek filmed prolog, tells the audience that not everyone is susceptible to the "tingling" forces, thus leaving an "out" for fewer motors than seats.

"Percepto" itself is effective, not so much because of the "tingle" but because it "menacingly" moves closer and closer in waves and, coupled with a whirring noise and sound-track heartbeats and screams, puts the filmgoer in the midst of the horror. Castle additionally has incorporated a second trick, bringing the film to a halt and the house lights up, at which point star Vincent Price calms the audience via a side speaker and two hasty gentlemen rush down the aisle with stretcher in hand to pick up a shrieking female who supposedly has fainted from fright. House lights will go up in all theatres, according to present plans, with the little play to be enacted in the key situations.

"Tingler" was written by Castle's associate, Robb White, and the screenplay is adeptly constructed to let the gimmicks sneak in unobtrusively. Most effective is a hairraising sequence in which a bathtub full of blood blares out in all its rich sanguinary color amid the remaining blacks and whites. When things are on the move — gimmicked or otherwise—White's script is fine, as is Castle's direction. On occasion, however, the film tends to become excessively "talky" and, until the wild moments begin, there is more than one obvious contrivance.

"The Tingler" tells of a pathologist who is curious about fear, theorizing it has force to produce tension which, if not relieved through screaming, can kill. From a deaf mute who dies of fright because she can't wail, the doctor extracts a living creature which had formed around the victims backbone, snapping it in two. The isolating and eventual handling of the creature constitutes the picture's main action.

Castle assembled a good cast for these sort of doings. Price appears perfectly sinister, and, when it's found he's not really bad after all, it becomes obvious he has left just the right loopholes in his actions and personality. Judith Evelyn is excellent as the deaf mute, speaking with her hands and her eyes,

and fine performances also are turned in by Darryl Hickman as Price's assistant and Patricia Cutts as his wandering wife. Pamela Lincoln, as Miss Cutts' younger sister, is a standout in displaying warmth and feeling. Philip Coolidge, as the mute's husband, often seems unfittingly cold, a quality that, at film's end, turns out to be the right one.

The technical side of "Tingler" is quite well done, most particularly Von Dexter's musical score. Photography by Wilfrid M. Cline, art direction by Philp Bennett, editing by Chester W. Schaeffer and sound by Harry Mills are first-rate. Only the creature itself appears improperly molded, looking unimaginatively more like an extended lobster than the embodiment of fear. But, as is the case with most horror films, there is considerable room for amusement, and its presence here just adds one more tingle. *Ron.*

The Boy and the Bridge
(BRITISH)

Offbeat and prolonged film with some pleasant touches of originality but unlikely to make much of a stir outside of arty houses.

London, July 28.

Columbia release of a Xanadu (Kevin McClory) production. Stars Ian MacLaine, Liam Redmond. Directed by Kevin McClory. Screenplay, Geoffrey Orme, McClory, Desmond O'Donovan, from story by Leon Ware; editor, Jack Slade; camera, Ted Scaife; music, Malcolm Arnold. At Columbia Private Theatre, London. Running time, **91 MINS.**

Tommy Doyle .... Ian MacLaine
Pat Doyle .... Liam Redmond
Tugboat Skipper .... James Hayter
Tugboat Engineer ..... Norman Macowan
Bridge Master .... Geoffrey Keen
Market Porter .... Jack MacGowran
Evangelist .... Royal Dano
Bridge Mechanics ..... Bill Shine, Arthur Lowe, Jocelyn Britton
Organ Grinder ..... Andress Malandrinos
Publican of the Globe ... Stuart Saunders
Publican's Wife .... Chili Bouchler
Landlady .... Rita Webb
Yeoman Warder ..... Meadows White
Tourist .... Winifrede Kingston
Punch and Judy .... Jimmy Herbert
Bridge Engineer .... Jack Stewart

Kevin McClory, an ebullient young Irishman, who had both John Huston and Mike Todd as his film mentors, has now set up in business on his own account. He is producer, director and helped in scripting of "The Boy and the Bridge." The pic, which is an official British entry for the Venice Film Fest, also got the Royal nod at its charity preem. It would be pleasant, but scarcely true, to say that the film lives up to its advance drum-beating. It may serve in arty houses, but misfires on several cylinders. And it is evident that McClory has not yet obtained the experience to put over such a slim, offbeat film.

Story is based on an American yarn and was set around the Golden Gate bridge of San Francisco. It now has been switched to London and the Tower Bridge. It concerns a youngster who sees his father arrested after a brawl, mistakenly believes that he is on a murder rap, runs away and without permission sets up house in the Bridge. This pleasant but flimsy idea is insufficient to stand up for 91 minutes.

The first 45 minutes (during which the youngster has not a single word to say) is largely devoted to establishing the bridge and its surroundings. Later the yarn perks up but by then the whimsey is beginning to be repetitive.

Star of the film is a tough, grave little youthful Cockney lad who makes his film debut. Young Ian MacLaine certainly makes a remarkable debut and is both amusing and occasionally moving as the boy for whom the bridge develops a personality of its own. But, as with most child actors, audiences will be conscious of the technical wheels going round. Nevertheless young MacLaine's performance is a fine tribute to the patience of director McClory and it's a pity that he has let technique get in the way of human emotion. Of the other performers, Liam Redmond does a workmanlike job as the kid's father and James Hayter, Geoffrey Keen, Arthur Lowe and Bill Shine also have their moments.

McClory's direction includes a great deal of somewhat self-conscious and arty-crafty camera angles, but Ted Scaife's lensing takes full advantage of the river scene and offers some easy-on-the-eye visual effects. Not so successful is Malcolm Arnold's music which leans to the celestial-choir mood and is often highly obtrusive. McClory is likely to become a considerable figure in British films and though this effort misfires it is an honorable attempt at getting away from routine fare. *Rich.*

Le Fric
(The Coin)
(FRENCH)

Paris, July 28.

United Artists release of CIL-IAL production. Stars Raymond Rouleau, Eleonora Rossi-Draga, Jean-Claude Pascal; features Roger Hanin, Pascale Roberta. Directed by Maurice Cloche. Screenplay, Guy Magenta, Andre Tabet, Cloche; camera, Roger Fellous; editor, Fanchette Mazin. At Balzac, Paris. Running time, **100 MINS.**

Williams .... Raymond Rouleau
Jacques .... Jean-Claude Pascal
Ellie .... Eleonora Rossi-Drago
Girlfriend .... Pascale Roberts
Bob .... Roger Hanin

The influence of "Rififi" is still apparent in this pic. This one is about how a couple of gangs fight over some uncut diamonds. Film is too moralistic, and its familiar plot, and lagging action and characterizations slant this primarily for the home market.

A young man, with a demanding girl, gets dragged into this fight only to be saved by the love of another girl and the gang's destruction of each other. Acting, direction and technical are par. *Mosk.*

Surrender—Hell!

War programmer based on fact, technically good, dramatically poor, but interesting because of authentic Philippines background.

Hollywood, July 22.

Allied Artists release of an Edmund Goldman production. Stars Keith Andes, Susan Cabot, Paraluman, Nestor De Villa. Producer, Edmund Goldman; director, John Barnwell. Screenplay, Barnwell, based on "Blackburn's Headhunters," book by Philip Harkins; camera, Miguel Accion; editor, Hugo Grimaldi; music, Francisco Buencamino Jr.; art direction, Richard Abelardo. Previewed at the studio, July 21, '59. Running time: **85 MINS.**

Donald D. Blackburn ...... Keith Andes
Delia .... Susan Cabot
Pilar .... Paraluman
Major Bulao .... Nestor De Villa

Based on the real-life adventure of a U.S. Army lieutenant who organized Filipino headhunters into a guerrilla outfit during the Japanese occupation, "Surrender—Hell!" despite an inept screenplay, is an interesting war programmer because of its subject and the fact that it was filmed entirely on location in the Philippines.

There are some exploitable ad possibilities in a number of scenes: lovely Filipino actress Paraluman washing down muscular Keith Andes in a shower stall; Paraluman in various stages of dishevelment as a result of brushes with the Japanese conquerors; realistic battle scenes; headhunters; Andes and Susan Cabot in a hayloft, and the like.

Preoccupied with these scenes, the script rambles from episode to episode, loosely tracing Lt. Donald D. Blackburn's (portrayed by Andes) flight from the Japanese, his reluctant acceptance of the leadership of civilian resistance in a mountain village, his strategic retreat to headhunter territory in the interior, his capture of certain Filipino provinces and his eventual assistance in Gen. MacArthur's invasion. It also sketches a brief romance with Miss Cabot and a more extended one with Miss Paraluman.

The principals do well enough within the limits of the script which is shot with cliches, uninspired speeches, silly dialog and two-dimensional characterizations; e.g., the Japanese are hissing caricatures which audiences haven't believed in several years.

The saving grace is that executive producers Paul Schriebman and Newton P. Jacobs and producer Edmund Goldman have succeeded in getting a lot of production value on the screen: there are numerous Filipino street scenes, interiors, jungle scenes and vistas of landscapes beautifully photographed in high key by Filipino cinematographer Miguel Accion; there are large numbers of Filipino extras; headhunter backgrounds are exotic and interesting and there's a touch of spectacle as a result of using these elements.

Francisco Buencamino Jr.'s score is sometimes inappropriate (violins during staff conferences) and sometimes just right (oboes and weird flutes backgrounding a headhunter festival). It's funny to hear headhunters apparently singing "Fight or Die," song by Constantcio de Guzman and Charles Martin, as if they were the Yale glee club. But editor Hugo Grimaldi's frequent use of lap dissolves, tastefully inserted, enhances the film. Most pleasant surprise is that the film, although made almost entirely in the Philippines, is completely up to Hollywood technical standards. *Glen.*

Bobbikins
(BRITISH-'SCOPE)

Max Bygraves, Shirley Jones and an appealing moppet in a comedy with songs which has to struggle to keep ticking.

London, July 28.

20th-Fox (Oscar Brodney) production and release. Stars Max Bygraves, Shirley Jones. Directed by Robert Day. Screenplay, Oscar Brodney; camera, Geoffrey Faithfull; editor, Ralph Kamplen, Stanley Hawkes; music, Philip Green. At Rialto, London. Running time, **90 MINS.**

Benjamin Barnaby .... Max Bygraves
Betty Barnaby .... Shirley Jones
Bobbikins .... Steven Stocker
Lydia .... Billie Whitelaw
Valerie .... Barbara Shelley
Dr. Phillips .... Colin Gordon
Luke .... Charles Tingwell
Gregory Mason .... Lionel Jeffries
Sir Jason Crandall .... Charles Carson
Jock Fleming .... Rupert Davies
Nurse .... Noel Hood
Hargreave .... David Lodge
Johnson .... Murray Kash
LeFarge .... Arnold Diamond
Stebbins .... Charles Lloyd-Pack
Rogers .... Bill Nagy
Cavendish .... Trevor Reid
Admiral .... John Welsh
Naval Petty Officer ..... Michael Ripper
Sailor Joe .... Ronald Fraser
Sailor Jones .... John Downing

Despite its coy title, the stellar duo of Max Bygraves and Shirley Jones, plus the emotional havoc which an appealing moppet invariably creates among femme audiences, should steer "Bobbikins" to a healthy b.o. reception in family houses. Whether it will do much to advance Bygraves' promising film career, however, is open to grave doubt.

Pic is based on a featherweight wheeze which the makers worry with the tenacity of a terrier at grips with a favorite bone. The likeable personalities of Bygraves and Miss Jones and the irresistible baby-stuff of young Steven Stocker help to relieve the banal screenplay and dialog of Oscar Brodney.

Bobbikins is the 14-month-old son of Bygraves and Miss Jones. Pop comes back from the navy to resume a show biz career, but when things go wrong and family life is disrupted, the babe decides to take a hand. He develops a habit of talking, but only to his father, which, considering some of the dialog, is rather considerate of him. Since Bygraves can't convince other people that Bobbikins is loquacious he lands on a psychiatrist's couch.

But Bobbikins' completely unexplained talent is turned to good use when he and his father meet and become friendly with the Chancellor of the Exchequer. Bobbikins passes on information from the Chancellor and as a result Bygraves becomes a hefty tycoon in the stock market. But young Bobbikins realizes that money and success is spoiling dad and breaking up the happy home. So he double-crosses him with a false tip, Bygraves loses all his cash and ends up again in show biz, happy with his wife.

There is nothing much to be done with this rigamarole except to admire the patience with which director Robert Day and lenser Geoffrey Faithfull have captured some cute expressions from Baby Bobbikins. Adult dialog emerging from the youngster is at first amusing but soon palls. Bygraves's relaxed personality is a great help and Miss Jones is a comely stooge.

Of the supporting players, Colin Gordon, as the psychiatrist; Lionel Jeffries, as a shady stockbroker, Charles Carson, as the Chancellor of the Exchequer; and Barbara Shelley, as Jeffries' flashy girlfriend, have the most opportunity of infusing some life into the singularly uninspired proceedings.

There are four songs, "Funny Little Clown," "Bobbikins Lullaby" and "Last Night I Dreamed," all authored by Bygraves and a ballad, "World Of Dreams," by Wilson Stone. Bygraves and Miss Jones put these over more than adequately and one or two of them should be clicks in the pop music world. "Bobbikins" needs far more wit and punch to be a more-than-average film but the performers should be more than enough to attract the patrons. *Rich.*

The Bridal Path
(BRITISH—COLOR)

Comedy of a Scot in search of a wife; fair measure of yocks but a rather parochial job.

London, July 28.

British Lion release of Frank Launder-Sidney Gilliat production. Stars Bill Travers, Bernadette O'Farrell. Directed by Launder. Screenplay, Launder and Geoffrey Willans, from novel by Nigel Tranter; camera, Arthur Ibbetson; editor, Geoffrey Foot; music, Cedric Thorpe

Davie. At Leicester Square Theatre. Running time, 95 MINS.
Ewan McEwan .... Bill Travers
Finley .... Alex Mackenzie
Archie .... Eric Woodburn
Hector .... Jack Lambert
Angus .... John Rae
Murdo .... Roddy McMillan
Katie .... Fiona Clyne
Siona .... Bernadette O'Farrell
Margaret .... Patricia Bredin
Isobel .... Dilys Laye
Sarah .... Joan Fitzpatrick
Craigie .... Pekoe Ainley
Barmaid .... Joan Benham
Good-Looking Waitress .. Annette Crosbie
Hotel Waitress .... Nancy Mitchell
Bank Clerk .... Lynda King
Sergeant Bruce .... George Cole
Constable Alec .... Gordon Jackson
Inspector .... Robert James
Constable Donald .... Terry Scott
Sergeant .... Duncan Macrae
Constable .... Jameson Clark
Neal .... Vincent Winter
Kirsty .... Elizabeth Campbell

The Launder-Gilliat team again has used their contract star, Bill Travers, in the sort of film in which he made his name, "Geordie." But this time, though there's a fair amount of fun in "Bridal Path," the joke wears a shade thin. It will provide a useful booking in family houses but, as with "Geordie," it is likely to have its greatest success in its home area, Scotland.

Travers plays a shy, dour Scot living on a remote island. The island elders decide that there must be no more consanguinity—the marriage of first cousins—so Travers is sent to the mainland to find a wife. He reaches Oban with "ten commandments" which are a blue print of what he must look for, and avoid, in his search for a bride. He becomes involved with various comely young women and there are a number of complications which result in his being chased by the police, a hazard which was perhaps too well and too lately dealt with in Scotland in the film, "The 39 Steps."

Without being a natural comedian, Travers has a likeable personality and helps to carry the pic to a pleasant conclusion. He is helped mightily by Launder's direction and by Arthur Ibbetson's lensing of the Scottish scenery. There are also a number of attractive young women on hand, notably Fiona Clyne, Bernadette O'Farrell, Patricia Bredin and Annette Crosbie. George Cole and Gordon Jackson put in excellent work as two of the cops tailing Travers and Jack Lambert. Eric Woodburn and Alex Mackenzie fit in admirably as some of the islanders who set the young man off on his romantic trail.

The screenplay by Launder and Geoffrey Williams is a deft job but tends to move rather leisurely and predictably. *Rich.*

Un Vaso De Whisky
(A Glass of Whiskey)
(SPANISH)

Locarno, July 28.

Mundial Film release of PEFSA-ESTE production. Stars Rossana Podesta, Arturo Fernandez; features Yelena Samarina, Maruja Bustos, Jorge Rigaud. Directed by Julio Coll. Screenplay, Germain Huici, Coll; camera, Torres Garriga; editor, Emilio Rodriguez. At Locarno Film Fest. Running time, 90 MINS.
Maria .... Rossana Podesta
Victor .... Arturo Fernandez
Laura .... Yelena Camarina
Inspector .... Jorge Rigaud

This is a heavy morality tale pounding home the fact that selfishness and immorality do not pay. It is too academic and sacrifices character for preaching. But it does denote a nice film sense behind it. Pic has enough movement plus its theme to slant it for Hispano language houses abroad.

A Don Juan-type male lives off women and leads to a suicide of one and his comeuppance at the hands of a boxer who loved the latter. Action is passable. Director Julio Coll has a good sense of composition and for getting in telling bits. But he has failed to get life into the characters. It is technically proficient while a drunken orgy scene that could be utilized for exploitation. Otherwise it is a limited entry for any undue offshore interest. *Mosk.*

Messieurs Les Ronds De Cuir
(The Bureaucrats)
(FRENCH)

Paris, July 28.

Discifilm release of Cinelor production. Stars Noel-Noel, Pierre Brasseur; features Jean Poiret, Michel Serrault, Jacques Grello, Micheline Dax, Philippe Clay. Directed by Henri Diamant-Berger. Screenplay, Diamant-Berger based on play by Georges Courteline; camera, Andre Germain; editor, Francine Diot. At Triomphe, Paris. Running time, 95 MINS.
Negre .... Pierre Brasseur
Leheminier .... Noel-Noel
Lahrier .... Jean Poiret
Curator .... Michel Serrault
Clerk .... Jacques Grello
Gaby .... Micheline Dax

Turn-of-century stage farce is done extremely stagily here. This concerns doings in a Civil Service office and milks one little misunderstanding dry. Cast of top comedians cannot overcome the stilted direction. Hence, this emerges primarily a local item on its verbiage and antique jokes.

Cast is in character, but below par technical work and an obvious quickie budget-militate against it for any export chances. *Mosk.*

Ilya Mourometz
(RUSSIAN—COLOR-SCOPE)

Paris, July 28.

Mosfilm production and release. With Boris Andreiev, A. Abrikossov, N. Vedviedeva, N. Vychkova. Directed by A. Ptuchko. Screenplay, V. Kotochnev; camera (Sovcolor), A. Renkov, B. Travkine; editor, E. Svidetele. At Studio De L'Etoile, Paris. Running time, 95 MINS.
Ilya .... Boris Andreiev
Vladimir .... A. Abrikossov
Princess .... N. Vedicdeva
Vassilisa .... N. Vychkova

Though this pic deals with an old Russki legend, it is a chest-beating theme of saving Russia from any invaders. But, aside from this oft-stated aspect, it has some stunning special effects and a simplicity that could make this an okay action entry abroad.

It takes place in the 13th Century when Russia is threatened by an invading Mongol army. It is saved by a massive giant who can uproot trees, slay three-headed dragons, etc. However, his wife is captured by the Mongols and his son is brought up by the Mongol king. After a 14-year truce, the son is sent out to fight his father in a titanic struggle. But a ring brings recognition and the defeat of the Mongol.

Film has impressive settings and battle scenes plus some songs worked into this naive folk drama. Technical and special effects are exemplary as is the color. With all the pontificating cut out, it could make a sort of okay sci-fi entry abroad. *Mosk.*

The Idiot
(RUSSIAN-COLOR)

Paris, July 28.

Mosfilm production and release. With You Iakovlev, Y. Borissova, N. Podgorni, L. Parkhomenko. Directed by Ivan Pyriev. Screenplay, Pyriev from novel by Feodor Dostoyevsky; camera (Sovcolor), V. Pavlov; editor, S. Volkov. At La Rotonde, Paris. Running time, 95 MINS.
Prince Mychkine .... You Iakovlev
Nastassia .... Y. Borissova
Gania .... N. Podgorni
Rogogine .... L. Parkhomenko
Aglae .... R. Maximova

Film is part one of a two-part film based on the Dostoyevsky novel. Now that Dostoyevsky is off the Soviet index, the Russians denote they have not lost their flair for depicting his world where people reflect their souls in everyday activity. This penchant for Slavic introspective ravings and dramatics will make this more difficult for general situations abroad, but its fine adapting, acting and the Dostoyevsky name could make this a good arty entry for some offshore spots.

This details the arrival of the epileptic, impoverished Prince Mychkine in old St. Petersberg in 1860, where his visit with relatives unleashes all the smoldering dramas. It details his strange, sacrificial love for the hardheaded, wronged Nastassia.

Color is uneven and even garish but it fits the baroque decoration. Acting properly captures the feverish feelings of these obsessed people. Its heightened dramatic line makes this seem theatrical at times. Technical credits, aside from the unbalanced color, are good. *Mosk.*

L'Ambitieuse
(The Ambitious One)
(FRENCH-COLOR)

Locarno, July 28.

Silver Films release of Chrysaor-Sud Pacifique-Atel-Silver Films production. Stars Andrea Parisy, Edmond O'Brien, Richard Basehart; features Nicole Berger, Nigel Lovell, Jean Marchat, Denise Vernac. Directed by Yves Allegret. Screenplay, Rene Wheeler from novel "Manganese" of F. Ponthier; camera (Eastmancolor), Carl Kayser; editor, Albert Jurgensen. At Locarno Film Fest. Running time, 90 MINS.
Dominique .... Andrea Parisy
Bucaille .... Edmond O'Brien
Georges .... Richard Basehart
Claire .... Nicole Berger
Andre .... Nigel Lovell
Uncle Albert .... Jean Marchand
Aunt Edwige .... Denise Vernac

There is secondary marquee appeal for the U.S. in this via the names of Richard Basehart and Edmond O'Brien. However, this tale of ruthless ambition is somewhat plodding, making it primarily for dual spots in the U.S.

An ambitious girl pushes her good, if simple husband into helping to doublecross their boss on a phosphate mine in Tahiti. She gives in to the boss' amorous designs while her husband takes over some mine deeds that the boss has permitted to elapse. Following their climb to riches, the husband falls for another girl, and ultimate tragedy.

Yves Allegret's direction is listless. O'Brien, as the boss, and Basehart, as the weak husband, can not do much with their stereotyped roles while Andrea Parisy is incapable of giving animation to the complicated character of the ruthless character. Also she is badly lensed making her less than the desirable type she is interpreting. Color is par while technical values are good. Some added appeal is the on-the-spot Tahiti lensing. There is some Australian money in this pic and also an English version which could be used for supporting fare in America. *Mosk.*

Pillow Talk
(C'SCOPE; COLOR; SONGS)

Sock b.o. comedy from U.

Hollywood, Aug. 7.

Universal release of Arwin production. Stars Rock Hudson, Doris Day; costars Tony Randall, Thelma Ritter. Produced by Ross Hunter and Martin Melcher. Directed by Michael Gordon. Screenplay, Stanley Shapiro and Maurice Richlin; based on a story by Russell Rouse and Clarence Greene; camera (Eastman Color), Arthur E. Arling; music, Frank DeVol; editor, Milton Carruth. Previewed at the Westwood Village Theatre, Aug. 7, '59. Running time, 105 MINS.
Brad Allen .... Rock Hudson
Jan Morrow .... Doris Day
Jonathan Forbes .... Tony Randall
Alma .... Thelma Ritter
Tony Walters .... Nick Adams
Marie .... Julia Meade
Harry .... Allen Jenkins
Pierot .... Marcel Dalio
Mrs. Walters .... Lee Patrick
Nurse Resnick .... Mary McCarty
Dr. Maxwell .... Alex Gerry
Mr. Conrad .... Hayden Rorke
Eileen .... Valerie Allen
Yvette .... Jacqueline Beer
Tilda .... Arlen Stuart
Mr. Walters .... Don Beddoe
Mr. Graham .... Robert B. Williams
Entertainer .... Perry Blackwell
Fat Girl .... Muriel Landers
Hotel Clerk .... William Schallert
Miss Dickenson .... Karen Norris
Jonathan's Secretary .... Lois Rayman

Universal has a sock boxoffice comedy in "Pillow Talk." It is a sleekly sophisticated production that deals chiefly with s-e-x. Although broad, it is tastefully handled, and Ross Hunter, who produced with Martin Melcher, has given it a production dripping with the trappings of glamor. The premise is dubious, but an attractive cast, headed by Rock Hudson and Doris Day, give the good lines the strength to overcome this deficiency. It plays.

The film follows the current trend in romantic comedies of being about as broad as the traffic allows these days. The principals seem to spend considerable time in bed or talking about what goes on in bed, but the beds they occupy are always occupied singly. There's more talk than action natch.

Hunter has used the split screen to give this action added emphasis, and uses it in one sequence for a split-screen bathtub effect that is both interesting and amusing. The talk and action take place on the happy hunting ground where boy-chases-girl and the reverse — or, vice versa — but nothing really happens.

The plot (slight) of the amusing screenplay by Stanley Shapiro and Maurice Richlin, from a story by Clarence Greene and Russell Rouse, is based on the notion that a telephone shortage puts Miss Day and Hudson on a party line. This idea may seem somewhat "dated" in most inflated localities, but the Shapiro-Richlin handling is as bright and up-to-date as a magenta-colored telephone. conclusion.

It helps that two established stars of first boxoffice rank are cast somewhat against type. Playing under Michael Gordon's perceptive direction and fine timing, both respond. Hudson, usually the lovable, overgrown boy, is here a sophisticated man about town. Miss Day discards her casual hair-style, displays a brace of smart Jean Louis gowns, and delivers crisply.

There are some really good songs, smartly integrated. The title tune and a novelty, "Roly Poly," seem like certain hits. Another good one is "Possess Me," which Miss Day sings behind the screen while registering quite a different attitude on-screen. There is a good deal of this sort of cinema trickery in "Pillow Talk." There are the split screens, as noted; spoken

thoughts by the main characters, and even introduction of background music orchestration for a laugh. It all registers strongly. The songs are by Buddy Pepper and Inez James, Joe Lubin and I. J. Roth, and Elsa Doran and Sol Lake. They are all good.

Tony Randall and Thelma Ritter are also top-lined in the cast and they deliver with authority, contributing a hefty proportion of the laughs. Nick Adams, Mary McCarty, Alex Gerry, Arlen Stuart, Marcel Dalio and Lee Patrick likewise rack up amusing values. Karen Norris shows an unusual flair for comedy in a brief, but important scene. In her key scene, singer Perry Blackwell is a standout.

Frank DeVol's bouncy score is an important asset. Since backgrounds play an important part in "Pillow Talk," art directors Alexander Golitzen and Richard H. Riedel, with set decoration by Russell A. Gausman and Ruby R. Levitt, have had a field day. Editing, by Milton Carruth, and sound by Leslie I. Carey and Robert Pritchard, are first-rate. Arthur Arling's Eastman color camera work highlights the mood, whether romance or comedy. The print shown for review was a work print so all color had not been brought into balance, but the finished portions were exceptionally fine. *Powe.*

The Devil's Disciple

Star cast in wobbly scripting of Shaw comedy.

Hollywood, Aug. 7.

United Artists release of Brynaprod and Hecht - Hill - Lancaster production. Stars Burt Lancaster, Kirk Douglas, Laurence Olivier. Produced by Harold Hecht. Directed by Guy Hamilton. Screenplay, John Dighton and Roland Kibbee; based on George Bernard Shaw's play; camera, Jack Hildyard; editor, Alan Osbistion; music, Richard Rodney Bennett. Previewed at the Academy Awards Theatre, Aug. 3, '59. Running time, **82 MINS.**

Anthony Anderson	Burt Lancaster
Richard Dudgeon	Kirk Douglas
General Burgoyne	Laurence Olivier
Judith Anderson	Jeanette Scott
Mrs. Dudgeon	Eva LeGallienne
Major Swindon	Harry Andrews
Lawyer Hawkins	Basil Sydney
British Sergeant	George Rose
Christopher Dudgeon	Neil McCallum
Rev. Maindeck Parshotter	Mervyn Johns
William	David Horne
Essie	Jenny Jones

"The Devil's Disciple" by George Bernard Shaw is better than this film version would indicate to those unfamiliar with the stage original. The final third of the picture is superb Shawmanship, but the major portion preceding it is fumbling and unsatisfactory. Considering the stature of those associated in the making of the United Artists release, its finished state is doubly disappointing.

That all is not lost may be credited almost entirely to Laurence Olivier. Although his role is relatively minor, once he gets onscreen for good, Olivier takes over. His character, that of General "Gentleman Johnny" Burgoyne, is a witty, mocking figure and mouthpiece for Shaw's wicked shafts into convention and history, in this case the American Revolution. Olivier certainly gets most of the good lines. But few players could equal his bland under-playing, his sunny urbanity in the face of British Military atrocities.

The other two stars, Burt Lancaster and Kirk Douglas, fare less well. Lancaster is Anthony Anderson, the peace-spouting person who eventually becomes a fiery rebel. Douglas is Dick Dudgeon, self-proclaimed a shameless, cowardly scoundrel, who in turn displays the truest Christian attitudes. These paradoxes are the basis for much of Shaw's humor.

Since both Lancaster and Douglas are conscientious, thoughtful actors, and since both had a hand in the making of the film (a joint Brynaprod and Hecht-Hill-Lancaster production), their hearts were obviously in the effort. But something went wrong.

Shaw's play, as adapted for the screen by John Dighton and Roland Kibbee, is the ironic Irishman's version of how the British, bumbling and fumbling, lost the American colonies. The reason, says Shaw; is that due to the long British weekend, someone at the War Office forgot to notify Lord North to join forces with General Burgoyne and pinch off the Colonials. It's an amusing notion and when this resolution comes it gets the response it deserves.

It's the build-up that is lacking in something, something that could be at fault in the writing or the editing or the direction. Character, motivation and mood are never set early in the film so response to the irony and humor is tentative and unsure. The film is exceptionally short for a major effort, 82 minutes. This would not, in itself, be lamentable. But the time used is not always employed for the sharpest effect.

Directors were changed in mid-filming on "The Devil's Disciple," and there seems in the finished product to be a division of style. Guy Hamilton is the director credited. He must bear the blame for the uncertain mood and pace. There are several scenes were timing is almost audibly off, just a beat, but enough to blunt the Shavian edge.

Janette Scott plays Lancaster's wife, but does not show herself well. Most of her scenes are annoyingly shrill. Eva LeGallienne is wasted as Douglas' mother, left with only a few lines and no recognizable characterization. Others who occupy prominent roles and who occasionally score include Harry Andrews, Basil Sydney, David Horne and Jenny Jones.

There are sporadic laughs in the early part of the film, and heavy and sustained laughter in the final third or so. But despite the intensity of playing by both Lancaster and Douglas, the film as a whole does not jell. At this late date, it is likely to raise some questions about what all the shooting was about, back there in 1777.

Jack Hildyard's camera work is up to his customary excellence, and Richard Rodney Bennett's musical score is bright. Settings seem to be a little sophisticated for 18th Century America. *Powe.*

The Bat

An unmysterious mystery. Exploitation should be heavy, as is film.

Hollywood, Aug. 3.

Allied Artists release of a C. J. Tevlin production. Stars Vincent Price and Agnes Moorehead. Directed by Crane Wilbur. Screenplay, Wilbur, based on a play by Mary Roberts Rinehart and Avery Hopwood; camera, Joseph Biroc; art director, David Milton; editor, William Austin; music, Louis Forbes. Previewed at the studio, Aug. 3, '59. Running time, **80 MINS.**

Dr. Malcolm Wells	Vincent Price
Cornelia Van Gorder	Agnes Moorehead
Lt. Anderson	Gavin Gordon
Warner	John Sutton
Lizzie Alen	Lenita Lane
Dale Bailey	Elaine Edwards
Judy Hollender	Darla Hood
Mark Fleming	John Bryant
Carter Fleming	Harvey Stephens
Jack Bailey	Mike Steele
Mrs. Patterson	Riza Royce
Detective	Robert B. Williams

The mystery that made a classic out of Mary Roberts Rinehart's "The Bat" in the 1920's has been all but muffled in this sluggish film version produced by C. J. Tevlin and released by Allied Artists. Flight of "The Bat" is apt to be low and slow. What is missing is definition, both of character and incident. The film unspools in nondescript touches, leaving the viewer to care only little about the victims and, for that matter, about the identity of the Bat himself.

Writer-director Crane Wilbur updated Miss Rinehart's story (originally titled "The Circular Staircase," before dramatized in association with Avery Hopwood), but despite this vehicle still creaks.

"The Bat" is a one-clawed, no-face gent who goes around ripping jugular veins. His prey isn't only blood, however, and he has more than a passing interest in $1,000,000 worth of bank securities which he thinks are hidden in a haunted-type house considerately stocked with assorted females. Main thread of the story revolves around the unmasking of the Bat, a feat that could have been, but isn't suspenseful.

As in nearly every other film he's made in the past two years, Vincent Price casts enough furtive glances to register as the ghoul when, indeed, he isn't. This time, however, he does turn out to be a murderer, and he plays the role with his skill and polish. Agnes Moorehead co-stars as a successful mystery writer and, if somewhat over-active, is at least interesting. Elaine Edwards, as the wife of an accused embezzler, is the best of the supporting cast, with competent work from Gavin Gordon, John Sutton, Lenita Lane, Darla Hood, John Bryant, Harvey Stephens, Mike Steele, Riza Royce and Robert B. Williams.

Most effective in the fright department is "The Bat" theme, a wierd set of notes played on the electric guitar by Alvino Rey. David Milton's art direction makes the film look a trifle more expensive than it likely is, and other technical credits are stock. *Ron.*

Ghost of Dragstrip Hollow

Inane juve programmer booked with "Diary of a High School Bride"; tunes may help sell it.

Hollywood, Aug. 4.

American International release of a Lou Rusoff production. Stars Jody Fair, Martin Braddock, Russ Bender; with Leon Tyler, Elaine DuPont, Henry McCann, Sanita Pelkey, Dorothy Neuman, Kirby Smith, Jean Tatum, Jack Ging, Nancy Anderson, Beverly Scott, Bill St. John, Judy Howard, Tom Ivo, Paul Blaisdell, George Dockstader, Marvin Almars, Rosemary Johnston, Marilyn Moe. Directed by William Hole Jr.; screenplay, Lou Rusoff; camera, Gil Warrenton; songs by Nick Venet, Jimmie Maddin, Charlotte Braser, Bruce Johnston and Judy Harriet; music, Ronald Stein; editors, Frank Keller and Ted Sampson; art direction, Dan Haller. Previewed at Stanley-Warner Building projection room, Hollywood, July 31, '59. Running time, **65 MINS.**

Lois	Jody Fair
Stan	Martin Braddock
Tom	Russ Bender
Bonzo	Leon Tyler
Rhodo	Elaine Dupont
Dave	Henry McCann
Amelia	Sanita Pelkey
Anastasia	Dorothy Neuman
Wesley	Kirby Smith
Alice	Jean Tatum
Tony	Jack Ging
Nita	Nancy Anderson
Hazel	Beverly Scott
Ed	Bill St. John
Sandra	Judy Howard
Allen	Tom Ivo
Monster	Paul Blaisdell
Motor Cop	George Dockstader
Leon	Marvin Almars
Lois's ouble	Rosemary Johnston
Nita's Double	Marilyn Moe

"Ghost of Dragstrip Hollow" is a juvenile programmer whose only utility is to fill time and marquee space next to "Diary of a High School Bride."

Producer Lou Rusoff, who also receives scripter credit, collected a mishmash of hotrods, ghosts, parrots, monsters and rock-and-roll and tied them flimsily together with threads of plot.

The idea was apparently to make a comedy, judging from the silly dialog. The gag, which is also the plot, is this: a hotrod club loses its garage and moves into a haunted house; the haunt turns out to be an actor left over from monster pictures. There's also a feud with a rival club and some nominal romances.

The adolescent market at which the film's aimed will charge it off as an adult inanity, but the juves's will probably dig some of the musical numbers, which are unsubtly inserted as plugs for American International Records: "Charge," "Ghost Train," "Geronomo," "Tongue Tied" and "He's My Guy," some of which are catchy and have the right beat.

In this case it's virtually impossible to assess individual actors since the script is so poor and the directing so perfunctory. The editing is choppy and abrupt but it's unlikely that this is the editors' responsibility. Otherwise the technical side is satisfactory. Whoever got some of the props together (e.g., the Thinking Hotrod) probably had some fun. *Glen.*

That Kind of Woman

Sophia Loren and Tab Hunter in Big City romance. Only mild b.o. indicated.

Hollywood, Aug. 6.

Paramount release of a Carlo Ponti-Marcello Girosi production. Stars Sophia Loren and Tab Hunter; co-stars Jack Warden, Barbara Nichols, Keenan Wynn, George Sanders. Directed by Sidney Lumet. Screenplay, Walter Bernstein, based on a story by Robert Lowry; camera, Boris Kaufman; editor, Howard Smith; music, Daniele Amfitheatrof. Previewed at the Fox Wilshire Theatre Aug. 6, '59. Running time, **92 MINS.**

Kay	Sophia Loren
Red	Tab Hunter
Kelly	Jack Warden
Jane	Barbara Nichols
Harry Corwin	Keenan Wynn
The Man	George Sanders

Despite several brilliant touches, "That Kind of Woman" is not satisfactory film drama. The Carlo Ponti-Marcello Girosi production seems to slide along the surface, only infrequently slicing into what could be an interesting relationship between an idealistic young man and another man's mistress. It has Sophia Loren and Tab Hunter for marquee bait, but, in all, the Paramount pic's salable elements are questionable.

Director Sidney Lumet is responsible for most of the noteworthy shadings in "That Kind of Woman," and his direction of individual sequences — particularly aboard a New York-bound train— is superb. Walter Bernstein's screenplay of a story by Robert Lowry contains literate dialog as well as some rather thought-pro-

voking values. But the tale, as it stands, is better suited to True Confessions than to serious film-making.

Hunter is a young (23) paratrooper about to go overseas during World War II. Aboard a train taking him for a last visit home, he meets Sophia Loren, an exotic female being kept by a wealthy New Yorker. He falls in love with her, and, despite her attempts to dismiss him, he stays around long enough to win her love. The ultimate conflict pits the luxury of her life as a mistress against the love she would enjoy with Hunter. While her decision to forsake riches and go with Hunter seems too pat, there would have been no story—only an episode—had she remained.

Miss Loren is quite good, especially in her more sensitive scenes, but Hunter does little more than gazingly look hurt. Highlight of the picture undisputedly is Jack Warden. As a scheming G.I., whose battle wounds crop up at propitious intervals, he is responsible for the film's most amusing moments and, for that matter, its best drama. Barbara Nichols plays what could be termed a second-team mistress, "a good time that no one wants to marry," and her feelings create a sympathetic portrayal. Keenan Wynn is fine and suitably cold as the ladies' escort, and George Sanders is his suave self as "The Man."

Boris Kaufman's photography is outstanding, and the use that he and director Lumet made of their New York locations is extraordinary. From a technical point of view, the film rings audibly true, and first-rate assists come from fine editing by Howard Smith, top sound by James Gleason and Charles Grenzbach, realistic art direction by Hal Pereira and Roland Anderson and an interesting musical score by Daniele Amfitheatrof.
Ron.

The Miracle of the Hills
(C'SCOPE)

Inspirational western for Bible Belt market.

Hollywood, Aug. 4.

20th-Fox release of Associated Producers production. Stars Rex Reason, Nan Leslie, Betty Lou Gerson. Features Theona Bryant, Charles Arnt, Jay North, June Vincent, Paul Wexler, Ken Mayer, Kelton Garwood, Claire Carleton, Tom Daly, Tracy Stratford, Gil Smith, I. Stanford Jolley, Gene Roth, Gene Collins, Cecil Elliott, Pat O'Hara, Vince Townsend Jr. Producer, Richard E. Lyons. Director, Paul Landres; screenplay, Charles Hoffman; editor, Betty Steinberg; camera, Floyd Crosby; music, Paul Sawtell, Bert Shefter; art director, Lyle R. Wheeler, John Mansbridge. Previewed at the studio, July 29, '59. Running time, 73 MINS.

Scott Macauley	Rex Reason
Alison Wingate	Theona Bryant
Davey Leonard	Jay North
Mark Leonard	Gilbert Smith
Laurie Leonard	Tracy Stratford
Sheriff Crane	Gene Roth
Dr. Tuttle	I. Stanword Jolley
Silas Jones	Gene Collins
Seth Jones	Kelton Garwood
Sam Jones	Paul Wexler
Milo Estes	Kenneth Mayer
Mrs. Leonard	June Vincent
Lucky	Pat O'Hara
Mike	Tom Daly
Miss Willowbird	Cecil Elliott
Fuzzy	Charles Arnt
Sally	Claire Carleton
Joanne Tashman	Nan Leslie
Kate Peacock	Betty Lou Gerson
Harry	Vincent Townsend Jr.

"The Miracle of the Hills" is a budget inspirational western made with the "Bible Belt" primarily in mind. However, it's good enough not only to do well in that market but also to fill programs in more sophisticated situations.

Rex Reason portrays a rugged Episcopal minister who takes over a run-down parish in a western mining town during the 1880s. A former prostitute (limned by Betty Lou Gerson) has inherited the town's only means of livelihood, an anthracite coal mine, and, motivated by vengeance, has become the town's malevolent despot.

The preacher alternately fights for improvements and defends the mine owner against a mob. Ultimately, she has a change of heart when three lovable children, whom her vengeance has indirectly orphaned, are trapped in a mine flood. The "miracle" is the children's rescue when an earthquake unjams a safety door which closes, causing the water to subside.

The numerous side plots and episodes include the minister's love interest with a nice dancehall girl, warmly portrayed by Nan Leslie; the death of the children's widowed mother, played with stark realism by June Vincent; reformation of the town drunk (Charles Arnt) and of the town bullies (Kelton Garwood, Paul Wexler and Gene Collins) all of whom do well.

Miss Gerson, a vet trouper, turns in her customarily strong characterization and numerous bit players are given chances to shine in imaginatively conceived roles. Reason's natural portrayal comes across effectively. Charles Hoffman's script, corny though the overall concept may be, is full of bright dialog and the morality play neatness to which the screenplay is fated is modified by Hoffman's intelligent and gutsy character construction. Theona Bryant does well as the niece.

Director Paul Landres, assisted by cinematographer Floyd Crosby, has provided some nice extra touches (e.g., a grave digger humanely pauses until the bereaved is out of view) which are uncommon in pictures of this budget level. Producer Richard Lyons makes full use of the facilities of the 20th-Fox lot to pack a lot of production value onto the screen, helped by first-rate art direction by Lyle R. Wheeler and John Mansbridge. It's welded together neatly by editor Betty Steinberg.
Glen.

Yellowstone Kelly
(COLOR)

Television names in a well-made western meller add up to good prospects.

Hollywood, Aug. 7.

Warner Bros. production and release. Stars Clint Walker, Edd Byrnes, John Russell; features Ray Danton, Andra Martin, Claude Akins, Rhodes Reason, Gary Vinson, Warren Oates. Directed by Gordon Douglas. Screenplay, Burt Kennedy, from book by Clay Fisher; camera, Carl Guthrie; music, Howard Jackson; editor, William Ziegler. Previewed at Academy Awards Theatre, Beverly Hills, July 28, '59. Running time, 91 MINS.

Kelly	Clint Walker
Anse	Edward Byrnes
Gall	John Russell
Sayapi	Ray Danton
Sergeant	Claude Akins
Maj. Towns	Rhodes Reason
Wahleeah	Andra Martin
Lieutenant	Gary Vinson
Corporal	Warren Oates

"Yellowstone Kelly" is a well-made western with three top television names as boxoffice bait: Clint "Cheyenne" Walker, John "Lawman" Russell and Edd "Kookie" Byrnes of "77 Sunset Strip." Byrnes in particular has developed a following among teenagers, a fact which should help the picture.

The story, although somewhat unusual, is not distinguished, and the film is compounded of elements familiar on television. Indeed, the picture must face competition from one or another of the three principals on ABC-TV on Friday, Sunday and Monday nights.

The added factor on which the picture's success largely depends is the feature filming art itself, for Warner Bros. and director Gordon Douglas have loaded this picture with craftsmanship in every department and displayed the three tv heroes in a production framework not approachable in telefilming. Boxoffice response to this picture will provide more data on the question of whether stars developed in teleseries can draw paying customers on the strength of their names rather than the tv characters they portray. It's a good bet that they will, especially in this combination.

The story concerns a fabled fur trapper, Kelly, who is on good terms with the Sioux Indians. He refuses to help the U.S. Cavalry's punitive expedition of 1876 but ultimately has to help the arrogant white men after they have been trounced by the righteous red men.

Kelly and his tenderfoot helper also become involved in the attempts of a non-Sioux Indian girl to escape from her Sioux captors.

At fadeout, the chief, who loves the girl, lets Kelly have her after a cruel brave, also a suitor, has killed Kelly's helper and has, in turn, been killed by Kelly.

Director Douglas moves the story along with a speed sufficient to cover up weak plot points and extracts some solid characterizations not implicit in the script: Walker, as Kelly the trapper, is a laconic, gargantuan woodsman; Russell is a magnetically powerful and believable chief; Ray Danton's a handsome swine of a brave; Andra Martin is fetchingly and helplessly lovely as the Indian girl, and Byrnes, although he's not "kookie," enlists sympathy as the tenderfoot.

Excitingly staged action scenes flow rapidly past Carl Guthrie's alert color camera, and editor William Ziegler, by using multiple lap dissolves, has melded the footage into a slickly finished whole. Firm thesping support is provided by Claude Akins, Rhodes Reason, Gary Vinson and Warren Oates. The picture gets strong assists from Stanley Fleischer's art direction, Howard Jackson's music, M. A. Merrick's sound, Marjorie Best's costumes and Gordon Bau's makeup (particularly in regard to Russell).
Glen.

The 30 Foot Bride of Candy Rock

Okay fantasy spoof for family and children's market starring the late Lou Costello.

Hollywood, Aug. 6.

Columbia Pictures release of a D.R.B. production. Stars Lou Costello; co-stars Dorothy Provine, Gale Gordon; with Jimmy Conlin, Robert Burton, Lenny Kent, Charles Lane, Will Wright, Ruth Perrott. Producer, Lewis J. Rachmil. Director, Sidney Miller; screenplay, Rowland Barber and Arthur Ross based on a story by Lawrence L. Goldman; editor, Al Clark; camera, Frank G. Carson; music, Raoul Kraushaar; art director, William Flannery. Previewed at the Iris Theatre, Hollywood, July 31, '59. Running time, 75 MINS.

Artie Pinsetter	Lou Costello
Emmy Lou Raven	Dorothy Provine
Raven Rossiter	Gale Gordon
Magruder	Jimmy Conlin
Stanford Bates	Charles Lane
First General	Robert Burton
Pentagon General	Will Wright
Sergeant	Lenny Kent
Aunt May	Ruth Perrott
Bill Burton	Peter Leeds
Bank Manager	Robert Nichols
Jackie Delaney	Veola Vonn
Pilot	Jack Straw

"The 30 Foot Bride of Candy Rock" is a mildly amusing fantasy spoof which stars the late Lou Costello. It should strengthen double bills and do best in drive-ins and at children's matinees.

Costello plays a somewhat straighter role than when he was paired with Bud Abbott in that long, successful series of pix in which they met nearly every villain from Captain Kidd to The Mummy.

Instead of the sober-faced Abbott, he has a thinking machine named "Max," which looks like a bird cage in a pepper mill, and when the going gets tough he calls for Max instead of the familiar "Ab-buuht!"

Despite the fact that the joke around which the story revolves is "What does a man do with a 30-foot-tall bride?" the picture is family entertainment, children included, since the picture is done in good taste.

Costello portrays Artie, the rubbish collector in the town of Candy Rock. Except for Artie's business, the town's entirely owned by a humorously despotic gubernatorial candidate named Uncle Raven (Gale Gordon). Artie, of course, love's Raven's niece, Emmy Lou, portrayed by Dorothy Provine.

Artie, with the help of a photographic memory, is a self-taught scientist and his invention, Max, should be able to do practically anything, except that it has Artie's confused personality.

When Emmy Lou inexplicably—there's some nonsense about a mysterious cave—grows to phenomenal height, the machine's too confused to help. Misunderstanding Artie's explanation that Emmy Lou is "bigger," Uncle Raven orders him to marry the girl, which he gladly does.

Before Max gets unconfused and gets Emmy Lou back to the proper size for a bride, the girl frightens the town, attracts a farcical military action against herself and generally is the subject of various photographic stunts. Artie, meantime, goes through a number of fairly funny slapstick maneuvers to protect his little woman.

The photographic effects are satisfactory, the screenplay's pretty well organized, direction and supporting thesping is adequate, Miss Provine and Gale Gordon provide strong support and Costello comes across with his usually competent performance, one which will please the fans who will be catching the last glimpse of him.

The film is technically slick but one is left wondering what "Wonderama and Mattascope" are. Presumably a matte process is used for the trick shots. Whatever it is, it produces no new and startling effects and it evidently isn't adaptable to a point where direct contact between monster and normal-sized persons is possible—a minus factor—but the present production didn't need this particular effect.
Glen.

Diary of a High School Bride

Good bet meller aimed at femme teenagers. Exploits rather than illuminates boy-girl marriages.

Hollywood, Aug. 8.

American International release of Burt Topper production. Stars Anita Sands, Ronald Foster, Chris Robinson; with Wendy Wilde, Louise Arthur, Barney Biro, Richard Gering, Peggy Miller, Elvira Corona, Clark Alan, Joan Connors, Al Laurie, Glenn Hughes, Dodie Drake, Lili Rosson, Luree Nicholson, Loretta Nicholson, Laura Nicholson, John Hart, John Garrett, Don Hix, Larry Shuttleworth,

Gloria Victor. Producer-director, Burt Topper; screenplay, Topper, Mark and Jan Lowell; editor, Richard Sampson; camera, Gil Warrenton; music, Ronald Stein; art direction, Dan Haller. Previewed at Stanley Warner Building projection room, July 31, '59. Running time, **72 MINS.**

Judy	Anita Sands
Steve	Ronald Foster
Chuck	Chris Robinson
Gina	Wendy Wilde
Mrs. Lewis	Louise Arthur
Mr. Lewis	Barney Biro
Richie	Richard Gering
Patty	Peggy Miller
Dancer	Elvira Corona
Guitarist	Clark Alan
Madge	Joan Connors
Tony	Al Laurie
Beatnik	Glenn Hughes
Beatnik	Dodie rake
Lydia	Lili Rosson
Verna	Luree Nicholson
Jerry	Loretta Nicholson
Edie	Laura Nicholson
Policemen	John Hart, John Garrett, Don Hix
Truck Driver	Larry Shuttleworth
Wife of Truck river	Gloria Victor

Producer-director Burt Topper's "Diary of a High School Bride" is an exploitable item aimed at drawing the femme teenage market. Packaged with "Ghost of Dragstrip Hollow" as a sop to the male side, "Diary" will go as far as its advertising campaign pushes it.

There's a pious note in the opening titles which asserts that the producers intend to elaborate on an urgent social problem, high school marriages. Since the film is designed to cash in on this problem rather than to clarify it, the claim is pretentious.

The story, which follows the tried-and-true pattern of "true" confession romance mags, has two principle lines: a minor one, in which the parents of a 17-year-old bride try to alienate her affection for her husband, aged 24, by giving the couple gifts which the husband's pride prohibits him from accepting, causing a quarrel; and the major story line, in which the girl's former beau maliciously tries a number of tricks to separate the couple. The jilted boyfriend is accidentally killed during a rape attempt on the girl and the pair, which had been briefly separated, is reunited.

The screenplay doesn't add any substance to the story since the characterizations are two-dimensional and the dialog is shallow.

The happy surprise is that in Anita Sands AIP has a lovely, warm, young actress, who with proper grooming may develop into a boxoffice attraction. She's aided in her screen debut by Chris Robinson who portrays with genuine menace the athlete-son of a Hollywood studio owner and by Ronald Foster who portrays with becoming naturalness the girl's husband.

Most adults will find the picture dreary and trite, but the very oversimplicity of the screenplay will appeal to the target market. There's also an excellent fight scene and a fairly good chase sequence filmed with Amco Studios as the background.

Tony Casanova's singing of "Diary of a High School Bride" and "When I Say Bye Bye" should prove reciprocally valuable to both picture and record.

Technical work is satisfactory for a picture of this type and supporting players are adequate.

Glen.

San Sebastian Fest

Salto a la Gloria
(Leap to Fame)
(SPANISH)

San Sebastian, Aug. 4.

C. B. Films release of Aspa Films production (Mardid). Stars Alfredo Marsillach, Asuncion Sancho; co-stars Jose Marco Davo, Mario Morales, Isabel de Pomes and Mercedes Munoz Sampedro. Directed by Leon Klimovsky. Screenplay, Vicente Escriva and Pombo Angulo; camera, Godofredo Pacheco; music, Isidro Maiztegui. At Teatro Victoria Eugenia, San Sebastian Film Festival. Running time, **96 MINS.**

Legit actor Adolfo Marsillach won best performance laurels in the role of Dr. Ramon y Cajal, Nobel prize winner for research in nerve cells. Actor breathes life into a role weighted down by an essentially narrative script in which the dramatic values of scientific discovery are missing.

In tracing the life span of Ramon y Cajal, from early childhood to the white-bearded savant's late acclaim, authors capture him colorfully as a mischievously imaginative moppet. As a career and research medic, little of transcendental screen interest emerges from his rapports with wife, children and microscope.

Budgeted modestly, this primarily features a distinguished cast. Direction and technical credits are fair.

Werb.

800 Leguas Por El Amazonas
(800 Leagues on Amazon)
(MEXICAN—COLOR—MEXISCOPE)

San Sebastian, Aug. 4.

Pelimex release of Producciones Corsa S.A. production. Stars Carlos Lopez Moctezuma, Rafael Bertrand, Elvira Quintana, Maria Duval, Beatriz Augirre, Raul Farell, Enrique Aguilar. Directed by Emilio Gomez Muriel. Adapted from Jules Verne by Julio Alejandro; screenplay by Jaime Salvador, Emilio Gomez Muriel; camera, Jack Draper. At San Sebastian Film Fest. Running time, **106 MINS.**

Gomez Muriel's treatment of Jules Verne's straight adventure story is a blend of vaudeville, gaslight thesping and an undeft touch of the infantile. Juan Garral, a respectacle landowner and family man with a turbulent, buried past is harried by an unscrupulous adventurer on a long journey down the Amazon into facing trial for an unsolved 26-year old murder. Death of the rash stranger leads to Garral's acquital.

Opening jungle sequence scores. After that the tuneful rancheros break the spell and it's low "Show Boat" spectacle with kiddie episodes interspersed and tediously assembled.

Werb.

La Petite
(Little One)
(BULGARIA—COLOR)

San Sebastian, Aug. 4.

Bulgarian State Films production and release (Sofia). Stars Margarita Ilieva, Anani Yavashev, Ivan Dimov, Stefan Guooularov, Georgi Kaloyanchev, Emil Grecov, Lilyana Bocheva. Directed by Nikolai Korabov. Screenplay by Lyuben Stanev; camera, Konstantin Yanakiev; music, Parashkev Hadjiev. At San Sebastian Film Fest. Running time, **91 MINS.**

Directing his first film, Nikolai Korabov crowds the screen with unrelated situations to burden the central story of a high school senior in rebellion against Dad-knows-best restraint after she debuts in love.

Maiden's firm stand contaminates her submissive brothers who stage a mass walkout on the overdomineering parent. Film aften detours from this ample pattern. Transition from girl to young woman is expressively performed and lensed. Cast and technical credits are good. Color is feeble.

Werb.

Cain Adolescente
(Adolescence of Cain)
(VENEZUELA)

San Sebastian, Aug. 4.

A Hilario Gonzalez production. Stars Carlota Ureta, Milagros del Valle, Edgar Jimenez; co-stars Orangel Delfin, Enrique Aizugaray, Rafael Briceno, Pedro Hurtado. Written and directed by Roman Chalbaud. Camera, Ramiro Vega; music, Eduardo Serrano. At San Sebastian Film Fest. Running time, **130 MINS.**

Clarity is not the strong point of this long, unusually slow-paced offering from Venezuela. Out of young writer-director Chalbaud's travail comes the admonition against tearing up roots in the soil for life in the big city.

A widow, on the far side of middle-age, makes this mistake to give her son the opportunities only a metropolis offers. Sequence after sequence depicts the seamy, dissolute, squalid existence in their hilltop shack slum overlooking Caracas. There is no redeeming note until the mother, who goes berserk sexually and alcoholically, dies and the son returns to his pueblo.

Below grade in all departments. Interesting only as a partial sociological document of modern-day Caracas.

Werb.

Zamach
(Partisan Mission)
(POLISH)

San Sebastian, Aug. 4.

Film Polsky production (Warsaw). With Bozena Kurowaka, Grazyna Staniszewska, Zbigniew Cynkutis, Roman Klosowski, Andrzej Kostenko, Tadeusz Lomnicki, Andrzej May, Stanislaw Mikulsky. Directed by Jerzy Passendorfer. Screenplay, Jerzy Stawinski; camera, Jerzy Lipman; music, Adam Walacinski. At San Sebastian Film Fest. Running time, **83 MINS.**

Dramatic tension in this highly-praised festival entry is touched off almost in the opening frame and maintains tingling suspense to the end.

Setting is occupied Warsaw, where a student resistance group executes the hated SS General Kutscher. In three main movements, the mission is carefully prepared, the attack is successfully staged and the German manhunt is launched. A very brief epilogue shows the survivors in action again.

Accent is on youth. Passendorfer, in his second film chore, plus a young cast make this an airtight, unembroidered celluloid yarn with pace and impact. Lensing, editing and music all contribute.

Werb.

Sam
(Alone)
(YUGOSLAV)

San Sebastian, Aug. 4.

Avala Film (Belgrade) production. Stars Nikola Simic, Milan Puzic, Pavle Vujisic, Radmila Radovanovic, Severin Bijelic. Written and directed by Vladimir Pogacic from Mihailo Renovcevic's novel of same name. Camera, Aleksandar Sekulovic; music, Bojan Adamic. At San Sebastian Film Fest. Running time, **94 MINS.**

A small band of partisans, guarding the retreat of main guerrilla troops, are cut off in the desolate Sutjeska Gorges. Sense of isolation and exhausted supplies demoralize the weak and tax the fibre of the detachment's leaders, left with no choice but a breakthrough against overwhelming German armed might.

Story is related with unremorseful realism. Psychological choice between resistance and despair ends implacably in death but "Sam" makes the point that there is a way to die as there is to live.

Cast, setting and low-key lighting are all very effective. Radmila Radovanovic, as the enceinte partisan, is lovely but her role as written is superfluous and slows a vivid war tale, otherwise neatly directed.

Werb.

Parmi les Decombres
(Shadows of the Past)
(EGYPTIAN)

San Sebastian, Aug. 4.

Orient Film Co. release of Ezz El Din Zulfikar production (Cairo). Stars Faten Hamama, Emad Hamdy, Safia Sarwat, Salh Zulfikar; co-stars Hussein Riad, Rawhia Khaled, Samiha Ayoub, Fouad El Mohandess, Salah Nazmi. Directed by Ezzeldin Zulficar. Screenplay, Yousself El Sebaii camera, Wahid Farid; music, Andre Ryder. At San Sebastian Film Fest. Running time, **140 MINS.**

What commences as a gay romantic comedy in a modern Cairo university setting, swings abruptly into an interminable flashback introducing a new set of characters and an entirely different film.

Marriage between a young college prof and co-ed fiancee is held up for two hours of screen time while a parental melodramatically romantic menage is slowly analyzed to determine whether the young couple are pre-announced brother and sister. In the lengthy recap, a brilliant author is torn between the attraction for a beautiful Egyptian maid and an invalid wife. Tempest of dialogue ultimately clears up doubts and marital obstacles to a new generation removed.

Safia Sarwat's early co-ed comedy performance pleases in this below-par entry.

Werb.

Smrt V Sedle
(Death in the Saddle)
(CZECHOSLOVAKIA-COLOR)

San Sebastian, Aug. 4.

Ceskoslovenksy Film production (Prague). Stars Rudolf Jelinek, Jana Kásanova; co-stars R. Lukavsky, E. Dubsky, J. Sovak. Directed by Jindrich Polak from original story and screenplay by Jiri Cirkl and Jindrich Polak. Camera, Ludvik Milic. At San Sebastian Film Fest. Running time, **85 MINS.**

Effect of Hollywood westerns on Czech stud farm jockeys is given a farce treatment during half of this film but mid-way in pic director Jindrich Polak changes style to wind up a cops-and-robbers production.

An avid reader of western pulp, the hero irks his fellow jockeys by pretending he is the original Beaver Kid. Determined to discourage his prairie pipe dream, they stage a mock outlaw raid. In the course of extended horseplay, the farm paymaster is killed and payroll looted. Early reels have some amusingly foolish moments and a scent of adolescent charm, best expressed by the young leads. Otherwise, no outstanding qualities except the above-average exterior color.

Werb.

Ari No Machi No Maria
(Ragpickers' Angel)
(JAPANESE-COLOR)

San Sebastian, Aug. 4.

Shochiku (Kiyoshi Takamura) Co. Ltd. (Tokyo) production and release. Stars Kakuko Chino, Shizue Natsukawa, Shinji Namzara, Fumio Watanable, Shuji Sano. Directed by Heinosuke Gosho. Screenplay by Keiji Hasebe. At San Sebastian Film Fest. Running time, **110 MINS.**

Film closely follows the real life

story of Maria Isabel Kitahara, daughter of a Japanese university professor, who was converted by Spanish Basque nuns. Her missionary zeal among the slum dwellers outside Tokyo inspired Toro Matsui's book on which the script is based.

Contrast in movement between the porcelain-like missionary sans habit and the primitive energy of junk scavengers living on the fringe of extinction, gives the film an unreal quality that defies sustained interest. Maria's long, drawn-out illness and ultimate sacrifice might be reminiscent of Kabuki legit but pace is taxing on audience.

Afgacolor tints and lensing excel. Inspirational value makes it a possible for special religioso slotting, if substantially pruned.
Werb.

Procesado 1,040
(Prisoner 1,040)
(ARGENTINA)
San Sebastian, Aug. 4.
Argentina Sono Film production (Buenos Aires). Stars Narciso Ibanez Menta, Walter Vidarte; co-stars Alicia Bellati, Tito Alonso, Carlos Estrada, Josefa Goldar, Betto Gianola. Directed by Ruben Cavallotti. Screenplay, Wilfredo Jimenez from book by Juan Carlos Patron. Camera, Alberto Etchebehere; music, Juan Ehlert. At San Sebastian Film Fest. Running time, 85 MINS.

Merit of this entry is its appeal for discernment in the administration of justice. To accent this, screenwriter Jimenez has contrived situations beyond credulity —taking a lovable old man from his pearl wedding party and almost drowning him in the quagmire of law and penal institutions.

Fortunate coincidence in the prison sequences, pairs this pillar of condemned innocence with a crafty young delinquent, Little Fox, who saves dad from the longest sentence ever imposed for a misdemeanor. W a l t e r Vidarte turns the cagey young felon role into a standout performance. Others play it much too broadly.
Werb.

Noci I Jutra
(Nights and Days)
(YUGOSLAVIAN)
Pula, Aug. 4.
Bosna Film (Sarajewo) production. With Marija Kohn, Vlastimir Stoiljkovic, Milan Srdoc. Directed by Pjer Majhrovski. Screenplay, Mesa Selimovic; camera, Stevo Landuo. At Pula Film Fest. Running time, 98 MINS.

Not much rings true in this partisan picture. Put the blame on a hardly convincing story and old hat character portrayals. If there's much suspense it's because of a partly impressive camera-work.

Story sees the commander of a partisan group falling into the hands of the Germans. A number of partisans, disguised as German soldiers, set out to free their commander. But they arrive too late the commander has been shot. Unquestionably, a lot of energy and ambition was put into this production, yet it looks as though the right technicians weren't at work here.
Hans.

Zvezda Putuje Na Jug

(The Star Goes to the South)
(YUGOSLAV-CZECH-COLOR)
Pula, Aug. 4.

Lovcen Film (Budva) and Barandova (Prague) production. With Gordana Miletic, Rudolf Hruscinski, Joza Gregorin. Directed by Oldrih Lipski. Screenplay, Jirzi Sila and Lipski; camera, Ferdinand Pecenka; music, Jirzi Baur. At Pula Film Fest. Running time, 93 MINS.

A harmless East European musical made by Titoland's Lovcen Film in conjunction with the Czech Barandova outfit. It has the Karel Vlacha orch, top band in the CSR, as the big attraction. Film is a welcome departure from the abundance of war and partisan pix still produced around here. This rates, at least for Yugo and Czech tastes, as top entertainment. Since there's a good deal of rhythmical music along with a number of nice gags in this film, latter may interest some foreign buyers. The Vlacha orch deserves praise. Technical credits are okay.
Hans.

Viza Zla
(The False Passport)
(YUGOSLAVIA)
Pula, Aug. 4.
Vardar (Skopje) production. Directed by France Stiglic. With Ilija Dzuvalekovski, Slobodan Perovic, Metka Ocvirk, Aco Jovanovski. Screenplay, Slavko Janevski; camera, Branko Mihajlovski; music, Bojan Adamic. At Pula Film Fest. Running time, 102 MINS

France Stiglic, creator of well-remembered film, "Valley of Peace," comes along with another interesting pic which may be given some exploitation chances despite the fact that it's a far cry from being a great production.

Subject guarantees some amount of suspense, but the drawbacks are too much talk and dull moments. The most interesting part about this is the camerawork. There are some unusually impressive shots. Acting is fine.

Pic calls itself a contemporary psychological drama about men who attempt to make some easy money via smuggling narcotics over the border. A routine love story is woven in. The evildoers are arrested as the climax.
Hans.

Dubrovsky
(YUGO-ITALIAN)
(COLOR-TOTALSCOPE)
Pula, Aug. 4.
Vardar Film (Skopje) and Hesperia Film (Rome) co-production. Stars John Forsythe, Rossana Schiaffino; features Wiliam Dieterle, Jan Sid, Paul Dahlke. Directed by William Dieterle. Screenplay, Akos Tolny and De Sanchis, after novel by A. S. Pushkin; camera (Eastmancolor), Aldo Gordani; music, Carlo Ruscelli. At Pula Film Festival. Running time, 115 MINS.

Disappointing costume adventure yarn adapted from Pushkin's novel of same name. Direction follows the most old-fashioned pattern. It's disappointing to see that William Dieterle is responsible for this. Not even the mass scenes which he once knew how to handle so masterly come off.

Commercially, the title and cast, headed by American John Forsythe and beautiful Rossana Schiaffino, may stir some interest. Dieterle enacts the role of Kirila Petrovitch, the unscrupulous owner of the Pokroskoe estate, with hardly impressive results. Support is adequate. Color photography occasionally is an advantage.
Hans.

Vrata Ostaju Otvorena
(The Door Remains Open)
(YUGOSLAVIAN)
Pula, Aug. 4.
Bosna Film production. With Radomir Vergovic, Milena Dravic, Teodora Arsenovic. Directed by Frantisek Cap. Screenplay, Vladimir Paskaljevic; camera, Janez Kalisnik; music, Borut Lesjak. At Pula Film Fest. Running time, 98 MINS.

This film benefits mainly from the skillful direction of Czech-born Frantisek Cap, one of the more

experienced pic creators of Yugoslavia. His handling of the players is fine. Plot isn't exactly exciting and occasionally is thin, but he makes the most of it. This well-made production has export possibilities.

Yarn touches the lost youth problem. A young lad, who lost his parents during the war, gets into bad company and becomes a crook. He's put into jail but escapes. He intends to continue his criminal life, and sneaks into a family home with the aim of robbing. The family's care, devotion and love for him mend his ways. Film's technical credits are fully satisfactory.
Hans.

Vetar Je Stao Pred Zoru
(The Wind Stops Blowing)
(YUGOSLAVIAN)
Pula, Aug. 4.
Avala Film (Belgrade) production. With Steven Stukelja, Radmila Radovanic, Branko Plesa. Directed by Rados Novakovic. Screenplay, Aleksander Vuco; camera, Nenad Jovicic. At Pula Film Fest. Running time, 102 MINS.

Avala Film, top producing outfit in Titoland, contributed four pix to this year's Pula fete and each of them dealt with war (mostly Partisan) subjects. This partisan pic is of better quality although also being very much on the cliche side.

Imaginative lensing is a definite plus. Also the acting comes up to fine standards. Direction is okay. As it's often the case with Yugoslavian pix, this is much too talky. Looms as a good suspense item domestically, with foreign possibilities regarded as moderate if there are any.
Hans.

Tri Cetvrtine Sunca
(Three Quarters of a Sun)
(YUGOSLAVIAN)
Pula, Aug. 4.
Triglav Film (Ljubljana) production. With Bert Sotlar, Pero Kvrgic, Nikola Popovic, Antun Vrdoljak. Directed by Joze Babic. Screenplay, Leopold Zahola; camera, Rudi Vavpotic; music, Bajon Adamic. At Pula Film Fest. Running time, 98 MINS.

This deals with people who return from Nazi concentration camps after the last World War. Pic is based on human interest material but suffers from slow-paced direction and sketchy character portrayals.

This basically interesting plot could have been exploited to much better advantage. In its present form, film has only slim export chances. Technical credits are fine.
Hans.

Pukotina Raja
(Heaven Without Love)
(YUGOSLAVIAN)
Pula, Aug. 4.
Jadran Film (Zagreb) production. With Ljubica Jovic, Milan Puzic, Severin Bijelic. Directed by Vladimir Pogacic. Screenplay, Pogacic, Milan Tutorov; camera, Milorad Markovic; music, Bojan Adamic. At Pula Film Fest. Running time, 109 MINS.

Jadran Film, producer of "Train Without Time-Table," here has a pic that's beyond the domestic average. It's a mixture of several different film categories, but well done and very interesting at the start. Screenplay is overloaded with situations but director Vladimir Pogacic manages to give it an entertaining slant combined with enough depth to cause the viewer to think.

It's the story of a young marriage. The egoism of the husband

drives the wife to death. Technical credits are adequate. Though not much for export, film deserves a good classification.
Hans.

Pogon B
(Factory B)
(YUGOSLAVIAN)
Pula, Aug. 4.
Ufus (Belgrade) production. Directed by Vojislav Nanovic. With Pavle Vujisic, Dragan Lakovic, Milivoje Zivanovic, Desa Beric. Screenplay, Vojislav Nanovic; music, V. Simic; camera, Milorad Markovic. At Pula Film Fest. Running time, 109 MINS.

Okay meller centering around the search for oil. Until latter is found, there are the usual familiar complications and situations mingled with substantial comedy relief. Latter comes on account of Palve Vujisic, a beardy driller called "Caracas," who received his drilling experience in America.

Pic found a receptive (domestic) audience here and will probably loom as a satisfactory b.o. contender at home. For western release, it's somewhat dull and overlong. Direction and script reach only fair standards. Technical credits are adequate.
Hans.

It Started With a Kiss
(C'SCOPE; COLOR)

Glenn Ford and Debbie Reynolds in a sexy romp in Spain. Boxoffice should be bright.

Hollywood, Aug. 11.

Metro release of an Arcola Production. Stars Glenn Ford, Debbie Reynolds; co-stars Gcstavo Rojo, Eva Gabor, Fred Clark; with Edgar Buchanan; also Henry (Harry) Morgan, Robert Warwick, Francis Bayier, Netta Packer, Robert Cunningham, Alice Backes, Carmen Phillips and Joi Lansing. Produced by Aaron Rosenberg. Directed by George Marshall. Screenplay, Charles Lederer, from a story by Valenetine Davies; camera, Robert Bronner; editor, John McSweeney Jr.; music, Jeff Alexander. Previewed at the Egyptian Theatre, Aug. 11, '59. Running time, 103 MINS.

Sgt. Joe Fitzpatrick .... Glenn Ford
Maggie .... Debbie Reynolds
Marquesa de la Rey .... Eva Gabor
Antonio Soriano .... Gustavo Rojo
Gen. O'Connell .... Fred Clark
Cong. Tappe .... Edgar Buchanan
Charles Meriden .. Henry (Harry) Morgan
Cong. Muir .... Robert Warwick
Mrs. Tappe .... Francis Bavier
Mrs. Muir .... Netta Packer
The Major .... Robert Cunningham
Sally Meriden .... Alice Backes
Belvah .... Carmen Phillips

"It Started With a Kiss" winds up in bed—a half dozen of them, spread from New York to Madrid, in this highly amusing, sex-motivated study of two physically suited newlyweds getting to know each other. The Aaron Rosenberg production, brightly directed by George Marshall, is aimed at the adult, and the combination of its borderline humor and Glenn Ford and Debbie Reynolds to deliver it should stack up in romantic returns for the Metro film.

There are few double-entendres in Charles Lederer's racy screenplay which leaves no doubt as to the intent of its ideas, and the action is as broad and obvious as the "do not disturb" sign on a honeymoon couple's hotel door. The Valentine Davies story runs on one line, offering a maximum of appealing misunderstanding and a minimum of contrivance. And director Marshall has taken advantage of every possibility for a laugh, winding up with a chunk of fun that is as maturely infatuating as any Hollywood has come up with to date.

In a smart merchandising tie-in, producer Rosenberg uses the Lincoln Futura, a bright-red Buck Rogerish automobile, as a fulcrum for much of the film's action. It's a useful gimmick for the picture itself and is quite capably set up as a potent source of promotion, both for the car and the film.

That's not all that's smart about "It Started With a Kiss," for the property is enchanced unlimitedly by its stunning Spanish settings. There's no cheating here, and cameraman Robert Bronner's panoramas of Spain are exquisite use of CinemaScope and Metrocolor.

Ford plays an air force sergeant, and Miss Reynolds plays a nightclub dancer who wants to marry a millionaire, which Ford is not. After one kiss, however, she judges he's worth a million dollars and within a few hours, they are man and wife. The next day he's moved out to Spain, and she follows, bringing along the $40,000 automobile he won in a raffle. On misunderstanding after she arrives, she's convinced their marriage is solely for physical reasons, and she demands a 30-day test during which time no bed tactics will be allowed. Main stem of the film has Ford, the husband, trying to convince Miss Reynolds, the wife, that man and wife just don't sleep on separate pieces of furniture. There's hearty confusion before the end, but he finally wins his point.

Ford and Miss Reynolds make an appealing twosome, at odds for most of the film's 103 minutes but with considerable "togetherness" before its wrap-up. As the befuddled sergeant, Ford is somewhere between the boy and the man, and he perfectly establishes his instincts and desires as always deserving of sympathy. Miss Reynolds does much to make the audience despise her gold-digging ways, a far contrast from her sweet norm, and, at her moment of realization, she has no trouble at all in winning everyone back. She's a delightful actress with a bright, breezy approach to comedy that puts her just about in a class by herself.

The Arcola Production is additionally assisted by fine performances from Eva Gabor as a beautiful marquesa, who goes after Ford, Gustavo Rojo as a wealthy bullfighter who goes after Ford's Lincoln and Ford's wife, and Fred Clark as an understanding if somewhat irritated general who just wants to be left alone. Edgar Buchanan, Henry (Harry) Morgan, Robert Warwick, Francis Bavier, Netta Packer, Robert Cunningham, Carmen Phillips and Joi Lansing round out the good cast, with an excellent performance from Alice Backes as an airman's wife.

In addition to Bronner's exceptional lensing, the film benefits from first-rate work by art directors Hans Peters and Urie McCleary, editor John McSweeney Jr. and recording supervisor Franklin Milton. Jeff Alexander's score is as full of whimsy as the film itself. But the Rudy Render-Charles Lederer title song, sung over the main titles by Miss Reynolds, is not apt to add any passion to "Kiss." *Ron.*

The FBI Story
(COLOR)

Federal agents "humanized" in good b.o. prospect.

Los Angeles, Aug. 14.

Warner Bros. release produced and directed by Mervyn LeRoy. Stars James Stewart and Vera Miles. Screenplay, Richard L. Breen and John Twist; based on the book by Don Whitehead; camera, (Technicolor) Joseph Biroc; music, Max Steiner; editor, Philip W. Anderson. Previewed at the studio, Aug. 11, '59. Running time, 149 MINS.

Chip Hardesty .... James Stewart
Lucy Hardesty .... Vera Miles
Sam Crandall .... Murray Hamilton
Geo. Crandall .... Larry Pennell
Jack Graham .... Nick Adams
Jennie Hardesty .... Diane Jergens
Anna Sage .... Jean Willes
Anne Hardesty .... Joyce Taylor
Mario .... Victor Millan
Harry Dakins .... Parley Baer
McCutcheon .... Fay Roope
U.S. Marshal .... Ed. Prentiss
Medicine Salesman .... Robert Gist
Mike Hardesty .... Buzz Martin
Salesman .... Kenneth Mayer
Suspect .... Paul Genge

Mervyn LeRoy has taken the factual material of Don Whitehead's best-selling "The FBI Story" and made of it a tense, exciting film story told in human terms. The Warner Bros. release is not the same as the book, because it is a romantic melodrama, not a documentary. The method used is to show the work of the FBI through the life of one of its agents, James Stewart, a familiar enough device, but correct and rewarding in this instance. This approach should pay off in strong boxoffice returns.

For those who did not read the book, the fine screenplay by Richard L. Breen and John Twist, is a reminder that the FBI does more than tail communists. As the film shows, it has at various times, taken on the Ku Klux Klan, Dillinger and Ma Barker, oilmen exploiting the American Indian, Bundists and Nazi spies during World War II, and young men who blow up airplanes to collect insurance on their mothers.

The purpose of the Breen-Twist screenplay, for theatrical purposes as well as to explore the FBI itself, is to show that FBI agents are not cold, silent, GPU-like grey men, but human beings with faults, frailties and families. Without getting soggy or silly, it humanizes a police service and gives to its members personal dignity. In this oblique way ,it distinguishes between patriotism and chauvinism. It is an honest, sympathetic revelation of the FBI, but it is also a fine film drama.

The fictional story used as a framework for the introduction of the FBI and its work sounds conventional enough. Stewart and his wife, Vera Miles, are torn between his dedication to his job with the FBI and the fact that he could give his family a more rewarding life outside the bureau. But Stewart believes what J. Edgar Hoover tells his agents when he takes over the service, that its men must be imbued not only with the service of justice but the love of justice. In the end, there can be no question that Stewart has served this ideal.

The intelligence of the screenplay, and its inventions, cannot be underestimated. The dialog is exemplary, economical in words despite the film's length, because every line seems to have a purpose, for exposition, to advance or highlight the action, for humorous relief. Too, the story does not run out of plot. It plunges directly into a revelatory incident before the main titles, and one of the most suspenseful sequences, a fine chase through New York streets, is used for the final crisis.

There are uses of understatement, such as a tootling arrangement of "Yankee Doodle" for a bridge theme and a fadeout of unusual poignancy. There is plenty of direction action, gunfights, sleuthing, slugging. There is good humor, and an adult love story of depth. Mervyn LeRoy's direction cannot be faulted, and his restraint is admirable.

Stewart gives a restrained performance, wry and intelligent, completely credible as the film covers a span of about 25 years to show both the fledgeling agent and the older man. Miss Miles, who plays particularly well with Stewart, synchronizes her more direct attack smoothly with his underplaying. Her role is vital in conveying the feminine attitude towards a man in this work, and her success contributes importantly to the film.

Murray Hamilton is memorable as Stewart's fellow agent, felled by gangsters. Larry Pennell and Diane Jergens supply the young love interest believably, and Buzz Martin is good as Stewart's son, killed in World War II. Nick Adams is effective in a brief, important sequence, and others who register include Jean Willes, Joyce Taylor, Fay Roope, Robert Gist, Kenneth Mayer and Paul Genge, latter in an important but almost non-speaking role.

Joseph Biroc's camera work, in Technicolor, is thoughtful and dramatic, where needed. Max Steiner's score avoids jingoism, but understates its points, in good orchestrations by Murray Cutter. Other technical credits are good, although some of the interiors in the later portion of the film seem a trifle lavish for the income scale of an FBI man. *Powe.*

I'm All Right, Jack
(BRITISH)

Standout performance by Peter Sellers as a union official in a smartly funny comedy that cocks an irreverent snoot at industry, unions, workers and employers indiscriminately.

London, Aug. 18.

British Lion release of a Boulting Brothers (Roy Boulting) production. Stars Ian Carmichael, Peter Sellers, Terry-Thomas. Directed by John Boulting. Screenplay, Frank Harvey, John Boulting from novel by Alan Hackney; camera, Max Greene; editor, Anthony Harvey; music, Ken Hare. At Leicester Square Theatre, London. Running time, 105 MINS.

Stanley Windrush .... Ian Carmichael
Fred Kite .... Peter Sellers
Major Hitchcock .... Terry-Thomas
Sidney de Vere Cox
Richard Attenborough
Bertram Tracepurcel ...... Dennis Price
Aunt Dolly .... Margaret Rutherford
Mrs. Kite .... Irene Handl
Cynthia Kite .... Liz Fraser
Windrush, Snr. .... Miles Malleson
Mr. Mohammed .... Marne Maitland
Waters .... John Le Mesurier
Magistrate .... Raymond Huntley
Knowles .... Victor Maddern
Dai .... Kenneth Griffiths
Charlie .... Fred Griffiths
Shop Stewards ...... Sam Kydd, Cardew Robinson, Bruce Wightman
Hopper .... Ronnie Stevens
Num Yum's Executive .... Martin Boddey
Appts. Bd. Exam. .... Brian Oulton
TV Panel Chairman .. Malc. Muggeridge
Detto Exec. .... John Glyn-Jones
Missiles Drector ...... Maurice Colbourne
Reporters ...... Michael Ward, Stringer Davis
Spencer .... Esma Cannon
Crawley .... Terry Scott
Workman .... Wally Patch
Tv producer .... Alun Owen
Tv announcer .... Muriel Young
B.B.C Announcer .... Frank Phillips
Card players .... David Lodge, Keith Smith, Kenneth Warren
Minister of Labor .... Basil Dignam
Trade Union Official .... Harry Locke

The Boulting Brothers specialize in poking shrewd, unmalicious but penetrating fun at various British institutions. Latest target is British factory life, trade unionism and the general possibility that everybody is working for one person—himself. A brilliantly observed performance by Peter Sellers, plus a standout supporting cast insures that "Jack" will clean up in U. K. It may well be that American trade union problems are rather different. But, even so, there will be no lack of yocks from U. S. audiences given the chance of seeing this slick, funny piece of satire. It brings the Boulting Brothers back to their own splendid standard which, on a couple of occasions recently, has tended to slip.

Ian Carmichael plays his by now over-familiar role of a misplaced, genial, young idiot who sparks off a number of situations without realizing why or how. In this instance he is an ex-university type who wants to get an executive job in industry. Instead, he is given a job as a factory worker by his uncle who wants him in as a stooge for a secret, dirty financial deal. From then on, it's no holds barred against employers and workers alike. The Boultings' premise, and rightly or wrongly it's highly amusing, is that everybody's working exclusively for their own ends. Nobody is spared and the producers refuse to make any decision as to who is right.

Carmichael becomes the unwitting cause of a factory strike that

swells to nationwide proportions. Gradually he begins to realize that he has been taken for a ride and on a BBC tv discussion program blows his top. Even then, though, he's the fall guy and is put on probation for a breach of the peace.

Carmichael slides smoothly through his performance, but it is Sellers, as the chairman of the factory's union works committee, who makes the film. With a make-up that subtly suggests Hitler, he brings rare humor and an occasional touch of pathos to the role. Sellers' strength is that he does not deliberately play for laughs. He produces them from the situations and sharp dialog provided by screenplay scribe Frank Harvey.

Dennis Price and Richard Attenborough as shady employers and Terry-Thomas as a bewildered personnel manager also provide rich roles. The pic is liberally provided with fine supporting artists who add to the fun. Among these are Margaret Rutherford, in a guest appearance: Victor Maddern, Sam Kydd and Fred Griffiths, as workers who are smart in getting a good wage packet for the minimum labor; Marne Maitland, as a contriving foreign minister with an eye for a slick deal; Irene Handl, as Sellers' long suffering wife and a promising newcomer, Liz Fraser, as his addle-pated, well-shaped daughter.

The film is sharply written, edited and lensed and keeps up a neat level of wit and caustic comment. *Rich.*

The Oregon Trail
(C'SCOPE-COLOR)

Fred MacMurray starrer which should do well in oater situations.

Hollywood, Aug. 10.

Twentieth-Fox release of a Richard Einfeld production. Stars Fred MacMurray, William Bishop, Nina Shipman; also stars Gloria Talbott, Henry Hull, John Carradine; with John Dierkes, Elizabeth Patterson, James Bell, Ralph Sanford, Tex Terry, Arvo Ojala, Roxene Wells, Gene N. Fowler, John Slosser, Sherry Spalding, Ollie O'Toole, Ed Wright. Directed by Gene Fowler Jr. Screenplay, Louis Vittes and Gene Fowler Jr., from a story by Vittes; camera, Kay Norton; editor, Betty Steinberg; music, Paul Dunlap. Previewed at the studio Aug. 10, '59. Running time, **82 MINS.**

Neal Harris .... Fred MacMurray
Capt. George Wayne...... William Bishop
Prudence Cooper .... Nina Shipman
Shona Hastings .... Gloria Talbott
Seton .... Henry Hull
Zachariah Garrison....... John Carradine
Gabe Hastings .... John Dierkes
Maria Cooper .... Elizabeth Patterson
Jeremiah Cooper .... James Bell
Mr. Decker .... Ralph Sanford
Brizzard .... Tex Terry
Ellis .... Arvo Ojala
Flossie Shoemaker......... Roxene Wells
Richard Cooper .... Gene N. Fowler
Johnny .... John Slosser
Lucy .... Sherry Spalding
James G. Bennett............ Olie O'Toole
Jesse .... Ed Wright

The low-hanging dust at the beginning of 20th-Fox's "The Oregon Trail" thickens toward the end in a high-flying flurry of mid-19th Century pioneering hazards, turning this first Richard Einfeld Production into a good bet for action houses.

Excitement hits its peak in a final Indian raid that sends a fusillade of arrows at the intended human targets, and interest along the way is sustained in clearly etched characters as screenplayed by Louis Vittes and Gene Fowler Jr. from Vittes' original story. Fowler directed "Oregon Trail" with a sure hand, and his pace and feel are very effective with the fast action.

The single most important element in the film is Fred MacMurray's portrayal of a New York reporter sent West to dig up a story. Through the actor's adroit sense of timing and humor, the entertainment values of "Oregon Trail" are increased considerably. He receives good support from William Bishop's fine performance and from Nina Shipman, 20th contract actress who gets better with each film. Pic also benefits from a fine portrayal by Gloria Talbott as an Indian girl and from good performances by Henry Hull, John Carradine, John Dierkes, Elizabeth Patterson and James Bell.

The story that MacMurray is to dig out is for New York Herald editor James Gordon Bennett, who believes President Polk is sending military troops to the Oregon territory in the disguise of pioneers. MacMurray gets his story, but sending it home is another matter, and he's taken prisoner by Indians in the attempt. Helped to escape by a beautiful Indian maiden, MacMurray ends up joining the troops to fight the Redskin onslaught. He resigns his journalistic post and, with the squaw, rides off as another pioneer.

The DeLuxe Color-CinemaScope production makes good use of film from other pix, thus keeping its own budget in hand. But bits of the new footage—particularly a sequence in front of a hill-and-dale backdrop—are embarrassingly phony.

The musical score by Paul Dunlap is very good, and assets include "Ballad of the Oregon Trail" by Dunlap and Charles Devlan and "Never Alone" by Will Miller. Indian technical adviser is Iron Eyes Cody, and in two instances the Indian make-up by Del Aceredo is of special note. *Ron.*

But Not for Me

Mild Clark Gable comedy romance of age-vs.-youth.

Hollywood, Aug. 14.

Paramount release of William Perlberg-George Seaton production. Stars Clark Gable, Caroll Baker, Lilli Palmer, Lee J. Cobb, Barry Coe. Directed by Walter Lang. Screenplay, John Michael Hayes; based on the play, "Accent On Youth," by Samson Raphaelson; camera, Robert Burks; music, Leith Stevens; editor, Alma Macrorie. Previewed at the Fox Wilshire theatre, Aug. 10, '59. Running time, **105 MINS.**

Russell Ward .... Clark Gable
Eleanor Brown .... Carroll Baker
Kathryn Ward .... Lilli Palmer
Jeremiah MacDonald........ Lee J. Cobb
Gordon Reynolds .... Barry Coe
Demetrios Bacos .... Thomas Gomez
Atwood .... Charles Lane
Montgomery .... Wendell Holmes
Roy Morton .... Tom Deggan

"But Not For Me," a romantic comedy based on Samson Raphaelson's old stage play "Accent on Youth," has its bright spots but it does not click as a whole. The concept, of the William Perlberg-George Seaton production is clever, but the realization does not always pay off. The Paramount release has some marquee values and supplementary production assets which it will need to pull at the boxoffice.

There have been considerable changes in the original play, first filmed by Paramount more than 20 years ago. The screenplay by John Michael Hayes brings the plot up to date. Where Raphaelson, writing for an adult Broadway audience, had his aging producer successful in his love affair with a younger woman, this film version, with today's young audiences in mind, has youth stick to youth.

Clark Gable plays the producer who feels his age creeping up on him at a galloping pace. The fact that he is past his prime is used in both the romantic and professional problems of the story. His angels hesitate to subscribe funds for his new Broadway production because they feel he has lost his touch. Gable himself feels his wrinkles when he falls in love with a much younger woman.

There is considerable fun in a star of Gable's vintage kidding himself in the role. As the producer he looks and acts a vigorous man, although he gives his age, variously, as 44, 46, 52 and 56. There is an amusing scene where his ex-wife, Lilli Palmer, cattily honors him with a birthday party and a huge cake comes in ablaze with what seems scores of candles.

Walter Lang's direction is generally well-paced although he sometimes seems to have Gable playing at such a breathless rate that it sacrifices diction. Hayes' screenplay could have jettisoned more of the original idea than it did. Such scenes as the pre-curtain jitters, on opening night, of tyro actress Carroli Baker have been done and over-done.

Miss Baker makes an appealing younger woman and Miss Palmer gives a breezy portrayal. Lee J. Cobb, in the role of a drunken playwright rehabilitated by Gable, is pleasant but less forceful than this actor usually is. Barry Coe makes a nice juvenile. Thomas Gomez is amusing as a Hollywood film tycoon of Greek origin, and Charles Lane and Wendell Holmes wind up the important supporting roles.

The title song is beautifully sung by Ella Fitzgerald behind the main titles, and its recording may be a plus selling value. Leith Stevens' score is bright. Edith Head's costumes may provide distaff appeal. Technical credits are generally capable. *Powe.*

Bal de Nuit
(Night Dance Hall)
(FRENCH)

Paris, Aug. 11.

CFF release of CFPC production. With Pascale Audret, Claude Titre, Sophie Daumier, Jany Clair, Micheline Francey, Bernadette Laffont. Directed by Maurice Cloche. Screenplay, Andre Tabet, Cloche; camera, Jacques Mercanton; editor, Fanchette Mazin. At Avenue, Paris. Running time, **90 MINS.**

Martine .... Pascale Audret
Gilles .... Claude Titre
Lalou .... Sophie Daumier
Louise .... Jany Clair
Mother .... Micheline Francey
Nicole .... Bernadette Laffont

This follows the plight of an unloved young adolescent girl who runs off and gets mixed up with a bunch of delinquents. Pic is somewhat sentimental, old fashioned and preachy. So it looks like mainly for local consumption.

The girl follows a rugged odyssey compounded by faulty parents, poverty and juvenile restlessness. Director Maurice Cloche ploddingly puts this on film carefully but without a true feeling for the milieu. It is technically okay. *Mosk.*

For the First Time
(COLOR; TECHNIRAMA; SONGS)

Lots of music in Lanza's latest. Will attract his regular fans.

Hollywood, Aug. 14.

Metro release of Corona Film Production. Stars Mario Lanza, ZsaZsa Gabor. Produced by Alexander Gruter. Directed by Rudi Mate. Screenplay, Andrew Solt; camera (Technicolor), Aldo Tonti; music supervisor-conductor, George Stoll; editor, Gene Ruggiero. Previewed at the studio, Aug. 6, '59. Running time, **97 MINS.**

Tonio Costa .... Mario Lanza
The Countess .... Zsa Zsa Gabor
Christa .... Johanna von Koczian
The Impresario .... Kurt Kasznar
Prof. Bruckner .... Hans Sohnker

Mario Lanza fans will probably welcome "For The First Time," but otherwise its appeal will be limited though there's lots of music. It's the tenor's first since "The Seven Hills of Rome," released more than a year ago.

Filmed entirely in Europe, "For The First Time" has Lanza as an unpredictable opera singer whose career is threatened by his nonchalance towards his singing engagements. Andrew Solt's screenplay is an attempt to get a little more reality into the usual story of a singer than is usually supplied by plots designed only to bridge the spaces between songs.

Screenplay has Lanza undergoing a change of personality after he meets a pretty young girl, Johanna Von Koczian, who is deaf. He falls in love with her and devotes himself to finding a surgeon who can cure her. There is an obvious basis for drama in the girl's deafness and Lanza's singing, and it is handled with taste and some subtlty.

Despite Rudy Mate's generally able direction, in which he tries to make the star's handicaps work for him, Lanza's delivery remains operatic whether he is singing Verdi or speaking Solt. He is fine when he stands up and belts out an aria—the big voice seems better than ever—but he is insecure on the speaking lines. The story is not helped, either, by some clumsy construction.

Opera scenes, filmed at the Rome Opera House are lavish and colorful and suited to the film's Technicolor and Technirama. These portions include scenes from "Rigoletto," "Pagliacci," "Cosi Fan Tutti," "Othello" and "Aida." Also included are some lighter songs, the Bavarian drinking song, "Munchen Lied," and "O Sole Mio," "Ich Liebe Dich," and two originals by musical supervisor-conductor George Stoll, "Capri, Capri" and "Pineapple Picker." There is also a good title song, sung in both Italian and English, that could be a strong promotional assist to the film.

Zsa Zsa Gabor plays a running part in the Alexander Gruter production, but the role—or Miss Gabor's conception of it—doesn't contribute much to the film. Kurt Kasznar has a comedy characterization that is mildly amusing. Young Miss Von Koczian is a different type than is usually seen in romantic roles in films, lacking glamor but with a certain innocence that has appeal.

Aldo Tonti's photography, of Capri, Rome, Salzburg and other markedly photogenic sites, is another asset, and Gene Ruggiero's editorial supervision has inspired a smooth film. *Powe.*

Upstairs and Downstairs
(BRITISH-COLOR)

Simple, rather uneven, yet amiable comedy about troubles of a young couple searching for a maid. Safe entry for U.K. houses, but short on stars for U.S.

London, Aug. 11.

Rank release of a Betty Box-Ralph Thomas production. Stars Michael Craig, Anne Heywood, Mylene Demongeot, James Robertson Justice. Directed by Ralph Thomas. Screenplay, Frank Harvey from Ronald Scott Thorn's book; camera,

Ernest Steward; editor, Alfred Roome; music, Philip Green. Previewed at R.F.D. Private Theatre, London. Running time, 101 MINS.

Richard	Michael Craig
Kate	Anne Heywood
Ingrid	Mylene Demongeot
Mansfield	James Robertson Justice
Maria	Claudia Cardinale
P. C. Edwards	Sidney James
Rosemary	Joan Hickson
Blodwen	Joan Sims
Farringdon	Joseph Tomelty
Mrs. Farringdon	Nora Nicholson
Wesley	Daniel Massey
McGuffey	Austin Willis
Mrs. McGuffey	Margalo Gillmore
Parson	Reginald Beckwith
Guard	Cyril Chamberllain
Agency Girl	Dilys Laye
Large Woman	Irene Handl
Kingsley	William Mervyn
Mario	Eric Pohlmann
First Old Lady	Jean Cadell
Second Old Lady	Barbara Everest
Mary	Barbara Steele
Paul	Stephen Gregson
Harry	Nicholas Phipps
Frank	Jeremy Burnham
Brian	Nicholas Parsons
Sgt. Tuck	Madge Ryan
Bridget	Betty Henderson

The problems of two likeable newlyweds in their attempt to get a domestic servant is the basis of a slender yarn, which, while simple, makes a cheerful enough diversion. The stars and the presence of a long list of familiar feature players make this a very brisk prospect for U.K. houses. But it is light on marquee value for the U.S. It's 60 minutes before Mylene Demongeot shows up, and then the film takes on a different shape. It becomes a more sentimental light comedy, with the slapstick largely abandoned.

Briefly, while John Gregson and Anne Heywood are on honeymoon in Italy, her father installs an Italian maid in their new house. They return to find that the fiery young woman has been entertaining half the United States Navy. The newlyweds arrive to find a drunken party going on. Exit the maid. Then starts their troubled attempts to find a replacement and disaster piles up. The next one introduces a sheepdog into the house, gets loaded on gin and ruins an important dinner party. No. 3, on her first venture out of her native Wales. The fourth attempt brings in a distinguished pensioned couple who use the job as cover for robbing the bank next door.

Finally, from Switzerland, comes a girl who is wonderful around the house and with the children, but falls mildly for the husband, plays havoc with all his married friends, stands up a musican at the altar and decides to return to her boy friend at home.

This chain of events brings in some obvious but quite funny comedy. Other situations are dragged in with more enthusiasm than logic but since there is never any intention of anyone being expected to take the pic seriously, no great harm is done. Frank Harvey's screenplay is uneven and his situations more effective than his fairly stereotyped dialog. Ralph Thomas briskly keeps the action moving except towards the end.

Most of the fun comes from the performances, many of them exaggerated but hilarious. For instance, Joan Hickson, as the tipsy maid trying to serve dinner has a standout yock scene, and Joan Sims turns in another of her sure cameos as the reluctant Welsh maid. Of the principals, Gregson and Miss Heywood contribute straightforward but very agreeable stints. James Robertson Justice as the father-in-law blusters cheerfully through his role. Miss Demongeot is an attractive French miss and it is easy to see why she causes devastation in the Gregson social circle. But some of her mannerisms are akin to coyness. Daniel Massey is also very much a hand as a cello-playing American, who nearly gets her to the altar.

Among other notable jobs done by old reliables are Sidney James, as a music-loving cop; Reginald Beckwith, as a fussy parson; Dilys Laye, a refined, acid agency clerk; Joseph Tomelty and Nora Nicholson, as the unlikely bank robbers, and Nicholas Phipps, as a silly admirer of Miss Demongeot.

"Upstairs And Downstairs" does not rate as highly as some of the comedies from the Box-Thomas stable. But with some good color lensing by Ernest Steward as a nice addition, it should prove a worthwhile booking for family audiences.

Rich.

La Nuit Des Espions
(Spies' Night)
(FRENCH)

Paris, Aug. 11.

Gaumont production and release. Stars Robert Hossein, Marina Vlady. Written and directed by Robert Hossein. Camera, Pierre Robin; editor, Gilbert Natot, Preemed in Paris. Running time, 85 MINS.

Peter	Robert Hossein
Helene	Marina Vlady

Film is primarily a gimmick pic since most of it deals with a femme and male spy isolated in a little cabin together in occupied France during the last war. They can either both be English, both German, or mixed, or one French and one English or German. Plot hinges on this scramble of nationalities.

But it is somewhat unclear and the two actors lack the weight to make their constant suspicions, love interludes and unremitting interrogations progressively dramatic. Some actors are rung in at the beginning to set up the premise, they also appear midway and at the end of the production.

Robert Hossein has taken on too much as star, director and writer. Constant camera movements do not help the film progress as it should. Marina Vlady's lack of expression makes her ambiguous, and she never really projects different facets of personality and thought to make the trick denouement plausible.

This pic looks chancey in the foreign market except for possible dualer or exploitation chances on its two-actor aspect and some long love scenes. It is so rambling and indefinite that it is a dubious entry for arty spots.

Mosk.

Christ in Bronze

Special Japanese film with special angles of interest.

Hollywood, Aug. 14.

Harpole Productions release of Shochiku production. Features Osamu Takizawa, Hitomi Nozoe, Isuzu Yamada, Akira Ishihama, Kyoko Kagawa, Eiji Okada. Produced by Kiyoshi Takamura. Directed by Minoru Shibuya. Screenplay, Ryosuke Saito; based on the novel by Yoshiro Nagayo; camera, Hiroyuki Nagaoka; music, Toshiro Mayuzumi. Previewed in Hollywood, Aug. 14, '59. Runnng time, 78 MINS.

Yusa Hagiwara	Eiji Okada
Tomi	Kazuko Okada
Christofa Ferrera	Osamu Takizawa
Tamon Fujita	Shinobu Araki
Monica	Kyoko Kagawa
Kichisaburo	Akira Ishihama
Kimika	Isuzi Yamada
O-Cho	Hitomi Nozoe
Choji	Shunj Sakai

An unusual subject for a Japanese film marks "Christ In Bronze," which tells of the persecution of Christians in Japan some 300 years ago. The film, being released here with English subtitles by Harpole Productions, is sketchy in its present form, presumably suffering from editing for the American market. Nonetheless as a special product for special handling, it should find its own audience.

The title comes from the manner in which the Japanese, fearing Catholic missionaries meant to spread western influence generally as well as western religion, tried to stamp out Christianity. They forced suspected converts to step on a picture or plaque of Christ. The believers, of course, refused and showed themselves Christians.

It's not clear whether the story, from a novel by Yoshiro Nagayo, is literally true. The central figure is a Portuguese priest who succumbs to police torture and becomes an informer on native Christians. Eventually he is shamed by the steadfastness of his converts and returns to his faith, but in the meantime is responsible for the torture and death of many who die rather than renounce their new faith.

If the story is not literally true, or even if it is, there might be some resentment among Catholics to the unflattering, if human, portrait the film paints of the missionary. He is shown degraded by a prostitute and in various ways the least admirable of the Christians. Osamu Takizawa is a believable Occidental, but his emotional portrayal seems broad by western standards. Isuzu Yamada has dignity as the prostitute, and Eiji Okada is good as the artist who creates the "Christ in Bronze."

The film winds with a visually impressive scene of a mass crucifixion of Japanese Christians by the authorities. Otherwise, however, the film quality of the print shown for review was poor. Lighting is dim and editing confusing. The frequent head-cropping leads to the belief that the film was shot in conventional dimension although shown wide-screen.

Powe.

Det Svanger Pa Slottet
(The Castle Is Swinging)
(SWEDISH)

Stockholm, Aug. 11.

Svensk Filmindustri production and release. With Alice Babs, Sven Lindberg, Yvonne Lombard, Lars Lonndahl, Gunnar Bjornstrand, Karl-Arne Holmsten. Directed by Alf Kjellin. Screenplay, Stig Olin, Hasse Ekman; camera, Gunnar Fischer; music, Bengt Hallberg. At Spegel, Stockholm. Running time, 97 MINS.

Inga	Alice Babs
Svante	Sven Lindberg
Sophie	Yvonne Lombard
Psychiatrist	Gunnar Bjornstrand
Conke	Karl-Arne Holmsten
Kurre	Lars Lonndahl
Simon	Simon Brehm
Madame Rochelle	Hjordis Petterson
Blide	George Funkquist
The Baroness	Bullan Weijden
Mrs. Brick	Sif Ruud
Adelaide	Lena Granhagen
Sixten	Ulf Johansson
The Baron	John Norrman
Ulrik Neuman	Ulrik Neuman
Little Gerhard	Karl Gerhard Lundquist
The Priest	Ingvar Kjellson

The housing shortage in Sweden is the talk of this country. Against this background, Hasse Ekman and Stig Olin, both leading actors and directors, have set the romance of a shy scholar who works at repairing old paintings. Sven Lindberg is the scholar while Alice Babs sings in a jazz band. Unable to get married because having no apartment, they separate but keep their own jobs. Miss Babs gets a good offer for a summer tour with the band and Svante (Sven Lindberg) is ordered to work on paintings in a castle where the young daughter is attracted to him. The comedy develops when the shy man is captured by this young Baroness Sophie (Yvonne Lombard). The mixup carries the couple to the altar but the actual ceremony is halted. And he goes back to Miss Babs, when an apartment is obtained.

"Castle" is entertaining but too much is devoted to Miss Babs' singing (she is Sweden's equivalent to Doris Day). Fact that she photographs poorly is a handicap. It is one of the better comedies for the home market, but it does not warrant export.

Fred.

Moscow Films

Tegnup
(Yesterday)
(HUNGARIAN)

Hunnia release and production. With Zoltan Maklary, Tibo Bitskey, Ferenc Ladanyi, Sandor Pecsi. Directed by Marton Keleti. Screenplay, Imre Dobozy; camera, Barnabas Hegyi; editor, G. Szabo. At Moscow Film Fest. Running time, 89 MINS.

This film treats with the 1956 Hungarian uprising. It naturally takes sides against the insurgents but does to a degree present both sides before making its point. Theme limits it for all but Bolsheviki belt. Setting is a small town (not Budapest, note) where revolutionaries storm a local garrison. Soldiers are divided on action. It also concerns a collective farm which an ex-landlord tries to recover. A revolutionary heavy is an unidentified man from abroad. Russians are absent from the picture except for an inkling via sounds of tanks rumbling in the end.

Well mounted and played, the film converts its gruesome history into a simplified adventure yarn. Conscience is given short shrift and the dilemma a shortcut solution.

Mosk.

Mer
(The Ball)
(RUMANIAN)

Difilm release and production. With Lazar Vrabie, Ion Bodeneau, Andrei Codarcea, Lucia Mara Dabija. Directed by Sinisa Iveticí, Andrei Blaier; screenplay, Francisco Munteanu, Iveticí, Blaier; camera, L. Ulmeni; editor, A. Vieru. At Moscow Film Fest. Running time, 70 MINS.

Depression yarn in pre-war Rumania concerns an unemployed school teacher who develops "social consciousness." Bleak tale of humiliations. Man attempts to raise money to buy his crippled son a ball.

Film has a visual flair and a beguiling performance by a Roumanian moppet.

Mosk.

The Red Line
(FINNISH)

Fenanda Film release and production. With Holger Salin, Liisa Nevalainen, Rakel Laakso. Written and directed by Matti Kasilia. Camera, Esco Nevalainen; editor, O. Lindeman. At Moscow Film Fest. Running time, 95 MINS.

Heavyhanded naturalism in a plodding feature about a poor farmer living in abject poverty in Finiand under Czarist Russia in the early 20th century. Film overdoes the primitivism and talks too much in its depiction of the coming of political age of the farmer who is only to die via a prowling bear.

Technical credits are good and acting and dream sequences somewhat theatrical.

Mosk.

The Unforgettable Road
(JAPANESE-C'SCOPE-COLOR)

Daiei release and production. With Fujiko Yamamoto, Takayoshi Wanami, Kaoru Kuroiwa. Directed by Kcji Shima. Screenplay, Kiniyuki Hasegawa, Shima; camera (Eastmancolor), George O'Hara; editor, S. Iwa. At Moscow Film Fest. Running time, 90 MINS.

Slickly made tearjerker is about a young blind boy who desires to become a great violinist like his late father. However leukemia strikes and he dies after meeting with a pen pal from the Vienna Boy's Choir. His work is carried on by a little sister who had not been allowed to develop a natural talent so as not to hurt him.

Pic tastefully keeps the pathos in hand and it emerges of possible general release calibre abroad on its fine technique and skillful tugging on the heart strings. Color and scope are well utilized.
Mosk.

A Man's Hunger
(MEXICAN)

Alfa Film release and production. Stars Pedro Armendariz, Rosita Quintana; features, Ignacio Lopez Tarzo. Directed by Rogelio Gonzales. Screenplay, Janett Alcor; camera, Victor Herrera; editor, G. Carrion. At Moscow Film Fest. Running time, 90 MINS.

This one resembles "Born Yesterday" but done seriously. A vulgar show girl moves in with a grasping, exploiting merchant, who corners a town's kidney bean output to scalp prices to poor people. The girl gets socially conscious via a progressive young doctor but she returns to the speculator when he too realizes the error of his ways.

Picture has some good touches and interplay of characterizations but its thematics are naive and telegraphed. It is well made and probably a good bet for Spanish lingo spots in the U.S. most notably it suggests a budding talent in director Rogalio Gonzales. *Mosk.*

Msdhumati
(INDIAN)

Roy production and release. Stars Dilip Kumar, Vyjayantimala; features, Johnny Walker. Directed by Bmal Roy. Screenplay, Shailendra; camera, A. Nasar; editor, S. Chowdhcry. At Moscow Film Fest. Running time, 110 MINS.

Sentimental love story works in a theme of reincarnation. A young man comes to an old house and feels he had been there before. A tale is then unfolded of his love for a girl while he worked as a foreman on a rajah's plantation. The rajah covets the girl who is killed trying to elude him.

Plot hinges on a scheme to trap the rajah via a girl who looks like the dead one. Then the boy finds a girl who looks exactly like the one from his obsession for a happy end. Songs and dances are adroitly worked into it. It is a limited international playoff possibility but has a sincerity and a solidity in mounting and progression that might make this an arty entry with some shearing.
Mosk.

Yugoslav Festival

Pet Minuta Raja
(Five Minutes of Paradise)
(YUGOSLAVIAN)

Pula, Aug. 11.

Bosna Film production. With Stevo Zigon, Lojze Rozman, Mira Nikolic. Directed by Igor Pretnar. Screenplay, Vitomil Zupan; camera, Eduard Bogdanic; music, Bojan Adamic. At Pula Film Fest. Running time, 105 MINS.

This Yugoslavian pic is a departure from the domestic cliche. It chiefly benefits from the highly interesting script by Vitomil Zupan. Direction by Igor Pretnar, a pupil of the late Eisenstein, is perhaps too much on the theatrical side but is still interesting. Mixture of realism, grotesque and symbolism makes this a somewhat controversial item, yet it looks to have the ingredients for some foreign arty situations.

Story sees two Yugoslavian concentration camp inmates used by the SS to disarm an unexploded plane bomb in the luxurious house of a retired German general. Here the two men find elegant evening suits which they put on, champagne, cigarets and last but not least, a young French deportee. They feel temporarily like they're in paradise. Talk centers around a philosophy of life. There's naturally a tragic end when one of the men gets killed in a gun duel with an SS man.

Acting is static. Technical credits are okay. Despite several drawbacks, this is a memorable film, mainly because of the ambitious script.
Hans.

Osma Vrata
(The Eighth Door)
(YUGOSLAVIAN)

Pula, Aug. 11.

Avala productions with Milivoje Zivanovic, Nada Skrinjar, Neva Rosic, Rada Djuricin, Ljiljana Krstic, Jovan Milicevic. Directed by Nikola Tanhofer. Screenplay by Miodrag Djurdjevic; camera, Misa Stojanovic; music, Dragutin Savin. At Pula Film Fest. Running time, 93 MINS.

This film, which teed off this year's Pula Festival, turned out somewhat disappointing because it was directed by Nicola Tanhofer of whom more was expected. Direction by Tanhofer, creator of "H 8" (winner of last year's Pula festival), is swiftly moving but too much on the conventional side, with too much repetition and cliche handling of players. Since the script is not flawless, also the writer must share the blame for vehicle's shortcomings. Film has little interest for foreign market.

Story revolves around a university professor who, at the time of the Nazi occupation, gets innocently involved with the political police. Story offers some suspense at the start, but later begins to drag. Technical credits are fine. Lensing is, as often in Yugoslav films, mostly outstanding. *Hans.*

Dobri Stari Pianino
(Good Old Piano)
(YUGOSLAVIAN)

Pula, Aug. 11.

Triglav Film production. With Vida Kuharjeva, Bert Sotlar, Vekoslav Janko, Kristijan Muck. Directed by France Kosmac. Screenplay, Vitomil Zupan, Igor Pretnar, France Milcicki; camera, France Gerar; music, Marijan Lipovsek. At Pula Film Fest. Running time, 103 MINS.

Best thing about this partisan pic is its music which was given a prize at the festival here. Story shows some originality but rather weak treatment and direction plus not too believable performances make this a second-rate item. Its outcome is infantile. Since there are quite a number of battle sequences in this, it contains chances for the local action market. Export chances are very slim.

Time is the German occupation era and the main role is played by an old piano. Latter is first in the possession of a composer. He's arrested by the Germans who confiscate the piano for their music loving SS officer. Then the piano gets into the hands of partisans and finally ends up in a church. However, it helped in beating the enemy. Technical credits are average.
Hans.

Miss Stone
(TotalScope-Color)
(YUGOSLAVIAN)

Pula, Aug. 11.

Vardar Film (Skopje) production. With Olga Spiridonovic, Ilija Milcin, Marija Tocineski, Dragan Ocokoljie. Directed by Zika Mitrovic. Screenplay, Dordi Abadziev, Trajoe Popov; camera (Eastmancolor), Ljube Petkovski; music, Ivan Pupnik. At Pula Film Fest. Running time, 105 MINS.

Historical adventure yarn is Yugoslavia's first TotalScoper in Eastmancolor. It's fairly well made with enough action and sufficient humor to hold the not too fastidious patron interest. As a western-styled actioner, pic stands a chance to sled into foreign markets, notably the Latin-American. Subject may create U.S. interest since much of its dialog is in English.

It's the story of Miss Stone, an American protestant missionary, who, at the beginning of this century, fell into the hands of Macedonian freedom fighters. Latter badly needed money to buy arms for their fight against the Turks, so they kidnapped the U.S. woman and asked for ransom.

Cast, headed by Olga Spiridonovic as Miss Stone, Marija Tocinoski and Petre Prlicko, comes along with nice performances. Technically the film represents a good standard.
Hans.

Campo Mamula
(Mamula Camp)
(YUGOSLAVIAN)

Pula, Aug. 11.

Avala production. With Dragon Lakovic, Pavle Vuisic, Ljuba Tadic, Petar Vujovic, Dusan Djordjevic. Directed by Velimir Stojanovic. Screenplay, Ratko Djurovic; camera, Aleksander Sekulovic; music, Bojan Adamic. At Pula Film Fest. Running time, 104 MINS.

Avala Film, which specializes in war pix, here has an item that's slightly beyond the average standard of similar pix seen here recently. Plot is not too interesting but creates a good deal of suspense. Stojanovic's direction is skillful but the character portrayals, chiefly the Germans (again the villians in this), lack conviction. Probably a good domestic bargain, yet not much for export.

Plot concerns Yugoslavian partisans in an Italian prison. When the war is over for the Italians, the Germans take over the command. They force the prisoners to remove mines from the sea. The prisoners attempt an outbreak but most of them are killed. Technically, the lensing is once more the best thing about this Yugoslav film. *Hans.*

Foreign Films

Meine Tochter Patricia (My Daughter Patricia). (AUSTRIAN). Neue Film Verleih release of OEFA-Schoenbrunn production. Features Martin Held, Gerlinde Locker, Marianne Schoenauer, Chariklia Baxevanos, Gerhard Riedmann, Edith Elmay, Hans Thimig, Horst Beck. Directed by Wolfgang Liebeneiner. Screenplay by H. F. Koellner; camera, Walter Partsch; music, Heinz Neubrand. At Loewen Kino, Vienna. Running time, 90 MINS

This lightweight picture, mostly funny, seems to have its main aim in keeping people happy for two hours. Then it can be forgotten. Gerlinde Locker as Patricia, just out of a Swiss boarding school, as well as Chariklia Baxevanos are very good in their roles. Both love the same man, Gerhard Riedmann but later change their minds several times. Wolfgang Liebeneiner directs at a nice pace. Camerawork by Walter Partsch is very good. Heinz Neubrand supplies smooth music.
Maas.

Paris, Aug. 11.

Un Temoin Dans La Ville (Witness in the City) (FRENCH). Gaumont release of SNEG-France London-Zebra Film production. Stars Lino Ventura; features Francoise Brion, Franco Fabrizzi, Jacques Berthier. Directed by Edouard Molinaro. Screenplay, Boileau, Narcejac, Andre Tabet, Gerard Oury; camera, Henri Decae; editor, Robert Isnardon. At Colisee, Paris. Running time, 90 MINS.

This suspense item has a man killing the murderer of his wife, her ex-lover. However, a taxi driver had seen him and the man becomes a confirmed killer as he tracks down the witness to kill him, too. Pic has some okay suspense values but piles everything on too thickly sans enough substance to make this more than a local screen bet.

It is well mounted and technically good, but only for possible dualer chances abroad. *Mosk.*

Des Femmes Disparaissent (Women Disappear) (FRENCH). Sirius release of Jacques Roitfeld production. Stars Robert Hossein; features Philippe Clay, Magali Noel, Jacques Dacqmine, Estella Blaine. Directed by Edouard Molinaro. Screenplay, Albert Somonin, Moriss-Dumoulin; camera, Robert Juillard; editor, Laurence Mery. At Normandie, Paris. Running time, 90 MINS.

This familiar tale has a young man saving his girl from a group of sadistic white slavers. Pic goes in for savoring violence and has flagellations, violent fisticuffs and the usual cynical array of thugs and panderers. Its main utilization overseas would be for exploitation purposes since fairly well made.

It also has a competent cast. Technical values are fine. *Mosk.*

Pourquoi Viens-Tu Si Tard? (Why Do You Come So Late?) (FRENCH). Cinedis release of Ulysee production. Stars Michele Morgan, Henri Vidal, Claude Dauphin; features Marc Cassot, Francis Blanche. Directed by Henri Decoin. Screenplay, Pierre Rostaing, Claude Brule, Albert Valentin; camera, Christian Matras; editor, Claude Durand. At Balzac, Paris. Running time, 100 MINS.

Pic makes comedy and drama, and does not quite come off; hence, it is a chancey item for oveseas. It concerns a femme lawyer who drinks trying to defend a youth who has killed his alcoholic father. Love sees her through her crises.

This is slickly made but does not go deeply enough into the drama or exploit its romantic angles. It is neatly acted and produced.
Mosk.

L'Increvable (The Indistructible) (FRENCH—SONGS). Columbia release of Cyclope production. Stars Darry Cowl, Line Renaud; features Michel Galabru, Francis Blanche, Armontel. Directed by Jean Boyer. Screenplay, Jacques Vilfrid, Robert Coffin; camera, Charles Suin; editor, Jacqueline Brachet; music, Loulou Gaste. At Triomphe, Paris. Running time, 85 MINS.

Columbia has an amusing entry which shapes mainly for local chances. It is about a zany waiter who is insured for his life, and the attempts by many to kill him. However, he comes through and the others are knocked off.

This has some funny bits thanks to Darry Cowl's mummery, but it is

familiar and not adroit enough for much overseas' chances. Line Renaud gets a chance to belt over a few catchy tunes. *Mosk.*

Ca N'Arrive Qu'Aux Vivants (It Only Happens to the Living) (FRENCH). Imperia release of Marivaux production. Stars Raymond Pellegrin, Giselle Pascale; features Magali Noel, Marc Valbel. Directed by Tony Saytor. Screenplay, Pierre Larey, Jean Cosmos from book by Peter Cheney; camera, Pierre Petit; editor, Monique Kirsanoff. At the Latin, Paris. Running time, 100 MINS.

Usual tale about a good guy framed by gangsters and his tracking them down, lacks the snap and offbeat values to make this more than a local filler with overseas chances very uneven. Technically and thespically, it is passable. *Mosk.*

Les Noces Venetiennes (Venetian Honeymoon) (FRENCH; TOTALVISION; COLOR). Cinedis release of Cinetel production. Stars Martine Carol, Vittorio De Sica; features Philippe Nicaud, Andre Versini, Jacques Sernas. Directed by Alberto Cavalcanti. Screenplay, Jean Ferry, Claude-Andre Puget from book by Abel Hermant; camera (Eastmancolor), Gianni De Venanzo; editor, Yvonne Martin. At Berlitz, Paris. Running time, 93 MINS.

This tinter has a well-worn tale of an adventuress and an adventurer who are caught up by love and find it is better than dough after all. It has some good production values in the Venetian backgrounds, and some neatly paced scenes, but this is mainly for dualer chances abroad.

It has the Martine Carol and Vittorio De Sica names for exploitation values, too. It is technically sumptuous. *Mosk.*

Paris, Aug. 11.
Nora Inu (Stray Dog) (JAPANESE). Shintoho production and release. Stars Poshiro Mifune, Takashi Shimura. Directed by Akira Kurosawa. Screenplay, Ryuzo Kikujima, Kurosawa; camera, H. Kusada; editor, Y. Sugihara. Preemed in Paris. Running time, 120 MINS.

Overlong suspense pic has enough assets to be worth pruning for possible special or dualer slotting in foreign marts. It concerns a rookie detective who has his gun stolen and then used by a murderer. Plot concerns his attempts to get it back.

Director Akira Kurosawa, who made "Rashomon," gives fine treatment and pacing. His look at various aspects of Tokyo, nightlife, and the final bout with the killer, are firstrate. Acting and technical credits are tops. *Mosk.*

Asphalte (FRENCH). Filmel release of Francis Lopez production. Stars Francoise Arnoul; features Massimo Girotti, Marcel Bozzuffi, Georges Riviere, Jean-Paul Vignon. Directed by Herve Bromberger. Screenplay, Jacques Sigurd; camera, Roger Hubert; editor, Gilbert Natot. At Triomphe, Paris. Running time, 95 MINS.

Soapy tale concerns a poor girl who has married a rich man. Bored with the life she drifts back to the old street one night and finds that her old flame is a delinquent. Attempted blackmail finds her torn between her old life and new.

This is fluffy and mainly for local fare. It is competently directed but lacks the flair to make it convincing. Francoise Arnoul is right as the winsome heroine but gets little aid from the story. Technical credits are okay. *Mosk.*

Paris, Aug. 11.
Le Petit Prof (The Little Professor) (FRENCH). Marceau production and release. Stars Darry Cowl; features Yves Robert, Beatrice Altariba, Francis Blanche, Christiane Barry. Written and directed by Carlo Rim; camera, Nicolas Hayer; editor, Robert Isnardon. At Normandie, Paris. Running time, 95 MINS.

Vehicle for comic Darry Cowl is an excuse for a series of sketches tracting the life of two bespectacled, stuttering teachers. There are some funny patches but this is too one-dimensional and slight for anything but local chances.

Cast is okay and Cowl is intermittently funny, but he has yet to find the right role to take advantage of his talents. Technical credits and direction are good. *Mosk.*

Les Seigneurs De La Foret (Masters of the Forest) (BELGIAN; DOCUMENTARY; C'SCOPE; COLOR). 20th-Fox release of FIL production. Written and directed by Heinz Seilman, Henry Brandt; commentary, Max-Pol Fouchet, spoken by Jean Desailly, Georges Aminel. Camera (Eastmancolor), Kurt Neuberg, Andre Lebeck; editor, Louis Linzee. At Saint Michel, Paris. Running time, 90 MINS.

Competent documentary on the animal and native life in the Belgian Congo has turned out to be a surprise hit here. Though native customs may be restaged, it has taking photographic qualities, excellent animal work and a well-knit commentary. It deals with the verdant forest and the dry plains on either sides of a volcanic range. Footage is well edited. Here is a documentary with probable foreign exploitation chances. *Mosk.*

The Blue Angel
(C'SCOPE—COLOR—SONGS)

Remake with Curt Jurgens and May Britt in the original Emil Jannings-Marlene Dietrich roles. Action updated to 1956-59 in present-day Western Germany. Fair boxoffice.

20th-Fox release of Jack Cummings production. Stars Curt Jurgens and May Britt. Directed by Edward Dmytryk. Screenplay, Nigel Balchin based on German screenplay (1930) by Karl Zuckmayer, Karl Vollmoeller & Robert Liebmann, from novel by Henrich Mann. Camera (DeLuxe Color), Leon Shamroy; music, Hugh Friedhofer, conducted by Lionel Newman; songs, Frederick Hollander, Jay Livingston & Ray Evans, Mack Gordon & Harry Warren; dances, Hermes Pan; special effects, L. B. Abbott, James B. Gordon; editor, Jack W. Holmes; asst. director, Joseph E. Rickards; art, Lyle R. Wheeler & Maurice Ransford; sets, Walter M. Scott & Paul S. Fox; costumes, Adele Balkan; orchestrations, Karlo Hagen; color consultant, Leonard Doss. Tradeshown N.Y., Aug. 21, '59. Running time, 107 MINS.

Prof. Immanuel Rath	Curt Jurgens
Lola-Lola	May Britt
Kiepert	Theodore Bikel
Principal Harter	John Banner
Rolf	Fabrizio Mioni
Prof. Braun	Ludwig Stossel
Clown	Wolfe Barzell
Gussie	Ina Anders
Keiselsack	Richard Tyler
Mueller	Voyiek Dolinski
Ertzum	Ken Walken
Lohmann	Del Erickson
Emilie	Edit Angold

When UFA made "Der Blaue Engel" it catapulted Emil Jannings, Marlene Dietrich, producer Erich Pommer and director Josef Von Sternberg into international repute. Later that year ('30), Paramount dubbed an English version and "Legs" Dietrich was on the road to Hollywood renown. This Jack Cummings-produced remake, his first indie for 20th-Fox release, may not be as electric an end-result but it will do much to further Germany's Curd (now Curt) Jurgens' and Sweden's May (pronounced "My") Britt's repute in the global film market generally and with Yank fans particularly. Both, of course, are no strangers to U.S. audiences, with good Hollywood credits already garnered.

As a boxoffice commodity "The Blue Angel" will be a fair entry. It will not be the rocker that the Jannings-Dietrich impact made and, while suffering inevitable comparison, neither Jurgens nor Miss Britt need be ashamed of their performances. Perhaps counting the most against them is the somewhat familiar plot motivation—the femme fatale and the destruction of the German professor who succumbs to her wiles —plus the indelible impact Jannings and Miss Dietrich made in their earthier approach to the same plot. In its era it was pretty daring stuff. The shocker also came from Jannings' complete professional and physical degradation as the crazed, disillusioned, lovesick former professor whom Lola-Lola and the impresario of this nondescript magico-girlesque had metamorphosed into becoming a cheap, abject clown.

Jannings was a sort of Teutonic forebear of the Rev. Davidson school of respectability. His were feet of clay, too, the moment he dropped his dignity. In the UFA original (in those days Paramount had an American correspondence-business exchange with the German film cartel) Jannings went berserk and insane. In the 1959 remake scripter Nigel Balchin and director Edward Dmytryk gave Professor Immanuel Rath (Jurgens) a somewhat "happier" ending. He, too, seeks to choke the floozy that he had married in insane jealousy but the kindly high-

school principal is the steadfast old colleague who indicates that the pedagogue - turned - buffoon would soon regain his professional position once he was "cured" of the faithless marriage and the indignities he had experienced.

But the prime shortcoming may prove to be the decision producer Jack Cummings, et al., made to give this saga a post-midcentury topicality in present-day Western Germany. The fantasy of the staid professor of botany is something that keys better in modern acceptance to another period.

Miss Britt is an eyeful as the seductress. Her shoulder-length blonde hair; her saucy mien and manner; the Dietrichesque style of straddling the chairs, which she utilizes as props, showing off her saucy gams, are eyefuls in every department. She handles two vocal reprises of Frederick Hollander's "Falling In Love Again" (which has served as Miss Dietrich's personal theme song over the years, and which also brought the composer-musician from Germany to Hollywood) and also projects the new thematic, "Lola Lola," which Jay Livingston and Ray Evans fashioned for her. The nondescript but still not too undecorative chorus also reprises an old Mack Gordon-Harry Warren tune, "I Yi Yi."

Jurgens proves a flexible performer in the Jannings original. He disguises his masculine attractiveness under an authentic German academician's mien, personating the unworldly schoolmaster with conviction. He makes the transition from the professor of botany, peering behind academic glasses, to the awkward swain of the capricious Lola-Lola, to her general factotum as a sort of house-broken stooge, and later her lowly luggage-carrier and still lowlier buffoon. His Pagliacci is not of a romantic concept as he permits eggs to be cracked on his clownish noggin while he emits the ridiculously embarrassing rooster's crows, under the proddings of the knavish Bikel (the magico), capping with the climactic attempt to strangle the faithless Lola-Lola.

Film was part-shot in Bavaria and the interiors in Hollywood. Support is authentic from the rowdiest students to Theodore Bikel as the machiavellian impresario-magician of this itinerant troupe. John Banner is stolid as the school principal; Italo newcomer Fabrizio Mioni is a new sleek type of juvenile; and the others are more than adequate in their roles.

"Blue Angel" ran 99 minutes 30 years ago and was deemed a shade too long then. Its present 107 minutes also leaves that conclusion despite the expanded canvas of the cinematurgy. *Abel.*

Blind Date
(BRITISH)

Better-than-average yarn of a cop's attempt to pin a murder rap on a young artist, with fine performance by Stanley Baker; worthwhile for all houses.

London, Aug. 18.
Rank release of a Julian Wintler-Leslie Parkyn (David Duetsch) production for Sydney Box Associates. Stars Hardy Kruger, Stanley Baker, Micheline Presle. Directed by Joseph Losey. Screenplay, Ben Barzman and Millard Lampbell, from novel by Leigh Howard; camera, Christopher Challis; editor, Reginald Mills; music, Richard Bennett. At Odeon, Lei-

cester-Square, London. Running time, 95 MINS.

Jan Van Rooyen .... Hardy Kruger
Inspector Morgan .... Stanley Baker
Jacqueline Cousteau ..... Micheline Presle
Sir Brian Lewis .... Robert Flemyng
Police Sergeant .... Gordon Jackson
Westover .... John Van Eyssen
Postman .... Jack Macgowran
Police Constable .... George Roubicek
Police Doctor .... Redmond Phillips

Here's a taut, well-written pic which gets away to a good, tense start and works up to a neat payoff. Very well acted by a small cast, "Blind Date" should be a brisk proposition for all types of audiences. Though there are several flashbacks they do not hold up the action which motivates from the discovery of a woman's body in a fashionable cottage. A Dutch painter (Hardy Kruger) is discovered in the house, admits that he was there to keep a rendezvous with the dead woman, agrees that he was in the house at the time the crime must have happened, but vehemently denies his guilt.

Detective Stanley Baker does not believe this filmsy yarn and by tough grilling eventually gets from Kruger the full story of how an accidental meeting with the wealthy and stylish French girl led over the weeks to a passionate affair, which had to be kept secret because of her marriage and position in society. But when Baker reveals that she was not married, but the mistress of a high-ranking diplomat the plot becomes thicker. Eventually Baker is convinced that Kruger is innocent but who did kill the mystery woman and why? Not till the last few minutes is it revealed, with a surprise switch.

The screenplay provides suspense. In the flashback scenes, there's some fairly torrid lovemaking between Kruger and Micheline Presle. The dialog is convincing and the police station and London sequences are authentic. Christopher Challis' camerawork proves very effective. Joseph Losey has kept his direction crisp and handled the flashbacks without fuss.

Baker, as the Welsh cop with a temper, a cold in the head, a passion for cold milk and a determination to get his man, gives a powerful and intelligent performance belying the old tag of London policemen being so courteous. Since Kruger has to spend most of his scenes either being grilled by Baker, making love to Miss Presle or quarreling with her, he does well to get so much variety into his performance, though much of his charm is masked by boorish and sullen behavior. She is cool, poised and elegant even when being slapped down by Kruger. Richard Bennett's music is unduly obtrusive and loud, but Reginald Mills' cutting both fit handily into a better-than-average British suspense drama. *Rich.*

Wir Wunderkinder
(Aren't We Wonderful)
(GERMAN)
(With Narration & Subtitles)

Humorously clever, remarkably candid study of the German character in relation to Nazism and the postwar period. One of the best from Germany since the war.

I. G. Goldsmith presentation of Kurt Hoffmann (Filmaufbau) production of Constantin Film, directed by Hoffmann. Stars Johanna von Koczian, Hansjorg Felmy, Wera Freydtberg, Robert Graf; features Elizabeth Flickenschildt, Ingrid Pan, Ingrid van Bergen, Jurgen Goslar, Tatjana Sais, Liesl Karlstadt, Michl Lang. Screenplay, Heinz Pauck and Gunther Neumann from Hugo Hartung novel; camera, Richard Angst; music, Franz Grothe. Previewed in N.Y., Aug. 19, '59. Running time, 120 MINS.

Kirsten .... Johanna von Koczian
Hans Boeckel .... Hansjorg Felmy
Wera .... Wera Frydtberg
Bruno Tiches .... Robert Graf
Frau Meisegeier .. Elizabeth Flickenschildt
Doddy .... Ingrid Pan
Evelyne .... Ingrid van Bergen
Schally .... Jurgen Goslar
Frau Haflingen .... Tatjana Sais
Frau Roselieb .... Liesl Karlstadt
Herr Roselieb .... Michl Lang
Narrators:
Erklarer .... Wolfgang Neuss
Hugo .... Wolfgang Muller

The Germans are not normally credited with much of a sense-of-humor, particularly when holding up the mirror to themselves in films. In "Wir Wunderkinder" (Aren't We Wonderful), recent winner of the Gold Medal award at the Moscow film festival, this tendency has been radically reversed. It is a remarkably well-done picture, a humorous and yet bitingly cynical commentary on the German mind, employing astonishing insight and an absolute willingness to call a spade a spade.

"Wunderkinder" offers proof positive that the Germans are quite capable of seeing themselves realistically and of getting the proper slant on the Nazi period. Oddly enough, Kurt Hoffmann has managed to weave into the picture a tender and quite charming love story involving an anti-Nazi journalist and a Danish girl, played respectively by Hansjorg Felmy and Johanna von Koczian.

The two key figures in the film are Felmy, who dislikes the Nazis from the start, but never actively fights them (he'll go only as far as losing his job over the refusal to join the party) and Robert Graf as the Nazi bully, the boy without brains who joins the brownshirts to get power and work out his inferiority complex. Anti-Semitism and persecution of the Jews is touched upon in the film, but not extensively.

There are many fine touches in this picture, which starts with 1913 and carries through to today, when Graf is back as a captain of industry, employing the same arrogance and ruthlessness that got him to the top under the Nazis, and Felmy is in an important editorial position where he exposes Graf's past. Final scene has Graf falling down an elevator shaft, with the narrator expressing hope that more of his ilk might follow. But at his funeral, he is honored as a loyal "comrade."

Acting is excellent. A good deal of the action is silent, with an English narrator speaking over it. Much of the commentary on the Germans, their sentimentality and their devotion to militarism is devastating. Device of running the whole thing as a flashback on a small screen of the old silent type, with a pianist and narrator interrupting from time to time with sarcastic songs of the "Three Penny Opera" genre, is effective.

"Wunderkinder" is clever, distinctly offbeat and highly attractive fare. It'll probably have its main attraction in the arties, though it's a treat for any thinking American concerned with the German problem. Best thing about the film is that it manages to say so much, and so well, with a light touch. *Hift.*

Invitation to Monte Carlo
(BRITISH-COLOR)

Well-made, amiable short feature bringing in Prince Rainier and Princess Grace and exploiting Monaco scenery; sound supporting job.

London, Aug. 18.

Hillcrest release of Richmond Film (Euan Lloyd) production. Features Germaine Damar, Gilda Emmanueli, Katharine Page, Jefferson Clifford and voices of Leo Genn, Nicole Maurey, E. V. H. Emmett. Written and directed by Euan Lloyd. Commentary written by Jack Davies; editor, Terry Trench; camera, John Wilcox, Tony Braun, Egil Woxholt; music, William Hill Bowen. Previewed at Metro Private Theatre, London. Running time, 46 MINS.

Jacqueline .... Germaine Damar
Lindy .... Gilda Emmanueli
The Matron .... Katharine Page
The Postman .... Jefferson Clifford
Tosca .... Himself

Obviously designed as a boost for the Principality of Monaco, this easy-on-the-eye and pleasant travel feature pic stands up as good entertainment. Only 46 minutes in length, it is an agreeable supporting pic for most houses. It was made with the full cooperation of Prince Rainer and provides some interesting sidelights on Monte Carlo and neighborhood. The main gimmick is the work and play glimpses of Prince Rainier, Princess Grace and their baby. These are helped by excellent color photography and a slight but charming "fairy-tale" story, based on a true incident.

Gilda Emmanueli plays a British orphan child who is picked to take a present to the Royal babe. The present is Tosca, a kitten, and Gilda's adventures on the trip are the peg on which the travelog is hung. Prince Rainier in his private zoo, doing some slick underwater diving and playing with his child, proves himself a pleasant personality, and no mean actor. Shots of Princess Grace will remind audiences that Monaco's gain was distinctly Hollywood's loss. Even Frank Sinatra crops up in one scene.

Little Miss Emmanueli is a cute and promising moppet. Germaine Damar, a Luxembourg actress, play an air hostess who chaperones the child and reveals herself as a delightful, fresh performer. Katharine Page and Jefferson Clifford provide useful support.

Jack Davies' commentary is light and informative. It is put over well by Leo Genn, Nicole Maurey and E.V.H. Emmett. Lensed in Cinepanoramic and Technicolor, John Wilcox, Tony Braun and Egil Woxholt have done a very satisfactory job while William Hill Bowen's music, played by the George Melachrino orch. is just in the right mood for this vehicle.

As writer, producer and director, Euan Lloyd has pulled off a smooth treble. He can well be satisfied with the result of his brain child. *Rich.*

Les Rendez-Vous Du Diable
(Meetings With the Devil)
(FRENCH—DOCUMENTARY—COLOR)

Paris, Aug. 18.

UGC release of Jacques Constant production. Directed by Haroun Terzieff. Commentary, Paul Guimard, R. M. Arlaud; camera (Agfacolor-Kodachrome), Terzieff, Pierre Bichet, Aldo Scavarda, Wanwo Runtu; editor, Monique Fardoulis. At Marbeuf, Paris. Running time, 80 MINS.

This film deals with a voyage that takes in all the important live and extinct volcanos of the world. It has some daring footage alongside belching craters and symphonic montages of wholesale eruptions. Though repetitive, this has enough daring to hold interest throughout.

Its expert editing, commentary and general offbeat aspects could slant this for specialized commercial showings abroad or for schools use. Sheared a bit it could make an excellent medium length pic of an unusual art house program.

Film ends in a brilliantly conceived montage of a volcano in full eruption at night which adequately fits the title. Here is an off-beat documentary with exploitation possibilities. Color is good despite being blown up from 16m. *Mosk.*

Les Yeux Sans Visage
(Eyes Without a Face)
(FRENCH)

Paris, Aug. 18.

Lux release of Champs-Elysees production. Stars Pierre Brasseur, Alida Valli; features Juliette Maynie), Francois Guerin, Edith Scob. Directed by Georges Franju. Screenplay, Jean Redon, Claude Sautet, Pierre Gascar; camera, Eugen Shuftan; editor, Gilbert Natot. Preemed in Paris. Running time, 90 MINS.

Professor .... Pierre Brasseur
Louise .... Alida Valli
Edna .... Juliette Mayniel
Catherine .... Edith Scob
Jacques .... Francois Guerin
Paulette .... Beatrice Altariba

Ambitious horror pic depends on clinical operation scenes and the showing of deformed faces for its effect. It has some queasy scenes, but unclear progression and plodding direction give this an old-fashioned air. Main offshore possibilities would be for dualer and exploitation chances on its theme, with arty chances also possible if well sold.

A plastic surgeon daughter's face is destroyed in an accident. He gets young girls, lured in by a woman whose face he has saved, and tries to transpose their faces to that of his daughter. The operations fail and the daughter finally kills the woman.

Director Georges Franju has given this some suspense and not spared any shock details. But the stilted acting, asides to explain characters and motivations, and a repetition of effects lose the initial impact. Lensing is excellent and technical effects okay. The editing is too leisurely and lacking in snap for this type of film. *Mosk.*

Los Seite Pecados
(The Seven Sins)
(MEXICAN)

Mexico City, Aug. 18.

Peliculas Nacionales release of a Filmadora Panamericana (Jose Diaz Morales) production. Stars Lilia del Valle, Luz, Maria Aguilar, Linda Cristal, Emilia Guiu, Domingo Soler. Directed by Morales. Screenplay and adaptation by Jose Diaz Morales, Augusto Benedico, Jose Luis Galiana. At Olimpia Theatre, Mexico City. Running time, 85 MINS.

Idea behind this one are the seven capital sins, with the producer using seven attractive females from the star, down to aspirants to stardom to be the fleshly embodiment of the major mortal sins.

What with the censors, it would have been better if film had been titled, "The Seven Female Sinners," for the sins are somehow bogged down in the rambling story although the curvaceous sinners are always even present. As this is a picture with the typical stamp of producer-director Jose Morals,

the femmes never fail to parade their charms in as skimpy bathing suits as the censors allow, with here and there scenes getting in that would not pass the MPA code. Despite recent get-tough attitude of censors, the Mexican branch is not as finicky as their counterparts in Spain, the U.S. and England.

According to the script, the seven lovely sinners are models, thus giving them an excuse for exposing epidermis. About the most attractive of the lot is Linda Cristal, the close runner-up being Lilia del Valle. Emilia Guiu appears in a farewell performance here since she has foresworn the screen for life on an Arizona ranch.

Andrea Palma plays the female heavy or vixen in this off-pace story of sin. Domingo Soler in a father part and leading men Antonio de Hud, Augusto Benedico and Arturo Correa struggle with their roles. The film has one merit, judging from audience reaction: envisaged as a drama, this effort made the patrons laugh at many of the developing dramatic situations. *Emil.*

La Sentence
(The Verdict)
(FRENCH)

Moscow, Aug. 18.
Pathe release of Christine Gouze-Renal production. Stars Marina Vlady, Robert Hossein; features Roger Hanin, Beatrice Bretty, Lucien Raimbourg. Directed by Jean Valere. Screenplay, Georges Arnaud, Marcel Moussy from an idea by Robert Hossein; camera, Henri Decae; editor, Leonide Azar. At Moscow Film Fest. Running time, **80 MINS**.

Catherine .... Marina Vlady
Georges .... Robert Hossein
Antoine .... Roger Hanin
Jeanne .... Beatrice Bretty
Francois .... Lucien Raimbourg

Five people, three men and two women, are herded into the cellar of a house on a beach to await execution in an hour after killing an important German officer during the last war. The condemned people are resistance workers and the time is just before the Allied landings.

Pic then follows the agonizing wait and their final execution as attempts to free them, and the delayed Allied landing, are too late. Direction fails to infuse this with the needed tension, and the forced characterizations make this lag in spite of a series of agitated bits sifted in with the wait and sudden character revelations.

Quickie aspects, with all military actions appearing off, and a lack of plausibility combine to cut the edge and heroics of the pic. Acting is theatrical and also is saddled with banal dialog. Film looms chancey in offshore markets except for possible arty slotting on its theme. *Mosk.*

Filles de Nuit
(Girls of the Night)
(FRENCH)

Paris, Aug. 18.
Warner Bros. release of CEC-Constantin-Prora Film production. Stars Georges Marchal, Nicole Berger; features Gil Vidal, Claus Holm, Kay Fischer, Renato Baldini. Directed by Maurice Cloche. Screenplay, Andre Tabet, Georges Tabet, Cloche; camera, Jacques Mercanton; editor, Fanchette Mazin. At Latin, Paris. Running time, **99 MINS**.

Charlie .... Georges Marchal
Neda .... Nicole Berger
Paul .... Gil Vidal
Father Herman .... Claus Holm
Marlene .... Kay Fischer
Marco .... Renato Baldini

Warner Bros. has an okay exploitable item in this pic about how some prostitutes are reformed by a zealous priest. There are plenty of torrid scenes and, if somewhat overdidactic in its moral preachment, this emerges an actioner with exploitable handles on theme and treatment for offshore placement.

A priest creates a refuge for prosties and tries to win them away from their panderers. They come to grips over a young girl coveted by one of the hoodlums. Then she, her fiance and the priest, helped by repentant joy girls, win a moral and physical victory over the gangsters. *Mosk.*

Jet Storm
(BRITISH)

Workmanlike suspense drama with some excellent acting cameos by an all-star cast; despite loose ends, it is a useful b.o. prospect.

London, Aug. 25.
British Lion release of a Britannia (Steven Pallos) production. Stars Richard Attenborough, Stanley Baker, Hermione Baddeley, Bernard Braden, Diane Cilento, Barbara Maskell, Harry Secombe, Elizabeth Sellars, Sybil Thorndike, Mai Zetterling, Marty Wilde. Directed by C. Raker Endfield. Screenplay, Endfield and Sigmund Miller from Miller's original story; camera, Jack Hildyard; editor, Oswalde Hafenrichter; music, Thomas Hajna. Previewed at Studio One, London. Running time, **90 MINS**.

Ernest Tilley ...... Richard Attenborough
Capt. Bardow .... Stanley Baker
Mrs. Satterly .... Hermione Baddeley
Otis Randolf .... Bernard Braden
Angelica Como .... Diane Cilento
Edwina Randolf .... Barbara Kelly
Dr. Bergstein .... David Kossoff
Pam Leyton .... Virginia Maskell
Binky Meadows .... Harry Secombe
Inez Barrington ...... Elizabeth Sellars
Emma Morgan .... Sybil Thorndike
Carol Tilley .... Mai Zetterling
Billy Forrester .... Marty Wilde
Mulliner .... Patrick Allen
George Towers .... Paul Carpenter
Rose Brock .... Megs Jenkins
Clara Forrester........... Jackie Lane
Colonel Coe .... Cec Linder
"Gil" Gilbert .... Neil McCallum
Jane Tracer .... Lana Morris
James Brock .... George Rose
Victor Tracer .... Paul Eddington
Michaels .... Glyn Houston
Gelderen .... Peter Illing
Jeremy Tracer .... Jeremy Judge

"Jet Storm" explores, once again, the not over-original idea of a bunch of strangers sharing a common danger in an enclosed space. The pic is built on their various reactions to this sticky situation. Though the film lacks pace and has several loose ends, there are so many excellent acting jobs from an impressive cast that it is sound entertainment and should prove a worthwhile b.o. proposition both in Britain and the U.S.

The film has been trimmed down from 99 minutes to 90. Though this may account for some of the loose ends, the trimming was a sound idea. Otherwise the film might have seemed almost as long as the transatlantic flight which is its theme. The yarn has a rather tense central core. One of the passengers of a jet plane bound from London to New York suddenly accuses another of being the hit-and-run driver who killed his child in an auto accident. The accuser (Richard Attenborough) is obviously mentally sick but insists that he is going to bump off the guilty driver. Also, in a burst of religious fervor, he accuses the whole human race of being equally guilty.

Cold dread breaks out among the passengers. Will Attenborough attempt murder and if so how will their own safety be affected? It transpires that Attenborough has smuggled a bomb aboard and the problem is whether he is serious in his threat. And if so, can the tragedy be averted in time. Here's a melodramatic situation which, while feasible, could almost become parody unless the writing, direction and acting stand up. Well, while it's all fairly talky, much of it is sound and amusing talk. Only occasionally will the audience become restless and ponder how few really dramatic highlights there are.

This is largely because of the skillful way in which director Endfield has handled a really fine cast. There are so many, that few have much chance of developing their characterizations. They have to rely on swift impact. Attenborough has a tough chore in making credible the fanatical avenger. Several others have good opportunities in their various ways. Stanley Baker, one of Britain's busiest actors, turns in another sound job as the captain of the plane who is faced with a group of temperamental passengers.

Among the actors particularly deserving of mention are Hermione Baddeley, Patrick Allen and Peter Illing, who are determined that strong arm methods are the only way to deal with Attenborough; George Rose, as the potential victim; Elizabeth Sellars, as a blase society woman who is afraid but considers it bad form to show it; Diane Cilento, as a blunt young woman who helps to keep the passengers from panic; Bernard Braden and Barbara Kelly, as a couple who philosophically play gin rummy while discussing their potential divorce; David Kossoff, as a doctor; Cec Linder, as a U.S. Army officer; and Mai Zetterling, as Attenborough's distraught wife. Standout comedy relief is provided by Harry Secombe and Sybil Thorndike, a most unlikely combination which, nevertheless, combines like bacon and eggs. Virginia Maskell, as an air hostess and Neil McCallum, as a cheerful second officer, also turn in valuable stints.

Photography and direction are extremely sound considering the hampered limits imposed by 95% of the action taking place aboard the plane. If there is a main disappointment in the pic, it is the way some of the characters fade out at the end once they have served their usefulness plus a contrived ending. *Rich.*

Carry on Teacher
(BRITISH)

Latest in profitable "Carry On" series of slapstick comedies successfully explores the scholastic field in search of b.o. yocks.

London, Aug. 25.
Anglo Amalgamated release of a Peter Rogers production. Stars Kenneth Connor, Charles Hawtrey, Leslie Phillips, Joan Sims, Kenneth Williams, Hattie Jacques, Rosalind Knight, Ted Ray. Directed by Gerald Thomas. Screenplay, Norman Hudis; camera, Reginald Wyer; editor, John Shirley; music, Bruce Montgomery. At Studio One, London. Running time, **86 MINS**.

William Wakefield .... Ted Ray
Gregory Adams .... Kenneth Connor
Edwin Milton .... Kenneth Williams
Sarah Allcock .... Joan Sims
Michael Bean .... Charles Hawtrey
Grace Short .... Hattie Jacques
Alf .... Cyril Chamberlain
Alistair Grigg .... Leslie Phillips
Felicity Wheller .... Rosalind Knight
Robin Stevens .... Richard O'Sullivan
Penny Lee .... Diana Beevers
Billy Haig .... George Howell
Pat Gordon .... Jacqueline Lewis
Harry Bird .... Roy Hines
Sheila Dale .... Carol White
Atkins .... Paul Cole
Irene .... Jane White
Boy .... Larry Dann

Third entry in Peter Rogers' sock "Carry On" series likely will emulate the success of "Carry On, Sergeant" and "Carry On, Nurse." Virtually the same team has combined to use the same yock-raising formula, this time in the scholastic field, and the laughs come readily. Here's a safe booking for most cinemas. "Carry On, Teacher" is an unabashed collection of uninhibited gag situations and dialog, but this time screenplay writer Norman Hudis has developed a slightly stronger story line and made the characters more credible.

Ted Ray is the acting headmaster of a school who, after 20 years, has set his heart on the headmastership of a new one in the country. Much

depends on the report put in to the Ministry of Education by a visiting inspector and a child psychiatrist. Because they don't want the popular master to leave, the students decide to sabotage his chances and start a well-planned campaign of bad behavior to influence the visiting inspectors. The little ruffians employ every possible farcical trick from itching powder to booby traps. They blow up the laboratory, ruin the school play and no master or mistress is safe from their pranks.

Some of the gags are telegraphed but the cheerful impudence with which they are dropped into the script is completely disarming. Gerald Thomas's direction has a pace that gives the audience little time to assess just how funny any particular bit of business really is. He is helped by a cast which has had years of experience in attacking an audience's funny-bone.

Ray, playing straighter than most of his colleagues, gives a pleasant performance as the headmaster whose job is in jeopardy. His staff is composed mainly of eccentric characters who are nicely assorted and all have plenty of "fat" without being on the screen long enough to become tedious. There's Kenneth Connor giving a fine performance as a nervous science master, Kenneth Williams and Charles Hawtrey, as a couple of precious masters in charge of literature and music respectively; Hattie Jacques as the formidable mistress who wages war on the saboteurs, and Joan Sims in her usual inimitable form as a games mistress.

Leslie Phillips is the psychiatrist and Rosalind Knight is the inspector who is ill-disposed towards the school until she falls for the science master. They turn in agreeable comedy performances. Richard O'Sullivan is sound as the ringleader of a credible bunch of schoolkids. Cyril Chamberlain also scores as the school janitor.

Satisfactory lensing by Reginald Wyer and competent editing round off a picture which knows precisely what target it is aiming at and, within its simple terms of reference, is a winner. *Rich.*

Stomach In, Chest Out!
(Vatsa Sisaan, Rinta Ulos!)
(FINNISH)

Suomen Filmiteollisuus (SF) release of T. J. Sarkka production. Stars Helge Herala, Tommi Rinne, Marjatta Kallio; features Elsa Turakainen, Pentti Irjala, Kullervo Kalske, Santeri Karile, Aarne Laine. Original story and direction, Aarne Tarkas; camera, Olavi Tuomi; music Toivo Karki. At Rex and Tuulensuu, Helsinki. Running time, 92 MINS.

Helsinki, Aug. 25.

This is a record-breaking local hit here despite a record heat wave. It looms as one of the biggest b.o. hits ever in Finland.

Story tells of a woman-hating army captain who, ordered to hold a civil defense lecture at a boarding school for girls, becomes the victim of the girls' shrewdness. He finally has to spend the night inside the school disguised as a cleaning woman. Meanwhile, the screwball of the company starts playing captain and winds up by saving the garrison during a general's surprise inspection.

Directed with an eye for comedy gags and having a fast pace, this contains many laughs. It is spiced by two sexy scenes—the school girls' shower bath scene and a similar situation with the pretty

femme gym instructor. Helge Harala is good as the suffering captain while Marjatta Kallio not only is pretty but has an excellent figure. She is the gym instructor. Tommi Rinne, as the screwball, excels via his clever delivery. The school girls are comely. Pic may have exploitation possibilities in many countries. *Tuus.*

Venice Films

En La Ardiente Obscuriadad
(In Burning Darkness)
(ARGENTINIAN-SCOPE)
Venice, Sept. 1.

Sono Film production and release. Stars Mirtha Legrand, Lautauro Murua; features Duilio Marzio. Directed by Daniel Tynaire. Screenplay, Buero Vallejos, Eduardo Borras; camera, Alberto Etchebero; editor, Jorge Garate. At Venice Film Fest (shown out of competition). Running time, 110 MINS.

This film deals with an institution for the blind. Main complication is the entrance of a tortured man who fights against the acceptance of his lot and need for love. Love comes via a blind inmate and appeasement of his hurt. Subject pulls out the dramatic stops. But it has an offbeat topic for possible lingo situations in the U.S.

It is well handled but somewhat conventional in its treatment. The acting and technical aspects are good but the theme seems gratuitous rather than revealing. *Hawk.*

Shinel
(The Overcoat)
(RUSSIAN)
Venice, Sept. 1.

Lenfilm production and release. With R. Rykov, I. Tolubeëv, A. Erkina. Directed by A. Batalov. Screenplay, L. Soloviev from story by Gogol; camera, G. Marangian. At Venice Film Fest (shown out of competition). Running time, 93 MINS.

Still another remake of Gogol's widely-known tale about the little clerk whose life becomes his new overcoat and how it goes with the theft of the coat. Set in the St. Petersburg of the 19th century, this takes whacks at bureaucracy. Film has the right amount of expressionistic mounting, acting and direction to match. It does justice to the tale but appears somewhat old fashioned and shapes mainly for arty chances abroad on the story and treatment. Otherwise it is obviously limited.

Technical credits are good. A deft use of sound and savvy editing remove some of the sting of the passe techniques. Acting of R. Rykov, as the unfortunate clerk, is the highspot of the film. *Hawk.*

V Tvoi Rukah Jizn
(Life in Your Hands)
(RUSSIAN)
Venice, Aug. 25.

Russian release of a Lenfilm production. Features Oleg Strijenox, Kutianski, V. Chekmariov, Clara Louchko, Youchka, Strijenova. Directed by N. Rosantsev. Screenplay, L. Agranovio. Camera, K. Rijov. Music, O. Karavanich. At Venice Film Fest. Running time, 90 MINS.

Captain Doudine..........Oleg Strijenov
Stepanovich .... Kutianski
Polkoviek .... Chekmariov
Nastia .... Clara Louchko

Denoting western influences despite its party-lining content, pic is basically a suspense yarn concerning the discovery and removal

of a giant bomb cache hidden by the retreating Germans in the midst of a now-flourishing city. A group of volunteers succeeds in freeing city of its nightmare after the long and painstaking neutralization task, which is interspersed with near-tragic moments when task appears impossible and an explosion inevitable.

Suspense is often very effectively highlighted and retained almost throughout action for an okay audience effect, with effective editing overcoming the more obvious mechanics of the story. Acting, in the emphatically understated Russian manner, is generally good, with Oleg Strijenov effective as the leader of the group of volunteers and Clara Louchko okay as the widow of the first bomb victim. Despite the yarn's tension, pic is dubious export entry. Credits are good, with a special nod to the musical score. *Hawk.*

The Crimson Kimono

Exploitable combo of murder mystery and racial romantics.

Hollywood, Sept. 4.

Columbia release produced, directed and written by Samuel Fuller. Stars Victoria Shaw, Glenn Corbett, James Shigeta. Camera, Sam Leavitt; music, Harry Sukman; editor, Jerome Thoms. Previewed at Screen Directors' Guild, Aug. 27, '59. Running time, 81 MINS.

Christine Downes ...... Victoria Shaw
Detective Sgt. Charlie Bancroft
.... Glenn Corbett
Detective Joe Kojaku .... James Shigeta
Mac .... Anna Lee
Casale .... Paul Dubov
Roma .... Jaclynne Greene
Hansel .... Neyle Morrow
Sugar Torch .... Gloria Pall
Mother .... Barbara Hayden
Willy Hidaka .... George Yoshinaga
Nun .... Kaye Elhardt
Sister Gertrude .... Aya Oyama
Karate .... George Okamura
Priest .... Rev. Ryosho S. Sogabe
Yoshinaga .... Robert Okazaki
Shuto .... Fuji

In "The Crimson Kimono," Samuel Fuller tries to wrap up a murder mystery with an inter-racial romance. Although Fuller's attempts to probe racial prejudice were undoubtedly motivated by a worthy desire, it doesn't work out very well. The mystery melodrama part of the film gets lost during the complicated romance, and the racial tolerance plea is cheapened by its inclusion in a film of otherwise straight action. Fair b.o. indicated.

Fuller has some brilliant picture-making touches in "Crimson Kimono," and some counterbalancing moments of extreme naivete. There is a breathless, pellmell quality about the film's opening scenes that gives it original impact but do not sustain. A technique of sharp inter-cutting, with hardly a single fade or dissolve, creates pace and mounting tension. It is a dangerous device, however, unless the story is carefully plotted. This one is not. The result is that the device ultimately creates confusion. Also, some of the medium and closeup shots do not match.

Fuller's story has Glenn Corbett and James Shigeta as officers of the L.A. Homicide Squad, buddies since they were fellow-soldiers in the Korean War. When they meet artist Victoria Shaw, they're investigating a murder. Corbett first falls in love with Miss Shaw, then Shigeta succumbs. The climax has Shigeta, a Nisei, bitter when he feels Corbett, a Causasian, objects to his romance because Miss Shaw is a Caucasian. Everything is eventually resolved in a burst of brotherhood.

Fuller's plea for racial understanding is presented inadequately, without proper dramatic introduction. Shigeta becomes embittered because he believes Corbett is "disgusted" at the idea of an Oriental in love with a Caucasian. There is no "disgust" apparent to the spectator, so Shigeta's actions seem contrived. It seems a deliberate contrivance set atop the murder mystery that provides the film's chief motivation, and the result is to make the auditor disturbed and uneasy at what seems commercialism of a delicate problem.

The three principals bring credibility to their roles, not too easy during moments when belief is stretched considerably. Anna Lee, Paul Dubov, Jaclynne Green and Neyle Morrow are prominent in the supporting cast.

Sam Leavitt's camera work has the proper realistic feel about it and Jerome Thoms' editing is technically proficient. *Powe.*

Web of Evidence

Routine British whodunit for program market.

Hollywood, Sept. .2

Allied Artists release of Maxwell Setton-John R. Sloan production. Stars Van Johnson, Vera Miles, Emlyn Williams, Bernard Lee, Jean Kent, with Moultrie Kelsall, Ralph Truman, Jameson Clark, Oliver Johnson. Directed by Jacj Cardiff. Screenplay, Ken Taylor, based on novel, "Beyond This Place," by A. J. Cronin, adapted by Kenneth Hyde; camera, Wilkie Cooper; editor, Ernest Walter; music, Douglas Gamley. Previewed Aug. 28, '59. Running time, 87 MINS.

Paul Mathry	Van Johnson
Lena Anderson	Vera Miles
Enoch Oswald	Emlyn Williams
Patrick Mathry	Bernard Lee
Louise Burt	Jean Kent
Chief Inspector Dale	Moultrie Kelsall
Sir Mathey Sprott, Q.C.	Ralph Truman
Swann	Jameson Clark
Prusty	Oliver Johnson
McEvoy	Leo McKern
Prison Governor	Geoffrey Keen
Ella Mathry	Rosalie Crutchly
Lady Catherine Sprott	Joyce Heron

Through more adept exposition "Web of Evidence" could have been a topnotch whodunit; as it stands, this British import is confusing, its premise not sufficiently developed and suitable only for the less discriminating program market. Names of Van Johnson and Vern Miles may help its chances, but subject misses the boat.

Based on A. J. Cronin novel, "Beyond This Place," the Maxwell Setton-John R. Sloan production unfolds in Liverpool, where Johnson, now living in America since being taken to the States during World War II by his mother, was born. Johnson has returned to learn about his family background, only to discover the father he thought died a hero's death was a convicted murderer. Stumbling upon evidence which convinces him his father is innocent, plottage twirls around his efforts to prove this innocence and turn up the real murderer.

Johnson delivers straightforwardly enough and Miss Miles is a librarian who helps him in his quest. Remaining characters are somewhat over-Britishly enacted, including Emlyn Williams, the real killer who circulated a petition to keep his father from the gallows; Bernard Lee, the father; Moultrie Kelsall, police inspector out to obstruct, for some obscure reason, the American in learning the truth of the case; Ralph Truman, prosecutor of the 20-year-o'd case who fears that a reinvestigation will endanger his forthcoming election to Parliament.

Jack Cardiff's direction of the Ken Taylor screenplay fails to overcome script deficiencies, but Wilkie Cooper's photography sometimes limns interesting Liverpool backgrounds. Technical credits otherwise are stock. *Whit.*

Julie La Rousse
(FRENCH)

Paris, Sept. 1.

Pathe release of Metzger-Woog-Marignan production. Stars Pascale Petit, Daniel Gelin; features Rene-Louis Lafforgue, Margo Lion, Jean Ozenne, Liliane Patrick. Directed by Claude Boissol. Screenplay, Paul Andreota, Boissol; camera, Roger Fellous; editor, Louis evaivre. At Lord Byron, Paris. Running time, 95 MINS.

Julie	Pascale Petit
Jean	Daniel Gelin
Max	Rene-Louis Lafforgue
Mother	Margo Lion
Uncle	Jean Ozenne
Tamara	Liliane Patrick

Mildly entertaining situation comedy is too pat and familiar for much chances outside of France. It lacks the sparkle and inventiveness needed to make the telegraphed tale diverting. It is smoothly made and played, but the eclat is only in isolated passages.

A rich man leaves his factory to a woman he jilted. His son tries to seduce the heiress, the woman's daughter, to get back the factory. It leads to both trying to trick the other until love comes along. It has been seen before, and better, in Yank comedies of this genre. *Mosk.*

Le Confident de Ces Dames
(The Womens' Confidant)
(FRENCH)

Paris, Sept. 1.

Pathe release of Cyclope-Dama production. Stars Fernandel; features Silva Koscina, Denise Grey, Ugo Toniasi. Directed by Jean Boyer. Screenplay, Serge Veber, Jean Manse, Boyer; camera, Charles Suin; editor, Roberto Cinquini. At Balzac, Paris. Running time, 90 MINS.

Veterinarian	Fernandel
Doctor	Silva Koscina
Countess	Denise Grey
Nephew	Ugo Toniasi

Fernandel vehicle is a quickie in production value, but garners a few yocks on its tale of a veterinarian. Latter ends up becoming a specialized femme doctor. Women come to his small town from all over the country after he saves a film star who has been in an accident.

It gives Fernandel a chance for his knowing double takes, rages and wily dramatics as he shows up a fortune hunting type and gets his girl, the local doctor. Pic stacks mainly for dualer chances abroad with main value the Fernandel name.

Direction wisely gives Fernandel the ball and he takes the film over its banal spots. It is somewhat talky and telegraphed. But its mixture of situation comedy, macabre humor; and a theatrical approach make this a good local bet. It's also a possibility abroad if given a hard sell. *Mosk.*

Babette S'En Va-T-En Guerre
(Babette Goes to War)
(FRENCH—COLOR—C'SCOPE)

Brigitte Bardot as draw.

Moscow, Aug. 18.

Columbia release of Iena-Raoul Levy production. Stars Brigitte Bardot; features Jacques Charrier, Francis Blanche, Hannes Messemer, Yves Vincent, Ronald Howard, Pierre Bertin. Directed by Christian-Jaque. Screenplay, Gerard Oury, Raoul Levy, Michel Audiard; camera (Eastmancolor), Armand Thirard; editor, Jacques Desagneaux; music, Gilbert Becaud. At Moscow Film Fest. Running time, 100 MINS.

Babette	Brigitte Bardot
Gerard	Jacques Charrier
Schultz	Francis Blanche
D'Arcy	Yves Vincent
Fitzgerald	Ronald Howard
Duke	Pierre Bertin

Shown out of competition, this pic scored highly with Russian audiences and officials. It also looks ripe for general distrib in the western orbit on the Brigitte Bardot name and the diverting progression and comedies. It's a natural for dubbing abroad.

However, it can be tightened for offshore spots where more pace is usually associated with comedies. Its leisurely movement will do for the Continent. Here, B.B., now an international entity, is embroiled in the last war when she ends up in England accidentally during the exodus in France in 1940.

Her perverse innocence and disarming pouting soon have her working with the Free French Forces and off on a mission to kidnap a German general to hold up the proposed invasion of England by making the Germans think he is a British agent. B.B. bungles through and is soon working for the Gestapo and manages to end all right and heroically.

B. B. displays a feeling for comedy and does not strain to give form or outline to the role. Director Christian-Jaque has wisely let her have her head and the appeal is there in her ingenuous winning through by the wiles and appeal forced on her by others.

She is always fully clothed in this and morally impeccable in spite of her harebrained attitude toward men, war, intrigue and action. B.B. is now a definite star personality and can do anything in any pic on her own attributes alone. Pic will have no censor troubles and is more in "The Parisienne" line than "God Created Woman."

This means much will depend on her standing abroad at this time and the savvy hypoing and placement of the pic. Its lush production values, well sustained risible tone, and comic war aspects are all plus assets as is Francis Blanche's excellent satirical portrait of a blustering, bloodthirsty Gestapo man. Jacques Charrier is acceptable and boyish as the male lead and supporting fare is fine.

Color is crisp and catching and a clever musical score also helps. A little pruning to get into the main theme earlier will help. This looks like a winner on entertainment values heightened by the still potent B.B. monicker. *Mosk.*

Venice Films

Hunde, Wollte Ihr Ewig Leben
(Inferno)
(GERMAN)

Venice, Aug. 29.

Transocean release of a Deutsche Film Hansa production. Features Joachim Hansen, Wilhelm Borchert, Peter Carsten, Armin Dahlen, Horst Frank, Paul Hoffmann, Carl John, Alexander Kerst, Ernst v. Klipstein, Carl Lange, Gunnar Moilar, Richard Muench, Gunther Pfitzmann, Wolfgang Preiss, and Sonia Ziemann. Directed by Franz Wisbar. Screenplay, Wisbar, Frank Diemen, Heinz Schroeter, from novel by Fritz Woess; camera, Helmut Ashley; music, Herbert Windt. At Venice Film Fest (shown in competition). Running time, 111 MINS.

1st Lt. Wisse	Joachim Hansen
General Paulus	Wilhelm Borchert
Kraemer	Peter Carsten
Stanescu	Armin Dahlen
Boese	Horst Frank

Elaborate, well-directed, and realistic recount of the German 6th Army's defeat at Stalingrad. Hollywood-styled item looks a good grosser in home country and European market, with overseas chances proportional. Names mean nothing outside Germany, so success burden must go to action-war aspects.

Based on a novel, "inferno" follows a few characters through the last stages of the battle of Stalingrad, where the German forces under Gen. Paulus were surrounded and defeated in the 1942 Russian winter offensive. More than following an isolated group of G.I.'s, pic tries and generally succeeds in taking in the overall picture via use of key characters in commanding and related ranks. Unoriginal and somewhat jarring to pic's realistic quality is the addition of sole femme character, a Russian girl played by actress Sonia Zieman, who befriends a German officer and by rare filmic coincidence meets him again in midd of battle ground, helping him to escape from the Red-controlled zone.

On the plus side of pic, which is more an act of accusal than a straight war pic, are some excellent battle scenes expertly fused by director Frank Wisbar (who lived in Hollywood for 17 years) with documentary clips. Acting is excellent throughout, with cast providing strong performances. Miss Ziemann is wasted in brief appearance as the friendly Russian girl. Lensing, music, and other credits are fine. *Hawk.*

Il Generale Della Rovere
(General della Rovere)
(ITALO—FRENCH)

Venice, Aug. 31.

Cineriz release of a Zebra Film (Morris Ergas)-Gaumont co-production. Stars Vittorio De Sica. Features Hannes Messemer, Sandra Milo, Anne Vernon, Vittorio Caprioli, Giovanna Ralli, Lucia Modugno, Luciano Picozzi. Directed by Roberto Rossellini. Story and screenplay, Sergio Amidei, Diego Fabbri, and Indro Montanelli, from novel by Indro Montanelli; camera, Carlo Carlini; art direction, Piero Zuffi; music, Renzo Rossellini. At Vienna Film Fest (shown in competition). Running time, 160 MINS.

Della Rovert	Vittorio De Sica
Colonel Mueller	Hannes Messemer
Banchelli	Vittorio Caprioli

Roberto Rossellini has made his first saleable film in years. That it is also a picture which will please the critics, or at least stimulate them to animated debate as to merits and defects, merely accentuates this remarkable two-pronged comeback by the controversial director.

This combination of circumstances, coupled with its Venice Festival exposure and the marquee value of Vittorio De Sica and to a lesser degree other cast names, plus word-of-mouth, should send "Della Rovere" off to healthy grosses in Italy and France. In other areas, including the U.S., pic has okay chances in a more restricted specialized release.

Sober and sombre story, based on fact, concerns a petty blackmarketeer and swindler whom the German occupation forces send to Milan's San Vittore jail (under false name of Italo "General della Rovere") to ferret out Italian resistance leaders. Once there, he slowly grows into his part, eventually assuming the leadership of the Italian prisoners who look up to him for comfort and guidance.

He decides, after all, not to betray the cause of his country and his fellow Italians. For this he is shot, in a shattering finale which harks back to the impact of "Open City." In fact, the entire picture deliberately recalls the atmosphere of that film and of "Paisan." While the immediacy of those classics has been lost in this dramatic recreation of those days, Rossellini obviously feels this material more than any he has touched since, and the result is often intriguing, often gripping, often moving, sometimes even amusing, but always significant picture.

Indro Montanelli's story is a natural. It also provides an ideal vehicle for Vittorio De Sica, who gives his best performance in years as the fake general. Topnotch performances are also contributed by Hannes Messemer as the SS Colonel, and by Vittorio Caprioli, measured and effective as a tortured fellow-prisoner of the general. Also good are Giovanna Ralli, in a brief role, and Sandra Milo, as a prostitute once befriended by the "General," as well as others in the populated cast. Throughout, however, it's unquestionably the strong hand of the director which gives a unity of style and tone to this document of its time.

Nevertheless, there's no doubt

that pic is far too long at its current 160 minutes. Much will have to be sliced (or sacrificed) before it's accessible to the general public. (As a matter of fact, director was still cutting pic on night before its Venice unveiling.) In other sectors, Rossellini has had expert assistance from Piero Zuffi, who in his first film art direction effort (he's a stage designer) has come up with a realistic and functional portrait of Genoa and the Milan jail during the war years and from Renzo Rossellini, who wrote the effective music score.

Withal, pic is a remarkable production achievement, not only for producer Morris Ergas, but for Rossellini himself who finished it in a record (for him) six-weeks. It's a comforting return which bids well for a future reprise of Italian film quality.   *Hawk.*

A Double Tour
(Double Twist)
(FRENCH—COLOR)
Venice, Sept. 8.

CCFC release of Paris Film-Panitalia production. With Antonella Lualdi, Jeanne Valerie, Bernadette Lafont, Jacques Dacqmine, Jean-Paul Belmondo, Madeleine Robinson. Directed by Claude Chabrol. Screenplay, Paul Gegauff from the novel by Stanley Ellin; camera (Eastmancolor), Henri Decae; editor, Jacques Gaillard. At Venice Film Fest (shown in competition). Running time, 105 MINS.
Leda .... Antonella Lualdi
Therese .... Madeleine Robinson
Elisabeth .... Jeanne Valerie
Julie .... Bernadette Lafont
Henri .... Jacques Dacqmine
Laszlo .... Jean-Paul Belmondo

Sleek whodunit is dressed up with a group of unsavory characters. It has good camerawork and tricky direction. But its downbeat qualities and lack of character development, plus overblown treatment, relegate this for art houses abroad with exploitation chances for more general situations on a hypo basis.

A middleaged man is having an affair with a young girl who lives next door to his house situated in the south of France. His authoritative, insensitive, climbing wife knows it as well as his unbalanced son and marriageable daughter. Attached to this family is a freewheeling Hungarian courting the daughter. A sensuous maid makes up the entourage.

Pic is decked out with lush color and story is told with sudden flashbacks and artful camerawork. But emphasis on technique robs this of telling motivations, suspense and a true feeling for the love, hatred and conflicting outlooks of this eerie family.

Feature looks headed for biz here. Director Claude Chabrol, one of the first of the "new wave," again displays his dexterity. Production gloss of Raymond and Robert Hakim is a plus value for this offbeater. Color is fine and editing snappy, with acting good.

But the characters seem to exist in a vacuum. Their hatreds and hopes are not clearly defined enough to make this sordid affair revelatory or taking. It will have to be sold on its outspoken, brash characters and treatment. *Mosk.*

Hadaka No Taisho
(The Nude General)
(JAPANESE—COLOR—TOHOSCOPE)
Venice, Sept. 8.

Toho release and production. With Gneiju Kobayashi, Aiko Mimasu, Yasuko Nakada, Daisuke Kato. Directed by Hiromichi Horikawa. Screenplay, Yoko Mizuki; camera (Eastmancolor), Asaichi Nakai; editor, Y. Kato. At Venice Film Fest (shown out of competition). Running time, 95 MINS.

Based on the life story of a contemporary, feeble-minded artist, noted for his tableaus made via pastings of colored bits of paper, this pic is solidly entertaining. It gets a lot of laughs by sustaining a high note of low comedy, satire and clever slapstick throughout.

Perhaps too many of its darts are aimed at internal Japanese foibles, which makes this primarily for special situations abroad. But more general chances are in store, with a simple shearing of some ambiguous spots.

The artist is a part-time tramp living off the land. But in his travels he manages to get into various scrapes and do many jobs.

The excellent etching of the artist by Keiju Kobayashi has him as the inspired and taking simpleton. Direction sustains the comic tone throughout. Color and scope are well utilized. A good comedy, this is one of the most generally exploitable pix for western marts to come out of the Japanese studios in some time.   *Mosk.*

Paradies Und Feuerhofen
(Paradise and Melting Pot)
(WEST GERMAN — DOCUMENTARY—COLOR)
Venice, Sept. 8.

Ifag Film release and production. Direction and commentary by Herbert Viktor. Screenplay, Rolf Vogel; camera (Agfacolor), Heinz Holscher; editor, Viktor. At Venice Film Fest (shown out of competition). Running time, 85 MINS.

Full length documentary was made by a West German team on Israel today. Aside from the delicacy of such a collaboration, the film does not have any undue exploitable aspects. It has good color, but is rather routine in its views of the country.

Accompanied by a fairly pompous, didactic commentary, it moves too rapidly and rarely allows for a true savoring and feel of the country. A dragged-in episode of Interpol capturing some drug smugglers on camels is ludicrous in a documentary of this kind.

Its main value for offshore spots is on its well lensed look at various points of interest in this dynamic little country. A tightening up in editing, and a smoother commentary could have made this a good supporting feature in U.S. art programs.   *Mosk.*

Pervy Den Mira
(The First Day of Peace)
(RUSSIAN)
Venice, Sept. 1.

Gorki Studio release and production. With V. Vinogradov, L. Butienina, P. Scerbakov. Directed by J. Seghel. Screenplay, I. Olscianski, N. Rudnieva; camera, B. Dulienkov; editor, M. Fradkin. At Venice Film Fest (shown out of competition). Running time, 95 MINS.

The time is the last days of the war as the oncoming Russian soldiers have a group of Germans under siege in a church in a German town. All surrender except three SS men. Pic then details how the escaping SS men kill a young Russo soldier fleeing from a Soviet nurse he loves.

Though the pic might be a bit paternalistic via a doctor who suffers for all the ills of his men and patients, and the pleas for peace are solidly couched and spoken, it is well directed. The acting is excellent throughout. Care is taken in giving credit to all other nationalities, and even an

American major who makes a speech at a victory banquet.

In short, this picture has more heart and film knowhow than most Soviet product. It may be a good art house entry for offshore spots via its well contained action aspects. Its character perception also slants it for more general chances too.   *Mosk.*

Bari Trekey Paliye
(The Runaway Boy)
(INDIAN)
Venice, Sept. 1.

L. B. Films release and production. With Param Bhattarak, Padma Dovi, Gyanesh Mukherjee. Written and directed by Ritwik Ghattak. Camera, Dinen Gupta; editor, S. Choudhury. At Venice Film Fest (shown out of competition). Running time, 90 MINS.

Film concerns a mischievous eight-year-old who runs off to the city after trouble with his father. Here he runs into many adventures and gets mixed up with the sordid side of urban life. He finally returns home to try for an understanding with his father and attempt the painful process of growing up.

Pic mixes too many styles and is somewhat repetitive in the boy's odyssey. It emerges primarily a moppet pic for kids on the ingenuous adventures and resolutions sans the insight for art chances abroad.

Technical aspects are uneven as is direction. But good performances manage to sustain interest most of its running time.   *Mosk.*

Third Man on Mountain

Fine mountain-climbing yarn, with Disney's name indicating good b.o.

Hollywood, Sept. 11.

Buena Vista release of a Walt Disney production. Stars Michael Rennie, James MacArthur, Janet Munro and James Donald; with Herbert Lom, Laurence Naismith; features Lee Patterson, Walter Fitzgerald, Nora Swinburne, Ferdy Mayne. Produced by William H. Anderson. Directed by Ken Annakin. Screenplay by Eleanore Griffin, based on James Ramsey Ullman's "Banner in the Sky." Camera, Harry Waxman; music, William Alwyn; editor, Peter Boita. Previewed at the Academy Theatre, Hollywood, Sept. 11, '59. Running time, 107 MINS.
Capt. John Winter..... Michael Rennie
Rudi Matt .... James MacArthur
Lizbeth Hempel .... Janet Munro
Franz Lerner .... James Donald
Emil Saxo .... Herbert Lom
Teo Zurbriggen ......Laurence Naismith
Klaus Wesselhoft ...... Lee Patterson
Herr Hempel .... Walter Fitzgerald
Frau Matt .... Nora Swinburne
Andreas .... Ferdy Mayne

"Third Man on the Mountain" is a majestic ascent up the Matterhorn, a story of a boy's supreme challenge unfolded in rich, colorful tones. It has the sort of high altitude thrills to send the viewer cowering deep in his seat and the sort of moving drama to put him on the edge of it. The "Walt Disney Presents" tag, the exploitation via Disney's television series and the tie-in with Disneyland's Matterhorn replica will help sell what, first of all, is a good film, and the Buena Vista release should strike lofty returns.

The film is a potent blending of all-around values by producer William H. Anderson. The mountain locations are among the best ever recorded, and in no scene does the feeling ring anything but true. Ken Annakin's direction is vivid, maintaining excitement and pace, building climaxes with changing character and slipping toeholds. Special nods are rated by cinematographer Harry Waxman, mountain unit director Gaston Rebuffat and mountain unit photographer Georges Tairraz. They have put an exalted atmosphere on film.

Eleanore Griffin's screenplay, based on James Ramsey Ullman's "Banner in the Sky," is well constructed, putting emphasis on the correct characters and conflicts. The writer has adeptly pitted man against nature, man against man, man against youth and, indeed, youth against itself.

What will be most appealing, particularly to Disney's young followers, is the challenge of the film's 18-year-old hero. Played with enthusiasm and concern by James MacArthur, he lives in the shadow of his dead father, the greatest Alpine guide of all time. It was on the Citadel, most foreboding of Switzerland's peaks, that the man, Josef Matt, lost his life 16 years earlier. His widow fears losing her only son to the mountain and with the help of her brother tries vainly to keep the lad from its peaks. There is perhaps an inherent cliche in the film's theme: "Man must do what he is meant to do, or he isn't a man." But it is developed carefully and tastefully enough to overcome the obvious, and when the boy shows the way to the first conquerors of the mountain, it is fitting drama.

Michael Rennie stars as a British climber, intent on reaching the Citadel's top, turning in an expert performance. Playing opposite MacArthur with youthful romance is Janet Munro, a charming British

actress whose warmth, coupled with zest, adds much to the film. James Donald, as the boy's uncle, creates a sharp portrayal of a man knowing the dangers of the mountain, and Herbert Lom, as a rival guide, adroitly marks the epitome of pride. Laurence Naismith is excellent and most appealing as an ex-guide, and Nora Swinburne is fine as the boy's mother. Good performances are turned in by Lee Paterson, Walter Fitzgerald and Ferdy Mayne. And MacArthur's real mother, Helen Hayes, can be seen in a passing spot, as can author Ullman, if you know what he looks like.

The Technicolor production, designed by John Howell, benefits from fine editing by Peter Boita and excellent sound by Chris Greenham. The musical score by William Alwyn, conducted by Muir Mathieson, is stirring complement to the action, and a bright moment or two comes from songs, "Climb the Mountain" by Franklyn Marks and "By" Dunham, "Good Night Valais" by G. Haenni and Tom Adair. *Ron.*

Day of the Outlaw

This slow horse opera will have to ride on names—Robert Ryan, Burl Ives, Tina Louise, David Nelson.

Hollywood, Sept. 11.

United Artists release of Security Pictures production. Stars Robert Ryan, Burl Ives, Tina Louise. Produced by Sidney Harmon. Directed by Andre De Toth. Screenplay, Philip Yordan; camera, Russell Harlan; editor, Robert Lawrence. Reviewed at the Hawaii Theatre, Sept. 9, '59. Running time: 91 MINS.

Blaise Starrett	Robert Ryan
Jack Bruhn	Burl Ives
Helen Crane	Tina Louise
Hal Crane	Alan Marshall
Dan	Nehemiah Persoff
Ernine	Venetia Stevenson
Vic	Donald Elson
Vivian	Helen Wescott
Tommy	Robert Cornthwaite
Tex	Jack Lambert
Pace	Lance Fuller
Denver	Frank De Kova
Vause	Paul Wexler
Shorty	Jack Woody
Gene	David Nelson
Clay	Arthur Space
Preston	William Schallert
Bobby	Michael McGreevy
Doc Langer	Dabbs Greer
Mrs. Preston	Betty Jones Moreland
Larry	Elisha Cook
Lewis	Dan Sheridan
Clagett	George Ross

Intended to provoke suspense, "Day of the Outlaw," succeeds only in demanding audience endurance. The Security Pictures' production for United Artists has a top cast and many talented hands in the making of it. But it does not come off and it will be suitable only for double-bills on the strength of the cast names.

Philip Yordan's screenplay takes a "Desperate Hours" kind of theme and transfers it to the frontier west. A troup of Army renegades led by Burl Ives takes over a small mountain town. The Ives men intend to rape the women and murder the men unless someone gets them out. Robert Ryan offers to, on the ruse of knowing an escape route to safety. Ives realizes Ryan is leading the men to their death, but he accedes to the plan. Ives is dying anyway of a gunshot wound and he is inclined to be chivalric about sparing the town.

Andre De Toth's direction fails to create any definite characters and it does not establish any mood. Jeopardy is the single important ingredient of a suspense film, such as this was intended to be, but it is not achieved initially and, with no early momentum, the picture never grasps the interest or emotions.

Yordan's screenplay has interest. It is based, in part, at least, on fact. There was such a character as Ives, an army officer who was responsible for a dreadful massacre in the waning days of the frontier west. Ives gives his role his customary forcefulness. Ryan seems too intellectual for a charactization that has been given no background to support sensitivity. Others in the cast who occasionally register include Alan Marshal, Nehemiah Persoff, Dabbs Greer and Betsy Jones-Moreland.

Russell Harlan's black-and-white camerawork often catches better than the story the desolate snow country in which the film's set, and the effect of this icy terrain on the characters. The locations must have been arduous. *Powe.*

Venice Films

La Grande Guerra
(The Great War)
(ITALO-FRENCH-C'SCOPE)

Venice, Sept. 8.

Dino DeLaurentiis Distribuzioni release of a DeLaurentiis-Gray Film (Paris) coproduction. Stars Vittorio Gassmann, Alberto Sordi, Silvana Mangano; features Folco Lulli, Bernard Blier, Romolo Valli. Directed by Mario Monicelli. Screenplay, Monicelli, Age, Scarpelli, Vincenzoni; camera (C'Scope), Giuseppe Rotunno; music, Nino Rota; editor, Adriana Novelli. At Film Festival, Venice. Running time, 140 MINS.

Giovanni	Vittorio Gassmann
Oreste	Alberto Sordi
Bordin	Folco Lulli
Castelli	Bernard Blier
Costantina	Silvana Mangano

Well-made war picture combining commercial and artistic quality for top entertainment. Human and spectacular values transcend lingual barriers, and while film should garner hefty figures in its home country, this parlay should help it to good results elsewhere as well. Cast names are an additional assist in Italy.

Episodic story in this fresco of the Italian front during World War I concerns two reluctant soldiers, well played with dialect overtones by Vittorio Gassmann and Alberto Sordi, who do their best to stay out of trouble—and the front lines. First part, which chronicles their various attempts to avoid responsibilities and combat, is very amusing. But towards finale, the tone changes and culminates in tragedy as the pair is seized by the Austrians and, hurt in pride as Italians, prefer to be shot rather than to betray their comrades.

Script by Age, Scarpelli, and Vincenzoni in collaboration with director Mario Monicelli, contains excellent dialogue. Much of it is rich in dialect and regional flavor (which however, may be lost in foreign versions). While including a number of war film cliches, it manages to avoid the banal, giving the picture a subdued, heroic patina effectively different from the run-of-the-mill combat chronicle.

Gassmann and Sordi are fine as the garrulous duo, both giving boisterous and believable performances. It's only in the very last shots that Sordi doesn't quite manage the difficult step from comedy to tragedy. But the responsibility there is more the fault of a script which leaves audience totally unprepared for the switch, coupled with the fact that Sordi is currently somewhat of a national hero, so that shooting him in this way is like shooting Santa Claus.

Some fiery thesping is also contributed by Silvana Mangano, as a camp follower befriended by Gassmann in ignorance of her true profession. Rest of cast, including a number of (locally-known) names drawn from various fields (singer Nicola Arigliano, tv actor Mario Valdermarin, ex-prizefighter Tiberio, Mitri, Himalayan climber-guide Achille Compagnoi) give the fresco a colorful backdrop. Bernard Blier, Folco Lulli, and especially Romolo Valli, are fine in other key roles.

Mario Monicelli has directed with good feeling for pace, especially in opening and closing sequences and his battle scenes are very effective. In between there are a few slow spots where trimming could pare footage of 140-minute pic down. CinemaScope lensing by Giuseppe Rotunno, assisted by Roberto Gerardi, takes advantage of the spectacular values of dramatic and pictorial battleground sweeps. Other technical credits, including Nino Rota's music, adapted from w.k. World War songs, are top-drawer. Throughout the film, the imprint of Dino De Laurentiis' production values are evident in a film exemplifying a new vitality in the Italo industry. *Hawk.*

The Savage Eye

Venice, Sept. 15.

Edward Harrison release of a City Film Corp. production. Features Barbara Baxley, Herschel Bernardi, Jean Hidey, Elizabeth Zemach, with commentary spoken by Gary Merrill. Camera, Jack Couffer, Helen Levitt, Haskall Wexler; music, Leonard Rosenman. At Film Festival, Venice (shown out of competition). Running time, 68 MINS.

Fascinating and uncompromising semi-documentary impressively put together as an obvious labor of love by three talented American film-makers, Ben Maddow, Sidney Meyers and Joseph Strick. Good offbeat entry for specialized art spots, with pairing important due to its relatively short footage. Word of mouth and, for the aficionados, the fact that this won an award at the recent Edinburgh Festival should help it.

Story of a divorced woman's attempts to readjust to a single life affords an excellent opportunity to dissect some frightening and depressing panoramas of modern existence. From the woman's first arrival at a big-city airport (site of most of shooting is Los Angeles, but it could have been made almost anywhere, and purposely, no effort has been made to establish a specific locale), pic moves into her first visual impressions of the city, its seamy side, its bars and drunks, its beauty parlors lined with elderly women, its store windows, and above all, its people.

Subsequent portions of the film feature among other things, the detailed horror of a nose-bobbing operation, the bloodthirsty behaviour of men and women at boxing and wrestling matches, a detailed and critically observed striptease sequence, complete with leering spectators, a cruelly fascinating sequence shot during a faith-healing service, surely one of the best documents of its kind, and a narrowing and nightmarish bit depicting a pervert's party.

Wealth of material is linked by presence of the key character, caught on her search for warmth and companionship, and by a spoken commentary (well-mouthed by Gary Merrill) in the form of a dialogue between the woman and an imaginary poet. Latter's oft-flowery material, however, is sometimes uncomfortably pretentious. Windup of film, after the woman has been driven into a nervous condition by an affair with married man and by the shock of the surroundings, finds her slowly warming up to a semblance of new life.

Footage, shot over a span of several years, boasts much expertly and realistically photographed (some of it hidden-camera) material. It's slickly integrated and matched with recreated sequences to bring about a true-looking patina. With exception of a few overlong sequences, editing job is likewise tops. Acting by Barbara Baxley as the woman is very good. Other credits, including an apt musical scoring by Leonard Rosenman, are in keeping.

Undeniably, there's enough material in this 68-minute item to shock even the mature spectator. Many will undoubtedly find some of the footage distasteful and much of it depressing, certainly disconcerting. Yet there's no question that the three filmmakers' intentions are sincere. This reasoning applies as well to the striptease footage which, though obviously exploitable per se, becomes relatively tame when seen in the brutally critical context of "The Savage Eye." *Hawk.*

Jazz on a Summer's Day
(COLOR-SONGS)

Venice, Aug. 30.

Galaxy Prod. release of a Raven Film production. Features Bert Stern, Harvey Kahn, Allan Green, Aram Avakian, Louis Armstrong Trio, George Shearing Quintet, Gerry Mulligan Trio, Mahalia Jackson, Jimmy Giuffre Trio, Thelonious Mank, Anita O'Day & Trio, Dinah Washington & Trio, Chico Hamilton Quintet, Sonny Stitt, Big Maybelle and Duo, Eli's Chosen Six. Directed by Bert Stern. Commentary by Albert D'Annibale and Arnold Pearl. Camera (Eastmancolor) Bert Stern, Ray Phelan, Courtney Hafela; music, Hoagy Carmichael, Duke Ellington, Count Basie, Seymour Simons, Gerald Marks, Thelonious Monk, Chuck Berry. Editor, Aram Avakian. At Film Festival, Venice (shown out of competition). Running time, 78 MINS.

Outstanding feature-length documentary centered around the Newport Jazz Festival with excellent chances in specialized slotting. A natural for jazzophiles, but has enough additional vaules to win over plenty of fringe customers as well. European chances, among other areas, are excellent with film likely to ride crest of current jazz popularity wave abroad. Adroit chanelling and selling are needed for maximum impact.

Pic is doubtlessly one of the greatest films on jazz ever made. But it is more than that. It's a document of the medium, spanning most of the jazz styles and including a rich selection of top performers and material. It's Americana, and a document of its time as well via observation of audiences and the life surrounding the Newport event, not least the neatly-integrated footage concerning the America Cup Yacht Races.

It's a stylist's delight and a rich emotional experience, thanks to spectacular color lensing, rich visual and aural material, plus skilled and tasteful editing. There have been few if any films, which have so impressively mirrored the impact of jazz, or even other forms of music, on spectators and on the musicians themselves.

Structure of the film basically follows that of the two-day event around which it centers, with occasional digressions, over the jazz soundtrack, to other nearby scenes such as the cup races, children playing, wave and water effects, reflections, all neatly matched to mood of motif being played. Juxtaposition is sometimes humorous, sometimes ironic, at others merely illustrative, but always deft.

Nor is there a lag in the material selected from among that performed by the jazz luminaries. The Jimmy Giuffre Trio plays "Train and the River," Thelonious Monk performs his own "Blue Monk"; "Sweet Georgia Brown" and "Tea for Two" are rendered in inimitable fashion by Anita O'Day, the George Shearing Quintet is in for "Rondo" while Dinah Washington sings "All of Me." Two windup spots are reserved for Louis Armstrong, who sings and plays "Rockin' Chair" with Jack Teagarden, then segues with "Lazy River," "Tiger Rag," and his standard "Saints Go Marching In."

On-the-spot (Eastmancolor) lensing under difficult lighting conditions, both daytime and nighttime, is often incredibly good. Some unprecented effects are achieved by cameramen Bert Stern, Ray Phelan, and Courtney Hafela (under Stern's imaginative and stylish guidance) despite fact that basic lensing taboos are broken by shooting into lights, etc. for one of the best color efforts in recent years. Similar plaudits must also go to editor Aram Avakian and those responsible for an outstanding (magnetic) sound recording job, all part of near-perfect teamwork on pic.

Undoubtedly, while this beautifully tooled and crafted effort is made to order for the jazz set, many others in the general audience category will not go for either its length or its jazz-rich contest. Hence a basic and reasoned consideration (remainding one that it is, after all, a documentary) must point to special handling and slotting despite its many values. While in some areas it will be able to run as is, in others some cuts will regrettably be necessary to fit programming habits and local tastes. *Hawk.*

Enjo
(Flame of Torment)
(JAPANESE)

Venice, Sept. 2.

Daiei release of a Daiei Production. Stars Raizo Ichigawa; features Ttasuya Nakadai, Ganjiro Nakamura, Yoko Uraji, Michiyo Aratama, Tamao Nakamura, Yoichi Funaki, Kinzo Shin, Tanie Kitabayashi. Directed by Kon Ichigawa. Screenplay, Natta Wada, Keiji Hasebe, from novel by Yukio Michima; camera, Kazuo Miyagawa; music, Toshio Mayuzumi. At Film Festival, Venice. Running time, **96 MINS.**

Stylish film version of Yukio Mishima's bestselling novel "The Temple of the Golden Pavillion" boasting fine acting and photography (by cameraman of "Roshomon," Kazuo Miyagawa), but emotionally distant from western concepts. Outside of Japanese situations, this is a doubtful commercial commodity, even in arty spots.

Film tells of the inner torment of a stuttering temple servant who burns down the shrine—the thing he most loves in this world—to prevent its being deviled by the commercialism of modern times. He then commits suicide. There's much more to it than that, of course. But much of the plotting and reasoning behind it will appear remote to western eyes and ears.

Lenser Kazuo Miyagawa uses his wide screen beautifully, also assisting director Kon Ichigawa in orig inal flashback effects. In the leading role, Raizo Ichigawa gives a sensitive portrayal of the tormented youth. Technically pic is first-rate. *Hawk.*

Sonatas
(MEXICAN—SPANISH—COLOR)

Venice, Aug. 30.

Unset release of a Producciones Barbachano Ponce-Unindis co-production Stars Maria Felix; Francisco Rabal, Aurora Bautista; features Fernando Rey, Carlos Rivas. Written and directed by Juan Antonio Bardem. Camera (Eastmancolor), Gabriel Figueroa. Cecilio Paniagua; music, Isidoro Maiztegui, L. Hernandez Breton. At Film Festival, Venice. Running time, **95 MINS.**

Bradomin .... Francisco Rabal
Concha .... Aurora Bautista
Nina Chole .... Maria Felix
Casares .... Fernando Rey

Based on the Spanish work by Ramon Maria del Valle-Inclan, "Sonatas" is an elegant and handsome period piece which will find general audience favor in many areas. There's a natural accent on Spain and Latin America, where star names and literary origin provide an extra fillip. Some censorship is to be expected in Spain, especially on some (exploitable) amorous passages.

Basically, two stories are told, one in Spain and other in Mexico, with a single main character bridging the gap. Film centers on description of a Marquis of Bradomin who is twice aroused from an apparently comfortable and uneventful life by affairs with a married Spanish noblewoman and with the mistress of a Mexican dictator. Both spur him on to bravery almost despite himself, and he eventually abandons the easy life and rides off to one of the battles marking the Mexican revolution. Pic has been stylishly directed by Juan A. Bardem. He gets a major assist from his two cameramen and the Spanish and Mexican settings. Film is often a visual delight while its romantic and action footage should please both male and distaff customers. Francisco Rabal walks off with acting honors as the Marquis, while Aurora Bautista appears miscast and overhealthy as his sickly first amour. Maria Felix overplays her role as the Mexican mistress. Both she and rest of cast are the victims of the emphatic acting style predominant (and popular) in Latino areas. Tehnical credits are firstrate. *Hawk.*

Come Back Africa

Offbeater made by a Yank indie in South Africa with art chances on its explosive theme and daring. Needs strong sell.

Venice, Sept. 8.

Rogosin release and production. With Lewis N'Kosi, Bloke Modisane, Dube-Dube. Written and directed by Lionel Rogosin. Camera, Ernest Artaria, Emil Knebel; editor, Carl Lerner. At Venice Film Fest (shown out of competition). Running time, **95 MINS.**

Yank indie Lionel Rogosin, who made "On the Bowery," went into South Africa to turn out this explosive film on race relations in a segregated society. It shapes as an offbeat exploitation item for art spots with special situations also in store if well handled and exploited. Word-of-mouth and critics could also be a plus factor.

Rogosin, as in "Bowery," has instilled a feel of the country into his imagery and woven a story into the fabric. It concerns a man who comes from a native reservation to Johannesburg to earn money for his family. He does a series of jobs marred by the touchy attitudes of the whites and his easy-going nature which jars relations with his employers.

His wife and children come to stay with him and tragedy ensues when his wife is killed by a violent fellow native whom he has a brush with. Spliced in the story are scenes of the native bustle of the city's slum area. They're contrasted adroitly with the brightly built white sections.

Rogosin secured natural, easy performances from his leads. In well poised scenes, he gets the feeling of impending violence in the natives plus the more moderate attempts to find a way of living in this artificially segregated world. A telling native musical score underlines the potent imagery.

There is some diffuseness in the subordination of the story to the many documentary explorations of the city. But it is one of the most telling expositions of the African native mind to be put on film. It should get plenty of attention on its unusual theme and treatment.

Despite the troubles that were probably encountered in making the film, it is of high order technically. Expert editing has welded all this picturesque and absorbing material into an off-the-beaten path entry that needs a hard-sell. But it could be worth it in its inherent controversial aspects. *Mosk.*

Le Testament Du Docteur Cordelier
(The Will of Doctor Cordelier)
(FRENCH)

Venice, Sept. 8.

Pathe release of SOFIRAD production. Stars Jean-Louis Barrault; features Michel Vitold, Terry Bilis, Jean Topart. Gaston Modot. Written and directed by Jean Renoir. Camera, Georges Leclerc; editor, Renee Lichtig. At Venice Film Fest (shown out of competition). Running time, **90 MINS.**

Dr. Cordelier .... Jean-Louis Barrault
Severin .... Michel Vitold
Joly .... Teddy Bilis
Desire .... Jean Topart
Blaise .... Gaston Modot

Jean Renoir made this film for a one-shot video appearance financed by the government. It was also made with an eye on theatrical distrib and has been taken for this purpose by Pathe. However, it bears the tv stamp of gray lensing, simple setups and economic production. Primarily of dualer value abroad on its old horror theme, this is an updating of the "Dr. Jekyll and Mr. Hyde" tale.

Here the doctor's changes are done via cuts and sans any special effects. Jean-Louis Barrault does some fine pantomiming as the clownish monster who is the evil in the doctor and his other self when released by a drug he has invented. But other actors are left to fend for themselves. Direction is simple and unassuming which makes the film lag and lose tempo at times.

Renoir has tried to make a pic to please both mediums and hasn't quite brought it off. But the well-wearing tale could make this film worth slotting in a tv horror series for the U.S. or for use in secondary situations. It lacks the weight and technical standards for art chances. *Mosk.*

Popiol I Diament
(The Ashes and the Diamond)
(POLISH)

Venice, Sept. 8.

Polski State Film release and production. With Zbigniew Cybulski. Ewa Krzyzanowska, Waclaw Zastrzezynsky. Directed by Andrzej Wajda. Screenplay, Jerzy Andromowicz, Wajda; camera, Jerzy Wocjik; editor, R. Mann. At Venice Film Fest (shown out of competition). Running time, **100 MINS**

Taut thriller about immediate postwar Poland also has a heavier theme of the futility of killing and violence. Its technical knowhow, fine acting and directorial prowess make this an above average drama with arty chances abroad. It has even more general chance on its pacing and action.

It concerns two men told to kill a top communist on the last day of the war. They represent the prewar Polski ruling forces. Film details the eventual murder and the ironic death of the murderer.

Director Andrzej Wajda is masterly in composing atmosphere and gets fine performances, especially from Zbigniew Cybulski as the erratic young killer. But it is somewhat overdone in expressionistic bravura. However, sharp direction, theme and insight into a changing Poland of the period lend it additional hypo factors. *Mosk.*

Kiku and Isamu
(JAPANESE—'SCOPE)

Venice, Sept. 8.

Daito release and production. With Emiko Takahashi, George Okunoyama, Tanie Kitabayashi. Directed by Tadashi Imai. Screenplay, Yoko Mizuki; camera, Shunichiro Nakao; editor, Masao Oki. At Venice Film Fest (shown out of competition). Running time, **117 MINS.**

Film deals with a boy and girl fathered by Negro American soldiers in Japan. It raises no controversy but simply shows their troubles with other children due to their color. It has insight and tenderness in outlining the plight of the moppets.

But film is overlong and has a tendency to repeat effects. Character bits and story points. It could have some exploitation qualities abroad, if sheared somewhat, on its theme and simple treatment of the subject. Acting and technical qualities are an asset. *Mosk.*

Menschen Im Netz
(Man in the Net)
(WEST GERMAN)

Venice, Sept. 8.

Bavaria Filmkunst release and production. With Hansjorg Felmy, Johanna Von Koczian, Inge Schoener Hans Messemer. Directed by Franz Peter Wirth. Screenplay, Herbert Reinecker; camera, Gunther Senftleben; editor, Claus Boro. At Venice Film Fest (shonw out of competition). Running time, **98 MINS.**

Slickly made actioner concerns an East German spy ring in West Germany using promises to free relatives of East Germans to get state secrets in the West. Film is expertly turned out if primarily a familiar suspense yarn.

A man returns from an East German prison to the West to find his wife murdered. She had been working for the eastern ring to free him. He tracks down the killers and breaks up the ring with police help.

This is reminiscent of Yank detective thrillers except for the political angles. Primarily for dualer use abroad due to obvious scripting, it's technically well done and thesped. *Mosk.*

Akiket A Pas Cirta Elkisert
(For Whom The Larks Sing)
(HUNGARIAN)
Venice, Sept. 8.
Hunnia Film release and production. With Klari Tolnay, Eva Papp, Geza Tordy, Gabor Agardy, Joszef Bihari. Directed by Laszlo Ranody. Screenplay, Joszef Darvas; camera, Istvan Paszter; editor, Endre Szervansky. At Venice Film Fest (shown out of competition). Running time, 100 MINS.

Peasant drama takes place in 1922. It concerns a young male servant who covets his employer's wife, but finally realizes his lot is with an adoring fellow servant he has made pregnant. Film has a fine feel for the period and emotional relations.

It is excellently lensed, edited and acted with the direction threading all into an above average drama. But being Hungarian, and of the land, it shapes mainly a lingo entry for abroad. *Mosk.*

Almatlan Evek
(Sleepless Years)
(HUNGARIAN)
Venice, Sept. 1.
Hungarofilm release of a Hunnia Filmstudios (Budapest) production. Features Eva Ruttkai, Geza Tordy, Zoltan Maklary, Mari Torocsik, Ferenc Zenthe, Eva Vass, Gabor Agardy, Elma Bulla; Directed by Felix Mariassy. Screenplay, Judith Mariassy; camera, Gyorgy Illes; music, Imre Vinze. At Film Festival, Venice. Running time, 106 MINS.

Episodic item telling the stories of several inhabitants of industrial Csepel Island, south of Budapest, site of an ammunition factory. Fragments concern party-lined examples of imperial, capitalist, and fascist oppression of workers when the tide finally begins to turn for the cause espaused in obvious terms by the film. Its export chances, at least in western areas, are nil.

Within a conventional framework, totally lacking in the warmth and charm of certain even recent Hungarian films. This entry plods its bleak way through a series of propagandistic cliches. Technical credits are average. *Hawk.*

Jago Hua Savera
(Day Shall Dawn)
(PAKISTANIAN)
Venice, Sept. 8.
Nauman Taseer release and production. With Tripti Mitra, Zurain Rakashi, Ances Ama, Kazi Khakiq. Written and directed by Asejay Kardar. Camera, Walter Lassally, Sadhan Roy; editor, Bill Bovet. At Venice Film Fest (shown out of competition). Running time, 100 MINS.

Pic took the third top award, a golden medal, at the recent Moscow Film Fest. For a first pic from Pakistan this is of high calibre. It's sombre, simple and effective technically and emotionally. However, its theme of poverty and exploitation, in spite of its poetic shafts and truth, slant this only for art chances abroad.

It concerns a poor family in a fishing village and their attempts to buy a boat which are stymied by lack of money and a greedy moneylender. It is well made and has a feeling for the lives and emotions of these people. *Mosk.*

La Encrucijada
(The Crossroad)
(SPANISH)
Venice, Sept. 8.
Jam release and production. Stars Jean-Claude Pascal; features Analia Gade, Roberto Camardiel. Directed by Alfonso Balcazar. Screenplay, Miguel Cussos, Balcazar; camera, Alfredo Fralle; editor, Juan Oliver. At Venice Film Fest (shown out of competition). Running time, 91 MINS.

This is one of those Spanish pix that uses the Spanish Civil War of 1936 as a background. It's primarily about a priest, hounded by the Red Loyalists, who makes a group of fleeing people, cognizant of their responsibilities to themselves.

Film is drawn-out with long scenes slowing the action and impact. Technical credits are good, and story, background and acting okay, to make this a possibility for Hispano language spots abroad. *Mosk.*

Sed D Amor
(Thirst For Love)
(MEXICAN-C'SCOPE)
Venice, Sept. 8.
Sotomayor release and production. Stars Silvana Pampanini, Peedro Armendariz; features Ana Luisa Peluffo, Jaime Fernandez. Directed by Alfonso Corona Blake. Screenplay, M. Fernandez; camera, Raul Martinez Solares; editor, Raul Lavista. At Venice Film Fest (shown out of competition). Running time, 85 MINS.

Mixing a religioso theme and sex in familiar melodramatic terms, this is only for Hispano exploitation lingo spots abroad. An impoverished fishing village has a girl who can suddenly work miracles. But her sister, a widow thirsting for a man, is in the power of a sinister individual who wants to corner the girl's miraculous powers.

When the villain tries to attack the miracle worker the widow kills him and rides off with his body. Acting is as broad as the exploited themes. But there are enough low cut gowns, torrid love scenes and axe fights to hypo action chances. *Mosk.*

They Came to Cordura
(COLOR; C'SCOPE)

Realistic, controversial action drama. Top names in top performances.

Los Angeles, Sept. 18.
Columbia release of William Goetz production. Stars Gary Cooper, Rita Hayworth, Van Heflin, Tab Hunter; features Richard Conte, Michael Callan, Dick York, Robert Keith. Directed by Robert Rossen. Screenplay, Ivan Moffat and Robert Rossen; based on the novel by Glendon Swarthout; camera (Eastmancolor), Burnett Guffey; music, Elie Siegmeister; editor, William A. Lyon. Previewed at the Screen Directors Guild, Sept. 10, '59. Running time, 123 MINS.
Major Thomas Thorn .... Gary Cooper
Adelaide Geary .... Rita Hayworth
Sgt. John Chawk .... Van Heflin
Lt. Wm. Fowler .... Tab Hunter
Cpl. Milo Trubee .... Richard Conte
Pvt. Andrew Hetherington .. Michael Callan
Pvt. Renziehausen .... Dick York
Colonel Rogers .... Robert Keith
Arreaga .... Carlos Romero
Capt. Paltz .... James Bannon
Colonel DeRose .... Edward Platt
Mexican Federale .... Maurice Jara
1st Correspondent ...... Sam Buffington
2nd Correspondent ...... Arthur Hanson

A bitter and realistic drama of the wry twists life can work on men when they are thrown into situations beyond their control—in this case the 1916 border action between U. S. troops and Pancho Villa's Mexican rebels — "They Came To Cordura" is an important and impressive film.

Its story is so provocative there will be some who will be antagonized by it, but there's no question it is compellingly told. The William Goetz production for Columbia is action on a vast scale, and in some ways is the most disturbing picture dealing with the psychological aspects of war since "Bridge on the River Kwai."

"Cordura" shows five American soldiers, all candidates for the Congressional Medal of Honor for heroism in action, acting the meanest and most contemptible of men. Before the film is over, the four most active (one is unconscious most of the time) have displayed sadism and treachery, among other vices. They have attempted rape, mutiny and murder.

The screenplay by Robert Rossen and Ivan Moffat from Glendon Swarthout's book, takes its theme from the title. Cordura is the name of the Texas town the principals are bound for. It is also the Spanish word for courage. The moral is that what's called courage is sometimes a question of interpretation, of accident, or of momentary abberation. Real courage, the film says, is that which is established quietly, sometimes doggedly, but with forethought and reason.

Gary Cooper is the U. S. Army officer detailed to lead five Medal of Honor candidates back from the front lines of the 1916 war with Pancho Villa's rebels. Cooper has been made Awards Officer after showing cowardice in battle. The son of an Army general and himself a career officer, Cooper is desperately interested in the five heroes because they have what he lacks—or so he thinks. Also on the party is Rita Hayworth, the disillusioned and dissolute daughter of a disgraced politician.

Before the party gets to Cordura, the five heroes have all but disintegrated. Although the ending is somewhat obscure, possibly deliberately so, it leaves the impression that sometimes life's cowards are more nearly its heroes and the reverse.

Robert Rossen, who directed as well as co-writing the screenplay, is purposely careful in laying in his touchy story. The screenplay goes to considerable lengths to make sure that early incident on which later action hangs is explicitly established. Rossen also deliberately understates some of his earlier climaxes to save most of his steam for his final one, which, when it comes, is a crusher.

Gary Cooper is very good as the central figure, although he is somewhat too old for the role. It is a little hard to believe that a man of his maturity would only then be finding out the things about himself which Cooper explores as part of his character. Miss Hayworth, looking haggard, drawn and defeated, gives the best performance of her career. If she shows only half the beauty she usually does, she displays twice the acting.

Van Heflin does a brilliantly evil job as one of the "heroes," and Richard Conte, as his malevolent side-kick, is almost equally impressive. Tab Hunter, as a weakling officer who crumbles under the stress of the trek to Cordura, is another who does probably the best acting of his film career. Michael Callan and Dick York are fine in important roles. In support, Robert Keith, Carlos Romero, James Bannon, Edward Platt, Sam Buffington and Arthur Hanson all contribute.

Burnett Guffey's CinemaScope photography in Eastman Color is artistically framed and technically fine. Use of the new Panavision lenses eliminates the distortion formerly common on closeups. The print shown for review, however, was uneven in color balance and not always as sharp as Guffey's photography would be, apparently a flaw in the developing.

Elie Siegmeister's score, orchestrated by Arthur Morton and conducted by Morris Stoloff, is a good one, composed of offbeat themes and unusual orchestrations. William A. Lyon's editing keeps the film paced and in mood, and John Livadary's sound maintains the out-door feel. James Havens directed the second unit and Frank G. Carson photographed it, making their contribution. *Powe.*

The Man Who Understood Women
(COLOR—C'SCOPE)

Uneven satire on film folk and their erratic romance. Leslie Caron, Henry Fonda for marquee. Needs special handling.

20th-Fox release of Nunnally Johnson production. Stars Leslie Caron, Henry Fonda, Cesare Danova; features Myron McCormick, Marcel Dalio, Conrad Nagel, Edwin Jerome, Harry Ellerbe. Directed by Johnson. Script, Johnson, from Romain Gary novel, "The Colors of the Day"; camera (color), Milton Krasner; music, Robert Emmett Dolan; song, "A Paris Valentine," Dolan and Paul Francis Webster; editor, Charles LeMaire. Previewed in N.Y. at the Academy of Music Theatre, Sept. 16, '59. Running time, 135 MINS.
Ann .... Leslie Caron
Willie .... Henry Fonda
Marco Ranieri .... Cesare Danova
Preacher .... Byron McCormick
Le Marne .... Marcel Dalio
G. K. .... Conrad Nagel
Baron .... Edwin Jerome
Kress .... Harry Ellerbe
Milstead .... Frank Cady
Soprano .... Bern Roffman
French Doctor .... Ben Astar

For the first half hour, "The Man Who Understood Women" looks as if it might pan out into a clever and hilarious spoof about Hollywood where Henry Fonda is a producer without a job and Leslie Caron a charming French lass trying to make the grade. The pace is fast, the lines funny and the overtones of romance promising.

What happens after that is something of a mystery. As if Nunnally Johnson, in his triple capaci-

ty of producer, director and writer couldn't make up his mind in which direction to proceed, the film fusses and fumes, roams between long and dull stretches and then back to exquisitely acted and staged sophistication and humor.

When the comedy is good, and the situation jells, the picture becomes hilarious, combining touches of farce and genuine feeling. But, more often than not, "The Man Who Understood Women" strains credulity, is vague in what it's trying to say, and makes one wonder whether the man who undersood women shouldn't first have tried to understand himself. The Fonda character, a key part, is both diffuse and obvious. This isn't Fonda's fault—in fact, he turns in a thoroughly enjoyable performance that mingles aspects of comedy and tragedy—but must be blamed on the script, which lets the picture down.

Story has Fonda helping Miss Caron to get a job with a studio. They fall in love, get married and she becomes a big star in films produced by him. But, from the wedding night on down, the marriage is never consummated and when they go to the Riviera to shoot a film, Miss Caron falls for Cesare Danova and has a lengthy affair with him.

Fonda has them shadowed, his jealousy aroused. Eventually, falls from a cliff, Danova up and quits Miss Caron, and the principals—a little worse for wear but still in love—are reunited. The sudden lapses from high comedy to deep drama are confusing and disturbing, even irritating. One never knows whether Johnson means it or he doesn't.

Miss Caron is delightful, though her constant changes of mood—as directed—are hard to take. She photographs exquisitely. Fonda handles himself with aplomb in a —for him—unusual role. Danova is handsome but little more. Myron McCormick is given some juicy lines as Fonda's assistant. Bern Hoffman and Edwin Jerome are at times very amusing as the old pair whom Fonda hires to shadow his wife (Hoffman is a Sicilian and Jerome a desiccated British count who's in a cigar-puffing stupor most of the time). Conrad Nagel is seen briefly as a Hollywood producer.

Johnson's direction has a great flair, particularly in the farcical and satirical scenes and he has a way of pulling delightfully impish surprises on the audience. Some of the dialog lines are very funny, which makes it the more surprising that other passages of the film are so tedious.

Milton Krasner's lensing is good and the colors are vivid, though the sound in this one, stressing its stereophonic quality, fails to integrate smoothly. Charles LeMaire's editing is smooth. The picture could stand cutting. *Hift.*

Five Gates to Hell

Well-made war film; can be exploited for good b.o.

Hollywood, Sept. 17.

Twentieth-Fox release of a James Clavell production. Stars Dolores Michaels, Patricia Owens and Neville Brand; co-stars Ken Scott; also starring Nobu McCarthy, Benson Fong; featuring Nancy Kulp, John Morley, Gerry Gaylor, Shirley Knight, Greta Chi, Linda Wong, Irish McCalla. Produced, written and directed by James Clavell. Camera, Sam Leavitt; editor, Harry Gerstad; music, Paul Dunlap. Previewed at the studio, Sept. 17, '59. Running time, **98 MINS.**

Chen Pamok .... Neville Brand
Gung Sa .... Benson Fong
Dr. John Richter .... Ken Scott
Dr. Jacques Minelle .... John Morley
Athena .... Dolores Michaels
Joy .... Patricia Owens
Greta .... Gerry Gaylor
Chioko .... Nobu McCarthy
Yoette .... Greta Chi
Susette .... Nancy Kulp
Ming Cha .... Linda Wong
Sister Magdalana .... Irish McCalla
Sister Maria .... Shirley Knight

In "Five Gates to Hell," writer-producer-director James Clavell has made a war film that is both commercial and artistic. He has used careful thought, good judgment and a first-rate storytelling ability to overcome the restrictions of a low budget, and the film, which will appeal to both men and women, should reap considerable profit for 20th-Fox.

During World War II, Clavell spent five years as a prisoner of the Japanese, and the imprint of this experience must have had an indelible effect on his approach to "Five Gates." This feeling appears to have resolved itself in unique values and honest action, creating something beyond the proportions of a run-of-the-mill war melodrama. Clavell impresses in all three creative departments. His story is exciting, and his screenplay, while paced a bit slowly at the end, is literate. His direction is sensitive and his production, especially considering its low cost, is highly proficient.

The setting is Indo-China, and Sam Leavitt's excellent CinemaScope camera work makes the Malibu mountains look the part. A team of Red Cross workers, including two doctors and seven nurses, are taken prisoner by a war lord's guerrilla band. The war lord is dying, and the medics are ordered to save him, a feat that proves impossible. The women are made to undergo intimacies with the Indo-Chinese soldiers, finally escaping by sheer use of their sexual prowess. The doctors are killed, as are most of the women and all the guerrillas, but Clavell's handling of the massacre results in much that transcends violence.

There are hard-hitting scenes—crucifiction of a nun, the stabbing of a man undergoing surgery—and there is sympathy, even with the villainous heavies.

The actresses build their characterizations with skill, the emotions including Dolores Michaels' sensitivity, Patricia Owens' cynicism, Nobu McCarthy's warmth, Gerry Gaylor's strength, Shirley Knight's concern, Greta Chi's love and Nancy Kulp's unhappiness. Neville Brand is excellent as the heir to the war lord's dynasty, succeeding in creating a portrayal of many shades. Ken Scott, as the doctor, should receive much noteworthy attention with this strong performance. Also are Benson Fong, John Morley, Linda Wong and Irish McCalla.

Technically, the film is bolstered by fine editing by Harry Gerstad, good art direction by Lyle R. Wheeler and John Mansbridge and a highly effective musical score by Paul Dunlap. *Ron.*

Les Liaisons Dangereuses

(The Dangerous Meetings)
(FRENCH)

Paris, Sept. 22.

Marceau release of Marceau-Cocinor production. Stars Gerard Philipe, Jeanne Moreau; features Annette Vadim, Jeanne Valerie, Simone Renant, Jean-Louis Trintignant. Directed by Roger Vadim. Screenplay, Roger Vailland, Claude Brule, Vadim from the novel by Chaderlos De Laclos; camera, Marcel Grignon; editor, Victoria Mercanton. At Colisee, Paris. Running time, **108 MINS.**

Valmont .... Gerard Philipe
Juliette .... Jeanne Moreau
Cecile .... Jeanne Valerie
Marianne .... Annette Vadim
Volange .... Simone Renant
Danceny .... Jean-Louis Trintignant

Based on an 18th century classic that has been having censorship trouble to this day, this updated film version is sure to follow suit. It has already been cut for release here and still has no export visa, though permission is considered imminent.

Pic is a glossy study of an immoral couple who get their comeuppance. So, in spite of its probing frankness on this score, its retribution aspects could help this entry in censor wrangles abroad. It looks to do well here on the controversy it has stirred up and looms an art entry abroad, with more general chances on its surely controversial career.

A young diplomat and his wife have found a perfect harmony. He allows her to have all the affairs she wants and she helps him in his conquests. Both seem content until love comes into this completely immoral household to bring on tragedy.

Film has fine lensing, production dress and mounting, but takes on a literary sheen as tale is spun out via the couple's letters to each other. She sets her husband onto his 17-year-old cousin because the latter has snagged her present lover. The husband succeeds in the seduction via a tape smuggled in from the man the girl really loves and breaks her down while she listens to it.

But then comes a pure, virtuous young mother and the hero falls for her. The wife, who realizes that their union is threatened, breaks it off with the girl over his weak protests and the latter goes mad. Recrimination leads to the husband being killed by his cousin's fiance when the wife informs him what has happened. His mate is disfigured when she tries to burn the incriminating letters on their life.

Film is somewhat long and tightening would help for export purposes. Gerard Philipe plays the eternal Don Juan in a pasty way and rarely elicits an understanding of his character and drive. But Jeanne Moreau is perfect as the cat-like, steely wife who lives mainly off the emotions of others. Annette Vadim lacks the expression to make her pure wife role taking, and her poorly done mad scene can be cut.

Picture also has plenty of erotica with undressing cunningly suggested via carefully concealed parts of the anatomy. This makes it both exploitable and also able to pass customs nude tests.

Though done in a mixture of styles via satire, comedy of manners and drama, the film rarely settles on one plane. However, it has that offbeat, controversial quality which makes it a contender for big b.o. at home and abroad. *Mosk.*

Maigret et L'Affaire St. Fiacre

(Maigret and the St. Fiacre Case)
(FRENCH)

Paris, Sept. 22.

Cinedis release of Intermondia production. Stars Jean Gabin; features Valentine Tessier, Michel Auclair, Robert Hirsch, Michel Vitold. Directed by Jean Delannoy. Screenplay, R. M. Arlaud, Michel Audiard, Delannoy from the novel by Georges Simenon; camera, Louis Page, editor, Henri Taverna. At Paris, Paris. Running time, **100 MINS.**

Maigret .... Jean Gabin
Countess .... Valentine Tessier
Count .... Michel Auclair
Priest .... Michel Vitold
Lucien .... Robert Hirsch

Jean Gabin again interprets the Georges Simenon literary figure, Inspector Maigret. Like its predecessor, this is short on suspense but long on solid characterization, atmosphere and talk. It looms a fine entry here with chances in art spots abroad, like the first one. But more general placing is difficult due to its insistence on psychology over action and tension.

Gabin returns to his old home town where the local countess, a woman he loved as a boy, has been threatened. Pic delves into his reactions to his former life. It also depicts the countess' murder and its deft but slow solving by Gabin. Shot in a small town, the local color helps the film's probing mood.

Supporting players are good. But they're subordinated to Gabin's quizzical figure of the plodding but shrewd detective who unknots the tangled skeins of provincial avarice and intrigue rather than arrive at a solution by slick police work. Technical credits are good. Director Jean Delannoy has done well in balancing the literary against the imagery to to make this interesting throughout despite the obviousness of the killer's identity. *Mosk.*

Yesterday's Enemy

(BRITISH)

Strong, uncompromising drama of the Burmese campaign with excellent thesping by Stanley Baker and others, plus suspenseful situations. Good b.o.

London, Sept. 14.

Columbia release of a Hammer Films production Stars Stanley Baker, Leo McKern, Guy Rolfe, Gordon Jackson. Producer, Michael Carreras. Directed by Val Guest. Screenplay, Peter R. Newman, from his own play; camera, Arthur Grant; editor, Alfred Cox. Previewed at Columbia Theatre, London, Sept. 14, '59. Running time, **95 MINS.**

Captain Langford .... Stanley Baker
Padre .... Guy Rolfe
Max .... Leo McKern
Sgt. McKenzie .... Gordon Jackson
Doctor .... David Oxley
2nd Lt. Hastings .... Richard Pasco
Brigadier .... Russell Waters
Yamazaki .... Philip Ahn
Dawson .... Bryan Forbes
Informer .... Wolf Morris
Suni .... Edwina Carroll
Perkins .... David Lodge
Turner .... Barry Lowe
Bendish .... Alan Keith
Davies .... Howard Williams
Simpson .... Timothy Bateson
Patrick .... Arthur Lovegrove
Elliott .... Donald Churchill
Orderly .... Nicholas Brady
Brown .... Barry Steele

Here is a soundly made, toughly uncompromising war film set in Burma in 1942. The old argument will be tossed around as to whether war pix are now oldhat as entertainment, but "Yesterday's Enemy" is a tense, workmanlike job which should rate as a useful entry in average houses. It's a shade light on stellar appeal for the U.S., but some tried, tested British performers keep the acting at a good level and milk best out of a sincerely written script.

The tired, bedraggled remnants of a British brigade, led grimly by Captain Langford (Stanley Baker) is desperately trying to join up with its divisional h.q. They wipe out the defenders of a small village and Baker's wary when he finds that among the small contingent of dead Japs there's a high-ranking Jap officer. Why? he argues, and ruthlessly interrogates a captured Burmese.

When the man refuses to talk

about either the Japanese or the significance of a field map, he threatens to shoot two Burmese villagers in cold blood. He carries out his threat to the disgust of his fellow officers. But the Burmese talks. Subsequently, the little band of Britishers is captured by a Japanese patrol and Baker finds himself on the receiving end of a similar situation. When he refuses to talk, he is killed and the survivors of his brigade are executed.

The character of the British captain who obstinately contends that war cannot be carried out to kid glove rules, and that any means that insures the end that his own men shall survive are justified, however brutal and heartless, is an interesting one. Clearly shown are the pitiless loneliness of command and the terrible moral issues that can bring a man to near breaking point. Baker gives a fine performance as the man prepared to sacrifice his own conscience and scruples for the sake of duty. Some of the star's actions and dialog seem a trifle over-melodramatic, but his acting is powerful and authoriative.

Guy Rolfe has a tricky task as the padre who himself is confused as to what is really right in wartime, and is too stolid. But, in fairness, his role is the least well written. Leo McKern as a war correspondent, Gordon Jackson as a sergeant toughly loyal to Baker, David Oxley as a doctor and Richard Pasco as a junior officer wrestling with fear also give useful performances, as do Percy Herbert, David Lodge, Bryan Forbes and Arthur Lovegrove as convincing "other ranks." Philip Ahn gives a suave and arrogantly sinister portrayal of the adamant Japanese major.

One of the film's best features is that the soldiers all seem to act, think and invariably talk like soldiers and not actors and so the smell of fear, blood, mud and sweat communicates itself to the audience. Philip Newman's screenplay (he adapted it from his own play) poses some interesting questions and offers some exciting situations. His dialog is best when it is straight-forward and some of his fancy probings into moral issues seem stilted and immature.

But Val Guest (probably the best thing he has done) has directed with a sure touch. The settings are remarkably credible considering that the film was shot in the studio and not in authentic locations, and Arthur Grant's "jungle" lensing helps a great deal. Sound has been used imaginatively. *Rich.*

Apur Sanshar
(The World of Apu)
(INDIAN)

Paris, Sept. 15.

Satyajit Ray release and production. With Soumitra Chatterji, Sarmila Tagore, Alkoe Chakravarty, Swapan Mookerji. Written and directed by Satyajit Ray from the novel, "Aparajito," by Bhibuti Banerji. Camera, Subrata Mitra; editor, Dulal Dutt; music, Ravishankar. Previewed in Paris. Running time, 100 MINS.

Apu .... Soumitra Chatterji
Aparna .... Sarmila Tagore
Kajal .... Alkoe Chakaravarty
Pulie .... Swapan Mookerji

Film is the final one of a trilogy on Indian life in the 1930s, following the life of a young boy and his family. This entry compares with its predecessors in knowing insight, poetics and ability, but surpasses them in craftsmanship. Thus, it is an art house bet abroad with chances for wider distribution via its treatment and storyline.

Here the boy, Apu, is seen after he has finished his schooling at 23. Hazy bureaucracy keeps him from getting a decent job. In a visit to his cousin's wedding he is talked into marrying the girl himself when the bridegroom, who has been arranged for the 15-year girl sight unseen, has a fit during the ceremony. Indian custom would have had the girl remaining a spinster if someone had not married her immediately.

Script then deals with the love that grows between the newlyweds, the wife's death in childbirth, the husband's anguish and wanderings and refusal to see his son, and finally his determination to win the boy over after some years.

Story appears simple, but its delineation of character makes this a timeless, placeless story of love and adjustment. In spite of the seemingly exotic, old fashioned customs that still exist in some parts of India, the human relationships transcend all this to make it a solid international prospect.

Director Satyajit Ray, with greater technical means, makes the truth of his relationships and the revelation of India today the main trumps of the film. Wit, tenderness and intrinsic human revelations illuminate this unusual film.

The boy, in spite of his timidness and poverty, becomes a figure of depth and stamina as he eventually assumes his responsibilities. The girl glows with charm, petulance and wisdom to make their love a real palpable thing. Besides the depth of the pic, Ray also shows a flair for the comic and tender.

Technically excellent, with nonactors giving absorbing performances, this is an art entry to follow "Pather Panchali" and "Aparajito" and surpass them with its transcendent poignance. Being Indian, film still needs a hard sell but word-of-mouth and critics are sure to be plus factors.

Ed Harrison will distribute this in the U. S. as he did "Panchali" and "Aparajito." In spite of its opening in other countries, Cannes will probably make a special dispensation to have "Apur Sanshar" an entry in '60. *Mosk.*

The Night We Dropped A Clanger
(BRITISH)

London, Sept. 11.

Corny war comedy which flops dismally and is an unlikely venture except for easily pleased auidences.

Rank release of a Sydney Box Associates Production. Stars Brian Rix and Cecil Parker; with William Hartnell, Hattie Jacques, Leslie Phillips. Producer, David Henley; director, Darcy Conyers; screenplay, John Chapman; editor, Sid Stone; camera, Ernest Steward; music, Edwin Braden. At Rank Private Theatre, London, Sept. 11, '59. Running time, 86 MINS.

Atwood, Blenkinsop .... Brian Rix
A. V. M. Bukpasser .... Cecil Parker
Sergeant Bright .... William Hartnell
Squadron Leader Thomas .. Leslie Phillips
Belling .... Leo Franklyn
Squadron Leader Grant .... John Welsh
Flight Lieutenant Spendal .. Toby Perkins
Lulu .... Liz Fraser
Madame Grilby .... Vera Pearce
W. A. A. F. Hawkins .... Sarah Branch
Air Commodore Turner Oliver Johnstone
Farmer .... Larry Noble
Ada .... Hattie Jacques
Wing Commander .... John Chapman
Corporal .... Gilbert Harrison
Wing Commander Jones .... Arnold Bell
Wing Commander Priestley
 David Williams
Monty's Double .... Geoffrey Denys
Llulu's Mum .... Irene Handl

Brian Rix, London's youngest actor-manager, has put the Whitehall Theatre on the map with a series of longrunning farces. Two of his acting team are Larry Noble and Leo Franklyn. Author of Rix's current legit click is John Chapman. So when these became involved in a film it could be optimistically expected to turn out a yock-raiser. Not so. In fact, "The Night We Dropped A Clanger" emerges as one of the unfunniest screen comedies in several years.

Chapman's screenplay is contrived and strains desperately for laughs which not even a very competent cast can provide on account of lack of fuel. Daroy Conyer's direction is plodding and again depends largely on material that just isn't there. Maybe the public will fall for this trite, lumbering stuff but one way and another the whole affair is a disaster.

It gives Rix a dual role. He's a bombastic but heroic Air Force officer who is going to France on a secret mission which vaguely concerns a flying missile. To hoodwink the Nazis it's arranged that a double should be sent to Cairo. The double, played, of course, by Rix, is a stupid oaf who is discovered as the latrine orderly in an Air Force Camp. The two characters land on the wrong planes with obvious and not very funny results. Dialog is labored and cheap; situations are predictable. So the whole thing fizzles out.

Rix does a workmanlike job in two very different roles and clearly has a screen future as a light comedy actor even though the idiot type is now becoming slightly out-of-date. Cecil Parker is wasted as a fatuous, absent-minded high-ranking Air Force officer, and Leslie Phillips, Liz Fraser John Welsh and William Hartnell are others who struggle in vain against their material. *Rich.*

Die Ideale Frau
(The Ideal Woman)
(GERMAN-COLOR)

Berlin, Sept. 8.

Bavaria release of Utz Utermann production. Stars Ruth Leuwerik. Features Martin Benrath, Boy Gobert, Friedrich Domin. Directed by Josef von Baky. Screenplay, Walter Forster, Joachim Wedekind, Hildegard Bruecher; camera (Agfacolor), Werner Krien; music, Georg Haentzschel; settings, Fritz Maurischat. At Zoo Palast, Berlin. Running time, 107 MINS.

Fanny Becker .... Ruth Leuwerik
Axel Jung .... Martin Benrath
Jaroslav Martini .... Boy Gobert
Lawyer Becker .... Friedrich Domin
Frau Jung .... Agnes Windeck
Nickelmann .... Heinrich Gretler
Rechnitz .... Paul Hoffmann

This romantic comedy, starring Ruth Leuwerik, Germany's top femme screen personality, will hardly contribute prestige for this country's film-making. It's a moderate item of typical German escapist fare with few export possibilities. Domestically, of course, the Leuwerik name will guarantee okay returns, primarily with second-run houses.

Miss Leuwerik portrays a mayoress of a fancy German small town called Rosenburg. Mediocre fun stems from the fact that she's secretly married to a town-councillor (Martin Benrath) who reps the opposition in the town's parliament. Her ambition is to organize a music festival in Rosenburg, her hubby is against it. After a series of quarrels, the whole thing ends happily.

Director Josef von Baky's experienced hand is obvious in many scenes. But, he can't save the pic from becoming considerably dull. The plot is too thin and old-hat to create interest. Miss Leuwerik contributes the kind of charm that has made her popular with the German public. Cast includes several character actors such as Friedrich Domin, Heinrich Gretler and Paul Hoffmann who turn in their usual dependable performances.

Technical credits are average. There are some nice Agfacolor shots of the French Riviera (Monte Carlo), where the couple eventually spend their holidays. *Hans.*

Los Desarraigados
(The Uprooted)
(MEXICAN)

Venice, Sept. 8

Intercontinental SA release and production. Stars Pedro Armendariz, Ariadna Welter; features Augustin De Anda, Sonia Furio. Directed by Gilberto Gazcon. Screenplay, Raul Andra, Gazcon; camera, Rosilo Solano; editor, M. Esperon. At Venice Film Fest (shown out of competition). Running time, 110 MINS.

Film concerns a Mexican family who live in a small American town on the border. The father longs for the old country, an older son is a reformed drunkard, a younger son sells dope and the daughter tries to enter Yank society via marrying a rich American boy who only seduces her and leaves her. Problem aspects of the script are stacked and the racial theme and social aspects are played mainly for exploitation use rather than trying to get a true perspective of the difficulties of adjustment. Thus this is mainly an exploitation film for home use with offshore chances mainly for Hispano lingo spots on a hypo basis. *Mosk.*

Pet Z Milionu
(Five in a Million)
(CZECHOSLOVAKIAN)

Venice, Sept. 8.

Czech State Film release and production. With Ludek Munzar, Karla Chadimova, Valentina Thislova. Written and directed by Zbynek Brynych. Camera, J. Curikl; editor, J. Laskowski. At Venice Film Fest (shown out of competition). Running time, 110 MINS

Czech pic goes through some slice-of-life incidents concerning how a couple of workers become friends after one saves the other during an accident. Depicted are a girl's first love, a married couple's annual reprise of courtship and other sequences, scenes are too flimsy and cursory to get much insight into the characters. Thus the production lags in spite of good technical aspects and fairly interesting mounting. Foreign chances look nil. *Mosk.*

The Wonderful Country
(COLOR)

Realistic, well-made adult western with a moody theme. Robert Mitchum and Julie London for the marquee.

Hollywood, Sept. 23.

United Artists release of a D.R.M. (Robert Mitchum) Production. Stars Robert Mitchum, Julie London; co-stars Gary Merrill, Pedro Armendariz; features LeRoy "Satchel" Paige, Jack Oakie, Albert Dekker, Charles McGraw. Produced by Chester Erskine. Directed by Robert Parrish. Screenplay, Robert Ardrey, based on novel, "The Wonderful Country," by Tom Lea; camera, Floyd Crosby, Alec Philipps; editor, Michael Luciano; music, Alex North; art director, Harry Horner; sound, Del Harris; assistant director, Henry Spitz. Previewed at Goldwyn Studios, Sept. 22, 1959. Running time, **96 MINS.**

Martin Brady	Robert Mitchum
Ellen Colton	Julie London
Major Colton	Gary Merrill
Governor Castro	Pedro Armendariz
Travis Hight	Jack Oakie
Captain Rucker	Albert Dekker
General Castro	Victor Mendoza
Doc Stovall	Charles McGraw
Elder Sterner	John Banner
Tobe Sutton	LeRoy Paige
Peebles	Tom Lea
Diego Casas	Jay Novello
Pancho Gil	Mike Kellin
Ludwig Sterner	Max Slaten
Stoker	Joe Haworth
Gallup	Chuck Roberson
Rascon	Chester Hayes
Captain Verdugo	Mike Luna
Santos	Anthony Caruso
Ruelle	Claudio Brook
Entertainer at Fiesta	Judy Marsh

"The Wonderful Country" is a wonderful western. The color photography is beautiful, the casting is accurate, the writing is tasteful and realistic and the characterizations are unusual. Robert Mitchum and Julie London provide the marquee value. Yet it will take selling, because it's moody.

The film's based in Tom Lea's novel set (and filmed) in Mexico and Texas and the time is just following the Civil War. It concerns an American, portrayed by Mitchum, who has practically grown up in Mexico, whence he fled as a boy after killing his father's murderer.

Now a gunman for a Mexican overlord (portrayed by Pedro Armendariz) he re-crosses the border to buy contraband guns but is delayed in a Texas border town when he breaks his leg. More Mexican than American, he refuses information to the U.S. Army in combatting the Apaches who are protected by the overlord. But his hostile feelings against "gringos"—there's no prettifying of the conflict between Mexicans and North Americans—are melted somewhat by a friend doctor (Charles McGraw), a naive immigrant (Mac Slaten), an amiable Texas Ranger (Albert Dekker) and a hot-eyed housewife (Miss London).

In self defense, he kills a man who has brutally murdered the immigrant and flees again across the border, only to find that the rulers of his adopted country are fickle, and, after considerable intrigue, he finds himself in the run from practically every side, ironically because he refuses to kill the overlord's brother.

He also has an illicit love affair with the housewife but, since her Army officer husband (Gary Merrill) dies, they are free to make it moral—which, at fade-out, it's clear they will. It's also clear, as he kills his horse—named "Lagrimas" which means "tears"—and drops his gun, that he will cease being a gunman and will return to his native land and probable amnesty.

What makes this story live is the honest dialog and characterization. For example, Mitchum's hero-gunman is consistently a mere hireling who feels quite comfortable, hat in hand, addressing the Mexican satrap as "patron." His English even shows traces of a Latin accent and he's as hygienically unsound as any other low-caste Mexican in the film.

Miss London succeeds in being immensely appealing without having a single really sexy scene and Merrill does very well as the husband she respects but does not love.

Cameo characterizations are limned by LeRoy "Satchel" Paige, who portrays a Negro sergeant heading a platoon of Negro U.S. Army soldiers; Jack Oakie, an irrepressibly cheerful railroad promoter; and others previously mentioned, such as the immigrant and his uncle (Max Slaten) who is a naturalized American working for the Mexicans.

Robert Ardrey's screenplay packs a lot of action and drama into 96 minutes, abetted by highly imaginative direction by Robert Parrish and superb Technicolor photography by Floyd Crosby and Alec Philipps. Alex North has provided an exciting musical score which heightens the impact of many scenes which are already powerful. Use of scenes at an actual Mexican fiesta are edited in with a deft hand to great effect.

The picture's a credit to the taste of producer Chester Erskine and of Robert Mitchum, for whose D.R.M. banner it was filmed. It compellingly conveys a sense of the period and the country. The fear here, however, is that the sadness—even wretchedness—of the main characters and the melancholy mood that pervades the film will not please the public. It'll probably be wise to sell the film on the sex, the Apaches and the brutal violence, which are really incidental in this earnestly made film. *Glen.*

Operation Petticoat
(COLOR)

Good Cary Grant-Tony Curtis service farce shapes as top b.o.

Hollywood, Sept. 25.

Universal release of Granart Production. Stars Cary Grant and Tony Curtis; features Arthur O'Connell, Joan O'Brien, Dina Merrill, Gene Evans and Dick Sargent. Produced by Robert Arthur. Directed by Blake Edwards. Screenplay, Stanley Shapiro and Maurice Richlin; suggested by a story by Paul King and Joseph Stone; camera, (Eastman Color) Russell Harlan; music, David Rose; editors, Ted J. Kent and Frank Gross. Previewed at the Westwood Village Theatre, Sept. 22, '59. Running time, **124 MINS.**

Sherman	Cary Grant
Holden	Tony Curtis
Dolores	Joan O'Brien
Barbara	Dina Merrill
Molumphrey	Gene Evans
Tostin	Arthur O'Connell
Stovall	Richard Sargent
Major Edna Hayward	Virginia Gregg
Henderson	Robert F. Simon
Watson	Robert Gist
Hunkle	Gavin MacLeod
The Prophet	George Dunn
Harmon	Dick Crockett
Lt. Claire Reid	Madlyn Rhue
Lt. Ruth Colfax	Marion Ross
Ramon	Clarence E. Lung
Dooley	Frankie Darro
Fox	Tony Pastor Jr.
Reiner	Robert Hoy
Kraus	Nicky Blair
Williams	John W. Morley

Already set as the Radio City Music Hall's Christmas attraction, Universal's "Operation Petticoat" is a slick holiday attraction that will attract top boxoffice. It has no more weight than a sackful of feathers, but it has a lot of laughs and the kind of situations that create good word-of-mouth. The stars, Cary Grant and Tony Curtis, are excellent. Produced by Robert Arthur, the film has been directed by Blake Edwards with a slam-bang pace.

Comedies about the armed services, especially when the setting is wartime, ask a certain suspension of reality. "Operation Petticoat" demands total suspension. The time is December, 1941, and the locale is the Philippines. For anyone old enough to remember what was going on there just 18 years ago, it is not the ideal setting for tricks and jokes. It might have been better to use fictitious place names, as Tom Heggen did in "Mr. Roberts."

Accepting this convention, however, that there can be comedy in chaos, Stanley Shapiro and Maurice Richlin (who wrote "Pillow Talk") have taken a story by Paul King and Joseph Stone and made a bright, diverting script of it. This team is equally good at a comedy line or a gag situation.

Cary Grant is the commander of a wheezy old submarine which he gets underway and operational through his conniving junior officer, Tony Curtis. In a series of improbable but acceptable situations, the sub takes on as passengers five army nurses, a couple Filipino families (including expectant mothers) and a goat. Some of the situations are predictable, such as those arising when chesty nurses meet seamen in a sub's narrow corridors. But Edwards' direction is light-handed and what risque material there is gets tasteful handling.

For some reason, "Operation Petticoat" is shot with an opening and closing flashback. The comedy runs more than two hours and could be cut. These scenes don't mean much, although otherwise the film is rich in humorous device and most of it plays well.

Cary Grant is a living lesson in getting laughs without lines. In this film, most of the gags play off him. It is his reaction, blank, startled, etc., always underplayed, that creates or releases the humor. Tony Curtis is a splendid foil, one of the two or three best young comedians around, and his different style of playing meshes easily with Grant's. Arthur O'Connell gives a solid performance and others who score include Joan O'Brien, Dina Merrill, Gene Evans and Dick Sargent.

David Rose's score is especially bright, helping the comedy without getting coy. Russell Harlan's Eastman color photography is top-drawer and other technical credits are fine. *Powe.*

Girls Town

Crude and vulgar exploitation item. Appeal to some boxoffice elements.

Hollywood, Sept. 25.

Metro release of Albert Zugsmith production. Features Mamie Van Doren, Mel Torme, Paul Anka, Ray Anthony. Directed by Charles Haas. Screenplay, Robert Smith; from a story by Robert Hardy Andrews; camera, John L. Russell; music, Van Alexander; editor, Leon Barsha. Previewed at the Academy Awards Theatre, Sept. 23, '59. Running time, **92 MINS.**

Silver Morgan	Mamie Van Doren
Fred Alger	Mel Torme
Jimmy Parlow	Paul Anka
Dick Culdane	Ray Anthony
Mother Veronica	Maggie Hayes
Singer	Cathy Crosby
Serafina Garcia	Gigi Perreau
Mary Lee Morgan	Elinor Donahue
Vida	Gloria Talbott
Sister Grace	Sheilah Graham
Charley Boy	Jim Mitchum
Stan Joyce	Dick Contino
Chip Gardner	Harold Lloyd Jr.
Joe Cates	Charles Chaplin Jr.
Themselves	The Platters
Flo	Peggy Moffitt
Gloria Barker	Jody Fair
Michael Clyde	Peter Leeds
Carhop	Nan Peterson
"Skin"	Grabowski

This Albert Zugsmith production is blatantly crude and vulgar. There is a patina of fake piety spread over some of the proceedings by putting part of the action at an institution run by Catholic nuns. Notwithstanding, or because it is likely to be offensive to Catholics. Yet there's always been a market of sorts for this type of film, so presumably there's one for "Girls Town."

The screenplay of the film is as flimsy as a G-string, and designed for somewhat the same purpose. It includes all the staples of the exploitation film, a drag race, a necking party, the flip and shallow conversation of a segment of youth, the slight and unconvincing nod to conventional morality at the ending.

According to the film, Mamie Van Doren is unjustly accused of the accidental death of a young man. She is sent to a "Girls Town" operated by Catholic nuns for rehabilitation. Although rehabilitation is said to be the purpose of the home, the inmates apparently control the institution on an underground basis with strong-armed sadism. There is no evidence of any program being followed that could conceivably lead to rehabilitation. On the contrary, as an example of "improvement" there is the character portrayed by Gigi Perreau. Although obviously the victim of a serious mental aberration, Miss Perreau's problems are said to be solved by making her a novice of the order of nuns who run the home. This solution would be incredible to anyone at all familiar with religious orders of any faith.

There are other disturbing scenes or approaches to scenes. The party scene which opens the film, for instance, is clearly intended to be as stimulating carnally as is possible. Scenes of Miss Van Doren in the tightest of costumes exchanging badinage with nuns are in dubious taste, to say the least. At a time when Hollywood is facing a rising storm of opposition about films with adult themes and adult treatment, it cannot help but be ammunition for the opposition. In the case of "Girls Town," there is not a mitigating ounce of artistry or the pretense of it.

The large cast has been chosen chiefly for its exploitation value. There are numerous names, Mel Torme, Paul Anka, Ray Anthony, Sheilah Graham, Jim Mitchum, Harold Lloyd Jr., Dick Contino, Cathy Crosby, Charles Chaplin Jr., that provide hooks for audience awareness and potential patronage. The cast, including Miss Van Doren, Maggie Hayes, Miss Perreau, Elinor Donahue, Gloria Talbott and Peggy Moffitt, is competent. Technical credits are adequate. Ars gratia artis. *Powe.*

Career

James Lee off-Broadway play has names and an interesting, albeit humorless, scenario. Dean Martin, Anthony Franciosa, Shirley MacLaine and Carolyn Jones do man-sized jobs. Show business exploitation angles could help it.

Paramount release of Hal Wallis production. Stars Dean Martin, Anthony Franciosa, Shirley MacLaine, Carolyn Jones; features Joan Blackman, Robert Middleton, Donna Douglas. Directed by Joseph Anthony. Screenplay, James Lee, from his off-Broadway play; camera, Joseph La Shelle; editor, Warren Low. Tradeshown in N. Y., Sept. 20, '59. Running time, 105 MINS.

Maury Novak	Dean Martin
Sam Lawson	Anthony Franciosa
Sharon Kensington	Shirley MacLaine
Shirley Drake	Carolyn Jones
Barbara	Joan Blackman
Robert Kensington	Robert Middleton
Marjorie Burke	Donna Douglas

In these days of epic-sized productions, Hal Wallis offers a feature so limited in production scope as to suggest the possibility that he was out to save money the hard way—that is, stinting on the pictorial values. But a closer look is reassuring, for it genuinely appears that the producer, in placing on the screen James Lee's off-Broadway play of the same name, and director Joseph Anthony were bent on preserving the intimacy of the original.

It's a show business story done in honest-to-goodness fashion. It centers on the ambition-driven but nonetheless agreeable aspiring actor, and the X-ray on this individual is no strain on logic. Whether he's maladjusted husband or insignificant waiter he's where he is because, in his free time, he's out to become a star and his other roles in life are unimportant.

With Anthony Franciosa in this pivotal role, and with Dean Martin, Shirley MacLaine and Carolyn Jones in the other major parts, Wallis, Anthony and Lee have put together an interesting picture that has salability, granting a flaw or two along the unspooling.

It's a serious theme, to be sure, but somewhere there must have been opportunity to get a little lighthearted. If such opportunities arose, either Lee or Anthony refrained from availing. Be that as it may, the Martin-Franciosa-Mac-Laine-Jones combo of marquee stuff, plus the frank and gimmickless handling of usually a good comeon story situation, rooted in the show world scheme of things, ought to provide a respectable payoff. The picture lends itself to the kind of sell that will be required.

A couple of Lee's story angles hardly seem to fit in, and this is no help in the secondary last-half that follows the attention-getting earlier episodes. Franciosa's call to the Korean war, with a brief glimpse of same, is not correctly integrated. Neither is the exposure of Martin, as a smalltime director on the way up, as a onetime Communist because, as he puts it, "I was ambitious." These bits seem to come from left, no pun, field and are disconcerting.

Otherwise, Franciosa and Martin, however sombre their parts, perform convincingly. Miss MacLaine as a producer's free-wheeling daughter has some misfitting dialog and story situations to cope with but gets across all right and Miss Jones, playing it straight as an agent, draws for herself a pleasant switch from her zany stint in the recent "Hole in the Head."

Joan Blackman, Robert Middleton and Donna Douglas are substantial citizens in second-billing parts.

Editing, music and other technical credits all good, with a particular nod to Joseph La Shelle's camera job that gets considerable movement from closeup scenes.

This is not one of Wallis' outstanding productions but, in its offbeat way, it could make good progress at the old meaningful b.o.
Gene.

Felicidad
(Happiness)
(MEXICAN—COLOR)

Mexico City, Sept. 15.
Peliculas Nacionales release of a Cinematografica Nacional, S.A. production. Stars Gloria Lozano and Carlos Lopez Moctezuma; features Fanny Schiller, Armando Saenz and Elsa Cardenas. Directed by Alfonso Corona Blake. Screenplay, Emilio Carballido; camera, Rosalio Solano; music, Raul Lavista. At Real Cinema, Mexico City. Running time, 90 MINS.

After being held up for more than a year this picture, which denounces errors in Mexican bureaucracy, finally premiered last week. Produced by actress Gloria Lozano, it attacks red tape and innefficiency in the Treasury Department. Opening of the film was delayed by the former head of the treasury in the past administration.

Picture, which also treats of difficulties of treasury employees to obtain their salaries, is shown without any cuts. Background for the film criticism of bureaucracy is a love story between Miss Lozano and Carlos Lopez Moctezuma, both playing roles of government employees having a tough time to make ends meet.

Moctezuma turns in his usual efficient performance. Miss Lozano gives a warm portrayal of a federal worker harrassed by her job and official incompetence. Director Alfonso Blake has used restraint in developing the main theme, and work is on par with his "The Road of Life" and "The Marble Tower," both of which concerned social problems.

Current administration, incidentally, has not impeded the film's exhibition. When first announced for showing, politicos tried to get higher-ups to ban it but the Film Bureau turned a deaf ear and granted a permit. This gave the film industry hope that greater leeway in production of social themes may now be in store.
Emil.

Inside the Mafia

Based on headlines of Sicilian crime brotherhood. Exploitable yarn for program market.

Hollywood, Sept. 24
United Artists release of Robert E. Kent production. Stars Cameron Mitchell; costars Robert Strauss, Grant Richards, Jim L. Brown, Elaine Edwards. Directed by Edward L. Cahn. Screenplay, Orville H. Hampton; camera, Maury Gertsman; editor, Grant Whytock. Previewed Sept. 10, '59. Running time, 75 MINS.

Tony Ledo	Cameron Mitchell
Anne Balcom	Elaine Edwards
Sam Galey	Robert Strauss
Doug Blair	Jim L. Brown
Augie Martello	Ted De Corsia
Johnny Lucero	Grant Richards
Chink Dayton	Richard Karlen
Julie Otranto	Frank Gerstle
Beery	Sid Clute
Rod Balcom	Louis Jean Heydt
Raycheck	Steve Roberts
Molina	Hal Torey
Dave Alto	Carl Milletaire
Sandy Balcom	Carol Nugent
Dan Regent	Edward Platt
Buzz	Michael Monroe
Joe, The Barber	Jack Daley
Corino	Jim Bannon
Morgan	Raymond Guth
Kronis	Anthony Carbone
Vince DeMao	Jack Kenney
Marty Raven	House Peters Jr.
Dyer	Sheldon Allman
Bob Kalen	Tony Warde
Manicurist	Donna Dale
Police Sergeant	John Hart

Familiar plot device of a household being terrorized and held captive by gangsters is drawn on for a Mafia caper in this exploitation entry which probably will be ballyed for fair returns in program market. Twist is sufficiently novel and topical to provide okay action fare, particularly in light of the Sicilian crime syndicate's present headline status.

Certain actual events spark Orville H. Hampton's story unfoldment, teeing off with the murder several years ago of kingpin Albert Anastasia in a Gotham barber's chair. From this, Hampton proceeds to the now-famous meeting of Mafia toppers from all sections of the country in a luxurious mountain lodge at Apalachin, N. Y., referred to in film as Apple Lake. Narrative is built then upon a fight for control of the syndicate. Film is not sparing in brutality and killings, and may meet with certain censor resistance.

Most of the movement unravels at a small emergency air field near the lodge in upper New York State, where the mobsters await arrival of the Mafia chief who was deported 10 years previously and now is due to make a secret visit to this country to solve the complex problems of the ring. Cameron Mitchell, chief aide to a Mafia topper who was gunned down—but not killed —for attempts to take over the syndicate, is also awaiting the chief's arrival, but for another purpose. His plan calls for him to kill the returning gangster as he descends from his plane, thus paving the way for his own chief to make another effort to seize control. He meets with unexpected interference from the airport manager and his two daughters, and is forced to hold them, along with several others, in their house at the field.

Edward L. Cahn gets good performances from his cast via sharp direction and Grant Whytock's sharp editing makes for fast pace. Mitchell is hard-hitting in his characterization, and has the benefit of Robert Strauss and Richard Karlen to back him in killer roles as they wait for Grant Richards, quietly proficient as the returning Mafia chief. Louis Jean Heydt as airport manager, Elaine Edwards and Carol Nugent in daughter roles, Ted De Corsia as the gunned gangster and Edward Platt as another Mafia member stand out.

Maury Gertsman's camera work and Bill Glasgow's art direction are further technical assists. *Whit.*

Miss Cuple
(SPANISH—COLOR)

Madrid, Sept. 20.
Chamartin release of a P.E.F.S.A. production. Stars Mary Santpere; co-stars Carlos Miguel Sola, Maria Mahor, Maria Ladron de Guevara and Marta Flores. Directed by Pedro Lazaga; screenplay by Arozamena and Mas Guindal; cameraman (Agfacolor), Federico Larraya; music, Augusto Alguero. At Cine Capitol, Madrid. Running time, 93 MINS.

"Miss Cuple" is a tortured story of an out-sized, ugly lass whose ludicrous stage-struck effort to sing turn-of-the-century tunes straight broadens into a routine of clownish caricature audiences love. Comedy evaporates when she falls for her girl friend's beau and from there in, it becomes an uncomfortable "laugh, clown, laugh" situation.

Seasoned comedienne Mary Santpere is only as good as her material which limits her to some effective mimicry but just barely reveals the untapped talent this Spanish Fanny Brice possesses. Her personal appearance turn onstage for first-nighters was much more successful. *Werb.*

Odds Against Tomorrow

Sometimes crude, violent crime suspense melodrama. Good names, good pic, good b.o.

Hollywood, Oct. 2.

United Artists release of Harbel production. Stars Harry Belafonte, Robert Ryan, Shelley Winters; features Ed Begley, Gloria Grahame. Produced and directed by Robert Wise. Associate producer, Phil Stein; screenplay, John O. Killens; based on a book by William P. McGivern; camera, Joseph Brun; music, John Lewis; editor, DeDe Allen. Previewed at the Fox Wilshire Theatre, Sept. 25, '59. Running time, **96 MINS.**

Ingram	Harry Belafonte
Slater	Robert Ryan
Lorry	Shelley Winters
Burke	Ed Begley
Helen	Gloria Grahame
Bacco	Will Kuluva
Coco	Richard Bright
Moriarity	Lou Gallo
Cannoy	Fred J. Scollay
Kitty	Carmen DeLavalade
Annie	Mae Barnes
Ruth	Kim Hamilton
Eadie	Lois Thorne
Soldier	Wayne Rogers
Girl	Zehra Lampert
Bartender	William Zuckert
George	Burtt Harris
Policeman	Clint Young
Hotel Clerk	Ed Preble
Operator	Mil Stewart
Fan With Dog	Ronnie Stewart
Ambulance Attendant	Marc May
Garry	Paul Hoffman
Fra	Cicely Tyson
Captain of Waiters	Lou Martini
Guard	Robert Jones
Solly	Floyd Ennis
Bank Guard	William Adams
Bank Manager	Fred Herrick
Bank Secretary	Mary Boylan
Clerk	John Garden
Police Chief	Allen Nourse

On one level, "Odds Against Tomorrow" is a taut crime melodrama. On another, it is an allegory about racism, greed and man's propensity for self-destruction. Not altogether successful in the second category, it still succeeds on its first. Produced and directed by Robert Wise with an alert eye and ear to sooty realism, the United Artists release is an absorbing, disquieting film that should draw good response.

The point of John O. Killens' screenplay, based on a novel of the same name by William P. McGivern, is that the odds against tomorrow coming at all are very long unless there is some understanding and tolerance today. The point is made by means of a crime anecdote, a framework not completely satisfactory for cleanest impact.

Harry Belafonte, Robert Ryan and Ed Begley are the principals of the narrative. They form a partnership with plans to rob a bank with a haul estimated to total $150,000. For each the sum represents what it will take to get him out of hock and into security. An ill-matched trio, their optimistic plans are dependent on the closest teamwork.

Belafonte, a horse-playing night club entertainer, is something of an adolescent. His addiction to pleasure and the ponies wrecked his personal life and threatens to end it. His mobster creditor has warned him that unless he pays off, his family faces injury or death. Ryan is a psychotic. His hatred of the world smoulders barely controlled. Tension and responsibility erode this control. He actually hates all men, but his festering malignancy is focussed against Negroes. Begley, an ex-cop fired for crookedness, has learned from this experience only not to get caught.

Killens' screenplay is violent, rather crude and often blunt in dealing with crime and sex. One of the henchmen of the mobster harrying Belafonte is an obvious homosexual. The script uses the word "ofay," a derogatory Negro term for whites seldom heard in films. Ryan's relationship with his girl friend. Shelley Winters, is explicitly discussed. But none of these bolder elements is used simply for shock or sensation. On the other hand, the home life of Belafonte's estranged wife is a unique view (for films) of a normal, middle-class Negro home — with an integrated Parent-Teachers Assn. meeting going on.

The trouble with the allegory is that it does not always sustain. The bank job is a bloody fiasco, torpedoed by Ryan's volatile temperament. All three men are killed because Ryan won't trust Belafonte, a Negro. The final shot is somewhat too pat. Both Ryan and Belafonte are burned to death. An ambulance attendant notes it is impossible to tell which is which. In death the Negro and the white man are indistinguishable.

Most of the parts of "Odds Against Tomorrow" are acceptable on both levels. It is the key episode, the bank holdup job, which is hard to equate with a general life situation. Otherwise, the suspicion, the anxiety, the fears, all point up the fact that a single captious action can destroy everyone. All these elements fuse. It is only the choice of the dramatic mechanism that creates confusion and dilutes the implications.

Wise has drawn fine performances from his players. It is the most sustained acting Belafonte has done. Ryan makes the flesh crawl as the fanatical bigot. Begley turns in a superb study of a foolish, befuddled man who dies, as he has lived, without knowing quite what he has been involved in. Shelley Winters etches a memorable portrait, and Gloria Grahame is poignant in a brief appearance. Others who contribute to the excitement include Will Kuluva, Richard Bright, Lou Gallo, Mae Barnes, Carmen DeLavallade, Wayne Rogers and Mil Stewart. Almost the entire cast, it should be noted, was recruited in New York, and a remarkable cast it is.

Joseph Brun's black and white photography catches the grim spirit of the story and accents it with some glinting mood shots. John Lewis' music backs it with a neurotic, edgy, progressive jazz score. *Powe.*

Counterplot

Meller set in Puerto Rico; okay as filler.

United Artists release of Kurt Neumann production. Stars Forrest Tucker, Allison Hayes, Gerald Milton; features Jackie Wayne, Miguel Angel Alvarez, Edmundo Rivers Alvarez, Charles Gibbs. Directed by Neumann. Screenplay, Richard Blake. Tradeshown in N.Y., Oct. 2, '59. Running time, **76 MINS.**

Brock	Forrest Tucker
Connie	Allison Hayes
Bergmann	Gerald Milton
Alfred	Edmundo Rivera Alvarez
Manuel	Jackie Wayne
Spargo	Miguel Angel Alvarez
Girl	Rita Tanno
McGregor	Charles Gibbs
Murdock	Richard Vernie
Dugan	Art Bedard
Nibley	Ulises Brenes
Police Chief	Guardo Albani
Messenger	Raul Davila
Bartender	Eed Smith
Maid	Yvonne Peck

There are some fair-enough story angles to be considered in this meller about a robust, handsome Yank on the lam for a murder rap in the States who finds refuge in Puerto Rico in the company of a native boy who knew him when they both went fishing in earlier and happier days. Unfortunately some of the plot potential is dissipated by mediocre performances.

"Counterplot" is billed as an A. J. Harold Odell Production, produced and directed by Kurt Neumann. Their entry, as scripted by Richard Blake, shapes as a mild meller that's fitting for a modest market groove. That is, the lower half for the dual billers.

Name values obviously are limited. Forrest Tucker is the American in trouble—until he convinces himself that the man he slugged in New York actually was murdered by the victim's business partner. The job thereupon is to expose the real criminal.

All sorts of slippery and heavy characters participate in the proceedings, and as things turn out the nefarious ones get their proper comeuppance and Tucker gets himself cleared.

For the romance angle there's Allison Hayes, who stays by Tucker despite his predicament. The youngster of the island is Jackie Wayne (who does an effective job), and the principal heavies are Gerald Milton, Miguel Angel Alvarez and Richard Vernie. Charles Gibbs is the agent for an insurance company which issued an important policy on the murdered man.

Camera work, music and other technical credits are acceptable. *Gene.*

Nacida Para Amar
(Born To Love)
(MEXICAN; COLOR)

Mexico City, Sept. 29.

Peliculas Nacionales release of Clasa Films Munciales, S.A. release. Stars Ana Luisa Peluffo and Wolf Rubinskys; features Cuco Sanches, Raul Meraz, Aldo Monti. Amparo Arozamena and Abel Salazar. Directed by Rogelio A. Gonzalez Jr. At Metropolitan Theatre, Mexico City. Running time, **90 MINS.**

While Clasa has exploited the angle as to the identity of the real life counterpart of this story of a top Mexican entertainer of the '20s, with names of Lupe Velez, Maria Condesa, Maria Tubau and Celia Montalvan widely advertised, the yarn about the rise and fall of a star isn't based on fact.

Film develops the "darling" of the public from the heights. Ana Luisa Peluffo, in the star role, once again proves she is capable of more than just displaying her charms in the raw before the cameras. Based on her performances in recent films, it's evident that she is being groomed to become one of Mexico's top female film personalities.

Story is developed via flashback technique, and director Rogelio Gonzalez Jr. has presented this fictitious biography of a boxoffice personality with realism. A number of songs by Agustin Lara give a picture of development of popular and sentimental music from the '20s to the present. *Emil.*

A Summer Place
(COLOR)

Slick, frank filmization of Sloan Wilson's bestseller about troubled teenagers, and their equally troubled parents. Spotty as drama but augurs b.o.

Warner Bros. release of Delmer Daves production. Stars Richard Egan, Dorothy McGuire, Sandra Dee, Arthur Kennedy, Troy Donahue; features Constance Ford, Beulah Bondi, Jack Richardson, Martin Eric. Directed by Daves. Screenplay by Daves, from Sloan Wilson novel; camera (Technicolor), Harry Stradling; music, Max Steiner; editor, Owen Marks. Previewed at the RKO 58th St. Theatre, N.Y., Sept. 16, '59. Running time, **130 MINS.**

Ken Jorgenson	Richard Egan
Sylvia Hunter	Dorothy McGuire
Molly Jorgenson	Sandra Dee
Bart Hunter	Arthur Kennedy
Johnny Hunter	Troy Donahue
Helen Jorgenson	Constance Ford
Mrs. Hamble	Beulah Bondi
Claude Andrews	Jack Richardson
Todd Hasper	Martin Eric

There is going to be a good deal of discussion about this screen adaptation of "A Summer Place." It's one of those big, emotional, slickly-produced pictures that bite off a great deal more than they can chew and neatly dispose of their intense, highly-dramatic melange by dropping their characters into slots clearly marked "good" and "bad."

Thrown in for good measure is a provocative story in which there's some tragic happening every few minutes and some equally provocative dialog. What results is an uneven, superficial film that has all the trappings of soap opera imposed on what essentially is an adult, serious theme.

As a commercial property with highly exploitable angles and a kind of blunt force with shock value, "A Summer Place" shapes as a major boxoffice contender. There's no question that, with all its platitudes, passionate romance and corny situations, it offers the kind of identification that general audiences seek and appreciate.

In his capacity as writer and director, Delmer Daves has missed the mark by a mile. His characters, anguished most of the time, are unreal and totally devoid of depth. The film runs at least 20 minutes too long and has a tendency to use dialog to "preach" what should be implied, to be harsh where it should be sensitive, and it makes the most of Hollywood's newly-discovered freedom to display the voluminous vocabulary of sex. There'd be nothing wrong with this had Daves coupled his frankness with taste and had he made his play for emotion less obvious.

With the single exception of Dorothy McGuire, who comes through with a radiant performance and is lovely to look at, the cast does an average job. Richard Egan is wooden. Young Sandra Dee has a conventionally pretty face, but it's only in one scene (when she becomes hysterical) that the director gets her to emote. Troy Donahue is handsome, but little more. Arthur Kennedy is good as a combination snob and drunk, but he fights some pretty tough lines. Constance Ford really isn't given much more than a chance to look nasty as the opportunistic, narrow-minded bigot, and Beulah Bondi is effective in a small role.

The script, with its curious inability to get inside of the people in the story, sticks fairly closely to the book. It's all there—the loveless marriages, the teenage romance, the luckless affair which ends in a double divorce and a remarriage troubled by hostility and guilt feelings. A couple of years ago, "A Summer Place" wouldn't have been made. Today, with the relaxed Code, the punishments for "sin" have become subtler, but subtlety obviously isn't Daves' forte.

Millionaire Egan, his wife (Miss Ford) and daughter (Miss Dee) arrive on a small island off the New England coast where, 20 years ago, Egan was a lifeguard and had an affair with Miss McGuire, who subsequently married Arthur Kennedy, the impoverished owner of a summer mansion. Egan has an affair with Miss McGuire, which is

discovered, and divorces result. Meanwhile, Miss Dee and Kennedy's son (Donahue) have fallen in love but are broken up by Miss Dee's mother who, at one point, has a doctor examine the girl when she and Donahue are stranded and spend the night on the beach.

Egan and Miss McGuire marry, and while spending a weekend at their parents' home, Miss Dee and Donahue resume and Miss Dee becomes pregnant. After futile attempts to get married, they finally confess and, with the blessings of Egan and Miss McGuire, they tie the knot. There's a good deal of sermonizing and weepy sentiment in the film, which certainly appears pitched primarily to the women's audience, though the love-sex angle won't drive the males away.

Film is attractively mounted, expertly photographed by Harry Stradling and the Technicolor hues aid, at least when it comes to the scenic shots. Max Steiner's music is lush, as befits this kind of popular fiction, and Owen Marks' editing is smooth. The picture could easily be tightened up by judicious cutting, particularly when it comes to some of those lengthy dialog scenes. The sets are handsome. While "A Summer Place" doesn't rate as a major achievement, it may well make up for that by turning into a major moneymaker. It's a shame that it couldn't have been both. *Hift.*

Venta De Vargas
(Vargas Inn)
(SPANISH-COLOR)

Madrid, Sept. 15.

Filmax release of a Pecsa Films-Jose Carreras Planas production. Stars Lola Flores, Ruben Rojo; co-stars Maria Navarro, Antonio Gonzalez, Antonio Almoros, Jesus Tordesillas, Felix Defauce, Carmen Flores. Directed by Enrique Cahen Salaberry. Screenplay, Luis Lucas, Jose Gallardo, A. de Foxa; camera (Eastmancolor), Mario Pacheco; music, Guillermo Cases; songs, Leon y Quiroga, Tellerias, A. de Foxa. At Roxy "A," Madrid. Running time, 92 MINS.

In his literary work, "National Episodes," Perez Galdos left endless volumes of exciting historical drama relating to Spain's War of Independence against Napoleon. But while Galdos gathers dust, "Venta de Vargas" comes along to increase the cycle of shoddy musical melodramas cloaked in this historical context.

Lola Flores is more than a match for "Jacobin" French armies. She outwits them at every turn — guiding the courier (her husband, guitarist Antonio Gonzalez) through enemy lines and saving the Spanish general for his big victory. She does it all without missing a tune in her cabaret repertoire.

Audience never sees the battle, getting a word-of-mouth account from the two contesting generals. Economy of time and money is lavished on Miss Flores, whose dynamic impact seems to diminish with age. Director Enrique Salaberry tries, but the script impedes him. Other credits and color are fair. *Werb.*

Un Hecho Violento
(Violent Fate)
(SPANISH)

Madrid, Sept. 29.

Hispano Foxfilm release of a Nervion Films production. Stars Richard Morse, Adolfo Marsillach, Mabel Karr; co-stars Rafael Luis Calvo, Carlos Mendy, Anastasio Aleman. Directed by Jose Maria Forque. Screenplay, Paul Burton-Mercur, adapted by Alfonso Sastre and Jose Maria Forque; camera, Antonio Ballesteros; music, Miguel Arbo. At Palacio de la Prensa, Madrid. Running time, 96 MINS.

Brutality and chain-gang violence border on sadism in this Spanish-made adaptation of an American screenplay based on an alleged true-to-life incident in Florida. Miscarriage of justice sends an innocent youth to the rock-pile and to torture at the hands of a cruelly demented warden. In the original circumstance, boy's death aroused the national conscience. Writers save him at the point of death.

Young New York stage and tv actor Richard Morse performs creditably as the guiltless victim in his first role. So does Adolfo Marsillach as the warden. Director Jose Maria Forque, however, weakens their efforts in attempting clinically to reach a hairline point where physical torture can destroy human defiance. Prison break and manhunt sequences are nevertheless well staged.

Story is too dated to have much appeal for the U.S. market. Lensing is good and technical credits okay. *Werb.*

12 Maedchen und 1 Mann
(12 Girls and One Man)
(AUSTRIAN-MUSIC-COLOR)

Vienna, Sept. 29.

Sascha Film Co. release (world distribution through UFA). Stars Toni Sailer; features Margit Nuenke, Gunther Philipp, Joe Stoeckl. Directed by Hans Quest. Screenplay, Kurt Nachmann, Helmut Andics, based on Wolfgang Ebert's comedy, "The Gangsters of Valence;" camera, Hannes Staudinger; music, Franz Grothe; editor, Dr. Herbert Gruber. Tradeshown Kosmos Kino, Vienna, Sept. 15, '59. Running time, 92 MINS.

Set in the Tyrolean Alps, this is a comedy that may have some possibilities in the international market. The Kurt Nachmann-Helmut Andics screenplay concerns 12 comely girls on a ski tour who meet Olympic champ Toni Sailer.

Sailer, cast as a police inspector, captures a smuggling ring and a bride as well. Comic relief is ably supplied by Ernst Waldbrunn as a police chief. Scenery has been expertly lensed by Hannes Staudinger's color camera. Direction of Hans Quest is good as are Franz Grothe's musical numbers. *Maas.*

4D Man
(COLOR)

Fair Pennsylvania-shot science-fantasy exploitationer. Moderate response for this market.

Hollywood, Oct. 2.

Universal release of Fairview production. Features Robert Lansing, Lee Meriweather, James Congdon, Robert Strauss, Edgar Stehli. Produced by Jack H. Harris. Co-produced and directed by Irvin Shortess Yeaworth Jr. Screenplay, Theodore Simonson and Cy Chermak; based on an idea by Jack H. Harris; camera (De Luxe Color), Theodore J. Pahle; music, Ralph Carmichael; editor, William B. Murphy. Previewed at the studio, Oct. 1, '59. Running time, 85 MINS.

Scott Nelson .... Robert Lansing
Linda Davis .... Lee Meriweather
Tony Nelson .... James Congdon
Roy Parker .... Robert Strauss
Carson .... Edgar Stehli

Whether there remains much of a market for the science fiction-fantasy exploitation film is debatable. Assuming there is, this Universal release should do moderately well. It is not offensively gruesome and has a fairly interesting gimmick. Produced as an independent production by Jack H. Harris, and shot at his Valley Forge, (Pa.) studios, Universal has bought U.S. and Canadian distribution rights.

The screenplay by Theodore Simonson and Cy Chermak is concerned with a research scientist who discovers a secret for penetrating solid matter. The scientist gets the power to do this by using some kind of electric motor to soup up his brainwaves. The effort, however, uses up his "life force." To replenish his "life force," and keep from aging prematurely, he has to draw "life force" from others. This works fine for him but kills the others.

This general theme has been the focus of several other films, but the mechanical aspects of it are given some novelty in Harris' production and occasionally achieves genuine excitement. The acting, under Irvin S. Yeaworth's direction, tends to be over-wrought, and the editing is not always consistent. Color of the DeLuxe print shown for review was very blue, and this was partly the fault of the lighting and partly that of the art director who had an unusual number of settings with that dead, dark color for background. The outdoor shots were very nice.

Cast is mostly made up of New York actors, interesting for their freshness, at any rate. The principals are Robert Lansing, Lee Mertweather, James Congdon, Robert Strauss and the radio veteran, Edgar Stehli.

Ralph Carmichael's musical score is capable, although the jazz background for films of any and all types is getting to be somewhat overdone. *Powe.*

Carmen La De Ronda
(Carmen of Granada)
(SPANISH-COLOR)

Madrid, Sept. 29.

Filmayer release of a Benito Perojo production. Stars Sarita Montiel, Jorge Mistral and Maurice Ronet; special appearance of Amadeo Nazzari; co-stars German Cobos and Maria Angeles Hortelano; features Jose Marco Davo, Felix Fernandez and Santiago Rivero. Directed by Tulio Demicheli. Screenplay by Arozamena, Mas Guindal and Tulio Demicheli; cameraman (Eastmancolor), Antonio Ballesteros; art director, Enrique Alarcon; music, Gregorio Segura. At Torre de Madrid Cine. Running time, 98 MINS.

After reigning as Spanish marquee queen for several years on the strength of tunes and times in the musical biog "El Ultimo Cuple" and the potboiler musical "La Violetera," Sarita Montiel returns as "Carmen" in an impact switch to melodic folklore.

Only tenuously related to the Prosper Merimee original, this costume musical takes place in Andalucia's picturesque clifftop pueblo of Ronda during Spain's historic resistance to the Napoleonic invasion. Actually, it's a war within a war as principals Jorge Mistral, Amadeo Nazzari, German Cobos and Maurice Ronet struggle violently for the open-bosomed cabaret belle breaking house records at the Inn of the Moor.

After rigging the libretto to expose La Montiel's carnal combustion and thrushing in every sequence, producer Benito Perojo surrounds his popular star with rugged hombres, gives her carefully-chosen vintage gypsy tunes immortalized a decade ago by Imperio Argentina, and provides beautifully-lensed Ronda backgrounds, bright costuming and lots of musketry.

In short, a savvy aggregate of elements for its destined Spanish-language market, where it should pull a great gate. *Werb.*

The Last Angry Man

Heart-warming, strong drama with Paul Muni. An answer to sadistic trend. Good b.o. though may open slow.

Hollywood, Oct. 9.

Columbia release of Fred Kohlmar production. Stars Paul Muni and David Wayne; features Betsy Palmer, Luther Adler, Claudia McNeil, Joby Baker. Directed by Daniel Mann; screenplay, Gerald Green, from his own novel; adaptation, Richard Murphy; camera, James Wong Howe; music, George Duning; editor, Charles Nelson. Previewed at the studio, Oct. 1, '59. Running time, 100 MINS.

Dr. Sam Abelman .... Paul Muni
Woodrow Wilson Thrasher .. David Wayne
Anne Thrasher .... Betsy Palmer
Dr. Max Vogel .... Luther Adler
Myron Malkin .... Joby Baker
Alice Taggart .... Joanna Moore
Sarah Abelman .... Nancy R. Pollock
Josh Quincy .... Billy Dee Williams
Mrs. Quincy .... Claudia McNeil
Lyman Gattling .... Robert F. Simon
Ben Loomer .... Dan Tobin
Nobody Home .... Godfrey Cambridge
Lee Roy .... David Winters
Miss Bannaham .... Helen Chapman

"The Last Angry Man" is a film as pungent and indelible as Brooklyn on a hot summer afternoon. It has faults; it does not live up to all its early promises. Technically it is sometimes patchy and uneven. But it is possible to overlook whatever imperfections stud Fred Kohlmar's Columbia production because so much of it is so good and, add, so rare.

The film is taken from Gerald Green's best-selling novel about a Jewish doctor, a character based on Green's own father. Green did the screenplay with an adaptation by Richard Murphy. The script is rich in strong, vital characterizations and the dialog crackles with imagery, acidic humor and glancing, controlled pathos.

Director Daniel Mann had his problems in getting the story on film, shooting much of it on Brooklyn locations, but the finished product is worth the labor. It is a singular story for these "violent" days, with its message of love and devotion to principle. With sentiment and honesty, it works a vein of rugged individualism that is as American as Mom's apple strudel, with international implications and appeal.

Although "The Last Angry Man" has none of the names customarily listed as top boxoffice draws, the picture could develop into a strong attraction. It may open slow, but its word of mouth should be unusually favorable. It is a film that will require nursing but may prove rewarding if it is given special handling.

The conflict in the story arises from the lifetime of selfless service by the doctor portrayed by Paul Muni when placed in conjunction with the commercial demands of contempory television. Television wants to exploit the Jewish doctor, to associate with him so it can claim some of his virtues. Muni is an immigrant who has absorbed his Americanism from Jefferson, from Emerson and Thoreau, and he believes what they said. Although he agrees to do the tv program more or less as a personal favor to the producer, David Wayne, in the end he walks out without a backward glance because one of his patients needs him.

What has motivated him is what Wayne tries to find out. He asks Muni, blustering, denying philanthropy, why he does it. The doctor is astounded at the question. *"Because they're my patients,"* he replies. To point up this attitude there is another doctor, superbly played by Luther Adler, who spe-

cializes in the latest machines to impress the paying customer, more interested in the profits of medicine than in the people who are benefitted.

The screenplay has some caustic things to say about commercialism in both medicine and television. It backs away at the end, tossing some small bouquet at each, that vitiates its astringency. But loss-of-nerve cannot completely blunt cutting edge, and through the strength of its speech and the performances of its leading characters, the impact remains sharp.

Muni gives a superlative performance. Someone chides him at one point for thinking of himself as an Albert Schweitzer. A Schweitzer he isn't, but in Muni's character delineation it's apparent it's the men like him who keep the world going. Muni's acting is both old-time European grand-scale and as Methodical as anything by today's youngsters. David Wayne, as his abrasive agent, is allowed no histronics, but his conviction must be absolute. Wayne is as persuasive as his narrow lapels and button-down collars.

Since the story is mostly the contest between these two men, the rest of the cast is subsidiary. Luther Adler, however, is brilliant, and Joby Baker creates an appealing figure of young manhood. Betsy Palmer is helpful as Wayne's wife, and Nancy Pollock is moving as Muni's wife. Young Billy Dee Williams is vivid as the Negro boy who is Muni's most difficult patient. Others who score include Joanna Moore, Claudia McNeil, Robert F. Simon and Dan Tobin.

James Wong Howe's black and white photography is graphic, both in its subtle implications and its actual compositions. George Duning's sparing score is discreetly helpful. Charles Nelson seems to have had his work cut out in editing the film. There is wide use of the reaction shot, apparently to cover gaps where the prime shot could not be obtained. There is some dubbing and apparent use of wild lines, to bridge patches. But these are technical deficiencies that will bother only the technicians.

The Legion of Decency has already given "The Last Angry Man" an unusual accolade as a film of positive good. It is the kind of motion picture that will do more for Hollywood than a corps of public relations experts. *Powe.*

North West Frontier
(BRITISH-C'SCOPE-COLOR)

Grandscale action drama set at turn of century, about perilous journey to save Indian boy prince from tribesmen. Overlong, but sock contender for b.o. honors.

London, Oct. 13.

Rank release of a Marcel Hellman production. Stars Kenneth More, Lauren Bacall, Herbert Lom. Directed by J. Lee Thompson. Screenplay, Robin Estridge; camera, Geoffrey Unsworth; editor, Frederick Wilson; music, Mischa Spoliansky. Previewed at Odeon, London. Running time, **129 MINS.**

Captain Scott .... Kenneth More
Catherine Wyatt .... Lauren Bacall
Van Leyden .... Herbert Lom
Bridie .... Wilfrid Hyde White
Gupta .... I. S. Johar
Lady Windham .... Ursula Jeans
Peters .... Eugene Deckers
Sir Thomas Windham .... Ian Hunter
Brigadier Ames .... Jack Gwillim
Prince Kishan .... Govind Raja Ross
ADC .... Basil Hoskins
Havildar .... S. M. Asgaralli
2d Indian Soldier .... S. S. Chowdhary
British correspondent ... Moultrie Kelsall
American correspondent .. Lionel Murton
Indian correspondent ...... Jaron Yalton
Indian correspondent ...... Homi Bode
Rajah .... Frank Olegario
Staff Colonel .... Ronald Cardew

From a smash opening to quietly confident fade, "North West Frontier" has what it takes to make a sock b.o. impact within most frontiers. Basically it's the ageless chase yarn, transferred from the prairie to the sun-baked plains of India and done with a spectacular flourish. It suffers faults, including some shakiness in characterization and overlength.

But the characterization sets out to be more than the stereotyped, and it'd be difficult to suggest where cuts might be made. At once a picture for the mass audience, it also carries incidental commentaries on outlooks and behaviors that lift it to a higher plane.

Handled with tremendous assurance by J. Lee Thompson, the film is reminiscent of the same director's "Ice Cold In Alex," with an ancient locomotive replacing the ambulance in that desert war story and with hordes of be-turbaned tribesmen substituting for the Nazi patrols. The differences are marked, though, if only in the scope of the action sequences. Some of the attack scenes are tops. Geoffrey Unsworth's location camerawork has captured a breadth and sweep that couldn't have emanated from any studio lot.

Time is the turn of the Century when the English still held sway in India. Kenneth More plays an officer ordered to take a boy prince, sacred figurehead to the Hindus, to safety in the teeth of Moslems. In company with an assorted group, More makes his getaway from a besieged citadel in a makeshift coach drawn by a worn-out locomotive. Many hazards happen en route, including the discovery of an enemy in the passengers' midst. Highlights include, besides the attack stuff, the train's nocturnal breakout from the besieged fortress, a suspenseful scene where the traitor shows his hand, another tense sequence of crossing a blown-up bridge, and yet another wherein More repairs the track under fire.

Throughout, the cast serves the job expertly, More coming through as solid and dependable if a shade too unemotional. Lauren Bacall scores with a keen delineation of the prince's outspoken nurse. Herbert Lom is first-rate as a journalist. I. S. Johar is acutally the hit of the picture as the Indian railroad man. Wilfred Hyde White is polished as an old servant while Eugene Deckers puts in good work as an armament salesman. Young Govind Raja Ross proves as an appealing prince while Ursula Jeans and Ian Hunter contribute excellently. **This is one of the best large-scale productions from British studios in recent times.** *Earn.*

Battle of the Coral Sea

World War II action feature; well-made, with average b.o. indicated.

Hollywood, Oct. 13.

Columbia release of a Morningside Production. Stars Cliff Robertson and Gia Scala; with Teru Shimada, Patricia Cutts, Gene Blakely; also, Rian Garrick, L. Q. Jones, Robin Hughes, Gordon Jones, Tom Laughlin. Produced by Charles Schneer. Directed by Paul Wendkos; screenplay, Daniel Ullman and Stephen Kandel, from a story by Kandel; camera, Wilfrid Cline; editor, Chester W. Schaeffer; music, Ernest Gold. Previewed at the Studio, Oct. 8, '59. Running time, **86 MINS.**

Lt. Comm. Jeff Conway .. Cliff Robertson
Karen Phillips .... Gia Scala
Comm. Mori .... Teru Shimada
Lt. Peg Whitcomb .... Patricia Cutts
Lt. (s.g.) Len Ross ...... Gene Blakely
Al Schechter .... Rian Garrick
Yeoman Halliday .... L. Q. Jones
Major Jammy Harris ...... Robin Hughes
Torpedoman Bates .... Gordon Jones
Ensign Franklin .... Tom Laughlin
Oshikawa .... Eiji Yamashiro
Capt. Yamazaki .... James T. Goto
CPO Connors .... K. L. Smith
Admiral McCabe .... Carlyle Mitchell
Army Major .... Larry Thor
Simes .... Patrick Westwood

A war film of no unique values, "The Battle of the Coral Sea" nonetheless is an interesting, nicely-made account of a World War II submarine crew and its escape from a Japanese-held island. Producer Charles Schneer has invested the film with an appearance that surpasses its budget, and the Columbia release should show reasonable boxoffice strength for a picture of its class.

Most of the film's action precedes the actual battle, one of the major campaigns in the war with Japan, and the film's heroes do not directly take part in it. The tight Daniel Ullman-Stephen Kandel screenplay, based on Kandel's story, instead places emphasis on a submarine crew which scouts the enemy's position prior to the fighting. Using a camera on the periscope, the sub's officers accomplish their mission and on their return home, are detected, seized and taken to a prison camp on a Japanese island. Through the help of a Eurasion "neutral" on the island, three of the officers manage to escape on a Japanese torpedo boat to provide the Navy with the information it needs to demolish the enemy.

Paul Wendkos' direction is sharp, making the most of the action and the human relations that help create it. Cliff Robertson, who stars with Gia Scala, maintains a somber character as the sub's captain, indicating his concern over all that he's up to. Miss Scala is believable in a surprisingly small but important role. Teru Shimada is excellent as the sympathetic Japanese commander, never letting weakness intrude on compassion. Patricia Cutts, as an Australian nurse, and Gene Blakely, as a navy lieutenant, are good.

Battle scenes—a combination of stock footage and miniature work —are skillfully accomplished. Wilfrid Cline's photography makes San Diego and the San Fernando Valley look like the South Pacific, and other technical assets are Robert Peterson's art direction, Chester W. Schaeffer's editing and Harry Mills' sound. Ernest Gold's rousing musical score is adequately spiced with patriotism and action. *Ron.*

Timbuktu

Routine program adventure yarn Victor Mature and Yvonne De Carlo for the marquee.

Hollywood, Oct. 9.

United Artists release of Imperial Pictures Inc. production. Stars Victor Mature, Yvonne De Carlo; features George Dolenz, John Dehner, Marcia Henderson, Robert Clarke, James Foxx. Director, Jacques Tourneur; screenplay, Anthony Veiller, Paul Dudley; camera, Maury Gertsman; art direction, William Glasgow; set decoration, Darrell Silvera; music, Gerald Fried; editor, Grant Whytock; sound, John Kean. Previewed at Goldwyn Studios, Oct. 9, 1959. Running time: **91 MINS.**

Mike Conway .... Victor Mature
Natalie Dufort .... Yvonne De Carlo
Colonel Dufort .... George Dolenz
Emir .... John Dehner
Jeanne Marat .... Marcia Henderson
Capt. Girard .... Robert Clarke
Lt. Marat .... James Foxx
Suleyman .... Paul Wexler
Mohamet Adani .... Leonard Mudie
Maj. Leroux .... Willard Sage
Capt. Rimbaud .... Mark Dana
Dagana .... Larry Perron
Nazir .... Steve Darrell
Ahmed .... Larry Chance
Sgt. Trooper .... Allan Pinson

This one is neither better nor worse than a solid program adventure picture such as can be seen nightly on the late late show, only Victor Mature's a little older now. (Edward Small, the producer, has dropped his own name from credits).

Screenwriters Anthony Veiller and Paul Dudley, with assistance from director Jacques Tourneur, have avoided most of the opportunities for unintentional humor.

For the record, the story concerns the conflict of the French Foreign Legion against the Taureg tribes of the French Sudan, about the time France was falling to the Germans—but it could have been any time over the past 30 years. Specifically, it deals with an American trader (Mature) who aids the commander of the French garrison at Timbuktu and falls for the commander's wife (Yvonne De Carlo). Considerable sympathy is set up for the commander, played with sensitivity and insight by George Dolenz. Thus, when the commander dies a hero's death releasing the unfaithful wife to the American adventurer, it doesn't seem much like the happy ending the filmmakers doubtless intended.

Yvonne De Carlo is beautiful and John Dehner urbanely wicked as the evil emir. Mature, of course, is competent in his customary role.

The action—there's lots of it, shot against a western American desert which resembles the Sahara —is primarily concerned with getting a Moslem holy man to Timbuktu so that he can quell the uprising. Leonard Mudie, who plays this key role, looks and acts more like an amiable sourdough. Marcia Henderson scores as the wife of one of the Legionaires.

Maury Gertsman's photography is sharp, William Glasgow and Darrell Silvera's art work is satisfactory, Gerald Fried's music was generally effective (although the bongos seemed out of place), and the technical aspects are well handled. *Glen.*

Rough and the Smooth
(BRITISH)

Sex melodrama with sizzling situations, though lacking sufficient conflict for true power.

London, Oct. 6.

Renown release of a George Minter-Siodmak production. Stars Nadja Tiller, Tony Britton, William Bendix, Natasha Parry. Directed by Robert Siodmak. Screenplay, Audrey Erskine-Lindop and Dudley Leslie; based on novel by Robin Maugham; camera, Otto Heller; editor Gordon Pilkington; music, Douglas Gamley. Previewed at Rialto Cinema, London. Running time, **100 MINS.**

Ila Hansen .... Nadja Tiller
Mike Thompson .... Tony Britton
Reg Barker .... William Bendix
Margaret Goreham ..... Natasha Parry
David Fraser .... Norman Wooland
Lord Drewell .... Donald Wolfit
Jack .... Tony Wright
Jane Buller .... Adrienne Corri
Mrs. Thompson .... Joyce Carey
Dr. Thompson .... John Welsh
Piggy .... Martin Miller
Head Waiter .... Michael Ward
Willy Catch .... Edward Chapman
Barman .... Norman Pierce
Hotel Manageress .... Beatrice Varley
Bobby Montagu-Jones ...... Myles Eason
Taxi Driver .... Cyril Smith
Ransom .... Geoffrey Bayldon

Aiming to offer the kind of torrid, adult love scene that helped make "Room At The Top" such a success not only at home but in the U.S., "The Rough And The

Smooth" is a story of passion and betrayal. It makes as frequent use as the situations allow of the fireside settee and the bedroom. And when it does employ these settings, it oft-times breeds an atmosphere of sex that's as powerful as any to emanate from British studios. The trouble with this pic is that it presents the love stuff in the course of a story that, one feels, could almost have been drummed up for that purpose alone.

With characterization, too, suffering distortion for the sake of dramatic revelations when the climax is looming, the result is often unsatisfactory, especially as there's a lack of dramatic conflict that's also a weakness..

Major attributes, and considerable compensations, are the stunningly seductive personality of Nadja Tiller, and the charm and skill of Tony Britton. The two make a standout team. William Bendix, too, makes a hit in the role of a vulgarian which provides comedy switching latterly to hokey pathos.

Britton plays an archaeologist living in the uppercrust world of London who throws over his fiancee for Miss Tiller, whom he has met by chance and about whom there's an alluring air of mystery. Britton's jealousy of Bendix is allayed on finding that the latter is an elderly dealer for whom his sweetheart works as secretary. But doubts are re-aroused during a would-be idyllic stay in a country hotel, it then beginning to emerge that the girl is nothing much better than a strumpet. Miss Tiller's attempts to find $4,000 to help the brutal crook she really loves precipitates Bendix's suicide, for he's her slave, prepared to let her commit all sorts of infidelities in order to have her around.

Robert Siodmak gives the whole proceedings a sure touch, even though he's often thrown back on small conversational groupings outside the superbly handled love scenes. Supporting players do exceedingly well, notably Natasha Parry, as the spurned fiancee; Norman Wooland, as a loyal friend, and Donald Wolfit, who has the ripe role of a Napoleonic proprietor of a muck-raking newspaper. Production qualities are tops, with a special nod to the editing. *Earn.*

The Best of Everything
(COLOR—C'SCOPE)

Illicit amours on a grand scale in N. Y.'s white collar set. Superficial, but looks like good b.o.

Hollywood, Oct. 9.
Twentieth-Fox release of Jerry Wald production. Stars Joan Crawford, Louis Jourdan, Hope Lange, Stephen Boyd, Suzy Parker, Martha Hyer, Diane Baker, Brian Aherne, Robert Evans. Directed by Jean Negulesco. Screenplay, Edith Sommer and Mann Rubin; based on the novel by Rona Jaffe; camera (DeLuxe Color) William C. Mellor; music, Alfred Newman; editor, Robert Simpson. Previewed at the Studio, Oct. 6, '59. Running time, 122 MINS.

Caroline Bender	Hope Lange
Mike	Stephen Boyd
Gregg	Suzy Parker
Barbara	Martha Hyer
April	Diane Baker
Mr. Shalimar	Brian Aherne
Dexter Key	Robert Evans
Eddie	Brett Halsey
Sidney Carter	Donald Harron
Mary Agnes	Sue Carson
Jane	Linda Hutchings
Paul	Lionel Kane
Ronnie Wood	Ted Otis
David Savage	Louis Jourdan
Amanda Farrow	Joan Crawford
Brenda	June Blair
Judy Masson	Myrna Hansen
Girls in Typing Pool	Alena Murray
	Rachel Stephens
	Julie Payne
Scrubwoman	Nora O'Mahony

While Jerry Wald's "The Best of Everything" might be considered a little over-optimistic in its title, there's no doubt it contains ingredients which usually add up to boxoffice. He has recently specialized in turning out multi-charactered, multi-plotted films, and this one is in the same genre as "Peyton Place" and "The Long Hot Summer." "The Best" is slick and glossy, like a color still on coated stock, and with no more depth, yet as popular entertainment it sustains interest and should sell.

A subtitle for "The Best of Everything" might be "Except Men —Who Are Beasts." Joan Crawford, a successful career woman in the book-publishing field that is the film's setting, is having an unsuccessful affair with a married man (unseen). One of Miss Crawford's co-workers, Martha Hyer, is also involved in an affair with another married man, fellow-editor Donald Harron. Suzy Parker, one of the firm's secretaries, is having an affair with stage producer Louis Jourdan, who jilts her to take up (extra-maritally, of course) with Myrna Hansen.

To continue, Diane Baker becomes pregnant (out of wedlock) by Robert Evans, who proposes they solve this problem by visiting an abortionist. Hope Lange is jilted by Brett Halsey for a rich girl, but he suggests that he and Miss Lange set up housekeeping on the side. Brian Aherne, a senior editor, also plays it catch as catch can. Sex, it will be seen, occupies a large part in this film.

The screenplay by Edith Sommer and Mann Rubin is not as blatant as all this sounds. It has taken Rona Jaffe's novel and simmered it down somewhat. Words like "damn" and "hell" are used with greater frequency than is customary, but the script also contains a high percentage of graceful lines and some sharp phraseology. If not wit, it is still several cuts above office wisecracking.

Still, none of this carrying on can be taken very seriously. To anyone familiar with the environs of Rockefeller Center and Madison Avenue, the sexual relationships are not impossible. But by compressing the multiplicity of plot into two hours of film, they become lop-sidedly important and incredible.

The performances are generally good, although there is no real chance for development. Miss Crawford uses her own great authority to give vividness and meaning to a role that is sketchy at best. Hope Lange and Diane Baker create some involvment. Stephen Boyd is pleasant, and Martha Hyer endows her brief appearances with glamor. Robert Evans seems unnecessarily unpleasant and Donald Harron is allowed only a hint of his acting ability. Suzy Parker, burdened with the most difficult emotional role, is least successful. Although the camera obligingly tilts for her mad scene to indicate emotional duress, and green spots are thrown in for good measure, Miss Parker is simply not up to it. Around, and attractive, are Louis Jourdan, Brett Halsey, Sue Carson, Linda Hutchings, Ted Otis, Lionel Kane, June Blair and Al Austin.

Jean Negulesco's direction is firm-handed at keeping the over-wrought story from getting overheated and at setting character as well as he can in such a crowd.

Technical credits are slick, and there is a title tune for exploitation, by Alfred Newman and Sammy Cahn. *Powe.*

The Jayhawkers
(V'VISION; COLOR)

Big, but unexciting, period western. Mild b.o. indicated.

Hollywood, Oct. 16.
Paramount release of Norman Panama-Melvin Frank production. Stars Jeff Chandler, Fess Parker, Nicole Maurey; features Henry Silva. Directed by Melvin Frank. Screenplay, Frank, Joseph Petracca, Frank Fenton, A. I. Bezzerides; camera (Technicolor), Loyal Griggs; music, Jerome Moross; editor, Everett Douglas. Previewed at the studio, Oct. 8, '59. Running time, 100 MINS.

Darcy	Jeff Chandler
Cam	Fess Parker
Jeanne	Nicole Maurey
Lordan	Henry Silva
Governor Clayton	Herbert Rudley
Evans	Frank DeKova
China	Don Megowan
Jake	Leo Gordon
Marthe	Shari Lee Bernath
Paul	Jimmy Carter

"The Jayhawkers" is a big, colorful, expensive but essentially empty period western. Having taken an intriguing and little explored subject to deal with, the Norman Panama-Melvin Frank production then neglects to make much of its novelty value, settling instead for a conventional narrative of love and revenge. There is considerable smoke but very little fire in the Paramount release. Commercial prospects look mild.

The screenplay, by Frank, Joseph Petracca, Frank Fenton and A. I. Bezzerides, is named for the bands of raiders—originally honestly anti-slavery in conviction—who operated in Kansas territory prior to the Civil War and before admission of Kansas to the Union (per John Brown). The slavery issue and the bitterness it then engendered is never made clear, although there are glancing references. Story develops instead into a personal narrative about a would-be Napoleon of the plains, Jeff Chandler, who is using the Jayhawker movement to enthrone himself in his own private empire. He is opposed, purely on personal grounds, by Fess Parker. Chandler was responsible for the downfall and death of Parker's wife while Parker was in jail. Things are resolved when Parker sees the danger of Chandler's ambitions, knocks off Chandler and finds a new romance with Nicole Maurey, a widowed Frenchwoman.

As producers, Panama and Frank have endowed their film with handsome pictorial values, and Frank has directed with perception and an awareness of pace within the constricted frame. Theme got lost somewhere along the way, possibly in all those writing credits. As the presentation now stands, there just isn't any particular point to it, and there isn't enough depth to the main characters.

Jeff Chandler creates a certain amount of dynamic interest as the Jayhawker chieftain, although his pretensions to power are empty without the background to give them substance. Fess Parker has some nice moments, particularly one in which (with homespun accent) he attempts to teach Miss Maurey's French-speaking "English." He conjugates "a-going" for them, "I'm a-goin', you're a-goin'," etc. Miss Maurey is attractive and others who figure prominently include Henry Silva, Leo Gordon and the youngsters, Shari Lee Bernath and Jimmy Carter.

Loyal Griggs' Technicolor photography in VistaVision is rich and gets a great deal of mileage out of Paramount's western street. The interiors are particularly striking,

thanks to art directors Hal Pereira and Roland Anderson. Everett Douglas' editing is able, and Jerome Moross' score achieves a restless rhythm that is helpful.

Powe.

Tarzan, the Ape Man

Lots of adventure to exploit.

Hollywood, Oct. 13.

Metro release of an Al Zimbalist production. Stars Denny Miller, Cesare Danova, Joanna Barnes, Robert Douglas. Directed by Joseph Newman; screenplay, Robert Hill. based on characters created by Edgar Rice Burroughs: camera, Paul C. Vogel; music, Shorty Rogers; editor, Gene Ruggiero. Previewed at the studio, Oct. 13, '59. Running time, 82 MINS.

Tarzan .... Denny Miller
Holt .... Cesare Danova
Jane Parker .... Joanna Barnes
Col. Parker .... Robert Douglas
Riano .... Thomas Yangha

Metro has remade its 1932 Johnny Weissmuller - Maureen O'Sullivan starrer, "Tarzan, the Ape Man" with the knowledge that Tarzan's jungle exploits continue to stir boxoffice action from one side of the globe to the other. The story is even more implausible than it was 27 years ago, but the Technicolor feature sprouts end-on end thrills, and a sales push that highlights these thrills should swing the film into profits.

In recent years Tarzan has encountered everything from Amazons and slave girls to mermaids and she-devils, but never has he met anything quite like Jane. In "Tarzan, the Ape Man" he meets her, falls in love with her, wins her love and ultimately takes her as his wife. It's quite a feat considering he's unable to mutter even, "Me Tarzan!"

To be sure, there will be snickers when Jane, the rapacious but gentle Englishwoman, gives up the riches of ivory to spend her life in a paradise of crocodiles. And Tarzan's yell has by this time become satire. But producer Al Zimbalist has made sure the adventure along the way is furious enough and the dangers overpowering enough to result in an entertaining, fast-moving film.

Denny Miller has his first to-do with the Tarzan character and is able to get by without revealing whether or not he is as strong as an actor as he is a tree-swinger. He's a good-looking, well-built youngster who at least is capable of seeming alternately happy and sad, but his thesping prowess remains obscure. Joanna Barnes makes a fetching Jane, proving herself to be a better actress than this part demands. Cesare Danova is fine as a rather ruthless fortune seeker, and Robert Douglas is very good as Jane's father. Also good is Thomas Yangha as a giant Watusi.

The Robert Hill screenplay, based on Edgar Rice Burrough's characters, gives free rein to the jungle and its inhabitants. Its weakness is in allowing insufficient time for Jane to get to know Tarzan before giving her all to him. Joseph Newman's direction is excellent, sustaining interest even in exposition, and his handling of two chimps and an elephant is exceptional.

Viewers either will feel cheated by the film's production values or be amazed at the resourcefulness of its producer. Zimbalist apparently has garnered his jungle footage from a myriad of sources. He has some fine original color footage, photographed with excellence by Paul C. Vogel, and he has made good use of other tinted animal film. Not quite so effective, however, are black-and-white cut-ins from previous jungle films, and one underwater fight looks suspiciously like another Tarzan, perhaps Weissmuller himself. Most of the special effects by Lee LeBlanc and Robert R. Hoag are well done. Editor Gene Ruggiero skillfully maintained movement in a film gleaned from so many sources. Art directors Hans Peters and Malcolm Brown created interesting looking jungles. Franklin Milton's sound is most competent.

The musical score was composed and conducted by contemporary artist Shorty Rogers. His sound is a whole lot more modern than the film's period, but the interest overcomes the anachronism. *Ron.*

Das Schoene Abenteuer

(The Beautiful Adventure)
(GERMAN-COLOR)

Berlin, Oct. 13.

Constantin release of Georg Witt production. Stars Liselotte Pulver and Robert Graf. Directed by Kurt Hoffman. Screenplay, Heinz Pauck, and Guenter Neumann, after a novel by Antonia Ridge; camera (Agfacolor), Guenter Anders; music, Franz Grothe; editing, Hilwa von Boro. At Zoo Palast, Berlin. Running time, 102 MINS.

Dorothee Durand .... Liselotte Pulver
Marius Bridot .... Robert Graf
Pierre Bridot .... Oliver Grimm
Francoise .... Bruni Loebel
Catherine .... Eva-Maria Meineke

A nice, harmlessly entertaining film which, however, disappoints inasmuch as it's been made by Kurt Hoffman. One expected more of the creator of "Wunderkinder" and some other above-average German pix.

The director's light hand is obvious in several scenes, particularly in details, yet the whole film lacks pace and originality. Moreover, the locality in which this "beautiful adventure" occurs, the Provence in Southern France, is remarkably un-French. Commercially, the Liselotte Pulver name and that of the director will create interest, yet it is doubtful whether the boxoffice returns will be satisfying.

The plot is as thin as the various gags this film has to offer. It concerns an English school teacher of partly French descent who travels to Southern France to search for her relatives she hasn't heard from in years. She not only finds them, but also a husband.

Miss Pulver is at home in her role of the teacher while Robert Graf, owner of a little hotel, is refreshingly natural as the man of her life.

Technical credits are fine. There are a number of beautiful outdoor shots. Another asset is Franz Grothe's score. *Hans.*

Libel

(BRITISH—METROSCOPE)

Stylish and compelling court-room drama, with stellar value, excellent supporting performances and glossy settings. Worthwhile booking for most houses.

London, Oct. 20.

Metro release of an Anatole De Grunwald production. Stars Dirk Bogarde, Olivia de Havilland; features Paul Massie, Wilfrid Hyde White, Robert Morley. Directed by Anthony Asquith. Screenplay by Anatole De Grunwald and Karl Tunberg from Edward Wooll's play; camera, Robert Krasker; editor, Frank Clarke; music, Benjamin Frankel. Previewed at Metro Private Theatre, London. Running time, 100 MINS

Sir Mark Loddon,
Frank Welney,
Number Fifteen .... Dirk Bogarde
Lady Loddon .... Olivia de Havilland
Jeffrey Buckenham .... Paul Massie
Sir Wilfred .... Robert Morley
Foxley .... Wilfrid Hyde White
Gerald Loddon .... Anthony Dawson
Judge .... Richard Wattis
Himself .... Richard Dimbleby
Dr. Schrott .... Martin Miller
Maisie .... Millicent Martin
Guide .... Bill Shine
Admiral Loddon .... Ivan Samson
Michael Loddon .... Sebastian Saville
Butler .... Richard Pearson
First Photographer .... Robert Shaw
Second Photog .... Geoffrey Bayldon
Maddox .... Gordon Stern
Car Salesman .... Arthur Howard
Miss Sykes .... Joyce Carey
Mrs. Squires .... Josephine Middleton
Fitch .... Kenneth Griffith
Barmaid .... Barbara Archer
Man ot Bar .... Anthony Doonan
Girl in Street .... Vanda Hudson

Courtroom dramas are usually fairly good value as screen entertainment, and "Libel" stands up among the best. Based on a 25-year-old play, it has been turned into a stylish and holding film by Anatole De Grunwald which seems likely to be a winner. With Dirk Bogarde and Olivia De Havilland heading a cast composed of some of the slickest performers in British pictures, this is a worthwhile booking for all but the most moronic patrons. Its pace is fairly leisurely but flashbacks help to relieve any possible tedium from the inevitable static play in the courtroom. Interest is well sustained, partly as a result of Anthony Asquith's sensitive direction and good, polished acting plus a literate screenplay dreamed up from the central idea.

This idea is simple enough. Is Sir Mark Loddon (Dirk Bogarde), owner of one of the stately homes of England, really Loddon or an unscrupulous imposter, as alleged by a wartime comrade? A certain amount of coincidence and occasional implausibility crop up, but the film achieves excellently its object of keeping the audience undecided as to Loddon's guilt or innocence.

The libel case is sparked off when a young Canadian airman sees a tv program introducing Loddon. He is convinced that he is really Frank Welney, a small part actor. The three were in prison camp together and he is confident that Loddon was killed during a prison break. The fact that Loddon and Welney bore a striking likeness to each other adds to his conviction that Welney has pulled off a con trick, and taken the dead Loddon's place. He exposes the alleged phoney in a newspaper and Loddon is persuaded by his wife to sue. The accused's faulty memory and other damning evidence is brought out in evidence but, skillfully, suspicion switches to and fro, with the audience kept in a state of indecision.

Bogarde carries much of the onus in this film since he plays both Loddon (during the war and at the time of the trial) and Welney. He also makes a third appearance during the slick climax. Bogarde does a standout job, suggesting the difference in the two characters remarkably well with the aid of only a slight difference in hair style. Bogarde handles the varying moods of the two characters subtlely. In this, he contributes one of the best performances he ever has pulled off. Paul Massie gives a likeable, though somewhat even-key performance as the young man whose suspicions trigger the drama. Olivia de Havilland, as Bogarde's wife, has two or three very good scenes which she handles well. But, in the courtroom scenes, she has little to do but react to the proceedings, and Miss de Havilland is fine in this tricky chore.

Light relief is mainly provided by the cut and thrust exchanges of the two leading counsel. Robert Morley is for Bogarde and Wilfrid Hyde White leads the defense. These parts are written with wit and this sound casting does much for the trial sequences.

Richard Wattis, subduing his usual slightly fatuous style, is an offbeat but successful choice for the judge. Other effective minor roles are given okay treatment by Anthony Dawson, Millicent Martin, Martin Miller and Bill Shine. One quarrel, however, with director Asquith. His Fleet Street photographers are the usual ill-mannered caricatures, and it is a pity that more authenticity was not introduced in their roles.

Robert Krasker has done some fine lensing. Because much of the off-court scenes were actually shot at Woburn Abbey, stately home of the Duke of Bedford, the production is given much budget-value. "Libel" is a firstclass combination of writing, direction and acting, despite some occasionally far-fetched tricks. *Rich.*

The Navy Lark

(BRITISH-C'SCOPE)

Easygoing farce with predictable, but useful, yocks. Based on a BBC radio series, it should provide plenty of fun for all but eggheads.

London, Oct. 13.

20th-Fox release of a Wilcox-Neagle Production. Stars Cecil Parker, Ronald Shiner, Leslie Phillips. Directed by Gordon Parry. Screenplay, Sid Colin and Laurie Wyman, based on BBC Radio Show by Laurie Wyman; camera, Gordon Dines; editor, Basil Warren; music, James Moody and Tommy Reilly. At Carlton, London. Running time, 82 MINS.

Commander Stanton R.N. .... Cecil Parker
C.P.O. Banyard .... Ronald Shiner
Lieut. Pouter R.N. .... Leslie Phillips
Leading Wren Heather .... Elvi Hale
Capt. Povey R.N. .... Nicholas Phipps
Lieut. Binns, R.N. .... Cardew Robinson
Leading Seaman Johnson .... Gordon Jackson
Gaston Higgins .... Harold Kasket
Fortune Teller .... Hattie Jacques
C.N.I. .... Reginald Beckwith
Brown .... Kenneth Warren
Mabel .... Wanda Ventham
Lieut. Bates R.N. .... Richard Coleman
Admiral Troutbridge .... Llewelwn Rees
Rear Admiral .... Clive Morton
Group Captain .... Gordon Harris
Fred .... Van Boolen
Commander .... Gordon Whiting
Naval Commander .... Tom Gill
Naval Captain .... Walter Hudd

There seems no end to the boxoffice potential of light-hearted, screen farces, based on improbable happenings in the British services. With "The Navy Lark," the senior service gets another brisk, irreverent going-over. Pic is based on a click BBC radio series. Herbert Wilcox has insured golden returns by sticking to a winning formula. He's hired a stock company of accomplished comedy performers and insisted that his writers and director should provide recognizable gag situations and dialog which telegraph predictable upcoming jokes without any subtlety.

The yarn is the oldie about a "forgotten" naval base on an island off the South Coast of Britain. They're having a high old

time feathering their nests with illicit smuggling and other rackets. Discipline has gone haywire. The skipper's involved in fishing. His No. 1 yen is a pretty Wren officer's blonde charms.

Suddenly higher authority decides that the minesweeping unit is redundant and from then on chaos breaks out as they scheme to avoid being posted elsewhere. The various shenanigans eventually lead to a "hoax revolution" being fixed with the natives of the island, who demand Home Rule. There's no point in spotlighting the various situations which are trotted out with disarming enthusiasm.

Scriptwriters Sid Colin and Laurie Wyman keep their yarn moving from one improbability to another and only occasionally does the comedy creak. Then director Gordon Parry has the good fortune to have on hand some skilled performers who hold the fort. These include Cecil Parker, a master of the art of bumbling; Nicholas Phipps, as the probing senior officer constantly on the receiving end of indignity; Ronald Shiner, who boisterously can play a wily petty officer in his sleep; Cardew Robinson, extremely good as an over-diligent war correspondent, and Leslie Phillips, as a philandering second officer. Phillips is unluckily forced to carry a shade too much of the obvious corn but he deals with it in smooth, flippant style. Harold Kasket, Richard Coleman, Llewelyn Rees and Gordon Jackson are also on hand to help out with the chuckles.

On the distaff side there are a number of comely femmes who are mostly around to decorate the scene. Elvi Hale, as a Wren officer who causes the love light in Phillips' eye, has the brightest opportunity and provides another reminder that she is one of Britain's liveliest contenders for femme stardom. Gordon Dines' lensing is, as usual, topnotch.

A minor bleat is the music which is so determinedly based on familiar sea-shanties that it quickly palls. Altogether, an unpretentious but amusing film for those prepared to spend an hour or so in familiar surroundings. *Rich.*

La Valse Du Gorille
(Gorilla's Waltz)
(FRENCH)

Paris, Oct. 20.

Pathe release of Raoul Plcquin-Pathe production. Stars Roger Hanin, Charles Vanel; features Yves Barsacq, Jess Hahn, Michel Thomass, Suzanne Dehelly, Micheline Gary and Ursula Herwig. Directed by Bernard Borderie. Screenplay, Antoine Dominique, Jacques Robert, Borderie from a novel by Dominique; camera, Claude Renoir; editor, Christian Gauuin. At Balzac, Paris. Running time, 105 MINS.

Le Gorille	Roger Hanin
Le Vieux	Charles Vanel
Berthier	Yves Barsacq
Ted	Jess Hahn
Boris	Michel Thomass
Hortense	Suzanne Dehelly
Blonde	Micheline Gary
Luisa	Ursula Herwig

Snappy secret service actioner has French, American and Russian spies battling to get an invention by a West German scientist which is able to lead to the recovery of all space missiles. Main offbeat accent is the emergence of a West German Secret police, who guard this secret avidly, though the inventor wants to give it to NATO. Otherwise this is an above-average actioner with dual and playoff possibilities abroad. It lacks the individual approach and characterization for any arty or specialized foreign chances.

The third in a popular series, the film looks to repeat here. It shows a Herculean French undercover man, The Gorilla, who is always forced back to work when he tries to leave—by a crusty, caustic aging superior. Here the scene is West Germany and all the agents are scrambling for the secret which is finally handed to NATO. The Russian and German undercover people are killed while the Frenchman (super hero), and the American finishing okay but not above trying to knock off the Frenchman when he feels he has been crossed by him.

Direction speeds this along but can not quite sustain interest over the long footage. Fights are well done and the acting is good with a new Gorilla, Roger Hanin, replacing Lino Ventura.

It has good technical and production values. *Mosk.*

Un Eroe Dei Nostri Tempi
(A Hero of Our Times)
(ITALIAN)

Rome, Oct. 13.

Galatea release of a Guiliana Scappino production. Features Marina Berti, Massimo Tonna, Guido Paradisi, Margherita Autuori, Livia Contardi, Marco Radaelli. Directed by Sergio Capogna. Screenplay, Capogna, from a novel by Vasco Pratolini; camera, Domenico Scala; music, Giovanni Fusco. Previewed in Rome. Running time, **130 MINS.**

Promising first effort by young writer-director Sergio Capogna, this pic is faithful screen adaptation of the bestseller by Vasco Pratolini. It tells of the shabb postwar heroics of a youngster whose main exploit, later regretted, lies in making an older widow fall for him, robbing her and then leading to her suicide. Extreme slow-paced and repetitious with its sequences, though mood-setting and okay in artistic, this indicates a need for drastic editing at times before a commercial release should be considered.

Acting by Marina Berti and Massimo Tonna, latter a non-pro, is excellent almost throughout, making the story believable. Surrounding cast of unfamiliar faces complete the picture. While some sequences are not quite brought off by director, others show brilliance of concept and dedication which bid well for his future career.

Deliberately grey and drab lensing by Domenico Scala is another major plus in pic while Giovanni Fusco's music captures the mood in his usually expert fashion. Other credits are good. *Hawk.*

Diego Corrientes
(Diego Corrientes)
(SPANISH—COLOR)

Madrid, Oct. 13.

Hispano-Foxfilm release of an Isasi production. Stars Jose Suarez, Marisa de Leza; co-stars Eulalia del Pino, Jesus Colomer, Jose Marco, Milo Quesada, Rafael Bardem. Directed and produced by Antonio Isasi-Isasmendi. Screenplay, Luis Colomeron, Jorge Ilia, A. Isasi-Isasmendi; camera (Eastmancolor), Salvador Garriga; music, Xavier Montsalvatge. At Palacio de la Musica, Madrid. Running time, **104 MINS.**

Opening reel exposes a wealth of faithfully lensed countryside and picturesque Andalucian towns but the distinguishing note in this tale of a legendary, golden-hearted outlaw is the amount of time actors spend in the saddle to get movement.

Action palls as director sends a generally below-par cast into a series of time-worn westerns and costumers. Addition of uninspired flamenco folklore, which many producers here consider indispensable commercial lure, is also of little help.

Jose Suarez, as the outlaw, is ruggedly handsome on a white charger. Sound track is faulty, and film is overlong. *Werb.*

La Gran Senora
(April in Portugal)
(SPANISH—COLOR

Madrid, Oct. 13.

Hispamex release of a D.I.A. production. Stars Alberto Closas, Zully Moreno; co-stars Isabel Garces, Yvette Lebon; features Manuel Diaz Gonzalez, Jose L. Lopez Vasquez, Jesus Tordesillas. Directed by Luis Amadori. Screenplay, Luis Marquina, Luis Amadori; camera (Eastmancolor), Jose Agualo. At Cine Coliseo, Madrid. Running time, **92 MINS.**

Despite a rash of screen values, this sentimental-romantic comedy gets cluttered up with an overdose of mistaken identity and repetitious farce. Not only does Alberto Closas, in a dual role, play a polished count and a lovable ne'er-do-well twin brother, but Zully Moreno doubles as a mannequin and fake countess.

Vet legit actress Isabel Garces gives a fine performance in her first film role as instigator of uneven flowing comic situations. Topflight cast, behind-scenes in Madrid's haute couture and scenic settings of Estoril stand out in the mad-ball confusion of who's who. Songstress Mona Bell impresses in a chorus of "April in Portugal." Color is good. *Werb.*

Gringalet
(ARGENTINE)

Buenos Aires, Oct. 13.

Argentina Sono Film production in Panoramic Vision. Features Walter Vidarte, Graciela Borges, Raul Rossi, Beatriz Taibo, Juan Carlos Barbieri, Maruja Gil Quesada. Directed by Ruben Cavalotti. Screenplay, Rodolfo M. Taboada, from play by Paul Vandenberghe; camera, Alberto Etchebehere; editor, Jorge Carate; music, Tito Rivero. At Monumenta, B.A.

An artificial production, this film attempts to cash in on what was a fairly successful play some years back. However, adaptation of the story to local atmosphere doesn't ring true. It will do fairly well in the domestic market and in Latin America, but isn't of the quality that will build a global demand for Argentine product.

Yarn concerns a light hearted youth in poor circumstances whose fortune improves. But he's discontent in a wealthy atmosphere and returns to his original background to recapture his former happiness. Script is unrealistic and strikes a falsely, sentimental note. There are occasional touches of unsubtle humor.

Walter Vidarte is miscast as Gringalet, the humanitarian Bohemian. Other players, for the most part, are merely adequate. The Boca, Buenos Aires' port area, is used as the youth's environment when he was a struggling factory worker. *Nid.*

A Bucket of Blood

Above average exploitation horror film with comedy elements; aimed at youth market. Top-billed with "Giant Leeches.'

Hollywood, Oct. 24.

American International release of a James H Nicholson and Samuel Z. Arkoff Production. Stars Dick Miller, Barboura Morris, Antony Carbone; with Julian Burton, Ed Nelson, John Brinkley, John Shaner, Judy Bamber, Myrtle Domerel, Burt Convy, Jhean Burton. Produced and directed by Roger Corman; screenplay, Charles B. Griffith; camera, Jack Marquette; editor, Anthony Carras; music, Fred Katz; art director, Dan Haller. Previewed at the Iris Theatre, Oct. 23, '59. Running time: **66 MINS.**

Walter	Dick Miller
Carla	Barboura Morris
Leonard	Antony Carbone
Brock	Julian Burton
Art Lacroix	Ed Nelson
Will	John Brinkley
Oscar	John Shaner
Alice	Judy Bamber
Mrs. Surchart	Myrtle Domerel
Lou Raby	Burt Convy
Naolia	Jhean Burton

"A Bucket of Blood" is a 66-minute joke compounded of beatniks and gore. It's too comic to be a typical horror film and the horror is too explicit for it to be a comedy, but for the youth market at which it's aimed, the feature looks like a winner.

An inept busboy yearns to be an artist like the arty phonies who frequent the beatnik expresso house where he works. In a frightful but hilarious scene the gentle lad accidentally impales a cat he's trying to rescue from a wall, and, to cover up the deed, he moulds clay around the poor animal's corpse.

Intoxicated with success when the beatniks hail the dead cat as a work of art, the formerly scorned lackey is soon embarked on the predictable career of immortalizing his contemporaries in clay—with them inside, of course.

During the first half of the picture, while this situation is being set up, there are many opportunities for gruesome humor, of which writer Charles B. Griffith takes full advantage. In the latter half the humor becomes lost as the filmmakers concentrate more on the horror and as it becomes necessary to punish the lovable maniac for his crimes.

Dick Miller's ability to sustain a sense of poignancy while acting conceited and committing atrocities is responsible in large part for the picture's appeal. With other actors—notably Barboura Morris, Antony Carbone and Julian Burton—producer-director Roger Corman has made equally happy casting choices. Corman has expertly captured the expresso house atmosphere and peopled it with accurate characters, the real-life counterparts of which should wince.

Technical aspects of the film are good, although some interior sets are substandard. Fred Katz' music, which includes a saxophone solo by Paul Horn, is particularly apt and helps the picture considerably.

It's perhaps idle to speculate on what Gorman might have come up with had he had more time and money for the film and had he not been bound by the necessity of providing the bucket of blood promised in the title (a man's head is severed with a circular saw and ichor drips into a bucket from a corpse's hiding place in the rafters—all pretty sickening).

The film will sell as is. But it might have been a very satisfying satire. *Glen.*

S.O.S. Pacific
(BRITISH)

Contrived but often exciting meller which has useful stellar value; packs enough punches to make for good business in most houses.

London, Oct. 20.

Rank release of a Sydney Box Associates' (John Nasht-P. Filmer-Sankey) production. Stars Richard Attenborough, Pier Angeli, John Gregson, Eva Bartok, Eddie Constantine; features Clifford Evans, Jean Anderson. Directed by Guy Green. Screenplay by Robert Westerby; camera, Wilkie Cooper; editor, Arthur Stevens; music, Georges Auric. At Leicester-Square Theatre, London. Running time, **91 MINS.**

Whitey .... Richard Attenborough
Teresa .... Pier Angeli
Jack .... John Gregson
Maria .... Eva Bartok
Mark Reisener .... Eddie Constantine
Miss Shaw .... Jean Anderson
Dr. Strauss .... Gunnar Moller
Peterson .... Clifford Evans
Willy .... Cec Linder
Monk .... Harold Kaskett

The Rank organization has insisted on alternative endings for "S.O.S. Pacific," a competent and often suspenseful thriller, with a cast that gets the most out of some meaty, if contrived, situations. The version seen here and the one intended for British consumption, despite protests by the producers, has an incredibly illogical happy ending. The U. S. will see a trimmed unhappy climax which to an adult audience will make sense. "S.O.S. Pacific" probably set out to be a serious drama with a message about the H-bomb. But it settles for a brisk adventure yarn. Despite many obvious holes, this should satisfy the average patron.

A decrepit seaplane sets off from a small Pacific port carrying a strange load of mixed humanity. It runs into hurricane trouble, catches fire, the pilot is injured, the co-pilot killed and the plane plunges into the sea. They are cast on a remote island which they discover is all set to be the scene of a nuclear test.

There are just five hours left for the survivors to get out of trouble. Can the fatal explosion be neutralized in time? That's the improbable, but nail-biting situation. But the fellow who pulls off the heroic deed survives to clasp his loved one to his bosom in the British version. In the Yank pic he is killed, which seems rather natural for anyone tampering with H-bombs at close quarters.

Apart from the climactic thrill, there are others such as the plane being at the mercy of the storm and on fire and the pilot being attacked by sharks, plus some minor gun-play. But the main interest is in the characters themselves who, though never fully developed, tangle with satisfactory results. The owner-pilot is a bitter man with a yen for the bottle. The air hostess is a goodlooker with a yen for the bottle while the co-pilot is a lazy character who appears to like nothing very much. The passengers are the usual odd lot including a tough sea-skipper being brought back to face trial for smuggling, a prim middle aged spinster, a shapely deported tart and a shy young German scientist.

With a couple of exceptions these are all very well played. Surprisingly, John Gregson gives a sub-standard performance as the surly pilot while Pier Angeli coasts along as the lovelorn stewardess who eventually falls for the dauntless sea-skipper. Eddie Constantine plays this with a tough offbeat charm and virility which gives a punch to the proceedings.

Best performances come from Richard Attenborough, who supplies a shrewd edge to the role of the informer, and from Jean Anderson, as the spinster who has guts beneath her bleak, snobbish exterior. Eva Bartok makes the most of limited opportunities as the goodtime girl while Clifford Evans, as the dick, and Gunnar Moller, as the scientist, fit snugly into the situations.

The film was shot in the Canary Islands, with the exception of the plane interiors, and cameraman Wilkie Cooper has got the best out of the locale. The shark sequences, filmed in a tank and from library shots, are effective. Guy Green's direction is sharp and devoid of frills.

Robert Westerby's screenplay is unashamed melodrama. He has dreamed up some tingling spots and his dialog is crisp and neatly blended with the humor. *Rich.*

Le Bel Age
(The Wonderful Age)
(FRENCH)

Paris, Oct. 20.

Pathe release of Centaure-Son Et Lumiere-Pathe-Films D'Aujourd'hui production. With Marcel Pagliero, Gianni Esposito, Loleh Bellon, Jacques Doniol-Valcroze, Alexandra Stewart, Francoise Brion, Ursula Kubler, Boris Vian. Directed by Pierre Kast. Screenplay, Jacques Doniol-Valcroze, Alberto Moravia, Kast; camera, Ghislain Cloquet; editor, Yannick Bellon. Previewed in Paris. Running time, **90 MINS.**

Stef .... Marcel Pagliero
Claude .... Gianni Esposito
Loleh .... Loleh Bellon
Jacques .... Jacques Daniel-Valcroze
Alexandra .... Alexandra Stewart
Carla .... Francoise Brion
Ursula .... Ursula Kubler

Extremely personal pic was made on the margin of the general film setup here. It is an exercise in that old Gallic theme of "cherchez la femme." A group of men relate their adventures with women, with the women allowed to give their side of each episode. Mostly narrated, this is somewhat fragile. Film shapes primarily an arty entry abroad, with little chance for general runs because of its verbose qualities.

Three men run a book store which seems to be visited by a bevy of pretty girls. All get their due until a new bookkeeper is wanted by all. One gets the inside track only to suddenly feel he is too old for her. Another sketch is about a sensitive poet whose affairs are mostly pain and suffering.

Last episode is about four girls who try to plan the sharing of four boys. But sudden emotions break up the project. Pic is neatly photographed but the acting is only passable. Characters are never alive. It looms primarily as a local item. For an inexpensive film, the production and technical credits are fine. *Mosk.*

Sign of the Gladiator
(COLOR-COLORSCOPE)

Unsatisfactory imported "spectacle" must depend upon American International's sales technique. In that connection could be good.

Hollywood, Oct. 19.

American International Pictures release of a Glomer Film Production. Stars Anita Ekberg, Chelo Alonso, George Marshall, Jacque Sernas; also, Folco Lulli, Lorrella De Luca, Alberto Franese, Mimo Palmara, Alfredo Varelli, Sergio Sauro, Paul Muller, Gino Cervi. Produced by Guido Brignine. Directed by Vittorio Musy Glori; story and screenplay, F. Thellung, F. De Feo, S. Leone, G. Mangione, G. Brignone; camera, Luciana Trasatti; music, A. Francesco La Vagnino; editor, Nino Baragli. Previewed Oct. 19, '59. Running time, **84 MINS.**

Zenobia .... Anita Ekberg
Marcus Valerius .... George Marshall
Semanzio .... Folco Lulli
Erika .... Chelo Alvonso
Julian .... Jacque Sernas
Bathsheba .... Lorrella De Luca
Marcel .... Alberto Farnese
Lator .... Mimo Palmara
Ito .... Alfredo Varelli
Tullius .... Sergio Sauro
Head Priest .... Paul Muller
Emperor Aurelian ... . Gino Cervi

"Sign of the Gladiator" is a crudely-made spectacle. The "deepest" thing about it is Anita Ekberg's cleavage. That's about all anyone will talk about. American International Pictures, which purchased the French-German-Yugoslav co-production for release, is apt to put more spectacular scenes into its ads than the filmmakers did into the picture. Commercial return could be disproportionately high.

The costumes and sets are lavish, but the production is chopped to bits and what should have been told in 120 swift minutes is told in 84 draggy ones. Basically, the story makes sense and with logic could have become an interesting film. As it is, however, the characters hurry and scurry from temple to tent with no apparent purpose. The viewer may be hard put to tell who is who, what they're doing and why, and by the time the picture gets down to action, it's too late to care.

Five writers—F. Thellung, F. De Feo, S. Leone, G. Mangione and G. Brignone—are responsible for the story and screenplay, and it might be properly assumed their intent is only slightly satisfied by the final print. The film is dubbed, and because the voices do not always seem to represent what the actors or director Vittorio Musy Glori might have had in mind, it's difficult to evaluate the performances. Miss Ekberg is voluptuous. George Marshall comes across as a strong Roman general. Lorrella De Luca is gentle as the virgin Bathsheba and, from her poise and appearance, may have a solid film future ahead. Jacque Sernas is fine as a Roman centurion, and Folies Bergere dancer Chelo Alonso swivels in a sensuous dance that results in the quickest movement seen throughout the entire film.

The time is 217 A.D., and Queen Zenobia (Miss Ekberg) heads the kingdom of Palymra which, having broken with the Roman Empire, is out to do it in. A Roman general (Marshall) deliberately is taken prisoner, feigns hatred of Rome, is taken into the queen's confidence and into her bedroom. All goes well, the Romans win and the queen is taken prisoner. But the general has fallen in love with the beauty and convinces the Roman senate that her deeds were calculated by a fiendish counsellor. She's freed to spend the remainder of her life with her Roman lover.

Guido Brignone produced, and the top assets are Vitt. Nino Novarcese's costumes and Ottavio Scotti's settings. Riccardo Freda's direction of the battle sequences has some spirit but is highly repetitious. The color (Eastman) in the print reviewed was disconcertingly bad. It didn't match from one scene to the next, or, for that matter, within a single take. *Ron.*

Warrior and Slave Girl
(SUPERCINESCOPE-COLOR)

Italian-made chariot opera; Romans vs. Armenians. Reasonable action for the exploitation market.

Hollywood, Oct. 23.

Columbia release of Alexandra Production. Stars Gianna Maria Canale, Georges Marchal, Ettore Manni. Produced by Virgilio De Blasi. Directed by Vittorio Cottafavi. Screenplay, Ennio De Concini, Francesco De Feo, Cian Paolo Callegari, Francesco Thellung. Previewed at the studio, Oct. 21, '59. Running time, **82 MINS.**

Princess Amira .... Gianna Maria Canale
Asclepio .... Georges Marchal
Marcus Numidius .... Ettore Manni
Lucanus .... Rafael Calvo
Zahar .... Vera Cruz

Armenians take the place of the Comanches and the Roman legions substitute for the U.S. Cavalry in "The Warrior and the Slave Girl," an Italian production being released in U.S. by Columbia.

Aside from some implausible dubbing, a plot that has been hacked to pieces by editing, and some acting so elementary that in spots it is barely noticeable, film has its points. The Eastman color is exceptionally good, and even throughout. "The "SuperCinescope," a frame of about Cinema-Scope proportions, is sharp and has unusual depth of field. Camera work (uncredited) is good.

The film passes up some standard staples of its kind. There are no "orgy" scenes, although there is plenty of opportunity. But there are some good, big action scenes, notably of the Roman cavalry charging, that satisfactorily fill the wide frame. Some of the contests in the gladitorial arena are genuinely exciting, one particularly tingling of a contest between a gladiator and a very healthy looking lion.

The plot has to do with the efforts of the Romans to clean up their Empire, in this case, the province of Armenia. There is a wicked Armenian queen, Gianna Maria Canale, who is trying to poison her youthful brother, the rightful king. She is trying to sell out her country to the Scythians and is only prevented by the timely arrival of Roman troops headed by Tribune Ettore Manni, who teams with the Armenian underground led by Georges Marchal to defeat the villains and villainesses and restore law and order.

The cast is capable to the demands placed on it, and Vittorio Cottafavi's direction is remarkably efficient at taking most advantage of the latent excitement within various scenes. *Powe.*

Caravan to Russia
(RUSSIAN-COLOR)

Paul Delmer Associates release of Central Documentary Film Studios of Moscow production. Produced in collaboration with the Ministry of Culture of the U.S.S.R. and Delmer. Directed by Delmer and Maria Pankina. Music, Alexander Zorov. Photographed in Sovcolor. English narration. At the Cameo, N.Y., starting Oct. 24, 1959. Running time, **85 MINS.**

For those who fancy travelogues in large dosage, and about the Russian people and several of their key cities, "Caravan To Russia" should please. At David Fine's Eighth Ave. Cameo Theatre it appeared film has real appeal for Russia-derived people. Add the intense interest in the Soviets of late.

Production is the result of a 16-week trek by Paul Delmer through Russia. Unlike some Russo pix of

this variety, this shows more historical landmarks and better known cultural leaders. It also has a camera close-up of Paul Robeson, plus a sequence in which he sings at a Soviet youth camp.

Moscow is the focal point for much of the footage, but Delmer also has taken his camera and his lens crew probably supplied by Soviet Russia) to Yalta, resorts along the Black Sea, a ride on that sea and to Leningrad and Minsk. Latter city is revealed as quite an industrial center, with giant tractors (Russian-made) rolling off the assembly line.

Delmer does a resourceful job of sustaining interest in what obviously could have been a tiresome travel film. If anything, the criticism from a photographer's point of view, would be that he tried to take in too many subjects and did not permit his camera to rest long enough on some of them in order to fully tell the story. Otherwise he has done an excellent job of giving a real close-up of Russian life.

There's a plea for more cultural, excange, mouthed by the unbilled narrator, at the end. *Wear.*

125 Rue Montmartre
(FRENCH)
Paris, Oct. 20.
Pathe release of Orex production. Stars Lino Ventura; features Andrea Parisy, Dora Doll, Robert Hirsch, Jean Desailly. Directed by Gilles Grangier. Screenplay. Jacques Robert, Andre Gillois. Michel Audiard, Grangier from novel of Gillois; camera, Jacques Lemare; editor, Jacques Douarinou. At Balzac, Paris. Running time, 85 MINS.

Pascal	Lino Ventura
Catherine	Andrea Parisy
Didier	Robert Hirsch
Memene	Dora Doll
Dodelot	Jean Desailly
Barrachet	Alfred Adam

This film is about a rugged, self-sufficient newspaper vendor who gets involved with a man who tries to drown himself. He is used by the man to pin a crime on him. Picture has some twists but its mixture of slice-of-life realism and suspense do not quite jell. This makes it an okay local bet and is chancey abroad.

Lino Ventura plays the simple hero with too many antics. His boorishness and violence make for a loss of sympathy and a falling off in interest. The murder plot is telegraphed. It is technically workmanlike with okay supporting work. *Mosk.*

Il Moralista
(The Moralist)
(ITALIAN)
Rome, Oct. 20.
Warner Bros. release of a Napoleon Film production. Stars Alberto Sordi; features Maria Percy, Vittorio DeSica, Franca Valeri, Leopoldo Trieste. Directed by Giorgio Bianchi. Screenplay by E. M. Margadonna, Corda, Sonego, Talarico, from story by Margadonna and Corda; camera, Alvaro Mancori; music, Carlo Savina. At the Splendore, Rome. Running time, 120 MINS.

Agostino	Alberto Sordi
Il Presidente	Vittorio DeSica
Monique	Maria Percy
Virginia	Franca Valeri
Giovanni	Franco Fabrizi

Highly amusing, well-written and acted comedy with top b.o. potential on the Italo market where the Alberto Sordi name is a surefire draw. Indicated for linguaters abroad.

Story tickles local risibilities in spoofing moral-censorial committees with jurisdiction over shows, garbing of performers, offensive-ness of posters, etc. in telling the story of one such organization headed by Vittorio DeSica but actually run by his factotum, Alberto Sordi. Naturally, despite their official function, both have decided leanings towards the opposite sex, with pseudo-bigoted Sordi turning out to be no less than a shady nitery enterpreneur in the end. Meanwhile, there are plenty of occasions for laughable scenes, most of them thanks to Sordi, with a healthy assist from DeSica.

Maria Percy is easy on the eyes as a stripper, while Franca Valeri runs off with several sequences as DeSica's man-hungry daughter. Other credits are all good. *Hawk.*

Solomon and Sheba
(TECHNIRAMA 70—COLOR)

Long, colorful Bible story with extravagant spectacle. Title and stars provide good marquee value. Big b.o.

London, Oct. 27.
United Artists release of Edward Small's presentation of King Vidor (Ted Richmond) production. directed by Vidor. Stars Yul Brynner, Gina Lollobrigida; also George Sanders, Marisa Pavan. David Farrar. Screenplay, Anthony Veiller, Paul Dudley, George Bruce from story by Crane Wilbur; camera, Freddie Young; editor, John Ludwig; music, Mario Nascimbene. At Astoria, London, Oct. 27, '59. Running time, 141 MINS.

Solomon	Yul Brynner
Sheba	Gina Lollobrigida
Adonijah	George Sanders
Pharoah	David Farrar
Abishag	Marisa Pavan
Joab	John Crawford
Herzrai	Laurence Naismith
Ahab	Jose Nieto
Sittar	Alejandro Rey
Baltor	Harry Andrews
Zadok	Julio Pena
Bathseba	Maruchi Fresno
Nathan	William Devlin
Egyptian General	Felix De Pomes
Takyan	Jean Anderson
Josiah	Jack Gwillim
David	Finlay Currie

London landed the world preem of "Solomon And Sheba" and it looks good for a long, prosperous run at the Astoria where it is set for an unlimited season of twice-daily showings. With its title out of scripture and time and stellar value its world b.o. potential is obviously big. The tab for this expensive production was unexpectedly hiked when Tyrone Power died in mid-production (although insurance covered much) and the subsequent hiring of Yul Brynner necessitated new writing as well as new shooting. A figure of over $5,000,000 has been named as the cost of the King Vidor feature and, judging by the spectacle, color and location expenses in Spain the sum seems a reasonable one.

When it is accepted that this epic is mainly a feast for the eye with a number of standout production spots its faults in story and dialog can be more readily forgiven. Film is in Technicolor and Super Technirama 70 and makes full use of both, in sweep and grandeur. Yet, the more intimate scenes are not dwarfed.

The story, which is developed straightforwardly and without pretensions to subtlety, concerns the clash between Solomon and his brother Adonijah when King David crowns the poet-philosopher instead of the warrior. From then on it's a story of political intrigue on the one hand, with Egypt conniving with Sheba to bring down the then prosperous and peaceful Israel, which is flourishing under the wise rule of Solomon who walks in the path of one God, Jehovah, and the treacherous manner in which the Queen of Sheba undermines Solomon but falls in love with him in the process.

The fascinating clash between the two brothers is only spasmodically developed and, inevitably, plays second fiddle to the relationship between the Queen and her infatuated target. This is handled interestingly but is not given the passion of brooding tragedy. This is due mainly to the fact that the dialog is often banal, and bromides rub uneasy shoulders with Biblical quotations. Often what should have been a moving, gripping romance turns out to be little more than an affair between a couple of people at the local golf club.

For this the writers must be faulted. To select one example at random, Sheba's prime minister comes out with a startlingly anticlimactic remark after the Temple of Jehovah has been struck by lightning, Solomon has been virtually forsaken by God, and Abishag has been sacrificed for Solomon's sins: Says Baltor to Sheba. *"We've been living under a great strain these last few days."*

But against these faults can be listed much to be admired. There are some magnificent production scenes. Three startlingly effective battle sequences, the stoning of Sheba, her arrival in Jerusalem, the terrifying wrath of God which razes the Temple of Jehova and Sheba's God of Love, the scene where Solomon gives judgment over the baby, the sight of the plains of Israel made bleak and arid and, above all, the startling dance-ritual to the God of Love which develops into an orgy of writhing, lustful bodies and which is the final crushing cause of the Israelites turning against their King.

Thousands of extras and soldiers were used in these scenes and the battle sequences are little miracles of patient direction and planning. The pagan dance orgy was choreographed and staged by Jaroslav Berger, of Switzerland's Berne Theatre, who has done a topnotch job in drilling the dancers into a turbulent rhythmic pattern. The action of the film is necessarily episodic but Vidor has kept an even balance between the action scenes and the quieter ones. He took on a mighty job and comes out of it well.

The clash of accents is sometimes a shade disturbing but Vidor has, on the whole, been well served by his thesps. Gina Lollobrigida virtually portrays three different Shebas. First, the arrogant, fiery, ambitious Queen intriguing to consolidate her queendom against enemies; then the voluptuous, wily, seductress cunningly determined to ruin Solomon by making him prisoner to her silken tresses and sleek arms; finally, the Sheba who involuntarily falls in love with the King and risks all by denouncing her own gods and becoming converted to Jehovah in order to save her lover at his moment of destiny.

Miss Lollobrigida not only looks stunning, with costumes to enhance her many charms, but shows the Queen to be a woman of sharp brain as well as sensual beauty. Brynner, surprisingly subdued, also does a fine job in presenting a Solomon who credibly suggests a singer of songs, a man of wisdom and of action when needed, a religious man and yet, finally, a man of ordinary flesh and blood who cannot resist Sheba though he recognizes in her a symbol of disaster.

Less happy is George Sanders as Solomon's ambitious, jealous, treacherous brother. Sanders' precise accent hardly fits his role and rarely does he appear to be anything more than Sanders in costume. Marisa Pavan is charming in a colorless role as the girl who loves Brynner. Among many minor roles, David Farrar also seems uneasy as the King of the Pharoahs, but William Devlin as Nathan, Prophet of Doom, Harry Andrews as Sheba's adviser, Finlay Currie, splendid as the dying King David, Jean Anderson as Sheba's maid, Jose Nieto, Alejandro Rey and John Crawford, as a virile Joab, all contribute telling performances.

Sound is mainly good, though

some of Mario Nascimbee's music is given an "echo chamber" effect which is disconcerting. Freddie Young's lensing is outstandingly good. Also there must be praise for the heavy chores of art directors Richard Day and Alfred Sweeney. Finally, a benevolent nod for production manager Richard McWhorter, property master Robert Goodstein and continuity girl Elaine Schreyeck. Ted Richmond, King Vidor and Edward Small can be proud of the achievements of their entire production team. Between them they have produced an eye-compelling film containing spectacle, romance, intrigue, color, treachery and action which despite certain faults, should entertain millions.   *Rich.*

Deux Hommes Dans Manhattan
(Two Men In Manhattan)
(FRENCH)

Paris, Oct. 27.
Columbia release of Belfort-Alter Films release. With Pierre Grasset, Jean Daracante, Jean Lara, Jerry Mengo. Written and directed by Jean-Pierre Melville. Camera, Nicolas Hayer; editor, Monique Bonnot. At Marignan, Paris. Running time, **85 MINS.**

Delmas	Pierre Grasset
Moreau	Jean-Pierre Melville
Rouvier	Jean Darcante
Bob	Jean Lara
Leslie	Jerry Mengo
Miss Nelson	Ginger Hill

New York at night is well utilized as the exterior backdrop of this French film with a manhunt as its motivation. It emerges a fairly slick pic with its theme keeping it moving through the NY night. But sans entirely adequate character motivation, and only surface observation of the milieu, this is primarily for dualer chances abroad with good payoff possibilities.

A good part of this vehicle is in English and it easily gets over the hurdle of a French pic made in the U.S. by using both lingos where necessary since the heroes are French newsmen looking for a French diplomat who has disappeared from the UN. They finally find he has died in the apartment of a mistress. The photog wants to use these pix for a big money scoop but the other insists they mask the affair.

The cynic finally decides to throw away his films and walks off into the N.Y. dawn laughing. The sudden switch in character is out of keeping, but director Jean-Pierre Melville has kept this slight production moving plus some assured bits of native Americana for okay results. Acting is generally fair. Pierre Grasset, as the opportunist, is standout. Technical credits are good. Yank exteriors and Paris interiors are well matched.   *Mosk.*

Happy Anniversary
(SONGS)

Slick picturization of legiter "Anniversary Waltz." High comedy and tuned for audience response. But no Seal.

Hollywood, Oct. 29.
United Artists release of Ralph Fields production. Stars David Niven, Mitzi Gaynor; co-stars Carl Reiner, Loring Smith, Monique Van Vooren, Phyllis Povah, Patty Duke; with Elizabeth Wilson, Kevin Coughlin. Directed by David Miller. Screenplay, Joseph Fields, Jerome Chodorov; based on their play, "Anniversary Waltz"; camera, Lee Garmes; editor, Richard Meyer; music, Sol Kaplan, Robert Allen; songs, "I Don't Regret a Thing," "Happy Anniversary." music, Allen, lyrics, Al Stillman; production de-

signer, Paul Heller; assistant director, Tony La Marca; sound, James Gleason. Previewed at Fox Beverly Theatre, Beverly Hills, Oct. 28, 1959. Running time, **83 MINS.**

Chris Walters	David Niven
Alice Walters	Mitzi Gaynor
Bud	Carl Reiner
Mr. Gans	Loring Smith
Jeanette	Monique Van Vooren
Mrs. Gans	Phyllis Povah
Debbie	Patty Duke
Millie	Elizabeth Wilson
Okkie	Kevin Coughlin

"Happy Anniversary" is a situation farce on the racy side, premarital relations of its two principals forming the basis for comedic complications of the plot. Chock full of laughs and suavely handled, the result is top entertainment of its kind. But film hasn't yet received an MPAA Production Code Seal (United Artists didn't get one, either, for its earlier "The Moon Is Blue") and consequently the UA release may encounter certain booking and Catholic difficulties. (UA will appeal Code Administrator Geoffrey Shurlock's nix, but will release pic regardless of outcome).

Joseph Fields and Jerome Chodorov, who authored original Broadway "Anniversary Waltz," doubled in brass on screenplay and come up with a binder which seldom slackens its fast pace. Film ends somewhat abruptly, but as directed by David Miller the punch carries through most of footage and producer Ralph Fields has peopled his cast with experts in art of fun-making.

David Niven and Mitzi Gaynor costar as a happy couple about to celebrate their 13th wedding anni, living in the happy knowledge that for a full year previous to marriage date they enjoyed the benefits of marital bliss. This blissful recollection, though, when indiscreetly confided by the tipsy Niven to his wife's parents after the anniversary dinner and overheard by young couple's two precocious children, becomes a nightmare, particularly when daughter, believing her parents on the verge of divorce after a quarrel, goes on a tv juve panel show and reveals the family scandal. Yarn winds on a happy note when wife discovers she's pregnant again and relents in her intention of divorce.

Both Niven and Miss Gaynor sock over their comedy with fine timing, and Patty Duke and Kevin Coughlin are amusing in moppet roles. Loring Smith and Phyllis Povah likewise score heftily as wife's parents, and excellent support is afforded by Carl Reiner, as Niven's law partner; Monique Van Vooren, their wealthy divorcee client; and Elizabeth Wilson, a maid. Femme star's chirping of "I Don't Regret a Thing" is a further performance asset.

Technical credits are expertly handled, standouts here including Lee Garmes' photography, Paul Heller's production designing, Richard Meyer's editing and music score by Sol Kaplan and Robert Allen.   *Whit.*

Hound-Dog Man
(COLOR-C'SCOPE-SONGS)

Neatly boxed showcase for teenaged fave Fabian. Appeal to juves and family trade.

Hollywood, Oct. 30.
Twentieth-Fox release of Jerry Wald production. Stars Fabian, Carol Lynley, Stuart Whitman, Arthur O'Connell, Dodie Stevens. Produced by Wald. Directed by Don Siegel. Screenplay, Fred Gipson and Winston Miller; based on Gipson's novel; camera (DeLuxe, Color) Charles G. Clarke; songs, Ken Darby, Frankie Avalon and Sol Ponti, Robert Marcucci and Pete De Angelis, Doc Pomus and Mort

Shuman; music, Cyril J. Mockridge; editor, Louis Loeffler. Previewed at the Picwood Theatre, Oct. 27, '59. Running time, **87 MINS.**

Clint	Fabian
Dony	Carol Lynley
Blackie Scantling	Stuart Whitman
Aaron McKinney	Arthur O'Connell
Nita Stringer	Dodie Stevens
Cora	Betty Field
Fiddling Tom Waller	Royal Dano
Sussie Bell	Margo Moore
Hog Peyson	Claude Akins
Doc Cole	Edgar Buchanan
Grandma Wilson	Jane Darwell
Dave Wilson	L. Q. Jones
Amy Waller	Virginia Gregg
Spud Kinney	Dennis Holmes
Rachael Wilson	Rachel Stephens
Terminus Dooley	Jim Beck
Jewell Crouch	Hope Summers
Sol Fikes	Harry Carter

"Hound-Dog Man" is a good example of how to use a singing personality in a theatrical film, displaying the star to favorable advantage and at the same time making a picture with general appeal. Not very much happens of importance in this Jerry Wald production for 20th-Fox, but what does transpire is amusing, heartwarming and consistently entertaining. "Hound-Dog Man," although having obvious special teenage appeal through its star, Fabian, is also an excellent family film.

The screenplay by Fred Gipson and Winston Miller, from Gipson's novel, is a bucolic tale about a boy and his dog. The boy, delightfully played by young Dennis Holmes, is taken on a hunting trip by his older brother, Fabian, and a friend, Stuart Whitman. Fabian is at an age when he is just beginning to learn about girls. Whitman, somewhat older, has already learned, his problem now is to avoid the marriage noose.

After a hunting trip which ends when the young men discover a neighbor whose leg has been broken while hunting, after a square dance and some drama when Whitman walks out with a married woman, all ends cozily with the boys allowed to make stabs at growing up, and the family of Fabian and young Holmes is knit more tightly than ever.

The screenplay by Gipson and Miller is colloquial without getting cute, and without achieving any terribly intense emotional moments, it creates effective contrast. Don Siegel's direction rides a slack rein on his stars, so that there is a feeling of spaciousness and unhurried ease within the relatively brief running time (87 minutes) of the film. At the same time, he has some chase scenes that are splendid cooperative efforts of direction and editing (Louis Loeffler was the editor), creating a tumbling, breathless reality that are exciting in their own right as well as advancing plot. Siegel has also staged the singing numbers so they are part of the film, and involve others than the two principals chiefly known for song, Fabian and young Dodie Stevens.

There are eight songs, including the title tune, all pleasant, all naturally part of the production. They are "What Big Boy?" "This Friendly World," "Pretty Little Girl," "Single," "I'm Giving Up," "Hill-Top Song" and "Hay Foot, Straw-Foot." Authors are Ken Darby, Frankie Avalon and Sol Ponti, Robert Marcucci and Pete De Angelis, Doc Pomus and Mort Shuman. Cyril J. Mockridge has wound them into a breezy, bouncy score that is conducted in high spirit by Lionel Newman.

While Fabian may not really be an actor at all, he is a clean-looking youngster who handles himself with grace and some charm. He carries conviction. Carol Lynley does a good job, continuing to

fulfill all her early promise. Stuart Whitman carries vitality and virility in his touchy role, the most interesting in the film. Arthur O'Connell, Dodie Stevens, Betty Field, Royal Dano, Claude Akins, Edgar Buchanan, Jane Darwell, Virginia Gregg and Rachel Stephens are among the others in the large cast who register effectively.

Charles G. Clarke's DeLuxe photography, especially his lighting in the sun-glinting forest scenes, is another valuable asset.   *Powe.*

La Casa de la Troya
(College Boarding House)
SPANISH: COLOR)

Madrid, Oct. 27.
Filmax release of a Coral production. Stars Ana Esmeralda, Arturo Fernandez; co-stars Jose Rubio, Julio Riscal, Rafael Bardem, Felix de Pomes and Candida Losada. Directed by Rafael Gil. Screenplay (based on novel by Perez Lugin) by Rafael Serrano; cameraman (Eastmancolor), Michel Kelber; art director, Enrique Alarcon; music, Maestro Parada. At Carlos III, Madrid. Running time, **95 MINS**

Popularity of Perez Lugin's sentimental, romantic novel, read by each succeeding generation of adolescents, and the rentability of nostalgia, make prospects for this bright in the Spanish-language market.

Ne'er-do-well Gerardo, packed off unwillingly to college in Santiago de Compostela, warms to the Gallegan capital city and to student hi-jinks as practiced in the late 19th Century. When he falls for a local beauty, fellow roomers and the student Tuna (traditional guitar and song choral marching society) conspire with him to circumvent parents' dislike of student suitors, and win Carmina's hand.

Fourth film version of the novel since 1924. Rafael Gil's is one of the sprightliest and most faithful to the original source. Ana Esmeralda, Arturo Fernandez and a cast of promising young actors give heart to the romance and make the university jump. Film is also helped by Michel Kelber's expert color lensing of picturesque Santiago, Parada's music score and Alarcon's sets.   *Werb.*

Li'l Abner
(SONGS—V'VISION—COLOR)

Click film version of the hit legit musical.

Hollywood, Oct. 30.
Paramount release of Panama-Frank production. Stars Peter Palmer, Leslie Parrish, Stubby Kaye, Howard St. John, Julie Newmar, Stella Stevens. Produced by Norman Panama. Directed by Melvin Frank. Screenplay, Panama and Frank, from their own stage musical based on Al Capp's characters; camera (Technicolor) Daniel L. Fapp; Music and Lyrics, Gene De Paul and Johnny Mercer; editor, Arthur P. Schmidt. Previewed at the Academy Awards Theatre, Oct. 26, '59. Running time, **113 MINS.**

Li'l Abner	Peter Palmer
Daisy Mae	Leslie Parrish
Marryin' Sam	Stubby Kaye
General Bullmoose	Howard St. John
Stupefyin' Jones	Julie Newmar
Appassionata Von Climax	Stella Stevens
Mammy Yokum	Billie Hayes
Pappy Yokum	Joe E. Marks
Earthquake McGoon	Bern Hoffman
Evil Eye Fleagle	Al Nesor
Romeo Scragg	Robert Strauss
Available Jones	William Lanteau
Senator Jack S. Phogbound	Ted Thurston
Moonbeam McSwine	Carmen Alvarez
Mayor Dawgmeat	Alan Carney
Rasmussen T. Finsdale	Stanley Simmonds

Paramount has a likely moneymaker in "Li'l Abner," the Norman Panama-Melvin Frank filmization of their Broadway hit. The musical is lively, colorful and tune-

ful, done with smart showmanship in every department.

While there's going to be a majority opinion in favor "Li'l Abner," there is also likely to be a dissenting minority. For this disenchanted group, the musical based on Al Capp's comic strip is going to seem one extended play a single joke. the stupidity and naivite of the title character.

The plot of the Panama-Frank screenplay is slight and intended only as a framework with which to festoon gags, songs and musical numbers. According to the script, Congress plans to use li'l Abner's hometown of Dogpatch for an atom bomb testing ground, it being the most worthless locale in the U. S. Dogpatchers must prove the town has some value so it will be spared. The item found is Mammy Yokun's Yokumberry Tonic, a stimulant to health and wealth and romance. The plot then thickens as private enterprise and the U. S. government compete for the celebrated syrup.

The plimsoll mark on Alvin Colt's costumes for the female members of the cast is notably low throughout, and some of the humor is strongly Chic Sale. It's generally done with a slapdash good humor, however, that kids sex rather than encourages leers. The songs, by Gene De Paul and Johnny Mercer, are not the kind that usually become popular hits, but they are breezy and amusing. The music gets a bouncy, infectious scoring and conducting by Nelson Riddle and Joseph L. Lilley. Lilley also did the vocal arrangements.

DeeDee Wood's dances, based on Michael Kidd's stage choreography, move more freely than usual, unconfined by conventional limits, and have considerable dazzle. The vocal numbers tend to get bunched up, as if the missing stage footlights were still imposing their limitations.

Panama's production and Frank's direction keep the film in a comic never-never land. Characterizations are as deliberately unreal as the costumes and the Hal Pereira-J. McMillan Johnson settings. It cuts down interest, however, to have characters who are plainly real-life cartoons.

Because of this, the principals don't have much chance to display anything but the broadest sort of caricature. Peter Palmer, who created the role on Broadway of "Li'l Abner," repeats his assignment here. Leslie Parrish, a delectable dish, essays Daisy Mae, and although delectable, the dish could do with a dash of spice. Stubby Kaye, another Gotham original, creates the most fun with a brisk portrayal of Marryin' Sam. Howard St. John, still another of the originals, has the best scene in the film as General Bullmoose. ("What's good for General Bullmoose is good for the country.") Julie Newmar and Stella Stevens are handsome and amusing as sexy sirens, Billie Hayes and Joe E Marks good as the elder Yokums, and others in the large cast who stand out include Carmen Alvarez, Al Nesor, Robert Strauss and Ted Thurston.

Daniel L. Fapp's Technicolor photography in VistaVision handles the big screen with imagination and grace. Sound by Harold Lewis and Charles Grenzbach is good, although sound level at the preview was so low it undermined some of the film's effectiveness. Editing by Arthur P. Schmidt is especially fine in the dance sequences, a great example of how film choreography can be plotted in editing as much as in the dance studio.

Powe.

Behemoth, Sea Monster
(BRITISH)

Routine science-fiction yarn, suitable as average dualer for undemanding audiences.

London, Nov. 3.

Eros release of a David Diamond (Ted Lloyd) production. Stars Gene Evans, Andre Morell. Directed by Douglas Hickox and Eugene Lourie. Screenplay by Eugene Lourie; camera, Desmond Davies; editor, Lee Doig; music, Ted Astley. Previewed at Studio One, London. Running time, **72 MINS.**

Steve Karnes .... Gene Evans
Professor James Bickford .. Andre Morell
Jeanie .... Leigh Madison
Tom .... Henry Vidon
John .... John Turner
Dr. Sampson .... Jack McGowran
Submarine Officer ... Maurice Kaufmann
Scientist .... Leonard Sachs

Here is a modestly made, routine science-fiction yarn which cannot be regarded as more than a useful dualer for average audiences. Apparently made on a lowish budget, its production value, in proportion, is very good and it is soundly acted. Unfortunately, variable photography and uneven matching rather takes the gloss off some good artwork and special effects.

Yarn concerns the tracking down by a couple of scientists of a giant sea-monster, called Behemoth, after the Biblical reference. This sea-monster is radioactive and is polluting the coast of Britain, causing violent atomic burns on its victims. Occasionally it come ashore spreading mighty destruction and panic. The creature is eventually disposed off by a torpedo from a midget submarine, but not before it has wrecked Westminster Bridge, the Woolwich ferry boat and roamed the terror-stricken streets of South London.

Apart from the first moment, when an agonized victim is struck down by the unknown creature, there's not much horror and precious few thrills in this pic. And when eventually the audience sees the giant creature the effect is largely an anti-climax. Apart from its size, towering over nearby buildings, and a habit of snarling fiercely before letting lose its radioactive breath, Behemoth looks the sort of cute working model that, reduced to about a foot, would be a wow with children at Christmas.

Some of the artwork and special effects are ingenious. Directors Douglas Hickox and Eugene Lourie can be complimented on playing the film seriously and not for laughs. But it's rather difficult to work up many yoks in a screenplay that consists largely of technical talk and action which must be mumbo-jumbo to most audiences. Gene Evans, Andre Morell, Jack McGowran, Leigh Madison and Maurice Kaufmann are among those who conscientiously do their thesping stints with as much serious intent as if they were all in the line for Oscars.

Rich.

The Wreck of the Mary Deare
(C'SCOPE—COLOR)

Sea mystery, realistically done up and excitingly filmed. With Gary Cooper and Charlton Heston as stars, this shapes as a high-grade adventure picture. Good b.o. prospects.

Metro release of a Julian Blaustein production. Stars Gary Cooper, Charlton Heston; features Michael Redgrave, Emlyn Williams, Richard Harris, Virginia McKenna, Ben Wright, Alexander Knox, Cecil Parker. Directed by Michael Anderson; script, Eric Ambler, from Hammond Innes novel; camera (color), Joe Ruttenberg; music, George Duning; editor, Eda Warren. Preview at Loew's 72nd St., N.Y. Oct. 14, '59. Running time, **105 MINS.**

Gideon Patch .... Gary Cooper
John Sands .... Charlton Heston
Nyland .... Michael Redgrave
Sir Walter Falcett ...... Emyln Williams
Chairman .... Cecil Parker
Petrie .... Alexander Knox
Higgins .... Richard Harris
Janet Taggart .... Virginia McKenna
Mike Duncan .... Ben Wright
Gunderson .... Peter Illing
Yules .... Walter Burke
Burrows .... Ashley Cowan
Frank .... Terence de Marney

The mystery of a "ghost" ship looming suddenly out of the night, with only a crazed and battered captain aboard, is solved skillfully and with a good deal of suspense in "The Wreck of the Mary Deare," which Julian Blaustein produced from the Hammond Innes novel originally published in the Saturday Evening Post back in 1956. It's the kind of adventure yarn which, thanks to intelligent treatment and topnotch photography, comes off with a bang and makes for a very entertaining film.

This being Blaustein's first entry at Metro, he and the studio have reason to congratulate themselves. Picture has been kept in a tight frame and, as should be, parts of it are told visually. Scenes of the Mary Deare" looming out of the stormy night and almost colliding with a little salvage ship, the wrecking of the ship on the reefs and, in the end, the underwater exploration of the sunken vessel, **are done with an expert eye for maximum tension and for the possibilities of the wide CinemaScope screen.**

Gary Cooper is cast as Gideon Patch, the captain who's been the victim of foul play but stands accused himself of negligence. And Charlton Heston plays the skipper of a salvage boat who becomes innocently involved in the mystery of the Mary Deare and, in the end, helps solve it. Both men are prefectly cast in rugged roles and Cooper particularly conveys a surprisingly range of emotion and reaction considering his usual, taciturn self in most of his previous pictures.

In the smaller (almost bit) parts, Michael Redgrave and Emlyn Williams are very British as they participate in the London Court of Inquiry. Richard Harris is the snarling villain. Ben Wright is comfortable as Heston's partner. Alexander Knox appears briefly as the ship owner doing business with Red China and Virginia McKenna, one of Britain's top actresses, is literally wasted in a nothing kind of part.

Story has Heston boarding the Mary Deare, which seems abandoned, in the hope of a rich prize. The ship flounders in a stormy sea and, aboard her, Heston finds only Cooper, dazed and quite determined to wreck the ship on the treacherous Minkies. Cooper tells Heston his story and the latter half believes him. At the London inquiry, all goes against Cooper. Eventually, the captain and Heston go on a dangerous under-water expedition inside the hull of the Mary Deare to come up with Cooper's exhoneration.

Eric Ambler's script gives cameraman Joe Ruttenberg plenty of opportunity to whip up excitement with excellent shots. Color is very good. There's a letdown in pace at the middle of the film when the Court of Inquiry appears stacked against Cooper, whose evidence is slim and whose past seeks against him. But the climax comes off with bangup effects that'll have audiences at the edge of their seats. Blaustein has produced a picture that will enjoy a wide and appreciative audience.

Hift.

The Mistress
(JAPANESE)

Strictly for the arties.

Hollywood, Oct. 30.

Edward Harrison release of Daiei production. Stars Hideko Takamine, Hiroshi Akutagawa, Eijiro Tono, Jurichi Uno. Produced by Masaichi Nagata. Directed by Shiro Toyoda. Screenplay, Masashige Narusawa; based on the novel "Gan," by Ogai Mori; camera, Mitsuo Miura; music, Ikama Dan; editor, Masanori Tsujii. Reviewed at Vagabond Theatre, Oct. 24, '59. Running time: **106 MINS.**

Otama .... Hideko Takamine
Okada .... Hiroshi Akutagawa
Suezo .... Eijiro Tono
Kimura .... Jukichi Uno
Osan .... Choko Iida
Zenzo .... Eiza Tanaka
Otsune .... Kumeko Urabe
Oume .... Miki Odagiri
Osada .... Kuniko Miijake
Oshige .... Rieko Himeji
Fish dealer's wife .... Hiroko Machida

For those "art" house still showing art films, "The Mistress," a Daiei production being released here by Edward Harrison, is a probable bet. It's a delicate and muted study of a classic theme—the mistress who wants to become an honest woman—handled in the Italian neo-realism manner. It's not consistently engrossing but it achieves considerable interest and pathos.

Based on a novel by Ogai Mori, the screenplay by Masashige Narusawa is laid in Japan in the early 1900's. Hideko Takamine plays the title role, a young woman ruined for marriage (according to the custom of the time) by a previous seduction. She is talked into becoming the mistress of a wealthy man by a procuress who promises he will eventually marry her. When she discovers this is, not so, she walks out on the life of comparative luxury although there is no indication she will be able to make any kind of comfortable life for herself in the harsh economics of those days.

Shiro Toyoda's direction is low key throughout, understating and suggesting. He creates a mood of emotional desolation, of individuals so numbed by the harsh economic facts of life that communication is all but shut off. It is difficult, surehanded direction.

Miss Takamine is a subtly delicate contrast to her usurious master, Eijiro Toro. So ingenuous are the actors that the film has the documentary quality that reinforces its candid theme. Others in the cast who are memorable include Kumeko Urabe, Miki Odagiri, Kuniko Miijake, Hiroko Machida and Choko Iida.

English subtitles by Donald Richie are good except for some spelling and typographical errors.

Powe.

The Bloody Brood
(CANADIAN)

Toronto, Nov. 3.

Allied Artists release of a Key Film Production; produced and directed by Julian Roffman; associate producers, Ralph Foster and Yvonne Taylor. Stars Jack Betts, Barbara Lord, Peter Falk; features Robert Christie, Ronald Hartman. Original script, Anne Howard Bailey; screenplay, Elwood Ullman, Ben Kerner; director of photography, Eugen Shuftan; editor, Robert Johnson; music, Harry Freedman. Trade shown at Twinex screen-

ing room, Toronto, Oct. 20, 1959. Running time, 80 MINS.

Cliff .... Jack Betts
Ellie .... Barbara Lord
Nico .... Peter Falk
Detective McLeod .... Robert Christie
Francis .... Ronald Hartmann
A Model .... Anne Collins
Studs .... William Brydon
Ricky .... George Sperdakos
Dave .... Ronald Taylor
Weasel .... Michael Zenon
Roy .... Billy Kowalchuk
Louis .... Sammy Sales
Paul, the Poet .... Kenneth Wickes
Blonde Neighbour .... Carol Starkman
Stephanex .... Rolf Colstan

Working with a nearly impossible story, director Julian Roffman has skillfully fashioned a low-budget crime melodrama for the action market in this, his first feature for Meridian studios of Toronto, with world-wide distribution by Allied Artists.

The only justification for making this sordid tale of supposed beatniks who commit a thrill killing is that it should have no difficulty earning back its $100,000 budget, and thus enable Roffman (former documentary film maker) and his partner, Ralph Foster, to go ahead with better stories and set up production on a steady and profitable basis—something not yet achieved in Canadian feature film making. Financing for the Brood was provided by Meridian, Allied and the N. A. Taylor Associates of Toronto.

Everything about this production is efficiently "sick" in the post-Freudian way, including the titles, the characters, the sets and music. The script and its dialogue however, by Anne Howard Dailey, Elwood Ullman and Ben Kerner, is itself pathetically sick and obscure, and only Roffman's virile direction and deft editing, together with the—under the circumstances—convincing portrayals of the cast, prevent the entire production from collapsing into comic absurdity.

Jack Betts gives a pleasant performance as a likeable and "normal" young man trying to find the murderers of his young brother, who had been fed a hamburger with ground glass. In a weird, "beatnik" hangout, he meets Nico, a smooth crook and psychopath, with his sissy companion, Francis. With the aid of Ellie, a mixed-up girl, he discovers how they staged the killing of his brother. Before the police arrive, however, Nico is conveniently killed by his henchmen, Studs and Weasel (whom he had tried to double-cross) in a well-staged knife sequence.

Nico is played with cold, Brando-like impassivity by Peter Falk, Ronald Hartmann is a suitably weak Francis, Ellie is attractively portrayed by Barbara Lord, and among the remainder of this mixed American-Canadian cast, Anne Collins, Ronald Taylor and the other "beatniks" play their parts with high spirits. Robert Christie has some impossible dialogue to cope with as the ineffective police inspector and William Brydon and Michael Zenon, as the henchmen, look like future candidates for a Hammer horror.

Shot in 16 days, film is abstract as to time and place, and except for a glimpse of Canadian money changing hands, the story has no discernible Canadian background—which is probably just as well. It's not related to life in any way, only to stereotypes of stereotypes.

Harry Freedman's jazz themes have been carefully added to the soundtrack by music director Louis Applebaum and they blend effectively with the on-scene music, the action and sound effects. Eugen Shuftan's lighting and photography are highly effective, disguising the economy and restrictions of the sets.

Strange though it may sound, "The Bloody Brood" is almost entirely free from sex, rape and suggestive dialogue, contenting itself with being just sordid and violent. *Pratley.*

Costa Azzurra
(Cote D'Azur)
(ITALIAN-COLOR-DYALISCOPE)

Rome, Oct. 27.

Euro International release of a Glomer (Enzo Merolle) production. Stars Alberto Sordi; features Rita Gam, Elsa Martinelli, Georges Marchal and Franco Fabrizi, Lorella DeLuca, Georgia Moll, Giovanna Ralli and Alberto Ciffariello. Directed by Vittorio Sala. Screenplay, Sala, Sonego, Alessi, Guerra; Camera, (Eastmancolor), Alberto Albertini; music, Roberto Nicolosi; editor, Anna Baragli. At Galleria, Rome. Running time, 105 MINS.

Pic is one of those "vacation" pix with intertwined stories framed by similar setting, in this case a colorful French Riviera. Title and above all the marquee value of Alberto Sordi, Italy's star of the moment, should lead this to big grosses here. Export chances shape as more on the spotty side.

Film is especially worth seeing thanks to another acting gem by Sordi, here seen as a Roman fruit peddler whose wife has received a film offer for a Riviera-localed pic. She loses her job, but he steps in, mistaking the director's interest in him as recognition of talent until his wife wises him up and drags him home. Other episodes are more conventional, though one in which Georgia Moll shares a honeymoon trip with a fanatically jealous (Sicilian) husband has its moments.

Thesping is generally uninspired and color often uneven on the copy seen, but the setting and Sordi win one over in the long run. Very lightweight but amusing. *Hawk.*

Ossessione
(Obsession)
(ITALIAN)

Paris, Nov. 3.

Cocinor-Marceau release of ICI production. Stars Massimo Girotti, Clara Calamai; features Elio Marcuzzo, Juan De Landa, Vittorio Duse. Directed by Luchino Visconti. Screenplay, Pietrangeli, Giuseppi De Santis, Mario Alicata, Gianni Puccini, Visconti from "Postman Always Rings Twice" by James M. Cain; camera, Aldo Tonti, Domenico Scala; editor, Mario Serandrei. At Caumartin - Cinema D'Essai, Paris. Running time, 112 MINS.

Gino .... Massimo Girotti
Giovanna .... Clara Calamai
Husband .... Juan Da Landa
Espanol .... Elio Marcuzzo
Detective .... Vittorio Duse

Though made in 1942 during the war, this is the first official foreign release of this film based on James M. Cain's "The Postman Always Rings Twice." It ran afoul of Fascist blue pencils and was radically cut before release. Copyright troubles, for the Cain novel was owned by Metro, kept it shelved until this year. It emerges a grim tale that rings true in character and might be a good arty house entry abroad.

Director Luchino Visconti has made this essentially Yank hard-boiled tale completely Italian by unfolding it without any recourse to suspense or glibness. Its personages are brought into their tragic position by their own characters and their impoverished milieu. The original storyline is followed as a semi-literate tramp falls for the young wife of an old tavern keeper. This leads to their murdering him, and they turn to distrusting each other to a final ironic climax.

Stark lensing and excellent acting give this banal slice-of-life tale almost tragic proportions. There are some patchy spots because footage is still missing. But this adds up to deep adult fare which could pay off in some spots. Another drawback might be its dated air since the dress is of a certain period in Italian history. Sound is not up to par but other technical credits are. Acting is exemplary. *Mosk.*

En Lektion I Karlek
(A Lesson In Love)
(SWEDISH)

Paris, Nov. 3.

Telecinex release of Svensk Filmindustri production. Stars Eva Dahlbeck, Gunnar Bjornstrand, Harriet Andersson; features Yvonne Lombard, Ake Gronberg. Written and directed by Ingmar Bergman. Camera, Martin Bodin, Bengt Nordwall; editor, Lennart Wallin. At Ursulines-Cinema D' Essai, Paris. Running time 90 MINS.

Marianne .... Eva Dahlbeck
David .... Gunnar Bjornstrand
Nix .... Harriet Andersson
Suazanne .... Yvonne Lombard
Carl Adam .... Ake Gronberg

Nowadays when the name, Bergman is mentioned in film circles it usually means Ingmar not Ingrid. The former, a Swedish film director-writer, has broken into regular distrib here and now means something on the art circuits of the U.S. and England. This is another of his earlier pix brought here for release.

This is a light comedy on marriage and concerns a gynecologist and his wife whose marriage is breaking up after 17 years. The good and bad are deftly brought into focus. It all ends in a wild foray into the lower depths of Denmark where the couple is reconciled.

Bergman keeps this moving with shrewd insight glances into character. However, there is a tendency to go in for too much talk and epigrams on the frailties of love and marriage. But cohesive acting, knowing direction and the right balance between character and complications make this an above-average situation comedy. It could have arty theatre chances abroad on the Bergman name and the film's sparkle. It has too much talk for more general spotting. Technical credits are fine. Bergman again shows he can make ideas quite entertaining filmically. *Mosk.*

Edge of Eternity

Well-made meller set in the beauty of the Grand Canyon. B.O. could be reasonably good.

Hollywood, Oct. 30.

Columbia release of a Thunderbird (Kendrick Sweet) production. Stars Cornel Wilde, Victoria Shaw, Mickey Shaughnessy; with Edgar Buchanan and Rian Garrick; also Jack Elam, Alexander Lockwood, Dabbs Greer, Tom Fadden, Wendell Holmes. Directed by Donald Siegel; screenplay, Knut Swenson and Richard Collins, from a story by Ben Markson and Swenson; camera, Burnett Guffey, editor, Jerome Thoms; music, Daniele Amfitheatrof. Previewed at the studio, Oct. 22, '59. Running time, 81 MINS.

Les Martin .... Cornel Wilde
Janice Kendon .... Victoria Shaw
Scotty O'Brien .... Mickey Shaughnessy
Sheriff Edwards .... Edgar Buchanan
Bob Kendon .... Rian Garrick
Bill Ward .... Jack Elam
Jim Kendon .... Alexander Lockwood
Gas Station Attendant .... Dabbs Greer
Eli .... Tom Fadden
Sam Houghton .... Wendell Holmes
The Dealer .... George Cisar
Pilot .... Buzz Westcott
Suds Reese .... Ted Jacques

"Edge of Eternity" is a tightly made melodrama which, for mood and excitement, takes sparkling advantage of Arizona's Grand Canyon. Its makers are to be commended for turning out a moderately budgeted film that is entertaining, slickly produced and to the point. The Columbia release should return an ample profit.

Producer Kendrick Sweet conceived the action with the Canyon in mind, thus accounting for the perfect fit. And with thrills spanning 9,000 feet across a gorge big enough to swallow a mountain, the final reel unspools in a staggering, heart-corroding climax. Knut Swenson (who really is Marion Hargrove) and Richard Collins wrote the screenplay from a story by Swenson and Ben Markson. While not entirely devoid of meller cliches, it is far from pedestrian as it handsomely weaves the plot in and out of the natural setting and turns what essentially is a cops-and-robbers yarn into a carefully and skillfully concocted film.

Director Don Siegel made the Canyon the star, kept the action believable, made sure ultimate solution was a surprise and held the dangers at a furiously high level.

Cornel Wilde plays an up-to-date sheriff's deputy who must solve a murder to re-establish his reputation as an able law officer. The victim is an executive of a gold mine who discovers his gold is being stolen for shipment to Mexico where it brings $50 an ounce instead of the paltry $35 an ounce on the domestic market. When two of the thieves bite the dust, either from internal or external strife, the remaining culprit, Mickey Shaughnessy, takes Victoria Shaw hostage and races off in a brand new Thunderbird (which just happens to be the name of Sweet's independent company). Wilde chases the pair straight into the "dancing bucket," a bright yellow tram car which rides a high cable from one canyon wall to the other. And, at this point, may a laurel of kudos be unreeled for Hollywood stunters Guy Way, Chuck Couch and Rosemary Johnston, who play in and hang from the perilous bucket as if they were enjoying the safety of a sandbox.

Wilde's performance is westernly subtle, his appearance and manner at once establishing him as the ultimate hero. His good performance is matched by a high-spirited one from Miss Shaw and Shaughnessy makes a trickly villain. Edgar Buchanan is good as the sheriff, as is Rian Garrick as a youthful dipsomaniac.

Burnett Guffey's photography (Eastman Color by Pathe) is exceptional, making fine use of the browns of the canyon and the blues of Arizona skies. His subjective camera, allowing the audience to ride through the giant chasm, is excellent. Robert Peterson's art direction keeps the real location feeling, with adept work from film editor Jerome Thoms and soundman George Cooper. Daniele Amfitheatrof's musicale score is very good, particularly the use of the whimsical bassoon.

The "dancing bucket" belongs to the United States Guano Corp., a firm that has found it profitable to extricate bat manure from the canyon. A closing credit expresses the film company's appreciation to the Guano firm "without whose cooperation this picture could not have been made." Undeniably, the

producers were taking a chance with such a credit, but the film is good enough to withstand any snide references. *Ron.*

The Miracle
(TECHNIRAMA; COLOR)

Max Reinhardt's old auditorium spectacle. Splashy, lavish religioso. Good b.o. despite sub-standard early 19th Century saga.

Hollywood, Nov. 6.
Warner Bros. production and release. Stars Carroll Baker, Roger Moore, Walter Slezak, Vittorio Gassman, Katina Paxinou, Dennis King, Gustavo Rojo. Produced by Henry Blanke. Directed by Irving Rapper. Screenplay. Frank Butler; based on the play by Karl Vollmoeller as staged by Max Reinhardt; camera (Technicolor), Ernest Haller; music, Elmer Bernstein; editor, Frank Bracht. Previewed at the studio, Oct. 20, '59. Running time, **121 MINS.**

Teresa	Carroll Baker
Michael Stuart	Roger Moore
Flaco	Walter Slezak
Guido	Vittorio Gassman
La Roca	Katina Paxinou
Casimir	Dennis King
Cordoba	Gustavo Rojo
Reverend Mother	Isobel Elsom
Carlitos	Carlos Rivas
Wellington	Torin Thatcher
Sister Dominica	Elspeth March
Gata	Daria Massey
Bolting	Lester Matthews

Warner Bros.' multi-million dollar spectacle, "The Miracle" though laid in 19th Century is a "biblical" subject with elements and approach, of such films. Should be a commercial success.

Henry Blanke's production has bullfights, military battles, lavish ballroom parties, music, dancing, gypsies and vaulted cathedrals echoing to choirs of nuns. It has about everything, in fact, except a genuinely spiritual story. For the studio and the producer that made "The Nun's Story" this is notable.

"The Miracle" was a costume special of the late German stager Max Reinhardt. Its theme is the recurrent one in religious legend, of the god, goddess or angel who assumes human shape to intervene directly in the affairs of men.

According to Frank Butler's screenplay, based on Karl Vollmoeller's old play, Carroll Baker is a postulant at a Spanish convent when she falls in love with Roger Moore, a soldier in the future Duke of Wellington's Army, then battling Napoleon in Spain. When she leaves the convent to follow Moore, "The Miracle" occurs. The statue of the Virgin in the convent chapel comes down from its pedestal and assumes the form of the postulant.

Miss Baker is off on various adventures. She becomes betrothed to gypsy Vittorio Gassman, but departs when he is killed by his jealous brother, Carlos Rivas. She becomes the sweetheart of bullfighter Gustavo Rojo and is taken under the "protection" of nobleman Dennis King. Rojo is killed in the bullring. She finally meets Moore again in Belgium, just before Waterloo, but having found him, renounces him to return to the convent.

Irving Rapper's direction is effective in the spacious exteriors, moving massed groupings with force and interest. It is less perceptive in the handling of individuals and their inter-action. Granted that characterizations in films of this sort tend to fall into stereotypes, there could still be more reality and diversity than Rapper and Butler have achieved. As for the theme itself, it is not exactly clear what "The Miracle" is supposed to do, other than give Miss Baker a chance to gallivant about Europe in a variety of costumes.

Although there isn't much room for character subtlety in this sort of pictorial grandeur, still Carroll Baker might have attempted to register with more warmth or, lacking that, less detachment. Miss Baker too often seems merely sullen. The men are pretty much of a pattern. Roger Moore is a big, handsome Englishman; Vittorio Gassman, a big, handsome gypsy; Gustavo Rojo, a big, handsome Spaniard. Walter Slezak tries a light-handed touch as a larcenous gypsy and makes it pleasant. Dennis King has elegance, and Katina Paxinou smoulders through a couple of scenes that generate some excitement.

Ernest Haller's photography in Technicolor and Technirama is one of the film's strongest assets, creating some striking visual effects. Technical aspects are generally good. *Powe.*

La Vida Aldredor
(Life Around Us)
(SPANISH)

Madrid, Nov. 3.
Mercurio release of Tecisa production. Stars Fernando Fernan Gomez, Analia Gade; co-stars Manolo Moran, Carmen de Lirio, Francisco Camoiras, Felix Fernandez. Directed by Fernan Gomez. Screenplay by Gomez, Manuel Pilares and F. Soria; cameraman, Alfredo Fraile; music, Rafael de Andres. At Cine Callao, Madrid. Running time, **92 MINS.**

Continuation of a previous Fernan Gomez success, "Life Ahead," this "Life Around Us" follows the same Italio-inspired neo-realistic comedy pattern. But it falls short on sustained humor and situation.

Gag-laden dialogue in opening reels effectively spoofs with everyday household dilemma of making both ends meet on meagre earnings as a baby is born. Husband essays a variety of added part-time jobs, finally uses his law training to defend petty lawbreakers. Wife plies her newlyborn with modern child training and raises extra coin teaching the subject to neighbors.

Script creaks and sputters about midway, becoming talky sans mirth. A good cast including Fernan Gomez, Analia Gade, Manolo Moran and Francisco Camoiras, is not good enough to carry the film on performance alone. Technical credits are fair. *Werb.*

House of Seven Hawks

Well-made suspense mystery.
Hollywood, Nov. 6.
Metro release of David E. Rose production. Stars Robert Taylor, Nicole Maurey; features Linda Christian, Donald Wolfit. Directed by Richard Thorpe. Screenplay, Joe Eisinger; based on Victor Canning's novel, "House of Seven Flies"; camera, Ted Scaife; music, Clifton Parker; editor, Ernest Walter. Previewed at the studio, Nov. 6, '59. Running time, **91 MINS.**

John Nordley	Robert Taylor
Constanta	Nicole Maurey
Elsa	Linda Christian
Hoff Commissar Van Der Stoor	Donald Wolfit
Wilhelm Dekker	David Kossoff
Capt. Rohner	Eric Pohlmann
Charlie Ponz	Philo Hauser
Inspector Sluiter (Mr Anselm)	Gerard Heinz

One of Metro's British productions, "House of Seven Hawks" is a skillfully made film in all departments, well written, acted, and directed. The David E. Rose production is not important enough in today's market to attract substantial business on its own, but it is a creditable picture all the same, and will make for healthy twin-billing.

Jo Eisinger's crisp, humorous and exciting screenplay is based on a novel by Victor Canning, "House of Seven Flies." In its film form, it concerns an American, Robert Taylor, who operates a charter boat service out of a British port. In trouble with the British authorities because of his casual attitude about shipping regulations, Taylor gets in serious trouble when one of his passengers turns up dead.

The screenplay traces a maze of events starting with the last days of World War II in Holland, and the disappearance then of a substantial treasure. Taylor gets on the trail of the loot, a sackful of cut diamonds worth millions of dollars, in trying to give the police a satisfactory explanation for why his passenger died, murdered, as it turns out.

Richard Thorpe's direction is adroit in taking advantage of the British and Dutch locations, in spotting and highlighting the bizarre characters who liven the narrative and advance the story. There is, in Thorpe's casting and direction, more than a suggestion of some of the best American mystery melodramas of 15 or 20 years ago, "The Maltese Falcon" and others.

Taylor does a good job with his characterization, assisted by two leading ladies, Nicole Maurey and Linda Christian. Donald Wolfit, David Kossoff, Eric Pohlmann and Philo Hauser are outstanding as the leading figures in the mystery, distinctive, intriguing characters, unusual in such a film.

Camera work by Ted Scaife is good, shadowy enough to sustain the atmosphere of mystery, but clear enough for any projection. Music by Clifton Parker is sparing but effective. *Powe.*

Arrangiatevi!
(You're On Your Own)
(ITALIAN)

Cineriz release of a Cineriz production. Features Toto, Laura Adani, Peppino DeFilippo, Franca Valeri, Vittorio Caprioli, Cristina Gaioni, Cathala Caro, Mario Valdemarin. Directed by Mauro Bolognini. Screenplay by Nenvenuti-DeBernardi, from the story, "Casa Nova, Vita Nova," by Mario DeMajo and Vinicio Gioli; camera, Carlo Carlini; music, Carlo Rustichelli; editor, Roberto Cinquini. At Bernini, Rome. Running time, **110 MINS.**

Fragile story erected on a single gag, a family in desperate search of a home, settles down unwittingly in a closed-down bordello. Innumerable double-entendres ensue, with family father, played by Peppino DeFilippo, who is the only one to know the original use of long hoped-for home. He desperately seeks to keep the truth from the eyes and ears of remainder of the family. It's mostly for local consumption, where the cast names will help.

Director Mauro Bolognini all too often allows humor to get too heavy and sometimes even untasteful in milking his single situation through an overlong running time. Sound track is loud and confused. Credits generally good. *Hawk.*

Strictly Confidential
(BRITISH)

Corny little comedy that can only hope to touch the best b.o. in undiscriminating houses.

London, Nov. 3.
Rank release of an Alliance-Twickenham (Guido Coen) production. Stars William Kendall, Richard Murdoch, William Hartnell. Directed by Charles Saunders. Story and screenplay by Brock Williams; camera, Jimmy W. Harvey; editor, Peter Pitt; music, Malcolm Lockyer. Previewed at RFD Private Theatre, London. Running Time, **62 MINS.**

Commander Binham-Ryley	Richard Murdock
Major Rory McQuarry	William Kendall
Maxine Millard	Maya Koumani
Grimshaw	William Hartnell
Warder	Colin Rix
Captain Sharples	Ellis Irving
Barman	Larry Burns
Inspector Shearing	Bruce Seton
Rizzi	Paul Bogdan
Muspratt	Norman Pitt

Basil Wantage .... Neil Hallatt
Elsie .... Jean Trend
Mellinger .... Llewellyn Rees
Hot Dog Man ....Harry Ross

There's presumably a market for this type of corny comedy, but it's a pity to see such a practised professional as producer Guido Coen, director Charles Saunders and some competent performers involved in a trifle that cannot hope to be more than a barely adequate filler in minor houses. Charles Saunders' direction gets little help from the story and screenplay cf Brock Williams, which touches the limits in feeble dialog. The odd thing is that Coen and Saunders have been responsible for some useful pix in the past.

The brief anecdote involves William Kendall (ex-Army) and Richard Murdoch (ex-Navy) as two conmen who have just been tossed out of the cooler. They team up and think they're on easy street when a rich young widow hires them as joint managing directors of her factory. Stupidly, she doesn't realize that they're ex-convicts. They, equally stupidly, don't realize that they're stooges in a shady deal which juggles with shares. The whole affair misfires limply.

This tepid little yarn plods along, mercifully, for only 62 minutes. Meanwhile, Murdoch and Kendall, plus William Hartnell as a crusty works manager, struggle heroically but unsuccessfully with naive dialog and foreseeable situations. Maya Koumani is in for sex-appeal. She's a goodlooker but has no chance to prove whether she also can act.

Jimmy Harvey's camerawork is okay, and the sets and location shots are authentic. But, all in all, this is a little number that should be forgotten for the sake of all the talent involved.   Rich.

La Passe du Diable
(The Devil's Pass)
(FRENCH-C'SCOPE-COLOR)
Paris, Nov. 3.
20th-Fox release of G. Beauregarde production. Directed by Jacques Dupont, Pierre Schoendoerfer. Screenplay and commentary, Joseph Kessel; commentary done by Jean Negroni; camera, Eastmancolor), Raoul Coutard; editor, Marcelle Lioret. At Raimu, Paris, Running time, 80 MINS.

Documentary-type film works in a storyline fairly laboriously to make this only a possible dualer item abroad on its color and Cinemascope unveiling of little known Afghanistan. It is about a young boy who follows his brother to an annual meet in which riders compete and fight in a central ring. He is helped to get there by a mysterious stranger, and is killed when he tries to warn his brother of a bad strap on his saddle.

Film has some colorful views of the country but is stretched and lacks the insight to make this of any unusual interest. C'Scope and color are good and non-actors acceptable.   Mock.

Labyrinth
(GERMAN-ITALIAN)
Berlin, Nov. 3.
UFA release of UFA and Cei-Incom (Rome) production. Stars Nadja Tiller, Peter van Eyck, Amadeo Nazzari. Directed by Rolf Thiele. Screenplay, Gregor von Rezzori and Thiele, after a novel by Gladys Baker; camera, Klaus von Rauthenfeld; music, H. M. Majewski; editor, A. Schoennenbeck. At Atelier am Zoo. Running time, 94 MINS.
Georgia .... Nadja Tiller
Ron Stevens .... Peter von Eyck
Dr. de Lattre .... Amadeo Nazzari
Marjorie .... Nicole Badal
Frau Gretzer ...... Elisab Flickenschild

Sir Agamemnon ..... Harald Kreutzberg
Dr. Beckmeier .... Benno Hoffmann

The best that can be said about this UFA release is that it's well made and optically interesting. Otherwise, it's a strange mixture of psychological drama, satire and social-criticism. What Rolf Thiele, creator of the successful "Girl Rosemarie," intended for this pic will remain a puzzle to most cinemagoers. Mild boxoffice looms.

Thiele attempted a serious theme, handled with a light satirical touch, but he exaggerated the satirical elements so much that much of it does not become involuntarily funny; also the message gets lost.

Localed in a Swiss sanitarium where there are all sorts of people, mainly from the alcoholic genre and all from high society. Central figure is a rich American authoress who wants to get cured from her mania for drinking and mental depressions. Her case looks hopeless but a shock created by the suicide of a young girl in the home leads her back to the right path.

Nadja Tiller (of "Rosemarie" fame), Peter van Eyck and Amadeo Nazzari head the cast. Acting is not overwhelming. There are several good supporting players.
                Hans.

Ben-Hur
(CAMERA 65—COLOR)

Blockbuster to top all previous blockbusters.

Metro release of Sam Zimbalist production. Stars Charlton Heston, Jack Hawkins, Stephen Boyd, Haya Harareet, Hugh Griffith, Martha Scott, Sam Jaffe and Cathy O'Donnell. Directed by William Wyler. Screenplay, Karl Tunberg from the novel by Gen. Lew Wallace; camera (Camera 65-Technicolor), Robert L. Surtees; editor, Ralph E. Winters and John D. Dunning; music, Miklos Rozsa. At Loew's State, N. Y., Nov. 16, '59. Running time, 212 MINS.
Judah Ben-Hur .... Charlton Heston
Quintus Arrius .... Jack Hawkins
Messala .... Stephen Boyd
Esther .... Haya Harareet
Sheik Ilderim .... Hugh Griffith
Miriam .... Martha Scott
Simonides .... Sam Jaffe
Tirzah .... Cathy O'Donnell
Balthasar .... Finlay Currie
Pontius Pilate .... Frank Thring
Drusus .... Terence Longden
Sextus .... Andre Morell
Flavia .... Marina Berti
Tiberius .... George Relph
Malluch .... Adi Berber
Amrah .... Stella Vitelleschi
Mary .... Jose Greci
Joseph .... Laurence Payne
Spintho .... John Horsley
Metellus .... Richard Coleman
Marius .... Duncan Lamont
Aid To Tiberius .... Ralph Truman
Gaspar .... Richard Hale
Melchoir .... Reginald Lal Singh
Quaestor .... David Davies
Jailer .... Dervis Ward
The Christ .... Claude Heater
Gratus .... Mino Doro
Chief of Rowers .... Robert Brown
Rower No. 42 .... John Glenn
Rower No. 43 .... Maxwell Shaw
Rower No. 28 .... Emile Carrer
Leper .... Tutte Lemkow
Hortator .... Howard Lang
Captain, Rescue Ship ..... Ferdy Mayne
Doctor .... John Le Mesurier
Blind man .... Stevenson Lang
Barca .... Aldo Mozele
Starter at Race .... Thomas O'Leary
Centurion .... Noel Sheldon
Officer .... Hector Ross
Soldier .... Bill Kuehl
Man in Nazareth .... Aldo Silvani
Villager .... Diego Pozzetto
Marcello .... Dino Fazio
Raimondo .... Michael Cosmo
Cavalry Officer .... Aldo Pini
Decurian .... Remington Olmstead
Galley Officer ...... Victor De La Fosse
Galley Officer .... Enzo Fiermonte
Mario .... Hugh Billingsley
Roman at Bath .... Tiberio Mitri
Pilate's Servant .... Pietro Tordi
The Corinthian .... Jerry Brown
The Byzantine .... Otello Capanna
Syrian .... Luigi Marra
Lubian .... Cliff Lyons
Athenian .... Edward J. Auregui
Egyptian .... Joe Yrigoyan
Armenian .... Alfredo Danesi
Old Man .... Raimondo Van Riel
Seaman .... Mike Dugan
Sportsman .... Joe Canutt

The $15,000,000 bet Metro topper Joseph R. Vogel and his associates put on a chariot race should result in the biggest payoff in the history of film business. "Ben-Hur" is a majestic achievement, representing a superb blending of the motion picture arts by master craftsmen. "Gone With the Wind," Metro's own champion all-time top grosser, will eventually have to take a back seat.

The big difference between "Ben-Hur" and other spectacles, biblical or otherwise, is its sincere concern for human beings. They're not just pawns reciting flowery dialog to fill gaps between the action and spectacle scenes. They arouse genuine emotional feeling in the audience.

This has been accomplished without sacrificing the impact of the action, panoramic, and spectacle elements. As a matter of fact, the famous chariot race between Ben-Hur, the Prince of Judea, and Messala, the Roman tribune — a trademark of the Gen. Lew Wallace

classic—will probably be preserved in film archives as the finest example of the use of the motion picture camera to record an action sequence. The race, directed by Andrew Marton and Yakima Canutt, represents some 40 minutes of the most hair-raising excitement that film audiences have ever witnessed.

Wisely, however, the film does not depend wholly on sheer spectacle. The family relationship between Ben-Hur and his mother, Miriam, and his sister, Tirzah; his touching romance with Esther, the former slave; his admiration of the Roman consul, Quintus Arrius, whom he rescues after a sea battle; his association with the Arab horseowner, Shiek Ilderim; and his struggle with Messala, the boyhood friend who became his mortal enemy, make moving and hearttugging scenes. And overshadowing these personal intimacies and conflicts is the deeply religious theme involving the birth and cruxification of Christ.

That the story is never trite or corny, factors that have detracted from previous biblical films, is a tribute to the script and director William Wyler. A veteran director, although new to the spectacle film, latter succeeded superbly in bringing out every nuance of each individual scene and in eliminating the artificiality that is too often apparent in topical conversations between biblical characters.

Karl Tunberg receives sole screen credit, although such heavyweight writers as Maxwell Anderson, S. N. Behrman, Gore Vidal and Christopher Fry, also worked on the film. Fry, a respected British poet-playwright, was present on the set throughout the production in Rome.

Well-chosen cast contributes greatly to final achievement. Charlton Heston, the Moses of "The Ten Commandments," is excellent as the brawny yet kindly Ben-Hur who survives the life of a galley slave to seek revenge of his enemy Messala and the Roman conquerors of Judea. Haya Harareet, the Israeli actress making her first appearance in an American film, emerges as a performer of stature. Her portrayal of Esther, the former slave and daughter of Simonides, steward of the House of Hur, is sensitive and revealing. Wyler presumably deserves considerable credit for taking a chance on an unknown. She has a striking appearance and represents a welcome departure from the standard Hollywood ingenue.

Jack Hawkins, as Quintus Arrius, the Roman consul who adopts Ben-Hur, adds another fine depiction to his acting career. Stephen Boyd, as Ben-Hur's enemy Messala, is not the standard villain, but succeeds in giving understanding to his position in his dedication to the Roman Empire.

Martha Scott and Cathy O'Donnell are fine as Ben-Hur's mother and sister who are miraculously cured of leprosy after they witness the cruxification of Christ. Hugh Griffith, as the Sheik Ilderim under whose colors Ben-Hur participates in the chariot race, is one of the standouts of the film. Other good portrayals are given by Sam Jaffe, as Simonides; Frank Thring, as Pontius Pilate, Finlay Currie, as the Egyptian who followed the star to Bethlehem, and Andre Morell, as Sextus. Credit is also due the rest of the large cast and the thousands of extras who appeared in the film.

The film, which took 10 months to complete at Rome's Cinecitta Studios, was photographed by Robert L. Surtees in Metro's new Camera 65 process. The new process, shown in 70m, achieves a clarity and color definition that has been rare in film presentations. Surtees has accomplished wonders in filming the intimate scenes as well as the chariot race, the sea battle, the birth and cruxification of Christ, Caesar's welcome of the hero Quintus Arris, and the various outdoor scenes of Rome and Judea.

The 300 sets, constructed under the supervision of art directors William Horning and Edward Carfagno, are one of the highlights of the film, particularly the massive arena for the chariot sequence. The musical score by Miklos Rozza is another factor that contributes to the overall excellence of the giant project.

Not to be forgotten in the credits is the late Sam Zimbalist, who died of heart attack in Rome when the film was near completion. "Ben-Hur" is a fitting climax to Zimbalist's career as a producer.

Metro undertook the venture at a time when the company was at its lowest ebb. The result is a complete vindication of the policies of Vogel and his management team.

The film runs three hours and 32 minutes with a 15-minute intermission. *Holl.*

Passeport Pour Le Monde

(Passport For The World)
(FRENCH—DOCUMENTARY—COLOR)

Paris, Nov. 10.

Pathe release of Jesse Hartman production. Directed by Victor Stoloff. Written by and with Peter Townsend; commentary, Henri Champetier spoken by Claude Dauphin; camera (Eastmancolor), Andre Bac; editor, Marcelle Lioret. At Calypso, Paris. Running time, 100 MINS.

Film is a restaging of the trip of Group Commander Peter Townsend around the world, after his break with the Princess Margaret. Its main interest would stem from any public curiosity in seeing him after the Princess episode and his recent engagement. Otherwise, this is a grabbag of conventional shots of various places around the world, with Townsend driving or walking through them.

He emerges, stolid, good natured and a good sportsman. There are some glimpses of Peru, the Sahara Desert and the U.S. which are well observed. Lensing is good and color okay, but this is mainly for a medium feature cutdown or television use abroad. ***Mosk.***

Beloved Infidel

(COLOR—C'SCOPE)

Slick, not very convincing, Gregory Peck, Deborah Kerr for insurance. A woman's picture.

20th-Fox release of Jerry Wald production. Stars Gregory Peck, Deborah Kerr, Eddie Albert; features Philip Ober, Herbert Rudley, John Sutton, Karin Booth, Ken Scott. Directed by Henry King; screenplay, Sy Bartlett, based on book of same title by Sheilah Graham and Gerold Frank; camera (Color by DeLuxe), Leon Shamroy; music, Franz Waxman; song, "Beloved Infidel," by Paul Francis Webster and Waxman; editor, William Reynolds. Previewed at 20th homeoffice, N.Y., Nov. 16, '59. Running time, 123 MINS.

F. Scott Fitzgerald .... Gregory Peck
Sheilah Graham .... Deborah Kerr
Carter .... Eddie Albert
John Wheeler .... Philip Ober
Stan Harris .... Herbert Rudley
Lord Donegall .... John Sutton
Janet Pierce .... Karin Booth
Robinson .... Ken Scott
Dion .... Buck Class
Johnson .... A. Cameron Grant
Miss Bull .... Cindy Ames

The protracted and stormy Sheilah Graham-F. Scott Fitzgerald romance in the 1930's is brought to the screen by producer Jerry Wald, taking Miss Graham's autobiographical book—"Beloved Infidel"—as his jumping off point. Judging by the book, Fitzgerald, despite his drinking and his eccentricities, was a fascinating personality, a tortured genius from Princeton who ran aground in Hollywood. Miss Graham didn't paint herself in quite so favorable a light.

In the picture, possibly for reasons of audience appeal, the tables have been turned. It is the columnist, played by Deborah Kerr, who suffers nobly and "serves" sympathetically. It is Fitzgerald who is portrayed as a weak, moody, spoiled child with little more to his credit than the attractive looks of Gregory Peck.

Unquestionably, there is a femme audience for this pictorially interesting and at times emotionally moving picture. But producer Wald, writer Sy Bartlett and director Henry King have turned out a kind of "elevated soap opera" that doesn't quite register. The romantic involvement of Peck and Miss Kerr has tenderness and plenty of ups and downs, but like those repeated shots of the surf pounding in, it runs out of juice and becomes static. At the end, it's difficult to maintain interest in a couple consisting of two uninteresting people.

This is primarily a film about a sharp, aggressive film columnist who falls in love with a man who is her intellectual superior by miles and who, through the association with him, attains a new human stature. It is also a film in which the characters go mostly unexplained, and this makes for a superficiality which deprives them of sympathy. What's more, the acting, while excellent and persuasive in parts, is shallow and artificial in others.

Problem is primarily with Peck, who brings to Fitzgerald the kind of cleancut looks and youthful appearance that conflict with the image of a has-been novelist, whacking away at a studio typewriter to make a living and to meet his family obligations. Peck's most dramatic moments come when he's drunk and insecure and whose disappointment over failure express themselves in attacks on Miss Graham. Whatever or whoever at fault, he just doesn't bring it off. All that remains is the pleasant Peck personality, which conflicts with the concept of Fitzgerald.

Miss Kerr is a beautiful woman with a very special kind of warmth. She can express a great deal with a slight movement of her head or a gesture of the hand, and her torment and despair when Peck goes on a binge make for good cinematics. But she, too, can't overcome the artificiality of the part or the situation, and after a while the affair just peters out and becomes dull. Miss Kerr starts out one way and changes her whole approach when she meets Peck. This is explained in the book, but not in the film. And it definitely needs explanation, much as other aspects of her history need clarifying.

In the smaller roles, Eddie Albert is okay as the family friend. Philip Ober does a competent job as the North American Newspaper Alliance boss who hires Miss Graham. Herbert Rudley is good as the producer and Karin Booth registers in a brief part as a star.

Bartlett's script tries to capture the spirit of the book, which was quite eloquent when it came to Miss Graham's relationship with Fitzgerald. Unfortunately, there's nothing inspired about the dialog and, of necessity, there is an overabundance of talk. Henry King directed in a routine way.

Leon Shamroy's camera work, in DeLuxe color, is good and in certain scenes quite excellent. Shot of the two principals huddling on the beach after Miss Kerr has confessed her humble beginnings to Peck, is memorable and beautiful. Color texture and effects are tops.

Paul Francis Webster and Franz Waxman wrote the musical theme, which wells up richly. Waxman wrote the general background score. William Reynolds did the editing. Picture runs over two hours, which is too long. It could have been tightened without any loss to anyone. "Beloved Infidel" can and will be sold as an unusual love story. Its two principals are attractive, but the action and the conflict are insufficient to set spark to the flame. *Hift.*

El Dia de Los Enamorados

(St. Valentine's Day)
(SPANISH—EASTMANCOLOR)

Madrid, Nov. 10.

An As Films release of an As Films-Asturias Films coproduction. Stars Tony Leblanc, Antonio Casal, Conchita Velasco, Jorge Rigaud, Katia Loritz, Angel Aranda, Mabel Carr, Manuel Monroy, Maria Mahor. Directed by Fernando Palacios. Screenplay, A Vich, P. Maso, R. J. Salvia; cameraman, Alejandro Ulloa; music, Augusto Alguero. At Palacio de la Musica, Madrid. Running time, 95 MINS.

In this technically well-made sentimental comedy dealing with young lovers on St. Valentine's Day, authors are prudishly unaware that a kiss expresses more than a thousand words of dialogue. While comedy accent stands out and some patter has a racy local flavor, audience is fed large patches of unexciting, ultra-moral gab on a subject that must have more than one hue. Dubious for foreign market.

St. Valentine sends an emissary earthwards to make it a big Feb. 14 for lovers and talks one couple to the altar, another to the engagement ring counter and a third off to a promising start. For good measure (or bad), there is a corny Miss Lonelyhearts fourth pair formed by a poor rich girl and med student who wants her, not her money.

Sturdy direction gives wordy script more than a breath of spirited conduct as well as a pleasant blend of local character and well-lensed Madrid sites. Generally, the cast fulfills in this technically good-looking film. *Werb.*

Five Out of a Milion

(CZECH)

San Francisco, Nov. 14.

Ceskoslovensky Film production. Stars Jaroslav Marvan, Jan Cifka, Frantisek Kreuzmann, Vlastimil Brodsky, Valentine Thielo Va, Eman Fiala, Fanda Mrazek, Karla Chadovova, Dudek Munzar. Written byVladimir Kalina and Zbynek Brynych. Directed by Zbynyk Brynycgh. Camera, Jan Curik. Music, Jiri Sternwald. At Metro Theatre, San Francisco. Running time, 110 MINS.

This is a big, somewhat pretentious production giving five "slices of life" in modern Czechoslovakia. It starts out well with a vignette about an older, master tile-layer and his apprentice—they save each other's lives in a hair-raising accident atop a tall cathedral. But from that point on the film runs downhill, through vignettes of a neglected grandfather, a couple's fifth anniversary, a pair of hobo musicians and a little tale of young love.

There is no unifying thread. The camera simply pans to a new scene and a set of new characters. This would be confusing with English dialog; it's nearly maddening with only English subtitles (and very oddly spelled ones, at that).

Camera work, generally, is good, though some of it tends to resemble some of the gaudier German productions of the 1930's. Players appear to be sensitive, especially the older man and his apprentice (Jaroslav Marvan and Jan Cifka) in the first vignette and the young girl (Karla Chadovova) in the final sequence. But by the time final vignette is reached, audience is squirming with disinterest.

This has little or no chance in the U.S. *Stef.*

The House of Intrigue

(COLOR-C'SCOPE)

Fast World War II spy melodrama based upon actual incidents.

Hollywood, Nov. 6.

Allied Artists release of Duilio Coletti production. Stars Curt Jurgens, Dawn Addams, Folco Lulli; features Dario Michaelis, Philippe Hersent, Rene Deltgen. Directed by Coletti; screenplay, Coletti, Ennio De Concini, Giuseppe Scoponi, Massimo Mida; based on H. J. Giskes novel, "London Calling North Pole"; camera (Ferranlacolor), Gabor Pogany; editor, Vittoria De Fazio Vigorelli; music, Nino Rota; art director, Franco Lolli. Previewed Nov. 6, '59. Running time, 94 MINS.

Bernes .... Curt Jurgens
Mary .... Dawn Addams
Kaarden (Gorilla) .... Folco Lulli
John ....—............... Dario Michaelis
Landers .... Philippe Hersent
Hermann .... Rene Deltgen
Matt .... Albert Lieven
Henry .... Giacomo Rossi Stuart
Chris .... Matteo Spinola
Herbert .... Ludovico Ceriana
Allan .... Adriano Uriani
Mac .... Alphonse Mathis
Felix .... Chris Hofer
Gerda .... Edith Jost
Wilhelm .... Stephen Garret

What purports to be the most amazing hoax ever perpetrated upon a major power and claimed as a true World War II episode is the basis for this action-packed spy melodrama. An Italian import, this feature is high in production values, good acting and of considerable interest for the hardy market where war dramas still are acceptable. Telling against film is lack of r e c o g n i z a b l e names, only two known to American audiences, and a title wholly undescriptive of the plot. Film is well dubbed in English.

Story, taken from H. J. Giskes' novel, "London Calling North Pole," concerns the deception German Intelligence practices upon the English, after Nazis capture a key British espionage agent whose duty is to communicate daily via wireless from Amsterdam with London. Germans continue these daily messages, unknown to the British, leading to numerous British agents being flown in and captured, as well as other catastrophes. Strong narrative suffers somewhat from a weak ending, but during the unfoldment it's top spy stuff.

Lensed in the Italian Ferrania-

color (prints by Technicolor) in actual story sites, producer-director Duilio Coletti has made handsome use of such backgrounds as Amsterdam, Barcelona and other locations and has drawn persuasive performances from a talented cast. Curt Jurgens enacts the high German Intelligence officer who directs the hoax, and Dawn Addams plays an English servicewoman who is smuggled into the Netherlands to check on the supposed operations of the British spy ring. Folco Lulli makes a convincing leader of the Dutch underground.

Technical credits are all exceptionally well executed, topped by Gabor Pogany's artistic color camera work, Vittoria De Fazio Vigorelli's sharp editing and Franco Lolli's lush art direction. *Whit.*

Il Magistrato
(The Magistrate)
(ITALO-SPANISH)
Rome, Nov. 10.

Titanus release of a Titanus-Hispamex Production. Stars Jose Suarez; features Francois Perier, Jacqueline Sassard, Massimo Serato, Ana Mariscal, Geronimo Meynier, Maurizio Arena, Claudia Cardinale, Louis Seigner, Francesco Casaretti. Directed by Luigi Zampa. Screenplay, Zampa, P. F. Campanile, Massimo Franciosa; camera, Gabor Pogany; editor, Mario Sernadrei. Previewed in Rome. Running time, 91 MINS.

Andrea Morandi	Jose Suarez
Luigi Bonelli	Francois Perier
Carla Bonelli	Jacqueline Sassard
Ugo	Massimo Serato
Emilia Bonelli	Ana Mariscal

Well-made picture treating important material in an honest, unemotional manner. Mild b.o. prospects here, though co-producing Spanish areas offer a better market.

Frequently-stated point is that a person accused of a crime is never alone the guilty one: circumstances, society and other influences likewise play a determining part and bear their share of guilt. No one, says the film, is able to shape own life and existence. This theme is well presented and the point brought home in flashback tale of family ruined by an overambitious mother. Pic is patchwork of little nuances, lacking intensity but achieving many moments of truth especially in showing the suffering of youth burdened by the problem of elders.

Best work is turned in by French actor Francois Perier, as the harried father. Jacqueline Sassard is excellent as his daughter. Jose Suarez is too much of a passive observer as the young judge while rest the remainder of the cast performs capably. Luigi Zampa's direction is perhaps too understated for audience impact, though he makes his point soberly and well. Lensing by Gabor Pogany on Genoese and Madrid locations is tops. *Hawk.*

The Snow Queen
(COLOR-SONGS-DUBBED)

Topnotch Russian cartoon feature based on Hans Christian Andersen tale; good prospects for American market.

Hollywood, Nov. 5.

U release of Soyuzmultfilm production. English dialog version featuring voices of Sandra Dee, Tommy Kirk, Patty McCormack, prolog featuring Art Linkletter; producer, Robert Faber; prolog, adaptation written by Alan Lipscott, Bob Fisher; prolog director, Phil Patton; editor, Hugo Grimaldi; music, Frank Skinner. Previewed Nov. 5 '59. Running time, 70 MINS.

Prolog:—Art Linkletter, Tammy Marihugh, Jennie Lynn, Billy Booth, Rickey Busch.

Gerda	Sandra Dee
Kay	Tommy Kirk
Angel	Patty McCormack
The Snow Queen	Louise Arthur
Ol' Dreamy	Paul Frees
The Raven	Paul Frees
Court Raven	June Foray
The Princess	Joyce Terry
The Prince	Richard Beals
Granny	Lillian Buyeff

Russian film animators show know-how in this first Soviet feature-length cartoon to hit the American theatrical market. Based upon Hans Christian Andersen's classic, "The Snow Queen," its 64-minutes' animation running time displays fine style and certain Old World charm which should prove a natural for young audiences and evoke considerable interest among adults as well.

Originally skedded as a Christmas release by Universal, which will distribute in U.S. and Canada, a six-minute Yuletide prolog starring Art Linkletter and a group of moppets was prepped to introduce the fairy tale. Release was set back to Easter, however, due to Columbia slating another cartoon feature, UPA's "1001 Arabian Nights," for Christmas.

"Snow Queen's" present opening, with its patent Yule atmosphere, consequently may be somewhat out of place. Once the footage gets into its actual story, though, the spell of Denmark's great story-teller is socked over.

Made by Soyuzmultfilm Productions of Russia, it set Robert Faber as producer of its English dialog version, with Sandra Dee, Tommy Kirk and Patty McCormack undertaking the voices of the principal characters. Animation and quality stack up well with American standards and the fine and subdued use of color (Eastman) is a definite added asset. Film's comparative short length should meet with exhib approval.

Story, told tersely and appealing to American audiences, follows two young children, a boy and a girl in a quaint European town of yore, and the wicked Snow Queen who turns the lad into an evil boy and takes him to her ice palace in the north. When the boy fails to return, the girl starts to search for him, a quest which takes her through many adventures until she finds him in the Snow Queen's palace. Yarn is presented imaginatively and with skill.

Trio of original songs, cleffed by Diane Lampert and Richard Loring and one of them, "Do It While You're Young," sung by Sandra Dee, lend musical enjoyment, to which Frank Skinner's score further contributes. Dialog written by Alan Lipscott and Bob Fisher and supervised by Hugo Grimaldi, who also does slick editing, is natural and in good sync,

and Dave Fleischner handled technical supervision. Phil Patton directed prolog. *Whit.*

Raubfischer in Hellas
(Search of Chorefto)
(JUGOSLAVIAN)
Vienna, Nov. 6.

Columbia Film release of Carl Szokoll (Tele Film Munich and Dubrava Film, Zagreb, Jugoslavia) production, in cooperation with Michael Arthur productions. Stars Maria Schell and Cliff Robertson; features Cameron Mitchell, Peter Carsten, Fritz Tillmann, Ivan Kostic, Nikola Popovic, Duja Vujsic. Directed by Horst Haechler. Screenplay by Jeffrey Dell and Jo Eisinger after book by Werner Helwig; camera, Kurt Hasse; music, Friedrich Meyer. At Forum, Vienna. Running Time, 103 MINS.

Mana	Maria Schell
Clements	Cliff Robertson
Psarathanas	Cameron Mitchell
Panagos	Peter Carsten
Stassi	Fritz Tillmann
Samsarello	Ivan Kostic
Barbanji	Nikola Popovic
Pope	Duja Vujsic

This is the world preem of an American motion picture in the German language here in Vienna (it was shot bilingually on a Jugoslavian island) with an Austrian star. Since it has a human-political leaning, Austria's new Foreign Minister headed the list of guests. This dramatic, tragic story of rivalry, fear and suspicion could be applied to family life.

It is heavy-handed naturalism and abject poverty. While the fishermen of Kalymnos lay nets, a war, unnoticed by the world, is started.

Cliff Robertson, as seaman Clements, not aware of the facts, arrives, on Kalymnos with the intention of settling down as a sponge diver. But Maria Schell, as "Mana, girl from Kuluri," steals all his money; hence, Robertson cannot buy the intended boat. Robertson is warned to follow her to Kuluri, where Cameron Mitchell (Psarathanas) terrorizes the population. But he does anyway, and they fall in love. He kills Psarathanas in a fight and then he and Miss Schell decide to leave the island for Chorefto, a spot existing only in Mana's dreams. The tragic end finds Robertson convincing the Kuluri "barbarians" that humanity comes first. They attempt to save the lives of their "enemies." The would-be rescuers are killed by those they try to save.

Robertson gives a restrained performance, completely credible and well tempered. Maria Schell, defiant and loyal, has visions of peace at Chorefto. She gives a memorable performance.

The role of Psarathanas is brilliantly portrayed by Cameron Mitchell. Peter Carsten, as Panagos as well as the remainder of the cast are very good.

There are flaws in Horst Haechler's otherwise good directing. Because the entire picture was shot on a Jugoslavian island, he employed its population, but it seems unlikely that there are only old men and ugly old women there. The storm scenes are not very credible. The dialog is unclear and the sound sometimes bad. He also overdoes the macabre life of the islanders.

Cameraman Kurt Hasse made full use of the scenery, both beautiful and ugly.

Friedrich Meyer used old Greek folkmusic. Other technical credits are good, except the editing. *Maas.*

Las Locuras de Barbara
(The Follies of Barbara)
(MEXICAN)
Mexico City, Nov. 17.

Columbia Pictures release of an Alfa Films and Filmax production. Stars Silvia Pinal; features Ruben Rojo, Antonio Casal, Marta Padovan, Juan Calvo, Gisia Paradis. Directed by Tulio Demichelli. Screenplay by Miguel Cuso and Tulio Demicheli from an original by Julio Porter. Camera, Frederico G. Larraya; music, Casas Auge and Francesco Lavignino. Previewed in Mexico City. Running time, 90 MINS.

Silvia Pinal, dieted down, interprets the comedy role of a calculating lass, spoiled and beautiful, and the troubles she falls into by virtue of her bad conduct.

Film had high intent to be a witty farce. While it starts off well, this misses the mark. The story line is far from original, involving as it does the heroine in a circle of admirers. Then when it narrows down to the one, there is the irrascible father, the "misunderstandings" and the final clinch.

Miss Pinal does the best she can with material and turns in her usual natural performance. She does photograph better than in earlier films when the plumpness was beginning to show.

Pace of film is good and Federico Larraya's photography is well done. Tullio Demichelli, director, has milked all he could from several gag sequences bordering on slapstick. *Emil.*

The Hidden Fortress
(JAPANESE)
San Francisco, Nov. 16.

Toho production. Stars Toshiro Mifune, Misa Uehara, Minoru Chiaki, Hamatari Fujiwara. Directed by Akira Kurosawa. Screenplay, Ryuo Kikushima, Hideo Oguni, Shinobu Hashimoto and Kurosawa; camera, Ichio Yamazaki; music, Masuru Sato. At Metro Theatre, San Francisco. Running time, 137 MINS.

This long, interesting, humor-laden picture of medieval Japan evidently was made for domestic consumption, but might find limited appeal in U.S. arties if trimmed a bit.

Story concerns efforts of a beaten warlord (Toshiro Mifune) to sneak his defeated princess (Miss Uehara) out of enemy territory, where their hidden fortress is situated, into a friendly province with the family's gold. They're aided and distracted, alternately, by two greedy yokels (Minoru Chiaki and Kamatari Fujiwara) who stumble on the gold and their hiding place.

Chiaki and Fujiwara are very funny as the yokels, and Mifune is properly heroic as the warlord. The beautiful Miss Uehara does a nice acting job, too.

But the picture is really director Akira Kurosawa's, who takes what could have been a terribly unwieldy subject and makes it believable and highly entertaining. Ichio Yamazaki's camera work is first-rate. Film's main trouble is that it contains certain built-in assumptions about the audience which Western audiences simply wouldn't savvy. *Stef.*

The Rookie
(C'SCOPE)

A "New Faces" in comedy launching proves unfunny, dated comedy. Will have to fight for bookings.

Hollywood, Nov. 19.

Twentieth-Fox release of Tommy Noonan production. Stars Tommy Noonan, Pete Marshall, Julie Newmar; costars

Jerry Lester; features Claude Stroud, Norman Leavitt, Joe Besser. Directed by George O'Hanlon. Screenplay, O'Hanlon, Noonan; camera, Floyd Crosby; editor, Harry Gerstad; music, Paul Dunlap. Previewed Nov. 17, '59. Running time, 84 MINS.

Colonel Taylor .... Claude Stroud
Major Dr. Evert .... Norman Leavitt
Medic .... Joe Besser
Janitor .... Vince Barnett
Lieut. Sumner .... Herb Armstrong
1st MP .... Richard Reeves
Cook .... Don Corey
Janitor .... Rodney Bell
Gen. Bechtel .... George Eldredge

The intent was fine but the execution didn't take place. Idea for formation of a new comedy team—with none now on the screen—made sense but material handed combo fails to come off as entertainment for today's market. "The Rookie," pairing Tommy Noonan and Pete Marshall, has an okay story springboard but handling is of the genre which went out years ago. Reception will be confined to less discriminating audiences who don't mind situations old-hat and unimaginative. Trimming of a good 20 minutes might help.

Plottage revolves around small-town, patriotic Noonan who on V-J Day insists that the army draft him, as per his summons. Through a crazy mixup the local camp which has discharged practically the entire personnel is ordered to remain open to give draftee his basic training. Among the few remaining is Master Sergeant Marshall, anxious to leave so he can marry buxom starlet Julie Newmar, and it's up to him to see that proper military routine is observed and followed. Romantic complications arise when starlet, who likes her publicity front-page, arrives with her demon press agent, Jerry Lester, to cash in on publicity surrounding Noonan. Noonan and Marshall are sent to Japan, with femme also on steamer, but en route trio fall overboard and end upon a desert island, where the last two wartime Japanese also land. After further adventures, they're rescued.

George O'Hanlon's direction of his and Noonan's script frequently goes overboard, with result both Noonan and Marshall overplay throughout, although in their dual roles of the Nips they draw a few chuckles. Miss Newmar wears skin-tight gowns well, plus some stripping, and Lester gives what he thinks is a flack's impersonation. Balance of cast try hard for laughs. Floyd Crosby's camera work is on the plus side. *Whit.*

The Proper Time

San Francisco, Nov. 22.

Business Administration Co. production (no release set). Stars Tom Laughlin; features Nyra Monsour, Norma Quine. Directed by Loughlin. Screenplay, Laughlin; camera, James Crabe; music, Shelly Manne. At Metro Theatre, San Francisco. Running time, 75 MINS.

This attempted tour de force by young actor-writer-director Tom Laughlin almost comes off. It may fall into a void somewhere between a real film and an exploitation picture.

Story focuses on a UCLA student, from a nice home, who stammers badly—except when he's with girls. Among girls this youth (Laughlin), handsome, beautifully muscled, is tremendously attractive. He finds himself rejected by a fraternity because of his speech problem but becomes very friendly with a charming blonde coed (Norma Quine). Shortly Miss Quine's rich, brunette roommate (Nyra Monsour), gets her claws into the boy, they sleep together and become engaged.

All along the boy's parents have urged him to go to the campus speech clinic for help, but when he gets there he finds the clinic won't help those who are only half-hearted about trying to remedy their defect. The boy eventually discovers he isn't alone in the affections of his brunette, breaks up with her in a brutally powerful scene, finds the sympathetic blonde still sympathetic and goes to the speech clinic of his own volition.

Picture's title concerns the proper time for sexual relations — that is, after marriage. Because the boy has been hooked by the brunette mainly as result of the sex act, he is supposed to be deeply disturbed.

A second false note is that the speech clinic is never brought into the film until the halfway point: the clinic needs considerably more underscoring but this would deprive the picture of some of its exploitation angles.

Miss Quine tends to be a bit too sweet in her role, while Miss Monsour leans the other way — obvious. Laughlin appears to be a "method" disciple, hardly sunny-dispositioned.

Laughlin's script has some cliche-laden dialogue, but his direction is good, as is James Crabe's camera work. Shelly Manne's music sounds as if it might have been written for "77 Sunset Strip" originally.

The climactic scene is a knockout, and some others, in which raw sex is implied but never made explicit, are presentable. Overall, rather uneven. *Stef.*

(The Green Mare) (FRENCH—COLOR) (FRANSCOPE)

Paris, Nov. 17.

Gaumont release of SPAC-Star Presse-SNEG-Costellazione production. Stars Bourvil; features Francis Blanche, Julien Carette, Yves Robert, Zavatta, Guy Bertil, Sandra Milo, Valerie Lagrange. Directed by Claude Autant-Lara. Screenplay, Jean Aurenche, Pierre Bost from novel by Marcel Ayme; camera (Eastmancolor), Jacques Natteau; editor, Madeleine Gug. At Ambassade-Gaumont, Paris. Running time, 95 MINS.

Haudoin .... Bourvil
Maloret .... Yves Robert
Deodat .... Zavatta
Marguerite .... Sandra Milo
Juliette .... Valerie Lagrange
Ferdinand .... Francis Blanche
Franc-Tireur .... Guy Bertil

This film is a determined effort to turn out a bawdy, Rabelaisian romp. It does not quite come off because of uneven scripting and direction. However, it has some bucolic frankness that could win some foreign arty theatre bookings. Talkiness and uneven quality will call for a hard sell.

Plot spots a partisan hiding under his bed when Prussians (it is the Franco-Prussian War of 1870) are looking for him and hearing his mother seduced by a Prussian officer on said bed. Then there is attempted rape and seduction; more coarse language, and the hero seducing the wife of his enemy with the son under the bed.

Bourvil is excellent as the sensual, romping hero. Others are okay but skimpily characterized at best. Color is fair and Franscope, a C'Scope process, passable. Film lacks a real feel for place, people and the times but has a brittle, ribald quality that could lead to chances abroad. Film was given a lot of publicity here since almost banned at the last minute. However, it opened on time.

In toto, this is like a "Ma and Pa Kettle" opus seen through the Kinsey Report and naturally done more frankly. *Mosk.*

A Non-Scheduled Train (YUGOSLAV)

San Francisco, Nov. 18.

Jadran Film production. Stars Ivica Pajer, Milan Milosevic, Inge Ilin, Lia Rho-Barbier. Directed by Veljko Bulajic. Screenplay, Bulajic, Ivo Braut, Stjepan Perolc, Elio Petri; camera, Kreso Grcevic; music, Vladimir Kraus-Rajteric. At Metro Theatre, San Francisco. Running time 120 MINS.

"A Non-Scheduled Train" has a few interesting aspects, but it's too long and slow to have a chance in U.S. arties.

Train takes poor residents of a Dalmatian hamlet to a rich interior plain, where they'll be given good farmland by the government—the overtones of politics are obvious.

Journey includes an oddly assorted lot, and camera follows the lives of a number of these people—a sailor, a pretty widow, two down-at-the-mouth oldsters, an engaged young girl, a young couple expecting a child, etc. Players are satisfactory—several better—but director-scripter Veljko Bulajic has maintained a far too leisurely pace, with far too much talk, not enough action.

Kreso Grcevic's camera work would have been benefited by better lighting. Film is very similar to another Yugoslav epic, "The Road A Year Long," and, like it, is pretty tiresome. *Stef.*

Four Fast Guns (1:2.35 Wide Screen)

Phoenix indie's program western. Fair story, poorly told.

Hollywood, Nov. 20.

Universal release of a Phoenix Film Studio production (Kenneth Altose-William Hole Jr.). Stars James Craig, Martha Vickers, Edgar Buchanan; features Brett Halsey, Paul Richards, Richard Martin, Blu Wright, John Swift. Directed by Hole; screenplay, James Edmiston and Dallas Gaultois; camera, John M. Nickolaus Jr.; editors, Reginald Brown, Harold Wooley, Henry F. Salerno; sound, Dale Knight; music, Alec Compinsky; assistant directors, Lee Lukather, Edward Haldeman. Previewed at U., Nov. 19, '59. Running time, 72 MINS

Sabin .... James Craig
Mary .... Martha Vickers
Dipper .... Edgar Buchanan
Johnny Naco .... Brett Halsey
Hoag .... Paul Richards
Farmer Brown .... Blu Wright
Quijano .... Richard Martin
Zodie .... John Swift
Bartender .... Paul Raymond

This everybody-either-starred-or-featured film is of interest primarily because it demonstrates the production facilities of the new Phoenix Film Studio in Arizona. The picture, however, is slow and downbeat, and has no redeeming feature to elevate it above the anchor spot on second-run double bills.

Producer-director William J. Hole Jr. has used a 1:2.35 aspect ratio (not called CinemaScope) to take maximum advantage of the colorful landscape around Phoenix and of the good-sized outdoor sets peopled with numerous local extras. This production value is the picture's main asset.

The story concerns Sabin, a man wanted for a murder he didn't commit, whom circumstances force into becoming "towntamer" of the Arizona town of Purgatory in 1873. As unofficial marshal he vies with the town menace, a cripple who owns the town saloon. The naive but visible premise is that the cripple's infirmity makes him immune to gun-slinging justice under the code of the West.

Out of admiration at first, then because of love, the wealthy cripple's wife tries to intercede as the saloon owner successively sends three gunmen to kill the towntamer, each of whom is killed instead. The last gunman turns out to be Sabin's brother, who provokes the reluctant Sabin to draw on him when it becomes clear that Sabin will be dishonored if he doesn't. Since the brother kills the cripple before being shot himself, the wife is conveniently free to marry Sabin and probably will at fadeout.

Screenplay is frankly inept. And, although James Craig (Sabin), Edgar Buchanan (the town drunk), Brett Halsey (Sabin's brother) and Richard Martin (the likeable Mexican gunslinger) make a valiant attempt at turning in pro performances, the script's too much for them. Some of the other performances are decidedly substandard.

Technical aspects are okay, but the camera work tends to be static and the music added very little. It's academic to speculate on how much could have been salvaged by direction, but Hole surely should have stepped up the pace. *Glen.*

2 Corazones y Un Cielo (Two Hearts and One Heaven) (MEXICAN)

Mexico City, Nov. 17.

Peliculas Nacionales release of Rosas Priego, S.A. Production. Stars Demetrio Gonzalez, Lalo Gonzalez ("Piporro"—Bassoon), Rosa de Castilla; features Carlos Orellana, Rose Elena Durgel, Carlos Agosti. Directed by Rafael Balendon. Screenplay by Rafael Baledon and Carlos Orellana from an original by Raul Zenteno. At Olimpia Theatre, Mexico City. Running time 80 MINS.

Only reason for this picture, in a weak-scripted love story involving an Italian gal (Rosa Elena Durgel) and a Spanish lover (Carlos Agosti), is to serve as a vehicle for one song after another by Demetrio Gonzalez, Lalo Gonzalez and Rosa de Castillo. It turns out to be a monotonous musical marathon, long on song and short on script. Film has at least 16 song numbers, these bursting on the scene at the slightest provocation. The leading lady falls in love, a song; the girl leaves the hero, a song; the hero is hungry, a song; the hero is dying of a broken heart, a song, and so on—indefinitely.

Comedy bits are handled by Lalo Gonzalez (The Bassoon) but his efforts are weak. But he no longer resorts to the crude vulgarities of some of his earlier films and performances. *Emil.*

On the Beach

Gripping, grim meller on after-effects of H-bomb with the world slowly expiring, all life doomed. Strong campaign to help b.o.

United Artists release of Stanley Kramer production. Stars Gregory Peck, Ava Gardner, Fred Astaire, Anthony Perkins, Donna Anderson. Directed by Kramer. Screenplay, John Paxton; based on the book by Nevil Shute; camera, Giuseppe Rotunno; music, Ernest Gold; editor, Frederic Knudtson. Previewed at the Screen Directors Guild theatre, Nov. 25, '59. Running time, **134 MINS.**

Dwight Towers	Gregory Peck
Moira Davidson	Ava Gardner
Julian Osborn	Fred Astaire
Peter Holmes	Anthony Perkins
Mary Holmes	Donna Anderson
Admiral Bridie	John Tate
Lieut. Hosgood	Lola Brooks
Farrel	Guy Doleman
Swain	John Meillon
Sundstrom	Harp McGuire
Benson	Ken Wayne
Davis	Richard Meikle
Ackerman	Joe McCormick
Davidson	Lou Vernon
Froude	Basil Buller-Murphy
Port Man	Paddy Morgan
Dr. Forster	Kevin Brennan
Salvation Army Captain	John Casson
Morgan	Grant Taylor

The unusual pre-release promotion campaign given Stanley Kramer's "On The Beach" has stressed the urgency and importance of its theme: that man may trigger the destruction of his own planet when he pushes the button to detonate the H-bomb. This is part of United Artists' campaign to make the film what's termed "a status symbol," meaning something to be seen despite its grim nature.

That's a realistic sales approach, at any rate, and a switch from making a tough picture and then selling scared; promoting romantic elements having little to do with the film in question. But it might be a good idea to note that "On The Beach" is a solid theatrical film of considerable emotional, as well as cerebral, content. It will need all possible emphasis on this fact, as well as on the star names involved, to make it a success.

Because the fact remains that the final impact of "On The Beach" is as heavy as a leaden shroud. In death there may be hope, but in a world dying—which is what this film's concerned with—there is no relief from depression. The spectator is left with the sick feeling that he's had a preview of Armageddon, in which all contestants lost.

John Paxton, who did the screenplay from Nevil Shute's novel, has avoided the usual cliches. There is no sergeant from Brooklyn, no handy racial spokesmen. Gregory Peck is a U. S. submarine commander. He and his men have been spared the atomic destruction because their vessel was submerged when the bombs went off.

The locale of the action is Australia and the time is 1964. Nobody remembers how or why the conflict started. "Somebody pushed a button," says nucelar scientist Fred Astaire. Australia, for ill-explained reasons, is the last safe spot on earth. It is only a matter of time before the radiation hits the continent and its people die as the rest of the world has died.

In addition to Peck and Astaire, the other chief characters include Ava Gardner, a pleasure-bent Australian; and a young Australian naval officer and his wife, Anthony Perkins and Donna Anderson. All the personal stories are well-presented. The trouble is it is almost impossible to care with the implicit question ever-present — do they live?

The answer is "No." The dying is not heroic. There is little effort, no matter how ineffectual, to devise some means of combatting the last, great plague. To soften the passing of the human race, the government passes out suicide pills. A great deal of the story seems concerned with those involved persuading each other the pills should be used.

There has been some speculation that this suicide aspect would provoke church condemnation. Actually, suicide is only superficially condoned. The real point of this emphasis on self-destruction is that the conditioning that leads to its acceptance is the same fatal lassitude that allowed men the use of such dangerous weapons as the H-bomb without aggressive opposition. Man, the story says, was doomed before he pushed the button.

The cast is almost uniformly excellent. Peck and Miss Gardner make a good romantic team in the last days of the planet. Perkins and Miss Anderson evoke sympathy as the young couple. Fred Astaire, in his first straight dramatic role, will attract considerable attention. Others who stand out include John Tate, Lola Brooks, Basil Buller-Murphy, Harp McGuire and Joe McCormick.

Giuseppe Rotunno's camera work is excellent, never neglecting opportunities for softening touches to the relentless story. Ernest Gold uses the Australian song, "Waltzing Matilda" for the theme melody and for background music throughout, in a dozen variations. It is a haunting score.

"On The Beach" deserves to be seen. It is honest and provoking picture. *Powe.*

Le Dejeuner Sur L'Herbe
(Dinner On the Grass)
(FRENCH-COLOR)

Paris, Dec. 1.

Pathe release of Jean Renoir Co. production. Stars Paul Meurisse; features Catherine Rouvel, Fernand Sardou, J. P. Grandval, O'Brady, Micheline Gary. Written and directed by Jean Renoir. Camera (Eastmancolor), G. Leclerc; editor, Renee Lichtig. At Marignan Paris. Running time, **95 MINS.**

Etienne	Paul Meurisse
Nenette	Catherine Rouvel
Nino	Fernand Sardou
Brother	J. P. Grandval
Rodolphe	O'Brady
Marguerite	Micheline Gary
Rouuseau	Jean Claudio

Director-writer Jean Renoir has brought off a light-hearted, philosophic romp based on the scientific, dedicated mind against nature, love and the supernatural. It is somewhat tenuous at times, but Renoir's visual flair, fine pacing and verve keep this bouncing along and over the rough spots of repetition. It could be an arty bet abroad but careful hard sell is in order.

Though it calls for shrewd handling, this pic has an entertaining quality which might also make this worth dubbing and for playoff chances in foreign spots. Color is well used. Plot concerns a leading scientist who advocates artificial insemination for the future of mankind. He feels that love eventually will give way to true eugenic propagation of the race.

At a country dinner, he announces his engagement to a world Girl Scout leader and also his decision to run for the head of an all-European scientific congress. However, a sensual country girl, who is direct in her femininity and feelings, and a country-side sorcerer brings on a change of heart in the intellectual via plain erotic appeal and some magic. He has an idyll with the girl and decides that science is not enough. It has to enhance and help the life force but not replace it.

Director-writer Renoir has given this fine color and a whimsical touch that makes it beguiling and rarely upsets the applecart of ideas mouthed quite freely through the film. It might be a difficult film. But its characters are well detailed and seem real as well as spokesmen and symbols of the various ways of life. It has lyric moments, downright farcical and slapstick bits. This is an unusual film that will have to be carefully handled but could be a grosser on its freshness, movement and fine direction and theme.

Paul Meurisse is excellent, as the scientist who is humanized by love, while Catherine Rouvel is a find as the zesty, loving country girl. Her nude bathing scene is worthy of a painting of Renoir's great painter father. No censor troubles here. *Mosk.*

De Espaldas a la Puerta
(Back To the Door)
(SPANISH)

Chamartin release of Halcon production. Stars Emma Penella, Amelia Bence, Luis Prendes, Elisa Loti, Luis Pena, Irene Lopez Heredia, Jose Maria Vilches, Jose Lopez Vasquez. Directed by Jose Maria Forque. Story by Los Arcos. Screenplay by Alfonso Paso, Los Arcos, J. M. Forque; cameraman, Enrique Guerner; music, Ramon Vives. At Cine Coliseo, Madrid. Running time, **92 MINS.**

Despite a routine police adventure yarn at his disposal and limited low-budget decor for his film narration, director Jose Maria Forque has come up with a well-rounded production that adds to growing maturity of film-making in Spain. Standout is the neat integration of a flamenco dance sequence starring La Chunga and the Goyesque Palao brothers. This heightens the action where suspense is most needed.

Who tried to murder the young nightclub hostess? Police inspector Luis Prendes and his aide, popular Lopez Vasquez provide the answer after sealing a packed nightclub and moving in on the usual assembly of latespot characters to ferret out the lawbreaker. Suspense is present, if not always pulsating, but the situations are old.

Cast is hand-picked. Though Prendes and Vasquez lack flatfoot-visages, their display of crime detection satisfies. First-rate performances **are registered by legit First Lady Irene Lopez Heredia, Emma Penella, Argentine's Amelia Bence, Luis Pena and the auspiciously-debuting Elisa Loti.**

Technical departments are above average. Replacement of censored kisses and dubbing give "Espaldas" a chance as a late tele film filler. ***Wear.***

Goliath and the Barbarians
(EASTMANCOLOR—TOTALSCOPE—DUBBED)

Blood - and - thunder period spectacle with male pulchritude. Trite yarn, but may prosper via exploitation.

American-International release of a Standard Production. Stars Steve Reeves; features Chelo Alonso, Bruce Cabot, Giulia Rubini, Livio Lorenzon, Luciano Marin, Arturo Dominici, Furio Meniconi, Fabrizio Capucci, Andrea Checci, Gino Scotti. Directed by Carlo Campogalliani; original story by Emimmo Salvi and Gino Mangini; screenplay by Campogalliani, Mangini Nino Stresa and Giuseppe Taffarel; sound, Piero Ortonali and Bruno Moreal; music, Les Baxter; assistant directors, Romolo Girolami and Sergio Bergonzelli. Running time, **85 MINS.**

Emiliano	Steve Reeves
Londo	Chelo Alonso
Alboyna	Bruce Cabot
Sabina	Giulia Rubini
Igor	Livio Lorenzon
Svevo	Luciano Marin
Delfo	Arturo Dominici
Marco	Furio Meniconi
Bruno	Fabrizio Capucci
Agnese	Andrea Checchi
Count Daniele	Gino Scotti

Despite an economy of production values and a trite story, "Goliath and the Barbarians" shapes as a solid exploitation entry for the teenage market. For cast in the title role is Steve Reeves, the much-publicized "Hercules," whose name will be a marquee lure for audiences with a yen for action and derring-do.

Aside from Reeves, however, and Bruce Cabot as the barbarian leader the cast of this American International release in relatively unknown to U. S. filmgoers. But that's scarely a liability since the picture's overall spectacle should overcome that deficiency.

On the other hand, this Italian-made film which was turned out as a co-production with Standard Productions has little appeal for adults. Its Eastmancolor and wide-screen undeniably provides a handsome frame for the panoply of a big spectacle. However, it fails to hide some so-so acting and the predictable story by Emimmo Salvi and Gino Mangini.

Yarn evolves as little more than an excuse for lensing some savage bloodletting. The gore is alternated with male pulchritude per topliner Reeves, whose massive physique takes the play from his distaff vis-a-vis. In this case she's Chelo Alonso, a Gina Lollobrigida type who has ample opportunity to display her charms.

Tale is set in the Italy of 568 A.D., when Bruce Cabot, as king of the Longobards, leads his rapist-murderers into Verona, a mistake since one of the inhabitants is bicep-bulging Reeves. Latter's scheme for repelling the invaders includes getting up as a strange beast and swooping down from the forest to do single-handed combat with bands of the barbarians. Thus he comes to be tagged "Goliath."

Miss Alonso, as the dancing daughter of one of Cabot's lieutenants, falls for Goliath and is instrumental in freeing him after his capture. When the bad guys are finally whipped, she and Reeves ride off to a new life in a scene almost as old as picture-making.

With the exception of Reeves and the veteran Cabot (in a minor role, actually), cast is all-Italo and, save for Miss Alonso's curves, of no consequence to domestic marquees. Performances generally match the thin yarn and aren't helped any for audiences by the dubbing. Neither Reeves or Cabot speaks for himself in the anglicized print, which is annoying. Reeves is no more than a tower of physical strength, while Miss Alonso is a cheesecake posturer now and then called on for some hackneyed melodramatics. Best of the supporting parts is Livio Lorenzon's licentious Igor, one of the barbarian leaders.

For all its "bigness," film conveys a sense of scenic economy, and Carlo Campogallini has directed with stubborn indifference. The color tends to underline the already arch characterizations. Bulk of the score (available in an A-I album) is by Les Baxter and doesn't rise above the overall qualitative level. *Pit.*

Ivan the Terrible, Part II

(The Revolt of the Boyars)
(RUSSIAN-MADE)

Janus Films release of a USSR Central Cinema Studio production. Stars Nikolai Cherkassov; features Serafima Birman. Directed by Sergei Eisenstein. Screenplay, Eisenstein; camera, Eduard Tisse, Andrei Moskvin; music, Sergei Prokofieff. Previewed N.Y. Nov. 20, '59. Running time, **87 MINS.**

Ivan IV .... Nikolai Cherkassov
Boyarina Efrosinia Staritzkaya .... Serafima Birman
Vladimir Andreyevich .. Piotr Kadochnikov
Malyuta Skuratov ...... Mikhail Zharov
Philip, Metropolitan .. Andrei Abrikosov
Pimen, Bishop ...... Alexander Mgebrov
Prince Andrei Kurbsky .. Nakolai Nazvanov
Alexei Basmanov .... Alexei Buchma
Fyodor .... Mikhail Kuznetsov
Piotr Volynets .... Vladimir Balashov
King Sigismund Augustus of Poland .... Pavel Massalsky

Long withheld by Soviet officials, "Ivan the Terrible, Part II" is hardly an entertaining film. But it is well worth the time of students of history and the cinema. This market alone should assure the Russian-made import some art house bookings. Its prospects in more general situations loom as meagre.

Ivan the Terrible, the first Russian czar, concededly was a wicked 16th century ruler. However, historians point out that he often sympathized with the commoners and loathed the boyars. They were members of an aristocratic order who had many privileges. How Ivan subdued a revolt of these boyars is the story peg for this Sergei Eisenstein production.

Originally, Eisenstein planned a trilogy on Ivan but he died in 1948 after completing only two of the films. His first, released in the U.S. in 1947, contained an abundance of "heavy-handed propaganda" according to reviewers. Ivan's cruel character was largely whitewashed and he was depicted as a saint.

In sharp contrast to Part I is the second film where Eisenstein apparently chose to forget the party line and concentrate upon a searching character study of the czar who even killed his own son. His "indecisive" approach caused him to become the target of an officially inspired critical attack and Part II was banned—a ban which lasted 12 years.

Eisenstein subsequently "confessed" that he had been "ideologically defective." One of the top creative artists in the cinema, he has written and directed a compelling portrait of the hated czar which often takes on the qualities of a Greek tragedy. There are plots and counterplots. Ivan comes off unscathed, but as much cannot be said about his victims.

Nikolai Cherkassov, who portrays the title role, aptly conveys the tragic struggle from within that Ivan was unable to cope with. Less impressive is Serafima Birman's performance as the czar's aunt who plotted his death. Her wooden interpretation makes it heavy-going for audiences. Piotr Kadochnikov is suitably doltish as an unwilling candidate for the czar's throne. Other players help sustain the film's overall grim mood.

Eisenstein as the director shows advantageously in a banquet scene, photographed in color (balance of footage is black-and-white). Choreography in the sequence is a striking backdrop for the czar's crafty machinations. As a writer, however, he seems rather "indecisive"—to use the word of his Communist superiors. Throughout the film is a fine score by Sergei Prokofieff. *Gilb.*

The Angry Red Planet

(COLOR)

Ordinary sci-fi horror item, but juve trade may respond.

Hollywood, Nov. 27.

Sino Production produced by Sid Pink and Norman Maurer. Features Gerald Mohr, Nora Hayden, Lee Tremayne, Jack Kruschen. Directed by Ib Melchior; screenplay by Melchior and Pink; based on a story by Pink; camera (Eastman Color), Stanley Cortez; music, Paul Dunlap; editor, Ivan J. Hoffman. Previewed at Hal Roach studios, Nov. 3, '59. Running time, **83 MINS.**

O'Banion .... Gerald Mohr
Iris Ryan .... Nora Hayden
Prof. Gettell .... Les Tremayne
Sgt. Jacobs .... Jack Kruschen
Gen. Treegar .... Paul Hahn
Prof. Weiner .... J. Edward McKinley
Dr. Gordon .... Tom Daly
Gen. Prescott .... Edward Innes

The red planet is Mars. It's angry because it has been landed upon by scientists from Earth. If this production from Sid Pink and Norman Maurer has little to recommend it, it could all the same make a stir in the juvenile market. At present the film has no release but is being exhibited here to see what interest can be aroused.

Chief publicity concerning "The Angry Red Planet" has to do with a gimmick called "Cinemagic." Advertised as a process, it isn't that, at least not in the CinemaScope, VistaVision, etc., term of reference. It is a kind of photographic trick that produces the effect of a negative. Shown in pinkish-colored tones, shadings are reverse; light's dark, dark's light. While it may take considerable ingenuity to produce this effect, the result isn't really worth it.

The story of the film, from a screenplay by Pink and Ib Melchoir, latter of whom directed, is routine. A space ship takes off for Mars, ands on Mars, fights off unfriendly fauna, and takes off again for Earth. Principal menace is a giant amoeba.

Acting is capable under the circumstances. Leading thesps are Gerald Mohr, Nora Hayden, Les Tremyane and Jack Kruschen. Technical credits, topped by Stanley Cortez' camera work and Paul Dunlap's planetary musical background, are good. *Powe.*

Expresso Bongo

(BRITISH)

Sharp, amusing glimpse at the more seamy side of U.K.'s Tin Pan Alley, disk world and starlet exploitation; Laurence Harvey's presence helps the marquee.

London, Dec. 1.

British Lion release (in association with Britannia Films) of a Val Guest production. Stars Laurence Harvey, Sylvia Syms, Yolande Donlan; features Cliff Richard. Directed by Guest. Screenplay by Wolf Mankowitz from his own play; editor, Bill Lenny; camera, John Wilcox; music and lyrics, Julian More, Monty Norman, David Heneker, Robert Farnon, Val Guest, Norrie Paramor, Paddy Roberts, Bunny Lewis. At Carlton Theatre, London. Running time, **111 MINS.**

Johnny Jackson .... Laurence Harvey
Maisie King .... Sylvia Syms
Dixie Collins .... Yolande Donlan
Bongo Herbert .... Cliff Richard
Mayer .... Meier Tzelniker
Lady Rosemary ..... Ambrosine Philpotts
Leon .... Eric Pohlmann
Gilbert Harding ..... Gilbert Harding
Penelope .... Hermione Baddeley
Rev. Tobias Craven ... Reginald Beckwith
Mr. Rudge .... Wilfrid Lawson
Kakky .... Martin Miller
Mrs. Rudge .... Avis Bunnage
Beast Burns .... Barry Lowe
Charlie .... Kenneth Griffith
Cynthia .... Susan Hampshire
Cynthia's Boy Friend .... Peter Myers
Chinese Rose .... Lisa Peake

Soho, with its atmosphere of sleazy stripperies, gaudy coffee bars and frenetic teenagers, is the setting for this amusing satire on how a little talent can be boosted overnight as the result of a successful disk and a click tv appearance. Wolf Mankowitz's story is slight and not particularly original, but it has pungency, wit and a sharp sense of observation. There are problems, of course. It isn't easy to parody something which, in itself, is a parody. And it's possible that teenage filmgoers will not relish seeing their own entertainment idols mocked, however shrewdly.

However, with Laurence Harvey as the star and a first-rate supporting cast, "Expresso Bongo" adds up to a film which is likely to be far more popular than the play with music from which it's been adapted.

Harvey is a cheap, opportunistic promoter, always on the lookout for an easy buck. He's a glib, flashy bluffer with a ready talent for the double-cross. In a Soho Expresso bar, he picks up an amateur singer and bongo player, signs him up on a dubious contract and boosts him to what is now regarded as stardom. All's well until it's discovered that the contract isn't valid, because the artist is a minor. That, in brief, is the thin story line. But what gives the film its merit are the characters and the authentic atmosphere.

Harvey gives a brashly amusing, offbeat performance as the small-time operator while Sylvia Syms, who has been mostly seen in prim roles before, is unexpectedly cast as a stripper with aspirations towards stardom as a singer. She turns in one of her best pieces of thesping to date.

Expresso Bongo is played by Cliff Richard, currently the teenagers' singing idol. And promising as Richard is as a performer, this was probably a wrong piece of casting. The songs with which he is provided are intended to spoof the whole business of pop crooning but they come over, in Richard's larynx, as completely feasible entries into the pop market. Richard shows signs of developing into a pleasant actor. Yolande Donlan is also in good form as a slipping American tv artist who has a more than sisterly eye on Richard.

Among the smaller roles that stand out are those of Ambrosine Philpotts, as a society publicity flack; Eric Pohlmann, cast as a coffee bar proprietor, and Hermione Haddeley, as a short-sighted tart. Meier Tzelniker plays the part which he did so well on the stage. He's boss of a disk company and here's an excellent characterization—flamboyant, garrulous and only slightly exaggerated.

The songs are unlikely to make the hit parade but they all fit admirably into the pattern of the film. "Nausea," "Shrine On The Second Floor" and "I've Never Had It So Good" are witty and original.

Location scenes and those in the strip club are smoothly lensed while Val Guest's direction is brisk and lively. "Expresso Bongo" is a neat job of work all round whether it be taken just as fun or whether it is regarded as a shrewd piece of social satire. *Rich.*

Never So Few

(C'SCOPE—COLOR)

Colorful, action-filled war romance. Good names for good b.o. Anti-Nationalist China and war morality issues may be troublesome.

Hollywood, Dec. 4.

Metro release of Canterbury production. Stars Frank Sinatra, Gina Lollobrigida; features Peter Lawford, Steve McQueen, Richard Johnson, Paul Henreid, Brian Donlevy, Dean Jones. Produced by Edmund Grainger. Directed by John Sturges. Screenplay, Millard Kaufman; based on Tom T. Chamales' novel; camera (MetroColor), William H. Daniels; music, Hugo Friedhofer; editor, Ferris Webster. Previewed at the studio, Dec. 2, '59. Running time, **126 MINS.**

Capt. Tom C. Reynolds ...... Frank Sinatra
Carla Vesari .... Gina Lollobrigida
Capt. Grey Travis .... Peter Lawford
Bill Ringa .... Steve McQueen
Capt. Danny De Mortimer .... Richard Johnson
Nikko Regas .... Paul Henreid
Gen. Sloan .... Brian Donlevy
Sgt. Jim Norby .... Dean Jones
Sgt. John Danforth .... Charles Bronson
Nautaung .... Philip Ahn
Col. Fred Parkson .... Robert Bray
Margaret Fitch .... Kipp Hamilton
Col. Reed .... John Hoyt
Capt. Alofson .... Whit Bissell
Mike Island .... Richard Lupino
Billingsly .... Aki Aleong

"Never So Few" is a gaudy Christmas package from Metro that will alleviate concern among exhibitors who might have felt that, with all the fuss about "Ben-Hur," the normal flow to distribution were being neglected. The Edmund Grainger production, directed with theatrical flourish by John Sturges, is also loaded with good young stars. It will be a good boxoffice attraction.

While the film glistens agreeably, it is far from being pure gold. Its story is a patchy affair, and the narrative opens a Pandora's box of moral and political questions. Although the screenplay attempts to clamp the lid shut on these queries before winding to its conclusion, it leaves dangling ends.

"Never So Few" is one of those films in which individual scenes and sequences play with verve and excitement. It is only when the relation of the scenes is evaluated, and their cumulative effect considered, that the threads begin to unravel like an old, worn sock.

The locale of the Millard Kaufman screenplay, based on Tom T. Chamales' book, is Burma during World War II. Frank Sinatra is the iconoclastic, ruggedly individualistic commander of a small British-American task force. The bulk of his force is made up of native Kachin troops. He is idolized by them and his Occidental troops, being a tough and tender character in equal if unpredictable quantities.

Chief action of the film has Sinatra leading a foray against a Japenese position near the Chinese border in which some of his men are ambushed by a Nationalist Chinese group out for plunder. When Sinatra discovers this duplicity by the supposed allies, he leads his men into Chiang Kai-Shek's China to wipe out the treacherous Chinese.

There is a lot of good, tough humor in Kaufman's screenplay, and his characters are well-defined. Sturges' direction sets the people and their purpose in tight, economical scenes. His transitions from the jungles to the sumptuous world behind the lines are skillfully handled. He gets a lot of excitement into his big raid scene and suspense in lesser actions.

The film stumbles on Sinatra's role. Sinatra handles his part with conviction and sympathy, but the script creates for itself a dangerous labyrinth of war morality and it

does not entirely extricate itself or its leading players. Sinatra at one point kills his servant because the man is fatally wounded and there is no medical help. Later, Sinatra orders the wholesale execution of the Chinese who murdered his American-British-Kachin comrades. There is provocation and even reason for these actions, but to condone them for ordinary consumption is beyond the powers of the narrative.

The wrap-up generally is too tidy and, at the same time, unsatisfactory. Sinatra is cleared of all accusations, including that of disturbing relations with Chiang Kai-Shek. His romantic interest is Gina Lollobrigida, looking like about $15,000,000, who has been the pampered mistress of mystery man Paul Henreid. She will abandon her plush life with Henreid and go back to Indianapolis with Sinatra, she says. She and Henreid were Allied agents all the time, she adds. Neither the explanation nor the offer are plausible.

The film may provide a catapault to stardom for Steve McQueen, hitherto known principally as a television actor. He has a good part, and he delivers with impressive style. Richard Johnson, a British actor, is also a standout. Peter Lawford, Paul Henreid, Brian Donlevy and Dean Jones are strong in important roles, and others who register include Charles Bronson, Philip Ahn, Robert Bray, Kipp Hamilton and Isabelle Cooley.

"Never So Few" did its principal photography on the Metro lot and on domestic locations, but it has some effective Ceylon photography that is neatly blended with the closer shots in Ferris Webster's editing. William H. Daniels' camera work is an effective ally of the story, and Hugo Friedhofer's score is a notable one. Helen Rose has given Miss Lollobrigida a slew of gowns that will have the ladies and gentlemen drooling, although for different reasons. *Powe.*

Journey to the Center of the Earth
(C'SCOPE—COLOR)

Tongue-in-cheek version of Jules Verne story. Good b.o. likely since appeal is mainly to the young trade.

20th-Fox release of Charles Brackett production. Stars Pat Boone, James Mason, Arlene Dahl and Diane Baker. Features Thayer David and Peter Ronson. Directed by Henry Levin. Screenplay, Brackett and Walter Reisch, based on the novel by Jules Verne; camera (C'Scope), Leo Tover; editor, Stuart Gilmore and Jack W. Holmes; music, Bernard Herrmann; special songs by James Van Heusen and Sammy Cahn. Previewed at Paramount Theatre, N.Y., Dec. 4, '59. Running time, **132 MINS.**

Alec McEwen .... Pat Boone
Prof. Oliver Lindenbrook .. James Mason
Carla .... Arlene Dahl
Jenny .... Diane Baker
Count Saknussemm .... Thayer David
Hans .... Peter Ronson
Groom .... Robert Adler
Dean .... Alan Napier
Prof. Bayle .... Alex Finlayson
Paisley .... Ben Wright
Kirsty .... Mary Brady
Chancellor .... Frederick Halliday
Rector .... Alan Caillou

Jules Verne, the father of science fiction writing, has usually been good boxoffice. His "Around the World in 80 Days" and "20,000 Leagues Under the Sea" were solid successes. So there's every reason to believe that 20th-Fox's experience with the film version of Verne's "Journey to the Center of the Earth" will be a money maker. It seems a natural entry for the upcoming Christmas holiday period since its appeal will be mainly to the young. It has a built-in teenage attraction in the person of Pat Boone, who draws the non-delinquent elements of the juve trade.

The Charles Brackett production, written by Brackett and Walter Reisch, takes a tongue-in-cheek approach to the Verne story, but there are times when it is difficult to determine whether the filmmakers are kidding or playing it straight. At theatre preview caught, it appeared on a number of occasions that the audience was laughing at and not with the picture. The true-blue sci-fi fan may find aspects of the picture ludicrous, but if one is willing to accept the film as one big spoof, it can turn out to be a fairly amusing entry.

The performances, directed by Henry Levin, are in the lighthearted tradition and the actors neither take themselves nor the picture seriously, which is all on the plus side. The story concerns an expedition, led by James Mason, who plays a dedicated scientist, to the center of the earth. Among those who descend to the depths with Mason are Boone, one of his students; Arlene Dahl, the widow of a Swedish geologist who steals Mason's information and tries to beat him to the "underworld"; and Peter Ronson, an Icelandic guide and jack-of-all-trades.

The descent is a treacherous one, filled with all kinds of dangers—underground floods, unusual winds, excessive heat, devious paths. However, the intrepid explorers succeed in the mission, discovering that the center of the earth consists of an ocean. Before reaching their goal, they confront pre-historic monsters, a forest of mushrooms, a cavern of quartz crystals, and a salt vortex. A volcano, an erruption of Stromboli miraculously lifts the group to the earth surface and they are fished out of the sea off the coast of Italy after starting their descent on the side of a crater in Iceland.

The special photographic effects by L. B. Abbott, James B. Gordon and Emil Kosa Jr. and the cinematography of Leo Tover contribute to a sense of excitement.

Boone is given an opportunity to throw in a couple of songs, but the moments selected for Boone to exercise his tonsiles, were among the occasions when the audience laughed at the picture. Romance has not been neglected. Waiting at home in Edinburgh for Boone is Diane Baker, Mason's niece. And it's obvious that Mason and the widow Dahl would end up in a clinch despite their constant bickering during the expedition.

Brackett has provided topnotch production values and Bernard Herrman comes through with an appropriate musical background. *Holl.*

The Village on the River
(DUTCH)

San Francisco, Dec. 1.

N.V. Nationale Filmproductie Maatschappij production. Stars Max Croiset. Written by Hugo Claus. Directed by Fons Redemakers. Camera, Eduard V. Der Enden. Music, Jurriann Andriessen. At Metro Theatre, San Francisco. Running time, **95 MINS.**

This is the Netherlands' first feature-length film shown in the U.S., and figures to be the last for some time after this offering.

It concerns a slightly whacky doctor in a provincial Dutch village around the turn of the century. He befriends common people, makes enemies of the leading townsmen, including the burgomaster, is eventually driven out of town after his wife dies and he buries her in his garden to keep her besides him.

The story is meandering, creates few real climaxes. Fons Rademakers' direction and Eduard V. Der Enden's camera work are decidedly dated, though Max Croiset, as the doctor, appears interesting and could make an impression in a more lively vehicle. Rest of the cast—doggedly peasant types—can do little with heavy-handled material.

An unlikely entry. *Stef.*

Cash McCall
(COLOR)

Improbable and prettied account of hi-jinx in capital gains high finance. B.o. rests on stars and romantic story.

Hollywood, Dec. 11.

Warner Bros. release of Henry Blanke production. Stars James Garner, Natalie Wood; features Nina Foch, Dean Jagger, E. G. Marshall, Henry Jones. Directed by Joseph Pevney; screenplay, Lenore Coffee and Marion Hargrove; based on the novel by Cameron Hawley; camera (Technicolor), George Folsey; music, Max Steiner; editor, Philip W. Anderson. Previewed at the studio, Nov. 30, '59. Running time, **102 MINS.**

Cash McCall .... James Garner
Lory Austen .... Natalie Wood
Maude Kennard .... Nina Foch
Grant Austen .... Dean Jagger
Winston Conway .... E. G. Marshall
Gil Clark .... Henry Jones
Will Atherson .... Otto Kruger
General Danvers .... Roland Winters
Harrison Glenn .... Edward C. Platt
Mr. Pierce .... Edgar Stehli
Miriam Austen .... Linda Watkins
Harvey Bannon .... Parley Baer

Today's world of high finance is a jungle, according to Warner Bros.' "Cash McCall," and it is populated largely by predators. This view of big business is a long way from Horatio Alger's "Sink Or Swim," and the clean, stalwart, hard-working success myth in America. According to Cameron Hawley's novel, if you've got any talent for business you start at the top and leave the details to the old-fashioned cruds.

The Henry Blanke production can't be taken too seriously as an accurate picture of contemporary finance, even though the former ad chief of Armstrong Cork, Cameron Hawley, knows his capital gains. Release will have appeal in its handsome stars, James Garner and Natalie Wood, and their romantic story. Joseph Pevney's direction is generally able.

The screenplay by Leonore Coffee and Marion Hargrove has Garner as a wonder boy of modern pyramid-and-equities finance. He doesn't seem to have any knowledge of any special business or any affinity for a specific product or service. His are the methods of finding a dying business, merging it with a thriving one, and using the first company's carry-forward losses and its demise for tax relief on the healthy concern. A standard practice today, this could be explored with considerable interest. The expository passages don't go much beyond explaining Garner buys a business for $2,000,000 and promptly sells it for $3,000,000, which will seem pretty dazzling to the hourly worker, but also leave the average picturegoer uninstructed as to "how."

Garner, as the title character, has an unpleasant business reputation for juggling deals of this kind, but it's hard to see why in the telling of the story where he's made an ingratiating personality, considerate of widows and orphans, who not only enriches himself with every transaction but uplifts others financially, as well. The plot turn that supplies the conclusion has him abandoning this life of a Robin Hood of high finance to settle down with Natalie Wood.

The script suffers from pulling its punches in delineating McCall so it's hard for the viewer to understand the opposition he faces from other businessmen. It also borders on the ridiculous in piling on the number and kind of his multifarious enterprises.

Characterizations are stock and, in some cases, foolish. Nina Foch suffers from an undeveloped role in which she performs as the "other woman" who spurs Miss Wood's jealousy. There is an unconvincing scene that is the crux of the romantic story, in which Miss Wood, shortly after being introduced to Garner, strips her clothes off and offers herself to him. This sequence, including a scene in which Miss Wood is ostensibly nude, showing her naked back to drive the point across, is as tasteless as it is pointless.

Still for audiences willing to accept a surface story for romantic shenanigans, the picture will suffice. Garner deserves better, and so does Miss Wood. They are both intelligent actors capable of handling more incisive material. Others in the cast can't manage much individuality. Miss Foch, Dean Jagger, E. G. Marshall and Henry Jones limp stock characterizations with professional skill.

George Folsey's Technicolor photography is able. The music by Max Steiner is rich and melodious. Malcolm Bert's art direction has a field day with lush settings, ably abetted by set decorator George James Hopkins. Editing by Philip W. Anderson is good, and so is Stanley Jones' sound.

1001 Arabian Nights

Clever animated telling of the story of Aladdin and his lamp. Mister Magoo stars in pic which is best for kids, indicating good b.o.

Hollywood, Dec. 4.

Columbia release of a UPA Production. Produced by Stephen Bosustow. Directed by Jack Kinney. Screenplay, Czenzi Ormonde; story, Dick Shaw, Dick Kinney, Leo Salkin, Pete Burness, Lew Keller, Ed Nofziger, Ted Allan, Margaret Schneider; production design, Robert Dranko; layout, Shirley Silvey, Gene Miller; color design, Jules Engel, Bob McIntosh; background, Barbara Beggs, Boris Gorelick, Rosemary O'Conner; animation director, Abe Levitow; sequence directors, Rudy Larriva, Gil Turner, Osmond Evans, Tom McDonald, Alan Zaslove; animators, Harvey Toombs, Phil Duncan, Clarke Mallery, Bob Carlson, Hank Smith, Ken Hultgren, Jim Davis, Casey Onaitis, Sanford Strother, Ed Friedman, Jack Campbell, Herman Cohen, Rudy Zamora, Stan Wilkins; editors, Joe Siracusa, Skip Craig, Earl Bennett; camera supervisor, Jack Eckes; sound, John Livadary, Marne Fallis; music, George Dunning; songs, Dunning and Ned Washington; conductor, Morris Stoloff; orchestration, Arthur Morton. Stars the voices of Jim Backus, Kathryn Grant, Dwayne Hickman, Hans Conried, Berschel Bernardi, Daws Butler, Alan Reed and the Clark Sisters. Running time, **76 MINS.**

Magoo .... Jim Backus
Princess Yasminda .... Kathryn Grant
Aladdin .... Dwayne Hickman
The Wicked Wazir .... Hans Conried
The Jinni .... Herschel Bernardi
The Sultan .... Alan Reed
Omar the Rug Maker .... Daws Butler
Three Maids From Damascus
Clark Sisters

After tripping through 53 one-reelers in 11 years, the Nearsighted Mister Magoo has hopped aboard a full-length magic carpet accompanied by a cat he thinks is a dog. While "1001 Arabian Nights" is not the kind of perceptive material that made Magoo a favorite of all ages,

it abounds in enough animated fun and evil to lure more children than the Pied Piper. The UPA film, being released this Christmas by Columbia, is a brightly wrapped present which, when opened, should reveal a profitable treasure.

UPA topper Stephen Bosustow produced the 75½-minute feature, keeping all the fables of Baghdad alive. All are there—Aladdin, the beautiful princess, the sultan, the wicked wazir, the jinni—and only Magoo, in the fullmyopic glory, has been added. The art work, now a trademark of UPA, is a blend of realism and impressionism which often results in amusing caricatures. The production is inventive, the colors gay and cheerful and George Dunning's musical score a gem.

The Czenzi Ormonde screenplay, based on a story credited to nine writers, makes Magoo an important but not the central figure. As a lovable lamp seller named Abdul Azziz Magoo, he's around to trigger good action and bad in his efforts to marry his young nephew to the beautiful princess.

Voices are well chosen to support the rollicking sounds of Jim Backus as Magoo. Kathryn Grant makes an enchanting princess, Dwayne Hickman a lively Aladdin and Hans Conried a terrifyingly sinful wazir. Alan Reed's voice is perfectly suited to the Sultan, as is Daws Butler's to Omar the rug maker. The Clark Sisters are heard as the Three Little Maids from Damascus.

Twenty-eight persons are credited with the visual creation of "1001 Arabian Nights" under the effective over-all direction of Jack Kinney. Major credit goes to production designer Robert Dranko, layout heads Shirley Silvey and Gene Miller, color designers Jules Engel and Bob McIntosh and animation director Abe Levitow.

Dunning and Ned Washington wrote three special tunes to complement the score, the best being "You Are My Dream," a romantic ballad sung by a chorus behind an imaginative lover's meeting. Audio portion of the film, with sound by John Livadary and Marne Fallis, is exceptionally crisp. *Ron.*

Take a Giant Step

Well-intended but not so well-made study of a teenaged Negro boy. Johnny Nash will add b.o. draw.

Hollywood, Dec. 4.

United Artists release of Hecht-Hill-Lancaster production. Stars Johnny Nash and Estelle Hemsley; features Ruby Dee and Frederick O'Neal. Produced by Julius J. Epstein. Directed by Philip Leacock. Screenplay, Louis S. Peterson and Julius J. Epstein; based on Peterson's play; camera, Arthur Arling; music, Jack Marshall; editor, Frank Gross. Previewed at Goldwyn studio, Dec. 1, '59. Running time, **99 MINS.**

Spencer Scott	Johnny Nash
Grandma	Estelle Hemsley
Christine	Ruby Dee
Lem Scott	Frederick O'Neal
Carol	Ellen Holly
Violet	Pauline Meyers
May Scott	Beah Richards
Rose	Royce Wallace
Poppy	Frances Foster
Bobby	Dell Erickson
Tony	Dee Pollack
Gussie	Frank Killmond
Johnny	Joseph Sonessa
Alan	Sherman Raskin

This is a "well-intentioned" film, an effort to examine the problems of a teenaged Negro boy and on another level than the depressed economic scale in which Negroes are usually shown. Unfortunately, its handling is not equal to its aims. The Hecht-Hill-Lancaster production will have appeal to younger audiences, however, and this draw will be enhanced by the casting of singer Johnny Nash in the leading role.

The screenplay by Louis S. Peterson and Julius J. Epstein, based on Peterson's play, is concerned with young Nash's growing awareness of his status as a Negro in a white world. Feeling rebuffed by his white friends, he seeks the Negro community, but finds as little help there. Unable to communicate with his parents, he eventually finds solace with the family maid, Ruby Dee. This experience, clearly a sexual one in the play, but ambiguous in the film, enables him to make the "Giant Step" from adolescence to manhood.

It is a quickening theme and one with universal acceptance, since the boy's problems are actually the same in substance of any teen-aged boy. They are special in kind for a young Negro, of course, fringed with bitterness and danger. But the growing up of a young man by his exposure to a mature woman is a recurrent and valid dramatic theme.

Director Philip Leacock, however, has not handled his story with compelling excitement or humanity. The characters, despite their genuine problems, remain cold and static. The screenplay may be partly to blame in this respect, as it is in others. The language used for instance, with such words as "bastard," "Prostitute," "behind," numerous "damns" and "hells," may be sound realistically. But because they are not so commonly heard on the screen, their use could give the impression they are inherent only to Negro households, an inaccurate impression and surely not the author's intention.

Some of the situations designed to expose Nash's problems and the solutions are not fresh, except that the central figure is a Negro. A crucial scene with three prostitutes is pseudo-O'Neill. The scenes between Nash and his white friends are awkward and stagey without real insight. The conclusion is unclear and appears to recommend an "Uncle Tom" philosophy.

Nash makes a nice bow. He is a good-looking youngster and indicates sensitivity. The veteran Negro actress Estelle Hemsley is warming as his understanding grandmother. Frederick O'Neal and Beah Richards are fine as Nash's misunderstood and misunderstanding parents. Ruby Dee is the most moving of the cast as the compassionate servant girl, and Ellen Holly is vivid in a brief appearance. Pauline Meyers, Royce Wallace and Frances Foster are colorful as the ladies who attempt to further Nash's education.

Julius J. Epstein produced, as well as co-authoring the screenplay. There will be a title song sung by Nash with words and music by Jay Livingston and Ray Evans, but it had not been added to the score at the time of preview. *Powe.*

Behind the Great Wall
(AromaRama)
(DOCUMENTARY—COLOR—TOTALSCOPE)

The sweet smell of success—via novelty; unenduring values.

Continental Distributing release of Astra Cinematografica-Leonardo Bonzi production. Directed by Carlo Lizzani: AromaRama process conceived and directed by Charles Weiss: written and adapted for AromaRama by Sidney Kaufman and Thomas Orchard: Narrator, Chet Huntley; camera (DeLuxe Color), Pierludovico Pavoni; editor, Mario Serandrei; AromaRama editor, Lou Rothstein: music, A. Francesco Lavagnino. Reviewed at DeMille Theatre, N.Y., Dec. 8, '59. Running time, **97 MINS.**

A feature-length documentary focusing on Red China, made by Italian producer Leonardo Bonzi a few years ago, "Behind the Great Wall" beckons trade attention now for it is being used to introduce AromaRama. Film unveiled (or uncorked?) New York's refurbished Mayfair, now the DeMille Theatre.

The prolog makes a comparison of this scent-yielding process with such cinematic milestones as sound, color and widescreen, and this simply is unrealistic; there's no new screen dimension added, such as provided by Cinerama. But the immodesty can be forgiven, for the presentation in good part does live up to its you-must-breathe-it-to-believe-it promises. Effective smells permeate the theatre, as emitted through airconditioning ducts, and are synchronized with the screen goings-on with remarkable precision.

Net result is a travelog with a good commercial one-shot gimmick.

Opening is a talk by commentator Chet Huntley, reminiscent of Lowell Thomas introducing "This Is Cinerama." And thereupon the public gets a view of a bowl of oranges, the halving and squeezing of one of them, and along with this the unmistakable aromatic pleasure of an honest-to-goodness orange.

From this point the audience is invited to poke its nose sniffingly into modern China. The documentary on its own is interesting, if somewhat uneven in terms of continuity. It copped the "best film" and "best photography" awards at a Brussels Film Exposition. This nasal-sprayed adaptation, as being put on by circuit operator-film importer Walter Reade, perhaps left out a scene here and there with the view of concentrating on the footage that especially lent itself to AromaRama.

The tour behind China's Great Wall provides cues for the transmission of numerous odors, ranging from the offensive waterfront, to the most agreeable grazing land, to sharp spices to the varying sweetnesses of jasmin and incense. Indeed, there's an over-abundance of different smells, with many of them undiscernable to the average person, and this becomes disconcerting. Too, there are instances where the machine-made olfactory flavors don't correspond with what's on view.

Interesting is the rapid removal of one aroma from the theatre to make way for another, as engineered with a purification air flow. However, there's a bargain-basement perfume fragrance that is injected frequently and gets too darn persistent. This has got to go.

There's no new screen dimension within the milestone frame of reference in AromaRama. It's hardly likely to remain a part of the picture business scene, on the basis of this first exposure (perhaps Mike Todd Jr.'s upcoming Smell-o-Vision may enhance the chemistry to a more significant cinematic level).

But there's a lot of built-in talk-about in "Behind the Great Wall" as a single entity—enough to assure a nice payoff for the Reade company. *Gene.*

I Magliari
(The Magliari)
(ITALIAN

Rome, Dec. 8.

Titanus release of Franco Cristaldi production for Vides. Stars Alberto Sordi; features Belinda Lee, Renato Salvatori, Linda Vandal, Aldo Giuffre, Nino Vingelli, Nino di Napoli, Pasquale Cenammo, Aldo Buffi Landi, Carmine Ippolito. Directed by Francesco Rosi. Camera, Gianni di Venanzo; music, Piero Piccioni; editor, Mario Serandrei. Previewed in Rome. Running time, **132 MINS.**

Totonno	Alberto Sordi
Mario	Renato Salvatori
Paula Mayer	Belinda Lee

Meller boasting excellent location work in Germany has marquee value in Alberto Sordi and Beiinda Lee names for local impact. Though overlong footage is partly justified for atmospheric reasons, pic needs cutting for a crisper pace. Spotty export chances.

In a story pattern very similar to that of director Francesco Rosi's first pic, "The Challenge," this tells of the attempt by a younger leader of swindlers to break into older boss' racket. All the action is in north German (Hamburg and Hannover) areas where expatriate Italians pass off cheap cloth for the real thing. Intruder gets his comeuppance, while in a semi-romantic subplot, a basically honest outsider is convinced he must ask out.

While the atmosphere is expertly captured and the film's mechanics (except for distracting by slow spots here and there) click in like fashion, pic somehow fails to convince, resolving self in stylistic exercise. Standout performance is again given by Alberto Sordi, as the upstart while Belinda Lee does some of her best work to date as the love interest. Renato Salvatori, on the other hand, lacks stature and the conviction of his role. Remainder of colorful cast, especially Nino Vingelli and Pasquale Cenammo, is outstanding.

Special nod must go to lenser Gianni di Venanzo, who under difficult location conditions, has come up with some of the year's finest footage. Other technical credits bear the Titanus quality stamp. *Hawk.*

The Gazebo

Cheerful murder-can-be-fun comedy. Glenn Ford and Debbie Reynolds star. Good b.o.

Hollywood, Dec. 15.

Metro release of an Avon production. Stars Glenn Ford, Debbie Reynolds; co-stars Carl Reiner; with John McGiver, Mabel Albertson, Doro Merande, Bert Freed, Martin Landau, Robert Ellenstein, Richard Wessel Herman. Produced by Lawrence Weingarten. Directed by George Marshall. Screenplay by George Wells, based on the play by Alec Coppel, from a story by Myra and Alec Coppel; camera, Paul C. Vogel; music, Jeff Alexander; editing, Adrienne Fazan. Previewed at Grauman's Chinese Theatre, Dec. 11, '59. Running time, **102 MINS.**

Elliott Nash	Glenn Ford
Nell Nash	Debbie Reynolds
Harlow Edison	Carl Reiner
Sam Thorpe	John McGiver
Mrs. Chandler	Mabel Albertson
Matilda	Doro Merande
Lieut. Joe Jenkins	Bert Freed
The Duke	Martin Landau
Ben	Robert Ellenstein
Louis, the Louse	Richard Wessel
The Pigeon	Herman

Atop the current crest of sophisticated comedies and sexy romps comes "The Gazebo," an old-fashioned film farce of amusing and often spirited proportions. The core of its fun is murder, and its makers—producer Lawrence Weingarten, director George Marshall and screenwriter George Wells—successfully have handled it with a light, breezy touch. Glenn Ford and Debbie Reynolds star in the Avon Production and should prompt good boxoffice for the Metro release.

"Gazebo" is based on the Alec Coppel play which starred Walter Slezak and Jayne Meadows on Broadway and Tom Ewell and Jan Sterling on the road. In its transfer to the screen, scripter Wells has spiced the often far-fetched devices of the play with a number his own delicacies, including a gregarious pigeon named Herman. Director Marshall, achieving a frisky blend of suspense and tomfoolery, put it all together with a bright, well-timed hand.

Ford, in his first non-uniform, non-cowboy role in his last eight films, plays a television writer who is married to a Broadway star (Miss Reynolds). Several years earlier, Miss Reynolds posed without proper attire, and now the possessor of said photographs is blackmailing Ford. Murder is his only out, Ford reasons, and in a carefully laid out plan, which includes two tranquilizers, a miner's hat and a shower curtain, he invites the blackmailer to his home and shoots him. He hides the body on the spot where a gazebo (summer house) is about to be positioned the following day. But when everything's done, the blackmailer shows up dead somewhere else, and with Ford pointing to the gazebo and crying, "Who the hell is out there?," the fun begins.

This film is nearly all Ford, and he's up to every scene, earning both sympathy and laughs as he muddles through his farcical "crime." Miss Reynolds is excellent, but her talents are beyond what her limited role requires. The part on Broadway was very minor and has not changed much. Carl Reiner, as the couple's district attorney friend, is good but also beyond the part. John McGiver is perfect as the builder in a delightful performance. Doro Merande, as the loud maid, is fine, and Herman is good for a healthy share of chuckles. Also in the cast are Mabel Albertson, Bert Freed, Martin Landau, Robert Ellenstein and Richard Wessel.

Paul C. Vogel's photography is crisp, with good work by art director George W. Davis and Paul Groesse, recording supervisor Franklin Milton and musical scorer Jeff Alexander. Adrienne Fazan's editing is excellent. *Ron.*

Suddenly, Last Summer

Homo whose mama is his procurer. A weirdo by any standard. Hepburn and Taylor chief b.o. bait.

Hollywood, Dec. 11.

Columbia release of Sam Spiegel production. Stars Elizabeth Taylor, Montgomery Clift, Katharine Hepburn; features Albert Dekker, Mercedes McCambridge, Gary Raymond. Directed by Joseph L. Mankiewicz; screenplay, Gore Vidal and Tennessee Williams; based on Williams' play; camera, Jack Hildyard; music, Buxton Orr and Malcolm Arnold; editors, William W. Hornbeck and Thomas G. Stanford. Previewed at the studio, Dec. 10, '59. Running time, **112 MINS.**

Catherine Holly	Elizabeth Taylor
Mrs. Venable	Katharine Hepburn
Dr. Cukrowicz	Montgomery Clift
Dr. Hockstader	Albert Dekker
Mrs. Holly	Mercedes McCambridge
George Holly	Gary Raymond
Miss Foxhill	Mavis Villiers
Nurse Benson	Patricia Marmont
Sister Felicity	Joan Young
Lucy	Maria Britneva
Hockstader's Secretary	Sheila Robbins
Blond Interne	David Cameron

Perversion and greed, Tennessee Williams' recurrent themes, are worked over again in "Suddenly, Last Summer," latest of Williams' plays to be filmed. Sam Spiegel production for Columbia is possibly the most bizarre film ever made by any major American company. In the play it was concerned with homosexuality and cannibalism. The cannibalism has been dropped, or muted, in the film version. Still it is like lifting the roof on Hell to see these characters in action. The film has some very effective moments, but on the whole it fails to move the spectator.

Perhaps the reason is that what was a long one-act play has been expanded in the screenplay, by Williams and Gore Vidal, to a longish motion picture. Nothing that's been added is an improvement on the original; the added scenes are merely diversionary. They stretch the seams of the original fabric without strengthening the seamy (sic; or, sic, sic, sic) aspects of the story. The play in its brevity introduced horror and then closed the books on it before it could be challenged by reason. The film gives the spectator a chance for disbelief, and this is fatal to Williams' grotesque fancies.

Despite these reservations, "Suddenly, Last Summer," directed by Joseph L. Mankiewicz, has its redeeming aspects, Williams' language, rich in vivid and poetic imagery, has a shimmering lustre. His construction (although marred in the screenplay) has some of the fascination of the suspense mystery melodrama. It even has a conventional "third act" when all the principals are gathered in one room while the "detective" recapitulates the mystery and elucidates it.

The story is that of a doting mother, Katharine Hepburn, and her son. The son was a homosexual and his mother his procuress. When she had passed the age when she could function effectively in this capacity, he enlisted the services of his beautiful cousin, Elizabeth Taylor. This nightmare ends when the young man's corruption provokes the primitive reaction of some of those he has debased, and he is torn to pieces by a mob of young men.

The question is whether Miss Taylor, in her description of the event, is fancifully insane or ruthlessly sane. Miss Hepburn wants a lobotomy performed on Miss Taylor, to excise the memory of the son's death, by detaching a portion of the brain. It is the job of Montgomery Clift, as the neuro-surgeon who would perform the operation, to decide if Miss Taylor is deranged as Miss Hepburn insists.

Miss Hepburn, with her surer techniques, is dominant, making her brisk authority a genteel hammer relentlessly crushing the younger woman. Miss Taylor is most effective in her later scenes, although these scenes have been robbed of their original theatricality in transfer from stage to screen. Clift is adequate, although he is little more than straight man to the two ladies. Mercedes McCambridge and Gary Raymond are fine as two typically Williams' "Menagerie" relatives. Albert Dekker is capable in a thankless role.

Although Mankiewicz' direction is inventive in giving the essentially static narrative some movement and rhythm, it is less successful in evoking sympathy or perception for the characters. He must be faulted, too, for blunting Miss Taylor's final scene so it fails to match Miss Hepburn's opening monolog. (The play was actually only two monologs of almost equal power and length.)

Jack Hildyard's camera work is superb, prowling about the actors like a questing eye, moving in for full, great closeups.. rich in atmosphere and meaning. The musical score is at times annoyingly obtrusive, and at others seems to emphasize, rather than contracting, as it should, the similarity of the film's atmosphere to the routime horror film. *Powe.*

Masters of the Congo Jungle
(C'SCOPE—COLOR)

Award calibre documentary with good art house b.o. potential.

20th-Fox release of International Scientific Foundation production, under auspices of Leopold III, King of Belgium. Produced by Henri Storck. Directed by Heinz Sielmann and Henry Brandt. Written by Joe Wilis; story by Sam Hill; music, Richard Cornu; narrators, Orson Welles and William Warfield. Previewed at studio, Dec. 10, 1959. Running time, **86 MINS.**

"Masters of the Congo Jungle" is a beautiful, unusual, feature-length documentary of Academy Award calibre, however misleading its title. Both artistic and informative, it deals with the stone-age natives of the northeastern Belgian Congo. Looks like a promising entry for the art houses.

The CinemaScope-De Luxe Color footage brought out by producer Henri Storck, directors Heinz Sielmann and Henry Brandt and a half dozen cameramen (not credited) includes magnificent vistas of jungles and volcanoes, close, dramatic views of birds and animals and, most important, captures the daily lives of the people.

No travelog, the film doesn't seek mere curiosity but faithfully follows a theme. King Badouin of Belgium, under whose auspices the International Scientific Foundation made the picture, states the theme in a title card: "There is a communion between the man of the forest and his natural surroundings which inspires in us a sense of respect, a recognition of spiritual heritage."

The voices of Orson Welles and William Warfield alternate at narrating Joe Wilis' dialog (Sam Hill's story). It's subtly written and the great voices give it a poetic quality. Welles seems to speak as a scientist, learned but humble in a quest for truth, and Warfield speaks as a native, secure and dignified in a world he understands in his very bones.

The world of the natives (related to Pygmies) is first shown in a superb, mood-setting animated sequence (not credited). Then, following the course of a wise man's lecture to the village warriors, the camera picks out each subject as the narrators relate each myth to fact.

For example, traditional dances and rites are shown and the bird or animal which inspired them is spot-lighted; the belief in the volcano god is made plausible through artfully selective photography and narrative.

Among the many notable animal scenes are: a little "night heron" gruesomely capturing and killing a larger bird's chick; a family of gorillas charging, almost at the camera. The scenes are the more remarkable because of the consistent studio quality of the photography.

The film editor and the sound man (not credited) did outstanding jobs and Richard Cornu produced a fine score—all of which was part of a rare harmony among all departments in this film. *Glen.*

Rue Des Prairies
(FRENCH)

Paris, Dec. 8.

Cinedis release of Ariane-Intermondia production. Stars Jean Gabin; features Marie-Jose Nat, Claude Brasseur, Roger Dumas, Paul Frankeur. Renee Faure, Roger Treville. Directed by Denys De La Patelliere. Screenplay, Michel Audiard, De La Patelliere; camera, Louis Page; editor, Jacqueline Thiedot. At the Paris, Paris. Running time, **90 MINS.**

Henri Neveu	Jean Gabin
Odette	Marie-Jose Nat
Loulou	Claude Brasseur
Fernand	Roger Dumas
Friend	Paul Frankeur
Lawyer	Renee Faure
Suitor	Roger Treville

This is a Jean Gabin vehicle. In it he gets a chance to play drunk, noble and angry, thus running his well-oiled gamut. He's always helped by his expert timing, sincerity and pro aplomb. As a widower bringing up three children, (his wife died while he was a prisoner of war), Gabin has a meaty role and brings this series of family incidents together for a good local item.

For foreign situations, it will depend mainly on the Gabin name because this is a talky film, with plenty of intrinsically French aspects. But the basic problem is international, and it has the conventional earmarks and sentiment for a family film playoff.

Director De La Patelliere has let this wisely rest on Gabin, and it averts being sudsy by his knowing thesping. Technical credits are good as is the supporting playing, but this vacillates between problem film, drama and comedy to make an itme needing careful handling. *Mosk.*

Vice Raid

Exploitation melodrama that could return a profit.

Hollywood, Dec. 9.

United Artists release of an Imperial Production. Stars Mamie Van Doren and Richard Coogan; co-stars Brad Dexter, Frank Gerstle, Barry Atwater; also, Carol Nugent, Joseph Sullivan, Chris Alcaide, Jeanne Bates, Juli Reding, Shep Sanderms, George Cisar, Nestor Paiva, Jack Kenney, Russ Bender, Tom McKee, George Eldredge, John Zaremba, Alex Goda, John Hart, Lester Dorr, Evans Davis. Produced by Robert E. Kent. Directed by Edward L. Cahn. Screenplay, Charles Ellis; editor, Grant Whytock; music, Paul Sawtell and Bert Shefter. Previewed at Goldwyn Studios, Dec. 8, '59. Running time, **71 MINS**

Carol Hudson	Mamie Van Doren
Sgt. Whitey Brandon	Richard Coogan
Vince Malone	Brad Dexter
Lt. Brennan	Frank Gerstle
Phil Evans	Barry Atwater
Louise	Carol Nugent
Ben Dunton	Joseph Sullivan
Eddie	Chris Algaide
Marilyn	Jeanne Bates
Gertie	Julie Reding
Mugsie	Shep Sanders
Marty Heffner	George Cisar
Frank Burke	Nestor Paiva
Leo Dempsey	Jack Kenney
Lawyer Drucker	Russ Bender
Doctor	Tom McKee
Police advocate	George Eldredge
City prosecutor Marsh	John Zaremba
Officer Hennessy	Alex Goda
Tom	John Hart

Man at Desk	Lester Dorn
Policeman	Evans Davis

In United Artists' 'Vice Raid," Mamie Van Doren plays a prostitute. That's exploitable, and the double-billing of the film with "Inside the Mafia" should earn fair boxoffice for the low budgeters. Outside the package, it's a sexy second feature.

Except for the prostie angle, there's not much difference between the Imperial Pictures production and television's 30-minute cops-'n'-robbers yarns. The intrigue is the same, and so is the action. The screenplay is by Charles Ellis and, while weak in some story points, is a workmanlike job. Producer Robert E. Kent has put together a competent production, and director Edward L. Cahn keeps most of it alive.

Miss Van Doren has a few moments of rather believable acting as a Detroit callgirl imported to New York to frame Richard Coogan, a member of the vice squad. By the film's windup, she becomes disillusioned with the Syndicate and helps the fired policeman crush the entire girlie racket.

Coogan, recognizable via his tv exposure on last season's "The Californians," is good as the cop, as are Brad Dexter as the boss, Barry Atwater as a hood and Frank Gerstle as a bribed officer. Carol Nugent makes a lively, cute-looking teenager.

Technical work—Stanley Cortez' photography, Bill Glasgow's art direction, Grant Whytock's editing and Al Overton's sound—is capably accomplished. The musical score by Paul Sawtell and Bert Shefter is good and occasionally striking. *Ron.*

Blood and Steel

Old hat World War II melo for minor markets only.

Hollywood, Dec. 10.
Twentieth-Fox release of Gene Corman production. Stars John Lupton, Ziva Rodann, Brett Halsey; features James Edwards, John Brinkley. Allen Jung. Directed by Bernard L. Kowalski; screenplay. Joseph C. Gillette: camera, Floyd D. Crosby; editor, Anthony Carras; music, Calvin Jackson. Previewed Dec. 9, '59. Running time, **62 MINS.**

Dave	John Lupton
George	James Edwards
Jim	Brett Halsey
Cip	John Brinkley
Lead Jap	Allen Jung
Native Girl	Ziva Rodann
Jap Draftsman	James Hong
Sugi	Bill Saito

"Blood and Steel" is a minor entry, formula war stuff and rather a strange offering now since subject matter is strictly old hat and has been done previously, and better. Feature's for the smaller program market, where its short 62 minutes' running time won't tell against it.

Considerable repetition mars the unfoldment of the Joseph C. Gillette screenplay of four Seabees landed on a Jap-held South Pacific isle to survey for a possible U.S. air base, and their chase by the Japanese. Although action is familiar, some of it provides a thrill or so because direction by Bernard L. Kowalski is properly realistic, and he draws hard-hitting performances from his cast.

John Lupton is leader of the quartet, others being Brett Halsey, John Brinkley and James Edwards, the latter left by his comrades after receiving critical leg wounds and forced to make his way back to the raft they've hidden. Ziva Rodann, as a native girl who helps Edwards and is mistakenly killed by one of the fleeing Seabees, is lost in her role. Allen Jung is okay as a Jap captain directing the pursuit of the Americans.

Floyd D. Crosby's photography is excellent. *Whit.*

The Gene Krupa Story

Competent biofilm, cast out of chronological sync. Teenage b.o. should be good.

Hollywood, Dec. 18.
Columbia release of a Philip A. Waxman production. Stars Sal Mineo, Susan Kohner, James Darren; with Susan Oliver, Yvonne Craig, Lawrence Dobkin, Celia Lovsky; and Red Nichols. Bobby Troup, Anita O'Day, Shelley Manne and Buddy Lester. Directed by Don Weis. Screenplay by Orin Jannings. Camera, Charles Lawton Jr.; editors, Maurice Wright and Edwin Bryant; music, Leith Stevens. Previewed at the Hawaii Theatre, Dec. 18, '59. Running time, 102 MINS.

Gene Krupa	Sal Mineo
Ethel Maguire	Susan Kohner
Eddie Sirota	James Darren
Dorissa Dinell	Susan Oliver
Gloria Corregio	Yvonne Craig
Speaker Willis	Lawrence Dobkin
Mother	Celia Lovsky
Red Nichols	Red Nichols
Tommy Dorsey	Bobby Troup
Anita O'Day	Anita O'Day
Davey Tough	Shelly Manne
Buddy Lester	Buddy Lester
Blues Singer	Ruby Lane
Ted Krupa	Gavin MacLeod
Father	John Bleifer

Columbia's "The Gene Krupa Story" at times is as bouncy as a drumhead and often just as thin. The Philip A. Waxman production was conceived for teenagers—to wit, the casting of juvenile-looking Sal Mineo in the title role—and while this conception may pay off at the boxoffice, it also weakens believability in the film.

Not that Mineo isn't up to the role. He's excellent, fresh and alive, a frenzied whiz at the drums. As the Krupa of 18, he's real. As the Krupa of 34, he's asked to create too great an illusion.

Orin Jannings' screenplay has its share of biographic cliches. Krupa's father wants him to become a priest, not a lowdown drummer. Krupa tries, can't make it and turns to jazz. Along the way, he neglects his girl, alienates his mother, almost loses his best friend and gets involved with the wrong kind of woman. He also smokes a reefer or two, is framed into a jail term, struggles and finally makes a comeback. Several good story points are only slightly motivated, but Jannings has done a first-rate job with dialog, turning out a hard, brittle sound that fits the characters and fills with interest the plot's bare spots.

Director Don Weis has created the right mood and does well with the characterizations when not hampered by a feeling that these are kids playing dress-up.

Susan Kohner, as Krupa's girl, displays the most growth, from a silly kid to a mature, emotional woman. James Darren underplays adeptly as the drummer's best friend, showing good looks and basic talent. As a loose singer, Susan Oliver is not given the opportunity to apply much shading to her role. Often enough, however, she ignites a strong spark that could mean potential stardom. Yvonne Craig makes a youthful sexpot, Lawrence Dobkin a good agent and Celia Lovsky a loving but misunderstanding mother.

Jazz is given a good ride through Leith Stevens' striking scoring. Appearing the the film as themselves are Red Nichols, Anita O'Day, Shelly Manne and Buddy Lester, with pianist Bobby Troup donning glasses to play Tommy Dorsey. Drumming was recorded by Gene Krupa, and Mineo matched it skillfully

Charles Lawton Jr.'s camerawork is fine, as is Robert Peterson's art direction, Maurice Wright's and Edwin Bryant's editing and Jack Solomon's sound. Montage work by Donald W. Starling is a definite plus. *Ron.*

The Flying Fontaines
(COLOR)

Fast-moving circus melodrama with aerial thrills; good entry for intended market.

Hollywood, Dec. 8.
Columbia Pictures release of Sam Katzman production. Stars Michael Callan, Joan Evans, Evy Norland, Rian Garrick; costars Joe de Santis, John van Dreelen, Roger Perry, Jeanne Manet. Directed by George Sherman. Screenplay, Donn Mullally, Lee Edwin, camera (Eastman-color), Fred Jackman; editor, Saul A. Goodkind; music, Mischa Bakaleinikoff. Previewed Dec. 3, '59. Running time, 73 MINS.

Rick Rias	Michael Callan
Suzanne Fontaine	Evy Norlund
Jan	Joan Evans
Bill Rand	Rian Garrick
Roberto Rias	Joe de Santis
Paul Fontaine	Roger Perry
Victor Fontaine	John van Dreelen
Michele	Jeanne Manet
Margie	Barbara Kelley
Sally	Dorothy Johnson
Doctor	Pierre Watkin
Ring Announcer	Murray Parker

Sam Katzman uncorks fresh talent in this fast-moving circus yarn revolving around a troupe of aerialists—from which pic takes its tab —and their problems, romantic and otherwise. To be packaged with "1001 Arabian Nights" as Columbia's Christmas release, hefty returns are indicated in the minor-A market for which it is beamed.

Pic, lensed in fine Eastman-color which sets off the blatant and picturesque atmosphere of the big top, catches the spirit of this form of life and its people both in the Donn Mullally-Lee Erwin screenplay and direction by George Sherman, who hits a pace early and never lets down. Characterizations are persuasive, and thrills of the flying trapeze highlight the action to reach a high note of interest. The whole panorama of the circus is vividly portrayed for excellent effect.

Plotline follows the return of Michael Callan, star of the flying Fontaines when he entered the Army two years previously, to find his girl, Joan Evans, now wed to Roger Perry, catcher of the troupe. He also finds new romantic interest in Evy Norlund, another young member of the troupe who was only a girl when he went away. Rebuffed because she's interested in Rian Garrick, also an aerialist, Callan gets another setback when his father, a former star trapeze artist who has trained him from infancy to take his place, refuses to recommend him for a Ringling Bros. act until he regains his pre-Army greatness. Unfoldment, during which Callan is responsible for Garrick's fall and retirement from the act, builds to a spectacular climax when Callan himself falls and is seriously injured, but it's indicated not only will he return but will win his femme after all.

Callan acquits himself nicely and Miss Norlund, who was Miss Denmark in "Miss Universe" contest is an interesting newcomer. Miss Evans, only vet of the youthful array, turns in a good performance as a heavy; Garrick and Perry both undertake their roles capably; Joe de Santis scores as Callan's stern disciplinarian father; and John van Dreelen and Jeanne Manet as Miss Norlund's parents are first-rate. Bill Quinn is okay as circus owner.

Technical departments are well handled throughout, including Fred Jackman's speedy photography, Saul A. Goodkind's tight editing;

Paul Palmentola's art direction and Mischa Bakaleinikoff's atmospheric music. *Whit.*

Treasure of San Teresa
(BRITISH)

Routine meller which lacks punch till the brisk finale; moderate dualer for average houses.

London, Dec. 15.

British Lion release (in association with Britannia Films) of John Nasht-Patrick Filmer-Sankey production. Stars Eddie Constantine, Dawn Addams, Marius Goring, Christopher Lee; features Nadine Tallier, Walter Gotell. Directed by Alvin Rakoff. Screenplay, Jack Andrews from story by Jeffrey Dell; camera, Wilkie Cooper; editor, Jim Connock; music by Jeff Davis, and Don Banks. Previewed at Studio One, London. Running Time, 81 MINS.

General Von Hartmann	Willy Witte
Larry Brennan	Eddie Constantine
Hedi Von Hartmann	Dawn Addams
Mike Jones	Gaylord Cavallero
Bar Girl	Penelope Horner
Bar Girls In Fight	Tsai Chin
	Diana Potter
Station Sergeant	Steve Plytas
Rudi Siebert	Marius Goring
Maid at Billie's	Anna Turner
Billie	Georgina Cookson
Piano Player	Hutch
Truck Driver	Thomas Gallagher
Zizi	Nadine Tallier
Cemetery Keeper	Clive Dunn
Jaeger	Christopher Lee
Schneider	Hubert Mittendorf

Here's a routine meller which might make a useful second feature in average houses. But it rarely sparks to life, is pulled down by an unimaginative script and only flickers into real action at the end. It's competently acted and directed, but the over-all effect is rather dull. With little or no marquee value in its performers, "Treasure Of San Teresa" is unlikely to make much b.o. impact.

The plot concerns a jewel chase. As an O.S.S. man in the war Eddie Constantine has delivered a package of family heirlooms to a convent in Czechoslovakia, at the request of a German resistance general who commits suicide. After the war, Constantine, now a radio officer on a merchant ship, arrives in Hamburg.

He is approached by the general's aide (Marius Goring) with a scheme whereby Goring, Constantine and the general's daughter (Dawn Addams) can smuggle the jewels out of the Iron Curtain country. Needless to say Goring is not on the level and there's a great deal of double-crossing before he is rubbed out.

Constantine handles this stuff professionally but without much spark. Goring puts over another of his suave bits of villainy while Miss Addams is a cool, attractive heroine. Nadine Tallier as her roommate and Christopher Lee as another crook, with his eye on the baubles, are also around satisfactorily.

Authentic locations and some good lensing by Wilkie Cooper give the pic a lift. But it unmistakably bears the imprints of a run-of-the-mill job which never excites. *Rich.*

A Dog of Flanders
(COLOR—C'SCOPE)

Handsome, intelligent remake of the Ouida standard. Easter release; good prospects for the "Old Yeller" market.

Hollywood, Dec. 18.

Twentieth-Fox release of a Robert Radnitz production. Stars David Ladd, Donald Crisp, Theodore Bikel. Directed by James B. Clark. Screenplay, Ted Sherdeman; based on the novel by Ouida; camera (DeLuxe Color), Otto Heller; music, Paul Sawtell and Bert Shefter; editor, Benjamin Laird. Previewed at the studio, Dec. 17, '59. Running time, 97 MINS.

Nello	David Ladd
Daas	Donald Crisp
Piet	Theodore Bikel
Cogez	Max Croiset
Corrie	Monique Ahrens
Alois	Siobhan Taylor

As a poet once said about something else, but applicable here, if this film doesn't warm the cockles of the heart, the heart needs a new set of cockles. "A Dog of Flanders," Robert Radnitz' film bow as a producer, is an almost literal transplant from an old-fashioned novel, but instead of seeming out-of-date, it is as charming as a Victorian valentine.

At first, director Robert B. Clark's leisurely pace, his emphasis on character and background rather than the frantic action of today's films, seems slow. But it has a beguiling warmth and credibility that builds a mounting interest and a cumulative effect. The 20th-Fox release proves that Walt Disney needn't have a monopoly on this sort of wholesome film fare.

"A Dog of Flanders," filmed in CinemaScope and DeLuxe color on Netherlands locations, will be an Easter release.

Screenplay by Ted Sherdeman, based on the old Ouida novel, preserves the quaint language and spirit of the time, roughly turn of the century. There is a little Dutch boy, sensitively played by David Ladd, who is the central character. He lives in the estate once termed honorable poverty, with his grandfather, Donald Crisp. The pair make their living, such as it is, by delivering milk from the farms surrounding Antwerp, to the city.

The boy, influenced by Holland's great artistic tradition, wants to be an artist. The grandfather hasn't the ability to dream so high. When the grandfather dies, the boy and his cart-dog (Disney's "Old Yeller," trained by Frank Weatherwax) manage to survive until young Ladd is adopted by a real artist, Theodore Bikel.

Clark's direction does not have much in the way of crisis or conflict to build on. The situations and homely philosophy in which they are met, are almost all muted. But they seem real and vital, because Clark has taken the trouble to cast a mood that sustains them. The film is also a good example of locations well-utilized, the most notably being the closing scene of Rubens' three-panel "Crucifixion."

Young Ladd, happily, is one of those children who barely seems to be acting. Teamed with the veteran Donald Crisp and the latter's polished style, the two mesh nicely. Bikel is amusing, and with the winning Dutch actress Monique Ahrens, provides an adult love interest that is ingeniously threaded through the film. Even a scene of Miss Ahrens, posing bare-backed for artist Bikel, is done so innocently and correctively, its intent cannot be mistaken. Max Croiset and young Siobhan Taylor complete the important roles, all well cast.

Otto Heller's camera work is rich in tone and composition, and the music of Paul Sawtell and Bert Shefter is about the finest each composer has ever done. *Powe.*

Follow a Star
(BRITISH)

Slapstick farce, with sentimental coating, starring Norman Wisdom, a British comedy name; has Wisdom in his best form, and that's its chief recommendation.

London, Dec. 15.

Rank (Hugh Stewart) production and release. Stars Norman Wisdom; features Jerry Desmonde, June Laverick. Produced by Hugh Stewart. Directed by Robert Asher. Screenplay, Jack Davies, Henry Blyth, Wisdom; camera, Jack Asher; editor, Roger Cherrill; music, Philip Green. Previewed at Odeon, Marble Arch, London. Running time, 103 MINS.

Norman Truscott	Norman Wisdom
Judy	June Laverick
Vernon Carew	Jerry Desmonde
Dymphna Dobson	Hattie Jacques
Dr. Chatterway	Richard Wattis
Harold Franklin	Eddie Leslie
Birkett	John Le Mesurier
Pendlebury	Sydney Tafler
Lady Finchington	Fenella Fielding
The General	Charles Heslop
Stage Manager	Joe Melia
Violinist	Ron Moody

"Follow a Star" is the seventh Norman Wisdom film in his seven-year-contract with the Rank Organization. It's been a mutually profitable honeymoon and this picture, sticking largely to the fun-and-sentiment formula at which Norman Wisdom is adept, should prove a happy b.o. proposition. Not since the hey-day of "Lassie" have films been so carefully tailored to suit a star personality as those of Wisdom. He's the little fellow, constantly put upon, who suddenly rebels and strikes back at pomposity. He evokes sympathy, invariably gets the girl, falls down, sings some songs and most certainly in Britain, raises the yocks.

Jack Davies and Henry Blyth and Wisdom himself have dreamed up the current story. It's a simple one. Wisdom is a suit-presser who aspires to singing stardom. Jerry Desmonde is a fading vocal star who hires the gullible Wisdom as a servant under the thin guise of teaching him to sing, makes a comeback by the mechanical use of Wisdom's voice. Tv appearances? The disk player is being operated in the wings.

His singing instructor (Hattie Jacques) and his girlfriend, who, for an inexplicable reason except perhaps to play for sobs is stuck in a wheelchair, believes in Wisdom as a singing personality in his own right. Unfortunately, he has no confidence and cannot sing unless the girlfriend (June Laverick) is on hand to tinkle the ivories and give him some courage. This tiny story line hardly adds up to a film, but it gives the star ample opportunity to project his widely-known, likeable personality. It really consists of a number of revue sketches which are mostly very funny.

For instance, there's a psychiatrist couch sequence in which Wisdom sends Richard Wattis near crazy; then, under the hypnotic influence of Wattis, Wisdom is splendid as a Guards Officer who turns a ritzy West End club inside out. There's also a great piece of clowning when Wisdom takes over from Desmonde at the Palladium and everything, but everything, goes wrong. Sometimes the comic routines come apart at the seams. But on the whole this is a genial joke which has certainly provided the little man with a lot of useful material for future tele and vaude appearances.

He is surrounded with some sound performers. Jerry Desmonde, as the unscrupulous vocalist, has more opportunity than usual for straight acting, and grasps it avidly. Hattie Jacques, a big striking personality, is firstclass as the singing instructor who unmasks the villain. A number of others have small, limited chances but also make good impact.

For instance, Ron Moody is a puzzled violinist during Wisdom's Palladium act, John Le Mesurier is an outraged headwaiter and Charles Heslop is a pompous club member. All have brief, effective scenes. June Laverick is a comely heroine but has little chance to make much of a colorless role.

The film lacks wit but has good spirits throughout. It is briskly directed by Robert Asher and neatly lensed by Jack Asher. Four or five songs are pumped into the continuity and "I Love You," and the title song, both scribed by Wisdom, have the earmarks of pop hits. *Rich.*

El Lazarillo de Tormes
(The Ragamuffin of Tormes)
(SPANISH)

Madrid, Dec. 15.

Mercurio release of a Hesperia Films production. Stars Marco Paoletti, Juan Jose Menendez, Carlos Casaravilla, Memmo Carotenuto, Margarita Lozano, Antonio Molino and Emilio Santiago. Written and directed by Cesar Ardavin. Camera, Manuel Berenguer; art director, Torre de la Fuente; music, Ruiz de Luna; costumer, Humberto Cornejo. At Cine Calloa, Madrid. Running time, 109 MINS.

Cesar Ardavin has taken the four better-known chapters of this Spanish literary classic and has brought them to life almost without compromise in a production that teems with screen values. "Lazarillo" must have been a labor of love for the writer-director and his corps of skilled technicians who spent months on exterior doting this picaresque tale with splendid authenticity.

Lazarillo is a young, fatherless lad who hires out successively to a mean, blind beggar, a miserly sacristan, a phony noble without a doubloon in his doublet and finally, to a vagrant family of itinerant actors.

Italian moppet Marco Paoletti delivers a first-rate performance, handicapped by his sweet, girlish features that belie the boy's grim exploits. Supporting cast is excellent. Lenser Berenguer gets a special nod for resurrecting the tableaux quality of XVII century Castilla. Art director La Fuente, composer Luna and costumer Cornejo also lend an effective hand.

"Lazarillo" should do good business in Hispano-America. Judicious pruning of overlength 109 Mins. would give it "artie" possibilities in the U.S.A. *Werb.*

The Stranglers Of Bombay
(BRITISH)

Competent meller about 18th Century Indian thuggery; lacks stellar value but its offbeat theme could well make it a useful dualer prospect.

London, Dec. 15.

Columbia release of a Hammer (Anthony Hinds) production. Stars Guy Rolfe, Allan Cuthbertson, Andrew Cruickshank. Directed by Terence Fisher. Screenplay by David Z. Goodman; editor, Alfred Cox; camera, Arthur Grant; music, James Bernard. At London Pavilion. Running time: 80 MINS.

Lewis	Guy Rolfe
Connaught-Smith	Allan Cuthbertson
Henderson	Andrew Cruickshank
High Priest	George Pastell
Patel Shari	Marne Maitland
Mary	Jan Holden
Silver	Paul Stassino
Ram Das	Tutta Lemkow
Gopali	David Spenser

Flood	Michael Nightingale
Mrs. Flood	Margaret Gordon
Camel Vendor	Ewer Solon

Hammer Productions, which for some time has concentrated, with solid b.o. winnings, on horror has lately decided to grow up. True, Hammer is still delving in the horror market but current pix are not exploiting horror for the sake of it. The case of "Stranglers of Bombay" is typical. Here is a chance to bring in a few horrific moments but, mainly, the film is a straightforward melodrama, competently made but not shaping as much more than a useful dualer. It lacks star value and slick writing, but Terence Fisher has done a good directing job.

It seems that around 1829 the East India Company was plagued by losses of cargo and the mysterious disappearance of thousands of people.

Rolfe gives a good performance in a plodding role while Cuthertson provides a useful foil as the supercilious new officer whose main interest is in playing polo in Britain. Andrew Cruickshank, as the boss of the setup, is suitably obstinate. But it is the natives who have the best opportunities, with Marne Maitland stealing the film as an oily local diplomat. George Pastell plays the High Priest with venom. But the main highlights of this film are such moments as the "Thugs" rituals, the initiation of new youngsters as stranglers, the wholesale massacre of a large caravan of bearers and when the captured Rolfe is saved from death.

With sharper dialog and swifter direction this could have been a much better film than it is. But, within its own modest limits, it provides a measure of suspense and interest. Arthur Grant with his camera contributes rather more than screenplay writer David Z. Goodman to the total effect.
Rich.

Abschied Von Den Wolken
(Departure From the Clouds)
(GERMAN)

Deutsche Film Hansa release of CCC (in conjunction with Baverag) production. Stars O. W. Fischer, Sonja Ziemann, Peter Van Eyck; with Linda Christian and Horst Frank. Directed by Gottfried Reinhardt. Screenplay, Georg Hurdalek, after a story by Ladislas Fodor; camera, Klaus von Rautenfeld; music, Werner Eisbrenner; editing, Kurt Zeunert. Previewed at Filmbuehne Wien, Berlin. Running time, **103 MINS.**

Peter van Houten	O. W. Fischer
Carla	Sonja Ziemann
Pink Roberti	Peter van Eyck
Mischa Gomperz	Christian Wolff
Dr. Quartz	Paul Dahlke
Stella Valencias	Chariklia Baxevanos
Countess Colmar	Linda Christian
Richard Marshall	Horst Frank

Star of this pic, somewhat reminiscent of Hollywood's "High and the Mighty," is a Madrid-bound Latin American airliner on which practically the entire action takes place. Pic tries hard to be suspenseful but the outcome is rather routine. Locally, it may do well because of its cast stars as O. W. Fischer, Sonja Ziemann, Linda Christian and, incidentally, in a small role, Silvia Reinhardt, wife of Gottfried Reinhardt, who directed this.

"Clouds" has 27 parts and its authors don't seem to have forgotten any angle: Jealousy between pilot and co-pilot (both love the stewardess), political refugees (who eventually force the pilot to change his route), a not-so-happy couple on their second honeymoon (for comedy relief), two notorious

chess players (ditto), an expectant mother, a young violin virtuoso and a pretty songstress (for the romantic interest) and, last but not least, a nonchalant adventurer (of dubious background) who not only overthrows the villains but also (he happens to be a former pilot) manages to make a safe landing.

Too much rings untrue in this. The various characters exaggerate their parts with partly childish effects. Also, the technical credits are only moderate. One is nearly always aware that pic was made in a studio.
Hans.

The Story on Page One
Loose details, but suspenseful courtroom meller. Healthy b.o.

Hollywood, Dec. 25.
Twentieth-Fox release of Jerry Wald production. Stars Rita Hayworth, Anthony Franciosa, Gig Young. Written and directed by Clifford Odets; camera, James Wong Howe; music, Elmer Bernstein; editor, Hugh S. Fowler. Previewed at the Westwood Village Theatre, Dec. 22, '59. Running time, **122 MINS.**

Jo	Rita Hayworth
Victor Santini	Anthony Franciosa
Larry Ellis	Gig Young
Mrs. Ellis	Mildred Dunnock
Judge Nielsen	Hugh Griffith
Phil Stanley	Sanford Meisner
Nordau	Robert Burton
Lt. Mike Morris	Alfred Ryder
Mrs. Brown	Katherine Squire
Judge Carey	Raymond Greenleaf
Alice	Myrna Fahey
Morrie Goetz	Leo Penn
Francis Morriss	Sheridan Comerate
Eddie Ritter	Biff Elliot
Detective Capt. Kelly	Tom Greenway
Lauber	Jay Adler
Avis	Carol Seflinger
Dr. Kemper	Theodore Newton
Hauser	James O'Rear
Calvin	Richard LePore
Court Clerk	Dan Riss
Lt. Morris	Joseph McGuinn
Gallagher	Joe Besser
Jury Foreman	Leonard George
Lemke	William Challee

Being a courtroom me'odrama, "The Story On Page One" should be as tidily constructed as a coroner's report, but it shows more loose ends than the back view of a burlesque chorus line. Editing? Writing? To give it its due, it works up considerable suspense and excitement, and the courtroom scenes that make up its greatest part, are very good. Granting its faults, the Jerry Wald production for 20th-Fox still shapes up as a healthy boxoffice contender.

Clifford Odets wrote and directed the film. His title is tangential. He's really telling the story behind the story on page one. It's a sordid murder trial. Rita Hayworth and Gig Young, lovers, are charged with plotting and carrying out the demise of Miss Hayworth's husband. Anthony Franciosa is Miss Hayworth's attorney.

The audience knows almost from the beginning that the death was accidental. It is Odet's skill, as writer (with above excepting, and director, that prevents this knowledge from dissipating suspense. He peppers the narrative with incident and character, interesting both in their own right and weighted with significance to the whole. There is even some doubt, as the trial progresses, that the couple will be found innocent.

Odets' premise and conclusion, that this adulterous couple should be free to pursue their romance on acquittal, may be distasteful to family morality and theologians. However, it is sound dramatically, because Odets has given sufficient depth to the background that led them to the situation creating the trial.

The film suffers from editing. It is evident that some of the dangling plot threads meant something in the fabric of the narrative as Odets originally planned it. Franciosa, for instant, is initially presented as a cheap, boozing shyster. Without further delineation, he becomes a cagey, well-tailored and almost infallible counsel once he gets into court. The odds against his case are said to be formidable, yet he conducts the case with hardly a setback. There are others that remain to nag the spectator.

The cast is responsible to a considerable degree for the fact that "The Story On Page One" is as gripping as it frequently is. Miss Hayworth continues the strain of realism shown in "They Came to Cordura," and is very effective.

Franciosa, less exuberant than usual, is strong in restraint. Young could have been better directed to protect him against some of the comedy mannerisms that are so useful in another kind of story.

The whole cast is lit by the performance of Katherine Squire as Miss Hayworth's mother. Miss Squire achieves an intensity and credibility that is a thrill to watch. The film is exceptionally well cast in supporting roles. Mildred Dunnock Hugh Griffith, Alfred Ryder, James O'Rear and William Challee are fine.

James Wong Howe's black-and-white camera work gives the CinemaScope screen unusual flexibility. With Odets he uses an old trick, of reaction shots to pin-point or pin-prick what another character is saying, with deft, almost off-hand grace.

Elmer Bernstein's music, lyrical to counterpoint the already backgrounds, is imaginative. Hugh S. Fowler's editing is technically proficient, and more than that in his flashback scenes, where he dispenses with the dissolve. Sound quality was poor at the preview of the film.
Powe.

The Battle of the Sexes
(BRITISH)
Witty film version of James Thurber's short story, "Catbird Seat"; good b.o. with discriminating audiences.

London, Dec. 22.
British Lion release (in association with Bryanston Films) of a Monja Danischewsky production. Stars Peter Sellers, Robert Morley, Constance Cummings. Written and produced by Monja Danischewsky, from James Thurber's story, "The Catbird Seat." Directed by Charles Crichton; camera, Freddie Francis; editor, Seth Holt; music, Stanley Black. Previewed at Studio One, London. Running time, **84 MINS.**

Mr. Martin	Peter Sellers
Robert MacPherson	Robert Morley
Angela Barrows	Constance Cummings
Andrew Darling	Jameson Clark
Old MacPherson	Ernest Thesiger
Irwin Hoffman	Donald Pleasence
Graham	Moultrie Kelsie
Robertson	Alex Mackenzie
MacLeod	Roddy MacMillan
Detective	Michael Goodliffe
Nightwatchman	James Gibson
Mr. White	Noel Howlett
Mr. Meekie	Abe Barker
Mr. Munson	Gordon Phillott
Jock Munro	Norman MacGowan
"C.J."	Macdonald Parke
Jeannie MacDougall	Patricia Hayes
Wine shop proprietor	Eric Woodburn
Tobacconist	Donald Bissett
American wife	Aletha Orr
American Husband	Sydney Keith

It was a bold move to take James Thurber's slim, witty short story, "The Catbird Seat," and build it to a full-length feature pic. It has come off via "The Battle Of The Sexes" because of equally witty writing, excellent characterization and the practised direction of Charles Crichton. The screenplay writer (also the producer) Monja Danischewsky has ingeniously developed Thurber's central idea into a pleasant combination of light comedy and farce. Presence of Peter Sellers, one of Britain's hottest character actors and comedians, will be good enough for British audiences. If it is put over as a version of "The Catbird Seat," it should also attract American patrons.

The old established firm of tweed makers. The House of Mac-Pherson, is thoroughly disrupted when the son (Robert Morley) takes over the business on his return from America and installs an attractive American efficiency expert (Constance Cummings) to pep up the firm with modern methods. Particularly irritated at the new regime is the quiet, inoffensive head accountant who has

been with the firm for 35 years. He is so distracted that he decides to bump off the woman. But in the end he finds more cunning and effective means of putting her in her place by an elaborate trick which convinces everybody, including the enamored boss, that she is nuts.

Most of the film's mood is quiet, observed comedy. Its pace is slow, yet effective, until the moment that the employee embarks on his plot. There is then one frantic, frenzied and funny sequence which is almost like an extract from a French farce. Stealing a plot from a film about a perfect murder, the accountant visits the woman's flat to commit the deed. His plans go hopelessly astray and the scene ends in a wild chase around the flat.

But the good humor of the vehicle depends largely on the performances of the three stars plus a very capable supporting cast, who have been richly served by Danischewsky and smartly directed. Peter Sellers adds another to his gallery of shrewdly observed characters as the mild-mannered accountant. Softly throwing away his lines, gently blandishing his boss and the woman, Sellers gets his effects with the maximum of thought and the minimum of effort. He is aided skillfully though briefly by an unnamed character actress.

Robert Morley puffs and glowers through the role of MacPherson while Constance Cummings makes a welcome return to the British screen as the attractive, but maddening efficiency expert. Among the lesser roles which stand out are those of Ernest Thesiger, Morley's father; Donald Pleasence, Moultrie Kelsall, Roddy McMillan, Donald Pleasence, Noel Howlett and Abe Barker.

Freddie Francis's lensing and the editing are all okay. Sam Wanamaker supplies a brief commentary at the beginning and end of the film. The ending, incidentally, leaves the film rather up in the air, on the lines that though Sellers may have won one of the battles of the sexes he may still live to lose the war. *Rich.*

The Human Condition
(JAPANESE)

Brandon Films release of Shochiku Pictures (Shigera Wakasuki) production. Features Tatsuya Nakadai, Michiyo Aratama, Chikage Awashim, Ineko Arima. Directed by Masaki Kobayashi; screenplay, Zenzo Matsuyama and Masaki Kobayashi, based on novel by Jumpei Gomikawa; camera, Yoshio Miajima; music, Chuji Knioshita; editor, Keiichi Uraoka. At Little Carneie Theatre, N.Y., Dec. 14, '59. Running time, 138 MINS.

Kaji .... Tatsuya Nakadai
Machiko .... Machiyo Aratama
Jin Tung Fu .... Chikage Awashima
Yang Chun Lan .... Ineko Arima

"The Human Condition," first of the eight Japanese films which Brandon Films has packaged for special U.S. distribution, is unique as a social document but pretty slow going as film entertainment. Picture's main claim to fame is that it's the first to be seen this side which portrays the brutality of the Japanese war machine as seen by Japanese. The drama is candid and stark; unfortunately, it is also lightly motivated, overly long and haphazardly edited.

Story is set in 1943 with southern Manchuria as its locale. Protagonist is an idealistic young Japanese who takes a post as a labor overseer at an isolated mine (it looks like coal, but nobody ever says) to escape Army service. Troubles arise when the guy tries to improve the lot of the labor force and objects to treatment given to 600 Chinese POWs who are brought in to dig. Irony is that he eventually finds himself despised by his fellow countrymen and hated by the workers whom he has tried to help.

Valid theme is detailed to the point of tedium in the course of 138 minutes. Even at this length, the picture looks to have been substantially edited since the continuity is not too smooth. Film might be promoted for its basically noble and humanitarian theme or for its more sensational aspects. Latter include a couple of sequences featuring "comfort girls" (brought in to comfort the workers and thus to make them more docile) and one scene of the beheading of several prisoners which shows everything except the heads actually toppling into the dirt trenches.

Technically the picture is first rate. Widescreen black-and-white lensing is very good; performances by the all-oriental cast and the English subtitles are adequate. Director Masaki Kobayashi, producer Shigera Wakatsuki, Shochiki Pictures, and of course, Brandon Films deserve credit for trying. *Canb.*

Molokai
(Father Damian Story)
(SPANISH)

Madrid, Dec. 22.

Procines release of Europea de Cinematografia production. Stars Javier Escriba (as Father Damian), Roberto Camardiel, Gerard Tichy, Marcela Yurfa; co-stars Toni Hernandez, Carlos Casaravilla, Maria Arellano, Angel Aranda, Francisco Camoiras. Directed by Luis Lucia. Screenplay by Jaime Garcia-Herranz; cameraman, Manuel Berenguer; music, Ruiz de Luno; religious advisers, Rev. Leoz and Rev. Diez (Order of Sacred Heart). At Cine Gran Via, Madrid. Running time, 103 MINS.

There is a heaven and hell contrast with no intermediate shadings in this ambitious biopic of Father Damian, an Order of the Sacred Heart missionary, whose dedication to the leper colony on Molokai, Island of the Damned, stirred international compassion late in the past century.

The Garcia-Herranz script biog is an earnest, often dramatic effort to justify impending canonization of Father Damian, demonstrate the crusading fervor of the Catholic Mission and accentuate the principle of felicity through faith.

Trapped between the sublime saintliness of Father Damian and his apostles, and the festering horror of an eyesore leper colony, director Luis Lucia is hard put to strike a fictional film balance for wide audience appeal.

Over-all direction is creditable, achieving strong inspirational values and some sequences of penetrating emotion with the help of young stage actor Javier Escriva in a difficult film debut, as the leper priest and the sharply-etched supporting roles of Roberto Camardiel, Gerald Tichy and Carlos Casaravilla. But the big cast in general fails to rise above an impersonalized mass, already illuminated or waiting in turn for inevitable conversion.

Music is banal, but other technical credits are very good. Overlength, "Molokai" could easily be pared of abundant macabre realism that might flagellate spectators in other markets, where the film is definitely a good bet for special slotting. *Werb.*

Don't Panic Chaps!
(BRITISH)

Strained and only spasmodically funny army comedy which will entertain only undemanding patrons.

London, Dec. 22.

Columbia release of a Hammer-A.C.T. (Teddy Baird) production. Stars Dennis Price, George Cole, Thorley Walters; features Nadja Regin, Harry Fowler. Directed by George Pollock. Screenplay by Jack Davies from original story by Michael Corston and Ronald Holroyd; camera, Arthur Graham; editor, Harry Aldous; music, Philip Green. Previewed at Columbia Private Theatre, London. Running time, 85 MINS.

Krisling .... Dennis Price
Finch .... George Cole
Brown .... Thorley Walters
Ackroyd .... Harry Fowler
Elsa .... Nadja Regin
Mortimer .... Nicholas Phipps
Bolter .... Percy Herbert
Meister .... George Murcell
Schmidt .... Gertan Klauber
Babbington .... Terence Alexander
Voss .... Thomas Foulkes

Jack Davies is one of Britain's deftest comedy screenplay writers but he's not been able to do very much with this limp little comedy which can surely please only the most undemanding. The cast works energetically and conscientiously but neither the dialog nor the situations are sparkling enough to prevent a tiny little jest from sagging. George Pollock's direction is plodding, though technically the film is okay.

It's just before the Allied landings in Sicily. Four inept British soldiers are sent to an Adriatic island to set up an observation post. Forgotten by the submarine that's skedded to relieve them, they find they're in the same position as a small German unit. The difference is that the Krauts are comfortably ensconced in good quarters and with ample provisions. The two officers call a truce and the two units live in harmony together until, inexplicably, a glamorous European is cast up on shore. Then the squabbles break out afresh.

Dennis Price, Thorley Walters, Nicholas Phipps, Percy Herbert and Thomas Foulkes come out best in a cast that cannot compete with its dire material. This material is padded with unlikely situations and relies for one of its chief yocks on the sight of the bare behinds of two of the soldiers and on some arch references to sex when a pleasant, shapely young woman named Najda Regin arrives on the scene. But all the characters are caricatures and the original neat idea is belabored unmercifully. "Don't Panic" obviously relies on the fact that there has been a successful run of service comedies on the British screen recently. It is doubtful if this one is even in the same league. *Rich.*

Voulez-Vous Danser Avec Moi?
(Will You Dance With Me?)
(FRENCH-COLOR)

Paris, Dec. 28.

Sofradis release of Francos Film-Vides production. Stars Brigitte Bardot; features Henri Vidal, Dario Moreno, Noel Roquevert, Dawn Addams, Philippe Nicaud, Paul Frankeur, Serge Gainsbourg. Directed by Michel Boisrond. Screenplay Annette Wademant, G. Caps. J. C. Tachella; camera (Eastmancolor), Robert Lefebvre; editor, William Sivel. At Normandie, Paris. Running time, 90 MINS.

Virginie .... Brigitte Bardot
Herve .... Henri Vidal
Anita .... Dawn Addams
Albert .... Noel Roquevert
Flores .... Dario Moreno
Daniel .... Philippe Nicaud
Inspector .... Paul Frankeur
Leon .... Serge Gainsbourg

The main point about this murder mystery-comedy is that it is another Brigitte Bardot starrer. The fact that it is also entertaining, colorful and deft is so much added gravy. So with the B.B. draw still on, this looks like a neat U.S. playoff item, with dubbing in order.

Pic is in the vein of "The Parisienne," with Miss Bardot remaining moral and loyal to her spouse but getting into ticklish situations because of her looks and come-on innocence. However, it manages to expose much of her widely known epidermis in marital scenes plus her usual pouting, wet lips, kittenish mien and movements. There are plenty of the latter since she works in a dance school trying to track down the murderer of the owner in order to help her husband who is unjustly accused of the killing.

B.B. is at ease since she has only to be her fluffy, natural self. She displays a pert sense of comedy and easily bungles through and solves the crime while vamping a police inspector.

Pic gets good mounting, the right garish colors, and good acting and directorial support to make this a B.B. pic that will probably be big here as well as abroad. This whodunit comedy also manages to add a few surprise and twists and keeps its balance between comedy, sex manners and suspense. *Mosk.*

Morte Di Un 'Amico
(Death of a Friend)
(ITALIAN)

Rome, Dec. 22.

Warner Brothers release of an Universalcine (Sandro Ghenzi) production. Features Gianni Garko, Spiros Focas, Didi Perego, Angela Luce, Anna Mazzuchelli, Fanfulla, Andrea Scotti, Olimpia Cavalli. Directed by Franco Rossi. Screenplay, Franco Riganti, Ugo Guerra, Franco Rossi, from story by Riganti, Pier Paolo Pasolini, Oreste Biancoli, Giuseppe Berto; camera, Toni Secchi; music, Mario Nascimbene; editor, Otello Colangeli. Previewed in Rome. Running time, 95 MINS.

Aldo .... Gianni Garko
Bruno .... Spiros Fokas
Lea .... Didi Perego
Franca .... Angela Luce
Adriana .... Anna Mazzuchelli
DeAmicis .... Fanfulla

Courageous and uncompromising, made with obvious sincerity, this pic is nevertheless a limited entry via its depressing theme and downbeat ending. Word-of-mouth will help. It might rate an arty o.o. since it has some exploitation angles.

Gianni Garko and Spiros Fokas are two childhood friends who drift apart with age, especially as one becomes involved with petty thievery and lives off a prostitute. Latter, however, eventually succeeds in introducing his friend into his corrupt life, repenting only when latter is killed following a holdup. Brutally realistic approach makes for plenty of frankly unsavory footage especially in the opening portion of the pic, in which Garko gets a foretaste of the seamy existence led by the inhabitants of Roman low-life so dear to co-writer Pier Paolo Pasolini. His influence is felt on much of pic.

Director Franco Rossi has done a splendid job with his actors, almost all unknowns, and his touch is evident throughout the pic as

well. He's failed only in one important detail: to justify the great friendship between Garko and Fokas, and the eventual repentance. Only happy note in whole pic is the contrasted young love of Garko for a teenage neighbor, so remote from the sordid existence he leads. She's exceedingly well played by another newcomer, Anna Mazzuchelli.

Sequence in which Garko breaks with his streetwalker friend and yells out their whole secret to a shocked neighborhood is brilliantly brought off.

Remaining credits are all good, with Mario Nascimbene's music rating an extra nod.   *Hawk.*

He Nacido en Buenos Aires

(I Was Born In Buenos Aires)
(ARGENTINE)

Buenos Aires, Dec. 22.
Internacional release of Eduardo Bedoya and Celestino Anzuola production. With Mario Fortuna, Gilda Louseck, Enzo Viena, Santiago Arrieta, Maria Luisa Robledo, Alberto Argibay, Ignacio Quiros, and Isabel Munoz. Directed by Francisco Mugica. Screenplay, Rodolfo M. Taboada; camera, Ricardo Younis; music, Sebastian Piana; editors, Atilio Rinaldi, Ricardo Nistal. At Normandie, Buenos Aires. Running time, **110 MINS.**

Given a smaller buildup than other recent releases, this picture shapes as the best native feature pic since 1955.

Director Francisco Mugica has turned the trick for the new Internacional production outfit on the basis of crisp, natural dialog, and human interest. Parts of the picture may be corny, but it has laughs and tear jerker scenes. For one thing it has a Tango background, always a safe recipe for domestic success. A dozen famous tangos, orchestrated by Francisco Canaro (and played by his quartet) form most of the musical background, except for that by Sebastian Piana.

Set in the rich early 19's and 20's, and audiences will delight in hearing about times when a chicken cost 80 centavos.

Socialite extras were enlisted for sequences of a pre-1914 War party at which the Tango made its bow in polites society.

Exceptionally good performances are turned in by veteran players Mario Fortuna, Santiago Arrieta and Maria Luisa Robledo. The younger players — Gilda Lousek, Enzo Viena, Ignacio Quiros, Isabel Munoz and moppet Oscar Orlegui acquit themselves well. This is a sample of what good direction can do.

Plot has three youngsters from the same neighborhood, one grandson of the aristocratic politician Robirosa, another son to the family's laundress, the third son of a drunken laborer, who grow up together, united by a common love for tango or popular music. They set up their own band, are acclaimed at home as well as Europe, and build up fortunes.

Director Francisco Mugica has captured the authentic atmosphere of the time, the easy relations between all classes despite differences in politics.   *Nid.*

1960

Scent of Mystery
(SMELL-O-VISION—COLOR)

Diverting tale told with nostril-appeal. The odor cycle's second-comer. Okay gimmicks.

Chicago, Jan. 12.

Michael Todd Jr. presentation of his own production. Stars Denholm Elliot, Beverly Bentley Peter Lorre, Paul Lukas, with Diana Dors as guest star, and Elizabeth Taylor in unbilled appearance. Directed by Jack Cardiff. Screenplay, William Roos, based on an original story by Kelley Roos; additional situations by Gerald Kersh. Camera (Todd Process), John Von Kotze; osmologist, Hans Laube; music, Mario Nascimbene. Premiered at Cinestage Theatre, Chicago, Jan. 6, '60. Running time, 125 MINS.

Scrutable Englishman .. Denholm Elliott
A sodden derelict .. Liam Redmond
The trepid and rotund chauffeur
Peter Lorre
A devil of an advocate .. Peter Arne
A dark and glowering gentleman
Paul Lucas
A black-hearted wife .. Mary Laura Wood
The aficionado .... Leo McKern
An evil lorry operator .. Juan Olaguivel
The bizarre store keeper .. Maurice Marsac
A gainly damsel ...... Diana Dors
A not-so-gainly damsel .. Judith Furse
The blande lorelei ..... Beverly Bentley
A brunette herring .. Billie Miller
A vintage aviator .. Michael Trubshawe

Now that the second "smellie" process, Smell-O-Vision, has been "uncorked," it appears that the new dimension will be nothing more than a passing whiff. Except for providing a novelty value, the accompanying odors neither add nor detract to the basic enjoyment of a motion picture.

Fortunately for Michael Todd Jr., who unveiled "Scent of Mystery" at his Cinestage Theatre in Chicago, he has a diverting and entertaining mystery-chase picture that can stand on its own without odors.

The aromas provide the plus that gives the film an aura of importance and oddballness that can be exploited successfully for roadshow engagements. The offering, however, rates as a solid boxoffice attraction for general situations sans Smell-O-Vision.

"Scent of Mystery" has been carefully planned to synchronize scents with action in the film. Unlike Aromarama, which hit the market (in Manhattan) first, the "Scent of Mystery" script, written by William Roos, has been designed with the smells in mind. In the Aromarama presentation, a documentary dealing with Red China, the odors were added as an afterthought.

The dispensing systems are different. In Smell-O-Vision, developed by the Swiss-born Hans Laube, the odors are piped via plastic tubing—a mile of tubing at the Cinestage Theatre—to individual seats, the scents being triggered automatically by signals on the film's soundtrack. The Aromarama smells are similarly touched off, but are conveyed through the theatre's regular air ventilating system. The Smell-O-Vision odors seemed more distinct and recognizable and did not appear to linger as long as those in Aromarama.

Reaction of those at the Smell-O-Vision premiere was mixed. Of those queried, not all claimed to have whiffed the some 30 olfactions said to have been distributed during the course of the film. A number of balcony smellers said the aroma reached them a few seconds after the action on the screen. Other balcony dwellers said they heard a hissing sound that tipped off the arrival of a smell. Among the smells that clicked were those involving flowers, the perfume of the mystery girl in the film, tobacco, orange, shoe polish, port wine (when a man is crushed to death by falling casks), baked bread, coffee, lavender, and peppermint.

The picture has not only been tailored to employ smells, but has also been geared specifically for the 70m widescreen. As such, it can serve as an example to Cinerama as to how a story-line film can be shot in the king-sized process. Utilizing the Todd Process, a similar but technically different process than Todd-AO, the picture —with or without the smells—is a fun picture, expertly directed by Jack Cardiff. It has many elements that are derivative of a Hitchcock chase film, the late Mike Todd's "Around the World in 80 Days," and the Cinerama travelog technique.

It wanders all over the Spanish landscape, covering fiestas, the running of the bulls ceremony, native dances, street scenes of Spanish cities and towns. It is often breathtaking in its scenic splendor and will serve as a great assist for Spanish tourism. The travelog is neatly integrated as part of the chase as Denholm Elliott, as a very proper Englishman on Spanish holiday, plays a sort of Don Quixote character who boldly stumbles through the cities and countryside as a self-appointed protector of a damsel in distress. He is accompanied by a philosophical taxi driver, neatly portrayed by Peter Lorre. Paul Lukas is properly sinister as a mysterious hired assassin. Beverly Bentley is fine as blonde decoy, Leo McKern as a bullfight-happy pension keeper, Mary Laura Wood as his "black-hearted" wife, and Peter Arne as a villainous lawyer.

Elliot turns in a winning performance as the bumbling but brave Englishman. Cardiff has wisely directed the film with a tongue-in-cheek quality that is reminiscent of the style of "Around the World in 80 Days." Diana Dors is seen briefly (time and costume) on a Spanish beach and Elizabeth Taylor is present at the denouement in a non-speaking role. Although smell plays an important part in Elliott's uncovering of the villain, the audience need not necessarily be involved in the odor —the recognition of a man's tobacco.

John Von Kotze's photography is superb as it captures the scenes of numerous Spanish cities and the surrounding countryside. All other technical aspects are first-rate. The new Todd process gives the same effect as Todd-AO, although there are occasions when blurring is apparent. One can quarrel with the constant repetition of the road scenes as car chases car or follows car, but overall it's worth the ride.

Holl.

Las Dos y Media . . . Veneno
(Poison At 2:30)
(SPANISH—COLOR)

Madrid, Jan. 5.

A Radio release of a Cinematografia Hispanica production. Stars Jose Luis Ozores, Antonio Ozores, Elisa Montes, Fernando Rey, Fernando Delgado, Teresa del Rio, Felix Fernandez. Written and directed by Mariano Ozores. Camera (Eastmancolor), Manuel Merino. At Cine Pompeya, Madrid. Running time, 87 MINS.

The three hermanos Ozores banded together to produce "Veneno." Their initial entry, it also serves as the debut for the eldest, Mariano, as film director.

Not even the talents of Fernando Rey and Felix Fernandez succeed in bolstering the featherweight, haphazard story. The situations involve a living cadaver propped for a sea funeral by a couple of clumsy, amateur undertakers hired by insurance-hungry heirs.

Film is neither fish nor fowl. For those who like inane comedy, there's plenty of sheer absurdity, slapstick and broad, loud acting. "Veneno" opens with a series of imaginative titles. The remainder is anti-climactic.

Werb.

Who Was That Lady?

Good b.o. comedy. Curtis-Leigh-Martin for marquee.

Hollywood, Jan. 8.

Columbia release of Ansark-George Sidney production. Stars Tony Curtis, Dean Martin, Janet Leigh; features James Whitmore, John McIntire, Barbara Nichols. Writer-producer, Norman Krasna, based on his play, "Who Was That Lady I Saw You With?"; director, George Sidney; camera, Harry Stradling; music, Andre Previn; editor, Viola Lawrence. Previewed at the Academy Awards Theatre, Dec. 16, '59. Running time, 116 MINS.

David Wilson .... Tony Curtis
Michael Haney .... Dean Martin
Ann Wilson .... Janet Leigh
Harry Powell .... James Whitmore
Bob Doyle .... John McIntire
Gloria Coogle .... Barbara Nichols
Parker .... Larry Keating
Orenov .... Larry Storch
Belka .... Simon Oakland
Florence Coogle .... Joi Lansing
Girl .... Barbara Hines
Miss Mellish .... Marion Javits
Glinka .... Michael Lane
Lee Wong .... Kam Tong
Schultz .... William Newell
Joe Bendix .... Mark Allen

Fifty-Nine was the year that film comedy made a comeback, and Sixty has a promising start in the same vein with Columbia's "Who Was That Lady?" It is perhaps not the rouser it might have been, but it is an often hilarious romp made somewhat sedate only in a compromise between farce and romantic comedy. It will certainly ride the commercial tide of other recent top comedies, doing nicely right down the line.

George Sidney directed Norman Krasna's screenplay, which Krasna produced and wrote from his own play. Latter, incidentally, had the longer handle of "Who Was That Lady I Saw You With?" The story is concerned with Tony Curtis as an assistant professor of chemistry whose chief extra-curricular interest is biology. When Curtis' wife, Janet Leigh, catches him kissing a pretty student, she threatens divorce. In his desperation for an acceptable alibi, Curtis turns to a friend, Dean Martin, a television writer.

Martin's scheme is to have Curtis persuade his wife he is really an undercover FBI agent only embracing a woman in the line of duty. She was actually a suspect as a spy, so the yarn goes. Obviously this is going to lead to farce complications, and it does. Curtis and Martin are soon embroiled with real FBI agents, real foreign agents, and real dumb blondes.

The film version follows the play closely except for greater stress on the romance of husband Curtis and wife Leigh. They make a handsome couple, and their marital togetherness will probably be inspiring to married spectators. George Sidney apparently decided to sacrifice some comedy to romance, to broaden the appeal of his film. Be that as it may. It also slows down his pace and throws off his timing, so he has to work hard to recapture the farcical mood.

Curtis and Martin work nicely together, and much of the film depends upon their teamwork. Curtis continues to show again in comedy technique, and Martin strengthens the false impression that he isn't acting at all. It should be so easy! Miss Leigh is pretty and pert, what the role calls for.

James Whitmore, not ordinarily thought of as a comedian, gets the film's biggest single laughs, mostly on reaction shots of no lines, just looks. The role should open new avenues for this always solid actor. Barbara Nichols and Joi Lansing are acceptable as the very broad broads. Others in the cast who contribute to the general fun include John McIntire, Larry Keating, Larry Storch, Simon Oakland, Marion Javits and Michael Lone.

Harry Stradling's photography highlights the comedy, and Andre Previn's sprightly musical score counter-points it. Editing by Viola Lawrence is knowledgeable and Charles J. Rice's sound is accurate.

Powe.

Gunfighters of Abilene

Run-of-the-mill oater to fill double bills.

Hollywood, Jan. 8.

United Artists release of a Vogue Pictures production. Stars Buster Crabbe. Produced by Robert E. Kent. Directed by Edward L. Cahn. Screenplay, Orville Hampton; camera, Maury Gertsman; editor, Edward Mann; music, Paul Dunlap. Previewed at Goldwyn Studios, Jan. 8, '59. Running time, 66 MINS.

Kip .... Buster Crabbe
Seth .... Barton MacLane
Alice .... Judith Ames
Rigley .... Arthur Space
Raquel .... Eugenia Paul
Wilkinson .... Russell Thorson
Harker .... Kenneth MacDonald
Hendricks .... Richard Cutting
Ruger .... Richard Devon
Jud .... Lee Farr
Miguel .... Jan Arvan
Andy Ferris .... Hank Patterson

There's a heap of shootin' in United Artists' "Gunfighters of Abilene," but the outcome is about as dead as the victims. Except for the most remote hamlets in the dustiest hinterlands, the Vogue Pictures production will complete double bills with 66 minutes of filler.

Whatever excitement the film could have built up was dissipated from the start by the thousands of television westerns that came before it. The Robert E. Kent production, directed by Edward L. Cahn from a screenplay by Orville Hampton, does sustain reasonable interest for a spell, but the characters are just too stock to keep you guessing.

Buster Crabbe, who stars as gunslinger, proves he has vim and vigor yet, fighting a wealthy landowner (Barton MacLane) to clear the name of his slandered brother. It seems MacLane's daughter (Judith Ames) was in love with the brother, and the future son-in-law sided with the ranchers who threatened MacLane's dynasty. So MacLane frames him in a hold-up, then lynches him. In the end practically everyone dies, leaving Crabbe to pick up with his dead brother's fiance where the dead brother left off.

Miss Ames, a pretty blonde, is among the film's more pleasant elements. MacLane is a good heavy to Crabbe's heroism, and there are competent performances by Eugenia Paul, Russell Thorson, Lee Farr, Jan Arvan, Arthur Space, Kenneth MacDonald, Richard Cutting, Richard Devon, Reed Howes and Hank Patterson.

Technically, the film is a cut above average considering its

minimal budget. Maury Gertsman's camera work tops credits that include William Glasgow's art direction, Jack Solomo's sound, Edward Mann's editing and Paul Dunlap's music. *Ron.*

Tommy the Toreador
(BRITISH—TECHNICOLOR)

Disarming comedy with songs tailored for Tommy Steele fans. Good bet for family audiences.

London, Dec. 22.

Warner-Pathe release of Associated-British's presentation of a Fanfare film (in association with Nat Cohen and Stuart Levy). Stars Tommy Steele. Janet Munro. Features Noel Purcell, Sidney James, Virgilio Texera, Pepe Nieto. Producer, George H. Brown. Director, John Paddy Carstairs. Screenplay by George H. Brown & Patrick Kirwan: editor, Peter Bezencenet; camera, Gilbert Taylor; music, Stanley Black. At Warner Theatre, London, Dec. 21, '59. Running time, **90 MINS.**

Tommy	Tommy Steele
Amanda	Janet Munro
Cadena	Sidney James
Paco	Bernard Cribbins
Ship's Captain	Noel Purcell
Patilia	Virgilio Texera
Quintero	Pepe Nieto
Lopez	Ferdy Mayne
Jose	Harold Kasket
Vice-Consul	Kenneth Williams
Martin	Eric Sykes
Matador	Manolo Blazquez
Hotel Proprietor	Francis De Wolfe
Bootblack	Tutte Lemkow
Waiter	Warren Mitchell
Comez	Charles Gray

Tailored for the talents of Tommy Steele, "Tommy the Toreador" emerges as a brisk, disarming little comedy. It should be a worthwhile booking for family houses, with Steele proving that he is a useful actor as well as a slick purveyor of pop songs. The scriptwriters, Patrick Kirwan and George H. Brown (who also produced), have relied a little too much on Steele's personality and their screenplay might have been built up more tightly. But John Paddy Carstairs, who directed most of Norman Wisdom's films, is a shrewd hand at getting the maximum yoks out of slim situations.

Steele plays a young seaman who gets stranded in Spain and through a string of highly fortuitous circumstances gets conned into making a one-performance-only appearance as a toreador.

Janet Munro is Steele's girl friend in the picture. She has little to do that's demanding and "Tommy the Toreador" won't do much to advance her career, but she has a fresh, likable personality and strikes up a happy partnership with Steele. Major disappointment is that usually stalwart character comedian, Sidney James. This time he has little opportunity and, saddled with a broken Spanish accent, he seems justifiably unhappy with his role of a bullfight promoter. However, his partner, Bernard Cribbins, scores a distinct success.

Noel Purcell, Virgilio Texera, Ferdy Mayne, Harold Kasket and Kenneth Williams, in a small but telling cameo, are others who make their mark. Tommy Steele puts over half a dozen cheerful songs written by Lionel Bart, Michael Pratt & Jimmy Bennett. Two of them, "Little White Bull" and "Tommy the Toreador," are particularly suited to the film and the first one is already making impact on radio and tv. Gilbert Taylor's lensing is firstclass throughout. *Rich.*

Toby Tyler
(COLOR)

A boy, a chimp, the circus. Disney scores again.

Hollywood, Jan. 8.

Buena Vista release of Walt Disney production. Features Kevin Corcoran, Henry Calvin, Gene Sheldon, Bob Sweeney, Richard Eastham. Directed by Charles Barton. Screenplay, Bill Walsh and Lillie Hayward; based on the book by James Otis Kaler; camera, (Technicolor) William Snyder; music, Buddy Baker; editor, Stanley Johnson. Previewed at the Academy Awards Theatre, Jan. 8, '60. Running time, **95 MINS.**

Toby Tyler	Kevin Corcoran
Ben Cotter	Henry Calvin
Sam Treat	Gene Sheldon
Harry Tupper	Bob Sweeney
Col. Sam Castle	Richard Eastham
Jim Weaver	James Drury
Mademoiselle Jeanette	Barbara Beaird
Monsieur Ajax	Dennis Joel
Aunt Olive	Edith Evanson
Uncle Daniel	Tom Fadden
Bandleader	Ollie Wallace

It's a safe bet that you don't judge the entries without considering their bloodlines, and while "Toby Tyler" would be a warm-hearted, chucklesome film no matter what its background, it's got that three-word phrase to precede the title that usually makes all the difference. The phrase, of course, is "*Walt Disney Presents.*" With this kick-off, this nostalgic comic adventure about the circus at the turn of the century should stir the same kind of brisk business the pink lemonade concession once attracted on hot summer days.

Trends come and trends go, some years the Production Code comes in for more attention than others, but Disney just keeps tootling along, following his own unique lode of paydirt. "Toby Tyler" is another examination of basically a now familiar Disney situation, a boy and his pet animal. In this case the boy's young Kevin Corcoran and his simian pal is a personable chimp called Mr. Stubbs.

The screenplay by Bill Walsh and Lillie Hayward, based on the book of the same title by James Otis Kaler, is kept clean and fairly elementary for the kids in the audience. Although the greater part of the action takes place in the circus, there are, on the visual evidence, no freaks, no cooch dancers, not even any soiled sawdust. The conflict is involved with young Corcoran's runaway from home, his "adoption" by a scoundrelly concessionaire, Bob Sweeney. Sweeney is the villain of the piece, trying to keep Corcoran from realizing his aunt and uncle really love him and want him to come home. But he isn't really much of a villain, being funnier than he is fierce. All ends happily when the boy steps into a difficult circus stunt to save the show, then retires from his brief glory to reunite with his family.

The Walsh-Hayward script has a number of good laughs, and consistently maintains interest even for the more sophisticated adults. The chimp provides some good comedy, too, particularly on reaction shots adroitly plotted by director Barton and his editor, Stanley Johnson. Feeling of the period is ably recreated by art directors Carroll Clark and Stan Jolley, and captured in good Technicolor.

Young Corcoran is an engaging youngster, and Bob Sweeney's unctuousness is amusing as well as crooked, creating a standout characterization. Henry Calvin is helpful, and Gene Sheldon achieves a modulated performance of some delicacy as the friendly clown. Richard Eastham, as the circus owner, Barbara Beaird and Dennis Joel as moppet performers, and Edith Evanson and Tom Fadden as Corcoran's foster partents, all score. The novelty animal act, The Marquis Family, is used effectively for humor.

Buddy Baker's musical score is as bouncy as a calliope and there's a pleasant novelty song, "Biddle-Dee-Dee," by Diane Lampert and Richard Loring. *Powe.*

Our Man in Havana
(BRITISH)

Diverting version of Graham Greene's novel with excellent marquee value and a standout performance by Noel Coward.

London, Jan. 5.

Columbia release of a Carol Reed production. Stars Alec Guinness, Burl Ives, Maureen O'Hara, Ernie Kovacs, Noel Coward, Ralph Richardson, Jo Morrow. Directed by Carol Reed. Screenplay, Graham Greene from his own novel; camera, Oswald Morris; editor, Bert Bates; music, Hermand Deniz. At Odeon, Leicester Square, London. Running time, **111 MINS.**

Jim Wormold	Alec Guinness
Dr. Hasselbacher	Burl Ives
Beatrice	Maureen O'Hara
Segura	Ernie Kovacs
Hawthorne	Noel Coward
"C"	Ralph Richardson
Milly	Jo Morrow
Carter	Paul Rogers
Ciluentes	Gregoire Aslan
Lopez	Jose Prieto
Rudy	Timothy Bateson
MacDougal	Duncan Macrae
Navy Officer	Maurice Denham
Army Officer	Raymond Huntley
RAF Officer	Hugh Manning
Teresa	Maxine Audley
Striptease Girl	Yvonne Buckingham
Professor Sanchez	Ferdy Mayne
Dr. Braun	Karel Stepanck
Svenson	Gerik Schjelderup
Beautiful Woman	Elisabeth Welsh

Based on a widely known Graham Greene novel, scripted by that author, directed by Carol Reed, shot mainly in colorful Cuba and acted by a star-loaded cast headed by Alec Guinness, this film has all the ingredients for being a b.o. success. "Our Man In Havana" turns out to be polished, diverting entertainment, brilliant in its comedy but falling apart towards the end when undertones of drama, tragedy and "message" crop up. These are not easily wed with the slick, satirical humor. The film will provide surefire amusement for discriminating audiences.

Story concerns a mild-mannered and not very successful vacuum-cleaner salesman in Havana who needs extra money to send his daughter to finishing school in Switzerland. Against his will he is persuaded to become a member of the British secret service. A more unlikely spy would be diffifult to imagine. And to hold down his job, he is forced to invent mythical sub-agents and concoct highly imaginative, fictitious reports which he sends back to London.

They are taken so seriously that two assistants are sent to help him, and the web of innocent deceit that he has spun gradually mounts up to sinister and dramatic consequences. The briefing of Alec Guinness into the world of spydom sets the early pace of the film. His ham-handed efforts to keep up a facade also contribute to the fun. But when tragedy comes in the shape of suicide by one of the leading characters, murder and the threat of it from unknown sources, "Havana" becomes a different film atnd not as good one as promised at the beginning.

Greene has scripted his novel fairly faithfully, though the Catholic significance is only lightly brought into the film. Sir Carol Reed sometimes lets the story become woolly but has expert control of a brilliant cast. Guinness is a perfect choice for the reluctant spy role, giving one of his usual subtle, slyly humorous studies.

But the standout thesping comes from Noel Coward. From his first entrance, which is immediately after the credits, he dominates every scene in which he appears. When he is not on the screen, the audience is awaiting him. This may not be altogther what either the author or the director intended but the performance makes for rich entertainment. He plays the boss of the Caribbean network. Coward, with his dry, nonchalant voice, makes every word sound like an epigram. He is at his best when he is recruiting Guinness with true cloak-and-dagger mockery.

Another performance which steals a lot of thunder from Guinness is that of Ralph Richardson who is Coward's boss stationed in London. Between them, these two do a fine job of joshing Britain's M.I.5 organization.

Burl Ives is impressive as a philosophical doctor who gets caught up in the machinery invented by Guinness and comes to a sticky end. This character, well drawn in the novel, fits less snugly into the film. Another character, Guinness' daughter, is played by Jo Morrow. The role is not given anything but adequate help by Miss Morrow.

Ernie Kovacs, rather more serious than usual, gives a smooth, suave performance as a very polite, but ruthless Cuban police officer while Maureen O'Hara is poised and attractive as the girl sent out to help Guinness. Among the smaller roles there are some neat cameos by Paul Rogers, Gregoire Aslan, Duncan Macrae, Maxine Audley and Ferdy Mayne. Oswald Morris' photography is very good. Reed has built up the Cuban atmosphere not only by some shrewd direction of street and saloon sequences but by adroit use of local music composed by Hermanos Deniz and played by his Cuban Rhythm Orchestra. *Rich.*

A Touch of Larceny

Good comedy. Could have art house as well as general appeal.

Hollywood, Jan. 8.

Paramount release of an Ivan Foxwell production. Stars James Mason, Vera Miles, George Sanders. Directed by Guy Hamilton. Screenplay by Roger MacDougall, in collaboration with Hamilton and Foxwell, based on Andrew Garve's novel, "The Megstone Plot"; camera, John Wilcox; editor, Alan Osbiston; music, Philip Green. Previewed at the Academy Awards Theatre, Jan. 4, '60. Running time, **91 MINS.**

Commander Max Easton	James Mason
Sir Charles Holland	George Sanders
Virginia Killain	Vera Miles
Minister	Oliver Johnston
Larkin	Robert Flemyng
Tom (Husband)	William Kendall
First Special Branch Man	Duncan Lamont
Captain Graham	Harry Andrews
Sub Lt. Brown	Peter Barkworth
Clare Holland	Rachel Gurney
Clare Holland's Son	Martin Stephens
Clare Holland's daughter	Waveney Lee
Robert Holland	Charles Carson
Susan	Junia Crawford
Steward of Club	Reginald Smith
Wren Officer	Rosemary Dorken
Jason Parrish	Macdonald Parke
Adele Parrish	Mavis Villiers
Commander Bates	Ernest Clark
Admiral	John Le Mesurier
American Officers	Lionel Murton
	Guy Kingsley Poynter
Tom the Boatman	Sidney Vivian
Landlord	Harry Locke

"A Touch of Larceny" has more than a touch of whimsy, a fair share of solid laughs and a wild plot that borders amusingly on the preposterous. It's a good·film about a hoax and the lovable fraud who perpetrated it, and it should earn a hearty enough reception to overcome its rather melodramatic title. James Mason, Vera Miles and George Sanders star in the Ivan Foxwell production which Paramount is releasing.

Roger MacDougall, in collaboration with producer Foxwell and director Guy Hamilton, wrote the screenplay, based on Andrew Garve's novel, "The Megstone Plot." MacDougall has written among other films "The Man in the White Suit," and his newest effort has the same droll humor that has become almost synonymous with "White Suit" star Alec Guinness. It's a masterful script, slow in parts but normally tight, and loaded with bright, sharp dialog. Director Hamilton has molded it into a film of intriguing absurdities, carefully building suspense and poking fun at the same time.

The story is of a British sea commander (Mason) who finds himself landlocked to a desk at the Admiralty. When he falls for an American widow (Miss Miles) and judges that money—or the lack of it—is the only thing standing between them, he devises a plot to get rich. He acts suspiciously at the Russian embassy, hides a top secret file behind a cabinet, goes on a fishing trip but doesn't get there, shows up on a dock inquiring about a ship named the Karl Marx and hides out on a tiny island off the coast of Scotland. He figures his actions will trigger a smear campaign against him, citing him as the traitor of the century, and he's right. Mason's aim is to show up innocently, explain away everything and sue Britain's newspapers for libel. He has his troubles, and while things do manage to work out for him, he decides to get rich legally and, in so doing, wins the girl.

Mason is at once an appealing wolf and a conniving wizard, dead set on the woman of his heart. Dishonest as he may be, he has the audience pulling for him as if he were the world's savior. On the island, supposedly shipwrecked but taking in the sun, sipping champagne and supping on lobster, Mason—and director Hamilton—have created a buoyant sequence.

Miss Miles is properly beautiful and aloof, making an excellent object of Mason's involved deception. George Sanders is type-cast as a stuffed shirt, ably fulfilling the role's drab requirements. Oliver Johnston, Robert Flemying, Duncan Lamont, Harry Andrews, Peter Barkworth and William Kendall head a good supporting cast.

The film's sprightly approach is kept alive through the fine technique of cameraman John Wilcox, editor Alan Osbiston, art director Elliot Scott and soundman John Bramall. Philip Green's musical score is particularly effective, and the gowns which Edith Held designed for Miss Miles are a fashionable plus. *Ron.*

Hell Bent for Leather
(COLOR-C'SCOPE)

Routine entry for western market with names of Audie Murphy and Stephen McNally to help.

Hollywood, Jan. 8.
Universal release of Gordon Kay production. Stars Audie Murphy, Felicia Farr, Stephen McNally, Robert Middleton; features Rad Fulton, Jan Merlin. Directed by George Sherman. Screenplay, Christopher Knopf; based on novel by Ray Hogan; camera (Eastman-color), Clifford Stine; editor, Milton Carruth; music, William Lava, Irving Gertz. Previewed Jan. 7, '60. Running time, 82 MINS.

"Hell Bent for Leather" is a fair enough entry for its intended market though noticeably lacking in the sort of usual heroics that go to make an exciting western. Consequently, it must depend for draw on the marquee value of Audie Murphy and Stephen McNally. Film, however, is strong on pictorial outdoor appeal, which progresses the action, and topnotch performances are turned in right down the line.

George Sherman capably handles the direction of the Christopher Knopf screenplay, which presents a mistaken identity theme. Murphy, an honest cowpoke who buys and sells horses, is sought by a marshal's posse as a murderer, although the lawman, an unscrupulous opportunist, knows he isn't the real criminal, planning to kill him and thereby receive credit for his capture. Pursuit is a long and drawnout affair which would have benefitted by tighter editing.

Murphy, who occasionally engages in both gun and fist display, generally plays his role straight. McNally, in marshal role, is a good heavy. Felicia Farr scores as a girl whom Murphy uses first as a hostage in making his getaway, but turns to help him in his attempted escape. Robert Middleton likewise is a standout in a brief but effective role of a badman, and Jan Merlin properly heavy as the real murderer.

As producer, Gordon Kay endows film with plenty of physical attributes and Clifford Stine's color photography is excellent. Technical departments generally are well fulfilled. *Whit.*

Desert Mice
(BRITISH)

Warmhearted comedy about how some of Britain's lower-league entertainers pitched in to give the troops some shows; lacks stellar value, especially for U.S.

London, Jan. 5.
Rank release of a Welbeck Film (Basil Dearden) production. Stars Alfred Marks, Sidney James, Reginald Beckwith, Patricia Bredin, Dora Bryan, Dick Bentley, Irene Handl, Marius Goring. Directed by Michael Relph. Screenplay by David Climie; editor, Reginald Beck; camera, Kenneth Hodges; music, Philip Green. Previewed at Leicester Square Theatre, London. Running time, 83 MINS.

For some years the British film industry has milked war themes with some success. Few arms of the services have escaped being ribbed. Latest to get the treatment is ENSA in "Desert Mice." ENSA was the official goverment entertainment service set up to bring a bit of entertainment to the troops.

First, let it be recorded that ENSA did a whale of a job. The bouquet goes less to the established stars than to the little artists who beat their brains out and did their stuff in lonely, dangerous spots under most unglamorous conditions. Okay, sometimes they were terrible. It was said that the British soldier helped to win the war on guts and gags, and that more guts was needed to listen to ENSA gags than to face the enemy. But these were real people. They had heart.

"Desert Mice" is a joke about ENSA, but it's an affectionate one and screenplay writer David Climie, obviously writing from knowledge, persuades us to laugh with them as much as against them. The result is an engaging little film which rates a booking. In the U.S., it has no stellar value. Even in Britain the cast is not so well-known. It consists of sound, popular feature artists, despite the phoney billing of these players above the title. But they do a very sound job and the result is good, happy family fun.

The story's as thin as a chorine's waistline. It simply tells how the third-rate "Chuckles" concert party became the bane of a major's life and involves him, mainly through the thickheadedness of his right hand man and his own bovine foolishness, in a series of crises which culminate in them capturing the commanding officer of a German unit.

The fun is in the quiet, shrewd observation of author David Climie and how the producer, Basil Dearden, and the director, Michael Relph, have cast with equal shrewd observation. Sidney James, as the boss-comic, with terrible jokes and worse songs; Dora Bryan, superb as his wife-stooge; Dick Bentley and Joan Benham, as singers with a pre-war musicomedy repertoire; Irene Handl, as the wise old pianist; Reginald Beckwith, as a magician; and Liz Fraser, a hopelessly untalented soubrette who gives with the sex.

Alfred Marks, as the bewildered major; George Rose, as the keeper of an Algerian brothel; and Marius Goring, as the German officer who, for tactical reasons, poses as being more British than the British, also help to keep the jest moving briskly. Patricia Bredin puts over a couple of pop songs pleasantly and might steer them into the big-time. It would be foolish to pretend that "Desert Mice" is anything but a small comedy. Yet, somehow, it has an endearing quality.

Technical credits are okay, with a few desert scenes skilfully borrowed from other films and fitted in nicely. *Rich.*

Carmen Comes Home
(JAPANESE)

Brandon Films release of Shochiku Pictures (Kiyoshi Takamara) production. Stars Hideko Takamine; features Toshiko Kobayashi, Takeshi Sakamoto, Shuji Sano, Chishu Ryu. Directed and written by Keisuke Kinoshita; camera, Hiroyuki Kusuda; music, Chuji Kinoshita. Toshio May Uzumi. At Little Carnegie Theatre, N.Y., Dec. 28, '59. Running time, 87 MINS.

As directed by Keisuke Kinoshita, the film manages to suggest a lot more than meets the eye. For one thing, the rustic village setting, with a towering volcanic mountain always looming in the background, is stark realism, imparting to the foolish foreground events a touch of the grotesque. Also, there is something more tragic than comic about the villagers themselves, particularly about Carmen's stern old father, who is mortified by his daughter's neo-sophistication, which actually reflects all the worst aspects of an American jukebox culture.

It's hard to say whether "Carmen" has lost some of its essential comedy in the American subtitling process, or whether it was out of focus to begin with. As is, it is a film curio which, at its best moments, is reminiscent of "The Welldigger's Daughter." Limited art house bookings are indicated.

Hideko Takamine is effective as the pretty, empty-headed heroine. In principal support are Toshiko Kobayashi, as Miss Takamine's dancing friend, and Takeshi Sakamoto, as her father. The Shochiku picture was produced by Kiyoshi Takamura and director Kinoshita also wrote the original story and screenplay. Black and white lensing by Hiroyuki Kusuda is excellent.

Since many dramas fail to realize their deepest potential, "Carmen Comes Home," a Brandon Films import from Japan, turns out to be something of a reverse twist: a comedy more profound than its theme and, as a consequence, not quite so funny as it should be. The picture, made in 1951, is just now arriving in the U.S. as one of the nine Japanese films which Brandon has packaged for stateside distribution.

On the surface, "Carmen" is a small, frivolous tale of a pretty Tokyo stripper who decides to pay a visit to the country village where she was born and raised. Her gum-chewing, Big City ways and wardrobe knock her farmer father and the other yokels for a scandalized loop. She eventually learns, like Thomas Wolfe, that you can't go home again, but not before she and an ecdysiast pal have staged a benefit strip performance in an old barn and donated the proceeds to local good works. *Anby.*

The Purple Gang

Well-made crime meller indicates fine b.o.

Hollywood, Jan. 7.
Allied Artists release of a Lindsley Parsons production. Stars Barry Sullivan, Robert Blake, Elaine Edwards; features Marc Cavell, Jody Lawrance, Joseph Turkel; with Suzy Marquette, Victor Creatore, Paul Dubov, Kathleen Lockhart, Nestor Paiva, Lou Krugman, Maurits Hugo, Norman Nazarr, John Indrisano, Dirk London. Prolog by Congressman James Roosevelt. Directed by Frank McDonald; written by Jack DeWitt; camera, Ellis Carter; editor, Maurice Wright; music, Paul Dunlap; song, "Runnin' Wild," by Joe Gray, Leo Wood, A. Harrington Gibbs; art direction, David Milton; set

decoration, Frank Lombardo; sound, Tom Lambert; assistant director, Lindsley Parsons Jr. Previewed at the studio, Jan. 6, '60. Running time, 85 MINS.'

Bill Harley	Barry Sullivan
"Honeyboy" Willard	Robert Blake
Gladys Harley	Elaine Edwards
Hank Smith	Marc Cavell
Miss Mac	Jody Lawrance
Daisy	Suzy Marquette
Eddie Olsen	Joseph Turkel
Al Olsen	Victor Creatore
Burke	Paul Dubov
Nun	Kathleen Lockhart
Laurence Orlofsky	Nestor Paiva
Dr. Rioden	Lou Krugman
Licovetti	Mauritz Hugo
Ricco	Norman Nazarr
Castiglione	John Indrisano
Tom Olsen	Dirk London

This is a fast-moving, violent film about actual Detroit hoodlumism during the Prohibition Era. Skillful blending of newsreel and stock footage with excellent staged material gives it an atmosphere certain to engross and excite juve and adult audiences alike. It looks like a b.o. winner.

Director Frank McDonald has avoided horror, and, with greater taste, concentrated on terror. Violent deaths abound in countless numbers, but the more explicit details of cruelty are omitted. Since the victims are shotgunned, crushed, sealed in cement etc., it's a mercy.

It's too melodramatic to be a "semi-documentary," too episodic to be drama, and too superficial to be the deadly serious slice-of-life sermon on crime it purports to be, but it's a shocker.

Premise (somewhat withdrawn in the final scene) is that underage criminals should be treated as severely as their adult counterparts. Except for a few pedantic remarks made by cops and welfare workers, the premise is neither defended or explored.

In a prolog, Congressman James Roosevelt assures the audience that the incidents, based on fact, can happen again.

Barry Sullivan, as a police officer, and Robert Blake, as the youthful gang leader, do fine jobs as do a number of supporting players (including Marc Cavell and Joseph Turkel). Others tend to overact. Elaine Edwards does very nicely.

Jack DeWitt's script allows such inanities as, "What is this, a hijack?" when it's obvious to all that it is. At numerous points, characters lack sufficient motivation. Partly make-up's fault, the teenagers do not show any signs of growing older as they become adults.

But it's an action picture—despite its pretentions to social significance—and, as such, it's topnotch. Since the crimes aren't prettified and the criminals not glamourized, it should do no social harm either, however violent the film.

Dazzled by a flurry of fascinating montages and stunned by the relentless march of viciousness, the audience won't cavil at a few dramatic flaws.

Cameraman Ellis Carter and film editor Maurice Wright have done outstanding jobs. Paul Dunlap's music assists as does the tune "Runnin' Wild." David Milton, art director, did a craftsmanly job of attuning the sets to the stock footage. And, of course, producer Lindsley Parsons has done an ace job of collecting and coordinating these talents. *Glen.*

The Bramble Bush
(COLOR)

Sex and mercy killing in staid old New England. Could be (a) controversial and (b) good b.o.

Hollywood, Jan. 14.

Warner Bros. release of Milton Sperling production. Stars Richard Burton, Barbara Rush, Jack Carson; features Angie Dickinson, James Dunn, Henry Jones. Directed by Daniel Petrie. Screenplay, Milton Sperling and Philip Yorden; based on Charles Mergendahl's novel; camera (Technicolor), Lucien Ballard; music, Leonard Rosenman; editor, Folmar Blangsted. Previewed at the studio, Jan. 5, '60. Running time, 93 MINS.

Guy	Richard Burton
Mar	Barbara Rush
Bert	Jack Carson
Fran	Angie Dickinson
Stew Schaeffer	James Dunn
Parker Welk	Henry Jones
Larry	Tom Drake
Dr. Kelsey	Frank Conroy
Sam McFie	Carl Benton Reid
Betsy	Patricia Crest
Father Bannon	William Hansen
Colin Eustis	Phil Coolidge
Sheriff Witt	Russ Conway
Ida Primmer	Joan Potter
Pico Salazar	Bern Hoffman
Judge Manning	Grandon Rhodes

So-called "mercy killing" is the subject of "The Bramble Bush," but the principals have such a brisk sex life that the subject rather gets lost in the bedclothes. Milton Sperling's production for Warners, aside from the controversy surrounding euthanasia, takes such a candid view of extra and pre-marital sexual activity that "The Bramble Bush" will not qualify as family entertainment. But whatever reservations individuals may have about the film's principal subject, as a motion picture it is compellingly told.

The screenplay, by Sperling and Philip Yordan, from a novel by Charles Mergendahl, presents the doctor who performs the "mercy killing" as a sympathetic character. But, although the point may be too subtle, by indirection it suggests that most human beings are so emotionally involved with each that the Olympian decisions on life and death should not be theirs. At any rate, the film does not present a clear-cut case for or against mercy killing, which may be the point.

Setting of the film is one of those New England towns that seem to be a hotbed (sic) of sex. Richard Burton is a young doctor who returns to his home town to care for his best friend, Tom Drake, who is dying of Hodgkins Disease. Burton has a brief affair with Drake's wife, Barbara Rush, who becomes pregnant. Burton has left his hometown partly because his father, a doctor before him, committed suicide long before the action of the picture opens, on discovering his wife (Burton's mother) was having an affair with James Dunn. Other complications include nurse Angie Dickinson's unrequited torch for Burton. She compensates by an affair with Jack Carson, and then poses for nude photos by the town editor, Henry Jones, when he threatens to expose Carson and blast his budding political career.

Any story, of course, can be reduced to absurdity by unfair synopsis. But "The Bramble Bush" really tries to pack too much into the package. Call it something of a tribute to the Sperling-Yordan screenplay, and Daniel Petrie's direction, that the feverish activities of the principals never lapse into the absurd. Petrie, incidentally, a television and stage director, makes his film bow with "The Bramble Bush," and establishes himself immediately as a knowing

and imaginative addition to feature ranks.

The legal trial of Burton, as Drake's "mercy" killer, is disposed of on subsidiary issues, not the main one. Burton is legally freed, and the implication is that somewhere, sometime, he and Miss Rush will be reunited. An odd facet of the story is that all the chief characters are Catholics, or at least attend the only church shown, which is presided over by a Catholic priest. Nothing much is ever made of this aspect, although it obviously gives the whole situation, or series of situations, a special viewpoint. The pastor of the church does deliver a clinching sermon on "mercy" killing to Burton, a lapsed Catholic, but nothing at all is made of the busy adulterous lives of the others.

Burton is intense and intelligent as the doctor, although he is miscast as a New Englander of laconic cast. Miss Rush delivers a strong and sensitive performance, and Jack Carson is consistent. Angie Dickinson's warmth overcomes some script deficiencies, and James Dunn is interesting in a role not completely realized. Tom Drake is excellent. Others who stand out include Frank Conroy, Carl Benton Reid, William Hansen and Grandon Rhodes.

Lucien Ballard's photography, in clean Technicolor, is helpful, and Leonard Rosenman's musical score is unusually evocative. Art director John S. Poplin is expert at creating the New England atmosphere (out of what looks, on close inspection, to be local California coastline), and editing by Folmar Blangsted is good. *Powe.*

The Last Voyage
(COLOR)

Top-notch ship-sinking adventure-suspense item. One to get behind.

Hollywood, Jan. 15.

Metro release of Andrew and Virginia Stone production. Stars Robert Stack, Dorothy Malone, George Sanders, Edmond O'Brien. Written and directed by Andrew Stone. Camera (Metrocolor), Hal Mohr; music, Rudy Schrager; editor, Virginia L. Stone. Previewed at the studio, Jan. 13, '60. Running time, 91 MINS.

Cliff Henderson	Robert Stack
Laurie Henderson	Dorothy Malone
Capt. Robert Adams	George Sanders
2d Engineer Walsh	Edmond O'Brien
Tammy Marihugh	Jill Henderson
Lawson	Woody Strode
Chief Eng. Pringle	Jack Kruschen
3d Officer Ragland	Joel Marston
1st Officer Osborne	George Furness
Engineer Cole	Richard Norris
Radio Operator	Andrew Hughes
2d Mate Mace	Robert Martin
Youth	Bill Wilson

The year is young, and predictions at this stage are risky, but to be as cautious as possible, "The Last Voyage" will probably not be surpassed as pure excitement very often during the coming months. It is the best film Andrew Stone has made since "Julie," and it is better in some respects than that successful production. The current Metro release, if well sold, could do very well.

Stone as writer and director, and with his wife, Virginia Stone, as co-producer and film editor, is pursuing a path of production unmarked by any other Hollywood film-maker. Made almost entirely on location, with natural sound and often natural lighting, Stone's films are an attempt to utilize realism for dramatic purposes. They are not all unqualified successes. But when they do connect, when the story matches the treatment,

as it does here, the result is electric, as tingling as a game of hare and hounds, with the audience the hare.

Stone's sure-handed direction is not always matched by his hand at dialog, which tends to be elementary. There is also narration used in "The Last Voyage" that is on somewhat the same level as the dialog, pointing out vocally what the eye has already observed, an unnecessary and sometimes annoying underlining. Some of the plot turns are questionable.

But these weak parts, if they are weak, are more than overcome by the impact of the whole. By concentrating on action, exploiting the forward and inevitable thrust of his story, Stone achieves and almost unwaveringly maintains a momentum of involvement for the spectator that is very rare.

The plot is simple. A great luxury liner begins to come apart—from fire and explosions—in the first scene, before the main titles are concluded. It sinks in the last scene, behind the closing credit. The story proceeds on two levels. First is the general story, with efforts by the crew to prevent the vessel's capsizing and the passengers' disintegration. The personal story concerns a young family, a couple, Robert Stack and Dorothy Malone, and their young daughter, Tammy Marihugh. Their particular problem is that Miss Malone is trapped by falling debris and is only released as the great ship slips beneath the water.

Ordinarily actors are commended for their thespic skill. The cast of "The Last Voyage" deserves a hand for its stamina. All the principals, Edmond O'Brien and George Sanders, as well as Stack and Miss Malone, are battered, bruised, begrimed and thoroughly wetted down. Miss Malone plays almost entirely throughout with only her nose and occasionally her mouth above sea level. Each turns in a first-rate performance. Woody Strode is impressive as Stack's chief confederate in freeing Miss Malone. Others who stand out in the supporting cast include Jack Kruschen, Joel Marston, George Furness and Bill Wilson.

Stone's chief ally in a film of this sort is his cameraman, and he is fortunate to have Hal Mohr. Mohr's work is especially effective in the interiors of the boiler rooms, as the cataclysmic inferno begins to take shape. His fine backward dolly shot of the last survivors fleeing the ship along a deck partially under water gives the film's closing moments a needed hypo.

Mrs. Stone's editing throughout is a great example of building tension through swift contrasting shots. Other technical credits, including contributions by production manager Harold A. Weinberger and sound by Philip N. Mitchell, are good. *Powe.*

Seven Thieves
(C'SCOPE)

First-rate crime yarn with good chances in general market; high exploitation potential.

Hollywood, Jan. 15.

Twentieth-Fox release of Sydney Boehm production. Stars Edward G. Robinson, Rod Steiger, Joan Collins, Eli Wallach; features Alexander Scourby, Michael Dante, Berry Kroeger, Sebastian Cabot, Marcel Hillaire, John Berardino. Directed by Henry Hathaway. Screenplay, Boehm, based on novel, "Lions at the Kill," by Max Catto; camera, Sam Leavitt; music, Dominic Frontiere; editor, Dorothy Spencer. Previewed Jan. 13, '60. Running time, 100 MINS.

Theo Wilkins ...... Edward G. Robinson
Paul .... Rod Steiger
Melanie .... Joan Collins
Poncho .... Eli Wallach
Raymond Le May....Alexander Scourby
Louis .... Michael Dante
Huo Baumer .... Berry Kroeger
Director Monte Carlo....Sebastian Cabot
Duc di Salins .... Marcel Hillaire
Chief of Detectives......John Berardino
Governor .... Alphonse Martell
Seymour .... Jonathan Kidd
Governor's Wife....Marga Ann Deighton

This is a hard-hitting melo of a bold robbery of $4,000,000 in franc notes from the Monte Carlo casino's underground vaults. Makes strong entry for the general market. Backed by good names and slick production technique, film should garner better-than-average returns.

Sydney Boehm production, which Henry Hathaway directs skillfully from Boehm's own screenplay, is flavored with mounting suspense as the unheard-of coup is planned by Edward G. Robinson and finally undertaken to the accompaniment of tense and exciting action. Actual French Riviera and Monte Carlo backgrounds establish the scene to give color and realism, and appropriate sets lend additional conviction and atmosphere. Principals with Robinson are Rod Steiger, Joan Collins and Eli Wallach, all names to contend with in the film's intended market; Alexander Scourby, Michael Dante and Berry Kroeger complete the line-up of the seven thieves.

Based on Max Catto's novel, "Lions at the Kill," plot opens with the arrival of Steiger in Cannes, summoned by Robinson, a former scientist, who wants newcomer to complete the gang otherwise composed of figures Robinson doesn't entirely trust. As much for the money itself, the robbery is to satisfy Robinson's ego in accomplishing something that will make the world gasp at its daring. Steiger finally agrees to participate despite the extreme risk involved, and becomes the guiding genius in executing the plan of operation which Robinson has spent more than a year in working out.

Robinson lends quiet strength to his role, whose heart cannot take the successful completion of his long-dreamed-of plan and dies before the money can be divided. Plotline carries a surprise twist in which the coin is found to be unusable, and is returned to the casino. Steiger performs with dynamic force and Miss Collins dishes up a couple of stirring scantily-clad dances in addition to her straight work as the robbery is in process. Wallach fakes a suicide at the gambling table as a diversionary step, delivering soundly.

Scourby, as the casino director's secretary who arranges for gang's presence at the governor's ball; Dante as an expert cracksman; Kroeger as a top mechanic whose skill is necessary, are all excellent. One of the most suspenseful sequences in film is when Steiger and Dante edge their way around a narrow ledge to gain entrance to the casino director's rooms so they may take a private elevator to the vaults below containing the treasure. Standout support also is offered by Sebastian Cabot, as the director, and Marcel Hillaire, as a lecherous French duke.

Technical credits are all highly placed, standouts here the photography of Sam Leavitt; Dorothy Spencer's tight editing; art direction by Lyle R. Wheeler and John De Cuir; Dominic Frontiere's atmaspheric music score. *Whit.*

The Hypnotic Eye

Exploitable but chancy gimmick sole appeal of plodding horror meller.

Hollywood, Jan. 16.

Allied Artists release of Ben Schwalb production. Stars Jacques Bergerac, Merry Anders, Marcia Henderson, Allison Hayes, Joe Patridge; features Ferdinand W. (Fred) Demara, Lawrence Lipton. Produced by Charles B. Bloch. Directed by George Blair. Screenplay, Gitta and William Read Woodfield; camera, Archie Dalzell; music, Marlin Skiles, Eve Newman; editor, William Austin. Previewed at the Screen Directors' Guild Theatre, Jan. 14, '60. Running time, 77 MINS.

The Great Desmond....Jacques Bergerac
Dodie Wilson .... Merry Anders
Marcia Blane .... Marcia Henderson
Justine .... Allison Hayes
Det. Dave Kennedy.......Joe Patridge
Doctor .... Fred Demara
Poet .... Lawrence Lipton
Psychiatrist .... Guy Prescott

"The Hypnotic Eye" is a horror film with a built-in exploitation gimmick which may be somewhat dangerous: The supposed hypnotist on the screen tries, during a special sequence, to hypnotize the audience. Questions of ethics and taste ignored the gimmick may see the film to good b.o.

The "hypnotist" is only an actor (Jacques Bergerac) and the stunts attempted with the audience are apparently harmless. However, since Bergerac is convincing and since his role in the rest of the melodrama is that of a stage hypnotist who lures beautiful women into mutilating themselves, a highly suggestible minority conceivably could be adversely affected.

The majority of the juvenile audience will probably consider the gimmick a background for entertaining one another. The houselights are brought up and the "hypnotist" spends about eight minutes daring people to unclasp their hands etc. At one point they are told they can't lift the balloons they just blew up. The balloons, with eyes painted on them, are handed out at the door.

The rest of the film is a plodding tale of a detective (Joe Patridge) whose girl (Marcia Henderson) eventually leads him to a solution of the mutilation mystery by offering herself as a victim.

Allison Hayes, portraying Bergerac's beautiful assistant, mesmerizes the victims into self-disfigurement to avenge her own ugliness (she wears a life-like mask). The handsome hypnotist's cooperation in the gruesome venture is never explained, but that's only one of myriad holes in the script.

The acting is of good quality throughout. Value is added by Fred Demara, much-publicized imposter, portraying a doctor, and by a beatnik scene featuring Lawrence Lipton reciting an original poem. Technical aspects are up to standard.

The film's "psychiatrist" at one point is caused to advise the audience never to allow itself to be hypnotized for entertainment purposes—"not even in a movie." It's advice which should have been unnecessary. ***Glen.***

The Pusher

Manhattan-lensed meller on the dope problem. Exploitation bookings likely.

Hollywood, Jan. 15.

United Artists release of Gene Milford-Carlyle. Directed by Gene Milford. Asso-Sidney Katz production. Features Kathy ciate producer, Bernard Storper; screenplay, Harold Robbins; camera, Arthur Ornitz; music, Raymond Scott; editor, Sidney Katz. Previewed at Goldwyn studio, Jan. 11, '60. Running time, 82 MINS.

Laura .... Kathy Carlyle
The Pusher .... Felice Orlandi
Lt. Peter Byrne....Douglas F. Rodgers
Harriet Byrne .... Sloan Simpson
Steve Carella .... Robert Lansing
Maria Hernandez .... Sara Aman

Many New York-filmed motion pictures have a commendable quality of realism about them, and "The Pusher," shot entirely in Manhattan, has that. It doesn't have much else.

It is a routinely melodramatic story about drug addiction and some of its side effects, moral degradation, murder, general wretchedness. The Gene Milford-Sidney Katz production for United Artists is honest enough, in its unpretentious way, but it is not novel or original enough to make it special. It will probably fare best in the exploitation market.

Harold Robbins' screenplay, based on a novel by Ed McBain, has Douglas F. Rodgers and Robert Lansing as a pair of police officers investigating the murder of a youthful narcotics addict. In the course of their investigation, Lansing discovers his fiancee, Kathy Carlyle, who is also Rodgers' daughter, is an addict herself. Through her, they find the murderer, Felice Orlandi, who is the drug peddler of the title.

The screenplay is thoughtful, not a cheap effort to cash in on the horrors of addiction. It attempts to pin-point the unwitting and often unwilling susceptibility of narcotic victims to the temptation of drugs. It uses the framework of the Puerto Rican community in New York to show how social deprivation can weaken those who might otherwise resist narcotics. But the handling of the story isn't equal to its aims.

Orlandi makes a strong impression as "The Pusher." The role is interestingly conceived and the actor plays it well. Miss Carlyle is sympathetic, although her convulsions as she "kicks" the drug habit is a climactic sequence that has been dulled through over-use in many films. Rodgers, Lansing and Sloan Simpson, latter as the girl's mother, are capable. Sara Aman is effective in her one key scene.

Familiarity of the story's general outlines is not improved by dialog that is often naive and just as often fake, but Gene Milford's direction, by concentrating on photographic realism, minimizes these drawbacks. Arthur Ornitz' photography is able, and Raymond Scott's contemporary score is first-rate. *Powe.*

Estate Violenta

(Violent Summer)
(ITALIAN-FRENCH)

Rome, Jan. 12.

Titanus release of a Titanus (Silvio Clementelli)-SGC production. Stars Eleonora Rossi Drago, Jean Louis Tritignant; features Lilla Brignone, Raf Mattioli, Jacqueline Sassard, Enrico Maria Salerno, Xenia Valderi, Federica Ranchi, Cathia Caro, Giampiero Littera, Bruno Carotenuto. Directed by Valerio Zurlini. Screenplay, Zurlini, Suso Cecchi D'Amica, Giorgio Prosperi, from a story by Zurlini; camera, Tino Santoni; editor, Mario Serandrei; music, Mario Nascimbene. Previewed in Rome. Running time, 99 MINS.

Roberta .... Eleonora Rossi Drago
Carlo .... Jean Louis Tritignant
Rossana .... Jacqueline Sassard

Sensitively conceived and directed, second film by Valeiro Zurlini confirms this director's maturing talent. It's a prestige entry for the producer and the Italian industry, with okay chances on the home market and the elements of an arty success abroad, especially in France.

Set in the war year of 1943, this tells the love story of a youngster still unscarred by a distant conflict and an older widow. The two meet at a seaside resort. After various conflicts, their affair ends as the war finally catches up with him, and he begins to face reality. Despite a slow pace, the affair unfolds believably thanks also to top-quality acting by both Eleonora Rossi Drago, who has never been better; and Jean Louis Tritignant.

Also good are the sequences of resort life among the teenage set, and the scenes in which the youths are casually reminded there's a war on. Acting is universally good, as are the period backdrops. Technical credits are topnotch. This easily rates among best of the year here. ***Hawk.***

Swan Lake

(BUSSIAN—BALLET—COLOR)

Bolshoi Virtuostic Ballet but photographically uneven. Part of US-USSR cultural exchange.

Columbia release of Central Documentary Film Studio production. Stars Maye Plisetskaya and Nicolai Fadeyechev; features Vladimir Levashev, V. Khomyakov. Directed by Z. Tulubyeva; scenario, Tulubyeva and A. Messerer; music, Peter Ilyitch Tchaikowsky; camera (Eastman Color), M. Silenko and A. Kravchin; orchestra of the Bolshoi Theatre conducted by Yuri Faier. Reviewed at Normandie Theatre, N.Y., Jan. 14, '60. Running time, 81 MINS.

Odetta-Odillia .... Maya Plisetskay
The Prince .... Nicolai Fadeyechev
Evil Spirit .... Vladimir Levashev
Jester .... V. Khomyakov

Under the agreement between the private American film industry and the Soviet State calling for the reciprocal exhibition of feature productions, Columbia has taken on release of Tchaikowsky's "Swan Lake" in a colorful and provocative cinematic form. It was made in Moscow in 1957 under the direction of Z. Tulubyeva who also collaborated on the screenplay with A. Messerer.

If and to the extent ballet is acceptable in U.S. on film—and this is a ballet feature devoid of any backstage plot flourishes—then "Swan Lake" must be recognized as impressive. Russia's earlier "Romeo and Juliet" was a success d'entime with critics and eggies.

"Swan Lake" is a frequently enrapturing performance by soloists of the Bolshoi Theatre Ballet and Orchestra conducted by Yuri Faier, all "familiar" in States via Bolshoi (Sol Hurok) tour.

Unfortunately, it lacks vividness, and this despite the asserted fact that the company is photographed during an actual workout before an audience at Moscow's Bolshoi Theatre.

Maya Plisetskaya is utterly delightful as the Queen of the Swans. She gives the dance form emotional wallop in depicting the spellbound beauty who will be returned to a bird unless she finds a man who truly loves her. Nicolai Fadeyechev is the favored party, the prince charming who seeks out a bride and looks to the Swan Queen. His is a tender and beautiful, yet manly, execution of the role. Vladimir Levanshev is the Evil Spirit who wants the lovely Odetta to remain under his spell in Swan Lake. This is the part where sinisterism is carried to the

point of near-caricature but in the instance of this particular tale of love it is fitting.

The Tchaikowsky music is the classical mixture that runs the range from frolicsome to the dark and foreboding. It is given sensitive interpretation by the Bolshoi Theatre Orchestra.

Why the lack of vividness? The producers of the Central Documentary Film Studio seem to have been tripped up by the mechanics in getting their ballet on film. The photographic framing is unforgiveably out of line at times; the camera actually is off the footwork of the performers. Frequent focusing on the theatre audience is disconcerning, could very well be gotten along without. The color has a strange predominance of amber. The sound track is short of the high fidelity to which Hollywood film fans are accustomed.

Thus, technical flaws have impaired an otherwise touching and stimulating terp outing. It will do fine until something better comes along, and does point up the need for more skilled hands in cinematic technology when something so precious as "Swan Lake" is the subject matter.

It seems a certainty that considerable interest will be evinced by Americans in this Russian ballet, and consequently a good performance can be expected at the boxoffice of specialty theatres.

Gene.

The Royal Ballet
(BRITISH—EASTMANCOLOR)

Outstanding prestige picture, excellently executed and a certain winner for discriminating audiences.

London, Jan. 12.

Rank release of a Paul Czinner production. Stars Margot Fonteyn; features Michael Somes, Julia Farren, Rosemary Lindsay, Alexander Grant, Franklin White, Bryan Ashbridge. Directed by Paul Czinner. Editor, Philip Hudsmith; choreography, Frederick Ashton; camera, S. D. Onions; technical director, Alfred Travers. At Columbia Theatre, London. Running time, 132 MINS.

Paul Czinner's production of "The Royal Ballet" is not only an important British prestige picture but, even though its appeal is limited to balletomanes the b.o. prospects appear good. At 132 minutes, this may prove heavy going for those who aren't ballet addicts but even they will admire the color, the lensing and the technical virtues. Above all is the satisfying feeling that experts connected with this have given their best.

The film was shot in a day and a half on the stage of the Royal Opera House at Covent Garden. It consists of three ballets linked with audience applause. With the rise and fall of the curtain between ballets, the effect of watching an actual stage production is most realistic. Nevertheless, though Czinner has kept rigidly within the framework of a stage production, he has used his team of cameramen with imagination and with slick camera angles and closeups. Thus, he has largely avoided the static effect sometimes obtained when a stage presentation is simply filmed.

The selected ballets are pleasantly contrasted, kicking off with Margot Fonteyn as Odette and Michael Somes as Prince Siegfried in Act Two of Tchaikowsky's "Swan Lake." Centrepiece is Stravinsky's lively and colorful "Firebird." Her dancing "The Firebird" is a little miracle of grace and imagination.

Finale is "Ondine," a less known ballet, by Hans Werner Henz. Madame Fonteyn's artistry is admirably matched by Michael Somes and other members of the Royal Ballet company. Technically the film is a remarkable achievement, considerably the hazards that Czinner must have faced, with sound, color, editing and photography all of outstanding quality.

Thoroughly recommended not only as a perpetual record of this widely known company but as good entertainment. And for those for whom ballet is a completely blank spot, each ballet is preceded with captions that tell the story with complete simplicity.

Rich.

El Gafe
(The Jinx)
(SPANISH)

Madrid, Jan. 12.

A Filmayer release of a Procusa production. Stars Jose Luis Ozores, Antonio Garisa, Teresa del Rio, Julie Caba Alba; features Jose Marco Davo, Nicholas Perchicot, Ramon Elias and Mari Loli Cabo. Directed by Pedro Ramirez. Screen story by Vicente Escriva; screenplay by Pedro Ramirez; cameraman, Federico Larraya; music, Maestro Contreras. At Cine Capitol, Madrid. Running time, 85 MINS.

A minor vein, low-budget comedy that spoofs at spirits and the superstitious in a quantity of dialogue-laden, rapid sketches that draws lusty laughter. There are patches of slow, sentimental romance where comic Ozores is not at his best, but there is plenty of breezy, prankish mirth to augur handsome returns for "The Jinx" in the local market.

Comedy is themed to an unhappy bank clerk whose evil eye sets off a series of minor disasters. An astute, glib-tongued pal (Antonio Garisa) puts the jinx to work and both discover there's a market for hexlers. Along comes love and the jinx is hexed.

Promising young director Ramirez achieves a surprising degree of humor by pacing the situations to balance a talky script and putting a deft fun accent on the dialogue. Garisa is excellent in comic support. So is talented actress Julie Caba Alba. "The Jinx" has no great export value, but it deserves a place among those Spanish films that are providing a home gross tonic to the industry here. *Werb.*

Nathalie Agent Secret
(FRENCH)

Paris, Jan. 12.

CFDC release of Sirius-SFC production. Stars Martine Carol, Felix Marten; features Dario Moreno, Jacques Berthier, Dany Saval, Noel Roquevert, Andre Versini. Directed by Henri Decoin. Screenplay, Pierre Apesteguy, Jacques Robert, Henri Jeanson from novel by Franck Marshal; camera, Robert Le Febvre; editor, Claude Durand. At Balzac, Paris. Running time, 95 MINS.

Nathalie	Martine Carol
Inspector	Felix Marten
Pivoine	Dany Saval
Don Jose	Dargio Moreno
Jean	Jacques Berthier
Darbon	Noel Roquevert

Film is a sequel to the successful "Nathalie," about a zany, emotionally generous model who keeps butting into police business and solves the crime before they do. This is somewhat heavyfooted and lacks the zest and movement necessary to sustain it. It injects some undressing scenes gratuitously. Any foreign chances this may have will be on exploitation aspects.

Here Nathalie, in the classy chassis of Martine Carol, gets mixed up with spies trying to steal a great new French invention, an atomic motor that can be used in autos. She outwits the blundering inspector. This has enough amatory bits and narrow escapes to keep this easy on the orbs if not on credibility.

Henri Decoin has not been able to give his direction the lightness and ease it needs. Miss Carol is somewhat too mannered in her pouts and femininity and the males are just foils. Technical credits are good. *Mosk.*

Pretty Boy Floyd

Low-budget biography of a late public enemy. Good exploitation possibilities among uncritical audiences with a taste for violence.

Continental Distributing release of a Le-Sac (Monroe Sachson) Productions presentation. Stars John Ericson. Directed and written by Herbert J. Leder; editor, Ralph Rosenblum; camera, Chuck Austin; sound, Dick Cramaglia; costumes, Bill Walstrom; music composed by Del Sirino and William Sanford. Previewed at Movielab, N.Y., Jan. 18, '60. Running time, 96 MINS.

Pretty Boy Floyd	John Ericson
Al Riccardo	Barry Newman
Lil Courtney	Joan Harvey
Blackie Faulkner	Herb Evers
Curly	Carl York
Jed Watkins	Roy Fant
Ann Courtney	Shirley Smith
Baker	Phil Kenneally
Bill Courtney	Norman Burton
Neil Trane	Charles Bradswell
Mr. Whitney	Truman Smith
Grindon Jr.	Ted Chapman
Ed Courtney	Leo Bloom
Gail	Casey Peyson
Ma Parks	Effie Afton
Shorty Walters	Peter Falk
Mike Clouder	Paul Lipson
Machine Gun Manny	Al Lewis
Big Dutch	Jim Dukes
Oil Field Boss	Gene O'Donnell
Lonely Woman	Dina Paisner

This is a grim, almost sadistic reworking of the tale of the Oklahoma farm boy who won fame and ill-fortune in the early '30s as Pretty Boy Floyd. With John Ericson in the title role and enough violence in the script to pass for excitement, film should do okay in the exploitation market. It points a glib moral ("crime does not pay") without ever presenting anything more than a few superficial reasons for the phenomenon that Pretty Boy Floyd represented. Script says Floyd had a bad temper and was ignorant. Period.

Ericson does a good job in the role and is backed by a competent group of New York actors, few of whom have been on the screen before. (Film was shot entirely at Gold Medal Studios in the Bronx.) Low budget of the pic shows through from time to time, but actually seems to help create an appropriately seedy and sordid atmosphere.

Script by Herbert J. Leder, who also directed, first picks up Floyd when he is making a desultory attempt to go straight as an oil-field worker. Bounced when it's revealed that he served time for armed robbery in St. Louis, Floyd picks up a life of crime again with an old cellmate. He soon branches out on his own and becomes the terror of the Middle West, sticking up banks and killing with little provocation. Some bit of romance was added to his living legend by his generosity with his loot among the back country hill folk, who hid him from the law "between dates."

The film shows numerous of Floyd's bank holdups, as well as the famous "Kansas City Massacre," in which Floyd and two others gunned to death two FBI men and a policeman who were transferring a brother hood to prison. Same incident, as well as Floyd's eventual demise at the hands of the G Men, were featured in Warners' "The F.B.I. Story" last year.

In most prominent support are Barry Newman, as one of Floyd's brainier assistants, Joan Harvey, as a girl who loved Floyd not wisely but well (her husband had been one of his earlier victims); Carl York, as a simple-minded friend from the hill country; and Phil Kenneally, as another partner-in-crime. Miss Harvey and York come through with a couple of surprisingly sincere moments.

Director Leder keeps the pace fast, aided to no little extent by noisy, semi-progressive jazz score by Del Sirino and William Sanford. Costumes, cars and sets do much to evoke the period. Camera work and editing are satisfactory. A couple of old newsreel clips, showing plight of Okie farmers, add effectively to the generally dismal illusion. Monroe Sachson was producer. *Anby.*

A Matter of Dignity
(GREEK)

San Francisco, Jan. 19.

Finos Films production. Stars Ellie Lambetti, features Michel Nikolinagos, Eleni Zafiriou. Directed by Michael Cacoyyannis. Screenplay, Cacoyannis; camera, Walter Lassally; music, Manos Hadziakis. At Metro Theatre, San Francisco. Running time, 97 MINS.

Except for the leading lady, Ellie Lambetti, "A Matter of Dignity" might be a remake of dozens of "sophisticated" dramas of high life made in England and the U.S. during the 1930's.

Story concerns the beautiful daughter (Miss Lambetti) of a free-spending, nearly bankrupt Athenian family. The girl's mother eggs her into becoming engaged to a rich Greek-American, who is about as romantic as a goatskin. In the process the girl throws over a clean-cut young fellow and an older, suaver chap (Michel Nikolinakos). The subplot involves the family's faithful maid (Elani Zafiriou), who hasn't been paid in many months and needs the money to pay off bills accumulated when her little boy is hurt and stricken mute. In the climactic scene the girl's mother and the maid have a knock-down, drag-out fight over the overdue wages, the maid topples over dead from a heart attack and the daughter, repentant for her family's phoniness, fulfills the maid's vow to take the little boy to a shrine, where he may recover his voice. He does.

This trite yarn is further cheapened by scenarist-director Michael Cacoyannis observing every convention in the book. Nor has Walter Lassally brought any originality to his camera work.

Miss Lambetti is an enchanting-looking woman who gets little material here; Miss Zafiriou has a strong, handsome face, evidently can act and should be lifted out of her frumpy maid's costume as swiftly as possible. Rest of the cast has nearly nothing to do.

Chances in the U.S. seem to be nil. *Stef.*

Please Turn Over
(BRITISH)

Bright comedy with brisk opportunities for some of Britain's favorite feature players; excellent b.o. potential.

London, Jan. 12.

Anglo-Amalgamated release of a Peter Rogers' production. Stars Ted Ray, Jean

Kent, Leslie Phillips, Joan Sima, Julia Lockwood, Tim Seely. Directed by Gerald Thomas. Screenplay, Norman Hudis, based on Basil Thomas's play, "Book Of Month"; camera, Ted Scaife; editor, John Shirley; music, Bruce Montgomery. Previewed at Studio One, London. Running time, 87 MINS.

Edward Halliday	Ted Ray
Janet Halliday	Jean Kent
Dr. Henry Manners	Leslie Phillips
Beryl	Joan Sima
Jo Halliday	Julia Lockwood
Robert Hughes	Tim Seely
Jeweller	Charles Hawtrey
Millicent Jones	Dilys Laye
Ian Howard	Lionel Jeffries
Gladys Worth	June Jago
Maurice	Colin Gordon
Saleswoman	Joan Hickson
Smithy	Victor Maddern
Mr. Appleton	Robert Adam
Mr. Jones	Cyril Chamberlain
Removal Man	George Street
Mrs. Waring	Marianne Stone
Cashier	Leigh Madison
Mrs. Moore	Myrtle Reed

A bright comedy entry from the same stable that has turned out the popular "Carry On" series, "Please Turn Over" looks like an equally profitable biz bet. Gerald Thomas's direction is lively and Norman Hudis has provided a screenplay which deftly blends slapstick, light comedy and one or two dramatic moments. The cast is stacked with good British character and feature players, who have plenty of opportunities. Almost satisfactory job which should kindle a gleam in the eye of most exhibitors.

Yarn concerns the uproar in a peaceful little suburban town when a teenage girl writes a bestseller novel called, "Naked Revolt," which deals with scandalous goings on in suburbia. The neighbors identify all her characters as her relations and friends, and in the end even the persons themselves begin to wonder. As a result her father is regarded as an embezzler carrying on with his secretary, her aunt as a drunk, her mother and uncle as lovers, the local doctor as a lecher after his patients and the girl herself as illegitimate and about to embark on a career as a call girl.

The simultaneous reading of the book by father and mother provides the central core of the film. As they read, the pages come to life with very funny effect. This part of the film is sheer parody and exaggerated sometimes in the way that would be quite unacceptable in a serious film. But in this one it merely adds greatly to the comic effect. One sequence that deserves mention is that in which Lionel Jeffries gives Jean Kent a driving lesson. It's a masterpiece of comic reaction.

Ted Ray gives his best film performance as the father who, in the novel, turns into a rake while Miss Kent is poised and assured as his wife. Leslie Phillips plays the shy doctor with his usual sense of fun. Joan Sims is better as the cockney maid than when she becomes a French one in the novel. June Jago, Tim Seely, Colin Gordon, Joan Hickson, Ronald Adam and Charles Hawtrey are others who keep the good humor bubbling. Dilys Laye makes a particular impact as Ray's secretary, efficient in real life but a good time girl in the novel. Julia Lockwood, in her first major role, plays the teenager whose novel causes all the fuss. Daughter of Margaret Lockwood, she has inherited much of her mother's charm and talent. She makes the most of a double role.

There are several high comedy peaks in "Please Turn Over." When the slim story occasionally sags, writer Hudis is by no means unabashed in producing a few irrelevant slapstick sequences to keep the film moving.   *Rich.*

A Dog's Best Friend

Canine fodder. And filler.

Hollywood, Jan. 12.
United Artists release of a Premium Pictures production. Stars Bill Williams and Marcia Henderson; with Roger Mobley, Charles Cooper, Dean Stanton, Roy Engel, Jimmy Baird, Terry Ann Ross. Produced by Robert E. Kent. Directed by Edward L. Cahn. Screenplay, Orville H. Hampton; camera, Kenneth Peach; editor, Michael J. Minth; music, Paul Sawtell and Bert Shefter. Previewed at Goldwyn Studios, Jan. 12, '59. Running time, 70 MINS.

Wes Thurman	Bill Williams
Millie Thurman	Marcia Henderson
Pip Wheeler	Roger Mobley
Bill Beamer	Charles Cooper
Roy Janney	Dean Stanton
Dan Murdock	Roy Engel
Jimmy Thurman	Jimmy Baird
Amy Thurman	Terry Ann Ross

The best thing about Premium Pictures' "A Dog's Best Friend" is the dog. He barks on command, nuzzles on cue and takes everything, including the insipid name Silver King, in stride. The chance of the United Artists release escaping the lower half of double bills is as dry as a bone.

Orville H. Hampton screenplay wraps up nicely with fair action in the final minutes, but in the main it's too obvious. Still, it could have resulted in a reasonably good film had director Edward L. Cahn managed to fashion the tenderness which this sort of film desperately needs.

Bill Williams and Marcia Henderson star as a ranching couple who takes in an embittered youngster (Roger Mobley). The boy has no use for his foster parents, remaining aloof and spending all his time with a German Shepherd he finds wounded in a meadow. The dog, an ex-Marine canine, belonged to a rich hermit who has been murdered, and it used its training to steal the murder weapon and run away. The boy finds the gun, ultimately faces the murderer and is saved when the animal snatches a second gun from the murderer's hand.

Williams and Miss Henderson are sympathetic as the parents. Mobley tries hard as the youngster, but from appearances he has been handled badly. He comes across so mean and ornery that audiences will have trouble digging below the surface to find anything in him to like. In supporting roles, Charles Cooper, Dean Stanton, Roy Engel and Jimmy Baird are more than competent.

The best emotional tugs in the Robert E. Kent production probably will result from the Paul Sawtell-Bert Shefter musical score. Other credits—Kenneth Peach's photography, Bill Glasgow's art direction, John Kean's sound and Michael J. Minth's editing—are good.   *Ron.*

Pickpocket
(FRENCH)

Paris, Jan. 12.
Lux release of Agnes Delahaye production. With Martin Lassalle, Pierre Leymarie, Pelegri, Pierre Etaix, Marika Green. Written and directed by Robert Bresson. Camera, L. H. Burel; editor, Raymond Lamy. At Mercury, Paris. Running time, 80 MINS.

Michel	Martin Lassalle
Jacques	Pierre Leymarie
Inspector	Pelegri
Accomplice	Pierre Etaix
Jeanne	Marika Green

This is a strangely austere study of a pickpocket. Director-writer Robert Bresson eschews all adventurous aspects and tries to depict the spiritual side of a kleptomaniac. He shows the young man believing he is far enough above society to continue this work and stop when he wants to. Arrest and the discovery of love finally lead to his first human feelings and the possibility that he will give up stealing.

Pic tells its story through the hero writing his memoirs, commenting on them, and then showing the actual happenings. This makes it lack the familiar picaresque qualities, though depiction of the pickpockets at work has a deft documentary flair. It looms an offbeater with mainly arty theatre chances abroad.

Bresson, who made "Diary of a Country Priest" and "A Condemned Man Escaped," again uses non-actors to get exactly what he wants in trying to denote the inner workings of his characters. They speak flatly and without emotion, just walking through their roles phlegmatically sans the accepted limning of their parts. The result is a probing affair that shows the spirit of a pickpocket but rarely makes a statement on the whys or wherefores of it all.

Film is technically excellent with a forceful feeling for wedding images and sound, thus creating almost an extreme reality in its progression. This is another offbeat, unusual pic by Bresson may win film prizes and specialized critical kudos. But it may prove difficult commercially abroad except for arty and specialized spotting.   *Mosk.*

The Third Voice
(C'SCOPE)

Above-par suspense-exploitation item.

Hollywood, Jan. 22.
Twentieth-Fox release of Maury Dexter-Hubert Cornfield production. Stars Edmond O'Brien, Julie London, Laraine Day. Written and directed by Cornfield; screenplay based on Charles Williams' novel, "All the Way"; camera, Ernest Haller; editor, John A. Bushelman; music, Johnny Mandel. Previewed at the studio, Jan. 20, '60. Running time, 80 MINS.

The Voice	Edmond O'Brien
Corey Scott	Julie London
Marian Forbes	Laraine Day
Blonde Prostitute	Olga San Juan
Judge Kendall	George Eldredge
Desk Clerk—Hotel Bahia	
	Tom Hernandez
Police Inspector	Abel Franco
Carreras	Edward Colmans
Tourist at Bar	Tom Daly
Harris Chapman	Ralph Brooks
Mrs. Kendall	Lucile Curtis
Carreras' Secretary	Shirley O'Hara
Bank Official	Raoul De Leon
Cashier—Hotel Miramar	Sylvia Rey
Captain Campos	George Trevino
Carlos, the Cab Driver	Eddie Le Baron
Photographer	Alberto Monte
Bank Clerk	John Garrett
Bank Cashier	Francisco Ortega
Fishermen	Roque Ybarra, Ruben Moreno
Clerk—Hotel Palacio	Henry Delgardo
Clerk—Hotel Miramar	Andre Oropeza
Bellhop	Robert Hernandez
Waiter	Francis Ravel
Headwaiter	Manuel Serrano
Orchestra Leader	Mario Armenta

"The Third Voice" is about three-quarters of an excellent suspense film. The ending is a disappointment because it tries too hard to be clever. Despite this weakness, however, the 20th-Fox release is a credit to Hubert Cornfield, who wrote and directed it, and co-produced (with Maury Dexter). Aside from its other merits, "The Third Voice" is a superior exploitation film.

Based on the book, "All the Way," by Charles Williams, "The Third Voice," deals with murder and impersonation. Laraine Day is the secretary-mistress to a wealthy American. Spurned by him when he decides to get married, she connives with Edmond O'Brien to murder the boss and have O'Brien take his place long enough for both of them to get their hands on $250,000 of his money.

The screenplay is a straightforward account of the events, without going into any of the background. It suffers from an obstacle not of the writer's creation. American audiences are so conditioned to the Production Code, in which crime must always be punished, that there can be no real suspense in such a story as told in "The Third Voice." Audiences know what the outcome must be, but they don't know how it will come. Cornfield has partially met his problem by prolonging the suspense almost to the end. He falters in attempting to make the scheme's collapse too tricky. He would have been on surer ground in admitting his problem, not trying to disguise it, but slapping shut his story as quickly as possible once the crime is uncovered. Even though the Production Code eliminates the "what" of a crime story, the "how" can still be explored for advantage.

Cornfield recognizes this up to a point. He keeps things securely in hand, sketching the details of the deception, heightening excitement as the fraud touches more and more points of possible exposure, and becomes more dangerous. He is also adept at preventing his few characters from wearing thin.

Edmond O'Brien is in almost every frame of the film, and gives a performance of uncommon dexterity. Miss Day, in the offbeat

role of a hard woman, driven to murder by rejection, is convincingly chilly. Julie London is attractive in an enigmatic role. Others who contribute include Olga San Juan, Shirley O'Hara, George Eldredge, Tom Hernandez, Edward Colmans and Lucile Curtis.

Ernest Haller's camera effectively points up the mood of the film, and Johnny Mandel's music is good. John A. Bushelman's editing is first-rate. *Powe.*

The Immoral Mr. Teas
(COLOR)

Nude comedy with touches of art appeal. Can do very well in art-house run.

Hollywood, Jan. 22.
Pad-Ram Enterprises release of a P. A. De Cenzie production. Stars W. Ellis (Bill) Teas; with Marilyn Wesley, Ann Peters, Michele Roberts, Dawn Dinielle. Written, directed and photographed (Eastman Color) by Russ Meyer; music and narration, Edward Lasko. Reviewed at the Monica Theatre, L.A., Jan. 22, '60. Running time, **63 MINS.**

"The Immoral Mr. Teas" is sort of a perverted "Mr. Hulot's Holiday," saved from being entirely a burlesque film only by the reaction shots of Mr. Teas himself. There's nudity galore in the Los Angeles-made feature, and its female take-off artists should get the film high off the ground in special art house bookings. The Monica Theatre, where the picture is playing *"to unashamed adults only,"* reported its house record broken on opening night.

The allusion to "Mr. Hulot" is in form only, with "Mr. Teas" cavorting through life without a sound, backed by a whimsical musical score and taking an interested look at everything around him. He's actor W. Ellis (Bill) Teas, and he rides a bicycle, carries a brown bag containing somebody's mouth and generally has a ball daydreaming about undressed females. There's only a slight story line, and Mr. Teas supposedly is "common man" in a complex society, the comment apparently being that every man would like to get away from his work-a-day world to become a Peeping Tom.

Russ Meyer wrote, directed and photographed the film, and its physical values, particularly some artistic Eastman Color lensing, are amazingly good. His direction doesn't seem overly important in the face of bare bosoms and bottoms, but he and actor Teas have come up with a rather interesting and amusing character. The film partially is narrated, and the patter, at the very least, is informative. For instance, the audience is given the date rubber was invented while watching a nude swing back and forth in a suspended rubber tire. Edward Lasko's background music is properly arranged to maintain and heighten the mood. And the picture features the bodies of Marilyn Wesley, Ann Peters, Michele Roberts and Dawn Dinielle, who have all the necessary equipment for this sort of thing.

P. A. De Cenzie, said to be a San Francisco theatre owner, produced the PAD-RAM Enterprises picture. Depicting several days in Mr. Teas' life, the film runs 63 minutes. It would have come off far better as a subtle short subject depicting, say, one day in 20 minutes. But then, in that form it wouldn't have made much money, would it? *Ron.*

The Men Who Tread On The Tiger's Tail
(JAPANESE

Brandon Films release of Toho Co. production. Features Hanshiro Iwai, Susumu Fujita, Kenichi Enomoto, Denjiro Okochi. Directed and written by Okira Kurosawa; camera, Takeo Ito; sound, Keiji Hasebe; music, Tadashi Hattori. At Little Carnegie Theatre, N.Y., Jan. 19, '60. Running time, **60 MINS.**

This is the kind of picture that needs quite a few program notes to give it meaning, but if the art house exhibitor goes to that trouble, his efforts will not be wasted. Discriminating audiences, properly briefed, should find much of interest in this re-working of an old Kabuki tale, banned first by the Japanese war government in 1945 and then again by the Occupation powers in 1946. The Japanese themselves didn't see it until 1953, and the picture only now is reaching the U. S. as part of Brandon Films' package of nine Japanese imports.

"The Men Who Tread on The Tiger's Tail," one of the earliest directorial efforts of Akire ("Rashomon") Kurosawa to reach this side, was commissioned by the wartime Japanese government as a propaganda piece aimed at extolling the old conception of feudalism and obedience. Story, a favorite Japanese legend, concerns a 12th Century lord who is forced to flee his territory with only six dedicated retainers to guard him.

Kurosawa, however, supplemented this story of classic heroism and devation by introducing a low comedy servant. Latter bounces through the solemn proceedings ridiculing and satirizing militarists held so near and dear. For this reason, film was banned the first time. Occupation authorities, in turn, saw none of the humor and promptly banned it as being pro-feudal.

For the present-day U.S. audience, film offers a unique opportunity to see a Kabuki type of drama (a highly stylized presentation in which dance and song are used to move the plot along) translated in screen terms. Satirical or not, it also evokes a quaintly attractive mood of long ago and far away.

Seen in principal roles are Hanshiro Iwai, as the hunted lord; Susumu Fujita, as a magistrate who allows the lord to escape when he understands the extent to which Iwai's retainers will go to protect their leader; Kenichi Enomoto, as the low comedy character; and Denjiro Okochi, as the sage chief of the lord's retainers.

Production values and camera work are not spectacular, but quite adequate, especially considering the fact that when film was in production almost all of the Japanese homeland was being subjected to a daily drubbing by the U.S. Air Force. *Anby.*

The Rise and Fall of Legs Diamond

Well-made gangster biopic with average b.o. outlook.

Hollywood, Jan. 19.
Warner Bros. release of a United States Production. Stars Ray Danton, Karen Steele, Elaine Stewart. Produced by Milton Sperling. Directed by Budd Boetticher. Screenplay, Joseph Landon; camera, Lucien Ballard; editor, Folmar Blangsted; music, Leonard Rosenman. Previewed at the Hollywood Paramount Theatre, Jan. 19, '60. Running time, 101 MINS.
Legs Diamond .... Ray Danton
Alice .... Karen Steele
Monica .... Elaine Stewart
Leo Bremer .... Jesse White

Lt. Moody .... Simon Oakland
Arnold .... Robert Lowery
Fats Walsh .... Judson Pratt
Eddie Diamond .... Warren Oates
Chairman .... Frank DeKova
Sgt. Cassidy .... Gordon Jones
Matt Moran .... Joseph Ruskin
Dixie .... Diane Cannon
Vince Coll .... Richard Gardner

"The Rise and Fall of Legs Diamond" is an old-fashioned gangster melodrama, super-saturated with gunfire and fear, competently made but without the elements that spell "Al Capone" business. Producer Milton Sperling appears to have filmed the biography on a moderate budget, and if that be the case, it should turn a profit for Warner Bros.

There is more emphasis on the rise than on the fall as played by Ray Danton. Coldblooded and cunning, stealing from thieves to hoist himself up an infamous but lucrative ladder, that's Legsie. The film's ending proves crime doesn't pay, for the gangland leader embarrassingly is dispossessed of his power and then shot to death. But during most of the film he "takes care of" fellow gangsters who deserve "taking care of," and his precisely planned journey to the top often tends to be amusing, even in the face of mayhem and murder. Diamond, for instance, is dead serious when he lights a girl's dress afire to keep her out of a dance contest he wants to win, but the scene somehow builds to a laugh. While the film doesn't glorify Diamond, it takes a breezy approach to his rise, and audiences may see him as the hero as often as they do the villain.

Screenwriter Joseph Landon pictures Diamond as a psychopath, and perhaps in this way audiences will keep the character in his proper perspective. The script is constructed cleverly, and Landon's dialog is brisk and sharp. Budd Boetticher's direction could well have tipped the scales further in favor of the story's grimmer side, but in all it is good both in the light and hard tones.

Core of the screenplay puts Diamond into gangster Arnold Rothstein's fold and ultimately has him taking over when the leader is slain. Legs—he was a dancer—develops a reputation of being indestructible, gets rich by making bootleggers and gamblers pay off, but finally meets his match in a building crime syndicate.

Danton makes a smooth Diamond, believable as the man who used people as stepping stones. Karen Steele etches a sympathetic portrayal of the woman he eventually marries, and she helps the film's visual side as well. Elaine Stewart is appropriately sexy as the woman Diamond uses to get to Rothstein, and good performances are turned in by Jesse White, Simon Oakland, Robert Lowery, Judson Pratt, Warren Oates, Diane Cannon and Joseph Ruskin.

The United States Productions picture is ably put together, with Lucien Ballard's photography very effective and Jack Poplin's art direction catching the feel of the late 20's. Assets are Folmar Blangsted's editing, Samuel F. Goode's sound and Leonard Rosenman's music. *Ron.*

A Bout De Souffle
(Out of Breath)
(FRENCH)

Paris, Jan. 26.
Imperia release of SNC production. Stars Jean Seberg, Jean-Paul Belmondo; features Van Doude, Liliane David, Henri-Jacques Huet, Claude Mansard. Directed by Jean-Luc Godard. Screenplay, Francois Truffaut; camera, Rene Coutard; editor, C. Decugis. At Marignan, Paris. Running time, **90 MINS.**
Patricia .... Jean Seberg
Michel .... Jean-Paul Belmondo
Editor .... Van Doude
Minouche .... Liliane David
Antonio .... Henri-Jacques Huet
Inspector .... Claude Mansard

This film emerges as a summation of the so-called "new wave" trends here in that it is a first pic by a film critic, it shows the immediate influence of Yank actioners and socio-psycho thrillers. Also the film has no big French names, but has the Yank name of Jean Seberg and has its own personal style.

All of this adds up to a production resembling such past Yank pix as "Gun Crazy," "They Live By Night" and "Rebel Without a Cause." But it has local touches in its candor, lurid lingo, frank love scenes, and general tale of a young, childish hoodlum whose love for a boyish looking, semi-intellectual American girl is his undoing. Gal, incidentally sells papers in the street.

Pic uses a peremptory cutting style that look like a series of jump cuts. Characters suddenly shift around rooms, have different bits of clothing on within two shots, etc. But all this seems acceptable for this unorthodox film moves quickly and ruthlessly.

The young, mythomaniacal crook is forever stealing autos, but the slaying of a cop puts the law on his trail. The girl finally gives him up because she feels she does not really love him, and also she wants her independence. Film does not engender much feeling over the ironic death of the petty thug in the street, but none of the characters rarely feel anything.

There are too many epigrams and a bit too much palaver in all this. However, this does give a new view of a certain type of fed-up, stagnating French youth. It is picaresque and has enough insight to keep it from being an out-and-out melodramatic quickie. With the Jean Seberg name, plus the action, this could be a playoff possibility even worth dubbing.

But it looms more of an arty house bet. A "wave" film, with its grabbag mixture of content, satire, drama and protest, this will need the hard sell. Technique is okay but somewhat grimy because of the spot shooting. But this very grayness may be rated an asset. Miss Seberg lacks emotive projection but it helps in her role of a dreamy little Yank abroad playing at life. Her boyish prettiness is real help. Jean-Paul Belmondo is excellent as the cocky hoodlum. Though the revolt may be a little hazy, this is a fairly vital off-beater worth special handling. *Mosk.*

La Notte Brava
(Tonight's the Night)
(ITALIAN)

Rome, Jan. 19.
Euro International release of an AJACE (Antonio Cervi and Alessandro Jacovoni) production. Features Rosanna Schiaffino, Elsa Martinelli, Laurent Terzieff, Jean Claude Brialy, Anna Maria Ferrero, Franco Interlenghi, Antonella Lualdi, Mylene Demongeot, Thomas Milian. Directed by Mauro Bolognini. Story and screenplay, Pier Paolo Pasolini; camera, Armando Nannuzzi; music, Piero Piccioni. Previewed in Rome. Running time, **105 MINS.**
Ruggeretto .... Laurent Terzieff
Scintillone .... Jean Claude Brialy
Rossana .... Rosanna Schiaffino
Laura .... Mylene Demongeot
Anna .... Elsa Martinelli
Bella-Bella .... Franco Interlenghi
Supplizia .... Antonella Lualdi
Nicoletta .... Anna Maria Ferrero

Expertly fashioned exploitable and exportable art entry, this has good home-market impact on gen-

eral audiences. Star values in the large name cast are an added fillip for Italy, France and other neighboring markets.

Plot recounts the adventures of two petty thieves out for a night on the town and involves their encounters—mostly on the seamy side—with the denizens of Rome-by-night. Their dubious behavior often skirts criminality. While pic never directly condemns them, it does do so indirectly by showing the emptiness and futility of their existence, and the eventual desperate loneliness to which it leads.

The pessimistic outlook, as well as the depicted world of prostitutes and young no-goods, is conceived by writer-scripter Pier Paolo Pasolini. He is to be credited with providing a jarring look at this ugly side of life in the Eternal City and its breeding ground of senseless violence. Even more credit, however, must go to director Mauro Bolognini who, at least entertainment-wise, has made this item a strangely expert commodity, vastly amusing on the surface and pregnant with thought beneath. His elegant handling of action and actors confirm his young talent.

Laurent Terzieff and Anna Maria Ferrero stand out in a large and capable cast, with Jean Claude Brialy, Antonella Lualdi and Elsa Martinelli also performing ably. Mylene Demongeot is decorative in a brief bit while Rosanna Schiaffino appears ill at ease in her stint.

Armando Nannuzzi's lensing is another plus factor in a top-bracket production effort, with Piero Piccioni's music another valuable contribution. Questionable as its moral content may appear to its critics, "La Notte Brava" remains one of the best Italian productions of the year. *Hawk.*

The Shakedown
(BRITISH)

Modest-budget crime meller with some deft writing and good acting. Situations predictable but timely in showing the changes in Britain's prostie situation.

London, Jan. 19.

Rank release of an Alliance (Norman Williams) production. Stars Terence Morgan, Hazel Court, Robert Beatty; features Donald Pleasance, Bill Owen, Harry H. Corbett. Directed by John Lemont. Original story and screenplay, Leigh Vance, John Lemont; editor, Bernard Gribble; camera, Brendan J. Stafford; music, Phil Green. Previewed at Leicester Square Theatre, London. Running time, **92 MINS**

Augie Cortona .... Terence Morgan
Mildred Hyde .... Hazel Court
Jessel .... Donald Pleasance
Spettigue .... Bill Owen
Jarvis .... Robert Beatty
Gollar .... Harry H. Corbett
Zena .... Gene Anderson
George .... Eddie Byrne
Arnold .... John Salew
Miss Firbank .... Georgina Cookson
Miss Ogilvie .... Joan Maythorne
Nadia .... Sheila Buxton
Grace .... Dorinda Stevens
Skt. Kershaw .... Jack Lambert
1st Thug .... Larry Burns
2d Thug .... Laurence Taylor
3d Thug .... Jack Taylor
Pinza .... Charles Lamb
Sylvia .... Linda Castle
Photo Model .... Patty Dalton
Barman .... Arthur Lovegrove
Fat Drinker .... Paul Whitsun Jones
Estate Agent .... Timothy Bateson

The makers of "The Shakedown" have jumped nimbly on the topical bandwagon of undercover vice now that London's prosties have been driven off the streets. The result's a fairly tough, competently-made picture which will rely on its shock theme for b.o. impact but is not deliberately sensational. In America, it should prove a useful dualer. In Britain this should stand has an "X" tag which means its taboo for cinemagoers under the age of 16.

Leigh Vance and John Lemont, who also directs, have turned out a briskly written screenplay, but it's fairly straightforward and predictable, and could have used a few surprise twists. The yarn concerns a vicious young vice king who serves a stretch in the cooler, and comes out determined to pick up where he left off.

But he finds that his old contacts no longer want to know, that the prosties have gone under cover and that an old associate now rules the prostitution roost. He thinks up a new angle. He uses a model school and photographic studio as a front and in the evenings uses the premises for amateur photographers who want to photograph call-girls pornographically. With that setup, blackmail is able to add caviar to his bread-and-butter.

That is one story line and the other, intermingled, is the gang warfare between him and his rival. Lemont has directed crisply, though the story falls by the wayside from time to time. At least one character who is important at the beginning becomes unwisely expendable and is tossed away carelessly. London and Scotland Yard scenes are authentic and Philip Green has provided a harsh but effective musical score which helps the atmosphere.

With no major star names, the producer has wisely packed the film with first-rate character actors. The cast helps to keep the film moving even through its occasional soggy patches. Terence Morgan gives a vivid portrayal of suave evil, cloaked with spurious charm, as the chief racketeer. He's matched with a really topflight study by Harry H. Corbett as the sinister gorilla leading the rival mob. Hazel Court, now making a considerable name for herself in America, reveals again how much she has been wasted here with some neat thesping as a policewoman who joins Morgan's model class and helps to trap him. Robert Beatty and Jack Lambert are plausible and sympathetic Scotland Yard dicks while Bill Owen is usefully employed.

The best performance comes from Donald Pleasence as the down-and-out alcoholic photographer who is unknowlingly used by Morgan as a front. It's a subtle and telling piece of work, and it's a weakness of the film that two thirds of the way through he disappears. Somehow, somewhere, he should have been brought into the closing sequences and helped in unmasking of the vice racketeer. Among several other sound performances are those by John Salew, as the victim of Morgan's blackmailing; Gene Anderson, a bewildered tart; Eddie Byrne, as a bartender, and Dorinda Stevens and Linda Castle.

A night club sequence introduces Sheil Buxton, a known tv thrush overhere, whose only reason for existence in the film is to plug the title song. This is a pretty feeble ditty and it is difficult to see how a song called "The Shakedown" (colloquialism for blackmail) can masquerade as love serenade. *Rich.*

Visit to a Small Planet

Jerry Lewis as a spacenik. Script weaknesses but b.o. prospects okay.

Paramount release of Hal Wallis production. Stars Jerry Lewis; costars Joan Blackman, Earl Holliman, Fred Clark. Directed by Norman Taurog. Screenplay, Edmund Beloin and Henry Garson, based on the play by Gore Vidal; camera, Loyal Griggs; editor, Frank Bracht, music, Leigh Harline. Previewed at the Loyola Theatre, Jan. 15, '60. Running time, **85 MINS.**

Kreton .... Jerry Lewis
Ellen .... Joan Blackman
Conrad .... Earl Holliman
Major Roger Spelding .... Fred Clark
Delton .... John Williams
George Abercrombie .... Jerome Cowan
Bob Mayberry .... Gale Gordon
Rheba Spelding .... Lee Patrick
Desdemona .... Barbara Lawson

Paramount's "Visit to a Small Planet," a watered-down film version of Broadway romp by Gore Vidal, wraps up the 10-year association of producer Hal Wallis and Jerry Lewis. During that decade the pair has come up with 13 straight winners, and "Visit" should make it a sweep.

The play, which starred Cyril Ritchard as the frisky spaceman, has been altered for Lewis. But writers Edmund Beloin and Henry Carson, or whoever dictated the changes, gave neither the screenplay nor the star a fair shake. Vidal's original has a good deal of thoughtful commentary on the stupidity of war, hidden adeptly behind a facade of farce. The picture tries, with only moderate success, to replace that commentary and, indeed, the core of the play with a poor stab at romance.

As Kreton, the spaceman from X-47 who goes AWOL to Earth, Lewis keeps the farce moving within the limits of the weakened story. But he's up to much more, showing in rare spots that he can be as vigorous as he is carefree. Lewis indicates that, if given a meaty comedy role to sink his teeth into, he'd come up with a strong, sure bite. Still, as Jerry Lewis the clown, he turns in a good, laugh-evoking performance. And director Norman Taurog fires up a rocket of comedy through the hero's ability to make cars fly, cameras pop and animals talk.

The film opens somewhere in the clouds, with Kreton playing the Peck's Bad Boy of extra-galactic space. He hops to Earth in a flying saucer to observe all that is human and winds up in the home of a befuddled television commentator who has just reported to America that "Flying saucers? There just ain't no sech animal."

Kreton, whose planetary existence is devoid of pain and sex, has a field day on Earth, peeking in on the love-making of the commentator's daughter and her harebrained boyfriend. In fact, he becomes so absorbed with it all, his space leader, looking down from above, lifts his powers and lets him be human for a spell. At that point, Kreton finds what pain and love and jealousy are all about, realizes how mixed up Earth really is and hops aboard a return flying saucer without a fuss.

In support of Lewis, Joan Blackman, as the daughter, makes a lovable, engaging female. Earl Holliman, as her boyfriend, adeptly projects his light mentality, and Fred Clark, as the commentator, is very good in an alternately settled and upset role. Rounding out the cast in top performances are John Williams as the space leader, Gale Gordon as an anxious Civil Defense watcher, Lee Patrick as the commentator's wife and Jerome Cowan as a Madison Avenue executive. In a beatnik sequence, which finds the beat generation looking its kookiest best, Barbara Lawson dances up a storm with Lewis.

Wallis' production-script expected—is technically excellent, particularly Loyal Griggs' black-and-white photography, aided by John P. Fulton's special effects and Farciot Edouart's process work. Top benefits are art direction by Hal Pereira and Walter Tyler, set decoration by Sam Comer and Arthur Krams, editing by Frank Bracht, sound by Gene Merritt and Charles Grenzbach and special music by Leigh Harline. *Ron.*

Signe Arsene Lupin
(Signed Arsene Lupin)
(FRENCH)

Paris, Jan. 26.

Gaumont release of Chavane-SNEG-Lambor-Costellazione production. Stars Robert Lamoureux; features Alida Valli, Yves Robert, Roger Dumas, Michel Etcheverry, Gisele Grandpre, Jacques Dufilho. Directed by Yves Robert. Screenplay, J. P. Rappeneau; camera, Maurice Barry; editor, G. Natot. At George V, Paris. Running time, **100 MINS.**

Arsene Lupin .... Robert Lamoureux
Aurelia .... Alida Valli
Laballu .... Yves Robert
Isidore .... Roger Dumas
Collector .... Michel Etcheverry
Friend .... Gisele Grandpre
Albert .... Jacques Dufilho

This tale is the second one featuring the early 1920's gentleman burglar, Arsene Lupin. Pic is refreshingly told but leisurely paced. It looks in for good biz here with foreign playoff possibilities on its general entertainment values. Conventional aspects do not make this arty house material.

Here Lupin gets out of the army after the first World War and is soon involved in trying to track down a 15th Century treasure with indications that it's hidden in a trio of Flemish miniature paintings. He is at odds with a femme looker, also trying to get the treasure. Between kisses and bouts, Lupin outsmarts her.

Though the denouement is never in doubt, this sustains interest thanks to the suave playing of Robert Lamoureux, as the wily Lupin and a good cast. Fine technical aspects and production dress also enhance this above average commercial entry. *Mosk.*

Guns of the Timberland
(COLOR)

Okay action drama. Alan Ladd for b.o., with help from teenage fave Frankie Avalon.

Hollywood, Jan. 26.

Warner Bros release of a Jaguar Production. Stars Alan Ladd, Jeanne Crain, Gilbert Roland; introducing Frankie Avalon; also starring Lyle Bettger, Noah Beery. Produced by Aaron Spelling. Directed by Robert D. Webb. Screenplay by Joseph Petracca and Spelling, based on the novel by Louis L'Amour; camera, John Seitz; editor, Tom McAdoo; music, David Buttolph. Previewed at the Hollywood Paramount Theatre, Jan. 26, '60. Running time **91 MINS.**

Jim Hadley .... Alan Ladd
Laura Riley .... Jeanne Crain
Monty Welker .... Gilbert Roland
Bert Harvey .... Frankie Avalon
Clay Bell .... Lyle Bettger
Blackie .... Noah Beery
Aunt Sarah .... Verna Felton
Jane Peterson .... Alana Ladd
Sheriff Taylor .... Regis Toomey
Vince .... Johnny Seven
Amos Stearnes .... George Selk
Bill Burroughs .... Paul E. Burns
Logger .... Henry Kulky

When Alan Ladd leads his loggers into the Great Northwest for "Guns of the Timberland," the ground becomes covered with more corn than sawdust. The concept was fine, pitting woodman against rancher, but the execution

leaves much to be desired. Yet this Warner release should do well in action market with an added boost from teenagers via the screen presence of singing idol Frankie Avalon in his first role.

There are elements in the Jaguar Production that simply don't fit. The first kiss between Ladd and his costar, Jeanne Crain, is both unfounded and embarrassing. There's a departure from reality when Avalon sings in the midst of a meadow to full orchestral accompaniment. And, within the 1895 setting, Avalon warbles a tune that sounds suspiciously like rock-'n'-roll.

On the plus side, the Joseph Petracca-Aaron Spelling screenplay holds together well enough to make the characters sufficiently interesting to care about. The conflict between the lumbermen, who want to cut down the trees, and the ranchers, who fear their watershed will be ruined, is motivated, and it plays well. Director Robert D. Webb was a little broad with emotions, but he made the most of the action sequences, creating some good fight footage and a realistic forest fire.

As taken from the novel by Louis L'Amour, "Guns of the Timberland" has Ladd and Gilbert Roland partners in a logging concern which has a government contract to cut down the trees on mountains surrounding a ranching valley. Led by Miss Crain, who owns a healthy spread, the ranchers put up a good fight. Ladd fights legally, but Roland is all for violence, and when Avalon, a friendly member of the ranching side, is hurt seriously, Ladd gives in and removes his men. By this time, of course, he and Miss Crain have fallen in love, and she boards the logging train with him.

Ladd has looked better, and he's had better roles than this one. Roland makes a strong he-man, doing as much with the part as possible. Miss Crain comes across best, both in looks and characterization. For his first dramatic performance, Avalon turns in some respectable work. Verna Felton, in one of her few screen roles since tv's "December Bride," is very good, with fine support from Lyle Bettger, Noah Beery, Regis Toomey, Johnny Seven and Ladd's pretty 16-year-old daughter Alana.

Spelling produced "Guns," which has good Technicolor lensing by John Seitz. Creditable are Tom McAdoo's editing, Francis M. Stahl's sound, John Beckman's art direction and David Buttolph's music. A special nod goes to makeup supervisor Gordon Bau.

Songs include "Gee Whizz Whillikens Golly Gee" and "The Faithful Kind" by Mack David and Jerry Livingston and "Cry Timber" by Sy Miller. The David-Livingston tunes are fine, even if they are used poorly. Miller's song at least fits. *Ron.*

Pantalaskas
(FRENCH)

Paris, Jan. 26.

Contact release of Pavox-Alter films production. Features Carl Studer, Albert Remy, Jacques Marin, Bernard Lajarrige, Ana-Maria Cassan, R. J. Chauffard, Hubert Deschamps. Directed by Paul Paviot. Screenplay, Paviot, Jacques-Laurent Bost from novel by Rene Masson; camera, L. H. Burel; editor, F. Grubert. Previewed in Paris. Running time, 90 MINS.

Pantalaskas .... Carl Studer
Policeman .... Jacques Remy
Hotel Owner .... Jacques Marin
Schoolteacher.........Bernard Lajarrige
Streetwalker...........Ana-Maria Cassan
Brigadier .... Hubert Deschamps

Pic attempts an ambitious theme about man's need to be humane and help his fellowman via three ordinary citizens saddled with a Lithuanian who cannot speak French and who wants to commit suicide. It is an all night trek thorough Paris as they try to find someone who speaks the language.

Pic slavishly follows the wanderings but the director, Paul Paviot, has not been able to give it a depth or breadth. Result is that the vehicle tends to lag and does not quite make its point. However, its offbeat theme and well shot aspects of an impoverished Paris and everyday people could slant this for art chances.

Each character is clearly etched but their loyalties, fatigue and eventual awakening to a human need to help each other is implicit in the dialog rather than the progression.

Result is that the film plods somewhat. Acting too is uneven. Carl Studer, a Yank, is clay-like as the Lithuanian. Others are okay but this voyage to understanding thorough the night misses the insight and revelation to make it an offbeater with a noble purpose. *Mosk.*

Two-Way Stretch
(BRITISH)

Crazy prison farce with Peter Sellers again leading a first-class supporting cast in yocks; good laughter booking for all types of audience.

London, Jan. 26.

British Lion release of a George and Alfred Black (M. Smedley Aston) production. Stars Peter Sellers, Wilfrid Hyde White. Directed by Robert Day. Story and screenplay by John Warren and Len Heath; additional dialog, Alan Hackney; camera, Geoffrey Faithfull; editor, Bert Rule; music, Ken Jones. Previewed at Studio One, London. Running time, 87 MINS.

Dodger Lane .... Peter Sellers
"Rev" Basil Fowler..Wilfrid Hyde White
Jelly Knight .... David Lodge
Lennie Price .... Bernard Cribbins
Prison Governor .... Maurice Denham
Sydney Crout .... Lionel Jeffries
Mrs. Price .... Irene Handl
Ethel .... Liz Fraser
Warder Jenkins.....George Woodthorpe
Warder George........Cyril Chamberlain
Warder Charlie .... Edwin Brown
The Lawyer .... John Glyn-Jones
Miss Pringle .... Beryl Reid
Miss Meakin .... Noel Hood
Miss Prescott .... Myrette Morvern
Colonel Arkwright......Thorley Walters
Rev. Butterworth..........Walter Hudd
Dustman .... Joe Gibbons
The Captain .... John Wood
Police Supt. .... Robert James
Jones .... Mario Fabrizi

Peter Sellers, one of Britain's hottest drawing cards, gives another of his deft, very funny performances in "Two-Way Stretch." In this goofy jail comedy he is supported by many of the character actors who expertly help to make this kind of comedy-farce currently indigenous to British production; and with highly profitable results. In the U. K. this will be a certain winner but it should also click with most audiences in the U. S. Few will fail to respond to the whacky situations and lively dialog.

The thin story line is padded with many gag situations which are telegraphed with the regular predictability, but invariably with yock-raising results. Story and screenplay, by John Warren and Len Heath, are jerky and contain several holes. This is obviously due to cutting, made necessary by scenes and ideas building up on the set. But since the objective is laughter it must be acclaimed a success.

This concerns a free-and-easy prison run by a governor who is more interested in gardening than discipline. The rigors of rockbreaking are not for his prisoners. Instead, there are rehabilitation classes in fretwork, carpentry, gardening, pottery and so on. Occupying a cell, which is far more like a luxury bed-sitting room, are three partners in crime—Sellers, David Lodge and Bernard Cribbins. They have the prison completely sewn up with the amiable assistance of easygoing wardens.

Posing as a clergyman, an outside partner arrives with a scheme for stealing $5,000,000 in diamonds. It needs the trio to break jail the night before their release, pull off the job, return to prison with their loot, and next morning walk out free men and with a perfect alibi. The arrival of a tough new chief warden frustrates their plans.

Ramifications of these operations are too complicated and implausible for serious discussion. They involve hefty slapstick and hilarious ingenuity, backed by racy dialog that fits the characters excellently. Much of the dialog was supplied by Alan Hackney and, almost certainly, by Sellers himself. Success of this film depends largely on the actors and Robert Day's brisk direction. Sellers has himself a ball as the leader of the crafty trio of crooks while Lodge and Cribbins make perfectly contrasted partners.

Wilfrid Hyde White, as Soapy, the crook who poses as a parson, is his usual, bland self and is particularly funny when he is directing the snatch operation with all the detail of an Army maneuver. Irene Handl, as Cribbins' mother, and Liz Frazer, as Sellers' blonde, shapely girl friend, also have many amusing opportunities.

A long list of tried, handpicked performers chip in when required, but among the standout performances are those of Maurice Denham, as the clottish, benevolent governor; George Woodthorpe as an amiable warden and Lionel Jeffries, as his complete opposite, a tough, vicious chief warden, who is in constant battle with the Sellers' gang.

Opening of the pic is merely to set the atmosphere of the jail and characters, and is perhaps overlong. Nevertheless, it contributes largely to the genial atmosphere which barely lets up throughout. The artwork and lensing is okay. There is more facetiousness than wit in "Two-Way Stretch" for it is an old blend of comedy and farce. But the enthusiastic and energetic search for yocks comes off brightly and this is recommended for anyone seeking an evening of escapist relaxation. *Rich.*

La Verte Moisson
(Green Harvest)
(FRENCH)

Paris, Jan. 26.

Gaumont release of Caravelle production. Features Claude Brasseur, Jacques Perrin, Francis Lemonnier, Dany Saval. Directed by Francois Villiers. Screenplay, Rene Forlani, Jean-Pierre Aumont, Villiers; camera, Paul Soulignac; editor, Edouard Berne. At George V, Paris. Running time, 95 MINS.

Robert .... Claude Brasseur
Olivier .... Jacques Perrin
Jean-Louis .... Francis Lemonnier
Dany .... Dany Saval

This film concerns a group of teenagers involved in a resistance movement of their own during the Occupation of the last World War. It draws the line sharply. The Germans are all brutal and the French youths all good except for a few gradations of character which do not matter when the chips are down. This shapes a clean-cut, well-done actioner with foreign changes indicated but sans the offbeat, deeper aspects for arty theatre chances.

The group begins their activities as a game and then get serious when they kill a German soldier to get arms to free a resistance man. An ironic twist has them picked up and tortured and finally with two taking the rap for the others. Acting is excellent. Director Francois Villiers has given this good visual effects and punched up the action scenes. If conventional, this keeps up interest throughout. It is aided by good production polish and technical gloss. *Mosk.*

Poedino
(The Duel)
(RUSSIAN)

Paris, Jan. 26.

Mosfilm production and release. With Irina Skobtseva, Youri Pouzirev, Andre Popov, Mikhail Nasanov. Directed by Vladimir Petrov. Screenplay, Petrov from story by Alexandre Kounrine; camera, I. Kalsati; editor, C. Veriokova. At Pagode, Paris. Running time, 95 MINS.

Chorotchka .... Irina Skobtseva
Romachov .... Youri Pouzirev
Nazansky .... Andrei Popov
Nilolaiev .... Mikhail Nasnaov

This is a tale of a military garrison in a small Russian town back in 1904. It depicts the empty, dreary military life. The officers are shown reacting against the dullness via drunken brawls and so-called duels of honor. Into this is woven the love of a young officer for another's wife which ends in tragedy via a duel.

Pic is somewhat academic since it employs commentary to tell its tale. It is also too slanted to show the suffocating atmosphere of Czarist times. But it has some visual force and solid characterizations.

The lensing resembles old prints and is helpful in creating the mood. The acting is good if somewhat too soulful for western tastes. This appears only for some arty house chances abroad because its style and overdone satire and drama would not fit in regular runs. Technical credits are fine. *Mosk.*

La Fievrè Monte A El Pao
(The Fever Rises in El Pao)
(FRENCH-MEXICAN)

Paris, Jan. 26.

Corona release of Groupe Des Quatre-CICC-Filmex production. Stars Gerard Philipe, Maria Felix; features Jean Servais. Directed by Luis Bunuel. Screenplay, Louis Sapin, Bunuel from novel by Henri Castillou; camera, Gabriel Figueroa; editor, James Cuenet. Previewed in Paris. Running time, 97 MINS.

Vasquez .... Gerard Philipe
Agnes .... Maria Felix
Alexandre .... Jean Servais

Pic is an offbeat look at the personal dramas behind a Latin American revolution. These happenings are not too well linked to the upheavals to make this somewhat overly melodramatic. It has some deft erotic gambits and looks mainly a Spanish lingo or exploitation entry abroad.

On an island off the coast of a Latino country, which is run by a strong man, an assassination has the governor's secretary put in charge. This fellow, who has vague liberal leanings, wins the murdered man's wife. They find themselves pitted against the new sadis-

tic governor who also covets the beauteous woman. Latter is played with some fire and some deftly done undressing scenes by Maria Felix.

Director Luis Bunuel has given this a rigorous visual look but the involved tale rarely makes its theme clear. Gerard Philipe is listless as the vacillating hero but Jean Servais manages to give bite to his role as the treacherous governor. Technical qualities are fine.

Mosk.

Malaga
(Moment of Danger)
(BRITISH)

Plodding chase drama that misfires despite efforts of Trevor Howard and Dorothy Dandridge; two mixed-up ideas in script dent b.o. prospects.

London, Jan. 26.

Warner-Pathe release of a Cavalcade Films (Thomas Clyde) production (in association with Douglas Fairbanks Ltd.). Stars Trevor Howard, Dorothy Dandridge, Edmund Purdom. Directed by Laslo Benedek. Screenplay by David Osborn, Donald Ogden Stewart, from Donald MacKenzie's novel; camera, Desmond Dickinson; editor, Gerald Turney-Smith; music, Matyas Seiber. At Warner Theatre, London. Running time, 95 MINS.

John Bain	Trevor Howard
Gianna	Dorothy Dandridge
Peter Curran	Edmund Purdom
Inspector Farrell	Michael Hordern
Montaya	Paul Stassino
Cecil	John Bailey
Shapley	Alfred Burke
Pawnbroker	Peter Illing
Corrigan	Barry Keegan
Airport Guard	Brian Worth
Spanish Woman	Thelma d'Aguiar
Gigolo	Neville Becker
Sir John Middleburgh	Martin Boddey
Waiter	Peter Elliott
Lady Middleburgh	Helen Goss

It's remarkable that a director of the calibre of Laslo Benedek should become involved in such a disappointing picture as "Malaga." "Malaga," incidentally, is the U.S. name for the film. It's meaningless except that Malaga is where some of the action takes place in Spain. Not that the original title, "Moment of Danger," means much. Just a cliche, like so much of a film which will satisfy only easygoing patrons and will rely very much on the names of its three stars, Trevor Howard, Dorothy Dandridge and Edmund Purdom, to whip up activity at the wickets.

Film falls down mainly because it cannot make up its mind whether it's a study of the relationship of two interesting people or a straightforward crime-chase yarn. Director Benedek seems more interested in the Freud stuff. Be that as it may, the crime story line keeps on obtruding without ever whipping up a lather of excitement.

Pic starts off splendidly. For around 15 absorbing minutes, two crooks, Howard and Purdom, pull off an audacious jewel robbery. Neither speaks. Only a couple or three lines of irrelevant dialog from the owners of the robbed house are allowed to break the tense silence. It seemed like this could be a winner.

The plot then starts and everybody starts yapping with unrewarding results. Howard, an embittered locksmith with a jail record, has been conned into rocks-robbery by Purdom, a suave felon who unscrupulously doublecrosses Howard and the girl with whom he's living (Dorothy Dandridge). Howard and Miss Dandridge, a persistent hanger-on, set off for Spain to catch up with Purdom. It takes too long to catch Purdom.

By then Howard and Miss Dandridge are thataway about each other, though at first the deadpan Howard cannot quite forgive the fact that Miss Dandridge sells her sinuous body in Madrid in order to raise funds.

Crime element in this in unbelievably unexciting. Gradual development of the relationship between the rather bored-looking Howard and the dusky Miss Dandridge offers greater hope, but is bogged down by drab dialog. Not even the fact that they inocuously share a bedroom through their tedious venture across Spain sparks hardly a glimmer of interest. Here is a clear case of two separate ideas warring, and both losing out.

Casting of Howard and Purdom in the same film is ridiculous. It's like matching a heavyweight against a flyweight. With almost boring ease Howard steals every scene from Purdom. Miss Dandridge tries hard but is beaten by the script. The color problem is never raised and there's no reason why it should be. Nobody else gets a look in, except that Michael Hordern has one short, well-executed scene as a police inspector. Camerawork and art direction are adequate, but rarely has Spain's exciting background been tossed away so tritely.

This is a sad misfire of a film. Apart from a brilliant opening, there are only a couple of scenes which defeat torpor. Both of these gainfully employ Howard and Miss Dandridge and involve them in some discussion of their past and future hopes. But they are not enough even for such talented thesps.

Rich.

Yo, Pecador
(I, Sinner)
(MEXICAN-COLOR)

Mexico City, Jan. 26.

Peliculas Nacionales release of a Brooks production. Stars Libertad Lamarque, Pedro Armendariz, Christiane Martel, Pedro Geraldo; features Sara Garcia, Andres Soler, Camela Rey, Nadia Haro Oliva, Enrique Rambal, Manola Saavedra and Xavier Gomez. Directed by Alfonso C. Blake. Screenplay, Eduardo Enrique Rios, based on autobiography of Friar Jose Fco. de Guadalupe Mojica, of Franciscan Order; camera, Jack Draper. Preemed day-date in five first-run theatres, Mexico City, Mexico.

Producer Oscar Brooks has turned out a good Mexican film with religious overtones but without phoney, hackneyed moralizing nor any apologetics for the actions of persons presented in the story. Pic looks like a gold mine for its producers. Pedro Geraldo, making his film debut, is excellent in the role of Jose Mojica, entertainer turned Franciscan friar. Added to which, his likeness to the real life Mojica is striking.

Director Blake has shown considerable skill and firmness in handling the theme, without letting it become maudlin or offend the actual religious position of the subject of the film biog.

There is no pulling of punches in the development of the life of Friar Mojica, and the steps that lead to his ultimate forswearing the world to go into the monastery.

This is the story of an arrogant, intemperate personality, as marked by Mojica's youth, when he was the public's darling.

But in this life, there eventually dawns a desire to seek something more than a superficial life. Fostered by a growing faith, there is a regeneration of the man pointed up.

Geraldo gives realism to his interpretation in all its phases. Libertad Lamarque is excellent as the mother and Pedro Armendariz as well as the others contribute in recreating personalities touched by Mojica.

Armendariz, Lamarque and Martel are billed as stars for exploitation purposes, but it is young Pedro Geraldo who wins the honors in this one for a very human performance. The Raul Lavista score adds to the film's worth as does Jack Drayer's photography.

Emil.

Drunken Angel
(JAPANESE)

Brandon Films release of Toho Co. (Sojiro Motoki) production. Stars Toshiro Mifune, Takashi Shimura, Reizaburo Yamamoto. Directed by Akira Kurosawa. Screenplay, Keinosuke Uegusa and Akira Kurosawa; camera, Takeo Ito; music, Fumio Hayasaka. At Little Carnegie Theatre, N.Y., Jan. 8, '60. Running time, 102 MINS.

Matsunaga	Toshiro Mifune
Dr. Sanada	Takashi Shimura
Okada	Reizaburo Yamamoto
Nanse	Michiyo Kogure
Miyo	Chieko Nakakita
Gin	Horiko Sengoku
Old Maid Servant	Choko Iida

"Drunken Angel," made by director Akira Kurosawa in 1948 (several years before he was acclaimed this side for "Roshomon"), is certainly one of the most effective and searching views of contemporary Japanese life to reach these shores. Picture is one of the nine which Brandon Films has packaged for distribution in the States.

In technique and style, "Angel" would seem to owe a lot to some of the great neo-realist films which came out of post war Italy. The sharp eye of the camera delights in catching the details of squalor, of oppressive heat and creeping disease, but the details are carefully selected and integrated to contribute to the single overall theme, which is one of human nobility in a chaotic, amoral world.

Story concerns an alcoholic doctor who runs a shabby little clinic in a big city-slum and his attempts to save the life of a young hood who is dying of TB. Doctor sees his own lost youth in the younger man and tries desperately to save him. It's a lost battle from the start, but director Kurosawa seems to be saying that the attempt, and not necessarily the conclusion, is the important thing.

Film is beautifully acted by Toshiro Mifune and Takashi Shimura (both of whom starred in "Roshomon") as, respectively, hoodlum and doctor. Story moves swiftly in a series of hard-hitting scenes which vividly delineate a milieu that would have been God-forsaken without the noble old doctor.

"Drunken Angel" deserves serious consideration by art houses in search of truly significant cinema work. Photography and music are first rate. English subtitles are adequate.

Anby.

Un Maledetto Imbroglio
(An Ugly Mess)
(ITALIAN)

Rome, Jan. 26.

Cineriz release of a RIAMA (Giuseppe Amato) Production. Stars Pietro Germi; features Claudia Cardinale, Franco Fabrizi, Cristina Gajoni, Claudio Gora, Eleonora Rossi Drago, Saro Urzi, Gianni Musy. Directed by Pietro Germi. Screenplay, Germi, Alfredo Giannetti, Ennio DeConcini, from a novel by C. E. Gadda; camera, Leonida Barboni; music, Carlo Rustichelli, editor, Roberto Cinquini. Previewed in Rome. Running time, 97 MINS.

Inspector Ingravallo	Pietro Germi
Liliana Banducci	Eleonora Rossi Drago
Assuntina	Claudia Cardinale
Virginia	Cristina Gajoni
Remo Banducci	Claudio Gora
Saro	Saro Urzi
Valdarena	Franco Fabrizi

One of the most satisfying releases of the year, this pic combines fine entertainment facets with top quality for a parlay which should please both spectators and critics. Rates fine home-market chances and looks like a good export bet.

Detective story plot tells how Inspector Ingravallo solves a puzzling murder case. But it's much more than a mere crime film, with the puzzle only an excuse (though a good and suspenseful one in its own right) for a fascinating study of people and mores. Acting, starting with a first-rate supporting effort by Claudio Gora as the widower of the murder victim, is excellent. Many fine cameos are contributed by a large cast.

Proceedings, however, are dominated by actor-director Pietro Germi in one of his finest performances as the very human police inspector who often lets personal likes and dislikes becloud his vision and judgment of the case. Throughout, also, is the director's fine taste for human relationships and he unintellectualized everyday existence which gives the pic a warm, believable trueness, and an additional dimension rarely found in films of its kind.

It is also coincidentally the first successful crime picture ever made in this country. Direction and editing are tight, lensing by Leonida Barboni excellent, music (Carlo Rustichelli) catching and production values highly satisfactory.

Hawk.

Menschen Im Hotel
(Grand Hotel)
(GERMAN)

Berlin, Jan. 26.

Gloria release of CCC production. Stars O. W. Fischer, Michele Morgan, Heinz Ruehmann, Sonja Ziemann, Gert Froebe. Directed by Gottfried Reinhardt. Screenplay by Hans Jacoby and Ladislaus Fodor, after novel by Vicki Baum; camera, Goeran Strindberg; music, Hans Martin Majewski; settings, Rolf Zehetbauer and Gottfried Will; editor, Kurt Zeunert. At Marmorhaus, Berlin. Running time, 106 MINS.

Baron von Gaigern	O. W. Fischer
Grusinskaja	Michele Morgan
Kringelein	Heinz Ruehmann
Flaemmchen	Sonja Ziemann
Preysing	Gert Froebe
Driver Max	Wolfgang Wahl
Suzanne	Dorothea Wieck

Twentyeight years ago, Metro did "Grand Hotel" which was a boxoffice hit. This updated German screen version of Vicki Baum's successful multi-character yarn, will hardly walk off with many laurels. But it may pay off commercially because of its star-studded cast headed by O. W. Fischer and France's Michele Morgan, latter in the famous Greta Garbo role.

The characters in this CCC production have remained very much the same, ditto their interlocking stories in a German hotel. But any similarity with the Hollywood classic stops there. While the old film did wonders for its stars, the new one disappoints with most of its acting, with the exception of Gert Froebe, as Preysing, the role Wallace Beery played once. At least his scenes ring true.

This can't be said of the other performers—partly a fault of the second-rate dialog sequences furnished by the script, but chiefly it's the fault of Gottfried Reinhardt's little adroit direction.

Reinhardt, incidentally, took over the directorial assignment for Curtis Bernhardt when the latter had to resign because of a heart ailment.

Reinhardt shows little directorial

imagination. And many of the actors reflect it, particularly O. W. Fischer whose portrayal of Baron von Gaigern, the chain-smoking, irresistable charmer and hotel thief, is a rare mixture of old-fashioned overacting, cliches and routine emotions. Also Miss Morgan isn't very convincing. She may be regarded as a better actress than Greta Garbo but she can't make one forget the latter's performance.

Reinhardt added what he thinks is sex to the plot. But the scene in which Sonja Ziemann, the stenographer, is "bought" by Froebe borders on the tasteless. Heinz Ruehmann, as the ailing Kringelein, takes care of some comedy relief, often inadequate in this.

In toto, this "Grand Hotel" could have been a truly cosmopolitan picture with sterling performances. A secondary script and little imaginative direction made it a rather dull picture. Compliments go only for its technical side.   *Hans.*

Les Yeux de L'Amour
(The Eyes of Love)
(FRENCH)
Paris, Jan. 26:
Pathe release of Pomereu-Borel Films production. Stars Danielle Darrieux, Jean-Claude Brialy; features Francoise Rosay, Bernard Blier, Eva Damien. Directed by Denys De La Patelliere. Screenplay, Roland Laudenbach, Michel Audiard from a story by Jacques Antoine; camera, Pierre Petit; editor, Georges Alepee. At Paris, Paris. Running time, 100 MINS.
Jeanne .... Danielle Darrieux
Pierre .... Jean-Claude Brialy
Jacques .... Bernard Blier
Mother .... Francoise Rosay
Denise .... Eva Damien

Novelettish pic is primarily a distaffer because of its tale about a love affair between a 24-year-old blind boy and a middle-aged spinster during the last war. This melodrama is talky, and emerges mainly for local use with foreign chances only for specialized spotting.

Escaping from the Germans, the blind boy is housed by a spinster in her home. Love blossoms but is almost ruined by a harridan mother who has convinced the daughter she is ugly. Actually the daughter is played by Danielle Darrieux, who still looks too good to believe that she is a hopeless mess. An eye operation leads to her fleeing but final meeting with the boy again for a happy clinch.

Director Denys De La Patelliere has played this slowly and allowed the literary dialog to take precedence over movement and visual display. Miss Darrieux plays this for all out drama and slightly overdoes her role. Jean-Claude Brialy also overplays the boy. Remainder of the cast is okay except for apparent overacting by Francoise Rosay as the selfish mother. Technical credits are par.   *Mosk.*

Die Bruecke
(The Bridge)
(GERMAN)
Berlin, Jan. 26.
Deutsche Film Hansa (DFH) release of Fono (Hermann Schwerin) production. Directed by Bernhard Wicki. Screenplay, Michael Mansfeld and Karl-Wilhelm Vivier, after novel of same name by Manfred Gregor; camera, Gerd von Bonin; editor, C. O. Bartning. At Zoo Palast, Berlin. Running time, 106 MINS.
Hans Scholten .... Volker Bonnet
Mutz .... Fritz Wepper
Forst .... Michael Hinz
Borchert .... Frank Glaubrecht
Horber .... Karl Michael Balzer
Hager .... Volker Lechtenbrink
Bernhard .... Guenther Hoffmann
Franziska .... Cordula Trantow
Heilmann .... Guenther Pfitzmann

One of the most remarkable Ger-

man pictures in many months if not in many years. This war film may be compared in many details, particularly its anti-war message and compromiseless realism, with "All Quiet On Western Front." It's the most hard-hitting, and authentic German war pic turned out since 1945.

Production has been directed by Swiss-born actor Bernhard Wicki, and it's his first directorial job on a feature film. And an outstanding one.

Although "Bridge" has no marquee names, it may emerge as a stout moneymaker in this country. Excellent reviews, word-of-mouth, the rating of "particularly valuable" (which means considerable tax relief) and the fact that it's been recommended by numerous domestic institutions will be a big help at the boxoffice. Pic has real foreign chances, too. Incidentally, it's going to participate in the upcoming Oscar derby.

Story concerns seven 16-year old German high school boys who have to join the army during the last war (it's April, 1945). A well meaning officer wants them to escape the last phase of the war. He gives them a guarding job on a strategically unimportant bridge.

A grim twist of fate brings American tanks, not expected to show up here, across this bridge. The young boys, still more children than soldiers, taught to obey their "Fuehrer" with all their hearts, do the senseless thing—they defend this bridge to the utmost. Result is that one after the other is killed Only one escapes.

Wicki's handling of the young players is excellent. He also shows much feeling for realistic atmosphere and in the fight sequences. A special word of praise goes to cameraman, Gerd von Bonin. Also other technical credits are fine. In all, a very impressive German film, and the surprise hit of the season.   *Hans.*

Le Chemin des Ecoliers
(Students' Road)
(FRENCH)
Paris, Jan. 26.
Gaumont release of Franco London-SPCE-Mondex-Tempo-Zebra Film production. Stars Francoise Arnoul, Bourvil, Lino Ventura, Alain Delon; features Jean-Claude Brialy, Pierre Mondy, Madeleine Lebeau, Sandra Milo. Directed by Michel Boisrond. Screenplay, Jean Aurenche, Pierre Bost from novel by Marcel Ayme; camera, Christian Matras; editor, Louisette Taverna. At Am-Bassade-Gaumont, Paris. Running time, 85 MINS.
Yvette .... Francoise Arnoul
Michaud .... Bourvil
Tiercelin .... Lino Ventura
Antoine .... Alain Delon
Paul .... Jean-Claude Brialy
Lulli .... Pierre Mondy
Flora .... Madeleine Lebeau

Film takes place in that rarely explored time, filmically, of the Occupation during the last war. It deals with the loosening of moral fibres among teenagers and adults alike in the persons of two French families. This has some frank comments on the habits of the times. But most of its harshness is blunted. This will have to be sold on its theme abroad.

It lacks the grim drive, ironic edge and bawdy humor of another Occupation pic made from a Marcel Ayme tale, "Four Bags Full." Ayme also wrote the original for this pic but it has been watered down and the recreation of place and atmosphere is not quite effective enough for complete acceptance.

A 17-year-old is having an affair with a married woman whose husband is a prisoner of war. She wants money and gets him into the

black market. His father, a simple, upright but ineffective man, finds out and is berating him when a prostitute with whom he has had a weak moment throws herself around his neck.

Bourvil has the right edge of gentleness and human weakness to make the father a telling portrait. Others are good but the prevalence of talk, the sudden ending sans enough satisfactory character resolution, make this a pic with arty chances abroad mainly on theme and locale. Technical credits are good and direction dextrous except for a tendency to underplay the inherent irony. Acting is good right down the line.   *Mosk.*

Once More, With Feeling
(TECHNICOLOR)

Excellent film version of the Harry Kurnitz Broadway play. Yul Brynner and late Kay Kendall for marquee bait. Top b.o. indicated.

Hollywood, Jan. 28.
Columbia release of a Stanley Donen production. Stars Yul Brynner, Kay Kendall; costars Gregory Ratoff. Screenplay, Harry Kurnitz, based on his play; camera, Georges Perinal; production designer, Alex Trauner; editor, Jack Harris. Previewed at Stanley Warner Beverly Theatre, Jan. 28, '60. Running time, 92 MINS.
Victor Fabian .... Yul Brynner
Dolly Fabian .... Kay Kendall
Dr. Hilliard .... Geoffrey Toone
Jascha Gendel .... Maxwell Shaw
Mr. Wilbur .... Mervyn Johns
Bardini .... Martin Benson
Chester .... Harry Lockhart
Maxwell Archer .... Gregory Ratoff

The bright, entertaining touches of producer-director Stanley Donen breeze through "Once More, With Feeling" like an allegro, making a good Broadway play into a better motion picture. It's a smart, perfectly cast comedy that will put the impressive sight of Yul Brynner and Kay Kendall on the screen and the welcome sound of profits on Columbia's ledger.

Miss Kendall died less than three months after "Once More" was completed. There will be tugs of the heart with her last performance, but they will only serve to highlight the remembrance of a lively, exciting personality. Her eyes clouded with tears, Miss Kendall blows away a kiss in her final scene, the sentiment seeming peculiarly prophetic. However, the picture of the actress through the rest of the film is one of life and of a spirited performer who symbolizes the grace, the complexities, the unpredictabilities and the beauty of woman.

As a pompous symphony conductor with a love of fine music that surpasses his participation in mundane existence, Brynner turns in perhaps his best performance since the successive "The King and I" and "Anastasia." In his hands, the character has strength and humor, with Brynner adeptly playing sly appeal against defiant arrogance. Together, he and Miss Kendall make an overwhelming screen couple.

Harry Kurnitz wrote the screenplay from his own play, moved the setting from the United States to Europe and came up with a scriptful of witty dialog and amusing situations. There's one gag which occasionally is overextended, but the repetition is infrequent, and it's mainly a tight screenplay that moves well. Donen and Kurnitz have added imaginative bits of business to the basic story and are most successful with more than a dozen works of art bearing Brynner's likeness. The maestro's personality is reflected directly by the paintings and busts, with every camera angle uproariously tuning in a different facet of the character.

Unfortunately, there's another bit of business that doesn't turn out quite so well when a violinist, seeking sympathy for his neurotic hand, unintentionally makes a vulgar hand sign that sent the preview audience into embarrassed titters. While the scene detracts from the picture, it more likely should be chalked up to poor judgment than bad taste.

The conflict of "Once More, With Feeling" finds Brynner at

odds with the world. He makes great music, but he can't get along with his musicians or the orchestra's board of trustees, and his pretty wife, Miss Kendall, must soothe feelings all the way around. Eventually she has enough of her egomaniac husband, leaves him and decides to marry a physicist. Only it seems she and Brynner never really bothered to tie the knot officially, and now, to avoid notoriety, they must be married so she can get a divorce and be free to wed the physicist. The conductor agrees in exchange for several more days' togetherness while he leads the London Festival Orchestra, and it's enough to get them back together for good.

In support of the stars, Gregory Ratoff is excellent as the agent, prone to absurd comparisons and remarkably able to keep the warring mates in hand. Geoffrey Toone is good as the physicist, Maxwell Shaw funny as the violinist, Martin Benson and Harry Lockart fine as the orchestra manager and conductor's assistant respectively. Mervyn Johns, as the symphony's key backer, is very good, cracking over with one of the film's best lines when, seeking the man who leads the orchestra, he rushes up to a musician and says, "Take me to your leader."

The Donen production is a lavish film, sparkling with Alex Trauner's design and Georges Perinal's Technicolor photography. Donen's direction maintains a swift style that is continued adeptly by editor Jack Harris. Sound by Joseph De Bretagne is fine, and Muir Mathieson ably conducted the music which integrates with Brynner's leading the music of Beethoven, Liszt, Wagner and Sousa among others. Femme patrons will get an added kick out of the wardrobe designed for Miss Kendall by Givenchy. And everyone will get a kick out of the clever main titles designed by Maurice Binder.

Ron.

Tall Story

Mild Josh Logan collegiate farce. B.o. rests on stars Anthony Perkins and newcomer Jane Fonda.

Hollywood, Feb. 5.

Warners release produced and directed by Joshua Logan. Stars Anthony Perkins and Jane Fonda; features Ray Walston, Marc Connelly and Anne Jackson. Associated producer, Ben Kadish; screenplay, J. J. Epstein; based on the play by Howard Lindsay and Russel Crouse taken from Howard Nemerov's book, "The Homecoming Game"; camera, Ellsworth Fredericks; music, Cyril Mockridge; editor, Philip W. Anderson. Previewed at the studio, Feb. 2, '60. Running time, 91 MINS.

Ray Blent .... Anthony Perkins
June Ryder .... Jane Fonda
Leo Sullivan .... Ray Walston
Charles Osman .... Marc Connelly
Myra Sullivan .... Anne Jackson
Coach Hardy .... Murray Hamilton
President Nagel .... Bob Wright
D. A. Davis .... Bart Burns
First D. A. Man .... Karl Lukas
Connie .... Elizabeth Patterson

The way the ball bounces in "Tall Story," a collegiate basketball story, is not very high. While the Warners release has its diverting moments, it is trivial considering the highpowered talents connected with it. Joshua Logan produced and directed the film which stars Anthony Perkins and Jane Fonda, latter in her film bow. Despite its mild nature, "Tall Story" will probably be a good attraction for younger audiences.

This one began as a novel by Howard Nemerov, satirical in its treatment of the collision that occurs when academic freedom must compete with "practical" collegiate concerns, i.e., a winning athletic team. This seriousness was partially lost in the stage play by Howard Lindsay and Russel Crouse made from the novel, called "The Homecoming Game." It has been completely dumped in the film version by J. J. Epstein.

An ethics professor's devotion to ethics, which had a forlorn but admirable dignity in Nemerov's original, has now been thinned to mere intellectual foolishness when confronted with the important things of the world (a), intercollegiate sports and (b) sex urges of the young.

There's nothing wrong, of course, with making a farce out of a satire, and Epstein's screenplay might have played with actors and a director better keyed to this form than those involved in "Tall Story." The greatest disappointment about the film is the lack of freshness and invention displayed by Logan, often a perceptive director. His use of closeups is good and has some novelty in this era of the big, busy screen. The sex humor, however, stems directly from burlesque and having it played by clean, young people does not make it fresh. Even a running gag of a young man in a shower, something of a Logan trademark, does not play for the humor intended.

The slim plot has to do with Perkins' romance with Miss Fonda. Although he is a third-year man in college, he is thrown mentally by the stimulation her presence causes him, so he flunks an ethics exam. Another mental hazard is the fact that some gamblers are trying to get him to throw an important basketball game. The opposing team, for no apparent reason, plot or comedy, is a visiting Russian quintet. The climax is devoted to getting Perkins past the exam and into the game.

Perkins, while physically attractive, does not vary his performance a great deal, beyond alternating a full-toothed grin to indicate artless charm and a tensing of the cheek muscles to indicate cogitation or mental distress. Miss Fonda makes an appealing film bow, but no evaluation of her talents is possible on the superficial character she has to work with. Ray Walston and Marc Connelly, two expert farceurs, get the chief laughs. Anne Jackson, as Walston's wife, has a nice quality and is helpful. Among the other players, moppet Phil Phillips is a standout.

Ellsworth Frederick's photography is helpful, as is art direction by Jack Poplin. Philip W. Anderson's editing is deft. There is a title song, by Dory Langdon, and Andre Previn and Shelly Manne, sung behind the main title by Bobby Darin, which may be a promotion plus.

Powe.

Home From the Hill
(COLOR; C'SCOPE)

Full-blooded melodrama with good new and established star names. Good b.o.

Hollywood, Feb. 5.

Metro release of Sol C. Siegel production. S..rs Robert Mitchum and Eleanor Parker; features George Peppard, George Hamilton, Everett Sloane, Luana Patten. Produced by Edmund Grainger. Directed by Vincente Minnelli. Screenplay, Harriet Frank Jr. and Irving Ravetch; based on a novel by William Humphrey; camera (Metrocolor), Milton Krasner; editor, Harold F. Kress; music, Bronislau Kaper. Previewed at the studio, Jan. 27, '60. Running time, 150 MINS.

Capt. Wade Hunnicutt..Robert Mitchum
Hannah Hunnicutt........ Eleanor Parker
Rafe Copley .... George Peppard
Theron .... George Hamilton
Albert Halstead .... Everett Sloane
Libby Halstead .... Luana Patten
Sarah Halstead .... Anne Seymour
Opal Bixby .... Constance Ford
Chauncey .... Ken Renard
Dr. Reuben Carson .... Ray Teal

A full-blown melodrama, high-octane in situations and characters, Metro's "Home From the Hill" shapes as a major boxoffice contender. Like an over-taxed engine, the production throws a plot rod or two in its final moments, but when the Sol C. Siegel production is concluded the spectator is at least aware he has seen something. The film is, overall, a powerful and absorbing story, and its production has the added interest of creating a vital and promising young star, George Peppard.

Even though the Harriet Frank Jr.-Irving Ravetch screenplay, from William Humphrey's novel, is florid and complicated, in the customary Deep South literary manner, it does not neglect humor and the lighter touches. Vincente Minnelli's direction is rich and satisfying, especially adroit in the creation and direction of a fistful of important characters.

Illicit and illegitimate romance in two generations occupy the principals of "Home From the Hill." Setting is Texas, a town of which Robert Mitchum is not only the richest citizen but the busiest stud. The latter characteristic has iced his marriage to Eleanor Parker since the birth of their now-grown son, George Hamilton. Mitchum has another son, George Peppard, born out of wedlock at about the same time as Hamilton. Hamilton has been so marked by his parents' relationship that when he falls in love with Luana Patten he lacks the courage to marry her. Completing the cycle, Peppard marries the girl and gives her child—by Hamilton—the father he, Peppard, never had.

Despite the intricacies, the story plays well, due to a fine cast and Minnelli's sure-handed direction. Only the closing sequences, when Miss Patten's avenging father, Everett Sloane, misguidedly shoots Mitchum to death, and young Hamilton, in revenge, kills Sloane, do things get out of hand. Minnelli uses a technique he previously tried in "Some Came Running," of pacing his film like an orchestral composition, with a thunderous and complex climax. It does not altogether come off.

Among the things that do come off are some stunning travelling shots by Minelli and his cameraman, Milton Krasner, of Hamilton on a boar hunt; the race through the vine-clotted forest is superb. A scene where the two young men, Peppard and Hamilton, acknowledge they are brothers, is a touching and unusual vignette of manly tenderness. A small point is that the characters all attempt at least an approximation of regional speech patterns, something too often neglected in films.

Mitchum delivers his strongest performance in years, and Miss Parker handles her end of the conflict well, too, although her role is less interesting. Hamilton gives a sensitive portrayal, continuing to fulfill his earlier promise. Miss Patten is fine. Sloane, Constance Ford, Anne Seymour, Ken Renard and Ray Teal are importantly cast and effective.

But it is Peppard from the N.Y. stage, who shines through. Having to portray a long-suffering, essentially good and gentle young man is not the easiest assignment, and to keep it from saccharine. Peppard does more than that, giving virility a warm and gentle connotation. He is a welcome addition to a small company of important newcomers.

Filmed on location in Mississippi and Texas, "Home From the Hill" is authentic in all departments.

Powe.

Oklahoma Territory

Routine western with minor appeal

Hollywood, Feb. 5.

United Artists release of Robert E. Kent production. Stars Bill Williams, Gloria Talbott; costars Ted de Corsia, Grant Richards; features Walter Sande, X Brands, Walter Baldwin, Grandon Rhodes. Directed by Edward L. Cahn. Screen, Orville H. Hampton; camera, Walter Strenge; editor, Grant Whytock; music, Albert Glasser. Previewed Feb. 3, '60. Running time, 67 MINS.

Temple Houston .... Bill Williams
Ruth Red Hawk .... Gloria Talbott
Buffalo Horn .... Ted de Corsia
Bigelow .... Grant Richards
Rosslyn .... Walter Sande
Running Cloud .... X Brands
Ward Harlan .... Walter Baldwin
Blackwell .... Grandon Rhodes

"Oklahoma Territory" is burdened with an overly-contrived plot but stacks up fairly okay for the less discriminating oater market. A slow pace militates against much interest in a story line that telegraphs ahead.

Robert E. Kent production twirls around plot of a railroad agent to stir the Cherokees to war through the arrest of their chief, accused of murdering the Indian Commissioner. Treaty of 1867 stipulates that should war be declared by the Indians their land will then be available for free right-of-way to the railroad.

As a fast-shooting district attorney, Bill Williams prosecutes the case against the man he's known all his life, winning a conviction, then arranging for chief's escape when new evidence reveals his innocence. Plotline takes an unbelievable turn when Williams, with guns drawn, forces a Federal judge to reopen case in courtroom and gains an acquittal.

Williams delivers a stock performance and Gloria Talbott, his costar, is the chief's daughter, looking about as much like an Injun as Ted de Corsia, the chief, who doesn't. Grant Richards undertakes the heavy role satisfactorily, and Walter Sande as a U.S. marshal, X Brands the chief's son and Walter Baldwin a newspaper editor handle their roles capably.

Edward L. Cahn's direction of the Orville H. Hampton screenplay is inclined to the leisurely but Walter Strenge's camera work is competent. Technical credits are okay.

Whit.

Los Tigres Del Desierto
(Desert Tigers)
(MEXICAN)

Mexico City, Feb. 2.

A Peliculas Nacionales release of a Producciones Zacarias, S.A. production. Stars Viruta y Capulina; features Donna Behar, Lorena Velazquez, Rodolfo Landa. Written and directed by Agustin P. Delgado, with special comedy routines supplied by the stars. At Real Cinema, Mexico City. Running time, 105 MINS.

Viruta y Capulina are the most popular comics in Mexico today, borrowing liberally from the routines of Laurel and Hardy and Abbott and Costello especially. However, they fall far flat of the efforts of their American counterparts.

The pat formula used by the comics on tele are repeated in the film: a dumb goon as the stooge, and an equally dumb, but slightly smarter partner. With Algiers in

the news, producers set the background action there as a horseless sort of horse-adventure opera. Comics fight a band of criminals and come out on top in the last scene after a series of absurd, slapstick situations, often reminiscent of The Three Stooges, when not of the other Hollywood comics mentioned.

Script is neither strong on comedy or adventure element, and there are some oldie jokes going back to the Mexican Joe Miller, too. But the audience loves these two clowns so the script is secondary to their antics.

Donna Behar sings a few songs in Arab and Spanish, and provides love interest with Lorena Velazquez. Latter is somewhat more covered up than usual for this is a "family" picture Rodolfo Landa, for the serious side, is a French official in the uniform of a Mexican army man of the times of Pirfirio Diaz. But this is unimportant since the bandits register fear whenever he heaves into sight—and he is a striking dashing figure in his uniform.

Emil.

This Rebel Breed

Exploitation film dealing somewhat carelessly with racial issues. Debatable impact.

Hollywood, Feb. 5.

Warner Bros. release of William Rowland production. Features Rita Moreno, Mark Damon, Gerald Mohr. Executive producer, Robert H. Yamin; director, Richard L. Bare; screenplay, Morris Lee Green; story, William Rowland and Irma Berk; camera, Monroe Askins; music, David Rose; editor, Tony Martinelli. Previewed at the studio, Feb. 1, '60. Running time, **90 MINS.**

Lola	Rita Moreno
Frank	Mark Damon
Lt. Brooks	Gerald Mohr
Papa	Jay Novello
Rudy	Eugene Martin
Muscles	Tom Gilson
Buck	Richard Rust
Don	Douglas Hume
Manuel	Richard Laurier
Jimmy	Don Eitner
Wigles	Diane Cannon
Winnie	Kenny Miller
Satchel	Al Freeman
Scratch	Charles Franc

"The Rebel Breed" is a flattering title for the jungle creatures portrayed in this Warners release. Another in the studies of this generation's juvenile depravity, present release is concerned with the conflicts creating separate and warring gangs of young Latins, Negroes and—in the film's word—"Anglos." Its aims may be lofty, to promote some racial common sense through horrible example, but its narrative means are suspect. A brief lecture at the film's conclusion does not quite wash away repeated use of crude racial terms or explicit scenes of inter-racial cruelty and violence.

Mark Damon plays a half Negro-half Mexican police officer who is teamed with Douglas Hume, a white police officer, to go underground in joining high school gangs. Their purpose is a break-up of narcotics rings pandering to the high school trade, but this story gets somewhat lost in subsidiary plots. A romance develops between Rita Moreno, a Mexican girl, and Damon, after a romance between Miss Moreno and one of the "Anglos" is ended with his death in a gang fight.

A combination of naivete and ineptness does not help the film. In the former category is a scene in which a marijuana pusher forces his wares on a trio of small Negro boys (aged about six years). The idea that these youngsters would be financially worthwhile customers for his evil wares would be chilling, if it were not so silly. Another scene which makes the film's high purposes suspect is the final sequence, a house-wrecking rumble by the three gangs. The spirit of this sequence is standard western roughhouse, nothing else.

Miss Moreno, despite drawbacks, is quite touching at moments, with an appealing fragility. Damon is inflicted with greasepaint an absurd dark (to emphasize, apparently, that he is partly Negro) but manages some conviction. Jay Novello, as Miss Moreno's father, and Gerald Mohr, as the police superior, achieve sincerity. Others who contribute include Hume, Diane Cannon, Richard Laurier, Eugene Martin and Tom Gilson.

Richard L. Bare's direction is generally first-rate, considering what he has to work with, and Morris Lee Green's screenplay, aside from the lapses noted, has some effective moments. *Powe.*

Conspiracy of Hearts
(BRITISH)

An all-out, wartime tear-jerker. Its religious background may limit its appeal but the moppets should woo femme patrons. Dialog and performances are often stilted, making it an "iffish" b.o. bet.

London, Feb. 2.

Rank release of a Betty E. Box—Ralph Thomas production. Stars Lilli Palmer, Sylvia Syms, Yvonne Mitchell, Ronald Lewis; features Albert Lieven, Peter Arne. Directed by Ralph Thomas. Screenplay by Robert Presnell Jr.; editor, Alfred Roome; camera, Ernest Steward; music, Angelo Lavagnino. Previewed at RFD Private Theatre, London. Running time, **113 MINS**

Mother Katharine	Lilli Palmer
Sister Mitya	Sylvia Syms
Sister Gerta	Yvonne Mitchell
Major Spoletti	Ronald Lewis
Colonel Horsten	Albert Lieven
Lt. Schmidt	Peter Arne
Sista Tia	Nora Swinburne
Father Desmaines	Michael Goodliffe
Sister Constance	Megs Jenkins
The Rabbi	David Kossoff
Sister Honoria	Jenny Laird
Petrelli	George Coulouris
Sister Elisaveta	Phyllis Neilson-Terry
Anna	Rebecca Dignam
Joseph	Joseph Cuby

Standout success of "The Nun's Story" proves that there's nothing fundamentally wrong with a convent-angled pic, but "Conspiracy Of Hearts," played mainly in an Italian convent in wartime, tries, sometimes uneasily, to make the best of two worlds, the serenity of religion and the starkness of war. Since the film has to do with the welfare of war-stricken waifs, it must have considerable femme appeal. Director Ralph Thomas has pulled out all the stops to make it the complete carpet-drencher.

But the dialog is often stilted, some of the performances overwritten and overplayed. It all works up to such a frenzied, melodramatic climax that it cannot be regarded as a fully satisfactory job. Its chances in the U.S. appear limited.

The scene is Italy in 1943. A convent near a transit camp mainly houses young Jewish children whose parents have been killed by the Nazis. Mother Katharine (Lilli Palmer) and her nuns help the children to escape from the camp and, from the convent to safety and comfort with foster-parents. Their work is dangerous but less so because the camp commandant, an Italian major (Ronald Lewis) is sympathetic enough to turn a blind eye to their work. Things get tougher when a Nazi colonel and his sadistic lieutenant take over the camp. It all builds up to a rather hysterical showdown when the nuns' underground activities are disclosed and three of them are ordered to be executed, the payoff being switched in a somewhat contrived manner.

There are a few poignant scenes with the little children and one or two that fit with difficulty into the script.

Ralph Thomas has directed with considerable sincerity but two thirds of the way through his theme gets away from him. Both he and the scriptwriter obviously have had difficulty in deciding how to tidy matters up. Location and artwork are okay and Ernest Steward's camerawork is very effective.

There are some good contrasting performances by the various nuns, with Lilli Palmer carrying the greatest weight as the poised, dedicated Mother Superior. Sylvia Syms also scores heavily as a young novice who is swayed between her devotions and her worldly feelings for Lewis, the Italian major. Yvonne Mitchell has a tough role as an embittered nun. Megs Jenkins and Phyllis Neilson-Terry have lesser but equally effective roles.

Albert Lieven and Peter Arne, as German officers, are almost entirely without sympathy. Lewis as the Italian officer makes quite a lot of a role which is mainly second fiddle to the Germans. George Coulouris and Michael Goodliffe also have two or three worthy scenes as a partisan and priest respectively.

The children, of course, have ample scene-stealing opportunities, especially Rebecca Dignam and Joseph Cuby. It says a great deal for Miss Syms that she holds her own on three or four occasions with the grave-eyed, pathetic little Miss Dignam. *Rich.*

The Prime Time

Low-budget meller for teen market. No names but exploitable theme as programmer.

Chicago, Feb. 1.

Essanjay release of a Mid-Continent production. Stars Jo Ann LeCompte, Frank Roche, James Brooks, Ray Gronwold. Directed by Gordon Weisenborn. Screenplay, Robert Abel; camera, Andrew Costikyan; editor, Elsie Kerbinhathorn; music, Martin Rubenstein and Buddy Frye. Previewed in Chicago, Dec. 30, '59. Running time, **76 MINS.**

Jean	Jo Ann LeCompte
Det. McKean	Frank Roche
Tony	James Brooks
The Beard	Ray Gronwold
Gloria	Maria Pavelle
Shorty	Robert Major
Painted Woman	Karen Black
Ruthie	Betty Senter

A modest picture by any and all standards, "The Prime Time" deals with the comeuppance of a bad girl, and was shot entirely in the Chicago area with an Actors Equity no-names cast. It's the first title from Chi's new Mid-Continent Films, which has talked of slating two or three specific market features a year, an ambition that may hinge on the boxoffice of this initialer.

For its thin budget and relatively inexperienced (before the cameras) players, "Prime Time" still looks to be an acceptable neighborhood programmer for the juve trade which fancies excitement, oddball characters, etc., as a young way of life. Sex and action are abundant ingredients, and the pace is made to seem quick per people coming and going, auto doors slamming, etc.

Yarn has to do with a bored 17-year-old femme's flight from her comfortable home in quest of kicks. She disappears into the clutches of a villainous beatnik artist, and the search for her is led separately by a clean-cut boyfriend and a hard-as-nails young detective. Some tangled story threads link the cop and sexually, and in the end she uses such evidence to blackmail the detective into marriage to escape being returned to her parents. Cop has to consent, but promises she'll rue the bargain, which implies ample punishment for her.

Its offbeat aspects and patent modesty furnish the film with a curious fascination. In addition, scripter Robert Abel and director Gordon Weisenborn have managed a surprising amount of suspense in an otherwise predictable tale.

Film faults mainly in its rather jagged telling, and some self-conscious direction and thesping. Cast, however, is often interesting to look at, with best performances being Jo Ann LeCompte's as the runaway girl, and Ray Gronwold as the sinister beatnik ultimately hoist with his own petard. *Pit.*

The Flesh and the Fiends
(BRITISH)

Competent remake of hoary old yarn of Burke and Hare, 19th Century Edinburgh bodysnatchers. Not particularly horrific but sufficiently suspenseful.

London, Feb. 2.

Regal International release of a Triad (Robert S. Baker-Monty Berman) production. Stars Peter Cushing, June Laverick, Donald Pleasence; features Dermot Walsh, George Rose, Renee Houston, Billie Whitelaw, John Cairney, Melvyn Hayes. Directed by John Gilling. Story by Gilling; screenplay, Gilling and Leon Griffiths; camera, Monty Berman; music, Stanley Black; editor, Jack Flade. At Rialto, London. Running time, **97 MINS**

Dr. Robert Knox	Peter Cushing
Martha	June Laverick
William Hare	Donald Pleasence
Dr. Mitchell	Dermot Walsh
Helen Burke	Renee Houston
William Burke	George Rose
Mary Patterson	Billie Whitelaw
Chris Jackson	John Cairney
Daft Jamie	Melvyn Hayes
Magie O'Hara	June Powell
Old Davey	Geoffrey Tyrrell
Old Angus	Beckett Bould
Blind Man	George Bishop
Dr. Ferguson	George Woodbridge
Dr. Elliott	Philip Leaver
Rev. Lincoln	John Rae
Inspector McCulloch	Andrew Foulds
Aggie	Esma Cannon
Baxter	Raf De La Torre
Drunken Sailor	Michael Balfour
Barman	George Street
Undertaker	Michael Mulcastel
Stallholder	Jack McNaughton

This latest version of the story about Dr. Robert Knox, the 19th Century Edinburgh anatomist, and Burke and Hare, the notorious bodysnatchers and murderers, has nothing very new to offer. But it is competently filmed, has some very good performances and though given an adults-only "X" certificate, hardly enters into the horrific class. There are one or two strong-meat scenes, but it should go down well and profitably with the big, varied audiences that go for this sort of fare.

As recalled, the yarn concerns a dedicated surgeon and university lecturer who believes that nothing is important enough to stand in the way of medical research. Bodies are needed for anatomical research and the need breeds a ghoulish race of bodysnatchers, who filch graves almost before the corpses are cold. Two such rascals, Irishmen Burke and Hare, decide to cut out the middle men, by murdering lonely, unknown and drunken riff-raff and selling the bodies to the academy. Knox, without particularly encouraging such methods, turns a blind eye to their activities. For him, the end justifies the means.

The lucrative racket of Burke

and Hare goes along steadily until they make an over-reach and murder one of the doctor's own pupils, his girl friend and a young well-known character in the town.

They are brought to trial. Burke is hanged and Hare, who has turned King's Evidence, gets off only to face the wrath of the crowd who, in a lynching, burn out his eyes in retribution. Meanwhile, Doctor Knox faces the jealousy of his collagues who try to pin the scandal of collusion on to him. Peter Cushing, playing Knox, is an expert in this sort of role. He knows that any parody is fatal and so he plays the part with as much straight-forward sincerity, dignity and authority as he would "Hamlet." The result is a most effective study in singleminded integrity which knits the film together admirably.

Dernot Walsh as the doctor who deplores Cushing's methods but also admires him personally also plays "straight," with equal effect, though the role is a colorless one. June Laverick also has an insipid role as Cushing's pretty niece and she, too, plays without frills. The other performers, in contrast, tend, to ham it up. Donald Pleasance and George Rose, as Hare and Burke respectively, are a couple of oily rogues with Pleasence particularly having himself a ball as the cunning instigator of the crimes. Renee Houston also helps the crimes.

But of all the other parts the one that most gives the pic a kick is that of Billie Whitelaw as the young streetwalker who ensnares the student (John Cairney) with her voluptuous charms before falling a victim to the bodysnatchers.

Miss Whitelaw is a fairly new entry into the world of films and looks to be a very useful bet for the future. She has fire and a sinuous grace which contrasts admirably with a few poignant moments thrown in for good measure. Melvyn Hayes, George Woodbridge, Esma Cannon and John Rae head a large supporting cast. John Gilling has directed conscientiously and makes a good point in his contrast of the academic atmosphere with that of the evil sleaziness of the 19th Century Edinburghs slums, brothel and taverns. Cushing's scenes in the lecture hall, his bitter exchanges with the medical tribunal, the roistering sequences in the inn and the brothel and the final near-lynching scenes all come off fairly well. *Rich.*

Le Travail C'Est La Liberte
(Work is Freedom)
(FRENCH

Paris, Feb. 2.
CFF release of CFPC production. With Raymond Devos, Gerard Sety, Sammy Frey, Jacques Dufilho, Judith Magre. Directed by Louis Grospierre. Screenplay, Jacques Lanzmann, Grospierre, Françoise Mallet-Joris; camera, Marcel Grignon; editor, Leonide Azar. At Triomphe, Paris. Running time, 85 MINS.
Emile .... Raymond Devos
Eugene .... Gerard Sety
Luigi .... Sammy Frey
Cop .... Jacques Dufilho
Jeanne .... Judith Magre

This pic is about three convicts who are sent out on a garbage detail during a strike. It relates their attempts to meet their girl friends, abetted by their two guardian cops, the strike etc. It lacks the pace to give this any comic vitality or satiric relief. Result is a lagging pic mainly for the home market with little foreign possibilities.

Good comedians are wasted because of the lacklustre writing

and direction. As another example of the "new wave," this is another mark against it. *Mosk.*

Le Secret Du Chevalier D'Eon
(FRENCH—COLOR DYALISCOPE)

Paris, Feb. 2.
Disfilm release of Paris-Elysees production. Stars Andree Debar; features Gabriel Ferzetti, Dany Robin, Isa Miranda, Bernard Blier. Directed by Jacqueline Audry. Screenplay, Cecil Laurent, Pierre Laroche; camera (Eastmancolor), Marcel Grignon, Henri Alekan; editor, Yvonne Martin. At Triomphe, Paris. Running time, 100 MINS.
Eon .... Andree Debar
Bernard .... Gabriel Ferzetti
Czarina .... Isa Miranda
Exeter .... Bernard Blier
Monval .... Dany Robin

Costumer of 17th Century skulduggery in Russia while France and Prussia vie for a treaty with the Czarina, revolves around a girl who has had to pose as a boy all her life. The French king sends the girl (a boy in the French army) to the Russo court to slip a letter to the Czarina to show up the Prussians.

Whole affair revolves around the single joke of this girl having to masquerade as a boy to get her father his inheritance from a crusty uncle who wanted a male heir. The joke wears thin.

Film lacks the action, acting or mounting to make it more than a possible dualer in the foreign market. Technical credits are good but this sacrifices spectacle for boudoir bits, attempts at royal jokes and mistaken identity. Acting is ordinary except for Isa Miranda's candid picture of an aging, lusty Czarina. *Mosk.*

Kidnapped
(COLOR)

Authentic, if rather dull, re-creation of the Robert Louis Stevenson adventure classic. Only fair b.o.

Hollywood, Feb. 12.
Buena Vista release of Walt Disney production. Features Peter Finch, James MacArthur, Bernard Lee, John Laurie. Associate producer, Hugh Attwooll. Writer-director, Robert Stevenson; adapted from Robert Louis Stevenson's public domain book; camera (Technicolor), Paul Beeson; editor, Gordon Stone; music, Cedric Thorpe Davie. Previewed at the studio, Feb. 12, '60. Running time, 97 MINS.
Alan Breck Stewart .... Peter Finch
David Balfour .... James MacArthur
Captain Hoseason ...... Bernard Lee
Shuan .... Niall MacGinnis
Uncle Ebenezer .... John Laurie
Cluny MacPherson ...... Finlay Currie
Robin Oig MacGregor.... Peter O'Toole
Mr. Rankeilor .... Miles Malleson
Mr. Campbell .... Oliver Johnston
The Highlander .... Duncan MacRea
Cabin Boy .... John Pike
Colin Roy Campbell
.... Andrew Cruickshank
Donald Dhu MacLaren........ Abe Barker
Jennet Clouston .... Eileen Way
The Ferryman .... Alex MacKenzie

Walt Disney's newest live-action feature is a faithful recreation of the Robert Louis Stevenson classic, "Kidnapped," and seems assured of a fair response for a Disney production. The film itself is sluggish because its story line is not clear enough and for other reasons does not arouse any great anxiety or excitement in the spectator, so it will not be as general a favorite as Disney's productions usually are.

James MacArthur plays the young 18th Century Scottish boy cheated of his inheritance by a conniving uncle, in the adaptation of Stevenson's story which has been written and directed by Robert (no relation) Stevenson. The boy is kidnapped by a cruel shipsmaster for sale as an indentured servant in the Carolinas. He escapes through the aid of a dashing fellow Scotsman, Peter Finch, and after various adventures makes his way back to his home town where the wicked uncle is foiled and all is set right.

A good deal of the plot revolves around the resistance by the Scots to the Hanovarian kings, and the Scots' devotion to the Stuarts. This part of history is apt to be pretty dim to most Americans (and possibly a good many Britons) and since the speech of the film is a commendable effort at consistency in speaking with the Highland burr, a good many of the fine points are altogether lost on the American ear. From a story point of view, the screenplay is weak. It is never clear what the aim of the principals is, so there is not much for the spectator to pull for. Individual scenes play, but there is no mounting or cumulative effect.

"Kidnapped" was photographed on location in Scotland and at Pinewood, London. The locations pay off richly, with an authentic flavor. Perhaps, as noted above, too richly, with accents as thick as Scotch oatmeal.

Peter Finch as the swashbuckling follower of the exiled Stuart kings is a tremendous aid to the production. James MacArthur, as the boy, gives a sturdy performance, handicapped by little opportunity for flexibility of character. It would have been nice to give him some lightening of mood. The film is short on humor. Others of the authentic Highland (and Lowland) types are well portrayed by Bernard Lee, John Laurie, Niall Mac-Ginnis, Finlay Currie, Peter O'Toole and Andrew Cruickshank. *Powe.*

Too Soon to Love

Teenage problems, drably presented. But with exploitation angles.

Hollywood, Feb. 12.
Universal release produced and directed by Richard Rush. Features Jennifer West and Richard Evans. Executive producer, Mark Lipsky. Original story and screenplay, Laszlo Gorog and Richard Rush; camera, William Thompson; editor, Stefan Arnsten; music, Ronald Stein. Previewed at the studio, Feb. 9, '60. Running time, 85 MINS.
Cathy Taylor .... Jennifer West
Jim Mills .... Richard Evans
Mr. Taylor .... Warren Parker
Hughie Wineman .... Ralph Manza
Buddy .... Jack Nicholson
Irene .... Jacqueline Schwab
Mrs. Jefferson .... Billie Bird
The Doctor .... William Keen

Although its story deals with teenagers who get into trouble, both sexual and legal, the theme of "Too Soon to Love" is certainly moral. The wages of sin, in this Universal release, are both grim and dreary. This is the strongest recommendation that can be made for the film, which is otherwise an inept retelling of a familiar story. With the title and the story, however, Universal has a picture that will at least lend itself to exploitation.

The apparent point of the screenplay by Laszlo Gorog and Richard Rush, produced and directed by Rush, is that parental obtuseness and lack of sympathy can be an important cause of juvenile desperation, leading to delinquency. While this can be a legitimate point of inquiry, its handling in "Too Soon To Love," almost proves just the opposite.

Jennifer West and Richard Evans are the young couple being kept apart by the girl's stern father, who is convinced the association will lead to no good. The boy and girl defy the father and promptly get picked up by the cops for necking in public; the girl becomes pregnant; the boy attempts a robbery to pay for it; the girl then attempts suicide. The film ends when the young people decide to face their accumulated problems by getting married. It brings on the reflection that the girl's father was right about the whole thing, pig-headed as he may have seemed.

Evans and Miss West are capable young actors, but both are damaged by lack of sharper directorial control. Evans plays too many lines punctuated with an over-abundance of "uhs," and nervous laughs, neither of which have any motivation or meaning. Miss West is allowed to be excessively teary, so what should be poignant is finally tiresome. Others in the cast who contribute include Warren Parker, Ralph Manza, Jack Nicholson, Jacqueline Schwab, Billie Bird and William Keen.

Rush made his film independently and then concluded a deal with Universal for its release. Hollywood needs young filmmakers confident enough of their ability to take this kind of chance, but it would be more encouraging if the material chosen had more freshness and variety. *Powe.*

The Atomic Submarine

Substandard sub-sci-fi pic with horror elements for exploitation.

Hollywood, Feb. 8.
Allied Artists release of Gorham (Alex Gordon) Production. Features Arthur Franz, Dick Foran, Brett Halsey, Tom Conway, Paul Dubov, Bob Steele, Victor Varconi, Joi Lansing; with Selmer Jackson, Jack Mulhall, Jean Moorhead, Richard Tyler, Sid Melton, Ken Becker. Associate producer, Henry Schrage; di-

recteʊ by Spencer G. Bennet; written by Orville H. Hampton; camera, Gilbert Warrenton; art direction, Don Ament, Dan Heller; set decoration, Harry Reif; editor, William Austin; music. Alexander Laszlo, Neil Brunnenkant; sound. Ralph Butler; assistant director. Clark Paylow. Previewed at the studio, Feb. 5, '60. Running time, 72 MINS.

Reef	Arthur Franz
Wendover	Dick Foran
Carl	Brett Halsey
Sir Ian Hunt	Tom Conway
Dave	Paul Dubov
Griff	Bob Steele
Kent	Victor Varconi
Julie	Joi Lansing
Admiral	Selmer Jackson
Murdock	Jack Mulhall
Helen	Jean Moorhead
Carney	Richard Tyler
Chester	Sid Melton
Powell	Ken Becker

The exploitation value of the title is about all this one has to recommend it, though it's based on a fairly good science fiction-monster story idea. The directing is sluggish, special photography loses effectiveness by repetition of scenes and the screenplay wanders aimlessly.

Clips of present-day atomic submarines and other vessels are used, but the story is set at some future time when atomic freight-and passenger-submarines are regularly sailing under the north polar ice cap. The plot (dismissing inconsequential subplots dealing with half-hearted personal conflicts) concerns the search by a U. S. Navy atomic sub for the cause of numerous undersea disasters around the pole. The cause is a flying (in this case it's swimming) saucer tenanted by a bug-eyed monster who's ultimately destroyed.

None of the featured players has marquee value but most have records of competence, e.g.: Arthur Franz, Dick Foran, Brett Halsey, Tom Conway, Paul Dubov, Bob Steele, Victor Varconi, Joi Lansing. In this film, director Spencer G. Bennet has them smiling incongruously, floundering in stage waits and moving without haste or seeming concern as alarm bells clang disaster.

Some of the special effects are good, but one atomic vessel passes the same iceberg at least three times. The monster—a clump of tentacles and weeds with one Cyclops eye on a central stock—is quite satisfactory. The importance to the film of the monster and the untidy deaths it inflicts on some mariners would indicate the film's title isn't apt—suggesting as it does a story about present-day war craft. There are, of course, newsreel clips (one is used at least twice) of present-day atomic subs and freighters, but one is supposed to believe them to be identical to future craft in design.

A typical error found in Orville Hampton's hasty script is to have learned scientists solemnly proclaiming that the Magnetic North Pole is identical with the Geographical North Pole.

Alexander Laszlo provides some satisfactory electronic sounds. Technical aspects, except as previously noted, are okay. *Glen.*

La Dolce Vita
(The Sweet Life)
(ITALO-FRENCH)

Rome, Feb. 10.
Cineriz release of a RIAMA (Giuseppe Amato)-Pathe (Paris) co-production. Stars Marcello Mastroianni, Anita Ekberg, Anouk Aimee, Yvonne Fourneaux, Alain Cuny, Annibale Ninchi, Magali Noel, Lex Barker, Jacques Sernas, Nadia Gray; features Walter Santesso, Valeria Ciangottini, Polidor, Mino Doro, Riccardo Garrone, Harriet White, Alain Dijon, Giulio Girola, Nico Otzak, Audrey MacDonald, Renee Longarini, Enzo Cerusico, Enzo Doria, Carlo di Maggio, Adriana Moneta, Domino, Sondra Lee, Enrico Glori, Gloria Jones, Guilio Paradisi, Lilli Granado, Massimo Busetti, Carlo Musto, Laura Betti, Ida Galli. Directed by Federico Fellini, from a story by Fellini, Tullio Pinelli, and Ennio Flajano. Screenplay, Fellini, Finelli, Flajano and Brunello Rondi. Camera, Otello Martelli. Sets and costumes, Piero Cheradi. Music, Nino Rota. Editor, Leo Catozzo. At Cinema Fiamma, Rome. Running time. 180 MINS.

Marcello Rubini	Marcello Mastroianni
Sylvia	Anita Ekberg
Emma	Yvonne Fourneaux
Maddalena	Anouk Aimee
Robert	Lex Barker
Marcello's Father	Annibale Ninchi
Steiner	Alain Cuny
Paola	Valeria Ciangottini
Paparazzo	Walter Santesso
Steiner's Wife	Renee Longarini
A Producer	Carlo di Maggio
Police Inspector	Giulio Girola

Director Federico Fellini shows basic rottenness and immorality, yet his film in ultimate analysis is a very moral one. High and low life in modern Rome are seen through the eyes of a reporter, Marcello (Marcello Mastroianni), whose beat brings him into contact with a world-famous film star (Anita Ekberg), with an unhappy and over-rich nymphomanic society girl (Anouk Aimee), with a false miracle "announced" by two lying children and exploited by press and TV, with the suicide of an intellectual (Alain Cuny) whom he's always idolized, with a debauched and tired party in a nobleman's castle peopled by ghosts of past and present, and finally, with an orgy (complete with a strip tease performed by the hostess) staged in a futile search for excitement by a grotesque assortment of youths and grownups of all sexes. All the while, the reporter refuses the advances of the only woman (Yvonne Fourneaux) who really loves him and, perhaps, could lead him away from the easy, "sweet," but empty life to which he is slowly but surely succumbing.

Only a few of the characters show positive humanity in this downbeat picture: significantly, one is the newsman's provincial father (Annibale Ninchi) whose oldfashioned ways exemplifying the rich full life that was contrast stridently with the apocalyptic setting he finds on a visit to his big-city son. But his offspring has neither the courage nor any longer the desire to react to this stimulus, nor does he react when a young girl (Valeria Ciangottini), the image of innocence, reminds him of the good and simple life and the basic human values he has abandoned and could, conceivably, regain.

Fellini's direction is a matured talent of poetic stature. To be sure some, perhaps many spectators will squirm at the three-hour length of the film or of some of its sequences (though Fellini cut some 30 minutes from "his" final print), yet others will never notice they've sat that long.

The performances are uniformly excellent, most of actors outdoing themselves. Marcello Mastroianni is perfect in the key role of the basically good and honest boy who succumbs to the sweet life. Anita Ekberg is a revelation as the visiting star, while Yvonne Fourneaux almost runs off with the picture as the reporter's instinctive, possessive mistress. A fine bit is turned in by Annibale Ninchi as the father, another by Magali Noel as a dancer he befriends, another by Lex Barker as Ekberg's slightly inebriated, slightly separated spouse; Anouk Aimee is fine as the society girl who craves company, as is Alain Cuny as Marcello's craggy-faced intellectual friend. And there are many more, both from and pro and non-pro ranks.

A further nod must go to Otello Martelli's mood-full black and white lensing, an important assist, while Nino Rota's musical scoring is another vital plus. All credit, finally, must also go to producers Giuseppe Amato and Angelo Rizzoli for believing in Fellini and helping him, with an open budget, to make a film which, controversial or not, understood or not, honors the Italian film industry. *Hawk.*

Sink the Bismarck
(C'SCOPE)

Exciting re-creation of a memorable naval crisis. Good b.o.

Hollywood, Feb. 10.
Twentieth-Fox release of John Brabourne production. Stars Kenneth More, Dana Wynter; features Carl Mohner, Laurence Naismith, Geoffrey Keen, Karel Siepanek, Michael Hordern. Directed by Lewis Gilbert; screenplay, Edmund H. North; based on C. S. Forester's book; camera, Christopher Challis; editor, Peter Hunt; music. Clifton Parker. Running time, 97 MINS.

"Sink The Bismarck!" is a first-rate film re-creation of a thrilling historical event. Concentrating almost entirely on the hare-and-hounds aspect of the great sea chase, the 20th-Fox release mounts considerable excitement and suspense. The British film, produced by John Brabourne and starring Kenneth More and Dana Wynter, should draw well.

The screenplay, by Edmund H. North, is taken from a book by C. S. Forester. It concentrates almost entirely on three playing areas. These are the subterranean London headquarters of the British admiralty, where the battle is plotted and directed; aboard the Germans' "unsinkable" battleship, the Bismarck; and on board the various British vessels called into pursuit of the Nazi raider.

The film opens with the chilling news that the Bismarck has escaped the British naval blockade and is loose in the North Atlantic. After it sinks the Hood, considered the greatest battleship in the world, it appears nothing can stop it from rendezvousing with its sister ships holed up at Brest.

Much of the conviction for this kind of film drama depends on the miniature work. This aspect is proficient, but its acceptance requires a certain amount of conditioning. Better used in stock battle footage adroitly blended with staged scenes. Cameraman Christopher Challis purposely gives some of his staged scenes a blurry quality to heighten this realism and complement the genuine battle film.

Some of the dialog is a little high-flown, with the British at times too aware of the historical importance of the event. The Germans, on the other hand, tend to be Nazi caricatures. It may very well have been this way, but for dramatic purposes it makes the definition between the opposing forces too sharp.

Kenneth More plays the British captain who directs the battle to catch the Bismarck with his customary and effective taciturnity. Dana Wynter is a helpful note as the WREN officer who is his aide. Carl Mohner manages some character as the German officer commanding the Bismarck. Others who contribute include Laurence Naismith, Geoffrey Keen, Karel Stepanek and Michael Hordern.

Lewis Gilbert's direction is surehanded on all levels. *Powe.*

Katia
(FRENCH—COLOR)

Paris, Feb. 16.
Cinedis release of Speva production. Stars Curt Jurgens. Romy Schneider; features Monique Melinand. Pierre Blanchar, Gabrielle Dorziat, Michel Bouquet, Alain Saury. Francoise Brion. Directed by Robert Siodmak. Screenplay, Charles Spaak, Georges Neveux from novel by Princess Bibesco; camera (Eastmancolor), Michel Kelber; editor. Henri Taverna. At Berlitz, Paris. Running time, 95 MINS.

Katia	Romy Schneider
Czar	Curt Jurgens
Koubaroff	Pierre Blanchar

Czarina .... Monique Melinand
Sophie .... Francoise Brion
Bibesco .... Michel Bouquet
Revolutionary .... Alain Saury

Robert Siodmak has done all that can be done with this curiously old-fashioned, romantic and historical drama. It is slow and familiar, and looks to have only possible playoff possibilities abroad on the story of Alexandre II, the 19th Century Czar of Russia, and the names of Curt Jurgens and Romy Schneider.

Otherwise, this is a soapy tale of the good-hearted Czar who's balked in his attempts at reform by conniving ministers. His new love, a young girl, tries to help him make his peace with the growing Communist hordes but the ministers cross everything up.

Period is rarely properly depicted, and it could be the Austrian court as well as the Russian. Jurgens and Miss Schneider are acceptable in their roles of unhappy but ardent lovers. But the slim, turgid storyline makes this lag. Production values are not big enough to give this a sheen and size for greater hypo chances abroad. *Mosk.*

Comanche Station
(C'SCOPE—COLOR)

Firstrate western.

Hollywood, Feb. 19.

Columbia release of Randown (Harry Joe Crown) Production. Stars Randolph Scott; features Nancy Gates. Produced and directed by Budd Boetticher. Screenplay, Burt Kennedy; camera (Eastmancolor), Charles Lawton; editor, Edwin Bryant; music, Mischa Bakaleinikoff. Previewed at the studio, Feb. 18, '60. Running time, **74 MINS.**

Jefferson Cody .... Randolph Scott
Mrs. Lowe .... Nancy Gates
Ben Lane .... Claude Akins
Frank .... Skip Homeier
Dobie .... Richard Rust
Station Man .... Rand Brooks
Mr. Lowe .... Dyke Johnson
Comanche Lance Bearer..... Foster Hood
Comanche Chief .... Joe Molina
Warrior .... Vince St. Cyr
Boy .... P. Holland

The feature western of any category grows scarcer and scarcer, and the medium budget film of this genre has practically disappeared. So rare, indeed, are these examples of the once predominant staple of the Hollywood screen, that one such as "Comanche Station" even has some novelty value. There must be an audience left for these films, despite the plethora of such fare on television, an audience now with little from which to choose.

This Columbia release is made by a trio, Randolph Scott, Harry Joe Brown and Budd Boetticher, which has collaborated on a series of good middle-budget westerns. It would seem that there would be a way of capitalizing on this record. Unhappily, "Comanche Station," despite its values, is more likely to slip out unheralded and unsung. Its title could be livelier. But however it is shown, it will be a more than satisfactory feature. It is by any standard, a good picture.

Without straining, with apparently a conscious attempt to create "boxoffice" features, the screenplay by Burt Kennedy, also a sometime collaborator, is true to western traditions and at the same time conscious of audience appeal factors. There is romance, although not a conventional love story. There are younger actors prominently featured, and criminal elements for suspense, mystery and excitement. Kennedy does not rely on casting for characterization. The dialog is sparse, but colorful, and humor is not neglected. Such brutality as there is, for menace, is not overly-explicit.

Randolph Scott plays one of those loners of the old West, who is bringing back to her husband a settler's wife, Nancy Gates, who has been captured by Comanches. Accompanying them are a trio of bad ones, Claude Akins, Skip Homeier and Richard Rust. Jeopardy is compounded by danger from within the party and from without by Comanches trailing the group.

All of this is resolved with neat, but not pat, solutions. The characters are vivid and Boetticher's direction of his good cast keeps interest high. It is obvious that Miss Gates' Indian captors have, as the saying goes, had their way with her. The issue is not dodged, or is it falsely emphasized.

Scott gives a characteristically stolid but convincing performance. Miss Gates is satisfactory as the story's focal point. Akins, Homeier and Rust are particularly valuable for their roles, which give color and even poignancy to the script.

Charles Lawton Jr.'s CinemaScope camera catches some superb exteriors (there are no interior scenes at all) on the rugged location, and creates some striking personal compositions. The Eastman color is not always true, and in the print shown for review, color balance was sometimes off. Mischa Bakaleinikoff's music is unobstrusive, but effective. *Powe.*

Justice and Caryl Chessman

Technically good documentary on California gas chamber candidate. Exclusive footage of Chessman. B.o. possibilities.

Hollywood, Feb. 23.

Sterling World Distribution release of Terrence W. Cooney production. Directed by John Jacobs. Written by Jules Maitland! narrated by Quentin Reynolds; editor, Ed Spiegel; camera, David Shore. Reviewed in Hollywood, Feb. 22, '60. Running time, **45 MINS.**

Worldwide front page news buildup gives this special its booking and public appeal, helped by fact that exclusive footage of Caryl Chessman is included and that the 45-minute subject is well produced technically. Meantime the "hero" of the film, Chessman—the convicted rapist turned legal and literary celebrity—is living on another 60 days of borrowed time. As a screen personality he is interesting but disappointing since he is steadily pokerface and his voice is never heard. An enigmatic guy, showing sharp intelligence, he "stares" straight at camera much in the style of a couple of stars who shall go unnamed here.

Policeman who nabbed Chessman in L. A. 12-odd years ago, prosecutor who sent him down the lane to the gas chamber, mother of a girl he raped, a juror, and Chessman's court-appointed lawyer all are in the film. The soundtrack is pro-Chessman.

Timeliness assures this film playoff. Its qualities are not always encountered in such obvious exploiteers. *Glen.*

The Threat

Mediocre low-budget crime film. For twin-bills.

Hollywood, Feb. 19.

Warner Bros. release produced and directed by Charles R. Rondeau. Features Robert Knapp, Linda Lawson, Lisabeth Hush, James Seay, Mary Castle. Story and screenplay, Jo Heims; camera, Edward Cronjager; editor, Howard Epstein; music, Ronald Epstein. Previewed at the studio, Feb. 16, '60. Running time, **66 MINS.**

Steve Keenan .... Robert Knapp
Gerri .... Linda Lawson
Sandy .... Lisabeth Hush
Harry Keenan .... James Seay
Laura .... Mary Castle
Lucky .... Barney Phillips
Chessner .... Richard S. Cowl
Smiley .... Lew Brown
Mousie .... Art Lewis
Junior .... Tom Gilson
Duncan .... Emile Meyer

Low-budget film makes the mistake of starting out to tell one story and winding up with another. This switch deprives it of a tautness that is requisite to a crime melodrama, and results in confusion of purpose and a deflated windup. The Warner Bros. release, produced and directed by Charles R. Rondeau, will be an adequate feature for double-billing.

Robert Knapp plays a police detective in Jo Heims' screenplay. Knapp kills a bigtime underworld character while the latter is resisting arrest. From then on Knapp is hounded by a mystery man seeking revenge for the gang leader's death.

Quite a lot is made, early in film, of Knapp's supposed reputation for tough dealing with criminals. But this part of the story is dropped about mid-way through for the mystery theme. A romance theme is also played for intrigue towards the end but since nothing has been done to establish it sooner, it doesn't have much value.

Rondeau's direction is competent, and takes good advantage of L.A. locations. Most of the film was shot outside a studio.

Cast, headed by Knapp, performs well. Others prominent include Linda Lawson, Lisabeth Hush, James Seay, Mary Castle, Barney Phillips, Richard S. Cowl and Lew Brown.

Edward Cronjager's photography is good, and Ronald Stein's jazz score is a strong plus. *Powe.*

Jungfrukallan
(The Virgin Spring)
(SWEDISH)

Stockholm, Feb. 16.

Swensk Filmindustri production and release. Stars Max von Sydow, Birgitta Valberg, Gunnel Lindblom, Birgitta Petterson, Axel Duberg, Tor Iseral; Ove Porath. Directed by Ingmar Bergman. Screenplay by Ulla Isaksson, based on a 14th Century ballad; camera, Sven Nykvist; music, Erik Nordgren; editor, Oscar Rosander. Opened at Roda Kvarn, Stockholm, Feb. 8, '60. Running time, **90 MINS.**

Toro .... Max von Sydow
Mareta .... Birgitta Valberg
Ingeri .... Gunnel Lindblom
Karin .... Birgitta Pettersson
Thin One .... Axel Duberg
Tongueless One .... Tor Isedal
The Beggar .... Allan Edwall
Little Boy .... Ove Porath
Bridge Watchman .... Axel Slangus
Frida .... Gudrun Brost
Simon .... Oscar Ljung
First Farmhand .... Tor Borong
Second Farmhand...... Leif Forstenberg

Ingmar Bergman was inspired by a 14th Century ballad of innocence, rape, murder and revenge for his latest film. It is set against a background of Christianity and heathendom. At this period, Christianity had moved into Sweden, but the people were still in the grip of heathendom in many ways. Based on this ballad, the strength of which lies in its condensed form, Bergman and scriptwriter Ulla Isaksson (a Swedish novelist who also wrote the screenplay for "Brink of Life") have made a film rich with details which sometimes are boring.

Karin is to make the virgin's ride to church. A spoiled child, Karin persuades her mother, Mareta to let her wear a gown that is the work of 15 virgins. She also persuades her father, Tore, (who owns a large farm) to let Ingeri, who is bearing an illegitimate child, join her part of the way.

The two girls ride to the edge of the forest where they are met by the bridge watchman. From here Karin rides on alone against Ingeri's protests. As Ingeri rests at the watchman's house. Karin encounters three herdsmen in the forest. She offers them food. After eating some of her food, the two full-grown herdsmen rape Karin while their little brother looks on. Ingeri has followed Karin later through the woods, but is unable to intervene when she sees the rape. One of the herdsmen beats the weeping, torn Karin to death with a pole. Then they steal her fine clothing.

Later in the evening, the herdsmen reach Tore's farm, not knowing that he is Karin's father, and ask for shelter and food. During the night, a scream from the frightened, upset little boy (one of the herdsmen) awakens Mareta. He offers her the virgin's bloodstained gown as a gift, saying it belonged to his sister. Recognizing the garment, Mareta locks up the herdsmen and awakens her husband.

Tore seeks revenge. He meets Ingeri who tells him what happened in the forest. Tore takes a slaughtering knife and murders the herdsmen as they sleep.

Then Tore and Mareta find the body of their dead daughter in the forest. Tore turns to God wondering why he allowed the rape and murders. Tore promises to build a church with his own hands right at this spot. Then Tore lifts Karin's body and a spring rushes forth from where her head has laid.

"Spring" is loaded with the theme of guilt. And there is no main character. Bergman has carefully mixed Christianity with Odin's raven, a toad, and heathen figures and symbols. Sven Nykvist's photography of the forest is excellent. Using the sounds of nature, Bergman has used a minimum of music and no tones from medieval ballads.

The acting of Birgitta Valberg, as Mareta; Max von Sydow (Tore), Gunnel Lindblom, as Inger, and Tor Isedal (Tongueless One) is superb. Bergman's most recent find, Birgitta Pettersson, as Karin, is very good, as Ove Porath and Axel Duberg.

This is an extremely powerful film, possibly Bergman's strongest. However, it lacks the human warmth of "Wild Strawberries" and the majesty of "Seventh Seal." Audiences likely will leave the theatre torn and shattered by an unpleasant experience. This is a technical masterpiece and will be loved by the technically minded. *Flei.*

Life Is a Circus
(BRITISH)

Slim, slapstick yarn exploiting that ageless British institution, the Crazy Gang, packed with gags and situations which will satisfy unsophisticated audiences.

London, Feb. 16.

British Lion release of a (M. Smedley Aston) Vale production. Stars Crazy

Gang (Bud Flanagan, Nervo and Knox, Naughton and Gold, "Monsewer" Eddie Gray), Shirley Eaton, Michael Holliday. Features Lionel Jeffries, Eric Pohlmann, Joseph Tomelty, Chesney Allen. Directed by Val Guest. Screenplay, Guest; editor, Bill Lenny; camera, Arthur Graham; music, Phil Green. Previewed at Studio One, London. Running time, 84 MINS.

Bud	Bud Flanagan
Sebastian	Teddy Knox
Cecil	Jimmy Nervo
Goldie	Jimmy Gold
Charlie	Charlie Naughton
Eddie	Eddie Gray
Ches	Chesney Allen
Shirley Winter	Shirley Eaton
Carl Rickenbeck	Michael Holliday
Genii	Lionel Jeffries
Joe Winter	Joseph Tomelty
Rickenbeck	Eric Pohlmann
Mr. Deaken	Fred Johnson
Hassan	Harold Kasket
Rose of Baghdad	Maureen Moore
Driver	Edwin Richfield
1st Hand	Peter Glaze
Removal Man	Sam Kydd
Policeman	Geoffrey Denton

The Crazy Gang, a British stage institution for years and still going strong, has fought shy of pictures for some years. Though their re-appearance will provide their fans with a lot of nostalgic fun, it's easy to see why they have been reluctant .to make make many films. Their warm, ebullient personalities do not register as strongly as over the footlights. It is rather obvious that they miss the communication with the Victoria Palace audience. "Life Is A Circus" however will register well with unsophisticated audiences.

Val Guest, who also directs, has dreamed up a simple story, the sole purpose of which is to provide a framework for slapstick situations and the Gang's outrageous puns. The Gang are circus hands in a travelling tent show that is up against it financially compared to a more spectacular rival. The Gang makes loyal but fruitless attempts to save the show. But nothing goes right until Bud Flanagan comes across an old lamp in a pile of junk. The story then goes slap into the "Alf's Button" stable. Rubbing the lamp releases a Genii ("I once worked for Aladdin") who assists the gang (sometimes with many mishaps) to put on a show which saves the circus.

The Gang introduces a great deal of their familiar stuff, including a "black mike" routine from one of their shows. They have made free use of gags that have served them well for years. There are several very funny sequences, notably one when Nervo and Knox do a trapeze act.. The dialog is largely uninhibited, fairly vulgar in a completely inoffensive manner, and unabashedly corny.

Flanagan mostly takes the lead in the revels, but Nervo and Knox, and Naughton and Gold complete the team as skilfully as on the stage. Eddie Gray manages to squeeze in his juggling act and some phoney magic. Lionel Jeffries plays the genii amusingly but finds it difficult to sustain the role. Joseph Tomelty as the unsuccessful circus proprietor and Eric Pohlmann as his rival lend solid support.

A tenuous love interest is introduced (with an eye to the younger cinemagoers). This is pleasantly put over by vivacious Shirley Eaton and Michael Holliday, a tv singer, who makes an agreeable debut and shows promise. They sing "For You, For You" amiably, but this and the title song, "Life Is A Circus," though just right for the film, are plugged unmercifully.

Val Guest allows the comedians mainly to have their way. Editing is also a shade slaphappy. But

Arthur Graham has done a very good job with his camera, with quite a lot of trick photography.
Rich.

I Passed for White

Romantic meller based on a mixed racial romance. Exploitable.

Hollywood, Feb. 26.
Allied Artists release produced, directed and written by Fred M. Wilcox. Features Sonya Wilde and James Franciscus. Based on the novel by Mary Hastings Bradley; camera, George Folsey; editor, George White; music, Jerry Irving. Previewed at the studio, Feb. 23, '60. Running time, 91 MINS.

Bernice Lee, Lila Browneil	Sonya Wilde
Rick	James Franciscus
Sally	Pat Michon
Mrs. Leyton	Elizabeth Council
Mr. Leyton	Griffin Crafts
Bertha	Isabelle Cooley
Jay	James Lydon
Dr. Merrett	Thomas B. Henry
Mr. Gordon	Max Mellinger
Nurse	Phyllis Cole
Eddie	Calvin Jackson
Chuck	Lon Ballantyne
Gram	Freita Shaw
Character	Ed Hashim
Bartender	Ray Kellogg
Woman	Elizabeth Harrower

Despite its True Confessions' title, "I Passed for White" is a low pressure inquiry into a legitimate social situation. The Allied Artists release, written, produced and directed by Fred M. Wilcox, is only a superficial probing of the reasons and reactions of the Negro girl who "passes." It is actually a romantic melodrama in which racial problems are a factor. While tasteful, if unrevealing, film's best chances will be as an exploitation item.

Sonya Wilde plays the young woman of the title, whose race is not apparent in her color. She believes she can make her best adjustment by leaving her community and Negro family and "passing." She discovers this means the exchange of one set of problems for another, when she falls in love and marries a white man without disclosing to him her background.

The young woman is presented as intelligent and sensitive, yet she goes into the precarious deception without any plan. She is trapped repeatedly by simple questions about her background and she is remarkably inept in extricating herself. Taking this premise, the untruths multiply rapidly, leading the heroine and the story away from any real exploration of the basic problems of the situation. The ending has Miss Wilde leaving her husband to vanish back into the Negro world from which she came.

Wilcox's screenplay, within its limits, is candid without being vulgar or offensive to any parties, although its climactic moments are likely to strike the younger generation, at least, as pretty old hat. (The heroine's chief concern is that she will bear a "black baby.") A good deal of the film's potential is wasted in diversionary scenes that have no application to the theme, and in other sequences where the points could be made more succintly. The direction, of the results of it, are often cursory.

Miss Wilde, making he film bow, displays an attractive and considerable talent. James Franciscus, as the husband, is handicapped by a character of no depth or shadings. Others in the cast who are prominent and helpful include Pat Michon, Elizabeth Council, Isabelle Cooley, Thomas B. Henry and Lon Ballantyne.

George Folsey's camera work is skillful.
Powe.

Carry on Constable
(BRITISH)

Another slapstick farce in a format that has reaped a golden biz harvest in Gt. Britain; plenty of yocks for the undemanding.

London, Feb. 23.
Anglo-Amalgamated release of a Peter Rogers production. Stars Sidney James, Eric Barker, Kenneth Connor, Charles Hawtrey, Kenneth Williams, Leslie Phillips, Joan Sims, Hattie Jacques. Shirley Eaton. Directed by Gerald Thomas. Screenplay by Norman Hudis, from an idea by Brock Williams; camera, Ted Scaife; editor, John Shirley; music, Bruce Montgomery. At Plaza Theatre, London, Feb. 22, '60.

Sergeant Wilkins	Sidney James
Inspector Mills	Eric Barker
Constable Constable	Kenneth Connor
Constable Gorse	Charley Hawtrey
Sergeant Laura Moon	Hattie Jacques
Constable Potter	Leslie Phillips
Policewoman Passworthy	Joan Sims
Constable Benson	Kenneth Williams
Sally Barry	Shirley Eaton
Constable Thurston	Cyril Chamberlain
Mrs. May	Joan Hickson
Distraught Woman	Irene Handl
Herbert Hall	Terence Longdon
Policewoman Harrison	Jill Adams
1st Crook	Freddie Mills
Store Manager	Brian Oulton
Criminal Type	Victor Maddern
Matt	Michael Balfour
Honoria	Diane Aubrey
1st Shop Assistant	Mary Law
Young Woman	Dorinda Stevens

Despite their terrific b.o. success, producer Peter Rogers is wise in announcing that he is going to ease up on his "Carry On" series. The format could easily wear thin. Rationed, there seems no reason why the pix shouldn't last for ever. The latest, "Carry On Constable," should prove as profitable as its predecessors.

This is simply an anthology of police gags and situations, with, for example, one of the cops being named Constable Charlie .Constable. It's easy to see how script-writer Norman Hudis has milked that joke for a couple of yocks.

Insofar as there is a story line, this concerns a flu-stricken police station which is reinforced by four fledgling cops straight from the police school. Their green behavior provides simple but surefire laughter. Of course, in the end the hapless quartet distinguishes itself by rounding up, in improbable fashion, a bunch of crooks.

The producer has brought back most of the team of stalwarts that has been on parade in the four previous "Carry On" films. Kenneth Connor, Kenneth Williams, Charles Hawtrey and Leslie Phillips are the four zany cops; Hattie Jacques and Joan Sims are two policewomen and Shirley Eaton and Jill Adams provide the glamour and slight touch of romance.

Eric Barker is excellent as the inefficient inspector in charge of the station while Sidney James, a newcomer to the team, is in his usual first-class form as the sergeant who is annoyed with the recruits.

The range of slapstick is proved by the fact that there is even one scene when, literally, a character falls down by slipping on a banana peel. The script is spiced with inoffensive vulgarity and much play upon words. At times it seems that the team is hard put to it to keep up the laughter pressure but, all in all, this achieves its objective of providing harmless merriment.
Rich.

Le Bossu
(The Hunchback)
(FRENCH—COLOR—DYALISCOPE)

Paris, Feb. 23.
Pathe release of Globe-PAC production. Stars Jean Marais, Bourvil; features Sabina Selman, Hubert Noel, Jean Le

Poulain. Directed by Andre Hunnebelle. Screenplay, Jean Halain, Pierre Foucaud from novel by Paul Feval; camera (Eastmancolor), Marcel Grignon; editor, G. Levy. At Richilieu-Gaumont, Paris. Running time, **115 MINS.**

Lagardere .... Jean Marais
Passepoil .... Bourvil
Aurore .... Sabina Selman
Nevers .... Hubert Noel
Gonzague .... Francois Chaumette
Killer .... Jean Le Poulain

This, an easygoing 18th Century costume actioner, shapes as a French western. It is a simple, romantic tale, having enough action and production dress to make for good returns here, and possible playoffs abroad. However, the familiar plot calls for the hard sell.

An adventurer and his comic sidekick help a nobleman. A conniving courtier has the nobleman killed, but the adventurer brings up the nobleman's baby daughter and then comes back to avenge his friend.

This has plenty of horseplay and duels. Jean Marais is correctly dashing as the avenger who masquerades as a hunchback to get into the enemy's graces. He displays rare acting ability as well as acrobatic knowhow. Supporting players are fine. Director Andre Hunnebelle has given this a good feel for the period and a light treatment of the romantic aspects to come up with a breezy affair. Bourvil is an asset as the comical, cowardly helper. Sabina Selman is attractive even though she has little to do. *Mosk.*

La Vache Et Le Prisonnier
(The Cow and the Prisoner) (FRENCH)

Paris, Feb. 23.

Pathe release of Cyclope production. Stars Fernandel; features Pierre Louis, Richard Winckler, Albert Remy, Rene Harvard, Francisca Kinz. Directed by Henri Verpeuil. Screenplay, Henri Jeanson, Jean Manse, Jacques Antoine; camera, Roger Hubert; editor, Gabriel Rongier. At Balzac, Paris. Running time, **120 MINS.**

Antoine .... Fernandel
Nasil .... Pierre Louis
Benno .... Richard Winckler
Franz .... Albert Remy
Gusti .... Rene Havard
Inge .... Francisca Kinz

Here Fernandel is a prisoner of war who escapes to make his way back to France during the last World War by leading a cow and maintaining he is a farm worker. Pic has some bawdy barracks room beginnings. But the gimmick is somewhat stretched with some okay invention but little comedy and mainly a playoff item abroad on the Fernandel monicker and the fairly offbeat theme.

Fernandel does his usual clever mugging of fear and canniness. The cow proved a good foil, but the over use of stock shots and few really inventive bits makes this a hard sell item.

The general style of the pic vacillates between realism, farce and situation comedy. This is just another Fernandel vehicle with main chances on his pull. *Mosk.*

When Comedy Was King

Sequel to same producer's "Golden Age of Comedy" compilation of silent footage.

Hollywood, Feb. 26.

Twentieth-Fox release produced and written by Robert Youngson. Narrator: Dwight Weist; music, Ted Royal. Cast: Fatty Arbuckle, Wallace Beery, Billy Bevan, Charlie Chase, Charlie Chaplin, Andy Clude, Chester Conklin, Vernon Dent, Stuart Erwin, Jimmy Finlayson, Madeline Hurlock, Keystone Cops, Keystone Teddy, Buster Keaton, Edgar Kennedy, Harry Langdon, Laurel & Hardy, Charlie Murray, Mabel Normand, Snub Pollard, Daphne Pollard, Gloria Swanson, Al St. John, Mack Swain, Sennett Girls, Ben Turpin, Bobby Vernon. Previewed at the studio, Feb. 25, '60. Running time, **90 MINS.**

Success of "When Comedy Was King" may be commensurate to response for "The Golden Age of Comedy," a similar compilation of clips from early silent films which the same producer, Robert Youngson, put together. Its appeal would seem to be chiefly to those who remember with nostalgia this great era of comedy, but perhaps younger audiences will find some fun of discovery. Twentieth-Fox is releasing this presentation.

Collection of several comedy samples of the silent days, many complete one or two-reelers embraces Charlie Chaplin and Mabel Normand; Laurel & Hardy and Jimmy Finlayson (in a short directed by Leo McCarey and photographed by George Stevens); Ben Turpin and the Sennett Girls; Wallace Beery, Gloria Swanson and Bobby Vernon; Harry Langdon, Fatty Arbuckle, Stu Erwin, Edgar Kennedy, Buster Keaton.

Response to the narration, written by Youngson and narrated by Dwight Weist, will vary. To this reviewer it often sounded condescending and cute, since the almost purely physical comedy stands on its own merits without need of explanation or elaboration. It seemed unnecessary to go into Chaplin's subsequent political adventures when showing a 1914 comedy. There is a tendency, also, to note personal decline from heights of popularity. This lugubrious foot-noting is not always accurate and it certainly isn't conducive to present laughter. The musical background is not very imaginative, either.

Still, it is a fast 90 minutes of film that Youngson has assembled. The narrator notes at one point that much silent footage has been lost.

Youngson has had the good sense to keep this film in the old aspect ratio (1.66) in which it was shot. Present-day film-goers, if they notice, may be surprised to see how much action and information it is possible to get into this frame, smaller, but not necessarily inferior, to current wide, wide screens. *Powe.*

Le Testament D'Orphee
(The Will of Orpheus) (FRENCH)

Paris, Feb. 23.

Pagode release of EC production. Written by, starring and directed by Jean Cocteau. Camera, R. Pontoiseau; editor, M. J. Yoyotte. At Pagode, Paris. Running time, **80 MINS.**

Probably only in France can a film like this be made as a commercial venture. Besides having a regular producer, a great deal of the money was raised from friends and well wishers. So it is a combo patronage-industry pic which allows Jean Cocteau, now 70, poet-writer-playwright filmmaker, to make a film in which he tries to explain the meaning of a poet's life and, incidentally, his own.

Full of his own symbolism, aphorisms and thoughts, playing himself as an errant poet who roams through the ages, this is naturally a highly personalized pic mainly for the arty set and those who care for or know his works and symbols. It is distinctly offbeat film fare.

This film is mainly for arty spots abroad but word-of-mouth could get in enough of the curious to give it a specialized run in some big city spots or at universities. His mythical "Orphee" is now in its seventh year at a West Berlin house. Hence, the right booking and patience could have this in for limited but possibly okay biz. But it needs personal handling.

Cocteau subtitles his pic, "And Don't Ask Me Why." He is an 18th Century poet who scares a few people.

Cocteau still has a flair for provoking strange moods in ordinary landscapes as well as utilizing simple trick effects effectively and judiciously. He ribs himself at times but is quite clear in his summation that a poet is rarely recognized in his time. But, overall, it is too murky, talky and self indulgent to be anything but a precious, unusual pic for the so-called "happy few."

Lensing is good and Cocteau is personable if sometimes quaint. Popping up throughout are familiar local actors plus Yul Brynner, Picasso, Serge Lifar, Luis Dominguin and others. This is his final film fling and will probably end as a museum piece. It can be analyzed, interpreted, but it emerges the meandering musings of a talented man out of kilter with his times. *Mosk.*

L'Eau a la Bouche
(The Mouth Waters) (FRENCH)

Paris, Feb. 23.

Cocinor release of Films Pleiade production. With Bernadette Lafont, Michel Galabru, Francoise Brion, Alexandra Stewart, Paul Guers, Jacques Riberolles. Written and directed by Jacques Doniol-Valcroze. Camera, Marcel Weiss; editor, C. Negri. At Mercury, Paris. Running time, **95 MINS.**

Prudence .... Bernadette Lafont
Cesar .... Michel Galabru
Milena .... Francoise Brion
Robert .... Jacques Riberolles
Fifine .... Alexandra Stewart
Jean-Paul .... Paul Guers

Ballyhooed as the first comedy of the so-called "new wave," the pic is actually only a familiar comedy of manners and sex habits. Set in a deserted chateau, it plays out the reassortment of two couples, plus that of a pair of servants. It is slickly done, with an insight into the surface maneuverings of its people. Film has enough bally angles via the love scenes to make this a possible Yank arty house entry, but a hard sell called for.

A girl, living with a fashionable photographer, finds she has inherited something from an old aunt and goes to an old chateau to hear the will. Her lover, who has a free arrangement with her as far as side love activities go, comes to see her and lets himself be taken for her brother, who is due to arrive later.

Then he falls for the beauteous cousin while his girl goes for the young lawyer who reads the will. In the background is a lovesick valet trying to seduce a coy maid. All get paired off. But the lawyer turns out to be a skirt chaser which almost causes a tragedy because the hysterical, naive girl runs off to possibly commit suicide. But she fails to take her own life.

Jacques Doniol-Valcroze, a film critic, has given this shrewd mounting but has relied somewhat too much on dialog. If the characters remain rather tepid, they are surrounded by photogenic aspects and there is a production plus in on the spot lensing in a colorful old chateau. Technical credits are good. Actors and actresses are fresh and sleek. *Mosk.*

. . . Und Noch Frech Dazu!
(. . . And Saucy At That!) (GERMAN)

Berlin, Feb. 23.

UFA production and release. With Helga Schlack, Horst Janson, Marianne Borck, Michael Verhoeven, Peter Gross. Directed by Rolf von Sydow. Screenplay, Max Colpet and Thomas Keck; camera, Ted Kornowicz; music, Ernst Simon; settings, Hanns H. Kuhnert and Wilhelm Vorwerg; editing, Ilse Voigt. At UFA Pavillon, Berlin. Running time, **97 MINS.**

Fred .... Horst Janson
Shortie .... Wolfgang Koch
Susanne .... Marianne Borck
Helga .... Ilse Page
Rockie .... Michael Verhoeven
Richard .... Peter Gross
Karin .... Helga Schlack
Ingrid .... Barbara Frey
Bulle .... Klaus Loewitsch
Baron .... Guy Gehrke
Bix .... Michael Weichberger
Boris .... Thomas Keck

This UFA production is to give newcomers, both before and behind the camera, a break. But if this is Germany's answer to the "new wave," it better had forget about it. There's little new or exciting about this film which, at best, is just a poor imitation of what people have been doing in Hollywood. Plot is unbelievably thin, situations familiar and acting mostly stereotyped. If pic shapes here as an okay grosser, it likely is because there is a strong interest in juve pix on the part of youthful audiences.

Roughly, this centers on a motorcycle gang which clashes with a bunch of young jazz fanatics. If this is to show the problems of today's youth, an essential subject has been wasted.

Rolf von Sydow, one of Germany's youngest directors, tried apparently hard to lead some of the young players to worth-while performances but the outcome is not very convincing. Positive exceptions: Michael Verhoeven in the role of a boy on the verge of gangsterism and Ilse Page as a beatnik's moll. Latter reveals some comedy talents.

Best about the pic is its background music contributed by a number of top-notch jazz musicians, including Americans Oscar Pettiford, Benny Bailey, Joe Harris, Sweden's Jack Lidstroem, England's Stud Hamer and others. Technical credits are okay. *Hans.*

Ein Mann Geht Durch Die Wand
(A Man Goes Through the Wall) (GERMAN)

Berlin, Feb. 23.

Deutsche Film Hansa release of Kurt Ulrich production. Stars Heinz Ruehmann; with Nicole Courcel, Rudolf Vogel, Hubert von Meyerinck, Peter Vogel. Directed by Ladislao Vajda. Screenplay, Istvan Bekeffi and Hans Jacoby, after novel "Le Passe Muraille" by Marcel Ayme; camera, Bruno Mondi; music, Franz Grothe. At Zoo Palast, Berlin. Running time, **98 MINS.**

Herr Buchsbaum ....Heinz Ruehmann
Yvonne Steiner .... Nicole Courcel
Painter .... Rudolf Rhomberg
Fuchs .... Rudolf Vogel
Hirschfeld .... Peter Vogel
Pickler .... Hubert v. Meyerinck
Holtzheimer .... Hans Leibelt

Ladislao Vajda's sensitive direction, an outstanding cast headed by Heinz Ruehmann and an amusing, heartwarming story make "Wall" one of the best German pix in recent years. This enjoyable film is a refreshing departure from

so many Teutonic cliche productions seen in the past year. Although this comedy is on the offbeat side, it should find a receptive audience here. It also has foreign chances since it contains something that this country's film comedies so often lack, real charm.

The title can be taken literally. It centers about a little, modest revenue officer (Ruehmann) who suddenly discovers that he has the ability to go through walls. He widely exploits his ability, resulting in numerous witty situations.

Director Vajda skillfully avoids corny slapstick but manages to give this comedy a human and sophisticated touch. In a way. "Wall" can be compared with his delightful Spanish-Italian venture, "Un Angelo Paso por Brooklyn."

Ruehmann masterfully makes the most of the title role. Not only does he garner laughter but he also knows to touch the heart. Support is tops also. French Nicole Courcel plays the girl next door. Hubert von Meyerinck is seen in a fine satirical study of Ruehmann's superior. Rudolf Vogel and Peter Vogel register strongly as his office colleagues.

Camera (there is some fine cinema trickery), imaginative music and editing come up to praiseworthy standards. The vehicle's production dress indicates a "little" film. But this noses out nearly all of this country's so-called expensive pix in the past year. It's a film of which Hungarian-born Vajda can be proud. *Hans.*

Wenn die Glocken Hell Erklingen

(When the Bells Sound Clearly)
(AUSTRIAN—COLOR—MUSIC)

Vienna, Feb. 23.

Neue Film Verleih release of Donau Film (Eduard Hoesch) production. With Willy Birgel, Annie Rosar, Rudolf Carl, Hermann Thimig, Ellen Schwiers and Teddy Reno. Directed by Eduard von Borsody. Screenplay, Kurt E. Walter and Borsody; camera, Hans Heinz Theyer; music, Willy Mattes. At Loewen Kino, Vienna. Running time, 90 MINS.

Guenther v. Warttenberg	Willy Birgel
Susanne Weiden	Ellen Schwiers
Mario Pucci	Teddy Reno
Alma	Annie Rosar
Michael	Michael Ande
Hanna Warttenberg	Loni Friedl
Maria Warttenberg	Senta Wengraf
Policeman	Rudolf Carl
Maxl	Alfred Costas
Poldi	Gerald Hayer
Fatty	Gustav Bauer
Mrs. Roesner	Lola Urban-Kneidinger
Mayor	Paul Horn
Dr. Mersmann	Hermann Thimig

This is another Vienna Singing Boys adventure opus with plenty of action and singing. Most of the story is laid in Hinterbiechl in East Tyrol, the vacation home of the boys. Michael Ande acts sharply in his part when accused of stealing. This time his innocence is proven by a medallion.

Willy Birgel, as his grandfather, again proves his high acting ability. Teddy Reno, in the role of the teacher, is very good. His opposite, Loni Friedl, displays varied emotions in their romance.

Director Eduard von Borsody approached this pic with serious intent. Willy Matte's music further moved the film through its paces. Hans Heinz Theyer's camera has captured the beautiful Alpine surroundings. *Maas.*

Heller in Pink Tights

(COLOR)

Good technique in filming an average story. B.o. prospects okay.

Hollywood, Feb. 29.

Paramount release of a Carlo Ponti-Marcello Girosi Production. Stars Sophia Loren, Anthony Quinn; costars Margaret O'Brien, Steve Forrest; with Eileen Heckart, Ramon Novarro, Edmund Lowe; and George Mathews, Edward Binns, Warren Wade, Frank Silvera, Robert Palmer, Leo V. Mafranga, Cal Bolder, Taggart Casey, Howard McNear. Directed by George Cukor. Screenplay, Dudley Nichols and Walter Bernstein, based on a novel by Louis L'Amour; camera (Technicolor), Harold Lipstein; editor, Howard Smith; music, Daniele Amfitheatrof. Previewed at the studio, Feb. 29, '60. Running time, 100 MINS.

With "Heller In Pink Tights," director George Cukor put tongue in cheek to turn an ordinary story into a gaudy, old-fashioned western satire with gleeful touches of melodrama. It's bright execution of a film whose boxoffice outlook is about average. Sophia Loren and Anthony Quinn star in the Carlo Ponti-Marcello Girosi production for Paramount.

Taken from a novel by Louis L'Amour and screenplayed by Walter Bernstein and the late Dudley Nichols, "Heller" follows The Great Healy Dramatic and Concert Co. in two red wagons through the wilds of Wyoming. The traveling theatre is fighting for its survival, and Miss Loren and Quinn put up a strong enough battle to make things interesting and amusing. It's when the film's plottage dissolves into pure western that it becomes somewhat commonplace.

Miss Loren donned blonde tresses for the role of an actress who has a knack for getting into situations. She looks fine with golden head and turns in a respectable, most believable performance. Quinn, as head of the Healy company, adeptly projects as the heman, yet properly building a tender, calm characterization.

Eileen Heckart just about steals the whole shootin' match as an actress who has given up a "promising" career for her daughter's chances on stage. It's real comedy, and Miss Heckart carries it off with polish. Steve Forrest makes a lovable villain, evil but never evil enough to lose his attraction. He's a good actor, versatile and appealing. Margaret O'Brien is fine in a role that offers her more chances to be seen than heard; Edmund Lowe is very good as a "Shakespearean" actor; and Romon Novarro is aptly sinister as a well-heeled banker.

Director Cukor filled many of his scenes with full-blown diversion, others with high action, and his skill blends the two without weakening either of them. It's fun when Miss Loren bets herself against a poker pot, showing four 7's but losing herself to Forrest, a professional gunman who has four Jack's. And it's exciting when Forrest saves the traveling group from the funniest band of Indians since the original cigar store redskin. But Cukor's ability can only keep things going so long, and more than once the 100-minute film bogs down.

The production itself is excellent, the Harold Lipstein Technicolor photography a striking composition of color and movement. Art directors Hal Pereira and Eugene Allen outdid themselves, particularly with the theatre settings, and the second unit work of director Arthur Rosson and cameraman Irmin Roberts takes full advantage of fine Arizona settings.

Daniele Amfitheatrof's musical score boosts the satire considerably, and definite bonuses are the result of expert work by costumer Edith Head, set decorators Sam Comer and Grace Gregory, editor Howard Smith and soundmen John Wilkinson and Winston Leverett. *Ron.*

Die Wahrheit Ueber Rosemarie

(The Truth About Rosemarie)
(GERMAN)

Berlin, March 1.

Union release of Rapid-Film (Wolfgang Hartwig) and Dieter Fritko production. Stars Belinda Lee; features Walter Rilla, Paul Dahlke, Jan Hendriks, Hans Nielsen. Directed by Rudolf Jugert. Screenplay, J. Joachim Bartsch; camera, Georg Krause; music, Willy Mattes; editing, Herbert Taschner. At Zoo Palast, Berlin. Running time, 101 MINS.

Rosemarie	Belinda Lee
Woltikoff	Walter Rilla
Reimer	Paul Dahlke
Salzmann	Jan Hendriks
Bernbeil	Hans Nielsen
von Riedendank	Karl Schoenboeck
Fred Guttberg	Claus Wilcke
Frau Huber	Lina Carstens

The second Teutonic pic about Rosemarie Nitribitt, Germany's famous postwar courtesan who was found strangled in her Frankfurt apartment, is not up to the first "Rosemarie" pic. While the first film, "The Girl Rosemarie," with Nadja Tiller in the title role, had a sharp satirical slant, this is more documentary type of feature pic. Its accent is on realism. As a matter of fact, the creators of this even had in mind to let a certain Pohlmann, suspect in the murder case but later acquitted, play himself in this production, but this idea was abandoned after a protest from the German film industry.

The Wolfgang Hartwig and Dieter Fritko production surpasses general expectations. It's remarkably well directed and excellently acted. Doubtful whether this film will become as stout a grosser as its predecessor. But it does have substantial b.o. possibilities abroad.

Best thing about the pic is the top-notch acting by England's Belinda Lee whose voice was dubbed by a German actress. Her portrayal of the girl Rosemaries who sells herself for money is unusually convincing. Director Rudolf Jugert also led the supporting players to fine performances. Even the minor characters come alive. Technical credits are nice, too. *Hans.*

Vivir del Cuento

(Living By One's Wits)

Mexico City, March 1.

A Peliculas Nacionales release of a Cinematografica Filmex, S.A. production. Stars Tin-Tan, Luz Maria Aguilar and Carlos Cores; features Pancho Cordova, Celia Viveros, Marcelo Chavez, Rita Rangel, Jose Jasso and Elena Julian. Directed by Rafael Baledon. Screenplay, Francisco Cordova based on original by Julio Porter. At Real Cinema, Mexico City. Running time, 90 MINS.

This is another in the series of Tin-Tan pictures in which the comic repeats old jokes and situations. Actor has a certain following in Mexico, is touted as second best to Cantinflas, but unlike the latter he draws heavily on standard comic patter in developing the story of a central character whose mode of earning daily expenses is from telling stories.

Tin-Tan falls far short of giving a film portrayal of a believable Mexican character. Strong point of Mexican comics is always to take off from a type identifiable by the masses like a doorman, a shoeshine boy, a lottery ticket peddler, fireman, elevator operator, and build up comedy by all sorts of situations that might feasibly be connected with his daily work. Add a dash of maudlin sentiment, a more or less flaming love affair, and the comics have a picture.

But this latest film will only appeal to Tin-Tan's nucleus of fans in Mexico and possibly in some Spanish-speaking areas. *Emil.*

Kajikko

(Angry Island)
(JAPANESE-COLOR)

Hollywood, March 2.

Bentley Films release of Mac Krim production, produced by Masafumi Soga. Features Kazuo Suzuki, Shigeo Tezuka, Teruo Shibata, Yasuo Tauchiya, Shigeaki Goto. Directed by Seeji Hisamatsu. Screenplay, Yoko Mizuki, from original story, "The Rowers," by Yoko Mizuki; camera (Eastman-color), Seiichi Kizuka; music, Yasushi Akatagawa. Previewed at Beverly Canon Theatre, March 1, '60. Running time, 90 MINS.

Tetsu Nakaya	Kazuo Suzuki
Teizo Terada	Shigeo Tezuka
Mitsuo Ito	Teruo Shibata
Kotaro	Yasuo Tsuchiya
Taichi	Shigeaki Goto
Susumu	Yukio Akiyama
Tadashi	Kiyoshi Komiyama
Kazuo	Sankichi Ishihara
Naoji	Gen Sato
Kinuko	Terumi Futagi
Yoshikawa	Mosao Oda
Izo	Saburo Ukida

"Angry Island" is based upon true incidents which happened in 1931 on an island in the Inland Sea of Japan, when authorities discovered that boys taken from reformatories were sold into virtual slavery for the back-breaking task of rowing boats for fishermen who beat and starved their unwilling and unhappy charges. Produced by the same filmmaker, Masafumi Soga, who previously turned out the well-remembered "Rashomon" and "Gate of Hell," it is a powerful entry for the art house trade which may gain by word-of-mouth.

Acquired for worldwide release, outside the Communist countries, by Mac Krim, during a recent visit to Japan, distribution will be handled by Bentley Films of N.Y. Feature benefits immeasurably by beautiful color photography and lovely land and seascapes, and careful casting for a well developed screenplay lends high conviction to subject matter. Most of the interest centers in the actions of the pitiful rower boys, under constant cruelty by their masters. After one of them has been killed by his owner, several of the boys escape to the mainland, where they're picked up and the conditions on Itoshi Island made known for the first time.

Cast is headed by Kazuo Suzuki, a rower boy who instigates the revolt, persuasive in a difficult role. Direction by Seiiji Hisamatsu is fine in its approach and encompassment of subject, well scripted by Yoko Mizuki, and color camera work by Seiichi Kizuka is superb. *Whit.*

Infierno de Almas

(Lost Souls)
(MEXICAN)

Mexico City, Feb. 23.

A Peliculas Nacionales release of a Filadora Mexicana, S.A. production. Stars Christiane Martel, Ramon Armengod and Sonia Furio; features Tito Junco, Yerye Beirute, Jose Baviera, Fernando Fernandez. Directed by Benito Alazraki. At Real Cinama, Mexico City. Running time, 90 MINS.

Director Benito Alazraki, who some years back turned out the prize winning "Raices" (Roots), here has been restricted in working on a three week shooting

schedule and a rigidly limited budget.

Picture suffers from the obvious speed in production evident even in dance scenes of Sonia Furio. Story takes place in Algiers, and has the usual quota of criminals, police, loves and intrigues, a Pepe le Moko sort of central character (played by Ramón Armengod who returns to the screen after a long absence), and a lovelorn policeman interpreted by Tito Junco. Yerye Beirute plays a decent, lovable sort of bandit. It all adds up to the usual hokum.

Were it not for the Alazraki touch, this would not have passed muster. As it is, the director has given picture a certain interest and suspense.

Yerye Beirute, as the bandit, milks the love scenes with sundry ladies. He wears a dried humming bird over his heart, and this is supposed to make the ladies lose the heads and hearts to him infallibly.   *Emil.*

Impaciencia del Corazon
(Impatient Heart)
(MEXICAN)

Mexico City, March 1.
A Peliculas Nacionales release of a Filmadora Chapultepec and Galindo Hnos. production. Stars Martha Mijares, Christiane Martell and Armando Silvestre; features Andres Solar, Miguel Manzano, Manuel Arvide, Genaro de Alba. Directed by Tito Davison. Screenplay by Tito Davison and Edmundo Baez from novel by Stefan Zweig; camera, Gabriel Figueroa; music by Raul Lavista. At Variedades Theatre, Mexico City. Running time, **90 MINS.**

This Mexican version of the novel by Stefan Zweig, covering the love affair of an invalid for an officer of the Mexican revolutionary forces, can best be described as being a satisfying spectacle. The photography of Gabriel Figueroa, ace cameraman, has captured the natural beauty of Guanajuato, where action develops.

However, the actors do not put across their lines nor make their characters convincing. Fault seems evenly divided between talent, direction and adaptation.

What was planned as a romantic tear jerker turns out flat and at times even bad taste.   *Emil.*

Marie Des Iles
(Maries of the Isles)
(FRENCH-COLOR)

Paris, Feb. 23.
Radius production and release. Stars Belinda Lee; features Magali Noel. Alain Saury, Folco Lulli, Jacques Castelot, Dario Moreno, Noel Roquevert. Jean Tissier. Directed by Georges Combret. Screenplay, Pierre Maudru, Combret from novel by Robert Gaillard; camera (Eastmancolor), Pierre Petit; editor, C. Laboreur. At Ambassade-Gaumont. Paris. Running time, **105 MINS.**

Marie	Belinda Lee
Julie	Magali Noel
Duparquier	Alain Saury
Lefort	Folco Lulli
Saint Andre	Jacques Castelot
Baracuda	Noel Roquevert
Fauvel	Jean Tissier

Tale of skullduggery and piracy on some tropical isles in the 17th century is statically mounted, acted and unfolded. It shapes mainly as a local item.

A conniving nobleman has the governor of an island kidnapped by pirates. But he escapes to come back to save his friends from the upstart's gallows and his girl from a fate worse than death. This lacks production value and proper thesping with little export chances.
                                         Mosk.

Los Desarraigados
(The Uprooted Ones)
(MEXICAN)

Mexio City, Feb. 23.
A Peliculas Nacionales release of a Cinematografica Inter-Continental, S.A. production. Stars Pedro Armendaris, Ariadne Welter, Agustin de Anda; features Sonia Furio, Jose Elias Moreno, Dolores Tinoco, Quintin Bulnes and Emily Lee. Screenplay by Raul de Anda and Gilberto Gazcon, based on play by J. Humberto Robles. Directed by Gilberto Gazcon. At Cine Roble, Mexico City. Running time, **95 MINS.**

An adaptation of the stage play by J. Humberto Robles, this improves on the dramatic work because of greater flexibility of the film camera, and the use of exterior scenes. The action takes place in San Antonio, Texas, in 1911, the uprooted being those who have fled the revolution north of the border, with their children born in the U.S. The second pic to be directed by Gilberto Gazcon, it is better than average film entertainment.

Problems of children born outside of their homeland, who deny their fatherland and their parents, form gist of story. Sometimes the language becomes quite strong. In this one, Mexicans gleefully have a chance to paint the gringos in uncomplimentary terms. Gazcon's first pic was "The Boxer," which won critical acclaim.

Sonia Furio, moving up, co-stars and essays a dramatic role instead of his usual song and dance, undress routines. Agustin de Anda, in his second film, shows improvement; Adriadne Welter is convincing and Pedro Armendariz, as the older brother, is better than he has been in recent efforts.

Jose Elias Moreno and Dolores Tinoca are the parents who do not forget their native land. Miss Tinoca's first appearance in pictures, she gives a realistic performance as the mother. Quintin Bulnes has a secondary role which does not require any special efforts.
                                         Emil.

Can-Can
(TODD-AO; TECHNICOLOR)

Serviceable filmusical. Sinatra, MacLaine, Chevalier and Jourdan spark b.o. which should be good.

Twentieth-Fox release of a Jack Cummings Production. Stars Frank Sinatra, Shirley MacLaine, Maurice Chevalier, Louis Jourdan. Produced for Suffolk-Cummings Productions by Jack Cummings. Director, Walter Lang; associate producer, Saul Chaplin; screenplay, Dorothy Kingsley and Charles Lederer, based on the musical comedy by Abe Burrows; songs, Cole Porter; musical arranger-conductor, Nelson Riddle; vocal supervision, Bobby Tucker; choreography, Hermes Pan; costumes, Irene Sharaff; camera, William H. Daniels; editor, Robert Simpson; art direction, Lyle Wheeler and Jack Martin Smith; set decoration, Walter M. Scott and Paul S. Fox; sound, W. D. Flick. Previewed at the Carthay Circle Theatre, Hollywood, March 8, '60. Running time, **134 MINS.**

Francois Durnais	Frank Sinatra
Simone Pistache	Shirley MacLaine
Paul Barriere	Maurice Chevalier
Philippe Forrestier	Louis Jourdan
Claudine	Juliet Prowse
Andre-Headwaiter	Marcel Dalio
Orch. Leader	Leon Belasco
Bailiff	Nestor Paiva
Photographer	John A. Neris
Judge Merceaux	Jean Del Val
Chevrolet	Eugene Borden
Recorder	Jonathan Kidd
Severe Woman	Ann Codee
Adam	Marc Wilder

"Can-Can" is neither as bad as the remarks of Khrushchev would indicate nor is it as good as the drumbeating of the 20th-Fox ballymen would have you believe. It falls somewhere in between. It's a serviceable musical and it will have no difficulty in attracting large droves of the general audience. The more discriminating film-goers will find it wanting.

It'll probably be a tremendous grosser despite the flaws in its execution. The marquee value of Frank Sinatra, Shirley MacLaine, Maurice Chevalier and Louis Jourdan, the Cole Porter songs, the publicity value of the Soviet Premier's comments, and the Todd-AO production represent solid b.o. ingredients. However, the film lacks the true stature of a roadshow entry.

It's Las Vegas, 1960; not Montmartre, 1896. The Jack Cummings production, as directed by Walter Lang, somehow conveys the feeling that Clan members Sinatra and Miss MacLaine would soon be joined by other members of the group for another "summit" meeting.

Miss MacLaine is bouncy, outgoing, scintillating, vivacious and appealing—but French she ain't. Sinatra is, well, Sinatra, complete with the ring-a-ding-ding vocabularly of the insiders. The juxtaposition of Sinatra and Miss Mac-Laine on the one hand, and authentic Parisians Maurice Chevalier and Louis Jourdan on the other is jarring.

Even if you accept "Can-Can" as a tongue-in-cheek offering, the basic premise is still hard to swallow. It has something to do with the banning of the can-can dance on the ground that it is "lewd and lascivious." The dance, as presented in the film, is spirited, well-executed and among the high points of the terp routines, but it is difficult to understand how it could have ruffled the sensibilities of Khrushchev or the fictional moralists of the film.

As the proprietor of cafe that pays off the gendarmes so that the imbibers can witness the illegal dance, Miss MacLaine has the op-

portunity to indulge in uninhibited and brash clowning and frenzied dancing. Sinatra is her wisecracking playboy-lawyer who aptly handles her legal and private affairs. Both Chevalier and Jourdan, who clicked so strongly in "Gigi," are wasted in thankless roles as corruptible and incorruptible judges, respectively.

The Dorothy Kingsley - Charles Lederer screenplay has been obviously spiced up with risque material and scenes. None of it is offensive, but it's occasionally labored, as the takeoff on the girl's name "Virginia," for example. The musical score has been enhanced with three Cole Porter songs that were not in the original Broadway musical—"Let's Do It," "Just One of Those Things" and "You Do Something to Me." The best tune from the original, as sung by Sinatra, is still "C'est Magnifique." "I Love Paris" is merely employed as background music. The Chevalier and Jourdan duet of "Live and Let Live" is merely so-so. Sinatra tallies nicely with "It's All Right With Me."

The dance numbers, for the most part, are the highlights of the film, particularly Miss MacLaine's Apache dance. The famous "Adam and Eve" ballet falls somewhat flat, although it does show off to good advantage Marc Wilder and Juliet Prowse. The can-can is fun, but about as lewd and lascivious as a Maypole dance.

The production is sumptuous and the costumes are lavish. These aspects are expertly captured by William H. Daniels' Todd-AO photography. Tom Keogh's titles, patterned after Tullouse-Lautrec, provide fine lead-in material.
                                         Holl.

Circus Stars

Culture exchange documentary on Russian circus. Pretty good.

Hollywood, March 1.
Paramount release of Central Documentary Film Studio production. Features Oleg Popov, Vladimir Durov, Alexander Serge, Vladimir Davaiko, the Diomkin Group, the Pavlovnov Group, Margarita Nazarova, Constantinovsky Rabadan Abarkoroff, Boris and Natasha Mazilhi, the Polifronov, Lavazinski, Valentin Filatov. Directed by L. Kristy; screenplay, V. Komissarzhevsky, L. Kristy; camera, I. Gutman, P. Rusanov, V. Vorontsov. Previewed at the studio, March 3, '60. Running time, **61 MINS.**

"Circus Stars" brings to American audiences a thorough (almost too thorough) account of what goes on under the Russian big top. It comes to States as part of the Jan. 27, 1958 U.S.-U.S.S.R. agreement on reciprocal exhibition of motion pictures. While it is a competent documentary of Russian circus skills, and certainly a welcome import, it doesn't figure to have hefty impact on our unsentimental capitalist boxoffice for the simple reason reason that it is the everyday Russian himself, not his circus, that has the natural appeal here.

As a circus picture, it is a straightforward, accurate study of that colorful world, and is ample evidence that the Russian version of America's 30-odd circuses contains elements of skill and excitement that are absent here. Although the tang, the imminent peril, the suspense of the circus can seldom be properly captured on celluloid, this film does have a candid pictorial quality, a sense of unrehearsed production that is appropriate in a circus picture. All the acts do not run smoothly. Minor mishaps occur that give the film an added dash of authenticity.

Audiences here should enjoy the many shots of Russian spectators as much as the acts themselves, latter running the gamut of well-known circus features—from educated wild animals to dazzling acrobats and aerial performers to the inevitable clown (the renowned and talented Oleg Popov, in this instance). All the performers are impressive, except the husky lady acrobats (no glamorous elephant girls here). There's a pretty tiger-trainer, Margarita Nazarova. Speedy acrobatic work of Vladimir Davaiko and his partners, is standout, ditto—educated bears of Valentin Filatov.

Technically the film is far from awe-inspiring, by our own cinematic standards. Sides of the screen tend to be fuzzy in certain shots and color is not always vivid and true. But there's plenty of energetic camera work and a fine musical background to complement the action. Other than the music and natural circus noises such as applause, laughter and whip-cracking, the only sound is that of the rather uninspired English narration—informative, but colorless.

"Circus Stars" is directed by L. Kristy, who collaborated on the scenario with V. Komissarzhevysky. It's good children's fare, but for the adult American world it's just too Ed Sullivanesque, too cautious a shipment (as if the Russians are holding back the real McCoyovitch). *Tube.*

Sergent X
(Sergeant X)
(FRENCH)

Paris, March 8.

Marceau production and release. Stars Christian Marquand, Noelle Adam, Paul Guers; features Renaud Mary, Rene Havard, Lutz Gabor, Daniel Cauchy. Directed by Bernard Borderie. Screenplay, Ivan Loukaoh, Jacques Robert, Andre Tabet; camera, Claude Renoir; editor, Christian Gaudin. At Normandie, Paris. Running time, 95 MINS.

Michel .... Christian Marquand
Francoise .... Noelle Adam
Henri .... Paul Guers
Captain .... Rene Havard
Friend .... Lutz Gabor
Card Player .... Daniel Cauchy

This remake, updated, of a prewar actioner still seems old fashioned. It is overplotted, with overdone coincidences, sans the characterizations, acting or mounting to make it acceptable. Film looms mainly a local item on its Sahara oil locale. Pic lacks the movement and pace for offshore chances.

An ex-paratrooper gets into an accident trying to bring back a hot truck from Morocco. His girl thinks he has left her and marries her boss. He ends up in the foreign Legion and all face each other on a Saharan oil site. Outcome is foreshadowed and pace is plodding. Acting is ordinary with production and technical aspects good. *Mosk.*

Because They're Young
(SONGS)

Topnotch high school drama with Dick Clark name to boost to heavy returns.

Columbia Pictures release of Jerry Bresler production. Stars Dick Clark; costars Michael Callan, Tuesday Weld, Victoria Shaw; guest stars, James Darren, Duane Eddy and Rebels, Bobby Rydell; features Roberta Shore, Warren Berlinger, Doug McClure, Linda Watkins, Chris Robinson, Rudy Bond, Wendell Holmes, Philip Coolidge, Bart Patton, Stephen Talbot. Directed by Paul Wendkos. Screenplay, James Gunn; story, John Farris, camera, Wilfrid Cline; editor, Chester W. Schaeffer; music, Johnny Williams. Previewed March 3, '60. Running time, 97 MINS.

Neil .... Dick Clark
Griff .... Michael Callan
Anne .... Tuesday Weld
Joan .... Victoria Shaw
Ricky .... Roberta Shore
Buddy .... Warren Berlinger
Jim .... Doug McClure
Frances McCalla .... Linda Watkins
Patcher .... Chris Robinson
Chris .... Rudy Bond
Mr. Donlan .... Wendell Holmes
Mr. Rimer .... Philip Coolidge
Kramer .... Bart Patton
Eric .... Stephen Talbot
Mrs. Wellenberg .... Kathryn Card
Pekarek .... Paul Genge
Plump Girl .... Susan Odin
Girl Friend .... Frances Karath

Dick Clark's swingover from television (temporary) to motion pictures for his film bow is a happy event for a ready-made teenage audience. The appeal that has made him a tv fave and spokesman for this particular bracket brightens an interesting and refreshing feature as Clark scores heavily. Boff returns may be expected in many situations, and good biz predicted wherever shown.

"Because They're Young" was made for Columbia release under Clark's own Drexel Productions banner, and benefit of tailored craftsmanship tells right down the line. Production duties by Jerry Bresler, direction by Paul Wendkos, scripting by James Gunn are standouts. What is obviously a handpicked cast persuasively delineates true-life characters in such a way that the full ensemble merits attention as a better-than-average motion picture.

Sparked by exploitation values, feature further profits from the guest-starring of pop fave James Darren, warbling the title song, and Duane Eddy and the Rebels beating out "Shazam" for top effect. Bobby Rydell also is a plus in his rendition of "Swingin' School."

Plottage twirls around Clark, as a new high school teacher, his personal life and influence on students in his history class. There's the personal problems of his students, too, solved directly or indirectly through contact with Clark, all tossed in the hopper to emerge a straightforward yarn and a natural for younger as well as more seasoned audiences. Spirit of high school life is well caught and music inserted logically.

Clark displays an ease and warmness which gets over to the audience, and Victoria Shaw, as secretary to high school principal, is in for romantic interest, a part well played. Michael Callan registers dramatically as a semi-delinquent and prospective troublemaker who comes under Clark's influence, and Tuesday Weld plays a sexpot ably. Strong support also is provided by Warren Berlinger, beset with a guilt complex because of his mother's infidelities, a role competently portrayed by Linda Watkins; Chris Robinson, toughie from another school who tries to kill Callan; Wendell Holmes, principal.

Technical credits provide good backing, including Wilfrid Cline's camera work; Chester W. Schaeffer's editing; Robert Peterson's art direction; Johnny Williams' music score. *Whit.*

Never Take Sweets From a Stranger
(BRITISH)

Excellent, restrained film dealing with an unpleasant, but urgent topic. Shrewd exploitation could build this up to a b.o. winner

London, March 8.

Columbia release of a Hammer Film (Anthony Hinds) production. Stars Felix Aylmer, Gwen Watford, Patrick Allen. Features Bill Nagy, Alison Leggatt, Michael Gwynn, Janina Faye. Directed by Cyril Frankel. Screenplay by John Hunter, from Roger Garis's original story; camera, Freddie Francis; editor, Jim Neels; music, Elizabeth Lutyens. At London Pavilion, London, March 4, '60. Running time, 81 MINS.

Sally .... Gwen Watford
Pete .... Patrick Allen
Olderberry Senior.......... Felix Aylmer
Defence Counsel........Niall MacGinnis
Martin .... Alison Leggatt
Olderberry Junior .... Bill Nagy
Judge .... Macdonald Parke
Crown Prosecutor........Michael Gwynn
Jean .... Janina Faye
Lucille .... Frances Green
Dr. Stevens .... James Dyrenforth
Eunice Kalliiuke .... Estelle Brody
Tom Demarest .... Robert Arden
Mrs. Demarest .... Mrs. Cook

Hammer Films has made a corner in horror pix and earned a few "X" certificates (no kids under 16 can see it) that have reaped a golden b.o. harvest. This time, this "X" certificate film is a sincere, worthy, restrained and exceedingly well done job which should be seen by every parent and every child. The "X" certificate prevents this. Anyway, if every parent sees it and tries to convey the message of the title ("Never Take Candy From A Stranger" for the U.S.) to their children, it could help to minimize the danger of a current social scourge.

The yarn is set in Canada. Though filmed in Britain, the Canadian atmosphere is remarkably well conveyed. It deals with a senile, psychopathic pervert with a yen for little girls. When he persuades two innocent little girls to dance naked in front of him in exchange for candy, the English parents of one of them decide to take him to court. Unfortunately, they do not realize that he is the local big shot, the man who has helped to build the Canadian town to its prosperity and power, and they find that they cannot whip up local conscience. He is acquitted and not until, towards the end of the film, he starts his tricks again and eventually murders a child, are the parents in the clear.

John Hunter's screenplay is firstclass and Cyril Frankel's direction sure and honest, with the acting excellent. This sort of thing goes on, but there is no reason why people should not be reminded so that the sore may be healed. It's doubtful whether a child would be scared by seeing the film. It's worth the risk since seeing the film may hammer home the lesson more effectively than 100 embarrassed chats between parent and child.

Gwen Watford and Patrick Allen, as the distraught parents, and Alison Leggatt, as a wise, understanding grandmother, leads a cast which is directed with complete sensitivity by Cyril Frankel. Both Miss Watford and Allen are completely credible while Miss Leggatt, well-served by Hunter's script, is outstanding.

Felix Aylmer, who doesn't utter a word throughout the film, gives a terrifyingly acute study of crumbling evil, while Bill Nagy, as his son, is equally effective. There are other penetrating pieces of acting, including Michael Gwynn and Niall MacGinnis as respective counsels.

The courtroom sequence, the climax when the kids flee through the woods to avoid their tormenter, who somehow creates sympathy as well as aversion, and the scene where the parents first learn how nearly their child has been debauched are written, directed and acted with considerable skill. "Never Take Candy From A Stranger" is a very good film. *Rich.*

Le Main Chaude
(The Itchy Palm)
(FRENCH)

Paris, March 8.

Gaumont release of Franco-London-Gibe-Mira Film production. Stars Jacques Charrier; features Macha Meril, Paulette Dubost, Alfred Adam, Franca Bettoja. Directed by Gerard Oury. Screenplay, J. C. Pichon, J. C. Tachella, Oury; camera, Andre Villard; editor, Paulette Robert. At Colisee, Paris. Running time, 95 MINS.

Michel .... Jacques Charrier
Yvette .... Macha Meril
Madame Lacoste .... Paulette Dubost
Lecuyer .... Alfred Adam
Christiane .... Franca Bettoja

This pic concerns a group of fairly grimy people playing at love, and also doing each other dirt. Characterizations remain sketchy and it lacks dramatic impact. However, it has some suggestive love scenes and the usual social frankness to give it the hypo needed for an arty house entry.

An 18-year-old blonde is living with a middle-aged waiter whose wife and kids are away. She feigns pregnancy to get money from him for an abortion. He gets the coin from a love-starved widow to whom he has made overtures. The girl, in turn, loses it to her young boyfriend who is taken in by a conniving girl. So they all get bilked in their desires.

Director Gerard Oury, an actor-turned-filmmaker gives this fairly competent mounting but can't instill enough life into it. It is technically good with acting lacklustre except for Alfred Adam, as the middle-aged rake. *Mosk.*

Too Young to Love
(BRITISH)

Routine juvenile delinquency drama, with some sensitive performances; fair prospects.

London, March 8.

Rank release of a Welbeck Film (Herbert Smith) production. Stars Thomas Mitchell, Pauline Hahn, Joan Miller; features Austin Willis, Cec Linder, Vivian Matalon. Directed by Muriel Box. Screenplay by Sydney and Muriel Box from "Pick-Up Girl," a play by Elsa Shelley; editor, Jean Barker; camera, Gerald Gibbs; music, Bruce Montgomery. At New Victoria, London. Running time, 89 MINS.

Judge Bentley .... Thomas Mitchell
Elizabeth Collins .... Pauline Hahn
Mrs. Collins .... Joan Miller
Mr. Collins .... Austin Willis
Larry Webster .... Vivian Matalon
Ruby Lockwood.........Sheila Gallagher
Peter Marti .... Jess Conrad
Mrs. Marti .... Miki Iveria
Mr. Elliott .... Alan Gifford
Mr. Brill .... Cec Linder
Mrs. Busch .... Bessie Love
Owens .... Cal McCord
Kellerer .... Robert Henderson
Waiting Room Man ...... Charles Farrell
Miss Porter .... Ilona Ference
Records Clerk .... Roma Miller
Court Attendant .... Bill O'Connor
Society Matron .... Bee Duffell
First Sailor .... Robert Desmond
Second Sailor .... Tom Gerrard

Based on Elsa Shelley's play, "Pick-Up Girl," this pic shows its stage pedigree only too clearly, being wordy and static. It is set in New York and, on the whole, the atmosphere of a N.Y. juvenile delinquency court is put over authentically. Without overmuch marquee value, the film will depend largely on its sex theme for success at the boxoffice. And it may have a struggle.

The yarn explores the well-worn theme of kids becoming juve delinquents because of lack of care by poor, harassed parents. In this instance, father is employed in California and the mother works into the late hours of the night as a cook in N.Y. Their 15-year-old daughter gets into bad company, is picked up by a sailor, has an abortion, and then subsequently is picked up by the cops when she is found in bed with a middle-aged

man. The film, apart from a few flashbacks, is mainly devoted to the hearing of her case in the juvenile court and the problem of whether or not she should be sent away to a reform school.

All this takes a whale of a time to work out. It is largely due to the performance of Thomas Mitchell as the understanding judge that interest is held. A well-rounded and well-written role, he handles it with skill. Pauline Hahn plays the girl, who is obviously not a bad kid and a victim of unfortunate circumstances. She does it with considerable sincerity, refusing to make the part as mawkish and embarrassing as it might well have been.

The role of the distraught mother is played by Joan Miller, who created it on the British stage. It gives Miss Miller several opportunities for the hysterical outbursts which she handles in the all-out manner with which she is associated in most of her performances. Austin Willis is excellent as the confused father, while Vivian Matalon, Sheila Gallagher, Cec Linder, Jess Conrad, Bessie Love and Alan Gifford are all usefully employed.

This is a sincere effort but it never moves. The producer must thank Mitchell in the main that the picture is gripping. *Rich.*

Othello

Russian-feature in color with State Dept.-dictated dubbing. A hodgepodge.

Universal release of Mosfilm production. Stars Sergei Bondarchuk, Irina Skobtseva, Andrei Popov, Vladimir Soshalsky, E. Vesnik, A. Maximova. Directed by Serge Yutevich. Screenplay, Yutevich, based on William Shakespeare's "Othello"; camera, E. Andrikanis; editor, G. Mariamov; music, Aram Khachaturian. English dubbing adapted by Nina Maguire, edited by Maria Moruzzi, recorded by Wally Milner, directed by William De Lane Lea. Previewed in N. Y. March 10, '60. Running time, 108 MINS.

Othello	Sergei Bondarchuk
Iago	Andrei Popov
Desdemona	Irina Skobtseva
Cassio	Vladimir Soshalsky
Roderigo	E. Vesnik
Emilia	A. Maximova
Brabantio	E. Teterin
Doge of Venice	M. Troyanovsky
Montano	A. Kelberer
Lodovico	N. Brilling

English Voices

Othello	Howard Marion Crawford
Iago	Arnold Diamond
Desdemona	Katherine Byron
Cassio	Patrick Westwood
Roderigo	Richard Warner
Emilia	Nancy Nevinson
Brabantio	Michael Moore
Doge	Oliver Burt
Lodovico	Roger Snowdon
Bianca	Ybanne Churchman

Imagine, if you can, a Shakespeare play converted into a Russian-language film and then presented with dubbed-into-English dialog. This incomprehensible tampering with the Soviet cultural exchange film, "Othello," transforms what might have been an excellent example of the Russian film art into a distracting hodgepodge.

Universal, which is releasing the film in the U.S., is eschewing the blame for the emasculation, contending that it is handling the production as the State Dept. desired. The English thesps who provided the voices are not at fault either. They recite the Shakespeare lines with clarity and with a genuine understanding of the characters.

The difficulty lies in synchronizing the Bard's words with the Russian mouthings of the Soviet actors. The languages are so dissimilar that this technical achievement is apparently an impossibility. The result is downright annoying. Voices are heard when lips do not move or lips move without a sound being heard. There's been no explanation why the dubbing method was employed instead of English sub-titles.

Despite the topnotch Soviet production, the picture is neither fish nor foul. It appears valueless for both general situations and for art houses. Presented in Russian and aided by English sub-titles, it could have been a most favorable art house attraction.

The Mosfilm production is a meticulous and eyefilling spectacle. The producers have admirably succeeded in taking the Shakespeare tragedy out of the narrow confines of the theatre and truly opening it up. The color photography, the costuming, the sets, and the outdoor locations are superb. The Russians have equalled, and perhaps surpassed, Laurence Olivier's film translation of Shakespeare's "Henry V." And they have accomplished this without detracting from the tragedy of the Moor who "loved not wisely but too well." The acting, on the basis of the physical aspects and facial expressions, is for the most part good, although Andrei Popov tends to be hammy as the villainous Iago. Sergei Hondarchuk's Othello is mostly standout, but becomes too broad when he reaches the state of uncontrollable jealousy. Irina Skobtseva is a lovely Desdemona and she plays the part with a quality that has become standard with British and American actresses. A. Maximova is a spirited Emilia.

However, it is the production values of the Soviet film that stand out. A prolog before the main titles presents a capsule version of Othello's adventures before he arrives in Venice. There's well-staged sea battle, a wreck at sea and Othello's escape from a slave ship. Khachaturian's score is also a strong asset, including two songs, which fortunately are sung in Russian. *Holl.*

Thirteen Fighting Men
(C'SCOPE)

So-so Civil War yarn. Lower-half billing.

Hollywood, March 15.

Twentieth-Fox release of an Associated Producers Inc. production. Stars Grant Williams, Brad Dexter, Carole Mathews. Produced by Jack Leewood. Directed by Harry Gerstad. Screenplay, Robert Hamner and Jack Thomas; camera, Walter Strenge; editor, John Bushelman; music, Irving Gertz. Previewed at the studio, March 15, '60. Running time, 70 MINS.

Forrest	Grant Williams
Major Boyd	Brad Dexter
Carole	Carole Mathews
Lt. Wilcox	Robert Dix
Prescott	Richard Garland
Loomis	Richard Crane
Sgt. Yates	Rayford Barnes
Corp. McLean	John Erwin
Pvt. Jensen	Bob Palmer
Root	Rex Holman
Lee	John Merrick
Sgt. Mason	Mark Hickman
Pvt. Pike	Dick Monahan
Col. Jeffers	Walter Reed
Pvt. Ebb	J. Stanford Jolley
Pvt. Harper	Ford Dunhill
Ives	Mauritz Hugo
Sgt. Wade	Stephen Ferry
Pvt. Fowler	Brad Harris
Corey	Fred Kohler
2nd Soldier	Earl Holmes
Jimmy	Dick Jeffries
Samuel	Ted Knight
Pvt. Connors	Bill Browne
Sentry	Jerry Mobley

The trouble with "Thirteen Fighting Men" is that their fight isn't worth the spoils. They've already won the Civil War, these Union soldiers, and now they're risking their lives to protect a box of government gold which won't be theirs even if they win. The Associated Producers Inc. picture, being released by 20th-Fox, stacks up as a routine programmer.

Where the film misses is in its emphasis on the battle between Grays and Blues over the $50,000 in gold, an approach that makes "Thirteen Fighting Men" just another batch of "shoot-'em-up. Screenwriters Robert Hamner and Jack Thomas hint at and ultimately develop the dissension among the Unionites themselves. Had they fully realized the potential of such discord, sparked by the desire for gold, they would have had a neat little psychological drama on their hands. As is, the characters are one-dimensional, and director Harry Gerstad isn't able to pierce the surface to offer much insight into them. He does manage to keep the action conflict at a reasonably dramatic point. Producer Jack Leewood made the film look better than its low budget would have indicated possible.

Grant Williams, Brad Dexter and Carole Mathews are starred, supported by 22 actors of varying talents. The topliners go through their paces well, and the remaining cast members keep the Civil W[illegible] an interesting looking pair of antagonists. Rex Holman, as an almost skeletonized fighter, distinguishes himself both in weird appearance and actions. His philosophy, too, is notable: "If you can't eat it, make love to it or wear it, forget it."

Walter Strenge's camera is capable. Irving Gertz' musical score is professional, though his climactic use of "The Battle Hymn of the Republic" is somewhat prententious. *Ron.*

Please Don't Eat The Daisies
(COLOR-C'SCOPE—SONGS)

Topnotch comedy based on Jean Kerr humorous essays with biz in kind.

Hollywood, March 19.

Metro release of Joe Pasternak production. Stars Doris Day, David Niven; co-stars Janis Paige, Spring Byington, Richard Haydn; features Patsy Kelly, Jack Weston, John Harding, Margaret Lindsay, Charles Herbert, Stanley Livingston, Flip Mark, Baby Gellert, Hobo. Directed by Charles Walters. Screenplay, Isobel Lennart; based on book by Jean Kerr; camera (Metrocolor), Robert Bronner; editor, John MacSweeney; music, David Rose. Previewed March 16, '60. Running time, 111 MINS.

Kate Mackay	Doris Day
Lawrence Mackay	David Niven
Deborah Vaughn	Janis Paige
Mrs. Suzie Robinson	Spring Byington
Alfred North	Richard Haydn
Maggie	Patsy Kelly
Joe Positano	Jack Weston
Rev. Dr. McQuarry	John Harding
Mona James	Margaret Lindsay
David Mackay	Charles Herbert
Gabriel Mackay	Stanley Livingston
George Mackay	Flip Mark
Adam Mackay	Baby Gellert

"Please Don't Eat the Daisies" is a light and frothy comedy, and boff family fare. Doris Day and David Niven in top roles will liven its excellent chances in all bookings, with plenty of word-of-mouth book's readership during 50 weeks on national bestseller lists due to further spark biz.

Pic is episodic—as was the book—a series of highly amusing incidents strung together by a rather loose story thread, but this circumstance doesn't militate against interest. Yarn launches with a couple of belly laughs, and this high degree of merriment is sustained more or less through its entire 111-minutes' running time, long for a comedy but so well turned out here that it's seldom in need of shearing. Charles Walters' direction maintains terrific pace.

For further assurance of comedic values, producer Joe Pasternak brings back Patsy Kelly after a 16-year absence and casts Spring Byington in an understanding mother-in-law role. Janis Paige is in for some memorable funstering, and Pasternak has also lined up four moppets who are immense as the problem children of Niven, turning from his Columbia U professorship to become a firststring New York newspaper dramatic critic as pic opens, and Miss Day, his ever-loving wife who holds the family together through the storms and tempests of their rather insane existence. Screenplay by Isobel Lennart catches the flavor which Miss Kerr socked over so well in her book, and is fluffy stuff expertly edited by John MacSweeney. Femme star embellishes footage musically with a couple of songs, title number and "Any Way the Wind Blows," done in her customary clicky style.

Plotline is based on the adventures of Miss Day and Niven after he turns to criticking—and sometimes believing in his own great wit—during which they are forced out of their Gotham apartment and buy a monstrosity in the country—70 miles from Broadway—where Miss Day takes on community life while trying to modernize and make their new home livable. Miss Paige enters scene as a Broadway actress whom Niven pans in his very first review, which also incurs the enmity of his best friend, producer Richard Haydn. The whole adds up to slick entertainment.

Miss Day adds to her laurels as a light comedienne, delivering lustily in a role right down the audience alley, and Niven makes hay with his critic's portrayal, for whom Miss Paige goes on the make in a big way. For this actress, it's a standout performance which should win her both fans and future roles. Miss Byington scores roundly as Miss Day's mother, Patsy Kelly as the maid, Haydn the touchy producer.

Jack Weston also is good as a play-writing cabby, and the four boys who are sometimes the bane of their parents' existence are well played by Charles Herbert, Stanley Livingston, Flip Mark and Baby Gellert. The dog, a big one of the sheep type, is in for some hilarious scenes, too.

Technical departments are expertly executed, including Robert Bronner's color lensing, David Rose' musical score, George W. Davis and Hans Peters' art direction. *Whit.*

Beast From Haunted Cave

Good cast and interesting locales lift horror meller above routine.

Hollywood, March 18.

Filmgroup release of a Gene Corman production. Features Michael Forest, Sheila Carol, Frank Wolff, Richard Sinatra, Wally Campo. Directed by Monte Hellman; screenplay, Charles Griffith; camera, Andy Costikyan; editor, Anthony Carras. Reviewed at Hollywood Theatre, Hollywood, March 16, '60. Running time, 65 MINS.

Gill	Michael Forest
Gypsy	Sheila Carol
Alex	Frank Wolff
Marty	Richard Sinatra
Byron	Wally Campo

Gene Corman has provided "Beast From Haunted Cave" with a good cast and some very interesting locales, and, if there's still a market for horror pix, it should do fairly well.

Shot in the Black Hills of South Dakota, the film picks up the freshness of snowy landscapes and the coziness of winterproofed cabins—all of which should heighten the horror when the cobwebby monster appears from its cave. But we've grown inured to monsters and hardly blink when this one guzzles its customary quota of blood.

Sheila Carol is brightly and warmly blonde, a pleasure to watch, and Michael Forest is good opposite her as the skier-hunter who is tricked into assisting a gang of gold bullion thieves who use his isolated cabin as a rendezvous with a plane which will fly the stolen gold to Canada. Frank Wolff does a nice job as the main menace; Richard Sinatra is good as his lieutenant and Wally Campo does well as the comic crook.

Cameraman Andy Costikyan probably had the most fun, since he had some fine backgrounds to work with. Monte Hellman's direction is satisfactory as is Anthony Carras' editing. Charles Griffith's screenplay is an honest piece of work for the most part, considering the exigencies of this sort of film: e.g., the monster is caused to menace illogically from widely separated points.

It's being released on a double-bill with "The Wasp Woman." *Glen.*

The Wasp Woman

Unexciting but exploitable horror film.

Hollywood, March 18.

Filmgroup release of a Roger Corman production. Features Susan Cabot, Fred Eisley, Barboura Morris; with Michael Marks, William Roerick, Frank Gerstle. Directed by Roger Corman; screenplay by Leo Gordon; art direction, Daniel Haller; editor, Carlo Lodato; music, Fred Katz. Reviewed at Hollywood Theatre, Hollywood, March 16, '60. Running time, 66 MINS.

Janice	Susan Cabot
Bill	Fred Eisley
Mary	Barboura Morris
Zinthrop	Michael Marks
Cooper	William Roerick
Hellman	Frank Gerstle

The idea in this one is that the "royal jelly" used in women's face creams is great so long as it comes from bees but that the stuff that comes from wasps can make a person sprout antennae and behave abominably. Film has interesting points and looks polished but it's pretty slow and not very frightening. It's exploitable, though.

First thing that's hard to buy is that Susan Cabot, portraying the head of a cosmetics company, looks too old. Since her glamour is the key to the company's success, she undergoes treatments developed by an amiable quack (Michael Marks) and becomes lovelier.

The pseudo-scientist too late discovers that the treatments turn the subjects into wasp-like creatures and the lovely executive murders three or four of her employees before being shoved through a window to her death.

Leo Gordon's script, though it mentions the fascinatingly horrid habits of the female wasp, doesn't cause the heroine-monster to behave like one—that would involve paralysing them and eating them alive, at leisure. The monster just bowls them over and sucks a little blood. Perhaps it's just as well.

Daniel Haller makes the sets look smart and producer-director Roger Corman has them nicely peopled with probable characters who act fairly convincingly. It's interesting to note that Frank Wolff, who has a lead role in the companion feature, "Beast From Haunted Cave," has a walk-on in "Wasp Woman," in a cheerfully different character.

Miss Cabot is very good as are Fred Eisley and Barboura Morris, limning two of her staff. Gordon's screenplay does provide them all with a gentle believable, humanity which is a pleasant relief. But when Miss Cabot's character is killed, it just seems senseless. Ads will hint that the character develops unnamed appetites for males following her treatments, but it's not in the picture. *Glen.*

The Mountain Road

James Stewart in not-too-exciting war film. B.o. prospects mild.

Hollywood, March 17.

Columbia release of a William Goetz production. Stars James Stewart; costars Lisa Lu, Glenn Corbett, Henry (Harry) Morgan. Director, Daniel Mann; screenplay, Alfred Hayes, based on the novel by Theodore White; camera, Burnett Guffey; editor, Edward Curtiss; music, Jerome Moross. Previewed at Screen Directors Guild, March 17, '60. Running time, 102 MINS.

Major Baldwin	James Stewart
Sue-Mei	Lisa Lu
Collins	Glenn Corbett
Michaelson	Henry Morgan
Kwan	Frank Silvera
Niergaard	James Best
Miller	Rudy Bond
Prince	Mike Kellin
Ballo	Frank Maxwell
Lewis	Eddie Firestone
General Loomis	Alan Baxter
Colonel Li	Leo Chen
Colonel Magnusson	Bill Quinn
Chinese Colonel	Peter Chong
Chinese General	P. C. Lee

Despite an earnest effort, William Goetz's "The Mountain Road" doesn't go very far. It raises considerable dust, wending its way through battle-torn China, but when the haze settles, it reveals nothing new in the way of a World War II film. Outside the action market—where the picture is a fair entry — only James Stewart will help the boxoffice, and it's not likely he can carry "Mountain Road" by himself.

Aside from the presence of Stewart, a long line of Chinese extras and the wholesale destruction of expensive props, the film is more than passingly similar to a host of low-budget war films that precede it. Director Daniel Mann effected a certain air of authenticity, etching a Chinese setting out of Arizona's hinterlands, but the picture never builds the importance it should. It does not set a course that can carry it smoothly and dramatically to a satisfying conclusion.

"Mountain Road" focuses on an eight-member American demolition team that, at leader Stewart's discretion, stalls the invading Japanese army by blowing up airstrips, bridges and ammunition dumps. **Alfred Hayes' screenplay, based on a novel by Theodore White, offers two significant pieces of dialog which, if carried through, would have provided "Road" with a backbone. In the beginning, Stewart says he asked for the assignment as new leader of the demo team because, even in retreat, he wants a command.** In the end, after using that command to destroy an entire Chinese village, he declares the power of command possessed him and was too much for him. But the screenplay allows little change between Stewart's prolog and his epilog. He seems like the thousands of screen commanders who came before him, a better leader than some, a worse one than others. When he's goaded into retaliating against the village because Chinese bandits have murdered two of his men, his action somehow seems humanly appropriate. And with the power to transport his men to immediate safety, he wrestles ably with the knowledge that he's exposing them to danger at his own discretion. As played strongly by Stewart, the American major holds the film together, though it's difficult to see where he went wrong if, indeed, he did.

Lisa Lu, as the Chinese girl who bears her own ideology to the American, turns in a sensitive portrayal. She is believable as she tries to instill in him her own compassion. She is convincing when, following Stewart's destruction of the village, she refuses to go with him. The love between the two, however, never seems to come across.

Columbia contractee Gleen Corbett is very good as a G.I. who has developed a love for China and gives his life in an act of mercy to its people. Studio seems to have a fine potential in this young actor. Henry (Harry) Morgan, as the demolition team's sergeant, is tops, extending his talents far beyond his work on television's "December Bride." Good work also comes from Frank Silvera, James Best, Rudy Bond, Mike Kellin, Frank Maxwell and Eddie Firestone.

Burnett Guffey's black-and-white photography is adept, as is art direction by Cary Odell, editing by Edward Curtiss and sound by Harry Mills. Of special note is Jerome Moross' musical score, reminiscent in orchestration of his superb work for "The Big Country." His brass themes and accenting French horns alternate skillfully with melodic strings, and Moross' work stands out as a highly important contribution to Goetz' film. *Ron.*

Plein Soleil
(Broad Daylight)
(FRENCH-COLOR)

Paris, March 22.

CCFC release of Robert and Raymond Hakim production. Stars Alain Delon, Marie Laforet, Maurice Ronet; features Elvira Popesco, Erno Crisa, Frank Latimore, Bill Kearns, Ave Nichi, Viviane Chantel. Directed by Rene Clement. Screenplay, Paul Gegauff, Clement from novey by Patricia Highsmith; camera (Eastmancolor), Henri Decae; editor, Francoise Javet. At Colisee, Paris. Running time, 110 MINS.

Tom	Alaine Delon
Marge	Marie Laforet
Philippe	Maurice Ronet
Popova	Elvire Popesco
Riccordi	Erno Crisa
O'Brien	Frank Latimore
Freddy	Bill Kearns
Gianna	Ave Nichi

Rene Clement has proved he is an excellent film craftsman in such pix as "Walls of Malapaga," "Forbidden Games" and "Gervaise." And now, he keeps this tale of how a murderer is finally ironically trapped interesting for almost two hours. Film's main appeal is in its fine workmanship, colorful Italian locales, technical prowess and fine production dress.

All human aspects are pushed into the background to detail the suspense by carefully denoting how the murderer goes about capitalizing on his acts. The how-come is the main thing as a have-not covets what the rich possess.

The killer supposedly has been sent by the victim's father to get his playboy son back to the U.S. The two go on a yacht with the latter's girl. The shrewd conniver evokes a fight between them and the girl is put ashore. Then he carries out his scheme, with the actual killing extremely well done and a harrowing bit of film that belongs in the who's who of adroit filmic scenes.

Then he goes ahead getting the dough and the girl. He even manages to put his second killing on the doorsteps of the dead man. And he almost gets away with it, save for the final twist.

The Eastmancolor is excellent. Alaine Delon is properly cold and pasty as the killer while Maurice Ronet etches an excellent portrait as the victim. Marie Laforet is an offbeat looker who shows future promise. This is her first pic.

Richly mounted pic has enough visual solidity and filmmaking savvy to give it exploitation handles. *Mosk.*

The Angry Silence
(BRITISH)

Topnotch film which tackles an urgent industrial problem and doesn't compromise either in writing, direction or acting. Deserves to be a click with any adult audience.

London, March 15.

British Lion release of a (Richard Attenborough-Bryan Forbes) Beaver Films Production. Stars Richard Attenborough, Pier Angeli, Michael Craig, Bernard Lee. Directed by Guy Green. Screenplay by Bryan Forbes from original story by Michael Craig, Richard Gregson; camera, Arthur Ibbetson; editor, Anthony Harvey; music, Malcolm Arnold. At Plaza Theatre, London. Running time, 95 MINS.

Tom	Richard Attenborough
Anna	Pier Angeli
Joe	Michael Craig
Connolly	Bernard Lee
Travers	Alfred Burke
Pat	Penelope Horner
Green	Michael Wynne
Eddie	Brian Bedford
Gladys	Brian Murray
Davis	Geoffrey Keen
Miss Bennett	Noel Hood
Martindale	Laurence Naismith
Harpy	Edna Petrie
Howarth	Lloyd Pearson
Seagrave	Norman Shelley
Daniel Farson	Himself
Alan Whicker	Himself

Beaver Films is a new name on the British filmscape and it's made an immediate impact. Headed by Richard Attenborough, Bryan Forbes and Guy Green, the outfit represents a group of film personalities who have rebelled at some of the film chores they've been compelled to do.

But make no mistake, this is no arty-crafty lark. It stands out as one of the best British films made for years. If "The Angry Silence" is a sample, then Beaver will become a major force. It should be a major b.o. click in Britain and, even in America, where perhaps the problems of its plots are slightly different in detail, it should command tab-buying respect.

It details the impact of industrial unrest on individuals, told with passion, integrity and guts, but without false theatrical gimmicks. Yes, this has a message, and it's put over honestly. But, apart from the message, there is a solid core of entertainment produced by taut writing, deft direction and topnotch acting.

Plot concerns a worker in a factory where there has been no trouble until a political troublemaker moves in. Insidiously he stirs up unrest, makes one of the workers his catspaw, creates a wildcat strike and then quietly moves on to spread his poison in other factories. The main victim of the strike is played by Richard Attenborough who, because he refuses to be pushed around, is sent to Coventry (a malicious practice which occasionally crops up in British factories, whereby a man is shunned by his workmates) and is beaten up, and his family intimidated. It ends with the workmen, bewildered and ashamed, but with nobody quite knowing who has won the victory.

Fundamentally, it is a story of human beings swept up, in various ways, by the frenetic ambitions of a few opportunists. A handful of people, not knowing much about politics or union affairs, just sense that there is something wrong with the way this backstage troublemaking is being organized. And, resenting it, they are the victims of physical and mental violence.

Original story by Richard Gregson and Michael Craig has been skillfully written for the screen by Bryan Forbes the end is slightly contrived, but a film has to end somewhere and the close of this pic is one that leaves the audience thinking. Guy Green has directed with quiet skill, leaving the film to speak for itself without bringing in any necessary melodrama. Arthur Ibbetson's camerawork is also first-class.

Mainly, it is the allround good acting that helps to put over this film and make it such a very absorbing job. Richard Attenborough, as the quiet little man who just wants to be left alone to grapple with his home problems, has done nothing better on the screen for a long time. That goes, too, also for Pier Angeli as his wife. Miss Angeli has often been wasted in superficial roles. Here she is a creature of flesh and blood, unhappily involved in a problem that she cannot understand. Michael Craig, as Attenborough's best friend, is also in his best form.

Of the lesser, but equally significant roles, a few stand out prominently, notably Alfred Burke, as the rabble-rouser; Bernard Lee, as the man who is Burke's tool; Geoffrey Keen, as the factory foreman, and Laurence Naismith cast as the boss. But the acting throughout achieves a high standard worthy of a film which fully compensates for a great deal of the twaddle that comes out of British studios. Watch Beaver Films. It has got away to a sparkling start with this film. *Rich.*

The Unforgiven
(COLOR)

"Adult" western with Burt Lancaster and Audrey Hepburn. Directed by John Huston. Big b.o. potential.

United Artists release of James Productions (Hecht-Hill-Lancaster) picture produced by James Hill. Stars Burt Lancaster and Audrey Hepburn. Co-stars Audie Murphy, John Saxon, Charles Bickford, Lillian Gish, Albert Salmi, Joseph Wiseman and June Walker. Directed by John Huston. Screenplay, Ben Maddow; based on a novel by Alan Le May; camera (Technicolor) Franz Planer; editor, Hugh Russell Lloyd; music, Dimitri Tiomkin. Previewed in N.Y. March 24, '60. Running time, **125 MINS.**

Ben Zachary	Burt Lancaster
Rachel Zachary	Audrey Hepburn
Cash Zachary	Audie Murphy
Johnny Portugal	John Saxon
Zeb Rawlins	Charles Bickford
Matilda Zachary	Lillian Gish
Charlie Rawlins	Albert Salmi
Abe Kelsey	Joseph Wiseman
Hagar Rawlins	June Walker
Georgia Rawlins	Kipp Hamilton
Jude Rawlins	Arnold Merritt
Lost Bird	Carlos Rivas
Andy Zachary	Doug McClure

Although "adult" westerns have by now become commonplace on the screen and in television, United Artists still has a potent entry in "The Unforgiven." With Burt Lancaster and Audrey Hepburn as top marquee bait and John Huston as the director, the film has what the industry likes to call the "chemistry" of a b.o. hit. Moreover, it's obvious that careful attention has been given to the casting so as to provide favorites for audiences of all age groups. For example, there's John Saxon and Audie Murphy for the younger groups and Lillian Gish and Charles Bickford for the senior citizens.

There are many aspects of "The Unforgiven" that will elicit comparison with "Shane," particularly in regard to the composition of the scenes and the photography. Huston and his cameraman Franz Planer have teamed to provide a physical production that is a credit to the art of motion picture making. It's not an obtrusive artsy-craftsy exercise, but an intelligent use of the photographic medium for eye-pleasing effects.

The Ben Maddow screenplay from a novel by Alan Le May—although many parts are better than the whole—provides a good framework for the talents of Huston and his performers. Miss Hepburn, who has been nominated for an Academy Award for her performance in "The Nun's Story," gives a shining performance as the foundling daughter of a frontier family. As her foster brother, obviously desperately in love with his "sister," Lancaster is fine as the strong-willed, heroic family spokesman and community leader.

The scene is the Texas Panhandle immediately after the Civil War at a time of unbending hatred between the white settlers and the local Kiowa Indians. The antagonism is marked by senseless massacres and excesses on the part of both sides. In the midst of this tension, it's discovered that Miss Hepburn is actually a full-blooded Indian. The desire of the Indians to recover their own "blood," the resentment of the settlers in having an "enemy" in their midst, and the determination to hold on to the girl who has been a member of the family almost since birth provides the crux of the conflict.

Until Miss Hepburn's origin is brought out into the open, an aura of mystery and suspense is conveyed effectively. It begins with the arrival of an eccentric old man on horseback brandishing a sabre. The old man, excellently played by Joseph Wiseman, turns out to be a former settler bent on revenge. He spreads the word both in the Indian and white camps about Miss Hepburn ancestry.

The situation, of course, provides the setting for a pitched battle between the Lancaster household and the Indian tribe. The Redmen, in the tradition of cowboy-Indian films, bite the dust. Between the Indian fights and the verbal battles among the settlers, there's opportunities to show cattle roundups and a horse-taming session.

Miss Gish, a silent film favorite, is okay as the mother who guards the secret of her foundling daughter. However, she has a tendency to over-react emotionally. There are good performances by Charles Bickford, as the head of another frontier family; June Walker, as his wife; Albert Salmi, as his son who courts Miss Hepburn; Kipp Hamilton, as his daughter, and Doug McClure, as Lancaster's youngest brother. Audie Murphy is surprisingly good as Lancaster's hot-headed brother whose hatred of Indians causes him to abandon his family. John Saxon is fine in an undeveloped role of an enigmatic half-breed.

Filmed on location in Mexico, the Hecht-Hill-Lancaster production, produced by James Hill, is technically excellent in all aspects. Dimitri Tiomkin's music tends to telegraph the action. *Holl.*

Les Heritiers
(The Heirs)
(FRENCH)

Paris, March 22.

Unidex release of Contact-SEC-PIP production. Stars Jean-Marc Thibault, Roger Pierre; features Jacqueline Maillan, Claude Vega, Brigitte Barbier. Directed by Jean Laviron. Screenplay, Thibault, Pierre, Laviron; camera, Marc Fossard; editor, Denise Baby. At Normandie, Paris. Running time, **90 MINS.**

Roger	Roger Pierre
Marc	Jean-Marc Thibault
Chantal	Jacqueline Maillan
Cousin	Claude Vega
Evelyne	Brigitte Barbier

Fairly well made slapstick comedy has a pair of popular local comics being chased by both sides of a family because they are the deciding links in a fabulous heritage. Slapstick abounds but it all seems somewhat forced and without any inventiveness. This pic lacks the pace to make this a truly risible or distinctive comedy.

Result is that pic is sporadically funny. It looks like an okay local entry but export possibilities are chancy. Technical qualities are good. This renews the Mack Sennet traditions without the genius of the latter. *Mosk.*

El Supermacho
(The Super He-Man)
(MEXICAN-COLOR)

Mexico City, March 22.

A Peliculas Nacionales release of a Cinematografica Intercontinental production. Stars Manuel "Loco" Valdes, Sonia Furio, Teresa Velazquez; features Oscar Pulido, Joaquin Garcia, Sergio Barrios. Directed by Alejandro Galindo. Screenplay by Raul de Anda and Pancho Cordova from original story by Rafael Garcia Traves; camera, Rosalio Solano; music, Sergio Guerrero. At Mariscala and Opera Theatres, Mexico City. Running time, **80 MINS.**

This is a superficial story based on a weakling turned into a super-superman by a scientific investigator (Oscar Pulido). Comic "Crazy" Valdes gets a chance to go through a series of his screwy routines but his style is hampered by lack of originality in story, trite situations and repetition of oldie Mexican Joe Miller jokes.

Valdes, who is one of most versatile Mexican tv comedians, suffers in his film appearances where he has to hew to script line instead of extemporaneous comedy. He plays the part of a student, a waiter working to pay for his tuition, hopelessly in love with a frivolous gal played by Sonia Furio.. His chance comes when scientist goes through rigamarole which turns him into a superman who can do anything, withstand anything and attain anything.

In Eastmancolor and Mexiscope, this picture has comic bits with Kippy Casado, Richard Lemus and Lucy Fabery Fellove. Teresa Velazquez shows off her figure well. This sort of low comedy might have some appeal in the Spanish language market. *Emil.*

Fin de Fiesta
(End of the Party)

Paris, March 22.

Angel Film production and release. With Arturo Garcia, Lautaro Mura, Graziella Borges, Leonardo Favio. Directed by Leopoldo Torre-Nilsson. Screenplay, Beatrice Guido; camera, Ricardo Uyounis; editor, Jose Serra. At Cinematheque Francaise, Paris. Running time, 100 MINS.

Braseras	Arturo Garcia
Guastarino	Lautaro Murua
Maria	Graziella Borges
Adolfo	Leonordo Favio

Film combines the difficulties of youth in a puritanical household in Argentina of the 1930's with the more corrupt aspects of politics. It tries to handle too many themes and this makes it somewhat overstuffed and primarily for language spots abroad.

A tyrannical political boss, who rules by force, hoodlums and extortion, is extremely rigid with a group of young grandchildren. Story revolves around the fall of the grandfather and the assuming of social conciousness and maturity by one of his grandsons. The film has a tendency to ramble and mix stark shafts of violence with more romantic, novelettish aspects of youth bridling at its thwarted physical and emotional needs.

Director Leopoldo Torre-Nilsson displays a good technical skill and a feeling for the times which might seem somewhat old-fashioned for some foreign audiences. The acting is persuasive but the many themes and lack of a clearcut stand make the characters ambiguous and weaken the impact of this well-made pic. *Mosk.*

Wake Me When It's Over
(C'SCOPE—COLOR)

Strong comedy. Needs initial selling but should return big coin when word-of-mouth starts.

Hollywood, March 18.

Twentieth-Fox release of a Mervyn LeRoy production. Stars Ernie Kovacs, Margo Moore, Jack Warden, Nobu McCarthy; features Dick Shawn. Director, Mervyn LeRoy. Screenplay, Richard Breen, based on the novel by Howard Singer; camera, Leon Shamroy; editor, Aaron Stell; music, Cyril J. Mockridge. Previewed March 18, '60. Running time, 126 MINS.

Captain Stark	Ernie Kovacs
Lt. Nora McKay	Margo Moore
Doc Farrington	Jack Warden
Ume	Nobu McCarthy
Gus Brubaker	Dick Shawn
Sgt. Warren	Don Knotts
Sam Weiscoff	Robert Strauss
Marge	Noreen Nash
Col. Hollingsworth	Parley Baer
Joab Martinson	Robert Emhardt
Hap Cosgrove	Marvin Kaplan
Pvt. Jim Hanigawa	Tommy Nishimura
General Weigang	Raymond Bailey
Col. Dowling	Robert Burton
Major Biglow	Frank Behrens
Kaiko	Linda Wong
Mrs. Hollingsworth	Caroline Richter
Connorton	Robert Peoples
Hawaiian Singer	Ron Hargrave
Capt. Arthur Finch	David Bedell
Col. Mulhern	Jay Jostyn
Major Horace Tillman	Byron Morrow
Capt. John Guevara	Michael Quinn

Into "Wake Me When It's Over," Mervyn LeRoy has injected all the wacky adventures that made his "Mister Roberts" and "No Time For Sergeants" two of Hollywood's most memorable service comedies. Absence of a surefire boxoffice cast means 20th-Fox must use full strength in getting this picture off the ground, but once properly launched, "Wake Me" can stand alone, banking on a beaucoup laughs to make it a dream of a grosser.

"Wake Me When It's Over" is the story of Gus Brubaker, a self-labled shnook, a sympathetic veteran who's re-drafted by mistake and sent to Shima, a lonely Pacific island, before he can straighten out the Government error. A barkeeper by trade and a hotel owner by desire, he boosts island morale by conceiving a luxury resort to be built out of useless war surplus. The hotel becomes the talk of the Far East and ultimately of Congress when a jealous journalist tags it the vice center of the Orient. A court-martial follows for Gus, who finally is saved by the very Government error that got him re-drafted in the first place.

The fascination of Richard Breen's screenplay lies in the writer's ability to resolve real absurdities into realities without defeating either the humor or the drama of the story. He has come through with dialog that is sharp and funny. The combined work of LeRoy and Breen results in some of the best sight gags on film, marking a hilarious representation of a humorous book. A few vacancies in plot likely are the result of final trimming, cutting the film to its sufficient two-hour-and-six-minute length. The flaws are minor.

What the cast lacks in names, it makes up for in adept handling of the comedy. In his film bow, Dick Shawn fills shnook Gus' shoes with the same warmth that has made him a top nitery talent. Judging from first exposure, his film horizon is broad. His timing is excellent, his abilities versatile and his appearance and personality an apt combination to establish him as a lighthearted leading man.

Ernie Kovacs' comic strength is appropriate for the role of the island's commander. He is excellent. Margo Moore is efficient as the flight nurse, but her coolness sometimes is overdone. Jack Warden aids the drama, particularly convincing in his defense of Shawn at the court-martial. Nobu McCarthy matches her outstanding beauty with a compassionate, enlivened performance as an island girl. Top comedy performances come from Don Knotts, Robert Strauss and Marvin Kaplan, with sprightly touches from Tommy Nishimura, as a Yiddish-speaking Oriental. Noreen Nash looks fine and performs well as Shawn's wife, and good work is turned in by Parley Baer and Robert Emhardt.

The picture is one of the best-looking DeLuxe Color films to come out of 20th in some time. In technique, LeRoy sets a classic example of how best to integrate the many elements of film production, making each a part of the story as well as the production. Leon Shamroy's color lensing is first-rate, and the art direction by Lyle R. Wheeler and John Beckman is stunning. Beckman and Wheeler have done a masterful job of putting together a hotel set from actual surplus parts, and set decorators Walter M. Scott and Ralph H. Hurst skillfully filled it. Top credit additionally goes to editor Aaron Stell, whose work keeps the comedy roaring to a peak, to costume designer Bill Thomas and soundmen Bernard Freericks and Harry M. Leonard.

Cyril J. Mockridge's musical score melds the environment of the Orient and the march tempo of the military, whimsically playing up the action. What may be a major bonus in selling the film, particularly in the beginning, is Andy Williams' Cadence disk of the jumping title tune by Sammy Cahn and James Van Heusen. *Ron.*

Summer of 17th Doll
(BRITISH)

Warmly exciting pic version of a lusty Australian play; several standout performances should insure brisk b.o. reaction.

London, March 22.

United Artists release of a Hecht-Hill-Lancaster (Australia) (Leslie Norman) production. Stars Ernest Borgnine, Anne Baxter, John Mills, Angela Lansbury. Features Vincent Ball, Ethel Gabriel, Janette Craig, Dana Wilson. Directed by Leslie Norman. Screenplay by John Dighton from Ray Lawler's play; camera, Paul Beeson; editor, Gordon Haies; music, Benjamin Frankel. At Pavilion, London, March 19, '60. Running time, 93 MINS.

Roo	Ernest Borgnine
Olive	Anne Baxter
Barney	John Mills
Pearl	Angela Lansbury
Dowd	Vincent Ball
Emma	Ethel Gabriel
Bubba	Janette Craig
Spruiker	Deryck Barnes
"Atomic Bomber"	Tom Lurich
Cane-Cutter	Al Thomas
Little Girl	Dana Wilson
Cane-Cutter	Al Garcia
Cane-Cutter	Frank Wilson
Nancy	Jessica Noad

Not having visited Australia this reviewer can only guess that producer-director Leslie Norman has done a more-than-adequate job of capturing the atmosphere of that uninhibited country. Anyway, "Summer Of Seventeenth Doll" emerges as a lusty, hearty pic with comedy skillfully balancing the poignancy. With several standout performances from stellar names, it should be an instant click in most situations.

The play brought a gust of fresh air into a recent London theatre season and the film has just that little edge on the play which comes from being able to take the camera to the beaches of Sydney. Incidentally, Paul Beeson, one of the better lensers in the British film industry, has done a remarkably vivid job in reflecting not only the moods of the artists but the locale of the story.

Simple plot concerns a couple of buddies who for most of the year work as sugar-cane cutters in North Australia. At the annual layoff, they descend on Sydney loaded with coin to pick up the happy, illicit lovelife with their two girl friends. It's been the custom of one of them (Ernest Borgnine) to bring his paramour a little doll each summer and it's come to mean a great deal to her. But the 17th summer produces a snag. He's had a bad season at work and arrives proud but broke. His chum (John Mills) finds that his girl-friend has married and her successor, a prim widow, is not easily persuaded to play.

Meanwhile, a younger man looks set to take over from Borgnine, which doesn't add to the gaiety of the summer layoff. It all adds up to a poignant comedy-drama about adults living in a dream world and refusing to accept the unpalatable fact that people grow up and what was fun in a person's teens is a shade embarrassing in later years.

Leslie Norman has directed with rare skill. He lets John Dighton's excellent screenplay speak for itself, with the comedy, the drama and the emotion emerging naturally.

He is also served brilliantly by half a dozen thesps. Borgnine, as a puzzled ox of a man, brings a touch of the Marty to his characterization of a man who refuses to accept that he's not the power he once was. Audiences will be happy when, at the end, he accepts the issue and decides to throw it all up and marry his girl. Mills gives one of his perkiest and most confident performances as his cocky little friend who lives only for the present and is still kidding himself that he's the great lover.

The femmes, too, are fine. Anne Baxter, stridently taking on an Australian accent, plays Borgnine's love-partner and there's something quite pathetic in the way that she, too, refuses to believe that the annual summer layoff can be anything but as sweet as the year before.

But the best performance probably comes from that skilled actress, Angela Lansbury, who plays the unwilling stand-in for Mills' absent girl-friend. Miss Lansbury brings a comic and sometimes sad dignity to bear on the role of the woman who is caught up in some odd proceedings, doesn't like them very much, but is not persuaded till the end of the film that this alfresco summer romance is not for her. *Rich.*

Get Outta Town

Shoestring production with some interesting points but not many prospects.

Hollywood, March 14.

MCP release of Charles Davis-Douglas Wilson production. Features Doug Wilson, Jeanne Baird, Marilyn O'Connor, Tony Lewis; with Frank Harding, Steve Bradley, Beppi De Vries, Edith Claire, Frank Mecully, Lee Kross, Tommy Holden, Sam Chiodo, Fred Chiodo, Robert Biggers, John O'Hara. Executive producer, William Hale; associate producer, Dale Jenks; directed by Charles Davis; screenplay, Bob Wehling; camera, Larry Raimond; 2d unit, Meridith Nicholson; editors, Richard Llewellyn, Davis and Wilson; music, Bill Holman. Reviewed at Hollywood Centre Theatre, March 14, '60. Running time, 63 MINS.

Kelly Olesen	Doug Wilson
Jill	Jeanne Baird
Claire	Marilyn O'Connor
Rico	Tony Lewis
Sgt. Wills	Frank Harding
Officer Kemper	Steve Bradley
Kelly's Mother	Beppi De Vries

The trade screening of this film suffered from amateurish projection (mediocre equipment and bungling by the operator) so the technical aspect cannot be assessed with certainty. Presuming these to be satisfactory, the film amounts to an earnest but ill-fated effort, whose exploitation value is questionable.

MCP's endcard reads "An Exclusive MCP Roadshow Attrac-

tion, probably indicating selective bookings in product-hungry smaller towns, though it has already played briefly in Los Angeles and Portland. It may return its costs.

Originally titled "The Day Kelly Came Home," plot deals with an ex-safecracker (portrayed by Doug Wilson) who returns to L.A. after three-year absence because his brother's been murdered. Police put the roust on him and the syndicate man behind the murder (Tony Lewis) has hoods beat him up—making for some good scenes of violence.

Kelly's mother, in which role Beppi De Vries is physically miscast, turns him in to the cops (he hasn't been hiding and cops decided to let him go in two minutes). And Kelly's girl (Jeanne Baird), having regained faith in him, gets outta town with him, since the police still think he's a crook despite fact they've just shot the murderer and have learned of Kelly's reformation.

Robert Wehling, in attempting to be offbeat and authentic, has succeeded in being obscure and disappointing. Bill Holman's jazz score is fine. Director co-producer Charles Davis has selected some interesting L.A. locales. Larry Raimond and/or Meridith Nicholson provide refreshing flashes of good photography.

Wilson's fairly good most of the time; Miss Baird is interesting and feminine; Lewis is satisfactory or better; Marilyn O'Connor (Mrs. Charles Davis) is polished as the syndicate man's unfaithful wife; Frank Harding and Steve Bradley are good as cops; Tommy Holden has some good moments in a small role; supporting players generally have the student-actor stamp. But, though Wehling provides some fair dialog at points, he has neither story to tell nor sufficient action to make up for the lack.   *Glen.*

Let's Get Married
(BRITISH)

Trivial comedy-drama with songs; despite upcoming b.o. appeal of Anthony Newley, cast is not strong enough to carry poor dialog and situations.

London, March 22.
Eros release of a Viceroy (John R. Sloan) production. Stars Anthony Newley, Anne Aubrey, Bernie Winters. Hermione Baddeley; features Lionel Jeffries, Diane Clare, John Le Mesurier, Joyce Carey, Sydney Tafler, Victor Maddern. Guest star, James Booth. Directed by Peter Graham Scott. Original screenplay, Ken Taylor; camera, Ted Moore; editor, Ernest Walker; music. Edwin Astley. At Carlton, London. Running time, 91 MINS.
Dicky .... Anthony Newley
Anne Linton .... Anne Aubrey
Bernie .... Bernie Winters
Mrs. O'Grady........Hermione Baddeley
Photographer .... James Booth
Marsh .... Lionel Jeffries
Glad .... Diane Clare
Dean .... John Le Mesurier
Works Manager .... Victor Maddern
Miss Finch .... Joyce Carey
Pendle .... Sydney Tafler
Miss Kaplan .... Betty Marsden
Salesman .... Cardew Robinson
Schutzburger .... Meier Tzelniker
R.A.F. Officer .... Nicholas Parsons
Uncle Herbert........Paul Whitson-Jones

Anthony Newley has been making a name for himself as a supporting comedian and character actor. Cashing in on this and the fact that Newley, to his self-confessed surprise, has crashed the Top 10 with a couple of disks, he has been elevated to stardom with "Let's Get Married." Whether he is yet ripe for such promotion is difficult to say on the strength of this. Neither Newley nor the rest of the cast can do much with the

---

grim dialog and erratic situations. During its West End run, Newley and other members of the cast will be staging a live show in support of the film. It certainly needs something to give it a lift.

Newley is a nervous medical student who takes a temporary job as a laundry delivery man in order to mix with people and gain confidence. He befriends a fashion model who is going to have a baby by a man who has deserted her. Newley gets her a job, marries her so that the baby can have a name and because everybody believes the child is his, anyway. Eventually he finds confidence as a doctor when, in an emergency, he has to deliver the girl's baby.

This corny setup blends uneasily with slapstick that is crashed home whenever the plot is sagging plus with two or three songs brought in extraneously and not very well put over. In fact, so many different styles have created a flat hodgepodge instead of the lighthearted lark that was obviously expected.

Equal blame must be apportioned to the director, Peter Graham Scott, who never seemed to know what kind of film he was supposed to be directing and to screenplay writer, Ken Taylor, who never appeared to know what sort of a film Graham Scott thought he was directing. Under the circumstances, the cast obviously went about its chore loyally.

Newley, as well as doing his fair share in trying to keep the film light and breezy, also has several serious moments which he handled well. But it was as a throwaway comedian with charm that he is most likely to score. To team him up with Bernie Winters was an error of judgment. With his brother Mike, Winters is the slapstick half of a successful vaude and tv team. On his own, as a character comedian, his zaniness quickly palls. Anne Aubrey is a pretty but as yet inexperienced as a leading lady. The pertness of Diane Clare, as Winters' girl friend, fits better into the pattern.

With Hermione Baddeley valiantly overacting as a garrulous landlady, Leslie Jeffries, as the laundry boss; and various other feature actors such as John Le Mesurier, Victor Maddern, Joyce Carey, Sydney Tafler and Cardew Robinson on hand it is fair to say that "Let's Get Married" had the actors to get the pic off the ground. But the material proved too formidable. Newley sings a couple of numbers, "Do You Mind" and "Let's Get Married," of which the former stands a sound chance of clicking. Miss Aubrey also gives with the credit title song, "Confessions."

Camerawork and editing are adequate but the entire affair proves a great disappointment.
Rich.

Bluebeard's Ten Honeymoons
(BRITISH)

Dull meller based, loosely, on career of Landru, French massmurderer; a dubious dualer.

London, March 22.
Warner-Pathe release of an Anglo-Allied (Roy Parkinson) production. Stars George Sanders, Corinne Calvet, Jean Kent, Patricia Roc, Maxine Audley, Greta Gynt. Directed by W. Lee Wilder. Screenplay, Myles Wilder; camera, Stephen Dade; editor, Tom Simpson; music. Al-

---

bert Elms. Previewed at Corner Theatre, London. Running Time; 90 MINS.
Landru .... George Sanders
Odette .... Corinne Calvet
Mme. Guillin .... Jean Kent
Mme. Dueaux .... Patricia Roc
Jeanette .... Greta Gynt
Cynthia .... Maxine Audley
Giselle .... Ingrid Hafner
Mme. Boyer .... Selma Vaz Dias
Lefevre .... Peter Illing
Lacoste .... George Coulouris
Pepi .... Sheldon Lawrence
Station Master ...... Paul Whitsun-Jones
Estate Agent .... Keith Pyott
Concierge .... Jack Melford
Bank Clerk .... Robert Rietty
Advertising Clerk ...... Mark Singleton
Librarian .... Milo Sperber
Neighbor .... C. Denier Warren
Jeweler .... Harold Berens
Attorney .... Ian Fleming
Hardware Store Owner .. Dino Galvani

This is a dull, preposterous yarn, allegedly based on the notorious career of Henri Landru, the French mass-killer. It drags tremendously, is acted only adequately, is written in cliches and directed with no sense of drama. In short, it's a sad little flop which is unlikely to make the grade even as a dualer. Not even the marquee value of George Sanders and Corinne Calvet can hide the fact that by all standards this one is a turkey.

Landru himself was a small, respectable, insignificant little man who killed women for money for the sake of his wife and family. In "Honeymoons," he emerges as an aristocratic, debonair antique dealer whose crimes are committed —still for money—but to satisfy the greed of a gold-digging nightclub singer with whom he is infatuated. He is thus able to be played by George Sanders, who wanders through the proceedings, but never satisfies the most trusting audience that he would go to all this trouble for the sake of the very obvious charms of Miss Calvet.

The screenplay writer and director have pulled off a remarkable feat in making the usually interesting theme of murder so desperately dull. The Paris settings reek of the studio. The acting is as good as can possibly be expected from a pic which presents all the characters as complete cardboard figures. Sanders, for once, is completely bogged down by his material. The only interesting performance comes from a screen newcomer, Ingrid Hafner, the sister of one of Sanders' gullible victims, who shows plenty of potential. Among Sanders' varied victims are Greta Gynt, Maxine Audley, Jean Kent and Patricia Roc. These are all experienced actresses and they pull off their inconsiderable chores satisfactorily.

But, in this day and age, there is absolutely no excuse for the cinema thinking it can combat tele with such tepid material.   *Rich.*

Bottoms Up
(BRITISH)

Straightforward slapstick pic based on popular British tv series starring Jimmy Edwards. Unsubtle, but providing plenty of mirth. U.S. boxoffice doubtful.

London, March 15.
Associated-British release of a Mario Zampi production. Stars Jimmy Edwards; features Arthur Howard, Martita Hunt, Raymond Huntley. Sidney Tafler, Reginald Beckworth, Melvyn Hayes. Directed by Mario Zampi. Screenplay by Michael Pertwee; additional dialog, Frank Muir, Denis Nordern; camera, Gilbert Taylor; editor, Richard Best; music. Stanley Black. At Warner Theatre, London March 8, '60. Running time, 89 MINS.
Prof. Jim Edwards.......Jimmy Edwards
Pettigrew ....Arthur Howard
Lady Gore-Willoughby......Martita Hunt

Sid Biggs.................Sidney Tafler
Garrick Jones.........Raymond Huntley
Bishop Wendover.....Reginald Beckwith
Matron ....Vanda Hudson
Cecil Biggs.............Melvyn Hayes
Wendover ....John Mitchell
Hamley ....Donald Hewlett
Colbourne ....Richard Briers
Prince Hassid..........Paul Castaldini
Swarthy Man...........George Pastell
1st Man ....George Selway
2nd Man ....Richard Shaw
Police Officer ....John Stuart

Here is a piece of genuine slapstick with purely local appeal, but which should do well in British cinemas if only from the support of popular tv comedian, Jimmy Edwards. "Bottoms Up" is based on Edwards' tv series, "Whacko," in which he plays the headmaster of a boys' school largely inhabited, it seems, by potential juvenile delinquents. Fault of film is that it is virtually a 30-minute tv program spun out to around 90 minutes. Hence, often the gags and the situations have to be flogged to produce the frequent yocks.

"Flogged" is, perhaps, the operative word since Edwards, headmaster of Chiselbury School, wages war against his preposterous pupils by shouting at them and wielding a cane with mock ferocity. The thin story line on which this pic is hung concerns the way Professor Jim Edwards quells a revolt among his pupils which starts, in some bewildering way, because of the arrival of a young prince from a trouble-torn Middle European state to attend school. For devious purposes, Edwards has already been forced, under blackmail, to bring in a young tough who is impersonating the prince.

It's pointless to go on. It is sufficient that the situation is ample to provide the sort of slapstick situations and dialog with which the "Whacko" series has established itself on tv. Edwards, a larger-than-life character, has not made a film for some years and he may well ponder the advisability of getting away from the schoolmaster character in order to broaden his opportunities for lusty character comedy.

Arthur Howard appears effectively as Pettigrew, Edwards' downtrodden assistant. Martita Hunt, Raymond Huntley, Reginald Beckwith, Melvyn Hayes, Sidney Tafler and John Mitchell add to the farcical confusion of what might well be re-titled "The Cane Mutiny." Direction by Mario Zampi is fast and uninhibited. Gilbert Taylor's lenswork is okay.   *Rich.*

Three Came to Kill

Crime melodrama with an exploitably newsy, documentary approach, but too outmoded in style to hold up strong when word-of-mouth catches up with it.

Hollywood, March 28.

United Artists release of Premium Pictures production. Stars Cameron Mitchell; costars John Lupton, Steve Brodie, Lyn Thomas; with Paul Langton, Logan Field, King Calder, Jan Arvan, Jean Ingram, Tom McKee, Ron Foster, Jack Kenney, Shep Sanders, Cecil Weston, Frank Lackteen. Producer, Robert E. Kent; directed by Edward L. Cahn; screenplay, James B. Gordon; story, Orville H. Hampton; camera, Maury Gerstman; editor, Grant Whytock; art director, Bill Glasgow; music, Paul Sawtell, Bert Shefter. Reviewed at Goldwyn Studios, March 28, 1960. Running time, **71 MINS.**

What with no self-respecting head of state content to stay at home anymore in this era of globe-trotting diplomacy, United Artists might be able to kick up something of a fuss about the timely, quasi-documentary aspects of this film, but public is likely to undo all the hard work, once the word gets around about "Three Came To Kill." Actually the picture is little more than graduate school "Dragnet," the sort of fare that no longer has any real business being in a theatre. As a potentially lower-berth attraction, it will have to depend on its exploitable elements of violence and gangsterism (given a sort of respectability by the "right out of yesterday's newspaper" approach) if it's to be of any help at all to itself or to twin-bills it's part of.

James B. Gordon's screenplay, brewed from a story by Orville H. Hampton, deals with a gang of thugs attempting to rub out a premier visiting Los Angeles. It strongly resembles, to cite at least one predecessor, the 1954 film, "Suddenly." The assassination job is royally botched, no thanks to the hapless efforts of the L.A. police, whom this film is supposed to be glorifying.

Edward L. Cahn's direction is pretty ragged, indicating greater than average haste on the part of producer Robert E. Kent to get this one in the can. There are all sorts of rough edges and loose ends, dramatically, physically, even technically.

It's difficult for any of the performers to attain any degree of credibility. Cameron Mitchell, a sound actor, labors in vain as the chief antagonist. To mention just a few of the others who seem to be trying most earnestly to create something of value, there are John Lupton, Steve Brodie, Lyn Thomas and Paul Langton, plus a strong physical assist from Jean Ingram.

Tube.

Five Branded Women

Distaff guerillas in a salable, well-made war film.

Hollywood, March 28.

Paramount release of Dino DeLaurentiis production. Stars Silvana Mangano, Van Heflin, Vera Miles, Barbara Bel Geddes, Jeanne Moreau, Carla Gravina, Richard Basehart, Harry Guardino, Steve Forrest, Alex Nicol, Pietro Germi, Romolo Valli; with Sid Clute, Teresa Pellati, Guido Celano, Franca Dominici, Gerard Herter, Aldo Silvani, Tiberio Mitri, Giacomo Rossi Stuart, Carlo Hinterman, Gerard Landry, Ewrin Strahl, Bob Cunningham, Tonio Selwart, Vera Fusek, Nona Medici, Lina Rogers, Cyrus Elias. Directed by Martin Ritt. Screenplay, Ivo Perilli, based on novel by Ugo Pirro; camera, Giuseppe Rotunno; editor, Jerry Webb; music, Francesco Lavagnino. Previewed March 28, '60. Running time, **100 MINS.**

Jovanka	Silvana Mangano
Daniza	Vera Miles
Marja	Barbara Bel Geddes
Ljuba	Jeanne Moreau
Mira	Carla Gravina
Capt. Reinhardt	Richard Basehart
Branco	Harry Guardino
Sgt. Keller	Steve Forrest
Svenko	Alex Nicol
Partisan Commander	Pietro Germi
Mirko	Romolo Valli
Velko	Van Heflin

Dino De Laurentiis' "Five Branded Women" is a grim account of the Yugoslavian partisans' fight against the invading Nazi army during World War II. The film occasionally plots an overly familiar conflict, but it catches the fervency of the resistance movement. Director Martin Ritt illuminates it with an appropriately integrated set of shocks. The shedding of hair by its five female stars, as a stigmata of their fraternization with a German officer, is an exploitable hook which can be used in selling the film. Coupling this exploitation with a potentially active word-of-mouth, the picture should be a moneymaker for Paramount.

The film's strength lies in Ritt's direction. If his story bogs down, he is quick to follow with a storm of action, gripping in tone and adventurous in concept. A jarring weakness in the film is its contrived ending, a "moment of truth" which tries in one abrupt minute to erase the dissensions built up through the 99 minutes that come before it.

The horrors of war are hammered out with serious intentions by screenwriter Ivo Perilli, who adapted the film from an unpublished novel by Ugo Pirro. He describes the partisans as savages, willing to execute their own members if necessary, because it is this savagery that ultimately will destroy the Nazis. Scene by scene, the Yugoslavs are depicted as cruel, inhuman fighters who are, in fact, less sympathetic than their German enemy. But their fight is to defend their home, and the film slowly but carefully obliterates their role as antagonist.

The women are Silvana Mangano, Vera Miles, Barbara Bel Geddes, Jeanne Moreau and Carla Gravina. Not all the roles are long, but they are universally rewarding, and the five actresses successfully fashion contrasting personalities.

Van Heflin stars as a partisan leader in one of his better recent roles. He is a standout, barking orders with sure authority and philosphizing with an assuring note. Richard Basehart is excellent as a captured German officer, more aware of his captors' problems than his own. Steve Forrest is the German soldier whose love-making is responsible for the branding of the women, and he scores with an electrifying scene, shouting of his mutilation by the partisans. Harry Guardino makes a thoroughly reckless resistance fighter, and good performances are turned in by Alex Nicol, Pietro Germi and Romolo Valli.

De Laurentiis' film is an able blend of European and American filmmaking, particularly effective in its use of locations. Guiseppe Rotunno's camera moves skillfully in and out of the action, highlighted by two good boom shots and fine snow footage. Francesco Lavagnino's music is a warlike background score, making full use of trumpets and drums set against the occasional romantic strings. Jerry Webb's editing is tight. Sound effects are used well, but the studio recording of dialog is antiseptic, too clean and not in keeping with the film's basic realism.

Ron.

Your Money or Your Wife
(BRITISH)

Feeble comedy about a young couple trying to fake a divorce to collect a legacy; possible filler for U.K. houses, but America can pass this one up.

London, March 29.

Rank release of an Alliance (Norman Williams) production. Stars Donald Sinden, Peggy Cummins. Features Richard Wattis, Peter Reynolds, Georgina Cookson, Gladys Boot, Barbara Steele. Directed by Anthony Simmons. Screenplay, Ronald Jeans; camera, Brendan J. Stafford; editor, Bernard Gribble; music, Philip Green. At New Victoria, London. Running Time, **91 MINS.**

Pelham Butterworth	Donald Sinden
Gay Butterworth	Peggy Cummins
Hubert Fry	Richard Wattis
Theodore Malek	Peter Reynolds
Thelma Cressington	Georgina Cookson
Mrs. Compton Chamberlain	Gladys Boot
Juliet Frost	Barbara Steele
Janet Fry	Betty Baskcomb
Mrs. Withers	Olive Sloane
The Judge	Ian Fleming
The Maid	Candy Scott
The Chauffeur	Noel Tregarthen

Here is an inept little comedy of unremitting silliness, showing nothing of the wit of which the screenplay writer, Roland Jeans, has shown himself capable of in the past. Popularity of the stars, Donald Sinden and Peggy Cummins, may make it a useful filler for undiscriminating British houses. But on the whole the entire project can be written off as a sad mistake.

The thin joke concerns a young married couple who, expecting a legacy, get themselves up to their eyebrows in debt. They find that there's a snag. The wife, under the terms of the will, gets only a pittance a week. The husband has to die or else they must be divorced before she can collect a lump sum. To make ends meet they take in a mixed bunch of lodgers, but unfortunately none of them pays the rent. In desperation they decide to fake a reason for a divorce and then to re-marry. But things go awry and the young wife decides that there is a very real reason for divorcing her husband. A predictable twist tidies up the piece cosily.

Director, lenser, editor and cast give "Your Money Or Your Wife" far more loyalty than the film deserves for it is practicably impossible for anybody to make anything of the frail story. Donald Sinden and Peggy Cummins acquit themselves as well as possible. Also, there are some neat performances by Richard Wattis, Georgina Cookson, Peter Reynolds, Gladys Boot and Barbara Steel as the oddly-assorted lodgers. Miss Steele is an attractive young woman and it is to be hoped that she will soon be given an opportunity of proving whether or not she can also act.

Rich.

The Boy and the Pirates
(COLOR)

Fantasy aimed to please juve taste for period action-adventure. Not too palatable for more sophisticated audiences, but lively enough to insure ample b.o. reaction from kiddies alone.

Hollywood, March 30.

United Artists release of Bert I. Gordon production, directed by Gordon. Stars Charles Herbert, Susan Gordon, Murvyn Vye; with Paul Guilfoyle, Joseph Turkel, Archie Duncan, Than Wyenn, Al Cavens, Mickey Finn, Morgan Jones, Timothy Carey. Screenplay, Lillie Hayward, Jerry Sackheim; camera, Ernest Haller; editor, Jerome Thoms; assistant directors, Bill Forsyth, Joe Boyle; sound, Alfred Fruzlin; are director, Edward L. Ilou; music, Albert Glasser. Reviewed at Goldwyn Studios, March 30, '60. Running time, **84 MINS.**

As long as boys will be boys, a market will exist for this kind of picture. A picturesque, picaresque throwback to the screen's light-hearted era, Bert I. Gordon's "The Boy and the Pirates" is a swash-buckling fantasy aimed directly at children, and raises sufficient cain to raise sufficient boxoffice coin, primarily from the less sophisticated, under-13, juve audience. The United Artists release is a natural for Saturday kiddie matinee exploitation—it's something youngsters don't find on their tv sets.

Childish in appeal, the film is equally childish in story. The Lillie Hayward-Jerry Sackheim screenplay hardly begins to explore the possibilities inherent in the situation they have created, very likely a compromise on their part in favor of marketable simplicity. Story is about an impressionable contemporary youngster who, with the aid of a likeable, though malevolent, pint-sized genie, transports himself back through time to Blackbeard's pirate vessel. There are a series of typical pirate skirmishes at sea, plenty of dialog of the yo-ho-ho-avast-yelubbers variety, and lots a swordplay and double-dealing, but eventually the youngster and his ladyfair (sort of the Errol Flynn and Olivia de Havilland of the carriage trade) make it to safety after several narrow escapes. The film's best scenes occur when the lad introduces to his newfound picaroon society the latest in 20th-century necessities: matches and bubblegum. Screenplay doesn't even begin to milk this classic situation.

It's a rough assignment for the two youths tackling the central roles. Considering the demands of their parts, both youngsters (Charles Herbert and Susan Gordon) manage quite admirably, although adult spectators may be forgiven an occasional wince or cringe for having to put up with plenty of mechanically-spoken dialog and robot-like reactions. Producer-director Gordon has obtained some solid, colorful performances from his pirate people, particularly Murvyn Vye, as a curiously hapless "Blackbeard"; Joseph Turkel, a robust genie; Paul Guilfoyle, a kindly mate; Archie Duncan, a menacing ship's cook; and Timothy Carey, an angry crewman.

Attractively tinted in Eastman hues, the production is handsomely mounted, benefitting from several striking special effects and generally proficient craftsmanship, notably Albert Glasser's lively music, Ernest Haller's agile camera work and Jerome Thoms' taut editing. This film is certainly no masterpiece, but it's a piece masters and junior misses should enjoy.

Tube.

The Cossacks
(I Cosacchi)
(ITALIAN—COLOR)

Italian spectacle dubbed into English. Action elements may appeal to less discriminating audiences. Mild b.o. anticipated.

(Italian-Made, Dubbed Into
English)
Universal release of Vanguard film
produced by W. Tourjansky. Stars Edmund Purdom, John Drew Barrymore,
Georgia Moll and Pierre Brice. Directed
by Giorgio Rivalta. Camera (Totalscope).
Massimo Dallamano; music. Giovanni
Fusco. Previewed in N.Y., April 1, '60.
Running time. 114 MINS.
Shamil .... Edward Purdom
Giamal............John Drew Barrymore
Tatiana .... Georgia Moll
Boris .... Pierre Brice
Patimat .... Elena Zareschi
Casi .... Erno Crisa
Alina .... Grazia Maria Spina
Alexander II .... Massimo Girotti
Voronzov .... Mario Pisu
Ferguson .... Laura Carli

There may be action elements in
this Italian-made spectacle that
will satisfy the less discriminating
general U.S.-Canada audience, but
otherwise this Universal release
dubbed into English, can serve
only as a time filler in a period of
a product shortage. Universal will
back the release with a bally
campaign, so there's a chance that
some money can be made via hit-and-run saturation bookings.

Italian filmmakers are turning
out these films on what seems like
an assembly line basis. It's apparent that U.S. film companies,
faced by astronomical budgets for
quality product, are latching on to
these specs to maintain the pace of
their distribution programs. If the
trend, started by Joseph E. Levine
with "Hercules," continues to any
extent, audiences who have been
lured back to the theatres may
return to their television sets.

Essentially "The Cossacks" is a
mediocre action drama reminiscent
of the stuff Hollywood turned out
perhaps 25 to 30 years ago. The
picture's only saving grace is the
cavalry battle scenes showing hundreds of horsemen. The story takes
place in Russia in the 1850's during
the reign of Alexander II and concerns the conflict between the Circassians, a Moslem tribe in the
Caucasas, and the Russians.

As a truce measure, the Circassian chief is forced to give up his
12-year-old son as a hostage. The
son is taken to St. Petersburg
where he is sent to the Imperial
School of Cadets. He becomes a
stalwart officer, torn between two
societies—the Russian aristocracy
and the tribal culture of the Caucasas. His period as a cadet and officer provide the opportunity for
scenes of Imperial balls and lush
living in and around the Czar's
palace. However, when his hot-tempered father renews his war
against the Russians, the young
man returns to his homeland to
convince his father of the folly of
such a war. Failing his mission, he
reluctantly joins his father in the
war against his new friends.

On the basis of the screenplay by
an uncredited writer, the performers, Edmund Purdom, as the Circassian chief, and John Drew
Barrymore, as his son, do the best
they can, Georgia Moll, an extremely pretty girl who looks like
Brigitte Bardot, deserves a better
break than her role as the love-stricken Russian princess. It's not
fair either to judge the other performances in a film that has been
dubbed. Dubbing, at its best, is distracting and there are many instances where the dialog and lip
movements are out of sync. Purdom and Barrymore obviously did
their roles in English, but it's frequently noticeable that their
voices were post-synchronized.

Giorgio Rivalta's direction hasn't
missed a single cliche and there
are a number of occasions when
U.S. audiences will laugh at what
are supposed to be serious scenes.
There's some really ludicrous stuff
on the battle field when the camera
focusses on dying men to catch
their last words.   Holl.

Charleston
(MEXICAN—COLOR)

Mexico City, March 29.
A Peliculas Nacionales release of an
Orofilms Mexico production. Stars Silvia
Pinal, Alberto Closas; features Lina Canalejas, Pastor Serrador. Directed by
Tulio Demichelli. At Real Cinema, Mexico City. Running time, 90 MINS.

This is supposedly a Mexican-Spanish coproduction for it boosts
Silvia Pinal and Italian director
Tulio Domichelli. But it is more
Spanish than Mexican in atmosphere, characters depicted,
scenery and supporting players.

Story is based on a comedy by
writing team of Arniches and
Abati, originally titled, "Don't Be
Offended, Beatriz." Beatriz, who
lives in the era of the frenzied '20s,
has an official fiance, a sort of
Casper Milquetoast character who
is an aficionado of abstract art, and
a second wolfish sort of boy friend.
Dialog and situations of this
central theme follow the classic
lines of Spanish comedy—jealousy,
misunderstandings and tender love
scenes.

Action is uniformly held to interior scenes with the Charleston
dance numbers in diversified variations including semi-ballet
sequences. Demichelli's direction
does not draw out the comic talents
of Silvia Pinal and the overall
effect is somewhat flat and off key.
Perhaps the fault lies in unilateral
use of interiors and restrictions
this imposes.

This is one of the films Miss
Pinal made in Spain and which are
now to be exploited here. Unfortunately the talents and versatility of star have not been fully
utilized in this one. Alberto Closas
plays the role of a libertinate playboy without effort while Pastor
Serrador is the timid fiance.

Picture is not pretentious and is
destined as top half of double feature exploitation in Spanish markets. Lina Canalejas, who contributes to the comedy, does an excellent bit of business with her featured number, "Oh, Madame."
Emil.

Operation Amsterdam
(BRITISH)

**World War II suspense film
that's fairly exciting.**

Hollywood, April 1.
Twentieth-Fox release of J. Arthur
Rank Production. Stars Peter Finch, Eva
Bartok; features Tony Britton, Alexander
Knox; with Malcolm Keen, Jim Turner,
John Horsley, Melvin Hayes, Christopher
Rhodes. Producer, Maurice Cowan; directed by Michael McCarthy; screenplay
by Michael McCarthy, John Elridge; based
on book, "Adventures in Diamonds," by
David E. Walker; camera, Reginald Wyer;
editor, Arthur Stevens; music, Philip
Green; assistant director, David Orton;
art director, Alex Vetchinsky. Reviewed
at the studio, April 1, 1960. Running time,
105 MINS.
Jan Smit .... Peter Finch
Anna .... Eva Bartok
Major Dillon .... Tony Britton
Walter Keyser .... Alexander Knox
Johan Smit .... Malcolm Keen
Dutch Lieutenant.......... Jim Turner
Commander Bowerman.....John Horsley
Willem .... Melvin Hayes
Alex .... Christopher Rhodes

"Operation Amsterdam" is a
doubtful commodity on this side
of the Atlantic. The J. Arthur
Rank film, imported from England
by 20th-Fox, is a fairly exciting
World War II suspense yarn, but
it's too long for comfortable lower-berth status, and too weak on several vital counts to aspire to
greater heights in the domestic
market. It appears to be a near
miss.

The Michael McCarthy-John Elridge screenplay, based on "Adventures in Diamonds," a book by
David E. Walker, deals with the
efforts of three men and one
woman to get about $10,000,000
worth of industrial diamonds out of
Amsterdam and across the English
Channel before the Nazis take over
the city. Some sort of record for
lucky breaks is established by this
quartet, consistently weakening the
element of suspense until, near the
end of the picture, the audience
hardly fears for their lives anymore, so certain is the onlooker
that they will safely accomplish
their mission. Nazi fifth-columnists are seen expiring like flies, but
the ones that survive appear to
rank among the poorest marksmen in history. Patriotism is fine,
but this incredible lack of balance
hampers the impact of the film.

There are some familiar, and respected, names in the cast, but none
of sufficient marquee weight in this
country to make a big difference
in the film's boxoffice prospects.
Peter Finch's quietly efficient performance is a standout. Eva Bartok gives a good account of herself,
although the character she is playing is uneven. As Finch's heroic
mates, Tony Britton and Alexander
Knox do well, particularly the former as the group's stern leader.
Outstanding support is generated
by Malcolm Keen and Melvin
Hayes.

The Maurice Cowan production
has been handled deftly by director
Michael McCarthy, particularly the
action sequences, which contain
some flashy stuntwork and realistic
explosions. The sharp, swift editing of Arthur Stevens is another
valuable assist, as are Reginald
Wyer's lensmanship, Alex Vetchinsky's art direction and Philip
Green's effective integration of
hurdy-gurdy music as a vital part
of the plot.   Tube.

Kindan No Suna
(Forbidden Sands)
(JAPANESE—COLOR)

Hollywood, March 16.
Cory Films release of Shochiku production. Stars Kyoko Izumi, Minoru Ohki,
Reiko Hitomi, Akira Ishihama; features
Yoko Katsuragi, Kurumi Yamabato, Keijiro Morozumi. Directed by Manao Horiuchi. Screenplay, Osamu Takahashi,
Tamon Okada; based on novel by Keitaro
Kondo; camera (Eastman-Shochiku Color),
Masao Obara; music, Chuji Kinoshita.
Previewed March 15, '60. Running time,
84 MINS.
Nagi .... Kyoko Izumi
Sakuji .... Minoru Ohki
Otaka .... Reiko Hitomi
Isamu .... Akira Ishihama
Kaoru .... Yoko Katsuragi
Toshi .... Kurumi Yamabato
Goro .... Keijiro Morozumi

This Japanese import, beautifully turned out photographically
but too alien for American tastes,
is strictly for the offbeat art house
trade. Slow-moving and sometimes
difficult to follow via English
titles, it's one of the less impressive
Far East films to hit the U.S. market, although its subject of femme
sea divers and their sometimes
dishabille may provide certain exploitation value.

Setting is a fishing village where
the lives of all are centered in the
daily catch of the divers. Story
line is tragic, based on hopeless
love, the three principals a once-champion diver who now returns
after a five-year absence to continue his romance with the village's
champ femme diver, a seductress
who has another young frogman on
the string. By American standards
plotline is antiquated, and treatment devoids it of much interest.
Somewhat eye-catching is a native
dance, with a song thrown in; and
a fight between two femme divers
and diving action itself lend
certain interest.   Whit.

The Fugitive Kind

Sex drama based on Tennessee Williams' play, "Orpheus Descending." Exploitable but still a questionable boxoffice entry.

Hollywood, April 8.

United Artists release of Jurow-Shepherd-Pennebaker production, produced by Martin Jurow, Richard A. Shepherd. Stars Marlon Brando, Anna Magnani, Joanne Woodward. Features Maureen Stapleton, Victor Jory, with R. G. Armstrong, Emery Richardson, Spivy, Sally Gracie, Lucille Benson, John Baragrey, Ben Yaffe, Joe Brown Jr., Virgilia Chew, Frank Borgman, Janice Mars. Directed by Sidney Lumet. Screenplay, Tennessee Williams, Meade Roberts, from Williams' play "Orpheus Descending"; camera, Boris Kaufman; editor, Carl Lerner; music, Kenyon Hopkins; assistant director, Charles H. Maguire. Reviewed at Directors Guild of America, April 8, '60. Running time 119 MINS.

Val Xavier	Marlon Brando
Lady Torrance	Anna Magnani
Carol Cutrere	Joanne Woodward
Vee Talbott	Maureen Stapleton
Jabe Torrance	Victor Jory
Sheriff Talbott	R. G. Armstrong
Uncle Pleasant, the Conjure Man	Emory Richardson
Ruby Lightfoot	Spivy
Dolly Hamma	Sally Gracie
Beulah Binnings	Lucille Benson
David Cutrere	John Baragrey
Dog Hamma	Ben Yaffee
Pee Wee Binnings	Joe Brown Jr.
Nurse Porter	Virgilia Chew
Gas Station Attendant	Frank Borgman
Attendant's Wife	Janice Mars

Another helping from Tennessee Williams' seemingly inexhaustible closet of mixed up southern skeletons is being exposed here with only occasional flashes of cinematic power. No doubt the playwright's adaptation (with an assist on the screenplay by Meade Roberts) of his theatre piece, "Orpheus Descending," will stimulate some morbidly curious audiences. However, this picture is not likely to be as strong a boxoffice attraction as, for example, his "Cat on a Hot Tin Roof" or the current "Suddenly, Last Summer."

"The Fugitive Kind" is not basically one of Williams' better works and, as directed by Sidney Lumet, it sputters more often than it sizzles. Aside from the fact that the screenplay is overlength and untidy at two hours, less one minute, the combination of Marlon Brando and Anna Magnani fails to generate the electricity hoped for by the young producer team of Martin Jurow and Richard A. Shepherd. Some of the characters are inadequately motivated. Joanne Woodward, looking like a battered fugitive from skid row, pops in and out of the story to provide a distasteful and often ludicrous extra dash of degeneracy. The scene in a cemetery where she attempts a carnal relation with Brando reaches a new low in suggestive animalism. (Shades of "Hatrack" in the old American Mercury.)

The only fully rounded character provided by Williams in the drama's collection of anguished and spiritually empty souls is that of Lady Torrance portrayed by Miss Magnani with a faded veneer of lustfulness. At least one can understand her frustration and loneliness, being married to a dying older man she doesn't love, and her bitterness toward fellow townsfolks, her father having died trying to save his wine garden set afire by vigilantes because he sold liquor to Negroes. Moreover, she bore secretly out of wedlock a child (dead) fathered by a leading rich citizen who married another more socially acceptable.

Brando's role as a disillusioned guitar-singer, who becomes involved, as hired hand and lover, with Lady in a small Mississippi town while trying to put aside the wild life he experienced in New Orleans hot spots, is less clearly defined. Presumably one is supposed to accept him as a manifestation of the Orpheus legend with a strange and powerful romantic charm. The weakness of the picture may not be so much in the writing, although that can't be dismissed, as due to the failure of Miss Magnani and Brando as directed to overwhelm the spectator with theatrical fireworks.

Some of Williams' dialog is strong and frank, as when Brando tells Miss Woodward he doesn't intend to serve her as a convenient "stud"; as when he at first rebukes Miss Magnani by declaring contemptuously that he sees her as "a not-so-young and not-so-satisfied woman that hired a man off the highway to do double duty without paying overtime."

Brando is back to mumbling with marbles in his mouth too often, and Miss Magnani's English is not always as distinguishable as could be desired. Frequently it is a strain to catch dialog and that doesn't help. Victor Jory as the vengeful, dying husband; Maureen Stapleton, R. G. Armstrong and John Baragrey, as the kiss-and-run-to-the-bottle rich man, hand'e their comparatively small roles satisfactorily. Miss Woodward does well by her role, considering that she floats in and out of the picture with much sound and fury.

Much of the picture was filmed on location in Milton, New York, and at the Gold Medal Studios in the Bronx. Boris Kaufman's photography is good. The general level of the production reflects professional competence, but as an entertainment experience "The Fugitive Kind" is a disappointment.

Pyro.

Killers of Kilimanjaro

African adventure piece on familiar trails, but with enough action and pictorial quality to rack up o.k. biz.

Hollywood, March 31.

Columbia release of a Warwick Film production. Stars Robert Taylor, Anthony Newley, Anne Aubrey; with Gregoire Aslan, Allan Cuthbertson, Martin Benson, Orlando Martins, Donald Pleasence, Martin Boddey, Earl Cameron, Harry Baird, Anthony Jacobs; introduces John Dimech. Producer, John R. Sloan. Directed by Richard Thorpe. Screenplay, John Gilling; screen story, Richard Maibaum, Cyril Hume; from the book, "African Bush Adventures," by J. A. Hunter and Dan P. Mannix; camera, Ted Moore; editor, Geoffrey Foot; assistant director Ted Sturgis; music, William Alwyn; art director, Ray Sim. Reviewed at the studio, March 31, '60. Running time, 91 MINS.

Adamson	Robert Taylor
Hooky	Anthony Newley
Jane	Anne Aubrey
Ben Ahmed	Gregoire Aslan
Saxton	Allan Cuthbertson
Ali	Martin Benson
Chief	Orlando Martins
Captain	Donald Pleasence
Pasha	John Dimech
Gunther	Martin Boddey
Witch Doctor	Earl Cameron
Boraga	Harry Baird
Mustaph	Anthony Jacobs

"Killers of Kilimanjaro" doesn't go beating around "the bush" in search of a new dramatic path through Africa. It simply forges relentlessly down the same old cliche-infested trail traveled by so many past film safaris. Luckily, though, it's stripped for action, an approach that's never gone out of style at the boxoffice. Add to this the vicarious appeal of touring the dark continent via CinemaScope and technicolor, and you have entertainment that will more than hold its own in America's ticket-stub jungle.

When the film isn't pausing to admire the usual mobile zoo of African wildlife, it's plunging recklessly into scenes depicting savage fights for survival. The John Gilling screenplay, from a screen story by Richard Maibaum and Cyril Hume, drawn in turn from the book, "African Bush Adventures," by J. A. Hunter and Dan P. Mannix, wastes little time on pretentious bwana philosophy or romantic monkey business. Plot traces the attempts of an engineer (Robert Taylor) to pave the way through treacherous veldt terrain for the first East African railway.

To do it, he's forced to put up with charging rhinos, noisy lions, hungry crocs, playful hippos, the vicious WaArusha cannibals, thirst, ambush from a rival gang of railblazers, and the hazardous presence in his own unit of one lady redhead and a couple of dozen hired jailbirds. Being a hero in the grand tradition of truly epic heroes, Taylor seems ill-at-ease only when he's alone with the redhead.

Anne Aubrey (the redhead) is decorative in the grand tradition of redheads in African color films. Taylor gives a competent performance, and brings commercial star stature to the picture. Anthony Newley, as the hero's whimsical sidekick (in the grand Sancho Panza tradition) steals the show with a boisterously appealing performance. The film introduces young John Dimech, a sort of latter-day Sabu. He gives a good account of himself, serving as a kind of one-man Berlitz school for his unprepared bwana friends. Orlando Martins, who's made a career out of this sort of thing, exhibits poise as a sociable tribal chief. There's able support from Gregoire Aslan, Allan Cuthbertson and Martin Benson.

John R. Sloan's production is endowed with a vigorous pace and a business-like attitude by director Richard Thorpe. Art director Ray Sim has selected some striking locales for the location sequences, and provided some fine imitations for interior scenes at England's Shepperton Studios. Ted Moore's CinemaScope photography is skillful, and Geoffrey Foot's editing careful. There is some difficulty on several occasions, however, when cuts from wild animal footage to performer reaction shots don't quite match in hue or clarity.

William Alwyn's unobstructive score is conducted spiritedly by Muir Mathieson. Cliff Richardson contributes some tidy special effects. Interesting backgrounds by Giselle Rocco spruce up the main titles.

Tube.

The Trial of Sergeant Rutledge
(COLOR-SONG)

Race-bias angle added to strong John Ford melodrama, needs selling.

Hollywood, April 4.

Warner Bros. release of John Ford (Willis Goldbeck & Patrick Ford) production. Stars Jeffrey Hunter, Constance Towers, Billie Burke. Directed by John Ford. Screenplay, James Warner Bellah and Willis Goldbeck; camera, Bert Glennon; editor, Jack Murray; music, Howard Jackson; song, "Captain Buffalo," Mack David and Jerry Livingston. Previewed at Warner Bros. studio, April 4, '60. Running time, 111 MINS

Lieut. Cantrell	Jeffrey Hunter
Mary Beecher	Constance Towers
Mrs. Fosgate	Billie Burke
Braxton Rutledge	Woody Strode
Skidmore	Juano Hernandez
Major Fosgate	Willis Bouchey
Captain Shattuck	Carleton Young
Lieut. Mulqueen	Judson Pratt
Captain Dwyer	Bill Henry
Captain MacAfee	Walter Reed
Captain Dickinson	Chuck Hayward
Nellie	Mae Marsh
Chandler Hubble	Fred Libby
Dr. Eckner	Charles Seel
Lucy Dabney	Toby Richards

Give John Ford a troop of cavalry, some hostile Indians, a wisp of story and chances are the director will come galloping home with an exciting film. In Warner Bros.' "Sergeant Rutledge," writers James Warner Bellah and Willis Goldbeck (latter also co-produced with Patrick Ford) provided an extra plus factor in the form of an offbeat and dramatically intriguing screenplay which deals frankly, if not too deeply, with racial prejudice in the post-Civil War era. Director Ford expertly blends the action-pictorial and the story elements to create lively physical excitement as well as sustained suspense about the fate of a Negro trooper who is accused of rape and double murder.

Original tag on this picture was "Captain Buffalo." With a serviceable song using that title composed by Mack David and Jerry Livingston it is questionable that the new label represents any improvement from the standpoint of exploitation. It will take aggressive selling to assure this film the kind of audience it deserves since there are no so-called big marquee names in the cast. However, the script offers plenty of opportunities for stimulating interest among virtually all types of audiences, excepting the young who should not be exposed to the sordid rape denouement.

While star billing goes to Jeffrey Hunter, Constance Towers and Billie Burke, it's actually Woody Strode who dominates. As the giant-sized Negro 1st sgt. who is eventually proven to be a victim of circumstantial evidence, Strode gives an unusually versatile performance. Ford uses his camera to accent the actor's natural physical strength, to build an image of a man of action and heroic proportions while Strode fills out the design with many subtle shadings of character.

The screenplay is said to have a historical basis in that the U.S. 9th and 10th Cavalry of Negro troopers, commanded by white officers, fought skirmishes with the Apaches in Arizona after the Civil War. Whether the actual incident which forms the plot structure—the murder of the Commanding Officer of the 9th Cavalry and the rape-murder of his daughter—also is factual is not quite as important as that it plays well. Story unfolds via a series of flashbacks from the court martial of Strode as witnesses describe his friendship with the dead white girl, his panicky desertion, the circumstances of his capture by the Lieutenant (Hunter) who later volunteers as defense counsel.

Most of the action flows out of the testimony of Miss Towers, the only sympathetic witness, whom Strode has saved from an Indian ambush. Ford makes strikingly effective use of a stage technique by gradually blacking out the screen so that only the figure of Miss Towers remains in the camera eye as her words fade into actions. When the picture is not pounding along as an Indian war party ravages the countryside, Ford sees to it that the court martial pro-

gresses with mounting suspense, tempered with a few touches of broad comedy. These are provided chiefly by Miss Burke as the gabby, but outwardly prim wife of the president of the court; Willis Bouchey as her annoyed and embarrassed spouse, and Judson Pratt as a member of the trial board.

Carleton Young has several opportunities for bravura acting as the cruelly vindictive prosecuting attorney and plays them to the hilt, revealing a forcefulness that this reviewer, at least, had not previously suspected. Hunter's role is more subdued, but he does a commendable job both in the role of attorney and soldier on horseback. Miss Towers is easy to look upon and performs with easy grace what is required of her. Juano Hernandez brings quiet dignity to his part as an aged trooper who was born slave and has no idea how old he actually is.

While the climax of the story has a distinctly melodramatic flourish, it carries considerable force. The scenarists and Ford apparently were striving for shock effect—and they have it. Although the revelation that the rape and murders were committed by the lusting father of a boy the girl knew takes "Sergeant Rutledge" out of the category of recommendable family entertainment, it is handled in good taste for adult viewing. Fred Libby, as the degenerate attacker, is required to display considerable emotion when he is exposed, but Ford permits him to chew the scenery with too much relish for comfort.

Technical credits, including editing by Jack Murray, sound by M. A. Merrick, are all good and Bert Glennon has used his color camera expertly to capture the majestic natural scenic values of Monument Valley, which always manages to look new and fresh and exciting in a John Ford picture.

Pyro.

Man On a String

Cloak-and-dagger for twin-bills, helped by some good overseas footage. Based on Boris Morros' espionage experiences.

Hollywood, April 5.

Columbia release of a Louis de Rochemont RD-DR production. Stars Ernest Borgnine, Kerwin Mathews; with Colleen Dewhurst, Alexander Scourby, Glenn Corbett, Vladimir Sokoloff, Friedrich Joloff, Richard Kendrick, Ed Prentiss, Holger Hagen, Robert Iller, Reginald Pasch, Carl Paffe, Eva Pflug, Michael Mellinger. Producer, Louis De Rochemont. Directed by Andre De Toth. Screenplay, John Kafka, Virginia Shaler; adapted in part from "Ten Years a Counterspy" by Boris Morros. Charles Samuels; camera, Charles Lawton Jr., Albert Benitz, Gayne Rescher, Pierre Poincarde; editor, Al Clark; art director, Carl Anderson; set decorator, James M. Crowe; assistant directors, Eddie Saeta, Jean Hoerler; sound, Lambert Day; music, George Duning. Reviewed at Fox-Wilshire Theatre, April 5, '60. Running time, 92 MINS.

Boris Mitrov	Ernest Borgnine
Bob Avery	Kerwin Mathews
Helen Benson	Colleen Dewhurst
Vadja Kubelov	Alexander Scourby
Frank Sanford	Glenn Corbett
Papa	Vladimir Sokoloff
Nikolai Chapayev	Frienrich Joloff
Inspector Jenkins	Richard Kendrick
Adrian Benson	Ed Prentiss
Hans Gruenwald	Rolger Hagen
Hartmann	Robert Iller
Otto Bergman	Reginald Pasch
People's Judge	Carl Jaffe
Rosnova	Eva Pflug
Detective	Michael Mellinger

Columbia's "Man On A String" is a presentable lower-berth prospect. Some intimate footage of actual Moscow and Berlin activity takes it just beyond the routine spy-suspense genre, but not far enough beyond to enable it to step rewardingly out of secondary status. "String" is simply hamstrung from taller theatrical aspirations by competitive television's well-known voracious appetite for just such fare.

The John Kafka-Virginia Shaler screenplay, loosely adapted from Boris Morros' autobiog, "Ten Years A Counterspy," is one of those you-can't-tell-the-villains-without-a-concealed-microphone affairs. Ernest Borgnine stars as a Moscow-born U. S. citizen who's been filling in his spare time by helping some sneaky Russian spies accomplish their mischief. Caught in the act by U. S. Central Bureau of Intelligence agents, he's persuaded to change sides, promptly finds himself in Moscow snooping on the Russians.

The cast is handicapped by plenty of platitudinous dialog ("In this business you have to forget every human feeling except your love for your country"), but most of the players are capable cloak-and-dagger-o-types. Borgnine carries on gamely in the central role, more than matching the dimension of the part. Kerwin Mathews is able as his top aide-de-enemy-camp. Colleen Dewhurst endows her rather shabby role with some life-giving spirit. Others who attract more than passive interest are Alexander Scourby, Vladimir Sokoloff, Friedrich Joliff, Ed Prentiss, Eva Pflug, Reginald Pasch and Glenn Corbett. Andre De Toth's direction springs to life in the action sequences, labors a little when dealing with exposition and family relationships. Clete Roberts' narration fills in the expository blank spaces.

The film's chief impact comes from its overseas footage—principally the work of cameramen Albert Benitz in Berlin and Pierre Poincarde in Moscow. Good domestic lensing is chipped in by Gayne Rescher in New York, Charles Lewton Jr. here in Hollywood. Editing by Al Clark is brisk, and music by George Duning heightens the tension of Louis De Rochemont's widespread production.

Tube.

Le Trou
(The Hole)
(FRENCH)

Paris, April 5.

Cinedis release of Play Art-Filmsonor-Titanus production. With Philippe Bancel, Jean Keraudy, Raymond Meunier, Marc Michel, Michel Constantin. Directed by Jacques Becker. Screenplay, Jose Giovanni, Jean Aurel, Becker from book by Giovanni; camera, Ghislain Cloquet; editor, Marguerite Renoir. At Marignan, Paris. Running time, 145 MINS.

Manu	Philippe Bancel
Geo	Michel Constantin
Traitor	Marc Michel
Monseigneur	Raymond Ceunier
Oldtimer	Jean Keraudy

The late Jacques Becker has left behind a solidly built film, based on a true story of a jailbreak. Using non-actors, including one who authored this Becker story, picture tells a tale of human endeavor and cooperation that transcends its actual locale. It is taut sans trying for any untoward suspense gambits because of its feeling for its people, place and motivations.

It is more than two hours long but this is hardly noticed. Five men awaiting sentence break through their cell floor, enter the insides of the prison, and get to the sewer system from where they can break into the regular sewage setup and freedom. But the best laid plans are foiled by a newcomer who turns them in.

The characters are neatly etched but the true criminal types are not given much backgrounding. Yet they have their own code and friendships and the intricate break and digging aspects are dynamically detailed. The rugged sets have the feel of a cement and iron prison. The acting is uncannily clear for non-actors, and it gives an added quality to the pic.

The uncomfortable aspects of prison life with the overcrowded cell, bad sanitary facilities and the harsh treatment of the prisoners, also play a part in this tale. In spite of the lack of background, the prisoners are all well depicted and acceptable.

Becker, sans music, holds the tensions and progression firmly in hand and has made an unusual escape pic. Unlike another French prison break pic before it, "A Condemned Man Escaped," Becker was interested only in the men and their strengths and weaknesses.

Its inflexible insistence on showing every aspect of the escape, peg this mainly an arty house film for abroad with playoff chances needing a hard sell. This has a knowhow in mounting, and a well sustained mood and action that could make this of foreign interest if properly handled. Technical credits are excellent.

Mosk.

Pollyanna
(COLOR)

Mostly on the strength of Hayley Mills portrayal of the title character, a potential b.o. smash for Disney.

Hollywood, April 1.

Buena Vista release of Walt Disney production. Stars Jane Wyman, Richard Egan, Karl Malden, Nancy Olson, Adolphe Menjou, Donald Crisp, Agnes Moorehead, Kevin Corcoran; presents Hayley Mills; features James Drury, Reta Shaw, Leora Dana, Anne Seymour, Edward Platt, Mary Grace Canfield, Jenny Egan, Gage Clarke. Written and directed by David Swift; based on novel by Eleanor H. Porter; camera (Technicolor), Russell Harlan; editor, Frank Gross; music, Paul Smith; assistant director, Joseph Behm; art directors, Carroll Clark, Robert Clatworthy. Reviewed at Academy Award Theatre, April 1, '60. Running time, 133 MINS.

Aunt Polly	Jane Wyman
Dr. Edmond Chilton	Richard Egan
Reverend Paul Ford	Karl Malden
Nancy Furman	Nancy Olson
Mr. Pendergast	Adolphe Menjou
Mayor Karl Warren	Donald Crisp
Mrs. Snow	Agnes Moorehead
Jimmy Bean	Kevin Corcoran
George Dodds	James Drury
Tillie Lagerlof	Reta Shaw
Mrs. Paul Ford	Leora Dana
Mrs. Amelia Tarbell	Agnes Seymour
Ben Tarbell	Edward Platt
Angelica	Mary Grace Canfield
Mildred Snow	Jenny Egan
Mr. Murg	Gage Clarke
Mr. Neely	Ian Folfe
Mr. Thomas	Nolan Leary
Mr. Gorman	Edgar Dearing
Pollyanna	Hayley Mills

Walt Disney's "Pollyanna" is a personal triumph for Hayley Mills. As soon as the word starts circulating about her performance in the title role, this picture is going to take off at the boxoffice. It's a sure-fire hit, but it really needed that one major effort to aspire to such glad prospects.

Miss Mills' work more than compensates for the film's lack of tautness and, at certain points, what seems to be an uncertain sense of direction. It starts strong, begins to sag and hesitate in the mid-section, temporarily losing sight of an overall dramatic goal, but picks up again and roars on to a climax that will leave hardly a dry eye in the house. That the incredibly pre-World War I confectionery character of "Pollyanna" (the glad girl, she was called) emerges normal and believably lovable is a tribute to Miss Mills' exceptional ability and to writer-director David Swift's sane, sensible approach to the familiar character from Eleanor H. Porter's "New Thought" novel.

"Pollyanna," of course, is the tale of the little 12-year-old girl who plays "the glad game" so well that she's soon got everyone she knows playing it. She's an orphan who lives with her aunt (Jane Wyman), the richest, most influential woman in a town which bears her name and sheepishly takes her advice and her charity. That is, until "Pollyanna" arrives. Led by this pint-sized dynamo with the sunny philosophy, the town rebels and is just beginning to enjoy its freedom when its heroine is paralyzed in the legs from a fall. For the climax, the grateful townspeople all turn out to cheer her up, and auntie sees the light.

With this performance, Miss Mills seems headed toward a great career. Rarely have the attitudes and mannerisms of a child been reflcted so expertly on the screen. A cast consisting largely of veterans has been assembled for this picture, but even these poised troupers are completely overshadowed by the youngster's excellence. Miss Wyman, Richard Egan, Donald Crisp, Adolphe Menjou, Agnes Moorehead and Karl Malden are more than competent in key roles. Nancy Olson makes a spirited return to the screen. Young Kevin Corcoran does a nice job as Miss Mills' little playmate. Outstanding supporting work is fashioned by Mary Grace Canfield and Reta Shaw. Others who attract favorable attention are James Drury, Leora Dana, Anne Seymour and Edward Platt.

Physically and technically, the film is typical of the high calibre of these departments in most Disney pictures. The handsome settings and tasteful, appropriate furnishings are a tribute to the handiwork of art directors Carroll Clark and Robert Clatworthy and set decorators Emile Kuri and Fred Mac Lean. Apt, colorful costuming is provided by Chuck Keehne and Gertrude Casey. Paul Smith's music, rousingly orchestrated by Franklyn Marks, adds character to the telling of the story. Russell Harlan's sure camera work and Frank Gross' editing are other vital contributions.

All these crafts hit a peak late in the film when they combine to create a "bazaar" sequence that's the best of its kind since "Picnic."

Tube.

Private Property

Adult film which should do well in special houses. Sex exploitable tale of couple of moral delinquents who get their comeuppance.

Hollywood, April 1.

Citations Films release of Kana Productions picture produced by Stanley Colbert; Lou Brandt associate producer & asst. director. Stars Corey Allen, Warren Oates, Kate Manx, Robert Wark, Jerome Cowan. Directed and written by Leslie Stevens. Camera, Ted McCord; editor, Jerry Young. Previewed in Los Angeles, April 1, '60. Running time, 79 MINS.

Duke	Corey Allen
Boots	Warren Oates
Ann Carlyle	Kate Manx
Roger Carlyle	Robert Wark
Ed Hogate	Jerome Cowan

A fellow named Marty once proved that an important film is not always a big film. Kana Production's "Private Property" is

not a big film, but a unique set of circumstances makes it possibly one of the year's most arresting American films. An uncompromising treatment of a normally taboo subject—the planned and detailed seduction of a young housewife—it is one of the few "Hollywood" films ever to be released without the code seal.

No doubt it will be called everything from dirt to art; what is certain is that it will be called something, that it will be talked about and that it will be watched by a curious Hollywood. Brought in by producer Stanley Colbert and writer-director Leslie Stevens for under $60,000, it should recoup its cost in a handful of engagements.

Citation Films' release pattern initially puts "Private Property" into top art houses (e.g., Paris Theatre, N. Y., starting April 18), then into general release. Immediate success depends on whether or not American art house audiences will accept an American art house film. Its long-range success is practically assured by a sex angle that is as exploitable as it is hard-hitting.

The picture is not flawless in execution, but it shows amazingly little strain from its tight pocketbook. Writer-director Stevens keeps the first 60-minutes in low key—one sometimes gets the feeling too low key—but with each scene, each probing, each bit of comic relief he builds fascinatingly to a wild, staggering final 20 minutes that will leave audiences in a sweat, whether they were excited by or repelled by what they had seen.

The picture is a psycological study of a young hoodlum, his suspiciously homosexual friend and a housewife frustrated by an inattentive husband. The hoodlum (Cory Allen) promises to "get" the housewife (Kate Manx) for the friend (Warren Oates) so he can "make" it for the first time. The subject mater is daring, but the treatment can hardly be called immoral, for it consistently expresses the degeneracy of the youths and because they ultimately are destroyed by their own doing. The responsibility shown by Colbert and Stevens ends with the adult mind; they did not make "Private Property" for children.

The story has strong interest because it stands out from the pile of hash and rehash that audiences have wearied of. Stevens' screenplay is crisp in dialog, full in implications; and his direction sharply explores his characters. Majority of the film rings true, though the relationship between the husband (Robert Wark) and the wife is weakly developed. Wark is not suited for the role, and thus the tone between sensuous Miss Manx and her spouse is difficult to believe.

As the smooth lover who lures the female, Allen is excellent, his best film role to date. Oates makes a striking contrast as the weak, simple friend who finds he can't take advantage of the woman. Miss Manx is a natural actress, underplaying admirably as the sensitive wife. Jerome Cowan, in a small role, is fine.

Biggest asset in the film's good looks is the firstrate photography by Oscar-winning Ted McCord, who captured an exciting mood and provided some interesting camera techniques. Jerry Young's editing is nicely done, particularly the inter-cutting. Lou Brandt, as associate producer and assistant director, had much to do with the production. It might be noted that sound, uncredited, has a dubbed effect, not always synchronized in the review print.

"Private Property" already has won a healthy share of national news breaks, many pointing out that Colbert and Stevens (each in his early 30s) are the start of America's "new wave" of filmmakers.

Whatever that means, Colbert and Stevens, indeed, are the makers of an unusual, exploitable film that has a certain look of art. Now under contract to 20th-Fox, where they'll adapt Stevens' Broadway play, "Marriage-Go-Round," they combine a serious approach with a commercial sense. "Private Property" is their first film, and whether or not they are the start of a new wave, they're certain to make significant contributions to the old one. *Ron.*

In Wake of a Stranger
(BRITISH)

Second-rate murder melodrama. Bleak prospects.

Paramount release of Crescent Film production. Features Tony Wright, Shirley Eaton, Danny Green, Harry H. Corbett, Willoughby Goddard; with Barbara Archer, Vanda Godsell, Tom Bowman, Alun Owen, James Ottaway, Peter Sinclair, Peter Carver, Frank Pemberton, Patricia Dean, David Hemmings, Jemma Hyde, Vera Lennox, Betty Anderson. Producer, John Penington; directed by David Eady; screenplay, John Tully; from novel by Ian Stuart Black; camera, Eric Cross; editor, John Seabourne; sound, Ken Cameron, Bill Bulkley; music, Edwin Astley. Reviewed at Paramount Studio, March 24, '60. Running time, 69 MINS.

The British, too, are capable of concocting strictly second-rate murder melodramas. Stateside prospects are bleak for this bundle from Albion. Outside of a few fresh faces and a certain atmospheric authenticity, Paramount has little of either artistic or market value to exploit in this film.

Its unwieldy title is typical of the unsound, loosely-woven construction that prevails within the yarn itself. "In the Wake of a Stranger," adapted for the screen by John Tully from a rather uninspired tome by Ian Stuart Black, is an incredibly puerile tale of a sailor who gets tangled up in the murder of a bookie. In many ways imitative of the lesser gangster products whipped up by American filmmakers in the past, the plot follows the sailor's series of misadventures as he wraps himself in a web of circumstance that is, at all times, illogical. There is a love story running parallel to the central plot that not only slows up the film, but is never very plausible. Both the dramatic and the romantic situations are resolved unconvincingly, if happily.

Under the burden of irrational plotwork, neither Tony Wright nor Shirley Eaton can give much weight to their key portrayals. He manages to give his role a certain hapless charm now and then, and she is a very attractive girl with a promising flair for sophistication.

Supporting cast is a colorful conglomeration of scoundrels, boobs and rapscallions, best of which are Danny Green, Harry H. Corbett and Willoughby Goddard. There's some seafaring music that's not always appropriate, but does give the picture an arty essence at times.

Technically and physically, John Penington's production is sound, lending an authentic backdrop quality that deserves a more respectable yarn up front. David Eady's direction makes the most of all plus values, but manages little headway with the waferweight story. *Tube.*

Peter Voss, Der Held Des Tages
(Peter Voss, Hero of the Day)
(GERMAN-COLOR)

Berlin, April 5.

UFA release of Kurt Ulrich production. Stars O. W. Fischer, Linda Christian; features Peter Vogel, Ingmar Zeisberg, Peter Mosbacher. Directed by George Marischka. Screenplay, Curt J. Braun and Peter Dronte; camera (Eastmancolor), Klaus von Rautenfeld; music, Erwin Halletz; editor, Hermann Haller. At Zoo Palast, Berlin. Running time, 110 MINS.

Peter Voss	O. W. Fischer
Grace McNaughty	Linda Christian
Prince Jose Villarossa	Peter Vogel
Dolly	Ingmar Zeisberg
Baron de Clock	Peter Mosbacher
Mary de la Roche	Helga Commerfeld
Perrier	Ludwig Linkmann
Charley	Ralf Wolter
Bobby Dodd	Walter Giller

"Peter Voss, Thief of Millions" emerged as one of the stoutest German picture grossers last season. So producer Kurt Ulrich didn't waste much time to come along with a sequel. As most frequently with sequels, this one falls quite short of the first one. Its intended tongue-in-check humor is considerably on the banal if not naive side, situations are farfetched, etc. Despite this, the pic will shape as a brisk money-maker here, guaranteed via the name of O. W. Fischer and helped by the fact that domestic audiences like this sort of escapist fare.

Peter-Voss (O. W. Fischer), globetrotter and happy-go-lucky fellow, in this is out to recapture eight tiny Ming horses, Chinese woodcarvings valued at several thousand dollars which have been stolen by an international gang. As the gangsters have distributed the precious horses among themselves, Voss has to chase around the world to North Africa, India, and even Las Vegas.

This is a natural for Fischer who's more at home in this pic than with his emotion-loaded films. Here he is given the opportunity to show up in several masks (he has to disguise himself) and he widely exploits this opportunity. He's an old servant, a clumsy waiter, a distinguished Chinese, a dashing police officer, a Castro-style revolutionary, a French professor and an Indian coolie. With the exception of Walter Giller, who enacts a private detective, others don't come off to much advantage in this. Linda Christian (her second German pic), incidentally, portrays a rich American "lady" in her usual fashion.

George Marischka has given the whole thing a swift, often overly fast gait. Eastmancolor is used to good advantage. Other technical credits are average. *Hans.*

Strafbataillon 999
(Penalty Battalion 999)
(GERMAN)

Berlin, April 5.

Union release of Willy Zeyn production. With Sonja Ziemann, Georg Thomas, Werner Peters, Ernst Schroeder, Heinz Weiss. Directed by Harald Philipp. Camera, Heinz Hoelscher; music, Willy Mattes; editor, E. Kleinert. At UFA Pavillon, Berlin. Running time, 110 MINS.

Julia Deutschmann	Sonja Ziemann
Ernst Deutschmann	Georg Thomas
Master Sergeant Kruell	Werner Peters
Dr. Kukill	Ernst Schroeder
Lieutenant Obermeier	Heinz Weiss
Captain Barth	Kurd Pieritz
Schwanecke	H. E. Jaeger
von Bartlitz	Werner Hessenland
Wiedeck	Georg Lehn
Lieutenant Bevern	Claus Kindler
Tanja	Judith Dorneys

Another outstanding German war film of nearly "Bridge" calibre. It's artistically not as clear-cut as "Bridge" but, on the whole, hardly less, impressive. In lensing and acting, it's even more effective. Since this is an honest and convincing picture about an especially brutal chapter of the last World War, it has definite U. S. chances.

This Union release dedicates itself to the many socalled "penalty companies" for various reasons. It centers less on a story but more on several individuals. Pic shows via the latter the brutality of war and how tough and inhuman human beings can get. In the "999" unit we find all sort of convicts: An officer who ignored an unscrupulous order to save his men, a soldier who didn't return to his unit in time, a bacteriologist who was accused of alleged self-mutilation to escape the army and a dubious character who stole during an air raid.

These men are shown as exposed to the chicanery of inhuman superiors and later used on the East Front: Here they are forced to remove (without technical equipment) mines and when the Russian offensive sets in, they are left without arms. Save the master-sergeant, one of their tough superiors, a coward basically, none of this unit survives.

This has been brought to the screen without concessions. Director Philipp used much sense on atmosphere and hard-hitting realism. He leads some of the players to top performances, such as Werner Peters (master-sergeant), Claus Kindler (Nazi officer), Heinz Weiss (human officer), and H. E. Jaeger, Lehn, Hessenland and Georg Thomas, as penalty soldiers. Less rewarding are the two femme roles: Sonja Ziemann, as Thomas' wife (in Berlin) and Judith Dorneys as Russian girl.

Special praise goes for the camera work of Heinz Hoelscher. Rarely has one seen in a German war film such realistic and skillfully staged battle sequences. Exteriors, incidentally, were shot in Yugoslavia. Original Russian tanks were borrowed from Tito's Army. *Hans.*

Dos Hijos Desobedientes
(Two Disobedient Sons)
(MEXICAN)
(Eastmancolor)

Mexico City, April 5.

Peliculas Nacionales release of Producciones Corsa production. Stars Pedro Armendariz, Antonio Aguilar, Elvira Quintana and Maria Duval; features Jose Elias Moreno, A. Soto Lamarina, Joaquin Garcia, Federico Curiel, and Jaime Fernandez. Directed by Emilio Gomez Muriel. Screenplay, Jaime Salvador; camera, Jack Draper. At Olimpia Theatre, Mexico City. Running time, 90 MINS.

Mexico's top boxoffice draw, Pedro Armendariz, mounts a horse in this one and goes through the motions of the typical Mexican western musical cowboy. Plot is slight, involving two rivals who slug it out over differences of opinion, for the love of a lady and for the sheer fact of being "muy macho" (he-men). But all this was done with a spirit of camaraderie. In all the fighting and shooting, nobody gets hurt.

It is difficult to understand why Armendariz ever got involved in this pic. They've been making the same story for years, involving two men, friends or enemies, disputing for love of a woman, getting drunk, even the traditional stalk, but without one of the principals biting the dust. Pictures of this sort have been a gold mine, however, for Mexican producers aiming at the tastes of lower class and rural public. And this one has the advantage of Eastmancolor to set off Armendariz in charro costumes.

Tony Aguilar, the younger mem-

ber of the pair, not much as an actor, is undoubtedly a better horseman by virtue of the many musical oaters in which he has appeared. But he does shine in the song number. Elvira Quintana and Maria Duval add the femme interest. For comedy relief the picture draws on talents of Borolas, Pichirilo and El Chicote, characters well fixed in the minds of patrons who dote on low comedy and song, and don't care too much for action. *Emil.*

League of Gentlemen
(BRITISH)

Smooth, suspenseful comedy thriller about a bank robbery. Happily cast for topline U.K. boxoffice and U.S. patrons likely also will find this an agreeable night out.

London, April 5.

Rank release of an Allied Film Makers (Michael Relph-Basil Dearden) production. Stars Jack Hawkins, Nigel Patrick, Richard Attenborough, Roger Livesey; features Bryan Forbes, Kieron Moore, Robert Cocte. Directed by Basil Dearden. Screenplay by Bryan Forbes from John Boland's novel; camera, Arthur Ibbotson; editor, John Guthridge; music, Philip Green. At Odeon, Marble Arch, London. Running time, 116 MINS.

Hyde	Jack Hawkins
Race	Nigel Patrick
Mycroft	Roger Livesey
Lexy	Richard Attenborough
Porthill	Bryan Forbes
Stevens	Kieron Moore
Bunny Warren	Robert Coote
Rupert	Terence Alexander
Peggy	Melissa Stribling
Weaver	Norman Bird
Wylie	Patrick Wymark
Elizabeth	Nanette Newman
C.S.M.	David Lodge
Molly Weaver	Doris Hare
Capt. Saunders	Gerald Harper
Grogan	Bryan Murray

This first entry from Allied Film Makers, a new setup here, has the look of a winner. AFM consists of actors Jack Hawkins, Richard Attenborough and Bryan Forbes, producer Michael Relph and director Basil Dearden. All five have had a hand in "A League Of Gentlemen," and it's a smooth piece of teamwork which shows what can be done when professionals get together. Skillfully written, acted and directed, it develops slowly but gathers momentum. Film has enough wit and suspense to make it an excellent evening's entertainment on both sides of the Atlantic.

The yarn is a novel twist on the ancient theme of an attempted bank robbery. The only snag is that according to film law, crime mustn't be allowed to pay off so that audiences will know that the gang will slip up and the main problem at the end is how. Rarely have audiences wished more fervently for the criminals to get away with it.

Jack Hawkins, disgruntled at being axed from the army which he has faithfully served for many years, decides to have a go at a bank robbery. He picks up the idea from an American thriller and recruits seven broke and shady ex-officers, all experts in their own line in the army. He forms a team to conduct the robbery as a strict army maneuver. The gang goes into hiding while every phase of the operation is planned down to the last detail. It involves explosives, weapons, radio jamming, smoke screens and split-timing. As a military exploit, the entire gang would have earned medals. As it is pulled off they are eventually tripped up by a slight, unforeseen happening.

The actual raid is short and, curiously, rather less exciting and interesting than the preparation leading up to the big robbery. Particularly amusing and gripping is an impudent raid made on an army depot under cover of a phoney camp inspection during which the gang help themselves to weapons and explosives.

Bryan Forbes has written a strong, witty screenplay from John Boland's novel. It takes time to get under way, but once the gang is formed, the situations pile up to an exciting and funny finale. Basil Dearden's direction is sure and Arthur Ibbotson has turned in some excellent camerawork. The eight members of the gang all give smooth, plausible performances, with Hawkins and Nigel Patrick, as his second-in-command, having the meatiest roles. Both acquit themselves very well. Richard Attenborough, Terence Alexander, Bryan Forbes, Norman Bird, Kieron Moore and, particularly, Roger Livesey, as a con-man posing as a parson, provide splendid contrasting styles. Livesey is especially effective playing the phoney brigadier.

Among the other roles well handled are David Lodge, as a sergeant major; Gerald Harper, as a nervous young officer and Brian Murray, the soldier who is rash enough to criticize the food. Toward the end, Robert Coote makes a sudden appearance and an explosive impact as a bumbling ex-brigadier who butts in Hawkins' house just as the gang are celebrating their success and setting off to their various destinations. Coote is expert in this sort of role, and it was a smart move to introduce the character and give the climax a lift.

It would have been possible for "A League Of Gentlemen" to have been written and played entirely for thrills and suspense, almost on the lines of "Rififi" or "Seven Thieves." But by electing to infuse a lot of comedy into the film, the producer have broadened its appeal and made it a thoroughly entertaining couple of hours. *Rich.*

Valley of the Redwoods

Lower-berth crime meller about a clumsy robbery in lumber country.

Hollywood, April 12.

Twentieth-Fox release of an Associated Producers Inc. production. Stars John Hudson, Lynn Bernay, Ed Nelson; with Michael Forest, Robert Shayne, John Brinkley, Bruno Ve Soto, Hal Torey, Chris Miller. Producer, Gene Corman. Directed by William N. Witney. Screenplay, Leo Gordon and Daniel Madison, from a story by Gene Corman; camera, Kay Norton; editor, Marshall Neilan Jr.; sound, Bill Bernds; art director, Daniel Haller; music, Buddy Bregman; assistant director, Richard Dixon. Reviewed at the studio, April 12, '60. Running time, 62 MINS.

Wayne Randall	John Hudson
Jan Spencer	Lynn Bernay
Dino Michaelis	Ed Nelson
Dave Harris	Michael Forest
Captain Sid Walker	Robert Shayne
Willie Chadwick	John Brinkley
Joe Wolcheck	Bruno Ve Soto
Philip Blair	Hal. Torey
Charlotte Walker	Chris Miller

"Valley of the Redwoods" offers audiences brevity, a dash of suspense, and some pulsating jazz background music—little else. It will suffice as secondary fare in situations where product is aimed at less mature tastes.

There's far more bark than bite to this lumbering account of loggers at loggerheads, concocted by Leo Gordon and Daniel Madison from a paperweight yarn by producer Gene Corman. Screenplay traces the misadventure of a trio of thieves (two men, one woman) who attempt to make off with an $81,000 lumber company payroll. The job, a complete botch, is further burdened by unconvincing romantic complications.

The three principal characters are to weak and incompletely drawn to arouse sufficient sympathy or concern. They are so pitifully inadequate, both at their task and in their relations with each other, that the audience begins to lose patience when it should be getting curious.

There's evidence of a considerable amount of care taken with the production—far more than the yarn merits. Kay Norton's black-and-white CinemaScope lenswork captures the picturesque flavor of lumber country as it follows the hoods into the woods. Other plus values are contributed by film editor Marshall Neilan Jr. and art director Daniel Haller. Some rousing logger-rhythms by Buddy Bregman help the film immeasurably. These factors bring an aura of surface tension and excitement to a film that needs all the help it can get.

Acting ranges from mechanical to competent. Ed Nelson, as the pro of the safecracking trio, comes off best. The script makes a sorry spectacle of John Hudson, forces him to writhe about in disabled agony from a wound for most of the footage. Lynn Bernay is capable and attractive as the third member of the lawbreaking party. In support, Bruno Ve Soto, as a watchman, registers most effectively. Michael Forest shows promise, but is gagged by some stiff romatic dialog as he blindly pursues the wicked Miss Bernay. Others in the cast are acceptable. Director William N. Whitney obtains best results when the actors are on the move. *Tube.*

Peeping Tom
(BRITISH—COLOR)

Offbeat, chilly yarn about a psychopathic killer. Saved from unpleasantness by shrewd direction and excellent photography. Above level horror pic.

London, April 12.

Anglo-Amalgamated release of Michael Powell production. Stars Carl Boehm, Moira Shearer, Anna Massey, Maxine Audley. Directed by Michael Powell. Story and screenplay by Leo Marks; camera, Otto Heller; editor, Noreen Ackland; music, Brian Easdale. At Plaza, London. Running time, 109 MINS.

Mark	Carl Boehm
Vivian	Moira Shearer
Helen	Anna Massey
Mrs. Stephens	Maxine Audley
Arthur Baden	Esmond Knight
Mr. Peters	Bartlett Mullins
Diane Ashley	Shirley Ann Field
Don Jarvis	Michael Goodliffe
Dora	Brenda Bruce
Doctor Rosan	Martin Miller
Milly	Pamela Green
Inspector Gregg	Jack Watson
Sergeant Miller	Nigel Davenport
Tony	Brian Wallace
Lorraine	Susan Travers
Publicity Chief	Maurice Durant
Assistant Director	Brian Worth
Miss Simpson	Veronica Hurst
Elderly Gentleman	Miles Malleson
Store Detective	Alan Rolfe

Anglo-Amalgamated has dipped into its till and unloaded around $560,000 on making "Peeping Tom," the biggest load of coin that Anglo has ever invested in one picture. It's as well, for stripped of its color and some excellent photography plus imaginative direction by Michael Powell, the plot itself would have emerged as a shoddy yarn. As it is, the title lends itself to shrewd exploitation. Despite a muddled script, this pic is above the level of the run-of-mill horror film and has obvious boxoffice potential.

Story concerns a young man who, as a boy, was used as a guinea-pig by his father, a noted professor studying the symptoms of fear. The boy grows up to become an insane killer obsessed with the desire to photograph the terror on the faces of his victims as he kills them. He also has an unhealthy craving for peeping at young lovers, hence the title. In between these activities, he has a regular job as an assistant cameraman in a film studio and a spart-time job of photographing saucy pictures for sale on a seedy newsstand.

This mixed up young man is played rather stolidly by Carl Boehm, a goodlooking young German actor. Actually, it is more the fault of the screenplay than the actor himself that one gets only a very superficial glimpse into the workings of his diseased mind. Anna Massey is charming as the girl who is one of his tenants and befriends him before she realizes that he is a killer. Maxine Audley, as her blind mother, tackles a difficult, unrewarding role very well. The presence of this character is largely extraneous and tends to hold up the action to little good purpose.

Brenda Bruce has a few good moments at the beginning of the film as a streetwalker who is his first victim while Moira Shearer is effective as another of his victims, an ambitious bit player who is murdered while he is pretending to give her a screen test on a deserted studio lot. Other useful pieces of thesping come from Esmond Knight, as a temperamental film director; Shirley Ann Field, as a film star; and Jack Watson,

the cop in charge of the murder inquiries.

Michael Powell has directed with imagination but he might well have tightened up the story line. The standout feature of "Peeping Tom" is some fascinating photography by Otto Heller, particularly in the film studio sequences. His use of color and shadow is most effective. Heller has done much to give "Peeping Tom" a veneer which the story by Leo Marks does not entirely deserve. *Rich.*

Frau Warren's Gewerbe
(Mrs. Warren's Profession)
(GERMAN)

Berlin, April 12.
Europa release of Real-Film production. Stars Lilli Palmer, O. E. Hasse, Johanna Matz; features Helmut Lohner, Rudolf Vogel, E. F. Fuerbringer. Directed by Akos von Rathory. Screenplay, Eberhard Keinforff and Johanna Sibelius, after legit play by George Bernard Shaw; camera, Albert Benitz; music, Siegfried Franz. At Zoo Palast, Berlin. 103 MINS.
Mrs. Warren .... Lilli Palmer
Sir Crofts .... O. E. Hasse
Vivie .... Johanna Matz
Frank Gardner .... Helmut Lohner
Samuel Gardner .... Rudolf Vogel
Pread .... E. F. Fuerbringer
Mother Warren...Elisabeth Flickenschild
Liz .... Ernie Mangold

It speaks well for George Bernard Shaw that this film, an adaptation from his nearly 60-year-old stage work comes across on the screen as an enjoyable item. It also speaks highly for the players who make much of their juicy roles. Otherwise, this is a film which neither directorially nor optically deserve any special compliments. It's conventionally filmed theatre. Cast and plot will make it a stout b.o. contender locally. Internationally, it has to depend on the Shaw subject, with possibly the Lilli Palmer name an exploitation help.

This revolves around Mrs. Warren who, at the turn of the century, makes a dubious yet very lucrative living via her various European "hotels" (brothels, that is). When her daughter, who lives in England, learns of her activities, it becomes a conflict which leads to a split of the two.

Miss Palmer, very much of a lady, is a far cry from being a genuine Mrs. Warren. In fact, she seems rather miscast, ironically enough, her performance never disappoints.

Johanna Matz, her daughter, too is pleasant and comely. Her acting (she's a member of the Viennese Burgtheatre) reveals considerable talent.

The most powerful performance is by O. E. Hasse who's much at home with GBS roles. His portrayal of the greedy and unscrupulous Sir Crofts, Miss Palmer's business partner, is an acting masterpiece. Good support is provided by Helmut Lohner and Rudolf Vogel as Frank and Samuel Gardner. *Hans.*

L'Amerique Vue Par
Un Francais
(America Seen By A Frenchman)
(FRENCH-COLOR-D'LSCOPE)

Paris, April 12.
Gaumont release of Films Pleiade production. Written and directed by Francois Reichenbach. Camera (Eastmancolor), Marcel Grignon, Reichenbach; editor, Albert Jurgenson. Preemed in Paris. Running time, 90 MINS.

This C'Scope-size pic is a fond look at the U.S., mainly through its foibles, fads and general surface aspects by a Frenchman who travelled all over the U.S. with his camera. Though sketchy, this has a feeling for imagery and observation, helped by expert editing which keep this engrossing throughout. It looms a likely offbeat arty entry abroad. It might also serve as a dualer though its content will be quite familiar to average audiences. A brisker commentary instead of the present literary one would help.

Picture skirts around San Francisco and the western area. It shows the breadth of the land and its myriad rodeos, mixed populations, religioso sects, etc. Film cannily picks out incidents which throw some light on a rich nation. A prison which stages a rodeo makes for incisive contrasts as do quick looks at teenage doings, advertising hocus-pocus, ghost towns, Disneyland and the face of New York's amazing architectural frontage.

Perhaps too much is pat and journalistic in this essay, but it does give an unusual closeup of the many sides of sprawling America that may have been seen before but not quite in this light of sympathetic curiosity.

This adds up to a different-type documentary of interest for special handling on a "how others see us" peg. It looms of tv interest, too, with technical credit excellent. Film will probably be one of the three French entries at the Cannes Film Fest. *Mosk.*

Cada Quien Su Vida
(To Each His Life)
(MEXICAN)

Mexico City, April 12.
A Peliculas Nacionales release of an Ismael Rodriguez production. Stars Kity de Hoyos, Ann Luisa Peluffo; features Emman Fink, Carlos Navarro, Barbara Gil, Linda Porto, Noe Murayama. Directed by Julio Bracho. Screenplay adaptation by Julio Bracho, based on play by Luis G. Basurto. Camera, Jack Draper. Music, Raul Lavista. At Mexico and Mariscala Theatres, Mexico City. Running time, 90 MINS.

This is virtually a faithful translation to the screen of Mexican dramatist's hit play which chalked up 1,000. The dialogue has been cleaned up and certain suggestive sequences cut out, including a fight scene in which Linda Porto is stripped from waist up. The Mexican Film Bureau is now strictly adhering to rule of no nudes or semi-nudes in national films.

Plot presents the seamier side of life in low grade Mexican dives, actually the development of a series of sequences unfolding the cupidity of a deputy, the ladies of the evening hunting male prey, the harried night club owner interested only in money and women, and the "honest" cop who becomes blind to everything when his palm is crossed. First half of picture, with stress on vulgarities and immoralities of the night belt are excellent and run close to real life. But then the inevitable moralizing and the switch to the happy end in an aura of piousness spoils the effect.

Cast is adequate, with Ana Luisa Peluffo as "Gold Heel," habitue of club, and Kitty de Hoyos as "Dorita," interpreting characters of night life lovelies with assurance. These two are the only changes from the original legit cast, with director Julio Bracho getting realism even from bit players. Picture falls apart when it wanders on to ultimate redemption of characters.

The Raul Lavista score is good as always and Jack Draper's black-and-white photography captures the sordid night club atmosphere well. *Emil.*

Normandie Nieman
(FRENCH-RUSSIAN)

Paris, April 12.
Cinedis release of Franco London-Alkam-Mosfilm production. Features Marc Cassot, Giani Esposito, Pierre Trabaud, Georges Riviere, Gerard Buhr, Jean-Claude Michel, Clement Thierry. Directed by Jean Dreville. Screenplay, Elsa Triolet, Charles Spaak, Constantin Simenov; camera, Jacques Natteau; editor, Borys Lewin. At Paris, Paris. Running time, 10 MINS.
Marcellin .... Marc Cassot
Lemaitre .... Giani Esposito
Chardon .... Pierre Trabaud
Benoit .... George Riviere
Flavier .... Jean-Claude Michel

Justified thematically, French Russian coproduction deals with the barely fictionalized story of the French pilots who fought with the Russians against the Germans during the last war. However, in spite of its background, on the spot shooting in Russia, and liberal use of good stock footage, this remains a familiar, stereotyped wartime airforce pic. It lacks the freshness and treatment for foreign art appeal but might do as a dualer on its theme.

After the Armistice many French pilots escape into Russia where they are formed into a squadron. It is overlong and falls into repetition via the eventual loss of most of the men. It also goes into the conflicting political aspects of the divided France of the time.

A cast sans big names is adequate and Russians and French are well used with a good handling of the lingo problems. Air footage is okay. Technical credits are good. Director Jean Dreville has made a competent, albeit conventional, war tale that might be in for biz here. *Mosk.*

Il Bell'Antonio
(Handsome Antonio)
(ITALO-FRENCH)

Rome, April 12.
Cino Del Duca release of a Cino Del Duca-Arco (Alfredo Bini)-Lyre Cinematografique production. Stars Marcello Mastroianni; features Claudia Cardinale, Pierre Brasseur, Rina Morelli, Tomas Milian, Fulvia Mammi, Patrizia Bini. Directed by Mauro Bolognini. Screenplay, Gino Visentini, Pier Paolo Pasolini, based on novel by Vitaliano Brancati. Camera, Armando Nannuzzi. Music, Piero Piccioni. Editor, Nino Baragli. Previewed in Rome. Running time, 97 MINS.

Extremely well-made film version of Vitaliano Brancati's controversial novel boasting topnotch direction, fine acting, a nice feeling for setting and a provocative bit of subject matter. Looks like a good U.S. arty bet.

It's taken 10 years, and various fights with the censor, for Brancatti's novel to reach the screen. And it's easy to see why, dealing as it does with the mental anguish of a temporarily impotent Sicilian who is unable to satisfy his young wife, though fathering a son by his servant girl. Problem is discussed frankly and openly in pic which alternates comic with tragic and dramatic moments, not missing every chance to poke ironic fun at "Don Juan"-ism and other popular foibles especially evident in the story's Sicilian locale.

Marcello Mastroianni is excellent as the handsome hero who becomes the object of scorn when his partial failing is known in the neighborhood. Pierre Brasseur tops other performances as Antonio's pompous father. Claudia Cardinale is fine in a limited role, while Fulvia Mammi, Patrizia Bini, Rina Morelli, and Tomas Milian back ably. Gino Visentini and Pier Paolo Pasolini have succeeded in the difficulty task of shaping an acceptable yet provocative screenplay from Brancati's explosive material. Mauro Bolognini has directed his best film to date with his usual elegance of style and fine sense for timing.

Armando Nannuzzi's expert lensing has moments of great beauty in his closeups of the Sicilian scene. Piero Piccioni's musical score is apt. One of the year's top pictures. *Hawk.*

Pay or Die

Hard-hitting 1909-era Mafia melo, based on true-life story of Lieut. Joseph Petrosino of N.Y. Police Dept.'s Italian Squad; hefty prospects.

Hollywood, April 20.
Allied Artists release of Richard Wilson production. Stars Ernest Borgnine, Zohra Lampert, Alan Austin; features Renata Vanni, Bruno Della Santina, Franco Corsaro, Robert F. Simon, Robert Ellenstein, Howard Caine, John Duke. Directed by Wilson. Screenplay, Richard Collins, Bertram Millhauser; production designer; Fernando Carrere; camera, Lucien Ballard; editor, Walter Hannemann; music, David Raksin. Previewed April 19, '60. Running time, 111 MINS.
Lt. Joseph Petrosino....Ernest Borgnine
Adelina Saulino .... Zohra Lampert
Johnny Viscardi .... Alan Austin
Mama Saulino .... Renata Vanni
Papa Saulino........Bruno Della Santina
Vito Zarillo .... Franco Corsaro
Commissioner .... Robert F. Simon
Luigi Di Sarno .... Robert Ellenstein
Enrico Caruso .... Howard Caine
Lupo Miano .... John Duke
Caputo .... John Marley
Loria .... Mario Siletti
Nun .... Mimi Doyle
Mrs. Rossi .... Mary Carver
Mayor ....~.............. Paul Birch
Simonetti .... Vito Scotti
Palumbo .... Nick Pawl
Fabraka .... Vincent Barbi
Giula De Sarno .... Sherry Alberoni
Girl at Bombing .... Leslie Glenn
Botti .... Sal Armetta
Don Cesare' .... Carlo Tricoli
Nicolo .... Bart Bradley
Girl from Opera........ Marian Collier
Sorgente .... Joseph D. Sargent
Rossi .... Sam Capuano
Marisa Rossi .... Judy Strangis

"Pay or Die" is a highly exploitable follow-up to Allied Artists' last year's top grosser, "Al Capone," which should garner plenty of additional playdates on the strength of current resurgence of headlined stories of the perennially unbusted Mafia. Lieut. Joseph Petrosino, head of the N.Y. Police Dept.'s Italian Squad who attempted to smash the Sicilian terrorist society in Manhattan's "Little Italy" and was assassinated for his zeal while abroad in 1909 is the basis for a grim, realistic, unrelenting account of brutality's most successful lodge.

Produced and directed by Richard Wilson, who did "Capone," the rather long but exciting melo stars Ernest Borgnine as the heroic Petrosino who tried to bring honor upon his people in America by erasing the evil power which held them in terror. He's virtually the only known name in cast, the balance being composed mostly of Italian thesps specifically assigned for their characters and who lend added conviction to yarn's unfoldment.

The Richard Collins-Bertram Millhauser screenplay is episodic, unreeling between 1906 and 1909, but editing by Walter Hannemann is so expert there is no appreciable letup as various sequences are brought together. Wilson's tight-reined direction builds telling suspense, particularly where Borgnine, marked for death, is cut down in Sicily by the Mafia, but not before he has mailed positive proof of the Mafia's existence in the U.S. and identity of its leader.

Borgnine delivers strongly as the hard-fisted upholder of the law, whose exploits among others include saving Enrico Caruso from a bomb trap outside the Metropolitan. Persuasive in his romance with an Italian girl whose father he also rescues from death. Zohra Lampert, in this role, gets her first big film break persuasively enacting femme who proposes to the detective after he holds back

thinking she is in love with another.
Alan Austin, also starred, handles this latter part competently, as one of Borgnine's squad. Top support likewise is contributed by Robert F. Simon, the commissioner; Renata Vanni and Bruno Santina, femme's parents; Robert Ellenstein, Mafia's mouthpiece whose daughter is killed in one of its bombings; Franco Corsaro, org's leader; John Duke, an enforcer; Vincent Barbi, bomber.

Technical credits are in kind, including Lucien Ballard's photography, Fernando Carrere's production designing, David Raksin's music score. *Whit.*

Le Baron De L'Ecluse
(The Baron of the Locks)
(FRENCH)

Paris, April 26.
Cinedis release of Intermondia-Filmsonor production. Stars Jean Gabin, Micheline Presle; features Jean Desailly, Jacques Castelot, Blanchette Brunoy, Jean Constantin. Directed by Jean Delannoy. Screenplay, Maurice Druon, Michel Audiard from story by Georges Simenon; camera, Louis Page; editor, Henri Taverna. At Berlitz, Paris. Running time, 90 MINS.
Baron .... Jean Gabin
Perle .... Micheline Presle
Maurice .... Jean Desailly
Villamayor .... Jacques Castelot
Maria .... Blanchette Brunoy
Prince Saddokan........Jean Constantin

Film is mainly another Jean Gabin vehicle which allows the vet thespian to play a broke Baron who lives by his wits, name and class consciousness. Gabin is good, but the pic is somewhat talky and conventional, making this primarily a local b.o. bet. Foreign chances seem to rest on the Gabin monicker, which is a real plus factor.

Gabin wins a boat in a card game and goes off on a trip with an ex-flame. They break down in a small town and the girl finds a rich suitor. Then the Baron (Gabin) almost settles down with a local cafe owner, an aging but comely femme. However, he is on his way again when a fresh bundle of money comes in.

Direction is acceptable but with little inventiveness with the story sketchy and resting largely on Gabin's dexterity in playing a number of scenes calling for different moods. Supporting cast is good and technical credits okay, but other production aspects are skimpy. *Mosk.*

Il Rossetto
(The Lipstick)
(ITALO-FRENCH)

Cino del Dica release of a Europa-Explorer-C.F.P.C. (Paris) coproduction. Stars Pierre Brice, Georgia Moll, Laura Vivaldi, Pietro Germi; features Bella Darvi, Ivano Staccioli, Nino Manchetti, Renato Mambor, Lia Angelieri. Directed by Damiano Damiani. Screenplay, Damiani and Cesare Zavattini. At Capitol, Rome. Running time, 100 MINS.

Well-made psychological crime film with good scripting and acting, this is a promising initial directing effort by Damiano Damiani. Okay returns for home markets, but has slight appeal for U.S. market.

Story involves a young girl of 13 in a crime, in which she turns out to be a key witness in the accusation of a murderer. Pic manages to maintain suspense throughout while at the same time aptly integrating story-lined elements with psychological byplay as seen from teenager point of view. The hand of vet scripter Cesare Zavattini is plainly seen in this.

Pietro Germi once more gives his role of the police inspector depth and understanding while Laura Vivaldi is very good as the moppet. Pierre Brice makes for a suitably charming villain. Georgia Moll has little to do as the latter's fiancee. Others are all good, as are technical credits in an interesting pic cut some notches above the norm. *Hawk.*

Las Rosas del Milagro
(The Miracle Roses)
(MEXICAN)

Mexico City, April 19.
Peliculas Nacionales release of Julian Soler production. Stars Jorge Martinez de Hoyos, Armando Silvestre, Crox Alvarado, Jaime Fernandez; features Andrea Soler, Francisco Jambrina, Miguel Manzano, Manuel Calvo, Lilia del Carmen Camacho, Arturo Soto Ranger, Enrique Garcia Alvarez. Story and screenplay, A. Patino Gomez. Directed by Julian Soler. At Mariscala Theatre, Mexico City. Running time, 90 MINS.

A number of films have been made about the appearance of the Virgen de Guadalupe, patron saint of Mexico, to humble Indian Juan Diego. This one has much stronger impact than former versions because of the careful direction of Julian Soler and excellent characterization of lead role by Jorge Martinez de Hoyos. Other members of cast also turn in creditable performances. Cinemascope and color are particularly effective in scenes of the indigenous rites.

With the blessing of high church dignitaries and the Legion of Decency, this religious picture is slated to do good business locally as well as in the Spanish language market. This one may also be released with subtitles or dubbed sound in the U.S. and foreign markets. *Emil.*

The Rat Race
(COLOR)

A mature, smooth screen version of Garson Kanin's play about life, love and the dog-eat-dog pursuit of happiness in the big city. Very bright b.o. prospects.

Hollywood, April 22.
Paramount release of Perlberg-Seaton production. Stars Tony Curtis, Debbie Reynolds; costars Jack Oakie, Kay Medford, Don Rickles; features Joe Bushkin, Sam Butera, Gerry Mulligan; with Marjorie Bennett, Hal K. Dawson, Norman Fell, Lisa Drake. Directed by Robert Mulligan. Screenplay, Garson Kanin, based on his play; camera, Robert Burks; editor, Alma Macrorie; sound, Hugo Grenzbach, Winston Leverett; art directors, Hal Pereira, Tambi Larsen; set decorators, Sam Comer, Frank McKelvy; music, Elmer Bernstein; assistant director, Richard Caffey. Reviewed at Pantages, April 22, '60. Running time, 105 MINS.
Peter Hammond Jr. .... Tony Curtis
Peggy Brown .... Debbie Reynolds
Mac .... Jack Oakie
Soda .... Kay Medford
Nellie .... Don Rickles
Frankie .... Joe Bushkin
Carl .... Sam Butera
Gerry .... Gerry Mulligan
Edie Kerry .... Marjorie Bennett
Man .... Hal K. Dawson
Phone Repairman........Norman Fell
Girl on Davenport...........Lisa Drake

"The Rat Race," Garson Kanin's play about two decent young people who survive Gothamania by sheer unadulterated togetherness, has been brought to the screen skillfully and tastefully in this Perlberg-Seaton production for Paramount. The film is sturdier in its parts than as a whole, but when it's good it's very good, thanks mostly to Kanin's witty, adult dialog and Robert Mulligan's perceptive direction. It should be a strong boxoffice draw.

Considerable marquee impetus is added by the film's costars, Tony Curtis and Debbie Reynolds, as well as several casting improvisations of specialized appeal to jazz and nitery aficionados, primarily in the nation's metropoli.

Curtis is presented as a clean-cut, leaguish sax player from Milwaukee who arrives in the big city to make his fortune by proving his talent. It's one of the flaws of Kanin's screenplay that he does neither—leaving much of the interest aroused in the character early in the film unfulfilled. At any rate, Curtis meets Miss Reynolds, a penniless young dancer-aspirant ("Miss Cha-Cha-Cha of 1957"), platonically shares a room with her (a la "It Happened One Night," complete with curtain), and proceeds to fall in love with her. The courtship is complicated by several professional mishaps, but the "rat race" for survival obviously has strengthened the bond between the two youngsters at happy fadeout.

There are a number of excellent scenes, but also one or two that demonstrate a lack of subtlety—a curious inconsistency but luckily one in which the credits outweigh the debits. The film hits a refreshing note of realism when newcomer Curtis is hosed down by a group of neighborhood brats on his Gotham arrival, enjoys a touching interlude when naive Curtis is bilked out of his precious instruments by three musically-talented thieves (stylishly enacted by Joe Bushkin, Sam Butera and Gerry Mulligan), and hits comic highs in the characterization of Kay Medford, one of those hard-on-the-outside but all-heart-on-the-inside types popular in drama set in New York.

Lesser moments occur in a scene in which Miss Reynolds is forced to strip to her slip on orders of

her sadistic employer (vigorously played by Don Rickles in an off-beat piece of casting), and in a sequence at a police precinct wherein an officious cop forces sax-man to sign for a bull fiddle. The strip scene is fuzzily-motivated, and the other is making a keen, pertinent, humorous observation, but runs itself into the ground by sheer length (making a moron out of the cop). Another glaring discrepancy occurs when the poverty-stricken Miss Reynolds, having just persuaded a phone company man not to disconnect her phone, promptly goes across the street to make a toll call.

Unfortunately for Curtis, the character he is playing is inconsistent—hip one moment, boob the next. But he does manage to create a likeable, sympathetic hero. Miss Reynolds exhibits a keen sense of restraint and thespic maturity. Much of the credit for this must go to director Mulligan, whose character helmsmanship sensibly avoids stereotype pitfalls without taking the fun out of his people. He also has not allowed his film to lapse into maudlinity in several areas where the temptation may have been strong.

In the supporting department, there are several noteworthy contributions in addition to the ones already touched upon. One is Jack Oakie's, as a lovable neighborhood bartender. Another is Norman Fell's, in a sharply amusing bit as a phone repairman. Others who register are Lisa Drake, Marjorie Bennett and Hal K. Dawson.

A racy score by Elmer Bernstein brightens things up considerably. Realistic backdrops have been erected and furnished by art directors Hal Pereira and Tambi Larsen and set decorators Sam Comer and Frank McKelvy. Flashy camera work by Robert Burks and neat editing by Alma Macrorie are vital assists to the production, as are Edith Head's appropriate costuming and the careful skills of makeupman Wally Westmore and hairstylist Nellie Manley. Another refreshing facet of the William Perlberg-George Seaton production is the tasteful, sensible manner in which it deals with sex—never indulging in it purely for its own sake. *Tube.*

Les Regates De San Francisco

(The Regattas Of San Francisco)
(FRENCH—COLOR—C'SCOPE)

Paris, May 3.

Columbia Films release of Iena-CEIAP production. Features Laurent Terzieff, Daniele Gaubert, Suzy Delair, Folco Lulli, Dominique Blondeau, Francois Nocher. Directed by Claude Autant-Lara. Screenplay, Jean Aurenche, Pierre Bost; camera (Eastmancolor), Armand Thirard; editor, Madeleine Gug. At Ermitage, Paris. Running time, **90 MINS**

Eneo	Laurent Terzieff
Lidia	Daniele Gaubert
Ario	Dominique Blondeau
Father	Folco Lulli
Mother	Suzy Delair
Brother	Francois Nocher

Producer Raoul Levy and director Claude Autant-Lara are reported to have a five-second shot in this pic, a close-up of the panties of a 15-year-old girl. Levy felt it was unnecessary and repugnant, and so Autant-Lara took his name off the pic. The film is like that, full of suggestive scenes, and rarely making its sexy or love scenes plausible.

Though steeped with a peeping-tom approach, this rarely has any true exploitable scenes. The rambling script, surface characterization and unsavory treatment make this mainly a bally pic abroad.

This is a gross tale of a crafty 15-year-old girl who sets out to be seduced by a local Don Juan in his 20's. There is the girl's peeping at a man in his shower, her enticing the young boy, etc.

Acting is flat, and raises some chuckles in dramatic scenes. Laurent Terzieff has some presence as the seducer but Daniele Gaubert is gauche and strained as the girl. Folco Lulli is loutish as the father. Color is uneven with production and technical angles only par. Abroad, this may attract the curious, but it lacks enough depth for many arty house chances.

The producers probably set out to do another "God Created Woman" but this lacks the free wheeling, kittenish appeal of Brigitte Bardot. Film is confused, tasteless, one track and one dimensional. It may have some biz here on the publicity stirred up by the producer-director row. Censor troubles could help this overseas. Title refers to the young boy's father who went off to row at the regattas in San Francisco and never came back. Pic emerges curiously old-fashioned and melodramatic. *Mosk.*

La Corde Raide

(The Tight Rope)
(FRENCH)

Paris, April 26.

Sirius release of Panda Film production. Stars Francois Perier, Annie Girardot; features Gerard Buhr, Genevieve Brunet, Hubert Deschamps. Henri Cremieux. Directed by Jean-Charles Dudrumet. Screenplay, Roland Laudenbach. Dudrumet from novel by Michel Lebrun; camera, Pierre Gueguen; editor, Janine Verneau. Running time, **90 MINS.**

Daniel	Francois Perier
Cora	Annie Girardot
Henri	Gerard Buhr
Isabelle	Genevieve Brunet
Pierre	Georges Descrieres
Lawyer	Hubert Deschamps
Doctor	Henri Cremieux

Lagging suspense item is somewhat too telegraphed to keep the needed tenseness and suspended disbelief in the twists. Acting doesn't get around the feeble characterizations either. However, this has okay technical credits and some exploitable love scenes for possible dualer or exploitation use abroad. It seems dubious for arty dates.

A woman is cheating on her husband. The wife and brother decide to kill the husband but the brother is knocked off by mistake and the denoument shows it was the lover after all. Hence, the adulterous wife and jealous husband are reunited.

As a first pic, this has acceptable mounting but does not display any untoward talents via director Jean Charles Dudrumet. Acting is okay with Annie Girardot managing to give an edge to her conniving, sensual wife. The men are trapped in their stereotype roles. *Mosk.*

Raymie

Acceptable, and likely profitable; tale of a boy and a fish. Low budget film for family audiences.

Hollywood, April 27.

Allied Artists release of A. C. Lyles production. Stars David Ladd, Julie Adams, John Agar, Charles Winninger, Richard Arlen; features Frank Ferguson, Ray Kellogg, John Damler, Jester Hairston; with Vincent Padula, Ida Smeraldo, Christy Lynn, Brent Wolfson, Shirley Garner, Marianne Gaba, Leslie Glenn, Vance Skarstedt, Doak Roberts. Directed by Frank McDonald. Screenplay, Mark Hanna; camera, Henry Cronjager; editor, George White; sound, Ralph Butler, Burdicks S. Trask; music, Ronald Stein; assistant director, Clark Paylow. Reviewed at the studio, April 27, '60. Running time, **72 MINS.**

Raymie	David Ladd
Helen	Julie Adams
Ike	John Agar
R. J. Parsons	Charles Winninger
Garber	Richard Arlen
Rex	Frank Ferguson
Neil	Ray Kellogg
John	John Damler
Ransom	Jester Hairston
Veulo	Vincent Padula
Carmen	Ida Smeraldo
Ellen	Christy Lynn
Brent	Brent Wolfson
First Girl	Shirley Garner
Second Girl	Marianne Gaba
Camera Girl	Leslie Glenn
Blake	Vance Skarstedt
Mike	Doak Roberts

An unpretentious and frankly sentimental "fish story" about a boy and a barracuda, "Raymie" will be an attractive item for the so-called family trade. Buttered up with homely philosophies and workaday symbolisms, it's a sort of minor variation on "The Old Man And The Sea." Being short (in length and budget scale) and sweet (in disposition), the Allied Artists release stacks up as a versatile, and potentially profitable, attraction.

David Ladd stars as an impressionable lad determined to hook a legendary giant barracuda. Mark Hanna's screenplay plants him in the midst of a curiously childish group of fishermen on a California pier. In the group there is a lovable old man (Charles Winninger) who urges the boy to continue his pursuit of the elusive fish-ideal. Darned if, at the climax, the lad doesn't actually hook the monster, only to cut the line and give the big fish back his freedom when all the assembled adults, led by Winninger, begin comparing the consequences of the boy's potentially prize-winning catch with the unhappy "fruits of war" and the premature ruination of an ideal. It's a dash of conclusive irony that is a mild letdown in terms of action on-screen, but it's also the sort of moral lesson that parents will be happy to have their children exposed to.

Master Ladd does a more than competent job, managing a quiet, respectfully restrained, believably youthful portrayal. Julie Adams and John Agar adeptly supply the film's romantic interest. Winninger gives a fine, tender performance as the aged angler, and Richard Arlen is effective as the owner of the pier. Frank Ferguson plays a crusty old heavy (a sterotype of the "family" film) with flair, and effective support is fashioned by Jester Hairston, Ray Kellogg and John Damler.

Director Frank McDonald, obviously in an attempt to please younger, less sophisticated tastes, has had it played broadly, letting the sentiment and stereotype fall where they may. The A.C. Lyles production, despite the limited budget, is highly competent, physically and technically, utilizing, among others, the efficient talents of lensman Henry Cronjager, editor George White and special effects men Milt Olsen and Max Luttenberg. There's a title ballad, sung pleasantly by Jerry Lewis both during the main title and at an appropriate point within the story, that's memorable enough to catch on. If it does, it will be a helpful boost to the film's prospects. *Tube.*

Ski Troop Attack

Top half of World War II action package. Okay b.o. prospects.

Hollywood, April 26.

Filmgroup release of Roger Corman production. Features Michael Forest, Frank Wolff; with Wally Campo, Richard Sinatra, Sheila Carol. Directed by Corman. Screenplay, Charles Griffith; camera, Andy Costikyan; editor, Anthony Carras; music, Fred Katz. Reviewed at Warner Hollywood Theatre, April 26, '60. Running time, **63 MINS.**

Factor	Michael Forest
Potter	Frank Wolff
Ed	Wally Campo
Herman	Richard Sinatra
Ilse	Sheila Carol

Ticketed for dual-billing opposite "Battle of Blood Island" as a Filmgroup package, "Ski Troop Attack" should just about hold its own in situations where war action is strong. With hot weather coming, the skiing aspect could be exploitably timely as an off-season visual magnet and refresher.

The Roger Corman production follows (rather crudely, much of the time) the adventures of a small U.S. ski patrol unit behind Nazi lines, and its successful attempt to blow up a vital bridge (but for bridges, war fiction would be in trouble). When the picture sticks to the action, it gets by. But when Charles Griffith's screenplay goes probing for deeper meanings and dimensional characterization, the cliches fly out thick and fast (particularly the one about the hard-bitten regular-army sergeant who resents the attitude of the young O.C.S. lieutenant—principal conflict in the piece). The absence of proper establishing shots and long-range pans to give the audience a perspective of depth and distance seriously blunts the impact of the all-important battle scenes. Responsibility for this flaw rests on the shoulders of director-producer Corman, who otherwise has managed a reasonably picturesque production, with the assistance of cameraman Andy Costikyan.

Acting is competent. Cast is headed by Michael Forest, a handsome and fairly promising young actor (as the looie), and Frank Wolff as the tough, but consistently wrong, sarge. Richard Sinatra, Wally Campo and Sheila Carol create characters of some substance. *Tube.*

Bumerang

(Boomerang)
(GERMAN)

Berlin, April 26.

UFA release of Roxy (Luggi Waldleitner) production. Stars Hardy Krueger, Martin Held, Mario Adorf, Horst Frank. Directed by Alfred Weidenmann. Screenplay, Herbert Reinecker, after novel by Igor Sentjuro; camera, Kurt Hasse; music, Hans-Martin Majewski; settings, Wolf Englert and Ernst Richter; editor, Lilian Seng. At Marmorhaus, Berlin. Running time, **92 MINS**

Robert Wegner	Hardy Krueger
Georg Kugler	Mario Adorf
Willy Schneider	Horst Frank
Police Inspector	Martin Held
Else	Ingrid van Bergen
Police Sergeant	Peer Schmidt
Helga	Cordula Trantow

Teutonic filmakers seldom have had luck when it comes to cops-and-robbers pix. This UFA release has the realistic approach, a competent director and a couple of talented players but, again, it still falls considerably short of similar foreign pix, notably American and French. Cast and theme will make it a good bet domestically, but international chances are hardly better than average.

The greater part of "Boomerang" has been shot against actual Berlin backgrounds which gives this

film an interesting documentary flavor. There's also a certain plus in Alfred Weidenmann's tight direction but Weidenmann can't save the pic from losing much of its conviction via a script that doesn't consequently follow the realistic pattern. Not only that several situations are far-fetched, but also, the script has its flaws via the dialog and character motivations.

Story sees three young fellows out to crack a safe in Rififi style. One of them informs, for reasons of jealousy, the police and the gang get bust. The boss of the trio is tracked down after a wild chase.

Hardy Krueger, Horst Frank and Mario Adorf play the three criminals. Adorf leaves much to routine, but is still the most convincing actor of the trio. Krueger, who portrays the boss, appears much too sympathetic in his role. Frank again overacts his part. Better polished performances are turned in by Martin Held as police inspector; Peer Schmidt, one of Held's subordinates, and Ingrid van Bergen, as Frank's moll.

Technically, this is a very good film. Kurt Hasse's lensing is outstanding and the same can be said of the score. *Hans.*

Les Arrivistes
(The Opportunists)
(FRENCH-EAST GERMAN)
Paris, April 25.
Pathe release of Pathe-DEFA production. Stars Madeleine Robinson, Jean-Claude Pascal; features Clara Gansard, Erika Pelikowski, Gerhard Biener, Harry Riebauer. Directed by Louis Daquin. Screenplay, Philippe Heriat from novel by Honore De Balzac; camera, Philippe Brun; editor, Claude Nicole. Running time, 115 MINS.
Philippe .... Jean-Claude Pascal
Blore .... Madeleine Robinson
Mariette .... Clara Gansard
Agathe .... Erika Pelikowski
Rouget .... Gerhard Biener
Max .... Harry Riebauer

Talky costumer deals with the fortunes of a fallen Bonapartist officer during the Restoration in France back in 1830's. It shows his unfortunate love affair which goads him to climb to the top in a corrupt society, only to get his comeuppance. Slow moving and fairly literary, this remains mainly a local bet.

Acting is acceptable but direction rarely gives it much movement. Mounting and production values are good but it is sans the flair and progression to give it any exploitation handles. Technical credits are fine. *Mosk.*

12 Hours To Kill

Uneven cops 'n' robbers meller. Lean support for double bills.

Hollywood, April 25.
Twentieth-Fox release of John Healy production. Stars Nico Minardos, Barbara Eden, Grant Richards, Russ Conway; with Art Baker, Gavin MacLeod, CeCe Whitney, Richard Reeves, Byron Foulger, Barbara Mansell, Ted Knight, Shep Sanders, Charles Meredith, Stewart Conway, Don Collier, Donald Kerr, Ed Sheehan, Bernard Kates, David Thursby, Sid Kane, Kitty Kelly. Directed by Edward L. Cahn. Screenplay, Jerry Sohl, based on SatEvePost serial, "Set Up For Murder," by Richard Stern; camera, Floyd Crosby; editor, Betty Steinberg; art director, John Mansbridge; music, Paul Dunlap; assistant director, Harry M. Slott. Reviewed at studio, April 25, '60. Running time, 83 MINS.
Martin .... Nico Minardos
Lucy .... Barbara Eden
Jim .... Grant Richards
Willie Long .... Russ Conway
Capt. Johns .... Art Baker
Johnny .... Gavin MacLeod
Clara .... CeCe Whitney
Mark .... Richard Reeves
Shelby Gardner .... Byron Foulger
Cynthia .... Barbara Mansell
Denton .... Ted Knight
Russo .... Shep Sanders
Druggist .... Charles Meredith

Bert .... Stewart Conway
Andy .... Don Collier
Neighbor .... Donald Kerr
Gas Attendant .... Ed Sheehan
Desk Editor .... Bernard Kates
Cab Dispatcher .... David Thursby
George .... Sid Kane
Woman .... Kitty Kelly

"Twelve Hours to Kill" is a weak lower-berth entry; an incredibly awkward cops 'n' robbers account of the perils experienced by an eyewitness to murder. At times the going gets so bumpy and unreal that the story seems on the verge of lapsing, unintentionally, into a parody of itself.

Based on a SatEvePost serial by Richard Stern, Jerry Sohl's screenplay traces the problems of a young Greek national (Nico Minardos) who, after ogling a murder, is ushered off into the relatives "safety" of suburban obscurity by the police, unaware that he is being double-crossed by a crooked gendarme.

Edward L. Cahn, the director, must also shoulder responsibility for much of the film's rigid, unbelievable appearance. Under these circumstances, it is impossible for any of the actors to attain any dimension. Minardos and Barbara Eden are an attractive pair, but they can do nothing with their roles. Others who labor in vain, but noticeably so, are Grant Richards, Russ Conway, Art Baker, Gavin MacLeod, CeCe Whitney and Richard Reeves.

John Healy's production for 20th has been capably mounted (art director: John Mansbridge), is photographically good (camera: Floyd Crosby), and musically okay (Paul Dunlap). The competence ends there. *Tube.*

Les Bonnes Femmes
(The Good Girls)
(FRENCH)
Paris, May 3.
Paris Film release of Robert and Raymond Hakim production. Features Bernadette Lafont, Lucile Saint Simon, Clothilde Joano, Stephane Audran, Mario David, Jean-Louis Maury, Sacha Briquet. Directed by Claude Chabrol. Screenplay, Paul Gegauff; camera, Henri Decae; editor, Jacques Gaillard. At Normandie, Paris. Running time, 105 MINS.
Jane .... Bernadette Lafont
Rita .... Lucile Saint Simon
Jacqueline .... Clothilde Joano
Ginette .... Stephane Audran
Ernest .... Mario David
Marcel .... Jean-Louis Maury
Henri .... Sacha Briquet
Albert .... Dinan

First "New Waver" Claude Chabrol is not a regular part of the industry as he churns out one pic after another. This is a look at four little working girls and their sad attempts to find love. None of them do and Chabrol has treated this in a mixture of tones from comic, cynical through tragic but rarely infuses life in these creatures.

There is also a lot of uneven padding via a caricatured boss who lectures the girls on morality while making lecherous passes, an old woman with a secret fetish and a drawn-out visit to a zoo.

One girl is a vulgarly vampish, a type whose lot is usually sordid pickups, another is going to marry into a drab shopkeeper family, the third sings secretly in a pop music hall and the fourth is a sentimental, romantic type followed all through the pic by a muscular motorcyclist.

This is a slice of life treating with some neatly observed scenes and a sleazy closeup of so-called "Gay Paree" and the working class. The inevitable strip tease is also there. Chabrol is a clever craftsman but he shows no definite attitude towards his poor puppet girl victims.

Bernadette Lafont stands out as the blase, careless girl whose life will be a series of endless pickups while Clothilde Joano is effective as the langorous romantic whose one love ends in sordid death. This pic seems somewhat like early pre-war Yank films of this sort without the more incisive feel. Technical credits are fine. *Mosk.*

The Adventures Of Huckleberry Finn
(C'SCOPE—COLOR)

Handsome, but lacklustre filmization of the Mark Twain classic, handicapped by direction and weakness in the title role. But timeless appeal and juve pull should create lively b.o. stir.

Hollywood, April 29.
Metro release of Samuel Goldwyn Jr. production. Stars Tony Randall, Eddie Hodges; introduces Archie Moore; features Patty McCormack, Neville Brand, Mickey Shaughnessy, Judy Canova, Andy Devine, Sherry Jackson, Buster Keaton; with Finlay Currie, Josephine Hutchinson, Parley Baer, John Carradine, Royal Dano, Dolores Hawkins, Sterling Holloway, Dean Stanton. Directed by Michael Curtiz. Screenplay, James Lee, from Mark Twain's book; camera, Ted McCord; editor, Frederic Steinkamp; art directors, George W. Davis, McClure Capps; set decorators, Henry Grace, Robert Priestley; music, Jerome Moross; assistant director, L. V. McCardle Jr. Reviewed at Academy Award Theatre, April 29, '60. Running time, 90 MINS.
The King .... Tony Randall
Huckleberry Finn .... Eddie Hodges
Jim .... Archie Moore
Joanna .... Patty McCormack
Pap .... Neville Brand
The Duke .... Mickey Shaughnessy
Sheriff's wife .... Judy Canova
Mr. Carmody .... Andy Devine
Mary Jane .... Sherry Jackson
Lion Tamer .... Buster Keaton
Capt. Sellers .... Finlay Currie
Widow Douglas .... Josephine Hutchinson
Grangerford Man .... Parley Baer
Slave catcher .... John Carradine
Sheriff .... Royal Dano
River Boat Singer ..... Dolores Hawkins
Barber .... Sterling Holloway
Slave catcher .... Dean Stanton

Mark Twain's "Huckleberry Finn" is all boy. Eddie Hodges' "Huck" isn't. Therein lurks the basic reason Samuel Goldwyn Jr.'s production of the Twain classic is not all it could, and should, be. The Metro release nonetheless figures to be a healthy boxoffice commodity, if only for the simple reason that there's a whole new generation presumably ready for a king-sized visual crack at "The Adventures of Huckleberry Finn." Most parents, who got to know "Huck" when they were young, will want their children to become acquainted with the original All-American boy, and many will decide to re-acquaint themselves in the process. A great many of these people, young and old, will be disappointed.

There is something artificial and self-conscious about young Hodges' all-important portrayal of "Huck," a lack of actor-character chemistry for which he's certainly not wholly responsible. An equal share of the rap must be shouldered by director Michael Curtiz, not only for the youthful star's shortcomings in the role, but for a general slack, a disturbing shortage of vitality noticeable at several key junctures of the film.

Hodges exhibits a disquieting tendency to posture cutely (particularly in closeup shots), a passable characteristic on a stage but an uncomfortable quality in the more intimate close-up medium of the motion picture. He fails to convey with full force the pre-adolescent confidence and ingenuity of the universally boyish "Huck" character. In his behalf, though, it must be stressed that the role is an extremely demanding one, and that his performance is not without its admirable attributes, principally an infectious rapport with Archie Moore, who makes his screen bow in the role of the runaway slave who shares a raft and an enriching experience with "Huck."

James Lee's screenplay has simplified Twain's episodic tale, eras-

ing some of the more complex developments and relationships, presumably for the benefit of the young audience. Some of the more sinister, frightening aspects of the story have been forgotten. It is director Curtiz, rather than scripter Lee, who seems largely responsible for the disappointment factor. There is a lot of shock for shock's sake (such as the sudden crash of a beam, narrowly missing the hero), but the intense concern that ordinarily accompanies such passages as Huck's brush with his fiercely drunken father has gone out of the story, and several of the more amusing bits of business are not as funny as they might be.

On the brighter side of the ledger, there are some stimulating performances and the handsome physical production itself. An extremely colorful and experienced cast has been assembled. There is Tony Randall, whose work as the roguish "King" is a delightful balance of whimsy and threat. There is Moore, the light heavyweight champion of the world, who brings the story its only moments of real warmth and tenderness. Seemingly a little ill-at-ease in the early rounds, Moore grows stronger as the contest moves along and scores a knockout in the last round, his poetic parting with "Huck."

There is the solid supporting work of Neville Brand (as Huck's father), Mickey Shaughnessy (the "Duke"), Andy Devine (the circus owner), Buster Keaton (the lion tamer), Finlay Currie (the steamboat captain), Royal Rano (the sheriff), Sterling Holloway (the barber) and Josephine Hutchinson (the widow).

Acceptable work is turned in by Sherry Jackson, Parley Baer, John Carradine, Dolores Hawkins and Dean Stanton. Patty McCormack is a bit abrupt and severe, and Judy Canova does not do all she might have in her single scene with "Huck," potentially a memorable one.

Credit art directors George W. Davis and McClure Capps with capturing the unique flavor of Mississippi River country, whether for selecting proper on-the-spot locales or good imitations in more western regions. Equally rewarding are the colorful interior sets, authentically furnished and trimmed by set decorators Henry Grace and Robert Priestley. A major factor in quickening the film's pace and creating a mood of latent excitement is the score, composed and conducted by Jerome Moross (reminiscent of his sweeping, ultra-American score for "The Big Country").

The Metrocolor (consultant Charles K. Hagedon) comes up with some stunning hues, particularly in the red-orange range of the spectrum. Ted McCord's lenswork is inventive, Frederic Steinkamp's editing not as tight as it should be, A. Arnold Gillespie's special effects workable. In short, most of the necessary values for cinema magic are present, but the excitement built into the book never really asserts itself in the film. *Tube.*

Platinum High School

Minor military academy entertainment with names of Mickey Rooney, Dan Duryea and Terry Moore for draw. Thin prospects.

Hollywood, May 3.

Metro release of Red Doff production. Stars Mickey Rooney, Terry Moore, Dan Duryea; with Yvette Mimieux, Conway Twitty, Warren Berlinger, Jimmy Boyd, Richard Jaeckel, Harold Lloyd, Jr., Jack Carr, Christopher Dark, Elisha Cook Jr. Directed by Charles Haas. Screenplay, Robert Smith, based on story by Howard Breslin; camera, Russell Metty; editor, Gene Ruggiero; music, Van Alexander. Previewed May 2, '60. Running time, **95 MINS.**

Steven Conway	Mickey Rooney
Jennifer Evans	Terry Moore
Maj. Redfern Kelly	Dan Duryea
Billy Jack Barnes	Conway Twitty
Crip Hastings	Warren Berlinger
Lorinda Nibley	Yvette Mimieux
Bud Starkweather	Jimmy Boyd
Hack Marlow	Richard Jaeckel
Joe Nibley	Jack Carr
Charley Boy Cable	Harold Lloyd Jr.
Vince Perley	Christopher Dark
Harry Nesbit	Elisha Cook Jr.

"Platinum High School" (title-misnomer) is minor melo entertainment, not slated to cause much of a stir in the program market where all the draw of Mickey Rooney, Dan Duryea and Terry Moore, the principals, will be needed to just get by. Its problems spring from a script that talks out much of the action and failure to properly develop a premise which might have emerged a firstclass suspense yarn.

The Albert Zugsmith Productions-Fryman Enterprises joint effort, produced by Red Doff, seldom achieves a sense of reality as the Robert Smith screenplay follows Rooney as a father dedicated to solving the mysterious death of his son. Plot is laid on a small island off the California coast, site of an expensive military school whose students not only come from wealthy families but are hardened delinquents sent to this academy when they are ousted from every other institution. Come to pay his last respects to the son he never knew, separated from him early by divorce, Rooney learns that instead of the boy having been accidentally killed he was murdered in a hazing caper. Every obstacle is placed in his path by hostile school authorities and students before the truth outs and he summons the police.

Rooney plays a somewhat offbeat role for him, but delivers well, even in those scenes in which he's forced to battle three of the school's officers, all past Marines, with rifle stocks. Duryea as the commandant is never completely believable, the character going back to early-day heavies, and Miss Moore also plays a heavy. Warren Berlinger passes as the dead boy's roommate who exposes the crime to Rooney, and Conway Twitty and Jimmy Boyd, name singers, are in for teenage lure, the former composing and warbling the title tune. Yvette Mimieux lends distaff interest in a bikini.

Charles Haas handled direction, and Russell Mitty's camera work suffices. Technical credits are okay. *Whit.*

Crack In the Mirror
(C'SCOPE)

Vivid but cold Zanuck melodrama well acted by three stars, each in a dual role. Needs hefty sell to make b.o. impact.

Twentieth-Fox release of DFZ production produced by Darryl F. Zanuck. Stars Orson Welles, Juliette Greco, Bradford Dillman. Directed by Richard Fleischer. Screenplay, Mark Canfield, based on novel by Marcel Haedrich; music, Maurice Jarre; camera, William C. Mellor; art director, Jean d'Eaubonne; editor, Roger Dwyre; assistant director, Paul Feyder; sound, Jacques Carrere. Reviewed at N. Y. home office, May 6, '60, Running time **97 MINS.**

Hagolin Lamorciere	Orson Welles
Eponine Florence	Juliette Greco
Larnier Claude	Bradford Dillman
President	Alexander Knox
Mother Superior	Catherine Lacy
Kerstner	William Lucas
Doctor	Maurice Teynac
Hurtelaut	Austin Willis
Murzeau	Cec Linder
Magre	Eugene Deckers
Prosecutor	Yves Brainville
Young man at Buvette	Vivian Matalon
Watchman	Jacques Marin
Doctor's Wife	Martine Alexis

Producer Darryl F. Zanuck and director Richard Fleischer, who collaborated so effectively on "Compulsion," have turned out another vivid melodrama in "Crack in The Mirror," beautifully acted by Orson Welles, Juliette Greco and Bradford Dillman, each of whom plays two roles. As a promotion gimmick and as an opportunity to let the stars show their stuff, the dual-role bit is a great idea. However, it also tends to belabor the film's small point and to distract audience interest from any central situation.

Mark Canfield's screenplay, based on a novel by Marcel Haedrich tells two parallel stories, both age-old triangle situations in which a not-so-young woman throws over her elderly lover for a much younger man. The first situation involves three working class people and the second, three members of Paris' **haute monde.** The stories come together when the working class dame and her young paramour are brought to trial for the murder of the older man. The lady is defended by an ambitious young lawyer who is currently carrying on with the mistress of one of France's most respected criminal lawyers, with the latter defending the boy.

By casting Welles as both the tyrannical old construction worker who is murdered and as the cuckolded lawyer, Miss Greco as the mistress in both situations and Dillman as the young laborer and the young lawyer in-a-hurry, Zanuck and Fleischer have obviously intended to make some pertinent statements about guilt and the ironies of justice: the working class couple is eventually packed off to prison for their deeds while their upperclass counterparts go scott free following the elderly lawyer's death. Latter occurs following the climactic trial when he has a heart attack after learning of his own mistress's affair with his young protege.

This irony, however, is telegraphed early in the film when the audience first is let in on the fact that the two stories are essentially the same. Another problem is that about halfway through, film's focal point switches from the working class triangle to the problems of the upperclass trio, with the result that audience interest and emotional involvement are put to a severe test. Picture then becomes a rather cold and not terribly profound intellectual exercise, with all six characters eventually being revealed as quite shoddy types.

Although it aspires to a meaning greater than it possesses, picture is never dull or (despite the dual castings) confusing. Tale unfolds swiftly and surely in a series of sharply etched scenes that catch the gamey, earthy flavor of Paris working class quartiers as well as the bored, somewhat jaded sophistication of successful salon life. It's only after the final fadeout that one realizes that there has been no particular revelation which might have given the sordid story, and the tricky treatment, significance. Picture features a couple of aggressively candid love scenes between Dillman and Miss Greco, particularly when they are enacting the working class lovers just before they garrot her former lover. This is quite a scene, with Dillman and Miss Greco thrashing around on a bed next to one in which the lady's children are sleeping. In a moment of sexual excitement they move into the kitchen (where Welles is sleeping) to put the old guy out of his misery.

Welles is fine as this drunken old slob and close to superb as the elderly lawyer. Dillman is also good as the two young men, both equally opportunistic. However, it's Miss Greco who comes off best—whether it's because of performance or the projection of a unique cinema personality, is hard to say. In any case, she provides the picture with the closest thing it has to a couple of warm, understandable and sympathetic characterizations, whether (as the poor dame) she is going after Welles with a crowbar, or (as the expensively dressed demimondaine) she is renouncing her lover at the fadeout. She's all-girl.

The three stars completely dominate the picture, but Alexander Knox is good in a brief, undemanding role as president of the court, and Catherine Lacy smooth and dignified as a mother superior who counsels the troubled murderess. William C. Mellor's black-and-white CinamaScope photography is excellent and Zanuck's sure, showmanly hand can be seen behind the fine editing job of Roger Dwyre. Produced entirely in Paris, picture has a thoroughly French look and sound.

"Mirror" is an intriguing film, but ultimately, like its central characters, unappealing, not likely to stir wide b.o. sympathy without some hard exploitation sell. *Anby.*

Circus of Horrors
(BRITISH—COLOR—SONG)

Horror film with a circus background; good exploitation entry for the secondary market.

American International release of a Julian Wintle-Leslie Parkyn production presented by James H. Nicholson and Samuel Z. Arkoff. Stars Anton Diffring, Erika Remberg, Yvonne Monlaur; features Jane Hylton, Kenneth Griffith, Conrad Phillips. Directed by Sidney Hayers. Original screenplay, George Baxt; camera (Eastman Color), Douglas Slocombe; editor, Reginald Mills; music, Franz Reizenstein and Muir Mathieson; song, "Look for a Star," Mark Anthony. Previewed N.Y. May 6, '60. Running time, **88 MINS.**

Doctor Goethe	Anton Diffring
Elissa	Erika Remberg
Nicole	Yvonne Monlaur
Vanet	Donald Pleasence
Angela	Jane Hylton
Martin	Kenneth Griffith
Inspector Ames	Conrad Phillips
Supt. Andrews	Jack Gwillim
Magda	Vanda Hudson
Melina	Yvonne Romain
Evelyn Morley	Colette Wilde
Doctor Morley	William Mervyn
Edward Finsbury	John Merivale
Nicole (child)	Carla Challoner
Inspector Knopf	Peter Swanwick
Von Gruber	Walter Gotell
Ringmaster	Chris Christian
Luis	Sasha Coco
Chief Eagle Eye	Jack Carson
Barker	Glyn Houston
Elderly Man	Malcolm Watson
1st Roustabout	Kenneth Warren
2nd Roustabout	Fred Haggerty

A British import distributed by American International, "Circus of Horrors" is aptly titled. For this Julian Wintle-Leslie Parkyn production is replete with blood and gore in the best "Dracula" tradition. While the film is hardly suitable for moppets, it has a wealth of exploitable values which could lure teenagers.

No artistic gem, "Circus" is the type of picture that lends itself to saturation campaigns and bookings. With proper selling, there's no reason why this entry can't mop

up in the secondary market—especially drive-ins. For horror and sex are parlayed, and they're a proven b.o. combo.

George Baxt's original screenplay is a fanciful tale of a renegade plastic surgeon who takes over a one-ring circus. It's a legitimate outfit to begin with, but under the physician's aegis the big top soon becomes a front for his sadistical hobbies.

Portrayed by Anton Diffring, the surgeon devotes his talents to restoring the facial graces of beautiful women who were scarred in one way or another. Curiously, most of these femmes have criminal backgrounds which the medico uses as a whip to hold them as his concubines. At the same time they're star performers in the circus.

When Diffring tires of a girl, she's eliminated in an "accident" during a performance. Naturally, the police eventually become suspicious and the surgeon, too, meets a gruesome fate. Diffring, who seems to have a flair for the role, is a realistic circus "Bluebeard."

Cast as the victims is an array of busty beauties which include Erika Remberg, Vanda Hudson and Yvonne Romain, among others. Before meeting their fates they provide plenty of visual excitation. Yvonne Monlaur, a femme who's curiously spared, is an added asset as an equestrienne ballerina.

Sidney Hayers' direction at times overdoes the macabre touch. Co-producers Julian Wintle and Leslie Parkyn mounted the entry with good physical values. They also give due credit to Billy Smart's Circus for use of latter's facilities. Douglas Slocombe's Eastman Color camerawork is standard as are other technical credits.

Somewhat incongruous is the use of a rock 'n' roll number heard frequently on the soundtrack. Written by Mark Anthony, it's called "Look for a Star." Garry Mills sings it and it's a catchy tune. But it's hardly in keeping with either a horror film or a circus picture. The Franz Reizenstein-Muir Mathieson score, however, is more conventional. *Gilb.*

Head Of a Tyrant
(Judith and Holophernes)
(ITALIAN—COLOR—TOTALSCOPE)

Head is served, per Scripture, to Judith's people, after love does not conquer all. Another Italo spec dubbed into English for the action trade.

Universal release of Vic Film, Rome and C.E.C., Paris coproduction. Stars Massimo Girotti, Isabelle Corey, Renato Baldini, Yvette Masson. Directed by Fernando Cerchio. Screenplay, Cerchio, Damiano Damiani, Gian Paola Callegari and Guido Malatesta; camera, Pierludovico Pavoni; music, Carlo Savino. Previewed in N. Y. May 4, '60. Running time 94 MINS.
Holophernes .... Massimo Girotti
Judith .... Isabelle Corey
Arbar .... Renato Baldini
Rispa .... Yvette Masson
Ozia .... Gianni Rizzo
Belial .... Camillo Pilotto
Servant Girl .... Lucia Banti
Isaac .... Riccardo Valle
Gabriele .... Leonardo Botta
Galaad .... Franco Balducci
Iras .... Luigi Tosi
Brother .... Gabriele Antonini
Naomi .... Daniela Rocca
Daniel .... Enzo Doria

Hordes of people and animals. Italian-made spectacle, spiced with English dubbing, prompts the quip, Italy must be running a sale on these films. "Head of Tyrant," the Universal acquisition, apparently serves a utilitarian purpose:

to provide U's distribution organization with product until its own planned-as-blockbusters product is available.

Originally titled "Judith and Holophernes," this one is based on an incident from Holy Scripture. As a costume drama more than an action film, the entry will likely appeal to the less exacting filmgoer and prove an okay entry for vacationing school kids.

It deals with an Assyrian effort to overrun all of Asia Minor and the relationship of the cruel Assyrian general, Holophernes, and the Judean girl, Judith. The girl sets out deliberately to entice the tyrant and kill him, thereby hoping to save her city from destruction. A strong love, however, develops between the general and the girl, a factor that deters her from carrying out her plan. She makes an effort to dissuade him from his purpose by reasoning, but the general, whose power is built on terror and the god-like worship of his army, fears that a sign of weakness would be his undoing. The girl eventually subjugates her love, cuts off her lover's head, and saves her people.

Massimo Girotti, as Holophernes, and Isabelle Corey, as Judith, are both attractive individuals and meet the demands of the roles. Fernando Cerchio's direction is standard. The dubbing job is a good one, and the lack of synchronization between the lip movements and the sound is not as obvious as in most dubbed pictures. *Holl.*

On N'Enterre Pas Le Dimanche
(One Does Not Bury Sunday)
(FRENCH)
Paris, May 10.
Gaumont release of Port Royal Films production. With Philippe Mory, Christina Bendz, Hella Petri, Albert Gilou, Marcel Cuvelier, Frederic O'Brady. Written and directed by Michel Drach from novel by Fred Kassak. Camera, Jacques Tournier; editor, Genevieve Winding. At Studio Publicis, Paris. Running time, 95 MINS.
Philippe .... Philipe Mory
Margaretha .... Christina Bendz
Mrs. Courtales .... Hella Petri
Mr. Courtales .... Albert Gilou
Inspector .... Marcel Cuvelier
Editor .... Frederic O'Brady

A first feature by documentary maker Michel Drach, this was made on the margin of the industry for about $50,000 and copped the top film critic award of the year. Film is a competently-made drama about the love affair between a young Negro and a Swedish girl which is destroyed by an unstable art milieu, and personal weaknesses.

Director Drach goes in for a lot of symbolism and smart visual effects which give the pic a gloss. But at times it prevents the relationships from expanding and the characters from becoming full-blooded. Result is a polished film that has art possibilities on its theme and style but would need hard-sell for subsequents.

Production keeps characters isolated. The hero works inside a large-sized bottle which he parades around Paris as an ad. This underlines his isolation while his viewing of loving couples points up his need for love. It finally comes via a Swedish girl but she refuses to give in. They become engaged but her employers, a fickle literary and a sluttish wife, are his undoing.

He is made jealous by the wife. Then he is seduced by the same wife, with a slaying to build a dubious climax.

Acting is only competent but Drach keeps things moving via deft editing. Some of the motivations are cloudy but this has exploitation handles and fine technical aspects. *Mosk.*

The Apartment

Billy Wilder touches, together with Jack Lemmon and Shirley MacLaine, make this comedy a top boxoffice contender.

Hollywood, May 4.
United Artists release of Billy Wilder production and Mirisch Co. presentation. Stars Jack Lemmon, Shirley MacLaine, Fred MacMurray; costars Ray Walston; with Jack Kruschen, David Lewis, Naomi Stevens, Hope Holiday and Edie Adams; also Joan Shawlee, Johnny Seven, Frances Weintraub Lax, Joyce Jameson, Willard Waterman, David White, Benny Burt, Hal Smith. Directed by Billy Wilder. Screenplay, Wilder and I.A.L. Diamond; camera (Panavision),, Joseph LaShelle; editor, Daniel Mandell; music, Adolph Deutsch. Previewed at the Village Theatre, Westwood, May 4, '60. Running time, 124 MINS.
C. C. Baxter .... Jack Lemmon
Fran Kubelik .... Shirley MacLaine
J. D. Sheldrake .... Fred MacMurray
Mr. Dobisch .... Ray Walston
Mr. Kirkeby .... David Lewis
Dr. Dreyfuss .... Jack Kruschen
Sylvia .... Joan Shawlee
Miss Olsen .... Edie Adams
Margie MacDougall .... Hope Holiday
Karl Matuschka .... Johnny Seven
Mrs. Dreyfuss .... Naomi Stevens
Mrs. Lieberman .... Frances Weintraub Lax
The Blonde .... Joyce Jameson
Mr. Vanderhof .... Willard Waterman
Mr. Eichelberger .... David White
The Bartender .... Benny Burt
The Santa Claus .... Hal Smith

Billy Wilder has furnished "The Apartment" with a one-hook plot that comes out high in comedy, wide in warmth and long in running time. As with his smash hit, "Some Like It Hot," the broad handling is of more consequence than the package. Wilder's cinematic skill and the lure of Jack Lemmon, Shirley MacLaine and Fred MacMurray insure acceptance of the Mirisch Co. picture. "The Apartment" should return substantial rentals to its landlord, United Artists.

The story is simple. Lemmon is a lonely insurance clerk with a convenient, if somewhat antiquated, apartment which has become the rendezvous point for five of his bosses and their amours. In return, he's promoted from the 19th floor office pool to a 27th floor wood-paneled office complete with key to the executive washroom. He's a phony Horatio Alger, and knowledge of this fact weighs heavily on his idealistic conscience. When he falls in love with Miss MacLaine, an elevator girl who's playing Juliet to top executive MacMurray's Romeo, he turns in his washroom key and all that goes with it in exchange for peace of mind. In the process, he wins the girl.

The screenplay, by Wilder and I.A.L. Diamond, fills every scene with touches that spring only from talented, imaginative filmmakers. But where their "Some Like It Hot" kept you guessing right up to fade-out, "Apartment" reveals its hand early in the game. Second half of the picture is loosely constructed and tends to lag as the rakes go through their paces in over-extending the major plot angle. Most of the time, it's up to director Wilder to sustain a two-hour-plus film on treatment alone, a feat he manages to accomplish more often than not, and sometimes the results are amazing.

The dialog, and its execution, are frank. There is no hiding that full-fledged lovemaking is going on in these quarters. To Wilder's striking credit, the picture has atmosphere, it creates a feeling about people, and, along the way, it makes a few pertinent comments about big businessmen and their infidelities.

"Apartment" is all Lemmon, with a strong twist of MacLaine. The actor uses comedy as it should be

used, to evoke a rainbow of emotions. He's lost in a cool world, this lonely bachelor played by Lemmon, and he is not so much the shnook as the well-meaning, ambitious young man who lets good be the ultimate victor.

Miss MacLaine, again in pixie hairdo, is a prize that's consistent with the fight being waged for her affections. Her ability to play it broad where it should be broad, subtle where it must be subtle, enables the actress to effect reality and yet do much more. Rather than a single human being, Miss MacLaine symbolizes the universal prey of convincing, conniving married men within the glass walls of commerce.

MacMurray is strong as the two-way player, sympathetic but usually the heel. Edie Adams, as his secretary, is good but of substantially more talent than this role requires of her. Same can be said about Ray Walston, used sparingly as one of the loving executives.

Jack Kruschen, as a philosophical doctor, is one of the film's hits. Top work also is done by David Lewis, Joan Shawlee, Naomi Stevens, Joyce Jameson in a fine "Marilyn Monroe" bit and Hope Holiday in a very funny representation of a tipsy femme.

Joseph LaShelle's Panavision camera states its case skillfully with low-key work for loneliness, brightness for the efficient office sequences. Art director Alexander Trauner and set decorator Edward G. Boyle have effectively recreated a Gotham apartment house and a business office that is spectacular in its scope. Film editor Daniel Mandell maintains smooth pace, and sound by Fred Lau is tops.

Adolph Deutsch's background score incorporates his own "Lonely Room" and Charles Williams' "Jealous Lover." Latter, through cooperation of Mills Music, is aptly being retitled "Theme From the Apartment" for commercial recording. Title change will halt confusion with a recent and more well-known tune of the same name and could well boost the film's b.o. even further. *Ron.*

A Terrible Beauty
(BRITISH)

This oldie yarn about the Irish troubles makes fair entertainment largely because of Robert Mitchum, who's more Irish than the Irish; sound booking.

London, May 10.

United Artists release of a Raymond Stross—D.R.M. production. Stars Robert Mitchum, Anne Heywood, Dan O'Herlihy, Cyril Cusack; features Richard Harris, Marianne Benet, Niall McGinnis. Directed by Tay Garnett. Screenplay by Robert White Campbell from Arthur Roth's book; editor, Peter Tanner; camera, Stephen Dade; music, Cedric Thorpe Davie. At London Pavilion, May 2, '60. Running time, 90 MINS.

Dermot O'Neill ....Robert Mitchum
Neeve Donnelly ....Anne Heywood
Don McGinnis ....Dan O'Herlihy
Jimmy Hannafin .... Cyril Cusack
Sean Reilly ....Richard Harris
Bella O'Neill ....Marianne Benet
Neil O'Neill ....Niall McGinnis
Patrick O'Neill ....Harry Brogan
Kathleen O'Neill .... Eileen Crowe
Sergt. Crawley ....Geoffrey Golden
Father McCrory .... Hilton Edwards
Quinn ....Wilfred Downing
Malone ....Christopher Rhodes
Corrigan .... Eddie Golden

Those who argue that the Irish troubles have been more than adequately dealt with on screen and stage have to admit that there have been plenty of screen vehicles on the American Civil War without the subject apparently being yet exhausted. Unfortunately, there seem to be no new permutations of the story of the Irish Republican Army. It crops up as the same old yarn, in the same old settings and, largely, with the same old cast.

Current contender, "A Terrible Beauty," comes hard on the downtrodden heels of "Shake Hands With The Devil," which in itself faced a whale of a lot of competition from memories of "The Informer," "Odd Man Out" and others. However, it's a workmanlike job which should be a useful booking, largely because of its star, Robert Mitchum.

Shot in Dublin, in and around the Ardmore Studios, the picture marshals that rich, but perhaps over-familiar gallery of Irish types, played by what can now be referred to as the Irish Stock Company. Stephen Dade and his camera have, like his predecessors, found the Irish scenery a fruitful background for some excellent black-and-white photography. The screenplay scripter, however, has found himself bogged down in the same corny cliches of dialog and situation.

Some dialog, however, is exempt from criticism. Unfortunately, little of the dialog remotely shapes up to a high original standard. Instead, it wallows around in the pseudo philosophy of show biz Irishmen.

The story can be briefly dismissed. It's that one about the wild young Irishman who gets caught up, patriotically, in the I.R.A. and then sees the light and wants no part of it. But by then he's up to it in his neck and finds he's an outlaw among his own buddies. All this to the accompaniment of endless drinking and periodic bursts into "Oirish" song.

Robert Mitchum holds the film together with his performance. Tough when required, it's mainly an underplayed piece of thesping with a neat sense of humor. He seems far more Irish than all the genuine ones surrounding him. Although he can do little with the dialog, he makes quite a lot of a routine role. Dan O'Herlihy, as a clubfooted, bitter fanatic leader of the local rebels, also makes his mark. Richard Harris, as Mitchum's harum-scarum pal, and Cyril Cusack, as the local cobbler, stand out against a competent set of performers such as Niall McGinnis, Christopher Rhodes, Harry Brogan and Eddie Golden, who have little to do but behave like all Irishmen do in this sort of film. Anne Heywood, as Mitchum's sweetheart, is a conventional colleen. Marianne Benet gets the best chance as a young, sharpish girl who gets bumped off by error.

Tay Garnett's direction is sound but stereotyped. The cutting sometimes is a bit flabby. *Rich.*

The Leech Woman

Lower-berth horror item about a lady Ponce de Leon. Not horrible enough to be very potent.

Hollywood, May 10.

Universal release of Joseph Gershenson production. Stars Coleen Gray, Grant Williams, Philip Terry, Gloria Talbott; with John Van Dreelen, Estelle Hemsley, Kim Hamilton, Arthur Batanides. Directed by Edward Dein. Screenplay, David Duncan, from story by Ben Pivar, Francis Rosenwald; camera, Ellis Carter; editor, Milton Carruth; art directors, Alexander Golitzen, Robert Clatworthy; music, Irving Gertz; assistant director, Joe Kenny. Reviewed at the studio, May 10, '60. Running time, 77 MINS.

June Talbot ....Coleen Gray
Neil Foster ....Grant Williams
Dr. Paul Talbot ....Phillip Terry
Sally ....Gloria Talbott
Bertram Garvay ......John Van Dreelen
Old Malla ....Estelle Hemsley
Young Malla ....Kim Hamilton
Jerry ....Arthur Batanides

How not to grow old gracefully is the subject explored haphazardly in "The Leech Woman," a lower-berth horror item out of Universal. Ticketed for coupling with Hammer Films' "Brides of Dracula," it does not shape up as a particularly companionable co-feature for a shock package owing to the superficiality of its all-important horror element and a tendency to meander into lengthy, irrelevant passages. Standout ingredient of the film is Bud Westmore's striking makeup work in creating some sorry-looking prune faces.

David Duncan's screenplay, drawn out of a story by Ben Pivar and Francis Rosenwald, traces the degeneration of a woman from loveless alcoholic to psychopathic murderess. Taken to Africa by her endocrinologist-husband, who is seeking a mysterious serum for perpetual youth, she discovers she is to be the guinea pig for her mate's experiment. Having none of this, she takes advantage of a curious tribal ritual by ordering the murder of her husband to resurrect her own beauty. Since the secret ingredient of this transformation is the hormone from the pineal gland of a live human male, she is forced to kill continually in order to retain the fickle beauty she has re-created. Her mistake is the murder of a woman, whose hormone is deficient in the vital youth-juice.

Coleen Gray plays the central character extremely well, sharing thespic honors with Estelle Hemsley who, as the aged leader of the tribe, reminds one vaguely of the late Mme. Ouspenskaya. Others who play important roles are Grant Williams, Phillip Terry, Gloria Talbott, John Van Dreelen and Kim Hamilton.

Edward Dein's direction adds no novel flair or approach to horror, but is mechanically sound. Unfortunately for its pace, the Joseph Gershenson production tends to get sidetracked in some uninspired sequences of old African wild animal footage. Ellis W. Carter's camera work and Milton Carruth's editing are proficient. Shock atmosphere is strengthened by Alexander Golitzen's and Robert Clatworthy's art direction and Irving Gertz's music. *Tube.*

Battle of Blood Island

Two-character study of survival and brotherhood of a Pacific atoll. Weaker, slower half of a World War II action package.

Hollywood, April 26.

Filmgroup release of Stan Bickman production. Stars Richard Devon, Ron Kennedy. Directed and screenplay by Joel Rapp; camera, Jacques Marquette; editor, Carlo Lodato. Reviewed at Warner Hollywood Theatre, April 26, ½60. Running time, 64 MINS.

Moe ....Richard Devon
Ken ....Ron Kennedy

How two GI's of different faiths and dispositions learn togetherness on a deserted Pacific isle during and after World War II is the subject of this film. Luckily for "Battle of Blood Island," it contains two fairly strong performances (by Richard Devon in particular, and Ron Kennedy). Otherwise, it's a rather plodding, questionable addition to a Filmgroup package headed into the action market.

The Stan Bickman-Joel Rapp production, produced by the former, written and directed by the latter, opens on a Japanese-held island where Devon and Ron Kennedy are the sole survivors of an unsuccessful Allied invasion. Concealing themselves in a cave, the two men later witness mass hara-kiri, indicating to the audience that the war has ended (although time is never clear in the film).

At this point, troubles really begin for the two men who, no longer forced to whisper, begin to snarl openly and incessantly at each other. Finally (and unaccountably) Kennedy erupts, terms Devon a "lousy Jew," promptly fires a bullet into his own pitching arm (he's Class C in the Yankee chain) in remorse. The two men are rescued just in time to avoid perishing in an atomic test blast ticketed for the island.

None of this is too plausible, let alone touching, and it's too slow and calm to be very suspenseful or exciting. Rapp's screenplay has some fair lines of dialog here and there, and his direction stirs up a couple of reasonably lively performances, but there's little beyond that to arouse a spectator who's bought his ticket hungering for action. Physical and technical credits are capable. *Tube*

The Brides of Dracula
(BRITISH-COLOR)

Exploitation entry that should appeal to the horror trade.

Universal release of Hammer Film Production produced by Anthony Hinds. Stars Peter Cushing, Freda Jackson, Martita Hunt, Yvonne Monlaur. Features Miles Malleson, David Peel, Mona Washbourne, Henry Oscar, Victor Brooks, Michael Ripper, and Andree Melly. Directed by Terence Fisher. Screenplay, Jimmy Sangster, Peter Bryan, Edward Percy. Camera (Technicolor), Jack Asher; editor, Alfred Cox; music, Malcolm Williamson. Previewed in N. Y. May 12, '60. Running time, 85 MINS.

Dr. Van Helsing ....Peter Cushing
Baroness Meinster.........Martita Hunt
Marianne ....Yvonne Monlaur
Greta ....Freda Jackson
Baron Meinster .... David Peel
Dr. Tobler...............Miles Malleson
Herr Lang................. Henry Oscar
Frau Lang............Mona Washbourne
Gina .... Audrey Melly
Hans ....Victor Brooks
Cure .... Fred Johnson
Coachman ....Michael Ripper
Landlord ....Norman Pierce
Landlord's Wife............. Vera Cook
Village Girl.............Marie Devereux
Severin .... Harold Scott

Horror films, for reasons best known to psychologists, continue to fascinate a large segment of the picture-going public. Consequently, "The Brides of Dracula," another sequel in the seemingly endless series, will undoubtedly prove a fairly successful exploitation offering during the summer months when vacationing teenagers are searching for ways to spend their time, if not improve their minds.

Hammer Films, the British company which specializes in these goose pimple diversions, has turned out a technically well-made film embellished with color. However, if the true aficiando of the horror cult is seeking a real eerie experience, he'll be disappointed.

"The Brides of Dracula" covers familiar ground and rehashes the vampire and undead legends of the mythical "mittel" Europe country popularized in the pic-

tures starring the late Bela Lugosi.

His modern day counterpart, as depicted by David Peel, hardly achieves the same degree of terror. Moreover, color—although considered an advance—detracts rather than adds to the horror aspects. It would have been considerably more scary if it had been filmed in old-fashioned black and white.

As the Baron Meinster, a young, handsome noble, Peel has somehow inherited the nefarious qualities of Count Dracula. His mother, aware of his affliction, keeps him locked up in the family castle and caters to his needs by procuring his victims. It catches up with her eventually, as she becomes one of his undead disciples.

Peter Cushing, the physician summoned by the local priest, is aware of the customs of the vampires and knows how to combat them with religious symbols and the wooden stake through the heart. Yvonne Monlaur, as a pretty school teacher, helps the Baron escape from his confinement in the castle and almost marries him, but she is saved from a vampire's fate by the timely intervention of Cushing.

There are the usual scenes of bats flapping outside windows, of corpses slowly emerging from coffins, and of the undead inflicting the fatal bite on their victims. The undead, supposedly drained of blood, are depicted as extremely pale-faced individuals who grow fangs as soon as they become members of the vampire colony.

The screenplay by Jimmy Sangster, Peter Bryan and Edward Percy adds little to the Dracula legend and follows formula horror gimmicks. Terence Fisher's direction treats the proceedings seriously and avoids ludicrous moments.

The cast, which also includes Freda Jackson and Martita Hunt, performs its function as if it believed in what is happening in the film. Technical aspects are fine.

Universal is backing the release with a strong exploitation campaign, a factor that should aid the b.o. in situations where the patrons go for these type of films.

Holl.

The Gallant Hours

Robert Montgomery as producer. Admiral Halsey biopic told tastefully. Unusually mature approach.

Hollywood, May 6.

United Artists release of Cagney-Montgomery production. Stars James Cagney; with Dennis Weaver, Ward Costello, Richard Jaeckel, Les Tremayne, Robert Burton, Raymond Bailey, Carl Benton Reid, Walter Sande, Karl Swenson, Vaughn Taylor, Harry Landers, Richard Carlyle, Leon Lontoc, James T. Goto, James Yagi, John McKee, John Zaremba, Carleton Young, William Schallert, Nelson Leigh, Sydney Smith, Herbert Lytton, Selmar Jackson, Tyler McVey, Maggie Magennis. Produced and directed by Robert Montgomery. Screenplay, Beirne Lay Jr. and Frank D. Gilroy; camera, Joe MacDonald; editor, Frederick Y. Smith; art director, Wiard Ihman; music, Roger Wagner; assistant director, Joseph C. Behm. Reviewed at Academy Award Theatre, May 6, '60. Running time, 115 MINS.

Adm. William F. Halsey	James Cagney
Lt. Comdr. Andy Lowe	Dennis Weaver
Capt. Harry Black	Ward Costello
Lt. Comdr. Roy Webb	Richard Jaeckel
Capt. Frank Enright	Les Tremayne
Maj. Gen. Roy Geiger	Robert Burton
Maj. Gen. Archie Vandegrift	Raymond Bailey
Adm. Ghormley	Carl Benton Reid
Capt. Horace Keys	Wanter Sande
Capt. Bill Bailey	Karl Swenson
Cmdr. Mike Pulaski	Vaughn Taylor
Capt. Joe Foss	Harry Landers
Father Gehring	Richard Carlyle
Manuel	Leon Lontoe
Adm. Isoroku Hamamoto	James T. Goto
Rr. Adm. Jiro Kobe	James Yagi
Lt. Harrison Ludlum	John McKee
Maj. Gen. Harmon	John Zaremba
Col. Evans Carlson	Carleton Young
Capt. Tom Lamphier	William Schallert
Adm. Callaghan	Nelson Leigh
Adm. Scott	Sidney Smith
Adm. Muray	Herbert Lytton
Adm. Chester Nimitz	Selmar Jackson
Adm. Ernest J. King	Tyler McVey

With dignity and good taste, "The Gallant Hours" tells the story of a short, critical period in the life of Admiral William F. Halsey Jr. Unfortunately, some are bound to feel that the story is being told with too much dignity and good taste, for it is a long picture and, though dealing with war, contains no footage whatsoever of battle action. This unusually adult, sophisticated approach may not hypo boxoffice but the enthusiastic support of more discriminating theatregoers should, eventually, make it a profitable venture.

Penetratingly written by Beirne Lay Jr. and Frank D. Gilroy, the screenplay studies Halsey as Commander of the Third Fleet during the few decisive weeks in the fall of 1942, when the complexion of the Pacific war was altered. At the core of the story is the strategic duel between Halsey and the crafty Japanese Admiral, Isoroku Hamamoto, a duel won by Halsey with the Allied victory at Guadalcanal and the death of his military rival.

An accurate, incisive portrayal of Halsey is created by James Cagney. The veteran actor has managed not only a correct physical suggestion of the admiral, but has successfully subordinated his own electric personality in striving for, and achieving, far more than a mere surface delineation of the character. It is a fine performance.

The casting of Dennis Weaver as Halsey's aide was a smart move, for this actor brings to the film just the warmth and whimsey it needs when the going begins to get a little too cold and sober. Others who command most favorable attention in supporting roles are Ward Costello, Richard Jaeckel, Lee Tremayne, Robert Burton, Raymond Bailey, Carl Benton Reid and Walter Sande. The treatment of Japanese characters is intelligent and, for a change, they speak in their native tongue as narration (by Art Gilmore) interprets the gist of their discussions. "Hamamoto" is played skillfully by James T. Goto.

Narration is excellent, not only supplying offbeat personal insights (of Hamamoto: "excellent poker player, especially good at bluffing"), but doing it always with a sense of humor.

Producer-director Robert Montgomery has brought to the production grace, integrity and a sensible point-of-view. But in one or two decisions he appears to have stumbled over his own artful aims, particularly in his offbeat use of choral music as background. Not that the Roger Wagner Chorale doesn't do some superbly disciplined chanting, but this sort of backing only serves to make even more sombre and ponderous a rather wordy film that can stand all the subsidiary excitement it can get.

Another flaw is the length at which certain scenes run on, principally one long, fuzzy sequence towards the end in which Cagney ponders alone over the gravity of the situation.

One of the outstanding facets of the production is the editing (editorial supervision by Frederick Y. Smith), which ranges from appropriately sharp cuts to slow dissolves that create desirable overlapping studies. A pair of other plus factors are Joe MacDonald's camera work and Wiard Ihman's sets.

Tube.

Macumba Love
(COLOR)

Jungle voodoo stuff for the summer exploitation trade.

United Artists release of Douglas Fowley production. Executive producer, M. A. Ripps with Steve Barclay. Stars Walter Reed, Ziva Rodann, William Wellman Jr., and June Wilkinson. Directed by Fowley. Screenplay, Norman Graham; camera, Rudolfo Icsey; music, Enrico Simonetti. Previewed in N. Y. May 13, '60. Running time, **86 MINS.**

Weils	Walter Reed
Venus de Viasa	Ziva Rodann
Sarah's husband	William Wellman Jr.
Sarah	June Wilkinson
Mama Rataloy	Ruth de Souza

The coming of the warm weather season appears to coincide with the film industry's prediliction to unleash gimmick or exploitation pictures. These pictures, usually made at low budgets or acquired cheaply from enterprising independent entrepeneurs, lend themselves to standard and often-repeated bally techniques.

"Macumba Love," which United Artists acquired from drive-in operator M. A. Ripps and Steve Barclay, falls in that category. Dealing with the voodoo rites allegedly practiced in parts of South America, the film provides the basis for numerous stunts and macabre displays of theatre fronts and lobbies. To be sure, there's an audience for these films, so theatre operators willing to expend the necessary exploitation energy will likely rack up a fair amount of wicket trade.

There's an added exploitation gimmick in June Wilkinson, the well-endowed model whose assets have been unbrassiered in Playboy Magazine, In the film, Miss Wilkinson is content to show considerable cleavage.

Filmed in Brazil, the film deals with a writer's efforts to unmask the practioners of voodoo. His probing of several unsolved murders, which he attributes to the voodooists, places his own life in danger. The voodoo angle provides the opportunity for some frenzied, uninhibited dancing by performers depicting natives. A couple of songs, identified as calypso, are thrown in from left field, although it is never explained how calypso got to this area of South America.

The color photography is quite good, considering the rest of the absurdities. Except for Ziva Rodann, the acting of Miss Wilkinson, Walter Reed, as her father, and William Wellman Jr., as her husband, are almost amateurish. Miss Rodann, however, emerges as an attractive and fiery performer who has a chance to make an important impact in future films. "Macumba Love's" chief asset is its service as a vehicle for the display of Miss Rodann's talent. The Israeli actress plays a mysterious heiress who becomes an unwilling instrument of the voodooists.

Douglas Fowley, better known as Doc Holliday of the Wyatt Earp tv series, produced and directed. He does the best he can with the story and the talent he had to work with. He does, however, get an outstanding performance from Miss Rodann. Technical aspects are okay.

Holl.

The Giant of Marathon
(ITALIAN-COLOR-D'LSCOPE-TOTALSCOPE)

Gaudy spectacle "based" loosely on the exploits of Greek hero Pheidippides. More beefcake heroics by Steve Reeves. Should have rapid, but respectable b.o. impact in U. S.

Hollywood, May 4.

Metro release of Bruno Vailati production. Stars Steve Reeves, Mylene Demongeot; with Daniela Rocca, Ivo Garrani, Philippe Hersent, Sergio Fantoni, Alberto Lupo, Daniele Varga, Miranda Campa, Gianni Loti. Drected by Jacques Tourneur. Screenplay, Ennio de Concini, Austo Frassinetti, Vainati, from idea of Alberto Barsanti, Raffaello Pacini; camera, Mario Bava; editor, Mario Serandrei; art director, Marcello Del Prato; music, Roberto Nicolosi; assistant directors, Ottavio Oppo, Odoardo Flory, Armando Govoni. Reviewed at the studio, May 4, '60. Running time, **90 MINS.**

Philippides	Steve Reeves
Andromeda	Mylene Demongeot
Karis	Daniela Rocca
Creuso	Ivo Garrani
Callimaco	Philippe Hersent
Teocrito	Sergio Fantoni
Milziade	Alberto Lupo
Dario, King of Persians	Daniele Varga
Un'Ancella	Miranda Campa
Teucro	Gianni Loti

. "The Giant of Marathon" offers contemporary audiences the opportunity to escape for 90 minutes from today's complex, impersonal society into an improbable, but perhaps enviable world where history could be altered by the flex of a biceps. Add to this lure the promises of Totalscope, Dyaliscope, Eastman Color and Olympian physiques amply displayed and what emerges is a film (from Italy) that **should make a brief, but sufficient clatter at the American boxoffice for Metro.**

Lurking behind all these purely physical excesses is an incredible, almost laughably absurd yarn that toys ingloriously with an intriguing slice of ancient history. The "Giant" is "Pheidippides," the memorable Greek marathoner who in 490 B.C. ran some 26 miles, 385 yards from Marathon to Athens to bring glad tidings of Greece's victory over Persia, then promptly expired upon reaching his goal. But none of this fascinating tale is depicted in the picture, screenplayed by Ennio de Concini, Augusto Frassinetti and producer Bruno Vailati from "an idea of" Alberto Barsanti and Raffaello Pacini.

"Idea" may have been to weave a yarn around Pheidippides' exploits, but what has been woven instead is a loose, uneven account of how the hero (re-dubbed "Philippides" and played by Steve Reeves) almost single-handedly wrecks the entire Persian army and navy. Once the story gets moving into matters military (and it takes its time about it), there is enough sheer war and gore to keep the customers entranced, although many will stir uneasily at the abundance of bloodshed, all bathed in vividly rubicund Eastman tint.

Reeves manages capably with the title role, although his Herculean physique tends to be distracting, drawing attention away from that minor portion of his performance which depends upon facial expression. In some instances, that's all for the better. Romantic interest is supplied attractively by Mylene Demongeot. Performances of considerable spirit are chipped in by Daniela Rocca, Sergio Fan-

toni and Ivo Garrani. Dubbing sound levels often are inaccurate, which doesn't help any of the performers.

It is in the filming of scenes depicting primitive warfare that the picture hits its stride and serves its cardinal purpose as audience escape via cinema craftsmanship. Director Jacques Tourneur has managed some well-disciplined but sufficiently spontaneous land battle sequences utilizing hordes of extras. He also has gotten the most out of some striking underwater photography (Totalscope lenses) and special effects by Mario Bava. But not for one moment are these heroic exploits of land and sea warfare to be taken seriously.

Further physico-dramatic aid comes from Mario Serandrei's editing, Marcello Del Prato's sturdy sets, Massimo Tavazzi's colorful decorations, Roberto Nicolosi's fitting music and Marisa Crimi's costumes which, if not entirely authentic, do reveal the proper amount of femme pulchritude and male muscle. Some rousing stuntwork heightens the impact of the battle scenes. *Tube.*

Hell Is A City
(BRITISH)

Great police yarn with authentic backgrounds, taut screenplay and firstclass performances, notably by Stanley Baker. Should prove topnotch b.o. winner.

London, May 10.

Warner-Pathe release of a Hammer (Michael Carreras) production. Stars Stanley Baker; features Donald Pleasence, Billie Whitelaw, John Crawford, Maxine Audley, Joseph Tomelty, George A. Cooper. Directed by Val Guest. Screenplay by Guest from Maurice Proctor's novel; editor, John Dunsford; camera, Arthur Grant; music, Stanley Black. At Warner Theatre, London. Running time, 98 MINS.

Inspct. Martineau .... Stanley Baker
Don Starling .... John Crawford
Gus Hawkins .... Donald Pleasence
Julia Martineau .... Maxine Audley
Chloe Hawkins .... Billie Whitelaw
Furnisher Steele .... Joseph Tomelty
Doug Savage .... George A. Cooper
Devery .... Geoffrey Frederick
Lucky Lusk .... Vanda Godsell
Clogger Roach .... Charles Houston
Tawny Jakes .... Joby Blanshard
Laurie Lovett .... Charles Morgan
Bert Darwin .... Peter Madden
Bragg .... Dickie Owen
Cecily .... Lois Daine
Comc. Traveller .... Warren Mitchell
Silver Steele .... Sarah Branch
Sam .... Alastair Williamson
Superintendent .... Russell L. Napier

There's nothing new about the idea of "Hell Is A City," which makes it all the more invigorating that such an absorbing film has been made of a conventional cops and robbers yarn. Val Guest's taut screenplay, allied to his own deft direction, has resulted in a notable film in which the characters are all vividly alive, the action constantly gripping and the background of a provincial city put over with authenticity. One of the best British films for sometime, it will certainly do well in U. K. It lacks stellar value for the U. S. but should do much to consolidate a growing opinion that Stanley Baker is among the first half dozen British film thesps.

The film was shot largely in Manchester. Arthur Grant's camerawork has arrestingly caught the feel of the big city with its grey, sleazy backstreets, its saloons, the surrounding factory chimneys, the bleakness of the moors and the bustle of the city. Indeed, it is this which helps to give the picture its sharp flavor, together with the use of a number of newish faces.

A slight problem arises here in that the local dialect may fall a bit strangely on the ears of foreigners. Two or three of the more salty bits of dialog in Guest's fast moving screenplay have been trimmed for U. S. consumption but the dialog remains credible and often amusing.

The yarn has Stanley Baker as a detective inspector who, married to a bored, unsympathetic wife (Maxine Audley) spends most of his time on his job. In this instance he is concerned with a dangerous escaped convict who, he suspects, will be returning to Manchester to pick up the stolen jewels that sent him to the cooler. When the girl clerk of a local bookie is attacked while on the way to the bank with a bagful of money and then found murdered on the nearby moors, Baker suspects that the crook and a small gang are the criminals.

Doggedly he starts to track them down. Patiently the clues begin to fit in, suspects are grilled and he breaks down the resistance of people who refuse to give information because of intimidation by the jailbird. Eventually everything clicks into shape and he captures three of the four men responsible for the murder. Only the ringleader is missing, loose in Manchester. But where? The film builds up to a sock climax. Refreshingly the film resists the temptation of a happy ending.

From the moment when the killer (John Crawford) makes his sudden surprise entrance and sets the wheels of the robbery in motion, suspense rarely lets up. The robbery itself is briskly pulled off, there is a firstrate scene on the moors when the police raid an illegal gathering of gamblers and some down-to-earth police station sequences, with Baker pulling no punches in his determination to get at the truth.

Acting all round is admirable. Baker presents the cop as a very human guy, tough but likeable and with a sense of humor. His strained relationship with his wife, neatly played by Maxine Audley, which occasionally crops up in the film is not obtrusive and in fact helps to give depth to his characterization. Crawford matches Baker in authority and makes the chief villain a dangerous thug.

There are a number of other interesting performances. Charles Houston, Joby Blanshard and Charles Morgan score as Crawford's assorted henchmen. George A. Cooper is fine as a shifty saloonowner. Joseph Tomelty shapes sound as one of the men Crawford tries to involve and Donald Pleasence, as usual, bringing shrewd observations to the role of a testy bookmaker. On the femme side there are three useful performances. Billie Whitelaw, Pleasence's flighty wife and an ex-girl friend of Crawford, brings some sexy piquancy to the scene where she is forced to harbor the killer for the night. Vanda Godsell gives a warmly sympathetic piece of acting as a barmaid who falls for Baker. A newcomer, Sarah Branch, has a tricky role as a deaf and dumb girl who is attacked by Crawford. A very pretty young woman, Miss Branch suggests potential.

"Hell Is A City" is a very satisfying film, with allround okay credits, including music by Stanley Black. *Rich.*

Noose For a Gunman

Old fashioned western for markets where westerns are indiscriminately accepted.

Hollywood, May 4.

United Artists release of Premium Pictures production. Stars Jim Davis, Barton MacLane; features Lyn Thomas, Ted de Corsia, Leo Gordon, Harry Carey Jr.; with Walter Sande, Lane Chandler, John Hart, Bill Tannen, Jan Arvan, Bob Tetrick, William Remick, Kermit Maynard, William Challee, Cecil Weston. Producer, Robert E. Kent. Directed by Edward L. Cahn. Screenplay, James B. Gordon, from story by Steve Fisher; camera, Al Cline; editor, Grant Whytock; art director, Bill Glasgow; sound, Ben Winkler; assistant director, Herbert S. Greene. Reviewed at Goldwyn Studios, May 4, '60. Running time, 90 MINS.

Case Britton .... Jim Davis
Della Haines .... Lyn Thomas
Cantrell .... Ted de Corsia
Tom Evans .... Walter Sands
Carl Avery .... Barton MacLane
Jim Ferguson .... Harry Carey Jr.
Ed Folsey .... Lane Chandler
Barker .... John Hart
Link Roy .... Leo Gordon
Willetts .... Bill Tannen
Hallop .... Jan Arvan
Anders .... Bob Tetrick
Man on Stage Coach .... William Remick
Carter .... Kermit Maynard
Gorse .... William Challee
Mrs. Franklyn .... Cecil Weston

With the output of theatrical westerns down considerably since television went sagebrush-happy, this unpretentious item out of the United Artists stable should be welcomed in situations where people gather to witness westerns on a big screen. There's absolutely nothing in "Noose For A Gunman" that's new or different in the western genre. Leaving the "adult" tag and the psychological overtones to the tv oater-makers, producer Robert E. Kent obviously is out to pacify the tastes of western "purists" and "classicists" who like their villains garbed in black and their heroes tall and tight-lipped.

Jim Davis stars in James B. Gordon's screenplay, from Steve Fisher's story, about a decent, peace-loving "fast gun" who is implicated in a complicated robbery-revenge situation. He returns to the town from which he has been banished unjustifiably (for killing the two sons of a wealthy land baron who caused the demise of his brother) in order to tip off an impending robbery by a notorious gunman he believes to be in cahoots with his arch enemy, the aforementioned baron. It's all true. The robbery is attempted, the baron is in chahoots with the thieves, and the hero's banishment is a travesty of justice. But it's all rectified in a series of showdowns and gun battles.

The hero is played by Davis in the classically cold, calculating, awe-inspiringly bold and brave style that is almost mandatory for essaying such a role in such a picture. Romantic interest is supplied with more than customary animation by Lyn Thomas. Ted de Corsia makes an almost likeable ogre out of the colorful gangleader —a nice performance. Portrayals of some interest are etched by Barton MacLane, Walter Sande, and Leo Gordon, and others noticeably on the scene are Harry Carey Jr., Lane Chandler, John Hart, Bill Tannen, Jan Arvan and Bob Tetrick.

The film is directed with businesslike simplicity by Edward L. Cahn—no nuances, no tricks. Audiences will be able to anticipate most of the action, gestures and character decisions, but they will have a rough time figuring out most of the motivations, if they bother to be discriminating about it all. Capable craftsmanship is supplied in the photographic area by lensman Al Cline. Film editing by Grant Whytock is sluggish only in one or two instances, and art director Bill Glasgow's work is adequate. *Tube.*

Rosen Fuer Den Staatsanwalt
(Roses For the Prosecutor)
(GERMAN)

Berlin, May 10.

NF release of Kurt Ulrich production. Stars Martin Held, Walter Giller, Ingrid van Bergen. Directed by Wolfgang Staudte. Screenplay, Georg Hurdalek; camera, Erich Claunigk; music, Raimund Rosenberger. At UFA Pavillon, Berlin. Running time. 98 MINS.

Wilhelm Schramm, prosecutor .... Martin Held
Rudi Kleinschmidt .... Walter Giller
Lissy .... Ingrid van Bergen
Hildegard Schramm .... Camilla Spira
Haase .... Werner Finck
Hessel .... Ralf Wolter
Kugler .... Werner Peters

A German film, with a sharp satirical accent, concerns the Nazi time and postwar period. This Kurt Ulrich production stands a solid chance abroad. Imaginative direction and acting contribute to make it one of the better and more interesting German pix of the year.

Story centers around a prosecutor and a humble street-vendor. Latter had been sentenced to death during the last war days for a minor offense. Through a fluke, he escapes the punishment. Years later, he happens to run across the wild Nazi who condemned him to die. He's again in a high position, a prosecutor in a German small town. It so happens that the street-vendor comes again before court. The end sees the prosecutor's unholy Nazi past revealed.

Perhaps most remarkable fact about "Prosecutor" is that its makers succeeded in making a highly enjoyable item out of a basically grim tale. Some of the more fastidious crix may complain that a "hard-hitting" subject has been sacrificed for the sake of a satirical farce. Commercially speaking, producer Ulrich was right. The film's appeal is now more universal. And as to its message, it still comes off, saying much with a light touch.

Although he hasn't created an artistic masterpiece, Staudte still deserves much praise. Direction is always swift and remarkably imaginative. A splendid bit of acting is turned in by Martin Held in the title role. He practically steals the show. Although he quite often comes close to exaggeration, one doesn't get tired of watching him. Next worth mentioning is Walter Giller who, as the street-vendor, also has a number of fine scenes. Support also is of high standard. A particularly efficient performance is contributed by Ingrid van Bergen, a sexy blonde, who is cast as a hotel-restaurant proprietress. Technical credits are excellent. *Hans.*

Il Mondo Di Notte
(The World at Night)
(ITALIAN)
(Songs—Color)

Rome, May 10.

Warner Bros. release of a Julia Film production. With Alfredo Alaria and his ballet, Tiller Girls, Kiyokawa Geisha House, Rapha Temporel and Dodo D'Hambourg, Fraternity Brothers, Apollo Theatre Gospel Show, The Nitwits, Wee Willy Harris, Whales of Marineland, the Lido de Paris and the Bluebell Girls, Tokyo's Queen Bee, Hong Kong Chinese Opera Company, Ricky Renee, the Las Vegas Rhythmettes, others. Directed by Luigi Vanzi. Camera (Technirama-Technicolor), Tonino delli Colli; music, Piero Piccioni; edited by Mario Serandrei. At the Adriano, Rome. Running time, 120 MINS.

WB has a winner in this handsome documentary of night life

around the globe, with healthy grosses predictable almost anywhere it plays. Though abridged in the local version, its accent on sex is nevertheless a major sales point, while its adroit spoofing as well as the appealing and varied remaining fare should please general audiences. Also, there's no dubbing or adaptation problem other than a lingual switch in the spoken commentary, making for savings in that sector.

Luigi Vanzi, who assisted Alessandro Blasetti in the successful "Europe by Night," is on his own here and comes up with generally fascinating fare in what is basically a pot-pourri of nitery turns around the world. Main difference is that while "Europe" comprised several top names, "World" has fewer, but manages to generate almost as much excitement and eye-appeal. There is no pretense at a consistent link between numbers beyond the commentary. But the formula should continue to click with audiences.

There are few letdowns in the entire collection, which varies from the neatly lensed whale ballet at Marineland and frenzied dances of Alfredo Alaria's troupe to the precision terping of the Lido's Bluebell line and the busy gambling interiors lensed at Las Vegas. One of the best bits, incidentally, is contributed by the Las Vegas Rhythmettes, an unusually sock bit also thanks to a perfect musical backdrop, as the girls march through the neon-lit streets of the gambling city. And there are many more, linked by a tongue-in-cheek commentary written by Gualtiero Jacopetti.

Final credit must go to a new fast Technicolor-Technirama stock which gives a new on-the-spot reality to certain sequences which would heretofore have required artificial lighting assists. This promises to provide future productions using the system with innumerable advantages. The technical credits are fine, and Piero Piccioni's music is apt. *Hawk.*

My Dog, Buddy

Low budget, Texas-made animal adventure pic. Appeal only to younger children.

Hollywood, May 3.

Columbia release of B. R. and Gordon McLendon production. Stars London; introduces Travis Lemmond; features Ken Curtis, Ken Knox; with James H. Foster, Jane Murchison, Bob Thompson, Jo Palmie. Producer, Curtis. Directed and screenplay by Ray Kellogg; camera, Ralph Hammeras; editor, Aaron Stell; sound, "Wee" Risser, L. Gianneschi, B R. Blackwood; music, Jack Marshall; assistant directors, Horace Hough, David Salven; set decorator, Louise Caldwell. Reviewed at the studio, May 3, '60. Running time, **76 MINS.**

Buddy .... London
Ted Dodd .... Travis Lemmond
Dr. Lusk .... Ken Curtis
Dr. White .... Ken Knox
Jim Foster .... James H. Foster
Jane Foster .... Jane Murchison
Salizar .... Bob Thompson
Nurse Lewis .... Jo Palmie
Special Detective ...... Judge Dupree
Patrol Officer .... Chuck Eisenmann
Elizabeth Lynch .... Gerry Johnson
George Lynch .... Don Keyes
Junior Lynch .... Bart McLendon
Junkyard Owner .... Honest Joe
Artist Fuller .... Bob Euler
Kolinzky .... Desmond Dhooge
Mr. Dodd .... C. B. Lemmond
Mrs. Dodd .... Lilla Lemmond

"My Dog, Buddy," frankly a film for children, will succeed in tickling the vulnerable fancies of the very young, and thereby carve a reasonably profitable niche for itself in the strictly moppet marketplace. Any broader appeal the Columbia release might have had (and there is an indication that such potential existed) is victimized by a tendency to stray off on irrelevent tangents and to indulge in some disconcerting gimmickry purely for its own sake.

The picture was made by the McLendon Co. radio station entrepreneurs in Dallas, reportedly for $73.000. It did such big business in the Southwest that Columbia is releasing nationally.

Essentially, "Buddy" is a short, sweet, simple tale of a boy, a dog, and their blinding devotion to each other. Ray Kellogg's yarn, an original for the screen, isolates them from each other in the wake of an auto tragedy in which the boy's parents are killed. The balance of the film is devoted to the dog's efforts to locate the hospitalized youngster, his only clue being the sound of the siren that accompanied the lad's departure, making him sort of a Pavlov's dog with a soul.

When it sticks to the central issue, the film has its suspenseful and touching moments. But writer-director Kellogg has not been content just to stick to the central issue. He has cluttered the picture with so many flashback repetitions and sequences foreign to the plot (principally one long, strained scene at a dog show in which the canines "talk") that by the time the situation is resolved it has been anticipated too frequently to make for a fully effective climax.

If nothing else, dogdom attains new stature in this film. London, the superbly trained German shepherd (owned and trained by Chuck Eisenmann, and formerly star of "The Littlest Hobo") who essays the title role, manages some remarkably skillful maneuvers for a dog. He has all the best of it over the humans involved, several of whom are depicted as frightfully base and sadistic, and fair game for an ASPCA investigation. Travis Lemmond, in his screen bow, is effective as the boy. Supporting work is generally adequate.

The film, produced by Ken Curtis, has a candid pictorial quality, almost "home-movieish" in appearance but actually deceptively well-lensed by Ralph Hammeras. A taut editing job by Aaron Stell is another valuable asset. Sound plays an important role in this picture, and is handled delicately by a trio of audio craftsmen—"Wee" Risser, Larry Gianneschi and B. R. Blackwood. The main title ditty, penned by Jack Marshall, is utilized throughout as backing and is difficult to erase from the mind, even hours after leaving the theatre.

There is one jarring aspect of the film that might better be snipped right now—an unwelcome throwback to the Stepin Fetchit days of Negro stereotype in motion pictures—with several scenes depicting some infamous eyeball-rolling, scaredy-cat antics by Negro cast in menial parts. That kind of "Uncle Tom" condescension to the Negro is now bitterly resented.

Tube.

Prisoner Of The Volga
(FRENCH-ITALIAN-COLOR)

Colorful production of a bulky, contrived period adventure yarn about a Russian army captain's struggle for justice. Unsuitable for healthy U. S. booking.

Hollywood, April 21.

Paramount release of Transmonde-Fides production. Stars John Derek, Elsa Martinelli, Dawn Addams; with Charles Vanel, Gert Froebe, Rik Battaglia, Wolfgang Preiss, Nerio Bernardi, Ingmar Zeisberg, Jacques Caetelot. Directed by W. Tourjansky. Screenplay, Salka Viertel; camera, Mario Montuori; editor, Robert Cinquini; music, Norbert Glanzberg; assistant director, Robert Martin. Reviewed at the studio, April 21, '60. Running time, **102 MINS**

Alexey .... John Derek
Mascha .... Elsa Martinelli
Tatiana .... Dawn Addams
Ossip .... Charles Vanel
Professor .... Gert Froebe
Lisenko .... Rik Battaglia
Gorew .... Wolfgang Preiss
Elagin .... Nerio Bernardi
Olga .... Ingmar Zeisberg
Jakowlew .... Jacques Caetelot

A certain gamey, quasi-cultural quality of production is about all that distinguishes this French-Italian co-effort. Too long and bulky in structure for comfortable pairing, too weak and contrived in content for loftier commercial aspirations, the Paramount release is an unlikely prospect for U. S. theatres.

"Prisoner of the Volga," screenplayed by Salka Viertel, awkwardly and ploddingly traces the experiences of a dashing young captain in the Russian Czar's army (John Derek) who is stripped of rank and ushered off to prison in Siberia for slugging a general who, he has discovered, has compromised his bride (Dawn Addams). Miss Addams, a courageous lass, is slain assisting Derek in a successful escape. Chased by Cossacks, he joins a band of Volga boatmen and becomes comrades with a snappy gypsy item (Elsa Martinelli). Following a contrived showdown with the villainous general, Derek is pardoned, restored to rank, and gets the girl as bonus.

Easily the oustanding feature of the film is its atmosphere—vivid, earthy, Czarist Russian. This, thanks to the sharp Eastman hues, some striking sets, furnishings and costumes, Norbert Glanzberg's vital music, and Mario Montuori's able camera work.

There's little else of merit. W. Tourjansky's direction is anything but taut. Any sense of participation the audience might feel is dulled by the dubbing aspect. The stiff dialog imposes a terrible burden upon the performances of Derek, Miss Martinelli and Miss Addams. Being attractive, they manage to be sympathetic. Supporting work is colorful, particularly that of Gert Froebe. *Tube.*

Cone of Silence
(BRITISH)

Sound, well-made drama of civil aircraft disasters, with excellent performances by George Sanders, Elizabeth Seal, Bernard Lee.

London, May 10.

British Lion release of a Aubrey Baring (Bryanston) production. Stars Michael Craig, Elizabeth Seal, Peter Cushing, Bernard Lee, George Sanders. Directed by Charles Frend. Screenplay by Robert Westerby from David Beaty's novel; camera, Arthur Grant; editor, Max Benedict; music, Gerald Schurmann. Previewed at 20th-Fox private theatre. Running time, **92 MINS.**

Captain Dallas .... Michael Craig
Captain Judd .... Peter Cushing
Captain Gort .... Bernard Lee
Charlotte Gort .... Elizabeth Seal
Sir Arnold Hobbes ...... George Sanders
Captain Manningham .... Andre Morell
Captain Bateson .... Gordon Jackson
Captain Braddock .... Charles Tingwell
Nigel Pickering .... Noel Willman
Joyce Mitchell .... Delphi Lawrence
Mr. Robinson .... Marne Maitland
First Officer .... William Abney
First Officer .... Jack Hedley
Navigator .... Simon Lack
Navigator .... Hedger Wallace
Steward .... Charles Mylne
Steward .... Howard Pays
Commissioner .... Ballard Berkeley
Commissioner .... Charles Lloyd Pack
Controller .... Homi Bode
Controller .... Anthony Newlands

Despite the attractive presence of Elizabeth Seal and Delphi Lawrence, "Cone Of Silence" is a bit short on glamor. It relies for its effectiveness on a sound basic idea and the clash of well-contrasted male personalities. This is likely to appeal more to male than femme filmgoers. It's an honest, absorbing pic which should have reasonable boxoffice potential.

Yarn concerns a veteran pilot who crashes a Phoenix jet airliner and is hauled before a Court of Inquiry, the question on the agenda being whether he is guilty of pilot error. He is found guilty, rapped over the knuckles and given a special test which he passes with honors. Nevertheless some highups still consider he is not fit to handle jets, especially when he again fatally crashes a plane. At a second Court of Inquiry, it comes down to a straight test of whether the pilot is at fault or whether the accidents are due to some flaw in the aircraft.

Only Miss Seal, playing the daughter, is really convinced of her father's innocence, but she convinces Michael Craig, playing a training officer. And between them, they manage to clear the pilot's name. Bernard Lee puts up a strong performance as the man on a spot. Craig, as the training officer, and Peter Cushing, convinced of Lee's guilt, provide sound contrasting acting.

Showiest role is that of George Sanders as the suave and deadly Queen's Counsel conducting the Courts of Inquiry. Sanders handles it with his usual aplomb. Miss Seal has been too tied up with the stage to do much screen work and more's the pity, for she shows in this one that she's got what it takes in the way of brains and personality.

Among an array of useful minor parts are those of Noel Willman, as a pompus aircraft designer, and Gordon Jackson and Charles Tingwell, as flying officers.

Charles Frend has directed with complete sureness of touch and flying effects. This plus slick lensing add greatly to the authenticity of the film. *Rich.*

Cannes Festival

Ballada O Soldatie
(Soldier's Ballad)
(RUSSIAN)

Cannes, May 17.

Mosfilm production and release. With Volodia Ivachov, Janna Prokhorenko, Anton Maximova, Nicolas Krioutchkov, Evgueni Ourbanski. Directed by Grigori Chukhray. Screenplay, V. Ejov, Chukhray; camera, V. Nikolaiev, E. Savelieva; editor, B. Nemetchek. At Cannes Film Fest. Running time, **85 MINS**

Soldier .... Volodia Ivachov
Girl .... Janna Prokhorenko
Mother .... Antonia Maximova
General .... Nicolas Krioutchkov
Wounded Man .... Evgueni Ourbanski

This film is in "The Cranes Are Flying" vein in that it is a war film done in a poetic style and a purported pacifistic outlook. It emerges a warm, simple film that could well be an art possibility abroad as well as possibly a more general entry.

It is tenuous but able to be sentimental without being mawkish. A 19-year-old Russian soldier, during the last war, is trapped by a couple of tanks which he manages to knock out in spite of his fear. He gets a four day pass and

sets out for his home to see his mother and fix the roof. But he gets into a series of adventures and manages to get home only for a few minutes to talk to his mother.

On this slim thread, the director has woven a series of tender sketches emphasizing the lurking terror, uselessness and hopelessness of war. It also shows that all Russo soldiers were not brave, that there were shirkers and that there were women who cheated on their husbands. But its main treatment is in a lyrical style with excellent camera work, direct acting and deft character blocking. This plus technical effects all combine to make this a touching pic.

Mosk.

The Young One
(MEXICAN—In English)
Cannes, May 17.

Olmec producton and release. Stars Zachary Scott; features Bernie Hamilton, Key Meersman, Grahan Denton, Claudio Brook. Directed by Luis Bunuel. Screenplay, H. B. Addis. Bunuel; camera, Gabriel Figueroa; editor, Carlos Savage. At Cannes Film Fest. Running time, 95 MINS.

Miller	Zachary Scott
Traver	Bernie Hamilton
Evalyn	Key Meersman
Jackson	Grahan Denton
Fleetwood	Claudio Brook

Made in Mexico, this still has the tang of a Yank film since it was written by an American screenwriter and directed by the widely known filmmaker, Luis Bunuel. It is a simple story that transcends its one locale and five characters to emerge a humane tale of people in crisis. Film deals in bigotry and emotional needs.

Its incisive, frank treatment of the Negro and the bigotted whites, and the relations between a 13-year-old girl and an older man, are explosive themes. But they are handled with an understanding which makes this an important human document besides being an extremely well-made and gripping film. This looks in for difficulty in the U.S. but could be of arty calibre for special situations and more general spotting in northern areas, with the south probably closed to it.

A laconic, middleaged man (Zachary Scott) lives on an island owned by some company off one of the South Atlantic states of the U.S. The 13-year-old girl lives with her grandfather, while in another shack, lives the handyman. But her grandfather's death has the two alone until a Negro arrives fleeing from a lynch crowd because suspected of rape.

The latter finds the girl alone while Scott (the handyman) is on the mainland. He gets food, a gun and gasoline from the girl, and he gives her money. Scott returns and tries to kill the Negro, but finds he had not molested the girl. He finally allows him to stay.

A series of complications arise as another man arrives with a church worker who wants to take the girl to a home. They bring news about a Negro wanted for rape and realize it is the one on the island. He is tracked down but finally freed when Scott is made to realize the Negro may be innocent. Then Scott affirms that he will marry the girl.

Bunuel has made this simple story in a masterful way and easily handles the characters and relations as well as notating everything with a firm technical grasp. It goes to the heart of bigotry. The scenes with the girl are done with taste.

This is an offbeater that will

have to be handled carefully. It is an unusual pic that might be worth the special effort. Film also looks in line for a prize at this festival.

Scott and fellow Yank Negro actor Bernie Hamilton are understanding and suited for their roles. The others in the small supporting cast of three are also well utilized and integrated into this fine pic.

Mosk.

Kagi
(The Key)
(JAPANESE—COLOR—C'SCOPE)
Cannes, May 17.

Daiei release of Masaichi Nagata production. Stars Machiko Kyo; features Ganjiro Nakamura, Junko Kano, Tatsuya Nakadai, Tanie Kitabayashi, Ichiro Sugai. Directed by Kon Ichikawa. Screenplay, Natto Wada, Keiji Hasebe, Ichikawa from book by Junichiro Tanizaki; camera (Agfa), Kazuo Miyagawa; editor, Hiroaki Fujii. At Cannes Film Fest. Running time, 107 MINS.

Ikuko	Machiko Kyo
Kenmochi	Ganjiro Nakamura
Toshiko	Junko Kano
Kimura	Tatsuya Nakadai
Hana	Tanie Kitabayashi
Massager	Ichiro Sugai

Warner Bros. has taken this unusual pic for distrib worldwide outside of Japan. This may prove a hot potato because this cold, dispassionate study of the sexual perversions of an aging man, and its disastrous effect on the weak, unpredictible people around him, could make ordinary audiences titter nervously. It remains an arty bet with special handling required.

This is enveloped in brilliant technical aspects and smart acting. Director Kon Ichikawa denotes a mastery of composition, the use of color and the spaciousness of C'Scope despite its confined, restricting theme. A respected, aging antique are specialist finds his sensual powers waning and his beautiful, younger wife becoming cold but still obedient to him. He makes his daughter's suitor a witness of his wife's drinking and fainting in hot baths.

But the wife is enamored of the youth, and finally leads to her husband's death by luring him on against doctor's orders.

The deft treatment, taste and firm control keep this from being scabrous. But the confines of the film and the overanalytical style do not bring the characters to full life. This is a difficult offbeater but might be worth the trouble as art tastes lean more and more towards the adult in the treatment of sex. English title for this obsessive pic is rightly "Odd Obsession."

Mosk.

Deveti Krug
(The Ninth Circle)
YUGOSLAVIAN
Cannes, May 17.

Jadran Film production and release. With Dusica Zegarac, Ervina Dragman, Boris Dvornik. Directed by France Stiglig. Screenplay, Zora Direnbach; camera, Ivan Marincek; editor, Zeljko Zagota. At Cannes Film Fest. Running time, 104 MINS.

Ruth	Dusica Zegarac
Iwo	Borie Dvornik
Makdo	Desnaka-Beba Loncar
Zvonko	Dragan Milojevic

Film concerns a young Jewish girl hidden by the gentile friends of her family when they are all deported during the last war. To help her, they arrange a marriage of reason to their young son. It leads to final love between them which is ultimately destroyed because of the madness, cruelty and horror of the times. This oft-treated theme bears repetition, especially when it is done with the tact, talent and moderation which this pic gets.

Sombre tale manages to adroitly tell a story of growing love and human consciousness. The boy finds he loves the girl but she is finally caught and deported when she goes out alone.

The characters are well drawn and it makes its case well by astute observation and progression. The bravura action at the end somewhat mars the pic but it looms a possible art film entry abroad, with hard sell and proper handling needed. It is not grim but is treated soberly in technical aspects and the acting is simple and unaffected. Title is the name of a concentration camp where the girl is sent.

Mosk.

Paw
(DANISH-COLOR)
Cannes, May 17.

Laterna Films production and release. With Jimmy Sterman, Edvin Adolphson, Sacha Wamberg, Asbjorn Andersen, Ninja Thostrup. Directed by Astrid Henning-Jensen. Screenplay, Bjarne and Astrid Henning-Jensen; camera (Eastmancolor), Henning Bendtsen; editor, Henning-Jensen. At Cannes Film Fest. Running time, 100 MINS.

Paw	Jimmy Sterman
Anders	Edvin Adolphson
Count	Sacha Wamberg
Daughter	Asbjorn Andersen
Aunt	Ninja Tholstrup

Film concerns a boy fathered by a Danish father with an Indian mother in the Antilles. Lad is returned to Denmark to stay with an aunt in a little town. Pic is made with entertainment appeal via a positive attitude towards human nature.

This looms a good moppet vehicle on its adventurous tale. It also holds appeal for adult audiences. The boy is enamored of nature but runs into bigotry at school, with his one refuge among the animals. He escapes from an orphanage and lives in the forest until all is resolved.

The nature work is excellent, the boy's life in the woods and with the animals is the best part of the pic. Color is good and acting natural with director Astrid Henning-Jensen getting knowing performances from the children. Technical assets are also positive. This is a fresh film with okay playoff probable.

Mosk.

Jakten
(The Chasers)
(NORWEGIAN)
Cannes, May 17.

ABC Film production and release. With Benedikte Liseth, Rolf Soder, Tor Stokke. Written and directed by Erik Lochen. Camera, Tore Breda Thoresen; editor, Jan Erik During. At Cannes Film Fest. Running time, 94 MINS.

Guri	Benedikte Liseth
Bjorn	Rolf Soder
Knut	Tor Stokke

A slight tale of a husband and wife whose best friend tries to win over the wife is puffed up out of all proportion in this slow moving pic. It mixes interior dialog, asides to the audience, etc.

In a dream the measured, slow progression might be acceptable but, in all, this emerges a fairly arty affair with limited foreign chances. Technical credits are acceptable. Acting is fair in spite of the lack of characterization and smothering via over-elaborate direction and too much of close-ups.

Mosk.

Tchien Gnu You Houn
(The Enchanting Shadow)
(FORMASAN—COLOR)
Cannes, May 17.

Shaw Ltd. production and release. With Lo Tin, Chao Lei, Yang Chih-Ching, Marguerite Tong Jo-Ching, Li Kuo-Hua.

Directed by Li Han-Hsiang. Screenplay, Wang Yueh-Ting; camera (Eastmancolor), Ho Lu-Ying; editor, Chen Chi-Jui. At Cannes Film Fest. Running time, 85 MINS.

Traveler	Lo Tin
Girl	Chao Lei
Yen	Yang Chih-Ching
Phantom	Marguerite Tong Jo-Ching

Ghost story is about a traveler who helps free the phantom of a dead girl from the hands of an evil sorceress. The defeat of the witch reincarnates the girl for a happy ending, with love triumphing over all. It is simply done and manages to keep fairly engrossing throughout because of its lack of pretention and the appeal of a good ghost tale. This lacks the depth, pacing and level for any untoward art or general chances abroad, but might be a natural for lingo circuits.

Color is good and the acting and costuming are just right for this naive supernatural tale. The director has paced this well and it unfolds smoother than most Formosan pix seen at festivals.

Mosk.

Wild River
(C'SCOPE—COLOR)

Outstanding screen achievement, largely because of Elia Kazan's indelible stamp. Word-of-mouth should exert strong b.o. pull.

Hollywood, May 18.

Twentieth-Fox release of Elia Kazan production. Stars Montgomery Clift, Lee Remick; costars Jo Van Fleet; with Albert Salmi, Jay C. Flippen, James Westerfield, Barbara Loden, Frank Overton, Malcolm Atterbury, Robert Earl Jones, Bruce Dern. Directed by Kazan. Screenplay, Paul Osborn, based on novels by William Bradford Huie and Borden Deal; camera, Ellsworth Fredricks; editor, William Reynolds; art directors, Lyle R. Wheeler, Herman A. Blumenthal; music, Kenyon Hopkins; assistant director, Charles Maguire. Reviewed at the studio, May 18, '60. Running time, **115 MINS.**

Chuck Glover .... Montgomery Clift
Carol .... Lee Remick
Ella Garth .... Jo Van Fleet
Hank Bailey .... Albert Salmi
Hamilton Garth .... Jay C. Flippen
Cal Garth .... James Westerfield
Betty Jackson .... Barbara Loden
Walter Clark .... Frank Overton
Sy Moore .... Malcolm Atterbury
Ben .... Robert Earl Jones
Jack Roper .... Bruce Dern

"Wild River" is an important motion picture. In studying a slice of national socio-economic progress (the Tennessee Valley Authority of the early '30's) in terms of people (those who enforced vs. those who resisted), it has caught something timeless and essential in the human spirit and shaped it in the American image. Since producer-director Elia Kazan has accomplished this with cinematic mastery, the 20th-Fox release, in spite of the absence of surefire marquee allure, will generate comment along the lines of Academy Award speculation and, resultantly, should whip up a hot boxoffice.

Sturdy foundation for Kazan's artistic indulgences and a number of exceptional performances is Paul Osborn's thought-provoking screenplay, erected out of two novels, "Mud on the Stars" by William Bradford Huie, and "Dunbar's Cove" by Borden Deal. It is the tragic tale of an 80-year-old "rugged individualist" (Jo Van Fleet) who refuses to give ground (a small island on the Tennessee River smack dab in TVA's dam-building path) to an understanding, but equally firm, TVAgent (Montgomery Clift). In the process of successfully separating the grand old lady from her precious, but doomed, slice of real estate, Clift gets into several scrapes with the local Tennessee bigots over his decent treatment of Negroes and squeezes sufficient romance into his tight schedule to wind up the spouse of the old woman's pretty granddaughter (Lee Remick).

Where the film soars is in its clean, objective approach to the basic conflict between progress and tradition ("electricity and souls," as Osborn puts it). Through this gentle veil of objectivity, a point-of-view unmistakably stirs, but never emerges to the point where it takes sides just to be taking sides. The result is that rare element of tragedy, in the truly classical sense of the word, where an indomitable individual eventually must fall helpless prey to an irresistible, but impersonal edict designed for universal good.

If there is a flaw, it is in relative emphasis. Too much of the film centers on the romantic story at the expense of the stronger central issue, but this is not overly damaging.

It is Kazan's direction that brings the film its special, unforgettable qualities. With cameraman Ellsworth Fredricks, he has created a number of indelible pictorial images, including a striking newsreelesque opening. Under his direction, incidental characters (many of them non-pro Tennessee folk) convey a natural, casual air rarely captured in films. And from his principals Kazan clearly has coaxed all the talent and integrity they can offer their roles.

Miss Van Fleet steals the show with a magnificent portrayal of the aged holdout, a performance with "Oscar" written all over it. Close behind is Miss Remick, whose splendid work in a difficult role establishes her as one of the most gifted young actresses in films today. Clift, although burdened with the stigma of glassy-eyed "sensitivity," a characteristic with which he unfortunately has become identified, gives a performance of merit, an intensive delineation of a man devoted to duty but aware of the gravity and responsibility of his assignment. A standout in support is Albert Salmi, backed up by consistently fine work from Barbara Loden, Jay C. Flippen, James Westerfield, Frank Overton, Malcolm Atterbury, Robert Earl Jones and Bruce Dern.

To single out but a few of the invaluable departmental contributions to this memorable film, there is the stimulating music by Kenyon Hopkins, the sure, steady editing of William Reynolds, the vivid sound work of Eugene Grossman and Richard Vorisek, the De Luxe color artistry supervised by Leonard Doss, and art direction by Lyle R. Wheeler and Herman A. Blumenthal that has distinctively captured the mood and flavor of America in the '30's. *Tube.*

Strangers When We Meet
(C'SCOPE—COLOR)

Handsomely filmed but vapid exploration of suburban marriage-on-the-rocks. Strong marquee names make good b.o. likely.

Hollywood, May 19.

Columbia Pictures release of Bryna-Quine production. Stars Kirk Douglas, Kim Novak, Ernie Kovacs, Barbara Rush; features Walter Matthau, Virginia Bruce, Kent Smith, Helen Gallagher; with John Bryant, Roberta Shore, Nancy Kovack, Carol Douglas, Paul Picerni, Ernest Sarracino, Harry Jackson, Bart Patton, Robert Sampson, Ray Ferrell, Douglas Holmes, Timmy Molina, Sue Ane Langdon. Producer and directed by Richard Quine. Screenplay, Evan Hunter, based on his novel; camera, Charles Lang Jr.; editor, Charles Nelson; art director, Ross Bellah; music, George Duning; assistant director, Carter De Haven Jr. Reviewed at the studio, May 19, '60. Running time, **117 MINS.**

Larry Coe .... Kirk Douglas
Maggie Gault .... Kim Novak
Rober Altar .... Ernie Kovacs
Eve Coe .... Barbara Rush
Felix Anders .... Walter Matthau
Mrs. Wagner .... Virginia Bruce
Stanley Baxter .... Kent Smith
Betty Anders .... Helen Gallagher
Ken Gault .... John Byrant
Linda Harder .... Roberta Shore
Marcia .... Nancy Kovack
Honey Blonde .... Carol Douglas
Gerandi .... Paul Picerni
Di Labbia .... Ernest Sarracino
Bud Ramsey .... Harry Jackson
Hank .... Bart Patton
Bucky .... Robert Sampson
David Coe .... Ray Ferrell
Peter Coe .... Douglas Holmes
Patrick Gault .... Timmy Molina

A pictorially attractive but dramatically vacuous study of modern-style infidelity, "Strangers When We Meet" is easy on the eyes but hard on the intellect. Nevertheless, the Columbia release has a boxoffice look about it, mostly on the basis of its star-studded cast.

A bunch of maladjusted suburbanites are thrown together in Evan Hunter's screenplay (from his novel), and what comes out is an old-fashioned soap opera. Brilliant architect Kirk Douglas is upset because his spouse, Barbara Rush, is overly concerned with balancing the family budget. Meanwhile, housewife Kim Novak is disturbed over being taken for granted by her undersexed mate, John Bryant. Out of this germ of marital instability, a feverishly passionate affair blossoms between Douglas and Miss Novak via a series of trysts. But unstable, sharp-eyed neighbor Walter Matthau, putting two and two together and coming up with an odd number, decides to even things up by getting into the act; promptly puts in a clumsy, unsuccessful pitch for some extra-curricular sexual attention from the wronged Miss Rush. Apparently learning his lesson from this display of moral fiber by his spouse, Douglas discontinues his pursuit of happiness with Miss Novak, returns home to his better half and kiddies. Miss Novak, it is assumed, is doing likewise.

It is a rather pointless, slow-moving story, but it has been brought to the screen with such photographic and atmospheric skill by producer-director Richard Quine and his battery of CinemaScopic experts that it charms the spectator into an attitude of relaxed enjoyment, much the same effect as that produced by a casual daydream fantasy. Most noteworthy assists to Quine in achieving this veneer of quality come from Charles Lang Jr.'s agile, energetically-angled camera setups and Ross Bellah's striking art direction, the latter's principally in his co-design with Carl Anderson of an interesting hilltop house that is in the process of erection throughout the picture. Editing by Charles Nelson is sharp, music by George Duning suitably romantic, and the Eastman color is positively hypnotic.

Douglas does well by his role, and Miss Novak brings to hers that cool, up-to-date, style-setting attitude that has become her trademark. Ernie Kovacs' sole function is to supply comedy relief and, being a gifted actor-comic, he does extremely well by some pallid material. Miss Rush gives a believable account of herself as the maltreated mate. Among the supporting players, most effective work is turned in by Virginia Bruce, with capable assistance from Matthau, Kent Smith, Helen Gallagher, Bryant, Roberta Shore, Paul Picerni, Ernest Sarracino, Harry Jackson, Bart Patton, Robert Sampson and moppets Ray Ferrell, Douglas Holmes and Timmy Molina, plus amusing bits by Nancy Kovack and Sue Ane Langdon. *Tube.*

Sons and Lovers
(C'SCOPE—BRITISH)

Conscientious adaptation of D. H. Lawrence's famous novel; needs careful promotion for maximum results.

20th-Fox release of a Jerry Wald production. Stars Trevor Howard, Dean Stockwell, Wendy Hiller, Heather Sears, Mary Ure. Directed by Jack Cardiff. Screenplay, Gavin Lambert and T. E. B. Clarke, based on D. H. Lawrence's novel; camera Freddie Francis. Reviewed at 1960 Cannes Film Fest. Running time, **99 MINS.**

Morel .... Trevor Howard
Paul Morel .... Dean Stockwell
Mrs. Morel .... Wendy Hiller
Clara Dawes .... Mary Ure
Miriam .... Heather Sears
William .... William Lucas
Baxter Dawes .... Conrad Phillips
Pappleworth .... Donald Pleasance
Hadlock .... Ernest Thesiger
Louisa .... Rosalie Crutchley
Mrs. Leivers .... Ruth Dunning
Mrs. Radford .... Elizabeth Begley
Mrs. Anthony .... Edna Morris
Mrs. Bonner .... Ruth Kettlewell
Rose .... Ann Sheppard
Arthur .... Sean Barrett
Doctor Ansell .... Philip Ray
Betty S .... Susan Travers
Fanny .... Dorothy Gordon
Polly .... Sheila Bernette
Collie .... Vilma Ann Leslie

Jerry Wald's production of "Sons and Lovers" was the official British entry at the Cannes Fest, and certainly did not let the side down. It is a well-made and conscientious adaptation of D. H. Lawrence's famed novel, smoothly directed by Jack Cardiff and superbly acted by a notable cast. By the very nature of the subject, however, the pic will call for thoughtful promotion to insure maximum returns in the U.S.

Gavin Lambert and T. E. B. Clarke have collaborated in producing a literate screenplay, though not entirely recapturing the atmosphere of the Nottinghamshire mining village so vividly described in the original. Also, there has been a tendency to portray the mother as an overly selfish, possessive and nagging woman. And even Wendy Hiller's flawless performance cannot make her a sympathetic character.

Many of the exteriors were filmed on location outside Nottingham, and their authenticity is a plus factor. Against the background of the grimy mining village is unfolded the story of a miner's son with promising artistic talents, who is caught up in continual conflict between his forthright father and possessive mother. Because of the overpowering maternal influences, he sacrifices a chance to study art in London, gives up the local farm girl he loves, and eventually becomes entangled with a married woman separated from her husband.

Easily the outstanding feature of the production is the powerful performance by Trevor Howard, as the miner. Always a polished actor, Howard has rarely been better, giving a moving and wholly believable study of a man equally capable of tenderness as he is of being tough. He looks the character, too. Rean Stockwell puts up a good showing as the son, and makes a valiant try to cope with the accent.

Miss Hiller's professionalism is always in evidence in her interpretation of the mother. Mary Ure is first class as the married woman while Heather Sears hits the right note of sincerity as the young girl who is taught to be ashamed of love. There is excellent support, too, from the big cast, notably Conrad Phillips, William Lucas, Donald Pleasance, Ernest Thesiger and Rosalie Crutchley.

Technically, the pic is first-rate. Jack Cardiff, who alternates between directing and lensing, has taken fullest advantage of the black-and-white CinemaScope screen, aided by Freddie Francis' excellent camerawork, and fluent editing. *Myro.*

Oscar Wilde
(BRITISH)

Stimulating court scenes in this honest, compelling story of the tragic downfall of the homosexual poet-playwright. Sound b.o. proposition.

London, May 20.

20th-Fox release of a Vantage production. Stars Robert Morley, Ralph Rich-

ardson, Phyllis Calvert, Alexander Knox, John Neville. Producer, William Kirby. Director, Gregory Ratoff. Screenplay, Jo Eisinger; camera, Georges Perinal; editor, Tony Gibbs; music, Kenneth V. Jones. At Carlton Theatre, London, May 22, '60. Running time, **98 MINS**

Oscar Wilde .... Robert Morley
Constance Wilde .... Phyllis (
Lord Alfred Douglas......John Neville
Sir Edward Carson .... Ralph Richardson
Robert Ross .... Dennis Price
Sir Edgar Clarke.........Alexander Knox
Marquis of Queensberry
Edward Chapman
George Alexander .... Martin Benson
Justice Henn Collins.......Robert Harris
Justice Wills .... Henry Oscar
Solicitor-General........ William Devlin
Cobble .... Stephen Dartnell
Lionel Johnson........Ronald Leigh-Hunt
Inspector Richards........ Martin Boddy
Richard Legalliene........Leonard Sachs
Clerk of Arraigns............Tom Chatto

There's been a neck and neck race between two film companies to come in first with the story of Oscar Wilde, the poet-playwright-wit whose tragic downfall on homosexual charges was a scandal in Victorian times. In an atmosphere of legal hassle Vantage Productions (release by 20th-Fox) and Viceroy Films for Warwick Productions (release by Eros) have battled it out and the black-and-white version of Vantage has hit the screens just five days before Warwick's color job. While it is doubtful if two versions of the Wilde story are strictly necessary it has provided a useful boxoffice talking point and stimulated interest in both.

The black and white film, here under review, was produced swiftly but shows no signs of technical shoddiness, even though it was being edited up to a couple of hours before screening for the press. Georges Perinal's lensing is effective and the atmosphere of Victorian London, Paris and the court scenes has been faithfully caught. Jo Eisenger has produced a literate screenplay in which he has drawn heavily on both Wilde's own epigrams and wisecracks but also on the actual documented evidence in the two celebrated court cases.

The picture starts unsatisfactorily but comes vividly to life when the court proceedings begin. The opening sequences are very sketchy and merely set the scene of Wilde as a celebrated playwright and his first meeting with the handsome father-hating young Lord Alfred Douglas, an association which was to prove his downfall. Eisinger is content merely to use Wilde's epigrams to suggest that he was a man of wit, but the character of Wilde is, early on, insufficiently rounded off, so that the subsequent downfall of the man does not compel sufficient understanding or compassion.

But the film sparks off from the moment Wilde is accused by Lord Alfred's father of "posing as a sodomite" and is unwisely baited into suing the Marquis of Queensberry for criminal libel. The court sequences make excellent screen drama. First, the merciless breaking down of Wilde by cross examination so that the libel case has to be stopped. Then the subsequent trial of Wilde on a charge of gross indecency which led to him getting two years' hard labor and the subsequent withering of his career in Paris.

Gregory Ratoff, as director, swiftly gets into his stride after the aforesaid uneasy start and, though the film is over-talky and over-stagey, it is a good and interesting job of work. Until the "rival" film is shown in a few days time it is impossible to make comparisons but there are certain performances which will need a great deal of brilliance to surpass.

Robert Morley, who once made an effective stage Oscar Wilde, looks perhaps a little too old for the role but he gives a very shrewd performance, not only in the rich relish with which he delivers Wilde's bon mots but also in the almost frighteningly pathetic way in which he crumbles and wilts in the dock. The final sequence when, in a Paris bistro, he sums up the tragedy of his life is most moving. Morley gives the role stature, dignity and pathos.

Sir Ralph Richardson is also in memorable form as the brilliant Queen's Counsel, Sir Edward Carson, who mercilessly strips Wilde in court with his penetrating questions. This is one of the most subtle and intelligent performances seen for many years. Only the less worthy because of more limited opportunity is the quiet thesping of Alexander Knox as Wilde's counsel.

John Neville makes his screen debut as the handsome, hedonistic Lord Alfred Douglas who used Wilde as a weapon in a savage family row against his father. He is also a little too old for the role but he does as well as is probably possible with such a difficult part. Dennis Price is charmingly convincing as Wilde's most loyal friend and Phyllis Calvert pleasantly handles the shadowy part of Wilde's faithful, bewildered wife. As the truculent, vindictive Marquis of Queensberry Edward Chapman pulls out all the stops and at times makes the figure a caricature. Robert Harris, William Devlin and Martin Benson also turn in minor but useful contributions.

Oscar Wilde is now only a legendary figure to many film goers, especially the younger generation, but he was a man of great personality and ability and the story of his downfall by homosexuality, caused mainly through his supreme egotism, is a compelling one. In this instance it has been presented with integrity, tact and good taste and the verbal duel between Morley and Richardson is alone well worth the price of a ducat. *Rich.*

The Day They Robbed The Bank of England
(BRITISH)

Sound crook yarn, devoid of comedy, and moving a little too slowly in early stages; fair booking for routine houses.

London, May 17.

Metro release of a (Jules Buck) Summit film. Stars Aldo Ray; features Elizabeth Sellars, Peter O'Toole, Hugh Griffith, Kieron Moore, Albert Sharpe. Directed by John Guillermin. Screenplay by Howard Clewes from John Brophy's novels adapted by Howard Clewes, Richard Maibum; camera, Georges Perinal; editor, Frank Clarke. At Liecester Square Theatre, London. Running time, **85 MINS.**

Norgate .... Aldo Ray
Iris Muldoon .... Elizabeth Sellars
O'Shea .... Hugh Griffith
Fitch .... Peter O'Toole
Walsh .... Kieron Moore
Tosher .... Albert Sharpe
Green .... John Le Mesurier
Cohoun .... Joseph Tomelty
Dr. Hagen .... Wolf Frees
Asst. Curator .... Miles Malleson
Gamekeeper .... Michael Golden
Piers .... Peter Myers

Odd how legend eventually becomes fact in the minds of some people. "The Day They Robbed The Bank of England" is based on just such a legend. There's never been any real evidence that the Bank of England ever did get looted but, one way and another, the story's been built up. Jules Buck's imagination was fired by conversation, reading and research. The result is a sound but not wholly convincing drama which will satisfy easily pleased tab buyers in average houses. There are some useful performers in the pic but not enough stellar value to help much. Maybe it's just as well because theatre managers will find the title itself rather cumbersome to use on marquees.

The story, certainly more fiction than fact, has Aldo Ray leading a bunch of Irish patriots in a 1901 raid on the Bank's bullion vaults to raise money for their struggle for Home Rule. By conscientious planning and by hefty physical labor in a disused sewer running below the bank, they practically pull off the job. But they are foiled by the Guards officer whose job is to protect the gold bars from robbers. The story unwinds very laboriously, having little of the suspense and thrill needed for this sort of farfetched crook yarn. Worse, it is practically devoid of wit or urgent dialog. John Guillermin has directed in a painstaking manner which, for long stretches of the film, is practically documentary. Georges Perinal has contributed some useful photography and the artwork is sound.

Though the cast goes through with their chores soundly, it is mainly a losing battle. It is difficult, in the first place, to take Aldo Ray, the American who's the brains of the plot seriously. Ray is excellent in later scenes when physical strength is needed to carry out the robbery, but he never impresses as a thinker.

Most interesting of the performances is from one of Britain's newest and best young actors, Peter O'Toole, as the Guards officer who unwittingly helps Ray and then unmasks him. But here again O'Toole is too intelligent to be convincing as a goof of a Guards officer, and he becomes the thinker far too glibly. Nevertheless, O'Toole has style and authority, and clearly is going to be a major acting property in films.

Elizabeth Sellars has a few moments as an Irish widow for whom Ray has an eye beyond the calls of bank-robbery duty but she gets little scope to develop the character. Hugh Griffith, Miles Malleson, Joseph Tomelty and John Le Mesurier make brief, but not very rewarding appearances. Kieron Moore plays a sulky, hotheaded member of the gang with the air of a man who remembers that recently he appeared in a far slicker bank robbery film. Wolf Frees is suitably enigmatic as the mathematical brains of the operation. Some much needed wry humor is contributed by Albert Sharpe as an old drunk.

More tenseness, more twists, more wit and more pace are needed in this good idea gone wrong, seemingly in the scriptwriting department. *Rich.*

The Electronic Monster

Passable lower-berth meller with a commercial sci-fi twist.

Hollywood, May 19.

Columbia Pictures release of Alec C. Snowden production. Stars Rod Cameron, Mary Murphy; features Meredith Edwards, Peter Illing, Carl Jaffe, Kay Callard, Carl Duering, Robert Huby; with Felix Felton, Larry Cross, Carlo Borelli, John McCarthy, Jacques Cey, Armande Guinle, Malou Pantera, Pat Clavin, Alan Gifford. Directed by Montgomery Tully. Screenplay, Charles Eric Maine; camera, Bert Mason; editor, Geoffrey Muller; art director, Wilfred Arnold; assistant director, Peter Crowhurst. Reviewed at the studio, May 19, '60. Running time, **72 MINS.**

Jeff Keenan .... Rod Cameron
Ruth Vance .... Mary Murphy
Doctor Maxwell........Meredith Edwards
Paul Zakon .... Peter Illing
Doctor Hoff ....Carl Jaffe
Laura Maxwell .... Kay Callard
Blore .... Carl Duering
Verna Berteaux .... Roberta Huby
Commissaire .... Felix Felton
Brad Somers .... Larry Cross
Signore Kallini .... Carlo Borelli
Claude Denver .... John McCarthy
French Doctor .... Jacques Cey
French Farmer .... Armande Guinle
Receptionist .... Malou Pantera
Receptionist .... Pat Clavin
Wayne .... Alan Gifford

"The Electronic Monster" offers one or two novel twists to an old cinema standby, the one about the diabolical scientist-sorcerer who creates disciples by toying with human brains. Since modern audiences seem intrigued with dramati-clinical sorties into the mysteries of the human thought mechanism, the Columbia release generates a certain pseudo-scientific appeal that should qualify it for comfortable second-billing. Outside of this quality and the fact that it has been produced with cinematic skill, it's a strictly routine melodrama.

Charles Eric Maine's screenplay dispatches an American insurance investigator (Rod Cameron) to Europe to investigate the mysterious death of a matinee idol. His snooping leads him to a psychotherapy clinic where "people who want to get away from life for awhile" undergo short or longterm (as long as six weeks at a clip) electronic hypnosis during which they are filed away in cabinets to dream via controlled, tape-recorded electronic stimuli. What Cameron discovers is that the Nazi-inspired owner of the clinic is altering the dreams into nightmares to suit his own evil, empire-building purposes. Needless to say, Cameron brings that nonsense to an abrupt halt, although since the police aren't interested he must do it single-handedly.

The dream sequences give the picture a curious dash of sex. As the coldstorage subjects sleep, they dream of scantily-clad femmes (uniform of the day; Freudian slips) prancing about and smooching with bare-chested males as the clinic-owner choreographs the fantasy. These scenes, directed by David Paltenghi and lensed by Teddy Catford, give the film an extra exploitable aspect.

Cameron is coolly competent in the pivotal role. Mary Murphy adeptly supplies romantic interest, and there is a fine performance by Meredith Edwards as a good scientist trapped in the wicked scheme. Others who contribute gamely are Peter Illing, Carl Jaffe, Kay Callard, Carl Duering, Roberta Huby, Felix Felton, Larry Cross, Carlo Borelli and John McCarthy.

Montgomery Tully's direction is efficient, and so are Bert Mason's camera work, Geoffrey Muller's editing and Wilfred Arnold's art direction. Electronic music by Soundrama provides appropriate bridges and accents to the drama. *Tube.*

The Challenge

Routine meller with useful star value in Jayne Mansfield and some brisk excitement in the climax.

London, May 17.

Rank release of a (John Timple-Smith) Alliance production. Stars Jayne Mansfield, Carl Mohner, Anthony Quayle. Direction, story and screenplay by John

Gilling. Camera, Gordon Dines; editor, John V. Smith; music, Bill McGuffie. At Odeon, Marble Arch, London. Running time, 93 MINS

Billy	Jayne Mansfield
Jim	Anthony Quayle
Kristy	Carl Mohner
Buddy	Peter Reynolds
Spider	John Bennett
Ma Piper	Barbara Mullen
Joey	Peter Pike
Bob Crowther	Robert Brown
Inspector Willis	Dermot Welsh
Det. Sgt. Gittens	Edward Judd
Rick	John Stratton
Max	Patrick Holt
Mrs. Rick	Lorraine Clewes
Shop Steward	Percy Herbert
Stripteaser	Liane Marelli
Nightclub pianist	Bill McGuffie
Dr. Westerley	Lloyd Lamble
School inspector	John Wood
Landlord	Arthur Brough
Ticket collector	Wally Patch
Sergeant	Bryan Pringle
Hostess	Marigold Russell
Foreman	Victor Brooks
Farm laborer	Bill Shine
Lorry drive	Richard Shaw
Policeman	David Davenport

This is a fairly conventional melodrama but, though it won't advance Jayne Mansfield's career overmuch, her presence in the cast, together with Anthony Quayle, Carl Mohner and some reliable British stock actors, should make it a useful b.o. prospect. It isn't easy to see why Miss Mansfield should have elected to stay on in Britain to appear in this film. It can only be brought that the role sounded meatier than it has turned out.

The blonde thesp, disguised in the early stages with a black wig, plays the ruthless leader of a gang of crooks. She is handicapped by some of the corny dialog usually associated with second-rate Hollywood crook mellers. But she manages to be persuasive enough to entice an infatuated widower (Anthony Quayle) to join in a large-scale bullion raid and stash away the loot while Miss Mansfield decoys the police.

However, Quayle is caught and goes to the cooler for five years. He emerges bitter and things don't look any more pleasant to him when he finds that in his enforced absence the gang have become prosperous and that Miss Mansfield has transferred her affections to another member of the gang (Carl Mohner).

The yarn then hinges on Quayle's attempts to keep the money, so that he can bring up his young son respectably, and the gang's determination to get it from him. The moll-leader has now lost most of her influence and can't restrain the gang from snatching Quayle's kid to force his hand. The leisurely film builds up to a brisk climax when the father and the police are just in time (natch!) to prevent the child's murder.

"The Challenge" suffers because it doesn't gather momentum fast enough and the story line is spasmodic and loosely contrived. Only Quayle, of the principal characters, emerges as much more than a cardboard figure and he gives a good performance of stolid determination and fear. Miss Mansfield does little for her role though she seems happier in the later sequences than as the tough gang leader. She also breathes the title song in a nightclub sequence and it is only fair to the composer, Bill McGuffie, to admit that as Miss Mansfield renders the ditty the lyric is strictly expendable. Carl Mohner occasionally registers as the tough member of the gang. Peter Reynolds is okay as the sadistic one who handles the child, pleasantly played by Peter Pike.

Dermot Walsh and Edward Judd handle the cops' roles soundly. Others who contribute useful performances are Lorraine Clewes, John Bennett and Barbara Mullen, very effective as Quayle's distraught mother. Settings are good and Gordon Dines has turned in some striking lensing particularly in the night shots.

John V. Smith's editing is often jerky and John Gillin has directed his own screenplay soundly but sluggishly at first and with insufficient thrills. *Rich.*

Never On Sunday
(GREEK)
(In English)

Cannes, May 17.

United Artists release of Melina Film production. Stars Melina Mercouri, Jules Dassin; features Georges Foundas, Titos Vandis, Mitsos Liguisos, Despo Diamantidou. Written and directed by Jules Dassin. Camera, Jacques Natteau; editor, Roger Dwyre; music, Manos Hadjikaris. At Cannes Film Fest. Running time, 97 MINS.

Ilya	Melina Mercouri
Homer	Jules Dassin
Tonio	Georges Foundas
Jorgo	Titos Vandis
Captain	Mitsos Liguisos
Despo	Despo Diamantidou
Ashcan	Dimos Starrenios

United Artists has a catchy comedy in this philosophical romp about an intellectual but prudish American who tries to reform a jolly Greek prostitute. It has some fine scenery and elicits enough entertainment, plus a colorful offbeat locale, to make this a probable overseas bet.

Though having no names, pic serves to establish Greek actress Melina Mercouri who might well become an international star via her work in this pic. Miss Mercouri has a temperament that comes over well. Although no beauty, she has a definite allure and finely planed face that goes well with the camera. She displays an excellent range. It is a brilliant execution of a larger than life character which is the anchor and very reason for the pic.

Yank director Jules Dassin also wrote and played the feckless American who almost ruins the life of this contented woman, and the simple people around her. Dassin is better with his behind-the-camera work because he does not quite instill the right note of naivete into his role. But he is adequate, with the Greek actors all natural and effective in other parts.

The Yank is a Greek buff who decides that this attractive joy girl is the symbol of the fall of ancient Greece since the senses and feelings have taken all precedence over the mind and spirit. He persistently keeps after her and finally gets her to agree to a twoweek experiment in which he will open her eyes to the better things in life. Her friends sadly stand by while she gives up her work and busies herself with improving her gray matter. But habit has her resuming her regular ways soon enough.

All is resolved and there is a hint that maybe love will save her from the oldest profession while the Yank goes home chastened. Dassin has given this a light touch and managed to keep the theme simple and not too cluttered except for some pat bits of business during her transformation.

The racy, jangling music score, with the local instruments, the bazookies, is also an asset. Technical credits are good. The tactful treatment should probably avoid any possible censorship troubles. Film is mainly in English with some Greek talk bits. *Mosk.*

Cannes Festival

Dama S Sobatchkoi
(The Woman With the Dog)
(RUSSIAN)

Cannes, May 24.

Lenfilm production and release. With Alexis Batalov, Ia Sawina, Ala Chostakowa. Written and directed by Josef Heifitz from a story by Anton Checkhov. Camera, Andrei Moskvine; editor, D. Meskhiev. At Cannes Film Fest. Running time, 90 MINS.

Gourav	Alexis Batalov
Woman With Dog	Ia Sawina
Wife	Ala Chostakowa

To commemorate the 100th anni of the birth of the playwright-novelist-story writer Anton Checkhov, the Russians have come up with a perfectly transcribed version of one of his short stories. The mood is faithfully rendered and it emerges a film possibly good for are situations abroad. But it is limited because of its delicate style and deliberate slowness. It might also be a good university film.

When more specialized fare has its place in the U.S., this would loom a good entry. It concerns the Russia of the 1900's where the upper and middle classes were bored but where propriety stifled any chance of escape.

A married man meets a married woman during a stay in Yalta. They have an affair and part. So he goes to see her again. She then comes to visit him in his town, but they know there is no way out of their impasse. Subtle direction evokes the inner states of the characters, and shows boredom without being boring.

Lensing is virtually perfect in bringing out the gray somnolent aspects of the Russia of the times. The feelings are intermingled with fine acceptable visual metaphors. Director Josef Heifitz has not tried to impose a personal viewpoint and wisely kept the full feeling of the Checkhov tale. It is a successful pic, but somewhat too talky and slow for general chances abroad. *Mosk.*

Zesowate Szczescie
(Cockeyed Happiness)
(POLISH)

Cannes, May 24.

Polski State Film production and release. With Bogumil Kobiela, Barbara Wwiatkowska, Edward Dziewonski. Directed by Andrzej Munk. Screenplay, Jerzy Stawinski; camera, Jerzy Lipman; editor, Jadwiga Zajicek. At Cannes Film Fest. Running time, 120 MINS

Piszczyk	Bogumil Kobiela
Yula	Barbara Kyiatkowski
Warden	Edward Dziewonski
Prisoner	Tadeusz Janczar

This film is the odyssey of a little man through the Poland of 1930 to 1950. It shows his attempts to cope with a changing world which seems to have no place for him. He has no consciousness of any kind but is always on the verge of turning into a more coherent human being only to be slapped down. It is a deft satirical affair that may have some more meaning for Poles. However, pic has an overall comic vein and knowing treatment that could make this a possible arty bet with some shearing.

It begins with the man's childhood. Then comes his first love marred by his unwitting embroilment in fascist politics, his being taken for a Jew because of his nose, his decision to join the army to charm girls, the war and his capture, and a nervous breakdown with a final plea to stay in the sanatorium where he has found some surcease.

Director Andrzej Munk keeps up his probing through the whole piece, aided by the expert acting of Bogumil Kobiela, as the little man. This is a witty, revealing epic comedy that could have foreign following if tightened and handled well on its theme and general offbeat tenure. Technical credits are good and a fine supporting cast helps Bogumil Kobiela's tour de force playing. *Mosk.*

L'Avventura
(The Adventure)
(ITALIAN)

Cannes, May 24.

Cino Del Duca release of PCE production. Stars Gabriele Ferzetti, Monica Vitti. Lea Massari; features Dominique Blanchar, James Addams, Renzo Ricci, Esmeralda Ruspoli. Directed by Michaelanglo Antonioni. Screenplay, Antonioni, Elio Bartolini, Tonino Guerra; camera, Aldo Scavarda; editor, Eraldo Da Roma. At Cannes Film Fest. Running time, 155 MINS.

Sandro	Gabriele Ferzetti
Claudia	Monica Vitti
Anna	Lea Massari
Patricia	Dominique Blanchar
Senator	Renzo Ricci

This film comes on the heels of Federico Fellini's "The Sweet Life," which also castigated the emptiness and decadence of Italian high life. However, this one is more personal and less symbolical. Pic tells its tale through characters which are more alive and responsible than in the other film. But it is long, grave and sometimes over-emphatic. This makes it an item with mainly art. chances abroad. Theme and treatment could possibly make this an exploitable item. It would probably need plenty pruning.

A group of idle rich go off on a cruise. Sandro (Gabrielle Ferzetti) is a sort of lady's man who is involved with the business interests and placements of his monied friends. He is loved by an erratic, mystical girl who showers him with love. But she is discontent and not ready to marry, and disappears when they land on a barren island.

It is not clear whether she has committed suicide or gone off on a boat of some cigarette smugglers. Her lover tries to follow her trail, being accompanied by the missing girl's friend, a poor girl. A love affair develops but seems doomed as the Don Juanish man goes off with still another girl. But there is some hope because the two try to find some meaning for each other.

Director Michaelangelo Antonioni has given this a good beginning as he incisively blocks out the characters and the lack of roots in a life where emotion and love have been lost in an almost meaningless chain of attempts at love.

The photography is clear and spacious. This does not go in for obvious symbolism and a series of orgies to make its points. This is a difficult audience film since characters are sometimes left ambiguous. The stark beginning does not quite blend completely with the second half.

The acting is always kept under control, with Monica Vitti standing out as the poorer girl whose

hope is that this affair is more than an adventure.

Here is a film that will probably find tough boxoffice going. But a tightening may make it okay for special runs. But this calls for the hard-sell and excellent handling.
Mosk.

Moranbong
(FRENCH-DYALISCOPE)

Cannes, May 17.

Film D'Aujourd'Hui-Ombre Et Lumiere production and release. With Oem Do-Soun, Ouan Djung-Hi. Directed by Jean-Claude Bonnardot. Screenplay, Armand Gatti; camera, Pak Gûioeun; editor, Sylvie Blanc. At Cannes Film Fest. Running time, 90 MINS.

Tong-Il .... Oem Do-Soun
Yang-Nan .... Ouan Djung-Hi

This was made in North Korea about the Korean war as seen via a love affair which is split up by the warfare only to be reunited again after the cease-fire. Pic is banned for local showing as well as export. It is uneven, and mixes documentary with fiction via stock shots.

It has some speeches about the rightness of the Northern side but rarely goes far probing into it. Film is competently made, but slow and uneven.

The propaganda is softpedalled but this looks like a chancey export item at best, even if it does get its visas. Technical credits are good and the acting acceptable. Title refers to a thearte in which the heroine works.
Mosk.

Parvi Urok
(The First Lesson)
(BULGARIAN)

Cannes, May 17.

Bulgare Film production and release. With Cornelia Bojanoa, Gueorgui Naoumov, Gueorgui Gueorguiv, G. Kaloyantchev. Directed by Ranguel Valtchanov; camera, Dimo Kolarov; editor, Maria Ivanova. At Cannes Film Fest. Running time, 95 MINS.

Pesho .... Gueorgui Naoumov
Violetta .... Cornelia Bojanova
Brother .... Gueorgui Gueorguiv
Teacher .... G. Kaloyantchev

This pic is about the love affair between a young worker and an upper class girl under the occupation in Bulgaria during the last World War. It shows how their idyll broken by the incompatibility of classes and has him joining the party and taking up in the resistance.

It is technically crude though the acting is fresh. But all is too subordinated to the message. The Bulgars seem to be lagging behind other Eastern countries in handling film subjects. It remains of little interest for anything but home consumption. A Bulgar-East German pic, "Stars," won a top prize at the last Cannes Fest. But this looks to have little chance.
Mosk.

Sujata
(INDIAN)

Cannes, May 24.

Bimal Roy Productions production and release. Directed by Bimal Roy. Screenplay, Subodh Gosh; camera, Kamal Bose; editor, Sudendhu Roy. At Cannes Film Fest. Running time, 140 MINS.

Sujata .... Nutan
Arid .... Sunil Dutt
Rama .... Shashikala
Mother .... Lalita Pawar
Father .... Tarun Bose
Grandmother .... Sulochana

This deals tastefully, if somewhat sentimentally, with the plight of the untouchables still existing in India today. It makes its plea via the tale of an untouchable girl brought up by an upper class family, and how she is finally accepted through love.

The family takes the girl when her own is wiped out by a plague. They try to send her off for the stigma of her low caste is still strong. After some overdone plotting, all realize that things must change and she is accepted as an equal.

Director Bimal Roy has gotten acceptable characterizations and never made this preachy. It is an eloquent plea against bigotry and obviously important and meaningful in its own country.

Film is mainly a specialized entry abroad on its slowness and tendency to melodrama. But this is a good film of its kind with only specialized foreign chances possible. Technical credits are good.
Mosk.

Le Dialogue Des Carmelites
(FRENCH—DYALISCOPE)

Cannes, May 24.

Lux release of Jules Borkon production. Stars Jeanne Moreau, Alida Valli, Pierre Brasseur; features Pascale Audret, Anne Doat, Pierre Bertin, Claude Laydu. Written and directed by R. L. Bruckberger and Philippe Argostini from book by Gertrud Von Le Fort and play by Georges Bernanos. Camera, Andre Bacs editor, Gilbert Natot. At Cannes Film Fest. Running time, 110 MINS.

Sister Marie .... Jeanne Moreau
Mother Therese .... Alida Valli
Commissaire .... Pierre Bertin
Sister Blanche .... Pascale Audret
Sister Constance .... Anne Doat
Mother Superior .... Madeleine Renaud
Father .... Pierre Bertin
Brother .... Claude Laydu
Mime .... Jean-Louis Barrault

A group of Carmelite nuns are guillotined during the French Revolution for disobeying orders because of their faith and beliefs. A drama of a young girl who is afraid to die and who finds refuge in the Carmelite Order to finally find faith and die for another who can carry on the order is the story of this film.

Pic unwinds slowly and emerges primarily a specialized item for foreign spots. The main theme only intermittently coincides with the larger one to make this somewhat slow until the final execution of the nuns.

This film could have benefitted from more detailed analysis of the nun's life and rituals which is surprisingly skimpy although one of the directors, R. L. Bruckberger, is a Dominican. Technical credits are good and production okay, with acting uneven except for the top roles. Jean-Louis Barrault adds a good bit as a fairground mime.

This may have a specially exploitable aspect since several nun films have captured considerable boxoffice of late. But this is so leisurely that will need hard-sell.
Mosk.

Los Golfos
(The Delinquents)
(SPANISH)

Cannes, May 17.

Pedro Portabella Films production and release. With Manuel Zarzo, Luis Marin, Oscar Cruz, Juanjo Losada, Ramon Rubio, Rafael Vargas, Maria Mayer. Directed by Carlos Saura. Screenplay, Mario Camus, Daniel Sueiro, Saura; camera, Juan Julio Baena; editor, Pedro Del Rey. At Cannes Film Fest. Running time, 90 MINS.

Juan .... Manuel Zarzo
Leader .... Luis Marin
Romero .... Oscar Cruz
Paco .... Juanjo Losada
Lisi .... Maria Meyer

Now Spain comes up with a film on drifting delinquents who exist in a rather poor neighborhood and live via petty thefts. They decide to pull bigger jobs to launch a friend as a bullfighter. This leads to the death of one in a flight from some victims and the novice bullfighter's bad first performance as it ironically winds up with impending arrest.

This has a good feel and a plus factor in the location shooting. But it has way of meandering and rarely gives a real insight into the boys' characters and motives. Pic looms mainly a foreign language entry, not more than an average for this type of pic.

Acting is adequate but there is a tendency to repeat things, and the production shows that it had some cuts made before being allowed out of Spain. Abrupt scene endings are often noticeable. Technical credits are good.
Mosk.

Si Le Vent Te Fait Peur
(If The Wind Frightens You)
(BELGIAN)

Mannes, May 17.

Spirafilm production and release. With Elisabeth Dulac, Guy Lesire, Henri Bilien. Written and directed by Emile Degelin. Camera, Frederic Geisful; editor, M. Boehm. At Cannes Film Fest. Running time, 80 MINS.

Claude .... Elisabeth Dulac
Pierre .... Guy Lesire
Stranger .... Henri Bilien

This is a mannered tale of a brother and sister on the verge of incest and fighting against it. It is slow, turgid and too pretentious in its drawnout connotations on their attempts to make liaisons with other people, only to be drawn back together again.

Pic rarely allows them to be more than symbolical figures. The bleak, dark lensing also is no help. The acting cannot overcome the essential static, literary characterizations and dialog. Only a possible arty exploiter effort on its theme can be in store for this. Otherwise it looks like strictly a local item.
Mosk.

Macario
(MEXICAN)

Cannes, May 17.

Clasa Films Mundiales production and release. With Ignacio Lopez Tarso, Pina Pellicer. Directed by Roberto Gavaldon. Screenplay, Gavaldon from novel by B. Traven; camera, Gabriel Figueroa; editor, Raoul Lavista. At Cannes Film Fest. Running time, 90 MINS.

Macario .... Ignacio Lopez Tarso
Wife .... Pina Pellicer

This deals with a poor, always hungry peasant with a wife and seven children who dreams of someday eating a turkey by himself. His wife finally steals one to assuage his desire, but before eating it he is tempted by the Devil, God and Death to give some to Death, become a rich healer, but then succumb in his turn.

Film is well made and has the proper lush lensing and production dress to make this old fable palatable. But its moralizing is all too pat and familiar. Also it lacks the insight and flair for raising this morality tale to an item with enough distinction for art or general chances abroad. Film appears more likely as a lingo entry there. It has an okay period aspect, with acting and technical credits good.
Mosk.

The Trials Of Oscar Wilde
(BRITISH-TECHNICOLOR)

Second version of the story of Oscar Wilde. This one in color and Technimara. Several superior performances and more mature allround coverage.

London, May 23.

Eros release of a Warwick Film Production (in association with Viceroy Films). Stars Peter Finch, Yvonne Mitchell, James Mason, Nigel Patrick, John Fraser. Features, Lionel Jeffries, Maxine Audley, Emrys Jones, James Booth. Executive producers, Irving Allen & Albert R. Broccoli. Producer, Harold Huth. Director, Ken Hughes. Screenplay, Ken Hughes from John Fernald's play, "The Stringed Lute" and Montgomery Hyde's "Trials Of Oscar Wilde." Camera, Ted Moore; editor, Geoffrey Foot; music, Ron Goodwin. At Studio One, London, May 23, '60. Running time, 123 MINS.

Oscar Wilde .... Peter Finch
Constance .... Yvonne Mitchell
Carson .... James Mason
Sir Edward Clarke .... Nigel Patrick
Marquess of Queensberry .. Lionel Jeffries
Lord Alfred Douglas .... John Fraser
Lady Wilde .... Sonia Dresdel
Ada Leverson .... Maxine Audley
Wood .... James Booth
Robbie Ross .... Emrys Jones
Charles Humphries .... Lloyd Lambie
Frank Harris .... Paul Rogers
Arthur .... Ian Fleming
Prince of Wales .... Laurence Naismith
Lily Langtry .... Naomi Chance
Auctioneer .... Meredith Edwards
First Clerk .... Anthony Newlands
Second Clerk .... Robert Perceval
Charles Gill .... Michael Goodliffe
Willie Wilde .... Liam Gaffney
Lord Ashford .... William Kendall
Lord Sonning .... Ronald Cardew
Lord Percy Douglas .... Derek Aylward
Inspector .... Cambell Singer
Justice Collins .... A. J. Brown
Justice Charles .... Charles Carson
Justice Wills .... David Ensor
Landlady .... Gladys Henson
Cafe Royal Manager .... John Welsh
Lady Queensberry .. Cicely Paget-Bowman

With the black-and-white version of the Oscar Wilde story firmly launched, a second rival version, in color and Technirama, has followed a day or so afterwards, so comparisons between the two films are inevitable. It is an intriguing situation and both films should be profitable and worthwhile bookings. Color and wide screen are a sock asset to "The Trials of Oscar Wilde" and, on balance, it has the greater stellar appeal.

Main difference in the two films is that where the black and white version starts at the first meeting of Wilde and Lord Alfred and moves pretty quickly into the excellent court scene, the color job starts where the scandalous friendship is well established and spends much more time setting the atmosphere of the time of the turn of the century. Also rather more time, and this is a distinct advantage, in showing the relationship not only between Wilde and Lord Alfred but also his family life. So that when the time of the disaster is reached audience will have a keener perception of the character of this talented, vain playwright and wit.

The color film also introduces Wilde's re-trial and, in one brilliant scene at Brighton, shows Wilde's anguish when he first realizes that he is merely being used by his young friend as a weapon in his vindictive struggle with his brutal father. But all in all the story is very much the same and is too wellknown to need elaboration here. The important thing is how the characters are written into the script and how they are played and, in most instances, "The Trials of Oscar Wilde" scores

over its black-and-white opposition.

Peter Finch gives a moving and subtle performance as the ill-starred playwright. Before his downfall he gives the man the charm that he undoubtedly had. The famous Wilde epigrams could well have been thought up by Finch. Morley's crumbling in the face of disaster is flamboyant and effective. Finch's disintegration is quieter, dignified and no less effective.

John Fraser as handsome young Lord Alfred Douglas is suitably vain, selfish, vindictive and petulant and the relationship between the two is more understandable. There is a firstclass study in malignant near-insanity by Lionel Jeffries as the Marquess of Queensberry and Yvonne Mitchell provides a brilliantly understated and understanding performance as Wilde's wife. Emrys Jones and Maxine Audley as his two most loyal friends are also unselfishly unobtrusive, while James Booth is a sharply drawn picture of an opportunistic young blackmailer.

Where "The Trials of Oscar Wilde" suffers in comparison with the black-and-white film is in the remarkable impact of the libel case court sequence. Though the dialog does not vary a great deal since most of it is based on the actual court proceedings, Sir Ralph Richardson's performance as Queen's Counsel is an incisive, superbly drawn piece of thesping in the first film, while James Mason, in a hewn-down role, never provides the strength and bitter logic necessary for the dramatic cut-and-thrust when Wilde is in the witness box. Neither is Nigel Patrick entirely right as Wilde's counsel, since Patrick is essentially an actor of modern times rather than period.

Ted Moore's lensing is firstclass, especially in such extravagant scenes as the theatre and the Cafe Royal sequences, while the art work is excellent throughout. Ken Hughes, both as script-writer and director, has allowed himself some padding and a few dramatic fireworks that don't always help the story, but mainly he has done a good, intelligent job.

With two versions of the yarn available for cinemagoers it's a case of them paying their money and taking their choice. Whereas "Oscar Wilde" concentrates largely on the trials, paradoxically "The Trials of Oscar Wilde" dwells much more on the man's personality and way of life and, in a summing up, must win the honors by a close margin. *Rich.*

Der Liebe Augustin
(The Dear Augustin)
(GERMAN-COLOR)
Berlin, May 24.
UFA production and release. With Mathias Fuchs, Nicole Badal, Veronika Bayer, Ina Duscha, Rudolf Forster. Directed by Rolf Thiele. Screenplay, Barbara Noack and Gregor von Rezzori, after a novel by Horst Wlfram Geissler; camera (Agfacolor), Guenther Anders; music, Bernd Kampka; settings, F. Smetana and Arno Richter. At Marmorhaus, Berlin. Running time, **97 MINS.**
Augustin Sumser .... Mathias Fuchs
Friederike .... Nicole Badal
Susanne .... Veronika Bayer
Lady Ann .... Ina Duscha
Dr. Mermer .... Rudolf Forster
Franz von Gravenreuth
                     Dietmar Schoenherr
Baron Gravenreuth .... Walter Rilla
Baroness Gravenreuth .. Margaret Hruby

"Augustin" looks to be acclaimed the most romantic Teutonic pic of the season. Adapted from H. W. Geissler's bestselling novel of the same name, this pic offers a lot of sentiment and love along with some historical ingredients plus bits of satire. Rolf Thiele directed this with obvious care, and the idea of creating something away from the cliches. Pace is not too important in a film like this, but his overly deliberate direction is responsible for a number of dull moments.

Commercially, "Augustin" is a real guess. Since it has no marquee names, film has to depend on its contents. Within its homegrounds the vehicle may get some help via its bestselling title. International prospects are on the slim side.

Augustin is a sort of sentimental Casanova, who lived around 1800 in the area near Lake of Constance. Three bitter-sweet tales are depicted: First is a quick romance that sees the young lad landing in the arms of a spiteful lady (Ina Duscha). The second romance has him deeply in love (and vice versa) with a pretty princess (Nicole Badal), but this amour is a bust because of difference in rank. Third romance (with Veronika Bayer, a simple girl) leads him into marriage.

Mathias Fuchs, still a comparatively unknown German player, has the title role. Although it's not too memorable a performance, Fuchs is believable, representing a lovable character in this. The three young girls, all very comely, come through with okay performance. The most impressive one in the cast is Rudolf Forster, Augustin's old fatherly friend.

Camerawork is fine and presents a number of beautiful shots. Score adds nicely to the mood. *Hans.*

And Quiet Flows the Don
(RUSSIAN-COLOR)

Big. One of the better Soviet cultural exchange films.

United Artists release of a Gorky film studio production. Stars Ellina Bystritskaya and Pyotr Glebov. Directed by Sergei Gerasimov. Screenplay, Gerasimov; based on the novel by Mikhail Sholokhov; camera, Vladimir Rappoport; music, Yuri Levitin. At Plaza Theatre, N.Y., May 25, '60. Running time, **107 MINS.**
Aksinya .... Ellina Bystritskaya
Grigory .... Pyotr Glebov
Natalya .... Zinaida Kirienko
Pantelei Melekhov...... Danilo Ilchenko
Pyotr .... Nikolai Smirnov
Darya .... Lyudmila Khityayeva
Dunyashka ...... Natalya Arkhangelskaya
Stepan Letakhov.. Alexander Blagovestov
Yevgeni Listnitsky .... Igor Dmitriev
Shtockman .... William Shatunovsky

(In Russian; English subtitles)
"And Quiet Flows the Don," based on a novel by Mikhail Sholokhov, is one of the better Soviet cultural exchange films. It presents a panoramic view of a section of pre-World War I Russia. It's a blockbuster in the sense that its scope is comparable to America's "Gone With the Wind" or perhaps the more recent "Giant."

As part of an ambitious trilogy, however, it may have a feeling of incompleteness, but it does nevertheless offer an effective and interesting insight of the life of the Cossacks just before and including the outbreak of war in 1914. The seeds of the Communist revolution are planted, but its inclusion is not as heavy handed as has been the practice in past Soviet films.

A carpenter working among the Cossacks is carted off by the authorities and presumably banished to Siberia. There is some discussion among the Cossacks about a guy named Marx, but they're unaware who he is or what he stands for. There are indications that the hero is beginning to question the lot of the people of Russia and he shows signs of revolt. Apparently much more will be heard from him in the later segments of the trilogy.

Generally, the story is one of illicit love within the background of the Cossacks and the historical period. A young Cossack takes up with wife of a neighbor while the latter is off on Cossack army maneuvers. Later he runs off with the wife, and while he himself is called up for army duty and engaged in the 1914 war, the femme switches her attention to an aristocratic officer.

The personal story serves merely as the framework for the broad picture of life among the Cossacks and the seething unrest brewing in Russia at the time. Sergei Gerasimov, who wrote the screenplay and directed, has succeeded admirably in capturing all the nuances of the period. He is aided considerably by a remarkable cast. All the performances, and particularly that of Ellina Bystritskaya and Pyotr Glebov in the leading roles, are superb. Miss Bystritskaya, not a leading lady in the true western sense, gives an earthy quality to her portrayal that is outstanding.

The technical aspects are all on the plus side, including the fine color photography. *Holl.*

The Music Box Kid

Exploitable lower-berth crime meller.

Hollywood, May 24.
United Artists release of Robert E. Kent production. Stars Ronald Foster, Luana Patten, Grant Richards; with Johnny Seven, Carl Milletaire, Dayton Lummis, Bernie Fein, Carleton Young, Hugh Sanders, Phil Jackson. Directed by Edward L. Cahn. Screenplay, Herbert Abbott Spiro; camera, Maury Gertsman; editor, James Blakeley; art director, Bill Glasgow; music, Paul Sawtell, Bert Shefter; assistant director, Herbert S. Greene. Reviewed at Goldwyn Studios, May 24. '60. Running time, **74 MINS.**
Larry Shaw .... Ronald Foster
Margaret Shaw .... Luana Patten
Chesty Miller .... Grant Richards
Tony Maldano .... Johnny Seven
Pat Lamont .... Carl Milletaire
Father Corman .... Dayton Lummis
Biggie Gaines .... Bernie Fein

Following a proven formula— cold-blooded violence plus lukewarm budget equals hot boxoffice return—producer Robert E. Kent has assembled a workman-like, exploitable lower-berth attraction in "The Music Box Kid." On the assumption that mushrooming civic-minded concern over a rising wave of crime and bloodshed in entertainment (a reaction springing from television's preoccupation with violence) has not yet appreciably altered the public's dependably insatiable appetite for this sort of fare, the United Artists release apears a shoo-in for black boxoffice ink in situations where king-sized thuggery is consistently in demand.

The "Music Box" of the title is a tommy gun, conspicuously wielded by Ronald Foster, who plays a ruthless killer working his way up through a bootlegging syndicate stationed in the Bronx in the 1920's. A married man, he fails to reckon with the conscience of his pregnant wife (Luana Patten), an oversight that brings his flamboyant career in crime to an abrupt and inglorious climax, but not before he has intimidated communities on both sides of the law into meek, ineffectual (and dramatically illogical) submission.

Foster successfully conveys the flashy, but uncomplicated, psychosis of the central character. Miss Patten gets sufficient anguish into a difficult introspective role. The balance of the cast is shackled with roles of a strictly stereotyped nature, but the key stereotypes are played with spirit by Grant Richards, Johnny Seven, Carl Milletaire and Dayton Lummis.

Edward L. Cahn's direction is swift, efficient and suitably unsophisticated. Attuned to this technique are Maury Gertsman's camera work and James Blakeley's editing, with proper atmospheric assists from art director Bill Glasgow and music men Paul Sawtell and Bert Shefter. *Tube.*

Brennender Sand
(Blazing Sand)
(GERMAN—ISRAELI—COLOR)
Berlin, May 24.
Aero-Film (Berlin) production. made in conjunction with Ran-Film (Israel). With Daliah Lawie, Gert Guenter Hoffman and Abraham Eisenberg. Directed and written by Raphael Nussbaum. Camera (Eastmancolor), Wolf Goethe, Mimisch Herbst; music, Siegfried Wegener; settings, Amiram Schamir. Previewed in Berlin. Running time, **105 MINS.**
Dina .... Daliah Lawie
Rosen .... Gert Guenter Hoffman
Zadek .... Abraham Eisenberg
David .... Uri Zohar
Mike .... Oded Kottlar
Hanna .... Gila Almagor
Police commissioner .... Nathan Cogan
Medico .... Abraham Ronai

"Sand" commands some special attention because it's the first joint feature film effort between a German and an Israeli outfit. This angle may attract the curious. Other exploitation angles are pic's outdoor shots (actual Israeli backgrounds), which benefit much from remarkably good Eastmancolor. Then there is a young Israeli beauty, Daliah Lawie, who's the femme lead in this. She's new to the screen.

There's nothing too exciting about Miss Lawie's acting, but she's an extremely sexy looker and the type of bombshell who might explode. She's mostly seen here in shorts which reveal plenty. Distribs may be well advised to bally this miss.

Otherwise, this is just a common adventure meller, with acting and character motivations on the flat side. Story and dialog sequences come close often to being corny.

This concerns the ancient Jordanian temple town of Petra, some 65 miles from the Israeli border. Miss Lawie (Dina), an Israeli girl, tries to persuade four men to save her lover, who lies helpless in one of the tombs at Petra. This nearly means suicide since Israel and Jordania live in feud with each other and tough border patrols on both sides shoot at every suspicious person. Miss Lawie,

typed here as a selfish girl, and her men manage to get to Petra but, except for one of the men, none returns. They become victims of their own adventure.

Raphael Nussbaum wrote, directed and produced "Sand." Pic has been shot in English, German and Hebrew versions. *Hans.*

Cannes Festival

Moderato Cantabile
(Soft Singing)
(FRENCH-C'SCOPE)

Cannes, May, 24.
Paramount release of Raoul J. Levy production. Stars Jeanne Moreau, Jean-Paul Belmondo; features Didier Haudipin, Valeric Dobuzinsky, Pascale De Boysson. Directed by Peter Brook. Screenplay, Marguerite Duras, Gerard Jariot, Brook from the novel of Miss Duras; camera, Armand Thirard; editor, Albert Jurgensen. At Cannes Film Fest. Running time, 90 MINS.

Anne	Jeanne Moreau
Chauvin	Jean-Paul Belmondo
Son	Didier Haudepin
Killer	Valeric Dobuzinsky
Patronne	Pascale De Boysson
Miss Giraud	Colette Regis

Muted tale of a would-be adulteress depends mainly on atmosphere to spin out its web of awakening emotions and dissatisfactions. This all ends in a return to the stifling bourgeois life which an unformed, self-indulgent mother and wife of an important business man briefly has tried to escape.

This film is wordy, repetitive and deals with a woman who witnesses a murder of passion in a worker's bar. This disturbs her obviously, and she returns to the seedy bar where she meets a mysterious young man who builds up the background of the killing for her. She slips out more and more to see him and tries to stave off her growing desire for the man. Then one night she runs off to be with the stranger only to be refused by him. She returns to her supposedly dreary upper crust life.

Jeanne Moreau does display an inkling about the stirring of unnamed emotions in the woman, but can not quite overcome the literary quality of the dialog. Slowness of direction really drags out the story rather than revealing much visually. Film's tasteful handling and offbeat aspects could slant this for arty spots abroad.

This was written by the woman who wrote "Hiroshima, Mon Amour" and has the same novelettish tang. It needs extra special handling. Technical credits are good if the editing is desultory, and the progression and actual characterization patchy. *Mosk.*

Telegramele
(Telegrams)
(RUMANIAN-COLOR)

Cannes, May 24.
Bucharest Film production and release. With Grigore Vasiliubirlic, Carmen Stanesco, Jules Cazaban, Costache Antoniu. Directed by Gheorghe Nagy, Aurel Miheles. Screenplay, Mirca Stefanesco from novel by Ion Luca Carariale; camera (Ansco), Ion Cosma; editor, Mircia Chiriac. At Cannes Film Fest. Running time, 90 MINS.

Prefect	Grigore Vasiliubirlic
Divorcee	Carmen Stanesco
Opposition	Jules Cazaban
Raoul	Costache Antoniu

Theatrical film is about a progressive and reactionary party in turn-of-the-century Rumania trying to use each other's private foibles in an election. Plot finally shows the two together finally when the feds butt in after each has sent many telegrams.

This is played in a farcical way and offers little interest for foreign dates. Color is uneven, playing overpuffed and technical credits only adequate. *Mosk.*

Kam Cert Nemuze
(When the Woman Butts In)
(CZECHOSLAVAKIAN-COLOR)
Czech State Film production and release. With Miroslav Hornicek, Jana Hlavacova, Jiri Sovak, Vlastimir Brodsky. Directed by Zdenek Podskalsky. Screenplay, Frantisek Daniel, Milos Kratochvil; camera (Ansco), Jiri Safar; editor, Z. Liska. At Cannes Film Fest. Running time, 80 MINS.

Faust	Miroslav Hornicek
Girl	Jana Hlavacova
Friend	Jiri Sovak

Cannes, May, 24.
Comedy starts off slowly but builds to some good situation and slapstick laughs. But the familiar tale of a man who thinks he is a reincarnation of Faust and mistakes a live girl for a cat, etc., untill love ends it all is somewhat tenuous for anything but local chances.

Technical aspects are good. This is played lightly with direction vacillating but getting down to business half way through to make this an okay item. *Mosk.*

The Story of Ruth
(C'SCOPE—COLOR)

Tasteful, but slow-moving embellishment of the biblical passage. A "woman's picture," it should register okay at the b.o., but needs lots of ballyhoo.

Hollywood, June .2
Twentieth-Fox release of Samuel G. Engel production. Stars Stuart Whitman, Tom Tryon, Peggy Wood, Viveca Lindfors, Jeff Morrow; introduces Elana Eden; with Thayer David, Les Tremayne, Eduard Franz, Leo Fuchs, Lili Valenty, John Gabriel, Ziva Rodann, Basil Ruysdael, John Banner, Adelina Pedroza, Daphna Einhorn, Sara Taft, Jean Inness. Berry Kroeger, Jon Silo, Don Diamond. Directed by Henry Koster. Screenplay, Norman Corwin; camera, Arthur E. Arling; editor, Jack W. Holmes; art directors, Lyle R. Wheeler, Franz Bachelin; music, Franz Waxman; assistant director, Eli Dunn. Reviewed at the studio, June 2, '60. Running time, 132 MINS.

Boaz	Stuart Whitman
Mahlon	Tom Tryon
Naomi	Peggy Wood
Eleilat	Viveca Lindfors
Tob	Jeff Morrow
Ruth	Elana Eden
Hedak	Thayer David
Elimeiech	Les Tremayne
Jehoam	Eduard Franz
Sochin	Leo Fuchs
Kera	Lili Valenty
Chilion	John Gabriel
Orpah	Ziva Rodann
Shammah	Basil Ruysdael
King of Moab	John Banner
Iduma	Adelina Pedroza
Tebah	Daphna Einhorn
Eska	Sara Taft
Hagah	Jean Inness
Huphim	Berry Kroeger
Tacher	Jon Silo
Yomar	Don Diamond

Samuel G. Engel's production of "The Story of Ruth" is a refreshingly sincere and restrained Biblical drama, a picture that in its elaboration on the romantic, political and devotional difficulties encountered by the Old Testament heroine earnestly contemplates character development and ignores the customary preoccupation with sex exhibitionism. Yet, for all its obvious high purpose, bolstered by several fine performances, there is a sluggishness that is disturbing.

Picture, however, lends itself to colorful exploitation and there's reason to believe that it will be a profitable investment for 20th-Fox, which is releasing of an exclusive engagement but not hard ticket basis. In initial openings, at least, "Story of Ruth" will have to overcome the boxoffice disadvantages of a cast not firmly identified in the public memory and the possible exhaustion of Biblical spectacles among more avid filmgoers.

Norman Corwin's screenplay describes the heroine's activities from her youthful indoctrination as a Moabite priestess through her marriage to the Judean, "Boaz." Along the way it dramatizes her romance with the kindly "Mahlon," his violent death, her conversion to Judaism and flight with Mahlon's mother, "Naomi," to Bethlehem, where she encounters religious persecution and becomes embroiled in a romantic triangle.

Corwin's screenplay is sound and careful in its construction of character growth and relationships, but it has a slight tendency to be incoherent, to lose sight of an overall objective as it meanders slowly from episode to episode. The 132-minute route is a strain on a drama based on such a short biblical passage. The tale lacks the variety and color to remain crisp and absorbing over such a span.

Although Corwin wisely has avoided archaic phrases, director

Henry Koster has not always succeeded in side-stepping stereotyped biblical-pic posturing and mannerisms among his players, and is inclined to anticipate mysterious character knowledge in a few instances. But he has coaxed several very effective portrayals out of his principals, all the more notable a feat considering the absence of much thespic experience in one or two cases. The film introduces to the screen Elana Eden in the title role. She gives a performance of dignity, projecting an inner strength through a delicate veneer—just the interpretation required of the character, although a shade more animation here and there may have made her "Ruth" more believable and interesting.

The picture is helped by Peggy Wood's excellent characterization of Naomi. The veteran Miss Wood demonstrates an instinctive ability to generate proper reactions, and her timing is always sharp. Tom Tryon, who has attained popularity as a tv star for Walt Disney, here establishes himself as a pleasing screen personality with a vigorous delineation of Mahlon. Stuart Whitman is impressive as Boaz, and Viveca Lindfors seems to get a charge out of her participation as the wicked high priestess of Moab. Jeff Morrow gives an aggressive, strong performance as Tob, a rival for Miss Eden's affections, but at times he overemotes a bit. There is competent support from virtually all others involved, most noticeably so in the cases of Thayer David, Les Tremayne, Leo Fuchs and Ziva Rodann.

The CinemaScopic spectacle benefits from Arthur E. Arling's agile lensmanship, but Jack W. Holmes editing is not always as helped as it might be in advancing the pace of the picture. The De Luxe color and art directors Lyle R. Wheeler's and Franz Bachelin's settings are more natural than spectacular, which is a way in refreshing for this sort of film. Franz Waxman's music is typically biblical in tone and tempo. *Tube.*

Hannibal
(SUPERCINESCOPE—COLOR—ITALIAN)

Bulky historical adventure spectacle from Italy and vicinity. Elephantine in scope and pace, but showy enough to make the b.o. grade if the public hasn't tired of this sort of fare.

Hollywood, June 1.
Warner Bros. release of Ottavio Poggi production. Stars Victor Mature; with Rita Gam, Gabriele Ferzetti, Milly Vitale, Rik Battaglia, Franco Silva, Mario Girotti, Mirko Ellis, Andrea Aureli. Directed by Edgar G. Ulmer. Screenplay, Mortimer Braus, from story by Poggi based on treatment by Alessandro Continenza; camera, R. Masciocchi; editor, R. Cinquini; art director, E. Kromberg; music, Carlo Rustichelli; assistant director, N. Zanchin. Reviewed at the studio, June 1, '60. Running time, 103 MINS.

Hannibal	Victor Mature
Sylvia	Rita Gam
Fabius Maximus	Gabriele Ferzetti
Danila	Milly Vitale
Hasdrubal	Rik Battaglia
Maharbal	Franco Silva
Quintilius	Mario Girotti
Mago	Mirko Ellis
Varro	Andrew Aureli

The boxoffice fate of this Warner Bros. release depends, to a great extent, on whether or not a saturation point has been reached in the thus-far affectionate rela-

tionship between the American filmgoing public and the stream of loosely historical spectacles that have been arriving with regularity from Italy. Although this version of the noted Carthaginian general's military and romantic activities near Rome in 218 B. C. is dramatically crude and ponderously paced, it contains enough sheer spectacle, gore and quasi-historical action to excite those still willing to meet such films on their own primitive level.

As depicted in the Mortimer Braus screenplay from producer Ottavio Poggi's story, "Hannibal," no dramatic newcomer to 20th century cinema, was a man unable to isolate his personal and sexual life from the battlefield. Eventually this personality conflict leads to his downfall after a series of successful skirmishes that presaged a flashier outcome. The film gets off to an interesting start in scenes illustrating the difficult and costly crossing of the snowy Alps by Hannibal's army, but slows down to an elephant's pace in the romantic passages at the heart of the picture. Except for the one major battle scene, momentum is never regained.

Victor Mature brings physical command to the central role, but turns wooden in the romantic going, as does Rita Gam as his doomed wartime paramour. Best support is chipped in by Gabriele Ferzetti as the patriotic senator, Rik Battaglia as Hannibal's ill-fated brother and Mario Girotti as a young, impetuous Roman warrior.

Director Edgar G. Ulmer has not accomplished battle sequences and bloodshed very smoothly or persuasively. His work is most effective in the early "transportation" passages. The film benefits most from careful dubbing of sound and dialog and Carlo Rustichelli's score. R. Masciocchi's "supercinescope" camera work seems no more "super" than normal. Editing by R. Cinquini and art direction by E. Kromberg are competent.

Tube.

Bells Are Ringing
(C'SCOPE—COLOR)

The hit Broadway musical, transposed with fervor and finesse to film. With Judy Holliday to lead the way, should be a bell-ringer at the b.o.

Hollywood, June 3.

Metro release of Arthur Freed production. Stars Judy Holliday, Dean Martin; with Fred Clark, Eddie Foy, Jean Stapleton, Ruth Storey, Dort Clark, Frank Gorshin, Ralph Roberts, Valerie Allen, Bernie West, Steven Peck, Gerry Mulligan. Directed by Vincente Minnelli. Screenplay, Betty Comden, Adolph Green, based on their musical play; camera, Milton Krasner; editor, Adrienne Fazan; art directors, George W. Davis, Preston Ames; music, Jule Styne; assistant director, William McGarry. Reviewed at Pantages Theatre, June 3, '60. Running time, **126 MINS.**

Ella Peterson	Judy Holliday
Jeffrey Moss	Dean Martin
Larry Hastings	Fred Clark
J. Otto Prantz	Eddie Foy
Sue	Jean Stapleton
Gwynne	Ruth Storey
Inspector Barnes	Dort Clark
Blake Barton	Frank Gorshin
Francis	Ralph Roberts
Olga	Valerie Allen
Dr. Joe Kitchell	Bernie West
1st Gangster	Steven Peck
Ella's Blind Date	Gerry Mulligan

Better Broadway musicals than "Bells Are Ringing" have come to Hollywood, but few have been translated to the screen so effectively. Since cinemusicomedies have become scarce commodities of late, and since this one is not only a good one but has Judy Holliday as its star, it's unquestionably going to stir up a merry boxoffice commotion for Metro.

"Bells" is ideally suited to the intimacy of the film medium. Where it might have a tendency in several passages to become dwarfed on a big stage, it's always bigger than life onscreen, which actually is a desirable factor in broad, free-wheeling comedy such as this. In incorporating CinemaScope, Metrocolor and Panavision, producer Arthur Freed has not allowed his film to become gaudy and cumbersome, but has been faithful to the buoyant spirit and whimsical personality of the original.

The Betty Comden-Adolph Green screenplay, based on their book musical, is not by any means the sturdiest facet of the picture, but it's a pleasant yarn from which several rather inspired musical numbers spring. Of the selections, "Just In Time" and "The Party's Over" have enjoyed the most popularity and are delivered smoothly by Dean Martin and Miss Holliday. The latter's outstanding turn, however, occurs near the end of the picture, when she demonstrates her verve and versatility on the amusing "I'm Goin' Back" (Where I Can Be Me, at the Bonjour Tristesse Brassiere Factory). She's also a delight on the telephonesque "It's a Perfect Relationship" and in a riotous Hollywood party routine tagged "Drop That Name."

Martin has a chance to get in some solid licks on the alcoholically-inspired "Do It Yourself" and in a traffic-stopping, crowd elbowing street sequence labelled "Hello." A real show-stopper is a production number with symphonic overtones presided over dynamically by Eddie Foy.

Vincente Minnelli's graceful, imaginative direction puts spirit and snap into the musical sequnces warmth and humor into the straight passages and manages to knit it all together without any traces of awkwardness in transition, a frequent stumbling block in filmusicals. Jule Styne's bright score has been vibrantly adapted and conducted by Andre Previn. The Comden-Green lyrics are smooth and workable, rarely intricate. Charles O'Curran's choreography is outstanding, making even Martin appear a fairly accomplished heel-and-toe'r. Physical, decorative and technical credits are uniformly solid, notably Milton Krasner's energetic camera maneuvers, Adrienne Fazan's crisp editing, Walter Plunkett's becoming costumes and George W. Davis and Preston Ames' tasteful art direction.

As for the cast, it is Miss Holliday who, as might be expected, steals show with a performance of remarkable variety and gusto as a girl who takes her switchboard and humanity seriously. Martin is excellent as her writer friend, displaying more animation than customary of his work. Foy is a comedy standout, as always. Also outstanding are Frank Gorshin as a beatnik who wants to be an actor and Bernie West as a dentist who wants to be a songwriter. Others who score favorably are Fred Clark (in a surprisingly straight role), Jean Stapleton, Ruth Storey, Dort Clark, Ralph Roberts, Valerie Allen, Steven Peck and Gerry Mulligan.

Tube.

Walk Like a Dragon

Low budget adult western that inspects old U.S. frontier prejudice vs. Orientals. Exploitable.

Hollywood, May 23.

Paramount release of James Clavell production. Stars Jack Lord, Nobu McCarthy, James Shigeta, Mel Torme; features Josephine Hutchinson, Rudolph Acosta, Benson Fong, Michael Pate; with Lilyan Chauvin, Don Kennedy, Donald Barry, Natalie Trundy. Directed by Clavell. Screenplay, Clavell, Daniel Mainwaring; camera, Loyal Griggs; editor, Howard Smith; are directors, Hal Pereira, Ronald Anderson; music, Paul Dunlap; assistant director, Richard Caffey. Reviewed at the studio, May 23, '60. Running time, **95 MINS.**

Linc Bartlett	Jack Lord
Kim Sung	Nobu McCarthy
Cheng Lu	James Shigeta
The Deacon	Mel Torme
Ma Bartlett	Josephine Hutchinson
Sheriff Marguelez	Rudolph Acosta
Wu	Benson Fong
Will Allen	Michael Pate
Mme. Lili Raide	Lilyan Chauvin
Masters	Don Kennedy
Cabot	Donald Barry
Susan	Natalie Trundy

In attempting to dramatize the unarguable doctrine that slavery is an ugly, unwelcome visitor in a free society, producer-director-writer James Clavell, in "Walk Like a Dragon," has somehow wound up with the curious "message" that clannish conformity is the logical path to peaceful coexistence for foreigners to pursue in America. Since Clavell wisely has set his story in the conveniently unprovocative and usefully primitive atmosphere of the old west, and has utilized some interesting, offbeat historical data in the process, the film fits snugly into the "adult western" genre, a category of proven commercial value in contemporary entertainment. Being a low-budget effort it can, with aggressive salesmanship, better than break even.

A maze of incomplete, often contradictory, character motivations gnaws away destructively at the roots of the screenplay by Clavell and Daniel Mainwaring. It is based on a three-ply conflict, an interracial romantic triangle consisting of one tall, strapping American (Jack Lord); one proud, rebellious Chinaman (James Shigeta); and one frail, would-be Chinese slave girl (Nobu McCarthy). Rescuing the latter from the perils of enforced prostitution, Lord promptly bumps into mass discrimination and an emotional duel with Shigeta when he brings the girl to live in his home. This situation evolves, in an unlikely fashion, into a showdown between the two men for the legal affections of the girl. The romantic rapport between Lord and Miss McCarthy is never plausibly established nor, for that matter, is the victorious relationship of the two young Chinese people.

Although shackled with a superficially-drawn role, Lord constructs a sympathetic characterization. Miss McCarthy, an attractive actress, lacks the subtle variety required for her role. Shigeta, too, manages only a shallow, one-note portrayal of the defiant Oriental. Mel Torme, cast as a gun-totin', scripture-spoutin' "deacon," plays the offbeat role with a flourish, but appears bewildered (as will the audience) by the nebulous nature of the character. There is capable support by Josephine Hutchinson as Lord's sensitive mother, Rudolph Acosta as a peculiarly ineffectual sheriff, Benson Fong as a diplomatic Chinese laundryman, Michael Pate as a preacher, and Lilyan Chauvin as a French lady of ill repute who owns up to having Indian blood.

As director, Clavell is adept in his handling of the film's more provocative moments, notably an exploitable scene wherein the heroine is stripped to the waste in the slave market. But his overall approach tends to form predictably repetitive patterns such as following each soft, tender sequence with an explosion of gunfire to open the next one. Loyal Griggs' sensitive camera work adds dramatic visual qualities to the film, and Paul Dunlap's music brings appropriate audible rewards. Art direction by Hal Pereira and Roland Anderson is believably late-19th century western in appearance, and Howard Smith's editing is smooth.

Tube.

Portrait in Black
(COLOR)

Contrived murder meller. Star-studed cast will hypo b.o., but prospects appear doubtful.

Hollywood, May 31.

Universal release of Ross Hunter production. Stars Lana Turner, Anthony Quinn, Sandra Dee, John Saxon, Lloyd Nolan, Richard Basehart; features Ray Walston, Virginia Grey, Anna May Wong; with Paul Birch, John Wengraf, Richard Morris, James Nolan, Robert Lieb, John McNamara, Charles Thompson, George Womack, Herold Goodwin, Jack Bryan, Elizabeth Chan, Henry Quan. Directed by Michael Gordon. Screenplay, Ivan Goff, Ben Roberts, from their play; camera, Russell Metty; editor, Milton Carruth; art director, Richard H. Riedel; music, Frank Skinner; assistant director, Phil Bowles. Reviewed at Screen Directors Guild Theatre, May 31, '60. Running time, **112 MINS.**

Sheila Cabot	Lana Turner
Dr. David Rivera	Anthony Quinn
Catherine Cabot	Sandra Dee
Blake Richards	John Saxon
Howard Mason	Richard Basehart
Matthew Cabot	Lloyd Nolan
Cob O'Brien	Ray Walston
Miss Lee	Virginia Grey
Tani	Anna May Wong
Peter Cabot	Dennis Kohler
Detective	Paul Birch
Dr. Kessler	John Wengraf
Mr. Corbin	Richard Morris
1st Detective	James Nolan
2nd Detective	Robert Lieb
Minister	John McNamara
Sid	Charles Thompson
Foreman	George Womack
1st Patrolman	Herold Goodwin
2nd Patrolman	Jack Bryan
Chinese Dancer	Elizabeth Chan
Chinese Headwaiter	Henry Quan

Universal has a shaky proposition on its hands in "Portrait in Black." The Ross Hunter production is topheavy with strong, established boxoffice names, but that doesn't appear to be enough to offset its severe artistic shortcomings.

The Ivan Goff-Ben Roberts screenplay (from their stage play) is a contrived murder melodrama with psychological character interplay that is more psycho than logical. The drama is set in motion

when an invalid shipping magnate (Lloyd Nolan) is murdered by his physician (Anthony Quinn), in cahoots with the tycoon's wife (Lana Turner). Since Nolan's death is accepted as the result of natural causes, the lovers appear safe until an anonymous letter arrives to congratulate Miss Turner on the success of the murder.

This unscheduled complication paves the way for a series of the usual suspicions, a second murder, and a near-miss on a third before Quinn and Miss Turner pay the inevitable price for onscreen homicide. A climactic disclosure concerning the identity of the unknown letterwriter who led the lovers to their doom is intended as a surprise ending. It comes not only as no great shock, but as a totally unconvincing revelation.

The screenplay is incomplete and frequently preposterous, but Michael Gordon's direction must be considered at least an equal partner in the deficiencies of the enterprise. Under his guidance, much of the acting has all the subtlety of a hypodermic needle. For some ill-advised reason, Gordon has restored an outmoded style of stiff, self-consciously awkward posturing that emerges ludicrously crude by contemporary dramatic standards, unintentionally amusing the audience at several vital junctures of the film.

Paradoxically, these distorted thespic attitudes and gestures provide just the sex-shock aura that makes for attractive photographic stills, a valuable exploitation assist for the film, whose primary appeal and draw should rest with the more impressionable femme teen audience. Basically a "woman's picture," it is not likely to please more mature women, who will be disappointed at the absence of motivation for the passionate central romance.

The familiarity of her personality and endurance of her beauty enables Miss Turner to come off reasonably well in an unbelievable role. But Quinn is uncomfortably miscast as the villainous physician, while John Saxon and Sandra Dee seem mechanical in "grown-up" roles of lovers trapped in the emotional turmoil. Ray Walston, as Miss Turner's insecure chauffeur, seems consistently on the verge of breaking out into some diabolical tune, and Anna May Wong, in returning to the screen after a 17-year absence, has chosen a thankless vehicle for the move—the unnecessary part of a suspicious housekeeper.

Most convincing performances in the film are fashioned by Nolan, Richard Basehart and Miss Turner's unrequited lover, Virginia Grey as a faithful secretary, and young Dennis Kohler as Miss Turner's perceptive charge.

Frank Skinner's music, built around recurring dramatic piano crescendos, is corny and predictable, particularly when it veers Oriental every time Miss Wong appears. Russell Metty's camera work is capable, making the most of some striking soft lighting effects and the Eastman color, and Milton Carruth's editing is graceful. Jean Louis' gowns for the star are obviously expensive but consistently non-functional. First-

rate contributions are Richard R. Riedel's art direction and Julia Heron's set decorations, a dash of elegance for a film that needs it.
Tube.

Ice Palace
(COLOR)

From Edna Ferber's saga of Alaska is derived as unusually strong human-conflict drama backed by potent pictorial values. This is a big one.

Warner release of Henry Blanke production. Stars Richard Burton, Robert Ryan, Carolyn Jones, Martha Hyer, Jim Backus; features Ray Danton, Diane McBaine, Karl Swenson, Shirley Knight, Barry Kelley, Sheridan Comerate, George Takei, Steve Harris. Directed by Vincent Sherman. Screenplay, Harry Kleiner, from novel by Edna Ferber; camera (Technicolor and widescreen), Joseph Biroc; editor, William Ziegler; music, Max Steiner. Previewed at WB's N.Y. homeoffice June 13, '60. Running time, **143 MINS.**

Zeb	Richard Burton
Thor	Robert Ryan
Bridie	Carolyn Jones
Dorothy	Martha Hyer
Dave Husack	Jim Backus
Bay	Ray Danton
Christine	Diane McBaine
Scotty	Karl Swenson
Grace (Age 16)	Shirley Knight
Einer Wendt	Barry Kelley
Ross	Sheridan Comerate
Wang	George Takei
Christopher (age 16)	Steve Harris

Total of 143 minutes of running time is an abundant amount of celluloid but in Henry Blanke's forceful production of "Ice Palace" it's not excessive, for the reason that there's an abundance of story to be told. Edna Ferber's sweeping saga of Alaska over a period of 40 years is peopled with numerous strong individuals encountering crisis after crisis.

There's steady flow of excitement and emotional charge in the fine screenplay contributed by Henry Kleiner. Of those 143 aforementioned minutes there's not a dull one. And with director Vincent Sherman casting a knowing camera's eye on the scenic values of the territory involved, plus the added background of the salmon packing industry, "Ice Palace" rates as an important production in terms of general audience acceptance and consequent boxoffice. It can't miss being big.

The Ferber novel goes year by year from the end of World War I to Alaska's 49th statehood. Pivotal character, played in brooding but nonetheless effective fashion by Richard Burton, is an embittered Saturday's children type who rises to the top in the cannery business and nearly destroys everyone with whom he comes in contact.

The yarn has a full quota of ironic twists. Burton, as "czar" of the Alaskan region, is a bigot, focusing some of his hatred on the natives, only to find that his daughter has eloped with a half-breed.

Also his own marriage, motivated only by monetary advantages, brings him lifetime grief for he has denied himself the woman he truly and lastingly loves.

In a role allowing for more dimensional histrionics, Robert Ryan is standout. He's rugged and yet compassionate, forever engaging in a vendetta with Burton, whom he had earlier befriended, and full of zeal in leading the crusade for Alaska's admission to the States. It's an interesting twist that these bitter enemies, Burton and Ryan,

sould one day have a mutual granddaughter.

Carolyn Jones shows remarkable versatility and insight as the local hotel owner's daughter first engaged to Ryan, then enamored of Burton, only to be abandoned by him. Martha Hyer portrays the hurt wife with sufficient conviction, and Jim Backus properly conveys Burton's more-or-less stooge business associate.

Ray Danton, Diane McBain, Karl Swenson, Shirley Knight, Barry Kelley, Sheridan Comerate, George Takei and Steve Harris round out the overall competent cast.

It's a credit to Kleiner's screenplay and Sherman's beautifully organized direction that there are so many characters involved, all fully participating, and yet "Ice Palace" unwinds smoothly and completely devoid of any blurriness as to story detail. The pacing is consistently good and the many dramatic wallops are developed logically.

Photography in Technicolor and widescreen has wrung out splendid values from the location sites, Max Steiner's music is fitting and, on its own, has built-in drama. Sets and settings are precisely appropriate and the editing (William Ziegler) is tight.

Perhaps in this "adult" era it should be noted that "Ice Palace" is innocent of anything that could offend even the most sensitive. It's a mature work, but sans rough stuff. And, to repeat, it's big.
Gene.

Dinosaurus
(C'SCOPE—COLOR)

A funny fantasy in which two dinosaurs and one friendly caveman fail to maintain peaceful coexistence with modern man. Potentially profitable surprise package for unsuspecting audiences with a sense of humor.

Hollywood, June 2.
Universal release of Jack H. Harris production. Stars Ward Ramsey, Paul Lukather, Kristina Hanson, Alan Roberts, Gregg Martell; features Fred Engelberg, Wayne Tredway, Luci Blain, Howard Dayton, Jack Younger, James Logan. Directed by Irvin S. Yeaworth Jr. Screenplay, Jean Yeaworth, Dan E. Weisburd, from original idea by Harris; camera, Stanley Cortez; editor, John A. Bushelman; art director, Jack Senter; music, Ronald Stein; assistant director, Herbert Mendelson. Reviewed at Pantages Theatre, June 2, '60. Running time, **85 MINS.**

Bart Thompson	Ward Ramsey
Chuck	Paul Lukather
Betty Piper	Kristina Hanson
Julio	Alan Roberts
Prehistoric Man	Gregg Martell
Mike Hacker	Fred Engelberg
Chica	Luci Blain
Jasper	Jack Younger
Dumpy	Wayne Tredway
Mousey	Howard Dayton
O'Leary	James Logan

"Dinosaurus" is, above all, a comedy. Presumably the Jack H. Harris production is meant to be funny, although there are times when the intent is questionable. Its humor, which ranges from low comedy to high satire, probably will catch audiences unawares unless Universal elects to tip off the unusual approach with some sort of quip in its advertising. Should Universal continue instead to plug it as an action-fantasy spectacle (actually a subsidiary aspect), word-of-mouth figures to spur greater-than-average curiosity.

Handled properly, it could very well turn out to be an unusually profitable venture.

Conceived by Harris, penned by Jean Yeaworth and Dan E. Weisburd, the offbeat yarn begins with the return to life of three prehistoric creatures: a carniverous tyrannosaurus rex, a herbiverous brontosaurus, and a whimsical neanderthal man who gives the film a shot in the funnybone. The serious passages of the picture are concerned with eventually successful efforts to destroy the deadly man-eater. The comedy relief is supplied by the caveman's brushes with modern civilization.

Much of the comedy may be crude, but its charm ranges from pie-in-the-face capers reminiscent of the Keystone Kops to sophisticated satire. An example of the latter occurs when the caveman and a modern woman whose face is covered with makeup suddenly come upon each other—and both flee in fright and disbelief. This is but one of a number of gags with thinly-veiled satiric points-of-view that should keep audiences roaring happily.

Although the sympathetic, likeable caveman (Gregg Martell) steals the show with a memorably comic performance, the special photographic effects by Tim Baar, Wah Chang and Gene Warren command attention in the sequences depicting dinosaur activity. Although their grunts remind one of a car with a weak battery starting up and their savage battle brings to mind Kukla and Ollie having a spat, these dinosaurs will be real enough for youngsters, who may miss the subtlety of the tongue-in-cheek approach. Worthy assists are contributed by cameraman Stanley Cortez, art director Jack Senter and editor John A. Bushelman.

With the exception of Martell, the acting is uncannily rigid, although this may be the result of a conscious overall aim for ridiculous merriment at the expense of believability. There is, for instance, a boy (Alan Roberts) who befriends the vegetarian brontosaurus and speaks to him in much the same stiff, matter-of-fact manner as Sabu used to address his favorite elephant. There is a hapless villain (Fred Engelberg) who is so villainous he will have audiences hissing.

For the success of the film's mirthful approach, director and co-producer Irvin S. Yeaworth Jr. deserves a large share of the credit, although at times one wonders whether his tongue was consistently in cheek. *Tube.*

Tarzan the Magnificent
(COLOR)

The new, and less flashy, ape man, sans "Jane," "Boy," et. al., in a sluggish bout with African criminal elements. Jet-age "Tarzan" may not pack as potent a wallop at the b.o.

Hollywood, June 9.

Paramount release of Sy Weintraub-Harvey Hayutin production. Stars Gordon Scott, Jock Mahoney, Betta St. John; features John Carradine, Lionel Jeffries, Alexandra Stewart; introduces Gary Cockrell. Directed by Robert Day. Screenplay, Berne Giler, Day, based on Edgar Rice Burroughs' characters; camera, Ted Scaife; editor, Bert Rule; art director, Ray Simm; music, Ken Jones; assistant director, Clive Reed. Reviewed at Beverly Theatre, June 9, '60. Running time, **82 MINS.**

Tarzan	Gordon Scott
Coy Banton	Jock Mahoney
Fay Ames	Betta St. John
Abel Banton	John Carradine
Ames	Lionel Jeffries
Lori	Alexandra Stewart
Johnny Banton	Gary Cockrell

In updating their "Tarzan" to fit what they seem to feel are modern specifications, producer Sy Weintraub and his associate Harvey Hayutin have taken most of the charm and vigor out of the character. Their jet-age "Tarzan" has lost his identity, and emerges anything but "The Magnificent" in this film. Instead, audiences will discover a rather glum, earthbound, unexciting version of the ape man in a slow-moving picture. Except for some fine African scenery and the fact that a "Tarzan" film invariably does a respectable job of selling itself, the Paramount release does not shape up as a paramount boxoffice prospect.

Also a victim of jet-age accessibility is the once fascinating and mysterious primitive appeal of the Dark Continent. In this Berne Giler-Robert Day screenplay, it has become the setting for a routine chase that might, save for an occasional lion or crocodile, just as easily have occurred in a western. It is concerned with Tarzan's efforts to bring a criminal to justice through treacherous jungle terrain, pursued by the criminal's evil family and slowed up by the haggling of his own entourage, which includes a cowardly Britisher whose unstable wife is sexually attracted to the captive.

Only briefly, near the climax, does the reckless, tree-swinging Tarzan of old emerge. The return to character will bring cheers from the audience—cynical cheers, to be sure, but tinged with a kind of nostalgic affection for the dear departed spirit of the original Edgar Rice Burroughs character.

The acting in this film surpasses the material, although Gordon Scott, as "Tarzan," seems uncomfortable in the role and brings it little more than an ample physique. There is good work from Jock Mahoney as the captive, Lionel Jeffries as the irascible husband, Betta St John as the roving wife, John Carradine as the captive's blackguard father, Alexandra Stewart as the most attractive member of the wary safari, and screenewcomer Gary Cockrell as Carradine's younger, mischevous son. Director Day hasn't made things easy on his cast. In striving for realism he has immersed them neck-deep in swamp mud during several passages.

Sound, always a key ingredient in a "Tarzan" film, has been vividly reproduced here through the combined efforts of supervisor John Cox, recorders Buster Ambler and Bob Jones, and editor Ted Mason. Art director Ray Simm has selected some striking African locations, and these have been capably lensed by Ted Scaife. Bert Rule's editing and Ken Jones' music are helpful contributions. *Tube.*

Sans Tambour Ni Trompette
(Without Trumpet or Drum)
(FRENCH-WEST GERMAN)
(Color)

Paris, June 14.

UFA release of CAPAC-UFA production. Stars Jean Richard, Hardy Kruger, Dany Carrel; features Francoise Rosay, Theo Lingen, Lucien Nat. Directed by Helmut Kautner. Screenplay, Jean L'Hote, Kautner from novel by L'Hote; camera (Eastmancolor), Jacques Letellier; editor, Kurt Doodenbach. At Biarritz, Paris. Running time, **90 MINS.**

Leon	Jean Richard
Fritz	Hardy Kruger
Marguerite	Dany Carrel
Grandmother	Franciose Rosay
Colonel	Theo Lingen
Captain	Lucien Nat

One of the first official French-West German coproductions chooses a war theme, but a harmless war or so the 1870 French-Prussian war is portrayed in this pacifistic comedy. Sentiments seem okay but the pic is fairly obvious and so slow that it looms mainly a Continental item. There seems to be some playoff chances abroad possible on its theme and color. It does not appear to have the weight and lightness for arty chances.

A French and German soldier change uniforms by mistake when one is taking a swim. They meet at a farmhouse where they become pals. The two help a flirtatious girl and her grandmother until some Prussians barge in, almost leading to tragedy. This ends on a comedy note. Director Helmut Kautner has been somewhat heavy-handed and pic becomes repetitious. But it does make its point about all men being alike and war being silly.

Acting is acceptable and color is an asset with technical credits fine. Lingos are well handled with subtitles where necessary. This is a coproduction which is justified and the begging of probable future French-West German film-making. *Mosk.*

The Last Days of Pompeii
(SUPERTOTALSCOPE—COLOR—ITALIAN)

Sin, blood and volcanic ash in one of the more spectacular spectaculars from Italy. Big, quick b.o. splash indicated.

Hollywood, June 9.

United Artists release of Paolo Moffa production. Stars Steve Reeves; features Cristina Rauffman, Barbara Carroll, Anne Marie Baumann, Fernando Rey, Mimmo Palmara, Angel Aranda, Guillermo Marin; with Mario Berroatua, Mario Morales, Angel Ortiz. Directed by Mario Bonnard. Screenplay, Ennio De Concini, Sergio Leone, Duccio Tessari, Sergio Corbucci; camera, Antonio Ballesteros; editor, Eraldo Da Roma; music, Angelo Francesco Lavagnino; assistant director, Tessari. Reviewed at Goldwyn Studios, June 9, '60. Running time, **103 MINS.**

Glaucus	Steve Reeves
Ione	Cristina Kauffman
Nydia	Barbara Carroll
Julia	Anne Marie Baumann
Gallinus	Mimmo Palmara
High Priest	Fernando Rey
Leader of Christians	Carlo Tamberlani
Antonius	Angel Aranda
Second Consul	Mino Doro
Askinius	Guglielmo Marin
Praetorian Guards	Mario Berroatua, Mario Morales, Angel Ortiz

For sheer spectacle, even the new practiced Italians will be hard put to top this new production of "The Last Days of Pompeii." Its crude dramatic approach and shallow characterizations can, should and will be lightly regarded as but a minor flaw of a film that is designed specifically to overpower the spectator with its physical magnitude and technical prowess. The promise of an erupting Vesuvius, an abundance of sex ex machina and gore galore, as well as the presenee of the now well-established Steve Reeves as its star, guarantees the United Artists release a swift, but tidy, domestic boxoffice impact.

The screenplay, as adapted by a battery of four (Ennio De Concini, Sergio Leone, Duccio Tessari and Sergio Corbucci), is little more than an excuse to knit the film's highly exploitable bursts of spectacle together. It is a frankly preposterous account of the hero's efforts to rid Pompeii of its bloodiest parasites, a band of Ku-Kluxian hoods posing as Christians.

As energetically portrayed by be-muscled Beowulfman Reeves, he is a fellow who can subdue a lion, a crocodile and 18 armed warriors at once with his bare biceps, and this despite a severe chest wound that would have laid Paul Bunyan low. Mark down as the superfluous request of the century the heroine's words as Reeves swims through a wall of fire at the climax: "Oh, help him, dear Lord —give him strength."

Under Mario Bonnard's direction, the film's violently spectacular elements have been accomplished with vigor. Fights have been staged with choreographic imagination. Reeves' battles with a lion and a crocodile have been lensed and edited skillfully. And when the time comes for the climactic eruption, the sparks really fly. Bathed in brilliant Eastman hues and helped by some sizzling special effects, the last minutes of Pompeii are depicted as a fireworks display to rival a Chinese New Year, U.S. Fourth of July and French Bastille Day put together.

Film has been produced in a new process dubbed "Supertotalscope." Since earlier arrivals from Italy were modestly fashioned out of mere "Totalscope," it will come as no shock should the next Neapolitan cinematic arrival be mounted in "Superduper-total-scope." *Tube.*

Battle in Outer Space
(TOHOSCOPE—COLOR—JAPANESE)

Cinematically skillful but outmoded sci-fi-fare. So-so prospects.

Hollywood, May 26.

Columbia Pictures release of Yuko Tanaka production. With Ryo Ikebe, Kyoko Anzai, Minoru Takada, Koreya Senda, Len Stanford, Harold Conway, George Whitman, Elise Richter, Hisaya Ito, Yoshio Tsuchiya, Hiro-O Kirino, Kozo Nomura, Fuyuki Murakami, Ikio Sawamura, Jiryd Kimagaya, Katsumx Tesuka, Mitsuo Isuda, Tadashi Okabe, Osran Yuri, Malcim Pearce, Leonard Walsh, Heimz Bolmer, Roma Corlson, Yasuhisa Tsutsumi, Kisao Hatamochi, Koichi Sato, Tatsuo Araki, Rinsaku Ogata, Keisumy Yamada, Yokikose Kamimera, Yutaka Oka, Snigro Kato, Saburo Kadowaki, Yusihiko Goxoo, Shinjiro Hirota. Directed by Inoshiro Honda. Screenplay, Shinichi Sekizawa, from original story by Jotaro Okami; camera, Hajime Koizumi; editor, Kazuji Taira; art director, Teruaki Andoi music, Akira Ifukube; assistant director, Koji Kajita. Reviewed at the studio, May 26, '60. Running time, **90 MINS.**

A naturally mandatory requirement of sci-fi films is that they be at least a little ahead of their time in point-of-view. "Battle In Outer

Space" isn't. In fact, outside of some sporadic flashes of technical and photographic skill, this Japanese-made item is as dated in concept as a Buck Rogers serial and frequently as futuristic in appearance as one of the less imaginative space exhibits in Disneyland. As such, the Columbia release is not likely to create much stir in the domestic sci-fi mart outside of the ripples of enthusiasm and attitudes of awe it may generate in children's sections.

The aimless, witless screenplay, by Shinichi Sekizawa from an "original" yarn by Jotaro Okami, drums up the dependable and thoroughly saturated idea that the peace-loving earth is about to be attacked by "other beings whose intelligence is superior to ours." In Sekizawa's variation, this occurs in the nearby year 1965, which is okay, except that our retaliation is so scientifically advanced it is entirely unbelievable. A few accurate blasts of that venerable weapon, the trusty ray gun, and the English-speaking invaders have been vanquished. But it's not the victory, it's how we play the game, that attracts the spectator's attention in this picture. For instance, the USSR is conspicuously absent from the UN conference table as earthmen convene to mull counter-attack strategy.

Although the expendable scenery has a cardboard look about it, there are one or two realistic destruction scenes in miniature, notably one in which the Golden Gate Bridge is demolished by a "space torpedo." For the effectiveness of these passages, major credit belongs to special effects man Eiji Tsuburaya and art director Teruaki Ando. Optical photography by Hinnsaburo Araki is accomplished, and use of color is an impressive embellishment. Dubbing, by Bellucci Productions, is capable. Most of the acting is over-acting, which says little, from a western cultural standpoint at any rate, for Inoshiro Honda's direction. *Tube.*

Never Let Go
(BRITISH)

Well made, but over-violent thriller, showing Peter Sellers in yet another new phase; will satisfy those with strong stomachs.

London, June 7.

Rank release of a Julian Wintle-Leslie Parkyn (Peter de Sarigny) production. Stars Richard Todd, Peter Sellers, Elizabeth Sellars; features Adam Faith, Carol White. Directed by John Guillermin. Screenplay, Alun Falconer, based on story by Peter de Sarigny and John Guillerman; editor, Ralph Sheldon; camera, Christopher Challis; music, John Barry. At Odeon, Leicester Square, London. Running time, 91 MINS.

John Cummings .... Richard Todd
Lionel Meadows .... Peter Sellers
Anne Cummings .... Elizabeth Sellars
Tommy Towers .... Adam Faith
Jackie .... Carol White
Alfie Barnes .... Mervyn Johns
Inspector Thomas .... Noel Willman
Cliff .... David Lodge
Alec Berger .... Peter Jones
MacKinnon .... John Bailey
Regan .... Nigel Stock
Pennington .... John Le Mesurier
Station Sergeant .... John Dunbar
Cyril Spink .... Charles Houston

Peter Sellers' determination to prove his versatility is becoming almost an obsession. It is leading him into making too many films and almost recklessly playing any type of part offered, provided it is different from the one before. His name, and that of Richard Todd, will attract the patrons. But they may be in for a shock when they find Sellers playing a thoroughly vicious, sadistic crook who runs a highly organized car-stealing racket. It is a remarkably effective performance but, having got it off his chest, it's to be hoped that this gifted performer will quickly return to the kind of shrewd, observant character comedy that has made him so popular.

"Never Let Go" is a tough, well-made film with more unpleasant violence than is needed. In fact, towards the end there is so much piled up that it tends to lapse into burlesque. There are four or five vicious beatings up, a hint of rape, and the choice instance when Sellers grinds a boy's hand under a heavy weight. All this is a pity, since on a less tough note, the pic would still have been a gripping drama.

Richard Todd plays an unsuccessful cosmetics salesman who buys a car in order to boost his business prospects. It is uninsured against loss and when it is stolen by a young hoodlum, Todd makes it a personal vendetta. In his determination to get the car back he treads on the toes of the police, loses his job, nearly loses his wife and suffers a couple of merciless beatings-up by Sellers and his gang.

Alun Falconer's screenplay is brisk and John Guillermin has directed with equal verve. Christopher Challis' lensing does much to bring out the sleazy atmosphere of London's backstreets. John Barry's music is also extremely effective.

Sellers, as the sleek, utterly callous crook is spasmodically good, and particularly useful in his quieter moments. Richard Todd, on the other hand, is excellent throughout. Playing a downtrodden near-failure is quite a departure for him but he is persuasive throughout. His relationship with his wife is an interesting side issue of the main plot and it might have been developed more, giving greater scope to Elizabeth Sellars, who has little to do but look long-suffering.

Offbeat casting is that of Adam Faith, a young pop singer-idol, who makes his debut (soundly, too) as a straight actor in the role of a tough, young hood. He also sings the title song.

Another newcomer is Carol White, a young blonde, who plays Sellers' mistress. Here again is a performance that suggests that Miss White has a future. Noel Willman's ice-cold, "stick-to-the-rules" cop, is a steely piece of thesping. David Lodge, as Sellers' bodyguard, and Mervyn Johns, as an old newsvendor who gets mixed up in the contretemps, both contribute strong performances. *Rich.*

Les Jeux de L'Amour
(GAMES OF LOVE)
(FRENCH)

Paris, June 14.

Cocinor release of AJYM production. With Genevieve Cluny, Jean-Louis Maury, Jean-Pierre Cassel. Directed by Philippe De Broca. Screenplay, De Broca, Cluny, Daniel Boulanger; camera, Jean Penzer; editor, Laurence Mery. At Balzac, Paris. Running time, 87 MINS.

Victor .... Jean-Pierre Cassel
Suzanne .... Genevieve Cluny
Francois .... Jean-Louis Maury
Client .... Robert Vattier
Consumer .... Claude Cerval
Driver .... Pierre Repp

The ebbing "New Wave" of filmmakers here has belatedly given its first true comedy in this fresh treatment of an old situation. Pic looms a surefire local item with art and playoff possibilities abroad indicated on its liveliness, theme and mounting.

A young girl, living with an irrepressible young painter, longs for at least a child to cement their affair. He refuses since happy in his present status. A best friend takes a hand by offering marriage but the flightly one finally sees the way and promises a wedding.

However, it is all in how told that puts this across. The love scenes are witty and infectious. Sudden scenes of improvised dance and even singing are well welded. Like all good situation comedies this has a dash of seriousness, well assimilated and observed. For once a "Waver" has made a pic carefully with a fine technical sheen and solid acting.

Jean-Pierre Cassel is unveiled as a much-needed leading man here with a catching gaiety, timing and personality. He is well seconded by Genevieve Cluny and Jean-Louis Maury as the girl and friend who bring him around to taking a position in life. Film is reminscent of the pre-war Yank romantic comedies. However, this has a frankness and clarity that is quite Gallic in tone and should help it in foreign spotting. The right handling could make this pay off. Irwin Shapiro, of Films-Around-the-World, a Yank foreign film distribution indie, already has it set for the U. S. *Mosk.*

Meurtre en 45 Tours
(Murder at 45 RPMs)
(FRENCH)

Paris, June 7.

Metro release of Cite-Films production. Stars Danielle Darrieux, Michel Auclair, Jean Servais; features Henri Guisol, Jacqueline Dano. Directed by Etienne Perier. Screenplay, Albert Valentin, Dominique Fabre, Perier; camera, Marcel Weiss; editor, Robert Isnardan. At the Paris, Paris. Running time, 105 MINS.

Eve .... Danielle Darrieux
Jean .... Michel Auclair
Faugere .... Jean Servais
Meloit .... Henri Guisol
Florence .... Jacqueline Dano

Fairly slick suspense item throws suspicion around as to whether a famous composer has been really killed in a car crash and is haunting his wife and her lover. Pace and tactics are fairly obvious. This rarely gets a true original feel into this oft-told tale so as to make it primarily a local item or a possible dualer item abroad on its theme and the name of Danielle Darrieux.

A famous singer has fallen in love with a younger man and her husband is supposedly killed in a car crash. Then he starts sending her records in which both are tormented. It finally seems that her husband's editor has engineered the affair. The direction is sleek but uses the usual dark effects with hooting owls for its suspense. Acting is acceptable and technical credits good. *Mosk.*

Tendre et Violente Elisabeth
(Tender and Violent Elizabeth)
(FRENCH)

Paris, June 7.

Gaumont release of Ceres-Marly-SNEG production. Stars Christian Marquand, Lucile Saint-Simon; features Marie Dea, Clement Thierry, Paulette Dubost. Directed by Henri Decoin. Screenplay, Mireille De Tissot, Decoin, Henri Troyat from novel by Troyat; camera, Pierre Petit; editor, Claude Durand. At Ambassade-Gaumont, Paris. Running time, 105 MINS.

Elisabeth .... Lucile Saint-Simon
Christian .... Christian Marquand
Patrice .... Clement Thierry

Film begins like "Junior Miss" and ends like a soap opera. It is conventional and lacks a comedic flair. Pic thus looms a gloomy, distaff entry primarily for local use with only dualer foreign chances indicated on the exploitation peg of some fairly lucid love scenes.

A young girl, daughter of the owners of a ski resort hotel, after fighting off advances of young boys is quickly seduced by a dashing handsome immoralist who wants only pleasure and not romance. She rebels and marries a young pianist. But the call of the flesh has her back with the first love.

Lucile Saint-Simon denotes presence but can still not evoke the needed girlish charm or more lusty character. However, she shows future promise. Pic is slickly if unimaginatively put together by oldtimer Henri Decoin. Technical credits are good with a usual stock of stereotypes backing the young actors. *Mosk.*

Les Scelerats
(The Wretches)
(FRENCH)

Paris, June 7.

Cocinor release of Marceau-Lopez production. Stars Michele Morgan, Robert Hossein; features Perrette Pradier, Olivier Hussenot, Jacqueline Morane, Frank Latimore, Robert Porte. Directed by Robert Hossein. Screenplay, Frederic Dard; camera, Jacques Robin; editor, Louisette Hautecoeur. At Colisee, Paris. Running time, 90 MINS.

Thelma .... Michele Morgan
Jess .... Robert Hossein
Louise .... Perrette Pradier
Father .... Olivier Hussenot
Mother .... Jacqueline Morane
Ted .... Frank Latimore
Inspector .... Robert Porte

Glossy drama is somewhat overdone for anything but possible dualed situations abroad. It is dragged out.

A couple of Americans move into a modern, glass walled house in a beat-up Paris neighborhood. Only one family seems to live next door and the daughter gets a job as maid as the couple are shown to be unhappy due to the death of a son in an auto accident some time ago. The wife drinks and the husband broods while the maid falls for him.

It ends with an accident in which the wife is killed and the maid makes him think the wife thought he did it deliberately. This lacks a lot, and the forced thesping of star Michele Morgan relegates it to dualers mainly or possible tele use. Technical credits are good but direction is draggy. *Mosk.*

La Brune Que Voila
(There is the Brunet)
(FRENCH)

Paris, June 14.
CFDC release of Film D'Art-Panoramas Film production. Stars Robert Lamoureux; features Christian Alers, Michele Mercier, Francoise Fabian, Ginette Pigeon, Pierette Pradier, Yves Robert, Jean-Pierre Marielle. Written and directed by Robert Lamoureux; cafera, Robert Lefebvre; editor, Denise Natot. At Ermitage, Paris. Running time, 80 MINS.
Germain .... Robert Lamoureux
Louis .... Christian Alers
Sonia .... Michele Mercier
Christine .... Francoise Fabian
Anne-Marie .... Ginette Pigeon
Sophie .... Pierette Pradier
Sutiro .... Jean-Pierre Marielle
Husband .... Yves Robert

This film is adapted from a boulevard comedy and is still too talky for film use. It concerns a rake carrying on with four married women who receives a call from one of their husbands and is warned to cease and desist, but does not know which one has phoned. Film follows its predictable course and seems mainly a local item with too many static qualities for any good foreign chances.

Robert Lamoureux is a smart comedian but as a director he relies too much on palaver. Hence, this lags. Technical credits are okay.   *Mosk.*

Recours en Grace
(Petition for Pardon)
(FRENCH)

Paris, June 7.
Cocinor release of Marceau- Laetitia production. Stars Raf Vallone, Emmanuele Riva, Annie Girardot; features Fernand Ledoux, Renaud Mary. Directed by Laslo Benedek. Screenplay, Henri Calef, Claude Brule, Benedek from novel by Calef; camera, Michel Kelber; editor, Marinette Cadix. At Ambassade-Gaumont, Paris. Running time, 100 MINS.
Mario .... Raf Vallone
Germaine .... Emmanuele Riva
Lilla .... Annie Girardot
Priest .... Fernand Ledoux
Foreman .... Renaud Mary

A familiar story of a man on the run gets some weightier treatment by bringing in the problems of desertion, old loves, conflicts between maternal and sensual love. This is primarily an arty possibility for any foreign chances. It is somewhat talky and sometimes sacrifices movement for ideas. But it is bolstered by a fine trio of actors for an added asset.

An Italian, who has become French, suddenly turns himself in as a deserter from the army after 15 years when a chance encounter with an old friend reveals he has been using another name and he cannot face the woman with whom he has been living for years. When she does not come to see him, he escapes and then goes through the hands of many people before being shot down by the police.

Laslo Benedek has given this a controlled mounting, relying on close-ups and acting to spin his tale of hopelessness. It tackles worthy themes but bogs it down in dialog. However, Raf Vallone, as the hounded fugitive; Annie Girardot, as an old love; and Emmanuelle Riva, as the muddled mistress give this a fair measure of quiet force. But it would need a hard sell abroad. Technical credits are good.   *Mosk.*

La Millieme Fenetre
(The Thousandth Window)
(FRENCH)

Paris, June 7.
UGC release of Ulysse production. Stars Pierre Fresnay, Jean-Louis Trintignant, Barbara Kwiatkowska, Carette, Francoise Fleury, Michel De Re. Directed by Robert Menegoz. Screenplay, Jacques Lanzmann, Menegoz; camera, Jean Penzer; editor, Ginnette Boudet. At Normandie, Paris. Running time, 90 MINS.
Armand .... Pierre Fresnay
Georges .... Jean-Louis Trintignant
Ania .... Barbara Kwaitkowska
Billois .... Carette
Annie .... Francoise Fleury
Tourtet .... Michel De Re

Well-meaning pic deals with an old rugged individualist who is holding up a big housing program by refusing to leave his old home. Young love buds around him and he finally capitulates when he finds he is being used by the entrepreneurs who do not have enough dough to finish it.

Film unfolds in a manner reminiscent of the early Yank situation comedies with many colorful characters. However, this lacks the snap, invention and precision to make it stand out in its genre. Though fairly entertaining, it is telegraphed and obvious with chancy possibilities abroad if an okay local item.

Pierre Fresnay is good as the crusty holdout while Polish actress Barbara Kwiatkowska has the looks, presence, intelligence and timing which should make her heard from soon. Ditto new director Robert Menegoz who portrays a good visual flair in his first vehicle, but is somewhat hampered by the talky and conventional script. Technical credits are good. On-the-spot lensing is also an asset.   *Mosk.*

La Caperucita Roja
(Little Red Riding Hood)
(MEXICAN—EASTMANCOLOR)

Mexico City, June 7.
Peliculas Nacionales release of Peliculas Rodriguez, S.A. production. Stars Maria Garcia, Manuel "Loco" Valdez, Midget Santanon, Prudencia Grifell, Beatriz Aguirre, G. Alvarez Bianchi and Irma Torres. Story and songs by Fernando Morales Ortiz; adaptation, F. Morales Ortiz and R. Garcia Traves; camera (Eastmancolor), Alex Phillips. At Roble Theatre, Mexico City. Running time, 09 MINS.

Mexican producers have discovered gold in fields of children's fairy tales, with the rich vein first struck with "Tom Thumb." In this adaptation of "Little Red Riding Hood," which scored at the recent Argentine Film Fest it's irregular at times since writers Ortiz and Traves have taken certain liberties.

The big bad wolf is not such a bad guy after all and is "regenerated" to become a stalwart citizen and helpmate of the woodchoppers of the little village in which the story is laid.

There are song and dance numbers while settings have been carefully prepared both on location and in the studio.

Maria Garcia, selected after a weeding out of hundreds of aspirants for the name role, shows promise. "Loco" Caldez obviously enjoys himself as the not-so-ferocious wolf. Midget Santanon, as the Lovelorn Fox, was written into script to avoid monologs by the Wolf. Veteran actress Prudencia Grifell interprets her role with sympathetic understanding, aiming at the kids in audience.

Background music, with no credit given, is good. Alex Phillips may not be very happy about way his photography turned out for colors because it's not uniform at times. There are lapses in story continuity, and a tendency to be over lavish with some sets. But the over-all effect is a better than average program picture for kiddies trade that should do good business.   *Emil.*

Vildfaglar
(Wild Birds)
(SWEDISH)

Paris, June 7.
Svensk Film production and release. With Maj-Britt Nilsson, Per Oscarsson, Ulf Palme, Ulla Sjoblom, Gertrud Fridh. Directed by Alf Sjoberg. Screenplay, Bengt Anderberg, Sjoberg; camera, Martin Bodin; editor, Lennart Wallen. At Pagode, Paris. Running time, 100 MINS.
Lenn .... Maj-Britt Nilsson
Nisse .... Per Oscarsson
Chief .... Ulf Palme
Ulla .... Ulla Sjoblom
Esther .... Gertrud Fridh

After Ingmar Bergman, the Swedish pic director with the most international renown probably is Alf Sjoberg. But he does not write his own material and his symbols, interpretations and attitudes are sometimes too surface, rarely letting the subject expand.

This one is a good, if familiar, tale of two lovers from different segments of society who take their own lives when all conspires against their being together. Sjoberg has tried to give this too heavy an air of finality and tragedy with a resultant lack of true poignance. But it has deft visual flair, excellent acting and an engrossing air which finally make its point.

The hero is a petty criminal and the heroine a middle-class girl not content with her approaching marriage and afraid of growing old. Their love is swift, violent and beautiful but they finally take their own lives. It is technically good except for the obvious studio feel of the interiors.

This looms only for arty chances abroad. It also has some exploitation pegs on its excellent portrayal of low life and the yearnings and questionings of youth. But its dovetail of all to the theme of pessimism and hopelessness robs it of real feeling.   *Mosk.*

Battle in Outer Space
(JAPANESE—COLOR)

Lusty sci-fi meller geared for top grosses in the juve market; strong exploitation values.

Columbia release of a Toho (Tomoyuki Tanaka) production. Features Ryo Ikebe, Kyoko Anzai, Leonard Stanford, Harold Conway, George Whyman, Elise Richter. Directed by Inoshiro Honda. Screenplay, Shinichi Sekizawa, based on story by Jotaro Okami; camera (Eastmancolor), Hajime Koizumi; editor, Kazuji Taira; special effects, Eiji Tsuburaya. Previewed N.Y., May 27, '60. Running time, 90 MINS.

Filmed as a co-production by Columbia and Japan's Toho company, "Battle in Outer Space" is a rousing exploitation entry for the youngsters as well as adults who dig sci-fi pix. It tops "Godzilla, King of the Monsters," another Toho production with which Joe Levine's Embassy Pictures

---

struck a b.o. bonanza some four years ago.

This Japanese import is tailor-made for saturation openings. If backed by a heavy tv spot announcement campaign and razzle-dazzle bally aimed at the kids, the multiple preems are bound to clean up at the wicket. Cast, comprised primarily of Japanese players, is unknown to American audiences.

But the lack of marquee names is no liability for the star of this entry is its imaginative story and special effects. Based on a story by Jotaro Okami, the Shinichi Sekizawa screenplay unreels an absorbing tale of how the nations of the Earth unite in a common cause to fight off an invader from outer space.

Picture has a number of flaws including some stereotyped performances and a dubbing (into English) job that isn't always synchronized with the players' voices. However, the Saturday matinee trade probably won't even be aware of these deficiencies.

Eiji Tsuburaya's special effects are particularly effective in sequences where two space ships from the Earth land on the Moon to destroy the invaders' base. There's also lotsa action and suspense as the Earth men utilize their heat ray guns to disintegrate their adversaries' flying saucers. Curiously, although the base is obliterated, the invaders' attack on the Earth proper comes anyway.

Eastman Color lensing of Hajime Koizumi adds realism to the yarn while Kazuji Taira edited the footage to a tight 90 minutes. Direction of Inoshiro Honda draws ample tension from the action scenes. There, incidentally, are the major interest and personalities are secondary.

Mixed cast of Japanese players and others who apparently are Americans have little to do with exception of manning the intricate equipment. Columbia's credit sheet is no help in identifying the players' roles. Producer Tomoyuki Tanaka, who also turned out "Godzilla," helped the credibility of "Space" with some lavish physical backgrounds.   *Gilb.*

Song Without End
(C'SCOPE—COLOR)

Cinematic know-how glosses over sketchy dramatization of the Franz Liszt story. Best for older audiences and classical buffs. Needs aggressive trade and consumer campaign to repeat Chopin biofilm click.

Hollywood, June 6.

Columbia Pictures release of William Goetz production. Stars Dirk Bogarde; features Capucine, Genevieve Page, Patricia Morison. Directed by Charles Vidor. Screenplay, Oscar Millard; camera, James Wong Howe; editor, William A. Lyon; music, Harry Sukman; asst. director, Carter DeHaven Jr. Reviewed at Academy Award Theatre, June 6, '60. Running time, **145 MINS.**

Franz Liszt .... Dirk Bogarde
Princess Carolyne .... Capucine
Countess Marie .... Genevieve Page
George Sand .... Patricia Morison
Prince Nicholas .... Ivan Desny
Grand Duchess .... Martita Hunt
Potin .... Lou Jacobi
Prince Felix Lichnowsky .... Albert Rueprecht
Chelard .... Marcel Dalio
Richard Wagner .... Lyndon Brook
Archbishop .... Walter Rilla
Czar .... Hans Unterkirchner
Thalberg .... E. Erlandsen
Chopin .... Alex Davion
Anna Liszt .... Katherine Squire

With a burst of cinematic energy and skill, the William Goetz production of "Song Without End" dramatizes the story of pianist-composer Franz Liszt. It is a must-see motion picture for music lovers, an enriching experience for "family" audiences, and a particularly compelling attraction for social security eligibles. Only question is whether the relatively unfamiliar cast and classical music may find resistance among a sizeable portion of the regular film-going mass public. However, Columbia turned the tide overwhelmingly in its favor 15 years ago with a similar, but not as well done, music treatment of Chopin. "A Song to Remember," so the time could be ripe for a boxoffice encore.

Columbia hasn't forgotten the doubts that at first surrounded the earlier hit and is prepared to give "Song Without End" the vigorous selling which should promote the enthusiasm and economically gratifying response it merits.

Oscar Millard's screenplay stumbles. A complex central character, Liszt is depicted as a man tragically embroiled in overlapping romantic, religious and professional conflicts. His relations with the opposite sex are stormy, illicit and ill-fated. Discarding the irreligious mother of his two children, he discovers happiness and the germ of artistic fulfillment during his affair with the devout wife of a Russian prince, only to have it dissolve abruptly on the eve of their wedding when the church refuses to annul her marriage. The film concludes on a dramatic note when the troubled Liszt seeks solace in a monastery for his secular wounds and sins.

Where the screenplay is never quite clear is in its concept of Liszt's creative ability. Peerless keyboard technician and interpreter of the genius of his contemporaries, he is regarded as "a victim of his own virtuosity and the urge to display it" when he pursues a more creative bent. And yet he is seen emerging triumphant as a composer. A more consistent point-of-view would have made for a better picture. Outside of this reservation and a tendency to follow standard procedure in musical biography, Millard's scenario is sturdy, particularly in the barbed wit and capsule commentaries of its dialog.

It is in the production itself that the film attains stature. Producer Goetz has created a striking spectacle filmed in fascinating, authentic Continental locales sure to enthrall the spectator. It is a feast of sight and sound put together by a battery of expert cinema craftsmen.

A masterpiece of sheer audio proportions has been fashioned by sound man Lambert Day out of the superb musical teamwork of adaptor Harry Sukman, consultant Abram Chasins, coordinator Victor Aller, recorder Earl Mounce, conductor Morris Stoloff, the Los Angeles Philharmonic and the Roger Wagner Chorale. Likewise, art director Walter Holscher has utilized a striking succession of concert hall, theatre and palace interiors to express the ornate culture of mid-19th century Europe. Lensman James Wong Howe has zeroed in on these authentic settings with athletic dexterity, quickening the tempo and increasing the visual interest of a series of "recital" sequences which otherwise have a tendency to grow monotonous. William A. Lyon's editing dramatically punctuates and coordinates the interrelationship of soundtrack with images.

All these skills have been integrated into an impressive physical whole by directors Charles Vidor and George Cukor, but they were not as uniformly successful in commandeering a matching dramatic spirit from the cast. Vidor died June 4, 1959, having filmed about 15% of the pictures. He gets full director's title at request of Cukor who took a smaller screen credit. That portions of the drama emerge more andante than allegro is at least partially the result of one or two less than convincing performances.

An exception is Dirk Bogarde, a fine English actor who plays the vain, impertinent, dynamic central character. Although there's a tendency to exaggerate a swagger (he even swaggers into the monastery at the climax), Bogarde delivers a vigorous portrayal of Liszt, and his mock keyboard fingerwork is a positively brilliant match to the exciting pianistics of soloist Jorge Bolet.

The film introduces former Parisian fashion model Capucine to the screen. Her acting lacks the required warmth and animation (there are moments when she appears to be posing for a Vogue cover), but she brings an unusual, strikingly mature facial beauty to films. More comfortably equipped with thespic talent is Genevieve Page, although at times she inserts a little too much wild-eyed fervor into her delineation of Liszt's mistress.

Favorable supporting characterizations are delivered by Martita Hunt and Lou Jacobi. Patricia Morison is more of a caricature than a character in the role of "George Sand." *Tube.*

A Matter of Morals
(SWEDISH)

Stockholm, June 14.

Sandrew Film release of Fortress Productions (Steve Hopkins and John Hess) production. Stars Patrick O'Neal, Maj-Britt Nilsson, Mogens Wieth; features Eva Dahlbeck, Claes Thelander, Lennart Lindberg, Vernon Young, Gosta Cederlund, Hampe Faustman. Directed by John Cromwell. Screenplay by John Hess; camera, Sven Nykvist; music, Dag Wiren. Previewed in Stockholm. Running time, **98 MINS.**

Alan Kennebeck .... Patrick O'Neal
Anita Anderson .... Maj-Britt Nilsson
Erik Walderman .... Mogens Wieth
Eva, his wife .... Eva Dahlbeck
Bjornson .... Claes Thelander
Sven Arborg .... Lennart Lindberg
Henderson .... Vernon Young
Eklund .... Goesta Cederlund
Kronstad .... Hampe Faustman

Here is the much discussed Swedish-American coproduction or better said American-Swedish since English is the main language.

Plot is simple, dealing with a big international financial genius, Eklund. He has a factory in Stockholm, and since he wants to expand his financial kingdom, he has asked a bank in Milwaukee for a huge loan. The bank sends a man to Sweden to have a look at the factory. This is Patrick O'Neal, who is taken care of by Mogens Wieth. Nobody discovers that Wieth (Eklund's right-hand man) and some others at the Stockholm office is working hard to ruin Eklund and take over his kingdom.

Wieth arranges so that his sister-in-law, Anita Andersson (Maj-Britt Nilsson) becomes the hostess of O'Neal during his Swedish stay. The two fall in love. Kennebeck with his American ideas of fair play, decides that what he can do is return to the U.S., and get a divorce from his wife. But Anita, on other hand, realizes that no matter if she loved him, they are too different, and that she might become a handicap to him in his career.

O'Neal is talked into cooperation with Wieth and joins the plan to ruin Eklund.

This develops into an ordinary crime thriller, but it leaves a lot to be desired. The action is too slow but it is a film which has been made for the arty houses of America. If cleverly exploited, it might do very good business.

O'Neal, as the American who runs into trouble in Sweden, is very good. Maj-Britt Nilsson as his girl sweetheart, also does an outstanding job. Wieth, Danish actor, plays Erik Walderman, the man who is the center of the plot. His role is dominating. Eva Dahlbeck as Walderman's wife, gives evidence of her talent. Goesta Cederlund, as the financial genius, has little to do except commit suicide at the end.

Camerawork (in AgaScope) by Sven Nykvist is first-class, particularly when he is on location in the small streets of Stockholm's old town. *Wing.*

Psycho

Alfred Hitchcock formula: Shock meller, with a couple of particularly lurid scenes. Unelaborate production. Well done, doubtless will succeed.

Paramount release of Alfred Hitchcock production. Stars Janet Leigh, Vera Miles, Anthony Perkins; features John Gavin, Martin Balsam, Simon Oakland. Directed by Hitchcock. Screenplay, Joseph Stefano, from novel by Robert Bloch; camera, John L. Russell; editor, George Tomasini; music, Bernard Herrmann. At DeMille Theatre, N.Y., June 16, '60. Running time, **109 MINS.**

Norman Bates .... Anthony Perkins
Marion Crane .... Janet Leigh
Lila Crane .... Vera Miles
Sam Loomis .... John Gavin
Milton Arbogast .... Martin Balsam
Sheriff Chambers .... John McIntire
Dr. Richmond .... Simon Oakland
And Frank Albertson, Pat Hitchcock, Vaughn Taylor, Lurene Tuttle, John Anderson and Mort Mills.

Anyone listening hard enough, might almost hear Alfred Hitchcock saying, "Believe this, kids, and I'll tell you another." The rejoinder from this corner: Believability doesn't matter; but do tell another.

Producer-director Hitchcock is up to his clavicle in whimsicality and apparently had the time of his life in putting together "Psycho." He's gotten in gore, in the form of a couple of graphically-depicted knife murders, a story that's far out in Freudian motivations, and now and then injects little amusing plot items that suggest the whole thing is not to be taken seriously.

The "Psycho" diagnosis, commercially, is this: an unusual, good entertainment, indelibly Hitchcock, and on the right kind of boxoffice beam. The campaign backing is fitting and potent. The edict against seating customers after opening curtain (as observed at New York's DeMille Theatre) if respected may add to the intrigue. All adds up to success.

Hitchcock uses the old plea that nobody give away the ending—"it's the only one we have." This will be abided by here, but it must be said that the central force throughout the feature is a mother who is a homicidal maniac. This is unusual because she happens to be physically defunct, has been for some years. But she lives on in the person of her son.

Anthony Perkins is the young man who doesn't get enough exorcise (repeat exorcise) of that other inner being. Among his, or her, victims are Janet Leigh, who walks away from an illicit love affair with John Gavin, taking with her a stolen $40,000, and Martin Balsam, as a private eye who winds up in the same swamp in which Miss Leigh's body also is deposited.

John McIntire is the local sheriff with an unusual case on his hands, and Simon Oakland is the psychiatrist who recognizes that Perkins, while donning his mother's clothes, is not really a transvestite; he's just nuts. Vera Miles is the dead girl's sister whose investigation leads to the diagnosis of what ails Perkins.

Perkins gives a remarkably effective in-a-dream kind of performance as the possessed young man. Others play it straight, with equal competence.

Joseph Stefano's screenplay, from a novel by Robert Bloch, provides a strong foundation for Hitchcock's field day. And if the camera, under Hitchcock's direction, tends to over-emphasize a story point here and there, well, it's forgiveable. Further, the audience's indulgence is not too strained with the inevitable appearance of Hitchcock himself. He limits himself to barely more than a frame.

Saul Bass' titles are full of his characteristic trickiness, Bernard Herrmann's music nicely plays counter-point with the pictorial action and editing seems right all the way. *Gene.*

El Esqueleto de la Senora Morales
(The Skeleton of Mrs. Morales)
(MEXICAN)

Mexico City, June 14.
Columbia release of Alfa Films production. Stars Arturo de Cordova, Amparo Rivelles; features Elda Peralta, Guillermo Orea. Directed by Rogelio A. Gonzalez Jr. Screenplay, Luis Alcoriza from "Islington Mystery," by Arthur Machen; camera, Victor Herrera; music, Raul Lavista. At Chapultepec Theatre, Mexico City. Running time, 90 MINS.

With this film, Mexican motion picture elements reveal a capacity to produce imaginative films, far removed from the quickies that have been turned out for years. Based on Arthur Machen's "The Islington Mystery," Luis Alcoriza's adaptation has followed the original story line more or less faithfully. Director Rogelio A. Gonzalez has preserved the measure of cruelty, even grotesque mockery of religion, but with Mexican audiences in mind he put the author's points across without substantially molesting religious beliefs of this intensely Catholic country. It proves to be a delicate matter of toning down some of the story highlights.

The ending had to be changed, but Alcoriza and Gonzalez have displayed considerably ingenuity in presentation of the police thriller with farce overtones, centering about the character of Dr. Morales, accused with having done away with his spouse. Arturo de Cordova, as the doctor portrays the person of a tormented, but good person at heart, with considerable skill. Amparo Rivelles is an excellent foil to de Cordova as Mrs. Morales, "a demon in skirts."

Victor Herrera's photography does excellent work in building up suspense and atmosphere of the picture. But there some images at times were out of focus. This is not, however, a criticism of the cameraman, one of the ablest in Mexico today. Recently, in first-run houses, Mexican pictures appear to be projected badly. Projectionists claim it is not their fault, but that of laboratories. And labs place the blame on cameramen.

This is doing excellent business at the Chapultepec, and the film may be readied for a big play in markets other than the usual Latin circuit, with addition of subtitles and/or dubbed sound. *Emil.*

12 to the Moon

Lower-half science-fantasy item in which a dozen good eggs from earth tangle with some righteous, but misdirected, luna-tics. Timely, but crude and cliche-laden.

Hollywood, June 14.
Columbia Pictures release of Fred Gebhardt production. Stars Ken Clark, Michi Kobi, Tom Conway, Tony Dexter, John Wengraf, Anna-Lisa, Phillip Baird, Roger Til, Cory Devlin, Tema Bey, Bob Montgomery Jr., Richard Weber, Francis X. Bushman. Directed by David Bradley. Screenplay, DeWitt Bodeen, from story by Gebhardt; camera, John Alton; editor, Edward Mann; art director, Rudi Feld; music, Michael Andersen; assistant director, Gilbert Mandelk. Reviewed at the studio, June 14, '60. Running time, 74 MINS.

Captain Anderson	Ken Clark
Dr. Murata	Michi Kobi
Dr. Orloff	Tom Conway
Dr. Luis Vargas	Tony Dexter
Dr. Heinrich	John Wengraf
Dr. Bromark	Anna-Lisa
Dr. Rochester	Phillip Baird
Dr. Martel	Roger Til
Dr. Makonen	Cory Devlin
Dr. Hamid	Tema Bey
Roddy Murdock	Bob Montgomery Jr.
Dr. Ruskin	Richard Weber
Narrator	Francis X. Bushman

"12 To the Moon" advances the wishful notion that man's initial flight to the moon will be conducted on a cooperative international basis, with representatives of both sexes and 12 nations blissfully zooming into space together.

DeWitt Bodeen's screenplay, from producer Fred Gebhardt's story, contains some very impressive-sounding, but doubtful, scientific mumbo-jumbo. Its characters, however, are straight out of the funnybook pages. There are occasional flurries of excitement as the space ship maneuvers through meteoric showers and microscopic dust formations, and an ironical twist when the moon-people turn out to be benevolent, peace-loving creatures, scared to death that earthlings will contaminate their civilization, snugly ensconced under the lunar crust. They want no part of us, and proceed (though benevolent and peace-loving!) to freeze North America to prove they're anti-social.

David Bradley's direction overlooks some of the now well-known characteristics of space flight. Under his guidance, the emoting is extremely stiff and postured. Among those chiefly involved are Ken Clark as the flight captain, Tom Conway as a pesky Russian, John Wengraf as the repentant son of a Nazi, Richard Weber as an Israeli scientists whose parents were murdered by Wengraf's father, Anna-Lisa as a glamorous Swedish research chemist who makes beautiful chemistry on the moon with Tema Bey, as a Turkish biologist, and Francis X. Bushman as director of the project.

Special effects, photographic and explosive, are accomplished, as is John Alton's camera work. Michael Andersen's score is effective, Rudi Feld's are direction appropriate, Edward Mann's editing capable. *Tube.*

The Subterraneans
(C'SCOPE—COLOR)

Look, ma, we're beatniks. Lacklustre screen invasion of Jack Kerouac's coffee-shop-worn fad.

Hollywood, June 15.
Metro release of Arthur Freed production. Stars Leslie Caron, George Peppard, Janice Rule, Roddy McDowall. Directed by Ranald MacDougall. Screenplay, Robert Thom, based on Jack Kerouac's novel; camera, Joseph Ruttenberg; editor, Ben Lewis; art directors, George W. Davis, Urie McCleary; music, Andre Previn; assistant director, William Shanks. Reviewed at the studio, June 15, '60. Running time, 89 MINS.

Mardou Fox	Leslie Caron
Leo Percepied	George Peppard
Roxanne	Janice Rule
Yuri Gligoric	Roddy McDowall
Charlotte Percepied	Anne Seymour
Adam Moorad	Jim Hutton
Julien Alexander	Scott Marlowe
Arial Lavalerra	Arte Johnson
Analyst	Ruth Storey
Bartender	Bert Freed
Joshua Hoskins	Gerry Mulligan
Herself	Carmen McRae
Himself	Andre Previn
Themselves	Shelly Manne, Red Mitchell, Art Farmer, Dave Bailey, Buddy Clark, Russ Freeman Art Pepper, Bob Enevoldsen, William R. Perkins, Frank Hamilton

Those who have suspected all along that beatniks are dull, have proof in Metro's "The Subterraneans." How the Arthur Freed production will fare financially depends to a great extent on whether beatnikism has sustained enough of its initial attention. Odds are that even young people will find this version unappealing and uninteresting. Since youth appears to be the prime audience target, both the film and the fad seem headed for ho-humsville.

Jack Kerouac's novel is the basis for Robert Thom's screenplay, which pokes around the off-beaten path of San Francisco's North Beach and dredges up some bargain-basement philosophy, B (eat)-girls and bed ruminations. Its hero (George Peppard), an ex-Olympic gold medal winner and Columbia honor grad now a nervous novelist, beats it when his mom chants the square cliche, "you need a nice girl."

Cruising around the Bay Area in search of meaning, he finds his home-away-from-home with the local coffee-house colony, promptly develops a crush on its most mixed-up member (Leslie Caron), an analyst's darling whose Freudian slip shows every time she submits frigidly to the sexual advances of her pals. Warming up to Peppard's amorous attentions, she is promptly with child, leading to a happy ending in which both decide to "go straight."

Miss Caron seems uncomfortable in this environment. Her fragile gamin charm is all but smothered under the character's unattractive, sickly veil. An apparent shortage of sensitivity makes handsome George Peppard rather unsuitable for his role.

Among the assorted beatniks, flashiest work is performed by Roddy McDowall as a kind of benevolent zen-mother who sleeps standing up, Janice Rule as a beat beaut with a complexion complex, and Arte Johnson as a paid-up member whose sizeable left bank-roll stems from literary sales to Hollywood. Respectable support is generated by Anne Seymour, Jim Hutton, Scott Marlowe, Bert Freed and Gerry Mulligan.

There is a lot of music in the picture, all of the modern jazz variety. Created by Andre Previn and interpreted by experts at the idiom such as Mulligan, Red Mitchell, Shelly Manne and Carmen McRae, it is the outstanding aspect of this film, which is also aided to a lesser extent by Joseph Ruttenberg's camera work and the George W. Davis-Urie McCleary art direction, both capturing the beatnik quality without overdoing it.

Moss Mabry's costumes, however, are surprisingly alien to the normal garb of the beat.

Ben Lewis' editing is competent.

The acting often has a "look ma —we're beatniks!" aura about it, and group scenes are self-conscious and stagey. This, of course, is no testimonial to Ranald MacDougall's direction. *Tube.*

Elmer Gantry
(COLOR)

The Old-Time Religion's a good racket for no-good evangelist. Powerhoused if potentially troublesome release.

Hollywood, June 16.
United Artists release of Bernard Smith production.. Stars Burt Lancaster, Jean Simmons; features Jagger, Arthur Kennedy, Shirley Jones, Patti Page. Directed by Richard Brooks. Screenplay, Brooks, from Sinclair Lewis novel; camera, John Alton; editor, Marge Fowler; music, Andre Previn; asst. director, Tom Shaw, Rowe Wallerstein, Carl Beringer. Reviewed at Goldwyn studio, June 16, '60. Running time, 146 MINS.

Elmer Gantry	Burt Lancaster
Sister Sharon Falconer	Jean Simmons
William L. Morgan	Dean Jagger
Jim Lefferts	Arthur Kennedy
Lulu Bains	Shirley Jones
Sister Rachel	Patti Page
George Babbitt	Edward Andrews
Reverend Pengilly	John McIntire
Pete	Joe Maross
Reverend Brown	Everett Glass
Reverend Phillips	Michael Whalen
Reverend Garrison	Hugh Marlowe
Reverend Planck	Philip Ober
Reverend Ulrich	Wendell Holmes
Captain Holt	Barry Kelly
Preacher	Rex Ingram

One of the more frequent criticisms of recent years is that too many small stories are being committed to the big screen. In filming Sinclair Lewis' contentious study of a scandalous evangelist, "Elmer Gantry," Richard Brooks has conversely framed a big story and one of the boldest religioso subjects Hollywood yet tackled for the old-fashioned rectangular screen (aspect ratio, (1.33x1) that was standard before CinemaScope.

This was a daring decision by writer-director Brooks and his producer Bernard Smith. But it should pay off by stimulating added conversation, if not debate, about a picture that aspires to be as provocative as was the book in 1927. Audiences may experience some initial strangeness in adjusting to the "Postage stamp" screen; some may even be expecting the picture momentarily to spread horizontally as late as the excitingly climactic destruction by fire of The Waters of Jordan Tabernacle. This sequence might well have been more spectacular on the broad screen. One thing is certain, however. It will be a rare viewer indeed that is not arrested, perhaps even agitated, by this sharply etched exhibition, albeit limited, of tawdry showmanship in revivalism.

Brooks has honored the spirit of Lewis' cynical commentary on circus-type primitive exhortation with pictorial imagery that is always pungent. He also has written dialog that is frank, biting and is apt to disturb, or even shock many particularly in the frequent use of the name of Jesus, rarely heard on the screen.

From the standpoint of technique this production plays like a symphony, with expertly ordered pianissimo and fortissimo story passages which build to a smashing crescendo in the cremation of Sister Sharon Falconer, an evangelist of questionable sincerity and propriety. She is caught in her own hell on earth as the crowning glory of her career burns fiercely while the blatantly corrupt Gantry is spared to head into an uncertain future.

The film ends roughly about the half-way mark in Gantry's life, whereas in the book he went on to become an influential Methodist minister, who married and raised

a family but continued to indulge in the carnal pleasures he denounced vehemently from the pulpit. Thus Brooks has softened the story, yet it is doubtful that "Elmer Gantry" will escape agitating the Bible Belt.

Burt Lancaster pulls out virtually all the stops as Elmer Gantry to create a memorable characterization. He acts with such broad and eloquent flourish that a finely balanced more subdueld performance by Jean Simmons as Sister Sharon seems pale by comparison. This was inevitable since the accent is on Gantry all the way and Brooks' adaptation, moreover, invests Sister Sharon with more sincerity of purpose. Lancaster's facial expressions are exaggerated and toothsome, yet colorfully characteristic of a type of fire and brimstone gospel spieler as he stalks the screen—hypocritically leading vice raids, wrecking saloons—with demonical fury, arrogance and cunning to create a character monsterously frightening his mesmerising effect upon women he desires, including Sister Sharon, as well as groups hungering for "salvation."

Third in importance in the cast is Arthur Kennedy as concerns size of role, yet this actor manages, as he does so frequently, to make an impression that is second to none. In the book Jim Lefferts (Kennedy) was a devil's advocate classmate of Gantry at the Baptist Terwillinger College. For purpose of dramatic convenience Brooks has transformed Lefferts into a skeptical, materialistic newspaper reporter who debunks Sister Sharon's crusade but is backed into a corner by Gantry, who succeeds in turning the journalistic attack into a prestige builder for the evangelist. Shirley Jones makes the most of several good scenes as Lulu Bains, a girl who falls into prostitution after being despoiled by Gantry in his first undergraduate ministerial service. (Brooks has altered the role of Lulu considerably). Also impressive are Patti Page, making her dramatic debut as featured singer in Sister Sharon's choral group, and Dean Jagger as the general manager of the gospel enterprise.

Edward Andrews has a fat part as George Babbitt, who is blackmailed into promoting Sister Sharon's show against the opposition of a group of substantial ministers who are represented nicely by Hugh Marlowe, Everett Glass, Michael Whalen, Philip Ober and Wendell Holmes. Barry Kelly also does well as the police captain.

Considering the size of the book and the many repetitious sins of Gantry, Brooks in choosing to concentrate on the association with Sister Sharon has done an extremely effective job of distilling the essence in truncating the novel. He has used the camera expertly to create a picture which surges with power, excitement and color. He had top cooperation from cinematographer John Alton, art director Ed Carrere, set director Frank Tuttle and costume designer Dorothy Jeakins in recreating the 1920s.

Andre Previn's music contribution measurably, too, providing an extra dimension of sensory excitement to the visual presentation which smoothly and with keen pictorial emphasis as a result of expert cutting by film editor Marge Fowler.

"Elmer Gantry" runs 146 minutes, but the ultimate tribute to Brooks and his cast is that one is too preoccupied to become conscious of the film's length. *Pry.*

La Estrella Vacia
(The Empty Star)
(MEXICAN-EASTMANCOLOR)

Mexico City, June 21.

Peliculas Nacionales release of Producciones Corsa production. Stars Maria Felix; features Carlos Lopez Moctezuma, Enrique Rambal, Ignacio Lopez Tarso, Ramon Gay, Carlos Navarro, Rita Macedo, Wolf Rubinskis, Tito Junco. Directed by Emilio Gomez Muriel. Screenplay, Julio Alejandro from novel by Luis Spota. Camera, Gabriel Figueroa: music, Gustavo Cesar Carrion At Alameda, Continental and Polanco Theatres, Mexico City. Running time, **105 MINS.**

This is a starring vehicle showing off Maria Felix as a clothes horse, with the usual trappings of gowns, furs and jewels plus an array of adoring males. Theme of film is the intimate life of a screen star, along the pattern of "A Star Is Born." She is the ambitious Olga Lang, this being a film biopic showing her rise in the world of films, acquiring fame and fortune until she is a celebrated star but an "empty" one. Pic is slated for the Latin American markets.

Luis Spota, a technically perfect novelist on the Mexican literary scene, wrote the book on which this is based. It has captured a political and social era of Mexico as well as the atmosphere of the local cinema world.

Director Emilio Gomez Muriel, one of Mexico's best professionals, leads the players through their roles with security and achieves the false glitter and phoney atmosphere of the haves and have-nots of the film world.

While theme is not new, the director milks it for dramatic impact. Although Maria Felix appears to dominate every scene, she turns in a creditable performance, with some moments where she makes the central character seem real and human.

Carlos Lopez Moctezuma, film vet, turns in his usually competent performance. The male butterflies and characters, as portrayed by Enrique Rambal, Ignacio Lopez Tarso, Ramon Gay (shot in a real life drama by an enraged husband), Carlos Navarro and Tito Junco, are life like.

Music is based on some of the better, older Agustin Lara numbers. Gabriel Figueroa's camera work is excellent with color technically perfect. *Emil.*

Patterson-Johansson

Unied Artists release of TelePrompter production. Narrated by Chris Schenkel. Running time, **21 MINS.**

Fight films, of course, are usually about as good as the match that has been photographed. In the Teleprompter-filmed account of Floyd Patterson's five-round knockout of Inegmar Johansson to become first ex-champ to regain his heavyweight crown, United Artists, which is releasing the pix, has an entry as powerful as the left hook that dropped Ingo to the canvas for the full count.

The plus, so far as the b.o. potential is concerned, is the fact that the fight was restricted to closed-circuit television, leaving a vast world-wide audience for the films.

The account, running 21 minutes and narrated by Chris Schenkel, shows the full five rounds and includes usual slow-motion reprise of the knockdowns and the final count-out. The camera has caught every nuance of the exciting battle, including the reflex quiver in Johansson's foot as he lay prone on the canvas. Also recorded is a full-face view of Johansson as he took the nine-count after the first knockdown. The excitement in the ring after Patterson's victory has also been captured.

UA so far has booked the films in 7,500 theatres which, according to sales chief William J. Heineman, represents the highest number of theatres ever to play a championship fight film. 20th-Fox is distributing the film abroad. *Holl.*

House of Usher
(C'SCOPE—COLOR)

A not altogether faithful, but nonetheless striking elaboration on Poe's short story. Should appeal to wide range of tastes, and score soundly at the b.o.

Hollywood, June 17.

American International Pictures release of Roger Corman production, directed by Corman. Stars Vincent Price, Mark Damon, Myrna Fahey; features Harry Ellerbe. Screenplay, Richard Matheson, based on Edgar Allan Poe's "The Fall of the House of Usher"; camera, Floyd Crosby; editor, Anthony Carras; music, Les Baxter; asst. director, Jack Bohrer. Reviewed at Pathe Labs, June 17, '60. Running time, **79 MINS.**

Roderick Usher	Vincent Price
Philip Winthrop	Mark Damon
Madeline Usher	Myrna Fahey
Bristol	Harry Ellerbe
"Ghosts"	Bill Borzage, Mike Jordon, Nadajan, Ruth Oklander, George Paul, David Andar, Eleanor Le Faber, Geraldine Paulette, Phil Sylvestre and John Zimeas

It's not precisely the Edgar Allan Poe short story known to high school English that emerges in "House of Usher," but it's a reasonably diverting and handsomely mounted variation. In having taken several liberties with the original, the American International release may aggravate Poe purists and scholars, but the shrewd alterations, since they pursue a romantic course, should prove popular with the bulk of the modern audience.

It is a film that should attract mature tastes as well as those who come to the cinema for sheer thrills. It's also a potent, rewarding attraction for children. All things considered, pro and con, the fall of the "House of Usher" seems to herald the rise of the House of AIP.

In patronizingly romanticizing Poe's venerable prose, scenarist Richard Matheson has managed to preserve enough of the original's haunting flavor and spirit. The elaborations change the personalities of the three central characters, but not recklessly so.

The film has been mounted with care, skill and flair by producer-director Roger Corman and his staff. In fact, in their dedicated efforts to construct a decaying mansion of evil to match Poe's moody specifications, these aesthetic craftsmen have tended almost to minimize the chilling story housed within their art. But the essential character of Poe's brooding, melancholy tale shines through the flashy production.

In Poe's tale, the first-person hero is a friend of Roderick Usher, not his enemy and the romantic wooer of his doomed sister, the Lady Madeline. Matheson's version, however, accomplishes this alteration without ruining the impart of the chilling climax, in which Madeline (Myrna Fahey), buried alive by her brother (Vincent Price) while under a cataleptic trance, breaks free from her living tomb to destroy her brother as the decaying "House of Usher" cracks asunder and settles into the rotten tarn of the region while the hero (Mark Damon) escapes.

Price is a fine fit as Usher, and Miss Fahey successfully conveys the transition from helpless daintiness to insane vengeance. Damon has his better moments when the going gets gory and frenzied, but lacks the mature command required for the role. Harry Ellerbe is outstanding as an old family retainer.

Those whose combined efforts have succeeded in mounting a flamboyant physical production include special effects man Pat Dinga and production designer Daniel Haller. Their cobweb-ridden, fungus-infected, mist-pervaded atmosphere of cadaverous gloom has been photographed with great skill by Floyd Crosby and enhanced further by Ray Mercer's striking photographic effects and the vivid color, most notably during a woozy dream sequence. Editor Anthony Carras has crisply knit these images, and the action together. Burt Schoenberg's interesting paintings dress up the set and convey an extra dash of madness. The haunting sounds of the place have been captured vividly by Phil Mitchell, and Les Baxter's music makes the overall mood that much more evil and tense. At the helm, producer-director Corman has turned out a go at Poe that is certain to inspire several more cinematic excursions into this author's extremely commercial literary realm. *Tube.*

Village Of The Damned
(BRITISH)

Strange, sick film with little marquee value; interesting idea gone awry, result being just a mediocre filler.

London, June 16.

Metro (Ronald Kinnock) production and release. Stars George Sanders, Barbara Shelley; features Laurence Naismith, Michael Gwynn. Directed by Wolf Rilla. Screenplay, Stirling Silliphant, Wolf Rilla, George Barclay, based on "Midwich Cuckoos," novel by John Wyndham; editor, Gordon Hales, camera, Geoffrey Faithfull; music, Ron Goodwin. Previewed at Metro Private Cinema, June 15, '60. Running time **77 MINS.**

Gordon Zellaby	George Sanders
Anthea Zellaby	Barbara Shelley
David Zellaby	Martin Stephens
Alan Bernard	Michael Gwynn
Doctor Willers	Laurence Naismith
Harrington	Richard Warner
Mrs. Harrington	Jenny Laird
Evelyn Harrington	Sarah Long
James Pawle	Thomas Heathcote
Janet Pawle	Charlotte Mitchell
Milly Hughes	Pamela Buck
Miss Ogle	Rosamund Greenwood
Mrs. Plumpton	Susan Richards
Vicar	Bernard Archard
P. C. Gobbey	Peter Vaughan

George Sanders' name is not enough to sell this rather tired and sick film which starts off very

promisingly but soon nosedives. It stands up as merely a moderate filler for undiscriminating audiences.

Plot kicks around what is not an uninteresting idea. A little British village comes under the spell of some strange, supernatural force which first puts everybody out for the count. Then the villagers come to and find that every woman capable of being pregnant is.

Snag is that all the children are little monsters. They all look alike —fair haired, unblinking stare and with intellects the equivalent of adults, plus the knack of mental telepathy. George Sanders, a physicist, is intimately involved, since his wife is the mother of the leader of the little gang of abnormal moppets. Sanders decides to probe the mystery and finishes up by blowing them all to perdition, including himself.

If there had happened to be any hint of why this remarkable business should have occurred, the film would have been slightly more plausible. As it is, this just tapers off from a taut beginning into soggy melodrama. Wolf Rilla's direction is adequate, but no more. Geoffrey Faithfull's lensing is very sound. Rilla's use of far too many solo closeups helps Faithfull's job, but doesn't give the film much imaginative lift.

It's not easy to get worked up about the cast. Sanders wanders through the film with the air of a man who long ago gave up wondering what the screenplay is all about. Barbara Shelley, as his wife, again reminds audiences that she is an actress of both intelligence and charm though she has little here with which to prove it. Michael Gwynn and Laurence Naismith labor conscientously in ill-written roles and, among the army of horrifying kids, Martin Stephens shines. But the question must cross any tab-buyer's mind why moppets be used in such an unpleasant pic?

Rich.

The Savage Innocents
(BRITISH-TECHNICOLOR)

Beautifully colored Eskimo-set drama, with fairly simple incident and dialog.

London, June 21.

Rank release of a Joseph Janni-Maleno Malenotti production. Stars Anthony Quinn, Yoko Tani. Directed by Nicholas Ray. Screenplay, Nicholas Ray, from Hans Ruesch novel, "Top of World"; editor, Ralph Kemplen; camera, Aldo Tonti, Peter Hennessy; music, A. V. Lavagnino. At Odeon, Leicester Square, London, June 21, '60. Running time, 111 MINS.

Inuke .... Anthony Quinn
Aslak .... Yoko Tani
2nd Trooper .... Carlo Justini
Powtee .... Marie Yang
Anarvik .... Andy Ho
Imina .... Kaida Horiuchi
Lulik .... Yvonne Shima
Ittimangnerk .... Lee Montague
Trading Post Boss.... Francois De Wolff
Missionary .... Marco Guglielmi
Kidak .... Anthony Chin
Hiko .... Anna May Wong
Undik .... Michael Chow
Pilot .... Ed Devereau

"The Savage Innocents" is a polyglot pic and that's maybe the understatement of the month, if not of the year. Financial responsibility is carved up between Britain, America and Italy. Rank chipped in with a third of the $1,500,000 budget and the Pinewood studios and British technicians were used; Italy, through producer Maleno Malenotti, has a third stake; America, (Paramount release) supplied the remainder. There's a Yank director and screenplay writer, Nicholas Ray. America's Anthony Quinn is the main star while the femme lead Yoko Tani comes from Paris.

Remainder of the cast is drawn from various countries. Shooting, apart from Pinewood took place in Hudson Bay and Greenland. Somewhere along the line Denmark gets an honorable mention among the credits. The result is a strange offbeat drama which will need some careful putting over to tease the run-of-mill patrons.

Two undeniable things stand out. Art director Don Ashton and editor Ralph Kemplen have done a standout job in matching and cutting so that it is virtually impossible to decide where Pinewood began and Canada came in. Secondly, the chief lensers, Aldo Tonti and Peter Hennessy, have turned out some brilliant camerawork with color sweeping superbly across the widescreen.

The problem appears to be whether the yarn stands up. For long sessions it is a documentary of life in the Eskimo belt. Animals, the simple natives, local customs all lift interest when the fairly conventional story tends to sag. The story line is simple. It concerns a powerful, good humored hunter (Anthony Quinn) who spends the early stages of the film deciding which of two young women he wishes to make his wife. Second half becomes melodrama when he accidentally murders a missionary, is tracked down by troopers, saves the life of one of them in a snowstorm and eventually is allowed to get away in a contrived ending.

The memorable moments are those of Quinn hunting down foxes, bears, seals, walruses and the majesty of the bleak wastes, the ice, the storms and primitive living conditions. The human element doesn't come out of it quite so well mainly because Ray's screenplay contains some pretty naive lines rubbing shoulders with out-of-character talky-talk.

However, anyone wishing to study the private life of an Eskimo will learn (in addition to the w.k. gag that Eskimoes never kiss but are happily content with nose-rubbing) that the femme is subservient to the male, that one of their favorite dishes is raw seal-meat which, on wide screen and in color, can be quite a shock to a patron's stomach, and that it is courtesy for an Eskimo to offer his wife to a friend.

Anthony Quinn, mainly talking pidgin English-cum-Eskimo, comes out as an authentic Eskimo. Yoko Tani is a delight as the woman. Francis De Wolff, Anthony Chin and Marie Yang are among several others who acquit themselves well. The latter is particularly moving in a scene where (per Eskimo custom) she is sent out to die because there is no room for a passenger in the frozen North. Peter O'Toole, one of Britain's outstanding new actors, in firstrate as a tough trooper. But he gets up credit, at his own wish. He objected to his voice being dubbed. There are many superb sequences in this strange film, but they are bogged down often by some very bad ones. The result is an iffy adventure and b.o. results will likely prove the same.

Rich.

From the Terrace
(C'SCOPE-COLOR)

Has chance for popular success, but as a film it's lower case John O'Hara.

20th-Fox release of Mark Robson production, directed by Robson. Stars Paul Newman, Joanne Woodward, Myrna Loy, Ina Balin and Leon Ames. Screenplay, Ernest Lehman; based on novel by John O'Hara; camera, Leo Tover; editor, Dorothy Spencer; music, Elmer Bernstein. Previewed in N. Y. June 22, '60. Running time, 144 MINS.

Alfred Eaton .... Paul Newman
Mary St. John .... Joanne Woodward
Martha Eaton .... Myrna Loy
Natalie .... Ina Balin
Samuel Eaton .... Leon Ames
Sage Rimmington .... Elizabeth Allen
Clemmie .... Barbara Eden
Lex Porter .... George Grizzard
Dr. Jim Roper .... Patrick O'Neal
MacHardie .... Felix Aylmer
Fritz Thornton .... Raymond Greenleaf
George Fry .... Malcolm Atterbury
Mr. St. John .... Raymond Bailey
Mr. Benziger .... Ted de Corsia
Duffy .... Howard Caine
Mrs. St. John .... Kathryn Givney
Mrs. Benziger .... Dorothy Adams
Frolick .... Lauren Gilbert
Nellie .... Blossom Rock
Josephine .... Cecil Elliott

At 20th-Fox the title "Peyton Place" has a magic ring. It's obvious that in the decision to transform John O'Hara's sprawling "From the Terrace" to the screen the powers-that-be at 20th dreamed of another in the "Peyton Place" groove. But while "From the Terrace" has a number of basic commercial elements, it hasn't the stamina to equal or come near the b.o. success of "Peyton Place."

The O'Hara name, the attention the novel received although considered pedestrian O'Hara by the literary reviewers, the marquee value of Joanne Woodward, Paul Newman and Myrna Loy, and the promise of some hot sex scenes that goes with almost any O'Hara work may make the picture a popular success, but the more discriminating film-goer will find "From the Terrace" seriously deficient.

Whether the fault lies with O'Hara's basic material or Ernest Lehman's screenplay is difficult to assay by a reviewer who skipped the novel. It's apparent, however, that Lehman faced a Herculean task in condensing O'Hara's fat novel to the exigencies of the screen. On the assumption that Lehman followed the O'Hara story closely, the blame must be placed squarely on the novelist, for "From the Terrace" builds up to one big cliche.

The picture is the study of one man's pursuit of success and money. During his climb up the Wall Street ladder, he neglects his wife, sacrifices his integrity, and unrelentlessly pursues his goal. But in keeping with our popular culture, he is overcome at end by the moment of truth. The climax takes place in the board room of a large Wall Street firm. Facing his superiors just as he is about to be made a full partner, our hero denounces his boss, berates the success goddess system, walks out on his career, dumps his society wife, and goes off to join his true love, a simple, warm, understanding smalltown girl.

Mark Robson's old-fashioned approach to the direction is no help. He has his characters speaking in sepulchral tones, particularly in the scenes between Paul Newman and Ina Balin, as if to give their conversations a world-shaking meaning. They seem to be reciting blank verse in a background of soft hearts-and-flowers music.

In between Newman's discharge from the Navy and his ascendency in Wall Street, O'Hara attempts to give a picture of the mores of the very rich. There are numerous parties on Long Island, discussions of the "right" marriage as part of the social snobbery of a particular group and uninhibited extra-marital activities.

An obvious effort is made at being "adult" in the sex scenes as Joanne Woodward, playing Newman's neglected wife takes on a lover. Then Newman and Miss Balin are caught in a hotel room by photographers hired by a jealous business rival. And there's the philosophy of Newman's boss. Divorce is out of the question, even for infidelity, if it is to affect the career of a young executive.

The early part of the film tries to provide the motivation for Newman's actions. He hails from the Pennsylvania region that O'Hara has made familiar. His father, a steel mill owner, is a stern, unloving man who denies his son fatherly affection because of his love for an older son who had died. His mother is an incurable drunkard who takes on a lover.

Why the picture tries to depict Miss Woodward as some sort of villainess is unclear. She is wholly devoted to her husband until it becomes clear that he is uninterested in her. Yet Newman, playing the leading role in a weltschmertz manner, emerges as the hero. It is only near the end that she is willing to accept the success setup when it becomes obvious that she cannot keep her husband any other way.

Newman plays the success-seeker as if he were carrying the weight of the world's problems on his shoulders. Despite the slight insight into his background, it's difficult to comprehend the reasons for his actions. He seems more like a pawn being pushed than an individual who knows what he is doing.

Miss Woodward is excellent as the wife who married Newman despite the objections of her socially-prominent family. There is a strong indication that the marriage is based more on sexual attraction than on deeper love.

Miss Balin, a dark-haired beauty, makes a nice contrast to blond Miss Woodward. However, she plays her role with such a dedicated seriousness that it is difficult to believe. Good performances are rendered by Myrna Loy, as the alcoholic mother; Leon Ames, as the unfeeling father; Felix Ayler, as the success-minded boss; George Grizzard, as a fun-loving wealthy playboy; Patrick O'Neal, as Miss Woodward's lover, and Ted de Corsia, as a rival on the success ladder.

The technical aspects are first-rate, including Leo Tover's photography, and the art direction of Lyle R. Wheeler, Maurice Ransford, and Howard Richman. Elmer Bernstein's music is on the syrupy side.

Holl.

Paris Nous Appartient
(Paris Belongs To Us)
(FRENCH)

Paris, June 28.

SEDIF release of AJYM-Carrosse Films production. With Betty Schneider, Giani Esposito, Francoise Prevost, Daniel Crohem, Francois Maistre, Jean-Claude Brialy, Noelle Leiris. Directed by Jacques Rivette. Screenplay, Jean Gruault, Rivette; camera, Charles Bitsch; editor, Denise De Casabianca. Preemed in Paris. Running time, **140 MINS.**

Anne ....Betty Schneider
Gerard ....Giani Esposito
Terry ....Francoise Prevost
Philip ....Daniel Crohem
Pierre ....Francois Maistre
Jean-Marc ....Jean-Claude Brialy
De Georges ....Jean-Marie Robain

The last of the "New Wave" films, in that it is the final one from the group of highbrow pic critics-turned-filmmakers, this may end all "Wave" talk. It uses a vague suspense theme and budding love story around a tale of a supposedly perking world totalitarian takeover by some sort of secret organization. This turns out to be a fiction in the mind of a psychotic American ex-journalist who had to leave the U. S. for political reasons. All this is overblown, making it pretentious, slow-moving and fairly confused.

This would need plenty of pruning because it takes much too long to tell its over-complicated story. It does have a fairly sleek mounting. If well cut, it might be an arty entry abroad but that is about all since this pic lacks the clarity, feeling and depth for more specialized distrib, with general chances extremely limited.

A young girl comes to Paris and her brother intros her into a Bohemian group. She is taken by an intense young theatrical director trying to put on a Shakespearean play with practically no money. She joins the troupe and hears he is in danger from some sort of organization. Pic then follows the girl's quest to find out what the danger is.

The emptiness and sordidness of the group is supposedly shown up through this search. Director Jacques Rivette does have a film grasp for isolated sequences but has not learned how to tighten up a scene or make suspense direct and dramatic. Too much palaver seems to have made this bog down and miss its point.

Rivette took two years to make the production and was given money by fellow "wavers" to finish it. Technically it does have uneven lensing at times, but, all in all, the pic has a fairly good production envelope for a vehicle that was made on a shoestring and the hard way. Acting is uneven with Betty Schneider not up to conveying the anguish and emotions of a fairly innocent young girl caught up in a big city. Others acquit themselves adequately with Giani Esposito especially effective as the idealistic if weak theatrical man.

Mosk.

Murder, Inc.
(CINEMASCOPE)

Exploitable gangster yarn, but lack of marquee lures may hamper its b.o. prospects.

20th-Fox release of Burt Balaban production; co-producer, Larry Joachim. Stars Stuart Whitman, May Britt, Henry Morgan, Peter Falk; "introduces" Sarah Vaughan. Directed by Balaban and Stuart Rosenberg. Screenplay, Irve Tunick and Mel Barr, from book "Murder, Inc." by Burton Turkus and Sid Feder; camera, Gaine Rescher; editor, Ralph Rosenblum; music, Frank De Vol. Previewed N. Y. June 23, '60. Running time, **103 MINS.**

Joey ....Stuart Whitman
Eadie ....May Britt
Turkus ....Henry Morgan
Reles ....Peter Falk
Lepke ....David J. Stewart
Tobin ....Simon Oakland
Bug ....Warren Fennerty
Mendy Weiss ....Joseph Bernard
Joe Rosen ....Eli Mintz
Laslo ....Vince Gardenia
Alpert ....Josip Elic
Rose ....Helen Waters
Louis ....Lou Polan
Anastasia ....Howard I. Smith
Panto ....Joseph Campanella
Loughran ....Leon B. Stevens
Betty Shaw ....Dorothy Stinnette
Sadie ....Sylvia Miles
Receptionist ....Barbara Wilkens
Teenagers ....Seymour Cassell & Paul Porter
1st Detective ....David Kerman
Sal ....Harold Gary
Eadie's Killer ....Bill Bassett
Johnny ....Ed Simon
Policeman ....Peter Gumeny
Bailiff ....Kent Montroy
Victim ....Ricky Colletti
2nd Detective ....Ed Wagner
Lodge Dancer ....Adrienne Mills
Walter Sage ....Morey Amsterdam
Sarah Vaughan ....Herself

Based on the book of the same name, "Murder, Inc." obviously has lotsa built-in exploitation values. These may help offset the lack of marquee lures in the lengthy cast of this Burt Balaban production. Among its better known players are May Britt and Henry Morgan while disk name Sarah Vaughan is "introduced."

Professional killers of the crime syndicate headed by the late Albert Anastasia and Louis "Lepke" Buchalter were a scourge in the depression era. They later became known as Murder, Inc.—a label so celebrated that its story has a solid boxoffice potential. But whether this will be realized is questionable.

For the Irve Tunick-Mel Barr screenplay takes a leisurely approach to its subject. The ultimate demise of the killers-for-hire is spelled out chronologically in the 103 minutes running time. But the pace is too slow, the suspense only occasionally gripping. Moreover, the overall production lacks the zing and tension required to assure it of top returns in deluxe situations.

On the other hand 103 minutes is overlong for many houses which rely upon a quick turnover. There are a number of sequences that either could be judiciously pruned in the interest of brevity or eliminated entirely. Among them is a nitery scene where Sarah Vaughan has a song stint. It's apparent that she's used merely as window dressing.

Amidst the tawdry backgrounds of Brooklyn's Brownsville section, the script recounts how Lepke and the syndicate shook down the garment district, trucking business and sundry other legitimate enterprises through goon squads and hired killers. Caught in this vicious crime ring through little fault of their own are a young couple — dancer May Britt and singer Stuart Whitman.

As the script develops, the fiendish machinations of Lepke and his No. 1 killer, Abe Reles; the fears of their victims and the inept investigations of the police are all seen through the eyes of Miss Britt and Whitman. The pair are kept in line as accomplices of the ring through beatings and threats until an aggressive Brooklyn district attorney along with ex-N. Y. Gov. Thomas E. Dewey finally crack Murder, Inc.

With the possible exception of Peter Falk's portrayal of Reles, scarcely any of the cast's performances could be rated as dynamic His delineation sharply defines the brutal nature of the thug who was killed in a "fall" from Brooklyn's Half Moon Hotel while in "protective" custody of the N. Y. police.

Whitman appropriately cringes as helpless man dominated by the killers. His role excites little audience sympathy. Miss Britt has a few sexy scenes but for the most part seems curiously inanimate. In an offbeat piece of casting, radio-tv's Henry Morgan is seen as Brooklyn D. A. Burton Turkus. He lends a subdued touch to the part.

David J. Stewart is too studied and laconic to impress as Lepke. Morey Amsterdam is mostly himself as a nitery operator who becomes a mob victim. Simon Oakland is a typical detective while fair support is contribbed by Warren Fennerty, Joseph Bernard, Eli Mintz and Vince Gardenia, among others.

Producer Balaban co-directed this 20th-Fox release with Stuart Rosenberg. They've achieved a mood and atmosphere of the early 1930s with some interesting character studies and realistic backgrounds. But their reining has failed to bring out the tautness and crackling melodrama inherent in the yarn.

Gaine Rescher's black-and-white CinemaScope camerawork has a low key effect that emphasizes the grim nature of the subject. Editing of Ralph Rosenblum could have been tighter as aforementioned. Frank De Vol's score is standard as are Dick Sylbert's art direction and other technical credits. Location work on this made-in-New York entry provides an authentic touch.

Gilb.

13 Ghosts

Fair, but not very scary, horror film in which spectators are invited to capture the spirit by utilizing a "ghost viewer" gimmick. Should attract enough juve trade to score at the b.o.

Hollywood, June 16.

Columbia Pictures release of William Castle production. Stars Charles Herbert, Jo Morrow, Martin Milner, Rosemary De Camp, Donald Woods; with Margaret Hamilton, John Van Dreelen. Directed by Castle. Screenplay, Robb White; camera, Joseph Biroc; editor, Edwin Bryant; art director, Cary Odell; music, Von Dexter; assistant director, Max Stein. Reviewed at Academy Award Theatre, June 16, '60. Running time, **85 MINS.**

Buck ....Charles Herbert
Medea ....Jo Morrow
Ben Rush ....Martin Milner
Hilda ....Rosemary De Camp
Cyrus ....Donald Woods
Elaine Zacharides....Margaret Hamilton
E. Van Allen ....John Van Dreelen

Another example of producer William Castle's penchant for cinematic trickery is on display in "13 Ghosts," a workmanlike, but not very frightening, horror film. The gimmick this time is a "ghost viewer," a visual aid with two windows: a red one that enables the spectator to ogle ghost activity on the screen, and a blue one ("ghost remover") that erases the ghastly ghostly images for those who "don't believe."

The idea is sound and exploitable, but in execution doesn't fully come off. As a result, the boxoffice fate of the Columbia release depends on how fast the kid wickets move. Since ghost pictures are in short supply these days, this one figures to get by.

Minus the showmanship, the yarn is pretty thin. Robb White's lean screenplay plants a happy, attractive, but impoverished family of four in a haunted house where 12 spooks gad about in search of a 13th member to join their party. There are two questions: who'll be number 13, and whose diabolical plot is it that that there'll be a 13? The mystery, never at all mysterious, is resolved neatly when the mastermind becomes his own victim.

It is a flaw of the picture, as it frequently has been with other shock films, that the spooks are far less scary when witnessed than when their presence is merely suggested. Unseen evil packs the real wallop. The ghosts assembled here lack personality and aren't frightening, so that there isn't sufficient tension in the sequences during which the "ghost viewer" comes into play.

The acting is capable. Donald Woods is fine and likeable as the head of the terrorized brood, and Rosemary De Camp is competent as his wife. As their children, young Charles Herbert is very good and Jo Morrow is decorative. Martin Milner does a nice job as the bad guy, Margaret Hamilton is her usual threatening self as the haunted housekeeper, and John Van Dreelen is adequate as Woods' scholarly boss.

The film is black-and-white with the exception of the main titles and "viewer" passages, for which Eastman color is utilized. Photographic color effects by Butler-Glouner Inc. are, of course, vital to the production, but are not as sharp, clear and workable as one might wish. Harry Mills' chilling sound work is a standout. Other crafts, including Joseph Biroc's lensing, Edwin Bryant's editing, Cary Odell's art direction and Von Dexter's music, are respectably represented. In addition to producing and directing, Castle appears onscreen to give instructions about his visual device. It seems superfluous.

Tube.

Austerlitz
(FRENCH-ITALIAN-YUGOSLAV)
(COLOR)

Paris, June 28.

Lux release of CFPI-Lyre-Galatea-Dubrava Films production. Stars Rossano Brazzi, Claudia Cardinale, Martine Carol, Orson Welles, Leslie Caron, Maria Ferrero, Ettore Manni, Jean Marais, Georges Marchal, Jack Palance, Vittorio De Sica, Michel Simon and Pierre Monday (as Napoleon). Written and directed by Abel Gance. Camera (Eastmancolor), Henri Alekan; editors, Leonide Azar, Yvonne Martin. At Gaumont-Palace, Paris. Running time, **170 MINS.**

Lucien Bonaparte .... Rossano Brazzi
Pauline ....Claudia Cardinale
Josephine ....Martine Carol
Mlle. De Vaudey ....Leslie Caron
Elise ....Maria Ferrero
Murat ....Ettore Manni
Carnot ....Jean Marais
Lannes ....Georges Marchal
Weirother ....Jack Palance
Pope ....Vittorio De Sica
Grognard ....Michel Simon
Robert Fulton ....Orson Welles
Napoleon Bonaparte ......Pierre Mondy

The 70-year-old French film pioneer Abel Gance, whose silent pic "Napoleon Bonaparte," in 1927 was a French film milestone, now has made his second film since the last World War. It is a sort

of sequel to his first Napoleon pic, taking the great soldier from the Treaty of Amiens to his great victory at Austerlitz in 1802.

The first film took the "Little Corporal" through the revolution to his command of the French forces and his victories in Italy. This one has him taking the powers of government and then proclaiming himself Emporor on the advice of people around him, plus his battle against the English, Russians and Austrians when the English betray the Treaty of Amiens.

This vehicle deals with the personal life of Napoleon at the time and the international intrigues which sent him into battle again. The first portion remains trained on his amorous activities, dealings with subordinates and family and manages to create a full-bodied character of Napoleon. Pierre Mondy has the flair, presence, rages and insight to portray the mighty little warrior though he does not quite give it the dimension of greatness in his moments of decision.

Production is long but well plotted with the more intimate first-half opening out into the battle scenes. Pic is full of cameo bits by pic names with Orson Welles sputtering in to offer Napoleon the steam boat only to be ironically turned down; Jack Palance, as an Austrian general, Leslie Caron, as a Napoleonic mistress; Martine Carol as Josephine, etc. They can be used for name handles. Pic has a decided patriotic aspect in its drumbeating for the glory of old France and the well meaning of Napoleon. But it is never blatant.

Color is good and the widescreen (Dyailscope) is adroitly used at the beginning and is an asset for the battle scenes. Production values are excellent and the battle scenes, if confused at times, are manned with vitality.

It is a fitting and hopeful return for Gance who gave the French film some of its earliest world renown in the silent days. With this coherent, witty look at Napoleon and the times, Gance displays a still solid filmic grasp and force. Napoleon may be carried another step in his historic career because this looks in for biz here, and could well be a sound playoff property abroad on its scope, taste and treatment. 20th-Fox has taken it for the U.S. It will probably be dubbed for general distribution. *Mosk.*

Stop! Look! and Laugh!

Another dose of Three Stooges slapstick, re-working the "Original" trio's one-reelers plus new footage. Profitable kidstuff.

Hollywood, June 21.

Columbia Pictures release of Harry Romm production. Stars The Original Three Stooges (Moe Howard, Larry Fine, Curly Howard), Paul Winchell (with Jerry Mahoney, Knucklehead Smiff); features The Marquis Chimps, "Officer" Joe Bolton. Directed by Jules White; editor, Jerome Thoms; music, Mischa Bakaleinikoff; assistant director, Milton Feldman. Reviewed at the studio June 21, '60. Running time, 76 MINS.

The durable lolli-popularity of The Three Stooges is being put to the theatrical test again by Columbia in "Stop! Look! And Laugh!" Instead of whipping up some new variations on the trio's pie-eyed slapstick, producer Harry Romm has thriftily spliced together some of the old shorts made years ago by the "Original" threesome and tied them in with some new footage featuring ventriloquist Paul Winchell and The Marquis Chimps. It's just the sort of utter nonsense that will make a handy attraction for Saturday matinees and for double-billing into kiddie packages, indicating a tidy profit margin for Columbia.

One of the major problems in a film of this nature is linking the various short subjects together with some semblance of unity. This has been accomplished respectably here by utilizing Winchell as something of a commentator to introduce each Stooges reel with an apt remark after clowning through his own comedy routines with one or the other of his two dummies, Jerry Mahoney and Knucklehead Smiff. Winchell is an amiable and versatile comedian, but too much of his approach stems from the thoroughly saturated Charlie McCarthy-Mortimer Snerd style. However, kids won't mind.

The "Original" Stooges, Larry Fine and Moe and Curly Howard (latter has been replaced by Joe De Rita in recent years), are featured in some 10 sequences during which they run the slapstick gamut. Their brand of comedy reminds one of an animated cartoon come to life (extreme physical punishment followed by remarkably rapid recovery, repeated over and over again), and therein lies its timeless kiddie appeal, strikingly illustrated by its tv rebirth over the past few years.

The Marquis Chimps are seen in one sequence late in the film when they become involved in some "Cinderella" monkeyshines produced and written by Sid Kuller and directed by Lou Brandt. The sight of monkeys playing "Cinderella" is sure to get its share of laughs, but the visual opening impact isn't quite strong enough to sustain the idea all the way.

Jules White served as overall director for Romm, and did a workmanlike job of pasting it all together, with the aid of editor Jerome Thoms and Mischa Bakaleinikoff's music. Individual "Stooges" segments were written, produced, lensed and edited by a wide variety of people, too numerous to recount in this space.

Paul Winchell passages were directed ably by Don Appell, with William Steiner manning the camera. *Tube.*

Cage Of Evil

Satisfactory lower-berth crime-does - not - pay - except - at-boxoffice meller.

Hollywood, June 23.

United Artists release of Robert E. Kent production. Stars Ronald Foster, Pat Blair; features Harp McGuire; with John Maxwell, Preston Hanson, Doug Henderson, Hugh Sanders, Helen Kleebs, Robert Shayne, Owen Bush, Ted Knight, Howard McLeod, Eva Brent, Joe Hamilton, Pat Miller, Ralph Sanford, Ralph Neff, Jack Kenney, Jack Tesler, Gregg Martell, Abel Franco, Henry Delgado. Directed by Edward L. Cahn. Screenplay, Orville H. Hampton, from story by Hampton and Alexander Richards; camera, Maury Gertsman; editor, Grant Whytock; art director, Serge Krizman; music, Paul Sawtell; sound, John Keans; assistant director, Herbert S. Greene. Reviewed at Goldwyn Studios, June 23, '60. Running time, 70 MINS.

Scott Harper	Ron Foster
Holly Taylor	Pat Blair
Murray Kearns	Harp McGuire
Dan Melrose	John Maxwell
Tom Colton	Preston Hanson
Barney	Doug Henderson
Martin Bender	Hugh Sanders
Mrs. Melton	Helen Kleebs
Victor Delmar	Robert Shayne
Sgt. Ray Dean	Owen Bush
Ivers	Ted Knight
Romack	Howard McLeod
Lucille Baron	Eva Brent
Dewey	Joe Hamilton
Ozzie Bell	Pat Miller
Bar Man	Ralph Sanford
Plumber	Ralph Neff
Lewis	Jack Kenney
Francen	Jack Tesler
Mick Borden	Gregg Martell
1st Mexican Cop	Abel Franco
2nd Mexican Cop	Henry Delgado

United Artists has a respectable running mate in "Cage of Evil." The Robert E. Kent production attempts, with practiced and appropriate economy, to prove anew the old, reliable dramatic maxim that crime does not pay (for criminals) but is a paying proposition (at the boxoffice).

Orville H. Hampton's screenplay, based on a story he wrote with Alexander Richards, tells of a Los Angeles police detective (Ronald Foster) who secretly turns hood when the force thrice nixes his bid for promotion to lieutenant. In cahoots (and in love) with a dazzling blonde babe (Pat Blair) involved in a gem robbery which he has been assigned to investigate, Foster conspires to make off to Mexico with Miss Blair and the jewels by bumping off, "in the line of duty," the crook who possesses the costly cargo. It doesn't quite work out that way. Foster is gunned down, leaving Miss Blair snug as a thug in the jug.

It is a mistake to witness this film with too critical an eye, for it has more than its share of unaccountable character behavior, and has a tendency to bypass established fact for purposes of dramatic convenience. Full enjoyment for the average filmgoer is contingent upon only surface appraisal of what is transpiring, a trick audiences have learned to employ in viewing second features.

Foster handles the central role with ease and authority. Miss Blair throws her weight around admirably and exhibits thespic skill as his moll. Support is effective, chiefly that of Harp McGuire, Preston Hanson, Hugh Sanders and Helen Kleebs. Edward L. Cahn's direction is competent.

Among the journeyman background assists are Maury Gertsman's adept camera work, Grant Whytock's smooth editing and Serge Krizman's businesslike sets. *Tube.*

Inherit the Wind

Outstanding screen achievement. Looms as big boxoffice attraction.

Hollywood, June 23.

United Artists release of Stanley Kramer production. Stars Spencer Tracy, Fredric March, Gene Kelly; features Florence Eldridge, Dick York, Donna Anderson, Harry Morgan, Elliott Reid, Philip Coolidge, Claude Akins, Paul Hartman, Jimmy Boyd, Noah Beery Jr., Gordon Polk, Ray Teal, Norman Fell, Hope Summers, Renee Godfrey. Directed by Kramer. Screenplay, Nathan E. Douglas-Jerome Lawrence-Robert E. Lee; camera, Ernest Laslo; production design, Rudolph Sternad; editor, Fredric Knudtson; sound, Joe Lapis; music, Ernest Gold; asst. director, Ivan Volkman. Reviewed at Screen Directors Guild June 23, '60. Running time: 126 MINS.

Henry Drummond	Spencer Tracy
Matthew Harrison Brady	Fredric March
E. K. Horbeck	Gene Kelly
Mrs. Brady	Florence Eldridge
Bertram T. Cates	Dick York
Rachel Brown	Donna Anderson
Judge	Harry Morgan
Davenport	Elliott Reid
Mayor	Philip Coolidge
Reverend Brown	Claude Akins
Meeker	Paul Hartman
Howard	Jimmy Boyd
Stebbins	Noah Beery, Jr.
Sillers	Gordon Polk
Dunlap	Ray Teal
Radio Announcer	Norman Fell
Mrs. Krebs	Hope Summers
Mrs. Stebbins	Renee Godfrey

It's front and center for Stanley Kramer, Fredric March, Spencer Tracy and the writing team of Nathan E. Douglas and Harold Jacob Smith. Individually and ensemble they are in top form in "Inherit the Wind." This United Artists release, produced and directed by Kramer, is a rousing and fascinating motion picture. Virtually all the elements that make for the broadest range of entertainment satisfaction—drama, comedy, romance, social significance, even suspense—are amply present.

Contributions of Gene Kelly, Dick York, Donna Anderson, Florence Eldridge, Harry Morgan and Claude Akins are not less worthy; in the overall development of the story there is not as much emphasis on their roles. Each, however, plays an important part and does so with telling effect.

Kramer has held the action in tight check, whether in a stifling country court or recording the swelling emotion of mob religious fervor, indignation and fury. One suspects it needed a strong hand to restrain the forensics of Tracy and March as defense and prosecution attorneys in this drama inspired by the 1925 trial in Dayton, Tenn., of a young high school teacher, John T. Scopes, for daring to teach Darwin's theory of evolution. Roles of Tracy and March equal Clarence Darrow and William Jennings Bryan who collided on evolution.

Pairing of Tracy and March was a master stroke of casting. They go at each other on the thespic plane as one might imagine Dempsey and Louis. Both men are spellbinders in the laudatory sense of the word. If they aren't top contenders in the next Academy sweepstakes, then Oscar should be put in escrow for another year. March actually has the more colorful role as Matthew Harrison Brady (Bryan) because, with the aid of face changing makeup, he creates a completely different character, whereas Tracy is not so benefited and has to rely solely upon his power of illusion. That is a most persuasive power indeed.

Without consulting the play, it is not possible to figure how much

of the dialog may have been transferred from the Jerome Lawrence-Robert E. Lee original. This is no reflection on the Douglas-Smith scenario. Their adaptation, which broadents the scope of the play, is a most commendable job of film construction. It is shot through with dialog that it florid, witty, penetrating, compassionate and sardonic. A good measure of the film's surface bite is contributed by Gene Kelly as a cynical Baltimore reported (patterned after Henry L. Menken) whose paper comes to the aid of the younger teacher played by Dick York. Kelly demonstates again that even without dancing shoes he knows his way on the screen.

But there can be little room for doubt that the underlying force in "Inherit the Wind" springs from Kramer's handling of the story and the people. Ernest Laszlo's camera speaks eloquently, too, picking up revealing expressions of principals and extras in crowd sequences. The Scopes case, popularly known as "The Monkey Trial," was fanned as a contest between Darwin and the Bible, intellectual progress and standpatism. The film doesn't soft peddle these issues. In fact, it emphasizes the religion angle to a point that arouse resentment among some audiences, particularly since a minister, whose daughter is in love with the teacher, is so carried away with righteous wrath that he nearly brings on mob fury.

Ernest Gold's music score, utilizing such familars as "Old Time Religion" and "Battle Hymn of the Republic," kicks up a sound track storm that gives the film added excitement. Bud Westmore merits a nod also for makeup, Rudolph Sternad for the flavorsome design of the production and Fredric Knudtson for editing.

Appearance of Miss Eldridge as wife of Brady marks her seventh film role opposite March, her husband. She invests the role with nuances that are magnificent—a gesture, a look, as she comforts the shell of a once great man who can't resist plaudits of the crowd, any crowd. Harry Morgan as the judge also is remarkably good and Philip Coolidge has his telling moments in a picture which runs 126 minutes. *Pry.*

Trapped in Tangiers
(SUPERCINESCOPE)

Lower-lower class crime meller that will be a severe handicap for double bills.

Hollywood, June 22.

Twentieth-Fox release of Antonio Cervi production. Stars Edmund Purdom, Genevieve Page, Gino Cervi; with Jose Guardiola, Mario Moreno, Felix DeFrauce, Amparo Rivelles, Antonio Molino, Luis Pena, Enrique Pelayo. Directed by Riccardo Freda. Screenplay, Alessandro Continenza, Vittoriand Petrilli, Paolo Spinola, Freda; camera, Gabor Pogany. Reviewed at the studio, June 22, '60. Running time, 77 MINS.

"Trapped in Tangiers" is an apt title for this crude concoction from the European theatre of cinematic operations, being released in this country by 20th-Fox. "Trapped" is precisely how audiences will feel enduring this lower-berth number to get at the film they will have come to see. Twin-bills will be extremely burdened by its presence.

About the best that can be said for the Antonio Cervi production is that its costars, Edmund Purdom and Genevieve Page, are attractive people. The screenplay, which is the work of no less than four writers (Alessandro Continenza, Vittoriand Petrilli, Pao'o Spinola and director Ricardo Freda), is an incredibly absurd study of a federal agent's efforts to bare and destroy an international dope ring. While in the process he becomes enamoured of no less a personage than the adopted daughter of the dope ringleader, a complication resolved with a bullet into the latter's black heart. These spy-story cliches have, of course been pursued many times in the past, but rarely with such lack of insight, grace and cinematic know-how.

Purdom, Miss Page, Gino Cervi and the others involved are up against too much bad material to attain any measure of thespic success. These difficulties are further complicated by the dubbing aspect. Freda's direction is extremely sluggish, with the exception of fight scenes which, unaccountably, he has sped up a la Keystone Kops. Camerman Gabor Pogany is listed, but most of the other craftsmen who operated on this film remain anonymous on the main titles and on 20th's credit sheet. It is a merciful gesture. *Tube.*

Le Pain Des Jules
(Jules' Breadwinner)
(FRENCH)

Paris, July 5.

Fernand Rivers release of Film Artistique production. With Christian Mery, Bella Darvi, Henri Vilbert, Cora Camoin, Georgette Anys, Yves Massard. Directed by Jacques Severac. Screenplay, Ange Bastiani, Severac; camera, Pierre Levent; editor, Monique Lacombe. At Balzac, Paris. Running time, 95 MINS.

Sauveur	Christian Mery
Gina	Bella Darvi
Assunta	Cora Camoin
Zoe	Georgette Anys
Toussaint	Henri Vilbert
Pascal	Yves Massard

The gangster milieu in southern France is touched on via this talky tale of an aging hood who is done in because of his yen for a young strumpet. Production is skimpy, pic is talky, and this hardly generates enough action or insight into its theme to make it anything but a local bet. Foreign chances are slim at best.

Acting is only fair and its legit sources are too evident. The director is unable to get more visual feeling into this long-winded affair which mixes comedy and tragedy. Technical credits also show a tight budget. *Mosk.*

It Started in Naples
(V'VISION-COLOR)

Naughty, pungent comedy-travelog. Funny, though a one-joke film. Sex, striking color-camera qualities and a cast in fine fettle will help win the b.o. battle.

Hollywood, June 13.

Paramount release of Melville Shavelson-Jack Rose production. Stars Clark Gable, Sophia Loren, Vittorio De Sica; with Marietto, Paolo Carlini, Claudio Ermelli. Directed by Shavelson. Screenplay, Shavelson, Rose and Suso Cecchi D'Amico, from story by Michael Pertwee and Jack Davies; camera, Robert L. Surtees; editor, Frank Bracht; art directors, Hal Pereira, Roland Anderson; music, Alessandro Cicognini, Carlo Savina; assistant director, Eric Rattray. Reviewed at Academy Award Theatre, June 13, '60. Running time, 100 MINS.

Michael Hamilton	Clark Gable
Lucia Curcio	Sophia Loren
Mario Vitale	Vittorio De Sica
Nando Hamilton	Marietto
Renzo	Paolo Carlini
Luigi	Claudio Ermelli

"It Started in Naples" is probably the best thing that ever happened to Naples. A more dazzling Neapolitan travelog is difficult to envision. Within this charming pictorial study weaves a frothy, frank and irreverent comedy that stumbles, sputters and stammers when it stretches its one basic gag —American puritanism vs. Italian moral abandon—too far, but partially restores its equilibrium with a parting shot of irony (from a U.S. standpoint) when it is the American who succumbs to the Italian point-of-view.

Since the film's candid approach opens up several exploitably naughtly avenues of human behavior, but generally knows when to pull down the shade, Paramount should rake in just enough Yankee dollars to commercially justify the enterprise. But the boxoffice battle won't be won easily.

The screenplay, by director Melville Shavelson, producer Jack Rose and Suso Cecchi D'Amico from a story by Michael Pertwee and Jack Davies, deposits Philadelphia lawyer Clark Gable in Naples to settle the estate of his brother, recently deceased via an auto accident. What Gable discovers is that his brother's extra-legal spouse also perished in the mishap, leaving their 10-year-old son (Marietto) in the care of the wife's sister (Sophia Loren).

While debating (in and out of court and courtship) the relative merits of a Philadelphia and Neapolitan environment for the child, Gable and Miss Loren fall in love and he eventually decides to make her his signora and stay on in Naples. Just how he plans to pursue his legal career is neither stated nor of concern to this light-hearted entertainment.

American audiences, accustomed to hearing every word clearly in their cinema pursuits, will have great difficulty attuning their ears to the preponderance of Italian inflection. The strain will be particularly aggravating in the cases of Master Marietto and Vittorio De Sica. Actually, it is important only to get the drift of their words, not to capture every verbal nuance, but it is a nonetheless disturbing aspect of the production.

Both the script and Shavelson's direction try too hard to make the film uproariously funny and risque. This will disturb a great many spectators. When the wit flows naturally, it is a delight; when it strains, it pains. One of the most memorable lines of comedy crops up when tired tourist Gable, wandering the noisy streets of Capri at 1:15 a.m., asks a waiter, "How are people supposed to sleep on this island?" "Together" is the matter-of-fact reply.

Gable and Miss Loren are a surprisingly effective and compatible comedy pair. The latter, more voluptuous than ever, is naturally at home in her native surroundings and gives a vigorous and amusing performance, even tackling a couple of nightclub song-and-dance routines with gusto. Although she is supposed to be a stripper, her numbers carefully conceal the fact (with ample clothing).

De Sica is suave as Gable's roving-eyed, pulchritudinously-influenced Italian attorney. Young Marietto, as the orphaned waif who smokes ciggies, guzzles wine and ogles the babes, is occasionally the victim of director's apparent desire to overpower the spectator with overly cute postures and smart quips. When allowed to be himself, little Marietto has a boyish charm rarely exhibited by American screen moppets. He should go far in filmdom. Paolo Carlini and Claudio Ermelli add prominent local color to the picture.

Robert L. Surtees' agile, inventive camera work, in combination with some unusually striking Technicolor tints (particularly some luscious greens and blues) brighten the proceedings considerably. Art directors Hal Pereira and Roland Anderson and set decorators Sam Comer and Arrigo Breschi have fashioned and filled several authentic interiors to match the preponderance of outside, on-the-spot activity.

Frank Bracht's editing is smooth and sharp. In addition to the score by Alessandro Cicognini and Carlo Savina, there are four songs, penned by Italian composers, two of which have been fortified with English lyrics for the occasion. All the music is fine and fitting. Leo Coleman's choreography makes a flashy, if not overly graceful, dancer of Miss Loren. *Tube.*

The Lost World
(C'SCOPE-COLOR)

Old Conan Doyle story about a modern expedition to a strip of prehistoric jungle on the Amazon. Production oomph softens major dramatic shortcomings, enough to indicate hefty teenage appeal for probable b.o. strength.

Hollywood, June 27.

Twentieth-Fox release of Irwin Allen production. Stars Michael Rennie, Jill St. John, David Hedison, Claude Rains, Fernando Lamas; with Richard Haydn, Ray Stricklyn, Jay Novello, Vitina Marcus, Ian Wolfe, John Graham, Colin Campbell. Directed by Allen. Screenplay, Charles Bennett, Allen, from Sir Arthur Conan Doyle's novel; camera, Winton Hoch; editor, Hugh S. Fowler; art directors, Duncan Cramer, Walter M. Simonds; music, Paul Sawtell, Bert Shefter; sound, E. Clayton Ward, Harry M. Leonard; assistant director, Ad Schaumer. Reviewed at the studio, June 27, '60. Running time, 97 MINS.

Lord Roxton	Michael Rennie
Jennifer Holmes	Jill St. John
Ed Malone	David Hedison
Professor Challenger	Claude Rains
Gomez	Fernando Lamas
Professor Summerlee	Richard Haydn
David	Ray Stricklyn
Costa	Jay Novello
Native Girl	Vitina Marcus
Burton White	Ian Wolfe
Stuart Holmes	John Graham
Professor Waldron	Colin Campbell

Watching "The Lost World" is tantamount to taking a trip through a Coney Island fun house. Like the latter, the Irwin Allen production should appeal primarily to teenagers which, what with the World War II and post-war birth rate, is a good group to be appealing to these days, from a fiscal standpoint. Although basically as plodding and cumbersome as its dinosaurs, the 20th-Fox release contains enough exploitable spectacle and innocent fun to generate a respectable boxoffice response.

The picture's chief attraction is its production gusto. Emphasis on

physical and pictorial values makes up, to some extent, for its lack of finesse in the literary and thespic departments.

In translating the Sir Arthur Conan Doyle story to the screen for the second time (after a lapse of 36 years since the first, silent version), Allen and Charles Bennett have constructed a choppy, topheavy, deliberately-paced screenplay that labors too long with exposition and leaves several loose ends dangling. Only when it turns the film over to the production department for a rousing theatrical safari through a region resembling red hell does the scenario make a smart move. But, until then, "Lost World" is a familiar place, loaded with romantic platitudes and ludicrous situations.

Although he has instilled a certain lighthearted spirit into portions of the dramatic proceedings, Allen's direction is not only sluggish but has somehow gotten more personality into his dinosaurs than into his people.

Among the curious individuals who venture into this treacherous hidden area at the headwaters of the Amazon are Claude Rains, overly affected as Doyle's popular stet character, Professor George Edward Challenger, a bit wooden as a titled playboy with a notorious reputation; Jill St. John, ill-at-ease as an adventuress who chooses tight pink capri pants as suitable garb for an Amazonian exploration; David Hedison, bland as a newsman-photog; and Fernando Lamas, unconvincing as a Latin guitar-player and helicopter-operator. Others whose thespic energies are spent in a dramatic vacuum are Richard Haydn, Ray Stricklyn, Jay Novello, Vitina Marcus and Ian Wolfe.

With the exception of one or two mighty ineffectual prehistoric spiders and a general absence of genuine shock or tension, the production is something to behold. The dinosaurs are exceptionally lifelike (although they resemble horned toads and alligators more than dinosaurs) and the violent volcanic scenery (like hot, bubbling chili sauce) and lush vegetation form backdrops that are more interesting and impressive than the action taking place in front of them.

For the superior craftsmanship evident in the production, credit art directors Duncan Cramer and Walter M. Simonds, set decorators Walter M. Scott, Joseph Kish and John Sturtevant, and the special photographic effects team of L. B. Abbott, James B. Gordon and Emil Kosa. Energetic Cinema-Scope lenswork by Winton Hoch and appropriately out-of-this-world music by Paul Sawtell and Bert Shefter are helpful ingredients. Hugh S. Fowler's editing is somewhat unsteady. *Tube.*

Thunder in Carolina
(COLOR)

Low-budget entry about stock car racing. Has exploitation value because of mounting interest in the sport. Mediocre, however, as a film, but probably okay for second feature and neighborhood playdates.

Howco release of J. Francis White production. Stars Rory Calhoun, Alan Hale, Connie Hines and John Gentry. Directed by Paul Helmick. Screenplay, Alexander Richards; camera, Joseph Brun; editor, Rex Lipton; music, Walter Green. previewed in N.Y. June 29, '60. Running time, 92 MINS.

Mitch Cooper ....Rory Calhoun
Buddy Schaeffer ....Alan Hale
Rene York ....Connie Hines
Les York ....John Gentry
Reichert ....Ed McGrath
Kay Hill ....Troyanne Ross
Eve Mason ....Helen Downey
Stoogie ....Van Casey
Myron Webb ....Trippie Wisecup
Tommy Webb ....Carey Loftin
Peaches ....Billie Langston
Singer ....Ann Stevens
Junior Thorsen ....George Rembert, Jr.
Motel Manager ....Olwen Roney
Higgins ....Richard Taylor
Roy Greenleaf ....William Sprott
Deputy ....Wes Stone
Minister .....Rev. Thomas M. Godbold
Announcer "Southern 500"...Ray Melton
Dirt Track Announcer..Raymond Caddell
Maid ....Edith Scott
"Miss Southern 500".... Carolyn Melton
Grand National Race Drivers ... Joe Weatherly, Buck Baker, Curtis Turner, Neil Castles, Joe Caspolich Shep Langdon, Joe Eubanks

With the interest in hot rods and stock car racing mounting, "Thunder In Carolina," a low-budget entry dealing with "Southern 500," an auto racing event that attracts some 100,000 people every Labor Day to Darlington, S. C., may have exploitation values that can be translated into okay boxoffice. But as a motion picture, it's an anachronistic entry reminiscent of the dozens of "B" pictures that teamed Richard Arlen and Chester Morris.

Financed by a group of southern exhibitors who apparently were influenced by the promotion aspects, "Thunder in Carolina" is a mediocre film that is heightened somewhat by some good action footage of an actual "Southern 500" race. Alexander Richards' screenplay purports to deal with the lives and loves of the dedicated drivers and their girls, but what emerges is a stilted story.

Rory Calhoun, who in addition to Alan Hale is only recognizable name in the film, is seen as femme-chasing veteran driver. He latches on to young gas station operator and the latter's wife. Under Calhoun's influence, the grease monkey, played by John Gentry, abandons his garage and turns to stock car racing. Calhoun makes passes at Gentry's wife, but she's faithful. However, when her husband achieves success, Connie Hines, the wife, seems more inclined to accept Calhoun's advances since Gentry is being pursued by a swelled head and another woman.

The climax, of course, sees Calhoun turn softie. He deliberately crashes his car to save the life of his former protege, allowing the latter to win the big race. A reconciliation follows. Gentry and his wife make up, and Calhoun goes off to race somewhere again.

Actual scenes for the preparation of the race, a pageant through the streets of Darlington, and the race, partly filmed from a speeding car, lend a degree of authenticity to the proceedings. Joseph Brun's color photography is first-rate in capturing the racing and some speedy practice driving on South Carolina mountain roads. There is a flaw in the sound recording, however. There is a hollow sound in the dialog, as if it had been filtered through an echo chamber.

The performances meet the needs of the script. In addition to the Calhoun - Gentry - Hines triangle, there's Hale as an injured driver turned mechanic, Ed McGrath, as a wealthy car owner, and Helen Downey as a girl on the loose. Actual participants in the Southern 500 are seen in the film. Paul Helmick's direction is static, particularly in the staging in one of the pre-race events during which the drivers and their girls stand around listlessly to listen to a singer. Technical aspects are okay. *Holl.*

Les Mordus
(The Fanatics)
(FRENCH)
Paris, July 5.

Jason release of Floralies-Jad-Jason production. Stars Sacha Distel; features Danik Patisson, Daniel Cauchy, Bernadette Lafont, Michel Galabru, Rene Dary, Philippe Hersent, Bernard Andrieu. Directed by Rene Jolivet. Screenplay, Jolivet, Lise Bodard; camera, Michel Kelber; editor, Suzanne De Troye; music, Distel. At Paris, Paris. Running time 110 MINS.
Bernard ....Sacha Distel
Francoise ....Danik Patisson
Mado ....Bernadette Lafont
Fischer ....Bernard Andrieu
Lane ....Philippe Hersent
Legoff ....Rene Dary
Fred ....Michel Galabru
Mosco ....Daniel Cauchy

Film seems to have been made mainly to intro the popular singer Sacha Distel. He is still gauche on the acting and is not lensed too well. This appears of little export value.

It is about a young delinquent who goes straight only to be almost pulled back into a gangster mob again. He is saved by friends and the love of a good girl. Story is pat and obivous. Direction, technical values and acting are only fair. Distel will need another time around before he can be judged for thesp talents. *Mosk.*

Las Hermanas Karambazo
(The Karambazo Sisters)
(MEXICAN)
Mexico City, June 21.

Columbia release of Jose Luis Calderon production. Stars Manuel "Loco" Valdez, Flor Silvestre, Irma Dorantes; features Manuel Capetillo, Roberto G. Rivera and Olivia Michel. Directed by Benito Alazraki. Screenplay, Jose Luis Calderon. At Orfeon Theatre, Mexico City. Running time, 90 MINS.

This is first starring vehicle for television comic "Loco" Valdes. And director Benito Alazraki has injected more quality than usual in Mexican pictures built around comics.

The sisters are Flor Silvestro, Irma Dorantes and Olivia Michel who, apart from acting as female bait for comic Valdes, sing a few numbers pleasantly and look attractive.

Although the picture was made with the usual speed, a threeweek shooting schedule, comic Valdes who is truly "crazy" on his television shows, is held on a tight rein by director so that comedy situations don't get out of hand.

A better than average effort with comic's antics causing most Mexican patrons to give out with laughs as comedy situations are milked for all they are worth, with these often obvious and sometimes grotesque.

Picture could have been a major comedy effort if director Alazraki, one of the best down here, had had more time to spend in development of situations and toning down overacting bits by his cast. *Emil.*

Our Last Spring
(GREECE)
Berlin, July 5.

Warner Bros. release of a Michael Cacoyannis production (Athens). Stars Alexander Matamis and Marie Ney. Directed by Cacoyannis. Screenplay, Cacoyannis and Jane Cobb from Cosmas Politis' novel, "Eroica"; camera, Walter Lassally; music, Argyris Kounadis. At Zoo Palast, Berlin, June 28, '60. Running time, 120 MINS.

Michale Cacoyannis is one of the most interesting directors in Europe. And there's evidence of his talents in this English-speaking Greek picture, but it is a ponderous, over-emphatic and overlong treatise on the subject of youth. It needs slashing, rather than editing, to have much of a chance in the commercial market.

The young people depicted in "Our Last Spring" are intense and highspirited boys and girls, all still at school, and all seeking an outlet for their emotions. Their high spirits droop after one of the youths is accidentally killed. From then on the youngsters behave mainly in abnormal fashion, seeking vengeance not only from the person responsible but from society itself. The subject-matter, however, is strangled by its own intensity.

Apart from the obvious deficiencies of the script, the weakest feature is the lax editing at least 30-40 minutes need to be scissored out of the finished print to make it palatable. Camerawork, however, is first class, and the acting is acceptable. *Myro.*

Men of Rio
(BRAZIL)
Berlin, June 28.

Moral Rearmament (Rio de Janiero) production and release. Directed. starring and written by Nelson Marcellino de Carvalho, Otto Lopes Barbosa, Carlos Anselmo. Camera, Edgar Eichhorn; music, Remo Usai. At Zoo Palast, Berlin, June 25, '60. Running time, 70 MINS.

There's a message in this pic, as is to be expected in a production sponsored by Moral Rearmament. But it is presented with maximum naivety, making it a slender commercial prospect.

The setting is the port of Rio, and the theme describes a clash between rival union leaders. The bad man is eventually persuaded to see the error of his ways. As he agrees to join the honest forces in organizing port labor, his crippled daughter manages to walk unaided for the first time in her life.

Direction and acting are in line with the spirit of the script. It's hard to understand, however, how this entry succeeded in being shown at a Class "A" international film festival. *Myro.*

Jokyo
(Woman's Testament)
(JAPAN—COLOR-C'SCOPE)
Berlin, June 28.

Daiei (Tokio) production and release. Directed by Yasuzo Masumara, Kon Ichikawa and Kazaburo Yoshimura. Stars Ayako Wakao, Fujiko Yamamoto, Machiko Kyo. Screenplay, Shofu Muranmatsu and Toshio Yazumi; camera, Hiroshi Murai, Setsuo Kobayashi, Kazuo Miyagawa; music, Yasushi. At Zoo Palast Berlin, June 26, '60. Running time, 94 MINS.

A three-part story, told with three separate casts, using a trio of directors and technical teams, "Jokyo" is an offbeat subject which attempts to depict the morality code of a trio of immoral women. It could have limited art chances Stateside.

First of the three women works in a Tokyo night club, and has an uncanny knack of extracting money from gullible men, which she shrewdly invests in a company of which the owner's son is her immediate target. The next is employed by a realty agent to lure equally gullible men into buying worthless property. Her particular gimmick is to invite the men to her room, urge them to take a bath while she washes their backs while quite naked. Something, she explains, her late husband enjoyed, and that helps to recapture the happy days. The third is an ex-Geisha girl, who inherits a prosperous restaurant from her husband, has problems with his family, but falls sincerely in love with a forger, and decides to wait for him until he's served his time.

The treatment is frank, but in good taste. The three starring girls are considerable lookers. The pic is fine technically, with excellent color and first-class anamorphic photography. *Myro.*

Venner
(Struggle for Eagle Peak)
(NORWAY)

Berlin, June 28.
A/S Nordsjofilm (Oslo) production and release. Directed by Tancred Ibsen; screenplay, A. Overland, T. Ibsen; camera, Ragnar Sorensen; settings, Grethe Hejes; music, Maj Sonstevold. At Zoo Palast, Berlin, June 26, '60. Running time, 90 MINS.

For a country with very limited producing facilities, "Venner" is a commendable effort, though it's somewhat too naive and melodramatic to make much of an impact with more sophisticated audiences. It looks an unlikely U. S. prospect but can probably recoup its investment in the Scandinavian market.

It's a story of two friends who attempt to climb the Eagle peak. At first, only one returns, and he claims the prize as the first to reach the summit, but the other comes back later, challenges his friend's claim, and accuses him of attempted murder. The Alpine Club conducts an inquiry, and the hearings are illustrated by constant flashbacks.

Production qualities are fair, acting adequate, and direction simple and straightforward. *Myro.*

In Love, But Doubly
(FINNISH)

Berlin, July 5.
Oy Suomen Filmiteollismus (Helsinki) production and release. Stars Wesa Enne. Directed by Willie Salminen. Screenplay and lyrics, Reino Helismaa; camera, Kalle Peronkoski; music, Toiwo Karki; choreography, Airi Saila. At Zoo Palast, Berlin, June 29, '60. Running time, 87 MINS.

It is a bold idea for a small producing nation to try its hand at a filmusical, and it must be admitted that this Finnish production is a tame effort. Film will have little appeal to audiences accustomed to the more polished article that comes from Hollywood. It may have some success in Scandinavian

territories where the players are known, but has only limited chances beyond.

The story line is completely unpretentious. And though the running time is restricted to 87 minutes, the action has to be padded with a specialty routine which has nothing to do with the plot. Theme concerns two young men who fall in love with the same girl; they not only lose out to their far richer boss, but get fired in the bargain. One then turns his attentions to a pop singer, and the other to the sister of a boxer.

Music and lyrics are unexceptional, the choreography is dated and the acting is barely adequate.
Myro.

Faja Lobbi
(Ardent Love)
(DUTCH)

Berlin, July 5.
Herman van der Horst production. Production, direction, screenplay, camera, settings and music by van der Horst. At Zoo Palast, Berlin, June 30, '60. Running time, 70 MINS.

As a one-man effort, this feature-length documentary pic is a thoroughly commendable job. Herman van der Horst has shown a real feeling for his subject, and has kept the footage down to a reasonable length to make it an acceptable supporting film. Instead of the more conventional type travelog, van der Horst has successfully tried his hand at presenting a profile of a primitive community in Sumarin, a Dutch possession on the northern coast of South America. It has no commentary, relying solely on visual means for telling its story.

Though there is inevitably some repetition in the subject matter, this picture of a community that still lives by the bow and arrow, and uses that weapon for hunting and fishing, has considerable appeal. First-rate color is one of its assets. *Myro.*

The Bellboy

Series of farcical episodes about a bumbling bellhop knit together into an uninspired film. Jerry Lewis name alone must make it a b.o. contender.

Hollywood, July 5.
Paramount release of Jerry Lewis production. Stars Jerry Lewis; features (no characters named) Alex Gerry, Bob Clayton; with Sonny Sands, Eddie Shaeffer, Herkie Styles, David Landfield, Bill Richmond, Larry Best, Cary Middlecoff, The Novelites, Joe Levitch, Stanley Allan, Duke Art Jr., Eddie Barton, Murray Barton, Howard Brooks, Ricki Dunn, Jack Durant, Jimmy Gerard, Matilda Gerard, Paul Gerson, Paul Gray, H. S. Gump, Jack Henkins, Elise Jayne, Dick Lynne, Pat Mack, John G. Morgan, Larry K. Nixon, B. S. Pully, Guy Rennie, Maxie Rosenbloom, Benny Ross, Joe E. Ross, Frankie Scott, Roy Sedley, Sammy Shore, Sarah Smith, Art Stanley, Hal Winters, Mike Zetz. Directed and written by Lewis; camera, Haskell Boggs; editor, Stanley Johnson; art directors, Hal Pereira, Henry Bumstead; music, Walter Scharf; sound, Gene Merritt, Charles Grenzbach; assistant director, Ralph Axness. Reviewed at Westwood Village Theatre, July 5, '60. Running time, 72 MINS.

Paramount has what appears to be a safe boxoffice proposition in "The Bellboy," an episodic farce written, produced and directed by and starring Jerry Lewis. As a midsummer attraction for vacationing schoolchildren, it's a natural. But, from an artistic standpoint, "Bellboy" is minor-league screen comedy, the victim of its energetic star's limited craftsmanship.

The picture is, as it admits in an introductory disclaimer, a "series of silly sequences" with "no story, no plot." It follows Lewis, as a bellboy at Miami's fashionable Fontainebleau Hotel, through a number of zany misadventures in which he speaks not a word of dialog. Several of the sequences are amusing, but too many are dependent upon climactic sight gags anticipated well in advance of the punch. The film has a tendency to grow repetitious, one of the major reasons for this being Lewis' strict adherence to the sort of physical exaggeration (the palsied movement and distorted facial maneuvers) that has become his trademark.

There is reason to suspect that the character of "The Bellboy" had the potential of turning into a memorable vehicle for Lewis. There are latent elements of Charlie Chaplin's little tramp, Jacques Tati's "Hulot," Danny Kaye's "Mitty" and Harpo Marx's curiously tender child-man, but the execution falls far short of such inspiration. Under Lewis' direction, the "Bellboy," for all of his "lovable underdog" possibilities, emerges a two-dimensional portrait, a clown without a soul, a funnyman to be laughed at, but not rooted for.

Lewis has surrounded himself with some exceptionally vigorous talents for this film and, as director, he has enlisted from them a controlled enthusiasm he himself has not matched. Among the standouts in the large, relatively unfamiliar supporting cast are Alex Gerry, Bob Clayton, Bill Richmond (in a Stan Laurel takeoff that is likely to inspire audience cheers) and the Novelites, who fashion one of the picture's comedy peaks. Milton Berle puts in a surprise guest appearance.

Cinematically, "Bellboy" is a satisfactory achievement. Chief among its generally strong depart-

mental contributions are Haskell Boggs' agile camera work, Stanley Johnson's sharp and tricky, but sensitive, editing (making the most of John P. Fulton's striking special photographic effects), and Walter Scharf's particularly vital musical punctuation of episode endings and use of instruments to represent characters.

Since all the action takes place at the actual Fontainebleau, and no well-known names other than Lewis grace its cast roster, "Bellboy" undoubtedly was brought in on an unusually small budget. The combination of economy, timing and Lewis' juve draw should be sufficient to insure profit. *Tube.*

Les Etoiles De Midi
(Stars at Noon)
(FRENCH-COLOR)

Paris, July 12.
CFDC release of Filmartic-Requin Films production. Directed by Marcel Ichac. Screenplay, Gerard Herzog, Ichac; camera (Eastmancolor), Georges Strouve, Rene Vernadet; editor, Pierre Gillette. At Biarritz, Paris. Running time, 78 MINS.

Well-made feature documentary enacts some true escapades among some of the top French mountain climbers. Though re-enacted it has a solid treatment and some eye-catching scenes and derring-do. It looms mainly a special feature pic for an arty house. Or this could be cut down for solid supporting fare or secondary playoff spots abroad.

Color, lensing and incidental acting by real mountaineers are all good. Though familiar overall, this has some originality via its war tale of a German escape, the saving of a couple of lost climbers and the agility and knowhow involved in this sport. *Mosk.*

Light Up the Sky
(BRITISH)

Lightweight yarn about fun, games—and a spot of tragedy—on a British searchlight site during the war. Good for U.K. but chancey in U. S.

London, July 5.
British Lion release (in association with Bryanston Films) of a Lewis Gilbert production. Stars Ian Carmichael, Tommy Steele, Benny Hill. Directed by Lewis Gilbert. Screenplay, Vernon Harris, from Robert Storey's play, "Touch Of Light"; editor, Peter Tanner; camera, John Wilcox; music, Douglas Gamley; song, "Touch It Light," by Lionel Bart and Michael Pratt. At Plaza, July 5, '60. Running time, 90 MINS.
Lt. Ogleby .... Ian Carmichael
Eric McCaffey .... Tommy Steele
Syd McCaffey .... Benny Hill
Ted Green .... Sydney Tafler
Lance Bombardier
 Tomlinson .... Victor Maddern
Roland Kenyon .... Harry Locke
Leslie Smith .... Johnny Briggs
"Spinner" Rice .... Cyril Smith
Harry (driver) .... Dick Emery
Compere .... Cardew Robinson
Jean .... Susan Burnet
Theatre act .... Sheila Hancock
Mr. Jennings .... Fred Griffiths

"Light Up The Sky" is the latest entry in a long line of Britain's war pix. This one's a comedy, which perhaps unwisely also brings in undertones of pathos and, in the end, tragedy. It deals with a searchlight unit manned by such incompetents that must make the average audience wonder how the 1939-1945 skirmish didn't end in disaster. From the U. K. point of view the casting of Ian Carmichael, Tommy Steele and Benny Hill, with firstrate support, makes

it a likely b.o. winner. America may find this too insignificant for serious consideration.

Though much of the military detail is suspect the atmosphere of the unit, the behavior of its members and the dialog is almost embarrassingly authentic, allowing for the fact that this has been concocted as a comedy and therefore exaggerated. Snags are that the story is straggly, and director Lewis Gilbert has slipped too easily into snapping up some quick vaudeville yocks, largely from ribald dialog.

This has no real plot, being simply the byplay of various members of the unit. There's the girl-chasing soldier who gets himself into a jam with a local girl. The older soldier whose son is killed in Egypt. The shy one who deserts in order to find his girl friend and clear up some misunderstanding. The comedy cook. The understanding, but vapid officer.

From the thesping angle, the most interesting point is that this is the first time Tommy Steele has played a straight role which has not been custom-made for him. He is surprisingly well disciplined in a part that is no bigger than the next man's. Benny Hill, a talented tv comedian, who has so far not clicked in films has still to find his way in pictures. In getting laughs he still remains himself, and not a character.

Ian Carmichael flips gaily through the role of a pleasant inefficient officer. Among the other performances that give yeoman service to this flimsy film are those of Victor Maddern, as a grouchy lance-bombardier in charge of the site; Harry Locke, as a cigarette-smoking Cockney cook; Johnny Briggs, as the lovelorn youngster who gets bumped off, and Sydney Tafler, as the older man who is like a father to his messmates. Cyril Smith, Susan Burnet, Dick Emery and Cardew Robinson are also occasionally employed to some effect.

There is one scene dragged in which gives Steele and Hill a chance to parody the sort of song-dance act which was one of the major sufferings that every soldier had to endure during the war. They do it well, but it doesn't help much.

Direction, lensing, editing and artwork are all adequate, but this is a surprisingly unambitious effort from Lewis Gilbert, who has been responsible for such notable pix as "Sink The Bismarck!" and "Reach For The Sky." This one looks rather like the sort of chore he might have tossed off during a seven days' leave. *Rich.*

Three Penny Opera
(Die Dreigroschenoper)
(GERMAN)

Brandon Films release of G. W. Pabst production. With Rudolph Forster, Lotte Lenya, Carola Neher, Ernst Busch, Fritz Rasp, Reinhold Schuenzel. Directed by G. W. Pabst. Screenplay adapted by Leo Lania, Ladislas Vajda, Bela Belaz, from play written by Berthold Brecht with music by Kurt Weill; music, Kurt camera, Fritz Wagner; settings, Andre Adnreiv; musical direction, Theodore Mackeben. Reviewed at Museum of Modern Art, N. Y., June 21, '60. Running time, 112 MINS.

Mackie Messer ....Rudolph Forster
Jenny ....Lotte Lenya
Polly ....Carola Neher
Street Singer ....Ernst Busch
Peachum ....Fritz Rasp
Tiger Brown ....Reinhold Schuenzel

The venerable English sardonic "Beggar's Opera" was adapted by Kurt Weill (music) and Berthold Brecht (libretto) into "Three Penny Opera," a much-produced stage work these last decades. Meanwhile the Nazis suppressed the 1931 film version, and it has taken 10 years of patience on the part of Tom Brandon to collect prints from foreign sources. From these he has re-recorded and equalized the soundtrack. Work, done by James Townsend with musical supervision by Henry Schuman, is technically notable.

Film was seen here briefly in 1931, in a cut version and without complete English titles, and created no stir whatsoever. It's easy to understand why — it was at least 30 years ahead of its time in point of view. Like the successful Marc Blitzstein American stage adaptation, which has been running for over five years off-Broadway, the film is a sophistication, cynically jaunty look at a seamy society. It's only moral: crime does pay—if you're clever enough.

Despite the tremendous general popularity of film's "Mack The Knife" theme, which might be expected to interest many filmgoers who do not ordinarily seek out the esoteric, picture will be most appreciated by art house audiences and, particularly, by cinema buffs interested in film techniques. As directed by G. W. Pabst, picture is a successful translation of a highly stylized stage work to the realistic screen medium, a problem which film producers continue to wrestle and seldom successfully.

Pabst, getting great help from the Weill score and settings by Andrei Andreiev, succeeds in creating a thoroughly believeable never-never land, that is, a turn-of-the-century London as imagined by a German who has lived through the post-war chaos of his own land. Within this frame, the Berthold Brecht tale of the notorious cut-throat, Mackie Messer, unfolds with complete honesty and a lot of wild, hard-as-nails social satire. The social satire, in fact, is pretty blunt and much of the so-called humor, as translated by the subtitles, is heavy.

But the inter-relationships of the three main characters, or rather the relationship of Mackie with his one true love, Polly Peachum, and with the prostitute, Jenny, are defined with reality and insight. This is due, not only to the performances of Rudolph Forster as Mackie, Carola Neher as Polly and Lotte Lenya as Jenny, but, of course, to the Weill music. The 1931 Miss Lenya (Mrs. Weill in private life) is especially appealing with her odd and haunting "Pirate Jenny" number.

Camerawork by Fritz Wagner is firstrate, even by today's standards. While the film is chiefly interesting as a museum piece, it is an often lively one that stands to attract a lot of interest in "selected" dates. *Anby.*

Le Panier a Crabes
(The Crab Basket)
(FRENCH)

Paris, July 12.

Dispat Film release of Lisbona film production. With Pierre Michael, Anne Doat, Anne Tonietti, Michel Bardinet, Paul Frankeur, Henri Vilbert. Written and directed by Joseph Lisbona: dialog, Henri-Francois Rey; camera, Pierre Petit; editor, Georges Alepee. At Monte Carlo, Paris. Running time, 90 MINS.

Charles ....Pierre Michael
Chantal ....Anne Doat
Liliane ....Anne Tonietti
Jacques ....Michel Bardinet
Clavier ....Paul Frankeur
Dorel ....Henri Vilbert

Pic deals with an idealist whose broken first love leads to his flunking out of college, getting into the film game and making a first pic but ankling for parts unknown after the film is a triumph because of his refusal to make concessions. Film is somewhat surface in handling and its indulging in the soft underbelly of pix producing here makes it somewhat regional in implications. This looms mainly a local item with foreign biz chances only on its theme and possible interest in French film matters.

This is the first for Joseph Lisbona who has given it sketchy but sincere mounting. The first part lacks enough insight into the growing love affair to make the second portion a seemingly different tale. It is a production that shows Lisbona may be heard from again in the film biz here.

Acting by a young troupe is adequate sans enough character depth to make the drama more cohesive. But it is a solid opus which ran into trouble with the governmental Centre Du Cinema here on its frank look at the corrupt side of filmmaking. Technical credits are good and the pic has a fine production gloss. *Mosk.*

Das Glas Wasser
(The Glass of Water)
(GERMAN-COLOR)

Berlin, July 12.

Deutsche Film Hansa release of a Georg Richter-Helmut Kautner production. Adapted from Eugene Scribe's stage play. Direction, screenplay and lyrics by Kautner. Camera, Gunther Anders; music, Bernard Eichhorn and Roland Sonder-Mahken; editor, Klaus Dudenhofer. At Zoo Palast, Berlin, July 5, '60. Running time, 84 MINS.

Sir Henry St. John....Gustaf Grundgens
Queen ....Liselotte Pulver
Lady Churchill................Hilde Krahl
Abigail ....Sabine Sinjen
Arthur Masham..............Horst Janson
Marquis de Torcy........Rudolf Forster
Butler ....Hans Leibelt
Beichvater ....Herbert Weissbach
Lord Avondale............Joachim Rake

Helmut Kautner is one of West Germany's best directors with an imposing list of credits, but he seems to be out of his depth in this English period piece. Though he has made striking use of his color cameras, he has hissed the light touch that is such an essential quality in restoration comedy. While it tries hard to be gay, frivolous and inconsequential, the over-heavy Teutonic touch is all too frequently in evidence.

Although it is encouraging and welcome to see the German industry breaking away from the more conventional type of postwar production, "Glass of Water" is more distinguished for its technical achievements than for its story content. Apart from the exceptional color contrasts (black and white are blended with vivid hues), it also breaks new ground by the use of ultra modernistic decor for a period piece, though the costumes have the genuine early 18th Century appearance.

The original stage play, which lightly deals with intrigue and backstage shenanigans in the English Court in 1710, has been refurbished to meet the needs of the motion picture, and a few bright lyrics (written by Kautner) have been added to the script. They're okay in German, but it's questionable whether they would translate into the English language.

A fundamental weakness of the entire production is the inability of the cast, experienced though it is to capture the mood and period of the subject. Gustaf Grundgens, for example, makes a tremendous effort as the dashing, debonair and witty Sir Henry St. John, but the performance just misses. Liselotte Pulver doesn't quite hit it off as the Queen, even though there is an inherent charm in her portrayal. Hilde Krahl is nearer the bullseye as the crafty Lady Churchill. Sabine Sinjen and Horst Janson offer an element of naive sincerity as the ingenue leads.

Among the technical credits, full marks go to the camera work. Brisk editing is a plus feature. *Myro.*

Nianchan
(My Second Brother)
(JAPANESE—C'SCOPE)

Nikkatsu Corp. (Tokyo) production and release. Stars Hiroyuki Nagato, Chigusa Takayama. Directed by Shohei Imamura. Screenplay, Sueko Yasumoto, Ichiro Ikeda, Inamura; camera, Masahisa Himeda; music, Toshiro Mayuzumi. At Zoo Palast, Berlin. Running time, 100 MINS.

A sombre, depressing story of life in a Japanese mining town, "Nianchan" may have only limited chances overseas, though it is a well-made pic, sensitively photographed in black and white C'Scope.

This is a tale of poverty and hunger among a depressed community, told almost without relief. The central characters are four orphan children who are eventually compelled to separate, even though willing neighbors are prepared to share their last spoonful of rice. Shohei Imamura's direction is painstakingly sincere. The acting is more than competent, though the subject compels all the players to maintain an almost constant expression of misery. *Myro.*

Le Signe Du Lion
(The Sign of the Lion)
(FRENCH)

Paris, July 12.

AJYM production and release. Stars Jesse Hahn; features Van Doude, Michele Girardon, Christian Alers, Jean Le Poulain, Gilbert Edard. Written and directed by Eric Rohmer. Camera, Nicolas Hayer; editor, Y. Yoyotte. Preemed in Paris. Running time, 90 MINS.

Pierre ....Jess Hahn
Reporter ....Van Doude
Girl ....Michele Girardon
Paul ....Christian Alers
Tramp ....Jean Le Poulain
Photographer ....Gilbert Edard

This "New Wave" film, made by a highbrow critic, has yet to get a release here. It deals with a foreigner living in Paris who finds himself caught sans money one summer and his way down to becoming a tramp before he is saved by friends and an inheritance.

The beginning is heavyhanded and ambiguous, but the film picks up via the study of the hero's

downfall and endless treks through a cold Paris. It is an offbeater mainly with only arty possibilities abroad on its slowness and one-track progression. But it does show another side of the so-called "Gay Paree."

Lead role is played by Yank actor Jess Hahn who is cast as some sort of foreigner living and studying music in Paris who comes into money. But then it seems it was all a mistake, and he finds himself with debts and alone. His slow degradation is done with insistence but insight. However, Hahn is somewhat too big and gruff to suggest a supposed artistic type using Paris as a Bohemian abode.

Director-writer Eric Rohmer displays a flair for showing the ungenerous qualities of Paris but rarely imbues this with the dramatic pitch to make the plight either moving or meaningful. Hence, the happy ending loses its needed ironic point. But the pic is unusual enough to merit arty chances abroad.

Technical credits are good. It is one of the early "New Wave" entries that has yet to be released anywhere.   *Mosk.*

The Thief In the Bedroom
(SWEDISH—COLOR)
Berlin, July 5.
Europa production and release. Stars Jarl Kulle, Gaby Stenberg. Direction and screenplay, Goran Gentele; camera, Karl Erik Alberts; settings, Arne Akermark; music, Harry Arnold. At Zoo Palast, Berlin. Running time, **100 MINS.**

An out-of-competition entry at the Berlin festival, this Swedish comedy is a light-hearted trifle, with a few amusing though often-contrived situations. It's a safe bet for the Scandinavian territories, and will also have some appeal in other countries. But it's an unlikely prospect for the U. S.

The screenplay puts the focus on a rich widow and a poor writer who first meet in an aeroplane and then become involved in a series of complications. The plot develops mainly on farcical lines. There's an amusing, though overlong, sequence in which the writer and a thief are in the widow's bedroom at the same time.

Though completely unpretentious, this has been handsomely mounted and photographed in color. Gaby Stenberg is striking as the widow and Jarl Kulle does okay as the romantic male lead.
                                  Myro.

My Slave
(THAILAND—COLOR)
Berlin, July 5.
Ubol Yugala production. With Vilaiwan Wattanaphanich, Prasitsukda Singhara, Supan Burapin, Adul Dulyarat, Arsa Israngkul. Directed by Ubol Yugala. Screenplay, Vanasiri; camera, Plong Sangsophon. At Berlin Film Fest. Running time, **135 MINS.**

This one commands some special attention because it's Thailand's first entry at a western film festival. It's an item primarily for home consumption, but might lure some curio-seekers outside its homegrounds.

Story centers around a farmer's daughter who has been sold to a rich nobleman because of the fact that her father accumulated debts which he was unable to pay. She

arouses the envy of her master's former favorite who tries everything to bring her into discredit. Justice is meted out in the end.

Film lacks suspense mainly because too long. Direction by Ubol Yugaa is routine while the acting is a bit on the primitive side. Vilaiwan Wattanaphanich, who enacts the title role, is quite a beauty who, incidentally, had a small part in Columbia's "River Kwai."
                                  Hans.

The Time Machine
(COLOR)

H. G. Wells' fantasy about a time-wanderer with a conscience, translated to the screen with taste, flair and inventiveness. A delightful experience. Absence of big cast names shouldn't deter b.o. success.

Hollywood, June 10.
Metro release of George Pal production. Stars Rod Taylor, Alan Young, Yvette Mimieux; with Sebastian Cabot, Tom Helmore, Whit Bissell, Doris Lloyd. Directed by Pal. Screenplay, David Duncan, based on H G. Wells' novel; camera, Paul C. Vogel; editor, George Tomasini; art directors, George W. Davis, William Ferrari; music, Russell Garcia; assistant director, William Shanks. Reviewed at Academy Award Theatre, June 10, '60. Running time, **103 MINS.**
Time Traveler .... Rod Taylor
Filby .... Alan Young
Weena .... Yvette Mimieux
Dr. Hillyer .... Sebastian Cabot
Anthony Bridewell .... Tom Helmore
Walter Kemp .... Whit Bissell
Mrs. Watchett .... Doris Lloyd

George Pal's production of "The Time Machine" is 103 minutes enchanting adaptation and materialization of H. G. Wells' provocative story. Metro release is a film for people of all ages, one that can be appreciated at various intellectual strata while being enjoyed on the common ground of pure escapist fantasy. If its artful, inventive cinematic values are exploited with a taste and imagination matching the product, the absence of established boxoffice names won't be a negative factor. "Time Machine" should prove a noteworthy success.

In utilizing contemporary knowledge to update Wells' durable novel, scenarist David Duncan has brought the work into modern focus. The point-of-view springs properly from 1960 rather than from the turn of the century, at which period Wells penned his farsighted tome. The social comment of the original has been historically refined to encompass such plausible eventualities as the physical manifestation of atomic war weapons. But the basic spirit of Wells' work has not been lost.

The film's chief flaw is its somewhat palsied pace. Forging its way through vital initial exposition, it perks to a fascinating peak when the "Time Traveller" (Rod Taylor) plants himself in his machine and begins his enviable tour of time. His "visits" to World Wars I, II, and III, and the way in which the passage of time is depicted within these "local" stops give the picture its most delightful, indelibly enchanting moments.

But things slow down to a walk when Taylor arrives at the year 802,701 and becomes involved generally with a group of tame, anti-social towheads (the "Eloi") and specifically with their loveliest and most sociable representative (Yvette Mimieux), with whom he falls in love. But dramatic sparks start sizzling again when Taylor unearths the reason for their apathetic behavior—a cannibalistic underworld element (the "Morlocks") which has enslaved the Eloi. There is wholesale horror in these passages of the film, highly exploitable shock material and a particularly vivid but not overly frightening experience for children. After stirring up a revolt (in a suspenseful scene), Taylor returns to 1900, only to select three books (identities of which are tan-

talizingly withheld) and return to his 802,701 romance.

With this portrayal, Rod Taylor definitely establishes himself as one of the premium young talents on today's screen. His performance is a gem of straightforwardness, with just the proper sensitivity and animation. A standout in support is Alan Young, in a gentle, three-ply role. Miss Mimieux is well cast. Innocent vacancy gleams beautifully in her eyes. Others who give favorable impressions are Sebastian Cabot, Tom Helmore, Whit Bissell and Doris Lloyd.

Pal's direction can be faulted only for its pace. In every other way, both in conception (as producer) and interpretation (as director), he has done a remarkable job. But it is a film which owes more than is customary to departmental crafts and skills such as Paul C. Vogel's first-rate lensing and, particularly, George Tomasini's meticulously intricate editing.

An absolutely essential contribution is the fascinating "special photographic effects" conjured up by Gene Warren and Wah Chang, in particular the unforgettable impressions of nature-on-the-move during time-machine transition passages. In a film that explores several eras and civilizations, art direction and set decoration are of cardinal importance. These two facets of the production have been handled with accuracy, insight and good taste by George W. Davis and William Ferrari (in the former category), Henry Grace and Keogh Gleason (in the latter). Russell Garcia's music, employing metallically futuristic sounds, adds to the mood.   *Tube.*

Follow That Horse
(BRITISH)

Lighthearted, flimsy comedy with little marquee value; genial yocks from a script which tends to skim rather than build up.

London, July 12.
Warner-Pathe release of a (Thomas Clyde) Associated-British Cavalcade production. Stars David Tomlinson, Cecil Parker, Richard Wattis; features Dora Bryan, Mary Peach. Directed by Alan Bromly. Screenplay, Alfred Shaughnessy, with additional scenes by William Douglas Home, from adaptation by Howard Mason of own novel, "Photo Finish"; editor, Gerald Turney-Smith; camera, Norman Warick; music, Stanley Black. At Warner Theatre, London, July 11, '60. Running time, **80 MINS.**
Dick Lanchester.........David Tomlinson
Sir William Crane.......... Cecil Parker
Hugh Porlock .... Richard Wattis
Susan Turner .... Mary Peach
Miss Bradstock .... Dora Bryan
Special Chief Branch..Raymond Huntley
Farrell .... Sam Kydd
Hammler .... George Travua
Major Turner .... John Welsh
Garrod .... Peter Copely
Spiegel .... Cyril Shaps
Blake .... Victor Brooks
Riley .... Vic Wise
Rudd .... George A. Cooper
Harriet .... Alison Fraser
Auctioneer .... Arthur Lowe
American Delegate ...... John Phillips
German Delegate .... Guy Deghy
Pilot .... John Crewdson

This gentle little comedy relies considerably on some smart thesping by some popular British funsters going through familiar antics. Completely inoffensive, it will be enjoyed by most people who see it. Those who fail to get around to seeing it will find no compulsive urge to search it out later. In short, a routine comedy item, with none of its ingredients

being sufficiently decisive to make it standout.

David Tomlinson, a skilled practitioner in the throwaway art of silly comedy, is a vapid young diplomat who is given the job of escorting an atomic scientist to a NATO conference. Said scientist turns out to be a spy. He escapes with some filmed Top Secret papers. The roll of films (for reasons which could only exist in the world of farce) is eaten by a racehorse. Tomlinson catches up with the horse, the spies and the film just in time to avert an international crisis.

Alfred Shaughnessy's screenplay and Alan Bromly's direction are both brisk in essential, but occasionally take time off to pursue some irrelevant situations which provide laffs but hold up the action. The pic builds up to a splendid chase sequence. But in the main it is rather too woolly.

Standout sequences are those in which Tomlinson bids for the auctioned horse while trying on the phone to convince the Treasury that the expenditure is essential; a House of Parliament sitting when the Minister of Atomic Energy waffles along when faced with telling the government opposition what has happened to the missing spy, and the final sequence when, in a mad auto race Tomlinson and the police head off a plane which is about to flee the country with the spies aboard. Also skillfully put over is the sequence where the urgent film roll is rescued from the horse's belly.

Tomlinson dithers delightfully. Cecil Parker, as the atomic Minister, and Richard Wattis, as his assistant, put over their now familiar, but always acceptable, brand of underplayed comedy. Mary Peach, a new entry in the glamour stakes, looks charming and is completely adequate as the young heroine. John Welsh, Sam Kydd, Vic Wise, Cyril Shaps, Victor Brooks and George Pravda also weigh in with helpful performances.

Two cameos stand out. A youngster, Alison Fraser, chips in with a tiny spot as the owner of the pony which is switched by the villains in order to get their mitts on the vital racehorse. Dora Bryan contributes a rollicking scene as the coy owner of a home for dumb animals. Miss Bryan, bespectacled numbskull, is irresistibly funny in an episode which does little to help the film along but provides a few minutes of comedy.

Stanley Black's music is gaily madcap. Photography and artwork are both completely competent.

Rich.

Doctor In Love
(BRITISH-COLOR)

Mixture as before in this latest of a profitable series; amiable blend of romance and comedy cameos make this a safe lightweight booking.

London, July 13.

Rank release of a Betty E. Box-Ralph Thomas production. Stars Michael Craig, James Robertson Justice, Virginia Maskell, Carole Lesley, Leslie Phillips; features Joan Sims, Liz Frazer, Reginald Beckwith. Directed by Ralph Thomas. Screenplay, Nicholas Phipps from Richard Gordon's novel: camera, Ernest Steward: editor, Alfred Roome: music, Bruce Montgomery. At Odeon, Leicester Square, London, July 12, '60. Running time, **97 MINS.**

Dr. Richard Hare .... Michael Craig
Dr. Nicholas Barrington .. Virginia Maskell
Dr. Tony Burge .... Leslie Phillips
Sir Lancelot Spratt
James Robertson Justice
Kitten Strudwick .... Carole Lesley
Wildewinde .... Reginald Beckwith
Dr. Clive Cardew ..... Nicholas Phipps
Leonora .... Liz Fraser
Dawn .... Joan Sims
Lady Spratt .... Ambrosine Philpotts
Professor MacRitchie ..... Irene Handl
Dr. Hinxman .... Nicholas Parsons
Sally Nightingale ...... Moire Redmond
Harold Green .... Ronnie Stevens
Mrs. Tadwich .... Fenella Fielding

Nobody's going to beat down the theatre doors to see this amiable, lightweight comedy. But it should do as well as its three predecessors in this disarming series, and they were all very good at the boxoffice. Only one character has survived all four pix, James Robertson Justice as the bellowing, bearded Sir Lancelot Spratt. This film follows much the same familiar format of gags, gaiety and gals.

Freely adapted by Nicholas Phipps from Richard Gordon's novel, there's only the slightest story line. But on a thin pretext of a plot, Phipps has adroitly hung some diverting situations which enable a variety of characters to pull off comedy cameos and then disappear without cluttering up the film. The Phipps' dialog is also neatly tailored to suit the various performers—including himself.

The humor doesn't pretend to be anything but simple. One of the girls, a nurse, is named Sally Nightingale, which sparks off a couple of irrelevant cracks.

Briskly directed by Ralph Smart and well enough photographed, story concerns Michael Craig as a young doctor who falls for his nurse while a patient in his own hospital. His chum, Leslie Phillips, stands in for doctor until he breaks his leg and is in turn replaced by a woman doctor (Virginia Maskell), with whom Craig falls in love.

Woven into this frail plot-line are such happy irrelevancies as when the two hardup young doctors volunteer as guinea pigs at an "Anti-Cold Research Unit," where they become involved with two strippers, a police station sequence involving drunkenness tests; a mixup by which Sir Lancelot turns up at a West End strippery instead of at a Medical Conference and the only comedy finale when the irascible surgeon insists on supervising his own operation.

Most formidable performance as usual in this series comes from the huge, blustering Justice. Craig is a likeable hero while Leslie Phillips gives another of his splendidly fatuous showings as a silly ass ladykiller. Nicholas Phipps plays the country doctor with suave comic timing. There's also Reginald Beckwith as an eccentric dispenser who has nothing much to do with the plot but steals most of the three or four comedy scenes he's in.

Virgina Maskell disappoints as the heroine. She looks pretty enough but Miss Maskell's attempts at comedy are not so good. Moira Redmond impresses in the small role of Craig's nurse. Liz Fraser and Joan Sims have no difficulty with the uninhibited roles of a couple of striptease dancers. Carole Lesley coasts along as a sexy receptionist. Ambrosine Philpots, Irene Handl, Ronnie Stevens, Fenella Fielding, Mary Mackenzie and John Le Mesurier are others who crop up from time to time to lend a hand successfully to the carefree proceedings.

Rich.

All The Fine Young Cannibals
(C'SCOPE—COLOR—PANAVISION)

Absurd romantic drama about two young couples who learn to share a mutual offspring after having a deuce of a time deciding who loves whom. Teen-appeal of its four young stars might rescue this pic at the b.o.

Hollywood, July 8.

Metro release of Pandro S. Berman production. Stars Robert Wagner, Natalie Wood, Susan Kohner, George Hamilton; features Pearl Bailey; with Jack Mullaney, Onslow Stevens, Anne Seymour, Virginia Gregg, Mabel Albertson, Louise Beavers, Addison Richards. Directed by Michael Anderson. Screenplay, Robert Thom, suggested by Rosamond Marshall's novel, "The Bixby Girls"; camera, William H. Daniels; editor, John McSweeney Jr.; art directors, George W. Davis, Edward Carfagno; music, Jeff Alexander; assistant director, Al Jennings. Reviewed at the studio, July 8, '60. Running time **112 MINS.**

Chad Bixby .... Robert Wagner
Salome Davis .... Natalie Wood
Catherine McDowall ...... Susan Kohner
Tony McDowall .... George Hamilton
Ruby Jones .... Pearl Bailey
Putney Tinker .... Jack Mullaney
Joshua Davis .... Onslow Stevens
Mrs. Bixby .... Anne Seymour
Ada Davis .... Virginia Gregg
Mrs. McDowall .... Mabel Albertson
Rose .... Louise Beavers
Mr. McDowall .... Addison Richards

Modern youth takes it on the chin again in Metro's "All the Fine Young Cannibals." The studio, having just proven in "The Subterraneans" that Bay Area beatniks are colossal bores, now aims its sights at some idle rich specimens operating out of Dallas, and discovers that their sole means of communication is physical contact, preferably of the sexual variety.

Pandro S. Berman's handsome prouction surrounds a ludicrous "Modern Romances" sort of screenplay by Robert Thom, which has been suggested by Rosamond Marshall's novel, "The Bixby Girls." Under scrutiny is the accelerated world of troubled contemporary youth where a one-night stand invariably results in pregnancy, fame or attempted suicide. More specifically, the scenario explores the affairs of two young couples (Natalie Wood-George Hamilton and Robert Wagner-Susan Kohner) who eventually learn to live with the fact they share a mutual tax-deduction in the form of a bouncing babe who bounced out of the pre-marital union of one-half of each partnership (Wagner and Miss Wood).

Director Michael Anderson attempts to establish and link the individual personalities of the central foursome by flashing rapidly to and fro from family to family. The technique backfires in that, by attempting to take in too much too swiftly, it leaves the audience out of focus on all four individual sets of motivations. The picture does benefit from some flashy interiors by art directors George W. Davis and Edward Carfagno and set decorators Henry Grace and Rudy Butler, and generally agile, inventive lens positioning by the team of director Anderson and cameraman William H. Daniels. Jeff Alexander's music is unobtrusively unexciting, and John McSweeney Jr.'s editing does little to speed up the film's sluggish pace.

"Cannibals" is an unfortunate vehicle for the four young people who are its costars. Miss Wood is a very pleasant young lady to behold, even though a pained expression is about all she is required to project here. Miss Kohner is not very convincing in her efforts to appear alternately gay, bored and distressed. Even less at ease are Wagner and Hamilton in a pair of incredibly unmasculine roles.

Best emoting is done by Pearl Bailey, but even she can barely cope with a preposterous role of a celebrated blues singer who dies of a broken heart when jilted by "that man who played horn for her." Fortunately, the plot takes a brief break to enable Miss Bailey to render one or two numbers in her inimitably casual, well-timed and phrased style.

Generally satisfactory support is contributed by Jack Mullaney, Onslow Stevens, Anne Seymour, Virginia Gregg, Mabel Albertson, Louise Beavers and Addison Richards.

Tube.

Kirmes
(The Fair)
(GERMAN)

Berlin, July 12.

Europa release of a Wolfgang Staudte production. Stars Juliette Mayniel and Gotz George. Directed by Staudte. Screenplay, Staudte, based on idea by Claus Hubalek; camera, George Krause; settings, Ellen Schmidt and Olaf Ivens; music, Werner Pohl; editor, Lilian Sing. At Zoo Palast, Berlin, July 2, '60. Running time, **105 MINS.**

Annette ....Juliette Mayniel
Robert Mertens .... Gotz George
Paul Mertens ....Hans Maunke
Geo. Holcheft ......Wolfgang Reichmann
Martha Mertens ....Manja Behrens
Priest ....Fritz Schmiedel
Eva Schumann .... Erika Schramm
Innkeeper's Wife.......Elisabeth Goebel
Innkeeper ....Benno Hoffmann
Else Mertens .... Irmgard Kieber
Erika ....Hansi Jochmann
Gertrud ....Solveig Loevel
Capt. Menzel ......Rudolf Birkenmeyer
Lt Wandray .... Reidar Muller
Young Soldier ....Horst Niendorf

"Kirmes" is one of the better grade postwar German pictures, and though it is somewhat overlong and treated a little leisurely, its subject matter may command interest and attention in the foreign markets. It has a literate and sympathetic script, is ably directed but the camera work in some of the earlier scenes is surprisingly out of focus in depth shots.

Wolfgang Staudte, who also produces and directs, has written a script based on an actual event first recorded by Claus Hubalek. It is a war story, unsympathetic to the Nazis, describing the experiences of a young deserter who goes on the run when the tide is running against the Germans and the Nazis are retreating.

The story opens in the present day at a fun fair, where the jollity is marred by the discovery of a soldier's skeleton. From that point, there's a prolonged flashback describing all that happened to the young boy who escaped and the suffering of his family and a priest who gave him shelter. There's a contrived femme angle, depicting a young French girl. She works at the local inn, is quite free

with her favors to the German soldiers, and then provides shelter and love to the escaped soldier.

There's a striking contrast between apparent gaiety of the opening fair sequences and the earnest subject matter that follows. The cruel and cynical attitude of the local Nazi commander and the Gestapo is strongly stressed, and there's evidence of the resistance to the Nazi war policy by many of the villagers.

Wolfgang Staudte's direction is bold, sincere and authoritative although a more forthright attitude in editing would have been a positive help. Apart from the blurs in some of the opening sequences, the lensing is excellent, and other technical qualities are up to general standards.

The acting, too, is superior in quality to that of most recent German films. Juliette Mayniel infuses an air of fresh sincerity and the cynism into the proceedings with her interpretation of the French girl. Gotz George is appropriately nervous and apprehensive as the young German soldier on the run. There is also a sturdy performance by Hans Mahnke as his father, though Manja Behrens is rather too emotional a personality as the mother. The remainder of the cast lends admirable support to the proceedings to make "Kirmes" a worthwhile festival entry. *Myro.*

Une Fille Pour L'Ete
(A Girl For the Summer)
(FRENCH-COLOR)
(DYALISCOPE)

Paris, July 12.
Cinedis release of Boreal-SPA Films production. Stars Pascale Petit, Michel Auclair, Micheline Presle; features Georges Poujouly, Claire Maurier, Aime Clariond, Balpetre. Directed by Edouard Molinaro. Screenplay, Maurice Clavel, Molinaro; camera (Eastmancolor), Jean Bourgoin; editor, Robert Isnardon. At Marignan, Paris. Running time, 92 MINS.
Manette .... Pascale Petit
Philippe .... Michel Auclair
Paule .... Micheline Presle
Michel .... Georges Poujouly
Viviane .... Claire Maurier
Rosenkrantz .... Aime Clariond
Poet .... Balpetre

In a C'Scope-like process and with color, this deals with a blase young artist who hires a girl for the summer to visit in a resort town with friends. But she is really not that kind and it ends in tragedy. Pic is somewhat too mannered and unclear in motivations and characterizations to make this convincing. Film emerges mainly an exploitation item in its look at callous youth on vacation.

The artist picks up the girl in a bar, and then runs off to visit with a middle-aged but still glamorous woman.

As the summer wanes, the artist and girl find life impossible, and the boy escapes to Israel. All this is punctuated with pointless wild parties.

Direction is too heavy to make anything out of the relations or make a point about the whole affair. Color is okay. Film does have some exploitable handles via the erotic escapades. That is about all because the acting is listless and the storyline muddled. Technical values are good. *Mosk.*

Les Loups Dans La Bergerie
(The Wolves in the Sheepfold)
(FRENCH)

Paris, July 12.
Discifilm release of Madeleine Films production. With Jean-Marc Bory, Pascale Roberts, Pierre Mondy, Jean-Francois Peron, Jean Babilee. Directed by Herve Bromberger. Screenplay, Frederic Grendel, Bromberger from a novel by Jean Heckert; camera, Jacques Mercanton; editor, D. Natot. Preemed in Paris, July 7. Running time, 85 MINS.
Director .... Jean-Marc Bory
Wife .... Pascale Roberts
Jasmin .... Jean Babilee
Charlot .... Pierre Mondy
Alain .... Jean-Francois Peron
Francis .... Jacques Moulieres
Micou .... Guy Deshays
Rouquin .... Jacques Bonnard

This film is reminiscent of the Dead End Kids pix because detailing how a group of gangsters on the run hole up in a detention home and show the delinquents they are cowards and abject killers which destroys them as hero images. Pic is deftly paced and played. However, it emerges a conventional vehicle in this vein, slanting mainly for secondary or playoff possibilities abroad on its pace and treatment.

The home for adolescents is run by a young man and his wife sans bars. The killers come in and take over. The killings lead to an eventual turnabout of the most hardened strayed youngsters. Director Herve Bromberger has given this brisk pacing but has not been able to overcome the essentially familiar qualities of the plot. Acting, technical credits and production values are all good. *Mosk.*

Le Huitieme Jour
(The Eighth Day)
(FRENCH)

Paris, July 12.
Art and Science production and release. Stars Emmanuelle Riva, Felix Marten; features Jose Vareta, Lucienne Bogaert, Marcel Andre. Directed by Marcel Hanoun. Screenplay, Gilbert Guez, Hanoun; camera, Marcel Fradetal; editor, Nicole Marco. At Calypso, Paris. Running time, 85 MINS.
Francoise .... Emmanuelle Riva
Georges .... Felix Marten
Alain .... Jose Varela
Mother .... Lucienne Bogaert
Father .... Marcel Andre

Tale of a sensitive girl who can't seem to accept the advances of a boorish but loving suitor in spite of her loneliness and isolation in Paris is too mannered and cold to make this moving. It looks only likely for arties abroad.

Film dwells on the girl's lone evenings and her Sundays at a race track where she seems to get some emotional kick. These scenes are even done in color. But the vague literary quality has permit this to lag and become repetitive. Acting can not overcome the quality of the characters. Direction is uneven but technical aspects shape okay. *Mosk.*

Anna Na Ulee
(Cross of St. Anne)
(RUSSIAN-COLOR)

Paris, July 19.
Sovexport release of Gorki Studio production. With A. Lalenova, M. Jarov, A. Vertinski. Written and directed by I. Annenski from a short story by Anton Checkhov. Camera (Sovcolor), G. Reishof; editor, M. Richor. At Panthenon, Paris. Running time, 90 MINS.
Anna .... A. Lalenova
Modeste .... M. Jarov
Prince .... A. Vertinski

This remains true to a Anton Checkhov short story in depicting the fading upper classes of the turn-of-the-century Russia. It also makes the middle classes out to be climbers and connivers, too. But this is slow action, with the colors uneven and garish. Makes this a dubious item abroad except for some arty spots or for school showings.

A comely, young girl marries a climbing old civil servant in order to help her family. But when she clicks with high society, she soon leaves him and her family behind to get as much of the so-called high life as she can.

Direction is somewhat theatrical as is the acting. But the times ring true as are some of the characters. Technical credits are good but the film appears curiously old fashioned. Other recent Russo Checkbov adaptations have had more dash, movement and mounting. *Mosk.*

In the Nick
(BRITISH)

Unpretentious farce about prison life, corn situations and performances will raise plenty of laughs among easygoing audiences.

London, July 12.
Columbia release of a Warwick (Harold Huth) production. Stars Anthony Newley, Anne Aubrey, Bernie Winters, James Booth, Harry Andrews. Directed by Ken Hughes. Screenplay, Ken Hughes, from story by Frank Norman; camera, Ted Moore; editor, Geoffrey Foot; music, Ron Goodwin. At Odeon, Marble Arch, London, July 6, '60. Running time, 105 MINS.
Dr. Newcombe .... Anthony Newley
Doll .... Anne Aubrey
Jinx .... Bernie Winters
Spider .... James Booth
Chief Officer Williams .... Harry Andrews
Prison Governor .... Niall Macginnis
Dancer .... Al Mulock
Mick .... Derren Nesbitt
Screw Smith .... Victor Brooks
Ted Ross .... Ian Hendry
Screw Jenkins .... Barry Keegan

"In the Nick"—British slang for in the cooler—suffers somewhat since it explores a joke only recently perpetrated successfully in "Two Way Stretch." This is about the easygoing progressive prison without bars and the comic way in which the prisoners react to the privileges. It lacks star value for the U. S., but U. K. audiences will find it an amusing enough diversion.

Warwick has poured its small stock company into the pic and augmented its with some well-tried thesps. Ken Hughes' direction is straightforward and brisk. His screenplay, based on a story by Frank Norman, has the authenticity expected in view of the fact that Norman has become a lively, successful author after several years spent on and off in jails. The story lags towards the end but when it sticks to situation gags it is okay for yocks.

The yarn concerns four tough young lads who are, astoundingly, sent to this progressive prison, the manner in which they take over the jail, their rivalry with another prison gang, the attempts of a young prison psychologist-doctor to get them through the girl friend of the ringleader and, unconvincingly, of this ringleader's eventual reformation. One or two of the situations misfire, particularly a pantomime put on by the prisoners, but it is a useful enough vehicle for the respective talents of the leading players.

A major error is the casting of Anthony Newley as the serious-minded young psychologist. Newley is a very able comedian who also has aspirations to do serious roles. This he may be able to do. But here his role falls between straight and light comedy, and Newley would have fared better as one of the gang members. Anne Aubrey, apart from one acutely coy striptease routine in a nightclub sequence, has little to do but is pretty and does her little quite adequately.

The four members of the gang are excellently contrasted and keep the fun stirring. The leader is James Booth, one of Britain's most promising young actors. His is a striking personality that should be harnessed to more serious roles. Bernie Winters, who specializes in slapstick, is given plenty of scope. Al Mulock and, particularly Derren Nesbitt, impress.

It was a shrewd idea by the producers to bring in Harry Andrews as the tough, yet likeable chief warder. Andrews has rarely been guilty of an off performance, and with this one he holds the film together by making the warder a credible character among all the farfetched material. Dialog is crisp and bright while Ted Moore's lensing is okay. Geoffrey Foot's editing at times seems jerky but this is due to the episodic format of the film with certain gags and situations being brought into the action and then rightly being tossed away before they pall. Lionel Bart has provided a couple of songs, one of which, "Must Be," seems a likely contender for some recognition. *Rich.*

Studs Lonigan

Arty, but unsatisfactory screen translation of James T. Farrell's tome. Book's reputation may help prospects. Doubtful b.o. candidate.

Hollywood, July 20.

United Artists release of Philip Yordan production. Stars Christopher Knight; costars Frank Gorshin, Venetia Stevenson, Carolyn Craig, Jack Nicholson, Robert Casper, Dick Foran, Katherine Squire, Jay C. Flippen; with Helen Westcott, Kathy Johnson, Jack Kruschen, Suzi Carnell, Mme. Spivy, James Drum, Ben Gary, Rita Duncan, Stanley Adams, Steven Ritch, George Keymas, Darlene Hendrix, Josie Lloyd, Suzanne Sidney, Kathie Browne, Judy Howard, Elaine Walker, Lorelei Vitek, Opal Eurard, Mavis Neal, Phil Arnold, John Graham, Don Garrett, Casey MacGregor, Brian O'Hara, Val Hidey, Snubby Pollard, Marty Crail.. Directed by Irving Lerner. Screenplay, Philip Yordan, based on James T. Farrell's novel; camera, Arthur H. Feindel; edtor, Verna Fields; art director, Jack Poplin; music, Garrald Goldsmith; sound, Ben Winkler; assistant directors, Louis Brandt, Eugene Anderson Jr. Reviewed at Golywyn Studios, July 20, '60. Running time, **103 MINS**

Studs Lonigan	Christopher Knight
Kenny Killarney	Frank Gorshin
Lucy Scanlon	Venetia Stevenson
Catherine Banahan	Carolyn Craig
Weary Reilly	Jack Nicholson
Paulie Haggerty	Robert Casper
Patrick Lonigan	Dick Foran
Mrs. Longan	Katherine Squire
Father Gilhooey	Jay C. Flippen
Miss Julia Miller	Helen Westcott
Frances Lonigan	Kathy Johnson
Charlie the Greek	Jack Kruschen
Eileen	Suzi Carnell
Mother Josephine	Mme. Spivy
Jm Doyle	James Drum
Various roles	Ben Gary
Kitty	Rita Duncan
Gangsters	Stanley Adams, Steven Ritch, George Keymas
Mrs. Reilly	Opal Eurard
Mrs. Haggerty	Mavis Neal
Dentist	Phil Arnold
Judge	John Graham
Policemen	Don Garrett, Casey MacGregor
Funeral Mourner	Brian O'Hara
Stripper	Val Hidey
Vendor	Snubby Pollard
Bartendner	Marty Crail

New Year's Eve Party Girls: Darlene Hendrix, Josie Lloyd, Suzanne Sidney.

Girls at Wild Party: Kathie Browne, Judy Howard, Elaine Walker, Lorelei Vitek.

Compressing James T. Farrell's respected trilogy into a 103-minute film ranks as one of the more courageous screen efforts of recent times. Sad to relate, it doesn't come off. Philip Yordan's production of "Studs Lonigan" is an earnest attempt gone wrong, partially in overly-artistic conception, but principally through incoherent execution complicated by undisciplined histrionics. To spell it out more plainly, Yordan's approach is too artsy-craftsy and Irving Lerner's direction fails to curb the uninhibited affectations of his inexperienced star, Christopher Knight.

Where this leaves "Studs" in the boxoffice tournament is debatable in view of the film's innate areas of exploitation and the book's provocative reputation. Since word-of-mouth figures to be decidely negative, the United Artists release may have difficulty locating a receptive audience. On the surface, it appears to be art house fare, but arty patrons are not ikely to be impressed. On the other hand, general audiences may be annoyed by its offbeat form and unstable content.

Yordan's scenario is quite faithful to Farrell's book which, of course, centers its attention on the essentially decent hero who struggles against slum life of Chicago's South Side district in the 1920's. Knight, as the hero, has a disquieting tendency toward facial contortion and responsive exaggeration, a serious flaw in the film. The role is an extremely demanding one for any actor, let alone a newcomer to the screen. Sterner direction than Lerner seems to have offered was an absolute necessity in this instance.

The three standouts in the large cast are Frank Gorshin, Helen Westcott and Dick Foran. Gorshin has an instinctive ability to generate a natural reaction. He's one of the most promising young actor-comics on the screen today. Miss Westcott creates a figure of pathos and dimension, despite the fact that Yordan's screenplay leaves the character she is playing—the loveless schoolteacher who becomes Stud's secret counsel and companion — essentially undeveloped and unexplored. Foran comes through admirably in the role of Stud's decent father—an abrupt departure in casting for this veteran actor. Others prominently cast, but generally less effective, are Venetia Stevenson, Carolyn Craig, Jack Nicholson, Robert Casper, Katherine Squire and Jay C. Flippen.

A great deal of cinematic artistry and technical inventiveness have gone into this product. Together with helmsman Lerner, lensman Arthur H. Feindel and special photographic consultant Haskell P. Wexler have chosen an unusual assortment of sharp, tilted angles at which to place the camera. In combination with some unusual shading effects, this emphasis on startling composition is clever, but frequently distracting. The production definitely captures the look of the '20s through Jack Poplin's perceptive art direction and the props and costumes, but Yordan's dialog seems a little up-to-date to be fully consistent with that era, Verna Fields' editing tends to be choppy. As a result of this and the staccato pace commandeered by Lerner, the viewer never gets the proper feeling of passage of time. Scenes that are supposed to be widely spaced in time to form a quick, atmospheric image of general activity seem instead to be happening right on top of one another, creating a ludicrous sequence of disconnected behavior. It's a serious miscue.

Gerrald Goldsmith's variable score is interesting, but at times diesn't jell snugly with the action onscreen. *Tube.*

The Nights of Lucretia Borgia

Handsome costume "epic" from Italy. More subdued and less exciting than most of its predecessors. May rate a quick, but ample, response.

Hollywood, July 21.

Columbia Pictures release of Fides-Musa production. Stars Belinda Lee, Jacques Sernas, Michele Mercier; features Arnoldo Foa, Franco Fabrizi; with Marco Tulli, Lily Scaringi, Germano Longo, Nando Tamberlani, Raf Baldassarre, Gianni Loti, Stelio Candelli. Directed by Sergio Grieco. Screenplay and Original Story, Mario Caiano, Aldo Segri; camera, Massimo Dallamano; music, Alexander Derevitsky. Reviewed at the studio, July 21, '60. Running time, **108 MINS**

(No character name credits supplied)

History, which gradually is being rearranged by the Italian filmmakers to supply modern audiences with an unbroken flow of escape spectacles, takes another beating in "The Nights Of Lucretia Borgia." Loosely, but decoratively, built around the early 16th century activities of the big, bad Borgias, Cesare and his wicked sister, Lucretia, it rambles on for an overlong 108 minutes of sword-play, horseplay and boudoir-play, with the emphasis on the latter. One of the less enthralling arrivals of its genre, but the initial domestic response should be brisk enough for Columbia's fiscal satisfaction.

Belinda Lee draws the title role and fills its physical and temperamental specifications more than amply. Her principal quarrel is with dashing Jacques Sernas, a young swordsman employed by her brother. She finds him irresistible, but he is enamoured of the Borgia's arch-rival, attractive Michele Mercier, who in turn appeals to brother Borgia.

After a great deal of derring-do by Sernas and derring-don't by the Borgias and their legion of scoundrels, everything falls into place for the expected "happy" ending. Enroute, only one vial of Lucretia's famous poison comes into play, instantly felling its victim. That should pacify the natural anticipations of those aware of the lady's hobby.

The acting is generally competent under Sergio Grieco's direction, within the absurd screenplay by Mario Caiano and Aldo Segri and the dubbing factor. The physical production, under the helm of Carlo Caiano, is impressive. Key embellishments are Alexander Derevitsky's music, as played by the Rome Philharmonic, Massimo Dallamano's adept camera work, and the eye-pleasing Eastman Color. *Tube.*

Belles and Ballets
(FRENCH—EASTMANCOLOR)

Chicago, July 20.

Excelsior Pictures release of a Cella Film (Paris) production. Features members of Ballet de L'Etoile, Paris. Directed by Louis Cuny; camera, Jacques Mercanto, Jacques Ledoux. World Playhouse, Chicago, July 20, '60. Runnng time, **92 MINS.**

French entry makes the cinematographic most of its specialized subject matter, the classic dance form. It faces a limited U.S. market, even on the arty circuit, but with sagacious selling could do well enough, particularly in areas where ballet has popularity. Fact that the Ballet de L'Etoile company has never been to U.S. shores is balletomane bait that shouldn't be overlooked.

Film is a thin representation of a day of studio rehearsal. While dancers go through exercise paces, gimmick dissolves are used to launch dance segments. Poignancy, humor, symbolistic drama and sensuality are choreographed to often arresting effect, and set to scores by, among others, Rossini, Aaron Copland and Villa-Lobos.

Some French words are soundtracked in a few sequences, but there's no character dialog as such. There's compelling, if sometimes self-conscious, use of camera. Color is excellent and at one point offers interesting mood use of monochromatic tints. *Pit.*

Mi Madres es Culpable
(My Mother is to Blame)
(MEXICAN)

Mexico City, July 19.

Peliculas Nacionales release of Cinematografica Filmex production. Stars Marga Lopez, Carlos Baena; features Domingo Soler, Miguel Angel Ferriz, Luis Beristain, Francisco Jambrina, Dolores Camarillo, Guillermo Orea, Antonio Raxel, Herbert Wallace Foronda. Directed by Julian Soler. Screenplay by Julio Alejandro. At Alameda and Continental Theatres, Mexico City. Running time, **90 MINS.**

Central theme of this film is the controversial subject of euthanasia with a distraught mother finally making the difficult decision of mercy death for an adored son.

Marga Lopez, as the mother, gives one of the most brilliant performances of her career, interpreting a difficult role with restraint. Carlos Baena, as the husband, gives credence to the family scenes. The doomed boy, played by new discovery Herbert Wallace Foronda, is standout. All actors underplay the central problem as carefully prepared by writer Julio Alejandro, culminating in anguished decision to give painless release to a lad doomed to agonizing death.

This is one of the few Mexican pictures that has dared to present a controversial theme of this type. Film was previewed by panelists and medical men before public release and given a clean bill of health.

With the skillful direction of Julian Soler who avoided the pitfalls of ham situations in tearjerker cliches, this one has been doing excellent business at two houses here. It is one of the better product for export to the Spanish language market. *Emil.*

La Chatte Sort Ses Griffes
(The Cat Shows Its Claws)
(FRENCH)

Paris, July 19.

Discifilm release of Paris-Elysee-Balar-Metzger and Woog coproduction. Stars Francoise Arnoul; features Horst Frank, Harold Kay, Francois Guerin, Jacques Fibbri. Directed by Henri Decoin. Screenplay, Jacques Remy, Eugene Tucherer, Decoin; camera, Pierre Montazel; editor, Claude Durand. At Ambassade-Gaumont, Paris. Running time, **100 MINS.**

Cora	Francoise Arnoul
Von Hollwitz	Horst Frank
Charles	Harold Kay
Louis	Francois Guerin
Gustave	Jacques Fabbri
Marie	Francoise Spira
Maud	Anne Tonietti

This is a sequel to a successful actioner of last year which detailed the underground activities of a femme resistance worker called "La Chatte" during the occupation of France in the last World War. Here she is captured by the Germans and brainwashed and turned loose to betray her friends. But she finally comes through for and not against them.

Slickly made, this is still conventional and the suspense is telegraphed. It thus looms mainly an action or dualer item abroad. Technical credits are good and it has a handle on the brainwashing development. Francoise Arnoul can not do much with an ambiguous role that is unclear without knowledge of the first pic.

Supporting cast is okay but direction overdoes the suspense to make characters shallow. Direction is competent but uninspired. *Mosk.*

Nacht Fiel Ueber Gotenhafen
(Darkness Fell On Gotenhafen)
(GERMAN)

Berlin, July 26.
Deutsche Film Hansa production and release. With Sonja Ziemann, Gunnar Moeller, Erik Schumann, Brigitte Horney, Mady Rahl. Directed by Frank Wisbar. Screenplay, Wisbar and Victor Schuller; camera, Willi Winterstein, Elio Carniel; music, Hans-Martin Majewski; editor, Martha Duehber. At Zoo Palast, Berlin. Running time, 101 MINS.
Maria Reiser .... Sonja Ziemann
Kurt Reiser .... Gunnar Moeller
Hans Schott .... Erik Schumann
Generalin von Reuss....Brigitte Horney
Edith Marquardt .... Mady Rahl
Vater Marquardt .... Erich Dunskus
Vater Reiser....Edith Schultze-Westrum
Dr. Beck .... Wolfgang Preiss
Meta .... Tatjana Iwanow
Gaston .... Dietmar Schoenherr

This is, after "Sharks and Little Fish" and "Inferno," Frank Wisbar's third film that deals with the last World War theme. While the first two pix centered around men in action, "Gotenhafen" is dedicated to the women who suffered hardly less during the war. War films have lately been doing remarkably well in this country. "Gotenhafen" won't be an exception. As per its subject, film stands a good chance to do well in foreign markets despite not being an extraordinary vehicle.

Pic depicts one of the major tragedies during the final phase of the last war—the sinking of "Wilhelm Gustloff," German luxury liner turned refugee ship, by a Soviet submarine on Jan. 31, 1945, in the Baltic Sea. Of the more than 6,000 people, mostly helpless women and children from Russian invaded East Prussia, that were on board of this ship, only 928 were rescued.

Screenplay contains a strong anti-war message but latter, unfortunately, loses much of its conviction by overly philosophical talk. In its present form, "Gotenhafen" has its shocking impact. It also takes a clear anti-Nazi stand via a scene which shows the brutal arrest of a hidden Jew. Acting is generally okay. Pic's highlight is the sinking of the ship. Latter's staging has technically been well made and is the best thing in this film. *Hans.*

Classe Tous Risques
(Consider All Risks)
(FRENCH)

Paris, July 19.
Cinedis release of Mondex-Odeon Zebra-Filmsonor production. Stars Lino Ventura; features Jean-Paul Belmondo, Sandra Milo, Dalio, Jacques Dacqmine, Claude Cerval. Directed by Claude Sautet. Screenplay, Jose Giovanni, Pascal Jardin, Sautet; camera, Ghislain Cloquet; editor, Albert Jurgenson. At Paris, Paris. Running time, 110 MINS.
Abel .... Lino Ventura
Eric .... Jean-Paul Belmondo
Liliane .... Sandra Milo
Gibelin .... Dalio
Blot .... Jacques Dacqmine
Fargier .... Claude Cerval

Neatly made gangster pic follows the last days of a gangster on the run. It concerns his loss of family and his revenge and his finding of friendship before the police close in on him. Somewhat too diffuse, and with too many side complications, this is still a well-done pic with possible dual possibilities abroad. It lacks the individuality for more arty chances.

Lino Ventura is the professional gangster at the end of his rope. He plays it with the right resignation. When he is trapped in Italy, his old French friends, who he had helped set up in business, are afraid to help him and hire a young hoodlum to do it. A friendship springs up between these two and they get back to France where Ventura has it out with his cowardly friends before he is also taken.

New director Claude Sautet shows a good feeling for pacing, characterization and action in his first film. He should be heard from again soon. But overplotting and lack of names will hurt its American chances. Technical credits are very good as is the acting. *Mosk.*

Faith, Hope And Witchcraft
(DANISH-COLOR)

Berlin, July 19.
Nordisk Films (Copenhagen) production and release. Stars Bodil Ipsen, Louis Miehe-Renard, Birte Bang. Directed by Erik Balling. Screenplay, William Heinesen and Balling; camera, Poul Pedersen; music, Svend Erik Tarp. At Zoo Palast, Berlin, July 2, '60. Running time, 96 MINS.

Set in one of the smallest of the Faroe Islands, with a community of only five inhabitants, this is a light-hearted comedy of people who have some faith, limited hope and practice a little witchcraft on the side. It's a safe bet for the Scandinavian market, and should have some chance in Europe, though a dubious bet for the U. S.

The plot concerns the oldest inhabitant who is determined to find a bride for his grandson, a naive and inexperienced young man who is scared of the opposite sex. It's a thin story, but there is a refreshing naievety about it which is thoroughly acceptable. Choice of locale provides an attractive background to the story, and the scenic views are enhanced by Eastmancolor photography. Pic is a little slow, but the acting is quite adequate. Other technical credits are okay. *Myro.*

One Foot in Hell
(C'SCOPE—COLOR)

An above-average western, spawned in television, about a galoot with a king-sized grudge. Has some serious shortcomings, but should be popular with the somewhat neglected followers of theatrical westerns.

Hollywood, July 28.
Twentieth-Fox release of Sydney Boehm production. Stars Alan Ladd, Don Murray, Dan O'Herlihy; features Dolores Michaels, Barry Coe; with Larry Gates, Karl Swenson, John Alexander, Rachel Stephens, Henry Norell, Harry Carter, Ann Morriss. Directed by James B. Clark. Screenplay, Aaron Spelling and Boehm, from story by Spelling; camera, William C. Mellor; editor, Eda Warren; art directors, Duncan Cramer, Leland Fuller; music, Dominic Frontiere; sound, Frank Webster Sr.; Harry M. Leonard; assistant director, Arthur Lueker. Reviewed at the studio, July 28, '60. Running time, 89 MINS.
Mitch .... Alan Ladd
Dan .... Don Murray
Harry Ivers .... Dan O'Herlihy
Julie Reynolds ...... Dolores Michaels
Stu Christian .... Barry Coe
Doc Seltzer .... Larry Gates
Sheriff Olson .... Karl Swenson
Giller .... John Alexander
Ellie Barrett .... Rachel Stephens
Caldwell .... Henry Norell
Mark Dobbs .... Harry Carter
Nellie .... Ann Morriss

"One Foot in Hell" began in television two-and-a-half years ago as "The Last Man," a "Playhouse 90" collaboration of Martin Manulis, John Frankenheimer and Aaron Spelling. In its transfer to the theatre screen it remains a gripping, powerful piece of western storytelling, but one still hindered by a few small, but disproportionately serious flaws. With major motion picture westerns the scarce commodity they have become since tv began its steady saturation of the field, the 20th-Fox release figures to be a welcome arrival in situations where large-screen sagebrushers are appreciated. On the whole, it's an above-average western.

Spelling, who penned the "90" version which costarred his wife, Carolyn Jones and Sterling Hayden, has collaborated with producer Sydney Boehm on the screenplay. Alan Ladd has taken on the pivotal role essayed formerly by Hayden and Dolores Michaels plays the part rendered on tv by Miss Jones.

Drama is based on an all-consuming grudge harbored by Ladd against the people of a small western town in which his pregnant wife perished as a result of his lacking $1.87 to pay for a vital medicine. Accepting a job as deputy sheriff in the town, he secretly plots revenge. Gathering around him a band of unsociable types he proceeds to set the machinery in motion for the slaying of those who contributed to his wife's untimely demise.

The plot, which includes robbery of $100,000 to plunge the town into economic depression works beautifully until Ladd unaccountably trains venom on the members of his own organization. A budding love affair between two of them (Don Murray and Miss Michaels) cuts short his dastardly intentions and puts the fellow out of his misery. It is in these final scenes that the picture stumbles. There is no sound motivation for Ladd's decision to wipe out those who assisted him in his foul scheme. Apparently the reason is a lofty one—something of the nature that they are not fit to continue living in this world. It's an unlikely reason for attempted quintuple homicide.

Ladd's delineation of the deranged central character is an intense, interesting one, hampered only by the perpetual, and rather disconcerting, faint smile he wears. It is Murray whose work catches the eye in this film. His portrayal of the proud, alcoholic rebel artist swept into the despicable scheme by bitterness over personal loss in the Civil War is virile and colorful. Miss Michaels is a bit reserved when events demand a more aroused reaction, but on the whole performs competently. Dan O'Herlihy creates an absorbing figure as a latently ornery Englishman, and Barry Coe, in an abrupt change of pace, essays a typical western fast-draw in lively fashion. Bringing up the rear of the cast effectively are Larry Gates Karl Swenson, John Alexander, Rachel Stephens Henry Norell Harry Carter and Ann Morriss.

James B. Clark's direction keeps the 89-minute film fast-paced. Without resorting to cinematic trickery, he gets the story told with considerable tension and pictorial variety. One of the chief contributions to the picture is Dominic Frontiere's music, underlining the action with a deliciously sinister note. Other capable assists are those of cameraman William C. Mellor editor Eda Warren and art directors Duncan Cramer and Leland Fuller. *Tube.*

The Entertainer
(BRITISH)

Uneven, raw, but vital and holding version of the John Osborne play; recent controversy could heft this as a b.o. bet, but it will need shrewd exploitation.

London, July 26.
British Lion release (in association with Bryanston) of a Woodfall (Henry Saltzman) production. Stars Laurence Olivier; features Brenda De Banzie, Roger Livesy, Joan Plowright. Directed by Tony Richardson. Screenplay, John Osborne, Nigel Kneale, from John Osborne's play; camera, Oswald Morris; editor, Alan Osbiston; music, John Addison. At Odeon, Marble Arch, July 25, '60. Running time, 96 MINS.
Archie Rice .... Laurence Olivier
Phoebe Rice .... Brenda De Banzie
Jean .... Joan Plowright
Billy .... Roger Livesey
Frank .... Alan Bates
Graham .... Daniel Massey
Mick Rice .... Albert Finney
Soubrette .... Miriam Karlin
Tina .... Shirley Anne Field
Mrs. Lapford .... Thora Hird
Mr. Lapford .... Tony Longridge
TV Star .... McDonald Hobley
Columnist .... Charles Gray
Hubbard .... Geoffrey Toone
Brother Bill .... Gilbert Davis
Interviewer .... Anthony Oliver

There's been a bit of a hassle over "The Entertainer," what with arguments with the censor, the film having to be re-dubbed and cut from 104 to 96 minutes; held over for three months before its West End showing, and switchings of West End showplace and general release circuit. But all this controversy could add up to considerable public interest. With shrewd exploitation this version of John Osborne's play could click. It's raw, but vital stuff, which tabbuyers will either like or loathe.

The yarn is mainly a seedy character study of a broken-down, disillusioned vaude artiste with more optimism than talent, and of the various members of his family and their reactions to his problems. So it depends mainly on the thesping and the direction.

Tony Richardson, the director, is still a fledgling film director, and he makes several mistakes. But he has a sharp perception of comera angles, stimulates some good performances and, particularly, whips up an excellent atmosphere of a smallish British seaside resort. In all, Richardson has done a fair job, backed up by Osward Morris's fine comerawork. The main problem was that of sound. Location noises originally marred some of the dialog's clarity, but this has been removed. Editing also has been a second-thought problem, but nothing that has been taken out harms the flow of the simple story.

Mainly, the interest is held by the acting and here there is a lot to praise, if some that may be condemned. The stage sequences in which the third-rate comedian, Archie Rice (Laurence Olivier) has to put over some tatty material in a broken down show, does not come over as effectively as it did on the stage.

Olivier cannot be blamed. He goes into sub-standard song, dance and patter with tremendous insight. But he is far happier in other sequences. The way he allows his sleazy facade to slip by a twist of the mouth, a throwaway line or a look in the eyes is quite brilliant. He is supported excellently, too.

Joan Plowright brings warmth and intelligence to the role of the loyal daughter while Roger Livesey, as Olivier's father, is sympathetic and completely believable Brenda De Banzie's role, as Olivier's wife, is at times irritating. as the oldtime vaude comedian. She is made to be too gabby, but nevertheless handles both comedy and pathos with assure touch. As the young beauty queen for whom Olivier falls, Shirley Anne Field is no more than adequate. Thora Hird, Albert Finney, Alan Bates and Miriam Karlin are others who turn in worthwhile supporting performances.

"The Entertainer," summed up, is a pic that lacks warmth, often disappoints but is well worth seeing. It is a film that will be talked about by those who do see it, but also it's one that could have been infinitely better if it had been handled by people apparently less in awe of the big names involved.
Rich.

For the Love of Mike
(C'SCOPE—COLOR)

Sugary but marketable item about a boy and his horse and building a church. Not for sophisticated audiences.

Hollywood, July 27.

Twentieth-Fox release of George Sherman production. Stars Richard Basehart; introduces Danny Bravo; features Stu Erwin, Arthur Shields, Rex Allen: with Armando Silvestre, Elsa Cardenas, Michael Steckler. Directed by Sherman. Screenplay, D. D. Beauchamp; camera, Alex Philips; editor, Fredrick Y. Smith; art director, Roberto Silva; music, Raul La Vista; sound, Manuel Topete; assistant directors, Henry Spitz, Mario Cisneros. Reviewed at the studio, July 27, '60. Running time, 87 MINS.

Father Phelan .... Richard Basehart
Doctor Mills .... Stu Erwin
Father Walsh .... Arthur Shields
Tony Eagle .... Armando Silvestre
Mrs. Eagle .... Elsa Cardenas
Ty Corbin .... Michael Steckler
Rex Allen .... As Himself
Michael .... Danny Bravo

An overdose of sweetness and light cloys an otherwise entertaining initial production effort by Shergari Corp. in "For The Love Of Mike." The new company, helmed by exhibitors Ted R. Gamble and F. H. Ricketson Jr. in partnership with the film's producer-director, George Sherman, obviously has set out to produce a picture for the "family" audience, but in so doing has burdened its product with an assortment of too-good-to-be-true stereotypes. Easily predictable dramatic situations result in loss of tension in scenes that need it.

Nevertheless, it is a film to be reckoned with commercially, particularly in that "small" area of the United States between the extremes of N.Y. and L.A. Also, it should be a picture of considerable appeal for children. Although it will not be a popular with more sophisticated urban audiences, the 20th-Fox release ought to prove profitable without their support. Its relatively brief length makes it potentially versatile—able to carry a bill in rural areas or bring up the rear effectively in city playdates.

D. D. Beauchamp is responsible for the screenplay, a slight yarn about a 12-year-old Indian lad (Danny Bravo) who nurses a quarter horse (white, naturally) to eventual victory in the local sweepstakes, paving the way for construction of a new church for his friends, irascibly sweet old Father Walsh (Arthur Shields) and likeable young Father Phelan (Richard Basehart). Only heavy on the premises is a rather cooperative mountain lion who stalks Master Bravo in the film's final passages, but keeps a respectable distance until help arrives in the nick of time. The dialog has some mirth of the aren't-we-cute-for-men-of-the-cloth variety.

Young Bravo, making his screen debut after several tv appearances, does nicely. Stu Erwin is especially fine as a local doctor. Shields does a first-rate job, as does Basehart. There is competent support from Armando Silvestre, Elsa Cardenas, Michael Steckler, and particularly Rex Allen, who plays himself and renders an effective vocal on the tune, "Charro Bravo."

Sherman's direction is a bit repetitious in spots, but generally sustains a light, gentle tone to the production, for which Mexican backgrounds were utilized. A straightforward, uncluttered cinematic approach marks the efficient work of lensman Alex Philips, editor Fredrick Y. Smith and art director Roberto Silva. Raul La Vista's music has a wide-open-spaces charm.
Tube.

Nijushi No Hitomi
(24 Eyes)
(JAPANESE)

Paris, July 19.

Shochiku production and release. With Hideko Takamine, Yumeji Tsukioka, Takahiro Tamura, Toshiko Kogayashi. Directed by Keisuke Kinoshita. Screenplay, Kinoshta from a novel by Sakae Tsuboi; camera, Kiroyuki Kusada; editor, C. Chujn. At Studio De L'Etoile, Paris. Running time, 110 MINS.

Hisako .... Hideko Takamine
Husband .... Yumeji Tsukioka
Girl .... Takahiro Tamura

Film slowly unfolds the tale of a teacher on a small island who at first looked down on because of her modern ways, but finally is accepted. In the background are the various colonial wars and then second World War. Film has perception and displays a feeling for youth and changing outlooks of the times. It is a limited, fragile film but has the understanding of human nature which could make it possible art house bet.

Direction is fluid and fine in its revelation of character. Nothing much happens directly but world events are aptly mirrored in the growing students and times. The teacher is expertly played by Hideko Takamine, and emerges a figure of stature. The expressly languid progression makes it a highly specialized item for foreign spots but worth personal handling on its true picturization of basic human qualities. Technical credits are fine with an eye-catching pictorial style an asset.
Mosk.

All the Young Men

Superficial study of Korean War anxiety within a small unit of uneasily-integrated U.S. troops. Marquee value of cast will help in spots, but b.o. stature uncertain.

Hollywood, July 19.

Columbia Pictures release of Hall Bartlett production. Stars Alan Ladd, Sidney Poitier; features James Darren, Glenn Corbett, Mort Sahl, Ana St. Clair; introduces Ingemar Johansson; with Paul Richards, Dick Davalos, Lee Kinsolving, Joe Gallison, Paul Baxley, Charles Quinlivan, Michael Davis, Mario Alcalde, Maria Tsien. Directed and screenplay by Bartlett; camera, Daniel Fapp; editor, Al Clark; are director, Carl Anderson; music, George Duning; sound, James Flaster; assistant director, Lee Lukather. Reviewed at Stanley-Warner Beverly Hills Theatre, July 19, '60. Running time, 86 MINS.

Kincaid .... Alan Ladd
Towler .... Sidney Poitier
Cotton .... James Darren
Wade .... Glenn Corbett
Crane .... Mort Sahl
Maya .... Ana St. Clair
Bracken .... Paul Richards
Casey .... Dick Davalos
Dean .... Lee Kinsolving
Jackson .... Joe Gallison
Lazitech .... Paul Baxley
Lieutenant .... Charles Quinlivan
Cho .... Michael Davis
Hunter .... Mario Alcalde
Korean Woman .... Maria Tsien
Torgil .... Ingemar Johansson

Racial prejudice at the front during the Korean War is explored in the Hall Bartlett production of "All The Young Men." The examination is neither dramatically plausible nor philosophically stimulating, at least one of which it ought to be. As such, the picture's commercial appeal rests squarely on the marquee calibre of its cast headed by Alan Ladd and including the ex-champ, Ingemar Johansson. It's boxoffice is debatable.

Bartlett's screenplay plants a handful of Marines in the unenviable position of defending a strategic Korean farmhouse against the recurring attacks of a superior enemy. Fortunately, the enemy's superiority is solely numerical — not an ounce of military sense seems to guide its feeble maneuvers. Marines have much more difficulty ironing out their own internal emotional instability.

Dissension within the ranks flares up when the last lieutenant dies, leaving a Negro sergeant (Sidney Poitier) in command. Although it strains credulity to suppose that race prejudice would be so strong and open a factor in a bitter battlefield struggle for survival, the bickering continues until, rather unaccountably, it is snuffed out by a simple blood transfusion in which Poitier's blood keeps chief antagonist Alan Ladd alive. Just about this time. Allied aid arrives with predictable nick-of-time precision.

Of all the players, Poitier is the most convincing, but even he is not as his best under the circumstances. Ladd's performance is rather mechanical. Mort Sahl, the only one of the bunch who does not look as if he has just shaved and showered, rattles off a couple of monologs, Crescendo-style. Darting to and fro among the grinning faces of Sahl's compatriots for spot reaction shots, Daniel Fapp's camera capers (quick and alert in battle scenes) illustrate the two-dimensional tone of Bartlett's character direction. The aura of war is rarely captured by the expressions of these men.

Others who most noticeably share the front line premises are James Darren, Glenn Corbett, Ana St. Clair, Paul Richards and Ingemar Johansson. Latter, who, as subsequent events proved, should have been training for the second Patterson fight about the time he indulged in this enterprise, proves that acting is not his line.

The Korean farmhouse designed by art director Carl Anderson and furnished by set decorator Bill Calvert is not a convincing central site for the action, resembling a delicate Japanese tearoom more than a strategic rural abode smack dab in the midst of the Korean chaos. Glacier National Park, site of the exterior locationing, is a passable replica of the rugged terra-firma near the 38th parallel sore spot.

James Flaster's sound conveys the ferocity of war. Editing by Al Clark is at its best in battle scenes. An easily-forgettable title song by George Duning (music) and Stanley Styne (lyrics) is incorporated into the story.
Tube.

Der Jugendrichter
(The Judge For the Young)
(GERMAN)

Berlin, July 26.

UFA release of Kurt Ulrich production. Stars Heinz Ruehmann. Features Karin Baal, Lola Muethel, Hans Nielsen, Rainer Brandt, Michael Verhoeven. Directed by Paul Verhoeven. Screenplay, Hans Jacoby and Istvan Bekeffi; camera, Erich Claunigk; music, Raimund Rosenberger; editor, Hermann Haller. At Gloria Palast, Berlin. Running time, 95 MINS.

Dr. Ferdinand Bluhme . Heinz Ruehmann
Inge Schumann .... Karin Baal
Elisabeth Winkler .... Lola Muethel
Schmittler .... Hans Nielsen
Kurt .... Rainer Brandt
Bill .... Peter Thom
Fred .... Michael Verhoeven
Paula Burg .... Lore Schulz
Police Sergeant .... Willi Rose
Vogel .... Erich Fiedler

Another contribution to the juve delinquency theme. Another surefire vehicle for Heinz Ruehmann whose portrayal of the title role is an acting masterpiece. His name means plenty in Germany, so there's no worry about this film's commercial outcome locally. It should do well also in some foreign areas.

As usual with a Ruehmann starrer, realism isn't the big thing

in this. It's sacrificed for the sake of heart-warming sentiment and entertainment. In a way, this UFA release comes close to a modern fairy-tale since Ruehmann is actually more a "dear good uncle" than a true-to-life judge here. But this was intended by film's makers and one may add that they did a skillful job. Film has considerable entertainment values, some suspense, and also a serious message that comes off.

Ruehmann has the role of a judge who believes that, for psychological reasons, one shouldn't punish the juve delinquents too severely but to give them a chance to mend. Here, action concentrates on a teenage girl who's been used as a decoy by a gang of juvenile racketeers. Ruehmann gets the girl a job as housemaid and manages to lead her back to the path of decency.

Of course, this is Ruehmann's film and his acting is again a fine mixture of pleasant humor, some tongue-in-cheek, lovable wit and real heart-warming thesping. Karin Baal plays the young girl, this being her top role to date. Fine support is supplied by Hans Nielsen, Lola Muethel and Willi Rose and a handful of promising youngsters of whom Michael Verhoeven, son of Paul Verhoeven, who directed this with much knowhow, is a standout.

Technical credits are good. It's a film that belongs to the better productions turned out by the Germans in recent past months.
Hans.

Culpable
(ARGENTINE)
Buenos Aires, July 26.
Araucania production and release. Stars Hugo del Carril; features Roberto Escalada, Elina Colomer, Miriam de Urquijo, Maria Aurelia Bisutti, Ernesto Blanco, Diana Ingro, Maria Esther, Duckse and Carlos R. Costa. Directed by Del Carril. Screenplay, Eduardo Borras from Del Carril play; camera, Americo Hoss; editor, Jose Serra. At the Ocean, Buenos Aires. Running time, **90 MINS.**

The Screen Institute tried to give this grim, humorless melodrama a boxoffice lift, via several awards, but this caused no rush to the boxoffice. Del Carril, customarily a stilted player, seems to communicate this woodenness to the entire cast.

At the start the impression is gained about a good whodunit, but this branches off into melodramatics which only reveal confused thinking. It shows Del Carril's customary slant against "injustices," though with twists which may point a return from fellow-travelling. The yarn tries to show that the gangster who blames his crimes on his status as a fatherless, nameless foundling, when given a second chance with advantages of wealth and education, inevitably turns to crime. So the moral of this story appears to be that man alone is master of his own destiny.

Though the psychology and characterization are confused, this is commendable striving at higher things in film production here.

This probably will do well in the domestic provinces and some Latin-American markets. Praise is due cameraman Americo Hoss. *Nid.*

Hell to Eternity

Overlong, but frank and exciting war film based on true story of Japanese-reared U.S. Marine hero who went to war against Japan. Strong male pull indicated, and b.o. prospects encouraging.

Hollywood, July 25.
Allied Artists release of Irving H. Levin production. Features Jeffrey Hunter, David Janssen, Vic Damone, Patricia Owens, Richard Eyer, John Larch, Miiko Taka, Sessue Hayakawa. Directed by Phil Karlson. Screenplay, Ted Sherdeman, Walter Roeber Schmidt, from story by Gil Doud; camera, Burnett Guffey; editors, George White, Roy V. Livingston; music, Leith Stevens; asst. director, Clark Paylow. Tradeshown at Academy Award Theatre, July 25, '60. Running time, **132 MINS.**

Guy Gabaldon	Jeffrey Hunter
Bill	David Janssen
Pete	Vic Damone
Sheila	Patricia Owens
Guy (as boy)	Richard Eyer
Capt. Schabwe	John Larch
Ester	Miiko Taka
General Matsui	Sessue Hayakawa
Leonard	Bill Williams
Mother Une	Tsuru Aoki Hayakawa
Sono	Michi Kobi
Kaz	George Shibata
Famika	Reiko Sato
Sullivan	Richard Gardner
Papa Une	Bob Okazaki
George (as boy)	George Matsui
Semperi	Nicky Blair
George	George Takai

Allied Artists has some pretty salable merchandise in "Hell To Eternity," a war picture with an unusual point-of-view. In constructing this film out of the true experiences of Marine hero Guy Gabaldon, it appears that certain concessions were made for the sake of commercialism, reducing its overall artistic stature, but the end product is one that is bound to please and excite the average filmgoer, particularly the average male. With the additional impetus of some attractive and promising young players to go along with its sex-and-war exploitation values, the ambitious Atlantic Pictures production should pay off solidly at the boxoffice.

The screenplay by Ted Sherdeman and Walter Roeber Schmidt from a story by Gil Doud is one of sharp contrasts—almost three separate stories loosely assembled into one package. Lacking a flowing tempo and complete dramatic unity, the 132-minute film may seem overlong to many spectators. The first phase of the picture relates the experiences of Gabaldon as a virtually homeless boy (sensitively played by Richard Eyer) "adopted" and reared by a Japanese family. The second major passages begins with Pearl Harbor and its impact upon the hero (now grownup into Jeffrey Hunter) and the Coast Japanese community in which he has been raised. These scenes, although rather awkwardly illustrated in spots, do bring to modern audiences a deeper understanding of the war's ironical impact upon this country's Nisei residents. This middle passage culminates in a raucous, but not wholly convincing, drunken orgy scene in which Hunter and his Marine buddies David Janssen and Vic Damone successfully seduce (or are seduced by?) Patricia Owens, Michi Kobi and Reiko Sato.

The third, and major, section of the film is the "war" part, the description of Gabaldon's exploits on Saipan in which, via his acquired knowledge of their native tongue, he coaxes a staggering number (as much as 800 at a clip) of defeated but holdout Japanese to surrender peacefully. Was this not based on fact, it would be difficult to swallow.

Hunter delivers a thoroughly believable characterization of Gabaldon, playing the role with sincerity and conviction. Unquestionably one of the standout portrayals in this picture is that of Janssen as Hunter's hard-bitten, war-wise Marine buddy. The prime quality of his success in the actually commonplace, almost stereotyped, role is the fact that he virtually flings himself at the character, giving it zest and life and color.

A somewhat less enthralling but equally likeable character is created by Damone as another "buddy." Miss Owens' physical endowments certainly complement her thespic abilities in tackling the brief, but torrid sequence in which she joins Miss Sato in a modified version of a living room strip (choreographed by Roland Dupree) enroute to more serious sexual pursuits in other rooms. The picture is quite frank, both in this area and in its colorful language (which includes an appropriate front-line inspired "lousy bastard").

Very convincing in important roles are John Larch, Bill Williams, Sessue Hayakawa (making a virtual career of his "Kwai" typecasting), George Shibata and George Matsui. Competent support is contributed by George Takai, Richard Gardner, Bob Okazaki, Miss Sato and Nicky Blair. Hayakawa's wife, Tsuru Aoki, gives a warm portrayal of Gabaldon's "mother." Miiko Taka and Miss Kobi are attractive in support.

Phil Karlson's direction is vigorous, most notably in the extremely realistic battle sequences (a pulsating beachhead and stimulating close contact shots). Much of this footage was shot on Okinawa, with military cooperation. It shows.

Vital production assists are Burnett Guffey's camera dexterity, David Milton's accurate art direction, the neat editing by George White and Roy V. Livingston and the sensitive sound by Ralph E. Butler and John Bury Jr. Leith Stevens' music brings added dramatic emphasis to the action. Augie Lohman's special effects are yet another convincing facet of Irving H. Levin's hard-hitting major production. *Tube.*

The High-Powered Rifle

Private-eye fare efficiently filmed. Passable lower-berth crime meller.

Hollywood, July 25.
Twentieth-Fox release of Maury Dexter production. Stars Willard Parker, Allison Hayes; with Dan Simmons, John Holland, Shirley O'Hara, Terrea Lea, Lennie Geer, Clark Howat, A. G. Vitanza. Directed by Dexter. Screenplay, Joseph Fritz; camera, Floyd Crosby; editor, Edward Dutko; assistant directors, Ralph Slosser, Willard Kirkham. Reviewed at the studio, July 25, '60. Running time, **62 MINS**

Dancer	Willard Parker
Sharon Hill	Allison Hayes
Lt. "Mac" McDonald	Dan Simmons
D.A.	John Holland
Jean Brewster	Shirley O'Hara
Terrea Lea	Terrea Lea
Gus Alpert	Lennie Geer
George Markle	Clark Howat
Little Charlie Roos	A. G. Vitanza

That seemingly inexhaustible source of modern melodramatics, the private-eye, is the center of attention once again in this swift, efficient, but uninspired program item out of 20th by Capri Productions. In many ways, it's no more and no less than an extension of the sort of super-sleuthing that can be found all over the network airwaves, but there are several areas in which it is a cut above the average for a film of its genre. As lower-half fare, "The High-Powered Rifle" is just about on target.

Willard Parker stars as the gumshoe who survives a brace of attempts on his life by thugs hired by an unknown killer. His investigations lead him into an affair with the lady friend of the principal suspect. The lady (Allison Hayes) turns out to be the would-be killer.

The film benefits from Parker's crisp, professional portrayal of the sleuth, and from producer Maury Dexter's restrained, economical direction, an approach abandoned only in a ludicrous shoot-'em-up climax. Another aid is the occasionally glib dialog of the screenplay by Joseph Fritz.

In addition to the decorative Miss Hayes, others who emote satisfactorily are Dan Simmons, John Holland, Shirley O'Hara, Lennie Geer, Clark Howat and A. G. Vitanza. The plot takes breathers twice to permit Terrea Lea to sing a pair of lengthy folk songs. She renders them well, but one swift chorus of each would have been a sufficient change of pace.

Floyd Crosby's camera work is mobile and skillful, and Edward Dutko's editing is sharp. *Tube.*

Yves Montand Chante
(Yves Montand Sings)
(FRENCH-RUSSIAN)

(Songs)
Paris, July 26.
Sovexport Film release of Dauphine production. Newsreel footage of Yves Montand's 1956 trip to Russia, edited in France by Leonide Azar with commentary by Montand, Simone Signoret. At the Cluny, Paris. Running time, **70 MINS**

Footage from some Soviet newsreels on Yves Montand's singing trip around Russia in 1956, as part of the cultural exchanges between France and the USSR forms the bulk of this pic. It is thus fragmentary with clips of Montand and his wife, Oscar-winning actress Simone Signoret, visiting cities or being entertained. But mostly it is concerned with Montand's own singing. It is the latter that makes this of possible video interest in the U.S. since his click there or cut down for supporting fare.

Montand's numbers are well lensed before workers or in sports stadiums or theatres. His impressive songalog, range, mime, thespian and even acting ability all come through in spite of being pegged in different surroundings. Miss Signoret makes some pointed comments and emerges the faithful companion, coach and aid of her husband though a known actress in her own right. Photographic quality is acceptable.
Mosk.

Locarno Fest

Mein Schulfreund
(My School Chum)
(WEST GERMAN)

Locarno, Aug. 2.
Gloria release of Siodmak-Divina production. Stars Heinz Ruhmann; features Robert Graf, Hertha Feiler, Ernst Schroder, Mario Adorf, Loni Von Friedel. Directed by Robert Siodmak. Screenplay, J. M. Simmel, R. A. Stemmle from play by Simmel; camera, Helmuth Ashley; editor, Walter Boos. At Locarno Film Fest. Running time, **95 MINS.**
Fuchs .... Heinz Ruhmann
Rosi .... Loni Von Friedel
Kuhn .... Ernst Schroder
Sander .... Alexandre Kirst
Neidermoser .... Mario Adorf
Strohbach .... Hans Leibelt

Robert Siodmak has deftly put this contrived tale on film, but it still retains a theatrical air despite the well interpolated ironic looks at a devasted Germany with Hitler's booming promises on the sound track. Its anti-Nazi theme is stated verbally but rarely worked into a deeper look at the times. But this film has some hypo factors for chances abroad and is a definite foreign language entry.

Heinz Ruhmann plays a little resigned postman who finally gets angry near the end of the last war in Germany when he feels that it is now killing children. He writes a letter to an old school friend who happens to be Field Marshall Hermann Goering himself. Subordinates intercept the letter and he is thrown into prison but orders are given to find him insane and get him exempt from any possible execution because he has stated in the letter that the war is lost.

Petty cowardices of the Nazis at the time, are shown as the film traces this man's troubles. His madness certicate keeps him from working and going to America with his daughter. The film may have important overtones in Germany but may seem somewhat familar for foreign spots where many of the illusions may be too sectional. The tirade against Nazism is gotten in while the hero simulates madness. While this may be symbolically meaningful, it is dramatically weak.

Ruhmann cleverly ambles through the pic and etches a personal portrait even if the motivations are somewhat vague. Siodmak has given this a good mounting and presented some telling scenes about the postwar repercussions of Nazism plus the lack of consciousness of their errors by ex-Nazis.

Well hypoed and handled on this aspect, it might be okay for special foreign spots. But since many films on the grisly side of Nazism have been made, this might seem a little tame and the few attempts at humor in the Nazi setup do not quite keep in line with the broader theme of the pic. Production quality is excellent and supporting players good. *Mosk.*

Vyssi Princip
(Mr. Superior Principle)
(CZECHOSLAVAKIAN)

Locarno, Aug. 2.
Czech State Film production and release. With Jana Brejchova, Frantisek Smolik, Otomar Misirik, Marie Vasova, Hanjo Hasse. Directed by Jiri Krejcik. Screenplay, Jan Drda, Krejcik; camera, Jaroslav Tuzar; editor, Josef Dobrichov-

sky. At Locarno Film Fest. Running time, **105 MINS.**
Malek .... Frantisek Smolik
Skala .... Otomar Krejca
Daughter .... Jana Brejchova
Vlastik .... Ivan Mistrik
Mother .... Marie Vasova
Worliezk .... Hanjo Hasse

This film story is laid in a small town of Czechoslovakia during the occupation and brutal Nazi reprisals after the assassination of the hangman of Prague, R. Heydrich. It concerns an old professor's realization that tyranhy must be fought with violence and concerns the arrest and execution of three students. Pic is extremely well mounted and handled and looms worthy of specialized chances abroad. However, it is limited on its classic form and progression which shows only one side of the affair in a measured manner.

The students jokingly put a beard on a picture of the dead Heydrich in a newspaper but an informer turns it in for money. This leads to the arrest and execution of the three boys despite the old professor's pleading with the local Gestapo head. He believes that even Nazis have a certain moral base, but finds out differently. Pic is a moving denunciation of Fascist violence and morals.

Film is starkly made, director Jiri Krejcik slowly building a tragic pattern. Lensing is appropriately sharp while the editing, pacing and acting all help to make this a sombre if compelling tale of the coming of consciousness and men's heroism as well as cowardice in the face of danger. *Mosk.*

Der Herr Mit Der Schwarzen Melone
(The Man In the Black Derby)
(SWISS)

Locarno, Aug. 2.
Prisma release of Urania production. With Sabina Sesselmann, Walter Roderer, Gustav Knuth, Hubert Meyerinck, Charles Regnier. Directed by Karl Suter. Screenplay, Alfred Bruggmann, Hans Gmur, Suter; camera, Rudolf Sandtner; editor, Rene Martinet. At Locarno Film Fest. Running time, **90 MINS.**
Christine .... Sabina Sesselmann
Hugo .... Walter Roderer
Meissen .... Gustav Knuth
Russian .... Hubert Meyerinck
Seelisberg .... Charles Regnier

Stolidly made Swiss comedy, this is about a little man who pulls off a daring robbery to win a rich girl. But all this is telegraphed. It lacks the flair and pacing to make it more than a local pet.

Swiss serenity is lampooned as well as international groups, nobility and other things. But this all adds up to a comedy sans edge. Lensing is flat and direction does not punch up the progression enough. This looks like an okay entry for the Germanic market. too. Acting is adequate. *Mosk.*

Kolybjelnaja
(Lullabye)
(RUSSIAN)

Locarno, Aug. 2.
Mosfilm release of Moldave production. With Lioubov Tchernoval, Nikolai Timofeev, Vladimir Ratomski. Directed by Mikhail Kalik. Screenplay, Avenir Zak, Issai Kouznetsov; camera, Vadime Derbenev; editor, Kalik. At Locarno Film Fest. Running time, **95 MINS.**
Aourika .... Lioubov Tchernoval
Lassiev .... Nikolai Timofeev
Shoemaker .... Vladimir Ratomski

After the war a father searches for his daughter when he hears that many children were saved in his old home town, supposedly

razed by the war. Pic details his quest with flashbacks showing how his daughter was saved and grew up before they finally meet.

Pic is sentimental but well mounted. It emerges mainly a programmer since conventional in treatment. Film looms only for dualers abroad.

It is technically good and well played with some touching scenes concerning a group of babies saved during the war. The children are exceptionally good. *Mosk.*

Hagringen
(The Mirage)
(SWEDISH)

Locarno, Aug. 2.
Weiss - Mandal - Helge Bylund - Edouard Laurot production and release. With Staffan Lamm, Gunilla Palmstierne. Directed by Peter Weiss. Screenplay, Helge Bylund, Weiss, Laurot; camera, Gustav Mandal; editor, Weiss. At Locarno Film Fest. Running time, **70 MINS.**
Boy .... Staffan Lamm
Mirage .... Gunilla Palmstierne

Avant-garde entry takes a young man into the city looking for work and being followed by the mirage of a young girl. There are a flood of city images and some striking effects, but this also is repetitive. This is only for film clubs or specialized showings abroad.

Director Peter Weiss has some flair for imagery but this personalized, tenuous pic seems somewhat old fashioned today. Sometimes the illusions of the non-conformist, idealistic man are there but there is also too much padding and unclear episodes. Imagery is good as is editing with some successful, concrete music and sound backgrounding. *Mosk.*

Wspolny Pokoj
(The Boarders)
(POLISH)

Locarno, Aug. 2.
Polski Film release of Kamera production. With Mieczyslaw Gajda, Gustaw Holoubek, Adam Pawlikowski, Anna Lubienska, Beata Tyskiewicz, Irena Netto. Written and directed by Wojciech J. Has; based on novel by Zbigniew Unilowski; camera, Stefan Matyaszkiewicz; editor, S. Zylewicz. At Locarno Film Fest. Running time, **90 MINS.**
Salis .... Mieczyslaw Gajda
Dziadzia .... Gustaw Holoubek
Zygmunt .... Adam Pawlikowski
Leopard .... Anna Lubienska
Teodozja .... Beata Tyszkiewicz
Stukonisawa .... Irena Netto

This depicts a group of boarders living in a cluttered flat in the poor section of Warsaw before the last war. They are mostly poet failures, students, etc. They drift around aimlessly trying to find a meaning to the emptiness of their own lives and the things about them. The only hope seems to be in a young Communist who is arrested. Though this is pessimistic and bleak, it has an insight into the people and a flair for narrative. However, the export chances look limited and for special situations primarily.

Director Wojciech J. Has has a talent for revealing character and recreating the past even if he shows only one side of it. Expert lensing, acting and editing also help give this dense, literary story balance and clear progression. It is an interesting look at the "sweet life" of the drifters of pre-war Poland. But it is a limited film for Western consumption. *Mosk.*

Foma Gordeev
(RUSSIAN)

Locarno, Aug. 2.
Mosfilm release of Gorki Studio production. With Gueorgui Epifantsev, Serguel Loukianov, Pavel Tarassov, Marina Strijenova, Alla Labetskaia. Directed by Marc Donskoi. Screenplay, Baris Bialik, Donskoi from novel by Maxim Gorki; camera, Marguerite Pilikhina; editor, S. Donskoi. At Locarno Film Fest. Running time, **95 MINS.**
Foma .... Gueorgui Epifantsev
Ignat .... Serguel Loukianov
Parrain .... Pavel Tavassov
Assa .... Marina Strijenova
Girl .... Alla Labetskaia

Turn-of-the-century Russia is well depicted in this didactic tale of the merchant class of the times and one man's revolt against it. Somewhat academic, this has brilliant mounting. However, it rarely breathes true life into the yarn which makes it somewhat cold. This looms only for some arty spots as well as Russo language houses.

Foma Gordeev is the son of a dynamic merchant who begins to choke in this closed world. His attempt to tell off the rapacious merchants ends in his being tied up like a dog, his spirit broken. Woven in this are some telling bits that are expertly handled by director Marc Donskoi, aided by outstanding solid production dress and fine acting.

Death of the hero's father in a nightclub where the floor is spun by men underneath it, wild parties, and the solid characters are all plus factors. Camera work is also good. But there is a tendency to make each character a symbol. The fine technique sometimes falls into sheer bravura making this a polished pic with only specialized chances in the West. *Mosk.*

Ocean's Eleven
(COLOR—PANAVISION)

Uninhibited romp about a whopping crime caper in which five Vegas strip hotels are stripped of all their casino funds by 11 clannish ex-paratroopers. Despite number of serious weaknesses in both material and interpretation, should rake in chips, thanks to cast.

Las Vegas, Aug. 4.

Warner Bros. release of Lewis Milestone production. Stars Frank Sinatra, Dean Martin, Sammy Davis Jr., Peter Lawford, Angie Dickinson, Richard Conte; guest stars Red Skelton, George Raft; features Cesar Romero, Patrice Wymore, Joey Bishop, Akim Tamiroff, Henry Silva; with Ilka Chase, Buddy Lester, Richard Benedict, Jean Willes, Norman Fell, Hank Henry. Directed by Milestone. Screenplay, Harry Brown, Charles Lederer, based on story by George Clayton Johnson, Jack Golden Russell; camera, William H. Daniels; editor, Philip W. Anderson; art director, Nicolai Remisoff; music, Nelson Riddle; sound, M. A. Merrick; assistant director, Ray Gosnell Jr. Reviewed at Fremont Theatre, Las Vegas, Aug. 4, '60. Running time, **127 MINS.**

Danny Ocean	Frank Sinatra
Sam Harmon	Dean Martin
Josh Howard	Sammy Davis Jr.
Jimmy Foster	Peter Lawford
Beatrice Ocean	Angie Dickinson
Anthony Bergdoff	Richard Conte
Duke Santos	Cesar Romera
Adele Ekstrom	Patrice Wymore
"Mushy" O'Conners	Joey Bishop
Spyros Acebos	Akim Tamiroff
Roger Carneal	Henry Silva
Mrs. Restes	Ilka Chase
Vincent Massier	Buddy Lester
"Curly" Steffens	Richard Benedict
Mrs. Bergdorf	Jean Willes
Red Skelton	Himself
George Raft	Himself

"Ocean's Eleven" figures to be a moneymaker in spite of itself. Although basically a no-nonsense piece about the efforts of 11 ex-war buddies to make off with a multi-million dollar loot from five Vegas hotels, the film is frequently one resonant wisecrack away from turning into a musical comedy. Laboring under the handicaps of a contrived script, an uncertain approach and personalities in essence playing themselves, the Lewis Milestone production never quite makes its point, but romps along merrily unconcerned that it doesn't. Where the Warner's release no doubt will make the desirable number is at the wicket windows, thanks to the boxoffice magnetism of its cast.

Coincidence runs rampant in the Harry Brown-Charles Lederer screenplay, based on a story by George Clayton Johnson and Jack Golden Russell. Set in motion on the doubtful premise that 11 playful, but essentially law-abiding wartime acquaintances from all walks of life would undertake a job that makes the Brink's hoist pale by comparison, it proceeds to sputter and stammer through an interminable initial series of scrambled expository sequences.

It is principally in these passages that the personalities of several of the stars clash with the characters they are attempting to portray. Acting under the stigma of their own flashy, breezy identities, players such as Frank Sinatra, Dean Martin, Sammy Davis Jr. and Peter Lawford never quite submerge themselves in their roles, nor try very hard to do so.

At any rate, the pace finally picks up when the daring scheme is set in motion. Just when all appears to be coming off as planned, a professional racketeer (Cesar Romero) deduces what the boys are up to. This discovery leads to an amusingly ironical climax that will pack a punch for audiences.

There is a plentiful amount of humor in the film, but much of it is largely for its own self-conscious sake and not consistent with or vital to the characterizations. The dialog is sharp, but not always pertinent to the story being told. And director Milestone has failed to curb a tendency toward flamboyant but basically unrealistic behavior, as if unable to decide whether to approach the yarn straight or with tongue-in-cheek. In trying to blend both approaches, he has succeeded in contradicting one with the other.

Likeable, but not very convincing, performances are turned in by Sinatra, Martin, Davis and Lawford. Angie Dickinson is attractively superfluous in a brief scene with Sinatra. Richard Conte gives one of the better portrayals, a heartfelt enactment of the band's ace, but doomed, electrician. Romero, another standout, delivers a commanding performance as the alert-minded gent who fouls up the super scheme.

Akim Tamiroff snares comedy honors, closely tailed by Joey Bishop, Buddy Lester and Martin. Others who perform favorably are Henry Silva, Patrice Wymore, Ilka Chase, Richard Benedict, Jean Willes, Norman Fell, Clem Harvey, Hank Henry and guest stars Red Skelton, George Raft and Shirley MacLaine, latter in an unbilled drunk bit.

Chief among the competent craft credits are William H. Daniels' photography, Philip W. Anderson's editing, Nelson Riddle's score, and Nicolai Remisoff's art direction. Several appealing but not particularly exciting tunes by Sammy Cahn and James Van Heusen crop up along the way. Main titles by Saul Bass are as clever as anything that follows. *Tube.*

The Hound That Thought He Was a Raccoon
(COLOR)

Amusing variation on an aged theme. A companionable and attractive Disney featurette.

Hollywood, Aug. 5.

Buena Vista release of Winston Hibler production. Directed by Tom McGowan. Screenplay, Albert Aley, from original story by Rutherford Montgomery; camera, Robert Brooker; editor, George Gale; music, Buddy Baker, William Lava; sound, Robert O. Cook. Reviewed at Academy Awards Theatre, Aug. 5, '60. Running time, **48 MINS.**

Long-standing camaraderie between individuals of enemy animal camps is nothing novel in the way of a dramatic theme ("Androcles and the Lion," "Sequoia," "Romulus and Remus," etc.), but "The Hound That Thought He Was A Raccoon" ("and nearly starved to death tryin' to eat like one") is a charming new variation. The 48-minute Disney featurette is certain to be a popular added attraction wherever it plays, particularly where "family" audiences flock.

Engagingly narrated (country style) by Rex Allen from Albert Aley's screenplay out of Rutherford Montgomery's story, the film describes the problem of a lost pup who, in infancy, takes up with a brood of 'coons. Later returned to his owner, he finds himself in the ironical role of a coon-hunt dog pack leader, but rises to the occasion by fighting off his own kind when they threaten his old playmate.

So patiently is the action blocked out by director Tom McGowan, lensman Robert Brooker and editor George Gale that some members of the audience (particularly the younger ones) won't even be aware that the story has been designed and constructed by people, and wasn't just happening when producer Winston Hibler, his staff and crew chanced upon it. As is typical of such efforts by Disney, music is a key ingredient in establishing personality and adding notes of humor and tension.

The score was penned by Buddy Baker and William Lava, and is well-orchestrated by Franklyn Marks. Color, sound and additional technical credits are more than satisfactory. *Tube.*

Young Jesse James
(C'SCOPE)

Another remake of America's favorite outlaw, this time as a visionary youth. Amounts to a weak lower-berth western.

Hollywood, Aug. 1.

Twentieth-Fox release of Jack Leewood production. Stars Ray Stricklyn, Willard Parker, Merry Anders; features Robert Dix, Emile Meyer; with Jacklyn O'Donnell, Rayford Barnes, Rex Holman, Bob Palmer, Sheila Bromley, Johnny O'Neill, Leslie Bradley, Norman Leavitt, Lee Kendall. Directed by William Claxton. Screenplay, Orville H. Hampton, Jerry Sackheim; camera, Carl Berger; editor, Richard C. Meyer; art directors, Lyle Wheeler, John Mansbridge; music, Irving Gertz; assistant director, William Kirkham. Reviewed at the studio, Aug. 1, '60. Running time, **73 MINS.**

Jesse James	Ray Stricklyn
Cole Younger	Willard Parker
Belle Starr	Merry Anders
Frank James	Robert Dix
Quantrill	Emile Meyer
Zerelda	Jacklyn O'Donnell
Pitts	Rayford Barnes
Zack	Rex Holman
Bob Younger	Bob Palmer
Mrs. Samuels	Sheila Bromley
Jim Younger	Johnny O'Neill
Major Turnbull	Leslie Bradley
Folsom	Norman Leavitt
Jennison	Lee Kendall

The public's seemingly insatiable appetite for the dramatized exploits of likeable outlaw Jesse James is being put to the test again in this supporting number from 20th-Fox. But western fans and aficionados of JJ's cantankerous career will find little to grow enthused over in Jack Leewood's production. Mrs. James' son, Jesse, has, through overexposure, become a caricature of himself. It is an easy matter now for an educated audience to anticipate his reactions—an element of familiarity that ought to curb future filmland inclinations to tackle the hackneyed story.

"Young Jesse James" examines Jesse (Ray Stricklyn) and brother Frank (Robert Dix) in the formative stages of their careers, during and just following the Civil War period in which they joined up with Quantrills Raiders. The Orville H. Hampton-Jerry Sackheim screenplay explores a heretofore untapped vein of mysticism in Jesse's youth, finds him beset by psychological pangs and Merlinesque visions of evil-to-come (hanging up the familiar "God Bless Our Home" sign on the wall of his home, he is overcome by an "unaccountable" fit of fear). Only other difference between this version of Jesse and his predecessors is that this one is a shade more venomous and unreasonably brutal.

Stricklyn does a fairly commendable job of delineating the junior-sized variation on the well-known "hero." Dix is reserved in the role of the rather ineffectual brother, Willard Parker ably plays Cole Younger, and Merry Anders is on for a brief, unnecessary scene as the inevitable Belle Starr. Rex Holman's snappy portrayal of a sadistic young tough puts some life into the film. Another effective performance is Emile Meyer's as Quantrill. Jacklyn O'Donnell is earnest and pretty as Jesse's young missus.

William Claxton's direction fails to avert the uneven pacing inherent in the script, which gets off to a fast start, labors interminably in the middle, and winds with a parting shot of action. Richard C. Meyer's editing is a bit choppy, and Carl Berger's lenswork fuzzy in spots. There is a listenable title ballad by Irving Gertz and Hal Levy that frames the story with some imagination. *Tube.*

Jungle Cat
(COLOR)

Another of Disney's true-life adventure pix. Expertly lensed and put together, but not always as fascinating or disarming as prior forays into the off-the-beaten-path terrain. Prospects favorable.

Hollywood, Aug. 5.

Buena Vista release of Walt Disney production. Written and directed by James Algar; camera, James R. Simon, Hugh A. Wilmar, Lloyd Beebe; editor, Norman Palmer; music, Oliver Wallace; sound, Robert O. Cook. Reviewed at Academy Awards Theatre, Aug. 5, '60. Running time, **70 MINS.**

Somewhat less astonishing, considerably less amusing, but equally as meticulous and painstakingly filmed as Walt Disney's previous true-life adventure pieces, "Jungle Cat" pokes around in the lush rain forests of Brazil and comes up with some splendidly photographed shots of wildlife in its best survival-of-the-fittest form.

Although the film lacks a desirable beginning-middle-and-end approach, it's both an interesting zoological chronicle and an entertaining motion picture for fanciers of four-legged, who-eats-whom shenanigans.

The "jungle cat," or jaguar, is the star and pivotal character of the picture, but plenty of other beasts cross the screen, a few of them (such as peculiar "sloth") obscure and fascinating. Prominent among others caught at work or play are the boa constrictor, the crocodile (or caiman), the great anteater, the lesser (but not by much) anteater, the iguana (a prehistoric lizard that bears a strong resemblance to the "dinosaurs" recently seen in 20th's "Lost World").

The jungle itself, stunningly photographed (as are all the creatures that cavort within it) by James R. Simon, Lloyd Beebe and the late Hugh A. Wilmar, is rewarding to behold in striking Technicolor hues.

Where there is a forest filled with bird and animal life, sound is always a vital ingredient, and it has been vividly reproduced here

by Robert O. Cook. Imaginatively punctuating the action and emphasizing humor or fear where each is apropos is Oliver Wallace's score, carefully orchestrated by Clifford Vaughan. The narrative, which is excellent and informative until a typically pedestrian "as the sun sinks in the west—such is the way of the jungle" climax, is the product of director James Algar, who has done a journeyman job of assembling all the footage into an attractive 70 minutes. Winston Hibler narrates listenably. Other key contributions are Norman Palmer's taut editing and skillful animation effects the familiar Disney paintbrush strokes) by Joshua Meador and Art Riley. *Tube.*

Pula Festival

Tri Ane
(Three Girls Named Anna)
(YUGOSLAV-TOTALVISION)
Pula, Aug. 2.
Vardar (Skopje) production. With Dusan Stefanovic, Svetlana, Miscovic, Marija Kon, Dubravka Gal. Directed by Branko Bauer. Camera, Branko Blazina; music, Bojan Adamic. At Pula Film Festival. Running time, **92 MINS.**

A postwar drama centering around an old man on the search for his daughter whom he lost during the chaotic war years and whom he believes still alive. Basically this is a humanly interesting and touchy story which hasn't been exploited to best advantage. Too talky for U. S. market.

Technically, it commands some attention as made in so-called Totalvision, a system comparable to CinemaScope. Good lensing is evident. Besides the inadequate direction and script work, fault lies also with the acting. Latter is not too impressive. *Hans.*

Drug Pretsednik Centafor
(Comrade President Centre-Forward)
(YUGOSLAV)
Pula, Aug. 2.
UFUS (Belgrade) production. With Mija Aleksis, Olivera Markovic, Pavle Vujusic, Tatjana Beljakova, Peter Kvrgic. Directed by Zorz Skrigin. Camera, Velibor Andrejevic; music, Bojan Adamic. At Pula Film Fest. Running time, **92 MINS.**

The showing of this gave evidence of two facts: That the Yugoslavs are also able to produce worthwhile comedies and that local audiences are receptive to them. It's a nice comedy which teems with many old and new gags. However, this is strictly local stuff.

As the title indicates, football (European soccer) plays an essential part in it. Director Skrigin showed a fine sense for amusing situations. Cast includes a number of sexy looking gals. *Hans.*

Rat
(War)
(YUGOSLAV-TOTALSCOPE)
Pula, Aug. 2.
Features Eva Krizevske, Anton Vrdoljak, Zlatko Madunic, Ljubisa Jovanovic, Ita Rina, Janez Vrhovec. Directed by Veljko Bulajic. Screenplay, Cesar Zavattini; camera, Kreso Grcevic; music, Vladimir Kraus. At Pula Film Fest. Running time, **80 MINS.**

Picture's theme (reminiscent of Stanley Kramer's "On The Beach"), the names of C. Zavattini (widely known Italian screenwriter) and of Eva Krizevska (Polish actress recently given a French prize as best actress of year) as well as the fact that "War" looms as one of the most expensive ($400,000) made this an eagerly awaited film at this festival. But it looms as one of the most disappointing feature pix of the Pula Fest. The fact that "War" walked off with second prize at Pula put the latter's jury in a not too favorable light.

"War" is another Yugoslav film about warfare but this one centers around a future war dealing with the utilization of atomic weapons and playing in a fancy state. It contains a strong anti-war message. Pic aims at telling that mankind would face terrible disaster.

Subject can hardly be taken seriously. Its treatment is too much on the naive if not primitive side. Cesar Zavattini's screenplay is weak. Bulajic, who last year directed "Train Without Time-Table" is another disappointment. Both he and Zavattini must share most of the blame for this film's considerable shortcomings.

Their biggest mistake was to combine satire with realism. This just doesn't mix. The acting in this isn't too impressive. What had been intended to be a shocking picture was nothing much more than a second-rate humoresque.

Noteworthy are the technical credits. That Yugoslavs can do special effects like nobody else was evidenced in this. Incidentally, Tito's Army contributed substantial assistance to this film. *Hans.*

Akjica
(Operation)
(YUGOSLAV)
Pula, Aug. 2.
Triglav (Ljubljana) production. With Lojze Rozman, Stane Potokar, Branko Plesa, Josko Lukeza, Arnold Tovarnik. Directed by Jane Kavcic. Camera, Franc Cerar; music, Aloiz Srebotnjak. At Pula Film Fest. Running time, **89 MINS**

"Operation" is another picture about the last war, depicting the courage of Tito's partisans. However, the producers tried a departure from the partisan cliche by showing a psychological study of these freedom fighters. The outcome of this isn't exactly positive. It's basically not too bad a picture. Has slim export possibilities.

After a battle between partisans and German occupation soldiers, most of the former are either killed or taken prisoner. Only seven partisans manage to escape. Technically, the film comes up to an okay standard. *Hans.*

Partizanske Price
(Partisan Stories)
(YUGOSLAV)
Pula, Aug. 2.
Ufus (Belgrade) production. With Boris Buzancic, Milan Milosevic, Branko Plesa, Janez Vrhovec, Nikola Popovic. Directed by S. Jankovic. Screenplay, S. Jankovic; camera, Jovan Jovanovic; music, Bojan Adamic. At Pula Festival. Running time, **105 MINS.**

The best thing about this film is the camerawork which includes a number of impressive shots. And there's a also a certain plus factor in the score by Bojan Adamic. But otherwise this is a rather disap-

pointing production. Put the blame on an utterly inplausible script, inadequate direction and ditto the acting. Nothing here for the U. S. market.

Pic presents two stories both dealing with episodes from Titoland's partisan era. Technically, the film reaches a good standard but remains a far cry from being an acceptable offering because of other drawbacks. *Hans.*

Kapetan Lesi
(Captain Leshi)
(YUGOSLAV-COLOR)
Pula, Aug. 2.
Slavija Film (Belgrade) production. With Aleksandar Gavric, Marija Tocinoska, Selma Karlovac, Petre Prlicko. Directed by Zivorad Mitrovic. Screenplay, Mitrovic; camera, Branko Itatovic; music, Redzo Mulic. At Pula Film Fest. Running time, **90 MINS.**

Film follows much the Hollywood action pattern and may be acclaimed as a good "domestic western." Z. Mitrovic has directed with remarkable skill and imagination. In its category, it's a praiseworthy commercial item that has above-average foreign possibilities. Many scribes here found "Leshi" the best directed and most competently-made film of the festival.

Film concerns the end of the last World War, and centers around Captain Leshi, who became an idol of the partisans for his courage and bravery. There is lots of fighting in this. The villains, of course, are the German Occupation soldiers and Yugoslavs who collaborated with the Germans. Yet it's not a political pic but an actioner whose main aim is to keep the viewer on edge. Lensing, colors, scenery and other credits contribute to give "Leshi" a good rating. *Hans.*

Izgubljena Olovka
(The Lost Pencil
(Yugoslav)
Zora-Film (Zagreb) production. Directed by Fedor Skubonja. Screenplay, Stanislava Berisavljevic; camera, Hrojove Saric; music, Miroslav Belamaric. With Mira Nikolic and Boska Gasevic. At Pula Film Fest. Running time **48 MINS.**

Pula, Aug. 2.
Artistically, this medium-length feature may be acclaimed as the best pic (of the 11 entries) offered at the 1960 Pula festival. With Mira Nicolic, one of the better known Yugoslav screen actresses, in the role of a teacher, film centers around children. Fedor Skubonja has brought a number of interesting studies of moppets before the camera. Film could be an attractive accompanying feature abroad.

Film's psychological message aims at showing that children need a particularly careful treatment. Skubonja's handling of the young players is excellent and also the camera work is a plus. *Hans.*

Spijun X-25 Javlja
(Agent X-25 Reports)
(YUGOSLAV)
Pula, Aug. 2.
Triglav Film (Ljubljana) production. Stars Dusko Janicijewic, Tamara Miletic, Stevo Zigon, Rolf Wanka, Nikola Simic. Directed by Frantisek Cap. Camera, Janez Kalisnik. Screenplay, Frantisek Cap, after novel by Milan Nikolic. At Pula Film Fest. Running time, **92 MINS.**

Frantisek Cap, one of Yugoslavia's most dependable film directors practically always spells an adequate production. This one is a competently made espionage thriller playing during the Nazi occupation in Yugoslavia. There's quite a bit of suspense in this pic. Unlike so many other Yugoslav films of the same calibre, "Agent" has the right pace. It may possibly do for some foreign markets.

Story sees the Germans hire a Yugoslav who they think is one of their followers, and train him as a spy. However, this man takes the job only in order to pass on information to the partisans. Acting is good. Technically, it's even a very solid film. Czech-born Cap tried to make a commercial film without dedicating himself too much to the cliche and has succeeded. *Hans.*

Kota 905
(Point 905)
(YUGOSLAV)
Pula, Aug. 2.
Jadran (Zagreb) production. With Dusko Bulajic, Hermina Pipnic, Ilija Dzuvalekovski, Stane Potokar, Milan Milosevic. Directed by Mate Relja. Camera, Tomislav Pintar; music, Danilo Danev. At Pula Film Fest. Running time, **85 MINS.**

This one is laid several months after the end of the last World War. Nevertheless, it offers considerable machine-gun fire. Storywise, pic develops a certain amount of suspense but this is dulled by the fact there's nothing new about the plot. Film's international chances are mild. Not only are cinema audiences somewhat tired of grim war tales but this isn't a good film.

Attention is focused on a group of Cetniks who during the war collaborated with the Germans, and later continued their activity via terrorizing the population. An officer of Tito's army joins the group by pretending he's one of them. He leads them into a trap so they are liquidated.

Acting is so-so. A nice performance is given by the girl in this, Hermina Pipinic, a promising talent. Camerawork is good. *Hans.*

Dilizansa Snova
(Dreams Came By Coach)
(YUGOSLAV-COLOR)
Pula, Aug. 2.
Avala Film (Belgrade) production. With Olivera Markovic, Ljubinka Bobic, Renata Ulmanski, Slobodan Perovic. Directed by Soja Jovanovic. Camera (Eastmancolor), Nenad Jovicic; music, Borivoje Simic. At Pula Film Fest. Running time, **102 MINS.**

"Coach" is one of two Yugoslav comedies show at the Pula festival, and it's nicely done. But the story is rather confusing so a western viewer will have a tough time making it all out. Pic may have some minor Continental chances if cut down.

Screenplay is based on three tales by the late classical Serbian writer, J. S. Popovic. It concerns an imposter who comes into a little town where he turns everything

ar.d everybody upside down. There's quite a bit of amusing romancing along the line. With fewer characters and complications, "Coach" could have been a really enjoyable pic.

Director S. Jovanovic (a woman) seems to have lost control near the middle of the picture. Acting in this is beyond Yugoslav average. Technical credits are fine. *Hans.*

Locarno Fest

Geisterland Der Sudsee
(The Fabulous South Seas)
(W. GERMAN-DOCUMENTARY-COLOR)
Locarno, Aug. 2.
Globus Films production and release. Written, lensed and edited by Eugen Schuhmacher in Agfacolor. Commentary spoken by Wolf Ackva. At Locarno Film Fest. Running time, 95 MINS

This documentary deals with the almost stonge-age life of the aborigines of New Guinea in the South Seas and with their penchant for killing birds of paradise for their plumage. It is well-made but adds nothing unusual for this type of pic. This is mainly for possible specialized use abroad if cut drastically or possibly for video usage.

Color is well balanced while editing is acceptable. Natural sound plus music accomp is an asset. It is somewhat repetitious but has unique features. Commentary is flat and would have to be cut and pepped up for foreign spots. *Mosk.*

Denize Inen Sokak
(The Road to the Sea)
(TURKISH)
Locarno, Aug. 2.
Sel Film production and release. With Ulvi Uraz, Ayfer Feray, Gulderin Ece, Sadettin Erbi. Written and directed by Attila Tokatili. Camera, A. Ustili; editor, Isak Dilman. At Locarno Film Fest. Running time, 85 MINS.
Ali Bey .... Ulvi Uraz
Perihon .... Ayfer Feray
Sister .... Gulderin Ece
Student .... Sadettin Erbi

Film is probably the first Turkish production to play a major film festival since the war. It may not be a forerunner for others because it is technically primitive and slow moving as well as repetitious. But this tale of a middle-aged landowner, who tries to get out in the world and finally does walk out on his dried-up family and life, may have more meaning in Turkey. This is not the stuff for any export chances except for possible foreign language theatres.

Though irregular in pacing, it does make its point about a man's need for activity and belonging. Also it furnishes a look at Turkey and its outlook. Technical credits are crude and acting below par. *Mosk.*

Questo Amore Ai Confini Del Mondo
(This Love at the End of the World)
(ARGENTINIAN-ITALIAN)
(C'SCOPE-COLOR)
Locarno, Aug. 2.
Italcaribe release of IC-Austral Film production. With Antonio Cifariello, Dominique Wilms, Fausto Tozzi, Egle

Martin, Nino Parsello, Conrado Diana. Directed and written by Giuseppe Scotese. Camera (Ferramicolor), Umberto Peruzzi; editor, Roberto Cinquini. At Locarno Film Fest. Running time, 95 MINS.
Walter .... Antonio Cifariello
Francoise .... Dominique Wilms
Claudio .... Fausto Tozzi
Mecha .... Egle Martin
Bigotes .... Nino Persello
Nicolas .... Conrado Diana

This Argentine-Italo western type pic has the familiar tale about a rancher who brings back a show girl after a trip abroad. This alienates a mistress and the wife does not love him. She takes up with a wild and wooly friend until a showdown and her running off with the friend. Film lacks the production values or originality for anything but lingo situations abroad.

Color is uneven and dark. Techniques are standard, with direction rarely infusing this with life or believable action. The playing also lacks plenty. *Mosk.*

Altas Variedades
(The Big Show)
(SPANISH)
Locarno, Aug. 2.
Este release of Este-Jad production. Stars Christian Marquand, Agnes Laurent; features Angel Aranda, Marisa De Leza, Vicky Lagos. Directed by Rovira Beleta. Screenplay, Manuel Salo; camera, Mario Pacheco; editor, Maria Rosa Ester. At Locarno Film Fest. Running time, 100 MINS.
Walter .... Christian Marquand
Illona .... Agnes Laurent
Rudolf .... Angel Aranda
Lita .... Marisa De Leza
Rosita .... Vicky Lagos

This is about a circus sharpshooter who makes a partner out of a pretty Hungarian refugee. But his love turns to hate when she falls for a friend after their engagement. He plots to have them kill each other, but relents at the last moment. Film is overlong and emerges a meller with too skimpy motivations to bring it off. Pic is mainly for lingo spots abroad via its theme.

Vehicle is solidly mounted but too reminiscent of pre-war German film themes. Acting is okay as are technical values. Two French actors, who play the leads, are well dubbed and pass as Spanish and Magyar types. *Mosk.*

Le Farceur
(The Joker)
(FRENCH)
Locarno, Aug. 2.
Mondex release of AJYM production. With Anouk Aimes, Genevieve Cluny, Jean-Pierre Cassel, Anne Tonietti, Palau, Francois Maistre. Directed by Philippe De Broca. Screenplay, Daniel Boulanger, De Broca; camera, Jean Penzer; editor, Laurence Mery. At Locarno Film Fest. Running time, 90 MINS.
Helene .... Anouk Aimes
Pilou .... Genevieve Cluny
Edouard .... Jean-Pierre Cassel
Olga .... Anne Tonietti
Theodose .... Palau
Andre .... Francois Maistre

"New Waver" Philippe De Broca managed to bring off the first inventive comedy among this group with his initial pic, "Games of Love." But his second, "The Joker," lacks the verve of the first effort, making it somewhat deliberate which permits the comedy to lag. This is a chancy export item except for special situations where its plot about the life of a ladies' man might be a hypo factor.

Pic is reminiscent of pre-war Yank comedies. A zany family harbors a fantasy-ridden young

man who has brought home two illegitimate children, married his first wife off to his older brother and romances the maid.

Into this setup comes a rich married woman whom the young man thinks he loves. After disrupting her life, he leaves for another flirt. However, this has too much talk.

Director De Broca still shows a flair for carefree Bohemian life, but this is sans the insight to make it click. Jean-Pierre Cassel is somewhat mannered which takes the edge off his Don Juan character while Anouk Aimee does not measure up as the rich woman. Others are bogged down with surface characteristics. Technical credits are good. And De Broca still looms as a comedy director not to be considered lightly. *Mosk.*

The Enemy General

Familiar, but fast-moving war meller. Stout supporting number for twin bills.

Hollywood, Aug. 2.
Columbia Pictures release of Sam Katzman production. Stars Van Johnson, Jean-Pierre Aumont, Dany Carrel; with John Van Dreelen, Francoise Prevost, Hubert Noel, Jacques Marin, Gerard Landry, Edward Fleming, Paul Bonifas, Paul Muller. Directed by George Sherman. Screenplay, Dan Pepper, Burt Picard, from Pepper's story; camera, Basil Emmott; editors, Gordon Pilkington, Edwin Bryant; art director, Gaston Medin; music, Mischa Bakaleinikoff; sound, Antoine Petitjean; assistant director, Ottavio Oppo. Reviewed at the studio, Aug. 2, '60. Running time, 75 MINS.
Lemaire .... Van Johnson
Durand .... Jean-Pierre Aumont
Lisette .... Dany Carrel
Gen. Bruger .... John Van Dreelen
Nicole .... Francoise Prevost
Claude .... Hubert Noel
Marceau .... Jacques Marin
Navarre .... Gerard Landry
Sgt. Allen .... Edward Fleming
Mayor .... Paul Bonifas
Major Zughoff .... Paul Muller

Nothing very novel about war in general or World War II in particular turns up in "The Enemy General," but the Sam Katzman production does generate some genuine suspense and arouse audience concern for several of its characters. The Columbia release lacks the originality and thought-provoking substance necessary to successfully top a double-bill, but it will be a strong supporting attraction.

If it was Katzman's conception to avoid probing for philosophical meaning, but to keep his project crammed with brisk movement, he has succeeded. The Dan Pepper-Burt Picard screenplay presents some interesting strokes of irony, but doesn't bother to mull over their psychological manifestations. The irony finds O. S. S. agent Van Johnson aiding in the escape to London of the treacherous Nazi general (John Van Dreelen) who was responsible for the cold-blooded murder of his bethrothed (Dany Carrel) and 11 other innocent French hostages. Doggedly pursuing his dangerous mission despite the threatening protestations of his compatriots and his own deep misgivings, Johnson eventually realizes that the general's promise of vital info for the Allies is the invention of the Nazi high command, a counter-espionage plot to fake the enemy into serious military blunders. He then deals with the enemy general as one might suspect he would.

Johnson's heroically compelling performance is backed up by the persuasive support of Jean-Pierre Aumont, the pretty Miss Carrel, Francoise Prevost, Hubert Noel, Jacques Marin, Gerard Landry, Edward Fleming, Paul Bonifas and Paul Muller. Although the title character he is playing is a familiar two-dimensional type of villain (the "dumbkopf!" kind of Nazi officer), Van Dreelen brings the role some interesting expressive characteristics.

George Sherman's direction succeeds in developing tension, but cannot justify pictorially several of the script's demands, such as the incredible survival of the general after what appears to be a

point-blank ambush in the film's initial scene.

Departmental assists are capable, with the exception of Antoine Petitjean's sound, which fails to maintain proper distance prespectives in a number of passages. The European scenery selected and/or erected by art director Gaston Medin has the authentic flavor.

Basil Emmott's photography and the Gordon Pilkington-Edwin Bryant editing are strong assists, and music by the late Mischa Bakaleinikoff is stimulating, particularly the martial beat of drums behind the main titles. *Tube.*

Make Mine Mink
(BRITISH)

Pleasant, light comedy about a crazy gang of amateur crooks that turns out amusingly. Lacks U. S. marquee value but is a safe booking.

London, Aug. 9.

Rank release of a Hugh Stewart production. Stars Terry-Thomas, Athene Seyler, Hattie Jacques, Billie Whitelaw. Directed by Robert Asher. Screenplay, Michael Pertwee from Peter Coke's play, "Breath of Spring"; camera, Reg Wyer; editor, Roger Cherrill; music, Phillip Green. At Odeon, Edgware Rd., London. Running time, **101 MINS.**

Major Albert Rayne	Terry-Thomas
Dame Beatrice Appleby	Athene Seyler
Nanette Parry	Hattie Jacques
Lily	Billie Whitelaw
Elizabeth Pinkerton	Elspeth Duxbury
Madame Spolinski	Irene Handl
Jim Benham	Jack Hedley
Hon. Fred Warrington	Kenneth Williams
Warrington's Secretary	Caroline Leigh
Cafe Proprietor	Denis Shaw
Thin Man	Michael Peake
Sinister Man	Derek Sydney
Fat Man	Steven Scott
Lionel Spanager	Sydney Tailer
1st Old Porter	Gordon Philpott
2nd Old Porter	Ron Foody
Gertrude	Penny Morrell
Mrs. Spanager	Joan Heal
Old Mrs. Spanager	May Hallatt
Ruby Golding	Claire Golding
1st Shop Assistant	Felicity Young
Jean	Dorinda Stevens
Inspeceor Pape	Raymond Huntley
Drunk	Freddie Frinton
Butler	Michael Balfour
Burglar	Noel Purcell
Super't.	Wensley Pithey

Terry-Thomas' recent drumbeating visit to the U. S. was rated a big success, and may well boost the marquee value in America for "Make Mine Mink." Because the shortage of stellar impact is the main fault of this amiable, lighthearted farce which is a safe booking for audiences geared to escapist entertainment. It is based on Peter Coke's West End comedy, "Breath of Spring," and naturally has been able to eke out the verbal comedy with some broader visual situations. The yarn is good for plenty yocks.

Plot concerns the blundering excursions into crime of a bunch of pinheaded amateurs, who specialize in lifting valuable furs and devoting the loot to charity. Dame Beatrice Appleby (Athene Seyler) takes in lodgers to help out her income and also to provide money for her charitable work. The idea of crimes comes to her when she is able safely to return a fur which has been given to her as a present by her devoted maid (Billie Whitelaw), a reformed thief who is now going steady with a policeman. Argues Miss Seyler: "If stolen goods can be returned easily they should be able to be lifted just as safely."

Her "gang" consists of Terry-Thomas, a retired officer who plans the raids along strictly military lines, a daffy spinster (Elspeth Duxbury), and Hattie Jacques, a heavyweight teacher of deportment. This unlikely quartet carry off several daring raids, their exploits blessed by luck rather than judgment, and the escapades provide some amusing preposterous slapstick.

The humor is episodic, but a typical sequence is when Terry-Thomas goes to London's East End in search of a fence, landing up in a sinister saloon which turns out to have been taken over by the Salvation Army.

Robert Asher has directed Michael Pertwee's lively screenplay briskly enough, and the camerawork is okay. The four members of the gang do their chores admirably, with Athene Seyler outstanding, but the role calls for it. Terry-Thomas, to his advantage, has to play as part of a team. Billie Whitelaw, in a colorless role, confirms recent impressions of her deftness.

With such tried thesps as Noel Purcell, Michael Balfour, Raymond Huntley, Joan Heal, Sydney Tafler, Irene Handl, Kenneth Williams and Freddie Frinton on hand to chip in with useful fun cameos, the acting serves to skate over the occasional periods when this thin idea tends to lag. *Rich.*

Morte Di Un Amico
(Death of a Friend)
(ITALIAN)

Locarno, Aug. 9.

Warner Bros. release of Continental Films production. With Gianni Garko, Spiros Focas, Didi Petego, Angela Luce, Anna Mazzucchelli, Fanfulla. Directed by Franco Rossi. Screenplay, Giuseppe Berto, Oreste Biancoli, Pier Paolo Pasolini, Franco Rignati; camera, Toni Secchi; editor, Otello Colangeli. At Locarno Film Fest. Running time, **95 MINS.**

Aldo	Gianni Garko
Bruno	Spiros Focas
Lea	Didi Perego
Franca	Angela Luce
Adriana	Anna Mazzucchelli
De Amicis	Fanfulla
Il Francese	Andrea Scotti

This film concerns two friends who lead to each other's undoing and redemption of one, most delinquent of the pair via the tragic death of the other after a holdup. Pic is solidly made but is predictible and conventional. This looms mainly for language spots abroad. It does not have the tang for arty theatre chances.

One pal is a delinquent who lives off a joy girl and who gets the other to do the same. But the latter meets a good girl and tries to go to work. But all is ruined by the appearance of the prostie. The young man helping his friend in a robbery is killed.

Pic is sombrely directed. Acting is acceptable and technical credits are good. On its theme and okay execution, it might also be an okay offshore dual entry. *Mosk.*

Let's Make Love
COLOR-C'SCOPE)

Marilyn Monroe and Yves Montand great in a cheerful, light-weight comedy-with-music which stands to be one of year's b.o. smashes. A stylish, sophisticated production makes a creaky Cinderella vehicle shine like new.

20th-Fox release of Jerry Wald production. Stars Marilyn Monroe, Yves Montand, Tony Randall; guest stars Bing Crosby, Gene Kelly, Milton Berle; with Frankie Vaughan, Wilfred Hyde White, David Burns, Michael David, Mara Lynn, Dennis King Jr., Joe Besser, Madge Kennedy, Ray Foster, Mike Mason, John Craven, Harry Cheshire. Directed by George Cukor. Screenplay, Norman Krasna; additional material, Hal Kanter; camera (DeLuxecolor), Daniel L. Fapp; songs, Sammy Cahn, James Van Heusen; musical numbers staged by Jack Cole; music direction, Lionell Newman; asst. director, David Hall; editor, David Bretherton. Reviewed at Paramount, N.Y., Aug. 18, '60. Running time, **118 MINS.**

Amanda	Marilyn Monroe
Jean-Marc Clement	Yves Montand
Howard Coffman	Tony Randall
Tony Danton	Frankie Vaughan
John Wales	Wilfrid Hyde White
Oliver Burton	David Burns
Dave Kerry	Michael David
Lily Nyles	Mara Lynn
Abe Miller	Dennis King Jr.
Lamont	Joe Besser
Miss Manners	Madge Kennedy
Jimmie	Ray Foster
Yale	Mike Mason
Comstock	John Craven
Minister	Harry Cheshire
Bing Crosby	Himself
Gene Kelly	Himself
Milton Berle	Himself

With Marilyn Monroe and Yves Montand to ride the top of the marquee, producer Jerry Wald has what stands to be one of the box-office smashes of the year in "Let's Make Love," a cheerful lightweight comedy-with-music very familiar in form but still delightful in execution. Picture is overly long and has its dull patches, but those facts may be of interest only to academicians, not to the fans. It's like this:

After the film has been underway about 12 minutes, the screen goes suddenly dark (the scene is rehearsal of an off-Broadway show) and a lone spotlight picks up Miss Monroe wearing black tights and a sloppy wool sweater. She announces, with appropriate musical orchestration, that her name is Lolita and that she isn't allowed to play (pause) with boys (pause) because her heart belongs to daddy (words and music by Cole Porter). This not only launches the first of a series of elegantly designed (by Jack Cole) production numbers and marks one of the great star entrances ever made on the screen, but is typical of the entire film—which has taken something not too original (the Cinderella theme) and dressed it up like new.

Miss Monroe, of course, is a sheer delight in the tailor-made role of an off-Broadway actress who wants to better herself intellectually (she is going to night school to study geography), but she also has an uniquely talent co-star in Montand. Latter, seen here previously in such dramatic imports from France as "The Wages of Fear" and "Witches of Salem," gives a sock performance, full of both heart and humor, as the richest man in the world who wants to find a woman who'll love him for himself alone.

Although film could have benefited by letting Montand do more singing and dancing (he only gets a chance to do two small bits), picture indicates that he'll be one of big new stars on the U. S. scene. His is a very special quality that's sure to get to the femmes with something of the same impact Maurice Chevalier had a couple of generations back—and still has, for that matter.

The framework for this poor girl-rich boy romance is an original screenplay by Norman Krasna (with additional material by Hal Kanter) that focuses on the struggles of an off-Broadway troupe trying to stage a musical revue. Background affords easy opportunity for songs, dances and gags in reference to the contemporary New York scene. Montand, as a billionaire-playboy, gets involved in the revue when he learns (via VARIETY article) that he's going to be satirized in the show along with Maria Callas, Van Cliburn and Elvis Presley. Plot complications follow when Montand, to be near chorine Monroe, lets himself be hired (incognito) by the producers to portray himself.

This is, indeed a fragile frame, predictable in design, but it has been put together by experts. Under the direction of George Cukor, Miss Monroe and Montand give performances of warmth and appeal that are hardly suggested in the script. Then, too, whenever the story threatens to intrude with tedium, there's a knockout Cole musical number. In addition to "My Heart Belongs to Daddy," film introduces four new songs by Sammy Cahn and Jimmy Van Heusen, the best of which are the title song and something called "Specialization," which Miss Monroe and British rock 'n' roller Frankie Vaughan tear off with gusto.

Another highlight is a comedy sequence in which Montand brings on Milton Berle, Bing Crosby and Gene Kelly (playing themselves) to coach him in the musical comedy arts.

Aside from these gimmicks, picture gets solid support from Tony Randall, cast as Montand's worried p.r. man. It's not an exceptionally funny part, but because he plays it so straight, Randall gets a boff comedy reaction. Also prominently seen are the aforementioned Vaughan, making his U. S. film debut as star of the show-within-the-show; British character actor Wilfred Hyde White, as Montand's aide-de-camp, and David Burns, as producer of the revue.

Physical production is exceptionally fine, particularly Daniel L. Fapp's De Luxe color photography and the art direction of Lyle R. Wheeler and Gene Allen. Latter also designed the amusing prologue which, via lithographs, shows how Montand's forebears lived and died, making money and pursuing busty women. Lithos set the wry tone for all that comes after. *Anby.*

As the Sea Rages
(GERMAN)

Smattering of Adriatic culture in a sluggish, hazy melodrama. Fair art house possibilities on strength of star names, but doubtful starter in regular situations.

Hollywood, Aug. 11.
Columbia Pictures release of Carl Szokoll production. Stars Marie Schell, Cliff Robertson. Cameron Mitchell; with Peter Carsten, Fritz Tillmann, Ivan Kostic, Jovan Janecijevic, Duje Vujsic, Nikola Popovic. Directed by Horst Haechler. Screenplay, Jeffrey Dell, Jo Eisinger, based on original German of Walter Ulbrich, from novel, "Raubfisher in Hellas," by Werner Helwig; camera, Kurt Hasse; editor, Arndt Heyne; art directors, Otto Pischinger, Harta Hareiter, Tihomir Piletic; music, Friedrich Meyer; assistant directors, Ernest Hofbraver, Dragoljvb Stojanovic. Reviewed at the studio, Aug. 11, '60. Running time, 76 MINS.

There is a certain ethnic quality about "As The Sea Rages" that may interest Western Hemisphere customers to some degree. That and the presence of some familiar, and respected, players such as Maria Schell, may make this import a mild attraction in art house circles, but its appeal is otherwise decidedly limited in this country. The difficulty is basically one of communication, or the lack of it. The average American audience would be baffled and/or bored by the Columbia release.

It appears as if the Jeffrey Dell-Jo Eisinger screenplay (from a novel by Werner Helwig) is making an effort to convey something profound as it describes the perils encountered by a young, heroic seaman (Cliff Robertson) when he becomes entangled in a small, but bitter, war between Grecian fishing communities. But whatever symbolic overtones there are in the tale have been lost in the telling. After ridding one of the communities of an ugly dictatorial element (in the person of Cameron Mitchell), Robertson gives his life in a noble gesture to establish peace with the enemy. Left to mourn his passing is the maiden (Maria Schell) with whom he was preparing to leave the region of chaos for a supposed better world beyond the usual horizon.

Miss Schell, as a l w a y s, is luminously feminine, which is about all she is required to be. Robertson's otherwise sound delineation of the hero is spoiled by his failure to erase the cocky smile he wears whenever mortal combat looms. It doesn't look like fun at all.

The outstanding quality of the picture is Friedrich Meyer's plaintive music, based on original Greek motives. Kurt Hasse contributes some interesting camera work, particularly in long establishing shots of the bleak, but picturesque, region (the mountains of Morkengro and the Adriatic Sea). Dubbing and English translation leave a great deal to be desired. Horst Haechler directed rather sluggishly for Carl Szokoll, who produced the film in cooperation with Michael Arthur Film productions. *Tube.*

The Crowded Sky
(COLOR)

Slick but corny account of skyhigh traffic jams and romantic chaos in the jet age. Okay b.o. prospects.

Hollywood, Aug. 15.
Warner Bros. release of Michael Garrison production. Stars Dana Andrews, Rhonda Fleming, Efrem Zimbalist Jr., John Kerr, Anne Francis, Keenan Wynn, Troy Donahue, Joe Matell; with Patsy Kelly, Donald May, Louis Quinn, Edward Kemmer, Tom Gilson, Hollis Irving, Paul Genge, Jean Willes, Frieda Inescourt, Nan Leslie, Karen Green. Directed by Joseph Pevney. Screenplay, Charles Schnee, from the novel by Hank Searls; camera, Harry Stradling Sr.; editor, Tom McAdoo; art director, Eddie Imazu; music, Leonard Rosenman; sound, M. A. Merrick; assistant director, Chuck Hansen. Reviewed at the studio, Aug. 15, '60. Running time, 105 MINS.

Dick Barnett .... Dana Andrews
Cheryl Heath .... Rhonda Fleming
Dale Heath ....Efrem Zimbalist, Jr.
Mike Rule .... John Kerr
Kitty Foster .... Anne Francis
Nick Hyland ....Keenan Wynn
McVey ....Troy Donahue
Louis Capelli ....Joe Mantell
with
Gertrude Ross .... Patsy Kelly
Norm Coster .... Donald May
Sidney Schreiber .... Louis Quinn
Caesar .... Edward Kemmer
Rob Fermi .... Tom Gilson
Beatrice Wiley .... Hollis Irving
Samuel N. Poole .... Paul Genge
Gloria Panawek .... Jean Willes
Mrs. Mitchell .... Frieda Inescourt
Bev ....Nan Leslie

Warner Bros.' "The Crowded Sky" is a kind of jet-propelled variation on the studio's 1954 aerial excursion, "The High And The Mighty." Since that earlier effort proved that flying so high with a pic in the sky is not exactly the public's idea of nothing to do, this latter day altitudinous rumpus is likely to establish Warner Bros. Airlines as "the only way to fly."

But stowed away beneath the veneer of its something-for-everybody cast, visually diverting approach and fasten-your-seat-belts-it's-going-to-be-a-rough-ride tone lurks a melodramaful of the familiar neurotic kooks who invariably populate big movie shows in the sky but seem to be in hiding at one's favorite real-life airport. Gone, too, in this exercise is that great dramatic virtue, simplicity—wafted away in vapor trail of disjointed flashbacks. Also lost in the general preoccupation with multi-exposition is an all-important philosophical point-of-view. Yet, slick popular entertainment manages to crawl out of the creative wreckage.

Charles Schnee's screenplay, erected with mechanical professionalism out of the pages of Hank Searls' novel, explores the attitudes and personalities of a dozen or so romantically-distorted individuals aboard two aircraft destined for an untimely rendezvous aloft in "The Crowded Sky." It is this underlying note of impending doom and disaster that gives the film its wait-until-the-end vigor, but the interrupting flashbacks begin to grow tedious through sheer quantity. Additional defects are Joseph Pevney's patronizing directorial touches (zooming in on individual players for intimate personal observations that are at once obvious to the audience) and a good deal of artificially hip dialog manufactured by Schnee and/or Searls ("I'm an ex-tramp and I know myself—one kiss and then blast off"). There is, however, a certain wallop at the point of aerial impact that is likely to keep an audience vicariously spellbound as props are feathered, switches are pulled, passengers are buffeted about (a few star members of the troupe even meet their heavenly comeuppance in the process) and airports are soaked down with suds.

Michael Garrison's healthy-looking production, bathed in some brilliant orange-and-blue aviation-inspired Technicolor tints, has been captured vividly through Harry Stradling's lens, knit together with skill by editor Tom McAdoo, artistically designed by art director Eddie Imazu and embellished with a good 22,000-feet-up sounding score by Leonard Rosenman.

Pevney has put the cast through its paces in a commercial, if not overly believable manner. Dana Andrews handles the role of the pilot with juve-delinquent-son problems in his affably levelheaded fashion. Rhonda Fleming justifies her participation visually as the scheming spouse of Efrem Zimbalist Jr., who plays the doomed pilot of the other craft. Zimbalist, of tv's "77 Sunset Strip," reminds one of an animated George Raft. He dispatches his role attractively. John Kerr casually polishes off the angry young co-pilot niche, with the paired-off-with assistance of "stewardess" Anne Francis, whose striking good looks and brisk, businesslike approach to a role make her a valuable screen commodity. Keenan Wynn is interesting as a roue-writer who shares a rather inane romantic duel of avoid-the-altar egos with Jean Willes, who plays her offscreen-voice role mostly by ear. Troy Donahue, a winner for the teenage set, holds up his end of the dramatic fireworks nicely. Joe Mantell is especially good as a perishable flight engineer. Satisfactory support is generally less-than-enviable parts is constructed by Karen Green, Nan Leslie, Donald May, Louis Quinn, Edward Kemmer, Tom Gilson, Hollis Irving, Paul Gange and Frieda Inescourt. *Tube.*

Dentist In the Chair
(BRITISH)

Corny, slapstick farce which plays unabashedly for yocks; should be a big grosser in U.K. but lacks star value for U.S.

London, Aug. 16.
Renown release of a Bertram Ostrer production. Stars Bob Monkhouse, Peggy Cummins, Kenneth Connor, Eric Barker. Directed by Don Chaffey, Screenplay, Val Guest; additional dialog, Bob Monkhouse and George Wadmore; editor, Bill Lenny; camera, Reginald Wyer; music, Ken Jones. Previewed at Hammer Theatre, London. Running time, 88 MINS.

David Cookson .... Bob Monkhouse
Peggy Travers .... Peggy Cummins
Sam Field .... Kenneth Connor
The Dean .... Eric Barker
Brian Dexter .... Ronnie Stevens
Michaels .... Vincent Ball
Ethel .... Eleanor Summerfield
Mr. Watling .... Reginald Beckwith
Inspector Richardson .. Stuart Saunders
Dentist .... Ian Wallace
Miss Brent .... Peggy Simpson
Lucy .... Jean St. Clair
Woman in Surgery .. Charlotte Mitchel
Young Man in Surgery .. Philip Gilbert
Instructor .... Jeremy Hawk
Porter .... Harry Hutchinson
Wrestler .... Alfred Dean
Jayne .... Sheree Winton

Here's another in the currently successful boxoffice vogue of British slapstick farces which takes a tiny idea and wrestles with it energetically to produce yocks. "Dentist In Chair" disdains any pretension to subtlety. It hits home its comic points in a succession of ham situations, many irrelevant. An uneven cast manages to keep the fun bubbling precariously. In U.K., the thesps involved are sufficiently well known to be welcome, but none is big enough to make this a likely bet in the U.S.

Val Guest has provided a thin story line on a subject that on the surface hardly lends itself to merriment, dentistry. The plot is eked out by a string of sequences that seem like vaude sketches. Extra dialog has been provided by Bob Monkhouse and George Wadmore, and this is mainly used by Monkhouse himself as one of the leads. Unfortunately, he points most of the patter as if unleashing a radio script. However, some of it evokes guffaws from an indulgent audience.

Monkhouse and Ronnie Stevens are a couple of madcap dentistry students who, unwittingly, get involved with a smalltime burglar (Kenneth Connor). They find they are receivers of stolen property in the shape of burgled dentistry equipment. Their attempts to get rid of the hot loot before falling into the hands of the police provide a series of adventures.

Don Chaffey's direction tends to let the screenplay take care of itself but, helped by some energetic overplaying, the result is amiable minor league entertainment.

Kenneth Connor, as the crook who has to masquerade as a dentistry student, works hard and succesfully. He provides lots of amusement, even though he is left rather too much to his own resources. Eric Barker, as the dean of the hospital, shows a neat line in throwaway humor while Reginald Beckwith, playing a precise lecturer, as so often, rises above his material. Monkhouse and Stevens are adequate as the young students involved in the crime crisis. Vincent Ball, Eleanor Summerfield, Stuart Saunders and Harry Hutchinson turn in useful supporting performances. Peggy Cummins, as the heroine, has little to do but look pretty, a not to difficult task for her.

Dialog is largely facetious and relies overmuch on innuendo. Technically this modest comedy is okay. *Rich.*

The Half Pint

Lower berth number about a boy, a chimp and a hobo. Should be popular with juve audiences.

Hollywood, Aug. 19.
Sterling World Distribution Corp. release of Erven Jourdan production. With Pat Goldin, Tommy Blackman, Ray Cordell, Douglas Lockwood, Dinke. Directed by Jourdan; editor, Carl Mahakian. Reviewed at Consolidated Film Industries, Aug. 19, '60. Running time, 73 MINS.

The Tramp .... Pat Goldin
The Half Pint .... Tommy Blackman
Grandpa .... Ray Cordell
Sandy .... Douglas Lockwood
Tinker the Chimp .... Dinke

"The Half Pint," an itinerant study of a boy, a chimp and a hobo on the loose in Los Angeles, is a low-budget supporting item tailor-made for bring-the-whole-family situations and Saturday matinee playdates. It ought to go over big in children's sections, but wider appeal is limited by the absence of tighter construction via about 10-minutes worth of judicious snipping.

Erven Jourdan's production attempts to extract some humor, tension and mild pathos out of the path-crossing adventures of a hungry hobo, a runaway chimp and a six-year-old lad believed to be kidnapped. Humor is generated mostly

by juxtaposition of characters. The boy is pursuing the lost chimp, the chimp is pursuing the starving hobo who reverses his field to pursue the chimp when it swipes a bunch of bananas, and the police are pursuing all three of them. Jourdan, who directed the film, has a keen eye for interesting geometrical angles and patterns, a talent that helps his picture considerably.

Pat Goldin brings certain Chaplinesque touches to the role of the tramp, particularly in no-dialog business during the earlier portions of the film. Agreeable performances are chipped in by Tommy Blackman as the boy, Ray Cordell as his grandpa, Douglas Lockwood as a friend, and Dinke, the chimp. *Tube.*

Man Who Couldn't Walk
(BRITISH)

Modest, competent London crime yarn. Useful program filler with a main feature pic.

London, Aug. 16.

Butcher's release of a Bill and Michael Luckwell (Jock MacGregor-Umesh Malik) production. Stars Eric Pohlmann, Pat Clavin, Peter Reynolds, Reed De Rouen. Directed by Henry Cass. Story and screenplay, Mallik; editor, Robert Hill; camera, James Harvey; music, Wilfred Burns. Previewed at Celluloid Theatre, London. Running time, 65 MINS.

The Boss	Eric Pohlmann
Keefe	Peter Reynolds
Carol	Pat Clavin
Luigi	Reed De Rouen
Cora	Bernadette Milnes
Enrico	Robert Shaw
Beppo	Martin Cass
Maria	Margot van der Burgh
Lou	Martin Gordon
Joey	Maurice Bannister
Johnny	Andre Muller
Watchman No. 1	Owen Berry
Watchman No. 2	John Baker

Produced for a modest figure, this unpretentious crime yarn is intended strictly as a second feature and competently fulfils its mission. It might have been an even smoother job had it run longer than 65 minutes, but it has suffered one or two minor clippings from the censor. However, it's still a safe bet as a dualer.

This is a straightforward story of a young cracksman who joins up with a gang, dabbling in larceny and dope peddling, run by a sinister chairbound crook. It proceeds in fairly routine style, but builds up to an acceptable climax. Dialog is brisk and locations and sets look to be worth rather more than the coin invested. Editing is occasionally woolly, but James Harvey's lensing is okay while Wilfred Burns has turned in a lively score.

Thesping is in safe hands, with the dependable Eric Pohlmann, as the boss man and Peter Reynolds giving a cool, efficient performance as the young safecracker. Bernadette Milnes, Reed De Rouen, Andre Muller and Margot van der Burgh are among those who come up with useful roles. The film also gives the audience a first view of a new young leading lady, Pat Clavin. She is often at sea when it comes to emoting; but she has an interesting face and figure. And she has made a promising start, considering that the film was turned out in less than three weeks. Director Henry Cass has played safe and, after a slowish start, has kept the action moving at a commendable pace. *Rich.*

The Angel Wore Red

Unappealing meller about a mixed-up priest and a forthright prostitute thrown together at the outbreak of the Spanish Civil War. Contains some philosophical merit, but just not boxoffice stuff.

Hollywood, Aug. 24.

Metro release of Goffredo Lombardo production. Stars Ava Gardner, Dirk Bogarde, Joseph Cotten, Vittorio De Sica; with Aldo Fabrizi, Arnoldo Foa, Finlay Currie, Rossano Rory, Enrico Maria Salerno, Robert Bright, Franco Castellani, Bob Cunningham, Gustavo De Nardo, Nino Castelneuvo, Aldo Pini. Directed and screenplay by Nunnally Johnson; camera, Giuseppe Rotunno; editor, Louis Loeffler; art director, Piero Filippone; music, Bronislau Kaper; assistant directors, Mario Russo, Carlo Lastricati. Reviewed at the studio, Aug. 24, '60. Running time, 99 MINS.

Soledad	Ava Gardner
Arturo Carrera	Dirk Bogarde
Hawthorne	Joseph Cotten
Gen. Clave	Vittorio De Sica
Canon Rota	Aldo Fabrizi
Insurgent Major	Arnoldo Foa
Bishop	Finlay Currie
Mercedes	Rossano Rory
Capt. Botargas	Enrico Maria Salerno
Father Idlefonso	Robert Bright
Jose	Franco Castellani
Mac	Bob Cunningham
Major Garcia	Gustavo de Nardo
Capt. Trinidad	Nino Castelneuvo
Chaplain	Aldo Pini

It's hard to tell who are the bad guys and who are the good guys in "The Angel Wore Red," a love story of sorts set against the grim backdrop of the Spanish Civil War. Americans audiences, not fond of being either confounded or depressed are not likely to be attracted to this film, sexy ad campaign or no. Actually, there is considerable merit to both screenplay and execution, cardinal sin being simply that the Metro release is not quite good enough to be commercial. More than likely, it will wind up as a long, but strong, bottom half of double bills.

Nunnally Johnson's screenplay contains some perceptive dialog and sharp observations of the ironies of war. It describes the tribulations encountered by a disillusioned priest (Dirk Bogarde) who forsakes his vows just as civil war breaks out between the devout Falangist rebels and anti-church loyalists. While being pursued by the latter, he encounters and falls in love with a brave, kindhearted prostitute (is there another kind?), played by Ava Gardner. Both eventually are taken prisoner, and suffer considerable hardship in attempting to remain mum on the whereabouts of a holy relic which is vital to the loyalist cause from a morale standpoint. In the process, Bogarde chooses the church over his deep feelings for Miss Gardner, who sacrifices her life in a noble parting gesture for the rebel cause. While the love story is unfolding front and center, loyalists and Falangists and taking turns as background villains. A spectator is never really certain for whom he is supposed to be rooting. He feels obliged to take sides because the romance is dragging and Bogarde's eventual preference of church over sex is clearly predictable.

The director half of Johnson hasn't made the most of his material. There are several tedious passages, principally the romantic ones. There are inconsistencies in the relationship between casting importance and roles, notably in the case of Joseph Cotten, who is costarred in a virtually irrelevant part that could well have been eradicated entirely, which may reflect back to a decision by producer Goffredo Lombardo.

The acting is strong. Miss Gardner and Bogarde give good romantic accounts of themselves. Cotten is capable as a one-eyed American newscaster with four glass eyes, suitable for all occasions. Vittorio De Sica does fine as a disenchanted old-style general who views victory in modern warfare as "successful dirty tricks." Unfortunately, his voice has been replaced with a jarringly incompatible dubbed version, presumably for purposes of clearer articulation. Aldo Fabrizi stands out in the supporting cast, with favorable key efforts by Finlay Currie and Arnoldo Foa.

There is capable camera work by Giuseppe Rotunno, editing by Louis Loeffler, and art direction by Piero Filippone. Music by Bronislau Kaper has an appropriately romantic Spanish flavor. *Tube.*

La Grande Vie
(The High Life)
(W. GERMAN—FRENCH—ITALIAN)

Paris, Aug. 23.

Pathe release of Pathe-Capitole-Novella production. Stars Giulietta Masina, Hannes Messemer; features Gert Froebe, Ingrid Von Bergen. Directed by Julien Duvivier. Screenplay, Rene Barjavel, R. A. Stemmle from novel by Irmgard Keun; camera, E. Clunick; editor, W. Boos. At Paris, Paris. Running time, 100 MINS.

Doris	Giulietta Masina
Ernst	Hannes Messemer

Tripartite pic is a vivid example of what can happen in a coproduction when the various national talents employed do not quite jell. The French glibness and direct statement (director Julien Duvivier), the Italian penchant for overplaying (Giulietta Masina), and the heavy German attitude towards satire (script and supporting players), hamper this slice-of-life film. Make this film a dubious export item except for possible hypo on the name of Miss Masina.

Miss Masina is a slightly silly innocent on the screen for a man. It ends in a long succession of interludes. She emerges not quite so innocent in callously taking men from friends or deluding herself when she is kept woman. It is somewhat like the simple-minded character she played in "La Strada" with an element of sex added. The series of adventures are only intermittently amusing or revealing. Actually, Miss Masina has a tendency to mugg rather than act and it is hard to believe that she is physically appealing to the myriad of men in her life even though she has a piquant charm.

Director Julien Duvivier has given this a slick mounting but rarely makes this satire telling in its attempt to outline the difficulties of finding a man for the emancipated woman of today. Technical credits are good. However, this heavyhanded affair is a chancey item at best. *Mosk.*

El Impostor
(The Imposter)
(MEXICAN)

Mexico City, Aug. 23.

Peliculas Nacionales release of Clasa Films production. Stars Pedro Armendariz, Silva Derbez; features Amanda del Llano, Jaime Fernandez, Jose Elias Moreno. Screenplay, Emilio Fernandez from play by Rodolfo Usigli. Directed by Emilio Fernandez. At Cine Olimpia, Mexico City. Running time, 90 MINS.

This controversial film, withheld from exhibition for a number of years, finally achieved a brief run. Based on Rodolfo Usigli's "El Gesticulador" (The Demagogue), and covering the rise to power of Cesar Rubio (admirably played by Pedro Armendariz), this film is a bold denouncement of Mexican politics, its vices, faults and errors. Still, the film version is greatly toned down from the dramatic work which was first presented in this capital in 1947, and caused a sensation for its faithful depiction of certain Mexican politicians.

Though it lacks the courage and vigor of the dramatic work, the film still manages to hit below the belt and trample on the feelings of certain politicos. For this reason it is unpopular with some, but as a segment presenting dirty politics in all its aspects, and the ruthless rise to power of an ambitious man and his ultimate fall, it hews to the truth.

Emilio Fernandez, director of the picture, owes part of his unpopularity for his faithful presentation of Mexican political dirty linen, as far as they would let him. He had fought for a faithful reproduction on the screen of the Usigli work, and lost.

Silvia Derbez, as an ambitious young lady, and Jaime Fernandez, as an idealist, are convincing. Amanda del Llano is surprisingly good in a character role.

Because of its theme, this one may be but a poor moneymaker in Mexico. Pressure too will be exerted to keep it from being exhibited abroad. *Emil.*

Fast and Sexy
(FRENCH-ITALIAN-TECHNIRAMA-COLOR)

Flashy variation on a creaky romantic formula. Marquee oomph of Lollobrigida and tv star Dale Robertson will help, but foreign vintage and superficial nature of pic indicate domestic b.o. reluctance.

Hollywood, Aug. 18.

Columbia Pictures release of Milko Skofic production. Stars Gina Lollobrigida, Dale Robertson, Vittoria De Sica; with Carla Macelloni, Gabriella Pallotti, Luigi De Filippo, Mario Girotti, Clelia Matania, Augusta Ciolli, Renzo Cesana, Gigi Reder, Marso Tulli, Carlo Rizzo, Ruth Wolner, Molly Robinson, Amedeo Nazzari, Peppino De Filippo. Directed by Reginald Denham. Screenplay, E. M. Margadonna, Luciana Corda and Joseph Stefano, from original story by Margadonna and Dino Risi; camera, Giuseppe Rotunno; editor, Eraldo Da Roma; art director, Gastone Medin; music, Alessandro Cicognini and Vittorio De Sica; sound, Renato Cadueri; assistant directors, Luisa Alessandri, Carlo Lastricati, Anna Gruber. Reviewed at the studio, Aug. 18, '60. Running time, 99 MINS.

Made-in-Italy-by-Italians irreverence and gusto puts just enough pizza-cato into "Fast and Sexy" to counteract the predictable, deliberate formulese of its central boy-meets-girl storyline. Sporadic flashes of spicy wit and snappy dialog keep it alive and kicking whenever the tired basic premise seems on the verge of triumph. The names of its romantic leads may strike a certain responsive sexual chord among more avid filmgoers, but the Columbia release will need strong companion help to break

down domestic boxoffice resistance to nonspectacle arrivals from overseas.

The E. M. Margadonna-Luciana Corda-Joseph Stefano screenplay goes gagging around a slight central storyline in which a young, wealthy widow (Gina Lollobrigida), burning her Brooklyn "Brigidas" behind her, returns to her native Italian village and proceeds to charm all the eligible bachelors but one, the handsome, pithy village smithy (Dale Robertson). Given this premise, anyone familiar with popular romanticomedies can immediately deduce the outcome and relax for an amusing romp that only spasmodically materializes, almost exclusively when the town's confession-conscious but gossipy parish priest (engagingly played by Vittorio De Sica) takes over.

Some minor additional merriment is generated by the star attraction's three chief suitors, a deflated baron (Renzo Cesana), an impressionable mayor (Peppino De Filippo), and an enterprising film exhibitor-sheepman (Amadeo Nazzari). Miss Lollobrigida seems relaxed in her native environment, but Robertson most of the time appears homesick for the old Wells Fargo.

Dubbing handicap is not severe, with English dialog neatly incorporated by Stefano. Reginald Derham's direction for producer Milko Skofic keeps things moving along at a bright pace. Music by Alessandro Cicognini and De Sica takes charge in establishing the proper mood for each new scene—an important plus value. "Fast and Sexy" is a good-looking film, ably lensed by Giuseppe Rotunno and decked out in vivid Technicolor. *Tube*.

Tirez Sur le Pianiste
(Shoot the Pianist)
(FRENCH-DYALISCOPE)
Paris, Aug. 23.
Cocinor release of Pleiade production. Stars Charles Aznavour; features Nicole Berger, Marie Dubois, Michele Mercier, Albert Remy, Claude Mansart, Daniel Boulanger. Directed by Francois Truffaut. Screenplay, Truffaut, Marcel Moussy from novel by David Goodis; camera, Raoul Coutard; editor, Cecile Decugis. Preemed in Paris. Running time, 80 MINS.
Charlie ....Charles Aznavour
Theresa ....Nicole Berger
Lena ....Marie Dubois
Clarisse ....Michele Mercier
Chico ....Albert Remy
Momo ....Claude Mansart
Ernest ....Daniel Bulanger

Francois Truffaut, an ex-highbrow film critic, was responsible for one of the most touching among the "New Wave" pix with his "400 Blows." This second film is done with the same freewheeling, inventive quality. But with adult heroes the plot is less clear and has a tendency to skirt its theme story line, too, goes off in too many directions and moods.

Truffaut still displays an unusual visual flair. The production is strewn with excellent scenes and revealing, incisive statements. But it floats between a gangster opus and a tale about a timid young man whose inability to act leads to the destruction of the women in his life.

Charlie (Charles Aznavour) is a pianist in a little bar. The waitress, who loves him, reveals she knows he was once a noted concert pianist before his inability to for-

give his wife, who had had an affair with his sleazy impresario. He is content to play in the bar until his brother brings in two gangsters whom he has doublecrossed.

The gangsters take out after Charlie and eventually slay the waitress. Charlie also inadvertently kills his boss in self-defense. He goes back to his piano and a new serving girl after it is all over.

Truffaut leaves too much that is not clear as he concentrates on individual scenes. Using a C'Scope-like process, Dyaliscope, he still manages to give this a terse quality in keeping with the hero's own prison he has created within himself. But the meandering script only intermittently makes its point. However, his offbeat technical aspects still give this enough quality to make it a possible arty theatre entry abroad. The aimless progression may make it more difficult for subsequent-runs.

Aznavour is excellent as the pianist in making himself felt despite the negative quality of his timidity. Truffaut still seems one of the most endowed among the "Wavers." And when he gets down to more uncluttered plots, he should be an important part of the film scene here.

Technical credits are good with on-the-spot lensing a help. *Mosk*.

Le Bois Des Amants
(Lovers' Woods)
(FRENCH)
Paris, Aug. 16.
Cocinor release of Hoche-Dama production. Stars Laurent Terzieff, Erika Remberg; features Horst Frank, Gert Froebe, Jean Verner, Francoise Rosay. Directed by Claude Autant-Lara. Screenplay, Jacques Remy, Rene Hardy; camera, Jacques Natteau; editor, Madeleine Gug. At Colisee, Paris. Running time, 95 MINS.
Charles ....Laurent Terzieff
Herta ....Erika Remberg
Von Stauffen ....Horst Frank
General ....Gert. Froebe
Interpreter ....Jean Verner
Parisot ....Francoise Rosay

Contrived war film gives enough insight into its characters caught in the web of the last World War to make it unusual enough for much export value. It might be okay for the Continent, but pic emerges somewhat too talky and forced for arties abroad.

A German girl forges a pass to see her officer husband in occupied France. She is lodged in an isolated house and her husband cannot join her because of the hunt for a Frenchman parachuted in by the English. All this, even if it is Xmas Eve.

Director Claude Autant-Lara has rarely infused the true feeling of muddled enemies into this. The story is not helped by callow acting, flat dialog and heavyhanded direction. Technical credits are good but this seems old fashioned. *Mosk*.

Venice Films

Holubice
(The White Dove)
(CZECHOSLOVAKIAN)
Venice, Aug. 26.
Czechoslovenski Film Production. Features Katerina Irmanovova, Hans-Peter

Reinicke, Karel Symczek, Vjaceslav Irmanov, Gustav Puttjer. Directed by Frantisek Vlacil. Story, Otakar Kirchner. Camera, Jan Curik. Music, Zdenek Liska. At Venice Film Festival. Aug. 25, 1960. Running time, 76 MINS.

Stylized, splendidly lensed item with many qualities of mood and feeling, but very limited audience possibilities outside the specialized orbit. General audiences will find this in-competition pic's esthetic digressions, for all their visual charm and beauty, very tedious and somewhat old hat.

Story tells of a white carrier pigeon which loses it way home to a Baltic island and lands instead on a Prague rooftop where, injured, it's saved by a young paralyzed child. Curing the bird also cures the child, and it eventually makes its way back to its home perch. Embroidery on this basic plot skein makes up bulk of the pic, and it's here that director Frantisek Vlacil (on his first film) and cameraman Jan Curik combine to produce some of the most beautiful images seen on the screen for a long time in depicting the effect of the dove's absence or presence on one or the other of the two drastically different environments in the pic.

It's a remarkable first effort, but a limited one audience-wise. Acting ably fits the mood and pace imposed, and technical credits, especially the above-mentioned lensing, are excellent. *Hawk*.

Un, Deux, Trois, Quatre!
(One, Two, Three, Four!)
(FRENCH-TECHNIRAMA 70M-COLOR-DANCE)
Venice, Aug. 24.
British Lion release of GPC-Talma Films-Doperfilme-Joseph Kaufman production. Stars Cyd Charisse, Moira Shearer, Zizi Jeanmaire, Roland Petit; features Dick Sanders, Hans Van Manen, George Reich. Directed by Terence Young. Choreography and ballets by Roland Petit; music, Georges Bizet, Jean-Michel Damase, Maurice Thiriet, Marius Constant; sets and costumes, Georges Wakhevitch, Andre Clave, Bazarte, Yves Saint Laurent; camera (Technicolor, 70m), Henri Alekan; editor, Francoise Javet. At Venice Film Fest. Running time, 140 MINS.

Roland Petit, whose mixture of sensuous movement, musical comedy and decorative flair revved up the classic ballet scene internationally some years ago has had four of his ballets filmed and bundled into a pic with such names as Cyd Charisse, Zizi Jeanmaire and Moira Shearer for marquee value. But this is an overlong purely dance pic in spite of diversity in moods and content.

There is color and production value in the bigscreen 70m pic, and this could obviously have some potent possibilities for ballet fanciers; this makes it primarily an art entry abroad, with probable roadshow aspects called for by virtue of its scope and size. For more general auds it will need a hard sell since it is all terp.

Maurice Chevalier is used as an emcee to intro each segment and give some storyline detail when necessary. This he does with his usual charm and suggestiveness. First up is a fantasy of a diamond-eating pickpocket gal in the market section of Paris who is finally tamed by a truck driver; then comes a version of "Cyrano De Bergerac," a merry widow bit in turn-of-the-century Paris and a torrid adaptation of "Carmen."

First one seems somewhat theatrical and does not quite get the inventive handling it needs. "Cyrano" has some dash and color and its romantic, more classical aspects at times give it a colorful note. The third one is a frothy tale of a widow who can not resist going on the town, and "Carmen" has a flashy, eye-catching quality that transcribes the tragic lovers well.

Director Terence Young has concentrated on the dance with primarily head-on shots with some happy slow motion bits at times. But this makes the ordinary ballet company a hindrance with mainly the principals shining. Petit's choreography ranges from graceful to staccato to acrobatic but only intermittently gives the film a quality that blends action, visual flair and decors. However he denotes a solid mime and thespic flair as well as a good dance style to make his various characters in the ballets, and especially "Cyrano," gather dimension and personality.

Miss Charisse is the widow with worldly ideas and has zest while Miss Shearer is a willowy, graceful Roxane in "Cyrano" but not up to a combo of the girlish guile and womanliness needed for the part. Miss Jeanmaire has a sinewy sensual grace in "Carmen" that make her hold on the hapless soldier acceptable in spite of her gamin looks. She does a solid stint as the diamond eater.

Color is good with some uneven patches that can be corrected since this is a first print for out-of-competition participation at the Venice Fest. Costumes and sets are expansions of theatrical sets, and music is fitting for this cross section of Petit's ballet work. British Lion has invested in this pic for Anglo rights and may act as go-between for U. S. spotting. It has the earmarks of a fine video spectacular after theatre runs. *Mosk*.

Shadows
Venice, Aug. 25.
Maurice McEndree-Pnico Papatakis release and production. With Lelia Goldoni, Ben Caruther, Tony Ray, Hugh Hurd. Directed by John Cassavetes. Screenplay, improvised by cast and director; camera, Eric Kolmar; editor, Len Appleson; music, Charles Mingus. At Venice Film Fest. Running time, 84 MINS.
Lelia ....Lelia Goldoni
Ben ....Ben Caruther
Tony ....Tony Ray
Hugh ....Hugh Hurd

First made in 16m as an exercise in improvisation by a group of actors directed by John Cassavetes, a w.k. thesp himself, "Shadows" was then filled out and blown up to 35m under the supervision of two producers. It came in for $40,000, and a recent showing at the British Film Institute got it raves and an advance from British Lion of $25,000. It has edge and insight and looms a good art entry in its home country the U. S., plus a possible playoff bet since its theme and treatment overcome the direct purposely simple technical aspects.

A brother and sister who look white have a brother who is completely Negro. The film dwells on the dramatic interludes in their lives and the inevitable race problems. The girl is 20 and unsure of her emotions until her first affair is marred by a cowardly reaction to the revelation of her col-

or by her lover. The white looking brother drifts through various adventures with too unanchored white friends, and the Negro brother is a singer accepting his fate of trying to work in low dive shows and getting along with his edgy sister and brother.

There are explosions of anger and maladjustment as well as moments of self realization and insight. The girl finds some measure of undrestanding with a Negro, the drifting brother, after a fight over an attempted pickup, gets some glimmer of a need to choose a way of life, and the singing brother goes on his way trying to find his place, bolstered by the friendship of his agent.

Nothing rings false in the film. Though the narrative is rambling it strikes solid truths and dimension in showing people living and reacting in a manner which is dictated from within rather than forced on them by a script. Pic, in its improvised form, has actors working from general situations within an agreed outline. Dialog comes over as right and with sting and wit. A party, a trip to a museum by the three fringe characters, a sudden, violent fight over some girls, the flareup of race tensions are all handled well and give the pic punch and drive.

The grainy film is an asset to the theme, and though made without a real script, there are not many jump cuts but a brash, unorthodox cutting technique that helps put across the reactions of its protagonists. Acting is of a piece in spite of the technique, for all have built their characters beforehand and played them in various scenes with control. The jumpy, nervous jazz background music is also an asset.

Lelia Goldoni has nervous charm, guile and vulnerability as the girl, Ben Caruther possesses the sullen violence of solitude and indecision, and Hugh Hurd has warmth and understanding as the breadwinning brother. Here is a case where an unusual approach has paid off with a pic that gives an incisive picture of human tensions and problems without preaching or proselytizing. Cassavetes has given this form and a point of view without trying to solve anything but letting the characters express themselves. There is no attempt at technique but the story and action carries itself and New York is an essential part of this unique film.

The "New Wave" tag has been overworked on certain French films and U. S. pix made outside the established industrial Yank trends. But "Shadows" is new in its bite, drive and intensity and its insistence on content over form. It needs special handling but its theme and potency could make this an offbeater with potential. It got a fine response in an out-of-competish spot in the Info Section at the Venice Fest. *Mosk.*

Vers L'Extase
(Towards Ecstasy)
(FRENCH)

Venice, Aug. 25.
Pathe release of Matignon production. Stars Pascale Petit; features Giani Esposito, Lysiane Rey, Monique Melinand, Michel Ardan. Directed by Rene Wheeler. Screenplay, Wheeler, Charles Spaak; camera, Christian Matras; editor, Renee Lichtig. At Venice Film Fest. Running time, **90 MINS.**
Catherine .... Pascale Petit
Jerome .... Giani Esposito
Woman .... Lysiane Rey
Man .... Michel Ardan
Priest .... Michel Etcheverry
Mother .... Monique Melinand

Film concerns a young, exalted girl looking for grace and communion with God. She gets married, though fearing it, to leave her petty family and goes to live in Morocco. Here she leaves her husband to get a job as a maid and humble herself. She does not succeed and goes back to her husband.

Pic is confused and static and can not convey the theme with clarity and depth. Result is a slow-moving affair that looms of little export value. Pascale Petit cannot do much with this foggy role and others are sketchy. Technical credits are fair but, in all, this is an attempt at depicting a search for belief and grace that does not come off. Miss Petit, a promising actress, has had three bad ones in a row and needs a good pic, if her possibilities are not to be lost. *Mosk.*

Under Ten Flags
(U.S.-ITALIAN)

Strong screen translation of World War II sea experiences of Nazi raiding vessel commander Bernhard Rogge, bolstered by first-rate acting but hampered by unnecessary subplots. Domestic b.o. response depends largely on extent of favorable word-of-mouth.

Hollywood, Aug. 29.
Paramount release of Dino De Laurentiis production. Stars Van Heflin, Charles Laughton; features Mylene Demongeot, John Ericson, Cecil Parker, Folco Lulli, Alex Nicol, Liam Redmond, Eleonora Rossi Drago, Gregoire Aslan. Directed by Duilio Coletti. Screenplay, Vittoriano Petrilli, Coletti, Ulrich Mohr, based on original diaries by Bernhard Rogge; camera, Aldo Tonti; editor, Jerry Webb; art director, Mario Garbuglia; music, Nino Rota; sound, Piero Cavazzuti; assistant directors, Mario Maffei, Davide Carbonari. Reviewed at Paramount, Aug. 29, '60. Running time, **92 MINS.**
Commander Reger .... Van Heflin
Admiral Russell ...... Charles Laughton
Zizi .... Mylene Demongeot
Krueger .... John Ericson
Col. Howard .... Cecil Parker
Paco .... Folco Lulli
Knoche .... Alex Nicol
Windsor .... Liam Redmond
Sara .... Eleonora Rossi Drago

When it sticks to its central issue—the tactical military duel between a foxy but humanitarian Nazi commander (Van Heflin) and a determined Churchillian admiral (Charles Laughton)—"Under Ten Flags" is a Grade A war film, a gripping, intriguing glimpse into one of World War II's most fascinating sea stories. But the Dino De Laurentiis production is tarnished by a tendency to stray off on irrelevant and undernourished character tangents and incidental sexploitation stuff that might better have been left on the cutting room floor (as indeed, most of it seems to have been, judging by the film's herky-jerky pace).

Fortunately, the basic story is dominant and, embellished by some acting of the first magnitude, ought to appeal to American cinematic appetites as good war films invariably do. So, although the Paramount release, being of largely foreign vintage, is no boxoffice shoo-in, it has the dramatic quality to spur enthusiasm among those who take it in—and can do reasonably well if its supporters are talkative enough.

The screenplay by Vittoriano Petrilli, Duilio Coletti and Ulrich Mohr is based on the diaries and autobiographical tome by Bernhard Rogge. Film deals chiefly with the exploits of the Nazi masquerraiding surface vessel, "Atlantis," captained by the surprisingly decent and scrupulous Rogge, portrayed by Heflin. As the British admiralty, headed by Laughton, desperately strives to pinpoint its position, the Atlantis proceeds to play cat and mouse with British shipping, posing as a friendly freighter under any one of a number of "personalities" it easily adopts via a complete array of flags, costumes and quick-change artistry until the enemy ship is caught unawares within range of its hidden artillery. The story is distinguished by the character of Captain Rogge, a man "full of ideas like fighting a clean war." Eventually the schizophrenic ship he commands is destroyed by the successful efforts of British intelligence to unscramble a vital Nazi code.

The abrupt departure from Nazi stereotype here is liable to disturb some filmgoers who will stand for no association between Nazism and decency, but the authentic nature and objective tone of the film ought to curb any such partisan outrage. Far more disturbing is the picture's patchwork quality when it deals with secondary characters. Even the important element of time is jumbled once or twice. Director Duilio Coletti appears to have had his troubles coordinating the project with De Laurentiis—deciding what to leave in, what to take out and, with editor Jerry Webb, where to splice in what was left of the original footage. Aldo Tonti's camera work is competent, Mario Garbuglia's art direction authentic and seaworthy. Nino Rota's music is adequate and dubbing is barely noticeable when incorporated.

Heflin gives a solid account of himself in the central role—a sincere, soft-spoken, sensitive portrayal. The comic overtones of Laughton's staunch performance make his character that much more interesting—a sort of merger of the characteristics of Captain Bligh and Churchill. John Ericson and Mylene Demongeot are stuck with unenviable roles, and can do little to make them three-dimensional. Distinguished support is fashioned by Cecil Parker, Alex Nicol, and Liam Redmond, with solid assistance from Gregoire Aslan and decorative aid from Eleonora Rossi Drago. *Tube.*

I Aim at the Stars

Generally exciting but occasionally evasive account of the life and times of scientist Wernher von Braun. B.o. prospects depend on extent of public curiosity about controversy surrounding the man.

Hollywood, Sept. 1.
Columbia Pictures release of Charles H. Schneer production. Stars Curt Jurgens, Victoria Shaw, Herbert Lom, Gia Scala, James Daly; with Adrian Hoven, Gerard Heinz, Karel Stepanek, Peter Capell, Hayden Rorke, Austin Willis, Alan Gifford, Helmo Kindermann, Lea Seidl, John Crawford. Directed by J. Lee Thompson. Screenplay, Jay Dratler, from story by George Froeschel, U. Wolter, H. W. John; camera, Wilkie Cooper; editor, Frederick Wilson; art director, Hans Berthel; music, Laurie Johnson; sound, Walter Ruhland; assistant directors, Karl Elsner, Hans Sommer. Reviewed at Columbia, Sept. 1, '60. Running time, **106 MINS.**

The timely and provocative story of Wernher von Braun is tackled tastefully in Charles H. Schneer's production of "I Aim At The Stars." Although the film has a tendency to aim too much at the stars and too superficially into the man, it sheds some worthwhile light on a new variation of an age-old philosophical puzzler—is genius exempt from the ethical and moral codes that govern man's behavior?

It is the sort of topic certain to spur debate and controversy (as, indeed, it has already within the industry), an argument factor that will be an important boxoffice stimulus, and is likely to mean the difference between profit and loss for Columbia.

Terse comments and perceptive observations abound in Jay Dratler's screenplay from a story by George Froeschel, U. Wolter and H. W. John, but several of the most vital junctures in von Braun's

complicated life are sloughed over unsatisfactorily. The film gets off to an explosive start, laboring little with unnecessary exposition, sweeping the spectator right into the heat of Nazi V-2 base Peenemunde, where the hero (Curt Jurgens) comes into focus as a nonpolitical instrument bullied into the Nazi cause by dint of his invaluable scientific genius. These scenes are the most arresting in the picture.

But from the point at which von Braun surrenders to U.S. authorities, an evasiveness is detectable. The reason for his choice of the U.S. over the USSR (certainly an enterprising one) is never fully clear, nor is America's hasty acceptance of Nazi scientists explored sufficiently. U.S. resentment of opposition to von Braun is embodied in one man (James Daly), a character of questionable motivation. Daly plays an army major embittered over the V-2 death of his wife and child in London. Just why an American would bring his wife and child to evacuated London at the apex of V-2 attacks is a jarring inconsistency of the plot. The character, a key one, emerges more of a symbolic device than a man as he leads a personal crusade against von Braun, whose attempts to shake the U.S. out of its postwar space lethargy make up the bulk of the latter half of the film. There is, of course, a pro-von Braun point -of-view, but it is subtly understated, never hurled at the viewer by Dratler's scenario.

Cinematically, it is an exciting, artfully constructed picture. Director J. Lee Thompson has instilled a whirlwind pace, making capital of the many rocket blastoffs (particularly some dandy launching pad fizles) which supply natural bridges between sequences. Frederick Wilson's editing successfully culminates Schneer's brisk, businesslike conception and Thompson's aggressive execution. Additionally helpful are Wilkie Cooper's sensitive camera work, Hans Berthel's accurate art direction and Laurie Johnson's stimulating music.

Jurgens plays the hero with quiet, persuasive intensity—a smooth, believable enactment. Victoria Shaw agreeably supplies his love interest. The major romance of the picture, however, takes place between one of von Braun's chief aides (Herbert Lom) and his secretary (Gia Scala), who is actually a spy for the Allies. It is a rather fuzzy relationship, but both skillfully execute their roles. Daly gives an earnest portrayal, making the most of a one-note character. Support is of uniformly high calibre. *Tube.*

End of Innocence
(ARGENTINE)

Kinsley International release of Mayron Pictures presentation and Argentine Sono Film production. Stars Elsa Daniel; features Lautaro Murua, Guillermo Battaglia, Jordana Fain, Berta Ortegosa, Barbara Mujica, Alejandro Rey, Lili Gacel. Directed by Leopoldo Torre Nilsson. Screenplay, Beatriz Guido, Nilsson, Martin Rodriguez Mentasti, based on novel by Miss Guido; camera, Anibal Gonzalez Paz; musi, Juan Carlos Paz. Reviewd at Paris Theatre, N. Y., Aug. 9, '60. Running time, 76 MINS.

(English Subtitles)

Here is a fascinating film worthy of the best playing time which discriminating art house exhibs can give it. "End of Innocence" (original title in Spanish: "House of The Angel") serves to introduce U.S. audiences to the fact that the Argentine film industry, almost unknown Stateside, can turn out pictures of firstrate quality, both technically and artistically. And, being the first such in this market, "Innocence" should create business-building interest and excitement among artie patrons on the lookout for the new and different.

Although film won a best-actress award for star Elsa Daniel at last year's Cannes film fest, "Innocence" is really a director's picture, a vivid, complex production that manages to tell a deeply subjective personal story that illuminates a whole time and place. For this reason, young Argentine director Leopoldo Torre Nilsson would seem to be a talent who will shortly rank alongside—if not ahead of—some of the more flashy and highly publicized of the French "new wavers."

Story is deceptively simple in outline: a sweet and innocent 16-year-old girl, reared within the strict confines of a fantastically Catholic household in Buenos Aires, is traumatically stripped of that innocence when she is seduced by her father's best friend. Life goes on and she is left only with a memory that is, in effect, a permanent scar. The film, however, is a good deal more than just another she-had-to-go-and-do-it item. Tale is told against the background of wealth, ignorance and political turmoil in the Argentina of the late 1920s.

With cinematic economy, director Nilsson manages to suggest a political and social climate in details seldom seen outside of a novel. This is all the more amazing since the film seldom leaves its central character, the little girl who is so protected that the nude statues on her father's estate are wrapped up in bedsheets when the children are around.

By means of quick, brilliantly drawn scenes such as one in the Argentine senate, where a debate on freedom of the press is going on, or another in which the heroine's mother argues religion with a taxi cab driver, film evokes a complete milieu which, in turn, makes the central situation totally believable and spiritually shattering.

Miss Daniel, who looks like a young Ingrid Bergman, is most appealing in the key role. Equally good, though, are Lautaro Murua as the well-meaning but callous seducer; Guillermo Battaglia as her noble old father, the kind of man who thinks the double standard was decreed by God, and Berta Ortegosa as the latter's wife, a cold and bitter woman for whom life is just one long preparation for the grave.

While somewhat literary in effect, picture is completely cinematic in form, beautifully edited and photographed, and, after the introductory scenes, swift in pace. Nilsson, Martin Rodriguez and Beatriz Guido did the screen adaptation from Miss Guido's novel. English subtitles are perfectly adequate. *Anby.*

Venice Films

Le Voyage En Ballon
(Voyage in a Balloon) (FRENCH-RYALISCOPE—COLOR

Venice, Aug. 30.

Cinedis release of Filmsonor-Montsouris production. With Maurice Baquet, Andre Gille, Pascal Lamorisse. Written and directed by Albert Lamorisse. Camera (Eastmancolor), Maurice Fellous, Guy Tabary; editor, Pierre Gillette. At Venice Film Fest. Running time, 85 MINS.

Pascal	Pascal Lamorisse
Grandfather	Andre Gille
Aide	Maurice Baquet

Albert Lamorisse has made two half hour shorts, "White Mane" and "The Red Balloon," which got festival kudos in the past and emerged boxoffice draws despite their length. His first feature is somewhat tenuous but with enough of the whimsy, assiduous workmanship and fringe poetics of his first films to make this stay the route and emerge a probable arty house entry abroad. It has enough entertainment angles for possible depth spotting.

In his previous pix, young boys finally fled the world of cruel and unthinking adults via a white horse disappearing into the sea or being carried away by a balloon. In this, a youth takes a trip around France in a balloon with his eccentric grandfather, finally to have it run away with him but in his escaping when the balloon takes out alone over the sea.

Lamorisse constructed a special non-vibrating camera setup to allow for some stunning helicopter shots around Paris and France. He seems to be enamored of old unchanging things and the grandfather appears anachronistic as he builds a Jules Vernetype balloon today for his trip during which his grandson stows away.

The balloon intrudes on a stag hunt, covers a forest fire, scales Mount Blanc, delves into Paris for some new, beautiful aspects of this much filmed capital city, and, in general, manages to include enough surprises to keep this from being repititious. It might seem precious in this jet age but has the repose, inventiveness and hard work to make this an unusual film with word-of-mouth a probable added plus factor.

Color is excellent and lensing adroit while it keeps the film progressive without any resort to back ground projection. Comic relief is added by an aid following the balloon in an old car that can take off by itself when necessary.

Actors are acceptable but it is the lensing conception and execution that make the film. *Mosk.*

I Delfini
(The Dauphins) (ITALIAN)

Venice, Sept. 6.

Lux Film release of a Lux-Vides production. Stars Claudia Cardinale, Gerard Blain, Annamaria Ferrero, Betsy Blair, Sergio Fantoni, Tomas Milian, with Claudio Gora, Antonella Lualdi. Directed by Francesco Maselli. Screenplay, Maselli, DeConcini, Aggeo Savoli, Alberto Moravia. Camera, Gianni di Venanzo; music, Giovanni Fusco; editor, Ruggero Mastroianni. At Film Festival, Venice. Running time, 110 MINS.

Fedora	Claudia Cardinale
Anselmo	Gerard Blain
Chere'	Betsy Blair
Marina	Annamaria Ferrero
Mario	Sergio Fantoni
Alberto	Tomas Milian
Ridolfi	Claudio Gora
Elsa	Antonella Lualdi

Elegantly produced by Franco Cristaldi, this in-competition pic looks a good boxoffice entry for the home (Italo) market, where combo of names, exploitable story elements and a distant affinity with "La Dolce Vita" will help it on its way. Export chances appear more limited, though the European market offers spotty possibilities.

Story deals with the empty lives lived by some rich young provincial bluebloods, the "Dauphins" of the title, and of the attempts of an outsider, Claudio Cardinale, to crash into the group of friends in an Italian small town where everyone knows everyone else. Several plot skeins are intertwined, replete with secret and wide-open love affairs, adulterous and otherwise, with nary a good sentiment showing on the winning side in this sharp accusal of hinterland mores. It's a slick third effort by young director Francesco Maselli, showing his increased maturity but at the same time a loss of feeling for his material, which as a result projects coldly and matter-of-factly events and feelings which should hit out with a strong emotional impact.

Acting is on a similar competent level, often badly served by indifferent, only at times pungent, material by a crew of scripters which includes novelist Alberto Moravia. Sergio Fantoni, Tomas Milian, Claudo Gora, and Annamaria Ferrero come off best in the thesping race, though Claudia Cardinale registers in many scenes on looks and performance and definitely headed up. Betsy Blair performs creditably but appears miscast, and Gerard Blain and Antonella Lualdi rarely have a chance to shine through an opaque script. Superior elements in the pic are certain sequences in which Maselli, greatly aided by lenser Gianni di Venanzo's expert lighting effort, unerringly depicts the uneventful and drab provincial life and its backdrops, and a jarring sequence in which actor Milian takes his temporary amour, Miss Cardinale, for a violent thrill ride in his Ferrari. Added nod to Giovanni Fusco for his musical scoring. All other credits in this production are top drawer. *Hawk.*

Krzyzacy
(Knights of the Teutonic Order) (POLISH)

Venice, Sept. 6.

Film Polski release of a Studio production. Features Urszula Modrzynska, Grazyna Staniszewska, Andrzej Szalawski, Henryk Borowski, Aleksander Fogiel, Mieczyslaw Kalenik, Emil Karewicz, Tadeusz Kosudarski. Directed by Aleksonder Ford. Screenplay, Ford, Jerzy Stawinski, from novel by Henryk Sienkefic; camera, (Eastmancolor-Dyaliscope). Mieczislaw Jahoda; music, Kazimierz Serocki; editor, Miroslawa Garlicka. At Venice Film Fest. Running time, 180 MINS.

Jaglenka	Urszula Modrzynska
Danusia	Grazyna Staniszawska
Jurand	Andrzej Szalawski
Zygrfyd de Lowe	Henryk Borowski
Macko	Aleksander Fogiel

Gigantic production effort of this Polish color epic is unfortunately not equaled by like entertainment values, despite some exciting battle and duel sequences which constitute its high points. The remainder is generally tedious

and talky pastiche telling of the rivalry between Poles and the Teutonic Knights in 14th and 15th Century Poland.

It culminates in the victory of the home forces after a spectacular battle. Its expert chances are all in the general market via dubbed form. However, heavy trimming is needed to slash the three-hour stretch to more reasonable footage.

Director Alegsander Ford obviously has taken Olivier and Eisenstein as his examples in shaping this one, yet the pic has neither the grandeur of latter's "Alexander Nievski" nor the warm vibrance of former's "Henry V."

Plus elements are often the splendid color lensing by Mieczyslaw Jahoda, especially in exteriors and battle scenes. Costumes and some interiors are too garish. Thespic aspects fit the needs of such a pic, with competent acting in all sectors of a large and varied cast.

Script rarely wavers from a propagandistic position in which Poles are painted white and (Germanic) Teutonic Knights and their religious fervor hued blacker than black. Pic looks a likely top grosser in Poland and perhops some other Eastern countries. *Hawk.*

Alaztosan Jeletem
(A Certain Major)
(HUNGARIAN)

Venice, Aug. 30.

Hungaro Film release of Hunnia production. With Miklos Gabor, Adam Szirtos, Tivadar Uray, Gyorgy Palos, Eva Ruttkay. Directed by Mihaly Semes. Screenplay, Laszlo Boka; camera, Ferenc Szecsenyi: editor, Eva Tormassy. At Venice Film Fest. Running time 100 MINS.

Major	Miklos Gabor
Sergt.	Adam Szirtes
Adjutant	Tivadar Uray
General	Gyorgy Uray
Bella	Eva Ruttkay

This concerns a career military man in the Hungarian army before the last World War under the dictator Horthy. It shows his closed mind in the midst of corruption and his final demise when the German's slaughter mutinying Magyars during the later days of that war. But the pic is somewhat one-sided and ends on a propagandist note for the Russian cause.

This vehicle thus looms of little export value. It has some insight into blind army ways, and denotes a telling flair for subtle human relations. It is well mounted and acted but seems mainly a bet for Hungary. *Mosk.*

El Cochecito
(The Little Motor Bike)
(SPANISH)

Venice, Sept. 6.

Portabella Films release and production. With Jose Isbert, Pedro Porcel, J. Lopez Vazquez, Luisa Ponte, Lepe. Directed by Marco Ferreri. Screenplay, Rafael Azcona, Ferreri; camera, Juan Julio Baena; editor, Pedro Del Rey. At Venice Film Fest. Running time. 81 MINS.

Anselmo	Jose Isbert
Carlos	Pedro Porcel
Alvarito	J. Lopez Vazquez
Matilde	Luisa Ponte
Luces	Lepe

Dealing with a theme, complications and people which could be morbid, sentimental or distasteful, this successfully emerges a mordant, ironic comedy with deft human and social insight and with all the earmarks of possible art spotting. It could also make general booking abroad if well handled and well dubbed.

An old man has a friend who is crippled and goes about in a little motor bike specially made for him. He becomes friendly with some people who use similar bikes and decides he is handicapped without one and demands one from his son, a tightfisted lawyer. The family refuses and he finally poisons them all to buy and keep his bike.

Director Marco Ferreri displays a firm feeling for satire and there is never any self-pity or bad taste evident in handling the crippled people. And the conflict between the old man's desire for liberty and friendship and the grasping, unseeing family is locked out with humor, timing and perception.

Jose Isbert is a natural comic figure as the old mumbling grumbling good hearted little man who only wants to be with the people who have accepted him. On-the-spot lensing helps and technical credits and thesping fit the spirited aspect of the pic. Some of the sudden moves of the old man, like poisoning the family, may jolt but are worked well into the fabric of this offbeater. *Mosk.*

Mikkai
(Secret Meeting)
(JAPANESE-SCOPE)

Venice, Sept. 6.

Nikkatsu production and release with Yoko Katsuragi, Seiji Miyyaguchi, Yuko Chikakao Hosokawa. Directed by Ko Nakasira. Screenplay, Akira Yoshimura; camera, Yoshihiro Yamazakia; editor, Masonari Tsujii. At Vence Film Fest. Running time, 74 MINS.

Kikuko	Yoko Katsuragi
Yuichiro	Seiji Miyaguchi
Sayo	Yuko Chiyo
Chikako	Noriko Hosokawa

Japanese film is reminiscent of the many Yank dramas in which adulterous couples end up with each other's undoing. This is slickly made and patly put together, but is not original enough for anything but dualer chances abroad.

A woman married to an older professor has an affair with one of his students. At one of their trysts in a park one night, they witness a murder. When he decides to go the police, she pushes him under a train in desperation because of her fear of scandal. Acting is good and direction gives this pace. The technical credits are fine. This also has a nice jazz music backgrounding. *Mosk.*

La Lunga Notte Del '43
(That Long Night in 1943)
(ITALIAN)

Venice, Aug. 30.

Euro International release of an Ajace-Euro production. Stars Belinda Lee, Gabriele Ferzetti, Enrico Maria Salerno, Gino Cervi; features Andrea Cecchi, Nerio Bernardi, Raffaella Pelloni, Isa Querio, Alice Clements, Loris Bazzocchi, Carlo di Maggio, Silla Bettini. Directed by Florestano Vancini. Screenplay, Vancini, Pier Paolo Pasolini, Ennio De Concini from story by Giorgio Bassani; camera, Carlo di Palma. At Venice Film Fest. Running time, 110 MINS.

Anna	Belinda Lee
Barilari	Enrico Maria Salerno
Franco	Gabriele Ferzetti
Aretusi	Gino Cervi

Well-made straightforward vehicle which brings to life once more some of the more dramatic moments in recent Italian history and the months towards the end of the last World War when Italians cruelly fought Italians behind the lines of battle. Major impact, however, is on the local ticketbuyer who is able to catch nuances and the import of dialog, scenes, and action. Expert values appear to indicate specialized slotting only.

Florestano Vancini has directed his first feature in creditable fashion, with a good feeling for period atmosphere. He has had his actors underplay most scenes to good effect. Yet this same understatement keys a certain lack of drama which results in long stretches of tedium where crisper handling would have won a wider audience. For a production treating such heartfelt problems, the pic rarely grips nor is the illicit love affair moving or believable.

Basic plot line has a woman betray her paralyzed husband for her younger ex-fiance. On one of her nightly absences, she's caught up in a Fascist roundup and while she and the lover escape the latter's father is brutally executed with other innocent citizens. Pic here becomes an anti-Fascist pamphlet, gist of which is that guilty onetime Fascist terrorists are still present in Italian society. Acting is competent in all sectors, special nod perhaps being due for Enrico Maria Salerno's performance as the semi-paralyzed husband who watches the doings through the years from a window position. Lensing by Carlo di Palma is especially good in capturing foggy-grey wartime years in the Po Valley where action takes place. Other technical credits are tops. *Hawk.*

Les Annees Folles
(The Mad Years)
(FRENCH-DOCUMENTARY)

Venice, Aug. 30.

Pathe production and release. Compiled by, and commentary with editing by Mirca Alexandresco, Henri Torrent. Commentary spoken by Serge Reggiani. At Venice Film Fest. Running time, 90 MINS.

A pic montage, sagely chosen from old newsreel footage and films from 1919 to 1929, this adroitly sums up these hectic years of change, abandon and sudden sobering. Not preachy, this is an objective, as far as possible, compilation with an informative commentary plus good editing.

The first World War is summed up and then the modes and happenings of the world are shown with the return to a Paris in the gaudy time of change, flappers, Charleston, art fads, etc. The personalities of the day, the heroes, Lindberg's trip and many other events build this into an engrossing looksee at the times. Though this has seldom seen sequences, it is not unique enough for anything but specialized supporting fare.

Editing is good. Besides a look at Paris, it delves into the world happenings during that gawdy period. It shows again that old film adroitly packaged with a good compact outline and commentary can be entertainment as well as educational fodder. It also illustrates that there is still gold in those old film cans if intelligently mined. *Mosk.*

The Dark at the Top of the Stairs
(TECHNICOLOR)

Excellent film version of William Inge's fine play. Needs selling but has quality to come through handsomely.

Hollywood, Sept. 6.

Warner Bros. release of Michael Garrison production. Stars Robert Preston, Dorothy McGuire; costars Eve Arden, Angela Lansbury, Shirley Knight; features Lee Kinsolving, Frank Overton, Robert Eyer, Penney Parker, Ken Lynch. Directed by Delbert Mann. Screenplay, Harrit Frank Jr. and Irving Ravetch, from play by William Inge; camera, Harry Stradling Sr.; art director, Leo K. Kuter; editor, Folmar Blangsted; music, Max Steiner; sound, Stanley Jones; assistant director, Russell Llewellyn. Reviewed at the WB, Sept. 12, '60. Running time, 123 MINS.

Rubin	Robert Preston
Cora	Dorothy McGuire
Lottie	Eve Arden
Mavis	Angela Lansbury
Reenie	Shirley Knight
Sammy	Lee Kinsolving
Morris	Frank Overton
Sonny	Robert Eyer
Flirt	Penney Parker
Harry Ralston	Ken Lynch

In just a few minutes more than two hours, Warner Bros.' "The Dark at the Top of the Stairs" recounts the frustrations of a lifetime. There's an unusual kind of something for-everybody in this probing, sentimental essay, making you feel better by proving the other fellow feels worse. The picture poses a peculiar selling problem in which fair-to-good pre-sold values must be bolstered by word-of-mouth. The fine Michael Garrison prdouction, ably directed by Delbert Mann, has in it the spirit to spark that word-of-mouth, and commercial prospects could be high.

The William Inge play on which the picture is based is a poignant study of an Oklahoma family torn by internal conflicts. It provides a salable title that should start the b.o. ball rolling uphill; it provides a moving story, skillfully adapted by Harriet Frank Jr. and Irving Ravetch, that should sustain the drive.

"Dark" falls somewhere between family and adult entertainment. Its relationships are barred with perception and penetration, and the problems of a young girl finding love and a young boy finding security are aspects of the film that should be noted by every youngster. The problems of the picture's parents, described in frank terms but handled in good taste, center on the bed and the activities which do, or more accurately, do not, take place in it.

The film is well cast and persuasively acted. Its chief cast value lies in Robert Preston, whose newly-won fame via "The Music Man" can be used to spur boxoffice for the WB picture. Easily detectable is the similarity in manner and speech between Harold Hill of "Music Man" and Rubin Flood of "Dark," both as portrayed by Preston. Each is a high-powered salesmen—one flamboyant, the other serious. But there's a strength and an independence that's the same. Preston is excellent as Flood, just as he was as Hill.

Dorothy McGuire is tops as the mother caught between devotion to her children and the knowledge she must sever the cord. With sensitivity, she is believable through all phases of her role. Eve Arden is convincing and highly effective as the sister, performing with spirit and proving she could have done

even more with her "big scene" if given the chance. Angela Lansbury plays one of her better and more sympathetic roles as the woman who wants Rubin, and she fills it well.

Shirley Knight is fine as the daughter, graphically showing signs of development. This part should boost Miss Knight's career considerably. Lee Kinsolving is first-rate as the ill-fated suitor. Frank Overton is effective as the brother-in-law, as are Robert Eyer as the son, Penney Parker as a bubbling friend and Ken Lynch as a rich oilman.

"Dark" is Garrison's second film, establishing him as a talented, tasteful producer and a filmmaker to watch. The picture additionally is another fine screen achievement for director Mann, in whose hands the excellent Frank-Ravetch screenplay becomes a human, compassionate drama balanced by warm comedy. The makers of this film have created a sense of honesty which, while sometimes overbearing in its unhappiness, sweeps real characters through a real world.

Harry Stradling Sr.'s Technicolor photography is rich, with art director Leo K. Kuter and set decorator George James Hopkins accurately catching the spirit of the period. Max Steiner has added a flowing musical score, aiding the film's emotional triggers. Film editor Folmar Blangsted kept a brisk pace going, and Stanley Jones' sound is tops, as are Marjorie Best's costumes. *Ron.*

Seven Ways From Sundown

Well-made oater with Audie Murphy and Barry Sullivan for okay marquee.

Hollywood, Sept. 8.

Universal-International release of Gordon Kay production. Stars Audie Murphy, Barry Sullivan; features Venetia Stevenson, John McIntire. Directed by Harry Keller. Screenplay, Clair Huffaker from his own novel; camera, Ellis Carter; editor, Tony Martinelli; art direction, Alexander Colitzen, William Newberry; music, William Lava, Irving Gertz; sound, Waldon O. Watson, William Russell; assistant director, Thomas J. Connors Jr. Reviewed at U-I, Sept. 6, '60. Running time, 86 MINS.

Seven Jones	Audie Murphy
Jim Flood	Barry Sullivan
Joy Karrington	Venetia Stevenson
Sergeant Hennessey	John McIntire
Lieutenant Herly	Kenneth Tobey
Ma Kerrington	Mary Field
Graves	Ken Lynch
Lucinda	Suzanne Lloyd
Fogarty	Ward Ramsey
Duncan	Don Collier
Beeker	Jack Kruschen
Gilda	Claudia Barrett
Jody	Teddy Rooney
Dorton	Don Haggerty
Eavens	Robert Burton
Chief Waggoner	Fred Graham
2nd Wagoner	Dale Van Sickle

"Seven Ways From Sundown" is a well-made oater which, despite story flaws, should do nicely at the top of the bill in its own market and lend solid support to double bills in the general market, thanks to well-meshed production elements brought together by producer Gordon Kay and to picture's good cast, headed by Audie Murphy and Barry Sullivan.

Murphy portrays a tyro Texas Ranger apprenticed to an elder Ranger (John McIntire) in search of a daring and debonair outlaw, Jim Flood, portrayed by Sullivan. Flood bushwhacks the elder Ranger but is subsequently captured by the tyro, named Seven-Ways-From-Sundown Jones (result of odd parental humor).

What's fine about the film is the consistent high quality of acting by the aforementioned principals, all of whom turn in excellent characterizations, and the sturdy support given by Kenneth Tobey and others, notably Suzanne Lloyd, a looker who impresses in a barfly bith.

Director Harry Keller smoothly builds up a good deal of suspense and Ellis Carter, cinematographer, has done a first-rate job of Eastman Color photography, particularly in the attractive and realistic night scenes. Except for some story flaws, screen writer Clair Huffaker has done an interesting and effective job on his own novel. Tony Martinelli has cut the footage effectively and all other departments are up to par. *Glen.*

Desire In the Dust
(CINEMASCOPE)

Sex and violence in the Deep South. Exploitable but silly imitation of Faulkner involving fratricide, insanity, adultery and suggestions of incest. Sensational elements could pay off.

20th-Fix release of A.P.I. production, produced by William F. Claxton. Stars Raymond Burr, Martha Hyer, Joan Bennett; features Ken Scott, Brett Halsey, Anne Helm, Jack Ging. Directed by Claxton. Screenplay, Charles Lang, based on novel by Harry Whittington; camera, Lucien Ballard; editor, Richard Farrell; sound, Jerry Trayler. Reviewed in N.Y., Sept. 9, '60. Running time, 102 MINS.

Colonel Ben Marquand	Raymond Burr
Melinda Marquand	Martha Hyer
Mrs. Marquand	Joan Bennett
Lonnie Wilson	Ken Scott
Dr. Ned Thomas	Brett Halsey
Cass Wilson	Anne Helm
Peter Marquand	Jack Ging
Luke Connett	Edward Binns
Maude Wilson	Maggie Mahoney
Zuba Wilson	Douglas Fowley
Sheriff Otis Wheaton	Kelly Thordsen
Burt Crane	Rex Ingram
Nora Finney	Irene Ryan
Thurman Case	Paul Baxley
Virg	Robert Earle
Nellie	Patricia Snow
Conductor	Elemore Morgan
Frank	Audrey Moore
Roy (Bartender)	Joseph Sidney Felps
Deputy	Joe Paul Steiner

Here's another sexy and violent turn through the red clay country which has served both William Faulkner and 20th-Fox so well in times past ("The Long Hot Summer" and "The Sound and The Fury". "Desire in The Dust," however, is a pale imitation of those earlier works, a synthetic, essentially pointless tale of greed and lust in the backwaters of the present-day South. Sensational plot elements, including fratricide, adultery, insanity and suggestions of incest, might well pique boxoffice interest among the indiscriminating fans.

Picture has a good cast headed by Raymond Burr, Martha Hyer and Joan Bennett, plus a number of promising young players, but they are all stymied by Charles Lang's overcharged and cliche-ridden screenplay from a Harry Whittington novel which contains enough plots for three films. Physical production, fortunately, is excellent, particularly Lucien Ballard's crystal-clear black and white CinemaScope camera-work, which creates a mood and authentic atmosphere never reflected in melodrama itself.

Hero of the piece is a young scrub farmer (Ken Scott), who returns to his home town after serving six years in the chain gang on a manslaughter charge of which he is innocent. It quickly turns out that he took the rap for Miss Hyer, with whom he was having an affair at the time of the "accident" and whose wealthy daddy, Raymond Burr, has aspirations to be governor and didn't want a scandal. Seems that the victim of the accident was Miss Hyer's little brother, the four-year-old son of Burr and Miss Bennett, and that Miss Bennett, who witnessed the accident has been insane ever since.

Scott returns to town with every intention of resuming with Miss Hyer, which he does for one night, after which he learns that while he has been gone she has married the young doctor treating her mother. And Miss Hyer is the kind of brazen dame who, when upbraided by Scott for infidelity to him, suggests, in all seriousness, that "half a loaf is better than none." Like any noble young perjurer, Scott is furious and eventually succeeds in exposing both daughter and father who, in the end, are left with just each other, which seems to suit them fine. They have a "close" relationship.

Though producer-director William Claxton has succeeded in injecting quite a bit of surface excitement in the film, none of it is more than skin-deep. Thus Miss Bennett, looking as lovely as ever, is saddled with a silly illness and preposterous, split-second recovery of her senses when the accident in which her son was killed is reenacted by a couple of amateur psychiatrists. Miss Hyer and Burr also are strictly papier-mache.

The newcomers in the cast—Scott, Anne Helm, Jack Ging, Brett Halsey—fare better, perhaps because they don't have to strike such melodramatic attitudes. Also contributing good support are Ed Binns, as a crusading newspaper editor; Kelly Thordsen, as a crooked sheriff; and Maggie Mahoney and Douglas Fowley, as a couple of earnest cracker types. *Anby.*

Beyond the Time Barrier

Uninspired sci-fi meller-with-a-message. Usual sex science-and-spectacle hard sell could rack up ample b.o.

Hollywood, Aug. 31.

American International release of Robert Clarke production. Stars Clarke, Darlene Tompkins; with Arianne Arden, Vladimir Sokoloff, Stephen Bekassy, John van Dreelen, Red Morgan, Ken Knox, Don Flournoy, Tom Ravick, Neil Fletcher, Jack Herman, William Shapard, James Altgens, John Loughney, Russell Marker. Directed by Edgar G. Ulmer. Screenplay and original story, Arthur G. Pierce; camera, Meredith M. Nicholson; editor, Jack Ruggiero; music, Darrell Calker; sound, Earl Snyder; assistant director, Leonard J. Shapiro. Reviewed at Stanley-Warner Hollywood Theatre, Aug. 31, '60. Running time, 75 MINS.

Major William Allison	Robert Clarke
Trirene	Darlene Tompkins
Markova	Arianne Arden
The Supreme	Vladimir Sokoloff
Karl Kruse	Stephen Bekassy
Dr. Bourman	John van Dreelen
The Captain	Red Morgan
Colonel Martin	Ken Knox
Mutant	Don Flournoy
Mutant	Tom Ravick
Air Force Chief of Staff	Neil Fletcher
Dr. Richman	Jack Herman
General York	William Shapard
Secretary Patterson	James Altgens
General LaMont	John Loughney
Colonel Curtis	Russell Marker

That familiar world of the future, the one with the antiseptic underground civilization governed by a benevolent despot who has a sexy daughter and a wicked right hand man, turns up again in American International's "Beyond the Time Barrier."

The only ingredient that distinguishes this effort from its many predecessors is the presence of a timely political message—lay off the nuclear testing 'cause the cosmic rays will get you if you don't watch out. This preach-peace aspect is put over with some impact via the absence of the expected happy ending, but it is preceded by too much quasi-scientific mumbo-jumbo and melodramatic absurdity to register with a desirable degree of conviction. Nevertheless, the promise of sex, science and spectacle (the three big S's of the exploitation pic) ought to do the customary effective job of selling this less-than-awe-inspiring picture for AIP in the market for which it is intended.

According to Arthur G. Pierce's screenplay, an early space explorer (Robert Clarke, who doubles as producer-star) crosses the fifth dimension via the speed of light and a resultant "relativity paradox," winds up in the year 2024, finds mankind paying the fee (everybody is sterile save the leader's daughter) for its 1960-71 nuclear meddling. Object is that he get back to 1960 by reverse "relativity paradox" so he can tip off contemporary powers about what's to become of mankind if man isn't kinder, to fellow man, pronto.

Clarke, the actor, does some of the more capable emoting in Clarke, the producer's, picture. Any doubts that glamour won't exist in 2024 are dispelled by Darlene Tompkins, who plays the head man's daughter, a deaf-mute with ESP and sex appeal. Key roles are dispatched in mechanical fashion by Arianne Arden, Vladimir Sokoloff, Stephen Bekassy and John van Dreelen. Director Edgar G. Ulmer fares favorably when the action is set in 1960, but his conception of 2024 behavior leaves a lot to be desired.

The film is technically and artistically sound, if uninspired. Meredith M. Nicholson's lenswork is accomplished, Ernst Fegte's production design familiar but workable, and Darrell Calker's music futuristically electronic-sounding, embellished with the inevitable bleep-bleeps and swoops of the sound department. Editor Jack Ruggiero utilizes a technique popular in filmdom's early serials, cutting in and out of scenes via geometrical wipes. It makes the picture seem that much more dated, which is a deadly factor in science-fiction. *Tube.*

Pancho Villa y la Valentina
(Pancho Villa and Valentina)
(MEXICAN-COLOR)

Mexico City, Sept. 6.

Peliculas Nacionales release of Ismael Rodriguez production. Stars Pedro Armendariz, Elsa Aguirre; features Carlos Moctezuma, Humberto Almazan; guest appearances by Domingo Solor, Emilia Guiu, Arturo Martinez. Directed by

Ismael Rodriguez. Screenplay, Ismael Rodriguez. At Mariscala Theatre Mexico City. Running time, **90 MINS.**

This year celebrates the 50th anni of the Mexican Revolution and the motion picture industry has made a series of productions on the revolutionary era, with many of them centering around the legendary figure of Pancho Villa who may be a bandit in American eyes but who, in the last two years, has attained the stature of a Mexican hero.

Pedro Armendariz interprets Villa and makeup department has made a real resemblance to the bandit-revolutionary. This one treats of the love life of Villa with Elsa Aguirre, in her farewell film appearance, playing the role of Valentina, femme revolutionary.

Story is pure fantasy, with little regard for historical events. And instead of a true picture of Villa's personality, there is more stress on anecdote and improbability than on reality. Villa turns out in this one as bandit at times, high-minded lover of his country in others; then a naive country bumpkin and in other sequences as one of Mexico's geniuses of the revolution.

But with the current public popularity of Pancho Villa, the picture has been well received. In isolated scenes at least, this gives a slight inkling of the man outside of legend. *Emil.*

September Storm
(STEREOVISION-C'SCOPE-DE LUXE COLOR)

Trite treasure hunt saga with 3-D and some exciting scenics for main draw. Routine story shapes as an okay programmer with some juve trade appeal.

Chicago, Sept. 9.

Twentieth-Fox release of Edwin L. Alperson production. Stars Joanne Dru, Mark Stevens, Robert Strauss, Asher Dann; features Jean Pierre Kerien, Claude Ivry, Vera Valmont, G. Ariel, Adam Genette. Directed by Byron Haskin. Screenplay, W. R. Burnett; camera, Jorge Stahl Jr.; editor, Alberto Valenzuela; art director, Boris Leven; special effects, Jack Cosgrove; music, Edwin L. Alperson Jr., Raoul Kraushaar; underwater camera, Lamar Boren; underwater director, Paul Stader. Reviewed at Oriental Theatre, Chicago, Sept. 9, '60. Running time, **110 MINS.**

Another 3-D entry, this one called Stereo-Vision, and some prominent vistas of storied Majorca furnish the salient interest in Edwin L. Alperson's "September Storm," an otherwise routine adventure yarn that sends three men and a woman in pursuit of a multimillion dollar sunken gold horde.

The predictable storm at sea and some underwater shots for skin-diving fans breathe the only other life in this little-ado-about-nothing item in Cinemascope and De Luxe color.

As with earlier dimensional efforts, this one also requires those bothersome Polaroid spectacles, but for most audiences the generally sharp and realistic quality of Stereo-Vision should compensate. Unfortunately, process requires simultaneous use of both projectors, necessitating about a 10-minute intermission for which poor provision was made in the story line. Moreover, too little advantage has been made of the optic novelty in tracking the gold—a flaw in part due to Jorge Stahl Jr.'s stiff camera work. By the denouement, it's clear some 15-20 minutes could easily have been clipped.

Film introduces Asher Dann, an improbably handsome specimen who isn't likely to impress on anything but looks in this debut. However, in fairness, his role is too flat and corny to fairly gauge the depth of his talent; but his "new face" presence could be a selling point with the juve trade.

W. R. Burnett's screenplay concerns a couple of boat bums—Mark Stevens and Robert Strauss—who connive to get Dann to run them out on the classy yacht of his Parisian employer. Joanne Dru is aboard for the usual ambivalences vis a vis Stevens, and all three men pursue her.

There's good underwater lensing by Lamar Boren, and Alberto Valenzuela's editing is okay. Byron Haskin's direction is slow-paced and almost uninterested, though it's hard to see how he could have done much better under the script burden. The score by Edwin L. Alperson Jr. and Raoul Kraushaar doesn't intrude especially, and Ray Mercer draws credit for the "optical research." *Pit.*

Piccadilly Third Stop
(BRITISH)

Conventional, but quite brisk, thriller based on the "robbery - that - goes - amiss" idea; okay booking for popular houses.

London, Sept. 6.

Rank release of a Sydney Box Associates (Norman Williams) production. Stars Terence Morgan, Yoko Tani, Mai Zetterling, William Hartnell, John Crawford, Dennis Price. Directed by Wolf Rilla. Story, screenplay by Leigh Vance; camera, Ernest Steward; editor, Bernard Gribble; music, Philip Green. At Leicester-square Theatre, London. Running time, **90 MINS**

Dominic	Terence Morgan
Fina	Yoko Tani
Pready	John Crawford
Christine	Mai Zetterling
Colonel	William Hartnell
Edward	Dennis Price
Mouse	Ann Lynn
Toddy	Charles Kay
Albert	Douglas Robinson
Bride's Mother	Gillian Haude
Bride's Father	Trevor Reid
Police Sergeant	Ronald Leigh Hunt

There has been a recent spate of pix dealing with the activities of gangs of crooks whose daring robberies go astray and lead to a sock climax before justice is served. "Piccadilly Third Stop" hardly pretends to be in the first league with such films, but it's brisk enough with good performances. It should be a very acceptable booking for popular houses.

Leigh Vance's screenplay packs plenty of events, dialog is smooth and the final chase is sufficiently taut. Terence Morgan is a smooth petty crook who works with John Crawford, a tough smuggler. He introduces suckers to Dennis Price's gambling parties. He meets the naive daughter of a foreign ambassador in London (Yoko Tani), who innocently reveals that her father is out of the country and that in the embassy safe is $280,000 in cash. Morgan plans to steal the dough. He seduces Miss Tani who is so infatuated that she agrees to help Morgan in the robbery. He works it out in great detail.

Wolf Rilla's direction is crisp and straightforward while the thesping places no great strain on the cast. Morgan once again effectively plays smooth, dangerous playboy crook. Crawford makes a very heavy "heavy," but the role calls for it. Price is firstclass as the suave, ruthless gambling boss.

Best of the male performances comes from William Hartnell, as the vet safecracker. Hartnell gets a chance to play a middle-aged character part which requires amusing observation. The two women, the misses Mai Zetterling and Tani, are both comely but well wasted.

The London atmosphere is well done. Final sequences below the subway rate a nosegay for the art and production departments. Philip Green's music, as usual, plays an unobtrusive but colorful part in the proceedings. *Rich.*

The Night Fighters

Unexciting Irish war meller for program market with Robert Mitchum for the marquee.

Hollywood, Sept. 8.

United Artists release of a DRM-Raymond Stross production. Stars Robert Mitchum, Anne Heywood, Dan O'Herlihy, Cyril Cusack, Richard Harris; with Marianne Benet, Niall MacGinnis, Harry Brogan, Eileen Crowe, Geoffrey Golden, Hilton Edwards, Wilfrid Downing, Christopher Rhodes, Eddie Golden. Directed by Tay Garnett. Screenplay, Robert Wright Campbell, from book, "A Terrible Beauty," by Arthur Roth; camera, Stephen Dade; editor, Peter Tanner; art director, John Stoll; music, Cedric Thorpe Davis; sound, Roy Baker; assistant director, Frank Ernst; second unit camera, Lionel Baines. Reviewed at Goldwyn Studio, Sept. 8, 1960. Running time, **89 MINS.**

Dermot O'Neill	Robert Mitchum
Neeve Donnelly	Anne Heywood
Don McGonnis	Dan O'Herlihy
Jimmy Hannafin	Cyril Cusack
Sean Reilly	Richard Harris
Bella O'Neill	Marianne Benet
Ned O'Neill	Niall MacGinnis
Patrick O'Neill	Harry Brogan
Kathleen O'Neill	Eileen Crowe
Sergeant Crawley	Geoffrey Golden
Father McGrory	Hilton Edwards
Quinn	Wilfrid Downing
Malone	Christopher Rhodes
Corrigan	Eddie Golden

This Irish potato was apparently too hot for producer Raymond Stross and Robert Mitchum's DRM Productions to handle. Although overall production is good, the attempt to justify the hero without justifying his cause — Irish collaboration with the Nazis during World War II—confuses the story and undermines the actors. It looks like program bookings in secondary markets for this one.

Screenplay suffers, perhaps, from an embarrassment of riches: the omnipresent dreamy Irish atmosphere, Nazi saboteurs, political interference by the church, grinding poverty, IRA intrigue, age-old British-Irish conflict. Against this backdrop are played too many personal dramas to be handled effectively in 89 minutes.

The hero, Dermot O'Neill (Mitchum), is a powerful, sleeping giant of a man who, against his better judgment, joins the local contingent of outlawed Irish Republican Army to help harass the British out of Northern Ireland. He disapproves but tolerates the IRA's collaboration with Nazi Germany.

Attempt to deal with this and several subplots results in some scenes being brief to the point of unintentional humor; motivations and some problems are left unresolved. Tay Garnett's direction does little to mitigate this objection to the Robert Wright Campbell screenplay, yet there are touching love scenes between Mitchum and Anne Heywood and many scenes soak up the rich atmosphere of Ireland, where the film was shot. Total effect is that of unevenness.

Mitchum etches an absorbing portrait through most of the picture but, when the hero fails to be particularly heroic, the characterization languishes. Richard Harris, as the hero's buddy, and Miss Heywood, as the sweetheart, have some fine moments. Dan O'Herlihy's role is stereotyped but he conquers it from time to time. Cyril Cusack is skilled as always.

Technical aspects are satisfactory. *Glen.*

Sands of the Desert
(BRITISH-COLOR)

Charlie Drake, top tele comic, makes slapstick debut here; fun often is strained, but should satisfy Drake's fans. An "iffy" deal for the U. S.

London, Sept. 8.

Warner-Pathe release of an Associated British (Gordon T. Scott) production. Stars Charlie Drake, Peter Arne, Sarah Branch. Producer, Gordon T. Scott. Directed by John Paddy Carstairs. Screenplay by John Paddy Carstairs, from story by Robert Hall, Anne Burnaby; additional dialog, Charlie Drake; camera, Gilbert Taylor; editor, Richard Best; music, Stanley Black. Previewed at Pathe Equipment Studio. Running time, **92 MINS.**

Charlie Sands	Charlie Drake
El Jabez	Peter Arne
Janet	Sarah Branch
Bossom	Raymond Huntley
Sheik Ibrahim	Peter Illing
Abdullah	Harold Kasket
Adviser to Shiek	Marne Maitland
Hassan	Neil McCarthy
Pilot	Paul Stassino
Mamud	Derek Sydney
Mustafa	Alan Tilvern
Selim	Martin Benson
Scrobin	Eric Pohlmann
Nerima	Rebecca Dignam
Philpots	Charles Carson
Yasmin	Judoth Furse
1st Tourist	Robert Brown
British Consul	William Kendall
Fahid	Inia Wiata

Charlie Drake, a tubby, curly-haired little comedian, has become one of Britain's top tv comedians. This is his first screen effort under his longterm contract with Associated British. They've teamed him with director John Paddy Carstairs, a deft hand at comedy pix. Result is an unabashed slapstick farce. The fun is uneven. Whereas 30 minutes of Drake in his own tele show is okay with many, 92 minutes of such a specialized comedian tends to pall. However, "Sands of the Desert" should please the faithful Drake following.

This has Drake as a clerk in a travel agency who is sent to open a desert holiday camp. He runs into trouble with some thugs of a local sheik, who is determined the camp shall not open because it is on land which the sheik knows to contain oil. Eventually, the two warring tribes come together, Drake gets the camp opened, the oil is discovered and his employer hails him as a genius.

There's nothing wrong in bringing in such old friends. Drake energetically extracts the fullest quota of mirth from his material.

But, on this showing, he is a repetitious comic, and it may be difficult in the future to find fresh angles for his brand of comedy. He is surrounded by some competent performers who, playing it straight, help to exaggerate the farcical proceedings. Raymond Huntley, as Drake's pompous boss; Peter Arne, as the sheik who wants to stop the camp opening; Harold Kasket, Marne Maitland, Neil McCarthy, Derek Sydney, Alan Tilvern, Peter Illing and Eric Pohlmann all help build up the yarn. There's also a pleasant piece of work by a grave-eyed child, Rebecca Digman. Apart from the harem charmers, the only sizable femme part is that of Sarah Branch, as a newspaper reporter.

Color and lensing is good, but the editing, as so often in this sort of film where one situation rarely leads to another, is often erratic. "Desert" will do okay with undiscriminating audiences, but Drake might have been well advised to have thinned down on his role until he has gained greater big screen experience. *Rich.*

The Sins of Rachel Cade
(COLOR)

Religious scruples vs. sexual desires in a Belgian Congo setting. Earnest but generally uninspired meller. B.O. prospect slim.

Hollywood, Aug. 26.

Warner Bros. release of Henry Blanke production. Stars Angie Dickinson, Peter Finch, Roger Moore; with Errol John, Woody Strode, Juano Hernandez, Frederick O'Neal, Mary Wickes, Scatman Crothers, Rafer Johnson, Charles Wood, Douglas Spencer. Directed by Gordon Douglas. Screenplay, Edward Anhalt, based on novel, "Rachel Cade," by Charles Mercer; camera, J. Peverell Marley; editor, Owen Marks; art director, Leo K. Kuter; music, Max Steiner; sound, Francis M. Stahl; assistant directors, Russell Saunders, William Kissel. Reviewed at WB, Aug. 26, '60. Running time, 123 MINS.

Rachel Cade .... Angie Dickinson
Col. Henri Derode .... Peter Finch
Paul Wilton .... Roger Moore
Kula, Rachel Cade's Aide ... John Errol
Muwango, the Medicine Man
Woody Strode
Kalanumu, the High Priest
Juano Hernandez
Buderga .... Frederick O'Neal
Marie Grieux .... Mary Wickes
Musinga .... Scatman Crothers
Kosongo .... Rafer Johnson
Mzimba .... Charles Wood

One of filmdom's favorite stamping grounds, the Belgian Congo, is the setting for some familiar bwana monkeyshines in "The Sins of Rachel Cade." Although it is an earnest and workmanlike effort, nothing very novel or enlightening occurs in the Henry Blanke production, which is based upon Charles Mercer's popular novel about a spinster missionary. Even the tribal dances have a shopworn look about them. Without a so-called "boxoffice cast" to pave the way, the Warner Bros. release is not likely to be much of a grosser.

A few exchanges of snappy dialog crop up in Edward Anhalt's screenplay, indicating that he has done all he can, and more, to pump some vigor into a pretty tired yarn. Chief conflict of the film is the heroine's (Angie Dickinson) inner emotional turmoil in which her religious principles debate against her natural sexual impulses. Arriving in the Congo, she dramatically persuades the region's "left wing" element to adopt the Christian philosophy, but has a deuce of a time practicing what she has been preaching when a handsome American RAF doctor (Roger Moore) arrives by unscheduled plane crash.

Enacting "Rachel Cade" is an important assignment for Miss Dickinson, and she is generally persuasive, although a trifle too composed in spots. Finch, a convincing low-pressure performer, makes the most of his role. Moore is handsome, but far too British-sounding to score in the part of an American, even a Yank from Boston. Those playing African natives are at the mercy of a nagging inconsistency in which their adherence to superstitious tribal customs clashes with their extremely articulate English speech. Outstanding among this group is the sensitive performance of Errol John as the heroine's lovable aide. Others who carry on gamely are Woody Strode, Juano Hernandez, Frederick O'Neal, Scatman Crothers, Rafer Johnson (the Olympic decathlon champ) and Charles Wood, as well as Mary Wickes and Douglas Spencer.

Direction by Gordon Douglas is nowhere near as perceptive as it should be. There is also a distracting tendency to jam the lens right into the pupils of the heroine's eye. She has pretty eyes, but there is a limit to intimacy. Generally capable craftsmanship is otherwise exhibited by cameramman J. Peverell Marley, editor Owen Marks and art director Leo K. Kuter. Max Steiner's music is satisfactory. *Tube.*

French Mistress
(BRITISH)

Somewhat frail joke enlivened by performances by well-tried British thesps. Humor uneven, if harmless, but should find a profitable spot in easygoing theatres.

London, Sept. 6.

British Lion release of a Boulting Bros. production. Stars Cecil Parker, James Robertson Justice, Ian Bannen, Agnes Laurent, Raymond Huntley, Thorley Walters, Irene Handl. Directed by Roy Boulting. Screenplay by Roy Boulting and Jeffrey Dell, from Robert Monroe's play; editor, John Jympson; camera, Max Greene; music, John Addison. Previewed at Studio One, London, Aug. 25, '60. Running time, 98 MINS.

Headmaster .... Cecil Parker
Robert Martin ..James Robertson Justice
Colin Crane ....Ian Bannen
Madeleine Lafarge.......Agnes Laurent
Rev. Edwin Peake .....Raymond Huntley
Staff Sergeant Hodges..... Irene Handl
Matron ....Edith Sharpe
Mr. Meade ....Kenneth Griffith
Mr. Ramsay .... Robert Bruce
Colonel Edmonds ......Thorley Walters
2nd. Governor ....Henry Longhurst
3rd. Governeor ....Brian Oulton
Edmonds .... Scot Finch
Milsom .... Richard Palmer
Wigram ....Peter Greenspan
Baines ....Jeremy Bulloch
Beatrice Peake ...... Athene Seyler
Ambulance Attendant ..Cardew Robinson
Monsieur Fraguier........Paul Sheridan

Billed as a "romp," the Boulting Brothers' latest entry grapples tenaciously with a fairly frail joke which doesn't stand up to its early promise. Based on a stage comedy by Robert Monroe (better known as the late comedian, Sonnie Hale), it owes much to some determined comedy acting by well-tried British character thesps. The screenplay harps friskily on sex. Roy Boulting's direction is sufficiently light of touch to provide a reasonable quota of mild amusement. The title should help exploit this film.

Arrival of a comely, curvaceous young French mademoiselle as French tutor at Melbury boys' school causes an upheaval at the college. Stuffy members of the staff view her advent with alarm, others with relish. Discipline cracks when the scholars, in the throes of calf love, find the new arrival a considerable distraction. It all sorts out, but not before the boys stage a mutiny when they hear that the new femme tutor is being dismissed.

The juvenile reactions to the French mistress swiftly become tedious once the joke is first put over, but the adults provide rather more fun. Agnes Laurent, playing the French schoolteacher, is a newcomer to British films and she handles her role appealingly. Not that she has much to do except look charming and provocative, a task which Mlle. Laurent takes in her stride. Cecil Parker plays the bedevilled headmaster with his usual bland manner in which he can throw away a line and do a double take with skill.

Raymond Huntley, as a stuffy-minded clergyman; James Robertson Justice, as a bluff man-of-the-world schoolmaster, and Thorley Walters as a pompous colonel who is head of the governors, all handle their roles with their customary competence. Ian Bannen, cast as the young lover, again testifies to his skill and charm. The distaff side is also well served, with Irene Handl giving another of her inimitable studies as a caricature of a cook, Edith Sharpe excellent as an understanding matron and Athene Seyler chipping in with some telling work as Huntley's nosey, spinster sister.

Regarded as a team, the scholars are okay, with Scot Finch, Richard Palmer and Jeremy Bulloch having the best opportunities of making individual impact. The school atmosphere is well caught, with good lensing by Max Greene and smooth editing by John Jympson. "Mistress" is occasionally inclined to snigger at sex in a rather adolescent way, but, on the whole, it is a reasonable diversion for unsophisticated audiences. *Rich.*

There Was a Crooked Man
(BRITISH)

Popular British comic, Norman Wisdom, mainly carries this one, his best effort so far. An entertaining mixture of slapstick and character comedy, it's an obvious booking for Britain, and U.S. might well take a chance.

London, Sept. 6.

United Artists release of a Knightsbridge (John Bryan) production. Stars Norman Wisdom; features Alfred Marks, Andrew Cruickshank, Reginald Beckwith, Susannah York. Directed by Stuart Burge. Screenplay, Reuben Ship; camera, Arthur Ibberson; editor, Peter Hunt; music, Kenneth V. Jones. At Astoria, London, Aug. 31, '60. Running time, 90 MINS.

Davy Cooper ....Norman Wisdom
Adolf Carter ....Alfred Marks
McKillup ....Andrew Cruickshank
Station Master ....Reginald Beckwith
Ellen ....Susannah York
Freda ....Jean Clarke
Flash Dan ....Timothy Bateson
Restaurant Gentleman...P. Whitsun-Jones
Taxi Driver ....Fred Griffiths
Hospital Sister ....Ann Heffernan
Nurse ....Rosalind Knight
Dutchman ....Reed De Rouen
Ashton .... Brian Oulton
Prison Warden............Percy Herbert
Woman (Assembly Hall)......Edna Petrie
Police Sgt. ....Jack May
Gen. Cummins ....Ronald Fraser
American Colonel ....Ed Devereaux
Foreman ....Sam Kydd

Norman Wisdom, one of Britain's most reliable slapstick comedians, has been gradually enlarging his scope during his past few pix. "There Was A Crooked Man" is his first since he broke away from the Rank setup and it's a distinct step forward for the comic. Yarn is untidy, sometimes gets bogged down, suffers from too many contrasting styles and occasionally trips up over its own ideas. But despite these faults, it gives Wisdom a chance to act as well as bring in enough slapstick routine to make it a click for British audiences. American ducat-buyers could also enjoy its modest fun.

Director Stuart Burge, a tv director making his debut in feature films, has done a good job, considering the many traps that Reuben Ship's ingenious, though far-fetched, screenplay has laid. Ship has overloaded his story line but has produced an idea which holds interest.

Wisdom is a down-and-out who runs into a gang of crooks who want his help because he is a demolitions expert. Rather naively he is conned into assisting the mob into cracking a bank vault. He alone is caught holding the loot, and goes to jail. When he's let out after five years, he determines to keep straight and goes to take up a job in a Northern seaside factory. He soon finds out that the town is under the control of a swindler (Andrew Cruickshank) who is persuading everybody to buy up shares in the town's future, another of his nefarious schemes.

Wisdom enlists the help of his crook friends on a wild enterprise to outwit Cruickshank. The gang poses as a top scret American army unit with orders to buy up the town to build a rocket base. Cruickshank buys back the townspeople's shares, then Wisdom and the gang blow up the town, doublecross Cruickshank and ruin him. The U.S. government is forced to build a new one for Anglo-American relations, and Wisdom is hailed as a benefactor before being hauled back to the cooler.

There are so many holes in this yarn that it's like a fishing net, but the result is amiable comedy. The robbery, in which Wisdom and his pals pose as surgeons and tunnel from the operating theatre into the next door bank, is wildly funny. Wisdom getting caught up in a wool sorting machine, avoiding the cops, and finally blowing up the town has good clowning moments.

Wisdom, whether he's flirting, playing dumb, interfering at a town meeting or posing as a U.S. general with a southern drawl, carries the most weight in the cast, and mainly does it well. But there are other useful pieces of comedy acting, notably by Andrew Cruickshank, as the powerful villain; Alfred Marks, as the gang leader, Reginald Beckwith, as a stationmaster and Percy Herbert, as a prison warden. Susannah York, as the girl for whom Wisdom falls,

stakes her claim as a useful new juve. Jean Clarke offers some Monroe wiggles.

Despite the outrageously implausible ending, "Crooked Man" is happy-go-lucky entertainment, with good technical support in all departments. It will win new supporters for a comedian who until now nearly found himself trapped by type casting. *Rich.*

Venice Films

Le Passage Du Rhin
(The Crossing of the Rhine)
(FRENCH)

Venice, Sept. 13.
CFDC release of Franco London-Gibe-UFA- Jonnia Film production. Stars Charles Aznavour; features Nicole Courcel, Georges Riviere, Betty Schneider, Cordula Trantow. Directed by Andre Cayatte. Screenplay, Armand Jammot, Pascal Jardin, Maurice Auberge, Cayatte; camera, Roger Fellous; editor, Borys Lewine. At Venice Film Fest. Running time, 130 MINS.
Roger	Charles Aznavour
Florence	Nicole Courcel
Jean	Georges Riviere
Alice	Betty Schneider
Helga	Cordula Trantow

Film chronicles the adventures of a successful journalist and a little baker during the last war. It deals with the good Germans and their tribulations as well as the complicated French loyalties under the occupation. Pic is solidly told though somewhat rambling, and looms as an important art entry abroad on the basis of its selection as the Venice Fest winner.

The newsman goes in service to prove himself though he might have had an out while the little, timid baker is in the army because he has to. There are no war scenes and soon the two are prisoners of war. Stationed in a small town the former stalks women and escapes by seducing one while the other decides to stay because he feels beholden to the family they work for. Also he is smitten by the daughter.

Then follows their return to Paris and disillusionment for both. The newsman gains a top position on a liberation paper but looses the woman he loves because she was a collaborator. The baker finds his wife cold and only thinking of business, and decides to go back to the German town.

Characters are somewhat one dimensional. The newspaperman's idealism is hard to believe in his rather calculated actions while the baker is a reserved little man only wanting to be loved and finding it in an enemy village. Charles Aznavour does have a simplicity of appeal and a timing which makes his little man plausible. Georges Riviere is hard put to make his character acceptable since he seems more like a small time ladies' man than a crushing liberal.

Technical credits are par while stock footage is only passable on brief wartime aspects. Film is somewhat too broad in scope and touches on several themes without the epic sweep and insight to give this a surer more international outlook. It thus has to be sold on its story and few incisive looks at wartime sex and collaboration, plus its Venice exploitability. *Mosk.*

Rocco E I Suoi Fratelli
(Rocco and His Brothers)
(ITALO-FRENCH)

Venice, Sept. 6.
Titanus-Les Films Marceau coproduction. Stars Alain Delon, Renato Salvatori, Annie Girardot, Katina Paxinou; features Roger Hanin, Paolo Stoppa, Suzy Delair, Claudia Cardinale, Spiros Focas, Claudia Mori, Alessandra Panaro, Corrado Pani. Directed by Luchino Visconti. Screenplay, Visconti, Suso Cecchi D'Amico, P. F. Campanile, Massimo Franciosa, Enrico Medioli, from original by Visconti, Vasco Pratolini, D'Amico: based on novel, "Il Ponte Della Ghisolfa," by Giovanni Testori; camera, Giuseppe Rotunno: music, Nino Rota: editor, Mario Serandrei. At Venice Film Fest. Running time, 180 MINS.
Rocco	Alain Delon
Simone	Renato Salvatori
Nadia	Annie Girardot
Rosaria	Katina Paxinou
Morini	Roger Hanin
Impresario	Paolo Stoppa
Luisa	Suzy Delair
Ginetta	Claudia Cardinale
Vincenzo	Spiros Focas
Ivo	Corrado Pani

Prestige entry for Italy. With all its faults, this is one of the very top achievements of the year in this country. It's badly overlength and contains some scenes which will shock even the most hardened viewer. If these faults can be corrected via savvy editing, the film's sale potential will rise in proportion and, with aid of names in cast and exploitable bally, pay off in good grosses in Italy and the remainder of the Continent. Offshore chances are more limited, with the pic looming mainly as a specialized bet. This was shown in competition.

Plot deals with a south Italian family's trek to the big northern city of Milan, where it intends to start a new life, and of its slow disintegration as its members go their own way. It's plotted in the form of an epic poem, each stanza dedicated to a member of the group. Rocco is the all-good brother who falls for the same girl, Nadia, a prostitute, as his brother Simone does. He reluctantly gives her up, but the affair ends tragically anyway with Simone killing Nadia. Other brothers break off and live honest lives on their own while Rocco is tormented by the tragedy and wishes only to return to the land where he was born. There are many other facets to the plot, all of them serving the central motif.

Scripting shows numerous hands at work, yet all is pulled together by Visconti's dynamic and generally tasteful direction. The director must, however, be charged with two or three glaring as well as unusual lapses in taste, mainly in an overlong, over-realistic rape scene in which one brother rapes the other's girl in his presence. Another bad taste scene shows Simone repeatedly stabbing Nadia in too-graphic detail. Occasionally also, as in the near-final revelation to the family of Simone's crime, the action gets out of hand and comes close to melodrama.

Yet the impact of the main story line, aided by the sensitive, expertly guided playing by Alain Delon, as Rocco; Annie Girardot, as the prostie, and Renato Salvatori, as Simone, is great. Backing by the large cast is on an equally high plane, with Paolo Stoppa, Spiros Focas, Corrado Pani and Suzy Delair coming through strongly. Katina Paxinou at times is perfect, at others she is allowed to act too theatrically and off key.

Lensing by Giuseppe Rotunno must be credited with a very strong assist to Visconti's direction. His grey picture of the northern metropolis is realistically harsh in key with the action. Nino Rota contributed his usual savvy musical backing while a good nostalgic song properly sets off the start and finish of the pic. Production values on an elaborate scale are in the stylish tradition of producer Goffredo Lombardo. *Hawk.*

Baishey Stravana
(The 22d Day)
(INDIAN)

Venice, Sept. 5.
Kollal production and release. With Ganaes Mukerji, Madhabi Mukerji, Hemangini Debi, Sumita Dobi. Written and directed by Mrinal Sen; camera, Sailaja Chatterji; editor, Siddobh Roy. At Venice Film Fest. Running time, 98 MINS.
Man	Ganaes Mukerji
Wife	Madhabi Mukerji
Mother	Hermangini Debi
Artisan	Sunita Debi

Though India is the second largest film producing country numerically, in the world, not much is known about these pix in the Western countries. Satyajit Ray broke thru via fest kudos and made an art house dent with his "Pather Panchali," and lesser known filmmakers are Raj Kapoor ("Boot Polish") and Bimal Roy ("One Acre of Land"). Now comes a talented newcomer, Mrinal Sen, with a moving, human film that rates art consideration broad.

The film is fluid and deceptively simple as it recounts the important aspects of the life of a poor, thirtyish salesman. He marries a 16-year-old girl, loses his mother, begins to lose his knack at his job, and the coming World War II and famine, (it is 1943) bring on a nervousness and irritability that lead to a savage argument with his wife and her subsequent suicide.

In spite of its slow progression it gives deep insight into the human relations with telling scenes of awareness and discovery. The protagonist's misfortunes are never sentimentalized. The playing is natural and graceful and the technical aspects excellent with the plastically perceptive lensing an asset. The director has control of his subject and deftly displays the man's condition and changing personality.

Although this does not have the poetic moments to make a timeless comment it has a solidity and humanity that make this a likely specialized bet abroad but still difficult for general spots on its more limpid if penetrating style. A dramatic, tangling, knowing musical score also helps. *Mosk.*

Tunes Of Glory
(BRITISH-COLOR)

Powerful performances by Alec Guinness and John Mills as rival commanders in a Scottish regiment; looms as sturdy b.o.

Venice, Sept. 6.
United Artists release of a Colin Lesslie production. Stars Alec Guinness, John Mills; features Dennis Price, Kay Walsh, John Fraser. Directed by Ronald Neame. Screenplay, James Kennaway; camera, Arthur Ibbetson; editor, Anne Coates; music, Malcolm Arnold. At Venice Film Fest, Sept. 4, '60. Running time, 105 MINS.
Lt.-Col. Jock Sinclair	Alec Guinness
Col. Basil Barrow	John Mills
Second in Command	Dennis Price
Cpl. Piper Fraser	John Fraser
Morag	Susannah York
Mary	Kay Walsh
Capt. Jimmy Cairns	Gordon Jackson
Major Simpson	Alan Cuthbertson

Alec Guinness again plays a colonel in the British army, and after his memorable Oscar-winning performance in "Bridge of the River Kwai," provides an obvious and powerful exploitation angle for his latest film. But in "Tunes of Glory," which was the official British selection for the Venice Fest, he has to compete for acting honors against John Mills—and the honors are even.

Both Guinness and Mills are cast as colonels, the former a man of humble origin who had risen from the ranks, the other a product of Eton, Oxford and a classy military academy. It is the clash of personalities between the two that provides the main story thread, and the stimulating histrionic battle should help this to become a sturdy b.o. contender, particular in the U. S. where the Guinness name means something.

"Tunes" is the story of a Scottish regiment in peacetime commanded by Guinness. He's reasonably popular with his fellow officers, though a few appear to resent his rough-and-ready behavior in the mess. His is only an acting command, and when he is superseded by John Mills (whose grandfather had commanded the same regiment), the clash is inevitable. The new regimental commander sets about his tightening discipline and improving the administration, but as he does so he slowly realizes he is losing the confidence and sympathy of his fellow officers.

It's not only the rank and filers who suffer under the new regime. The officers, too, are put through their paces, and are exposed to a final indignity when all of them—Mills and Guinness included—are ordered to a pre-reveille parade for refresher dancing lessons. At the same time, there is a growing cleavage in the mess, with some of the officers openly siding with the old commander against the new, thus hypoing the unconcealed tension.

The struggle between the two colonels reaches its climax when Guinness finds his daughter in a public house with a young corporal, and strikes the soldier. That's a serious offense under military law, and though Mills has the power to deal with the case, he chooses to submit a report to higher authority, which would inevitably lead to a courtmartial. Only his second in command encourages him to pursue this line of action. The realization that the entire regiment is against him eventually leads to a change of mind—and to suicide when he recognizes he's failed in his job.

Ronald Neame's crisp and vigorous direction keeps the main spotlight on the two central characters, and no director could be better served by his stars. Nonetheless, the other characters are clearly established even though they play a comparatively minor role in pic. Arthur Ibbetson's camerawork,

Anne Coates' smooth editing and particularly Malcolm Arnold's music are plus technical credits. The Scottish regimental atmosphere is enhanced by the adroit use of pipers.

Though the film is technically excellent, it relies more than most do on its cast. Guinness, as always, is outstanding, and his performance is as forthright as it is subtle. He assumes an authentic Scottish accent naturally, and never misses a trick to win sympathy, even when he behaves foolishly. It's a tough assignment for Mills to play against Guinness, particularly in a fundamentally unsympathetic role, but he is always a match for his costar. The scene in which Mills is established as a paranoic is extremely moving. He plays it with considerable delicacy.

As always in British pix of this calibre, the feature cast is hand-picked. Such polished performers as Dennis Price, John Fraser, Gordon Jackson and Alan Cuthbertson lend distinguished support. Kay Walsh and Susannah York as the only two femme members of the cast maintain the high standard.
Myro.

El Lazarillo de Tormes
(The Valet of Tormes)
(SPANISH)

Venice, Sept. 13.
Hesperia Films production and release. With Marco Paoletti, Juan Jose Menendez, Carlos Casaravilla, Memmo Carotenuto. Directed by Cesar Ardavin. Screenplay, Ardavin based on a classic novel; camera, Manuel Berenguer; editor, J. Baena. At Venice Film Fest. Running time, 114 MINS.
Lazare .... Marco Paoletti
Blind Man .... Juan Jose Menendez
Sexton .... Carlos Casaravilla
Knight .... Memmo Carotenuto

This film won the top prize, the Golden Bear, at the Berlin Film Fest this year. It is difficult to see why since it is mainly a stolidly told narrative about the adventures of a little valet in 16th Century Spain. However, it is fairly diverting and could be an okay lingo bet with some specialized bookings abroad.

Based on a famous Spanish classic, this is somewhat like a morality tale as it shows a little boy's travels around Spain working for various adults who are all either vain, stupid, cupid, egotistic or self deceptive. He has to be shrewd and conniving to keep alive.

Marco Paoletti is somewhat mannered as the wily valet while the adults all contribute acceptable stylized performances. Technical credits are good. This is a costumer that does have some pointed satirical, morbid humor but is somewhat repetitious. A good hyping and handling could give this a chance abroad on its story. Production values are good. *Mosk.*

Maribel Y La Extrana Familia
(Maribel and the Strange Family)
(SPANISH)

Venice, Sept. 6.
Tarfe release of AS production. Stars Sylvia Pinal; features Adolfo Marsillach, Julia Caba Alba, Guadalupe Sampedro, Trini Alonso. Directed by Jose Maria Forque. Screenplay, Miguel Mihura; camera, Jose Aguayo; editor, Tibor Reves. At Venice Film Fest. Running time, 110 MINS.
Maribel .... Sylvia Pinal
Marcelino .... Adolfo Marsillach
Paula .... Julia Caba Alba
Mother .... Guadalupe Sampedro

This good idea gets fairly theatrical, pedestrian mounting to make it primarily a Hispano lingo entry abroad where its okay entertainment values might make it pay off. It does not maintain the original pace to fit it into regular playdating.

A timid widower meets a flashy girl in a bar. He brings her home to meet his family, a giddy mother and aunt who want to be up-to-date. They ask her to marry their son and nephew. There is some comedy in the conflict of generations, with some added dramatic twists, in the suspicion that the shy young man might have drowned his first wife. But it all turns out well.

Technical credits are good and acting acceptable if a bit mannered. The direction lacks the required snap. Hence, this is essentially a talky piece. *Mosk.*

Romeo, Julie A Tma
(Romeo, Juliet And Shadows)
(CZECHOSLAVAKI)

Venice, Sept. 6.
Czech State Film production and release. With Ivan Mistrik, Dana Smutna, Jirina Sejbalova, Frantisek Smolik, Jiri Kodet. Directed by Jiri Weiss. Screenplay, Jan Otcenasek, Weiss; camera, Vaclav Hanus; editor, F. Hasek. At Venice Film Fest. Running time, 95 MINS.
Pavel .... Ivan Mistrik
Hana .... Dana Smutna
Mother .... Jirina Sejbalova
Grandfather .... Frantisek Smolik
Vojta .... Jiri Kodet

A youth hides a Jewish girl in the family garret room during the occupation of Prague in the last World War. Love grows amid the hatred and danger only to be destroyed by human cowardice and misunderstanding. The subject has been done before but this has a power, tenderness and dramatic impetus which makes it worth saying again. It is a possible arty entry abroad but difficult for general chances except for lingo houses.

The girl has come to see a family recently sent off to a concentration camp and is hidden by the boy. Their fear is slowly dissipated as love grows, but is intensified when German reprisals grow after the murder of the Hangman of Prague. This leads to her discovery and sacrifice for the boy.

Director Jiri Weiss has given this a simple, firm mounting which allows the characters to grow while the terror of the war is omnipresent. Dana Smutna has poise and can give depth to her portrait of the doomed Jewish girl which is enhanced by a handsome and expressive face. All others perform well under the guidance of the director. This is another moving war film that transcends its theme in depicting love in wartime ruins and restrictions. Technican credits are topnotch. The film won the Grand Prix at the recent Saint Sebastian Film Festival in Spain. It is showing out of competition here. *Mosk.*

Vento Del Sud
(South Wind)
(ITALIAN)

Venice, Sept. 6.
Lux Film release of a Lux-Vides-Cinecitta production. Stars Renato Salvatori, Claudia Cardinale; features Rosella Falk, Annibale Ninchi, Franco Volpi, Laura Adani, Ivo Garrani, Salvatore Fazio, Giuseppe Cirino, Sara Simoni. Directed by

Enzo Provenzale. Screenplay, Mangione, Petri, Crispino, Provenzale, from story by Mangione and Provenzale; camera, Gianni di Venanzo; music, Gino Marinuzzi Jr.; editor, Ruggero Mastroianni. At Venice Film Fest. Running time, 100 MINS.
Antonio .... Renato Salvatori
Grazia .... Claudia Cardinale
Marquis .... Annibale Ninchi
Deoddata .... Rosella Falk

Slickly mounted picture dealing with the Sicilian Mafia problem on that island. Film has some star value here, but needs a hard-sell to overcome conventional material which predominates. It's exportable, but the chances are very spotty. Pic is being shown here out of competition.

Story deals with a young man who's charged by the Mafia with killing a man. He fails to summon up enough courage, and the organization begins its persecution, chasing him and a girl he befriends half way across Sicily until she commits suicide and he is killed by his pursuers.

Plot unfolds in a generally predictable fashion, with many points remaining unclear. Direction lacks force, though it takes good advantage of splendid backdrops elegantly lensed by Gianni di Venanzo, which give the production a veneer it otherwise lacks. Acting is competent but uninspired. Other credits measure up. *Hawk.*

Leningradskoe Nebo
(Leningrad Skies)
(RUSSIAN)

Venice, Sept. 6.
Soviet release of a Denfilm Production. Features Peter Glibov, V. Platov, M. Ulianov, R. Bykov. Directed by Vladimir Vengherov. Screenplay, Nikolai Chukovski; camera, G. Marnjan; music, M. Schwarz. At Venice Film Fest. Running time, 89 MINS.

This rhetorical war pic detailing some aspects of the last World War's defense of Leningrad, looks to have no export chances. It was shown in competition here.

Disjointed story line concerns members of an air squadron charged with defense of the city as well as some aspects of city life under wartime duress and hunger. One good sequence depicts the crossing of a frozen lake by a lifeline truck convoy under constant German shelling. Though some scenes have similar hard-hitting handling and lensing, the film adds nothing to an already heavy backlog of war pix except an unusually heavy dose of flagwaving for the Soviet cause.

Attempts at inserting human values are likewise doomed by overweighty handling, particularly noticeable in the wooden performances from all concerned. Air sequences are sometimes well rendered, but at other times blatantly reveal trick and process photography. Reenactment of bitter wartime air-sea battle in Leningrad Gulf by spick-and-span peacetime ships also clashes with reality of reconstruction. *Hawk.*

Adua E Le Compagne
(Adua and her Colleagues)
(ITALIAN)

Venice, Sept. 6.
Cineriz release of a Moris Ergas (Zebra Film) production. Stars Simone Signoret, Emmanuele Riva, Sandra Milo, Marcello Mastroianni, Gina Rovere; features Claudio Gora, Gianrico Tedeschi. Directed by Antonio Pietrangeli. Screenplay, Ruggero Maccari, Ettore Scola, Tullio Pinelli, Pietrangeli; camera, Armando Nannuzzi; music, Piero Piccioni; editor, Eraldo da Roma. At Film Festival, Venice. Running time, 150 MINS.
Adua .... Simone Signoret
Milly .... Gina Rovere
Lolita .... Sandra Milo
Marilina .... Emmanuele Riva
Ercoli .... Claudio Gora
Lawyer .... Ivo Garrani
Stefano .... Gianrico Tedeschi
Piero .... Marcello Mastroianni

This is a natural b.o. winner in Italy on its controversial theme, handling and star value. Elsewhere, it looks like a good import value on the strength of subject matter and, to a more limited degree, to the Signoret, Mastroianni and Riva names, with dubbing perhaps more indicated than a subtitled release. It has plenty of exploitable angles and costuming. But the need for cutting is obvious since a bit unwieldly at its current two and a half hours. This was shown in competition.

Director Antonio Pietrangeli has sensitively treated his topical story, which deals with the attempt at a new life by a quartet of ex-prostitutes thrown out of house and job by a law passed in Italy a few years ago abolishing prostie emporiums. Girls open a country tavern-restaurant. After several gauche attempts to acclime themselves to normal life and housekeeping chores they seem to have made the grade in a desperate search for true love and understanding. Then they are unceremoniously thrown back into their old existence as social outcasts.

With all its initial graphic detail, film treats the girls and their problems warmly and understandingly as one finds a new, if eventually no-good, love. Another reunites with her long-abandoned child, still another is loved sincerely for the first time in her life, etc. Some of the sequences have an obvious and telegraphed aspect, but generally the script and direction manage to overcome these hurdles tastefully. Opening third of pic likewise has a confused approach, but after that, character delineation becomes sharper.

Acting is excellent throughout, with Oscar winner Simone Signoret registering as Adua, the quartet's leader, and Emmanuele Riva ("Hiroshima Mon Amour") in for some strong bits as a neurotic companion. Sandra Milo as a birdbrain prostie nearly walks off with acting honors, however. Gina Rovere, the fourth gal, has some fine moments as the one who wants to go "straight."

Topnotch backing comes from Marcello Mastroianni, as an innocent-faced profiteer. Claudo Gora is likewise good, but somewhat stereotyped as the heavy in their lives while others add color and competence in the background.

Some of the more colorful sequences and bits of dialogue will probably run into censorship trouble here and there, but on the whole in view of the subject at hand, it's been handled with remarkable discretion, despite the sharp bite of certain scenes. Lensing is fine and Piero Piccioni's musical backing in a jazz mood is apt. Other credits are good. *Hawk.*

Onna Ga Kaidan O Agaru Yoki
(When a Woman Goes Upstairs)
(JAPANESE-SCOPE)

Venice, Sept. 13.
Toho production and release. Stars Hideko Takamine, Masayuki Mori; features Daisuke Kato, Tatsuya Nakadai. Directed by Mikio Narause. Screenplay, Ryuzo Kikushima; camera, Kasao Tamai; editor, H. Ito. Tt Venice Film Fest. Running time, 110 MINS.
Keiko .... Hideko Takamine
Fujisaki .... Masayuki Mori
Yuri .... Daisuke Kato
Boy .... Tatsuya Nakadai

Film deals with the bar girls who play hostess at the myriad of Tokyo night spots used by businessmen for meetings. Usually the girls are just for talk and entertainment, but some turn professional prostitutes. Pic deals with a head hostess and her tribulations. But this vehicle is not a sensation or exploitation opus, but a penetrating, tastefully done drama on one woman's attempt to cope with such a situation.

Drama is inherent in her relations with men on the job, with her family always pressing her for money. Direction is subtle and displays an understanding of female psychology. The slow, measured treatment makes this mainly an art entry for abroad and a specialized one at best.

Hideko Takamine ably portrays the woman forced into this work. She gives it an insight and passion that make her plight important but not hopeless as she goes on despite many rebuffs, use by married men and general difficulty of her position. Acting and technical credits are outstanding. *Mosk.*

Ceneri Della Memoria
(Ashes of Memory
(ITALIAN-COLOR)

Venice, Sept. 13.
Corona-CLM production and release. Written and directed by Alberto Caldana. Camera (Ferraniacolor), Carlo Ventimiglia; editor, Caldana; commentary, Caldana, Luigi De Santis, Tino Banieri. At Venice Film Fest. Running time, 54 MINS

Medium-length documentary is a tactful but forceful statement on last Christmas' resurgence of synagogue desecrations and anti-semitism around Europe. It shows today's Italian-Jewish community. And then it traces the terrible persecutions of Jews under Nazism via photos and film footage to make its eloquent objective statement against intolerance.

The present day scenes are shot in color. These filmic remarks have been made before but this summing up with the last outbreaks of this scourge is timely and taut. It could be a fine specialized supporting film abroad or a fine video program special. It is well mounted and commented. *Mosk.*

I-Ro-Ha-Ni-Ho-He-To
(Of Men And Money)
(JAPANESE-C'SCOPE)

Venice, Sept. 1.
Schochiku release and production. With Koiji Sada, Yunosuka Ito, Seiji Miyaguchi, Taiji Tonoyuma. Directed by Noboru Nakamura. Screenplay, Shinobu Hashimoto, Takeo Kunihiro; camera, Yushun Atsuta; editor, T. Mayuzumi. At Venice Film Fest. Running time, 109 MINS.
Amano .... Koiji Sada
Matsumoto .... Yunosuko Ito
Director .... Seiji Miyaguchi
Assistant .... Taiji Tonoyama

Film deals with some petty pitchmen and hoodlums who set up a securities corporation in which they invest money of people who give it to the org. Savvy handling of the dough and immunity from the law makes them all rich but a stock mart crash leads to their downfall at the hands of a plodding detective.

Pic effectively denotes corruption in high places and the detective's fight to avoid giving in to the lucrative payola. But it is all somewhat talky and didactic and lacks the dramatic insight that would have made this a more incisive tale of big business ethics and morality. As is it is slickly made but seems of dubious export value for possible dualer or lingo use. It has the earmarks and pace of Yank pix of this genre. Thesp and technical credits are good. *Mosk.*

Legy Mindhalalig
(Be So Till Death)
(HUNGARIAN)

Venice, Sept. 6.
Hungarofilm production and release. With Mari Toricsik, Iren Pseta, Tibor Bitskey, Ferenc Bossonyi. Directed by Laszlo Ranody. Screenplay, Josef Darvas from book by Zeigmond Moricz; camera, J. Bedel; editor, M. Reves. At Venice Film Fest. Running time, 90 MINS.
Girl .... Mari Toricsik
Misi .... Iren Pseta
Friend .... Tibor Bitskey
Professor .... Ferenc Bossonyi

In a Hungary of the 1930's a 12-year-old boy is smart enough to get a scholarship to school. This pic concerns his adventures as he is finally driven out of it by adult intrigues into which he is dragged in spite of himself. The film has a feeling for the period and children without being quaint. This is a good moppet pic, and has some lingo house possibilities abroad.

The boy here is bright and tries to please. But he's used by a young man as a go-between with a girl he elopes with. Then he is accused of stealing a lottery ticket. The adult incomprehension sends him out of school but into an acceptance of life.

School life is well portrayed and the children extremely well handled by director Lazlo Ranody. The technical credits are also good. This also was "out of competition." *Mosk.*

Toro Negro
(Black Bull)
(MEXICAN)

Venice, Sept. 6.
Matouk production and release. With Fernando Casanova, Terre Velasques, Miguel Manzano. Directed by Benito Alazraki. Screenplay, Luis Alcoriza; camera, Enrique Wallace; editor, Jaime Brachos. At Venice Film Fest. Running time, 90 MINS.
Gavino .... Fernando Casanova
Alice .... Terre Velanques
Jose .... Miguel Manzano

Behind-the-scenes bullfight tale deals with a would-be matador of poor background who does not make it because of a lack of talent rather than the fighting spirit. Though not penetrating enough in characterization this is briskly told. Film holds interest with lingo situations interested in this type of yarn. More general situations or chances abroad remain doubtful.

The young hero has a girl who

---

helps him, and friends, but simply fails to measure up on the big day, his first bull fight in a small town.

Director Benito Alazraki has a flair for incisive observation and denoting milieu but the film tries to make a small event too sweeping in import.

Acting and technical credits are good while the bullfight de-mystification is another okay hypo peg. *Mosk.*

Il Suffit D'Aimer
(It Is Enough To Love)
(FRENCH)

Venice, Sept. 13.
Edic-SENC-Tamara production and release. With Daniele Ajoret, Madeleine Sologne, Bernard Lajarrige. Directed by Robert Darene. Screenplay, Gilbert Cesbron; camera, Marcel Weiss; editor, Germaine Artus. At Venice Film Fest. Running time, 105 MINS.
Bernadette .... Daniele Ajoret
Mother .... Madeleine Sologne
Father .... Bernard Lajarrige

This details the story of Bernadette in an textbook manner which seems more acceptable for school and specialized bookings than for the commercial circuits. It is solidly made, with the story blocked out without any surprises. It looms only for restricted chances abroad.

Technical credits are fair, with the right luminous lensing quality. Daniele Ajoret, as Bernadette, has the proper ecstatic quality during her visions. Her final retreat and last days are also acceptably done. This is a solid religioso film to be handled accordingly. *Mosk.*

Stratford Films

The Rehearsal Goes On
(CZECHOSLOVAKIA)

Stratford, Ont., Sept. 1.
Ceskoslovensky Film production and release. Directed by Jaroslav Balik; script, Jiri Fried; camera, Rudolph Stahl; music, Ivan Rezac. Stars Ivan Palec, Zdenek Stepanek, Martin Ruzek. At the Stratford (Ont.) Film Festival, Sept. 1, '60. Running time, 104 MINS.
Frantisek Lukavec .... Ivan Palec
Jitka, his wife .... Miriam Hynkova
Mrs. Muller .... Irene Kacirkova
Director Suda .... Zdenck Stepanek
Professor Tuma .... Martin Ruzek
Karel Cizek .... Joseph Kemr
Dana Pelcova .... Jana Stepankova
Eva Malatova .... Nada Myskova
Standa Ruml .... Vladimir Hasek
Vasek Malat .... S. Zindulka
Tony Novak .... Milos Patocka

(In Czech: English Subtitles)

In their films the Czechs have shown themselves to be the most accomplished filmmakers in the Soviet bloc, excepting the Russians, and sophistication and good taste are usually to be found in their productions. In this picture however, rather oddly called "The Trial" at Stratford (although there is no reference to such a title on the film or in the official publicity) its interest in party politics has spoiled a good story. If, of course, this is a genuine picture of how political beliefs affect artistic values, then it's both revealing and disturbing.

This is a story of the theatre world in Prague and the problems of a young actor (Ivan Palec) who finds his growing popularity in films and television affecting his stagework and family life. In the play he's rehearsing, he comes up

---

against his old teacher (now an accomplished actor) whom he had once informed on in his days of youth.

Had the script been content to stay within these bounds it would have developed into a powerful and dramatic conflict of ambition and personality, but unfortunately the hero has difficulty in being a good Communist and in spite of giving spirited talks to his comrades and attending party meetings, he fails to realize, (until the happy fadeout that not until he understands what being a good Communist means can he also achieve artistic maturity as an actor. This sounds so unlikely and is expressed in such tiresome terms that one loses patience with the picture. Acting, direction and photography are all good, and the film presents some fascinating scenes of radio, television and theatrical activity in Prague. *Gera.*

Adam Becomes a Man
(LITHUANIAN)

Stratford, Ont., Sept. 23.
Lithuanian Film Studios production. Director, V. Zhalakyavichus; script, V. Siriss Gira; photo, A. Matskus; music, E. Balsis. Cast: V. Puodjukaitis, A. Boyarchute, S. Petronaitis. At the Stratford (Ont.) Film Festival, Aug. 25, '60. Running time, 83 MINS.

(In Lithuanian; English Subtitles)

While this is politically speaking a Russian entry, it has a style of its own and is not at all like Russian films. Neither is it as advanced as most of them.

The time is 1936, unemployment is widespread, the police are after the Bolsheviks and the city dwellers and peasants alike are selling their land and buying tickets from the Alfa travel agency which promises them a new life in Buenos Aires. Among them are Adam and his sweetheart who work hard to emigrate together. But the rogue who runs the travel agency (and there's a shadowy American involved in this somewhere) takes the money and the girl and speeds off on the night train to Nazi Germany.

What is Adam to do now? Join the party, become a man and work for a brighter future!

While it may not sound subtle, neither is this a heavy-handed yarn. It's a slow and solid O'Neill-like work with a confused storyline and under-developed characters who sit on the fog-laden dock and dream of other times. Only the restrained love scenes between Adam and his girl really come to life.

The settings however, have a true sense of period, and the production style of the film is of the early thirties, as though the producers had been studying Hollywood films of that era. Photography has a fine depth of focus and the music is highly effective. Acting is sometimes too theatrical, but seems to suit the style. *Gera.*

Serge
(RUSSIAN)

Stratford, Ont., Aug. 30.
Sovexportfilm release of Mosfilm Film Studios production. Stars Borya Barhatov, Serge Bondarchuk, S. Skobtseva; directed by Georgi Danela; script, V. Panova, G. Danela, I. Talankin; photo, Anatoli Nitochkin; music, Boris Chaikovsky. At

Stratford (Ont.) Film Festival, Aug. 30, '60. Running time, 80 MINS.

Seryozha	Borya Barhatov
Korostelev	S. Bondarchuk
Maryana	S. Skobtseva
Lidka	Matasha Chechotkina
Vaska	Seryozha Metelitsin
Zhenka	Ura Kozlov
Vaska's Mother	L. Sokolova
Uncle Kostya	V. Merkuryev

(In Russian; English Subtitles)

This is a delightful, utterly charming story of a small boy who is wise but never precocious, showing episodes in his daily life and his relationship with his parents. Serge Bondarchuk plays the small role of the father in charge of a cooperative farm with his customary skill, and is particularly good in a small scene showing him in a newsreel participating in a ceremony.

The little boy, played by Borya Barhatov, is so natural and winning at all times his performance is little short of astonishing, and a great tribute to director Georgi Danela. A gentle, peaceful child-study, introducing one slightly contrived note of the end when the parents plan to move away leaving the boy with an aunt for a few months, "Serge" comes as a welcome change from war stories and contains many fascinating glimpses of Russian life in the country today. While its commercial possibilities are not strong outside of specialized exhibition it should most certainly be included in the Soviet-American exchange. It will be shown in Canada as a matter of course. *Gera.*

Years of Youth
(RUSSIAN-COLOR)

Stratford, Ont., Aug. 29.

Sovexportfilm release of Dovzhenko Kiev Studios production. Stars O. Zhivankova and V. Rudoi; directed by Alexsi Mishurin; script, A. Shaikevich; photo, A. Gerasimov; music, Platon Maiboroda. At Stratford (Ont.) Film Festival, Aug. 29, '60. Running time, 82 MINS.

Natasha	O. Zhivankova
Sergei	V. Rudoi
Volodya	V. Kulik
Dneprov-Zadunaiski	A. Hvilya
Natasha's Mother	E. Mashkara
Uncle Vasya	M. Yakovchenko
Director of the Culture Club	A. Sova

(In Russian; English Subtitles)

At the somewhat surprising request for "something lighter" by the festival administration, the Russians obliged with this tuneful, fast-moving but un-festival musical which seems to contain all the best things from the Hollywood musicals of the '30s.

A musical comedy involving two young Ukrainian dancers who meet on their way to Kiev where they hope to pass the entrance exams to a theatrical school, the plot contains such "novelties" as the girl and boy singing on top of a train, the girl posing as a boy and as her own sister, a "knowing" mother, a "show must go on" opening and many other familiar acts. The whole however, is put over with such zest, fast camera movement and smart editing that the time passes pleasantly enough *Gera.*

High Time
(C'SCOPE-SONGS-COLOR)

Lightweight Bing Crosby comedy with Fabian added as lure for teenagers.

Hollywood, Sept. 17.

Twentieth-Fox release of Charles Brackett production. Stars Bing Crosby; costars Fabian, Tuesday Weld, Nicole Maurey; features Richard Beymer, Patrick Adiarte, Yvonne Craig, Jimmy Boyd, Gavin MacLeod, Kenneth MacKenna, Nina Shipman. Directed by Blake Edwards. Screenplay, Tom and Frank Waldman, based on story by Garson Kanin; camera (DeLuxe Color), Ellsworth Fredricks; music, Henry Mancini; editor, Robert Simpson. Previewed Sept. 16, '60. Running time, 102 MINS.

Harvey Howard	Bing Crosby
Gil Sparrow	Fabian
Joy Elder	Tuesday Weld
Helene Gauthier	Nicole Maurey
Bob Bannerman	Richard Beymer
T. J. Padmanagham	Patrick Adiarte
Randy Pruitt	Yvonne Craig
Higgson	Jimmy Boyd
Thayer	Gavin MacLeod
President	Kenneth MacKenna
Laura	Nina Shipman
Crump	Paul Schreiber
Harvey Howard, Jr.	Angus Duncan
Bones McKinney	Dick Crockett
Tobacco Auctioneer	Frank Scannell

"High Time" is pretty lightweight fare for a star of Bing Crosby's proportions, and all the draw of the Groaner, who only trills twice, will be required to sell it. Beating on the promising premise of Crosby—51, father of two, a millionaire restaurant chain owner—enrolling in college as a freshman and continuing through four years to graduation, film depends on individual situations and gimmicks rather than on straight story line, consequently it doesn't have too much to sustain it.

Produced under the banner of Bing Crosby Productions with Charles Brackett as producer, a bit of whimsy and great attention to unusual special photographic effects and montages apparently were believed sufficient to bolster the episodic nature of the 102-minute film. It isn't, though the finished product is good fun at times, some of the situations near the belly-laugh stage. Brackett has given the overall handsome production mounting and Blake Edwards' direction is light and fluid as he catches the college spirit.

The Tom and Frank Waldman screenplay is based on a story by Garson Kanin.

Crosby handles his role in his usual fashion, perfectly timing his laughs, and delivers a pair of Sammy Cahn-James Van Heusen songs, "The Second Time Around" and "Nobody's Perfect."

Co-starring with him are Fabian and Tuesday Weld, students, former singing an old folksong effectively, and Nicole Maurey, as the French teacher whom Crosby romances. Patrick Adiarte and Richard Beymer score as Crosby's roommates, together with Fabian; Gavin MacLeod gets a few chuckles as a screwball faculty adviser; Yvonne Craig is cute as a co-ed; and Kenneth MacKenna is college prexy. Balance of cast play well.

Ellsworth Fredricks' color photography is outstanding, Henry Mancini's music score melodic and finely attuned to the demands of the action and art direction by Duncan Cramer and Herman A. Blumenthal lends class. Robert Simpson's editing also is sharp. *Whit.*

Let No Man Write My Epitaph

Well-produced translation of the bestseller but downbeat aspect. Needs hard selling.

Hollywood, Sept. 16.

Columbia Pictures release of Boris D. Kaplan production. Stars Burl Ives, Shelley Winters, James Darren, Jean Seberg, Ricardo Montalban, Ella Fitzgerald; features Rudolph Acosta, Philip Ober, Jeanne Cooper, Bernie Hamilton, Walter Burke, Francis DeSales, Michael Davis. Directed by Philip Leacock. Screenplay, Robert Presnell Jr., based on novel by Willard Motley; camera, Burnett Guffey; editor, Chester W. Schaeffer; music, George Duning. Previewed Sept. 15, '60; running time, 105 MINS.

Judge Bruce Mallory Sullivan	Burl Ives
Nellie Romano	Shelley Winters
Nick Romano	James Darren
Barbara Holloway	Jean Seberg
Louie Ramponi	Ricardo Montalban
Flora	Ella Fitzgerald
Max	Rudolph Acosta
Grant Holloway	Philip Ober
Fran	Jeanne Cooper
Goodbye George	Bernie Hamilton
Wart	Walter Burke
Magistrate	Francis DeSales
Nick (Child)	Michael Davis
Mike	Nesdon Booth
Eddie	Dan Easton
Whitey	Roy Jenson
Barney	Joel Fricano
Lee	Joe Gallison

"Let No Man Write My Epitaph" is powerful drama but the general subject, backgrounded against Skid Row and its seamy characters, lacks the appeal of a boxoffice hit. That it has been well produced and superbly enacted by a topflight cast there can be no question; its downbeat flavor and the unpleasant aspects of dope addiction which motivates a rather chilling climax look to militate against heavy acceptance by general audiences.

Boris D. Kaplan, the producer, and Robert Presnell Jr., scripter, have translated Willard Motley's novel of life in Chicago's South Side jungle with faithful regard to catching its sleazy atmosphere and limning the human ruins who populate the area and comprise the characters of plot. Direction by Philip Leacock, too, is compelling for most part as he persuasively handles his people, making of bums sometimes interesting persons and creating a suitable framework for yarn's unfoldment.

Plot twirls around the efforts of Shelley Winters, widow of a hoodlum who went to the chair, to rear their young son decently in their slum environment.

Acting honors are about evenly divided between Miss Winters and Ives, but James Darren registers impressively as the boy who fights to keep his head high and become a concert pianist despite his illegitimate background. Femme socks over a realistic performance, particularly during her hunger pains for dope, and Ives lends fine conviction to his "drunken scholar" role.

Montalban is smooth as a heavy, killed by Ives in the belief peddler has harmed the boy, and balance of cast contribute effectively. Jean Seberg is in briefly for a suggestion of romance with Darren and Philip Ober as her father. Miss Fitzgerald further scores with her warbling of several songs, includng "Reach for Tomorrow," cleffed by Jimmy McHugh and Ned Washington.

Technical credits are definite assets to film's unreeling, including Burnett Guffey's camera work, Chester W. Schaeffer's tight editing, Robert Peterson's art direction and George Duning's music score. *Whit.*

Three Moves to Freedom
(GERMAN)

Well made, but slowish and sometimes confused melodrama. Useful booking for specialized houses; risky for general consumption.

London, Sept. 8.

Rank release of a Luggi Waldleitner production. Stars Curt Jurgens, Claire Bloom, Jorg Felmy. Features Albert Lieven, Mario Adorf, Karel Stepanek, Alan Gifford. Produced by Luggi Waldleitner. Directed by Gerd Oswald. Screenplay by Harold Medford & Gerd Oswald from Stefan Zweig's novel, "The Royal Game." Camera, Gunther Senftleben; editor, K. M. Eckstein; music, Hans-Martin Majewski. At Leicester-square Theatre, London, Sept. 6, '60. Running time, 104 MINS.

(English Dialog)

Werner von Basil	Curt Jurgens
Irene Andreny	Claire Bloom
Hans Berger	Jorg Felmy
Mirko Centowic	Mario Adorf
Hartmann	Albert Lieven
Mac Iver	Alan Gifford
Rabbi	Dietmar Schonherr
Baranow	Karel Stepanek
Moonface	Wolfgang Wahl
Hotel Manager	Rudolf Forster
Scientist	Albert Bressler
First Officer	Jan Hendriks
Ballet Master	Harald Maresch

Somewhat confused, ponderous and overlong, though sensibly edited for commercial release, "Three Moves to Freedom" is an interesting melodrama which should do well with specialized audiences. However, it's a risky booking for the average house, despite the appeal of Curt Jurgens and Claire Bloom.

It's a flashback story concerned mainly with the effects of brainwashing.

The film, which was the official German entry in the Venice Film fest, is intelligently directed and has the benefit of a heavy but equally intelligent performance by Jurgens as a smuggler of art treasures out of the country for the benefit of the church. Miss Bloom plays a ballerina. Though the role is important, and offers the pic its slight love interest, the character never clearly comes to life. It's a fault of the screenplay rather than any complaint over Miss Bloom's acting.

Jorg Felmy as the Nazi and Albert Lieven as his boss also weigh in with forceful characterizations and Alan Gifford makes the most of scant opportunity as the Scotsman. Gunter Senftleben's lensing is satisfactory and editor K. M. Eckstein has done a sound stint. Without having seen the original German version it isn't possible to determine just where he has cut some 20 minutes, but the result is worth it. *Rich.*

The Criminal
(BRITISH)

Tough, well made crook film with compelling prison sequences and strong performances, particularly by Stanley Baker. Winner with audiences with strong stomachs.

London, Sept. 15.

Anglo-Amalgamated presentation of Merton Park production. Stars Stanley Baker; features Margit Saad, Sam Wanamaker, Gregoire Aslan. Producer, Jack Greenwood. Director, Joseph Losey.

Screenplay, Alun Owen; camera, Robert Krasker; editor, Reginald Mills; music, Johnny Dankworth. Previewed at RFD Private Theatre, Sept. 13, '60. Running time, **97 MINS.**

Johnny Bannion .... Stanley Baker
Mike Carter .... Sam Wanamaker
Frank Saffron .... Gregoire Aslan
Suzanne .... Margit Saad
Maggie .... Jill Bennett
Mr. Edwards .... Rupert Davies
Mr. Town .... Laurence Naismith
Formby .... John Van Eyssen
Prison Governor .... Noel Willman
Priest .... Derek Francis
Prison Doctor .... Redmond Phillips
Clobber .... Kenneth J. Warren
Chief Warder, Barrows .. Patrick Magee
Kelly .... Kenneth Cope
Sol .... Patrick Wymark
Scout .... Jack Rodney
Snipe .... John Molloy
Pauly Larkin .... Brian Phelan
Alfredo Fanucci .... Paul Stassino
Warder Brown .... Jerold Wells
Flynn .... Tom Bell
O'Hara .... Neil McCarthy
Hanson .... Keith Smith
Ted .... Nigel Green
Quantock .... Tom Gerard
Chas. .... Larry Taylor

There have been plenty of crime and prison screen yarns before, and "The Criminal" cannot claim to offer anything very new on the subject. But it is certainly one of the toughest, most uncompromising British pix of its kind and should compel the interest of audiences who like strong meat. This one is worth seeing both for a vigorous performance by Stanley Baker and the dank, sleazy, claustrophobic prison atmosphere built up by good art work, lensing and very skillful casting in minor roles.

The story never rises above the level of a conventional meller, but Alun Owen's screenplay projects the characters and his dialog always rings true. The opening is rather vague but fulfils its purpose in creating the prison atmosphere and the personality of Johnny Bannion, the arrogant, tough, bitter and yet often likeable crook played by Baker. During a three year spell in the cooler during which he has become top man among the prisoners he has planned the biggest robbery of his career, a $120,000 raid on a racetrack. The coup is pulled off (and this is a surprisingly unexciting sequence) but when Baker hears that his fence is upping his required percentage he decides to hide the cash until it's less hot. He buries it in a lonely field but helps himself to fifteen hundred bucks which he blows on a ring for his new girl friend (Margit Saad).

This doesn't please his ex-flame (Jill Bennett) who tips off the cops and Baker finds himself back in jail for 15 years. He refuses to say where the dough is, deciding to sweat out his sentence and come out a rich man. Through prison contacts his outside gang try to get Baker to tell where the money is. When that fails they use his moll as bait, plan a prison riot and Baker's escape and the crook falls for the trap by leading the gang to the field where the loot is hidden. But they, wipe him out too soon, and are left digging. Final chase has some tension but it is the prison sequences and the relationship of men and warders (who come out as a pretty sadistic lot) which is most interesting, plus a very rough riot scene.

Baker's performance dominates the film, but Sam Wanamaker as his doublecrossing righthand man gives a studied performance of oily corruption, while Gregoire Aslan, Patrick Wyman, Kenneth J. Warren, Brian Phelan, Tom Bell, Jack Rodney, John Molloy and Tom Gerard are prominent among the assorted crooks and thugs. On the side of the law Noel Willman's governor is coldly apt, while Patrick Magee (a prominent stage and tv actor), making his first big film performance is splendid as the vicious, conniving chief warder with an implacable hatred of Baker. Only two femmes have much prominence, Jill Bennett making her mark briefly but pointedly as Baker's ex-moll and a piquant German actress, Margit Saad, suggesting more saucy sexappeal than genuine thesp ability as his steady.

Owen's screenplay is his first effort, though he is one of Britain's most known tv dramatists. It is taut enough to suggest that when he can get his teeth into a story of his own origination he'll be a top-flight recruit.

Joseph Losey's hard hitting direction is right in the mood for the pic and he's been well served by cameraman Robert Krasker and art director Scott Macgregor.

Johnny Dankworth has both composed and conducted the music and again this is a useful "first time" effort. His wife, Cleo Laine, sings a "Prison Blues" which has a banal lyric but a haunting effectiveness in its melody. *Rich.*

The Boy Who Stole A Million

Well made comedy meller. Word-of-mouth should be good.

Hollywood, Sept. 14.

Paramount release of a George H. Brown production. Stars Virgilio Texera and Marrianne Benet; introduces Maurice Reyna. Directed by Charles Crichton. Story and original screenplay, Niels West-Larsen; scenario, John Eldridge and Crichton; camera, Douglas Slocombe; editor, Peter Bezencenet; art director, Maurice Carter; music, Tristram Cary; sound, John Michell; assistant director, David Orton. Previewed at the studio, Sept. 14, '60. Running time, **65 MINS**

Miguel .... Virgilio Texera
Maria .... Marianne Benet
Paco .... Maurice Reyna
Luis .... Harold Kasket
Bank Manager .... George Coulouris
Police Chief .... Bill Nagy
Pedro .... Warren Mitchell
Mateo .... Tutte Lemkow
Knife Grinder .... Xan Das Bolas
Blind Man .... Francisco Bernal
Commissionaire .... Edwin Richfield
Gang Leader .... Barta Barri
Organ Grinder .... Herbert Curiel
Reporter .... Gaylord Cavallaro
Desk Sergeant .... Paul Whitsun Jones
Detective .... Robert Rietty
Carlos I .... Mike Brendel
Carlos II .... Juan Olaguivel
Chico .... Victor Mojica
Currito .... Curt Christian
Bank Clerk .... Cyril Shaps
Assistant Organ Grinder . Antonio Fuentes
Shoemaker .... Andrea Malandrinos
Street Vendor .... Goyo Lebrero

In "The Boy Who Stole a Million," Paramount has picked up a tasteful little picture which is sensitively conceived and ably filmed. It's the kind that will play the lower half of a double bill, but it's not unlikely that more than one patron will go away proclaiming the second feature was better than the one they paid their money to see.

The brief (65 minutes) picture was filmed in Valencia, Spain, taking cinematic advantage of an infrequently used location. And director Charles Crichton has used the urban Spanish setting to its fullest. The film, whose writing credits go to Niels West-Larsen, John Eldridge and Crichton, subtly blends melodrama. comedy and heart. Director Crichton has put his tongue in his cheek, just as he did with "Lavender Hill Mob," and the George H. Brown Production turns into an entertaining, albeit short, film experience.

"Boy" of the title is Maurice Reyna, a 12-year-old Spanish youngster who works as a messenger in the Banco Nacional. His widower father has forfeited his taxi to a demanding mechanic, and the boy figures he, as do the bank's customers, can "borrow" 1,000,000 pesetas. Word of the robbery circulates through the town, and every hood in Valencia goes after the boy in quest of his loot. Crichton has done exceptionally well with the chase sequences, aided humorously by Tristram Cary's musical score, and the entire affair often looks more like a live action Tom and Jerry cartoon.

Reyna says little but moves a lot, performing admirably as the youngster. Virgilio Texera is excellent as his father, with fine support from Marianne Benet, Harold Kasket and a talented little dog, uncredited.

Sometimes jarring are the British accents in a normally Spanish environment. But for an off-the-cuff conversation in Spanish, the picture has been made entirely in English; if there's dubbing, it's well done.

Producer Brown has come up with a fine combination of British technique and European art. Douglas Slocombe's camera moves around Valencia with skill and feeling; Peter Bezencenet's editing is first-rate and tight; are director Maurice Carter found the right spots; sound by John Mitchell is tops. *Ron.*

Sunrise at Campobello

Superlative film bio of FDR, Worthy Two-a-day entry.

Hollywood, Sept. 13.

Warner Bros. release of Dore Schary production. Stars Ralph Bellamy, Greer Garson; features Hume Cronyn, Jean Hagen, Ann Shoemaker, Alan Bunce, Tim Considine, Zina Bethune, Frank Ferguson, Pat Close, Robin Warga, Tom Carty, Lyle Talbot. Directed by Vincent J. Donehue. Screenplay Dore Schary from his stage hit; camera, Russell Harlan; editor, George Boemler; music, Franz Waxman; director, Russell Saunders. Reviewed at studio Sept. 13, 1960. Running time, **144 MINS.**

Franklin D. Roosevelt .... Ralph Bellamy
Eleanor Roosevelt .... Greer Garson
Louis Howe .... Hume Cronyn
Miss LeHand .... Jean Hagen
Sarah Roosevelt .... Ann Shoemaker
Alfred E. Smith .... Alan Bunce
James Rooselvelt .... Tim Considine
Anna Roosevelt .... Zina Bethune
Dr. Bennett .... Frank Ferguson
Elliott Roosevelt .... Pat Close
Franklin D. Roosevelt Jr. .. Robin Warga
John Rooselvelt .... Tom Carty
Mr. Brimmer .... Lyle Talbot
Mr. Lassiter .... David White
Capt. Skinner .... Walter Sande
Marie .... Janine Grandel
Edward .... Otis Greene
Charles .... Ivan Browning
Senator Walsh .... Al McGranary
Daly .... Herb Anderson
Speaker .... Jerry Crews

Dore Schary has done it again. His film version of "Sunrise at Campobello" is a stirring drama. In the journey from stage to screen this chapter from the life of Franklin Delano Roosevelt has lost none of its poignant and inspirational qualities, none of its humor and pathos. Indeed, the scope and intimacy that the motion picture permits gives added dimensions to both the sense of loss suffered by a robust man crippled by infantile paralysis in the prime of life and his determination to triumph over his adversity.

Schary, as author-producer of the play and the film (being released by Warner Bros.) can take just pride in this grandslam feat. And this satisfaction is to be shared also by Ralph Bellamy, whose brilliant portrayal of Roosevelt, and Vincent J. Donehue, the director, clicked so resoundingly on Broadway. Latter more than atones for the shaky start he made on Schary's earlier pic, "Lonely Hearts."

"Campobello" is a class motion picture in every way, eminently worthy of the two-a-day (with intermission) policy for its key engagements. It may turn out to be an unexpectedly hot political potato, too. The Democratic Party comes up smelling like roses and a hard blow is struck at religious bigotry at a time when political sentiments are at the boiling point throughout the land. It would be most regretable, however, and shockingly shabby treatment of a remarkably mature and absorbing film, if party and/or religious factionalism should intrude at the boxoffice.

That Bellamy gives a warm, revealing, compassionate, yet always energetic performance, is hardly news. He comes as close as seems humanly possible in speech, mannerisms and expression to being the Roosevelt of the four-year span of this biography. The period is 1921, when polio shatters a joyous family vacation on the island retreat of Campobello, to 1924, when Roosevelt reemerged in public to put in Al Smith's name as a presidential hopeful at the Democratic convention and in the process, lit his own political star. By ending where it does, the picture avoids the treacherous waters of controversy that later surrounded Roosevelt the President, a monumental historical figure who, like Lincoln, seems destined to be idolized and deprecated. Schary expresses unashamedly, and with unerring dramatic instinct, affection and admiration for a man who, in his determination to overcome a devastating affliction, gave inspiration and hope to others and inspired the March of Dimes to mount a practical assault against polio.

Few scenes in motion picture history have touched the heart as does the climactic Democratic Convention sequence in "Sunrise at Campobello." It is noisy, boisterous, wonderfully exciting and eye-filling in Technicolor. It is almost overpowering in emotional punch when the vibrant man, who secretly learned to drag himself along the floor on his powerful arms for fear of being trapped by fire, finally stands, more through sheer will than the painful braces that encase his legs, triumphant at the lectern as the crowd roars and the band blares "Sidewalks of New York." **It's that smash ending directors and producers yearn for but only rarely achieve.**

If "Campobello" opened a new career for Schary as a playwright in 1958, shortly after he exited as production head of MGM, then it can be said with equal confidence that this film should mark the beginning of a new and brilliant career for Greer Garson. She comes through as Eleanor Roosevelt with a deeply moving, multifaceted characterization that reveals an understanding of emotions which transcends the point beyond which

It seems possible for a director or writer, with all due respect, to assist in the creation of a performance. Miss Garson succeeds astonishingly in submerging her own personality and, considering the distinctive voice of Eleanor Roosevelt, the total impression is all the more remarkable.

Miss Garson is a major source of interest, emerging from a shy, introspective wife and mother to suggest, as the film ends, the positive, humane and politically conscious woman now so well known to the world. The side of Eleanor Roosevelt revealed in this picture —the strengths of reserve she draws upon in tireless nursing and wifely devotion to a husband undergoing a trying psychological rebirth, the while giving patience, sympathetic understanding and love to five growing children and fending with a less than adoring mother-in-law—commands respect and affection.

The wonderful thing about "Sunrise at Campobello" is that it flows in the outdoors and the livingroom as a good motion picture should (for which cameraman Russell Harlan and editor George Boemler also are entitled to take bows). This is the kind of teamwork that complements splendid writing, direction and acting. In the last department there is a third tower of strength in the person of Hume Cronyn as Louis Howe, the wizened, asthmatic, devoted friend and political Svengali to Franklin Roosevelt. The latter's mother, sharply illumined in the performance of Ann Shoemaker, is openly hostile to chain-smoking Howe whom she suspects of being more intent about being the tail on her son's then questionable (and utterly outlandish in Sara Roosevelt's eyes at the time) political kite.

The part of Howe calls for many illuminating facets of personality and Cronyn invests the role with rich and compelling artistry. There is, considering the sober nature of the subject, a surprising amount of humor in "Campobello" and a good measure of it is deftly generated by Cronyn. Although only in two scenes, Alan Bunce (from the play cast) makes a strong impression as Al Smith, the "Happy Warrior," in whose behalf Roosevelt writes a stinging rebuke to groups opposing Smith because of his Roman Catholicism. The Roosevelt children are played with a nice dash of naturalness, particularly by Tim Considine and Zina Bethune. As Missy LeHand, the devoted secretary, Jean Hagen is delightful. Lesser roles are capably handled by Frank Ferguson, Lyle Talbot, David White, Herb Anderson and Otis Greene. Schary himself has a good moment as chairman of the Connecticut delegation who yields to New York on the convention floor.

Franz Waxman's score makes a big contribution, notably to the convention sequence. Pic begins with an overture, about eight minutes, of melodious oldtimers. Tunes, which perhaps will stir more emotions among the over-40 viewers, are a welcome mood-setter for a picture that should live long and fondly in the memory of most viewers   *Pry.*

Where The Hot Wind Blows

Post - dubbed Franco - Italian film with Gina Lollobrigida and Yves Montand. Comic and sexy. Promises fine b.o.

Hollywood, Sept. 15.
Metro release of Jacques Bar production (for The Group of Four and G.E. S.I. Cinematografica Titanus S.P.A.) Joseph E. Levine presentation. Stars Gina Lollobrigida, Yves Montand; features Pierre Brasseur, Marcello Mastroianni, Melina Mercouri, Paolo Stoppa. Directed by Jules Dassin. Written by Dassin from novel by Roger Vailland; dialog, Françoise Giroud; camera, Otello Martelli; music, Roman Vlad; song, "Where the Hot Wind Blows," by Jimmy McHugh and Buddy Kaye, sung by Ames Bros. Previewed at Metro, Sept. 14, '60. Running time, 120 MINS.
Marietta .... Gina Lollobrigida
Brigante .... Yves Montand
Don Cesare .... Pierre Brasseur
The Engineer ......Marcello Mastroianni
Donna Lucrezia .... Melina Mercouri
Tonio .... Paolo Stoppa
Francesco .... Raf Mattioli
Attilio .... Vittorio Caprioli
Pizzaccio .... Nino Vingelli
Guidice .... Teddy Billis
Giuseppina .... Lydia Alfonsi
Giulia .... Edda Soligo
Elvira .... Luisa Rivelli
Maria .... Anna-Maria Bottini
Balbo ...., Bruno Carotenuto
The Priest .... Marcello Giorda
The Swiss Tourist..Herbert Knippenberg
The Tourist's Wife....... Sonia Barbieri
Anna .... Anna Arena

The canny commercial sense of Joseph E. Levine is combined in this Franco-Italian import with the artistic acumen of writer-director Jules Dassin, the sex appeal of Gina Lollobrigida, the dramatic talent of Yves Montand and the Italian atmosphere to make a tragicomic romp which, despite post-dubbing, should do very well on the American market at which the Jacques Bar production is aimed.

Miss Lollobrigida depicts the virginal village temptress who's also a kind of female Fagin, inducing local youths to steal for her. Light-heartedly amoral, she's chaste merely to be chased and hopes to marry well—hence she steals in order to collect a dowry.

Montand portrays a scar-faced gangster who seeks power and social position, partly for the sake of his handsome son, limned by Raf Mattioli, but is opposed by the aristocratic - but - poor incumbent, portrayed by Pierre Brasseur.

Hat set for the eligible young engineer, Marcello Mastroianni, the temptress spurns the gangster —scarring his face further in an attempted rape—inherits the aristocrat's wealth and brings the hapless engineer to bay. Gangster is dishonored when he provokes his son's mistress (played by Melina Mercouri) to suicide and the lad deserts him.

Many of the scenes are frankly contrived so as to show the luscious Lollobrigida to best advantage. Besides, she acts with appealing zeal and a fine sense of the comic. Ladies are apt to be too absorbed with Montand to object.

Dassin's expert touch is everywhere felt, despite contrivances and devices. Camera wheels through carnival scenes, meanders down beaches, plummets with the suicide and keeps constant the sense of movement while simultaneously noticing provocative detail. He draws excellent performances from all concerned.

Title tune by Jimmy McHugh and Buddy Kaye and sung by the

Ames Bros. should help promotion some and technical aspects — except for single-level, poorly synced post-dubbing—are satisfactory.

Ten Who Dared
(COLOR)

Disappointing screen translation of the journal of Major John Wesley Powell. Easy, appealing way to learn some fifth-grade American history, but dramatically second-grade. Not one of Disney's better b.o. bets.

Hollywood, Sept. 23.
Buena Vista release of Walt Disney production. Stars Brian Keith, John Beal, James Drury; with R. G. Armstrong, Ben Johnson, L. Q. Jones, Dan Sheridan, David Stollery, Stan Jones. David Frankham, Pat Hogan, Ray Walker, Jack Bighead, Roy Barcroft, Dawn Little Sky. Directed by William Beaudine. Screenplay, Lawrence Edward Watkin, based on journal of Major John Wesley Powell; camera, Gordon Avil; editors, Norman Palmer, Cotton Warburton; art directors, Carroll Clark, Hilyard Brown; music, Oliver Wallace; sound, Harry M. Lindgren; assistant director, Russ Haverick. Reviewed at Academy Award Theatre, Sept. 23, '60. Running time, 92 MINS.
William Dunn .... Brian Keith
Major John Wesley Powell.... John Beal
Walter Powell .... James Drury
Oramel Howland .... R. G. Armstrong
George Bradley .... Ben Johnson
Billy Hawkins .... L. Q. Jones
Jack Sumner .... Dan Sheridan
Andrew Hall .... David Stollery
Seneca Howland .... Stan Jones
Frank Goodman .... David Frankham
Indian Chief .... Pat Hogan
McSpadden .... Ray Walker
Ashtishkel .... Jack Bighead
Jim Baker .... Roy Barcroft
Indian Woman .... Dawn Little Sky

"Ten Who Dared" is lower case Disney. Worthwhile as it is from a purely academic standpoint, the picture is doubly disappointing in dramatic terms—a surprisingly undistinguished attempt to illustrate the perils encountered by Major John Wesley Powell and nine boatmen in successfully navigating three small craft down the treacherous Colorado River for the first time in 1869—a feat recorded in Powell's journal, upon which the film is based. The promise of American history a la Disney will be a considerable drawing card, but youngsters may not find it exciting and fast-moving enough for their tastes, and more mature patrons are likely to detect a number of serious, disturbing flaws and contrivances. The Buena Vista release is no boxoffice shoo-in.

Judging from the conflicts depicted — principally personality clashes among the men, with man vs. nature decidedly secondary— the journal seems to be a rather lacklustre piece of literature.

Perhaps in an effort to spike the material with all the emotional sparks he could muster, Lawrence Edward Watkins has burdened his adaptation with a number of artificially theatrical elaborations. A major character clash between a deranged ex-Union Army man and an ex-Confederate is resolved in unrealistically sudden and highly cornball fashion when the two join in a folksy duet of a rebel song just after engaging in mortal combat.

A sequence or two involving a canine member of the party are contrived and predictable. There is a tendency to mislead the spectator near the end when three members of the expedition decide to finish the journey by land and seem to be successful until a narrative tag informs the audience that eventually they perished (off-screen). In fact, save for one or two rugged fistfights, a conscious

effort to avoid any violence or shock appears to have been made, as if prompted by recent public uproar over such things. Such avoidance is fine up to a point—the point where steering clear of physical turmoil results in a sort of fishy-washy negative approach.

Difficult as the production undertaking looks to have been, the pictorial aspect fails to compensate for other shortcomings. Actually, the journey is rather unexciting even in the photographic sense. Art directors Carroll Clark and Hilyard Brown obviously have chosen some remarkably picturesque locales in Grand Canyon and Arches National Monument, but the scenery generally comes up a boring brown on the film—a color monotony that cameraman Gordon Avil can do nothing to avoid. In filming the action sequences, notably over the river rapids, he has, however, done a splendid job. And editors Norman Palmer and Cotton Warburton have knit together the fruits of these painstaking photographic labors with great skill. Oliver Wallace's score accompanies the party down the river with some fine, sweeping strains.

The acting is excellent. Brian Keith steals the picture, emerging a wonderfully robust and comic figure as an astrologically-guided plainsman fond of teasing rattlesnakes. John Beal is firm as the one-armed Major Powell, although the character itself astonishingly does not come into sharp focus.

James Drury is quietly forceful as Powell's brother, the veteran of imprisonment in Andersonville whose venom so remarkably vanishes. The seven others, all of whom perform admirably, although the characters they play are generally underdeveloped, are R. G. Armstrong, Ben Johnson, L. Q. Jones, Dan Sheridan, David Stollery, Stan Jones and David Frankham. Additional support is fashioned ably by Pat Hogan, Roy Barcroft, Dawn Little Sky, Ray Walker and Jack Bighead. Although he is no doubt at least partially responsible for the rewarding tenor of the performances and the energetic nature of the production effort (along with associate producer James Algar in the case of the latter), director William Beaudine appears to have failed to sense and delete or sidestep some of the corny and/or hammy aspects inherent in the script.

Tube.

Un Guapo Del 900
(A Bravo of the 1900's)
(ARGENTINE)

Buenos Aires, Sept. 13.

Angel release of a Nestor Gaffet production. Directed by Leopoldo Torre Nilsson and Samuel Eichelbaum, from the adaptation by both of Eicheibaum's play of the same name. Features Arturo Garcia Buhr, Alfredo Alcon, Lidia Lamaison, Duilio Marzio and Elida Gay Palmer. Camera, Ricardo Younis; music, Hector Stamponi; editor, Jorge Garate. Preemed in a benefit for the Anti-Polio Assn., at the Gran Rex, Gaumont and 8 neighborhood theatres. Running time, 84 MINS.

This is another evocation of the Buenos Aires of 60 years ago, when national characteristics were more clearly defined. The charm of that era is over exploited in parts, with self - conscious reproduction of street cries and local color.

Samuel Eichelbaum's play, first staged several decades ago, has misplaced, unquestioning, instinctive loyalty as its theme. The picture is standout and a top grosser mainly because of the forceful acting of Alfred Alcon as Ecumenico Lopez, the "bravo." He conveys all the courage, sense of honor and queer chivalry, despite his savagery, which were characteristic of the Gaucho.

Lidia Lamaison, too stagily made up, but steeped in her part, plays "Natividad" the Bravo's staunch old Mother, a character almost out of Shakespeare. Arturo Garcia Buhr, as a political boss is more convincing, while Duilio Marzio and Elida Gay Palmer, as erring lovers, do what they can in stiltedly unreal roles.

This was an Argentine entry at Santa Margarita de Ligure, winning the best direction prize. It was also a succesful entry at the Argentine Rio Hondo Festival, where it won a number of awards.. It has distinct possibilities for other markets.

Nid.

Les Vieux de la Vieille
(The Old Chaps)
(FRENCH)

Paris, Sept. 27.

Cinedis release of Cite-Cinetel-Fides-Terra Film production. Stars Jean Gabin, Pierre Fresnay, Noel-Noel; features Mona Goya, Yvette Etievant, Yane Barry. Directed by Gilles Grangier. Screenplay, Rene Fallet, Michel Audiard, Grangier from the novey by Fallet; camera, Louis Page; editor, Paul Cayatte. At Paris, Paris. Running time, 90 MINS.

Jean-Marie .... Jean Gabin
Baptiste .... Pierre Fresnay
Blaise .... Noel-Noel
Catherine .... Mona Goya
Louise .... Yvette Etievant
Mariette .... Yane Barry

Three top French film character actors have a romp in this episodic tale of a trio of disgruntled, irascible old men who decide to leave their village and go into an old folks' home. However, they cause so much trouble that they have to be sent back. Full of overacting and slightly sketchy, this looms mainly as a local item.

Jean Gabin and Pierre Fresnay overdo their characters while Noel-Noel manages to get some wry wit and timing into his. Film is a series of set scenes in which each oldster has his bit to do. They play little tricks on people, gripe about the new generation and are a generally senile lot who do raise some laughs under Gilles Grangier's easy, sympahtetic direction.

Technical credits are par. This appears primarily for special situations, and lacks the more transcending qualities to make it more universal.

Mosk.

Freckles
(C-SCOPE-COLOR)

Amiable, mildly entertaining adaptation of old Gene Stratton-Porter novel, designed strictly for the juve trade.

20th Fox release of API production (Harry Spaulding). Stars Martin West, Carol Christensen; with Jack Lambert, Steven Peck, Roy Barcroft, Lorna Thayer, Ken Curtis, John Eldridge. Directed by Andrew V. McLaglen; screenplay, Harry Spaulding, based on Jean Stratton-Porter novel; camera (De Luxe Color), Floyd Crosby; editor, Harry Gerstad; music, Henry Vars. Reviewed in N.Y., Sept. 15, '60. Running time, 84 MINS.

Freckles .... Martin West
Chris .... Carol Christensen
Duncan .... Jack Lambert
Jack Barbeau .... Steven Peck
McLean .... Roy Barcroft
Miss Cooper .... Lorna Thayer
Wessner .... Ken Curtis
Mr. Cooper .... John Eldridge

Not for the first time Hollywood visits the Gene Stratton-Porter Limberlost country (Indiana) in CinemaScope and DeLuxe color, and the territory, well covered in previous "Freckles" films, again proves an especially photogenic locale for an amiable, mildly diverting drama designed strictly for the juve trade. Film also is an answer to those industry critics who think Hollywood has abandoned the family audience to tv. Picture is okay for the Saturday-Sunday matinee crowds, but will find pretty slim pickings elsewhere.

Produced by Harry Spalding and directed by Andrew V. McLaglen, this "Freckles" has, in addition to its production values, the benefit of a couple of new young faces who add a measure of freshness to film: Martin West, in the title role, and pretty Carol Christensen as the girl he woos and wins amidst only the slightest of complications.

It's this lack of any real complications, and thus excitement, which dogs Harry Spalding's screenplay and may even result in some kiddie patrons becoming a mite restless. Story tells of an earnest, 20-year-old orphan, West, who had lost one hand as a child, and how he finds a home for himself in the Limberlost country. Kid is hired by Roy Barcroft, rough, individualistic owner of a logging company to guard a 2,000-acre timber lease against lumber thieves.

Principal villian is a French-accented lumber man, Steven Peck, who challenges Barcroft's right to the timber and continues to take what he wants out of the Limberlost, trying, at the same time, to keep the young hero out of the fray. There is, however, a showdown in which West is forced to shoot it out with Peck and thus, it's indicated, becomes a man.

Though film generates very little suspense, there is a kind of appealing naivete about it, particularly in the depiction of a villian who is down deep, a good and noble soul. Under McLaglen's direction this simplicity is reflected in the performances which are wholesome and attractive but which don't give much indication of what the actors may be capable. Best things in the film are the vistas of rolling, rocky timberlands, caught so beautifully by Floyd Crosby's CinemaScope - DeLuxe color camerawork.

Anby.

Key Witness
(C'SCOPE)

Fast-moving, suspenseful crime meller with attractive young cast. Very exploitable, except in Dixie because of racial point.

Hollywood, Sept. 22.

Metro release of a Kathryn Hereford and Pandro S. Berman (Avon) Production. Features Jeffrey Hunter, Pat Crowley, Dennis Hopper, Joby Baker, Susan Harrison, Johnny Nash, Corey Allen; with Frank Silvera, Bruce Gordon, Terry Burnham, Dennis Holmes. Directed by Phil Karlson. Screenplay by Alfred Brenner and Sidney Michaels, based on novel by Frank Kane; camera (CinemaScope), Harold E. Wellman; editor, Ferris Webster; music, Charles Wolcott; art directors, George W. Davis, Malcolm Brown; sound, Franklin Milton; assistant director, Donald C. Klune. Previewed at the studio, Sept. 21, '60. Running time, 81 MINS.

Fred Morrow .... Jeffrey Hunter
Ann Morrow .... Pat Crowley
"Cowboy" .... Dennis Hopper
"Muggles" .... Joby Baker
Ruby .... Susan Harrison
"Apple" .... Johnny Nash
"Magician" .... Corey Allen
Det. Rafaey Torno .... Frank Silvera
Arthur Robbins .... Bruce Gordon
Gloria Morrow .... Terry Burnham
Phil Morrow .... Dennis Holmes

Market realities will cause Pandro S. Berman and Kathryn Hereford's hard-hitting, fast-moving, exciting little film to be beamed at the youth audience, but highly talented cast, plausible script and Phil Karlson's uncompromisingly realistic direction justify adult attention. Except for a blurred racial tolerance bit, it's a gem.

Story is the familiar yarn about gang pressure on a solid citizen who is the key witness to a murder, the terrorizing of his family etc. It's liberally laced with dope, sex, motorcycles, sports cars, switchblades and the like.

But scripters Alfred Brenner and Sidney Michaels have lined out some characters and dialog which the fine young cast, under Karlson's stimulation, make shockingly effective.

Jeffrey Hunter and Pat Crowley, a handsome pair, convincingly portray a well-heeled, suburbanite couple with two children. Hunter, as a realtor, stops in an L.A. slum district tavern to telephone and sees four young hoodlums surround and knife a boy. Naturally, he calls police then discovers that of all the witnesses to the crime, he's the only one who'll talk. (Hunter is due for future fame in Jesus Christ role "King of Kings," now completed in Spain.—Ed.).

Dennis Hopper is a chilling menace as the passionately vengeful young killer and Susan Harrison, as his girl, gives an absorbing study in exceeding far-outness—a stunning performance. Johnny Nash limns a believable, sensitive young tough and Joby Baker scores with a frightening mixture of beguiling hipness and mindless malice as a dope addict. Corey Allen gives solid support as fifth member of the youth gang.

Script doesn't attempt to explain motivations of individual members of the gang, but the very mystery this leaves in viewers' minds adds to the sense of terror—unrestrained by any recognizable values and hyped on dope, the gang could do anything. And they slug a cop to get the witness' address, bully the realtor with their car, rough up his wife, attempt to kidnap his son, etc. Karlson keeps it moving so fast that there's no time to wonder at small lapses in plot logic (why, at some points, people don't scream or call the police etc.).

Only important flaw is an unnecessary scene in which references are made to Nash's race, Negro. It's been established earlier that the Negro's the only decent one in the gang, so adding the realtor's racial prejudices into the conflict then promptly resolving them—all in a few final minutes—is dramatically unsound. It barely mars the windup, however. Frank Silvera, as a hardened detective, is among the supporting actors who add importantly to the film's tone.

Harold E. Wellman's Cinema-

Scope photography is one of the film's major assets, especially in the exciting chase sequences, and Charles Wolcott's latter-day rock music score is an important plus. Technical quality is consistently high and often superior; there was a fine unit on this one. *Glen.*

Meine Nichte tut das nicht

(My Niece Doesn't Do That)
(AUSTRIAN)

Vienna, Sept. 17.

Sascha Film release of Herbert Gruber production. Stars Conny Froboess; features Fred Bertelmann and Peter Weck; in cast, Margit Nuenke, Walter Gross, Rex Gildo, Gerti Gordon, Jack Finey, Susanne Engelhardt, Else Fambausek, Elisabeth Stiepl, C. W. Fernbach, Raoul Retzer, Ljuba Welitsch. Directed by F. J. Gottlieb. Screenplay by Janne Furch, Marie Osten-Sacken, Theo Mr. Werner; camera, Sepp Ketterer; settings, Fritz Juptner-Jonstorff and Alexander Sawszynski; music, Charly Niessen, Gerhard Froboess. At Flieger Kino, Vienna, premiere Sept. 2, '60. Running time, **90 MINS.**

Amusing comedy with good b.o. potential for the German language market, where Conny Froboess is a surefire draw.

Story concerns inside doings of a disk company, operated by ex-singer Fred Bertelmann. His niece Conny disguises in a contest. Wins of course. Peter Weck is put on her trail as detective, they fall in love and all ends well. Meanwhile there are many amusing scenes mostly thanks to the actress as her opposites, Bertelmann and Weck, fail to impress. Bertelmann, also a recording artist cannot act. Opera star Luba Welitsch was also miscast.

Charly Niessen and Gerhard Froboess contributed eight songs, all of them routine. "Jamaica" is perhaps best.

Considering the forced casting the direction of F. J. Gottlieb is efficient at taking advantages of the implicit humor, but lacks invention. Pic is neatly photographed by Sepp Ketterer.

For an inexpensive film, settings and technical credits are okay.

Maas.

Santa Claus

(COLORSCOPE)

Okay Christmas entry for the moppet trade.

K. Gordon Murray presentation of Walter Calderon production. Stars Joseph Elias Moreno. Directed by Rene Cardona. Narration by Ken Smith. Eastman Color. Filmed at Churubuso, Mexico. Musical director, Anthony Diaz Conde. Previewed in N. Y., Sept. 23, '60. Running time, **60 MINS.**

Appropriately-titled "Santa Claus" emerges as a fair entry for the juvenile trade during the Christmas season. The Mexican-made film, narrated and dubbed into English, is somewhat overlong at 94 minutes and contains a number of dull stretches, but it is not without appeal for St. Nick-believing youngsters.

Here is the traditional Yuletide gentleman with white beard, red ensemble, hearty laugh, twinkling eyes, and love for children. The Eastman color entry opens in far off space where Santa maintains his home and toy factory. Aided by youngsters of all nationalities, including Chinese Russian, Santa is busy putting the finishing touches to the gifts he is prepared to distribute. The youngsters of many nations are extremely appealing. Each group is dressed in native costumes and sings the songs of each country. Santa's factory is well equipped with modern gadgets, including an earscope, teletalker, cosmic telescope, master eye, and dreamscope. And Santa has the help of Marlin the magician who provides him with powders to keep children asleep, a golden key that opens everything, and a flower that makes him invisible.

Santa's mission to earth is frustrated by a disciple from Hades, garbed in a bright red devil's outfit. The devil's representative is charged with the task of luring children into mischief. A poor little girl is tempted to steal a doll. Three boys are persuaded to harrass St. Nick. But Santa finally outwits the devil's advocate—provides love for a poor little rich boy and a doll for the poor little poor girl.

The story is somewhat rambling and repetitious and might have been more effective if the footage had been cut. Nevertheless, children more attuned to the leisurely pace of fairy tales than to westerns and private eyes might find it diverting. It's mainly for the moppet trade.

Joseph Elias Moreno gives a good performance as Santa Claus. The dubbing job is acceptable for the film and some of the voices employed are especially fine. Technical aspects are first-rate. The film is the winner of the Golden Gate Award for the best family film at the 1959 San Francisco International Film Festival.

Holl.

Et Mourir de Plaisir

(And Die of Pleasure)
(FRENCH-ITALIAN-TECHNIRAMA-COLOR)

Paris, Sept. 26.

Paramount release of EGE-Documento Films production. Stars Mel Ferrer, Annette Vadim, Elsa Martinelli; features Serge Marquand, Marc Allegret. Directed by Roger Vadim. Screenplay, Claude Brule, Roger Vailland, Claude Martin, Vadim from novel by Sheridan Le Fanu; camera (Technicolor), Claude Renoir; editor, Victoria Mercanton. At Colisee, Paris. Running time, **87 MINS.**

Leopoldo	Mel Ferrer
Carmilla	Annette Vadim
Georgia	Elsa Martinelli
Judge	Marc Allegret
Guiseppe	Serge Marquand

Paramount has an arty, elegant vampire tale in this French-Italo film of Roger Vadim it has picked up for world release. Though pic has reportedly been pushed back on the Paramount U.S. calendar, local company reps claim it was because of too much product and had nothing to do with censor and code worries on some lesbian hints in it.

Not very scary, this is primarily an art entry with general chances mainly lower case. But there is a plus aspect in its fine color lensing.

Vadim, who made the Brigitte Bardot starrer, "And God Created Woman," takes the usual vampire legends and bring them up to date with a psychological explanation. However, he coyly intimates that they are probably so.

The descendants of a famed Germanic family, who are cousins, live in the old ancestral home. The man is to marry, but his cousin is in love with him. A doctor talks of the myths of vampirism connected with the family, and at a party the girl stumbles on the grave of the supposed vampire. Becoming possessed of the vampire, she sets out to kill the fiancee.

There is a long femme clinch as the girl gets blood on her lip from a pricked finger and the vampire goes for it. Lesbos intimations are evident and the further underlined in a dream sequence before the vampire tries for her blood.

But since her love for her cousin is the main motivation, the lesbian aspects may not offer any untoward censorship troubles. The dream symbols are also arty enough to be open to various interps. While the classic horror mold is followed, the film relies more on carefully laid out pictorial compositions and shots than in creating suspense moods.

Annette Vadim is an impassive actress whose cherubic, placid looks make it hard to take her for a vampire. Moreover, the film's vacillation between a horror opus and a tongue-in-cheek parody take the edge off the shock aspects. Mel Ferrer ad Elsa Martinelli are acceptable in the ill-defined roles of the lovers.

Vadim has given this venture visual appeal. A hard sell of the adult horror angles could make this a possible regular entry abroad. But it needs careful placing for best results. General prospects look spotty. Pic was originally called "Blood and Roses," which may be its Yank monicker. *Mosk.*

Watch Your Stern

(BRITISH)

Lighthearted with smooth performances. Made by the click "Carry On" team.

London, Sept. 14.

Anglo-Amalgamated presentation of Peter Rogers' production. Stars Kenneth Connor, Eric Barker, Leslie Phillips, Joan Sims, Noel Purcell, Hattie Jacques, Guest star, Sidney James. Features Spike Milligan, Eric Sykes. Producer, Peter Rogers. Director, Gerald Thomas. Screenplay by Alan Hackney & Vivian A. Cox, from Earle Couttie's play, "Something About a Sailor"; camera, Ted Scaife; editor, John Shirley; music, Bruce Montgomery. Previewed at Studio One, London, Sept. 14, '60. Running time, **88 MINS.**

O/S Blissworth	Kenneth Connor
Captain Foster	Eric Barker
Lt. Cmdr. Fanshawe	Leslie Phillips
Ann Foster	Joan Sims
Sir Humphrey Pettigrew	Noel Purcell
Agatha Potter	Hattie Jacques
Dockyard Matey	Spike Sullivan
Dockyard Matey	Eric Sykes
C.P.O. Mundy	Sidney James
Commander Phillips	Ed Devereaux
Security Sergeant	David Lodge
1st Sailor	Victor Maddern
Flag Lieutenant	Robin Ray
2nd Security Guard	George Street
Admiral's Secretary	Peter Howell
1st Security Guard	Michael Brennan
Coxswain	Arch Taylor
Officer of the Day	Richard Bennett
Wren Driver	Leila Williams
3rd Security Guard	Rory MacDermot
Engineer Officer	Eric Corrie

The team responsible for the clicko "Carry On" series are up to their profitable yock-raising larks again with "Watch Your Stern." The laughs come steadily and this is a safe booking for all types of audience. On the surface, this could be regarded as another "Carry On," but there is a stronger story line, characters are developed more roundly and director Gerald Thomas does not rely on a string of largely disconnected gags and situations. But the same formula of lighthearted, breezy comedy is used to very funny effect.

Screenplay by Alan Hackney and Vivian A. Cox produces some sound situations and dialog, and while occasionally corny, also comes up with some felicitous jokes and wisecracks. The yarn concerns a top secret test on an Acoustic Torpedo which, when fired, upsets arrangements by doubling in its tracks, missing the target raft and blowing up the firing ship. An Admiralty boffin is detailed to modify the torpedo, the plan gets destroyed, a copy mislaid and the destroyer's officers manage to bluff the Admiral with the plans of the ship's refrigeration plant. But it is essential that the Admiral should not meet the boffin until the right plan is at hand. This involves an electrically minded seaman being disguised, first as a Scottish scientist and then as a woman. The film is a jigsaw puzzle of mistaken identity, misunderstandings, bluffs and counter bluffs and, moving fast, the various complications keep the cheerfulness bubbling almost incessantly right up to a protracted but acceptable climax.

Acting is on a firstclass farcical comedy level, with Kenneth Connor as the unfortunate seaman projecting a likable personality and scoring heavily in his two disguises, especially when, as the "woman scientist," he has to cope with the attentions of the amorous Admiral. Connor never forces his laughs but treats his various appearances as character studies. Noel Purcell is in hearty form as the irascible Admiral and Eric Barker and Leslie Phillips as the ship's officers, responsible for nudging the plot along, keep well in character and mainly get the laughs by playing straight. Sidney James, guest-starring as a chief petty officer, enlivens his scenes as always and there is a standout cameo by Spike Sullivan and Eric Sykes as a couple of gabby electricians.

On the distaff side Hattie Jacques as a hefty woman scientist puts over her usual genial personality but Joan Sims, for once playing a straight role instead of a comedy character, nevertheless brings charm and humor to the role of Barker's sister. Jaunty music by Bruce Montgomery early sets the breezy tone of the pic and all other technical credits get the okay. This gay piece of escapist nonsense should certainly keep up the reputation of the Peter Rogers' team and the Anglo-Amalgamated stable from which they operate.

Rich.

Too Hot to Handle

(BRITISH—COLOR)

Seamy meller set in Soho's clipjoint stripperies. Jayne Mansfield's name may help this dubious entertainment at the wicket.

London, Sept. 21.

Warner-Pathe release of a Wigmore Films production. Stars Jayne Mansfield, Leo Genn, Carl Boehm. Producer, Selim Cattan. Directed by Terence Young. Screenplay, Herbert Kretzmer from an idea by Harry Lee; camera, Otto Heller; editor, Lito Carruthers; music, Eric Spear. Previewed at Studio One, Sept. 20, '60. Running time, **100 MINS.**

Midnight Franklin	Jayne Mansfield
Johnny Solo	Leo Genn
Robert Jouvel	Carl Boehm
Lilliane Decker	Danik Patisson
Novak	Christopher Lee
Cynthia	Kai Fischer
Inspector West	Patrick Holt
Mr. Arpels	Martin Boddey

Diamonds Dinelli ..... Sheldon Lawrence
Pony Tail .... Barbara Windsor
Moeller .... John Salew
Flash Gordon .... Tom Bowman
Pawnbroker .... Ian Fleming
Terry .... Penny Morrell
Melody .... Katharine Keeton
Marjorie .... Susan Denny
Maureen .... Judy Bruce
Jacky .... Elizabeth Wilson
Jungle .... Shari Khan
Piano Player .... Bill McGuffie
Tourist Guide .... Michael Balfour
Mouth .... Larry Taylor
Hostess .... June Elvin
Dinelli's Driver .... Morton Lowry
Muscles .... Harry Lane

Jayne Mansfield made a 6,000-mile journey to make this British meller, but the trip hardly seems worth it. It will need all her marquee value to sell this dubious and seamy piece of entertainment which is set among the flashy backgrounds of Soho's striptease joints.

Harry Lee is credited with the original idea, but the word "original" is flattering. Herbert Kretzmer's screenplay is hardly inspired and even that talented director, Terence Young seems dispirited with the matter on hand. Good color lensing by Otto Heller is about the most commendable aspect of a disappointing pic.

Yarn concerns the rivalry and mutual double crossing of two striptease club owners. It ends in both clubs being wrecked and one of the clubowners going to jail for his part in fixing a meeting between one of the under-age strippers and his rich backer, which results in the death of the girl. Also on hand is a French journalist who is writing a piece about the sleazy side of London nightlife.

The chief letdown is the offcolor thesping of Miss Mansfield as Midnight Franklin, star of the Pink Flamingo nightclub, who also eyes Leo Genn, a clubowner who likes to play a lone hand. Her acting is tepid and, at times, frankly ludicrous.

A fair example of the Mansfield superstructure is displayed. She also sings a couple of undistinguished numbers adequately, but in a far from pulse stirring fashion. Genn, a good actor, seems puzzled at finding himself in the film at all, and though he gives his best he cannot make the character of Johnny Solo more than a pasteboard figure.

Carl Boehm is straightforward as the journalist, Danik Patisson, a demure French actress, plays a mysterious stripper well enough, while Sheldon Lawrence as the rival club owner and Christopher Lee as Genn's treacherous right-hand man also provide useful support. Some of the nightclub girls provide neat cameos, particularly Barbara Windsor as the cute Pony Tail whose death brings about Genn's downfall.

The nightclub settings are flamboyant and overdone. Some of the production numbers come over reasonably well on the screen, though it is doubtful if they could be staged (even allowing for expense) in the average stripteasery. Dialog veers from dull to vulgar and there are many loose ends in an endeaver to provide authentic atmosphere. *Rich.*

The Magnificent Seven
(COLOR-PANAVISION)

Two-thirds sizzling, one-third fizzling western, but packs overall voltage, under John Sturges' artful guidance, to win the b.o. showdown.

Hollywood, Sept. 28.

United Artists release of John Sturges production. Stars Yul Brynner, Eli Wallach, Steve McQueen, Charles Bronson, Robert Vaughan, Brad Dexter, James Coburn; introduces Horst Buchholz; with Vladimir, Rosenda Monteros, Jorge Martinez de Hoyos, Whit Bissell, Val Avery, Bing Russell, Rico Alaniz, Robert Wilke. Directed by Sturges. Screenplay, William Roberts, based on Japanese film, "Seven Samurai"; camera, Charles Lang Jr.; editor, Ferris Webster; art director Edward FitzGerald; music, Elmer Bernstein; sound, Jack Solomon, Rafael Esparza; assistant directors, Robert Relyea, Jaime Contreras. Reviewed at Goldwyn Studios, Sept. 28, '60. Running time, 128 MINS.

Chris .... Yul Brynner
Calvera .... Eli Wallach
Vin .... Steve McQueen
Chico .... Horst Buchholz
O'Reilly .... Charles Bronson
Lee .... Robert Vaughn
Harry Luck .... Brad Dexter
Britt .... James Coburn
The Old Man .... Vladimir Sokoloff
Petra .... Rosenda Monteros
Hilario .... Jorge Martinez de Hoyos
Chamlee .... Whit Bissell
Henry .... Val Avery
Robert .... Bing Russell
Sotero .... Rico Alaniz
Wallace .... Robert Wilke

Until the women and children arrive on the scene about two-thirds of the way through, "The Magnificent Seven" is a rip-roaring, rootin' tootin' western with lots of bite and tang and old-fashioned abandon. The last third is downhill, a long and cluttered anti-climax in which "The Magnificent Seven" grow slightly too magnificent for comfort. The Mirisch-Alpha production for United Artists, with John Sturges at the creative controls, was an expensive picture to make. But it has the appealing elements for good grossing, and should rack up a profit.

Odd foundation for William Roberts able screenplay is the Japanese film, "Seven Samurai." The plot, as adapted, is simple and compelling. A Mexican village is at the mercy of a bandit (Eli Wallach), whose recurrent "visits" with his huge band of outlaws strips the meek peasant people of the fruits of their labors. Finally, in desperation, they hire seven American gunslingers for the obvious purpose. The villagers are trained for combat by these professional gunmen, a trap is laid for Wallach and his gang, and the strategy is partially successful. A number of Wallach's men are slain in the clash, but the leader and most of his band manage not only to escape to the hills but subsequently succeed in outfoxing and capturing the seven Americans while regaining control of the village.

At about this point, or just prior to it, the film begins to take itself too seriously and the pace slows to a walk. Suddenly there is a great deal of verbal thunder about fear, courage and the hopes and hazards of the gunslinging profession. Contrived, maudlin elements are introduced in a bid to shape some philosophical meaning. It is an abortive pitch for additional stature in that the simple point, intrinsically present, is patronizingly stated and labored. The seven heroes, temporarily defeated and escorted out of the village, realize that victory over Wallach and his band is no longer a mere professional matter, but has become one of affection and principle. They return and lead the villagers to victory.

There is a heap of fine acting and some crackling good direction by Sturges mostly in the early stages, during formation of the central septet. Wallach creates an extremely colorful and arresting figure as the chief antagonist. Of the big "Seven," Charles Bronson, James Coburn and Steve McQueen share top thespic honors, although the others don't lag by much, notably Horst Buchholz, who makes an auspicious screen bow in this country. Bronson fashions the most sympathetic character of the group. Coburn, particularly in an introductory sequence during which he reluctantly pits his prowess with a knife against a fast gun in an electrifying showdown, is a powerful study in commanding concentration.

McQueen, an actor who is going places, brings an appealing ease and sense of humor to his role. Yul Brynner, as the leader of the force, exhibits anew the masculine charm that has won him so many femme fans. The western setting does not appear to arouse the best in Robert Vaughn, but this fine young actor has his moments. Brad Dexter stylishly rounds out the seven. In the supporting cast, Rosenda Monteros, Jorge Martinez de Hoyos and Rico Alaniz are outstanding.

Strokes of photographic artistry aid the film, a tribute to the superior craftsmanship of director Sturges and his cameraman, Charles Lang Jr. Ferris Webster's smooth editing perfectly anticipates the visual desires of the audience. In selection of exact exterior Mexican locale and vision for texture, content and authenticity of interiors, there is true reward in Edward FitzGerald's art direction. Elmer Bernstein's lively, pulsating score, emphasizing conscious percussion, strongly resembles the work of Jerome Moross for "The Big Country." *Tube.*

Tosca
(ITALIAN—C'SCOPE—COLOR

Hollywood, Sept. 30.

Sol Hurok presentation of Cinecitta Studios (Rome) production. With Franca Duval, Franco Corelli, Alfro Poli, Vito De Taranto, Antonio Sacchetti, Aldo Corelli, Ferdinando Alfieri. Directed by Carmine Gallone. Story, Victorian Sardou, with adaptation and lyrics by Giuseppe Giacosa, Luigi Illica; camera, Giuseppe Rotunno; are director, Guido Fiorini; music, Giacomo Puccini; assistant director, Franco Cirino. Reviewed at Vista Continental Theatre, Sept. 30, '60. Running time, 112 MINS.

Floria Tosca (Sung by Maria Caniglia)
Franca Duval (Soprano)
Mario Cavaradossi..Franco Corelli (Tenor)
Scarpia .... Afro Poli (Baritone)
Sacristan .... Vito De Taranto (Baritone)
Angelotti ...... Antonio Sacchetti(Bass)
Sciarrone .... Aldo Corelli (Bass)
Spoletta ...... Ferdinand Alfieri (Tenor)

Tackling grand opera by means of the motion picture often has a way of bringing out the worst in both art forms. The opera is essentially a visually static art that relies on aural excellence for its impact. The cinema, conversely, is a visual medium dependent on scope and movement, far less concerned with the ear than the eye. Yet, in spite of this basic incompatibility, there is a great deal of merit and considerable (though naturally limited) appeal in this Italian-made motion picture version of Puccini's "Tosca." Bolstered by the support of opera buffs, presentation for which S. Hurok's name and prestige is borrowed, should enjoy a mild success in U.S. art house circles. (Typically Hurok gets a % for use of his name on art films.)

Supposedly, the film cost $2,000,000 to make, and there is certainly evidence of such expense. Lavish, elegant sets, furnishings and costumes keep the eye at attention throughout. Unfortunately the eye has other duties, principally the nagging act of scanning sub-titles as they explain what all the melodramatic and vocal hubbub is about. It would be extremely helpful if patrons (particularly those unfamiliar with "Tosca") were provided with a brief synopsis of the plot as they entered the theatre. Prior knowledge of the opera would make consultation of the titles less of a factor, and would increase general comfort and satisfaction.

Musically, this rendition of the opera is a delight. Sole drawback is the lack of spontaneity—the performers employ lip sync (all, with the exception of "Tosca" herself, to their own voices). But the singing is splendid, the orchestration vigorous, and the recording exceptionally sound. In addition to their musical and lip-matching efforts, the cast, under the artistic direction of Carmine Gallone, strives to avoid the stiff posturing common in onstage opera. Prominent among the players are tenor Franco Corelli (whose handsome looks indicate a bright future), Franca Duval (a soprano who plays "Tosca" while another soprano Maria Caniglia sings it offscreen), and baritone Afro Poli (as the villainous "Scarpia," who generates the tragedy). Orchestra and chorus of the Teatro Dell 'Opera of Rome is conducted masterfully by Oliviero De Fabritis.

Print witnessed at the preview screening was choppy, noisy and focally unstable, so that technical and photographic work could not properly be judged. *Tube.*

Girl of the Night

Exploration of the call-girl world. Hampered by an uncertain, slow-moving approach. Within adults-only limitations, should get by, but may draw the wrong customers for the wrong reasons.

Hollywood, Sept. 27.

Warner Bros. release of Max J. Rosenberg production. Stars Anne Francis, John Kerr, Lloyd Nolan, Kay Medford; with Arthur Storch, James Broderick, Lauren Gilbert; introduces Eileen Fulton, Julius Monk. Directed by Joseph Cates. Screenplay, Ted Berkman, Raphael Blau, based on "The Call Girl," psychoanalytical study by Dr. Harold Greenwald; camera, Joseph Brun; editor, Aram A. Avakian; art director, Charles Bailey; music, Sol Kaplan; sound, Ernie Zatorsky, Dick Vorisek; assistant director, Larry Sturhahn. Reviewed at the studio, Sept. 27, '60. Running time, 93 MINS.

Bobbie .... Anne Francis
Dr. Mitchell .... Lloyd Nolan
Rowena .... Kay Medford
Larry .... John Kerr
Jason Franklin Jr. .... Arthur Storch
Dan Bolton .... James Broderick
Mr. Shelton .... Lauren Gilbert
Lisa .... Eileen Fulton
Swagger .... Julius Monk

Another filmmaking taboo falls by the wayside in Warner's "Girl of the Night," a well-meaning attempt to shed some serious light on the dark doings of the call-girl

profession. Max J. Rosenberg's Vanguard production has a positive, uplifting thrust about it, as well as some frank, arresting passages, but has also a tendency to grow alternately vivid and fuzzy, to come in and out of focus as it examines the personal problem of one rather reluctant practitioner of big business sex. In groping for artistic eloquence, it hesitates for effect at vital junctures, slowing up the story, laboring and clouding the issue, creating an outside-looking-in aspect at odds with the cardinal purpose of character penetration.

All of which leaves the Warner release in a potential boxoffice quandry. Obviously aimed at an adults—only audience, it does not appear to be the artistic triumph that would spur the enthusiastic word-of-mouth or critical acclaim to draw the mature audience for which it is tastefully intended. Rather, it is an offbeat, fairly provocative and workmanlike effort that may have to rely heavily on the old-fashioned sex-sell to pull in the customers, many of whom may come secking cheap thrills they won't find. It should do well within its limitations, perhaps surprisingly well in certain situations.

"The Call Girl," a psychoanalytical study by Dr. Harold Greenwald, serves as foundation for the well-written screenplay by Ted Berkman and Raphael Blau. Anne Francis limns the title role, that of a girl who seeks the aid of psychologist Lloyd Nolan when she learns the long-range intentions of her boy friend (John Kerr) aren't exactly honorable. Under Nolan's influence she musters the moral courage to break free from Kerr's domination, under which she has been operating as call girl to provide his sole means of support under the naive pretext that financially-solvent marraige is their mutual goal. There are two sizzling scenes, both exceptionally well-handled, both subtly illustrating the actual call-girl operation.

Miss Francis really sinks her pretty teeth into the part, probably the most challenging and important of her career. She does a vigorous, persuasive job. The role of an out-and-out heel is a complete thespic depatrure for Kerr, up to now almost exclusively mired in "sensitive" characters. He indicates a flare for this type of emoting, but is forced to cope with a rather unrealistic character whose appeal (to the heroine) and approach to life are only vaguely suggested.

Nolan, who has little to do but look sympathetic and concerned while Miss Francis tells her troubles from the couch, does his usual dependable work. Kay Medford is a convincing and colorful madame. Arthur Storch and Lauren Gilbert are exceptionally disturbing as a couple of unsavory types and James Broderick is competent in one of the few likeable roles. The film introduces Julius Monk, who is interesting as the madame's personal parasite, and Eileen Fulton in a brief, but poignant enactment of a doomed newcomer to the call girl ranks. Miss Fulton looks particularly promising.

Joseph Cates' direction rises beautifully to the occasion when

the going gets hot and heavy. But he fails to maintain the desirable swift pace throughout. Parts of the film are tediously drawn out, presumably for atmospheric effect. Sol Kaplan's music is unusually melodic and consciously listenable. Accomplished craftsmanship is exhibited by lensman Joseph Brun and art director Charles Bailey. Aram A. Avakian's editing is occasionally sluggish, although it appears as if he was instructed to labor his fades to create a mood that may backfire by making audiences restless.   *Tube.*

L'Affaire D'Une Nuit
(A One Night Affair)
(FRENCH)

Paris, Oct. 4.
Pathe release of Progefi production. Stars Pascale Petit. Features Roger Hanin, Pierre Mondy. Directed by Henri Verneuil. Screenplay. Jean Aurenche, Henri Jeanson, Verneuil, from a novel by Alain Moury; camera, Robert Lefevbre; editor, Leonide Azar. At Balzac, Paris. Running time, **95 MINS.**
Catherine .... Pascale Petit
Michel .... Roger Hanin
Antoine .... Pierre Mondy

Tale of adultery uses a snide approach to the whole affair to make its satirical, comedic and ironic attempts bungle. Fun is labored, insight is meagre and it is mainly an exploitation item for foreign spots on its insouciant look at a one-night affair between a married man and the wife of an old friend.

A man, with two hours on his hands, meets an old school chum. He gets the chore of driving his friend's wife somewhere and a flirtation starts which ends in an all night affair which leads to troubles in the morning.

The husband decides to go off to join the army in Algeria while the philanderer is left with only a shallow quirk of conscience. Pic has too many local illusions and jibes in its dialog. The characters are plotted disagreeable and cynical without any true wit or insight into their lives or motivations to make this a fairly unpleasant comedy.

Pascale Petit and Roger Hanin lack the lightness and timing for their roles of the lovers while Pierre Mondy is much better and more human as the cuckolded husband. Direction is also heavy-handed, and there is a disrespect for its characters which makes this would-be racy situation comedy more waspish than naughty.

Technical credits are good. This is one of those adulterous comedies that has exploitation values but not the class for more arty chances.   *Mosk.*

Cresus
(FRENCH-FRANSCOPE)

Paris, Oct. 4.
Gaumont release of Giono Films production. Stars Fernandel. Features Marcelle Ranson, Rene Genin, Sylvie, Rellys. Olivier Hussenot, Helene Tossi. Written and directed by Jean Giono. Camera, Roger Hubert; editor, R. M. Isnardon. At Ambassade-Gaumont, Paris. Running time, **100 MINS.**

Jules .... Fernandel
Fine .... Marcelle Ranson
Pere .... Rene Genin
Teacher .... Sylvie
Paul .... Rellys
Agent .... Olivier Hussenot

Jean Giono is a noted French novelist from whose books Marcel Pagnol adapted many of his better pre-war pix like "The Baker's Wife," "Harvest," "Angele" and "Joffre." Giono has written some scripts and now turns writer-director to handle his first film in this capacity.

Result is a fairly sturdy peasant comedy but sans the scope, brashness, insight and bawdiness that Pagnol gave Giono's works. It is chancey abroad except for possible art spotting on its theme and the Fernandel monicker.

Fernandel is a sheepherder who is content to have a neighboring widow come over from time to time and feud with his suspicious, petty fellow herdsmen. He discovers a great cache of money and gives a big party at which he makes his fellowmen even more jealous.

He gets revenge by distributing the money among them and making them uneasy and edgy. But it turns out to be counterfeit currency which the Germans had wanted to use in retreat during the last war to upset French economy.

Fernandel is more subdued than usual and has some solid comic bits. Giono displays a good eye for scenery, though it is arid in a poor section of France, and a good use of character actors. But the film is familiar without the freshness and uniqueness to make its anecdote more penetrating or comic. It is technically good.   *Mosk.*

La Francaise Et L'Amour
(The French Woman and Love)
(FRENCH)

Paris, Oct. 4.
Unidex release of Metzger & Woog-Paris Elysee Film Production. **Stars** Sophie Desmarets, Dany Robin, Paul Meurisse, Jean-Paul Belmondo, Annie Girardot, Francois Perrier, Martine Carol, Robert Lamoureux, Simone Renant. Directed by Jean-Paul Le Chanois, Christian-Jaque, Henri Verneuil, Rene Clair, Michel Boisrond, Jean Delannoy, Henri Decoin. Screenplay, Felecien Marceau, Louise De Vilmorin, Jacques Robert, Annette Wademant, Clair, France Roche, Michel Audiard, Charles Speak, Marcel Ayme; camera, Robert Lefebvre; editor, Jacques Lebreton. At Normandie, Paris. Running time, **135 MINS.**
Dufieux .... Darry Cowl
Mother .... Sophie Desmarets
Nicole .... Dany Robin
Jean .... Paul Meurisse
Gil .... Jean-Paul Belmondo
Danielle .... Annie Girardot
Michel .... Francois Perier
Elaine .... Martine Carol
Desire .... Robert Lamoureux

Based on a love survey among a cross-section of French women, and launched with savvy publicity and a saleable title, this series of light sketches looks to be a good Continental entry. However, the sketches, which only use the interesting statistics as a jumping off point for familiar little bits, may have harder going abroad. But it has hypo qualities on theme, outlook and solid marquee names.

Seven sketches are destined to show femme comportment in childhood, adolescence, virginity, marriage, adultery, divorce or living alone. Seven directors handled these. Their segments differ in style but are mainly light, conventional and aim for comedy rather than any real insight into the female psyche.

A little girl asks where babies come from for a forced comedic item when she's told they come

from cabbages. An adolescent girl begins to kiss boys and worry her parents only to grow out of it in a skimpy sketch. A girl gives in to her fianceee's demands since they will marry anyway.

Two newlyweds have their first quarrel and decide to make concessions; an urbane husband neglects his wife but copes with her cheating on him for the most insouciant sketch since he has a mistress; a friendly divorce turns into bitterness due to conniving lawyers, and a Don Juan tries to bring love to two emancipated women only to end in prison, femme lawyer waiting for him when he gets out.

Acting is acceptable, and most stylish direction comes from old-timer Rene Clair in his knowing, light comic handling of a newly-wed couple. All the parts are outlines for situation sex comedies and seem fragile.

But with firm handling and ballyhoo, this could have some commercial mileage in it. All sketches are held together by a racy commentary and witty little animated strips with technical credits balanced and good.
            Mosk.

Una Cancion Para
Recordar
(A Song to Remember)
(MEXICAN-COLOR)

Mexico City, Sept. 27.
Peliculas Nacionales release of Cinematografica Latino Americana. S. A. production. Stars Evangelina Elizondo, Ana Bera Lepe; features Carlos Cores, Virma Gonzalez, Miguelito Valdes, Alejandro Algara. Directed by Julio Bracho. Camera, Rosalio Solano; music, Chucho Zarzosa. At Olimpia Theatre, Mexico City. Running time, **90 MINS.**

While this musical was made some time ago, its producers are cashing in on news value of the film's femme stars. Both were principals in recent murders of boy friends by ex-hubby and father, respectively, of Evangelina Elizondo and Ana Berta Lepe.

Although billed as star, Miss Lepe appears but briefly in some song and dance scenes. Julio Bracho does not add to his directing laurels with this one, though it is a fairly acceptable Mexican movie musical. Weak book features Miss Elizondo as gal with usual l'amour troubles, with these resolved in final clinch.

Sandwiched in the footage are dances, songs and rhythms featuring ditties best liked in Latin America. There is a comic bit by Virma Gonzalez who starred in Mexican stage version of "Redhead," and comedy turns by Miguelito Valdez and Alejandro Algara.

Technical quality is good. Top tunes of past and present are featured, "St. Louis Blues," "Aloha," "Babalu," "Brasil," "Ti-Pi-Ti-Pi-Tin," etc. Picture is slated for strong promotion in the Latin American market.   *Emil.*

Spartacus

SUPER TECHNIRAMA 70; COLOR)

Big Roman spectacle. Bloody and Powerful. A big money picture.

Hollywood, Oct. 18.

Universal release of Bryna Production. Stars Kirk Douglas, Laurence Olivier, Jean Simmons, Charles Laughton, Peter Ustinov, John Gavin, Tony Curtis; with Nina Foch, Herbert Lom, John Ireland, John Dall, Charles McGraw, Joanna Barnes, Harold J. Stone, Woody Strode, Peter Brocco, Paul Lambert, Robert J. Wilke, Nicholas Dennis, John Hoyt, Frederic Worlock, Dayton Lummis. Executive producer Kirk Douglas. Produced by Edward Lewis. Directed by Stanley Kubrick. Screenplay, Dalton Trumbo, based on Howard Fast novel; camera (Technicolor), Russell Metty; editor Robert Lawrence; music, Alex North; asst. director, Marshall Green. Reviewed at Directors Guild, Oct. 4, '60. Running time, **196 MINS.**

Spartacus .... Kirk Douglas
Crassus .... Laurence Olivier
Varinia .... Jean Simmons
Gracchus .... Charles Laughton
Batiatus .... Peter Ustinov
Caesar .... John Gavin
Helena .... Nina Foch
Tigranes .... Herbert Lom
Crisus .... John Ireland
Glabrus .... John Dall
Marcellus .... Charles McGraw
Claudia .... Joanna Barnes
David .... Harold J. Stone
Draba .... Woody Strode
Ramon .... Peter Brocco
Gannicus .... Paul Lambert
Guard Captain .... Robert J. Wilke
Dionysius .... Nicholas Dennis
Roman Officer .... John Hoyt
Laelius .... Frederick Worlock
As Antoninus .... Tony Curtis

It took a lot of moolah—U says $12,000,000—and two years of intensive work to bring "Spartacus" to the screen. Film justifies the effort. By this time next year Universal, which supplied the bankroll for this Bryna Production, should be happily contemplating a rich harvest of dividends.

"Spartacus" appears to have what it takes to satisfy the multitudes. There is more than a sufficiency of grandscale spectacle and thunderous physical commotion to satisfy elemental audience tastes. Moreover, there is solid dramatic substance, purposeful and intriguingly contrasted character portrayals and, let's come right out with it, sheer pictorial poetry that is sweeping and savage, intimate and lusty, tender and bitter-sweet.

This is one of those rare big pictures in which none of the performers gets lost, in which each, however limited or large his or her role, makes a positive contribution to the 196-minute (plus intermission) canvas composed under the direction of Stanley Kubrick. Kirk Douglas, executive producer, has the longest role as Spartacus and performs nobly, yet there are many rich moments that are made the most of by Laurence Olivier, Jean Simmons, Peter Ustinov, Charles Laughton, Tony Curtis, John Gavin, John Ireland and Woody Strode.

Behind them there is an army of featured and bit role players who contribute importantly, and there are unbilled extras who never speak a word but loom large, if fleetingly, as faces in the crowd—youngsters and old people—faces on which are graphically etched the agony, hopes and crushing despair of a lifetime.

Behind-the-camera brigade all rate a salute, particularly producer Edward Lewis, cinematographer Russell Metty, production designer Alexander Golitzen, art director Eric Orbom, set decorators Russell A. Gausman and Julia Heron, composer Alex North, assistant director Marshall Green, film editor Robert Lawrence and his assistants, Robert Schulte and Fred Chulak, and the sound crew composed of Waldon O. Watson, Joe Lapis, Murray Spivack and Ronald Pierce.

But the individual who emerges above all is Director Kubrick. At 31, and with only four other pix behind him—"Paths of Glory," "The Killing," "Fear and Desire" and "The Killer's Kiss"—Kubrick has out-DeMilled the old master in spectacle, without ever permitting the story or the people who are the core of the drama to become lost in the shuffle. He demonstrates here a technical talent and comprehension of human values.

True, he had a remarkably good screenplay with which to work, yet it was not at first entirely to his satisfaction and he worked it over several times during filming with the writer. Latter, of course, is Dalton Trumbo, whose name appears on film for the first time in about a decade since he served a prison sentence for contempt of Congress because he refused to declare whether he was or was not a member of the Communist party. While the question of Trumbo's political position may again become an issue here as in "Exodus," there is no ignoring that the man is a helluva craftsman.

"Spartacus" is a rousing testament to the spirit and dignity of man. Although it deals with a revolt by slaves against the pagan Roman Empire, the desire for freedom from oppression that motivates Spartacus has its modern counterpart today in areas of the world that struggle under Communist tyranny and it stands as a sharp reminder for all mankind that there can be no truly peaceful sleep whilst would-be conquering legions stand poised to suppress. Whether the picture carries out the intent and content as well of the Howard Fast (who has acknowledged his disillusionment with Moscow) novel, this observer can't report having found the book ponderous going for 152 pages.

Some will take exception to the brutal nature of "Spartacus" and not without cause in a couple of sequences. For instance, when Olivier as the voluptuary patrician General Crassus slits the neck of a gladiator and his face is spattered with the victim's blood, or in the savage climactic battle between the slaves and Roman legions when a warrior's arm is severed by a sword. Realism has its place, but there may well be a limit to the shock audiences can be expected to take in Technicolor and on the magnified 70m film.

There is more violence, more frank sex exposition per frame in "Spartacus" than has yet been put on the screen in any single picture. Yet it is overall not offensive, for it is part of a soaring pictorial canvas that is a harsh and convincingly honest representation of a debauched and all powerful, corrupt ruling order. Almost every sequence merits detailed, individual discussion. Nothing seen up to now on the screen, however, can quite match in savage excitement the training process for gladiators or the duel in which the towering Woody Strode, armed with triton and net, engages in mortal combat for the enjoyment of depraved female Roman nobles (Nina Foch and Joanna Barnes) with Kirk Douglas, wielding a stunted Thracian sword. And in terms of spectacle the clash between the slave army led by Douglas and the Romans commanded by Olivier is nothing short of flabbergasting.

In acting honors among the principals the fair decision would seem to be a draw, for each in his own way is exceptionally good. Douglas is the mainstay of the picture. He is not particularly expressive—not in contrast with the sophisticated Olivier, the conniving parasite of a gladiator ring operator portrayed by Ustinov, or the supple and subtle slave maiden represented by Miss Simmons. But Spartacus is, after all, an uneducated, searching man (though sometimes he speaks with astonishing depth and fluency). He is consumed and driven by a desire to be a free man, to walk with his head held high. Douglas succeeds admirably in giving an impression of a man who is all afire inside, and that is what was required to give stature and force to Spartacus. Ustinov emerges as an engaging rascal due to his adroit acting and thanks to some delightfully, sardonically humorous dialog supplied by Trumbo. Tony Curtis as the Italian slave, Antoninus, who serves as houseboy to Olivier before running away to join Spartacus, gives a nicely balanced performance in a role that calls for mercurial qualities and positive boldness.

Miss Simmons at times looks too pretty, under field camp conditions, as a slavey. However, that's a minor fault, for her performance has sincerity, heart and depth, especially in the climactic scenes when Olivier is trying to win her affection after crucifying hundreds of captured slaves on wooden crosses along the Appian Way. That, incidentally, is a truly horrendous scene. Laughton is superbly wily and sophisticated as a Republican Senator who is outwitted by Olivier in attempting to gain control of Rome through sponsorship of the young Julius Caesar. John Gavin plays the latter adequately.

Some 8,000 Spanish soldiers became Roman legionaires for the massive battle sequences filmd outside Madrid, but the rest of the picture was made in Hollywood. "Spartacus" is a whale of a motion picture. *Pry.*

Surprise Package

Yul Brynner, Mitzi Gaynor and Noel Coward provide far less fun than they seem to think in this takeoff on a deported American mobster.

Columbia release of Stanley Donen production, directed by Donen. Stars Yul Brynner, Mtz Gaynor, Noel Coward; features Eric Pohlmann, George Coulouris, Guy Deghy, Warren Mitchell, Lyndon Brook, Alf Dean. Screenplay, Harry Kurnitz; based on book by Art Buchwald; camera, Christopher Challis; editor, James Clark; music, Benjamin Frankel; song, "Surprise Package," Sammy Cahn and James Van Heusen. At Loew's 72d St. Theatre, Manhattan, Sept. 29, '60. Running time, **100 MINS.**

Nico March .... Yul Brynner
Johnny Stettina .... Bill Nagy
Gabby Rogers .... Mitzi Gaynor
Two U.S. Marshals ...... Lionel Burton, Barry Foster
Stefan Miralis .... Eric Pohlmann
King Pavel II .... Noel Coward
Dr. Hugo Panzer ...... George Coulouris
Igor Trofim ..... "Man Mountain" Dean
Klimatis .... Warren Mitchell
Tibor Smolny .... Guy Deghy
Stavrin .... Lyndon Brook

Players, director and writer all seem to assume they're pulling off something outrageously funny in "Surprise Package." The picture has that kind of air about it—a "look how impishly clever we are" attitude that's noticeable in the script, the staging and the thesp work. But it doesn't quite come off.

Takeoff on a big-deal mobster, deported by the U.S. Government to his native Greece, sometimes provides a chuckle via lines from the Harry Kurnitz screenplay.

Too often though the would-be satirical taking of what has been, basically, a reallife Napoleon-to-Elba situation a la Lucky Luciano misses out on genuine wit.

Perhaps the subject is simply nothing to be laughed at. Or, the drawback might be that only one individual on screen has any natural simpatico and he is killed (which is rather a tasteless turn for the film to take).

A book by Art Buchwald is credited as the original source material. The book presumably was Buchwald's "A Gift from the Boys" although this curiously is not listed in the Columbia fact sheet.

Yul Brynner is a caricature of a foreign-born denizen of the Stateside underworld, Mitzi Gaynor is a caricature of a dumb blond and Noel Coward plays Noel Coward playing a supercillious deposed king who lives regally on the small Grecian island to which Brynner is banished.

Buchwald's novel involved an Italian, now he's a Greek. Anyway, in "Package" he arranges for his cohorts to ship him a satchel of loot. But there's a doublecross and instead he gets a gift from the boys in the form of Miss Gaynor.

Eric Pohlmann is a cliche as a double-dealing local police chief. George Coulouris is a routine foreign intrigue type and Man Mountain Dean is positively goofy as Coulouris' oversized aide.

Warren Mitchell, Guy Deghy, Bill Nagy and Lyndon Brook round out the major part of the cast.

Under Stanley Donen's direction, "Package" moves fast but sometimes erratically and now and then with a story twist suddenly abandoned or not made clear. The editing in some instances is too abrupt. Christopher Challis' camera picked up some interesting views of historic ruins in the Grecian island (film actually was lensed on Rhodes) and otherwise rates as okay.

Title of the picture is the title of a song (and dance bit) done by Miss Gaynor and Coward. It's introduced like from right out of left field. It's a strange interlude. Add lots of cheesecake to the scenic values, what with Miss Gaynor in briefie lingerie (she finally marries Brynner so that part of it is all right) and the substantially undressed nifties who comprise Coward's "court." *Gene.*

Poima O More
(Poem of the Sea)
(RUSSIAN—COLOR)

Paris, Oct. 11.

Mosfilm production and release. With Zinaida Kirienko, Boris Livanov, Boris Andreev. Mikhail Tzarev. Directed by Julia Solnsteva. Screenplay, Alexandre Dovjenko; camera (Sovcolor), Gueorgui Eguiazarov; editor, Miss Solnsteva. At Caumartin, Paris. Running time, 110 MINS.
Girl .... Zinaida Kirienko
Boy .... Mikhail Tzarev
Father .... Boris Andreev
General .... Boris Livanov

The late Alexandre Dovjenko's silent film, "Earth," was a lyrical opus which was voted one of the 12 greatest films ever at the Brussels Greatest Films of All- Time Fest in 1958. Present pic was entirely scripted by him before he died. It was directed by his wife Julia Solnsteva, and it is a tribute to their relationship that the pic has his poetic stamp and feeling and transcends its politico outlook.

The story concerns a little town that is to be sacrificed by being covered by an inland artificial lake when a new dam is opened. Many people come back to take a last look at their home town. Some of the residents try to fight and stick to their land.

Sometimes the sentiment is almost garish and flamboyant as in a scene where a girl, jilted by a Don Juanish type, dreams of her own death. The color is uneven and some of the playing is affected and stilted.

Its extolling of the Russian way of life makes this a chancey item abroad, but by giving both sides could make this an arty item. It does infer that the Soviet way of life will eventually iron out all individual differences and the progress is more important for the masses than for those who can't cope with it.

This is a risky export item. The widescreen effect is well utilized.
Mosk.

Foxhole in Cairo
(BRITISH)

Confused, tepid thriller based on a real wartime spy episode; frigid b.o. prospect.

London, Oct. 4.

British Lion (in association with Britannia Films Distributors) release of an Omnia Film (Steven Pallos-Donald Taylor) production. Stars James Robertson Justice; features Albert Lieven, Adrian Hoven, Niall MacGinnis, Peter Van Eyck, Robert Urquhart, Neil McCallum, Fennella Fielding, Gloria Mestre. Directed by John Moxey. Screenplay by Leonard Mosley, Donald Taylor, from Mosley's book, "Cat and the Mice"; editor, Oswald Hafenrichter; camera, Desmond Dickinson; music, Wolfram Roehrig, Douglas Gamley, Ken Jones. At Odeon, Leicester-square, London, Oct. 4, '60. Running time, 80 MINS.
Captain Robertson D.S.O.
                    James Robertson Justice
John Eppler .... Adrian Hoven
Radek .... Niall MacGinnis
Count Almaszy......... Peter Van Eyck
Major Wilson .... Robert Urquhart
Sandy .... Neil McCallum
Yvette .... Fanella Fielding
Amina .... Gloria Mestre
Rommel .... Albert Lieven
Roger .... John Westbrook
Aberle .... Lee Montague
Colonel Zeltinger........... Henry Oscar
British Major..Howard Marion Crawford
S.S. Colonel .... Anthony Newlands
General .... Richard Vernon
Weber .... Michael Caine
Rommel's Aide .... Storm Durr
Signorina Signorelli......Nancy Nevison
1st Barman .... John Blythe

Newspaperman Leonard Mosley did a good, compelling job with his book, "The Cat and the Mice," which was based on a factual wartime spy story. But the book has not translated to the screen in any way to stir the pulse. War correspondent Mosley's yarn emerges as a tepid piece of espionage, confused to the point of dullness. Since Mosley collaborated with Donald Taylor on the screenplay, he must accept some responsibility for the outcome. But the major blame must be laid on John Moxey's desperately stolid direction, and editing by Oscar Hafenrichter which is so flabby that confusion is inevitable.

The story's set in Cairo of 1942, and tells how a German playboy named John Eppler is smuggled into Cairo to spy for Rommel. British counter-espionage captures Eppler just in time to prevent Rommel winning the Battle of Alamein. This simple factual story is tricked out with glamorous spies and a final climactic scrap which are all probably authentic, but don't look like it on the screen.

The dialog, fortunately, is sharp but the thesps have to go through some rather turgid situations.

Acting is mostly competent rather than inspired, with Albert Lieven, as a well-studied Rommel; Adrian Hoven, a lively but not very convincing Eppel and James Robertson Justice, as bluffly hearty as usual the boss of Britain's Naval counter - espionage service. There are also some useful cameos by Henry Oscar, Howard Marion Crawford, Niall MacGinnis and Neil McCallum. Robert Urquhart plays, with some skill, the unbelievable part of a weak British officer whose infatuation for a Cairo dancer nearly plays the British into Rommel's hands.

On the distaff side, Fanella Fielding, as a Jewish agent, gives poise and sharp authenticity to a cardboard role while Gloria Mestre, as a glamorous dancing Mata Hari, acts slightly better than she dances, which isn't at all well. Technically the film is okay, apart from some violent cutting, with some genuine newsreel battle scenes being introduced not too obtrusively. "Foxhole" obviously started off as a very alert idea for a film. Somewhere along the line it lost its way. The result is turgid fare.
Rich.

Comment Qu'Elle Est!
(What a Girl!
(FRENCH)

Paris, Oct. 11.

Prodis release of CICC production. Stars Eddie Constantine; features Francoise Brion, Francoise Prevost, Andre Luguet, Alfred Adam, Robert Berri. Directed by Bernard Borderie. Screenplay, Marc-Gilbert Sauvajon, Borderie from book by Peter Cheney; camera, Robert Juillard; editor, Christian Gaudin. At George V, Paris. Running time, 95 MINS.
Lemmy .... Eddie Constantine
Martine .... Francoise Brion
Isabelle .... Francoise Prevost
General .... Andre Luguet
Girotti .... Alfred Adam
Dombie .... Robert Berri

Eddie Constantine, the Yank singer-actor who became a star here playing a hardboiled U.S. G-Man in French film mellers, now is back to these pix after some years' absence making films in Great Britain and West Germany. This is the usual sleek item of this kind sans any distinguishing characteristics to make this anything but a dualer or video entry abroad.

Here, Constantine is a G-Man sent to help the French secret police catch a spy. He drinks gallons of Scotch, meets plenty of willing girls, mercilessly slugs people around but emerges victorious and unruffled after it all is over. Constantine is the impishly impudent, impolite but engaging character which made him a star in Europe. These vehicles are still substandard glossy renditions of like Yank entries and are of interest only on their exploitable sex and violence tags.

Supporting cast is okay as are technical credits, and fight scenes are better staged than in most French pix.
Mosk.

Que Bonito Amor
(Ah, Love Is Beautiful)
(MEXICAN)

Mexico City, Oct. 4.

Peliculas Nacionales release of Grovas Productions production. Stars Antonio Aguilar, Lola Beltran; features Joaquin Cordero, Luz Maria Aguilar. Directed by Mauricio de la Serna. Screenplay, Fernando and Jose Luis Galiana. At Mariscala Theatre, Mexico City. Running time, 90 MINS.

Lola Beltran and Antonio Aguilar are cast as would-be-weds before the altar, during the uniting ceremony. But when the officiating priest comes to the words signifying that the wife must obey hubby an argument ensues which breaks off ceremony. Two principals then set about proving that each is capable of dominating life, and each other, under married bliss status.

Antonio Aguilar is an old trouper in these light comedy turn films, added to which he bursts into song at regular intervals. Lola Beltran is competent too, but does not photograph too well, perhaps because of camera angles.

Unpretentious film fare, obviously aimed at nabe houses and markets in Latin America where both stars have a following. Feature, without being exceptional, has more originality than usual modest national efforts of this type.
Emil.

Mundo, Demonio y Carne
(The World, Flesh and the Devil)
(MEXICAN)

Mexico City, Oct. 4.

Peliculas Nacionales release of Calderon Films production. Stars Columba Dominguez, Luz Maria Aguilar, Olivia Micheli; features Cesar del Campo, Marisa Prado, Jorge del Campo, Tony Carbajal, Augusto Benedico. Directed by Jose Diaz Morales. Screenplay, Jesus Cardenas; music, Antonio Diaz Conde. At Orfeon Theatre, Mexico City. Running time, 90 MINS.

With nudity in Mexican films prohibited by federal legislation, boxoffice success is sometimes sought by accenting morbid, sensational and sexy themes.

Luz Maria Aguilar is the beautiful "devil" whose perverseness destroys lives of all who touch her. She becomes "saved" by viewing and praying to a holy image in a church at the end. There is also a long-winded sermon by a priest on the follies of the flesh.

This is billed "for adults only." But it falls far short of an attempt to emulate Frenchmen who turn out pix with audacious themes. There are "sexy rhythm" dances of abandon by shapely senoritas in costumes scantier than usual, featuring Leon Escobar and his group. There's also frenzied music sensually played by Mario Patron's combo.

While frowned on by the Legion of Decency and authorities, this sort of effort aimed at nabe houses is lapped up by public. It probably will do fair business in Latin America, too.
Emil.

Midnight Lace
(COLOR)

Artistically mounted but contrived mystery meller. Bolstered by presence of Doris Day and beaucoup elements to attract femme patrons, upshot should be b.o. click in the Ross Hunter tradition.

Hollywood, Sept. 26.

Universal release of Ross Hunter-Martin Melcher production. Stars Doris Day, Rex Harrison, John Gavin, Myrna Loy, Roddy McDowall; features Herbert Marshall, Natasha Parry, John Williams, Hermione Baddeley; with Richard Ney, Anthony Dawson, Rhys Williams, Richard Lupino, Doris Lloyd. Directed by David Miller. Screenplay, Ivan Goff, Ben Roberts, from the play, "Matilda Shouted Fire," by Janet Green; camera, Russell Metty; editors, Russell F. Schoengarth, Leon Barsha; art directors, Alexander Golitzen, Robert Clatworthy; music, Frank Skinner; sound, Waldon O. Watson, Joe Lapis; assistant directors, Phil Bowles, Carl Beringer, Doug Green. Reviewed at Academy Awards Theatre, Sept. 26, '60. Running time, **108 MINS.**

Kit Preston .... Doris Day
Anthony Preston .... Rex Harrison
Brian Younger .... John Gavin
Aunt Bea .... Myrna Loy
Malcolm .... Roddy McDowall
Charles Manning ...... Herbert Marshall
Peggy Thompson .... Natasha Parry
Dora .... Hermione Baddeley
Inspector Byrnes .... John Williams
Daniel .... Richard Ney
Ash .... Anthony Dawson
Victor Elliott .... Rhys Williams
Foster .... Richard Lupino
Nora .... Doris Lloyd

Doris Day is off and running again in "Midnight Lace," a contrived and not very mysterious mystery melodrama that most audiences will love. The Ross Hunter-Arwin production spends most of its time purposely misleading the spectator, steering him into a motivational maze, casting suspicion on everyone but the proper party. But, for all of its vagaries, the Universal release is so craftily manufactured, so luxuriously mounted and so artistically framed that audiences will have a fine time. Hunter, U, Marty Melcher, Day & Co. appear to have themselves another hit.

As in most of Hunter's recent efforts, the emphasis is on visual satisfaction. His idea, successful up to now, seems to be to keep the screen attractively filled. First and foremost, it is mandatory to have a lovely and popular star of Miss Day's calibre. She is to be decked out in an elegant wardrobe and surrounded by expensive sets and tasteful furnishings. This is to be embellished by highly dramatic lighting effects and striking hues, principally in the warmer yellow-brown range of the spectrum. The camera is to be maneuvered, whenever possible, into striking, unusual positions.

Basis of the fuss is, preferably, to be a melodrama, but a light, sophisticated comedy is an acceptable alternative. That it works so well in this film is a credit to the cinema skills of people such as cameraman Russell Metty, art directors Alexander Golitzen and Robert Clatworthy, set decorator Oliver Emert, editors Russell F. Schoengarth and Leon Barsha, and gown designer Irene, all operating under Hunter's enthusiastic surveillance.

In "Midnight Lace," which Ivan Goff and Ben Roberts have adapted from Janet Green's play, "Matilda Shouted Fire," Miss Day is victimized by what seems to be a crank on the telephone. Informed by a nagging, mysterious, persistent caller that her life is in jeopardy, she works herself into such a lather that others, Scotland Yard included, begin to believe her obsession is the myth of a neglected wife (husband Rex Harrison is constantly and unaccountably preoccupied with business matters).

Among the chief suspects are John Gavin, a construction gang foreman who makes phone calls in a neighborhood pub; Roddy McDowall, a spoiled young punk who can't keep his eyes off the heroine; and Herbert Marshall, treasurer in Harrison's firm who's having trouble paying off his bookie. There is the standard hokum of producers requesting that the "unique plot development" (another way to term "the ending") not be revealed. Actually, it's more preposterous than "unique." A less ingenious, more botched up plot to kill is difficult to envision.

The effervescent Miss Day sets some sort of record here for frightened gasps. As executed by her, even a gasp can be attractive. Harrison is capable, as are McDowall, Marshall, Gavin, Myrna Loy, Natasha Parry, Hermione Baddeley and Richard Ney. John Williams, type-cast as a Yard inspector, does quite well.

Director David Miller adds a few pleasant little humorous touches and generally makes the most of an uninspired yarn, building suspense with whatever device is handy, be it curtain to rustle, fireplace to crackle ominously or footstep to overhear. Frank Skinner's score unobtrusively heightens the tension. *Tube.*

G.I. Blues
(COLOR)

Elvis Presley returns in a flimsy, creaky military musical. Curiosity about the star should hypo b.o., but that vast teenage following has matured and the new crop of youngsters will find less to squeal about.

Hollywood, Oct. 14.

Paramount release of Hal Wallis production. Stars Elvis Presley, Juliet Prowse; with Robert Ivers, Leticia Roman, James Douglas, Sigrid Maier, Arch Johnson. Directed by Norman Taurog. Screenplay, Edmund Beloin, Henry Garson; camera, Loyal Griggs; editor, Warren Low; art directors, Hal Pereira, Walter Tyler; music, Joseph J. Lilley. Reviewed at Westwood Village Theatre, Oct. 14, '60. Running time, **115 MINS.**

Tulsa McCauley .... Elvis Presley
Lili .... Juliet Prowse
Cooky .... Robert Ivers
Tina .... Laticia Roman
Rick .... James Douglas
Marla .... Sigrid Maier
Sgt. McGraw .... Arch Johnson

"G.I. Blues" restores Elvis Presley to the screen in a picture that seems to have been left over from the frivolous filmusicals of World War II. On the logical assumption that the teenage following that catapulted Presley to the boxoffice top a few years back has grown older, wiser and more sophisticated in its tastes, the rather juvenile Hal Wallis "comeback" production may have to depend on younger, pre-teen age groups for its chief response. But if the Paramount release is to get by at the boxoffice, it will need the support of Presley's formerly ardent fans.

About the creakiest "book" in musicomedy annals has been revived by scenarists Edmund Beloin and Henry Garson as a framework within which Presley warbles 10 wobbly songs and costar Juliet Prowse steps out in a pair of flashy dances.

Plot casts Presley as an all-American-boy tank-gunner stationed in Germany who woos supposedly icy-hearted Miss Prowse for what starts out as strictly mercenary reasons (if he spends the night with her, he wins a hunk of cash to help set up a nitery in the States). Needless to say, the ice melts and amor develops, only to dissolve when Miss Prowse learns of the heely scheme. But everything turns out all right in the end, paving the way for a kiss-kiss-kiss finale that is straight out of the Sonja Henie ice age.

Responsibility for penning the 10 tunes is given no one on Paramount's credit sheet. Considering the quality of these compositions, such anonymity is understandable. Joseph J. Lilley is credited with scoring and conducting music for the film. It is not absolutely clear whether he had a hand in composing the pop selections, but it is doubtful. Presley sings them all as a slightly subdued pelvis.

Miss Prowse is a firstrate dancer and has a pixie charm reminiscent of Leslie Caron. She deserves better roles than this. A couple of promising, attractive actresses from abroad make their screen bows in this film: Leticia Roman from Italy and Sigrid Maier from Germany. Robert Ivers, as Presley's G.I. sidekick, is a comic standout, and should go places in films. James Douglas capably plays another buddy and Arch Johnson is involved as the inevitable dumb top sergeant.

Lenswork, under the capable control of Loyal Griggs, is adequate, as are the bulk of contributions in art and technical departments. *Tube.*

Siege of Sidney Street
(BRITISH)

Better-than-average crime thriller based on authentic London gangster crime; lacks marquee value for U.S., but it's a sound b.o. prospect.

London, Oct. 11.

Ragal Filfs International release of a Mid-Century (Robert S. Baker-Monty Berman) production. Stars Donald Sinden, Nicole Maurey, Peter Wyngarde, Kieron Moore; features Leonard Sachs, Tutte Lemkow, George Pastell, T. P. McKenna, Angela Newman. Directed, photographed and edited by Robert S. Baker & Monty Berman. Screenplay, Jimmy Sangster and Alexander Baron, from story by Jimmy Sangster; music, Stanley Black. Previewed at Studio One. Running time, **93 MINS.**

Mannering .... Donald Sinden
Sara .... Nicole Maurey
Yoska .... Kieron Moore
Peter .... Peter Wyngarde
Blakey .... Godfrey Quigley
Svaars .... Leonard Sachs
Dmitreieff .... Tutte Lemkow
Brodsky .... George Pastell
Nina .... Angela Newman
Lapidos .... T. P. McKenna
Gardstein .... Maurice Good
Hefeld .... James Caffrey
Hersh .... Harold Goldblatt
Police Commissioner . . Christopher Casson
Old Harry .... Harry Brogan
Police Inspector .... Alan Simpson

Because Robert Baker and Monty Berman produced, directed, photographed and edited "Siege of Sidney Street" themselves, it's a simple matter to decide where to dish out blame or praise. In this instance, it's praise since, within its modest limits, this turns out to be quite a lively version of a gangster episode that had the East End of London on its ears early in 1911. It's a re-vamp of the celebrated incident when a gang of Russians brought out the police and the army before they could be smoked out of their hideout in Sidney Street.

In straightforward fashion, this shows Donald Sinden as a dedicated police officer who patiently tracks down the gang of Russian patriots, led by a character named Peter the Painter (Peter Wyngarde). They robbed allegedly to gain funds for their cause, which was anarchy. By disguising himself as a down-and-outer, Sinden eventually gets the thugs penned up. The result was one of the bloodiest gangster scenes that London has ever known. The East End of London in 1911 is vividly brought to life, direction is sound without being over-emphasized while the final siege is an exciting sock climax. The actors may not have much stellar appeal for the U.S., but they all do a useful job, with one or two particularly deft performances.

Wyngarde gives an alert, strong portrayal of the quiet but ruthless top gangster. Kieron Moore, a trigger-happy lieutenant, and Leonard Sachs, as an older but equally devoted member of the cause, are also first-rate. Sinden, as the cop, tends to play much on some note, but his is a comparatively colorless role compared with those of the Russo thugs. Tutte Lemkow, T. P. McKenna, Godfrey Blakey and George Patell are others who provide useful thesping.

The femme side is less strongly represented, but Nicole Maurey and Angela Newman both fit in well. Miss Maurev plays an orphaned Russian refugee who gets drawn into the gang because of loneliness and her infatuation for Peter. She has one or two standout scenes, notably during a police grilling. She also handles a few touches of implied romance between her and Sinden, with discretion and charm. Miss Newman, as a tougher member of the gang, also registers decisively.

The Jimmy Sangster-Alexander Baron screenplay is sound and keeps tension to a high level, while offering the directors a splendid chance of bringing some dramatic vitality to the final siege. Gang, with the exception of Peter the Painter, who was never caught, are wiped out by fire. Sangster also has a realistic, cheeky cameo as the then Home Secretary (Winston Churchill) who personally conducted the final operations.

Stanley Black has provided adequate music and there is an intriguing Russian song, sung by Miss Maurey, in the East End social club, which has been neatly composed by David Palmer and U.S. newsman, Robert Musel. *Rich.*

The Two Faces of Dr. Jekyll
(BRITISH-TECHNICOLOR)

Sixth film version of the Stevenson chiller, sometimes crude but with an imaginative twist and enough horror to make it a good b.o. bet with bold exploitation.

London, Oct. 13.
Columbia release of Hammer Film production. Stars Paul Massie, Dawn Addams, Christopher Lee; features David Kossoff, Norma Marla, Francis De Wolff. Producer, Michael Carreras. Director, Terence Fisher. Screenplay, Wolf Mankowitz, from Robert Louis Stevenson's story; editor, Eric Boyd-Perkins; camera, Jack Asher; music and songs, Monty Norman & David Heneker. At Pavilion, London. Running time, **88 MINS.**
Jekyll/Hyde .... Paul Massie
Kitty .... Dawn Addams
Paul Allen .... Christopher Lee
Liauer .... David Kossoff
Inspector .... Francis De Wolff
Maria .... Norma Marla
Sphinx Girl .... Magda Miller
Clubman .... William Kendall
Girl in gin shop........Pauline Shepherd
Nannie .... Helen Goss
Coroner .... Percy Cartwright
Corinthia .... Joe Robinson
Cabby .... Arthur Lovegrove

This is the sixth film version of Stevenson's classic chiller. Decked out in Technicolor, with an interesting performance by Paul Massie in the dual role, and with script-writer Wolf Mankowitz's blood and lust this one has all the earmarks of being a b.o. winner, if shrewdly handled. Mankowitz has palpably distorted and, in fact, jettisoned Stevenson's original story and the affair becomes mostly a straight-forward horror yarn, but with the benefit of some good opportunities for characterization and a useful climax. There are some blatantly inserted spots of sadism.

Whereas in previous editions Dr. Jekyll, the experimenting scientist, has been seen being transformed with the aid of the makeup department into a hideous monster, this time the bearded Victorian doctor turns into a young clean-shaven handsome man around town as Mr. Hyde. Paul Massie, playing the double role, has had to imply horror, mainly through voice and eyes. Considering that Massie has only three films behind him and is a bit short on experience he does a remarkably adept job, aided by a screenplay which though invariably tongue-in-cheek does offer some good thesping chances.

The original yarn's too well known to need much recapping here. In new film Doctor Jekyll is trying to separate man's two distinct personalities, the decent and the evil. He experiments on himself and the suave and evil Hyde occasionally takes over and has a high old time, wallowing in sin around the nightspots of Victorian London. He murders a couple of people, drives Jekyll's wife to suicide and frames Jekyll's own suicide with a spot of arson. In the end the good doctor destroys Hyde, but in doing so destroys himself.

Terence Fisher's direction has crudities, but is done effectively with a few hold barred, the Victorian atmosphere is well put over and Jack Asher's camerawork is colorful and sure. Massie keeps the thesping side together and shows up even better as Hyde than as Jekyll. And there are two or three useful performances to help Massie. Christopher Lee, one of Hyde's victims (bumped off by a snakedancer's serpent), is assured as Mrs. Jekyll's lover, and Dawn Addams and Norma Marla, as Jekyll's wife and Hyde's moll, respectively, are both well cast. There is also a quiet little gem of observation from David Kossoff as Dr. Jekyll's worried, sympathetic friend.

Among the violent highspots are the murder of Lee with a snake, Miss Addams' death plunge, the strangling of Miss Marla during a bedtime frolic with the wicked Mr.

Hyde and some evocative glimpses of some of Victorian London's seamier joy spots. *Rich.*

The Alamo
(TODD-AO-COLOR)

Homespun, expensive version of the famous Texas battle. Some firstrate combat scenes. Much of picture submerged in talky platitudes and childlike horseplay. Good kid payoff.

Hollywood, Oct. 20.
United Artists release of John Wayne production. Stars Wayne, Richard Widmark, Laurence Harvey, Richard Boone; features Frankie Avalon, Patrick Wayne, Linda Cristal, Joan O'Brien, Chill Wills, Joseph Calleia, Ken Curtis; with Carlos Arruza, Jester Hairston, Veda Ann Borg, John Dierkes, Denver Pyle, Aissa Wayne, Hand Worden, Bill Henry, Bill Daniel, Wesley Lau, Chuck Roberson, Guinn Williams, Olive Carey, Ruben Padilla. Directed by Wayne. Screenplay, James Edward Grant; camera, William H. Clothier; editor, Stuart Gilmore; art director, Alfred Ybarra; second unit director, Cliff Lyons; music, Dimitri Tiomkin; sound, Jack Solomon; assistant directors, Robert E. Relyea, Robert Saunders. Reviewed at Carthay Circle Theatre, Oct. 20, '60. Running time, 192 MINS.
Col. David Crockett..... John Wayne
Col. James Bowie .....Richard Widmark
Col. William Travis.... Laurence Harvey
Smitty .... Frankie Avalon
Capt. James Butler Bonham
.... Patrick Wayne
Flaca .... Linda Cristal
Mrs. Dickinson .... Joan O'Brien
Beekeeper .... Chill Wills
Juan Seguin .... Joseph Calleia
Capt. Almeron Dickinson.. Ken Curtis
Lieut. Reyes .... Carlos Arruza
Jethro .... Jester Hairston
Blind Nell .... Veda Ann Borg
Jocko Robertson..........John Dierkes
Gambler .... Denver Pyle
Angelina Dickinson .... Aissa Wayne
Parson .... Hank Worden
Dr. Sutherland .... Bill Henry
Col. Neill .... Bill Daniel
Emil .... Wesley Lau
A Tennessean .... Chuck Roberson
Lieut. Finn .... Guinn Williams
Mrs. Dennison .... Olive Carey
General Santa Anna...... Ruben Padilla
Gen. Sam Houston .... Richard Boone

"The Alamo" which was shot in 91 days at a stated cost of $12,000,-000 has a good measure of money-making quality, viz. mass appeal, in its 192 minutes. But to get it, producer-director-star John Wayne and the creative staff have loaded the telling of the tale with happy homilies on American virtues and patriotic platitudes under life-and-death fire which smack of yester-year theatricalism rather than the realism of modern battle drama.

It is not until the straightforward, rip-roaring climax that the Batjac production for United Artists attains the universally-gratifying stature that might sell tickets the "hard" way.

Obviously Wayne and James Edward Grant, who penned the original screenplay, had an entertainment, not a history lesson, in mind. A desirable concept, of course, but in their zeal to reproduce a colorful, homespun account of what went on in the course of those 13 remarkable days in 1836, they have somehow shrouded some of the fantastic facts of the original with some of the frivolous fancies of their re-creation. The philosophy and personality of the Mexican force and its leaders are ignored in favor of repetitious exposition and establishment of internal conflict that fairly swallows up the entire first half of the film, and even seeps into the superior latter portion.

And yet, in spite of these painstaking attempts to explore the characters of the picture's three principal heroes (Bowie, Crockett, Travis), there is an absence of emotional feeling, of a sense of participation, from the vantage point of the audience. Somehow Grant's screenplay never seems to penetrate beneath these courageous facades into the real men.

It is almost as if the writer is willing to settle for the popular conception of familiar heroes such as Davy Crockett and Jim Bowie as sufficient explanation of their presence and activities. But developments have a way of backfiring dramatically, owing to insufficient characterization. A great deal of priceless footage is consumed in a questionable romance between Crockett (Wayne) and a Mexican girl (Linda Cristal), when the time might more wisely have been spent investigating the more interesting, pertinent personal problem of Bowie (Richard Widmark), who has left his Mexican wife to join the force at the Alamo to help protect his huge land investment in Texas. When news of his wife's death arrives later in the film, the sequence lacks the emotional wallop it might have had.

In all fairness to Grant's screenplay, however, there is no denying its broad, but ingratiating, sense of humor and crackerbarrel comment on history-in-the-making. The picture is too talkative at times, but at least the talk is snappy and childishly appealing. Kids will understand it (no small matter), and most adults will find most of it agreeable.

In undertaking production, direction and thespic participation in his expensive project, Wayne may have spread his talents out too thin for best results. As producer he has mounted a physically sound achievement, an historical spectacle that has the smack of fact. He has assembled some of the finest creators and craftsmen in Hollywood, and coaxed from them a number of sturdy contributions. As director of his picture, he has been less successful.

With the rousing battle sequence at the climax (for which a goodly share of credit must go to second unit director Cliff Lyons) the picture really commands the spectator's rapt, undivided attention. The first half labors through some interminable, out-of-place speechifyin' (particularly one peculiarly stilted exchange near the outset between Laurence Harvey and Ken Curtis).

In the second half, there is a rather embarrassing "birthday party" passage in which the film momentarily seems on the verge of dissolving into a family musical. In general, Wayne's direction bogs down in the more intimate areas. It is in scenes of military combat and maneuvers that his work is at its best. There are several spectacular views of General Santa Anna's immense army on the march, and equally impressive glimpses of this force encircling the mission-fort. Minor military skirmishes are excitingly executed, in particular those that take place under the blanket of night. And then, finally, there is the big one, the final fight to the death, a sequence in which the disposition of battle, the movement of groups, is kept in focus astonishingly well. Most gratifying is the absence of any corny strokes when the heroes perish. These are accomplished with great dignity and ample meaning through dramatic and directorial restraint.

It is as actor that Wayne functions under his own direction in his least successful capacity. Gen-

erally playing with one expression on his face, he seems at times to be acting like a man with 12 million dollars on his conscience. But it is doubtful that audiences will mind. His b.o. pull is long established, ditto his emoting style. Inspired, subtle histrionics on his part aren't really necessary, nor are they anticipated.

Both Widmark and Harvey are unusually appealing actors, and though both suffer minor lapses in their performances, there is vigor and color in them. Their personality conflict is the running thread that binds the film together, along with the underlying note of doom and disaster that is intrinsic in the subject.

Britisher Harvey's attempt at a southern accent is abortive and ill-fated, and he seems awfully young for commander of the garrison, yet his Travis is a dominant, interesting figure. As the only women with appreciable parts, both Miss Cristal and Joan O'Brien are capable as well as decorative.

Younger players Frankie Avalon and Patrick Wayne show spirit. Chill Wills is responsible for most of the film's hill-country good humor. Curtis carries on gamely, although forced to play something of a toy soldier as Harvey's aide. Veda Ann Borg has a fine moment or two as a blind woman, and Jester Hairston is sympathetic as Bowie's faithful slave. Among supporting players, Carlos Arruza (the noted matador), Joseph Calleia and John Dierkes linger most favorably in the mind. Richard Boone is a definite standout in his two scenes as General Sam Houston—a sincere, meaningful slice of acting.

William H. Clothier's Todd-AO camerawork is dexterous and aggressive in outdoor action passages, and exhibits interesting qualities of composition in interior shots. Editor Stuart Gilmore's work, most notably in combat cutting, heightens the excitement and keenly anticipates the audience's visual desires.

The full-scale reproduction of the Alamo and surrounding settlement is the accomplished achievement of art director Alfred Ybarra—an absolutely vital and tremendously skillful effort.

A distinguished score by Dimitri Tiomkin—incorporating and intertwining melodies of Latin and country-style-U.S.A. flavors—is an important contribution to the product. There are compelling choral passages and even a few pleasant little ditties, lyrics for which were penned by Paul Francis Webster. The picture's theme already has captured the nation's attention via pop recordings. *Tube.*

Butterfield 8
(C'SCOPE-COLOR)

Fairly gratifying translation to the screen of a lesser John O'Hara work. Plenty of sizzling sex and the marquee might and torrid emoting of Elizabeth Taylor indicate big boxoffice.

Hollywood, Oct. 12.

Metro release of Pandro S. Berman production. Stars Elizabeth Taylor, Laurance Harvey, Eddie Fisher, Dina Merrill; features Mildred Dunnock, Betty Field, Jeffrey Lynn, Kay Medford, Susan Oliver; with George Voskovec, Virginia Downing, Carmen Matthews, Whitfield Connor. Directed by Daniel Mann. Screenplay, Charles Schnee and John Michael Hayes, from John O'Hara's novel; camera, Joseph Ruttenberg, Charles Harten; editor, Ralph E. Winters; art directors, George W. Davis, Urie McCleary; music, Bronislau Kaper; assistant directors, Hank Moonjean, John Clarke Bowman. Reviewed at the studio, Oct. 12, '60. Running time, **109 MINS.**

Gloria Wandrous	Elizabeth Taylor
Weston Liggett	Laurence Harvey
Steve Carpenter	Eddie Fisher
Emily Liggett	Dina Merrill
Mrs. Wandrous	Mildred Dunnock
Mrs. Fanny Thurber........	Betty Field
Bingham Smith	Jeffrey Lynn
Happy	Kay Medford
Norma	Susan Oliver
Dr. Tredman	George Voskovec

Approximately all that could have been accomplished with John O'Hara's "Butterfield 8" in terms of the motion picture craft has been accomplished in this Pandro S. Berman production. The film's principal flaws are chiefly outgrowths and extensions of the raw material, its outstanding merits a matter of cinematic approach and execution. The fact that it manages to be a reasonably arresting experience even though it is carved out of a highly questionable melodrama can be attributed to the keen sense of visual excitement possessed by those who pooled their talents to put it on the screen. With Elizabeth Taylor to give it the boxoffice oomph it needs, "Butterfield," for all of its major shortcomings, seems certain to be a huge Metro goldwinner.

Alterations made on O'Hara's 1935 novel by scenarists Charles Schnee and John Michael Hayes (among other things, they have updated it from the Prohibition ear, spectacularized the ending and refined some of the dialog) have given it the form and pace it needs for best results on the modern screen, but the story itself remains a weak one, the behavior and motivations of its characters no more tangible than in the original work.

Under director Daniel Mann's guidance it is an extremely sexy and intimate film, but the intimacy is only skin deep, the sex only a dominating behavior pattern that dictates some strange, wild relationships and activities rarely rooted in logic. The spectator who attempts to unearth sound reasons for what he sees transpiring on the screen is doomed to bewilderment. Maximum enjoyment of "Butterfield 8" can be attained by adoption of an attitude similar to that of a young child reading a fairy tale.

"Butterfield," however, is far from child's play. It is the tragic tale of a young woman (Miss Taylor) tormented by the contradictory impulses of flesh and conscience. Victim of traumatic childhood experiences, a fatherless youth, a mother's refusal to face facts and, most of all, her own moral irresponsibility, she drifts from one illicit affair to another until passion suddenly blossoms into love on a six-day sex spree with Laurence Harvey, who's got the sort of "problems" (loving, devoted wife, oodles of money via marriage, soft, respectable job) non-neurotic men might envy. First indication of the impending love affair is a fierce battle of endurance in which Miss Taylor slowly jams the sharp heel of her shoe into Harvey's foot as he squeezes her wrist both tantalizingly increasing the pressure, both refusing to wince. It's an uneasy scene, to say the least.

Their peculiar personalities now firmly established, it is not long before they are battling again, this time over a mink coat which Miss Taylor earlier had removed from Harvey's swank New York City apartment in a fit of pique. Since the coat belongs to his wife, Harvey interprets it as thievery, calls Miss Taylor every name in the book, then regrets his words, chases after her on the way to Boston, corners her, professes his undying love.

After nearly weakening, she flees again, Harvey in hot pursuit. Careening through a highway barricade and over a cliff in a vivid, electrifying sequence, Miss Taylor commits what might be termed O'Hara-kiri, and Harvey returns to his wife, but not until he has senselessly bleated out his participation in the messy affair to a puzzled gendarme (unlike the novel, in which he remains sensibly but despicably mum). The wife (Dina Merrill), who certainly must rank as one of the most patient, understanding and/or implausible wives in recorded history, actually seems favorably disposed toward the reunion.

The picture's major asset, dramatically as well as financially, is Miss Taylor, who makes what is becoming her annual bid for an Oscar. While the intensity and range of feeling that marked several of her more recent endeavors is slightly reduced in this effort, it is nonetheless a torrid, stinging overall portrayal with one or two brilliantly executed passages within.

"Butterfield" is a picture thoroughly dominated by Miss Taylor. Harvey seems ill-at-ease and has a tendency to exaggerate facial reactions. Eddie Fisher, as Miss Taylor's long-time friend and father image, cannot unbend and get any warmth into the role. Miss Merrill's portrayal of the society wife is without animation or depth. But there is better work from Mildred Dunnock as Miss Taylor's mother and Susan Oliver as Fisher's impatient girl friend. Betty Field is a standout as Miss Dunnock's friend, particularly in one or two acid exchanges with Miss Taylor. Kay Medford is excellent as a verbose motel proprietress. Competent support is fashioned by Jeffrey Lynn, George Voskovec, Virginia Downing, Carmen Matthews and Whitfield Connor.

Panavision camerawork shared by Joseph Ruttenberg and Charles Harten makes the film a visually gratifying experience with several notable passages, among these the spectacular auto crash at the climax, masterfully edited by Ralph E. Winters. Other more-than-satisfactory contributions are music by Bronislau Kaper and tasteful art direction by George W. Davis and Urie McCleary. *Tube.*

Utamaro, Painter of Women
(JAPANESE-COLOR)

Hollywood, Oct. 16.

Ed Harrison release of Masaichi Nagata production. With (no character names) Kazuo Hasegawa, Chikage Awashima, Yasuko Nakada, Keiko Awaji, Hitomi Nozoe, Fujiko Yamamoto, Yuko Mori, Masumi Harukawa, Kyu Sazanka, Tamae Kiyokawa, Bontaro Miake, Seizaburo Kawazu, Gen Shimizu, Sonosuke Sawamura, Hideo Hongo, Osamu Maruyama, Seishiro Hara. Directed and screenplay by Keigo Kimura; camera, Hiroshi Imai; art director, Gizo Uesato; music, Hiroyoshi Ogawa. Reviewed at Monica International Theatre, Oct. 13, '60. Running time, **93 MINS.**

What clearer indication of the fate of "Utamaro, Painter of Women" in this country than the fact that printed matter adorning theatres exhibiting the picture alters the title to "Utamaro, Painter of Nudes"?

The film, of Japanese origin, deserves a somewhat more refined fate than it appears destined to receive here. The promise of an abundance of exposed flesh will attract mostly those patrons whose aesthetic appreciation is generally limited. For them, "Utamaro" will prove tedious. There's only one big "nude" scene, a mass fishing contest between two teams of bare-breasted maidens.

Bulk of the picture is devoted to the title character, late 18th century Japanese artist whose specialty was painting the ladies. Most of the ladies he paints seem to develop quite a crush on "Uta," but the artist in him forces him to give all such affectionate candidates the brush. Nature of his work makes him one of Japan's more commercial painters, but the hero is obsessed with becoming a great artist. Tragedy ensues when his gifted arm is deliberately crushed by a hired gang and he is deserted and forgotten by those he made famous through his portraits, all but one faithful "model" who darts from the altar on her wedding day to return forever to the stricken artist.

There are a few interesting glimpses of Utamaro's work, views embellished by the subtle, handsome tones of the Japanese Daieiscope and color processes. There is a surprisingly romantic western strain to the dramatic proceedings—seemingly somewhat alien to the popular conception of the Japan of a few centuries ago. But the heavy dose of sentiment ought to prove pleasing to conditioned western cinematic tastes. *Tube.*

Aventuras de Joselito y Pulgarcito
(Adventures of Joselito and Tom Thumb)
(MEXICAN—COLOR)

Mexico City, Oct. 18.

Peliculas Nacionales release of Cinematografica Filmex production. Stars Joselito, "Pulgarcito" (Tom Thumb), Enrique Rambal; features Oscar Ortiz de Pineda, Anita Blanch, Nora Veryan, Arturo Castro, Guillermo A. Bianchi, Alfredo W. Barron, Florencio Castillo and Manuel Capetillo. Directed by Rene Cardona. Screenplay, Rene Cardona and Adolfo Torres Portillo; camera (Eastmancolor), Alex Phillips. At Orfeon, Ariel and Soliseo Theatres, Mexico City. Running time, **90 MINS.**

Mexico has discovered gold in the series pictures, especially those aimed at children. In this one Spanish child actor Joselito is paired with Tom Thumb ("Pulgarcito") in a film featuring the love of a youngster for his dad and putting across the moral of human brotherhood and solidarity. The screenplay may be conventional, but it is geared strictly for the kiddie trade and as such combines a human story, funny situations and tenderness.

Plot centers around a Spaniard

who seeks fame in the bullring, goes to Mexico for this purpose, leaving his mother and son behind. When time passes and the head of the house sends no word, young Joselito decides to go search for his Dad, embarking in a fragile craft. He is picked up at sea, goes to the U.S. and finally to Vera Cruz where he meets Tom Thumb, with the latter aiding him in a successful search for his father.

Rene Cardona is a director who has specialized in turning out such kiddie pix, and he is adept with this one. The Alex Phillips photography in color is acceptable in general. This is one that will be pushed in all markets by producers Cesario Gonzalez and Gregorio Wallerstein. *Emil.*

The Crowning Experience
(COLOR)

Well-meaning Moral Re-Armament drama-with-songs based loosely on life of Negro educator Mary McLeod Bethune. Handsomely produced but tepid film fare lacking dramatic impact. Strictly for special situations.

Moral Re-Armament release of MRA production. Stars Muriel Smith, Ann Buckles; with Louis Byles, George McCurdy, William Pawley Jr., Phyllis Konstan Austin, Anna Marie McCurdy, Robert Anderson, Cecil Broadhurst. Directed by Marion Clayton Anderson. Screenplay, Alan Thornhill; camera (Technicolor), Richard Tegstrom; musical director, Paul Dunlap; original songs, Will Reed, George Fraser; sound, Jack Dickson. Reviewed at Warner Theatre, N.Y., Oct. 21, '60. Running time, **102 MINS.**

Emma Tremaine .... Muriel Smith
Sarah Miller Spriggs .... Ann Buckles
Charlie (as a man) .... Louis Byles
Charlie (as a boy) ..... George McCurdy
Mr. Spriggs ...... William Pawley Jr.
Mrs. Spriggs ...... Phyllis Konstan Austin
Julie .... Anna Marie McCurdy
Blaney .... Robert Anderson
Editor .... Cecil Broadhurst

Moral Re-Armament's "The Crowning Experience" is going to need all the help and support it can get from Pastor Buchman's followers (of which, apparently, there are lots) if it's going to make the grade in straight commercial competition. As well-meaning as it is, film is a tepid drama-with-songs, episodic in structure and lacking in the kind of sock emotional impact that should grow naturally out of the narrative itself.

Without meaning to be flip, it's like an extended tv commercial, full of endorsements for the product (MRA), and of the need for it, but which never defines the product except in the most general terms.

Screenplay by Alan Thornhill, apparently based on the life of Mary McLeod, tells of a Negro educator who succeeds in her dream of building a university but only at the expense of providing love and understanding to her immediate family. Eventually, through MRA, the lady sees the error of complete preoccupation with education as an answer to world problems and realizes the need for a reemphasis of more personal spiritual values. At the same time, her son-in-law, who has become a Communist agitator, mends his ways.

Except in its opening sequences, showing the educator (played by Muriel Smith) teaching in a little open-air school, film never quite touches the heart as it should, perhaps because the screenplay tries to cover too much ground in too great a hurry and hasn't time to develop interesting characterization. Struggles to build the university are never depicted nor are the reasons for the impact which the lady has on the world around her.

What vitality the film has comes almost entirely from Miss Smith's warm and dignified performance, and in her delivery of about six of the picture's 11 original songs. The best of these is a bouncy little item called "Sweet Potato Pie," which Miss Smith first sings in delightful chorus with a bunch of bright-eyed moppets at her hillside school. It's also reprised twice, both to good effect.

In addition to Miss Smith, the only other professional performance is that of pretty Ann Buckles, late of Broadway's "Pajama Game," seen as a spritely newspaper girl who follows Miss Smith's career from the start and eventually guides her into MRA. As outlined in the picture, this mean's "honesty, purity, unselfishness and love," and/or "putting right what's wrong."

For the most part, Marion Clayton Anderson's direction is as undramatic as the script, though the aforementioned opening sequence has charm. Otherwise there is the recurring impression that the essential drama, the primary conflicts and important thoughts, all are being expressed somewhere off-screen.

The physical production, however, is firstrate, especially Richard Tegstrom's Technicolor camerawork which, in scenes of bright, sunlit countrysides (Mackinac Island), captures a feeling of real spirituality.

Despite its dramatic shortcomings, "Crowning Experience" does provide a pretty, (if not profound) picture of the U.S., especially its race relations. Thus it could prove to be of value overseas in the west-east information war. *Anby.*

A Breath of Scandal
(COLOR—SONGS)

Some splendid views of the old country and of Sophia Loren in a listless romantic comedy about an Austrian princess who falls for a brash, dashing Yank.

Hollywood, Oct. 10.

Paramount release of Carlo Ponti-Marcello Girosi production. Stars Sophia Loren, Maurice Chevalier, John Gavin, Angela Lansbury, Milly Vitale, Roberto Risso, Isabel Jeans; with Tullio Carminati, Carlo Hinterman, Frederick von Ledebur. Directed by Michael Curtiz. Screenplay, Sidney Howard, based on play, "Olympia," by Ferenc Molnar; camera, Mario Montuori; editor, Howard Smith; art director, Hal Pereira, Eugene Allen; music, Alessandro Cicognini; assistant director, Mario Russo. Reviewed at studio, Oct. 10, '60. Running time, **97 MINS.**

Olympia .... Sopnia Loren
Philip .... Maurice Chevalier
Charlie .... John Gavin
Lina .... Angela Lansbury
Can-Can Girl .... Milly Vitale
Aide .... Roberto Risso
Eugenie .... Isabel Jeans
Albert .... Tullio Carminati
Ruprecht .... Carlo Hinterman
Sandor .... Frederick von Ledebur

'Tis a far, far better world audiences will escape to when they witness "A Breath of Scandal." Set against the exquisite Austrian countryside and some luxurious Hapsburg interiors, it plants the spectator in a fairytale world of benevolent despots, beautiful princesses and upstart American commoners so handsome and moral it hurts the intellect. But, outside of its pre escapist value, the Carlo Monti-Marcello Girosi production is a lifeless effort that plods along to a foregone conclusion.

The characters of Ferenc Molnar's stage comedy, "Olympia," never come alive in Sidney Howard's adaptation. Further burdened with a telescoped ending, the pace seems intolerably deliberate. In an attempt to put some up-to-date spice into the drab proceedings, there are occasional references to sexual matters and little bits of suggestive business, but these are tame, contrived and out of place. Apart from Isabel Jeans' witty, take-charge performance, none of the acting is very diverting or amusing. Director Michael Curtiz attains satisfactory results only when he has cameraman Mario Montuori train his lenses on the cooperative Continental scenery or on Sophia Loren's anatomy.

The slight tale is of an Austrian princess (Miss Loren) who must choose between loveless marriage to a Prussian prince (Carlo Hinterman) or romantic wedlock to an untitled, but amorous American mining engineer (John Gavin). From the first it is obvious that American engineering morality and respectability will triumph over European character laxity.

Pair of tunes of appropriate Viennese nature make film a little jollier by their presence. The title tune is a lilting waltz by Robert Stolz, American lyric by Al Stillman, and the other is a happy little intrusion by Sepp Fellner, Karl Schneider and Patrick Michael titled "A Smile in Vienna," sung briefly, in his inimitably cheerful fashion by Chevalier.

Miss Loren's performance is rather vacant. Gavin is stiff, but fills the role's visual specifications. Maurice Chevalier is Maurice Chevalier, never managing to submerge his own identity into the character he plays—Miss Loren's father. Nor does it matter. Others prominent and competent are Angela Lansbury, Roberto Risso, Tullio Carminati, Hinterman, Milly Vitale and Frederick von Ledebur.

In selection of exact locales, director Curtiz and art directors Hal Periera and Eugene Allen have given the film a much needed aesthetic shot in the arm. Studio sets masterminded by the latter pair (in Rome and Vienna) are a fine match to the pictorial splendor of the authentic backdrops. Elegant costumes (executed by Ella Bei and Knize of Vienna), complimented by some striking Technicolor, are sure to please the eyes of distaff customers. Howard Smith's editing is cleancut, and Alessandro Cicognini's music adds to the romantic mood, *Tube.*

The Millionairess
(BRITISH-COLOR)

Stylish, handsomely mounted vision of George Bernard Shaw's comedy; it has many yocks and glamor, but it's an offbeat, even with Sophia Loren, needing careful nursing for most houses.

London, Oct. 25.

20th-Fox release of a Dimitri De Grunwald (Pierre Rouve) production. Stars Sophia Loren, Peter Sellers; features Alastair Sim, Dennis Price, Gary Raymond, Vittorio De Sica. Directed by Anthony Asquith. Screenplay by Wolf Mankowitz, from Riccardo Aragno's adaptation of Shaw's play; camera (Eastmancolor), Jack Hildyard; editor, Anthony Harvey; music, George van Parys. At Carlton, London, Oct. 18, '60. Running time, **90 MINS.**

Epifania .... Sophia Loren
Doctor Kabir .... Peter Sellers
Sagamore .... Alastair Sim
Joe .... Vittorio De Sica
Adrian .... Dennis Price
Alastair .... Gary Raymond
Fish Curer .... Alfie Bass
Mrs. Joe .... Miriam Karlin
Professor .... Noel Purcell
Polly .... Virginia Vernon
Muriel .... Pauline Jameson
Butler .... Graham Stark
Whelk Seller .... Wally Patch
President .... Willoughby Goddard
Nurse .... Diana Coupland
Secretary .... Basil Hoskins

The witty plays of George Bernard Shaw, always provocative in thought but by now sometimes outdated, always have proved screen b.o. gambles. The b.o. reception of "The Millionairess" certainly will vary considerably in different houses. But with most discriminating audiences it should register strongly. Even the most run-of-the-mill patron should find a lot to entertain, for despite its several faults, this has much which that will attract patrons.

Primarily, this stylized pic has Sophia Loren at her most radiant, wearing a series of stunning Balmain gowns. Shaw's Shavianisms on morality, riches and human relationship retain much of their edge, though nudged into a practical screenplay by Wolf Mankowitz.

Anthony Asquith's direction often is slow, but he breaks up the pic with enough hilarious situation to keep the film from getting tedious. A major fault is that the cutting of a film, which is mainly episodic, is often needlessly jerky and indecisive. But against this, there are such credits as Paul Sherriff's handsome artwork and the relish with which Jack Hildyard has brought his camera to work on them. There's also Miss Loren. There's also an interesting piece of casting in co-star Peter Sellers, and some topnotch supporting thesping.

Briefly, the yarn concerns a beautiful, spoiled young heiress who has all the money in the world but can't find love. Her eccentric, deceased old man has stipulated that she mustn't marry unless the man of her choice can turn $1,400 into $42,000 within three months. She cheats. Her first marriage flops, she contemplates suicide and then sets her cap for a dedicated, destitute Indian doctor running a poor man's clinic. He's attracted to her, but scared of her money and power. He hopes to dodge wedding bells by dreaming up a clause in his mother's will. He mustn't wed unless the girl can take $5 and the clothes she's wearing and earn her own living for three months.

She does the job by taking over a "sweatshop" bakery and making it a huge, machine-run success. He fails miserably. But with some manipulating by the family lawyer, the two get together just before she decides to go into a convent. The story is only a sly excuse for some Shavian jabs at society, both in crisp dialog and situation. In short this is a mixture which will exasperate, baffle but always entertain.

Miss Loren, the Italian charmer, who recently revealed her comedy potential in "It Started in Naples,"

is irresistible. Whether in those eye-catching dresses or, provocatively half naked the predatory, Miss Loren is a constant stimulation. She catches many moods. Whether she's wooing the doctor brazenly, confiding in a psychiatrist, trying to commit suicide, upbraiding her lawyer or just pouting she is fascinating.

Sellers plays the doctor and it's another challenge in a career in which he is determined not to be typed. Though he plays it straight, apart from an offbeat accent, he still manages to bring in some typical Sellers comedy touches which help to make it a fascinating character study. He even injects a few emotional throwaways which are fine.

In the supporting roles there are two or three gems, notably the unctuous, scheming lawyer of Alastair Sim. Dennis Price is perfectly cast as the smooth, opportunistic couch-doctor. Noel Purcell revels in a small role as a tipsy professor while Alfie Bass scores in an amusing, if irrelevant, sequence. Miriam Karlin, Pauline Jameson, Vittorio De Sica and Graham Stark also contribute selling support.

This is a pic in which the audience has to play along with the thesps, the director and the writer. It's to be recommended. *Rich.*

School for Scoundrels
(BRITISH)

Dandy comedy based on Stephen Potter's sly, dry-witted spoofs of winning and losing in the game of life. Excellent performances by several top comedy players. Strong selective situation prospect.

Hollywood, Oct. 18.

Continental Distributing Inc. release of Hal E. Chester production. Stars Ian Carmichael, Terry-Thomas, Alastair Sim, Janette Scott, Dennis Price, Peter Jones; with Edward Chapman, John Le Mesurier, Irene Handl, Kynaston Reeves, Hattie Jacques, Hugh Paddick, Barbara Roscoe, Gerald Campion, Monty Landis, Jeremy Lloyd, Charles Lamb, Anita Sharp-Bolster. Directed by Robert Hamer. Screenplay, Patricia Moyes, Chester, based on series of books by Stephen Potter; camera, Edwin Hillier; editor, Richard Best; art director, Terence Verity; music, John Addison. Reviewed at Beverly Canon Theatre, Oct. 18, '60. Running time, **94 MINS.**

Heenry Palfrey .... Ian Carmichael
Raymond Delauney .... Terry-Thomas
Mr. S. Potter .... Alastair Sim
April Smith .... Janette Scott
Dunstan .... Dennis Price
Dudley .... Peter Jones
Gloatbridge .... Edward Chapman
Head Waiter .... John Le Mesurier
Mrs. Stringer .... Irene Handl
General .... Kynaston Reeves
First Instructress.........Hattie Jacques
Instructor .... Hugh Paddick
Second Instructress.....Barbara Roscoe
Proudfoot .... Gerald Campion
Fleetsnod .... Monty Landis
Dingle .... Jeremy Lloyd
Carpenter .... Charles Lamb
Maid .... Anita Sharp-Bolster

The gentle art of getting and remaining "one up" on the next fellow (if you're not one up, you're one down), so painstaking chronicled by British humorist Stephen Potter in his series of books, is engagingly translated to the screen in this delicate English comedy. Those familiar with Potter's spoofs ('Lifemanship," "Gamesmanship." "Oneupmanship") certainly will get the biggest boot out of "School for Scoundrels," but this by no means rules out enjoyment among the uninitiated. If release be one up on some Americans, it looms as a hot attraction on the art house circuit.

Although it is virtually impossible to capture Potter's many intimate ironies (among other things, his series is a rather scathing satire on the technique of textbook-writing itself, unwieldy footnotes and all), scenarists Patricia Moyes and Hal E. Chester (with the aid of Peter Ustinov's "screen adaptation") have successfully caught the essence of the author's maxim—"How to Win Without Actually Cheating!" (as the film is subtitled) and have woven Potter's wicked philosophy into a romantic triangle and capped it off with a climax likely to stun disciples of Potted-manship-namely the triumph of simple sincerity.

For the role of the cunning Mr. Potter himself the perfectly equipped actor was chosen, Alastair Sim. He personifies the master lifeman down to the minutest detail—a brilliant performance. Ian Carmichael is a delight as the pitifully inept wretch who undergoes metamorphsis at Sim's finishing school for social misfits, and Terry-Thomas masterfully plummets from one-up to one-down as his exasperated victim.

Janette Scott, a fresh, natural beauty, charmingly plays the object of their attention. Unfortunately for Dennis Price and Peter Jones, they are involved in the weakest passage of the film—a none-too-subtle used car sequence that will disturb Potter purists. But both lend it all the comic restraint and invention they're got, which is plenty. Additional support is excellent, right down the line.

Direction by Robert Hamer is not always as taut and sophisticated as desirable for the fragile material, as if he and the producers (exec Hal E. Chester and associate Douglas Rankin) might have been making concessions to mass taste for farcical exaggeration. But, on the whole, Hamer's is a perceptive job. Most satisfying of generally tip-top departmental contributions is John Addison's music, endowed with a lively sense of humor to match the product. *Tube.*

Le Propre de L'Homme
(The Right of Man)
(FRENCH)

Paris, Oct. 25.

Films 13 production and release. With Janine Magnan, Claude Lalouch. Written and directed by Claude Lalouch. Camera, Jean Boffety; editor, Monique Bonnot. At Cinematheque Francaise, Paris. Running time, **80 MINS.**

Made in 19 days on the streets of Paris by 22-year-old Claude Lalouch, this remains amateurish and looms of little export value with local chances also slim. It concerns an all-day date of a boy and girl ending finally in a hotel room with love transmuted into abstract color images and sounds.

The boy and girl drive and roam around Paris but are never brought to life. Instead the two are used as a pretext for a series of scenes and incidents around them done with a hidden camera. Some are clever but they are all dragged in and never help make the relationship clearer or even counterpoint it.

Technical credits are good. However, this is an offbeater sans the spark or talent to make it anything but an overdose of imagery without any viewpoint. *Mosk.*

Walk Tall
(C'SCOPE-COLOR)

Routine lower-half western, handsomely filmed and happily brief.

Hollywood, Oct. 14.

Twentieth-Fox release of Maury Dexter production. Stars Willard Parker, Joyce Meadows, Kent Taylor. Directed by Dexter. Story and screenplay, Joseph Fritz; camera, Floyd Crosby; editor, Eddie Dutko; music, Dick Aurandt; assistant directors, Frank Parmenter, Willard Kirkham. Reviewed at the studio, Oct. 14, '60. Running time, **60 MINS.**

Captain Ed Trask .... Willard Parker
Sally Medford .... Joyce Meadows
Ed Carter .... Kent Taylor
Colonel Stanton .... Russ Bender
Leach .... Ron Soble
Carlos .... Alberto Monte
Jake .... Bill Mims
Chief Black Feather........Felix Locher
Buffalo Horn .... Dave DePaul

Other than some agreeable picture-postcard views of the San Bernardino mountain country, there is little to distinguish this low-budget, trail-weary western, even in the programming category for which it is designed. "Walk Tall" brings not a single novel variation to a story grown stale through infinite repetition — the one where the indiscriminate Indian-killing outlaw is being brought to justice by the lawman, with both pursued by the outlaw's small band of 19th-century hooligans. Kids alone will find something to yip about. Brevity is its chief virtue as a twin-biller.

Willard Parker plays the lawman, an army captain bringing in Kent Taylor, whose raid on a small Indian community threatens to produce an uprising of "the entire Shoshone nation" unless he is brought to justice. Parker's chore is complicated by the presence of an Indian-hating young woman (Joyce Meadows), a case of snakebite, and the untimely arrival of Taylor's gang, but eventually he polishes off the job with the aid of some Shoshone warriors who turn up right on cue. The story and screenplay are credited to Joseph Fritz.

Parker does a respectable job as the big gun. Miss Meadows is suitably helpless as the lady. Taylor does a fairly colorful slice of acting as the head hood, and his three henchmen are played in lively fashion by Ron Soble, Alberto Monte and Bill Mims.

Producer Maury Dexter's direction, burdened with an extremely thin script, fails to keep the film from crawling at a deliberate, mechanical pace. Fortunately the scenery is interesting, as craftily captured through Floyd Crosby's lens and embellished by the values of CinemaScope and De Luxe Color, which give the film a premium look not captured in other departments. Eddie Dutko's editing is reasonably accomplished, but sound has a distracting tendency in spots of overlapping from scene to scene. *Tube.*

The Sundowners
(COLOR)

One of the year's finest films. Tale of Australian sheepman and his family, beautifully told. Poses some selling problems, both to trade and public, but has the stature to overcome them and click at the b.o.

Hollywood, Oct. 25.

Warner Bros. release of Fred Zinnemann production. Stars Deborah Kerr, Robert Mitchum, Peter Ustinov; features Glynis Johns, Dina Merrill; with Chips Rafferty, Michael Anderson Jr., Lola Brooks, Wylie Watson, John Meillon, Ronald Fraser, Mervyn Johns, Molly Urquhart, Ewen Solon. Directed by Zinnemann. Screenplay, Isobel Lennart, from novel by Jon Cleary; camera, Jack Hildyard; editor, Jack Harris; are director, Michael Stringer; second unit director, Lex Halliday; music, Dimitri Tiomkin; sound, David Hildyard; assistant directors, Peter Bolton, Roy Stevens. Reviewed at the studio, Oct. 25, '60. Running time, **133 MINS.**

Ida Carmody .... Deborah Kerr
Paddy Carmody ....Robert Mitchum
Vanneker .... Peter Ustinov
Mrs. Firth .... Glynis Johns
Jean Halstead .... Dina Merrill
Quinlan .... Chips Rafferty
Sean .... Michael Anderson Jr.
Liz .... Lola Brooks
Herb Johnson .... Wylie Watson
Bluey .... John Meillon
Ocker .... Ronald Fraser
Jack Patchogue .... Mervyn Johns
Mrs. Bateman .... Molly Urquhart
Halstead .... Ewen Solon

Warner Bros. release is a wonderfully warm, rich and compelling picture about truly flesh-and-blood people. And yet, the commercial success of "The Sundowners" appears to be another, and very delicate, matter. The problem is to convey to the public a marketable "image" that is also faithful to the film's high standards. That won't be easy, for this is a picture that won't "classify" easily in the public's imagination.

It is set in the Australia of the 1920s and, although its appeal is intrinsically universal and its characters identifiably human, it defies the advertising urge to pinpoint and sensationalize or clarify in terms of imminence or excitement. As such, its success hinges on the reputation of its producer Fred Zinnemann (in more discriminating circles, of course), the existing popularity of its stars and, most important of all, the extent of favorable word-of-mouth. On the hopeful assumption that a fine product normally finds a receptive market, "The Sundowners" should be a boxoffice success.

Jon Cleary's novel is the basic source from which Zinnemann's inspiration springs. Between Cleary and Zinnemann lies Isobel Lennart's perceptive, virile screenplay, loaded with bright, telling lines of dialog and gentle philosophical comment. But, fine as the scenario is, it is Zinnemann's poetic glances into the souls of his characters, little hints of deep longings, hidden despairs, indomitable spirit that make the picture the achievement it is. He has also managed a stimulating visuo-cultural expedience, particularly early in the film in nature scenes that seem to have popped to life right out of the pages of National Geographic magazine. In lesser hands these passages might have grossly lacked relevance and delayed the pace of the human story. Not so, under Zinnemann's aesthetic guidance.

On paper, the story sounds something short of fascinating. It tells of an Irish-Australian sheep-

drover (Robert Mitchum) whose fondness for the freedom of an itinerant existence clashes with the fervent hope of settling-down shared by his wife (Deborah Kerr) and his son (Michael Anderson Jr.). The wife, in an effort to raise funds for a down-payment on a farm, persuades her husband to accept stationary employment as a shearer. Then, in a petulant fit, he gambles away the entire family savings. His attempt to make amends backfires, but it provides the irony for a desirably natural ending.

Mitchum's rugged masculinity is right for the part. His thespic range seems narrow, but that can be deceptive, for there are moments when he projects a great deal of feeling with what appears to be a minimum of effort. This may be the finest work he has done in films. Miss Kerr gives a luminous and penetrating portrayal of the faithful wife, rugged pioneer stock on the outside, wistful and feminine within. There is one fleetingly eloquent scene at a train station, in which her eyes meet those of an elegant lady traveller, that ranks as one of the most memorable moments ever to cross a screen.

Peter Ustinov, as a whimsical, learned bachelor who joins the family and slowly evolves into its "household pet," gives a robust, rollicking performance. Glynis Johns is a vivacious delight as a hotelkeeper who sets her sights on matrimonially-evasive Ustinov. Young Anderson does a convincing job as the son, likewise Dina Merrill as a lonely wife befriended by Miss Kerr. The picture contains some wonderful supporting performances, one of the best of which is John Meillon's as an expectant father. Meillon accomplishes one of the best cockeyed drunk bits seen in years.

Art, photographic and technical skills are extremely well represented by the craftsmen assembled in the bush country of Australia and at Elstree Studios in London. There is evidence of painstaking camera work by Jack Hildyard. Editing by Jack Harris is tidy and sensible. Art director Michael Stringer's efforts are authentic and appropriate, and the same goes for wardrobe designer Elizabeth Haffenden and set dressers Frants Folmer and Terrence Morgan. Dimitri Tiomkin's music, heavy on the melancholy harmonica, backs up most of the action with listenably melodic tenderness, but flares up into more violent tempos and punctuations where necessary.

Zinnemann has resisted all petty tendencies to be theatrical at the expense of being real.   *Tube.*

The Secret of the Purple Reef
(C'SCOPE—COLOR)

Watered-down mystery meller about a naughty nautical caper on a tropical isle. Pleasing views of the Caribbean make it attractive for lower-berthing.

Hollywood, Oct. 19.
Twentieth-Fox release of Gene Corman production. Stars Jeff Richards, Margia Dean. Features Richard Chamberlain, Terence de Marney, Gina Petrushka, Phil Rosen, Robert Earl, Larry Markow,

Frank Ricco, Jerry Mitchell, Ben Blum. Directed by William N. Witney. Screenplay, Harold Yablonsky, from SatEvePost novel by Dorothy Cottrell; camera, Kay Norton; editor, Peter C. Johnson; art director, Juan Viguie; music, Buddy Bregman; sound, John L. Bury Jr.; assistant directors, Jack Bohrer, Robert Webb. Reviewed at API screening room, Oct. 19, '60. Running time, 80 MINS.
Mark Christopher .... Jeff Richards
Rue .... Margia Dean
Webber .... Peter Falk
Ashby .... Terence de Marney
Dean Christopher...Richard Chamberlain
Tobias .... Robert Earl
Grandmere .... Gina Petrushka
Henri .... Frank Ricco
Twine .... Phil Rosen
Priest .... Ben Blum
Kilt .... Larry Markow

Nothing dramatically novel or emotionally stimulating happens in "The Secret of the Purple Reef." But, as strictly Grade B mystery melodrama, it ought to please the tastes of those who will settle for several flurries of explosive combat in the foreground and a screenful of tropical sea water in the background. Since the views are embellished by some handsome CinemaScope-De Luxe Color photography, and the action is set against Caribbean locales, the Gene Corman production for 20th-Fox is suitable for programming as a companion piece, and might even make a small splash as a minor chief attraction in isolated rural areas where the natives don't grow restless if the drama is little more than an excuse for a waterlogged travelog.

Corman's "Reef"er springs from the SatEvePosted novel by Dorothy Cottrell, as efficiently screenplayed by Harold Yablonsky. It has to do with a young man's efforts to discover why a fishing vessel commanded by his late brother went to the bottom on a supposedly calm sea. The mystery is unearthed, or in this case dehydrated, in routine melodramatic fashion. The title hints there will be some underwater activity, but the action all takes place on the surface.

In addition to Kay Norton's scenic-minded camerawork, the film's chief asset is Buddy Bregman's music, alive with semi-atonalistic young ideas and appropriate tropical percussion rhythms. A good deal of footage could have been trimmed down or out by Corman and director William N. Witney. There are several unnecessary or strained passages, particularly a long pre-titles burial sequence. Mechanically, Peter C. Johnson's editing is adept.

Acting tends to be wooden among the younger principals, livelier among the character players. Jeff Richards plays the young man out to solve the mystery, Richard Chamberlain his brother and co-sleuth, Margia Dean a doomed casino proprietress. Slickest work is turned in by Peter Falk as the heavy and Terence de Marney as an alcoholic old salt, and there's a sympathetic portrayal of an elderly native islander by Robert Earl.   *Tube.*

Heaven on Earth
(COLOR)

Essentially a stunning travelog on the treasures of Rome and, particularly, the Vatican. Framed by an aggressively innocuous American-girl-meets-Italian-boy story. Nice for the arties.

JB Film Enterprises release of a Dominick Franco-Fulvio Lucisano production. Features Barbara Florian, Charles Fawcett, Gabriele Tinti, Arnoldo Foa. Directed and written by Robert Spafford. Camera (Eastman color), Rino Filippini; original story, Murray Hill Topman; music, Alberto Vitalini. Reviewed at 55th Street Playhouse, N.Y., Oct. 28, '60. Running time, 82 MINS.
Caroline Brent .... Barbara Florian
Henry Brent .... Charles Fawcett
Antonio Verbano .... Gabriele Tinti
Count Verbano .... Arnoldo Foa

Despite a woefully amateurish script that passes for a story, this Italian-U.S. coproduction venture should hold a good deal of interest for special U.S. situations and patrons who like to travel sitting down. At least 80% of the footage is pure travelog through Rome and the Vatican, featuring the classic ruins of the former and the magnificent art treasures of the latter. These scenes, photographed in often breathtaking color, are fine and informative.

All this, however, has been framed with some silly, artlessly acted and badly post-synched (English) fiction that has to do with a pretty American girl's visit to Rome with her ex-G.I. father. Her guide through the city is the Italian son of an old friend of her father's. It's boy meets girl, boy shows girl, boy gets girl. That's okay until, sandwiched in between a visit to the Sistine Chapel and the Vatican Museum, is a sidewalk cafe scene in which the heroine semi-rocks a little ballad called "At Seventeen" ("I'm seventeen and searching for love"). An audience, which moments before had been thrilled by the Sistine Chapel Choir and Lydia Aldini's singing of the "Ave Maria," is inclined to be struck totally dumb.

While Carol Danell gets program credit for singing "At Seventeen," nobody is cited as film editor, which may be just as well since the continuity is ragged in the extreme. Rino Filippini's camerawork is particularly good in the hard-to-photograph interiors, including the Sistine Chapel, the Catacombs of St. Sebastian, the Basilica of St. John The Lateran and St. Peter's.

As the youngsters, Barbara Florian and Gabriele Tinti are handsome enough to rate chances in another film which might show whether or not they have screen personalities. Robert Spafford's direction is uncertain, but he does rate a nod if he was responsible for getting permission to film inside the Vatican. Alberico Vitalini composed and conducted the score, played by the Rome Symphony Orchestra.   *Anby.*

Labbra Rosse
(Red Lips)
(ITALIAN—FRENCH)
Rome, Oct. 25.
Dino DeLaurentiis release of a Rotor Film (Carmine Bologna) Gray Film (Paris) coproduction. Stars Gabriele Ferzetti, Jeanne Valerie, Christine Kaufmann; features Giorgio Albertazzi. Directed by Giuseppe Bennati. Screenplay, Bennati, Paolo Levi. Federica Zardi; camera, Dino Santoni; music, Piero Umiliani; editor, Franco Fraticelli. At Trevi, Rome. Running time, 97 MINS.
Martini .... Gabriele Ferzetti
Irene .... Jeanne Valerie
Baby .... Christine Kaufmann
Carrel .... Giorgio Albertazzi

One of a series of nymphet-styled items currently making their appearance on the local market, this pic is a natural entry for the exploitation markets in dubbed form. It's handled fairly adroitly,

and if made with more care might have played to a wider market. This a very saleable export piece.

Film tells of the sudden infatuation of middle-aged father for a young teen-ager. He fights it for awhile. Just as he's about to give in, he's shocked to his senses by the discovery that his own young daughter has run off with a friend of his.

Jeanne Valerie plays her usual role as the baby-faced temptress while Gabriele Ferzetti and especially Giorgio Albertazzi perform capably as the two men.

Film boasts fine lensing by Dino Santoni. Other credits measure up.   *Hawk.*

San Francisco Fest

Nianchan
(The Diary of Sueko)
(JAPANESE)

San Francisco, Oct. 26.
Nikkatsu Corp. production. Stars Akiko Maeda; features Takeshi Okimura, Kayo Matsuo, Hiroyuki Nagato, Tanie Kitabayashi. Directed by Shohei Imamura. Screenplay, Ichiro Ikeda, Shohei Inamura; camera, Masahisa Himeda; music, Toshiro Miyazumi. At San Francisco Film Fest. Running time, 100 MINS.
Sueko Yasumoto .... Akiko Maeda
Koichi Yasumoto ...... Takeshi Okimura
Yoshiko Yasumoto .... Kayo Katsuo
Kiichi Yasumoto ....Hiroyuki Nagato
Granny Sakata .... Tanie Kitabayshi

This picture might also and more accurately be titled, "Hard Times Among Southern Japan's Coal Miners in 1953-54." This would be a way of saying that what might be a blockbuster in Japan is a total bust outside Japan, for the theme simply has little to interest any western audience.

Deep-rooted family ties, and all they imply, seem to have more significance to the Japanese than to westerners, and therefore this picture may seem more poignant to Japanese eyes than to western ones.

The picture depicts how four orphaned children of a mining family are forced to go their separate ways and manage to reunite during a local depression. This is supposed to be told through the eyes of a 10-year-old girl, nicely played by Akiko Maeda.

Well, life is difficult, but everyone survives and sub-plots abound —none of them too clear, even with English subtitles.

The script cliches are wholly predictable: the cheapskate storekeeper with a heart of gold, the upper-class social worker, the mine disaster, etc., etc. Along with the script cliches are the camera cliches, all looking as if they came out of a Hollywood program picture of 25 years ago. Another "western" touch is the zither musical background—more cliche. And on top of all this, the picture meanders for an hour and 40 minutes.

Not a bet in the U. S.   *Stef.*

En Fremmed Banker Paa
(A Stranger Knocks)
(DANISH)

San Francisco, Oct. 22

Flamingo Film Studio production. Stars Birgitte Federspiel, Preben Lerdorff Rye. Directed by Johan Jacobsen. Screenplay, Finn Methling; camera, Ake Borglund, Johan Jacobsen; music, Eric Fiehn. At San Francisco Film Fest. Running time, 87 MINS.

She .... Birgitte Federspiel
He .... Preben Lerdorff Rye
Man From Village.. ......Victor Montell

This brooding, explosive and superbly fabricated Danish film has only one obvious flaw: it is simply too explicit for exhibition in the U.S.

The picture starts in a very low key, with a hunted man (Preben Lerdorff Rye) seeking shelter in a cottage on a lonely stretch of land along the North Sea in 1947. A seemingly cold, expressionless woman (Birgitte Federspiel) lets him in, feeds him and allows him to sleep by her hearth.

Gradually, her story comes out: she is the widow of a Resistance hero. She has lived in this cottage, alone, for three years, mourning her husband, who was murdered by brutish collaborators.

The hunted man sees the setup is wonderful for him. He determines to hide out and, further, to make love to the woman. He does and she opens up, like a flower meeting the sun. But slowly details of her husband's murder seep out—the telltale detail is that the murderer was supposed to have had a scar "like an animal's mouth" on his right arm.

In an utterly shocking climactic scene, the woman is at the height of erotic passion when she espies the scar on her lover's arm. In the film's last 25 minutes she plays with the man, wrings a coward's confession from him and finally shoots him as he tries to escape.

This is a conscious updating of the Cain and Abel story, with this quote from Genesis thrown on the screen at the film's start: "And the Lord set his mark upon Cain lest any finding him should kill him. Therefore whosoever slayeth Cain, vengeance shall be taken from him sevenfold."

There can be no doubt that the woman, having erased the stain of the man by killing him, bears within herself the greater guilt of murder.

Johan Jacobsen's direction lends this Gothic theme great validity, and the Jacobsen-Ake Borglund black-and-white camera work is impeccable, while Eric Fiehn's incidental music is just right.

Miss Federspiel etches an unforgettable character and Rye offers a finely balanced portrayal of maleness, cowardice and cunning.

Indeed, this is a highly moral film—but the candor of its two seduction scenes makes France's "The Lovers" seem like a Disney family special. Unfortunately, these two scenes—especially the latter one—are indispensable to the film's dramatic integrity, and therefore it appears unlikely that many, if any, U.S. art houses would want to take a chance on "A Stranger Knocks." *Stef.*

Flight
(U.S.)

San Francisco, Oct. 25.

San Francisco, Inc., production. Stars Efrain Ramirez. Directed by Louis Bispo. Screenplay, Barnaby Conrad, from a John Steinbeck story; camera, Verne Carlson; music, Laurindo Almeida. At San Francisco Film Fest. Running time, 72 MINS.
Pepe .... Efrain Ramirez
Mother .... Esther Cortez
Sister .... Maria Gonzales
Brother .... Andrev Cortez
Old Man .... Ed Smith
Young Girl .... Susan Jane Darby
Hunters......Richard Crommie, Edward O'Brien, Barnaby Conrad

"Flight" never gets off the ground. Though the John Steinbeck story, from which the film was made, is simple enough—a Mexican-American youth kills a drunk in a Monterey, Cal., bar, circa 1900, flees to the hills and eventually is caught and shot by a lynching party—the picture fails to build much tension and fails to evoke much sympathy for the youth (Efrain Ramirez).

Among reasons for this failure are:

(1) Barnaby Conrad's remarkably childish scripting;

(2) Unclear motivation of the lynch party—they may be "bad men" but why are they bad?

(3) Insufficient odds in favor of the youth—he's badly wounded right at the start of the chase, and it's mostly a case of waiting till he's finished off;

(4) Over-realism—that is, the youth appeared to be living in such grinding poverty at the film's start that perhaps he's better off dead.

Relatively minor flaws include over-acting, which may be director Louis Bispo's fault or may result from the fact that most of the players either came straight from legit or had no acting experience whatever, and some of the most over-emphasized makeup seen on the screen since the early 1930s.

On the credit side is a good score by Laurindo Almeida and some superb photography of the Big Sur area south of Monterey by Verne Carlson. These credits aren't enough to pull this "art" picture through. *Stef.*

Chin Nu Yu Hun
(The Enchanting Shadow)
(HONG KONG)

San Francisco, Oct. 23.

Shaw Brothers (HK) Ltd. production. Stars Chao Lei, Betty Loh Tih; features Margaret Tong, Yang, Chi-Ching. Directed by Li Han-hsiang. Screenplay, Wang Yueh-ling; camera, Ho Lu-Ying; music, Chi Hsiang-tang. At San Francisco Film Fest. Running time, 81 MINS.
Hsiao Chien .... Betty Loh Tih
Nin' a ai-chen .... Chao Lei
Lo Mu .... Margaret Tong
Yen .... Yang Chi-Ching

The Shaw Brothers' Hongkong studio has come up with an interesting and, at times, exciting Eastmancolor picture in this old Chinese legend.

Story revolves around a haunted temple, where a young scholar (Chao Lei) beds down one night. An exquisite maiden (Betty Loh Tih) appears and tries to seduce him, but because he is a highly moral fellow, he rejects her advances. Gradually, he understands that she is a ghost and is trying to set him up to be killed by her ghostly aunt. Only so long as he is morally upright will he be able to save his life. Rest of the film carries out this theme, with temptations spread along the path of the young scholar—in final frames the murderous ghost is done in.

As a fairy tale, this is delightful, with director Li Han-hsiang keeping things moving at a nice, scary clip, the cast giving good performances and Ho Lu-Ying's color camera work pleasing the eye immensely.

It is a question whether this would fit in more than a few U.S. situations, though it might have one definite possibility: with an English soundtrack it might make a pretty good kids' picture.

But whether it plays the Western Hemisphere or not, the Shaw Brothers ought to clean up with the "Overseas Chinese" throughout Southeast Asia. *Stef.*

Les Jeux de L'Amour
(The Love Game)
(FRENCH)

Films Around the World release of AJYM production. Stars Genevieve Cluny; features Jean-Pierre Cassel, Jean-Louis Maury. Directed by Philippe Le Broca. Screenplay, Genevieve Cluny, Philippe De Broca, Daniel Boulanger; camera, Jean Penzer. At Frisco Film Fest. Running time, 83 MINS.
Victor .... Jean-Pierre Cassel
Suzanne .... Genevieve Cluny
Francois .... Jean-Louis Maury
Client .... Robert Vattier
Consumer .... Claude Cerval
Driver .... Pierre Repp

This brioche may be just what the baker ordered in France, but it falls pretty flat in the U.S., with or without translation.

It is supposed to be a French romp—and contains plenty of romping, though a sophisticated U.S. audience could hardly imagine what U.S. Customs was worried about in holding up its importation.

Story centers on a girl (Genevieve Cluny) in her mid-20's who wants to marry the artist (Jean-Pierre Cassel) she's been living with two years. He doesn't buy until his best friend (Jean-Louis Maury) starts making goo-goo eyes at the girl. Then he agrees.

The trouble with all of this is the men. They posture outrageously, indeed, almost sickeningly.

Occasional individual scenes are funny, and Miss Cluny is an arch and pleasant actress. Jean Penzer's camera work in and around Paris is stunning. Doubtful bet even for U.S. art houses. *Stef.*

Era Notte a Roma
(Night in Rome)
(ITALIAN)

San Francisco, Oct. 21.

International Golden Star-Film production. Stars Giovanni Ralli, Sergei Bondarschuk. Leo Genn, Peter Baldwin; features Renato Salvatore, Hannes Messemer. Directed by Roberto Rossellini. Screenplay, Roberto Rossellini, Diego Fabbri, S. Amidei, B. Rondi; camera, Carlo Carlini; music, Renzo Rossellini. At Frisco Film Fest. Running time, 138 MINS.
Esperia .... Giovanni Ralli
Fyodor Nazukov......Sergei Bondarschuk
Michael Pemberton...........Leo Genn
Peter Bradley .... Peter Baldwin
Renato .... Renato Salvatore
Commandant .... Hannes Messemer

Roberto Rossellini's latest essay on World War II is about a third too long, but with judicious cutting and tightening might be successful in U.S. specialty houses or, conceivably, could go into general release.

Picture concerns plight of three Allied prisoners who have escaped after the 1943 Italian surrender. The three—an American (Peter Baldwin), Englishman (Leo Genn) and Russian (Sergei Bondarschuk) —are aided by a beautiful, young black marketeer (Giovanni Ralli) and smuggled into a Roman attic.

Germans, assisted by informers, still control the city and the underground has to hide the soldiers until they can escape to Allied lines. Bulk of the film's occupied with the soldiers' and girl's close calls.

Eventually, the Russian is killed, as is the girl's fiance (Renato Salvatore). In final scenes the Briton kills the informer who caused death of the Russian and the girl's fiance—the informer is in the midst of trying to seduce the girl. Final frames show the Allies entering Rome.

Picture is quadro-lingual, which is interesting. Chunks of English, Russian and German are used, together with the predominant Italian. But too many scenes simply are too long and have too much talk for what, essentially, must be an action picture, no matter what "message" Rossellini's trying to put over (message, lousy). Some blame for length and script's turgidity must be placed on Rossellini.

On the other hand, the acting is excellent, especially among the Italians—the Yank, Briton and Russian tend to be stereotyped. And Rossellini has injected some interesting business about a princely Roman family and about the church's part in the underground. Furthermore, there are plenty of the old, arty Rossellini touches and Carlo Carlini's camera work is splended. Sound dubbing on this particular print is poor, but presumably can be corrected.

This could go—IF the proper cutting's done, and it has some exploitation possibilities. *Stef.*

North to Alaska
(C'SCOPE-COLOR)

A noisy "northern" action-comedy romp starring John Wayne and sparked by three memorabaly bruising mob brawls that will stimulate the kind of talk the picture must get to score at the b.o.

Hollywood, Nov. 3.

Twentieth-Fox release of Henry Hathaway production. Stars John Wayne, Stewart Granger, Ernie Kovacs, Fabian, Capucine; with Mickey Shaughnessy, Karl Swenson, Joe Sawyer, Kathleen Freeman, John Qualen, Stanley Adams, Stephen Courtleigh, Douglas Dick, Jerry O'Sullivan, Ollie O'Toole, Frank Faylen, Fred Graham, Alan Carney, Peter Bourne, Fortune Gordien. Directed by Hathaway. Screenplay, John Lee Mahin, Martin Rackin, Claude Binyon, based on 'Birthday Gift," play by Laszlo Fodor, adapted from idea by John Kafka; camera (De Luxe color), Leon Shamroy; editor, Dorothy Spencer; art director, Duncan Cramer, Jack Martin Smith; music, Lionel Newman; sound, Alfred Bruzlin, Warren B. Delaplain; assistant director, Stanley Hough. Reviewed at Village Theatre, Westwood, Nov. 3, '60. Running time, 122 MINS.

Sam McCord .... John Wayne
George Pratt .... Stewart Granger
Frankie Canon .... Ernie Kovacs
Billy Pratt .... Fabian
Michelle "Angel" .... Capucine
Boggs .... Mickey Shaughnessy
Lars .... Karl Swenson
Commissioner .... Joe Sawyer
Lena .... Kathleen Freeman
Lumberjack .... John Qualen
Breezy .... Stanley Adams
Duggan .... Stephen Courtlegh
Lieutenant .... Douglas Dick
Sergeant .... Jerry O'Sullivan
Mack .... Ollie O'Toole
Arnie .... Frank Faylen
Ole .... Fred Graham
Bartender .... Alan Carney
Olaf .... Peter Bourne
Lumberjack .... Fortune Gordien

"North to Alaska" is a good-humored, old-fashioned, no-holds-barred, all-stops-out northern, a kind of rowdy second cousin to a not-very-adult western. It's the sort of easygoing, slaphappy entertainment that doesn't come around so very often anymore in films, a product that wins friends without influencing people. Viewed with the discriminating eye of sophisticated-at-all-costs maturity, the running joke may seem to slow down to a walk. The Henry Hathaway production must be accepted in absolutely the right spirit to be fully appreciated.

As a boxoffice attraction the 20th-Fox release will pick up steam from word-of-mouth about its several uninhibited, knock-down-drag-out free-for-all's, unquestionably the highlights of the picture. These sequences, together with the diversified appeal of the cast, ought to be just enough to counter the negative effects of recent saturation of the Alaskan setting in entertainment (particularly in television), and do the wicket-moving job.

The John Lee Mahin-Martin Rackin-Claude Binyon screenplay (based on "Birthday Gift," an unproduced play by Laszlo Fodor, adapted from an idea by John Kafka) takes an instantly recognizable yarn and wisely plays it for laughs. It's the story of the successful Alaskan gold prospector who transports a girl from Seattle north-to-Alaska for his lovesick partner, then proceeds to fall in love with her, she with him. Any seasoned filmgoer gets the message right from the start, but the message isn't the important thing in this picture. The fun is in the execution and, under Hathaway's free-wheeling direction, there's just enough of it to count.

The three brawls Hathaway has staged are classics of the cinematic art of make-believe pugilistics. Just about every trick in the "How to be a Motion Picture Stuntman" book is utilized, with telling comedy results. The first, at the outset of the film, is danced off amidst a barroom full of gushing beer keys. Second, highlighted by a mistaken piece of strategy in which star John Wayne unleashes a rail wagon down a steep incline at his foes but forgets to get out of it himself, is staged in a thorough water setting. Third at the tail-end of the picture, is one big mud-bath, with most of the mud winding up in and around Ernie Kovacs' eye.

Wayne and Kovacs share comedy honors. Wayne displays a genuine flair for the light approach, is far more animated than is his custom. Kovacs, apparently sensing instinctively that the shortest path to humor is to seem to be playing it seriously, is the best of the lot. The others, obviously less knowledgable at the comedy trade, tend to play it too broadly, to adopt a see-how-funny-this-is attitude instead of letting the humor flow naturally out of the situations.

Director Hathaway ought to have curbed some of the excess zeal exhibited, particularly by Fabian and Stewart Granger. Both, however, are amiable types and have their better moments. Capucine does an attractive, spirited job, but has a few things to learn about the comic nuances of the English language. Supporting work is lively and colorful, most impressionably in the cases of Mickey Shaughnessy, Karl Swenson, Joe Sawyer and Kathleen Freeman.

The film was shot a long way from the Klondike, but captures the flavor of the far north, principally through the gratifying art direction of Duncan Cramer and Jack Martin Smith who have selected some fine Alaskan-looking sites in four areas of California and dressed them up with sets faithful to the popular notion of that northern frontier at the turn-of-the-century.

Credit editor Dorothy Spencer with some exceptionally perceptive cutting of the battle-royal passages, a major contribution to the comic impact of these three scenes. Leon Shamroy's lens maneuvers are both polished and energetic. Lionel Newman's music captures the flavor of the region. The title tune, as sung by Johnny Horton, has proven catchy enough to attract national attention via his recording.

Fabian croons one ballad, "If You Knew," by Russell Faith, Robert P. Marcucci and Peter DeAngelis. It's not much of a tune, but he sings it well. *Tube.*

Ship Dae Eui Ban Hang
(The Unheeded Cries)
(KOREAN)

San Francisco, Oct. 31.

Hyup-E Motion Picture Co. production. Stars Whang Hae Nam; features Uhm Aing Nam, Cho Mi Ryung, Ahn Sung Kee, Park Noh Shik. Directed by Kim Kee Yung. Screenplay, Oh Yung Jin; camera, Duk Jin Kim; music, Sang Ki Han. At San Francisco Film Festival, Oct. 30, '60. Running time, 90 MINS.

Kil Nam .... Whang Hae Nam
Bong Sun .... Uhm Aing Nam
Pil Nyuh .... Cho Mi Ryung
Keun Sun .... Ohn Sung Kee
Wang Cho .... Park Noh Shik

The first Korean film to get a U.S. screening is a sort of Seoul-slanted "Blackboard Jungle," depicting the life and times of a gang of modern-day juvenile pick-pockets in a Korean slum.

It has esoteric interest for two reasons: (1) It is a native Korean effort to come to grips with some of that nation's problems in a motion picture, and (2) it shows the deep influence on Oriental life today of American culture, and especially Hollywood films.

The story focuses on the gang's leader (played by Whang Hae Nam), who looks, acts and dresses like a young Marlon Brando, right down to the leather motorcycle jacket of "The Wild One." He is quite unregenerate most of the picture, but eventually a pre-adolescent (played by Ahn Sung Kee) wheedles his way into the tough kid's heart of gold, and everything comes out okay. Subplots abound, most of them cliches harking as far back as Dickens.

Surprisingly, the technical work on this one, especially Duk Jin Kim's camera, is good. Picture has very little possibility in any U.S. market but might stand up quite well in the Japanese and Southeast Asian markets. *Stef.*

Le Pillole di Ercole
(Hercules' Pills)
(ITALIAN)

Dino DeLaurentiis release of a Maxima Film production. Stars Nino Manfredi, Sylva Koscina, Jeanne Valerie; features Francis Blanche, Mitchell Kowal, Vittorio DeSica, Andreina Pagnani. Directed by Luciano Salce. Screenplay, Salce, Maccari, Scola, Baratti, based on play by Maurice Hennequin and Paul Bilhaud; camera, Enrico Menczer; music, Armando Trobajoli; editor, Roberto Cinquini. At Metropolitan, Rome. Running time, 105 MINS.

Nino .... Nino Manfredi
Silvia .... Sylva Koscina
Col. Cuocolo .... Vittorio DeSica
Odette .... Jeanne Valerie

Rome, Nov. 2.

Fragile but highly amusing bedroom farce, with many saleable points, will make this a surefire entry at home and of good export value for certain markets where its piquancy can be exploited.

Story is one of those intricate affairs involving miraculous Chinese pills whose aphrodisiac effects are soon noted on the various denizens of an Italian resort hotel. It gets plenty of laughs, thanks to a well gagged script, nicely paced direction by Luciano Salce, and risible performances by Nino Manfredi, Vittorio DeSica and Mitchell Kowal. Male audiences will find Sylva Koscina and Jeanne Valerie must-see added attractions as faithful wife and French mistress, respectively.

Technical credits, including Armando Trovajoli's functional musical scoring, are good. *Hawk.*

Last Woman on Earth
(VITASCOPE—COLOR)

Slim lower-berth melodrama about three unappealing survivors of a deadly worldwide phenomenon.

Hollywood, Nov. 2.

Filmgroup release of Roger Corman production. Stars Antony Carbone, Betsy Jones-Moreland, Edward Wain. Directed by Corman. Screenplay, Robert Towne; camera (Eastman color), Jack Marquette; editor, Anthony Carras; music, Ronald S. Stein; assistant director, Jack Bohrer. Reviewed at Orpheum Theatre, Los Angeles, Nov. 2, '60. Running time, 71 MINS.

Harold .... Antony Carbone
Evelyn .... Betsy Jones-Moreland
Martin .... Edward Wain

Sad to relate, "The Last Woman on Earth" turns out to be the center of a typical romantic triangle, according to this Roger Corman production. Neither she nor the two last men on earth prove to be very appealing people. The result is an unappealing picture. Paired, in current citywide L.A. openings, with "Journey to the Lost City" (see adjoining review), the Filmgroup release is a weak supporting attraction.

Robert Towne's two-dimensional screenplay proceeds to wipe out all human life, with the exception of the aforementioned trio, via a sudden reduction in the oxygen content of the atmosphere. The three lucky ones survive because they happen to be deep sea diving at the time of the swiftly-passing, deadly phenomenon, which is never properly explained. The rest of the film is childish melodrama, concerned chiefly with the efforts of the two men to win the woman, when they ought to be doing something constructive. The possibilities inherent in the premise are never pursued.

Betsy Jones-Moreland plays the last woman, Antony Carbone and Edward Wain the last men. None is convincing, nor do they have a chance to be under the circumstances. The picture, filmed in Puerto Rico, is equally routine in areas of photography (save one good underwater sequence), art work and music. Corman's direction is generally lacklustre. *Tube.*

Swiss Family Robinson
(COLOR-PANAVISION)

Standard long-ago novel, restored to the screen in an overstuffed Disney version. Wholesome family fare aimed at children, and that spells b.o.

Hollywood, Nov. 8.

Buena Vista release of Bill Anderson production. Stars John Mills, Dorothy McGuire, James MacArthur, Janet Munro, Sessue Hayakawa, Tommy Kirk, Kevin Corcoran, Cecil Parker; with Andy Ho, Milton Reid, Larry Taylor. Directed by Ken Annakin. Screenplay, Lowell S. Hawley, based on novel by Johann Wyss; camera (Technicolor), Harry Waxman; editor, Peter Boita; music, William Alwyn; assistant director, Rene DuPont. Reviewed at Academy Awards Theatre, Nov. 4, '60. Running time, 126 MINS.

Father .... John Mills
Mother .... Dorothy McGuire
Fritz .... James MacArthur
Roberta .... Janet Munro
Pirate Chief .... Sessue Hayakawa
Ernst .... Tommy Kirk
Francis .... Kevin Corcoran
Captain Moreland .... Cecil Parker
Auban .... Andy Ho
Big Pirate .... Milton Reid
Battoo .... Larry Taylor

The rather modest 147-year-old Johann Wyss tale of the "Swiss Family Robinson" has been blown up to prodigious proportions in this Walt Disney effort. The essence and the spirit of that simple, intriguing story of a marvelously industrious family is all but snuffed out, only spasmodically flickering through the ponderous approach. But that isn't likely to keep the family trade from flocking to see it. The Buena Vista release is a zoo-lulu for the kiddies,

specifically tailored to their tastes.

As reconstructed by scripter Lowell S. Hawley and executed under the guidance of director Ken Annakin, it is almost as if a Disney cartoon fantasy has come to life. The vital statistics and the element of hardship, intrinsically important aspects of the tale, have been stripped away. What emerges is a kind of glorious tropical Disneyland overrun with hapless pirates and happy beasts.

The Robinson family seems to be enjoying a standard of living that would be the envy of the average family of today. Their famous tree house is almost outrageously comfortable (running water, no less), and seems to pop up overnight with virtually no effort. In fact, the element of time and realistic effort, so vital to the overall perspective, is consistently vague in this version. It seems to be happening in a matter of days, not decades.

The climactic scrape with a band of Oriental buccaneers is the crushing blow to any semblance of credulity that has managed to strain through.

Photographically, it is a striking achievement. Through Harry Waxman's lens have been captured some compelling Technicolor views of Tobago island in the West Indies. Also on display is an array of animals to rival the beastly populations of most zoos. Editing by Peter Boita and music by William Alwyn are plus ingredients. Several sequences have a heap of genuine excitement, particularly the opening raft scene in which the family battles treacherous ocean currents to get from wrecked ship to island. These aspects add excitement and interest to the Bill Anderson production, but don't make up for the all-important loss of the story's basic values.

The acting is generally capable, but hardly memorable. John Mills and Dorothy McGuire are pleasant as mother and father Robinson. James MacArthur and Tommy Kirk are energetic and appealing as their older sons, but Kevin Corcoran is a bit too vociferously squeaky for comfort along about the latter stages. Janet Munro brings freshness and sparkle to her character. That excellent British actor, Cecil Parker, does extremely well by a small role. Sessue Hayakawa plays the leader of the pirates.

In its effort to avoid gore or vivid violence, the picture is guilty of one of the most ineffectual battle sequences on record. Huge boulders and logs dispatched downhill by the Robinson's at their corsair adversaries are so obviously cardboard that the scene just about lapses into sheer slapstick for everyone but tots. From the standpoint of comedy, that may be desirable. But "Swiss Family Robinson" is something more than comedy. *Tube.*

Journey to the Lost City
(COLORSCOPE)

Striking scenery of India hidden behind some crude, familiar melodramatics. Will attract only those willing to accept visual thrills indiscriminately.

Hollywood, Nov. 2.

American International release of Fritz Lang production. Stars Debra Paget; features Paul Christian, Walter Reyer, Claus Holm, Luciana Paluzzi; with Inkihinoff, Sabina Bethman, Rene Deltgen. Directed by Lang. Screenplay, Werner Joerg Luedecke, based on original story by Thea Von Harbou; camera, Richard Angst; editor, Walter Wischniewski; art directors, Willi Schatz, Helmut Nentwig; music, Michel Michelet. Reviewed at Orpheum Theatre, Los Angeles, Nov. 2, '60. Running time, 95 MINS.

Seta .... Debra Paget
Alan Burton .... Paul Christian
Prince Chandra .... Walter Reyer
Ramigani .... Claus Holm
Barani .... Luciana Paluzzi
Modani .... Inkihinoff
Irene .... Sabina Bethman
Rhodes .... Rene Deltgen

Some fascinating views of the province of Rajastan in India are on display in Fritz Lang's production of "Journey to the Lost City." The picture's value ends there. Dramatically, it is as crude a sex-and-sand spectacle as one can imagine. The American International release is strictly for those who are willing to settle for sheer visual escape as an excuse for visiting the cinema. Judging by the considerable popularity of this type of fare in recent years, this is no small group.

The film, directed by Lang with Werner Joerg Luedecke's screenplay as a guide, describes the perils encountered by a young western architect in the "lost city" of Eshnapur, a place teeming with sealed-off lepers, cruel princes, luscious dancing girls and loyal untouchables. The government is split into rival factions (neither very desirable), and there is a social eruption just in time to save the architect from an untimely denouement.

The players, led by Debra Paget, are burdened with dialog that is positively Ali-Babble all the way (sample: *"The prince is pleased. Your dancing has relieved his melancholy"*). Most of it is post-dubbed, adding to the discomfort.

Lang's direction is physically successful when he steers the lenses away from the actors and concentrates on the scenery. For this visuo-ethnic relief, some credit is due cameraman Richard Angst and art directors Willi Schatz and Helmut Nentwig. *Tube.*

Saturday Night and Sunday Morning
(BRITISH)

Powerfully directed, acted drama about a young rebel. Authentic Midlands background, frank sex. Little U. S. marquee values, but success of the novel may pre-sell this to most audiences.

London, Nov. 1.

British Lion release of a Bryanston presentation of a (Tony Richardson-Harry Saltzman) Woodfall production. Stars Albert Finney, Rachel Roberts, Shirley Anne Field, Hylda Baker. Directed by Karel Reisz. Screenplay by Alan Sillitoe from his own novel; camera, Freddie Francis; editor, Seth Holt; music, Johnny Dankworth. At Warner Theatre, London. Running time, 89 MINS.

Arthur .... Albert Finney
Doreen .... Shirley Anne Field
Brenda .... Rachel Roberts
Aunt Ada .... Hylda Baker
Bert .... Norman Rossington
Jack .... Bryan Pringle
Robboe .... Robert Cawdron
Mrs. Bull .... Edna Morris
Mrs. Seaton .... Elsie Wagstaffe
Mr. Seaton .... Frank Pettitt
Blousy Woman .... Avis Bunnage
Loudmouth .... Colin Blakeley
Doreen's Mother .... Irene Richmond
Betty .... Louise Dunn
Civil Defense Officer .... Anne Blake
Drunken Man .... Peter Madden
Mr. Bull .... Cameron Hall
Policeman .... Allister Williamson

Alan Sillitoe's novel has had such a fine paperback success that there should be no difficulty in luring tab-buyers to the film. It's produced, directed and acted with integrity and insight. This is a good, absorbing but not very likeable film. There's some bold dialog and some seamy sex stuff.

The real problem, which only patrons can decide, is whether or not the "angry young man" theme is frayed at the edges. It's an amoral, rather than immoral picture, but it well earns its "X" certificate. This is a product of the school of realism, adult in approach, slightly reminiscent of "Look Back In Anger." The approach is adult, but when analyzed, it says nothing new or profound.

The hero is a Nottingham factory worker who refuses to conform. He hates all authority but protests so blunderingly. His attitude is simple; "What I want is a good time. The remainder is all propaganda." Through the week he works hard at his lathe. In his spare time—Saturday night and Sunday morning (and a couple of evenings)—he comes into his own. Liquor and women. But what he is trying to prove is difficult to decide. He has an affair with the wife of a workmate until she is pregnant. Meanwhile, he picks up with a girl who won't play till she has a ring on the significant finger. Then he's beaten up by some pals of his workmate, and decides to settle down but is grimly determined not to stop fighting.

This thinnish story is mostly a vehicle for several first-class character parts. None of the people in the film is a particularly pleasant type, but all are real, devised and portrayed with keen insight and honesty. They speak in a peculiar Midland accent which is not always entirely comprehensible and a certain amount of dubbing in more acceptable English has been deemed necessary for the U. S.

Sillitoe has done a good job with his first screenplay, though, necessarily, much of the motive and the thinking of his characters has been lost in the adaptation. Director Karel Reisz has graduated from documentaries and his experience in that field has enabled him to bring a sharp tang and authenticity to the film. The locations and the interiors have caught the full atmosphere of a Midland industrial town. Seth Holt's editing and Freddie Francis' camerawork also do full justice to a film that is always holding.

The author and director can hardly have wished for better service from this cast. The central figure is cocky, violent and selfish yet at times almost pathetically likeable. This role is played by Albert Finney. Finney is a young, 24-year-old actor of immense promise and this, his first major screen performance, marks him as a man to watch. He handles scenes of belligerence and one or two torrid love scenes with complete confidence and is equally effective in quieter moments.

On a par is the performance of Rachel Roberts as the married woman carrying on a hopeless affair with Finney. With this performance, she immediately reaches star status.

Shirley Anne Field, as the conventional young woman who eventually snares Finney, is appropriately pert. Hylda Baker, a vaude and tv comedienne, making her debut in a straight part, has some good moments as the aunt to whom Finney and Miss Roberts go for help. Bryan Pringle, as Miss Roberts' weak husband; Norman Rossington, as Finney's cousin and best friend, Edna Morris, as a nosey neighbour and Robert Cawdron, a factory foreman, are others who give fine support.

It would be of help if the author had given a little more clue as to his message. But viewed as straightforward drama there is much to admire in both the writing and the production. "Saturday Morning And Sunday Night" is a mature, absorbing pic. *Rich.*

The Plunderers

Juve delinquency in the old west. Short of "A" quality or "B" pace. Timely aspect of yarn and presence of several fresh young faces will have to do rescue job at the b.o.

Hollywood, Oct. 31.

Allied Artists release of Joseph Pevney production. Stars Jeff Chandler, John Saxon, Dolores Hart, Marsha Hunt, Jay C. Flippen, Ray Stricklyn, James Westerfield, with Dee Pollock, Roger Torrey, Harvey Stephens, Vaukhan Taylor, Joseph Hamilton, Ray Ferrell, William Challee, Ken Patterson, Ella Ethridge. Directed by Pevney. Screenplay, Bob Barbash; camera, Eugene Polito; editor, Tom McAdoo; art director, David Milton; music, Leonard Rosenman; sound, Ralph Butler; assistant director, Bob Saunders. Reviewed at Academy Awards Theatre, Oct. 31, '60. Running time, **94 MINS.**

Sam .... Jeff Chandler
Rondo .... John Saxon
Ellie Walters .... Dolores Hart
Kate Miller .... Marsha Hunt
Sheriff McCauley .... Jay C. Flippen
Jeb .... Ray Stricklyn
Mike Baron .... James Westerfield
Davy .... Dee Pollock
Mule .... Roger Torrey
Doc Fuller .... Harvey Stephens
Jess Walters .... Vaughn Taylor
Abilene .... Joseph Hamilton
Billy Miller .... Ray Ferrell
1st Citizen .... William Challee
2nd Citizen .... Ken Patterson
Mrs. Phelps .... Ella Ethridge

"The Plunderers" is a rather classic example of a picture that falls into that gray market area between the top and bottom half of a double bill. Essentially, it is neither. The Joseph Pevney production appears to be aspiring for the number one position, but it falls considerably shy of that goal. It would be a strong supporting attraction save that it is a trifle too long, a bit pretentious, and too slow-moving for secondary standards. If the Allied Artists release is to get by, it will have to impress upon the public that it is telling a timely story (juvenile delinquency) in an old west setting, and that there are some fresh and promising young people in the cast, in addition to star Jeff Chandler. Being a medium-budgeted effort, it might have a long-shot chance.

The Bob Barbash screenplay contains several highly dramatic passages and provides most of the performers with plenty of high-voltage emoting room, but leaves too many motivational questions unanswered and seems to avoid the normal paths of inter-character communication. It is almost as if the people involved in Barbash's screenplay go out of their way not to discuss and reason things out in the accepted human fashion, with the result that the climaxes emerge artificial. The

drama concerns four unsociable young drifters who, sensing the fear they inspire in a small village peopled by peace-loving types, proceed to take over. Eventually they are overhauled one by one, primarily through the efforts of a one-armed Civil War hero (Chandler), who is in the process of regaining his courage and confidence.

Chandler gives a straightforward delineation, a sensible approach to the character. He leaves the emotional sparking to the younger people in the cast, some of whom come through admirably. Ray Stricklyn brings immature menace to the role of the leader of the young rat pack, and Roger Torrey is a standout as his giant lieutenant, an irrational but awe-inspiring hulk of a boy-man. Dolores Hart is pretty and capable as the girl who loves Chandler (in spite of the jarring discrepancy in age). There is solid character playing by Marsha Hunt, Jay C. Flippen and James Westerfield.

Dee Pollock is not altogether convincing as the brightest and most decent of the sinister quartet. Least successful of the players is John Saxon, although his failure is partially a result of some extremely obvious directorial touches by Pevney, predictable bits of business such as the villainous leer when eyeing the innocent young girl. Saxon's interpretation of a dangerous vaquero is far too exaggerated for belief.

Cinematically, the approach is simple and uncluttered. A level of journeyman competence is attained by lensman Eugene Polito, art director David Milton, editor Tom McAdoo, composer-conductor Leonard Rosenman. *Tube.*

Via Margutta
(ITALIAN)

Rome, Nov. 1.

Cineriz release of a Documento Film production. Features Antonella Lualdi, Gerard Blain, Franco Fabrizi, Yvonne Fourneaux, Cristina Gaioni, Spiros Focas, Claudio Gora, Walter Brofferio, Corrado Pani, Marion Marshall and Alex Nicol. Directed by Mario Camerini. Story and screenplay, Franco Brusati, Camerini, Ennio De Concini, Ugo Guerra; camera, Leonida Barboni; music, Piero Piccioni. At Corso Cinema, Rome. Running time, **108 MINS.**

Stefano .... Gerard Blain
Marta .... Yvonne Fourneaux
Donata .... Antonella Lualdi
Giosue .... Franco Fabrizi
Marco .... Spiros Focas
Maid .... Cristina Gaioni

Fragmentary expose of artists life and troubles along Rome's Via Margutta, local painters row, this often hits the mark but just as often misses its target. It's a spotty item which must rely on a strong, adroit sell, coupled with a large and likeable cast roster, for full effect.

Screenplay denotes the presence of too many different contributors, and generally tries to ring in too many elements and problems. These include the fashionable phony artist, the talented one who makes good, the foreign dabbler who is in Via Margutta for kicks alone (an escape from his dominant wife), the homo art dealer who helps along his protegees, the pure and innocent housemaid and the opportunist who lives off the work of others.

The result is perforce superficial character development not aided by strangely, uninvolved direction by Mario Camerini. The pic has its moments, however, and a good re-editing job would help.

The acting is better than the material, with Alex Nicol walking off with most honors, followed by Antonella Lualdi, Yvonne Fourneaux and others. Claudo Gora and Franco Fabrizi repeat previous roles, while the usually competent Gerard Blain appears ill at ease in his role as the dedicated painter. Homosexual aspects are rendered in unflinching manner here, but the handling is honest and straightforward. It got by the local censor as is.

Technical credits, from Piero Piccioni's good score to Leonida Barboni's expert camerawork on colorful Roman locations, are all first-class. *Hawk.*

They Were Ten
(ISRAELI

San Francisco, Oct. 30.

Orb Films, Ltd., and Scopus, Inc., production. Stars Ninette Dinar, Oded Teomi; features Leo Filer. Directed by Baruch Dienar. At San Francisco Film Festival, Oct. 29, '60. Running time, **108 MINS.**

Manya .... Ninette Linar
Josef .... Oded Teomi
Zalman .... Leo Filer

This picture tells the story of 10 settlers from an Eastern European ghetto in Galilee near the end of the 19th Century. Nine are men, the 10th the wife (Ninette Dinar) of one (Oded Teomi). The 10 are forced to scrape a farm out of a racky, barren hillside, fight unfriendly Arabs for water and lebensraum and face down the land's Turkish rulers. They also must put down dissension in their own ranks, and the wife has to put off another too-ardent settler. Among the picture's predictable facets are the birth of a child, a grim drought and, at the film's end, the woman's death and a heavy rain.

The whole picture was shot in the hills of Galilee by an unknown cameraman with the all-Israeli cast speaking Hebrew. It is a nice try at a peasant epic but really doesn't come off because Baruch Dienar's direction is erratic and it follows a much too familiar pattern. Performances of the leading players are quite good, though the characters tend to be stock.

Film probably has art house market in New York, Chicago, Los Angeles, Boston and Philadelphia, also has exploitation possibilities as the first all-Israeli production to be shown in U.S. *Stef.*

Bis Dass Das Geld Euch Scheidet
(Until Money Departs You)
(GERMAN)

Constantin release of Alfa production. Stars Luise Ulrich and Gert Froebe; features Corny Collins, Wolfgang Lukschy, Christiane Nielsen. Directed by Alfred Vohrer. Screenplay, Heinz Oskar Wuttig, after novel of same name by Angela Ritter; camera, Kurt Hasse; music, Herbert Trantow; editor, Ira Oberberg. At Marmorhaus, Berlin. Running time, **99 MINS.**

Lisbeth Grapsch .... Luise Ulrich
Jupp Grapsch .... Gert Froebe
Heidi Grapsch .... Corny Collins
Berni Grapsch .... Manfred Kunst
Nina Sonntag .... Christiane Nielsen
Manfred Grothe ...... Wolfgang Lukschy
Dr. Plauert .... Leon Askin
Dr. Giller .... Hans Hessling
Fritz Hassen .... Herbert Tiede
Poldi .... Peter Parak

As per its subject this is one of the more ambitious recent German pix. It makes an attempt to criticize West Germany's newly rich society. Pic's intended social-criticism, however, lacks a good deal of conviction, and the whole thing borders too much on the novelettish. While foreign prospects are rather problematical, film's domestic chances look satisfactory, undeniably helped by the name of Luise Ulrich, one of few German screen actresses who's managed to keep a star status for more than 20 years.

Film tries to show that money is often the root of all evil. Here is projected a couple who lived happily while they had to struggle along with financial difficulties. Thanks to the German economic boom, the man struck it rich and became an industrial tycoon. That evidently spoils his character in this vehicle. All that he has now in his mind is to get rid of his wife for the sake of a younger woman. Film's ending sees the man deserted by all, even by the girl for whom he gave up his wife and children.

As often with German pix of this type, this one suffers from an inadequate script. Situations, story development and character motivations are too conventional to make an impression. Although much of their acting rings untrue in this, the players are still the best thing about this film.

This particularly applies to Gert Froebe whose portrayal of the spoilt-by-money hubby, is worth watching. Luise Ulrich, his wife, has to exaggerate her naivete but she too has a number of good scenes. Cute Corny Collins turns in an acceptable performance as their daughter, a modern-type girl. Christiane Nielsen is believable as the sexy femme for whom the man falls. Wolfgang Lukschy contributes a crook who specializes on fake grounds for divorce.

Alfred Vohrer's direction is usually too broad and reveals some lack of routine. But it's his first adult film after a series of pix that revolved aroung teenagers. Herbert Trantow's score is good while the lensing is average as are the film's other technical credits. *Hans.*

Djavulens Oga
(The Devil's Eye)
(SWEDISH)

Stockholm, Nov. 1.

Svensk Filmindustri production and release. With Jarl Kulle, Bibi Anderson, Nils Poppe, Gertrud Fridh, Sture Lagerwall, Stig Jarrel, Gunnar Bjornstrand, Georg Funkquist, Gunnar Sjoberg, Allan Edwall. Directed by Ingmar Bergman. Screenplay, Bergman; camera, Gunnar Fischer; music, Domenico Scarlatti; editor, Ocar Rosander. At Roda Kvarn, Stockholm. Running time, **90 MINS.**

Don Juan .... Jarl Kulle
Britt-Marie .... Bibi Anderson
The Priest .... Nils Poppe
Renata .... Gertrud Fridh
Pablo .... Sture Lagerwall
Satan .... Stig Jarrel
The Actor .... Gunnar Bjornstrand
Count .... Georg Funkquist
Marquis .... Gunnar Sjoberg
Eared Devil .... Allan Edwall

Ingmar Bergman's new comedy, "The Devil's Eye," is based on the Irish proverb that "a virgin is a sty in the devil's eye." In the pit of hell, one day Satan's eyelid began to swell and experts informed him that the cause was the untouched 20-year-old daughter of a country priest. In order to set things straight again, Satan decides to dispatch Don Juan, his most experienced seducer to earth.

On his journey to seduce the young girl, Don Juan was accompanied by his servant, Pablo. Defying orders, Pablo promptly set out to seduce the frustrated wife of the priest. The priest was kind and had a childish faith in the goodness of mankind. Don Juan managed in causing a momentary breach between the daughter, Britt-Marie, and her fiance and breaking down her resistance. Previously, Don Juan was always the indifferent lover who had awakened the passions of women, but Britt-Marie's reaction was indifference. And on this occasion Don Juan fell in love.

Bergman's story is a fanciful one set in the world of the comedy of manners, with the music of Scarlatti backgrounding. Although the film belongs to his lighter works, his favorite serious subjects, God, the devil and sex, play dominating roles.

Gunnar Fischer's photography is tops, but this time Bergman has related his story largely through words and less through pictures. However, there are a number of amusing photographic tricks. On the whole, the acting is superb. Top honors go to Bibi Andersson, Gertrud Fridh and Nils Poppe. One of the best scenes occurs when the priest captures a devil in his cupboard.

"Eye" may not be one of Ingmar Bergman's greatest masterpieces, but it is a well-made film with a fair amount of racy dialog that can be humorous if not hilarious. It should be a boxoffice tantalizer. Some of the arty audiences may be disappointed, but should find material to dissect. *Fred.*

Komisario Palmun Erehdys
(Mysterious Case of Rygseck Murders)
(FINNISH)

Helsinki, Nov. 1.

Suomen Filmitelollisuus (SF) production and release. Screenplay and directed by Matti Kassila after a novel by Mika Waltari. Stars Joel Rinne, Elina Pohppanpas, Matti Ranin; features Jussi Jurkka, Elina Salo, Saara Ranin, Aino Mantsas, Leevi Kuuranne, Leo Jokela and Pentti Siimes. Camera, Olavi Tuomi; music, Osmo Lindeman; editor, Elmer Lahti. At Rex and Tuulensuu, Helsinki. Running time, **109 MINS.**

Mika Waltari, who is the widely-known author of such bestsellers as "The Egyptian," "The Adventurer," has given a solid literary basis for this thriller-type modern picture. However, the yarn is turned over to images and sounds with such an exceptional filmatic verve that the picture must be considered the best for director Matti Kassila.

Plot is told on two time levels simultaneously. Never before has any director managed to drive this way of telling to such extremes as here without losing in clarity or pace. An abundance of humor, sometimes sarcastic, keeps up the balance with a rather grim main story line. The impact of the overall effect is tremendous. There are almost no breaks in the tension. This is due to clever editing by Elmer Lahti.

Film's star, Joel Rinne, plays an amiable detective, Inspector Palmu. All the others are exceptionally

good. Elina Pohpanpas is a suspected young girl; Elina Salo plays a girl in the net of a blackmailing relative; while Pentti Siimes is the drunken brother. Leo Jokela is very funny as one of the detectives. A special laurel goes to Matti Ranin as Rinne's assistant, his role being mostly without dialog.

Camera work of Olavi Tuomi provides brilliant depth and shadows. The music by Osmo Lindeman is a definite asset. Other technical credits are good.

Competently dubbed, this picture should have fine possibilities in any country. At home, it is surging to top b.o. results.   *Tuus.*

Watan
(Motherland)
(PAKISTANI)

San Francisco, Oct. 31.
Shah Noor Studios of Lahore production. Stars Kamal; features Ejaz, Musarrat Nazir, Bahar, Ilyas. Directed by Anwar Kemal. Screenplay, Anwar Kemal; camera, Rashid Lodhi; editor, M. Akram; music, Inayat Hussain. At San Francisco Film Fest, Oct. 30, '60. Running time, **92 MINS.**
Javed .... Kamal
Masud .... Ejaz
Reshman .... Musarrat Nazir
Jenny .... Bahar
Seth Mansoor .... Ilyas

As an example of the impress of western — and especially Hollywood—culture on the Middle East, this first Pakistani film to be screened in the U.S. is rather interesting. But that's all.

Picture centers on stepbrothers, one from poor, heroic family, other from rich family, who seek the hand of the daughter of a government official. Poor boy wins, of course, after many harrowing experiences, all of which have been lifted from 30-year-old Hollywood scripts, it would seem. Pace is slow and film is technically weak from every standpoint by western standards.

This film has only curiosity value and no chance whatsoever in any European or American market.   *Stef.*

Legions of the Nile
(ITALIAN—C'SCOPE—COLOR)

Cleopatra and Mark in a dub-dud though some good derring-do scenes.

Twentieth-Fox release of Virgilio De Blasi-Italo Zingarelli production. Stars Linda Cristal. Cast (no character names given) includes Georges Marchal, Ettore Manni, Maris Mahor; with Conrado Sanmartin, Alfredo Mayo, Daniela Rocca, Mino Doro, Juan Majan, Andrea Aureli, Stefand Terra, Stefano Oppedisano, Salvatore Furnari, Rafael Duran, Tomas Blanco, Jany Clair, Mary Carillo. Directed by Vittorio Cottafavi. Screenplay, Cottafavi, Giorgio Cristallini, Arnoldo Marrosu, Ennio De Concini; camera, Mario Pacheco; editor, Giulio Penna; art director, Antonio Simont; music, Renzo Rossellini; sound, Luis Buch, Oscar De Arcangelis; assistant directors, Antonio Ribas, Tsetso Zamurovich. Reviewed at the sudio, Oct. 28, '60. Running time, **90 MINS.**

Add "Legion of the Nile" to the list of quasi-historical adventure spectacles manufactured on the Italian assembly line and post-dubbed on these shores for quick, easy domestic digestion. Within the regrettable limitations of such international reconditioning, the film has a certain cultural merit that attracts attention and a child-like quality of epic heroism to capture the imagination of younger patrons and fanciful adults who can stand the sight of blood and the contrivances of two-dimen-

sional melodrama. The 20th-Fox release, bolstered by CinemaScope and De Luxe Color, figures to make the usual swift, but ample dent on the accommodating American boxoffice.

The last days of Cleopatra and Mark Antony are under surveillance. With Cleopatra also the object of a far more ambitious enterprise being undertaken by this studio, it is understandable that 20th is rather hastily pressing this into release, more or less to get it out of the way before any conflict or confusion might arise. Actually the examination of these two well-known historical figures is extremely superficial and unconvincing in this film, occupying a subsidiary position behind the spectacular perils encountered by one Curridius, a Roman envoy who has been sent to Alexandria to persuade Antony to avert the disaster of a battlefield tangle with the home office. He falls, but in the process falls in and out of amor with the doomed Cleopatra.

Scenes of derring-do are pretty exciting, and there are several diverting passages of gladiatorial action, underwater combat and feats of archery. Linda Cristal, as Cleopatra, is not exactly the woman of infinite variety Shakespeare had in mind, but she's easy to look at. Ettore Manni is handsome and swashbuckling as Curridius. All of the acting suffers from the rub-a-dub-dubbing. Vittorio Cottafavi's direction keeps it moving along briskly for co-producers Virgilio De Blasi and Italo Zingarelli. The film, lensed in and around Rome and Madrid, is for the most part artistically authentic and photographically efficient.   *Tube.*

Le Capitan
(The Yokel)
(FRENCH—COLOR DYALISCOPE)

Paris, Nov. 1.
Pathe release of Pathe-Dama Films production. Stars Jean Marais, Bourvil; features Elsa Martinelli, Pierrette Bruno, Annie Anderson. Directed by Andre Hunebelle. Screenplay, Jean Halain, Pierre Foucaud, Hunebelle from novel by Michel Zavaco; camera (Eastmancolor), Marcel Grignon; editor, Jean Feyte. At Marignan, Paris. Running time, **115 MINS.**
Francois .... Jean Marais
Cogolin .... Bourvil
Gisele .... Elsa Martinelli
Maid .... Pierrette Bruno
Beatrice .... Annie Anderson
King Louis .... Christian Fourcade

Andre Hunebelle had a successful pic with his "The Hunchback" and now repeats with another swashbuckling costumer that should follow in its predecessors' hoofprints. However, this appears somewhat too naive and familiar for anything but playoff or moppet use abroad.

Pic is amply mounted. It has a fair share of good swordplay and acrobatics by Jean Marais while the needed comic relief comes from funnyman Bourvil. It concerns a country nobleman trying to defend himself and his king from a usurping regent. He also gets a girl in the bargain. The fights are well staged and characters are the usual sawdust variety. This is all passable entertainment but lacks the originality or robustness for wide Yank chances. Its wordiness and nationalist drumbeating also make this more of a Continental item.

It all transpires in the 17th Century as Marais saves young Louis XIII from his conniving regent. Costumes, color and C'Scope size are all plus values.   *Mosk.*

World of Suzie Wong
(COLOR)

Good hot boxoffice looms for this screen translation. But gay life of prostitution may draw civic protests.

Hollywood, Nov. 7.
Paramount release of Ray Stark production. Stars William Holden, Nancy Kwan, Sylvia Syms, Michael Wilding; with Jacqui Chan, Laurence Naismith. Directed by Richard Quine. Screenplay, John Patrick, adapted from novel by Richard Mason and play by Paul Osborn; camera, Geoffrey Unsworth; editor, Bert Bates; art director, John Box; music, George Duning; sound, Roy Baker; assistant director, Gus Agosti. Reviewed at the studio, Nov. 7, '60. Running time, **130 MINS.**
Robert Lomax .... William Holden
Suzie Wong .... Nancy Kwan
Kay .... Sylvia Syms
Ben .... Michael Wilding
Gwennie .... Jacqui Chan
O'Neill .... Laurence Naismith

The advantage of on-the-spot geography does a great deal for the screen version of "The World of Suzie Wong." The ultra-picturesque environment of teeming Hong Kong brings a note of ethnic charm to the Ray Stark production, and amounts to a major improvement over the legit translation of Richard Mason's novel. The cause is further aided by the intimacy of film and the advanced maturity of the leading man. Against which assets the basic story being told remains simply mild diversion, and nothing more. The shortcomings of the original work, which led to the shortcomings of the play, have carried over to the picture, and in a few instances have been compounded.

Commercially, the Paramount release appears to be in good shape. First off, there is the pre-sold audience familiar with Mason's tome. Secondly, there is that legion of femme fans of William Holden, who hasn't exactly suffered from overexposure lately. Additionally, there is the publicity surrounding the leading lady, Nancy Kwan, who stepped into the role under unusual circumstances and has since received no minor national buildup. Finally, there is the picture itself, a compelling and exploitable east-meets-west love story. Boxoffice success seems assured.

The touchy subject of sex will be a key factor in the film's reception. Its frank discussions and examinations of matters sexual, acceptable in its book and play form, are a ticklish business in its transfer to the screen, where a wider variety of ages, outlooks and temperaments are to be exposed to it. For moppets, it is unsavory fare. Unsuspecting mothers who bring their children to the theatre are likely to regret it. For teenagers, particularly the younger ones, it will be an uncomfortable experience and may plant some strange, wild ideas in more impressionable youthful minds. In treating prostitution as a rather delightful "profession" (almost a milk-and-honey world), it conceivably could influence some femme youngsters to consider the "merits" of the occupation. After all, the bar-girls of the film seem to be having a fairly agreeably time at their trade. Boxoffice is going to reflect the moral stance of the filmgoing public. There is likely to be some controversy stirred up, and the result will be a stimulus to adults and a caution to parents.

"Suzie Wong" is the story of an artist (Holden) who has come to Hong Kong to devote one year to "learning something about painting and something about myself." Before long, he is also learning a great deal about Suzie (Miss Kwan), a kind of titular leader of a band of lovable, warmhearted prostitutes (are there any other kinds?). After resisting temptations of the flesh and giving her the brush for an admirable period, Holden eventually succumbs to the yen. Complications ensue when it develops Miss Kwan has a child, but harmony once again prevails and east-west relations are cemented following a rather spectacular rainstorm during which the child perishes and Hong Kong seems to be coming apart at the seams.

Scenarist John Patrick's attempt to enhance the romance by laying in some additional social significance is, for the most part, abortive. His little glimpses into western prejudice do not quite ring true with three-dimensional insight. But the love story makes much more sense with the substitution of the mature Holden for the younger hero of the play. It is far more understandable that an older man would fall deeply in love with the little Oriental bargirl, and that she would return that affection.

That and the scenery are the major improvements. On the decidedly negative side of Patrick's adaptation are three passages in which realism is virtually abandoned for theatrical effect. These are scenes in which (1) Miss Kwan, beaten up by a sailor, proudly displays her bloody lip to the girls as a token of Holden's jealousy, (2) Miss Kwan and Holden dine on salad dressing so as not to reveal her illiteracy to a "stuckup" waiter, and, (3) Holden impulsively tears Miss Kwan's dress off when she turns up in his room looking like the western version of what she is.

Utilizing the intimacy of the camera, director Richard Quine has been able to add several humorous touches to the action. He also seems to have extracted the best possible work from his cast, particularly in choice of when to zero in for tight closeups and when to pull back and away. In this respect, credit is also due editor Bert Bates. With cameraman Geoffrey Unsworth, Quine has added interest and mobility through several strokes of dramatic lens-positioning such as a sudden glimpse of the bedroom from a darkened and elevated vantage point. Unsworth's shutterwork is most notable for the subtle photographic qualities of his smoky barroom views.

Interior sets designed by John Box smack of authenticity and are a fine complement to the enchanting shots of Hong Kong itself. There are several passages of sheer travelog, worthwhile glimpses of culture-in-action. Audiences unfamiliar with the city will marvel at them. George Duning's music is unobtrusively gratifying.

Holden gives a first-class performance, restrained and sincere. He brings authority and compassion to the role. Miss Kwan, a most agreeable-looking creature, is not always perfect in her timing of lines (she has a tendency to anticipate) and appears to lack a full range of depth or warmth when the occasion calls for an extreme degree of emotional reaction, but on the whole she manages a fairly believable portrayal. She will be a valuable commodity whenever Eurasian parts are to be filled in films.

Michael Wilding is capable in a role that has been trimmed down somewhat in importance from the play version, in which the character seemed less appealing. For purposes of contrast, it should have remained less appealing. Sylvia Syms does exceedingly well by the comparatively thankless role of the "other woman," and Laurence Naismith is excellent as her liberal-minded father. Jacqui Chan is convincing as a B-girl sans sex appeal, only one of the group (outside of the heroine) left with an identity in the screen translation.

Tube.

De tal Palo, tal Astilla

(Chip On the Shoulder) (MEXICAN)

Mexico City, Nov. 8.

Peliculas Nacionales release of Filmadora Chapultepec production. Stars Luis Aguilar, Lalo Gonzales ("Piporro" Bassoon); features Flor Silvestre, Marina Camacho. Directed by Miguel M. Delgado. Screenplay, Alfredo Varela Jr., from original by J. Maria Fernandez Unsain; camera, Agustin Jimenez; music, Manuel Esperon. At Cine Orfeon, Mexico City. Running time, **90 MINS.**

Attempt in this one was to poke fun at the typical American western. But even though singer Luis Aguilar and comic Lalo Gonzalez ("Piporro") swagger around with traditional six shooter trappings, give a version of the stalk, and use the word "sheriff" for the Mexican upholder of law and order (played by Aguilar), it just doesn't come off.

Sum total is neither a Mexican western, although it has the necessary number of shooting scenes and the inevitable singing, nor a lampoon of the Hollywood potboilers.

Both actors play double roles of father and son, and story centers around differences of opinion of two old timers in the Mexican village, and a "switch" of offspring of both where the "good guy" has the "bad man's" child and vice versa. Situations this develops have been used before in other films.

Audience liked the show, laughing at the conventional stock comedy situations. It all winds up in a stirring quartet achieved by trick dubbing, with warring old timers burying the hatchet, the mixup of sons cleared up and love interest provided by Flor Silvestre and Marina Camacho. These latter don't sing, only look on adoringly as the two stars give forth with gusto in their quartet finale.

Producers obviously intend to build up Aguilar and Gonzalez as a team for the home and Latin American markets.

Emil.

The Facts of Life

Lively, witty romp sparked by spirited work of Bob Hope and Lucille Ball as a pair of frustrated extra-marital lovers. Bright b.o. prospects.

Hollywood, Nov. 9.

United Artists release of Norman Panama-Melvin Frank production. Stars Bob Hope, Lucille Ball, Ruth Hussey, Don De Fore, Louis Nye; with Philip Ober, Marianne Stewart, Peter Leeds, Hollis Irving, William Lanteau, Robert F. Simon, Louise Beavers, Mike Mazurki. Directed by Frank. Screenplay, Panama and Frank; camera, Charles Lang Jr.; editor, Frank Bracht; art directors, J. Macmillan Johnson, Kenneth A. Reid; music, Leigh Harline; sound, Joseph Edmondson; assistant director, Jack Aldworth. Reviewed at Grauman's Chinese Theatre, Nov. 9, '60. Running time, **103 MINS.**

Larry Gilbert	Bob Hope
Kitty Webster	Lucille Ball
Mary Gilbert	Ruth Hussey
Jack Webster	Don De Fore
Charlie Busbee	Louis Nye
Doc Mason	Philip Ober
Connie Mason	Marianne Stewart
Thompson	Peter Leeds
Myrtle Busbee	Hollis Irving
Airline clerk	William Lanteau
Motel clerk	Robert F. Simon
Gussie	Louise Beavers
Man in motel room	Mike Mazurki

The vanishing art of bedroom comedy is revived in the Panama and Frank production of "The Facts of Life." Thanks to the comic know-how of a couple of pros, Bob Hope and Lucille Ball, the effort is highly successful, and the boxoffice is going to reflect that success in spite of the fact that Hope and Miss Ball are so frequently accessible for free on television.

The humor in "Facts" ranges from rapid-fire gag lines to out-and-out farce, but hits its peak in a couple of situations that are telling takeoffs on contemporary family relations. These scenes have an immmediate communicative impact on audiences. They hit home. But the United Artists release is mostly light, harmless romantic fluff of the bedroom-hopping variety, and is liable to launch a trend by putting some fun back into filmdom's bedroom, site of so much no-nonsense dramatic activity in recent times.

The sharp, fast-moving screenplay, collaborative effort of producer Norman Panama and director Melvin Frank, pairs off Hope and Miss Ball in an extra-marital romantic affair. Both, taken for granted by their respective spouses and children, seek escape from humdrum suburban family life in each other's arms, but the affair swiftly expires when the red-tape and heartbreak involved in a clean break with the past become apparent. Obviously there is an underlying serious strain to the proceedings, but this serves primarily as a sound, solid springboard for some of the year's best screen humor.

Both of the stars are in exceptionally fine form. Hope exhibits refreshing restraint in his approach, admirably underplaying to his costar but rattling off gags and handling reaction business as only he can. Miss Ball returns to the screen after a rather lengthy absence and proves anew that she's one of the top comediennes around, a fact with which tv audiences are quite familiar. Somewhat more subdued than her well-known "Lucy" image, Miss Ball thoroughly brightens up the comedy, be it farce, slapstick, sophisticated or satire, all of which are incorporated into the picture.

Ruth Hussey and Don De Fore are disarmingly unpleasant as the non-romantic mates of the roving couple. Louis Nye is a delightful bounder. Among the supporting players, Peter Leeds gives a particularly amusing performance as a sharp-eyed laundryman and Robert F. Simon puts over some memorably unimpressed visual attitudes as a motel clerk who isn't buying the husband-wife registration stance of Hope and Miss Ball. Additionally agreeable support is generated by Philip Ober, Marianne Stewart, Hollis Irving, William Lanteau, Louise Beavers and Mike Mazurki.

Frank's direction is a gem of comic perception, with only one or two lapses in which bits of business initially uproarious are repeated until the life has been sapped out of them. Only other criticism is the fact that a large amount of dialog is drowned out beneath waves of audience laughter over the lines preceding them. Presumably the dialog lost is unimportant, but seeing lips move without hearing what is being said is thoroughly frustrating.

Workmanlike camera capers by Charles Lang Jr., cutting by Frank Bracht and art direction by J. Macmillan Johnson and Kenneth A Reid are vauable contributions to a film that is unpretentious by physical and photographic standards. Leigh Harline's score adds a light, effervescent note, and there is a lilting, literate title ditty by Johnny Mercer, sung by Eydie Gorme and Steve Lawrence as the Saul Bass titles unravel.

Tube.

Man in the Moon

(BRITISH)

Amiably amusing, but mainly disappointing Kenneth More comedy. This spoof on science fiction ambles along to rather gimmick ending. Excellent production work, and More's name should suffice.

London, Nov. 8.

Rank release of (Michael Relph & Basil Dearden) Allied Film Makers' production. Stars Kenneth More; features Shirley Anne Field, Michael Hordern, Noel Purcell. Directed by Basil Dearden. Screenplay, Michael Relph, Bryan Forbes; camera, Harry Waxman; editor, John Guthbridge; music, Philip Green. At Odeon, Leicester Square, London, Oct. 31, '60. Running time, **99 MINS.**

William	Kenneth More
Polly	Shirley Anne Field
Herbert	Norman Bird
Dr. Davidson	Michael Hordern
Dr. Wilmot	John Glyn-Jones
Professor Stephens	John Phillips
Leo	Charles Gray
Rex	Bernard Horsfall
Roy	Bruce Boa
Prosecutor	Noel Purcell
Storekeeper	Ed Devereaux
Dr. Hollis	Newton Blick
1st Doctor	Richard Pearson
2d Doctor	Lionel Gamlin
Woomera Director	Russell Waters
Lorry Driver	Danny Green
Jaguar Driver	Jeremy Lloyd

The popularity of Kenneth More will insure safe b.o. reaction at popular houses, but considering the amount of talent on the bandwagon for "Man In The Moon," this is a mild disappointment. It's an amiable spoof on science fiction but is rarely as funny as its original idea promises. It ambles along towards a gimmick ending which is not strong enough to justify the word "climax." There are quite a number of yocks but the film is a tame return for More to the type of comedy that he can handle so well.

He plays a medical guineapig who, at the start of the film is working on field tests for the Common Cold Research Centre. But More is a person of such equable temperament that he's completely immune from violent emotions. And, apparently, from colds, too. Anyway, he's fired by the Research Centre.

But next door, at the National Atomic Research Centre they're looking for a man to train as a pathfinder to the moon, before sending off a rocket containing a

team of supermen. They decide that More's the man—healthy, with no ties, unworried, expandable. The financial carrot's satisfactory to him and he agrees, but there's one flaw in the plan.

They neglect to tell him that he's destined for the moon and con him into thinking that he's still a guinea pig. When he discovers the truth and that there's a reward of $280,000 for being the first man on the moon, he decides to go through with it, figuring the cash will be useful for marrying a stripteaser for whom he's fallen. But, in the finale, the test fizzles out and so, in fact, does the film.

The most fun comes in the rivalry of More and the three supermen, excellently played by Charles Gray, Bruce Boa and Bernard Horsfall. Shirley Anne Field competently provides the brief romantic trimmings. Michael Hordern, John Glyn-Jones and John Phillips are soundly amusing.

Basil Dearden's direction is uneven as, indeed is the script by Michael Relph and Bryan Forbes. The whole affair has the air of a serious film into which comedy has been rather desperately pumped. More's affable personality is relaxed and pleasant as always, but in this instance the character seems insufficiently rounded for full impact. Harry Waxman has done a good job with his lensing.
Rich.

'Beat' Girl
(BRITISH)

Cheap little dualer about a London kid who gets mixed up with beatniks, a striptease murder and problems with her father and stepmother; may click with undiscriminating audiences.

London, Nov. 8.
Renown release of a George Minter (George Willoughby) production. Stars David Farrar, Noelle Adam, Christopher Lee, Adam Faith; features Shirley-Anne Field, Delphi Lawrence, Gillian Hills. Directed by Edmond T. Greville. Story and screenplay by Dail Ambler; camera, Walter Lassely; editor, Gordon Pilkington; music, John Barry. Previewed at Renown Theatre, London. Running time, 86 MINS.
Paul Linden .... David Farrar
Nichole .... Noelle Adam
Kenny .... Christopher Lee
Jennifer .... Gillian Hills
Dave .... Adam Faith
Greta .... Delphi Lawrence
Dodo .... Shirley-Anne Field
Tony .... Peter McEnery
Honey .... Claire Gordon

It's difficult to know quite how to deal with this film. It's probably no worse than many others that have been specifically designed to appeal to a certain market. But it's a shade puzzling to know how such a market can exist. Some good performers strive valiantly, but with little success, to resource writing, direction and production all of which seem equally uninspired.

The story concerns a young girl who resents the arrival of her new stepmother, a French girl just married to her father (David Farrar). She seems a nice kid, if a little sullen, but she's apparently leading a double life by mixing with Soho beatniks. When young mum tries to influence her the youngster discovers that the French girl (Noelle Adam) was once a stripteaser and, maybe, even worse. It takes an attempted

---

seduction by a nightclub lecher and a murder before the child is brought to her senses.

Dialog may be authentic to the beatnik atmosphere, but it grates on the ear. Adam Faith, a top pop singer, is brought into a film which, with an "X" certificate, bans his own following. Farrar, Miss Adam, Christopher Lee and Delphi Lawrence bring professionalism to cardboard parts while a new girl, Gillian Hills, is clearly not sufficiently experienced to cope with the unpleasant role of the rebel teenager. John Barry and his Seven play some numbers that are adequate but unmemorable.

Briefly, a British film in which the local industry can take little pride.
Rich.

I Piacieri del Sabato Notte
(The Pleasures of Saturday Night)
(ITALIAN)

Rome, Nov. 8.
Dino DeLaurentiis release of a Donati-Carpentieri production. Features Jeanne Valerie, Andreina Pagnani, Maria Pershy, Roberto Risso, Pierre Brice, Romolo Valli, Scilla Gabel, Jean Murat, Renato Speziali, Elsa Martinelli, Corrado Pani. Directed by Daniele D'Anza. Screenplay, Oreste Biancoli, D'Anza, Giuseppe Mangione, Mino Guerrini; music, Armando Trovajoli; editor, Roberto Cinquini. At Trevi, Rome. Running time, 101 MINS.

Slickly made item with several exploitation pegs, notably a topical call-girl theme which coupled to a comely cast should make this a saleable item in many foreign areas. Bally aspects apply to Yank possibilities as well.

Call-girl operation is successful until an elderly client dies of a heart attack while on a rendezvous with one of the girls. Attempt to cover up by removing his body merely starts off a chain of complications involving the girl in a murder rap and her father's subsequent suicide.

Thesping is okay, with Jeanne Valerie creditably handling her key role, and Maria Perschy, Scilla Gabel, Pierre Brice, Corrado Pani, and others backing her. The girls are all lookers.

Daniele D'Anza's direction is functional and lagless, denoting his video background while other credits measure up in kind.
Hawk.

CinderFella
(COLOR)

Variation on the fairy tale, with Jerry Lewis as the male counterpart of the famous heroine. Should rake in enough kiddie coin to count.

Hollywood, Nov. 10.
Paramount release of Jerry Lewis production. Stars Lewis, Ed Wynn, Judith Anderson, Anna Maria Alberghetti; with Henry Silva, Count Basie, Robert Hutton. Directed and screenplay by Frank Tashlin; camera, Haskell Boggs; editor, Artie Schmidt; art directors, Hal Pereira, Henry Bumstead; music, Walter Scharf; sound, Gene Merritt; assistant director, C. C. "Buddy" Coleman. Reviewed at Academy Awards Theatre, Nov. 10, '60. Running time, 88 MINS.
Fella .... Jerry Lewis
Fairy Godfather .... Ed Wynn
Wicked Stepmother .....Judith Anderson
Princess Charmein
          Anna Maria Alberghetti
Maximilian ....·.... Henry Silva
Count Basie .... Count Basie
Rupert .... Robert Hutton

The "F" in "CinderFella" should stand for Fiscal and the "C" for Comfort, as far as Paramount is concerned. Although it isn't likely to break the Academy barrier against comedy, this sexual switch on the familiar fairy tale should do for the simple reason that the name Jerry Lewis on a marquee represents the kind of product parents aren't afraid to send their kiddies off to see. And for the oldsters, either one goes with Lewis all the way, or has reservations, which in this case could be considerable.

Lewis, who produced, stars as the male variation on Cinderella in Frank Tashlin's screenplay. Tashlin also directed the picture and, along with his star-producer, must share the rap for failure of the mirthful to materialize into consistent merriment.

There seems to have been a dearth of comic inspiration. Bits of funny business that do show instant promise are milked to extremes. Lewis, in fact, depends almost exclusively on the art of cumulative mugging, but often misjudges the breakoff point. The pace engineered by Tashlin is uncomfortably deliberate for a comedy. Breaks for song tend to labor the issue instead of brightening the tempo. This despite some artistic staging by Nick Castle and inventive camera angling by Tashlin and lensman Haskell Boggs on these numbers.

Lewis puts all he's got into the effort, which is considerable. The facial gyrations will keep the moppets amused but, with the exception of a couple of clever sequences and the star's adept hoofing and rubbery footwork, others aren't likely to find much to roar about.

Ed Wynn is whimsical as the fairy godfather. Judith Anderson plays the wicked stepmother, Henry Silva and Robert Hutton the mercenary stepbrothers. They are competent, but the roles are rather choppy, vague and incomplete. Anna Maria Alberghetti is dazzling as the princess.

Art directors Hal Pereira and Henry Bumstead have provided a number of lavish, elegant sets. Coupled with some interesting lighting effects and enhanced by Technicolor, the result is a visual feast. But editor Artie Schmidt seems to have had his problems coping with the fantasy aspects of the tale. Scenes such as that of a

---

chauffeur turning back into a fish at the stroke of midnight are fuzzily handled, failing to come up with the intended fun.

Walter Scharf's score does a lot toward making the pace seem brighter than it is. There are three songs by Harry Warren and Jack Brooks. None of them comes off very well, but that seems to be a result of the manner in which they are delivered rather than a commentary on their intrinsic quality. The numbers, two of them warbled in uncertain fashion by Lewis (with some help by Wynn and Miss Alberghetti) are titled "Somebody," "Princess Waltz" and "Let Me Be A People." The big ball sequence at the climax is enlivened by the driving jazz music of Count Basie's band.

Credit Edith Head with some striking costumes, neatly matching the decor of the sets. Incidentally, director Tashlin seems to have a "thing" about backs. On several occasions, he zeroes in on his performers from the rear and maintains the vantage point. It's a unique approach.
Tube.

The Great Impostor

Amazing real-life assumed-identity feats of F. W. Demara Jr. are basis for a funny, though superficial, biopic. Factual aspect will spur word-of-mouth. Despite flaws, favorable b.o. prospects.

Hollywood, Nov. 11.
Universal release of Robert Arthur production. Stars Tony Curtis, Edmond O'Brien, Arthur O'Connell, Gary Merrill, Joan Blackman, Raymond Massey, Robert Middleton, Karl Malden. Directed by Robert Mulligan. Screenplay, Liam O'Brien, based on book by Robert Crichton; camera, Robert Burks; editor, Frederic Knudtson; art directors, Alexander Golitzen, Henry Bumstead; music, Henry Mancini; sound, Waldon O. Watson, Frank Wilkinson; assistant director, Joseph Kenny. Reviewed at Fine Arts Theatre, Nov. 11, '60. Running time, 112 MINS.
Fred Demara .... Tony Curtis
Captain Glover........... Edmond O'Brien
Warden Chandler.......Arthur O'Connell
Pa Demara .... Gary Merrill
Catherine Lacey .... Joan Blackman
Abbot Donner .... Raymond Massey
Brown .... Robert Middleton
Ma Demara .... Jeanette Nolan
Eulalie .... Sue Ane Langdon
Cardinal .... Larry Gates
Thompson .... Mike Kellin
Barney .... Frank Gorshin
Wac Lt. .... Cindi Wood
Hotchkiss .... Richard Sargent
Fred Demara Jr........Robert Crawford
Farmer .... Doodles Weaver
Exec. Officer Howard......Ward Ramsey
Dr. Hammond .... David White
Hun Kim .... Philip Ahn
Senior Officer .... Herbert Rudley
Defense Lt. .... Jerry Paris
Dr. Joseph Mornay......Harry Carey Jr.
Lt. Thornton .... Willard Sage
Father Devlin .... Karl Malden

The incredible story of Ferdinand Waldo Demara Jr., "The Great Impostor" whose masquerading exploits make Walter Mitty's imagination uninspired by comparison, has been turned into a sprightly comedy by Universal. Were it not for the foundation of fact, most people would dismiss the plot and the picture as utterly unbelievable. It is this factual basis that will make the difference in wicket window traffic. The Robert Arthur production will stimulate comment and should net a tidy profit.

Yet the film, for all of its merry moments, is a disappointment. There are two principal reasons for this. One is the fact that, in striving primarily for brisk, boisterous comedy, director Robert Mulligan has had to sacrifice penetration into the fascinating person-

ality of his subject. Demara's curious drives and motives remain, for the most part, hidden and unexplored.

He emerges in Liam O'Brien's screenplay (from Robert Crichton's book) as a kind of jolly one-upman who's not truly content until he's two-up on the next fellow. The other major flaw is the casting of Tony Curtis, who's simply not the man for the part of Demara. It is a role that someone of Guinnessian versatility (like Guinness, for instance) could have made a classic. As delineated by Curtis, the character is merely pleasant, handsome and likeable.

Demara's story, as depicted here, is a career of assumed identities. He is seen as a schoolteacher, a novitiate in a Trappist monastery, an assistant to a prison warden and a surgeon lieutenant in the Canadian Navy, all without the benefit of formal education, prior experience or anything resembling proper qualifications. In the course of these varied pursuits, he indulges in three romantic affairs. Since Demara is still "at large" (although having been apprehended several times, as described in the film), there is no "end" to the yarn, and this fact is whimsically illustrated by Curtis' coy smile when that deathless legend, "The End," shows up on the screen.

Mulligan's otherwise slick direction, along with some stickout performing by several gifted veterans of the screen, is responsible for some memorably humorous passages. In accomplishing this, he has had to forsake credulity for the sake of a shock or a laugh. There is one truly hilarious scene in which Curtis, in the guise of naval medic, shoots so much novocaine into the jaw of ship skipper Edmond O'Brien prior to pulling his tooth that O'Brien's entire body is reduced to rigidity. O'Brien steals the picture in this sequence.

Going down the list of fine character performances, there is Karl Malden as Curtis' parish priest and confidante, Raymond Massey as a wise old Abbot, Gary Merrill in a small part as Curtis' father, Jeanette Nolan as his mother, Arthur O'Connell as a hapless prison warden, Mike Kellin as a grateful convict, Frank Gorshin as a perennial time-server, Doodles Weaver as a jug-guzzling farmer, Robert Middleton as a guard. Others who attract brief, but favorable attention are Larry Gates, Richard Sargent, Ward Ramsey, David White, Philip Ahn, Herbert Rudley, Jerry Paris, Harry Carey Jr. and Willard Sage.

The three lady-loves are enacted by Joan Blackman, Sue Ane Langdon and Cindi Wood. The striking Miss Blackman is stuck with some extremely syrupy, unrealistic lines. The exuberant Miss Langdon creates a strong comic impression as the warden's uninhibited daughter. Miss Wood, a pretty miss, does well by the role of a WAC looie. Robert Crawford, a brown-eyed youth, plays the blue-eyed Curtis as a child. Crawford plays it with enthusiasm, but the part and the expository passage itself seem superfluous.

Robert Burks' camera work is skillful, making particularly valuable use of the zoom maneuver. Some adept editing touches by Frederic Knudtson, such as scene transition in the middle of a sentence, brighten the pace. Henry Mancini's music is light, romantic, melodic. Art directors Alexander Golitzen and Henry Bumstead, undaunted by Demara's occupational versatility, have kept pace beautifully with some authentic settings.

Tube.

Wir Kellerkinder
(We Cellar Children)
(GERMAN)

Stella release of Hans Oppenheimer production. Directed by Jochen Wiedermann. Screenplay, Wolfgang Neuss. Camera, Warner Lenz; music, Peter Sandloff. With Wolfgang Neuss, Wolfgang Gruner, Jo Herbest, Willi Rose, Hilde Sessak, Ingrid van Bergen, Karin Baal, Achim Strietzel, Rudi Schmitt, Paul Westermeier. At Atelier am Zoo, Berlin. Running time, 90 MINS.

This film is currently causing a real row in Germany in view of its boycott by West Germany's exhibitor associations. Latter hold to the principle that a film that has been shown on television must never be given a theatrical run. "Cellar Children" was originally planned as a theatrical film. Wolfgang Neuss, the author, tried to find a producer but failed because of domestic filmites' reluctance towards his story material. Neuss finally interested SFB (Berlin) and NWRV (Hamburg) for whom Hans Oppenheimer produced it as a joint telecast. "Cellar Children" was on the West German tele last June.

Film cost about a quarter of what a German pic normally does. Author Neuss, who also plays a principal role in "Children," is coinvestor in the production. Pic comes off much better via widescreen than tv. Foreign possibilities are a special guess.

It doesn't exactly belong to the easy-to-understand type of film. Most of it is narration, with much wordplay and political gags and jokes of strictly German calibre. A few German patrons will find a tough time understanding the film's meaning or message. "Children" is cleverly written and teems with amusing dialog sequences but requires a receptive audience. It'll probably be enjoyed mostly by the intellectual set.

Film has only to do with Germans and spans a period from the '30's up to the present time. It satirically shows how many Germans changed their political views under the different rulers. There's a former Nazi functionary who later manages to find an equally influential job in what became Communist Germany after 1945.

There's former notorious Commie who had it tough under the Nazis who later gets a topflight position in East Germany only to flee that regime because he realizes that this sort of communism is a far cry from what he expected. The swastika smearings in West Germany find substantial mention, ditto the newly rich and those who "can't remember" what happened under Hitler.

In the main, this is a Neuss picture. His satirical writing talents as well as his cabaretist acting abilities come off to good advantage here. Cast includes members of Berlin's Porcupines, a local literary cabaret ensemble, with standout performances by Jo Herbst and Wolfgang Gruner, both pals of Neuss; and Achim Striezel, as a Commie. Fine support is supplied by Willi Rose, Hilde Sessak (parents of Neuss), Ingrid van Bergen and Karin Baal, among others. Technically, the film is okay. Production dress reveals the modest budget, but this is of little importance here.

Hans.

Os Bandeirantes
(The Pioneers)
(FRENCH-BRAZILIAN-COLOR)

Paris, Nov. 15.

Cinedis release of Manzon-Terra-Cinetal-Cite-Cormoran-CICC-Titanus Films production. With Raymond Loyer, Elga Andersen, Lourdes De Oliveira, Lea Garcia. Directed by Marcel Camus. Screenplay, Louis Sapin, Camus; camera (Eastmancolor), Marcel Grignon; editor, Andree Feix; music, Henri Crolla. At Marignan, Paris. Running time, 115 MINS.

Jean	Raymond Loyer
Elga	Elga Andersen
Suzana	Lourdes De Oliveira
Herminia	Lea Garcia
Baija-Flora	Almiro de Espiritu Santo

Marcel Camus has gone back to Brazil for this film after his prize-winning "Black Orpheus," made there. This lacks the Orpheus myth basis which gave his former pic some dramatic structure as well as color and spirit in its Brazilian tempo and locale. It emerges mainly a romanticized documentary on the little-known hinterlands of Brazil, with a bare storyline used to make some points on vengeance, humanity and true happiness.

It has a tendency to meander in characterization, plot and story as it lovingly savors the bounty, simple zest and human wisdom of the natives. Most of the film's comments are made via homilies and well-meaning platitudes spoken by its characters. But it has a richness in incident and a sincere sentimentality which keep it beguiling and cohesive. It's also helped by an eye for landscapes, the people and the dances.

Film has are exploitation chances abroad on its offbeat looks at Brazil, but will be more chancey for general spotting. The renown of "Orpheus" is also a selling point.

An adventurous Frenchman, mining diamonds, is shot down by a supposed friend and partner, but recovers to seek vengeance. This takes him on a trip into the more primitive parts of Brazil. Religious processions, fights and fiestas abound together with a series of interludes with women. The Frenchman picks up a German cabaret singer who knows his enemy's whereabouts. However, later he falls for a native girl, gives up his quest, and even saves the killer's life in a contrived ending.

Raymond Loyer is somewhat stiff but acceptable as the Frenchman. Elga Andersen is passable as the German girl. But it is the vital, dynamic and earthy Brazilian players who give the film its main tang and feeling. His visuals are excellent as usual but he lacks a good scripter to weld all into a more satisfying pic. This looks to do well here, but will need the hard sell abroad. It is in French and Portuguese.

Mosk.

Terrain Vague
(The Waste-Land)
(FRENCH)

Paris, Nov. 22.

Cinedis release of Gray, Jolly Films production. With Daniele Gaubert, Maurice Caffarelli, Constantin Andrieux, Jean-Louis Bras, Dominique Dieudonne, Roland Lesaffre, Denise Vernac. Directed by Marcel Carne. Screenplay, Henri-Francois Rey, Carne from novel, "Tomboy," by Hal Ellison; camera, Claude Renoir; editor, Marguerite Renoir. At Berlitz, Paris. Running time, 105 MINS.

Dan	Daniele Gaubert
Lucky	Maurice Caffarelli
Marcel	Constantin Andrieux
Barar	Jean-Louis Bras
Raleur	Dominique Dieudonne
Hans	Roland Lesaffre
Mother	Denise Vernac

The "Waste-Land" consists of lots and half-demolished buildings around new housing projects where a young gang has its headquarters. From cabalistic youths they almost become delinquents because of the influence of a criminal type, but tragedy and love prevent it. This is a familiar tale. However, it is stolidly told here to make this of local interest but lacking the clarity, characterizations and depth for many arty chances abroad. Film looks to have more general exploitation possibilities via its theme.

A tomboyish girl leads a gang which steals lesser things. It meets in a broken-down factory. Into this setup comes a character escaped from a reform school who promises them big money. But one decides against the move as love grows between him and the now feminine tomboy. It leads to a knockdown fight and the death of a young boy.

Oldtime director Marcel Carne has directed this with a heavy hand. He has made a romantic tale of something which needed revelation and compassion. Flight from the neighborhood seems the only solution and parents are again vaguely guilty figures in the background. Playing is mainly stiff and technical credits glossy.

Mosk.

Esther And The King
(C'SCOPE—COLOR)

Heap of sex and spectacle in a muddled meller loosely based on the biblical tale. Commercial approach may redeem the formula despite the casting and production flaws.

Hollywood, Nov. 18.

Twentieth-Fox release of Raoul Walsh production. Stars Joan Collins, Richard Egan; with Daniella Rocca, Folco Lulli, Denis O'Dea, Sergio Fantoni, Rick Battaglia, Renator Baldini, Gabriele Tinti, Rosalba Neri, Robert Buchanan. Directed by Walsh. Screenplay, Walsh, Michael Elkins; camera (Technicolor), Mario Bava; editor, Jerry Webb; are director, Giulio Giovannini; music, Francesco Lavagnino, Roberto Nicolosi; sound, Giulio Tagliacozzo; assistant director, Ottavia Oppo. Reviewed at the studio, Nov. 18, '60. Running time, 110 MINS.

Esther	Joan Collins
King Ahasuerus	Richard Egan
Mordecai	Denis O'Dea
Haman	Sergio Fantoni
Simon	Rick Battaglia
Klydrathes	Renato Baldini
Samuel	Gabriele Tinti
Keresh	Rosalba Neri
Hegai	Robert Buchanan
Queen Vashti	Daniella Rocca
Tobiah	Folco Lulli

That the tale of Esther is one of the more aesthetic and narratively skillful passages of the Bible is never apparent in the Raoul Walsh production of "Esther and the King." The absorbing incidents that occur in the biblical story have been exaggerated and expanded into a crude melodramatic hodgepodge, its believable characters twisted into stereotyped shapes to fit the formulese of the film's dramatic pattern. And yet the presence of that double-barrelled boxoffice standby, sex-and-spectacle, may justify the project commercially. The 20th-Fox release, filmed in Italy by Americans and Italians, should have an impact here similar

in nature to that of the many other Italian-made historical and biblical epics that have been flooding the U.S. cinemarketplace with increasing regularity.

Joan Collins stars as Esther in the Walsh-Michael Elkins screenplay. To the biblical tale about her persuasive influence upon King Ahasuerus in combatting the Jew-baiting tactics of his wicked minister, Haman, has been added, among other things, a side love interest that only serves to cloud the central issue and use up valuable time that might better have been spent focusing attention on the principals.

The screenplay is written in an extremely archaic style that rings comical to the modern ear and intellect. Walsh's direction is responsible for some pretty candid sexmanship and smatterings of military spectacle, but he has breathed no life and hardly any visual sense into the personal drama. The origin of the Jewish Feast of Purim is little more than an afterthought in the film.

Miss Collins brings physical beauty to the role, but is not convincing as Esther. Richard Egan hasn't much life as the King. As Haman, Sergie Fantoni wears a perpetual smile. Perhaps fortunately he has no mustache to twist as he leers. Daniella Rocca makes quite a display of her chest measurements as the evil Queen Vashti. Others prominent but no more histrionically successful are Denis O'Dea, Rick Battaglia, Renato Baldini and Robert Buchanan.

There are some fairly diverting shots of old ruins and flashy palaces whipped up by art director Giulio Giovannini and lensed competently by Mario Bava. Jerry Webb's editing is workmanlike, Tito De Luc's choreography attractively naughty, and the Francesco Lavagnino-Roberto Nicolosi score routinely biblical in tone. *Tube.*

Faust
(GERMAN—COLOR)

Berlin, Nov. 15.

Gloria release of Divina production. Stars Gustaf Gruendgens, Will Quadflieg, Elisabeth Flickenschild. Directed by Peter Gorski. Adapted from "Faust," tragedy by Wolfgang von Goethe; camera, Guenther Anders; music, Mark Lothar; editor, Walter Boos. At Zoo Palast, Berlin. Running time, **127 MINS.**

Faust	Will Quadflieg
Mephisto	Gustaf Gruendgens
Gretchen	Ella Buechi
Marthe	Elisabeth Flickenschildt
Theatre Director	Herman Schomberg
Wagner	Eduard Marks
Valentin	Max Eckard
Pupil	Uwe Friedrichsen
Frosch	Heinz Reincke
Altmayer	Hans Irle
Brander	F. G. Backhaus
Siebel	K. H. Wuepper

Gloria has in "Faust" a true piece of art as well as real prestige item. It's a top-flight presentation of the most renowned work of German stage literature, impressively performed by the ensemble of Deutsches Schauspielhaus, Hamburg. Since this filmization is a departure from the ordinary, its commercial prospects are somewhat in doubt. However, helped by the name of Gustaf Gruendgens, the top German stage personality, it may emerge as a surprise hit in this country. Film even may result in the making of more such filmizations of classical German stage works. Internationally, it recommends itself for many arty spots.

Gustaf Gruendgens, who also acted as artistical supervisor, aimed at finding exactly the middle between filmed theatre and conventional films. It was shot within 21 days using 480 camera shots at a cost of about $240,000.

It runs two hours and seven minutes as contracted with the original stage presentation which runs three hours and 10 minutes, the latter including the various intermissions. Minor dialog has been cut for the sake of the contents. The filmic possibilities (closeups, mass scenes, etc.) have been exploited to good advantage.

Of course, such an enterprise finds its opponents, especially on the part of those who opine that film and theatre will always be two things that cannot be put together. But even they would admit that this "Faust" filmization is a highly commendable document. It gives are followers everywhere an opportunity to see on the screen, one of the finest German stage ensembles in one of the most powerful presentations the domestic theatre ever has performed.

In the main, this is Gruendgens' film. Gruendgens, head of the Hamburg Schauspielhaus and theatre genius, is seen here as Mephistol, his most famous stage role which he has portrayed hundreds of times. Cast includes Will Quadflieg, as Faust; Swiss-born Ella Buechi, as Gretchen; Elisabeth Flickenschildt, as Marthe, all talented stage players. Camerwork, color, costumes and settings contribute to make this an impressive offering. *Hans.*

Zazie Dans le Metro
(Zazie In the Subway)
(FRENCH-COLOR)

Paris, Nov. 15.

Pathe release of Nouvelles Editions De Films production. With Catherine Demongeot, Philippe Noiret, Jacques Dufilho, Hubert Deschamps, Annie Fratellini, Carla Marlier. Directed by Louis Malle. Screenplay, Jean-Paul Rapponeau, Malle from novel by Raymond Queneau; camera (Eastmancolor), Henri Raichi; editor, Kenout Peltier. At Mercury, Paris. Running time, **90 MINS.**

Zazie	Catherine Demongeot
Gabriel	Philippe Noiret
Turandot	Hubert Deschamps
Mado	Annie Fratellini
Gridoux	Hubert Deschamps
Albertine	Carla Marlier

After his stylized, sensual "The Lovers," which was quite a hit, youthful director Louis Malle essays his first comedy which is a sort of intellectual slapstick entry. It has some risible bits but is, in all, somewhat diffuse. Film looms mainly as an arty theatre entry abroad.

Zazie (Catherine Demongeot) is a 12-year-old girl whose mother leaves her with an uncle when she comes into Paris from the country for a day with her latest lover. Zazie has never seen the subway and wants to ride in it but it's on strike. Next morning she is off on a round of adventures in a weird, colorful Paris. Zazie is shrewd, clever, innocent deadly and honest as a strange gallery of characters whirl past her.

There is a man who changes guise frequently and is either a policeman or a satyr. Her uncle is a pompous, self-indulgent type who dances in a nitery in travesty. Then there are assorted characters to keep up this pic that has obviously been influenced in style by the better Yank animated pix and Mack Sennett comedies.

But instead of springing full blown from the inventiveness of the makers this has been reworked for the screen. Result is an uneven texture that runs from inspired scenes to repetitive bits and overstraining in the symbolism of the story.

It does take potshots at certain French penchants for not washing, making sex just a meaningless group of gestures and at hard-headed pettiness. It also warns of the dangers of fascism under the continuing French general mistrust of each other and foreigners. It also flays the so-called "Gay Paree" of tourism and ends with a free-for-all sauerkraut battle to replace pies.

Malle has shown a wealth of invention and has used color artfully. Traffic jams, a visit to the Eiffel Tower, and chase sequences are expertly manned.

Catherine Demongeot is a sassy, pert character. This vehicle moves at whirlwind pace and is a comedic offbeater that could be of art interest if well handled. Its satire, though national in format, is universal in meaning. *Mosk.*

Jazz Boat
(C'SCOPE)

Comedy-crime caper with a jazz background. Sudden intrusions of song-and-dance passages result in chaos. Occasionally amusing. Acceptable lower-berther with drive-in biz value.

Hollywood, Nov. 22.

Columbia Pictures release of Irving Allen-Albert R. Broccoli production. Stars Anthony Newley, Anne Aubrey, Bernie Winters, James Booth, Leo McKern; introduces Jean Philippe; with Lionel Jeffries, Al Mulock, David Lodge, Joyce Blair, Liam Gaffney, Henry Webb. Directed by Ken Hughes. Screenplay, Hughes and John Antrobus from original story by Rex Rienits; camera, Ted Moore; editor, Geoffrey Foot; art director, Ray Simm; music, Kenneth V. Jones, Ted Heath; sound, Wally Milner; assistant director, Ted Sturgis. Reviewed at the studio, Nov. 10, '60. Running time, **96 MINS.**

Bert	Anthony Newley
The Doll	Anne Aubrey
Sgt. Thompson	Lionel Jeffries
Holy Mike	David Lodge
The Jinx	Bernie Winters
Spider	James Booth
The Dancer	Al Mulock
Rene	Joyce Blair
Inspector	Leo McKern
Jean	Jean Philippe
Spider's Father	Liam Gaffney
Barman	Henry Webb

An odd assortment of romance, jazz, musical comedy and youthful crime is poured into "Jazz Boat," latest effort of England's Warwick Film firm to arrive on these shores. What comes out is largely chaos, though some of it is infectiously amusing. Mostly it's vague, disjointed and purposeless. Director Ken Hughes may have been making some sort of an attempt at parody of American crime pix.

Although the Irving Allen-Albert R. Broccoli production serves as an interesting glimpse into the lesser attitudes of English youth, the Columbia release lacks the cohesion, care or substance to fit properly into the U. S. art house scheme. It will double up acceptably in regular runs, and may cause a mild stir in the drive-in circuit, where it will be appreciated by the more rebellious youth.

The screenplay, by Ken Hughes and John Antrobus from an original story by Rex Rienits that isn't so very original, deals with a decent lad who is roped into a robbery caper by an amateurish band of young hoodlums when he brags he is a big-time crook. Sudden jarring, uncalled-for bursts into song and tipsy terpsichore make it a kind of "Bloaks and Babes" version of "Guys and Dolls," utterly destroying the mood and pace. Some of the comedy is quite funny, but there isn't enough of it to save the day. The story itself is routine, the execution careless.

Anthony Newley is likeable as the nice lad. Anne Aubrey, as an unwilling moll, is a miracle of cleavage, and amply illustrates the fact. Lionel Jeffries adds a strong impression of a semi-sadistic, mooching cop to the list of first-rate characterizations. There is a slick portrayal of a young heavy by James Booth, some amusing efforts as his henchmen by Al Mulock and David Lodge, and good support by Bernie Winters and Joyce Blair.

Camera work by Ted Moore, editing by Geoffrey Foot and art work by Ray Simm are adequate. Most of the music is of the jive- and jazz-variety by Ted Heath and his swinging band. Specialty numbers, ranging from r 'n' r to ballads, were scored by Joe Henderson, with additional lyrics by Newley and Hughes. They're not bad but don't fit snugly into the context here. There's also a Gallic selection by Huberg Giraud and Michael Julien, sung with Montand-like charm by a promising vocalist named Jean Philippe. *Tube.*

Suspect
(BRITISH)

Modest, well-made dualer deliberately shot on a shoestring. Writing, acting and direction all add up to a smart, smooth peace of film-making which should be safe booking in any house.

London, Nov. 15.

British Lion release of a Boulting (John Boulting) Bros. production. Stars Peter Cushing, Ian Bannen, Virginia Maskell, Tony Britton; features Raymond Huntley, Donald Pleasence Thorley Walters, Kenneth Griffith, Spike Milligan. Directed by Roy Boulting. Screenplay by Nigel Balchin, from his novel, "A Sort of Traitors," with additional scenes and dialog by Jeffrey Dell, Roy Boulting; editor, John Jympson; camera, Max Greene; music by Chopin and Schriabin, arranged and played by John Wilkes. At Queen's, Bayswater Road, London. Running time, **81 MINS.**

Bob Marriott	Tony Britton
Lucy Byrne	Virginia Maskell
Professor Sewell	Peter Cushing
Alan Andrews	Ian Bannen
Sir George Gatling	Raymond Huntley
Mr. Prince	Thorley Walters
Brown	Donald Pleasence
Arthur	Spike Milligan
Dr. Shole	Kenneth Griffith
Levers	Ronald Bruce
Parkin	Anthony Booth
Dr. Childs	Basil Dignam
Director	Brian Oulton
Slater	Sam Kydd

The old theory that a second feature can get away with being shoddily written, directed and produced is not true. The challenging Boulting Brothers set out to prove it with this deliberately designed dualer, "Suspect." Shot in 17 days, it skimps on nothing except possibly running time. This is adapted from Nigel Balchin's novel, "A Sort of Traitors."

The Boultings have lined up a fine cast of firstclass established artists and top technical boys. The writing and direction are taut (perhaps a shade too taut towards the

end). Under Roy Boulting's direction, the cast has done excellent stints and obviously did not need too much time for re-takes. "Suspect" may well be a model of the pre-planning that saves coin, and within its modest limits is a very sound job. Certainly a useful booking for any theatre.

Story concerns a small team of research medical scientists who have patiently dug out the virulent germ that can dispose of typhus and bubonic epidemics. The boss (Peter Cushing) is shocked when he is told by the Minister of Defense (Raymond Huntley) that their findings cannot be published under the Official Secrets Act.

Reluctantly, they buckle down to authority—all except one member of the team (Tony Britton). Not for financial gain, but purely in the interest of humanity, he nearly commits treason when he arranges for the findings of the experiment to be published. He's egged on by a maimed pilot who has a grudge against the country which has left him in his armless plight. Britton is saved from his folly in the nick of time.

There's nothing pretentious about this film, but it is entertaining and literate. In the hands of less experienced people, both technicians and thesps, weaknesses might show up through lack of development of characters. But here there are a number of topnotch performances. Tony Britton, as the weak young man; Donald Pleasance, as an insidious spy; Virginia Maskell, the femme link in the research team, Kenneth Griffith, Raymond Huntley, and Peter Cushing could hardly be bettered.

Thorley Walters, as an apparently vague security officer, adds to his fast growing reputation as a character actor while Ian Bannen, as the embittered ex-pilot who engineers the near-treason, enhances his rep as one of Britain's most significant young actors.

Lensing, artwork and editing are all satisfactory. There's no sense in hailing "Suspect" as anything more than a competent and useful program filler. But if talent can continue to be harnessed to move in swiftly, snap up temporary studio space, and turn out little pix like "Suspect," then there's some sanity in a world of million-dollar efforts. May it happen more often, for here's a "tv play" which has just that extra polish and knowhow that distinguishes the small box from the big screen.　　　　*Rich.*

Peligros de Juventud
(Dangers of Youth)
(MEXICAN)

Mexico City, Nov. 15.
Peliculas Nacionales release of Calderon Films production. Features Elvira Quintana, Teresa Velazquez, Fernando Lujan, Aida Araceli, Roberto G. Rivera, Manuel (Loco) Valdes, Guillermina Tellez Giron, Hector Godoy, Xavier Loya and Guillermo Mayaudon. Directed by Benito Alazraki. Screenplay, Julio Alejandro from "Las Cosas Simples" by Hector Mendoza.

Play from which this film was made ran over 1,000 performances in restaurant presentation, where paying customers were also drawn into action of drama. Film is a faithful reproduction of the play, with action centering around a street walker and a young man who wants to make her his wife.

Drama unfurls in a cafe set where actors (and there are few stars in this one since featuring some of Mexico's new faces) go through their paces. There is no overplaying, with the general effect being that of everyday occurrences in the life of cabaret habitues.

Elvira Quintana makes a good looking femme of easy virtue and shows that she is capable of taking on more serious acting. For comedy relief "Loco" Valdes interprets a screwball character.

Director Benito Alazraki has turned in one of his best film efforts which may be dubbed in English as well as exploited in European markets.　　　*Emil.*

La Verite
(The Truth)
(FRENCH)

Paris, Nov. 15.
Columbia release of Iena Films production. Stars Brigitte Bardot; features Charles Vanel, Paul Meurisse, Sami Frey, Marie Jose Nat, Louis Seigner, Jean-Louis Reynols, Andre Oumansky. Directed by H. G. Clouzot. Screenplay, Clouzot, Michele Perreins, Christiane Rochefort, Simone Marescat; camera, Armany Thirard; editor, Albert Jurgenson. At Colisee, Paris. Running time, **130 MINS.**
Dominique .... Brigitte Bardot
Annie .... Marie Jose Nat
Gilbert .... Sami Frey
Guerin .... Charles Vanel
Prosecutor .... Paul Meurisse
Judge .... Louis Seigner
Michel .... Jean-Louis Reynols
Ludo .... Andre Ourmansky

Using the background of a murder trial, director H. G. Clouzot has given a series of slice of life sketches, via flashbacks, detailing the modern French youth today. It does not preach but gives various sides in detailing its downbeat tale of a young provincial girl's adventures in Paris and the eventual murder of her lover and her own suicide. It stars Brigitte Bardot, forced into one of her most dramatic roles by director Clouzot.

Star's suicide attempt may help this here. It has the Bardot name and news interest abroad, too. But the pic is overlong and quite plodding. Hence, it will need hard-sell. It shapes an arty entry on its relentless exposure of youthful morals today. This goes further in frankness and pictorial treatment than is usually the case in these type pix.

Miss Bardot is a dissatisfied smalltown girl who goes to Paris. Instead of working, she sinks into a Bohemian life and first affairs with intellectual characters. Her sister's boyfriend falls for her but she is capable of having other affairs while theirs is on. But in time she becomes faithful to him.

They finally fight and part. But she realizes it is love and tries to come back to him only to end in her killing him and trying suicide again.

Miss Bardot is her morally blind, pleasure-ridden sexy self in most of the production and is then called on to have big dramatic moments. Though they are mainly outbursts, but she seems to have been whipped into shape by Clouzot.

Clouzot has given this a solid mounting, but the depiction of youth seems strangely flat. It does take swipes at a justice that can be unfeeling. But this rarely gives more than the life of a childish sexpot whose sudden determination to love leads to her complete destruction.

It is sound technically, but could use some tightening for foreign chances. The theme and Bardot name are the main assets for foreign use. His study of the younger generation is a stereotyped look at delinquency that has been seen before. Miss Bardot looks as sex kittenish as ever, however, and has some savvily done nude and love scenes. These, of course, are hypo factors.　　　*Mosk.*

Where The Boys Are
(C'SCOPE—COLOR—PANAVISION)

Potential boxoffice whopper on basis of unusually strong appeal for young people. Showcase for several of Hollywood's more promising younger players. Pictures updated college snakes.

Hollywood, Nov. 16.
Metro release of Joe Pasternak production. Stars Dolores Hart, George Hamilton, Yvette Mimieux, Jim Hutton, Barbara Nichols, Paula Prentiss; introduces Connie Francis; with Frank Gorshin, Chill Wills, Rory Harrity, Ted Berger, John Brennan, Vito Scott. Directed by Henry Levin. Screenplay, George Wells, based on novel by Glendon Swarthout; camera (Metrocolor), Robert Bronner; editor, Fredric Steinkamp; art directors, George W. Davis, Preston Ames; music, George Stoll; assistant director, Al Jennings. Reviewed at Westwood Village Theatre, Nov. 16, '60. Running time, **99 MINS.**
Merritt Andrews .... Dolores Hart
Ryder Smith .... George Hamilton
Melanie .... Yvette Mimieux
TV Thompson .... Jim Hutton
Lola .... Barbara Nichols
Tuggle Carpenter .... Paula Prentiss
Angie .... Connie Francis
Police Captain .... Chill Wills
Basil .... Frank Gorshin
Franklin .... Rory Harrity
Stout Man .... Ted Berger
Dill .... John Brennan
Maitre D' .... Vito Scotti

A number of Hollywood's fresh, young up-and-coming players are given a chance to cut loose and show their thespic wares in Metro's "Where the Boys Are." The more studious collegian may cringe in horror at this adult eye-view of modern undergrads at play, but the Joe Pasternak production is going to pay off big at the boxoffice.

It's a long way from Andy Hardy to "Where the Boys Are" today. "The Boys" of today, according to George Wells' screenplay out of Glendon Swarthout's novel, are generally in irresponsible sexual orbit and it is up to the girls of today to bring them down to earth. The Andy Hardy peck-on-the-cheek and woo-woo are utterly passe—they have been replaced by the illicit bedtime story. These young people are far more mature than their forerunners, but they are also far less savory. The illusion of wholesome youth becomes the latest illusion to be stripped away as filmdom's mushrooming preoccupation with illicit sex continues.

Wells' scenario is set in Fort Lauderdale, Florida, site of an annual spring invasion by Easter-vacationing collegians from all over the East and Midwest, most of the males apparently from the Halls of Ivy (or Yalies," as they are precociously referred to once too often here). Most of the girls manage to avoid the primitive passion, but there is an occasional casualty, in this case Yvette Mimieux who winds up walking the white line on a Florida highway after getting in too deep with a pair of these unscrupulous "Yalies" (who weren't "Yalies" after all, she comments from her hospital bed). Following this slice of melodrama, the other girls limp back to dear old nothing - ever - happens - on - campus U. and Miss Mimieux is on her way home to recuperate.

Among the "pairs" on view are Dolores Hart and George Hamilton. They make beautiful music together. Miss Hart's fresh all-American-girl beauty and budding dramatic talent herald a

bright future for her in films. Hamilton is a little wooden. It appears to be an attempt at suave, mature masculinity, which is desirable but requires a shade more warmth and animation.

Miss Mimieux, in a demanding role, gets by dramatically. Visually she is a knockout, and has a misty, quality that will spring her parts as soon as the casting department draws a bead on her appeal. Paula Prentiss, making her screen debut, will be a big hit with audiences in this vehicle. Her approach is of the Rosalind Russell-Eve Arden mold, and stamps her as a valuable commodity for Hollywood. Recording star Connie Francis also makes her screen debut. Because of a less appealing role, it is less auspicious, but she does get to sing two selections, and renders them with zip and style. The tunes, by Howard Greenfield and Neil Sedaka, are pleasant but unexciting.

In other key roles Jim Hutton is affable, Barbara Nichols flashy (as a dumb blonde in an exaggerated swimming-tank sequence), Frank Gorshin animated and amusing, and Chill Wills effective. Others favorably on display are Rory Harrity, Ted Berger, John Brennan and Vito Scotti.

Director Henry Levin has whipped up some merry mob scenes, but is responsible for several extremely artificial touches. Among these are a phonily-staged back-to-back love scene between Hamilton and Miss Hart and unrealistic passages in the tank and on the highway. Robert Bronner's camera work, embellished by Metrocolor, is attractive, Fredric Steinkamp's editing generally smooth. Art directors George W. Davis and Preston Ames have made the most of the Fort Lauderdale locale on exteriors and matched the tropical holiday mood with some smart interiors of motels, bars and boats. Pete Rugolo's "dialectic" jazz adds a prominent youthful note. George Stoll's score fills in the musical balance adequately. Producer Joe Pasternak deserves a thank-you for giving all this young talent an opportunity to show off. He'll be all the better for it when the returns are in. This one has smash potential.

Studio and picture's producer both say "it's in Cinemascope with Panavision lenses." Panavision veep Meredith Nicholson says privately that Metro hasn't used C'Scope for a long time but is contractually required to use the name. Joe Pasternak says "Boys" just used Panavision lenses but picture's in C'Scope, as the credits say.

Without getting too technical, C'Scope is same as Panavision 35 except for lenses used. Now, it would seem, if Pan lenses are used, it's Panavision. But studio credits say C'Scope. *Tube.*

Fortunat
(FRENCH)

Paris, Nov. 29.

Cinedis release of Silver Film-Cinetel-PCM production. Stars Bourvil, Michele Morgan; features Rosy Varte, Teddy Bilis, Frederic Robert, Patrick Millow, Gaby Morlay. Written and directed by Alex Joffe. Dialog and screenplay by Joffe, Pierre Corti from novel by Michel Breitman; camera, Pierre Petit; editor, Erick Puet. At Ambassade-Gaumont, Paris. Running time, 130 MINS.

Fortunat	Bourvil
Juliette	Michele Morgan
Mrs. Falk	Rosy Varte
Mr. Falk	Teddy Bilis
Maurice	Frederic Robert
Pierre	Patrick Millow
Miss Massillon	Gaby Morlay

Overlong pic serves as a vehicle for stars Bourvil and Michele Morgan as a strangely assorted couple brought together by the trials of the occupation during the last World War. It is well carpentered but conventional with tearjerker aspects. This appears mainly a local item since a surface comedy-drama sans the characterization or feeling for the time to make it much of an arty possibility.

Miss Morgan has to be spirited into the French free zone when her husband, an important resistance man, is arrested. Bourvil gets her across with her two children posing as her husband. He then becomes indispensable and love grows causing problems with the older son. There are side complications of a deported neighbor Jewish family and life under the occupation.

Miss Morgan is svelte but plays in her usual too well made up and studied manner to make her position in this situation acceptable. Bourvil does the peasant character in love with a fragile upper class woman for laughs. Alex Joffe has given this standard treatment without trying to make the relations more revealing. *Mosk.*

Los Fanfarrones
(The Braggarts)
(MEXICAN)

Mexico City, Nov. 22.

Columbia release of Alfa Films production. Stars Miguel Aceves Mejia, Flor Silvestre, Julio Aldama; features Mauricio Garces, Irma Dorantes, Veronica Loyo, Joaquin Garcia. Directed by Rogelio A. Gonzalez. Screenplay, Alfredo Varela Jr. from original story by Jose Maria Fernandez Unsain; camera, Ezequiel Carrasco; music, Jesus Zarzosa. At Cine Orfeon, Mexico City. Running time, 90 MINS.

The tale of three wild and wooly characters who ride into the usual Mexican replica of a dusty cowpoke town, is nicely done here. They fall in love and set things aright in town, to the accompaniment of fisticuffs, gunplay and much singing. Still this simple sort of musical western goes good with the nabe house audiences.

Miguel Aceves Mejia, who covets the throne of the late Jorge Negrete, is in good ranchero voice (strong and loud), aided and abetted by Julio Aldama, who wishes to become a singing cowboy in films. Lesser aid is supplied by Mauricio Garces who is better in straight acting roles. *Emil.*

The Grass Is Greener
(TECHNIRAMA-COLOR)

Verbose, only occasionally gratifying comedy about some Anglo-American scuffling in and around England's "stately homes." Powerful cast will make the desirable difference at the b.o.

Hollywood, Nov. 18.

Universal release of Stanley Donen production. Stars Cary Grant, Deborah Kerr, Robert Mitchum, Jean Simmons; with Moray Watson. Directed by Donen. Screenplay, Hugh and Margaret Williams, from their play; camera (Technicolor), Christopher Challis; editor, James Clark; art director, Paul Sheriff; music, Noel Coward; sound, John Cox; assistant director, Roy Stevens. Reviewed at Screen Directors Guild Theatre, Nov. 18, '60. Running time, 105 MINS.

Victor Rhyall	Cary Grant
Hilary Rhyall	Deborah Kerr
Charles Delacro	Robert Mitchum
Hattie	Jean Simmons
Sellers	Moray Watson

Merry old England is the site of this not-always-so-merry comedy about a romantic clash between a British Earl-ionaire and an American oil-ionaire. It will take all the cumulative magnetism of its appealing cast to bail it out at the boxoffice. But bail it out the cast probably will for Universtal and Grandon Productions, latter the company in which the picture's star, Cary Grant, and its producer-director, Stanley Donen, are partnered.

The Hugh and Margaret Williams screenplay, adapted from their London stage hit, takes an outrageous premise, has some sophisticated fun with it for awhile, then slowly evolves into a talky and generally tedious romantic exercise, dropping the semi-satirical stance that brightens up the early going.

At the start, it appears the film will have something novel and interesting to say about the tourist Americans and enterprising British who make up opposite halves of the "stately homes" business in which England's titled gentry rather unwillingly fling open the doors of their historically-significant houses to curious Yanks for a stipend ("Nowadays an English home is not his castle, it's his profit"). Observations on this issue soon peter out, whereupon the story swerves toward some sharp and outspoken comments on the difference between being Anglo and being American.

While this is going on, a romantic triangle is developing among the Earl (Grant) his wife (Deborah Kerr), and a "rip-roaring Grade A romantic" American millionaire (Robert Mitchum) who wanders off-limits into milady's drawing room during the tour and promptly and preposterously falls in love with her, she with him. Balance of the picture is concerned with Grant's efforts to woo his wife back to his side and, except for his own polished performance and Miss Kerr's, has little to offer in the way of light comedy, which appears to be the objective of all concerned.

Grant, as noted, is in good form. It is a tribute to his once-a-generation flair for light comedy that every time he wanders out of eye-and-ear range, the comedy sputters, stammers and stalls. The uninspired screenplay has its staunchest ally in Grant, whose stiffest comedy competition comes not from his three costars but from Moray Watson, who so agreeably plays the butler, a fellow who admits he's too normal, happy and well-adjusted to succeed in his ambition to be a novelist. Exchanges between Grant and Watson are the highlights of the film.

Miss Kerr gives a sturdy performance as the object of this abundance of affectioin. Jean Simmons, decked out in purposely exaggerated makeup and several high-styled gowns by Christian Dior, manages reasonably well in the role of a madcap ex-girl friend of Grant's, a kind of British Zsa-Zsa. Weakest link in the romantic and comedic give-and-take is Mitchum. He's pretty sluggish on the comedy end and thoroughly unconvincing in his relationship with Miss Kerr, never really projecting the implied passion, or even interest.

There are some thoughtful, inventive directorial touches by Donen (significant empty chairs and bedroom doors softly closing), but for the most part he has failed to translate static stage techniques into cinema terms. The picture fairly talks itself to death, and the dialog isn't consistently amusing enough to bring it back to life for more than fleeting moments. There are some compelling views of the English countryside ("The Grass" does seem a lot "Greener" over there), and some striking interiors of the old house, for which art director Paul Sheriff rates a bow. As does director of photography Christopher Challis for the charming way in which his camera regards these scenic attractions. James Clark's editing cannot be faulted, and the incorporation of some of Noel Coward's memorable tunes gives matters a lift, particularly his "Stately Homes of England," lyrics and all.

An outstanding achievement is that of Maurice Binder, whose use of babies at play to match the main title credits is a stroke of originality. In fact, audiences may enjoy the titles as much as the picture proper. *Tube.*

Faces In The Dark
(BRITISH)

Implausible, but smooth meller, with a chilling climax. Worthwhile booking in any house.

London, Nov. 22.

Rank release of a Welbeck (Jon Penington-Eady) production. Stars John Gregson, Mai Zetterling, John Ireland, Michael Denison, Tony Wright. Directed by David Eady. Screenplay by Ephraim Kogan, John Tully; camera, Ken Hodges; editor, Oswald Hafenrichter; music, Edwin Astley. At Leicester Square Theatre, London. Running time, 85 MINS.

Richard Hammond	John Gregson
Christiane Hammond	Mai Zetterling
David Merton	Michael Denison
Max	John Ireland
Clem	Tony Wright
Janet	Nanette Newman
French Doctor	Rowland Bartrop
1st Nun Nurse	Colette Bartrop
French Surgeon	John Serret
Miss Hopkins	Valerie Taylor

There are holes in this meller, but it's a smooth, compelling piece of work that sustains interest and leads up to fairly obvious but chilling climax. Despite modest marquee value, this is a useful booking for any house. Right from the outset director David Eady sets out to create atmosphere, with stylized cloud sequences and off-beat music by Edwin Astley. Cast helps to build up suspense through intelligent readings of the occasionally loose screenplay.

John Gregson plays a brusque, ambitious electric light bulb factory owner, who is experimenting on a bigger and better bulb. On the day his wife goes to the factory to tell him that she is leaving him, Gregson is involved in a laboratory accident and is blinded. She sticks with him, but between bouts of

self pity and the belief that he may be going mad, Gregson has a rough time.

With a blind man's extra perception he senses that something screwy is going on, but what? He eventually discovers that his wife and his partner, her lover, are planning to kill him, but when and how is an unpleasant dilemma for a blind man. Eventually they show their hand, but in a sock climax it is they, not he, who get their comeuppance.

There are one or two glaring holes in the plot. For instance the wife flies him to France instead of Cornwall and has had his country house almost identically reconstructed. But tiny differences make him suspicious of his fading memory. Could such a plot fool even a blind man? The convenient death of his brother helps the murder plot along, but it is straining credulity to believe that the blind man would have discovered that a temporary cross bearing his name, instead of the brother's, had been stuck in the prepared grave.

However, these are minor points, as are other red herrings, which don't rob the film of its interest. Gregson plays an unlikeable boor, which makes it somewhat difficult to be very sympathetic with his dilemma. However, he gives a very effective performance as a blind man, always a difficult task. Mai Zetterling is cool and attractive as the conniving wife while Michael Denison is an equally cool, suave villain. John Ireland's role as Gregson's brother put little strain on the thesp's capabilities. Tony Wright, as a chauffeur with a past and Nanette Newman as a pert maid, round out the important roles in the cast.

Ken Hodges' lensing is okay while the sets are lush and appropriate. "Faces In Dark" is certainly good for 85 minutes of drama, which might have been helped by a little light and share humor in a rather dogged screenplay.

Of Love And Lust
(SWEDISH)

Hollywood, Nov. 22.
Films Around the World Inc. release of Europa production. With Mai Zetterling, Anita Bjork, Anders Henrikson, Gunnel Brostrom, George Fant, Elsa Carlson, Edvin Adolphson, Gerda Lundquist, Hjordis Petterson, Torsten Lilliecrona. Directed by Henrikson. Screenplay, Katherine and Tage Aurell, adapted from August Strindberg's stories of Married Life; camera, Karl Eric Alberts; music, Herbert Sandberg. Reviewed at Beverly Canon Theatre, Nov. 22, '60. Running time, 109 MINS.

In spite of one basic error of theatrical judgment, "Of Love and Lust" is an exceptional attraction for the more literate U. S. filmgoer and ought to enjoy a fair measure of success in the art theatre circuit. The subtitled Swedish picture consists of two stories by August Strindberg, effectively transplanted into cine-dramatic terms by scenarists Katherine and Tage Aurell and director Anders Henrikson. The error is in the order of arrangement.

Both halves of the bill are concerned with the same basic issue —internal marital conflict arising from sexual attitudes of the mates —one treating it lightly and satirically, the other seriously and dimensionally. As arranged (oppo-

site to the order stated in the title), the comedy follows the tragedy and comes as an anticlimax. Had the lighter half preceded the weighty tale, each would have benefitted, the first from absence of audience anticipation, the second from natural progression of frivolity to deep involvement, whereby an audience is prepared and ready to digest meatier matter after a light appetizer.

The stories, adapted from Strindberg's tales of Married Life, are "On Payment," which delves into the tragic affair of an anti-sexual wife and her sexually-uncertain spouse, and "A Doll's House," not Ibsen's, but Strindberg's spoof of it. There are three outstanding principal performances and a flock of worthy character portrayals. The three that linger in the memory are those of Anita Bjork and Anders Henrikson (who directed the film) in "Payment" and lovely Mai Zetterling as the doll in "Doll's House."

Cinematically, there are flashes of photographic and directorial inspiration but the picture is not always sharp and clear and the subtitles are a source of considerable aggravation. There is, however, no arguing with the film's literary worth. This is an easy, diverting way to tackle Strindberg. *Tube.*

Mein Kampf
(SWEDISH—DOCUMENTARY)

Paris, Nov. 28.
Rene Thevenet release of Minerva Films production. Old newsreel and war footage compiled and edited by Edwin Leiser; commentary written and spoken by Leon Zitrone. At Avenue, Paris. Running time, 100 MINS.

Tautly edited footage traces the background to the rise of Adolph Hitler and then the horrors brought to the world by his rule and eventual defeat. It is objective and incisive, and has a wealth of rarely seen material firmly salvaged from archives and newsreels by Erwin Leiser. The story is known but here it is given more depth and interest in its visual form. This looms of theatrical interest abroad as well as for school, tv and special showings.

It is even more meaningful as swastikas again break out in hate programs from time to time. Photos, newspaper clips and footage are all tied together to tell this infamous story. The commentary is clear and a good counterpoint, in its sombreness and taste, to the harrowing events it unfolds. It also has weight in giving a rounded picture of the times that helped lead to the rise of Hitler and his nefarious aides as well as their eventual snuffing out.

Editing is expert while the quality of the images is very good. It again shows the power of the film as a document and witness of its time when put together with intelligence, insight and feeling. Some recently found footage of the horrible Warsaw Ghetto gives the film tragic weight.

This is being shown in German theatres and to German youth to make them cognizant of their past and responsibilities.

This direct, harsh picture of Hitler and his cronies shows them in all their eerie tricks and tirades. It would be almost comic if it did

not mean the terrible carnage and lowering of mankind's dignity in that these men could lead a nation and a world into chaos. Guilts are there in this thought-provoking pic. *Mosk.*

Cimarron
(C'SCOPE-METROCOLOR)

Good blending of action and personal drama should give wide audience appeal to this second telling of Edna Ferber's novel of Oklahoma land rush of 1889. Not so certain for limited hardticket intro dates.

Oklahoma City, Dec. 1.
Metro-Goldwyn-Mayer (Edward Granger) Production. Stars Glenn Ford, Maria Schell, Anne Baxter; features Arthur O'Connell, Russ Tamblyn, Mercedes McCambridge, Vic Morrow, Robert Keith. Directed by Anthony Mann. Screenplay, Arnold Schulman from Edna Ferber's novel; camera, Robert L. Surtees; special effects, A. Arnold Gillespie, Lee LeBlanc, Robert R. Hoag; editor, John Dunning; art directors, George W. Davis, Addison Hehr; music, Franz Waxman; title song, Paul Francis Webster, Waxman; assistant director, Ridgeway Callow; sound, Franklin Hilton; costumes, Walter Plunkett. Reviewed at Midwest Theatre, Oklahoma City, Dec. 1, 1960. Running time, 140 MINS.

Yancey Cravet	Glenn Ford
Sabra Cravet	Maria Schell
Dixie Lee	Anne Baxter
Tom Wyatt	Arthur O'Connell
The Kid	Russ Tamblyn
Sarah Wyatt	Mercedes McCambridge
Wes	Vic Morrow
Sam Pegler	Robert Keith
Yountis	Charles McGraw
Jess Rickey	Henry (Harry) Morgan
Sol Levy	David Opatoshu
Mavis Pegler	Aline MacMahon
Felicia Venable	Lili Darvas
Mr. Johnson	Edgar Buchanan
Mrs. Johnson	Mary Wickes
Ike Howes	Royal Dano
Millis	L. Q. Jones
Hoss	George Brenlin
Jacob Krubeckoff	Vladimir Sokoloff
Lewis Venable	Ivan Tissault
Cim Cravet	Buzz Martin
Suggs	John Cason
Arita Red Feather	Dawn Little Sky
Ben Red Feather	Eddie Little Sky

Edna Ferber's novel of the first Oklahoma land rush (1889) shapes up in its second film translation as a potentially big money winner for Metro-Goldwyn-Mayer. "Cimarron," as produced by Edmund Grainger and directed by Anthony Mann, maintains a good balance between rousing action and the marriage of Glenn Ford and Maria Schell as Yancey and Sabra Cravet. New adaptation of the book (made by RKO in 1931 with Irene Dunne and Richard Dix) is the work of Arnold Schulman.

Majority of today's audience will be seeing "Cimarron" for the first time, and its appeal, moreover, for European market should be heightened by marquee value there of Miss Schell. Pic also should set her up big in this country. She creates a sharply defined characterization of Sabra. There are many subtle shadings in her performance as she transforms over period of 25 years from adoring, lovable bride to embittered, abandoned wife, successful newspaper publisher and bigoted mother-in-law when son Cim marries a childhood friend Indian girl. Latter and her mother were taken into the Cravet family by Yancey during the homestead run when the father was lynched by an Indian-hating scoundrel, played in grand bullboy style by Charles McGraw.

Glenn Ford emerges a strong and thoroughly likeable adventurer-idealist as the restless rover, Yancey, who is loving and devoted after his own fashion and spurns opportunity to become governor by helping to defraud Indians of their oil rights. Ford's portrait is in the mold of the pioneer spirit, the type of legendary American associated with the growth of the United States. Pic pulls no punches, however, in pointing up the greed that discovery of black gold brought

out in the rags-to-riches Oklahoma pioneers.

Whereas most pix hold the big action in abeyance, "Cimarron" starts off with a bang. Spectacle of thousands of land seekers lined up in Conestoga wagons, buckboards and even a surry with the fringe on top, straining to dash into the new territory at high noon on April 22, 1889, is masterfully handled by director Mann. This is grand scale action in spades when the odd assortment of conveyances and men charge pell-mell into a future that holds death for many even before they can stake land claims. Although Mann and Grainger put a lot of ingenuity into the preparation of this tumultuous sequence, they needed expert assistance of unheralded stuntmen, special effects wizards A. Arnold Gillespie, Lee LeBlanc and Robert R. Hoag; assistant director Ridgeway Callow; cinematographer Robert L. Surtees and editor John Dunning. Latter contrbiutes some shrap intercutting to bring into focus emotions of men, women and children without losing any of the overall actionful impact.

Fortunately Schulman's adaptation doesn't let the performers down after the whirlwind start. Otherwise there wouldn't be much Ford, Miss Schell and Anne Baxter could do about sustaining the remainder of the two hour-20 minutes film. Miss Baxter's role is surprisingly short. However, she makes a vibrant contribution as the Red Light belle, Dixie Lee, particularly in her pathetic play to share Yancey at least with his wife and, this time with sardonic flippancy, when she is confronted by Sabra for news about the husband she hasn't heard from in a couple of years.

Although "Cimarron" is not without flaws—thoughtful examination reveals a pretentiousness of social significance more than valid exposition—the script as a whole plays well. As was the case with the filmed "Oklahoma!" of Rodgers-Hammerstein, "Cimarron" was color photographed on location in Arizona. And producer Grainger, apparently being more concerned about pictorial composition than actual topography, has permitted mountains to show in backgrounds alien to Oklahoma. The discrepancy, however, most likely will not be recognized by the majority.

Next to the stars, David Opatoshu, as a Jewish peddler who overcomes ridicule to become a prosperous merchant; Arthur O'Connell and Mercedes McCambridge, as impoverished parents of a brood of ten youngsters who are helped by open-hearted Yancey on the way to the land rush, and become greedy oil barons, have the choicest roles. They each do extremely well. Good performances also are turned in by Aline MacMahon, Robert Keith, Russ Tamblyn, Vic Morrow, Henry Morgan, Edgar Buchanan, Eddie and Dawn Little Sky, Royal Dano, Vladimir Sokoloff and Buzz Martin as the grown up Cimarron.

Paul Francis Webster and Franz Waxman (he also composed the complementary music score) provde an agreeable, though not distinguished, title song. Metrocolor is used most advantageously by cameraman Surtees in panoramic and intimate shots. There is a rich, but not overpolished, quality to interiors that abet contributions of art directors George W. Davis and Addison Hehr; set decorators Henry Grace, Hugh Hunt and Otto Siegel and the attractive costumes designed for Miss Schell and Miss Baxter by Walter Plunkett. Sound recording supervised by Franklin Milton is firstrate.

Metro's giving "Cimarron" limited hardticket start, as a prestige-builder for general pop policy runs Eastertime. It's by far the shortest entry in the two-a-day sweepstakes, a relief not to be denied. Wisdom of this exhibition policy will be evident soon, but it appears a safe bet that in regular run "Cimarron" will contribute importantly to sutdio's financial well being in 1961. *Pry.*

Un Couple
(A Couple)
(FRENCH)

Paris, Nov. 29.

Discifilm release of Balzac Film production. With Juliette Meyniel, Francis Blanche, Nadine Basile, Jean Kosta, Danielle Godet, Christian Duvaleix. Directed by Jean-Pitrre Mocky. Screenplay, Mocky, Raymond Queneau; camera, Eugene Schuftan; editor, Borys Lewin. Previewed in Paris. Running time, **85 MINS.**

Annette .... Juliette Meyniel
Pierre .... Jean Kosta
Boss .... Francis Blanche
Girl .... Danielle Godet
Alex .... Christian Duvaleix
Clara .... Nadine Basile

Comedy-drama mixes themes unevenly and emerges a hothouse item depicting the difficulties of lives in which sex has lost meaning. But this rarely settles down to treat thoroughly any of the incidents in the lives it touches. Result is an unbalanced pic but has possible arty chances.

Film leaves its meanings open and is literary in making most of its points verbally. The young director Jean Pierre Mocky shows he is not afraid to treat unusual themes and take slaps at certain segments of society. But he has a tendency to ramble and repeat effects.

A young married couple, after three years, has the husband confessing that sex with his wife has lost all meaning. Yet he tries to be true to her. She at first tries to woo him back but finally falls easy prey to a ladies' man who's a neighbor. Then she walks out on her hubby.

Several savory satirical characters bring out the theme of passionless sex. It does have some hypo pegs via its frankness, but unfortunately is minus a strong point of view. It is well lensed and played, and has a plus value in on-the-spot filming. ***Mosk.***

The 3 Worlds of Gulliver
(SUPERDYNAMATION-COLOR)

Acid of Swift's satirical tome neutralized to suit family audience tastes. Plenty of fun left in live-action fantasy-adventure. Striking visual effects. A novel attraction in today's market. Should do very well.

Hollywood, Nov. 25.

Columbia Pictures release of Charles H. Schneer production. Stars Kerwin Mathews, Jo Morrow, June Thorburn; features Lee Patterson, Gregoire Aslan, Basil Sydney, Sherri Alberoni; with Charles Lloyd Pack, Martin Benson, Mary Ellis, Marian Spencer, Peter Bull, Alec Mango. Directed by Jack Sher. Screenplay, Arthur Ross, Sher, based on "Gulliver's Travels" by Jonathan Swift; camera (Eastman), Wilkie Cooper; editor, Raymond Poulton; art directors, Gil Parrendo, Derek Barrington; music, Bernard Herrmann; special visual effects, Ray Harryhausen; assistant directors, Eugenio Martin, Paul Ganapoler. Reviewed at the studio, Nov. 25, '60. Running time, **98 MINS.**

Gulliver .... Kerwin Mathews
Gwendolyn .... Jo Morrow
Elizabeth .... June Thorburn
Reldresal .... Lee Patterson
King Brobdingnag .... Gregoire Aslan
Emperor of Lilliput .... Basil Cydney
Makovan .... Charles Lloyd Pack
Flimnap .... Martin Benson
Queen Brobdingnag .... Mary Ellis
Emperor of Lilliput .... Basil Sydney
Lord Bermogg .... Peter Bull
Galbet .... Alec Mango
Glumdalclitch .... Sherri Alberoni

From Jonathan Swift's durable 18th-century fantasy-satire, producer Charles H. Schneer has erected a live-action screen translation with enormous appeal for younger children and family audiences. Swift's stinging four-part satire has been considerably softened and drastically romanticized, but enough of its telling caustic comment remains and applies to the present to give it the added stature of philosophical importance that spells the difference between acceptable kiddie fare and a worthwhile full-fledged family attraction. The Columbia release will have impact in today's market, where a film of this nature is the exception to the rule.

Scholars may scoff at the liberties taken with Swift's respected novel, but experienced filmgoers will recognize the sugar-coating technique as merely showman's insurance. The mass family trade appreciates a healthy dose of romance and sentiment in its film diversion, and scenarists Arthur Ross and Jack Sher have managed to provide these elements without severely stripping the story of its thought-provoking qualities. The original four-part work has been trimmed to the more familiar twosome of Lilliput, land of little people, and Brobdingnag, where the natives are as tall in proportion to Gulliver as the Lilliputians are short. The hero's wife and family of Swift's tome have been dropped in favor of a fiery fiancee who shares his misadventure in Brobdingnag. Gulliver, thankfully, still goes it alone in Lilliput, according to the film.

The picture is notable for its visuo-cinematic achievements and its bold, bright and sweeping score, latter by Bernard Herrmann, the Columbia Workshop's old standby, who conducts the London Symphony Orchestra. Special visual effects expert Ray Harryhausen, whose Superdynamation process makes the motion-pictured Gulliver plausible and workable, rates a low bow for his painstaking, productive efforts. Perspectives, optical variations and split-screen synchronization effects are gratifying and invaluable. Camera work by Wilkie Cooper is another sizable assist to the production and soundwork, although uncredited on Columbia's printed roster of craftsmen, is equally sensitive and perceptive. Raymond Poulton's editing is accomplished.

The artistic, discerning eyes of art directors Gil Parrendo and Derek Barrington are responsible for some excellent sets, drawn neatly to scale for a film in which scale and physical specifications are unusually important requirements. Director Sher, together with Schneer, has succeeded in incorporating all this specialized cinematic craftsmanship into the product without overpowering the story itself. The physical technique serves the drama, which is as it should be.

Kerwin Mathews, generally reserved and persuasive, makes a first-rate Gulliver. Among the more arresting performances are those of Basil Sydney as the **pompous emperor of Lilliput, Martin Benson as its conniving minister of finance, Marian Spencer as the vain empress, Mary Ellis and Gregoire Aslan as king and queen of Brobdingnag.**

Other vigorous portrayals are chipped in by Lee Patterson, Charles Lloyd Pack, Peter Bull and Alec Mango. Jo Morrow is decorative as one of the more becoming Lilliput-terers, Sherri Alberoni very pretty but a bit synthetically sweet as a Brobdingnag maiden. June Thorburn is high-spirited and attractive as Gulliver's girl. *Tube.*

The Wackiest Ship In The Army
(C'SCOPE-COLOR)

Lively naval romp sparked by Jack Lemmon's jolly performance and a sharp script. Good b.o. bet.

Hollywood, Nov. 15.

Columbia Pictures release of Fred Kohlmar production. Stars Jack Lemmon, Ricky Nelson; features John Lund, Chips Rafferty, Tom Tully, Joby Baker, Warren Berlinger, Patricia Driscoll; with Mike Kellin, Richard Anderson, Alvy Moore, Joe Gallison, Teru Shimada, George Shibata, Richard Torrence, Naaman Brown. Directed by Richard Murphy. Screenplay, Murphy, from screen story by Herbert Margolis and William Raynor, based on story by Herbert Carlson; camera, Charles Lawton Jr.; editor, Charles Nelson; art director, Carl Anderson; music, George Duning; sound, George Cooper; assistant director, Sam Nelson. Reviewed at Stanley Warner Beverly Hills Theatre, Nov. 15, '60. Running time, **99 MINS.**

Lt. Rip Crandall .... Jack Lemmon
Ensign Tommy Hanson .... Ricky Nelson
Commander Vandewater .... John Lund
Patterson .... Chips Rafferty
Capt. McClung .... Tom Tully
Josh Davidson .... Joby Baker
Sparks .... Warren Berlinger
Maggie .... Patricia Driscoll
Chief Mate MacCarthy .... Mike Kellin
Lt. Foster .... Richard Anderson
Johnson .... Alvy Moore
Cameo .... Joe Gallison
Major Samada .... Teru Shimada
Capt. Shigetsu .... George Shibata
Horse .... Richard Torrence
Goroka .... Naaman Brown

"The Wackiest Ship in the Army" is see-worthy. An extremely witty screenplay by Richard Murphy and an instinctively deft and cogent comic performance by Jack Lemmon are its strong points.

Murphy's screenplay had its origin in a World War II yarn by Herbert Carlson, later adapted into screen story form by Herbert Margolis and William Raynor. It has nothing to do with the "Army," as the revised title indicates.

The story, loosely based on an actual incident in the war, offers Lemmon as the skipper of a laughably unwarlike vessel (there appears to be a run of these in films) commissioned to transport an Australian scout through treacherous enemy waters to a Japanese-occupied area where he is to spy on ship movements. The going gets tense in spots, but never serious enough to interfere with the primary funny business. The improbable nature of climactic de-

veleopments adds a farcical note to the film, but most of the humor is surprisingly sophisticated and delightfully perceptive in its irreverent regard of military ways and means.

In addition to his stout scripting effort, Murphy directed the picture. As director he has added several inventive comic touches and coaxed some jovial performances out of his cast. Among the funnier ones are Mike Kellin's as the conscientious chief mate of the decrepit but game U.S.S. Echo and Warren Berlinger's as its radio operator, a young fellow with the absurdly apropos real name of Sparks. Other effective enactments are contributed by John Lund (too rarely seen in films these days), Chips Rafferty, Tom Tully, Joby Baker, Patricia Driscoll, Richard Anderson, Alvy Moore, Joe Gallison, Teru Shimada, Richard Torrence and Naaman Brown. George Shibata adds some offbeat amusement as a UCLA-educated Japanese captain. Costar Ricky Nelson is more-than-capable as a young ensign, and warbles one selection adequately. But this is Lemmon's picture, his eminent domain. His restraint is admirable, his comic invention a joy to behold.

Camera work by Charles Lawton Jr. is generally skilled and agile, particularly some expert underwater photography. Only several process shots are not quite up to snuff. But there are some dandy sea battle shots in vivid Eastman hues. Adept editing by Charles Nelson and sensitive sound by George Cooper are valuable assists.

Filmed in Hawaii, the picture captures that wartime South Pacific feel through Carl Anderson's knowledgeable art direction. Among the most rewarding contributions is George Duning's music. His keenly clever, humorous tuning is never more apparent than when the good ship Echo is tensely circling through a mine field. Duning's accompanying ditty: "Here We Go 'Round the Mulberry Bush." *Tube.*

The Marriage-Go-Round
(C'SCOPE-COLOR)

Faithful, but tedious screen translation of the Broadway play.

Hollywood, Nov. 29.

Twentieth-Fox release of Leslie Stevens production. Stars Susan Hayward, James Mason, Julie Newmar; with Robert Paige, June Clayworth, Joe Kirkwood Jr., Mary Patton, Trax Colton, Everett Glass, Ben Astar. Directed by Walter Lang. Screenplay, Stevens, from his play; camera (DeLuxe), Leo Tover; editor, Jack W. Holmes; art directors, Duncan Cramer, Maurice Ransford; music, Dominic Frontiere; sound, E. Clayton Ward, Frank W. Moran; assistant director, Eli Dunn. Reviewed at Grauman's Chinese Theatre, Nov. 29, '60. Running time, **98 MINS.**

Content .... Susan Hayward
Paul .... James Mason
Katrin .... Julie Newmar
Dr. Ross .... Robert Paige
Flo .... June Clayworth
Henry .... Joe Kirkwood Jr.
Mamie .... Mary Patton
Crew Cut .... Trax Colton
Professor .... Everett Glass
Sultan .... Ben Astar

Something appears to have gone wrong somewhere between Broadway, where "Marriage-Go-Round" sustained itself as a hit play from Oct., 1958, to Feb., 1960, and Hollywood, where it has just become a rather tame and tedious film. At any rate, there isn't a great deal of novelty or merriment in the Leslie Stevens production, which Stevens has adapted for the screen from his own stage play. Wickets are likely to be stickier than 20th may have been led to anticipate.

Preoccupation with sex has evolved into a sort of national entertainment pastime of late. It may be that the shock of '58 is the yawn of '60. So, instead of boasting that he had retained 95% of the play's original dialog, it appears that scripter Stevens ought to have been updating the wit. Humor is a perishable inspiration.

"Marriage - Go - Round" rotates laboriously around one joke—the idea that an amorous Amazonian doll from Sweden would match endowments, gene for gene, with a brilliant cultural anthropology professor from the U.S.A. Since the prof is a happily-married monogamist, Miss Sweden's forward pass is intercepted right in the shadow of the goal (or bed) posts. The central joke is peppered with a series of rapid-fire gags, all of the same pseudo-suggestive mold. Sample: (He) "What she needs is a good spanking." (She) "You keep your hands to yourself."

In the role of the professor, James Mason is competent, managing to stay reasonably appealing in a perpetual state of mild flabbergastedness. Susan Hayward does exceptionally well in the role of the wife. Julie Newmar, who won the Antoinette Perry Award as best supporting actress for her Broadway performance as the gregarious glamorpuss from Scandinavia, appears to have misplaced her award-winning attributes. The intimacy of larger-than-life celluloid reveals a queen-sized heap of overacting from the blonde bombshell. Robert Paige is effective as a handy language prof summoned as occasional interpreter - understanding friend. Others on the premises are June Clayworth, Joe Kirkwood, Jr., Mary Patton, Trax Colton, Everett Glass and Ben Astar.

Brisk direction by Walter Lang fails to enliven the general tedium by much. There is also some structural confusion; choppy flashback transitions that indicate something has been lost of the play's novel staging technique.

The main set, Florida home of college prof Mason, resembles more the abode of a film star than an educator. It's the handiwork of art directors Duncan Cramer and Maurice Ransford. There is adequate lenswork by Leo Tover, editing by Jack W. Holmes and music by Dominic Frontiere.

Tony Bennett does well by the title tune, a lilting but lyrically lacklustre, ditty by Alan Bergman, Marilyn Keith and Lew Spence. *Tube.*

Jalsaghar
(The Music Room)
(INDIAN)

Paris, Nov. 29.

Ray production and release. With Chabi Biswas, Ganga Pada Basu, Kali Sarkar, Padma Devi, Tusli Lahari. Written and directed by Satyajit Ray. Camera, Subrata Mitra; editor, Dulai Ditt. Previewed in Paris. Runnng tme, **100 MINS.**

Bshamber .... Chabi Biswas
Servant .... Ganga Pada Basu
Son .... Kali Sarkar
Wife .... Padma Devi
Friend .... Tusli Lahari

Satyajit Ray, who made the noted prizewinning trilogy of "Pather Panchali" and "World of Apu," did this pic in between his previous pix. It is a perceptive study of a decaying nobleman. Done in a slow but incisive manner, this looms mainly an arty bet abroad with its visual beauty an aid.

A man sits in his once-great home, now beginning to fall to ruin. He reminisces on his past life, and his great parties as well as the loss of his son and wife. His inability to adapt himself to the changing scene about him are subtly blocked in. He is shown as one of those once powerful men whose failure to cope with the times has made him a recluse. He is a dilettante and seems to be more engrossed in simple social duties rather than in life about him. He gives one last party, tosses away all his money and dies in a fall from a horse.

Ray knows how to depict the slow passing of time, character and place without making the film static. It delves deeply into the man and though he is pathetic there is never any pity for him but an acceptance as a human being out of kilter with the times.

Pic is excellently lensed. The acting is good with the direction blending all into a keen study of a character. It is slow but deeply revealing. Well handled this could be a fine arty house bet. Music is also an excellent aspect of this tender, penetrating film. *Mosk.*

Mit Himbeergeist Geht Alles Besser
(It Goes Better With Raspberry-Juice)
(AUSTRIAN)

Vienna, Nov. 29.

Sascha Film (Herbert Gruber) production. Stars O. W. Fischer; features Marianne Koch, Jackie Lane, Petra Schuermann. Drected by Georg Marschka. Screenplay, Hans Jacogy and Willibald Eser from novel by Johannes Mario Simmel; camera, Guenther Knuth; settings, Fritz Jueptner-Jonstorff and Alexander Sawczynski; costumes, Gerdago; music, Johannes Febring. At Forum Kino, Nov. 18, '60. Running time, **90 MINS.**

Philipp Kalder .... O. W. Fischer
Hilde v. Hessenlohe .... Marianne Koch
Chou-Chou .... Jackie Lane
Suzie .... Petra Schuermann
Captain .... Bill Ramsay

Despite the awkward title, this motion picture should do good b.o. in the German language countries. Star O. W. Fischer is, in this instance, very natural in depicting the ups and downs of a prisoner of war (first French, than U. S., from where he fled) and his role afterwards on the black market, crowned by honorary citizenship of the city he supplied with goods, illegally obtained.

A clear satire on the conditions of 1945-50. Marianne Koch, his opposite, is also excellent. She, too, has the necessary "connections" on the black markets. Idea of plot: for hero first to use her for his "dark purposes," than to fall in love, is hardly new, but well constructed.

In the supporting cast, all do nicely. George Marischka directed and showed good sense in speeding up the early scenes, setting bad times of 1945. Cameraman Guenther Knuth did a good job.

Johannes Fehring supplied a few songs. *Maas.*

Le Caid
(The Boss)
(FRENCH)

Paris, Dec. 6.

Prodis release of CICC production. Stars Fernandel; features Barbara Laage, Georges Wilson, Claude Pieplu, Francois Darbon, Albert Michel. Directed by Bernard Borderie. Screenplay, Jean-Bernard Luc from novel by Claude Dorval; camera, Robert Juillard; editor, Christian Gaudin. At Aubert Palace, Paris. Running time, **90 MINS.**

Migonnet .... Fernandel
Rita .... Barbara Laage
Monsieur A. .... Georges Wilson
Oxner .... Claude Pieplu
Amedee .... Francois Darbon
Filatre .... Albert Michel

Fernandel is a philosophy teacher in this film. He gets mixed up with gangsters and molls when a big wad of money is dropped into his lap by an escaping holdup artist. He bluffs his way through this, but the complications and plotting are stereotyped and familiar.

This has only the Fernandel monicker for offshore chances, and hence they seem slight in this pic. Technically it is below par with a quickie look.

Supporting cast is subordinated entirely to Fernandel but Georges Wilson, as a sinister gangleader, manages to make his presence felt. It looks like a local item primarily. *Mosk.*

Das Erbe von Bjoerndal
(Heritage of Bjoerndal)
(AUSTRIAN-COLOR)

Vienna, Nov. 29.

Sascha Film release of Wiener Mundus Film production. Stars Britt Nilsson, Hans Nielsen, Carl Lange, Franz Messner. Directed by Gustav Ucicky. Screenplay, Per Schwenzen after novel by Trygve Gulbranssen; camera, Elio Carniel; music, Rolf A. Wilhelm. At Flieger Kino, Vienna. Running time, **90 MINS.**

Adelheid .... Maj-Britt Nilsson
Tante Elo .... Brigitte Horney
Gunvor .... Ellen Schwiers
Dag .... Joachim Hansen
Major Barre .... Hans Nielsen
Herr von Gall .... Carl Lange
Aslak .... Hans Christian Blech
Dag's son .... Michael Hinz
Lorenz .... Franz Messner
Jungfer Kruse .... Elisabeth Epp
Barbara .... Gertraud Jesserer
Kaufmann Holder .... Franz Schafheitlin
Pfarrer Ramer .... Hintz Fabricius

Appropriately titled "Heritage," this emerges as a fair entry for German and Norwegian language countries. This Norwegian-Austrian film is a continuance of a novel by Trygve Gulbranssen, cleverly turned into a screen vehicle by Per Schwenzen. It depicts the worries of farmers who stay on their soil today, and always. The intrigue of bad neighbors is the basis for the film's plot.

Dramatic events, however, are not overloaded with fantasy by the author or scripter. Young Dag (Joachim Hansen) at the end courts another girl.

Hansen is convincing as is his opposite Maj-Britt Nilsson as Adelheid. Brigitte Horney makes a fine comeback as Aunt Elo. Ellen Schwiers is excellent as the woman who spoils all peace efforts. The remainder of the cast is okay.

Though there is not much suspense, directing by Gustov Ucicky deserves praise. Camerawork by Elio Carniel is a major asset, especially the outdoor scenes shot in most northern sectors of Norwegia.

The Vienna Symphonic orch plays the smooth music by Rolf A. Wilhelm. All other technical credits are par. *Maas.*

L'Homme A Femmes
(Ladies' Man)
(FRENCH)

Paris, Dec. 6.

Pathe release of Cyclops production. Stars Danielle Darrieux, Mel Ferrer; features Claude Rich, Alan Scott, Catherine Deneuve, Pierre Brice. Directed by Jacques Cornu. Screenplay, Maurice Clavel, Alain Cavalier, Cornu from novel by Patrick Quentin; camera, Jacques Tournier; editor, Andre Feix. At Triomphe, Paris. Running time, **95 MINS.**

Gabrielle	Danielle Darrieux
George	Mel Ferrer
Vaillant	Claude Rich
Marc	Alan Scott
Catherine	Catherine Deneuve
Laurent	Pierre Brice

Loosely constructed whodunit has neither the characterization or treatment to keep this suspenseful. The unimaginative direction does not help either. It is mainly a local item.

A blackmailer, who has wooed Mel Ferrer's wife, Danielle Darrieux, and niece, is found dead. Various motives are sorted out by a taciturn police inspector to solve this tame meller.

The acting cannot do much with the surface personages. Technical credits are only fair. *Mosk.*

Hem Hayu Asara
(They Were Ten)
(ISRAELI)

Tel Aviv, Nov. 29.

ORB Film release of Baruch Dinar production. Stars Ninett Dinar and Oded Teomi. Directed by Baruch Dinar. Screenplay, Baruch Dinar, Gavriel Dagan and Menachem Shuval, based on story by Baruch Dinar; camera, L. Banes; editor, Helga Krenston; music, Gerd Bertini. Previewed at Chen, Tel Aviv.

Manya	Ninett Dinar
Josef	Oded Teomi
Zalman	Leo Filler
Shimon	Josef Safra
Avraham	Israel Rubinchik
Margin	Gavriel Dagan
Asher	Nisim Azikari
Yoel	Jichak Bareket
Berl	Josef Zur
Shmuel	Amnon Kahanovitz
Dr. Weiss	Jehuda Gabai
Mrs. Weiss	Shlomit Kaplansky
Turkish Officer	Moshe Yari
Arab Sheik	Moshe Kedem

This pic, which cost $100,000, fails to measure up to the great things expected of it. Made under difficult circumstances, the difficulties are visible throughout. Lack of money, absence of technical experience and a rather amateurish script make for a too slow film. Never compelling, the pic, however, has some poetic beauty. And it will appeal particularly to Jewish audiences. Oded Teomi is a sensitive actor and Ninett Dinar a delicate actress.

A group of young European Jews, one woman and nine men, gave up studies, merchandise, etc. and left the Old Continent determined to build up an agricultural settlement in the Promised Land. That's the basic plot.

They get a deserted building and a small piece of rugged land, bought from the Arabs with Jewish funds. The young settlers don't know how to handle a plough, they sow against the wind, they have to learn how to build a fireplace and how to ride a horse. The neighboring Arabs won't let them use the well and the Turkish policeman doesn't allow them to rebuild the house. Two men leave because they think the struggle is hopeless, and the woman dies. But the others survive.

Essentially, this unfolds the story about the start of the Jewish State. But the production never really makes the point. *Lapid.*

Exodus
(Super-Panavision 70; Technicolor)

Important human drama. Boffo boxoffice results strongly indicated.

United Artists release of Otto Preminger production, directed by Preminger. Stars Paul Newman, Eva Marie Saint, Ralph Richardson, Peter Lawford, Lee J. Cobb, Sal Mineo; features John Derek, Hugh Griffith, Gregory Ratoff, Felix Aylmer, David Opatoshu, Jill Haworth. Screenplay, Dalton Trumbo, from novel by Leon Uris; camera (Technicolor), Sam Leavitt; editor, Louis R. Loeffler; art director, Richard Day; music, Ernest Gold; assistant directors, Gerry O'Hara, Otto Plaschkes, Yoel Silberg, Larry Frisch, Christopher Trumbo. Reviewed at Rivoli Theatre, N. Y., Nov. 17, 1960. Running time, **212 MINS.**

Ari Ben Canaan	Paul Newman
Kitty Fremont	Eva Marie Saint
Gen. Sutherland	Ralph Richardson
Major Caldwell	Peter Lawford
Barak Ben Canann	Lee J. Cobb
Dov Landau	Sal Mineo
Taha	John Derek
Mandria	Hugh Griffith
Lakavitch	Gregory Ratoff
Dr. Lieberman	Felix Aylmer
Akiva	David Opatoshu
Karen	Jill Haworth
Von Storch	Marius Goring
Jordana	Alexandra Stewart
David	Michael Wager
Mordekai	Martin Benson
Reuben	Paul Stevens
Sarah	Betty Walker
Dr. Odenheim	Martin Miller
Sergeant	Victor Maddern
Yaov	George Maharis
Hank	John Crawford
Proprietor	Samuel Segal
Uzi	Dahn Ben Amotz
Colonel	Ralph Truman
Dr. Clement	Peter Madden
Avidan	Joseph Furst
Driver	Paul Stassino
Lt. O'Hara	Marc Burns
Mrs. Hirshberg	Esther Reichstadt
Mrs. Frankel	Zeporah Peled
Novak	Philo Hauser

With a reported record advance sale of $1,000,000, Otto Preminger's "Exodus" is off to a fast boxoffice start. Its commercial success assured. (Estimated cost of pic is $3,50,000-$4,000,000). Whether bulk of earnings will be reaped from the upped two-a-day admissions policy for this United Artists release, or come through later general run at pop prices, is a tossup in view of signs of stiffening public attitude toward premium price pix. In any event, this picture has the ingredients for mass audience pull: fresh, exciting pictorial (Technicolor) atmosphere, pulse-quickening action and agreeable romantic interest. "Exodus," taken from the Leon Uris book, is by and large a fine and important motion picture, which, unfortunately, falls somewhat short of artistic greatness.

Preminger, as producer-director, and scenarist Dalton Trumbo have created a dramatization of the birth pangs of a new nation, Israel, that is frequently soul-stirring, charged with savage action and punctuated by cunning enterprise which often is indeed stranger than fiction. A real hair-raising, worth-the-b.o.-tariff, sequence is the plotting and execution of the escape of a fanatic Irgun leader, brilliantly portrayed by David Opatoshu, from a British military prison.

In this and other intermittent interludes in the three hour-32 minutes (plus intermission) production, Preminger is at his directorial best. His action is strong and purposeful. He is not nearly as consistently successful, and neither is Trumbo's adaptation, in exploring and giving three-dimensional depth to personal relationships. A notable example is the character of the young, dedicated Hagana leader Ari Ben Canaan. Technically Paul Newman gives a sound performance, but he fails to give the role the warmth and deep humanity that would give the character distinguished stature. Far more communicative in this respect are Ralph Richardson, Eva Marie Saint, Lee J. Cobb, Sal Mineo, John Derek and a promising newcomer named Jill Haworth. This young lady has a haunting personality and given the benefit of experience should become a star. At present she often is guilty of over-projecting, a weakness Preminger should have controlled.

Transposing Uris' hefty novel to the screen was not an easy task. It is to the credit of Preminger-Trumbo that they have done as well as they have. One can, however, wish that they had been blessed with more dramatic incisiveness. **The picture wanders frequently in attempting to bring into focus various political and personal aspirations that existed within the Jewish nationalist movement itself as well as in regards to Arab opposition to the partitioning of Palestine and the unhappy role that Great Britain played as custodian of the status quo while a young United Nations pondered the fate of a new nation.**

One of the truly overwhelming moments, not only in this film but in screen history, is played aboard a rusty old freighter in which 611 Jews of all ages, from all over the face of Europe and spirited out of an internment camp on Cyprus under the nose of the British, attempt to sail to Palestine. Gregory Ratoff appears briefly, yet gives perhaps the finest performance of his career as an elder who can contribute nothing more than unswerving determination to support a hunger strike designed to expedite UN action and break the British blockade at the harbor entrance. The whole spirit that brought Israel into being is reflected in this particular sequence toward the end of the first part of the film. It's a real dramatic gem.

The 70m Super-Panavision lensed camera supervised by Sam Leavitt takes full advantage of intimate as well as largescale scenes, and for those familiar with the topography of southern California there is a striking similarity. Art director Richard Day in his contribution to the production design integrated sets and authentic buildings with such ingenuity that probably only those who worked the picture could spot the difference. The first assistant director, Gerry O'Hara, and his former colleagues had their hands full in coping with the background involving large crowds at times and served Preminger well. Ernest Gold's score is a strong plus factor and through its use of minor chords provides a flavorsome blending of ancient Hebraic strains with the modern surge of a people on the march.

The romance that develops slowly between Newman and Miss Saint, as a widowed American who contributes her nursing abilities to Jewish refugees on Cyprus and later in Palestine, as Arabs attack the new settlers, is conventional. But perhaps this relationship should not be of special import, since what happens to two individuals is secondary to the broader scope of the drama. Miss Saint has several good scenes and makes the most of them, as does Richardson, a sympathetic British general, who calmly gives the lie to rumors that his attitude is due to his Jewish ancestry. Only unfavorable British note (aside from country's role as policeman) in picture is reflected by Peter Lawford as a major and aide to the commander who is patently anti-Semitic. The character is at best fatuous and Lawford brings it off as the script required.

Lee Cobb gives his customary dependable, thoroughly professional performance as a conservative elder Hagana community leader father of Newman and brother of the fanatical violence advocate played by Opatoshu. The brothers' silent meeting after years of separation through a barred slot in a prison door is great pictorial drama. Sal Mineo as a loyal Irgun youngster, who has been brutalized by the Nazis, is excellent and John Derek stands out too as an Arab whose friendship for Newman and his family goes back to boyhood. Other fine acting contributions are made by Hugh Griffith, Felix Aylmer, Marius Goring, Peter Madden, Martin Benson, Martin Miller, Betty Walker, and Alexander Stewart.

While "Exodus" may have a special appeal to Jews, it is an inspiring picture of a great human struggle and every effort should be made through exploitation to avoid any attachment of a special interest label. That the picture may not satisfy all Jews as being a thoroughly accurate reflection of the struggle for national identification seems just as inevitable as the chances are that not all readers of the Uris book will agree with the film adaptation. There is room to criticize "Exodus"—its length might be shortened to advantage; perhaps Preminger tried to crowd too much incident from the book for dramatic clarity, and some individual scenes could be sharpened through tighter editing. But the good outweighs the shortcomings. Preminger can take pride in having brought to the screen a Twentieth Century birth of a nation. *Pyr.*

Herod The Great
(ITALIAN-TOTALSCOPE-COLOR)

Heavy, sullen account of the Tetrarch of Judea in the twilight of his wicked career. Slightly more penetrating, but probably less appealing to U.S. b.o. tastes for a biblical costume pix.

Hollywood, Dec. 5.

Allied Artists release of Gian Paolo Bigazzi production. Stars Edmund Purdom, Sylvia Lopez; with Sandra Milo, Alberto Lupo, Massimo Girotti. Directed by Arnaldo Geroino. Screenplay, Damiano Damiani, Federico Zardi, Fernando Cerchio, W. Tourjansky, from story by Damiani and Tullio Pinelli; camera (Eastman), Massimo Dallamano; editor, Antoinetta Zitta; music, Carlo Savina; sound, Umberto Picistrelli, Manlio Urbani; assistant director, Sergio Bergonzelli. Reviewed at the studio, Dec. 5, '60. Running time, **93 MINS.**

Herod	Edmond Purdom
Miriam	Sylvia Lopez
Sarah	Sandra Milo
Aaron	Alberto Lupo
Octavius	Massimo Girotti

Slowly, but surely, the Italian film industry appears to be piecing together a sort of history of the

ancient world on 20th century celluloid, draining the last ounce of melodrama out of the sacred scriptures and historical records of the period just B.C. In "Herod The Great," a grim, ponderous account of the ravings and cravings of that mad monarch, a key piece in this quasi-biblical, quasi-historical jigsaw is fit into place for the modern filmgoer who seeks periodic escape in these oversexed, overstuffed costume epics.

Yank reaction to this one may not be quite as favorable as recent response to several of its more dashing, more sexy, less introverted predecessors which raked in some quick U. S. coin. Somewhere along the way, a point of saturation is going to be reached, and Allied Artists, which is unleashing "Herod," is liable to encounter faint evidence of an ebb tide in public disposition toward the costume import.

The film, complicatedly labelled "A Samuel Schneider Presentation" and "A Film Of W. Tourjansky" exec produced by Gian Paolo Bigazzi, traces the twilight career of the confused and wicked Herod between his defeat in alliance with Antony at the hands of Rome and his insane demise following the birth of Christ. There is a literate quality to the screenplay (by Damiano Damiani, Federico Zardi, Fernando Cerchio and Tourjansky), but the entire film is played on one note of treachery, remorse and general gloom. It is too much for any audience and hardly can be termed "escape," although that is the anticipated tonic that will draw its audiences.

Under the handicap of post-dubbing, none of the players can prosper. Best of the lot is Edmund Purdom in the title role. He plays with integrity, albeit too much fervor is spots.

Arnaldo Genoino's direction appears postured and artificial. Sets and costumes are rich and lavish, music (by Carlo Savina) alternately plaintive and heavily emotional. Scene transitions are rough and choppy, frequently dramatically confusing. But the root of the film's failure is the uniformly unappealing nature of its characters. When the picture ends with the spoken-offscreen moral that "There must be a place in the world for love, rather than hate," one irresistibly wishes such a place had been found in the film just witnessed. *Tube.*

Boulevard
(FRENCH)

Paris, Dec. 13.

Pathe release of Orex Film production. Stars Jean-Pierre Leaud; features Monique Brienne, Magali Noel, Pierre Mondy, Jacques Duby, Robert Pizani. Directed by Julien Duvivier. Screenplay, Rene Barjavel from novel by Robert Sabatier; camera, Roger Dormoy; editor, Paul Gayatte. At Paris, Paris. Running time, 95 MINS.

Georges	Jean-Pierre Leaud
Marietta	Monique Brienne
Jenny	Magali Noel
Dicky	Pierre Mondy
Pittore	Jacques Duby
Paulo	Robert Pizzani

Vet director Julien Duvivier has taken the adolescent hero of the "New Wave" hit pic, "400 Blows," Jean-Pierre Leaud, for this vehicle, only here he is 16 years old. In "Blows" he was nearly 14. This is a series of episodes in the boy's life, alone in the colorful Pigalle section of Paris. Picture looms as almost a sequel to "Blows."

This lacks the feeling of a youthful world. Duvivier has been content to allow a lot of contrived, superfluous episodes thrown in for color and exploitation values around this story of a teenager who has left his father.

His crush on a hefty stripteaser, budding puppy love with a pretty neighbor, two homos pawing him in a scene and his enmity with a mean, punchy fighter make up the narrative. This displays him getting soured on people and the world.

Leaud sometimes shows the insight of "Blows" but mostly this does not ring completely true. Supporting roles are good, especially Magali Noel, as the big stripper, but all is subordinated to Leaud in an attempt to milk his performance in "Blows." This will need a hard sell. *Mosk.*

The Wizard of Baghdad
(C'SCOPE-COLOR)

Generally witless spoof of typical harem-scarem film fare. Should score moderately well during the holiday b.o. season.

Hollywood, Dec. 9.

Twentieth-Fox release of Sam Katzman production. Stars Dick Shawn, Diane Baker, Barry Coe; with John Van Dreelen, Robert F. Simon, Vaughn Taylor, Michael David, Stanley Adams, William Edmonson, Leslie Wenner, Michael Burns, Don Beddoe, Kim Hamilton. Directed by George Sherman. Screenplay, Jesse L. Lasky Jr., Pat Silver, based on story by Samuel Newman; camera (De Luxe), Ellis W. Carter; editor, Saul A. Goodkind; art directors, Duncan Cramer, Theobold Holsopple; music, Irving Gertz; sound, Alfred Burzlin, Harold A. Root; assistant director, Jack R. Berne. Reviewed at Beverly Theatre, Dec. 9, '60. Running time, 92 MINS.

Genii-Ali Mahmud	Dick Shawn
Princess Yasmin	Diane Baker
Prince Husan	Barry Coe
Julinar	John Van Dreelen
Shamadin	Robert F. Simon
Norodeen	Vaughn Taylor
Meroki	Michael David
Kvetch	Stanley Adams
Asmodeus	William Edmonson
Princess Yasmin (as a child)	Leslie Wenner
Young Prince Husan	Michael Burns
Raschild	Don Beddoe
Teegra	Kim Hamilton

"The Wizard of Baghdad" will have some boxoffice impact during the holiday season. Beyond that, it does not figure to cause any appreciable stir. The Sam Katzman production for 20th-Fox is designed as a satire of the typical Arabian Night-mare, but the mockery is superficial and relies more on pun-laden allusions to modern-day absurdities than to the subject it is supposed to be spoofing.

The Jesse L. Lasky Jr.-Pat Silver screenplay, based on a story by Samuel Newman, pits a kind of ineffectual "junior genie-man" (Dick Shawn) against a wicked sultan (John Van Dreelen) in an effort to occupy the throne of ancient Baghdad with the handsome prince (Barry Coe) and the beautiful princess (Diane Baker). Shawn is aided in his effort by a talking horse, but the animal doesn't utter a single clever or amusing line. (Have talking horses, too, become bores?) The screenplay's main attempt at humor is of the play-on-word variety, principally injections of television vernacular ("It takes a thinking man to filter out smoke where there's a fire") into the Baghdad environment.

Shawn, from cafes, is agreeable as the genie, but the film does not give him much of a chance to exercise his comic ability. Miss Baker and Coe are virtually wasted in stiff, preposterous roles. Neither's budding career benefits from this sort of casting. Van Dreelen does well as the bad sultan. Most prominent and effective support comes from Robert F. Simon, Vaughn Taylor, Stanley Adams and Don Beddoe. George Sherman's direction is not always all it should be, notably in a distractingly lethargic battle sequence.

Lenswork by Ellis W. Carter is adequate. Sets fashioned by art directors Duncan Cramer and Theobold Holsopple are colorful. There is an unusual editing approach by Saul A. Goodkind in which a kind of visible blur (accompanied by a repeated musical bridge) crosses the screen for each of the many scene transitions. It succeeds in conveying a sense of dramatic direction, but its overuse also imparts a sense of monotony. Music by Irving Gertz is unobtrusive. Shawn renders a pair of vocals, one of which ("Eni Menie Geni" by Diane Lampert, Peter Farrow and David Saxon) he delivers in a sort of semi-Danny Kaye style over the main titles. **Neither of the tunes (one is uncredited) is distinguished. Special photographic effects by L. B. Abbott and Emil Kosa Jr. are generally accomplished and are responsible for most of the available merriment. One disconcerting feature of their work, however, is the obvious visibility of wires on which the flying carpet is suspended.** *Tube.*

Hand In Hand

Appealing, moving drama about two moppets who solve an adult religious problem through their own devices. Woman producer's low budget film should be a strong item both as an arty and in later general release.

Hollywood, Dec. 8.

Columbia Pictures release of Helen Winston production. Stars John Gregson, Sybil Thorndike, Finlay Currie; introduces Loretta Parry, Philip Needs; with Miriam Karlin, Derek Sydney, Kathleen Byron, Martin Lawrence, Arnold Diamond, Barry Keegan, Barbara Hicks, Dennis Gilmore, Peter Pike, Susan Reid, Eric Francis, Stratford Johns, Donald Tandy, Madge Ryan. Directed by Philip Leacock. Screenplay, Diana Morgan, based on adaptation by Leopold Atlas of story by Sidney Harmon; camera, F. A. Young; editor, Peter Tanner; art director, Ivan King; music, Stanley Black; assistant director, Doug Hermes. Reviewed at the studio, Dec. 8, '60. Running time, 78 MINS.

Rachel Mathias	Loretta Parry
Michael O'Malley	Philip Needs
Father Timothy	John Gregson
Lady Caroline	Sybil Thorndike
Mr. Pritchard	Finlay Currie
Rabbi Benjamin	Derek Sydney
Mrs. Mathias	Miriam Karlin
Mr. Mathias	Arnold Diamond
Mrs. O'Malley	Kathleen Byron
Mr. O'Malley	Barry Keegan
The Cantor	Martin Lawrence
Miss Roberts	Barbara Hicks
Tom	Dennis Gilmore
Harry	Peter Pike
Priscilla	Susan Reid
Newsboy	Eric Francis
Farmer	Stratford Johns
George	Donald Tandy
George's wife	Madge Ryan

"Hand In Hand" is an unpretentious, universally appealing and unusually affecting "little" picture. It marks an auspicious bow as producer for Helen Winston, who has brought it in at an enviably tidy sum (reportedly under $200,000). Filmed in England and released by Columbia, it is ticketed for the art house circuit, where it should do very well when the word gets around. Being a short film, it should also be a valuable double-bill attraction in general release and conceivably could be one of the year's real "sleepers," for addition to being a compelling, heart-warming picture it also has something important to say and says it astonishingly well.

People will talk about the two children who play the central roles. The too youngsters, both of whom are making their screen debut, are Loretta Parry and Philip Needs. Not only are they handsome, charming tykes, but they are gifted players. The success of the film is linked perilously with their efforts, and they have come through beautifully (with only occasional minor lapses of overzealousness) under the careful, artful guidance of director Philip Leacock.

Without bombarding audiences with its preachment, "Hand" delivers an effective denouncement of religious intolerance, especially the way in which it can interrupt the normal character growth of children. Diana Morgan's screenplay, based on an adaptation by Leopold Atlas of a story by Sidney Harmon, describes the close bond that develops between a seven-year-old Jewish girl and her seven-year-old Roman Catholic playmate in spite of the discord that threatens to interrupt their friendship when a senseless age-old religious platitude filters down from the adult world.

The going, fortunately, never gets heavy or too obvious, although there are one or two moments when the film is on the brink of mild overlovableness in its regard of local men of the cloth. Actually, there is an extraordinary amount of humor, notably during the passage in which the lad is almost frightened to death when he participates in synagogue services, the girl likewise as an observer of Catholic Mass. The humor arises irresistibly from the serious point being made that unfamiliarity with other people's customs engenders a kind of primitive fear in the unindoctrinated beholder.

In addition to the captivating work of the two youngsters, there are fine performances by John Gregson, Sybil Thorndike, Finlay Currie, Derek Sydney, Miriam Karlin, Arnold Diamond, Kathleen Byron and Barry Keegan. Some of the camera work by F. A. Young is exceptionally sensitive. **Editing by Peter Tanner and art direction by Ivan King are major assists, and there is a moving and listenable score by Stanley Black. But it is Leacock's extremely perceptive direction that gives the picture its special quality.** *Tube.*

Pepe
(Color-Panavision-CinemaScope)

George Sidney's long-awaited production has color, class and rich comedy, an outstanding comedian in Cantinflas, music, dancing and fun. But too long.

Columbia release of George Sidney production. Stars Cantinflas; costars Dan Dailey, Shirley Jones; features Carlos Montalban, Vicki Trickett, Matt Mattox, Hank Henry, Suzanne Lloyd, Carlos Rivas and "guest stars." Directed by Sidney. Screenplay, Dorothy Kingsley and Claude Binyon; screen story, Leonard Spigelgass and Sonya Levien; based on play by L. Bush-Fekete; camera, Joe MacDonald; photographic lenses by Panavision, print by Technicolor, special sequences photographed in CinemaScope; editors, Viola Lawrence and Al Clark; music editor, Maury Winetrobe. Previewed at Criterion Theatre, N. Y., Dec. 19. Running time **195 MINS.**

Pepe	Cantinflas
Ted Holt	Dan Dailey
Suzie Murphy	Shirley Jones
Auctioneer	Carlos Montalban
Lupita	Vicki Trickett
Dancer	Matt Mattox
Manager	Hank Henry
Carmen	Suzanne Lloyd
Carlos Rivas	Carlos Rivas
Jewelry Salesman	Stephen Bekassy
Waitress	Carol Douglas
Priest	Francisco Reguerra
Charro	Joe Hyams

GUEST STARS

Maurice Chevalier, Bing Crosby, Michael Callan, Richard Conte, Bobby Darin, Sammy Davis Jr., Jimmy Durante, Zsa Zsa Gabor, Judy Garland (voice), Greer Garson, Hedda Hopper, Joey Bishop, Ernie Kovacs, Peter Lawford, Janet Leigh, Jack Lemmon, Jay North, Kim Novak, Andre Previn, Donna Reed, Debbie Reynolds, Edward G. Robinson, Cesar Romero, Frank Sinatra, Billie Burke, Ann B. (Schultzy) Davis, William Demarest, Jack Entratter, Col. E. E. Fogelson, Jane Robinson, Bunny Waters, Charles Coburn.

Embedded in the trend toward marathon productions are pitfalls; to state it simply, running time can so easily become excessive. "Pepe," which has a wealth of entertainment, has dull spots that should (or must) be cut.

This is a honey of a show; done up in showmanly style. There can be no doubt that Columbia and George Sidney will come out on top, along with their exhibitor accounts. The exploitation possibilities are vast, and to be noted particularly are some big names who have given themselves to "cameo" performances that are truly gems. Most of all, it's fun.

Story line, about a Hollywood director, a near has-been because he is overly fond of whiskey, and the tramp-like character who straightens him out in all directions, has moderate weight, certainly not enough to provide impact throughout three hours and 15 minutes of footage plus intermission. But compensating for this deficit are the wonderful bits.

Maurice Chevalier sings "September Song"; Jimmy Durante is an exasperated Las Vegas sharpshooter who can't outdraw the yokel; then, too, Bing Crosby, Michael Callan, Richard Conte, Bobby Darin, Sammy Davis Jr., Zsa Zsa Gabor, Greer Garson, Joey Bishop, Hedda Hopper, Ernie Kovacs, Peter Lawford, Janet Leigh, Tony Curtis, Jack Lemmon, Jay North, Kim Novak, Andre Previn, Donna Reed, Debbie Reynolds, Cesar Romero and Frank Sinatra.

Guest star listing also has Edward G. Robinson but actually his appearance, as a bigtime operator in Hollywood, is far more extensive and important than the casual billing would indicate.

George Sidney, as producer and director, and the multi-combinationed writing credits (Dorothy Kingsley and Claude Binyon, screenplay; Leonard Spigelgass and Sonya Levien, screen story, and L. Bush-Fekete, original play) obviously have taken a cue or more from the late Mike Todd's "Around the World in 80 Days." They patterned their show after a hit, rather than originating one, but nonetheless they collaborated on a hit.

Boldface scorecard is needed to determine who did what so far as other credits are concerned. The song and music acknowledgments are numerous; suffice to say that Johnny Green was the supervisor and did the background. Technicolor provided the print, the photographic lenses were Panavision and some special sequences were lensed in Cinemascope. The off-the-set observer can only note that the camera work is excellent, the tinted photography exquisitely nailing down beautiful sets and backgrounds in Beverly Hills, Vegas and Mexico. Edith Head's costumes are another significant plus.

The major consideration of "Pepe" must center on Cantinflas, who's a delight as a performer hailing from Mexico way. Temptation is to call him Chaplinesque, but actually he has his own style of quiet and quick facial movement delivery. Owner of a fine horse whom he calls his son, parleyor of a piggy bank into a fortune at Vegas, partner in bigscale filmmaking, and weeping loser in love, Cantinflas is a tactful comedian of high order. The job he does has substance, point and, most important, simpatico.

Unhappily, the script gets stickey for "Pepe" toward the finale as he comes to realize that his yen for Shirley Jones is unrequited. And there's an overly-pathetic concern about his losing his horse. Let's call in a doctor with scissors.

Jack Lemmon does a femme impersonator bit like in "Some Like It Hot," Janet Leigh and Tony Curtis are amusing in a tiny part, Kim Novak registers nicely (meaning very pretty) as a bystander who surreptitiously helps Cantiflas as "Pepe," buy a marriage ring, Judy Garland is heard offscreen, Crosby is heard onscreen, and there's Hank Henry of Vegas fame and Jack Entratter of ditto.

Too, songs and dances intertwined, the title tune being an ingratiating one and some expert choreography and execution.

Dan Dailey is all right as the film director (as per script) on the verge of skid row and Miss Jones makes for an appealing gal trying for the bigtime in pictures. It ought to be said about here that there's no need for the romantic rough stuff as Dailey makes a play for Miss Jones; it doesn't seem fitting.

Sidney has provided an obviously expensive and impressive production—but too much. Suburban commuters will get home awfully late. *Gene.*

Spring Affair

Low-budget indie about a henpecked husband who strays. Resources too limited for smooth treatment of demanding topic, but at least pic sidesteps lower-berth formula.

Hollywood, Dec. 14.

Geo. Bagnall Associates release of Bernard "B.B." Ray production. Stars Lindsay Workman, Merry Anders; with Yvonne White, Don Kennedy, Albert Carrier, Ron Kennedy, Coleman Francis, Oween Cameron, Shawn Mallory, Ellen Marty, Cecile Rogers, Brad Olson, Charles Calvert, Terry Loomis, Pat Wiles. Directed and screenplay by Ray; camera, Elmer Dyer, Roland Price; editor, George Merrick; music, Manuel Francisco; assistant director, Art Hammond. Reviewed at Consolidated Film Labs, Dec. 14, '60. Running time, **79 MINS.**

Wilbur Crane	Linssay Workman
Dorothy	Merry Anders
Martha	Yvonne White
Dan	Don Kennedy
Arthur	Albert Carrier
Ted	Ron Kennedy
Smith	Coleman Francis
Elsie	Oween Cameron
Model	Shawn Mallory
Waitress	Ellen Marty
Registrar	Cecile Rogers
Instructor	Brad Olson
Tailor	Charles Calvert
Imaginary Blonde	Terry Loomis
Counter Blonde	Pat Wiles

For a minimal-budget film tailored to fit into the rear half of a twin-bill, "Spring Affair" is an astonishingly ambitious project, unlike the average lower-berther being ground out these days by studios with more at their disposal. Unfortunately, in its bid to veer away from programming story formulese, the film, written-produced-directed by Bernard "B.B." Ray, is dealing with subject material it cannot quite handle gracefully and dimensionally within its limited range and resources. But at least it is an attempt to break the "B" barrier of safe conformity, and this alone may enable it to rack up an extra playdate or two.

The picture, which is dedicated to the producer's late wife (50% of the profit is to be donated to the Cancer Fund), describes a rather lecherous henpecked husband's extra-curricular affair with a hooker, an affair resolved happily when it suddenly turns out to be a bad dream. There is an underlying attempt to treat the story lightly and humorously (particularly with some jarringly merry musical backing), but there is really nothing very amusing about the pathetic people involved in the tale.

Lindsay Workman limns the straying husband, and creates a pitiful figure of incredible naivete. He does get a good deal of whimsy into the character, however. Merry Anders does well by the role of his lady friend. Others who attract passing attention are Don Kennedy, Yvonne White, Albert Carrier, Ron Kennedy, Coleman Francis, Oween Cameron, Shawn Mallory, Ellen Marty, Cecile Rogers, Brad Olson, Charles Calvert, Terry Loomis and Pat Wiles. Diane Dauncey and Dan Talbot warble a tune or two composed by Irving Bibo.

Considering the shoestring budget, art, technical and visual contributions are game and creditable. *Tube.*

No Kidding
(BRITISH)

Pleasant, but not very high-powered comedy from the click "Carry On" stable.

London, Dec. 13.

Anglo-Amalgamated release of a Peter Rogers production. Stars Leslie Phillips, Geraldine McEwan, Julia Lockwood, Noel Purcell; features Irene Handl, Joan Hickson, June Jago. Directed by Gerald Thomas. Screenplay, Norman Hudis and Robin Estridge from Valerie Estridge's book, "Beward of Children"; camera, Alan Hume; editor, John Shirley; music, Bruce Montgomery. Previewed at Studio One, Londn. Running time, **87 MINS.**

David Robinson	Leslie Phillips
Catherine Robinson	Geraldine McEwan
Vanilla	Julia Lockwood
Tandy	Noel Purcell
Mrs. Spicer	Irene Handl
Cook	Joan Hickson
Matron	June Jago
Colonel Matthews	Cyril Raymond
District Nurse	Esma Cannon
Edgar Treadgold	Alan Gifford
Mr. Rockbottom	Sydney Tafler
Vicar	Bryan Oulton
King	Eric Pohlmann
Will	Brian Rawlinson
Henri	Michael Sarne
Mrs. Rockbottom	Joy Shelton
Queen	Patricia Jessel
Angus	Martin Stephens
Eileen	Millicent Kerr

The capable, talented team of producer Peter Rogers and director Gerald Thomas occasionally indulges itself. It strays away, rather half heartedly, from its click "Carry On" formula. There have been times when by roaming into a less slapstick comedy field there has been equal boxoffice results. But not, it would seem, in this film. With not much change of policy or script, this could have been yet another "Carry On." But, in its own right, this flounders a bit. This amiable hybrid is not quite farce, not quite comedy and not quite romantic comedy. In the sagging frail story line, there's a feeling that somewhere, ever so gently, has misfired.

The idea here is a good one and, if anybody wants to use that idea seriously, "No Kidding" hasn't remotely absorbed its prospects. A young couple, saddled with a white elephant of a country house, turn it into a vacation resort for the unfortunate offspring of rich people who are too busy living it up to have any time for their moppets. These over-privileged youngsters are brought to Chartham Place, run by Leslie Phillips and his young wife, Geraldine McEwan.

Theory rubs shoulders with fact. Most of the youngsters are spoiled, bored brats. Miss McEwan thinks they need freedom. But Phillips quickly discovers that they need discipline. Meanwhile a local, interfering official (Irene Handl) is sabotaging the young couple's efforts because she wants the house for under-privileged kids. That's about all there is to it.

Just a little comedy with a series of amiable but not highly original situations, which end up in the children liking the place so much that they refuse to go home until their parents agree not to ignore them. The finale, contrived as a tear-jerker, doesn't blend with what's gone before.

Phillips, his usual brisk self, is as likeable as ever, while Miss McEwan, not used enough in pix, seems lacking in confidence. She has good moments, but some are erratic. June Jago as an over-efficient matron; Joan Hickson, an alcoholic cook; Irene Handl, Noel Purcell, Esma Cannon, Brian Rawlinson, Sydney Tafler and Julia Lockwood, the last-named as a teenager with more sex appeal and imagination than food for her, all chip in with useful comedy performances. *Rich.*

Der Hauptmann Von Köln
(The Captain From Cologne)
(EAST GERMAN-COLOR)

Paris, Dec. 13.
Defa production and release. With Rolf Ludwig, Christel Bodenstein, Erwin Geschonneck, Else Wolz. Directed by Slatan Dudow. Screenplay, Henryk Keisch, Michael Tchesno-Hell, Dudow; camera (Agfacolor), Werner Bergmann; editor, Eric Schmidt. At Floride, Paris. Running time, 120 MINS.
```
Hauptmann .................. Rolf Ludwig
Hannelore .......... Christel Bodenstein
Hans Albert ........ Erwin Geschonneck
Rich Girl ..................... Else Wolz
```

This East German pic probably can't be shown in the U.S. under present diplomatic conditions. Its subject tends to make it a chancey item. Though heavyhanded, this does take pot shots at remnants of Nazism in Germany today and has a fairly diverting plot and thesping except for some repetition and is overlong for a comedy.

A little waiter gets mistaken for an ex-Nazi and is picked up by a group of sympathizers. He becomes an important man and is unmasked when the real Nazi shows up. Pic naturally is one sided.

Acting fits in with the satire but color is somewhat harsh and runny. Direction is a bit stolid relying on its lampooning for effect. It is an example of a propaganda film that has some insight into its subject. *Mosk.*

The Bulldog Breed
(BRITISH)

Typical Norman Wisdom. Scrappy, but yock-providing naval yarn. Good light booking for family houses.

London, Dec. 13.
Rank production and release. Stars Norman Wisdom; features Ian Hunter, David Lodge, Robert Urquhart, Edward Chapman, Liz Fraser. Produced by Hugh Stewart. Directed by Robert Asher. Original screenplay, Jack Davies, Henry Bligh. Norman Wisdom; camera, Jack Asher; editor, Gerry Hambling; music, Philip Green. At New Victoria, London, Dec. 13, '60. Running time, 100 MINS.
```
Norman Puckle ........ Norman Wisdom
Admiral Blyth ............. Ian Hunter
C. P. O. Knowles........... David Lodge
Commander Clayton... Robert Urquhart
Mr. Philpotts ......... Edward Chapman
P. O. Filkins ............... Eddie Byrne
Diving Instructor .......... Peter Jones
Prosecuting Counsel.. John Le Mesurier
Defending Counsel...Terence Alexander
Speedboat Owner ........ Sydney Tafler
Naafi Girl ................... Liz Fraser
Marlene ............... Penny Morrell
Mr. Ainsworth ............ Brian Oulton
Greenfield ............... Joe Robinson
Girl on Yacht ............ Claire Gordon
Yachtsman ............ Leonard Sachs
Polynesian Girl .......... Julie Shearing
Gym Instructor .......... Glyn Houston
Landlord .............. Cyril Chamberlain
Doris ................... Sheila Hancock
Peggy ................ Rosamund Lesley
```

It may be unadventurous, but it's obviously sound business to stick to a proved formula for Britain's No. 1 slapstick comedian, Norman Wisdom, the little chap up against problems which he can never quite tackle, yet somehow muddling through.

Jack Davies and Henry Bligh, with assistance from Wisdom himself, are credited with having written this script. It would be fairer to say that they, with the producer, the director and, who knows, maybe the cameraman, the props and even the continuity girl have chipped in to concoct a vehicle for the likable, energetic little star.

Series of situations, pegged to a thin story line, offer a lot of yocks

even at their most contrived and this will certainly be popular entertainment among out-for-escapist-entertainment audiences.

Without bothering with logical reasons, Wisdom tries to commit suicide for love of a haughty cinema cashbox blonde. As in everything in life he fails horribly, is rescued and persuaded to join the Navy, where he continues to make a hash of everything. But, for a reason known only to the admiral, he is chosen, as the newest recruit, to be the first man sent into space in the "Interplanetary Projectile Bosun." He is so obviously the wrong man for the job that even obstinate Admiral has to admit it. But by a farcical mix-up he does make the space journey and blunders back successfully.

The film stands or falls by Wisdom and though the actor, as always, seems to be trying rather too hard, his general good humor and energy carry him through the various situations entertainingly. Whether he's flirting with a dame, getting into the hair of senior officers, pricking pomposity, suffering indignities in the gymnasium or in special trainng he is always the amiable gump, who retains the audience's sympathy even when they're ribbing him. There is one scene when he is court-martialled which offers a lot of shrewd fun, and the scene when he is let loose in the space bound projectile is amusing, even though the results come mainly from some slick trick photography.

Robert Asher has directed briskly and the screenplay, while a bit short on wit, has several hilarity situations. Wisdom is surrounded by some very capable performers, notably Ian Hunter as the pompous admiral, Edward Chapman as an even more pompous character and David Tafler, Robert Urquhart, Peter Jones and Eddie Byrne also turn in some telling cameos. The girl angle is less fully served, but Liz Fraser, Julie Shearing and Penny Morrell show that Britain at least has its fair share of good looking young thesps. Technically, it's a capable job.

For how long it will be possible to get away by shrugging and saying "it's another typical Norman Wisdom job" is a problem that this successful comedian may well have to consider very seriously soon. Till then, "The Bulldog Breed" serves its undemanding purpose.
Rich.

Flaming Star
(C'SCOPE—COLOR)

Familiar, but diverting hoss opera with action for the moppets, Presley for the teens, and white man-Indian bloodline conflict for the adults. Good b.o. prospects.

Hollywood, Dec. 15.
Twentieth-Fox release of David Weisbart production. Stars Elvis Presley, with Steve Forrest, Barbara Eden, Dolores Del Rio, John McIntire. Directed by Don Siegel. Screenplay, Clair Huffaker, Nunnally Johnson, based on novel by Huffaker; camera (De Luxe), Charles G. Clarke; editor, Hugh S. Fowler; art directors, Duncan Cramer, Walter M. Simonds; music, Cyril J. Mockridge; sound, E. Clayton Ward, Warren B. Delaplain; assistant director, Joseph E. Rickards. Reviewed at the studio, Dec. 15, '60. Running time, 92 MINS.
```
Pacer ................... Elvis Presley
Clint .................... Steve Forrest
```

Roslyn Pierce .... Barbara Eden
Neddy Burton .... Dolores Del Rio
Pa Burton .... John McIntire
Buffalo Horn .... Rudolph Acosta
Dred Pierce .... Karl Swenson
Doc Phillips .... Ford Rainey
Angus Pierce .... Richard Jaeckel
Dorothy Howard .... Anne Benton
Tom Howard .... L. Q. Jones
Will Howard .... Douglas Dick
Jute .... Tom Reese
Ph'sha Knay .... Marian Goldina
Ben Ford .... Monte Burkhart
Hornsby .... Ted Jacques
Indian Brave .... Rodd Dedwing
Two Moons .... Perry Lopez

"Flaming Star" has Indians-on-the-warpath for the youngsters, Elvis Presley for the teenagers and socio-psychological ramifications for adults who prefer a mild dose of sage in their sagebrushers. The plot—half-breed hopelessly involved in war between white man and Redman—is disturbingly familiar and not altogether convincing, but the film, attractively mounted and consistently diverting, will entertain and absorb the audience it is tailored for. There's good business in store for the 20th-Fox release, produced by David Weisbart.

Presley plays the half-breed, pivotal character in the conflict between a group of Texas settlers and the angry Kiowa tribe. Part of a heterogeneous family (full-blooded Indian mother, white father, half brother) resented and tormented by whites, taunted and haunted by Indian ties, Presley is buffeted to and fro between enemy camps by the prevailing winds of prejudice and pride, sees his father and mother die, eventually perishes alone in his private no-man's land. Except for a contrived ending and an occasional lapse or misjudgment, the Clair Huffaker-Nunnally Johnson screenplay, based on a novel by Huffaker, is taut, plain and gripping.

The role is a demanding one for Presley. The film relies heavily on his reactions as an explanation for its dramatic maneuvers and thematic attitudes. But, at this stage of his career, Presley lacks the facial and thespic sensitivity and projection so desperately required here. Physically, however, he is thoroughly believable in the half-breed role and athletically he is well-endowed for the part's masculine demands. And one other thing can be said for Presley's approach—he's never guilty of overacting.

The standouts are the veterans, Dolores Del Rio and John McIntire. Miss Del Rio, durably lovely, ever feminine, brings dignity and delicacy to the role of Presley's full-blooded Indian mother. McIntire adds nobility and compassion as the father of the doomed household. Steve Forrest is competent as the brother, Barbara Eden decorative as his girl. Rudolph Acosta plays the Kiowa chieftain with a flair. There is vigorous supporting work by Karl Swenson, Richard Jaeckel, Ford Rainey, Anna Benton, L. Q. Jones, Douglas Dick, Tom Reese, Marian Goldina, Monte Burkhart and Ted Jacques.

Director Don Siegel has packed plenty of excitement into the picture, notably some realistically-staged fistfight, battle and chase passages. But there are a few equally unrealistic-looking scenes.

Charles G. Clarke's camera work is alert and sensitive, Hugh S. Fowler's editing skilled. Outdoor backdrops have a vast, frontier flavor, and interiors are suitably rugged and humble, under the perceptive

supervision of art directors Duncan Cramer and Walter M. Simonds.

Music by Cyril Mockridge, very important in this film (there isn't a great deal of dialog), unobtrusively mixes plaintive Indianesque and action themes. Presley capably renders two songs. One is the rather uninspired title tune by Sherman Edwards and Sid Wayne. The other, "A Cane and a High-Starched Collar," is a lively country ditty by Sid Tepper and Ray Bennett. *Tube.*

Pierrot La Tendresse
(Pete The Tender)
(FRENCH)

Paris, Dec. 20.

Gaumont release of Caravelle productin. Stars Michel Simon; features Dany Saval, Claude Brasseur, Marie Daems, J. P. Marielle. Directed by Francois Villiers. Screenplay, Charles Exbrayat, Yvan Audouard, Jean Serge; camera, Paul Soulignac; editor, Edouard Berne. At Balzac, Paris. Running time, 85 MINS.

Pierrot .... Michel Simon
Marie .... Dany Saval
Tony .... Claude Brasseur
Micky .... Marie Daems
Emile .... J. P. Marielle

This film marks the comeback of the character actor Michel Simon after three years of illness and bad roles. Meandering pic about a tender-hearted gangster who sacrifices all for his ward lacks the characterization and snap to make this primarily a local entry with chancey foreign possibilities.

Simon is an aging killer with a heart of gold. His last job is to find the loot hidden by a young hoodlum who had served time after running out on the others with the swag of a holdup. The boy uses the ward, who falls for him, to foil Simon. But the latter gets the money from him, turns it over to the police and makes the boy settle down with the girl.

Simon is properly crotchety, tender and with flashes of deadliness. But he is not helped by a lacklustre script, ordinary direction and uneven acting around him. The plot lacks the satirical note to make this unusual. Technical credits are only par. Simon still needs a vehicle to bring his fading career into focus again. *Mosk.*

The Pure Hell of St. Trinian's
(BRITISH)

Typical adventure of Ronald Searle's monstrous but funny schoolgirls; sure winner in family houses.

London, Dec. 20.

British Lion release of a Gilliat-Launder production. Stars Cecil Parker, George Cole, Joyce Grenfell; features Eric Barker, Sidney James, Thorley Walters, George Cole, Irene Handl, Dennis Price. Directed by Frank Launder. Screenplay (inspired by Ronald Searle' original St. Trinian's drawings) by Sidney Gilliat, Frank Launder & Val Valentine; editor, Thelma Connell; camera, Gerald Gibbs; music, Malcolm Arnold. At Odeon, Marble Arch, London. Running time, 94 MINS.

Professor Canford .... Cecil Parker
Sgt. Ruby Gates .... Joyce Grenfell
Flash Harry .... George Cole
Butters .... Thorley Walters
Culpepper-Brown .... Eric Barker
Miss Harker-Packer .... Irene Handl
Alphonse O'Reilly .... Sidney James
Gore Blackwood .... Dennis Price
Judge ..... Raymond Huntley
Superintendent Kemp-Bird . Lyold Lamble
Miss Partridge .... Liz Fraser
Emir .... Elwyn Brook-Jones
Octavius .... Monty Landis
Major .... Nicholas Phipps
Captain .... Cyril Chamberlain
Prosecuting Counsel ..... Mark Dignam
Defense Council .... George Benson
Chief Constable .... Wesley Pithey
V.I.P. .. .. Clive Morton
British Consul .... Harold Berens
Minister .... John Le Mesurier
Rosalie .... Julie Alexander
Millicent .... Maria Lennard
Jane .... Dawn Berret
Lelita Chatterley...... ... Ann Wain
Minnie Hen ...... Gilda Emmanuelli
Maud Birdhanger .... Sally Bulloch

Ronald Searle's familiar cartoon characters come to life in yet another St. Trinian's School romp, which is well up to standard. It will please all addicts of Searle's monstrous school children. Those who saw the previous St. Trinian's pix will know precisely what to expect of this one, an outrageaus frolic which throws logic overboard. Frank Launder and Sidney Gilliat know that the girls are their trump card, but wisely surround them with a long cast of experienced character actors, even in parts that are the merest cameos.

Current yarn gets off to a flying start with the girls burning down the school and being brought to trial at the Old Bailey. But to the horror of the police and the Ministry of Education they are acquitted. This is partly because the judge has a roving eye and does not miss the most beautiful blonde in the Sixth Form (Julie Alexander), but also because of the intervention of a strange professor who offers to start a new St. Trinian's and give the girls a fresh start. He turns out to be a dubious character mixed up with a racket for supplying glamor girls to an Oriental Emir as wives for his numerous sons. Ostensibly off on a cultural tour of the Greek Isles, the sixth formers finish up in Arabia. The army is alerted but, of course it is the fourth form of St. Trinian's which comes to the rescue and routs the enemy.

The Old Bailey sequence, the fire scenes and several in the desert notably when the girls lock themselves out of reach of the eager young men of the Emir's Palace all provide ready yocks. Dialog is brisk and the film is directed at a sufficiently swift pace to keep the fun moving steadily.

In a large cast, Cecil Parker, as the professor; Irene Handl, as his assistant, Dennis Price, Thorley Walters, Eric Barker and Raymond Huntley all provide the type of polished comedy studies which audiences have come to expect. Joyce Grenfell is once again the prim policewoman in love with the superintendent. George Cole repeats his familiar performance as Flash Harry, who runs a matrimonial agency on behalf of the Sixth Form.

Julie Alexander, Maria Lennard, Erica Rogers, Shirley Lawrence and Dawn Berret are the nucleus of a shapely bunch of Sixth Formers. Miss Alexander is particularly decorative. Art work is good, the "location" scenes, all done in the studio, being convincing. "Pure Hell" is very much a specialist farce. Audiences who dig the characters will have a lively 90-minutes, for there's no doubt that, within its self-imposed bounds, it's a slickly done job. *Rich.*

The Three Treasures
(JAPANESE—TOHOSCOPE—COLOR)

Lavish spectacle built around Japanese mythology. Striking photographic effects and cultural values make it an impressive arty attraction.

Hollywood, Dec. 27.

Toho Co. release of Sanezumi Fujimoto-Tomoyuki Tanaka production. Stars Toshiro Mifune; with Yohko Tsukasa, Kyoko Kagawa, Kohji Tsuruta, Takashi Shimura. Directed by Hiroshi Inagaki. Screenplay, Toshio Yasumi, Ryuzo Kikushima; camera (Agfacolor), Kazuo Yamada; special effects director, Eiji Tsuburaya. Reviewed at Toho La Brea Theatre, Dec. 20, '60. Running time, 111 MINS.

Prince Yamato Takeru....Toshiro Fifune
Princess Tachibana........Yohko Tsukasa
Princess Miyazu...........Kyoko Kagawa
Younger Kumaso......... Kohji Tsuruta
Elder Kumaso............Takashi Shimura

Toho Co. of Japan has, in "The Three Treasures," mounted a lavish, visually meticulous account of Japan's mythological heritage. Western audiences, although by now so acclimated to cinematic spectacle that there is a tendency to regard them with a sophisticated shrug, will have to admire the artistry and painstaking photographic mastery of the craftsmen who designed and manufactured this film.

Already noted for their miniature, color and special effects work, these Japanese artisans have set a new standard for themselves with this effort. The film should attract art house attention beyond the Japanese sphere and, being physically and culturally superior to recent costume imports from Europe, could even, with proper handling make some sort of a showing as a general theatrical attraction.

The epic story, almost operatic in dramatic style, describes the personal tragedy of Japan's mythological hero, Prince Yamato. Yamato, vigorously enacted by leading Toho player Toshiro Mifune, undergoes an episodic series of romantic and political misadventures, eventually perishes in battle but is instantly reincarnated as a magical swan to destroy his enemies and fly off to the gods.

Several players who make impressions are the lovely Yohko Tsukasa, Kyoko Kagawa and Kohji Tsuruta. Although passage of time, scene trnsition and sense of direction seem occasionally fuzzy or irregular, Hiroshi Inagaki's direction breathes life and vitality into the drama, particularly in scenes of combat and notably in the enthusiasm of crude Oriental swordplay.

Kazuo Yamada's lenswork is agile and alert. But it is Eiji Tsuburaya's special effects that steal the picture. His execution of the story's demanding visual aspects (eight-headed dragon, erupting volcano, flood, molten lava, earthslides and brush fires) are spectacularly lifelike. These purely cinematic achievements may be the lesser art to the philosophical stature of a simple, human story, but within the narrow horizon of technical physique, "The Three Treasures" is a fine accomplishment. *Tube.*

Die Junge Suenderin
(The Young Sinner)
(GERMAN)

Berlin, Dec. 20.

Europa release of Kurt Ulrich production. Stars Karin Baal, Rudolf Frack, Vera Tschechowa, Paul Hubschmid, Grethe Weiser. Directed by Rudolf Jugert. Screenplay, Maria von der Osten-Sacken, Peter Berneis; camera, Ekkehard Kyrath and Werner Lenz; music, Ernst Simon. At UFA Pavillon, Berlin. Running time, 92 MINS.

Eva Reck .... Karin Baal
Carola Ortmann .... Vera Tschechova
Werner Ortmann.......... Rudolf Prack
Alfred Schott .... Paul Hubschmid
Robert .... Rainer Brandt
Anna Reck, Eva's mother. .Grethe Weiser
Franz Reck, Eva's father.... Georg Lehn
Ludwig Reck .... Peter Thom
Iso Sensbach .... Lore Hartling
Erich Kolss .... Peter Vogel
Businessman .... Hans Richter

If this is one of the films with which Teutonic producers aim at combatting the menacing inroads of television, it looks like the new medium shapes as a winner. This film, produced by Kurt Ulrich, one of this country's top producers, lacks about everything that could hope to lure the big clientele. If it nevertheless emerges as an okay grosser, it will be because wide segments of the German populace still have no tele sets. Modestly budgeted black-and-white pic has only slim export potential.

Screenplay by Maria von der Oston-Sacken is astonishingly superficial. It centers around a teenage girl, daughter of a workman, whose attractive looks interest wealthy men. She has to go through a number of delicate situations until she lands, free of sin, at the altar. She gives up a student whom she loves for the sake of her girl friend who also loves the young man. Her hubby turns out to be a man who's much older than she is, but a millionaire.

More or less the really positive thing about this unimportant film is 19-year old Karin Baal in the title role. After some second-string acting years. Miss Baal has emerged as a convincing thespian.

Rudolf Prack and Paul Hubschmid (he worked in Hollywood under the name of Paul Christian) play the male roles in a routine manner. As often in German pix, smoother performances are given by supporting players. Grethe Weiser, Miss Baal's mother, is one of the standouts in the supporting cast.

This is a "social" film without any depth or imagination. Rudolf Jugert, some years back one of the more promising German directors, directed this but his abilities are hardly evident here. Technically, there's a certain plus in the lensing by vet cameraman Ekkehardt Kyrath. *Hans.*

Division Brandenburg
(GERMAN)

Berlin, Dec. 20.

Union release of Willy Zeyn productin. With Wolfgang Reichmann, Peter Neusser, Klaus Kindler, Hans E. Joeger. Directed by Harald Philip. Screenplay, Philip; camera, Heinz Hoelscher; music, Hans Martin Majewski; editor, Liesbeth Kleinert. At Albrechtshof, Berlin. Running time, 104 MINS.

Ungerland .... Wolfgang Reichmann
Pflug .... Peter Neusser
Czerny .... Klaus Kindler
Jonas .... Hans E. Jaeger
Kugelmann .... Helmut Oeser
Nina .... Gudrun Schmidt
Doerner .... Heinz Weiss
Popoff .... Bert Sotlar
Mitropoulos .... Stanislav Dedinek

The Germans have produced a number of good war pix this year, some being even outstanding. Harald Philip, creator of "Penalty Battalion," one of these, now comes along with another war film, "Brandenburg." Latter falls short of his first war effort, but Philip achieves war mood and hard-hitting realism. The first half is rather confusing, because of too many characters, but the second part is clearer and contains good suspense. The players turn in fine performances via Philip's directing abilities.

Division Brandenburg was an elite special assignment corps of the German Wehrmacht. It performed a number of daredevil deeds, mostly disguised in enemy uniforms or as partisans behind enemy lines. Film's narrator, in the beginning, tries to make it seem plausible that officers of Division Brandenburg were not heroes, but blind idealists. This in an attempt not to glorify these men. Also that they were misused by a criminal (Nazi) system.

Financially, this production stands for good returns in the

country, especially since large segments of German film patrons again have taken a fancy to war pix. Film also looks to have solid foreign chances.

This Union release depicts two operations of "Brandenburg." The first one, "Operation Brassiere," concerns a special command in Roumania to protect the oil coming into Germany. The second one, "Operation Barbarossa," takes place in Russia behind enemy lines where a group attempts to seize a bridge. None of this unit returns.

Cast is composed of lesser-known actors but nearly all turn in brilliant performances. The most effective performances are contributed by Peter Neusser, Wolfgang Reichmann, Hans E. Jaeger, Heinz Weiss and Helmut Oeser. Neusser and Reichmann dominate many scenes.

Technically, the film is not as clearly cut as Philip's "Battalion," but it is still fine. There are some impressive camera shots.

Ingeborg
(GERMAN)
Berlin, Dec. 20.

UFA release of Roxy (Luggi Waldleitner) production. Stars Ingrid Ernest, Rudof Vogel, Walter Giller. Directed by Wolfgang Liebeneiner. Screenplay, Curt Goetz and Willibald Eser, after the comedy, "Ingeborg," by Goetz (treatment by Karin Jacobsen); camera, Guenther Senftleben; music, Peter Thomas; editor, Lilian Sng. At Marmorhaus, Berlin. Running time, 88 MINS.
Ingeborg .... Ingrid Ernest
Herr Konjunktiv .... Rudolf Vogel
Aunt Ottilie .... Fita Benkhoff
Ottokar .... Walter Giller
Peter .... Dietmar Schoenherr

This is an adaptation of a comedy of the same name by the late Curt Goetz who, together with Willibald Eser, turned out the screenplay. The stage work was one of Goetz' most successful ones. Unfortunately, the film version falls short of the original. Nevertheless, this film stands good boxoffice chances domestically. But there's nothing special about this film to give it better than moderate possibilities in the foreign field.

Plot involves the old triangle of one woman and two men. The trouble is that she loves both men. One is her husband, while the other man is an idol of her youth. There are the usual complications stemming from jealousy, alleged unfaithfulness, etc.

The dialog is often remarkably frank and certainly nothing for the prudish. Yet it's still the best thing about this film which otherwise is a bit on the dull side. Wolfgang Liebeneiner's expert directorial hand is evident throughout but his direction could have been more brisk. Also the picture could have stood some more sophisticated and satirical touches. The whole thing has been handled too deliberately.

Title role is played by Ingrid Ernest. Considering that it's her first big screen role, her performance is satisfactory. The two men are Walter Giller, her husband, and Dietmar Schoenherr. Both give adequate performances. The most polished performances, however, are turned in by Fita Benkhoff, as Aunt Ottilie, and Rudolf Vogel, as the butler. They account for most of the comedy. Technically, this film is very good, especially for the editing and lensing.   *Hans.*

La Hermana Blanca
(The White Sister)
(MEXICAN)
Mexico City, Dec. 20.

Peliculas Nacionales release of F. Mier prduction. Stars Jorge Mistral, Yolanda Varela; features Prudencia Griffel, Antonio Carbajal, Augusto Benedico, Aurora Walker, Andrea Palma, Rodolfo Landa. Directed by Tito Davison. Screenplay, Tito Davison, inspired by "The White Sister." At Alameda Theatre, Mexico City. Running time, 105 MINS.

In this Mexican version of "The White Sister," director Tito Davison, also responsible for the adaptation, has transferred the locale to Mexico to give it typical Mexican atmosphere. A clergyman acted as technical advisor on the film, suggesting cuts of all controversial material that might be contrary to religious precepts.

Otherwise, the picture more or less follows original pattern, with Yolanda Varela doing a creditable job in the name role. Jorge Mistral, as a young soldier, reported dead in action and this causing his intended bride to enter a religious order, is also acceptable in a starring role.

With religious pictures always enjoying a good boxoffice south of the border, this one is already showing that it will make an excellent return on production investment.   *Emil.*

Der Teufel hat gut lachen
(The Devil May Well Laugh)
(SWISS)
Zurich, Dec. 17.

Praesens-Film Zurich release of Gloria-film Zurich (Max Dora) production. Directed by Kurt Frueh; screenplay, Frueh, Max Haufler; camera, Emil Berna; music, Walter Baumgartner; editor, Hans Heinrich Egger. At Apollo Theatre, Zurich, Dec. 15, '60. Running time, 107 MINS.
Barbarossa .... Max Haufler
Clown .... Ruedi Walter
Duerst .... Zarli Garigist
Elke .... Grit Boettcher
Juergen Luedecke .... Horst Janson
The Devil .... Walter Morath
Hotel Manager .... Theo Lingen
Erich Fuellgrabe .... Gustav Knuth
Helga Fuellgrabe .... Trude Herr
Phyllis Knightsbridge Littleton
                              Voli Geiler
Il Colosso .... Ettore Calla
Bernasconi .... Max Warner Lenz
(*In Swiss dialect and German*)

This new Swiss feature is a modern comedy-fantasy about three penniless bums who are tempted by the Devil via a well-filled wallet. Succumbing to the temptation at first and getting into all kinds of mischief and ticklish situations, they end up as poor as before, but just as happy and carefree.

As a new variation on the familiar money-is-the-root-of-all-evil theme, this hardly offers many new aspects on a fairly worn-out subject. It lacks the pace or originality to lift it above standard comedyfare, despite a remarkably witty opening sequence in bright comedy style which is not maintained. And episodic screenplay and lack of continuity are to blame.

Although this hardly looms as an export vehicle for overseas, it looks like a reasonably safe commercial bet in Switzerland and maybe Germany-Austria due to a cast of mostly familiar local and German names. Swiss comedians Max Haufler (who also co-scripted), Reudi Walter and Zarli Carigiet are amusing as the three hoboes, and German screen thesps Theo Lingen, Gustav Knuth and Trude Herr contribute importantly.
                              Mezo.

1961

Cry For Happy
(C'SCOPE—COLOR)

Contrived romantic comedy about four sailors and four geisha girls living platonically under the same Japanese roof. Disappointing.

Hollywood, Jan. 6.

Columbia Pictures release of William Goetz production. Stars Glenn Ford, Donald O'Connor, Miiko Taka, James Shigeta, Miyoshi Umeki; with Michi Kobi, Howard St. John, Joe Flynn, Chet Douglas, Tsuruko Kobayashi, Harriet E. MacGibbon, Robert Kino, Bob Okazaki, Harlan Warde. Directed by George Marshall. Screenplay, Irving Brecher, based on novel by George Campbell; camera (Eastman), Burnett Guffey; editor, Chester W. Schaeffer; art director, Walter Holscher; music, George Duning; sound, Lambert Day; assistant director, George Marshall Jr. Reviewed at Picwood Theatre, Jan. 6, '61. Running time, 110 MINS.

Andy Cyphers .... Glenn Ford
Murray Prince ....Donald O'Connor
Chiyoko .... Miiko Taka
Suzuki .... James Shigeta
Harue .... Miyoshi Umeki
Hanakichi .... Michi Kobi
Admiral Bennett ......Howard St. John
McIntosh .... Joe Flynn
Lank ....Chet Douglas
Koyuki ..... Tsuruko Kobayashi
Mrs. Bennett......Harriet E. MacGibbon
Endo .... Robert Kino
Izumi .... Bob Okazaki
Chaplain ....Harlan Warde
Miss Cameron ....Nancy Kovack
Lt. Glick ....Ted Knight
Lyman .... Bill Quinn
Keiko ....Chiyo Nakasone

An undercurrent of ethnic information, a suggestion of sex, some humor and one or two fairly dependable boxoffice names should make Columbia's "Cry for Happy" a mildly paying proposition. But, sad to relate, the information is sparse, the sex is artificial, the humor is uneven and largely low, exaggerated or obvious, and the stars have little to sink their thespic teeth into. Producer William Goetz's Nipponese-flavored follow-up to his successful "Sayonara" is a disappointment.

Irving Brecher's screenplay, which he assembled from the novel by George Campbell, meanders along rather aimlessly and deliberately to a conclusion telegraphically familiar to filmgoers (romantic alteration to altercation to altar). The story concerns four members of a naval photographic unit who, while recuperating in Japan from a Korean combat mission, quarter themselves in a Geisha establishment inhabited by a convenient quartet of G-girls. At first mistaking the G for an earlier letter in the alphabet, the boys soon learn that Geisha does not imply easy virtue. After some difficulty over the mistaken notion of their superiors that they are operating an orphanage, harmony once again prevails at the finish when two of the lads wed two of the girls, leaving the remaining unwed foursome in an aura of implied romantic bliss of a less conclusive nature.

Glenn Ford is quite adequate as the officer-in-charge of this cozy little group. Donald O'Connor comes off particularly well in the most romantic role, but one irresistibly wishes this talented performer had a chance to exercise his more premium song-and-danceman gifts.

James Shigeta and newcomer Chet Douglas are capable as the other two amorously-entangled chaps. The four girls are Miiko Taka, Miyoshi Umeki, Michi Kobi and Tsuruko Kobayashi, all pretty, all delicately charming, but all rather blandly predictable. Among those in support, Howard St. John, Joe Flynn, Harriet E. MacGibbon and Robert Kino are most valuable for comedic purposes.

Although very cautious, almost self-consciously naive, in its approach to matters sexual, the film is peppered with suggestive one-liners ("He's so full of it" . . . "We won the war and lost the piece") that conceivably could offend the very patrons it seeks to appease with its otherwise careful tone. It's a case of misguided values.

Director George Marshall has done a commendable enough job, making the most of the screenplay's more humorous situations and filling in the expositional gaps smoothly. The picture's most amusing sequence is a Japanese western takeoff. Burnett Guffey's camera work is competent, his best effort occurring early in the film during a brief naval action sequence. Walter Holscher's sets are colorful, notably the intricate, adjustable abode of the Geishas. Other journeyman credits are George Duning's melodic Oriental-toned score and Chester W. Schaeffer's neat editing. The title tune, by Duning and Stanley Styne, sung by Miss Umeki, is pleasant and has a contagious quality. It will help the picture's chances.

Tube.

Sword Of Sherwood Forest
(MEGASCOPE-COLOR)

Further adventures of Robin Hood, adequately told and handsomely produced. Traditionally solid moppet appeal should make it versatile addition to general bills.

Hollywood, Jan. 5.

Columbia Pictures release of Sidney Cole-Richard Greene production. Stars Greene, Peter Cushing; features Niall MacGinnis, Richard Pasco, Jack Gwillim, Dennis Lotis; with Sarah Branch, Nigel Green, Vanda Godsell, Edwin Richfield, Charles Lamb Directed by Terence Fisher. Screenplay, Alan Hackney; camera (Eastman), Ken Hodges; editor, Lee Doig; art director, John Stoll; music, Alun Hoddinott; sound, John Mitchell, Harry Tate; assistant director, Bob Porter. Reviewed at the studio, Jan. 5, '61. Running time, 80 MINS.

Robin Hood ....Richard Greene
The Sheriff .... Peter Cushing
Friar Tuck ....Niall MacGinnis
Earl of Newark ....Richard Pasco
Hubert Walter .... Jack Gwillim
Marian Fitzwalter ....Sarah Branch
Little John ....Nigel Green

Robin Hood, who ranks with America's Jesse James as the screen's most exploited and marketable outlaw, is worth shaking out of theatrical mothballs at least once a decade for each new crop of moppets to admire. "Sword of Sherwood Forest" accomplishes that task satisfactorily. The British Hammer-Yeoman Films co-production, a Columbia release, should be a versatile, companionable attraction wherever general, easygoing audiences assemble for traditional, uncomplicated entertainment.

Richard Greene, unquestionably the most experienced "Robin" of them all through his stet tv portrayal of the character, doubles as the gallant hero and co-producer (with Sidney Cole) in this enterprise. Although the lyrical charm and cultural strain of the anonymous original ballads have virtually vanished through commercial erosion, there's plenty of life left in the characters, whose conflicts are communicable to the modern mind.

In this workmanlike variation, Robin and his affable Hood-lums boldly rescue the ever-present, ever-captivating maid, Marian, and the good Hubert Walter (Archbishop of Canterbury) from the ambitious treachery of the Earl of Newark, one bad fellow, and that most dependably foul of villains, the Sheriff of Nottingham. It hardly matters that the Merry Men are not really very merry and that the business of taking-from-rich, giving-to-poor etc., is not much of an issue in this depiction.

Greene is a pleasant, if not very dashing, Robin. Although no longer the factor—he once was on a U. S. marquee, younger tv-viewing fans will accept him as the rightful Robin. Peter Cushing plays the sheriff the way the sheriff should be played—wickedly with a trace of hapless exasperation. Sarah Branch is a delectable Marian. Richard Pasco is particularly valuable as the evil Earl. Others involved prominently are Niall MacGinnis, Jack Gwillim, Nigel Green and Vanda Godsell. There is an awfully lethargic battle sequence, but Terence Fisher's direction is otherwise generally competent.

MegaScope camera work is alertly dispatched by Ken Hodges, and embellished by the lush Eastman Color interpretation of the Irish countryside passing for Sherwood Forest. A few quaint ballads by Stanley Black are a colorful addition to the film's score by Alun Hoddinott. John Stoll's artwork and Lee Doig's editing are capable assists to the eye-appealing production built around Alan Hackney's scenario, to which the obvious adjective doesn't quite apply.

Tube.

A Fever In The Blood

Workmanlike courtroom meller about politicos and judiciaries angling for high office. Lively scriptwork and appealing cast should give it some initial oomph, but lacks the substance or cinematic flair to be solid b.o. contender.

Hollywood, Dec. 22.

Warner Bros. release of Roy Huggins production. Stars Efrem Zimbalist Jr., Angie Dickinson, Jack Kelly, Don Ameche, Ray Danton, Herbert Marshall, Andra Martin; with Jesse White, Rhodes Reason, Robert Colbert, Carroll O'Connor, Parley Baer, Saundra Edwards, June Blair. Directed by Vincent Sherman. Screenplay, Huggins, Harry Kleiner, from the novel by William Pearson; camera, J. Peverell Marley; editor, William Ziegler; art director, Malcolm Bert; music, Ernest Gold; sound, Robert B. Lee; assistant director, Sergei Petschnikoff. Reviewed at the studio, Dec. 22, '60. Running time, 117 MINS.

Judge Hoffman......Efrem Zimbalist Jr.
Cathy Simon .... Angie Dickinson
Dan Callahan .... Jack Kelly
Sen. A. S. Simon............Don Ameche
Marker .... Ray Danton
Gov. Thornwall.........Herbert Marshall
Laura Mayberry .... Andra Martin
Mickey Beers .... Jesse White
Walter Thornwall .... Rhodes Reason
Thomas Morely .... Robert Colbert
Matt Keenan .... Carroll O'Connor
Bosworth .... Parley Baer
Lucy Callahan .... Saundra Edwards
Paula Thornwall .... June Blair

Some of Warner Bros. appealing young contract players are given a chance to cut up theatrically in this complicated study of modern political corruption and judicial hanky-panky. Their presence in the cast and some fairly literate dialog by producer Roy Huggins and Harry Kleiner, who collaborated in adapting William Pearson's novel for the screen, may lend the moderately-budgeted film some mild boxoffice mileage, but "A Fever In The Blood" lacks the dimension or visual excitement to be a hot wicket contender.

The gubernatorial aspirations of three candidates, a judge, a district attorney and a senator, are placed in jeopardy in the course of a provocative murder trial in which all three become entangled. The senator (Don Ameche), whose wife is an ex-flame of the judge (Efrem Zimbalist Jr.), attempts to bribe the latter into a Federal Court judgeship. The judge, to prove his righteous resistance, almost costs the innocent defendant his life by withholding evidence of the bribe attempt. The D.A. (Jack Kelly) is an unscrupulous, bad type whose shady character eventually reveals itself to the voters. Ultimately the senator, whose reckless ambition and coronary weakness don't mix, expires of a heart attack, paving the way for a hasty, contrived ending in which Zimbalist is swept into office

Zimbalist, a calm, persuasive actor, makes a young, but sympathetic judge, and will further aid the film's prospects through the support of his tv ("77 Sunset Strip") following. The extent of such support, however, is a moot point in this instance since the picture is little more than an extension of a fairly good tv courtroom drama, and not the sort of fare likely to lure a great many people away from their home receivers.

The beauty of Miss Dickinson will be another plus commercial factor, although she has little to do but look alternately loyal and potentially disloyal. What she does, she does well, however. Kelly, ordinarily a likeable actor, has a rather bad time of it as the d.a., a distasteful role. Ameche, who returns to the screen after a 12-year absence, gets in a few good licks as the doomed senator. Ray Danton plays the defense attorney with force and sincerity, but Herbert Marshall seems a bit lost and bewildered at the absurdity of his character, rather unconcerned uncle of the defendant and overly zealous supporter of Zimbalist-for-guv. Andra Martin is sympathetic and pretty as the girl friend of the man on trial. Good support is generated among Jesse White, Rhodes Reason, Robert Colbert, Carroll O'Connor, Parley Baer, Saundra Edwards and June Blair.

Considering the complexity of the plot, director Vincent Sherman has done a decent job of keeping it all as taut and playable as possible for producer Huggins, who has since ankled his WB post for the top tv niche at 20th-Fox. J. Peverell Marley's busy, tight camera work is similar in technique to tv, with its preponderance of close-ups, a style further reflected in William Ziegler's abrupt editing. Music by Ernest Gold has a tendency to crop up in passages where it doesn't seem fully appropriate to the mood. Malcolm Bert's art direction has an authentically modest stamp.

Tube.

Wilhelm Tell
(SWISS; COLOR)

Zurich, Jan. 3.

Beretta-Film A.G. Zurich release of Urs-Film Buochs (Josef Kaelin) production. Directed by Michel Dickoff. Screenplay, Dickoff; Music, Hans Haug; camera (color), Hans Schneeberger. At Corso Theatre, Zurich. Running time, 98 MINS.

Wilhelm Tell	Robert Freitag
Walter Fuerst	Alfred Schlageter
Melchtal	Hannes Schmidhauser
Stauffacher	Leopold Biberti
Stauffacherin	Maria Becker
Attinghausen	Heinz Woester
Rudenz	Georges Weiss
Berta von Bruneck	Birke Bruck
Gessler	Wolfgang Rottsieper
Baumgarten	Zarli Carigiet
Baumgartnerin	Hellen Hesse
Jester	Peter Schmitz
Reding	Raimund Bucher
Priest	Alfred Lohner
Abder Halden	Max Knapp
Ruodi	Paul Buehlmann
Hedwig Tell	Trudy Moser
Wolfenschiessen	Karl Pistorius
Armgard	Verena Furrer
Landenberg	Arnold Putz

Although the story of Swiss national hero William ("Wilhelm" to the natives) Tell has been treated cinematically 12 times, dating from as far back as 1898, it's never been done on the homeground, i.e., in Switzerland and with Swiss talent. This latest Swiss entry obviously hoped to remedy that. With a $580,000 budget, this is the costliest Swiss pic ever.

Mentioning that the pic was shot chiefly on location at historical sites in Central Switzerland in widescreen and with Eastman color by vet cameraman Hans Schneeberger is pointing out its chief assets. Because apart from the sometimes breathtakingly beautiful photography, there's not much left to boast about here. Originally planned as big-style with possibly international importance, this is sadly lacking in almost every department except the lensing.

Direction by a young Swiss newcomer, Michel Dickoff, who also scripted (based partly on the Friedrich Schiller classical German drama, partly on historical research in old chronicles and period records), is clumsy and uninspired. There's a definite lack of continuity, an insistence on negligible details while some key sequences are hastily reeled off, plus several blatant cases of miscasting. Such spectacular highlights as the Sermon of Freedom on the Ruetli, the shooting of the apple by Tell off his own boy's head, the boat-ride on Lake of Lucerne during a tempest and the tyrant Gessler's assassination by Tell are neither uplifting nor even very professionally handled.

In the lead is Swiss thesp Robert Freitag as William Tell who is physically adequate, but barely gets by histrionically. Gesseler is fairly convincing, but little more, as played by Wolfgangf Rottsieper. All others in the unusually large cast (including many extras) never get a real chance.

Music by Hans Haug is obtrusive at times and has a tendency to over-dramatize. Considering that Swiss circles cried havoc when the late Errol Flynn teed off his own William Tell project (which was abandoned mid-way for lack of funds), fearing that a Hollywood-style treatment might hurt sensitivities here, this failure to turn out an "authentic" and artistically gratifying Tell film is all the more deplorable. *Mezo.*

Das Spukschloss Im Spessart

(The Haunted Castle)
(GERMAN-SONGS-COLOR)

Berlin, Jan. 3.

Contantin release of Georg Witt production. Stars Liselotte Pulver. With Heinz Baumann, Hubert von Meyerinck, Ernst Waldow, Hanne Wieder, Curt Bois, Elso Wagner, Herbert Huebner. Directed by Kurt Hoffmann. Screenplay, Guenther Neumann and Heinz Pauck; camera (color), Guenther Anders; music, Friedrich Hollaender; editor, Hilwa van Boro. At Gloria Palast, Berlin. Running time, 98 MINS.

Charlotte	Liselotte Pulver
Martin	Heinz Baumann
Von Teckel	Hubert von Meyerinck
Yvonne	Elsa Wagner
Uncle Ernst August	Ernst Waldow
Prince	Hans Clarin
Hugo	Curt Bois
Max	Georg Thomalla
Katrin	Hanne Wieder
Hartog	Herbert Huebner
Sophie	Veronika Fitz
Toni	Paul Esser
Jockel	Hans Richter

Taking into consideration that Germans have not been very successful when it comes to light musical fare, this production is a remarkable achievement. It has its flaws but again, for German standards, this is an outstanding film. Kurt Hoffmann, often known as this country's most gifted filmmaker, succeeds in producing a competent musical. As he did in his most successful pic, "Aren't We Wonderful," this has depth with a light touch.

"Castle" is an admittedly strange but amusing mixture of music, comedy, slapstick, satire and cabaret. Some critics may accuse him of putting too much into this film (the effects, to be sure, are sometimes confusing), but all will undoubtedly admit that he is never tasteless. This film is the more remarkable for its charm and imagination, something that German pix often lack. There are brilliant gags and, in particular, highly effective optical tricks.

Technically, this is perhaps the best film the Germans have turned out in years. With a fine cast headed by popular Swiss-born Liselotte Pulver, word-of-mouth and good reviews, this film should be a b.o. smash in this country. Foreign prospects are, however, dubious. A great part of the amusement relies on the dialog. There are an abundance of typically German word-plays plus political and social-critical gags in "Castle." It would be difficult to translate these into foreign lingo.

Hoffmann is helped by such creative talents as Guenter Neumann and Heinz Pauck, who delivered the fresh texts, and old-timer Friedrich Hollaender who wrote the catchy score. Credit goes also to the top-notch camerawork by Guenther Anders. Liselotte Pulver sparkles in the leading role as castle countess. Memorable performances are turned in by Hubert von Meyelnck, Ernst Waldow, Curt Bois, Hans Richter, Georg Thomalla and Hanne Wieder, of whom the last, a sexy ghostess, is a real standout.

Story is of minor importance. It takes place in an old castle which is heavily in debt and in which suddenly an ensemble of ghosts appear. Latter help Miss Pulver, the beautiful countess, to solve her financial dilemma and also help her get a man. Much fun is poked at current political personalities and topics. Occasionally, the fun is far-fetched but one cannot deny that the whole thing is witty and intelligent. Another film of which Kurt Hoffmann can well be proud. *Hans.*

El Correo Del Norte

(Northern Courier)
(MEXICAN)

Mexico City, Jan. 3.

Peliculas Nacionales release of Universal, S.A. production. Stars Luis Aguilar, Rosa de Castilla, Fernando Fernandez; features Rosario Galvez, Salvador Flores, Sergio Murriata, Fernando Oses. Directed by Zacarias Gomez Urquiza. Screenplay, Luis Manrique. At Orfeon Theatre, Mexico City. Running time, 70 MINS.

A so-so effort which has the Mexican Revolution as a background and a masked superman character who fights the "good fight" against "bad Mexicans" of the era. This turns out to be sort of a glorified yarn about a caped hero who virtually wins the revolt single-handed. Story line is weak, more for the kiddie trade and nabe house audiences.

Only aside on this is that the Film Bureau has been making a big thing of the defamatory presentation of aspects of Mexican history. This one is replete with scenes that can't be called favorable, yet the picture has been passed by censors. *Emil.*

Go Naked In The World

Another examination of the good works of the modern call-girl. Some snappy melodrama plus able-bodied Gina Lo'lobrigida, hard-working cast and compelling title should make it fair b.o. candidate, but public disenchantment with overworked theme may be factor.

Metro release of Aaron Rosenberg production. Stars Gina Lollobrigida, Anthony Franciosa, Ernest Borgnine; with Luana Patten, Will Kuluva, Philip Ober, John Kellogg, Nancy R. Pollock, Tracey Roberts, Yale Wexler, Rodney Bell, John Gilaudet, Chet Stratton, Maggie Pierce, Bill Smith. Directed by Ranald MacDougall. Screenplay, MacDougall, based on novel by Tom T. Chamales; camera (Metrocolor), Milton Krasner; editor, John McSweeney Jr.; art directors, George W. Davis, Edward Carfagno; music, Adolph Deutsch; assistant director, Williom Shanks. Reviewed at the studio, Jan. 11, '61. Running time, 103 MINS.

Giulietta Cameron	Gina Lollobrigida
Nick Stratton	Anthony Franciosa
Pete Stratton	Ernest Borgnine
Yvonne Stratton	Luana Patten
Argus D'avolos	Will Kuluva
Jack Kebner	Philip Ober
Cobby	John Kellogg
Mary Stratton	Nancy R. Pollock
Diana	Tracey Roberts
Charles Stacy	Yale Wexler
Parkson	Rodney Bell
Rupert	John Gallaudet
Jack	Chet Stratton
Girl	Maggie Pierce
Boy	Bill Smith

Hollywood, Jan. 12.

The screen's obsession with ladies of ill-repute is prolonged in "Go Naked In The World," a plodding account of a call-girl's romantic disaster. There are some magnetic personalities in the cast, some flashy melodramatic scenes and a provocative title, and these should make the Metro release a fair boxoffice contender. But the Aaron Rosenberg production may have to weather a mounting wave of opposition to the astonishing quantity of recent pictures glorifying the shady lady of the night. This certainly has been a banner year for the call-girl, who has supplanted the pink-cheeked girl-next-door as filmdom's reigning heroine.

It is Gina Lollobrigida's turn to play the trollop with the heart of gold and bank account to match. She shares an ill-fated love affair with Anthony Franciosa, rebellious son of a dominant, self-made construction tycoon (Ernest Borgnine).

Ranald MacDougall's screenplay (from the novel by the late Tom T. Chamales) adds a novel twist and a new dimension to the now classic story of hooked and hooker in that father, like son, has shared intimate relations with the girl. When the lad, incredibly naive, finally becomes aware that his woman has racked up considerable sexual mileage, he flies into a rage, but soon repents and makes up with her, only to have her end it all by leaping from an Acapulco balcony in a supreme, unselfish gesture to save him from a life of matrimonial embarrassment and suspicion. Most of the basic issues, however, remain unresolved at the climax.

The character Miss Lollobrigida is playing lacks depth. She brings to it her exciting sensual beauty, and this is a most desirable addition, but the character never comes into focus. Franciosa gives an earnest, virile performance, but there are moments when his unrelenting intensity begins to grow disconcerting and uncomfortable for the spectator. Emoting honors belong to Ernest Borgnine, who creates a

hearty and colorful, if essentially disagreeable character as the gregarious dad. His pathetic wife is played capably by Nancy R. Pollock, his daughter attractively by Luana Patten. Others who make impressions are Will Kuluva, Philip Ober and John Kellogg.

MacDougall's screenplay has some sharp, sizzling, up-to-date verbal exchanges, particularly in the superior early portion of the film. But the yarn thins out and grows so interminable in the latter stages that the spectator finds himself losing interest in the conflict.

As director, MacDougall has embellished his writing effort with some inventive, arrestingly dramatic touches, but in his zeal to pack a pictorial wallop he is also guilty of failing to curb a tendency toward some overly-theatrical histrionics. Emotional flareups occur so frequently that one beings to wince in anticipation of violence. The screenplay is loaded with declarations of love, but the characters have a peculiar way of exhibiting it with a shove, a slap or an out-and-out slug. The lack of communication is frightening.

There is some exceptionally intimate camera work by Milton Krasne and attractive artwork by George W. Davis and Edward Carfagno. John McSweeney Jr.'s editing punctuates the action with good dramatic sense, and Adolph Deutsch's score backs it up meaningfully without intruding. Helen Rose's elegant costumes are flattering to Miss Lollobrigida, who is easily flattered by clothes. *Tube.*

One Hundred And One Dalmatians
(COLOR)

Bright, wholesome family attraction, especially for the kiddies. Not quite in a league with Disney's most memorable full-length cartoon efforts of bygone years, but good enough to score favorably at the b.o.

Hollywood, Jan. 13.

Buena Vista release of Walt Disney production. With voices of Rod Taylor, J. Pat O'Malley, Betty Lou Gerson, Martha Wentworth, Ben Wright, Cate Bauer, Dave Frankham, Fred Worlock, Lisa Davis, Tom Conway, Tudor Owen, George Pelling, Ramsay Hill, Sylvia Marriott, Queenie Leonard, Marjorie Bennett, Mickey Maga, Barbara Beaird, Mimi Gibson, Sandra Abbott, Thurl Ravenscroft, Bill Lee, Max Smith, Bob Sevens, Paul Wexler, Mary Wickes, Barbara Luddy, Lisa Daniels, Helene Stanley, Don Barclay, Dal McKennon, Jeanne Bruns. Directed by Wolfgang Reitherman, Hamilton S. Luske, Clyde Geronimi. Screenplay, Bill Peet, based on book by Dodie Smith; art direction and production design, Ken Anderson; editors, Donald Halliday, Roy M. Brewer Jr.; music, George Bruns; sound, Robert O. Cook: directing animators, Milt Kahl, Marc Davis, Ollie Johnston, Frank Thomas, John Lounsbery, Eric Larson; layout, Basil Davidovich, McLaren Stewart, Vance Gerry, Joe Hale, Dale Barnhart, Ray Aragon, Dick Ung, Homer Jonas, Al Zinnen, Sammy June Lanham, Victor Haboush: layout styling, Don Griffith, Erni Nordli, Collin Campbell; color styling (Technicolor), Walt Peregoy; character styling, Peet, Tom Oreb; character animation, Hal King, Cliff Nordberg, Eric Cleworth, Art Stevens, Hal Ambro, Bill Keil, Dick Lucas, Les Clark, Blaine Gibson, John Sibley, Julius Svendsen, Ted Berman, Don Lusk, Amby Paliwoda. Reviewed at the studio, Jan. 13, '61. Running time, **79 MINS.**

Children are certain to get a big boot out of "One Hundred and One Dalmations," which marks Walt Disney's return to the sort of product for which probably he is most renowned, the full-length cartoon feature. While not as indelibly enchanting or inspired as some of the studio's most unforgettable animated endeavors of years ago, it is nonetheless a painstaking creative effort and certainly a valuable and welcome addition to the current theatrical scene. Wholesome family fare of this nature, especially that bearing the "Disney Presents" label, is certain to have considerable impact in the contemporary market.

There are some adults for whom 101—count 'em—101 dalmations is about 101 dalmations too many, but even the most hardened, dogmatic pooch-detester would likely be amused by several passages in this story. Bill Peet's screen yarn, based on the book by Dodie Smith, is set in London and concerned with the efforts of Blighty's four-legged population to rescue 99 dognapped pups from the clutches of one Cruella De Ville, a chic up-to-date personification of the classic witch. The concerted effort is successful thanks to a canine sleuthing network ("Twilight Bark") that makes Scotland Yard an amateur outfit by comparison. Cruella winds up in the doghouse, and for the pups, every last syrupy-sweet one of them, it's arf-arf ever after.

Film purportedly is the $4,000,000 end product of three years of work by some 300 artists under the astute generalship of art director-production designer Ken Anderson and directors Wolfgang Reitherman, Hamilton S. Luske and Clyde Geronimi. It benefits from the vocal versatility of a huge roster of "voice" talents (see above credits). Background artwork by Al Dempster, Ralph Hulett, Anthony Rizzo and Bill Layne is exceptional, as is the subtly-shaded color styling of Walt Peregoy. Animation, both character and effects, are effective. Editing by Donald Halliday and Roy M. Brewer Jr. is sound and smooth, music by George Bruns (as orchestrated by Franklyn Marks) a fitting complement to the action. There are three songs by Mel Leven, best and most prominent of which is "Cruella De Ville," which sounds infectious enough on first hearing to attain considerable popularity beyond the realm of the film. *Tube.*

I Like Mike
(Surprise Party)
(ISRAELI)

Tel Aviv, Jan. 10.

GEVA-IFA production. Written and directed by Peter Frye. Screenplay, Edna Shavit, based on play by Aharon Meged; music and song, Arie Levanon: camera, Leon Nissim; editor, Nelly Bogor. Reviewed at "HOD" cinema, Tel Aviv. Running time, **110 MINS.**

Yaffa Arieli .... Batya Lancet
Benjamin Arieli .... Gidon Singer
Yaakov .... Zeev Berlinsky
Tamar Arieli .... Ilana Rovina
Tzip Arieli .... Meira Shor
Mike .... Seymour Gitin
Mikha .... Chaim Topol
Nili .... Geula Nuni
12 characters .... Albert Chizkiyahu

To avoid political connotations this pic, called in Israel "I Like Mike," will be marketed abroad as "Surprise Party." Story is as plain as apple pie, represented by Mike, twentyish son of a Jewish millionaire from Texas. He comes to visit Israel, because his father likes only money while Mike mostly admires horses, preferably Jewish horses. He is taken from Lydda airport to Tel-Aviv by a cab-driver, who is as instructive as any of his New York colleagues. To escape the attention of a nudging girl, Mike leaves the hotel and accepts driver's invitation to stay with his family.

This family consists of a dominating sister, her husband and two daughters. The mother decides to enhance Israeli-American friendship, by catching the young millionaire for her Tamar. But Tamar already has a boy friend, Mikha, a captain in the Israeli army. And Mike is in love with a girl-sergeant in the same army, but he's seen her only on a magazine cover.

Mother uses every known device to promote the betrothal. While the party is going on, Mike is in the Negev desert, guest of the Bedouin tribe of Suleiman. They eat rice, drink black coffee, sing and dance. Of course, Mike meets Nili, the mag cover girl. Mike marries Nili, Mikha weds Tamar and they all stay in a kibbutz where people are all equal, even sons of millionaires.

Story is based on a play which a few years ago was quite a success at the Habima Theatre. Peter Frye, a former New Yorker, is a much respected legit director in Israel, and all the actors participating in the film are theatrical people. This makes the pic more theatrical than good cinema.

The pic gets out of hand in an unnecessarily long, symbolic sequence. And the story never quite recovers.

Acting is good, partly because of expert directing. Batya Lancet, starring as the mother, makes the best of a two-dimensional part. Albert Chizkiyahu makes a tour de force, playing in a dozen different character roles, depicting various Israeli "types." Mike is played believably by a young American, Seymour Gitin, who in private life happens to be a student of theology at the Hebrew University in Jerusalem. *Lapid.*

The Singer Not The Song
(BRITISH—COLOR)

Good performances by John Mills and Dirk Bogarde keep together a loosely-knit but holding drama with religious theme plus trimmings; Catholic problems may make exploitation tricky.

London, Jan. 10.

Rank release of a Roy Baker Production. Stars Dirk Bogarde, John Mills, Mylene Demongeot. Directed by Roy Baker. Screenplay by Nigel Balchin from Audry Erskine Lindrop's novel; camera, Otto Heller; editor, Roger Cherrill; music, Philip Green. At Odeon, Leicester Square, London. Running time, **132 MINS.**

Anacleto .... Dirk Bogarde
Father Keogh .... John Mills
Locha .... Mylene Demongeot
Old Uncle .... Laurence Naismith
Police Captain .... John Bentley
Father Gomez .... Leslie French
Presidente .... Eric Pohlmann
Vito .... Nyall Florenz
De Cortinez .... Roger Delgado
Phil Brown .... Philip Gilbert
Chela .... Selma Vaz Dias
Pablo .... Laurence Payne
Dona Marian .... Jacqueline Evans
Pepe .... Lee Montague
Josefa .... Serafina Di Leo

As a dialectic discussion hinged on the Roman Catholic religion, this can only be accepted as flippant. As a romantic drama, it must be agreed that is it glossy, but over-contrived. Yet, somehow, the thesping of the two principals, John Mills and Dirk Bogarde, prevents the screen version of Audrey Erskine Lindrop's novel from falling between these two spacious schools. In fact, the overall effect is compelling. Roy Baker, who produced and directed, has done so with obvious affection for the yarn.

But because he has failed to use enough local actors the result is often like a British or a Hollywood film shot in uneasy circumstances. In this instance, the film was shot in Spain, which is probably so near to Mexico in spirit and terrain that it makes little difference.

In Britain the stellar value is big, but elsewhere it may be dubious. However, the Roman Catholic angle may make this one a difficult selling proposition in many markets, and obviously in the U. S.

John Mills is a dedicated Roman Catholic priest who comes to the tiny community of Quantana to replace an older priest who is worn out from battling with the murderous, marauding gang of bandits led by Anacleto (Dirk Bogarde). To intimidate the newcomer, Bogarde's gang sets out on a series of murders by the alphabetical method. Thus, when somebody whose name begins with "E" is bumped off, it clearly unsettles the nerves of anybody whose monicker begins with "F."

Priest Mills, resolutely deciding to break Bogarde's power, shows a struggle in which the two gain mutual respect, though their religious opinions clash badly. The unscrupulous, cynical bandit realizes, though in a manner not explained very convincingly, that a local belle (Mylene Demongeot) is in love with the priest and he with her. He uses this knowledge to create a situation that puts the priest in a moral dilemma. The film boils up to gunplay and the death of the two adversaries.

Title is explained by the dying decision of the bandit, a confirmed atheist, that the Catholic religion is put over by good men rather than the religion creating good men, a point of view that is bound to rouse controversy.

Mills and Bogarde have some excellent acting encounters, though their accents, like those of many others, strike odd notes in the Mexican atmosphere. Mills gives an honest, intelligent performance while the latter is cool, cynical and impressive in a role that might well have been hammed up badly. Mylene Demongeot, usually regarded as a sexpot in films, essays a rather more serious role, but seems strangely out of place. John Bentley, as a police officer and Laurence Naismith, cast as an alcoholic middleaged henchman of Bogarde are among those who give excellent support to the main trio of actors.

Otto Heller's lensing takes full advantage of some colorful backgrounds, Roger Cherrill's editing is okay and Philip Green's music fits happily and unobtrusively into the film. "The Singer Not The Song" has its faults, but mainly it provides smooth, intelligent entertainment. *Rich.*

Touchez Pas Aux Blondes
(Lay Off Blondes)
(FRENCH)

Paris, Jan. 10.

CFF release of Robert De Nesle production. Stars Philippe Clay, Dario Moreno; features, Maria Riquelme, Jany Clair, Anne Carrere. Directed by Maurice Cloche. Screenplay, Cloche from the book by Carter Brown; camera, Jacques Mercanton; editor, Fanchette Mazin. At Biarritz.. Paris. Running time, 95 MINS.

Al .... Philippe Clay
Alexis .... Dario Moreno
Pickpocket .... Jany Clair
Secretary .... Maria Riquelme
Drusilla .... Anne Carrere

Exteriors of this detective tale were done in Los Angeles and it is billed as the Yank-type actioner that does away with subtitles. Resultant quickie lacks Yank bounce, tautness and progression. Tale of call girl murders seems strictly for grind or sexploitation.

A cadaverous ladies' man detective, played by gaunt, little sympathetic singer Philippe Clay, does his share of scotch drinking, loving and killing as he unravels the murders of some call girls by a procurer who hides behind a funeral parlor front.

Direction is static and unimaginative, French interiors hardly match the real Yank exteriors in feeling. There are some undraped lookers, plenty of corpses and a telegraphed unmasking of the murderer. Technical credits are below par. *Mosk.*

Not Tonight Henry
(COLOR)

Old-fashioned "adults only" burlesque peep show translated to celluloid. Artistically zero, but should attract the bare-babe-oglers wherever theatres cater to such whims.

Hollywood, Dec. 30.

Foremost Films release of Ted Paramore-Bob Heiderich production. Stars Hank Henry; features Valkyra, Babe McDonnell, Daurine Dare, Marge Welling, Betty Blue, Joanne Berges, Genii Young, Little Jack Little; introduces Brandy Longi with Joni Day, Doris Gohlke, Margo Gahlke, Lisa Drake, LaLanne Francis, Shirley Sweet, Joyce Wagner, Gene Bianco, Doc Boyc-Smith, Don Mathers, Jim Elsner, Wally Johnson, Walt Hoffman, Milo Reckow, Myrin Griffin, Susan Woods. Directed by W. Merle Connell. Screenplay, Paramore, Heiderich; camera (Eastman), Connell; editor, William Brown; music, Hal Borne; assistant director, Mike Henry. Reviewed at Monica International Theatre, Dec. 30, '60. Running time, 70 MINS.

Theatres that cater to the most broad-minded of adult male clientele no doubt will generate a fairly brisk wicket response with this attraction. But a pip of a peep show "Not Tonight Henry" isn't. It's simply unabashed sex ex machina (motion picture machina, that is), burlesque artificially translated to celluloid for voyeuring Toms, Dicks and Harrys.

Vegas vaudeville's Hank Henry and a bevy of bosom companions participate in this risque sexercise, which was written and produced by Ted Paramore and Bob Heiderich, directed and lensed (at an approximate average aspect ration of 38-24-36 to 1) by W. Merle Connell. The premise is that a matriarchal society has developed, with the male of the species relegated to the role of mere procreator. By way of demonstrating the point, Henry assumes the identities of various heroic figures such as Napoleon and Samson, only to be dominated in each case by a woman.

The "plot" is a poor, generally humorless excuse for regular displays of chest cleavage and bare derrierres, mostly in skinny-dipped Eastman color. Bulk of the activity is of the no-dialog variety, accompanied by a tedious narration stuffed with puns and plays-on-words. *Tube.*

The Private Lives Of Adam & Eve
(COLOR)

Revised version of the Garden of Eden farce-fantasy "condemned" last year by Legion of Decency. Generally harmless, as adjusted, but also ragged and tasteless. Cast and controversy may stir up some initial b.o. reaction.

Hollywood, Jan. 11.

Universal release of Red Doff production. Stars Mickey Rooney, Mamie Van Doren, Fay Spain, Marty Milner, Cecil Kellaway, Tuesday Weld, Paul Anka; with Ziva Rodann, Theona Bryant, June Wilkinson, Phillipa Fallon, Barbara Walden, Toni Covington, Nancy Root, Donna Lynne, Sharon Wiley, Miki Kato, Andrea Smith, Buni Bacon, Stella Garcia. Directed by Albert Zugsmith, Rooney. Screenplay, Robert Hill; camera (Spectacolor), Phil Lathrop; editor, Eddie Broussard; art directors, Alexander Golitzen, Richard Riedel; music, Van Alexander; sound, Walden O. Watson, Frank Wilkinson; assistant directors, Phil Bowles, Carl Beringer. Reviewed at Hawaii Theatre, Jan. 11, '61. Running time, 86 MINS.

Nick Lewis (Devil)..... Mickey Rooney
Evie Simms (Eve)......Mamie Van Doren
Lil Lewis (Lilith)............. Fay Spain
Hal Sanders .... Mel Torme
Ad Simms (Adam)......... Marty Milner
Doc Bayles .... Cecil Kellaway
Vangie Harper .... Tuesday Weld
Pinkie Parker .... Paul Anka
Passiona .... Ziva Rodann
The Devil's Familiars .. Theona Bryant, June Wilkinson, Phillipa Fallon, Barbara Walden, Toni Covington.
Satan's Sinners .. Nancy Root, Donna Lynne, Sharon Wiley, Miki Kato, Andrea Smith, Buni Bacon, Stella Garcia

As presumably adjusted, "The Private Lives Of Adam & Eve" is a tasteless, if harmless farce, bulk of which is devoted to a dream sequence burlesque of Genesis. In view of the sacred nature of the topic spoofed, and the trouble same subject once got Mae West into the original choice of vehicle was ill-advised, a dubious decision borne out by the reaction of the Catholic Legion of Decency about a year ago, just as the Albert Zugsmith production was hitting the market (Legion branded the picture with a C-Condemned-rating, terming it "blasphemous and sacreligious," following which U and Zugsmith hastily recalled 150 prints for some judicious snipping and alterations).

In its revised state, the film, an obvious parody, is less morally objectionable than artistically chaotic. While not particularly advisable for attendance by impressionable children, it is difficult to see where anyone might draw any serious conclusions whatsoever from witnessing this rambling romp. Chances are that, partially as a result of the notoriety it has obtained and partially because of its risque nature and diversified collection of familiar marquee names, there will be a fairly brisk initial boxoffice reaction, largely from unaccompanied males at matinee time and teenage dating parties in the evening.

The disjointed yarn, for which Robert Hill draws screenplay credit, deals with a group of romantically-disturbed people bound for Reno via bus. They are stranded in a church by a flash flood, proceed to dream their little satire of the Garden of Eden, and awake supposedly cleansed and refreshed. Originally, there was some question whether the film properly conveyed the illusion that it was a dream fantasy. There is no mistaking that fact now. The audience is reminded of it so persistently that it begins to grow tedious and patronizing.

Mickey Rooney makes a puckish Satin, Mamie Van Doren a naive Eve. Marty Milner a Tarzanesque Adam, Fay Spain a torrid temptress. Mel Torme and Tuesday Weld have so little to do they are merely irrelevant. Paul Anka, as a hot-rodder, is guilty of overacting, but did utilize his more natural talents to pen the extremely commercial title ditty, which he sings enthusiastically. Cecil Kellaway is involved as the bus driver.

Zugsmith and Rooney collaborated on the direction. Red Doff is producer. Cinematically it is a passable job, largely through Phil Lathrop's lensing (about a third of which is in Spectacolor), imaginative artwork by Alexander Golitzen and Richard Riedel, and music by Van Alexander. Editor Eddie Broussard certainly had his work cut out for him. *Tube.*

Blueprint For Robbery

Serviceable crime - suspense drama based on Brink's robbery. Good programming entry, especially where action is emphasized.

Hollywood, Jan. 13.

Paramount release of Bryan Foy production. With Jay Barney, J. Pat O'Malley, Robert Gist, Romo Vincent, Marion Ross, Henry Corden, Tom Duggan, Sherwood Price, Robert Carricart, Robert Wilke, Johnny Indrisano, Paul Salata, Joe Conley. Directed by Jerry Hopper. Screenplay, Irwin Winehouse, A. Sanford Wolf; camera, Loyal Griggs; editor, Terry Morse; art directors, Hal Pereira, Al Roelofs; music, Van Cleave; sound, Hugo and Charles Grenzbach; assistant director, C. C. Coleman Jr. Reviewed at the studio, Jan. 9, '61. Running time, 88 MINS.

Red Mack .... Jay Barney
Pop Kane .... J. Pat O'Malley
Chips McGann .... Robert Gist
Fatso Bonelli .... Romo Vincent
Young Woman .... Marion Ross
Preacher Doc .... Henry Corden
Dist. Attorney .... Tom Duggan
James Livingston
Gus Romay .... Sherwood Price
Gyp Grogan .... Robert Carricart
Capt. Swanson .... Robert Wilke

Paramount has a serviceable product in "Blueprint For Robbery," a crime drama that roughly parallels the renowned Brink's caper. Although it misses on several key counts, it is a type of film fare that is perennially popular with male patrons, yet has not turned up in abundance of late. As such, the modestly budgeted Bryan Foy production should be a respectable programming commodity in the current market, of particular value wherever action-suspense tastes are catered to.

There is a businesslike tone about the entire production, and that is good. Frills, nuances and high-toned philosophical clutter do not delight enthusiasts of this sort of picture. Aficionados of scientific crime prefer the objective approach, so that they can draw their own conclusions. The Irwin Winehouse-A. Sanford Wolf screenplay describes mechanically the planning of the big heist, the preparatory stages (best part of the film), the $2,700,000 stickup itself and the deterioration of the plot through greed, impatience and inability to resist temptation for petty pilfering on the part of members of the gang. The thoroughly familiar "moral" of the story: stealing is bad, but stooling is worse.

The screenplay itself, while straightforward, is the weakest link in the production. It is a bit obvious and telegraphic in the latter stages, and tends to be repetitious and somewhat inconsistent. The best moments are the ones without dialog, notably one shatteringly suspenseful sequence in which two of the thugs indulge in a bit of inside reconnaissance, carefully avoiding a night watchman and a maze of alarms and electric eyes to obtain the necessary impressions for a chore of key-making. Director Jerry Hopper, with the aid of a sharp editing job by Terry Morse, has manufactured a snappy scene here of some 15-minutes duration.

There are no star names in the cast. The acting is generally capable, with J. Pat O'Malley attracting the most attention in the key part of an old man persuaded to participate in the one final caper prior to embarking for the "old country" (Ireland), his last fervent wish. The wish materializes when his disciple, Jay Barney, bitter over inner-gang treachery, turns stoolie on condition the old man be set free, wrecking the plot just before the statute of limitations is to expire. Barney does an able job. Others who make vivid impressions are Romo Vincent, Henry Corden, Sherwood Price, Robert Gist and Marion Ross. Tom Duggan plays the d.a.

Suitably dingy sets by Hal Pereira and Al Roelofs, brisk, alert lenswork by Loyal Griggs and an unobtrusively tension-generating score by Van Cleave are plus factors. *Tube.*

Circle Of Deception
(BRITISH)

Mildly intriguing, but somewhat outdated spy drama of the last war. Sound performances by Bradford Dillman and Harry Andrews in yarn that never fully convinces.

London, Jan. 10.

20th-Fox production (Tom Monohan) and release. Stars Bradford Dillman, Suzy Parker, Harry Andrews. Directed by Jack Lee. Screenplay by Nigel Balchin & Robert Musel from story by Alec Waugh; camera, Gordon Dines; editor, Gordon Pilkington. At Rialto, London. Running time, 100 MINS.

Lucy Bowen .... Suzy Parker
Paul Raine .... Bradford Dillman
Captain Rawson .... Harry Andrews
Major Spence .... Paul Rogers
Major Taylor .... John Welsh
Captain Stein .... Robert Stephens
Frank Bowen .... A. J. Brown
Henry Crow .... Martin Boddey
Ayres .... Charles Lloyd Pack
Abelson .... Ronald Allen
Cure .... Jacques Cey
Captain Ormerod .... John Dearth
Carter .... Norman Coburn
Small Boy .... Hennie Scott
German Colonel..........Richard Marner
Lohmann .... Andre Charise
His assistant .... Jean Briant
Liebert .... Richard Shaw
Ballard .... Duncan Lamont

German Officer............George Mikell

The fact that while "Circle Of Deception" is neatly enough acted, written and directed, it seems only a mildly intriguing entry probably stems from the fact that patrons may have had their fill of spy yarns. However, it measures up to a fair booking and the recent rise in stature of Bradford Dillman should help. Nigel Balchin and Robert Musel's screenplay is based on a story by Alec Waugh. Told largely in flashback, it is an adventure in occupied Normandy before the invasion.

British intelligence decides to drop an agent in Normandy to feed the enemy false information. Captain Rawson (Harry Andrews), boss of Intelligence, decides the scheme will be more convincing if an agent is sent who does not know he is a catspaw, a man who will keep mum until the breaking point and then reveal the information which he does not know to be false. Rawson's assistant, Lucy Bowen (Suzy Parker), points out that this could lead to the man's death but she is reminded that the sacrifice of one man's life is worth it if thousands are saved.

The girl is instructed to become friendly with a young Canadian officer whose courage is suspect. It's felt that he mightly certainly break down at the critical moment. She falls in love with him but duty being duty is unable to warn him of the mission's real object. He is captured, tortured, gives away the information and is then rescued after a raid on the prison by the local Maquis. But sickened by the thought that he has been a coward and betrayed his country, the young man is spending the postwar months drinking himself stupid in Tangiers, his mind full of self-bitterness. The girl finds him and convinces him that so far from being a coward he behaved like a hero, "the one man on his own against both sides."

The chase before the officer is captured and the storming of the prison has some tenseness, but the torture scenes are unnecessarily brutal and revolting.

Jack Lee's direction is straightforward and Gordon Dines' lensing sound. A weakness of the film is that it is revealed at the beginning that the hero gets through his ordeal safely.

Bradford Dillman gives a likeable performance as the double-crossed officer and the differences between his amiable personality before the job, his toughness while in captivity and his bitterness at the end of the film are subtle. Harry Andrews is also firstclass as the ruthless Intelligence chief, to whom war is an unpleasant job but one which must be carried out whatever the cost. Less successful is Suzy Parker as the girl. Miss Parker is a stunning looking young woman, but she has yet to prove that she has the range necessary to carry the entire distaff weight of a film. Maybe it is being thrust into uniform that cramps her style, for she is certainly more convincing in her boudoir scenes with Dillman.

Among the lesser roles Paul Rogers, Duncan Lamont and, notably, Robert Stephens, as a suave, cunning, supercilious German officer, stand out. Production is smooth and special effects are fine. "Deception" is a curious sort of film. It never quite comes to full life or excitement, yet the ingredients are on tap throughout.

Rich.

Division Brandenburg
(GERMAN)

Berlin, Jan. 10.

Union release of Willy Zeyn Production. With Wolfgang Reichmann, Peter Neusser, Klaus Kindler, Hans E. Jaeger. Directed by Harald Philip. Screenplay, Harald Philip; camera, Heinz Hoelscher; music, Hans-Martin Majewski; editor, Liesbeth Kleinert. At Albrechtshof, Berlin. Running time, **104 MINS.**

Ungerland .... Wolfgang Reichmann
Pflug .... Peter Neusser
Czerny .... Klaus Kindler
Jonas .... Hans E. Jaeger
Kugelmann .... Helmut Oeser
Nina .... Gudrun Schfidt
Doerner .... Heinz Weiss
Popoff .... Bert Sotlar
Mitropoulos .... Stanislav Ledinek

The Germans have produced a number of good war pix this year. "The Bridge" and "Penalty Battalion 999" even might be called outstanding. Harald Philip, who has "Penalty" to his credit, now comes along with this war film. However, it falls short of his previous effort, but, again, Philip achieves a convincing war mood and hard-hitting realism. Film's first half is rather confusing because of too many characters, but the latter part is clearer, with a good portion of suspense. The cast turns in fine performances because of Philip's direction.

"Division Brandenburg" was an elite, special group of the German Wehrmacht. It was under the direction of Admiral Canaris and performed numerous dare-devil deeds mostly in the disguise of enemy uniforms or as partisans behind enemy lines. Film's narrator tries to make it seem plausible that the officers of Division Brandenburg were not heroes but blind idealists. This in an attempt not to glorify these men. Also, they were misused by a criminal (Nazi) system. The pic has the sympathies belonging involuntarily to the heroes on the screen.

This stands to get good returns in this country, especially since large segments of German cinema patrons have taken a fancy to war pix. Pic also seems to have solid foreign chances, especially if the title can be shortened.

This Union release depicts two operations of the "Brandenburg," the first concerning a special command in Roumania to protect oil coming to Germany; the second taking place in Russia behind enemy lines where a group attempts to seize a bridge.

Cast is composed of lesser-known actors but nearly all turn in brilliant performances. The most effective performances are contributed by Peter Neusser, Wolfgang Reichmann, Hans E. Jaeger, Heinz Weiss and Helmut Oeser. Both Neusser and Reichmann should be worth watching.

Technically, film is fine. There are also some impressive camera shots.

Hans.

La Pyramide Humaine
(The Human Pyramid)
(FRENCH-COLOR)

Paris, Jan. 10.

Films Pleiade release and production. Written and directed by Jean Rouch using amateur actors around an improvised theme. Camera (Eastmancolor), Louis Miaille, Rouch; editor, Marie-Josephe Yoyotte. Previewed in Paris. Running time, **90 MINS.**

Unusual experimental-improvisation film, made by anthropologist-filmmaker Jean Rouch, has a timely theme which could make this of interest for foreign art situations or definitely for university and specialized showing. Film concerns an integrated school in Abidjan in the Ivory Coast of Africa where French whites and local Negroes go to school together and how they decide to try to fraternize socially and the troubles, frictions, friendships, understandings and decisions that come out of it.

Rouch took a group and told them they would be enacting certain roles in this film. Then near the end of the film there is a talk on what each character, now him or herself, got from it and a planned dramatic bit to see how they would now react with what was garnered from their experience. Film thus does get somewhat strained and overlong. But the body of the film abounds with fine observation as blacks and whites display their respective attitudes, prejudices and lack of them, and learn how to live together.

Blown up from 16m Kodachrome it is acceptable in color. Commentary adroitly blends with the simple imagery as love brings on problems and they all begin to act and react on and to each other to gain a definite experience from it. As the commentator says it does not make much difference whether it is well directed, acted etc but that these people learned what racism was and how to deal with it. Commercially in U.S. this could be a hard film due to its break with regular film aspects and its many discussion periods. But it is a worthwhile film that could make its way if personally and carefully handled and sold. Rouch shows a decided filmic flair as well as human insight.

Mosk.

An Heiligen Wassern
(Sacred Waters)
(SWISS-GERMAN—COLOR)

Zurich, Jan. 10.

Stamm-Film Zurich release of Cine Custodia A.G. Zurich (Henryk Kaestlin) production. Stars Hanspoerg Felmy; features Cordula Trantow, Hanns Lothar, Gisela von Collande, Karl John, Gustav Knuth, Margit Rainer, Leopold Biberti. Directed by Alfred Weidenmann. Screenplay, Herbert Reinecker, based on J. C. Heer novel; camera (color), Otto Heller; music, Hans Martin Majewski. At Capitol Theatre, Zurich. Running time, **98 MINS.**

Roman Blatter .... Hansjoerg Felmy
Binia Waldisch .... Cordula Trantow
Thoeni Grieg .... Hanns Lothar
Seppi Blatter .... Karl John
Fraenzi Blatter......Gisela von Collande
Presi .... Gustav Knuth
Cresenz Waldisch .... Margrit Rainer
Garde .... Leopold Biberti
Vroni Blatter .... Uta Kohlhoff
Chaplain Johannes......Walter Ladegast
Village Priest .... Fritz Schulz
Lemmy .... John Bentley

This Swiss-German co-production, based on a popular novel by Swiss author J. C. Heer, was mass-released in some 100 German-Austrian-Swiss situations as a holiday offering. Though falling somewhat short artistically, it looms as a saleable product with good b.o. prospects in German-language territories. The novel's wide popularity, solid performances and workmanlike technical credits, notably the topnotch Eastman color photography by British cameraman Otto Heller, are important assets.

Story is set in the Swiss mountain canton (state) of Valais where avalanches threaten to interrupt the all-important water supply every winter. Lots are drawn to single out a man bound to repair the destroyed water-channels high up in the mountains, thereby risking his life. When one of the villagers is persuaded by the town's president, to whom he is indebted, to volunteer for the job and falls to his death, his son emigrates to India. He returns three years later as an engineer, trying to initiate more modern methods on building of channels. These are violently fought by the conservative townsfolk. Progress wins out, however, and so does the young engineer's romance with the president's daughter, jeopardized at first by a rival suitor's intrigues.

German director Alfred Weidenmann has done a commendable job holding together the story's many threads, aided by Herbert Reinecker's skillful, though at times uninspired, script. Performances by a predominantly German cast are generally satisfactory, with Hansjoerg Felmy, as the victim's son, Gisela von Collande, as his mother, and Gustav Knuth, as the president, especially standout. Music by Hans Martin Majewski is too intruding at times. Exteriors were shot in the Valais last fall and interiors at Germany's Munich-Baldham studios.

Mezo.

Der Brave Soldat Schwejk
(The Good Soldier Schweik)
(GERMAN)

Berlin, Jan. 10.

Gloria release of CCC-Film (Arthur Brauner) production. Stars Heinz Ruehmann; features Ernst Stankowski, Ursula Borsodi, Senta Berger. Directed by Axel von Ambesser. Screenplay, Hans Jacoby, after novel of same name by Jaroslav Hasek. Camera, Richard Angst; music, Bernhard Eichhorn; editor, Angelica Appel. At Marmorhaus, Berlin. Running time, **96 MINS.**

Schwejk .... Heinz Rushmann
Lieutenant Lukas.... Ernst Stanknowski
Kathi .... Ursula Borsodi
Grell .... Senta Berger
Baroness .... Erika von Thellmann
Woditschka .... Franz Muxeneder
Sergeant Flanderka .... Hugo Gottschlich

"Schwejk" is one of the better German films but hardly can be termed a big film. Commercially, it shapes as a solid grosser in this country, and foreign b.o. prospects may surpass the German average. The anti-military story, adapted from the world-famous novel of the same name by Jaroslav Hasek, is of wide appeal and will be understood by all. Heinz Ruehmann may not be an ideal Schwejk but his portrayal of the title role is not disappointing. He delivers a heart-warming performance and his acting gives the film a nice lift.

Although "Schwejk" has its merits, one feels that the theme could have been exploited to better advantage. Director Axel von Ambesser avoids corny slapstick but his direction is overly deliberate and lacks temperament. Also the script could have been more imaginative. As a result, the slow-moving pic cannot escape boredom at times.

There are various witty scenes, situations and amusing gags. Supporting cast is well chosen. Ernst Stankowski contributes a dashing lieutenant, Erika von Thellmann eacts an amusing baroness while cute Senta Berger shows promising talents as one of the girls.

The widely known story is set in Bohemia. At that time, it still belonged to the Austrian-Hungarian monarchy. Schwejk, a little dog dealer, gets into the treadmill of the military and the first World War, but masters all the situations his own way because he is not quite sane. Whether he is mentally really narrow-minded or just pretends being it, doesn't quite come off. Films aim is to ridicule military obedience. Schwejk shows that total obedience has much in common with idiocy, but it ridicules every superiority.

Technically, film is okay. However, lensing is only conventional. *Hans.*

Goliath And The Dragon
(COLORSCOPE)

Ponderous costume spectacle from Italy for a market crowded with similar efforts. May stir mild initial reaction, but has no staying power. Lean b.o. prospects.

Hollywood, Jan. 18.
American International release of Achille Piazzi-Gianni Fuchs production. Stars Mark Forest, Broderick Crawford, Eleonora Ruffo; with Phillipe Hersent, Sandro Maretti, Federica Ranchi, Gaby Andre. Directed by Vittorio Cottafavi. Screenplay, Marco Piccolo, Archibald Zounds Jr.; camera (Colorscope), Mario Montuori; editor, Maurizio Lucidi; music, Les Bexter; sound, Franco Groppini. Reviewed at Pix Theatre, Jan. 18, '61. Running time, **90 MINS.**
Goliath .... Mark Forest
King Eurystheus ..... Broderick Crawford
Dejanara .... Eleonora Ruffo
Illus .... Phillipe Hersent
Ismene .... Sandro Maretti
Thea .... Federica Ranchi
Alcinoe .... Gaby Andre

Only the most avid fans of these blood-and-thunder escape epics out of Italy will derive satisfaction from "Goliath and the Dragon," which resembles, but is not to be confused with, "Sword and the Dragon," the recent import from the Soviet Union. To the average filmgoer, for all of its fire-breathing monsters and displays of muscular prowess, it will amount to little more than a supercolossal bore. Since the domestic market already is overstuffed with films of this nature, prospects are slim for the American International release, which isn't likely to generate anything more than a mild opening splash.

The yarn by Marco Piccolo and Archibald Zounds Jr. pits Goliath (Mark Forest) against a series of lethal devices unleashed by his ambitious adversary, King Eurystheus (Broderick Crawford). Among them: a three-headed, flame-spitting dragon dog, a giant killer bat, a king-sized bear, a bull elephant with an inclination to crush, a pitful of venomous snakes and a flesh-eating dragon of the more traditional one-headed variety. These monsters have one trait in common: they are extraordinarily ineffectual, particularly the dragon who resembles a mechanical rubber toy and sounds like a vacuum cleaner. Whenever Goliath isn't tangling with these bloody beasts, he is spouting or ripping up scenery, presumably to show off his beef stroganoff.

Forest is the right man for the prop-busting part. Crawford and Sandro Maretti are haplessly adequate as heavies in these circles. Eleonora Ruffo, Federica Ranchi and Gaby Andre are the decorative ladies-in-distress. Les Baxter's music helps, but photographic and color qualities are inconsistent. Film was directed by Vittorio Cottafavi for co-producers Achille Piazzi and Gianni Fuchs.

Gorgo
(COLOR)

Highly exploitable monster spectacle about a mother dragon infuriated by modern commercialism when her 65-foot high baby is put on display by a London circus. Misses on several counts, but b.o. prospects are favorable.

Hollywood, Jan. 18.
Metro release of Wilfred Eades production. With Bill Travers, William Sylvester, Vincent Winter, Christopher Rhodes, Joseph O'Conor, Bruce Seton, Martin Benson, Maurice Kauffman, Basil Dignam, Barry Keegan, Thomas Duggan, Howard Lang, Dervis Ward. Directed by Eugene Lourie. Screenplay, John Loring, Daniel Hyatt; camera (Technicolor), F. A. Young; special photographic effects, Tom Howard; editor, Eric Boyd-Perkins; art director, Elliott Scott; music, Angelo Lavagnino; assistant director, Douglas Hermes. Reviewed at the studio, Jan. 18, '61. Running time, 79 MINS.
Joe .... Bill Travers
Sam .... William Sylvester
Sean .... Vincent Winter
McCartin .... Christopher Rhodes
Prof. Hendricks .... Joseph O'Conor
Prof. Flaherty .... Bruce Seton
Dorkin .... Martin Benson
Radio Reporter ...... Maurice Kauffman
Admiral .... Basil Dignam
Mate .... Barry Keegan
1st Naval Officer .... Thomas Duggan
1st Colonel .... Howard Lang
Bosun .... Dervis Ward
Stunt Artists .... Connie Tilton, David Wilding, Michael Dillon Peter Brace, Peter Perkins

Its intrinsic exploitation factor should catapult "Gorgo" into the successful boxoffice sphere for King Bros. and Metro. The film will do particularly well in situations geared and most favorably inclined to properly ballyhoo its lavish spectacle and implied terror.

But, in spite of the painstaking physical artistry of the assembled cinema-technicians and the presence of an aquatic dragon that, in sheer physique and destructive capacity, makes a meek monkey out of "King Kong," this one fails in its attempt to add a new human dimension to the now-classic monster story of the theatrical screen, only medium truly equipped to meet its gaudy requirements.

"Gorgo," according to the conception by scenarists John Loring and Daniel Hyatt, is a 65-foot high heap of prehistoric violence urged out of the sea surrounding Ireland by volcanic activity. After roughing up the Irish coastline, it is captured by a pair of enterprising, but not very idealistic, boatmen and promptly placed in exhibition by a London circus. The sudden astonishing discovery: "Gorgo" is only a baby beast. Now along comes mama, a 250-foot tall mass of impregnable dragon-flesh, to rescue her precious infant from us mercenary homo sapiens who have no concern for the domestic tranquility of our animal friends. Mama proceeds to tear the traditional London scenery to shreds, rescues her "tot" and strides off peacefully to her ocean habitat.

Scenes of the destruction of London, while faintly monotonous through length and repetition, are rewardingly realistic, a credit to the superb special photographic effects work of Tom Howard and the accompanying contribution of art director Elliott Scott. The picture's attempt to squeeze in some sort of message about man's mercenary motivations at the expense of his appreciation of the finer things in life (such as respecting the mother love of a dragon for her offspring) is largely abortive. Another shortcoming of the film is its failure to exploit the potential element of genuine fear and horror. Mama and Gorgo are impressive monstrosities, but they lack the personality to frighten an audience. Bill Travers and William Sylvester are capable as the mercenary mariners. Young Vincent Winter, of "Little Kidnappers" fame, gives an expressive performance as the only person truly appreciative of what's ailing the monsters. Supporting work is passable.

Director Eugene Lourie has done an exceptional job of handling mob panic scenes and military retaliatory action. Eric Boyd-Perkins' editing is generally proficient, slipping only in the monotonous aspects of the London destruction passage. F. A. Young's Technicolor photography has, in some of the early scenes, an odd, smoky quality about it, but he has met with skill the pictorial demands of the picture, notably several underwater sequences. Angelo Lavagnino's score underlines the dramatic action with appropriate transitions in mood, tempo and tone.

Film, produced by Wilfred Eades under the aegis of Frank and Maurice King, was shot in England and Ireland. *Tube.*

Shunko
(ARGENTINE)

San Justo production and release. Directed by Murua. Stars Lautaro Maura. Story by Jorge W. Abalos, adapted by Augusto Roa Bastos; camera, Gicente Cosentino, Alberto Curchi; editor, Jose Serra. With Raul del Valle, Fanny Olivera, Orlando Sacha, Gabriela Schoo, Angel Greco (Shunko), Graciela Rueda, Martha Roldan. Running time, 76 MINS.

This has the wild, rocky, dust-laden background of one of Argentina's poorest, most backward provinces, and is authentic enough to be termed a documentary. One can feel the dust parch one's throat. Lautaro Murua has done a remarkable job of directing the children of that district in a poignant and stark portrayal of all the poverty, superstition and innate goodness of the Santiaguenos, known as among the hardest-working of Argentina.

Murua, who is starred, is a young school teacher from the city, who finds his school consists of a few battered desks under the burning sun, his pupils must be brought in against their parents' hostility. He has only the Comisario's (sheriff's) authority to help him. A love of nature binds him to his pupils and they come to welcome the learning he instils. Medical skill in emergencies wins over the parents, who cooperate to build him the little shed he yearned for. As in the case of Sarmiento, the great educator, he shares poverty and sorrow with all.

Murua directed with sincerity, though the dialog may be faulted for its over simplicity. As always his acting is forceful. To make this his first picture, he ignored the important role of Ecumenico in "El Guapo del 900," which won for Alfredo Alcon the highest local honors.

The director found the moppets, customarily difficult to handle in kind of animal gimmickry common to pictures about beasts.

"Nautical," the star of this film, is no horse of a different color. He doesn't talk. He doesn't get on his high horse and fly away a-la-Mobilgas. He doesn't change jockeys in midstream. He doesn't even give us too much of the old horse laugh. In short, he's a horse, which is a refreshing thing for a picture-star horse to be these days. "Horse With The Flying Tail" is a kind of equestrian Horatio Alger story, a horseblanket-to-Olympic silks variation on the old rags-to-riches theme. Springing from

humble beginnings, forced to endure a succession of odd jobs, and suffering his share of maltreatment in the process, "Nautical," a naturally gifted jumper, survives a career of frustrations to become a world champion hurdler, winning the King George V cup event in London. Pictorially most gratifying attribute of this handsome golden palomino is the peculiar mannerism of his tail which, unlike his competitors', has a way of swishing straight up whenever he clears a barrier. The taller the obstacle, the more erect the tail. Thus, the title.

An otherwise diverting featurette is marred only by an overpowering burst of patriotic zeal at the climax (complete with flag and the strains of "America, the Beautiful") and a tendency to make villains of the first magnitude out of horse-neglecting businessmen. Children may be caught up in the spirit of these exaggerations, but some adults will squirm.

Otherwise it is a fine little film, with a surprisingly emotional impact for a story about a steed. Its most rewarding touch is the use of actual newsreel footage (in sepia tones) showing Nautical winning the coveted cup.

Lansburgh's effort is first-rate. Helpful assists are Janet Lansburgh's screenplay, William Lava's music, Warren Adams' editing and Groucho-Marxman George Fenneman's narrating. *Tube.*

The Horse With The Flying Tail
(COLOR)

Champion jumping horse. Companionable Disney featurette in Technicolor.

Hollywood, Jan. 13.

Buena Vista release of Larry Lansburgh production. Narrated by George Fenneman and Dorian Williams. Directed by Lansburgh. Screenplay, Janet Lansburgh; editor, Warren Adams; music, William Lava. Reviewed at the studio, Jan. 13, '61. Running time, 47 MINS.

Fresh out of the Walt Disney stable, this not-so-short horse-and-jockey short should add plenty of commercial horsepower to whichever of the studio's product it is teamed up with (ticketed for initial pairing with "101 Dalmatians"). In illustrating the biography of a champion jumper, producer-director Larry Lansburgh and staff have exhibited plenty of theatrical horse sense, stressing characterization instead of horsing around with the that isolated district, easy to direct. In a country which loves its children inordinately, this picture should prosper at the boxoffice. Foreign distributors at the Mar del Plata Festival, at which it was the official entry and won the local critics' award for the best picture of 1960, are showing interest in handling it. *Nid.*

Chi No Hate Ni Ikuru Mono
(The Furious Sea)
(JAPAN)

Mar Del Plata, Jan. 17.

Toho Company Ltd. release of Morishige production. Directed by Seiji Jisamatsu. With Hisaya Morishige, Yoko Tsumasa, Mitsuko Kusabue and Jun Funato. Screenplay, Musuaki Saegusa and Seiji Hisamatsu from novel, "The Old Man of the Okhotsk Sea," by Yubio Togawa; camera, Seiichi Endo.

This semi-documentary, in color, depicts the hard life of fisher folk in the northern isles of Japan. It is produced with quality and color, photography values being excellent.

As cinema entertainment, it is overly long and slow in action. Cast gives fine performances, but the subject is very grim. Story is told in flashback by the oldster who guards year-round the huts on an ice-bound isle in the north, being alone for months against the hard cruelties of nature. He relives his life as a successful fisherman, with his beloved wife, three sons and his own fishing fleet. The furious sea takes each son in turn, and the wife dies from exposure.

Best sequence is the tortous journey by sleigh vainly trying to get the wife to an outpost where penicillin can save her. Story carries a message pleading for return to Japan of islands ceded to Russia after the last world war.

Carthage In Flames
(TECHNIRAMA-COLOR)

Fiery melodramatic account of the Roman-Carthaginian argument Circa 200 B.C. Production know-how wasted on absurd story. Lukewarm b.o. candidate, at best.

Hollywood, Jan. 12.

Columbia Picture release of Guido Luzzato production. With Anna Heywood, Jose Suarez, Pierre Brasseur, Daniel Gelin, Ilaria Occhini, Paolo Stoppa, Erno Crisa, Cesare Fantoni, Ivo Garrani, Mario Girotti, Edith Peter, Aldo Silvani, Gianrico Tedeschi. Directed by Carmine Gallone. Screenplay, Gallone, Ennio de Concini, Duccio Tessari, from book by Emilio Salgari (in _____ technicolor). Piero Portalupi; editor, Niccolo Lazzari; art director, Guido Fiorini; music, Mario Nascimbene; sound, Renato Cadueri; assistant director, Franco Cirino. Reviewed at the studio, Jan. 12, '61. Running time, 111 MINS.

While the artists and producers of this pyromaniacal Franco-Italian enterprise were usying themselves playing with matchsticks, their neglected melodrama was allowed to go up in emotional smoke. It is a shame to see so much production ingenuity spent on so imitative and undistinguished a story effort.

The romantic tale weaving within the spectacle of warfare between Rome and Carthage in 200 B.C. concerns a quartet of stubborn lovers: two warriors enamored of the same maiden, two maidens enamored of the same warrior. The superfluously-wooed pair survives and sails off to bliss while Carthage burns to a cinder and the unrequited lovers perish. The rather jumbled screenplay is the work of director Carmine Gallone with Ennio de Concini and Duccio Tessari, and springs from the book by Emilio Salgari.

The film contains a most impressive battle at sea aboard a pair of ancient warships whose skillful design and construction reflects credit on the men who guided the artwork for this Guido Luzzato production. Sets are the handiwork of Guido Fiorini; naval consultant was Salvatore Prinzi. Director Gallone has not had a great deal of success in the film's intimate passages, but his work shows a flair for action and spectacle.

Anne Heywood, as the long-suffering heroine, plays with sincerity.

Jose Suarez is dashing as the heroic warrior who won't give her a tumble. Best support comes from Daniel Gelin and Pierre Brasseur. Columbia Pictures is releasing, and may encounter opposition in touchy Dixie because of a prominent interracial romantic angle (white man-colored woman). *Tube.*

Three Blondes In His Life

Drab lower-case private-eye melodrama.

Hollywood, Jan. 18.

Cinema Associates release of George Moskov production. Cast: Jock Mahoney, Greta Thyssen; with Jesse White, Elaine Edwards, Anthony Dexter, Valerie Porter. (No character names). Directed by Leon Chooluck. Screenplay, Moskov; camera, Ernest Haller; editor, Maurice Wright; art director, Theobold Hotsopple. Reviewed at Pix Theatre, Jan. 18, '61. Running time, 86 MINS.

Akin, but in many ways inferior, to the crop of routine private-eye melodramas that have saturated television in recent years, "Three Blondes in His Life" is suitable for lower-berthing only and that in the most unsophisticated of theatrical situations. The Cinema Associates release, paired with "Goliath and the Dragon" in local opening playdates, is a generally plodding, frequently ludicrous account of the efforts of a traditional gumshoe to uncover the puzzling reasons behind the demise of a colleague.

Jock Mahoney stars as the sleuth in the minimal-budgeted Golden Film production, produced by George Moskov. He plays the part with the smirk-and-swagger technique typical of actors playing private eyes. There is, however, one vicious fistfight sequence in which he dips into his accomplished bag of stuntman tricks and rises above the norm. Jesse White agreeably plays an aide. Greta Thyssen, Elaine Edwards and Valerie Porter are attractive as the central femme threesome, objects of numerous profile closeups not necessarily of the facial variety. Film, among other things, is a sad commentary on contemporary marital relations —there isn't a faithful wife or husband in the bunch.

Leon Chooluck served as director of the enterprise, which was penned by producer Moskov. Level of cinematic craftsmanship is generally routine. *Tube.*

La Carcel de Cananea
(Cananea Prison)
(MEXICAN-COLOR-MEXISCOPE)

Mexico City, Jan. 17.

Peliculas Nacionales release of Cinematografica Continental production. Stars Pedro Armendariz, Agustin de Anda, Sonia Furio, Teresa Velazquez; features Andres Solor, Carlos Lopez Moctezuma, Felix Gonzales. Directed by Gilberto Gazcon. Screenplay, Fernandez Mendez Jr. and Aldo Monti; camera, Rosalio Solano. At Alameda Theatre, Mexico City. Running time, 90 MINS.

Pedro Armendariz plays the role of a federal policeman in this oater, who follows and captures the fugitive, played by the late Agustin de Anda. And as story develops a growing bond develops between the lawman and the criminal.

While the central theme is not original, this one is outstanding for Rosalio Solano's color camerawork, the acting of the stars and the development of a western with more care than usually accorded this type of film fare here.

The end result is a better than average picture which should do well not only here but in Spanish speaking areas. It also can be shown in American and foreign markets with even dubbed versions. Director Gazcon, with a sure hand, has happily thrown aside all sentimental references to Mexican folklore, and false delineation of his central characters. Armendariz and the young de Anda, with an able assist from veterans Carlos Lopez Moctezuma and Andres Soler, are well defined as men who live with and know how to use guns.

In the past the so-called action westerns in Mexico have been impeded by singing cowboys and cowgirls, with the action dragging in the dust. But in this one, a creditable realism is achieved and this may well be the beginning of the new era of quality in westerns in the republic.

Armendariz, as the lawman, turns in an excellent portrayal as the tough but good-hearted rural policeman. Young de Anda is also convincing as the youthful fugitive. Sonia Furio effectively plays a mute, doing her talking with her eyes. Color is a little off but not glaringly so, with the photography capturing some of the most impressive scenery in Mexico. *Emil.*

The Misfits

Clark Gable's last film. Hot b.o. a foregone conclusion. A stirring adventure pic on the surface, but psychological overtones are a bit murky.

Hollywood, Jan. 23.

United Artists release of Frank E. Taylor production. Stars Clark Gable, Marilyn Monroe, Montgomery Clift; features Thelma Ritter, Eli Wallach, James Barton. Directed by John Huston. Screenplay, Arthur Miller; camera, Russell Metty; editor, George Tomasini; art directors, Stephen Grimes, William Newberry; music, Alex North; sound, Philip Mitchell; second unit director, Tom Shaw; assistant director, Carl Beringer. Reviewed at Screen Directors Guild Theatre, Jan. 23, '61. Running time, 124 MINS.

Gay Langland	Clark Gable
Roslyn Taber	Marilyn Monroe
Perce Howland	Montgomery Clift
Isabelle Steers	Thelma Ritter
Guido	Eli Wallach
Old Man	James Barton
Church Lady	Estelle Winwood
Raymond Taber	Kevin McCarthy
Young Boy	Dennis Shaw
Charlie Steers	Philip Mitchell
Old Groom	Walter Ramage
Young Bride	Peggy Barton
Cowboy	J. Lewis Smith
Susan	Marietta Tree
Bartender	Bobby LaSalle
Man	Ryall Bowker
Ambulance Attendant	Ralph Roberts

At face value, "The Misfits" is a robust, high-voltage adventure drama, vibrating with explosively emotional histrionics, conceived and executed with a refreshing disdain for superficial technical and photographic slickness in favor of an uncommonly honest and direct cinematic approach. Those who accept it on this basis will enjoy it thoroughly.

Within this wholesome, compelling framework, however, lurks a complex mass of introspective conflicts, symbolic parallels and motivational contradictions the nuances of which may seriously confound general audiences and prove dramatically fallible for patrons unable to cope with author Arthur Miller's underlying philosophical meanings.

Where "The Misfits" fits most snugly is into the current boxoffice picture. Certain to have a profound influence over its commercial fate is the fact that the John Huston-Seven Arts production marks Clark Gable's farewell to the screen. And a most gratifying aspect of the film's nature is that it enabled Gable to tackle with his customary zeal and virility a character tailor-made for his special gifts as an actor.

Gable essays the role of a self-sufficient Nevada cowboy, a kind of last of the great rugged individualists—a noble misfit improvising an unnaturally natural existence on the free, non-conformist fringe of modern society. Into his life ambles a woman (Marilyn Monroe) possessed of an almost uncanny degree of humanitarian compassion, an instinctive appreciation of the natural order of things in their free, desirable state. Their relationship matures smoothly enough until Gable goes "mustanging," a ritual in which wild, "misfit" mustangs are rudely roped into captivity—a kind of survival of the (mis)fittest contest that underlines the drama with an ironic parallel.

Revolted by what she regards as cruel and mercenary, Miss Monroe, with the aid of yet another misfit, itinerant, disillusioned rodeo performer Montgomery Clift, strives to free the captive horses. Gable, since he is already perplexed over the less commendable aspects of his endeavor, reacts violently to this impassioned attack on his identity, desperately engaging and defeating the lead stallion of the pack in a breathtaking duel of physical endurance only to set his adversary free once he has subdued it. Having asserted his will and proved his point ("I don't want nobody makin' up my mind for me—that's all"), Gable rejoins the perceptive Miss Monroe on an eye-to-eye, heart-to-heart basis.

The film, produced by Frank E. Taylor, is somewhat uneven in pace and not entirely sound in dramatic structure. Character development is choppy in several instances. The one essayed by Thelma Ritter is essentially superfluous and, in fact, abruptly abandoned in the course of the story. Eli Wallach's character undergoes a severely sudden and faintly inconsistent transition. Even Miss Monroe's never comes fully into focus.

But these shortcomings are, for the most part, erased by the genuine excitement generated in the final third of the picture. The flashy, informative "mustanging" sequence is a gem of filmmaking from start to finish. And it is here that Gable really shines, meeting the brutal physical demands of the action with the masculine grace, ardor and dexterity of a young man.

Miss Monroe never quite fully submerges her own identity into the character, which in terms of fragile sensitivity yet basic naivete might easily be construed as a rough takeoff on her own personality or public image, especially since it was written by Miller. In spite of any such similarities that may be observed, Miss Monroe's familiar breathless, childlike mannerisms have a way of distracting, of drawing attention away from the inner conflicts and complexities of the character itself.

Clift is excellent. He displays a respect for and a thorough understanding of his character, conveys effectively its rather perverse wit, gamely meets its physical challenge. Wallach is another who comes through in a difficult role, that of a frail character who thrives on sympathy. Miss Ritter is her usual dependable, gently caustic self. James Barton does what comes naturally to him—the high-spirited old westerner routine, but he plays second fiddle in this instance to young Dennis Shaw, who enjoys a moment of memorable humor as a lad stunned by alcoholic intake. Balance of the supporting work is vigorous.

Some of Miller's scenario contains deeply penetrating insight into human behavior under emotional stress. But several of his lines and situations ring false, and it appears as if some of his expository material wound up on the cutting room floor for there are one or two instances when the people of his screenplay reveal knowledge not compiled in the natural course of events witnessed by the audience. Sequence of exposition is also questionable now and then. The artistic touch of director John Huston gives the United Artists release its special quality, an unusually lifelike character almost New-Waveish in mood and technique, stirring in impression. But he has failed to instill an even tempo and there are some unaccountably awkward passages such as one in which a carload of people stop everything apparently to eavesdrop on a phone booth conversation between Clift and his mother. It isn't natural.

An outstanding contribution is Alex North's score, melodically listenable, dramatically potent. George Tomasini's editing is exceptionally quick in mechanical transition. Lenswork of Russell Metty conveys that almost crude, this-is-life photographic quality, and art direction by Stephen Grimes and William Newberry is accurately modest in interior settings, interesting in exterior locale and characteristic. *Tube.*

The Executioners

Uninspired documentary study of Nazi atrocities.

Hollywood, Jan. 21

Continent Films production. Directed by Felix Podmanitzky. Written by Joe J. Heydecker and John Leeb. Commentary, Jay Willke. Reviewed at Hollywood Theatre, Jan. 21, '61. Running time, 77 MINS.

"The Executioners" is a needlessly repulsive reminder of the atrocities in Germany. Illustrated in documentary style through old newsreal clips, the study is pegged on the Nuremberg trial, each defendant's history traced rather roggedly through the rise and fall of Nazism. The film, produced by Continent Films and "presented" by Sig Shore and Joseph Harris, is of little value in the current market. Several television documentaries and dramas in the past few years have dealt more nobly and successfully with the subject.

Developed and written by Joe J. Heydecker and John Leeb, directed by Felix Podmanitzky, the film suffers most from incoherent construction. There is a tendency to ramble into irrelevant issues instead of sticking to the trial principals under central surveillance. The tone of the narrative is emotional, where it should, for best results, be absolutely objective, informative and penetrating.

There is a tendency to be carried away on tangents for their sheerly sensational pictorial aspects. Among these are a brutally lengthy and graphic examination of the victims of atrocities (piles of corpses etc., same clips shown in court to the accused at Nuremberg) and a long passage in which Eva Braun is observed indulging in gymnastics and aquatic recreation, latter in the nude as the audience can plainly see. *Tube.*

The Young One

Offbeat melodrama dealing with sex and bigotry in the deep South. Doesn't fit snugly into domestic b.o. scheme.

Hollywood, Jan. 21.

Valiant Films release of George Werker production. With Zachary Scott, Kay Meersman, Bernie Hamilton, Claudio Brook, Crehan Denton. Directed by Luis Bunuel. Screenplay, H. B. Addis, Bunuel, based on story by Peter Matthiesen; camera, Gabriel Figueroa; editor, Carlos Savage; art director, Jesus Bracho; sound, James Fields; music, Leon Dibb. Reviewed at Hollywood Theatre, Jan. 21, '61. Running time, 94 MINS.

Miller	Zachary Scott
Evie	Kay Meersman
Traver	Bernie Hamilton
Rev. Fleetwood	Claudio Brook
Jackson	Crehan Denton

"The Young One" is an odd, complicated and inconclusive attempt to interweave two sizzling contemporary themes—race prejudice in the deep South and an almost "Lolita"-like sex situation with Tennessee Williams overtones—into an engrossing and salable melodramatic fabric. The offbeat project, lensed in Mexico under the production aegis of George Werker, artistic jurisdiction of writer-director Luis Bunuel, is likely to be more popular abroad, where slice of life and modest dramatic environments are more warmly received, than domestically, where more penetrating social probes are required for art houses, more marquee might and slicker, clearer stories are the preferable ticket for general situations.

"Travelin' Man," a short story by Peter Matthiessen, is the origin for Bunuel's screenplay, which he set down in collaboration with H. B. Addis. The story takes place on an island wild game preserve off South Carolina occupied by an unsavory gamekeeper (Zachary Scott) and a 13 or 14-year-old orphan girl whose handyman-grandfather has just expired. Into this potentially explosive scene drifts a hip-talking Negro (Bernie Hamilton) falsely accused of rape and on the run. The girl is unwillingly compromised by the gamekeeper, the Negro engaged in a hypothetical debate in which he counters the white man's overuse of the term, "nigger," with his own inevitable recourse to salutations of the "white trash" variety. It's a very unrealistic, academic discussion, considering the locals and the nature of circumstances. Eventually a Reverend arrives from the mainland and helps resolve both the sexual and racial predicament.

Scott is convincingly unpleasant, Hamilton equally believable and sympathetic. Kay Meersman cuts a rather pitiful figure as the innocent, nymphet-like nature girl creature involved helplessly in the emotional turmoil. A detestable southern bigot is essayed neatly by Crehan Denton. The Reverend is played acceptably by Claudio Brook.

Bunuel has done an alert, perceptive job of directing, succeeding in getting the Carolina geographical flavor out of the Mexican location. He has incorporated the skilled assistance of lensman Gabriel Figueroa, art director Jesus Bracho and editor Carlos Savage. But these vigorous efforts are lamentably diluted by the unsatisfactory nature of the story they are attempting to translate into the cinematic drama form. *Tube.*

Tess Of The Storm Country

Sentimental drama based on the Gráce Miller White character last seen on the screen 29 years ago. Low-budget pic will appeal to easygoing audiences. B.o. prospects favorable in appropriate situations.

Hollywood, Jan. 27.

Twentieth-Fox release of Everett Chambers production. Stars Diane Baker, Lee Philips, Wallace Ford; with Jack Ging, Robert F. Simon, Archie Duncan, Bert

Remsen, Grandon Rhodes, Nancy Valentine. Directed by Paul Guilfoyle. Screenplay, Charles Lang, from novel by Grace Miller White and dramatization by Rupert Hughes; camera (De Luxe), James Wong Howe; editor, Eddy Dutko; art director, John Mansbridge; music, Paul Sawtell, Bert Shefter; sound, John Ke–n; assistant director, Willard Kirkham. Reviewed at API projection room, Jan. 27, '61. Running time, **83 MINS.**

Tess Mac Lean .... Diane Baker
Peter Graves .... Jack Ging
Eric Thorson .... Lee Philips
Hamish Mac Lean .... Archie Duncan
Teola Graves .... Nancy Valentine
Mike Foley .... Bert Remsen
Fred Thorson .... Wallace Ford
Mr. Foley .... Grandon Rhodes
Mr. Graves .... Robert F. Simon

Wherever heavy doses of uncomplicated screen sentiment are warmly welcomed, wherever easy-going audiences congregate, "Tess of the Storm Country" will be received enthusiastically. The 20th-Fox release is not much of an attraction for the busy, sophisticated urbanite, but it should have special impact in rural areas and lure the family trade in most situations. Considering its modest budget, the Everett Chambers production ought to rack up more than an ample number of playdates.

"Tess" is, of course, no new heroine to seasoned filmgoers. The role was essayed by Janet Gaynor in 1932, Mary Pickford prior to that. Charles Lang's scenario retains hardly even the plot skeleton of the Grace Miller White novel and Rupert Hughes dramatization upon which it is based." The revised tale involves "Tess" (Diane Baker) in a three-ply country feud among farmers, the owners and operators of an undesirable chemical plant contaminating the waters of the region and killing the stock, and a Mennonite family that created the ugly situation by selling land to the chemical company.

In the midst of this turmoil, two Romeo-Juliet affairs are conducted between farmerette Tess and Mennonite lad Jack Ging, chemical foreman Bert Remsen and Mennonite maiden Nancy Valentine.

Miss Baker plays the heroine with spirit. Ging rings pretty true in his part. Miss Valentine has the proper fragile, delicate quality. Remsen and Lee Philips are competent. There's a good deal of colorful character work, notably from Archie Duncan, Wallace Ford, Grandon Rhodes and Robert F. Simon. Director Paul Guilfoyle keeps most of it rolling along gently. That several of the scenes are rather stiff and artificial seems as much a fault of the dialog as the direction.

The scenery in and around Sonora, Calif., where the film was shot in becoming De Luxe Color, looks far more lovely through the James Wong Howe lens, which is equally flattering to the players. Capable assists to the production are fashioned by editor Eddy Dutko, art director John Mansbridge and musicmen Paul Sawtell and Bert Shefter. *Tube.*

The White Warrior
(DYALISCOPE—COLOR)

Ponderous, undistinguished adventure meller framed against war between Czarist Russia and its Caucasus tribes. Lean b.o. prospects.

Hollywood, Jan. 26.

Warner Bros. release. Stars Steve Reeves; with Georgia Moll, Renato Baldini, Gerard Herter, Nicola Popovic, Scilla Gabel. Directed by Richard Freda. Screenplay, Gino DeSanctis, Akos Tolney, from novel by Leo Tolstoy; camera (Technicolor), Mario Bava; art director, Alexander Milovic; music, Robert Nicolosi. Reviewed at the studio, Jan. 26, '61. Running time, **86 MINS.**

Ordinarily these Italo-originated costume epics can be forgiven their lean premises, exaggerated melodramatics and transparent characterizations thanks to the saving grace of some furious quasi-historical combat spectacle production savvy. No such virtue rescues "The White Warrior," latest and one of the poorest arrivals in a seemingly endless surge of brawny European spectacles currently clotting U.S. cine-market arteries and making motion picture ad pages resemble a nightmare out of Muscle Beach. The Warner Bros. release is a doubtful boxoffice candidate.

Even the work of the late, great Russian novelist, Leo Tolstoy, has not been spared the painful process of hasty adaptation, his novel being the basis of this undistinguished film. The stuffy Gino DeSanctis-Akos Tolnev scenario deals with a mid-19th century dispute between Czarist Russia and the Caucasus mountain tribes under his sovereign rule. The "White Warrior" is the young leader (Steve Reeves) who successfully defends his tribe against Czarist tyranny while surmounting all sorts of political and romantic intrigue within his own domain.

Reeves delivers the usual muscular performance, and looks dashingly blank in his white play-war outfit. Romantic interest is supplied by Georgia Moll and Scilla Gabel, villainous passion by Renato Baldini and Gerard Herter. Richard Freda's direction is sluggish. There is surprisingly little action for what basically is an adventure film.

Photography, artwork and music are, at best, routine. In short, there is little to recommend "White Warrior" to a public saturated with similar post-dubbed endeavors of livelier tempo and more diverting content. *Tube.*

The Mark
(BRITISH)

Overlong, occasionally plodding but honest yarn about a social problem, with likeable performances by Stuart Whitman, Rod Steiger, Maria Schell. Worthwhile booking for adults.

London, Jan. 24.

20th-Fox release of a Raymond Stross-Sidney Buchman production. Stars Maria Schnell, Stuart Whitman, Rod Steiger; features Brenda de Banzie, Donald Wolfit, Maurice Denham, Paul Rogers, Donald Houston. Directed by Guy Green. Screenplay by Sidney Buchman & Stanley Mann, from the novel of Richard Israel; camera, Douglas Slocombe; editor, Peter Taylor; music, Richard Bennett; At Carlton, London. Running time, **127 MINS.**

Ruth .... Maria Schell
Jim Fuller .... Stuart Whitman
Dr. McNally .... Rod Steiger
Mrs. Cartwright .... Brenda de Banzie
Austin .... Donald Houston
Clive .... Donald Wolfit
Milne .... Paul Rogers
Arnold .... Maurice Denham
Janie .... Amanda Black
Ellen .... Marie Devereux
Mr. Fuller .... Bill Foley
Mrs. Fuller .... Anne Monaghan
Patricia .... Josephine Frayne
Acker .... Eddie Bryne
Inez .... Bandana Das Gupta

Producer Raymond Stross in the past has made a number of pix which have tended to rough up sex in equal mixtures of naivete and sleaziness. With "The Mark," Stross still clings to an undeniable belief in sex as an ingredient that interests adult filmgoers. But, this time, he's set his sights higher. Result is an overlong, sometimes plodding, but honest, interesting glimpse at a sex dilemma, the circustances of which could be regrettably topical in the U.K. these days. It should prove a good booking for audiences not in sheer escapist mood, though it needs some careful exploitation.

Filmed at Ardmore Studios in Eire, "The Mark" has marshalled some sound all-round talent in writing, technicians and acting. Rod Steiger, Stuart Whitman and Maria Schell form a useful marquee pull for the U.S. There are one or two obvious flaws in the story line and some of the flashbacks are irritating. But quietly it makes engrossing impact.

Whitman is on parole after serving a three-year sentence for a crime committed when he was sick, during which time he has undergone therapy and has now been declared well. He continues the weekly therapy with a psychiatrist (Steiger) but is not fully convinced that he is now a fit man. It's some time before the audience discovers why he was jugged. Through talks with the psychiatrist and flashbacks to prison life, it's revealed that his childhood, with a weak father, dominating mother and as youngest of a family consisting of five sisters, has given him a complex leading to a sickness which makes him doubt whether he can have normal relationship with women. It also leads him to the cooler when he is found guilty of abducting a 10-year-old girl with a view to rape. Though not guilty of the actual crime, he is so horrified by the thought that it was in his mind that he puts up no defense, and prefers to be put away until he shakes off his instability.

He builds up a good career in a new town, gradually falls in love with a young widow and is all set to lick his problem when he is crucified by an unscrupulous local newspaperman. It leads to humiliation, a near breakdown and an eventual ending with the young widow which suggests a rosier future. This seems far-fetched, yet nobody knows enough of the complexities of crimes that make ruthless headlines. The screenplay is intelligently written, but there's one glaring problem, notably the fact that no newspaper, under law, could behave in such irresponsible fashion.

The early constant flashbacks are sometimes jerky and irritating. But throughout, the audience will feel compassion for the hero's dilemma, since the screenplay offers a real man and not just a cardboard figure sketched out to provide a few dramatic pegs. Stuart Whitman gives a rather downbeat but absorbing and likeable performance as the victim while Maria Schell as the young widow is a pleasant character. Whitman's scenes with the eccentric yet understanding psychiatrist, played with sharp incisive wit by Rod Steiger, are highlights.

Donald Wolfit as a shrewd employer, Brenda de Branzie and Maurice Denham, as the couple with whom he lodges; Donald Houston, as the reporter; Paul Rogers as the man he supplants in the firm and Amanda Black as Miss Schell's appealing moppet daughter are all very sound. Eddie Byrne has his moments as a prison-mate. Both Marie Devereux and Miss Schell have brief, sexy scenes with Whitman which make impact.

Director Guy Green (himself an ex-ace lenser) and Douglas Slocombe, on camera, have turned out some imaginative shots. They have taken full advantage of both urban and country locations, while the art work is first-class. The reason for Whitman going early off the rails is not convincingly explained, especially in view of his manly bearing. But he treads the delicate tightrope of self-confidence, personal doubts, optimism and acute depression admirably. "The Mark," without being a totally significant social document, shows how easily it is for a man to be trapped, despite himself, by his past. As such, it is good, commendable drama. *Rich.*

Like Father Like Son

First portion of a projected trilogy by Tom Laughlin. No release deal set yet. Has some artistic merit, but b.o. calibre doubtful.

* * *

Hollywood, Jan. 25.

Tom Laughlin production. With Laughlin, Taffy Paul, William Wellman Jr., Jim Stacey, Chris Robinson, Dennis O'Flaherty, Bob Colonna, Chuck Siebert, Roxanne Heard, Charles Heard, Dorothy Downey, Linda March, Ed Cook, John Burns, Jack Starrett. Directed and written by Laughlin; camera, James Crabe; editor, Don Henderson; music, Shelly Manne; sound, LeRoy Robbins; assistant director, Herb Willis. Reviewed at 20th-Fox projection room, Jan. 25, '61. Running time, **90 MINS.**

Christopher Wotan .... Tom Laughlin
Ginny Miller .... Taffy Paul
John .... William Wellman Jr.
Art .... Jim Stacey
Bobby .... Chris Robinson
Marty .... Dennis O'Flaherty
Harry .... Bob Colona
Lee .... Chuck Siebert
Joan Meyers .... Roxanne Heard
Mr. Wotan .... Charles Heard
Mrs. Wotan .... Dorothy Downey
Tury Martin .... Linda March
Coach Webster .... Ed Cook
Coach Ferguson .... John Burns
Coach Jennings .... Jack Starrett

"Like Father Like Son" is the first installment of what its producer-director-writer-star, Tom Laughlin, has ambitiously and rather optimistically designed as a trilogy ("We Are All Christ"). No releasing commitment has yet been firmed for completed Part I.

That Laughlin has potential in more than one of those departments cannot be denied. He brings an aggressively youthful perspective and some fresh ideas in film-making to Hollywood, which certainly can utilize and absorb, and ought to encourage, budding new creators with offbeat points-of-view. But Laughlin has not yet learned to harness or fully develop his native talent. This film has a lot that is right, but too much that is wrong and awkward. In its present condition, it simply isn't a very marketable commodity, either by art house or general audience tandards.

Laughlin's story, or at least the first third of his story, is about an essentially decent, extremely sensitive and high-strung high school athlete who just can't seem to avoid trouble. Victimized by a rather sadistic coach, in and out

of romantic and sexual difficulties, he more or less seems to be following in the uncertain footsteps of his liquor-beaten failure-father.

It is as director that Laughlin seems most gifted. He has succeeded in bringing to the film several artistic touches, notably linking romantic interludes shot from a distance. But he has also failed to instill an even tempo, particularly in his incorporation of two lengthy "humorous" passages (a speech class and a drunken spree sequence) that are sufficiently natural as separate entities, but almost totally irrelevant and painfully detrimental to the central story.

Major shortcomings of Loughlin's approach to his tale are his failure to instill dimension into any of the characters save his own and the unlifelike nature of his female characters. It is also not quite clear just what he is trying to say. Perhaps that clarity would come in Parts II and III but, after all, Parts I must speak for itself. As writer, he hasn't succeeded in properly focusing the issue. And several lines ("you dirty mother" and—to sacred church symbols—"you're a pig"), while emotionally honest, are in questionable taste.

As an actor (his own star, a strain and potential pitfall even for seasoned helmsmen), Laughlin has a keen sense of timing and a kind of rugged, natural youthful appeal. But he lacks great variety, resorting inevitably to three general expressions: the sulk, wild glee, and utter anguish. Those are widely divergent emotions, but Laughlin does not fill in the subtle gaps between too expressively. He also seems a trifle too old for the part of a high scholar.

Most of the players are competent, considering the undernourished roles they must contend with. Most vivid in the memory are John Burns and Taffy Paul. Level of cinematic craftsmanship is above average for a film of this nature. Great credit, particularly, is due cameraman James Crabe for his perceptive views. Music, largely rhythmic percussion and/or sentimental string passages, was composed and conducted by Shelly Manne. *Tube.*

His and Hers
(BRITISH)

Neat comedy idea that misfires and becomes flabbily confused; Terry-Thomas and the others work hard earning spasmodic yocks.

London, Jan. 24.
Eros Films release of a Sabre (Hal E. Chester) production. Stars Terry-Thomas, Janette Scott, Wilfrid Hyde. Nicole Maurey. Directed by Brian Desmond Hurst. Screenplay, Stanley Mann, Jan & Mark Lowell; camera, Ted Scaife; editor, Max Benedict; music, John Addison. At Studio One, London. Running time, **90** MINS.
Reggie Blake .... Terry-Thomas
Fran Blake .... Janette Scott
Charles Lunton ...... Wilfrid Hyde White
Simone Rolfe .... Nicole Maurey
Baby .... Billy Lambert
Hortense .... Joan Sims
Harold .... Kenneth Connor
Policeman .... Kenneth Williams
Felix McGregor .... Meier Tzelniker
TV Announcer .... Colin Gordon
Phoebe .... Joan Hickson
Poet .... Oliver Reed
Woman .... Barbara Hicks
Wanda .... Francesca Annis
Dora .... Dorinda Stevens
Stunning Wife .... Marie Devereux

"His and Hers" starts off with a reasonable idea for a comedy, but the writing and the direction is haphazard. Screwy situations and gags are popped in with little relevance and the players, with the sole exception of the urbane Wilfrid Hyde White, all seem to work so desperately hard that the result is a flabby hotch-podge. It earns spasmodic laughs, but, overall, can be recommended only to easygoing audiences.

Terry-Thomas plays an explorer-author whose success as writer of bestsellers has been largely built up by outrageous stunts dreamed up by his publisher. But there's nothing phoney about him being lost in the desert just before publication of his latest book, "I Conquered the Desert." He really is lost and has been living with a tribe of Bedouins before being rescued. During this period he "finds" his true self and has written a book on his adventure which his publisher turns down as trash. He has also adopted Bedouin dress and habits, and expects his wife to conform.

This could have been the springboard for a neat satirical comedy, but instead the pic floats uneasily into farce. The two fight so much that they decide, fatuously, to divide the house, and household duties in two—"His" and "Hers."

Though this provides the opportunity for yock situations, such as the husband involved with domestic duties and the wife settling down to write a book giving the lowdown on her husband called "I Was Conquered By a Middle-Aged Monster," it is about here that the comedy starts to flounder precariously.

A pretty French camera-girl becomes involved with the husband, there's talk of divorce and, in the end, the bachelor publisher has to patch things up, during which time he gets a taste for women.

Tighter writing, firmer direction could have helped this inconsequential comedy but as it is, this relies mainly on the artists. Terry-Thomas, who is an acquired taste as a comedian, carries most of the burden of "His and Hers," and is more consistently funny than in many of his previous pix. Janette Scott is prettily adequate as his wife while Nicole Maurey is decoratively effective as the other woman. Wilfrid Hyde White ambles through the film in his bland, polished way taking advantage of at least two scenes which help his contribution, without adding much to the film. One is when he finds himself alone with the glam French girl, in her apartment, and the other at a beatnik party.

Joan Hickson plays the inevitable Cockney daily help and artists like Kenneth Williams, Kenneth Connor, Joan Sims and Colin Gordon are roped in as "guest stars" for parts which could have been played perfectly well by talented feature players. Director Brian Desmond Hurst's excellent past record does not show evidence that farcical comedy is his natural bent, and this one does nothing to disprove the fact. Ted Scaife's photography is okay, but Max Benedict's editing is not taut enough to cope with a jumpy script. *Rich.*

Der Gauner Und Der Liebe Gott
(The Swindler and the Lord)
(GERMAN)

Berlin, Jan. 24.
Gloria release of Divina production. Stars Gert Froebe and Karlheinz Boehm. Directed by Axel van Ambesser. Screenplay, Curth Flatow and Stefan Gommermann; camera, Oskar Schnirch; music, Norbert Schultze. At Bavaria Film-Studio, Berlin. Running time, **92 MINS.**
Paul Wittkowski .... Gert Froebe
Father Steiner .... Karlheinz Boehm
Maria Holzmann .... Ellen Schwiers
Peter Holzmann ...... Manfred Kunst
Mrs. Nestle .... Lucie Englisch
Miss Mauer .... Barbara Gallauner
Baumberger .... Rudolf Vogel
Therese .... Toni Treutler
Helga .... Rosemarie Kirstein
Richard .... Gerd Seid
Sergeant Franke ...... Hans J. Diedrich
President of Court .... Walter Jacob

Axel von Ambesser is one of the few German directors who can achieve the subtle touch. This film also displays his charm and imagination the result is one of the most enjoyable German pix in years. As per its budget, it's not a big film, but this one has heart and enough sentiment. Film looks like a fine grosser in this country. It also has foreign possibilities. Screenplay by Curth Flatow contains some improbabilities but are of minor importance. This is a tastefully created film with many amusing situations and lovable characters.

The crook here is a safe cracker who has spent many years in prison. Again he is caught but this time he is innocent and sentenced to eight years in prison. He succeeds in escaping. In a church where he hides he steals a cassock and continues his flight in the disguise of the clergy. He seeks shelter in a house which happens to be a clergyman's house. Many of the later situations develop because one is a genuine and the other a pseudo clergyman. The former eventually finds out about the latter, but he is a man with a big heart and leads the crook back to the path of decency.

Gert Froebe, one of Germany's busy character players, is seen here in his first big starring role. He will garner many kudos from crix. Excellently led by director Ambesser, Froebe never overdoes his role and skillfully avoids slapstick. It's a top-notch portrayal which will further his career, Karlheinz Boehm enacts the genuine clergyman, his performance being very impressive. It is one of his best performances to date.

Supporting cast includes such fine players as Rudolf Vogel, as an unscrupulous businessman; Ellen Schwiers, as an attractive widow, and Lucie Englisch, cast as Boehm's maid.

All credits are fine but the biggest compliment should go to Axel von Ambesser who has here created one of the most enjoyable German comedies of the year. *Hans.*

La Proie Pour L'Ombre
(Prey For the Shadows)
(FRENCH)

Paris, Jan. 24.
Marceau-Cocinor production and release. Stars Annie Girardon, Christian Marquand, Daniel Gelin; features Michele Girardon. Written and directed by Alexandre Astruc. Dialog, Claude Brule. Astruc: Camera, Marcel Grignon; editor, Denise Casablanca. Previewed in Paris. Running time, **95 MINS.**
Anna .... Annie Girardon
Eric .... Daniel Gelin
Bruno .... Christian Marquand
Anita .... Michele Girardon

Alexandre Astruc was the first film critic to turn director long before the "new wave." But he passed into the film ranks with one medium-length pic and two feature film. The first two got awards at film fests but none did much box-office, and he languished till this sleek, sophisticated vehicle about a married woman hungering for independence was made.

Her husband allows her to run an art gallery but keeps strings on her, really believing a woman's place is in the home. A love affair with a lonely man frees her physically but he, too, can't seem to give her everything she needs. She loses both men as she gets complete control of her gallery and goes off to a supposedly unfulfilled life. Though dealing apparently with basic needs, the film is glossy and slowly unfolds the characters in well-modulated scenes of love, explanation and dramatic decisions.

Astruc's complete control manages to make the characters more than symbols. He has telling notations on love, sensuality, as well as marital and love relations. It looms mainly an arty theatre film on its almost austere unfoldment but has enough to make this a more profound distaff film that will appeal to adult audiences.

Annie Girardon is expressive and appealing as the woman striving to prove herself as a person as well as a love object while the men are forcibly depicted by Daniel Gelin, as the reserved husband, and Christian Marquand, as the romantic lover.

Technical credits are excellent. This smoothly-made pic is muted and sensitive, seeming to lack only a fillip of warmth to make the characters more alive. Some daring love episodes are done with taste and tact. This vehicle has some exploitation handles via these scenes. This is a novel entry with specialized treatment and handling a must. *Mosk.*

Candide
(FRENCH)

Paris, Jan. 24.
Pathe release of CLM-Pathe production. Stars Jean-Pierre Cassel, Pierre Brasseur; features Dahlia Lavi, Michel Simon, Nadia Gray, Louis De Funes, Jean Tissier. Written and directed by Norbert Carbonneaux from book by Voltaire. Camera, Robert Lefevbre; editor, Paulette Robert. At Marignan, Paris. Running time, **93** MINS.
Candide .... Jean-Pierre Cassel
Pangloss .... Pierre Brasseur
Cunegonde .... Dahlia Lavi
Nanar .... Michel Simon
Dame .... Nadia Gray
Gestapo Man .... Louis De Funes
Jacques .... Jean Tissier

Voltaire's 18th Century satire on optimism, inspired by the Lisbon earthquake which killed 30,000, has been updated for its film form in the light of the Atom Bomb which did away with 300,000. The film keeps its original shell as it follows the adventures of a blindly innocent and candid hero, Candide, through the last war, concentration camps, into the U.S. and Russia to the happy ending.

Candide, taught by his connivingly simple professor, Pangloss, that all is for the best in the best of all possible worlds, carries this credo through obviously well meaning by this silly code in the face of facts. This gives the film its ironic edge. It sometimes gets almost grisly in its comedy but manages

to bring it off through its forth-right attitude, treatment and pace.

However, the pic touches on many things and much has a sketchy, revue-like feeling. Comedy makes its point in isolated episodes but rarely keeps building. The use of a commentary, drawings and stock shots to overcome more difficult visuals also sometimes keeps this literary rather than complete-ly filmic.

But the film has enough insight to make it of arty house value abroad with exploitation handles. More general usage would entail a harder sell. Technical credits are good.

Jean-Pierre Cassel has the open face and movements for the hero while Pierre Brasseur is a savory professor. Pretty Dahlia Lavi is somewhat gauche but helped by this very facet in the role of inno-cent Cunegonde, who is continuous-ly raped and used by brutal Ger-mans. French black marketeers and others.

Candide goes through army training and gets involved with military bungling to be taken prisoner and then allowed to escape by a German but captured when turned in by a Swiss guard. He is then tortured and turned into a German because he is from the German-speaking part of France. Candide is also involved in inspect-ing a concentration camp decked up for a visiting Swiss doctor, and then into adventures in the Asia-tic colonies and in the U.S.

This is a fairly sprightly film romp, if somewhat talky and filmsy at times. It has enough bite for hypo possibilities. So far it has no export visa. *Mosk.*

Lebensborn
(Fountain of Life)
(GERMAN)
Berlin, Jan. 24.

FTR-DFG release of Alfa production. With Emmerich Schrenk, Harry Meyen, Maria Perschy, Joachim Hansen and Joachim Mock. Directed by Werner Klingler. Screenplay, Paul Markwitz and Max Vorwerg, after a magazine series by Will Berthold; camera, Igor Oberberg; music, Gerhard Becker. Previewed at CCC Studios, Berlin. Running time, 91 MINS.
Meyer Westroff ...... Emmerich Schrenk
Dr. Hagen .... Harry Meyen
Doris Korff .... Maria Perschy
Steinbach alias Adameit..Joachim Hansen
Kempe .... Joachim Mock
Hellmich .... Waldemar Tepel
Mertens ....Gert Guenter Hoffman
Koss .... Lothar Mann
Guehne .... Michael Welchberger
Nietermann .... Helmuth Lange
Irmgard .... Eva Bubat

As per its topic, this Alfa pro-duction may very well be acclaimed as one of the most unusual Teu-tonic pix of the season. "Lebens-born" was the title of a macabre operation founded by Heinrich Himmler in the '30's. The SS chieftain's notion was to "breed" a Germanic noble race. To accom-plish this, he had choice German girls selected and brought to-gether with equally choice German males. Their only purpose was the birth of children for the great Fuehrer.

This pic is fairly well made but it lacks real conviction. This is not due to the Nordic eugenics theme of Hitler's race phobia era but to the story which has been woven in for the sake of suspense and entertainment. Also, the question may be asked whether the filmiza-tion of this macabre theme was not superfluous.

Subjectwise, "Lebensborn" may emerge as a big grosser in this country as it may attract a lot of the curio-seekers in addition to the general public. For the same rea-son, the film may also stir interest outside the country. The film pro-ducers tried hard to make this an important film.

Lineup of drawbacks contain an unconvincing script and cliche character portrayals. Acting in-deed varies. While some players are satisfactory, others tend to exaggerate their portrayals. Wer-ner Klingler, an ex-German whose passport reads American, directed this. His direction doesn't com-mand particular attention. The score is fine while there's also cer-tain praise due the camera work. Some outdoor shots are quite impressive. *Hans.*

Ravissante
(Ravishing)
(FRENCH)
Paris, Jan. 24.

Prodis release of CICC production. Written, directed by and starring Robert Lamoureux. Features Sylva Koscina, Philippe Noiret, Lucille Saint-Simon. Jac-ques Dacqmine. Camera, Robert Lefebvre; editor, Christian Gaudin. At Paris, Paris. Running time, 75 MINS.
Thierry .... Robert Lamoureux
Maurice .... Philippe Noiret
Francoise .... Lucille Saint-Simon
Evelyne .... Sylva Koscina
Marc .... Jacques Dacqmine

Robert Lamoureux is an engag-ing comedian but he is lacklustre as a director and scripter. This is a familiar situation comedy which might be an okay local bet but sans the invention or appeal for off-shore chances.

A ladies' man pilot is called in by a friend to chasten a friend's wife who has sluffed off his ad-vances. But his own wife is taken for the victim. All is finally cleared up.

Film is a theatrical and verbose, with complications quite obvious. It is technically flat. *Mosk.*

Sniper's Ridge

Brisk, businesslike low-budget lower-berth war drama. Will be a strong companion feature.
Hollywood, Jan. 31.

Twentieth-Fox release of John Bushel-man production. Stars Jack Ging, Stanley Clements, John Goddard, Douglas Hen-derson; features Gabe Castle, Allan Mar-vin; with Anton Vanstralen, Mason Curry, Mark Douglas, Scott Randall, George Yoshinaga, Albert C. Freeman Jr.; Henry Delgado, Thomas A. Sweet, Joe Caw-thon, Richard Jeffries. Directed by Bush-elman. Screenplay, Tom Maruzzi; camera, Ken Peach; editor, Carl Pierson; art direc-tor, John Mansbridge; music, Richard La Salle; sound, Carl Zint; assistant director, Ira Stewart. Reviewed at API projection room, Jan. 31, '61. Running time, 61 MINS.
Scharack .... Jack Ging
Tombolo ....John Goddard
Pumphrey .... Stanley Clements
Peer .... Gabe Castle
Sweatish .... Doug Henderson
Wardy .... Allan Marvin
Bear .... Anton Vanstralen
Young Soldier .... Joe Cawthon
Soldier .... Scott Randall
Soldier .... Dick Jeffries
Bo-Bo .... Mark Douglas
Mongolian .... George Yoshinaga
Gwathney .... Albert Freeman, Jr.
David .... Mason Curry
Tonto .... Hank Delgado
Stunt Double .... Tom Sweet

Resourcefulness and talent went into the making of this modest war picture, proving anew that the quality of a product need not be determined by the extent of pro-duction funds. "Sniper's Ridge," to be sure, has its dramatic limita-tions, but it is a snappy action-combat item, certain to appeal to the tastes of masculine audiences, and absorbing enough to its fringe psychological ramifications to keep anyone attentive through its crack-ling 61-minute span. The API through 20th-Fox release will make a strong lower-berth program booking.

Tom Maruzzi penned the screen-play, which is a little fuzzy around the motivational edges (a forgive-able failure considering the obvi-ous aim to keep it taut) but tangy and true in terms of its trench-line dialog. Yarn deals with an in-cident on the front lines in the final hours before cease fire in the Korean War. Principals are a neu-rotic captain (John Goddard) and a rebellious, war-weary corporal (Jack Ging) overdue for rotation. In spite of the imminence of truce, the captain orders a dangerous last-minute patrol. However, patrol action is averted when the captain accidentally sets foot on a "bounc-ing Betty" mine and freezes on the spot (bouncing Bettys explode when you step *off* the plunger). He is rescued by Ging, who is serious-ly wounded in the process. The ending has a let's-wrap-it-up-quick-ly aspect, but the conclusive mine sequence is suspenseful and nerve-tingling.

The film, taut, swift and engross-ing, is a credit to producer-direc-tor John Bushelman. Under his crisp guidance, the acting is un-usually firm and businesslike. God-dard is a standout. Ging exhibits clearly that he's a young actor with a bright future. Other solid key per-formances are fashioned by Stan-ley Clements, Douglas Henderson, Gabe Castle and Allan Marvin, and support is efficient.

Strong additional aids are Ken Peach's lenswork and Carl Pier-son's editing. Art director John Mansbridge has made a game at-tempt to make California resemble Korea. Richard La Salle's music is a bit too busy in spots. *Tube.*

The Long Rope

Adequate lower-berth western that will sustain greatest in-terest among less discriminat-ing audiences.
Hollywood, Jan. 30.

Twentieth-Fox release of Margia Dean production. Stars Hugh Marlowe, Alan Hale, Robert Wilke, Lisa Montell; with Chris Robinson, Jeffrey Morris, David Renard, Medeline Holmes, John Alonzo, Jack Powers, Kathryn Harte, Jack Car-lin, Scott Randall, Stephen Welles, Linda Cordova, Alex Cordellis. Directed by William Witney. Screenplay, Robert Hamner; camera, Kay Norton; editor, Peter Johnson; art director, John Mans-bridge; music; Paul Sawtell, Bert Shef-ter; sound, Vic Appel; assistant directors, Col. Harold E. Knox, Ira Stewart. Re-viewed at API projection room, Jan. 30, '61. Running time, 60 MINS.
Jonas Stone .... Hugh Marlowe
John Millard .... Allan Hale
Ben Matthews .... Robert Wilke
Maria .... Alvarez Lisa Montell
Reb Gilroy .... Chris Robinson
Will Matthews ....Jeffrey Morris
Louis Ortega .... David Renard
Dona Vega .... Madeleine Holmes
Manuel Alvarez .... John Alonzo
Luke Simms .... Jack Powers
Mrs. Creech .... Kathryn Harte
Henchman .... Jack Carlin
Henchman .... Scott Randall
Mexican Waitress .... Linda Cordova
Jim Matthews .... Stephen Welles

A routine, unpretentious west-ern, "The Long Rope" will be an adequate twin-bill filler. Whipped out in a week with the greatest of economy, the Margia Dean pro-duction through API for 20th-Fox will be most companionable wher-ever audience taste for frontier conflicts and primitive themes flourishes. But its market value as a running mate with diminish if paired with too premium an attrac-tion. Care should be taken to avoid burdening more selective au-diences with such a modest, cursory morsel of dramatic entertainment.

The film runs only half-a-minute beyond an hour, an unusually short span in today's market, even for a second feature. Written by Robert Hamner, the yarn is concerned with the stalwart efforts of a federal circuit judge in the early west to conduct a respectable trial in a lawless town for a poor Mexican shopkeeper falsely accused of mur-dering the brother of an influen-tial, tyrannical land baron. It de-velops that the Mexican's deranged mother-in-law is the guilty party, having planned the murder as a frame in order to make her daugh-ter re-available for matrimony to the baron, thus restoring the fam-ily's pride and wealth. The story is full of motivational holes, but it manages to sustain interest and mild concern.

Acting is generally competent. Prominently involved, and effec-tive, are Hugh Marlowe (as the judge), Alan Hale, Robert Wilke, Lisa Montell (attractive as the de-fendant's spouse), Chris Robinson, Jeffrey Morris, David Renard, Mad-eleine Holmes (the mother-in-law) and John Alonzo (the accused). Considering the rush factor, direc-tor William Witney has done a re-spectable job, as have cameraman Kay Norton, editor Peter Johnson, art director John Mansbridge, and score collaborators Paul Sawtell and Bert Shefter, along with "in-cidental" music contributor (theme strains) Frankie Ortega. *Tube.*

Gold Of The Seven Saints
(Warnerscope)

Absorbing western adventure

drama along the order of "Treasure of Sierra Madre." Weak ending dilutes overall flavor, but pic answers a b.o. need for good medium-budgeted westerns.

Hollywood, Jan. 27.
Warner Bros. release of Leonard Freeman production. Stars Clint Walker, Roger Moore; features, Leticia Roman, Robert Middleton, Chill Wills, Gene Evans. Directed by Gordon Douglas. Screenplay, Leigh Brackett and Freeman, from novel by Steve Frazee; camera, Joseph Biroc; editor, Folmar Blangsted; music, Howard Jackson. Reviewed at the studio Jan. 25, '61. Running time, 89 MINS.
Jim Rainbolt .... Clint Walker
Shawn Garrett .... Roger Moore
Tita .... Leticia Roman
Gondora .... Robert Middleton
Doc Gates .... Chill Wills
McCracken .... Gene Evans
Armenderez .... Roberto Contreras
Ames .... Jack C. Williams
Ricca .... Arthur Stewart

Obviously figured the time is ripe and the public is ready for another adventure drama in the tradition of "Treasure of Sierra Madre," Warner Bros. has hatched a chubby offspring, "Gold of the Seven Saints." By gold-and-rod western standards, the Leonard Freeman production is no "Treasure" by a long shot, but it's a darned good imitation-heir apparent, expertly written and colorfully enacted by a polished cast headed by Clint Walker and Roger Moore. Since the sagebrush fever hit tv, there has been a diminishing supply of well done westerns in the moderate budget classification for the theatrical market. This production plugs the gap nicely, and its boxoffice should reflect that value.

A strong screenplay by producer Freeman and Leigh Brackett is the firm foundation upon which the picture remains erect and engrossing until its disappointingly shaky conclusion. Working with a novel by Steve Frazee, they have penned some frisky dialog and constructed several gripping situations. Walker and Moore are cast as trapping partners who strike it rich, and are chased persistently over the sprawling desert and through craggy hill country by several marauding parties who have one thing in common—total disdain for the golden rule. In the end, as in its unforgettable predecessor to the screen, nobody wins but everyone grins at the common misfortune. In the desperate battle for the booty, the gold is washed away down some churning rapids.

Unlike "Treasure," this film lays a golden egg through the unconvincing nature and transparent spirit of the climactic laughing jag, for the gold did not corrupt these heroes as it did the gentlemen of "Sierra Madre." The loss does not convey the same irony. It is plainly no joking matter. Under Gordon Douglas' otherwise apt and spirited direction, an absorbing film concludes on a hollow, phony, imitative note.

Utilizing his customary heroically-reserved approach Walker does well by the role of anchor man. Moore, as his faithful but emotionally-unsettled Irish mate, gives what appears to be his best and most colorfully compelling screen characterization to date. His work heralds a promising career in films. Chill Wills does his usual expert character work, and Robert Middleton and Gene Evans are excellent in top support. Leticia Roman adequately conveys the brief ro-

mantic interest.

Some marvelously picturesque red-rock Utah scenery is unaccountably sacrificed to the black-and-white lens, presumably for economic reasons. It seems an example of misjudged thrift. Warner-Scope succeeds partially in improving the pictorial aspect. Art director Stanley Fleischer has helped select some eye-appealing locales and designed a fine Spanish hacienda for the single key interior scene. Other positive factors are Joseph Biroc's camera angles, Folmar Blangsted's editing, Howard Jackson's score. *Tube.*

La Grande Olimpiade
(THE GREAT OLYMPIAD)
(ITALIAN-COLOR)
Rome, Jan. 31.
Cineriz release of a film produced by the LUCE Institute for C.O.N.I., 17th Olympic Games Committee. Directed by Romolo Marcellini. Story and screenplay, Marcellini, Niccolo Ferrari, Daniele G. Luigi. Commentary, Sergio Valentini, Corrado Sofia, Donato Martiucci; camera (Eastmancolor), Aldo Alessandri, Francesco Attenni, Libio Bartoli, Cesare Colo, Mario Damicelli, Renato del Frate, Vittorio della Valle, Angelo Filippini, Rino Filippini, Maro Fioretti, Angelo Jannarelli, Luigi Kuweiler, Emanuel Lomiry, Angelo Lotti, Erico Mencer, Ugo Nudi, Emanuele Piccirilli, Marco Scarpelli, Antonio Secchi, Renato Sinistri, Carlo Ventimiglia, Fausto Zuccoli, Mario Damicelli. Editor, Mario Serandrei. Jolanda Benventi, Aleblivo Verdejo. Music, A. F. Lavagnino, with Armando Trovajoli. Previewed at Rome Opera House, Rome.. Running time, 142 MINS.

A magnificently exciting human and pictorial document of the 17th Olympic Games has been put together by a large Italian team led by Romolo Marcellini. It gives everyone a peerless up-front seat at the 1960 Olympics, whether they have witnessed the event or not. It should pay off handsomely in all markets for the obvious effort and expense which went into its making. It's a special item, of course, but rates high in its class.

Structurally, it begins with views of Rome, harks back briefly to Greece and the torch-lighting ritual, then follows the flame on its trip to Rome overland and oversea. Whole villages in southern Italy turn out to see a runner flash by with the torch. Pic segues with opening ceremonies, then flashes into action with various events. Approach is necessarily selective, and some events are missed though all sports are touched upon. The highlights in track, swimming, cycling, etc., are rendered in some detail and capture the excitement and pathos of victory and defeat both in closeup and long shot.

Print viewed naturally had an accent on Italo feats, with much footage dedicated to cycling, where local medals topped others, but remainder is remarkably well balanced. Nevertheless, an Anglo-U.S. version is also being readied with slightly varied content. Japan (where pic is already sold), will edit its own version. On all, however, the Italo Olympic Committee has final okay to see that nothing is distorted.

Two dozen lensers have done a firstrate job to make this one of the finest sports documents in history, often going beyond mere reportage into the realms of human emotion or pictorial beauty sometimes bordering on the surreal. Thus such memorable mementos as the close-up views of javelin thrower Cantello's eliminating toss, or high-jumper Thomas' defeat, or

the duel between decathloners Johnson and Kwan. Pure sport buffs may object to accent on faces rather than muscles as the athletes go through their paces, but the film gains much from this switch.

Other highlights are Wilma Rudolph's runaway wins, the (elaborately produced) nighttime marathon triumph of the barefoot Abyssinian, Bikila. Above all, the brotherhood-of-nations aspects of the Games are given an oft-moving accent throughout this stirring production effort, for which a giant team deserves much credit.
Hawk.

Le Chien de Pique
(THE JACK OF SPADES)
(FRENCH)
Paris, Jan. 31.
Cocinor release of Belmont-Ares production. Stars Eddie Constantine; features Raymond Pellegrin, Pierre Clementi, Marie Versini, Douking. Directed by Yves Allegret. Screenplay, Albert Vidalie, Allegret; camera, Michel Kelber; editor, Maurice Serein. At Biarritz, Paris. Running time, 90 MINS.
Patrick .... Eddie Constantine
Robert .... Raymond Pellegrin
Zefra .... Marie Versini
Paco .... Pierre Clementi
Manuel .... Douking

Eddie Constantine is the Yank singer-actor who became a European star playing hard-drinking American G-Men in local parodies of the genre. Now he appears in the first attempt at a Gallic western. It follows the familiar American patterns but is just too small-scale to emerge as much of anything but a local bet.

Constantine is a reformed gangster who has bought a ranch in the plains section of France where he raises bulls. Into this comes an old pal on the run and also trouble with rice planters who infringe on his grazing grounds. A young girl enamored of Constantine brings on troubles when the pal makes passes. But all is straightened out to end on a tragic note as he kills the friend who has led his young sidekick into robbery and death.

Countryside is sufficiently good, but fights, action and characterizations are just too sparse. And the actors cannot do much with the stereotypes. Technical credits are okay. *Mosk.*

Shadows

Powerful, provocative improvised drama imaginatively reined by John Cassavetes. Brings fresh, raw, naturalistic approach to U.S. filmdom. Might kick off cycle of similar homemade efforts.

Lion International release of Maurice McEndree-Seymour Cassel production. With Ben Carruthers, Lelia Goldoni, Hugh Herd, Rupert Crosse, Tony Ray, Tom Allen, Dennis Sallas, Davey Jones, David Pokitillow. Directed by John Cassavetes. Camera, Erich Kollmar; editor, McEndree; sets, Randy Liles, Bob Reeh; music, Charlie Mingus, Shifi Hadi; sound, Jay Crecco; asst. director, Al Giglio. Reviewed at Paramount Studio Theatre, Feb. 6, '61. Running time, 81 MINS.
Benny .... Ben Carruthers
Lelia .... Lelia Goldoni
Hugh .... Hugh Herd
Rupert .... Rupert Crosse
Tony .... Tony Ray
Tom .... Tom Allen
Dennis .... Dennis Sallas
Davey .... Davey Jones
David .... David Pokitillow

"Shadows" is a "significant" motion picture. If it creates the stir domestically that it did overseas, where it walked off with awards and critical superlatives, it may well be the standard bearer for a radical swerve in U.S.-manufactured screen entertainment. And there is every reason to believe it will be a smash success in this country's art theatres, for this is a film that tangles and tingles with life.

Produced by Maurice McEndree and Seymour Cassel via the most modest of cinema expenditures (reportedly $40,000), released by Lion International and ticketed for domestic bow March 21 at New York's Embassy Theatre, the release establishes John Cassavetes, already well-known as actor and occasional television director ("Johnny Staccato"), as a gifted, inventive, perceptive director.

In "Shadows," Cassavetes has accomplished something all too often forgotten, disregarded or unattained by many of his veteran colleagues. He has succeeded in utilizing the motion picture as it rarely has been utilized since the era of the silent screen putting drama in visual terms, telling the story in pictures, thus reducing the improvised dialog of his actors to secondary status. There are moments, in fact the film's most vital and arresting passages, when the actors do not say a word, yet all that has to be said is said through the expressions in their eyes, producing the enchanting effect of a montage of unforgettable snapshots.

The technical quality of "Shadows" is crude. At times the audience can barely hear or even see what is going on, but one can always feel the impulse of excitement generated by the picture. Its very crudeness captures the spontaneity, the unpredictability, the raw, unruly pattern of human behavior.

But what separates, what ultimately distinguishes "Shadows" from several other recent, abortive screen attempts at dramatic improvisation is the substance of its characters. The underlying drama is pegged on the tragedy of a pair of fair-skinned Negroes, free souls adrift in the never-never no-man's land between the overlapping white and colored social jungles of New York. One, the girl, has an ill-fated love affair with an un-

aware white boy, abruptly terminated when he is confronted by her dark-skinned brother in her apartment, the film's most remarkable, and unforgettable, scene. His sincere, but clumsy attempts at apology for dashing off in shocked confusion produce another noteworthy passage.

Other story, the boy's, is told in a somewhat lighter vein as he romps about with his white buddies in search of stimulation, only to emerge physically beaten (in a very natural fistfight sequence) but spiritually unbowed in spite of the social chaos and confusion that is to be his lot.

There are a number of sharp, vivid performances in spite of the acute uncertainty engendered by improvisation. The actors all have their momentary lapses, but they have done an exceptional job and, in concert, the effect is quite overpowering.

Among those who excite special attention are Ben Carruthers (the boy), Leila Goldoni (the girl), Tony Ray (her white lover), Hugh Herd (their brother), Rupert Crosse (his manager), Tom Allen and Dennis Sallas (Ben's buddies). An important factor in the exciting chemistry of this film is the improvised music by Charlie Mingus and Shifi Hadi, effectively split among a moody sax and a driving string and tympany. *Tube.*

The Full Treatment
(BRITISH)

Psychiatric meller which holds a morbidly gripping interest, though the climax is contrived and obvious. Rather too chatty, but a strong sex angle and good performances by a sound cast makes this easily exploitable.

London, Feb. 9.
Columbia release of a Val Guest production (in association with Falcon Films). Stars Claude Dauphin, Diane Cilento, Ronald Lewis, Francoise Rosay. Features, Bernard Braden. Produced and directed by Val Guest; screenplay, Val Guest & Ronald Scott Thorn, from the latter's novel; camera, Gilbert Taylor; editor, Bill Lenny; music, Stanley Black. At New Victoria, London, Feb. 7, '61. Running time, 109 MINS.
David Prade .... Claude Dauphin
Denise Colby .... Diane Cilento
Alan Colby .... Ronald Lewis
Madame Prade .... Francoise Rosay
Harry Stonehouse........ Bernard Braden
Connie .... Katya Douglas
Nicole .... Anne Tirard
Baroness de La Vaillon. Barbara Chilcott
Dr. Roberts .... Edwin Styles
Mr. Manfield .... George Merritt

There's not a great deal of star value in this rather gabby psychiatric melodrama, but it is well played and directed with force. With a strong sex streak in it, "The Full Treatment" should be easily exploitable and is a worthwhile booking. Excellent locations in the South of France should add to its interest for many people. The film is often rather confused, but the somewhat tortuous events curiously add to the pic's suspense value.

Under the credit titles the film opens with a bang, when an auto crashed into a truck. Hurt in the accident is the International racing driver (Ronald Lewis) just off on his honeymoon with Diane Cilento. It takes a year for his wounds to heal and he sets off on his delayed honeymoon in the South of France.

But though physically he is fit he still suffers from mental blackouts. He finds to his horror that every time he goes to make love to his wife he has an irresistible urge to strangle her, which hardly makes for a happy honeymoon.

The meet a psychiatrist who promises to help readjust Lewis if he will put himself in his hands. But Lewis is suspicious, moody and jealous of the psychiatrist's interest in his young wife. It eventually transpires that Lewis is walking into a trap set by the psychiatrist whose mind is even more disturbed than his patient's. The twist is kept pretty well to the end, but it is fairly predicable and the climax does not come with the necesary punch. However, the acting and direction is vigorous and effective and "The Full Treatment" adds up to a well-produced, holding entertainment with two or three highly sexy sequences, notably one where the hero makes love to his wife in the bathtub.

There are five important acting roles and all are handled effectively. Lewis, though tending to play rather sullenly, is a goodlooking and virile hero and he well conveys his varying moods of passion, despair, jealousy and the like. Diane Cilento, though handicapped by a phoncy-seeming Italian accent, gives an engaging performance. She looks pleasant yet sexy and the pair make an attractive young married couple.

Claude Dauphin tackles the important role of the psychiatrist with bland assurance and for quite awhile excellently kids the audience into believing what he is not. Francoise Rosay, as his deaf mother, is dignified and sympathetic, though this talented artist isn't given scope. Bernard Braden, as an auto-driver buddy of Lewis's, makes a rare appearance on the screen and is perfectly natural in the way he handles his few breezy scenes.

Val Guest's direction of an offbeat script (which he partially wrote) holds the suspense well until the pic falls apart at the end and camerawork and art work are both firstclass. *Rich.*

Sanctuary
(C'SCOPE)

Another flashy, provocative sex epic in a story loaded with shady heroines. Too clumsily transposed from the Faulkner prose to rate quality label that, along with big campaign and risque reputation, would spell huge, sustained b.o. But should attract enough attention for hot start and fair showing.

Hollywood, Feb. 15.
Twentieth-Fox release of Richard D. Zanuck production. Stars Lee Remick, Yves Montand, Bradford Dillman; features Harry Townes, Odetta. Directed by Tony Richardson. Screenplay, James Poe, based on novels and play by William Faulkner; camera, Ellsworth Fredricks; editor, Robert Simpson; art directors, Duncan Cramer, Jack Martin Smith; music, Alex North; sound, Charles 'eck, Harold A. Root; assistant director, David Hall. Reviewed at the studio, Feb. 15, '61. Running time, 90 MINS.
Temple .... Lee Remick
Candy .... Yves Montand
Gowan .... Bradford Dillman
Ira Bobbitt .... Harry Townes
Nancy .... Odetta
Governor ....Howard St. John
Norma .... Jean Carson
Reba .... Reta Shaw
Dog Boy ....Strother Martin
Lee .... William Mims
Flossie ....Marge Redmond
Swede .... Jean Bartel
Mamie .... Hope Du Bois
Jackie .... Enid Janes
Connie .... Dana Lorenson
Cora ....Pamela Raymond
Randy .... Linden Chiles
Gus ....Robert Gothie
Tommy ....Wyatt Cooper

Little more than the skeleton of its complex but perceptive, sensational but poetic, source material remains in the Richard D. Zanuck production of William Faulkner's "Sanctuary." Major liberties have been taken with the novel and its subsequent appendage, "Requiem For a Nun," to make the frank original often shockingly incisive and appalling in its thorough, penetrating examination of the South's (and some of humanity's) dirty underwear, suitable for the screen. The deletions are understandable and often mandatory, but too much has gone out of "Sanctuary." Not enough of the original flavor and vitality has been retained. Film emerges essentially a dubious "entertainment" in the lighter sense of the word.

How well "Sanctuary" will hold up as a boxoffice attraction is linked perilously with the prevailing climate of the motion picture marketplace, currently in a state of peculiar contradiction and uncertain flux. It is to hit the screen at a time when frank, "adult" themes are more and more abundant in spite of pressures exerted by powerful domestic audience factions to curb filmdom's inclination to depict the raw, seamy side of life.

"Sanctuary" is not a picture for children but, on the heels of a brisk, expensive campaign launched by the company, the 20th-Fox release should stimulate enough attention in the adult world to stir up a sharp initial wicket reaction. However, the picture does not have the stature to attain prestige proportions, and that will narrow its ultimate boxoffice horizon.

Rearranging and simplifying Faulkner's minute sensitive prose into a sound and clear dramatic screen structure was the almost herculean task faced by scenarist James Poe in sifting through the author's novels and his play, formerly adapted for the stage by Ruth Ford. That a gifted writer such as Poe somehow lost the dominant spirit and biting observation of Faulkner's basic tale illustrates the complexity, and almost argues against the feasibility, of the undertaking itself. In consolidating a number of Faulkner's individual, and widely divergent, characters into composite shapes, Poe has created inconsistencies in his people and unlikelihoods in relationships and situations. For instance, Yves Montand and Odetta are each a composite of three separate Faulkner characters of varying, almost contradictory, personalities. They do not stand up well in their revised form, and this is a major shortcoming of the screenplay.

Lee Remick stars as Temple Drake, the flexible young heroine of Faulkner's story. She is a more savory person in Poe's version, which eliminates some of the baser acts she commits in the novel. Screen sheds far less light upon her complicated moral makeup and upon the significance and ironies of her relationships with other characters.

In the screen story, Miss Remick experiences a rude sexual awakening at a remote country still to which she has stupidly been brought by a spoiled, superficial college lad (Bradford Dillman) following an unfulfilled one-sided fit of passion (his). It is here she encounters and is seduced in a corn bin by bootlegger Montand, then becomes his kept woman in a New Orleans brothel. When Montand is reported killed fleeing the law, Miss Remick resumes the life she led prior to her fall, is wed by the repentant Dillman, who feels responsible but refuses to face reality.

When Montand shows up five years later Miss Remick, now the mother of two but disenchanted with her marriage, prepares to run off with him, but is prevented from so doing when her maid (Odetta), aware of the consequences, slays Miss Remick's baby. The entire story is told in flashback from the point a night before Odetta is to hang for the crime, for which Miss Remick feels a sense of guilt and responsibility.

Miss Remick dispatches her role persuasively and vigorously, and conveys especially well the transition of the character through the abrupt changes in her life. It is not a perfect, not an unforgettable, piece of acting, but she is suited for the part, carries it off well enough, and further establishes herself as one of Hollywood's most important young talents.

The part played by Dillman has almost no dimension. Under this handicap, this fine young actor is stymied in his earnest attempts. Montand suffers equally, but for a different reason. His character, a three-ply composite, is vague and inconsistent, too self-contradictory to make sense. Odetta is another snowed under by character complication—on the one hand acknowledged to be drug addict and past prostie, on the other an unbelievably perceptive, self-sacrificing, almost motherly person. Harry Townes and Howard St. John are

competent in major roles and support is good, notably in the cases of Strother Martin and William Mims.

Tony Richardson's direction is generally sound and even. The tempo does get a bit sluggish in spots, but that is mostly a result of a wordy, rather static, script.

Richardson handles the flashback aspect very neatly and crisply. Much of Faulkner's perception of nature's detail has been caught by the craftsmen on this picture. The Duncan Cramer-Jack Martin Smith sets, notably the repulsive still and its immediate environment, capture to a great degree the mood and atmosphere of the original work, a quality enhanced by the sensitive work of the sound team (Charles Peck and Harold A. Root) and cameraman Ellsworth Fredricks. Robert Simpson's editing is mechanically expert, but the drama itself has a tendency to lurch and swerve rather abruptly, indicating some anxious snipping to trim the film to 90 minutes.

Alex North's score underlines the story with a sinister, moody, macabre strain that fits. *Tube.*

Arretez Les Tambours
(Stop the Drums)
(FRENCH)

Paris, Feb. 14.

Jacques Letienne release of Bourdonnaye-Co. Lyonnaise production. Stars Bernard Blier, Lucille St. Simon; features Lutz Gabor, Anne Doat, Daniel Sorano, Beatrice Bretty, Paulette Dubost. Directed by Georges Lautner. Screenplay, Pierre Laroche from novel by Richard Prentout; camera, Maurice Fellous; editor, Michele David. At Paris. Running time, **100 MINS.**

Mayor .... Bernard Blier
Catherine .... Lucille St. Simon
Major .... Lutz Gabor
Dany .... Anne Doat
Germaine .... Beatrice Bretty
Toulousain .... Daniel Sorano
Widow .... Paulette Dubost

War film treats a small town in occupied France where people show their true colors in helping or washing their hands of resistance during the last World War. Cheap production has too much utilization of stock footage, and its familiar unfolding makes this mainly of dualer use abroad sans the depth for arty houses.

Film is about an easy-going middleaged mayor who helps people but finally emerges a hero when the chips are down. Director Georges Lautner cannot give it the punch or humanity to make it more than a conventional war film. Technical credits are okay with acting honors going to Bernard Blier for his deft portrayal of the decent mayor. *Mosk.*

The Absent Minded Professor

In the "Shaggy Dog" tradition, another boxoffice whopper for Disney. Enjoyable as an absurd, uncomplicated comedy-fantasy, but discerning film-goers may discover deeper, more significant humorous nuances.

Hollywood, Feb. 17.

Buena Vista release of Walt Disney production. Stars Fred MacMurray, Nancy Olson, Keenan Wynn, Tommy Kirk; features Ed Wynn, Leon Ames, Elliott Reid, Edward Andrews, David Lewis, Jack Mullaney, Belle Montrose; with Wally Brown, Don Ross, James Westerfield, Charlie Briggs, Alan Hewitt, Wendell Holmes, Wally Boag, Forrest Lewis, Alan Carney, Gage Clarke, Raymond Bailey, Leon Tyler. Directed by Robert Stevenson. Screenplay, Bill Walsh, based on story by Samuel W. Taylor; camera, Edward Colman; editor, Cotton Warburton; special photographic effects, Peter Ellenshaw, Eustace Lycett; art director, Carroll Clark; music, George Bruns; sound, Dean Thomas; assistant director, Robert G. Shannon. Reviewed at the studio, Feb. 17, '61. Running time, **90 MINS.**

Prof. Ned Brainard .... Fred MacMurray
Betsy Carlisle .... Nancy Olson
Alonzo Hawk .... Keenan Wynn
Biff Hawk .... Tommy Kirk
President Rufus Daggett .... Leon Ames
Shelby Ashton .... Elliott Reid
Fire Chief .... Ed Wynn
Defense Secretary ...... Edward Andrews
General Singer .... David Lewis
Air Force Captain .... Jack Mullaney
Mrs. Chatsworth .... Belle Montrose
Coach Elkins .... Wally Brown
1st Referee .... Alan Carney
Officer Kelly .... Forrest Lewis
Officer Hanson .... James Westerfield
Reverend Bosworth .... Gage Clarke
General Hotchkiss .... Alan Hewitt
Admiral Olmstead ...... Raymond Bailey
General Poynter .... Wendell Holmes
Lenny .... Don Ross
Sig .... Charlie Briggs
T. V. Newsman .... Wally Boag

On the surface, Walt Disney's "The Absent Minded Professor" is a comedy-fantasy of infectious absurdity, a natural follow-up to the studio's successful "Shaggy Dog" story of last year, and a picture that is going to mop up at the nation's boxoffice. But its mass appeal goes deeper than that.

For beneath the preposterous veneer lurks a comment on our time, a reflection of the plight of the average man haplessly confronted with the complexities of a jet age civilization burdened with fear, red-tape, official mumbo-jumbo and ambitious anxiety. Deeply rooted within associate producer Bill Walsh's screenplay, is a subtle protest against the detached, impersonal machinery of modern progress. It is an underlying theme with which an audience today can identify. It is the basic reason why this film is going to be an enormously popular attraction.

The "Professor" (Fred MacMurray) is an easygoing, likeable small-town practical chemist who comes up with a practical discovery—a gooey substance endowed with the elusive quality of anti-gravity. He dubs it "flubber" (flying rubber) and proceeds to put it to use in incongruous ways.

In the film's most hilarious passage, he applies it at half time to the gym shoes of a basketball team hopelessly outclassed by its opponents' height, whereupon the beaten boys promptly stage a bouncy aerial second half ballet climaxed by a winning point in which both ball and player go through the basket. He plants it in the engine of his Model T and goes zooming off to the clouds. Eventually he sky-drives to Washington where he plans to let the Federals in on his secret discovery, but the latter don't trust this flying flivver.

MacMurray, a seasoned film comedian, is ideally cast as the car-hopping prof, and plays the role with warmth and gusto. The preposterous spectacle of a grown man (and his dog) swooping through the air in old tin lizzie while the populance looks on in matter-of-fact acceptance is, in itself, a stroke of comic perception that somehow expresses all the absurdity of modern scientific acceleration, incomprehensible and beyond the intellectual scope of the normal individual. It is progress reduced to its simplest essentials—a Model T aloft via a bouncing rubber ball principle in reverse (the ball gains, rather than loses, altitude with each bounce).

Nancy Olson attractively supplies romantic interest. Keenan Wynn is a delight in a delicious satirical role—that of a money-mad loan tycoon who would sell his own alma mater for a buck (as he tells his son, "what do you want, some total stranger to close the college down, or a loyal alumnus?"). The son is played exceptionally well by Tommy Kirk.

Ed Wynn has a suitable bit as a fire chief, along with a long list of fine supporting performances, prominent among which are those of Leon Ames, Elliott Reid, Edward Andrews, David Lewis, Jack Mullaney, Belle Montrose, Wally Brown, Alan Carney and James Westerfield, latter in a classic bit of comic repetition as a down-to-earth cop.

The comedy is deftly and expertly handled by director Robert Stevenson, who has received tremendously skilled assists from lensman Edward Colman, editor Cotton Warburton, art director Carroll Clark, composer George Bruns and soundman Dean Thomas.

A lion's share of the credit for a film so dependent on the fantasy aspect must go to the special photographic effects team of Peter Ellenshaw and Eustace Lycett and to Joshua Meador's animation effects. This picture is a winner in every department. It is profoundly easy to enjoy, and there is more in it to enjoy than meets the casual eye. *Tube.*

Black Sunday
(ITALIAN)

Italo shock package, long on production, short on scriptwork. Since mood, tension and visual implication count most in a horror pic, this exploitable item should fare well at b.o., primarily with junior wicketeers.

Hollywood, Feb. 9.

American International release of Massimo de Rita production. Directed by Mario Bava. Screenplay, Ennio De Concini, Bava, based on "The Vij" by Nikolai Gogol; camera, Bava, Ubaldo Terzano; editor, Mario Serandrei; art director, Giorgio Giovannini; music, Les Baxter; assistant director, Vana Caruso. Reviewed at Screen Directors Guild Theatre, Feb. 9, '61. Running time, **83 MINS.**

Witch Princess Katia ..... Barbara Steele
Dr. Gorobec .... John Richardson
Prince .... Ivo Garrani
Dr. Choma .... Andrea Checchi
Javutich .... Arturo Dominici
Constantin .... Enrico Olivieri
The Pope .... Antonio Pierfederici
Innkeeper .... Clara Bindi
His Daughter .... Germana Dominici
Nikita .... Mario Passante
Ivan .... Tino Bianchi

There is sufficient cinematographic ingenuity and production flair in "Black Sunday" to keep an audience pleasantly unnerved. This in spite of a screenplay that reads, in translation from the original Italian, like a grade school imitation of Poe. Still, American International's little dish of Italo-concocted ghoul-ash is exploitable and entertaining enough to get a good play and reap a tidy profit, especially in the domain of the teenage dating party.

There's nothing very novel about the spooky setup in "Sunday," which was lifted, rather recklessly it might safely be conjectured, from "The Vij," a story by the noted 19th century Russian author, Nikolai Gogol. As confusingly and inconsistently pieced into melodrama by Ennio De Concini and Mario Bava, the film follows the exploits of a vain vampire witch and her undead henchman as they emerge from a two-century siesta to indulge in some bloodsucking in an eerie old Russian castle inhabited by a few descendants against whom they nurture a long-standing family grudge. After painstakingly vamping 'til ready for the prize transfusion, Miss Vampira succumbs to that age old occupational hazard of the plasma-gulping profession—crucifixation.

Most of the suspense and excitement stirred up in the Massimo de Rita production is accomplished by means of photography and artwork. The lens, under the perceptive guidance of director Bava, keeps zooming, swooping and snooping in and out of dark, forbidding corners of the castle and surrounding forest to hold the spectator's nerves at attention. And art director Giorgio Giovannini has supplied just the proper scenery and atmosphere to keep the screen alive with implied horror around every bush and behind every door.

Barbara Steele, in the dual role of the witch and her intended victim, at times seems a bit confused as to which of the two characters she is supposed to be at a given moment. She bears a strong resemblance to Jackie Kennedy and manages to be attractive in both parts, which may not have been the original intention. Others prominently entangled are John Richardson, Ivo Garrani, Andrea Checchi, Arturo Dominici and Enrico Olivieri, all of whom are competent.

Les Baxter's chilly score and Mario Serandrei's jumpy but suspense-inducing editing contribute to the prevailing funeral mood. *Tube.*

No Love For Johnnie
(BRITISH)

Excellent pic based on a controversial novel; glimpse of Houses of Parliament chicanery. Good, strong adult stuff which should prove sound b.o.

London, Feb. 14.

Rank (Betty E. Box) production and release. Stars Peter Finch; features Stanley Holloway, Mary Peach, Billie Whitelaw, Donald Pleasance. Directed by Ralph Thomas. Screenplay, Nicholas Phipps and Mordecai Richler, based on novel by Wilfred Fienburgh; camera, Ernest Steward; editor, Alfred Roome; music, Malcolm Arnold. At Leicester-Square Theatre, London. Running time, **111 MINS.**

Johnnie Byrne .... Peter Finch
Fred Andrews .... Stanley Holloway
Pauline .... Mary Peach
Roger Renfrew .... Donald Pleasence
Mary .... Billie Whitelaw
Tim Maxwell .... Hugh Burden
Alice .... Rosalie Crutchley
Dr. West .... Michael Goodliffe
Charlie Young .... Mervyn Johns
Prime Minister .... Geoffrey Keen
Sydney Johnson .... Paul Rogers
Flagg .... Dennis Price
Henderson .... Peter Barkworth

Wilfred Fienburgh, a Socialist member of Parliament wrote a novel, "No Love For Johnnie," just before he was killed in an auto crash. It was heady, controversial stuff and the film of his book adds up to just that. It can be taken as a cynical peek at what

goes on behind the scenes in Britain's House of Commons or can be regarded as a scathing profile of a careerist who throws away all chances of personal happiness in pursuit of power. The film slickly combines both angles. Though not sensational in treatment, it has some earthy sex angles and is a strong, adult film which should hold intelligent audiences. Though it has no obvious stellar value for the U.S., "No Love For Johnnie" is a film worth the attention of any out-of-the-rut booker.

The hero is a heel. He is returned to Parliament for a drab, North of England constituency, but is disgruntled because he is not given his coveted job in the government. He is estranged from his wife, spurns the affection of the adoring girl in the apartment above, falls for a young blonde half his age, ruins his career because of his blind devotion to her, loses her, engages in a shabby plot to undermine his political party and finishes up with a tawdry hint of power by getting a minor government job.

Peter Finch, as the Member of Parliament, dominates the pic with a persuasive, plausible performance. Yet, the thesp's own likeable character projects a shade too much for him to be completely convincing as the arrogant opportunist. This is a man which the audience should detest, but only occasionally does. Nevertheless, with a great supporting cast, Finch steers this witty, knowledgeable script excitingly through some intelligent, dramatic moments.

There are some brisk, sexy sequences, such as when he is in bed with his young love. The parliamentary atmosphere is portrayed with skilled insight. There's a superbly captured episode at an offbeat Bohemian party. There also is a moment of tragedy when he is rejected by his constituents. Always there is an alertness in the direction by Ralph Thomas which provides some vivid entertainment.

Director Thomas has an extremely competent cast, apart from the sterling acting by Finch. Mary Peach is a newish, young blonde, who is slightly out of her league as the young love in his life. Yet but she still has enough charm to be acceptable. The other women in his life, Rosalie Crutchley, as his incompatible wife; and Billie Whitelaw, as the girl who yearns for him, are both firmly portrayed.

But it is in the smaller performances that the film's strength is revealed. Geoffrey Keen, as the Prime Minister; Paul Rogers, as his private secretary; Stanley Holloway, as a vet politician; Peter Barkworth, as a new member; Donald Pleasence as a political trouble-raiser and Hugh Burden, as his accomplice, all help the Parliamentary angle most stickly. Dennis Price, as a disillusioned photographer, and Fenella Fielding, as a scatty Bohemian party hostess, both contribute striking cameos.

These actors merely contribute, effectively, to a film that has been written, directed and photographed with a sense of purpose. There is an uneasy feeling that the producers have not quite made up their mind whether the pic is to be a savage commentary on political life or a shrewd portrait of a man at war with himself. But the end product is absorbing. ***Rich.***

Hoodlum Priest

A low budget exploitation effort that zoomed out of its class to merit big picture treatment from UA. Biopic of ex - con rehabilitator Rev. Charles Dismas Clark is somewhat distorted and uneven, but is an earnest, hard-hitting film and satisfactory b.o. sleeper.

Hollywood, Feb. 21.

United Artists release of Don Murray-Walter Wood production. Stars Murray; features Larry Gates, Keir Dulles, Logan Ramsey, Don Joslyn; introduces Cindi Wood; with Sam Capuano, Vince O'Brien, Al Mack, Lou Martini, Norman MacKaye, Joseph Cusanelli, Bill Atwood, Roger Ray, Kelley Stephens, William Wardord, Ralph Petersen, Jack Eigen, Walter L. Wiedmer, Warren Parker, Joseph H. Hamilton. Directed by Irvin Kershner. Screenplay, Don Deer, Joseph Landon; camera, Haskell Wexler; editor, Maurice Wright; art director, Jack Poplin; music, Richard Markowitz; sound, William C. Bernds; assistant directors, George Batcheller, Eddie Bernoudy. Reviewed at Goldwyn Studios, Feb. 17, '61. Running time, **100 MINS.**

Rev. C. D. Clark, S. J.	Don Murray
Louis Rosen	Larry Gates
Ellen Henley	Cindi Wood
Billy Lee Jackson	Keir Dulles
George Hale	Logan Ramsey
Pio Gentile	Don Joslyn
Mario Mazziotti	Sam Capuano
Asst. District Attorney	Vince O'Brien
Judge Garrity	Al Mack
Angelo Mazziotti	Lou Martini
Father Dunne	Norman MacKaye
Hector Sterne	Joseph Cusanelli
Weasel	Bill Atwood
Detective Shattuck	Roger Ray
Genny	Kelley Stephens
Asst. D. A.'s Aide	William Wardord
Governor	Ralph Petersen
A Prisoner	Jack Eigen
Father David Michaels	W. L. Wiedmer
Warden	Warren Parker
Prison Chaplain	Joseph H. Hamilton

"Hoodlum Priest" certainly merits the revision it has inspired in United Artists' campaign blueprint. For out of the original concept of a modest exploitation feature there has arisen, through the intelligence and cinematic savvy of cowriter-coproducer-star Don Murray and staff, a film that is dedicated and uncompromising in its efforts to make a worthwhile point on the issue of society's stance toward the ex-convict and the condemned man. Though, in making its impassioned plea, the film is guilty of occasional distortion, it is earnest and hard-hitting enough to captivate, persuade, and even arouse an audience. Its relentlessly grim, depressing nature may be a negative factor with some customers, but there is sufficient emotional meat here to make it a successful boxoffice candidate and, in view of its minimal cost, a nice gift package for UA.

Biographically based on the offbeat activities of the Rev. Charles Dismas Clark, a Jesuit priest in St. Louis noted for his rehabilitation work with ex-cons, the screenplay by Don Deer (Murray's nom-de-plume) and Joseph Landon pinpoints Clark's problems against the tragedy of a confused, but far from hopeless youth who pays with his life for crimes of which he is not solely responsible. Along the way, Murray and Landon illustrate the necessity of meeting ex-cons on their own terms to urge them away from a life of crime, and even take a swipe at capital punishment, going right into the gas chamber to do so in the film's most powerful scene.

The picture, largely photographed in St. Louis, is burdened with loose motivational ends and has a tendency to skip over key expository details, demanding the audience take for granted developments that require elaboration to ring true. But it is a case of the whole justifying its parts. The moving parts are erratic, but the machine does its job.

Murray gives a vigorous, sincere performance in the title role. But the film's most moving portrayal is delivered by Keir Dulles as the doomed lad. Larry Gates manages to be effective as an attorney whose motivations aren't quite clear.

Good prominent supporting work is etched by Don Joslyn, Sam Capuano and Lou Martini. Most others in minor support are competent. Logan Ramsey is stuck with the film's most stereotyped character, a detestable journalist who accuses the hero of furthering crime. Cindi Wood, introduced to the screen in this picture, is a trifle uncertain in her romantic byplay.

Irvin Kershner's direction sustains a flow of excitement and expectation, and is particularly effective in its technique of handling transition without dialog. Richard Markowitz' music is unusually valuable in these speechless packages. The picture is alertly and discerningly lensed by Haskell Wexler, tautly edited by Maurice Wright. The lifelike settings, chosen and/or designed by Jack Poplin, are an integral part of the story's meaning. *Tube.*

L'Ours
(The Bear)
(FRENCH-COLOR)

Paris, Feb. 14.

Cinedis release of Intermondia-Filmsonsor-Titanus production. Stars Renato Raschel, Francis Blanche; features Daniel Lecourtois, Gaucha. Directed by Edmond Sechan. Screenplay, Roger Mauge, Sechan; camera (Eastmancolor), Andre Villard; editor, Jacqueline Thiedot. At Balzac, Paris. Running time, **85 MINS.**

Medard	Renato Raschel
Chappius	Francis Blanche
The Bear	Gaucha
Director	Daniel Lecourtois

Edmond Sechan made the prize-winning 10-minute short about a boy and a goldfish "The Goldfish," and now for his first feature does a tale about a talking bear and his helpful keeper in a zoo. But this lacks enough whimsy and invention to sustain it. Hence, it looms mainly an okay kiddie pic. It does not have the stamina for some arty chances, but looms mainly as good supporting holiday fare.

A self effacing zoo keeper, harried by a tyrannical chief, one day finds a bear that can talk. Nobody believes him and he eventually has the bear, lovesick one, have an evening of love with a neighboring polar bear before getting his sadistic boss fired when he hears the bear talk.

Work is painstaking but inercuts with a man in bearskin and the real one, though a well-trained Russian circus animal, are obvious. Budget also looks strained for promising material on the animals being let loose are skimped over in a few shots. Renato Raschel is acceptable as the keeper while Francis Blanche overcharges his role as the bullying head man. Color is okay as are technical values. *Mosk.*

El Fantasma de la Opereta
(The Phantom of the Operetta)
(MEXICAN)

Mexico City, Feb. 14.

Peliculas Nacionales release of Producciones Brooks production. Stars Tin-Tan, Ana Luisa Peluffo; features Marcelo ChavezVitola, Antonio Brillas, Julian de Meriche, Armando Saenz, Eduardo Alcaraz, Luis Aldas. Directed by Fernando Cortes. Screenplay, Alfredo Ruanova. At Orfeon and Coliseo Theatres, Mexico City. Running time, **90 MINS.**

This is a Tin-Tan spoof of "The Phantom of the Opera," with the comic relying heavily on his stock-in-trade comedy tricks, aimed at kids and simple folk. In some ways, Tin-Tan, is actually the people's comic here, now that Cantinflas has gone on to bigger things in Hollywood. He has a slick approach and timing that could be used to better advantage if more attention was paid to scripting and comedy situations.

In an atmosphere of song and dance plus comedy, the funster faces up to ghosts, ruffians, madmen and monsters. Ana Luisa Peluffo graces this one for female interest, and the cast is on the whole acceptable in spoofery. Exceptional standout is Vitola who, in her first role before the cameras, shows a deft ability for comedy.

Comic Tin-Tan turns out pictures one after the other, is building up his following at home and abroad. This type of fare is sure-fire to recoup budget investments in Mexican and Latin American markets. *Emil.*

Les Nymphettes
(FRENCH)

Paris, Feb. 21.

Thanos Film production and release with Christian Pezey, Colette Descombes, Claude Arnold. Written and directed by Henry Zaphiratos. Dialog, Bernard Chesnais, Roland Guinier; camera, Roger Duculot; editor, S. Frankiel. At Rotande, Paris. Running time, **85 MINS.**

Lucien	Christian Pezey
Joelle	Colette Descombes
Mireille	Claude Arnold
Philippe	Jacques Perrin
Mario	Mario Pilar
Mother	Adrienne Serventie

Main hypo factor about this is the title which Vladimir Nabakov rendered known via his novel "Lolita." But girls in this are 16 to 20 years old without any of the offbeat allure of a Lolita. Film is a lacklustre tale about an idealistic young boy's search for a nice girl without the characterization, feeling or depth to make it of export value.

At best, this is an exploitation item. Direction cannot point up any true relationships. Technical credits are only passable with acting just fair. This looms primarily a local entry. *Mosk.*

Underworld, U.S.A.

Gangster meller about a moody, but essentially "decent" thief on a king-sized campaign to slay the four murderers of his father. Strong saturation entry.

Hollywood, Feb. 16.

Columbia Pictures release of Samuel Fuller production. Stars Cliff Robertson, Dolores Dorn, Beatrice Kay; features Paul Dubov, Robert Emhardt, Larry Gates, Richard Rust, Gerald Milton; with

Allan Gruener, David Kent, Tina Rome, Sally Mills, Robert P. Lieb, Neyle Morrow, Henry Norell. Directed and screenplay by Fuller; camera, Hal Mohr; editor, Jerome Thoms; art director, Robert Peterson; music, Harry Sukman; sound, Josh Westmoreland; assistant director, Floyd Joyer. Reviewed at the studio, Feb. 16, '61. Running time, **98 MINS.**

Tolly	Cliff Robertson
Cuddles	Dolores Dorn
Sandy	Beatrice Kay
Gela	Paul Dubov
Connors	Robert Ehhardt
Driscoll	Larry Gates
Gus	Richard Rust
Gunther	Gerald Milton
Smith	Allan Gruener
Tolly (12 years)	David Kent
Woman	Tina Rome
Connie	Sally Mills
Officer	Robert P. Lieb
Barney	Neyle Morrow
Prison Doctor	Henry Norell

"Underworld, U.S.A." is a slick gangster melodrama made to order for filmgoers who prefer screen fare explosive and uncomplicated. In this picture, the "hero" sets out on a four-ply vendetta of staggering proportions and accomplishes his mission with the calculation and poise of a pro bowler racking up a simple four-way spare. As in most gangster films, it is the tone of the acting and the tautness of the direction that count, and it is here that Samuel Fuller's Globe Enterprises production tallies its winning points. The Columbia release is ideally suitable for saturation booking.

Written and directed by Fuller, the yarn follows the wicked career of supposedly decent but hate-motivated, revenge-consumed fellow who, as a youngster, witnessed in horror the gangland slaying of his father by four budding racketeers. Through various hitches in an orphanage, a reformatory and prison, he matures into bitter manhood and ultimately embarks on his furious and primitive revenge. Working on both sides of the law, he succeeds masterfully in his deadly undertaking, but comes a cropper when he goes after an underworld kingpin for reasons removed from his original emotional scheme. Basically this is all conventional, traditional stuff, the type that will appeal to conventional, traditional audiences.

As the central figure, Cliff Robertson delivers a brooding, virile, finely balanced portrayal. It's a first-rate delineation atop a cast that performs expertly. Dolores Dorn supplies romantic interest with sufficient sincerity, and Beatrice Kay is persuasive as the decent, compassionate woman whose fervent, but unfulfilled, desire for motherhood gives rise to a vague mother-son relationship with Robertson. There are three top-notch gangster portrayals by Paul Dubov, Robert Emhardt and Richard Rust, a telling characterization of a top cop by Larry Gates, and a more than competent personification of Robertson as a lad by David Kent.

Fuller's screenplay has its lags, character superficialities and unlikelihoods, but it is crisp with right-sounding gangster jargon and remains absorbing. As director, he has whipped his cast into businesslike shape and kept his camera (deftly manned by Hal Mohr) probing for character, even to the extent of considerable eyeballing.

Robert Peterson's sets range pertinently from slum squalor to penthouse luxury. Jerome Thoms' editing is tight and sure. The film's score by Harry Sukman underlines the story with meaning, including a prominent "Auld Lang Syne" theme via music box, a fitting ditty linked with the hero's personality.

Tube.

Les Grandes Personnes
(The Adults)
(FRENCH)

Paris, Feb. 14.

Fernand Rivers release of Pomereu-International Films production. Stars Jean Seberg, Micheline Presle, Maurice Ronet; features Francoise Prevost, Annibal Ninchi. Directed by Jean Valere. Screenplay, Roger Nimier, Valere from novel by Nimier; camera, Raoul Coutard; editor, Leonide Azar. At Mercury, Paris. Running time, **95 MINS.**

Michele	Micheline Presle
Ann	Jean Seberg
Philippe	Maurice Ronet
Gladys	Francoise Prevost
Severin	Annibal Ninchi

Sleek, stilted film is about a 19-year-old Yank girl who comes of emotional age while visiting with a doctor uncle in Paris. She gets mixed up with a worldly crowd. Her education is mainly in cropping her hair, dressing correctly and in the sex department. Surface characterization, over literary dialog and a soapy aspect make this primarily for exploitation use abroad. It might find hard going in arty theatres, but could conceivably be a hypo entry.

American girl, played by U.S. actress Jean Seberg, nurses a career woman back to health after an attempt at suicide over her sweetheart, a melancholy playboy who is trying to rekindle a defunct auto factory he owns. She adores the woman and hates the man, but naturally falls for him and has her first affair. Then it develops he really belongs to the woman. The American girl then goes home to Nebraska with her down-to-earth fiancee still dreaming of the love she found.

Characters are futile and uninteresting. Director Jean Valere and scripter Roger Nimier have been unable to display an insight into what makes them tick. It is all handled in a glossy, conventional manner except for a torrid love scene which could be a hypo peg. Acting cannot do much with the one dimensional characters. Editing helps give the pic a punch at times. Technical credits are very good.

Mosk.

The Night We Got The Bird
(BRITISH)

Broad slapstick comedy made to a formula that often clicks with undemanding audiences in U. K. Lacks marquee appeal for U.S.

London, Feb. 14.

British Lion release of a Rix-Conyers production. Stars Brian Rix, Dora Bryan, Ronald Shiner; features Leo Franklyn, Liz Fraser, Irene Handl, John Slater. Directed by Darcy Conyers. Screenplay, Ray Cooney, Tony Hilton and Darcy Conyers from Basil Thomas' play, "The Love Birds"; camera, S. D. Onions; editor, Thelma Connell; music, Tommy Watts. At Studio One, London. Running time, **82 MINS.**

Bertie Skidmore	Brian Rix
Julie	Dora Bryan
Victor	Leo Franklyn
Ma	Irene Handl
Fay	Liz Fraser
Wolfie Green	John Slater
Chippendale Charlie	Reginald Beckwith
Dr. Vincent	Robertson Hare
Mr. Warre-Monger, J.P.	Kynaston Reeves
Clerk of the Court	John Le Mesurier
Cecil Gibson	Ronald Shiner
P. C. Lovejoy	Terry Scott
Bus Conductor	Basil Lord

Actor-manager Brian Rix has, in the last 10 years, made a corner in British stage farce at the Whitehall Theatre. Now, with a similar corny, unpretentious formula dedicated to raising slapstick yocks, he is moving into the pix business. "Night We Got the Bird" is the second in a series which promises to run quite awhile. Gags and situations are hit home with sledge-hammer wallops. Family audiences in Britain will revel in the cockeyed goings-on. With no marquee value for the States, this farce may be difficult to sell in America.

This one is based on a stage play, "The Love Birds," and has Ronald Shiner, for no valid reason, returning after his death, in the guise of a South American parrot, to haunt his widow and her new spouse. Shiner was a shady fixer of antique furniture which provides a hinge for the honeymoon of Rix and Dora Bryan to be constantly interrupted while they attempt to find a phony antique bed which Shiner sold under false pretenses. All this to escape the wrath of a local gangster. The "plot" needs no more explanation. In fact, precious little more could be provided.

It's simply an excuse for people to lose their trousers, Rix and Miss Bryan to pose as schoolchildren, a crazy car chase, a lot of jokes about sex, characters bumping into others, people falling into the sea, and so on.

The snare about this sort of film is that it cannot rely on the timing that can be given to similar material on the stage. So sometimes the gags misfire, but on the whole there is a fair amount of honest, vulgar laughter. Rix has wisely gathered around him some expert farceurs such as Shiner, Leo Franklyn, the inevitable Irene Handl, John Slater, Robertson Hare and Reginald Beckwith. John Le Mesurier and Kynaston Reeves, as clerk of a magistrate's court and a deaf, bumbling magistrate, respectively, provide some quieter fun to the knockabout stuff.

Technical credits are all satisfactory.

Rich.

La Giornata Balorda
(The Strange Day)
(ITALIAN-FRENCH)

Paris, Feb. 14.

UFA release of Transcontinental-Euro Film production. With Jean Sorel, Lea Massari, Jeanne Valerie, Rik Battaglia, Isabelle Corey, Paolo Stoppa. Directed by Mauro Bolognini. Screenplay, Pasolini, Moravia, Visconti from story by Moravia; camera, Aldo Scavarda; editor, Boris Lewyn. At Paris, Paris. Running time, **85 MINS.**

David	Jean Sorel
Mistress	Lea Massari
Amie	Jeanne Valerie
Sabine	Isabelle Corey
Trucker	Rik Battaglia
Lallus	Paolo Stoppa
Freja	Lea Massari

French producer Paul Graetz made this pic in Italy where it has been forbidden showing; hence, he promptly preemed it here. Film is a day in the life of a youth looking for work and finding mainly corruption and misery. However, this lacks the true rage and insight to make its irony moving, and it looms mainly as an exploitation bet.

Director Mauro Bolgonini, as is customary, has done this all in real settings. A 20-year-old good-looking boy has a child by a neighbor and goes out one day to find money to buy a job to have the child baptized and to marry the youngster's mother.

He hopes to get work through a shifty uncle who sends him to a shady jobber. Latter only gives him a job because of the insistence of his mistress who has a yen for the boy.

He finally nabs a ring from a dead man's finger to pay for his job, with a hopefully ironic ending as he plays with his child and future wife. Pic has a tendency to amble along with its social and economic critique somewhat blunted by Jean Sorel's one register thesping as the boy. But the girls and characters he meets are well limned. This would need a hard sell but its theme and general solidity could make it worthwhile. Technical aspects are fine.

Mosk.

Lola
(FRENCH)
(Franscope)

Paris, Feb. 14.

Unidex release of Rome-Paris Films production. Stars Anouk Aimee; features Marc Michel, Elina Labourdette, Alan Scott, Annie Duperoux, Jacques Harden, Margo Lion. Written and directed by Jacques Demy. Camera, Raoul Coutard; editor, M. Georges. Previewed in Paris. Running time, **90 MINS.**

Lola	Anouk Aimee
Roland	Marc Michel
Desnoyers	Elina Labourdette
Frankie	Alan Scott
Cecile	Annie Duperoux
Michel	Jacques Harden
Jeanne	Margo Lion

Still another first pic with the "new wave" characteristics of on-the-spot lensing, little known names and an improvised look. Its tale of small town bordedom and attempts to escape its grasp is done in a serio-comic manner and scattered shafts of insight do not quite bring off the tongue-in-cheek happy ending. But it has enough candor for foreign arty house possibilities.

A young man floats through jobs and hopes to leave a stultifying little town. He meets an old flame who dances in a club and has half-hearted affairs with Yank sailors while waiting for her first lover and father of her illegitimate son to come back. The boy falls for her again but up pops her old lover for a wry happy ending while the young man goes forth into the world.

A fading middleclass woman and her 14-year-old daughter looking for love are also entwined in these series of sketches that intermingle to give a cross section of life and desires.

But the mixture of melodrama, satire and poetics does not entirely jell. It is offbeat, with shafts of tender feeling and truth. But trying to touch on too many subjects make the film uneven.

Anouk Aimee has a pathetic quality as the mythomaniacal dancer who finally finds happiness while Marc Michel is properly aimless as the boy. But other roles are mainly one dimensional types. Lensing has the proper gray quality for this pleasant unusual pic.

Mosk.

Offbeat
(BRITISH)

Slick little dualer which shapes up excellently as one of new-look British second features. No U.S. marquee value here, but still a worthwhile booking as secondary pic.

London, Feb. 26.

British Lion release of M. Smelley Aston production. Stars William Sylvester, Mai Zetterling; features Anthony Dawson, John Meillon, John Phillips, Victor Brooks. Directed by Cliff Owen. Original story and screenplay, Peter Barnes; camera, Geoffrey Faithfull; editor, Antony Gibbs; music, Ken Jones. At Studio One, London. Running time, **72 MINS.**

Layton/Steve Ross.....William Sylvester
Ruth Lombard .... Mai Zetterling
Johnny Hemick .... John Meillon
James Dawson .... Anthony Dawson
Leo Farrell .... Neil McCarthy
Gill Hall .... Harry Baird
Superintendent Gault......John Phillips
Inspector Adams .... Victor Brooks
Maggie Dawson .... Diana King
Jake .... Gerad Heinz
J. B. Wykenham .... Ronald Adam
Pat Ryan .... Neil Wilson

British producers in general, and those working for British Lion in particular, are doing a worthwhile job in trying to raise the stature of low-budget second feature pix. Typical example of this is "Offbeat," which was brought in for around $70,000. It is a compact little crime yarn, well acted, and briskly written and directed. A very useful dualer for Britain, this could well click in the U.S. though it has no names known to American audiences.

It has William Sylvester as a Scotland Yard undercover man who is recruited to pose as a crook, then join a gang and find out for the police about a new type of criminal in the underworld, the men who run crime on strictly business level.

He is accepted by a gang whose boss runs a small export firm as a front. A big robbery is planned in which Sylvester is the main brains. But he has become involved with a young widow in the gang and also finds that his friendship for the crooks is growing, so that he is loath to betray them. The widow discovers that he has connections with the police but he persuades her that he is now on their side and has broken with the police. But when a fence exposes him as an impostor he unwittingly plays into the police's hands and the gang is rounded up.

This is a neat story. But it is a pity that a wholly unnecessary "prologue" before the credit titles partly gives away the ending. Production and direction are smooth, dialog and characterization plausible and technically it measures up to many pix from far more ambitious producers.

Sylvester gives a strong performance as the sleuth. Mai Zetterling is appealing as the widow while John Meillon and Anthony Dawson, as the two principal crooks, are both sound. Victor Brooks and John Phillips fill their chores as limbs of the law very competently. There are some shrewd touches in the way the "new wave" of criminals plan their crimes like a respectable, law abiding business. *Rich.*

Das Wirtshaus im Spessart
(The Spessart Inn)

Casino Film Exchange release of Constantin-Film production. Stars Liselotte Pulver, Carlos Thompson; features Ina Peters, Herbert Huebner, Guenther Lueders, Otto Storr, Helmut Lohner, Hans Clarin. Directed by Kurt Hoffman. Written by Heinz Pauch and Liselotte Enderle, based on story by Wilhelm Hauff; camera, Richard Angst; music, Franze Grothe. Previewed at Bonded Film Storage screening room Feb. 15, '61. Running time, **99 MINS.**

The only thing to complain about in this new German import directed by Kurt Hoffman is that it is years behind the times in terms of subject matter. The performance is a good one and the cinematic techniques are right up to date. The tinted photography is professional, the pacing is brisk, and sound, editing, etc., all first-rate.

Unfortunately, these talents were lavished upon thematic material of a bygone era. It's billed as a spoof of the story anent robbers of the forest kidnapping titled young lady along with her apparently in adequate spouse-to-be for purposes of ransom.

Captain of the robbers is the one to whom the countess eventually turns for purposes of romance. But before this, with the idea of deceiving the highwaymen, the countess poses as a male and her newly-found young male friend (who takes up with her maid) poses as the countess.

These and other of the characters on and off break out into song with Teutonic gusto.

Well done, and parts of it are fun but hardly fitting all the way for the taste of modern times.
Gene.

El Gato
(The Cat)
(MEXICAN)

Mexico City, Feb. 21.
Columbia Pictures release of Alfa Films production. Stars Joaquin Cordero, Lucha Moreno; features Angel Infante, Andres Solcer, Chucho Salinas, Ramon Bugarini, Salvador Terroba, Carlos Leon. Directed by Miguel M. Delgado. Screenplay, Alfreda Varela Jr., from original by Jose Ma. Fernandez Unsain; camera, Victor Herrera; music Raul Lavista. At Nacional and Tlacopao Theatres, Mexico City. Running time, **80 MINS.**

Main point about the preem of this one is that it opened in two nabe houses, with an oldie Pedro Infante film as the second feature.

Based on American westerns, an attempt is made to present a western badman always ready with an itchy trigger finger. But it turns out flat and even the action scenes including fist fights and gun duels are overplayed and exaggerated.

"The Cat" gets his in the end but it all adds up to a very poor imitation of a cowboy meller. *Emil.*

Paloma Brava
(Brave Pigeon)
(MEXICAN)

Mexico City, Feb. 21.
Peliculas Nacionales release of Churubusco production. Stars Rosita Quintana, Miguel Aceves Mejia, Sara Garcia; features "Beto the Pharmacist," Alfredo Varela Jr., Guillermo "Lobe." Manuel Vergara "Mamber," Jose Galvez. Directed by Rogelio Gonzalez. Screenplay, Janet Alcoriza; camera, Victor Herrera; music, Gustavo Cesar Carrion. At Orfeon Theatre, Mexico City. Running time, **90 MINS.**

Rosita Quintana as the brave

pigeon who copes with assorted situations in this comedy with oater overtones deserves better roles because she is capable of handling roles better than one in this quickie. Veteran Sara Garcia also is miscast in a picture which follows pattern of getting together boxoffice names for a quick recoup of production investments via exhibition in nabe houses.

Director Rogelio Gonzalez is also worthy of better things than this feeble commercial effort. *Emil.*

Ca Va Etre Ta Fete
(It's Your Birthday)
(FRENCH)

Paris, Feb. 28.
Unidex release of GEF-Belmont Film-Contact production. Stars Eddie Constantine; features Barbara Laage, Claude Cerval, Stephen Schnabel, Medina, Lloyd Kerber. Directed by Pierre Montazel. Screenplay, Clarence Weiss, Montazel; camera, Michel Kelber; editor, Raymond Lamy. At Balzac, Paris. Running time, 90 MINS.
Jarvis .... Eddie Constantine
Michele .... Barbara Laage
Chief .... Claude Cerval
Bargarian .... Stephen Schnabel

After making films in other countries, Eddie Constantine is back in France with his action vehicles in the American detective genre. Pic has a lame script but enough movement, fights and gags to make it an okay entry here but shapes mainly of dualer calibre for any possible Yank chances. But Constantine has a flock of these pix behind him which could be bundled into a tv series.

Here he is on a mission for the U.S. Secret Service to unearth a double agent in Lisbon which he does by setting himself up as a decoy. Constantine has his usual casual charm and drinks less than in other pix with not too many femmes dropping into his arms.

Accent is on intrigue and gags in this one. It is well paced with okay technical credits. *Mosk.*

The Police Dog Story

Routine cops 'n' robbers meller with a fairly novel canine story twist that makes it especially serviceable as kiddie draw.

Hollywood, Feb. 23.
United Artists release of Robert E. Kent production. Stars James Brown, Merry Anders; with Barry Kelley, Milton Frome, Vinton Hayworth, Francis De Sales, Brad Trumbull, Pat McCaffria, Joe Flynn, Charles Waggenheim, Jack Mann, Ray D. Barwick, Elvin Frazier, Henry Y. Coul, Lawrence E. Weatherwax, George Sawaya, Jerry Todd, Rocco. Directed by Edward L. Cahn; camera, Maury Gertsman; editor, Arthur Hilton; art director, Serge Krizman; sound, John Kean; assistant director, Herbert S. Greene. Reviewed at Goldwyn Studios, Feb. 23, '61. Running time, 62 MINS.
Norm Edward .... James Brown
Terry Dayton .... Merry Anders
Bert Dana .... Barry Kelley
Todd Wellman .... Milton Frome
Commissioner .... Vinton Hayworth
Capt. Dietrich .... Francis De Sales
Bill Frye .... Brad Trumbull
Keith Early .... Pat McCaffria
Collins .... Joe Flynn
Firebug .... Charles Waggenheim
Mattson .... Jack Mann
Royce .... Ray D. Barwick
Adams .... Elvin Frazier
Davis .... Harry Y. Coul
Fallon .... Lawrence E. Weatherwax
Driver .... George Sawaya
Helper .... Jerry Todd
Wolf (dog) .... Rocco

Concentrating on the canine element in their story, the Zenith Pictures team of producer Robert E. Kent and director Edward L. Cahn have constructed a serviceable lower-berth item out of an essentially standard, insipid cops 'n' robbers melodrama. For best results, the United Artists release should be programmed in double bills aimed at a moppet audience.

Orville H. Hampton's screenplay dwells at length on the training routine prescribed for rookie contenders of the police K-Nine Corps, then veers into a routine pattern in which policeman and policedog round up a gang of insurance-motivated arsonists. Star of the picture is Rocco (redubbed "Wolf," a handle more befitting a pooch of such heroic proportions), a husky German Shepherd who can growl, arf-arf, hurdle a fence and chew up a trousers leg with the best of 'em. That the dog is more impressive than the two-legged characters in this film can be attributed at least partially to the stiff, mechanical dialog penned by Hampton, delivery of which "Wolf" alone is spared.

James Brown capably essays the role of the rookie cop assigned to train the dog. Romantic interest is dispatched by Merry Anders. Adequate support is contributed by Barry Kelley, Milton Frome, Vinton Hayworth and Francis De Sales. Cahn's direction has a tendency toward repetition, but he has succeeded in minimizing the maudlin aspects that so easily can seep into a picture in which an animal is the hero.

Various crafts are dispatched in an unpretentious, businesslike manner. Among these assists are Maury Gertsman's camera work, Serge Krizman's sets and Arthur Hilton's editing. *Tube.*

Konga
(SPECTAMATION-COLOR)

Fairly exploitable fantasyspectacle of a familiar nature —the mad scientist and his

rebellious monster.

Hollywood, Feb. 24.

American International release of Herman Cohen production. Stars Michael Gough, Margo Johns, Jess Conrad, Claire Gordon. Directed by John Lemont. Screenplay, Aben Kandel, Cohen; camera, (Eastman), Desmond Dickinson; editor, Jack Slade; art director, Wilfred Arnold; music, Gerard Schurmann; sound, Ronald Abbott; assistant director, Buddy Booth. Reviewed at Goldwyn Studios, Feb. 24, '61. Running time, 90 MINS.

Dr. Charles Decker	Michael Gough
Margaret	Margo Johns
Bob Kenton	Jess Conrad
Sandra Banks	Claire Gordon
Dean Foster	Austin Trevor
Superintendent Brown	Jack Watson
Professor Tagore	George Pastell
Bob's Mother	Vanda Godsell
Inspector Lawson	Stanley Morgan
Miss Bernesdell	Grace Arnold
Bob's Father	Leonard Sachs
Daniel	Nicholas Bennett
Mary	Kim Tracy
Eric	Rupert Osborne
Janet	Waveney Lee
Comm. Garland	John Welsh

Herman Cohen's production of "Konga" is essentially a combination of three other monster spectacles of the screen. It is akin to "Frankenstein" in theme (mad scientist and superhuman creation), "King Kong" in physique (the oversized gorilla), and "Gorgo" in locale of destruction (London). But "Konga," regrettably, is not quite the equal of any one of the three. American International Pictures will have to bank on the film's intrinsic exploitation qualities to arouse the filmgoing public's curiosity. Lacking the novelty, names and thought-provoking values that spur word-of-mouth, the picture is a logical candidate for the swift saturation method of exhibition.

That the film is as diverting as it is from time to time reflects credit on director John Lemont, who has managed to keep his actors disciplined and concerned; cameraman Desmond Dickinson, whose Eastman-tinted views of plant, animal and human monstrosities are often intriguing; and art director Wilfred Arnold, who has designed some admirably ornate and employable sets and objects for the occasion.

Producer Cohen penned the screenplay in collaboration with Aben Kandel. Basis for the existence of their mutant monster is discovery of a link in the evolutionary barrier between plant and animal life by a botany professor who returns to London after a year in the jungles of Africa. The professor, unfortunately, is mad. Injecting a chimp (Konga) with a phenomenal growth serum extracted from the roots of an ultra-carnivorous plant, he creates a gorilla of super proportions, hypnotizes it and sets it loose on a campaign of murder and destruction.

Film is burdened with verbose, repetitious scientific gobbledegook, but ultimately boils down to the inevitable skyscraper-hopping climax in which the army puts an abrupt end to Konga's messy monkeyshines in the vicinity of Big Ben.

Of additional aid is the fact that the actors are British. Somehow the London tongue lends a certain extra degree of persuasiveness to a fantasy such as this, at least to the American ear.

A process dubbed Specta-Mation is utilized to accomplish the spectacle aspects. Jack Slade's editing is skilled, Gerard Schurmann's score stimulating.

Just why the professor is so unfavorably disposed toward his fellow man is never clear, but Michael Gough plays the part with style and fervor. Margo Johns is earnest as his ill-fated housekeeper. Claire Gordon is a shapely addition to the cast as a student over whom Gough goes romantically wild.

Tube.

Saint Tropez Blues
(FRENCH-COLOR)

Paris, Feb. 28.

Champs-Elysees release of Jules Borkon production. With Marie Laforet, Fausto Tozzi, Jacques Higelin, Pierre Michael, J. M. Riviere, Monique Just. Written and directed by Marcel Moussy. Camera (Eastmancolor), Pierre Lhomme; editor, Denise Natot; music, Henri Crolla. Previewed in Paris. Running time, 90 MINS.

Anne-Marie	Marie Laforet
Trabu	Fausto Tozzi
Jean-Paul	Jacques Higelin
Francois	J. M. Riviere
Veronique	Monique Just

Film is the first "New Wave" pic by ex-scripter Marcel Moussy. It attempts to treat the freer sex habits of the youth of today in comedy fashion. He is also the first to use color. Localed in the Riviera resort of Saint Tropez, the virginal heroine manages to remain chaste through a myriad of temptations and mild orgies. It is lightly done but meanders somewhat, with flimsy characterizations. This primarily is an exploitation item on its frankness and youthful pranks.

A bookish girl, who is supposed to be home catching up on her studies, goes off to a summer resort with a childhood friend. The friend is a free-wheeling boy and they are soon involved with the free-living art colony of the place. She manages to come out of it intact and realizes she loves the old friend. So they open a nitery together and will presumably live happily ever after.

Director Moussy takes some potshots at the quaint morals of the place but the film rarely settles down to real situation comedies or a true feeling for the problems and escapades of the gilded youth and youth-seeking elders. It has okay acting by a flock of new actors. Marie Laforet is somewhat mannered but Jacques Hegelin denotes a true serio-comic flair as the irrepressible young boy in love.

Mosk.

The Canadians
(BRITISH—COLOR)

Plodding drama about the Canadian Mounties, competently performed by Robert Ryan and others, but lacking any real dramatic spark. Tepid b.o. prospect.

London, Feb. 28.

20th-Fox production (Herman E. Webber) and release. Stars Robert Ryan. John Dehner, Torin Thatcher; features Teresa Stratas. Directed by Burt Kennedy. Screenplay, Burt Kennedy; camera, Arthur Ibbetson; editor, Douglas Robertson. At Rialto, London. Running time, 85 MINS.

Inspector Gannon	Robert Ryan
Frank Boone	John Dehner
Master Sergeant McGregor	Torin Thatcher
Contable Springer	Burt Metcalfe
Superintendent Walker	John Sutton
Greer	Jack Creley
Ben	Scott Peters
Billy	Richard Alden
The White Squaw	Teresa Stratas

The first British quota picture to be shot solely in Canada is a plodding, tepid drama about Canada's Mounted Police. It is short on high dramatic notes and on humor. Main virtue of pic is the sweeping Canadian scenery but even this is fuzzily photographed, especially in long shots. Despite a dogged performance by Robert Ryan as one of those Mounties who always gets his man and the introduction of singer Teresa Stratas there is nothing much about this one to give a kick to the boxoffice. This seems a safe booking for undemanding audiences, but that's its limit.

General Custer has been wiped out at Little Big Horn and the Sioux have entered Canada to escape the U.S. Cavalry. Ryan and two men are sent to meet the Injuns and tell them that they will be left in peace so long as they remain peaceful. But the Sioux camp is invaded by an American rancher searching for his stolen horses and his three gunhands. The Indians are massacred and the Americans abduct a white squaw as "proof" that they were rescuing a white woman. Nevertheless, Ryan and his two buddies take in the crooks and set off to take them to the Mounties' post. The audience plods along with the little band until the Indians stampede the villains over a high cliff.

That's about all, it takes a tedious time to happen.

A dull script is played out conscientiously but without much spirit by Ryan and this fellow thesps. The only really dramatic scene is when the Sioux take charge and stampede the horses but even this is patently faked. The Sioux are wasted after a promising start. Ryan, expressionless as his horse, gives a stolid performance as the dedicated Mounty who falls gently for the white squaw. Torin Thatcher and Burt Metcalfe are his two men and such slight humor as there is, brought out by the clash between the hard-bitten sergeant (Torin Thatcher) and the rookie.

John Dehner, Jack Creley, Scott Peters and Richard Alden are the heavies and, though they snarl a great deal, they don't add up to much a menace. Teresa Stratas, making her screen debut, sings a couple of songs charmingly but her acting is strictly minor league. Most disappointing aspect of this pic is the way the wonderful Canadian scenery is often wasted through apparent fuzziness in the lensing. It sometimes has the air of 16m film having been blown up.

Rich.

Five Guns To Tombstone

Routine lower-berth western. Best fit for the moppet brigades.

Hollywood, Feb. 24.

United Artists release of Robert E. Kent production. With James Brown, John Wilder, Walter Coy, Robert Karnes, Della Sharman, Joe Haworth, Quent Sondergaard, Boyd Morgan, Jon Locke. Directed by Edward L. Cahn. Screenplay, Richard Schayer, Jack De Witt, from story by Arthur Orloff; camera, Maury Gertsman; editor, Bernard Small; art director, Serge Krizman; music, Paul Sawtell, Bert Shefter; sound, Robert Post; assistant director, Herbert S. Greene. Reviewed at Goldwyn Studios, Feb. 24, '61. Running time, 71 MINS.

Billy Wade	James Brown
Ted Wade	John Wilder
Ike Garvey	Walter Coy
Matt Wade	Robert Karnes
Hoke	Joe Haworth
Hank	Quent Sondergaard
Hoagie	Boyd Morgan
Kolloway	Jon Locke
Arlene	Della Sharman

Just about par for the supporting feature course, "Five Guns to Tombstone" will pad a twin-bill adequately wherever filmgoers still prefer two for the price of one, no matter the fluctuation in A-to-B calibre. There is, however, nothing here for the discriminating audience, and that should be kept in mind when pairing decisions are made. Even incurable western buffs will find nothing novel in the way of plot or character in the Zenith Pictures offering, but they may cotton to its sustained flow of action. The United Artists release will spur its most appreciative response from childrens' sections.

Robert E. Kent's modest production features James Brown as a reformed gunslinger framed into renewed lawlessness by his brother, an escaped convict hired for a huge heist on condition his brainy brother participate. Secretly in cahoots with the authorities, Brown plays along with the baddies and ultimately outfoxes and outguns their leader, whose greed proves his undoing.

Scenarists Richard Schayer and Jack De Witt, working over a yarn by Arthur Orloff, obviously haven't fretted over motivational nuances, choosing, understandably so under the circumstances, to stress action elements. Nor has director Edward L. Cahn labored long with explanatory details in his zeal for action. When a gun is fired and a man is killed in a balcony room of a quiet gambling saloon, none of the poker-playing customers even blinks. Apparently they are too intent on their own killings to notice.

Brown gives a reserved portrayal of the hero. John Wilder delivers an earnest delineation of his confused nephew. One of those laughing boy heavies is essayed in assured fashion by Walter Coy. About all that is required of the femme lead is that she be pretty. Della Sharman is just that.

Supporting work is efficient, as are the unostentatious contributions of cameraman Maury Gertsman, editor Bernard Small, art director Serge Krizman and tuners Paul Sawtell and Bert Shefter.

Tube.

Une Aussi Longue Absence
(Such a Long Absence)
(FRENCH)

Paris, March 7.

Procinex production and release. Stars Alida Valli; features Georges Wilson, Amedee, Blavette, Jacques Harden. Directed by Henri Colpi. Screenplay, Marguerite Duras, Gerard Jarlot; camera, Marcel Weiss; editor, Jasmine Chasney. Previewed in Paris. Running time, 95 MINS.

Therese	Alida Valli
Tramp	Georges Wilson
Trucker	Jacques Harden
Michel	Amedee
Client	Blavette

For his first pic as a director, film editor Henri Colpi ("Hiroshima Mon Amour" was edited by him) won the coveted French critic's prize, the Prix Louis Delluc. Film is a measured, atmospheric tale that tries to reveal the interior needs and aspects of its characters much in the vein of "Hiroshima" which was also written by Marguerite Duras who penned this script. Result is a slow, deliberate comment on a woman's need to find or relive old love, and war's

place in this scheme. This appears mainly an arty theatre bet without the depth of its predecessor, "Hiroshima."

A woman (Alida Valli), who runs a cafe, thinks she sees her supposedly dead husband, killed in deportation during the last war, when a new tramp appears in her neighborhood. He turns out to be an amnesiac and she tries everything to try to make him remember only to have him run off.

Miss Valli is heavier than previously but still handsome and displays an interior intensity and poise that are not quite right for the cafe-owner role. But the pic only uses these real surroundings to detail this woman's longing for her first real love and a chance to experience it again.

Director Colpi has managed to build up tension and flow of catching images. Film just lacks the tie with life to make it truly arresting and gave it the tingle of life which it does not quite achieve.

Miss Valli gives her role an inner intensity while Georges Wilson is effective as the man without a memory. The ending is a brilliant tour-de-force as she tries to bring back his past by sitting before a gawdy jukebox on which she has put a classical record he on once liked.

This is a difficult film but one that might be worth the trouble as art and more general tastes seem to swing to the more personalized, literary-type distaff pix. But it needs specialized handling. Technical credits are excellent.

Mosk.

The Trapp Family
(AUSTRIAN-COLOR)

Sentimental family portrait of the angelically warbling Austrian brood. Too outmoded in style to score in today's market, but clears the boards for 20th's future Trapp musical, "Sound Of Music."

Hollywood, Feb. 28.

Twentieth-Fox release of Wolfgang Reinhardt-UTZ Uterman production. Stars Ruth Leuwerik; with Hans Holt, Josef Meinrad, Maria Holst, Friedrich Dumin, Hilda Von Stolz, Michael Ande, Knut Mahlke, Ursula Wolff, Monika Wolf, Angelika Werth, Ursula Ettrich, Monika Ettrich. Directed by Wolfgang Liebeneiner. Screenplay, Herbert Reinecker, based on book by George Hurdalk and memoirs of Baroness Maria Von Trapp; camera (De Luxe), Werner Krien; editor, Margot von Schlieffen; art directors, Robert Herlth, Gottfried Will; music, Frank Grothe; sound, Hans Endraulat, Martin Mueller; assistant director, Zlata Mehlers. Reviewed at the studio, Feb. 28, '61. Running time, **97 MINS.**

"The Trapp Family" is a sweet, old-fashioned picture for sweet, old-fashioned people. Once upon a (more innocent) time, say a quarter of a century ago, the Wolfgang Reinhardt-UTZ Uterman production, lensed in Austria, m i g h t have been quite a hit with the filmgoing public. But the screen and its audience are presumably made of sterner, slyer, more perceptive stuff these days.

The domestic fortunes of this film are somewhat partially dependent upon the extent of the reactionary, back-to-peaches-and-cream movement spurred by the boldness of theme and provocation of content that has characterized the screen's most important new efforts. Whether this ideological reaction will translate into an appreciable market in this instance is highly doubtful, especially since the product in question is of foreign vintage, is post-dubbed, bears not a single name (other than "Trapp" itself) that carries any weight at the U. S. boxoffice, and is too long and cumbersome for graceful pairing.

The screenplay, penned by Herbert Reinecker from a book by George Hurdalek, is based on the memoirs of the still-living Baroness Maria Von Trapp, which also formed the basis of the Broadway musical, "The Sound of Music," picture rights to which have been purchased by 20th-Fox which, in quickly releasing this version, thus clears the decks for the major undertaking to come. The story traces the activities of this model Austrian brood from the point at which it is joined by its inspirational force—a devoted young convent novice who undertakes the duties of governess of its seven children, later to become their stepmother—up through its flight from Nazi oppression and overseas to America, where its natural choral gifts enable it to catch on in the touring concert circuit and establish happy residence in Vermont.

The film's uncomprisingly sentimental nature has a tendency to slop over into naivete. A more lovable, less dimensional crop of characters is difficult to envision. On top of that, all of the conflicts are predictable and the pace commandeered by director Wolfgang Liebeneiner and supplemented by editor Margot von Schlieffen is ponderous in tempo, lopsided in emphasis. Sole virtue untarnished by dubbing translation is the choral warbling of the children, a delight to the ear and an assault on the heartstrings. Fact they sing like trained angels first time they raise their voices in concert is questionable, to say the least, but then everything wonderful comes pretty easy in this story.

Ruth Leuwerik, who bears a slight resemblance to Claudette Colbert, plays the novice-come-baroness. The character is not sufficiently developed, so that her charming innocence occasionally borders on the artificial, but on the whole she does a persuasive job. As the baron, Hans Holt cuts a handsome, impressively blank figure as a rather hapless example of obsolete nobility in a compressing society giving way to the commoner. The seven children form an attractive unit, individual personality flashing out only in the singing passages.

Frank Grothe's melodious music is an outstanding aspect. The Robert Herlth-Gottfried Will sets, especially the baron's home, are sturdy and elegant, and are appreciatively regarded through Werner Krien's camera via De Luxe Color. *Tube.*

Walk The Angry Beach

Stark study of lower-depth element on Hollywood fringe in which the glamor capital itself is depicted as the heavy. An earnest, passionate, but undisciplined, rather immature film lacking sufficient b.o. value by arty or general standards.

Hollywood, March 2.

John Patrick Hayes production (no release set). Stars Anthony Vorno, Rue McClanahan. Directed and screenplay by Hayes; camera, Vilis Lapenieks; editor, Esther Poche, Ronald Thorne; music, Bill Marx. Reviewed at General Film Labs, March 2, '61. Running time, **74 MINS.**

Tony .... Anthony Vorno
Sandy .... Rue McClanahan
Nick .... Paul Bruce
Ernest .... Ernest Macias
Tom .... John Barrick
Shakespearean.........Leslie Moorhouse
Fitz .... Doug Rideout
Patti .... Joanne Stewart
Mrs. McVea .... Lea Marmer

Hollywood's wilder, more sordid elements are the basis for an undisciplined, emotionally bitter "Expose" in "Walk the Angry Beach." Few will deny the baser instincts of mankind are as much a reality in the film capital as they are anywhere but, in implying that the corrupt nature of the community itself is responsible for the tragic death of his hero, a basically decent but confused young man who lacks the self-control or perception to avoid his own destruction, writer-producer-director John Patrick Hayes is guilty of a distorted perspective that tarnishes a no doubt sincere effort.

Although the very earnestness of Hayes' glum, acid point-of-view and the passion with which he presents his case merit industry and community observation, if only to witness the extent to which Hollywood can be held in low esteem, this film is not going to be a favorite down at the Chamber of Commerce nor is it likely to snare very easily the release commitment it is now without, at least from the major Hollywood distribution points. Way shy of respectable art house calibre, far too offbeat and specialized for popular general run, and entirely too risque in its present state to pass the puritan pressure barrier, it is a doubtful prospect for the current domestic cinemarketplace.

Hayes' angry young picture of Hollywood is pegged on the experiences of a young fellow (Anthony Vorno) who: 1) is abandoned by his wife, 2) fails in his junkyard business, 3) tangles with a prospective employer in his bid for a job, 4) joins a pair of crooks in a waterfront heist, 5) falls in love with a mixed-up peeler (Rue McClanahan) who wants to be an actress, but is a sucker for a bedroom "casting" pitch, 6) dies in her arms after he is knifed by one of the theives.

By refusing to give Hollywood, or mankind for that matter, the benefit of the doubt, preferring instead to poke around in all the dark, corrupt corners of human nature, Hayes' never makes it quite clear just what he is saying or proposing, if anything. It is as director that he seems most gifted—particularly in the course of several discerningly-lensed passages (with the aid of his cameraman, Viles Lapenieks). Editing by Esther Poche and Ronald Thorne has a tendency to be too abrupt and to take too much for granted. Original jazz score by Bill Marx, featuring Bud Shank, adds drive and the proper note of agitation.

Vorno does a commendable job as the hero. Miss McClanahan does exceptionally well as his stripper girl friend. General tone of thespic support is satisfactory. *Tube.*

The Long And The Short And The Tall
(BRITISH)

Gripping war yarn with some standout performances. Lacks women thesps but if public's not now sated by war pix, this one should do well.

London, Feb. 28.

Warner-Pathe release of a Michael Balcon production for Associated-British. Stars Laurence Harvey, Richard Todd, Richard Harris; features David McCallum, Ronald Fraser, John Meillon, John Rees, Kenji Takaki. Directed by Leslie Norman. Screenplay, Wolf Mankowitz, from Willis Hall's play; camera, Edwin Hillier; editor, Gordon Stone; music, Stanley Black. At Corner Theatre, London. Running time, **105 MINS.**

Sgt. Mitchem .... Richard Todd
Private Bamforth ...... Laurence Harvey
Corporal Johnstone ..... Richard Harris
Lance-Corporal Macleish .. Ronald Fraser
Private Whitaker ...... David McCullum
Private Smith .... John Meillon
Private Evans .... John Rees
Tojo .... Kenji Takaki

Director Leslie Norman and scriptwriter Wolf Mankowitz have **not been able to resist the temptation to take a great deal of Willis Hall's war play into the open air of the jungle. This is a pity. It loses the sense of pent-in suspense that marked the play so effectively and it also shows up the fact that the Elstree "jungle" is rather phoney. Nothing can detract from the powerful interest of this war yarn, however, for the characters and their sparking are well contrived. Only snag is that there have been many war films and public interest may be satisfied by now.** There's reasonably good stellar value in Laurence Harvey and Richard Todd. This measures up as a good boxoffice prospect.

Film depends on characterization rather than on the thinnish plot. It's set in the Far East jungle during the Japanese campaign. A small patrol led by a sergeant (Richard Todd) is cut off. Suddenly "sparks" makes radio contact and jabbering Japanese voices nearby cause them to realize that they're in a spot.

A lone Japanese scout moves into their position and Todd insists that they must get him back to base alive as a source of information. The remainder want to bump him off with the solitary, surprise exception of a loudmouthed and brash private (Laurence Harvey). The drama of the film comes from the private hatred, misunderstanding and bitterness that each man holds for the other. There are not many highlight physical situations. The pic depends on the dialog which is candid, raw and completely authentic, and also on the conventional but blended characters and their reactions to each other and their plight. There's also an ironic climax.

Standout performance comes from Harvey. It is dramatic license that enables him to behave a way that would undoubtedly have had him up on a charge in a real situation. He is bombastic, amusing and, in scenes with the Jap, remarkably gentle and deserving with sympathy.

The bewildered Jap, subtly played by Kenji Takaki, is another very sound performance.

In fact there is no weak link in the cast. Todd is a dogged, worried sergeant; Richard Harris shapes very good as his righthand man and Ronald Fraser is fine as

a dour Scot, David McCallum, John Meillon and John Rees competently make up a cast that is handpicked to put over the author's message.

Edwin Hillier's lensing, is okay, as are the other technical credits, except for the too obvious certainty that the film was shot in a studio. But that's a minor moan. Director Leslie Norman has helped to raise an orthodox and rather wordy war adventure to quite a pitch of excitement.   *Rich.*

20,000 Lieues Sur La Terre
(20,000 Leagues Across Earth) (FRENCH-RUSSIAN) (COLOR)

Paris, Feb. 21.

UFA release of Procinex-Trident-Gorki production. Stars Tatiana Samoilova; features Jean Gaven, Jean Rochefort, Ludmila Martchenko, Leon Zitrone, Yuri Bielov, Valentin Zoubkov. Directed by Marcel Pagliero. Screenplay, R. M. Arlaud, M. Cournot, Serge Mikhalkow, I. Zorine. Camera (Sovcolor), J. Penzer, I. Rappaport; editor, Victoria Mercanton. At Miramar, Paris. Running time, **90 MINS.**

Natacha .... Tatiana Samoilova
Macha .... Ludmila Martchenko
Leon .... Leon Zitrone
Gregoire .... Jean Gaven
Pernand .... Jean Rochefort
Andre .... Yuri Bielov
Nicolas .... Valentin Zoubkov

A vague storyline is used as an excuse to work in a lot of documentary footage on Moscow and various other sectors of Russia. This is simple and unassuming but sans any character or newness in approach for any foreign chances except for possible cutting down for filler use or as tv fodder. Too much Russo stuff has hit Yank screens for this to have much curio value either.

A French video crew float around with one looking for an old wartime friend, and also doing programs about the country. Interludes with girls and a story of finding the financee of the interpreter's girl who has run off due to a misunderstanding, also give excuse for some other traveling footage.

Characters are fairly engaging if one dimensional. Some of the scenic values are okay. But the color is drab and pic overlong for its framework.   *Mosk.*

Frontier Uprising

Adequate supporting fare for western buffs. Good production values.

Hollywood, Feb. 23.

United Artists release of Robert E. Kent production. Stars James Davis, Nancy Hadley, Ken Mayer. Directed by Edward L. Cahn. Screenplay, Owen Harris, from story by George Bruce; camera, Maury Gertsman; editor, Kenneth Crane; art director, Serge Krizman; music, Paul Sawtell, Bert Shefter; assistant director, Herbert S. Greene. Reviewed at Goldwyn Studios, Feb. 23, '61. Running time, **68 MINS.**

Jim Stockton .... James Davis
Consuela .... Nancy Hadley
Beaver .... Ken Mayer
Montalvo .... Nestor Paiva
Kilpatrick .... Don O'Kelly
Ben Wright .... Stuart Randall
Lopez .... David Renard
General Torena .... John Marshall
Lieutenant Ruiz .... Eugene Iglesias
Chief Taztay .... Herman Rudin
Commander Kimball ... Addison Richards

"Frontier Uprising" rises slightly above lower-berth western standards in terms of physical proportion, but sings slightly below the norm in story and screenplay values. Upshot is secondary fare of appreciable appeal only to the most easygoing of sagebrush enthusiasts. United Artists is releasing the Zenith Pictures offering, produced by Robert E. Kent.

Jim Davis, star of the syndicated tv series, "Rescue 8," stars in this film as a rugged frontier scout embroiled in the early struggle for California among Yanks, Mexicans and the American Indian. Owen Harris has constructed his screenplay (from the story, "Kit Carson," by George Bruce) to allow for several lively battle passages and one novel sequence in which hero and heroine share a common bath, semi-Japanese style, in a partitioned pool, but his attempts to inject whimsy are clumsy and the dialog is creaky. The film is notable for some sweeping panoramic views of craggy desert country captured through Maury Gertsman's lens under Edward L. Cahn's observant direction, an unusually expansive quality for such a modest picture.

Davis plays agreeably and heroically. Nancy Hadley poses prettily for the camera, but that is a shortcoming of her performance. She seems to be posing, more than performing. Able support is chipped in by Ken Mayer, Nestor Paiva, Don O'Kelly, Eugene Iglesias, Stuart Randall, David Renard, John Marshall, Herman Rudin and Addison Richards.

The film benefits from the journeyman efforts of editor Kenneth Crane, art director Serge Krizman and cleffers Paul Sawtell and Bert Shefter.   *Tube.*

Five Golden Hours
(BRITISH)

Only spasmodically amusing comedy, with too much weight on Ernie Kovacs' shoulders. Unusually heavy-handed production and direction by Mario Zampi. Useful marquee value, but mainly a misfire.

London, Feb. 28.

Columbia and Fabio Jenner release of a Mario Zampi production. Stars Ernie Kovacs, Cyd Charisse, George Sanders; features Kay Hammond, Dennis Price. Directed by Zampi. Original story and screenplay, Hans Wilhelm; camera, Christopher Challis; editor, Bill Lewthwaite; music, Stanley Black. At Odeon, Marble Arch, London. Running time, **89 MINS.**

Aldo Bondi .... Ernie Kovacs
Baroness Sandra .... Cyd Charisse
Mr. Bing .... George Sanders
Martha .... Kay Hammond
Raphael .... Dennis Price
Rosalia .... Clelia Montania
Dr. Alfieri .... John Le Mesurier
Father Superior .... Finlay Currie
Brother Geronimo .. Reginald Beckworth
Beatrice .... Avice Landone
Alfredo .... Sydney Tafler
Enrico .... Martin Benson
1st Lady Guest .... Hy Hazel
2nd Lady Guest .... Joy Shelton

It's easy to see how the idea of "Five Golden Hours" would appeal to Mario Zampi's impish sense of humor. But something has misfired badly in this comedy which he produced and directed. It is gabby, protracted and largely tedious despite a very sound cast. The names may drag in some customers, but they are likely to be disappointed at the result. Technically the film is okay but Hans Wilhelm's script is not as witty as it may have read and too much onus is flung on the shoulders of Ernie Kovacs, a talented comedian, but one who is more acceptable in smaller doses.

He plays a professional mourner and pallbearer whose racket is to console rich, bereaved widows. This way he lives in considerable comfort. But he really falls for a baroness (Cyd Charisse) despite the fact that she's allegedly penniless. To help her out he persuades **three rich widows to lend him money which he claims he can turn into a fortune by playing on the difference in time between Rome and New York—hence the title.**

But when the baroness disappears with the loot, he is faced with the problem of explaining to the cheated widows. Kovacs decides to bump them off but when the plan goes haywire, he decides to feign madness. Eventually he marries Miss Charisse, but it seems fairly certain that she has her roving eye on his fortune and that it won't be long before he is attending another funeral, as the principal of the event.

This idea needs a far more nimble touch and wit than it has received. Though the cast works gamely their efforts, with the exception of those of George Sanders, swiftly become tedious. Kovacs tackles the funeral fun and games with huge gusto and earns a few yocks but there is far too much of him.

Sanders is suavely debonair as a fellow inmate of the looney bin while Miss Charisse looks charming as the baroness but has little into which she can get her teeth. Kay Hammond, Clelia Mantania and Avice Landone are the three merry widows.

Some small but telling contributions by Dennis Price, Martin Benson, Hy Hazel, Joy Shelton, John Le Mesurier and Finlay Currie support the principals. But it is the muddled, heavy script that causes the slight joke to go sour.   *Rich.*

La Recreation
(FRENCH)

Paris, March 7.

Columbia release of Elite Films production. Stars Jean Seberg, Christian Marquand; features Evelyne Kerr, Francoise Prevost. Directed by Francois Moreuil, Fabien Collin. Screenplay, Daniel Boulanger, Moreuil, based on story by Francoise Sagan; camera, Jean Penzer; editor, Rene Le Henaff. At Ermitage, Paris. Running time, **87 MINS.**

Kate .... Jean Seberg
Philippe .... Christian Marquand
Wife .... Francoise Prevost
Friend .... Evelyne Kerr

Yank actress Jean Seberg stars in her fourth French pic with this, and it is a first directorial effort by Francois Moreuil. It is also a Francoise Sagan original and has a fresh and airy progression and unpretentious tang that could have this worth an arty theatre spotting abroad with more general usage inherent in it via its entertainment qualities.

Moreuil has been content to let this simple tale amble along via the impetus of its actors which helps give it a feeling for incident and human relations. However, its Saganesque tale of people trying to love, and an older man's brief affair with a young girl is slight overall. It is pleasant but lacks a forthright conception.

Film is thus sketchy. An American teenager, Miss Seberg spies on a sculptor and his wife from her school. She also sees a hit and run driver too and does not know it is the sculptor until she falls for him. She has an affair with him and then leaves him. Pic is not wicked, but somewhat condescending to the bored upper crust it pictures while the hardheaded American girl, in a French boarding school, eagerly finds her first love in this listless group.

But it is well observed, with a racy American style dialog that manages to go over in French. The defensive wisecracks also score. This is a tenuous pic but has flair and impact in spite of its almost amateurish technical approach. This is a help in not insisting on relations and letting them grow and ripen, and then fade away.

Miss Seberg's aspects also fit as her developing love turns her into a female who has learned a lesson. Christian Marquand and Francoise Prevost are properly vapidly charming as the married couple. Moreuil shows a decided feel for situation comedy and may be heard from in the future. It is good natured and even tender but its almost sentimental indulgence of whim and surface feelings does not give it the needed penetration so this calls for the hard sell on its good points.   *Mosk.*

The World in My Pocket
(GERMAN)

Munich, March 7.

Constantin-Omnia release of Corona (Alexander Grueter) production. Features Nadja Tiller, Rod Steiger, Peter Van Eyck, Jean Servais, Ian Bannen. Directed by Alvin Rakoff. Screenplay, Frank Harvey, based on novel "The World In My Pocket" by James Hadley Chase; camera, Vaclav Vich. Running time, **90 MINS.**

The Marseilles setting and the "Rififi" style treatment alone would have made this hardly more than just another version of the much-used Brink's story. But an ingenious turn to the diabolical-comical lets pic come off as delectable fare with strong b.o. potential.

For in the end it is not the police who are spelling doom to the gangster quintet's excruciating efforts to appropriate the armored truck with the $1,000,000 loot, nor the amateur sleuth (this time, amusingly, a juvenile), nor even the familiar falling out among the robbers. It is an inanimate object, the strongbox on wheels itself, which merely has to employ its own inbuilt defense and safety mechanism to reduce to mincemeat what has been prepared and even executed as a perfect crime.

After its capture it goes right on broadcasting its respective location on every point of the further trip. When this is taken care of by cutting a wire, it just continues refusing to let itself be opened by force of explosives, blowtorches, etc., or to give away more than two of the seven code numbers necessary to handle the dial.

Thus defeated by the quasi-demonic power of a mechanical thing the truck's hijackers are losing their minds. First to crack is the safe-dial specialist with the hypersensitive finger touch, then all others. Their fate is played straight and for all its genuinely tragic effects. However, reminding of the kidnappers in the O. Henry story whom their bad boy victim drives crazy to a point where they die to get rid of him without the least bit of ransom, they are at

the same time a screamingly funny lot.

The finish, set in the Southern France counterpart of "High Sierra" (on the surface repeat'ng the end of the Bogart-Lupino film classic of the '40s) makes the most of this tragicomic contrast: seven corpses, two from the "good side," the rest comprising the entire team of evildoers, and an armored truck passing back into the hands of its owners, hardly scratched and with its contents intact.

Excellent performances throughout: Austrian Nadja Tiller is the appealing girl who masterminds the robbery attempt. Rod Steiger, past master in the gangster boss line, reveals quite a few new facets; Jean Servais, French veteran of the "Rififi" series, ex-Hollywood's Peter Van Eyck, now a German star and rightly so; and Britain Ian Bannen, remarkable young new lover, type. Terse, underplaying direction by Alvin Rakoff and Vaclav Vich's outstanding camerawork do much to make this one of the more noteworthy pix of this season. *Jok.*

Les Amours De Paris
(Paris Loves)
Paris, Feb. 28.

Pathe release of Film Matignon production. Stars Darry Cowl, Francois Perier; features Harold Kay, Perrette Pradier, Nicole Courcel, Bernard Veringer. Directed by Jacques Robin; editor, Jacques Lesaganeoux. At Marignan, Paris. Running time, 100 MINS.

Maurice	Francois Perier
Florist	Darry Cowl
Doctor	Harold Kay
Francoise	Perrette Pradier
Nicole	Nicole Courcel
Jacques	Bernard Voringer

Situation comedy criss-crosses three couples, a cheating married man with a wife who's likewise, a young skirt chaser and a marrying-minded model, and a bumbling, zany couple. All ends happily after many complications, but this does not have the snap for characterization, and the inventiveness to make it of anything but primarily local fodder. Film looms unlikely for foreign marts.

The married man worries only about seeing his wife in the hospital while she has eyes for the doctor; the Don Juan finally marries the girl, and the madcap couple also find romance. Acting is acceptable but without the brightness and necessary sound story to really make their antics funny or beguiling.

New director Jacques Poirenaud seems assured but without the individuality and flair to have all this jell. Technical credits are good. *Mosk.*

One-Eyed Jacks
(V'VISION—COLOR)

Stirring adventure tale masterfully directed by Marlon Brando. Striking settings and camera work. Sizzling b.o. looms.

Hollywood, March 9.

Paramount release of Frank P. Rosenberg production. Stars Marlon Brando, Karl Malden. Katy Jurado; introduces Pina Pellicer; Directed by Brando. Screenplay, Guy Trosper, Calder Willingham, based on novel, "The Authentic Death of Hendry Jones," by Charles Neider; camera (Technicolor). Charles Lang Jr.; editor, Archie Marshek; art directors, Hal Pereira, J. McMillan Johnson; music, Hugo Friedhofer; sound, Hugo and Charles Grenzbach; assistant directors, Francisco Day, Harry Caplan. Reviewed at the studio, March 9, '61. Running time, 137 MINS.

Rio	Marlon Brando
Dad Longworth	Karl Malden
Louisa	Pina Pellicer
Maria	Katy Jurado
Bob Amory	Ben Johnson
Lon	Slim Pickens
Modesto	Larry Duran
Harvey	Sam Gilman
Howard Tetley	Timothy Carey
Redhead	Miriam Colon
Bank Teller	Elisha Cook
Leader of the Rurales	Rudolph Acosta
Bartender	Ray Teal
Bearded Townsman	John Dierkes
Flamenco Dancer	Margarita Cordova
Doc	Hank Worden
Margarita	Nina Martinez

With "One-Eyed Jacks," Marlon Brando adds another character to his list of respected histrionic achievements, but this time he has ranged beyond the limited sphere of the actor to assume directorial controls and guide an entire process of creative interpretation with meticulous, dynamic intensity and integrity. In striving above all for clarity, honesty and dimension of characterization, he has constructed a compelling experience out of a serviceable work of adventure fiction.

With a reputed $5-$6,000,000 at stake Brando gives Paramount's full-house prospect for its gamble. The Pennebaker production, produced by Frank P. Rosenberg under the executive aegis of George Glass and Walter Seltzer, is, in short, of whopping wicket potential.

The production, framed against the turbulent coastline of the Monterey peninsula and the shifting sands and mounds of the bleak Mexican desert, is notable for its visual artistry alone. There is an appreciation of color and of nature that is a credit to the remarkable VistaVision-Technicolor camera virtuosity of Charles Lang Jr. The superior visual aspect is backed up formidably by the balance of the film's photographic crew: second unit photographer Wallace Kelley, special photographic effects man John P. Fulton and process photographer Farciot Edouart. Comparable plaudits must go to the art directing team of Hal Pereira and J. McMillan Johnson for the flavor and authenticity they have instilled in their interior sets and for the part they have played in selection of outdoor locale.

Charles Neider's novel, "The Authentic Death of Hendry Jones," is the source from which Guy Trosper and Calder Willingham penned their tellingly direct screenplay. It is the brooding, deliberate tale of a young man (Brando) consumed by a passion for revenge after he is betrayed by an accomplice (Karl Malden) in a bank robbery, for which crime he spends five years (1880-1885) in a Mexican prison. His vengeful campaign leads him to the town of Monterey, where

Malden has attained respectability and the position of sheriff, but romantic entanglements with Malden's stepdaughter (Pina Pellicer) persuade Brando to abandon his intention until the irresistibility of circumstance and Malden's own irrepressible will to snuff out the living evidence of his guilt draws the two men into a showdown that is fatal to the latter.

It is an oddity of this film that both its strength and its weakness lie in the area of characterization. Brando's concept calls, above all, for depth of character, for human figures endowed with overlapping good and bad sides to their nature. In the case of the central characters—his own, Malden's, Miss Pellicer's—he is successful. But a few of his secondary people have no redeeming qualities—they are simply arch-villains. It is here that Brando appears to contradict his basic purpose.

In spite of the familiarity of his mannerisms as an actor, in spite of the handicap of serving as his own director, Brando creates a character of substance, of its own identity. It is an instinctively right and illuminating performance. The character makes sense, and undergoes a considerable transition of nature in the course of the film, which has captured to an astonishing degree the gradually changing quality of events in a novel.

Another rich, vivid variable portrayal is the one by Malden. Katy Jurado is especially fine as Malden's wife. Outstanding in support are Ben Johnson as the bad sort who leads Brando to his prey, Larry Duran as Brando's doomed Mexican buddy, and Slim Pickens as a sadistic deputy. Others who score in prominent secondary roles are Sam Gilman, Timothy Carey, Miriam Colon, Elisha Cook, Rudolph Acosta and Ray Teal. Pretty Miss Pellicer, who makes her screen bow in this film, does a sensitive, sympathetic job.

"Jacks" is a long film, but it is credibly and tautly knit by editor Archie Marshek. Hugo Friedhofer's melodically romantic strains are a delight to the ear. Soundwork by Hugo and Charles Grenzbach is excellent. *Tube.*

Le President
(FRENCH)
Paris, March 14.

UFA release of Cite-Fides-Terra-CESI Films production. Stars Jean Gabin; features Bernard Blier, Renee Faure, Louis Seigner, Henri Cremieux, Alfred Adam. Directed by Henri Verneuil. Screenplay, Michel Audiard from novel by Georges Simenon; camera, Louis Page; editor, Jacques Desagneaux. At Paris, Paris. Running time, 110 MINS.

Emile	Jean Gabin
Philippe	Bernard Blier
Milleran	Renee Faure
Governor	Louis Seigner
Minister	Henri Cremieux
Francois	Alfred Adam

This film is mainly a vehicle for actor Jean Gabin. After a happy tramp, an old drunkard, a broke Baron, now he is an elder statesman in this pic. Living in retirement, he has one last chance to make himself felt by preventing somebody from taking office before passing into history. Film is stolid and talky, but has some solid characterizations and an interesting look at pre-war French politics. But it looks like a limited foreign item.

Gabin's solid thesping and the

crusty, crochety, sincere quality of the character weld well to have him dominate this sketchy pic and make it the main appeal. He is shown via flashbacks in a few situations of government and in his retirement receiving visitors or writing his memoirs. A young aide who had crossed him is kept from forming a new cabinet by Gabin's wrath and his past perfidy.

Film is overlong and verbose but in its favor are the restricted use of stock shots and isolated acting strength. Director Henri Verneuil has subordinated all to Gabin's powerful presence. It looms a good entry here. Technical credits are fine. *Mosk.*

Operation Eichmann

Heavyhanded study of one Nazi chieftain's infamous deeds. Mild b.o. splash via saturation is likely, but unsatisfactory film's impact should be short-lived.

Hollywood, March 2.

Allied Artists release of Samuel Bischoff-David Diamond production. Stars Warner Klemperer, Ruta Lee, Donald Buka. Directed by R. G. Springsteen. Screenplay, Lewis Coppley; camera, Joseph Biroc; editor, Roy Livingston; art director, Rudi Feld; music, Alex Alexander, June Starr. Reviewed at Screen Directors Guild Theatre, March 2, '61. Running time, 92 MINS.

Adolf Eichmann	Werner Klemperer
Anna Kemp	Ruta Lee
David	Donald Buka
Sara	Barbara Turner
Rudolf Hoess	John Banner
Frau Hoess	Hanna Landy
Kurt Kessner	Lester Fletcher
Jacob	Steve Gravers
David (as boy)	Jim Baird
Sara (as girl)	Debbie Cannon
Jacob (as boy)	Jackie Russo
Lopez	Paul Thierry
Sanchez	Rudolfo Hoyos Jr.
Uri Goldmann	Norbert Schiller
Heinrich Himmler	Luis Van Rooten
Kuwait Ch. of Police	Oscar Beregi Jr.
Felsner	Theodore Marcuse
Rostich	Otto Reichow
Eichmann's Driver	Walter Linden
Hans	Hans Hermann
Klaus	Hans Gudegast
Ben (Pilot)	Robert Christopher
Cafe Singer	Carla Lucerne

In their haste to capitalize on a topic of global import and immediacy, producers Samuel Bischoff and David Diamond have failed to come up with the sort of distinguished, meticulous and penetrating analysis that would justify a decision to risk aggravating the desirable climate of objectivity sought for the imminent trial. "Operation Eichmann" is a heavyhanded film that sheds virtually no insight on the character of the man and fails to convey the air of authenticity that is mandatory for a picture dealing so intimately with an inflammatory slice of modern history. It emerges a rather unsavory attempt at fast-buck exploitation.

Since it is ticketed for mass exhibition shortly before the outset of the trial itself, the Allied Artists release seems certain to generate some swift, though likely short-lived, wicket activity. But customers will go to see the film primarily out of curiosity to learn something of the man behind the beast, and it is here that "Operation Eichmann" will prove most unsatisfactory to them for, not only does it fail to penetrate, it has an emotional tendency to distort the issue. This factor may have a somewhat damaging effect on the picture's ultimate boxoffice.

The film, written by Lewis Coppley, begins with a questionable

"prologue" in which Eichmann, played by Werner Klemperer, rants and raves at the audience in Hitleresque fashion over the travesty of justice, the "circus" of a trial he must endure before a smug world. First half of the picture is devoted to illustrating his activities as the grotesque monster responsible for extermination of 6,000,000 Jews in two years, second half centering on his post-war efforts to sustain Nazism while feverishly avoiding capture by the Jews. The film ends with the ultimate capture.

The hasty nature of the project is all too apparent in the patchwork dramatic quality. There are long, verbose lags and a number of mechanical oversights or inconsistencies. Film clips of shocking atrocities are incorporated for no absolutely pertinent reason, giving the picture, directed by R. G. Springsteen, an even more staccato pace. And most of the characters are so nebulous, so superficially drawn, that they defy audience identification. This is particularly damaging in the cast of the Israeli pursuers, who are almost entirely devoid of personality.

Klemperer, in undertaking a role of frighteningly distasteful proportions, acquits himself well. So does Ruta Lee as his mistress, in spite of the fact the character never comes into focus. Donald Buka is passable in the bland role of Eichmann's most tenacious pursuer. Others who attract attention, more or less favorably, are Lester Fletcher, John Banner, Hanna Landy, Jim Baird, Luis Van Rooten, Paul Thierry and Rudolfo Hoyos Jr.

Of the crafts, Joseph Biroc's camera efforts and Rudi Feld's art direction are most proficient. Roy Livingston's editing is not always as taut and smooth as desirable. The Alex Alexander-June Starr score is unobtrusive, and there is additional music in the form of a brief cabaret song by Franz Steininger and Gustav Heimo and a prayer sung by Cantor Sholom Katz. *Tube.*

L'Enclos
(The Enclosure)
(FRENCH)

Paris, March 7.

Clavis film production and release. With Herbert Wochinz, Jean Negroni, Christian Blech, Jean-Marie Serreau. Directed by Armand Gatti. Screenplay, Gatti, Pierre Joffroy; camera, Robert Juillard; editor, Yvonne Martin. Previewed in Paris. Running time, 100 MINS.

Karl	Herbert Wochinz
David	Jean Negroni
Lieutenant	Christian Blech
Doctor	Jean-Marie Serreau

There has been increased filmmaking interest in the Nazi crimes during the last war. This is a French film that deals with an ideological struggle between a young French Jew and a German anti-Nazi in a concentration camp. It is a reserved look at the camp horrors and dwells on the outlook of these martyred men. It looms a downbeat affair with mostly specialized chances but is of interest and worth careful placement in the light of the importance and treatment of this subject.

The camp's destruction of human values is depicted and then it concerns a cruel plot to make a hardened German anti-Nazi talk about a resistance plot among the prisoners by throwing him into an enclosure with a young Jew and telling the two that if only one survives he will not be killed.

The film covers the attempts to help them by the resistance group as well as the growing awareness of each other culminating in the Jew's sacrifice to help the German escape. If this lacks the epic sweep to make its human point more forceful, it at least has a harsh, sharp flair for men-in-crisis and makes a point about the infamy of Nazi terrors. Its stark lensing and location shooting in Yugoslavia also help.

Acting is good except that sometimes the roles become symbols rather than humane in great crisis. But this is forceful and not evasive. *Mosk.*

Posse From Hell
(COLOR)

Classic chase western hampered by moral and social overtones that slow the action and make types of the characters. Striking scenic views and star names should make it successful b.o. candidate.

Hollywood, March 7.

Universal release of Gordon Kay production. Stars Audie Murphy, John Saxon. Directed by Herbert Coleman. Screenplay, Clair Huffaker, from his novel; camera (Eastman), Clifford Stine; editor, Frederic Knudtson; art directors, Alexander Golitzen, Alfred Sweeney; music, Joseph Gershenson; sound, Waldon O. Watson, Joe Lapis; assistant director, Ray Gosnell Jr. Reviewed at the studio, March 7, '61. Running time, 89 MINS.

Banner Cole	Audie Murphy
Seymour Kern	John Saxon
Helen Caldwell	Zohra Lampert
Crip	Vic Morrow
Capitain Brown	Robert Keith
Marshal Webb	Ward Ramsey
Johnny Caddo	Rudolph Acosta
Uncle Billy	Royal Dano
Burt Hogan	Frank Overton
Benson	James Bell
Jock Wiley	Paul Carr
Leo	Lee Van Cleef
Larson	Ray Teal
Dr. Welles	Forrest Lewis
Hash	Charles Horvath
Russell	Harry Lauter
Chunk	Henry Wills
Luke Gorman	Stuart Randall
Burl Hogan	Alan Lane

Universal's "Posse From Hell" is a picture-postcard western in which the picture, a sweeping Eastman Color Panorama of Lone Pine country where Mt. Whitney rises out of Death Valley, is eminently superior to the postcard. Release bogs itself down with sociological implications instead of sticking to action essentials.

Although Gordon Kay's handsome production is shy the story and character stature or novelty to please the discriminating patron, it will be appetizing fare for that legion of less selective, less critical filmgoers for whom escape and pictorial majesty are enough of a cinematic virtue. The names and performances of Audie Murphy and John Saxon should be an additional wicket stimulus to boost the film into a satisfactory boxoffice sphere.

Clair Huffaker adapted the screenplay from his own novel. Murphy plays a young gunslinger-turned-deputy who leads a small posse from a town named Paradise (despite the "Hell" of a title) in pursit of a quartet of killers who murdered some of the townspeople, robbed the bank and departed with the prettiest girl on the premises, Zohra Lampert. For one reason or another, the posse dwindles to a threesome, which nonetheless proves sufficient for the task of destroying the astonishingly inept foursome of baddies, who unaccountably but helpfully elect to double back to the scene of their crime instead of (logically) high-tailing it out of the territory with their booty.

Huffaker's screenplay dwells at length on issues such as prejudice, cowardice, false fronts and moral courage. It attempts to glorify the classically humble, soft-spoken, regular-guy approach to life, which is fine but, in so doing, creates a filmful of distorted character stereotypes to make its point. Thus an earnest attempt to bring additional meaning to an essentially simple western backfires and becomes ludicrous.

Murphy, whose heroic exploits in real life make him ideally suitable for, and extra-believable in, super heroic roles, does his usual commendably restrained job. Saxon is outstanding here, creating the picture's most colorful character as a saddle-sore dude from New York who rises to the perilous occasion. Miss Lampert is pretty, but not consistently persuasive, as a fallen woman "had" by all four thugs. Among those in support, most lasting impressions are made by Rudolph Acosta, Ward Ramsey, Royal Dano, Lee Van Cleef and Vic Morrow, latter utilizing a kind of neo-classic Brando scowl to good effect as a heavy.

Herbert Coleman's direction rises in partnership with Clifford Stine's astute and agile lensmanship, but falls in association with Huffaker's uneven source material. It is Coleman's bow as a motion picture helmsman and there is evidence he has an uncompromising taste for realism, notably in the explosive way in which his characters are shattered by gunfire and the gasping way in which they die.

Frederic Knudtson's editing is efficient, and sets designed by Alexander Golitzen and Alfred Sweeney have the proper frontier flavor. *Tube.*

The Secret Partner

Absorbing but deviously-plotted mystery. Lacks premium b.o. attributes, but will fit fine as a supporting number.

Hollywood, March 1.

Metro release of Michael Relph production. Stars Stewart Granger, Haya Harareet. Directed by Basil Dearden. Screenplay, David Pursall, Jack Seddon; camera, Harry Waxman; editor, Raymond Poulton; art director, Alan Withy; music, Philip Green; assistant director, George Pollock. Reviewed at the studio, March 1, '61. Running time, 92 MINS.

John Brent	Stewart Granger
Nicole	Haya Harareet
Det. Supt. Hanbury	Bernard Lee
Charles Standish	Hugh Burden
Det. Insp. Henderson	Lee Montague
Helen Standish	Melissa Stribling
Alan Richford	Conrad Phillips
Clive Lang	John Lee
Ralph Beldon	Norman Bird
Strakarios	Peter Illing
Lyle	Basil Dignam
Brinton	William Fox
Vickers	George Tovey
Dock Foreman	Sydney Vivian
Man in Street	Paul Stassino
Girl in Car	Colette Wilde
Hotelkeeper	Willoughby Goddard
P. C. McLaren	Peter Welch
Brent's Secretary	Joy Wood
Dentist's Receptionist	Dorothy Gordon

Considering its great popularity as paperback and television fare, there has been a surprising scarcity of mystery fiction on the theatrical screen of late. Since Metro's "The Secret Partner" falls into that rather neglected category, it would appear to be a promising candidate for boxoffice success. But it isn't. The British-vintage Michael Relph production is engrossing, but is neither ingenious enough nor tidy enough in retrospect to fully satisfy or excite an audience as an "A" attraction. The picture appears destined for the rear end of twin bills where, in spite of its 92-minute bulk, it will serve as above-average support.

The rather wobbly yarn is the original screenplay effort of David Pursall and Jack Seddon. Stewart Granger essays its central role, that of an ex-con, now shipping exec, who is pinned with the rap for a $250,000 robbery of his firm's vault.

Balance of the film details Granger's, and the law's efforts to uncover the masked thief, introducing several likely candidates in the persons of suitors of Granger's estranged wife (Haya Harareet), who is revealed as working in cahoots with the crook. The surprise ending fails to properly justify the crime schematic in terms of strength of motivation, soundness of anticipation, or ultimate decision to own up to the law. Equally disturbing in retrospect is the fact that when the thief is not attempting to baffle the police, he appears to be purposely misleading the audience, which is an unpardonable pitfall into which film mysteries seem irresistibly inclined to fall.

Although a bit lax in minor detail (which can be anything but minor in a mystery picture), director Basil Dearden has done a generally businesslike job, even to the extent of injecting an occasional dash of humor. But some of his attempts to heighten tension have a contrived "pulp" look about them. Slicker qualities are incorporated through Harry Waxman's lensmanship, Raymond Poulton's editing and Alan Withy's art direction, but Philip Green's music has a tired and intrusive "Dragnet" air about it.

Granger does a thoroughly competent, polished, aggressive job in the key role. There is outstanding support from Bernard Lee as the sharp and conscientious chief sleuth, and others whose featured efforts are beneficial to the film are Hugh Burden, Lee Montague, Melissa Stribling, Conrad Phillips, John Lee and Norman Bird. Miss Harareet is a disappointment. She plays with one rather blank, frozen expression, as if the slightest glint in her pretty eyes or tilt of the head will give the whole mystery away. *Tube.*

Azahares Rojos
(Red Blossoms)
(MEXICAN—COLOR)

Mexico City, March 7.

Peliculas Nacionales release of Rosas Priego production. Stars Francisco Rabal, Teresa Velazquez; features Hector Goddy, Silvia Fournier, Roberto Canedo, Domingo Solar, Maria Eugenia San Martin. Directed by Alfredo B. Crevenna. Screenplay, Julie Alejandro and Edmundo Baez; music, A. Diaz Conde. At Roble and Coliseo theatres, Mexico City. Running time, 90 MINS.

This picture is based on a novel "My Frivolous Wife," written by an unknown writer whose pen name was "The Audacious Gentleman." Tome caused adolescents to blush here some two decades ago.

Translated to the screen, under the capable direction of Alfredo Crevenna, story turns out to be a rather good comedy based around the yarn of a young miss who calculatingly marries for gain, without love. The borderline passages of the book were cleaned up by writers Julio Alejandro and Edmundo Baez. But film still has a "for adults only" classification.

Tere Velazquez, being groomed for starring parts, still lacks assurance and experience. But she does what she can with the role of the girl who marries the man of money (Francisco Rabal) who has been formerly her very good friend. She embarks on this matrimonial venture to save her family from financial reverses. Story line is developed against the background of Mexico City high society. Situation comedy and misunderstandings are quite good. A rather melodramatic finale leading up to the birth of true love is the only jarring note.

Technically, the picture is high grade, has good atmosphere, city backgrounds, excellent and luxurious sets. Rabal performs in his usual competent manner, with this possibly showing the acting inexperience of Miss Velazquez. She is very comely, however. As for the others, Roberto Canedo overacts just a shade, while Domingo Soler, Hector Godoy, Silvia Fournier and Maria Eugenia San Martin do good work in their roles.

A more ambitious film than many other light comedy attempts, this has been doing good business and appears to be slated as a moneymaker in Latin American and possibly in European markets.
                                        Emil.

Days Of Thrills And Laughter

Third in Robert Youngson's series of silent screen tidbits. A diverting collection, serviceable as a spot filler attraction.

Hollywood, March 10.
Twentieth-Fox release of Robert Youngson production of old silent clips. Narration written by Youngson; music, Jack Shaindlin; sound effects, Alfred Dahlem, Ralph F. Curtiss; narrated by Jay Jackson. Reviewed at the studio, March 10, '61. Running time, **93 MINS.**

A fascinating reminder of the screen's speechless, but anything but tranquil era, "Days Of Thrills And Laughter" is the third in producer Robert Youngson's series of antique celluloidal compilations, first of which appeared early in '58, second earlier this year. There is no reason to suspect just yet that Youngson may be overplaying his hand, for he is dealing in cinematic art and automatic nostalgia, a powerful combination.

Among giants of filmdom's great comedic period who are on display in this collection are Charlie Chaplin, Douglas Fairbanks, Stan Laurel and Oliver Hardy (prior to their merger), Houdini, Pearl White, Harry Langdon, Ben Turpin, Charlie Chase, Snub Pollard, Fatty Ar-

buckle, Mack Sennett and his Keystone Kops and Bathing Beauties. Chaplin's pre-eminence is undeniable, but there's no shortage of talent and inspiration in any of the many* clips that have been bound together in a valuable volume and spared disintegration on the dusty shelves of time. Included in this anthology are a montage of serial climaxes and several reels of the hair-raising variety to go along with the purely comic samplings from the past. The thrillers, however, emerge just as funny as the comedies, thanks to the sophistication of retrospect.

Although the narration, written by Youngson and delivered by Jay Jackson, has considerable explanatory value, there is simply, too much of it. Intrusive, superfluous and condescending verbal descriptions of the action (which almost invariably speaks for itself) will annoy many patrons. Jack Shaindlin's score, orchestrated by Ted Royal, effectively incorporates the styles and musical themes of the bygone time on display, but lacks distinction and genuine creativity. Sound effects by Alfred Dahlem and Ralph F. Curtiss seem to take something away from the original charm rather than adding to it.

Over and above its value as a cross-section of the early cinema, "Days Of Thrills and Laughter" is an enchanting glimpse of the frenetic, light-hearted personality of a far more comprehensible world than the one we live in now. It also brings closer to us the identity of today's 70-year-old, for whom these vestiges are something more than curiosities. *Tube.*

Flucht Nach Berlin
(Escape to Berlin)
(GERMAN)

Berlin, March 7.
Stun-Film production. With Christian Doermer, Susanne Korda and Narziss Sokatscheff. Directed and written by Will Tremper. Camera, Guenter Haase; music, Peter Thomas; editor, Ulivelli and Dayan. Previewed in Berlin. Running time, **112 MINS.**

Claus Baade .... Christian Doermer
Doris Lange .... Susanne Korda
Hermann Gueden .... N. Sokatscheff

In some respects, "Escape" is an unusual German pic. It was made without the backing of a distributor but financed by the American firm, Unexcelled Chemical Corp., and its Swiss affiliate, Unexcelled International, Zurich. Stun-Flim, producer of the film, is a subsid company of the latter. This has a theme usually regarded as taboo by West German filmites the divided Germany. Subject has been considered as boxoffice poison here.

"Escape" is based on actual happenings, the flight of East Germans to West Berlin. Within the postwar years, nearly 3,000,000 Germans have fled the Commie regime in East Germany. Politically speaking, "Escape" is no doubt the most anti-Communist West German film since 1945.

Whether the German cinema patrons will appreciate this subject remains to be seen. But apart from being a political film, this is also a thriller. Hence, large segments of the action trade may go for it. Lacking star* names, pic needs selling on its plot, which can be exploited. Film has good foreign selling points, too.

Technically, this is well made and the score by Peter Thomas (who contributes the theme song, a catchy march) and camerawork by Guenter Haase are praiseworthy. Artistically, the film commands less attention. Although 32-year old Will Tremper directed this film (incidentally, his first directorial job) with obvious care and devotion, he concentrated chiefly on its thrilling elements. There are some implausibilities in Tremper's script and some character motivations are sketchy. But it is a suspenseful and politically interesting film.

"Escape" has only three principal players: Christian Doermer, as a young East German Commie functionary, Narziss Sokatscheff, as an East German farmer and Susanne Korda as a Swiss femme journalist. Doermer comes with other Commies into an East German village whose inhabitants, all farmers, have not still "voluntarily" surrendered to the Soviet-style colchos (collective) system. Sokatscheff has quarrels with Doermer and flees. On his flight to West Berlin, he is given a lift by Miss Korda on the highway. Doermer for some reason is dropped by his Commie friends and decides also to head for Berlin. The three principal characters run into each other shortly before they reach Berlin.

Unusual angle of this film also is that the cast is composed mostly of amateurs. In fact, almost everyone who's associated with this production appears in it. Of the professional players, Doermer is the best known, with a dozen pix to his credit. As a young Commie, he turns in a believable performance. Sokatscheff, the farmer, a newcomer, is a handsome and talented chap who should go places. Miss Korda is less effective but is saddled with the least rewarding role in the film. Film only cost around 500,000 D-Marks ($125,000). It could stand some cutting but not particularly necessary. *Hans.*

The Rebel
(BRITISH—COLOR)

Funny first appearance of one of Britain's top tele comedians; stylish comedy which though slow at times earns plenty of laughs. Little doubt of it being a big U.K. success, but American audiences may need time to appreciate Tony Hancock.

London, March 7.
Warner-Pathe release of an Associated-British (W. A. Whittaker) production. Stars Tony Hancock; features George Sanders, Paul Massie, Margit Saad, Gregoire Aslan, Dennis Price. Directed by Robert Day. Screenplay, Alan Simpson, Ray Galton, based on an original by Hancock, Simpson and Galton; camera, Gilbert Taylor; editor, Richard Best; music, Frank Cordell. At Plaza, London. Running time, **105 MINS.**

Anthony Hancock ...... Tony Hancock
Sir Charles Broward.... George Sanders
Paul .... Paul Massie
Margot .... Margit Saad
Carreras .... Gregoire Aslan
Mrs. Crevatte .... Irene Handl
Manager London art gallery .... Mervyn Johns
Manager Paris art gallery ...... Peter Bull
Office Manager .... John Le Mesurier
Waitress .... Liz Fraser
Josey .... Nanette Newman
Madame Laurent .... Marie Burke
Yvette .... Marie Devereux
Bar Attendant .... Mario Fabrizi

The slideover from tv stardom to success on the bigger screen has been a hazardous one for many of Britain's television comedians. Tony Hancock, one of U.K.'s hottest tv comics, has waited his moment cautiously. Apart from a minor appearance in an unimportant farce some years ago, he has shuffled uneasily away from pix. But, with "The Rebel," his takeover bid can be rated a reasonable success. In Britain, his reputation is such that, though this film is a fairly lightweight affair, it should be a big boxoffice click. He may not find immediate stardom abroad as a result of "The Rebel." But a U.S. booking should find plenty of word-of-mouth support. One adverse point, the title hardly suggests a comedy.

Hancock's tv writers, Alan Simpson and Ray Galton, have scripted this, and they know their man's idiosyncracies intimately. Hancock is a wry, deprecating personality. He's not simply a comedian but a very good actor who sparks off humor from an ordinary situation or verbal gag. He's the little man, slightly at war with himself and his fellows, but quick to grasp an opportunity for getting on.

In "Rebel," he is a downtrodden London city clerk, fed up with the daily round, and with a yen to be a sculptor. Unfortunately, he's very unskilled. Eventually, he blows his top, throws up his job and sets up shop as an existentialist painted in Paris. He talks himself into being accepted on the Left Bank as the leader of a new movement in art. Then an art connoisseur boobs. He exhibits the paintings of Hancock's roommate, thinking they are Hancock's work. The misfit becomes a national figure till, in the end, everything blows up. And, contented, he returns to obscurity in London and his private daubing.

This is a sly dig at some of the fakes who pretend they understand the avant-garde work of the untalented, and the flimsy framework is mainly an excuse for some orthodox situations to which Hancock lends his shrewd sense of character-comedy.

Among several amusing scenes are those when Hancock revolts against his office boss, an existentialist Left Bank party, Hancock's visit to the yacht of a Greek millionaire where he is commissioned to sculpt the tycoon's vamp wife, a colorful carnival party aboard the yacht and Hancock "painting" a picture by daubing paint on a canvas and then bicycling over it.

Well photographed mainly in Paris and on the Riviera, "The Rebel" is a good technical job except that the ending shows signs of over-ruthless cutting.

The ever-dependable George Sanders is a debonair figure as the art connoisseur and critic. Gregoire Aslan plays the millionaire with sure touch. Irene Handl is a tower of strength. Margit Saad whips the sex-appeal around with abandon. Paul Massie, as the frustrated artist with whom Hancock shares a garret, has an almost completely straight role and plays it with charm.

Among the minor roles, Mervyn Johns, Peter Bull, John Le Mesurier, Marie Burke and Nanette Newman give useful support. Dennis Price is a standout in a smallish, irrelevant role which looks sus-

piciously as if it had been based on the eccentricities of Salvador Dali. *Rich.*

Parrish
(COLOR)

Glossy translation to screen of Mildred Savage's tome about the contest for power in Connecticut's tobacco leaf industry. Pictorially pleasing but overlong, superficial and unexciting. Rising and appealing young players in cast will spur curiosity and should advance b.o. prospects into passable sphere.

Hollywood, March 14.
Warner Bros. release of Delmer Daves production. Stars Troy Donahue, Claudette Colbert, Karl Malden, Dean Jagger, Connie Stevens, Diane McBain, Sharon Hugueny. Directed and screenplay by Daves; camera (Technicolor), Harry Stradling Sr.; editor, Owen Marks; art director, Le K. Kuter; music, Max Steiner; sound, Stanley Jones; assistant directors, Chuck Hansen, Russell Llewellyn. Reviewed at the studio, March 14, '61. Running time, **140 MINS.**

Parrish McLean	Troy Donahue
Ellen McLean	Claudette Colbert
Judd Raike	Karl Malden
Sala Post	Dean Jagger
Lucy	Connie Stevens
Alison Post	Diane McBain
Paige Raike	Sharon Hugueny
Teete Howie	Dub Taylor
Edgar Raike	Hampton Fancher
Wiley Raike	David Knapp
Evaline Raike	Saundra Edwards
Eileen	Sylvia Miles
Rosie	Bibi Osterwald
Addie	Madeleine Sherwood
Tom Weldon	Hayden Rorke

Delmer Daves' production of "Parrish" is a long, plodding account of man vs. monopoly in Connecticut's tobacco game. Although slickly produced, charming to the eye in its pictorial appreciation of New England's scenic beauty and carefully cast with a mixture of solid veteran troupers and a host of pretty, mostly blue-eyed, colts and fillies weaned in Warner Bros. television-indoctrinated stable, the film, for all of its length, rarely gets beneath the skin of its characters and eventually begins to get under the bulk of too many climaxes followed by too many dramatic plateaus. One comes away from the 140-minute experience with far keener insight into the growing process of the tobacco plant than into the peculiar breed of people who do the growing in this picture.

"Parrish" does not even remotely figure to be an overpowering box-office attraction, but has elements that indicate a mild success, not the least of which is its likely strong appeal to younger audiences, who may be able to identify to some extent with the growing pains of its central characters as they encounter the initial responsibilities of maturity. Also going for the Warner Bros. release is the fact that there are a number of rising young players in the cast, attractive performers who will arouse curiosity among filmgoers.

Based on the highly "Parrish" able novel by Mildred Savage, Daves' screenplay is something of a cross between a rich man's "Tobacco Road" and a poor man's "A Place in the Sun." Troy Donahue essays the title role of a poor young man who emerges from a laborer's toil in the Connecticut tobacco fields to challenge the dynasty of mighty land baron Karl Malden, an inconceivably ruthless and greedy tycoon who would put another man's lifelong labor in his pipe and smoke it in order to gain control of the entire tobacco valley.

A number of romantic entanglements crop up to complicate this basic conflict, not the least of which are Donahue's bat-of-an-eyelash love affairs with Malden's daughter (Sharon Hugueny), his arch rival's (Dean Jagger's daughter (Diane McBain) and a loose field girl (Connie Stevens) who gives illegitimate birth to the child of Malden's son (Hampton Fancher). Then there is the supreme complication: Malden's marriage to Donahue's mother (Claudette Colbert). At any rate, Donahue proceeds to walk out on an enviably-salaried position as his stepfather's aide, acquires the last remaining strip of land in the valley independent of Malden's control and scuttles the latter's last-ditch attempt to beat him down.

Donahue is handsome and has his moments, but lacks the animation and projection that is required to bring the title character, curiously vacant and elusive as written, into clearer focus. It is a serious setback to the film, which revolves dependently around the personality of its hero. The picture's three principal veterans—Miss Colbert, Malden and Jagger—do well, particularly Malden in spite of the exaggerated nature of his role. Pretty Miss Stevens displays a nice feel for intimate romantic byplay. The strikingly beautiful and glamorous Miss McBain is effective as Jagger's spolled daughter. Other young people who make vivid impressions are Miss Hugueny, Fancher and David Knapp. Dub Taylor pitches in with a nice character performance, and the balance of support is more than adequate.

There is a certain class stereotype about the characters—coldness and decadence among the rich, lovableness and camaraderie among the poor—that Daves has not managed to erase either as scenarist or director. It seems a rather dated concept in these socially-flattened times. Harry Stradling Sr.'s astute photography is extremely flattering to the players, particularly the young ladies who benefit enormously in close-up from the soft, careful regard of his lens. Leo K. Kuter's artwork is accurately and perceptively geared to the social status of the parties whose habitats are on display. Editor Owen Marks has done a respectable job of knitting this long film. Max Steiner's score is soft, romantic and melodic, similar in theme to that of his score for Daves' "A Summer Place." *Tube.*

Look In Any Window

Tasteless, unpleasant meller about a junior-grade peeping Tom. Exploitable aspects may entice some, but overall b.o. prospects are lean.

Hollywood, March 13.
Allied Artists release of William Alland-Laurence E. Mascott production. Stars Paul Anka, Ruth Roman, Alex Nicol, Gigi Perreau, Carole Mathews, George Dolenz, Jack Cassidy; with Robert Sampson, Dan Grayam. Directed by Alland. Screenplay, Mascott; camera, W. Wallace Kelley; editor, Harold Gordon; art director, Hilyard Brown; music, Richard Shores; sound, Charles Schelling; assistant director, Charles W. Bohart. Reviewed at the studio, March 13, '61. Running time, **87 MINS.**

Craig Fowler	Paul Anka
Jackie Fowler	Ruth Roman
Jay Fowler	Alex Nicol
Eileen Lowell	Gigi Perreau
Betty Lowell	Carole Mathews
Carlo	George Dolenz
Gareth Lowell	Jack Cassidy
Lindstrom	Robert Sampson
Webber	Dan Grayam

Out of the nine leading characters in "Look In Any Window," seven are thoroughly unsavory types. Included in this unpleasant cast of characters in this extremely unpleasant picture are an emotionally-disturbed teenager who is a peeping Tom on the side, a shiftless alcoholic, an unscrupulously opportunistic widower, two unfaithful wives, a wealthy and decadent businessman and a righteous, sadistic cop. In other words, not exactly wholesome, bring-the-whole-family-to-the-theatre entertainment.

Obviously a film peopled with characters of such a sensational nature has a certain air of exploitation about it, the kind that might entice a thrill-seeker to the neighborhood ozoner. But the Allied Artists release amounts to film-making at its most distasteful level, and the bulk of the general public is discerning enough not to support such fare. Such pictures are a discredit to Hollywood and a gross distortion of the American way of life.

The film was produced by William and Laurence E. Mascott, written by the latter and directed by the former. Teenage singing favorite Paul Anka essays the pivotal role, that of the demented youngster from a broken home who asserts his latent masculinity by donning a mask and spying on the ladies of the sub-bourbon community. The picture gets tangled up in irrelevant issues but ultimately gets to the crux of the matter and suggests a happy eventuality when the boy's parents agree to make a fresh go of it and the lad, caught in the act and unmasked, is ticketed for psychiatric care. No novel point is made through all this melodramatic fuss, except perhaps that people who live in glass houses shouldn't get stoned but had better draw their blinds at night.

Anka, a nitery performer and composer of some note, does not seem well-suited to the business of acting, but gives it a valiant try. He sings the lacklustre title ditty, which he wrote. Ruth Roman contributes a sultry, sexy performance as Anka's naughty mama. Alex Nicol turns in an effective portrait of his alcoholic papa. Others involved are Gigi Perreau, Carole Mathews, George Dolenz, Jack Cassidy, Robert Sampson and Dan Grayam.

Editing is haphazard, even to the extent that sound from one scene overlaps into the next. There is journeyman camera work by W. Wallace Kelley, art director by Hilyard Brown. *Tube.*

The Secret Ways

Outmoded cloak - and - dagger meller. Weak wicket candidate.

Hollywood, March 10.
Universal release of Richard Widmark production. Stars Widmark; features Sonja Ziemann, Charles Regnier, Walter Rilla. Directed by Phil Karlson. Screenplay, Jean Hazlewood, based on novel by Alistair MacLean; camera, Max Greene; editor, Aaron Stell; art directors, Werner and Isabella Schlichting; music, Johnny Williams; sound, Kurt Schwarz; assistant directors, Andre Farsch, Erich von Stroheim Jr. Reviewed at Westwood Village Theatre, March 10, '61. Running time, **112 MINS.**
Michael Reynolds......Richard Widmark

Julia .... Sonja Ziemann
The Count .... Charles Regnier
Jansci .... Walter Rilla
Colonel Hidas .... Howard Vernon
Elsa .... Senta Berger
Minister Sakenov .... Heinz Moog
Hermann Sheffler. Hubert von Meyerinck
The Fat Man .... Oskar Wegrostek
Border Official .... Stefan Schnabel
Olga .... Elisabeth Newmann-Viertel
Janos .... Helmuth Janatsch
Jon Bainbridge .... John Horsley
Peter .... Walter Wilz
Special Agent .... Raoul Retzer
Language Professor....... Georg Kovary
Sandor .... Adi Berber
The Commandant..... Jochen Brockmann
Waitress .... Brigitte Brunmuller
The Count's Men... Reinhard Kollderoff, Rudolf Rosner

"The Secret Ways" is a serious film at which, regrettably, discerning audiences are likely to laugh. Cause of the unscheduled merriment is its thoroughly outmoded style and a pack of visual cliches. It emerges a ludicrous, imitative, unintentional parody of dozens of cloak-and-dagger pictures that have preceded it to the screen. Filmed in Europe by producer-star Richard Widmark, the Heath production amounts to a sort of poor man's "Third Man." Totally lacking in appeal outside of the Widmark name, the Universal-International release is a depressingly weak boxoffice contender and, additionally, is much too long for comfortable pairing as a supporting attraction.

The undistinguished, astonishingly uninformative screenplay was adapted by Jean Hazelwood from the novel by Alistair MacLean. Widmark stars as an American adventurer-for-hire who hires out to rescue a noted scholar from behind the Iron Curtain in Hungary. He has a running skirmish with the Budapestiferous AVO (Hungarian Secret Police), but ultimately gets his man. As directed by Phil Karlson, there are a few lively chase sequences but most of the film is burdened with suspicious eye-balling and unrealistically theatrical behavior.

The way Widmark plays the central character—with a sort of smugly, ugly Americanese swagger—one never becomes concerned about his chances for survival. There is, however, some good character work by Charles Regnier and capable enough support by Walter Rilla, Howard Vernon, Heinz Moog, Hubert van Meyerinck and Oskar Wegrostek, although each of these people and most of the bit players have been encouraged to behave like classic spy picture, strictly-from-Hungary types. The film brings a pair of delightfully good-looking young European ladies to the American screen: handsome Sonja Ziemann and a well-proportioned blonde bombshell with the culinary-sounding name of Senta Berger, latter in a preposterously irrelevant role incorporated into the film apparently for purely decorative reasons.

Max Greene's photography has an energetic bent in the run-run-run passages that comprise seemingly a good half of the film. That the picture seems overly long and repetitious is not a favorable commentary on Aaron Stell's editing. Art directors Werner and Isabella Schlichting have imported the ornate style of European architecture. Johnny Williams theme music adds an appropriately ominous note. *Tube.*

Cuando Regree Mama
(When Mother Returns)
(MEXICAN)

Mexico City, March 14.

Peliculas Nacionales release of Alameda Films (Cesar Santos Galindo) production. Stars Ofelia Montesco, Maria Duval, Rafael Bertrand, Pedro de Aguillon; features Hortensia Santovena, Alejandro Chianguerotti Jr., Lucero Taboada, Rocio Rosales, Rafaelito Banquells, Enrique Edwards. Directed by Rafael Baledon. Screenplay, Ramon Obon. At Variedades Theatre, Mexico City. Running time, 90 MINS.

This is an unabashed sentimental tear-jerker centering about four children who become orphans and have the truth hidden from them for a long time. Plot concerns a pious older brother who remains silent, attempting to withhold the truth from the children. These gradually learn of the death of their parents. The ultimate acceptance of this fact is rather ingeniously presented by the youngest child.

Lucero Taborda, Rocio Rosales, Rafaelito Banquells and Enrique Edwards, the quartet of kids around whom film revolves, do quite well in their roles. And with action taking place around Christmas time, there are many festive scenes likely to be appreciated by kiddies in the audience.

Picture is about evenly divided between laughter and tears. Thanks to the sure direction of Rafael Baledon, the transition never gets out of hand. While the script is conventional, acting is on the whole convincing. This one will have a long life of many years in nabe houses in reruns, and is fitting fare for Spanish speaking area markets. *Emil.*

Macario
(MEXICAN)

Mexico's "Best Foreign Film" Oscar nominee, a moving and illuminating allegory about a poor woodsman's spiritual bout with Death and material bout with hunger. On heels of nomination, a favorable arty prospect.

Hollywood, March 16.

Azteca Films release of Armando Orive Alba production. Stars Ignacio Lopez Tarso, Pina Pellicer; with Enrique Lucero, Jose Galvez, Jose Luis Jiminez, Mari Alberto Rodriguez. Directed by Roberto Gavaldon. Screenplay, Emilio Carballido, Galvandon, from story by Bruno Traven; camera, Gabriel Figueroa; art director, Manuel Fontanals; music, Raul Lavista. Reviewed at Azteca studio projection room, March 16, '61. Running time, 91 MINS.

Macario .... Ignacio Lopez Tarso
Macario's Wife .... Pina Pellicer
Death .... Enrique Lucero
The Devil .... Jose Galvez
God .... Jose Luis Jimenez
Don Ramiro.... Mario Alberto Rodriguez

In "Macario," the Mexican film industry has produced one of the finest films of 1960. A charming, touching allegory expressed with primitive power and spiritual significance, the Clasa Films Mundiales production, produced by Armando Orive Alba, is also a film of ethnic value, providing as it does an insight into the cultural traditions of the country and their impact on its people. Since, additionally, its artistry has been rewarded in this country with an Academy Award nomination for "Best Foreign Film," "Macario" is certain to attract a good deal of attention in the art house circuit, where it should be most favorably received.

Ignacio Lopez Tarso contributes a memorable performance as "Macario," a kind, decent, but ever-hungry woodman whose wish to have, for once in his life, one thing all to himself (a turkey which he will not share with his impoverished family) leads to his destruction when he shares his feast, instead, with Death, receiving in return the power to cure. In a symbolic chain of events he becomes renowned for his magical abilities to determine the life or death of his patients, until he is confronted with an ultimatum from the Inquisition to cure a viceroy's son (which he cannot) or pay with his own life. His wife (Pina Pellicer) finds him expired in the forest, his half of the symbolic turkey (representative of all the hunger of his life) intact, suggesting the consequences of refusal to share, no matter the extent of personal motivation.

Within this complicated but compelling framework there are several passages of great emotional force and indelible beauty. The early scenes of the family's utter poverty amidst a ceremony in which rich foodstuffs are offered to the dead has great impact. Then, too, sly humor has been instilled into the passages in which Death determines, often to Macario's astonishment, which patients shall survive and which shall perish.

The film is masterfully directed by Roberto Gavaldon. The moving screenplay by Gavaldon and Emilio Carballido was adapted from a story by Bruno Traven. It benefits from the adept photography of Gabriel Figueroa, aware and meticulous art direction of Manuel Fontanals, capable special effects of Juan Munoz Ravelo, and expressive music of Raul Lavista. In addition to Tarso's exceptional portrayal, Miss Pellicer is luminous and compassionate as his wife, Enrique Lucero commanding and impressive as Death. Also fine are Jose Galvez as the Devil, Jose Luis Jimenez as God, and Mario Alberto Rodriguez as a wealthy townsman. *Tube.*

All In A Night's Work
(COLOR)

Periodically witty script, keen direction and a merry performance by Shirley MacLaine.

Hollywood, March 14.

Paramount release of Hal Wallis production. Stars Dean Martin, Shirley MacLaine; features Cliff Robertson, Charlie Ruggles; Norma Crane. Directed by Joseph Anthony. Screenplay, Edmund Beloin, Maurice Richlin, Sidney Sheldon, based on story by Margit Veszi and play by Owen Elford; camera (Technicolor) Joseph LaShelle; editor, Howard Smith; art directors, Hal Pereira, Walter Tyler; music, Andre Previn; sound, Gene Merritt, Charles Grenzbach; assistant director, Daniel J. McCauley. Reviewed at Grauman's Chinese Theatre, March 14, '61. Running time, 94 MINS.

Tony Ryder .... Dean Martin
Katie Robbins .... Shirley MacLaine
Dr. Warren Kingsley Sr. Charlie Ruggles
Warren Kingsley Jr .... Cliff Robertson
Marge Coombs .... Norma Crane
Oliver Dunning .... Gale Gordon
Sam Weaver .... Jerome Cowan
Lasker .... Jack Weston
O'Hara .... Ian Wolfe
Mrs. Kingsley Sr. ...... Mabel Albertson
Miss Schuster .... Mary Treen
Carter .... Rex Evans
Albright .... Roy Gordon
Colonel Ryder .... Charles Evans
Baker .... Ralph Dumke
Harry Lane .... John Hudson

A surprisingly high reading on the laugh meter is recorded in this essentially predictable, featherweight comedy. The Hal Wallis production never really soars to any sustained comic crescendos and has plenty of barren patches between the fun but, thanks to the flashes of wit in the screenplay and the surges of zany merriment for which director Joseph Anthony and costar Shirley MacLaine are chiefly responsible, there is a presentable degree of humor and diversion to be found. With Dean Martin and Miss MacLaine as potent marquee bait, the Paramount release should prove to be a fairly respectable, though not dynamic, boxoffice attraction.

Other than a vague comment on how the most innocent circumstance can spur suspicion of foul play in today's complex, impersonal business world, there is no satiric profundity in screenplay by Edmund Beloin, Maurice Richlin and Sidney Sheldon. Consolidated from a story by Margit Veszi and a play by Owen Elford, their scenario describes with disarming disregard for reality the development of a romantic attachment between the heir to a publishing dynasty (Martin), and a girl (Miss MacLaine). She's suspected of having enjoyed intimate relations with his uncle-benefactor just prior to the latter's smiling death in bed. The entire yarn is fabricated on the false notion shared by Martin and his board of directors that Miss MacLaine is blackmailing the firm, which is seeking an important bank loan dependent on the good name of its deceased leader. As expected, everything comes clean in the end.

Miss MacLaine is still playing the sweet, naive, tanglefooted kook she began a few years back in "Some Came Running," but she plays it with such innocent sincerity and comic gusto that she thoroughly succeeds in winning over the audience and gives the film a much-needed shot in the funnybone.

Never for one moment is Martin believable in the role of the youthful publishing tycoon, but his easygoing manner and knack for supplying the comedy reaction gets him by. Then, too, there is a lamentable shortage in Hollywood of younger romantic leading men who can play it for laughs.

Cliff Robertson, in an "other guy" role, is miscast. A fine dramatic actor, he seems ill-at-ease in this lightweight environment. The film benefits from a number of exceptional supporting comic performances, prominent among which are those of Norma Crane, Jack Weston (especially good), Charles Ruggles, Gale Gordon and Jerome Cowan. Anthony's direction is outstanding—beautifully timed to get the most out of a punch line or sight gag and unusually perceptive in its incorporation of extra little bits of funny business to spank over a joke.

Joseph LaShelle's Technicolor photography is vivid and alert. Credit art directors Hal Pereira and Walter Tyler with a number of attractive, colorful sets. Sharp editing of Howard Smith is especially rewarding in its flashback technique — conveying the apt quality of a swift revolving stage to

isolate past from present. Most of Andre Previn's listenable score has a classical air about it, notably the refreshingly different theme melody.   *Tube.*

A Raisin In The Sun

Fine, stirring film and stout b.o. contender. A few elements have been lost in translation.

Hollywood, March 28.
Columbia Pictures release of David Susskind-Philip Rose production. Stars Sidney Poitier. Directed by Daniel Petrie. Screenplay, Lorraine Hansberry, from her play; camera, Charles Lawton Jr.; editors, William A. Lyon, Paul Weatherwax; art director, Carl Anderson; music, Laurence Rosenthal; sound, George Cooper; assistant director, Sam Nelson. Reviewed at Screen Directors Guild Theatre, March 9, '61. Running time, **127 MINS.**
Walter Lee Younger..... Sidney Poitier
Lena Younger .... Claudia McNeil
Ruth .... Ruby Dee
Beneatha .... Diana Sands
Asagai .... Ivan Dixon
Mary Lindner .... John Fiedler
George Murchison .... Louis Gossett
Travis .... Stephen Perry
Bobo .... Joel Fluellen
Willie Harris .... Roy Glenn
Bartender .... Ray Stubbs
Taxi Driver .... Rudolph Monroe
Employer .... George DeNormand

A blaze of truth and perception lights up Lorraine Hansberry's marvelous tale of a frustrated but indestructible Negro family in Chicago. A great play, it has now become a fine motion picture. Yet something has gone out of "A Raisin in the Sun" in its translation from the stage to the cinema, and that something is the rapport, the direct and stirring communication that binds together colored actors in person on the stage with the ordinarily predominantly white audiences on the other side of the footlights. It is an interracial bond of understanding that, to some extent, vanishes when the drama is enacted via the more impersonal medium of celluloid. There simply isn't the same reassuring togetherness about the experience, and that is the crux of its legit potency.

But it is a tribute to Miss Hansberry's creation that, although it shows to better advantage on the boards, it is still a powerful and moving drama on the screen. The David Susskind-Philip Rose production, released by Columbia, will be successful at the boxoffice because it is an important, worthwhile, timely social document and because, most of all, it is simply a good film, one that deals with genuine, everyday people who will be universally understoood. Since it arrives on the screen at such a critical juncture in U. S. white-colored relations, and is certain to penetrate areas denied the legit production, it is bound to influence people who can use some influencing in the business of living together.

Miss Hansberry has adapted her own play to fit the specifications of the screen. The changes are few. It is the touching tale of a Negro family stirred into emotional flux when the proud matriarch of the household (Claudia McNeil) receives a $10,000 life insurance payment. They plan to move into a small home in a white suburban neighborhood but when the restless, impatient son (Sidney Poitier) squanders two-thirds of the sum in a get-rich-quick scheme, the dream is apparently destroyed. Further complications ensue when the residents of the white neighborhood dispatch a "welcoming" representative whose "welcome" is a plea for them to abandon their intentions, but it is at this critical point that the son emerges from the depths of despair, attains ma-

turity, and rallies the family back into unity and action. Undaunted, unbowed, they move.

Seven members of the original Broadway cast repeat their roles in the film. Poitier gives a striking, commanding performance. There is a poetry in the very expression of his body movements—wild, desperate gestures and thrusts of arm and restless, almost choreographic floor-pacing gyrations that convey physically but clearly the inner turmoil, the years of denial that the character has had to seal within himself. Miss McNeil repeats her towering stage portrayal of the devout, loyal, courageous matriarch. It is an enactment shining with warmth, dignity and compassion, one that is sure to be remembered next Oscar time.

Ruby Dee, as Poitier's sweet, hard-working wife, is a wistful, fragile figure, one audiences will understand and one with which distaff customers can easily identify. A sharp, up-to-date character is created by Diana Sands as Poitier's enlightened student sister. She is a standout. Others who fashion memorable moments are Ivan Dixon, John Fiedler, Louis Gossett, Stephen Perry, Joel Fluellen and Roy Glenn.

Director Daniel Petrie, working with a vehicle far more favorably suited to the dimensions and characteristics of the stage than to the motion picture, has nevertheless succeeded in instilling a sense of movement and variety into some unusually cramped quarters. Miss Hansberry has transferred several scenes to a neighborhood bar but, by and large, all of the action takes place in the family's small apartment. Petrie has kept his camera, manned astutely by Charles Lawton Jr., moving, and has positioned it at a number of interesting vantage points. However, the film seem to have lost some of the spirit of the play's humorous passages, and this may very well have something to do with the fact that much of the merriment (notably an African drum ritual) has the quality of a spectacle, and needs to be regarded from a distance to be properly appreciated. Petrie, a bit unwisely, has chosen to play these scenes in tight, thus missing some of the fun contained in details of the movement and interplay.

Carl Anderson's sets carry the appropriate flavor of lower middle class respectability but economic reality. Editing by William A. Lyon and Paul Weatherwax is true. There isn't a great deal of background music, but what there is —principally Laurence Rosenthal's theme strain—is heart-tugging and listenably melodic.   *Tube.*

La Notte
(The Night)

Rome, March 21.
Dino DeLaurentiis release of Nepi (Rome)-Sofitedip-Silver Film (Paris) coproduction. Stars Marcello Mastroianni, Monica Vitti, Jeanne Moreau; features Bernard Wicki, Maria Pia Luzi, Rosi Mazzacurati, Guido Aimone Marson, Vincenzo Corbella, Gitt Magrini Corbella, Ugo Fortunati. Directed by Michelanglo Antonioni. Story and screenplay, Antonioni, Ennio Flajano, Tonino Guerra; camera, Gianni di Venanzio; music, Giorgio Gaslini; editor, Eraldo da Roma. At Fiamma, Rome. Running time, **125 MINS.**
Giovanni .... Marcello Mastroianni
Lidia .... Jeanne Moreau
Valentina .... Monica Vitti
Tommaso .... Bernard Wicki

Resy .... Rosy Mazzacurati

Only a few years ago, this engrossing film might have been shrugged off as boxoffice poison by most exhibitors. Now, pix of this kind ("Hiroshima, Mon Amour" and this same author's previous "Avventura"), which require full spectator participation, seem to have found their niche. And the niche is constantly widening. This one needs careful handling in both sales approach and foreign lingual versions, but can pay off handsomely in almost all areas where quality pix are sought.

Story is a superficially simple one. After 10 years of marriage, a popular writer and his wife begin to realize their affair is nearing the breaking point. She's bored, has had an extra-marital fling with a family friend who has just died suddenly, leaving her even more despondent. Outwardly successful, he knows he's a failure, is looking around desperately for another woman to inspire him again. More than misunderstanding, here it's a question of lack of communication between two beings—a theme which the director has developed before. Pic covers one day and a night. And when dawn breaks up the party which the couple is attending, habit, fear, loneliness and sorrow bring them together again in one last desperate act of love.

Jeanne Moreau walks off with acting honors in a carefully modulated, masterful performance as the wife, Monica Vitti is fine as a would-be distraction for the husband. Latter is played well by Marcello Mastroianni, though the range of the role is more limited, the script giving the wife the choicest acting morsels. A brief but effective cameo is contributed by Bernard Wicki as the dying friend whose death triggers the couple's thoughts and actions. Others are ably selected for a colorful backdrop which always rings true to life.

Slow pace adopted by Antonioni may irk some customers, but it fits the mood admirably. And here he has his most accessible but also his most personal film, in which intelligent dialogs and a similar script come to grips with significant material. The technical credits, from the mood-setting lensing by Gianni di Venanzo to the apt music by Giorgio Gaslini, are outstanding in this difficult but stimulating picture.   *Hawk.*

Portrait Of A Mobster

Two - dimensional account of prohibition era activities of the unsavory "Dutch" Schultz. Should attract gangster pic buffs in sufficient numbers to get by at the b.o.

Hollywood, March 21.
Warner Bros. production and release. Stars Vic Morrow, Leslie Parrish, Peter Breck. Directed by Joseph Pevney. Screenplay, Howard Browne, from book by Harry Grey; camera, Eugene Polito; editor, Leo H. Shreve; art director, Jack Poplin; music, Max Steiner; sound, M. A. Merrick; assistant director, Charles Hansen. Reviewed at the studio, March 21, '61. Running time, **108 MINS.**
"Dutch Schultz" .... Vic Morrow
Iris Murphy .... Leslie Parrish
Frank Brennan .... Peter Breck
Bo Wetzel .... Norman Alden
Michael Ferris .... Robert McQueeney
Lt. D. Corbin .... Ken Lynch

Anthony Parazzo	Frank de Kova
Guthrie	Stephen Roberts
Vincent Coll	Evan McCord
Steve Matryck	Arthur Tenen
Louise Murphy	Frances Morris
John Murphy	Larry Blake
Joe Noe	Joseph Turkel
Matty Krause	Eddie Hanley
Lou Rhodes	John Kowal
"Legs" Diamond	Ray Danton

The enduring popularity of gangster fare, especially the quasi-documentary recollection of underworldliness in the flamboyant era of prohibition, seems to insure "Portrait Of A Mobster" of a respectable, if short-lived, boxoffice showing. For the aficionado of crime, for whom the rat-a-tat symphony of the tommy gun, the black sedan and the concealed booze distillery are the symbols of exciting entertainment, the film should be a magnet. But the Warner Bros. release appears to be nearing the point of diminishing returns—the point at which the tried and true formula suddenly begins to lapse into the overworked and shopworn parody.

The absence of novelty, depth or surprise about "Portrait Of A Mobster" indicates that a change of approach may be due if prospects for such pictures in future are to remain at the safe-and-sound commercial level.

The foundation and/or suggestion of fact that characterizes this film allows less latitude for character creation. It hems in the creator, restricts him to events and personalities explored before. In dealing with known people and incidents, in working without the freedom of pure fiction, he must manage to retain authenticity yet establish audience concern for and involvement with his despicable, but after all human, "heroes." In "Mobster," scenarist Howard Browne, tackling the book by Harry Grey, fails to accomplish this.

"Dutch" Schultz, the central character in the film, although essayed with dynamic intensity by Vic Morrow, emerges a hollow figure, and this is the crux of the picture's shortcoming. In tracing Schultz's career in crime, Browne has shed no true light on the inner nature of the man—the factors that warped his personality, shaped his destiny, formed the foul killer. The audience therefore must accept the man the way he is, and since "the way he is" is utterly distasteful, no sense of understanding is established, no insight into the base thought processes that govern his behavior. The "Portrait" thus becomes more of a snapshot.

Lovely Leslie Parrish plays Morrow's mistress, who temporarily is lured away from marriage to a weak, but decent, policeman (Peter Breck) when the latter is framed and enrolled into the Schultz organization. Miss Parrish starts off very nicely but has some difficulty conveying the latter (disillusioned and alcoholic) aspects of the character. Again, however, the character itself is superficial. Although Morrow has murdered her father, and virtually everyone on the premises is at least vaguely cognizant of the fact, the truth never occurs nor is it suggested to the astonishingly naive young women played by Miss Parrish. It strains credulity.

Breck gives a capable performance, as do most of those in support. Ray Danton is an interesting figure in his re-creation of the "Legs" Diamond role. Norman Alden does an excellent job as Morrow's faithful aide who, betrayed but unaware of it, unintentionally kills his boyhood buddy in the end.

The production, a "house" effort for which no individual producer receives credit, is ably reined by Joseph Pevney, within the Scope cited Newsreel footage has been incorporated smoothly to heighten authenticity. Eugene Polito's camera work is straightforward, Max Steiner's music unobtrusively mood-building, Jack Poplin's art direction an authentic reflection of period fads and styles.

In a film of this nature, editing must often account for the precise movements of several persons converging on an appointed spot for conflicting reasons. It requires some swift and tricky transitions, which Leo H. Shreve has managed without destroying mood or continuity. *Tube.*

The Fiercest Heart
(C'SCOPE-COLOR)

Routine action-adventure meller fabricated from mid-19th century flight of Boer people in South Africa. Promising material, but stock approach.

Hollywood, March 22.
Twentieth-Fox release of George Sherman production. Stars Stuart Whitman, Juliet Prowse, Ken Scott, Raymond Massey, Geraldine Fitzgerald, Rafer Johnson. Directed by Sherman. Screenplay, Edmund H. North, based on novel by Stuart Cloete; camera (De Luxe), Ellis W. Carter; editor, Richard Billings; art directors, Duncan Cramer, George Van Marter; music, Irving Gertz; sound, Alfred Bruzlin, Warren B. Delaplain; assistant director, Jack R. Berne. Reviewed at the studio, March 22, '61. Running time, **91 MINS.**
Bates	Stuart Whitman
Francina	Juliet Prowse
Harry Carter	Ken Scott
Willem	Raymond Massey
Tante Maria	Geraldine Fitzgerald
Nzobe	Rafer Johnson
Barent	Michael David
Hugo Bauman	Eduard Franz
Sarah	Rachel Stephens
Peter	Dennis Holmes
Madrigo	Edward Platt
Major Adrian	Alan Caillou
Hendrik	Hari Rhodes
Mrs. Adrian	Katherine Henryk
Klaas	Oscar Beregi

Programmed into situations where African adventure is more likely to be appreciated on a purely escape basis, "The Fiercest Heart" will have entertainment value for the more easygoing customer. But overall boxoffice prospects aren't very bright for this tame, rather antiquated-in-style description of the northward trek of the Boer people through the Dark Continent along about 1837.

The 20th-Fox release has some good names and capable actors in its cast, and these will aid its fortunes, but George Sherman's production unwisely flounders in contrived, predictable melodrama at the expense of the story's loftier, more worthwhile historical values, an interesting facet which it tends to dismiss. There is a smattering of action (a pair of Zulu raids), but director Sherman has not quite managed to instill the desirable tension or realism into these passages.

The screenplay by Edmund H. North is diluted from the novel by Stuart Cloete. Stuart Whitman plays a footloose escapee from a British South African stockade who joins a band of Boer farmers journeying to their "promised land." It is the stock, but compelling theme of the self-centered adventurer who through involvement with the cause of underdog people, slowly develops ideals, undertakes a new identity, heroically leads the folks to attainment of their goal when the chips are down, and takes up with the prettiest and most desirable girl in the party (Juliet Prowse), who helps tame him into a respectable pulp.

Whitman and Miss Prowse do all that is required of them, which, histrionically speaking, isn't a great deal. They are handsome people. Veterans Raymond Massey and Geraldine Fitzgerald give presentable accounts of themselves. Ken Scott is all that a heavy should be and more. Rafer Johnson, the Olympic decathlon champ, does fine, albeit with little to say or do until the climactic moment when he utilizes his athletic prowess to good advantage by tossing a spear with javelinesque ease and precision into the heart of the Zulu gangleader, thus routing the inept enemy force with one fell swoop. There is key support of a skilled nature from Eduard Franz and Michael David, although both are anchored in stereotyped roles, Franz the "wise man," David the "other man" in the romantic triangle.

Stock African animal footage (the usual zoo-ology-romping zebra, contented giraffe, et.al.) is incorporated for no really pertinent reason. The Duncan Cramer-George Van Marter art direction conveys an aura of space and expanse where there isn't any.

Efficiency is exhibited by Ellis W. Carter's CinemaScope-De Luxe Color lenswork and Richard Billing's editing. The Irving Gertz score is sometimes more dramatic than the drama it is accompanying. *Tube.*

La Ragazza con la Valigia
(Girl with a Suitcase)
(ITALIAN)

Rome, March 21.
Titanus release of a Titanus (Maurizio Lodi-Fe) production. Stars Claudia Cardinale; features Jacques Perrin, Corrado Pani, Renato Baldini, Luciana Angelillo, Riccardo Carrone, Romolo Valli. Directed by Valerio Zurlini. Screenplay, Zurlini, Piero de Bernardi, Leo Benvenuti, from a story by Valerio Zurlini. Camera, Tino Santoni; music, Mario Nascimbene; editor, Mario Serandrei. At Metropolitan, Rome. Running time, 135 MINS.
Aida	Claudia Cardinale
Lorenzo	Jacques Perrin
Marcello	Corrado Pani
Priest	Romolo Valli
Mother	Luciana Angelillo

A mature film cut several notches above the norm, with sensitive handling of adolescent love plus fine performances. Good value for home market and rates export attention as well. Word-of-mouth will help it build, though it needs special care and proper slotting. Some trimming in the latter part would help this over some rough spots.

Story has a familiar ring, but has been given adroit twists both in plotting and lensing to make it just that different. Sans the trimmings, it's about a young girl, Claudia Cardinale, who's had all the bad breaks in life. Left with a child by a man who abandons her, she's picked up while singing with a cheap dance band by a rich young aristocrat, who in turn after a fling soon drops her by the wayside. She traces him to his home, where he sends his younger brother, Jacques Perrin, to steer her off his track. A sensitive sixteener, he falls for her — and she for him—without even realizing it until the film's windup. When they both catch on, knowing it can't be, they leave one another, saddened but enriched by the experience.

For about two thirds of the way, director Valerio Zurlini has guided story and participants unerringly, slowly unfolding his sensitive and pure love story. Then, there's a sharp break in rhythm and style when the girl goes back to her old life, which jars the spectator, until the boy reappears and the story takes up where it left off. Zurlini takes his time in developing his affair, almost resists letting tenderness set in as though in fear of the banal and the expected.

Miss Cardinale has never been better in her instinctive portrayal of Aida, an animal-like creature with a strange morality all her own, while Perrin is excellent as the boy whom her appearance awakes to first love, jealousy, responsibilities, and eventual disappointment. Remainder of the cast is well chosen. Technical credits are all top quality, with apt music arrangements by Mario Nascimbene rating special mention. *Hawk.*

La Menace
(FRENCH)

Paris, March 21.
Gaumont release of Franco London-Paris Union-Gaumont-Continental production. Stars Robert Hossein; features Marie-Jose Nat, Paolo Stoppa, Elsa Martinelli, Philippe Caster, Henri Tissot. Directed by Gerard Oury. Screenplay, Frederick Dard, Oury from novel by Dard; camera, Andre Villard; editor, Genevieve Vaury. At Ambassade-Gaumont, Paris. Running time, **80 MINS.**
Savary	Robert Hossein
Josepha	Marie-Jose Nat
Cousin	Paolo Stoppa
Stephane	Philippe Caster
Girl	Elsa Martinelli
Jerome	Henri Tissot

This mixes up a sex murderer, a lonely, pretty 18-year-old orphan girl and a group of budding delinquents for an inconclusive affair. This is completely without characterization or acceptable motivation. Hence this, at best, is only a possible exploitation item abroad.

The girl wants desperately to be a part of the cabalistic young crowd. To prove herself, she accuses a druggist, who has made a pass at her, of being a sex murderer. Slaying of a young girl is unsolved at the time of her charge. But the crowd hops to the police and then she retraces this and gives up this silly crowd of adolescents only to have the druggist turn out to be the murderer. He almost kills her.

Director Gerard Oury has given this a flat tone, without allowing it to build and develop through character. While making it melodramatic, this lags in the suspense. Marie-Jose Nat is properly straight-laced and bewildered as the girl while Robert Hossein just looks sickly as the sex murderer. Technical qualities are okay. However, **this has an old-fashioned, shallow look about it.** *Mosk.*

All Hands On Deck
(C'SCOPE—COLOR)

Shopworn service comedy with songs. Boxoffice fate depends on extent of kiddie appeal and teen pull of Pat Boone.

Hollywood, March 29.

Twentieth-Fox release of Oscar Brodney production. Stars Pat Boone, Buddy Hackett, Dennis O'Keefe, Barbara Eden. Directed by Norman Taurog. Screenplay, Jay Sommers, based on novel by Donald R. Morris; camera (De Luxe), Leo Tover; editor, Frederick Y. Smith; art directors, Jack Martin Smith, Walter M. Simonds; music, Cyril J. Mockridge; sound, E. Clayton Ward, Frank W. Moran; assistant director, Stanley Hough. Reviewed at Westwood Village Theatre, March 29, '61. Running time, **98 MINS.**

Lt. Donald	Pat Boone
Garfield	Buddy Hackett
Lt. Comdr. O'Gara	Dennis O'Keefe
Sally Hobson	Barbara Eden
Ensign Rush	Warren Berlinger
Comdr. Bintle	Gale Gordon
Lt. Kutley	David Brandon
Bos'n	Joe E. Ross
Lt. Comdr. Anthony	Bartlett Robinson
Mulvaney	Paul von Schreiber
Nobby	Ann B. Davis
Lt. J. G. Schuyler	Jody McCrea
Gruber	Pat McCaffrie

If "All Hands on Deck" is to make the boxoffice grade, it will have to enlist the support of junior America. Only the moppets are likely to get much of a sustained charge out of producer Oscar Brodney's amiable naval rumpus. The 20th-Fox release should generate some teen response via Pat Boone, but for most grownup wicketeers it will amount to little more than a drab and predictable variation on dozens of service comedies that have preceded it to the screen.

Scenarist Jay Sommers' rub-a-dub hubbub is rather insecurely anchored to a novel by Donald R. Morris. The plot is elementary, for anyone in elementary school, that is. Lt. Donald (Pat Boone) falls instantly in love with newshen Sally Hobson (Barbara Eden). He wants to marry her, but his ship sails to the Aleutians. The voyage s complicated by the presence aboard of a Chickasaw Indian sailor (Buddy Hackett) who has grown attached to a stowaway turkey (Owasso), who in turn has grown attached to the captain (Dennis O'Keefe). Hackett solves this little everyday problem by smuggling aboard a pelican. Result: an unhatched turkey-pelican egg.

When the ship returns to port in Long Beach, there is an inspection by admirable admiral Gale Gordon. The main problem is to prevent the admiral from encountering: (1) the turkey; (2) the egg; ((3) Miss Eden who, impatient to see her lover, has slipped onboard concealed in an ashcan. The admiral discovers: (1) the turkey; (2) the egg; (3) Miss Eden, and is about to make his black report when it develops that Miss Eden is employed by a senator in charge of naval appropriations.

Boone, U.S. teendom's good humor man, smiles and warbles his way out of histrionic difficulty. His comedy reactions need work, but his clean-cut, youthful good looks go well with the naval officer's attire. Hackett's zany approach to merriment should go over with the types. O'Keefe, a pro at comedy, delivers competently. Miss Eden, equipped with a delectable figure and a face to match, is good to have around. There's a nifty comic performance by Pat McCaffrie and generally agreeable support by Warren Berlinger, Gordon, Ann B. Davis, David Brandon, Joe E. Ross, Bartlett Robinson, Paul von Schreiber and Jody McCrea. Norman Taurog has directed with a light touch, but the material leaves too much to be desired.

Leo Tover's photography is vivid and colorful (De Luxe), Frederick Y. Smith's editing snappy, Cyril J. Mockridge's score unobtrusively helpful. There are several listenable, but not very memorable, songs. Art direction by Jack Martin Smith and Walter M. Simonds conveys the appropriate nautical flavor. *Tube.*

Les Laches Vivent D'Espoir
(Cowards Live on Hope)
(FRENCH)

Paris, March 28.

UFA release of Athos production. With Gordon Heath, Francoise Giret, Aram Stephani. Written and directed by Claude-Bernard Aubert. Camera, Raoul Foulon; editor, Gabriel Rongier. At George V, Paris. Running time, **90 MINS.**

Daniel	Gorden Heath
Francoise	Francoise Giret
Professor	Aram Stephan

A Negro African student and a French white girl fall in love. The film details the various aspects of bigotry, prejudice and self doubts that almost break them up until a coming child leads to marriage and overcoming all the difficulties. This seems well meaning and sincere, but has a tendency to get preachy and one track. It looms mainly as an exploitation item abroad.

Love comes quickly to this couple and there are many scenes of them wandering happily through Paris and making love. Then comes the encroachment of her family's disgust and hatred, many little petty actions of people, and his growing anger and her bewilderment. There is also a professor who gives a course on racism and tries to get to its aimless, dangerous roots.

But all this is somewhat stilted. And the rage against this form of prejudice is rarely put into acceptable dramatic form. The result is a series of tableaus showing them reacting to the growing pressures but rarely do they seem really alive or to have the love needed to surmount their problems.

American actor Gordon Heath can not quite overcome the almost symbolic quality of his role as the loving but angry, proud Negro student. Francoise Giret is appealing as the girl.

Technical qualities are good but director Claude-Bernard Aubert has been too didactic rather than allowing his characters to grow within their crises. The love scenes naturally will keep this out of the south in the U.S. *Mosk.*

L'Amant De Cinq Jours
(Lover For Five Days)
(FRENCH)

Paris, March 28.

Cinedis release of Ariane-Filmsonor-Mondex-Cineriz production. Stars Jean Seberg, Jean-Pierre Cassel, Micheline Presle, Francois Perier; features Paolo Stoppa, Jean Poiret, Michel Serrault. Directed by Philippe De Broca. Screenplay, Daniel Boulanger, De Broca from novel by Francoise Parturier; camera, Jean Penzer; editor, L. Mery. At Marignan, Paris. Running time, **85 MINS.**

Claire	Jean Seberg
Antoine	Jean-Pierre Cassel
Madeleine	Micheline Presle
Georges	Francois Perier

Film is a situation comedy concerning adultery. Its people are stereotypes, and, though there are a few inventive moments, this is somewhat repetitive in its love scenes and never becomes very engaging. It is mainly for exploitation possibilities without the true insight for weightier chances.

Yank actress Jean Seberg, becoming a regular here, plays a wife of a rather dullish civil servant who is in the midst of an affair with a man she met by accident. He happens to be kept by her best friend, a snobbish couturier. Then things are uncovered and a party brings them all face-to-face.

She finally goes back to the husband, who will stand for her affairs, and the lover, who wanted to go to work and marry her, goes back to his position of gigolo. There is no feeling for place or time, and so this is like a pre-war comedy of saucy French sex manners.

Miss Seberg, looking like Shirley Temple in a wig, is hard put to give a lively knowing air to the wife while Jean-Pierre Cassel plays the gigolo in his usual airy manner. Micheline Presle and Francois Perier, as the cheated partners, are more in character. Direction segues between love, comedy and satire. He does not quite pin down a point of view on the whole thing, there being little flair to make all this bed hopping palatable. Technical aspects are okay. *Mosk.*

La Princesse De Cleves
(The Princess of Cleves)
(FRENCH—COLOR—DYALISCOPE)

Paris, April 4.

Cinedis release of Cinetel-Silver Films production. Stars Jean Marais, Marina Vlady; features Jean-Francois Poron, Annie Ducaux, Lea Padovani, Raymond Gerome, Pieral. Directed by Jean Delannoy. Screenplay, Jean Cocteau from novel by Madame De La Fayette; camera (Eastmancolor), Henri Alekan; editor, Henri Taverna. At Colisee, Paris. Running time, **115 MINS.**

Prince De Cleves	Jean Marais
Princesse De Cleves	Marina Vlady
Duc De Nemours	Jean-Francois Poron
Diane De Poitiers	Annie Ducaux
Catherine De Medecis	Lea Padovani
Henri II	Raymond Gerome
Dwarf	Pieral

Based on one of the first French literary classics of the 16th Century, this concerns a pure but tragic love affair in the court of the King Henri II of that era. It is somewhat static and resembles a series of well constructed tableaus. Though a faithful transposition of the book, it lacks a true feeling for recreating the period and stays mainly in formal court pageantry pattern. This makes it primarily a specialized entry abroad with little depth possibilities since it lacks action. However, its local chances look good.

A 16-year-old girl marries a 40-year-old prince only to fall in love at first sight with a young nobleman. Her purity and breeding keep her faithful to her husband who actually dies when told a false rumor about her infidelity. She still remains true to her husband's memory, and dies young.

Film has a rich sheen, with the court life well done. But director Jean Delannoy rarely has been able to give this a visual insight and breadth to have the times and emotions come to life. A jousting scene leading to the death of the king is one of the fairly actionful sequences. Court dances, intrigues and coincidences mark its literary antecedents.

Marina Vlady has the porcelain looks for the role of the ill-fated Princess while her star-crossed lover Jean-Francois Poron lacks the dash for his part. Jean Marais is acceptable as the suffering husband. Lesser characters are better blocked.

Production values are excellent and technical credits are high. This just misses in making this pic pulsate with life. Hence, this calls for special handling abroad and the hard sell on its nobility of purpose and theme. *Mosk.*

El Globero
(Balloon Man)
(MEXICAN)

Mexico City, March 28.

Columbia Pictures release of Jose Luis Calderon production. Stars Clavillazo and Pulgarcito; features Rodolfo Landa, Irma Dorantes, Rita Macedo, Roberto G. Rivera. Directed by Rene Cardona; music Antonio Diaz Conde; camera, Raul Martinez Solarez. At Palacio Chino, Mexico City. Running time, **90 MINS.**

While the Rene Cardona direction is good and comic Clavillazo turns in a better performance than recently, the sum total of this one is a weak carbon copy of Chaplin's "The Kid," and a number of films made here in the past.

Story revolves about son of a good family (played by Pulgarcito of "Tom Thumb" fame) who is lost and found by Clavillazo, who is a humble balloon vendor. He takes boy under his protective wing. The theme of a father without a son, and a son without a father is milked dry. But there are pathos and comedy touches.

Most important point to this film is fact that comic Clavillazo, who is contracted to churn out pictures like a sausage factory, displays considerable historic talent in straight dramatic acting. And in this one, he avoids the grimaces and bald slapstick of former roles. With the proper script and intelligent direction, Clavillazo shows he could become one of the top performers able to handle both comedy and straight roles capably.

This will do good business at nabe houses and throughout Latin America where the Clavillazo name is being built up. *Emil.*

Les Godelureaux
(The Wise Guys)
(FRENCH)

Paris, March 28.

Cocinor release of International-SPA production. Stars Jean-Claude Brialy, Bernadette Lafont; features Charles Belmont, Jean Tissier, Jean Galland, Sacha Briquet. Directed by Claude Chabrol. Screenplay, Eric Ollivier, Paul Gegauff from novel by Ollivier; camera, Jean Rabiex; editor, James Cuenet. At Marignan, Paris. Running time, **100 MINS.**

Ronald	Jean-Claude Brialy
Ambroisine	Bernadette Lafont
Arthur	Charles Belmont
President	Jean Tissier
Uncle	Jean Galland
Fiancee	Sacha Briquet

The most prolific "New Waver" (also the first), Claude Chabrol, again contributes a satirical pic about the French youth of today. It is sardonic but takes its potshots at hypocritical conformism. Film has some emotional passages plus a serio-comedic edge which could make this an arty theatre possibility abroad. However, it calls for the hard sell in general situations.

A free living youth has a run-in with an effeminate esthete who swears revenge. The former lives with a sensual, young tart from the provinces. They all become friends. Then comes several escapades as they break up phony art shows, seduce pompous people and show up some professional do-gooders. But the esthete takes over the boy's girl and shows her up.

Chabrol has a flair for comic routine but still has yet to get a point of view into his destructively themed pix. The usual orgies are more subdued in this and more attention is paid to these youths whose revolt against their elders is brazen. Yet nothing is introduced to put in its place. In some ways, it is reminiscent of U.S. slapstick films.

This has some bite and wit with Chabrol showing himself to be one of the most technically adept "wavers" in pix here: Jean-Claude Brialy is properly seductive as the rococo character while Charles Belmont is effective as the more serious youth. Bernadette Lafont is a revelation as the perfidious, ibpulsive girl.

Technical credits are good. While this is uneven it has enough exploitation handles and provocative subject matter for offshore chances.

Mosk.

Fuenf Tage - Fuenf Naechte
(Five Days—Five Nights)
(E. GERMAN-RUSSIAN)
(COLOR)

Berlin, March 28.

Progress release of coproduction of Defa (East German) and Mosfilm (Soviet). Directed by Lew Arnstam. Screenplay, Arnstam and Wolfgang Ebeling; camera, Alexander Schelenkow and Tschen Julan; music, Dmitri Shostakovich; editor, Tatjana Lichatschowa. At the Babylon, East Berlin. Running time, 103 MINS.

Paul Naumann ...... Heinz Dieter Knaup
Captain Leanow ..... Wsewolod Safanow
Sergeant Koslow ..... Wsewolod Sonajew
Katrin .... Annekathrin Buerger
Nikitina .... Jewgenija Kosirjewa
Luise Rank .... Marga Legal
Erich Braun .... Wilhelm Koch-Hooge
General .... Michael Majorow

This is the first East German-Soviet Russian coproduction. Both Defa, sole producing outfit in East Germany, and the Russian Mosfilm contributed about the same number of players and technicians, with Lew Arnstam, a Russian, handling the overall direction. Of can be said, both keep about in can be said both keep about in balance. Too much propaganda makes it an item of little interest for western release.

Story starts in 1945 in Dresden, a few weeks after this city's heavy destruction by Anglo-American bombers. It tells in semi-documentary form the rescue, safeguarding and restoration of Dresden's world-famous picture-gallery by Soviet soldiers.

Pic follows an extremely human tendency showing both Russians and the defeated Germans as friends although the war chaos is still at its peak. As well meant as this film probably is, its superhuman attitude gives it a flair of naivety throughout. Latter and frequent overly sentimental passages furnished by the script rob this film of a considerable part of its conviction.

While the script must be called the film's most essential deficiency, there are definite assets in the fine color photography and the score written by Dmitri Shostakovich. The acting is passable although everybody in this tends to wax sentimental. Technically, the pic reps a very good standard.

Hans.

La Mort De Belle
(Death of a Beauty)
(FRENCH)

Paris, March 28.

Lux release of Cinephonic-Chavane-Odeon production. With Jean Desailly, Alexandra Stewart, Monique Melinand, Marc Cassot, Yves Robert. Directed by Edouard Molinaro. Screenplay, Jean Anoulin from novel by Georges Simenon; camera, Jean-Louis Picavet; editor, Robert and Monique Isnardon. At Marbeuf, Paris. Running time, 100 MINS.

Stephane .... Jean Desailly
Belle .... Alexandra Stewart
Blanchon .... Monique Melinand
Policeman .... Marc Cassot
Barman .... Yves Robert

This whodunit is more interested in atmosphere, characterization and psychology than suspense. The oversimplified psycho aspects, and a lack of true insight into motives and place makes this primarily a dualer item abroad. Specialized spotting also is a possibility.

A withdrawn, shy professor, who has an uneventful life with his wife, suddenly finds himself suspected of the murder of an 18-year-old boarder, a comely American daughter of his wife's friend. Then it develops that she had secretly loved him and that she was a loose little girl who drank a lot. And the man begins to emerge from his cocoon of inhibition as the police hound him.

Ironic note is struck as the real murderer is caught. Acting is good. The direction is somewhat too stolid for the fairly routine analysis of the affair. The petty reactions of the townspeople are also cursory. Technical credits are good.

Mosk.

El Hombre de la Ametralladora
(Machine-Gun Man)
(MEXICAN)

Mexico City, March 28.

Peliculas Nacionales release of Alameda Films and Cesar Santos Galindo production. Stars Fernando Casanova, Rafael Bertrand. Silvia Fournier; features Alfonso Mejia, David Silva, Rocio Rosales, Lucero Tabaoda. Directed by Chano Urueta. Screenplay, Ramon Obon. At Cine Olimpia, Mexico City. Running time, 90 MINS.

A crime film with suspense overtones, with actor David Silva, usually cast in hero roles, turning in a highly realistic performance of a born killer, with henchman Rafael Bertrand equally villainous. Action revolves around the kidnapping of heroine Silvia Fournier and two children, played by child actors Rocio Rosales and Lucero Taboada.

Two-fisted Fernando Casanova is the law man who sniffs out the trail of kidnappers. It all leads to a smash end, after some tricky scenes where it looks as though the kidnappers will win, with the hero facing bad men only with his fists and vanquishing them.

Director Urueta has kept up suspense, mystery and action scenes in this one. Oddly enough the actors do not ham it up or overplay. Better than average Mexican effort of its type slated for good boxoffice business throughout Latin America.

Emil.

Greengage Summer
(BRITISH—COLOR)

Leisurely, romantic drama which should score with femme audiences. Persuasive performances by Kenneth More and a bright newcomer, Susannah York, are set attractively in French champagne counttry.

London, April 4.

Columbia release of a Victor Saville-Edward Small production. Stars Kenneth More, Danielle Darrieux, Susannah York, Claude Nollier. Directed by Lewis Gilbert. Screenplay, Howard Koch from Rumer Godden's novel; camera, Frederick A. Young; editor, Peter Hunt; music, Richard Adinsell. At Odeon, Leicester Square, London. Running time, 100 MINS.

Eliot .... Kenneth More
Mdme. Zisi .... Danielle Darrieux
Joss .... Susannah York
Mdme. Corbet .... Claude Nollier
Hester .... Jane Asher
Vicky .... Elizabeth Dear
Wilmouse .... Richard Williams
Paul .... David Saire
Renard .... Raymond Gerome
Mr. Bullock .... Maurice Denham
Monsieur Dufour .... Andre Maranne
Monsieur Prideaux ...... Harold Kaskett
Monsieur Joubert ...... Jacques Brunius
Mrs. Grey .... Joy Shalton

Here's a stylish, warm romantic drama which gets away to a flying start in that it's set in the leisurely champagne country of France. Cameraman Frederick A. Young has taken full advantage of this fact, with some enchanting color lensing. Pic is always a delight to the eye apart from its other qualities. This should readily appeal to femme audiences, particularly, and it's a worthwhile booking for most houses.

Kenneth More is a big attraction for home audiences, Danielle Darrieux and the location will help to take care of Continental appeal, but its marquee value in the U. S. is more doubtful. However, it virtually introduces a new young British actress who, on this showing, looks to have a bright future. The name's Susannah York, previously seen in a smaller role in "Tunes of Glory."

Howard Koch's screenplay, based on Rumer Godden's novel, works up to a holding emotional pitch. Lewis Gilbert has directed with an obviously affectionate care. Story concerns four English schoolchildren, the oldest (Susannah York) being just over 16. They are enroute to a holiday in France's champagne-and-greengage country when their mother is taken ill and is whisked off to hospital.

Alone and dispirited they arrive at the hotel which is run by Danielle Darrieux and managed by Claude Nollier, a Frenchwoman, despite the Christian monicker. The children get a frigid reception from Milles, Darrieux and Nollier. But Kenneth More, a debonair, charming, mysterious Englishman insists that they stay. He's having an affaire with Miss Darrieux and she cannot resist his whims.

During the long summer the atmosphere thickens. He annoys his mistress by taking the children under his wing. The teenager blossoms, and he begins to look at her in a less than patronly light. There is open antagonism between the girl and the older woman. The film builds up to a series of romantic developments during which it becomes clear that More is a notorious jewel thief.

The awakening teenager falls for his quite sincere charm. But when she thinks he has humiliated her, she unwittingly leads to his capture by the police. For him it means prison, for Miss Darrieux the end of love and for young Miss York it means hurt and disillusionment.

This could have turned out overly melodramatic and contrived, but it's mainly handled with delicacy and good taste. Even the dramatic scenes never jar. The early part of the film, when the relationship between More and the children in developing, is particularly charming and pleasantly staged. Miss York 20 progresses delightfully from the resentful, gawky schoolgirl to the young woman eager to live. She handles some tricky scenes (as when she gets drunk with champagne and when she is assaulted by an amorous scullery boy) with an assurance beyond her thesping experience. She has a fresh, wideeyed adolescent beauty which is most appealing.

More's friendly charm and light humor have never been more persuasive than in this film. His scenes with the moppets are great as are his rather more astringent skirmishes with Mlle. Darrieux. She plays the jealous, fading mistress on rather too much of one note, but with keen insight. And there is a subtly drawn relationship of hinted lesbianism between her and Mlle Nollier.

The three younger children are engagingly player, particularly by a red-haired, wise youngster named Jane Asher. David Saire has some overdrawn scenes as the scullery-boy but he, Raymond Gerome, Andre Maranne and Jacques Brunius all contribute useful support.

Dialog is largely unforced and this, with the smooth acting, helps director Gilbert to build up a sustained plausable atmosphere from the outset. He deserves plenty bouquet for his tactful drawing out of adolescent awakening. With sound allround technical okays, from the art work to Richard Addinsel's dainty, evocative music, "Greengage Summer" is a human production that, from time to time, will be remembered with affection for quite a number of sequences.

Rich.

Carry On Regardless
(BRITISH)

Latest in this Midas-touch slapstick series, which defies serious criticism. No coherent plot, but yocks galore; looks a sturdy b.o. prospect.

London, April 4.

Anglo-Amalgamated release of Peter Rogers production. Stars Sidney James, Kenneth Connor, Charles Hawtrey, Joan Sims, Kenneth Williams, Bill Owen, Liz Fraser, Terence Longdon. Directed by Gerald Thomas. Screenplay, Norman Hudis; camera, Alan Hume; editor, John Shirley; music, Bruce Montgomery. At Odeon, Marble Arch, London. Running time, 90 MINS.

Bert Handy .... Sidney James
Sam Twist .... Kenneth Connor
Gabriel Dimple .... Charles Hawtrey
Lily Duveen .... Joan Sims
Francis Courtenay.....Kenneth Williams
Mike Weston .... Bill Owen
Delia King .... Liz Fraser
Montgomery Infield.....Terence Longdon
Frosty-Faced Sister.......Hattie Jacques
Stanley Unwin .... Stanley Unwin
Miss Cooling .... Esma Cannon
Matron .... Joan Hickson
Club Manager .... Sydney Tafler
Mata Hari .... Betty Marsden
Trudi Trelawney.......... Julia Arnall
Penny Panting .... Fenella Fielding

Trevor Trelawney.....Terence Alexander
Wine Connoisseur........David Lodge
Martin Paul ....Jerry Desmond
Sinister Man ....Eric Pohlmann
First Sister ....June Jago
Mr. Delling ....Jimmy Thompson
Mrs. Delling ....Carole Shelley

Any serious criticism of "Carry On Regardless" is futile. Anglo-Amalgamated, through Peter Rogers and Gerald Thomas, have found a goldmine in this slapstick series. Shrewdly, they're going to continue turning them out until the whole formula falls on its face, but this could be quite a long time off. Every exhib who has clicked with any of the previous "Carry On" films will be standing in line for this one. It's a solid b.o. prospect.

The story, such as is, has Sidney James running "Helping Hand Ltd.," an agency prepared to take on any sort of job any time. On his staff are most of the trained imbeciles of previous "Carry On" films. Kenneth Williams, Joan Sims, Charles Hawtrey, Bill Owen, Terence Longdon, Liz Fraser and Kenneth Connor. Disaster winds up every job. Typical of these are scenes which involve Kenneth Williams in taking a chimp for a walk through London, Kenneth Connor baby-sitting (the baby turns out to be a married woman), and Charles Hawtrey deputizing for a pugilist with this weedy comedian getting the job of a nightclub bouncer. Joan Sims has to demonstrate a bubble bath, Liz Fraser finds herself modelling underwear. The good slapstick climax has the whole gang cleaning out a filthy, antiquated house.

Ingenuity of scriptwriter Norman Hudis is sometimes a bit strained, but he has come up with some sound comedy situations.

Hudis' dialog is also lively, relying a great deal on double meanings, saucy vulgarity and the various personalities of the lengthy cast. Even down to the smallest one, the roles are played by actors well experienced in jumping through the comedy hoops that director Gerald Thomas tosses deftly in the air.

Of the principals, Kenneth Connor and Kenneth Williams get the t chances, but Sidney Jam Joan Sims and Liz Fraser pull their weight. Esma Cannon has a high old time as James' assistant and Hattie Jacques, Fenella Fielding, Julia Arnall, Nicholas Parsons, David Lodge, Betty Marsden, Sydney Tafler, David Lodge and a dozen others all make a mark in brief cameos. Film also introduces Stanley Unwin, a tv and radio man who specializes in double talk. Technical credits are all okay.
                                    Rich.

Blast of Silence

Clinical downbeat study of a rubout that doesn't quite convince. Okay prospects, however, with canny handling.

Universal release of an Alfred Crown-Dan Enright production. Features Allen Baron, Molly McCarthy, Larry Tucker. Produced by Merrill Brody. Written and directed by Allen Baron; editor, Peggy Lawson; sound, John Strauss; camera, Erich Kollmar; music, Meyer Kupferman. Reviewed at Universal homeoffice, April 6, '61. Running time, **77 MINS.**

Frank Bono ....Allen Baron
Lorrie ....Molly McCarthy
Big Ralph ....Larry Tucker
Troiano ....Peter Clume
Petey ....Danny Meehan

Troiano's Girl ....Milda Memonas
Nightclub Singer ....Dean Sheldon
Contact Man ....Charles Creasap
Gangster ....Joe Bubbico
Sailor ....Bill DePrato
Bellhop ....Erich Kollmar
Building Sup. ....Ruth Kaner
Gangster ....Gil Rogers
Gangster ....Jerry Douglas
Lorrie's Boyfriend ....Don Saroyan
Waiter ....Jeri Sopanen
Drummer ....Mel Sponder
Troiano's Wife ....Betty Kovac
Gangster ....Bob Taylor
Gangster ....Ernest Jackson

With shrewd sell, Universal may have either a possible art house or lower berth conventional entry with this shoestring effort. Starkly grey, "Blast of Silence" is a quasi-analytical study of a contemporary hired gun, and is done in the neo-realist minor key of such films as "Savage Eye" and "Shadows."

Under the thin avant-garde veneer, however, it is a fairly conventional tale that doesn't quite come off. Fault basically is that it relies too much on over-emphatic narration and not enough on artful plot and characterization. As a consequence, the soundtrack not only works too hard, but is a hindrance in the film's cumulative effect.

An Alfred Crown-Dan Enright presentation, "Blast" was conceived and executed entirely in Manhattan by its producer, Merrill Brody, and director-scenarist Allen Baron, with latter also playing the hired gun. All but two members of the cast are reputed tyro thesps, but some surprisingly effective performances result notwithstanding.

Yarn follows a hood imported to kill a prominent mobster. Along the way, he's reunited with a hometown sweetheart who rejects him, and is forced to strangle a bizarre fat man who has arranged for the murder weapon. When he has finally knocked off the mobster, the gunman goes for his payoff on a deserted strip of beach, where syndicate thugs kill him in an ambush.

In development, the story wavers uncertainly between psychologizing (chiefly via the narration) and being reportorially taut. In seeking to meld the two approaches, "Blast" never really does. Despite this crucial flaw, though, film manages a fair amount of interest as the camera pounds the Gotham pavements.

Baron, as the hired killer, turns in an acceptable maiden stint, but without ever really exposing the thug's conflicting drives. Molly McCarthy as his onetime girl friend delivers her lines in flat fashion. She's one of two pros in the picture, other being Danny Meehan, who satisfactory limns her brother in a brief and familiar role.

Of the others, Larry Tucker, a former songwriters' agent, shows considerable promise as the corpulent, bearded and greedy lowlifer who arranges for the murder gun; and Peter Clune is seen but scarcely heard in the archly-conceived part of the marked mobster.

An echo of black list days is the no-credit for Lionel Stander's crisp-gravel narration, written in pulpish manner by Mel Davenport. Stander's reading is nicely pitched if to small avail.

Though it gets flamboyant in spots, Meyer Kupferman's score shapes as a plus, being a lucid, full-bodied jazz complement. Other technical credits, including Erich Kollmar's camera and Peggy Lawson's editing, are good.   *Pit.*

Taste Of Fear
(BRITISH)

Far-fetched but holding drama, which, despite many holes in the plot, builds up a chilly atmosphere and has a couple of socko twists. Good U. K. prospect, but Susan Strasberg's stellar value is the U. S. test.

London, April 4.
Columbia release of a Hammer (Jimmy Sangster) production. Stars Susan Strasberg, Ronald Lewis, Ann Todd. Features Christopher Lee. Directed by Seth Holt. Screenplay, Jimmy Sangster; camera, Douglas Slocombe; music, Clifton Parker; editor, Eric Boyd Perkins. At Warner Theatre, London. Running time, **82 MINS.**

Penny Appleby..........Susan Strasberg
Bob ....Ronald Lewis
Jane Appleby ....Ann Todd
Dr. Gerrard ....Christopher Lee
Spratt ....Leonard Sachs
Marie ....Anne Blake
Inspector Legrand............John Serret

Screenplay writer Jimmy Sangster takes his first stab at production with "Taste of Fear," and has done the script himself. The script can be shot to pieces for contrived implausibility but the overall effect, which is to keep audiences on edge, is well achieved. This looks to be a safe booking for Britain. Apart from Susan Strasberg, probably, and Ann Todd, possibly, there's no marquee kick for the States.

Columbia is peddling this one on a shrewd exploitation gimmick, that of asking patrons to see this from the start.

Plot is that one about a young woman who is being robbed of her sanity and her inheritance by some fairly odd malarkey. It's been done before, but this one drops in a couple of adroit twists towards the end which may surprise even students of this type picture.

The girl in the case this time is Susan Strasberg, pinned to a wheelchair, who, at the request of her father who she has not seen for 10 years, returns to his Riviera villa and meets, for the first time her stepmother (Ann Todd). But Dad is apparently away on a business trip. However, on the first night she wheels her way into a summer house and there sees her father sitting, dead, in a chair. Or did she? Next day, she has the same uncomfortable experience in the hall. Is she right or is she merely having hallucinations?

Her stepmother and the family doctor assure her that she is in the hallucination market. But she is not sure and neither is Ronald Lewis, her father's handsome young chauffeur. He comforts her and they search for her father's corpse, looking in several unlikely places (including the deep freeze) until they discover him floating in the swimming pool.

But, before they can tell the police, things happen fast. It turns out that Miss Strasberg is really the dead daughter's companion and that she is working in league with the doctor to expose the villains of the piece. These, who else?, are the stepmother and the chauffeur. Only cynics will spot early that the chauffeur is not all he makes himself out to be. The denouement, while predictable, is crisply and excitingly put over.

It is easy to pick a dozen logical objections to this plot. Film succeeds because suspense is skillfully built up, and Douglas Slocombe's lensing helps a great deal. Seth Holt's direction of the Sangster screenplay is always confident, never overdoing the creaking door angle.

Miss Strasberg, who is obviously hampered by being tied largely to her wheelchair, gives a useful performance of bewilderment, fear and near craziness. Ann Todd, stunning as the stepmother, provides enough charm to make people wonder for awhile whether or not she is the villainess of the piece. Ronald Lewis, the chauffeur, has got his first Hollywood break as a result of this film. He's a handsome, virile actor. Christopher Lee, usually associated with villainous roles, is obviously brought in as the reddest of red herrings as the doctor. He plays this straight role convincingly.

Leonard Sachs, Anne Blake, John Serret and Fred Johnson complete the cast effectively. The pre-credit titles sequence sets the atmosphere remarkably well and **it is a feature of this that Clifton Parker's music is used sparingly, and hence with greater impact.**
                                    Rich.

Mr. Topaze
(BRITISH—COLOR)

Slow moving, patchy but fascinating adaptation of Marcel Pagnol's play. Peter Sellers both stars and directs, which is an error. However, his name should insure useful b.o. support.

London, April 4.
20th-Fox release of a Dimitri De Grunwald production. Stars Peter Sellers; features Nadia Gray, Herbert Lom, Leo McKern. Written and produced by Pierre Rouve, from Marcel Pagnol's play. Directed by Peter Sellers. Camera, John Wilcox; editor, Geoffrey Foot; music, Georges Van Parys. At Carlton, London. Running time, **95 MINS.**

Topaze ....Peter Sellers
Suzy ....Nadia Gray
Castel Benac ....Herbert Lom
Muche ....Leo McKern
Baroness ....Martita Hunt
Roger ....John Neville
Ernestine ....Billie Whitelaw
Tamise ....Michael Gough
Colette ....Joan Sims
Blackmailer ....John Le Mesurier
Lilette ....Pauline Shepherd
Gaston ....Michael Sellers

Peter Sellers, a significant comedy actor in British pix, often expressed a yen to have a go at direction. But he was perhaps unwise to essay the tricky task of directing himself in "Mr. Topaze." There have been few standout examples of this two-hat approach coming off successfully and, though "Mr. Topaze" emerges as a stylish picture which, with the Sellers name should be a neat b.o. proposition, it's likely that his personal performance has suffered some. Judgment on his directing powers must be reserved until he can handle a subject without the extra headache of acting.

Sellers plays a kindly, dedicated and very poor schoolmaster in a little French town. His integrity is such that when he refuses to compromise over a pupil's report to satisfy the child's rich, influential grandmother he is fired by the arrogant headmaster. The gullible Sellers is soft-talked into becoming the front for a swindling business man, finds that he has been a pawn

but by then has discovered the wicked ways of the world. He decides to settle for becoming an even bigger "respectable" crook than his employer.

The film falls into sharply contrasting moods. The early stages, with Sellers as the gentle, honest schoolmaster is crammed with sly humor. The schoolroom scenes are well handled by director Sellers. His wooing of the pedagogue's daughter is also delightful, thanks to the completeness with which Sellers absorbs himself in the role.

When the scene switches to the big business sequences there are patchy moments when it seems that the players have embarked on an entirely different film. However, Sellers' acute observation carries him through almost till the end. Then something misfires and the audience is left feeling that it's been tricked. What has started out to be a quiet comedy has suddenly become an uncomfortably brittle, snide drama. Fortunately, that does not happen until near the fadeout.

Without ever being Sellers' most astute performance, it adds another to his fast-growing gallery of versatile characterizations. As a director he has brought out some slick performances from his colleagues. Leo McKern tends to overplay the headmaster. Yet his scenes with Sellers are lively exchanges. Billie Whitelaw, as the daughter, who Sellers shyly woos, has limited opportunities but does well with them. The other leading performances are those of Michael Gough, Nadia Gray and Herbert Lom. Gough is splendid as a seedy schoolmaster who is devoted to Sellers. Lom plays the con man flashily and effectively. Nadia Gray, as Lom's musicomedy mistress, brings a flamboyant touch of glamor to this role. Two other cameos that stand out are John Le Mesurier's furtive blackmailer and Martita Hunt's characteristic study of a rich, acid-tongued martinet.

Film is handsomely mounted and John Wilson's camera work is nice. Music by Georges Van Parys catches the right French mood. George Martin and Herbert Kretzner, who lately wrote the Sellers-Loren hit song, "Goodness, Gracious Me," have not come up with a similar winner with "I Like Money," a trite number put over tepidly by Miss Gray. Perhaps Pierre Rouve's script has kept too closely to the original play. This is by no means the Best of Sellers, but it's still an entertaining picture. *Rich.*

Atlantis, The Lost Continent
COLOR

Lesser fantasy effort by George Pal. Potentially fascinating subject sacrificed to the melodramatic gods. But sufficiently exploitable to make a presentable b.o. showing.

Metro release of George Pal production, directed by Pal. Screenplay, Daniel Mainwaring, based on play by Sir Gerald Hargreaves; camera (Metrocolor), Harold E. Wellman; editor, Ben Lewis; are directors, George W. Davis, William Ferrari; music, Russell Garcia; special effects, A. Arnold Gillespie, Lee LeBlanc, Robert R. Hoag; assistant director, Ridgway Callow. Reviewed at the studio, April 12, '61. Running time, **91 MINS.**

Demetrios	Anthony Hall
Antillia	Joyce Taylor
Sonoy	Frank de Kova
Zaren	John Dall
Xandros	Jay Novello
King Kronas	Edgar Stehli
Azor	Edward Platt
Petros	Wolfe Barzell
Surgeon	Harry Kroeger
Andes	Buck Maffei

Through proper exploitation, curiosity inspired by the subject and, to a certain extent, producer George Pal's reputation as a science-fantasy specialist, Metro's "Atlantis, The Lost Continent" should drum up fairly good business. But, though cinematically skillful, the film as a whole is strictly lower-grade Pal; far inferior, for example, to his outstanding production of a year ago, "The Time Machine."

After establishing legendary significance via an arresting prolog in which the basis for age-old suspicion of the existence of a lost continental cultural link in the middle of the Atlantic is discussed, scenarist Daniel Mainwaring promptly proceeds to ignore the more compelling possibilities of the hypothesis in favor of erecting a tired, shopworn melodrama out of Sir Gerald Hargreaves' source material. A few novel incidents turn up in the story, and these are eagerly embraced by the artisans and craftsmen working in the picture to provide its best moments. But by the large the film is peopled with thoroughly worn out character types—vicious henchmen, feeble rulers, heroic slaves, scrupulous but helpless royal damsels—whose attitudes and activities are predictable from start to finish.

The plot: Greek fisherman is wooed to Atlantis by roving princess, promptly enslaved, then via muscular prowess leads oppressed people to escape as entire decadent continent is submerged, drowning all the bad guys.

Actually, and rather surprisingly, the picture closely parallels in style and structure of content the sort of escapist screen entertainment being fashioned in great abundance by Italian filmakers over the past few years. There is an astonishing similarity to the stevereevesian spectacle that have been arriving on these shores with clockwork consistency. There is a Romanesque aura about the production, undeniably imitative of the vast number of films that have been set in that civilization. An "ordeal by fire and water" ritual conducted in a great, crowded stadium seems almost a replica of gladiatorial combat in the Colosseum. When Atlantis is burning to a cinder at the climax, one can almost hear Nero fiddling. Even Russ Garcia's score has that pompous, martial Roman air about it. And, finally, at least several of the mob spectacle scenes evidently have been lifted and incorporated from Roman screen spectacles of the past (the 10-year-old version of "Cuo Vadis" looks like the source), an example of some enterprising snipping by producer-director Pal, with the assistance of editor Ben Lewis.

The acting is routine. A pair of newcomers to the screen from the tv ranks, Anthony Hall and Joyce Taylor, undertake the leading romantic assignments, and neither fares particularly well under the burden of some stiff, mechanical dialog and the uneven nature of the screenplay, which is extremely untidy in detail, incomplete in exposition. Others in principal roles of shallow dimension are John Dall, Frank De Kova, Jay Novello, Edgar Stehli, Edward Platt, Berry Kroeger, Wolfe Barzell and a seven-foot, 408-pound hulk of a man named Buck Maffei who shares the film's most diverting dramatic sequence with hero Hall.

Harold E. Wellman contributes some pretty Metrocolor camera work. Gaudy, crystalline-dominated Atlantis is pictorially attractive through the efforts of art directors **George W. Davis and William Ferrari.** Its destruction is astutely managed via a combination of meticulous miniature work and the spectacularly explosive special effects operation (notably one awesome tidal wave) of A. Arnold Gillespie, Lee LeBlanc and Robert R. Hoag. A vital assist is fashioned by makeupman William Tuttle, whose transformation of human facial features into those of cows and asses brings to mind a similar arrangement in "A Midsummer Night's Dream." The similarity is purely physical. *Tube.*

Double Bunk
(BRITISH)

Trite mixture of comedy, farce which only rarely is genuinely funny; after a promising start, whole thing misfires badly.

London, April 11.

British Lion release of Bryanston-George H. Brown production. Stars Ian Carmichael, Janette Scott; features Sidney James, Liz Fraser, Dennis Price. Written and directed by C. M. Pennington-Richards; editor, John D. Guthridge; camera, Stephen Dade; music, Stanley Black; title song, Stanley Black, Jack Fishman, Michael Pratt. Previewed at Studio One, London. Running time, **92 MINS.**

Jack	Ian Carmichael
Peggy	Janette Scott
Sid	Sidney James
Sandra	Liz Fraser
Watson	Dennis Price
Harper	Reginald Beckwith
Mrs. Harper	Irene Handl
O'Malley	Noel Purcell
1st Conservancy Officer	Naunton Wayne
2d Officer	Bill Shine
Granville-Carter	Michael Shepley
Rev. Thomas	Miles Malleson
French Official	Jacques Frey
Flowerman	Graham Stark
Madame de Sola	Gladys Henson

C. M. Pennington-Richards' script has neither the wit nor the comedy invention to survive his own heavy-handed, predictable direction. As a result, "Double Bunk" is a rather tired comedy which is saved from complete defeat by a valuable piece of mugging by that reliable character, Sidney James. Somewhere along the line producer George H. Brown should have taken either Pennington-Richards, writer, or Pennington-Richards, director, by the scruff of the neck. Or maybe both. As it is, "Bunk" just plods along aimlessly and is unlikely to give much of a boot to any but unsophisticated audiences.

Newlyweds Ian Carmichael and Janette Scott, desperate for living accommodations, buy a houseboat and it is predictably obvious that they have been sold a leaky property. Their honeymoon night is ruined by rain, paint flaking off the walls and other headaches. Then Carmichael decides to move the boat and reluctantly Miss Scott agrees to a short trip up the river. They are joined by Sidney James, as navigator, and his dumb striptease girl friend (Liz Fraser).

They cause havoc among the fishermen and boaters on the Thames, they lose their course in a fog, spring yet another leak and land in France without any petrol. They "borrow" some from a nearby yacht owned by their landlord (Dennis Price) who taunts them into accepting a challenge to a race home. Thanks to Price's skipper getting drunk and turning back on his course Carmichael's party comes home winners.

Trite though this idea is, much more fun probably could have been obtained via sharper script and more positive performances.

Ian Carmichael is a pleasant enough hero but his role of the slightly ineffectual but well meaning young man has been played by him so often that it's in danger of wearing thin. Janette Scott still looks too young to be convincing even as a newlywed. And it's doubtful whether comedy is her forte.

James has pulled the rescue act on many pix, but even his valiant efforts can do little with this one. Liz Fraser is getting type cast as a dumb, wiggly blonde but she goes through the motions with a cute mixture of Cockney sharpness and naivete. She and James shape up as a click comedy team.

Noel Purcell, Reginald Beckwith, Naunton Wayne, Miles Malleson, Gladys Henson and Graham Stark are responsible for telling little cameos. Dennis Price, as the nouveau-riche, smart jerk of a yacht owner, gives a competent performance.

Direction on the Thames is done with some dexterity, John D. Guthridge's editing is jerky and Stephen Dade's lensing okay. The song "Double Bunk" is not very inspired, though Stanley Black's score is pleasant. *Rich.*

Nobi
(Fire on the Plains)
(JAPANESE)

Paris, April 11.

Pathe Overseas release of Daiei production. With Eiji Funakoshi, Mantaro Ushio, Yoshiro Hamaguchi. Directed by Kon Ichikawa. Screenplay, Natto Wada from novel by Shohei Ooka; camera, Setsuo Kobayashi; editor, Hiroaki Fujii. At Studio de L'Etoile, Paris. Running time, **100 MINS.**

Tamura	Eiji Funakoshi
Sergeant	Mantaro Ushio
Officer	Yoshihiro Hamaguchi
Soldier A	Osamu Takizawa
Soldier B	Micky Curtiso
Soldier C	Asao Sano

This goes much further than the

accepted war masterpieces in detailing for humanity in crisis, and the spark left in one man, have it transcend its plot to make this production one of the most searing pacifistic comments on war yet made. This is a downbeat but fervent pic that merits specialized foreign outlet attention. But it needs individual handling.

Story covers the defeat and rout of the Imperial Japanese army during the Philippine campaign in the last World War. A ragged remnant is left but they are warned the Americans will slaughter them and so start a trek through the jungles to the sea. It is all seen through one tubercular Japanese soldier whose approaching death has put him above it all. He manages to maintain a semblance of humanity to keep him from sinking to cannibalism like many of his fellow soldiers.

Taken from a novel published in the U.S., director Kon Ichikawa has knit this into a visual tour-de-force in which man's inhumanity to man is denoted as he sinks into an animal void. The soldiers cannot stop in their retreat with chaos and hallucination blended. The widescreen is well utilized and the acting is exemplary.

The only criticism might be a certain literary quality in the handling of the lead character, many of whose actions are not always clear. But it is a bone hard, forthright film. It is thus a difficult vehicle but one that should find its place. *Mosk.*

Qui Etes-Vous Mr. Sorge?
(Who Are You Mr. Sorge?)
(FRENCH-JAPANESE) (C'SCOPE)
Paris. April 18.

Cinedis release of Terra-Cormoran-Cinetel-Cite-Silver-Pat Film-Jolly Film-Shochiku production. With Thomas Holtzmann, Hans Otto Meissner, Keiko Kishi, Jacques Berthier. Directed by Yves Ciampi. Screenplay, Ciampi, R. M. Arlaud, H. O. Meissner; camera (C'SCOPE); editor, L. Alepee. At Balzac, Paris. Running time, 130 MINS.
Richard Sorge ...... Thomas Holtzmann
Hans Otto Meissner .... Himself
Baronne Sakurai .... Keiko Kishi
Serge De Branowski ....Jacques Berthier

This spy film is based on the exploits of Richard Sorge who was a Soviet spy operating through the German Embassy in Japan from about 1935 to 1943. It mixes documentary and straight dramatic story telling. However, the pic does not get enough character, depth and suspense into it to make either aspect able to carry it for over two hours. Result is a tale that could stand some pruning and then be of exploitation value abroad on its story. But it is not of arty house calibre.

It begins with historical personages telling what they know about Sorge and then segueing into his story. He is picked up in Japan where he is a newspaperman for a German paper with access to the German Embassy through friends. He is part German and part Russian, and has thrown in with the Soviets. He has formed a spy ring consisting of pacifistic and communist Japanese, two French people and another German.

Sorge manages to get out the news of the invasion of China by Japan, the fact that the Soviets would be invaded by Germany,

---

and that the Japanese would not attack Russia which allowed for the freeing of troops to help stop the Germans at Stalingrad. Some of Sorge's loves are brought in. The pic makes the point that his pride eventually passed his patriotic motives. Also that he was never really hung by the Japanese, and may be still alive. Plot has the ring broken up by an implacable Japanese security colonel.

Acting is solid but not much depth can be given the characters since historical precision and spy workings are the thing. Director Yves Ciampi has done the pic honestly but without either a real insight into the era or a firm dramatic flair. Stock footage is well utilized. *Mosk.*

Ojos Tapatios
(Mexican Eyes)
(MEXICAN—COLOR)
Mexico City, April 18.

Peliculas Nacionales release of Producciones Brooks production. Stars Christiane Martell, Luz Maria Augilar, Pedro Geraldo; features Julio Julian, Roberto Silva, Rodolfo Landa, Oscar Ortiz de Pinedo, Eduardo Alcaraz, Hortensia Santovena, Maria Eugenia San Martin, Judith Sierra. Directed by Gilberto Martinez Solares. Screenplay, Julio Porter and O. Jason: camera (Eastmancolor), Jack Draper. At Alameda Theatre, Mexico City. Running time, 90 MINS.

A singing academy in Mexico City is background for this musical, with principals leading a Bohemian sort of life while waiting for the big break. Roberto Silva is the professor of the academy. Story line is more or less reminiscent of others of this type picture, with the penniless student who gets emotionally involved with a wealthy girl, who of course does not say she is rich.

Christine Martell and Pedro Geraldo act out the main love yarn. As a contrast there are Julio Hulian and Luz Maria Aguilar who also are in love. Julio Julian and Pedro Geraldo have a chance to display their ability as singers. In dramatic moments, they are somewhat weak, but the whole emphasis of picture is on the musical side. Christiane Martell is as tall and stately and beautiful as ever, with Luz Marin Aguilar also a charming eyeful. Color work by Jack Draper is good, and best of all is the dubbing in of singing voices.

This is all around entertainment for Mexican and Latin American chains, and Spanish circuit markets in the U.S. *Emil.*

La Mascara de la Muerta
(The Mask of Death)
(MEXICAN)
Mexico City, April 11.

Peliculas Nacionales release of roducciones Universal production. Stars Luis Aguilar, Rosa de Castilla, Fernando Fernandez: features Jaime Fernandez, Rosario Galves, Salvador Flores, Sergio Murrieta, Fernando Oses. Directed by Zacarias Gomez Urquiza. Screenplay, Luis Manrique. At Olimpia Cine, Mexico City. Running time, 75 MINS.

This is a modest sort of effort, revolving around imaginary incidents of the Mexican Revolution, with the inevitable masked rider, a sort of Superman and The Shadow mixed in one, doing deeds of derring-do, overcoming the bad guys (also masked), saving the maiden in distress and doing his bit for his country.

There's no attempt at giving an atmosphere of truth in this one. It's all pure hokum, with a lot of wild riding, shooting and all the rest of the trimmings of a Mexican western. The kiddies will love it.

On the whole, this picture is well made, with the direction of Zacarias Gomez Urquiza surefire and the acting of Luis Aguilar and other principals geared to give excitement and suspense. Sure of being a hit in nabe houses of all Latin markets. *Emil.*

Pleins Feux Sur L'Assassin
(Lights on the Murderer)
(FRENCH)
Paris, April 11.

Metro release of Jules Borkon production. Stars Pierre Brasseur, Marianne Koch, Pascale Audret, Jean-Louis Trintignant; features Dany Saval, Jean Babilee, Philippe Leroy. Directed by Georges Franju. Screenplay, Boileau, Narcejac, Robert Thomas, Franju; camera, Marcel Fradetal; editor, Gilbert Natot. At Marignan, Paris. Running time, 95 MINS.
Herve .... Pierre Brasseur
Jeanne .... Pascale Audret
Edwige .... Marianne Koch
Jean-Marie ...... Jean-Louis Trintignant
Micheline .... Dany Saval
Christian .... Jean Babilee

Metro has an okay program pic in this whodunit. Concerned with a group of would-be heirs in an old chateau, and with one trying to kill off the others, this film is familiar in theme. But it is given a solid narrative flair, plus a grim humorous tinge, keeping it interesting throughout. Vehicle is a good dualer entry abroad with not quite the weight and uniqueness for art chances.

Director Georges Franju has done this honestly and made good use of the atmospheric and photographic aspects of an old chateau. A dying old man holes up in a secret niche in the chateau and his heirs find they can not get the right to sell the castle till his body is found. They decide to turn it into a tourist gambit via a light and sound setup. Then begin a series of accidents that finally point to murder.

Some twists perk it up as it bogs down about two-thirds the way through. Stereotype characters are given enough solidity to fit in with this tale. There are some offbeat touches, such as a risible quality to a funeral and a sexy widow, all of which combine to make this an entry with enough individual treatment to make it stand up.

Franju has brought off an entertaining melodrama. Technical credits are good. *Mosk.*

Am Galgen Haengt Die Liebe
(Love Hangs On The Gibbet)
(GERMAN)
Berlin, April 11.

Europa release of Rex (Berlin) production. Stars Carl Wery and Annie Rosar; features Bert Forell, Marian Mell, Paul Esser. Directed by Edwin Zbonek. Screenplay, Erna Fentsch, after stageplay, "Philemon and Baukis," by Leopold Ahlsen; camera, Walter Partsch; music, Ernst Roters. At Lohde-Studio, Berlin. Running time, 94 MINS.
Nikolaos .... Carl Wery
Marulja .... Annie Rosar
Alexandros .... Bert Forell
Alka .... Marisa Mell
Karl, German soldier..... Paul Esser
Petros .... Sieghardt Rupp
German lieutenant........ Michael Lenz
German captain .... Hannes Schiel
Jannis .... Michael Janisch

The 33-year-old Edwin Zbonek, former Austrian film critic, has created an attention-getting film with this vehicle. Directed for Rex Film, a small Teutonic outfit, "Gibbet" emerges as one of the more unconventional domestic feature pix of the season. Subjectwise, the film, a war drama, stands a good chance to make way into foreign markets.

Adapted from the prizewinning German stageplay, "Philemon and Baukis," by Leopold Ahlsen, action takes place in 1944 in German-occupied Greece. It centers about an elderly Greek couple who grant shelter to two German soldiers, of whom one is seriously wounded. They know that if the two fall into the hands of partisans, they'll be kilied. The old people put humanity above patriotic fanatism and are killed by their own countrymen.

Pic achieves a convincing war mood and benefits from impressive acting performances and brilliant lensing. Top acting honors easily go to Annie Rosar and Carl Wery who portray the old people. Miss Rosar's portrayal of a resolute but good-natured woman is as excellent as Wery's study of her patient husband. Both performances carry emotional impact. Cast includes several interesting faces such as Bert Forell, as a young Greek; Maria Mell, his sweetheart; Sieghardt Rupp, as a grim partisan leader, and Paul Esser, in a particularly fine performance as a German soldier.

Although the script appears contrived at times, this is a good film. It deserves a special compliment for being as compromiseless as possible and trying to avoid demagogical cliche and black-and-white treatment. Both sides, the Germans and Greek partisans, are shown as brutal as they were. Zbonek may be classified as a "new waver" because this ambitious pic marks his bow as a feature film director. *Hans.*

The Young Savages

Timely, but too shallow, examination of juve crime problem. Pulsatingly lensed and directed, should be sturdy attraction in big cities where such menace is intimate matter, but lacks dramatic logic and novelty to compel, enthrall more discerning filmgoer.

Hollywood, April 13.

United Artists release of Pat Duggan production. Stars Burt Lancaster, Shelley Winters, Dina Merrill; features Edward Andrews, Vivian Nathan, Larry Gates. Directed by John Frankenheimer. Screenplay, Edward Anhalt, J. P. Miller, based on novel by Evan Hunter; camera, Lionel Lindon; editor, Eda Warren; art director, Burr Smidt; music, David Amram; sound, Harry Mills; assistant director, Carter DeHaven Jr. Reviewed at Screen Directors Guild Theatre, April 12, '61. Running time, **103 MINS.**

Hank Bell .... Burt Lancaster
Karin Bell .... Dina Merrill
Mary di Pace .... Shelley Winters
Dan Cole .... Edward Andrews
Mrs. Escalante .... Vivian Nathan
Randolph .... Larry Gates
Lt. Richard Gunnison ...... Telly Savalas
Louisa Escalante .... Pilar Seurat
Angela Rugiello .... Jody Fair
Jenny Bell .... Roberta Shore
Walsh .... Milton Selzer
Judge .... Robert Burton
Barton .... David Stewart
Danny di Pace .... Stanley Kristien
Arthur Reardon ... John Davis Chandler
Anthony Aposto .... Neil Nephew
Zorro .... Luis Arroyo
Roberto Escalante .... Jose Perez
Gargantua .... Richard Velez
Soames .... William Sargent
Pretty Boy .... Chris Robinson
Lt. Hardy .... Stanley Adams
Capt. Larsen .... William Quinn
Maria Amora .... Linda Danzil
Jose .... Raphael Lopez
Pierce .... Henry Norell
McNally .... Jon Carlo
Turtleneck .... Bob Biheller
Diavalo .... Mario Roccuzzo
Doctor .... Harry Holcombe
Mrs. Patton .... Helen Kleeb
Mr. Abbeney .... Thom Conroy
Lonnie .... John Walsh
Officer Wohlman ...... Irving Steinberg
Whitey .... Clegg Hoyt
Clerk of the Court .... Joel Fluellen
Sullivan .... Robert Cleaves

"The Young Savages" is a kind of non-musical east side variation on "West Side Story." It is a sociological cussword puzzle, a twisted riddle aimed at detection of the true motivation for juvenile crime, as set against the backdrop of New York's teeming East Harlem district in which neighborhood nationalities mobilize into youthful raiding parties at the drop of a psychotic frustration.

Sad to relate, since there is reason to suspect that a deeply perceptive, fully convincing screen story lurks in this wild tenement region, the Harold Hecht production (produced by Pat Duggan) fails to arrive at any novel insight into the environmental mess, nor does it approach the subject with fully methodical logic or the calculating objectivity required for the dramatic job it sets out to do. Instead, it gets waylaid with a number of familiar stereotypes, cliches and convenient oversights, and eventually resolves the issue by pinning the blame for an unquestionably heinous and premeditated crime on that old, reliable whipping boy, society itself. A spectator comes away with a bad taste in his mouth, but no new dramatic potion with which to wash it out.

If the United Artists release scores at the boxoffice, and there is reason to believe it won't do poorly at the wicket windows, it will owe a principal share of its success to the timely nature of its theme. Juvenile crime is, of course, a very real, ticklish issue begging for attention. It is rich, ripe dramatic pasture for thoughtful, creative minds and a source of some concern for all Americans, especially those in large cities who can come into contact with the problem just by heading down the wrong street at the wrong time. For all of its shortcomings, this should be a magnetic attraction in the nation's big cities.

The picture is inventively, arrestingly directed by John Frankenheimer with the aid of cameraman Lionel Lindon. Together they have manipulated the lens to catch the wild fury of gang pavement warfare; twisting, tilting, pulling way back, zeroing in and composing to follow and frame the vicious excitement as if the theatre spectator was the immediate participant who happened by at an inopportune, dangerously insane moment and grew too excited and emotional to observe objectivity. The technique works to perfection in the opening sequence, in which the crime is committed that sets the stage for the story.

But there is nothing Frankenheimer or any of the craftsmen can do to make the yarn itself—concocted by Edward Anhalt and J. P. Miller out of a novel by Evan Hunter—stand tall as screen fiction. The story is that of three Italian lads (of 15, 16 and 17) who murder a blind Puerto Rican boy of 15 who is regarded as a top warlord of a rival gang. Immediate motivation: the blind boy acts as a kind of one-man arsenal for the Puerto Ricans who, when cornered by the police, deposit all their weapons on his person to avoid apprehension (a doubtful technique in that the lawmen would be a good bet to shake down this shadowy bystander, blind or not, as well as the others). At any rate, the case for the prosecution is taken over by scrupulous d.a.'s asst. Burt Lancaster whose search for truth and justice and familiarity with the law of the asphalt jungle (he grew up there) leads him to make a valiant courtroom stand on behalf of the boys he is supposed to be trying to convict, at the suggested expense of the political aspirations of his boss, a very shallow figure who seems less a man than the traditional symbol of empty, heartless ambition. The young toughs get off easy and society, that convenient intangible, gets the rap.

Lancaster smoothly and persuasively dispatches his chore. Shelley Winters is effective as the mother of one of the responsible lads (Stanley Kristien), whose mild one-year sentence seemingly disregards his undeniable participation in conspiracy to commit murder. Kristien does a good job. Dina Merrill is adequate as Lancaster's socialite wife. Edward Andrews plays the stereotyped d.a., a bit type-casting. Best of the supporting players are Luis Arroyo, Vivian Nathan, Pilar Seurate and Telly Savalas, with other standout portrayals by Chris Robinson, John Davis Chandler and Neil Nephew.

The flavor and chaos of the New York slum has been captured, both on-the-spot and through Burr Smidt's art direction. Eda Warren's editing is competent, David Amram's music most exciting when it is accompanying the action passages with driving, shrieking atonal chord thrusts. *Tube.*

The Pharoah's Woman
(EASTMANCOLOR—C'SCOPE)

Typical Italo costumer with all cliche stops out. Okay lower berth item for undemanding action enthusiasts.

Universal release of a Vic Film-Faro Production. Features Linda Cristal, Pierre Brice, Armando Francioli, John Drew Barrymore. Directed by W. Tourjansky. Screenplay by Ugo Liberatore from a story by Virgilio Tosi and Massimo Vitalo; photoplay, Pier Ludovico, music, Giovanni Fusco. Reviewed at Universal homeoffice, April 21, '61. Running time, **88 MINS.**

Sbaku .... John Drew Barrymore
Akis .... Linda Cristal
Ramsis .... Armando Francioli
Amosi .... Pierre Brice

Universal has itself a ho-hum but saleable sex-and-actioner in the now-familiar Italian spectacle genre. It's complete with the usual cheesecake dancing girls, a desert battle between two armies, and a crocodile kill by a doughty warrior in the muddy Nile.

Believability in these epics is scarcely tried as the yarn plays out its good-versus-evil theme, but doubtless there are plenty of customers around who won't be looking for anything more than the customary carnal carryings-on, power struggles, etc. Even by these standards, however, "The Pharaohs' Woman" is a rather pallid offering. While the pic has a couple of American names in Linda Cristal and John Drew Barrymore, they don't figure to drum up the trade. The appeal, such as it is, is obviously in the type of picture.

Miss Cristal is plenty figure-fetching in an otherwise vacuous part of the noblewoman-cum-slave girl desired by a pair of feuding Egyptian princes and a court physician. Barrymore dutifully glowers and snarls his way through one of the prince roles, and in the end is put to death. Armando Francioli portrays the triumphant prince okay, and Pierre Brice woodenly plays the physician who ultimately wins the girl.

Technical credits are par for the course and oke. The Eastmancolor is less garish than might be expected for this type of entry. *Pit.*

Ring Of Fire
(C'SCOPE—COLOR)

Exciting action-suspense drama about a kidnapping and a forest fire. Weak storyline overshadowed by hot, on-the-spot production. Fairly good b.o. looms.

Hollywood, April 18.

Metro release of Andrew and Virginia Stone production. Stars David Janssen, Joyce Taylor, Frank Gorshin; features James Johnson. Directed and screenplay by Andrew L. Stone; camera (Metrocolor), William H. Clothier; editor, Virginia L. Stone; special effects, Herman E. Townsley; music, Duane Eddy; sound, Franklin Milton; assistant director, Henry Spitz. Reviewed at the studio, April 18, '61. Running time, **90 MINS.**

Sergeant Steve Walsh.... David Janssen
Bobbie Adams .... Joyce Taylor
Frank Henderson .... Frank Gorshin
Deputy Pringle .... Joel Marston
Roy Anderson .... James Johnson
Sheriff Niles .... Ron Myron
Deputy .... Marshall Kent
Mr. Hobart .... Doodles Weaver

No moss has much of a chance to gather on filmdom's rolling Stones, Andrew and Virginia. Continuing their association with elements on bad behavior, they have shifted their imaginations and energies from the waterlogged "Last Voyage" to the firelogged "Ring of Fire" and, with the aid of a battery of cinematic experts and cooperative actors, pro and non-pro, have cooked up a full head of theatrical steam.

This is a motion picture of the old rip-roaring showmanship school, a "fun" film that keeps an audience alert and a trifle overwhelmed by the sheer production of the thing. As a display of sheer filmmaking know-how itself, it serves a definite entertainment function. There are major reservations, to be sure, in the area of its dramatic content, but these are sufficiently overshadowed by the pictorial excitement and technical flash that assaults an audience's senses from the screen. The Metro release, in which four relatively new talents are given an opportunity to cut loose, should be a handy, fairly successful attraction.

Stone's original screenplay is plenty hard to swallow; in fact it's downright indigestible in spots, but as the serviceable foundation or "excuse" for an ostentatious display of production prowess, it is exonerated. Director Stone, at any rate, certainly makes the inflammatory most of writer Stone's fickle fiction. The yarn would have one believe that an Oregonian police officer (David Janssen) who is counter-apprehended (or kidnapped) in the act of apprehending three less-than-wholesome young people (Joyce Taylor, Frank Gorshin, Jimmy Johnson) could manage to: 1) talk his captors out of a clean getaway in favor of forging through a forest to some nebulous destination, 2) re-apprehend them in an unguarded moment, 3) engage in a shadowy smooching spree with the girl, 4) get captured again, 5) persuade them to continue playing follow-the-leader, himself as leader, 6) lead them smack into a trap, 7) rescue an entire town from the clutches of a wild forest fire seconds after he stands accused of statutory rape relations with the girl, 8) fall in love with the girl.

Janssen gives further evidence that he may become one of Hollywood's top stars. He has the looks, the masculinity, the personality, and he can act. His reactions and his timing are keen. Miss Taylor scores, too, as the sultry, thrill-seeking girl in whom a spark of humanity lurks beneath the hardened veneer. Gorshin, switching from comedy to drama, is explosive and convincing as the head menace, and Johnson, in his first screen exposure, is true as his unstable henchman. There are other sound enactments by Joel Marston, Ron Myron, Marshall Kent and Doodles Weaver and, in fact, the entire citizenry of the town of Vernonia, Oregon, participated actively in the film and

acquitted themselves well under Stone's astute surveillance.

William H. Clothier's photography is vivid and dexterous, bathed in sharp Metrocolor hues and shot from a variety of exciting angles, including some breathtaking aerial scrutiny of the fiery activity. The enormous forest fire that climaxes the film actually is made up mostly of footage taken last summer of a pair of legitimate blazes, one near Baker, Oregon, the other Truckee, California. Smokey Bear would be terrified by the proportion, but pleased as punch by the message (a casually discarded ciggie caused it all in the film). As editor, Mrs. Stone has employed sudden shock and humor to good effect as punctuation marks between the action. Herman E. Townsley's special effects heighten the magnitude of the flaming spectacle. There is a title tune penned and strummed by Duane Eddy, a twangy gee-tar melody that is infectious in a monotonous sort of way. *Tube.*

Very Important Person
(BRITISH)

Flippant POW comedy, with cliches and new touches blended; useful U.K. cast but not much to excite America despite amiable yocks.

London, April 25.

Rank release of an Independent Artists Picture (Julian Wintle-Leslie Parkyn Production). Stars James Robertson Justice, Leslie Phillips, Stanley Baxter; features Eric Sykes, Richard Wattis, Godfrey Winn, Jeremy Lloyd. Directed by Ken Annakin. Screenplay by Jack Davis, Henry Bligh; camera, Ernest Steward; editor, Ralph Sheldon; music, Reg Owen. At Leicester Square Theatre, London. Running time, **98 MINS.**

Sir Ernest Pease	James Robertson Justice
Jimmy Cooper	Leslie Phillips
Everett	Stanley Baxter
Major Stampfel	Stanley Baxter
Willoughby	Eric Sykes
Woodcock	Richard Wattis
Interviewer	Godfrey Winn
Briggs	Colin Gordon
Miss Rogers	Joan Haythorne
Grassy Green	John Forrest
Bonzo Baines	Jeremy Lloyd
Shaw	Peter Myers
Cynes	Ronald Leigh Hunt
Plum	John Ringham
Piggott	John Le Mesurier
Travers	Norman Bird
Hankley	Ronnie Stevens
Higgins	Vincent Ball
Webber	Ed Devereaux

Even those who think that yet another screenseye view of a German prisoner-of-war camp is by now very old hat should still get some amiable yocks out of "Very Important Person." Writer Jack Davies has dreamed up a lively enough yarn, Ken Annakin's direction is lighthearted and the thesping is flippantly cheerful. Though there's not enough marquee value to mean much in the U.S., the pic is loaded with the laffs and is a safe bet for average houses.

Film bows in and closes with a nifty parody of "This Is Your Life," the victim being a gruff, distinguished scientist (James Robertson Justice) who had a remarkable wartime experience. Posing as a naval public relations officer he is flown over enemy territory to see at first-hand the results of one of his radar experiments. He's shot down, flung into a POW camp and suspected by some of the prisoners of being a spy.

But when word comes through from War Office that he is a Very Important Person whose escape must be assisted in every possible way, the other prisoners give the job top priority. But it's the irascible, super-efficient professor who organizes his own escape in the most bland manner. This simple story line has been tricked out with some of the usual POW camp film cliches, notably the inevitable camp concert, the clashes between the irrepressible, facetious Royal Air Force types and the humorless Germans and the tunneling botch-ups.

The huge, bearded James Robertson Justice has a role right up his alley as the arrogant professor, the master of the withering squelch, the chap who suffers fools very ungladly. He is excellently cast. With only one previous film appearance behind him, in "Geordie," Scottish comedian Stanley Baxter, here eagerly grabs a useful chance of establishing himself. Baxter is a sound recruit to the screen. He plays a dour, suspicious prisoner of war dedicated to the art of tunneling.

Baxter doubles this with the role of the humorless, prissy German camp commandant, and the double comes off remarkably well. Further switch calls for Baxter to impersonate the camp commandant so that he is virtually responsible for a subtle treble.

Leslie Phillips, Jeremy Lloyd and Peter Myers romp through the parts of typical silly ass RAF officers. There are also familiar entries from such regulars as John Le Mesurier, Richard Wattis, Colin Gordon, Norman Bird and Eric Sykes. Justice Joan Haythorne makes brisk impact as a supercilious secretary. Gimmick casting is that of Godfrey Winn, prolific journalist and tv personality, as the tele interviewer. Winn, who used to be an actor many years ago, fulfils the chore ably.

"Very Importnt Person" is an agreeable, light comedy with sound allround technical credits and more cheerful good humor than wit. *Rich.*

Payroll
(BRITISH)

Straightforward crook drama which sometimes lapses into meller; dialog is insufficiently incisive, but the pic builds up to a neat climax and competent thesping compensates for lack of sock stellar value.

London, April 18.

Anglo-Amalgamated release of a Julian Wintle-Leslie Parkyn Lynx (Norman Priggen) production. Stars Michael Craig, Francoise Prevost, Billie Whitelaw, William Lucas. Directed by Sidney Hayers. Screenplay, George Baxy, from Serek Bickerton's novel; camera, Ernest Steward; editor, Tristram Cones; music, Reg Owen. Song, "It Happens Every Day" by Tony Osborne, sung by Eddie Ellis. At Plaza, London. Running time, **106 MINS.**

Johnny Mellors	Michael Craig
Katie Pearson	Francoise Prevost
Jackie Parker	Billie Whitelaw
Dennis Pearson	William Lucas
Monty	Kenneth Griffith
Blackie	Tom Bell
Bert Langridge	Barry Keegan
Det. Insp. Carberry	Andrew Faulds
Det. Sergt. Bradden	Edward Cast
Harry Parker	William Peacock
Frank Moore	Glyn Houston
Madge Moore	Joan Rice
Doll	Vanda Godsell
Bowen	Stanley Meadows
Brent	Brian McDermott
Mr. John	Hugh Morton
Alf	Keith Faulkner
Worth	Bruce Beeby
Billy	Murray Evans
Archie	Kevin Bennett

Here's a straightforward crook drama that makes no pretense to any particular subtlety but tells its flimsily-built story with punch. It builds up to a neat but fairly incredible climax. Could be that the dialog might have been a shade slicker and the criminal types are fairly familiar characters. But there are some useful performances, compensating for lack of top stellar value.

The pic has the virtue of topicality since, regrettably, payroll snatches have been a formidable entry in Britain's recent crime sheet. Yarn concerns a gang of smalltime crooks who are planning to snatch the payroll of the Kneale factory, loot valued at around $280,000. Inside man is a wages clerk.

But, after much planning, the gang hits a snag. Their catspaw is taken off the run and, worse, the factory introduces an armored van which is foolproof, according to the two men who devised it. Nevertheless, bandit Michael Craig is not put off. He forces the stooge to copy the layout of the van. The raid is pulled off (with the usual edginess caused by unexpected snags such as a traffic jam snarling up the timetable). During the raid, the driver of the armored car is killed, his mate badly injured and one of the four robbers also gets a fatal slug.

From then on its not only the police looking for the bandits but the vengeful young widow of the murdered driver also chipping in with anonymous phone calls and letters to the "inside man" determined to make him sweat and break down. He has his other problems, too, with a nagging wife who starts an affaire with the boss of the thugs and eventually doublecrosses not only her husband, but her lover and finally herself. Altogether, there's a great deal of skulduggery going on, with everybody putting the cross on everybody else.

The raid sequence is well done and so is a rather incredible but effective scene where the crook disposes of two of his henchmen in a bog.

Sidney Thayers' direction is straightforward and plenty of brisk cutting raises the tempo of the film whenever it shows signs of flagging. Ernest Steward's lensing is fine. Location scenes shot in and around Newcastle are authentic.

The characters are mainly conventional for this type of thriller and the chosen thesps fulfil their chores satisfactorily. Craig, for once playing a heavy, is a suitably dour, tough criminal with the necessary smoothness to impress the ladies. There's the weak, ambitious man drawn into crime by need of money and by the incessant nagging of his wife. William Lucas has some first-rate nervy moments in his role. Billie Whitelaw as the vengeful young widow, gives her usual shrewd performance, but here she's handicapped, since the character is never properly developed and though her objective is clear her method of reaching it is not. Francoise Prevost, as the Frenchwoman, has one or two effective displays of shrewish temper.

Kenneth Griffith, Tom Bell and Barry Keegan, as assorted crooks and Andrew Faulds and Edward Cast, as arms of the law, are nicely contrasted, with Griffith being particularly useful as a moody chicken-hearted little drunk. Glyn Houston, William Peacock, Joan Rice, Vanda Godsell and Bruce Beeby are others who contribute telling cameos.

"Payroll" is a conscientious crime yarn which, despite certain flaws and irregularities, keeps the cat-and-mouse atmosphere reliably alive. *Rich.*

They Were Ten
(Heym Hayu Assara)
(ISRAELI)

Earnest tale of Palestine pioneers. Effective, but limited prospects.

George Schwartz & Arthur Sachson release of Scopus oPrductions film by Baruch Dienar. Features Ninette, Oded Teomi, Leo Filler, Yosef Safra, Yosef Zur, Gavriel Dagan, Yisrael Rubintshik, Nissim Azikri, Amnon Kahanovitch, Yitchak Bareket, Yosef Bashi, Yehuda Gabai, Moshe Yaari, Mashe Kedem. Screenplay, Gavriel Dagan, Baruch Dienar, Menachem Shuval, based on story by B. Dienar. Directed by Baruch Dienar; camera, Lionel Banes; editor, Helga Cranston; music, Gari Bertini. Opened April 17, '61, at the Symphony Theatre, N.Y. Running time, **105 MINS.**

A trickle of Jews from eastern Europe arrived in Palestine toward the close of the last century, there to claim freedom and a new life. What happens to a small colony of such pioneers forms the basis for the Israeli film "They Were Ten."

Yarn is an earnest account of frontier hardship, the desperate battle to keep the colony going and bring a desolate land to blossom. Film is competently, if not artfully, rendered, with a specialized theme and content that makes it seem headed for limited play in the United States. Special handling in Jewish population centres, however could yield good runs. Dialog is Hebrew (with some French), with excellent English subtitling.

Pic follows eight men and a woman (a baby comes later, making the tenth of the title) who establish themselves in the midst of a hostile land and hostile Arabs. The adversity of the situation leads to conflicts as nerves fray, and as the settlers stand up to both environment and the Arabs. Ultimately the Jews triumph, and have double cause for celebration because the married couple among them has produced a child. The mother, however, dies soon after of malaria. Her burial coincides with a drought-breaking rain—the symbolic death and regeneration.

Baruch Dienar, who did the original story and produced and directed the Scopus Production, has arranged the tale in rather pat and oversimplified fashion, avoiding exploration of the Arab-Jew antagonisms, and without plumbing the principal characters, settling instead for straight forward storytelling that at moments becomes a bit arch. But at the same time he has contrived a frequenly affecting account of faith and tenacity.

Acting is uneven, but generally effective. Technical credits are all good, with Gari Bertini's score making eeffctive and charming use of some Yiddish-Hebraic folk themes. *Pit.*

Mexico Lindo y Querido
(Beautiful and Beloved Mexico)
(MEXICAN—COLOR)

Mexico City, April 18.

Peliculas Nacionales release of Cinematografica Latino Americana production. Stars Ana Bertha Lepe, Lola Beltran, Pedro Vargas, Evangelina Elizondo; features Ernestina Garfias, Raul Martinez. Directed by Julio Bracho. Screenplay, Alfonso Patino Gomez; camera, Rosalio Solano; music, Chucho Zarzoza. At Cine Orfeon, Mexico City. Running time, **90 MINS.**

Plot of this color musical centers around a foreign femme who comes to visit gay Mexico as a prelude to marriage. She becomes so enamored of the land and her attentive Mexican guide that she forgets all about wedding bells and decides to remain in Mexico indefinitely.

There are plenty of ditties ranging from folklore to popular tunes of the day, interpreted by Lola Beltran and Pedro Vargas in Chucho Zazoza's arrangements which accentuate the animated Mexican music. Costumes and ballet numbers are pleasing. Soprano Ernestina Garfias contributes more classical arias. The principals go through the light story demands without difficulty.

Julio Bracho's direction is sure while cameraman Rosalio Solano handles the color camera adequately. Only downbeat note is perhaps some rigidity in the settings, giving the effect that the vehicle is being presented on a stage instead of the wider film medium. Outside of this, the pic is a fair sort of musical that will click here and in Latin American areas where Lola Beltran's and Pedro Vargas' names are widely known. *Emil.*

Vive Henri IV, Vive L'Amour
(Long Live Henry the Fourth, Long Live Love)
(FRENCH—COLOR—DY'SCOPE)

Paris, April 8.

Gaumont release of Hoche DA-MA production. With Francis Claude, Daniele Gaubert, Roger Hanin, Bernard Blier, Jean Sorel, Armand Mestral, Melina Mercouri, Nicole Courcel, Pierre Brasseur, Vittorio De Sica, Francis Blanche, Simone Renant, Danielle Darrieux. Directed by Claude Autant-Lara. Screenplay, Jean Aurenche, Henri Jeanson; camera (Eastmancolor), Jacques Natteau; editor, Madeleine Gug. At Ambassade-Gaumont, Paris. Running time, **120 MINS.**

Henri IV .... Francis Claude
Charlotte .... Daniele Gaubert
Conde .... Jean Sorel
Ravaillac .... Roger Hanin
Bossompierre .... Armand Mestral
Ambassador .... Vittorio De Sica
Henriette .... Danielle Darrieux
Madame Tremoille .... Simone Renant
Montmorency .... Pierre Brasseur
Sully .... Bernard Blier
Jacqueline .... Nicole Courcel
Prieur .... Francis Blanche

Historical opus is played tongue-in-cheek as title infers. It covers the last year in the life of the 17th Century French King Henri IV who seemed more interested in women than any other aspect of ruling. The bedroom look has some risible moments and a zest of action plus fine production dress for probable good hiz here. But it is somewhat too talky for anything but exploitation chances abroad.

Henri IV has a harridan wife but has managed to have a flock of children out of wedlock with his many favorites. He brings all the children up together. He falls for a 16-year-old at 56 and marries her to one of his illegitimate sons who professes no interest in women.

There are plenty of epigrams and a goat-like performance from Francis Claude, as the lecherous king, with some good bits etched by several guest star names. The young couple are stiffly played by Daniele Gaubert and Jean Sorel.

But director Claude Autant-Lara has given this eye-catching color and mounting, and played it like a royal boudoir comedy. Technical credits are fine. *Mosk.*

Jakobli und Meyeli
(Jakobli and Meyeli)
(SWISS)

Praesens-Film A.G. Zurich release of Neue Film A.G. (Franz Schnyder) production. Directed by Schnyder. Screenplay, Schnyder and Richard Schweizer; camera, Konstantin Tschet; music, Robert Blum. At Urban Theatre, Zurich. Running time, **104 MINS.**

Anne Baebi Jowaeger .... Margit Winter
Hansli .... Ruedi Walter
Jakobli .... Peter Brogle
Meyeli .... Kathrin Schmid
Parson .... Edwin Kohlund
Sophie .... Annemarie Dueringer
Doctor .... Peter Arens
Maedi .... Margrit Rainer
Sami .... Fred Tanner
Vehhansli .... Max Haufler
Vicar .... Franz Matter
Haechler .... Hans Gaugler
Midwife .... Hedda Koppe
Maurer-Vreni .... Anneliese Egger
Vicar Streng .... Bernhard Enz
Court President .... Sigfrit Steiner

The second part of a two-part filmization of 19th Century Swiss poet Jeremias Gotthelf's popular peasant novel, "Anne Baebi Jowaeger," is superior in every way to the first one which was released here five months ago with moderate success. Although the subject matter limits its international chances, it looms as an interesting, if specialized arty theatre entry because of the quality of its cinematic values.

In this novel, Gotthelf took an angry stand against quacks and [illegible]stition poisoning the lives of Swiss countryfolk in the last century and barring the way of scientific medicine. This is exemplified in the story of young newlyweds, Jakobli and Meyeli, who lose their baby, and the groom's domineering mother who, thereupon, secludes herself in isolation, neglecting the farm and causing the family's near-destruction.

Paralleling this central yarn is the story of a young country doctor who tries in vain to break through the barrier of stubbornness and mistrust of his countrymen and dies prematurely.

Direction by Franz Schnyder, who also produced and co-scripted, holds a good balance between the prevailing sombre mood and occasional comic relief. It's a cleancut, tasteful job which avoids lagging spots. An important asset is the topnotch lensing by Konstantin Tachet. Robert Blum's music deserves credit for its unobtrusiveness.

Performances are generally well above par, including some high-[illegible], notably by Margrit Winter, as the mother; Peter Brogle and Kathrin Schmid (Mr. & Mrs. in real life), as the young couple; Peter Arens, as the unfortunate physician and Margrit Rainer, cast as a venomous servant. The actors speak the German language and in Swiss dialect. *Mezo.*

Viva Jalisco Que Es Mi Tierra
(Long Live Jalisco, My Natal Land)
(MEXICAN-COLOR)

Mexico City, April 18.

Peliculas Nacionales release of Producciones Pereda production. Stars Maria Antonieta Pons, Manuel Capetillo, Andrea Palma; features Ramon Pereda, Los Panchos, the Silva Brothers. Directed by Ramon Pereda. Screenplay, Ramon Pereda; camera, Agustin Jimenez; music, Manuel Esperon. At Mariscala Cine, Mexico City. Running time, **90 MINS.**

A song-and-dance musical western, with the book revolving around an orphaned daughter of an entertainer (Maria Pons), who seeks to become a star, and the son of a breeder of bulls whose dream is to become a torero. Naturally, both are in love. Plot complications concern the attempt by kinfolk to break up the love affair.

Atmosphere is typically Mexican. The highlight is the town fair photographed expertly in color by veteran cameraman Agustin Jimenez, who has trained his lens on the various facets of hinterland folklore at fiesta time. When the pair of lovers get to the big city, there are night club sequences featuring such performers as the Five Latins, The Panchos, The Tex Mex Trio, the Los Mexicanos Trio, and the Four Silva Brothers singing popular numbers.

Manuel Capetillo, who does well as the young man with a dream of torero fame, actually was a bullfighter who almost lost his life some years back when he was gored in the ring. Maria Antonieta Pons lends grace and beauty as the stagestruck young girl.

Although this one certainly will not win any prize awards, it is still the sort of film fare, which, without being original in story, development or technique, still manages to turn out as a tasteful blend of life south of the border. Production shows considerable understanding and compassion for Mexico and Mexicans.

This one should do well in foreign markets because it does give a true picture of life in the provinces. As a western, it does have its "killers," but this is not so important. What the film turns out to be is a rather authentic interpretation of Jalisco gayety as well as the song, laughter and vivacity of Mexico. *Emil.*

Les Mains D'Orlac
(The Hands of Orlac)
(FRENCH-BRITISH)

Paris, April 25.

CFDC release of Sovic-Riviera International-Pendennis production. Stars Mel Ferrer, Lucile Saint-Simon, Dany Carrel; features Christopher Lee, Balpetre, Felix Aylmer, Mireille Perrey. Directed by Edmond-T. Greville. Screenplay, Greville from novel by Maurice Renard; camera, Jacques Lemare; editor, J. Ravel. At Biarritz, Paris. Running time **100 MINS.**

Orlac .... Mel Ferrer
Louise .... Lucile Saint-Simon
Lila .... Dany Carrel
Nero .... Christopher Lee
Doctor .... Balpetre
Uncle .... Felix Aylmer
Landlady .... Mireille Perrey

Even with the name of Mel Ferrer, this shapes mainly as a dualer. It is a horror-psycho drama that does not build up the required suspense and is fairly lame in the direction, thesp and interest departments.

Tale was made as a silent German pic in 1924, with Conrad Veidt. It was later remade by Metro as "Mad Love" for Peter Lorre's first Yank pic. Both of these had the feeling of hallucination and terror which is absent in this remake. Maybe scientific advances make this tale, of a pianist who has an accident and thinks his hands have been replaced by those of a murderer executed that day, somewhat old hat.

Instead of playing on the pianist's psychological problems of believing his hands are taking over and turning him into a would-be killer, it introduces a petty magician who finds out and preys on the pianist's penchant and problems. Mel Ferrer can not do much with this uneven role and others are able to do even less. Mounting is lacklustre and dialog listless. Technical credits are acceptable. Hence, this is strictly program fare. *Mosk.*

La Famille Fenouillard
(The Fenouillard Family)
(FRENCH)

Paris, April 18.

Gaumont release of Cinephonic-Chavane-Fabre-SNEG production. With Sophie Desmarets, Jean Richard, Annie Sinigalia, Marie-Josee Ruiz. Directed by Yves Robert. Screenplay, Jean Ferry, Robert from book by Christoph; camera, Andre Bac; editor, Marie-Josephe Yoyotte. At Boul. Mich. Paris. Running time, **80 MINS.**

Mrs. Fenouillard .... Sophie Desmarets
Mr. Fenouillard .... Jean Richard
Older daughter .... Annie Sinigalia
Younger daughter .... Marie-Josee Ruiz

Based on a noted illustrated comic book of the turn-of-the-century, this film tries to emulate it by stylized sets, slightly speeded up movement and a general note of satirical fantasy with a big dose of slapstick. It has some clever moments but fails to sustain the humor and it becomes repetitious. This is mainly a local entry, with foreign chances dim.

A stuffy shopkeeping family takes off to see Paris from a small town in 1890 so that the father will develop some worldliness, and thus be able to run for mayor. But they get lost and end up on a ship and visit Brazil, get lost in the Antarctic, hit Japan and come back hereoes.

A slapstick cheese fight and some clever takeoffs on the chauvinistic closemindedness of the time get some laughs, but generally this is a series of revue sketches, and not all are successful.

Director Yves Robert has a flair for putting over a comic interlude but cannot extend it sufficiently enough to build and dominate the film. Actors fit in with the general conception. Technical credits are okay. But this is an extremely specialized entry at best on its attempt to bring back some of the tomfoolery of the silent comedies. *Mosk.*

Het Mes
(The Knife)
(DUTCH)

Amsterdam, April 18.

Nederlandse Filmproduction Maatshappij production. With Ellen Vogel, Paul Cammermans, Reitze van der Linden, Marie-Louise Videc, Mia Goossen, Hetty Beck, Elly van Stekelenburg, Cor Witschen, Henk Haselaar. Directed by Fons Rademakers; story and screenplay, Hugo Claus; camera, Eduard van der Enden; editor, Han Rust; music, Pim

Jacobs. At City Theatre, Amsterdam. Running time, **90 MINS.**

This is the story of 13-year-old boy, entering puberty, and jealousy of his mother who has taken a lover (tutor to her son) and friend of her late husband. "The Knife" looks spotty for the export market.

This is the second film produced by N.F.M., new outfit which wants to control continuous film production instead of a haphazard one as customary in Holland until now. The delicate subject has been treated with a mature outlook and is developed by director Fons Rademakers (this is his third pic) in a suitable poetic way.

Film misses, however, a tone of reality as characters and their inter-relation are badly drawn and never become quite real. Though one can see what the director meant this to be, he lacked the vision to make it either an arty item or a touching poetic story.
Saal.

The Guns Of Navarone
(BRITISH-COLOR)

Star-studded, spectacular war meller. Hefty investment involved, and rousing b.o. looms for this exciting piece of entertainment.

London, April 27.
Columbia release of Open Road (Carl Foreman-Cecil F. Ford) production. Stars Gregory Peck, David Niven, Anthony Quinn, Stanley Baker, Anthony Quayle, James Darren; features Irene Papas, Gia Scala, James Robertson Justice, Richard Harris. Directed by J. Lee Thompson. Screenplay by Carl Foreman from Alistair MacLean's novel; camera, Oswald Morris; editor, Alan Osbiston; music, Dimitri Tiomkin. At Odeon, Leicester Square, London. Running time, **157 MINS.**

Mallory	Gregory Peck
Miller	David Niven
Andrea	Anthony Quinn
Brown	Stanley Baker
Franklin	Anthony Quayle
Pappadimos	James Darren
Maria	Irene Papas
Anna	Gia Scala
Jensen	James Robertson Justice
Barnsby	Richard Harris
Cohn	Bryan Forbes
Baker	Allan Cuthbertson
Weaver	Michael Trubshawe
Grogan	Percy Herbert
Sessler	George Mikell
Mussel	Walter Gotell
Nicholai	Tutte Lemkow

A real heap of coin, labor, sweat, patience, tears, faith and enthusiasm has gone into the making of Carl Foreman's "The Guns Of Navarone." This needed some out-of-this-world cooperation by the Greek government and, through the sweet-talking of exec producer Foreman and producer Cecil F. Ford, it got it. It faced the problem of a director-switch in midstream. Film was a prolonged physical and mental endurance test which had everybody on edge right up to a few hours before the preview when a Technicolor print was finally delivered. But last Thursday (27) it got away to good notices and a glamour charity preem in front of the Queen and Prince Philip. Foreman and Columbia may now relax, for "Guns" looks likely to make sweet b.o. music everywhere and handsomely repay even the hefty investment of $6,000,000.

"Guns" is the sort of spectacular drama that can ignore any tv competition and, even with its flaws, should have patrons firmly riveted throughout its lengthy narrative. With a bunch of weighty stars, terrific special effects, several socko situations plus good camerawork and other technical okays, Foreman and director J. Lee Thompson have sired a winner.

Story, adapted by Foreman from Alastair MacLean's pop novel, is set in 1943. The Axis has virtually over-run Greece and its islands, except for Crete and the tiny island of Kheros, both a few miles from Turkey. Germany is trying to force Turkey into the war on its side and plans to storm Kheros. The only chance for the worn-out garrison of 2,000 men is evacuation by sea, through a channel between Kheros and another island. But this channel is impregnably guarded by a couple of huge, radar-controlled guns on Navarone. A small bunch of saboteurs is detailed to spike these guns. How they carry out this suicidal job against time and fantastic odds makes for tingling melodrama.

While the film sticks to the physical hazards, the tension rarely lets up. But the complications arising from the conflicting personal relationships between the members of the party only develop in spasms. Sometimes, between the slabs of excitement, Foreman's well-written screenplay has the cast bickering rather tentatively about the ethics of war, leadership and personal responsibility. But only occasionally does this become a near-trap. Usually, just in time, director Thompson gets his cast moving again towards the high adventure and excitement that tags the pic as major league. But for this, it would have been a different and perhaps not such a rewarding motion picture.

The film has lined up a fine array of talent, though, frankly, the thesps have to take second place to the situations and the great climax. The saboteur gang consists of Anthony Quayle, Gregory Peck, David Niven, Stanley Baker, Anthony Quinn and James Darren. They all turn in worthwhile jobs. Of this sextet, Baker, playing a dour, war-sick expert with a knife, and Darren, as a baby-faced killer, get rather less opportunity for impact than the others. Yet both do justice to their sketchy opportunities.

Quayle leads the expedition with conviction as the man who dreamed it up, a character who revels in war's danger kicks. Peck is suitably laconic yet authoritative as the officer who takes over when Quayle becomes a casualty. Quinn is a dominating figure as a Greek officer who is conducting all-out vendetta against the enemy and a half-hearted personal one against Peck.

And Niven, cast as a satirical corporal with a genius for handling high explosives, scores with most of the rare but wry humor in the film as well as rising well to a couple of dramatic moments. Two women have been written into the film who were not in the novel, a couple of Greek partisans played very well by Irene Papas and Gia Scala. Though one becomes a key character in the story line they don't add a great deal to the picture but fulfil their chores satisfactorily. Such competent actors as Albert Lieven, James Robertson Justice (who impressively speaks the prologue), Richard Harris, George Mikell and Allan Cuthbertson also contributes small but telling performances.

The cliff-scaling sequence, a scene when the saboteurs are rounded up by the enemy, a wonderfully directed and lensed storm segment and the final boffo climax are just a few of the nail-biting highlights. Apart from Foreman's visualization of the yarn, Oswald Morris's superb camerawork and Dimitri Tiomkin, respectively, there must be plaudits for the superb special effects engineered by Bill Warrington and Wally Veevers. In fact, it's a stint for which every technician can take a bow.

There are some implausibilities in "Navarone" (how, for instance, could the little knot of saboteurs from a fishing boat have blown up a German E-boat at close range without suffering a single scar?), but the overall reaction is that such points are unlikely to occur to audiences while the film is showing. From the start of the credits, patrons will be beguiled by an ambitious, splendidly produced piece of entertainment-plus.
Rich.

Der Letzte Zeuge
(The Last Witness)
(GERMAN)

Berlin, April 25.
Europa release of Kurt Ulrich production. Stars Martin Held, Hanns Lothar and Ellen Schwiers; features Juergen Goslar, Adelheid Seeck, Werner Hinz. Directed by Wolfgang Staudte. Screenplay, R. A. Stemmle and Thomas Keck; camera, Ekkehard Kyrath; music, Werner Eisbrenner. At Zoo Palast, Berlin. Running time, **102 MINS.**

Werner Rameil	Martin Held
Dr. Fox, lawyer	Hanns Lothar
Ingrid Bernhardy	Ellen Schwiers
Dr. Heinz Stephan	Juergen Goslar
Gerda Rameil	Adelheid Seeck
Council of the Court	Werner Hinz
Miss Ebeling	Lore Hartling
Police Inspector	Siegfried Wischnewski

Wolfgang Staudte, director of such pix as "Murderers Are Among Us" and "Roses For the Prosecutor," has with this film another better-grade German vehicle to his credit. It, however, is not his best effort. "Witness" is a courtroom drama with a new slant. The injustice of justice.

Staudte attempts to show how people can innocently get into the treadmill of a judicial system which he thinks needs reforming. Unfortunately, his well-meant effort is not too convincing. Nearly all the reps of justice (the police inspector, judge, prosecutor, even the council of the supreme court), have a flair of either narrow-mindedness or unscrupulousness in this. As a consequence, the whole thing doesn't ring true enough. A solid grosser domestically, treatment of the subject matter gives this foreign possibilities.

A four-month old baby has been strangled. The police sees in the illegitimate mother (Ellen Schwiers) the logical suspect and arrest her. A clever lawyer (Hanns Lothar), who believes in her innocence, sets out to discover the murderer on his own hook. Although he has an alibi, the murderer turns out to be the infant's father, a wealthy married businessman.

Staudte's direction is generally swift while his handling of the players is brilliant.

The most praiseworthy performances are turned in by Martin Held and Lothar. Also Miss Schwiers has many fine scenes. The outstanding support includes Juergen Goslar, as a young medico who innocently becomes a judicial victim; Lore Hartling, cast as Lothar's assistant; Werner Hinz, Adelheid Seeck and Lucie Mannhelm.

Technically, this is flawless. The imaginative lensing by vet cameraman Ekkehard Kyrath is especially noteworthy. In all, this courtroom drama shapes as one of the better German pix.
Hanz.

Return To Peyton Place
(C'SCOPE-COLOR)

Slick, soap-operatic followup to Jerry Wald's earlier hit. Carefully tailored for same audience. Should be a money attraction, though not quite the equal of its predecessor.

Hollywood, April 26.
Twentieth-Fox release of Jerry Wald production. Stars Carol Lynley, Jeff Chandler, Eleanor Parker, Mary Astor, Robert Sterling, Luciana Paluzzi, Brett Halsey, Gunnar Hellstrom, Tuesday Weld. Directed by Jose Ferrer. Screenplay, Ronald Alexander, based on novel by Grace Metalious; camera (DeLuxe), Charles G. Clarke; editor, David Bretherton; art directors, Jack Martin Smith, Hans Peters; music, Franz Waxman;

sound, Bernard Freericks, Warren B. Delaplain; assistant director, David Hall. Reviewed at Grauman's Chinese, April 26, '61. Running time, **123 MINS.**

Allison MacKenzie	Carol Lynley
Lewis Jackman	Jeff Chandler
Connie	Eleanor Parker
Roberta Carter	Mary Astor
Mike Rossi	Robert Sterling
Raffaella	Luciana Paluzzi
Ted	Brett Halsey
Lars	Gunnar Hellstrom
Selena Cross	Tuesday Weld
Dexter	Kenneth MacDonald
Peter White	Bob Crane
Mark Steele	Bill Bradley
John Smith	Tim Durant
Nick Parker	Casey Adams
Mr. Wadley	Pitt Herbert
Lupus Wolf	Warren Parker
Selectman	Arthur Peterson
Mrs. Jackman	Jennifer Howard
Mrs. Humphries	Joan Banks
Bud Humphries	Emerson Treacy
Dr. Fowlkes	Wilton Graff
Miss Wentworth	Laura McCann
Arthur	Hari Rhodes
Steve Swanson	Leonard Stone
Pierre Galante	Alex Dunand
Frank O'Roark	Reedy Talton
Postman	Jack Carr
Photographer	Tony Miller
Nevins	Max Mellinger
Mrs. Bingham	Collette Lyons
Counterman	Charles Seel
Interviewers	Carol Veazie, Helen Bennett

The same audience that devoured "Peyton Place" figures to embrace this sequel. Since the original was such a smash hit, both as a book and a motion picture, and since the sequel has attained bestselling proportions, the film would appear to be presold.

But "presold" is not necessarily the guarantee of success it is sometimes taken to be. It is an aid, not an absolute insurance policy. Fortunately for Jerry Wald's followup, the "presold" nature of the product has been fortified with dramatic restraint, shrewd casting, sound performances and the same slick production values that characterized the first effort. In accomplishing this, and yet never veering too far away from proven formula, Wald has fashioned a likely money picture for his company and his studio, 20th-Fox, although not quite the match of the original in this respect.

Basically, "Return to Peyton Place" is a high-class soap opera. Women, its chief prey, will respond with the most enthusiastic support. There will also be strong support from young people, who will identify with its indictment of parental over-possessiveness, and from civic-minded groups, who will cotton to its plea for tolerance and social reexamination. But the film is by no means universally appealing. It figures to strike the more intelligent, literate filmgoer as at least a trifle too condescending in its preachment, a mite too obvious and predictable in its dramatic construction, and slightly lethargic in its drift to foregone conclusions.

Ronald Alexander's screenplay preserves the nature of the novel, alternately building three or four separate but related story veins into individual crescendos, then welding the moving parts into a single grand climax in which everything falls neatly into place.

The basic stories are: (1) Carol Lynley's, as the tyro novelist whose close-to-home fiction produces civic repercussions and whose romantic relations with her editor-publisher, Jeff Chandler, accelerate her maturity; (2) Tuesday Weld's, as the emotionally-troubled girl whose past misfortunes are soothed when Miss Lynley's book sheds new light into the matter for the hypocritical citizens of the backward burg, who are undergoing a kind of civic metamorphosis; and (3) Mary Astor's, as a super-possessive Peyton Place mother whose attempts to wreck the marriage of her son, Brett Halsey, are curbed when her wretched nature is bared before the entire town in a powerful climactic sequence.

Jose Ferrer's direction of this material is deliberate, but restrained and perceptive. Always in control of his story, he unquestionably makes capital of the best of it and improves the worst of it.

The cast is a blend of polished veterans and promising young players. There are no towering marquee names, but there are a number of good performances, and that is vastly more important to a film that banks so heavily upon its story source for marquee impetus. The lovely Miss Lynley, who ripens into mature screen status with this role, establishes herself as a top candidate for important leading lady assignments in future films. She does a thoroughly capable job, although a shade more animation would have been desirable. Another whose talent blossoms and whose career take a forward spurt via this vehicle is Miss Weld. There are equally strong starring enactments by Chandler, Robert Sterling, Halsey, Eleanor Parker, Luciana Paluzzi and Gunnar Hellstrom, and solid support from a large, animated cast. But it is the veteran Miss Astor who walks off with the picture. Her approach to a taxing, essentially distasteful role is so skillful, so admirably restrained yet perceptively true and lucidly projected, that she succeeds remarkably in exciting audience compassion for the character.

"Return to Peyton Place" is an example of Hollywood production values at their glossiest. Contributing to this impeccable appearance and tone are Charles G. Clarke's De Luxe camera regard for both scenic and personal beauty, David Bretherton's keen editing touch, Franz Waxman's soaringly romantic score and the tasteful sets of art directors Jack Martin Smith and Hans Peters who, together with Clarke, have conveyed a picture-postcard New England in a Hollywood studio and the slopes of Mammoth, California. A song, "The Wonderful Season of Love" by Paul Francis Webster and Waxman, accompanies the main title. It is not an outstanding number, but sweet enough to attain considerable popularity. Rosemary Clooney works it over nicely.

Tube.

Io Amo, Tu Ami
(I Love, You Love)
(ITALIAN-FRENCH)
(Color-Songs)

Rome, April 25.

Dino DeLaurentiis release of a DeLaurentiis-Orsay (Paris) co-production. Features Marny Trio, Fattini, Cairoli, Don Jada's Japanese Revue, Las Hermanas Benitez, Obraszov and his Theatre, George Lafaye, Moiseev Ballet, Chaz Chase, Sophisticated Ballet, Veronique, Red Army Choir. Directed by Alessandro Blasetti, from an idea by Blasetti, Chiarini, Romano, Savignano. Camera (Technicolor-Ultrascope), Aldo Tonti. Music arranged by Carlo Savina. Editor, Tatiana Morigi. At Corso Cinema, Rome. Running time, **95 MINS.**

Pic is one of those currently popular vignette potpourris, with the difference that the usual melange of entertainment, spectacle, sex, humor and music, has here been given an extra fillip or two: a central theme and an implied message. Theme is love in its four seasons, and in all its forms and manifestations, from the pure to the decadent, etc., namely childhood, adolescence, middle and old age. And love is witnessed in Italy, Britain, Russia, France, etc.

Filled with crowd-pleasing ingredients, splendidly lensed, this film is a highly saleable item, not the least for its many exploitable aspects. With an adroit "foreign" commentary and perhaps some reediting to smooth the continuity, it's also a fine export bet.

Director Blasetti and his partners have caught some insight-ful glimpses of the various forms their main subject matter assumes in various age groups, climes, and countries, (also that present-day Soviets are sentimentalists too) and viewed them satirically or lovingly as the mood struck them. Interspersed with such documentary annotations on manners and mores are such well-known entertainment staples as Chaz Chase, Veronique, Fattini, Obraszov's puppets and many more with Moisseev Ballet a highlight.

Edith Piaf's "Hymn to Love" backdrops an effective mood montage in a movingly sentimental vein which is unfortunately jarred at the end by an unfortunate editing justaxposition with the Red Army Choir. This in turn leads to pic's final message of peace and brotherhood which, though an effective curtainer, looks more like an afterthought as currently presented. **Patrons may find that other parts of the pic jump about too much, also, and a new editing effort might avoid this pitfall.**

This vehicle has been splendidly outfitted from all technical aspects, including a rousing musical selection arranged by Carlo Savina.

Hawk.

Master Of The World
(COLOR)

Fairly lavish production based on the Jules Verne fantasy, but sluggishly paced and loosely written. B.o. prospects depend on campaign.

Hollywood, April 19.

American International release of James H. Nicholson production. Stars Vincent Price, Charles Bronson, Henry Hull, Mary Webster, David Frankham. Directed by William Witney. Screenplay, Richard Matheson, based on "Master of the World" and "Robur, The Conqueror" by Jules Verne; camera (Magnacolor), Gil Warrenton; editor, Anthony Carras; art director, Daniel Haller; music, Les Baxter; sound, Glen Glenn; assistant director, Robert Agnew. Reviewed at Academy Awards Theatre, April 19, '61. Running time, **104 MINS.**

Robur	Vincent Price
Strock	Charles Bronson
Prudent	Henry Hull
Dorothy	Mary Webster
Philip	David Frankham
Alistair	Richard Harrison
Topage	Vito Scotti
Turner	Wally Campo
Weaver	Steve Masino
Shanks	Ken Terrell
Wilson	Peter Besbas

It is obvious that a great deal of care, expense and ingenuity went into the making of this picture, American International's most ambitious project to date. Therefore it is doubly disheartening that the finished product emerges watered-down Jules Verne, diluted by modern dramatic agents foreign to the nature of the author's original fantasy. Company wil have a battle recouping the considerable outlay that went into the production. Through clever exploitation of the character of the odd flying craft that is the crux of the picture, there is the possibility that sufficient curiosity will be aroused and imaginations haunted to stimulate a respectable turnout, particularly among younger film-going groups.

Richard Matheson's screenplay represents the dramatic consolidation of two of Verne's novels, "Master Of The World" and "Robur, the Conqueror." Robur, the would-be-master, is played by Vincent Price. He is the skipper of an impressive aerial craft, the Albatross, with which he aims to "end for all time the scourge of warfare by means of its invincible power." But, in his blueprint to subdue and disarm the outside world, he fails to reckon with retaliatory sabotage from within. He, his faithful crew and his beloved flying fortress ultimately are destroyed by four passengers whom he has held captive for discovering his craft in a crater, or repair pit.

Judging by Matheson's scenario, Verne's remarkable vision extended to language refinements. The dialog has the distracting ring of mid-20th century idiom and expression. There also is a heavy dose of the shopworn romantic triangle situation, disproportionately injurious to the character of this respected fantasy-fiction and preposterous to boost. And there is a certain element of monotony and repetition about the long ride in the air, a suspended lethargy that director William Witney has not been able to disturb too frequently.

Technically and visually, the James H. Nicholson production is a fairly astute job, notably the work of art director-production designer Daniel Haller, whose "Albatross" is an admirable flying machine in its interior, and Tim Barr, Wah Chang and Gene Warren (of Projects Unlimited), whose special effects make it equally fascinating when regarded from exterior vantage points. Further credit is due cameraman Gil Warrenton (although some of the MagnaColor hues are slightly too artificial), photographic effects specialist Ray Mercer (of Butler-Glouner Inc.), aerial photog Kay Norton, composer-conductor Les Baxter (whose work included a romantic title song, with the aid of lyricist Lenny Addelson) and the battery of "StereoSonic" sound experts. Pat Dinga's special props and effects are helpful. Some judicious sniping might have improved matters. Editor is Anthony Carras.

Acting isn't especially exciting, but it is thoroughly competent. Price can handle this kind of role with ease. The other principals—Charles Bronson, Henry Hull, Mary Webster and David Frankham—acquit themselves well, and support is adequate.

Actually the most inspired stroke in the production is its prolog of newsreel clips of early aerial disasters with crude, birdlike, would-be flying contraptions. This pass-

age basically transcends humor, but it will inspire audience howls.
Tube.

Mad Dog Coll

Superficial scrutiny of the infamous character's crime career. Introduces several promising young players. Serviceable supporting fare.

Hollywood, April 27.

Columbia Pictures release of Edward Schreiber production. Stars John Chandler, Kay Doubleday, Brook Hayward; features Neil Nephew, Jerry Orback, Vincent Gardenia, Telly Savalas. Directed by Burt Balaban. Screenplay, Schreiber, based on material by Leo Lieberman; camera, Gayne Reschner; editor, Ralph Rosenblum; art director, Richard Sylbert; music, Stu Phillips; assistant directors, Arthur Steckler, Ulu Grosbard. Reviewed at the studio, April 27, '61. Running time, **88 MINS.**

Vincent Coll .... John Chandler
Rocco .... Neil Nephew
Elizabeth .... Brooke Hayward
Caroline .... Joy Harmon
Joe .... Jerry Orbach
Lt. Dawson .... Telly Savelas
Harry .... Glenn Cannon
Ralphie .... Tom Castronova
Clio .... Kay Doubleday
Schultz .... Vincent Gardenia

The uproar against crime, bloodshed and brutality in American entertainment fare will hardly be soothed by Columbia's "Mad Dog Coll," a choppy and unpleasant chronicle of the deeds of a bootleg-era butcher. Edward Schrieber's production, his first, brings some interesting new people to the screen and offers several other young performers an opportunity to expand their histrionic horizons, but as a screen story it offers little insight into the machinations of the criminal mind and fails to arouse the necessary audience concern for its characters, whichever side of the law they happen to pursue. Liberally stocked with young actors, the picture is likely to attract the attention of youthful filmgoers, but it appears destined to evolve into a supporting attraction only.

Schreiber's screenplay, based on material by Leo Lieberman, traces Coll's activities from early childhood, when he is beaten unmercifully by his sadistic father who dubs him a "mama's boy," through several abortive romances and a fast-rising criminal career in which he challenges New York's mobster hierarchy, to his violent death at age 23. As played by John Chandler, Coll emerges a character instead of a person. Chandler's delineation is explosive and commanding, but it is a one-note performance.

Making their screen bow in the film are Kay Doubleday and Brooke Hayward. The former plays a naive stripper vivaciously. Latter, the lovely daughter of producer Leland Hayward and the late Margaret Sullavan, shows promise in her portrayal of a decent girl involved with Coll and a member of his gang (Jerry Orback), with whom she lays the groundwork for the leader's downfall. Neil Nephew gives a flashy account of himself as Coll's chief aide, albeit with a scowl and an attitude that is pure Brando. Others who sand out in support are Telly Savalas, Joy Harmon, Vincent Gardinia and Orback.

Burt Balaban's direction instills a good deal of authenticity into the character byplay but fails to overcome some clumpsy story construction, particularly in the use of narration by more than one participant, which results in some confusion and distraction. The film was shot in New York and appears faithful to both period and environment, partially through the efforts of art director Richard Sylbert. Gayne Reschner's photography is agile, Ralph Rosenblum's editing competent.

Stu Phillips' excitable score includes a title ballad (with lyrics by Eddie D. Trush), which seems designed to serve as a kind of exploitation Coll-ateral. It's sung by Hal Waters of Colpix Records.
Tube.

The Curse Of The Werewolf
(COLOR)

Topnotch monster fare. A class production surrounding a familiar topic. Good b.o. bet.

Hollywood, April 24.

Universal release of Anthony Hinds production. Stars Clifford Evans, Oliver Reed, Yvonne Romain, Catherine Feller. Directed by Terence Fisher. Screenplay, John Elder, based on novel by Guy Endore; camera (Eastman), Arthur Grant; editor, Alfred Cox; art director, Don Mingaye; music, Benjamin Frankel; sound, Jock May; assistant director, John Peverall. Reviewed at the studio, April 24, '61. Running time, **91 MINS.**

Alfredo .... Clifford Evans
Leon .... Oliver Reed
Servant Girl .... Yvonne Romain
Cristina .... Catherine Feller
Marques Siniestro ..... Anthony Dawson
Marquesa .... Josephine Llewellyn
Beggar .... Richard Wordsworth
Teresa .... Hira Talfrey
Priest .... John Gabriel
Pepe Valiente .... Warren Mitchell
Rosa Valiente .... Anne Blake
Dominique .... George Woodbridge
Old Soak .... Michael Ripper
Don Fernando .... Ewen Solon
Don Enrique .... Peter Sallis
Jose .... Martin Matthews
Rico Gomez .... David Conville
Gaoler .... Denis Shaw
Chef .... Charles Lamb
Senora Zumara .... Serafina Di Leo
Vera .... Sheila Brennan
Isabel .... Joy Webster
Yvonne .... Renny Lister

An elaborate yet meticulous production, a value characteristic of England's Hammer Film firm, lends an especially slick sheen to "The Curse Of The Werewolf," an outstanding entry of the horror picture genre. Although not a particularly frightening or novel story treatment of the perennial shock film topic (werewolves ranking second only to vampires in cinema), it is a first-class effort in other respects. Earmarked for exhibition as the lead attraction in a pairing with "Shadow Of The Cat" (see adjoining review) and ticketed for U.S. distribution during the coming summer vacation season, when its exploitability figures to exert its strongest influence, the Universal release seems assured of a good boxoffice showing.

John Elder's screenplay, based on the novel, "The Werewolf Of Paris," by Guy Endore, dwells at extraordinary length, even for a horror picture, on expository background—on the vile heritage responsible for the genesis of the story's monster. But it is a credit to Elder and all concerned that this lengthy "prolog" sustains equal, if not greater, interest than the film's principal story passages, which involve the personal plight of the actual wolfman himself. The drama unfolds soundly and logically, and leads to the inevitable demise of the beast by means of the customary silver bullet carved from a blessed crucifix.

There are no names in the cast that mean anything to American audiences, but stars are not vital to the success of a horror picture. More important, the level of performance is exceptional for a film of this nature. Especially convincing characters are created by Oliver Reed (who resembles Dirk Bogarde) as the compassionate werewolf, Clifford Evans, Anthony Dawson, Richard Wordsworth and Martin Matthews. Attractive distaff support is fashioned by Yvonne Romain, Catherine Feller and Josephine Llewellyn, and there is a restrained portrayal of the budding lycanthrope as a lad by young Justin Walters.

Principally the film is a triumph of the production artisans assembled by producer Anthony Hinds for the occasion. Under director Terence Fisher's obviously knowing surveillance, these experts have created a mood and a production appearance that is an example of horror filmmaking at its visual best. Among those who illustrate they are masters of their craft are cameraman Arthur Grant (whose vivid views and balanced compositions, tinted in Eastman Color, have a haunting character), art director Don Mingaye (whose sets are unusually sturdy, expansive and artistic) and makeupman Roy Ashton (who has created some of the vilest creatures imaginable).
Tube.

Two Loves
(C'SCOPE-COLOR)

Frigidity in the American female, with a New Zealand locale. Top production values and names, but dramatic loose ends.

Hollywood, April 27.

Metro release of Julian Blaustein production. Stars Shirley MacLaine, Laurence Harvey, Jack Hawkins. Directed by Charles Walters. Screenplay, Ben Maddow, based on novel, "Spinster," by Sylvia Ashton-Warner; camera (Metrocolor), Joseph Ruttenberg; editor, Fredric Steinkamp; art directors, George W. Davis, Urie McCleary; music, Bronislau Kaper; assistant director, William Shanks. Reviewed at the studio, April 27, '61. Running time, **100 MINS.**

Anna .... Shirley MacLaine
Paul .... Laurence Harvey
Abercrombie .... Jack Hawkins
Rauhuia .... Juano Hernandez
Mrs. Cutter .... Norah Howard
Whareparita .... Nobu McCarthy
Mark Cutter .... Neil Woodward
Seven .... Alan Roberts
Hinawaka .... Lisa Sitjar
Matawhero .... Edmund Vargas
Head Master Reardon...... Ronald Long

Frigidity is the subject broached by Metro's "Two Loves," a story of the reawakening of a spinster American schoolteacher in New Zealand. The Julian Blaustein production, based on Sylvia Ashton-Warner's novel, "Spinster," also takes a passing swipe at U. S. morality, examines the vigorous spontaneous way-of-life of the Maori natives and utilizes the "civilized" point-of-view of western-white values as a frame of reference. Unfortunately, the personal story emerges less lucid than its broader overtones.

Since the Metro release stars two currently hot boxoffice commodities, Shirley MacLaine and Laurence Harvey, and the gifted British actor, Jack Hawkins, it has a strong commercial head start and seems assured of a fairly good response. But it will have to overcome several negative factors to get a big play.

One is the fuzzy nature of the all-important central character, so vaguely defined that an audience never fully grasps the reasons behind her moral ailment. Another is that title. Rarely has a picture been re-dubbed with a blander handle. The original tag, "The Spinster," was not only more provocative and salable, it made more sense.

The physical production itself is first-class. In addition to being rich in cultural values, the George W. Davis-Urie McCleary sets have that elusive lived-in look. Director Charles Walters, with astute camera work by Joseph Ruttenberg and editing by Fredric Steinkamp, has kept the film visually hopping. He also has accomplished the most taxing assignment of supervising, controlling and extracting naturalism from the bedlam of 40-odd moppets who play a major role in a number of scenes, and has coaxed plenty of romantic excitement out of his principal players. And Ben Maddow's screenplay is fortified with some intelligent adult dialog. Yet, in spite of all these plusses, the picture misses.

Miss MacLaine plays a dedicated schoolteacher who has found her way to an isolated settlement in Northern New Zealand from Pennsylvania, although how and why is never clearly established. Her dogged innocence is threatened by the amorous advances of Harvey, a rather irrational and immature fellow teacher unhappy with his lot but unable to rise above it. Influenced by the primitive but practical morality of the Maoris, she seems on the verge of giving her all to Harvey when he (rather conveniently) comes to a violent end in a motorcycle mishap. On the rebound, she is coaxed out of self-guilt pangs by senior school inspector Hawkins, and abruptly gives her all to him.

Compassion for the central character is never truly aroused, partially out of expository vagueness, partially because she is presented as a self-sufficient woman seemingly quite content to thrust herself into her work, which she dispatches with a vigor and insight that is the byproduct of love and cannot be matched by her colleagues. Yet the story is bent on proving that she is an unhappy, incomplete woman. Unfortunately it attempts to do so by offering her a choice of males who would not necessarily tempt even a woman of easy virtue—one an irresponsible, self-destructive young boozer, the other a middle-aged married man. Frigidity is a serious problem tackled here as if it can be erased by one night with a man.

Miss MacLaine, although not ideally suited to the role, manages for the most part to rise above the miscasting and deliver an earnest, **interesting portrayal. But there is a degree of gravity and warmth**

missing in her delineation, making it slightly difficult to understand Harvey's passion and Hawkin's tender affection for her. Miss MacLaine is a full-of-fun actress who is at her best playing characters endowed with a dash of whimsy. There is something artificial about Harvey's playing here, but he does have several fine moments. Hawkins fares the best. This fine actor's reactions and attitudes are something to behold. Nobu McCarthy comes through with flying colors as a 15-year-old Maori girl delighted to bear Harvey's children out of wedlock. Juano Hernandez gives a fine performance, and the balance of support is tip-top, right down through the little army of children. Bronislau Kaper's score provides exciting emotional accompaniment, listenable on its own terms. *Tube.*

Cry Freedom
(FILIPINO)

Crude, but infectious rehash of World War II glory days of Filipino freedom fighters. Woven within is an intimate love story, valuable as a b.o. lure.

Hollywood, April 21.

Parallel Film Distributors release of Edith Perez De Tagle production. Stars Pancho Magalona, Rosa Rosal; with Tony Santos, Johnny Reyes, Jack Forster, Charles Kelly. Directed by Lamberto V. Avellana. Screenplay, Wolf Bayer; camera, Mike Accion; music, Restie Umali. Reviewed at NT&T projection room, April 21, '61. Running time, **93 MINS.**

Marking .... Pancho Magalona
Yay .... Rosa Rosal
Cabalhim .... Johnny Reyes
Sid .... Jack Forster
Lt. Stoddard................Charles Kelly
Juanito .... Tony Santos

There is a charming and infectious naivete that threads through "Cry Freedom," a simple, almost childlike vitality that forms an incongruous parallel with its subject, guerrilla combat in the darker days of the Philippine theatre of operations in World War II. The Filipino film, an award-winning import that copped six honors from that country's Academy of Motion Picture Arts and Sciences, is technically crude, frequently dramatically incoherent and motivationally unstable and impulsive, but it has a spontaneous vigor that tells a good deal about the character of this faraway land and its people, and is instilled with a sense of residual ultra-patriotism and nationalism that is invigorating and refreshing in this time of anxious, but sophisticated detachment.

However, its prospects as a box-office attraction in this country are uncertain, at best. Its abundance of combat sequences may attract the action fans, but there have been signs of filmgoing apathy with respect to pictures that rehash the glories of that 15-20 year-old war.

Point should be stressed that this is World War II through the eyes and point-of-view of the Filipino, that it is spoken in English not of the customary post-dubbed variety from abroad, and that it is also a personal story about a man and a woman who are bound together by the crisis and the cause of freedom. This latter, intimate angle is the one to sell, because people are interested in people. Their enthusiasm for decade-old causes has waned in the disenchanting course of the sobering post-war period.

Wolf Bayer's screenplay concerns a bus driver who takes command of a small band of courageous guerrillas at the time of Japanese occupation. In the band there is an educated Filipino girl with whom he falls in love. When the Americans invade and the process of total liberation begins, the young leader fears that, with war's end, his comparative lack of social standing and education will mean the loss of his lover. But, of course, the two young people have experienced too much together for a break to occur based on the trivia of upbringing or so, at least, it stands in the zeal of wartime.

Pancho Magalona gives a winning performance as the young man, impulsive, dominating, emotional and likeable. Rosa Rosal, as the girl, is equally, if not more persuasive. She exhibits a high degree of restraint and feminine dignity, even in the contradictory garb of the guerrilla fighter. Supporting work is fine.

Lamberto V. Avellana directed for producer Edith Perez De Tagle. *Tube.*

La Ragazza In Vetrina
(Girl in the Window)
(ITALO-FRENCH)

Rome, April 25.

Lux Film release of Nepi (Rome)—Sofitedip-Zodiaque (Paris) coproduction. Features Lino Ventura, Magali Noel, Marina Vlady, Bernard Fresson. Directed by Luciano Emmer. Screenplay, Emmer, P. P. Pasolini, Ennio Flajano, Martino, from story by E. Cassuto, Emmer, R. Sonego; camera, Otello Martelli; music, Roman Vlad. At the Barberini, Rome. Running time, **85 MINS.**

Else .... Marina Vlady
Federico .... Lino Ventura
Carrel .... Magali Noel
Vincenzo .... Bernard Fresson

Much has been trimmed out of this item by the local censors, ostensibly in key scenes which helped further character development. What remains, apart from jerky continuity, is (to stretch a point) mainly backdrop and bridging material. Mild chances, at least for this cut version, in most areas.

Plot deal with two Italian miners working in Holland who take two girls from Amsterdam's shopwindow redlight row (hence the title) for a weekend at a lake resort. The younger girl (Marina Vlady) predictably falls for her guy (Bernard Fresson) and makes him change his mind about returning to Italy. Magali Noel and Lino Ventura, as the other couple, walk off with acting honors. Beautiful Miss Vlady and her partner walk rather listlessly through their roles, the tenderness of their relationship only at times breaking through. Luciano Emmer has neatly backdropped his action in the Dutch mining area. His opening reels are firstrate documentation on working conditions there, but his more intimate scenes seem to lack that extra fillip which binds an audience.

Otello Martelli's lensing on actual Dutch locations is outstanding, with other credits matching up. *Hawk.*

Dr. Blood's Coffin
(COLOR)

Bloodbath shocker in which an idealistic scientist, in the grand "Robin Hood" tradition, takes from the evil and gives to the good. Trouble is, he is transferring human hearts. Visually quite distasteful, dramatically unstable, commercially doubtful.

Hollywood, April 25.

United Artists release of George Fowler production. Stars Kieron Moore, Hazel Court, Ian Hunter. Directed by Sidnie J. Furie. Screenplay, Jerry Juran, adapted by James Kelly, Peter Miller; camera (Eastman), Stephen Dade; editor, Tony Gibbs; art director, Scott MacGregor; music, Buxton Orr; sound, William Salter; assistant director, John Comfort. Reviewed at Goldwyn Studios, April 25, '61. Running time, **92 MINS.**

Peter Blood .... Kieron Moore
Linda Parker .... Hazel Court
Dr. Robert Blood .... Ian Hunter
Mr. Morton .... Fred Johnson
Sgt. Cook .... Kenneth J. Warren
Beale .... Andy Alston
Steve Parker .... Paul Stockman
Hanson .... John Romano
Sweeting .... Gerald C. Lawson

Repulsive is about the most congenial word for "Dr. Blood's Coffin," yet its very repellant nature figures to be its staunchest ally in luring the customers. The aptly-titled George Fowler production, an attraction for more impressionable tykes, nor would it be palatable fare for anyone who can't stomach the sight of blood. To compound the decidedly Rh-negative circulatory aspects of the sanguinary United Artists release, the picture does not even benefit from sound story construction. As the responsible British themselves might say, it's a bloody shame.

Jerry Juran's original yarn, adapted by James Kelly and Peter Miller, focuses on the irrational activities of a brilliant young biochemist (Kieron Moore) who, through the use of curare (a South American arrow tip poison), fixes it so that he can transfer the heart of a worthless person to the corpse of someone worthwhile, an idealistic notion that, of course is sheer lunacy in practice. For one thing, somebody has to die in the process, which does not forecast a healthy destiny for said medicine man. For another, there is no accounting for the behavior of a resurrected year-old corpse, who has a right to be confused, and may even hate doctors. At any rate, Moore, who has no trouble befuddling the most procrastinatory and blockheaded set of law enforcers extant, finally meets his comeuppance at the hands of his own Frankensteinian cadaver, whose first remark after coming back to life is "Linda, Linda" (what a memory!).

The story is loaded with inconsistencies and unaccountable behavior. Furthermore, it is utterly fuzzy in scientific detail and rather sluggishly directed by Sidnie J. Furie. Fortunately, there is some dexterous exterior lenswork by Stephen Dade and capable special effects by Leslie Bowie. Otherwise it amounts to the best argument yet against the medical search for the means to immortality.

Moore braves the dramatic absurdity as best he can. Hazel Court is attractive as "Linda," first woman ever involved in a triangle with a doctor and a corpse. Ian Hunter seems ill-at-ease as the doc's dad, and he can hardly be blamed. *Tube.*

The Minotaur
(ITALIAN-TOTALSCOPE-COLOR)

Melodramatic fabrication based on the Greek mythological monster. Uninspired but exploitable.

Hollywood, April 27.

United Artists release of Giorgio Agliani-Dino Mordini-Rudolphe Solmsen production. Stars Bob Mathias, Rosanna Schiaffino. Directed by Silvio Amadio. Screenplay, S. Continenza, G. P. Callegari, Daniel Mainwaring; camera (Technicolor), Aldo Giordani; editor, Nella Nannuzzi; art director, Piero Poletto; music, Carlo Rustichelli; sound, Mario Dal Pezzo; assistant director, Spartaco Conversi. Reviewed at Goldwyn Studios, April 27, '61. Running time, **96 MINS.**

Theseus .... Bob Mathias
Phaedra (Ariane) .... Rosanna Schiaffino
Chrysone .... Alberto Lupo
Demetrius .... Rick Battaglia
Gerione .... Nico Pepe
King Minos .... Carlo Tamerlani
King Egeo .... Nerio Bernardi
Queen Pasiphae .... Tina Lattanzi
Doctor .... Paul Muller
Elea .... Tiziana Casetti
Xanto .... Alberto Plebani
Amphitrite .... Susanne Loret

The Italian film industry, which for some time now has been rearranging history and legend to suit the specifications of the modern cinema, has done it again. In "The Minotaur," a film inspired by the Greek mythological tale of the notorious half-man, half-bull of Crete to whom periodic human sacrifices were made, the adaptors have succeeded in sacrificing a potentially fascinating screen topic to the melodramatic gods.

While there is ample action, sex, suspense and general production know-how to satisfy those who crave escape alone when they visit a film theatre, the United Artists release would be a disappointment for anyone who might expect a novel treatment of the source material. Nevertheless, it has the exploitation value to make a swift impression at the American box-office via the saturation method.

Only the skeleton of the legend remains in the S. Continenza-G. P. Callegari-Daniel Mainwaring screenplay and the accompanying production perspective. Even the established physical appearance of the beast itself has been disregarded. In place of the bull's-head-on-a-man's-body, the artisans have fashioned a Minotaur that is all bull, it's only apparent human characteristic being that it stands upright. It's a fearsome creature, but no Minotaur. Worse yet, the title character plays only a minor part in the production, appearing but for two or three minutes at the climax. The rest of the story is a run-of-the-mill fabrication, centering on the romantic and muscular prowess of its legendary hero, Theseus (Bob Mathias), who is credited with slaying the beast.

Ex-Olympic decathlon champ Mathias, through his athletic reputation, brings more credibility to the character's stupendous one-man feats than would the average leading man. His acting itself is not nearly so impressive, but then all performances in this film are tarnished by the handicap of post-dubbing. Rosanna Schiaffino manages a decent degree of contrast in her portrayal of twin sisters, one wicked, one sweet. Silvio

Amadio's direction fails to erase a stiff, unnatural aura about the love scenes, but he has achieved some gymnastic novelty in his choreography of man-to-man combat, and Mathias follows through admirably.

Contributions from the assembled crafts are thoroughly professional. *Tube.*

The Fabulous World Of Jules Verne
(MYSTIMATION)

Novel attempt to translate Verne to the screen that is astonishingly faithful to the author's image and style. Combines live action and animated elements in an unusual process dubbed Mystimation. Pic has arty possibilities, but Levine-Warner has other distribution ideas.

Hollywood, April 19.

Warner Bros. release of Joseph E. Levine Czechoslovakia import. With Louis Tock, Ernest Navara, Milo Holl, Francis Sherr, Van Kissling, Jane Zalata. Directed by Karel Zeman. Screenplay, Zeman, Francis Gross, based on novels by Jules Verne; camera, George Taran, B. S. Piccard, Antony Hora; art director, Zep Kopal; music, Sydney Fox; animation, Ernest Marchand, Henry Liss, Francis Kramm. Reviewed at the studio, April 19, '61. Running time, **83 MINS.**

Simon Hart	Louis Tock
Prof. Roch	Ernest Navara
Artigas	Milo Holl
Pirate Captain	Francis Sherr
Serke	Van Kissling
Jana	Jane Zalata

Certainly the oddest and essentially the most artistically authentic translation of the noted mid-19th century author's works to the screen, "The Fabulous World of Jules Verne" is a fascinating motion picture from Czechoslovakia, one that merits particular observation from members of the film industry in this country.

Novel in style, offbeat in technique and remarkably durable in story content, it conveys the image and flavor of Verne to an astonishing degree by means of combined live action and animation, through a mysterious but workable process dubbed Mystimation. Joseph Levine presentation and Warner Bros. release is ticketed for pairing (probably of a saturation nature) with "Bimbo the Great" (see adjoining review), but actually it merits a more respectable exhibitory fate.

Based on Verne's yarn, "The Deadly Invention," which is remarkably apropos in today's world, the film, directed by Karel Zeman and adapted by him and Francis Gross, preserves much of the spirit and fluent, flowery style of the author's prose. It concerns the capture of a naive scientific genius by a diabolic buccaneer and his gang for the purposes of utilizing the former's knowledge of explosives (he is working on a project roughly proportionate in 1860 to the A-bomb of 1690) to subdue and rule the world.

More than the story, it is the cinematic style here that captures the spectator's imagination and rivets his attention in spite of the crude dramatic nature of the proceedings. The film recreates some of the vigorous flavor of the silent screen and of early "talkie" serials, an aura enhanced by the photographic techniques of George Taran, B. S. Piccard and Anthony Hora and by Sydney Fox's enchantingly different score and sound effects through music.

But it is the sets, the animation and the artwork in general that give this picture its peculiar individuality, its unique character. One experiences the sense of witnessing the illustrations that accompany Verne's books come to life. It is as if one is looking at the picture through a layer, or photographic filter, of pin-striped horizontal (and sometimes vertical) lines, conveying both a quality of fantasy and a character that is Verne. This atmosphere is supplemented by pin-striped sets, props and drawings, thus linking live action and animation to a single pictorial theme. Happily, it is a black-and-white picture, in keeping with the period. A great variety of shading has been accomplished in those basic tones.

There is an introductory passage narrated by Hugh Downs. The acting is suitable and secondary. Post-dubbing hardly interferes. The true stars here, under Zeman's aegis, are animators Ernest Marchand, Henry Liss and Francis Kramm, artists Syd Ostrov and Joseph Zeman and set designer Zep Kopal. *Tube.*

The Snake Woman

Second-rate supporting number for a horror package.

Hollywood, April 26.

United Artists release of George Fowler production. Stars John McCarthy, Susan Travers. Directed by Sidnie J. Furie. Screenplay, Orville Hampton; camera, Stephen Dade; editor, Anthony Gibbs; art director, John G. Earl; music, Buxton Orr; sound, H. C. Pierson; assistant director, Douglas Hickox. Reviewed at Goldwyn Studios, April 26, '61. Running time, **68 MINS.**

Charles Prentice	John McCarthy
Atheris	Susan Travers
Col. Wynborn	Geoffrey Danton
Dr. Murton	Arnold Marle
Aggie	Elsie Wagstaff
Dr. Adderson	John Cazabon
Polly	Frances Bennett
Constable	Jack Cunningham
Inspector	Hugh Moxey
Barkis	Michael Logan
Martha	Dorothy Frere
Sheperd	Stevenson Lang

Bringing up the rear of a United Artists shock package is "The Snake Woman," which was fabricated by the same English producer-director team responsible for "Dr. Blood's Coffin" (see adjacent review), the lead attraction in the macabre doubleheader. Outside of production values, which favor the latter, the two features are about on a par, equally unsound in dramatic structure and equally unappealing in horror content. Together, they don't figure to cause any prolonged commotion at the boxoffice.

According to Orville Hampton's screenplay for producer George Fowler, a doctor in Northumberland, England restores his lunatic wife's sanity by injecting her with shots of snake venom, thus producing a cold-blooded female offspring who can turn into a poisonous reptile at the bat of an eyelash. The snake babe matures, plausibly enough as horror pictures go, into a most comely, attractive woman who responds pleasantly to the message of a snake charmer's flute, converses in the most articulate British tongue with any handsome young gentleman who happens into the moors, but turns into a regular hellion when someone comes looking for trouble. Eventually she turns into a snake once too often.

Hiss-trionically, Susan Travers never quite sinks her pretty fangs into the part of the sexy serpent, and the whole picture proceeds to fall apart when she breaks her ominously icy silence to chat amiably with the man from Scotland Yard, a character played personably by John McCarthy. Supporting performances are dispatched capably.

Director Sidnie J. Furie, with the aid of art director John G. Earl's gloomy settings, succeeds in instilling an eerie mood, but meets with little success in attempting to deal credibly with Hampton's filmsy fiction. At times the interpretation hovers about a step away from lapsing into a parody of itself, which might have been a more sensible concept to begin with. General level of the film's arts and crafts is adequate outside of the editing, which fails to convey, in visually convincing terms, the transformation of the woman into the snake and back again. *Tube.*

The Shadow Of The Cat

Adequate lower-berth horror item about a "catty"-cornered band of greedy British swindlers.

Hollywood, April 24.

Universal release of Jon Penington production. Stars Andre Morell, Barbara Shelley, William Lucas, Freda Jackson, Conrad Phillips. Directed by John Gilling. Screenplay, George Baxt; camera, Arthur Grant; editor, John Pomeroy; art director, Don Mingaye; music, Mikas Theodorakis; sound, Jock May; assistant director, John Peverall. Reviewed at the studio, April 24, '61. Running time, **79 MINS.**

Walter Venable	Andre Morell
Beth Venable	Barbara Shelley
Jacob	William Lucas
Clara	Freda Jackson
Michael Latimer	Conrad Phillips
Inspector Rowles	Alan Wheatley
Andrew	Andrew Crewford
Ella Venable	Catherine Lacey
Louise	Vanda Godsell
Edgar	Richard Warner

Installed as . :e companion attraction opposite Hammer Films' "Curse of the Werewolf," this British-produced chiller about a cantankerous tabby cat with the memory of an elephant and the disposition of a wounded panther rounds out a twin-bill with fairly promising domestic chances. Although decidedly the lesser of the Universal released pair, the Jon Penington production should keep horror aficionados reasonably, if not acutely, distracted and expectant.

No fewer than five persons succumb to meow-mania in George Baxt's catastrophic yarn about a feline with an unusually purr-nicious sense of vengeance. The puss swings into action following the murder of its beloved wealthy mistress by a group of greedy relatives who subscribe to the theory that where there's a will, especially a sizeable one, there's a way. But, one by one, they are victimized by tabby's uncanny tabulations.

The film, in spite of its distorted degree of felinearity, is prevented from growing monotonous or ludicrous by acting of a high order, mood-molding direction (John Gilling's) and considerable photographic ingenuity, notably cameraman Arthur Grant's device of distorting the picture to represent the cat's-eye-view of the dastardly vendetta. There's not a poor performance in the film, and that goes, as well, for the cat, trained for cinematic good behavior by John Holmes. From top to bottom, serious-minded, persuasive portrayals are delivered by Andre Morell, Barbara Shelley, William Lucas, Freda Jackson, Conrad Phillips, Alan Wheatley, Andrew Crawford, Catherone Lacey, Vanda Godsell and Richard Warner.

Additionally helpful to the production are Don Mingaye's art direction, Jock May's sound, John Pomeroy's editing and Mikis Theodorakis' score and orchestration. *Tube.*

Bimbo The Great
(COLOR)

Parade of big top cliches. Exploitation aspect of pic on circus life may help b.o. chances somewhat.

Hollywood, April 19.

Warner Bros. release of Alexander Gruter production (imported from Germany by Joseph E. Levine). With Claus Holm, Germaine Damar, Elma Karlowa, Marina Orschel, Helmut Schmidt, Paul Hartmann, Lisa Gussack, Loni Heuser. Directed by Harold Philipp. Screenplay, Hans Raspotnik, Philipp, Erich Kroehnke; camera (Eastman), Willy Winterstein; music, Theo Mackeben, Klaus Orgermann. Reviewed at studio, April 19, '61. Running time, **92 MINS.**

Bimbo Tagore	Claus Holm
Lilo	Germaine Damar
Yvonne	Elma Karlowa
Marianne	Marina Orachel
Kovacs	Helmut Schmidt
Williams	Paul Hartmann
Monica	Lisa Gussack
Circus Agent	Loni Heuser

Most of the cliches of circus life have crept into "Bimbo The Great." Were it not for its twin-billed association with another Joseph E. Levine import, the unusual and possibly attention-getting "Fabulous World of Jules Verne" (see adjoining review), "Bimbo" might just have wound up in theatrical limbo. But, as it is in the market realities of general saturation run, the inferior of the two attractions is just liable to get the bigger exploitation buildup. If so, the essentially incompatible Warner Bros. pairing is likely to make a less than impressive boxoffice impression.

"Bimbo," of German origin, is the story of a circus performer (an elephant trainer and trapeze expert) who loses his wife-partner in what is interpreted as an accident only by the characters in the film.

Incorporated is the usual variety of circus performing (although somewhat less than usual), the inevitable circus fire and a few limber, but irrelevant dance numbers. The entire effort is weighted down by predictability of story and a case of elephantiasis of pace.

Fortunately, there are some strikingly lovely leading ladies in the film although, alas, the loveliest (Marina Orachel) is the ill-fated wife, who departs for a better world no more than 10-minutes into the action. Most of the acting is adequate, with Claus Holm ("Bimbo), Germaine Damar, Elma Karlowa, Helmut Schmidt, Paul

Hartmann and young Lisa Gussack prominent.

The Alexander Gruter production, directed by Harold Philipp, is lensed in Eastman Color and post-dubbed. It is artistically, photographically and technically competent. *Tube.*

The Parent Trap
(COLOR)

Hayley Mills - Disney combo. Young star, playing twin sisters, carries the picture, which needs some carrying. Overlong and sticky in parts, but plenty of good comedy within. B.O. potential.

Hollywood, April 28.

Buena Vista release of Walt Disney production. Stars Hayley Mills, Maureen O'Hara, Brian Keith; features Charlie Ruggles, Una Merkel, Leo G. Carroll, Joanna Barnes; with Cathleen Nesbitt, Ruth McDevitt, Crahan Denton, Linda Watkins, Nancy Kulp, Frank De Vol. (No character name credits given. Directed by David Swift. Screenplay, Swift, based on book by Erich Kastner; camera (Technicolor), Lucien Ballard; editor, Philip W. Anderson; art directors, Carroll Clark, Robert Clatworthy; music, Paul Smith; sound, Dean Thomas; assistant director, ivan Volkman. Reviewed at Academy Awards Theatre, April 28, '61. Running time, **129 MINS.**

Thanks to Hayley Mills, "The Parent Trap" is a winner. This remarkably gifted young British actress, whose work in "Pollyanna" earned her a special Academy Award, illustrates anew that she is the number one child talent in films today and clearly indicates that mere adulthood is not going to curtail her blossoming career, as it has many other top juvenile stars in the past. It's a fortunate thing for the picture that she's in it, because the picture needs her as much as Amos needed Andy.

The combination of Miss Mills and "Walt Disney Presents" is going to be a mighty one on the nation's marquees. Parents and children alike and galore are going to fall into "The Parent Trap."

David Swift, whose writing, direction and appreciation of his young star's natural histrionic resources contributed so much to "Pollyanna," has repeated the three-ply effort on this excursion, with similar success. Swift's screenplay, based on Erich Kastner's book, "Das doppelte Lottchen," describes the nimble-witted method by which identical twin sisters (both played by Miss Mills) succeed in reuniting their estranged parents after a 14-year separation during which the sisters were parted, unbeknownst to them, in opposite parental camps.

When Miss Mills is not on the screen, the film labors, not because of any lack of comic savvy on the part of other members of the cast, but because the yarn is absolutely predictable from the outset and stretches itself interminably in the romantic passages, particularly in the final third of the picture during which the youthful star, for the most part, is spared key participation in some pretty sticky passages.

Much of the humor is of the slapstick, practical joke variety, an approach that will have younger audiences in stitches and adults plenty amused. But the best part

of the story occurs in the midsection, when the two sisters swap identities to meet the respective parent they've never known. There's both fun and heart in these long-overdue rendezvous.

Miss Mills is astonishingly natural, yet creatively so. She seems to have an instinctive sense of comedy and an uncanny ability to react in just the right manner. Her contribution to the picture is virtually infinite. Overshadowed, but outstanding in his own right is Brian Keith as her father. Already a respected dramatic actor, he reveals a bright flair for humorous roles. Maureen O'Hara's durable beauty makes the mother an extremely attractive character. Solid featured work is chipped in by Charlie Ruggles, Una Merkel, Leo G. Carroll and Joanna Barnes, and there are a number of excellent character performances in support.

Sizeable assists are fashioned by cameraman Lucien Ballard, special photographic effects expert Ub Iwerks, art directors Carroll Clark and Robert Clatworthy and composer Paul Smith. The 129-minute film certainly would benefit from some judicious snipping. Otherwise, Philip W. Anderson's editing is sound. There are three songs by Richard M. and Robert B. Sherman, largely in a kind of semi, latter day r 'n' r vein, and fairly infectious.

The title ditty might just catch on, and "Let's Get Together" would have been a good seller a few years back, when a rockin' jump beat and a casually wailed "yay, yay, yay" phrase were just about enough to insure pop success. *Tube.*

The Pleasure Of His Company
(COLOR)

Generally pleasurable translation of the hit play. Bolstered with good marquee cast, bright performances and snappy direction, should be solid b.o. candidate.

Hollywood, April 20.

Paramount release of William Perlberg production. Stars Fred Astaire, Debbie Reynolds, Lilli Palmer, Tab Hunter; features Gary Merrill, Charlie Ruggles. Directed by George Seaton. Screenplay, Samuel Taylor, based on the play by Taylor and Cornelia Otis Skinner; camera (Technicolor), Robert Burks; editor, Alma Macrorie; art directors, Hal Pereira, Tambi Larsen; music, Alfred Newman; sound, Hugo and Charles Grenzbach; assistant directors, Harry Caplan, Donald Roberts. Reviewed at Grauman's Chinese, April 20, '61. Running time, **114 MINS.**

Biddeford Poole	Fred Astaire
Jessica Poole	Debbie Reynolds
Katharine Dougherty	Lilli Palmer
Roger Henderson	Tab Hunter
James Dougherty	Gary Merrill
MacKenzie Savage	Charlie Ruggles
Toy	Harold Fong
Mrs. Mooney	Elvia Allman

As is the case with many a Broadway play translated to the screen, "The Pleasure of His Company" may strike some as verbose, static and confined for a "motion" picture. But the Perlberg-Seaton production happily retains most of the play's sophisticated pep—it's witty, fast-paced patter—and adds to this the intimacy of close-up reactions, an extra dimension that cannot be matched on a stage. So, despite its shortcomings, it is a winning entertainment—not especially original, not particularly exciting, but a winner nevertheless. And, of paramount importance to the studio that is releasing, it has the marquee punch and popular appeal to score the necessary points that are a pleasure for any film company.

Samuel Taylor's screenplay, based on the Broadway comedy Cornelia Otis Skinner and he concocted is the sort of property that rises or falls with the comic conduct of the cast and the calibre of the direction. Those departments, fortunately, are generally well represented in the film version. George Seaton's direction, for the most part, indicates verve and humorous perception, letting down only briefly in the picture's lethargic midsection.

Most of the performances are bright and keen-witted, and in one or two cases downright inventive. Fred Astaire plays the role originated by Cyril Ritchard on the stage, that of the prodigal, middle-aged playboy papa who returns after a 15-20 year absence to visit his wealthy ex-wife (Lilli Palmer) and daughter (Debbie Reynolds) just prior to the latter's wedding. Balance of the film consists of a contest of sorts in which Astaire more or less vies with his daughter's fiance for her affection over the protestations of the shrewd, knowing Miss Palmer and the vexations of her present husband, who has some misgivings about his wife's intentions with respect to the dashing interloper. Unlike the play in its original form, Astaire flies off alone in the end, leaving matters approximately the way they were in the beginning.

It is Miss Palmer who steals the show. Her reactions are responsible for the picture's strongest

comedy wallops, and she comes through equally fine during the weaker sentimental passages. She is an actress equipped with an enviable supply of grace, poise and general thespic know-how, and her mature good looks make her ideally suitable for this kind of role—the latently romantic but perceptively responsible woman of the world. It's an outstanding performance.

The venerable Astaire isn't very far behind. His legion of fans should be delighted at his portrayal. The role even enables him to indulge in a bit of ballroom strutting and casual crooning, and his familiar graceful mobility, even in walking or just standing there, suggests a kind of semi-dance, frequently backstopped by romantic music (Alfred Newman's) that seems on the verge of terpsichorean accompaniment.

The picture belongs to the veteran players. Gary Merrill is persuasive as the husband, Charlie Ruggles (recreating his legit role) fine as the bemused, tolerant grandfather. Miss Reynolds has many good moments, but actually she no longer is quite the ingenue required for the role. With her it seems to be a case of casting for the marquee rather than the story. Tab Hunter fits the part of her fiance, and Harold Fong inserts some fun as the Oriental servant.

"Pleasure" is a pretty picture, thanks to Robert Burks' Technicolor photography, the Hal Pereira-Tambi Larsen art direction, and the incomparable scenic wonders of San Francisco. Alma Macrorie's editing is competent. *Tube.*

Two Women
(ITALO-FRENCH)

Excellent performances distinguish this heavily downbeat art entry focused on wartime mother-daughter travail, including rape. Fine b.o. prospects.

Embassy Pictures release of Champion (Rome)-Les Films Marceau-Cocinor and Societe General de Cinematographie Paris (coproduction. Stars Sopria Loren; Belmondo, Eleanora Brown, Raf Vallone. Produced by Carlo Ponti. Directed by Vittorio DeSica. Screenplay by Cesare Zavattini from the novel by Alberto Moravia; camera, Mario Capriotti; editor, Adriana Novelli; music, Armando Trovajoli; assistant director, Lusia Alessandri. Previewed April 27, '61, in N.Y. Running time, **105 MINS.**

Cesira	Sophia Loren
Michele	Jean Paul Belmondo
Rosetta	Eleanora Brown
Giovanni	Raf Vallone

If only on the basis of Joe Levine's track record at the box-office—meaning his exploitation savvy—his maiden aegis of an art picture (acquired for domestic play at a reputed $300,000) might be figured a certain moneymaker. He has aligned a very probable b.o. click that is highly promotable.

"Two Women" has cinematic weaknesses, but it also has a heck of a lot going for it on the art circuit. Carlo Ponti, who produced, and Vittorio De Sica, who directed, are a potent one-two for the intelligentsia. French thesp Jean Paul Belmondo (who scored in "Breathless") must also be reckoned a wicket asset, with Spanish novelist Alberto Moravia's name lending literati lustre.

What may surprise the buffs, though, is the standout contribution of star Sophia Loren in her least glamorous but most impressive histrionic job to date.

Much Moravian epigram and aphorism have been re a ned in the screen translation of his novel. There are also moments of keen shock, including a double rape scene, but not of a nature likely to raise censor hackles. Throughout, the pic is laden with distaff-angled emotion, but the sentiment somehow never descends to the maudlin.

Cesare Zavattini's screenplay appears to have transferred Moravia with scrupulous adherence to the letter of the book, if not quite the spirit—the irony and hope. There is only unremitting horror and soul-trying for the two women —the mother (Miss Loren) and her 13-year-old daughter (newcomer Eleanora Brown)—as they reel from one wartime adversity to another, cresting with their marathon debauching by a band of Moroccan soldiers. It is the grim life in spades, and so bleak that audiences are apt to puzzle for a philosophic point.

This and overlength make for some tedium, but it probably will go unnoticed to the ladies since "Women" is definitely a moist outing for women. Still, one wishes Adriana Novelli had been more heartless at editing.

Yarn follows the mother and daughter when they leave Rome as bombing attacks increase and journey south to the older woman's girlhood village in the mountains. They join the villagers and other refugees, including Belmondo as a bespectacled and disillusioned young intellectual. He becomes smitten with the mother but hides the fact till shortly before some German troops requisition him as a guide. Many months later, frustrated by their existence and with Allied forces moving up the Italian boot, the mother decides they should return to Rome and their grocery shop. En route, they are ravished by the Moroccans in a scene set symbolically in a gutted church. The attack shocks the girl numb, and it is only at the end, when she hears of the death of Belmondo, whom she liked, that she is restored to normal grief.

There are numerous moments of emotional pitch in all this, mostly via their squalid situation and the strain imposed on their relationship. Miss Loren achieves what is easily her "finest hour" on the screen, faced with the need to be both woman and mother. Young Miss Brown shows an amazing insight to the awkward-age child—innocent, confused and emotionally scarred. An American, she delivers impressively in her debut and is certain to be heard from anon.

Belmondo, in a cliche role as the physically timid egghead, manages the part plausibly. And in a brief stint early in the film, Raf Vallone convincingly limns the Roman neighbor who agrees to be custodian of Miss Loren's grocery after he has his way with her.

DeSica has directed in a way that maximizes the anguish, yet is free of melodrama. Armando Trovajoli's music is a compassionate plus, and other technical aspects are of a polished calibre.

It may also be noted for exhibitors that "Two Women" was the official Italian entry this year at the Cannes festival, and before that won for Miss Loren Italy's "silver ribbon"—equivalent to a Hollywood Oscar.

While a cut below earlier postwar neo-realist Italo product, this one has performances and associated name value that bode brisk boxoffice. *Pit.*

The Little Shop Of Horrors

Lower-berth comedy relief for horror twin-bills. The comedy is low.

Filmgroup release of Roger Corman production. With Jonathan Haze, Jackie Joseph, Mel Welles, Myrtle Vail, Leola Wendorff, Dick Miller. (No character names given). Directed by Corman. Screenplay, Charles B. Griffith; camera, Archie Dalzell; editor, Marshall Nellan Jr.; art director, Daniel Haller; music, Fred Katz; assistant director, Richard Dixon. Reviewed at Pix Theatre, April 20, '61. Running time, **70 MINS.**

Reportedly only two shooting days and $22,500 went into the making of this picture, but limited fiscal resources haven't deterred Roger Corman and his game, resourceful little Filmgroup from whipping up a serviceable parody of a typical screen horror number. It makes a handy supporting attraction for shock features, supplying both comedy relief and offbeat diversion.

Actually, "Little Shop of Horrors" is kind of one big "sick" joke, but it's essentially harmless and good-natured and there's an audience for it. Written by Charles B. Griffith, the plot concerns a young, goofy florist's assistant who creates a talking, blood-sucking, man-eating plant, then feeds it several customers from skid row before sacrificing himself to the horticultural gods. This is low comedy, to be sure, and the percent of parody is considerably less than 50-50, but the film comes up with several good laughs via its wild disregard for reality and its wacky characterizations.

There is, for example, a fellow who visits the Skid Row flower shop to munch on purchased bouquets ("I like to eat in these little out-of-the-way places"). There is also the Yiddish proprietor, distressed by his botanical attraction ("we not only got a talking plant, we got one dot makes smart cracks"), but content to let it devour as the shop flourishes. And there are assorted quacks, alcoholics, masochists, sadists and even a pair of private-eyes who couldn't solve the case of the disappearing fly in a hothouse for Venus Fly-Traps. In short, the film is a sort of rowdy vegetable that hits the funnybone in about the same way that seeing a man slip on a banana peel does. It's absurd, but different.

Considering the minimal expense and time allotment, a high degree of technical proficiency is exhibited. The acting is pleasantly preposterous. Mel Welles, as the proprietor, and Jonathan Haze, as the budding Luther Burbank, are particularly capable, and Jackie Joseph is decorative as the latter's girl. Comic support is broad, sick and low, but it plays. Horticulturalists and vegetarians will love it, especially on Arbor Day. *Tube.*

Eve And The Handyman
(COLOR)

Peep show cloaked in what is intended to be a satire. Should do good biz in houses where sex is the big attraction.

Hollywood, May 5.
Pad-Ram Enterprises release of Russ Meyer production. Stars Eve Meyer, Anthony-James Ryan. Written and directed by Meyer; camera (Eastman), Meyer. Reviewed at Paris Theatre, May 5, '61. Running time, 64 MINS.

"Eve and the Handyman" is roughly the cinematic equivalent of one of the more sophisticated pose magazines. It is a slick slice of sex suggestion, an anatomical peepathon accompanied by that double-entendre narration that is the hallmark of caption poets from "Dude" to "Nugget" to "Playboy." More often than not, the intended satire sinks into double talk, vulgarity and low comedy, but the film is evidence that, given more reputable channels in which to direct his skill, producer-director-writer-photographer Russ Meyer (of "Mr. Teas" notoriety), who is responsible for this glorified hormone stimulant, might prove he is more than a mere flesh-in-the-pan impresario.

For its class, the picture is somewhat above average. It is superior in style and entertainment value to others of its ilk currently pulling big boxoffice at theatres that cater to the bare-babe-ogling customer, so it ought to score at least equally as well along Filmdom's "broad"way circuit.

Eve Meyer is the star attraction, undertaking a variety of roles, sole distinction among which amounts to the number and characteristic of garments in which she is frocked and/or unfrocked. Several other young ladies are intimately scrutinized, too. The degree of nudity in the film ranges from absolute zero (from an occasional aft vantage point) to form-fitting attire into which all forms fit admirably. Anthony-James Ryan is the handyman, and both he and Miss Meyer perform skillfully, considering the nature of their material.

Meyer has an affinity for extremely tight closeups. He will jam his lens right into someone's mouth for comic effect. Depending upon where he is jamming his lens, it is fairly effective. But Meyer would just as soon jam it into a ladies' toilet as he would into an eye. And some of his suggestive symbolism (notably a blast of explosives, sight gags and sound effects implying a sex act) appeals in the most arrested mentality way to the human animal's grosser sense of humor. *Tube.*

Odissea Nuda
(Nude Odyssey)
(ITALO-FRENCH)
(Color)

Rome, April 25.
Cineriz release of a P. C. Mediterranee-Cineriz (Rome)-Francinex (Paris) coproduction. Stars Enrico Maria Salerno; features Patricia Dolores Donlon, Venantino Venantini, Elisabeth Logue, Vaea Bennett, Natalie Gasse, Pauline Remy, Charles Mau, Jack Russell, Giulia Merserve, Arona. Directed by Franco Rossi. Screenplay, Rossi, Ennio DeConcini, Ottavio Alessi, from story by Rossi, DeConcini, and Golfiero Colonna. Camera (Eastmancolor-TotalScope), Alessandro D'Eva. Music, A. F. Lavagnino. Editor, Otello Colangeli. At Fiamma, Rome. Running time, 120 MINS.
Enrico .... Enrico Maria Salerno
Maeva .... Elisabeth Logue
Tepare .... Nathalie Gasse
Turere .... Vaea Bennett
Hinano .... Pauline Remy

A European finds a new purpose in life during a visit to the Polynesian Islands in this fine new film by Franco Rossi. Picture lacks marquee value and is deliberately slowpaced, but should find its audience among savvy filmgoers everywhere. This copy, as projected, appeared to be badly cut by censor.

Pic consists of diary-like notations, both visual and commented, of a documentarist's trip to Tahiti and nearby islands. At first, he succumbs to its carefree life (and women), later finds solace in its tranquility and contemplative solitude. In conclusion, however, he realizes that one cannot (or must not) escape life's responsibilities. And, so with new resignation and courage, he returns to the hectic everyday European existence.

Director Rossi sketches his tale in brief, rapid strokes at first, not sparing some biting comments on modern life. Then, as his character (well underplayed by Enrico Maria Salerno) is assimilated by his surroundings, the film gains stature and importance until the hero decides to break out and face the music once more. Occasionally, though, the pace lags too much. One feels that the island life has deeply affected the director-writer's thoughts, and it's a good guess that the original production idea was sharply modified after its makers had been exposed to the local scene.

Breathtaking lensing by Alessandro D'Eva are part and parcel of a tasteful and visually exciting pic which tries at all times to avoid banal tropic island-isms, the only concession being an over-dazzling array of beauties who populate the hero's Polynesian adventures. Music by A. F. Lavagnino is a further plus in this added feather in Italian cinema's cap. *Hawk.*

La Bride Sur Le Cou
(The Slack Reins)
(FRENCH-C'SCOPE)

Paris, May 2.
UFA-Comacico release of Jacques Roitfeld-Francos Film production. Stars Brigitte Bardot; features Michel Subor, Jacques Riberolles, Claude Brasseur, Mireille Darc. Directed by Roger Vadim. Screenplay, Jean Aurel, Claude Brule, Vadim; camera, Robert Le Fvebre; editor, Albert Jurgenson. At Paris, Paris. Running time, 85 MINS.
Sophie .... Brigitte Bardot
Alain .... Michel Subor
Philippe .... Jacques Riberolles
Claude .... Claude Brasseur
Barbara .... Jacqueline James

The main appeal and commercial chances abroad for this one depend on the continuing pull of star Brigitte Bardot. Otherwise, this as an uneven situation comedy which lacks the invention, zest,

pace and enough knowing thesping to keep it going. The result is a patchy work with some clever bits but most subordinated to Miss Bardot's undressing, pouting and sex kittenish carryings-on. However, she remains chaste until the last scene.

She is cast as a cover girl in love with her photographer. When she loses him to a rich American girl she decides to get him back by making him jealous via a suitor of hers. In the interim, she falls for the decoy, and it proves a happy ending for both couples. Miss Bardot gets to do a suggestive dance in a skintight, flesh-colored tights, busses her man quite thoroughly and displays her dim-witted but charming mannerisms as well as subtly concealed nudism.

Director Roger Vadim seems to lack the feeling for timing and characterization to make this silly story very acceptable. Miss Bardot sets out to shoot her rival but is dissuaded by her young flirt. Then follows some forced gags, with the trail leading to a ski resort, and some custard pie tossing.

Miss Bardot is properly and innocently immoral and willingly seduced for the film's main selling points. 20th-Fox has this for the U.S. and it looks like something for general distrib on the Bardot monicker. But arty chances seem limited. *Mosk.*

The Big Show
(C'SCOPE-COLOR)

Familiar big top melodramatics. Bulky pic will have to bank on vigorous selling campaign, top production values and customary family appeal of circus fare to cash in.

Hollywood, May 3.

Twentieth-Fox release of Ted Sherdeman-James B. Clark production. Stars Esther Williams, Cliff Robertson, Nehemiah Persoff, Robert Vaughn, Margia Dean; features David Nelson, Carol Christensen. Directed by Clark. Screenplay, Sherdeman; camera (De Luxe), Otto Heller; editor, Benjamin Laird; art director, Ludwig Reiber; music, Paul Sawtell, Bert Shefter; sound, Walter Ruhland, Don McKay; assistant director, Herman Goebel. Reviewed at the studio, May 3, '61. Running time, 113 MINS.

Hillary	Esther Williams
Josef	Cliff Robertson
Bruno	Nehemiah Persoff
Klaus	Robert Vaughn
Carlotta	Margia Dean
Eric	David Nelson
Garda	Carol Christensen
Hans	Kurt Fecher
Teresa	Renata Mannhardt
Fredrik	Franco Andrei
Vizzini	Peter Capell
Lawyer	Stephan Schnabel
Judge Richter	Carleton Young
Ringmaster	Philo Hauser
Frau Stein	Mariza Tomic
Prosecutor	Gerd Vespermann

A million dollars went into the making of "The Big Show," largest picture to stem from the 20th-Fox offspring wing operated by Robert L. Lippert. Being the type of product likely to attract a huge tyke turnout, fortified with what is purported to be a half-million-dollar ad coin outlay, and the target of exec producer Lippert's impassioned personal plea for a display of showmanship zeal on the part of its exhibitors, the picture has a fair chance, if everything jells properly, to make a flashy boxoffice showing, as most "big" circus cinespectacles have in the past. But if it does, it will by and large represent a triumph of salesmanship over product, the odds against which, in today's cautious, enlightened, "show me" world, are considerable, to say the least.

There is a lot that catches and captivates the eye in the Ted Sherdeman-James B. Clark production, but very little to tickle the mind or exercise the imagination. It is, simply, an old-fashioned "escape" picture which some will be content to escape into, while others would prefer to escape from.

Major circus films in the past have enjoyed great popularity, which no doubt helped prompt the choice of vehicle, but it is entirely questionable as to whether the public can be enticed again to respond wholeheartedly to an entertainment that is as familiar as it is, in this case, pretentious. The time may have arrived for the addition of new dramatic scope and insight into the "big" circus picture, if the once-healthy form of product is to continue to thrive.

Sherdeman penned the tale and Clark directed the picture. The former's scenario is a busy, shallow and far-fetched melodrama about the members of a European circus family. Punctuated by passages devoted to the customary serial and bestial big top specialties, three romantic yarns and a kind of overall saga unravel. The romances involve two sons (one good, one bad) and a daughter (good) of a domineering father (bad) blindly addicted to circus life. In the end, all the "bads" have neatly perished, thus assuring the "goods" of happily-ever-afterism.

The story, rather unnecessarily it seems, is told in flashback. The technique diminishes tension and ruins the impact of several story highlights by serving as a tipoff. Additionally, on the negative side, the film is awkward and heavily dependent on coincidence in its expository section, and its characters, particularly the ladies, are shy the desirable dimension. Moreover, the picture lacks a sense of humor and there is a lethargy about some of the romantic passages, several of which could either have been snipped or accelerated by director Clark. The circus acts themselves are diverting and, in one or two instances, quite suspenseful, notably the trapeze and highwire feats and a polar bear sequence. They are dexterously lensed by Otto Heller, whose De Luxe Color photography is the picture's outstanding element.

Esther Williams is decorative as a wealthy American girl who falls for Cliff Robertson, favorite son member of the morbid trapeze clan and the only rationally flexible flyer in the slay-ride. Robertson, a skillful actor, does what he can with the role. Nehemiah Persoff, another able player, limns the ferociously single-minded paper and manages to put some bite into the gummy role. Robert Vaughn instills first haplessness, then menace, into his part of the maltreated son driven into a demented craving for revenge. Carol Christensen adds youthful beauty as Persoff's daughter, who finds happiness with a shy U.S. serviceman amiably played by David Nelson. Others who attract more than passing attention are Peter Capell, Margia Dean, Kurt Pechner, Franco Andrei and Renata Mannhardt, latter especially interesting as the polar bear trainer.

Much of the film was shot in Munich, and the exteriors happily impart some of the character of that city, certainly improving the overall appearance of the film. Circus sets, arena and behind-the-scenes, reflect credit on the work of art director Ludwig Reiber. Benjamin Laird's editing is mechanically stable. Composers Paul Sawtell and Bert Shefter have installed the big top flavor into much of their score, abandoning that theme when the melodramatic fireworks demand broad musical expression. *Tube.*

The Right Approach
(C'SCOPE)

Shallow study of a heel in Hollywood. Cast lends some marquee value to otherwise lightweight prospect.

Hollywood, May 5.

Twentieth-Fox release of Oscar Brodney production. Stars Juliet Prowse, Frankie Vaughn, Martha Hyer, Gary Crosby, David McLean. Directed by David Butler. Screenplay, Fay and Michael Kanin, based on play by Garson Kanin; camera, Sam Leavitt; editor, Tom McAdoo; art directors, Duncan Cramer, Herman A. Blumenthal; music, Dominic Frontiere; sound, Arthur Kirbach, Frank W. Moran; assistant director, Ad Schaumer. Reviewed at the studio, May 5, '61. Running time, 92 MINS.

Ursula Poe	Juliet Prowse
Leo Mack	Frankie Vaughn
Anne Perry	Martha Hyer
Rip Hulett	Gary Crosby
Bill Sikulovic	David McLean
Brian Freer	Jesse White
Liz	Jane Withers
Helen	Rachel Stephens
Mitch Mack	Steve Harris
Granny	Paul von Schreiber
Horace	Robert Casper

"The Right Approach" is precisely what this picture required. In tracing the meteoric rise and downfall of a Hollywood heel, it overlooks the fact that even Hollywood heels are human. It amounts to a stereotypographical error that lurches the entire project out of focus. The Oscar Brodney production for 20th-Fox will have to rely primarily on its ample array of relatively fresh cast names for boxoffice stimulus. Otherwise, it's a pretty lean prospect.

Based on a play by Garson Kanin, the Fay and Michael Kanin scenario describes the method by which a slick and unscrupulous acting aspirant (Frankie Vaughn) arrives in the film capital and proceeds to: 1) break up the harmony of a bachelor establishment inhabited by five incredibly naive young gentlemen playing house, 2) wreck two potential love affairs, deliberately, 3) stoke a carhop into unwed motherhood, 4) chisel every last five spot he sights, 5) con his way onto the cover of a national mag.

Vaughn tries hard by the unsavory character, but doesn't get very far. His warbling of a couple of tunes reveals savvy and showmanship in selling a song, but nothing exceptional in the way of voice. Juliet Prowse and Martha Hyer supply the romantic interest, neither with a great deal of success. The five lads conned by Vaughn are Gary Crosby, David McLean, Steve Harris, Robert Casper and Paul von Schreiber. Each has some good moments. Jane Withers and Jesse White manage to insert some comedy relief.

David Butler's direction fails to instill the desirable fluidity into the film as a whole or into many of the individual scenes. Sam Leavitt's lenswork and Tom McAdoo's editing are adequate. Art directors Duncan Cromer and Herman A. Blumenthal have whipped up an interesting central set—a "South Seas" type of restaurant converted into a kind of bachelor barracks. Dominic Frontiere's background music, largely of a rhythmical pop nature, has a tendency to be distracting where it should be unobtrusive. Several pop style ditties are incorporated, catchiest of which is the title tune, sung over the main titles by the Kirby Stone Four, later by Vaughn. *Tube*

Romanoff And Juliet
(COLOR)

From Peter Ustinov's witty legit spoof of modern political cranky hanky-panky, a lively merry film only slightly diluted in translation to screen. Satisfactory b.o. looms.

Hollywood, May 4.

Universal release of Peter Ustinov production. Stars Ustinov, Sandra Dee, John Gavin, Akim Tamiroff. Directed and screenplay by Ustinov, based on his play; camera (Technicolor), Robert Kras-

Alexander Trauner; music, Mario Nascimbene; sound, Sash Fisher; assistant director, Gus Agosti. Reviewed at Fine Arts Theatre, May 4, '61. Running time, 103 MINS.

General	Peter Ustinov
Juliet Moulsworth	Sandra Dee
Igor Romanoff	John Gavin
Vadim Romanoff	Akim Tamiroff
Beulah Moulsworth	Alix Talton
Freddie	Rik Von Nutter
Hooper Moulsworth	John Phillips
Otto	Peter Jones
Evdokia Romanoff	Tamara Shayne
Marfa	Suzanne Cloutier
Patriarch	Edward Atienza
Randle Wix	John Alderson
Chief Executive	Thomas Chalmers
The Spy	Carl Don
President at U.N.	Tonio Selwart
Joseph the Pilot	Renato Chiantoni
Customs Officer	Booth Colman
Cook	Moura Budberg

Some of the satiric toxin has gone out of Peter Ustinov's "Romanoff and Juliet" in its cinemetamorphosis, but enough of the comic chemistry remains to induce a favorable reaction from any audience. If good pictures mean good boxoffice (and would that they invariably did), then the Universal release will be a profitable contender, although its gross potential figures to lie in the modest, as opposed to the blockbuster, range of the commercial spectrum.

Ustinov's own magnetic personality, his gifts not only as a performer-linguist-satirist but as an outstanding human being, and his shiny new Academy ward as "Best Supporting Actor" will serve as the film's ace lure, particularly for more discriminating individuals who will be attracted further by the reputation of the hit play itself. As a most important added come-on for general audiences, especially in this country, producer Ustinov has shrewdly cast Sandra Dee and John Gavin in the key romantic roles. The product itself should do the rest of the selling job.

In adapting and trimming "Romanoff" to 103 minutes of screen essentials, it appears as if

Ustinov has added a little ice water to his hot and slyly acid solution, presumably to make it more palatable for the not-quite-)-sharp mass audience that visits a film, where it will miss a play. The picture, as compared to its source, seems confusing in spots, and slightly lopsided, in the sense that its best moments occur in the first half.

But these are only minor reservations inspired by a profound respect for the Ustinov talent. For Ustinov has managed not only to retain the lion's share of his tongue-in-cheek swing at political hypocrisy, diplomatic pomposity and general 20th century lack of harmony or philosophical perspective, but he has added several noteworthy observations in the process of rearranging his play for the screen. Most significant of these additions occurs right at the outset, while the titles unravel. It is a delicious piece of inspired nonsense in which Ustinov does all the voices voting "yes" or "no" on a UN proposal. His remarkable variety of inflections and verbal attitudes makes a meaningful and hilarious commentary out of the two simplest words in any language. It is something memorable.

His performance as the general of Concordia, a tiny mock republic feverishly wooed by Russia and the U.S. to solicit its vital UN vote, is a beautiful blend of outrageous mugging and sly comment. When he's on, the picture's at its best. Miss Dee and Gavin costar as daughter and son of the U.S. and Russian ambassadors to Concordia, respectively, whose romance and marriage ultimately blots out the political crisis, representing Ustinov's love-and-laughter platform for harmonious international relations, which he underlines in the film with a curiously subdued and serious ending that seems just a mite too precious and obvious for what is essentially a satire that should convey its own conclusions without spelling them out.

Miss Dee does a commercial job. Gavin is not at all believable as a Russian, but fortunately such authenticity is almost superfluous and definitely secondary to the role's physical specifications, which he suits admirably.

Akim Tamiroff is a comedy standout as the Russ ambassador, and other prominent first-rate enactments are delivered by John Phillips, Tamara Shayne, Rik Von Nutter, Alix Talton, Suzanne Cloutier (Mrs. Ustinov), Peter Jones, Carl Don, Moura Budberg and Edward Atienza.

Under the surveillance of director Ustinov's keen discerning eye, the cinematic contributions as well as the performances are expert. This goes for Robert Krasker's rich Technicolor photography, Alexander Trauner's art direction (which succeeds in making Concordia out of Rome), Renzo Lucidi's editing and Mario Nascimbene's music. *Tube.*

Angel Baby

Heavyhanded meller dealing with Dixie faith healers, wheelers and dealers. Not much b.o. punch.

Hollywood, May 1.

Allied Artists release of Thomas F. Woods production. Stars George Hamilton, Mercedes McCambridge, Joan Blondell, Henry Jones, Burt Reynolds, Roger Clark; introduces Salome Jens. Directed by Paul Wendkos. Screenplay, Orin Borsten, Paul Mason, Samuel Roeca, from novel, "Jenny Angel," by Elsie Oaks Barber; camera, Haskey Wexler, Jack Marta; editor, Betty J. Lane; art director, Val Tamelin; music, Wayne Shanklin; sound, Al Overton; assistant director, Leonard Kazman. Reviewed at Academy Awards Theatre, May 1, '61. Running time, 97 MINS.
Paul Strand .... George Hamilton
Sarah Strand ....Mercedes McCambridge
Mollie Hays .... Joan Blondell
Ben Hays .... Henry Jones
Hoke Adams .... Burt Reynolds
Sam Wilcox .... Roger Clark
Otis Finch .... Dudley Remus
Ma Brooks .... Victoria Adams
Big Cripple .... Harry Swoger
Farm Girl .... Barbara Biggart
Little Boy .... Davy Biladeau
Angel Baby .... Salome Jens

The practice of faith healing, as it is questionably evoked in the deep South, is the tricky subject upon which some ponderous and heavyhanded melodramatics are heaped in Allied Artists' "Angel Baby." This is a topic that requires careful and serious scrutiny if it is to form the basis for valid, effective drama. It receives no such cogent consideration from the Thomas F. Woods production, a confusing and tastelessly sensational hodge-podge of hallelu-cinations. There will be superficial reminders of the evangelism of "Elmer Gantry."

It is difficult to see where "Angel Baby" will attain much of an intensity in the boxoffice spectrum. If that perennial stimulant, a hint of sex, is to characterize the ad campaign, then the picture will be enticing attendance from those very patrons for whom its rather implausible approach to an inflammatory subject may excite the most undesirable of impressions and conclusions.

After exposing some of the shadier implications of the faith-healing-for-money trade, the film proceeds to tear its own argument to tatters by resolving the issue with a parting burst of purely fanciful, artificial theatricality. The Orin Borsten-Paul Mason-Samuel Roeca scenario, constructed from the novel, "Jenny Angel," by Elsie Oaks Barber, tells the tale of a mute young lady (Salome Jens) in whom evangelistic fervor is instilled following restoration of her voice through the heaven-guided power of a young healer (George Hamilton).

Surviving some weighty romantic and sexual entanglements, Miss Jens promptly sets up her own prayer shop, but falls under the commercial influence of a shady operator who, unbeknownst to his naive star attraction, plants mock invalids in the throngs who flock to her for instant cure. Seriously shaken when the racket is exposed, Miss Jens wretchedly gravitates to a neighboring community, where her reputation is still unbesmirched, and immediately restores her own faith in herself by coaxing mobility out of a hopelessly lame child, with Hamilton hovering among the spectators for the inevitable reconciliation. Faith-healing has been credited with some startling displays of recovery, but the climactic feat exhibited here must stand in a class by itself. It is a moment of supreme contrivance where a more tangible illustration of the power of suggestion through

faith and prayer could at least have brought the film to a less dazzling, but far more sound, conclusion.

Miss Jens, in her initial screen exposure, plays the difficult role with sufficient intensity and integrity. Hamilton does generally well by his taxing assignment, but would have gone a thespic step further by instilling a slightly broader variety of expression into his characterization, principally in his dispatch of the romantic portions of his labor.

Accomplished veterans the likes of Mercedes McCambridge and Joan Blondell lend the project a special polish, and there is more than adequate featured support from Henry Jones, Bert Reynolds and Roger Clark. Director Paul Wendkos neatly evades some of the story's more melodramatic ramifications, but he's up against just too much emotional fire and brimstone for sustained dramatic comfort.

Camerawork by Haskel Wexler and Jack Marta, editing by Betty J. Lane and art direction by Val Tamelin are favorably discharged. Wayne Shanklin's score incorporates several appropriate spiritual ditties. *Tube.*

El Pandillero
(Gang Leader)
(MEXICAN)

Mexico City, May 2.
Peliculas Nacionales release of Cinematografica Filmex production. Stars Tin-Tan, Virma Gonzalez, Tito Junco; features Jose Galvez, Tito Novaro, Marcelo Chavez, Guillermo Rivas, Carlos Ancira, Carlos Nieto, Ramon Valdez, Fanny Shiller, Adolfo Aguilar, Francisco Sandoval. Directed by Rafael Baledon. Screenplay, Rafael Baledon, Alfredo Ruanova, Carlos Toscada; camera, Agustin Martinez Solares; music, Gustavo Cesar Carrion. At Orfeon Theatre, Mexico City. Running time, 80 MINS.

Comic Tin-Tan is popular with the Mexican public, and for all that he turns out one picture after the other, he has a certain comedy flair and versatility in interpreting different types. These range from a humble Indian to a sophisticated man of the world. Coupled with this is agility as a dancer and a more or less pleasing voice. Comic also has a pleasing personality and delivery worthy of better efforts than the hastily put together scripts assigned him.

In this one, he plays the role of a gangster, and embellishes it with his own special comic delivery and situations. Virma Gonzales, who appeared in the Mexican version of "The Redhead" on the stage, contributes the feminine fluff. Tito Junco, Marcelo Chavez and Jose Galvez add to the comedy.

Tin Tan in some ways is tops as a comedian with the humbler fans in nabe houses. And here, as well as in Latin American areas where his name is being built up, including the Spanish language circuit in the American southwest, this picture will garner fair boxoffice. *Emil.*

Le Ciel Et La Boue
(Sky and Mud)
(FRENCH-COLOR)

Cannes, May 9.
Rank rlease of Ardennes Film production. Written and directed by Pierre-Dominique Gaisseau; commentary, Gerard Elloye, Gaisseau; camera (Agfa), Gilbert Sarthe; editor, Georges Arnstam. At

Cannes Film Fest. Running time, 90 MINS.

This film is a true and affecting documentary on an exploration safari through some uncharted sections of the island of New Guinea. Primitive men and hardships are evoked without frills. Pic is a penetrating adventure film with arty chances in store. This has feeling for the place and peoples and a wry, incisive insight.

Group first goes by boat and encounters various villages of men still in the stone age era of life. Though headhunters and even cannibals, most of them are being slowly civilized. The group gets caught in a dry spell and has to trek overland. They are helped by periodic plane drops but the harrowing trek is told without false heroics and overtones but in a well realized adventurous and objective manner.

Nudity is acceptable here, being an essential part of these people. There is a definite feeling in the lensing, editing and conception of this absorbing film. Deft ironic notes of outside moon and space shots in this pre-historic setting also underline what man has yet to accomplish and what might have been lost in the benefits of civilization. Color is fine. This subject can take its place among the many outstanding documentaries in filmic history. A love and respect for exploration and the people pervades this unusual pic.

Of course, this needs careful handling but has the essentials for a good arty theatre. *Mosk.*

Cannes Festival

The Connection

Cannes, May 9.
Lewis Allen-Shirley Clarke production and release. With Warren Finnerty, Gary Goodrow, James Anderson, Jerome Raphael, Carl Lee, William Redfield, Barbara Winchester. Directed and edited by Shirley Clarke. Screenplay, Jack Gelber from his own off-Broadway play; camera, Arthur Ornitz; music, Freddie Redd. At Cannes Film Fest. Running time, 110 MINS.
Leach .... Warren Finnerty
Ernie .... Gary Goodrow
Sam .... James Anderson
Solly .... Jerome Raphael
Cowboy .... Carl Lee
Sister .... Barbara Winchester
Director .... William Redfield
J. J. Burden .... Roscoe Brown
Harry .... Henry Proach
Piano .... Freddie Redd
Sax .... Jack McLean
Bass .... Michael Mattos
Drums .... Larry Richie

Hollywood, U.S. art film distribs, foreign capitals and film festivals have been made aware in the last couple of years, of an interesting non-Hollywood independent filmmaking group developing in N.Y. This group has definitely arrived with the latest indie pic, "The Connection," which shows that America can make its own art films.

If by art film is meant one dealing with an unusual theme in a non-conventional and frank manner, this pic fits this description aptly. The tale of a group of junkies waiting for their fix also has an edge and tingle of life which could mean specialized depth

distrib as well as art slotting. It uses some off-color words, but they are part of the scene and never utilized for shock. Subject is treated objectively, and, though censor problems seem certain, it should have no trouble in some enlightened spots.

An arty documentary filmmaker is supposed to be making a film about a group of supposedly real drug addicts in the pad and Leach (Warren Finnerty) a fastidious, repressed homosexual. Their payment is the heroin that is to be bought by someone called Cowboy (Carl Lee). But the addicts do not take easily to the filmic attempts of the "square," that is the uninitiated filmite.

They walk, wrangle, joke and chafe during their wait. A group of musicians, also waiting, go into jazz pieces. The music is well meshed as both backgrounds and the sudden dramatic underline or break the tempo. Then Cowboy arrives bringing a Salvation Army woman who saved him from the police. He gives the shots in the uncomprehending woman's presence who finally thinks they are drinking in the bathroom, and exits.

The square filmaker takes his first shot to understand the results first-hand but only gets sick. One takes an overdose and nearly dies. Technique of a flim within a film keeps alive an awareness that these may be real addicts. So the justification of all lensing angles by the two would-be filmakers via lens changes and film breaks allow editor-director Shirley Clarke to exercise a complete control on this group of addicts.

There is no story but it is a successful, living experience. The characters, crisp lingo and wry wit get laughs, for their seeming reality and lack of preaching have them acceptable types that one can laugh with. There are no phony dramatics here. Many voice vague reasons for being what they are. One says that most people are hooked in some way, and they just happen to have an illegal vice.

The result is a jolting look at the hip and beat drug crowd. Miss Clarke shows a definite filmic flair in keeping this one room pic constantly revealing and absorbing. Tensions grow and ebb, revelations are made, and then the climax of a near-death leads to a rout of most of them to end it all on a muted note.

The moody music of Freddie Redd, Arthur Ornitz's atmospheric lensing, the expert set and, above all, Miss Clarke's virile handling of this group knits this into a unique vehicle.

"Shadows," "Come Back Africa" and "Wedding and Babies" all won out-of-competition prizes at foreign fests. "Connection" is the most technically perfect of the group, having been made by a minimum all-union crew for $170,-000. It has been invited by the Federation of French Film Authors in an out-of-competition spot at the present Cannes Fest. It is in the running for the International Film Critic's award.

Jack Gelber's (he scripted from his own play) flair for characters and mood are also a plus factor even if some of the final general reasons for the condition of the characters may be cursory. But the actors are all expert in giving these characters a density of life.

Finnerty's snarling, petty pad

owner; Lee's commanding, strong Cowboy; William Redfield's clumsy attempts as the filmmaker; Gary Goodrow's psychopathic member, James Anderson's talky addict and Jerome Raphael's more philosophical one are all standout. Miss Clarke, for her first feature, after making some prizewinning shorts, has turned out a tour de force.
Mosk.

La Viaccia
(The Bad Street)
(ITALIAN)
Cannes, May 9.

Titanus release of an Alfredo Bini production for Titanus-Arcofilm-Galatea. Stars Claudia Cardinale, Jean Paul Belmondo, Pietro Germi, Paul Frankeur; features Gabriella Pallotta, Romolo Valli, Gina Sanmarco, Franco Balducci, Emma Baron, Marcella Valeri, Gianna Giacchetti, Dante Posani, Nando Angelini, Aurelio Nardi, Giuseppe Tosi. Directed by Mauro Bolognini. Screenplay, Vasco Pratolini, P. F. Campanile, Massimo Franciosa, from novel, "L'Eredita," by Mario Pratesi; camera, Leonida Barboni; music, Piero Piccioni, with themes by Debussy. At Cannes Film Fest. Running time, **106 MINS.**
Amerigo .... Jean Paul Belmondo
Bianca .... Claudia Cardinale
Stefano .... Pietro Germi
Ferdinando .... Paul Frankeur
Carmelinda .... Gabriella Pallotta
Dante .... Romolo Valli

Elegant period drama with a top-notch cast and stylish direction by Mauro Bolognini for prestige impact at home and abroad. Despite its many qualities, this needs a hard sell to give it wider acceptance because it's more attuned to arty theatres.

Amerigo (J. P. Belmondo) is a farmer's son who prefers city life in the Florence of 1885 to work on his homestead. In love with a comely, young prostitute, he at first steals money from his uncle to be with her. When the family cuts him off, he even seeks employment in the call house where she works. Frustrated by her chill reactions to his proposals, and jealous of another one of her clients, he gets into a fight and is knifed. Repulsed once more by the girl, who feels she has suffered enough and doesn't want to be involved, he drags himself away and dies alone, within sight of his farm home.

Film is a stylist's delight, with costumes, sets, and lighting in general, literally reeking with period atmosphere. So much so that at times that the action bogs down to give way to pure setting. Hence, the audience may get the impression that nothing is really going on at all. But then director Bolognini adds a touch of humor or drama, and sets things rolling again.

Some trimming for pace would help, however. Claudia Cardinale is excellent as the voluptuous, hardened-by-life prostie, ably seconded by Jean Paul Belmondo as the farm boy. Pietro Germi contributes a neat cameo as his stubborn father, as does Paul Frankeur as his uncle. Also good are Gina Sanmarco, as the madam, and Gabriella Pallotta, as a younger sister. Many supporting players lend colorful assists.

Art director Pierro Tosi deserves a separate hand for his outstanding work in recreating period and place with dazzling efefct, with an added not to producer Alfredo Bini for a praiseworthy coordination effort on a difficult project.
Hawk.

L'Annee Derniere A Marienbad
(Last Year in Marienbad)
(FRENCH-DYALISCOPE)
Cannes, May 9.

Cocinor release of Terra-Cormoran-Precitel-Como-Argos-Tamara-Cinetel-Silver Film-Cineriz production. With Delphine Seyrig, Georgio Albertazzi, Sacha Pitoeff. Directed by Alain Resnais. Screenplay, Alain Robbe-Grillet; camera, Sacha Vierny; editor, Henri Colpi. At Cannes Film Fest. Running time, **90 MINS.**
Woman .... Delphine Seyrig
Man .... Sacha Pitoeff
Other Man .... Sacha Pitoeff

One of the favorites for repping France at the presently unspooling Cannes Fest, this film was passed over by Culture Minister Andre Malraux. It is a difficult, daring film and a definite festival pic but was not picked. It has been shown in the outside commercial setup of Fest. This looms a chancey entry on its uncompromising form and treatment, and an arty one at best.

However, Western world audiences have begun to show a penchant for offbeat pix. Ingmar Bergman is considered to have made it in arties. And Michaelangelo Antonioni's "Adventure," though booed at last year's Cannes Fest, went on to be a hit here and in some other spots. And director Alain Resnais (this is his second pic) found his first, "Hiroshima Mon Amour," going on to become a sound hit in the U. S. and in Europe despite its unusual theme. But this vehicle takes plenty of patience from any audience, including the most esthetic. Hence, it is a limited entry.

Where "Hiroshima" evolved on two planes, this film takes place on various levels of thought. It evokes the current literature of description with human memory, emotions hazy and strange things.

A man sees a woman in a fashionable German hotel that looks like an old chateau. He keeps asking her if she remembers last year and they are seen through the talk in different periods, mixing the present with the past and the varying versions of the past. All other characters, except a man who might be her husband, are seen as mere silhouettes, mouthing inanities or platitudes. Through this it slowly appears that maybe he had made advances to her last year at this resort, or some other place, and now she would leave with him.

This could have been a simple story but the director was not interested in that. His aim seems to be to lay bare the impossibility of true remembrance, and the action of these people. They are never made clear. But the director has given this a brilliant imagery and made the characters a part of the baroque surroundings of this castle-like hotel.

The actors have the faces that can be utilized in this maze-like tale. Delphine Seyrig looks like a pre-war romantic film heroine with her slender body and studied poses. The men are also done plastically.

Resnais again shows his cold feeling for expert images and at times some human attitude or feeling breaks through. It is not clear whether this is to show a decadent, rich fading class system in the late '30's, or if it is mainly about the difficulties of loving or communication. At any rate it will be talked about. This might be

that arty pic which could draw if well handled and spotted. But is seems a limited if worthy try.

Editing is outstanding, keeping its various layers of thought, action and posing fluid, and intact. Lensing too is exemplary. *Mosk.*

On the Double
(COLOR—PANAVISION)

Repeating the usual look-alike plot allows Danny Kaye to be funny only part of the time. Modest results.

Paramount release of Jack Rose production. Stars Danny Kaye, Dana Wynter; features Wilfrid Hyde White, Margaret Rutherford, Diana Dors. Directed by Melville Shavelson. Written by Rose and Shavelson; camera, Harry Stradling; editor, Frank Bracht; music, Leith Stevens; songs, Sylvia Fine. Previewed Loew's 83d Street Theatre, N.Y., May 9, '61. Running time, **92 MINS.**

Pfc. Ernie Williams .... Danny Kaye
Lady Margaret MacKenzie-Smith .... Dana Wynter
Colonel Somerset .. Wilfrid Hyde White
Lady Vivian .... Margaret Rutherford
Sergeant Bridget Stanhope Diana Dors
Captain Patterson .... Alan Cuthbertson
Corporal Joseph Praeger .... Jesse White
Colonel Rock Houston Gregory Walcott
Sergeant Colin Twickenham .... Terrence De Marney
General Carleton Browne Wiffingham .... Rex Evans
Oberkommandant .... Rudolph Anders
Blankmeister .... Edgar Barrier
General Zlinkov .... Ben Astar

Mel Shavelson and Jack Ross might have done better by Danny Kaye. Amiable, versatile comedian, in "On the Double," is too often, rather than himself, a crazy mixed-up zanyist. The intent clearly was to go all in broad farce.

Kaye has done wacky routines in past, of course, but somehow injecting expert subtleties with some depth. That's missing in "Double"—depth. It's just one-dimensional surface comedy.

The Shavelson-Rose production, Panavisioned and Technicolored, has Kaye as an American PFC in England pre-D Day. Allied Intelligence is concerned about the welfare of a British general who's a key figure in mapping the invasion. They find the Yank and the Britisher to be look-alikes. Kaye is assigned to the job of posing as the general, so that the genuine latter can be well hidden from harm and be free to give full time to the landing blueprint. Kaye plays the two parts, naturally, a la "Prison of Zenda" and umpteen other variations of the look-alike thing.

Wilfrid Hyde White and Gregory Walcott represent Intelligence. Diana Dors, flashily attractive, is the general's chauffeur and romantic intimate, although he's married to Dana Wynter, who happens to be out of the country, and who happens to return unexpectedly. She assumes the Yank soldier to be her husband but is not to be deceived too long.

The real general is killed (leaving Kaye and Miss Wynter to eventually become togetherness personified) and, Kaye is kidnapped. Among those shipping him off to Germany is Miss Dors. The chick is a Nazi spy.

Kaye escapes and the Gestapo pursuit of him provides the base for the burlesque shenanigans. In eluding his would-be captors, he's in one door and out the other of a German opera house, beerhall and a plane in flight. When he goes out the latter he's fortunate enough to have a parachute with him.

Kaye's role is more than a dual one. In trying to outwit the Germans he masquerades as Marlene Dietrich, or as close as he can get, in a throaty nitery song, as a Gestapo agent, as a Nazi pilot, and, indeed, even Hitler himself.

Kaye is expert comic talent, gets many laughs on and off in the zany (though somehow old-fashioned) chase and quick disguise madcap stuff. His takeoff on Miss Dietrich is a honey.

Some might wonder about the timeliness of the subject material, even if only done for laughs. An horrified era in world history has been greatly re-spotlighted of late via the Shirer book, Eichmann and "Nazi Beast" pictures. Does this background lend itself to spoofing?

The parts are played by pros down the line, including those aforementioned and Margaret Rutherford, Terrence De Marney, Allan Cuthbertson, Rex Evans and others.

Rose's production has interesting backgrounds via London locationing and Harry Stradling's photography (Technicolor and Panavision) is quick and on the beam. Shavelson's direction of a script by himself and Rose, along with the tight editing, stresses rapid-fire movement.

Two songs by Sylvia Fine, one a ballad, "My Darlin' Meggie," and the other tailored for Kaye's nimble-tongue delivery, titled "The Mackenzie Hielanders," fit in as entertainment assets and Leith Stevens' music backs up everything nicely.

All adds up to fair Kaye.

Gene.

David And Goliath
(ITALIAN—TOTALSCOPE—COLOR)

Exploitable adaptation of the Biblical story, satisfactory for general audiences, but a bit bulky and inaccurate for the more discriminating. Okay b.o. contender.

Hollywood, May 11.

Allied Artists release of Emimmo Salvi production. Stars Orson Welles: with Ivo Payer, Edward Hilton, Masimo Serato, Eleonora Rossi Drago, Giulia Rubini, Pierre Cressoy, Furio Meniconi, Kronos, Dante Maggio, Luigi Tosi, Umberto Fiz, Ugo Sasso. Directed by Richard Pottier, Ferdinando Baldi. Screenplay, Umberto Scarpeli, Gino Mangini, Ambrigio Molteni, Salvi; camera (Eastman), Carlo Fiore; editor, Franco Fraticelli; art director, Oscar D'Amico; music, Carlo Innocenzi; sound, Pietro Ortolani, Vruno Moreal; assistant director, France Baldanelle. Reviewed at the studio, May 11, '61. Running time, **95 MINS.**

King Saul .... Orson Welles
David .... Ivo Payer
Prophet Samuel. .... Edward Hilton
Abner .... Masimo Serato
Merab .... Eleonora Rossi Drago
Michal .... Giulia Rubini
Jonathan .... Pierre Cressoy
King Asrod .... Furio Meniconi
Goliath .... Krosnos
Cret .... Dante Maggio
Benjamin Di Gaba .... Luigi Tosi
Lazar .... Umberto Fiz
Huro .... Ugo Sasso

From the well-known passage in the Old Testament, the Italian film industry has mounted an exploitable attraction that, in terms of characterization and story development, is a cut above the average costume epic from that country. More discerning filmgoers will be dismayed over several liberties taken with key facets of the Biblical tale, and many will find the going ponderous owing to the familiarity factor inherent in this popular story, but the average easygoing customer for whom the film is designed and the hard-sell campaign geared to entice should discover ample entertainment value in the experience. The Allied Artists release should make a swift but satisfactory domestic impression.

The presence of Orson Welles no doubt will interest aficionados of the cinema, and should amount to an added lure for those who have closely followed this man's career through its ups and downs. Welles plays King Saul, bringing to the role his characteristic intensity and, to some extent, his respect for the grotesque magic of facial makeup. His approach, reserved, brooding and introspective, is successful in suggesting the psychological decline of the once-mighty monarch, but the role is not a particularly formidable challenge to his histrionic energy, latitude and invention.

Acting, in general, is on a higher plane than is customary in these post-dubbed Italo spectacle imports. Especially satisfactory are Edward Hilton as the Prophet Samuel, handsome Ivo Payer as David and Furio Meniconi as Asrod, the foul Philistine king. Kronos, a European circus and music hall figure, is ideally suited for the physical specifications of the Goliath role. Others in important parts are Masico Serato, Eleonora Rossi Drago, Giulia Rubini, Pierre Cressoy and Danta Maggio.

There is a smattering of sex, notably a scene in which Goliath is taunted by a ring of suggestively undulating dancing girls, but nothing compared to the usual Italian sex spectacle. Direction, a chore shared by Richard Pottier and Ferdinando Baldi, is measured, but soundly so. The quality and character of Carlo Fiore's Eastman Color photography varies with the location. The film was shot in Rome, Jerusalem and Yugoslavia. Artwork by Oscar D'Amico is authentically ornate, and other departmental duties are skillfully dispatched.

Tube.

The Steel Claw
(COLOR)

Superficial war film with a Philippines setting. For fanciers of uncomplicated action. Light prospect.

Hollywood, May 9.

Warner Bros. release of George Montgomery production. Stars Montgomery. Directed by Montgomery. Screenplay, Ferde Grofe Jr., Malvin Wald, Montgomery; camera (Technicolor), Manuel Rojas; editor, Jack Murray; music, Harry Zimmerman; sound, Jack Milner; assistant directors, Barri, Vincent Nayve, Jairo Mullin. Reviewed at Academy Awards Theatre, April 25, '61. Running time, 96 **MINS.**

Capt. John Larsen . George Montgomery
Lolita .... Charito Luna
Santana .... Mario Barri
Frank Powers .... Paul Sorensen
Christina .... Amelia De La Rama
Rosa .... Carmen Austin
Dolph Rodriguez .... Ben Perez
Commander .... John MacGloan
Himself .... Joe Sison
A Father .... Pedro Faustino
Child .... Oscar Keesee Jr.
Sergeant .... Al Wyatt

"The Steel Claw" is an action film of the strictly non-cerebral variety designed presumably to cater only to the most diehard of straight war adventure fanciers. In that respect, while no bull's eye, it is roughly on target. But the George Montgomery (Ponderey) production is weakened by ludicrous dialog, lack of character definition or substance and an essentially unrealistic tone that diminishes audience concern, so the question is whether it can compile sufficient boxoffice mileage from those willing to accept such films at absolute face value. Endowed with no semblance of timeliness or marquee might, with which it might attract the necessary additional attention from more mature filmgoers, the Warner Bros. release appears to be a lower-berth prospect.

Montgomery undertakes the taxing four-ply assignment of producer-director-writer-star, but is not particularly successful in any of those departments. His on-the-spot production conveys a certain sense of immediacy, and the locale (the Philippines) is visually interesting, but it is a risky endeavor in that, by modern market standards, it is too dated and impersonal an approach to wartime conflict. As director, he exhibits a taste for hard-fighting, hard-drinking, hard-loving behavior, but his perception of personal relationships is awkward and two-dimensional. As the hero of the bland screenplay (which he penned with Ferde Grofe Jr. and Malvin Wald), the character of a Marine captain handicapped by the loss of a hand (there is an interesting do-it-yourself passage in which he forges himself a steel claw, or hook), Montgomery etches a straightforward portrait of a thoroughly familiar "man's man" leatherneck type.

The screenplay is concerned with efforts of this latter-day Captain Hook to rescue a General from the clutches of the Japanese at the outset of the war. The General, it transpires, is dead, but the hero has a deuce of a time making it to safety himself, doing so with the aid of two bands of Filipino guerrillas and the handicap of a young, critically-wounded native girl who hasn't the presence of mind to suppress a cough in a crisis (unintentionally producing the film's funniest line: "You must stop this coughing so we can hear the ship").

Of the Filipino thespians assembled by Montgomery, Mario Barri, as a guerilla leader, gives the best performance. The rest of the playing is largely artificial. Journeyman assists are contributed by cameraman Manual Rojas, editor Jack Murray and composer-conductor Harry Zimmerman.

Tube.

L'Imprevisto
(Unexpected)
(ITALO-FRENCH)

Rome, May 9.

Columbia release of a Gianni Hecht Lucari production for Documento (Rome)—Orsay (Paris). Features Tomas Milian, Anouk Aimee, Jeanne Valerie, Raymond Pellegrin, Jacques Morel, Donatella Erspamer, Giuseppe Porelli, Arianna Gormi, Yvette Beaumont, Philip Dumas, Guy Trejean. Directed by Alberto Lattuada. Screenplay, Edoardo Anton, Claude Brule, Aldo Buzzi, Noel Calef, from story by Anton; camera, Roberto Gerardi; music, Piero Piccioni; editor, Leo Catozzo. At Metropolitan, Rome. Running time, **106 MINS.**

Tomas .... Tomas Milian
Juliette .... Jeanne Valerie

Claire .... Anouk Aimee
Serizeille .... Raymond Pellegrin
Police Insp. .... Jacques Morel

A well-writeen kidnapping tale has been made into a crackerjack suspense entry by director Alberto Lattuada. When equipped with functional topnotch foreign-language soundtracks, pic (which boasts a French original track and was dubbed into Italian for the version seen) should find ready acceptance in general situations in most countries. Unfortunate lack of true marquee bait keeps this out of the international big time, but will in part be compensated by word-of-mouth. Film should as a result travel plenty.

Tale concerns the prepping and carrying out of a "perfect" kidnapping attempt (and bears some striking similarities to the Peugeot case in France, though written well ahead of that headline case), carried out by a young smalltown professor and two femme assistants, respectively his wife and mistress. Without revealing the plot further, suffice it to say that it's all extremely cleverly done and continuously punctuated by effective bits of suspense to hold audience attention to the end.

Directed with a sure hand and ably acted by Tomas Milian (the professor), Anouk Aimee (his wife), Jeanne Valerie (the other woman), Raymond Pellegrin (the victim's father), and a host of aptly chosen character players, the film is more a straightforward, no-message entertainment than an arty entry. It has a class and veneer not usually found in this kind of film.

Technical credits, with special nod to editing job by Leo Catozzo, are all good, though photographic quality on copy seen, an early print, was slightly uneven and could be corrected.   Hawk.

Vyssi Princip
(The High Princip)
(CZECH)
Berlin, May 9.
Progress release of Czech State Film production. With Frantisek Smolik, Jana Brejchova, Hanjo Hasse. Directed by Jiri Krejcik. Screenplay, Jan Drda and Krejcik; camera, Jaroslav Tuzar; music, Zdenek Liska; editing, J. Dobrichovsky. At Colosseum, East Berlin. Running time, 106 MINS.
The old professor......Frantisek Smolik
The lawyer .... Otomar Krejca
The daughter .... Jana Brejchova
Vlastik .... Ivan Mistrik
SS chief .... Hanjo Hasse
Vlastik's mother .... Marie Vascova

One of the most impressive films the Czech have turned out in recent years. It also is one of the most gripping feature films on Nazi brutality. It could sled into foreign markets although perhaps primarily as an arty house entry.

The action takes place in 1942 in Nazi-occupied Czechoslovakia shortly after the assassination of Reinhard Heydrich, the mighty SS chieftain of that era. Film deals with the fear the common Czech people had of SS and Gestapo, and concentrates on an old professor and his students. Three students have been arrested by the SS and are sentenced to death for a minor delinquency which actually was only a joke. The old professor tries to save the young men by pleading with the town's Gestapo chief. But they are brutally executed along with many others, men and women, explained by the Nazis with reprisals for the death of Heydrich.

Director Jiri Krejcik succeeds in creating convincing atmosphere. The mood of the then tragic years in Czechoslovakia is compellingly caught. This realistic subject is also praiseworthy for its moving performances. Frantisek Smolik's portrayal of the old professor is a thespian masterpiece. Hanjo Hasse turns in an excellent study of a cynical SS leader. Young and comely Jana Brejchova portrays a student girl. Also technically, this Czech production deserves a good classification.   Hans.

House of Fright
(Megascope—Eastmancolor)

An uninspired Jekyll-Hyde meller sans much shock and with only fair b.o. outlook. Has usual Hammer Bros. "Finish."

American-International Pictures release of a Hammer Bros. film produced by Michael Carreras. Stars Paul Massie, Dawn Addams, Christopher Lee. Directed by Terence Fischer. Screenplay by Wolf Mankowitz, based on the Robert Louis Stevenson story; photography (Eastmancolor) by Jack Asher; music, John Hollingsworth. Reviewed in N. Y., May 10, '61. Running time, 80 MINS.

It's customary for Britain's Hammer Bros. to give their shock and sci-fi entries plenty of loving production care, and, for the most part, "House of Fright" meets this expectation. Unfortunately, the effort has been lavished on form but not enough on content in this film, so its wicket prospects shape merely fair—and that provided some hardsell backs up the American-International release. AIP, being exploitation-minded, doubtless will.

Company, incidentally, originally tagged the pic "Jekyll's Inferno" (the Hammer title was "Two Faces of Dr. Jekyll"), but switched to "House of Fright" for "commercial reasons." Decision seems wise, since the Jekyll-Hyde antics have been sufficiently worked over, and in theory any title tipping the split-personality theme would have discouraged patronage.

In this screen translation of the Robert Louis Stevenson tale, the shock aspects are rather tame. There is little to horrify audiences, of whatever age. There is, however, abundant flouting of the moral code — adultery, two rapes and the standard shocker genre violence—that make this anything but a kiddie's matinee film.

Yarn has the grist for an intriguing and awesome psychological study—certainly the basic premise is full of exciting promise along that line. Instead, the Wolf Mankowitz screenplay is superficial and surprisingly uninspired in both logic and suspense value. Some of the bygone hokum that characterized this idiom would have been welcome. Such plausibility as it pretends to isn't helped, for instance, when Jekyll's beard vanishes without explanation when the Hyde in him is dominant. There are also moments of unintended comedy that don't help.

Film's competently acted, though Terence Fischer's direction is as tacky as the script. (Cuts made in U.S. for Code and Legion?) Paul Massie, as Jekyll and Hyde, does better in capturing the doctor's self struggle than the producers had any right to expect. Dawn Addams as his faithless wife does as well as she can with a foolishly drawn part, and Christopher Lee as her paramour is good in a way reminiscent of an oily riverboat gambler.

Film's best moments are furnished in a can-can sequence that's given excellent pictorial play. Michael Hollingsworth's score is engagingly romantic, and other technical aspects are okay. Pic is in Eastmancolor and a widescreen process called Megascope.   Pit.

The Warrior Empress
(ITALIAN—C'SCOPE—COLOR)

Exploitably sexy, sumptuous but shallow adventure meller about political corruption and romantic intrigue on an ancient isle.

Hollywood, May 10.
Columbia Pictures release of Gianni Hecht Lucari production. Stars Kerwin Mathews, Tina Louise; features Riccardo Garrone, Susy Golgi, Alberto Farnesa, Enrico Maria Salerno. Directed by Pietro Francisci. Screenplay, Ennio De Concini, Francisci, Luciano Martino, from a story by Francisci; camera (Eastman), Carlo Carlini; editor, Nino Baragli; art director, Giulio Bongini; music, Francesco Lavagnino; assistant director, Pietro Nuccorini. Reviewed at the studio, May 10, '61. Running time, 101 MINS.
Phaon .... Kerwin Mathews
Sappho .... Tina Louise
Hyperbius .... Riccardo Garrone
Actis .... Susy Golgi
Laricus .... Alberto Farenese
Melanchrus .... Enrico Maria Salerno
Paeone .... Antonio Batistella
Priestess .... Strelsa Brown
Dyla .... Annie Gorassini
Cleide .... Lilly Mantovani
Man With Scar .... Aldo Fiorelli
Sappho's Nurse .... Elda Tattoli
Peasant Woman .... Isa Crescenzi

The stream of escapist sextravaganzas from Italy continues in "The Warrior Empress," an excessive, fanciful account of masculine goings-on and feminine comings-off in and around the notorious isle of Lesbos, circa 600 B.C. Like most of the recent costume capers in heavy Italics that have bombarded the domestic market, this one, released by Columbia, is suitable only for the hit-and-run school of contemporary theatrical exhibition—a slippery but sound technique better known as instant saturation.

Within the first 10 minutes mad montage includes one fierce ambush, one bloody passage of hand-to-hand saber combat, one skirmish between man and beast in a lion moat, one chariot race with ladies at the reins (Ben-Hurs), and an exotic boating and terpsichorean ritual conducted by a bevy of wispily-frocked Lesbosomy creatures who make the Goldwyn Girls seem adolescent by comparison.

Balance of the sit-back-and-relaxathon is concerned with the efforts of the underprivileged people of Mytilene to overthrow their decadent government and rid the impoverished monarchy of taxation without representation. Most of the action takes place in the Temple of Aphrodite, a kind of finishing school for high priestesses that more closely resembles in its gay and giggly character a dormitory for sexy showgirls, and the dialog is peppered with perennially puny profundities such as "when a woman is angry, she is even more beautiful."

The leading romantic players are dashing Kerwin Mathews and statuesque Tina Louise, who in their inability to communicate or woo in harmony suggests a 26-century-old variation on the Bickersons. All of the playing, given to stereotype, is further burdened by post-dubbing, but director Pietro Francisci has whipped up some divertingly violent and ingenious scenes to combat. Many of the lavish sets fashioned by art director Giulio Bongini resemble something inspired by a trip to Disneyland, and the fun house image is further conveyed by Carlo Carlini's Eastman Color photography. Francesco Lavagnino's score heightens the excitement, but Nino Baragli's editing is frequently jumpy.   Tube.

Vacasiones en Acapulco
(Vacations in Acapulco)
(MEXICAN—COLOR)

Mexico City, May 9.
Peliculas Nacionales release of Alameda Films (Cesar Santos Galindo) production. Stars Antonio Aguilar, Ariadna Welter; features Fernando Casanova, Sonia Furio, Rafael Bertrand, Mapita Cortes, Alfonso Mejia, Fernando Lujan. Directed by Fernando Cortes. Screenplay, Jose Maria Fernandez and Alfredo Varela Jr; camera (Eastmancolor), Jose Ortiz Ramos; music, Antonio Prieto and Navarro Brothers. At Cine Latino, Mexico City. Running time, 90 MINS.

Without any top stellar film names, this filmed musical comedy, with tourist overtones, is a pleasant enough effort in color. It is definitely big leap ahead of the so-called musical comedies made in Mexico where accent is on so-so ranchero or non-ranchero singers.

Jose Ortiz Ramos has used his color camera to good effect in depicting the tourist centers of Cuernavaca, Taxco and Acapulco. The script is not the main thing, but it revolves about a pair of newly-weds who go to Acapulco and return as a bored married couple, a long suffering father who goes vacationing with eight kids, an entertainer on the hunt for a millionaire; a girl from Chicago, of Mexican descent, who is in Acapulco to learn about her parent's native land; and the tired industrialist, who is prey for the gold digging entertainer.

The episodes are played against the colorful background of Acapulco's beaches, hotels and nightlife, with dozens of easy-to-look-at "Orquideas" (Orchids) of the national film industry (starlets) cavorting around in brief bathing costumes. Director Fernando Cortes has achieved a continuity and order in the various incidents. Therefore, the film escapes being merely a string of isolated incidents, interspersed with musical numbers, and comes out fairly interesting film fare.

On the travelogue side, apart from the scenic beauties, there are two nightclub scenes; the ski show; the "bat" man who soars into the air from a ski take off and other highlights of the port resort's life.

Players interpret their roles well, they simply play themselves. This is an agreeable sort of picture that is packing them in the Latino and cinemas in key areas, including Acapulco. This has better than average possibilities for Spanish markets, and may be spruced up as a tourist propaganda tour de force for English-speaking
                    Emil.

Cannes Festival

Domaren
(The Judge)
(SWEDISH)
Cannes, May 16.
Sandrews production and release. Stars Ingrid Thulin, Gunnar Hellstrom, Per Myrberg; features.Georg Rydeberg, Naima Wifstrand, Ulf Palmer. Directed by Alf Sjoberg. Screenplay, Vilhelm Moberg; Sjoberg from play by Moberg; camera, Sven Nykvist; editor, Lennart Wallen. At Cannes Film Fest. Running time, **110 MINS.**

Brita .... Ingrid Thulin
Arnold .... Gunnar Hellstrom
Krister .... Per Myrberg
The Judge .... Georg Rydberg
Teacher .... Naima Wifstrand
Psychiatrist .... Ulf Palmer

This picture concerns corruptive bureaucratic manipulating that drives a man into insanity and debases most of the people concerned. Played on an expressionistic level, with satiric, suspense and even ghost-like comic overtones, this is somewhat too involved to be able to make its point effectively. It appears a chancey foreign entry except for a few arty spots.

A rich, young man comes home from a stay in Italy with his new fiancee to find he has been ruined. The executor of his estate has milked him dry by forging documents and getting all his money tied up. The former is a mysterious judge who manages to block all his attempts to get justice, and the boy is finally driven insane. His fiancee tries to help and gets a young lawyer who wants to fight the judge. But he also sells out.

Though this has some deft suspense at the beginning when the boy is driven frantic by bureaucratic red tape, it gets too involved as it goes on. Picture makes its points in a too heavyhanded manner to have its condemnation of graft and power taken too seriously.

Alf Sjoberg, the director, has a good eye for imagery and handles his actors well. But this is all too worried and rambling to get across.

Pic would need specialized handling for off-shore chances plus some pruning of unnecessary hallucination scenes. *Mosk.*

The Wastrel
(ITALIAN)
(In English)
Cannes, May 16.
Lux release of Lux-Tiberia production. Stars Van Heflin, Ellie Lambetti; features Michael Stellman, Franco Fabrizi. Directed by Michael Cacoyannis. Screenplay, Cacoyannis. Frederic Wakeman from novel by Wakeman; camera, Piero Portalupi; editor, Alberto Gallitti. At Cannes Film Fest. Running time, **115 MINS.**

Duncan .... Van Heflin
Liana .... Ellie Lambetti
Rudi .... Franco Fabrizi
Cam .... Michael Stellman

This melodrama meanders somewhat and appears short in character portrayals. It concerns a rich playboy who early in life has learned to distrust women but falls in love and marries only to think he has been betrayed. This makes his wife's life a hell until

an adventure while adrift at sea with his young son brings on a probable change of heart.

A refusal to accompany his wife to a party leads to his going off on a boating trip with his son. The boat blows up and this leaves him alone with his boy on a little raft. As they try to make shore, a series of flashbacks shows how he met his wife, married her and loved her till a suspicion of betrayal led to a hellish continued union.

Film entered the Cannes Festival as a Cyprus pic though it was made in Italy for an Italo company, in English, with Yank star Van Heflin and Greek actress Ellie Lambetti. This consequently is a truly international film.

But the many temperaments have made this vehicle somewhat sluggish. The action and dialog is too simplified, lacking the depth of meaning so essential for this story.

Heflin turns in an acceptable performance as does Ellie Lambetti, as his wife. The latter has the looks and elegance which could spell a future in international pix. Technical credits are good, but this drama needs a little pruning to sift out some repetitious sea stuff. It then could possibly be an okay dualer bet or programmer for the U.S. on the Heflin name and its familiar love story. Arty theatre possibilities are chancey. *Mosk.*

Ototo
(Her Brother)
(JAPANESE-COLOR C'SCOPE)
Cannes, May 9.
Daiei production and release. Stars Keiko Kishi, Hiroshi Kawaguchi, Kinuyo Tanaka, Masayuki Mori; features Noburu Nakaya, Jun Hamamura. Directed by Kon Ichikawa. Screenplay, Yoko Mizuki; camera (Agfa), Kazuo Miyakawa; editor, T. Shimogawara. At Cannes Film Fest. Running time, **100 MINS.**

Gen .... Keiko Kishi
Hekiro .... Hiroshi Kawaguchi
Stepmother .... Kinuyo Tanaka
Father .... Masayuki Mori
Policeman .... Noburo Nakaya
Doctor .... Jun Hamamura

This film details a close relationship between a teenage brother and sister caused by negligent parents. The boy can only confide in his stalwart sister and uses her. He only begins to understand himself and life on his deathbed. Though meticulously done, this lacks a true connection with life. And it emerges a chancy foreign bet because of its slowness.

Director Kon Ichikawa has a deft flair for depicting character and quite a feeling for imagery. The production only takes dramatic moving form during the boy's illness. It transpires in 1926 when the old-fashioned family rituals of Japan are just beginning to take on a modern outlook. Color is splendid as is the use of Cinemascope, with acting and technical qualities outstanding.

The pic just tries to put too much emphasis and meaning on trivial aspects. *Mosk.*

Madalena
(GREEK)
Cannes, May 16.
Finos Films - Damaskinos - Michaelides production and release. Stars Dimitris Papamichael, Aliki Vouyouklaki; features Pantelis Zervos. Directed by Dinos Dimopoulos. Screenplay, Georges Roussos; camera, Walter Lassaly; editor, M. Zer-

vas. At Cannes Film Fest. Running time, **90 MINS.**

Madelena .... Aliki Vouyouklaki
Giorgas .... Dimitris Papamichael
Father .... Pantelis Zervos

Folksy comedy concerns a 17-year-old girl orphan with several brothers and sisters. She takes over the ferry of her defunct father on a little Greek island. She fights against a rival to keep her father's biz and support her charges. It divides the islanders but is finally settled by a marriage to the son of the rival ferry owner. Sentimental opus appears mainly for lingo situations aboard because it never transcends its conventional envelope.

However, this has a spirited, simple zest about it and has Greek star Aliki Vouyouklaki emerging as an engaging player whose mannerisms do not interfere with her charm. It is technically good. *Mosk.*

Piesen O Sivom Holubovi
(Song of the Gray Pigeon)
(CZECHOSLAVAKIAN)
Cannes, May 16.
Czech State Film production and release. With Pavel Polacek, Pavel Mattos, Karol Machata, Karla Chadimova. Directed by Stanislav Barabas. Screenplay, Ivan Bukovcan, Albert Marencin; camera, Vladimir Jesina; editor, W. Releden. At Cannes Film Fest. Running time, **98 MINS.**

Rudko .... Pavel Polacek
Vinco .... Pavel Mattos
Teacher .... Karol Machata
Natacha .... Karla Chadimova

Engaging moppet pic bundles five episodes during the last war as it affects three children. The terror of war is muted but ever present as the film unfolds. But it lacks the fillip of feeling to give it a sure atmosphere of the times. And some episodes are weak while others are too self-consciously preachy. This makes it a chancey item abroad except for a few special situations.

A 14-year-old and two more youthful ones are the heroes. At one stage, they meet a Russian soldier and save him from capture. Another time, they help partisans. They are present when a boy finds his father is a coward. They also meet with an escaped Russian girl guerilla, and finally find tragedy at the war's end in a mine field.

Some sketches are extremely perceptive, especially the one in which the 14-year-old gets his first taste of combat and the poignant ending. The pigeon is a bird with a crippled wing which is a pet of one of the boys. The children are well handled. Direction is intermittently successful in showing the war's colors through the eyes of the young. Technical qualities are good. *Mosk.*

Povestj Plamennykh Let
(Story of the Burning Years)
(RUSSIAN—COLOR)
Cannes, May 16.
Mosfilm production and release. With Nikolai Vingranovski, Svetlana Jgoun, Boris Andreev, Serguei Loukianov. Directed by Julia Solnsteva. Screenplay, Alexandre Dovchenko; camera (Sovcolor), Fyodor Provorov, Alexei Temerine; editor, Miss Solnsteva. At Cannes Film Fest. Running time, **85 MINS.**

Ivan .... Nikolai Vingranovski
Julia .... Svetlana Jgoun
General .... Boris Andreev
Professor .... Serguei Loukianov

For this Soviet pic there is a

step back to the heroic lyrical film of yore albeit with a step forward in the first use of 70m size film by the Russians. It is a stunning tribute to the will to survive of the soldiers and civilians during the last World War. Of course, the characters are larger than life and it all may seem like pamphleteering at times. So this is mainly an entry on its brilliantly conceived battle scenes for the foreign market. It is chancey but might be worth it on its exceptional technical qualities, direction and poetic conception.

One man symbolizes most of the soldiers and emerges a heroic figure doing almost superhuman deeds in his belief of a better life after the war.

The color is excellent and the 70m screen is fine for the massively conceived and executed battle scenes. This is based on a script by the late Russo director Alexandre Dovchenko, and was directed by his wife. It is a tribute to their relationship that the film has the lyrical stamp of Dovchenko. There is a feeling for the land, heroism and dedication that overcome the proselytizing at times. Film should be around comes time for prizes. *Mosk.*

Dan Cetrnaesti
(The 14th Day)
(YUGOSLAVIAN)
Cannes, May 9.
Lovcen production and release. With Nikola Popovic, Olga Spiridonovic, Karlo Bulic, Viktor Starcic. Directed by Zdravko Velimirovic. Screenplay, Borislav Petrovic; camera, Vladeta Lukic; editor, V. Raterjic. At Cannes Film Fest. Running time, **100 MINS.**

Timotije .... Nikola Popovic
Emilie .... Olga Spiridonovic
Zorz .... Karlo Bulic
Arsenije .... Viktor Starcic
Pavle .... Slobodan Pipinic

A Yugoslav law allows prisoners out for two weeks near the end of their terms. This film is about a few of them and their adventures on one of these sojourns. Film adds no deep insight into their return for a while to real life and is only a series of predictable episodes dominated by love. Film is a very chancey foreign item.

This has fairly spirited direction and acting but is just too sketchy and telegraphed to make much impact. Technical credits are par while the acting is good considering the one dimensional characters. *Mosk.*

Line
(NORWEGIAN)
Cannes, May 16.
Concord Film production and release. Stars Margrethe Robsahm, Toralv Maurstad. Directed by Nils Reinhardt Christensen. Screenplay, Axel Jensen; camera, Ragnar Sorensen, editor, M. Iversen. At Cannes Film Fest. Running time, **90 MINS.**

Line .... Margrethe Robsahm
Jacob .... Toralv Maurstad

Main theme is a young talented man coming of personal age and responsibility when he realizes that he has to learn to forgive others their faults. However, the unfoldment is fairly conventional and, though it sustains interest, looks mainly a Scandinavian entry with only exploitation chances

abroad via some nude swim scenes.

The youth comes home after years at sea with a novel and refuses to see his sick father who drove his mother insane and taunted him. He falls in love but almost kills the girl in a fit of jealous anger when self doubt and the refusal of his book undermine his logic.

Direction keeps this moving but never displays the insight to make the characters more than one dimensional. Acting is acceptable as are technical credits. *Mosk.*

Matka Joanna Od Aniołow
(Mother Jeanne And Angels)
(POLISH)

Cannes, May 9.
Polski State Film release of Kadr production. Stars Lucyna Winnicka, Mieczysław Voit; features Anna Ciepielewska, Maria Chwalibog, Kazmierz Fabisiak, Stanisław Jasiukiewicz. Directed by Jerzy Kawalerowicz. Screenplay, Tadeusz Konwicki, Kawalerowicz from novel by Jaroslaw Iwaszkiewicz; camera, Jerzy Wojcik; editor, W. Otocka. At Cannes Film Fest. Running time, 105 MINS.
Mother Jeanne .... Lucyna Winnicka
Abbe Suryn .... Mieczysław Voit
Sister Marguerite ....Anna Ciepielewska
Innkeeper .... Maria Chwalibog
Priest .... Kazmierz Fabisiak
Nobleman .... Stanisław Jasiukiewicz

This film is about bad and evil, darkness and light, and love and denial, set in the 17th Century in which a group of nuns supposedly possessed by demons make up the springboard of the plot. It creates a sobre impression, and looms mainly an arty entry abroad on theme and treatment.

A convent in a small town is being visited by high Catholic church officials trying to exorcise the nuns who seem to be in the grip of Satan. A local priest has been burned at the stake for supposedly creating this condition by sexual temptation of the nuns, especially the Mother superior who is supposed to bring on the collective hysteria of the group.

Into this setting comes a young priest who is also to help in the exorcism. His first meeting with the convent head, Mother Jeanne of the Angels, has her seemingly possessed by her demons and troubling the priest as she utters blasphemes and incites him.

She begs the priest to save her and help her to be a saint. To help her be free and go towards sainthood, he kills two innocent people to be forever a prey of the devil and thus allow her freedom.

Jerzy Kawalerowicz has given this sombre symbolical tale a real feeling for time and place. The acting of Lucyna Winnicka as the Mother Jeanne is exemplary as she vacillates between seeming madness and a need for faith and love. Mieczystaw Voit is powerful as the tortured priest while the remainder of the cast fits into the framework of this offbeat pic.

Its main problem abroad probably will be the fact that interpretations of the film's message may differ. There also could be Catholic objections, though the film seems to transcend its actual theme and place.

This film makes a point about withdrawal from life being dangerous. This is an offbeater with an arresting visual quality. But it is something that needs personalized handling and placement. As more specialized pix make their way into

U.S. arty theatre marts, this may be another that could pay off if wisely used. Technical credits and productcion dress are topnotch. *Mosk.*

La Peau Et Les Os
(Skin and Bones)
(FRENCH)

Cannes, May 16.
Pathe release of Raoul, Ploquin-Standard Film production. Stars Gerard Blain, Juliette Meyniel; features Rene Dary, Andre Oumansky, Julien Verdier. Written and directed by Jean-Paul Sassy, Jacques Panijel; camera, Georges Leclerc; editor, Pierre Gillette. At Cannes Film Fest. Running time, 85 MINS.
Mazur .... Gerard Blain
Michele .... Juliette Meyniel
Director .... Rene Dary
Charly .... Andre Oumansky
Buttiaux .... Julien Verdier

This prison pic vacillates between an attempt at a hardboiled depiction of the milieu and the story of a new prisoner who is helped by another out of sheer goodness. It lacks the tautness and virile qualities for the prison segments or the characterization and clarity. This is thus mainly a local item with only minor programmer chances abroad.

A newcomer in a prison leads to trouble when the leader tries to lord it over him. But in spite of persecution, the new man resists and then the ex-pesterers decide to help because they feel he is innocent. All this is contrived.

Direction is too soft and undecided to weld all this together while acting is only fair. Technical credits are also only passable. The film won a special French Film Critic's Award, the Prix Jean Vigo. It is difficult to see why. Pic played in the commercial section of the Cannes Festival. *Mosk.*

Snow White and the Three Stooges
(C'SCOPE—COLOR)

A tiresome excuse for a hokum vehicle that isn't funny. But the marquee values suggest good moppet biz.

Twentieth-Fox release of a Charles Wick production. Stars Three Stooges, Carol Heiss; features Edson Stroll, Patricia Medina, Guy Rolfe, Buddy Baer. Directed by Walter Lang. Screenplay, Noel Langley, Elwood Ullman, based on story by Charles Wick; camera, (DeLuxe color), Leon Shamroy; editor, Jack Holmes; art direction, Jack M. Smith, Maurice Ransford; songs, Harry Harris, Earl Brent; music supervision, Lyn Murray; assistant director, Eli Dunn. Reviewed at 20th-Fox homeoffice, N.Y., May 12, '61. Running time, 107 MINS.
Snow White .... Carol Heiss
Three Stooges .... Themselves
Prince Charming .... Edson Stroll
Queen .... Patricia Medina
Oga .... Guy Rolfe
Hordred .... Buddy Baer

First Columbia latched on to the Three Stooges after television revived their careers, and now it's the turn of 20th-Fox. At the same time, 20th is also bowing young Carol Heiss, the champion figure skater, in this anemic and overlong affair which is apt to have a difficult time keeping even moppets from fidgeting.

Exploiteers may be able to drum up some interest by promoting the filmic debut of Miss Heiss, but it's clearly the Stooges who will have to carry the boxoffice brunt, and their billing is enough to suggest okay prospects, though the pic is not much more than a passable dualer for the kiddies.

"Snow White and the Three Stooges" bears only slight resemblance to the venerable fairytale from which it derives. The casting necessarily required revisions, so there's no point carping with the liberties—just the stubborn insipidity.

The Charles Wick production in CinemaScope and DeLuxe color simply doesn't give the Stooges much chance to explode their eye-gouging propensities. Could be there was apprehension their brand of clowning might run into substantial resentment. The solicitude, if that was the case, is laudable—but ironically defeats the whole project. For without the free-wheeling style of their yesteryear fame, the Stooges haven't much else in the way of a comic gambit. In this pic they've been subdued to one or two brief physical eruptions, though there is a scene where pies collide with a character's face. But that's about it. (It's noteworthy that at the review screening, with a number of children on hand, whoops and laughs were conspicuous by their near absence.)

Miss Heiss is a fetching lass, and if she seems mostly marsh-mallowy midst all the greeting card settings, it is not her fault. The Noel Langley-Elwood Ullman paste-pot dialog makes it tough even for more experienced players. The skater does have a couple of opportunities to flash her blade prowess, naturally, and in this endeavor she is on far firmer footing. She also does some simple caroling in passable fashion, though of the four tunes (three by Harry Harris, one from Earl Brent), none is of lingering substance.

Film is generally tedious but does break out at a couple points

—with a chase, and the inevitable swordplay scene. But these are not comic in the sense one would associate with a Stooges picture. Also, while opportunities for sight gags abound, none is in evidence and it's as if the writers had no heart for such invention. Could be.

Patricia Medina is satisfactory as the wicked queen, and Edson Stroll gives an okay account of himself as Prince Charming. As the sinister adviser to the queen, Guy Rolfe rates a pat for understating a usually arch role. Buddy Baer is around as a huntsman torn by divided loyalties, and others in the cast are sufficient unto. Walter Lang's direction is only what the film deserves, and other technical aspects are oke.

All too plainly, this "Snow White" is dull grey. *Pit.*

Capture That Capsule

Heavyhanded cloak-and-dagger meller, but headline nature of title and topic makes it saleable merchandise on bottom half of twin-bills.

Hollywood, May 17.
Will Zens production. No stars. Directed by Zens. Screenplay, Zens, Jan Elblein; camera, Villa Lapenieke; editor, Bill Schaefer; art director, Cliff Bertrand; music, Arthur Hopkins; sound, Floyd Crow; assistant director, David Bradley. Reviewed at General Film Labs, May 17, '61. Running time, 75 MINS.
Ed Nowak .... Richard Miller
Al .... Dick O'Neil
Henry .... Richard Jordahl
Jack Reynolds .... Pat Bradley
Hamilton .... Carl Rogers
Mary .... Dorothy Schiller
Borman .... Ed Siani
Joe .... Doug Hughes
Mac .... Wylie Carter
Boy .... Michael David
Beach Girl .... Larae Phillips
Art .... Jack Treacy
Webster .... Ed Gangel
Persinger .... Richard Twohy
Party Girl .... Miriam Wilson
Boat Men .....Ron Wright, Lee Fortner
Game Officers..Gene Garner, Web Smith

The exploitably timely nature of its title and theme should make "Capture That Capsule" a fairly saleable lower berth program item. Beyond that, there is little of value in this heavyhanded account of a band of thoroughly hapless and unsavory fellow-travelers who are attempting to make off with a secret U.S. data capsule recovered after earthly re-entry from orbit. Picture, frankly and entirely commercial in design and resultantly contrived and ludicrous in execution, is the first of a projected four to be made by Riviera Productions, which will distribute through exchange areas on a states-rights basis.

Produced, directed and written by Will Zens, with aid in the latter capacity from Jan Elblein, the film is built on an extremely unstable story foundation in that the ring of Communists has been outwitted from the outset (the data capsule is a decoy, planted by U.S. agents who have chosen, for some ungodly reason, to play cat-and-mouse, resulting in three or four unnecessary murders). Tension is thus destroyed before it can be developed.

The acting is uncommonly stiff and artificial, especially in the characterizations of the "comrades," who are totally lacking in camaraderie and human decency, but display a remarkable affinity for American idiom ("you drive like a cotton-pickin' demon . . .

great balls of fire, let me outta here"). It is one thing to depict Communists as heavies. It is another to portray them as absolute buffoons and murderers. From top to bottom, it's a case of black-or-white stereotype. Zens' direction is confusing, particularly in the opaque expository section. Sporadic merit and visual interest is provided through Vilis Lapeniecks' lens maneuvers and Bill Schaefer's editing. *Tube.*

The Last Sunset
(COLOR)

Marquee cast will have to bail out shaky western yarn about a desperado with peculiar romantic problems. B.o. horsepower limited by contrived story.

Hollywood, May 8.
Universal release of Eugene Frenke-Edward Lewis production. Stars Rock Hudson, Kirk Douglas, Dorothy Malone, Joseph Cotten, Carol Lynley, Neville Brand. Directed by Robert Aldrich. Screenplay, Dalton Trumbo, based on novel, "Sundown At Crazy Horse." by Howard Rigsby; camera (Eastman), Ernest Laszlo; editor, Michael Luciano; art directors, Alexander Golitzen, Alfred Sweeney; music, Ernest Gold; sound, Waldon O. Watson, Don Cunliffe; assistant directors, Thomas J. Connors Jr., Nate Slott. Reviewed at Grauman's Chinese, May 8, '61. Running time, 112 MINS.

Dana Stribling ....Rock Hudson
Brendan O'Malley .... Kirk Douglas
Belle Breckenridge.....Dorothy Malone
John Breckenridge.......Joseph Cotten
Missy Breckenridge........ Carol Lynley
Frank Hobbs .... Neville Brand
Milton Wing .... Regis Toomey
Julesburg Kid .... Rad Fulton
Calverton .... Adam Williams
Ed Hobbs .... Jack Elam
Bowman .... John Shay
Jose .... Margarito De Luna
Rosario .... Jose Torvay

Some strong marquee display names have been assembled for "The Last Sunset," insulating the picture from the possibility of any extreme commercial misfortune. But the selling angles of the Eugene Franke-Edward Lewis production for Brynaprod S.A. are not matched on the screen, which is where any film's boxoffice destiny is ultimately determined. So, though emphasis on the cast is sure to be an important plus factor, the Universal release is shy the necessary additional values to make it a stout contender.

"The Last Sunset" is a large-scale western action melodrama penned by Dalton Trumbo from the pages of Howard Rigsby's novel, "Sundown At Crazy Horse." It is apparent that Trumbo has made an earnest attempt at three-dimensional characterization, at least insofar as the central character (Kirk Douglas) is concerned, but the tricky story he is attempting to bring to dramatic life is burdened with serious unlikelihoods, and the artificial strain is compounded by the fact a number of key scenes have a distractingly postured appearance and deliberate pace, a shortcoming for which director Robert Aldrich must take the rap.

Story centers on the plight of Douglas, an unstable gunman who, although acknowledged to be a killer, is also presented as a man of latent decency. Pursued across the border to Mexico by Rock Hudson, Douglas takes up with his childhood sweetheart, Dorothy Malone, with whom he shared an

abortive romance when she was only 16. There is a tipoff of events to come in that Miss Malone's daughter, Carol Lynley, is now a young lady of 16 herself. Enroute to the U.S. border, where a showdown is to occur, Hudson wins the contest for Miss Malone's affections and Douglas takes up romantically with Miss Lynley, only to discover she is his daughter. The studio has requested that the incest taboo ending not be revealed, but it's not likely to come as a surprise to seasoned filmgoers.

By far the acting standout of the picture is Joseph Cotten, who plays Miss Malone's doomed husband with a vigor and abandon that opens up a brand new vista of character parts for him. Douglas gives his characteristically intense portrayal. Hudson and Miss Malone are a bit wooden, Miss Lynley lovely to look at but uncertain in her characterization. Supporting performances are generally adequate.

An erratic work print witnessed at the screening made it difficult to properly evaluate Ernest Laszlo's Eastman Color photography. Editing by Michael Luciano and art direction by Alexander Golitzen and Alfred Sweeney are competent. Ernest Gold's listenable score is largely in the traditional western vein. A rather undistinguished ditty, "Pretty Little Girl in the Yellow Dress," was written for the picture by Dimitri Tiomkin and Ned Washington. *Tube.*

The Beast of Yucca Flats

Low budget indie meller about a scientist turned fiend by A-Bomb radiation. Bit crude, even for program double-billing.

Hollywood, May 18.
Anthony Cardoza-Roland Morin production. Stars Douglas Mellor, Larry Aten, Barbara Francis, Bing Stafford, Linda Bielima, Tor Johnson; features John Morrison, Tony Cardoza, Bob Labansat, Jim Oliphant. No character credits provided. Directed and screenplay by Coleman Francis; camera, John Cagle; editor, Francis; music, Irwin Nafshun, Al Remington; assistant director, Austin McKinney. Reviewed at Pathe Labs, May 18, '61. Running time, 60 MINS.

Filmaking at the $34,000-per level is of course fraught with production peril and artistic compromise. That sobering fact is all too clearly illustrated by "The Beast of Yucca Flats," an earnest but uncertain effort to tell a taut and different screen-story-with-a-message on discouragingly limited means. Picture, produced by Anthony Cardoza and Roland Morin and, as of now, shy the all importance release commitment, lamentably shapes up as somewhat crude even by lower berth program standards, which are, realistically, all it can aspire to.

Written and directed by Coleman Francis, the story centers around the plight of a noted scientist who, chased by Communist agents into an A-Bomb test area, is somehow transfigurated into an inhuman fiend through radiation after-effects.

Dialog is held to a bare minimum in favor of narration which is frequently too stilted, superfluous and condescending to be of much aid in advancing the story or

developing interest. There is definite menace in the behavior of the beast, but the activities of other characters are irrational and the direction often displays a jarring lack of geomorphic perspective, an important factor in a film so dependent upon the logic and nature of the chase. For instance, a good hundred errant bullets are fired at people, some almost at point-blank range. Credulity, in short, is strained throughout.

Camerawork and editing reflect the cut-corners character of the coin allotment, the former frequently so dark that one is squinting at silhouettes, the latter too jumbled for comfort.

All in all, this is a film that courageously attempts to lift itself out of the routine meller class by instilling a message (A-Bomb tests are history's pests) into the narrative, but the lifting requires greater resources and resourcefulness than these game cinemateers could quite muster this time out. *Tube.*

Nearly A Nasty Accident
(BRITISH)

Mildly amusing comedy which jerks a few yocks from slim, untidy story line; has amiable, unambitious appeal which rates it as a dualer, but no more.

London, May 16.
British Lion (in association with Britannia (Films) release of Bertram Ostrer production. Stars Jimmy Edwards, Kenneth Connor, Shirley Eaton. Directed by Don Chaffey. Screenplay, Jack Davies, Hugh Woodhouse; from play "Touch Wood," by David Stringer, David Carr; camera, Paul Beeson; editor, Bill Lenny; music, Ken Jones. Previewed at Columbia Theatre, London. Running time, 92 MINS.

Group Captain Kingsley. Jimmy Edwards
A.C.2 Alexander Wood. Kenneth Connor
Jean Briggs .... Shirley Eaton
Fl. Lt. Pocock .... Ronnie Stevens
Wagstaffe .... Richard Wattis
General Birkenshaw........Jon Pertwee
The Minister .... Eric Barker
Fl. Lt. Winters .... Peter Jones
Grogan .... Jack Watling
Warrant Officer Beech
                       Cyril Chamberlain
Miss Chamberlain .....Charlotte Mitchell
Lady Trowborough .... Joyce Carey

The success of a number of British comedies, notably the "Carry On" series, may be leading British film producers into the easy, complacent feeling that "anything goes." "Nearly a Nasty Accident" is yet another of the flimsy pix that strain a slim idea to the breaking point. It's amiable, produces a number of indulgent laughs, but has a "let's take a chance and see if it comes off" attitude. And this one does only occasionally.

Outline of the "plot" needs little space. It concerns a well-meaning, humble member of the air force who is crazy about anything mechanical, but is very accident-prone. He becomes a figure of national importance when he is reported missing and the Prime Minister orders that he must be found. He's costing too much money with his blunders. The story line is merely a thin excuse for a number of slapstick situations, most of which are heavily telegraphed and jump sloppily here and there without much purpose.

Don Chaffey has directed with somewhat heavy-handed touch and the scripters, Jack Davies and Hugh Woodhouse, have provided the cast with a few amusing lines and problems—but not consistently. The cast is a familiar one. Kenneth Connor is a better actor than some of his roles recently would suggest. He plays the airman with engaging charm, and certainly milks the situations of every possible glimmer of humor. His commanding officer is played energetically, but rather tediously, by Jimmy Edwards. He's a radio funnyman who has yet to find the right niche in films. A little of him goes a very long way. In this case, he has to carry much of the burden of the comedy and it's a hard fight for Edwards to survive.

Quite the best comedy performances come from Eric Barker, as the harassed Air Minister (scoring because he is also a very sound character actor). Richard Wattis scores as usual as a pompous civil servant while Charlotte Mitchell is in a brief role as a Bohemian artist. Jon Pertwee is effective as an eccentric, out-of-date general. Shirley Eaton has the main distaff role and this trimly shaped blonde again proves that winning smile is not enough to disguise somewhat shaky thesping ability. *Rich.*

Cannes Festival

La Mano En La Trampa
(The Hand in the Trap)
(ARGENTINIAN)

Cannes, May 16.
Angel Film production and release. Stars Elsa Daniel, Francisco Rabal; features Leonardo Favio, Maria Rosa Gallo, Bertha Ortegosa. Directed by Leopoldo Torre Nilsson. Screenplay, Beatriz Guido; camera, Alberto Etchbehere, Juan Julio Baena; editor, Pablo De Amo, Atilio Stampone. At Cannes Film Fest. Running time, 90 MINS.

Laura .... Elsa Daniel
Cristobal .... Francisco Rabal
Miguel .... Leonardo Favio
Ines .... Maria Rosa Gallo
Maria .... Bertha Ortegosa

Decorative pic about a young girl's assumption of maturity also has an expert dramatic flair and narrative flow. This makes the point about provincial, inbred society and its suffocating prejudices without sacrificing an insight into characters. Film has the style and quality for arty theatre chances abroad.

The girl in question comes home from school to her once-rich home now maintained by her aunt and mother's sewing. Someone is locked upstairs and it is supposed to be an idiot of the family. But it turns out to be an aunt who had been jilted by a local, rich playboy. She gets involved with him and ends up in the trap of becoming his mistress without any way out as long as she feels for him and he wants her.

Director Leopoldo Torre Nilsson has kept this fanciful tale from falling into predictable melodramatics, by an astute use of mood, character revelation and a feeling for smalltown life. Acting

is expert in conception and execution, especially with Elsa Daniel, as the troubled girl. Technical credits are also expert. *Mosk.*

Chronique D'Un Ete
(Summer Chronicle)
(FRENCH)

Cannes, May 16.

Argos Film release of Anatole Bauman, Philippe Lipschitz production. Written and directed by Jean Rouch and Edgar Morin. Camera, Raoul Coutard, Michel Brault; editor, Jean Ravel. At Cannes Film Fest. Running time, **90 MINS.**

Anthropologist-filmaker Jean Rouch and sociologist-film critic Edgar Morin refer to this pic as the "cinema-truth" in conception and intent. A series of interviews with several people, with some dramatic sequences played out by them, this hits solid moments of human revelation, outlook and depth. It is constantly interesting. However, its format and technique make this a limited film abroad. It might be worthwhile if properly and personally handled in specialized theatres.

Rouch supervised the filmic aspects which are alive with a flair for catching people in sudden moments of emotional verity or thoughtful revealing actions. A cover girl's thoughts on the sound track while showing her at work at a beach resort, some African friends trying to understand what the tattoo on the arm of a Jewish girl (deported during the last war) means, asking people in the street what happiness represents and whether unknown to them and a worker's sudden outburst are moving and exciting parts of this most unusual pic.

This gives an absorbing look into the lives of some French people. Of course, not all walks of life are touched on, but it does give weight and dramatic depth to people as they are or think they are. This is a definite offbeater but a unique and novel pic. *Mosk.*

Viridiana
(SPANISH)

Cannes, May 23.

Uninci release of Gustavo Alatriste production. Stars Silvia Pinal, Francisco Rabal, Fernando Rey; features Margarita Lozano, Victoria Zinny, Teresa Rabal. Written and directed by Luis Bunuel. Camera, Jose F. Aguayo; editor, Predro Del Rey. At Cannes Film Fest. Running time, **90 MINS.**

Jorge	Francisco Rabal
Viridiana	Silvia Pinal
Don Jaime	Fernando Rey
Ramona	Margarita Lozano
Lucia	Victoria Zinny
Rita	Teresa Rabal

Brilliantly carpentered offbeat pic is sure to be controversial, but it looms an arty theatre possibility on this alone besides its excellent conception. Theme is about charity and its uses and misuses, coupled with an insight into human reasons. Film will need careful handling but could be of interest abroad as the demand for unusual film grows.

A girl, who is about to take her vows to be a nun, pays a visit to a rich uncle. He sees in her an image of his dead wife who died on their wedding night. He begs her to be his wife, then drugs her and almost makes advances to her. He does not but claims he did in order to hold her. He finally confesses, and she leaves. He hangs himself, leaving his large estate to her and a son.

The would-be nun tries to become a useful saintly creature by bringing in a flock of poor derelicts and letting them sleep in an adjoining barn and house. But they get out of hand and almost rape her. And she finally decides to try and become a human being first before trying to be a selfless saint for which she is neither made nor capable of.

Director Luis Bunuel, formerly Spanish and now Mexican, returned to Spain for the first time since 1938 to make this film. He is known among motion picture buffs for his unusual pix. He displays a perfection in film flow and language in this relentless pic.

Atmosphere is invoked by a fluid feel for incidents which glide by before an explanation is given to heighten awareness of theme and character. Symbols abound but are never superflous or unclear. The tale of a novice nun not of the ability or humility for her vocation may also have this in for Catholic Legion difficulties.

But it does make its points that charity out of pride and humility and self abnegation out of vanity could lead to chaos. The etching of the uncle's lonely phobias are also extended to the other characters.

The wild orgy of the derelicts who sneak into the big house is handled with explosive humor and then a shattering burst of violence that makes the heroine realize her need for human understanding and acceptance before she can ever become a nun.

Technical credits are excellent. Director Bunuel has welded the thesping into a perfect whole that defies singling out any for special praise.

Pic had the biggest effect at the recently wound Cannes Film Fest, with many feeling it was the best film. But it aroused pros and cons and different interpretations. It is a picture that needs careful handling and placement but is unique enough to arouse plenty of interest. It calls for hardsell but could well be worth the trouble.

Mosk.

El Centroforward Murio Al Amanecer
(The Forward Center Dies At Dawn)
(ARGENTINIAN)

Cannes, May 23.

INC release of Rene Mujica production. With Raul Rossi, Luis Medina Castro, Didi Carli, Enrique Fava. Directed by Rene Mujica. Screenplay, Agustin Cuzzani; camera, Ricardo Younis; editor, Atilio Rinaldi. At Cannes Film Fest. Running time, **85 MINS.**

Catcho	Luis Medina Castro
Dancer	Didi Carli
Lupus	Raul Rossi
Aid	Enrique Fava

This film is an amusing fantasy that is sustained through familiar situations by inventiveness and ingenuity in directing and story form. But its symbolical aspects make this primarily a dualer or lingo film for foreign spots.

A young football player is bought by a mysterious man but he ends up as part of a millionaire's collection rather than in another club. The rich man wants the best in all walks of life but only as symbols and does not want to use them. The football player tries to escape and kills the rich man in the attempt.

Of course, political and social implications are evident in this fantasy but it does not press its points. Film manages to bring enough wit and simplicity to keep it engrossing. The sale of the footballer at an auction, a ballet dancer secretly dancing in the rain, a party to fete the coming marriage by the rich man who decides he wants to create new and perfect people are some of the scenes which have the most tang.

This is an offbeater with the right quality to bring it off. Technical credits are acceptable and the acting is keyed to the right stylization needed. Director Rene Mujica, for his first film, displays a good feeling for narrative and wit. He may be heard from in a more heavyweight pic in the future. *Mosk.*

Duvad
(The Beast)
(HUNGARIAN)

Cannes, May 16.

Hungarofilm release of Hunnia production. With Ferenc Bessenyei, Tibor Bittskei, Maria Medgyesi, Bela Barsi. Directed by Zoltan Fabri. Screenplay, Imre Carkadi; camera, Ferenc Szecsenyi; editor, Maria Szecsenyi. At Cannes Film Fest. Running time, **95 MINS.**

Sandor	Ferenc Bessenyei
Zsuzska	Maria Medgyesi
Janos	Tibor Bitskei

There is a good visual flair and dramatic bite in this story of an overbearing, selfish man who can't adjust to the new communal life in Hungary after the war. But the effect is somewhat dampened by an academic second half which makes him a vestigial symbol of pre-Communist privileges rather than a man. Hence, it is an unlikely export item.

The beast of the title has his fill of the girls around his farm and especially one he then discards. She marries a young man who runs the co-op farm the former joins. But the ex-landowner tries to win her back and alienates everybody and is finally shot down trying to force himself on the girl again.

Director Zoltan Fabri has a certain feel for the countryside and rustic sensuality, and keeps this a good dramatic affair through most of the film. But thesping varies from the flamboyantly mannered to the understated, and this too throws the pic off-balance. Technical credits are good.

Mosk.

Che Gioia Vivere
(The Joy of Living)
(ITALIAN-FRENCH)

Cannes, May 16.

Cineriz release of a RIRE (Rome)-Francinez (Paris) coproduction. Stars Alain Delon, Barbara Lass; features Ugo Tognazzi, Gino Cervi, Rina Morelli, Paolo Stoppa, Aroldo Tieri, Carlo Pisacane, Giampiero Littera, Didi Perego, Annibale Ninchi, Leopoldo Trieste, Nanda Primavera, Nando Bruno, Enzo Maggio, Graziella Durano, Luigi Giullani, Jacques Stanislawski, Stefano Valle, Franco Pseziali, Rosalba Neri. Directed by Rene Clement. Screenplay, Clement, Leo Benvenuti, Piero DeBernardi; from an idea by Gualtiero Jacopetti. Additional dialog, Pierre Bost; camera (Dyaliscope), Henri Decae; music, A. Francesco Lavagnino. At Cannes Film Fest. Running time, **120 MINS.**

Ulisse Cecconato	Alain Delon
Franca Fossati	Barbara Lass
Olinto Fossati	Gino Cervi
Gorgolano	Paolo Stoppa
Rosa Fossati	Rina Morelli
1st Anarchist	Ugo Tognazzi
2nd Anarchist	Aroldo Tieri

Amusing, bright and intelligent comedy-satire looks headed for a sparkling boxoffice future in Italy and France, its countries of origin, with other foreign chances proportionate and depending on careful lingual translation to maintain tongue in check spirit of the original. At two hour running time, pic also appears overlong. It could stand some trimming to further highlight its many droll moments, and avoid some slow points.

Story, set in the early Italian 1920's (and here a brief explanation of period's political trends to enlighten spectators might be appropriate in foreign versions), this deals with the adventures of a youngster who has just been released from army service, and looking for a job. He incautiously grabs the first one he's offered by a Fascist organization, but soon gets a better offer from a group of anarchists. He joins them without really knowing what he's getting himself in for.

Remainder of pic amusingly tells of anarchists' exploits, led by the unwitting heroics of the boy, and includes a romantic interlude with the anarchist leader's pretty daughter. Much of the humor has topical inferences which spell big laughs and general enjoyment in Italy, but other areas should respond almost as well. Writer-director Clement maintains a rollicking pace almost throughout. A series of visual gags and intelligently droll incidents are the films highlights. Towards the end, the action appears a bit confused, and some points are easily lost. A trimming job could help.

Under Clement's careful direction, Alain Delon is excellent as the unwitting anarchist while Barbara Lass is fine and winning as his girl. She rates important attention on looks and ability, and if properly guided could become a valuable marquee property.

Ugo Tognazzi and Aroldo Tieri are hilarious as a bomb-setting pair of agitators. Paol Stoppa and Rina Morelli are wasted in minor roles while Gino Cervi is good as the girl's father. Frequent scene-stealer is Carlo Pisacane, as the anarchist grandpa who's locked up in the attic to keep him out of trouble.

Francesco Lavagnino has some catchy backdrop music in a period vein for good effect, while Henri Decae's Dyaliscope lensing is another standout for the pic. Other credits fine.

Hawk.

Kozaki
(The Cossacks)
(RUSSIAN—COLOR)

Cannes, May 23.

Mosfilm production and release. With Boris Andreiev, Zina Kirienko, L. Goubanov, E. Bredoun. Directed by Vassili Pronine. Screenplay, Victor Chklovski from book by Leo Tolstoi; camera (Sovcolor), I. Guelein, V. Zakharov; editor, E. Severov. At Cannes Film Fest. Running time, **100 MINS.**

Erochka	Boris Andreiev
Marianne	Zina Kirienko
Olenine	L. Goubanov
Loukachka	E. Bredoun

Solidly carpentered film tells of profligate young nobelman who tires of his ways and goes to live among the Cossacks in a Caucasian outpost at the turn of the century.

There he learns of love, friendship and nature. Film is rich in character and good narrative values, but appears mainly an arty entry abroad since action is sacrificed for character and sound folk mores.

Taken from a semi-autobiographical novel of Leo Tolstoi, it is well acted and has a fine color envelope. The man leaves behind his first true love and friends to go home and try to live in a new way. The authentic period ring should help.   *Mosk.*

A Primeira Missa
(The First Mass)
(BRAZILIAN)

Cannes, May 16.
Ferdinando Aguiar production and release. With Jose Mariano Filho, Margarida Cardoso, Dionisio De Azevado. Written and directed by Lima Barreto from novel by Nair De Lacerda; camera, Henry Fowley; editor, G. Migliori. At Cannes Film Fest. Running time, **113 MINS.**

Boy .... Jose Mariano Filho
Man .... Dionisio De Azevado
Mother .... Margarida Cardoso

A priest thinks back on his youth and how and why he decided to become a priest. Film is well meaning but stereotyped and obvious in its unfolding and preaching. Child actors are mannered. However, this looms mainly for Latino language spots abroad.

Director Lima Barreto has given this some colorful incidents but lacks the flair for making the child's coming of awareness either meaningfull or absorbing. Film spouts too many platitudes which sakes it static and slow. Technical credits are good but the thesping is theatrical.   *Mosk.*

Les Mauvais Coups
(Foul Play)
(FRENCH-CINEGRAPHISCOPE)

Cannes, May 16.
20th-Fox release of Editions Cinegraphiques-Jean Thuillier production. Stars Simone Signoret; features Reginald D. Kernan, Alexandra Stewart, Marcel Pagliero, Serge Rousseau. Directed by Francois Leterrier. Screenplay, Roger Vailland, Leterrier from novel by Vailland; camera, Jean Badal; editor, Leonizde Azar. At Cannes Film Fest. Running time, **110 MINS.**

Roberta .... Simone Signoret
Milan .... Reginald D. Kernan
Helene .... Alexandra Stewart
Luigi .... Marcel Pagliero
Duval .... Serge Rousseau

This is a muted mood piece about a middleaged couple breaking up, and a young girl they both use for themselves and against each other. However, it is mainly a vehicle for a stunning acting performance by Oscar winner Simone Signoret. Otherwise, this film is somewhat literary and only intermittently taking and incisive. Picture looms as an arty entry abroad, with the hard-sell needed but with the Signoret name a plus. For depth possibilities, it has a distaff handle.

Miss Signoret plays an attractive but aging woman who has sacrificed all for her man, a morose, noted racing-car driver, now retired to the country. Here they begin to grate on each others nerves. A young, fresh girl comes into their lives, and she uses her to try to awaken her husband's past desires for her. He falls for the girl but does not crave her

because he feels it would only end disastrously.

All this leads to Miss Signoret's suicide. She gives the film its main life as her intense but thwarted needs are ever intensified in her many acts from drunkenness to deliberately beautifying the girl.

Direction wisely allows Miss Signoret to carry things but cannot quite fit the meandering tale and mood into a more revealing drama. Result is a slow, measured film with an asset in the arresting gray and moody lensing of Jean Badal. Reginald D. Kernan is too wooden as the husband. Alexandra Stewart has the ingenuousness for the young girl caught up in the involved life of a couple whose true needs and troubles are never clear enough to balance the pic.   *Mosk.*

Darclee
(RUMANIAN—COLOR)

Cannes, May 16.
Bucuresti production and release. With Silvia Popovici, Victor Rebenclue, Cristea Avram, Costache Antoniu. Directed by Matei Jacob. Screenplay, Constantin Cirjan, Ionel Hristea; camera (Agfa), Andrei Feher; editor, M. Teodoru. At Cannes Film Fest. Running time, **102 MINS.**

Darclee .... Silvia Popovici
Iorgu .... Victor Rebenciuc
Giraldoni .... Cristea Avram
Gounod .... Costache Antoniu

Pic had no business at an international competitive film festival, especially in the running. It is a stilted tale of the struggle in Rumania to get a good opera house and performers through the prestige of one of their leading singers.

Color is garish and runny, performances theatrical, and the story banal. There is some okay operatic work at times. Pic looms mainly of interest in Eastern countries.

Technical credits are below par.
                    Mosk.

Gidget Goes Hawaiian
(COLOR)

Attractive young players and polished vets bolster slickly-produced, but only sporadically amusing, sequel. Though limited in appeal, has the trimmings for satisfactory b.o.

Columbia Pictures release of Jerry Bresler production. Stars James Darren, Michael Callan; introduces Deborah Walley; features Carl Reiner, Peggy Cass, Eddy Foy Jr., Jeff Donnell. Directed by Paul Wendkos. Screenplay, Ruth Brooks Flippen, based on the Frederick Kohner characters; camera (Eastman), Robert J. Bronner; editor, William A. Lyon; art director, Walter Holscher; music, George Duning; sound, Lambert Day; assistant director, Jerrold Bernstein. Reviewed at the studio, May 24, '61. Running time, **101 MINS.**

Jeff Mather .... James Darren
Eddie Horner .... Michael Callan
Gidget .... Deborah Walley
Russ Lawrence .... Carl Reiner
Mitzi Stewart .... Peggy Cass
Monty Stewart .... Eddie Foy Jr.
Dorothy Lawrence .... Jeff Donnell
Abby Stewart .... Vicki Trickett
Judge Hamtlton .... Joby Baker
Larry Neal .... Don Edmonds
Wally Hodges .... Bart Patton
Barbara Jo .... Jan Conaway
Dee Dee .... Robin Lory
Clay Anderson .... Arnold Merritt
Stewardess .... Terry Huntington
Waiter .... Jerardo De Cordovier
Lucy .... Vivian Marshall
Bellboy .... Guy Lee
Johnny Spring .... Johnny Gilbert
Mr. Matsu .... Y. Chang

Some of the youthful effervescence of "Gidget" has vanished in this sequel, but the combination of extremely handsome young players in the foreground and seasoned comedy veterans in the background should help it win the battle of the boxoffice bulge. The Jerry Bresler production for Columbia Pictures is limited in its appeal, however.

Those who may have been surfbored with the Sandra Dee starrer of a few years back will find even less to cheer about in this follow-up. The film will enjoy its biggest draw among the vast teenage group, but it is not quite sophisticated enough in its depiction of the modern young person to win the favor of the older teenager and yet, in tangling uneasily with several ticklish adult issues, it won't make too satisfactory an attraction in spots for the younger teener. Fortunately, it is cast with fresh and promising young people whose looks make them likely targets for a barrage of fan mail and juvenile adulation. This, together with slick production, invigorating photography, insertion of a few musical breaks and several witty lines of dialog, should bail it out.

Ruth Brooks Flippen's screenplay, based on the Frederick Kohner characters, takes Gidget (now played by Deborah Walley, whom the picture introduces), severs her from the romantic ties that bind her to boy friend James Darren in California, and plants her in Hawaii, complete with parents and a gang of lads vying for her affection. Romantic complications ensue when Darren arrives on unscheduled flight, setting up a complicated situation of mix-ups and false accusations, chief antagonist being Vicki Trickett, a spoiled kind of Trader-vixen jealous of Miss Walley's instant popularity with the woo-woo brigade. It's all resolved in a rather flat finish.

Miss Walley has a future. She is cute as a button and displays a versatility not matched by the equally attractive Miss Dee in the

original. Her emoting is competent enough for the part. Darren is a definite candidate for top stardom—handsome as they come and a good singer, to boot. He plays with authority and in a few years should graduate into meatier adult roles. Michael Callan, an agile, gifted hoofer, has a chance to display his talent in a flashy, but not very inventive, specialty strut choreographed by Roland Dupree. He, too, should go places when the parts give him more latitude.

There are solid performances by Carl Reiner, New York's own Peggy Cass, Eddie Foy Jr. and Jeff Donnell, although one wishes they had more elbow room to cut up (the film proves that adults are a lot more fun than kids) especially on a Hawaiian vacash). Miss Trickett does adequately by a rather unenviable role. Joby Baker stands out among the supporting horde of youngsters, all of whom do well under the brisk surveillance of director Paul Wendkos, who also reined the original.

Eastman Color camera work, from splashy process shots of surf 'n' sand to warm interiors, is brightly dispatched by Robert J. Bronner. Walter Holscher's art direction and William A. Lyon's editing are major league. George Duning's score is modern and youthfully rhythmical, a big help. There are two tunes, one the title, the other "Wild About That Girl," both by Fred Karger and Stanley Styne. Both are in the traditional pop vein, and are stylishly warbled by Darren.   *Tube.*

Tam Na Koneene
(At the Terminus)
(CZECH)

Berlin, May 25.
Progress release of aSttni production. With Eva Ocenasova, Vladimir Raz and Martin Ruzek. Directed by Jan Kadar and Elmar Klos. Screenplay, Ludvik Askenazy; camera, Rudolf Stahl; music, Zdenek Liska. At East Berlin cinemas. Running time, **98 MINS.**

Olina .... Eva Ocenasova
Martinec .... Vladimir Raz
Pesta .... Martin Ruzek
Marona .... Jana Ditetova
Mrs. Mala .... Anna Meliskova

A Czech film which deserves a good rating. It tends toward sadness and is somewhat lengthy, but impressive acting and humanly interesting episodes provide compensation. Non-political pic qualifies itself for export on a limited (art house) basis.

As per mood and atmosphere, directors Jan Kadar and Elmar Klos followed the early Italian poetic realism executed of, say, De Sica. Yarn deals with the inhabitants of an apartment house, at the terminus of a streetcar line, in a Prague suburb. It centers on three episodes. Major situation concerns a young girl who has an affair with a lodger. The romance results in the girl's pregnancy and disillusionment when the man insists on abortion. The second episode has to do with a motherless moppet that's taken care of by friendly people, but there's a constant menace in the person of the child's father, a notorious drunkard, who wants the child for himself. Third story introduces a young nurse whose husband is in jail and who has now a would-be lover on her heels. Although feel-

ing desperate because of her loneliness, the woman resists the man.

Film's philosophy relates to human loneliness. It's shown how people live in the same house but hardly know anything about each other. Fadeout is more optimistic: The two young women get together and both realize that they are still able to laugh.

Players make the most of the material in a skilfully written script. Technically, film reps a good standard. *Hans.*

Niewinni Czarodzieje
(The Innocents)
(POLISH)

Paris, May 23.

Polski Film release of Kadr production. With Tadeusz Lomnicki, Katryn Strymkolska, Zbigniew Zybulski. Directed by Andrzej Wajda. Screenplay, Jerry Andrzejewski, Jerzy Skolimowski; camera, Krzysztof Winiewicz; editor, W. Otocka, A. Rut. At the Napoleon, Paris. Running time, **85 MINS.**

Andrzej .... Tadeusz Lomnicki
Girl .... Katryn Strymkolska
Edmond .... Zbigniew Zybulski

Film concerns itself with morally d'soriented youth and the difficulty of loving, but has an optimistic ending unlike many Western counterparts. It does denote life as somewhat gray, empty and loose in this Eastern country, with the ending probably a necessary censor sop. Otherwise, it is a neatly told interlude depicting the prevailing outlooks via a boy and girl who meet one night.

A certain archness in direction and playing make this loom mainly a language entry abroad. A young doctor is tired of being sought by women. He meets a pert young girl one night who all but forces herself into his room where they talk sagely of morals and love, and that's all. Bue he loses her when he goes out to see some friends and rushes madly around the city after her only to find she has returned.

Director Andrej Wajda has a flair for good observation and characterization. The actors project their characters through their presence as well as through words. The central situation is a little forced but it still is an interesting picture of Polish youth today. That could be its main arty theatre hypo peg abroad. Technical credits are good. *Mosk.*

Spare The Rod
(BRITISH)

Honest and often effective peek at certain problems of education; good b.o. potential for thoughtful audiences.

London, May 23.

British Lion release of (Victor Lyndon) Bryanston production. Stars Max Bygraves; features Donald Pleasence, Geoffrey Keen, Betty McDowall, Eleanor Summerfield and Worrell Street Mob. Directed by Leslie Norman. Screenplay, John Cresswell, from Michael Croft's book; camera, Paul Beeson; music, Laurie Johnson; editor, Gordon Stone. At Odeon, Marble Arch, London. Running time, **93 MINS.**

John Saunders .... Max Bygraves
Mr. Jenkins .... Donald Pleasence
Mr. Gregory .... Geoffrey Keen
Miss Collins .... Betty McDowall
Mr. Murray .... Peter Reynolds
Mrs. Pond .... Jean Anderson
Mrs. Harkness .... Eleanor Summerfield
Miss Fogg .... Mary Merrall
Mr. Bickerstaff .... Aubrey Woods
Mr. Richards .... Rory McDermott
Harkness .... Richard O'Sullivan
Margaret .... Claire Marshall
Angell .... Jeremy Bulloch
Doris .... Annette Robertson
Hoole .... Brian Lown

Michael Croft's book, "Spare the Rod," has caused a lot of controversy among educational authorities and he had a bit of an uphill fight to get it filmed. It was thought that the arguments regarding corporal punishment were a bit too tough and that the book did, and ipso facto, the film would show up the educational system in a rough light. Well, the film's toned down the book and there isn't overmuch controversy in it, at least not over the question of corporal punishment. But it does take an honest peek at some aspects of certain types of school and pupil, poses few questions and hints at a couple of answers.

Max Bygraves, a topline performer in nearly every other branch of show biz has not yet hit the jackpot in pix. He is a pleasant personality and a most effective professional. And here he gives a warm and mainly engaging performance. But somehow he cannot yet completely shape his personality to a part. However, he's progressing fast and this is certainly his best effort to date. Bygraves has a popular name and that, and the title, should make this a worthwhile risk for most houses.

Story line concerns a dedicated but inexperienced young teacher who finds himself in a school in a tough East London area, where most of his colleagues have given up the ghost. Bygraves believes that he can get through to them by sympathy and understanding. He is beginning to win out especially with one of them. Then he hits a snag and Bygraves gets several jolts to his theories before eventually he appears to have penetrated and got the message over.

The pros and cons of the efficacy of caning are not very clearly put over while the problem of the cause of this juvenile delinquency is more urgently posed. Conclusions are inevitably left to the individual.

Leslie Norman, the director, has extracted some very good performances from his cast and his handling of the many children in the Worrell Street Mob is first-rate, both individually and in the crowd scenes. Direction of classroom, playground and a riot sequence are excellently done. A weakness is that every one of the children seems a hopeless, useless young thug.

Richard O'Sullivan, as the one who interests Bygraves particularly, is an experienced young actor and gives an intelligent performance. Of the others, Brian Lown, Jeremy Bulloch and Claire Marshall show promise.

Apart from a small opportunity for Eleanor Summerfield, as O'Sullivan's mother, the other adult parts are those of the school staff. A very fine study comes from Donald Pleasence as an embittered headmaster. Pleasence builds up his role admirably. Geoffrey Keen has a meaty but not wholly convincing role as a bullying, loud-voiced master who believes that thrashing is the only possible way of getting anything into children's heads.

Betty McDowall has a wispy role as a teacher who agrees with Bygraves' methods while Peter Reynolds, Jean Anderson, Aubrey Woods, Rory McDermott and Mary Merrall are in support. The drab, shabbiness of the school is authentically portrayed, as is the surrounding slum neighborhood, thanks to some excellent lensing by Paul Beeson.

An interesting film which smacks of America's "Blackboard Jungle." If the points that the author and scripter John Cresswell put over are not tremendously exaggerated, then it's a topic to which other producers might well turn for another peek. *Rich.*

The Last Time I Saw Archie

Shaky service comedy, funny on the surface but weak at the core. Firstclass supporting performances put some sock into study of a slick Air Corps con man, but uncertain b.o. contender.

Hollywood, May 17.

United Artists release of Mark VII Ltd.-Manzanita-Talbot production. Stars Robert Mitchum, Jack Webb, Martha Hyer, France Nuyen; features Louis Nye, James Lydon, Del Moore, Joe Flynn, Richard Arlen, Don Knotts, Robert Strauss, Harvey Lembeck. Directed by Webb. Screenplay, William Bowers; camera, Joseph MacDonald; editor, Robert Leeds; art director, Feild Gray; music, Frank Comstock; sound, Frank Sarver; assistant director, Chico Day. Reviewed at Fort MacArthur, San Pedro, May 17, '61. Running time, **103 MINS.**

Archie Hall .... Robert Mitchum
Bill Bowers .... Jack Webb
Peggy Kramer .... Martha Hyer
Cindy .... France Nuyen
Pvt. Russell Drexel .... Joe Flynn
Pvt. Billy Simpson .... James Lydon
Pvt. Frank Ostrow .... Del Moore
Pvt. Sam Beacham .... Louis Nye
Colonel Martin .... Richard Arlen
Captain Little .... Don Knotts
Master Sgt. Stanley Erlenheim
Robert Strauss
Sergeant Malcolm Greenbriar
Harvey Lembeck
Lola .... Claudia Barrett
Daphne .... Theona Bryant
Carole .... Elaine Davis
Patsy Ruth .... Marilyn Burtis
Corporal .... James Mitchum
Bartender .... Gene McCarthy
Lieutenant Oglemeyer .... John Nolan
First Second Lieutenant.... Martin Dean
Soldier .... Bill Kilmer
First Soldier .... Phil Gordon
Soldier .... Dick Cathcart

Few institutions in modern life measure up to the military as a source of cinematic humor. Filmakers for years have enjoyed greater - than - average commercial security simply by aiming pot shots at martial pomposity. If the enduring popularity of the service comedy is any indication, "The Last Time I Saw Archie" should hold its own in the boxoffice scuffle. But, for a variety of reasons, such a conclusion is open to some debate.

There are several key factors going for the Mark VII Ltd.-Manzanita-Talbot production, not the least of which is the valuable presence in the supporting cast of some of Hollywood's most outstanding comedy talent. Then, too, there are a few names that mean something on a marquee. But, ultimaetly, it is the story itself that determines a picture's destiny, and it is here that the United Artists release is not all as it should be.

Line for line, William Bowers has cooked up a witty script and, take for take, director Jack Webb has seasoned it with an alert humor. But, in concert, the film does not jell, the running parts do not keep the machine humming along smoothly. Bowers' screenplay is based on true incidents in his life, but the incidents, frail to begin with as the basis for vigorous comedy, are treated too lightheartedly to register with the desirable force. A sharp audience will be able to sense punch-line developments ahead of time, a deadly factor in a comedy. Furthermore, the shred of plot on which the film is hooked, however true, however stranger than fiction, fails to register as a plausible, serious situation. And this is the sort of comedy in which the central premise must be hard as a rock to support the comic ramifications.

The story, sort of a buck-private's eye-view of the service, revolves around a cocksure, slick private (Robert Mitchum) in a World War II Civilian Pilot Training outfit who wields a clipboard and wears a swagger with such confidence and authority that he soon had his entire unit convinced not only that he is a G-2 general on assignment but that he's hot on the trail of a Japanese spy-ette (France Nuyen). The yarn ends abruptly with a quick segue into civvies, revealing Mitchum as the same smoothie on the outside. The fast finish after a long narrative that never really seems headed anywhere gives the film a lopsided feel.

Thanks to the casting and the playing, the picture has its rewards. Don Knotts and Louis Nye are outstanding. Not too far behind are Del Moore, James Lydon, Joe Flynn, Robert Strauss, Harvey Lembeck and Richard Arlen. Mitchum displays comic poise and solidity in the lead, Martha Hyer and Miss Nuyen are capable and decorative. Webb, as Mitchum's sidekick and first-person narrator, plays it a bit wooden. He has a tendency to direct his dialog to the camera instead of at the person with whom he is sharing a scene, perhaps illustrating the difficulty of serving as one's own director.

Robert Leeds' editing shows an adeptness with quick and tricky cuts, but is not always successful at advancing the story smoothly. There is agile lenswork by Joseph MacDonald, service-able art direction by Feild Gray and a sprightly stars-and-stripesy score by Frank Comstock that is especially good at building comedic momentum. *Tube.*

When The Clock Strikes

Contrived crime-suspense meller. Adequate for twin-billing.

Hollywood, May 23.

United Artists release of Robert E. Kent production. Stars James Brown, Merry Anders; with Henry Corden, Roy Barcroft, Peggy Stewart, Jorge Moreno, Francis De Sales, Max Mellinger, Eden Hartford, Jack Kenny. Directed by Edward L. Cahn. Screenplay, Dallas Gaultois; camera, Kenneth Peach Sr.; editor, Grant Whytock; music, Richard La Salle; sound, Dean Thomas; assistant director, Herbert S. Greene. Reviewed at Goldwyn Studios, May 23, '61. Running time, **72 MINS.**

Sam Morgan .... James Brown
Ellie .... Marry Anders
Cady .... Henry Corden
Sheriff .... Roy Barcroft
Mrs. Pierce .... Peggy Stewart

Martinez .... Jorge Moreno
Warden .... Francis De Sales
Postman .... Max Mellinger
Waitress .... Eden Hartford
Cafe Proprietor .... Jack Kenny

"When The Clock Strikes" is not one of the better supporting items turned out by United Artists' prolific program picture combo of producer Robert E. Kent and director Edward L. Cahn. Though only of 72-minute duration, a length ideal for the virtue of storytelling simplicity, it hurls a barrage of plot complications, coincidence, contrivance and confusion at an audience, until one is limp just trying to keep up with it. The UA release will suffice as a filler for those who prefer two-for-the-price-of-one and don't expect wonders from the bottom half of a theatrical double-header.

Dallas Gaultois' crime-suspense melodrama tangles with circumstances surrounding the execution of a murderer in a remote rural area to which several persons connected with the doomed man converge. Most of the plot is concerned with unlawful efforts by these persons to track down the hidden booty that was stashed away by the killer prior to his apprehension and conviction. It gets very involved, and the characters are consistently jumping to peculiar conclusions and saying and doing irrational things.

James Brown and Merry Anders, who are developing into something of a "team" in these Kent-Cahn features, play the romantic leads. If their performances seem a bit shaky in spots, it is understandable in view of the modest nature of the production. Actually they do quite well, considering, and so do Henry Corden, Roy Barcroft, Peggy Stewart, Jorge Moreno, Francis De Sales and Max Mellinger in key supporting roles.

Kenneth Peach Sr.'s camerawork and Grant Whytock's editing are efficient. *Tube.*

Tres Romeos y Una Julieta
(Three Romeos and a Juliet)
(MEXICAN)

Mexico City, May 30.
Columbia release of Jose Luis Calderon production. Stars Jorge Mistral, Antonio Badu, Elvira Quintana; features Irma Dorantes, Julio Aleman, Lorena Goubaud, Oscar Pulido. Directed by Chano Urueta. Screenplay, Adolfo Torres Portillo; camera, Raul Martinez Solares; music, Antonio Diaz Conde. At Orfeon Theatre, Mexico City. Running time, 90 MINS.

Despite the marshalling together of some top names in Mexican pictures, from acting talent, to director, cameraman and musical director, this one proves to be a so-so effort. Billed as the comedy of the year concerning a modern day Juliet and her avid suitors, picture falls far short of the mark. Comedy situations are strained and talents of Jorge Mistral, Antonio Badu and Elvira Quintana, as well as the supporting players is wasted on this one.

This may go well in nabe houses but for broader horizons its limitations, and sliding off into bad taste, are two strikes against it. *Emil.*

The Deadly Companions
(PANAVISION-COLOR)

Pathe-America's "first" release. Fairly engrossing western drama about four emotional frontier characters who converge on a ghost town to solve their respective problems. Well-acted, directed and photographed, should be satisfactory b.o. contender.

Hollywood, May 26.
Pathe-America Distributing Co. release of Pathe-America production. Stars Maureen O'Hara, Brian Keith, Steve Cochran, Chill Wills. Directed by Sam Peckinpah. Screenplay, A. S. Fleischman, from his novel; camera (Pathe), William H. Clothier; editor, Stanley E. Rabjon; music, Marlin Skiles; sound, Robert J. Callen. Reviewed at Academy Awards Theatre, May 26, '61. Running time, 90 MINS.

Kit .... Maureen O'Hara
Yellowleg .... Brian Keith
Billy .... Steve Cochran
Turk .... Chill Wills
Parson .... Strother Martin
Doctor .... Will Wright
Cal .... Jim O'Hara
Mayor .... Peter O'Crotty
Mead .... Billy Vaughan
Gambler .... Robert Sheldon
Gambler .... John Hamilton
Bartender .... Hank Gobble
Indian .... Buck Sharpe

As of now, "The Deadly Companions" represents the successful culmination of the first phase in the three-ply operation of Pathe-America, the new production-distribution-exhibition project predicated on the theory that exhibitors can sense better than anyone what their customers want on the screen. This initial product, to be sure, has its lapses and weaknesses, but on the whole it is an interesting and sufficiently novel slice of frontier fiction, one that western fanciers should enjoy while those who are not especially fond of tumblin' with the tumbleweed can find diverting, as well. It appears to be a sound commercial risk, albeit on a moderate, not stupendous, boxoffice scale.

The Carousel production, produced by Charles B. FitzSimons and directed by Sam Peckinpah, is constructed on A. S. Fleischman's screen adaptation of his own novel. The latter's scenario is the dramatic tale of four characters who encounter their respective moments of truth in a ghost town smack dab in the heart of Apache country. One (Maureen O'Hara) is a dancehall woman heading for the ghost town to bury her son next to her late husband, thus establishing her virtuous character and erasing the stigma of her shady reputation. Another is Brian Keith, whose motivation is revenge against Chill Wills, an unstable galoot with whom he has an old score to settle. Fourth member of the odd party is Steve Cochran, a gunslinger with eyes for Miss O'Hara. Keith and Miss O'Hara ultimately fall for each other in spite of the fact he accidentally killed her son in the course of upsetting a bank robbery. The other two men eliminate each other, cleansing Keith of his passionate five-year campaign to slay Wills.

Fleischman's screenplay is pretty far-fetched and relies heavily on coincidence but, for the most part, it plays. This thanks to superior emoting by the four principals and an auspicious debut as a director for the screen by Sam Peckinpah.

a fine tv helmsman. Keith plays with customary reserve and masculine authority a character refreshingly different from the usual impregnable western "tall man." Durably handsome Miss O'Hara comes through with a convincing performance, one of her best in some time. Cochran's characterization, somewhat of a departure from the type of role for which he is most renowned (the suave Roaring 20's thug), is truly outstanding. Wills, also in an offbeat assignment, acquits himself exceptionally well.

There's genuine idyllic beauty in much of William H. Clothier's Pathe Color photography — especially his moody views of solitary figures framed silhouette-like against the vast, splendid desert sky. Stanley E. Rabjon's editing soundly splices together the drama. Odd orchestration, assembled by Marlin Skiles, keynoted by the solo guitars of Laurindo Almeida and Robert Bain, and featuring a number of novel instruments including some Indianesque percussion, brings a most listenable air to the production. However, there are moments when the music grows too listenable, when its nature disconcertingly overlaps into the viewer's conscious and makes him feel that there are Indian percussionists and war dancers carrying on just over yon hill, which they aren't. A plaintive refrain, "A Dream Of Love" by FitzSimons and Skiles, is crooned by Miss O'Hara over the main titles. *Tube.*

Eichmann and the Third Reich
(SWISS)

Praesens-Film A.G. (Lazar Wechsler) production. Written and directed by Erwin Leiser, assisted by Miriam Novitch; camera, Emil Berna; editor, Hans Heinrich Egger. Opened at Wellenberg, Zurich, May 25, '61. Running time, 90 MINS.

(With German narration)
In the unbelievably short time of little over six weeks, Erwin Leiser, whose "Mein Kampf" has been the year's top grosser here as well as in other European countries and is currently piling up big takings in the U.S., has completed another documentary for Swiss Praesens-Film (Lazar Wechsler). It is presently being mass-released in Swiss and German cities to coincide with the Eichmann trial in Jerusalem. World distribution rights have been acquired by Columbia, and pic will be dubbed in 12 languages. In an unusual move, but perfectly befitting the subject matter, Praesens has decided to make this a non-profit venture, with all profits going to Jewish aid organizations and victims of the Nazi terror.

In sharp contrast to other current, fictionalized "Nazi beast" pictures, this one is a strictly authentic document sans actors. Absent, too, in German track is a "polemic" commentary. It contains original footage collected during many months from archives in Germany, Poland, France, Czechoslovakia and Israel, as well as excerpts from instruction films to the Nazis heretofore unpublished; original material recently filmed in Israel during the trial;

and witnesses to the Eichmann crimes now residing in Israel.

Leiser has again done a topnotch job, enhanced by the masterful editing by Swiss Hans Heinrich Egger, the lensing in Israel by Swiss vet cameraman, Emil Berna; and the valuable assistance by Miriam Novitch, herself a concentration camp escapee and now director of the Kibbutz Museum of Ghetto Fighters in Israel.

By choosing to let the horrible facts speak for themselves, the makers of this deeply stirring documentary have achieved a degree of objectivity which must be deemed admirable. For no one, except maybe the still remaining, most unyielding followers of the Nazi ideology, will remain unmoved before this relentless exposure of horror, sadism, shame and suffering. Hearing a sentence such as this, with which camp commanders "saluted" the incoming victims: "You are not coming to a sanatorium—you will leave this place only through the chimney!" suffices to freeze anyone's blood.

The hero-villain himself is not shown in live action during the Hitler reign of terror, though stills of him are included. There is a fair amount of footage of Eichmann as prisoner at the dock in Israel. The barely perceptible nervous twitch around the eyes, and the firm (or read cruel?) mouth carry their own drama. His voice in court pleading "pure heart and clear conscience" are part of the soundtrack.

The film shows the beginning of Nazism in 1933; the first bloody persecutions of all non-Aryans"; the establishment of the notorious Nuremberg race laws; the rise of Eichmann from a smalltime official to a powerful "executive" whose signature became synonymous with mass extinction; the invasion of Austria, Poland and Czechoslovakia; the atrocious revenge for the murder of Heydrich in Prague by shooting all male inhabitants of the village of Lidice; the skeleton-like victims of concentration camps and, as a terrifyingly cynical contrast, German propaganda films showing to the home front that the Jews in camps are "well taken care of" and getting sufficient food; and finally, the current Jerusalem trial during which Eichmann declares himself not guilty, minimizing his deeds as having merely executed orders. *Mezo.*

Morgan The Pirate
(EASTMAN-CINEMASCOPE)

Well-made adventure yarn. No acting award nominees but constant action. Good summer fare.

Joseph E. Levine presentation. Metro release, Lux - Adelphia co - production (Italy). Stars Steve Reeves. Features Valerie Lagrange, Armand Mestral, Chelo Alonso. Directed and written by Andre DeToth. Photography, Tonino and Franco Delli Colli. Effects, Eros Baciucchi; costumes, Fillippo Sanjust. Editor, Maurizio Lucidi. Reviewed in Metro projection room, N.Y. June 1, 1961. Running time 95 MINS.

Henry Morgan .... Steve Reeves
Dona Inez .... Valerie LaGrange
Dona Maria .... Lydia Alfonsi
Concepcion .... Chelo Alonso
L'Olonnais .... Armand Mestral

Any resemblance in "Morgan

the Pirate" to actual history may be considered slight. Still he's a well-advertised myth figure; like Robin Hood, and that will help with the kids. Add that the opulent Eastman color makes an ideal pictorial come-on for the drive-ins and summer trade generally. Strongest factor for the boxoffice is, of course, the almost constant action. Fists are forever plowing into the pow and rapiers into the viscera.

The story is not complicated by any iconoclastic thoughts on piracy itself, which in reality operated like Capone in Chicago with indispensable official cooperation, tips, warnings and sharings. Little of that is here beyond one hint. As impersonated by Steve Reeves this was the most genteel cutthroat who ever scuttled Spaniards on Caribbean trade routes. The pirate exhibits remarkable delicacy of feeling if no particular subtley of facial expression. At the end of his raid on the city of Panama with everybody else up to their scuppers in gore Reeves is still an honorable, clean-cut English chap who will legally marry the girl, though its left unclear whether he'll string up her father, the governor.

The incongruous immunity to corruption of the pirate captain no doubt is one of the picture's assets for the family trade since it is hard to object to or perhaps believe in such a decent murderer. No oaths, no impure pleasures, no eye-patch, and clean-shaven chest. Model youth! His mother is not in the picture but you know instinctively that he writes her regularly. Suffice that the lovely scenic effects in Eastman and CinemaScope are matched by the pirate's red-blooded physique and true-blue loyalty.

The production in general is first class. Especially splendid are the costumes of Fillippo Sanjust, the effects of Eros Baciucchi and the props provided by the production manager Aldo Pomilio. The ship scenes and island settings are exotically arranged. In the large cast are numerous interesting offbeat types. Of characterization in depth there is naturally none, for that would make Reeves look bad. He is called upon only to be handsome and healthy, never worried, the front cover of all the stag beauty magazines rolled into one. On galley chain gang, or with sword in hand, or giving a pep talk to his pirate crew from the bridge, he's a boy's dream of manhood. As previously implied, all this is boxoffice.

Don't ask for heavy-duty acting from either Reeves or his pretty-pretty Italian leading lady, Valerie Lagrangs, who feels—and kisses—with all the abandon of a banker reviewing a loan. The most arresting female in the cast is a half-breed camp follower who gets this separate screen credit: "And including the extraordinary participation of Chelo Alonso."

Her opportunites on screen are not extensive but enough to sample a sexburst of considerable tease value for another time. In the story she is groaning for the big hunk of beefcake who can't see her for Spanish dust. There is one meeting of lips far back from the campfires but then he says "I'm sorry" and walks off-camera, a gentleman to his teeth, intent only upon monogamy.

In managing his multitudes and playing the broad panorama of ships at sea, the boarding and raiding, the scaling of walls, the governor's banquet and all the rest Andre De Toth has kept the action steady and mostly believable. He and Joe Levine deliver the merchandize to Metro as contracted. But De Toth's script wobbles here and there and the editing is jerky now and then. The main faults lie in the post-production dubbing, not the voice matches or lip sync so much as the trite dialog on occasion and a handful of careless-seeming misfits as when the English ambassador, sound like a modern hood: *"We want a third of the take!"* or when the girl awakening on the field of carnage whimpers, *"Where am I?"*

It is not entirely fair yet there is an element of truth in the assertion that the production is superior to the direction in "Morgan The Pirate." The feeling will not go away that greater attention by De Toth to details would have enhanced net respect for the picture. Even so it is visibly superior to most swashbuckling stuff and its prospects under Joe Levine's saturation techniques of big ballyhoo and mass playoff seem certain to serve summer well.

Not the least arresting aspect of the production comes directly in the screen credits. They are large, they are many, they linger lovingly in frame. Even the assistant director takes a full solo bow. It's almost as if Italy wished to make a case, in passing, that it could match Hollywood, ego massage for ego massage. *Land.*

Schwarzer Kies
(Black Gravel)
(GERMAN)

Ufa production and release. With Helmut Wildt, Ingmar Zeisberg, Wolfgang Buettner, Peter Nestler. Directed by Helmut Kaeutner. Screenplay, Kaeutner and Walter Ulbrich; camera, Heinz Pehlke; editor, Klaus Dudenhoefer. At Filmbuehne Wien, Berlin. Running time, 113 MINS.

Robert Neidhardt	Helmut Wildt
Inge Gaines	Ingmar Zeisberg
John Gaines	Hans Cossy
Otto Krahne	Wolfgang Buettner
Elli	Anita Hoefer
Eric Moeller	Heinrich Trimbur
Bill Rodgers	Peter Nestler
Anni Peel	Edeltraud Elsner
Margot	Gisela Fischer
Loeb	Max Buchsbaum
Frau Marbach	Else Knott
Wiecher	Guy Gehrke

This is the pic against which the Central Council of Jews in Germany brought suit because of alleged anti-Semitic passages. Although the court exonerated director Helmut Kaeutner and UFA, latter decided to cut out the objectionable scenes.

What Kaeutner apparently had here in mind was to shoot a film that's realistic in every respect, including to let people talk like in real life, without mincing the matter. The results: As to the dialog, this is the most outspoken German film in years. Moreover, rarely has a German pic offered so many frank bedroom sequences. Along his ambition to create an utterly realistic film (with social-critical ingredients), Kaeutner has definitely gone overboard. Many scenes have a touch of tastelessness because they don't seem necessarily essential. Since also the story, quite apart from its "message" which is questionable, too, appears contrived, the whole film has a false ring and, in fact, disappoints.

Subjectwise, "Black Gravel" may be compared with the 1954 German feature pic, "Golden Pestilence." Set in a West German village, it shows how moral and ethical standards are turned upside down because of sudden wealth. Latter comes on account of a U. S. rocket base being built by Americans and Germans. "The world's richest milk cow," the U. S. Army, is being milked. Stables are turned into bars, dollars flow like wine, and there's prostitution and blackmarketeering.

The actual evildoers in this pic are Germans who smuggle black gravel destined for the rocket base to other outlets. But apart from unscrupulous materialism and prostitution, Kaeutner also shows people's fear of another war, their greedy thirst for pleasure, opportunism and inability for honest love. There's also a romance between a German truckdriver and the German wife of a U. S. major, a wild mixture of everything.

Kaeutner became a victim of himself: He just put too much into this film. And seemingly lost control. Some may admit that there's some golden footage too, such as some cleverly lensed outdoor shots and a number of good acting sequences. On the positive side is the discovery of Helmut Wildt, Berlin stage actor, who enacts here in his film debut the role of a German truckdriver. And there is a catchy jukebox song, "Fraeulein Schmidt," which could become a hit. *Hans.*

Nikki, Wild Dog Of The North
(COLOR)

Dogs, bears and Disney. Pleasant diversion for the family, and a satisfactory contender for the dog days of summer.

Hollywood, June 2.

Buena Vista release of Winston Hibler production. Directed by Jack Couffer, Don Haldane. Screenplay, Ralph Wright, Hibler, based on novel, "Nomads Of The North," by James Oliver Curwood; camera (Technicolor), Lloyd Beebe, Couffer, Ray Jewell, William W. Bacon III, Donald Wilder; editor, Grant K. Smith; music, Oliver Wallace; sound, Robert O. Cook; assistant directors, Phil Hirsch, Jerry Stoll. Reviewed at Academy Awards Theatre, June 2, '61. Running time, 74 MINS.

Andre Dupas	Jean Coutu
Jacques Lebeau	Emile Genest
Makoki	Uriel Luft
Durante	Robert Rivard
The Malemute	Nikki
The Bear	Neewa

Take one malemute dog (one-eighth part wolf, seven-eighths part husky) and one bear (100% bear), establish an incongruous friendship, set it against the picturesque wilderness of the Canadian Rockies, label it "Disney," and nature (human, American) will take care of the rest. The formula—dog meets bear, dog loses bear, dog wins bear—is familiar, but that doesn't figure to aggravate the mass moppet corps. Adults, too, should find "Nikki, Wild Dog Of The North" light and palatable entertainment. A family attraction, the Winston Hibler production should make a satisfactory showing during the "20 degrees cooler inside" cinema season.

The picture is a latitude North variation on the Disney featurette of a year ago, "The Hound That Thought He Was A Raccoon." The costarring coon is replacing by a costarring bear and the basset hound is replaced by a Malemute. The Hibler-Ralph Wright scenario from a novel by James Oliver Curwood brings the two together in their early youth, separates them from the dog's master and follows them through a series of mutual misadventures until the bear succumbs to hibernation instinct, at which point the dog is forced to grin and bear it solo in the unfriendly dog-eat-dog (or crow, or what have you) wilds of the North. After an unfortunate experience with a trapper who is a heavy to end all heavies (he mistreats everything), stouthearted Nikki relocates his master for a conclusion that is pure Log Cabin syrup.

Youngsters will learn a few things about animals from this film, including that nugget of knowledge about bear hibernation, probably the most oft-repeated grade school axiom in the education business. As for the photography, it is spectacularly colorful and dramatically perceptive (for the battery of lensmen, see above credit roster). Additionally helpful are Oliver Wallace's dramatic score, Jacques Fateux's instructive narration, Dwight Hauser's "additional" narration and Grant K. Smith's taut editing. A pair of directors astutely guided separate units (Cangary Ltd. and Westminster Films Ltd.) involved in three-ply production with the Disney people. They are Jack Couffer and Don Haldane. Two versions of the film were shot to avoid dubbing, one in French (for the French-Canadian mart), the other in English.

Nikki, a gifted barker, should be in the PATSY sweepstakes. Ditto Neewa, the bear. The people actors—Jean Coutu, Emile Genest and Uriel Luft—are less impressive. *Tube.*

The Ladies Man
(COLOR)

Likely Lewis moneymaker in which the uninhibited comic picks up where "Bellboy" and "Cinderfella" left off. Comedy is pretty scarce, but the customers won't be. Lavish production values.

Hollywood. June 1.

Paramount release of Jerry Lewis production coauthored, directed and starring Lewis; features Helen Traubel, Kathleen Freeman, Hope Holiday, Lynn Ross, Gretchen Houser, Lillian Briggs, Mary LaRoche, Madlyn Rhue, Alex Gerry, Jack Kruschen, Vicki Benet; guest stars, Buddy Lester, George Raft, Harry James Band, Pat Stanley. Screenplay, Lewis, Bill Richmond; camera (Technicolor), W. Wallace Kelley; editor, Stanley Johnson; art directors, Hal Pereira, Ross Bellah; music, Walter Scharf; sound, Charles Grenzbach; assistant directors, C. C. Coleman Jr., Ralph Axness. Reviewed at Picwood Theatre, June 1, '61. Running time, 106 MINS.

Jerry Lewis pictures make money, and "The Ladies Man" is not likely to be the exception. Despite those in the land who do not

cotton to his outrageous antics, the fact remains that, at the moment, Lewis is Hollywood's clown prince.

Actually "Ladies Man" is a kind of parlay of scraps and ideas apparently left over from Lewis' last two films, "The Bellboy" and "Cinderella." In its episodic nature, it resembles the former. In its lavish production and eye-appeal, it takes after the latter. And the central character is kind of a combination of the downtrodden "Fella" and the hapless "Bellboy." The slight plot, written by producer-director Lewis with the aid of Bill Richmond, concerns a girl-shy goof who becomes the houseboy in a sort of palatial girlatorium. Primarily the plot is little more than a limp excuse for a series of anything-goes slapstick sequences and sight gags punctuated by an occasional song or dance, an occasional romantic interlude and a lethal dose of the star's homely philosophy. Lewis will try anything for a laugh. It's a hit-or-miss proposition. When he hits, it's a belly laugh. But too often he misses.

The odd characteristic of this picture, and of many of Lewis' pictures, is its close resemblance to the style of an animated cartoon. It can be found in the technique of absurd facial exaggeration, the repetition, the insane body gyrations, the incongruous relationships of sight and sound, the trick effects, the abundance and short duration of scenes, the very fantasy of the thing.

Although he appears to be aging beyond the sphere of the dim-witted juvenile, Lewis gets by okay this time as the rubber-faced, rubber-legged, clumsy hero. For glamour, he is surrounded by 31 girls and an elaborate set, the exact likes of which has never been seen on the screen. It is the accomplished handiwork of art directors Hal Pereira and Ross Bellah, a complex three-story multiroomed, strikingly-tinted $350,000 creation that is something to behold. Ditto the $150,000 worth of props and furnishings chipped in by set decorators Sam Comer and James Payne.

The girls do all right, but they play second fiddle to the set, especially an all-white room that's a classic. Game and valuable comedy support is contributed by Helen Traubel, Kathleen Freeman, Doodles Weaver, Westbrook Van Voorhis and guest stars Buddy Lester and George Raft, among others. Pat Stanley makes an auspicious screen bow as Lewis' heart-throb.

Jockeying around that set required astute photography and sound, which it got from W. Wallace Kelley and Charles Grenzbach, respectively. Edith Head's wardrobe for the ladies is heavy on the pants and capris which, while authentic for the Hollywood scene, is lamentable, aesthetically speaking. Several songs by Harry Warren and Jack Brooks please the ear but leave the memory. Stanley Johnson's editing is geared to the comedy tempo, but a number of scenes should have been spliced out by Lewis for a tauter film. Walter Scharf's score discerningly punctuates the comedy. *Tube.*

Un Taxi Pour Tobrouk
(A Taxi for Tobruk)
(FRENCH—DYALISCOPE)

Paris, May 30.

Gaumont release of Franco London-Procusa-Continental Film-SEG production. Stars Lino Ventura, Charles Aznavour, Hardy Kruger; features Maurice Biraud, German Cobos. Directed by Denys De La Patelliere. Screenplay, Rene Havard, Michel Audiard; camera, Marcel Grignon; editor, Jacqueline Thiedot. At Marignan, Paris. Running time, 90 MINS.

Theo	Lino Ventuar
Samuel	Charles Aznavour
Ludwig	Hardy Kruger
Francois	Maurice Biraud
Jean	German Cobos

Crucible pic has four Free French soldiers lost in the African desert during the last World War. They capture a German truck with an officer in it, the film recounting their odyssey. This has humor and witty patter with the right smattering of pacifism and suspense. It thus appears mainly a playoff item on its deft construction rather than an arty entry.

The Frenchmen come to depend on and even like the German officer though one of them, who is Jewish, makes it clear he has accepted him but not forgiven him. The trip takes them through enemy territory and minefields till they are all killed except one when the German truck is blown up by an Allied tank.

Characters are familiar in the tough but good hearted sergeant, the mama's boy, the benign Jewish fellow, the more bitter one and the enemy but "good German." Direction keeps this moving, but the script and talk make them all fairly petty people. Only intermittently does the war, plight and action take on depth and meaning.

Charles Aznavour is reserved and effective as the Jewish boy while Hardy Kruger shows an adept talent in limning the German. Technical credits are good and this is an okay war pic with acceptable chances abroad if well placed and handled. Dubbing seems called for. *Mosk.*

Don't Bother To Knock
(BRITISH-COLOR)

Richard Todd's first indie production is a rather contrived, self-conscious little joke about the love problems of a young Scottish travel agent; difficult to visualize any stampedes at b.o. for this one.

London, May 30.

Warner-Pathe release of a (Frank Godwin) Richard Todd-Haileywood production. Stars Richard Todd, June Thorburn, Nicole Maurey, Judith Anderson, Elke Sommer. Directed by Cyril Frankel. Screenplay, Denis Cannan, Frederick Gotfurt from Clifford Hanley's novel; camera, Geoffrey Unsworth; editor, Anne V. Coates; music, Elisabeth Lutyens. At Plaza Theatre, London, May 29, '61; Running time, 88 MINS.

Bill	Richard Todd
Lucille	Nicole Maurey
Ingrid	Elke Sommer
Stella	June Thorburn
Guilio	Rik Battaglia
Maggie	Judith Anderson
Harry	Dawn Beret
Perry	Scott Finch
Mother	Eleanor Summerfield
Father	John Le Mesurier
Rolsom	Colin Gordon
Ian	Kenneth Fortescue
Fred	Ronald Fraser
Al	Tom Duggan
Spinster	Joan Sterndale-Bennett
Colonel	Michael Shepley
Neighbour	Kynaston Reeves
Taxi Driver	John Laurie

Richard Todd, who has scored many successes in fairly serious screen roles, has now branched out into production on his own account, and not unnaturally starring himself in his first effort. He has chosen a light, flippant comedy. It would be over-loyal to rate it as more than a qualified success. The film is amiable, harmless, but lacking in witty bite, with situations mostly predictable. Todd emerges as the pleasant man he is. But there is nothing about his comedy performance to suggest that Jack Lemmon, David Niven or Tony Randall need be unduly worried. The result is a slim entertainment that may do useful local trade but is unlikely to create much of a boxoffice stir internationally.

Main gimmick is that Todd has surrounded himself with glamorpusses and has also provided audiences with brief, vicarious glimpses of Edinburgh and some Continental pleasure spots. Both the gals and the scenery are easy on the eye though it is not difficult to decide which are the more artificial.

Storyline has Todd as an Edinburgh travel agent who goes off on a Continental business trip spree after quarreling with his fiancee (June Thorburn). He falls for a variety of charmers and hands out the key of his apartment to them with abandon. Having patched up his differences with his girl friend over the phone, he returns to Edinburgh and, of course, all the other feminine complications then arrive and take up residence. Unfortunately, none of the visitors to his apartment is as amusing as those who cluttered up the Lemmon resident in "The Apartment."

Here is the basis of a spry bedroom farce, but the dialog of Denis Cannan and Frederick Gotfurt is heavy-handed. And director Cyril Frankel has not been able to induce performances that disguise this sorry fact. Todd spends most of his time looking understandingly bewildered over the naive behavior of the character he is playing. Of the girls, Nicole Maurey is certainly the most attractive, June Thorburn the one who has to work hardest to make any effect and Elke Sommer the one who proves the biggest disappointment in view of a publicity buildup.

Ronald Fraser, Colin Gordon, Dawn Beret, Scot Finch and Tom Duggan all score on various occasions. Judith Anderson, as one of those American matriarchs who take the daughters of literary societies on tours of Europe, sails through the film with a determined dedication worthy of a better cause. But, overall, the main memory that this reviewer will retain of the performances in "Don't Bother To Knock" is that of John Laurie, who briefly plays a dour taxi-driver superbly.

The color is good, the lensing of Geoffrey Unsworth impeccable and the music and artwork okay. Todd, a fine professional, will not be satisfied with this initialler. But it's to be hoped that he will not be deterred and that his next fling will provide him with meatier opportunities.

Picture, incidentally, has the same title as the Richard Widmark-Marilyn Monroe starrer which 20th-Fox released in 1952. The stories, of course, are different. *Rich.*

Love In A Goldfish Bowl
(PANAVISION-COLOR)

Strictly teenage fare that misses the mark frequently, but has several values that might attract the attention of young people. Long shot chance as a summer entry.

Hollywood, June 1.

Paramount release of Martin Jurow-Richard Shepherd production. Stars Tommy Sands, Fabian; features Jan Sterling, Toby Michaels, Edward Andrews. Directed by Jack Sher. Screenplay, Sher; camera (Technicolor), Loyal Griggs; editor, Terry Morse; art director, Roland Anderson; music, Jimmie Haskell; sound, Frank McWhorter. Reviewed at the studio, June 1, '61. Running time, 88 MINS.

Gordon Slide	Tommy Sands
Guiseppi La Barba	Fabian
Sandra Slide	Jan Sterling
Blythe Holloway	Toby Michaels
Sen. Clyde Holloway	Edward Andrews
Dr. Frowley	John McGiver
Alice	Majel Barrett
Clara Dumont	Shirley O'Hara
Lieut. J. G. Marchon	Robert Patton
Gregory	Phillip Baird
Oscar Flegler	Denny Miller
Jenny	Susan Silo
Jackie	Elisabeth Macrae

Here's a dark horse entry for the summer vacation season, a picture for teenagers that might just cause a few traffic jams at the ozoners. Martin Jurow-Richard Shepherd production does come close to capturing teen-acity, '61, than most of the condescending, precocious confections about youth in recent years. Despite shortcomings the Paramount release, if it spurs discussion among the self-conscious high schoolers, could turn into a summer boxoffice sleeper.

Especially helpful, from an adolescent standpoint regarding marquees, are the names Tommy Sands and Fabian. Sands, his tresses bleached a Dobie Gillis shade of bright, shocking yellow (the question, "why?", pops to mind) is the central figure in the Jack Sher screenplay about two young, parentally neglected students (male and female) who retreat, with Thoreau-like intentions, to his mother's home in Balboa (while she's away) to innocently bone up on plane geometry during a two-week vacation span. All goes well (his and her bedrooms, etc.) until an amorous, though reasonably normal and clean-cut sailor (Fabian) makes a pitch for the girl (Toby Michaels), leading into a wild party sequence interrupted by the arrival of the parents, who jump to conclusions. It is at this point that the platonic relationship between Sands and Miss Michaels flowers (at last) into puppy romance, followed by parental understanding and enlightenment. For a moment it appears that Sands' mom (Jan Sterling), a frivolous widow, and Miss Michaels' dad (Edward Andrews), an unattached state senator, will succumb to cupid, too, in the tradition of happy romanticomedy endings, but this soggy cliche is neatly sidestepped, a welcome bit of writing restraint.

Much of this strains credulity (the audience is, in effect, asked to stand still for the notion that sex and romance isn't the main thing in life to youngsters of 18), a great deal of it sputters and misfires comedically and most of it can be anticipated, but Sher's scenario at least gives the benefit of the doubt to the kids, and regards them as young, occasionally irrational but ordinarily responsible human be-

ings, which is really somewhat refreshing. The point is made that parents be concerned, but not so concerned, that it overlaps into over-possessiveness or watchdogging. Sher's direction has the proper tang and hop, for the most part.

Sands, blonde locks and all, creates an amiable (though incredibly innocent) character, displays he is a competent actor. Fabian is a decorative addition for the autographed photo legions. Pretty, sweet and feminine Miss Michaels shows true potential. Andrews is outstanding, Miss Sterling polished and spirited. Others who contribute most favorably are John McGiver, Majel Barrett, Shirley O'Hara, Robert Patton and Elisabeth Macrae, with adequate support from Phillip Baird, Denny Miller and Susan Silo.

Capable camera work by Loyal Griggs, editing by Terry Morse and art direction by Roland Anderson are incorporated. Jimmie Haskell's score has youthful bounce and drive. There are two tunes in the teenage pop vein, at least one of which, the title ditty by Hal David and Burt Bacharach (sung by Sands) has the herky-jerky tempo and frenetic lyric ("yeah, yeah, yeah, yeah") to be a his contender. One thing is sure —it'll help sell the picture.
Tube.

Le Capitaine Fracasse
(Captain Fracasse)
(FRENCH—COLOR—DYALI-SCOPE)

Paris, May 30.
Unidex release of Plazza-Metzger & Woog-Paris Elysees Films-Hoche- Documento production. Stars Jean Marais; features Genevieve Grad, Gerard Barray, Louis De Funes, Anna-Maria Ferrero, Daniele Godet, Alain Saury. Directed by Pierre Gaspard-Huit. Screenplay, Albert Vidalie, Gaspard-Huit from novel by Theophile Gautier; camera (Eastmancolor), Marcel Grignon; editor, Louisette Hautecoeur. At Normandie, Paris. Running time, 105 MINS.
De Sigognac .... Jean Marais
Isabelle .... Genevieve Grad
Vallombreuse .... Gerard Barray
Scapin .... Louis De Funes
Marquise .... Anna-Maria Ferrero
Sophie .... Daniele Godet

French costume actioner mixes melodramatic skullduggery and some okay sword play. It has a good production dress but lacks the sprightliness, movement and invention to blend the two. This makes it loom an okay local item sans much exportation chances.

An impoverished nobleman takes up with a traveling acting troupe in 17th Century France. He falls for the ingenue who loves him but will not marry him. Then she turns out to be the half sister of a villainous young nobleman who has courted and kidnaped her. When she is saved she can marry her nobleman and forgive her chastened half brother.

Jean Marais has the dash for the hero and the action sequences are deft and fast. But there are too many slow courtly asides, and the concoction only jells intermittently. Technically it is first-rate.
Mosk.

Mumu
(RUSSIAN)

Artkino release of Mosfilm production. Features Afanasi Kochetkov, Nina Grebeshkova, Yelena Palevitskaya, Leonid Kmit. Directed by Anatoli Bobrovsky and Yevgeni Teterin. Screenplay, K. Kheson-

sky, based on story by I. Turgenev; camera, K. Petrichenko; music, A. Muravlyov. At Cameo Theatre, N.Y., June 3, '61. Running time, 65 MINS.
Gerasim .... A. Kochetkov
Tanya .... N. Grebeshkova
Lady of Manor .... Y. Palevitskaya
Kapiton .... I. Bezyayev
Gavrila .... I. Ryzhov
Khariton .... Y. Teterin
Stepan .... L. Kmit
Lyubimovna .... V. Myasnikova
Housekeeper .... A. Denisova
Ustinya .... A. Fyodorova

The unhappy lot of the serf under the Czarist regime emerges as a moving and touching film in "Mumu." A Mosfilm production based on an Ivan Turgenev story, this Russian import has little appeal to the average commercial house filmgoer but should prove an interesting feature for art houses. B.o. prospects are fair.

Decadence of the pre-revolution Russian aristocracy as mirrored by the Turgenev yarn has been caught none too subtly by this tale of a deaf mute giant who is taken from his rural surroundings by the whim of a wealthy "lady of the manor.' During his daily menial tasks as a janitor at her estate he falls in love with a pretty laundress and later becomes attached to a mongrel pup which he calls "Mumu."

But the heartless despotism of the manor's elderly ruler compels the laundress to wed a drunken cobbler. Her lack of consideration also forces the mute to drown the pup upon which he's lavished his affections in lieu of the laundress. Ironical aspects of the film are pointed up by the lady of the manor's remark, "How cruel these Russian peasants are," after she learns of the dog's drowning.

Some fine performances distinguish this import. Afanasi Kochetkov, cast in a difficult role, wins sympathy as the mute giant who's become a victim of circumstances. Nina Grebeshkova as the laundress gives a strong pathetic quality to her part while Yelena Palevitskaya is the epitome of a femme Czarist aristocat who delights in making her subjects miserable. They're aided by good support provided by I. Bezyayev, among others.

Direction of Anatoli Bobrovsky and Yevgeni Teterin helps accent the unpleasantness of the times while K. Petrichenko's camerawork adequately captures the sombre atmosphere surrounding the manor and its people. The A. Muravlyov score is an asset while other technical credits are standard. Black-and-white print, however, was somewhat grainy at screening caught.
Gilb.

By Love Possessed
(COLOR)

Heavy-handed, superficial screen adaptation of bestselling novel. Sexy reputation of the book, and personal appeal of the stars, will have to carry this at the b.o.

United Artists release of Mirisch Pictures-Seven Arts production produced by Walter Mirisch. Stars Lana Turner, Efrem Zimbalist Jr., Jason Robards Jr., George Hamilton, Susan Kohner, Barbara Bel Geddes, Thomas Mitchell; features Everett Sloane, Yvonne Craig, Jean Willes, Frank Maxwell, Gilbert Green, Carroll O'Connor. Directed by John Sturges. Screenplay, John Dennis, based on novel by James Gould Couzzens; camera (DeLuxe color), Russell Metty; music, Elmer Bernstein; title song lyricist, Sammy Cahn; editor, Ferris Webster; art director, Malcolm Brown; sound, Franklin Hansen; assistant director, Sam Nelson. Reviewed New York, May 31, '61. Running time, 115 MINS.
Marjorie Penrose .... Lana Turner
Arthur Winner .... Efrem Zimbalist Jr.
Julius Penrose .... Jason Robards Jr.
Warren Winner .... George Hamilton
Helen Detweiler .... Susan Kohner
Clarissa Winner .... Barbara Bel Geddes
Noah Tuttle .... Thomas Mitchell
Reggie .... Everett Sloane
Veronica Kovacs .... Yvonne Craig
Junie McCarthy .... Jean Willes
Jerry Brophy .... Frank Maxwell
Mr. Woolf .... Gilbert Green
Bernie Breck .... Carroll O'Connor

When, towards the climax of this Mirisch-Seven Arts production, Lana Turner strokes the brow of Efrem Zimbalist Jr., with whom she's just spent an adulterous interlude, and whispers, "I don't want this night to end," it's obvious that James Gould Couzzens' thoughtful, bestselling and (for him) sexy novel has been reduced to a complex soap opera of melodramatic cliches. The long-range boxoffice pull of "By Love Possessed" will have to depend on the interest created by the well-known title, plus the personal draw of Miss Turner, Zimbalist and the other performers.

In barest outline, the Dennis screenplay seems much like the source material: a look into the lives of a half-dozen socially prominent, well-to-do citizens in a small eastern town (switched, for no apparent reason, from Maryland to Massachusetts). The focal point is a successful lawyer, Efrem Zimbalist Jr., who, in the course of several climactic days, finds that his perfectly ordered life is, in reality, as full of self-deception and chaos as the lives of some of his less stable friends. The latter include his law partner, Jason Robards, who, after a crippling accident, refuses the love-pity of his wife, Miss Turner, who subsequently turns to double scotches and solace with Zimbalist.

Further complications involve Zimbalist's inability to understand his son, George Hamilton ("Dad, we sort of talk at each other. We don't communicate"), with the result that his son seeks release with the town hussy, who charges the boy with rape. There is also the problem of Hamilton's parentally-encouraged engagement to wealthy Susan Kohner, who promptly commits suicide (by

drinking cleaning fluid) when Hamilton rejects her.

Clearly, almost any one of these situations could have provided material for a feature all by itself. That's the major problem in the film. It tries to cover too much narrative ground, with the result that no one character or situation can be explored to the degree necessary for the audience to understand or be emotionally moved by their king-sized plights.

This flaw is emphasized by the manner in which director John Sturges has chosen to relate the story—a series of short, talky, inconclusive scenes which never permit the players to create anything but an approximation of a character.

Miss Turner looks beautiful in a great wardrobe, but can only suggest the ironic, gutsy dame the character might have been. Zimbalist spends most of his time looking thoughtful while chomping on his pipe, and Robards, with no help from the script whatsoever, just limps and looks pained.

Barbara Bel Geddes, as Zimbalist's understanding wife, almost overcomes the script with a warm performance tinged with humor. Somewhat lively, and likeable, too, is Thomas Mitchell, as Zimbalist's senior law partner, who eventually is unmasked as an arch-embezzler (though for reasons that would do credit to Robin Hood). Hamilton and Miss Kohner are as adequate as can be expected. Scoring nicely in a small, quite silly role, is Yvonne Craig, as the town trollop who persists in talking about herself in the third person.

The film has been handsomely produced by Walter Mirisch, with the lush settings, indoors and out, photographed in DeLuxe color. Elmer Bernstein's musical score is (perhaps intentionally) intrusive as it anticipates the action on the screen and, occasionally describes emotional crises of a depth hardly suggested by the performers.
Anby.

Wild In The Country
(C'SCOPE-COLOR)

Shaky, contrived portrait of Presley as a potential literary genius. His own following plus added marquee and production values should lend it necessary zip at the b.o.

Hollywood, June 7.
Twentieth-Fox release of Jerry Wald production. Stars Elvis Presley, Hope Lange, Tuesday Weld, Millie Perkins, Rafer Johnson, John Ireland. Directed by Philip Dunne. Screenplay, Clifford Odets, based on novel, "The Lost Country," by J. R. Salamanca; camera (DeLuxe), William C. Mellor; editor, Dorothy Spencer; art directors, Jack Martin Smith, Preston Ames; music, Kenyon Hopkins; sound, Alfred Bruzlin, Warren B. Delaplain; assistant director, Joseph E. Rickards. Reviewed at the studio, June 7, '61. Running time, 112 MINS.
Glenn .... Elvis Presley
Irene .... Hope Lange
Noreen .... Tuesday Weld
Betty Lee .... Millie Perkins
Davis .... Rafer Johnson
Phil Macy .... John Ireland
Cliff Macy .... Gary Lockwood
Uncle Rolfe .... William Mims
Dr. Underwood ..... Raymond Greenleaf
Monica George...... Christina Crawford
Flossie .... Robin Raymond
Mrs. Parsons .... Doreen Lang
Mr. Parsons .... Charles Arnt
Sarah .... Ruby Goodwin
Willie Dace .... Will Corry
Professor Larson .... Alan Napier
Judge Parker .... Jason Robards, Sr.
Bartender .... Harry Carter

Sam Tyler ....Harry Shannon
Hank Tyler ....Bobby West

For the easygoing, less discriminating patron of the cinematic arts, "Wild In The Country" should be acceptable as a slickly-produced, glamorously-cast hunk of romantic fiction that won't trouble the mind when one leaves the theatre. What with Elvis Presley's name to grace the marquee in company with three attractive and much-talked-about leading ladies who transmit a hint of amorous fireworks to the romantically-inclined filmgoer, the Jerry Wald production for 20th-Fox appears to be on safe commercial ground. But all this Simoniz cannot quite make a new car out of an old Model T.

Dramatically, there simply isn't substance, novelty or spring to this wobbly and artificial tale of a maltreated country boy (Presley) who, supposedly, has the talent to become a great writer, but lacks the means, the emotional stability and the encouragement until he comes in contact with a beautiful psychiatric consultant (Hope Lange) who develops traumas of her own in the process. The complications occur when the two spend an innocent night in a motel, innocent on the strength of their May (he)-December (she) respect for each other. The gap in romantic seasons is quickly bridged when their one-night relationship is misinterpreted by some of the incredibly foul and mischievous people who live in the town, leading to her near-suicide, his near-manslaughter-charge and an ultimate amicable parting of the lovers, he to college, she presumably to sit it out. Clifford Odets penned the screenplay, an adaptation of a novel by J. R. Salamanca. The writing has its occasional rewards.

It is difficult to accept the character as a "potential literary genius" and, for that matter, the lovely and sophisticated Miss Lange as a lonely, learned widow with surprisingly few male admirers but a penchant for resurrecting lost, young, boyish souls. It's a credit to both that they do as well as they do. Presley, subdued, uses what dramatic resources he has to best advantage in this film. Miss Lange, for the most part, plays intelligently and sensitively. Tuesday Weld, steadily improving as an actress, contributes a flashy and arresting portrait of a sexy siren enamored of Mr. P. A third romantic entanglement is portrayed adequately by Millie Perkins, who returns to the screen after an almost 30-month absence since her debut as "Anne Frank." Others promiment on the scene are John Ireland, Rafer Johnson and Gary Lockwood. There is an especially fine supporting performance by William Mims. Philip Dunne's direction is responsible for several vivid, engrossing sequences. But the whole canvas is not stable or uniform. Some of the key scenes seem rushed, some of the lesser ones protracted.

Story, set in the Shenandoah Valley, was filmed in the Napa Valley. The picturesque views through William C. Mellor's lens help erase some of the geographical make-believe, as does the discerning art direction of Jack Martin Smith and Preston Ames. Sensitive sound by Alfred Bruzlin and Warren B. Delaplain aids in conveying an authenticity to the production. Kenyon Hopkins' music has warmth and body. Sans wiggle, Presley croons four or five songs, one of which, the title tune by Hugo Peretti, Luigi Creatori and George Weiss, sounds destined for the big hit charts. The others are soft and sweet, with the exception of "I Slipped, I Fell," a mild rocker by Fred Weiss and Ben Weidman. Guitars rather mysteriously keep turning up on the premises, but E.P. leaves the plunking to Miss Weld. *Tube.*

Most Dangerous Man Alive

Columbia Pictures release of Benedict Bogeaus production. Stars Ron Randell, Debra Paget, Elaine Stewart. Directed by Allan Dwan. Screenplay, James Leicester, Phillip Rock, based on story, "The Steel Monster," by Rock and Michael Pate; camera, Carl Carvahal; editor, Carlos Lodato; music, Louis Forbes; sound, Joe Kavigan. Reviewed at the studio, June 1, '61. Running time, 82 MINS.

Eddie Candell ....Ron Randell
Linda ....Debra Paget
Carla Angelo...........Elaine Stewart
Damon ....Anthony Caruso
Lt. Fisher ....Gregg Palmer
Captain Davis ....Morris Ankrum
Dr. Meeker ....Tudor Owen
Devola ....Steve Mitchell
Franscetti ....Joel Donte

"Most Dangerous Man Alive" is a grade B melodrama designed for nightcapping purposes on Columbia's doubleheader packages. Even in that subsidiary capacity, the Benedict Bogeaus production will not be a very handy item to have around. In fact, it may be an unwelcome companion with which to burden major theatrical product aimed at enlightened 1961 audiences.

The James Leicester-Phillip Rock screenplay, based on "The Steel Monster," a story concocted out of the wild imaginations of Rock and Michael Pate, is concerned with the problem of a condemned, though innocent, man who, fleeing the law, wanders into a desert test site for a cobalt bomb explosion, becomes exposed to the rays of a mysterious cobalt element X and promptly turns into a steel chap. The rest of this shopworn, absurd and tasteless melodrama describes the iron man's campaign for revenge against those who have framed him, and the law's inept attempts to destroy him. Funniest line in recent screen annals occurs when the unfortunate fellow's bulletproof epidermis suddenly and unaccountably begins to revert to normal flesh as he is sprayed by gunfire. With happiness and relief, his beloved cries, "Eddie, you're bleeding!"

Allan Dwan's direction is sluggish and repetitious, Carl Carvahal's photography too dark and shadowy, Carlos Lodato's editing far from skillful, Joe Kavigan's soundtrack frequently noisy. Louis Forbes' score is unobtrusive.

All the actors labor in vain, especially Randell as the most curious by-product of U.S. Steel and Debra Paget and Elaine Stewart as bad girl and good girl, respectively. The only revealing things about the film are the negligees worn by these two young ladies. *Tube.*

Fanny
(COLOR)

Elaborate remake of the Marcel Pagnol perennial. A touching, thoroughly enjoyable entertainment for the whole family, with top performances and lovely pictorial values. Big b.o. in store.

Hollywood, June 9.

Warner Bros. release of Joshua Logan production; directed by Logan. Stars Leslie Caron, Maurice Chevalier, Charles Boyer, Horst Buchholz; features Salvatore Baccaloni, Lionel Jeffries, Raymond Bussieres. Screenplay, Julius J. Epstein based on play by S. N. Behrman and Logan, from the Marseilles Trilogy by Marcel Pagnol; camera (Technicolor), Jack Cardiff; editor, William H. Reynolds; art director, Rino Mondellini; music, Harold Rome; sound, Jean Monchablon, Richard Vorisek; assistant director, Michel Romanoff. Reviewed June 9, '61. Running time, 133 MINS.

Fanny ....Leslie Caron
Panisse ....Maurice Chevalier
Cesar ....Charles Boyer
Marius ....Horst Buchholz
Escartifique ....Salvatore Baccaloni
Monsieur Brun ......Lionel Jeffries
Admiral ....Raymond Bussieres
Louis Panisse ....Victor Francen
Honorine ....Georgette Anys
Cesario ....Joel Flateau

Marcel Pagnol's enduring creation has had a peculiar history. Center of a trilogy ("Marius," "Fanny" and "Cesar") penned some 30 years ago, it graduated from stage to screen in 1933 French film versions that, sans English titles, died after a week's exhibition in a New York theatre. Refurbished with titles and an additional 25-minutes in 1948, it became an unforgettable motion picture and an art house click in this country. Earlier, in 1938, Metro had produced a film (a Wallace Beery starrer titled "Port of the Seven Seas") based on the Pagnol yarn. Then, of course, there was the Broadway musical version in 1956. It is the presence of this latter factor that may result in some advance audience confusion, since many may be expecting a screen counterpart of the musical, which "Fanny" isn't. The only music in "Fanny"-1961 is the soaring, affecting and elaborate arrangement of the beautiful title song by composer Harold Rome, "adapted" by Harry Sukman and sensitively conducted by Morris Stoloff to provide a sweeping romantic underscore for the entire production.

Although the deep sentiment in Pagnol's tale constantly threatens to lapse into maudlinity in this film, it never quite does. The sentiment is wholesome and is made tolerable by the rapport between characters and audience established early in the picture. Pagnol's story, skillfully adapted by Julius J. Epstein out of the original Marseilles Trilogy and the legit book by S. N. Behrman and Logan, focuses upon four peoples: a thrifty waterfront bar operator (Charles Boyer); his son (Horst Buchholz), who has a yen to sail away to the "isles beneath the wind"; a fishmonger's daughter (Leslie Caron) in love with the wanderlustful lad; and an aging, wealthy widower (Maurice Chevalier), whose great wish is to add "& Son" to the sign above his shop. Buchholz sails off, leaving Miss Caron with a yet-unborn son. On the rebound she weds Chevalier, providing him with the heir he has so long been denied. Upon his death, with rather astonishable compassion and heart, he virtually bequeathes his wife and child to Buchholz, who has been pining away for his beloved on dry land after finding those cherished isles just so much "volcanic ash."

Through Logan's delicate direction, the combination of profoundly-touching pathos and lusty sense of humor is blended into a film rich in humanity and pictorial beauty, though perhaps not quite so spontaneously merry and charmingly simple as the superb trilogy that preceded it by so many years. There is, however, a fuzziness about the relationship of period and customs that may trouble some customers.

The contribution of cameraman Jack Cardiff is enormous, ranging from great, sweeping panoramic Technicolor views of the port of Marseilles and the sea to tight, intimate shots of the faces of the principles that turn the entire screen the color of flesh. His interior lighting has a beauty all its own, leaving the memory heir to a number of indelibly poetic images. There's an ACE of an editing job by William H. Reynolds, highlighted by quick cuts that punctuate scenes to establish the relevant state of action elsewhere. Art director Rino Mondellini's sets and artistic detail are authentic and atmospheric, and Anne-Marie Marchand's costumes are a perfect complement to personality and locale. Ben Kadish merits favorable mention in his post as associate producer.

Miss Caron, who certainly has an enviable win-place-and-show parlay of first names going ("Lili" to "Gigi" to "Fanny" — what a double-play combo!), employs that Gallic gamin quality to full advantage again, and scores with a warm enactment of the title character. Buchholz does a nice job as "Marius," playing the role with conviction and restraint. But a couple of old pros named Boyer and Chevalier walk off with the picture. Boyer, playing the "Raimu" role, does it with heart, gusto, humor and manliness—a colorful, compelling portrayal. Chevalier is Chevalier, surely one of the most infectiously lovable and evergreen personalities ever to hit the screen. There are a batch of stimulating character performances, especially those of Georgette Anys as Miss Caron's raffish, but respectability-obsessed mother; Raymond Bussieres as a cracked "old salt" who's spent his life in drydock but represents a kind of "spirit of the sea"; and Lionel Jeffries and Salvatore Baccaloni as a pair of rowdy chums who team with Boyer and Chevalier to supply the film with its humorous interludes. Joel Flateau is adequate as the youngster who enriches Chevalier's life but causes all the romantic fuss. *Tube.*

The Silent Call

Familiar story of wandering dog hunting for young master. Modest item, amiably told.

Hollywood, June 15.

Twentieth-Fox release of Leonard A. Schwartz production. Stars Gail Russell, David McLean, Roger Mobley. Directed by John Bushelman. Screenplay, Tom Maruzzi; camera, Kay Norton; editor,

Carl Pierson; art director, John Mansbridge; music, Richard D. Aurandt; sound, Larry Gannon; assistant director, Frank Parmenter. Reviewed at the studio, June 15, '61. Running time, **62 MINS.**

Guy	Roger Mobley
Joe Brancato	David McLean
Florie Brancato	Gail Russell
Art	Joe Besser
Muscles	Jack Younger
Moose	Rusty Wescoatt
Sid	Roscoe Ates
Johnny	Sherwood Keith
Mohammed	Milton Parsons
Old Man	Dal McKennon

The oft-told, but durably disarming, tale of the faithful dog that journeyed 1,000 miles in search of its departed and despandent young master is retold in "The Silent Call." As in most such boy-and-his-dog films, the Leonard A. Schwartz production (his first) fares better with the dog than it does with the boy, but the audience for whom the picture is unpretentiously designed should find it affectionate and easy to take. Lasting a short and sweet 62 minutes, the 20th-Fox release out of its API mill will make a satisfactory program companion for summer playdates, especially in theatres with well-populated children's sections.

Tom Maruzzi's simple yarn separates a lad (Roger Mobley) from his pet, Pete (formerly the "Dog of Flanders"), when his poor parents (Gail Russell and David McLean) move from Elko, Nev. to L.A. in a small economy car. Left behind with a rather unsavory neighbor, the pooch breaks away and follows the uncertain trail, encountering a series of misadventures enroute. Meanwhile, the unhappy, dogmatic child is moping around in his new home, making life generally miserable for his patient, indulgent parents. Finally the itinerant canine arrives, and it is instantly evident (as, actually, it had been all along) that this family will live happily-ever-arf-arfter.

The talented dog truly earns his Ken-L-Ration. Miss Russell and McLean are capable as the parents and Master Mobley is adequate as the boy. There are a flock of offbeat character portrayals (hobos, hermits and truckees encountered by the dog). Among these supporting players are Joe Besser, Roscoe Ates, Milton Parsons, Dal McKennon, Sherwood Keith, Jack Younger, Rusty Wescoatt and H. Tom Hart.

Director John Bushelman has done a generally commendable job, as have cameraman Kay Norton, editor Carl Pierson, art director John Mansbridge and composer Richard D. Aurandt, all making effective contributions on a modest scale. *Tube.*

Two Rode Together
(COLOR)

John Ford "adult" western that is often too childish for adults, too adult for children. Story of efforts to bring back whites from Comanche captivity, marked by James Stewart's fine performance and visual beauty. Has the marquee horsepower to score required b.o. points.

Hollywood, June 15.

Columbia Pictures release of Stan Shpetner production. Stars James Stewart, Richard Widmark, Shirley Jones; features Linda Cristal, Andy Devine, John McIntire. Directed by John Ford. Screenplay, Frank Nugent, based on novel by Will Cook; camera (Eastman), Charles Lawton Jr.; editor, Jack Murray; art director, Robert Peterson; music, George Duning; sound, Harry Mills; assistant director, Wingate Smith. Reviewed at Academy Awards Theatre, June 15, '61. Running time, **108 MINS.**

Guthrie McCabe	James Stewart
Lt. Jim Gary	Richard Widmark
Marty Purcell	Shirley Jones
Elena	Linda Cristal
Sgt. Darius P. Posey	Andy Devine
Major Frazer	John McIntire
Edward Purcell	Paul Birch
Mr. Wringle	Willis Bouchey
Quanah	Henry Brandon
Jackson Clay	Harry Carey Jr.
Abby Frazer	Olive Carey
Boone Clay	Ken Curtis
Ward Corbey	Chet Douglas
Belle Aragon	Annelle Hayes
Running Wolf	David Kent
Mrs. Malaprop	Anna Lee
Mrs. McCandless	Jeannette Nolan
Ole Knudsen	John Qualen
Henry Clay	Ford Rainey
Stone Calf	Woody Strode
Officer	O. Z. Whitehead
William McCandless	Cliff Lyons
Hannah Clay	Mae Marsh
Capt. Malaprop	Frank Baker
Woman	Ruth Clifford
Lt. Chase	Ted Knight
Post Doctor	Major Sam Harris

John Ford's new western is of the adult variety, a story of the ill-advised attempt to haul white prisoners back to civilized society in the 1880's after they have spent a decade or more suffering the slings and arrows of Comanche Indian captivity. This is fairly fresh sagebrush fiction, invading and surveying a relatively untapped corner of American history. From that standpoint, the film has validity and novelty. But somehow the Stan Shpetner production, directed by Ford, misfires in the process.

The difficulty seems to stem from an uncertainty as to basically for whom the film is designed. Being a western, it is more or less taken for granted that it will be appealing to children. And yet youngsters, fed visions of cowboys and Indians, are likely to be disappointed at the almost total absence of action or suspense and confused over the tricky matters (compromise, fallen women, even rape) upon which a great deal of the story dwells. Since the picture therefore falls rather squarely into the adult western classification, by virtue of the mature issues with which it is dealing, it requires a firm, adult approach. But this, regrettably, isn't consistently forthcoming.

Whereas parts of the film zoom into the heavy, psychological sphere of the ultra-modern western, others revert to the outmoded innocence and directness of a 30-year-old sagebrush style, as if intended as parody. This inconsistency, along with several patches of far-fetched theatricality and a certain lethargy in coming to the point may trouble some of the more restless, discerning adult customers.

There are, however, compensations, especially of a commercial nature. Not the least of these is the unusually practical, non-heroic nature of the central character, most disarmingly and authoritatively enacted by James Stewart. The great degree to which this character is a departure from the traditional variety of western "tall man" will attract attention, please those accustomed to less radical displays of substance in western heroes, and should stimulate favorable comment. Then, too, there is a fairly strong marquee cast, led by Stewart, Richard Widmark and recent Oscar winner Shirley Jones, plus the name of Ford as a creative backbone to the production. All aspects considered, the Columbia release has the values to hold its own.

As noted, Frank Nugent's screenplay, based on the novel by Will Cook, describes an attempt by two adventurers (Stewart and Widmark), on behalf of a group of generally despondent immigrants, to enter the Comanche camp and bring back, peacefully, sons, daughters and wives who have been captured in Indian raids years before. The task is basically hopeless because the prisoners either had been kidnapped too young and indoctrinated too thoroughly into the identity of the Indian to be restorable, or else too old to make an acceptable reverse transition.

Nevertheless, two prisoners are reclaimed and brought back. One, a young brave of 17, is too bewildered to adjust, reacts wildly and winds up lynched. The other, a Mexican maiden (Linda Cristal) five years the squaw of a Comanche chieftain, is given a rough time by the narrow-minded Officers' Club set, eventually rides off into the sunset for a better life with the equally disenchanted Stewart who, in the process of playing the unwilling hero, has lost his job, his financial prospects, and his patience.

Stewart far and away cops histrionic honors, employing and projecting all the casual charm, assurance and personal magnetism he has developed in the course of a long and distinguished career. It's a performance sure to delight his many fans. A level of competence is attained by most of the other players, prominent among whom are Misses Jones and Cristal, Andy Devine (slightly plumper but otherwise the same raspy-voiced, amiable character he was years ago) and John McIntire. Widmark does a respectable job, but somehow this skilled actor seems to lose much of his natural color and excitement in straight heroic parts such as this. Perhaps it's the auspicious way in which he vaulted to stardom as Tommy Udo, but he still seems most at home in the character of a heavy. Able support is contributed by John Qualen, Paul Birch, Willis Bouchey, Harry Carey Jr., Olive Carey, Ken Curtis, Annelle Hayes, David Kent, Jeannette Nolan, Henry Brandon and Woody Strode.

Director Ford, while no doubt considerably responsible for the aforementioned inconsistency of concept, does endow the film with the unmistakable stamp of his personality, both in the pictorial and dramatic areas. First-class aid he obtains from Charles Lawton Jr., whose Eastman Color views are frequently striking in shade and composition; editor Jack Murray, whose knitting is mechanically sound; art director Robert Peterson, whose sets correctly convey the period; and composer George Duning, whose pretty score gives body and tone to the action without intruding. *Tube.*

Ne Dokantchenee Pismo
(The Unposted Letter)
(RUSSIAN)

Paris, June 13.

Mosfilm production and release stars Tatiana Samoilova; features Innokenty Somtunovsky, Evgeny Urbansky, Vasily Livanov. Directed by Mikhail Kalatozov. Screenplay, V. Ossipov, Kalatozov; camera, Serguei Oussessky; editor, N. Anikina. At Lord Byron, Paris. Running time, **80 MINS.**

Tania	Tatiana Samoilova
Sabinine	Innokenty Smoktunovsky
Serguei	Evgeny Urbansky
Andrej	Vasily Livanov

Film was yanked from the Cannes Film Fest of 1960, and it is easy to see why. Because this both taunts and vaunts the Soviet penchant for worker heroics. A happier ending reportedly was finally added. At any rate, the film has some expert lyrical passages and a feel for people in crisis. On this it could be of some interest in foreign marts.

The same team, which made the prizewinning "Flying Cranes," was responsible. It has the same bravura, dexterous camerawork and the winning thesping of Tatiana Samoilova.

Four geologists are looking for diamonds in Siberia. There are three men and a girl. When they finally find them, a forest fire has them lost and then dying one by one as the winter sets in. Only one man makes it after a harrowing trek.

Love pokes its way into the quartet as a more elemental type tries to win the girl from her intellectual lover. But it is the trek back that is the main aspect of the film. From glory for the motherland, the return becomes just a hallucinated need to stay alive.

Film has a brilliant feel for the elements and man's place in them. For once the Russians are mainly human, and a sharp note of protest is noted as the radio talks of the great national feat they have accomplished when they are actually lost and dying.

The camera literally flies through the woods after them or soars in a helicopter. Lensing also has a stark contrast in keeping with the theme. *Mosk.*

Tammy Tell Me True
(COLOR)

Syrupy confection for popcorn munchers. Wholesome sequel graced with a new leading lady, should be lucrative vacash-season contender.

Hollywood, June 9.

Universal release of Ross Hunter production. Stars Sandra Dee, John Gavin; features Charles Drake, Virginia Grey, Julia Meade. Directed by Harry Keller. Screenplay, Oscar Brodney, based on novel by Cid Ricketts Sumner; camera (Eastman), Clifford Stine; editor, Otto Ludwig; art directors, Alexander Golitzen, Alfred Sweeney; music, Percy Faith; sound, Waldon O. Watson, Frank W. Wilkinson; assistant director, Joseph Kenny. Reviewed at Beverly Theatre, June 9, '61. Running time, **97 MINS.**

Tammy	Sandra Dee
Tom Freeman	John Gavin
Buford Woodley	Charles Drake
Miss Jenks	Virginia Grey
Suzanne Rook	Julia Meade
Mrs. Call	Beulah Bondi
Captain Joe	Cecil Kellaway
Judge Carver	Edgar Buchanan
Rita	Gigi Perreau
Della	Juanita Moore
Joshua Welling	Hayden Rorke
Caleb Slade	Ward Ramsey
Captain Armand	Henry Corden
Roger	Don Dorrell
Joan	Pat McNulty
Kay	Taffy Paul
John	Lowell Brown
Phil	Bill Herrin

Mrs. Bateman	Catherine McLeod
Professor Bateman	Ross Elliott
Dr. Stach	Ned Wever

Though certainly limited in appeal, "Tammy Tell Me True" is "limited" to that vast and responsive legion of filmgoers known vaguely but affectionately in the trade as the "family audience." This being the season when the "family audience" is in its most "family way," what with school being out, and in its most theatrical mood, what with theatres being 20-degrees cooler than the hot air outside of them and television being relegated to furniture status thanks to its annual affliction of rerunitis, the Ross Hunter production figures to make satisfactory boxoffice hay while the sun shines. But it is only fair to note that this is decidedly not the sort of entertainment calculated to whet the tastes of those who prefer Scotch to cherry cokes, charades to blind man's buff, and bridge to old maid. The Universal-International release is not designed for anyone who entertains even the slightest notion of sophistication.

The character, "Tammy," first appeared on the screen four years ago in the person of Debbie Reynolds. With Miss Reynolds having moved on to other things, the role has been taken over by Sandra Dee of "Gidget" fame, a character that she, like Miss Reynolds with "Tammy," has relinquished to a substitute. Sort of a Hollywood variation on musical chairs. Oscar Brodney, who penned the original "Tammy and the Bachelor" scenario, also has written the sequel. He has retained the spirit of the original character, a kind of composite of Pollyanna, Gidget, Lili and Liza Doolittle, with a little Ma Kettle thrown in for good measure.

According to Brodney's plot, Tammy docks her shantyboat on the shores of dear old Seminola U to get a little book larnin' so's she can measure up to boy friend Pete, who's also away at College. There she meets prof John Gavin, with whom she learns to forget all about good ol' Pete, and eccentric dowager Beulah Bondi, who leaves her manse to enjoy the simple life on the river in Tammy's floating version of home-sweet-home. The "joke" of the picture (there's really only one) is Tammy's personality clash with organized society. Her incredible naivete ("you mean they got pills for puttin' people to sleep?") covers a heart of pure gold, a disposition of pure sunshine, a mind of pure common sense insight, an identity of pure cornball.

Director Harry Keller has not overlooked a single opportunity to slip in sentiment. The going gets pretty sticky and lethargic. Several scenes have their moments, and the picture has its scenes, but any slightly discerning spectator will consistently be a hop, skip and jump ahead of the script.

Miss Dee does a fine job of submerging her personality and glamour within the character although, in effect, she is doing a kind of imitation of Debbie Reynolds imitating the all-American farmer's daughter. There is probably no more handsome actor on the screen today than Gavin. Pity that about all he's required to do here is roar with amusement over Miss Dee's antics. The character is little more than a substitute for canned laughter. Others besides Miss Bondi who are frequently noticeable are Charles Drake, Virginia Grey, Julia Meade, Cecil Kellaway, Edgar Buchanan and Gigi Perreau.

The photoplay by Clifford Stine is flattering. The colorful sets by Alexander Golitzen and Alfred Sweeney look like sets. Percy Faith's music is romantically stimulating. There's a title song, by Dorothy Squires, that's sung by Miss Dee. It's no "Tammy," but it's listenable. *Tube.*

Homicidal

Handy suspense melodrama with good returns indicated backed by strong exploitation campaign.

Hollywood, June 9.

Columbia Pictures release of William Castle production. Stars Glenn Corbett. Patricia Breslin. Eugenie Leontovich; features Jean Arless, Alan Bunce. Richard Rust, James Westerfield, Gilbert Green. Directed by Castle. Screenplay, Robb White; camera, Burnett Guffey; music, Hugo Friedhofer; editor, Edwin Bryant; sound, Lambert Day; art director, Cary Odell; assistant director, Al Shenberg. Reviewed at Academy Award Theatre, June 8, '61. Running time, **87 MINS.**

Karl	Glenn Corbett
Miriam Webster	Patricia Breslin
Emily	Jean Arless
Helga	Eugenie Leontovich
Dr. Jonas	Alan Bunce
Jim Nesbitt	Richard Rust
Mr. Adrims	James Westerfield
Lt. Miller	Gilbert Green
Olie	Wolfe Barzell
Mrs. Adrims	Hope Summers
Mrs. Forest	Teri Brooks
1st Clerk	Ralph Moody
2nd Clerk	Joe Forte

Producer-director William Castle lifts a choice morsel from headlines out of Scandinavia a decade ago to build the climax of his latest horror melo and backtrack his suspenseful narrative leading up to a surprise and chilling finish. Film, despite certain corny elements and a few misplaced laughs, has every appearance of a boxoffice hit in exploitation bookings where smart campaigns pay off. Castle again displays a forte for macabre entertainment in his handling of Robb White's definitive screenplay which carried all the ingredients for this type of fare.

As in all films of this nature, audience isn't asked to swallow a completely believable tale; accept it for what it is, argue about it later but take it straight during its unfoldment. There's a gimmick toward the end, a sudden interruption during a particularly suspenseful moment, in which a design is flashed on the screen with the words, "This is a fright break," in which the audience is given 45 seconds to contain themselves. It's good for laughs, probably intended by Castle and White, a good mood piece and showmanship which builds to even greater suspense.

Yarn opens on a mysterious note of murder, a bride killing a justice of the peace with a scalpel immediately after the ceremony, which isn't cleared up until the final wrap-up; then not too clearly. Plottage then takes the bride from Ventura, Calif., where she hires a hotel bellboy for $2,000 to be her groom for the moment, to Solvang, some distance away, and a gloomy old house where she lives with a paralyzed old woman unable to speak and the young man who owns the house but is seldom home. In a weird recital of events, it develops that bride registered at hotel under the name of the young man's half-sister, who owns a flower shop in Solvang; there's deep hatred between the murderess and the old woman ending in latter's violent death; and the half-sister is nearly murdered when she returns to the house with her brother. Ending cannot be revealed here because it would dissipate its shock element, but would have benefitted by clearer exposition.

Jean Arless makes her screen bow as the murderess, and is generally okay although there are occasions when her part doesn't ring true. Patricia Breslin delivers nicely as the half-sister, caught in a web which nearly destroys her, and Glenn Corbett handily enacts the druggist in love with her. Eugenie Leontovich as the old woman spins a neat characterization sans a word of dialog. Alan Bunce as a doctor, Richard Rust the bridegroom and James Westerfield the justice of the peace are competent.

Castle, who appears in a prolog to set the mood, delivers strongly in his double assignment as producer-director and gets top backing down through the technical credits. Edwin Bryant's editing is sharp and fast, Burnett Guffey's photography and Hugo Friedhofer's music first-rate and Cary Odell's art direction in keeping. *Whit.*

Misty
(C'SCOPE-COLOR)

Sweet, simple tale of a boy, a girl and a pony. Occasionally too sweet, but welcome fare for the neglected family trade. Good summer vacash prospects.

Hollywood, June 5.

Twentieth-Fox release of Robert B. Radnitz production. Stars David Ladd, Arthur O'Connelly. Directed by James B. Clark. Screenplay, Ted Sherdeman, based on book, "Misty of Chincoteague," by Marguerite Henry; camera (De Luxe), Leo Tover, Lee Garmes; editor, Fredrick Y. Smith; art directors, Duncan Cramer, Maurice Ransford; music, Paul Sawtell, Bert Shefter; sound, Bernard Freericks, Frank W. Moran; assistant director, Stanley Hough. Reviewed at the studio, June 5, '61. Running time, **92 MINS.**

Paul Beebe	David Ladd
Grandpa Beebee	Arthur O'Connell
Maureen Beebe	Pat Smith
Grandma Beebe	Anne Seymour
Eba Jones	Duke Farley

"Breakin's the quick way, gentlin's the sure way," remarks Arthur O'Connell in this film, as he considers the proper way to tame a wild pony. Employing the same horse sense in his attempt to tame a wild audience, producer Robert B. ("Dog Of Flanders") Radnitz has, in "Misty," succeeded in "gentling" a product specifically for those outspoken multitudes righteously indignant over the scarcity of recent film fare tailored for juvenile or "family" style consumption. Just in time for the school's-out swerve in audience proportion, this modest little pony tale do its mite to pacify the alarm among nervous parents bewildered by the neighborhood theatrical menu whenever they're about to shoo their little Kelloggers off to the matinee. That alone seems to assure the 20th-Fox release of a respectable summer showing. It's a sure-fire "matinee idyll."

The risk inherent in designing films point-blank at the family trade, is in going overboard in the sweetness and lovability departments. It is here that "Misty" occasionally grows too misty-eyed for adult comfort. But if Messrs. Radnitz, James B. Clark (the director) and Ted Sherdeman (the scenarist) are guilty of sporadic sugar-lumping, they are able to be commended for sidestepping temptations to resort to the screen's most inevitable cliche in an equestrian picture — the grand climax in which the horse-hero wins the big race.

Based on Marguerite Henry's tome, Sherdeman's screenplay describes the love of two youngsters for a wild pony they eventually acquire after a good deal of painstaking financial maneuvering and sentimental tension. Grooming the animal for the big race, they find themselves unable to deny any further its longing for the freedom of yon wild game preserve, where its stallion friend continually whinnies with a monogamous passion remarkable in stallions. Some filmgoers may be slightly "Misty"-fied by the abrupt fashion in which the picture thus changes horses in midstream, so to speak, but the ending is refreshing in that it catches an audience off guard.

The children are played by David Ladd and Pam Smith, both amiable and handsome. Director Clark, however, has failed to sense the element of repetition that marks his scene-endings where the youngsters are involved. Too often (four or five times), scenes are concluded with the children giggling happily over some development. It's tedious. Arthur O'Connell, as their grandpa, draws the meatiest lines and, with veteran instinct, plays them to the hilt. Anne Seymour is equally fine as their grandma. Almost all of the other parts are played by the citizens of Chincoteague, Va., site of the film.

The Leo Tover-Lee Garmes photography is, to the eye, like a tenement dweller's daydream of the country. Art direction (Duncan Cramer-Maurice Ransford) and editing (Fredrick Y. Smith) are professionally dispatched. There's pastoral beauty to the Paul Sawtell-Bert Shefter score (much of which is an elaborate arrangement of the old folk refrain, "Buckeye Jim"). Sound by Bernard Freericks and Frank W. Moran has an especially vivid quality. *Tube.*

King Of The Roaring 20's — The Story Of Arnold Rothstein

Choppy, superficial biopic of the infamous moneyman. Exploitation will help.

Allied Artists release of Samuel Bischoff-David Diamond production. Stars David Janssen, Mickey Rooney, Dianne Foster, Jack Carson, Dan O'Herlihy, Mickey Shaughnessy, Keenan Wynn, Joseph Schildkraut, William Demarest. Directed by Joseph M. Newman. Screenplay, Jo Swerling, based on book, "The Big Bankroll," by Leo Katcher; camera, Carl Guthrie; editor, George White; art director, David Milton; music, Franz Waxman; sound, Ralph Butler; assistant director, Lindsley Parsons Jr. Reviewed

at Academy Awards Theatre, June 12, '61. Running time, 106 MINS.

Arnold Rothstein	David Janssen
Carolyn Green	Dianne Foster
"Big Tim" O'Brien	Jack Carson
Madge	Diana Dors
Phil Butler	Dan O'Herlihy
Jim Kelly	Mickey Shaughnessy
Tom Fowler	Keenan Wynn
Abraham Rothstein	Joseph Schildkraut
Hecht	William Demarest
Williams	Mervyn Vye
Bill Baird	Regis Toomey
Lenny	Robert Ellenstein
Joanie	Teri Janssen
Johnny Burke	Mickey Rooney

Even the most devout aficionados of crime-a-la-cinema are likely to find the going pretty skimpy in this wobbly chronicle of the wretched-on-a-grand-scale career of one Arnold Rothstein. Besides being weighted down with the longest and most cumbersome title of the current screen year, the Samuel Bischoff-David Diamond production, in spite of some pregnant casting and several high-powered performances, is tediously mechanical in character and outrageously contrived in its embellishment of the "real life" story. Commercially, the Allied Artists release will go only so far as thorough exploitation can take it, which doesn't figure to be too far.

Pity of the matter is the fact that producers Bischoff and Diamond, director Joseph M. Newman and scenarist Jo Swerling, in dealing with one of the most provocative, mysterious figures in the annals of the upper-underworld, have somehow diluted him into a shallow, colorless, entirely unsavory vestige of a man. Out of a "King," they have created a crooked bookkeeper. Had they pinpointed, and elaborated upon, one key incident in his infamous career instead of endeavoring to cover the whole story (from Leo Katcher's book, "The Big Bankroll"), far more insight into his unique drive and personality might well have resulted. As it is, neither Rothstein nor any of the other characters associated with him in this choppy exercise emerge people of dimension. Relationships are fuzzy, motivations unclear and the romantic story (devoted wife, business-consumed husband, domestic void) shopworn.

The story traces Rothstein's rise, via a mind that is three-quarters IBM, one-quarter SOB, to riches and prominence among the chief chiselers, crooks and millionaires of his time. He meets an early demise as a consequence of some shady double-dealings in which he seals the violent fate of his best boyhood friend (Mickey Rooney). The film ends on an unbelievably phony note. All his life, Rothstein, according to the story, has hoped someday to be dealt a royal flush poker hand. He happens to be playing poker with the boys when suddenly he is shot to death, and it would be condescending to describe here the nature of the final hand he never got to play.

David Janssen, an actor rising to stardom, does not benefit from the title role, nor does he play it with much variety or animation. The standout of the picture is Rooney, who brings warmth, gusto and conviction to a a short, but explosive role. Others who do fairly well are Keenan Wynn, Mickey Shaughnessy and Jack Carson. But none of the characters are clearly defined, and this hampers all of the performances, including those of Dan O'Herlihy, Joseph Schild-

kraut and William Demarest. Dianne Foster is affected as Janssen's unhappy spouse. Diana Dors is on briefly, and others who appear momentarily are Murvyn Vye, Regis Toomey, Robert Ellenstein, Teri Janssen (sister of the star), Timmy Rooney (son of the costar) and Jim Baird.

Journeyman contributions in the arts and crafts are fashioned by cameraman Carl Guthrie, art director David Milton, editor George White and composer-conductor Franz Waxman. *Tube.*

La Croix Et La Banniere
(The Cross and the Banner)
(FRENCH)

Paris, June 13.

Films Saint-Germain productions and release. Stars Evelyne Eiffel, Michel Bardinet, Michel Galabru. Directed by Philippe Ducrest. Screenplay, Jean-Louis Curtis, Ducrest; camera, Marc Fossard; editor, Marie-Louise De Canters. Preemed in Paris. Running time, 90 MINS.

Wife	Evelyne Eiffel
Husband	Michel Bardinet
Thief	Michel Galabru

Hazard of destroying a devoted married couple is the theme of this pic. But it lacks the insight into character to make the irony acceptable. It is thus mainly a limited arty entry.

A woman buys a handbag in which a thief on the run has hidden a diamond necklace. She does not know it but the husband discovers it and begins to suspect her. The couple breaks up. When the thief and woman happen to meet, they are shot by the jealous husband.

Direction overdoes interior monologs and closeups to miss the tingle and life which might have given this more dramatic feeling. However, there is some know-how in the flashback techniques and clever symbolism. But stiff acting keeps it from coming off. Technical credits are good. *Mosk.*

Vacances En Enfer
(Vacation in Hell)
(FRENCH)

Paris, June 13.

Warner Bros. release of Madeleine Films-Gilbert De Goldschmidt production. With Catherine Sola, Michel Subor, Elina Labourdette, Georges Poujouly, Michel Vitold. Directed by Jean Kerchbron. Screenplay, France Roche, Maurice Clavel from novel by Jean Bommart; camera, Marcel Fradetal; editor, Suzanne Bon. At Avenue, Paris. Running time, 80 MINS.

Catherine	Catherine Sola
Andre	Michel Subor
Mme. Martel	Elina Labourdette
Jean	Georges Poujouly
M. Martel	Michel Vitold

This is an okay programmer about the war's end. Actioner pic makes some attempt at a deeper definition of loyalty and heroism. But characters remain somewhat fuzzy and a tacked-on commentary also waters things down. It seems mainly a dualer for foreign chances with okay Continental exploitation aspects.

A French youth has fought with the Germans against the Russians during the last World War and flees as the end nears and comes back to save a family he knew from being killed by false partisans. It leads to love with the daughter and her attempt to help him escape into Spain despite his past.

It is during this trek that the youth performs a heroic thing

though seemingly doing it out of disdain and a reluctant heroism. Direction overdoes the violence for shock effect and rarely gives a feel for the time or an insight into the characters.

Technical credits are acceptable. Acting lacks the spark to make these people more than cardboard figures. Film has exploitation handles on its love scenes and action sections. *Mosk.*

Voyage to the Bottom Of the Sea
(C'SCOPE-COLOR)

Sleek production values dress up fast-paced if dramatically unsound sci-fi adventure tale about a sub skipper bent on saving mankind from catastrophe, in spite of mankind's unwillingness to be saved. Bright b.o. prospect.

Hollywood, June 21.

Twentieth-Fox release of Irwin Allen production. Stars Walter Pidgeon, Joan Fontaine, Barbara Eden, Peter Lorre, Robert Sterling, Michael Ansara, Frankie Avalon. Directed by Allen. Screenplay, Allen, Charles Bennett, from story by Allen; camera (De Luxe), Winton Hoch; editor, George Boemler; art directors, Jack Martin Smith, Herman A. Blumenthal; music, Paul Sawtell, Bert Shefter; sound, Alfred Bruzlin, Warren B. Delaplain; special photographic effects, L. B. Abbott; assistant director, Ad Schrumer. Reviewed at the studio, June 21, '61. Running time, 105 MINS.

Admiral Nelson	Walter Pidgeon
Dr. Hiller	Joan Fontaine
Kathy	Barbara Eden
Emery	Peter Lorre
Capt. Crane	Robert Sterling
Alvarez	Michael Ansara
Chip	Frankie Avalon
Dr. Jamieson	Regis Toomey
Admiral Crawford	John Litel
Congressman Parker	Howard McNear
Dr. Zucco	Henry Daniell
Member of Crew	Skip Ward
Smith	Mark Slade
Gleason	Charles Tannen
Kowski	Delbert Monroe
Cookie	Anthony Monaco
Member of Crew	Michael Ford
Sparks	Robert Easton
Young	Jonathan Gilmore
Ned Thompson	David McLean
Dr. Newmar	Larry Gray
Lt. Hodges	George Diestel

Ace prospector Irwin Allen, who last year unearthed a tidy gold mine on an expedition to a "Lost World," has switched his course from eons to fathoms in undertaking a "Voyage to the Bottom of the Sea" on behalf of 20th-Fox. His findings may be unfathomable to the Scripps Institute cult, but the elaborate manner in which his production has been mounted, and the savvy demonstrated by the artisans and craftsmen who have designed and executed it, should pay off in dividends roughly equal to those of Allen's last sci-fi epic. There is no reason to suppose that "Voyage" won't appeal to the same audience that responded to "World."

Whatever reservations one may entertain with respect to Allen's newest excursion into fantasyland, and there are reservations aplenty, no one can accuse him of inducing his customers to fall asleep in the deep. "Voyage," which Allen produced, directed and wrote, enlisting aid only in the latter capacity from Charles Bennett, is a crescendo of mounting jeopardy, an fefervescent adventure in an anything-but-Pacific Ocean. The way the story goes, this brilliant admiral (Walter Pidgeon), commander of a marvelous atomic sub that resembles a smiling Moby Dick, devises a scheme to save mankind when life on earth is suddenly threatened by a girdle of fire caused when the Van Allen Belt of Radiation encircling the globe goes beserk and erupts. Trouble is mankind does not seem to want to be saved, and is unwilling to cooperate with the impulsive admiral who, with an astonishing display of patriotism, informs the United Nations that "my answer can come only from the President of the United States!"

Unable to contact the prez (golfing?), skipper Pidgeon takes the initiative, heads for a spot

near the Marianas where he plans to orbit a Polaris and explode the heavenly blaze (which is scorching the earth at a rate of two-degrees higher per day) out into space. After a series of mishaps in which the sub is sabotaged from within and torpedoed from without, the missile is dispatched, the day is is saved, and the admiral is off the hook, an outcome never for one moment seriously in doubt.

Actually the title is somewhat misleading. Customers who expect a kind of advanced course in oceanography will discover only an occasional giant squid and a lot of rubbery vegetation. For the most part, "The Bottom" of Allen's "Sea" is merely the setting for the kind of emotional calisthenics that might just as easily break out 100-feet from the tip of Mount Everest.

The acting is generally capable, about the best it can be under the trying dramatic circumstances. In addition to Pidgeon, those in prominent parts are Joan Fontaine as an attractive saboteuress; Barbara Eden as a conscientious, and equally attractive, secretary; Peter Lorre as a calm commodore; Robert Sterling as a misguided, but humanitarian, captain; Michael Ansara as a religious fanatic; Frankie Avalon as a lippy lieutenant. Support is efficient, special impressions made in this department by Regis Toomey, John Litel, Howard McNear, Mark Slade and Charles Tannen.

The cinematic wizardry of photographic effects expert L. B. Abbott plays a major part in the production, as do the efforts of cameraman Winton Hoch, underwater photog John Lamb, art directors Jack Martin Smith and Herman A. Blumenthal and editor George Boemler, all astute and inventive contributions that make the film visually explosive. As in any production in which much of the action takes place underwater, music and sound must play a vital role. These audio chores are accomplished skillfully by the sound team of Alfred Bruzlin and Warren B. Delaplain and composers Paul Sawtell and Bert Shefter. Paul Zastupnevich's costumes are seaworthy.

Avalon has a potential disclick and the picture has a strong salesman in the title tune, a mellow, romantic refrain by Russell Faith.

Tube.

Caperucita y Sus Tres Amigos

(Little Red Riding Hood and Her Three Friends)

(MEXICAN—COLOR)

Mexico City, June 20.

Peliculas Nacionales release of Peliculas Rodriguez production. Stars Maria Gracia, "Loco" Valdez, "Dwarf" Santanon; features Prudencia Griffel, Beatriz Aguirre, Guillermo Alvarez Bianchi, Manuel Pelayo, Armando Lujan; Enrique Edwards, Edmundo Espino, Leticia Roo, Eduardo Alcaraz, Consuelo G. de Luna, Roberto Meyer, Elvira Lodi. Directed by Roberto Rodriguez. Original story and screenplay, Roberto Rodriguez; camera (Eastmancolor), Jose Ortiz; music, Sergio Guerrero. At Variedades Theatre, Mexico City. Running time, **90 MINS.**

This is another in the pop series featuring the further rdventures of Little Red Riding Hood, interpreted by child player Maria Gracia. All the familiar standbys, including the "ferocious" wolf, played with zest by "Loco" Valdez, are in the film, obviously made for the kiddie trade.

Producer and director Roberto Rodriguez continues to mine gold in these film tales of fantasy for children. Here Eastmancolor adds to the effect. Story puts Little Red Riding Hood through her paces with her three friends, the wolf (Valdez), dwarf Santanon as the wily fox and "Duce," the dog. Script is light, and sometimes action stops for development of side sketches which have little to do with the main plot.

Actors Valdez and Santanon virtually steal the show with their caperings as the animal characters, shunting Maria Gracia to the background. She is the thin thread holding the story together. The large cast of secondary players contributes to the overall effect of a film made to please youngsters and it does.

This one will do good business everywhere and no doubt there will be a long series of Little Red Riding Hood pictures to come.

Emil.

Flame In the Streets

(BRITISH-COLOR)

This is a persuasive, though not highly original peek at the color problem; sound allround acting ,with John Mills in gcod form. Provides a useful booking.

London, June 21.

Rank release of a Roy Baker production. Stars John Mills, Sylvia Syms, Brenda De Banzie; features Earl Cameron, Ann Lynn, Wilfrid Brambell, Johnny Sekka, Meredith Edwards. Directed by Roy Baker. Screenplay, Ted Willis from his play, "Hot Summer Night"; camera, Christopher Challis; editor, Roger Cherrill; music, Philip Green. At Odeon, Leicester Square, London, June 20. Running time, **93 MINS.**

Jacko Palmer	John Mills
Kathie Palmer	Sylvia Syms
Nell Palmer	Brenda De Banzie
Gabriel Gomez	Earl Cameron
Peter Lincoln	Johnny Sekka
Judy Gomez	Ann Lynn
Old Man	Wilfrid Brambell
Harry Mitchell	Meredith Edwards
Visser	Newton Blick
Hugh Davies	Glyn Houston
Les	Michael Wynne
Jubilee	Dan Jackson
Dowell	Cyril Chamberlain
Mrs. Bingham	Gretchen Franklin
Billy	Harry Baird

Once again the question of racial discrimination gets a going-over. Although Ted Willis hasn't very much new to offer, he has come up with a thoughtful screenplay which avoids over-sensationalism and tries to show both sides of the issue. It is directed quietly and intelligently by Roy Baker, and firmly acted. Altogether a sound booking.

Story, which hasn't much dramatic bounce, concerns the dilemma of a staunch trade unionist who averts a threatened factory strike over a Negro foreman, swaying the staff by urging that the color of a man's skin is unimportant, only to find that his daughter has fallen in love with another colored man. How to reconcile his very different feelings over the two incidents is his problem.

John Mills makes a convincing figure as the father who has neglected his family because of his dedication to union work. He is honest, puzzled, genuinely moved when he realizes that he has let down his wife and daughter and is genuinely concerned about the girl's future. It's a straightforward character study by Mills, but charged with impact. Brenda De Banzie, his wife, bitter and intolerant about colored people, has two telling scenes, one with her husband and one with her daughter. And Miss De Banzie plays both of them with no holds barred.

Sylvia Syms, the schoolmistress daughter who outrages her parents by her determination to marry a young Negro schoolteacher, contributes a neat performance in a role which is not developed fully. But she plays intelligently and sympathetically. Ann Lynn has a couple of neat cameos as a white girl married to the colored foreman, played with dignity and assurance by Earl Cameron. The Negro hero is Johnny Sekka, and he, too, has enough charm, dignity and good breeding to make it appear quite logical that Miss Syms should fall in love with him.

Meredith Edwards, as an intolerant "spade-hater"; Wilfrid Brambell, as John Mills' father; Newton Blick, Dan Jackson and Glyn Houston are others who register in smaller roles. The fact that "Flame In the Streets" is derived from a play "Hot Summer Night" is always obvious. However, by staging the film on Guy Fawkes' Night, the director is able to get his cameras out into well-filled streets for atmosphere. And the fireworks and bonfires can presumably be interpreted as symbolism. The film builds up an accurate picture of a district very much involved in the color problem and the screenplay rightly shows that there are thugs and villains on both sides, white and black.

The street riot between the two factions is curiously anticlimactic, mainly because the film's appeal is largely the quietness of its direction and playing. Christopher Challis' color lensing is excellent and art director Alex Vetchinsky's artwork offers convincing interiors of Mills' small, neat house and the squalid rooming house inhabited by the colored folks.

Rich.

The Green Helmet

(BRITISH)

Pack of autoracing melodramatic cliches helped by fast action sequences aficionados of the sport will devour. Adequate lower berth item.

Hollywood, June 14.

Metro release of Charles Francis Vetter production. No star credits. Directed by Michael Forlong. Screenplay, Jon Cleary, based on his novel; camera, Geoffrey Faithfull; editor, Frank Clarke; art director, Alan Withy; music, Ken Jones; assistant director, Stan Strangeway. Reviewed at studio, June 14, '61. Running time, **89 MINS.**

Rafferty	Bill Travers
Bartell	Ed Begley
Richie Launder	Sidney James
Diane	Nancy Walters
Mrs. Rafferty	Ursula Jeans
Kitty Launder	Megs Jenkins
Taz Rafferty	Sean Kelly
Carlo Zaraga	Tutte Lemkow
Hastrow	Gordon Tanner
Rossano	Ferdy Mayne
Charlie	Peter Collingwood
George	Rolland Curram
Pamela	Diane Clare
Lupi	Harold Kasket
Jackie	Lyn Cole
Pit Manager	Glyn Houston
Jack Brabham	Himself

Here's one for the "Motor Trends" set, a modest little gasser from Britain about a big-time racing car driver with a foot of lead and a heart of marshmallow. Though packed with just about every auto racing film cliche in the book (a kind of "Porsche Faces Life" with grease smears), the Charles Francis Vetter production generates plenty of visual excitement when it gets behind the wheel, opens throttle and shifts into emotional overdrive. The Metro release will be a companionable supporting item and, though utterly star-shy by American standards, there may even be scattered situations, where male action fans assemble, where it would hold its own for about one lap in an economy run.

Jon Cleary's screenplay, based on his novel of the same title (which may have had some significance in the book, but the green means nothing in the black-and-white picture), retells the shopworn yarn about the vet driver who is losing his nerve after several near-fatal mishaps. He has the usual father who died a champion in a crash, the usual younger brother who's itching to get into the cockpit, the usual long-suffering mother, the usual fiancee worried about her lover's longevity, and the usual lovable mechanic friend who comes out of repair pit retirement long enough to get himself killed.

To compensate for the familiar story, the spectator is assaulted with the real feeling of enormous speed in the many noisy, breathtaking scenes shot from the cockpit. It's a kind of "Ben-Hur" in reverse, one big chariot race with occasional pauses for exposition. The light English Jaguar driven by the hero represents the white horses, the dark Italian Maserati being the equivalent of the black horses. Director Michael Forlong, with the aid of some good racing stock footage, some agile camerawork by Geoffrey Faithfull, and the skilled driving maneuvers of racing champ Jack Brabham, has woven in several spectacular crashes and mounted a number of excellent action scenes, a quality not matched when the film shifts into the neutral position.

Bill Travers is convincing as the troubled hero. But Sidney James, as the ill-fated mechanic, cops histrionic honors. Prominent parts are dispatched adequately by Ed Begley, Nancy Walters, Ursula Jeans, Megs Jenkins, Sean Kelly and Tutte Lemkow.

The production is improved by Frank Clarke's brisk editing of the race sequences, Alan Withy's authentic art direction and Ken Jones' aggressive score. *Tube.*

Come September

(C'SCOPE—COLOR)

Likely hot moneymaker. Romantic comedy bolstered with potent marquee bait, rich production values and some ripe comedy ideas brightly executed by attractive cast.

Hollywood, June 19.

Universal release of Robert Arthur production. Stars Rock Hudson, Gina Lollobrigida, Sandra Dee, Bobby Darin, Walter Slezak. Directed by Robert Mulligan. Screenplay, Stanley Shapiro, Mau-

rice Richlin; camera (Technicolor). William Daniels; editor. Russell F. Schoengarth; art director. Henry Bumstead; music. Hans J. Salter; sound. Waldon O. Watson, Sash Fisher; assistant director, Joseph Kenny. Reviewed at Beverly Theatre, June 19, '61. Running time, 112 MINS.

Robert Talbot	Rock Hudson
Lisa	Gina Lollobrigida
Sandy	Sandra Dee
Tony	Bobby Darin
Maurice	Walter Slezak
Margaret	Brenda De Banzie
Anna	Rosanna Rory
Spencer	Ronald Howard
Beagle	Joel Grey
Sparrow	Ronnie Haran
Larry	Chris Seitz
Julio	Cindy Conroy
Linda	Joan Freeman
Patricia	Nancy Anderson
Ron	Michael Eden
Carol	Claudia Brack

Universal has a hot money prospect in "Come September." The Robert Arthur production is not all it could or should be but its shortcomings are not likely to dim the big b.o. take.

Rich in marquee might, slick production and attractive stars, the romantic comedy also benefits from especially sharp performances by Rock Hudson. Gina Lollobrigida and Walter Slezak. Then, of course, there is the added lure of recent newlyweds Sandra Dee and Bobby Darin, whose presence as an on-screen romantic duo, the latter in his first cinematic exposure, is sure to be an attendance factor among young people. Add it up and it spells boxoffice.

Scenarists Stanley Shapiro and Maurice Richlin have dreamed up a bright premise for a comedy, to wit that a rich U.S. businessman (Hudson), who ordinarily spends only one month (September) annually at his Italian villa, abruptly puts in a July appearance to the dismay of his enterprising major domo (Slezak) who has been converting the private abode into a very public hotel for 11 months out of every year.

Even in the film's lesser spans there are occasional kicks and spurts of high good humor, but too often, in manipulating the plot for the purposes of introducing incongrous comedy spectacles (Hudson chasing after La Lollo at the wheel of a battered chicken truck, or the latter, garbed in full wedding gown regalia, chasing after the former in an old jeep), the writers seem inclined to telegraph, repeat and pile it on, director Robert Mulligan to stretch scenes too far. But this is not to say that the scripting and direction are poor. Far from it.

Under Mulligan's generally keen command. Hudson comes through with an especially jovial performance, perhaps his best to date. He reveals again the flair for comedy that marked his work in "Pillow Talk." Indeed, comedy appears to be his forte, which should make him an even more valuable leading man in Hollywood films.

Miss Lollobrigida need just stand there to generate sparks, but here she abets her eye-to-eye appeal with plenty of comedy savvy. Slezak is excellent. His scenes with Hudson are the best scenes in the picture. Miss Dee has the misfortune to be overshadowed in the glamor department here by Lady Lollo, who far and away draws the most form-fitting and revealing of the fashionable, flattering gowns designed by Morton Haack and has the form to fit and reveal something worth revealing. But the young actress is plenty decorative and capable in her own right.

Darin does a workmanlike job, and gives evidence he'll have more to show when the parts provide him with wider opportunity. Besides his acting, he penned the upbeat ditty, "Multiplication," which he warbles in the film, and composed the title tune (wordless background variety), which is invested with the typical Darinesque shuffle beat. Brenda De Banzie and Roland Howard (son of the late Leslie) make strong impressions in key parts, and the rest of the support is efficient.

Shot in Italy, the picture is graced with richly-tinted, maneuverable photography by William Daniels and smart, elegant sets by Henry Bumstead. Russell F. Schoengarth's editing adds punch to the comedy's brighter moments and Hans J. Salter's score is easy on the ear. *Tube.*

Berlin Festival

Description D'Un Combat
(ISRAELI-COLOR)

Berlin, June 27.
SOFAC release of Yitzhic Zohar production. Written and directed by Chris Marker. Camera (Eastmancolor), G. Cloquet; old footage, B. Hesse; editor, Eva Zora; commentary spoken by Jean Vilar. At Berlin Film Fest. Running time, 55 MINS.

An Israeli producer and a French filmmaker have put a filmic face on Israel, that new-old country. Fine observation, gentle wit and a deft combining of images and commentary make this an absorbing documentary with chances for special programming abroad of two medium length feature pix or for tele usage.

At first, the country is explored, and then the film gets close to people. It gives a background in old footage and makes statements about the various facets of this sturdy nation.

The different nationalities and faces, the kibbutz life, the Arab minority problem, the feeling of a cross-section of the people, the tourists, the residual ghetto of orthodox Jews, the work done to bring a country out of the desert and the promised land aspects all are expertly welded in this vehicle.

Color is excellent, editing adroit, and all technical aspects first-rate. The title "Description of a Combat" refers mainly to the combat every resident has to do with himself in the change from scapegoat and resigned man to a member of a new nation. There is a smartly done documentary about a country that makes for good viewing and interesting as well as provoking film fare. *Mosk.*

Goodbye Again

Anatole Litvak's stylish production of Francoise Sagan's Parisian soap opera. Fine performance by Ingrid Bergman. Strong distaff appeal indicates slick b.o.

United Artists release of Anatole Litvak production, directed by Litvak. Stars Ingrid Bergman, Yves Montand, Anthony Perkins. Screenplay, Samuel Taylor, based on novel "Aimez-Vous Brahms" by Francoise Sagan; camera, Armand Thirard; editor, Albert Bates; music, Georges Auric; lyrics, Dory Langdon; Asst. director, Paul Feyder. Reviewed June 26, '61, in N. Y. Running time, 120 MINS.

Paula Tessier	Ingrid Bergman
Roger Demarest	Yves Montand
Philip Van Der Besh	Anthony Perkins
Mrs. Van Der Besh	Jesse Royce Landis
Maisie I	Jackie Lane
Maitre Fleury	Pierre Dux
Maisie II	Jean Clarke
Gaby	Uta Taeger
Monsieur Steiner	Andre Randall
British lawyer	David Horne
Madame Fleury	Lee Patrick
Madeline Fleury	A. Duperoux
Jimmy	Raymond Gerome
Monsieur Cherel	Jean Hebey
Young Man in Club	Michel Garland
Waiter	Paul Uny
Asst. lawyer	Colin Mann
Singer	Diahann Carroll

In addition to guaranteeing a mint to United Artists, producer-director Anatole Litvak's "Goodbye Again" serves another function: to prove that soap opera life can be literate, if not beautiful. The secret storm raging within heroine Ingrid Bergman is vintage formula stuff (which man will she choose?), but here it's told in comparative adult, often witty terms. And, in the resolution of the triangle, there is a note of dispassionate irony that would do credit to sterner, more ambitious drama.

Taking as their text Francoise Sagan's short novel, "Aimez-Vous Brahms," Litvak and scripter Samuel Taylor have made a romantic, sentimental film about superficial people, told entirely from the heroine's extremely limited point of view. The ladies will love its surface chic and sophistication. Vicariously they will share beds—first with Yves Montand and then with Anthony Perkins. To give it all the look of modernity, especially in the eyes of that section of the distaff audience which has passed middleage, the film makes one tentative observation about love: there may be something more important than sexual fidelity. This nugget of wisdom, however, comes only after a good deal of high-style sinning.

High-style, in fact, is the keynote to Litvak's meticulous, handsomely photographed (black/white) production made entirely in Paris. Its heroine, a successful interior decorator, is dressed by Dior, and her two lovers drive high-powered sports cars. When they dine, it's usually at Maxim's, and when young Perkins goes out to get drunk, he winds up at a bistro being consoled by no less a chantootsie than Diahann Carroll. If you're going to have the old love-miseries, this is the way to have them.

Miss Bergman is cast as a beautiful (what else?), 40-ish woman-of-the-world, who, after five years of an affair with industrialist Montand, is beginning to feel "alone and not quite so young." Montand makes no secret of his extra-curricular liaisons with other, younger dames, but Miss Bergman and he tell each other they have too good a relationship to allow it to be destroyed by jealousy. They

also figure that marriage would destroy the freedom of their love.

However, when Montand leaves her alone for increasingly long intervals, the lady proves easy prey for a wealthy, gangling post-adolescent American, Tony Perkins, at least 15 years her junior and who suffers from a mighty lack of interest in anything except love. Because of their age differences, and because Miss Bergman still hankers for Montand, theirs is one of those "impossible" though passionate affairs. When Montand returns after six months and proposes marriage to Miss Bergman, she breaks the kid's heart, and accepts Montand. The aforementioned irony is that, shortly afterwards, Montand is up to his old tricks, and Miss Bergman again spending most of her evenings alone.

The beauty of Miss Bergman's performance illuminates, and adds validity to, the shallow fiction. Also Litvak's direction is carefully detailed, though seldom overstated. There is one beautiful scene in which the camera focuses on the face of the troubled heroine as she lies alone in bed, listening to some dissonant jazz while young Perkins, just arisen from her side, comments on the contents of her icebox. He notes that he feels like he hasn't eaten in a month.

The other performances seem either pale or overwrought alongside Miss Bergman's. Perkins, who won the top male acting prize at Cannes this year for "Goodbye," is overdoing his "coltishness" to the point of self parody, and Montand, with a not very attractive role, looks like a guy who has wandered into the powderroom by mistake.

Jessie Royce Landis is amusing as Perkins' addlebrained mother, and Jackie Lane piquant as one of Montand's series of doxies. Diahann Carroll sings one song in a charming manner, also handling a brief scene with equal competence. Georges Auric's score does more than any other single factor, except Armand Thirard's photography, to add a feeling of plush lushness to the physical production. Editing by Albert Bates is sharp and inventive. *Anby.*

20.000 Eyes
(CINEMASCOPE)

Robbery-in-a-museum crime-suspense meller. A compatible lower-berth entry.

Hollywood, June 29.
Twentieth-Fox release of Jack Leewood production. Stars Gene Nelson, Merry Anders, James Brown. Directed by Leewood. Screenplay, Jack Thomas; camera, Brydon Baker; editor, Peter Johnson; art director, John Mansbridge; music, Albert Glasser; sound, Lloyd Wyler; assistant directors, Frank Parmenter, Doc Joos. Reviewed at API studios, June 29, '61. Running time, 61 MINS.

Dan	Gene Nelson
Karen	Merry Anders
Jerry	James Brown
Kurt	John Banner
Girl	Judith Rawlins
Police Lt.	Robert Shayne
Ryan	Paul Maxey
High School Boy	Rex Holman
High School Girl	Barbara Parkins
Moore	Ollie O'Toole
Museum Guard	Bruno Ve Sota
Appraiser	William O'Connell
Policeman	Rusty Wescoatt
Museum Guard	Vince Monroe Townsend Jr.

Six days, $70,000 and "20,000 Eyes" later, producer - director Jack Leewood has managed to sur-

mount the challenging specifications of filmmaking within API's wholesale discount shop to bring in a competent supporting product for retail parent company 20th-Fox. Not everything focuses out 20-20 in "Eyes" but, stacked up against "B" calibre in recent times, it is a superior quickie that will hold an audience between main courses. (*This film though marked for July 3 review release has been playing off for some weeks in Manhattan.—Ed.*)

The picture, kind of a minor league "Asphalt Jungle" (there's even a minor league imitation of MM by a slinky blonde creature named Judith Rawlins) stems from an original screenplay by Jack Thomas that is a trifle foggy in the motivation area and not always rational in development, but does sustain suspense and concern for its characters. To these values have been added sufficient directorial aplomb (by Leewood in his first such helming stint) and capable performances by all involved to fashion passable nightcap entertainment.

The story opens fast with a young man of unexplained background (Gene Nelson) in jeopardy after swindling a retired mobster out of some stock, which he has used as collateral for a personal loan. Mortally threatened, he devises an elaborate scheme to pay back the money, but ends up by paying with his life. The best scenes are the how-to-commit-a-robbery footage in which Nelson executes his plan—a tricky caper in which he pilfers some rough, but valuable diamonds from an art museum display, replaces them with low-grade stones, uses the booty to obtain a tidy insurance sum, and then gets the genuine gems back into the case before the theft is discovered. Good suspense stuff.

Though weakly motivated Nelson does a better than businesslike job. Costars Merry Anders and James Brown, who have teamed up in many a lower berth rumble lately, do so again here, and demonstrate the savvy picked up by frequent exposure in filmdom's six-day wonders. They are reluctant aides in the robbery. Support is okay, John Banner standing out in this department.

Albert Glasser's music adds dramatic drive. Camera work by Brydon Baker, editing by Peter Johnson and art direction by John Mansbridge are journeyman contributions, though all reflect the realities of a production mounted on limited means. *Tube.*

Thief of Baghdad
(Italian-Made)
(EASTMAN COLOR—C'SCOPE)

Joe Levine-Steve Reeves-Arabian Nights parlay. Action and production values offset the inane dialog. Good drive-in bet and should enchant moppets.

Joseph E. Levine presentation. Metro release of Titanus (Italy) production. Stars Steve Reeves. Produced by Bruno Vailata. Directed by Arthur Lubin. Story and screenplay by Augusto Frassinetti, Filippo Sanjust, Vailati; camera Eastmancolor), Tonino Delli Colli; editor, Gene Ruggiero; special effects, Thomas Howard. Reviewed June 26, 1961, at MGM screening room, N.Y. Running time, 90 MINS.

Karim	Steve Reeves
Amina	Georgia Moll
Osman	Arturo Dominici
Kadeejah	Edy Vessel
Magician	George Chamarat

(English Dubbed)

The mixture as before. In "Morgan the Pirate" only a few weeks ago and now in "Thief of Baghdad" the American beefcake hero, Steve Reeves, appears in an Italian-made fantasy, or call it breach of reason, wherein a professional criminal is pictured as noble, brave, loyal and superbly, not to say incredibly, chaste. There is again, as before, the advantages of considerable action, Eastman-Pathe color and CinemaScope production values, arresting special effects, picturesque settings and costumes. Fine for drive-ins, Joe Levine has another boy's-dream-of-superman-come-true that will probably please its natural audience, if leaving cerebral types dumbstruck.

It is well, perhaps, to dispose immediately of the oldtimers' questions. This is not, by any stretch of charity, either echo or kin of the silent classic of the same title in which the late great Douglas Fairbanks appeared. True, Reeves scales a few walls, rope-swings over his pursuers' heads and so on. Absent is the jauntiness, the sense of qui vive of the old master of derring-do.

There is a slight variation from the Reeves format in that this time he does not conquer by sheer muscle and fearlessness alone. When cornered he resorts to a vanishing cloak or he rubs a magic ring and, presto, has a friendly army to command.

Whatever his seen or unseen enemies concoct he has the necessary physical and/or metaphysical counterblows. Whether it is quite sporting for him to be the champion wrestler of Mesopotamia and also Houdini need not delay our little essay.

The story, frankly Arabian Nights, moves with directness. There is a princess. The thief loves her on sight and she loves him. All he needs to square his criminal past, win the girl and become sultan-designate is a blue rose which lies at the end of a series of tests.

Special effectsman Thomas Howard puts Reeves through a night in an orchard where the trees crawl, into burning swamps, sudden floods, a love nest operated by a vindictive nymphomaniac. Reeves comes through without losing his sense of direction, virtue or breath.

As with "Morgan the Pirate" the Italian cast credits for "Baghdad" are strangely curtailed in New York. There is no identification of the nympho for instance, nor various of the nefarious palace courtiers.

Georgia Moll (the princess) is a mere child photographically and histrionically. There are a few deft light touches in characterization by the Sultan (Edy Vessel) and the Genii (George Chamarat). Which about takes care of the acting.

Arthur Lubin directed the fantasy against the colorful backdrop of oriental structures in Tunisia. There are arresting quick-cuts to street scenes and mobs. A good deal of plausible atmosphere is achieved.

During the hero's series of "tests" the story-telling pace slows somewhat, but is redeemed with the finale, an amusing battle between baffled broadsword cavalry and staff-wielding acrobats conjured up by the magic ring. It is easy to imagine kids hooting and hollering in delight at this free-for-all.

A strange melange of realistic effects and relationships and unabashed abracadabra, this picture will probably make out because what it has will outshine what it hasn't, bearing in mind the probable juvenile and family response it will draw in the first instance.

A professional reviewer is entitled to complaint here, as with "Morgan the Pirate," that the English dubbing is lumpy with starchy dialog—such Baghdadian colloquialisms, as *"Just don't stand there — do something!"* or the heavy who keeps repeating, *"I've had enough!"* Such inane lines unhorse the make-believe. *Land.*

The Boy Who Stole A Million
(BRITISH)

Amusing, occasionally touching yarn involving a boy, a dog and a chase. Excellent family entertainment despite frail marquee value.

British Lion release of a Bryanston presentation of a George H. Brown production. Stars Virgilio Texera, Marianne Benet, Maurice Reyna. Director, Charles Crichton. Scenario by John Eldridge & Charles Crichton from Niels West Larsen's story and original screenplay; camera, Douglas Slocombe; editor, Peter Bezencenet; music, Tristram Cary. Previewed at Columbia Theatre, London, June 27. Running time, 81 MINS.

Miguel	Virgilio Texera
Paco	Maurice Reyna
Maria	Marianne Benet
Luis	Harold Kasket
Currito	Curt Christian
Police Chief	Bill Nagy
Bank Manager	George Coulouris
Commissionaire	Edwin Richfield
Bank Clerk	Cyril Shaps
Pedro	Warren Mitchell
Gang Leader	Barta Barri
Mateo	Tutte Lemkow
Chico	Victor Majica
Organ Grinder	Herbert Curiel
Shoemaker	Andrea Malandridros
Blind Man	Francisco Bernal
Knife Grinder	Xan Das Bolas
Reporter	Gaylor Cavallaro
Desk Sergeant	Paul Whitsun Jones
Detective	Robert Rietty

It's difficult to go wrong with the combo of an appealing kid, the inevitable pooch and a chase in which the youngster's up against the world. This one is marred by some slightly uneasy dubbing and an occasional lapse into slapstick when only light comedy was needed, but overall it's a warm little piece which will give good value in most family houses.

Though a British film, it was mainly shot in authentic locations in Valencia, Spain, and director Charles Crichton and cameraman Douglas Slocombe have used the proffered canvas wisely. They have taken the chase over a wide area of Valencia and the camera has helped to brisk up the urgency of the chase very smartly.

The yarn, briefly, concerns a likeable youngster who lives with his widowed father and works as a bank messenger. He finds that his taxi-driver father needs money to get his cab out of hock and decides to borrow some from the bank. After all, he argues, that's what banks are for, surely? His haul, however, turns out to be a million pesetas (roughly $28,000) and that sets the city on its ears. At the drop of a peseta he is being chased by half the thugs in Valencia, the police and his father.

Bewildered, harassed, frightened, the kid keeps on the run. He and his faithful shaggy-haired dog miraculously escape capture in a series of adventures that sometimes smack too much of the Keystone Cops technique but are always holding. He gets involved in a fiesta and a couple of frightening and tensely directed sequences with a blind beggar and a sinister knife grinder. A gang of thugs, a strange organ grinder and a deaf shoemaker all play their parts in this fascinating little motion picture which required just a little more imagination by script writer and director to lift it in to the same class as "The Red Balloon"

Young Maurice Reyna, making his screen debut, has been described as a midget Cantinflas, and goes through the motions of thesping admirably. Harold Kasket is breezily effective as the friend of the kid's father, who is rather glumly played by Virgilio Texera. Marianne Benet provides a touch of unnecessary pulchritude, Billy Nagy is unusually uneasy as the cop in charge of the chase and there is a first class conglomeration of Spanish actors who score mightily as thugs and sinister characters. Of them, mention must justly be made of Francisco Bernal, as the evil blind man, Xan Das Bolas as the equally sinister knife grinder and Herbert Curiel who, though he doesn't say a word as the organ grinder, projects a load of potential.

Maurice Carter has grabbed and imagined some good artwork and locations, editing is smooth and Tristam's Cary's evocative music blends well with the screenplay. *Rich.*

The Naked Edge

Coop's last stand: a neatly directed suspense meller of conventional design about a woman who thinks her husband is a murderer. Nice b.o. outlook.

United Artists release of Pennebaker-Baroda production (Marlon Brando Sr. executive producer) produced by Walter Seltzer and George Glass. Stars Gary Cooper, Deborah Kerr; features Eric Portman, Diane Cilento, Hermione Gingold, Peter Cushing, Michael Wilding. Directed by Michael Anderson; screenplay, Joseph Stefano (based on Max Ehrlich novel, "First Train to Babylon"); camera, Edwin Hillier; editor, Gordon Pilkington; art director, Carmen Dillon; music, William Alwyn; sound, Norman Coggs; assistant director, Peter Bolton. Reviewed June 30, '61, at Victoria Theatre, N. Y. Running time, 99 MINS.

George Radcliffe	Gary Cooper
Martha Radcliffe	Deborah Kerr
Jeremy Clay	Eric Portman
Mrs. Heath	Diane Cilento
Lilly Harris	Hermione Gingold
Mr. Wrack	Peter Cushing
Morris Brooke	Michael Wilding
Mr. Claridge	Ronald Howard
Donald Heath	Ray McAnally
Manfridi	Sandor Eles
Mr. Pom	Wilfrid Lawson
Miss Osborne	Helen Cherry
Victoria Hicks	Joyce Carey
Betty	Diane Clare
Judge	Frederick Leister
Jason Roote	Martin Boddey
Chauffeur	Peter Wayn

The picture that winds up Gary Cooper's long list of credits is neatly constructed, thoroughly pro-

fessional little suspense meller that may seem anti-climactic only because it climaxes a great career. Leaving sentimentality aside, "The Naked Edge" is sheer escapism—director Michael Anderson's able exercise in how to get the most tension out of material that is somewhat short on invention and light on surprises. Names of Cooper and of his co-star, Deborah Kerr, indicate a nice b.o. outlook for the summer trade.

For most of its running time, "Edge" asks the audience to suspect that Cooper is a killer, not above dispatching his own beloved wife (Miss Kerr) should the need arise. "How long," he asks the nearly hysterical Miss Kerr at one point, "can a man live with a woman who might turn him in at any moment?" But, knowing that his wife suspects him, would he drive her out to the white cliffs of Dover and ask her to stand with him on the brink, if he had no motive other than giving her a view of the sea? The aroma of red herrings such as these linger on when the lights come up at the end.

Based on Max Ehrlich's novel, "First Train to Babylon," Joseph Stefano's screenplay casts Cooper as an American businessman living in London who, coincidently to the murder of his business partner (and the disappearance of a couple of hundred thousand dollars), happens to make a killing on the stockmarket, which funds he uses to make an even bigger fortune.

When, five years later, a blackmailer in the form of Eric Portman turns up to accuse her husband of the murder, Miss Kerr remembers that Cooper, after all, had been the key prosecution witness at the murder trial and had come into a lot of money quite suddenly. The lady's further investigations confirm her suspicions. Subsequently, as is the convention in such plots, the accused (Cooper) doesn't go out of his way to look anything but guilty.

Although the script thus is somewhat arbitrary in development, Anderson has directed it with imagination and a good deal of excitement. Flashbacks to earlier events, sometimes as recounted by untrustworthy witnesses, are artfully integrated with present action, helping to build to one of those corny, but still effective climaxes where in the heroine, alone late at night in the great house, is stalked by the unknown villain.

Anderson, his cameraman (Edwin Hillier) and editor (Gordon Pilkington) have put together a number of hair-raising sequences out of the comparatively modest material. There is a legitimate and stunning feeling of hysteria, for instance, when Miss Kerr becomes suddenly lost in a maze of lookalike tenement blocks. Even Hermione Gingold, as a somewhat looney patron of the arts, and Sandor Elcs, as her limp-wristed young protege, though they have nothing to do with the plot contribute to a mood that borders on madness.

Miss Kerr suffers very prettily in a highly emotional role. Cooper, perhaps because he must appear to be enigmatic most of the time, gives a less successful performance. He seems too solid a character to be the kind of scheming killer he

would have to appear to be to make the plot plausible.

The picture, filmed entirely in London, utilizes some fine British supporting people, including Diane Cilento, as the wife of the man Cooper wrongly sent to jail; Eric Portman, as a seedy disbarred attorney (and number one suspect); and Michael Wilding, as Cooper's fast-talking, opportunistic business associate.

George Glass and Walter Seltzer produced for Pennebaker-Baroda Productions and United Artists release. *Anby.*

Berlin Festival

Question 7
(U.S.)

Berlin, July 4.
Louis de Rochemont Associates release of Lothar Wolff-Lutheran Film Associates-Luther Film production. Features Michael Gynn and Margaret Jahnen. Directed by Stuart Rosenberg. Screenplay, Allan Sloane; camera, Gunter Senftleben; music, Hans-Martin Majewski. At Berlin Film Fest, June 25, '61. Running time, **107 MINS.**

Friedrich Gottfried.... Michael Gwynn
Gerda Gottfried ..... Margarete Jahnen
Peter Gottfried....Christian de Bresson
Martin Kraus .... John Ruddock
Herr Rettmann .... Leo Bieber
Rolf Starke .... Erik Schumann
Heinz Dehmert .... Fritz Wepper
Otto Zingler .... Edward Linkers
Marta Zingler ..... Marianne Schubarth
Anneliese Zingler .... Almut Eggert
Barber .... Philo Hauser
Karl Marschall ...... Rolf v. Nauckhoff
Luedtke .... Helmo Kindermann
Prof. Steffl .... Manfred Furst
Herr Durfel .... Lutz Altschul
Herr Kesselmaier.........Sigurd Lohde
A. A. Tritschler .... Erik Jelde
Bishop .... Ernst Constantin

"Question 7" was invited to the Berlin film festival for obvious political reasons. It is a story of religious persecution in Eastern Germany and is said to be based on actual incidents and documents. But like most blatant pieces of propaganda, it is treated without any subtlety. Pic was filmed on location in (Western) Germany with a European cast, the majority of which is little known internationally. Film calls for special exploitation, and needs support of churches and other organizations to get maximum results.

Allan Sloane's screenplay emphasizes the honesty, sincerity and conviction of the pastor who is troubled about his son's future, whereas Herr Rettmann, the commissar, is more treacherous than most screen heavies. The pastor's son is a budding pianist whose future studies are dependent on conformity to party doctrine. The test of same are answers to a party questionnaire, in which the seventh question asks: "What have been the predominant influences on my social development?" The youngster apparently gives the right answers so as not to miss the opportunity of going to the conservatoire, but escapes to the West when he realizes he's become a pawn in party propoganda.

There is ample dramatic content to the story, but the failure to add a touch of shading to the characterizations robs the plot of much of its conviction. Integrity on one side and sheer villainy on the other may, indeed, be a true picture of the religious scene in Eastern Germany, but on the screen it emerges as heavy-handed propa-

ganda, with entertainment values of secondary consideration.

Apart from that obvious failing, the vehicle is well enough made, though most of the performances are undistinguished. Michael Gwynn, as the pastor, Margarete Jahnen, as his wife, and Christian de Bresson, who plays their son give earnest, unsmiling portrayals. Leo Bieber is too clean-cut as the heavy. Stuart Rosenberg's direction is slow and painstaking, and other credits are up to standard. *Myro.*

Amelie Ou Le Temps D'Aimer
(Amelie or the Time to Love)
(FRENCH)

Berlin, July 4.
Port Royal Film-Prima-Indusfilm production and release. Stars Marie-Jose Nat, Jean Sorel; features Sophie Daumier, Jean Babilee, Clotilde Joano. Written and directed by Michel Drach from a novel by Michele Angot. Camera, Jean Tournier; editor, Genevieve Winding. Official French entry at Berlin Film Fest. Running time, **105 MINS.**

Amelie .... Marie-Jose Nat
Alain .... Jean Sorel
Emmannuelle .... Sophie Daumier
Fany .... Clotilde Joano
Pierre .... Jean Babilee
Loyse .... Louise De Vilmorin

This official French entry at the Berlin Film Fest is a moody tale of love in turn-of-the-century France. It displays a flair for decorative period as well as insight into its languid characters. As such, it appears a good arty entry for export.

A young orphan Amelie (Marie-Jose Nat) is in love with her cousin (Jean Sorel). They live in his house and she works in the dry goods store owned by his father. He has a penchant for her but dreams more of going off to sea. They live on a small island off the coast of France. Into this setting, comes a piquant actress who symbolizes adventure for the boy. He goes for her and drops Amelie. He tries to return to her when the actress drops him, it is too late. Finally, he goes off to sea and she finally dies.

Though this seems like familiar melodrama it is given depth by Michel Drach's sincere treatment of this muted love plus the freshness of the players. Miss Nat has the correct fragile looks and elan while most of the others are more than adequate. Technical qualities, costuming and on-the-spot lensing also help.

For this second pic, Drach shows a surety in using atmosphere and a sincerity in feeling that should make him a probable regular on the film scene in France. This film has a muted appeal that slants it more for specialized chances than for depth possibilities. *Mosk.*

The Marriage of Mr. Mississippi
(SWISS)

Berlin, July 4.
Ufa release of a CCC (Berlin) and Praesens Film (Zurich) coproduction. Stars O. E. Hasse and Johanna von Koczian. Directed by Kurt Hoffmann. Screenplay, Friedrich Durenmatt's from his own play; camera Sven Nykvist; editor, Hermann Haller; music, Hans-Martin Majewski. At Berlin Film Fest, June 24, '61. Running time, **95 MINS.**

Friedrich Durenmatt's political satire is a difficult subject to translate to the screen, and this

Swiss-German coproduction must be rated a valiant try, though a near miss. The opening title, which suggests that any similarity with events and living persons is intentional and not coincidental, sets the mood for the comedy treatment, but it's a difficult mood to sustain and there are occasional lapses into near-slapstick. Film has already been acquired for U.S. distribution by Times Films, and it may have fair chances in arty theatres.

Opening scene, with one signpost pointing to Oxford and another to Moscow, establishes the two principal male characters. Mississippi campaigns for the return of the laws of Moses, and Saint-Claude advocates world revolution. The central femme character has killed her husband with poison supplied by her doctor lover, but Mississippi, now attorney-general, uses the remains of the poison to murder his own wife, banishes the doctor, and forces the woman to marry him.

From then on, the plot goes off at various tangents, with revolution and counter-revolution being plotted in the woman's bedroom. Mississippi is finally put away in a mental home, the banished lover returns and is spurned, the counter-revolution succeeds, and Anastasia, the woman in the piece, winds up as the first lady.

Kurt Hoffman's confident direction keeps the action rolling, though not on an even keel. Occasionally, there are bursts of fine comedy passages, but the dialog is variable.

The two male lead roles are in the hands of O. E. Hasse (Mississippi) and Martin Held (Saint-Claude), and both are experienced performers. Johanna von Koczian, as Anastasia, is quite a looker and a very capable actress, though her role called for more fire than she puts into it. Supporting cast is okay, and ditto the technical credits. *Myro.*

Mabu
(The Stableman)
(KOREA)

Berlin, June 27.
Hwa Ryong Lee (Seoul) production. With Kim Seung-ho, Cho Mi-eyung, Shin Yong-kyam, Um Aeng-ran, Kim Chin. Directed by Dae Jin Kang; screenplay, Hee Jae Im; camera, Mun Beik Lee. At Berlin Film Fest. Running time, **120 MINS.**

This Korean entry manages to keep some interest thanks to the natural acting performances. It's the story of a 50-year-old stableman and his children who has a tough time to maintain his existence for he earns so little. Plot is rather naive—on one side, the thoroughly mean weathy, on the other one, the always good-hearted needy.

This contains a mammoth amount of sentiment, yet it's actually never dull. One takes a fancy to the people on the screen. Especially likeable is Kim Seung-ho as the stableman. Technically, film is primitive.

But in summing it up, "Mabu" surpasses expectations. *Hans.*

Teenagers
(UNITED ARAB REPUBLIC)

Berlin, July 4.
Magda Films (Cairo) production and release. Directed by Ahmed Dhiaa el Din.

Screenplay, Ali el Zorkani; camera, Wadid Serri; editor, Saied El Sheikh. At Berlin Film Fest, June 26, '61. Running time, 136 MINS.

The United Arab Republic is one of the backward areas filmically speaking, though there is presumably a local market for the naive-type pictures produced there. "Teenagers" is an attempt to do a modern-type story, but it's told in old-fashioned, simple terms, and cannot hope to have much appeal to the more sophisticated filmgoers of the West.

It's a story of three teenage girls of different walks of life who encounter the same sort of emotional problems, like strict parents, growing-up and, naturally, falling in love. It's a very predictable subject, and the screenplay makes no pretense towards subtlety.

Performances match the subject, direction is slow and detailed, and the editing is exceptionally slack. For the record, principal roles are played by Magda, Rouschidi Abaza, Dawlat Abyad, Omar Zulfukar and Hussein Riad.   *Myro.*

Dreamland of Desire
(Documentary)
(GERMAN—COLOR)
Berlin, July 4.
Columbia release of a Wolfgang Mueller-Sehn production.. Direction, screenplay, camera by Mueller-Sehn; commentary, Johannes Gaitanides; music, Manos Hadzidakis. At Berlin Film Fest, June 27, '61.. . Running time, 103 MINS.

Scenically and historically, it would be hard to find a more attractive locale for a documentary travelog than Greece and its surrounding islands. And this Wolfgang Mueller-Sehn production, which Columbia has acquired for world release, covers the territory thoroughly. Too thoroughly, in fact, because some of the camera-work is repetitive. The resultant length will surely militate against its widespread acceptance. If reduced to second feature film proportions, it could make a useful supporting attraction.

Mueller-Sehn spent more than two years making the film, covering thousands of miles of territory by car, boat and plane, and visiting all the classical centres as well as dwelling at some length on a guided tour of Athens. While much of the footage is of considerable interest, there is also an undue emphasis on the conventional, much of which could be eliminated with ease.

Making the film was obviously a labor of love for the producer, and this is obvious in the treatment. But the project was too much of a one-man operation, and outside editing would have helped. Eastmancolor lensing in Ultrascope is first-rate.   *Myro.*

The Bad Sleep Well
(JAPANESE)
Berlin, July 4.
Toho release of a Tomoyuki Tanaka-Akira Kurosawa production. Directed by Kurosawa. Screenplay, Hideo Oguni, Eijiro Kusaka, Kurosawa, Ryuzo Kikushima, Shinobu Hashimoto; camera, Yuzuru Aizawa; music, Sasaru Sato. At Berlin Film Fest, June 26, '61. Running time, 144 MINS.

Akira Kurosawa is Japan's most distinguished director, and several of his period pictures have been established as screen classics. But

"The Bad Sleep Well," a modern story of graft and corruption, despite occasional flashes of directorial brilliance, is a disappointment. However, the finished product could be immensely improved by a renewed and more determined attempt at editing.

With five writers credited for the screenplay, it is inevitable that there should be an uneven quality about the story. But that's a minor fault that could be corrected by keen editing. There is hardly a sequence that is not overlong, and the few that have been well cut stand out with surprising sharpness.

Opening scene of the film is the wedding of a government official's daughter to his private secretary, but the jollifications (if one may use that term for the solemn nuptials) are disrupted by the arrival of the police to arrest one of the guests.

From then on, the production goes into a prolonged flashback recalling another scandal within the **same governmental department a few years previously, involving suicides, bribery and murder. It's a powerful subject, and the director has obtained good allround performances.**

Masayuki Mori, as the government official, and Toshiro Mifune, as the groom, head the first-rate cast. Yuzuru Aizawa makes excellent use of the CinemaScope screen with his clearcut lensing.   *Myro.*

Antigone
(GREEK)
Berlin, July 4.
Norma Film Productions presentation. Stars Irene Papas. Directed by George Tzavellas from his own screenplay; camera, Dinos Katsourdis; music, Arghyris Kounadis. At Berlin Film Fest, June 27, '61. Running time, 93 MINS.

Sophocles' great tragedy has been brought to the screen for the first time via this Greek production, and a very worthy effort it is, too. Film is lavishly mounted, faithfully scripted and acted with intelligence. But this must be considered a dubious b.o. proposition except for the most artie of art theatres. It should have wide appeal, however, for high school and college students who are interested in high drama.

The production is the first venture of a new company in which an American exhibition (Sperie Perakos) is a guiding influence. Though it may seem a strange subject for a theatre owner to choose, it has been filmed with good taste and integrity, with none of the more familiar concessions to eventual boxoffice appeal.

Story is set in the pre-classical era of Greece in the seven-gated city of Thebes and, to recap the familiar plot, concerns the defiance by Antigone of the king after her two brothers are killed in a quarrel about their succession to the throne. For her defiance, Antigone is condemned to death by the king, even though she is betrothed to his son.

George Tzavellas' direction from his own screenplay is a model of strength and integrity. The scene in which Antigone meets her death by being buried alive in a cave, captures the essence of this great tragic play. Adding to the power-

house dramatics is the outstanding performance by Irene Papas in the title part. It is an impeccable interpretation of a classic role. Other noteworthy portrayals come from Manos Katrakis as the king, Maro Kontou, as Antigone's sister; Nikos Kazis, cast as the king's son, and Ilia Livikou, as the queen.   *Myro.*

Anuradha
(Love of Anuradha)
(INDIA)
Berlin, June 27.
Hrishikesh Mukerjee production. Directed by Hrishikesh Mukerjee. Screenplay, Sachin Bhownik, D. N. Bedi; camera, Jaywant Pathare; music, Pandit Ravi Shanker. At Berlin Film Fest. Running time, 120 MINS.

India's contribution to the Berlin Film Fest is another well-meant effort that doesn't quite come off. "Anuradha" is just another story of someone learning the real meaning of love. Plot is simple: Successful, talented girl vocalist marries a dedicated, simple country doctor but soon finds it difficult to adjut herself to the quiet village life. She feels she isn't appreciated and threatens to leave him. Marriage is saved at the last minute when Anuradha realizes he does need her, and that her love has spurred hubby to new medical discoveries.

Acting throughout is mediocre, and lacks vitality. Only bright spot is the little daughter whose impishness and sparkle provide some good laughs. In all, hardly a film for a festival. Technically, the pic doesn't command much attention either.   *Hans.*

Brainwashed

Slow-moving but interesting psychological suspense meller based on a Stefan Zweig novel about an intellectual's method of survival under Nazi brainwash treatment. Somewhat grim and ponderous.

Hollywood, June 26.
Allied Artists release of Luggi Waldleitner production. Stars Curt Jurgens, Claire Bloom, Jorg Felmy. Directed by Gerd Oswald. Screenplay, Oswald, Harold Medford, from an adaptation by Herbert Reinecker of Stefan Zweig's novel, "The Royal Game"; camera, Gunther Senftleben; art directors, Wolfe Englert, Ernst Richter; music, Hans-Martin Majewski; sound, K. M. Ecksteins assistant director, Jochen Weidermann. Reviewed at the studio, June 26, '61. Running time, 102 MINS.
Werner von Basil ....Curt Jurgens
Irene Andreny ....Claire Bloom
Hans Berger ....Jorg Felmy
Mirko Centowic ....Mario Adorf
Hartmann ....Albert Lieven
Mac Iver ....Alan Gifford
Rabbi ....Dietmar Schonherr
Baranow ....Karel Stepanek
Moonface ....Wolfgang Wahl
Hotel Manager ....Rudolf Forster
Scientist ....Albert Bessler
First Officer ....Jan Hendriks
Ballet Master ....Harald Maresch
Countess ....Dorothea Wieck
Berger's Secretary .....Ryk De Gooyer
Young Lady ....Susanne Kolber
Bishop Ambrosse ....Hans Sohnker

Buffs of the psychological drama will discover much to enthuse over in this screen adaptation of "The Royal Game," a fascinating novel by Stefan Zweig. Deftly and creatively directed by Gerd Oswald, who collaborated with Harold Medford in penning the scenario, the Luggi Waldleitner production is a deliberate, often plodding, yet suspense-holding piece that requires

a theatre audience to be as mentally alert and physically composed as mute spectators at a chess tournament.

But whether American audiences, accustomed as they are to the rat-a-tat tempo of modern society and the generally slam-bang tenor of its entertainment, will be entirely appreciative of such introspective matters and painstaking technique, especially in view of the drama's expository haziness, is extremely doubtful. Chances are the Allied Artists release won't be racking up any master points in the domestic boxoffice tournament.

It appears from the revised title (originally the author's title was used) as if Allied has an exploitation campaign in mind for this film. If so, trouble may loom. Those prone to respond to the traditionally sensual, sensational lure of exploitation figure to be the very ones unlikely to sit still while matters hinted at vaguely in come-ons fail to materialize as electrically as promised. On the other hand, those most likely to enjoy the noble, erudite touch of Zweig that has filtered through are liable to be repelled by a sledgehammer crash campaign. Tasteful handling might avert to some degree the eventuality of quick commercial checkmate for which such a film appears, on the surface, headed.

The picture was shot in Austria and Yugoslavia. It stars Curt Jurgens and Claire Bloom, two gifted players whose names have slight, though respected, marquee meanings in this country. Zweig's tale concerns the plight of a learned Austrian aristocrat (Jurgens) condemned to solitary confinement upon Nazi occupation of his nation. In the process of refusing to reveal vital secrets, he employs a makeshift pattern for mental survival by smuggling a book on chess into his cell and clinging tenaciously to the realm of the chessboard to maintain his sanity. When ultimately he cracks, it is all the way, rendering him a useless pawn to his captors. The body of the drama is told in flashback, following a passage in which we see the free man hold his own against the world's chess champion in an impromptu match.

There are holes and lapses in the drama, but it has its rewards, too, for those who appreciate the ironies of twisted destiny in troubled times. Many of the rewards lie in the characterizations, ranging from fine pivotal ones by Jurgens and the lovely, luminous Miss Bloom to meticulous supporting enactments by Jorg Felmy, Mario Adorf, Albert Lieven, Alan Gifford and Wolfgang Wahl.

Oswald's inventive direction—meaningful angling, tilting and positioning of the camera for dramatic effect—is a driving factor in an otherwise static, confined piece. In this he receives the astute aid of lensman Gunther Senftleben. Balance of the behind-the-scenes efforts are creative, too.   *Tube.*

Un Soir Sur La Plage
(One Night on the Beach)
(FRENCH)
Paris, June 27.
Cocinor release of Francis Cosne, Manic Films. Marreau production. Stars

Martine Carol; features Jean Desailly, Dahlia Lavi, Michel Galabru, Rellys, Genevieve Grad. Directed by Michel Boisrond. Screenplay, Annette Wademant, Boisrond; camera, L. H. Burel; editor, Claudine Bouche. At Marignan, Paris. Running time, **85 MINS.**
Georgina ....Martine Carol
Francis ....Jean Desailly
Marie ....Dahlia Lavi
Sylvie ....Genevieve Grad
Gardener .... Rellys
Inspector ....Michel Galabru

Who killed the langourous, beauteous nymphomaniac amidst an idle family and their visitors on the French Riviera? That's the theme of this pic. Though smartly made, this lacks the needed characterization, suspense and adroitness to make this mainly a dualer item for the foreign market.

A pretty, fortyish widow with two teenage children and a senile father-in-law, plus her secret beau, a German visiting student, and the gardener, the father of the murdered girl, are the suspects in the slaying. Besides slow progression, it is not difficult to spot the killer. Acting is acceptable in this kind of film while technical aspects are good. But plodding surface story and conventional directing do not get it out of the run-of-the-mill whodunit class. *Mosk.*

The Honeymoon Machine
(C-SCOPE-COLOR)

How an electronic brain can beat the roulette wheel. Merry romantic farce that misfires when it slips away from the central premise. But has the cast and imagination-appeal for respectable b.o.

Hollywood, June 28.
Metro release of Lawrence Weingarten production. Stars Steve McQueen, Brigid Bazlen, Jim Hutton, Paula Prentiss, Dean Jagger; features Jack Weston, Jack Mullaney. Directed by Richard Thorpe. Screenplay, George Wells, based on play, "The Golden Fleecing," by Lorenzo Semple Jr.; camera (Metrocolor), Joseph LaShelle; editor, Ben Lewis; art directors, George W. Davis, Preston Ames; music, Leigh Harline; assistant director, Ronald Florance. Reviewed at Picwood Theatre, June 28, '61. Running time, **88 MINS.**
Lt. Fergie Howard ....Steve McQueen
Julie Fitch ....Brigid Bazlen
Jason Eldridge ....Jim Hutton
Pam Dunstan ....Paula Prentiss
Adm. Fitch ....Dean Jagger
Signalman Burford Taylor Jack Weston
Ensign Beau Gilliam . Jack Mullaney
Inspector, Casino Games Marcel Hillaire
Russian Consul .... Ben Astar
Tommy Dane ....William Lanteau
Capt. James Angle .... Ken Lynch
Capt. Harvey Adam ......Simon Scott

Once again Metro is wagering its chips on fresh rookie talent and light romantic farce material. The combination paid off in "Where the Boys Are," and this one looks like a modest, but tidy, followup payoff. Although "Honeymoon Machine" is in need of a little lubrication on some of its running parts, and could have done with a few hasty repairs in the performance department, the Lawrence Weingarten production is dealing with a surefire premise that long has gripped the imagination of mankind—the infallible system for a "killing" at the roulette wheel—and is doing so via that most ultra-modern of devices, the mechanical brain. That should spur the necessary curiosity and, together with the participation of several rising young players, stimulate the necessary comment.

George Wells' in-and-out screenplay has two young naval officers (Steve McQueen and Jack Mullaney) and one civilian computer expert (Jim Hutton) concocting an elaborate scheme for fun and profit whereby they will utilize the services of an electronic brain (dubbed Max) onboard ship to digest and analyze roulette wheel data at a casino in Venice and then predict the winning numbers.

All goes well until ship-to-shore blinking messages are intercepted by an admiral (Dean Jagger) who, instead of pursuing a rational course of action (investigating the computer room on the ship), decides that the fleet is about to be attacked. This leads into a series of slapstick sequences and several romantic complications enroute to a happy fadeout in which Cupid triumphs over cupidity.

Since the real wallop looms in the basic premise, Wells' scenario is disappointing in that it has a tendency to get overly involved in side-show ramifications, not all of which sustain the merriment. Almost every scene, however, has a few good comic jolts, and there are other compensations. Among these are the performances of McQueen, who reveals a promising flair for romantic comedy, Jack Weston, who chips in a gregarious characterziation of a drunk to overcome some pretty brittle material, and Mullaney, who scores points as a hapless accomplice in the greedy scheme. Dean Jagger comes through nicely as the perturbed admiral. Brigid Bazlen, Chicagoan who did Solome in Bronston's "King of Kings," seems green and uneasy in her work here.

The picture re-teams "Boys Are" couple Jim Hutton and Paula Prentiss, who are in the process of further teamwork in Metro's "Bachelor In Paradise." It is time they were un-teamed. Hutton, who does a very capable job here in a role less corny and uninhibited than in "Boys," bares evidence he can go places in filmdom, and not necessarily in comedy. He's got the looks and style for straighter roles. Miss Prentiss, an effective clown-comedienne, is stuck with a part that is little more than a distaff imitation of the blind-as-a-bat character played by Frank Gorshin in "Boys." The gag is due for a moratorium out Metro way. Able-bodied support is delivered by Marcel Hillaire, Ben Astar, William Lanteau, Ken Lynch and Simon Scott. Director Richard Thorpe has milked the script for all its worth, sometimes more.

The George W. Davis-Preston Ames sets—from a lavish, ornate hotel suite to the complex gadgetry of the computer cabin—are a standout. Joseph LaShelle's CinemaScope-Metrocolor photography is handsome and flattering. Ben Lewis' editing and Leigh Harline's score are serviceable. A song, "Love Is Crazy," by Harline and Jack Brooks, is warbled over the titles. It's a routine ditty. *Tube.*

The Touchables
(COLOR)

Sexy capers and bare body gymnastics at a girl's ranch. Story a slim excuse for striptee-hees.

Hollywood, June 29.
Jay Sheridan production. No star credits. Directed by Sheridan and Monroe Manning. Screenplay, Monte Mann; camera, Bill Hines; sound, Leroy Robbins; Asst. director, Jay O. Lawrence. Reviewed at Nosseck Studios, June 29, 1961. Running time, **50 MINS.**
Jessie .... Claire Brennen
Fred Barf .... Billy Holms
Monk .... John Dennis
Louie .... Brad Logan
Marge .... Maureen Bryce
Kathy .... Elaine Jones
Hilda .... Margo Woods
Guard .... Rhea Walker
Cindy .... Nancy Lewis
Timmy .... Doris Gohlke

That flesh-flaunting has become a lucrative business in modern cinema circles cannot be denied, as witness the profitable tenures of sociologically dubious attractions such as "Not Tonite, Henry," "Immoral Mr. Teas" and "Eve And The Handyman" in Coast theatres loosely classified as "art" houses. To many it may not be cricket, but it does move many a wicked wicket. And so now we have another item in this venal vein, a creepy peepathon suggestively titled "The Touchables" that is often no more than a strap tug away from lapsing into a courteous, gentleman's stag film.

Pulling the purse, or "G" strings under the banner of Paheton International Pictures are exec producer John Shay and producer-director Jay Sheridan. Their picture has no release arrangement, but opened at Hollywood's Academy Theatre July 4, just in time for layman sexologists and roving-eyed, well-preserved sexagenarians to celebrate their "independence" with a revealing revelry of striptee-hees.

Film, written by Monte Mann and directed by Sheridan and Monroe Manning, plants a meek Mr. Peepers type accountant in a femme rejuvenation camp (Fat Chance Farm) to escape from a pair of inept mobsters who he has reported to federal authorities for tax evasion. There is ample latitude for Sennett-like chases and various misadventures in steam rooms, exercise emporiums and swimming pools, where bevies of uninhibited maidens are soaking up Vitamin D through just about every available pore, fore and aft. The time is 1932—the uniform of the day half a bikini. It may not be compatible but, scanto-logically speaking, that's "show" biz.

Billy Holms plays the four-eyed hero, an accurate personification of Barney Google with the goo-goo-googly eyes. The thugs are played with spirit by John Dennis and Brad Logan. Children would enjoy their antics, but this is no place for children. Holms' body-guardian angel is limned decoratively by Claire Brennen. The other sportsmanlike girls, all in reasonably good shape, are listed in the above credits. Arts, crafts, music and choreography are dispatched adequately. *Tube.*

Quai Notre-Dame
(FRENCH)

Paris, June 27.
Gaumont release of Eloi-SnEG production. Stars Anouk Aimee; features Jacques Dacqmine, Christian Pezey, Christian Alers, Genevieve Fontanel. Directed and written by Jacques Berthier. Based on book by Dominique Rolin; camera, Roland Pontoiseau; editor, Jacques Mavel. At Mercury, Paris. Running time, **80 MINS.**
Elle .... Anouk Aimee
Lormoy .... Jacques Dacqmine
Eloi .... Christian Pezey
Nenette .... Genevieve Fontanel
Fouille .... Christian Alers

A young junk dealer's love for a chic shop owner's wife is the theme of this slice of life film. It is depicted as platonic and impossible. Hence, this appears too sudsy and sentimental for arty theatre chances abroad.

The boy has a fiancee, daughter of the junk shop owner, and a pert little sister. He talks energetically, however, against love until he sees a svelte, elegant woman in a fancy shop. He then gets a job there but his love is calmly denied by the woman who sends him back chastened to his fiancee.

For his first production, actor-turned-director Jacques Berthier, still lacks the observation and pacing to make this revealing and poignant rather than sentimental. Acting is also unresolved. Technical credits are okay. *Mosk.*

Francis Of Assisi
(C'SCOPE-COLOR)

Restraint and good taste. And compelling pic for students of religion. But plodding and talky.

Hollywood, July 6.

Twentieth-Fox release of Plato A. Skouras production. Stars Bradford Dillman, Dolores Hart, Stuart Whitman. Directed by Michael Curtiz. Screenplay, Eugene Vale, James Forsyth, Jack Thomas, based on novel by Louis de Wohl; camera (De Luxe), Piero Portalupi; editor, Louis R. Loeffler; music, Mario Nascimbene; asst. director, Ottavio Oppo. Reviewed at studio, July 6, '61. Running time, **105 MINS.**

Francis	Bradford Dillman
Clare	Dolores Hart
Paolo	Stuart Whitman
Sultan	Pedro Armendariz
Cardinal Hugolino	Cecil Kellaway
Pietro	Eduard Franz
Aunt Buona	Athene Seyler
Pope	Finlay Currie
Brother Juniper	Mervyn Johns
Brother Elias	Russell Napier
Canon Cattanei	John Welsh
Bernard	Harold Goldblatt
Donna Pica	Edith Sharpe
Scefi	Jack Lambert
Father Livoni	Oliver Johnston
Bishop Guido	Malcolm Keen
Saracen Girl	Evi Marandi
Lucia	Manuela Ballard
Elfrida	Jole Mauro
Regina	Uti Hof
Friars	Paul Muller, John Karlsen, David Maunsell, Cyrus Elias, Curt Lowens, Renz, Walter Maslow

Taste, care, restraint and considerable expense (reportedly $3,000,000) went into the making of "Francis Of Assisi," an emotional film that is bound to be a favorite with students of religion, especially Catholics. But, from a cold, mercenary point of view, the Plato A. Skouras production for 20th-Fox appears destined for commercial instability. The absence of sustained dramatic friction and a reluctance to grapple with conflicts and climaxes in visual terms results in an aura of absolute serenity and a characteristic of-ponderous verbosity that may be true in spirit, tone and tempo to the tale of supreme devotion being told, but is unlikely to prove sufficiently palatable to modern audience tastes.

The Eugene Vale-James Forsyth-Jack Thomas screenplay, based on a novel by Louis de Wohl, is remarkably akin in event and circumstance to "Ben-Hur." There is a scene in a leper colony. There is a rivalry between the hero and an irreligious comrade, who turns enemy. There is a desert rendezvous with a sultan. There are other similarities, too, but no chariot race. There is precious little action, a change of pace the film desperately needs.

Bradford Dillman essays the title role. There is an opening burst of pageantry as the story follows him into youthful combat. But he is promptly lured away into the service of God by a heavenly voice, and the balance of the picture describes his hardships as the devout, humble and inspirational leader of a small new Catholic order, the Franciscans, that cannot easily match its founder's rigid tenets as it begins to grow and prosper.

Within this framework, a love story unfolds involving Dillman; Dolores Hart, daughter of an aristocratic family whose love leads her to follow Dillman into the church; and Stuart Whitman, a nobleman - warrior whose unrequited love for Miss Hart fosters a hatred for Dillman that expires only when the latter is dying.

Michael Curtiz' direction and the playing of the principals leave something to be desired. Outside of several enlightening and touching scenes, Curtiz direction has a tendency to repetition (especially in the romantic byplay) and, at least in one respect (the heavenly voice) lacks subtlety or imagination. The matter-of-fact method by which mystical heavenly call is conveyed does not register with the required impact. It might better have been illustrated by suggestion or extreme visual measures accompanied by a profound silence, a technique more favorably suited to the disposition of a more sophisticated filmgoer.

Dillman's portrayal of Francis lacks the depth or variety to sustain interest. The character may be a disappointment to those who have found fascination in the celebrated, but shadowy, saint of Assisi. Whitman cannot do a great deal with his rather nebulous characterization, nor can the pretty Miss Hart with hers. Fairly vivid supporting impressions are made by Eduard Franz, Pedro Armendariz, Cecil Kellaway, Finlay Currie and Mervyn Johns. Others competent and noteworthy in support are Athene Seyler, Russell Napier, John Welsh and Harold Goldblatt. Balance of the cast is satisfactory.

Cameraman Piero Portalupi has failed, more than likely owing to somewhat uncertain leadership, to take advantage of several dramatic opportunities. For example, there is a sequence in which a pair of ocelots attack St. Francis and are calmed by him that doesn't come across with punch largely because the camera rather studiously avoids the incident. This is obviously a difficult problem to overcome, but nevertheless cries for the theatrical savvy that makes a stirring film. Louis R. Loeffler's editing, too, lacks the required excitement at critical points.

There is a tedious repetition about Mario Nascimbene's score that contradicts its melodic beauty and distills its dramatic impact. Edward Carrere's artwork (in locales native to the story, interiors in Rome) is excellent, especially in its incorporation of Giotto frescos, beautifully lensed by Portalupi behind the main titles. Nino Novarese's costumes lend a splash of color to the pageantry.
Tube.

Mary Had A Little
(BRITISH)

Lower case farce concerning a wager that hypnotic suggestion during prenancy cannot produce a model infant. Pregnant idea, miscarries.

Hollywood, June 16.

United Artists release of George Fowler production. No star credits. Directed by Eddie Buzzell. Screenplay, Robert E. Kent, Jameson Brewer, from the play by Arthur Herzog Jr., L. Rosen and Muriel Herman; camera, Desmond Dickinson; editor, Bernard Gribble; art director, John Blezard. Reviewed at Vogue Theatre, June 16, '61. Running time, **83 MINS.**

Mary Kirk	Agnes Laurent
Dr. Malcolm Nettel	John Bentley
Scott Raymond	Jack Watling
Laurel Clive	Hazel Court
Burly Shavely	John Maxim
Duchess of Addlecombe	Rose Alba
Angie	Patricia Marmont
Pottle	Hoel Howlett
Dr. Liversidge	Trevor Reid
Hunter	Michael Ward
Taxi-Driver	Charles Saynor
Grimmick	Sidney Vivian
Hawkes	Mark Hardy
Tigg	Michael Madden
1st Woman	Margaret Bull
2nd Woman	Yvonne Ball
Park Keeper	Raymond Ray
Watkins	Clifford Mollison
Esther	Frances Bennett
Carney	Vincent Harding
Fitchett	John Cazabon
Shakespeare	Tony Thawnton
Police Sergeant	Terry Scott
1st Interne	John Ronane
2nd Interne	Stephen John

The knack for light, farce comedy, for which British filmmakers have come to be renowned in recent times, is scarcely evident in "Mary Had A Little." Some of the gags and situations are so creaky that one experiences at intervals the sensation that he is observing an old English film on a tv late-late show. Director is the American, Eddie Buzzell.

Primary assest of the George Fowler production are its exploitably suggestive title and the presence in its cast of a young lady named Agnes Laurent, whose attitude and endowments are roughly similar to those of one Brigitte Bardot. Since sex figures to be the film's principal boxoffice bait, Miss Laurent should prove a handy lure to have around. But the sparseness of humor in the United Artists release should relegate it to the hind half of twin bills.

The screenplay, penned by Robert E. Kent and Jameson Brewer, stems from the play by Arthur Herzog Jr., L. Rosen and Muriel Herman, which is founded on an absurd, but sufficiently pregnant premise for witty exploration in the idea of a wager between a producer and a psychiatrist that the latter cannot, via hypnotic suggestion, bring about the birth of a model baby. The subject chosen is Miss Laurent, who actually is not pregnant at all, but is laboring in cahoots with the producer. The lady, however, proceeds to fall in love with the doctor, ruining the scheme but leading to several sequences in which the principals take turns hiding under sofas and in bedrooms, and falling under hypnotic spells.

A jovial performance by Jack Watling as the producer is responsible for most of what fun there is. The other principals—Hazel Court, John Bentley, John Maxim, Rose Alba and Patricia Marmount—participate creditably under Eddie Buzzell's capable direction. The various behind-the-scenes arts and crafts are dispatched with ample skill. "Mary Had A Little," but not enough.
Tube.

Battle At Bloody Beach
(C'SCOPE)

Action meller describing a rescue operation in Japanese-occupied Philippines during World War II. Bites off more than it can chew dramatically, but satisfactory for lower-berthing.

Hollywood, July 5.

Twentieth-Fox release of Richard Maibaum production. Stars Audie Murphy, Gary Crosby, Dolores Michaels; introduces Alejandro Rey. Directed by Herbert Coleman. Screenplay, Maibaum, Willard Willingham; camera, Kenneth Peach; editor, Jodie Copelan; art director, John Mansbridge; music, Sonny Burke; sound, Frank McWhorter; assistant directors, Chico Day, George Batcheller. Reviewed at API studios, July 5, '61. Running time, **83 MINS.**

Craig Benson	Audie Murphy
Marty Sackler	Gary Crosby
Ruth Benson	Dolores Michaels
Julio Fontana	Alejandro Rey
Caroline Pelham	Marjorie Stapp
Pelham	Barry Atwater
Dr. Van Bart	E. J. Andre
Blanco	Dale Ishimoto
Delia Ellis	Lillian Bronson
Nahni	Miriam Colon
Camota	Pilar Seurat
M'Keever	William Mims
Tiger Blair	Ivan Dixon
Timmy Thompson	Kevin Brodie
Mrs. Thompson	Sara Anderson
Japanese Lieutenant	Lloyd Kino

"Battle At Bloody Beach" is a routine entry in the war-action melodrama genre, competently filmed on a limited production scale by the experienced programmers at Robert L. Lippert's API shop. The Richard Maibaum production is an adequate lower berth candidate but, except in widely scattered situations patronized by action buffs known to walk a mile for cine-matters martial, the 20th-Fox release hasn't the strength, importance, appeal or clarity to carry a twin-bill. Its staunchest ally, from a boxoffice standpoint, is the name of Audie Murphy atop the cast.

There are indications that producer Maibaum, who penned the screenplay with Willard Willingham, aspired to come up with something deeper, something more dimensional, than the average "B" program picture. But it appears that, in trimming his film to a snug 83 minutes, he had to make compromises detrimental to his aim. The picture is overcrowded with complicated characters wading through complicated emotional problems. Given wider dramatic latitude and longer running time, Maibaum might have been able to make something of them. But, under the circumstances, it would have been wiser to focus on the principals, heighten the suspense, concentrate on action, and eliminate some of the undernourished secondary melodrama. Simplicity is simply a must in a film of this nature.

Plot has Murphy, a civilian adventurer, rescuing a group of Americans and supplying arms to guerrilla fighters in the Philippine sector during Japanese World War II occupation of the islands. Within this framework, several romantic stories unravel, central one implicating Murphy, his wife and a guerrilla leader.

Murphy brings his usual authority to the pivotal character. Gary Crosby is effectively businesslike as his ill-fated accomplice, happily subduing some of the practiced Bing-like casualness that has seeped into most of his film work in the past. Dolores Michaels is persuasive as the center of the battlefield triangle. The film "introduces" Alejandro Rey, a capable young actor, as the guerrilla leader. Prominent in the large supporting cast are Marjorie Stapp, Barry Atwater, E. J. Andre, Dale Ishimoto, Lillian Bronson, Miriam Colon, Pilar Seurat, William Mims and Ivan Dixon.

Director Herbert Coleman has whipped up some brisk combat stuff, with the aid of cameraman Kenneth Peach, editor Jodie Copelan, art director John Mansbridge.

sound man Frank Mc Whorter and composer Sonny Burke. *Tube.*

Affaire Nina B
(The Affair Nina B)
(GERMAN-FRENCH)

Paris, July 4.

Cinedis release of Filmsonor-Cinealliance production. Stars Nadja Tiller, Pierre Grasseur; features Walter Giller, Jacques Dacqmine, Maria Meriko, Jose-Luis Villalonga. Directed by Robert Siodmak. Screenplay, Roger Nimier, Siodmak from novel by J. Mario Simmel; camera, Michel Kelber; editor, Henri Teverna. At Paris, Paris. Running time, 100 MINS.

Nina B	Nadja Tiller
Berrera	Pierre Brasseur
Holden	Walter Giller
Zern	Jacques Dacqmine
Mila	Maria Meriko
Kurt	Jose-Luis Villal

Sleek and familiar melodrama is touched up by skullduggery aspects of ex-Nazis become big industrialists. Otherwise, this looms mainly a local item with some playoff possibilities on its deft action and movement. Art chances are out.

A mysterious opportunist gets the upper hand in a big development plan for underdeveloped countries by getting the goods on past Nazi activities of the directors of a big engineering firm in West Germany. But his wife hates him and takes up with her chauffeur.

Acting is broad in keeping with the one-dimensional characters. Director Robert Siodmak has given this a glossy finish. Technical credits are okay but this coproduction, located in Germany, was filmed mainly in France because of the availability of actors, which also gives it a somewhat ambiguous quality. *Mosk.*

Alakazam The Great
(Japanese)
(COLOR-SONGS)

Pleasant Japanese cartoon feature about an arrogant little monkey who learns humility the hard way. Brightly reedited, dubbed and scored for the U.S. market. Good b.o. prospects.

American International Pictures release of Toei production. English dialog version produced by Lou Rusoff. Features voices of Frankie Avalon, Dodie Stevens, Jonathan Winters, Arnold Stang, .eeling Holloway. Screenplay, Lou Rusoff, Osamu Tezuka, Lee Kresel; editor, Salvatore Billitterin:::c, Les Baxter; camera Seigo Otsuka. H−−−nto Otsuka, Komel Ishikawa, Kenji Sugiyama; music coordinator, Al Simms. Previewed July 7, '61, in N. Y. Running time, 84 MINS.

∧¦−−∩m	Frankie Avalon
De De	Dodie Stevens
Sir Quigley Broken Bottom	
	Johnathan Winters
Lulipopo	Arnold Stang
Narrator	Sterling Holloway
(English Dubbed)	

Considering the dearth of product (other than Disney's) suitable for the moppet trade, this brightly reedited, dubbed and scored Japanese cartoon feature should do quite nicely at the summer b.o. Story is an oriental fairytale of universal appeal—about an arrogant little monkey who learns humility the hard way. Since almost all the characters possess at least a couple of magicial powers, it's fantasy of the kind of extraordinary proportions best handled by imaginative animators.

The Toei animators are imaginative, and while the pictorial style is hardly avant-garde, there is much that is attractive even to the adult eye. Producer Lou Rusoff's English version also has bounce of its own, with the voices of Frankie Avalon and Dodie Stevens singing a couple of jaunty—if not memorable—Les Baxter tunes, and Jonathan Winters and Arnold Stang providing the voices for several of the supporting characters. Winters is especially good when sounding off as Sir Quigley Broken-Bottom, a large, fat gluttonous pig who'll eat almost anything, "excepting, of course, ham."

Picaresque tale opens with Alakazam being named king of the animals, and thereby becoming a little more than somewhat bigheaded. He tricks Merlin the magician into revealing all his magic, and then sets out to conquer the world. For this arrogance, the local human king sentences the monkey to make a long pilgrimage to learn the moral facts of life. It's these misadventures which comprise the bulk of the film and provide it with the kind of surprises and suspense which don't permit the small fry time to become restless.

The color (Pathe) print viewed by this reviewer seemed of uneven quality, but producer reports that corrections now being made for the release prints. *Anby.*

Mujeres Enganadas
(Deceived Women)
(MEXICAN)

Mexico City, July 4.

Peliculas Nacionales release of Pelliculas Rodriguez production. Stars Rosita Arenas, Luz Maria Aguilar, Marina Camacho; features Cesar del Campo, Raul Meraz, Antonio Raxel, Mauricio Garces. Directed by Fernando Mendez. Screenplay by Roberto Rodriguez and Fernando Mendez from story by Roberto Romana; camera, Rosalio Solano; music, Sergio Guerrero. At Orfeon Theatre, Mexico City. Running time, 90 MINS.

Picture is billed as a reel portrayal of real life occurrences in the Mexican capital, where unwary senoritas with artistic aspirations for theatre, television, pictures and modeling careers, as well as those seeking to earn a living in office or retail store posts, are victimized by unscrupulous characters. These latter are shown preying on and perverting naive young ladies.

While the daily press here has recounted gimmicks of tricksters time and time again, film fails in giving documentary treatment and stresses sensational aspects as three chief interpreters, including Rosita Arenas (appearing in a thinly disguised version of what occurred to her in real life) fall into snares of the calculating villains.

Although laid for the most part in Acapulco, photography does not contribute much to this picture which has a tendency to lag and stumble along at times.

A sensational one for nabe houses, and possibly for Latin American exploitation, where the situation depicted is known. *Emil.*

Berlin Festival

Miracle of Malachias
(GERMAN)

Berlin, July 4.

Ufa Film Hansa release of a Bernhard Wicki production. Stars Horst Bollmann. (Foreign distribution through Transocean Films, Berlin). Directed by Wicki. Screenplay, Heinz Pauck and Wicki, from novel by Bruce Marshall; camera, Klaus von Rautenfeld and Gerd von Bonin; editor, Carl Otto Bartning; music, Hans Martin Majewski. At Berlin Film Fest, July 3, '61. Running time, 122 MINS.

Pater Malachias	Horst Bollmann
Dr. Erwin Glass	Richard Munch
Helga Glass	Christiane Nielsen
Rudolf Reuschel	Gunter Pfitzmann
Gussy	Brigitte Grothum
Nelly Moorbach	Karin Moorbach
Christian Kruger	Pinkas Braun
Bishop	Kurt Ehrhardt
Canon Kleinrath	Kurt Lauermann

Bernhard Wicki is widely recognized as one of Germany's top directors, and his newest production was hotly touted as a strong contender at the Berlin festival. It had been kept under wraps, as editing had been going on up to screening time. And on the first viewing, it became apparent there is adequate scope for more use of the scissors if this film is to make the maximum impact.

"The Miracle of Malachias" is essentially a satirical theme, but suffers in its present form from repetitive treatment which could well be corrected by thoughtful editing. Though the main character is sympathetic by virtue of his very naievete, it is really a bitter film, exposing the phoneys who prey on any incident, however sacred it may be, for the sake of making a fast buck. It is, in some ways, reminiscent of films which have been made in other countries, but has a personality of its own to commend it. However, it will need highly personalized handling and exploitation to make the grade in the U.S.

Father Malachias is a simple, honest and sincere priest, who prays for a miracle to happen. His prayers are immediately answered. A notorious bar is lifted bodily from its site in the centre of the city, together with all its customers, and planted on an island a few miles away. It's a latter-day sensation, of course, and is so treated by the press, by publicity hounds and by unscrupulous tradesmen who quickly turn the site into a profitable mecca for the hores of tourists who come flocking in from all over.

While the Bishops and Canons look for a more logical explanation, the simple father alone believes that God has performed the miracle at his behest. But the problems that arise from the miracle gradually get the better of him, until finally he prays all over again for the miracle to be undone, and for the bar to be restored to its original site.

When the story spotlights the sincerity of Father Malachias, it is warm and gentle, but the bitter, and more satirical mood sets in when the focus is on the exploiters. The satire should have been the most powerful feature of the film, but misses somewhat through over-emphasis. The point could well have been made by a more subtle and relaxed treatment.

Horst Bollman's interpretation of the title role is one of the high spots of the film. At all times he looks and behaves like a dedicated cleric, and is completely overwhelmed by the fame that has surrounded his exploit. Other top roles are ably played by a well-chosen cast, though these performances reflect the director's treatment of the subject. Technically, the pic is in the Grade A bracket. *Myro.*

Los Jovenes
(Young People)
(MEXICO)

Berlin, July 4.

Cinematografica Filmex, S.A. production. Directed and written by Louis Alcoriza. Camera, Agustin Martinex Solares. At Berlin Film Fest. Running time, 90 MINS.

Mexico's contribution to the Berlin film festival concerns juvenile delinquency. This one revolves around youngsters who revolt against the society code and set up their own gang. They beat up harmless young couples and, remarkably enough, one of the innocent girls falls for the velvet eyes of the juve chief. In the end, justice is meted out by brute fo   ·.

Film offers some suspense but both story-telling and the message lack conviction. Acting is not bad and the lensing good.

But direction and script are too primitive to make this a memorable entry. The brutality in this has been exaggerated to the extent that it creates involuntary laughter. *Hans.*

14,000 Witnesses
(NATIONALIST CHINA)

Berlin, July 4.

Overseas Chinese Film Co. production. With W. Hao, Chan Feng-hsia, Hsieh I-ching, Weih Ping-ao, Lei Ming. Directed by Wang Hoo. Screenplay, Pan Rai; camera, Hwa Hwei-yin; music, Chow Lan-ping, Chu Men-lian. At Berlin Film Fest. Running time, 128 MINS.

This one plays in a big prison camp right after the Korean war. Thousands of Red Chinese wait for their release. The prisoners are split in two groups, one being pro and the other anti-Communist. Near the end, nearly all prisoners decide not to return to Red China.

Film, which is said to be based on real life incidents, catches the depressive atmosphere of life behind the barbed wire. Pic has technical and directorial deficiencies but remains interesting because of several impressive faces. Film, incidentally, ran at the Berlin Fest outside competition, reportedly because it was submitted too late. *Hans.*

A Morte Comanda o Cangaco
(The End of the Cangaceiros)
(BRAZIL-COLOR)

Berlin, July 4.

Aurora Duarte Producoes Cinematograficas production, Soa Paulo. With Alberto Ruschel, Aurora Duarte, Milton Ribeiro, Maria Augusta Costa Leite, Gilberto Marques. Directed and written by Walter Guimares Motta. Camera (Eastmancolor), Georg Pfister. At Berlin Film Fest. Running time, 109 MINS.

This film proved a considerable disappointment for all those who still remembered Brazil's outstanding "O Cangaceiro," also shown at a Berlin festival several years ago. Film is overly brutal and sadistical, often to an unbearable degree.

It's a brute force and revenge story mingled with some tastelessly erotic sequences. If exported,

many scenes will hit the cutting room floor. The best thing about this Brazilian entry is the beautiful color photography. *Hans.*

Kirik Canaklar
(Nothing But Broken Dishes)
(TURKEY)

Berlin, July 4.
BE-YA Film Agaeami-Beyoglu (Istambul) production. Directed by Memdu Un. Stars Mualla Kaynak. Screenplay, Lala Oraloglu; camera, Turgud Oren. At Berlin Film Fest. Running time, 80 MINS.

This Turkish entry surpassed expectations. Everything tends to exaggeration in this film—especially the acting—and, in all it's a rather primitive offering. But it has the kind of fresh naivety that's disarming and amusing.

Story concerns marriage trouble and a neighbor who tries hard to separate the couple so that he ultimately can marry the woman. But everything ends up smoothly after a lot of misunderstandings. Technically, the film can't stand comparison with western productions. But this vehicle garners much laughter. Hardly passable for export. *Hans.*

Markers, Staakt Uw Wild Geraas
(If It Doesn't Come From Your Heart)
(HOLLAND)

Berlin, July 4.
Netherlands Film Productions. With Herums and Ellen Vogel, Guus Oster, Yoka Berretty, Jan Teulinks, Ank van der Moor, Hans van de Water. Directed by Fons Rademakers. Camera, Eduard van der Enden; screenplay, Jan Blokker. At Berlin Film Fest. Running time, 99 MINS.

Holland's Fons Rademakers is one of Europe's better known directors. However, he has done better films than this one. But this pic is slightly above average. It's been made with obvious care and devotion.

Plot concerns the Fest of St. Nicholas, December 5, Holland's most important festival of the Xmas season, and three couples who try to cast off their daily problems to make it a special day for their closest friends. Pic contains some humor and fortunately avoids corny sentiment. Although nothing special, film qualifies for some limited export situations. *Hans.*

Black Silk
(THAILAND-COLOR)

Berlin, July 4.
Ratana Pestonji, Bangkok, production. Written and directed by Ratana Pestonji, Ratanavadi Ratanabhand, Thom Iswachart. Camera (Eastmancolor), Pestonji Ratanabhand, Viswachart. At Berlin Film Fest. Running time, 118 MINS.

Thailand came to the Berlin festival with a remarkably bloody film. It makes an obvious attempt to follow the western pattern. As long as this pic has its own face, it's quite interesting. But it doesn't ring true when it tries to imitate western productions.

Story centers on a bar owner who's heavily in debt. Along with his cousin, he secretly buries his dead twin brother and plays the latter to get into the possession of his own life insurance. There's a

lot of action and pathos in this production which, all in all, is only something for the curio-seekers. *Hans.*

Tulipunainen Kyykkynee
(The Red Dove)
(FINLAND)

Berlin, July 4.
T. J. Sarkka production. With Tauno Palo and Gunvar Sandkvist. Directed by Matti Kassila. Screenplay, Juha Navalainen; camera, Kalle Peronkoski; music, Osmo Lindeman. At Berlin Film Fest. Running time, 85 MINS.

Finland's contribution to the Berlin show concerns a husband who finds a letter that's addressed to his wife in which she's asked for a date. The husband follows her, only to find his wife murdered. In order to escape suspicion, he sets out to find the murderer whom he kills.

Film offers a certain amount of suspense but direction and acting are not very convincing. But despite its flaws, this is the type of vehicle which is okay for foreign export. *Hans.*

La Patota
(Teddy Boys)
(ARGENTINE)

Berlin, July 4.
Instituto Nacional de Cinematografia (Argentine) release of a Daniel Tinayre-Eduardo Borras production. Stars Mirtha Legrand. Directed by Tinayre. Screenplay, Borras; camera, Ricardo Agudo; editor, Jorge Garate; music, Lucio Milena. At Berlin Film Fest, June 30, '61. Running time, 89 MINS.

Now Argentina has come along with a "Blackboard Jungle" theme. "Teddy Boys" is an absorbing type treatment of a wellworn theme, with some sharp exploitation possibilities. It looks a lightweight prospect for the arty trade, but might have chances as a dualer.

Mirtha Legrand, a sensitive actress, portrays a young teacher of psychology, who had had an expensive but unloved upbringing. She takes a teaching post in a slum neighborhood against the wishes of her father. She has a rough time with her students, is waylaid and raped by some of them, and then gets fired because she's pregnant — and unmarried. Twist to the plot is that the selfsame thugs who raped her foil her attempted suicide.

Though the rape scene is rough and tough, the whole subject has been honestly handled, and has been quite competently made. Its main weakness is that it has nothing to add socially or morally to a very familiar subject. Acting is on a good average level, direction is smooth and other credits are more than adequate. *Myro.*

I Faresonen
(Zone of Danger)
(NORWAY)

Berlin, July 4.
ABC Film production, Oslo. With Rolf Soeder, Roy Bjoernstad, Harald Aimarsen, Erik Bye and Fredrik Wildhagen. Directed by Bjoern Breigutu. Written by Ragnar Kvam, Arild Brinchmann and Breigutu; camera, Tore Breda Thoresen. At Berlin Film Fest. Running time, 56 MINS.

"Zone," a mixture of feature and documentary film, was Nor-

way's entry at the Berlin festival. It takes a stand against the misuse of alcohol, especially among Norwegian sailors.

While certainly well meant, but too conventional to make an impression. Subject could have been exploited to better advantage had the material been more substantial. On the plus side, there are some good camera shots. *Hans.*

Greyfriars Bobby
(BRITISH—COLOR)

This is another Disney family film hit and his name compensates for lack of thesp marquee value. True story of a pooch who became famous 100 years ago in Scotland; warm refreshing fare.

London, July 18.
Walt Disney production and release. Stars Donald Crisp, Laurence Naismith. Directed by Don Chaffey. Screenplay, Robert Westerby from book, "Greyfriars Bobby," by Eleanor Atkinson; camera, Paul Beeson; editor, Peter Tanner; music, Francis Chagrin. At Studio One, July 14, '61. Running time, 91 MINS.

John Brown	Donald Crisp
Mr. Traill	Laurence Naismith
Old Jock	Alexander Mackenzie
Mrs. Brown	Kay Walsh
Lord Provost	Andrew Cruickshank
Tammy	Vincent Winter
Magistrate	Moultrie Kelsall
Farmer	Gordon Jackson
Farmer's Wife	Rosalie Crutchley
Old Woman Caretaker	Freda Jackson
Constable	Jameson Clarke
Maclean	Duncan Macrae
Allie	Joan Buck
Farmer's Daughter	Jennifer Nevinson

Only the toughest, most snide cynic, or maybe a really dedicated dog-hater, will fail to be beguiled by Walt Disney's latest canny excursion into the warm-hearted field of easygoing humor and unabashed sentiment. "Greyfriars Bobby" sets out to melt the heart and does it skillfully. Saphisticates may sneer, but Disney knows what he's doing. And there are enough audiences tired of perpetual violence in pix to make this a sturdy b.o. prospect.

Central character is a little Skye terrier, and this engaging little animal is quite irresistible. He's a sort of Pollyanna Pooch. This one picture gives him a place in the Canine Hall of Fame, along with Rin Tin Tin, Lassie and Pluto. Story is a true one, set in and around Edinburgh some 100 years ago.

It tells of an old shepherd who died of old age, exposure and starvation, and was buried in the little Greyfriars Kirk in Edinburgh. From the day of the funeral Bobby resolutely refused to leave his beloved master. By day he'd frolic with the local slum kids, and beg food from the eating house where his master used to take a frugal lunch. But despite the irritation of the caretaker of the cemetery and the annoyance of the police who didn't care for a dog hanging around without a license or even collar, every night he would outwit them, sneak into the cemetery and sleep on his master's grave.

In the end he won over all the local burghers and was solemnly declared a Freeman of the City, handed a collar by the Lord Provost and adopted by the entire populace of Edinburgh. Yes, a true, if odd story, and there's a statue of Greyfriars Bobby in Edinburgh to prove it. The film could have turned out to be a piece of overcooked whimsey, but Robert Westerby's screenplay doesn't overplay the sentimentality while director Don Chaffey has steered the piece with a nice balance of fun and potential tear-jerking.

Patiently and brilliantly trained, Bobby wraps up the stellar honors for himself and the humans, knowing they don't stand a chance, wisely are content to play chorus.

Nevertheless, there are some very effective pieces of thesping, largely by Scottish actors. Laurence Naismith gives a strong, likeable performance as the kindly eating-house owner who takes Bobby under his wing but, by standing up for a principle, brings the facts of the dog's case into court. He is matched by Donald Crisp as the crusty cemetery caretaker who is won over by the little dog. The clashes between Naismith and Crisp provide a lot of the film's amusement.

There are also sound performances by Duncan Macrae, as a pompous cop, Andrew Cruickshank, Alexander Mackenzie, as the old shepherd; Moultrie Kesall, Freda Jackson and Kay Walsh. Vincent Winter and Joan Buck stand out among the slum children who also take Bobby to their hearts.

The film has the real authentic Scottish flavor so that patrons almost will smell the heather. The 18th Century Edinburgh has been devised by art director Michael Stringer with apparent authenticity. Paul Beeson's camerawork on Auld Reekie and its surrounding glens is a delight.

"Bobby" is such a very warm and human piece of work that only a professional grouch might complain that Disney has pulled off a cheeky confidence trick by producing a film about the problems of a wee, devoted mutt in an island where it is well known that animals have a status equal—and some people suggest even higher—than that of human beings. *Rich.*

En Cada Feria Un Amor
(A Love at Every Fair)
(MEXICAN)

Mexico City, July 11.
Columbia release of Alfa Films production. Stars Julio Aldama, Alfredo Sadel, Olivia Michel, Javier Solis; features Oscar Pulido, Evita Munoz, Kipy Casado, Aurora Alvarado, Gregorio Acosta, Alicia Moreno, Gerardo del Castillo, Aurora Zermena, Salvador Terroba. Directed by Rogelio A. Gonzalez. Screenplay, Alfonso Patino Gomez; camera, Jose Ortiz Ramos; music, Gustave Cesar Carrion. At Olimpia Theatre, Mexico City. Running time, 75 MINS.

Julio Aldama, Alfreda Sadel and Javier Solis are featured in this musical, a more or less carbon copy of three or four other musicals featuring singing stars and aimed at the nabe house trade. Nothing much more can be said for this pic, a minor effort centered around theme of three lover boys who, instead of being like sailors, having a love in every port, have a love in the continuous fairs held throughout Mexico.

Scriptwriter Alfonso Patino Gomez, who has turned out better things, is responsible for a weak screenplay which stresses impossible, often absurd situations plus jokes and scenes which are just this side of being in bad taste. A modest budget effort, the cast does what it can with material, but this is by no means a work of art.

Still, the names of the stars in this will bring in patrons, especially in nabe houses, and possibly in Latin American circuits where they have a following. *Emil.*

Les Moutons De Panurge
(Panurge's Sheep)
(FRENCH)

Paris, July 18.
20th-Fox release of Gallus Film production. Stars Darry Cowl; features Pascale Roberts, Jacques Dynam, Elena Cardy, Jean Piat. Directed by Jean Girault. Screenplay, Jacques Vilfrid, Francis Rigaud, Girault; camera, Raymond Letouzey; editor, Jean-Michel Gautier. At Marignan, Paris. Running time, 100 MINS.
Husband .... Darry Cowl
Wife .... Pascale Roberts
Seducer .... Jean Piat
Girl .... Elena Cardy

20th-Fox has largely a local programmer in this situation comedy about two young married people who almost stray, but actually do not. Combined is a satirical look at overcrowded conditions here. But this one lacks depth and the biting satire. In fact, the general conception is fuzzy.

Technical credits also make this look like a quickie. Acting is only acceptable. It does not have any earmarks indicating export chances. *Mosk.*

Der Teufel Spielte Balalaika
(The Devil Played the Balalaika)
(GERMAN—C'SCOPE)

Berlin, July 18.
UFA Filmhansa release of Peter Bamberger production. With Charles Millot, Goetz George, Rudolf Forster, Anna Smolik, Pierre Parel. Directed by Leopold Lahola. Screenplay, Heinrich Dechamps, Johannes Kai and Lahola; camera, Karl Schroeder; music, Z. Borodow; editor, Karl Aulitzky. At Marmorhaus, Berlin. Running time, 122 MINS.
Seidenwar .... Charles Millot
Peter Joost .... Goetz George
Admiral .... Rudolf Forster
Elena .... Anna Smolik
Fusow .... Pierre Parel
Ebermeier .... Peter Lehmbrock
Hintermoser .... Franz Muxeneder
Akimoto .... Oda Hiroki
Lauterbach .... Sieghardt Rupp
Gellert .... Guenter Jerschke

This is, like "Doctor of Stalingrad" and "Taiga," another German pic which deals with German POW's in Russian camps. Unlike the other two films, which were more commercial, this Peter Bamberger production reveals courage and ambition inasmuch as it has no star names and avoids conventional cliche. Also, it is remarkably objective. It has neither an anti-Soviet nor a pro-German slant. Film's b.o. prospects, hence, are dubious. It's actually nothing for the entertainment-conscious average patron. But it's the type of film that stirs foreign interest. It actually may do better biz outside of Germany.

What militates against the film's entertainment value is the fact that it has no story line. Action concentrates on the various individual characters. Principal figures are the tough but not mean camp commander, the mighty tolerant and mild political officer and the latter's officer-wife of the same sort and the young, honest and disillusioned POW. The Russian political officer is an idealist who believes in tolerance while the camp commander sticks to the strict discipline theory. The former, incidentally, is Jewish and his Jewish wife has been tortured in Nazi concentration camps. Humanity and goodwill instead of revenge and irreconciliation is the "message" of this film. Film's super-human attitude may lack conviction at times, but producer Bamberger, who also

worked on the script, insists that the characters in this are not fictitious. He was a German POW in Russia for many years himself.

Although Czech-born Leopold Lahola directed this film with obvious devotion and imagination, his well-meant creation suffers from several flaws. Too much talk goes at the expense of suspense. Also the film appears overlong.

Acting is excellent on the part of the Soviet officers and Goetz George, the young German POW. But there are others who tend to overdo their roles. In all, however, the creators of "Balalaika," which cost $300,000, deserve a compliment for having tried to achieve something different. *Hans.*

Un Pais Llamado Chile
(A Country Called Chile)
(CHILE-COLOR)

Berlin, July 11.
Emelco Chilena S.A.C. production. Directed and story by B. H. Hardy. Camera (Eastmancolor), Ricardo Younis. At Berlin Film Fest. Running time, 109 MINS.

This pic, a travelog done in 1960 just after the disastrous earthquake, is the Chilean entry at the Berlin festival. Pic contains several fine shots and gives audiences an interesting insight into the variety of life in Chile. Unfortunately, film is somewhat conventional and also overlong.

Then too, the film goes overboard with showing too many factories and other industrial scenes. It should have offered more original things that are typical of Chile. One of the good features is the musical score which supplies the mood. The German narrative proves good enough to keep audience interest at an average level. Technically, film is put together adequately. *Hans.*

Ada
(C'SCOPE—COLOR)

How folks can erase graft in state government. Throwback to the screen's political romanticomedy era. Farfetched story rescued by sharp dialog, fancy production and stars with marquee oomph. Promising contender.

Hollywood, July 12.
Metro release of Lawrence Weingarten production. Stars Susan Hayward, Dean Martin; features Wilfrid Hyde White, Ralph Meeker, Martin Balsam. Directed by Daniel Mann. Screenplay, Arthur Sheekman, William Driskill, based on novel, "Ada Dallas," by Wirt Williams; camera (Metrocolor), Joseph Ruttenberg; editor, Ralph E. Winters; art directors, George W. Davis, Edward Carfagno; music, Bronislau Kaper; assistant director, Al Jennings. Reviewed at Hollywood Paramount Theatre, July 12, '61. Running time, 109 MINS.
Ada .... Susan Hayward
Bo Gillis .... Dean Martin
Sylvester Marin....Wilfrid Hyde White
Colonel Yancey .... Ralph Meeker
Steve Jackson .... Martin Balsam
Ronnie Hallerton ...... Frank Maxwell
Alice Sweet .... Connie Sawyer
Speaker .... Ford Rainey
Al Winslow .... Charles Watts
Joe Adams .... Larry Gates
Warren Natfield ...... Robert S. Simon
Harry Davers .... William Zuckert

There's an unmistakable element of mass audience appeal about "Ada," a political drama that amounts to a kind of "Mr. and Mrs. Smith Go to Washington," only on a state government level. To a great degree, the Lawrence Weingarten production seems to come straight out of the lucrative and highly-regarded tropic of Capra-corn that dominated the screen a couple of decades ago, the good Deeds and Doe's era of the cinema when plain Joes and their plain Janes came out of the country farmhouse to liberate the nation from thriving political graft and corruption. The big difference about "Ada" is that its plain Jane is not exactly the apple-cheeked farmer's daughter but a full-fledged, albeit reformed, trollop.

But the rest of the formula remains virtually intact. The parasites of the piece are the selfish, narrow-minded members of the smart, wealthy social set, whose vested interests the cunning graftsmen seek to protect. The heroes are the young, relatively uneducated "greenhorns" of government, updated reflections of the Robin Hood image who are out to take the rich, give to the poor.

"Ada" is a thoroughly implausible story, but it does have redeeming qualities, not the least of which is some tart, caustic dialog by scenarists Arthur Sheekman and William Driskill, a value that frequently will win over an audience even when the incidents built around the conversation are lean and unconvincing. Then, too, the Metro release is fortified with hefty marquee cargo in the names of Susan Hayward and Dean Martin. It would come as no great surprise should the picture make a strong commercial showing.

Film is based on the novel, "Ada Dallas," by Wirt Williams. Miss Hayward is a prostie from down on the farm who appeals to bumpkin gubernatorial candidate Martin, so much so that he decides to defy the party of his choice by making the party of the first part his wife. Pretty soon the naive Martin is governor, and he is signing "authorizations for the commissioner

of finance" without looking. Alerted by his wife, he begins to suspect foul play, is promptly hospitalized by a bomb explosion, but not before little Ada, against his wishes, has become lieutenant governor. Whereupon the little lady proceeds to turn the state capital into a kind of reform-oratorium and starts her house cleaning with the House of Representatives. Martin returns from the hospital just in time to deliver an impassioned address to the assembly and reconciliate with his wife, as expected.

Martin, the likeable theatrical personality and singer, is pretty hard to swallow as the guv. His portrayal emerges as an imitation of Dean Martin imitating Bing Crosby imitating a governor. But he's a helluva good singer for a singing governor, as he proves when he croons "May the Lord Bless You Real Good," a fittingly homespun ditty by Warren Roberts and Wally Fowler.

Miss Hayward, an exciting actress to watch, puts a high-voltage charge into her lines, best in the picture, but the character is almost monotonously cocksure and triumphant, and her portrayal makes it more of an inverted snob than a true women—by far the sharpest prostitute ever to grace the screen.

There's a crack portrayal of a sly, wicked party leader by Wilfrid Hyde-White, a character inconceivably outfoxed by Miss Hayward, along with several supposedly sharp people also uncannily outwitted by the lady. Effective key support is dispatched by Ralph Meeker, Martin Balsam and Frank Maxwell. Others in the cast perform satisfactorily.

Daniel Mann's generally crisp, businesslike direction keeps the story moving along at a brisk, balanced pace, assisted by Joseph Ruttenberg's knowing lensmanship, Ralph E. Winters' cognizant editing. There is commendable art direction by George W. Davis and Edward Carfagno, who have instilled the atmosphere of a Southern state capital in the depression into a film shot against California prosperity. Meticulous set decoration, down to wall-to-wall butterfly collections, is the contribution of Henry Grace and Jack Mills. Bronislau Kaper's score is unobtrusive, except for the burst of campaign parade melody under the titles that deserves to be heard.

Helen Rose costumes look well on Miss Hayward, although they are not always precisely what one would expect the well-dressed first lady, ex-prostitute or not, to wear.
Tube.

En Busca de La Muerte
(Looking for Death)
(MEXICAN)
Mexico City, July 18.
Peliculas Nacionales release of Delta Productions production. Stars Armando Silvestre, Lilia del Valle; features Carlos Cores, Magda Guzman, Sergio Jurado, David Silva. Directed by Zacarias Gomez Urquiza. Screenplay, Alberto Ramirez de Aguilar and Carlos Ravelo; camera, Manuel Gomez Urquiza; music, Sergio Guerrero. At Orfeon Theatre, Mexico City. Running time, **90 MINS.**

This is a whodunit with screenplay by Alberto Ramirez de Aguilar, a crime reporter, and allegedly based on an actual case, murder of a man of affairs. Lilia del Valle

plays the role of mistress suspect. Story line revolves around clearing of her name by the crime reporter, who has her in his custody.

While there are the usual false clues and scenes developed for their shock value, picture is head shoulders above the ordinary whodunit fare. It has good photography, excellent sound effects and musical background. Armando Silvestre and Lilia del Valle, as crime reporter and suspect, do not overplay, but strive for realism in their interpretations of roles. Other players also contribute to the documentary-type approach, with the direction only showing a slight tendency to lag at times.

As usual in police dramas, the reporter character is not exactly true to life, with Silvestre representing a brash, pugnacious type. But as a whole, the picture does stand up, with the weaknesses of the mild sort. Second of a series by de Aguilar and collaborator Ravelo, it is doing good business. It should click in Latin American markets. And scriptwriter-producer team are planning further crime films. *Emil.*

Clear Skies
(RUSSIAN—COLOR)
Moscow, July 18.
Sovexport release of Mosfilm production. Stars Nina Drobysheva, Evgeny Urbansky, Oleg Tabakov. Directed by Grigary Chukhrai. Screenplay, Daniil Khrabrovitsky; camera, Sergei Poluyanov. At Moscow Film Fest, July 17, '61. Running time, **98 MINS.**

Grigary Chukhrai is one of the Soviet Union's most distinguished directors and the acclaim he has received internationally for his "Ballad of a Soldier" undoubtedly will be reflected in the results of his latest picture. "Clear Skies" is a significant work with considerable artistic merit-and with surprising political importance. It should be a profound success in the U.S. in arty situations and deserves international popularity on both counts.

More than anything else, the film reflects great political courage on the part of the Russians in washing their dirty linen in public and, in striking cinematic terms, underlines the political thaw that followed the death of Stalin. But it is by no means a straight propaganda piece, as it is also visually exciting, beautifully acted and strikingly directed. It has its faults, particularly in regard to a lazy use of the flashback technique. And it certainly needs re-editing to achieve maximum results and critical acclaim. That, however, is a technical detail that can be readily overcome.

Without its political overtones, "Skies" boils down to a boy meets girl story. A young factory worker casually meets a distinguished pilot for a few seconds at a party, and subsequently discovers his telephone number. She calls him up, makes a blind date and that is followed by a few days of hectic romancing before his leave from his unit expires.

He goes back to active service and she discovers she is to have a baby. But before the child is born, he is reported dead and posthumously decorated. The girl insists on remaining faithful to his

memory and turns down other suitors. Eventually her confidence is justified and he returns home. To their joint bewilderment he is denigrated for having surrendered to the enemy after being shot down, and as the years go by he takes to the bottle more and more. Then comes the news of Stalin's death and shortly thereafter he is rehabilitated, redecorated for gallantry and becomes a leading test pilot.

Technically, the production represents a substantial advance on the style displayed in "Ballad of a Soldier," and, more importantly, the story is narrated in warmer and more human terms. The direction is impeccable and there are several memorable scenes. There is one, for example, in which the girl is keeping her blind date with the hero and when she eventually plucks up courage to approach him, strides forward with the enthusiasm and determination of a Red Army soldier.

It would be difficult to better the performances. Nina Drobysheva gives a moving, tender and sincere portrayal as the girl. Her various moods, from the depths of despondency to complete elation, are reflected with integrity. Evgeny Urbansky plays the hero with warmth, conviction and authority, though there are moments of indecision in his interpretation during the prolonged period between his return from the war and his eventual rehabilitation. As already indicated, the pic needs some re-editing, but the camera work is absolutely first-rate and the color completely unobtrusive.
Myro.

(Editorial note: Above Soviet film was co-winner of the Grand Prize at the Moscow Festival, with a Japanese silent, "The Island." Review of latter not received at press time.)

San Sebastian Fest

Les Honneurs De La Guerre
(The Honors of War)
(FRENCH)
San Sebastian, July 18.
Fernand Rivers release of Ako Films production. With Danielle Godet, Alix Mahieuy, Gaby Basset, Albert Hehn, Erwin Strahl, Willi Harlander. Directed by Jean Dewewer. Screenplay, Jean-Charles Tacchella; camera, G. Cloquet; editor, G. Levy. At San Sebastian Film Fest. Running time, **85 MINS.**

A group of German soldiers have some French Resistance people holed up in a church in a small French town at the end of the last World War. Obviously intended as a pacifistic pic this lacks the intensity and compassion for the needed irony and the sweep to make its point. Result is a little war sketch with scanty foreign chances except for possible dualer use.

A bunch of assorted French types set out to help their beleagured countrymen trapped in the church. It turns into a sort of picnic when they hear the Germans intend to surrender. But a misunderstanding has the film ending in an attack on the Ger-

mans and the recommencement of fighting whereas the Germans had planned surrender to the oncoming Yanks.

Director Jean Dewewer has laced this with comic looks at people in war and the Germans turn out more humane than most of the French. This fits into the cycle of "good German" pix here. But the sarcasm of a French Fascist to his fellows, the twists that lead to needless carnage, neither transcend its cadre of the last war or make their point on war's uselessness.

Little known actors supply surface characterizations and technical qualities are okay. But the feel of the times, the impending Yank approach, or the actual tone of war are rarely present in this film.
Mosk.

Vaude Ziji Lide
(People Live Here Too)
(CZECHOSLAVAKIAN)
San Sebastian, July 18.
Czech State Film production and release. With Ivan Palec, Jana Hlavacova, Zdenek Stepanek, Jana Stepankova. Directed by Jiri Hanibal, Stepan Skalsky. Screenplay, Hanibal, Vera Kalabova, Jiri Marek; camera, Josef Strecha; editor, B. Moravec. At San Sebastian Film Fest. Running time, **95 MINS.**

Mirek .... Ivan Palec
Eva .... Jana Hlavacova
Dr. Mrazek .... Zdenek Steponek
Rehak .... Jana Stepankova

A young doctor learns to live with the people of a little town though yearning to get back to the big city because of a girl. It is a simple vehicle that skirts banality because of deft characterization and a feel for the subject. But this is a limited foreign export. Its look at collective farm life and its problems also is not sharp enough to merit offshore chances.

The young doctor is taken under the wing of an ailing, but astute and old country doctor. He becomes part of things and finally leaves his fiancee to stay on after the old man retires.

Acting is acceptable and extremely perceptive via Zdenek Stepanek's aging doctor. He manages to make a familiar character revealing. Others do not do as well.

Technical credits are good. This adds up to a pic that probably means more at home, where there are problems of keeping them down on the collective farm. It loses more international appeal on its calm but conventional unfoldment. *Mosk.*

Vancouver Fest

The Kitchen
(BRITISH)
Vancouver, July 25.
Lion International Films release of A.C.T. Films (Sidney Cole) production. Stars Carl Mohner and Mary Yeomans; features Eric Pohlmann and Tom Bell. Directed by James Hill. Screenplay, Sidney Cole, adapted from play by Arnold Wesker; camera, Reg Wyer; music, David Lee; editor, Gerry Hambling. At Vancouver Film Fest. Running time, **76 MINS.**

Peter .... Carl Mohner
Monica .... Mary Jeomans
Mr. Marango .... Eric Pohlmann
Paul .... Eric Pohlmann
Kevin .... Brian Phelan
Raymond .... Howard Greene
Michael .... James Bolan
Hans .... Scot Finch

Gaston .... Gertan Klauber
Max .... Martin Boddey
Dimitri .... Sean Lynch
Magi .... Josef Behrm/nn
Frank .... Frank Pettitt
Nick .... George Eugeniou
Chef .... Charles Lloyd Pack
Alfred .... Frank Atkinson
Mangolis .... Andreas Markos
Anne .... Patricia Greene
Hattie .... Jeanne Hepple
Bertha .... Jessie Robins
Winnie .... Fanny Carby
First Jiving Waitress .. Patricia Clapton
Second Jiving Waitress ... Lynn Barton
Fifth Waitress .... Claire Isbister
Sixth Waitress .... Veronica Wells
Eighth Waitress .... Gwen Nelson
Ninth Waitress ..... Jennifer Wallace
11th Waitress .... Joan Geary
17th Waitress .... Rosalind Knight
19th Waitress .... Ida Goldapple
20th Waitress .... Susan Field
21st Waitress .... Nilo Christian
23rd Waitress .... Madelaine Leon
34th Waitress .... Ruth Meyers
2d Porter .... Andreas Costantine
1st Dish Washer ..... Andreas Lysandrou

This is in the current trend of "angry- young man" drama from Great Britain, a sometimes witty and generally amusing comedy, as adapted from Arnold Wesker's play of the same name which is presently playing at London's Royal Court theatre. Film version preceded the stage play which opened June 27. Vancouver fest unreeling was a world preem.

Entire story, apart from one minor exterior scene, is played in the kitchen of a bustling London restaurant as it survives a day of cooking and serving 2,000 meals. Situation is intrinsically comic and director James Hill exploits it to create a diverting and often hilarious film.

Film is not, however, all fun and games. Beneath the frothy surface an attempt is made to convey a powerful social message, and the author seems to be trying to say that his kitchen represents the whole world, with its up-and-down pressures and tensions. This theme is never adequately developed but does serve to give a nervous edge to the wit.

What does come across as the hours of work go by in the kitchen and temperatures and tempo mount are the comic characterizations established by the polyglot kitchen staff. Their realism in gay, lusty or wistful roles provides a particular kind of earthy but brilliant humor. Perhaps this is a type of comedy best appreciated by British or Canadian auditors; undoubtedly much of the rich characterizations would be lost to a U.S. audience unaccustomed to British dialect and inflections. Pic would certainly do better in larger U.S. situations where patrons are more familiar with English flavor.

Hill has used a cast of young actors and actresses who give outstanding performances. Most of the parts are played by comparatively unknown players, many of whom are re-enacting the same roles that they did in the current stageplay. Of the few "names," Carl Mohner, as the rebellious cook, is a known German actor who has appeared in several continental films, and Eric Pohlmann, the nervous restaurateur, has chalked up numerous screen credits in previous British pix.

Production is enhanced by Gerry Hambling's crisp editing. William Kellner's set is effective throughout. David Lee's music is a plus but the song "Something's Cooking," written and composed by Les Vandyke, is unnecessary intrusion and obvious effort to cash in on

the popularity of singer Adam Faith.

With proper exploitation, pic offers good export possibilities.

Shaw.

Badjao
(The Sea Gypsies)
(PHILIPPINES)

Vancouver, July 25.
Parallel Film Distributors (Los Angeles) release of L.V.N. Pictures Inc. (Manila, P.I.) production. Stars Rosa Rosal, Tony Santos, Leroy Salvador, Joseph de Cordova, Vic Silayan. Directed by Lamberto V. Avellan. Screenplay, Rolf Bayer; camera, Miguel Accion; music, F. Buencamino Jr.; editor, Gregorio Carballo. At Vancouver Film Fest. Running time, **91 MINS.**
Bala Amoi .... Rosa Rosal
Hassan .... Tony Santos
Taosug Chief .... Leroy Salvador
Badjao Chief .... Joseph de Cordova
Taosug Warrior .... Vic Silayan

"Badjo," a Philippines version of the Romeo and Juliet theme, won seven awards in the Asian Film Fest including best direction, screenplay, photography and editing, has never been released in North America prior to this Vancouver Fest showing.

Plot concerns a youth and femme from rival Filipino tribes, the Badjaos and Taosugs, who break century-old traditions by marrying. The boy is from the Badjaos, who ply the sea for fish and pearls while girl is a Taosug, arrogant and economically-superior tribe of farmers and traders.

Tony Santos is effective as the idealistic young Badjao pearl-diver who believes passionately in the possibility of closer understanding between the two tribes. He accepts the ostracism of his own people and has the courage to carry his defiance of social taboos to the headman of the Taosug village to win the hand of his sweetheart, portrayed sympathetically by Rosa Rosal. The greed and cruelty of the Taosug chief is well conveyed by Leroy Salvador and is the rock against which the Badjao boy's mission founders.

The couple returns to the Badjaos and are ultimately accepted but only after the boy responds to ancient custom by throwing their baby into the sea and seeing the child live.

Film is of special interest for its treatment of two little-known cultures and its concern for understanding and friendship among all peoples. Direction and acting are more than adequate but the biggest plus for this pic is the technical excellence, with photography particularly good. Sub-titling is easily followed and in keeping with simplicity of theme and statement. *Shaw.*

A Cold Wind In August

Skillfully executed study of an experienced nympho-stripper's seduction of a green young lad. Yet another example of modern screen's almost morbid preoccupation with distorted sex. Pic lacks Code Seal, is strictly for special houses. Prospects debatable.

Hollywood, July 25.
Aidart Pictures release of Phillip Hazelton production. Stars Lola Albright, Scott Marlowe; features Joe de Santis, Herschel Bernardi. Directed by Alexander Singer. Screenplay, Burton Wohl, from his novel; camera, Floyd Crosby; editor, Jerry Young; music, Gerald Fried. Reviewed at Goldwyn Studios, July 25, '61. Running time, **79 MINS.**
Iris Hartford .... Lola Albright
Vito Perugino .... Scott Marlowe
Juley Franz .... Herschel Bernardi
Papa Perugino .... Joe De Santis
Harry .... Clark Gordon
Shirley .... Janet Brandt
Al .... Skip Young
Carol .... Ann Atmar
Alice .... Jana Taylor
Mary .... Dee Gee Green

No matter how well Vladimir Horowitz might play "Chopsticks," it would still be "Chopsticks." By roughly the same token, all the exceptional ability that went into the cinematic execution of Burton Wohl's "A Cold Wind In August" is levelled to the common denominator of its subject—a short course in the seduction, care and feeding of a healthy 17-year-old boy by a nymphomaniacal 28-year-old stripper.

Had all the directorial, photographic and histrionic savvy and ingenuity that is demonstrated in the chemistry of this film gone into a project of loftier merit and significance, something of special import and value might well have transpired. But, as in so many other pictures of recent vintage, the preoccupation is with sex in a distorted state, undeniably a part of life but blown out of all proportion, in modern, post-Freudian cinema times, to its natural status in society.

The commercial question rears its ugly head. What do you do with a hormone opera of considerable quality? This is no attraction for general runs. The Phillip Habelton (Troy Films) production and Aidart Pictures release must make its way in the art house sphere, where its fate will be determined by initial critical reaction and the disposition of arty clientele to the provocative siren song of cinema sensuality manufactured in America which, in the highbrow circuit, often rates second to the sexy art stuff shipped here from abroad.

Wohl's screenplay, from his novel, plants the handsome super's son (Scott Marlowe) in the flashy upstairs apartment of a sultry body-goddess (Lola Albright) who is on a kind of annual three-month vacation in respectable anonymity from the questionable life she leads the other nine. Passion matures into love, but the romance goes ker-plop for the lad when he discovers she is not the madonna he naively believed her to be, leaving the lady crestfallen, heartbroken and alone with her overactive libido.

The tenor of performance in this film is exceptionally high. Since uniformity of cast excellence is a definite sign of directorial prowess, the part played by director

Alexander Singer in coaxing top performances cannot be underestimated. Additionally, he has endowed his picture with a blunt and powerful realism. His actors seem perfectly at home in the N.Y. environment. Their language (via Wohl) is the language of hip New Yorkers, their actions (via Singer) the natural actions of the Manhattan street scene and private realms a few stories above or one flight below street level.

Another significant factor in the film's visual impact is the extraordinarily active, inventive camerawork by Floyd Crosby. There is a strip scene (Miss Albright as object) that rivals in sensuality any strip scene ever put on non-stag celluloid, not so much in what is revealed of the female anatomy but in how it is revealed—darting images of undulating sections of Miss Albright's partially exposed and admirable epidermis formation.

Miss Albright is in command of her difficult role all the way. It is a vigorous, intelligent enactment. She should be making more films, and it is a mystery why she hasn't been making them all along, in addition to her tv work. Marlowe delivers a racy, sensitive portrayal of the boy—average, innocent but ripely savage. He's got a future. There is a towering performance as the boy's perceptive, call-a-spade-a-spade super-father by Joe de Santis—a small part memorably well played.

Others who are outstanding are Herschel Bernardi, Clark Gordon, Janet Brandt and Skip Young. The picture is tautly edited by Jerry Young and contains an agitatingly moody score by Gerald Fried. Titles by Gene Grand and Leo Monahan assault the eye so flamboyantly that the credits themselves seem merely incidental. *Tube.*

Armored Command

Uneven World War II adventure hampered by over emphasized but unconvincing melodramatic facets. Modestly salable as an exploitation entry.

Hollywood, July 24.
Allied Artists release of Ron W. Alcorn production. Stars Howard Keel, Tina Louise, Warner Anderson. Earl Holliman. Directed by Byron Haskin. Screenplay, Alcorn; camera, Ernest Haller; editor, Walter Hannemann; art director, Hans Berthel; music, Bert Grund; sound, F. W. Dustmann, J. Rapp; assistant director, Frank Guthke. Reviewed at the studio, July 24, '61. Running time, **98 MINS.**
Col. Devlin .... Howard Keel
Alexandra Bastegar ... Tina Louise
Lieut. Col. Wilson .... Warner Anderson
Sgt. Mike .... Earl Holliman
Capt. Macklin .... Carleton Young
Skee .... Burt Reynolds
Arab .... James Dobson
Pinhead .... Marty Ingels
Tex .... Clem Harvey
Jean Robert .... Maurice Marsac
The Major .... Thomas A. Ryan
Little General .... Peter Capell
Capt. Swain .... Charles Nolte

In "Armored Command," writer-producer Ron W. Alcorn has attempted to weave an intimate melodrama into a cold, hard account of military strategy at a critical juncture during World War II. But his formula doesn't jell. Milady's bedroom becomes the strategic center of interest, (at

the expense of the film's potentially more compelling and rewarding combat facets. Exploitation should help bring out the action fans, but the Allied Artists release may prove a bit shopworn, sluggish and disjointed for the average war picture buff.

Alcorn's romantic story implicates a decent sergeant (Earl Holliman), an opportunistic private (Burt Reynolds) and a luscious Nazi spyette (Tina Louise) who has been dispatched by the enemy to determine and report just what the 7th U.S. Army has in mind to defend its precarious position in the Vosges Mountains.

While the boys are scrapping over her affections, Miss Louise makes her report and almost brings about Allied disaster. But not quite, thanks to hard-bitten, Patton-like Col. Devlin (Howard Keel), who saves the day. As the Yanks in tanks repulse the Germans, Miss Louise commits a kind of Mata-Hari-Kari by gunning down Reynolds in the midst of enemy attack to avenge his smaller-scale attack the night before. This is virtual suicide because Holliman is a witness to the treachery. Placing duty before love, he trains his machine-gun on her as she stares, Juliet-like, on a balcony, and fires away.

Keel is competent as the colonel, Holliman properly perturbed and convincing as the sarge. Reynolds adds color and excitement. The latter two engage in a beaut of a no-holds-barred brawl that gets the film out of the doldrums for a few moments. Visual interest is also hypoed by the presence of anything - but - teeny Tina L., wooden though she tends to be in her enactment. Carleton Young, Warner Anderson and Maurice Marsac perform creditably. Prominent among the stereotypes in Holliman's small squadron are James Dobson (Arab), Marty Ingels (Pinhead) and Clem Harvey (Tex.). It seems as if a war picture just wouldn't be complete without an Arab, a Pinhead and a Tex on the premises.

The film ends in a burst of combat, ably helmed by director Byron Haskin, lensed by cameraman Ernest Haller. Special effects by Augie Lohman invest the action passages with authenticity, and the bleak, snowy Continental countryside setting instills a realistic atmosphere into the overall proceedings. Bert Grund's score and Walter Hannemann's editing are satisfactory contributions. *Tube.*

Whistle Down The Wind
(BRITISH)

Hayley Mills faces stiff moppet competition in a fascinating film which could have been mawkish. This is sincere, touching, funny production done with taste and skill. It's a little gem, worthy of a b.o. chance.

London, July 25.

Rank release of Allied Film Makers presentation of a Richard Attenborough & Bryan Forbes' production. Stars Hayley Mills, Bernard Lee, Alan Bates. Directed by Bryan Forbes. Screenplay by Keith Waterhouse, Willis Hall, from Mary Hayley Bell's novel; camera, Arthur Ibbetson; editor, Max Benedict; music, Malcolm Arnold. At Odeon, Leicester Square, London. Running time, **99 MINS.**

Bostock .... Bernard Lee
The Man .... Alan Bates
Eddie .... Norman Bird
Miss Lodge .... Diane Clare
Salvation Army Girl. Patricia Heneghan
Teesdale .... John Arnatt
Auntie Dorothy .... Elsie Wagstaff
P. C. Thurstow .... Ronald Hines
Kathy .... Hayley Mills
Nan .... Diane Holgate
Charles .... Alan Barnes
Jackie .... Roy Holder
Raymond .... Barry Dean

Richard Attenborough and Bryan Forbes, the team that turned out "The Angry Silence," have created a remarkably good film in "Whistle Down the Wind." They have taken a modern, sentimental-religious subject and treated it with care, taste, sincerity, imagination and good humor. One of the best British pix to emerge from the British stable for some time, "Whistle" has Hayley Mills as its main marquee bait. This looms a first-rate prospect with any audience. Possible snag for American audiences is the authentic North country accents particularly of the children. But it's a risk worth taking.

Films which have a religious background must face the possibility of giving offense. But this one skillfully and tactfully avoids the pitfalls and a cinemagoer would have to be hyper-sensitive religious-wise to find anything with which to take exception.

The film was shot entirely on location in the bleak, raw countryside around Burnley in Lancashire. This harsh landscape has been superbly caught by Arthur Ibbetson's camerawork, which cheerfully and effectively even ignores the rain in certain sequences. Based on Mary Hayley Bell's novel, it is a slight but human story of faith seen through the eyes of children. Three small children, leading a lonely life on their father's farm, stumble on a ragged, unshaven man taking refuge in their barn. Startled when a terrified, Hayley Mills asks who he is, the stranger is so relieved at finding the intruder is merely a child that he involuntarily swears "Jesus . . . Christ."

The children take the remark literally. They believe he has returned to earth and make it their secret to protect him from the adults who they believe will crucify him again. In fact, the man is a murderer on the run. It may strain belief that modern children should accept such a naive theory, but it is written, directed and acted with such complete sureness that it all seems completely credible.

Keith Waterhouse and Willis Hall have fashioned a screenplay which combines humor, sentiment and tension with remarkable insight. There are many pieces of New Testament symbolism but they are introduced with subtlety and arise naturally from the action. For instance, the betrayal is innocently done by a child at a birthday party. The local bully twists a smaller boy's arm and three times makes him deny that the fugitive is, indeed, Jesus Christ. Finally, when the police close in and frisk him, he stands with arms raised quite naturally, but the implication of the Crucifixion is clear in the pose.

Bryan Forbes makes an auspicious debut as a director with this film which never falters into maudlin sentimentality. He has coaxed some outstanding performances from a bunch of local kids. Only their leader, young Miss Mills, ever saw a script before. Result is complete authenticity. Miss Mills, now a vet thesp of four films, is hard put not to have the film stolen from her by some of the youngsters. But she gives a thoroughly moving, likeable performance. Little Diana Holgate plays with assurance and Alan Barnes, a snub-nosed, knowing seven-year-old, in fact does steal most of the scenes in which he figures with his natural comedy.

Alan Bates as the mysterious stranger handles a very difficult role brilliantly. Bates is a well-known stage actor but virtually a newcomer to pix. Bernard Lee is splendid as the children's gruff father and Norman Bird amusing as a handyman. Others who impress in lesser roles are Elsie Wagstaff, as a stern aunt; John Arnatt, as a parson, and Diane Clare and Patricia Heneghan in two tiny cameos. Malcolm Arnold has contributed a haunting score.

Forbes, and all connected with "Whistle Down the Wind," earn the utmost for their work. In print, it is difficult to create its special flavor without overplaying the religious theme but this has a poignancy, delicacy and yet down-to-earth robustness which makes it holding entertainment. *Rich.*

After Mein Kampf

More Nazi atrocities via a splicing of old footage from various points. Exploitation angles could help—a little.

Release as yet unset for Joseph Brenner production. Written and directed by Ralph Porter. Narrator, Jonathon Farwell; editor, Stan Norvin. Screened in N.Y., July 27, '61. Running time, 74 MINS.

Latest compilation of library scenes of Nazi horrors plus some theatrically-staged footage reputedly reproducing actual incidents makes for an unimpressive continuation of a trend. "After Mein Kampf" proclaims for itself via the narration, a nobility of purpose in being a reminder of Third Reich beastiality. But it also, and more strongly, mirrors opportunistic motivation.

Producer Joseph Brenner has pieced together stock shots of marching German soldiers in joyous military song, Hitler tirading before multitudes of frenzied followers, gas chambers and crematories and the ghastly views of bodies.

Incorporated, too, are scenes apparently taken from theatrical features. One is a crude episode in which a German soldier rapes and kills a Norwegian girl who is shown in full view naked to the waist. Another revolting addition has prostitutes forced into an experiment concerning the resuscitation of a near-dead man through the warmth of contact with the girls' bodies.

Film also undertakes to be provocative by posing the question as to whether Hitler still is alive. That's pretty shabby even in this kind of commercial enterprise. *Gene.*

Juana Gallo
(MEXICAN—COLOR)

Mexico City, July 25.
Peliculas Nacionales release of Producciones Zacarias production. Stars Maria Felix, Jorge Mistral, Luis Aguilar, Christiene Martell, Ignacio Lopez Tarso; features Rita Macedo, Rene Cardona, Marina Camacho, Jose Alfredo Jimenez, Noe Murayama, Armando Saenz, Alberto Marcos, Antonio Raxel, Manuel Donde. Directed by Miguel Zacarias. Screenplay, Miguel Zacarias from his original; camera (Eastmancolor), Gabriel Figueroa; music, Manuel Esperon. At Roble, Mexico, Ariel theatres in Mexico City. Running time, **120 MINS.**

While critical comment in the Mexican press on this biopic of the legendary Zacatecan heroine of the Mexican revolution, Juana Gallo, who became a sort of Mexican Joan or Arc, is divided, the fact is that, within its limits, the film is a tribute to the ideals of the Mexican revolution and the personalities that played a part in this social upheaval.

There is a slight tendency to overact on the part of Maria Felix, in the title name role, but there are moments when she does portray the bitter, angered woman who becomes a leader because her man is slain by the forces of usurper Victoriano Huerta. Juana Gallo in real life fought on the side of constitutional forces, with victory culminating in the tremendous battle for Zacatecas, brought to the screen with full impact by director Miguel Zacarias.

Jorge Mistral, as a military man ruled by honor and duty; Luis Aguilar, cast as a man of the people turned warrior, and Ignacio Lopez Tarso, who represents a *compesino* (farmer) turned into a fighter, give the best performances. Christiene Martell is satisfactory as a saloon entertainer who turns many hearts. Rita Macedo, in a brief role, as an articulate villager who cries out against hunger and misery, is very effective and believable.

This is by no means a political picture or one that presents the doctrines of the Mexican Revolution. Hence, the press here in general claims that the "true motion picture depicting the Mexican revolution is still to be made." Director Zacarias was not looking for a significant film in capturing the spirit of the revolt, with ideals, faith, cruelty, self-abnegation, spiritual values, etc. of the upheaval. He took an episode, admittedly dressed it up fictitiously for greater impact. And he has turned out a production that is adapted to his leading lady Miss Felix, and the tastes of the Mexican public. While this picture does not have the stature of a film to win much festival acclaim, it is a stirring drama that entertains in its own right.

The splendid photography, as usual, of cameraman Gabriel Figueroa, adds to the dramatic scenes, especially the battle scene which, despite the fact that it makes no mention of Pancho Villa, Tomas Urbina, Filexe Angeles and other

generals who were part of this famous duel of arms, is one of the most exciting made in Mexico. No matter about its hewing to the line of truth, which obviously it does not.

As an aside, the real Juana Gallo died in poverty and obscurity in October, 1959. After having given her all for popular causes, she wound up a mere seller of "tacos" (tortillas filled with meat, cheese, etc.) in the railway station of Zacatecas. But she had become a legend, and a ballad of Juana Gallo was one of the popular Mexican songs. It was actually this ballad that touched off making this picture.

Picture is one of the most ambitious efforts to date, has a cast of top Mexican players, represents much work and money investment. Film will be a moneymaker for years to come, whatever the comments on its artistic merits.

Emil.

Locarno Fest

Rabindranath Tagore
(INDIAN—DOCUMENTARY)
Locarno, July 25.
Ministry of Information release of a Satyajit Ray production. Written and directed by Satyajit Ray. Camera, S. Roy; editor, Dulal Dutt. At Locarno Film Fest. Running time, 50 MINS.

Widely-known Indian director Satyajit Ray, who made the "Pather Panchali" trilogy, did this pic for the 100th anni of the birth of the great Indian poet Tagore. It is a tribute of a poet to a poet, and a revealing compilation of photos, actual footage and enacted segments. It is a telling documentary on a noted literary figure of the times. It looms mainly for specialized supporting fare abroad and might make a fine video pic.

Ray's talent for extracting character, emotion and interior life from his actors creates a notable passage on the youth of the poet and his subsequent personal crises and decision to write. They fit admirably with the true photos and footage.

A telling commentary, music, and the adroit combination of all facets make this a statement and tribute to a man instead of a didactic entry. It is also a tribute to Ray's film flair and ability. Though a recipient of the Nobel Prize, Tagore today is not as widely known in the West. *Mosk.*

El Brazo Fuerte
(The Strong Arm)
(MEXICAN)
Locarno, July 25.
Rebecca Salina-De Thomas-Norman Thomas production and release. With Claudio Morrett, Hermila Guerrero, Jorge Gonzalez. Directed by Giovanni Korporaal. Camera, Walter Reuter; editor, Korporaal. At Locarno Film Fest. Running time, 85 MINS.

Engineer .... Claudio Morrett
Nacha .... Hermila Guererro
Mayor .... Jorge Gonzalez

Forbidden in its home country, this film is a takeoff on smalltown politics and life. It has sting and insight if somewhat formalistic at times. This looms a possible arty entry or Latino lingo possibility for the US.

This manages to keep its spoofing always incisive and clear as it takes potshots at corruption, backwardness and selfishness in good visual terms. It may lack the depth and character to make the tale more rounded but makes its points in a firm manner.

A surveyor comes to a small town where he is first mocked. But a letter from the government, never disclosed, makes him a hero and he wins the girl of the town's richest man. He then takes over the town and becomes a ruthless exploiter to finally get his comeuppance in an accident.

For a first pic, Dutch-Italo filmmaker Giovanni Korporaal shows a biting imagery. Theme is clear enough for comprehension in any clime. Technical credits are good and playing properly broad with on-the-spot lensing. *Mosk.*

Quand Nous Etions Petits Enfants
(When We Were Children)
(SWISS)
Locarno, July 25.
SPN Films release of Harry Brandt production. Direction, screenplay, editing and camera by Harry Brandt. Commentary, E. A. Niklaus, E. Pidoux, J. P. Borel, narrated by Pierre Boulanger and Andre Pache. At Locarno Film Fest. Running time, 90 MINS.

This documentary covers a year in the Jura mountains district of Switzerland as seen via a group of school children. It is a tender look at the country. However, its length relegates this more for video use than for theatrical possibilities since it is a fragile pic without the sweep for wider chances. It is also in 16m and blowing it up to 35m might lose too much film quality for theatrical possibilities.

Director Harry Brandt shows a feeling for children and the seasons. Made for a teacher's org, it naturally tends to be paternalistic. Brandt's filmic flair and feel for the land and the people partly overcomes this. *Mosk.*

Der Zukunft Ist Palling
(The Future Is Finished)
(SWISS)
Locarno, July 25.
Houck production and release. Written and directed by Gunter Grawert, M. E. Houck. Camera, Verena Tobler; editor, Hanspeter Giger. At Locarno Film Fest. Running time, 65 MINS.

Avant garde pic is an attempt to show man's almost mechanical place in today's society. But it does it by so much repetition that it lapses into boredom. Lack of communication makes this tedious rather than revealing. It is only for film clubs or perhaps some arty chances abroad.

Camera interminably follows a salesman who is preceded everywhere by some one else. At other times he meets a girl. Film plods on and on, finally to make its point that everybody is guilty for this man's alienation. Camerawork is fair but editing cannot alleviate the boring progression. This appears old-fashioned. *Mosk.*

The Tai Woman Doctor
(RED CHINESE—COLOR)
Locarno, July 25.
Haiyen production and release. With Chin Yi Wei Ho-Ling, Kang Tai, Hsia

Tien. Directed by Hsu Tao. Screenplay, Chi Kang, Kung Pu; camera (Sovcolor), Lo Chung-Chou; editor, Hu Teng-Jen. At Locarno Film Fest. Running time, 100 MINS.

Haihan .... Chin Yi
Poman .... Wei Ho-Ling
Yenwen .... Kang Tai
Laoba .... Hsia Tien

Red Chinese pix are still in the phase of explaining the revolution and fighting superstition. Result is a simple didactic pic with only local chances in store. But this displays a step forward in film direction, pacing and technical qualities.

Melodramatic story concerns a wicked overseer still exacting taxes during the beginning of the revolution. He tries to have a girl, daughter of an enemy, branded as a witch, but a young Communist thwarts him and gets the girl. But not before many coincidences.

The girl tries to drown herself when run out of town but is saved and becomes a doctor in two years. She finally returns to her old land where she saves her ex-fiance. Of course, all the Communists are good but even vestigial capitalists are shown capable of change and humanity.

Red China has a long way to go to make pix palatable for Western tastes. In a few years, it could well turn to less propagandistic themes and possibly make films of more worldwide interest. *Mosk.*

Scano Boa
(ITALIAN—SPANISH)
Locarno, July 25.
Lombarda-Ara-Luvi production and release. Stars Jose Suarez, Carla Gravina; features Alain Cuny, Gianfranco Penzo, Emma Pennella. Directed by Renato Dall'Ar. Screenplay, Messers Benedetti, Moretti, Cavedon, Dall'Ara, Avanza, Pinelli; camera, Antonio Macasoli; editor, Armando Nalbone. At Locarno Film Fest. Running time, 90 MINS.

Baroncello .... Jose Suarez
Clara .... Carla Gravina
Cavarzran .... Alain Cuny
Sguerzin .... Gianfranco Santess
Buba .... Emma Pennella

Melodramatic look at an impoverished Italo fishing town called Scano Bon is sans the needed characterization, feeling and thesping. It lapses into a sudsy, unreal pic with little export chances except for Latino marts.

A young girl is taken by her father to the village and is raped by a local Don Juan. The lack of fish leads to poor days. Her father is killed. The birth of the child gives the rapist a change of heart and an acceptance of the girl.

Ordinary technical credits hint at a skimpy budget. Acting cannot do anything with the stereotyped roles except for a moppet. Otherwise, the players display forced dramatics. *Mosk.*

Proshaite Golubi
(Goodbye Dove)
(RUSSIA)
Locarno, July 25.
Sovexport release of Yalta Film production. With Alexei Loktev, Svetlana Savelova, V. Telegina, S. Plotnikov. Directed and written by Yakov Segel. Camera, Y. Iliakov; editor, T. Fradkine. At Locarno Film Fest. Running time, 90 MINS.

Guena .... Alexei Loktev
Tania .... Svetlana Savelova
Mother .... V. Telegina
Gas Man .... S. Plotnikov

Tender tale further points up the Russo film thaw. Propaganda is there but satirized. Its tale of young love has sentimentality

without being mawkish. Fairly lightweight, this is mainly a specialized entry for the foreign market.

A young apprentice gas man balks at the tip-taking of his boss and goes over his head to do his work sans eliciting money. He falls for a young medical student and finally becomes engaged to her before leaving on a trip as a member of a young Communist organization.

But it is the good-natured treatment and acting that give this its tone and appeal. The youthful couple's ingenuous love scenes are well etched. A series of comic interludes are directed with invention.

The technical credits are fair but this has a verve and freshness that make it a light, pleasing item. Director Yakov Segel looms a new director to give knowing emotional lightness to the usually sombre Soviet fare. Made in Yalta by a new company, it bodes a further change in Soviet films. *Mosk.*

Ludzie Z Pociagu
(Panic on the Train)
(POLISH)
Locarno, July 25.
Polski State Film release of Kadr production. With Janina Traczky, Andrzej May, Jerzy Block, Maciej Damiecki. Directed by Kazmierz Kutz. Screenplay, Marian Brandys, Ludwika Woznicka; camera, Kurt Weber; editor, T. Karwanski. At Locarno Film Fest. Running time, 90 MINS.

Anne .... Janina Traczyk
Pierre .... Andrzej May
Chief .... Jerzy Block
Boy .... Maciej Damiecki

A wartime incident serves as the framework of this crucible pic which has a feeling for character, pacing and action. This all goes to make this a taut, telling vehicle with possible arty chances abroad.

A train comes into a smalltown station and a group have to be left behind when two coaches are found unusable. While waiting for another train to take off for Poland, the local German station head gets drunk but gives an alarm before passing out. (It is 1943).

Pic concerns the attempts to get the passengers on a train before the Germans swoop down. The characters are mostly neatly blocked out.

There are the good and the bad, the heroic and cowardly. The Germans do come and find the German official missing, but it's all cleared up without any reprisals.

This points up that heroic people were not necessarily Communists. This solid pic looms a possibility for Yank arties. Kazmierz Kurt, a new director, keeps this tale suspenseful and honest. *Mosk.*

Mutter Courage Und Ihre Kinder

(Mother Courage and Her Children)
(EAST GERMAN—SCOPE)

Locarno, July 25.

DEFA production and release. With Helene Weigel, Angelika Hurwicz, Ekkehard Schall, Heinz Schubert, Ernst Busch, Wolf Kaiser, Regine Lutz. Written and directed by Peter Palitzach and Manfred Wekworth from play by Bertolt Brecht. Camera, Heins Ullrich, Bruno Schlicht, Gunter Muller; editor, Ella Kleberg-Ensink; music, Paul Dessau. At Locarno Film Fest. Running time, 150 MINS.

Mutter Courage	Helene Weigel
Kattrin	Angelika Hurwicz
Eilif	Ekkehard Schall
Schweizerkas	Heinz Schubert
Cook	Ernst Busch
Chaplain	Wolf Kaiser
Yvette	Regine Lutz

This was made by the East German Berliner Ensemble legit rep company of the late playwright Bertolt Brecht. It is primarily an attempt to put the direction of Brecht on film. So this epic tale of war profiteers remains essentially theatrical. Therefore it is somewhat lacking in pic interest but of curio value for possible specialized spotting and a definite video-type pic on its theme plus university chances.

Tale unfolds during the interminable 17th Century wars of Europe. It concerns an enterprising woman who follows all armies and sells them things. But in the process she loses her natural children begotten by many soldiers and ends up following the armies alone pulling her old and battered wagon.

Done in a studio, the original sets are still represented, if on a bigger scale. Film gets closer to the protagonists but still remains a strange cross between film and legit. It is mainly worthwhile via the brilliant thesping of Helene Weigel, as the crafty Mother Courage as well as that of some others. Not as forceful as on the stage, this still holds interest. Its length and form slant this for spotty film chances. Pic is technically excellent.

The strident, cutting songs of Paul Dessau and Brecht also effectively underline and comment on the action. Use of split screen tactics are also of note. But this is mainly a hybrid pic, neither filmic enough for theatres or theatrical enough to give the full idea of a play. But it has the poetics, bite and force of Brecht's original. *Mosk.*

Vancouver Fest

Cinderella
(RUSSIAN—COLOR)
Vancouver, July 25.

U.S.S.R. Ministry of Culture release of Gorky Film Studios production. Stars Raisa Struchkova, Gennadi Lediakh, Elena Vanke; features the Ballet Troupe and Orch of State Academic Bolshoi Theatre. Directed by Alexander Row, Rostislav Zhakarov. Camera, Alexander Gintsburg; music, Sergei Prokofyev; editor, V. Bitiukova. At Vancouver Film Fest. Running time, **80 MINS.**

Cinderella	Raisa Struchkova
Prince	Gennadi Lediakh
Stepmother	Elena Vanke
Haughty	Lesma Chadarain
Spiteful	Natalya Rizhenko
Cinderella's Father	Alexander Pavlinov
FAIRIES OF THE SEASON	
Spring	Yekaterina Maximova
Summer	Elena Riabinkina
Autumn	Marina Kolpakchi
Winter	Natalya Taborko

This late entry from the U.S.S.R. arrived unheralded to provide the Vancouver Film Fest with an unexpected North American preem and ballet buffs with a satisfying screen version of Serge Prokofiev's widely known ballet. Produced by the Gorky studios in Moscow, this film features the ballet troupe and orch of the State Academic Bol-

shoi Theatre. It is highlighted by two rising stars in the persons of Raisa Struchkova, as Cinderella, and Gennadi Lediakh, as her Prince Charming.

There are no deviations or innovations imposed on the venerable fairy story as it unreels with simplicity and charm. The beauty of the film lies in the stunning virtuosity of the choreography and the fidelity of sound track recording of Prokofiev's rich score. To a non-balletomane's jaundiced eye, this is far and away the best filmed ballet seen to date and surpasses all previous Russian efforts as well as British productions in this limited field.

Sovcolor lensing is both soft and brilliant to key the mood and pace created by the score and story line. Editing is sharp throughout. Camera work is particularly noteworthy as it catches intricate footwork unerringly. Although pic is in standard ratio, the wide sweep of the staging is never lost. And it is always apparent that this is ballet staged for filming, not a film version of a theatre presentation.

Subject matter obviously makes this a limited arty house import but for those who cater to the opera and ballet set, smart campaigning should pay off. *Shaw.*

Hollywood: The Golden Years
(U.S.)

Wolper-Sterling Productions, Inc. release of David L. Wolpert (Jack Haley Jr.) production. Directed by Wolper. Narrator, Gene Kelly. Cast includes Hollywood stars of the silent era, seen in sequences from some of their best-known films. Script, Sidney Skolsky, Malvin Wald; music, Elmer Bernstein; editor, Philip R. Rosenberg. At Vancouver Film Fest. Running time, **53 MINS.**

"Hollywood: The Golden Years" was submitted to the Vancouver Film Fest as a feature-length documentary of the silent era of pictures and proved to be a fascinating parade of the greats of yesteryear. Starting with "The Great Train Robbery" of 1907, film spans the years to the coming of the sound track in 1927, with Al Jolson's "The Jazz Singer."

There are reminders of Charlie Chaplin, Rudolph Valentino, Douglas Fairbanks, Mary Pickford, Gloria Swanson, Harold Lloyd, Greta Garbo and John Barrymore as they appeared in some of their most-known pix. Result is a melange of silent era.

Producer David Wolper and film editor Philip Rosenberg made sagacious selection of footage received from 20th Fox, Metro, Warners, Paramount, UA, Universal and others. Narration is by Sidney Skolsky and Malvin Wald. Sometimes fulsome but in the main factual and not overly sentimental. It gets a sympathetic reading from Gene Kelly, who appears on-camera only briefly, at intro and fadeout. Music by Elmer Bernstein is in keeping with nostalgic flavor of the pic and heightens the mood without being obtrusive.

Funny today is Rudolph Valentino's love making with Vilma Banky. Audience was awed by spectacular action of oldies "Birth of a Nation," "Intolerance" and the still-impressive chariot race from the 1926 "Ben-Hur."

"Golden Years" is slated for television exposure via NBC under sponsorship of Procter and Gamsponsorship of Procter & Gamble. *Shaw.*

Moscow Film Fest

Big Request Concert
(AUSTRIA)
Moscow, July 25.

Oster Film production and release. Stars Carlos Thompson, Linda Christian, Edmund Purdom. Directed by Arthur-Maria Rabenalt. Screenplay, Felix Lutzkendorf, Rolf Olsen; camera, Walter Tuch. At Moscow Film Fest. Running time, **115 MINS.**

Austria has one of the smallest film industries in Europe and has, with rare exceptions, not been noted for the quality of its productions. This is one of the below average films to come from that country. It did little credit to the Austrian industry and hardly merited a place in an international fest.

For the biggest part of two hours, the contrived screenplay describes how a little girl helps her widowed father, a distinguished conductor, to find happiness with the right woman. It is a cliche-ridden script, oozing with naive sentiment, leisurely directed and casually edited. The promine cast, headed by Carlos Thompson, Linda Christian and Edmund Purdom, vainly battle uphill against such undistinguished material. *Myro.*

A Revolutionary Family
(CHINA—COLOR)
Moscow, July 25.

Peking Studios production. Stars Youi Lan, Soun Dai-line, Tchjan-Lian. Directed by Coui Khoua. Screenplay Sia Yan and Choui Khoua; camera, Tsian Tsian. At Moscow Film Fest. Running time, **118 MINS.**

Not much is known in the West about Red China's film industry, but if its contribution to the Moscow festival is a typical example, there is not much to worry about. "A Revolutionary Family" is one of the poorest pictures ever to be entered at any fest. It is long, tedious and repetitious, loaded with propaganda cliches, and with an extremely naive script.

In great detail the plot describes the experiences of a single family during the prolonged Chinese civil war period. It pinpoints their growth of political consciousness towards the "Communist ideal." Film is undistinguished in almost every way, though the color is adequate. The technical level is just fair. *Myro.*

Tonight A Town Dies
(POLISH)
Moscow, July 25.

Film Polski (Warsaw) production and release. Stars Andrezej Lapicki, Beata Tyszkiewicz, Danuta Szaflarski. Directed by Jan Rybkowski. Screenplay, Leon Kruczkowski, Jan Rybkowski; camera, Boguslaw Lambach. At Moscow Film Fest. Running time, **92 MINS.**

There is a maturity about Polish productions which is reflected in this grim, but sincere story of a concentration camp inmate who escapes while being transported

to Dachau, and then hides out in Dresden. Unfortunately, the mood is not sustained. It starts out as an exciting chase story, but switches half way through to focus attention on the American bombing of the city. Though competently made and intelligently directed, the variation in plot robs the film of much of its dramatic impact. This emerges as a lightweight prospect for Western audiences.

The leading role is smoothly interpreted by Andrezej Lapicki. First part of the pic, when he is on the run from the Gestapo, is holding and dramatically exciting. The cat and mouse adventures with the authorities build up to an intense pitch, but suddenly it all falls flat when the emphasis is on the destruction of the city. There is a note of authenticity about the devastating raids on Dresden, but they are out of key, so far as the rest of the picture is concerned.

There is a touching performance by Beata Tyszkiewicz and also a worthy contribution by Danuta Szaflarska, who is one of Poland's best known actresses.

Technically the film is first-rate, with fluent direction, confident editing and smooth camerawork. However, the technical efforts are lost in the confused style of the finished picture. *Myro.*

San Sebastian Fest

La Carcel De Cananea
(The Cananea Prison)
(MEXICAN—COLOR)
San Sebastian, July 25.

CISA release of Raul De Anda production. Stars Pedro Armendariz, Augustin De Anda, Sonia Furia, Teresa Velasquez. Directed by Gilberto Gazcon De Anda. Screenplay, Fernando Mendez, I. Y. Aldo Monti; camera (Eastmancolor), Rosalio Solano; editor, S. Lozano. At San Sebastian Film Fest. Running time, **75 MINS.**

Pedro	Pedro Armendariz
Ramon	Augustin De Anda
Margarita	Sonia Furia
Rebeca	Teresa Velasquez

Though a familiar oater situation in its basic tale of a dedicated, almost cruel policeman bringing back an escaped prisoner, who is really a good man (innocent in this case), film has a snap and feel for character which makes its obvious unfoldment engrossing at times. It looms a good Latino circuit bet for the U.S., with enough action aspects for dualer use.

The policeman traps an escaped youth accused of killing the father of his fiance. On the way back they tangle and he tries to make various escapes only to be thwarted. But the byplay and building of feelings for the characters and types make this section a telling, progressive portion of this short taut pic.

The two become friends after battles, and saving each other, with a growing liking and mutual admiration. Then the real culprit is unmasked at the end. Pedro Armendariz is properly bluff and brutal as the policeman, while Augustin De Anda has a projective, canny quality which makes him both sympathetic and a man of stature as the innocent prisoner. Technical qualities are good and

locations well utilized. This is a small picture that misses being a unique entry by its concessions and patness. But there is enough bite, verve and intermittent insight to make this an okay entry on both sides of the border.

Mosk.

The Pit and The Pendulum
(C'SCOPE—COLOR)

Blood, sweat and torture in a 16th Century Spanish castle. A rococo elaboration of Poe's famous horror story. Stylish, imaginative production helps hide corny script and some wooden acting. Good exploitation possibilities.

American International Pictures release of Roger Corman production. Stars Vincent Price, John Kerr, Barbara Steele, Luana Anders. Directed by Corman. Screenplay, Richard Matheson, based on Edgar Allen Poe story; camera, Floyd Crosby; special effects, Pat Dinga; editor, Anthony Carras; music, Les Baxter; production design, Daniel Haller; assistant director, Jack Bohier. Reviewed Aug. 3, '61, in N.Y. Running time, **85 MINS.**

Nicholas Medina .... Vincent Price
Francis Barnard .... John Kerr
Elizabeth Barnard Medina
.... Barbara Steele
Catherine Medina ...... Luana Anders
Dr. Charles Leon ..... Anthony Carbone
Maxmillian .... Patrick Westwood
Maria .... Lynne Bernay
Nicholas (as a child)..... Larry Turner
Isabella .... Mary Menzies
Bartolome .... Charles Victor

Producer-director Roger Corman, who racked up a neat box-office record for AIP last year with his screen adaptation of Poe's "House of Usher," obviously hopes that lightning will strike again with "The Pit and the Pendulum." And it may. With Vincent Price again as star. Corman employed some of the same prop bolts and plot gimmicks, which illuminated the earlier film with good and eerie effect. "Pit and Pendulum" is an elaboration of the short Poe classic about blood-letting in 16th Century Spain. The result is a physically stylish, imaginatively photographed horror film which, though needlessly corny in many spots, adds up to a good exploitation bet.

The main problem with the picture is that Poe furnished scriptwriter Richard Matheson with only one scene—the spine-tingling climax—and Matheson has been hard put to come up with a comparably effective build-up to these last 10 or so minutes. He has removed the tale one generation beyond the time of the Spanish Inquisition (for reasons best known to himself) and contrived a plot involving an ill-fated nobleman slowly losing his mind because he thinks he accidentally buried his wife alive, just like his father did some years before—on purpose.

Actually Matheson's plotting isn't at all bad, but he has rendered it in some of the fruitiest dialog heard on the screen in a couple of decades. If audiences don't titter, it's only because veteran star Price can chew scenery while keeping his tongue in his cheek. "This room," says Price soothingly of the basement torture chamber, "was my father's life."

Costar John Kerr and the rest of the cast are not so experienced. As a young Englishman who has come to Price's castle to investigate the reported death of his sister, Kerr wanders through the proceedings with a grim stoicism, almost as if he refused to be surprised at the next line he'll be called upon to utter. ("Will you stay the night, Mr. Barnard?" "The night and more, sir, until I find out exactly what happened.")

What happened, in brief, is that Price's supposedly deceased wife, Barbara Steele, and his best friend, Anthony Carbone, have contrived the apparent death of Miss Steele as part of a plan to drive Price mad. Ironically, they succeed, but only to the point of making Price assume the identity of his late father, the most infamous of Spain's grand inquisitors. After killing Carbone, and locking Miss Steele in a handy iron maiden, the demented Price sets about to shave Kerr's chest with the giant, free-swinging razor which Dad employed on religious heretics.

While Matheson's script takes a good deal of time, including three extended flashbacks, to get to the denouement, it's almost worth it. The last portion of the film builds with genuine excitement to a reverse twist ending that might well have pleased Poe himself.

Adding much to the effectiveness of the film is Floyd Crosby's camerawork (in appropriately livid Pathe color) and the grandeur that once was one Spanish castle, designed by Daniel Haller. Les Baxter's music also contributes while editing is sharp and to the point.

Though her performance is limited by the range of the material, Miss Steele registers as a remarkably striking "new face" in Hollywood. Luana Anders, as prices innocent sister, looks as pained and glum as Kerr at finding herself in such garish circumstances.

Anby.

The Secret Of Monte Cristo
(DYALISCOPE—COLOR)

Shopworn adventure meller crammed with cliches. Adequate lower berth item for kiddies.

Hollywood, July 25.
Metro release of Robert S. Baker-Monty Berman production. Stars Rory Calhoun, Patricia Bredin; features John Gregson, Peter Arne, Sam Kydd, Ian Hunter, David Davies, Gianna Maria Canale. Directed by Baker and Berman. Screenplay, Leon Griffiths; camera (Eastman), Baker, Berman; editor, John Jempson; art director, Allan Harris; music, Clifton Parker; sound, W. Daniels; assistant director, Bert Batt. Reviewed at the studio, July 25, '61. Running time, **83 MINS.**
Capt. Adam Corbett.... Rory Calhoun
Pauline .... Patricia Bredin
Renato .... John Gregson
Boldini .... Peter Arne
Albert .... Sam Kydd
Colonel Jackson .... Ian Hunter
Van Ryman .... David Davies
Auclair .... Francis Matthews
Gino .... Tutte Lemkow
Innkeeper .... George Street
Cafe Proprietor .... C. Denier Warren
Carlo .... Endre Muller
Jenkins .... John Sullivan
Militia Officer .... Tony Thawnton
Ben .... Bill Cummings
Lucetta .... Gianna Maria Canale

"The Secret of Monte Cristo" is the British equivalent of the old-fashioned American western. The hero wears a starched collar instead of a 10-gallon chapeau and brandishes a sword instead of a six shooter. Otherwise the setting might just as well be 1860 Texas as 1815 England. Whereas, however, the American western has recently gone high hat, adult and psychological, this little number from Metro's British unit is a throwback to the non-cerebral adventure epic of yesteryear, complete with every cliche from runaway coach horses halted at cliffside to the comic manservant who

conks his master on the noggin with a barrel when aiming for the villain's bean in a titanic fistfight in yon inn. All of which makes it an ideal conglomeration of free-wheeling good-natured, lower berth pap for juniors with a healthy appetite for derring-do infrequently satisfied on the ever-more-sophisticated modern screen.

Hero of the piece is Capt. Adam Corbett (Rory Calhoun), soldier of fortune implicated in a mercenary pilgrimage to the Island of Monte Cristo for purposes of unearthing a hidden treasure chest via (what else?) treasure map. Bursts of mortal danger crop up at a rate of about two-a-minute in Leon Griffiths' screenplay. Bad guys can be spotted instantly by the tilt of their left eyebrow, but this dead giveaway escapes only heroine Pauline (Patricia Bredin), who refuses to trust Calhoun until he has littered the countryside with villainous rabble bent on inflicting perils upon Pauline. Ultimately, the treasure chest sinks to the bottom of the sea, but Calhoun and Miss Bredin have "found something greater than diamonds and pearls," and so forth and so on into the golden sunset.

Generally the actors do what is required of them in a film of this character, which isn't very much save to look scared (in the case of the girls and the man-servants), brave (in the case of Calhoun and the gentlemen on his side of the good-evil fence) or foolishly troublesome (you know who). Among those prominent in addition to the leads are John Gregson as a friendly outlaw ("ha-ha, this Corbett, I like him, he is one brave fellow"), Peter Arne as an unfriendly outlaw, Sam Kydd as the comedy relief lackey and Ian Hunter as Miss Bredin's father, whose every other line seems to be, "Corbett, again I'm indebted to you," until he runs out of indebtedness when he runs into a sword.

The film was produced, directed and photographed by Robert S. Baker and Monty Berman. From a purely cinematic standpoint, it is a creditable piece of filmmaking, with some especially pretty Eastman Color views of the countryside on the other side of the Atlantic.

Tube.

Magic Boy

(JAPANESE—COLOR)
Artistically adept but dramatically routine cartoon fantasy. Fast-paced number especially suited to tastes of tykes and trimmed to neat twin-billing essentials.

Hollywood, Aug. 2.
Metro release of Toei production. Executive producer, Hiroshi Okawa. Associate producer, Hideyuki Takahashi. Director of animation, Sanae Yamamoto. Screenplay, Dohei Muramatsu, from original story by Kazuo Dan; camera (Magicolor), Seigo Otsuka, Mitsuaki Ishikawa; editor, Shintaro Miyamoto; art supervisor, Seigo Shindo; music, Toru Funamura; sound, Hisashi Kase; animators, Akira Daikuhara, Hideo Furusawa, Yasuji Mori, Masao Kumagawa. Reviewed at the studio, Aug. 2, '61. Running time, **76 MINS.**

With "Magic Boy," the Japanese animators display their drawing and coloring prowess in a fast-paced, though dramatically unimaginative, full-length adventure-fantasy cartoon that probably will

appeal to the tykes of any land. Trimmed to a swift and snug 76-minutes, it should fit attractively into any package assembled and aimed at moppets by Metro, and is especially valuable as a lower-berther for summer distribution.

Famous for duplication, the Japanese artisans here again prove their skill as following a proven formula. With a forestful of sweet animals, a lovable little hero, a handsome prince and a wicked witch, their little tale is almost pure Disneyland with an Oriental accent. The scenario by Dohei Muramatsu, from an original story by Kazuo Dan, takes a normal, but especially courageous, Japanese boy, invests him with magic powers acquired during a three-year course given by a helpful hermit, and pits him against the forest's evil sorceress in a hectic great debate to the death.

Unlike the animal heroes of U.S. cartoondom, the animals of "Magic Boy" don't talk, which makes sense. They merely cheep, squeal, grunt and tug human arms to warn of neighborhood peril. Unfortunately, though, the animals bear a striking resemblance to the stuffed toys of the average department store, and little more in the way of personality. Luckily, the stress is on the human characters.

The artwork, while perhaps not as exacting as recent U.S. cartoon endeavors, is beautifully colored, and the animation, under the direction of Sanae Yamamoto, is smooth and expressive. Sound, engineered by Hisashi Kase, is vivid, and the novel music score by Toru Funamura is exciting and surprisingly international in theme (even incorporating a guitarish Latin flavor on occasion).

A title tune, written by Fred Spielman and Janice Torre and sung by Danny Valentino, tells the gist of the story in a melodic, tv-commercial way. Voice dubbing (the Japanese characters speak perfect English), naturally less of a problem in a cartoon, doesn't interfere at all. *Tube.*

Scream Of Fear
(BRITISH)

Contrived but expertly executed mystery shocker.

Hollywood, Aug. 4.

Columbia Pictures release of Jimmy Sangster production. Stars Susan Strasberg, Ronald Lewis, Ann Todd, Christopher Lee. Directed by Seth Holt. Screenplay, Sangster; camera, Douglas Slocombe; editor, Eric Boyd-Perkins; art director, Bernard Robinson; music, Clifton Parker; sound, James Groom; assistant director, David Tomblin. Reviewed at the studio, Aug. 4, '61. Running time, **81 MINS.**

Penny Appleby .... Susan Strasberg
Bob .... Ronald Lewis
Jane Appleby .... Ann Todd
Dr. Gerrard .... Christopher Lee
Ins. Legrand .... John Serret
Spratt .... Leonard Sachs
Marie .... Anne Blake
Father .... Fred Johnson
Gendarme .... Bernard Brown
Plain-clothes Sgt. .... Richard Klee
Swissair Hostess .... Mme. Lobegue

If ever a picture has been salvaged by expert cinematic execution, "Scream of Fear" is it. Thanks to the deft efforts of director Seth Holt, an earnest cast and the master craftsmen of mood and shock who work for Britain's Hammer Films, a holding and frightening suspense thriller has somehow been fashioned out of a devious, involved and thoroughly implausible morsel of mystery fiction by producer Jimmy Sangster.

As is the case with most mysteries erected on contrived foundations, everything hums along mysteriously but grippingly, then promptly falls apart at the moment of truth. Audiences may be dismayed by this barrage of contradictory and doubtful climactic revelations, but at least they will have enjoyed the 71-minute buildup to the 10-minute letdown, and that should make the Columbia release a salable programming commodity.

As the complex picture begins, a girl's body bearing an uncanny resemblance to Susan Strasberg is dredged from a lake. Then the viewer is immediately transported to a wealthy French Riviera estate, where Miss Strasberg, an invalid now, arrives to visit her father, whom she has not seen for 10 years. Father is "away on business," but pretty soon Miss Strasberg is bumping into his upright, new-you-see-it-now-you-don't corpse in every room. Are these merely hallucinations? Is she going insane?

As the plot unfolds, stepmother Ann Todd evolves into the chief suspect and Miss Strasberg accompanied by helpful chauffeur Ronald Lewis, is on her way to inform the gendarmes when suddenly Lewis steps out of the car into the arms of Miss Todd as the vehicle carrying the crippled Miss Strasberg and daddy plunges off yon cliff. The provisions of the will paint a very bright future indeed for Lewis and Miss Todd. But lo, whom should they encounter next day at the villa but the pesky Miss Strasberg, no invalid-daughter at all but rather a companion of the deceased sprig originally witnessed while being dredged from the lake at the outset. Foul play was suspected, and Miss Strasberg had been dispatched to investigate.

Miss Strasberg makes a sympathetic heroine, sure to bring out the protective instinct in every male spectator. Lewis and Miss Todd create subtle portraits of evil within surface kindness. Christopher Lee is excellent as the family doctor, and support is capable all around.

Credit the film's suspenseful mood and occasional crescendos of shock and terror mostly to the skilled assists of cameraman Douglas Slocombe, editor Eric Boyd-Perkins, composer Clifton Parker, art director Bernard Robinson and soundman James Groom, all operating under Holt's aggressively imaginative generalship. *Tube.*

Die Schatten Werden Laenger
(The Shadows Are Getting Longer)
SWISS-GERMAN)

Zurich, Aug. 1.

Praesens-Film AG. Zurich release of Praesens (Lazar Wechsler) and CCC-Film (Artur Brauner) production. Directed by Ladislao Vajda. Screenplay, Istvan Bekeffi, Heinz Pauck, Vajda; camera, Enrique Gaertner; music, Robert Blum; editor, Hermann Haller. At Rex Theatre, Zurich. Running time, **90 MINS.**
(IN GERMAN)

Frau Diethelm .... Luise Ullrich
Christa Andres .... Barbara Ruetting
Max .... Hansjoerg Felmy
Eriga Schoener .... Loni von Friedl
Dr. Borner .... Fred Tanner
Helene .... Helga Sommerfeld
Anni .... Renja Gill
Barbara .... Margot Philipp
Bessie .... Carola Rasch
Hilde .... Iris Erdmann
Paula .... Heidi Pawellek
Ruth .... Brit von Thiesenhausen
Steffie .... Elizabeth Roth
Susanne .... Erika Wolf
Vera .... Gabriele Adam
Yvette .... Bella Neri
Fritz Schmoll .... Michael Paryla

This Swiss-German coproduction, filmed on location in Zurich and interiors in Munich, has the commercial assets of a topical theme, slick production and generally above-par performances. Fate at the boxoffice for this depends on whether the public has not been somewhat overfed lately with tales of juvenile delinquency and the rehabilitation of morally rotten youngsters. Director Ladislao Vajda, whose former credits include the Swiss filmization of a Friedrich Duerrenmatt story, "It Happened in Broad Daylight" (which has been released in the U.S.), has done a commendable job in keeping a maudlin story from lapsing into over-sentimentality. The action takes place in a girls' education home and centers on a 16-year-old inmate, a seemingly hopeless case, and one of her educators, a young woman whose shadowy past runs somewhat parellel to the future of this teenager. The woman's desperate efforts to prevent the girl from re-living her own experience, are momentarily thwarted when her former lover and ruthless exploiter turns up and tries to renew his hold over her. She finally kills him, and her arrest causes the girl to realize her own errors at last.

Despite several serious flaws, notably because of lack of motivation (it's never explained how the woman managed to get such a highly responsible job without properly accounting for the time lapse during which she "provided" for the pimp), the story plays better than it reads. Vajda's directorial touch is responsible for this since there are several believable performances.

Topping the cast is Barbara Ruetting as the ex-prostitute-gone-straight. Avoiding the pitfalls of excessive dramatics inherent in such a cliche-ridden part, she offers a strong, convincing portrayal. Newcomer Loni von Friedl reveals remarkable talent as the tough teenager while Luise Ullrich, an old pro in German films, plays the home's matron with quiet dignity and understanding. The many individual girls' parts are all convincingly cast, partly with amateurs. Technical credits are okay. This is done in the German language. *Mezo.*

Shin Heike Monogatari
(The Sacreligious Hero)
(JAPANESE-COLOR)

Paris, Aug. 1.

Pathe Overseas release of Daiei production. With Raizo Ichikawa, Yoshiko Kiga, Michiyo Kogure. Directed by Kenji Mizoguchi. Screenplay, Yoshikata Yoda; camera (Eastmancolor), Kazuo Miyagawa; editor, F. Hayasaka. At Studio De L'Etoile, Paris. Running time, **104 MINS.**

Kiyomori .... Raizo Ichikawa
Tadamori .... Yoshiko Kiga
Mother .... Michiyo Kogure

Film is listed as the last of the late great Japanese director Kenji Mizoguchi. It has his flair for recreating period, in this case the 17th Century, and a feeling for the epic drama and man's place in it. If not as rigorous and finished as his other pix, this has a beauty in imagery and a solidity in characterization for specialized placement abroad.

Plot concerns the son of a samurai warrior who finds he might have another father. But he stays alongside the one he knows when adversity has his father arrayed against the corrupt leaders and monks of the era. He fights his doubts, and backs his father in problems of banishment and persecution by the warlike monks.

It ends with the son facing up to and defeating the monks and then vowing to make the reign of the debauched despots short-lived.

This is possible Mizoguchi may not have finished this pic but it has enough eye appeal and absorbing narrative to have this something worth personalized handling. Technical credits are expert all along the line, with solid production values also a help. *Mosk.*

Yugoslav Festival

Uzavreli Grad
(When the Fires Started)
(YUGOSLAV)

Pula, Aug. 1.

Avala Film (Belgrade) production. Directed by Veljko Bulajic. With Olivera Markovic, Ilija Dzuvalekovski, Bata Zivojinovic. Screenplay, Dragoslav Ilic, Radenko Ostojic, Bruno Barati and Veljko Bulajic; camera, Dusan Jericevic. At Pula Film Fest. Running time, **122 MINS.**

"Fires," which teed off the 1961 Pula Film Festival, falls considerably short of "Train Without Timetable," Veljko Bulajic's 1959 effort. But it's still better than same director's "War," his rather disappointing opus of last year. This shows Bulajic's directorial abilities in handling the players, but, as a whole, fails to make an impression because unconvincingly told. It's overly long, and fundamentally holds little interest for western audiences.

Film depicts how Yugoslav peasants became industrial workers right after the war. The building of the first melting furnace is shown. Action is focused on all sorts of characters—there's love, jealousy, intrigues, misunderstanding, etc. along the way.

Towards the end of the pic, there's a flood which threatens to destroy the melting furnace but the men and women get together to save it. There are some good performances while technical credits are satisfactory. *Hans.*

Carevo Novo Ruho
(The King's New Clothes)
(YUGOSLAV—COLOR)

Pula, Aug. 1.

Zora Film (Zagreb) production. With Zlatko Madunic, Ana Karic, Vanja Drach. Directed by Ante Babaja. Screenplay, Bozidar Violic; camera (Eastmancolor), Oktavijan Miletic; music, Andelko Klobucar. At Pula Film Fest. Running time, **78 MINS.**

Zora Film, which specializes in puppet and fairytale pix, comes along with a full-length fairytale adapted from a Hans Christian Andersen yarn. It's technically well made and imaginative but the film is somewhat confusing inasmuch as it's neither fish nor fowl.

The Andersen plot doesn't quite come off while the gags appear overly adult. Technically, the film

is interesting. It's played against a painted background with only few props. Despite these objections, the film qualifies for some special situations abroad. It could stand some cutting.

Story is set in a country called Great Puritania where the moral code is very strict. There's a minister who controls all the dreams. A vagabond is sentenced to death because he dreamed he saw someone naked. But then he dreams of invisible clothes and this dream, also caught by the minister, gives him the chance to escape death if he succeeds in making such clothes for the king. Of course, he does. The acting is competent. *Hans.*

Martin U Oblacima
(Martin in the Clouds)
(YUGOSLAV)
Pula, Aug. 1.
Jadran production. With Boris Dvornik, Ljubica Jovic, Joza Seb. Directed by Branko Bauer. Screenplay, Fedor Vidas; camera, Branko Blazina; music, Aleksandar Bubanovic At Pula Film Fest. Running time, **101 MINS.**

This is a harmless, little comedy charmingly acted and not without brilliant ideas. However, story appears a bit far fetched. For this type of comedy, this runs too long. This strictly commercial pic should do well in this country. If cutting could give it more pace, film may have some slight export possibilities.

Two young students, deeply in love with each other, dream of a flat of their own. In order to raise the necessary money, the boy rents the apartment of his landlord when latter goes with his wife on an extensive vacation. Thereafter he's constantly fearing that bad weather may make the apartment owners return earlier. The young principal players show possibilities. *Hans.*

Dan Cetrnaesti
(The Fourteen Days)
(YUGOSLAV)
Pula, Aug. 1.
Lovcen production. With Mira Stupica, Olga Spridonivic, Hermina Pipinic, Mira Nikolic Babovic. Directed by Zdravko Velimirovic. Screenplay, Borislav Petrovic; camera, Vladeta Lukic; music. V. R. Rajteric. At Pula Film Fest. Running time, **98 MINS.**

This is an interesting film. But the plot's possibilities haven't been exploited to the best advantage. So the picture is nothing much more than a Yugoslav average production. It has only some spotty chances abroad.

A law in this country gives prisoners the chance to take an annual 14 days' home leave provided, of course, they have shown good conduct in jail. This pic centers on four convicts who are granted such privilege and shows what they do on leave.

It contains a number of good sequences and also a good deal of comedy to balance with the more serious stuff. But, all in all, it lacks the necessary pace and is too talky. A more imaginative script and fluent direction could have helped much. As often in Yugoslav films, the lensing is very good while the acting is generally fine. *Hans.*

Signali Nad Gradom
(Signal Over the City)
(YUGOSLAV)
Pula, Aug. 1.
Jadran production. With Aleksandar Gavric, Marija Tocinoska, Dragan Ocokoljic. Directed by Zika Mitrovic. Screenplay, Slavko Goldstajn; camera, Branko Ivatovic; music, Bojan Adamic. At Pula Film Fise. Running time, **85 MINS.**

Jadran reportedly produced this film in memory of the 20th anni of the general uprising of the Yugoslav people against the Nazi occupation forces. But this is hardly a film to celebrate the event. It's nothing more than a common actioner, rather naive if not primitive in many respects. An okay item for this country's juve action trade, but there's nothing here for western release.

Plot sees two members of the illegal underground movement caught by the pro-German police. In the disguise of the pro-German Ustashi soldiers, their partisan friends march into the town and free one of them. There's a lot of gun fire in film's final sequences. Acting is routine. direction fair and technical credits are average. *Hans.*

Balada O Trubi I Oblaku
(A Ballad About a Trumpet And a Cloud)
(YUGOSLAV)
Pula, Aug. 1.
Triglav production. With Lojze Potokar, Angelca Illebce, Branko Miklavic, Rudi Kosmac. Directed by France Stiglac. Screenplay, Ciril Kosmac; camera, Rudi Vavpotic; music, Aloiz Srebotnjak. At Pula Film Fest. Running time, **75 MINS.**

This is, artistically speaking, one of the most ambitious Yugoslav pix of the season. It benefits from superb camerawork and some impressive acting. However, it fails to make the grade due to a confusing script and direction. Along with his efforts to be as uncompromising as possible, director Stiglac seemingly lost control at times. Film's outcome may be called vivid but it's too strange a mixture poetic realism, mediocre Ingmar Bergman and early (the snow scenes) Leni Riefenstahl. A doubtful export item.

Story takes place high in the Yugoslav mountains during the last World War. An old forester sets out on his own to warn a group of wounded partizans, who have hidden up there, of a Whiteguardist patrol which plans to liquidate them. The old man puts patriotic duty above all and succeeds in reaching his goal. However, he has to kill the three Whiteguardists and gets killed himself. All this is delivered in sort of a brutal fairytale with ghostly dream visions. It's occasionally hard to distinguish what's reality and what's the dream world. Pic also suffers from monotony. *Hans.*

Ples U Kisi
(Dancing in the Rain)
YUGOSLAV)
Pula, Aug. 1.
Triglav production. With Miha Baloh, Dusa Pockaj, Ali Raner, Rado Nakrst. Directed by Bostjan Hladnik. Screenplay, Hladnik; camera, Janez Kalinnik; music, Bojan Adamic. At Pula Film Fest. Running time, **100 MINS.**

Here is the most controversial Yugoslav film of the year. It's the type of feature pic that will garner the most varied reviews, ranging from bad to brilliant. Film both shocks and amuses, but also will thrill an audience. Nothing for the general public but an obvious bet for arties that specialize in offbeat items. Pic is original enough to qualify itself as an entry at festivals where it will lead to many discussions.

Some crix may object that director Bostian Hladnik (incidentally, his first full-length film) may have thefted too many directorial ideas from others. In fact, some scenes in "Rain" are very reminiscent of several big directors. Fellini, Chabrol, Welles, Cocteau, Clouzot, Hitchcock. They also may object that Hladnik hasn't found a clearcut style of his own because it's a mixture of realism, poetic realism, surrealism and expressionism.

However, this admittedly is an extremely interesting film and one that's technically well made. Although the pic is somewhat too long, it's never dull for one technical surprise follows the other. Obviously the film would have benefitted from some cutting. It seems as though Hladnik occasionally fell in love with symbolism and has lost control of his vehicle. But nevertheless, the film's outcome is extremely intriguing.

"Rain" is a modern psychological drama that centers around a couple that finds it tough to master the problems of daily life. He's a struggling painter, his wife a sensitive actress. Their marriage is a far cry from being happy. In fact, the man has become tired of his wife. Although she has the chance to turn to another man, she remains faithful.

But she feels that she cannot live without love and decides to take her life. Her death makes her husband realize what he has lost. Practically half of the film is composed of his or her day-dreaming.

Camerawork and editing of these sequences are particularly praiseworthy. Also the acting deserves praise. Especially impressive is the performance turned in by Dusa Pockaj, the woman in this unusual film. *Hans.*

Locarno Fest

Tire-Au-Flanc
(The Sad Sack)
(FRENCH-FRANSCOPE)
Locarno, Aug. 1.
SEDIF release of Carrosse-SEDIF-Anray Films production. With Christian De Tiliere, Jacques Balutin, Serge Davri. Directed by Claude De Givray. Screenplay, De Givray, Francois Truffaut from play by Mouezy-Eon, Sylvane; camera, Raoul Coutard; editor, Claudine Bouche. At Locarno Film Fest. Running time, 90 MINS.
Lerat .... Christian De Tiliere
Joseph .... Ricet-Barrier
Corporal .... Jacques Balutin
Colonel .... Serge Davri

French army comedy is a series of gags about new recruits. Though many are familiar, this has a pacing, tone and inventiveness which make them all risible enough. There is an adequate amount of originality in this comedy, making it likely for playoff for even specialized spots abroad.

A snobbish rich boy and his chauffeur are drafted. Follows the routine of breaking into this new life. What it does succeed in doing is looking at the army in an inventive manner with the gags eliminating any need for plot or more elaborate setting up.

Gray lensing enhances the atmosphere of the pic and newcomer actors are also a help. This is a highly amusing comedy on army life and the first one from France since the last war. It looks headed for biz here and proper handling and placement could make it a solid entry in the U.S. *Mosk.*

Fantasmi A Roma
(Ghosts In Rome)
(ITALIAN-COLOR)
Locarno, Aug. 1.
Lux release of Lux-Vides-Galatea-Franco Cristaldi production. Stars Marcello Mastroianni, Vittorio Gassman, Sandra Milo, Eduardo De Filippo, Belinda Lee. Directed by Antonio Pietrangeli. Screenplay, Messers Flaiano, Pietrangeli, Amidei, Scola, Maccari; camera (Technicolor), Giuseppe Rotunno; editor, N. Orota. At Locarno Film Fest. Running time, **100 MINS.**
Reginaldo .... Marcello Mastroianni
Flora .... Sandra Milo
Caparra .... Vittorio Gassman
Principe .... Eduardo De Filippo
Girl .... Belinda Lee

Ghost comedy concerns a bunch of eerie characters living in an old house with an eccentric prince. He cannot see them but is aware of these ghosts, and most of the comedies are based on this. Pic is quaint but bogs down after some inventive early passages. It looms more a dualer item abroad than for specialized chances.

Ghosts get panicky when the prince dies and a nephew decides to sell the house. But they manage to restore things and the prince becomes one of them to continue to live happily.

Special effects are good but without the film pacing to make them captivating throughout. Obvious phantoms soon get repetitive. Technical credits are good as is color and the performances. *Mosk.*

Nocni Host
(Night Guest)
(CZECHOSLAVAKIAN—SCOPE)
Locarno, Aug. 1.
Czech State Film production and release. With Jiri Vala, Jana Hlavacova, Rudolf Hrusinsky, Svetla Amortova, Martin Ruzek. Directed by Otakar Vavra. Screenplay, Ludvik Askenazy, Vavra; camera, Jaroslav Tuzar; editor, K. Semenen. At Locarno Film Fest. Running time, 90 MINS.
Emil .... Jiri Vala
Jana .... Jana Hlavacova
Huppert .... Rudolf Hrusinsky
Mother .... Svetla Amortova
Remunda .... Martin Ruzek

In these days of the Eichmann trial and renewed interest in the causes and meaning of Nazism, this pic has timeliness. It examines a case of a still active Nazi outlook of a West German today. But the film is somewhat unbalanced dramatically. So this is mainly for specialized situations abroad.

A West German, visiting the site of his family's former quarters in Czechoslavakia, stops at a roadside bar with a young Czech girl he has picked up. He speaks Czech and after some drinks sounds off with the philosophy of might making right and the right to kill off things less beautiful than those in power, etc. He is

shot at by the proprietor who had been in a concentration camp. Then the police come, and the German goes away as arrogant as ever.

Film uses a split screen effectively to evoke thoughts and past feelings in superimposition. The acting manages to keep this an essentially talky pic if fairly engrossing. The longing for speed and adventure of wayward youth is also worked in as well as some symptoms of discontent among some Czechs on their jobs. But all is too easily cleared up when faced by the incipient Nazi.

Somewhat loaded, this still makes its points and is neatly acted and directed. It is just too pat in its sentiments and symbolism to allow it to be told visually.
Mosk.

Cuba Baila
(Cuba Dances)
(CUBAN)

Locarno, Aug. 1.
ICAIC release of Manuel Barbachano Ponce production. With Raquel Revuelta, Alfredo Perojo, Vivian Gude, Humberto Garcia Espinosa, Wilfredo Fernandez. Written and directed by Julio Espinosa; screenplay, Barbachano Ponce, Alfredo Guevara; camera, Sergio Vejar; editor, Jose Fraga. At Locarno Film Fest. Running time, **80 MINS.**

Flora	Raquel Revuelta
Ramon	Alfredo Perojo
Marcia	Vivian Gude
Joseito	Humberto Garcia Espinosa
Augustin	Wilfredo Fernandez

For the first Cuban feature pic and first to be shown at a Western film fest, this is strangely unrevolutionary. It concerns family problems pre-revolutionary with some social notations on the times. Somewhat naive in conception, this looms mainly a Latino entry.

Cuban girls "come out" at the age of 15 and a big party was rated necessary. A little clerk just does not have the money for such an affair but his ambitious wife eggs him on to borrow from his boss or even slight his old friends to bring it off.

Some satire is aimed at the petty bureaucrats of the day. Also pointed up is the Cuban passion for dancing. Film also makes a point in the clerk's revolt and having the party in a public dance place, with the bureaucrats joining in.

The U.S. is only mentioned by some of the rich people at a dance as being a fine place for shopping. Technical credits are good and direction probing in spots but somewhat stilted in others. It shows a technical proficiency growing in Cuba but as yet a simple approach to film techniques and subject matter.
Mosk.

The Big Gamble
(C'SCOPE—COLOR)

Bountiful in production values, but generally undistinguished adventure drama concerning a young couple's strenuous efforts to found a trucking concern in Africa.

Hollywood, Aug. 10.
Twentieth-Fox release of Darryl F. Zanuck production. Stars Stephen Boyd, Juliette Greco, David Wayne. Directed by Richard Fleischer. Screenplay, Irwin Shaw; camera (Eastman), William C. Mellor; editor, Roger Dwyre; art director, Jean D'Eaubonne; sound, Max Olivier; assistant director, Paul Feyder. Reviewed at Grauman's Chinese Theatre, Aug. 10, '61. Running time, **98 MINS.**

Vic Brennan	Stephen Boyd
Marie Brennan	Juliette Greco
Samuel Brennan	David Wayne
Aunt Cathleen	Dame Sybil Thorndike
Kaltenberg	Gregory Ratoff
Father Fredrick	Harold Goldblatt
John Brennan	Philip O'Flynn
Margaret Brennan	Maureen O'Dea
Cynthia	Mary Kean
Naval Lieutenant	Alain Saury
Davey	Pergal Stanley
High Offical	Fernand Ledoux
Irish Truck Driver	J. G. Devlin
Hotel Manager	Jacques Marin

A short, but invaluable course in how not to drive a 10-ton truck through French Equitorial Africa is offered in Darryl F. Zanuck's production of "The Big Gamble." Outside of a heap of dramatic jeopardy and some interesting scenic views of the Dark Continent, there isn't a great deal in this picture to entice the average customer. Though an uncompromising display of filmmaking savvy and ingenuity, it lacks the importance of theme and story to justify all the obviously painstaking care that went into its making. Absence of both this premium value and a magnetic cast make the 20th-Fox release a shaky contender.

Irwin's Shaw's original screenplay launches itself in Dublin, where newlyweds Stephen Boyd and Juliette Greco are seeking funds from the former's family to finance a trucking ventue in Africa. They get the money, but they also inherit milquetoast bank clerk-cousin David Wayne who, for some intangible reason (apparently comedy relief, an artificial story device), decides to accompany them in order to "protect the family investment." Balance of the film depicts the trio's oversea and overland misadventures in reaching their destination, mostly problems of reading a road map, living in harmony and getting their rugged vehicle across any number of obstacles.

Their courage and conviction is admirable, but somehow the viewer is not profoundiy moved by the strictly-business reasons for their difficult endeavor. The sense of involvement is thus superficial, giving the overlapping crises an almost monotonous aspect and rendering the ending anti-climactic.

Boyd amply fills the physical specifications of the iron-willed, quick-tempered character he is portraying, but he has one or two dramatic lapses and fails to project much in the way of character growth, although he receives little aid from Shaw's scenario in this all-important respect. Miss Greco, too, has some uncertain moments and seems to change very little in the course of the perilous journey. It is suggested that Wayne is undergoing some emotional

growth, but this is inconclusive hearsay, and he seems unchanged at the climax. It must, however, be noted that all three leads really earned their pay on this excursion.

The physical hazards of the trip get pretty fierce in spots. The late Gregory Ratoff is convincing and colorful in an incidental part, and Dame Sybil Thorndike works with assurance as matriarch of Boyd's Irish brood. Others in the supporting cast, which includes players from the Abbey Theatre, Ulster Theatre and Comedie Francaise, are satisfactory.

The physical production is adeptly mounted and executed under the guidance of director Richard Fleischer. But his discipline and perception in some of the more intimate dramatic passages is less effective.

A great portion of the film was shot on location in the Ivory Coast of Africa, with other exteriors in Dublin and France, interiors in London and Paris. Ethnic, geographic and general pictorial values are interpreted admirably through William C. Mellor's Eastman Color photography and Jean D'Eaubonne's art direction, as well as via the efforts of the second unit, headed by director Elmo Williams and cameraman Henri Porsin. Roger Dwyre's editing is steady.

Miss Greco shows up in a pretty flashy dress to meet her staid in-laws. It's inconsistent with the perceptive person she turns out to be, and a curious error in Jean Zay's otherwise sensible wardrobe.
Tube.

Marines, Let's Go
(C'SCOPE—COLOR)

Band of leatherneck lugs adept at war but inept at amor. Exploitation values and coincidence of current military re-emphasis will help.

Hollywood, Aug. 7.
Twentieth-Fox release of Raoul Walsh production. Stars Tom Tryon, David Hedison, Tom Reese. Directed by Walsh. Screenplay, John Twist, based on story by Walsh; camera (De Luxe), Lucien Ballard; editor, Robert Simpson; art directors, Jack Martin Smith, Alfred Ybarra; music, Irving Gertz; sound, Bernard Fredricks, Warren B. Delaplain; assistant director, Milton Carter. Reviewed at the studio, Aug. 7, '61. Running time, **103 MINS.**

Skip Roth	Tom Tryon
Dave Chatfield	David Hedison
McCaffrey	Tom Reese
Grace Blake	Linda Hutchins
Russ Waller	William Tyler
Ina Baxter	Barbara Stuart
Newt Levells	David Brandon
Chase	Steve Baylor
Hawkins	Adoree Evans
Pete Kono	Hideo Inamura
Hank Dyer	Vince Williams
Song Do	Fumiyo Fupimoto
Yoshida	Henry Okawa

Raoul Walsh's production of "Marines, Let's Go" could not be hitting the market at a more opportune peacetime juncture, what with the current drive to hyke the U.S. military force. This burst of nationalism and the renewed interest spurred in military life and times, especially among young men eligible for duty, is sure to exert a favorable influence on the film's boxoffice. It's a fortunate circumstance indeed for the 20th-Fox release, which will need all the help it can get from the nervous history of current events.

The picture, produced, directed and based on a story by Walsh, is dated, corny, juvenile and predictable. Strictly an exploitable action entertainment tailored for those who come to the cinema seeking not enlightenment or dramatic sense, but simply emotional sensations in a noisy, busy escape package. (Any resemblance between Marine life depicted here and actual Marine life is purely coincidental).

John Twist's screenplay follows the activities of a platoon of leathernecks shifted from Korean War combat to regimental reserve status in Japan and then back again to combat in order that those suspected of cowardice (by the characters, never the audience) may prove otherwise in the heat of battle. This platoon is populated by all the instantly recognizable types indigenous to the war film: "the naive, bashful, likeable galoot from Texas"; the slick operator known as "the brain"; the "Back Bay aristocrat" who must prove he has guts; and Pfc. "Let's Go McCaffrey," who's been busted from sergeant to private, "but don't let that fool you he's the guy these men follow."

Most of the picture gravitates toward Marine's Marine McCaffrey, played with a masculine flourish by a young newcomer, Tom Reese, recently seen in "Shadows." Reese, a cigar-chomping, bulbous-nosed he-man, does very well by the role. Top-billed, but definitely lower-case in importance to Reese, are Tom Tryon (the brain) and David Hedison (the aristocrat), both of whom dispatch their stereotypes as effectively as possible under Walsh's broad, free-wheeling, staccato direction. Others who make prominent impressions are David Brandon (Newt, the Texas galoot), William Tyler, Steve Baylor, Peter Miller, Henry Okawa, Hideo Inamura and Vince Williams. Distaff chores are handled attractively, if uncertainly, by Fumiyo Fujimoto, Linda Hutchins, Barbara Stuart and Adoree Evans.

Combat scenes at the beginning and end are brisk and explosive, colorfully lensed in De Luxe hues by Lucien Ballard, crisply spliced into a few actual battle shots by editor Robert Simpson. Other capable contributions are made by art directors Jack Martin Smith and Alfred Ybarra and composer Irving Gertz.

The title tune (by Mike Phillips and George Watson, sunk by Rex Allen) sounds much like a collegiate pigskin fight song.
Tube.

Bridge To The Sun

Affecting screen treatment of Gwen Terasaki's misadventures as wife of a Japanese diplomat during World War II. Pic lacks penetration in spots, but on the whole a moving romantic drama, well executed. Needs advance bally-hoo beyond average.

Hollywood, Aug. 9.
Metro release of Jacques Bar production. Stars Carroll Baker, James Shigeta. Directed by Etienne Perier. Screenplay, Charles Kaufman, based on autobiography by Gwendolen Terasaki; camera, Marcel Weiss, Seiichi Kizuka, Bill Kelly; editors,

Robert and Monique Isnardon; art director, Hiroshi Mizutani; music, Georges Auric; assistant directors, Jacques Roufflo, Takashi Fugie, Olivier Gerard. Reviewed at the studio, Aug. 9, '61. Running time, 112 MINS.

Gwen Terasaki .... Carroll Baker
Hidenari Terasaki .... James Shigeta
Hara .... James Yagi
Jiro .... Tetzuro Tamba
shi .... Hiroshi Tomono
Mako Terasaki. Nori Elisabeth Hermann,
                        Emi Florence Hirsch
Fred Tyson .... Sean Garrison
Aunt Peggy .... Ruth Masters

The unusual and edifying experiences of Gwen Terasaki, as first related in her 1957 autobiography, have now been translated into a touching and fairly enlightening film. American audiences, especially women, will be engrossed and moved by this screen account of the profound challenges and conflicts met and surmounted by a courageous American girl and her Japanese husband placed in the precarious position of enduring World War II in Japan. The picture, produced by Jacques Bar, is often shy the clarity, penetration and boldness required for a fully satisfying treatment of such an intimate story, but there are compensations, principally histrionic and cinematic, to take up some of the slack and hold an audience even when the drama skipps over a vital issue or fails to clarify itself on a pertinent point of deep interest and concern.

"Bridge to the Sun" does not have a boxoffice cast. It is a film that will have to rely mostly on favorable word of mouth, a tasteful campaign by Metro and a warm initial reaction on the part of those whose opinions have been known to persuade large masses of filmgoers. It is the kind of picture that requires aggressive handling to trade and public.

Charles Kaufman penned the screenplay. Carroll Baker portrays the Tennessee girl whose devotion to her Japanese diplomat husband (James Shigeta) transcends personal caution and leads her to accompany her troubled mate back to Japan at the outbreak of war. The couple manages to survive one crisis after another, only to be parted by tragedy when the war is just over.

Since he is telling a large story encompassing many years and many subtle emotional ironics, Kaufman must convey a great deal in fleeting, individual scenes that depend less on dialog than on visual facets for audience understanding. Director Etienne Perier has come to his aid beautifully in this respect by dispatching exposition, maintaining dramatic perspective and advancing character and time in terms of impressions, such as one indelible moment when Miss Baker's eyes meet the searching, longing gaze of a young American POW in Japan as she passes slowly by on a train.

Screenplay is frequently slipshod on major issues. It evades matters of moment and importance. And, most injuriously, it somehow fails to truly get under the skin of its hero and heroine. We can appreciate their problem, but somehow we never really get to know these people, to understand the magnitude of their affection (especially at the development of their romance) and the profound loyalty of their mutual devotion.

It is there. We can see it and admire it, but we can never truly feel it, even as our tears accompany their tragedy.

This shortcoming is in no way due to the enactments of Miss Baker and Shigeta, both of whom play with sufficient sincerity and warmth. Members of the supporting cast—James Yagi, Tetzuro Tamba, Hiroshi Tomono, Sean Garrison, Ruth Masters, Nori Elisabeth Hermann and Emi Florence Hirsch—all participate creditably.

The black-and-white photography—split among Marcel Weiss, Seiichi Kizuka and Bill Kelly (the film, internationally staffed, was shot in Japan, Washington, D.C., and Paris)—is vivid, alert to the visual impact of a novel vantage point, and quite artistic in texture and composition. Editors Robert and Monique Isnardon, too, have done an astute job. Cultural values of East and West have been captured and transmitted by art director Hiroshi Mizutani, notably during the film's visit to Kyoto, focal point of Japanese culture.

Georges Auric's romantic score tastefully blends themes of both countries. War footage is masterfully executed, especially in a pair of frighteningly realistic air raid scenes, enlivened by Konji Inagawa's special effects. *Tube.*

World By Night
(TECHNIRAMA DOCUMENTARY-TECHNICOLOR)

Kaleidoscopic collection of world glamor spots, emphasizing European niteries, in a travelog design. Heavy selling needed, with European market and art houses looming as best booking possibilities.

Hollywood, Aug. 10.
Warner Bros. release of Julia Film production. Featuring portions of night entertainment throughout the world. Produced by Francesco Mazei and Gianni Proia. Directed by Luigi Vanzi; script, Gualtiero Jacopetti. Reviewed Aug. 8, '61, in Hollywood. Running time, 90 MINS.

Warner Bros. will have to do some hefty trade and consumer selling to coin appreciable profits from "World By Night." A kaleidoscopic collection of world glamour spots, with particular emphasis on European niteries, the film is one that could turn into a sleeper, but looks more like a loser. Too long for second billing and lacking sufficient international public identification to go out as a mainstem topper, it's best market appears to be art houses with more possibilities looming for foreign rather than U.S. bookings.

Francesco Mazei and Gianni Proia produced under the Julia Film banner, with direction credited to Luigi Vanzi from a script by Gualtiero Jacopetti. Premise is a tour of the world's most glamorous entertainers, with studio plugging it as "An entertainment tour around the world in 100 minutes." (Actual time is 90 min.).

Chief problem of the film, probably more evident in American markets, is its failure to properly represent the international field. U.S. is given only meagre Las Vegas showing, along with a unique section of the Harlem Gospel Show and, surprisingly, in view of the overall night time theme and California's Marineland whales. It embraces various media of entertainment, but never quite completes any of them. Perhaps sticking to the major nitery theme would have given it more solidity instead of forcing into bits and pieces of other fields.

The picture justifies listing as a camera tour. Technirama and Technicolor photography making its strongest impact in most areas, though a dreary bluish prologue in London, no doubt planned to convey the foggy weather, starts thing off on a dull note. Striking is Copenhagen's beautifully lighted Tivoli Gardens, while lavish extravaganzas featuring Paris' Bluebell Girls of the Club Lido and the Crazy Horse Saloon show, Las Vegas' Rhythmettes and the Tahiti Ballet are vivid and exciting. Considerable attention is given to girlie shows and there are several bits from various countries featuring strippers of all types.

Other areas feature a portion of The House of Geisha legit production, "Kiyokawa"; Britain's rock 'n' roller, Wee Willie Harris; the amazing sword artist, Marco; hilarious Nitwits, slapstick musicians, and vet American vaude act, Bob Williams and his dog, Louis.

Shot as a documentary in what is actually a travelogue design, film has a running line of narration kept to a minimum only for identification purposes. Occasional personal angles (lovers along the Paris waterfront, a stripper's boyfriend rushing her to work, etc.) lightly tie in the theme of showing people the world over playing at night. *Dale.*

The Magic Fountain
(ULTRASCOPE—EASTMAN COLOR)

Awkward handling of the Grimm fairy tale. Some good color shots of the Black Forest. Boxoffice fate depends upon the pulling power of off-screen names, Sir Cedric Hardwicke and Hans Conried.

Chicago, Aug. 9.
Classic World Films release of Allan David production, directed by David. Features Peter Nestler, Helmo Kinderman, Joseph Marz, Catherine Hansen, Osman Ragheb. Guest stars Sir Cedric Hardwicke, Hans Conried, Buddy Baer. Screenplay, John Lehman, based on the Grimm fairy tale, "Fountain of Life"; camera, Wolf Schneider; editor, Richard Hertel; music, Jacques Belasco; special effects, Weegee; sound, Riva Studios, Munich. Reviewed Aug. 9, '61 in Chicago. Running time, 82 MINS.

(Dubbed in English)

Chi tyro producer Allan David's adaptation of one of Grimm's fairy tales requires as much willing suspension of disbelief in the technical area as it does from a literary standpoint. The low-budget moppet entry is generally attractively photographed and makes the most of the Black Forest in Germany and two extremely handsome castles. There is also some b.o. potential in the names of Sir Cedric Hardwicke, Hans Conried and Buddy Baer, although Hardwicke is the narrator and never seen and Conried, also unseen, speaks through a stuffed owl.

Storyline has a king (Erik Jelde) dying (in what appears to be a fright wig). His three sons are gathered about him. Two of the princes (Helmo Kinderman and Osman Ragher) are patently villainous, while the youngest (Peter Nestler) is all heart. They decide to find the Magic Fountain, whose waters will bring the old man back to life. In their separate searches they run across a conjuring dwarf, an ingenious boy, a lovely princess and nine lovely maidens clad in medieval negligees. After some double-dealing by the elder princes, the youngest prince is cast into disrepute, but eventually proves himself, get's back into the king's good graces and embraces the princess who inhabits the castle of the Magic Fountain. The evil brothers see the light and all are reconciled.

John Lehman's screenplay is pedestrian (despite some scenes on horseback), and David's direction is hackneyed and trite. Biggest disappointments are Weegee's special effects. In one dream sequence, the jagged edge of a rippling dissolve cuts the princess in half. In another scene, intended to purvey excitement, Weegee shoots statically through a standard prism, producing an effect that might be mildly stimulating with a home kaleidescope.

Richard Hertel's editing is rough, and his scene changes are frequently jarring where they should be segued. Title song was written by Steve Allen and Don George. *Roth.*

Me Faire Ca A Moi
(Do That to Me)
(FRENCH)

Paris, Aug. 15.
Cocinor release of Area production. Stars Eddie Constantine, Bernadette Lafont; features Jean-Louis Richard, Pierre Grasset. Written and directed by Pierre Grimblat. Camera, Michel Kelber; editor, Francine Javet. At Balzac, Paris. Running time, 85 MINS.

Eddie .... Eddie Constantine
Anna .... Bernadette Lafont
Chief .... Jean-Louis Richard
Spy .... Pierre Grasset
Mercedes .... Rita Cadillac

Instead of being a G-Man, Yank star Eddie Constantine plays a reporter in this actioner. But there's the usual fisticuffs and women, with enough chase sequences and plot twists to make this an okay dual entry for action marts. But it doesn't seem good enough for arty or specialized consideration abroad.

Here Constantine is used as bait by the French Secret Service to find out who is leaking material from the French rocket bases. He has to do this in order to get out of a spy ra for trying to take unauthorized news photos.

Constantine meets some old flames and gets shot at, chased and fought with until the guilty ones are unmasked. For a first pic, director Pierre Grimblat shows a flair for pacing and movement. However, the hackneyed script still relegates this to second slot spotting.

Constantine is his usual dynamic self and supporting cast and technical credits are acceptable. *Mosk.*

The Young Doctors

Accurate, restrained and informative medical drama in which moments of great wisdom and reflection overrule several awkward passages. Respectable marquee and word-of-mouth should make it big money pic.

Hollywood, Aug. 11.

United Artists release of Stuart Millar-Lawrence Turman production. Stars Fredric March, Ben Gazzara, Dick Clark, Ina Balin, Eddie Albert; features Phyllis Love, Edward Andrews, Aline MacMahon. Directed by Phil Karlson. Screenplay, Joseph Hayes, based on a novel by Arthur Hailey; camera, Arthur J. Ornitz; editor, Robert Swink; art director, Jimmy Di Gangi, Angelo Laiacona. Reviewed at Screen Directors Guild Theatre, Aug. 11, 61. Running time, 103 MINS.

Dr. Joseph Pearson ..... Fredric March
Dr. David Coleman .... Ben Gazzara
Dr. Alexander .... Dick Clark
Cathy Hunt .... Ina Balin
Dr. Charles Dornberger .... Eddie Albert
Mrs. Alexander .... Phyllis Love
Bannister .... Edward Andrews
Dr. Lucy Grainger..... Aline MacMahon
Tomaselli .... Arthur Hill
Miss Graves .... Rosemary Murphy
Dr. Kent O'Donnell...... Barnard Hughes
Dr. Shawcross .... Joseph Bova
Dr. Roward .... George Segal
Dr. Rufus .... Matt Crowley
Operating Intern .... Dick Button
Dolph Sweet, Ella Smith, Nora Helen Spens, M.D.

"The Young Doctors" is an enlightening motion picture executed with restraint and clinical authenticity. Furthermore, in dissecting some of the ordinarily "closed shop" conflicts of the rather mysterious medical profession, it brings to its subject a point of view, making it an experience not easily erased from the mind when one leaves the theatre. The Stuart Millar-Lawrence Turman production has its dramatic failings, to be sure, but what is wrong within the picture is superseded and dominated by what is right about it.

Although there are bound to be those filmgoers who, in sizing up its value as entertainment, will find it more of a treatment than a treat, the United Artists release shapes up as a big moneymaker. Its cast makes a good impression on a marquee. Word-of-mouth and the picture itself will do the rest.

The screenplay, based on a novel by Arthur Hailey, was written by Joseph Hayes. Except for several expository passages in which it stumbles into some awkward behavior in attempting to establish personality and relationship and be quick about it, it's a generally brisk, literate and substantial piece of cinema writing marked by a few soaring bursts of thought-provoking philosophical wisdom as re-gards life, death and love.

Essentially the story represents an idealistic clash between two pathologists, one (Frederic March) the vet department head whose ideals and perspective have been mellowed and blunted somewhat by years of red tape and day-to-day frustration, the other (Ben Gazzara), his new assistant, young, aggressive, up-to-date and meticulous in his approach to the job.

The conflict is dramatically illustrated via two critical cases in which both are pretty intimately involved. On one of them, March makes a grievous error, promptly resigns his post. The ending is a bit abrupt, and the reasons for the error seem quite inconsistent with the sort of person March is portraying, but the point is made, and made with a minimum of the sort of emotional fuss, furor and frenzy that can be so tempting to a screenwriter and director. Both Hayes and director Phil Karlson are to be congratulated for the restraint and reason they have employed in molding and executing this facet of the film. Producers Millar and Turman, too, are to be commended for conceiving and fashioning a picture that is informative, arresting and topical.

Again the veteran March proves he's one of the finest actors to be found on the contemporary screen. It is a tribute to this man that one is barely aware or conscious of the fact he is acting. He creates a person, a character of dimension and compassion. Gazzara plays with great reserve and intensity, another fine portrayal. Dick Clark is persuasive as a young intern, Eddie Albert outstanding as a dedicated obstetrician. Ina Balin experiences a few uncertain moments in her enactment of a gravely ill young nurse in love with life in general and Gazzara in particular, but she comes through in the more demanding passages of her characterization. Phyllis Love's performance as Clark's pregnant wife (she's Rh negative, he's Rh positive, the combination that results in March's unaccountable goof) is tarnished by some of the screenplay's clumsier business, which she draws. Among the supporting players, Aline MacMahon and Edward Andrews are stickouts.

Camerawork by Arthur J. Ornitz is pretty uncompromising in the clinical sequences, doesn't spare the surgical scrutiny to save the squeamish witness in the audience. Pretty bold stuff, but one can't argue too strenuously against realism. It's a vivid, hard-hitting and aggressively-directed job of photography. Robert Swink's editing is clean-cut. There's excitement and dramatic virility to Elmer Bernstein's score, most noticeably so as it accompanies the main titles.

Tube.

Teenage Millionaire
(MUSICOLOR)

Rock 'n' rollathon strictly for teenagers. Exploitable enough to open well, but likely to evolve rapidly into supporting item.

Hollywood, Aug. 15.

United Artists release of Howard B. Kreitsek production. Stars Jimmy Clanton; songs by Chubby Checker, Dion, Bill Black's Combo, Marv Johnson, Vicki Spencer, Jack Larson. Directed by Lawrence F. Doheny. Screenplay, H. B. Cross, with additional dialog by Doheny; camera, Gordon Avil, Musicolor song sequences by Arthur J. Ornitz; editor, Jack Ruggiero; art directors, Rolland M. Brooks, Howard Hollander; song sequences by Paul Sylbert; assistant directors, Hal Klein; song sequences by Don Kranz. Reviewed at Goldwyn Studios, Aug. 15, '61. Running time, 84 MINS.

Bobby Chalmers .... Jimmy Clanton
Rocky .... Rocky Graziano
Aunt Theodora .... Zasu Pitts
Bambi .... Diane Jergens
Adrienne .... Joan Tabor
Sheldon Vale .... Sid Gould
Ernie .... Maurice "Doberman" Gosfield
Desidieria .... Eileen O'Neill

Extreme caution is advisable in the programming of this film. Exploitation values and teen appeal may give it some opening strength, but the Howard B. Kreitsek production lacks the quality to sustain itself for very long as a head attraction. Therefore, being of maneuverable 84-minute duration, there might exist the temptation to insert it haphazardly at the bottom half of general double bills, regardless of the calibre or character of the principal feature. This would be regrettable in any situation not thoroughly dominated by a teenage audience. Unaccompanied adults on the receiving end of "Teenage Millionaire" would be as out of sync as a 78 rpm disk on a 45 rpm turntable.

The United Artists release is the cinematic equivalent of a wild rock 'n' roll party, around which has been constructed a plot that is nothing more than an excuse to tie together the film's 11 musical breaks. H. B. Cross' patchy screenplay explains why a teenage lad (Jimmy Clanton) who has inherited a million clams is likely to be unhappy. Boy's got a yen to warble, but his aunt (Zasu Pitts) is bent on keeping him cooped up, and employs a bodyguard (Rocky Graziano) to keep him out of trouble. U.S. Army greeting solves the crisis.

The 11 songs that interrupt the plot (actually it's vice versa) are virtually all of the r 'n' r variety and they are all audibly insufferable for most anyone over 21, which is as good a sign as any that they have the makings for commercial success. The breaks are bathed in a process dubbed Musicolor, the crude quality fo which might suggest to the layman that it consists of nothing more than a colored cellophane lollipop wrapper placed in front of the lens. The colors, each one utilized for a separate break, range from racy chartreuse to outrageous orange to kimnovak lavender. The singers, virtually all of whom are lyrically at the extreme depths of romantic despair, are Chubby Checker, Vicki Spencer, Marv Johnson, Jack Larson and an especially gloomy lad fashionably tagged Dion.

Clanton, a pleasant-looking young fellow, Graziano and Miss Pitts persevere courageously. Sid Gould and Maurice (Doberman) Gosfield attempt comedy relief that refuses to materialize, let alone relieve. Diane Jergens, Joan Tabor and Eileen O'Neill improve the scenery. The picture was directed by Lawrence F. Doheny.

Tube.

One Plus One
(Exploring the Kinsey Reports)

Weak attempt to translate Kinsey sex survey statistics into episodic drama; too tame, inconsistent and uncertain in concept either to entertain or inform. Failure to appeal to one type of audience or the other marks it as dubious b.o. bet.

Hollywood, Aug. 15.

Selected Films Inc. release of Arch Oboler production. Stars Leo G. Carroll; with Hilda Brawner, William Traylor, Kate Reid, Ernest Graves, Richard Janaver, June Duprez, Austin Willis, Jane Rose, Truman Smith, Winifred Dennis, Rita Gardner, Jack Betts. Directed and screenplay by Oboler, based on his play, "Mrs. Kingsley's Report"; camera, George Jacobson; editor, Chester W. Schaeffer; music, John Bath; sound, Frank Orban, Abe Dicesare; assistant directors, Richard Dixon, Gordon Milligan. Reviewed at Screen Directors Guild Theatre, Aug. 15, '61. Running time, 114 MINS.

Leo G. Carroll as Professor Logan,
"Honeymoon" starring Hilda Brawner as
"Baby" starring Rita Gardner as Peggy Clare, William Traylor as Hollister, with Madeleine Christie.
"Homecoming" starring Kate Reid as Julia Bradley, Ernest Graves as John Bradley, Richard Janaver as Carlton, with Garrick Hagon and Toby Tarnow, Michael Stewart, Sharon Acker, Robert Christie, Alfred Scopp.
"The Divorcee" starring June Duprez as Margaret Gaylord, Austin Willis as Sam Tooray, with Peggy Loder, Douglas Rain.
"Average Man" starring Jane Rose as Mrs. Kingsley, with Winifred Dennis as Gertrude, Virginia MacLeod as Miss Pom, and Leslie Yeo.
"Baby" starring Rita Gardner as Peggy Cannon, Jack Betts as Bill Cannon, with Barbara Hamilton, Syd Brown, Susan Fletcher, Frances Tobias, Ruth Springford, and Judith Orban, Bena Schuster, William Ferguson, Alice Hill, Cal Whitehead, Sammy Sales.
"Lecture Hall": Arch McDonnell, Herman Ettlinger, Margot Christie, Norman Welsh, Daryl Masters, Eleanor Beecroft.

Arch Oboler's "One Plus One" is an uneven, uncertainly-conceived attempt to deal dramatically, as well as academically, with five primary patterns of sexual behavior statistically accredited with altering the ideal course of civilized mankind's self-imposed marital pair-off system. By proclaiming itself to be an exploration of the Kinsey Reports, as its sub-title so invitingly puts it, the film is likely to attract too many of the wrong people for the wrong reasons and yet disappoint too many of the right people owing to its failure to adhere to the serious, studious structure of its apparent intent. Thus, it will succeed in fully satisfying and entertaining neither sensation-seeked nor knowledge-seeker, and those will be the two types of audience whose interest will be aroused.

The picture, released by Selected Films, may enjoy some mild initial success on the strength of its natural curiosity value, but the response figures to be short-lived once word begins to circulate that it's somewhat of a sheep in wolf's clothing.

Oboler wrote, directed and produced "One Plus One," exercising the latter function under the aegis of Fluorite Ltd., a Swiss investment firm. His screenplay is an outgrowth of his play, "Mrs. Kingsley's Report," his filming location a wintry Toronto, and most of his players are drawn from the thespic ranks of the Canadian Broadcasting Co. The picture is episodic in structure, with five playlets linked to a seminar discussion of statistical findings of the Kinsey Reports. The meeting is presided over by a college professor (Leo G. Carroll), and in his audience are the individuals whose flashback musings translate the statistics into drama. The subjects explored are premarital relations, infidelity, divorce, middle-aged male promiscuity and abortion.

Unfortunately, Oboler's course is erratic and inconsistent. His episodes contradict one another in style. After his first three dramas pursue the subject in a serious vein, the fourth abruptly abandons realism for comic absurdity and the unrealistic aura thus introduced in midstream spills over, pervades and tarnishes the fifth. Then Oboler proceeds to cap it off with a preposterous and essentially irrelevant climactic stroke. The episode themselves are tediously stretched and morally and socially inconclusive.

There are a number of capable performances in the picture, however, prominent among which are those of Hilda Brawner, William Traylor, Kate Reid, June Duprez, Austin Willis, Jane Rose, Truman Smith, Winifred Dennis, Rita Gardner and Jack Betts. Carroll is well-equipped for and unaffected in the prof role.

Oboler's direction tends to slip up on detail, such as the altered condition of props upon change or camera angle. He also seems to have a penchant for inserting mysterious offscreen voices to build mood, an artificial gimmick that comes out ludicrous and monotonous in execution. But he has coaxed some sensitive performances and, with the aid of cameraman George Jacobson, extracted the vigor of his physical locale and pumped its brick flavor into his picture. Chester W. Schaeffer's editing seems abrupt in its initial flashback transition, but that is essentially because the audience is rather unprepared for the sudden dramatic swerve. John Bath's music is consistently helpful in building and sustaining mood, but sound by Frank Orban and Abe Dicesare is occasionally too crude, causing some dialog to be missed.
Tube.

Dondi

Wee, uncomfortably precious orphan lad from Europe who melts the heart of America. Intolerably sweet. Strictly a companion item.

Hollywood, Aug. 9.

Allied Artists release of Albert Zugsmith-Gus Edson production. Stars David Janssen, Patti Page, Walter Winchell, Mickey Shaughnessy, Robert Strauss, Arnold Stang, Louis Quinn; introduces David Korp. Directed by Zugsmith. Screenplay, Zugsmith, Edson, based on syndicated comic strip, "Dondi," by Edson and Irwin Hasen; camera, Carl Guthrie; editor, Edward Curtiss; art director, William Glasgow; sound, Ralph Butler; assistant director, William A. Calihan Jr. Reviewed at Wiltern Theatre, Aug. 9, '61. Running time, 80 MINS.
Dealey .... David Janssen
Liz .... Patti Page
Walter Winchell .... Walter Winchell
Sergeant .... Mickey Shaughnessy
Sammy Boy .... Robert Strauss
Peewee .... Arnold Stang
Dimmy .... Louis Quinn
Colonel .... Gale Gordon
Perky .... Dick Patterson
Lt. Calhoun .... Susan Kelly
Jo-Jo .... John Melli
Gladdy .... Bonnie Scott
Ted .... William Wellman Jr.
Candy .... Nola Thorp
Sally .... Joan Staley
Dondi .... David Kory

That forbidden point beyond which wholesome sentiment shatters into artificial saccharinity is crossed by "Dondi," a syrupy sweet concoction about a European orphan waif who is befriended and "adopted" by a group of GI's, smuggled into the U.S., misplaced, rediscovered and naturalized by act of Congress. The Albert Zugsmith production for Allied Artists, based on the syndicated comic strip by Irwin Hasen and Gus Edson (who co-produced), is marketable as a secondary item on double bills aimed at low pressure family situations dominated by kiddie audiences.

Originally dispatched at 100-minutes duration, the picture, written by Zugsmith and Edson and directed by the former, has now been trimmed to 80 minutes for lower berthing. As a result, the performances of a number of featured players seem to have been reduced to virtual walk-ons. Among those spotted most frequently are David Janssen (a promising actor who deserves a better fate than he's been getting lately), Patti Page, Walter Winchell, Mickey Shaughnessy, Robert Strauss, Arnold Stang, Louis Quinn, Gale Gordon and Dick Patterson. Most of these players are guilty of over-emoting, a condition for which, since it's so prevalent, director Zugsmith must be held greatly responsible.

The film introduces David Kory as Dondi. Lamentably, the child speaks as if he's got both a cold and a bagful of jelly beans in his mouth. Although the character's mastery of the English language and idiom is astounding for a five-year-old orphan discovered in Italy, his sentence structure and articulation are, to put it bluntly, abominable. The youngster tries hard and gets a few laughs and sighs, but the lovableness bit simply grows intolerable.

Economy is reflected by William Glasgow's sets and carl Guthrie's lenswork. Obviously, editor Edward Curtiss has been a busy man. There are two pop songs by Earl Schuman and Mort Garson, both routine. Tommy Morgan's harmonica backing adds to both the whimsical and melancholy qualities of the film.
Tube.

You Have To Run Fast

Adequate lower berth number about a doc hiding out from a murderer whom he has identified to police.

Hollywood, Aug. 14.

United Artists release of Robert E. Kent production. Stars Craig Hill, Elaine Edwards, Grant Richards. Directed by Edward L. Cahn. Screenplay, Orville H. Hampton; camera, Gil Warrenton; editor, Robert Carlisle; music, Richard La Salle; sound, Ralph Butler; assistant director, Herbert S. Greene. Reviewed at Goldwyn Studios, Aug. 14, '61. Running time, 73 MINS.
Roger Condon Frank .... Craig Hill
Laurie .... Elaine Edwards
Big Jim Craven.......... Grant Richards
Bert .... Shep Sanders
Stan .... John Apone
Deputy .... Brad Trumbull
Injun George .... Ken Mayer
Col. Maitland .... Willis Bouchey
Doc Rayburn .... Max Mellinger
Lt. Dan Corbo .... Jack Mann
Chuck .... John Clarke
Fran .... Claudia Barrett
Rocco .... Ric Marlow
Lou Miles .... Jack Kenny
Small Boy .... Joel Lewinson

"You Have To Run Fast" will more than suffice as a supporting item on a twin bill, provided said twin bill is designed to confront audiences less inclined to fret over a dip in quality from the "A" to "B" halves of the program. Wherever the demands are low pressure and audience taste favors police-suspense melodrama, this number, produced on an enterprisingly modest but realistic lower berth scale by the experienced Harvard Film Corp. tandem of producer Robert E. Kent and director Edward L. Cahn, will fit fine.

According to Orville H. Hampton's screenplay, a doctor (Craig Hill) is called upon to treat the victim of a thorough beating by hoodlums Grant Richards and Ric Marlow. When the victim expires, the doc is on the spot because he has identified the killers to the police. Rather impulsively and uncooperatively shunning police protection, and abandoning his practice for the duration, he hightails it out to hunting country where he hides out for a year as a sporting good's clerk, meanwhile falling in love with the local innkeeper's daughter (Elaine Edwards). Eventually, but rather mysteriously, he is sniffed out by the hoods. Refusing to run any further or faster (in spite of the title), he takes a firm stand and turns the tables on his pursuers.

There are holes aplenty in the yarn and some of the execution is awkward, but on the whole it's a businesslike job of "B" picture making—and so long as there must be B's, it is important they be done as well as possible, thankless and compromising though the task may sometimes be. The principals all do an adequate job under the circumstances, and support is satisfactory, with an especially persuasive performance by Willis Bouchey.

The level of competence extends to the crafts involved, including cameraman Gil Warrenton, editor Robert Carlisle, sound mixer Ralph Butler and musicman Richard La Salle.
Tube.

Reveille-Toi Cherie
(Wake Up Dear)
(FRENCH—COLOR)

Paris, Aug. 15.

CFDC release of Panda Films production. Stars Daniel Gelin, Francois Perier, Genevieve Cluny. Written and directed by Claude Magnier from his play. Camera (Eastmancolor), Pierre Gueguen; editor, Charles Bretoneiche. At Normandie, Paris. Running time, 92 MINS.
Masure .... Daniel Gelin
Jacquleine .... Genevieve Cluny
Robert .... Francois Perier

Filmed play still has too much theatrical playing and palaver to be effective in this film. It lacks a true visual subjugation of the obvious coincidences and complications. This looms mainly a local possibility.

A man's car breaks down and he goes into a house in the country. Taking some water that has a sleeping draught in it he lies down next to the lady of the house, already asleep. Then there are usual explanations to the returned husband, with a novel ending.

Color is good but the three characters play unevenly. Also, the overabundant dialog and telegraphed proceedings are a drawback. For a first pic, Claude Magnier still has to learn how to concentrate on visual rather than theatrical thesping and revelations.
Mosk.

Yugoslav Festival

DVOJE
(And Love Has Vanished)
(YUGOSLAV)

Pula, Aug. 15.

Avala production. With Beba Loncar, Miha Baloh, Milos Zutic, Borislav Radovic. Directed by Aleksandar Petrovic. Screenplay, Petrovic; camera, Nenad Jovicic. At Pula Film Fest. Running time, 85 MINS.

This is one of the two or three best films the Yugoslavs have turned out in the 1960-61 season. A simple boy-meets-girl story, but so imaginatively directed and beautifully photographed that it will be around a long time. Art-slanted film, which contributes much to the prestige of Yugoslav picture production, this looks okay for export. It's primarily an item for the arties.

A young man falls in love with a comely girl. She's at first reluctant but finally gives in. Their love lasts for a year but then the man loses interest in her. The transition from being a passionate lover to an indifferent and even rude partner on the part of the man appears somewhat quick, yet this is a minor flaw. Film teems with beautiful scenes of which the tender love scenes have a French flair.

Petrovic reveals remarkable directorial talents and a fine feel for genuine intimacy. Optically, the pic is superb. The two leading players turn in praiseworthy performances. *Hans.*

Mirno Leto
(A Quiet Summer)
(Yugoslav)

Pula, Aug. 15.

Vardar production. With Ljupka Dzundeva, Slobodan Perovic, Meri Boskova. Directed by Dimitrije Osmanli. Screenplay, Frida Filipovic; camera, Ljube Petkovski; music, Dragutin Savin. At Pula Film Fest. Running time, 88 MINS.

Harmless comedy of the seen-and-forgotten type. Film received many laughs here so it appears a good bargain for the domestic market. But there's nothing special about this to give it better than mild export possibilities.

A young couple is fed up with living among the many people in a big city and therefore they are very happy when the husband gets a job in the country. They hope to spend there a quiet summer far away from the big city. However, their joy doesn't last long since, by and by, their friends and relations show up there too, and gone is the chance to spend a quiet summer. Direction is average, acting pleasant and technical credits okay. *Hans.*

Pesma
(The Poem)
(YUGOSLAV)

Pula, Aug. 15.

Avala production With Vasa Pantelic, Zoran Milosavljevic, Spela Rozman, Rado Marcovic. Directed by Rados Novakovic. Screenplay, Novakovic; camera, Nenad Jovicic. At Pula Film Fest. Running time, 86 MINS.

Another Yugoslav film dealing with the Nazi occupation period. The atmosphere is well captured, with good camerawork and adequate acting. But the direction is too slow. Also, the pic is overloaded with dialog. This is chiefly an item for the native market, and possibly okay for release in East European countries.

It has to do with young Communists who plan to join the partizans and take along a famous poet with them. The poet is caught and beaten up by the Gestapo. The Communists are freeing the man but one of them, the youngest in

the group, pays with his life for his deed.

This has some good scenes, with a very effective ending. But the flaws are too big a handicap to make "Poem" much better than an average production. Technical credits are fine.   *Hans.*

Solunski Atentatori
(The Salonika Terrorists)
(YUGOSLAV)
Pula, Aug. 15.
Vardar production. With Aleksandar Garvic, Petre Prlicko, Joachim Mock, Marlies Behrens. Directed by Zika Mitrovic. Screenplay, Jovan Boskovski; camera, Ljube Petkovski; music, Dusan Radic. At Pula Film Fest. Running time, 105 MINS.

Another Yugoslav action film, but this one doesn't center around Tito's partizans. Macedonian revolutionaries are the heroes in this pic. The time is 1903 when these patriots stood up against the then Ottoman empire which kept the Macedonians down by brute force. Film seems a good bet for the native action trade and also may slip into foreign markets. But chances are slim for this is, as measured by western standards, since only a mediocre actioner. It lacks pace and it's too talky.

Plot has to do with a group of Macedonian highschool boys who plan the assassination of some of Ottoman's big shots. Also the blow-up of a bank is on their list. The greater part of the film deals with their preparations and is rather tiresome.

Direction by Zika Mitrovic is rather old-fashioned. Acting as well as technical credits are nothing special.   *Hans.*

Ne Diraj U Srecu
(Don't Meddle With Fortune)
(YUGOSLAV)
Pula, Aug. 15.
Lovcen production. With Slobodan Perovic, Irena Kolesar, Pavle Vujisic. Directed by Milo Dunkanovic. Camera, Aleksandar Sekulovic; music, Dusan Radic. At Pula Film Fest. Running time, 80 MINS.

The Yugoslavs now are turning out more comedies. This one garnered lots of laughter when screened here. It's a strictly Yugoslav escapist fare based on that country's problem, the housing shortage in big cities. A sure commercial success within its homegrounds. Export possibilities are limited to the East European market.

Story starts out in an apartment which is shared by a couple of families plus their relations. The hero in the film, one of the husbands, then has a dream which takes up a large part of the pic. This dream contains a number of amusing situations, and fortunately is not overly long. Acting, direction and technical credits are average.   *Hans.*

Nasilje Na Trgu
(Violence At the Square)
(YUGOSLAV)
Pula, Aug. 15.
Lovcen production. With Broderick Crawford, Branko Plesa, Valentina Cortese, Anita Bjoerk, Bibi Andersson. Directed by Leonardo Berkovici. Screenplay, Berkovich; camera, Aleksandar Sekulovic; music, Dusan Radic. At Pula Film Fest. Running time, 104 MINS.

This vehicle commands some special attention because its international cast includes such names as America's Broderick Crawford, Italy's Valentina Cortese and Sweden's Anita Bjoerk and Bibi Andersson. With the exception of Crawford, who's seen throughout the film, their roles are relatively small. Plot is quite interesting, with the atmosphere of a German-occupied city in 1944 well caught. But the unconvincing script and heavy-handed direction are considerable drawbacks; hence export chances are only moderate.

Crawford enacts a medico who's been ordered by the resistance movement, of which he's a member, to throw a bomb at a German officer. The bomb kills 30 Germans and as a reprisal measure, the Germans take 300 hostages who are to be shot if the man who threw the bomb doesn't surrender himself voluntarily. In order to save the hostages, Crawford does it against the movement's order. The end sees them all killed. Crawford's acting talents are evident but not too impressive because of constant underplaying for which the direction is to blame.
                    Hans.

Parce Plavog Neba
(A Piece of Blue Sky)
(YUGOSLAV)
Pula, Aug. 15.
Bosna production. With Rahela Ferari, Slavad Vujisic, Olivera Markovic. Directed by Toma Jancic. Screenplay, Vasa Popovic; camera, Eduard Bogdanic; music, Bojan Adamic. At Pula Film Fest. Running time, 88 MINS.

Another Yugoslav comedy dealing with human weaknesses. Film presents a series of amusing situations and has some amicable characters to offer. But this is too typically a domestic feature to go in other than Eastern markets.

Pic concentrates on various people living tightly together in a Serbian town. There's a notorious drunkard, a crippled boy, a pigeon breeder, a woman suffering from complexes, a girl who's looking for a husband, a student, an artist, etc. Director Toma Jancic has given the whole thing an optimistic slant. Acting is not bad and technical credits about average.   *Hans.*

Splendor In The Grass
(COLOR)

Young love in poignant romantic drama. Provocative theme may spur b.o.

Hollywood, Aug. 25.
Warner Bros. release of Elia Kazan production. Stars Natalie Wood, Pat Hingle, Audrey Christie, Barbara Loden, Zohra Lampert; introduces Warren Beatty. Directed by Kazan. Screenplay, William Inge; camera (Technicolor), Boris Kaufman; editor, Gene Milford; music, David Amram; assistant director, Don Kranze. Reviewed at the studio, Aug. 25, '61. Running time, 124 MINS.
Wilma Dean Loomis ...... Natalie Wood
Ace Stamper .... Pat Hingle
Mrs. Loomis .... Audrey Christie
Ginny Stamper .... Barbara Loden
Angelina .... Zohra Lampert
Bud Stamper .... Warren Beatty
Del Loomis .... Fred Stewart
Mrs. Stamper .... Joanna Roos
Juanita Howard .... Jan Norris
Toots .... Gary Lockwood
Kay .... Sandy Dennis
Hazel .... Crystal Field
June .... Marla Adams
Carolyn .... Lynn Loring
Doc Smiley .... John McGovern
Miss Metcalf .... Martine Bartlett
Glenn .... Sean Garrison

The sexual and psychological adjustment inherent in the transition from romantically idealistic, parentally guided (or, more aptly, misguided) youth to the reflective wisdom of self-governed adult maturity is the turbulent emotional business covered in "Splendor in the Grass." Elia Kazan's production of William Inge's original screenplay, directed by Kazan, covers this forbidding chunk of ground with great care, compassion and cinematic flair. It is an extremely intimate and affecting experience, a drama fashioned expressly for the screen and that, in turn, benefits enormously from compatibility with its medium.

Yet there is something awkward about the picture's mechanical rhythm. There are missing links and blind alleys within the story. Several times it segues abruptly from a climax to a point much later in time at which is encountered revelations and eventualities the auditor cannot take for granted. Too much time is spent focusing attention on characters of minor significance in themselves. It is a long film, telling as a whole experience, but its lengthy span has not always been used to advantage.

How the Warner Bros. release will fare is a question linked to the prevailing public preoccupation with sex themes on the screen. Sex is tastefully handled in "Splendor," never exploited for its own sake but completely, vitally and unalterably a part of the story. However, there should be caution not to project a shallow, overly racy image in the selling. What's more, the picture's theme is apt to be misconstrued as a preachment against chastity by those who attribute to sexual abstention the adverse consequences suffered by the hero and heroine.

Discerning filmgoers will be attracted by the Kazan-Inge legend. General audiences should be given some inkling that this is not a period piece, with sensational sensual overtones, but a very human, personal story with a timeless, uplifting theme. "Splendor in the Grass" may be no boxoffice whopper, but it should do better than satisfactory.

Inge's screenplay deals with a young couple deeply in love but unable to synchronize the opposite polarity of their moral attitudes. Their tragedy is helped along by the influence of parental intervention. The well-meaning parents (his father, her mother, both of whom completely dominate their more perceptive mates), in asserting their inscrutable wills upon their children, lead them into a quandary. The children, unable to maintain compatibility between the idealistic doctrines fostered in them by their elders and the tantalizing passion of their feelings, cannot consummate their relationship, either sexually or maritally. Their split is a near-disaster, and they do not recover until they mature, and can benefit reflectively from their own experience. But each must settle for less than each would have been able to offer the other, so the recovery, in essence, is hollow, a triumph of philisophy over reality.

Natalie Wood and Warren Beatty (whom the picture "introduces") are the lovers. Although the range and amplitude of their expression is not always as wide and variable as it might be, both deliver convincing, appealing performances.

The real histrionic honors, though, belong to Audrey Christie, who plays Miss Wood's mother, and Pat Hingle, as Beatty's father. Both are truly exceptional, memorable portrayals, and will be worth serious Oscar consideration when the time comes for such matters. Barbara Loden does an interesting job in a role (Beatty's flapper sister) that is built up, only to be sloughed off at the apex of its development. Fred Stewart is excellent as Miss Wood's father. Although the character is hazy and incomplete, he has one touching line, one moment at the end of the film, that registers more emotional impact than anything else in the picture, and Stewart does it beautifully. Rest of the players, all of whom have individually important passages, are more than capable. These include Zohra Lampert, Joanna Roos, Jan Norris, Gary Lockwood, Sandy Dennis, Crystal Field, Marla Adams, Lynn Loring, John McGovern, Martine Bartlett and Sean Garrison.

Boris Kaufman's photography is notable for its appreciation of beauty, human and nature's. Though responsibility for the gaps and staccato rhythm of the film may lie elsewhere, reservations must be entertained about Gene Milford's editing. Exteriors for the picture were shot in New York State, and the countryside looks a little lush for Kansas, which is the setting of the drama. But interiors designed by Richard Sylbert and furnished by Gene Callahan seem meticulously accurate. Composer David Amram's romantic theme is hauntingly beautiful. There's an exceptional job of costuming by Anna H. Johnstone. The clothes are not only faithful to the two eras (late '20s, early '30s) covered, but they are attractive on the people who wear them.   *Tube.*

Claudelle Inglish

Romantic miseries of poor Georgia sharecropper, his wife and irrational daughter. Heavy, gloomy going in which performances are ray of light.

Hollywood, Aug. 23.

Warner Bros. release of Leonard Freeman production. Star Diane McBain, Arthur Kennedy, Will Hitchins, Constance Ford, Claude Akins. Directed by Gordon Douglas. Screenplay, Freeman, from the novel by Erskine Caldwell; camera, Ralph Woolsey; editor, Folmar Blangsted; music, Howard Jackson; asst. director, William Kissel. Reviewed at Academy Award Theatre, Aug. 23, '61. Running time, **99 MINS.**

Claudelle Inglish	Diane McBain
Clyde Inglish	Arthur Kennedy
Will Hutchins	Dennis Peasley
Jessie Inglish	Constance Ford
S. T. Crawford	Claude Akins
Harley Peasley	Frank Overton
Linn Varner	Chad Everett
Rip Guyler	Robert Colbert
Rev. Armstrong	Ford Rainey
Josh	James Bell
Charles Henry	Robert Logan
Dave Adams	Jan Stine
Ernestine Peasley	Hope Summers

Nice guys finish last is the only discernible comment on human behavior furnished in "Claudelle Inglish," a sudsy and pessimistic romantic tragedy set in the deep South. The Leonard Freeman production, written for the screen by Freeman from Erskine Caldwell's novel, is apparently an attempt to illustrate dramatically why and how an essentially sweet girl can turn sour and destroy herself, as well as those most concerned with her welfare, but the film fails to make its point. Several fine performances and an attractive cast are the bright spots in the boxoffice picture.

"Heroine" Claudelle (Diane McBian), daughter of a poor tenant farmer (Arthur Kennedy) nagged incessantly by his bitterly unhappy wife (Constance Ford), ignores her mother's advice to accept the romantic proposals of wealthy, middleaged landowner Claude Akins, insteads becomes betrothed to poor, but handsome young neighbor Chad Everett, who promptly leaves for a two-year hitch courtesy Uncle Sam. Jilted by Everett, Miss McBain abruptly and defiantly evolves into the town's pushover. Upshot is a messy tragedy in which the boxscore reads two dead, one runaway wife (Miss Ford), and one decent, rational hardworking farmer (Kennedy) stripped of his entire family in one fell swoop. The dramatic ball is fumbled at the critical point in which Miss McBain changes from the faithful maiden to the town belle.

It must have taken courage for Freeman and director Gordon Douglas to avoid the temptation to sidestep the uncompromisingly gloomy ending they have retained. But this dismal, hopeless view of life leaves a spectator bewildered. All aware of man's inhumanity to man, but this painfully pessimistic picture seems to suggest not only that the primrose path leads irrevocably to tragedy, but that tragedy is the ultimate lot of the poor. It leaves a bitter taste.

Ralph Woolsey's camera, appreciative of beauty, finds a cooperative subject in Miss McBain, who delivers an earnest portrayal of an unappealing character. Kennedy, ever a dependable actor, gives a genuinely winning performance as the unfortunate farmer, and Miss Ford's enactment of his inflexibly shalow and disenchanted wife is rich in emotional projection and understatement. Akins is convincing as the awkward landlord with an unreasonably single-minded yen for Miss McBain. Will Hutchins is the most animated and believable of the host of young actors who participate in the leading lady's favors, a physically attractive and histrionically competent group made up of Chad Everett, Robert Colbert, Robert Logan and Jan Stine. Others strong in support are Frank Overton, Ford Rainey and Hope Summers. Director Douglas gets a lot out of his performers. Editing seems rather repetitious, espicially in the way the picture keeps panning to the swaying treetops every time Miss McBain gets naughty. *Tube.*

A Thunder Of Drums
(C'SCOPE-COLOR)

A green lieutenant and dashing cad learns to soldier and woo fairly on the Apache-jammed 1870 frontier. Superior action facets crowded out by laborious romantic angles and overdose of obscure, shaky exposition, but neglected cowboy-Indian buffs should respond in sufficient numbers.

Hollywood, Aug. 21.

Metro Release of Robert J. Enders production. Stars Richard Boone, George Hamilton, Luana Patten, Arthur O'Connell; features Charles Bronson, Richard Chamberlain, James Douglas; introduces Duane Eddy. Directed by Joseph M. Newman; screenplay, James Warner Bellah; camera (Metrocolor), William Spencer; editor, Ferris Webster; music, Harry Sukman; assistant director, Hal Polaire. Reviewed at the studio, Aug. 21, '61. Running time, **97 MINS.**

Capt. Maddocks	Richard Boone
Lt. Curtis McQuade	George Hamilton
Tracey Hamilton	Luana Patten
Sgt. Rodermill	Arthur O'Connell
Trooper Hanna	Charles Bronson
Lt. Porter	Richard Chamberlain
Trooper Eddy	Duane Eddy
Lt. Gresham	James Douglas
Laurie	Tammy Marihugh
Camden Yates	Carole Wells
Trooper Erschick	Slim Pickens
Trooper Denton	Clem Harvey
Trooper Baker	Casey Tibbs
Mrs. Scarbrough	Irene Tedrow
Mrs. Yates	Marjorie Bennett
Capt. Alan Scarborough	J. Edward McKinley

"A Thunder of Drums" bears out, at length and in detail, what every red-blooded American boy from Huckleberry Finn to Holden Caulfield has discovered en ronte to adolescence—that girls will only foul up a good game of cowboys and Indians. In expounding this primitive, but sound, philosophy in adult terms, the Robert J. Enders production (his first feature) tends to violate its own precept by laboring the romantic byplay while the cavalrymen and the Apaches are waiting patiently in the wings to go at each other. But, fortunately, the film has compensations of a strictly military, no-gush-no mush, nature with which it will divert the ardent student of hard life and times on the 1870 American frontier. The mass audience represented by this western adventure buff and the relative scarcity of recent theatrical product aimed in its lucrative, appreciative direction assures the Metro release of a satisfactory commercial history.

James Warner Bellah's screenplay describes the evolution of a headstrong, pampered, emotional young cavalry lieutenant into an officer and a gentleman. The "officer" he becomes in the course of a sustained debate with his rational, seasoned c.o. (Richard Boone) and a band of ornery neighborhood Apaches of the old screen school of all-bad Injuns. His metamorphosis into gentleman involves a second-time-around passion with an old flame (Luana Patten) affianced to a colleague, a triangle shattered by the convenient death of his competitor and the departure of his beloved, rendering him the sort of officer regarded as ideal by head man Boone, who ascribes to the theory that "bachelors make the best soldiers—all they have to lose is their loneliness."

The Boone-Hamilton clash is by far the most interesting and rewarding aspect of the film, and both actors handle their assignments skillfully, especially Boone, who projects a whole lot of humanity with a minimum of affectation. Miss Patten fails to loosen up in her characterization. Her love or concern for either of her two suitors is never truly conveyed to the audience through her performance. Arthur O'Connell and Charles Bronson contribute valuable, colorful character work. Most of the other characters are two-dimensional, with prominent support essayed by James Douglas, Richard Chamberlain, Carole Wells, Irene Tedrow, Slim Pickens, Clem Harvey, Duane Eddy and Tammy Marihugh.

The recent furor over excessive violence on the screen should be soothed considerably by this film. The concept engineered by producer Enders and director Joseph M. Newman is to "look the other way" when the going begins to get too brutal and bloody, as illustrated in the opening scene when the horrors of an Apache raid on a remote shed occupied by two women is witnessed through the petrified stare of a child in an adjoining room. The child sees only the reflected pattern on the ceiling of lust and struggle, and that's all the audience sees, too, which is fine. William Spencer's photography aids in this regard, as well as in its picturesquae scrutiny of the barren, but scenic Arizona desert. Ferris Webster's editing is an asset. The 1870 fortification designed by art directors George W. Davis and Gabriel Scognamillo seems correct and authentic. Harry Sukman has composed a vigorous, listenable score, especially rousing as it accompanies the main titles. *Tube.*

The Grass Eater

Full-length filibuster by a wild bore of a poet whose verbosity makes a mockery of his ideas. Pic has no release, its prospects for getting one dubious.

Hollywood, Aug. 24.

Paul Leder-William Norton production. With Leder, Rue McClanahan, Leon Schrier, Patricia Manning, Helen Goodman, Richard Villard, Ted Roter, Bernard Dukore, Bill Guhl. Directed by John Patrick Hayes. Screenplay, Norton; camera, John Morrill; editor, Thomas Conrad; Music, Jaime Mendoza-Nava. Reviewed at Cinema Theatre, Aug. 24, '61. Running time, **63 MINS.**

Pete Boswell	Paul Leder
Loraina	Rue McClanahan
Harvey	Leon Schrier
Mary	Patricia Manning
Melba	Helen Goodman
Bartender	Richard Villard
Waiter	Ted Roter
Bookstore Owner	Bernard Dukore
Man on Street	Bill Guhl

William Norton's awkward, immature, intolerably verbose play about a neonihilistic, picaresque poet, a local legit attraction last fall, has been turned into an awkward immature, intolerably verbose motion picture. Where, as a stage play, it had a certain passionately offbeat, avant garde value and appeal, as a film these qualities fail to materialize, owing at least partially to the strucure, design and purpose of the celluloid medium, into which "The Grass Eater" refuses to fit.

The Paul Leder-William Norton low budget indie production, directed by John Patrick Hayes, who also penned the screen treatment from Norton's play, is at the moment sans release commitment. Nor will getting one by easy, however desirable the opportunity to avail new voices of expression via the medium of film, especially Hollywood film, which is sorely in need of fresh, aggressive, new creative talent. Trouble is "The Grass Earter" is not the sort of product that can interest an art house audience or entertain a general audience. It contains too much that is meaningless and egotistically juvenile for the arty trade, and it is much too high-flown, windy and obscure for the easygoing general patron, who would not be likely to accept it even as a second feature.

What "plot" there is centers on the unorthodox behavior of hero Pete Boswell (played flamboyantly, but without depth, by coproducer Leder), a bohemian-like chap who wins back his "normal" girl's affections by unmasking the absurdity of an "average" married couple via seduction of the wife, reduction of the husband to an ignominious pulp. It is quite possible that flashes of wit and insight occur in the course of the heroe's 62-minuate filibuster—but these are drowned out by the plethora of quasi-philosophic drivel that pours incessantly and irritatingly from his endlessly wagging tongue.

The other characters are caricatures, entirely subservient to the leading man. Patricia Manning attracts the most favorable attention among this unfortunate mob, prominent in which are Rue McClanahan, Leon Schrier, Helen Goodman, Richard Villard and Bernard Dukore. Cinematically, it is a compentent example of filmmaking on limited means, a budget obstacle acceptably hurdled via John Morrill's photography, Thomas Conrad's editing, Ray Creevey's sets, Jaime Mendoza-Nava's music. *Tube.*

Invasion Quartet
(BRITISH)

Sporadically funny military farce, satirical takeoff on "Guns Of Navarone." Logjam of English comedies in U.S. arties blunts its arty prospects, but pic is highgrade supporting item for general runs.

Hollywood, Aug. 16.

Metro release of Ronald Kinnoch pro-

duction. Stars Bill Travers, Spike Milligan, John Le Mesurier, Gregoire Aslan; guest star, Eric Sykes. Directed by Jay Lewis. Screenplay, Jack Trevor Story, John Briley, based on story by Norman Collins; camera, Geoffrey Faithfull, Gerald Moss; editor, Ernest Walter; music, Ron Goodwin; asst. directors, George Pollock, Peter Price. Reviewed at Beverly Theatre, Aug. 16, '61. Running time, 87 MINS.

Freddie Oppenheimer	Bill Travers
Godfrey Pringle	Spike Milligan
Colonel	John Le Mesurier
Debrie	Gregoire Aslan
Dr. Barker	Maurice Denham
Kay	Millicent Martin
Cummings	Thorley Walters
Matron	Thelma Ruby
Col. Harbottle	Cyril Luckham
Brigadier	Alexander Archdale
Coding Officer	Bernard Hunter
Duty Officer	John Wood
Maquis Leader	David Lander
Naval Officer	Bill Mervyn
Gun Commander	Peter Swanwick
German Sergeant	Ernst Ulman
Band Conductor	Eric Sykes

The traffic jam of farce comedies from merry old England continues with "Invasion Quartet," a kind of "Guns Of Navarone" for laughs. Now it becomes a question of just how much such British-manufactured mirth the U.S. wicket traffic will continue to bear, what with daffy Englishmen carrying on all over the place in American theatres. If the answer, as it ought to be, is the quality of the comedy, then "Invasion Quartet" would seem to have as good a chance as several other in-and-out entries that made it in a big way over here. But there is such a factor as too much of an essentially good thing, and Ronald Kinnoch's production, released by Metro, appears to lack the essence of commercial magnetism that would enable it to rise above the adversity inflicted upon it by the current fad and crash through at the boxoffice.

"Invasion Quartet," then, downright funny as it is in spots, lacks the all-around charge to strike it rich on the arty circuit reserved for British comedies, in case Metro is entertaining such notions. The picture will be a dandy item, however, for inclusion on double bills.

The screenplay by Jack Trevor Story and John Briley, from a yarn spun by Norman Collins, has to do with a quartet of disabled limeys so anxious to return to active duty they sneak out of a Dover hospital, cross the Channel, and proceed to blow up a long-range cannon on the Coast of France utilized by the Nazis to keep the residents of the English coastline in a constant state of shell-shock. In skeletal synopsis, this sounds like pretty serious business, but not the way it's executed in this film.

For example, when a Nazi plane swoops low to scrutinize their modest boat as it chugs across the Channel, one of the passengers, obviously a crack duck or skeet shooter, takes aim with a mere rifle, mutters to himself, "three lengths in front of the beak," and fires. Down goes the aircraft. The mission is accomplished via a series of incidents comparable to this. Actually, it would have been a better comedy had its creators been able to sustain the on-the-level realism that marks the film's first half-hour, before it lapses into out-and-out farce. But whether that was possible, in view of the objective, is a moot point. Anyway, some of the farce is pretty funny farce, and director Jay Lewis has extracted every ounce of fun the script provides.

The jolly, dauntless quartet is essayed affably by Bill Travers, Spike Milligan, John LeMesurier and Gregoire Aslan. Chief romantic aid is contributed by Millicent Martin, comedy support by Maurice Denham, and there's an amusing speciality bit by Eric Sykes.

Ron Goodwin's score, full of high spirits, sound gimmicks and comic tuba tones, is important to the merriment. Artwork, editing and lenswork, including Tom Howard's photographic effects, are capably performed. *Tube.*

Yojimbo
(The Bodyguard)
(JAPANESE)

Venice, Aug. 20.

Toho release of a Kurosawa production. Directed by Akira Kurosawa. Stars Toshiro Mifune; features Eijiro Tono, Seizaburo. Screenplay, Kurosawa, Tomoyuchi Tanaka; camera (Tohoscope), Kazuo Myagawa; music, Masaru Sato. At Venice Film Fest. Running time, 110 MINS.

Sanjuro	Toshiro Mifune
Gonji	Eipiro Tono
Seibei	Seizaburo Kawazu

Rousing, good story, told with vigor and visual excitement by Akira Kurosawa, and splendidly acted by Toshiro Mifune, this has limited export possibilities. However, it has ideal remake material for a Yank company.

Tale set in 1800's concerns a wandering samurai who arrives in a village split into two rival and warring factions. He offers his services to one, then to the other gang leader. Both of the leaders are eager to have this able swordsman on their side. Lured by a big payoff, he almost joins one side, only to learn they want to kill him once he's won the battle for them. Going over to the rivals, he starts a series of fights, duels, kidnappings, until he unselfishly frees some prisoners giving them his money. Beaten up, he recoups forces and eventually defeats his enemies, and peace returns to village.

Against a period Japanese backdrop, the tale nevertheless is a natural for transposition to the Yank western scene, containing some of the ingredients of "High Noon," "Magnificent Seven" itself a remake of a previous Japanese film, and "The Gunfighter."

Though this lacks the epic stature of "Seven Samurai," Kurosawa here again shows his mastery of the medium in dramatic and visual terms, aided by a fine performance by the reliable Toshiro Mifune. His choice of backdrop characters is also adroit and colorful as in his ever-exciting use of the camera. Story itself as noted is a good one, but it's Kurosawa's vigorous hand which makes this an unusual actioner.

Music by Masaru Sato rates a special nod for the way it keys the serio-comic tone of various sequences. *Hawk.*

Namonaku Mazushiku Utsukushiku
(Happiness Is Within Us)
(JAPANESE-SCOPE)

Venice, Aug. 22.

Toho production and release. Stars Hideko Takamine; features Kejiu Kogayashi, Izumi Hara. Written and directed by Zenzo Matsuyama. Camera (Tohoscope), Maseo Tamai; editor, Y. Sabura. At Venice Film Fest. Running time, 130 MINS.

Akiko	Hidego Takamine
Michio	Kejiu Kobayashi
Son	Ibumi Hara

Tender tale of a deaf woman and her deaf mute husband is saved from mawkishness and sentimentality by its gentleness, sincerity and warmth of approach. Film might be too long for arty theatre abroad but looms worth a general or dualer release. It seems a language-spot natural.

A deaf woman, who can speak, marries a mute. Film concerns their problems and eventual understanding that they have been happy via each other in spite of their infirmities. Their silent world is well depicted by adroit direction, thesping and the use of sound around them.

Film tugs at the emotions without tearjerking techniques. Playing is expert all along the line. This emerges as a good acceptable melodrama. Technical credits are excellent. *Mosk.*

Samson
(Sampson)
(POLISH)

Venice, Aug. 22.

Film Polski release of Droga-Kadr production. Features Serge Merlin, Alina Janowska, Jan Ciecierski, Elzbieta Kepinska, Tadeusz Bartosik, Wladyslaw Kowalski, Beata Tyskiewicz, Irena Netto, Jan Ibbel. Directed by Andrzej Wajda. Screenplay, Wajda and Kazimierz Brandys, from novel by Brandys; camera (Dyaliscope), Jerzy Wojcik; music, Tadeusz Baird. At Venice Film Fest. Running time, 120 MINS.

Jakub Gold	Serge Merlin
Lucyna	Alina Janowska
Mr. Malina	Jan Ciecierski
Kazia	Elzbieta Kepinska

Grim entry from Poland's Andrzej Wajda, and not up to the potency of that director's previous "Kanal" or "Ashes and Diamonds." Properly trimmed of excess footage, this might shape as an arty entry in limited situations.

Story of racial persecution begins with a prewar manslaughter sentence given a Polish Jew, Serge Merlin, for the accidental killing of a schoolmate. War opens the prison gates, but Merlin is newly confined to the Ghetto, whence he escapes only to want to return. He's treated like a leper outside. Finally, he's offered a chance to fight and, Samson-like, regains moral and physical stature just before his death in the ruins of the building which he's sought to defend.

Pic is filled with symbolisms and shows the internal struggle of harried Jew, but is carried out at too slow a pace and is too lengthy to be completely effective. Despite this, the story is a good, powerful one. French thesp Merlin is very good in the key role. A large cast of Polish actors lend able support. Technical credits are good. This film is shown in competition. *Hawk.*

The Exiles

Venice, Aug. 22.

MacKenzie production and release. With Yvonne Williams, Homer Nish, Tommy Reynolds. Written and directed by Kent MacKenzie. Camera, Erik Daarstad, Robert Kaufman, John Merril; editor, Warner Brown. At Venice Film Fest. Running time, 80 MINS.

Yvonne	Yvonne Williams
Homer	Homer Nish
Tommy	Tommy Reynolds

After "The Little Fugitive," "On the Bowery," "Jazz on Summer's Day," "Savage Eye," "Shadows" and "The Connection," this foreign film festival unveils another budding indie U.S. filmmaking talent. Like the others, this looms a specialized entry needing careful handling.

Film concerns a group of American Indians, mainly young, who quit the reservations to come and live on a slum area of Los Angeles. They seem neither a part of the city or the homes they left. They flit about the city like temporary visitors trying to keep from feeling their state of exile within their own country.

But this is not pat problem pic. It evokes its situation with insight, technical means and understanding. A few are picked out and followed about during one day, showing what happens to them.

This has the tingle of life and a polish in technical qualities and visual presentation. On-the-spot lensing captures the immediacy of the Indians' wanderings, frustrations and sudden fits of violence or brooding. It winds with a sort of mock tribal, drunken dance on a hill overlooking L.A.

The film, like the others in this category, still needs individual booking methods. There is probably an audience for this sort of film if the distribs go out and find it through knowing placement.

Kent MacKenzie appears filmically gifted in his first pic and takes his place as a budding talent to be watched as indie production grows outside the Hollywood pattern.

Incidentally, this year these sort of pix have made dents at the Cannes and Locarno festivals. *Mosk.*

Banditi A Orgosolo
(Bandits at Orgosolo)
(ITALIAN)

Venice, Aug. 22.

Titanus release of a Vittorio DeSeta production. Features Michele Cossu, Peppeddu Cuccu, Vittorina Pisano and other Sardinian peasants. Directed by DeSeta. Screenplay, Vera Gherarducci, DeSeta; camera, DeSeta; music, Valentino Bucchi. At Venice Film Fest. Running time 98 MINS.

Michele	Michele Cossu
Peppeddu	Peppeddu Cuccu
Mintonia	Vittorina Pisano

Fine initial effort by young Italian filmmaker, Vittorio DeSeta, "Orgosolo" is a pic which while closely bordering on the documentary nevertheless has enough story elements to hold audience attention. Despite all recognized values, its chances will have to depend largely on the newly expanded absorption possibilities of the international arty and quality film market.

Plot tells of vain efforts of a Sardinian shepherd to escape from his fate. He is unjustly involved in a theft and murder episode, with the police hunting him and his flock of sheep over hill and valley. Animals die and the shepherd, already partly resigned, accompanies his brother to the village where they lived. Then he takes to the hills again, where circumstances now force him to steal others' sheep and become what to the outside world is merely a "bandit." However, the audience realizes he is a human being who becomes the unjust victim of circumstances.

It's a director's picture all the way, and a brilliant start for DeSeta who, though he doesn't entirely attain the stature of a (Robert) Flaherty, hits the mark

with his pure treatment of elemental themes of man and nature. His choice and direction of the Sardinian back country smacks of the uncanny, and the craggy rockhewn face of Michele Cossu as the shepherd is unforgettable.

There is little to tip the fact that these are not weathered pros living realistic roles. The only concession to realism is that they speak Italian, not the original local argot. Director has also outdone himself in handling his own camera, with lensing always fitting the mood as well as providing striking effects of its own.

Pace is keyed to setting and people, slow and not overly talkative, and may irk a general audience accustomed to more external action. This is, however, present here in the chase which runs nearly the length of the film. Music is unobtrusive and apt. Other technical credits highgrade. *Hawk.*

Pustolov Pred Vratima
(Adventure at the Door)
(YUGOSLAV)

Pula, Aug. 22.

Jadran production. With Ana Karlc, Zoran Ristanovic, Kutijaro Emil. Directed by Sime Simatovic. Screenplay, Simatovic; camera, Branko Blazina, music, Aleksandar Bubanovic. At Pula Film Fest. Running time, **75 MINS.**

This film is a departure from today's routine pix inasmuch as it is remarkably old-fashioned. This very slow moving pic is not without interesting sequences. It's not a bad film, yet its hardly something for western buyers.

Central figure is a woman who's lying mentally very ill in a sanatorium. She's never been in love and has never been loved. Then she has a dream, said dream taking nearly all the footage. She dreams that she is the wife of a good and kind man and leads a happy marriage. The dream ends tragically, and she's dead when the dream is over. Film, based on the drama by Yugoslav writer Milan Begovich, benefits artistically from good camerawork and especially impressive lighting. Acting performances are not very exciting. Technical credits represent good domestic average. *Mosk.*

Venice Films

Of Stars And Men
(ANIMATED—COLOR)

Venice, Aug. 22.

Storyboard production and release. Directed by John Hubley. Screenplay, Hubley, Faith Hubley, Harlow Shapley from book by Shapley; animation directors, William Littlejohn, Gary Mooney; commentary spoken by Shapley; musical director, Walter Trampler; camera (Eastmancolor), John Buehre; editor, Faith Hubley. At Venice Film Fest. Running time, **63 MINS.**

John and Faith Hubley have concocted a beguiling, absorbing animated look at man and his place in the universe in this medium length pic. With mainly aducational playoff distribution in store, this Yank pic also has the quality for art theatre placement with another shorter pic plus supporting fare probabilities.

Taken from Harlow Shapley's book, "Of Stars and Men," this displays a little man who becomes king of the earth by his dexterity and ability. Then he is faced with advances and comes to the conclusion he may not be the only human species in the universe.

Shapley's concise and friendly commentary, delivered by himself, and the clear and expert visuals make the points with eye appeal and investiveness. Humor is also laced into it.

Animation is deft as well as creative with a fine employment of color. It is an excellent use of the medium. Right handling could make this a commercial as well as cultural entry. Video possibilities also loom large. *Mosk.*

La Fille Aux Yeux D'Or
(Girl With the Golden Eyes)
(FRENCH)

Venice, Aug. 22.

Warner Bros. release of Madeleine Films-Gilbert De Goldschmidt production. Stars Marie Laforet, Paul Guera; features Francoise Prevost, Jacques Verlier, Francoise Dorleac. Directed by Jean-Gabriel Albicocco. Screenplay, Pierre Pelegri, Philippe Dumarcay from novel of Honore De Balzac; camera, Quinto Albicocco; editor, Georges Klotz. At Venice Film Fest. Running time, **90 MNS.**

Girl .... Marie Laforet
Henri ....(............. Paul Guers
Eleonore .... Francoise Prevost
Paul .... Jacqques Verlier
Katia .. .. Francoise Borleac

This pic looms mainly a specialized arty entry abroad. Its lesbo theme might help for bally but the slow unfoldment and muted, mannered treatment call for a hard sell.

An updated version of an Honore De Balzac story, this maintains a literary feeling in relying on a series of decorative scenes to spin out the essentially moody, atmospheric study.

The hero is a callow fashion photog noted for his seductions. He meets a mysterious girl who is capricious if a loving creature. It finally comes out that she is the kept friend of his associate, a woman. He then realizes that he really loves the girl. But the lesbo femme kills her before they can flee together.

Director Jean Garbiel Albicocco, for a first pic, displays a good feel for camera setups but possibly too much preciseness in his narrative. Result is an obscuring of any human feelings and a tendency towards repetitiveness.

Camerawork relies on strong backlighting and reflections with an overall crystallike effect that is in keeping with the general quality of the film. Albicocco is only 24, but displays a filmic flair.

The pic does have a gloss and exploitable handle. Acting is primarily posturing but fits the mood of this vehicle. Production values are fine. *Mosk.*

Sung Choonhyang
(Story of Choonhyang)
(KOREAN—COLOR—SCOPE)

Venice, Aug. 22.

Okk release and production. With Choi Eun Hi, Kim Jin Kyoo, Kum Bong. Directed by Shin Sang Okk. Screenplay, Im Hi Jai; camera (Agfa), Lee Hyong Pye; editor, Jyung Yoon Joc. At Venice Film Fest. Running time, **140 MINS.**

Lee Mong Yong .... Choi Eun Hi
Choonhyang .... Kim Jin Kyoo
Servant . ... Do Kum Bong

Although in widescreen and color, this remains a quaint, naive, old-fashioned pic. It is mainly for the record and for local Korean consumption. Film is technically acceptable, however.

It's a tale of 18th Century Korea where a liberal noble fails for a lower born girl. She is almost seduced by a wicked usurper only to be saved by the noble, who weds her.

It is only worth Information Section showing to give an idea of Korean film production. It has some color and dash but is geared for 14-year-old minds. *Mosk.*

Tu Ne Tueras Point
(Thou Shalt Not Kill)
(YUGOSLAV)

Venice, Aug. 22.

Columbia release of a Lovcen Film (Belgrade) and Gold Film Anstalt (Vaduz) (Morris Ergas) production. Stars Laurent Terzieff, Horst Frank, Suzanne Flon; features Mica Orlovic, Marjan Lovric, Ivo Jaksic, Vladeta Dragutinovic. Directed by Claude Autant Lara. Screenplay, Jean Aurenche, Autant Lara, Pierre Bost, from story by Aurenche; camera, Jacques Natteau; editor, Madeleine Gug. At Venice Film Fest. Running time, **125 MINS.**

Cordie .... Laurent Terzieff
Adler .... Horst Frank
Cordie's mother .... Suzanne Flon

A powerful message against war and in favor of concientious objection emerges from this controversial film. Controversy has never hurt boxoffice returns, and thus pic has the elements of an international hit, though its grimness and handling of religious angles are two elements which together with others must be weighed in balance before success is assured. There is no doubt that the film in its present form will have censorship difficulties in certain areas.

Story is about two men before the courts for what are only apparently similar charges. Laurent Terzieff is a concientious objector who has refused all compromise in his belief, engendered by his deep religious feelings, that he should not serve as a potential instrument of war. Horst Frank, on the other hand, is a priest, who during the war executed a partisan on orders from a superior officer and has ever since undergone intense moral suffering. After painstaking deliberation, court aquits the priest and condemns the objector.

Unfortunately for the production's unity, the issues are at times confused, with the religious angle particularly involved. Also, as in most message pix, the authors have loaded the dice to prove their point. And there is a contrived air about some of the proceedings and situations despite the director's claim that everything here is based on fact. Nevertheless, the total effect is undeniable. While doubts and uncertainties confuse the issue, few will quibble with the main arguments this expounds.

Acting is fine on the part of Terzieff, as the objector; and good by Frank, as the harried priest. A large number of players lend apt support.

A special nod must go to the song, sung by Charles Aznavour, in three reprises during the pic. Besides its effective anti-war content, it has a delivery and lilt which spell a hit. Technical credits are good. *Hawk.*

Victim
(BRITISH)

Smooth, holding combo of thriller-drama and social probe. Standout showing by Dirk Bogarde and all-round cast. Adult approach to homosexual and blackmail problems well handled; carefully exploited, this could be a top talking-point pic.

London, Sept. 1.

Rank release of Allied Film Makers' presentation of a Michael Relph & Basil Dearden production, produced by Relph, directed by Dearden. Stars Dirk Bogarde, Sylvia Syms; features Dennis Price. Original screenplay, Janet Green & John McCormick; camera, Otto Heller; editor, John Guthridge; music, Philip Green. At Odeon, Leicester-square, London. Running time, **100 MINS.**

Melville Farr .... Dirk Bogarde
Laura .... Sylvia Syms
Calloway .... Dennis Price
Lord Fullbrook .... Anthony Nicholls
Paul Mandrake .... Peter Copley
Harold Doe .... Norman Bird
Barrett .... Peter McEnery
Eddy .... Donald Churchill
Sandy Youth .... Derren Nesbitt
Det. Inspector Harris ...... John Barrie
Bridie .... John Cairney
Scott Hankin .... Alan MacNaughtan
Phip .... Nigel Stock
Barman .... Frank Pettitt
Madge .... Marvis Villiers
Henry .... Charles Lloyd Pack
P.H. .... Hilton Edwards
Mickey .... David Evans
Patterson .... Noel Howlett
Miss Benham .... Margaret Diamond
Frank .... Alan Howard
Sylvie .... Dawn Beret

Dirk Bogarde, long among the leading boxoffice propositions in British pix, has had a leanish time in his last three or four films. This time he has come up with a winner, as long lunchtime queues outside the cinema, despite the heatwave, testify. It needed some courage on Bogarde's part to tackle this offbeat role, that of a successful barrister with homosexual leanings, since he has a firm feminine following. Result is that he is in a film which has an adult theme. It has something pertinent to say about an urgent social problem but in its own right is a well-written, well-directed thriller-drama that is sustained entertainment. It should mean big b.o. among thoughtful audiences. However, filmgoers who drop in expecting any sensationalization of the homosexual problem are in for a disappointment.

Producer Michael Relph, director Basil Dearden and writers Janet Green and John McCormick (the team which produced "Sapphire," involving racial prejudice) have adopted a similar technique with "Victim." They've provided a taut, holding thriller about blackmailers latching on to homesexuals (90% of U.K. blackmail cases involve "queers") and at the same time have taken several critical swipes at the present British law which encourages the blackmailing by making homos criminal outcasts.

The authors do not condone homosexuality but merely recognize its presence and make a plea for greater tolerance for those caught up in it. They make a case for a change in the law which, while still coming down heavily on the debauching of youth, would recognize the right of consenting adults to live their own private lives. This tricky theme has been handled with commonsense and tact and it is difficult to see how anybody could find offense in it. Though provoking discussion the peek at the problem is hardly penetrating enough to change the views of anybody who has definite

opinions on the moral and legal aspects of the controversy.

Bogarde plays a successful barrister who is on the verge of becoming a Queen's Counsel. He is happily married to a wife who knew of his homo leanings when she married him but has successfully helped him to lead a normal life. He refuses to see a youth with whom he previously has had association because he fears possible blackmail. Instead the boy is trying to protect the barrister from blackmail. The youth commits suicide, Bogarde is caught up in enquiries by the cops and, from remorse, sets out to break the blackmailers even though he knows that if the facts come out it will ruin his marriage and his career.

Patiently, he tracks down others who are being blackmailed but none will admit who is putting on the squeeze. Eventually, he does expose them (and the exposure, incidentally, is the least satisfactory and convincing part of the film) and the pic ends, rightly, on an unhappy note. The homosexuals involved are not caricatures but are shown as varying human beings caught up, often against their will, in something that is probably more medical than criminal. There are a philanthropist peer, an actor, an aging barber, a hearty car salesman from a good family, a photographer, a bookseller and a factory clerk. The pic vividly reveals that all types occupy this half-world of darkness.

Relph and Dearden have cast with meticulous detail, so that even the smallest role is expertly played. The writing is taut, the direction firm and swift and Otto Heller's camerawork does full justice to the authentic London location. Those who have no pity but only contempt for these abnormal men have their say, but mostly the case is weighted against the law which provides "a blackmailer's charter."

Bogarde, as the barrister, gives what is probably the performance of his career to date—subtle, sensitive and strong. Sylvia Syms, as his wife, handles a difficult role with delicacy and there is one memorable scene when the two quarrel after she forces him to admit what she doesn't want to hear. This is telling, moving stuff.

Other top performances come from newcomer Peter McEnery as the youth who sparks off all the trouble, Dennis Price, Norman Bird, Charles Lloyd Pack, Nigel Stock and Anthony Nicholls as assorted homosexuals and Donald Churchill as McEnery's friend. Darren Nesbitt makes a distinct impression as the strongarm man of the blackmail ring, John Barrie and John Cairney are stolidly right as representatives of the law and Margaret Diamond, Dawn Beret, Noel Howlett, Hilton Edwards, Alan Howard, David Evans, Mavis Villiers, Frank Pettitt and Alan MacNaughtan are others who contribute useful performances.

Writing about the theme and plot of this film is tricky as it can easily give a false impression that the makers are cashing in on a controversial idea. This is not true. The film has been made with obvious sincerity and intelligence. It does not shock but it does stimulate some thought and cutting, music and decor all add to the merits of the scripting and thesping to provide stimulating entertainment. *Rich.*

Donde Estas Corazon?
(Where Are You Heart?)
(MEXICAN)

Mexico City, Aug. 22.

Columbia Pictures release of Alfa Films production. Stars Rosita Quintana, Lola Beltran, Amalia Mendoza, Miguel Aceves Mejia; features German Robles, Luis Aragon, Guillermo Orea, Mauricio Garces. Directed by Rogelio A. Gonzalez Jr. Screenplay, Rogelio A. Gonzalez from original by Isaac Diaz Araiza; camera, Victor Herrera; music, Manuel Esperon. At Mariscala Theatre, Mexico City. Running time, 90 MINS.

Film is a biopic treatment of the Garnica Asencio Trio, female unit, highly popular in the early 30's in Mexico, which specialized in romantic music.

Amalia Mendoza, billed as "La Tariacuri"; Lola Beltrañ and Rosa Quintana interpet the roles of the late flapper age trio. While the script takes inevitable liberties in twisting true happenings, in general this picture gives a rather good picture of that era. There are many good sentimental scenes, and the song delivery, especially by Miss Mendoza, Lola Beltran and Miguel Aceves Mejia, is excellent.

This one, despite its liberties with truth and tendency to exaggerate, is a better than average effort, more or less giving a summary of the so-called golden age of Mexican song. It is bound to be a moneymaker in all Latin American areas and Spanish language houses in the U.S. *Emil.*

Tres Tristes Tigres
(Three Sad Tigres)
(MEXICAN)

Mexico City, Aug. 22.

Peliculas Nacionales release of Cinematografica Jalisco production. Stars Luis Aguilar, Joaquin Cordero, Dagoberto Rodriguez; features Ariadne Welter, Irma Dorantes, Maria Eugenia. Directed by Gilberto Gazcon. Screenplay, Pancho Cordova and Gilberto Gazcoa, from story by Pancho Cordova and Eduardo Gazcoa; camera, Ignacio Torres; music, Gustavo Cesar Carrios. At Mariscala Theatre, Mexico City. Running time, 90 MINS.

This is a low budget, spotty quality film for nabe house trade. Its boxoffice will depend upon draw of singing star Luis Aguilar. Picture depicts the adventures of a trio of Romeos and their lasses. Contrived situations, which are used to carry a story along, are somewhat in bad taste.

But there's a market for coarse situation comedy and film will probably make money by continuous reruns in third string nabe houses. Good returns also loom in the provinces, where they like their fun rough and raw. *Emil.*

Venice Films

Summer and Smoke
(PANAVISION—COLOR)

Beautifully acted and distinguished screen version of Tennessee Williams play.

Venice, Aug. 30.

Paramount release of Hal Wallis Production. Stars Geraldine Page, Laurence Harvey; features Una Merkel, John MacIntire, Malcolm Atterbury, Rita Moreno, Thomas Gomez, Pamela Tiffin, Casey Adams, Earl Holliman. Directed by Peter Glenville. Screenplay, James Poe, Meade Roberts; based on play by Tennessee Williams; camera (Technicolor-Panavision), Charles Lang Jr.; sets, Hal Pereira, Walter Tyler; music, Elmer Bernstein. At Film Festival, Venice. Running time, 120 MINS.

John Buchanan	Laurence Harvey
Alma Winemiller	Geraldine Page
Doctor Buchanan	John MacIntire
Mrs. Buchanan	Una Merkel
Rev. Winemiller	Malcolm Atterbury
Rose Zacharias	Rita Moreno
Her Father	Thomas Gomez
Nellie Ewell	Pamela Tiffin
Roger Doremus	Casey Adams

Producer Hal Wallis and director Peter Glenville have fashioned a distinguished motion picture from the latest of Tennessee Williams' plays to be adapted for the screen. By the same token, however, it will take plenty of adroit salesmanship to make "Summer and Smoke" into a major b.o. contender. Critical recognition of its qualities should also help.

Peter Glenville, who guided play in Britain, gives this pic version a solid delineation, effectively guiding his cast, and giving several scenes heightened impact by cutting them off short, allowing effect to follow into next sequence. Throughout most of the first half, he has also successfully disengaged film from its stage format. In latter part, which often bogs down in some talky stretches and a less varied approach, one is more conscious of fact that "Summer and Smoke" was originally a play. The denouement, especially, seems a long time coming, and pic suffers as it searches for a solution.

Performances are almost uniformly excellent, though few will deny that Geraldine Page walks off with top honors in a repeat of her 1952 stage role as Alma Winemiller, the repressed spinster. It's an outstanding effort which will no doubt be rememberd when Oscar time comes round. Laurence Harvey, perhaps a bit young to play her opposite number, John, perhaps a bit too continental as a bayou boy, is nevertheless very good, and gives a solid and believeable rendering of the ne'er-do-well who reforms. Una Merkel (again a repeat of her stage role) cuts herself a memorable cameo in a relatively small part ,while Rita Moreno as the dance hall girl, Thomas Gomez as her father, John MacIntire as the boy's pa, all give their supporting roles an effective reading. Earl Holliman is standout in a brief one-sequence appearance as the traveling salesman in the finale. An extra nod must go also to Pamela Tiffin, who as Nellie adds a pro flair to dazzling youthful beauty to rate plenty of future attention. It's her first screen role.

Special plaudits must also go to camera work (Charles Lang Jr., and art direction (sets by Hal Pereira and Walter Tyler; costumes by Edith Head; furnishings by Sam Comer and Arthur Krams) with muted colors and lace-framed southern backdrops neatly suiting action. Music by Elmer Bernstein is apt. Other technical credits are outstanding, too. *Hawk.*

Myr Vodjaschemu
(Peace to Who Enters)
(RUSSIAN)

Venice, Aug. 29.

Mosfilm production. Features V. Avdjusko, A. Demjanenka, S. Hitrov, L. Shaporenko. Directed by Alekasnaver Alov and Vladimir Naumov. Screenplay, Alov, Naumov, Leonid Zorin; camera, A. Kuznetsov; music, N. Karetnikov. At Film Festival, Venice. Running time, 85 MINS.

Action, humor, pathos combine with other elements in this fine Russian film in which for once the Soviet message of peace and international understanding comes out in simple, human terms. Pic has all the ingredients of an international hit in the successful tradition of "Ballad of a Soldier" which it resembles in certain aspect.

Though set in last days of W.W.II, when the German army was being routed and Soviet and Yank troops about to meet on the Elbe, pic is not basically a war story. It tells of three men—a driver, a shellshocked and mute sergeant, and a youngster just graduated from officers school—who undertake a trip on a truck to take a pregnant German woman to a rear-line hospital and deliver a message to a command post. Various incidents slow the trip and first the driver and then the sergeant are lost along the way, with final portion bridged with aid of a U. S. Army truck and its Yank driver.

While "Ballad of a Soldier" was told in sweeping epic-poetic terms, this pic is more directly on human level. Yet its impact is nevertheless a strong one. The three main characters soon become unforgettable. To this trio must be added the faultless portrayal of an American G. I. who helps the group on last leg of trip. Not a word of dialog or single image mars this stint (by an unbilled Soviet thesp) characterizing the joviality and devil-may-care strength of the U. S. soldier instinctively drawn to his wartime ally, without a trace of implied criticism or propaganda.

Not the least of pic's virtues is the taste with which its young writer-directors have fashioned it, never overworking an effect, always maintaining a rapid pace and keeping a light touch, not an easy trick in a pic set during the war. Acting is topnotch in all cases, while other credits are likewise outstanding, including the perfect matching of wartime footage with excellent lensing by pic's A. Kuznetsov. As usual, the reconstruction by these Russian filmmakers of wartime scenes of devastation is impressive. *Hawk.*

Il Brigante
(The Brigand)
(ITALIAN)

Venice, Aug. 30.

Cineriz production and release. Features Adelmo di Fraia, Franceseo Seminaro, Serena Vergano, Mario Ierard, Anna Filippini, Giovanni Basile, Renato Terra. Directed by Renato Castellani. Screenplay, Renato Castellani, from novel by Giuseppe Berto; camera, Armando Nannuzzi; music, Nino Rota; editor, Jolanda Benvenuti At Film Festival, Venice. Running time, 175 MINS.

Michele Rende	Adelmo di Fraia
Nino Stigliano	Francesco Seminirao
Pataro	Mario Ierard
Fimiani	Giovanni Basile
Milella	Serena Vergano
Giulia Ricadi	Anna Filippini
Nino's mother	Elena Gestito
Bovone	Francesco Mascaro
Nino's grandmother	Angela Sirianni
Don Francesco Tomea	Salvatore Moscianese

An impressively mounted and expertly directed item, this pic is nevertheless overstated and far too long for proper general audience acceptance in its present unweidly

form. Requires sharp pruning effort to highlight action and tone down social criticism facets which weigh it down in its middle portion. Fine home market value and okay export fare if pared drastically.

Writer-director Renato Castellani has been given full rein in making of this item, and it shows in exaggerated length. Early portions of pic, roughly about one hour running time, are excellent as they show growing infatuation of a south Italian boy, Nino, for Michele Rende, the local hot-blood and sort of town hero. Unjustly accused of a local murder and jailed, he escapes and takes to the hills. From there he directs invasion and seizure of unused land by local farmers. He falls in love with Nino's sister, who goes to live with him until she is accidentally killed. Michele loses his mind, kills a man and goes to the village to vent his revenge, only to be shot down in the town square.

All portions of pic pertaining to growing realization of life and the human condition by the youngster are well-paced and sensitively rendered. It's the redundant intrusion of the poor peasant vs. rich landowner theme which mars the ealier tone of pic, often giving it melodramatic, rather than dramatic, overtones.

Castellani's guidance of his actors, most of them non-pros of the area in which pic was shot, is uncanny. The boy, Francesco Seminario, is a find, as are Adelmo di Fraia, playing the bandit, Giovanni Basile, who portrays an understanding gendarme, Serena Vergano, as the bandit's girl, and many others. Armando Nannuzzi has done his usual outstanding lensing job, making the most of colorful scenic backdrop (every foot of film was shot on location) and low-key lighting. Other credits are topnotch. *Hawk.*

Il Posto
(The Job)
(ITALIAN)

Venice, Sept. 2.

Titanus release of 24 Horses Production. Features Alessandra Panseri, Locedana Detto. Written and directed by Ermanno Olmi. Camera, Lamberto Caimi; Olmi; editor, Carla Colombo. At Film Festival, Venice. Running time, 98 MINS.

Domenico .... Alessandro Panseri
Antonietta .... Loredana Detto

This is a little jewel of a picture made (for $55,000) as his first feature effort by Ermanno Olmi. Players are all non-pros but they and other facets of pic form so winning a combo that item should get plenty of mileage both in Italy and in foreign situations where the qualities and innate charm of it can be appreciated. Word of mouth is guaranteed.

Story is extremely simple: a youngster has just finished school and leaves his town for the big city to seek a job. After an exam, at which he meets a young girl to whom he takes a teenage fancy, they are both admitted. He serves a period of apprenticeship, then finally is seated at a desk of his own. Plot is deceptively simple, but every frame of pic is rich with shadings and nuances. Olmi's keenly observant camera is of major assistance, as are his actors. His two leads, Alessandro Panseri and Loredana Detto, are almost incredibly good in their muted, underplayed roles, while all others in pic are equally well chosen and directed. Nor is pic the usual grim picture of workaday existence. On the contrary, it is filled with humorous passages and tongue-in-cheek observations of the daily scene. (There's a particularly funny sequence spoofing mental and physical tests by applicants.) To be sure, film is not shaped in completely orthodox way: Olmi's documentary origin is often revealed as he digresses for an apt sideline note, while towards the film's middle there's a slightly disturbing continuity offshoot which loses track of main characters to glimpse the home lives of boy's fellow workers. Pic also has no musical backdrop, an effective added note of realism.

Camera work is standout, whether in hidden-camera street shots or in close-ups at home or office. Midst the worldwide rash of teenage delinquency pix, "The Job" is an all too rare and refreshing change. *Hawk.*

The Square of Violence
(U. S.-Yugoslavia)

Venice, Aug. 30.

Lovcen release of Lovcen-Budva Production. Stars Broderick Crawford; features Valentina Cortese, Branko Plesa, Bibi Anderssen, Anita Bjork, Bert Sotlar, Dragomar Felsa. Directed by Leonardo Berkovici. Screenplay, Eric Berkovici, Leonardo Berkovici. Camera, Aleksandar Eekulovic; Music, Dusen Radic. At Venice Film Festival. Running time, 120 MINS.

Doctor Berfnardi .. Broderick Crawford
Mrs. Bernardi .... Valentina Cortese
German officer .... Branko Plesa
Mrs. Gambetta .... Anita Bjork
Pregnant woman .... Bibi Andersson

(In English)

Hard-hitting item made in Yugoslavia by Americans, in addition to substantial dramatic values boasts an invaluable original English-language soundtarck and a cast of known players headed by Broderick Crawford. Despite downbeat story, it rates definite stateside attention in general situations and the dualer market. Word-of-mouth should also be good.

"Square" in title is one in which Germans have herded 300 hostages in a wartime occupied town. They are to be shot on the spot unless the man who threw bomb killing 30 Germans gives self up. Though set in a Yugoslva community, pic was inspired by wartime incident in Rome. Pic's original impact consists in concentrating on the mental and physical anguish undergone by the wanted man, faced with several decisions, notably should he follow his sense of guilt and give himself up, though only possibly saving the hostages; or should he obey partisan orders and hide, thus avoiding probable torture and risk of revealing partisan setup? Various facets of man's predicament are dramatically explored by script written by two Berovicis, father and son. Pic story is also equipped with a suspense mechanism which maintains audience doubt until the ironic finale which sees man shot by partisans as he's giving himself up, followed by killing of all hostages by enraged Germans.

Crawford does his best work in years as the harried Doctor Bernardi. The 15-minute near-silent scene in which he prepares to throw bomb and those immediately following are especially standout. His major opponent, the Nazi officer, is likewise a topnotch stint by Branko Plesa, one of best-known Yugoslav players who should rate definite Yank attention for this portrayal. Valentina Cortese, Anita Bjork, and Bibi Anderssen have smaller roles, but especially Miss Anderssen contributes strongly via bit in which she gives birth to child while husband is awaiting death among the hostages. Almost all other roles are neatly filled, though in some the English voices dubbed on a few Yugoslav players don't quite ring true. Berkovici, whose first direction stint this is, has obvious flair for dramatic effect which draws full advantage from a linear and explicit script, though at times, especially in the calmer interludes of story, he permits too much rationalizing and talk to show. It's an impressive debut, nevertheless.

Camerawork and other credits in elaborate production also deserve credit, with an extra nod to an outstanding musical score by Dusen Radic. *Hawk.*

Accattone
(ITALIAN)

Venice, Aug. 31.

Cino del Duca release of an Alfredo Bini (Arco Film)-Cino Del Duca production. Stars Franco Citti; Corsini. Written and directed by Pier Paolo Pasolini. Camera, Tonino delli Colli; music, J. S. Bach, adapted by Carlo Rustichelli; editor, Nino Baragli. At Film Festival, Venice. Running time, 120 MINS.

Accattone .... Franco Citti
Stella .... Franca Pasut
Maddalena .... Silvana Corsini
Ascenza .... Paola Guidi
Nannina .... Adele Cambria
Balilla .... Mario Cipriani

This is a fascinating debut in direction by writer-director Pier Paolo Pasolini, who has scripted some interesting pix here in past few years, and who was only recently named one of Nobel Prize candidates in poetry. Strange and downbeat pic rates foreign attention for arty spots. In Italy, this low-budgeter could gross well, especially if given proper ad-pub launching.

Tale is essentially about Accattone, a sort of Roman rebel without a cause who lives from hand to mouth in the daily pursuit of the wherewithal to live, preferably accomplished without manual labor, and sometimes with the unsavory financial support of local prostitutes. This world of men and women who skirt legality, often flaunting laws and mores, is particular to Pasolini, and has been as much criticized as it has been praised. It's naturally repellent, but has a certain earthy poetry to it to make it acceptable to all but prudes. Basically, pic's story recounts Accattone's way of life, then introduces a new love (he's married, but has abandoned wife and kids) which influences him for better, drives him to work for a living, but ironically brings about his final demise and death just as he's determined to go straight, or as straight as one of his ilk can go. Pic's fascination—and its values—lie in the realism with which the writer-director has rendered setting and characters of his world, more than in the story line per se, and in the colorful, vulgar, gross, yet humorous and poetic dialog of these human beings reduced to lowest human condition.

His actors, practically every one of them taken from life (many are reenacting their slum selves) are all excellent, and a more colorful lot cannot be imagined, nor will their actions be viewed without some shock and distaste by some. Franco Citti is especially standout as the sleepy-eyed Accattone, a definite find. Dozens of others fill out the picture with almost equal ability, though here and there a naive stint tips its non-pro origins. Pic needs some trimming to heighten effect and tighten story, and it's likely that other passages and bits may prove too crude for censor tastes. The themes treated are likewise sizzlers, with implied and outspoken social criticism, and one may question the validity and logic of this one or that. Yet this is an illogical world that's being viewed, and the total effect is one of great impact. Technical credits are uneven, though acceptable, indicating low budget origins. A Bach musical adaptation effectively counterpoints action, especially in a fight scene.

Hawk.

Vanina Vanini
(FRANCO-ITALIAN)
(Color)

Venice, Aug. 28.

Columbia release of a Zebra Film-Orsay Film coproduction. Features Sandra Milo, Laurent Terzieff, Martine Carol, Paolo Stoppa, Isabelle Corey. Directed by Roberto Rossellini. Screenplay, Rossellini, Franco Solinas, Antonello Trombadori; from novel by Stendahl; camera (Technicolor), Luciano Trasatti; music, Renzo Rossellini. At Film Festival, Venice. Running time, 128 MINS.

Vanina .... Sandra Milo
Pietro .... Laurent Terzieff
Countess Vitelleschi.......Martine Carol
Prince Vanini .... Paolo Stoppa
Clelia .... Isabelle Corey

Lavish costumer based on novel by Stendahl constitutes a disappointing entry by director Roberto Rossellini. Mainly for dualers in the States, but needs much work before it can expect to impress public. Okay chances on home market where name and controversial story angles should boster possibilities.

Pic follows its literary antecedent in telling love story of young Italian revolutionary and a Roman princess. They first meet when, disguised as a woman, he seeks escape from chasing soldiers in the Vanini Palace. Love becomes passion and she eventually follows him when he's named to lead a revolutionary group in a northern province. However, when she begins to feel that his love is ebbing and that her lover is taking more interest in his political mission than in her, she betrays his fellow plotters. He gives himself up to authorities, lest it's thought that he himself betrayed his men for her sake. Vanina gets her influential friends in Rome and the Vatican to commute his death sentence to life imprisonment, but when he beats her with his prison chains on their last meeting, she flees to a convent as he's executed on the guillotine.

Potentially good story has been ineptly adapted for the screen. Result is strangely blended and uneven melange of patriotism and sex delivered in soapy words which make neither element en-

tirely believable, especially in several seemingly interminable bedroom scenes consisting almost entirely of long and violent political discourses infrequently interrupted by embraces. Intermittently also, some sharp barbs are thrown at Church behavior of the period, notably its interference in Italian politics and policing action, while there's also a confession scene between the heroine and a handsome young priest which borders on the objectionable. Other similar clerical references tip possible Church objections to pic in current form.

Sandra Milo, unflatteringly lensed, is not up to past performances, while Laurent Terzieff is in most scenes wooden. Martine Carol walks through a brief appearance, while Paolo Stoppa has little trouble in running off with whatever audience sympathy it engenders via a colorful and human rendering of role of Vanina's father.

Also on pic's plus side are some splendid mass scenes and action sequences. Luciano Trasatti's lens work (Technicolor) is good, but color quality was still off on what is apparently an early work print. *Hawk.*

Night Tide

Venice, Aug. 27.
Phoenix release of Virgo production. Stars Dennis Hopper, Linda Lawson; features Luana Anders, Gavin Muir. Written and directed by Curtis Harrington. Camera, Vilis Lapenieks; editor, Jodie Copelan. At Venice Film Fest. Running time, 95 MINS.
Johnny .... Dennis Hopper
Mora .... Linda Lawson
Murdock .... Gavin Muir
Girl .... Luana Anders

Curtis Harrington was at one time an avant garde filmmaker and has spent the last few years as an assistant to Jerry Wald. He has now made his first feature on an indie basis and it looms mainly a dualer bet in U.S. circuits.

Film mixes a love affair with the super-natural. Though neatly explained in the end it still leaves a glimmer of doubt. But, if Harrington displays a good flair for narration and mounting, his feel for mood, suspense and atmospherics is not too highly developed as yet.

A sailor on leave meets a girl who works as a mermaid in a side show on the amusement pier in Venice, California. It develops into love but there is a strangeness in her comportment.

Her guardian tells the sailor that he had found her on a Greek island and brought her to the U.S. and that she is really a mermaid. It also develops that two men she had been with were found drowned. The sailor is bewildered but when she almost kills him during skin diving he manages to escape while she disappears.

Then it develops she drowned and her guardian had filled her with the tale of her being a mermaid, until she was obsessed, to keep other men from having her. But the mystery of the strange woman remaining and the sailor goes off remembering his first love.

Certain nightmares, and the growing awareness of the girl's weirdness, are well handled but Harrington is better as a director

than a scripter. Dialog is flat and the story sometimes has to be forced to get in certain colorful backgrounds.

Dennis Hopper is acceptably bewildered by his plight while Linda Lawson has the exotic looks for the psychotic siren.

Harrington has made a pic cheaply and well with good dualer chances on its generally acceptable tale. *Mosk.*

Leviathan

(FRENCH)
Venice, Aug. 23.
Valois release and production. Stars Louis Jourdan, Lilli Palmer, Marie Laforet; features, Madeleine Robinson, Georges Wilson. Directed by Leonard Keigel. Screenplay, Rene Gerard, Julien Green, Keigel from the novel by Green; camera, Nicolas Hayer; editor, Armand Psenny. At Venice Film Fest. Running time, 92 MINS.
Paul .... Louis Jourdan
Angele .... Marie Laforet
Wife .... Lilli Palmer
Husband .... Georges Wilson
Mrs. Londe .... Madeleine Robinson

Sombre film deals with a man on the run but is more interested in the symbolism of his crime. Result is a pic with art house chances on its solidity in treatment and thesp aspects.

A man living in a small town with his wife has been there a few months. He lives by tutoring and has become obsessed with a young girl he follows about. He finally accosts her but he finds she has been the friend of the father whose son he tutors. In a pique he affronts her with this and she denies it. He makes a pass and she resists him; leads to his almost killing her and scarring her face. He kills an old man in flight and is hunted.

For a first pic director Leonard Keigel displays a feeling for narration and underlining the action with filmic observation. There is some sort of religioso and spiritual meaning in all this. Like the Biblical great fish, Leviathan, all the characters are already submerged and only a bit shows to make them not quite plausible enough. Technical credits are good and Louis Jourdan is a marquee value. He plays the unhappy hero with a sort of desperation that makes it acceptable if not clear. Others are adequate but Madeleine Robinson etches a character of greed, pettiness a firm bedrock.

Seven Arts has purportedly prepared an English version and invested in the pic with 20th-Fox to handle it abroad. It needs careful placement for best specialized possibilities. *Mosk.*

Piel De Verano

(Summer Swim)
(ARGENTINIAN)
Venice, Aug. 27.
Angel Film release and production. Directed by Leopoldo Torre Nilsson; Screenplay, Beatrice Guido, Torre Nilsson. camera, Oscar Melli; editor, Jacinto Cascales. At Venice Film Fest. Running time, 100 MINS.
Martin .... Alfredo Alacon
Marcela .... Graciela Borges
Joujou .... Franca Boni
Adela .... Luciana Possamay
Marcos .... Juan Jones
Director Leopoldo Torre Nilsson is one of those talents who owe growing worldwide recognition to film fests. First unveiled at Cannes four years ago, he finally won a prize there this year and

scored here with another pic which shows a still maturing but definite talent wtih a truly individual style and outlook.

Film needs special handling but could be an arty autry on its texture, treatment and theme. Once again the pic deals with the upper classes and a certain distortion of true feeling and a corruption of sentiments.

A young girl accepts a proposition from her youthful grandmother to be nice to a young man who is dying and in love with her. He is the son of the grandmother's man friend. She accepts a trip to Paris. Love on his part, and a seeming growing feeling of her own lead to what seems a miraculous recovery. But she tells him all and he kills himself.

Torre Nilsson's authoress-scriptwriter wife, Beatrice Guido, has a flair for pertinent, sharp dialog and a visual sense of construction. The film has a knowing sensual aspect too which is never vulgar or exploited for its own sake.

Technical cedits are an asset as well as Graciela Borges' sensitive emoting. *Mosk.*

Prisioneros De Una Noche

(Prisoners of the Night)
(ARGENTINIAN)
Venice, Aug. 30.
Angel Film release and production. Directed by David Jose Kohon. Screenplay, Carlos Latorre; camera, Alberto Etchbehere; editor, Anibal Di Salvo. At Venice Film Fest. Running time, 85 MINS.
Martin .... Alfredo Alcon
Elsa .... Maria Vaner
Brenda .... Osvaldo Terranova
Bebe .... Juan Jose Edeleman
Luisa .... Helena Tritek

As a first pic this denotes a new dirctorial talent in David Jose Kohon and another in the group of worthy pix coming out of Argentina of late as revealed at European film fests. This looms a solid Latin language prospect for the U.S. but sans the added fillip to make it a general art house bet.

Though somewhat familiar in theme, the pic has a concern for the characters and their plight to make this engrossing. It does have some excess bravura and a tendency to simplify things by making the heavy all too evil in this love drama.

A disillusioned dancehall hostess meets a young worker and love blossoms. But a pitchman, who has preyed on her and has the boy beaten up, tries to kidnap her and forces himself on the girl only to be killed by her. It ends on an ironic twist with the boy confessing his love and not knowing of the crime.

Characters are well limned and on the spot lensing gives this an added feel for reality. Script and acting are fine except for a tendency to take some shortcuts in plot complications. Technical credits are good. *Mosk.*

Maeva

(COLOR)
Venice, Aug. 24.
Cascade Films release of Umberto Bonsignori production. Directed and written by Umberto Bonsignori. Camera (Ansco), Alberto Baldecchi; editor, Bonsignori; commentary written by Maya Deren and spoken by Adienne De Joie. At Venice Film Fest. Running time, 95 MINS.
Maeva .... Tumata Teuiau
Guido .... Jean Kave

Pierre .... Oscar Spitz
Girl .... Pola

Yank pic deals with the life of a Tahitian girl in a dramatized documentary fashion filled out by a commentary. Though a little light in story value, it does have an exotic appeal and a rightness in its treatment that could make this a specialized entry.

A Tahitian girl is shown in her childhood when she first feels attached to a boy but already has a yearning to know other places besides her little island. Grown up, she begins to feel a need to understand the vague demands of her body and mind. She is raped, leaves home and goes to live near the harbor which fills her with a sense of adventure.

She has affairs with some white men, becomes a sort of tourist attraction and goes through a period of maladjustment before going home and finding a man of her own kind and realizing there is a life to be made even on her small island.

There is no dialog but Maya Deren's commentary points up the revelations and inner feelings and moods of the girl without being didactic or literary. It is a stream of consciousness effect which blends with the imagery.

Shooting is simple but has a bite and feeling. Actors living their parts while Tumata Teuiau is lovely and agile as the heroine called Maeva. Color is acceptable.

It has the usual dancing and gentle erotica of the islands. The throbbing musical score of Teiji Ito, plus the local songs, are also a help. *Mosk.*

Kde Reky Maji Slunce

(The Day the Tree Blooms)
(CZECHOSLOVAK)
Venice, Aug. 29.
Czechoslovensky Film production and release. Features Redrich Vrbsky, Karel Hlusika, Suzana Fisarskova. Jaroslava Ticha. Directed by Vaclav Krska. Screenplay, Krska, Jiri Criki, from novel by Maria Majerova; camera, Josef Illik; music, Jarmil Burghauser. At Venice Film Fest. Running time, 95 MINS.
Lenka .... Suzana Fisarskova
Borek .... Karel Hlusicka
Hladik .... Bedrich Vrbsky

Stylized, splendidly lensed period piece, based on bestselling novel, looks too old hat to have any export appeal. Cliche'd story is about a young girl who is persecuted by her father and whose family forbids her to marry the man she loves, preferring a rich landowner. She flees to the big city to join her beloved one, only to catch a brief glimpse of him as he rides off to the war. Pic intimates she'll wait and start a new life with him when he returns.

Film boasts a topnotch lensing effort by Josef Illik, to which director has added such expressionistic facets as blurred screen, titled with camera angles, etc., but the devices fail to give this that extra quality with which to stand out. Thesping by Suzana Fisarskova is okay, while others tend to overact in overstated general tones of the entire film. Technical qualities are outstanding. This pic is shown in competition. *Hawk.*

No, My Darling Daughter
(BRITISH)

Unpretentious, amiable, comedy which serves to introduce Juliet Mills to the screen.

London, Aug. 22.

Rank release of Betty E. Box-Ralph Thomas production. Stars Michael Redgrave, Michael Craig, Roger Livesy, Rad Fulton, Juliet Mills. Features Renee Houston, David Lodge, Joan Sims, Peter Barkowrth. Director, Ralph Thomas. Screenplay by Frank Harvey, based on the play, "Handful of Tangy," by Harold Brooke & Kay Bannerman; camera, Ernest Steward; editor, Alfred Roome; music, Norrie Paramor; title song, Herbert Kretzmer & David Lee. At Odeon, Leicester-Square, London. Running time, 97 MINS.

Sir Mathew Carr .... Michael Redgrave
Thomas Barclay .... Michael Craig
Gen. Barclay .... Roger Livesey
Cornelius .... Rad Fulton
Tansy .... Juliet Mills
Miss Yardley .... Renee Houston
2d Typist .... Joan Sims
Charles .... Peter Barkworth
Flanigan .... David Lodge
1st Typist .... Carole Shelley
Policeman .... Victor Brooks
Allingham .... Court Benson
Vicar .... Ian Fleming
Constable .... Terry Scott

Following Juliet Mills' successful stage appearances, in "Five Finger Exercise," both in the West End and on Broadway her screen debut has been awaited with more than average interest. Would she be able to keep up the screen tradition of father John Mills and her younger sister, Hayley Mills? Answer appears to be "Yes," though she has a fairly stereotyped role in a not outstanding pic. This, at best, is an unpretentious, amiable comedy. At worst it has to thrash around too energetically for the yocks.

Miss Mills has charm, freshness and an obvious sense of humor, but "Daughter" is too flimsy a vehicle for her performance either to laud or damn her. She plays one of those rollicking school teenagers who are more at home on the hockey field than in the lounge. Her business tycoon pop (Michael Redgrave) wants to launch her in Paris. Instead she launches herself into an innocent enough friendship with the teenage son of an American business associate of Redgrave's. While they meander around London, all's well. But when they take to gadding around Scotland on a motor bike scandal rears its interfering head. The fact that it's so highly platonic that she sleeps inside a tent and boy keeps guard outside doesn't matter. She's made a ward of court, the yarn hits the front pages and a teenage-girl-hunt is soon in full cry.

Miss Mills is brought back by Michael Craig, the son of Redgrave's British business associate. And, in the end, Miss Mills and Craig are last seen eloping in the general direction of Gretna Green. But this does not mean that the film, as a light, inconsequential comedy does not offer an escapist service. There are some intriguing glimpses of Scottish scenery; some determinedly bland and comic exchanges between Redgrave and the boy's father (Roger Livesey); a rather haphazard performance by Rad Fulton as the young man; a rather more dogged and shrewd one by Craig, who is becoming something of an expert in handling unrewarding roles; a sharp piece of thesping by Renee Houston as an efficient secretary; neat music by Norrie Paramor and pleasant photography by Ernest Steward.

Rich.

Die Ehe des Herr Mississippi
(The Marriage of Mr. Mississippi) (SWISS)

Zurich, Sept. 3.

Praesens- Film A. G. Zurich release of Praesens & CCC-Film Berlin production. Stars O. E. Hasse, Johanna von Koczian, Hansjoerg Felmy, Martin Held. Directed by Kurt Hoffmann. Screenplay, Friedrich Duerrenmatt, based on his play, "Fools Are Passing Through"; camera, Sven Nykvist; music, Hans-Martin Majewski; editor, Hermann Haller; executive producer, Max Dora. At Capitol Theatre, Zurich, Aug. 25, '61. Running time, 90 MINS.

Florestan Mississippi .... O. E. Hasse
Anastasia .... Johanna von Koczian
Graf Bodo von Uebelohe-Zabernsee
.... Hansjoerg Felmy
Saint-Claude .... Martin Held
Minister of Justice .... Charles Regnier
Van Bosch .... Max Haufler
McGoy .... Ruedi Walter
Santamaria .... Karl Lieffen
Schlender .... Hans Ernest Jaeger
Lukretia .... Edith Hanke
Prime Minister .... Otto Graf
Chatterley .... Karl Buecheler

The play which established Switzerland's Friedrich Duerrenmatt in international legit is "The Visit"; here is a Swiss-German screen version of one of his earlier plays which had a shortlived off-Broadway run in April '58 at the Jan Hus Theatre under the title, "Fools Are Passing Through." Although lacking the commercial stamina and provocativeness of "The Visit," this one still emerges an interesting venture with enough offbeat qualities to raise it above par. Times Films has acquired it for the U.S.

"Mississippi" is primarily a political satire, aiming at no particular side, but at politics and the "power of a woman" in general. The woman, in this case, is an unscrupulous female who (1) poisons her first husband; (2) is forced into marriage by Mississippi, a d.a. who wants to re-establish the Laws of Moses and has himself poisoned his wife, the mistress of the woman's husband; (3) has an affair with Mississippi's former accomplice, a Communist who wants to bring about a world revolution; (4) spurns her former lover, an idealistic doctor who had provided her with the poison; and (5) ends up as the first lady by teaming with the Minister of Justice, while Mississippi's confession of his and her crimes are regarded as a freak and he is thrown into an asylum. Pic ends on a cynical note, with the interned d.a.'s unheard plea: "One must change the world . . ."

Unpleasant in content, sharply intellectual in storyline and execution and with occasionally free-wheeling dialog, this shapes as high-level sophisticated fodder.

Director Kurt Hoffman, of "Aren't We Wonderful?" and other postwar hits, rates kudos for a sharply witty, uncompromising and tight-paced piece of work. He gets important assist from Sven Nykvist's (one of Ingmar Bergman's aces) superb lensing, Hans-Martin Majewski's satirical score and Swiss Hermann Haller's tight editing. Performances are generally topnotch, notably O. E. Hasse as the d.a., Charles Hegnier as the Minister of Justice and Martin Held as the Commie. Johanna von Koczian seems not quite at home in an offbeat characterization.

Mezo.

Venice Films

Leon Morin, Pretre
(Leon Morin, Priest) (FRENCH)

Venice, Sept. 1.

Rome Paris Film release and production. Stars Jean-Paul Belmondo, Emmanuelle Riva; features, Irene Tunc, Nicole Mirel, Marco Behar. Written and directed by Jean-Pierre Melville from the book by Beatrice Beck. Camera, Henri Decae; editor, Jacqueline Meppil. At Venice Film Fest. Running time, 130 MINS.

Leon Morin .... Jean-Paul Belmondo
Barny .... Emmanuelle Riva
Christine .... Irene Tunc
Sabine .... Nicole Mirel
Edelman .... Marco Behar
France .... Patricia Gozzi

Tale of a young agnostic woman's conversion to Catholicism and her physical love for a priest during the Nazi occupation of France is handled with tact and talent. Savvy handling could make this a worthwhile Yank bet.

The woman in question works in an office. One day in a fit of pique she decides to bait a priest but instead meets a young one who seems to be able to cope with her capriciousness. She begins to visit him and finds her true nature. All aspects of religion and attitudes are deftly treated in these well limned sequences.

Then comes the changing times of the war and her finding of religion and, at the same time, a carnal love for the priest. He understands it and even wards off an overt attempt of the woman with tact. A covetous dream she has is also handled tastefully.

Jean-Paul Belmondo, the feckless hoodlum of "Breathless," here displays a reserve and understanding of his role as progressive young priest that adds to his stature as an actor. Emmanuelle Riva, the heroine of "Hiroshima Mon Amour," is again an exalted, troubled woman and she gives the role an intensity that is acceptable in spite of some overdone personal tics and mannerisms.

Director Jean-Pierre Melville has adroitly underlined the talk with good visual rhythm and an expert recreation of the times. Technical credits are good, and, if it lacks a certain fervor and intensity, it has a reserve and intelligence.

Mosk.

Il Giudizio Universale
(The Last Judgment) (ITALO-FRENCH)

Venice, Sept. 2.

Dino DeLaurentiis release of a DeLaurentiis-Standard (Paris) coproduction. Features, in order of appearance, Vittorio Gassmann, Renato Rascel, Elli Davis, Fernandel, Akim Tamiroff, Franco Franchi and Ingrassia, Georges Riviere, Paolo Stoppa, Anouk Aimee, Don Jaime de Mora y Aragon, Melina Mercouri, Nino Manfredi, Vittorio DeSuca, Silvana Mangano, Jack Palace, Mike Bongiorno, Eleonora Brown, Elisa Cegani, Lino Ventura, Alberto Sordi, Ernest Borgnine, Jimmy Durante, Domenico Modugno, Marisa Merlini, Andreina Pagnani, Giuseppe Janigro, Alberto Bonucci, Sergio Iossa, Princess Karamann, Lilly Lembo, Maria Pia Casilio, Gaddo Treves, Mario Abussi, Remington Olmstead, Giuseppe Porelli, Nando Angelini, Edith Peters, Giacomo Furia, Regina Bianchi, Lamberto Maggiorani, Luigi Bonos, Ottavio Bugatti, Ugo D'Alessio, Eugenio Maggi, Teresa de Vita, Pietro de Vico, Enzo Petito, Luigi Reder, Agostino Salvietti, Giuseppe Iodice, Mario Passante, Nello Ascoli, Alfredo Melidoni, Vittorio Bottoni, Alberto Castaldi, Pasquale Cenammo, Nino di Napoli, Alberto Albani Barbieri, Pasquale Cutolo, others. Directed by Vittorio De Sica. Story and Screenplay, Cesare Zavattini; camera, Gabor Pogany; music, Alessandro Cicognini, with song by Modugno-Pugliese. Editor, Adriana Novelli. At Venice Film Fest. Running time, 98 MINS.

Elaborately staged latest product of the Vittorio DeSica-Cesare Zavattini team which has fashioned such hits as "Bicycle Thief," on down to their most recent "Two Women," "Last Judgment" actually best vaguely approximates their semi-surreal "Miracle in Milan" of some years ago in feeling. Pic rates hefty foreign attention on team's prestige value plus the marquee bait offered by scores of w.k. players and performers from various countries (i.e. Jimmy Durante, Jack Palance, Ernest Borgnine, Akim Tamiroff, repping the USA; Fernandel, Anouk Aimee, Georges Riviere, etc. from France and so on). Plus of course the unusual subject matter.

Parlay, if properly projected, is likely to overcome feeling that latest DeSica-Zavattini product is not up to their best work in past and that, here and there, inventiveness lags and the jokes fall flat. Admittedly, the subject is a challenging one for screen transposition. It asks one to imagine that one day, bustling Neapolitan life is interrupted and for a few hours by a mysterious voice which from the heavens announces that "The Last Judgment will start at 6 p.m." Not believed at first, it soon grips the fancy and fears of superstitious and God-fearing Neapolitans, influencing them in various manners, but mostly for the better. Many of them, for the first time, take stock of their lives, and begin to right their ways and repent. The Judgment hour never arrives, however, and the temporarily transfigured and cleansed populace, it's insinuated, will soon resume its previous selfish views of life until the next, and real day of reckoning.

There are some artful episodes in this DeSica-Zavattini potpourri while other vignettes fail to come off in their oft-humorous spoof of human manners and mores. The huge cast performs capably, some of the appearances (Jimmy Durante, for one) being merely one or two-shot affairs. Alberto Sordi, not unusually, steals the most attention. Direction by DeSica is very smooth and pace is lagless on 98 minute pic, though some last-minute cuts seem to have jarred continuity somewhat, leaving a few characters dangling with insufficient justification of their actions.

Technical credits on pic are outstanding, beginning with Gabor Pogany's lensing, black and white except for the Grand Ball windup scene which is in color, splendidly photographed in Naples Opera House. Alessandro's musical scoring is likewise a plus factor, while other technical and production credits reconfirm the unstinting high standard set by producer Dino DeLaurentiis.

Hawk.

Odwiedziny Prezydenta
(A Visit From the President) (POLISH)

Venice, Sept. 2.

Polski State Film release of Syrena production. Directed by Jan Batory.

Screenplay, Jerzy Zawieyski; camera, J. Lipmann; editor, R. Mann. At Venice Film Fest. Running time, 95 MINS.
Boy .... Janusz Pomaski
Mother .... Malgorzata Lorentowicz
Father .... Leon Niemczyk
Granny .... Beata Tyszkiewicz

Film mixes whimsy and insight to make for a look into the world of a child. In trying to depict the world through his eyes, and yet having it done by adults, it sometimes seems a bit stilted. But, overall, it is a moppet yarn for both kids and adults but looms mainly for specialized use abroad.

A boy of six is neglected by his newly remarried father. He retreats into a world where he is visited by a man he calls The President who helps him and talks to him. This visitor has the figure of his father before the divorce and their estrangement.

The parents are not mean but somewhat unable to understand the boy's needs. He is finally taken to a pyschiatrist who recommends treatment. But the parents' lack of understanding leads to a final loss of the boy's vision and his first setback on his way to growing up.

Technical credits are okay and direction mainly effective, especially with a dream sequence set in a zoo. Pic won the Special Jury Prize at the San Sebastian Film fest in Spain last July.   *Mosk.*

Tiro al Piccione
(Pigeon Shoot)
(ITALIAN)
Venice, Aug. 29.
Euro International release of an Alace-Euro International production. Stars Jacques Charrier, Francisco Rabal, Eleonora Rossi Drago. Directed by Guiliano Montaldo. Screenplay, Montaldo and others, based on novel by Giose Rimanelli; camera, Carlo di Palma; editor, Nino Baragli; music, Carlo Rustichelli. At Venice Film Fest. Running time, 125 MINS.
Marco Laudato .... Jacques Charrier
Elia .... Francisco Rabal
Anna .... Eleonora Rossi Drago

One of current rash of fascist-resistance tales, this item differs from the others in telling story from Fascist side. Nevertheless, approach and content are too locally-slanted for much impact abroad, especially as pic lacks power and universal stature. On the local market, if cut for pace, it should hit okay figures thanks also to controversial political angles.

Pic tells of internal struggles of young Fascist, Marco, to find himself, morally and politically, during the confused last days of Fascism, when allegiances to the blackshirt cause began to crumble. Wounded, he has an affair with a nurse (an obtrusive and badly handled interlude which distracts from story), then returns to the front where, bit by bit, he too sees the light which signals the end of the Fascist era. First for director Giuliano Montaldo, this has many fragmentary qualities but little unity. Opening mood-setting sequences are good, as is a near-finale execution bit in which Marco is forced to shoot his best friend. Jacques Charrier appears unequipped to the handle difficult lead, and gives it a two-dimensional reading. Francisco Rabal is fine as his best friend while Eleonora Rossi Drago unsuccessfully fights inadequate dialogue. Others back colorfully, with many fine supporting roles. Carlo Rustichelli's music is ob-

trusive while other credits are good.   *Hawk.*

The Sergeant Was A Lady
(ROMANTIC-COMEDY)

One-joke service comedy with chief attention on romance and playdown of comedy values.

Hollywood, Sept. 6.
Universal release of Twincraft Production, written, directed and produced by Bernard Glasser. Camera, Hal McAlpin; editor, John F. Lind; dances, Noel Parenti; asst. directors, Robert Farfan and Buddy Messinger. Reviewed at UI Revue Studio, Sept. 5, '61. Running time, 72 MINS.
Cpl. Gale Willard .... Martin West
Sgt. Judy Fraser ..... Venetia Stevenson
Col. House .... Bill Williams
Major Hay .... Catherine McLeod
Sgt. Bricker .... Roy Engle
Red Henning .... Gregg Martell

The one-joke service comedy is resurrected again without letting off any bright sparks in "The Sergeant Was a Lady," Twincraft Production written, produced and directed by Bernard Glasser. Chief attention plays down natural comedy development that could come from situation involving a GI mistakenly transferred to a base "manned" by 125 Wacs. More emphasis goes to romantic interest that doesn't give it any more value and only succeeds in negating appeal it might have had for youngsters in the comedy vein. Pic additionally has weak conflict that doesn't maintain interest.

Story situation is a war games competition with a neighboring island of soldiers. Gals want to show it's a women's as well as a man's army, though the array of Wacs depicted hardly look like disciplined lady soldiers.

Performances fail to add to the film. Venetia Stevenson is pretty but anything but a hardboiled lady sergeant, while Martin West plays the soldier with quiet naivete. Standout is pixieish Mari Lynn. Catherine McLeod and Bill Williams hold their own in stock roles. Francine York comes on strong as a sex-starved Wac, but remainder of cast has little to work with.

Filmically, picture is an average example of product on a limited budget. Pic includes stock war footage in games sequences, and editing fails to soften the insertion.   *Dale.*

Ganga
(The River)
(INDIAN)
Venice, Sept. 2.
Cine Art Productions release and production. Written and directed by Rajen Tarafder. Camera, Dinen Gupta; editor, A. Rajan. At Venice Film Fest. Running time, 105 MINS.
Bilas .... Niranjan Ray
Panchu .... Janash Mukherji
Himi .... Sandhya Ray
Damini .... Ruma Gangaly

Simple tale of a young fisherman wanting to follow his river to the sea for work, but blocked by fear and superstition, has a robust approach to reality and a feeling for the people and country. But it lacks the poetic and transcendant insight that made Satyajit Ray's films art possibilities abroad. This one would have harder going.

But there is a solidity in construction and a good visual narra-

tive and plastic talent that mark a name to be heard from in the growing Bengali filmmaking in India. Technical credits are good and acting sincere and vital.

Satyajit Ray's noted "Apu Trilogy" has paved a way for specialized audiences for Indian pix and this may cash in on this.   *Mosk.*

Animas Trujano
(MEXICAN-C'SCOPE)
Venice, Aug. 25.
Marco Males release of ARS-UNA production. Stars Toshiro Mifune, Columba Dominguez, Flor Silvestre. Directed by Ismael Rodriguez. Screenplay, Rodriguez from the novel by Regelio Rivas; camera, Gabriel Figueroa; editor, Pedro Del Rey. At Venice Film Fest. Running time, 100 MINS.
Animas .... Toshiro Mifune
Wife .... Columba Dominguez
Catherine .... Flor Silvestre

A good dash of folklorish exaggeration, brisk, bawdy acting, and sound technical values, make this a natural for the Hispano lingo circuit abroad. But its surface treatment makes this a chancier art entry.

It takes place among the Mexican Indians in a rural part of the country. Each year a man is elected to be the chief by the church. However it takes money. The hero dreams of someday becoming the chief, but lives off his wife and abuses their children.

He is also superstitious and tries all ways to get the money. He finally does succeed only to be looked down upon even though he is now the head man. His wife kills a local harlot he had taken up with and he suddenly makes a gesture in taking the blame.

Japanese actor Toshiro Mifune gives a crafty, picaresque and weighty limning of the peasant. He manages to fit into Mexican surroundings and has gotten away with the feat of playing it by learning the lingo phonetically. He is the plus factor in this sleek pic.   *Mosk.*

Yanco
(MEXICAN)
Venice, Aug. 28.
Yanco Productions release and production. With Ricardo Ancona, Jesus Medina, Maria Bustamante. Written and directed by Servando Gonzalez. Caomera, Alex Phillips Jr.; editor, Jesus Marin. At Venice Film Fest. Running time, 100 MINS.
Boy .... Ricardo Ancona
Old Man .... Jesus Medina
Mother .... Maria Bustamante

Engaging film could be a moppet entry abroad. It is somewhat sentimental but seems sincere and is bolstered by expert technical work.

A little boy with a highly developed aural sense and a growing musical genius can not stand the noises of his little town and runs off to the forest to play on a homemade violin. Then he meets and old candy vender who teaches him the violin.

On the old man's death the violin, called Yanco, is found in a pawn shop and the boy gets it out every night, via a secret entrance, and plays it. The superstitious villagers think it is an evil omen and try to track it down and kill it and the little boy is finally drowned in a whirlpool.

A whimsical feel for nature, if somewhat mannered and overdone,

expert camerawork and a feel for imagery make this an acceptable film. For a first pic it also shows a possible new talent in director Servando Gonzalez. Made on a shoestring outside the Mexican industry, pic has a certain charm and merit. There is almost no dialog in the pic.   *Mosk.*

I Katara Tis Manas
(The Promise)
(GREEK)
Venice, Aug. 23.
GD Films release of Pyrsos Films production. Stars George Foundas; features, Titos Vandis, Sonia Zoldou, Ilin Lyvicou. Directed by Basile Georgiadis. Screenplay, Nico Foscolo; camera, Nico Cardelis; editor, C. Capnissis. At Venice Film Fest. Running time, 110 MINS.
Tasso .... Georges Foundas
Chryssa .... Sonia Zoldou
Vayas .... Titos Vandis
Despos .... Ilia Lyvicou

Adventure tale, set within the framework of an old Greek legend, is mainly for language situations.

A group of hoodlums prey on a small town in the 1910's Greek countryside. One man opposes them but tries to avoid bloodshed only to finally kill them all off. Technical credits are only par and direction misses giving this a heightened flair and feeling to make the heroics more potent.   *Mosk.*

Nise Daigakusi
(The False Student)
(JAPANESE-SCOPE)
Venice, Aug. 29.
Daiel release and production. Written and directed by Yasuzo Masamura. Camera, M. Tamai; editor, H. Hasumi. At Venice Film Fest. Running time, 100 MINS.
Otsu .... Ayako Wakao
Girl .... Sachiko Murase
Boy .... Jerry Fugio
Leader .... Ikishi Itami

There is some curio value in this due to the student and leftist uprisings in Japan that stymied ex-U.S. President Eisenhower's trip there last year. It deals with these student circles and political activities. But the story is somewhat too sketchy and it emerges as a disjointed look at the subject.

A boy who can not pass an entrance exam still hangs around school and tries to convince his mother he is really there. He gets mixed up with a leftist group but is thought to be spy when it is found he is not enrolled in school. He is tied up and sequested by his former friends for three days. It leads to his eventual madness.

Technically it is well done and acting is adequate if not able to overcome the shallow figures.   *Mosk.*

Education of Love
(CHINESE)
Venice, Aug. 24.
International Film Co. release and production. With Jeannette Lin Tsui, Vang Yng, Kelly Lai Chen, Wang Lai. Directed by Chung Chi Wen. Screenplay, Cheng King Chin; camera, Fan Chiehi; editor, Chi Tang. At Venice Film Fest. Running time, 105 MINS.
Lin .... Jeannette Lin Tsui
Ching Yi .... Vang Yng
Father .... Kelly Lai Chen
Friend .... Wang Lai

Formosan pic is mainly for the record and only for language spots abroad. It is a sound little drama but without any unusual aspects. Formosa seems to make little mellers for its own consumption.

A young girl is first somewhat against her father's teaching vocation even though she has trained for it herself. But she is finally brought around to it. Moppet work is the most engaging part of this obvious pic. Technical credits and adult thesping are passable.

Mosk.

The Explosive Generation

Stratford, Ont., Sept. 3.

UA release of Vega (Stanley Colbert) production. Directed by Buzz Kulik. Screenplay, Joseph Landon; camera, Floyd Crosby; music, Hal Borne. At Stratford (Ont.) Film Festival, Sept. 2, 1961. Running time, **89 MINS.**

Peter Gifford	William Shatner
Dan Carlyle	Lee Kinsolving
Janet Sommers	Patty McCormack
Bobby Herman	Billy Gray

Also: Virginia Field, Steve Dunne, Phillip Terry, Edward Platt, Arch Johnson, Suzi Carnell, Jan Norris, Beau Bridges, Peter Virgo Jr., Judy Norton, Bruce Kerner.

This is a well-written, carefully considered and capably-filmed study of American youth which avoids the sensational aspects of Hollywood's similar pix. Based on a case in Chicago, Joseph Landon has devised a screenplay which allows for a natural progression of events showing how three high school students in California are instrumental in getting their teacher reinstated after he's been suspended for considering the discussion in class of sexual behavior.

His suspension is brought about by complaints from the students' parents who, while neglecting their proper responsibilities in such matters, are loud in their denunciation of the teacher. Being unable to talk to their parents, the students had brought up the matter at school because of their bewilderment as to how far they should go in their lovemaking.

Landon and Colbert create a genuine case of varying complexities and dramatic truth over the issue of academic freedom. Unfortunately, they almost destroy their good work by bringing in a last minute compromise ending which is obvious even to the most uncritical audience. This is when one parent learns that her daughter had not slept with her boy-friend, so everything turns out just fine and ends with smiles and happy tears all round; with the principal coyly handing back to the teacher the forbidden papers, etc.

Canadian actor William Shatner doesn't have a large role as the teacher, but he registers sympathetically and effectively. He has a pleasant screen personality and brings a moving power of oratory to his short speech about students "protesting all over the world."

Lee Kinsolving, Patty McCormack and Billy Gray are likable and intelligent as the students while, among the parents, Virginia Field, Steve Dunne and Phillip Terry give believable characterizations. Edward Platt turns in a reliable performance as the principal, and the remaining players add to the film's conviction.

Production values are modest but professional, with Floyd Crosby's photography bringing out the documentary realism of the settings. Hal Borne's music, employing a restrained jazz motif, is effective until the syrupy ending. In his quiet but firm direction, Buzz

Kulik (a recruit from television), maintains a sense of purpose and avoids, with writer Landon, familiar scenes of violence and sordid behavior. This impressive little picture might have won the Stratford Critics' Award had it not been for the wrong ending.

Prat.

The Sand Castle
(PART-COLOR)
(U.S.A.)

Stratford, Ont., Aug. 30.

Noel Productions, produced, written and directed by Jerome Hill. Camera (b&w & Eastmancolor), Lloyd Ahern; music, Alec Wilder. At Stratford (Ont.) Film Festival, Aug. 23, 1961. Running time, **70 MINS.**

Boy	Barry Cardwell
Girl	Laurie Cardwell
Artist	George Dunham
Fisherman	Alec Wilder
Shade Lady	Maybelle Nash
Sun Lady	Erica Speyer
Young Man	Charles Rydell
Young Girl	Allegra Ahern
Fat Man	Lester Judson
Frogman	Martin Russ
Priest	Ghislain Dussart
Voice of Shell	Mabel Mercer

This delightful, fanciful look at the world and its people as we might like them to be is the complete work of Jerome Hill who, a few years ago, made the notable documentary, "Albert Schweitzer." This picture is so different in every way that it hardly seems to be the creation of the same filmmaker.

Candid camera studies of people at work and play are commonplace but Hill's observations of people spending a day at the beach are striking and original in style. A little boy and his sister start the day's activities as their mother leaves them on the beach to play. Slowly but in ever-increasing numbers, other people begin to arrive: the painter (George Dunham) who must change his picture as the people obscure his view; the eccentric old lady (Maybelle Nash) who brings her bird in its cage and sits beneath a large canopy; the angler, the diver, the fat man and the blonde who worship the sun.

Oblivious to them all, the boy starts to build a large sand castle in the shape of a fort, helped by his sister who fetches driftwood and shells. The others gather round and admire his work. There is no dialog, only incidental and amusing conversation. A group of nuns playing baseball draw the crowd away from the boy, but soon all return to exclaim at the beauty and skill of his work.

Nothing is overstated and none of the characters is overdrawn or derivative. The mood is always one of gentleness, charm and tranquility. This public beach, it seems, is really a private world, a dream world for the filmmaker and for the audience which shares it with him.

As the afternoon ends everyone goes home and the boy and his sister fall asleep by their castle to dream (in color) of being within its walls where they meet cut-out puppets (also the work of Mr. Hill) of the people who were on the beach.

When they awake their mother is calling them and the tide is coming in, washing away their castle as gradually as the day is slipping away for ever. The work of both the boy and the artist is only of the day, but the impressions and the memories will always remain.

This unusual picture is best described as a beautiful experience: a fantasy that is at the same time very real. The people involved, especially the children, Barrie and Laurie Cardwell, are a pleasure to watch. It is a perfect family film, and Jerome Hill's inventive, delicate control of this fragile piece of makebelieve cannot be faulted.

Prat.

The Wayside Pebble
(JAPANESE)

Stratford, Ont., Sept. 1.

Produced by Tokyo Eiga Co. Ltd. Directed by Seiji Hisamatsu. Script, Keneto Shindo; camera, Shojiro Sugimoto; music, Ichiro Saito. At Stratford (Ont.) Film Festival, Aug. 31, 1961. Running time, **104 MINS.**

Goichi Aikawa	Hiroyuki Ohta
Oren, his mother	Setsuko Hara
Shogo, his father	Hisaya Marishige
Tsugino, his teacher	Tatsuya Mihashi
Churuke, the head clerk	Kyu Sazanka

(English Titles)

There is much of Dickens' social conscience and concern for humanity in this film, the theme of which is almost identical to that of Hungary's "Be Good Until Death."

The setting is a poor village in Japan in 1910. Goichi, a little boy with a brutal father and a careworn mother, has set his heart on going to a private school, but his parents cannot afford the cost. Although a kind bookseller befriends him, the father refuses to allow the boy to go to the school and apprentices him in the service of a callous merchant instead. After the death of his mother, Goichi refuses to be used further by his master's selfish family and sets out train to Tokyo to find a new life.

The script of "The Wayside Pebble" was written by Keneto Shindo (who wrote and directed "The Island," Japan's award-winning film at Moscow this year), and it bears a close affinity to the early part of the story of Apu, including the train symbol. Even so, it is firmly rooted in Japanese traditions and breathes its own character and life into the events. And these only go to point up what should be an obvious fact: that the theme of a child growing up in poverty and asking only for love and knowledge has a universal application.

Melodrama is not allowed to intrude into this recreation of Japan emerging from the feudal system. Under the direction of Hisamatsu, the details of Goichi's environment are carefully filled in as the story progresses. The boy is movingly and naturally played by Hiroyuki Ohta and the mixed emotions of a child growing up and becoming aware of grief and hardship are beautifully expressed.

In black-and-white and Tohoscope this sad yet engaging film should find an appreciative audience in art houses in North America. Unfortunately the Japanese write their subtitles in American phraseology. The terms "So long" and "okay" sound out of place for Japan of 1910.

Prat

When A Woman Loves
(JAPAN)

Stratford, Ont., Sept. 1.

Produced by Shochiku Co. Ltd., producer, Zengo Sakai. Director, Heinosuke Gosho; script, Toshio Yasumi; camera

(Eastmancolor), Haruo Takeno; music, Yasushi Akutagawa. At Stratford (Ont.) Film Festival, Aug. 28, '61. Running time, **97 MINS.**

Kiyo Mizushima	Ineko Arima
Reisaku Niizu	Shin Saburi
Yukiko (his wife)	Yatsuko Tan-ami
Hideya (a geisha)	Nobuko Otowa

(English Titles)

The veteran Japanese director, Heinosuke Gosho (who was represented at Stratford in 1958 with "The Yellow Crow"), has adapted this film from a celebrated novel, the story of a young girl's adolescent passion for a middleaged married journalist. The affair develops, as she grows up, into a mature and self-denying love.

The pace is slow and the technique uninspired. Ineko Arima gives a sincerely felt performance as the girl, but Shin Saburi as the man, goes through the picture without registering an emotion of any kind. A tearjerker, it seems that when a woman loves she suffers the agonies of hell. *Prat.*

Song of the Woods
(RUSSIAN)

Stratford, Ont., Aug. 25.

Produced at Dovzhenko Studio, Kiev. Written and directed by Viktor Ivtchenko. Based on story by Lesia Ukrainka; camera (Sovacolor). Alexey Prokopenko; music, Igor Shamo; special effects, V. Kuratch. At Stratford Film Festival, Aug. 24, 1961. Running time, **97 MINS.**

Cast: R. Nedashevskaya, V. Sydortchuk, P. Veskliarov, V. Rudin, V. Gubenko, R. Pirozhenko.

(English Titles)

This is a quaint, oldfashioned fairytale about a woodland sprite who falls in love with a human, only to be abandoned by him (an oafish farm hand) and left to spend the rest of eternity as a forest tree.

The color photography, goblins, witches and special effects are in the true spirit of makebelieve, the cast is convincing, and the dialog translated into gracious old English: example, "a star has fallen in my heart" and "I shall bring you roses and adore you like a queen."

This is not up to festival standards but in this case dubbing would be acceptable for children. It's an ideal picture for youngsters.

Prat.

Dimitri Gorin's Career
(RUSSIAN)

Produced by M. Gorky Film Studios, Moscow. Directed by F. Dovlatian & L. Mirsky; script, B. Medovoy; camera (Sovacolor), K. Arutiunov; music, A. Eshpay. At Stratford (Ont.) Film Festival, Aug. 29, 1961. Running time, **100 MINS.**

Cast: Tatiana Koniukhova, Alexandre Demianenko, V. Seleznev, V. Vysotsky, L. Kudriashov, N. Kazakov.

(English Titles)

The mystery of what happened to Dimitri Gorin at Venice has been solved. He was sent to Stratford instead, and this is probably the best place for him. With this film the Russians have a likeable entry, more for Stratford's tolerant audience than the sophisticates at Venice.

Russian pix dealing with contemporary life are seldom shown in North America mainly because their distributors have found that audiences prefer ballet, war stories or versions of classic books. This being so, Dimitri Gorin's Career" turned out to be a pleasing comedy with a present day setting.

Gorin is a bank clerk in a large city who becomes an unskilled laborer with the hydro system and goes to work erecting steel towers and power lines in the forests of the Ural mountains. In contrast to his city life he learns that in working with a group of men he must share and share alike and, trust his companions.

Deftly directed, the story is laid against contrasting backgrounds of city, rivers, forests and mountains and Dimitri's change from clumsy assistant into experienced worker is accompanied by charm, invention and humor, with scenes of how the people live. The color photography is outstanding, the score quite gay, and Alexander Demianenko gives a clever portrait of an inhibited citydweller turning into a robust outdoors character.

He falls in love with a hydro girl and the film ends with an heroic salute for the workers; the treatment, however, is breezy and cheerful and never obnoxious.

Prat.

See You Tomorrow
(POLISH)

Film Polski production. Directed by Januez Morgenstern. Script, Zbigniew Cybulski; camera, Jan Laskowski; music, Krzyztof T. Komeda. At Stratford (Ont.) Film Festival, Aug. 24, 1961. Running time, 89 MINS.
Marguerite .... Teresa Tuszynska
Jacek .... Zbigniew Cybulski
Joasia .... Grazyna Muszynska
Jurek .... Jacek Fedorowicz
Girl from Cafeteria. Barbara Baranowska
Also: W. Bielicki, R. Polanski, E. Kaluzynska, R. Freyer, T. Wojtych.

(English Titles)

Polish filmmakers montinue to experiment in styles, techniques and methods of storytelling, but director Morgenstern (whose first film this is in collaboration with actor Cybulski, who wrote the script) doesn't seem to have taken hold of this theme. The pace is exasperatingly slow and the events frequently confusing.

Cybulski (the doomed young man from "Ashes and Diamonds") plays the director of a group of "pantomimika" actors who meets and falls in love with the attractive daughter of a French diplomat. She is the more sophisticated of the two and knowing that they are of different worlds, wisely refuses to fall in love with him.

It now seems possible that the events did not take place after all; the director has dreamed up another sentimental sequence for his players to perform.

On the whole the film is sincere and often truthful in its more meaningful moments, but for the most part Cybulski has reduced himself to playing another of those tiresome young screen heroes who mope around in the throes of first-love. *Prat.*

The Young Lady's Fool
(GREEK)

Stratford, Ont., Sept. 1.

Produced by Roussopouloi Bros. Directed by Jhon Dal Dalianidis. Script, Nikos Tsiforos & Polyvios Vassilianis; camera, Dimos Sacellariou; music, Manos Hajidakis. At Stratford Ont.) Film Festival Aug. 29, 1961. Running time, 75 MINS.
Julia .... Tzeny Karezi
Grigori .... Dinos Iliopoulos
Caralis .... Dionyssis Papayannopoulos
Aliki .... Rica Dialyna
Manolis .... Stavros Xenidis

(English Titles)

This is not a film for any festival although it looks as if it would be a successful domestic comedy.

Taken from, and looking like, a play it's a frantic, overacted tale about the spoiled daughter of a wealthy industrialist who falls in love with one of her father's clerks. This unlikely hero is pleasingly played by Dinos Iliopoulos, who is popular in Greece.

Prat.

A Taste Of Honey
(BRITISH)

Compelling, offbeat slice of North Country life based on Shelagh Delaney's hit play. Intriguing performance by newcomer Rita Tushingham, imaginative direction by Tony Richardson and a down-to-earth approach should help this comedy-drama overcome its lack of marquee values.

London, Sept. 13.

British Lion-Bryanston release of a Bryanston presentation of a Woodfall film. Stars Dora Bryan, Robert Stephens, Murray Melvin, Paul Danquah, Rita Tushingham. Produced and directed by Tony Richardson. Screenplay, Shelagh Delaney and Tony Richardson from Miss Denaley's play; camera, Walter Lassally; editor, Antony Gibbs; music, John Addison. At Leicester Square Theatre, London, Sept. 12, '61. Running time, 100 MINS.
Helen .... Dora Bryan
Jo .... Rita Tushingham
Peter .... Robert Stephens
Geoffrey .... Murray Melvin
Jimmy .... Paul Danquah
Bert .... David Boliver
Doris .... Moira Kaye
Shoe Shop Proprietor.... Herbert Smith
Woman in Shoe Shop. Valerie Scarden
Nurse .... Rosalie Scase
Gladys .... Veronica Howard
Landlady .... Margo Cunningham
Ship's Mate .... Jack Yarker
Cave Attendant......... John Harrison
School Mistress .... Eunice Black

Shelagh Delaney's play, "A Taste of Honey," which clicked both in the West End and on Broadway, was a natural selection for the current vogue of down-to-earth British films exemplified by "Saturday Night and Sunday Morning." The result is compelling, offbeat job, imaginatively directed and produced.

It should have no difficulty in licking its two obvious handicaps, a cast that hardly rates in American marquee value and Britain's colloquial, North Country lingo which my prove an occasional strain on U.S. ears until they are attuned.

"Honey" has an earthy gusto and sincerity that lift its somewhat downbeat theme and drab surroundings. It has humor, understanding and poignance. Oddly enough the dialog, though pointedly couched in the semi-illiterate vernacular of the lower-class North Country working folk archives, at times, a halting and touching form of poetry.

The film faithfully follows the narrative of the play. But the camera effectively gets into the streets and captures the gray drabness of the locals as well as the boisterous vulgarity of Blackpool, saloons and dance-halls.

Yarn primarily concerns five people and their dreams, hopes and fears. They are Jo (Rita Tushingham); her flighty, sluttish neglectful mother; the fancy man her mother marries; a young Negro ship's cook with whom Jo has a brief affair which leaves her pregnant, and a sensitive young homosexual who gives her the tenderness and affection lacking in her relationship with her mother.

Nothing much happens. It is purely a well observed slice of life. The girl reaches out for the stars, has a brief spell of happiness and finds that her taste of honey is shortlived.

Tony Richardson's direction is sometimes over-fussy but he uses Walter Lassally's camera and Antony Gibbs' editing to exciting effect. Much of the camerawork was done via a candid technique and it produces a vivid realism and authenticity which smacks of the streets rather than the studio. Richardson has not been afraid to let his direction linger over his players' reactions, and an extensive use of close-ups has put a challenge to his cast which they have skillfully accepted.

Film introduces a 19-year-old newcomer, Rita Tushingham, as the 16-year-old school-girl. Her previous experience has been limited to a couple of years in stock and a small role in the play, "The Kitchen." Miss Tushingham has nothing of the conventional box-office prettiness about her. She plays with no makeup, her hair is untidy, her profile completely wrong by all accepted standards; but her expressive eyes and her warm, wry smile are haunting.

She handles comedy, drama and pathos with equal facility and, even though the film dwells overlong on her pregnancy she never allows it to become maudlin. How much of this is her own talent and how much the skilful work of the director is difficult to assess. But she brings a vitality to her role which clearly suggests a new successful entry into Britain's growing stable of fresh, exciting talent.

Dora Bryan, best known for a string of sharp comedy cameos in films and plays, tackles the role of the flighty, footloose mother with confidence and zest. The three men in the lives of daughter and mother are also played with keen insight by Robert Stephens, Paul Danquah and Murray Melvin.

Stephens gives a fine performance as the loud-mouthed, raffish lover of Miss Bryan, particularly in one brilliant scene when he is half proud and half embarrassed at the spectacle she makes of herself when singing in a lively saloon sequence. Danquah plays the young Negro lover of Miss Tushingham with charm and tenderness.

Perhaps the most difficult role is that of Melvin. He repeats the success he made of the part of the young homosexual in the play. The supporting players fit snugly into a film about real people, people, of whom audiences will probably not approve but who are alive and not puppets.

"A Taste of Honey" occasionally dawdles and the screenplay by Miss Delaney and Richardson does not offer anything particularly profound in philosophy or message. But it is a vital and absorbing piece of film-making both technically and performance-wise.

Rich.

What A Carve Up
(BRITISH)

Farcical spoof on the haunted house type of yarn. Some conscientious actors play the joke for rather more than it is worth; it's largely heavy-going.

London, Sept. 15.

Regal Films release of a New World Pictures production. Stars Shirley Eaton, Sidney James, Kenneth Connor, Dennis Price, Donald Pleasance. Features Michael Gough, Esma Cannon, Michael Gwynn.

Valerie Taylor, Philip O'Flynn. Produced by Robert S. Baker and Monty Berman. Directed by Pat Jackson. Screenplay, Ray Cooney and Tony Hilton from Frank King's novel, "The Ghoul"; editor, Jeanne Henderson; camera, Monty Berman; music, Neil Mathieson. At Hammer Theatre, London. Running time, 87 MINS.

Ernie .... Kenneth Connor
Syd .... Sidney James
Linda .... Shirley Eaton
Guy .... Dennis Price
Mr. Sloane .... Donald Pleasance
Fisk .... Michael Gough
Janet .... Valerie Taylor
Aunt Emily .... Esma Cannon
Dr. Edward .... George Woodbridge
Malcolm .... Michael Gwynn
Gabriel.
Arkwright .... Philip O'Flynn
Porter .... Timothy Bateson
Hearse Driver .... Frederick Piper

This is a farcical version of "The Ghoul," an oldtime Boris Karloff feature, and despite a good cast of experienced actors the attempt to josh the "haunted-house" type of spooky drama doesn't quite come off. However, hard work by the players ensures a fair quota of laughs. For undiscriminating audiences, this could be a useful second feature.

It concerns the goings on in a lonely mansion in the North of England when members of Uncle Gabriel's family are summoned to hear the reading of his will. They are a crackpot bunch consisting of a frightened little man who reads proofs of horror novels for a living and who persuades his bookmaker chum to go along with him for the ride.

Also on hand are the dead man's doctor-brother, his two sons, a dissolute, hard drinking Army officer and an eccentric pianist; his hard-bitten daughter and a simple old aunt who still thinks World War I is not yet ended. Mix this motley bunch with a sinister solicitor, and an even more sinister butler plus the dead man's pretty nurse and the characters are on hand for a night of murders and all the trappings of an eerie whodunit.

But the film never quite gets farcical enough or thrilling enough and the cast has to work tremendously hard to keep the tempo alive. Kenneth Connor and Sidney James provide most of the yocks, Shirley Eaton is a pretty diversion, Dennis Price is a suave Army officer and Donald Pleasence a forbidding solicitor. Valerie Taylor, Esma Cannon, Michael Gough and Michael Gwynn also are assets.

Unfortunately there is a mixture of styles, some playing straight, others going for the frolicsome. Direction by Pat Jackson is never controlled enough to decide quite the type of film he is trying to develop. But special effects camerawork and the general atmosphere of spookiness are sound.

Rich.

The Flight That Disappeared

Confusing programmer.

Hollywood, Sept. 12.

United Artists release of Robert E. Kent production. Stars Craig Hill, Paula Raymond, Dayton Lummis. Directed by Reginald LeBorg. Screenplay, Ralph and Judith Hart, Owen Harris; camera, Gilbert Warrenton; editor, Kenneth Crane; music, Richard Le Salle. Reviewed at Goldwyn Studios, Sept. 12, '61. Running time, 71 MINS.

Tom Endicott .... Craig Hill
Marcia Paxton .... Paula Raymond
Dr. Morris .... Dayton Lummis
The Examiner .... Gregory Morton
Hank Norton .... John Bryant
The Sage .... Addison Richards
Barbara Nielsen .... Nancy Hale
Joan Agnew .... Bernadette Hale
Walter Cooper .... Harvey Stephens
Jack Peters .... Brad Trumbull
Helen Cooper .... Meg Wyllie
Manson .... Francis DeSales
Announcer .... Carl Princi
Miss Ford .... Eden Hartford
O'Conner .... Ed Stoddard
Jamison .... Roy Engle
Ray Houser .... Jerry James
Garrett .... Jack Mann
ATC Official .... Stephen Ellsworth Crowley
Radio Operator .... Joe Haworth

Plot of "The Flight That Disappeared" goes beyond its depth in trying to propound an ethical premise on the planning of nuclear warheads which might devastate the entire earth. Action enters a realm which, though supposed to be fanciful, is too confusing for acceptance and film emerges a weak programmer.

Action takes place aboard an airliner en route from Los Angeles to Washington on which are a celebrated nuclear physicist, Dayton Lummis, his research assistant, Paula Raymond, and a rocket propulsion expert, Craig Hill. Scientists have been called to the Pentagon for an important meeting, assumed relating to a superbomb they have developed.

Plane starts climbing out of control, reaching altitudes far beyond normal mechanical possibilities, and all passengers except three principals lose consciousness when oxygen is exhausted. Trio discovers plane apparently has landed far beyond the earth's atmosphere on a cloud-shrouded plateau, where they are taken from craft by a mysterious figure and tried before a jury of generations yet to be born for the bomb which they destroy all future life. Script by Ralph and Judith Hart and Owen Harris lacks the finishing touches subject requires, and Robert E. Kent production leaves spectator as perplexed as the principals when they finally arrive in Washington after plane has disappeared for 24 hours.

Reginald Le Borg makes the most of his direction and cast capably play their roles. Gilbert Warrenton's lensing is first-class, but script was against Kenneth Crane's editing. *Whit.*

The Frightened City
(BRITISH)

Brisk gangster dualler about the protection racket in London. Some tough performances and some smooth direction. Useful b.o.

Anglo Amalgamated release of a Zodiac production. Stars Herbert Lom, John Gregson, Sean Connery, Alfred Marks, Yvonne Romain. Features Olive McFarland, Kenneth Griffiths, David Davies, Bruce Seton. Produced by John Lemont and Leigh Vance. Directed by Lemont. Screenplay by Leigh Vance from original story by Vance and Lemont; camera, Desmond Dickinson; editor, Bernard Gribble; music, Norrie Paramor; at Odeon, Marble Arch. Running time, 97 MINS.

Waldo Zhernikov .... Herbert Lom
Sayers .... John Gregson
Paddy Damion .... Sean Connery
Harry Foulcher .... Alfred Marks
Anya .... Yvonne Romain
Sadie .... Olive McFarland
Wally .... Kenneth Griffiths
Alf Peters .... David Davies
Ogle .... Frederick Piper
Hood .... Robert Cawdron
Tanky Thomas .... Tom Bowman
Frankie Farmer .... Patrick Jordan
Sanchetti .... George Pastell
Superintendent Carter .... Patrick Holt
Asst. Commissioner .... Bruce Seton
Wingrove .... Robert Percival
Miss Rush .... Joan Haythorne
Moffat .... Arnold Diamond
Tyson .... Jack Stewart
Salty Brewer .... Douglas Robinson
Barmaid .... Marianne Stone
Head Waiter .... Neal Arden
Pianist .... Norrie Paramor
Choreographer .... Malcolm Clare
Informer .... J. G. Devlin
TV Announcer .... John Witty

Just how frightened London need be of the "protection racket" exposed in "The Frightened City" is a moot point. But it has provided material for a conventional but brisk gangster yarn which could be a useful dualler in average U.S. houses. There's no obvious star value but, on the other hand, a solid allround cast keeps the entertainment value bubbling apart from a forced and overdramatic ending.

It is very much a two-man circus. Leigh Vance has written the screenplay from an original yarn by himself and John Lemont. The two co-produce and Lemont directs for their own indie company, Zodiac.

Accent of the film is tough and hard-hitting and concerns intergang warfare plus the clash between the cops and the crooks, the cops, as a spokesmen bitterly says, finding themselves hampered by out-dated laws. "We're trying to fight 20th century crime with 19th century legislation," he says.

Six main gangs are running the protection racket and a bent accountant hits on the idea of organizing the gangs into one all-powerful syndicate. All goes well for awhile but then the boss of the organization makes a successful play for a deal involving a $560,000 block of offices being built.

One of the gangsters fights shy of this bigger game, backs out of the organizations and re-forms his own gang. This sparks off gang warfare and the boss decides that the rebel gangleader must be rubbed out. The man detailed to do this cons the victim's best friend into betraying him and the climax comes with the friend bumping off the murderer and then exposing the top undercover man to the police.

That reliable "smoothie," Herbert Lom, plays the brains of the crooked organization with urbane villainy and an equally reliable actor, John Gregson, makes a solid, confident job of the dedicated cop. Alfred Marks, best known as a vaude, tv, and radio comedian, is cast offbeat as Lom's gangster lieutenant. Marks gives a rich, oily, sinister and yet often amusing portrayal of an ambitious thug who is prepared to turn killer to get his own way. A comparative newcomer, rugged Sean Connery, makes a distinct impression as an Irish crook, with an eye for the ladies, who kills Marks out of revenge and then helps to seal the doom of the organization by testifying against the crooks in court. Connery is a rangy, virile young man who combines toughness, charm and Irish blarney.

Olive McFarland, as Connery's steady, and Yvonne Romain as the ambitious night club singer for whom he falls, have the two principal distaff roles, but neither of the parts amounts to very much. Of the rest of a long cast there are useful studies of smalltime crooks by David Davies, Patrick Jordan and Kenneth Griffiths, while Frederick Piper, Patrick Holt and Bruce Seton help Gregson uphold the law. Joan Haythorne, Norris Paramor, J. G. Devlin, George Pastell and Vanda Godsell are others who chip in with useful supporting performances.

Director Lemont extracts the full sock out of the material on hand though the murder fight when Connery and Marks meet comes ridiculously near to parody and should have been ruthlessly edited. Desmond Dickinson's camera has caught the sleazy atmosphere of a certain section of London while the artwork in the interiors is up to scratch. *Rich.*

Le Gout De La Violence
(The Taste of Violence)

Paris, Sept. 19.

Gaumont release of Franco London Film-Continental-Gaumont production. Stars Robert Hossein, Giovanna Ralli; features Mario Adorf, Madeleine Robinson, Dany Jacquet, H. Neubert. Directed by Robert Hossein. Screenplay, Hossein, Louis Martin, Claude Desailly; camera, Jacques Robin; editor, Borys Lewin. At Marignan, Paris. Running time, 85 MINS.

Perez .... Robert Hossein
Maria .... Giovanna Ralli
Chamaco .... Mario Adorf
Bianca .... Madeleine Robinson
Isa .... Dany Jaquet
Chico .... H. Neubert

Supposedly taking place in a Latino country, "Le Gout de la Violence" was made in Yugoslavia with a French, Italo, German and Yugoslav cast. It remains too much a hybrid in spite of some okay approximations. Its simple tale and ordinary direction relegate it to bookings in action dualers abroad. Film is minus depth and meaning for art spots.

A revolutionary leader captures the daughter of the local dictator. In lugging her back to headquarters love grows. He ends up killing his followers who would use her for ransom or worse rather than for the cause. Romance naturally blooms between them before parting.

Director-writer-star Robert Hossein has obviously seen many Yank oaters and Mexican pix. His film imitates them and has little originality of its own. Lensing is good and acting acceptable if not of a Latino feeling. ***Mosk.***

La Fete Espagnole
(The Spanish Fiesta)
(FRENCH)

Paris, Sept. 19.

20th-Fox release of Univers-Jose Benazeraf production. Stars Peter Van Eyck, Dahlia Lavi; features Roland Lesaffre, Helmo Kindermann, Anne-Marie Coffinet. Directed by Jean-Jacques Vierne. Screenplay, Henri-Francois Rey and Vierne from the novel by Rey; camera, Raymond Lemogine; editor, Eric Pluet. At Ermitage, Paris. Running time, 100 MINS.

Georgenko .... Peter Van Eyck
Nathalie .... Dahlia Lavi
Nancini .... Roland Lesaffre
Walter .... Helmo Kindermann
Gina .... Anne-Marie Coffinet

Film handles a subject absent from the screen of late, namely a tale of a liberal in the Spanish Revolution of 1936. A love story is also placed into this 20th-Fox release. Though it lacks a directional punch, a feeling for the times and a good narrative style make this entry suitable for dualer use. Art chances abroad are chancier.

The liberal involved in the yarn runs up against some irritating Communist principles. A member of a brigade going to Spain, he misses his truck. On the way down

he meets an American girl and love blossoms.

Film has some well done love scenes which could be exploitable. The liberal decides to desert with the girl when he feels love is stronger than the revolution, but they are captured by an anarchistic group and he is brutally murdered.

Peter Van Eyck has the craggy looks and personality for the hero while Dalia Lavi brings mainly on attractive physique to her role of the American girl. The cruelty of the battles are well handled. However, director Jean-Jacques Vierne often lets things lose point and punch by not underlining the essentials more dynamically.

Its grayish lensing, stock shots and general depiction of tired and betrayed liberals give the film an atmosphere of the era. But it needs a hard sell for it smacks of the 1930s in characterization and point. For his first pic, director Vierne displays some ability in narration but as yet lacks a more distinctive, hard hitting style. *Mosk.*

Une Femme Est Une Femme

(A Woman Is Always A Woman) (FRENCH-COLOR-FRANSCOPE)

Paris, Sept. 19.

Unidex release of Rome Paris Films production. Stars Anna Karina, Jean-Claude Brialy, Jean-Paul Belmondo. Written and directed by Jean-Luc Godard. Camera (Eastmancolor), Raoul Coutard; editor, A. Guillemot. Preemed in Paris. Running time, 80 MINS.

Angela .... Anna Karina
Emile .... Jean-Claude Brialy
Alfred .... Jean-Paul Belmondo

Jean-Luc Godard, whose use of unusual cutting, fragmented pacing and cynical jocularity worked in his first film, "Breathless," has now tried to apply these techniques to a situation comedy. It does not come off as well and is only intermittently bright. Film's market in the U. S. appears limited, with subsequents more difficult on its sprawling aspects.

A stripteaser, living with a young bookseller, decides she wants a baby. He is againt it until they get married. She finally goes to his friend so that she can have her child and comes back and tells her beau who accepts the situation.

There are some good sequences in the strip parlor. Some witty dialog along with visual and sound jokes also are assets. But not enough of the material is effective and too many situation gags fall flat.

Godard has kept wife Anna Karina almost continually on screen. She is a fetching featherbrain, but is sometimes lost in the dead spots that call for girlish mugging. Actors Jean-Claude Brialy and Jean-Paul Belmondo are mainly foils, but acquit themselves well. Color is uneven. At times, however, it aids the story.

Too much homage to Yank musicals and comedies point up the lack of polish in this entry. It looms a difficult film that could still cash in on the growing interest for pix with offbeat approaches. It won the Special Jury Prize and thesp award for Miss Karina at the Berlin Film Fest this year. *Mosk.*

West Side Story

(SONG—PANAVISION 70—COLOR)

Smash picturization of Broadway musical with handsome prospects indicated.

Hollywood, Sept. 14.

United Artists release of Robert Wise production, presented by Mirisch Pictures, in association with Screen Arts Productions. Stars Natalie Wood, Richard Beymer, Russ Tamblyn, Rita Moreno, George Chakiris. Directed by Wise and Jerome Robbins. Screenplay, Ernest Lehman, based on stage play produced by Robert E. Griffith, Harold S. Prince, book by Arthur Laurents; music, Leonard Bernstein; lyrics, Stephen Sondheim; choreography, Robbins; production designer, Boris Leven; camera, Daniel L. Fapp; editor, Thomas Stanford. Previewed at Carthay Circle Theatre, Los Angeles, Cal., Sept. 13, '61. Running time, 153 MINS.

Maria .... Natalie Wood
Tony .... Richard Beymer
Riff .... Russ Tamblyn
Anita .... Rita Moreno
Bernardo .... George Chakiris
Lieutenant Schrank ..... Simon Oakland
Officer Krupke .... William Bramley
Doc .... Ned Glass
Glad Hand .... John Astin
Madam Lucia .... Penny Santon
Chino .... Jose De Vega
Pepe .... Jay Norman
Indio .... Gus Trikonis
Luis .... Robert Thompson
Rocco .... Larry Roquemore
Loco .... Jamie Rogers
Juano .... Eddie Verso
Chile .... Andre Tayir
Toro .... Nick Covacevich
Del Campo .... Rudy Del Campo
Ice .... Tucker Smith
Action .... Tony Mordente
Baby John .... Eliot Feld
A-Rab .... David Winters
Snowboy .... Bert Michaels
Joyboy .... Robert Banas
Big Deal .... Scooter Teague
Gee-Tar .... Tommy Abbott
Mouthpiece .... Harvey Hohnecker
Tiger .... David Bean
Anybodys .... Sue Oakes
Graziella .... Gina Trikonis
Velma .... Carole D'Andrea
Consuelo .... Yvonne Othon
Rosalia .... Suzie Kaye
Francisca .... Joanne Miya

"West Side Story" is a beautifully-mounted, impressive, emotion-ridden and violent musical which, in its stark approach to a raging social problem and realism of unfoldment, may set a pattern for future musical presentations. Screen takes on a new dimension in this powerful and sometimes fascinating translation of the Broadway musical to the greater scope of motion pictures. The Robert Wise production, said to cost $6,000,000, should pile up handsome returns, first on a roadshow basis and later in general runs.

The Romeo and Juliet theme, propounded against the seething background of rival and bitterly-hating youthful Puerto Rican and American gangs (repping the Montagues and the Capulets) on the upper West Side of Manhattan, makes for both a savage and tender admixture of romance and war-to-the-death. Technically, it is superb; use of color is dazzling, camera work often is thrilling, editing fast with dramatic punch, production design catches mood as well as action itself.

Even more notable, however, is the music of Leonard Bernstein and most of all the breathtaking choreography of Jerome Robbins, who in film is not limited by space restrictions of the stage. His dancing numbers probably are the most spectacular ever devised and lensed, blending into story and carrying on action that is electrifying to spectator and setting a pace which communicates to viewer. Bernstein's score, with Stephen Sondheim's expressive lyrics, accentuates the tenseness that constantly builds.

Ernest Lehman's screenplay, based upon Arthur Laurents' solid and compelling book in Robert E. Griffith and Harold S. Prince' Broadway production, is a faithful adaptation in which he reflects the brutality of the juve gangs which vent upon each other the hatred they feel against the world. Here is juvenile delinquency in its worst and most dangerous sense, and Wise, as producer and co-director with Jerome Robbins, catches the spirit in devastating fashion.

It is a preachment against j.d. even more potent than though it were a "message picture" and in a sense may lack popular appeal, but in the final analysis the overall structure is so superior that it should deliver mass impact. In his direction, Wise utilizes both the stage and screen technique; i.e., long holds on individual scenes and bits of action which suddenly switches to dynamic movement. Effect is stimulating.

Plottage focuses on the romance of a young Puerto Rican girl with a mainland boy, which fans the enmity between the two gangs and ultimately leads to the "rumble" which leaves both gang leaders dead of knife wounds and climaxing in the murder of the American swain by girl's Puerto Rican protector. Characters are excellently delineated, and members of the two gangs, recruited from various "Story" troupes, both Broadway and national, satisfactorily combine their menace with terrific dancing.

Natalie Wood offers an entrancing performance as the Puerto Rican who falls in love with Richard Beymer, forbidden by strict neighborhood ban against group intermingling, and latter impresses with his singing. Most colorful performance, perhaps, is offered by George Chakiris, leader of the Puerto Rican gang, the Sharks, and brother of femme lead, who appeared in London company in same role portrayed here by Russ Tamblyn, leader of the white Jets gang. Tamblyn socks over his portrayal and scores particularly with his acrobatic terping. Rita Moreno, in love with Chakiris, presents a fiery characterization and also scores hugely.

In rugged support, Tony Mordente stands out as a Jets member who wants action; Tucker Smith, another white gangster; Simon Oakland and William Bramley, police officers; Ned Glass as owner of the candy store where the two gangs hold their war council.

Musical numbers are topped by "America," lyrics pitting virtues of U.S. against those of Puerto Ricans' homeland and providing one of the most sensational production dances of entire pic. "Cool," by Tucker Smith, is background for another terrific dance routine, as is "Gee, Officer Krupke." Another spirited dance is the two gangs terping on neutral ground in the neighborhood gymnasium, fast and furious, and opening "Jet Song," led by Tamblyn, gives audience an impression of what is to come.

Half a dozen straight song numbers also lend melody and charm, including "Maria," sung by Beymer; two other singles by Beymer, "Something Comin'" and "Somewhere"; "I Feel Pretty," led by Miss Wood; "Tonight," duet by Beymer and femme; "I Have a Love," Wood; "A Boy Like That," Rita Moreno; "One Hand, One Heart," Beymer-Wood. Singer Marni Nixon dubs Wood's voice and so perfect is the effect that audience isn't aware it isn't actress' own voice.

Film, opening with a three-minute orchestral overture, has been expertly filmed by Daniel L. Fapp, whose aerial prolog, looking straight down upon Gotham as camera flies from the Battery uptown and swings to West Side, provides impressive views. Johnny Green conducts music score, which runs 51½ minutes; Thomas Stanford's tight editing maintains a generally rapid pace; Boris Leven scores as production designer; and Saul Bass is responsible for novel presentation of titles and credits. Irene Sharaff, who designed costumes for Broadway, repeats here. *Whit.*

Recordando

(Remembering)

Santiago, Sept. 14.

Producciones Cinematograficas Alfonso Nararjo. Directed and edited by Edmundo Urrutia. Script, Victoriano Reyes; music, Hector Carvajal; narrator, Gustavo Salgado. At Bandera Theatre. Running time, 85 MINS.

Put together from old newsreels and other films that were bought per kilo by director Edmundo Urrutia before they found their way to junk, this is a pic that evokes a mood of gentle nostalgia. Over half the total footage is pre-1925. It includes scenes from "Verguenza" a Chilean feature of 1922 vintage and from a German film on interplanetary travel exhibited in Santiago in 1917.

Newsreel clips have obvious historical interest. The most exciting are cerca 1910, and include celebrations of the first centennary of Chile's independence, one of the first planes to fly in Santiago and an excellently lensed 15-minute coverage of President Pedro Montt's funeral (also 1910) by French cameraman Jules Chavelains.

Well edited, with brief introductory and closing footage shot by Urrutia, "Recordando" also has a good atmosphere-creating score by Carvajal, but somewhat flat and reiterative text by Reyes.

Local box office prospects are excellent, but international appeal is less certain. *Chile.*

The Hustler

Plenty of exploitation needed for long, sordid story of a pool shark. Paul Newman, Jackie Gleason names as help.

Hollywood, Sept. 23.

Twentieth-Fox release of Robert Rossen production. Stars Paul Newman; features Piper Laurie, George C. Scott, Jackie Gleason. Directed by Rossen. Screenplay, Rossen, Sidney Carroll, based on novel by Walter S. Tevis; camera, Gene Shufton; editor, Deedee Allan. Previewed at Westwood Village Theatre, Sept. 22, '61. Running time, 134 MINS.

Eddie Felson .... Paul Newman
Minnesota Fats .... Jackie Gleason

Sarah Packard .... Piper Laurie
Bert Gordon .... George C. Scott
Charlie Burns .... Myron McCormick
Findlay .... Murray Hamilton
Big John .... Michael Constantine
Preacher .... Stefan Gierasch
Bartender .... Jake LaMotta
Cashier .... Gordon B. Clarke
Score Keeper .... Alexander Rose
Waitress .... Carolyn Coates
Young Hustler .... Carl York
Bartender .... Vincent Gardinia

"The Hustler" belongs to that school of screen realism that allows impressive performances but defeats the basic goal of pure entertainment. This Robert Rossen production accomplishes its purpose of providing a showcase for characterization, but by same token is shy on appeal. Prospects are spotty, lack of femme interest and film's subject matter requiring unusually hard selling.

Film is peopled by a set of unpleasant characters set down against a backdrop of cheap pool halls and otherwise dingy surroundings. Chief protagonist is Paul Newman, a pool shark with a compulsion to be the best of the lot; not in tournament play but in beating Chicago's bigtime player, Jackie Gleason. Unfoldment of the Rossen-Sidney Carroll screenplay, based on novel by Walter S. Tevis, is far overlength, and despite the excellence of Newman's portrayal of the boozing pool hustler the sordid aspects of overall picture are strictly downbeat.

Newman is entirely believable in the means he takes to defeat Gleason, and latter socks over a dramatic role which, though comparatively brief, generates potency. In some respects, the quiet strength of his characterization overshadows Newman in their scenes together. Piper Laurie establishes herself solidly as an actress as a hard-drinking floosie who lives with Newman, and George C. Scott scores as a gambler who promotes Newman and teaches him the psychology of being a winner. Myron McCormick as Newman's early manager and Murray Hamilton as a rich Lexington, Ky., billiard enthusiast lend able support.

Rossen has directed with a harsh hand, developing his theme satisfactorily and setting a pattern of grimness. Technical departments are in keeping with the mood, including Gene Shufton's photography, Harry Horner and Albert Brenner's art direction. *Whit.*

The Devil at 4 O'Clock
(COLOR)

Exciting tropical isle meller with Spencer Tracy and Frank Sinatra to spark b.o. attention.

Hollywood, Sept. 17.

Columbia Pictures release of Fred Kohlmar-Mervyn LeRoy production, produced by Kohlmar, directed by LeRoy. Stars Spencer Tracy, Frank Sinatra; features Kerwin Mathews, Jean Pierre Aumont, Gregoire Aslan, Alexander Scourby, Barbara Luna, Bernie Hamilton, Cathy Lewis, Martin Brandt. Screenplay, Liam O'Brien, from novel by Max Catto; camera (Eastman-color), Joseph Biroc; editor, Charles Nelson; music, George Duning. Previewed at Screen Directors Guild Theatre, Hollywood, Cal., Sept. 14, '61. Running time, **125 MINS.**

Father Matthew Doonan .... Spencer Tracy
Harry .... Frank Sinatra
Father Joseph Perreau .. Kerwin Mathews
Jacques .... Jean Pierre Aumont
Marcel .... Gregorie Aslan
The Governor .... Alexander Scourby
Camille .... Barbara Luna
Matron .... Cathy Lewis
Charlie .... Bernie Hamilton
Dr. Wexler .... Martin Brandt
Aristide .... Lou Merrill
Gaston .... Marcel Dalio
Paul .... Tom Middleton
Clarisse .... Ann Duggan
Corporal .... Louis Mercier
Margot .... Michele Montau
Fleur .... Nanette Tanaka
Antoine .... Tony Maxwell
Captain Olsen .... "Lucky" Luck
Louis .... Jean Del Val
Sonia .... Moki Hana
Napoleon .... Warren Hsieh
Constable .... William Keaulani
Fouquette .... Norman Josef Wright
Marianne .... Robin Shimatsu

"The Devil at 4 O'Clock," despite a meaningless title, stirs up enough suspense and excitement, backed by draw of Spencer Tracy and Frank Sinatra, to rate as a strong entry in the general market.

A small volcanic South Seas isle makes a colorful setting for this tale of heroism and sacrifice, but vying with interest in characterizations are the exceptional special effects of an island being blown to pieces, enhanced by potent useage of Eastman-color.

Fred Kohlmar produces and Mervyn LeRoy directs the Liam O'Brien screenplay, based on a novel by Max Catto, for definitely plus credits. Plot is off the beaten path for an adventure yarn, story of a priest (Tracy) who with three convicts (Sinatra, Gregoire Aslan, Bernie Hamilton) save the lives of the children in a mountain-top leper hospital by leading them through fire and lava flow to the coast and a waiting schooner after the volcano erupts and island is doomed to certain destruction.

Tracy delivers one of his more colorful portrayals in his hard-drinking cleric who has lost faith in his God, walloping over a character which sparks entire action of 125-minute film. Sinatra's role, first-class but minor in comparison, overshadowed in interest by Aslan, one of the convicts in a stealing part who lightens some of the more dramatic action. Third con, Hamilton, also delivers solidly as the strong man who holds up a tottering wooden bridge over a deep gorge while the children and others from hospital cross to safety.

In for romance with Sinatra, Barbara Luna is appealing and pretty and Cathy Lewis scores as hospital matron in a brief part. Also excellent are Alexander Scourby, governor of the island who orders its evacuation; Jean Pierre Aumont, pilot of plane which drops Tracy and convicts over hospital; Martin Brandt, hospital doctor; Kerwin Mathews, missionary who is replacing Tracy on island.

Special effects of Larry Butler and Willis Cook highlight the picture, filmed impressively in color by Joseph Biroc on the vivid island of Maui in the Hawaiian group. Closeups of a volcano in actual eruption, long shots and the devastation created by fire and lava are realistically presented in such a fashion that these sequences are among the most exciting in special effects history.

Charles Nelson's tight editing, John Beckman's suitable art direction and George Duning's musical score are further assets. *Whit.*

The Mighty Crusaders
(ITALIAN-DUBBED-COLOR-SUPERCINESCOPE)

Weak Italo spec entry.

Falcon Productions presentation of a Max Productions (Octavio Poggi) picture. Stars Francisco Rabal, Sylva Koscina; feature Gianna Maria Canale, Rick Battaglia, Philippe Hersent. Directed by Carlo Ludovicio Bragaglia. Screenplay, Alessandro Contienenza; English version, Frederica Nutter, A. Limentani; editor, Renato Cinquini; camera, Rodolfo Lombardi; music, Roberto Nicolosi. At the Palace, N.Y., Sept. 23, '61. Running time, **87 MINS.**

Tancrid .... Francisco Rabal
Glorinda .... Sylva Koscina
Armida .... Gianna Maria Canale
Renaldo .... Rick Battaglia
Geoffrey of Bouillon .... Philippe Hersent

While it's not very chic to find something good to say about the rash of Italo spec films seen this side recently, the fact is that of number of them have actually fulfilled their corny ad promises of gaudy, if primitive, cinematic excitement. In other words, within the limitations of the genre they can be successful. However, "The Mighty Crusaders" is a lethargic, stilted film with practically nothing to recommend it for any audience.

The confused tale, with a cast of tens, purports to recount how the Crusaders finally captured Jerusalem in the 11th Century. Seems all they had to do was put a couple of wobbly ladders against the walls, climb up, knock a few heads together and take over. Filling out the narrative is a tentative love affair between a crusading knight and the warrior-daughter of the King of Persia. Her penchant for donning armor and joining the battle results in the affair's tragic denouement: her lover, not recognizing her under all the tinplate, runs her through with his sword in the heat of the climatic battle. How's that for irony?

Performances by Francisco Rabal, as the knight, and Sylva Koscina, as the princess, are no better than the material. Color and camerawork are so-so. The English dubbed voices are hollow and often disembodied, but the arch dialog is sometimes good for a laugh. ***Anby.***

Le Temps Du Ghetto
(The Time of the Ghetto)
(FRENCH—DOCUMENTARY)

Paris, Sept. 25.

Films De La Pleiade release of Pierre Braunberger production. Written and directed by Frederic Rossif with additional commentary writing by Madeleine Chaptal; additional camera work, Marcel Fradetal; editor, Suzanne Baron. Preemed in Paris. Running time, **82 MINS.**

Pic is not just another mounting of the Warsaw Ghetto footage. Presumably only a small part of this footage has been seen in other films of this type. Painstaking research has unearthed enough to be able to show a more rounded picture of the infamous episode of 1943.

The herding into the Ghetto is depicted and then the daily life. It shows the attempts at first of trying to make it a sort of slave city with its own laws and enforcement agencies. The moves by some leaders to subjugate their own peoples, in a misguided notion it might save them, are also shown as well as their falling into their own trap of eventually persecuting their people. (This could lead to censor problems.)

Growing horror and loss of most human traits when the only desires left is to survive, are brought out as well as the final evacuation and revolt and complete destruction of the Ghetto.

Narration is well spoken by Nadine Alari and Jacques Perrot and the testimonials in closeup by survivors also attest. This is a film worth special handling and is explicit and shattering in its effect. *Mosk.*

Le Miracle Des Loups
(The Miracles of the Wolves)
(FRENCH-COLOR-DYALISCOPE)

Paris, Sept. 19.

Pathe release of PAC-DAMA production. Stars Jean Marais, Rosanna Schiaffino; features Roger Hanin, Jean-Louis Barrault, Annie Anderson, Jean Marchat. Directed by Andre Hunebelle. Screenplay, Jean Halain, Pierre Foucaud, Hunebelle from the novel by Henry Dupuy-Mazuel; camera (Eastmancolor), Marcel Grignon; editor, Jean Feyte. At Paris, Paris. Running time, **130 MINS.**

Robert .... Jean Marais
Jeanne .... Rosanna Schiaffino
Louis XI .... Jean-Louis Barrault
Charles .... Roger Hanin
Catherine .... Annie Anderson
Eveque .... Jean Marchat

Aging but still agile Jean Marais again defends king and girl in this 16th century tale of political skullduggery in France. Leaning on pageant, talk and court intrigues, with a good core of action, it will probably be a good grosser here but is somewhat too static for overseas spots unless wordier scenes are drastically cut.

With the jousting scenes, swordplay and naive love episodes, the film could be useful for dualers on its neat color, scope and costume aspects. The hero saves his girl as well as his king from the clutches of a would-be revolutionary vassal.

Marais does all his own stunts and is impressive in the heroic posturing. Jean-Louis Barrault gives a bit more weight to the cast lineup as the wily king. A miracle is also rung in as the heroine is saved from the heavies by a group of ferocious wolves who do not touch her. Production values are good as are technical credits. *Mosk.*

Paris Blues

Expatriate Yank musicians and vacationing U.S. girls in pursuit of happiness and all that jazz on the Left Bank. Slim story given some novelty via offbeat execution. Strong marquee cast will aid. Has angles for, and needs, advertising.

Hollywood, Sept. 20.

United Artists release of Sam Shaw production. Stars Paul Newman, Joanne Woodward, Sidney Poitier. Features Louis Armstrong, Diahann Carroll. Directed by Martin Ritt. Screenplay, Walter Bernstein, Irene Kamp, Jack Sher, adapted by Lulla Rosenfeld from novel by Harold Flender; camera, Christian Matras; editor, Roger Dwyre; music, Duke Ellington; asst. director, Bernard Farrel. Reviewed at Goldwyn Studios, Sept. 20, '61. Running time, **98 MINS.**

Ram Bowen .... Paul Newman
Lillian Corning .... Joanne Woodward
Eddie Cook .... Sidney Poitier
Wild Man Moore .... Louis Armstrong
Connie Lampson .... Diahann Carroll
Michel Duvigne .... Serge Reggiani
Marie Seoul .... Barbara Laage
Rene Bernard .... Andre Luguet
Nicole .... Marie Versini

Rum's Band:
Drums .... Moustache
Piano .... Aaron Bridgers
Bass .... Guy Pederson
Pianist .... Maria Velasco
Gypsy Guitarist ...... Rober Blin
Pusher .... Helene Dieudonne
Ricardo .... Niko

Pennebaker (George Glass-Walter Seltzer) production, produced by Sam Shaw and directed by Martin Ritt, reflects to some extent in form and technique the influence of the restless young Paris cinema colony, the environment in which the film was shot. But incongruously conspicuous within its snappy, flashy veneer is an undernourished romantic drama of a rather traditional screen school. The upshot is a choppy, shallow and discordant picture in which story runs a poor and distant second to style.

Though rich in marquee weight, the United Artists release may be a spotty attraction. It figures, for example, to fare better domestically in urban than in rural areas and in the North than in the South. The reaction of the Negro audience will be a factor. While this is likely to be largely favorable, since the film significantly erases some of the traditional color barrier of Hollywood product, it also might arouse some passive criticism from more radical quarters, where it may be felt that a potentially bold interracial theme has been abortively handled and cautiously diluted for mass consumption.

The Jack Sher-Irene Kamp-Walter Bernstein screenplay, based on a novel by Harold Flender, relates the romantic experiences of two expatriate U.S. jazz musicians (Paul Newman and Sidney Poitier) and two American girls (Joanne Woodward and Diahann Carroll) on a two-week vacation fling in Paris. The men fall in love with the girls, then must weigh their philosophies and careers against their amour. One decides to return to the U.S., the other remains in France.

Crux of the picture's failure is the screenplay's failure to bring any true identity to any of these four characters. As a result, their relationships are vague and superficial. Furthermore, except for sporadic interludes, none of the four players can achieve clarity, arouse sympathy or sustain concern. This is especially disappointing in view of the acknowledged calibre of performers such as Newman, Poitier and Miss Woodward.

The film is notable for Duke Ellington's moody, stimulating jazz score. The music is likely to seem just too obtrusive and dissonant for more conservative tastes, but there is no denying its importance as a driving factor in the sluggish dramatic proceedings and its intrinsic value as a jazz work. There are, however, scenes when the drama itself actually takes a back seat to the music, with unsatisfactory results insofar as dialog is concerned. Along the way there are several full-fledged passages of superior Ellingtonia such as "Mood Indigo" and "Sophisticated Lady," and Louis Armstrong is on hand for one flamboyant interlude of hot jazz.

Christian Matras' camera work is admirable for its artistic scrutiny of the Paris scene, especially several slow, sweeping panoramic shots and a number of strikingly composed interior scenes. As in most new wave films, a great deal of attention is given to faces in the crowd and fleeting impressions of objects and places, and director Ritt has attempted to duplicate that flavor in one or two scenes with his principals that have an almost improvisational aura.

Alexander Trauner's art direction faithfully conveys the character of the locale—artsy-craftsy, cluttered, Left Bankrupt. Roger Dwyre's editing is competent, Jo de Bretagne's sound clear. The picture has two strong supporting performances by Serge Reggiani and Barbara Laage.   *Tube.*

Deja Que Los Perros Ladren
(CHILEAN)
Santiago, Sept. 17.
Atlas Films release of Guido Vallejos production for Producine. Direction and screenplay by Naum Kramerenco. Camera, Ricardo Younis; music, Tito Le der Reviewed at Gina Pacifico. Running time, 87 MINS.
Father .... Ruben Sotocon
Mother .... Rakuel Luquer
Son .... Hector Noguera
Minister .... Roberto Parada
Editor .... Rafael Frontaura

This adaptation of a stage hit by Sergio Vodanovic adhered too closely to the original in its screenplay and Naum Kramarenco's direction also did little to remove legit flavor. Story deals with graft in government circles that triggers a father-son conflict. The son, unable to find a cause to believe in, gives in to environment's corruption but returns to the straight and narrow path thanks to a stand by the older generation which shows him that there decency and honesty are still worth fighting for.

Acting level is reasonable, with a good performance by Ruben Sotocon (Father).

Pic's importance on a local level is its professional approach. Technical credits are a considerable improvement on previous Chilean features, particularly Ricardo Younis' competent black and white lensing.

Filmed in 27 days at a cost of $40,000, "Deja que los Perros Ladren" (Let the Dogs Bark) stands a fair chance to recoup investment on local market. Foreign chances are limited.   *Chile.*

La Morte-Saison Des Amours
(The Dead Season of Loves)
(FRENCH)
Paris, Sept. 26.
Cocinor release of Jad Films production. Stars Francoise Arnoul, Daniel Gelin, Francoise Prevost, Pierre Vaneck. Directed by Pierre Kast. Screenplay, Kast, Alain Aptekman; camera, Sacha Vierny; editor, Yannick Bellon. At Pantheon, Paris. Running time, 100 MINS.
Genevieve .... Francoise Arnoul
Jacques .... Daniel Gelin
Francoise .... Francoise Prevost
Sylvain .... Pierre Vaneck

Two married couples have criss-cross affairs which end with one of the wives going off with the two men. Talky, mannered treatment leaves out any shock values and this is mainly an obscure bet at best abroad.

One couple is composed of a self-dramatizing writer who has run dry after one book and his mythomaniacal wife and the other of a youngish diplomat and his dry, hard wife. Both couples cheat on each other and then go for a settlement with the writer's wife getting both men and the diplomat's spouse the land and the running of it from her hubby.

Thesps are adequate but the vague and basically feckless and vapid characters soon wear thin, and this flaky, elegant attempt at a comedy of morals falls flat. Too much off-screen commentary and static direction also lose it the needed verve insight and insouciance to make it as impertinent as intended.

A pre-war pic of Ernst Lubitsch, "Design for Living" (Par), also had one woman deserving two men, but it had the wit and comedic balance to bring it off as a sprightly look at sophisticated mores while this pic is much too verbose and self consciously quaint to have it acceptable. It has mainly its thematic handle for offshore chances.   *Mosk.*

Forbid Them Not

Worthwhile documentary study of the young blind. Suitable for theatrical twin-billing, tv pubservice programming or educational exhibition.

Hollywood, Sept. 21.
Norman Kaplan and Associates (William A. Fraker, Robert L. Kimble, James C. Robinson) production. No character credits. Cast includes Michael Cole, Jean Gale, Patti O'Neil, John Ehrin, Herb Niccolls, John Beers, Ann Dashner, Alex Gal. Directed and screenplay by Kimble; camera, Fraker; editor, Kimble; music, Richard Berres; narrated by Jose Ferrer. Reviewed at 20th-Fox Studios, Sept. 21, '61. Running time, 67 MINS.

"Forbid Them Not" is an important and affecting examination of the sightless school-age child and his relationship with the "seeing" society prone to misunderstand and underestimate his capabilities. Essentially a documentary, but with an irresistible twist of drama, this physically modest but socially invaluable film, produced by Norman Kaplan, exec director of the Foundation for the Junior Blind, is certain to be an instructive and inspirational experience for all who see it.

Just who will see it is a moot point at the moment, for the picture has no theatrical release, but there is no question that it will soon be seen to advantage by people all over the world. Though the film lacks the commercial magnetism to draw patrons in sufficient numbers to theatres, art or otherwise, it can easily and effectively be inserted at the bottom half of a twin bill, and is ideally suitable for public service programming on television or for 16mm exhibition in the library-school and non-profit welfare circuit.

Written and directed by Robert L. Kimble, the film, some four years in the making, would have cost in the neighborhood of $100,000, but only $214 actually came out of the production team's pocket, thanks to the cooperation of the motion picture industry. The drama deals with the plight of a lad (Michael Cole) rendered blind following an accident, and his abortive attempts to adjust until he is taken in by the Foundation, an L.A. association which Kaplan hopes can be duplicated in other communities for whom this film will be exposed.

Both as drama and documentary, the picture has its shortcomings, to be sure, and these are essentially a result of the mixed concept itself, which can be pretty tricky in execution. The first half of the picture is primarily a drama, focusing on the boy and his personal tragedy. But when the film veers into the Foundation and its good work, the first person story is relegated to the background, giving the entire project a lopsided effect. Then, too, there is a tendency to get carried away with flowery inspirational prose and complicated imagery that make the picture, which should be light, direct and simple, a bit heavy in spots. But these are only minor shreds in a rich canvas.

The film's real punch lies in the fact that its star is not just acting —he is truly blind. That makes it a genuine emotional experience, and it will cause a great many seeing eyes to cloud over with tears. Master Cole does an excellent job in the role, and there is competent assistance from Jean Gale as his mother and Patti O'Neil as his sister. Also on view are Kaplan and many of the youngsters at the Foundation.

Most of the narration, written by Phillip Dunne, is crisp and to the point. Narrator is Jose Ferrer, wherein the producers have been fortunate in obtaining the services of one of the richest, most expressive "voices" in the business. Richard Berres' music adds dramatic impact. William A. Fraker's lenswork is first-rate, especially in a shattering carnival sequence. Kimble's editing is satisfactory.   *Tube.*

Le Puits Aux Trois Verites
(The Well of Three Truths)
(FRENCH)
Paris, Sept. 26.
Gaumont release of Caravelle-SNEG-Sicilia Film production. Stars Michele Morgan, Jean-Claude Brialy, Catherine Spaak; features Scilla Gabel, Jacques-Henri Duval. Directed by Francois Villiers. Screenplay, Remo Foriani, Henri Jeanson, Jean Canolle, Villiers from the novel by Jean-Jacques Gautier; camera, J. Robin; editor, Christian Gaudin. At Ambassade-Gaumont, Paris. Running time, 95 MINS.
Renee .... Michele Morgan
Laurent .... Jean-Claude Brialy
Daniele .... Catherine Spaak
Model .... Scilla Gabel
Man .... Jacques-Henri Duval

Youngish mother and her self-dramatizing daughter court tragedy via a youthful Bohemian painter. Surface characters and obvious, evasive unfoldment slant this as "soap opera," French style.

The mother is the chic Michele Morgan who is about to give in to a feckless charm boy, the painter in question, when her daughter shows up and love blossoms. Pair marry and come to live with mother. Then the boy gets out of hand, still yens the mother, and finally drives his wife to suicide.

Film is too pat in its characters and progression and it is hard to see why the irritating painter,

played too broadly by Jean-Claude Brialy, is so irresistible to women. The rest of the cast is also one-dimensional and, if technical credits are good, the picture is directed fairly listlessly with gloss taking the place of insight and feeling. *Mosk.*

Le Monocle Noir
(The Black Monocle)
(FRENCH)
Paris, Sept. 16.

Pathe release of Orex Films production. Stars Paul Meurisse, Bernard Blier, Elga Anderson; features, Pierre Blanchar, Marie Dubois. Directed by Georges Lautner. Screenplay, Jacques Robert, Pierre Laroche from a novel by Remy; camera, Maurice Fellous; editor, Michel mann. Art Director, Hector del Campo. David. At Balzac, Paris. Running time, 100 MINS.
Dromard .... Paul Meurisse
Martha .... Elga Anderson
Marquis .... Pierre Blanchard
Torunemire .... Bernard Blier
Catherine .... Marie Dubois

Spy story about a group of different nationality undercover people tracking down a neo-Nazi group is told tongue-in-cheek. Comedics and suspense grip only at intervals. Outlook overseas but so-so.

A half mad French nobleman is awaiting the supposedly still alive leader of the Nazi Youth. French, German and Russo spies are about but the ex-Nazi never shows for it seems he had really been dead and used by a hireling for personal prestige.

Director Georges Lautner does an acceptable job of keeping suspense alive for the first half but then loses control and gets heavyhanded at the end. Acting is acceptable with Paul Meurisse, sporting a black monocle, adding an elegant air to the proceedings as a French agent. Technical credits are good. *Mosk.*

Raising The Wind
(BRITISH-COLOR)

Cheerful comedy aimed at "Carry On" customers and put over by same production team and many of the "Carry On" players. Agreeable relaxation for middlebrow audiences.

London, Sept. 7.

Anglo Amalgamated release of a Peter Rogers production. Stars James Robertson Justice, Leslie Phillips, Sidney James, Paul Massie, Liz Fraser, Eric Barker. Produced by Peter Rogers. Directed by Gerald Thomas; original story, screenplay and music, Bruce Montgomery; editor, John Shirley; camera, Alan Hume. At Plaza Theatre, London. Running Time: 91 MINS.
Sir Benjamin..James Robertson Justice
Mervyn .... Leslie Phillips
Sid .... Sidney James
Malcolm .... Paul Massie
Harold .... Kenneth Williams
Morgan Rutherford .... Eric Barker
Miranda .... Liz Fraser
Jill .... Jennifer Jayne
Mrs. Deveens .... Esma Cannon
Sir John .... Geoffrey Keen
Alex .... Jimmy Thompson
Taxi Driver .... David Lodge
Harry .... Lance Percival

Peter Rogers and Gerald Thomas continue their successful boxoffice formula for Anglo Amalgamated and much the same team, before and behind the cameras, that have hit a long winning streak with the "Carry On" series. They again carry on in search of yocks with "Raising the Wind." The situations and gags are strung together on a thin, but sufficient story line, and exhibitions who have struck oil with the "Carry On" frolics should cut themselves in on this one.

Film concerns the adventures of some impecunious students at the London Academy of Music & Arts who are striving for the plum scholastic award of the year. That's about the lot plotwise except that one of them, when under the influence of hooch, finds he has sold a corny pop song to a couple of sharp publishers. This puts him in a spot with the academy and he and his pals nearly go nuts trying to raise enough cash to buy back the ditty.

Situations and dialog are fairly credible but garner a steady flow of yocks. There's the absent-minded professor, the deaf landlady, the irascible professor and various other stock characters all dropped lightheartedly into the loose fabric.

Where these "Carry On" films score consistently is that all the roles, even cameos, are played by expert performers and trained funny men. The result, briskly directed by Gerald Thomas and in color, is lively entertainment for the masses. Funniest situation is when Kenneth Williams, a cocky, supercilious student, conducts the orch for his examination.

James Robertson Justice bulldozes his way magnificently through the role of the hot-tempered professor and Eric Barker gives a remarkably amusing study of an absent-minded one. The main students are pleasant young people, except Williams, who skillfully repeats his characteristic performance of slightly mincing snobbery but which is now over-familiar.

Leslie Phillips is effective in a major role and Liz Fraser supplies her usual brand of come-hither sex appeal, though this time disguised behind some unlikely serious looking spectacles. Jennifer Jayne, a newcomer, also provides some pleasant femme interest and looks to be a discovery. Jimmy Thompson and Paul Massie also register as students.

Among others who participate in the proceedings are Sid James and Lance Percival as the bent music publishers, Esma Cannon as the deaf landlady, David Lodge, Geoffrey Keen, George Woodbridge, Brian Oulton and Victor Maddern.

The London Sinfonia orchestra plays Bruce Montgomery's score admirably and also does valiant work in the visual orchestral sequences.

This entry is bright amusement for those desiring a couple of hours' escapism. Whether or not the formula is beginning to wear thinnish can be answered only by the b.o. takings and it is unlikely that Anglo Amalgamated has much to worry on that score. *Rich.*

Secret Of Deep Harbor

Heavyhanded waterfront crime meller for cautious lower berthing.

Hollywood, Sept. 26.

United Artists release of Robert E. Kent production. Stars Ron Foster, Merry Anders, Barry Kelley. Directed by Edward L. Cahn. Screenplay, Owen Harris, Wells Root, based on novel, "I Cover the Waterfront," by Max Miller; camera. Gilbert Warrenton; editor, Kenneth Crane; music, Richard LaSalle; sound, Stanley Cooley; assistant director, Herbert S. Greene. Reviewed at Goldwyn Studios, Sept. 26, '61. Running time, 70 MINS.
Skip Hanlon .... Ron Foster
Milo Fowler .... Barry Kelley
Janey Fowler .... Merry Anders
Barney Hanes .... Norman Alden
Travis .... James Seay
Rick Correll .... Grant Richards
Frank Miner .... Ralph Manza
Mama Miller .... Billie Bird
Rita .... Elaine Walker
Doctor .... Max Mellinger

"Secret of Deep Harbor" is a ludicrously-plotted, ketchup-spattered, waterfront crime melodrama. The Robert E. Kent production for United Artists release is undistinguished secondary fare and, accordingly, should be carefully programmed so as not to burden exhibition of grade A product, especially in situations where more discriminating audiences gather for product they cannot obtain for free in their living rooms. This is simply one of the lesser efforts of the competent "B" filmmaking tandem of Kent and director Edward L. Cahn.

The Owen Harris-Wells Root scenario, from Max Miller's tome, "I Cover the Waterfront" (first filmed under UA banner in 1933), traces the grim story of a waterfront reporter (Ron Foster) who falls in love with the daughter of an old salt (Barry Kelley) who is smuggling mobsters out of the country for a crime syndicate. When the reporter exposes old dad, there is the usual romantic misunderstanding, and it all winds up in a warehouse, with the two men battling it out in a spitting, shooting and bloodletting match ("go ahead . . . try to shoot as straight as you can spit," grunts the old codger after he is out-expectorated by the younger man) more or less umpired by the girl. Obviously what the climax needed was more polish and less spit.

Foster, Kelley and Miss Anders are now veterans of the Kent-Cahn finishing school of one-week-at-a-shot melodrama, but can do nothing substantial with these roles. Neither can Norman Alden, James Seay, Grant Richards, Ralph Manza and Billie Bird, all momentarily prominent in support. Art, photographic, musical and technical contributions are dispatched adequately by those listed in the above section. *Tube.*

Susan Slade
(COLOR)

Another in the run of recent Warner releases dealing with the repercussions of illegitimate birth. A contrived soaper-meller. Slick production and a well-balanced cast spotlighting Connie Stevens will have to carry the b.o. burden.

Hollywood, Sept. 26.

Warner Bros. release of Delmer Daves production. Stars Troy Donahue, Connie Stevens, Dorothy McGuire, Lloyd Nolan, Brian Aherne, Grant Williams. Directed and screenplay by Daves, from novel by Doris Hume; camera (Technicolor), Lucien Ballard; editor, William Ziegler; art director, Leo K. Kuter; music, Max Steiner; sound, Stanley Jones; assistant director, Russell Llewellyn. Reviewed at the studio, Sept. 26, '61. Running time, 116 MINS.
Hoyt Brecker .... Troy Donahue
Susan Slade .... Connie Stevens
Leah Slade .... Dorothy McGuire
Roger Slade .... Lloyd Nolan
Stanton Corbett .... Brian Aherne
Conn White .... Grant Williams
Marian Corbett .... Natalie Schafer
Dr. Fain .... Kent Smith
Wells Corbett .... Bert Convy
Slim .... Guy Wilkerson

A May-December cast of handsome (a) young rising players and (b) seasoned veterans assembled by triple-threat man Delmer Daves will have to carry "Susan Slade" at the boxoffice. Though slickly produced and attractively peopled, the Warner Bros. release weighs in as little more than a plodding and predictable soap opera.

It is, however, a telling showcase for Connie Stevens, whose turn it is (just as it was Troy Donahue's turn in "Parrish," Diane McBain's in "Claudelle Inglish") to step up out of Warner Bros. stable and prance like a true thoroughbred.

The screenplay by Daves, who also produced and directed as is his custom, is from the novel by Doris Hume. Yarn has a chicken way of evading its real issues by ushering in devastatingly convenient melodramatic swerves at key moments. Miss Stevens enacts the innocent, virginal daughter of a devoted family man and engineer (Lloyd Nolan) who returns with his brood to luxury in the States after 10 years of service on a project in remote Chile. The girl promptly falls madly in love and finds herself with child but without husband when the irresponsible lad, a compulsive mountain climber, gets himself killed climbing Mt. McKinley (because it is there).

The family then tries a fake by moving to Guatemala, where Nolan dies and his wife (Dorothy McGuire) supposedly bears the child. The story returns to the U.S.A. and boils down to the inevitable triangle. Who is worthy of Miss Stevens love—junior tycoon Bert Convy or poor stable operator Troy Donahue? As anyone over 13 knows instantly, rich boys are shallow fellows and poor chaps always get the girl in the movies. "Susan Slade" is no exception to this golden rule. When the truth comes out that Susan slept here, Convy hightails it and Donahue (whose first novel has just been accepted for publication, the last straw in contrivance) wins the hackneyed, one-sided contest.

Pretty Miss Stevens comes on like gangbusters, and Lucien Ballard's misty, flattering close-up photography is her ally from start to finish. Donahue gives a wooden performance. Veterans Nolan and Miss McGuire, in characters that rank as the most understanding and unselfish parents of all time, emote with sincerity. Convy and Grant Williams, latter as the peak-a-boob, are good-looking newcomers and adequate actors. Brian Aherne, Natalie Schafer, Kent Smith and Guy Wilkerson round out the cast satisfactorily.

The film was lensed in dazzlingly scenic places such as the Carmel coastline and San Francisco. Leo K. Kuter's art direction and Dave's appreciation of visual beauty brings out the best of such places. Editor William Ziegler seems to have done his best to enliven an essentially lethargic and painstaking drama. Max Steiner's romantic score, heavy on the strings, is typical of the music that accompanies Daves' screen projects. Howard Shoup's costumes range from full-dress attire to casual outdoor garments for cool climes. The players look properly insulated against the weather and decorated for the event. *Tube.*

Snobs
(FRENCH)
Paris, Oct. 2.

UFA-Comacico release of Balzac Films production. With Francis Blanche, Veronique Nordey, Gerard Hoffmann, Jacques Dufilho, Max Montavon, Elina Labourdette, Noel Roquevert. Directed by Jean-Pierre Mocky. Screenplay, Mocky with dialog by Alain Moury; camera, Marcel Weiss; editor, Marguerite Renoir. Preemed in Paris. Running time, **85 MINS.**

Boss .... Francis Blanche
Girl .... Veronique Nordey
Courtin .... Gerard Hoffmann
Yachtsman .... Jacques Dufilho
General .... Noel Roquevert
Wife .... Elina Labourdette

Young director Jean-Pierre Mocky shows a lot of rancor against "the Establishment" in France. He has somewhat overloaded this satirical opus with heavyhanded parody which does not always bring out the irony he seeks. Some boxoffice value in France but release is dubious for export.

The director of a dairy cooperative drowns in a vat and four of the veepees start a campaign for getting his spot. This leads to a look at the corruption, pettiness and sordidness in just about everybody in town except a young girl who has a passion for one of the four, who finally gets the job.

Gritty emphasis on balding men, homosexuals, scatterbrained hostesses, suspected perverts of all kinds and shafts at retired army men, the Boy Scouts and other things are included.

Director Mocky does have something to say but leaps on the abuse. Stolid approach dulls many episodes. It is technically good but direction uneven. *Mosk.*

Pirates Of Tortuga
(C'SCOPE—COLOR)

This time Morgan the Pirate, the villian, is pursued and destroyed by a romantic British naval officer. Lightweight, fanciful corsair epic, fundamentally for the kiddies. Mild prospects.

Hollywood, Sept. 28.

Twentieth-Fox release of Sam Katzman production. Stars Ken Scott. Leticia Roman, Dave King, John Richardson, Rafer Johnson, Robert Stephens. Directed by Robert D. Webb. Screenplay, Melvin Levy, Jesse L. Lasky Jr., Pat Silver, based on story by Levy; camera (De Luxe), Ellis W. Carter; editor, Hugh S. Fowler; art directors, Jack Martin Smith. George Van Marter; music, Paul Sawtell, Bert Shefter; sound, E. Clayton Ward. Frank W. Moran; assistant director, Jack R. Berne. Reviewed at the studio, Sept. 28, '61. Running time, **97 MINS.**

Bart .... Ken Scott
Meg .... Leticia Roman

Pee Wee .... Dave King
Percy .... John Richardson
John Gammel .... Rafer Johnson
Morgan .... Robert Stephens
Phoebe .... Rachel Stephens
Montbars .... Stanley Adams
Sir Thomas Modyford....Edgar Barrier
Reggie .... James Forrest
Randolph .... Patrick Sexton
Bonnett .... Arthur Gould-Porter
Lola .... Hortense Petra
Kipper .... Malcolm Cassell
Fielding .... Maxwell Reed
Ringose .... Alan Caillou

"Pirates of Tortuga" is strictly an escape entertainment, a broad, thoroughly implausible romance-adventure epic calculated to cater to the uncomplicated tastes of juveniles and only the most easygoing of adults. The 20th-Fox release should find a niche for itself in kiddie matinees and similarly low-pressure situations, but its prospects as a principal feature are mild, at best. Perhaps the most favorable circumstance aiding the Sam Katzman production is the relative scarcity in recent times of the buccaneer picture.

Many moppets are liable to be confused by one facet of the Melvin Levy-Jesse L. Lasky Jr.-Pat Silver screenplay. Having just recently been exposed to a heroic variation of "Morgan the Pirate" with Joe Levine's Steve Reeves, they may be astonished to find an entirely different Morgan here, a villainous wretch of a fellow enacted by Robert Stephens. Hero in this instance is a British captain (Ken Scott) who has been dispatched to Tortuga to destroy Morgan and his crew of blackguards. The job is accomplished, but not until Scott and his men have overcome several outbursts of predictable treachery and a Liza Doolittle-Henry Higgins-style romance involving a Cockney stowaway (Leticia Roman).

Scott does a capable job, except for his artificially robust outbursts of laughter at Miss Roman's peculiar antics. She is guilty of consistent overacting, although apparently encouraged by director Robert D. Webb. Video personality Dave King adds a light, comic note to the proceedings, then surprisingly bites the dust in the climactic skirmish. Adequate top support is etched by Rafer Johnson, John Richardson, Robert Stephens, Rachel Stephens, James Forrest, Stanley Adams, Edgar Barrier and Patrick Sexton.

The back lot at 20th acceptably passes for the Caribbean area through the accomplished art direction of Jack Martin Smith and George Van Marter and De Luxe Color photography of Ellis W. Carter. Journeyman services to the production are also contributed by editor Hugh S. Fowler and composers Paul Sawtell and Bert Shefter. *Tube.*

Les Lions Sont Laches
(The Lions Are Loose)
(FRENCH—DYALISCOPE)
Paris, Oct. 3.

Gaumont release of Franco London, SNEG, Vides production. Stars Danielle Durrieux, Michele Morgan, Lino Ventura, Jean-Claude Brialy, Claudia Cardinale. Directed by Henri Verneuil. Screenplay, France Roche, Michel Audiard from the novel by Nicole; camera, Christian Matras; editor, Borys Lewin. At Colisee, Paris. Running time, **110 MINS.**

Albertine .... Claudia Cardinale
Cecile .... Michele Morgan
Marie-Laure .... Danielle Darrieux
Andre .... Lino Ventura
Didier .... Jean-Claude Brialy

Helene .... Denise Provence
Robert .... Darry Cowl

Laborious libertine comedy takes a well stacked, pretty provincial divorcee and sets her in the middle of the futile, petty Parisian high life called the "Tout Paris." With wit and points mainly local, this appears more a home item than a foreign bet. It does have some names in its high powered cast for U.S. attention.

Girl from the sticks becomes the prey of (1) a self indulgent writer who turns out to be important in the bedroom, and (2) the mistress of a society doctor who is ready to marry her.

Claudia Cardinale is the Italo looker who here essays her first big French role. She is pert and healthy but is not called on to emote much. Oldtime thesps Michele Morgan and Danielle Darrieux play the friend and snob respectively, while Lino Ventura as the doctor and Jean-Claude Brialy as the writer round out the cast.

Direction is somewhat listless and never gets the bite and edge into it to make it either a satire, drama or sleek situation comedy. *Mosk.*

La Reveur
(The Dreamer)
Paris, Sept. 19.

Ludmila Vlasto presentation of a two-act comedy by Jean Vauthier. Staged by Georges Vitaly; sets, Felix Labisse. Stars Jacques Dufilho, Claude Nicot; features, Monique Delaroche, Paul Gay. Opened Sept. 15, '61, at the Theatre La Bruyere, Paris; $3 top.

Simon .... Jacques Dufilho
Georges .... Claude Nicot
Laurette .... Monique Delaroche
Manasse .... Paul Gay

What might be called an intellectual farce, "Le Reveur" ("The Dreamer") is in the nature of the avant garde theatre of Iionesco and Beckett. Its shafts and points are only intermittently effective and it lacks the clarity for Broadway chances, but might do for off-Broadway because of its theme and treatment.

The title character is a fey young man who lives off his mother. One day he goes to see his high - pressure radio producer friend, and is taken by the latter's wife. A goofy situation develops as the producer's mistress keeps calling on the phone and the vague hero tries to declare his love to the wife.

Much of it is off-target and verbose but it does at times bite satirically into the commercial man who twists everything to his needs as well as slapping the wrist of the art-for-art's-sake types. Though well played and directed, this seems more like an expanded revue sketch than a stage play. *Mosk.*

Badjao
(FILIPINO)

Hollywood, Sept. 27.

Parallel Film Distributors release of Manuel de Leon production. Stars Rosa Rosal, Tony Santos. Directed by Lamberto V. Avellana. Screenplay, Rolf Bayer; camera, Mike Accion; editor, Gregorio Carballo; art director, Teody Carmona; music, F. Buencamino Jr.; sound, July Hidalgo. Reviewed at NT&T screening room, Sept. 27, '61. Running time, **100 MINS.**

Bal-Amai .... Rosa Rosal
Hassan .... Tony Santos
Asid .... Leroy Salvador
Datu Tahil .... Joseph de Cordova
Jikiri .... Vic Silayan
Pearl Dealer .... Oscar Keesee
Badjao Chief .... Pedro Faustino
Chief's Bodyguard .... Tony Dantes

The way of life of the sea-roving Badjao people of Sulu, southernmost province of the Philippines, is the foundation upon which this lively and meaningful drama of pride and passion has been constructed by several creative people in the budding Filipino film industry. The film, a multi-award winner created and executed largely by the same talent that fashioned "Cry Freedom."

Yet, for all its intrinsic value, both as an edifying academic examination of the customs and lore of these faraway peoples and as pure screen drama, the Manuel de Leon production is a dubious commodity for the U.S.-Canada market. For whatever limited response the picture is capable of eliciting, it will be necessary to impress upon art house audiences (its natural market sphere) that the film sheds light on the behavior and conflicts of primitive, but rational people in a remote corner of the world, and does so in emotionally moving and entertaining terms.

Romantic nucleus of Rolf Bayer's screenplay is but another variation on the well-exploited Romeo-Juliet situation. The son of the chieftain of the wandering, ocean-dwelling Badjaos must abandon his beloved tribe to win the hand of the niece of the leader of the land-inhabiting Moros, or Tausugs, who regard the Badjaos as their inferiors. After making the adjustment, with some difficulty and personal sacrifice, the hero is called upon to utilize his inherent ability as a Badjao pearl-diver for the monetary gain of his new people. Unable to thus live between two contradictory worlds, he returns with his wife to his nomadic tribe, and sails off.

The enchanting native rituals and ceremonies of these two tribes, the pagan Badjaos and the Moslem Morqs, are richly and expressively captured through Lamberto V. Avellana's skillful direction. Additionally, there is great texture and clarity in Mike Accion's photography, much of it conveying almost a National Geographic quality. The two leads, Rosa Rosal and Tony Santos, emote with power and conviction. *Tube.*

King of Kings
(70M SUPER-TECHNIRAMA TECHNICOLOR)

Samuel Bronston's highpowered re-do of Gospel. A big boxoffice picture, worldwide.

Metro release of Samuel Bronston production. Costars Jeffry Hunter, Siobhan McKenna, Robert Ryan, Hurd Hatfield, Ron Randell, Viveca Lindfors, Rita Gam, Carmen Sevilla, Brigid Balzan, Harry Guardino, Rip Torn, Frank Thring, Guy Rolfe. Screenplay by Philip Yordan. Directed by Nicholas Ray. Camera (Technicolor), Franz F. Planer, Milton Krasner, Manuel Berenguer; sets & costumes, George Wakhevitch; editor, Harold Kress; music, Miklos Rozsa. Previewed Sunday Oct. 8 at Loew's State, N.Y. Running time, **168 MINS.**

Jesus Christ	Jeffrey Hunter
Mary	Siobhan McKenna
Pontius Pilate	Hurd Hatfield
Lucius	Ron Randell
Claudia	Viveca Lindfors
Herodias	Rita Gam
Mary Magdalene	Carmen Sevilla
Salome	Brigid Bazlen
Barabbas	Harry Guardino
Judas	Rip Torn
Herod Antipas	Frank Thring
Caiphas	Guy Rolfe
Nicodemus	Maurice Marsac
Herod	Gregoire Aslan
Peter	Royal Dano
Balthazar	Edric Connor
John the Baptist	Robert Ryan
Camel Driver	George Coulouris
General Pompey	Conrado San Martin
Joseph	Gerard Tichy
Young John	Jose Antonio
Good Thief	Luis Prendes
Burly Man	David Davies
Caspar	Jose Nicto
Matthew	Ruben Rojo
Madman	Fernando Sancho
Thomas	Michael Wager
Joseph of Arimathea	Felix de Powes
Melchior	Adriano Rimoldi
Bad Thief	Barry Keegan
Simon of Cyrene	Rafael Luis Calvo
Andrew	Tino Barrero
Blind Man	Francisco Moran

Carefully, reverently and beautifully made this retelling of the ministry and agony of Jesus Christ is a major motion picture by any standard—as a production, as a script, for masterly management of scenes by its director, and as an entertainment with the stature and stamina of a roadshow. For ordinary purposes and people it surely steers a tactful course between Christian and Jew, dogma and drama.

Running 168 minutes, filmed in Technicolor 70m Super-Technirama, "King of Kings" has wisely substituted characterizations for orgies. Nicholas Ray has brooded long and wisely upon the meaning of his meanings, has planted plenty of symbols along the path yet avoided the banalities of religious calendar art. The total screening session contrasts with the three hours and 30 minutes of "Ben-Hur." This will make it easier on theatre managers and les derrieres.

The sweep of the story presents a panorama of the conquest of Judea and its persistent rebelliousness, against which the implication of Christ's preachments assume, to pagan Roman overlords, the reek of sedition. All of this is rich in melodrama, action, battle and clash. But author Philip Yordan astutely uses the bloodthirsty Jewish patriots, unable to think except in terms of violence, as telling counterpoint to the Messiah's love-one-another creed.

It is because "King of Kings" is inherently a powerful sermon contained in a melodrama that its boxoffice prospects are so good. There is excitement and there is compassion. Foremost among the players must be Jeffrey Hunter as the Saviour. Did he not carry conviction one may only imagine the embarrassment. But he does come remarkably close to being ideal. Here, of course, it is necessary to recognize the almost insuperable difficulties in casting and directing the role. There are more concepts of Christ than there are artists—ranging all the way from the brutal realism in a Mexican chapel to the blonde, almost choreographic vision of 20th Century modernity.

Hunter's blue orbs and auburn bob (wig, of course) are strikingly pictorial. The director and his cameraman, Franz F. Planer at the outset, later Milton Krasner and Manuel Berenguer, have obtained very tender and touching moments. The handling of the Sermon on the Mount which dominates the climax of the first part before intermission is wonderfully skillful in working masses of people into an alternation of faith and skepticism while cross-cutting personal movement among them of the Saviour and his disciples. The uneven terrain, rocky and barren in the foreground, yet with a broad vista beyond, captures and incorporates the sense of both history and [illegible]try. Of course, those in back[illegible]ound could hardly hear the sermon, sans microphones.

There is sure to be some denominational discussion of the miracles. These present an innate difficulty for the modern audience. Christian teaching is that not Christ alone but his followers in great numbers performed miracles during the early phase of the movement. The Yordan approach is camera-eye, what will photograph. This passes over the question of interior faith, from whence comes healings and presents the Saviour as having the cure in his hands and eyes and presence. One miracle is shown as a blind man shuffling along the street and accidentally colliding with the shadow of Jesus, the cure following without any act of faith whatever in the blind man, a sort of radioactivity kind of miracle. But these are questions for the religionists rather than the ticket-buying public. Suffice that Ray has respected reverence and taste.

Shrewdly selected excerpts from the Gospels have been telescoped into the Sermon on the Mount sequence. With the Beatitudes, the Lord's Prayer, and many a parable woven into a pattern of Christian doctrine, this tradepaper critic dares to forgive Yordan for the liberties, transitional devices and transpositions he has employed for he has been wonderfully faithful in spirit. Will all the clergy also forgive? One cannot guess.

The crucifixion has been photographed for the theatre screen on a variety of occasions, including recently in "Ben-Hur." As here handled the brutality of the punishment is not glossed over, and yet neither is the horror piled on, Latin fashion. The story-line is very successful in keeping the balance between Jewish zealotry, Roman severity, and the gentle (and little understood) gospel of universal brotherhood.

There are interesting touches during Christ's missionary, including the constant references to him as "Rabbi." (That may smite certain bigots rather hard.) It is made pictorially clear that crucifixion was routine in that day, the scene being a veritable orchard of crosses.

It will probably be remarked that "King of Kings" has no single scene comparable to the chariot race in "Ben-Hur." Against that are the mosaic of detail, the strong story-telling pace, the accumulation of performance values from the players. There is no scene-stealing but there are many scene-enriching performances. Siobhan McKenna as the Virgin Mary infuses a sort of strength-through-passivity, infinitely sad yet never surprised. The Irish actress and the director have been knowing indeed for Mary must meet the expectations of the Marians as well as the common run of spectators. She is close enough to the symbol at a million altars to satisfy (one presumes to think) the devout while contriving to be a recognizably warm, living woman. The Irish touch for the Jewish mother may have been one of the Bronston team's more inspired decisions.

When the Salome scene was shot at the Sevilla studios in Madrid in the summer of 1960 a great many protection shots were taken of the 16-year old Chicago schoolgirl, Brigid Bazlen, who had somewhat daringly been selected, it being her screen debut. The director's pains have paid off, with a suspected assist from film editor Harold Kress. To pun, they skirt the danger of the veils of opera. Actually the sequence is tightly controlled and Salome is a believable little itchibay. She's portrayed as a Biblical juvenile delinquent, who bellydances rather than jitterbugs. Entirely plausible, considering that she was the seed of the sensual Herodias (Rita Gam) and the product of the corrupt puppet court of her stepfather, Herod Antipas. Not a professional dancer, Miss Bazlen (she's the daughter of the Chicago gossip columnist, Maggie Daly) was able to seem precociously adept at bellydancing, thanks to the coaching of Betty Utey, who is Mrs. Ray.

Technicalities in the court, the royal kitchens, the streets of Jerusalem and the Judean villages all lend their usefulness to the unfoldment of the tale. George Wahhevitch rates the credit, and a major one it is, for sets and costumes. Music, too, plays a vital part as background and underscore for the physical action and the metaphysics, both. That's Miklos Rozsa's special bow.

Typically in a production of such immensity there are all sorts of wonderworkers behind scenes that do not get adequate notice. The special effects of Al C. Weldon and Lee LeBlanc should be remarked, though they cannot here be differentiated.

The spotlight must swing back to the producer, Samuel Bronston, who has made it big with this one. His associate producers are Alan Brown of the U.S. and Jaines Prades of Spain. (A considerable number of the production assistants were Spaniards.)

In the long cast "costarring" mention goes to 13 players. Of these the Misses McKenna, Gam and Bazlen have already been mentioned along with the Christ figure. Off-type for him is Robert Ryan as John the Baptist, and he makes an attractive character of the holy man who recognized the Redeemer on sight. The Spanish actress, Carmen Seville, is an effective Mary Magdalene, although the role is not fat.

For sheer villainy it is apparent that the Australian, Frank Thring, is the thing. He suggested as much when he played Pontias Pilate in "Ben-Hur." He's now seen as a kind of Jukes family potentate with strains of homicide, incest, superstition and plain nastiness. His old role of Pontius is played by Hurd Hatfield with a nice blend of aristocratic Roman boredom, ambition and detached amusement. He and his Claudia (Viveca Lindfors) are leaders of the career diplomacy set of their day. Their performances singly and jointly are always strong. It is one of Miss Lindfors' top exposures in some time.

There is something of a convention in melodramas of Scriptural origin of having one Roman commander with intimations of decency. This time the job belongs to Ron Randell. He is never converted but he is troubled. Meanwhile the actor impresses the viewer. The same may be said for the brutish, muscle-bound Barabbas of Harry Guardino, who makes a pretty good case that sedition frequently hurts only itself. The classic heel in Christendom, Judas Iscariot, has been written and is played by Rip Torn as a blundering boob seeking to test Christ's divinity quite as much as to betray him. (There are no 30 pieces of silver shown, a second significant omission along with the unseen head of John The Baptist.) Guy Rolfe is properly cowardly as the High Priest playing footsie with Rome.

Some special admiration may be owing to the dialog which compromises Scriptural and everyday speech with only one or two lines that fall falsely on the ear. Without having the verbiage count in hand as this review is written, it would seem probable that there is much more talk than is typical of epics, yet talkiness is avoided. In casting, the emphasis was on acting experience and it shows in the finished result.

The final tribute to "King of Kings" is not that it succeeds as spectacle. It does that, too. Rather it succeeds in touching the heart. Though everyone naturally knows the ending before it begins, there is surprising suspense.

In short, a big picture.

Land.

Town Without Pity

Rape and its repercussions in a German town, when the offenders are American GI's. Faulty direction fails to realize potential. But surface, provocative theme values for b.o. impetus.

Hollywood, Oct. 6.

United Artists release of Gottfried Reinhardt production. Stars Kirk Douglas. Directed by Reinhardt. Screenplay, Silvia Reinhardt, Georg Hurdalek, based on adaptation by Jan Lustig of Manfred Gregor's novel, "The Verdict"; camera, Kurt Hasse; editor, Hermann Haller; art director, Rolf Zehetbauer; music, Dimitri Tiomkin; sound, Helmut Ransch; asst. director, Eva-Ruth Ebner. Reviewed at Academy Awards Theatre, Oct. 6, '61. Running time, **112 MINS.**

Major Steve Garrett	Kirk Douglas
Major Jerome Pakenham	E. G. Marshall
Jim	Robert Blake

Bidle	Richard Jaeckel
Chuck	Frank Sutton
Joey	Mal Sondock
Inge	Barbara Rutting
Karin	Christine Kaufmann
Herr Steinhof	Hans Nielsen
Frau Steinhof	Karin Hardt
Trude	Ingrid van Bergen
Frank Borgmann	Gerhart Lippert
Mutter Borgmann	Eleanore van Hoogstraten
Dr. Urban	Max Haufler
Burgermeister	Siegfried Schurenberg

At face value, "Town Without Pity" appears to be a straight courtroom drama treatment of a gang rape case and its repercussions on a German community incensed over the fact that the rapists are American GI's and the victim a local girl. Obviously provocative, adult stuff that attracts attention, stirs controversy and stimulates attendance. But the Gottfried Reinhardt production is attempting to go much deeper than that, to probe into issues of human conduct at moments of stress, of human frailties impending the desired path of justice. In this it does not succeed and, in failing on its elevated thematic plane, it also betrays itself on the commercial level.

Being not the artful, lofty film it was intended to be, the Mirisch Co.-Gloria Films presentation, shot in Europe for United Artists release, will have to rely on its lesser sordid values for boxoffice strength.

The Silvia Reinhardt-Georg Hurdalek screenplay, based on an adaptation by Jan Lustig of Manfred Gregor's novel, "The Verdict," dramatizes the story of a military defense attorney who, in attempting to properly perform his task (defense of the four GI rapists facing a death penalty), must, against his will, bring about the destruction of an innocent victim (the raped girl) of her own human fallibility and the fallibility of German witnesses whose pride, hatreds and insecurities—all normal emotions—lead them to lie, exaggerate or conceal on the stand.

A picture that raises important, hypothetical moral and judicial questions must do so in terms of rounded, dimensional characters if it is to properly communicate its message or register with impact. "Town Without Pity" fails in this regard. The spectator never truly feels a strong sense of involvement with or without concern for the principal characters, most of whom never really come into focus. The directorial approach is simply too diffuse. More is bitten off than the story can devour. Side issues, some of considerable significance in themselves, others of absolutely no relevance, are introduced and dismissed. The audience is not permitted to zero in on the central characters, because too much time is wasted on incidental business. More than once the serious mood is upset by comedy stuff that serves no necessary function in the story.

Director Reinhardt is guilty of several unaccountable lapses, most destructive of which occurs during a sequence in which pathetically warped, but serious testimony is greeted by waves of idiotic laughter from the courtroom throng. The lack of perception is illustrated by the fact that the theatre audience is not finding this amusing.

Kirk Douglas does an able job as the defense attorney. Likewise E. G. Marshall as the prosecutor. There is an especially earnest and intense portrayal of one of the defendants by Robert Blake. The others—less prominent—are skillfully delineated by Richard Jaeckel, Frank Sutton and Mal Sondock. Christine Kaufmann, whose rare combination of sensual beauty and sensitivity mark her as an actress to watch, handles her assignment—the victim—with sincerity and animation. Other key roles are capably dispatched by Gerhart Lippert, Hans Nielsen, Karin Hardt, Ingrid van Bergen, Eleanore van Hoogstraten, Max Haufler and Siegfried Schurenberg. Barbara Rutting does reasonably well by an overemphasized part—an aggressive local newshen.

Among the generally competent behind-the-scenes contributions, one stands out, both favorably and unfavorably. That is Dimitri Tiomkin's music. His title tune, a rock 'n' rollish ditty with lyrics by Ned Washington (sung by Gene Pitney), is an astonishingly haunting refrain, a superior example of its usually lacklustre breed. But a point is reached where sheer repetition of this one melody begins to grate on the spectator's nerves. Too much of a good thing.

Tube.

Back Street
(COLOR)

Glamorous remake of the Fannie Hurst soaper, dressed to kill. Strictly for women. Promising b.o. candidate.

Hollywood, Sept. 21.

Universal release of Ross Hunter production. Stars Susan Hayward, John Gavin, Vera Miles; features Charles Drake, Virginia Grey, Reginald Gardiner. Directed by David Miller. Screenplay, Eleanore Griffin, William Ludwig, based on the novel by Fannie Hurst; camera (Eastman), Stanley Cortez; editor, Milton Carruth; art director, Alexander Golitzen; music, Frank Skinner; sound, Waldon O. Watson, Frank H. Wilkerson; assistant director, Phil Bowles. Reviewed at Screen Directors Guild, Sept. 21, '61. Running time, **107 MINS.**

Rae Smith	Susan Hayward
Paul Saxon	John Gavin
Liz Saxon	Vera Miles
Curt Stanton	Charles Drake
Janie	Virginia Grey
Dalian	Reginald Gardiner
Caroline	Tammy Marihugh
Paul Jr.	Robert Eyer
Mrs. Evans	Natalie Schafer
Miss Hatfield	Doreen McLean
Mr. Venner	Alex Gerry
Mrs. Penworth	Karen Norris
Charley Claypole	Hayden Rorke
Marge Claypole	Mary Lawrence
Airport Clerk	Joe Cronin
Hotel Clerk	Ted Thorpe
Proprietor	Joseph Mell
Sailor	Dick Kallman
Showroom Model	Joyce Meadows
Paris Airport Employee	Lilyan Chauvin
Harper's Bazaar Models	Vivianne Porte, Joarne Betay, Isabelle Felder, Melissa Weston, Bea Ammidown

This is the third time around on the screen for Fannie Hurst's old tearjerker. Thanks to the glamorous touch of producer Ross Hunter, boxoffice success seems assured. A woman's picture of the old sudsy school, the Universal release figures to bring out the hanky brigade. Ladies are apt to enjoy every moment of romantic misery but men who tag along may be miserable.

In a cinema era given to stark realism and brutally frank themes, Hunter is probably the most significant exception. A throwback to the days of the screen's glamour merchants, he has consistenely parlayed pictorial beauty, handsome people and production values. He has dressed "Back Street" to the teeth. The story is commercial, but it isn't necessarily the story that will attract the people. It's the almost outrageous glamour of the thing.

The Eleanore Griffin-William Ludwig screenplay has Susan Hayward (in the Irene Dunne-Margaret Sullavan role) and John Gavin (in the John Boles-Charles Boyer part) sharing the ill-fated, grand-scale, extra-curricular romance destroyed by the latter's cranky, alcoholic, but adhesive wife, Vera Miles. The yarn is never fully plausible, nor are the characters (especially the sour wife). Drama is full of coincidence, the dialog full of gush.

Miss Hayward emotes up a storm as the suffering heroine. Her fans will be pleased. The range of Gavin's expression is narrow, but he needn't fret. This handsome young man is well on his way to becoming a number one romantic lead in motion pictures. Miss Miles is a skillful, accomplished actress. She does all that is humanly possible with her role.

Support is quite satisfactory, most prominent assists coming from Charles Drake, Virginia Grey, Reginald Gardiner, Robert Eyer and Tammy Marihugh. David Miller's direction milks all the pathos possible out of the tale. The abundance of stagey clutches, clinches and climaxes may seem artificial, but Hunter's "Back Street" is, after all, an artificial world into which customers will be coming to escape. Miller has only done his job.

But the true stars of this picture are the artisans, designers and craftsmen behind the scenes. Cameraman Stanley Cortez has consistently kept his lens flattering to the players and astonishingly appreciative of the Eastman tinted scenery, be it seascape, still life or one of the sumptuous, luxurious sets designed by Alexander Golitzen and furnished by Howard Bristol.

Women are going to be impressed by the parade of high-fashion gowns designed by Jean Louis. The wardrobe will be talked about, and perhaps talked right into an Academy Award nomination.

Frank Skinner's rhapsodically romantic score is an important ingredient. Milton Carruth's editing knits the story with logic and proper pace.

Tube.

El Analfabeto
(The Illiterate One)
(MEICAN—COLOR)

Mexico City, Oct. 10.

Columbia Pictures release of Posa Films International production. Stars Mario Moreno (Cantinflas); features Lilia Prado, Angel Garaza, Sara Garcia; with Miguel Manzano, Daniel Herrera, Guillermo Orea, Carlos Agosti, Fernando Soto, Oscar Ortiz de Pinedo, Carlos Martinez Baena. Directed by Miguel M. Delgado. Screenplay, Jaime Salvador, from original by Marcelo Salazar and Juan Lopez; additional dialog, Carlos Leon; camera, Victor Herrera. At Roble, Mexico, Orfeon, Polanco theatres, Mexico City. Running time, **90 MINS.**

Mario Moreno (Cantinflas) has come back to the Mexican fold in this one, winning back the respect and admiration of his Mexican fans who had felt let down by the recent few efforts of their "common man" idol and clown.

This film shows beyond a doubt that Cantinflas is the top mimic and comic in Mexican pictures. It represents his best effort in the last few years. Also, it stands up well with his earlier buffoonery of about a decade back. The truth is that Cantinflas's Mexican fans (they are legion, as attested to by four houses doing peak biz with this) were somewhat disconcerted by his Dr. Jekyll-Mr. Hyde transformation of personality in recent screen roles.

First character switch was Mario Moreno's disassociation from Cantinflas, the comic, to become a man of business affairs, including diversified forays in fields far apart from motion pictures. The second, and rudest shock was his role in "Around the World in 80 Days," which his fans did not like or understand. They were also shocked by a sprucely dressed Cantinflas who spoke English, abandoning the incoherent double talk that has been his trademark in Mexican pictures ever since his early days. And then there's the third character still to be unfurled in Mexico, as exemplified in "Pepe."

Therefore, in more ways than one, this latest film is a revindication in the eyes of his Mexican fans. Once again Cantinflas is the representative of the poor but honest Mexican underdog, added to which he's an illiterate. It is true that Cantinflas does not wear the low-slung, baggy pants of his earlier efforts, but his costume does have enough raggediness about it to be acceptable. Obviously his sprucing up of the tattered sweat shirt and pants is a concession to his international prestige. And possibly plans have been made to dub this one in English.

Story line is unpretentious, yet in the development via the acting of Cantinflas and his supporting players, it comes out as a warm, human document with strong comic overtones which bring plenty of laughs. Cantinflas is a misfit saddled with the name of Inocencio Prieto y Calvo, and he gets a letter from the capital city advising him of a $160,000 legacy left him by his deceased uncle.

Only Inocencio cannot read. Discharged from a carpenter shop for inefficiency, and distressed by his inability to read and write, Inocencio decides that he will go to school and learn to read his own letter so that he need not submit it to prying eyes of strangers or neighbors. Lilia Prado comes into his life as the love interest, and the love scenes between the two have an innocent sort of naiveness that is charming.

Ultimately, Inocencio learns to read, only to find that the letter is lost. It had fallen out of his pocket in a bank where he had wheedled himself into a sort of porter's job; fallen into the hands of a crooked attorney via a bank employee who had it in for Inocencio since a practical joke aimed at the "illiterate one" misfired.

Inocencio and his Blanquita are falsely accused of stealing jewels of the bank president's wife. But there's the inevitable happy end

with the villian seeking to con Inocencio's money getting his come uppance, and Cantinflas getting the girl. And Inocencio pledges a good part of his fortune to build more rural schools.

Another good point about this film is that Cantinflas does not hog the camera, lets such good veteran actors as Angel Garaza and Carlos Martinez Baena contribute to the development of the story via their own scenes. Grandma Sara Garcia turns in an excellent job as a hard-working old aunt who takes in washing. Lilia Prado as the love interest is a charming partner to Cantinflas's shy lovemaking.

All in all, this is a production that the Mexican fan enjoyed, including bits of business with Cantinflas apeing a slinky walk, and his light terpsichore foot work in a dance scene. The Victor Herrera camera work in color is well done while the sound has no flaws.

This one will do bonanza box-office throughout the Spanish-language market. And indications in the way the pic is developed is a tip-off that Posa Films plans to dub it in English for worldwide release. *Emil.*

A Matter Of Who
(BRITISH)

Somewhat confused drama about the World Health Organization. Presence of Terry-Thomas in lead role has its problems for, though playing it reasonably straight, this comedian automatically produces some yocks which don't fit easily into a film hinged on a smallpox epidemic.

London, Oct. 3.

Metro release of a (Walter Shenson-Milton Holmes Foray Films production. Stars Terry-Thomas, Alex Nicol, Sonja Ziemann. Directed by Don Chaffey. Screenplay by Holmes; adapted by Patricia Lee, from story by Miss Lee, Paul Dickson; camera, Erwin Hillier; music, Edwin Astley; editor, Frank Clarke. Previewed at Metro Private Theatre, London. Running time, **92 MINS.**

Bannister	Terry-Thomas
Michele	Sonja Ziemann
Kennedy	Alex Nicol
Jamieson	Richard Briers
Sister Bryan	Honor Blackman
Ivanovitch	Guy Deghy
Beryl	Carol White
Hatfield	Clive Morton
Foster	Geoffrey Keen
Rahman	Martin Benson
Linkers	Eduard Linkers
Dr. Blake	Vincent Ball
Skipper	Michael Ripper
Cooper	Cyril Wheeler

The odd title of this item is explained by the fact that WHO stands for World Health Organization and the plots concerns a topic that is unlikely material for entertainment—a smallpox epidemic. As a straight drama this might be acceptable but the casting of Terry-Thomas in the lead automatically produces some uneasy yocks.

There is a lot of red herring, and the plot itself is confused. It does not add up as an entry likely to have much popular appeal. Though the wisdom of the Terry-Thomas casting is questionable, the thesp himself cannot be blamed. He plays the World Health Organization official, "a germ detective" as he describes himself, commendably straight. But the immaculate Eng-

lishan, derby-hatted and carrying an umbrella through all crises, is bound to be a figure of fun and Terry-Thomas, understandably, cannot resist getting as many yocks as possible. They don't fit in happily all the time with the smallpox theme.

The death of an oil man on a plane arriving at London Airport is traced to smallpox. Two men are vitally interested in the death, Terry-Thomas, because disease is his WHO business, and Alex Nicol, who is the man's partner. The latter cannot understand what has gone wrong with oil-drilling tests in the Middle East. The two join forces to find the germ-carrier because several other cases are reported in Europe and the two are convinced that there is a link. The dead man's new bride (Sonja Ziemann) and a tough oil and shipping magnate (Guy Deghy) are also involved in a complicated plot which leads to the Swiss Alps and an only slightly dramatic showdown.

Terry-Thomas's performance is skillfully smooth while Nicol plays a bewildered but determined American oil man with a firm touch. Miss Ziemann has little to do but look suspicious and attractive. She achieves both feats satisfactorily. Guy Deghy is an appropriately sinister tycoon while Honor Blackman, Richard Briers, Clive Morton, Geoffrey Keen and Vincent Ball are other proven thesps who are on hand in support.

Don Chaffey steers the film through its somewhat involved plot with a somewhat stolid touch which does not sufficiently hold the balance between drama and comedy. However, Erwin Hiller's lensing is admirable, and the artwork and editing are both sound. There is the inevitable pop song over the credit titles which has absolutely nothing to do with the film itself. Written by Bob Russell and sung by Roy Castle. It does not sound a likely candidate for the parade. *Rich.*

Breakfast At Tiffany's
(COLOR)

Kept boy wins kept girl in amoral Manhattan free spirit tale powderpuffed and purified for mass consumption. Sleek production values, bizarre story and some topnotch acting, especially by Audrey Hepburn, make it bright b.o. contender.

Hollywood, Oct. 5.

Paramount release of Martin Jurow-Richard Shepherd production. Stars Audrey Hepburn, George Peppard; features Patricia Neal, Buddy Ebsen, Martin Balsam, Mickey Rooney. Directed by Blake Edwards. Screenplay, George Axelrod, based on novel by Truman Capote; camera (Technicolor), Franz F. Planer; editor, Howard Smith; music, Henry Mancini; asst. director, William McGarry. Reviewed at studio, Oct. 5, '61. Running time, **115 MINS.**

Holly Golightly	Audrey Hepburn
Paul Varjak	George Peppard
"2-E"	Patricia Neal
Doc Golightly	Buddy Ebsen
O. J. Berman	Martin Balsam
Mr. Yunioshi	Mickey Rooney
Jose de Silva Perriera	Vilallonga
Tiffany Clerk	John McGiver
Mag Wildwood	Dorothy Whitney
Rusty Trawler	Stanley Adams
Librarian	Elvia Allman
Sally Tomato	Alan Reed
Stripper	Miss Beverly Hills
Sid Arbuck	Claude Stroud

Whitewashed and solidified for the screen, Truman Capote's "Breakfast at Tiffany's" emerges an unconventional, but dynamic entertainment that will be talked about and, resultantly, commercially successful. Out of the elusive, but curiously intoxicating Capote fiction, scenarist George Axelrod has developed a surprisingly moving film, touched up into a stunningly visual motion picture experience by the screen artisans assembled under the aegis of producers Martin Jurow and Richard Shepherd and surveillance of director Blake Edwards.

Capote buffs may find some of Axelrod's fanciful alterations a bit too precious, pat and glossy for comfort, but enough of the original's charm and vigor have been retained to make up for the liberties taken with character to erect a marketable plot.

What makes "Tiffany's" an appealing tale is its heroine, Holly Golightly, a charming, wild and amoral "free spirit" with a latent romantic streak. Axelrod's once-o over-lightly erases the amorality and bloats the romanticism, but retains the essential spirit ("a phony, but a real phony") of the character, and, in the exciting person of Audrey Hepburn, she comes vividly to life on the screen. Miss Hepburn's expressive, "top banana in the shock department" portrayal is complemented by the reserved, capable work of George Peppard as the young writer whose love ultimately (in the film, not the book) enables the heroine to come to realistic terms with herself.

Excellent featured characterizations are contributed by Martin Balsam as a Hollywood agent, Buddy Ebsen as Miss Hepburn's deserted husband, and Patricia Neal as Peppard's wealthy "sponsor." Mickey Rooney's participation as a much-harassed upstairs Japanese photographer adds an unnecessarily incongruous note to the proceedings. Others prominent and valuable in support are John McGiver, Vilallonga, Dorothy Whitney, Stanley Adams, Elvia Allman and Alan Reed.

Cinematically, the film is a sleek, artistic piece of craftsmanship, particularly notable for Frank F. Planer's haunting Technicolor photography and Henry Mancini's memorably moody score. The latter's "Moon River," with lyrics by Johnny Mercer, is an enchanting tune with great commercial prospects. Other ace contributions are those of are directors Hal Pereira and Roland Anderson, set decorators Sam Comer and Ray Moyer, editor Howard Smith and wardrobe designer (for Miss Hepburn) Hubert de Givenchy. *Tube.*

Three Tales of Checkhov
(RUSSIAN—COLOR)

Paris, Oct. 3.

Mosfilm production and release. With Klavdia Blokhina, Anatoli Adoskine, Euguenl Eustigneev, Mikhail Yanchine, Ludmilla Kasatkina, Sacha Barsov, Nikolai Plotnikov, Nikolai Nikitine. Directed by Marie Andjaparidze (Aniouta), Irina Poplavskaia (A Vengeance), Edouard Botcharov (Vanka). Screenplays, Miss Andjaparidze (Aniouta), Grigori Koltounov (Vengeance), Guenrikh Oganissian (Vanka) from tales by Anton Checkhov; camera, Nocolai Olonovski (Sovcolor), Piotr Emelianov, Piotr Katoev and Joseph Martov; editors, V. Dorman, S. Popov, K. Gordon. At Marignan, Paris. Running time, **76 MINS.**

ANIOUTA	
Aniouta	Klavdia Blokhina
Klotchkov	Anatoli Adoskine
Painter	Euguenl Eustigneev

A VENGEANCE	
Touramov	Mikhail Yanchine
Wife	Ludmilla Kasatkina
Degtiarev	Georgui Vitsine
Woman	Anastasia Guerguievaskia

VANKA	
Vanka	Sacha Barsov
Aliakine	Nikolai Plotnikov
Nikititch	Nikolai Nikitine

Three of Anton Checkhov's short stories are here adroitly adapted with one in color and two in black and white. Two are expert in creating incisive looks at people without pathos or ridicule while one overdoes the sentiment. It looms a possible special entry abroad, but limited as a sketch film. Best chances seem to be for separation and use as supporting fare or for tele.

All are made by different people. Two women come off best. "A Vengeance," of Irima Poplavskaia, concerns an oafish older man married to a younger woman whose attempt at avenging a friend courting his wife backfires, "Aniouat," of Marie Andjaparidze, is a slice of life in a rundown hotel. "Vanka," of Edouard Botcharov, is a tale of a little slavey mistreated by his employers.

"Vengeance" has a true comic sense that smites pettiness without becoming absurd or moralistic. "Aniouta" touches human misery in a knowing way. "Vanka" has has a flair for showing true childish hope and despair.

Acting and technical credits are fine. This is a well balanced episode picture. Color is used in the comedic "Vengeance" only. Checkhov's world of the petty and harsh is well drafted on to film without any untoward propaganda. *Mosk.*

Scarlet Sails
(RUSSIAN-COLOR-SCOPE)

Paris, Oct. 3.

Mosfilm production and release. With Ivan Pereversev, Serguei Martinson, Nicolai Volkov, Anna Orotchko, Antonia Kontcha kova. Directed by Alexandre Ptouchko. Screenplay, A. Yourivski, A. Nagorni from novel by Alexandre Grine; camera (Sovcolor), G. Tsekavyi, B. Yakouchev; editor, I. Moronov. At Marignan, Paris. Running time, **86 MINS.**

Longrene	Ivan Pereversev
Philippe	Serguei Martinsan
Aigle	Nicolai Volkov
Neighbor	Anna Orotchko
Mary	Antonina Kontchkova

Made for moppets, this is a simple tale with a moral. Good color work and technical values help. It looms only for juvenile showing abroad.

Supposedly taking place somewhere in England, it concerns a daughter of a toy maker and the son of a nobleman. She has been told, as a child, that her Prince Charming will come for her in a boat with red sails, and he leaves home to take to the sea. He becomes a captain, hears about the girl and falls in love with her. He puts up red sails and comes for her for the happy ending.

Film admits that man needs illusions and miracles but makes its point that these must be created with his own hands. But fairy tale, strictly not for adults. Color is more even in this than in most Russo pix. The scope is well utilized. Thesps play in a broad style. *Mosk.*

Alieskine Liubov
(The Love of Aliocha)
(RUSSIAN-SOVSCOPE)
Paris, Oct. 3.

Mosfilm production and release. With Leonide Bikov, Alexandra Zavialova, Youri Belov. Directed by S. Toumanov, G. Choukine. Screenplay, B. Metelnikov; camera, K. Petrichenko; editor, W. Rubin. At Marignan, Paris. Running time, 91 MINS.
Aliocha .... Leonide Bikov
Zina .... Alexandra Zavialova
Arcady .... Youri Velov

A simple, fresh film about a young worker's love affair, this is refreshingly free from heavy-handed propaganda. It attests to the growing, new individualistic Soviet film. Pic stands a chance for special situations abroad but does not seem to have the fillip for arty houses.

Aliocha (Leonide Bikov) is a worker with an outfit working the steppes of Russia in search of oil and minerals. He feels he does not quite belong. He's absentminded in his work, and a general sad sack. Then love smites via the person of a sharp-tongued, comely daughter of a stationmaster. He finally wins her after fighting a surly fellow worker.

While this has a sentimental approach, it is never mawkish, containing refreshing observation, movement and characterizations. The comedy pokes fun at cultural radio programs and over-dedicated workers though there is the aside about the glory of the work, etc.

Film is technically excellent. Done by two new directors, it shows a modern, spirited type of film. The hand of propaganda is light, this being an apparent proof of the thaw in Russo pic making.
Mosk.

Bellye Nochi
(White Nights)
(RUSSIAN-COLOR)
Paris, Oct. 3.

Mosfilm production and release. With Ludmilla Martchenko, Oleg Strijanov, M. Pekihoban. Written and directed by Ivan Pyriev from story by Feodor Dostoyevsky. Camera (Sovcolor), Valentin Pavlov; editor, Y. Fogel. At Marignan, Paris. Running time, 95 MINS.

Nashtenka .... Ludmilla Martchenko
Dreamer .... Oleg Strijanov
Roomer .... M. Pekihoban

Faithful transcription of a Feodor Dostoyevsky story, this relates the tale of a lonely dreamer whose brief interlude with a girl gives him the only solace in his lifetime. Though dramatically right and well acted, film is somewhat slow moving in its series of incidents. Hence, it appears mainly a specialized entry abroad on the Dostoyevsky name.

A young daydreamer meets a girl on a bridge one night in 19th Century St. Petersburg (Czarist Russia). They become friends and he sees her for five nights. The lad tells her about his dreams and she explains about a man she loves. Love blossoms for him and she almost accepts him. Then the other man finally shows up and he realizes he has wasted his life.

Oleg Strijanov as the dreamer has the right inflections while Ludmilla Martchenko is perfect as the romantic girl. Color has the right chromo aspect. Well handled, this

---

might find a niche for itself in the U.S. art sphere. *Mosk.*

Voskresenie
(Resurrection)
(RUSSIAN)
Paris, Oct. 3.

Mosfilm production and release. With Tamara Skomina, Eugeni Mateev, L. Zolothoukine, L. Joukovskaia, B. Sex. Directed by Mikhail Chveitser. Screenplay, Eugeni Gabrilovitch, Chveitser from novel by Leo Tolstoy; camera, E. Savelievi, editor, K. Aleeva. At Marignan, Paris. Running time, 100 MINS.
Katioucha .... Tamara Skomina
Nekhllodov .... Eugeni Mateev
Prosecutor .... L. Zolothoukine
Missy .... L. Joukovskaia

The Russians are tapping their pre-revolutionary literary heritage for film subjects and doing them with taste and flair plus a feeling for the times and characters. Already done by U. S. producers (three different versions), this Leo Tolstoy tale still holds dramatic flavor with possible arty chances abroad.

Main drawback is a tendency to treat this tale in a flashy modern camera style which sometimes makes the drama lose force. But its insight into character and its faithfulness to Tolstoy's work give this a solid base.

The black and white lensing has a fine crisp quality. Acting is excellent. Scenes of the seductions, with naked desire overruling all responsibilities, are done with a feeling for sensuality rare in Russo pix.

After fine filmic adaptations of Checkhov and Dostoyevsky, Tolstoy gets treated right here.
Mosk.

Judgment At Nuremberg

A film of great meaning and importance albeit overlong. Topheavy, star-struck casting.

United Artists release of Stanley Kramer production. Stars Spencer Tracy, Burt Lancaster, Richard Widmark, Marlene Dietrich, Maximilian Schell, Judy Garland, Montgomery Clift. Directed by Kramer. Screenplay, Abby Mann; camera, Ernest Laszlo; editor, Fred Knudtson; music, Ernest Gold; assistant director, Ivan Volkman. Reviewed at Directors Guild of America, Oct. 11, '61. Running time, 190 MINS.

Judge Dan Haywood .... Spencer Tracy
Ernst Janning .... Burt Lancaster
Col. Tad Lawson ...... Richard Widmark
Mme. Bertholt .... Marlene Dietrich
Hans Rolfe .... Maximilian Schell
Irene Hoffman .... Judy Garland
Rudolf Petersen ...... Montgomery Clift
Capt. Byers .... William Shatner
Senator Burkette .... Ed Binns
Judge Kenneth Norris
   .... Kenneth MacKenna
Emil Hahn .... Werner Klemperer
Gen. Merrin .... Alan Baxter
Werner Lammpe .... Torben Meyer
Judge Curtiss Ives .... Ray Teal
Friedrich Hofstetter .... Martin Brandt
Mrs. Halbestadt .... Virginia Christine
Halbestadt .... Ben Wright
Major Abe Radnitz ...... Joseph Bernard
Dr. Wieck .... John Wengraf
Dr. Geuter .... Karl Swenson
W. llner .... Howard Caine
Pohl .... Otto Waldis
Mrs. Lindnow .... Olga Fabian
Mrs. Ives .... Sheila Bromley
Perkins .... Bernard Kates
Elsa Scheffler .... Jana Taylor
Schmidt .. .. Paul Busch

The reservations one may entertain with regard to Stanley Kramer's production of "Judgment At Nuremberg," and major reservations are certainly entertainable, must be tempered with appreciation of the film's intrinsic value as a work of historical significance and philosophical merit. With the most painful pages of modern history as its bitter basis, Abby Mann's intelligent, thought-provoking screenplay is a grim reminder of man's responsibility to denounce grave evils of which he is aware. The lesson is carefully, tastefully and upliftingly told via Kramer's large-scale production.

Commercial aspects cannot be gauged by the customary entertainment yardstick. Presence of seven highpowered actors should help, of course. Fundamentally, however, the nature of the drama will be the determining factor rather than the personalities.

Picture demands unusually deep and sustained concentration from an audience. At 190 minutes it is more than twice the size of the drama as first witnessed early in 1959 as a concise, stirring and rewarding production on television's "Playhouse 90." A faster tempo by Kramer and more trenchant script editing before shooting would have punched up picture.

United Artists release has the stature and cast for financial success, but it is a heavy, demanding attraction that requires unusually deep and sustained concentration from its audience, perhaps more than most modern audiences will be willing to give over a deliberate, painstaking 190-minute course. The picture may have difficulty making its point the hard (ticket) way.

Mann's drama, of course, is set in Nuremberg in 1948, the time of the Nazi war crimes trials. It deals not with the trials of the more well-known Nazi leaders, but with members of the German judiciary who served under the Nazi

regime and went along with the infamous legal mandates of a period in which 6,000,000 innocent persons were murdered. The intense courtroom drama centers on two men: the presiding judge (Spencer Tracy) who must render a monumental decision, and the principal defendant (Burt Lancaster), at first a silent, brooding figure, but ultimately the one who rises to pinpoint the real issue and admit his guilt, which is the guilt of all who rationalized or ignored the inhuman acts of Nazism, which demanded the open denunciation of all rational people, especially those of extraordinary power and ability, such as the character portrayed by Lancaster.

There the stars enjoy greater latitude and length of characterization, such as in the cases of Tracy, Maximilian Schell and Richard Widmark (latter two as defense counsel and prosecutor, respectively, the element of personal identity does not interfere. But, in the cases of those who are playing brief, though vital, cameo-like roles, such as Judy Garland and Montgomery Clift, the familiarity intrudes on the spectator's conscious, and he has insufficient time to divorce actor from character. Although both Clift and Miss Garland bring great emotional force and conviction to their chores, he as a somewhat deranged victim of Nazi sterility measures, she as a German accused of relations with a Jew at a period when such an activity was forbidden and punishable by death for the Jew, the roles might better have been handed to lesser-known players.

As the presiding judge, Tracy delivers a performance of great intelligence and intuition. He creates a gentle, but towering, figure, compassionate but realistic, warm but objective—a person of unusual insight and eloquence, but also a plain, simple human being demandingly sandwiched between politics and justice. Tracy's gift for underplaying makes the character all the more winning.

Schell repeats the role he originated, with electric effect, on the tv program, and again he brings to it a fierce vigor, sincerity and nationalistic pride not easily forgotten. Widmark is effective as the prosecutor ultimately willing to compromise and soft-pedal his passion for stiff justice when the brass gives the political word (the cold war is on and the Germans must be wooed).

The casting of Lancaster as the elderly, respected German scholar-jurist on trial for his however-unwilling participation in the Nazi legal machine presents the actor with a taxing assignment in which he must overcome the discrepancy of his own virile identity with that of the character. This he manages to do with an earnest performance, but he never quite attains the cold, superior intensity that Paul Lukas brought to the part on tv. Marlene Dietrich is persuasive as the aristocratic widow of a German general hanged as a war criminal, but the character is really superfluous to the basic issue, and its introduction into the story slows up the film. The excess time spent on "outside" characters like this might better have been utilized to bring into sharper focus some of the key characters in the court-

room, such as the four defendants.

A number of fine players appear in support, and do strong jobs. Among the most prominent of these are William Shatner, Ed Binns, Werner Klemperer, Torben Meyer, Martin Brandt, Virginia Christine, Ben Wright, Howard Caine, Otto Waldis, Alan Baxter, Ray Teal, Kenneth MacKenna, Joseph Bernard, John Wengraf and Karl Swenson.

Any film confined to the interior of a courtroom for most of its length is susceptible to a static aura and a characteristic of tedious verbosity. This is avoided in "Judgment" by the skilled camera work of Ernest Laszlo. The photography brings both intimacy and mobility to a drama that needs both values. The frequent glides around the courtroom serve to vary the audience perspective, and the many sudden zooms into or away from the character of moment certainly heighten dramatic effect. Fred Knudtson's editing is crisp—no frills, no dissolves, just straight, clean and abrupt transitions. The German-English language obstacle of the trial is sidestepped beautifully.

Ernest Gold's music, unobtrusively helpful whenever it is incorporated into the film proper, is especially valuable in the short, rousing overture in establishing feeling and mood for the experience to come. Other important contributions are those of production designer Rudolph Sternad and sound engineer James Speak.

Tube.

Boy Who Caught a Crook

A boy, a tramp and a puppy outwit a crook. For supporting duty in easygoing dates.

Hollywood, Oct. 9.

United Artists release of Robert E. Kent production. Stars Wanda Hendrix, Don Beddoe, Roger Mobley, Richard Crane. Directed by Edward L. Cahn. Screenplay, Nathan Juran; camera, Gilbert Warrenton; editor, Robert Carlisle; music, Richard La Salle; assistant director, Herbert Greene. Reviewed at Goldwyn Studios, Oct. 9, '61. Running time, **72 MINS.**

Laura	Wanda Hendrix
Kid	Roger Mobley
Colonel	Don Beddoe
Rocky Kent	Johnny Seven
Sergeant	Robert Stevenson
Keeper	William Walker
Flannigan	Henry Hunter

Another supporting item from the Robert E. Kent-Edward L. Cahn assembly line of instant melodrama, "Boy Who Caught a Crook" is a flimsy, but bookable, filler-thriller for houses that cling to the double (feature) standard and cater to the less quality-concsious filmgoer.

The United Artists release, produced by Kent, directed by Cahn and written by Nathan Juran, is a routine utility "B" with more than the customary cargo of honey, but no sting in the tale. It's about a boy who finds a briefcase that belongs to a crook who has mislaid his booty while fleeing from the police. The boy is aided in his adventure by a tramp and a puppy dog. In fact, the extensive title might be extended even further to read, "the puppy who led the police who found a tramp who saved the boy who caught the crook." With that kind of lovable parlay going for it—puppies, tramps and boys—the picture seems on pretty safe ground.

The acting is superior to everything else in this draggy, deliberate, repetitious number. Roger Mobley drains every last drop of sentiment out of his part as the kid. Don Beddoe makes the kind of tramp one wouldn't mind having over for Sunday dinner. Wanda Hendrix plays the role of the mother earnestly. Richard Crane is capable as a newsman. Johnny Seven thoroughly hissable as the crook. Cinematically, it's an example of adequate filmmaking on a limited allotment.

Tube.

Seven Women From Hell

Small party of dolls chased across 1942 New Guinea by Japanese army. Absurd meller punctuated by unintentional witty flashes. But exploitable.

Hollywood, Oct. 6.

Twentieth-Fox release of Harry Spalding production. Stars Patricia Owens, Denise Darrel, Cesar Romero, Margia Dean, John Kerr. Directed by Robert Webb. Screenplay, Jesse Lasky Jr., Pat Silver; camera, Floyd Crosby; editor, Jodie Copelan; music, Paul Dunlap; asst. directors, Leon Chooluck, Willard Kirkham. Reviewed at the studio, Oct. 6, '61. Running time, **87 MINS.**

Grace	Patricia Owens
Claire	Denise Darcel
Luis Hullman	Cesar Romero
Mara	Margia Dean
Janet	Yvonne Craig
Mai-Lu	Pilar Seurat
Anna	Sylvia Daneel
Sgt. Takahashi	Richard Loo
Regan	Evadne Baker
Captain Oda	Bob Okazaki
Dr. Matsumo	Yuki Shimoda
Rapist Guard	Lloyd Kino
House Guard	Kam Fong Crun
Guard	Yankee Chang
Bill Jackson	John Kerr

Some of the funniest dialog of the year turns up in this 20th-Fox release. Unfortunately, it wasn't intended to be that way. The Harry Spalding production is, fundamentally, a serious melodrama about women fleeing a Japanese prison camp in New Guinea during the early part of World War II. But the end product is a ludicrous, childish film of limited appeal, though serviceable on the strength of its exploitation values.

Spalding has rounded up a number of attractive actresses for his enterprise, decked them out in tatters and subjected them to a screenplay (by Jesse Lasky Jr. and Pat Silver) that not for one moment can be taken seriously. Among the memorably absurd tokens of presumably unintentional wit that crop up in this picture are: (1) the reply of a Japanese guard to a woman prisoner who has just offered him a fountain pen in exchange for favoritism—"Hmm, made in Japan. No good. Not a Parker"; (2) the final two words in the film, best of their kind since the classic "Nobody's perfect" in "Some Like It Hot." Finally sighting Allied soldiers after their perilous trek through the jungle, the girls cry, "Yanks!" and the boys cry, "broads!"

The six-count 'em-six girls (apparently "Seven" reads better on a marquee) are Patricia Owens (an ornery ornothologist), Denise Darcel (a bosomy thief), Margia Dean (a waitress with Saks Fifth Ave. aspirations), Yvonne Craig (the pregnant one), Pilar Seurat (an Oriental nurse) and Sylvia Daneel (a Dutch girl looking for a plantation to run). Cesar Romero portrays an Argentine-German plantation owner who is collaborating with the Japanese until he runs [illegible] pays the price for underestimating her. John Kerr plays a Yank flier who bails out of a disabled plane over the remote New Guinea jungle, lands right smack in the lap of this bevy of beauties, and dies the next morning.

Robert Webb's direction is unobservant and erratic, and the latter characteristic applies as well to the level of technical performance exhibited in this picture.

Tube.

Le Cave Se Rebiffe
(The Victim Strikes Back)
(FRENCH)

Paris, Oct. 10.

UFA-Comacico release of Cite Films-PCCM production. Stars Jean Gabin, Martine Carol, Bernard Blier; features Francoise Rosay, Franck Villard, Maurice Biraud, Valpetre, Ginette Leclerc. Directed by Gilles Grangier. Screenplay, Albert Simonin, Michel Audiard, Grangier from novel by Simonin; camera, Louis Page; editor, Jacqueline Thiedot. At the Paris, Paris. Running time, **100 MINS.**

Le Dabe	Jean Gabin
Solange	Martine Carol
Charles	Bernard Blier
Eric	Franck Villard
Robert	Maurice Biraud
Lea	Ginette Leclerc
Lucas	Valpetre
Woman	Francoise Rosay

Jean Gabin again plays a retired gangster who comes back for a last job. This has a sleek mounting and acceptable suspense with a surprise ending. But it looms mainly a specialized entry because of its talky aspects and sketchy characterization. This seems more a local than foreign appeal pic.

Gabin comes back from an easy life in the tropics to work with three shifty characters in counterfeiting millions of Dutch guilders. Attempts to doublecross him end when he flies off with all the loot.

Dialog is local underworld jargon and is tossed off neatly. But there is too much extraneous straining for color and dialog with the film falling off after a witty beginning. Job is well documented but sacrifices too much for attempts at comedy.

Acting is good and technical credits okay but all rests on the veteran shoulders of Gabin who displays his usual solid, waspish and domineering presence.

Mosk.

Suicidate, Mi Amor
(Kill Yourself, My Love)
(MEXICAN)

Mexico City, Oct. 10.

Peliculas Nacionales release of Producciones Matouk production. Stars Tin Tan, Teresa Velazquez, Marina Camacho; features Beto el Boticario, Antonio Raxel, Erick del Castillo, Carl Hillos. Directed by Gilberto Martinez Solares. Screenplay, Luis Alcoriza; camera, Manuel Gomez Urquiza; music, Sergi Guerrero. At Mariscala Theatre, Mexico City. Running time, **90 MINS.**

This is the umpteenth Tin Tan picture, with the actor one of the busiest of the Mexican film world. But in this one he does an about face, eschews song, dance and grimacing or clowning to plug for laughs, and turns in a straight acting performance.

The end result is quite acceptable because Tin Tan, who has appeared in a number of quickies best forgotten, does have talent and technical skill. He puts it to work in this tale of an eccentric, picturesque Mexican millionaire who comes to the aid of the damsel in distress when she needs him most.

Picture definitely is not what the public expects from a mugging, slapstick Tin Tan, but it is by far one of his better efforts. And, strangely enough, because it is so, with patrons accustomed to his so-so efforts, there was talk of substituting this film with another after only a few days. It ran out its full exhibition week, however. But it may take time for the public to get used to Tin Tan as a straight comedian.

Emil.

Murder She Said
(BRITISH)

Rather wordy whodunit starring Margaret Rutherford as the Agatha Christie sleuth. Enough red herrings to satisfy the average murder mystery addict.

London, Oct. 3.

Metro (George H. Brown) production and release. Stars Margaret Rutherford, Arthur Kennedy, Muriel Pavlow, James Robertson Justice; features Thorley Walters, Charles Tingwell, Conrad Phillips, Ronald Howard. Directed by George Pollock. Screenplay, David Pursall, Jack Seddon from novel, "4.50 From Paddington" by Agatha Christie; camera, Geoffrey Faithfull; editor, Ernest Walter; music, Ron Goodwin. Previewed at Metro Private Theatre. Running time, **86 MINS.**

Miss Marple	Margaret Rutherford
Quimper	Arthur Kennedy
Emma	Muriel Pavlow
Ackenthorpe	James Robertson Justice
Craddock	Charles Tingwell
Cedric	Thorley Walters
Harold	Conrad Phillips
Alexander	Ronnie Raymond
Mrs. Kidder	Joan Hickson
Eastley	Ronald Howard
Librarian	Stringer Davis
Albert	Gerald Cross
Hillman	Michael Golden
Bacon	Gordon Harris
Lucy	Lucy Griffiths
Mrs. Stainton	Barbara Hicks

Agatha Christie's spinster sleuth is a natural role for Margaret Rutherford's eccentricities. Hence, this competent murder mystery gives the actress ample opportunity for exploiting the quivering powl, the roving eye and the characteristic voice which are so large a part of her stock in trade. David Pursall and Jack Seddon have made a reasonable job of condensing one of Miss Christie's complicated mysteries, "4.50 from Paddington," introducing enough suspects to satisfy most followers of the whodunit. Technically the film is okay, though George Pollock's direction sometimes wavers.

Miss Marple is returning from London on a train and is amusing herself by looking in at the carcaiges of another train going the same way on an adjacent track. A blind is suddenly jerked up and she sees a man throttling a girl as the train moves away. She reports it to the railway authority and the local police inspector but neither believes her. Both think she had an hallucination or seen a couple necking. After all, where's the

body? Only one person, the local librarian, believes her and agrees to help her find the missing torso.

She suspects that the body is in the grounds of nearby Ackenthorpe Hall, gets herself a job there as a ma[illegible] sets about looking for the victim and unravelling the mystery. The body is duly found but two more deaths complicate matters. Eventually Miss Marple deduces who is the killer.

Apart from Miss Rutherford's important contribution, there are several other useful characterizations. James Robertson Justice, as a bad-tempered hypochrondriac; Arthur Kennedy, as the local doctor, Thorley Walters, Conrad Phillips and Gerald Cross as Justice's no-good sons and Campbell Stringer, as the librarian, are standout. Ronald Howard, Ronnie Raymond, Joan Hickson, Michael Golden and Barbara Hicks are others in the sound cast. As Justice's daughter, Muriel Pavlow has little to do except look sweet which she does admirably while Charles Tingwell, who has a rep in tel here, makes an agreeable impression in the biggish role of the cop.

Astute mystery students will find the identity of the killer something of a surprise, but the secret is kept right to the bitter end.

Rich.

View From the Bridge
(Vu Du Pont)
(FRENCH)

Paris, Oct. 10.

Cocinor release of Transcontinental production. Stars Raf Vallone, Raymond Pellegrin, Jean Sorel, Maureen Stapleton, Carol Lawrence; features Morris Carnovsky. Directed by Sidney Lumet. Screenplay, Norman Rosten from play by Arthur Miller; camera, Michel Kelber; editor, Francoise Javet. Preemed in Paris. Running time, 110 MINS.

Eddie	Raf Vallone
Beatie	Maureen Stapleton
Marco	Raymond Pellegrin
Rodolfo	Jean Sorel
Katie	Carol Lawrence
Alfieri	Morris Carnovsky

(In English)

Though a French film, exteriors were made in New York, while the creative aspects of director and adaptor of the Arthur Miller play were American. The result is a faithful dramatic version of the play. There are no marquee names for the U.S. but monickers for Europe. Both versions are impeccable and the pic appears a weighty arty house contender.

It might easily overcome its lack of names with a plus via the Miller monicker. Its fringe aspects on the immigrant borderline of America also give it a reason for its accented players who mix well with the native talents.

There is a tendency to be theatrical in hewing close to a series of dramatic incidents rather than letting them grow more harmoniously from the characters and their plight. The photographic reality removes the Greek tragedy envelope of the play.

Raf Vallone, the Italian film star who made a name in Paris in the legit version of "Bridge," again essays the lead role. He is powerful and tortured as the docker whose guilty love for his 18-year-old niece leads to his neglect of his wife. There is the insane jealousy over an illegal immigrant that brings on his sinking low enough to turn him over to the authorities and his suicide after a public humiliation.

Maureen Stapleton in a passive role, as the wife who is losing her man, still impresses in her expression of inner torment. Carol Lawrence is acceptable as the confused niece. Jean Sorel, as the immigrant lover, and Raymond Pellegrin, as his brother, are stalwart in their parts.

The exteriors, shot in Brooklyn, and the interiors, made in Paris, are well welded. Film shows that in this age of growing blending of industries and production abroad, an acceptable American film can be made by a foreign producer, provided he avoids hybridization. The immigrant theme easily assimilates the mixture of accents and American talk. It is technically fine.

Attempt to create the aura of tragedy, by having all the characters already suffering within their emotional makeups gives the film a grim, downbeat look. Hence, this looms mainly an arty bet with not too much entertainment value for more extensive distrib which may be spotty. It thus needs hard-sell in subsequents. Walter Reade's Continental Distributing Co. has this pic for the U.S. via production investment.

Director Sidney Lumet has punched up the dramatic scenes with a theatrical result at times, but his handling of the big scene with the docker and his niece's suitor is right and tactful.

Mosk.

The Head
(GERMAN)

Exploitable, but shopwarn shocker. Tedious variation on the mad doctor premise.

Hollywood, Oct. 3.

Trans-Lux release of Wolfgang Hartwig production. No star credits. Directed and screenplay by Victor Trivas; camera, Otto Reinwald, Kurt Rendel; editor, Friedl Buckow-Schier; art directors, Herman Warm, Bruno Monden; music, Willy Mattes, Jacque Lasry; sound, Rudolph Kaiser. Reviewed at Boulevard Theatre, L.A., Oct. 3, '61. Running time, 92 MINS.

Dr. Ood	Horst Frank
Professor Abel	Michel Simon
Criminal Commissioner	Paul Dahlke
Irene	Karin Kernke
Laboratory Asst. Bert	Helmut Schmid
Lilly	Christiane Maybach
Paul	Dieter Eppler
Dr. Burke	Kurt Muller-Graf
Mrs. Schneider	Marie Stadler
Bartender	Otto Storr

"The Head" is a tedious and tasteless horror film of German origin. The Trans-Lux release, written and directed by Victor Trivas was actually produced some five years ago, but has yet to be seen in this country. Its boxoffice fortunes depend upon the impact of exploitation measures, to which the film most provocatively lends itself, but awkward post-dubbing, overlength and the shabby, shopworn nature of the story will narrow its acceptance, even among horror buffs.

"The Head" in question is that of a noted professor, severed from its body yet kept alive (via the inevitable serum X) by an unbalanced colleague, Dr. Ood. Ood then goes a step further by transplanting the lovely head of a hopeless lady hunchback on the admirable body of a stripper, disposing of the undesirable remainders. But the operation proves to be a big bust when the half-and-half girl reveals the source of her neckdown identity to the boy friend of the partially-deceased stripper, who instantly prefers the new variation of the woman he loves. This lack of gratitude on the part of his creation so unhinges Ood that he leaps to his death.

Horst Frank is a model of villainy as the demon doctor. The head of the professor is essayed in rather detached fashion by the late Michel Simon. Karin Kernke plays the hunchback, Christiane Mayback the stripper. Both have attractively interchangeable heads and bodies. Trivas' direction is heavy, choppy and disjointed, but there are one or two passages endowed with a desirably eerie quality via the art, music and photography department contributions.

On The Fiddle
(BRITISH)

Outmoded comedy set in the second World War. It's a lowerbracket yock-raiser with such names as rate in U. S. being employed in minor chores; an "iffy" prospect.

London, Oct. 10.

Anglo-Amalgamated release of an S. Benjamin Fisz production. Stars Sean Connery, Alfred Lynch; features Cecil Parker, Wilfrid Hyde-White, Stanley Holloway, Kathleen Harrison, Eleanor Summerfield, Eric Barker, Terence Longdon, Alan King. Directed by Cyril Frankel. Screenplay by Harold Buchman from R. D. Delderfield's novel, "Stop at a Winner"; camera, Edward Scaife; editor, Peter Hunt; music, Malcolm Arnold. At Preview Theatre, London. Running time, 97 MINS.

Horace Pope	Alfred Lynch
Pedlar Pascoe	Sean Connery
Gp. Capt. Bascombe	Cecil Parker
Mr. Cooksley	Stanley Holloway
T/Sgt. Buzzer	Alan King
Doctor	Eric Barker
Trowbridge	Wilfrid Hyde White
Mrs. Cooksley	Kathleen Harrison
Flora McNaughton	Eleanor Summerfield
Air Gunner	Terence Longdon
1st Airman	Victor Maddern
Huxtable	Harry Locke
MacTaggart	Lance Perceval
Hixon	John Le Mesurier
Sister	Viola Keats
Mr. Pope	Peter Sinclair
Police Constable	Jack Lambert
Ticket Collector	Cyril Smith
Sgt. Ellis	Graham Stark
WAAF Sergeant	Miriam Karlin
Corporal Gittens	Bill Owen
Lancing	Ian Whittaker
Conductor	Monty Landis
Mavis	Barbara Windsor
Ivy	Toni Palmer
Dusty	Kenneth Warren
Iris	Ann Beach
U. S. Snowdrop	Gary Cockrell

This little item will produce plenty of laughter among easygoing audiences. But overall it has the rather jaded air of a script that suggests that it has been kicking around so long that it is now hopelessly outmoded. It is a comedy harking back to the war years, rationing, air-raid sirens and the lot. Though it has a number of supporting names known to Americans, they are largely wasted.

Based on a novel by R. D. Delderfield, Harold Buchman's screenplay appears to have been assembled rather than written. Cyril Frankel's direction, while extracting the maximum laughs from the material at hand, fails to cover the fact that the film is mostly a string of episodes only loosely connected.

The story concerns two R.A.F. recruits, a one a sharp-witted unscrupulous wise boy (Alfred Lynch) and the other an amiable, slow-witted gypsy (Sean Connery). Lynch sees the service life as an ideal way of making a quick buck and he cons the unsuspecting Connery into going along with him as an accomplice. They are up to every racket, handling leave-passes, postings, service rations, and eventually reviving a village inn in order to swindle the local American troops. Eventually Lynch outsmarts himself. They land up in France and finish up as heroes.

Main purpose of this apparently is to launch Lynch and Connery and they make a useful team, mainly by contrast. Lynch, previously in the stage version of "The Hostage," is a performer with a nimble attack, but in this role he lacks a necessary streak of charm.

Connery, who made a hit in "The Frightened City," is a husky, virile actor with a presence which is rather bogged down in this role. But both Lynch and Connery are clearly very acceptable new recruits to British pix. There is a great deal of proven talent on hand both before and behind the cameras, but most of the long supporting cast have clearly been brought in to the film, used swiftly and dismissed even more swiftly. Among the better opportunities are those that befall Eleanor Summerfield, as a sex-starved WAAF officer; Stanley Holloway, as a butcher and Alan King, as an American sergeant.

Technically the film is okay. But what may have sounded like a very good idea in the talking stages seems to have gone sadly awry in action. Three or four amusing sequences in a film devoted to providing yocks are not enough.

Rich.

La Belle Americaine
(The Beautiful American)
(FRENCH)

Paris, Oct. 10.

CCFC release of Film D'Art-Panorama-Corflor production. Stars Robert Dhery, Colette Brosset; features Alfred Adam, Jacques Fabbri, Catherine Sola, Christian Morin. Directed by Robert Dhery. Screenplay, Dhery, Pierre Tonernin, Alfred Adam; camera, Ghislain Cloquet; editor, Albert Jurgenson. At Mercury, Paris. Running time, 95 MINS.

Marcel	Robert Dhery
Paulette	Colette Brosset
Simone	Catherine Sola
Alfred	Alfred Adam
Pierre	Christian Marin
Grocer	Jacques Fabbri
Inspector	Louis De Funes

Robert Dhery, who had a hit Broadway run with his comic revue, "La Plume de Ma Tante," now turns to films and comes up with a fairly engaging comedy. There are many risible sketches but film does not build in character and gags. However, this is easygoing and pleasant. It could find playoff possibilities on its general overall entertainment values, but arty spots look chancy.

Title here refers to a big white Cadillac that falls into a modest worker's hands for $100 because of a widow's desire to avenge herself on her late husband's mistress. After arousing the wonder of his friends, the worker loses his job because his bosses envy him. He gets into a series of adventures such as getting locked in the trunk for a night, forced into a governmental shindig and becoming a favorite of the minister.

Dhery plays the guileless hero with a gentleness and good timing and cheer. The cast is helpful especially the hard-hearted mugging of Louis De Funes in two roles as a foreman and a police inspector.

Dhery does not try for belly laughs but rather for adroit situation bits. He clocks plenty of laughs but the one joke sometimes wears thin. What was deft, fresh and witty on the stage, where the skits were fast and quickly replaced by another, does not always work out in this film.

But Dhery shows a flair for comedics and has come up with a diverting pic which should do well here and abroad if properly handled. He shows a talent for pacing *** *** *ags, *** with more heavyweight material should emerge a personalized new film comedy presence. *Mosk.*

Casi Casados
(Virtually Married)
(MEXICAN)
Mexico City, Oct. 10.

Peliculas Nacionales release of Alameda Films and Cesar Santos Galindo production. Stars Fernando Casanova, Rosita Arenas, Mauricio Garces; features Oscar Pulido, Pedro de Aguillon. Directed by Migueu M. Delgardo. Screenplay by Jose Maria Fernandez Unsain and Alfredo Varela Jr. At Cine Orfeon, Mexico City. Running time, 90 MINS.

This is bedroom farce entertainment with vaudeville gag routines tossed in. A modest mechanic accepts plea of a rich friend to pass himself off as the man of means while the latter goes off on an important business junket. The impostor gets caught up in a serio-comic, merry-go-round which has him getting married. And then the comedy scenes begin when the wealthy friend returns into this situation. There's nothing very exciting or new about the theme, there are some really funny sequences.

Unpretentious though it is this is what the patrons here like in no uncertain terms. Saving grace is that actors, all public favorites, really go all out in their roles and turn in creditable performances. Low budgeted, this one will be a moneymaker in Mexico and other Latin areas. *Emil.*

Simitrio
(MEXICAN)
Coronado, Oct. 14.

Azteca Films release of Corsa, S.A. production. Stars Jose Elias Moreno, Javier Tejada, Carlos Lopez Moctezuma. Directed by Emilio Gomez Muriel. Camera, Jack Draper. At Coronado International Fest of Films. Running time, 100 MINS.

This is Mexicorn which snaps, crackles and pops because of performances of Elias Moreno, moppet Javier Tejada and the smart direction of Gomez Muriel.

Sentimental picture concerns village's fight to keep a blinded veteran teacher from being retired by the state and the teacher's reciprocated love for the boys who constantly harass him. They desist finally when they realize the cruelty of their pranks.

This sounds hokey but the decent emotions involved are handled skillfully by Muriel, Elias Moreno, as the teacher, and Tejada, as the boys' leader. The film's in-

timacy is jarred by one scene of marching and singing boys plus courting couple also chirping which appears to be right out of a passe musical. Draper's photography sustains the mood and other technical credits are okay. *Meade.*

The Twilight Story
(JAPANESE)
Coronado, Oct. 10.

Toho release of Ichi Sato production. Stars Fujiko Yamamoto, Hiroshi Akutagawa. Directed by Shiro Toyada. Screenplay, Toshio Yasumi from book by Kafu Nagai. At Coronado International Fest. of Films. Running time, 150 MINS.

• Film is a long, tedious story of a familiar film figure, a prostie with a heart of gold. In the past year, she has "Suzie Wonged," "Butterfield Eighted" and "Gone Naked in World" via U. S. films, and it would be difficult to tabulate her appearances in all foreign product.

In this 1960 release in Japan (but not in U. S.), Miss Yamamoto is winning her scarlet letter in Tokyo's red-light district, having come from a small town to finance her mother's illnesses in the only way she knows how.

She pins her hopes for a good man to take her out of this on Akutagawa, a martially discontented teacher who tells her he is single. He is unhappy at home because his wife has born the child of her former master. Akutagawa returns to his wife and Miss Yamamoto is made even more unhappy when she learns that her uncle, Masao Oda, has squandered funds entrusted to him and her mother has died for lack of care. Miss Yamamoto is desperately ill and life continues its downward spiral in the red-light district. Film ends on this cheery note.

Miss Yamamoto is beautiful and a capable actress judging by her performance here. Akutagawa is okay as the teacher. Oda is fine as the unworthy uncle as are a number of the girls who have taken to the tenderloin. *Meade.*

Weekend Pass
Coronado, Cal., Oct. 13.

Pama (Paul von Schreiber) Production. Stars von Schreiber, Jane Wald and Suzi Carnell. Directed by John Howard. Screenplay, Robert Somerfield; camera, John Stevens; editor, Howard; music, Bill Marx; sound, Ted Gomillion; script supervisor, Liz Shannon. Reviewed at Coronado International Festival of Films. Running time, 40 MINS.

This initial production effort by Paul von Schreiber, a young Hollywood actor, premiered here to good audience reception and has power for the present and promise for the future. Long for a short and short for a feature, its hybrid length may hinder von Schreiber's search for a release. It is offbeat enough to draw comment and commercial enough to please customers.

Von Schreiber plays a hinterland sailor on weekend liberty in Los Angeles where, like any wandering, friendless stranger, most of what he sees is the garish neon sneer of the city and its derelicts. A Pershing Square pickup (Suzi Carnell) proves to be a religious fanatic who delivers a deranged harangue in a bar.

A dance hall girl (Jane Wald)

appears to be a loneliness cure, and is, until Von Schreiber, reminded he has forgotten something, learns it is a $10 fee, not a goodnight kiss.

Von Schreiber, Miss Wald and Miss Carnell are excellent in the lead roles and the city-street types, persuaded to be themselves for the camera, are arrestingly authentic as are the sights and sounds. Technical credits are okay. A wealth of ideas has offset paucity of budget in this entry by a group of talented youngsters. *Meade.*

Toys on a Field of Blue
Coronado, Cal., Oct. 13.

Independent production written, produced, directed and photographe by Richar Evans. Stars George Ashley and Paul and Mitchell Evans. Associate producer and editor, Gil LaVeque. Reviewed at Coronado International Festival of Films. Running time, 23 MINS.

Loneliness apparently is the forte of young independent producers for it is the topic of this initial effort previewed here just as it was in Paul von Schreiber's "Weekend Pass," screened earlier the same night.

Writer Evans has cast his own two boys as youngsters who cross the path of an impoverished wino, Ashley, still scarred by memories of World War I. Having missed an annual free holiday dinner for veterans, the only place he finds understanding, Ashley is rejected at an audition for department store Santa Clauses because he cannot laugh on cue.

After an afternoon of watching children play war with ingeniously contrived duplicates of adult weapons, Ashley is disturbed by the two boys while consoling himself with a bottle of cheap wine. When he tries to return an abandoned wagon to the frightened boys, his mind returns to a wartime experience of grenading two men. He flees in terror from the mindsight. The children arrive home breathless and find a toy missile under the Yule tree.

This is an excellent first effort revealing latent talent in Evans and LeVeque and is effectively played by Ashley and the boys. It has its laughs but they are bitter, more bile than smile. *Meade.*

The Purple Hills
(C'SCOPE—COLOR)

Satisfactory lower-berth western.

Twentieth-Fox release of Maury Dexter production. Stars Gene Nelson, Joanna Barnes, Kent Taylor. Directed by Dexter. Screenplay, Edith Cash Pearl, Russ Bender; camera (De Luxe), Floyd Crosby; editor, Jodie Copelan; music, Richard La Salle; assistant director, Frank Parmenter. Reviewed at Iris Theatre, Oct. 18, '61. Running time, 60 MINS.

Shepard	Gene Nelson
Barnes	Kent Taylor
Chito	Danny Zapien
Young Brave	Medford Salway
Deputy	Russ Bender
Amy Carter	Joanna Barnes
Martin	Jerry Summers
Beaumont	John Carr

"The Purple Hills" smoothly fulfills the companion function for which it has been designed. Action-packed, picturesquely photographed in CinemaScope and De Luxe Color, and trimmed to a sensibly snug 60-minutes, the 20th-Fox release makes a serviceable running mate, especially handy for pairing opposite attractions aimed at juvenile audiences. Customers looking for surprises or story subtlety won't find them in the modestly-budgeted Maury Dexter production (shot within a week), but, by lower-berth western fiction standards, the film is more than adequate.

Written by Edith Cash Pearl and Russ Bender, the plot is concerned with the efforts of a one-shot bounty hunter (Gene Nelson) to obtain the sizeable cash reward offered for his victim, whom he has buried after the shooting. His claim is complicated when the dead man's mercenary partner in crime (Kent Taylor) protests that it was he, not Nelson, who accomplished the desired killing. Then both are promptly confronted with the arrival of the victim's kid brother, whose aim is to kill the killer is frustrated by the twin claims. The confusion is resolved by a war party of Apaches, who manage to slay the right man (Taylor). After all his pains, Nelson decides he doesn't want the reward money after all, scrupulously but pennilessly rides off into the sunset with the kid brother and his attractive guardian (Joanna Barnes).

The three stars dispatch their roles competently, with the satisfactory support of Jerry Summers (the brother), Russ Bender (co-author of this piece), Danny Zapien, Medford Salway and John Carr.

The economy-minded savvy of producer-director Dexter is backed up by editor Jodie Copelan, art director John Mansbridge, composer Richard La Salle and cameraman Floyd Crosby, latter's De Luxe photography of the Apacheland, Arizona filmsite giving a special lift to the production. *Tube.*

Mr. Sardonicus

Another William Castle chiller, short on shock, but fairly suspenseful and more rational than most in the genre. Gimmick audience "poll" for exploitation; should do well enough.

Columbia release of a William Castle production. Features Oscar Homolka,

Ronald Lewis, Audrey Dalton, Guy Rolfe. Directed by William Castle. Screenplay, Ray Russell; camera, Burnett Guffey; editor, Edwin Bryant; music, Von Dexter. Reviewed in N.Y., Oct. 19, '61. Running time, 89 MINS.

Krull .... Oscar Homolka
Sir Robert .... Ronald Lewis
Maude .... Audrey Dalton
Sardonicus .... Guy Wolfe
Father .... Vladimir Sokoloff
Anna .... Lorna Hanson
Elenka .... Erika Peters

William Castle's latest excursion in fantasy-horror should please most chill-prone audiences and do okay at the b.o. It may, however, leave some craving for more blood and oldfashioned spookery than the producer has chosen to lens this time. Those who dig the shock-for-shock's-sake approach are apt to feel a little cheated, because Castle has woven the tale of "Mr. Sardonicus" with rather more intelligence than is usually accorded the genre, and the moments aimed at making audiences recoil are well-spaced and story-integrated with relative plausibility.

Credit for the more reasoned delineation must be shared with Ray Russell, who did the screenplay from his original story (in Playboy mag). For example, where the inevitable medical angles come into play, Russell has scorned the usual visual hokum; and his explanation for the tragedy that befell Sardonicus (facial disfigurement) is handled with simple logic rare for this type of exploitation product.

Well-mounted story deals with a British doctor's efforts to cure facially-disfigured Mr. Sardonicus, complicated by the fact the mistress of his Mittel Europa barony is the medic's former sweetheart. It develops (via flashback) that the nobleman's misfortune owes to shock and guilt over encountering the skeletonized features of his [illegible] e (he the nom-de-ghoul Sardonicus) after invading the old man's grave to claim a winning lottery ticket.

The doctor's cure is nothing more than a trick, the power of suggestion. It's enough to shock Sardonicus back to facial normality, but still leaves him without the ability to eat or speak. Enter producer Castle at this point to "invite" audiences to ballot on whether Sardonicus has or hasn't suffered enough. He hasn't, and some sweet and amusing revenge occurs to wind up the tale. Pertinent for exhibs, Columbia is furnishing gimmick ballot cards for lobby distribution. The word-of-mouth on [illegible] me otherwise indifferent patronage.

Picture succeeds nicely at the atmospheric level, and though Castle is not long on "shock," there are still some adroit moments of this type. The grave excavation, for one. Then there's the quick cut to a pretty maid, bound to a chair, while leeches "treat" her face—one of Sardonicus' efforts (others are simply suggested) to find a cure for his disfigurement. And there's also the critical moment audiences first glimpse his chilling face.

Guy Rolfe, as the title character, is quite efficient, and Ronald Lewis' limning of the London doctor is likewise convincing. His love, and Sardonicus' fear-fraught wife, is played satisfactorily by Audrey Dalton, while Oscar Homolka turns in a highly effective job as the nobleman's jack-of-all-trades, mostly evil. In lesser but well-handled appearances are Vladimir Sokoloff, Lorna Hanson and Erika Peters.

Castle's direction is restrained and tidy, and Burnett Guffey's photography is a strong contribution. Other technical credits also rate plus. *Pit.*

Ce Soir Ou Jamais
(Tonight or Never)
(FRENCH)

Paris, Oct. 17.

Pernand Rivers release of Elefilm-Ulysse production. With Anna Karina, Claude Rich, Jacqueline Dano, Anne Tonietti, Francoise Dorleac, Michel De Re. Directed by Michel Deville. Screenplay, Deville, Nina Companeez; camera, Claude Lecomte; editor, Miss Companeez. At Monte Carlo, Paris. Running time, 95 MINS.

Valerie .... Anna Karina
Laurent .... Claude Rich
Martine .... Jacqueline Dano
Anita .... Anne Tonietti
Danielle .... Francoise Dorleac
Alex .... Michel De Re

Fairly sprightly romantic comedy takes place in an apartment in which a group of young theatrical hopefuls are planning to put on a show. But seduction and criss-cross desires are the main thing. Pic is somewhat strident and shrill rather than witty. But it has a feeling for movement and displays a new talent for situation comedy, director Michel Deville.

This has that "New Wave" feeling in little known actor, seemingly off-the-cuff shooting, and an absorption in personal quirks rather than in coherent narrative. The couples mill about, dance and have flirtations. And through it all, a headstrong, childish, but sexually adult girl, gets the man she wants.

Actors are personable if somewhat too precious in their actions and speech. The tendency to improvise sometimes leads to good scenes but also to free-for-alls that are not too clear on the soundtrack. Anna Karina is fetching as the girl who gets her man. The others are adequate.

Chances abroad look limited because of the uneven treatment. But if properly handled and placed, its youthful exuberance could make this a possible specialized entry. *Mosk.*

The Queen's Guards
(BRITISH—COLOR)

Tribute to the Guards Regiments. Slight story but enough to prevent this becoming just a colorful documentary. There's a streak of snobbishness in the yarn and dialog that some may find hard to swallow; may be difficult to put over except in specialized situations.

London, Oct. 17.

20th-Fox release of Michael Powell production. Stars Daniel Massey, Raymond Massey, Robert Stephens, Jack Watson, Peter Myers; features Jess Conrad, Ursula Jeans, Frank Lawton, Anthony Bushell, Duncan Lamont, Ian Hunter, Jack Allen. Directed by Michael Powell. Story and screenplay by Roger Milner from an idea by Simon Harcourt-Smith; camera, Gerald Turpin; editor, Noreen Ackland; music, Brian Easdale. At Carlton Theatre, London. Running time, 110 MINS.

John Fellows .... Daniel Massey
Captain Fellows .... Raymond Massey
Henry Wynne-Walton .... Robert Stephens
Sergeant Johnson .... Jack Watson
Gordon Davidson .... Peter Myers
Mrs. Fellows .... Ursula Jeans
Commander Hewson .... Frank Lawton
Major Cole .... Anthony Bushell
Dankworth .... Jess Conrad
Photographer .... Cornel Lucas
Mr. Dobbie .... Ian Hunter
Susan .... Elizabeth Shepherd
Ruth .... Judith Stott
Major Wilkes .... Duncan Lamont
Brigadier Cummings .... Jack Allen
Farinda .... Laurence Payne
Mrs. Wynne-Walton .... Eileen Peel

Michael Powell's new production is a very British subject which may need careful exploitation except in specialized houses. Based on the belief among many people in Britain that, nowhere in the world is there such a great fighting force as the Guards Regiments, it is a kind of prolonged documentary sketchily pegged to a thin story line.

It runs the risk of being accused of snobbishness and snootiness. It is all very stiff upper lip and pukka. Yet, in a warming way, it does show something of the years of tradition and history that have gone towards making the Queen's Guards what they are. This may have more than mere curiosity value for foreign viewers and, certainly, it will enable Americans to view the Trooping of the Color in rather more detail and comfort than most have been able to do in London.

In fact, the ceremony of Trooping the Color is the framework for the film. It is told in a series of flashbacks going through the mind of a young Guards officer while on duty at the ceremony as leader of the escort to the Color. His thoughts take in his days of training at Sandhurst, his relationship with his father, his romances, his misery at the belief that his brother, killed during the war, had sacrificed his men through a blunder, his relief when he finds that in fact his brother died a hero and the memory of a recent brisk action in the desert when he lived up to the name of the brother he idolized.

Training sequences are sometimes slow but offer some superficial and amusing glimpses of backstage life in the Guards; the war sequence is credible and, though not urgently exciting, lifts the film to a firm climax. The Trooping of the Color sequences offer a piece of pageantry that, in CinemaScope and Technicolor, is fascinating to watch.

Powell has directed with meticulous attention to detail and, without getting bogged down too much in any one facet, has been able to present a welldrawn picture of the life and thoughts of the average Guards officer. Daniel Massey and Robert Stephens are two buddies who, with Duncan Lamont, Anthony Bushell and Peter Myers epitomize most people's impression of Guards officers. Jack Watson makes a stalwart sergeant.

It was a shrewd thought to cast Raymond Massey as the dyed-in-Guards-tradition, disabled father of Massey Jr. and Massey pere gives a sound performance in a rather overwritten and overdrawn role. Ian Hunter brings relief as a down-to-earth haulage contractor who is by no means impressed by Guards officers. Judith Stott and Elizabeth Shepherd do all they can with a couple of rather skimpy roles as the girl friends of Massey and Stephens. Ursula Jeans, Frank Lawton, Jack Allen, William Fox, Nigel Green and Laurence Payne bring polish to minor roles. Jess Conrad, a local pop singer, is also given a part, mainly as an excuse for him to sing a not very distinguished ditty, but he shows promise with his limited opportunities for acting.

Under Gerald Turpin, a half dozen cameramen have done a notable job with the Trooping of the Color ceremony and the other lensing and artwork are all up to scratch. Much of the film was actually shot at the Guards' barracks and hence has the right note of authenticity. The film is backed throughout by rousing military music given a lilting zest by the expertise of the Mounted Band of The Horse Guards and the Massed Bands, Drum and Pipes of the Brigade of Guards. Nothing but the best in this department. *Rich.*

On Friday At Eleven
(BRITISH)

Taut thriller about the hi-jacking of a payroll armored car. It wobbles somewhat once the plan goes haywire but still packs a wallop that will keep patrons on edge.

London, Oct. 17.

BLC release of a British Lion (Alexander Gruter) production. Stars Rod Steiger, Nadja Tiller, Ian Bannen, Peter Van Eyck, Jean Servais. Directed by Alvin Rakoff. Screenplay, Frank Harvey from James Hadley Chase's novel, "World In My Pocket"; camera, Vaclav Vich; editor, Alice Ludwig-Basch; music, Claude Bolling. At Plaza Theatre, London. Running time, 93 MINS.

Ginny .... Nadja Tiller
Bleck .... Peter Van Eyck
Gypo .... Jean Servais
Kitson .... Ian Bannen
Morgan .... Rod Steiger

Filmed partly in Germany, partly in the South of France with much of the technical work done in Britain and with a cast and crew recruited from several nationalities, "On Friday at Eleven" is a complete co-production hybrid. This thriller sags somewhat, particularly after the halfway mark, and ends in some improbable melodrama. But it is guaranteed to keep most patrons in a state of chilly expectancy, and is a reliable booking for most situations.

Story is the one about a ruthless gang's plan to hijack an armored payroll car containing a million dollars, how it inevitably goes wrong and how, equally inevitably, retribution falls on the crooks. It is directed by Alvin Rakoff with a sharp, hard intensity while Frank Harvey's screenplay adroitly keeps suspense drawn as tight as a drumskin.

Cast consists virtually of five people, the members of the gang. Boss is Morgan (Rod Steiger). The others are a quarrelsome, lecherous albino (Peter Van Eyck), a neurotic safecracker with an obsession about snakes (Jean Dervais) and an edgy driver (Ian Bannen). The gang is persuaded to try the scheme by the tongue of an ice-cold, beautiful Teutonic moll (Nadja Tiller), who originated the plan. The idea involves faking an auto accident which will cause the armored car to stop, persuade the guards to leave it, allow the gang to move in, hide the car in a trailer and travel to a caravan camp where, among holidaymak-

ers, they can set about the task of opening up the armor. It is an ingenious plan, and it is fascinating to watch it being evolved.

But, of course, things go wrong. The driver doesn't leave his charge and, though wounded, managed to kill one of the gang in a series of chilly suspense sequences. An over curious child at the caravan site alerts the police, and soon the gang and its haul is on the run. Right up to the time that the plan misfires this is fine, suspenseful stuff. But it seems to fall apart at the caravan site. Although it perks up to a very exciting climax, there is not the cold, clinical, nail-biting tautness at the end as in most of the first half.

Steiger plays the gang leader with tough compulsion while Bannen, Servais and Van Eyck provide contrasting types to produce four credible criminal characters. Miss Tiller gives a sullen, humorless performance and might occasionally have permitted herself a shade more emotion. But she makes fine impact in one sequence where the gang raids a night club and the girl reveals just how tough she is on the surface—but only on the surface.

Vaclav Vich's camerawork is spare and effective while Claude Bolling has provided useful background music which helps to point up the tension. *Rich.*

What A Whopper
(BRITISH)

Unpretentious farce which extracts plenty of humor from predictable situations. Introduces Adam Faith, local top pop warbler, in his first pic which should mean good British b.o.

London, Oct. 17.
Regal release of a Viscount (Teddy Joseph) production. Stars Adam Faith, Sidney James, Carole Lesley. Features Terence Longdon, Clive Dunn, Freddie Frinton, Marie France, Charles Hawtrey, Spike Milligan. Directed by Gilbert Gunn. Screenplay, Terry Nation; camera, Reginald Wyer; music, Laurie Johnson; editor, Bernard Gribble. Songs. "What a Whopper!" and "The Time Has Come," by Johnny Worth. At Rialto Theatre, London. Running time, 89 MINS.
Tony .... Adam Faith
Harry .... Sidney James
Charlie .... Carole Lesley
Vernon .... Terence Longdon
Mr. Slate .... Clive Dunn
Gilbert Pinner .... Freddie Frinton
Marie .... Marie France
Arnold .... Charles Hawtrey
Tramp .... Spike Milligan
Postie .... Wilfred Brambell
Mrs. Pinner .... Fabia Drake
Sammy .... Harold Berens
Jimmy .... Ewan Roberts
Macdonald .... Archie Duncan
Sergeant .... Terry Scott
Grace .... Anne Gilchrist
Jojo .... Lloyd Reckord
Policeman .... Lance Perceval
Teacher .... Mollie Weir
Commentator .... Fyffe Robertson
Man Lover .... Graham Stuart
Girl Lover .... Eileen Gourlay

The British appetite for this type of unpretentious, slapstick comedy appears to be insatiable. This latest example is a sound dualer, with no pretentions to wit, but which gets continuous yocks from predictable situations. A long, reliable cast of known names and faces helps with the producers having gone wisely in for added U.K. b.o. insurance by making this the first film of Adam Faith, a leading pop singer with a big local following.

Faith makes a commendable first appearance though obviously lacking thesp experience. He has a fresh charm, though a rather monotonous speaking voice. He also sings a couple of ditties which will please his public though neither seems destined for the Top 10. They are by Johnny Worth and give the singer little scope.

Acceptable premise for this type of comedy has Faith as an aspiring young writer living with some arty beatnik types—a surrealist painter (Charles Hawtrey), a sculptor (Lloyd Reckord), a composer (Terence Longdon) and a dumb socialite, blonde (Carole Lesley), who is in love with Longdon. They are relying on the publication of Faith's book about the Loch Ness Monster to make ends meet. When its thumbed down they hit on a resourceful idea. They make their own Monster, photograph it and then set off to Scotland to kid the locals that they have seen the Monster. In this way, Faith figures, the publisher's interest in the book will be revived.

From this situation springs a lot of cheerful malarkey, complications arising from a lot of climbing in and out of bedrooms and much losing of trousers and femme dresses. But though some of the lark is repetitious, the thesps hammer home the comedy enthusiastically. Gilbert Gunn keeps his direction on its toes.

Faith makes a likeable young hero while Terence Longdon provides amiable support as his buddy. Neither Miss Lesley nor a French newcomer, Marie France, has the technical knowhow to make the roles of the girl friends more than pretty puppets. There are some ripely funny performances by such well-tried troupers as Sidney James, as a get-rich-quick Loch Ness saloonkeeper; Freddie Frinton, for years a top exponent of comedy drunkenness, as the tipsy father, and by Wilfred Brambell, as the village postman. Spike Milligan also has a hilarious cameo as an eccentric hobo. Fabia Drake, Ewen Roberts, Terry Scott, Harold Berens, Charles Hawtrey and Archie Duncan also contribute amusingly.

A sharper, wittier screenplay by Terry Nation was all that was needed to raise "What a Whopper" a cut about its present standing, for the situation and the talent were both available. As it is, the film provides harmless good-humored amusement and a pleasant peek at Loch Ness, through Reginald Wyer's lens. *Rich.*

The Comancheros
(C'SCOPE—COLOR)

Big action western. Implausible story, but fine production values, popular cast, underlying sense of humor. Good b.o.

Hollywood, Oct. 27.
Twentieth-Fox release of George Sherman production. Stars John Wayne, Stuart Whitman, Ina Balin, Nehemiah Persoff, Lee Marvin. Directed by Michael Curtiz. Screenplay, James Edward Grant, Clair Huffaker, based on the novel by Paul I. Wellman; camera (De Luxe), William H. Clothier; editor, Louis Loeffler; music, Elmer Bernstein; assistant director, Jack R. Berne. Reviewed at the studio, Oct. 27, '61. Running time, 107 MINS.
Cutter .... John Wayne
Regret .... Stuart Whitman
Pilar .... Ina Balin
Graile .... Nehemiah Persoff
Crow .... Lee Marvin
Amflung .... Michael Ansara
Tobe .... Pat Wayne
Major Henry .... Bruce Cabot
Melinda .... Joan O'Brien
Horseface .... Jack Elam
Judge Bean .... Edgar Buchanan
Gireaux .... Henry Daniell
Estevan .... Richard Devon
Comanchero .... Steve Baylor
Bill .... John Dierkes
Bub Schofield .... Roger Mobley
Pa Schofield .... Bob Steele
Spanish Dancer .... Luisa Triana
Josefina ...... Iphigenie Castiglioni
Bessie .... Aiessa Wayne
Iron Shirt .... George Lewis

"The Comancheros" is a big, brash, uninhibited action-western of the old school, about as subtle as a right to the jaw. In spite of a plot that's as holey as Swiss cheese, it's a likeable piece of high adventure escape entertainment for anyone open-minded enough to overlook all the little improbabilities and inconsistencies, and just sit back. Kids will love it, because the George Sherman production is CinemaScopically big as all outdoors and action-packed to boot. Adult customers will appreciate the faint tongue-in-cheek strain that weaves through the entire film, a signal that if they aren't willing to take it seriously, that's all right too.

A blockbuster western "The Comancheros" is not. It lacks the depth or substance of story for such aspirations to be entertained. But the 20th-Fox release does have the marquee pull and the production magniture to make a bright and profitable boxoffice showing.

The James Edward Grant-Clair Huffaker screenplay, based on the novel by Paul I. Wellman, is a kind of cloak-and-dagger yarn on horseback. It is set against the Texas of the mid-19th century, a troubled time prior to its statehood when the Comanches were on the warpath and renegade white men, or "Comancheros," were aiding the Indian cause with fighting equipment. Against this setting, the film relates the story of a Texas Ranger (John Wayne) and an itinerant gambler (Stuart Whitman) who team up to detect and destroy the renegade, parasitic society. Among the incidental complications they also must solve are: (1) Wayne actually is bringing Whitman to justice for having killed a man (though fair and square in a pistol duel), (2) Whitman loves Ina Balin, who happens to be the daughter of the Comanchero chieftain. Both problems are overcome with consummate ease, considering their formidable nature.

Wayne is obviously comfortable in a role tailor-made to the specifi-

cations of his easygoing, square-shooting, tight-lipped but watch-out-when-I'm-mad screen personality. Whitman and Miss Balin are valuable talents on the rise, and will widen considerably their appeal and popularity via this vehicle. Both seem at home in the western idiom. Lee Marvin makes a vivid, indelible impression in a brief, but colorful, role as a half-scalped, vile-tempered Comanchero agent. Ben Nye's makeup job on Marvin's pate is masterfully gruesome.

Nehemiah Persoff creates an animated portrait of the invalid leader of the Comancheros. As in "The Alamo," the Wayne brood is well represented, with Pat and Aiessa on hand. Former is vigorous in a key part. Others who perform capably in prominent supporting roles are Michael Ansara, Bruce Cabot, Joan O'Brien, Jack Elam, Edgar Buchanan, Henry Daniell and Richard Devon.

Save for a few essentially irrelevant or slow-moving scenes, director Michael Curtiz has done a more than commendable job of keeping this large-scale production high-spirited, coherent and sufficiently intimate to sustain concern. He was fortunate in having aboard some excellent stunt men whose hard falls, leaps and maneuvers during the raid and battle sequences (directed by Cliff Lyons) are something to see. Their tactics help in diverting one's attention from dwelling too long on the annoying fact that neither Comancheros nor Comanches seem able to hit the side of a barn with their absurdly errant gunfire.

Cameraman William H. Clothier's sweeping panoramic views of the Moab, Utah site are something to behold. Unfortunately, some of the studio shots don't match (the brown hills turn purple). Louis Loeffler's editing is taut, art direction by Jack Martin Smith and Alfred Ybarra generally accurate-looking. Elmer Bernstein's score is stirring, and brings excitement and thrust to simple, establishing scenes. But it's an oddity that one comes out of the theatre humming his already familiar score for last year's "The Magnificent Seven." There's considerable similarity between the two, but it's a pleasant similiarity. *Tube.*

Bachelor in Paradise
(CINEMASCOPE— METROCOLOR)

A restrained but nonetheless quick-with-the-quip Bob Hope and a nifty looker Lana Turner in welldressed, frequently diverting adult comedy. Should be okay boxoffice.

Metro release of Ted Richmond production. Stars Bob Hope and Lana Turner; features Janis Paige, Jim Hutton, Paula Prentiss, Don Porter, Virginia Grey, Agnes Moorehead. Directed by Jack Arnold. Screenplay, Valentine Davies and Hal Kanter, from story by Vera Caspary; camera (CinemaScope and Metrocolor), Joseph Ruttenberg; music, Henry Mancini; title song, music by Mancini, lyrics by Mack David; editor, Richard W. Farrell. Previewed at Loew's 86th Street Theatre, N.Y., Oct. 25. Running time, 109 MINS.
Adam J. Niles .... Bob Hope
Rosemary Howard .... Lana Turner
Dolores Jynson .... Janis Paige
Larry Delavane .... Jim Hutton
Linda Delavane .... Paula Prentiss

Thomas W. Jynson .... Don Porter
Camille Quinlaw ...... Virginia Grey
Judge Peterson ..... Agnes Moorehead
Mrs. Pickering....... Florence Sundstrom
Rodney Jones .... Clinton Sundberg
Austin Palfrey .... John McGiver
Backett .... Alan Hewitt
Mrs. Brown .... Rita Shaw

Like through the years Bob Hope makes with the funny cracks, and Lana Turner who, like the years haven't gone by at all, is lovely to look at. This adds to agreeable romantic and comedic values in a handsome Ted Richmond production that ought to do all right for Metro.

It's engaging, humorous situation material that Valentine Davies and Hal Kanter have provided in their screenplay which, in turn, was taken from a Vera Caspary story. Hope is stocked with numerous funny lines and delivers them in his familiar flip-lip style. There's a little departure from Hope of past, however, for now he's showing a bit of restraint and it's particularly fitting in the story line that might have gotten out of hand in terms of good taste.

It's a no depth (but easy to take) yarn which has Hope as a writer whose business affairs are mismanaged with the result that he's in hock to Internal Revenue. He goes to a newly-developed California community to indite something on what makes American women tick.

The women in town, all young marrieds and pretty, take to him, either for his counsel on marital affairs or a flirtation walk now and then. Menfolk become suspicious, dope it out that the hero is showing too much muscle in the love department. Actually, though, Hope is innocent of any romantic hanky panky, eventually announces his love for Miss Turner, the only single girl in the vicinity.

Nothing special about the performances, but then not too much is demanded of the leads plus Janis Paige, Jim Hutton, Paula Prentiss, Don Porter and Virginia Grey. Suffice to say they all fit in well. Agnes Moorehead is in briefly as a judge in a courtroom scene and this vet showgal plays a rather wacky part to a whimsical turn.

Jack Arnold's direction maintains a breezy pace except for a few lulls which, it seems, could be eliminated by a closer editing job. Music, mainly the title song by Henry Mancini and Mack David (lyrics), is beaucoup agreeable. Joseph Ruttenberg's photography (CinemaScope and Metrocolor) is sharp throughout and takes proper note of the handsome wardrobe and set layouts. *Gene.*

Man-Trap
(PANAVISION)

Heavyhanded suspense meller of dual-bill quality in spite of fairly hefty marquee names, including Jeffrey Hunter from 'King of Kings.'

Hollywood, Oct. 11.

Paramount release of Edmond O'Brien-Stanley Frazen production. Stars Jeffrey Hunter, David Janssen, Stella Stevens. Directed by O'Brien. Screenplay, Ed Waters, from John D. MacDonald's novelette, "Taint of the Tiger"; camera, Lloyd Griggs; editor, Jack Lippiatt; music, Leith Stevens; assistant director, Tom Shaw. Reviewed at the studio, Oct. 11, '61. Running time, 93 MINS.

Matt Jameson .... Jeffrey Hunter
Vince Biskay .... David Janssen
Nina Jameson .... Stella Stevens
Liz Adams .... Elaine Devry
Cortez .... Arthur Batanides
Puerco .... Perry Lopez
Fat Man .... Bernard Fein
Ruth .... Virginia Gregg
Bobby-Joe .... Mike Vandever
E. J. Malden .... Hugh Sanders
Lt. Heissen .... Tol Avery

Melodramas the likes of "Man-Trap" can be found all over television. Long since relegated to supporting or hit-and-run exploitation status on the theatre screen, their popular appeal is limited to those who attend motion pictures either indiscriminately or for uncomplicated, sensual kicks. The presence of three up-an-coming thespic talents in the cast is the best boxoffice ally the Edmond O'Brien-Stanley Frazen-Tiger production has, but this won't be sufficient to offset the shopworn nature of the story and the tasteless, chaotic manner in which it has been executed under O'Brien's direction. The Paramount release appears destined for a swift commercial career, with sexy teaser promotional art honoring Stella Stevens' anatomical endowments the probable main bait for this "Man-Trap."

Ed Waters' screenplay, from John D. MacDonald's Cosmopolitan novelette, "Taint of the Tiger," offers Jeffrey Hunter as the miserable husband of an inexplicably spoiled alcoholic (Miss Stevens) in a sub-bourbon community where the neighbors shoot martini pistols at each other and play a parlor game called "Braille" (blindfolded husbands must identify their wives by feeling all the women) for kicks. Things look bad enough, but then along comes Hunter's old war buddy, David Janssen, to complicate matters even further with a wild scheme for pilfering three-million clams from a Latin syndicate. Since Hunter is in the employ of Miss Stevens' father and malcontent with his parasitical lot, he eventually goes along with the plot, with dire consequences for all involved. (This is a pretty weird role for Hunter following his Jesus in "King of Kings," now roadshowing.)

Earnest performances by all three of the leads are wasted. Waters' dialog is affectedly slick and tough, and the situations, though fast-paced and hard-hitting, are absurd. Support runs to stereotype, especially in the cases of the Latin hoodlums, but Elaine Devry tries hard as the only reasonably healthy individual implicated in this violent emotional mess.

Loyal Griggs' lenswork is capable, and so is Jack Lippiatt's editing, Al Roelofs' art direction and Leith Stevens' score. But it's a lost cause from the beginning. *Tube.*

The Mask
(CANADIAN)

Erratic horror item punctuated by 3-D passages.

Hollywood, Oct. 26.

Warner Bros. release of Julian Roffman (Canada) production. Directed by Roffman. Screenplay, Frank Taubes, Sandy Haver; camera, Herbert S. Alpert; editor, Stephen Timar; music, Louis Applebaum. Reviewed at the studio, Oct. 26, '61. Running time, 83 MINS.

Dr. Allan Barnes ..... Paul Stevens
Pamela Albright........ Claudette Nevins
Lt. Martin .... Bill Walker
Miss Goodrich .... Anne Collings
Michael Radin .... Martin Lavut
Dr. Soames .... Leo Leyden
Mrs. Kelly .... Eleanor Beecroft
Anderson .... William Bryden
Prof. Quincy .... Norman Ettlinger
Museum Guide .... Stephen Appleby
Lab Technician .... Ray Lawlor
Himself .... Jim Moran
Girl Who Is Killed ... Nancy Island
Dr. Barnes (in depth-dimension) Rudy Linschoten
Demon of the Mask ... Paul Nevins

Considering that it would make an especially handy Halloween attraction, it's rather astonishing that "The Mask" is ticketed to open Nov. 1 in L.A., Nov. 11 nationally. Whatever the reason, the Warner Bros. release is being denied exhibition on the one occasion when a horror-shocker of its nature enjoys a special boxoffice advantage. Missing this ideal opportunity, Julian Roffman's Canadian-made production does not figure to cause much of a stir in the cinemarketplace. An untidy execution of a flimsy horror yarn, the sole novelty of this attraction is the incorporation of depth-dimensional (3-D) special effects for the harem-scarem sequences.

"The Mask," according to the Frank Taubes-Sandy Haver scenario, enables the wearer to descend into "the hidden recesses of the human mind." These "hidden recesses" turn out (as the spectator discovers by putting on the 3-D peepers provided) to contain images of a kind of amusement park chamber of horrors character. Just why they inspire in the characters who don the mask an obsession to kill is the biggest mystery about the film. There is plenty of ghoul and gore in these passages, but no genuine chill and suspense of the sort that can only be created by the spectator's imagination, which is never activated by this film.

As directed by Roffman and edited by Stephen Timar, the dramatic action is jumpy, lethargic and inconsistent. Key facets are left dangling inconclusively, even at the climax. Assumptions

Compounding the erratic nature of the production is Herbert S. Alpert's photography, which is frequently too dark, particularly on daylight exteriors. The three LSD-like "trips" into the cadaverous vividly mounted by special effects expert Herman S. Townsley and special photographic effects man James B. Gordon, purportedly with the employment of a unique British camera here used for the first time. Louis Applebaum's music, into which electronic sounds have been incorporated, nicely complements the desired mood.

The actors, most of them relatively unknown to U.S. filmgoers, carry on gamely, notably those involved in the dream sequences. *Tube.*

West End Jungle
(BRITISH)

London, Oct. 24.

Competent, but not sufficiently pointed, documentary about West End vice since the streets were cleaned up by law.

Miracle Films release of Arnold Louis Miller, Stanley A. Long production. Directed by Long. Screenplay, Long and Miller; editor, Stanley Marks; narrator, David Gell; voices, Heather Russell, Tom Bowman. Previewed at Cameo-Poly, London. Running time, 55 MINS.

"West End Jungle" has run into censor trouble and, so far has not copped a certificate permitting allround public exhibitions. It is now being shown at a London film club. Pic also has had the benevolent nod from local authorities in Cardiff, Leeds and Coventry where permitting it to be shown with a certificate that okays this for viewing by anybody over the age of 16.

Producers have set out to make a film that is a "startling and controversial" study of how vice has gone underground in London since the Street Offenses Act of 1959 drove prosties off the street. This perhaps laudable aim has not come off. "Jungle" is a competently made documentary which only the very naive will find remotely startling. It has nothing important, urgent or new to say about its subject and leaves the edgy feeling that what it offers is very much the same thing that it purports to deplore.

This ranges a well-tilled field. It shows how call girls operate and how young women from the provinces are procured for vice. It shows the ramifications of alleged artists in masseuse, nightclub hostesses and prosties in clip near-beer joints. None of it is very edifying and none of it very revealing.

Film simply takes 55 minutes to tell audiences what they already know, that though streetwalkers are now, fortunately, not allowed to roam their beats vice can still be engaged in by any sucker who knows the ropes and has a few dollars.

Where "Jungle" chalks up a credit is that it is directed and written with an occasional sense of humor and also does not fall back on the old cliches of violence, junkies, pimps and so on. David Gell gives with the commentary excellently, the photography is okay and Heather Russell and Tom Bowman cope with various voices adequately. *Rich.*

Pocketful Of Miracles
(PANAVISION—COLOR)

Sentimental comedy based on a Runyon story and a 1933 Capra pic. Sweet and old-fashioned, runs hot and cold. But Capra touch should bring satisfactory b.o.

Hollywood, Oct. 13.

United Artists release of Frank Capra production. Stars Glenn Ford, Bette Davis, Hope Lange, Arthur O'Connell. Directed by Capra. Screenplay, Hal Kanter, Harry Tugend, based on screenplay by Robert Riskin and story by Damon Runyon; camera (Eastman), Robert Bronner; editor, Frank P. Keller; music, Walter Scharf; assistant director, Arthur S. Black Jr. Reviewed at Grauman's Chinese, Oct. 13, '61. Running time, 136 MINS.

Dave the Dude .... Glenn Ford
Apple Annie .... Bette Davis
Queenie Martin .... Hope Lange
Count Romero .... Arthur O'Connell
Joy Boy .... Peter Falk
Judge Henry G. Blake Thomas Mitchell
Butler .... Edward Everett Horton
Junior .... Mickey Shaughnessy
Governor .... David Brian
Steve Darcey .... Sheldon Leonard
Carlos Romero .... Peter Mann
Louise .... Ann-Margret
Police Commissioner..... Barton Maclane
Police Inspector .... John Litel
Mayor .... Jerome Cowan
Spanish Consul ..... Jay Novello
Newspaper Editors..... Frank Ferguson, Willis Bouchey
Pierre .... Fritz Feld

Soho Sal	Ellen Corby
Hotel Manager	Gavin Gordon
Flyaway	Benny Rubin
Cheesecake	Jack Elam
Big Mike	Mike Mazurki
Captain Moore	Hayden Rorke
Pool Player	Doodles Weaver
Mallethead	Paul E. Burns
Angie	Angelo S. Rossitto
Gloomy	Edgar Stehli
Shimkey	George E. Stone
Smiley	William F. Sauls
Herbie	Tom Fadden
Knuckles	Snub Pollard

Once upon a time, say a quarter of a century ago, a sweet, sentimental fairy tale like Frank Capra's "Pocketful of Miracles" would have been an odds-on shoo-in for a happy ending at the wicket windows. But today the tracks are faster, the stakes are stiffer, and the pot of gold more elusive. Yesteryear's favorite is today's long shot. The question is whether unabashed sentiment has gone out of style? The answer would probably be yes, save for the fact that the old master of mellow, firthful mayhem has not lost his unique touch. Hence the United Artists release should be a satisfactory boxoffice candidate, especially useful as a Yuletide season attraction. And, should it manage to do better than satisfactory, it could kick off a renaissance of 30's-type screen comedy.

The Hal Kanter-Harry Tugend scenario, which alternates uneasily between wit and sentiment, is based on the 1933 Columbia release, "Lady for a Day," which was adapted by Robert Riskin from a Damon Runyon story, and directed by Capra. It has to do with an impoverished apple-vender (Bette Davis) who would have her long lost daughter (Ann-Margret) believe that she is a lady of means. This is simple enough when the daughter is on the other side of the globe, but when she comes trotting over for a look-see, mama is in trouble. Enter mama's favorite apple-polisher, influential Dave the Dude (Glenn Ford), who hastily sets up an elaborate masquerade with the aid of a horde of typical Runyonesque hoodlums who are hard as nails on the surface, but all whipped cream on the inside.

The picture seems too long, considering that there's never any doubt as to the outsome, and it's also too lethargic, but there are sporadic compensations of line and situation that reward the patience. Fortunately Capra has assembled some of Hollywood's outstanding character players for the chore, some of whom haven't been seen too often in recent years. These people are pros, masters of things like the double take and the aside, and they play their material to the hilt. When the material cooperates, which it does only occasionally, some comedy sparks are generated.

For the romantic leads, Capra has Glenn Ford and Hope Lange. As a comedy team, they are no James Stewart-Jean Arthur (probably Capra's most formidable star-pairing), but they get by—particularly Ford. Miss Lange is more suitable for serious roles. Miss Davis has the meatly role of "Apple Annie" and, except for a tendency to overemote in closeups, she handles it with depth and finesse.

The best lines in the picture go to Peter Falk, who reveals a flair for comedy to go along with his reputation for gangster parts. Falk just about walks off with the film when he's on. Among the veterans who score prominent points are Arthur O'Connell, Thomas Mitchell, Edward Everett Horton, Barton MacLane, John Litel and Jerome Cowan. Sheldon Leonard comes out of tv-management limbo to spank home his renowned characterization of a lovable Runyon hood. Ann-Margret emotes with feeling. Mickey Shaughnessy clicks in a key role. Especially amusing in comedy bits are Fritz Feld and Jay Novello. Balance of support in the exceptionally large cast is generally solid.

Action onscreen is kept lively and attractive through Robert Bronner's camera work, with a strong assist from editor Frank P. Keller and art directors Hal Pereira and Roland Anderson. Walter Scharf's score is a little heavy on the "Nutchacker Suite," but otherwise unobtrusively helpful.

Tube.

Flight Of The Lost Balloon
(SPECTRASCOPE—COLOR)

Exploitation pic hampered by trite story and crude execution.

Hollywood, Oct. 23.

Woolner Bros. release of Bernard Woolner production. Stars Mala Powers, Marshall Thompson; features James Lanphier, Douglas Kennedy; with Robert Gillette, Felippe Birriel, A. J. Valentine, Blanquita Romero, Jackie Donoro. Directed by Nathan Jurgan. Screenplay and story, Juran; camera (Eastman), Jacques Marquette; editor, Rex Lipton; music, Hal Borne; assistant directors, Howard Alston, Jock Bohrer. Reviewed at Warner Hollywood, Oct. 23, '61. Running time, **91 MINS.**

Ellen	Mala Powers
Dr. Faraday	Marshall Thompson
Hindu	James Lanphier
Sir Hubert	Douglas Kennedy
Sir Adam	Robert Gillette
Gelan	Felippe Birriel
Giles	A. J. Valentine
The Malkia	Blanquita Romero
Native Dancer	Jackie Ronoro

Upon entering the theatre, customers who attend the "Flight of the Lost Balloon" are to be provided with a "motion sickness pill," the better to withstand the turbulance of the adventures depicted in the film. For any discriminating filmgoer who wanders in, a good old-fashioned sleeping pill might be equally as effective. At any rate, it is upon this sort of gimmickery that the boxoffice fortunes of the Woolner Bros. release seem totally dependent.

While it is difficult to determine the exact and ultimate thrust of exploitation, in this case it is probable that the commercial altitude attained will be severely limited by the hot air balloonacy of Nathan Juran's story and screenplay, the ludicrously disproportionate trigonometry of his physical direction, and the crude character of Bernard Woolner's game, but overburdened, production. Woolner's "Balloon" may launch promisingly off easygoing pads, but its life expectancy is as slim as a hydrogen bomb's in mid-air.

According to Juran's wild imagination, a member of the London Geographic Society is being held captive in a dungeon at the headwaters of the Nile by a wicked Hindu fellow who believes the explorer has discovered and hidden Cleopatra's lost treasure. The diabolical Hindu masterminds an elaborate scheme whereby a rescue party is dispatched from London by balloon. Aboard is the explorer's fiancee, whom the Hindu plans to torture in the presence of the explorer to get the desired info. But the villain hasn't reckoned with the frail character of the explorer, who treasures the treasure more than his lady love, remains mum even when milady is on a Spanish stretching rack. Eventually, all the good people escape and the bad people perish.

The disposition of hero Marshall Thompson's chapeau is not only of interest, but is a clue to the absurd nature of these dramatics. Thompson's tophat survives the windy currents of balloon travel, a swim across Lake Victoria and several skirmishes with condors, warriors and gorillas. It is momentarily lost in a chase, miraculously reappears in the next scene, and remains atop his crown until heroine Mala Powers playfully tosses it out of the balloon at the climax, to the great dismay of the witness who has learned to admire its cranial sticktoitiveness. After enduring incidents that would have felled Beowolf, Samson, even Steve Reeves, Thompson politely remarks, "it's been quite a morning." This surely ranks as one of the great understatements of our time.

Thompson's acting conveys a tongue-in-cheek flavor, an understandable approach for anyone who read the script. Miss Powers looks attractively perturbed. James Lanphier strikes a reserved, cunning figure as the Hindu. Douglas Kennedy is animated as the deranged explorer.

Exteriors were shot in Puerto Rico, not exactly a carbon of darkest Africa. Rex Lipton's editing, coupled with Juran's direction, cannot seem to avoid an erratic incompleteness about scene endings. Jacques Marquette's camerawork is colorful, but the crudeness and discernible outline shadows of the process photography tarnishes the illusion of balloon travel and may disturb the educated filmgoing eye.

Tube.

Les Trois Mousquetaires
(The Three Musketeers)
(FRENCH—COLOR—DYALISCOPE)

Paris, Oct. 14.

Prodis release of Films Broderie-Modernes-Film D'Art-Fonoroma production. With Gerard Barry, Georges Descrieres, Bernard Woringer, Jacques Toja, Mylene Demongeot, Perrette Pradiar, Jean Carmet, Daniel Sorano, Francoise Christophe, Henri Nassiet. Directed by Bernard Borderie. Screenplay, Jean Bernard-Luc, Borderie from novel by Alexandre Dumas; camera (Eastmancolor), Armand Thirard; editor, Christian Gaudin. At Balzac, Paris. Running time, **100 MINS.**

D'Artagnan	Gerard Barry
Athos	Georges Descrieres
Portos	Bernard Woringer
Aramis	Jacques Toja
Planchet	Jean Carmet
Milady	Mylene Demongeot
Constance	Perrette Pradier
Queen Anne	Francoise Christophe
Richilieu	Daniel Sorano
Treville	Henri Nassiet

Alexander Dumas' "The Musketeers" gets what is listed as the 20th screen adaptation. Story is assiduously followed with a good share of swashbuckling and swordplay. However, the talk and pageantry between fights is slow. This appears mainly for local consumption, with some actioner slotting abroad possible if sheared.

Director Bernard Borderie does this with tongue-in-cheek for sure moppet appeal. This concerns D'Artagnan's arrival in Paris and his joining the Musketeers of the king in 17th Century France along with helping to save the queen some embarrassment.

Film has been made in two parts with second to follow later as a separate entry. Production dress is good. Players perform with gusto even if some overact in trying to give this some substance.

Mosk.

Le Rendez-Vous
(FRENCH)

Paris, Oct. 24.

Cinedis release of Cinetel-Silver Films production. Stars Annie Girardot, Andrea Parisy, Odile Versois, Jean-Claude Pascal, George Sanders; features Philippe Noiret, Michel Piccoli, Jean-Francois Poron. Directed by Jean Delanney. Screenplay, Jean Aurenche, Pierre Bost; camera, R. Juillard; editor, Henri Taverna. At Le Francis, Paris. Running time, **125 MINS.**

Madeleine	Annie Girardot
Daphne	Andrea Parisy
Edith	Odile Versois
Pierre	Jean-Claude Pascal
J.K.	George Sanders
Paul	Michel Piccoli
Daniel	Jean-Francois Poron

This whodunit is much too long on build to keep suspense alive and lacks the more incisive feel for character to mix its enigmatic love and upper class looksees. Pic looms mainly a local entry with foreign chances calling for pruning. But this is sleekly mounted and acted and could be used for subsequents if well sheared.

An aspiring young photographer tries to blackmail himself into a rich family and is murdered. He had been the lover of the ex-wife of the man now married to a wealthy girl. The mystery unravels neatly to free him and have him back with wife No. 1.

Ordinary characterization and too many coincidences permit this to sag until near the end when a few surprise twists help. Even these are overworked as is the measured, uninspired direction of Jean Pelannoy.

The acting is the best part of this fairly laborious pic. George Sanders plays the ruthless, harsh rich man well while Annie Girardot stands out as the ex-wife. The other are just adequate.

Mosk.

The Wonders of Aladdin
(C'SCOPE-EASTMAN COLOR)

Probably oke potential, but artless hokum.

Metro release of a Joseph E. Levine presentation, produced by Lux Film, Italy. Stars Donald O'Connor. Features Vittorio De Sica, Noelle Adam, Aldo Fabrizi. Directed by Henry Levin. Screenplay, Luther Davis; camera (C'Scope), Tonino Delli Colli; music, Angelo Lavagnino; 2d unit director, Mario Bava. Reviewed in N.Y., Oct. 26, '61. Running time, **93 MINS.**

Aladdin	Donald O'Connor
Djalma	Noelle Adam
Genie	Vittorio De Sica
Sultan	Aldo Fabrizi
Zaina	Michele Mercier
Omar	Milton Reid
Prince Meluk	Mario Girotti
Grand Vizier	Fausto Tozzi
Fakir	Marco Tulli
Magician	Raymond Bussieres
Bandit Chieftain	Alberto Farnese
Vizier's Lieutenant	Franco Ressel

This is cornball escapism for which the audience potential never

seems to run dry. And with Metro ticketing the Embassy-Lux Film coproduction for a splurge of year-end holiday dates, the prospect is less glum than the footage from Tunisia and Rome might otherwise be.

Henry Levin, the director, and Luther Davis, credited with the screenplay, apparently have tried to bring off a spoof of the durable Aladdin legend. Better they should have summoned a genie. The result of their human labors is a pratfall-and-gag session dependent almost entirely on Donald O'Connor's famlar mugging, and projected almost consistently with a painful thud.

The farce is famished. Film piques the imagination to contemplate how the children's fantasy might have fared as a tongue-in-cheek exercise had it been kept more in character as satire, either sly or woolly.

Minarets and mules, decorous ladies and much epidermis, sardonic villainy and preposterous predicaments—these are all there, per vintage recipe, in color on the widescreen. If the intended comedy is generally labored, there is, still, a witty line here and there (for small solace). During a pitched battle, one warrior pulls an arrow from the hide of another, admonishing, *"Chew a little hashish—it will diminish the pain."* For audiences, gum will have to do.

As the day-dreaming boy Aladdin, O'Connor carbons himself as well as the script allows, and this is apt to suffice for kiddies. There is able support from a mostly Italian cast, including two top art circuit names—Vittorio De Sica and Aldo Fabrizi—whose talents have been squandered, especially De Sica's as the lamp-caged genie with three wishes to grant. French ballerina Noelle Adam, who wins O'Connor, is cute (physically). Others who appear to good effect include Marco Tulli, Raymond Bussieres, Alberto Farnese, Milton Reid, and Mario Girotti.

Levin's direction is at least equal to the film's concept, and all other technical credits are adequate.
Pit.

The Second Time Around
(C'SCOPE—COLOR)

Blend of comedy, romance, drama, farce, spoof and western. Genial for easygoing family audiences. Fair b.o. candidate.

Hollywood, Oct. 26.
Twentieth-Fox release of Jack Cummings production. Stars Debbie Reynolds, Steve Forrest, Andy Griffith, Juliet Prowse, Thelma Ritter, Ken Scott. Directed by Vincent Sherman. Screenplay, Oscar Saul, Cecil Dan Hansen, based on novel, "Star in the West," by Richard Emery Roberts; camera (De Luxe), Ellis W. Carter; editor, Betty Steinberg; music, Gerald Fried; assistant director, Jack R. Berne. Riviewed at Picwood Theatre, Oct. 26, '61. Running time, 98 MINS.
Lucretia .... Debbie Reynolds
Dan Jones .... Steve Forrest
Pat Collins .... Andy Griffith
Rena .... Juliet Prowse
Aggie .... Thelma Ritter
Sheriff John Yoss .... Ken Scott
Mrs. Rogers .... Isobel Elsom
Rodriquez .... Rudolph Acosta
Bonner .... Timothy Carey
Shack .... Tom Greenway
Mrs. Trask .... Eleanor Audley
Mrs. Collins .... Blossom Rock
Cissie .... Tracy Stratford
Tobey .... Jimmy Garrett
Mrs. Rodriguez .... Lisa Pons
Mr. Stone .... Nicky Blair

The trouble with "The Second Time Around" is that it's a little too much of everything in general and not enough of anything in particular. It's a western, but it's also a romance, a farce, a situation comedy, a drama and even a spoof. Customers may not know what to make of it, and the non-committal title won't help them any in making up their minds whether or not to indulge. The cast is fairly attractive but, except for Debbie Reynolds buffs, hardly overpowering. The upshot appears to be a fair boxoffice contender of special appeal to youthful, "family" audiences because of its genially inoffensive tone and "Tammy Goes West" character. More selective adults probably would find the 20th-Fox release too frivolous and too obvious for their tastes.

The screenplay by Oscar Saul and Cecil Dan Hansen stems from the novel, "Star in the West," by Richard Emery Roberts. Miss Reynolds plays a N.Y. widow who goes West in 1912 to Arizona in order to establish a new life for herself and her two children. Enroute to this "new life," she ascends incredibly from lowly ranchhand to town sheriff and, with the aid of the decent residents of the town, drives out the lawless elements.

Miss Reynolds is a natural at this sort of thing, and her fans will be delighted to find she hasn't yet lost that unspoiled, wholesome, Little Miss Fixit, girl-next-door quality. She really flings herself into this part, which requires unglamorous mud-splatting, falls and soakings beyond the call of duty. It's her show.

Steve Forrest plays the love interest smoothly, and amiable Andy Griffith lends an easygoing comic note as the romantic rival. Except for one brief, snappy Flamenco, all Juliet Prowse has to do is kind of hover in the unfocused background as Forrest's dancehall flame. She hovers well. Thelma Ritter creates her customary character—an exterior of steel covering up a heart of pure goo. Competent in top support are Ken Scott, Isobel Elson, Rudolph Acosta, Timothy Carey and Lisa Pons.

In guiding the Jack Cummings production, director Vincent Sherman has failed to sense the clash of the story's conflicting elements. Better to stress one facet and softpedal the other than to stir up a hodge-podge. For example, the farce and satire stuff neutralize each other, and the romantic drama is too much of an issue to meld gracefully with the comedy. It's a case of accentuate the positive, eliminate the negative and don't mess with Mr. In-Between or pandemonium is liable to walk upon the scene.

Ellis W. Carter's color photography is deluxe, and that's an adjective, not just a brand name. A few of the intra-scene cuts don't match perfectly, but that appears to be more of a directorial flaw than an editing one. Otherwise, Betty Steinberg's splicing is fine. The Jack Martin Smith-Walter M. Simonds art direction is true to period and locale, as are Don Feld's costumes Square dance strains are featured by Gerald Fried's score, which also makes use of Henry Mancini's tune from "High Time"

from which the title of this picture, curiously enough, was borrowed.
Tube.

Flower Drum Song
(PANAVISION—COLOR)

Uneven translation of the R&H musical but should be dependable b.o. candidate.

Hollywood, Nov. 1.
Universal release of Ross Hunter (in association with Joseph Fields) production. Stars Nancy Kwan, James Shigeta, Miyoshi Umeki. Directed by Henry Koster. Screenplay, Fields, based on the novel by C. Y. Lee; camera (Technicolor, Eastman), Russell Metty; editor, Milton Carruth; music, Richard Rodgers; assistant director, Phil Bowles. Reviewed at Academy Awards Theatre, Nov. 1, '61. Running time, 133 MINS.
Linda Low .... Nancy Kwan
Wang Ta .... James Shigeta
Auntie (Madame Liang).....Juanita Hall
Sammy Fong .... Jack Soo
Wang .... Benson Fong
Helen Chao .... Reiko Sato
Wang San .... Patrick Adiarte
Dr. Li .... Kam Tong
Frankie Wing .... Victor Sen Yung
Madame Fong .... Soo Yong
Professor .... Ching Wah Lee
Headwaiter .... James Hong
Dr. Chen .... Spencer Chan
Dr. Fong .... Arthur Song
Policeman .... Weaver Levy
Holdup Man .... Herman Rudin
Song Girl Friend.........Cherylene Lee
San's Girl Friend .... Virginia Lee
Mei Li .... Miyoshi Umeki

Much of the fundamental charm, grace and novelty of Rodgers & Hammerstein's "Flower Drum Song" has been "overwhelmed" by the sheer opulence and glamour with which Ross Hunter has translated it to the screen. As a film, it emerges a curiously unaffecting, unstable and rather undistinguished experience, lavishly produced but only sporadically rewarding. Still, while hardly an overpowering boxoffice contender, the Universal release is certainly a safe commercial risk, heir as it is to the reputation of Broadway success and the formidable R-H factor. The average film audience figures to overlook or at least dismiss its irregularities and lack of inspiration, and find ample diversion in both its score and story.

The dominant issue in Joseph Fields' screenplay, based on the novel by C. Y. Lee and adapted from the legit book by Fields and Hammerstein, is the clash of East-West romantic-marital customs as it affects the relationships of four young people of Chinese descent living in a state of social flux between two worlds in San Francisco's Chinatown. The four are Nancy Kwan, a gold-digging, husband-hungry nightclub dancer; Jack Soo, a kind of Chinese Nathan Detroit; James Shigeta, most eligible bachelor in Chinatown—the student prince of Grant Avenue; and Miyoshi Umeki, "picture (or mail-order) bride" fresh (and illegally) off a slowboat from China and ticketed for nuptials with Soo. None of the four adhere to the eastern custom of formal, pre-ordained marriages ascribed to by their elders. The romantic chaos is further complicated by overlapping affections, but ultimately all the pieces fall into place in an incredibly hasty double wedding ceremony.

There is something about the main "joke" of this musical that registers disconcertingly as just too precious for words. The humor

is derived from the spectacle of observing Orientals "adjusting to" or "adopting" American customs. It is as if we are being asked to note "how darling" or "how precocious" it is of them to undertake execution of American dances such as the charleston or the rock 'n' roll, to comprehend the science of baseball, or to grapple with U.S. idioms such as "American plan" or "filter, flavor, flip top box" or "that's bop, pop." This is a shopworn device for manufacturing mirth. It comes out hollow, occasionally even distasteful. Chinese-Americans do not figure to be very amused.

As in most R&H enterprises, the meat is in the musical numbers. There are some bright spots in this area of the film, but even here the effect isn't overpowering. It is not one of the team's towering or more memorable scores to begin with, and several of the numbers are not seen to advantage. Best results are obtained on "A Hundred Million Miracles," quaintly-rendered by Miss Umeki; "I Enjoy Being a Girl," striking demonstration, via three-way mirror, of Miss Kwan's rare beauty; and "Grant Avenue," flashy street strut led by Miss Kwan. Two elaborate numbers, "Love, Look Away" and "Sunday," emerge somewhat pretentious and overly-involved, tending to dwarf the activities of some talented dancers and the choreography of Hermes Pan. Scenery by Alexander Golitzen and Joseph Wright is colorful and imaginative, but occasionally tends toward an ornateness and splendor that overshadows the human element. Their replica of S.F.'s Chinatown, however, is pretty remarkable.

Miss Kwan, whose exciting looks herald a great future, demonstrates plenty of dance savvy, and gets by histrionically here. Shigeta handles his number one song role capably and exhibits vocal prowess. Miss Umeki re-creates her Broadway role with the same winning China-doll-like quality. Satisfactory in top supporting roles are Soo, Juanita Hall, Benson Fong, Reiko Sato and Kam Yong. Young Patricia Adiarte makes a vivid impression with his fancy dancing.

Tempo of Henry Koster's direction is somewhat choppy and lethargic. Russell Metty's photography hits the eye with impact, especially in its arrangement and regard of color. Both Technicolor and Eastman Color are utilized. Milton Carruth's editing is satisfactory, Irene Sharaff's costumes frequently ingenious. Music supervisor-conductor Alfred Newman has fashioned some rousing orchestrations, with the assistance of Ken Darby. Dong Kingman's water-colored title paintings are a delight. *Tube.*

Everything's Ducky

Two sailors and a talking duck. Skimpy comedy premise, sluggishly developed. Companion item for the tyke trade.

Hollywood, Oct. 30.
Columbia Pictures release of Red Doff production. Stars Mickey Rooney, Buddy Hackett; introduces Joanie Sommers; features Jackie Cooper. Directed by Don Taylor. Screenplay, John Fenton Murray, Benedict Freedman; camera, Carl

Guthrie; editor, Richard K. Brockway; music, Bernard Green; assistant director, Jerrold Bernstein. Reviewed at Loyola Theatre, Westchester, Oct. 30, '61. Running time, **80 MINS.**

Beetle McKay	Mickey Rooney
Admiral John Paul Jones	Buddy Hackett
Lieut. Parmell	Jackie Cooper
Nina Lloyd	Joanie Sommers
Capt. Lewis Bollinger	Roland Winters
Susie Penrose	Elizabeth MacRae
Lt. Comm. Kemp	Gene Blakely
Chief Conroy	Gordon Jones
Dr. Deckham	Richard Deacon
George Imhoff	James Millhollin
Misanthropist	Jimmy Cross
Duck Hunter	Robert B. Williams
Frank	King Calder
Nurse	Ellie Kent
Corpsman	William Hellinger
Wave	Ann Morell
Simmons	George Sawaya
Froehlich	Dick Winslow
Jim Lipscott	Alvy Moore
Mr. Johnson	Harold Kennedy

"Everything's Ducky" is marketable as a supporting item on double bills aimed either at youngsters or at adults with only the most easygoing dispositions and miniature mentalities. To go beyond that limited audience sphere would not be advisable. The Red Doff (Barbroo Enterprises) production, released by Columbia, is concerned with a talking duck and two quack-pot sailors with whom it shares a series of juvenile misadventures. Even those willing to tag along with this premise will not be rewarded with the kind of ingenious situation comedy development so necessary to sustain interest in a film based on such a skimpy, wild notion.

Written by John Fenton Murray and Benedict Freedman, this fowl play has Mickey Rooney and Buddy Hackett as a pair of simple-minded seamen who befriend the gabby mallard, only to discover it harbors a secret formula vital to the success of a naval satellite launching program. Eventually, all three wind up in the nose cone of a satellite as it circles the earth, and the film concludes in this state of unresolved suspension. Lighter moments are concerned with efforts to capitalize on the duck's gift for gab (frustrated by its martini-guzzling desire) or on attempts to instruct it in the arts of swimming and quacking.

The comic behavior of Rooney and Hackett will probably amuse children. Jackie Cooper is seen briefly as a psychiatrist. Joanie Sommers, a talented vocalist known for her work in the nitery and recording fields, makes her screen bow without warbling a note. As straight actress, she's a bit uncomfortable yet. Elizabeth MacRae adds further romantic interest, and there is competent comedy support from Roland Winters, Gene Blakely, Gordon Jones, Richard Deacon, James Millhollin, Larry Gates and Robert B. Williams. The duck's voice belongs to Walker Edmiston.

Director Don Taylor has done what he can to make capital of the lean material. There isn't much to work with. Editing, art, music and camera work are generally satisfactory. Studio credits list three new songs by Harold Spina, only one of which is heard (the title tune, as rendered by the Hi-Lo's), indicating some last-ditch snipping. *Tube.*

Too Late Blues

John Cassavetes' his first Hollywood pic, after scoring on his improvised indie. "Shadows," shows a flair for movement and character. Needs hard sell.

Paris, Nov. 7.
Paramount release and production. Stars Bobby Darin, Stella Stevens. Directed by John Cassavetes. Screenplay, Cassavetes, Richard Carr; camera, Lionel Lindon; editor, Frank Bracht; music, David Raksin; art director, Tanby Larson. Preemed in Paris. Running time, **100 MINS.**

Ghost	Bobby Darin
Jess	Stella Stevens
Benny	Everett Chambers
Charlie	Cliff Carnell
Red	Seymour Cassel
Shelley	Bill Stafford
Countess	Marilyn Clark
Nick	Nick Dennis
Reno	James Joyce

Paramount decided to release this John Cassavetes film—his first Hollywood-made project—in Europe before it hits the domestic (U.S. and Canada) theatres in January. It's primarily for the arties and lesser situations.

Cassavetes was encouraged by Par after his initial shoestring production of "Shadows," produced entirely in Manhattan. With Hollywood facilities at his command it is conventional although he does adhere to his refreshing approach and, also, he accents the "new faces."

"Shadows" was bought by British Lion and distributed in the U.S. by it. Film did better abroad but was a breakthrough for the New York bunch. If it was rough technically there was a feel and flow of life as the tale evolved from within the characters.

Working now from a script, Cassavetes shows certain flaws. This time he shows a tendency to force casebook psychology on the characters at a loss of spontaneity. Thus an idealistic small time jazz pianist and composer, Bobby Darin, loses his way when he is left by his girl due to a physically cowardly act. Used in an explanatory way there may be something psychologically right in this but it is somewhat too flat and contrived for acceptance in a film.

Same goes for the flashly, good looking would-be singer, Stella Stevens.

So everybody, a group of hip jazz musicians, has his articulate ideas about his state and life. Darin's group is shown playing engagements in orphanages and in a park where nobody comes. A chance for a record date is blown skyhigh when Darin's early insistence on doing what he wants is compromised by his girl's quitting him after his cowardly actions in a pool room brawl.

He becomes the gigolo of an aging woman but finds his spark dampened. He finally seeks out his old girl, now a tramp, and dusts off some elderly suitors and drags her to his old bunch, now playing a sleazy joint. Intimation at ending is that he will take up with them again.

Film never makes it clear whether the Darin character truly has talent or whether he should accept what he has and do his best at it. Ambiguity also robs the pic of a lot of punch. Cassavetes

shows at his best in party scenes where characters are deftly blocked good natured "getting-to-love-you" scenes.

Cassavetes does bring out new talents and other aspects in known people. Darin is effective and does not sing a note, though that is his specialty. His flaccid, unformed face and his fumbling idealism fuse well as he fails to give the needed love to his confused girl which is played with forceful anguish by Miss Stevens.

Others in cast score effectively and especially a non-actor—mainly a tv producer—Everett Chambers, as a vindictive, neurotic agent, stands out.

Party-liners might read into the basic situation a dictate of western culture for personal success, but the same pressures to excel are implicit in Russian life, and indeed universal to human ego, although Marxists chose to blame everything on economics. Nobody is more expert at "speed-up" than the Soviets.

"Too Late Blues" includes a neat jazz score by David Raksin. Dubbing for the musician-impersonating actors are Shelly Mann, Red Mitchell, Benny Carter, Uan Ramsey, Jimmy Bowles.

Still, Cassavetes looms a new director with a flair for atmosphere and an interest in newer themes and stories. His free wheeling insights are to be encouraged. Film has already played the London Film Festival and opens there soon with a probable Paris date in the near future. London fest reviews were fine. *Mosk.*

Los Jovenes
(The Young Ones)
(MEXICAN)

Mexico City, Oct. 31.
Peliculas Nacionales release of Cinematografica Filmex production. Stars Tere Velazquez, Julie Aleman, Adriana Roel, Rafael del Rio; features Dacia Gonzalez, Miguel Suarez, Fanny Shiller, Sonia Infante, Miguel Manzana, Lupe Carriles, Leopoldo Salazar, David Hayat, Oscar Cuellar, Rosa Maria Gallardo, Miguel Zaldivar; special appearances by Enrique Rambal and Carmen Montejo. Directed by Luis Alcoriza. Screenplay and adaptation by Luis Alcoriza. At Variedades and Coliseo theatres, Mexico City. Running time, **95 MINS.**

This is an all-out Luis Alcoriza production, with director doing the original story, screenplay and direction. The picture, a stirring screen indictment of rebellious youth, is based on a true incident a few years ago here.

Just for a prank, three society youths, of good family, one of them a senorita, obeying some compulsive inner emotional urge, stole a car in Mexico City, and sped off to Guadalajara. Federal highway police as well as state enforcement agencies were alerted. The youngsters soon ran out of ready cash, tried to sell the car, but car dealer's suspicions were aroused. So the frightened kids went on the lam again. This time across dirt roads and into country they did not know. And this brought about a tragic end. In a small village the police chief instructed his subordinates to "shoot to kill," and so the three youths were shot down by the cops.

Out of this raw material, Alcoriza has woven a well-paced, tight

action story which borders on the exceptional. Alcoriza's direction attempted to seek out the reason behind the anxious desire of the young to live intensely and dangerously. While there may be questioning of some strong scenes, brutal and realistic, the fact is that film does have vigorous strength and quality.

In black-and-white, pic is technically perfect, with Alcoriza highlighting dramatic moments by judicious camera work. All the actors, youngsters with little box-office stature, turn in exceptional performances. There are some slight defects and director Alcoriza, who wove strong realism in first half, weakens slightly towards the close. Spotty cutting is reflected in sequence jumps. Tere Velazquez, in the role of the young lady, still has a tendency to overact but she is improving.

But the virtues outshine the slight off-key notes. This one is good enough for the American market, if given a dubbed English sound track. And it is scheduled to have good boxoffice, hypoed by controversy, in the Spanish language market.   *Emil.*

Les Amours Celebres
(Famous Love Affairs)
(FRENCH-COLOR-DYALISCOPE)
Paris, Nov. 7.

Unidex release of Generale Europeenne Du Film-Unidex production. Stars Brigitte Bardot, Simone Signoret, Jean-Paul Belmondo, Alain Delon, Dany Robin. Edwige Feuillere, Marie Laforet; features Pierre Brasseur, Suzanne Flon, Jean Desailly, Pierre Vaneck. Directed by Michel Boisrond. Screenplay, France Roche, with four sketches by Pascal Jardin. Marcel Achard (first one), Françoise Giroud (second), Jacques Prevert (third), and France Roche. Michel Audiard (fourth): camera (Eastmancolor), Robert Lefebvre; editor, Raymond Lamy. Preemed in Paris. Running time, 115 MINS.
Agnes .... Brigitte Bardot
Jenny .... Simone Signoret
Albert .... Alain Delon
Torine .... Jean-Claude Brialy
Lauzan .... Jean-Paul Belmondo
Monaco .... Dany Robin
Raucour .... Edwige Feuillere
Deshenoys .... Annie Girardot
Eliane .... Marie Laforet
Ernst .... Pierre Brasseur
Ursula .... Susanne Flon
Baron .... Jean Desailly
Count .... Pierre Vaneck

After the success of the sketch film, "Love The Frenchwoman," now comes a group of tales based loosely on historical love affairs. It has the Brigitte Bardot and Simone Signoret names for the U. S. with a plus in its title. But it will need hard sell since the level is sketchy and skimpy with love and spectacle, backseated by slightly too much talk.

First up is tale of King Louis XIV being deprived of a new mistress by a dashing young cavalier. Here it is played in a boulevard comedy vein with pageantry and elegance that soon wears thin. It is helped by Jean-Paul Belmondo's dash and drive as the man who outwits the king by locking his secret door and keeping the mistress.

Then comes 19th Century melodrama about an aging coquette who has a lover but about to leave her. Simone Signoret is effective as the hardened but romantic woman who is showed up by a plodding if clever police inspector. Muted tinting helps the period flair but this lacks the punch to give the real melodramatics.

Brigitte Bardot appears in the guise of a medieval barber's comely daughter in Bavaria. She is coveted and won by the local prince. But Miss Bardot's pouting, kittenish sensuality is sadly amiss in old Bavaria. And her trial for witchcraft is unintentionally risible. The whole thing needed a tongue-in-cheek approach. It is only intermittently so.

End of pic has two waspish 19th Century actresses fighting over roles and a baron in the Comedie-Francaise of that period. Though played with vigor by Edwige Feuillere and Annie Girardot, this sketch wears thin in its repetitiveness.

Color is well used throughout with subtle differences in each period. But director Michel Boisrond tends to leave all this talky and flat in direction, depending mainly on his actors to put it across. This keeps things on a theatrical, almost comic-strip level because of the lack of pace and character buildup. Then, too, there is the papier-mache feeling of the period sets.

But this may cash in okay at the b.o. in France on the name values, insouciance and popularity of sketch pix. It has selling factors abroad, too, but seems better fitted for more general distribution than for arty house needs. Production coin seems to have gone more for marquee names than for spectacle.
Mosk.

A Majority Of One
(COLOR)

Choice play becomes choice pic. Offbeat casting results in colorful, interesting performances. Bright b.o. contender.

Hollywood, Nov. 9.
Warner Bros. release of Mervyn LeRoy production. Stars Rosalind Russell. Alec Guinness, Ray Danton, Madlyn Rhue. Directed by LeRoy. Screenplay, Leonard Spigelgass, based on his play; camera (Technicolor), Harry Stradling Sr.: editor, Philip W. Anderson; music, Max Steiner; assistant director. Gil Kissel. Reviewed at the studio, Nov. 9, '61. Running time, 156 MINS.
Mrs. Jacoby .... Rosalind Russell
Koichi Asano .... Alec Guinness
Jerome Black .... Ray Danton
Alice Black .... Madlyn Rhue
Mrs. Rubin .... Mae Questel
Eddie .... Marc Marno
Mr. McMillan .... Gary Vinson
Bride .... Sharon Hugueny
Noah Putnam .... Frank Wilcox
Amer. Embassy Rep. .. Francis De Sales
Mr. Asano's Sec'y .... Yuki Shimoda
Mrs. Putnam ...... Harriett MacGibbon
Capt. Norcross .... Alan Mowbray

Leonard Spigelgass' unabashedly sentimental, yet warm and compatible brew of schmaltz and sukiyaki, has now become an outstanding film. The Mervyn LeRoy production beautifully mounted and especially notable for the exciting results obtained from some bold, strikingly unconventional casting, will appeal to a wide audience and is a solid commercial prospect.

Few pictures that come to mind have ever embodied such natural appeal for the middle-aged or elderly patron. The response of the Serutan set, that segment of the audience largely neglected by the adult screen fare of recent years in favor of wilder, more provocative themes aimed at the young adult, will be a significant boxoffice factor. Furthermore, this is a choice and unusually substantial family attraction, with a penetrating scrutiny of deeply ingrained, passive prejudice. If it fails to attract the young adult audience, and there is reason to believe it will be least magnetic in this area of its draw, the Warner Bros. release should more than make up for that through its uncommonly potent charm for other age groups.

Rosalind Russell and Alec Guinness play the parts created on Broadway by Gertrude Berg and Cedric Hardwicke. Were lesser actors involved, the argument might have been advanced that, for purposes of absolute authenticity, the roles should have been awarded to a Jewish actress and a Japanese actor, or more reasonable facsimiles thereof. But Miss Russell and Guinness are artists, and their performances not only reflect that artistry but actually bring a vigor to the characters that might have been missing had the roles been cast purely for physical and/or verbal accuracy. Producer LeRoy is to be commended for his sense of dynamic casting and director LeRoy for following through with perceptive leadership in execution.

Miss Russell's Yiddish hex-cent. though at times it sounds like what it is—a Christian imitating a Jew —is close enough to the genuine article that, accompanied by acutely sensitive gestures, attitudes and mannerisms, it conveys the character almost to perfection. Even more astonishing is the way Miss

Russell has been completely deglamorized into a matronly woman. Orry-Kelly's costumes are a big help in this regard. In all ways, it's a deep, hearty performance, rich in humor and in understanding.

Guinness, even with eyes slanted and hair tightly drawn back, does not really look very Japanese. Rather he becomes Japanese through physical suggestion and masterful elocution It's a challenging role for this actor, but no one is better equipped to meet such a challenge.

Madlyn Rhue and Ray Danton play Miss Russell's daughter and son-in-law, latter the diplomat whose assignment to Japan paves the way for the unusual (Charley Chan's Jewish Rose) romance between middle-class Brooklyn widow and wealthy, influential Tokyo widower The characters limned by Miss Rhue and Danton are somewhat devoid of vigor, but the performances are sound. Mae Questel attracts attention with a portrayal of a Brooklyn neighbor that borders on. but never quite crosses completely over into, caricature. Marc Marno, a member of the original Broadway company, is a definite standout in an atypical part—an arrogant, opportunistic Japanese servant—that is a complete and welcome departure from the stereotype. Competent support is added by Gary Vinson, Sharon Hugueny, Frank Wilcox, Francis De Sales, Yuki Shimoda, Harriett MacGibbon and Alan Mowbray.

A prize job of art direction by John Beckman. accompanied by some equally astute set decoration by Ralph S. Hurst, really dresses up this film. The three main interiors (Miss Russell's Brooklyn apartment, Danton's cluttered diplomat quarters and the lavish Tokyo pad of Guinness) present striking contrasts and point up the purity, simplicity and functional sense of Japanese decor compared with the bulky chaos that can occur in a Western home. Harry Stradling Sr.'s camerawork is keenly conscious of humorous effect—very alert in the way it will draw back to spot. say, an awkward leg under a coffee table. But some of the process stuff aboard ship leaves something to be desired. Editing by Philip W. Anderson and music by Max Steiner are further assets to one of the finer films of the year.
Tube.

X-15
(PANAVISION—COLOR)

Confusing tale of the record-shattering aircraft, its test pilots and their women. Timely factor may put punch in openings.

Hollywood, Nov. 10.
United Artists release of Henry Sanicola-Tony Lazzarino production. Stars David McLean. Charles Bronson, James Gregory; features Ralph Taeger, Mary Tyler Moore, Patricia Owens, Lisabeth Hush, Brad Dexter, Kenneth Tobey. Directed by Richard D. Donner. Screenplay, Lazzarino, James Warner Bellah, from story by Lazzarino; camera (Technicolor), Carl Guthrie; editor, Stanley Rabjohn; music, Nathan Scott; assistant directors, Russ Haverick. Jay Sandrich. Reviewed at Academy Awards Theatre, Nov. 10, '61. Running time, 107 MINS.
Matt Powell .... David McLean
Lt. Col. Lee Brandon ....Charles Bronson

Major Ernest Wilde ... Ralph Taeger
Major Anthony Rinaldi ... Brad Dexter
Col. Craig Brewster .... Kenneth Tobey
Tom Deparma .... James Gregory
Pamela Stewart ..... Mary Tyler Moore
Margaret Brandon ..... Patricia Owens
Diane Wilde .... Lisabeth Hush
Mike Brandon .... Stanley Livingston
Col. Jessup .... Lauren Gilbert
Major McCully .... Phil Dean
Lt. Commander Joe Lacrosse ... Chuck Stanford
Susan Brandon .... Patty McDonald
B-52 Pilot .... Mike MacKane
Test Engineer .... Robert Dornam
Ed Fleming, ABC .... Himself
Lee Giroux, NBC .... Himself
Grant Holcomb, CBS .... Himself
Lew Irwin, ABC .... Himself
Security Policeman ...... Frank Watkins
Secretary .... Barbara Kelley
Nurse .... Darlene Hendricks
Narrator .... James Stewart

Even with the front pages of the nation's newspapers conducting what is tantamount to the perfect advance publicity campaign, "X-15" is a rather dubious prospect. Much too t[illegible] 'ved for the layman—at times it resembles a training film more than a popular entertainment—the Henry Sanicola-Tony Lazzarino production also tends to blur the human elements by focusing at length on mechanical cockpitfalls and control room-inations, with accompanying militarese mumbo-jumbo, thus failing to stimulate anything even remotely related to an emotional response in the audience. The United Artists release will simply have to depend on its up-to-the-minute, topical and highly patriotic nature for a boxoffice showing. Openings may be fairly strong, as a direct result of this timeliness and topicality, but [illegible] may quickly ground this aircraft.

Failure of "X-15" to emerge as satisfactory entertainment is doubly disheartening in that there is evidence that a potentially stirring and certainly significant story has been misplaced somewhere between outline paper and processed celluloid. The screenplay by Lazzarino and James Warner Bellah is hackneyed and confusing, and execution is awkward and frequently incoherent.

Story, simply enough, is concerned with the flight and domestic problems of the X-15's three test pilots. But none of the characters are endowed with any real identity or personality. Furthermore, it's never really made clear to the audience, until just prior to the climax, what the drama's ultimate objective is, with the result that the viewer never is able to get his bearings and establish perspective or sense of direction. It's all pretty baffling.

Equally disconcerting is the film's shaky start and its failure to resolve several side issues. We are introduced to too many people too quickly, and we are pushed into the thick of things before being given a chance to establish concern. Several individual scenes, as separate entities, have been directed capably by Richard D. Donner (a tv director here helming his first feature) but the whole is erratic and disjointed. Stanley Robjohn's editing leaves dramatic lapses and question marks. Both cameraman Carl Guthrie and special aerial photog Jack Freeman have had to cope with some formidable difficulties, such as shooting through glass and dodging reflections. Some of their photography is novel and invigorating, however. Music by Nathan Scott lacks that sense of dramatic thrust and explanation that can really aid and enliven an airplane picture. There's also a little too much "Nothing Can Stop the Army Air Corps" in Scott's score.

Under the circumstances, the actors don't have much of a chance to put any sock into their performances. Charles Bronson and James Gregory seem to fare the best, former as one of the three test pilots, latter as project test director. Other two pilots are played capably by David McLean and Ralph Taeger. Three suffering wives are portrayed by Mary Tyler Moore, Patricia Owens and Lisabeth Hush. James Stewart narrates.
Tube.

The Hellions
(BRITISH-TECHNICOLOR)

Violent yarn of outlaws terrorizing a South African veldt town'et; overemphasized performances but could ring the bell in many situations.

London, Nov. 7.

BLC release for Columbia of an Irving Allen-Jamie Uys (Harold Huth) production. Stars Richard Todd, Jamie Uys, Anne Aubrey, Marty Wilde, James Booth, Lionel Jeffries; features Ronald Fraser, Zena Walker. Directed by Ken Annakin. Screenplay by Harold Swanton, Patrick Kirwan, Harild Ruth, from Swanton's story; camera, Ted Moore; editor, Bert Rule; music, Larry Adler. At Odeon, Leicester Square, London. Running time, **80 MINS.**

Same Hargis .... Richard Todd
Priss Dobbs .... Anne Aubrey
Ernie Dobbs .... Jamie Uys
John Billings .... Marty Wilde
Luke Billings .... Lionel Jeffries
Jubal Billings .... James Booth
Mark Billings .... Al Mulock
Matthew Billings .... Colin Blakely
Frank .... Ronald Fraser
Julie Hargis .... Zena Walker
Malachi .... George Moore
Mike the Barman .... Bill Brewer
Jan Pretorius .... Jan Bruyns
Martha Pretorious .... Lorna Cowell
Billy Dobbs .... Freddie Prozesky

Clearly devised as a rough, violent picture designed to give a kick to audiences that relish raw meat, "The Hellions" certainly does that, and should hit a profitable market in popular situations. But, too often, this "Western," set in the South African veldt 100 years ago goes overboard in the unpleasantness of its studied violence, despite some obvious and wise trimming by the censor.

What this variation of the old-hat "High Noon" theme mainly lacks is the cold, menacing suspense that comes from atmosphere and understatement. Everything, acting, writing and direction, is exaggerated. The yarn concerns the arrival of "The Hellions," a band of murderous thugs consisting of Luke Billings (Lionel Jeffreys) and his four sons. They are out to get the local police sergeant (Richard Todd).

Todd finds that he can get no support from the other men in the township as the gang openly defies him. There comes the inevitable tussle with his conscience and his wife's appeal to toss in his job and save his skin. Eventually duty is rewarded—the timid local storekeeper is provoked into helping him and then the remainder of the village rallies, and the gang is duly wiped out.

Richard Todd is stiff upper lip and reliable as the sergeant, but, thanks to the stilted screenplay, the audience will feel more for his physical than his moral dilemma. Lionel Jeffreys leads the gangsters (James Booth, Al Mulock, Marty Wilde and Colin Blakely) with all stops out. Director Ken Annakin might have been well advised to tone down performances which, at times, borders on the ludicrous when not vicious. Jamie Uys does a commendable job as the craven storekeeper. There is a likeable performance by Ronald Fraser as the local saloon-keeper. Anne Aubrey and Zena Walker handle insignificant chores, as the wives of Uys and Todd respectively, with confident charm.

The color of the South African veldt has been well captured by cameraman Ted Moore. As an extra bonus for younger patrons, Mary Wilde briskly sings the song over the credits.
Rich.

Auguste
(Kolka, My Friend)
(FRENCH)

Paris, Nov. 7.

Cocinor release of Marceau production. Stars Fernand Raynaud, Valerie Lagrange, Jean Poiret; features Palau, Roger Carrel. Directed by Pierre Chevalier. Screenplay, Raymond Castans, Chevalier from play by Castans; camera, Marcel Grignon; editor, Gabriel Rongier. At Lord Byron, Paris. Running time, **90 MINS.**

Auguste .... Fernand Raynaud
Francine .... Valerie Lagrange
Publicist .... Jean Poiret
Banker .... Palau
Cousin .... Roger Carrel

An expert vaude and video mime, Fernand Raynaud is never well served in films. This attempt at satirizing publicity and film milieus is lacking in inventiveness and shows quickie production aspects. It is mainly a local item.

A timid bank clerk saves a starlet during a phony suicide attempt and becomes a hero. He is utilized by an unscrupulous publicist until he catches on and turns the tables and walks off with the starlet to cash in on his fame via freeloading.

Listless direction never can go from satire to pathetic shafts. Raynaud's clowning is wasted here. Technical credits are lacklustre and supporting cast, except for Jean Poiret's monstrous pub man, is below par.
Mosk.

Hadaka No Shima
(The Island)
(JAPANESE)

Paris, Nov. 7.

Cocinor release of Kindai Eiga Kyokai production. With Nobuko Otowa, Taiji Tonoyama, Shinji Tanaka, Masanori Horimoto. Written and directed by Kaneto Shindo. Camera, Kiyoshi Kuroda; editor, Toshio Enoki; music, Hikaru Hayashi. Preemed in Paris. Running time, **95 MINS.**

Toyo .... Nobuko Otowa
Senta .... Taiji Tonoyama
Taro .... Shinji Tanaka
Jiro .... Masanori Horimoto

An elemental tale of the life of a poor farming family on a small island, off the Japanese coast, without water, this is lifted by an unerring feeling for life and drama. This remains absorbing despite the fact that nobody in this family, father and mother and two small boys, says a word during the whole film. It is mainly an arty theatre bet on its style and treatment. Right handling could make this something that could do specialized biz in subsequents.

The parents make many trips to the mainland in a rowboat to get water. Their treks soon elevate this ritual to the mainstay of their lives. The boys fish and help with chores. One goes to school. Only sounds they make are cries of joy when a fish is caught.

Director-writer Kaneto Shindo has lovingly traced the daily routine of these hard working people. The silence is rarely forced. Only at intervals does the film cut away when something was about to be said.

Songs of children are the only things mouthed in this sincere, moving film. There is no pity or false bravura in it but the pleasure boats that ply by, and the one moment of the mother's revolt and hurt after the death of one of the boys, make it a human story.

Lensing is clear and does not glorify this harsh existence. This somber pic shared the grand prix at the Moscow Film Fest this year with the first anti-Stalinist Russo pic, "Clear Skies."

This is lifted from sentimentality and banality by its power and feeling for the place and its people. It is musically, technically and thespically tops.
Mosk.

Tout L'Or Du Monde
(FRENCH)

Paris, Nov. 14.

Cinedis release of SECA-Filmsonor-Cineriz production. Stars Bourvil; features Philippe Noiret, Claude Rich, Annie Fratellini, Colette Castel, Alfred Adam. Written and directed by Rene Clair. Camera, Pierre Petit; editor, Louisette Hautecoeur. At Ambassade-Gaumont, Paris. Running time, **90 MINS.**

Mathieu,
Toine .... Bourvil
Victor .... Philippe Noiret
Fred .... Claude Rich
Rose .... Annie Fratellini
Stella .... Colette Castel
Jules .... Alfred Adam

French director Rene Clair has turned out an updated look at that old theme of the city slickers and the hick. The film mixes satire, whimsy, fable and comedy unevenly. It gives the pros and cons of both sides, but pulls an ironic ending rather than letting it emanate from the people themselves. This is a weak link in this fairly sprightly if overstretched comedy.

On its polish and directing aspects this could be a good foreign bet. But the pic still has an old fashioned ring about its fantasy which slants it more for specialized chances than for depth possibilities.

Clair has such pre-war comedy classics to his credit as "Italian Straw Hat," "Under Paris Roofs," "A Nous La Liberte" and "Le Million." But since the war, his pix have been glossy and brilliant on the surface but lacking warmth. They have been doing well locally if spotty abroad.

Here, two high-pressure real estate operators decide to buy a sleepy little town, where people live long, and turn it into an immense new housing area featuring the lure of long life and a rejuvenating spring. The townspeople immediately sign over their property except for a cantankerous old man.

The city people try everything but it all misfires. The old man is finally killed tearing down one of the signs on his property.

However, this lad loves a town belle but his timidity is stalling the romance. The real estate man keeps up his endeavors and even ties him up with a publicity-seeking singer which allows for a look

at television, "New Wave" film-making and the general prob' s of urban life as opposed to rustic simplicity. He is packed home when he exposes the shady dealings of the big business men on a tele show.

Then the staving off of the final signing is somewhat dragged out with the invention of another brother and the final getting together of the peasant and his girl. But the real estate man dies of a heart attack at that moment and the whole project comes to nought.

Bourvil is a disarmingly clever actor who plays the father and son with fine timing. Other roles are stylishly right whether they represent rapacious big business or country types. But after a fast montage of city life, that brings laughs and anticipation, the film has only intermittent scenes of expert comedy.

Clair still shows a flair for working out gags but the whimsy and satire are somewhat surface without the exemplary pacing that marked his earlier efforts. This looks to do well here with chancier aspects abroad. Technical qualities are firstrate and Clair shows his usual aplomb. *Mosk.*

Drug Moi. Kol'ka
(RUSSIAN)
Paris, Nov. 7.

Mosfilm production and release. With Sasha Kobozhev, Anya Rodionova, A. Kuznetsov. Directed by Alexandre Salgtikov, Alexandre Mitta. Screenplay, A. Hmelik, C. Yermolinska; camera, V. Maslenikov; editor, A Zharenov. Preemed in Paris. Runnin time, 85 MINS.
Kolka .... Sasha Kobozhev
Masha .... Anya Rodionova
Rudenko .... A. Kuznetsov
Klava .... Tania Kuznetsova
Yura .... Alesha Borzhunov

A great popular success in Russia, this film was made by two graduate students of the Russo film school. Its twitting of formalistic, slogan-ridden Soviet education is its main plus factor. Otherwise this fresh, simple pic is only average. Chances abroad are limited except for special placement on its theme and diverting aspects.

Plot is familiar. But its slap at the conformism of party line teaching tactics, and the heady playing and direction, keep this moving along. It is technically good and another example of the thaw in Russo film subject matter.

In spite of its implied criticisms, there is the happy ending and the young pioneers go off in their truck singing the Young Communist song. *Mosk.*

Valley Of The Dragons

Corny caveman spec. OKay appeal for youngsters.

Hollywood, Nov. 15.

Columbia Pictures release of Byron Roberts production. Stars Cesare Danova, Sean McClory, Joan Staley; introduces Danielle De Metb. Directed by Edward Bernds. Screenplay, Bernds, from story by Donald Zimbalist based on Jules Verne's "Career of a Comet"; camera, Brydon Baker; editor, Edwin Bryant; music, Ruby Raksin; assistant director, George Rhein. Reviewed at the studio, Nov. 15, '61. Running time, 79 MINS.

Hector Servadac .... Cesare Danova
Denning .... Sean McClory
Deena .... Joan Staley
Nateeta .... Danielle De Metz
Od-Loo .... Gregg Martell
Tarn and Doctor .... Gil Perkins
Patoo .... I. Stanford Jolley
Anoka .... Michael Lane
Vidal .... Roger Til
Andrews .... Mark Dempsey
LeClere .... Jerry Sunshine
Mara .... Dolly Gray

With a splice here and a process shot there, the makers of "Valley of the Dragons" have assembled, for modest programming purposes, a corny caveman spectacle that is shopworn even by 20-year-old cinema standards. Unless the memory betrays, source of much of the footage appears to be "One Million B.C.," the 1940 Hal Roach production. Even the story here related is astonishingly similar to that fossiliferous fricassee of two decades ago, although its origin is traced to a yarn by Jules Verne. Upshot of this iguanachronism is a film that would divert only the very young, and it is that segment of the audience toward which the Byron Roberts production-Columbia release should be aimed and programmed.

According to Edward Bernds' screenplay, which stems from Verne's "Career of a Comet" by way of a story by Donald Zimbalist, two men are swept into space on a fragment of earth torn from its moorings by a straying 1881 comet. For some incredible, ill-explained reason, they emerge in a land inhabited by pre-historic paraphernalia such as mastodons, neanderthals and plateosaurs. Fortunately, though, they encounter two maidens more indigenous to Schwabs than the Stone Age and willing to play Jane to their Tarzan, proceed to correct a Hatfield-McCoy situation between two tribes of apemen, and settle down, with Flintstone-like togetherness, to enjoy the advantages of living paleontology. Their sole contributions to eolithic culture: gunpowder and the smooch.

Cesare Danova and Sean McClory manage to act this out with straight faces, albeit sometimes too straight under the circumstances. Joan Staley and Danielle De Metz are the Mesozoic glamour girls. Bernds' direction is mechanically capable, considering the patch-work aspect of his chore. Among the adequate assists are those of cameraman Brydon Baker, art director Don Ament, editor Edwin Bryant, soundman Lambert Day, special effects man Dick Albain and composer Ruby Raksin.
Tube.

The Day The Earth Caught Fire
(BRITISH)

Topical, absorbing yarn hinged on nuclear science and set against a newspaper background; worthwhile b.o. bet.

London, Nov. 14.

BLC release of a British Lion-Pax presentation of a Val Guest Production. Stars Janet Munro, Leo McKern, Edward Judd; features Gene Anderson, Edward Underdown, Michael Goodliffe, Arthur Christiansen, Bernard Braden, Reginald Beckwith, Austin Trevor. Directed by Val Guest. Screenplay by Wolf Mankowitz and Val Guest; camera, Harry Waxman; editor, Bill Lenny; music, Stanley Black. Previewed at Columbia Theatre, London. Running time, 99 MINS.

Jeannie .... Janet Munro
Bill Maguire .... Leo McKern
Peter Stenning .... Edward Judd
Night Editor .... Michael Goodliffe
News Editor .... Bernard Braden
Harry .... Reginald Beckwith
May .... Gene Anderson
Editor .... Arthur Christiansen
Sir John Kelly .... Austin Trevor
Angela .... Renee Asherson
2d Sub Editor....... Peter Butterworth
Foreign Editor ...... Charles Morgan
Sanderson .... Edward Underdown
1st Sub Editor .... John Barron
Holroyd .... Geoffrey Chater
Michael .... Ian Ellis
Nanny .... Jane Aird
Ronnie .... Robin Hawdon

Val Guest's latest production is as topical as today's newspaper headlines and, for that alone, it can be tagged an intriguing, worthwhile booking. But it also has a fascinating yarn, some very sound thesping and, for once, an authentic Fleet Street (newspaper) background. The screenplay by Guest and Wolf Mankowitz has some loose ends and a fairly contrived ending but, nevertheless, this will hold the customers, despite a few flaws.

By mischance, an American nuclear test at the South Pole is conducted on the same day as a Russian one at the North Pole. It first causes a sinister upheaval in the world's weather and then it is discovered that the globe has been jolted out of orbit and is racing towards the sun and annihilation. It's figured that four giant bombs exploded simultaneously might save the grave situation and the world's powers unite, for once, to help a possibly doomed civilization. On the day the bomb is detonated the world goes underground to await the verdict and it is a weakness of the film that the audience is left in the air virtually guessing whether or not the crisis had been arrested.

Drama of this situation is played out as a newspaper scoop. Picture was shot largely in the building of the Daily Express, one of Britain's top sheets. Moreover, Arthur Christiansen, ex-editor of the Express and acknowledged to be one of U.K.'s greatest editors, acted as technical advisor as well as playing the editor. It certainly is rare for a film to have such an authentic newspaper background which gives it added urgency and zest. There is also a sub-plot of a disillusioned reporter and his romance with a girl in the Meteorological Office who, unwittingly, spills the technical beans.

Guest's direction is brisk and makes good use of newsreel sequences and special effects, designed by Les Bowie. Not all the interpolated sequences blend completely harmoniously but their use is justified in giving the film

---

authoritative impact. Dialog is racy and slick without being too parochial for the layman. Harry Waxman's camerawork is fine.

The acting all round is effective. Edward Judd, making his first star appearance, clicks as the hero, the reporter who brings in the vital facts that make the story take shape. He shows rugged charm in his lightly romantic scenes with Janet Munro, who is pert and pleasant in the only considerable distaff role. Outstanding performance comes from Leo McKern, who is tops as a dependable gruff and understanding science reporter. Bernard Braden, Michael Goodliffe, Edward Underdown and Peter Butterworth play Fleet Street newspapermen with the right air of authority. Gene Anderson and Reginald Beckwith provide some light relief as the owners of a club frequented by newspapermen. *Rich.*

Yanco
(MEXICAN)
Mexico City, Nov. 14.

Peliculas Nacionales release of Producciones Yanco production. Stars Ricardo Ancona; Jesus Medina and Maria Bustamante. Written and directed by Servando Gonzalez; camera, Alex Phillips Jr. At Variedades Theatre, Mexico City. Running time, 95 MINS.

This is theatrical release of a controversial experimental films, the joint effort of writer-director Servando Gonzalez and youthful photographer Alex Phillips Jr. (son of Alex Phillips Sr., who was a cameraman originally in Hollywood). Original story, adaptation, editing, acting, and photography were made by non-professional, non-union elements. Director Servando Gonzalez, recently admitted to the director's union is also in hot water for turning out a non-union picture. But both he and Phillips Jr. indicate with this they will go far in motion pictures.

On its first commercial run at the Veriedades, this proved a revelation because its simple story revolves about a tiny lad Yanco, native of a tiny village called Mizquic, which forms part of the Xochimilco area on outskirts of Mexico City. Story centers around All-Saints Day (known as Day of the Dead) and the fact that in this tiny village a way of indigenous life with a blend of Catholic religion and paganism, is still practiced. And exemplified here by sensitive camera work that borders on poetry.

The scenes of the night celebration of the Day of the Dead, with the hundreds of flower-bedecked canoes crowding the lagoons, illuminated with torches, and laden with offerings and food for the departed, are exceptionally well done.

The naturalness of the amateur actors, the admirable montage work, and the agile direction as well as the gifted camera work of young Phillips has created a memorable film experience. It looks solid for Mexicans and the overseas trade.

Picture has virtually no dialog, and the scenes with sound are the least effective. Film was shot without sound, with background effects added in laboratory, under supervision of editor Raul Portillo.

Background music, uncredited, is also excellent. The firm hand of director Gonzalez, who worked for months without haste in the Mizquic area, make his amateur actors appear expert veterans.

This film perhaps shows that Mexico has a talented "New Wave" in technical aspects, that should be given a chance to be heard.

"Yanco" is an arty film, produced on an experimental basis. Yanco, the sensitive lad, and the old grandpappy who is his mentor, form the basic background for a picture that both touch and move the public. Despite some of its shortcomings, this is one of the best Mexican pictures produced in the republic in the past decade.

Emil.

Dynamite Jack
(FRENCH—COLOR)
Paris, Nov. 21.
Imperia release of J. P. Bertrand production. Stars Fernandel; features Eleonora Vargas, Adrienne Corri, Carl Studer, Lucienne Raimbourg. Directed by Jean Bastia. Screenplay, Jacques Ary, Jean Manse, Jacques Emmanuel. Bastia; camera (Eastmancolor). Roger Hubert; editor, Jacques Desagneaux. At Napoleon, Paris. Running time. **100 MINS.**
Dynamite Jack.
Antoine .... Fernandel
Dolores .... Eleonore Vargas
Pegeen .... Adrienne Corri

It was probably thought funny to put malleable-faced comic Fernandal in an American western-type film, simulated in France. Also that it would be a howl to have him playing two parts, a jumpy French visitor and a local gunman killer. The ideas do not quite come off. This pic is without the movement and pacing to have this parody successful. It is thus mainly a dualer item abroad with a plus on the Fernandel monicker.

Film apes a Yank yarn but the terrain seems too flat. The few comic moments are not enough. Fernandel uses his timing and comic terrors to advantage at times but the film is too detached and plodding to take much advantage of his abilities.

Color is okay, but the supporting cast is only ordinary. Technical qualities are par. It is not enough just to copy a Yank oater. There has to be knowhow in direction and mounting that eludes director Jean Bastia. *Mosk.*

Adieu Philippine
(So Long Philippine)
(FRENCH)
Paris, Nov. 14.
Rome Paris Film production and release. With Jean-Claude Aimini, Yvaline Cery, Stefanie Saba, Vittorio Caprioli. Written and directed by Jacques Rozier. Camera, Rene Mathelin; editor. Marc Pavaux. Preemed in Paris. Running time. **110 MINS.**
Michel .... Jean-Claude Aimini
Liliane .... Yveline Cery
Juliette .... Stefant Saba
Pachella .... Vittorio Caprioli

Film is in the "New Wave" idiom via gray lensing, erratic progression and an interest only in what its characters are doing, and not in what happens next. It has a tender tale of two 18-year-old girls and a boy and their comaraderie and growing love. While having a true ring, this is somewhat overlong, with mainly specialized chances abroad.

New director Jacques Rozier works in real settings and does not worry about setups, framing or storyline. It is the little world of youth that is important. In this, it comes across in its callowness, tenderness, growing awareness and simplicity. But this type of pic can lead to a dead end where it is not re-creation.

The girls in question meet a young tele worker and he courts both. They plot against him but one finally gives in. A neat look at vidfilm making, commercial ad pic work, group vacationing and the unfettered cruelty and gentleness of youth are the main plus factors.

The girls in this vehicle are fresh and vibrant while the youth arrogant and self-centered. Pro actor Vittorio Caprioli holds his own with the zesty beginners as a caddish ad film producer, and manages to be human rather than just a caricature. Director Rozier shows a feeling for mood, action and telling understanding of the young even if it tends-to be a bit indulgent at times. *Mosk.*

El Gato Con Botas
(Puss in Boots)
(MEXICAN—COLOR—SCOPE)
Mexico City, Nov. 14.
Peliculas Nacionales release of Peliculas Rodriguez production. Stars Rafael Munoz, Santenon, Humberto Dupeyron, Antonio Raxel, Armando Gutierrez, Rocio Rosales, Luis Manuel Pelayo. Directed by Roberto Rodriguez. Screenplay by Roberto Rodriguez from original story by Sergio Magana, inspired by Perroult fairy tale. At the Americas, Real Cinema, Olimpia and Ariel theatres, Mexico City. Running time, **90 MINS.**

Director-producer Roberto Rodriguez, who in past years has turned out a number of excellent films for children, has surpassed himself in this classic Mexican adaptation of the "Puss-in-Boots" tale by Frenchman Charles Perrault. Rodriguez exploits to the full all the spectacular phases of the original work such as the threatened castle, the Princess in danger and the ferrocious ogre. Dwarf Santanon plays the role of the Puss-in-Boots hero with verve. Abundant trick photography is excellently done.

All other participants in this kiddie trade production comport themselves well, despite the fact that many of them are in early stages of their careers. Amando Gutierrez is especially good as the fearful ogre.

The natural color (Eastmancolor) photography highlights the settings and careful costuming, with uncredited background music and songs adding to the overall effect.

Rodriguez has always shown a sure touch in translating children's fables to the screen, and here he has been helped by the story line worked out by young Mexican playwright Sergio Magana Esquival.

This pic is scheduled for a long, profitable run in Mexico and can be adapted for worldwide release with dubbed in sound. *Emil.*

The Golden Trumpet
(TAIWAN)
San Francisco. Nov. 14.
Shaw Taiwan Ltd., production. Features Fanny Fan. Paul Chang Chung. Li Haiang-chun. Fei Li, Yang-Shih-ching, Chiang Kwong-chao. Directed by Doe Ching. Screenplay, Doe Ching, camera, Tung Shao-yung; music, Chi Hsiang-tang. At Film Festival, San Francisco. Running time, **92 MINS.**

This is a special item which obviously will have some appeal in Southern Asia, but little elsewhere.

It concerns Hong Kong's best trumpet player—The Golen Trumpet—and his search for money. He's a simple fellow and loses cash as quickly as he gets it. Thus, while his wife is hospitalized waiting birth of a their baby, the horn player gets himself beaten up, seduced, becomes a party to a robbery, is suspected of kidnaping and has his trumpet lifted. He loves to gamble—indeed, arrived home broke to discover his wife needed a caesarean—and that's why he goes through these melodramatic incidents.

Film apparently is diverting to Chinese but its context is such that it doesn't mean much to occidentals—for example, hero goes to tremendous lengths to keep wife and a son away from free medical treatment, but western audiences can't understand why there's anything wrong with free medical treatment.

Paul Chang Chung is adequate as horn player and Fei-Li, as his son, steals most scenes in which he appears. Direction and technical credits are okay on this Shaw Bros. production. It has no chance in U.S.

Alba Regia
(HUNGARY)
San Francisco, Nov. 8.
Hunnia Film Studios production. Stars Tatiana Samoilova, Miklos Gabor; features Hedi Varadi, Imre Raday. Directed by Mihaly Szemes. Screenplay, Syorgy Palasthy; camera, Barnabas Hegyi; music, Sandor Szokolay. At Film Festival, San Francisco. Running time, **98 MINS.**

Russian actress Tatiana Samoilova delivered a memorable performance in the Soviet "Cranes Are Flying," but in this Hungarian production she delivers an easily forgettable one, looking calm, unruffled and uninterested throughout this World War II yarn.

Story involves a Hungarian surgeon in a Nazi-occupied town near the Danube. Surgeon, played well by Miklos Gabor, considers himself non-political and operates on wounded of any nationality. Mysterious, beautiful girl (Miss Samoilova) arrives with Russian forces and stays behind when Nazis drive Russians out of the town whose name in days of Roman Empire was Alba Regia. Doctor and girl set up a menage a deux and the girl, who turns out to be a Soviet signal corps infiltrator, also sets up a secret radio.

In combat-loaded finale, doctor saves girl's life by clobbering a Nazi and, as he is operating, Russians drive out Nazis. Instead of winning the girl, however, the surgeon loses her; duty calls her to new assignment in Berlin where, the audience is told she is killed.

Picture is loaded with Soviet-style propaganda, the moral being that one cannot be a humanitarian for humanity's sake but must make a political choice and become an "activist."

Film's also loaded with cinematic cliches, being told in one long flashback. Its characters are, for the most part, stock—the Nazi "beasts," for instance—and the finale's big battle scene is terribly stagey. Mihaly Szemes' direction tends to be draggy and Barnabas Hegyi's camera work is unimaginative. This isn't much of a bet in the U.S., on or off the art circuit. *Stef.*

Over The Odds
(BRITISH)
London, Nov. 14.
Rank release of a Jermyn Productions (Alec C. Snowden) film. Directed by Michael Forlong. Stars Marjorie Rhodes, Glenn Melvyn; features Thora Hird, Cyril Smith, Emma Cannon, Wilfrid Lawson, Frances Cuka. Screenplay by Ernest Player; editor, Reggie Beck; camera, Norman Warwick. At RFD Private Theatre. Running time, **65 MINS.**
Bridget Stone .... Marjorie Rhodes
George Summers .... Glenn Melvyn
Sam .... Cyril Smith
Alice .... Esma Cannon
Mrs. Carter .... Thora Hird
Willie Summers .... Wilfrid Lawson
Hilda Summers .... Frances Cuka
Mrs. Small .... Gwen Lewis
Butcher .... Rex Deering
Marilyn .... Patsy Rowlands
Fruit Vendor .... Fred Griffiths
Fishmonger .... Leslie Crowther
Blonde .... Sheena Marshe
Bridesmaid .... Erica Houen

"Over the Odds" is an unpretentious, slapstick comedy which aims to be nothing more than a nice stooge to a top film. And within its modest limits, this fills that bill. It shows signs of the script having been trimmed down remorselessly so that many scenes and characters have not been developed to full yock-potential, but it contains a plentiful quota of unsophisticated laughs.

Yarn concerns a middle-aged bookmaker whose wife has walked out on him. He decides to marry again and there comes a clash between his bride and his dragon of an ex-mother-in-law. All comes out right after a series of vaudeville gags.

The cast rightly hams up the proceedings without much subtlety. Glenn Melvyn, as the bookmaker, Marjorie Rhodes, as the belligerent ma-in-law, Cyril Smith as the bookie's runner; Wilfrid Lawson, as the bucolic father; and Esma Cannon, as a tippling scrubwoman wrest full value from the cheerful if simple action.

Michael Forlong has directed with straightforward aim. The camera-work is okay and the editing, though occasionally jerky, keeps the film moving within the confined limits of its small framework. *Rich.*

One, Two, Three

Topical, ultra-contemporary farce occasionally too quick-witted. Refreshing, delightful pic and stout b.o. candidate.

Hollywood, Nov. 16.

United Artists release of Billy Wilder production. Stars James Cagney, Horst Buchholz, Pamela Tiffin, Arlene Francis; features Lilo Pulver, Howard St. John, Hanna Lother, Red Buttons. Directed by Wilder. Screenplay, Wilder, I. A. L. Diamond; camera, Daniel Fapp; editor, Daniel Mandell; music, Andre Previn; assistant director, Tom Pevsner. Reviewed at Academy Awards Theatre, Nov. 16, '61. Running time, **115 MINS.**

MacNamara	James Cagney
Otto	Horst Buchholz
Scarlett	Pamela Tiffin
Phyllis	Arlene Francis
Ingeborg	Lilo Pulver
Hazeltine	Howard St. John
Schlemmer	Hans Lothar
Mrs. Hazeltine	Lois Bolton
Peripetchikoff	Leon Askin
Mishkin	Peter Capell
Borodenko	Ralf Wolter
Fritz	Karl Lieffen
Dr. Bauer	Henning Schluter
Count von Droste	Hubert von Meyerinck
Newspaperman	Til Kiwe
Zeidlitz	Karl Ludwig Lindt
Tommy MacNamara	John Allen
Cindy MacNamara	Christine Allen
Bertha	Rose Renee Roth
M.P. Corporal	Ivan Arnold
E. German Corporal	Helmut Schmid
E. German Interrogator	Otto Friebel
E. German Sergeant	Werner Buttler
Second Policeman	Klaus Becker
Third Policeman	Siegfried Dornbusch
Krause	Paul Bos
Tailor	Max Buchsbaum
Haberdasher	Jaspar von Gertzen
Stewardess	Inga de Toro
Pierre	Jacques Chevalier
Shoeman	Werner Hessenland
Jeweler	Abi von Hasse
M.P. Sergeant	Red Buttons

Billy Wilder's "One, Two, Three" is a 115-minute pause that refreshes; a fast-paced, high-pitched, hard-hitting, lighthearted farce crammed with topical gags and spiced with satirical overtones. Story of the mayhem that ensues when an emptyheaded Coca-Cola heiress on the loose in Berlin ties the knot with a card-carrying Communist, it's so up-to-date it's already dated in spots, and so furiously quick-witted that some of its wit gets snarled and smothered in overlap. But total experience packs a considerable wallop. As fresh, frank and funny a film as has come along in some time, the United Artists release should do Grade A Capitalist business.

Written, produced and directed by Wilder, in the former task with the aid of associate I. A. L. Diamond, the Mirisch Co presentation stars James Cagney as the chief exec of Coca-Cola's West Berlin plant whose ambitious promotion plans are jeopardized when he becomes temporary guardian of his stateside superior's wild and vacuous daughter. The girl (Pamela Tiffin) slips across the border, weds violently anti-Yankee Horst Buchholz, and before long there's a bouncing baby Bolshevik on the way. When the home office head man decides to visit his daughter, Cagney masterminds an elaborate frame and masquerade that backfires, nets Buchholz the choice and coveted company assignment earmarked for Cagney.

The Wilder-Diamond screenplay, based on a one-act play by Merenc Molnar, is outstanding. Sometimes it just can't seem to resist obvious puns that might better have been resisted, and sometimes it's so ferociously fast that even the cream of an audience will be hard-pressed to catch over 75% of the significance of the dialog on first hearing, but overall it's a sparkling script that pulls no punches and lands a few political and ideological haymakers on both sides of the Brandenburg Gate. Wilder's direction is sharp, sex-packed and furious, especially astute in the mounting and timing of sight gags and visual horseplay.

Cagney proves himself an expert farceur with a glib, full-throttled characterization. Although some of Buchholz delivery has more bark than bite, he reveals a considerable flair for comedy. Pretty Miss Tiffin scores with a convincing display of mental density. Lilo Pulver, a Swiss beaut, adds sex, glamour, sex, humor and sex as Cagney's all purpose secretary. Arlene Francis plays Cagney's understanding wife with special grace and aplomb. Howard St. John carries off the tycoon role admirably and Hanns Lothar is a consistent delight as a heel-clicking, Prussianesque right hand man. The large supporting cast is effective right down the line, with Leon Askin, Lois Bolton and Karl Lieffen particularly strong in key spots. Red Buttons makes a vivid impression in a brief bit as a shaken M.P.

Daniel Fapp's photography enlivens the talky sequences, of which there are many, via some novel setups, and really shows flair and imagination when things are on the move, such as during a car chase sequence that's almost pure Keystone Komedy. Daniel Mandell's fleet editing is a plus factor, too, in both these regards. Alex Trauner's art direction contributes importantly to the merriment, notably in a most amusing scene set in a smoky East Berlin nightspot. Another significant factor in the comedy is Andre Previn's score, which incorporates semi-classical and period pop themes (like "Saber Dance" and "Yes, We Have No Bananas") to great advantage throughout the film.

Further key assists are those of soundman Basil Fenton-Smith, special effects man Milt Rice and second unit director Andre Smagghe. *Tube.*

I Bombed Pearl Harbor
(JAPANESE—COLOR)

Sneak attack and Pacific war aftermath, from the Japanese point of view. Strictly action. No philosophy, no excuses. Curiosity value, timeliness and exploitation should give it swift b.o.

Hollywood, Nov. 17.

Parade release of Tomoyuki Tanaka production. Directed by Shue Matsubayashi; camera (Technicolor), Kazuo Yamada; editor, Hugo Grimaldi; music, Gordon Zahler, Walter Green. Reviewed at Fox Wilshire Theatre, Nov. 17, '61. Running time, **100 MINS.**

Lt. Koji Kitami	Yosuke Natsuki
Admiral Yamaguchi	Toshiro Mifune
Lt. Tomonari	Roji Tsuruta
Keiko	Miss Uehara
Sato	Aiko Mimasu
Capt.	Jun Tazaki
Lt. Matsuura	Makoto Sato
Tosaku	Takash Shimura

The outbreak and critical early stages of World War II in the Pacific theatre are seen from the point-of-view of the Japanese in "I Bombed Pearl Harbor," a highly-exploitable action film from the resourceful Toho filmmakers of Japan. The emphasis on action should make it a popular attraction for male customers. That, together with the novelty of the perspective and the timeliness of the release (approximately the 20th anni of the infamous attack) should give it a swift, short-lived, but sufficiently potent kick at the box-office, especially on a multi-opening, "spray-and-scram" basis.

Film brings no appreciable new insight into the Japanese war attitude or the reasons for their aggression. If anything, the picture proves only that war looks exactly the same from either side: revolting. Hero of the film, which has been dubbed into English, is a young Japanese flight lieutenant who tastes the tonic of victory at Pearl Harbor, the bitter pill of defeat at Midway. The screenplay does not penetrate very deeply into his thoughts or feelings. Action is stressed throughout.

Dubbing, though exceptionally well executed under the aegis of Riley Jackson, Robert Patrick and Hugo Grimaldi, may trouble the more discerning customer for the reason that the spectacle of English-speaking Japanese attacking Americans tarnishes the absolute authenticity required here for maximum audience involvement.

Most of the action is accomplished through miniature work, a field in which the Japanese screen artisans excel. But, impressive as this work is, these models simply cannot completely convey to the critical eye the illusion of reality. However, the Toho craftsmen have come about as close as possible to this elusive goal. It's quite an achievement.

The young lieutenant is played with zeal and conviction by Yosuke Natauki, a handsome lad. There is a performance of great reserve, strength and dignity by Toshiro Mifune as Admidal Yamaguschi. Supporting work is uniformly satisfactory Shue Matsubayashi's direction is vigorous and fast-tempoed. *Tube.*

Blue Hawaii

Elvis Presley back in stride, doing what comes easiest. Looks sure to please his natural constituency.

Hollywood, Nov. 28.

Paramount release of Hal Wallis production. Stars Elvis Presley; features Joan Blackman, Angela Lansbury, Roland Winters, Nancy Walters, John Archer, Howard McNear. Directed by Norman Taurog. Screenplay, Hal Kanter, based on story by Allen Weiss; camera (Technicolor), Charles Lang Jr.; editor, Warren Low; assistant director, Mickey Moore. Reviewed Nov. 25 at Iris Theatre, Hollywood. Running time, **103 MINS.**

Chad Gates	Elvis Presley
Maile Duval	Joan Blackman
Abigail Prentace	Nancy Walters
Fred Gates	Roland Winters
Sarah Lee Gates	Angela Lansbury
Jack Kelman	John Archer
Mr. Chapman	Howard McNear
Mrs. Manaka	Flora Hayes
Mr. Duval	Gregory Gay
Mr. Garvey	Steve Brodie
Mrs. Garvey	Iris Adrian
Patsy	Darlene Tompkins
Sandy	Pamela Akert
Beverly	Christian Kay
Ellie	Jenny Maxwell
Ito O'Hara	Frank Atienza
Carl	Lani Kai
Ernie	Joss De Varga
Wes	Ralph Hanalie

"Blue Hawaii" restores Elvis Presley to his natural screen element—the romantic, non-cerebral filmusical—one which he has departed for more dramatic doings in his last few films.

It is this sort of vehicle which the singing star seems to enjoy his greatest popularity, the kind his vast legion of fans seems to prefer him in, and Hal Wallis' production for Paramount should enjoy widespread boxoffice success over the short haul.

Hal Kanter's breezy screenplay, from a story by Allan Weiss, is the slim, but convenient, foundation around which Wallis and staff have erected a handsome, picture-postcard production crammed with typical South Seas musical hulaballoo. Plot casts Presley as the rebellious son of a pineapple tycoon who wants to make his own way in life, a project in which he succeeds after numerous romantic entanglements and misunderstandings.

Under Norman Taurog's broad direction, Presley, in essence, is playing himself—a role sure to delight his ardent fans. Romantic support is attractively dispatched by Joan Blackman and Nancy Walters, with stalwart comedy air provided by Angela Lansbury, Roland Winters and Howard McNear.

In a somewhat over-emphasized and incompletely-motivated role of an unhappy young tourist, pretty Jenny Maxwell emotes with youthful relish and spirit. Others able in key spots are John Archer, Flora Hayes, Gregory Gay, Steve Brodie, Iris Adrian, Darlene Tompkins, Pamela Akert and Christian Kay.

Enchancing the production are Charles Lang Jr.'s picturesque photography, Warren Low's snappy editing and Walter Tyler's colorful sets and natural backdrops. Musical numbers, about a dozen of them, are effectively staged by Charles O'Curran. Music is skillfully scored and conducted by Joseph J. Lilley. *Tube.*

Bachelor Flat
(C'SCOPE—COLOR)

Farce comedy of Anglo-American romantic errors. Adequate fare for easygoing customers.

Hollywood, Nov. 22.

Twentieth-Fox release of Jack Cummings production. Stars Tuesday Weld, Richard Beymer, Terry-Thomas, Celeste Holm. Directed by Frank Tashlin. Screenplay, Tashlin, Budd Grossman, based on play by Grossman; camera (De Luxe), Daniel L. Fapp; editor, Hugh S. Fowler; music, Johnny Williams; assistant director, Ad Schaumer. Reviewed at Lido Theatre, Nov. 22, '61. Running time, **92 MINS.**

Libby	Tuesday Weld
Mike	Richard Beymer
Professor Bruce	Terry-Thomas
Helen	Celeste Holm
Gladys	Francesca Bellini
Dr. Bowman	Howard McNear
Liz	Ann Del Guercio
Mrs. Roberts	Roxanne Arlen
Mrs. Bowman	Alice Reinheart
Paul	Stephen Bekassy
Moll	Margo Moore
Paul Revere	George Bruggeman

"Carry On Archaeologist" might be an apt sub-title for this frivolous, farcical concoction about a British bone specialist (dinosaur variety) who is irressistibly attractive to the predatory modern American female. In Terry-Thomas, the Jack Cummings production has a funnybone-fracturer of the first magnitude, and his ace clownsmanship, together with the film's slick, spicy, non-cerebral Schweppervescence, should attract

and divert the less selective,' less skeptical filmgoer seeking a cinematic escape valve from everyday pressure. But the 20th-Fox release is just a mite too risque and suggestive for the family trade and its humor too obvious and anticipatable for the more cautious celluloid sampler. It is not a very robust boxoffice prospect.

Frank Tashlin has directed from his own screenplay, written in collaboration with Budd Grossman, who wrote the play upon which it is based. Thomas is the archaeology professor situated in California, where he is on the verge of wedlock with a roving fashion designer (Celeste Holm) who is abroad on business as the nuptial date approaches. T-T's path to the altar is complicated by: (1) the unscheduled advent of Tuesday Weld, who is Miss Holm's daughter, unbeknownst to the prof; (2) regular invasions of his bachelor quarters by campus cuties hellbent on personally improving Anglo-American relations; (3) the irresponsible advice of cynical student-neighbor Richard Beymer, who has a crush on Tuesday; (4) the singleness-of-purpose of Beymer's dachshund, a typical bona-Fido determined to bury the professor's prize possession—a rare dinosaur bone.

Except for Thomas, whose comic intuition and creativity, abetted by director Tashlin's appreciation of same, is responsible for most of the merriment, it is the supporting cast, rather than the principals, that comes through on the comedy end. Neither Miss Weld nor Beymer seems comfortably at home yet in farce, especially in such fast company as that of Mr. T-T. Both of these young people tend to try too hard to be funny, and the strain often shows through. Miss Holm, a formidable light comedienne, is stuck, regrettably, in a rather bland role. Francesca Bellini, a well-constructed ballerina, shows a flair for comedy as an oversexed lush equipped with an instant martini kit and disposition to match. Dependable Howard McNear generates some comic aid as a rival archaeologist. Adequate support is fashioned by Ann Del Guercio, Roxanne Arlen, Alice Reinheart, Stephen Bekassay, Margo Moore, George Bruggeman and Robert Karnes.

Visually, it is a handsome production, capably designed and mounted by art directors Jack Martin Smith and Leland Fuller, flatteringly lensed by Daniel Fapp. Hugo S. Fowler's editing is satisfactory, although there is a slight lethargy about several scene endings during which he seems to have been somewhat hypnotized by Fapp's picturesque seascapes. Johnny Williams' score is an asset, accompanying the action with strains and rhythms appropriate to the comedy of the moment, such as a Latin rhumba beat for the sequence in which the dog is tugging his king-sized bone across the sand. The dachshund, incidentally, is an accomplished low comedienne.
Tube.

Wa Islamah
(Love and Faith)
(U. A. R.)

Ramses Naguib-Misr Society production. Features Lubna Aziz, Tahia Kariuka, Ahmed Mazhar, Emad Hamdy, Hussein Riad. Directed by Andrew Marton. Screenplay, Robert Andrews; camera, Waheed Farid; music, Fouad Elzahiry. At Film Festival, San Francisco. Running time, **110 MINS.**

This widescreen, color film is supposed to depict the Tartar invasion of Egypt, which is a relatively unknown and meaningless incident in history to Western people. Indeed, it is difficult to separate the "good guys" from "bad guys" in this picture—they all look alike. Actress Lubna Aziz plays Jihad, a sort of Egyptian Joan of Arc who rises from a harem girl to lead her people into battle to repel the invaders. Subplots abound and the story line, almost incomprehensible to start with, is further confused by yellow subtitles which keep jumping around the bottom of the screen.

To put it mildly, the acting is rudimentary. The direction, while having a certain sense of spectacle, fails to convey any pace or, indeed, meaning. Color camerawork is routine. Perhaps with dubbing and some profound cutting this could get a few U.S. playdates as the lower half of double bills but even that's extremely doubtful.
Stef.

El Cid
(70 M-SUPER TECHNIRAMA-TECHNICOLOR)

Spain's 11th century legendary hero paces a jousting, galloping, battling pictorial action romp. Promises big global playoff.

Allied Artists release of Samuel Bronston (and Dear Film) production. Stars Charlton Heston and Sophia Loren. Features Raf Vallone, Genevieve Page, John Fraser, Gary Raymond, Hurd Hatfield, Massimo Serato, Herbert Lom. Directed by Anthony Mann. Associate producers, Jaime Prades, Michael Waszynski. Screenplay by Fredric M. Frank and Phil Yordan; Photography, Robert Krasker; editing, Robert Lawrence; art direction, Veniero Colasanti, John Moore; musical score, Miklos Rozza. Previewed at Loew's State, N.Y., Dec 1, '61 Running time, **180 MINS.**

Rodrigo Diaz (El Cid)	Charlton Heston
Chimene	Sophia Loren
Ordonez	Raf Vallone
King Ferdinand	Ralph Truman
Sancho	Gary Raymond
Alfonso	John Fraser
Urraca	Genevieve Page
Gormaz	Andrew Cruickshank
Don Diego	Michael Hordern
King Ramioro	Gerard Tichy
Don Martin	Christopher Rhodes
Arias	Hurd Hatfield
Fanez	Massimo Serato
Bermudez	Carlo Giustini
Moutamin	Douglas Wilmer
Al Kadir	Frank Thring
Ben Yussuf	Herbert Lom

Samuel Bronston's second Broadway roadshow film, "El Cid," is a fast-action, color-rich, corpse-strewn, battle picture. It's deliberately engineered for international audiences with minimal dialog and characterization. Call it a "moving" picture in the oldfashioned sense of crowds, soldiers, clash, pageantry. Broadsword rings against broadsword, horses and men go down before brutal onslaught. The one reservation is that the action engages the eye rather than the mind. But there is little doubt of its boxoffice potential.

The Spanish scenery is magnificent with a kind of gaunt beauty. The costumes are vivid, the chain mail and Toledo steel gear impressive. Perhaps the 11th century of art directors Veniero Colastani and John Moire exceeds reality, but only scholars will complain of that. There is an obvious plus in the title and theme for all Latin lands since El Cid lived and died a hero and survives as a Hispanic legend. Spanish language and history classes in the U.S. are a special resource for theatre parties during the reserved seat phase.

Action rather than acting characterizes this film. The pictorial values throw the first spotlight to the camera work of Robert Krasker. The regalia of the age lends itself admirably to Technicolor just as the masses of fighting men cram the 70m Technirama screen. Because there is an almost constant series of small skirmishes and large battles some of the scenes become repetitious. Long columns of horsemen silhouetted against twilight or dawn lose dramatic impact in due course. The camera is always in the forefront of the beholder's consciousness, perhaps over-much so. Also the musical score of Miklos Rozsa is occasionally too self-assertive.

Yet the film creates respect for its sheer picturemaking skills. Director Anthony Mann, with assists from associate producer Michael Waszynski who worked closely with him, battle manager Yakima Canutt, and a vast number of technicians, have labored to create stunning panoramic images. This they have surely done.

(Incidentally the main credits on the film mention innumerable names not given on the reviewer's reprise from Allied Artists.)

Of acting there is less to say after acknowledging that Charlton Heston's masculine personality ideally suits the title role. His powerful performance is the central arch of the narrative. He not only makes "El Cid" a man's picture but gives it women appeal. Sophia Loren, as first his sweetheart and later his wife, has a relatively passive role, in the Spanish preference. Although she fights him at the outset when he slays her father in a brawl of honor, knight style, she is the devoted woman most of the way. That means she is spending most of her time in a convent while Heston is out doing the picture's business —fighting, fighting, fighting.

Miss Loren helps "El Cid" rather more than the other way round, giving the marquee its second strong name. There is evidence that the part was fattened up, at least pictorially, during principal photography. Still the glamorous Italian has little to do in the last half but keep the lamp in the window.

Two actors in "King of Kings" who remained over in Spain to appear in "El Cid" ended up as bit actors. Hurd Hatfield is the court herald in a couple of scenes, without personality identification. Frank Thring is a most unconvincing Moorish emir with a shaved noggin who lolls about in a harem registering a kind of sulky impatience.

It's a mixed American, British, Spanish and Italian cast as this is a coproduction of Yank, Iberian and Roman interests. Italy's Raf Vallone is the other man who never has a chance with Chimene. After betraying El Cid he is spared and, at a later period, becomes a follower only to die, tortured, by the invading North African monster, Britain's Herbert Lom. Lom has the curious, for an actor with special billing, experience of doing almost all his acting with his face covered to the eyes by a black mask.

Most provocative performance among the supporting players is that of Genevieve Page, as the self-willed princess who protects the weakling brother who becomes kind after she, sweet sibling, has the older brother slain. One more sequence of Miss Page and one less battle might have been to the picture's advantage. As the sniveling prince, John Fraser starts slowly but ends up creating some conviction.

There is a degree of confusion lurking in the difference between "good Moors" and "bad Moors." Where historic truth lies will not here be proved. The Moslem culture in Spain, which endured for hundreds of years, was a high one with religious tolerance and the script probably intends to hint as much. Hence the second-most-noble character after El Cid, and his good friend and ally, is a cultured Moor played with consider-

able aristocratic charm by Douglas Wilmer.

The direction or possibly Robert Lawrence's editing is a bit unsure at two points, one when El Cid's party is rescued from ambush by one set of Moors by the timely arrival of another. This is accomplished before the spectator quite knows what's what or who's who. Again when the film resumes after intermission El Cid displays an unexplained facial scar, a graying beard and gives the sense of constant warfare. While a good enough device for suggesting the passage of time, Miss Loren is still her pretty self when he stops at the convent to see her and their twin daughters.

Perhaps the strangest facet of the production comes at the end when the final battle is led by El Cid, presumably already dead and strapped to his horse. Just how this stunt could be carried off (legend says it worked) is not explained, nor is the audience explicitly told that the figure is dead. One is inclined to suspect that the version for the Spanish markets may be more pointed. Naturally it is inherently a weird dramatic situation.

In effect the picture carries a foreign title and some New York showmen express the opinion an explanatory subtitle may be desirable. "El Cid" means "The Lord."

That "El Cid" will be a moneymaker is not doubted. How much mileage it can rack up on hard-ducat is more of a question. The film has lots of production and length (three hours), melodrama aplenty, absolutely no humorous relief, two strong star names. The script concocted by Fredric M. Frank and Phil Yordan is knowing but not inspired.

Balance the advantages against the omissions and the verdict is a good action film, a kind of pictorially opulent Spanish Ivanhoe with meagre characterization. But a real fine eyefull.   *Land.*

The Errand Boy

Jerry Lewis at his best.

Hollywood, Nov. 28.

Paramount release of Ernest D. Glucksman production. Stars Jerry Lewis; features Brian Donlevy, Howard McNear, Dick Wesson, Robert Ivers. Directed by Lewis. Screenplay, Lewis, Bill Richmond; camera, W. Wallace Kelley; editor, Stanley E. Johnson; music, Walter Scharf; assistant director, Ralph Axness. Reviewed at Iris Theatre, Nov. 28, '61. Running time, 92 MINS.

Morty S. Tashman .... Jerry Lewis
Mr. T. P. .... Brian Donlevy
Dexter Sneak .... Howard McNear
The A.D. .... Dick Wesson
Miss Carson .... Pat Dahl
Miss Giles .... Renee Taylor
Singer .... Rita Hayes
Grumpy .... Stanley Adams
Mrs. T.P. .... Kathleen Freeman
Irma Paramutual .... Isobel Elsom
Baron Elston Carteblanche .. Sig Ruman
Serina .... Felicia Atkins
Man on Scaffold .... Doodles Weaver
Foreign Director ... Fritz Feld
Mr. Fumble ...... Kenneth MacDonald
Jedson .... Joey Forman
The Great Actress .... Iris Adrian
Mary & Paul Ritts ...... Themselves
Lance .... Dave Landfield
M.C. .... Del Moore

"The Errand Boy" is one of the best and funniest Jerry Lewis pictures to come along. Memory is a fickle and treacherous intangible, but it may even be the best and funniest, period. True, there are some vital breakdowns in the erratic comic machinery of this film, but there is an underlying streak of satire that indicates Lewis is maturing as an artist beyond the sphere of the madcap slapstick - and - sentiment. The cream-pies-in-the-kisser are now being flung and licked with more finesse.

Although there's never been much question about Lewis' commercial standing as a film comedian, there have always been reservations in sophisticated circles over his comic artistry and creativity. 'Errand Boy' not only will sustain his boxoffice reputation, but should reduce those reservations.

Like "The Bellboy" of last year, this Ernest D. Glucksman production for Paramount is a necklace of related comic situations—some of them cultured pearls of humor, some of them duds. Where "Errand Boy" is superior is in comment and observation. Here Lewis is spoofing something that can stand spoofing — the pretentiousness of certain aspects of filmdom. He is letting the air out of the hierarchy, ribbing the "great star," poking fun at yes-manism and pompous henchmen. As a comedy premise manufacturer, his gifts seem inexhaustible. Often he fails in development of his premises, too often he settles for the antique gag and the obvious or unfulfilled climax, but his film (which he directed and, with the aid of Bill Richmond, wrote) is a success as a whole.

The list of stout performances from those Lewis has enlisted for support is too long for individual comment here. Among those most prominently helpful are Brian Donlevy, Howard McNear, Dick Wesson, Robert Ivers, Pat Dahl, Kathleen Freeman, Felicia Atkins, Fritz Feld and Iris Adrian. Behind-the-scenes assistance is tiptop, too, notably W. Wallace Kelley's especially dexterous lens maneuvers, editor Stanley E. Johnson's perceptive sense of sequence, Walter Scharf's inventive musical accompaniment. But this is an entertainment thoroughly dominated by Lewis. And he's dominating well. Jerry Lewis movies are better than ever. Amen.   *Tube.*

The Innocents

(BRITISH)

High - quality, spine - chilling drama, with Deborah Kerr and director Jack ("Room at Top") Clayton as marquee-bait.

London, Nov. 28.

20th-Fox release of Jack Clayton's production. Stars Deborah Kerr; features Michael Redgrave, Peter Wyngarde, Megs Jenkins, Pamela Franklin, Martin Stephens. Directed by Jack Clayton. Screenplay by William Archibald and Truman Capote, based on Henry James' story, "Turn of the Screw"; adaptation by William Archibald and John Mortimer; editor, James Clark; camera, Freddie Francis. At Carlton, London. Running time, 99 MINS.

Miss Giddens .... Deborah Kerr
The Uncle .... Michael Redgrave
Quint .... Peter Wyngarde
Mrs. Grosse .... Megs Jenkins
Miles .... Martin Stephens
Flora .... Pamela Franklin
Miss Jessel .... Clytie Jessop
Anna .... Isla Cameron
Coachman .... Eric Woodburn

Jack Clayton has come up with another high quality film which will enhance the reputation he made with "Room at the Top." That rep plus the presence of Deborah Kerr in the cast should prove selling points for this offbeat psychological drama. "The Innocents," based on Henry James' story, "Turn of the Screw," catches an eerie, spine-chilling mood right at the start and never lets up on its grim, evil theme. Clayton has made full use of camera angles, sharp cutting, shadows, ghost effects and a sinister sound track. In fact, every trick is employed to keep the patrons' hands clammy with apprehension and anticipation.

This is by no means a pretty yarn but it certainly is a compelling one. Miss Kerr has a long, arduous role as a governess in charge of two apparently angelic little children in a huge country house. Gradually she finds that they are not all that they seem on the surface. Soon she is convinced that the young boy and girl share an evil secret which is corrupting them.

She discovers from the housekeeper that the previous governess and her employer's valet had had a passionate, sadistic love affair before they both died. She is now convinced that the two dead people have possessed the souls of the two children and are meeting again in this world through them. Her determination to save the two moppets' corrupted souls leads up to a tragic, powerful climax.

From this chilling plot, William Archibald and Truman Capote have built up a suspenseful screenplay with dark twists and an atmosphere of pending, brooding evil. Clayton's small but expert cast have done full justice to their tasks. Miss Kerr runs a wide gamut of emotions in a difficult role in which she has to start with an uncomplicated portrayal and gradually find herself involved in strange, unnatural goings-on, during which she sometimes doubts her own sanity. It is an excellent performance.

Clayton has also coaxed a couple of remarkable pieces of playing from the two youngsters. Martin Stephens and Pamela Franklin. Though the chances are that they didn't know much about what was going on, their performances are extraordinary blends of innocence and sophistry. Megs Jenkins weighs in with one of her usual dependable and thoughtful characterizations as the housekeeper who refuses to believe the horror that Miss Kerr unearths.

Peter Wyngarde and Clytie Jessop, though important to the story, get little chance of shining since they appear only fitfully and then as hazy figures. Michael Redgrave, in a guest spot as the children's uncle, is suavely effective. Since he disappears after the first few minutes, it might have been wiser to use a lesser player. As it is, audiences may be expecting Redgrave to play an important role in the plot, which doesn't happen. It is a letdown.

Freddie Francis' lensing is skilled, with the lighting and artwork gloomily atmospheric. The sound track and music are great assets in building up the mood of a powerful and gripping though sombre and disturbing picture.   *Rich.*

The Roman Spring of Mrs. Stone

(COLOR)

Tragedy of a fading, widowed actress devoured by Rome's opportunistic romance merchants and her own melancholy. Downbeat Tennessee Williams story of unsavory people, but Vivien Leigh's return to screen after long absence will help.

Hollywood, Nov. 24.

Warner Bros. release of Louis de Rochemont production. Stars Vivien Leigh, Warren Beatty. Directed by Jose Quintero. Screenplay, Gavin Lambert, adapted from novel by Tennessee Williams; camera (Technicolor), Harry Waxman; editor, Ralph Kemplen; music, Richard Addinsell; assistant director, Peter Yates. Reviewed at Academy Awards Theatre, Nov. 24, '61. Running time, 103 MINS.

Karen Stone .... Vivien Leigh
Paolo .... Warren Beatty
Meg .... Coral Browne
Barbara .... Jill St. John
Contessa .... Lotte Lenya
Young Man .... Jeremy Spenser
Mrs. Jamison-Walker ... Stella Bonheur
Lucia .... Josephine Brown
L. Greener .... Peter Dyneley
Baron .... Carl Jaffe
Tailor .... Harold Kasket
Julia .... Viola Keats
Singer .... Cleo Laine
Bunny .... Bessie Love
Mrs. Barrow .... Elspeth March
C. Kennedy .... Henry McCarthy
Giorgio .... Warren Mitchell
Tom Stone .... John Phillips
The Barber .... Paul Stassino
Stefano .... Ernest Thesiger
Mrs. Coogan .... Mavis Villiers
Mita .... Thelma D'Aguir

Vivien Leigh makes her first screen appearance in six years as the star of this gloomy, pessimistic portrait of the artist as a middle-aged widow. There will be considerable curiosity about her return, especially among filmgoing women. This curiosity factor surely will play a significant part in the fortunes of the Louis de Rochemont production, and could even avert the dubious boxoffice career for which the enterprise might otherwise be destined.

But, even with Miss Leigh atop the cast and rising young Warren Beatty as her leading man, the Warner Bros. release seems in for some tough sledding, principally because of the unhappy, unsavory characters dealt with in scenarist Gavin Lambert's adaptation of Tennessee Williams' only novel (published some years ago) characters with whom an audience will have enormous difficulties establishing compassion, let alone identification.

The two-time Academy Award winner here portrays a lonely, uncertain ex-actress who has given up her profession and her past to settle in Rome following the sudden death of her wealthy husband. However reluctantly, she soon falls prey to the foul interests of the fortune-hunting parasites and pimps of Rome who seek monetary rewards in return for romantic favors. But Miss Leigh has the misfortune to fall in love with her "young man" (Beatty), who convincingly feigns amour, then flutters away on another attractive assignment provided by agent-panderer Lotte Lenya. Shaken to despair, Miss Leigh invites in the shadowy, symbolic young man who, silently but ominously, has been

hounding her throughout the drama, waiting for just such an opportune moment. The film concludes on this stark, depressing typically Williamsian note.

Miss Leigh gives an expressive, interesting delineation—projecting intelligence and femininity, as always. "Mrs. Stone," however, is no Blanche DuBois. There's less to work with. Although every once in a while a little Guido Panzini creeps into his Italo dialect and Marlon Brando into his posture and expression, Beatty gives a fairly convincing characterization of the young, mercenary punk-gigolo. Miss Lenya, the noted German actress, is frighteningly sinister as the cunning pimpette—an excellent portrayal. Top supporting roles are capably executed by Coral Browne, Jill St. John and Jeremy Spenser.

Alert, inventive direction by Jose Quintero is helpful throughout. His prolog, or pre-title, scenes are especially well handled and his execution of passages involving Miss Leigh and Spenser—her ill omen shadow—is enthralling and imaginative. An important assist in these areas of the film is contributed by editor Ralph Kemplen.

There is top-notch camerawork by Harry Waxman, who has trained his lens on the players from some interesting vantage points and has captured, in association with Quintero, much of the leisurely pace and romantic antiquity of Rome. Herbert Smith's art direction, in company with John Jarvis' set decoration, shows perception—from the cluttered, ornate chaos of Miss Lenya's abode to the elegance of Miss Leigh's apartment.

Richard Addinsell's melancholy score is another valuable ingredient in the production, filmed in Rome and London. Balmain of Paris has created an attractive wardrobe for Miss Leigh, although one or two of the outfits are better advertisements for the designer than they are personally suitable to the diminutive proportions of the star. *Tube.*

The George Raft Story

Shallow but fairly diverting portrait of the noted and sometimes notorious actor-hoofer. Generally good b.o. looms.

Hollywood, Nov. 27.

Allied Artists release of Ben Schwalb production. Stars Ray Danton, Jayne Mansfield, Julie London, Barrie Chase, Barbara Nichols, Frank Gorshin, Margo Moore, Brad Dexter, Neville Brand. Directed by Joseph M. Newman. Screenplay, Crane Wilbur; camera, Carl Guthrie; editor, George White; music, Jeff Alexander; assistant director, Lindsley Parsons Jr. Reviewed at Academy Awards Theatre, Nov. 27, '61. Running time, **105 MINS.**

Raft .... Ray Danton
Lisa .... Jayne Mansfield
Sheila .... Julie London
June .... Barrie Chase
Texas .... Barbara Nichols
Moxie .... Frank Gorshin
Ruth .... Margo Moore
Benny .... Brad Dexter
Capone .... Neville Brand
Frenchie .... Robert Strauss
Frankie .... Joe de Santis
Sam .... Herschel Bernardi
Mrs. Raft .... Argentina Brunetti
Mr. Raft .... John Fleifer
M.C. (Team)... Pepper Davis, Tony Reese
Fitzpatrick .... Jack Lambert
Charleston Dancer .... Cecile Rogers
Mizner, The Wit .... Tol Avery
Harvey .... Robert H. Harris

The novel and curiously enthralling thing about "The George Raft Story" is that its subject is, first of all, very much alive, and secondly, an intimately familiar figure in the medium in which he is here impersonated by another actor. This gives the Ben Schwalb production an add sort of vigor and special curiosity value for film audiences. Although the Allied Artists release strikes one as a very glossy treatment, shy the boldness, penetration and complete frankness that registers as sound, serious and affecting biography, it should be an entertaining experience for the average easygoing filmgoer, diverting enough to do good business.

Were it not for the fact that it is based on life, Crane Wilbur's screenplay might seem too stuffed with biopic cliches to be convincing. But the reassuring image of the real-life Raft himself crowds into the viewer's conscious at these moments, and gives seeming artificiality and contrivance a kind of peculiarly life-like lustre. The story traces Raft from his early days as a New York hoofer on the fringes of the underworld, follows him to Hollywood, depicts his success as the "Scarface" coin-flipper, describes his mushrooming discontent with gangster part type-casting (a dilemma which hounded him throughout his career), shows him in the comparatively down-and-out latter stages of his life, and winds on the threshold of his "Some Like It Hot" comeback. Yet, it is a curiously one-sided portrait. The inside of the man remains a mystery. We see only the head of the coin.

Ray Danton is successful in the title role, paradoxically because he never seems to be trying to make himself a carbon copy, which, considering the absence of physical similarity, would have been an injurious approach. No one is going to confuse Danton with Raft (as one might, for examp'e, confuse Larry Parks with Al Jolson), but Danton has submerged his own mannerisms to a degree that they never interfere with the image of Raft that never really vanishes from the mind. Danton, then, is a black-and-white neutral through which the audience can color in Raft. Somehow, it works.

Five women are shown involved in Raft's life—each a shallow, shadowy, inconclusive interlude. They are played by Jayne Mansfield, Julie London, Barrie Chase, Barbara Nichols and Margo Moore. Their roles enable Miss Mansfield to display her astonishing physique, Miss London to croon a sultry vocal, Miss Chase to showcase her hoofing prowess (in partnership with Danton, who's no Raft as a dancer, but sufficiently graceful), Miss Nichols to render a flashy song-and-dance as Texas Guinan, and Miss Moore to snare histrionic honors from the other members of this good-looking quintet.

Capable playing in generally stereotypical character parts is contributed by Frank Gorshin, Brad Dexter, Neville Brand (in his familiar "Capone" guise), Robert Strauss, Joe De Santis, Herschel Bernardi, Argentina Brunetti and Jack Lambert. Comedy team of Pepper Davis & Tony Reese chips in with a fair nitery routine.

Joseph M. Newman's direction is workmanlike, although there are moments when the tempo slows and staggers and the actors have to strain. Newman is backed up by the journeyman efforts of cameraman Carl Guthrie, editor George White, art director David Milton, composer Jeff Alexander and choreographer Alex Romero.

One of the film's more interesting vignettes is the scene in which Raft, following his success in "Scarface," is summoned to the Chicago headquarters of Al Capone, portrayed once again by Neville Brand, who is making something of a career-within-a-career of portraying the character. This sequence, played with a kind of grave tongue-in-cheek, is especially curious for the manner in which it "humanizes" Capone. *Tube*

True Gang Murders

Dull array of newspaper photos of slaughtered gangsters from Jesse James to Roger Touhy. Historically inaccurate and gratuitously gory.

Chicago, Nov. 30.

Teitel Films release of Sagittarius Films production. Directed by Sherman Rosenfield. Produced and written by Dan Goldberg and Harry Mantel; associate producer, Charles Teitel; narrator, Dan Gordon; dialog, Rolf Forsberg; art director, Phil Lepinsky; music, Gene Martin. Reviewed at the Monroe Theatre, Chicago, Nov. 30, '61. Running time, **62 MINS.**

Chi newsman Harry Mantel grave-robbed the newspaper morgues for the series of gory stills pasted together for this patchwork poesy for necrophiles. As cliche-ridden as it is bullet-ridden, it alleges to limn the history of gang killings for a period starting with Jesse James and ending with Roger Touhy. However, it's apparent that the "history" was written to fit the photos available, and there are both important omissions and undue emphasis on several minor hoodlums where sufficiently bloody pictures were available.

Mantel's incomplete annals include photos of the Younger and Dalton brothers and bordello queens Victoria Shaw, then shows the freshly-slaughtered remains of Jim Colosimo ("he hungered for power and wealth"), Machine Gun Jack McGurn, Legs Diamond, Baby Face Nelson (neatly cross-stitched from naval to neck on an autopsy table), Pretty Boy Floyd, Ma and Fred Barker, John Dillinger, Dutch Schultz ("He stepped out of his house . . . It was the doorway to hell"), Bugsy Siegel, Willie Moretti and Albert Anastasia.

Conspicuous by their absence are many still-living mobsters involved in the slayings and, as in the case of Al Capone, anyone with a family who might sue. This makes for sticky going in explaining the St. Valentine Day massacre of the Bugs Moran gang in a Chi garage and precludes the inclusion of Jake "The Barber" Factor in its rundown on Roger Touhy. Factor, whose kidnapping resulted in Touhy's going to jail, is now a prosperous business man in Beverly Hills. An attorney for Capone is currently suing Allied Artists and CBS for their portrayals of the prohibition-era gang figure, and Factor is suing a Chi newspaper reporter for a book he wrote on the Touhy case.

Don Gordon's voice-of-doom narration is so hackneyed as to be comic, and Gene Martin's ratatatat drum and vibe accompaniment is intrusive and apparently randomly interpolated. *Roth.*

Babes In Toyland
(COLOR)

Cross between stagey Toyland and cartoonish Disneyland. Great for the moppets. Should be strong Xmas season attraction.

Hollywood, Dec. 1.

Buena Vista release of Walt Disney production. Stars Ray Bolger, Tommy Sands, Annette, Ed Wynn; features Timmy Kirk, Kevin Corcoran, Henry Calvin, Gene Sheldon, Mary McCarthy, Ann Jilliann, Brian Corcoran. Directed by Jack Donohue. Screenplay, Ward Kimball, Joe Rinaldi, Lowell S. Hawley, based on operetta by Victor Herbert and Glen McDonough; camera (Technicolor), Edward Colman; editor, Robert Stafford; music adaptation, George Bruns; assistant director, Austen Jewell Reviewed at Academy Awards Theatre, Dec. 1, '61. Running time, **106 MINS.**

Barnaby .... Ray Bolger
Tom Piper .... Tommy Sands
Mary Contrary .... Annette
Toymaker .... Ed Wynn
Grumio .... Tommy Kirk
Boy Blue .... Kevin Corcoran
Gonzorgo .... Henry Calvin
Roderigo .... Gene Sheldon
Mother Goose .... Mary McCarty
Bo Peep .... Ann Jilliann
Willie Winkie .... Brian Corcoran
Twins ..... Marilee & Melanie Arnold
Simple Simon .... Jerry Glenn
Jack-be-Nimble .... John Perri
Bobby Shaftoe .... David Pinson
The Little Boy .... Bryan Russell
Jack .... James Martin
Jill .... Ilana Dowding

Walt Disney's Christmas present for filmgoers this year is his first live-action musical, a lavish translation to the screen of Victor Herbert's operetta, "Babes In Toyland." It's an expensive gift, brightly-wrapped and intricately-packaged, and is certain to be a fast-selling item in the Yuletide marketplace. A choice attraction for the pre-teen set, it will be an especially big draw among those in the five-to-ten age bracket. But some of the more mature patrons may be distressed to discover that quaint, charming "Toyland" has been transformed into a rather gaudy and mechanical "Fantasyland." What actually emerges is "Babes In Disneyland."

The Disney concept of "Toyland," as written for the screen by Ward Kimball, Joe Rinaldi and Lowell S. Hawley, and engineered under the scrutiny of director Jack Donohue, falls somewhere in that never-never land where the techniques of the stage, the live-action screen and the animated cartoon overlap. The result leaves an audience in something of a state of suspension, uncertain whether it is supposed to hiss the villain and cheer the hero or just sit back and be content to admire the special effects, the sets and the talents of the artists. Only the tykes will be able to involve themselves in the ramifications of the plot. Others will just have to seek occasional rewards in the technical achievements, the melodic score, the buoyant dancing and several widely scattered twists of comic satire.

Ray Bolger is the standout mem-

ber of the cast. As the arch-villain out to dispose of Tommy (Tom, Tom, the Piper's Son) Sands in order to wed the heiress, Annette (Mary, Mary, Quite Contrary), he delivers a sly, rollicking, congenially menacing portrayal. His rubber-legged hoofing shows to special advantage on a "Castles in Spain" number, and he has some notably merry moments in the climactic sequence in which, as the target of an all-out toy-soldier attack, he proceeds to retaliate with a miniature cannonade of his own.

Sands and Annette are rather wooden as the young lovers, but each has an opportunity to display vocal prowess and capable choreographic footwork. Ed Wynn and Tommy Kirk score as toymaker and assistant, Henry Calvin and Gene Sheldon as Bolger's inept, mercenary aides. Pretty moppet Ann Jillana, as Bo Peep, impresses with her lovely singing voice. Others featured are Kevin and Brian Corcoran and Mary McCarty.

Modernization of Herbert's evergreen score to suit the new medium and the tempo of the times and the action has been accomplished smoothly by George Bruns. Mel Leven's new libretto and lyrics are clever, but some of the simple charm of the original words, such as in the delightful "I Can't Do the Sum," have been sacrificed for purposes of visual trickery. Tommy Mahoney's choreography is brisk and workable, with best results obtained in an exciting dance of gypsies.

Special effects by Eustace Lycett and Robert A. Mattey and animation effects by Joshua Meador are neatly integrated. Toy sequences by Bill Justice and **Xavier Atencio are impressive.** The skills of cameraman Edward Colman and editor Robert Stafford are evident throughout. The fantasy-on-a-stage nature of the concept is ably reflected in the cardboard and gingerbread sets of Carroll Clark and Marvin Aubrey Davis. But there is something faintly disconcerting about a stage technique when utilized on the screen, which is too realistic and fluid a medium for a rigid and confining theatre-like concept of action and design.   *Tube.*

Lover Come Back
(COLOR)

More 'Pillow Talk' with Doris Day, Rock Hudson and Tony Randall; colorful, somewhat risque comedy has lots of the boxoffice charm of the original.

Universal release of 7 Pictures-Knob Hill-Arwin production, produced by Stanley Shapiro and Martin Melcher, with Robert Arthur as exec producer. Stars Rock Hudson, Doris Day, Tony Randall; features Edie Adams, Jack Oakie, Jack Kruschen. Directed by Delbert Mann. Original screenplay, Shapiro and Paul Henning; editor, Marjorie Fowler; camera (Eastman Color), Arthur E. Arling; music, Frank DeVol; songs, "Lover Come Back," words and music by Alan Spilton and DeVol, and "Should I Surrender," lyrics by William Landman, music by Adam Ross. Sneak preview at RKO 58th St. Theatre, Dec. 5, '61. Running time, 107 MINS.

Jerry Webster	Rock Hudson
Carol Templeton	Doris Day
Peter Ramsey	Tony Randall
Rebel Davis	Edie Adams
J. Paxton Miller	Jack Oakie
Dr. Linus Tyler	Jack Kruschen
Millie	Ann B. Davis
Hadley	Joe Flynn
Brackett	Howard St. John
Kelly	Karen Norris
Fred	Jack Albertson
Charlie	Charles Watts
Deborah	Donna Douglas
Hodges	Ward Ramsey

Various of the talents who two years ago provided Universal with the major success, "Pillow Talk," are in hand with a follow-up. "Lover Come Back" is piracy of the original, but in commercial cinematic order.

Let there be compunctions registered about certain story twists which are overly reached for. And the play on sexicology mirrors a further bit of strain. But then the sauciness, while perhaps startling a few years ago, is not disagreeable within the context of "modern times," importantly considering that there's no disregard of good taste.

This is a funny, most-of-the-time engaging, smartly produced show. Farce has Rock Hudson as would-be conqueror of Doris Day, who as the victim of a who's-who deception plays brinkmanship with surrender. There's a bed scene but this is all right because the two, while not remembering the Maryland ceremony (due to being stoned under preposterous circumstances), were legally hitched. An annulment is followed nine months later by another marriage ritual as Miss Day enters the delivery room.

This kind of synopsis is inadequate in getting across the wit and color (and some off-color) content. A little more of the plot: Hudson and Miss Day are rival Madison Avenue ad account people. He deceives her into thinking he's a scientist working on an actually non-existent product called VIP. She undertakes to wrest the VIP account from the masquerading Hudson. He meanwhile is trying to maneuver her into romantic conquest.

Like "Pillow Talk" and other recent-vintage comedies, "Lover Come Back" has its girls beautifully gowned and its sets handsomely dressed. Miss Day's garb, via Irene, particularly offers the audience an eyeful. The production overall is rich and fitting with the story. A trio shares a top credit, Robert Arthur as executive producer and Stanley Shapiro and Martin Melcher as producers.

The script, an original by Shapiro and Paul Henning, has a divers array of characters, all of them ingratiating, and has too a good quota of sharp and humorous lines. Miss Day is strictly pinup material, and she can pout with the best of them. Hudson does right well with light comedy but while he's supposed to be lecherous he might have been so with a little less leer.

Tony Randall draws yocks consistently as head of an agency he inherited but doesn't really helm because he can't make decisions. His is a satirical situation and right in the groove for Randall.

Jack Oakie plays broadly and humorously the part of floor-wax maker who goes to the agency offering him the best girls and bourbon. Edie Adams clicks as a chorus girl trying to get ahead, and Jack Kruschen, as a partly screwball scientist, also wins laughs. Good support too is provided by Ann B. Davis, Joe Flynn, Howard S. Johm, Karon Norris, Jack Albertson, Charles Watts, Donna Douglas and Ward Ramsey.

Couple of songs, "Lover Come Back" (Alan Spilton and Frank DeVol) and "Should I Surrender?" (William Landan and Adam Ross) **are rendered pleasingly by Miss Day, and tucked behind the screen** action appropriately.

Director Delbert Mann keeps "Lover Come Back" on the go about 90% of the time. His pacing is commendable but nonetheless there are a few lags. Tighter editing might be in order. Adding to the fun is his skillfully worked-in appearances of a couple of sideline characters who make brief comments on Hudson's way with the girls.

Arthur E. Arling's photography (Eastman Color) is on the beam, contributing to the production richness, and DeVol's music is another plus.   *Gene.*

The Colossus Of Rhodes
(ITALIAN - SUPERTOTALSCOPE - COLOR)

Italo costume epics, impressively mounted but skimpily written. B.o. reaction should be brisk, but brief.

Hollywood, Nov. 30.
Metro release of Michele Scaglione (Procusa-Cineproduzioni Associates) production. Stars Rory Calhoun. Directed by Sergio Leone. Screenplay, Ennio De Concini, Leone, Cesare Seccia, Luciano Martino; camera (Eastman), Antonio Ballesteros; editor, Eraldo DaRoma; music, Angelo Francisco Lavagnino. Reviewed at the studio, Nov. 30, '61. Running time, 128 MINS.

Dario	Rory Calhoun
Diala	Lea Massari
Peliocles	Georges Marchal
Thar	Conrado Sanmartin
Koros	Angel Aranda
Mirte	Mabel Karr
Lissipo	Jorge Rigaud
Serse	Roberto Carmardiel
Ares	Mimmo Palmara
Careto	Felix Fernandez
Xenon	Carlo Tamberlani
Creonte	Alfio Caltaviano
Eros	Jose McVilches
Phoenician Ambassador	Antonio Casas
Mahor	Yann Larvor
Sirione	Fernando Calzado

Elaborately produced but dramatically two-dimensional epic from Italy, "The Colossus of Rhodes" should stimulate the customarily brisk, but short-lived, boxoffice reaction accorded these overstuffed, though diverting, ad-

venture spectacles that arrive regularly from that country. Certainly no one is going to accuse the producers of this film of creating a colossal bore, least of all moppets and easygoing males, the audience most likely to congregate wherever the Metro release is exhibited.

But scholars, Rhodes or otherwise, are bound to flinch at the liberties taken here with fact. The eighth wonder of the world is the knack Italo cinemateers have for mounting impressive historical pictures by studiously ignoring history.

According to the screenplay by Ennio DeConcini, Sergio Leone (the director), Cesare Seccia and Luciano Martino, the marvelous monument of the title stood intact and upright for a couple of days, then plunged into the Mediterranean during a storm, coupled with a popular revolt against the wicked men in power at the time (280 B.C.). Principal object of the Colossus, here depicted as a kind of second cousin to the almost impregnable cannons of Navarone, or all-purpose torture chamber within a false artistic front, apparently was to ward off the possibility of invasion by hurling molten lead at any intruder.

Rory Calhoun plays the Hollywood Yankee in King Serse's Court. His performance, along with those of the other featured players, is robust and spirited except when forced to contend with a heap of bad dialog, weakest link in the production.

It's a pretty impressive replica of the Colossus that Jesus Mateos has designed and Francisco Assensio has constructed. Considerable dexterity is displayed by cameraman Antonio Ballesteros in the way he has photographed the structure to create the illusion one is ogling the genuine article. Credit for the production's physical realism and for some fierce and lively mob scraps is due director Leone, though his intimate scenes leave much to be desired. The show is filmed in Supertotalscope, which is really kind of wide screen with superlatives. No pikers with scope, these Italians.   *Tube.*

Mysterious Island
(SUPERDYNAMATION—COLOR)

Another in a steady stream of Jules Verne tales to be translated into film. Escapist fare for easygoing audiences. Thorough exploitation should bring okay b.o. response.

Hollywood, Dec. 5.
Columbia Pictures release of Charles H. Schneer production. Stars Michael Craig, Joan Greenwood, Michael Callan, Gary Merrill, Herbert Lom. Directed by Cy Endfield. Screenplay, John Prebble, Daniel Ullman, Crane Wilbur, based on the novel by Jules Verne; camera (Eastman), Wilkie Cooper; editor, Frederick Wilson; music, Bernard Herrmann; assistant director, Rene DuPont. Reviewed at the studio, Dec. 5, '61. Running time, 100 MINS.

Capt. Cyrus Harding	Michael Craig
Marquisa Maria Labrino	Joan Greenwood
Herbert Brown	Michael Callan
Gideon Spilett	Gary Merrill
Captain Nemo	Herbert Lom
Elena	Beth Rogan
Sgt. Pencroft	Percy Herbert
Neb	Dan Jackson
Tom	Nigel Green

Captain Nemo rides again in Charles H. Schneer's resourceful production of Jules Verne's "Mysterious Island," latest in a long

line of that clairvoyant author's works to be translated to the screen in recent years. Although not in a league with the major cinematic efforts to materialize Verne's prose, and somewhat tarnished by the saturation point that appears to have been reached in the sheer rush by enterprising filmmakers to explore and reproduce his fiction, the picture will appeal to audiences seeking escape and easy diversion, and content to get along without dramatic nuance. Prospects are mildly favorable for the Columbia release, which lends itself wholeheartedly to exploitation measures.

Produced in England under Cy Endfield's vigorous direction, the film illustrates the strange plight that befalls three Union soldiers, a newspaperman and a Rebel who, in 1865, escape the siege of Richmond in the inevitable Verne balloon and return to land on an island in the remote South Seas, where they encounter, in chronological order: (1) a giant crab, (2) a giant bird, (3) two lovely shipwrecked British ladies of average proportions, (4) a giant bee, (5) a band of cutthroat pirates, (6) Captain Nemo's inoperative sub, (7) Captain Nemo.

The screenplay by John Prebble, Daniel Ullman and Crane Wilbur winds with a staple of the science-fantasy melodrama—an entire volcanic isle sinking into the sea as the heroes and heroines beat a hasty retreat, leaving, in this instance, the ideologically admirable but otherwise undesirable Captain Nemo behind in a lotta lava.

Dramatically the film is awkward, burdened with unanswered questions and some awfully ineffectual giant animals, but photographically it is noteworthy for the fashion in which the Superdynamation process and special visual effects by Ray Harryhausen have been employed by lensman Wilkie Cooper to couple incongruous, unbalanced elements on the screen with reasonable realism. Egil Woxholt's underwater photography is another asset, as is Bernard Herrmann's score played with fullbodied vitality by the London Symphony, and art director Bill Andrews' specifications for the offbeat "Island." Editor Frederick Wilson obviously had his work cut out for him, since one key member of the cast (Nigel Green) is "seen" in the picture only as a skeleton. Nigel Green is no skeleton.

Flesh-and-blood portrayals are dispatched with spirit by Michael Craig, Joan Greenwood (whose speaking voice is one of the wonders of the modern world), Michael Callan, Gary Merrill, Herbert Lom, Beth Rogan, Percy Herbert and Dan Jackson.   *Tube.*

Nuremberg

Usual documentary footage of Nazi Germany, into which has been woven a thin, personalized storyline that doesn't jell. Title is misleading. Lean prospect.

Hollywood, Dec. 8.
CR Enterprises Ltd production and release. With Lee Bonnell, Roy Bennett, Marta Mithovitch. Associate producer, Alan Kane. Reviewed at Academy Theatre, Dec. 6, '61. Running time, 75 MINS.

"Nuremberg" is a somewhat misleading title for this attempt to weave an intimate dramatic story into reams of generally stock, and by now rather shopworn, documentary footage illustrating the pomp and circumstances under which Germany was terrorized and hypnotized by Nazi leadership. The effort to personalize is largely abortive because the story is little more than an afterthought, a substitute for narration which might have been more eloquent and incisive. It is an illustration of the perils inherent in attempting to knit new dialog into old, objective pictures, a case of putting the cart before the horse. For dramatic sense, the story simply must come first, and the film should follow, not vice-versa as is the case in "Nuremberg."

The title, which has been the subject of a continuing legal squabble between CR Enterprises, producers and distributors of this film, and Stanley Kramer, producer of "Judgment At Nuremberg" (which world preems Dec. 14 in Berlin) fundamentally misleads in the sense that it implies to a prospective audience that the bulk of the film deals with the operations and activities of that tribunal, which actually it does not. True, the issue at stake in the drama which has been incorporated into the footage does deal with efforts to determine whether one woman was a member of the Nazi party. But the film, as a whole, is basically an illustrated study of Nazi Germany through documentary film clips, and the story of the woman at Nuremberg is roughly a linking device or dramatic "excuse" around which to parade the customary footage.

The point of the film, as it turns out, is that the woman, who protests her innocence so vehemently convincingly and slyly that she is freed, is actually a dyed-in-thewool Nazi, still afflicted with the cause. However, though she fools those who try her case in the film, she does not fool the audience, which can sense her obvious guilt through her words.

There is still morbid fascination in some of these film clips, but much of the footage has been seen too often at this point, and monotony becomes a factor due to the exhaustive length of several sequences, such as an enormous goose-stepathon that lasts almost 15 minutes.   *Tube.*

Then There Were Three

Satisfactory supporting item for audiences that prefer war mel'ers heavy on the action and suspense.

Hollywood, Nov. 29.
Parade release of Alex Nicol production. No character names. Cast includes Nicol, Frank Latimore, Barry Cahill, Sid Clute, Michael Billingsley, Frank Gregory, Fred Clark, Brenden Fitzgerald, Paola Falci. Directed by Nicol. Screenplay, Gregory, Allan Lurie; camera, Gastone Di Giovanni; editor, Manual del Campos; assistant director, Mauro Sarcopanti. Reviewed at Hollywood Theatre, Nov. 29, '61. Running time, 74 MINS.

Italo-filmed, but otherwise thoroughly Yankee, "Then There Were Three" is an absorbing action-suspense melodrama, modestly but re-

sourcefully produced and directed by American actor Alex Nicol under the auspices of Alexandra Films. Released by Parade distributors, it is a compatible and holding supporting item, a bit ragged in spots, but quite serviceable as a filler-in situations that cater to the male audience.

Sandwiched between its somewhat redundant start and slightly contrived climax is a dramatization of an interesting war incident wherein a small, detached party of American GI's seeking to rejoin the main body of Allied troops in Italy is joined by a Nazi spy whose orders are to slay a notorious Italian partisan left behind by the retreating Germans. Neither characters nor audience is aware of the spy's identity, so there is a lot of diverting guesswork before the mission is nipped in the bud.

A dearth of tight closeups and much too dark photography makes it difficult for the audience to establish and straighten out identities. But the Frank Gregory-Allan Lurie screenplay is brisklyconstructed and its characters have dimension, including the morbid sense of humor and the human strain of cowardice that strikes even the heroes of combat. There are competent performances by Nicol, Frank Latimore, Barry Cahill, Sid Clute, Michael Billingsley, Frank Gregory, Fred Clark, Brenden Fitzgerald and Paola Falci. The art, technical and musical contributions of the Italian staff and crew are generally adequate, considering the limited expenditure.   *Tube.*

The Children's Hour

Somewhat dated, but bold, brisk and faithful remake of Lillian Hellman's play. Adult fare, and so labelled. Strong contender.

Hollywood, Dec. 6.
United Artists release of William Wyler production. Stars Audrey Hepburn, Shirley MacLaine, James Garner; features Miriam Hopkins, Fay Bainter, Karen Balkin, Veronica Cartwright. Directed by Wyler. Screenplay, John Michael Hayes, from an adaptation by Lillian Hellman of her play; camera, Franz F. Planer; editor, Robert Swink; music, Alex North; assistant director, Robert E. Relyea. Reviewed at Directors Guild of America, Dec. 6, '61. Running time, 109 MINS.
Karen Wright .... Audrey Hepburn
Martha Dobie .... Shirley MacLaine
Dr. Joe Cardin .... James Garner
Mrs. Lily Mortar .... Miriam Hopkins
Mrs. Amelia Tilford .... Fay Bainter
Mary Tilford .... Karen Balkin
Rosalie .... Veronica Cartwright

Lillian Hellman's study of the devastating effect of malicious slander and implied guilt comes to the screen for the second time in this crackling William Wyler production of "The Children's Hour." Wyler, who directed the 1936 Samuel Goldwyn production (then titled "These Three"), which veered away from the touchier, more sensational aspects of Miss Hellman's Broadway play, this time has chosen to remain intimately faithful to the original source. As a result of this boldness and directness, the United Artists release bears a "not recommended for children" tag but, fortified with a Code Seal, an adult approach along with an exceptionally potent marquee cast and some superlative

acting, it has the makings of powerful boxoffice.

If there is a fault to be found with the new version, it is that the sophistication of modern society makes the events in Miss Hellman's play slightly less plausible in the 1961 setting into which it has been framed. But this is a minor reservation, overshadowed by the general excellence of Wyler's production and the durable power of the playwright's work.

Story, written for the screen by John Michael Hayes from the playwright's own adaptation, deals, of course, with an irresponsible, neurotic child who, as a result of surreptitious reading, coupled with flight from a punishment she deserves, creates and spreads a slanderous rumor of a Lesbian relationship between the two headmistresses of the private school for girls she attends. Ultimately, the ugly lie is exposed, but not before the scandal has reached such alarming proportions that it has resulted in a lawsuit, destruction of the school, devastation of the relationship between one of the women and her fiance, and suicide of the other, latently guilty in the mind, but not in deed.

The personalities of Audrey Hepburn and Shirley MacLaine, in the leading roles, beautifully complement each other. Miss Hepburn's soft sensitivity, marvelous projection and emotional understatement result in a memorable portrayal—one of potential Oscar nomination calibre. Miss MacLaine's enactment is almost equally rich in depth and substance. James Garner is effective as Miss Hepburn's betrothed, and Fay Bainter comes through with an outstanding portrayal of the impressionable grandmother who falls under the evil influence of the wicked child. The latter is played in the bad seed tradition by newcomer Garen Balkin. The only jarring note in the youngster's approach is its tight similarity to the manner in which Bonita Granville essayed the role in the earlier film. But the performance generates sparks. Young Veronica Cartwright, as another student implicated in the scandal, makes an especially vivid impression. Miriam Hopkins, who played Miss MacLaine's part in the 1936 production, scores here as the character's shallow aunt. Balance of support is fine.

Wyler's direction is arresting, penetrating and sensitive. There are several noteworthy strokes of artistry—small but acutely perceptive touches that might have been overlooked in lesser hands. Franz F. Planer's camerawork is intense and inquisitive, Robert Swink's editing notable for its cumulative impact and stability. Alex North's score, though not an extensive one, is always helpful when introduced, especially in atonal accompaniment to the film's more sinister passages.

Fernando Carrere's art direction is tastefully in keeping with locale.   *Tube.*

Hey, Let's Twist

Production hurry shows, but obvious timeliness helps. Fun for the cultists, entertainment for the curious. All in all, a showmanly quickie trip to market.

Paramount release of Harry Romm production. Stars Joey Dee, The Starliters, Teddy Randazzo, Kay Armen; features Zohra Lampert, Dino de Luca, Jo Ann Campbell. Directed by Greg Garrison. Screenplay, Hal Hackady; camera, George Jacobson; editor, Sid Katz; music, Henry Glover. At Paramount homeoffice Dec. 15, '61. Running time, **80 MINS.**

Himself .... Joey Dee
Themselves .... The Starliters
Rickey Dee .... Teddy Randazzo
Angie .... Kay Armen
Sharon .... Zohra Lampert
Papa .... Dino di Luca
Rore .... Richard Dickens
Piper .... Jo Ann Campbell
Themselves ...... Peppermine Loungers
The Doctor .... Alan Arbus

Call it showmanship, enterprise or just plain opportunism, the fact remains that Paramount, faster than you can say Peppermint Lounge is ready with a Twister, and it's tolerable. The finished product doesn't keep hidden the quickie nature of the 80-minute feature; producer Harry Romm evidently was in a frenzy to finish. But he has come up with an all right novelty—there are sufficient boxoffice good points—and it deserves serious consideration in the marketplace.

There's a story line that plays well, despite its schmaltziness, and an abundance of Twist music and terpery. Perhaps it should be mentioned up front that the kids drink only Cokes and chocolate frosteds between dances, there not being around a drop of the 80-or-plus-proof juices.

Joey Dee, the Starliters, Kay Armen and Teddy Randazzo are among those on view, and the Gotham lensing was done partly at the Lounge. These are seil plusses which go hand in hand with the robust campaign which has been in evidence the past several weeks.

Photography is barely adequate; a show of more flexibility would have helped nicely. Some of the group Twisting in "Hey, Let's Twist" shows about as much imagination as the afternoon dance sessions (with amateurs) on television. A Twist single by Jo Ann Campbell might have been real cool except that Miss Campbell is never entirely within the camera's cone of vision. Cameraman George Jacobson, further, seems preoccupied with uninspired femme derieres with the shakes.

Peppermint Lounge is Italo flavored in Hal Hackady's scenario. There's papa, Dino di Luca, who runs the place as an ice cream and soda dispensary. He wants his two sons, Joey Dee and Teddy Randazzo, to complete college. But they prefer to stay home introducing the Twist to the Loungers. A cafe society gal, Zohra Lampert, almost breaks them with her high-fallutin redesigning ideas. They return to their original no-minimum-no-cover modest scale of operation and win out.

The Starliters, Peppermint Loungers, Dee and Randazzo make with vocal and instrument interpretations in typically wild Twist fashion, and director Greg Garrison does well enough in interlarding song & dance with the plot. Editing and technical credits fair.

Gene.

The Continental Twist

Skimpy, shopworn story trimmings, but topical assault. Exploitable film for the short haul.

Hollywood, Dec. 11.

Maurice Duke production. Stars Louis Prima, June Wilkinson, Sam Butera and the Witnesses (Lou Sino, Rolly Dee, Morgan Thomas, Bobby Morris, John Nagy, Allen Seltzer); with David Whorf, Gertrude Michael, Hal Torry, Ty Perry, Fred Sherman, Dick Winslow, Gil Fry. Directed by William J. Hole Jr. Screenplay, Berni Gould; camera, Gene Polito; editor, John Durant. Reviewed at NT&T screening room, Dec. 11, '61. Running time, **76 MINS.**

Louis Evans .... Louis Prima
Jenny Watson .... June Wilkinson
Sam Butera .... Sam
The Witnesses .... Themselves
Letitia Clunker .... Gertrude Michael
Riffy .... David Whorf
The Mayor .... Hal Torry
Mr. Arturo .... Ty Perry
Julius .... Fred Sherman
M. Dubois .... Dick Winslow
Policeman .... Gil Fry

Fasten your seat belts, here they come! First twister to hit the Coast, and ticketed for subsequent funnelling Dec. 30 into 50 key U.S. burgs, is Keelou's "The Continental Twist," a rambunctious celluloid rumble into which a slim, shopworn story has been loosely constructed around periodic outbursts of the new dance. Obviously an opportunistic exploitation enterprise, the Maurice Duke production doesn't figure to have any appreciable staying power, but is apt to make the quick buck wherever it is first on the launching pad.

Berni Gould's original screenplay is a pretty lame excuse for several frenetic displays of the bathtowel wiggle, as sexecuted by Louis Prima, June Wilkinson, Sam Butera and a host of nervous torso wrenchers. The film, most of which centers around the bandstand, is little more than an extension of one of those musical short subjects popular in the late 30's or early 40's. Absurd storyline has Prima's nitery tenure in jeopardy owing to the abortive efforts of an upstairs painting counterfeit operation determined to rid the building of its jam sessions.

As a spectator sport, the twist suffers from an element of monotony. Esthetically, it has about as much charm as an exhibition at Vic Tanny's.

Prima, an adept showman and musician but hardly the accomplished actor, does what he can with the histrionic aspects of his role. He's most at home, of course, when music is the object, a chore he dispatches in company with Butera and the Witnesses in the course of some dozen "breaks" for swinging standards or new twist tunes. Miss Wilkinson's anatomical proportions are admirably suited to the machinations and undulations of this holds-barred slice of contemporary choreography.

Featured parts are dispatched uneasily by Gertrude Michael, David Whorf, Hal Torry, Ty Perry, Fred Sherman, Dick Winslow and Gil Fry under William J. Hole Jr.'s game, but erratic direction.

Rush-rush and cut-corners nature of the enterprise is evident throughout, in spite of the journeyman efforts of cameraman Gene Polito, editor John Durant, art director Gabe Scagnamillo.

Tube.

The Queen of Spades
(RUSSIAN—COLOR)

Paris, Dec. 12.

Mosfilm production and release. With Oleg Strijanov, Olga Krassina, Elena Polivitskaia, Valentina Koulik, Vadim Medvediev. Directed by Roman Tikhomirov. Screenplay, Gueorgui Vassiliev, Serguei Vassiliev, Pavel Vesibram, Boris Yaroustovski, Tikhomirov from the opera by Chaikovsky and the story of Alexandre Pushkin; camera (Sovcolor), Evgueni Svetlanov. At Pagode, Paris. Running time, **100 MINS.**

Guerman .... Oleg Stirjanov
Voice .... L. Andjaparitze
Lisa .... Olga Krassina
Voice .... T. Milachkina
Countess .... Elena Polivitskiai
Voice .... S. Preobrajenskaia
Ieletski .... Valentina Koulik
Voice .... E. Kibkalo
Tomski .... Vadim Medvediev
Voice .... V. Netchipailo
Polina .... Irina Gourzo
Voice .... L. Avdeieva

This filmed opera manages to get the eerie feel of this tale about an obsessed man whose need to win riches destroys him and his woman. When singing and real backgrounds get acceptable, this has the right expressionistic filmic flair, but it remains primarily for opera rather than film buffs.

A young officer, poor but ambitious, sweeps a young girl off her feet. But love is tempered by his need and greed. The girl's grandmother is supposed to have the secret of winning at cards. He tries to wrest the knowledge but frightens the old woman to death.

Good voices are well dubbed on the actors while the lyric form allows for expressionistic excesses. The weird goings-on at the end are especially effective. This looms primarily a highly specialized entry abroad.

Mosk.

The Outsider

Tragic biopic of Ira Hayes, the ill-starred Mt. Suribachi Indian hero. Lacks necessary clarity, objectivity and penetration to suit the thought-provoking tale, and that may blunt b.o. action.

Hollywood, Dec. 12.

Universal release of Sy Bartlett production. Stars Tony Curtis; features James Franciscus, Gregory Walcott, Bruce Bennett, Vivian Nathan. Directed by Delbert Mann. Screenplay, Stewart Stern, based on "The Hero of Iwo Jima" by William Bradford Huie; camera, Joseph LaShelle; editor, Marjorie Fowler; music, Leonard Rosenman; assistant director, Ray Gosnell Jr. Reviewed at Directors Guild, Dec. 12, '61. Running time, **108 MINS.**

Ira Hayes .... Tony Curtis
Sorenson .... James Franciscus
Kiley .... Gregory Walcott
General Bridges .... Bruce Bennett
Nancy Hayes .... Vivian Nathan
Jay Morago .... Edmund Hashim
Sgt. Boyle .... Paul Comi
Noomie .... Stanley Adams
Cpl. Johnson .... Wayne Heffley
Uncle .... Ralph Moody
McGruder .... Jeff Silver
Tyler .... James Beck
Bradley .... Forrest Compton
Mr. Alvarez .... Peter Homer Sr.
Chairlady .... Mary Patton

The tragic story of Ira Hamilton Hayes, the Pima Indian whose participation as one of the carefully-posed flag-raisers on Mt. Suribachi and inability to accept the hypocrisy of a heroism to which he never felt entitled combined to destroy him, is told in "The Outsider." At its roots, the Sy Bartlett production is an important, significant and profoundly moving experience, a biography of a man victimized by his heritage and sacrificed to symbolism. Yet, regrettably, the picture betrays its hero by introducing, but not penetrating into, mystifying elements in the story, by blurring the focal issue with an undercurrent of unresolved melodramatic artificiality.

As a direct result of this tendency to compromise with the story's intrinsic eloquence and natural, unaffected poignancy for purposes of dramaturgical broadening and flavoring, the Universal release is not apt to be the commercial success its story merits. Many filmgoers, more discriminating and otherwise, will sense that something has gone amiss, and that may prove an especially telling negative factor for a picture that demands absolutely straightforward telling to get the universal response such a story deserves.

Stewart Stern's screenplay, based on William Bradford Huie's "The Hero of Iwo Jima," traces the personal tragedy of Hayes from the point at which he leaves his Arizona reservation and enlists in the Marines to his death from exposure and alcoholism 10 years later. Tony Curtis portrays the hero. The first half of the film is briskly and convincingly executed, particularly the scenes of eager recruit Hayes in boot camp. But, as the hero begins to come apart at the emotional seams, so does the picture.

The crux of the project's weakness is the rather disproportionate depiction of a personal friendship as the essential cause of Hayes' destruction. Although it is quite feasible that an Indian be severely broken up over the sudden demise of his only true buddy in the white man's world, the relationship of the two men and its profound, lingering effect on Hayes has an uncomfortably unnatural ring here, one that adds an odd and baffling connotation to the story and that, through emphasis, blunts audience identification with the character and his problem. This curious element of the tale, incidentally, was not a factor in Merle Miller's earlier dramatization of the Hayes biography, an excellent television play titled "The American," and seen on "Sunday Showcase" early in 1960 with Lee Marvin as the hero.

Equipped with a re-shaped nose for physical suggestion of the character, Curtis gamely and valiantly attempts to submerge his personality into that of the person he is portraying. Although he is not altogether convincing as an Indian, perhaps through the sheer familiarity and unquenchable force of his own identity, the actor plays with conviction and sincerity and overcomes, to a great degree, a somewhat questionable bit of casting.

James Franciscus is strong and vigorous as the ill-fated buddy. Others effective in major roles are Gregory Walcott as a tough drill instructor, Bruce Bennett as a perceptive general, Vivian Nathan as the hero's mother, Edmund Hashim as chief of the tribal council of the underprivileged Pimas who must grind out a bleak existence on arid terrain, deprived

of precious water by broken government promises. Especially formidable in support are Paul Comi and Stanley Adams.

Director Delbert Mann has gotten the most out of his material, his cast and his crew. Many of the production backdrops are the actual sites of Hayes' life, lending the film an invaluable air of physical authenticity, a credit to Bartlett, Mann and art directors Alexander Golitzen and Edward S. Haworth. Lively, dexterous photography by Joseph LaShelle is a plus, as is the crisp, abrupt editing of Marjorie Fowler, the introspective, thought-reading score of Leonard Rosenman and the observant set decorations of Oliver Emert, to cite just a few of the contributions.

Highly effective incorporation of newsreel footage aids the production, both in combat passages and in a scene in which Hayes attends ceremonies surrounding dedication of the Mt. Suribachi monument in Washington. Latter passage is astutely managed in the way newsreel clips (spotlighting the appearance of Dwight D. Eisenhower) are neatly matched by "studio" recreations of the event (with Ike's "double" carefully but convincingly regarded from safe distances and vantage points). *Tube.*

Cause Toujours Mon Lapin
(Keep Talking Baby)
(FRENCH)

Paris, Dec. 12.

UFA-Comacico release of Jacques Roitfeld production. Stars Eddie Constantine; features Renee Cosima, Francois Chaumette, Alain Nobis. Directed by Guy Lefranc. Screenplay, Roger Boussinot, Yvon Samuel, Lefranc from novel by Day Keene; camera, J. L. Picavet; editor, Claude Durand. At Lord Byron, Paris. Running time, **90 MINS.**

Jackson	Eddie Constantine
Francoise	Renee Cosima
Simon	Francois Chaumette

After 10 years as a French and European pic star and the same type character in scores of films, Yank singer-actor Eddie Constantine is in a position where his pix could be named "Eddie Drives A Taxi," "Eddie the G-Man," etc. This one could be "Eddie the Ventriloquist Falsely Accused of Murder." It is an okay actioner with some inventive turns before it bogs down. It might be a dualer or video item for the U.S.

Constantine, though not a G-Man this time, is his usual phlegmatic, resourceful self, also irresistible to women. Again, he is a rugged in other films. When a crime is pinned on him in a boite in which he works, he manages to get out of prison and find the culprits.

It seems that the boite is a drug center. In the interim he has a little girl on his hands who the gang has used in blackmailing her mother into accusing Constantine of murder. It gives him a chance to sing a song for the lass.

Picture has some clever scenes but the suspense is lacking sans the characterizations to hold up the obvious proceedings. But Constantine has about perfected his easygoing screen personality. It looks to do well on the home grounds. Technical credits are okay. *Mosk.*

The Two Little Bears

Moppet fantasy, Marquee bait for teeners; the natural tyke appeal should combine to create a versatile pint-sized b.o. package, especially serviceable as support on kiddie packages.

Hollywood, Dec. 12.

Twentieth-Fox release of George W. George production. Stars Eddie Albert, Jane Wyatt; introduces Brenda Lee; features Soupy Sales, Donnie Carter, Butch Patrick, Jimmy Boyd. Directed by Randall F. Hood. Screenplay, George, from story by Judy and George W. George; camera, Floyd Crosby; editor, Carl Pierson; music, Henry Vars; assistant director, Willard Kirkham. Reviewed at the studio, Dec. 12, '61. Running time, **83 MINS.**

Harry Davis	Eddie Albert
Ann Davis	Jane Wyatt
Timmy Davis	Donnie Carter
Billy Davis	Butch Patrick
Tina Davis	Brenda Lee
Emily Wilkins	Nancy Kulp
Magda	Opal Euard
Janos	Ted Marcuse
Pat McGovern	Soupy Sales
Tom Provost	Dick Alden
Phil Wade	Jack Lester
Dr. Fredericks	Milton Parsons
Dr. Evans	Jack Finch
Grimshaw Wilkins	Emory Parnell
Jefferson Stander	James Maloney
Johnny Dillon	Jimmy Boyd
Mary Jergens	Charlene Brooks

"The Two Little Bears" is a cross between a fantasy for the moppet audience and a quasi-tunefilm that introduces Brenda Lee to the teenage screen audience. Artistically, the elements are fundamentally incompatible. They don't quite jell. Commercially, however, the cross-purposes are less injurious. In fact, the blend will probably widen the prospective audience, since tykes will not be troubled by the superfluous presence of Miss Lee and teenagers who would otherwise not be attracted may show up out of curiosity to see both one of their recording heroines (Miss Lee) and one of television's more popular and provocative "children's show" personalities (the uninhibited Soupy Sales) materialize on theatrical celluloid. All of which makes the modestly-budgeted George W. George production, fashioned under the auspices of Robert L. Lippert's API operation at 20th-Fox, a rather versatile little package. Most of its play, though, is likely to be as a supporting item on bills aimed at children, and so it should be.

Producer George's scenario is predicated on the theory that little boys can turn into little bears if they "believe" hard enough. This complicates the life and times of grammar school principal Eddie Albert, whose promotion is jeopardized by his insistence that his two offspring actually do accomplish the lycanthropic transition, a claim his superiors, who belong to the conservative "boys will be boys" school, are inclined to dismiss until they are present at one of the transfigurations.

Albert, a seasoned pro regardless of the nature of his roles, is excellent as the harassed papa. Here is an actor's actor. Jane Wyatt is fine as the mother. Donnie Carter and Butch Patrick are quite agreeable as the bearish youngsters, especially the latter. There is satisfactory supporting work from Jimmy Boyd, Nancy Kulp, Opal Euard, Ted Marcuse, Dick Alden, Jack Lester, Milton Parsons, Jack Finch, Emory Parnell, James Maloney and Charlene Brooks. Sales, who has been causing a good deal of commotion and comment in teenage circles, is employed here in a rather small, bland, subdued role of a helpful cop, but his name in the cast should be an attendance factor. Miss Lee, a skillful vocalist who warbles like a little league Kay Starr, has much to learn about acting. Her vocals ("Honey Bear" and "Speak to Me Pretty") are out of place in these proceedings, but she renders them with assurance and enthusiasm.

Although some of the going gets pretty syrupy, director Randall F. Hood on the whole has done a craftsmanlike job of assembling the incongruous elements into a respectably fluid package, in spite of economic realities. He has a keen sense of the visual. The production is quite tidy and orderly for a budget film, reflecting the savvy of cameraman Floyd Crosby, editor Carl Pierson, art director John Mansbridge, soundman E. C. Ward and composer Henry Vars. *Tube.*

Le Jeu De La Verite
(The Game of Truth)
(FRENCH—DYALISCOPE)

Paris, Dec. 12.

Cocinor release of Marceau-Cocinor production. Stars Robert Hossein, Francoise Prevost, Paul Meurisse; features Jean Servais, Nadia Gray, Thien-Huong, Jacques Dacqmine, Perrette Pradier, Georges Riviere, Marc Cassot, Jeanne Valerie, Jean-Louis Trintignant. Directed by Robert Hossein. Screenplay, Jean Serge, Robert Chazal, Louis Martin, Steve Passeur; camera, Christian Matras; editor, Gilbert Natot. At Marignan, Paris. Running time, **80 MINS.**

Inspector	Robert Hossein
Guylaine	Francoise Prevost
Borquere	Paul Meurisse
Verlat	Jean Servais
Solange	Nadia Gray
Girl	Thien-Huong
Florence	Perrette Pradier
Francine	Jeanne Valerie
Bernard	Georges Riviere
Guy	Jean-Louis Trintignant
Industrialist	Jacques Dacqmine
Husband	Marc Cassot

Sleek whodunit takes place in one room at a party bringing together a group of unsavory, futile people. Dialog is glib but overdone while the suspense is intermittent. Looms mainly for dualer use abroad with better chances locally.

A famed writer is holding a party with friends. In comes a sardonic acquaintance who waves an envelope which he claims is worth a lot of money and concerns somebody present. During a game of truth, when people ask each other qquestions with truthful answers demanded, he is killed.

A call for the police has one man walk in. It is hard to believe this group of hardboiled, crafty people think that the police travel alone. He turns out to be the killer who is trying to blackmail the one who hired him. There are a few switches before the killer is unmasked.

Direction is smooth but the lack of substance in characterization, the forced rapid cutting and camera movement to keep things moving, and the telegraphed ending has this bog down after a smart opening. Actors all do acceptably with their roles which are typed rather than real characters. *Mosk.*

Sail A Crooked Ship

Unevenly executed tale of band of zany, inept seagoing thieves. Could break even or better.

Hollywood, Dec. 7.

Columbia Pictures release of Philip Barry production. Stars Robert Wagner, Dolores Hart, Carolyn Jones, Frankie Avalon, Ernie Kovacs, Frank Gorshin. Directed by Irving Brecher. Screenplay, Ruth Brooks Flippen, Bruce Geller, from novel by Nathaniel Benchley; camera, Joseph Biroc; editor, Williab A. Lyon; music, George Duning; assistant director, Sam Nelson. Reviewed at Academy Awards Theatre, Dec. 7, '61. Running time, **88 MINS.**

Gilbert Barrows	Robert Wagner
Elinor Harrison	Dolores Hart
Virginia	Carolyn Jones
Rodney	Frankie Avalon
The Captain	Ernie Kovacs
George Wilson	Frank Gorshin
McDonald	Jesse White
Nickels	Harvey Lembeck
Sammy	Sid Tomack
Helmut	Guy Raymond
Finster	Buck Kartalian
Simon J. Harrison	Wilton Graff
Mrs. Chowder	Marjorie Bennett
Young Lady Pilgrim	Terry Huntingdon
1st Man	Graham Ferguson
2nd Man	Tom Symonds
Mr. Caldingham	Howard Wendell
Woman	Mary Young
Newsboy	Bru Mysak
Biddy	Hope Sansberry
Cop	Mark Myer

There has been a run of nautical comedies in recent years, per "Operation Petticoat," "Wackiest Ship in the Army." Columbia's "Sail a Crooked Ship," a Philip Barry production, has several highly amusing passages of an outrageous nature, but lacks the overall finesse and consistency to keep an audience thoroughly disarmed and beguiled. Fortunately, the Columbia release does not appear to have been produced on such an elaborate scale that it cannot break even at the boxoffice.

The "Crooked" of the title refers not to the ship shape but rather to the disposition of its crew. The Ruth Brooks Flippen-Bruce Geller screenplay, from the novel by Nathaniel Benchley, has a band of zany thieves commandeering a rejuvenated vessel from a mothball fleet for purposes of safe transport to and from Boston, where they plan to pull a bank heist. The blueprint is smudged by a sudden hurricane, navigational inadequacies (only a captive knows how to steer), and a very unscientific robbery (a Founders' Day turkey raffle is in progress at the bank).

Sprightliest humor in the film is obtained from a number of sight gags and a twist of satire. But both the scenarists and director Irving Brecher are guilty of over-repetition. Latching on to a good thing, they proceed to hammer away at it until it is no longer very funny (such as a running spoof of the Capt. Queeg ball-bearing routine and a sight situation in which the helmsmen are steered by the helm, instead of vice-versa).

The degree of comedy varies with the performer to whom an incident or gag is entrusted. In the cases of Ernie Kovacs and Frank Gorshin, both practiced and instinctive funnymen, the results are superior. But the approach is to let everyone try his hand at comedy, and not all are fully equipped for the assignment. There is a need for contrast, for

straight men off of whom the more adept comedians can bounce their slapstick skill.

Robert Wagner exhibits some flair for fun, and Carolyn Jones, in a sexier assignment than customary for her, has some nice moments. But pretty Dolores Hart sems a bit ill at ease in her role, and the scenes she shares with Miss Jones slow up the picture. Frankie Avalon is adequate, and delivers one vocal of a routine pop ditty ("Opposites Attract") with style and assurance. Top support is ably fashioned by Jesse White, Harvey Lembeck, Sid Tomack, Guy Raymond and Bud Kartalian.

The lens dexterity of Joseph Biroc helps convey the nautical feel, as do the sets designed by Robert Peterson. Film has been trimmed to a swift, snug 88-minutes by editor William A. Lyon. George Duning's score adds an effervescent note to the wobbly voyage. *Tube.*

Un Nomme La Rocca
(A Man Called La Rocca) (FRENCH)

Paris, Dec. 12.

Pathe release of Cyclope-DAMA production. Stars Jean-Paul Belmondo; features Christine Kaufman, Beatrice Altariba, Pierre Vaneck, Nico Papatakis, Jean-Pierre Darras, Mario David. Directed by Jean Becker. Screenplay, Jose Giovanni, Becker from novel by Giovanni; camera, Ghislain Cloquet; editor, Danise De Casabianca. At Paris, Paris. Running time, 105 MINS.

La Rocca	Jean-Paul Belmondo
Xavier	Pierre Vaneck
Genevieve	Christine Kaufman
Nevada	J. P. Darras
Moll	Beatrice Altariba
Charlot	Mario David

Film unfolds with a gangster and prison background in the South of France soon after the last war. This is somewhat leisurely paced and rarely makes its point about a couple of friends trying to get away from it all. Pic thus emerges primarily as a dualer or actioner possibility abroad.

Jean-Paul Belmondo has the presence of mind as a retired exhood, whose friend gets railroaded to prison, to come back to help him. But the character and times lack a crystallizing outlook and clarity. Instead this becomes a series of episodes rather than a coherent drama of awakening.

Belmondo goes to prison when he wipes out some blackmailing hoodlums who have deserted the American Army. There he meets his buddy and they are put on a detail to dig up mines. The friend loses an arm saving him and after serving their sentences they decide to buy a farm. But the friend does a little blackmailing which leads to the death of his sister and the loss of his only buddy.

Jean Becker, son of the late French director Jacques, for his first pic, shows a firm hand in visuals but this grabbing of gangster and prison scenes lacks the coherent drive to make it a specialized pic of its kind. Production is technically okay if mainly a local entry. However, it may mean a good new director on the scene here. *Mosk.*

Les Bras De La Nuit
(The Arms of Night) (FRENCH)

Paris, Dec. 12.

SNC release of Ares-Transfilms-Editions G.M. production. Stars Danielle Darrieux, Roger Hanin; features Pierre Destailles, Pierre Larquey. Written and directed by Jacques Guymont from a novel by Frederic Dard. Camera, Jean Tournier; editor, Charles Bretonneiche. At Le Bretagne, Paris. Running time, 90 MINS.

Daniele	Danielle Darrieux
Landais	Roger Hanin
Morel	Pierre Destailles
Belleau	Pierre Larquey
Dora	Eva Damien

A police inspector falls in love with a woman who murdered her husband and ironically covers up for her which leads to a useless further killing. Pic is somewhat talky and lacking the directorial punch or characterization to make it anything but a local entry.

Danielle Darrieux walks through her role of the wife while Roger Hanin is minus the projection to give the part of the lovestruck inspector the proper strain and revelations of love vs. duty.

Off-screen commentary is overdone, the picture plodding its way to an ironic end. Technical credits are okay but director Jacques Guymont shows too much discretion for his first vehicle. It needed a feeling and depth which he was unable to give. *Mosk.*

The Young Ones
(BRITISH—COLOR)

Bright, breezy musical zinging with youth.

London, Dec. 19.

Warner-Pathe release of an Associated British (Kenneth Harper) production. Stars Cliff Richard, Robert Morley. Features Carole Gray, Richard O'Sullivan, Melvyn Hayes, Sonya Cordeau. Directed by Sidney J. Furie. Original story and original screenplay by Peter Myers and Ronald Cass; editor, Jack Slade; camera, Douglas Slocombe; choreography, Herbert Ross; music and lyrics, Peter Myers, Ronald Cass; additional numbers by Roy Bennett, Sid Tepper, Shirley Wolfe, Sky Soloway, Bruce Welch, Hank B. Marvin, Peter Gormley, Norrie Paramor, Stanley Black; musical supervisors, Paramor and Black. At Warner Theatre, London. Running time, 108 MINS.

Nicky	Cliff Richard
Hamilton	Robert Morley
Toni	Carole Gray
Ernest	Richard O'Sullivan
Jimmy	Melvyn Hayes
Chris	Teddy Green
Barbara	Annette Robertson
Dorinda	Sonya Cordeau
Eddie	Sean Sullivan
Dench	Harold Scott
Watts	Gerald Harper
Chauffeur	Robertson Hare
Woman in Market	Rita Webb
The Shadows	Themselves

Britain hasn't produced a really effective filmusical since the war. Now producer Kenneth Harper has staked on youth and, with "The Young Ones," his gamble seemingly has come off. It's a naive, but gay pic which should sing its way into the heart of many boxoffices via its sheer exuberance. Harper signed up a 28-year-old Canadian director, Sidney Furie; a slick choreographer, Herbert Ross; and Cliff Richard, one of Britain's top pop singers, to play the hero. He then engaged a young, largely unknown cast and tossed them into a warm, jolly piece of escapism.

The idea won't win any Oscars for originality, but the songs, dancing and Furie's nimble direction keep the screenplay on zestful enough plane. Richard is the leader of a youth club whose humble little clubhouse is endangered when a millionaire property tycoon buys the land on which it is situated. Unbeknown to the other teenagers, the tycoon is Richard's father. They decide to fight him and this involves raising $4,000 to challenge the lease. It's decided the best way to do this is by taking over a derelict theatre to stage a show. This gives plenty of opportunity for musical numbers while rehearsing and in the finale, when the show is put on against great odds.

This frayed, slightly tired idea is given a lift by one or two inventive situations and by some young talent which augurs well for the future of British screen musicals. Of 13 song-and-dance numbers two have already hit the Top 10. Most of the others are production situations which help the film along.

It starts off briskly with the same offbeat informality that characterized "On the Town." "Friday Night," "What D'You Know We've Got a Show," "Lessons In Love" and "Girl In Your Arms," raise this film a cut above recent British musical pix.

The choreography of Ross is agile and sharp. Between them Norrie Paramor and Stanley Black have made best use of the musical side. Main fault of the film is that the screenplay and dialog are uneven.

However, Robert Morley, as the tycoon, does an impressive job in bringing some adult wit and irony to the screen. Richard is still inexperienced as an actor but has a pleasant charm, sings well within his range and will certainly attract his big public.

A new dancing girl, Carole Gray, is a youthful delight, though she too is happier when enjoying the exuberance of the numbers than when having to act. Melvyn Hayes and Richard O'Sullivan, two young child stars now growing up, offer some pleasantly shrewd comedy. Remainder of the young people give a fillip to the singing, dancing and comedy. Sonya Cordeau, as an oversexed, large-bosomed actress, Robertson Hare, as a chauffeur and Harold Scott, as an aged solicitor, help the pic with some welldone cameos.

Technical credits are okay, except that Douglas Slocombe's lensing sometimes suffers from overflorid color. *Rich.*

Cleo De 5 A 7
(Cleo From Five to Seven) (FRENCH)

Paris, Dec. 12.

Rome Paris Film production and release. Stars Corinne Marchand; features Antoine Bourseiller, Dorothee Blank, Michel Legrand, Dominique Davray. Written and directed by Agnes Varda. Camera, Jean Rabier; editor, Janine Verneau; music, Michel Legrand. Preemed in Paris. Running time, 90 MINS.

Cleo	Corinne Marchand
Antoine	Antoine Bourseiller
Dorothee	Dorothee Blank
Bob	Michel Legrand
Angele	Dominique Davray

A blonde, good-looking young femme singer is convinced she has cancer and is awaiting the results of a medical test. The film concerns the time she spends waiting and her moods, actions and final reaction to her predicament. There is a delicate balance of mood which is practically sustained throughout. Also this pic marks femme director Agnes Varda as a fine addition to French film ranks.

The girl is comely and tall. Nothing of her illness and fears show at the outset. She sings at a sesion with some zany songwriters, the songs displaying that she is good but not outstanding in this sphere. The gal is also somewhat shy and modest in spite of her looks. Then there is a busy businessman lover who never has time for her.

Director Agnes Varda is able to overcome the banality of the situation by a knowing visual feel for revelation and reflections of the girl's state via intelligent symbols. Sometimes invention falters as in the scene with the songwriters. But Miss Varda then easily picks up the threads and keeps alive interest in the girl and her plight.

She goes to a fortune teller, has a crying jag in public, buys a hat, sees her lover for a while who is loath to admit any sickness she may have, visits a model friend, sees a little film comedy which buoys her up—and finally meets a soldier who helps her face up to getting the test results.

Miss Varda is heralded a precursor by the New Wave for a feature pic she made six years ago. This one is better orchestrated and benefits from expert technical aspects in spite of almost all nonstudio shooting. Corinne Marchand is well utilized as the sick girl while others just lend silhouettes to her wanderings except for Antoine Bourseiller's knowing portrayal of the soldier.

This is an offbeater with enough feeling and depth to overcome its few flat sections. The girl's problem blends with things around her until she is finally able to face up to it and accept her illness and the attempts that will be made to help and cure her. *Mosk.*

The Best Of Enemies
(COLOR)

Wryly witty, offbeat wartime comedy with serious undertones. Stylish standout performances by David Niven and Italy's Alberto Sordi. Excellant bookings for all audiences.

London, Dec. 12.

BLC release of a Columbia presentation (Dino De Laurentiis) production. Stars David Niven, Alberto Sordi; features Michael Wilding, Harry Andrews, Amedeo Nazzari. Directed by Guy Hamilton. Screenplay by Jack Pulman from adaptation by Age Scarpelli and Subo Cecchi D'Amico from Luciano Vincenzomi's story; editor, Buri Bates; camera, Giuseppe Rotumno; music, Nino Rota. At Odeon, Leicester Square, London. Running time, 104 MINS.

Major Richardson	David Niven
Captain Blasi	Alberto Sordi
Burke	Michael Wilding
Major Fornari	Amedeo Nazzari
Captain Rootes	Harry Andrews
Bernasconi	David Opatoshu
Sergeant Todini	Aldo Giuffre
Soldier Moccacia	Tiberio Mitri
Lt. Thomlinson	Kenneth Fortescue
Sgt. Trevethan	Duncan Macrae
Lt. Hilary	Noel Harrison
Private Singer	Robert Desmond
Colonel Brownhow	Michael Trubshawe
Tanner	Bernard Cribbins
Prefect	Ronald Fraser

"The Best Of Enemies," produced by Italy's Dino De Laurentiis for Columbia, is not an Italian pic dubbed into English. It's an English-speaking production

shrewdly designed for an international market which it well merits capturing. Call it a hybrid. But it's a splendidly warm, wryly witty and amusing hybrid. Written by one Englishman and two Italians, it is directed by an Englishman (Guy Hamilton), has an Anglo-Italian star cast, with a few exceptions, (one being American David Opatoshu) and an Anglo-Italian crew. It was shot mainly in Israel, with some location and studio work in Italy. Israelites were used as extras. Some Abyssinians were imported to play abyssinians, and two trained gazelles were recruited in Frankfurt, Germany.

It all adds up to a smash combined operation which could well become one of the offbeat comedy clicks of 1962. It was launched first in Italy with acclaim. Then it bowed into London with a midnight gala preem. Presence of David Niven and Michael Wilding playing bland, light comedy roles, is enough to spark interest in terms of marquee. Yet it is an Italian actor, Alberto Sordi, who is likely to be most glowingly discussed. Such discussion, plus keen exploitation, should give "Enemies" its deserved b.o. potential.

It's a wartime comedy, with a gently serious undertone for those who seek it. Locale is the Ethiopian desert in 1941. Niven, a British major, and his pilot RAF officer Wilding, crash on a reconnaissance trip. They are captured by an Italian patrol, led by an Italian officer (Sordi). He releases them on condition that they let his patrol move freely to a nearby fort. Back in base, Niven is ordered to attack the fort and does so reluctantly. From then on it's an hilarious cat-and-mouse game, with captor and captive alternating as the fortunes of war sway.

From this wry shambles emerges a mutual respect and liking between the two enemies. The serious undertone? That war is crazy.

The screenplay is peppered with brisk jokes and unexpected offbeat situations which keep the proceedings light and easy. Hamilton has directed with a sure touch which brings out the characteristics of the two opposed nations admirably. The locations are authentic and Guiseppe Rotumno's color lensing okay.

Niven, debonair, nonchalant and skilfully underplaying, is matched, excellently by Sordi. Playing his first English speaking role, this Italian actor did the job parrot-fashion and scores a hit. He is a handsome young man, a comedian with a touch of pathos. Of a long supporting cast of British and Italian thesps, Michael Wilding, in a typical throwaway is casually effective; Harry Andrews, as a bewildered regular officer and Duncan Macrae, as a sergeant who treats the desert as if it were a military parade ground, are standouts.

"Best Of Enemies" emerges as a superior slice of entertainment. De Laurentiis deserves a shake of the mitt for resisting any attempt to introduce a phoney love-theme. Only femme faces seen are the photographs of their wives that Niven and Sordi carry with them.

Rich.

Something Wild

Confused, inarticulate drama about the rehabilitation of a rape victim. Strikingly photographed, sincerely played, it may make out in the arties.

United Artists release of Prometheus (George Justin) production. Stars Carroll Baker, Ralph Meeker. Directed by Jack Garfein. Screenplay, Garfein, Alex Karmel, based on novel, "Mary Ann," by Karmel; camera, Eugen Shuftan; music, Aaron Copeland; editor Carl Lerner; asst. director, Jim Digangi. Reviewed in N.Y., Dec. 19, '61. Running time, **112 MINS.**

Mary Ann .... Carroll Baker
Mike .... Ralph Meeker
Mrs. Gates .... Mildred Dunnock
Warren Gates .... Charles Watts
Shirley Johnson .... Jean Stapleton
Landlord .... Martin Koslek
Manager of 5 & 10.......... Ken Chapin
Detective Bogarde .... Clifton James
Girls in 5 & 10 ....Tanya Lopert, Margaret Shirley, Virginia Baker, Doris Roberts, Anita Cooper
1st Policeman..........George L. Smith
A young boy .... Duke Howard

Although George Justin and company obviously produced with loving care, "Something Wild" is a lugubrious drama of rape-and-rehabilitation that is ultimately as inarticulate as its central characters. The names of Carroll Baker and Ralph Meeker may help at the boxoffice; its best chance is for the arties where its technical brilliance (Eugen Shuftan's camerawork and Aaron Copeland's score) will be appreciated.

For most of its running time, "Something Wild" is a one-woman show as it focusses almost exclusively on Miss Baker and her ill-defined moods of shame, guilt, loneliness and utter desperation following her rape. A product of a rather joyless, middleclass New York home, the girl subsequently seeks to lose herself in the jungle of Manhattan. On the brink of suicide, she is saved by a sensitive but apparently dimwitted garage mechanic, Meeker, who takes her home and, after months of fumbling, persuades her to love him.

The film is trying to say something perceptive about human loneliness and the need for love, but because the characters played by Miss Baker and Meeker are almost totally tongue-tied, very little compassion is worked up for their dreary state. As a result, the film's main interest is furnished by the subsidiary characters—Miss Baker's weakgened "respectable" mother, played by Mildred Dunnock, and assorted New York types Miss Baker meets in her wanderings—and by the series of candid views of Manhattan life—sleazy and crystal-hard—caught by Shuftan's camera. The action at screen centre may be spiritless, but there is often throbbing life on the periphery.

Director Jack Garfein (Miss Baker's husband and partner in their Promethous Enterprisee, from which this comes) has nobly tried to tell his story with more pictures than words. That he has failed is probably because the main conflict faced by his heroine is "interior," with very little of it registering on the screen. This would also explain the eventual monotony in the two principal performances. They're all emotion, and in slow motion.

Aaron Copeland's score, on the other hand, while often intrusive is also lively and pointed, giving the film a point of view and direction it otherwise lacks.

Anby.

In The Doghouse
(BRITISH)

Medium comedy about veterinary surgeons mildly joshes the British passion for animals. A few yocks, but unlikely as a boxoffice hit.

London, Dec. 15.

Rank production (Hugh Stewart) and release. Stars Leslie Phillips, Peggy Cummins, Hattie Jacques, James Booth; features Dick Bentley, Colin Gordon, Joan Heal, Fenella Fielding, Esma Cannon, Richard Goolden. Directed by Darcy Conyers. Screenplay by Michael Pertwee from "It's a Vet's Life," novel by Alex Duncan; music, Philip Green; camera, Alan Hume; editor, Roger Charrill. At New Victoria, London. Running time, 93 **MINS.**

Jimmy Fox-Upton .... Leslie Phillips
Sally .... Peggy Cummins
Gudgeon .... Hattie Jacques
Bob Skeffington .... James Booth
Mr. Peddle .... Dick Bentley
Dean .... Colin Gordon
Mrs. Peddle .... Joan Heal
Miss Fordyce .... Fenella Fielding
Mrs. Raikes .... Esma Cannon
Mr. Ribart .... Richard Goolden
Miss Gibbs .... Joan Hickson
Mrs. Crabtree .... Vida Hope
Rita .... Jacqueline Jones
Sid .... Harry Locke

The Briton's passion for animals is taken for a gentle ride in "In the Doghouse," which offers a few yocks but is neither sharp nor lively enough to make it stand out as a very likely boxoffice bet. Film's advantage is that it has a skilled cast, well versed in the art of putting over this particular brand of British comedy. Thus people such as Leslie Phillips, Hattie Jacques, Fenella Fielding, Richard Goolden, Dick Bentley, Esma Cannon and Colin Gordon can jump through the comedy hoops with the greatest of ease. But Michael Pertwee's screenplay doesn't offer them many hoops.

Yarn concerns two young vet surgeons. One (Leslie Phillips) is a good veterinarian, fond of animals and in charge of a vet practice in a poor district. The other (James Booth) is a bad vet, who's in the business purely for money, and unscrupulously fleeces his wealthy clientele.

After a series of mishaps which involve Phillips with the pet lion of an eccentric and in chasing a performing chimp through a ladies' Turkish bath, Booth gets mixed up in a racket for exporting worn-out horses to the butchers of France. He tricks Phillips into taking on the job but, naturally, in time Phillips discovers the plot, breaks the racket and gets the girl (Peggy Cummins).

This simple stuff is taken at a reasonably bright pace by director Darcy Conyers, but there is more bark to the script than bite. Miss Cummins makes a comedy heroine while Hattie Jacques provides another of her pungent studies as an officer of the Royal Society for the Prevention of Cruelty to Animals.

Phillips is his usual lighthearted self, but Booth tends to ham up his role as the shady vet. Rosie the Lion and Chaka the chimp—(or vice-versa!)—stand up well to the human competition.

Technically, the film is okay and Philip Green has provided another distinctive score.

Rich.

Divorzio all'Italiana
(Divorce, Italian Style)
(ITALIAN)

Lux Film release of a Lux-Vides-Galatea production. Produced by Franco Cristaldi. Stars Marcello Mastroianni. Directed by Pietro Germi. Story and screenplay, Germi, Ennio DeConcini, Alfredo Giannetti. Camera, Leonida Barboni. Editor, Roberto Cinquini. Music, Carlo Rustichelli. Previewed, Rome. Running time, **108 MINS.**

Ferdinando .... Marcello Mastroianni
Rosalia .... Daniela Rocca
Angela .... Stefania Sandrelli
Carmelo Patane ...... Leopoldo Trieste
Don Gaetano .... Odoardo Spadaro
Sisina .... Margherita Girelli
Agnese .... Angela Cardile

This one may turn into a sleeper with word of mouth a probable major factor of film's success. Comedy with grotesque and satirical overtones, offbeat by usual Italian standards, it likewise has a strong foreign potential.

In its distinctive tongue-in-cheek way, film suggests a solution to unhappy couples unable to divorce under Catholic Italian law: kill your spouse—but make sure that your deed is recognizably in defense of your and your family's honor. In which case, under article 587 of Italian law, the murderer is penalized only 3 to 7 years in jail; no more, sometimes less. Needless to say, pic proves the absurdity of the archaic legislation, which had prompted—or excused—large number of similar "crimes of honor," especially in the Italian south.

Plot deals with a fed-up husband (Marcello Mastroianni) who plans several ways to get rid of his nagging wife (Daniela Rocca), finally decides to find a lover for her, spring on the couple and shoot her dead. After several clever plot twists, he does, going on to marry the girl next door while his entire village cheers him as it would a hero. But film must be seen, not told. Skillfully written, with a penetrating, almost brutal glimpse of Sicily and its antiquated way of life, it has been directed by Germi with lagless pace and consistent incisiveness, evoking constant chuckles rather than isolated guffaws.

Marcello Mastroianni gives an imaginative performance as the scheming wife-hater, showing great versatility in this change-of-pace role which is sure to be remembered by years-end award time. Daniela Rocca is excellent as his wife, Stefania Sandrelli at times unsure but well cast as his ideal girl, Leopoldo Trieste good as the wife's onetime suitor, while others in a vast and colorful cast provide topnotch backing.

Blending of Carlo Rutichelli's fine musical score with Roberto Cinquini's apt cutting job are other major plus factors, as is Leonida Barboni's oft-breathtaking camerawork, all on Sicilian locations. Franco Cristaldi's production credits (as well as his courage in tackling so offbeat a project) are in same quality niche.

Hawk.

Los Hermanos del Hierro
(Brothers of Iron)
(MEXICAN)

Mexico City, Dec. 19.

Peliculas Nacionales release of Cinematografica Filmex production. Stars Antonio Aguilar, Julio Aleman, Columba Dominquez; features Patrica Conde, Dominguez; features Eduardo Noriega, Ignacio Lopez Tarso, Victor Manuel Mendoza, Jose Elias Moreno, David Silva, Amanda de Llano, Pedro Armendariz. Directed by Ismael Rodriguez. Screenplay, Ricardo Garibay; camera, Rosalio Solano; music, Raul Lavista. At Alameda Theatre, Mexico City. Running time, 90 **MINS.**

Ismael Rodriguez, one of the more dedicated Mexican producers, who always inserts his personal touch by adapting original screenplays to his special style, has taken the basic idea of a tale of vengeance and family feuding, and turned this into a brutally realistic and cruel film. It relates depressing and true to life incidents still reported of "venganzas" (vengeance) in the Mexican hinterlands.

The director receives able help from his cast in developing this sordid tale of life, with exceptionally notable performances by Emilio "Indio" Fernandez, Julio Aleman, Antonio Aguilar and Columba Dominguez. Patrica Conde, introduced in this one, shows definite ability to handle a difficult role. Other actors, in spot scenes, contribute to the story development, with psychological overtones, as brought out by Rodriguez.

Rosalio Salono's black and white photography contributes to the sombre mood of film, with music by Raul Lavista also heightening the dramatic effect.

An excellent, if controversial theme, this above average Mexican effort is slated to have a good life in the domestic ma.ket as well as overseas. This one is a candidate for English dubbing. *Emil.*

Petticoat Pirates
(BRITISH-COLOR)

Despite energetic efforts by British tv idol, Charlie Drake, this remains a fairly limp naval spree, providing only intermittent yocks.

London, Dec. 19.

Warner-Pathe release of an Associated British Pictures (Gordon L. T. Scott) production. Stars Charlie Drake, Anne Heywood, Cecil Parker, John Turner; features Maxine Audley, Thorley Walters, Eleanor Summerfield, Victor Maddern. Directed by David MacDonald. Screenplay by Lew Schwarz from story by T. J. Morrison; additional material, Charlie Drake; editor, Ann Chegwidden; camera, Gilbert Taylor; music, Don Banks. At Warner Theatre, London. Running time, **87 MINS.**

Charlie .... Charlie Drake
Anne .... Anne Heywood
C-inC .... Cecil Parker
Michael .... John Turner
Superintendent .... Maxine Audley
Jerome .... Thorley Walters
Mabel .... Eleanor Summerfield
C.O.C. Nixon .... Victor Maddern
Admiral (U.S.N.) ...... Lionel Murton
P.T. Instructress ...... Barbara Hicks
Paul Turner .... Kenneth Fortescue
Sue .... Dilys Laye
Tug .... Michael Ripper
Alec .... Anton Rodgers
Kenneth .... Murray Melvin
Gunnery Officer .... Diane Aubrey
Mess Attendant .... Kim Tracy

Pocket-sized television comedian Charlie Drake, a wow on the small screen, is finding the transito the cinema a tricky one. "Petticoat Pirates" is his second attempt and the occasion is liable to strain the loyalty of even his most ardent admirers. Drake is a highly individual comic but he would probably be more effective in smaller doses. Though he doesn't carry the full burden in this pic, there's little doubt but that it was designed as a vechicle for him. And it doesn't come off, except occasionally.

Drake's name, and the many favorites in the supporting cast, should bring patrons to the Brit-ish cinemas, but the film is likely to meet stormy weather elsewhere.

Film has a flimsy, screwball but acceptable theme for a comedy-farce. Wren Officer Anne Heywood and the 150 girls under her command are piqued. On the grounds that anything men can do, Wrens can do better they maintain the right to serve at sea in warships. When the plan is turned down by the authorities they raid a frigate, imprison the skeleton crew and set off to sea, where they take part in an exercise between British and U.S. fleets, cover themselves with glory but eventually have to admit defeat when they hit a storm.

These goings on are mainly an excuse for Drake to masquerade as a Wren and for the main decks of the frigate to be turned into a sun-bathing parade, with the girls stripped down to their scanties. Drake has a few bright comedy situations and one notably unfunny one when, in a dream sequence, he appears as seven different naval types, which is reminiscent of an earlier Alec Guinness film, "Barnacle Bill," but far less subtly devised.

The screenplay is flabby and dialog mainly flat. It seems that director David MacDonald was trying not to let Drake monopolize the action, and the result is an uneasy mixture of slapstick and straight comedy. Of the remainder of the cast, Miss Heywood looks pretty, but unconvincing as the chief raider. Cecil Parker offers another of his well-timed studies in pomposity while John Turner makes a stalwart, pleasant hero. Among the many others who are valiant in support are Lionel Murton, Thorley Walters, Eleanor Summerfield, Dilys Laye, Victor Maddern, Maxine Audley, Murray Melvin and a host of shapely charmers who look stunning dressed or undressed, but they're practically indistinguishable.

Technically the film is okay with excellent lensing by Gilbert Taylor, authentic settings and a well-staged storm sequence. Music tends to harp on the "Life on the Ocean Wave" type of tune. Regrettably it must be recorded that "Petticoats Pirates" provides too few laughs on the ocean wave. *Rich.*

Salvatore Giuliano
(ITALIAN)

Rome, Dec. 19.

Lux Film release of a Lux-Video-Galatea (Franco Cristaldi) production. Features Salvo Randone, Frank Wolff. Directed by Francesco Rosi. Screenplay, Rosi, Suso Cecchi D'Amico, Enzo Provenzale, Franco Solinas; camera, Gianni di Venanzo; music, Piero Piccioni; editor, Mario Serandrei. Previewed in Rome. Running time, **125 MINS.**

Court President .... Salvo Randone
Pisciotta .... Frank Wolff

An outstanding film, sure to rank among the best of the season, has been fashioned by Francesco Rosi using the story of Sicilian bandit Giuliano as a pretext for a historical, political, and social document of its times (the late 40's and early 50's), and of the island setting (Sicily) which made it possible.

Though the pic has many moments of suspense and excitement as it tells the Giuliano story and all that went with it, it is by no means the usual bandit-gendarme yarn. In fact, one rarely if ever catches a closeup of the notorious outlaw who made national and international headlines in the post-war years. But we brilliantly get the feeling of Sicily—and Italy—of those days, of how the bandits, the police, the army, the gendarmes, the Mafia and the local politicians operated in knots, in an almost inextricable confusion of ideas, ideals and exploits.

Tale is told in flashback, beginning with a graphic reenactment of Giuliano's death (shot by his best friend, then again by the police, who claimed credit for the deed), and the ending when still another gang member, who betrayed, is shot during a recent Sicilian night. The flashback technique used by Rosi (it is his best film) is at times confusing to the non-Italian viewer, and this had best be kept in mind when pic is adapted for export. What is crystal-clear, in all its implications, to one who has lived through the era, is not as clear, at least on all levels, to non-initiates.

The director's handling of non-pro and pro players, as well as his cinematic and dramatic sense, make this a visually exciting picture above and beyond other considerations and values. Of the name players, Salvo Randone does an outstanding job as the judge charged with the impossible job of seeking clear-cut justice for those involved, gang members and not. Frank Wolff, an American, is standout as Gaspare Pisciotta, Giuliano's righthand man. Others, inward and act, are the image of Sicily.

Gianni di Venanzo's camera work is uniformly outstanding. All of the pic was shot on location in Giuliano's home territory. An extra nod must go also to Piero Piccioni's fine musical scoring, and outstanding asset of pic, which, if it can solve certain local censorship difficulties, should prove a truly heavyweight boxoffice contender. It has proportionately good export chances dependent on an adroit "foreign" adaptation. *Hawk.*

Twist Around The Clock

Another quickie effort to cash in on the Twist sweepstakes. Fairly presentable novelty item. Should hold its own in the Twist scramble.

Hollywood, Dec. 18.

Columbia Pictures release of Sam Katzman production. Stars Chubby Checker, Dion, Vicki Spencer, The Marcels; introduces Clay Cole. Directed by Oscar Rudolph. Screenplay, James B. Gordon; camera, Gordon Avil; editor, Jerome Thoms; assistant director, Floyd Joyer. Reviewed at the studio, Dec. 18, '61. Running time, **83 MINS.**

Chubby Checker .... Himself
Dion .... Himself
Vicki Spencer .... Herself
The Marcels .... Themselves
Clay Cole .... Himself
Mitch Mason .... John Cronin
Tina Louden .... Mary Mitchell
Debbie Marshall ...... Maura McGivney
Joe Marshall .... Tol Avery
Dizzy Bellew .... Alvy Moore
Georgie Clark .... Lenny Kent
Jimmy Cook .... Tom Middleton
Larry .... Jeff Parker
Headwaiter .... Ernesto Morelli
Mrs. Vandeveer .... Barbara Morrison
1st Dowager .... Ezelle Poule
Girl in Booth .... Renee Aubry
Harry Davis .... John Bryant
Harvey .... Barry O'Hara
Proprietor .... Dal McKennon

The Great American Twist Picture has yet to be made, but Columbia's version should more than hold its own in the current scramble to cash in on America's latest contribution to world culture while it is still a hot, fresh, sweepstakes issue. Sam Katzman production is attractively and resourcefully mounted and endowed with a reasonable sense of dramatic content and concern for characterization, so that it is not entirely a string of teen-geared nitery acts united without purpose or direction.

Written by James B. Gordon, the Twist comes out of the boon docks, where it is discovered in all its idyllic, virginal splendor by an enterprising but unemployed promoter who has become appraised of the lamentable fact that rock 'n' roll is dead, man, dead. The young man's problem, in bringing his find to national attention and benefitting financially therefrom, is a romantic one. The daughter of the head of yon big talent agency that can translate this back country wiggle into big business loves him, but the handsome promoter loves one of the wigglers. Eventually all is resolved for fun and profit.

In between this slim, but adequate, storyline fabrication, a dozen "musical interludes" occur. Among those who participate prominently are Chubby Checker, Dion, Vicki Spencer, The Marcels and Clay Cole. Checker, or "The King of the Twist" as he is grandly known, offers three pertinent exhibitions of his prowess at Twistcraft. Other able-bodied Twisters are Cole and Jeff Parker. But Dion, who wails three tunes, and Miss Spencer, who warbles a pair, apparently have been employed for purposes of teen marquee impetus. Their solo contributions neither advance story nor have anything to do with the essential business at hand—Twisting.

John Cronin and Mary Mitchell are an attractive pair as the romantic couple, and the latter does some competent twisting. Chief supporting players are Maura McGiveney, Tol Avery and Alvy Moore.

Man's face may be more beautiful than his backside, as a visiting official once noted, but Gordon Avil's bottoms-up photography does not exactly adhere to this view. Most of the choreographic action is regarded from below-the-belt, which, of course, is where the Twist really comes on strong. Generally it's a tidy, quite busy little production, consideraig the time and cost factors involved. Director Oscar Rudolph, editor Jerome Thoms, art director George Van Marter and other craftsmen involved have performed their labors with skill. *Tube.*

1962

Upstairs And Downstairs
(BRITISH-COLOR)

Servant problem in England, tediously scrutinized in overlong farce.

Hollywood, Dec. 28.
Twentieth-Fox release of Betty E. Box production. Stars Michael Craig, Anne Heywood, Mylene Demongeot; with Sidney James, James Robertson Justice. Directed by Ralph Thomas. Screenplay, Frank Harvey; camera (De Luxe), Ernest Steward; editor, Alfred Roome; music, Philip Green. Reviewed at Hollywood Theatre, Dec. 28, '61. Running time, **101 MINS.**

The laughs are few and far between in "Upstairs And Downstairs," an episodic British farce comedy that examines, at great length, the problems connected with locating reliable domestics in England. The Betty Box production, being released in the U.S. by 20th-Fox, has already played Manhattan nabe spots. It runs an excessive, ultimately oppressive, 101-minutes, far too lengthy for compatible pairing. Wisely, 20th has chosen not to plant it in the arties—as has been the custom with British comedy exports—for it is most assuredly not in a league with most of the English farce product. But considerable trimming is in order to make this number palatable as support in general U.S. twin-bill playdates.

Screenplay by Frank Harvey describes the plight of a young British couple beset with servant instability. The plot is divided into five sections—in each of which the hired domestic becomes the center of attraction. Of the five thus employed, the first is mad for sailors, the second mad for booze, the third frightened of death of civilized man, the fourth a thief, the fifth in love with her employer. There are patches of merriment in this episodic stew, but most of the time the film is obviously and elaborately laboring to set up punch situations that don't quite register with the intended impact, at least in this country, where domestics in a middle-class situation are pretty much obsolete. Moreover, the final, and lengthiest, episode takes itself seriously, an approach for which the audience is unprepared.

wood are the harassed employers. Neither character is endowed with much in the way of personality. The stars of the show actually are the domestics, but accomplished histrionic efforts in this department are, for the most part, blunted by writing mediocrity and rather ragged, sluggish editing. Key parts are dispatched with some skill by Mylene Demongeot, Sidney James and James Robertson Justice. A certain amount of visual ingenuity by director Ralph Thomas and cameraman Ernest Steward is of helpful comic value. The film is in color, and rather unnecessarily so.
Tube.

Sasom i en Spegel
(Through a Glass, Darkly)
(SWEDISH)
Stockholm, Dec. 26.
Svensk Filmindustri production and release. Stars Harriet Andersson, Gunnar Bjornstrand, Max von Sydow, Lars Pass-

gard. Directed by Ingmar Bergman. Screenplay by Ingmar Bergman; camera, Sven Nykvist; music, J. S. Bach; editor, Ulla Ryghe. At Roda Kvarn, Stockholm. Running time, **89 MINS.**
Karin .... Harriet Andersson
David .... Gunnar Bjornstrand
Martin .... Max von Sydow
Fredrik .... Lars Passgard

Ingmar Bergman in "Through a Glass, Darkly," tells a story that is in many ways reminiscent of "Long Day's Journey Into Night." Pic deals with four members of a family who are estranged from one another through their inability to express feelings for each other. The action is limited to 24 hours in the lives of the four. The time is the nightless Scandinavian summer and the setting is an isolated island in the Baltic. Not a pleasant film, it is a great one.

Main character is Karin, portrayed by Harriet Andersson, who is suffering from a mental ailment. Released from a mental institution, she seeks the security of her childhood, the love of her father (Gunnar Bjornstrand) and her 17-year-old brother (Lars Passgard). She turns more and more away from her husband Martin (Max von Sydow), a doctor and instructor at a medical school.

Martin has been told that she will probably get a relapse and there is little hope of her being cured. Martin sincerely loves her and wants to help, but she is no longer attracted to him. Her father, David, is a popular novelist who has never had any critical success. Younger brother, Fredrik, (Lars Passgard), is at the age when sexual inquisitiveness is awakening.

During the night after the family reunion, voices from Karin's mad world call her. She goes off to an abandoned house to have her mad meeting with the voices from another world. Afterwards she goes to her father's room for the protection of childhood. Her father is working on his latest novel and she soon falls asleep. When she wakes up, her father has gone out and she looks in his diary where she reads that her condition is hopeless. Also that her father is driven by an irresistible desire to study her deterioration

in a boat for a day of fishing, Karin and her brother confide inner secrets to one another. The day of youthful fun-making comes to a tragic end when Karin madly seduces her brother. Later, Karin only wants the peace of life in her world of unreality. The Bergman message comes at the end when David speaks personally to his son that he believes: "God exists in love, in every sort of love, maybe God is love."

L'Enlevement Des Sabines
(The Rape of the Sabines)
(FRENCH-ITALIAN-COLOR)
Paris, Jan. 2.
20th-Fox release of CFPI-FICIT production. With Mylene Demongeot, Folco Lulli, Roger Moore, Scilla Gabel, Georgia Moll, Francis Blanche, Jean Marais, Rossana Schiaffino. Directed by Richard Pottier. Screenplay, Carlo Infascelli, Edouardo Anton, Marc-Gilbert Sauvajon; camera (Eastmancolor), Adalberto Albertini; editor, R. Renoux. At Ermitage, Paris. Running time, **100 MINS.**
Vestal .... Mylene Demongeot
Romulus .... Roger Moore
Pheonecian .... Scilla Gabel
Father .... Folco Lulli
Girl .... Georgia Moll
Roman .... Francis Blanche

Though made in Italy and Yugoslavia, this is primarily a French coproduction. An attempt to get into the antique costumer series, it emerges a weak sister in this category with fast playoffs its main chances.

Early Rome has no women and the leader is the son of the God Mars. Neighboring Sabines have lookers and the Romans manage to get to them. Thus, a war is averted by the girls, now converted to Roman ways.

Direction lacks snap and the attempted recreation of time misfires with the modern dialog somewhat ludicrous. Neither comedy nor spectacle, this film will have to be sold via its cavorting girls, and the theme. Sets looks like production funds were held down. The acting goes off on all tangents.

Technical aspects are also uneven with color lacking snap.
Mosk.

Bonitas Las Tapatias
(Jalisco Gals Are Beautiful)
(MEXICAN)
Mexico City, Dec. 26.
Peliculas Nacionales release of Tele Talia Films production. Stars Elvira Quintana, Joaquin Cordero, Carlos Lopez Moctezuma, Barbara Gil; features Jaime Fernandez, Manola Saavedra, Felix Gonzalez, Arcelia Larranaga and Graciela Lara. Directed by Humberto Gomez Landero. Original story and screenplay, Humberto Gomez Landero. At Olimpia Theatre, Mexico City. Running time, **90 MINS.**

Elvira Quintana, comely star of this film, has the distinction of having intepreted more diversified roles than any other Mexican actress—a doctor, anthropologist, singer, femme fatale and female vampire. In this one, she essays the role of a western queen, but an active one. She pitches in to put the bad guys, headed by villain Carlos Lopez Moctezuma, in their place.

The story is simple without any beating around the bush. There's plenty of action and gunplay before Moctezuma is unmasked and gets his just deserts.

Moctezuma turns in his usually good performance as the hypocritical badman masquerading behind the skirts of respectability. Youngster Jaime Fernandez is an adept lieutenant, equally villainous, to the point where he actually steals some scenes. Miss Quintana not only is pleasing on the eyes but has a flair for acting. Barbara Gil is also adequate in her role. For beautiful window dressing there are Manola Saavedra, Arcelia Larranaga and Graciela Lara who don't get much opportunity except to display their charms to best advantage.
Emil.

Tender Is The Night
(C'SCOPE—COLOR)

Scott Fitzgerald's novel, intelligently but sluggishly translated to dramatic essentials in a long, elaborately mounted film. Good performances. Deliberate pace may dampen prospects, but rich, accurate production, thoughtful selling and some trimming could bring b.o. success.

Hollywood, Jan. 4.
Twentieth-Fox release of Henry T. Weinstein production. Stars Jennifer Jones, Jason Robards Jr., Joan Fontaine, Tom Ewell; features Cesare Danova, Jill St. John, Paul Lukas. Directed by Henry King. Screenplay, Ivan Moffat, based on the novel by F. Scott Fitzgerald; camera (De Luxe), Leon Shamroy; editor, William Reynolds; music, Bernard Herrmann; assistant director, Eli Dunn. Reviewed at the studio, Jan. 4, '62. Running time, **146 MINS.**
Nicole Diver .... Jennifer Jones
Dick Diver .... Jason Robards Jr.
Baby Warren .... Joan Fontaine
Abe North .... Tom Ewell
Tommy Barban .... Cesare Danova
Rosemary Hoyt .... Jill St. John
Dr. Dohmler .... Paul Lukas
Mrs. McKisco .... Bea Benaderet
Mr. McKisco .... Charles Fredericks
Dr. Gregorovious...... Sanford Meisner
Colis Clay .... Mac McWhorter
Louis .... Albert Carrier
Francisco .... Richard de Combray
Mrs. Hoyt .... Carole Mathews
Pardo .... Alan Napier
Topsy Diver .... Leslie Farrell
Lanier Diver .... Michael Crisalli
Piano Player .... Earl Grant
Sir Charles Golding. Maurice Dallimore
Mrs. Dunphrey .... Carol Veazie
Governess .... Arlette Clark

A combination of attractive, intelligent performers and consistently interesting. De Luxecolorful photography of interiors and exteriors—mostly the French Riviera—provide big plus qualities in this 20th-Fox adaptation of "Tender Is The Night." This may not be a 100 proof distillation of F. Scott Fitzgerald. Such is not possible of achievement since the essential beauty of the novel is the literary artistry of its prose. But "Tender Is The Night" is nonetheless on its own filmic terms a thoughtful, disturbing and at times absorbing romantic drama. Since the basic appeal is sufficiently broad to satisfy both younger adult and older audiences, its boxoffice prospects are bright and with a strong selling campaign aimed at stimulating both groups this Henry T. Weinstein production could well become an important moneymaker.

It has been some time since the screen has delivered a profoundly romantic film of this nature, thankfully devoid of the dark and baser sex connotations. This alone should come as welcome relief, even though scenarist Ivan Moffat has not succeeded altogether in clarifying the elusive meanings of the drama and director Henry King has been more resourceful in capturing atmosphere than in dissecting the principal characters. "Tender Is The Night" has been produced on an elaborate scale. Obviously a lot of painstaking care has gone into the mounting and carving. It is evident that the film's creative team has striven for physical authenticity and fidelity to plot, and these are important values. They provide a basic strength, which, however, might still be made even stronger by some judicious last-ditch trimming. A number of minor scenes might be sliced out altogether, others refined to expository essentials, to sharpen and accelerate the flow of the drama.

Novel and film depict the decay and deterioration of a brilliant and idealistic psychiatrist (Jason Robards Jr.), whose love for and marriage to a wealthy patient (Jennifer Jones) ultimately consumes, dissipates and destroys him by engulfing him in the meaningless motives and glamorous le'sure of upper social class Americans adrift in Europe in the prosperous 1920's. Moffat's screenplay emphasizes the point of transference of strength from doctor to patient, traces the reverse process in which heroine and hero travel in emotionally opposite directions as a result of their tragic relationship. That the climax, the wife's decision to divorce her husband, emerges less plausible in the film than in the novel is attributable to the less dimensional, less incisive examination of the two characters and their kinship within the necessarily naked form of drama.

Jennifer Jones, is the picture's strongest marquee value, although this outing is bound to boost Robards tremendously when word-of-mouth gets sufficient circulation. In short this looks like a film which should build at theatres. Miss Jones, absent from the screen since "A Farewell to Arms" in 1957, emerges a crisply fresh, intriguing personality and creates a striking character as the schizophrenic Nicole, Robards whose non - matinee-idol masculinity makes him an ideal choice for the role of the ill-fted doctor-husband, Dick Diver, plays with intelligence and conviction. John oFntaine is convincing as Nicole's shallow, older sister, performing with the right manifestation of frivoiity and bite that her part requires.

Tom Ewell is believably wry and boozily doomed in a somewhat watered-down version of the expatriate Broadway composer Abe North. Paul Lukas delivers an excellent portrayal of Dr. Dohmler, the discerning mentor who warns Diver of the pitfalls of marriage to Nicole. Jill St. John plays the role of Diver's youthful actress-admirer with a bit too much naivete. Cesare Danova is suave as the adventurer who eventually lures Nicole away from her husband. Especially notable in the generally satisfactory supporting cast are Charles Fredericks, Sanford Meisner and Bea Benaderet. Moppets Leslie Farrell and Michael Crisalli are attractive as the Diver children.

Cameraman Leon Shamroy has captured some invigorating panoramic views of Continental locales, though occasionally the scenery tends to overwhelm the human factor, and Pacific Title has contributed a mood of mixed light and sombre tone in the attractive main title. Sets by Jack Martin Smith and Malcolm Brown are elegant and true by geographical, social and period standards. Bernard Herrmann's score is rich and expressive, and the rhapsodically romantic and melancholy title song by Sammy Fain and Paul Francis Webster not only haunts the mind but plays a part in the drama. The refrain has a bright commercial future, and very likely will contend for the 1962 Oscar. Pierre Balmain's gowns for the three leading ladies—Misses Jones, Fontaine and St. John—are flattering and accurately stylish for the period. *Tube.*

L'Oro di Roma
(The Gold of Rome)
(ITALO—FRENCH)

Rome, Jan. 9.

Lux Film release of Sancro Film-Ager Film-Cirac (Rome)-Contact Organization (Paris) coproduction. Stars Gerard Blain, Anna Maria Ferrero, Jean Sorel; features Filippo Scelzo, Paola Borboni, Andrea Checchi, Enzo Petito, Umberto Raho, Ugo D'Alessio, Rainiero di Cenzo, Luigi Casellato. Directed by Carlo Lizzani. Story and screenplay, Lizzani, Lucio Battistrada, assisted by Cesare Zavattini, Alberto Lecco; camera, Enrico Menxczer; editor, Franco Fraticelli; music, Giovanni Fusco. At Capranica, Rome. Running time, 110 MINS.

Davide .... Gerard Blain
Giulia .... Anna Maria Ferrero
Massimo .... Jean Sorel
Giulia's father .... Andrea Checchi

This film reenacts the 1943 episode in which the German commandant of Rome offered the Eternal City's Jewish population their lives in exchange for 100 pounds in gold. Has good export possibilities in various areas on the strength of human conflict involved, and the underplayed way in which it's told. But some cuts are suggested for to help the pace.

Rather than on Nazi repression, the pic concentrates on efforts and internal conflicts of the Hebrew colony faced with what most feel will prove a life-saving barter, despite the warnings of (later proven correct) of a rebellious shoemaker who joins the partisans when the Germans go back on their promise and deport the Jews.

Inserted for good measure, but not nearly so effective, is the romance of a Jewish girl and a Catholic schoolmate. She becomes a Catholic in order to marry him, but at the fadeout joins her people and is deported.

Carlo Lizzani's direction is almost painstakingly detailed, with a resultant loss in pace and excitement which this needs. However, he does manage several vital points. Anna Maria Ferrero is the most believable character in the film, well backed by Andrea Checchi, as her father and Filippo Scelzo, as the head of the community. Gerard Blain is good as the shoemaker while Jean Sorel does his best with an insipid role as the girl's aristocratic suitor.

This production has semi-documentary flavor, and at its best (perhaps this was not in authors' intentions) when it depicts the community plight of Rome's wartime Ghetto. Other production credits are top level. ***Hawk.***

Moon Pilot
(COLOR)

Another Disney moneymaker, likely to gain b.o. momentum as it goes along. Amusing, frequently uproarious comedy-fantasy about a reluctant astronaut.

Hollywood, Jan. 12.

Buena Vista release of Walt Disney production. Stars Tom Tryon, Brian Keith, Edmond O'Brien; introduces Dany Saval; features Bob Sweeney, Kent Smith, Tommy Kirk. Directed by James Neilson. Screenplay, Maurice Tombragel, from SatEvePost serial by Robert Buckner; camera (Technicolor), William Snyder; editor, Cotton Warburton; music, Paul Smith; assistant director, Joseph L. McEveety. Reviewed at the studio, Jan. 12, '62. Running time, 98 MINS.

Capt. Richmond Talbot ...... Tom Tryon
Major Gen. John H. Vanneman
Brian Keith
McClosky .... Edmond O'Brien
Lyrae .... Dany Saval
Senator Henry McGuire .. Bob Sweeney
Secretary of Air Force ...... Kent Smith
Medical Officer .... Simon Scott
Agent Brown .... Bert Remsen
Celia Talbot .... Sarah Selby
Col. Briggs .... Dick Whittinghill
Walter Talbot .... Tommy Kirk

At first gulp, Walt Disney's "Moon Pilot" is a marvelous mixture of absolute nonsense, a thoroughly intoxicating, high-spirited and full bodied blend of moonshine and monkeyshine. A careful analysis of the ingredients, however, uncovers a more significant reason for its potent kick. For within the frivolous surface merriment of its stohy lurks a most disarmingly irreverent spoof of the current morbid preoccupation with reaching various heavenly bodies before anyone else beats us to it. It's a healthy country that can take time out to laugh at its most sacred, troublesome issues, and a healthy industry that supplies the tonic to ease such excess anxiety.

Filmgoers in general will accept this picture as light, gay, infectious diversion. For those who probe deeper and detect something more significant at the core, so much the better. The upshot, at any rate, appears to be another moneymaker for Disney, though sans surefire marquee names.

Maurice Tombragel's screenplay, based on a SatEvePost serial by Robert Buckner, jovially scans the earthbound predicament of an unwilling, altitude-shy astronaut-to-be on a three-day pass prior to his junket to the moon. Under strict orders not to divulge the nature of his mission, the young man (Tom Tryon) instead becomes embroiled in a see-saw struggle between a comely miss (Dany Saval) from a superior society in outer space and a frustrated government security agent (Edmond O'Brien) who is convinced the mysterious lady is a spy.

"Moon Pilot" is an excellent piece of screen writing by Tombragel, especially uproarious when it is being most disrespectful. For example, in a top level conference room full of logical, strapping young candidates for the maiden moonshot, not a single one is willing to volunteer. Tombragel's script has an inclination towards repetition, and it tends to get missile-bound in its rather flabby romantic midsection, but its virtues far outweigh its faults. The picture is even more notable for its calibre of performance and direction. Every comic nuance is expiored through James Neilson's deft, inventive direction.

Tryon accomplishes a winning portrayal of the reluctant spaceman. Here's an actor on the way up in filmdom, one of the few likely to bridge that historically discouraging gap between television and motion picture stardom.

For Miss Saval, a Gallic comedienne here making her U.S. film bow, it is a striking showcase. But the picture is thespically dominated not by the romantic leads but by two of Hollywood's most polished, versatile actors—Brian Keith and Edmond O'Brien. Keith, as a bombastic, hot-tempered Air Force general, plays with a sense of comic perception. His reactions to a stream of wild beatnik girls unconcernedly passing through a police lineup (one of the film's juiciest scenes) are worth the attention of any acting aspirant. O'Brien, as the exasperated govt. man, consistently gets the exactly correct flavor into his lines, occasionally turning an ordinary exchange of dialog into a wildly funny moment.

Others who perform with skill include Bob Sweeney, Tommy Kirk, Kent Smith, Simon Scott, Bert Remsen, Sarah Selby, Dick Whittinghill, Nancy Kulp and a most cooperative chimp who emerges unexpectedly from a space capsule at the climax of the film's elaborately clever opening scene.

The slick, attractive production is a reflection of filmmaking savvy in all areas, encompassing the compact, colorful art direction of Carroll Clark and Marvin Aubrey Davis, adroit photography of William Snyder, smoothly progressive editing of Cotton Warburton and vivid soundwork of mixer Harry M. Lindgren. A special joy is Paul Smith's score, which, by playing it straight, enhances the comic flavor. Had Smith attempted to compete by inserting his own comic musical comment, his score might have intruded. An additional bow to coproducer Bill Anderson and associate Ron Miller for a job well done. *Tube.*

Murder She Said
(BRITISH)

Margaret Rutherford out-Sherlocks Scotland Yard in an amiable, if improbable, murder mystery with a whimsical streak. Fine supporting item.

Hollywood, Jan. 10.

Metro release of George H. Brown production. Stars Margaret Rutherford, Arthur Kennedy, Muriel Pavlow, James Robertson-Justice; features Thorley Walters, Charles Tingwell. Directed by George Pollock. Screenplay, David Pursall, Jack Seddon, from an adaptation by David Osborn of Agatha Christie's novel, "4.50 from Paddington"; camera, Geoffrey Faithfull; editor, Ernest Walter; music, Ron Goodwin; assistant director, Douglas Hickox. Reviewed at the studio, Jan. 10, '62. Running time, 87 MINS.

Miss Marple ...... Margaret Rutherford
Dr. Quimper .... Arthur Kennedy
Emma .... Muriel Pavlow
Mr. Ackenthorpe
James Robertson-Justice
Inspector Craddock....Charles Tingwell
Cedric .... Thorley Walters
Harold .... Conrad Phillips
Alexander .... Ronnie Raymond
Mrs. Kidder .... Joan Hickson
Stringer .... Stringer Davis
Brian Eastley .... Ronald Howard
Albert .... Gerald Cross
Hillman .... Michael Golden
Bacon .... Gordon Harris
Lucy .... Lucy Griffiths
Mrs. Stainton .... Barbara Hicks
Ticket Collector .... A. N. Other

The spectacle of a grandmotherly amateur criminologist outsleuthing the skeptical, methodical professionals provides most of the fun in this somewhat unconvincing, but nonetheless engaging, murder mystery manufactured at Metro's British Studios in Borehamwood. Since the aged distaff Sherlock happens to be Margaret Rutherford, one of filmdom's foremost character comediennes, the

thread of humor weaving through the whodunit is in good histrionic hands. The upshot, insofar as U.S. exhibition is concerned, is a choice item for double billing purposes, though distinctly shy the voltage and lustre to carry the meat end of the bill.

According to the David Pursall-Jack Seddon screenplay, from an adaptation by David Osborn of the Agatha Christie novel, "4.50 from Paddington," Miss Rutherford witnesses a murder transpiring in the compartment of a passing train. Since the police do not believe her story, and being an avid reader of mystery fiction, she takes it upon herself to solve the case, planting herself as maid within the household of the chief suspects. After considerable personal jeopardy and two follow-up homicides, she brings in the killer—a medic (Arthur Kennedy) with a greedy eye for the family inheritance.

The George H. Brown production is weak in the motivation area (Kennedy's mercenary vendetta and his campaign tactics register as pretty implausible and far-fetched), and there's a sticky and unnecessary parting shot in which Miss Rutherford nixes an absurd marriage proposal from the stingy, irascible patriarch of the house (James Robertson-Justice), but otherwise matters purr along at a pleasant clip.

In addition to Miss Rutherford, who simply does what comes naturally (to comic actresses of her stature, that is), others who play prominent roles with flavor and assurance include Kennedy, Justice, Muriel Pavlow, Charles Tingwell, Thorley Walters, Conrad Phillips, Joan Hickson, Stringer Davis, Ronald Howard, Michael Golden and young Ronnie Raymond.

The picture is efficiently directed by George Pollock, with the skilled assistance of cameraman Geoffrey Faithfull, editor Ernest Walter, art director Harry White and composer-conductor Ron Goodwin. *Tube.*

Giorno per Giorno, Disperatamente

(Day by Day, Desperately)
(ITALIAN)

Rome, Jan. 9.

Titanus release of a Titanus-Vides (Franco Cristaldi) production. Features Tomas Milian, Nino Castelnuovo, Madeleine Robinson, Tino Carraro, Franca Bettoia, Riccardo Garrone, Isa Crescenzi. Directed by Alfredo Giannetti. Screenplay, Giannetti, Guido de Biase, from story by Giannetti; camera, Aiace Parolin; music, Carlo Rustichelli; editor, Ruggero Mastroianni. Previewed in Rome. Running time, **100 MINS.**

Dario	Thomas Milian
Gabriele	Nino Castelnuovo
Mother	Madeleine Robinson
Pietro	Tino Carraro
Marcella	Franca Bettoia

This is strong stuff, served up in uncompromising fashion by a promising new director, Alfredo Giannetti, and his first film. Pic will need a hard sell, both in Italy and abroad, to overcome initial resistance to its central theme: insanity, and to its downbeat approach. Paradoxically, word-of-mouth should prove a help.

Writer-director asks his audience to picture the plight of a family burdened with a desperate problem. This is that of putting up with a partially insane son whose presence and tantrums, condoned by an almost fanatically devoted mother, have made victims of the two other members of the household: the father and the demented boy's brother. The mother day by day hopes that after each fit her son will recover. When, after one final attack of fury, she realizes that this will never be, she dies in his arms.

Director, unfortunately for the film's unity, never chooses to concentrate on one or other of his two main themes: the mother's clinical attachment, and the father's mental suffering at his family's disintegration. Either one would have made for a top-notch picture.

As it is, the effect is diluted, though total impact, especially of mad scenes, is frighteningly brutal and chilling.

Thomas Milian is excellent as the insane brother, one of the most realistic renderings of its sort. He gets fine support from Nino Castelnuovo, as his brother, and from Tino Carraro as his father. Madeleine Robinson tends to overstrain her role at times. An interesting cameo is provided by Isa Crescenzi, as a girl friend of the father's. All in all, Giannetti displays a fine hand for his story and its setting, and should be heard from in the future.

Technical plaudits go to lenser Aiace Parolin, working on largely real-life settings, and to Carlo Rustichelli for his apt musical scoring. *Hawk.*

Les Nouveaux Aristocrats

(The New Aristocrats)
(FRENCH)

Paris, Jan. 9.

Sirius release of Chronos Film production. With Paul Meurisse, Charles Belmont, Maria Mauban, Yves Vincent, Catherine Sola, Mireille Dare, Janine Vila, Michel Galabru. Directed by Francis Rigaud. Screenplay, Rigaud, Jacques Vilfrid, Michel De Saint Pierre from novel by De Saint Pierre; camera, Jacques Robin; editor, Pierre Villette. At Normandie, Paris. Running time, **95 MINS.**

Father Maubrun	Paul Meurisse
Mother	Maria Mauban
Father	Yves Vincent
Denis	Charles Belmont
Mad	Catherine Sola
Milou	Mireille Dare
Sylvie	Janine Vila
Father Menuzzi	Michel Galabru

Tale of a well-to-do boy's moral dilemmas about God and love is too full of aphorisms and surface characterizations to make much point. Static direction and talkiness tag this mainly a local item with foreign chances somewhat chancey.

A teenage boy and his sister see their parents breaking up. The boy comes into battle with a new teacher in the Jesuit school he attends. When he is thrown out for writing a blasphemous editorial in a student paper, he tries to commit suicide but is saved by the teacher's words.

This is the main fault of the film. Everything is done by dialog instead of being revealed through visual aspects and the comportment of the characters. It makes this production add up to soapy fare since it lacks the insight into the dilemmas which are just sketchily presented.

Direction does not help build this drama and the shallow characters are helped to become somewhat real by some good but undirected actors. It is technically okay but another in the literary, verbose type of films springing up here. **It makes this questionable export fare.** *Mosk.*

Light In The Piazza

(C'SCOPE—COLOR)

Novel, touching romantic drama about a mother's struggle to locate happiness for her mentally retarded daughter. Artistically framed vs. lush Italo backgrounds, and skillfully enacted, especially by Yvette Mimieux. Good b.o. contender.

Hollywood, Jan. 3.

Metro release of Arthur Freed production. Stars Olivia de Havilland, Rossano Brazzi, Yvette Mimieux, George Hamilton, Barry Sullivan; with Isabel Dean, Moultrie Kelsall, Nancy Nevinson. Directed by Guy Green. Screenplay, Julius J. Epstein, based on story by Elizabeth Spencer; camera (Metrocolor), Otto Heller; editor, Frank Clarke; music, Mario Nascimbene; assistant director, Basil Rayburn. Reviewed at the studio, Jan. 3, '62. Running time, **102 MINS.**

Margaret Johnson	Olivia de Havilland
Signor Naccarelli	Rossano Brazzi
Clara Johnson	Yvette Mimieux
Fabrizio Naccarelli	George Hamilton
Noel Johnson	Barry Sullivan
Miss Hawtree	Isabel Dean
The Minister	Moultrie Kelsall
Signora Naccarelli	Nancy Nevinson

With "Light in the Piazza," first item out of its 1962 hopper, Metro has hit that elusive bull's-eye at which picturemakers inevitably aim—the film that achieves the rare and delicate balance of artistic beauty, romantic substance, dramatic novelty and commercial appeal, the latter being the natural end product of the first three. Discerningly cast and deftly executed under the imaginative guidance of director Guy Green, the Arthur Freed production, filmed in the intoxicatingly visual environments of Rome and Florence, is an interesting touching drama based on a highly unusual romantic circumstance created in prose by Elizabeth Spencer. The film has its flaws, but they are minor kinks in a satisfying whole. This is an especialy enticing picture for people who like pictures, and will be a special favorite with more mature distaff audiences.

Julius J. Epstein's concise and graceful screenplay, from Miss Spencer's story, examines with reasonable depth and sensible restraint the odd plight of a beautiful, wealthy 26-year-old American girl (Yvette Mimieux) who, as a result of a severe blow on the head in her youth, has been left with a permanent 10-year-old mentality. It is, too, the story of her mother's (Olivia de Havilland) dilemma—whether to commit the girl to an institution, as is the wish of her husband (Barry Sullivan), who superficially sees in the measure a solution to his marital instability, or pave the way for the girl's marriage to a well-to-do young Florentine fellow (George Hamilton) by concealing knowledge of the child's retarded intelligence. The lad is no mental pride himself, but he is a warmhearted, responsible boy. The mother pursues the latter course. As the newlywed couple leaves the church, she muses, "I did the right thing. I know I did." And the audience cannot help but feel the same way.

Lovely Miss Mimieux leaps to thespic stature and prominence with her enactment of this novel, afflicted character. Histrionically, it's her picture. Her career takes a resultant giant stride forward. The role requires an aura of luminous naivete mixed with childish vacancy and a passion for furry things and kind, attractive people. That's precisely what it gets from Miss Mimieux. Hamilton acceptably manages the Italian flavor and displays more animation than he normally has in the past. It's a good job.

Miss de Havilland's performance is one of great consistency and subtle projection. It is a pleasure to see her back on the screen after an extended absence. However, there seems to be a slight distortion in the concept of the character, for which the director, moreso than the actress, may be responsible. She is depicted as just a mite too endowed with bloodless aplomb in her own affairs of the heart, with a kind of pseudo-sexual oneupmanship that strips the character of the latently essential warmth indicated. It leaves gaps, question marks and discrepancies in the film's secondary romantic relationship, Miss de Havilland's with Hamilton's very-much-married father, Rossano Brazzi, who nevertheless plays with his patented Continental charm and persuasiveness. Sullivan is sound and true as the shallow husband, and there is top-notch support from Isabel Dean, Moultrie Kelsall and Nancy Nevinson.

Outside of that one reservation **of character concept, Green's direction is outstanding. His, and cameraman Otto Heller's, regard of the two Italian cities is rich in scenic splendor and aesthetic perception. And Green's device of** observing the development of love in the young couple through the eye-view of the mother brings the affair the right note of idyllic poetry, and avoids dull romantic shop talk. Frank Clarke's brisk, tidy editing is a plus, as is Frank White's discerning art direction and Mario Nascimbene's pleasing score. Christian Dior's gowns for Miss de Havilland are stylish and chic, but not always ideally suitable and complimentary to the durable prettiness of the vet actress. The concern, lamentably, seems more for fashion than for subject. *Tube.*

Tintin Et Le Mystere De La Toison D'Or

(Tintin And the Mystery of the Golden Fleece)
(FRENCH-COLOR-DIALISCOPE)

Paris, Jan. 9.

APCUP release of APC-Union Cinematographique-Telefrance Film production. With Jean-Pierre Talbot, Georges Wilson, Charles Vanel, Ulvi Uraz. Directed by Jean-Jacques Vierne. Screenplay, Andre Barret, based on comic strip by Herge; camera (Eastmancolor), Raymond Lemoigne; editor, Leonid Azar. At Balzac, Paris. Running time, **100 MINS.**

Tintin	Jean-Pierre Talbot
Haddock	Georges Wilson
Tournesol	Charles Vanel
Yefime	Ulvia Uraz
Papos	Dario Moreno
Angorapoulos	Dimitri Starenios

Mainly a moppet pic, this brings to life for the first time on the screen the most popular comic strip character in Europe. It has

color and simplicity even if it lacks the snap and inventiveness in direction for more depth possibilities abroad. But this could serve for kiddie shows.

Tintin, a cowlick-haired teenager, his dog and friend Captain Haddock, a cantankerous sea captain, go to Turkey to pick up a boat the latter has inherited. It turns out to be a leaky scow. But mysterious attempts to kill them have them keeping it and finally finding a treasure. Pic has colorful Greek and Turkish backgrounds.

Direction takes advantage of scenic aspects but lacks the briskness to give this a more adventurous drive. Technical aspects are okay and supporting cast is adequate with a plus in Georges Wilson's sputtering Captain. The dog is also good. *Mosk.*

Placido
(SPANISH)

Paris, Jan. 9.
Jet Films release of Alfredo Matas production. With Casto Sendra Cassen, Jose Lopez Vazquez, Elvira Quintilla, Manuel Alexandre. Directed by Luis Berlanga. Screenplay, Berlanga, Rafael Azcona, J. L. Colina, J. L. Font; camera, Francisco Sempere; editor, Antonio Rojo. Preemed in Paris. Running time, **90 MINS.**
Placido .... Casto Sendra Cassen
Quintanilla .... Jose Lopez Vazquez
Emilia .... Elvira Quintilla
Julian .... Manuel Alexandre
Martita .... Mari Carmen Yepes
Galan .... Amelia De La Torre
Zapater .... Jose M. Cafarell

Film satire looks at the type of charity that comes once a year and more from rote than actual human feelings. It walks the tightrope of good taste but comes out ahead via adroit direction and pacing. But this thin tale looms mainly a specialized entry abroad with foreign language house chances more probable than for arty house.

A poor truck owner, who has bought it on credit, works for a group in a small Spanish town. He is in danger of losing his truck because he is behind on his payments. He spends the time trying to get these arranged while getting mixed up with the charity drive backed by a local cooking utensil manufacturer.

The various troubles of the poor, such as one dying, another getting drunk and another oblivious to the good being ladled out to him, background the truckdriver Placido's finally regulating his payments.

Director Luis Berlanga could have used more bite. But he has the saving grace of doing clever characters and he depicts a tender but accusing humanity. He makes his points but sometimes the plot seems repititious.

Acting is homogeneous. The slaps at unctuousness and false charity and its lack of sentimentality kept this out of the Venice and London Film Fests this year where it was invited. But it is allowed export. Technical qualities are good. *Mosk.*

The Happy Thieves

Serious overtones and dramatic untidiness tarnish otherwise genial, diverting farce about a trio of ill-fated art thieves headed by a righteous pro. Hayworth and Harrison names and performances should generate some response.

Hollywood, Jan. 8,
United Artists release of Hillworth production. No producer credit. Stars Rita Hayworth, Rex Harrison; features Joseph Wiseman, Alida Valli, Gregoire Aslan. Directed by George Marshall. Screenplay, John Gay, based on Richard Condon's novel, "The Oldest Confession"; camera, Paul Beeson; editor, Oswald Hafenrichter; music, Mario Nascimbene. Reviewed at Goldwyn Studios, Jan. 8, '62. Running time, **88 MINS.**
Jim Bourne .... Rex Harrison
Eve Lewis .... Rita Hayworth
Jean Marie Calbert ..... Joseph Wiseman
Dr. Munoz .... Gregoire Aslan
Duchess Blanca .... Alida Valli
Cayetano .... Virgilio Texera
Mr. Pickett .... Peter Illing
Mrs. Pickett .... Brita Ekman
Senor Elek .... Julio Pena
Antonio .... Gerard Tichy
1st Guard .... Lou Weber
2nd Guard .... Antonio Fuentes
Inspector .... George Rigaud
Chern .... Barta Barri
Police Official .. Karl-Heinz Schwerdtfeger

"The Happy Thieves" belongs to that popular genus of film comedy depicting the zany misadventures of a band of lovably daring crooks who attempt to execute a bold, ingenious heist. In recent years, some notable screen success stories have been concocted out of this formula, generally of English origin and specifically several for which Alec Guinness attained international renown. Regrettably, this latest cinematic toast to the comic facets of larceny does not measure up to the standards and requirements of imaginative inspiration that must be realized by such a film in order for it to spur the enthusiastic word-of-mouth that attracts the more selective picturegoer.

As the first novel of former United Artists' overseas publicist "Oldest Confession" was notable for its bouncy prose style and grim moral implications, a life sentence for the hero, tragedy for everybody else. As a film the adaptation is an unpretentious, frivolous fresco-pade, with vivacious performances and the names of Rita Hayworth and Rex Harrison to adorn the marquee. Result should generate a mildly comfortable response.

Where the picture, filmed in Madrid, slips is in its instability of basic concept and in its misguided willingness to overlook and/or disregard important secondary plot ramifications, leaving the audience suspended, bewildered and frustrated and certain vital aspects of the story unresolved and ill-explained. In a film concerned with scientific criminal ingenuity, such lack of neatness is proportionately more disastrous.

John Gay's frequently amusing but rather awkwardly constructed screenplay, from Richard Condon's novel, "The Oldest Confession," describes the aborted operation of a trio of art thieves to pilfer an 8x11 Goya masterpiece (feet, not inches) from the Prado Museum in Madrid. Failure of the scheme to materialize as planned results from some unscheduled homicide and from the inescapable fact that the crime, like the picture, is anything but perfect.

In his best diabolically debonair tradition, Harrison carries off with aplomb his central role—the pro thief who rationalizes away the disfavor of his profession with the cozy philosophy that "there's a little touch of larceny in all successful men." Miss Hayworth, durably pleasing to the eye, is agreeably spirited as his unwilling spouse-accomplice, but the character introduces a serious overtone to the proceedings that is out of concert with the prevailing mood of farcical fun. Joseph Wiseman is endearing and amusing as the third member of the party, and especially effective aid is supplied by Gregoire Aslan, Virgilio Texera and Alida Valli, latter's presence missed in recent years by American screen audiences.

Director George Marshall has made the most of the merrier moments, but the film's basic uncertainty and tendency toward confusion and over-involvement have not been refined, a possibility through more adroit direction. Art, photographic and technical contributions are adequate. An infectious theme ditty by Mario Nascimbene, featuring a whistler and the odd comic tones of a jews-harp or some such "Boing-boing" sound-producing instrument, weaves purposefully and consciously through the film to punctuate and comment on the action. It is used so extensively that it lingers obtrusively in the mind long after one leaves the theatre. That's one way to get on the Top 40 Tunes list. *Tube.*

Le Comte De Monte Cristo
(The Count of Monte Cristo)
(FRENCH—COLOR—DYALISCOPE)

Paris, Jan. 16.
Gaumont release of Jean-Jacques Vital-SNEG-Cineriz production. Stars Louis Jourdan, Yvonne Furneaux; features Pierre Mondy, Franco Silva, Bernard Dheran, Claudine Coster, Henri Guisol, Henri Vilbert. Directed by Claude Autant-Lara. Screenplay, Jean Halain from novel by Alexandre Dumas; camera (Eastmancolor), Jacques Natteau; editor Madeleine Gug. At Gaumont Palace, Paris. Running time, **80 MINS.**
Edmond Dantes .... Louis Jourdan
Mercedes .... Yvonne Furneaux
Caderousse .... Pierre Mondy
Henri .... Bernard Dheran
Montcere .... Jean-Claude Michel
Faria .... Henri Guisol
Father .... Franco Silva
Girl .... Claudine Coster
Dantes .... Henri Vilbert

The old filmic war horse of Alexandre Dumas gets another production ride with this pic. This time it is somewhat overlong, with a tendency to bog down action with chatter. It looms mainly a local item with playoff possibilities abroad if pic is well sheared. It has the added assets of the Louis Jourdan name and color.

Young seaman Edmond Dantes (Louis Jourdan) is again railroaded to prison on his wedding day in early 18th Century France by three wily men each acting on his own. One for venal reasons, another because of his love for Dantes' wife, and the third to cover up his father's political activity. Dantes spends 17 years in prison and then escapes, finds a great treasure, and comes back to re-venge himself on his three enemies.

Script gets grandiloquent in its messages about vengeance and honor. It appears to be trying to make a modern parallel. But its lack of character depth, the forced coincidences, and the missing action fillip to make the melodrama more telling are against it. Jourdan is made to seem somewhat pompous in his posturings and posings.

Color is good but Claude Autant-Lara's direction is too heavyhanded to give this well-worn story the gait and racy mounting it calls for. Supporting roles are good. This was made as a big major production, but does not seem to measure up. *Mosk.*

Le Triomphe De Michel Strogoff
(The Triumph of Mchael Strogoff)
(FRENCH—COLOR—DYALISCOPE)

Paris, Jan. 16.
Films Modernes release of EmileNatan-Fono Roma production. Stars Curt Jurgens, Capucine; features Pierre Massimi, Inkijinoff, Claude Titre, Pierjac, Daniel Emilfork. Directed by W. Tourjansky. Screenplay, Marc-Gilbert Sauvajon; camera (Eastmancolor), Edmond Sechan; editor, Henri Taverna. At Ambassada-Gaumont, Paris. Running time, **120 MINS.**
Michael Strogoff .... Curt Jurgens
Tatiana .... Capucine
Prince .... Pierre Massimi
Shem .... Inkijinoff
Igor .... Claude Titre
Ivan .... Pierjac
Tarcasan .... Daniel Emilfork

The "Michael Strogoff" film, based on the Jules Verne novel, did sock biz here a few years ago. This is a sequel having the same cast and producers. It is played simply, with action aspects passable. Production emerges a good moppet pic with foreign playoff possible on its color, scope and the Curt Jurgens name.

Strogoff here is attached to a Russian Prince's company to protect him in a campaign against a border Tartar country in the days of Czarist Russia. He manages to turn the headstrong Prince into a man of honor, get a girl who belongs to the Tartar group though of Russian strain, and emerge the stalwart hero.

Jurgens, somewhat puffy, slogs through his role with the right solidity and righteousness while Capucine deadpans the enemy.

Remainder of cast is good. Also this gets nice production dress and technical assists from producer Emile Natan. It also has the right workmanlike direction from W. Tourjansky. Like any western, this has its black and white characters, obvious action and skullduggery. It might repeat the success of its predecessor over here, but remains mainly good as dualer fare in the foreign field. *Mosk.*

Jedermann
(Everyman)
(AUSTRIAN—COLOR)

Vienna, Jan. 9.
Bavaria Film release of Duerer production. Stars Walter Reyer; features Kurt Heintel, Ewald Balser, Almas Seidler, Wolfgang Gasser, Edward Cossovel, Viktor Braun, Ellen Schwiers, Paul Dahlke, Sonja Sutter, Heinrich Schweiger, Paula Wessely, Max Lorenz. Directed by Gottfried Reinhardt. Camera, Kurt Hasse; music, Ernst Krenek; choreography, Heinz Rosen. From Hugo von Hofmannsthal's play. At Forum Kino, Vienna. Running time, **105 MINS.**

Voice of God .... Ewald Balser
Death .... Kurt Heintel
Everyman .... Walther Reyer
His mother .... Alma Seidler
His journeyman .... Wolfgang Gasser
Overseer .... Eduard Cossovel
Cook .... Viktor Braun
Poor neighbor .... Helmut Janatsch
Prisoner for debt .... Karl Bluehm
His wife .... Roswitha Posselt
Paramour .... Ellen Schwiers
Fat Cousin .... Rudolf Rhomberg
Lean cousin .... Peter Jost
Mammon .... Paul Dahlke
Good deed .... Sonja Sutter
Faith .... Paula Wessely
Devil .... Heinrich Schweiger
Play inaugurator .... Max Lorenz
Servant .... Herbert Fux

This picture about the man, "who can't take it with him," Everyman, should do good biz in German language countries for which it is intended. But it's a dubious entry for the U.S. This is a German make with mostly Austrian stars.

Film revolves around the presentiments of death which Everyman, played by Walther Reyer, experiences. He finally repents, although at times he is not bad at heart. Reyer, who will be remembered for his excellent acting at Salzberg last season, repeats his performance in this. He is at his best in the scene when all his friends desert him. Kurt Heintel is "Death," and very good.

Ellen Schwiers' performance as "Paramour" is flawless as is Wolfgang Gasser as "Journeyman." Heinrich Schweiger plays the "Devil" with a human touch and really steals the pic. Alma Seidler as Everyman's Mother is impressive.

Director Gottfried Reinhardt is responsible for the actors looking into the camera too often. In legit this is okay but not in pictures since on the stage talking to the audience is common practice in this play.

The original Hofmansthal manuscript was used. The actors speak only in rhymes. Some of the rhymes are worse than rock-and-roll lyrics.

Ernst Krenek contributed lots of music, and there's a dance song that even has a melody.

Cameraman Kurt Hasse did a nice job. Heinz Rosen in charge of the choreography had a difficult task in getting his excellent dancers moving to the dance music by Krenek.

No new sets were used, which makes this seemingly high budgeted picture, a middle-budgeted one.

The Minister of Education gave this the top ranking classification but film patrons may not.

Maas.

Der Traum Von Lieschen Muller
(The Dream of Lieschen Mueller)
(GERMAN—COLOR—SONGS)

Berlin, Jan. 9.

Gloria release of Divina production. Stars Sonja Ziemann, Martin Held and Conny Froboess; features Helmut Griem, Peter Weck, Wolfgang Neuss. Directed by Helmut Kaeutner. Screenplay, Kaeutner; camera, Guenther Senftleben; music, Bernhard Eichhorn; editor, Klaus Dudenhoefer. At Zoo Palast, Berlin. Running time, **93 MINS.**
Lieschen Mueller .... Sonja Ziemann
Dr. Schmidt .... Martin Held
Jan .... Helmut Griem
Anni .... Conny Froboess
Paul .... Peter Weck
Chauffeur .... Wolfgang Neuss
Bank director Mayer........ Bruno Fritz
Hotel director .... Karl Schoenboeck

One cannot help feeling sorry for Helmut Kaeutner. Despite all his ambition, one failure follows the other. Germany's film director seems to have lost the knack of doing a good film. He appears to have tried too much and achieved too little. His latest, "The Dream of Lieschen Mueller," shows ambition and even imagination, but the outcome is neither fish nor fowl. And its a dull picture. Domestically, the attractive cast and film's title may provide sufficient playdates. However, this is a very dubious export item.

Lieschen Mueller is the nickname for the anonymous average German female cinema patron who is fond of seeing a dream world on the screen.

Lieschen Mueller is a bank employee in a small German town. A rich man wants to hire her as a temporary secretary. She'll have to travel around the world, elegant clothes will be bought her, etc. Then she falls asleep and dreams. Her dream (in color) makes up the greater part of the film. It shows Miss Mueller as a millionairess. There are numerous trick sequences. Then the dream ends and she decides not to take the job.

Kaeutner, who also wrote the script, seems to have gone overboard with everything. He parodized too much, picked too many topics, and seemingly fell in love with thick sequences.

The acting disappoints too. Sonja Ziemann may have been an ideal Lieschen Mueller some years ago, but not anymore. Martin Held (the rich man) gives evidence of the fact that he's a fine actor but in this his acting is mere routine. Helmut Griem is only a lukewarm Prince Charming.

Best thing about this is its color and trick photography. But these two assets are not enough.

Hans.

Der Luegner
(The Liar)
(GERMAN)

Berlin, Jan. 9.

Europa Filmverleih release of Real (Walter Koppel) production. Stars Heinz Ruehmann; features Julia Follina, Annemarie Dueringer and Gustav Knuth. Directed by Ladislao Vajda. Screenplay, Hans Jacoby and Istvan Bekefi; camera, Guenther Anders; music, Siegfried Franz. At Filmbuehne Wien, Berlin. Running time, **88 MINS.**
Sebastian Schumann....Heinz Ruehmann
Nicky .... Julia Follina
Annemarie Karsten
.... Annemarie Dueringer
Fraulein Kriese .... Blandine Ebinger
Rotbarth .... Gust: v Knuth
Sperber .... Werner Hinz
Police Inspector . Siegfried Wischnewski
Goliath .... Werner Schumacher
Beggar .... Joseph Offenbach

Hungarian-born Spanish Ladislao Vajda is one of the few Continental directors who is able to achieve something that has become rare in films, real charm. Vajda doesn't intend to make people laugh, but he does make them smile. Vajda's latest, "The Liar," is a mixture of comedy and modern fairy tale. Helped by the Heinz Ruehmann name, pic should do very well in this country. It also qualifies itself for export.

This is Vajda's third film to star Heinz Ruehmann, one of Germany's finest comedians. Ruehmann is at his best in this pic. He is a good-natured employee whom his wife deserted, leaving him alone with his little daughter. The eight-year old girl is all his happiness and he tells her one lie after the other to keep her from learning some of life's miseries.

But he gets deeper and deeper in trouble, loses his job and attracts the attention of youth authorities. Latter mistrust his educational abilities and are about to take the child away from him. But all ends happily.

Ruehmann adds another splendid performance to his lineup of credits. Little Julia Follina is the cute child while Annemarie Dueringer, as the young woman, is outstanding, too.

Script is unusually tight and imaginative. There's also some fine camerawork. But in the main, this is Vajda's picture. This is one of the few German pix of 1961 worth remembering. *Hans.*

I Sogni Muoiono all'Alba
(Dreams Die at Dawn)
(ITALIAN—SONG)

Rome, Jan. 9.

Cineriz release of a Franco Magli production. Features Lea Massari, Aroldo Tieri, Gianni Santuccio, Mario Feliciani, Ivo Garrani. Written and directed by Indro Montanelli. Assistant directors, Mario Craveri, Enrico Gras: camera, Marelli and Raffaldi; music, E. Lavagnino; editor, Eraldo da Roma. At Barberini, Rome. Running time, **95 MINS.**

Indro Montanelli's first film betrays its legit origins but is unlikely to repeat its success. Story showing the internal and dialectic conflict among several correspondents of different political schools holed up in a hotel during the abortive Hungarian revolution, has its tense moments and its valid sentiments. But as reflected on the screen, it seems overstated and strangely unexciting. This looks like a lukewarm entry.

Matter-of-fact portrayal of a situation, which moved millions, is diluted by lengthy programmatic speeches which are valid arguments all, and intelligently written. But here they lack proper impact.

Acting is likewise competent, but that's not enough. The result is a certain listlessness, relieved only here and there thanks to an engaging performance by Lea Massari, as a Commie who has seen the light. Other credits are okay.

Hawk.

Sergeants 3
(PANAVISION—COLOR)

"Gunga Din" in American west. Kidding reproduction, presided over by "Group" leader Sinatra. Likely moneymaker.

Hollywood, Jan. 18.

United Artists release of Frank Sinatra production. Stars Sinatra, Dean Martin, Sammy Davis Jr., Peter Lawford, Joey Bishop; features Henry Silva, Ruta Lee, Buddy Lester; introduces Phillip, Dennis and Lindsay Crosby. Directed by John Sturges. Screenplay, W. R. Burnett; camera (Technicolor), Winton Hoch; editor, Ferris Webster; music, Billy May; assistant director, Jack Reddish. Reviewed at Fox Wilshire Theatre, Jan. 18, '62. Running time, **113 MINS.**

Mike Merry .... Frank Sinatra
Chip Deal .... Dean Martin
Jonah Williams .... Sammy Davis Jr.
Larry Barrett .... Peter Lawford
Roger Boswell .... Joey Bishop
Mountain Hawk .... Henry Silva
Amelia Parent .... Ruta Lee
Willie Sharpknife......... Buddy Lester
Corporal Ellis .... Phillip Crosby
Private Page .... Dennis Crosby
Private Wills .... Landsay Crosby
Blacksmith .... Hank Henry
Col. Collingwood ...... Richard Simmons
Watanka .... Michael Pate
Caleb .... Ermand Alzamora
White Eagle .... Richard Hale
Morton .... Mickey Finn
Corporal .... Sonny King
Ghost Dancer .... Eddie Littlesky
"Ceffie" .... Herself
Irregular .... Rodd Redwing
Colonel's Aide .... James Waters
Mrs. Parent .... Madge Blake
Mrs. Collingwood .... Dorothy Abbott
Telegrapher .... Walter Merrill

"Sergeants 3" is warmed-over "Gunga Din," a westernized version of that screen epic, with American-style Indians and Vegas-style soldiers of fortune. The essential difference between the two pictures, other than the obvious one of setting, is that the emphasis in "Gunga" was serious, with tongue-in-cheek overtones, whereas the emphasis in "Sergeants" is tongue-in-cheek, with serious overtones. The revised concept, though it naturally dilutes the story, is fundamentally sound from a box-office standpoint, since adventure-happy moppet customers will take it seriously anyway, while most adult audiences will take one look at the cast and come prepared for the humorous approach.

Moreover, this being the first summit meeting on the screen since the board of directors convened for "Ocean's 11," the Frank Sinatra production is covered with ample "Group" insurance against the unlikelihood of any boxoffice accident. The United Artists release is, to use the appropriate vernacular, no gasser, but seems to have plenty of commercial horsepower.

Although, unaccountably, no mention is made of the obvious source in the screen credits, W. R. Burnett's screenplay not only owes its existence to that story, but adheres to it faithfully, with one noteworthy exception — "Gunga" does not die for his heroism. It's peaches and cream all the way.

The "Big Three" of Sinatra, Dean Martin and Peter Lawford reenact the parts played in the original by Cary Grant, Victor McLaglen and Douglas Fairbanks Jr. Of the three, Martin seems by far the most animated and comfortable. Sinatra and Lawford coming off a trifle too businesslike for the irreverent, look-ma-we're-cavalrymen approach.

Sammy Davis Jr. gives a likable, enthusiastic performance as a

jazz-came-up-the-river variation of the rootin', tootin' hornblower. Joey Bishop deadpans his way through his role, and has one good drunk scene. Henry Silva plays forcibly and believably as the baddest Injun on the premises, and Ruta Lee is attractive in the only important distaff role. It seems as if half the performing denizens of Vegas went along for the ride, among them Buddy Lester, Hank Henry and three of the Crosboys —Phillip, Dennis and Lindsay. Henry has a good card-playing bit. Balance of support is competent.

John Sturges' direction is brisk and humorously alert. The boisterous, slapstick brawls and battles of the first half of the picture contain some pretty amusing fistic choreography, explosive strategy and daring stunt maneuvers.

Winton Hoch's expansive, color-sensitive photography is invigorating. Great panoramic views of the Kanab and Bryce Canyon regions of Utah have a breathtaking picture-postcard flavor. Ferris Webster's editing is neat and quick, the latter attribute a sizeable assist to the humor. Frank Hotaling's art direction imparts authenticity, as does Vic Gangelin's carefully detailed set decoration. Other valuable ingredients are Billy May's inventive score and Harold Lewis' keenly balanced sound. Second unit director Al Wyatt and lensman Carl Guthrie merit praise. Exec producer was Howard W. Koch. *Tube.*

The Valiant
(BRITISH)

Somewhat protracted wartime suspense yarn based on real life incident. Sound performances by John Mills, Robert Shaw, Liam Redmond even if film lags.

London, Jan. 16.

United Artists release of a Jon Penington production. Stars John Mills. Features Ettore Manni, Robert Shaw, Roberto Rissi, Liam Redmond. Directed by Roy Baker. Screenplay by Willis Hall, Keith Waterhouse, based on Robert Mallet's play, "L'Equipage Au Complet"; camera, Wilkie Cooper; editor, John Pomeroy; music, Christopher Whelen. At Odeon, Leicester Square, London. Running time, 100 MINS.

Captain Morgan	John Mills
Luigi Durand de La Penne	Ettore Manni
Emilio Bianchi	Roberto Rissi
Lt. Field	Robert Shaw
Surg. Conim. Reilly	Liam Redmond
Commander Clark	Ralph Michael
Chief Gunner's Mate	Colin Douglas
Norris	Dinsdale Landen
Bedford	John Meillon
Rev. Ellis	Patrick Barr
Turnbull	Moray Watson
Medical Orderly	Charles Houston
Payne	Gordon Rollings
Admiral	Laurence Naismith

Once again John Mills gets into naval uniform, wears his widely-known stiff upper lip and copes with a problem based on a real life wartime incident. It would be foolhardy to suggest that the formula is wearing dangerously thin, but the suspicion is sound. The fact is that "The Valiant," despite its acceptable and suspensive core of an idea, does not rise to more than a routine drama in which patience is strained with many missed opportunities. The problem is over protracted but an all-male cast serves producer and director soundly.

The scene is Alexandria in 1941, and the battleship, The Valiant, is about to put to sea. Italian frogmen set out to mine the ship and two of them are captured. Item one. Did the Italians succeed in their mission? Item two. If so, where is the bomb based? Item three. How much time has the ship before it is blown up? Skipper Morgan (Mills) faces these problems with puckered brow and set chin. The two Italians should obviously be treated as prisoners of war. One of them is wounded and should have medical attention.

But, obstinately, Mills determines to break them and get the necessary information. He decides that they will sweat it out with the British crew. The Italians refuse to crack and Mills becomes more worried as he realizes that several of his officers find his methods unjustifiable.

This clash and mental struggle between two enemies who respect each other and also the inner struggles of all the men concerned should have built up an atmosphere of sweaty tension. But it doesn't. The brief tension fades ploddingly almost to anti-climax, which is the fault largely of the scripters, Keith Waterhouse and Willis Hall. Roy Baker has directed in fairly straightforward way but has, in doing so, dodged most of the moral issues.

Mills gives his usual confident performance in a role in which he could have had little heart. Liam Redmond makes a dour ship's medical officer and Robert Shaw has one of the more interesting roles, which is scarcely developed, of an officer with twin loyalties, since he is married to an Italian girl. Ettore Manni and Roberto Rossi are the two Italian frogmen, presented as pleasant, intelligent and sympathetic characters. In fact, they are indicative of the normal run of British war films. That war must be presented without hate. A very worthy theory but not necessarily conducive to the sock, stark type of film that makes top boxoffice.

Capable lensing by Wilkie Cooper, coupled with Egi Woxholt's underwater photography. Christopher Whelen's score and Wally Weevers' special effects are plus marks in a film which is worthy but, it is to be feared, will be strictly unmemorable. *Rich.*

The Three Stooges Meet Hercules

Typical Stooges slapstick. For the moppets.

Hollywood, Jan 11.

Columbia Pictures release of Norman Maurer production. Stars The Three Stooges (Moe Howard, Larry Fine, Joe De Rita). Directed by Edward Bernds. Screenplay, Elwood Ullman, from story by Maurer; camera, Charles W. Welborn; editor, Edwin Bryant; music, Paul Dunlap; assistant director, Herb Wallerstein. Reviewed at the studio, Jan. 11, '62. Running time, 89 MINS.

Moe, Larry, Curly Joe	The Three Stooges
Diane Quigley	Vicki Trickett
Schuyler Davis	Quinn Redecker
Ralph Dimsal	George N. Neise
Odius	George N. Neise
Hercules	Samson Burke
Ajax	Mike McKeever
Argo	Marlin McKeever
Shepherd	Emil Sitka
Thesus	Hal Smith
Ulysses	John Cliff
Achilles	Lewis Charles
Anita	Barbara Hines
Hecuba	Terry Huntington
Helen	Diana Piper
Simon	Gregg Martell

There always seems to be a niche in the moppet market for the Three Stooges, just about the last surviving practitioners of the clonk-on-the-noggin, custard-pie-in-the-kisser school of screen comedy. Aimed specifically at this audience, the Norman Maurer production and Columbia release should get by at the ticket windows.

The comic style of the Three Stooges bears a striking resemblance to the technique of the animated cartoon. Violence is heaped upon violence, yet not an ounce of blood is shed, nary a feature truly disfigured, with immediate recovery a foregone conclusion even in the face of apparent disaster. The natural audience, then, is precisely the one for whom the traditional cartoon short is designed — a group thoroughly dominated by children, but containing scattered easygoing adults. The nature of such comedy, however, makes it ideal for the brisk pace of a short subject. The sustained force of the slapstick is bound to be diffused over the feature length course, and this inevitably puts a strain on comic invention and limits appeal and response.

This one incorporates elements of "The Time Machine" and "Ben-Hur" as it turns the heroes loose in Ithaca, Greece, circa 961 B.C., where they engage the strong man and various other superhuman monsters in an effort to shape history in the accepted image. Elwood Ullman's screenplay, from a story by producer Maurer, provides ample excuse for the patented messy pratfalls of the starring trio.

In addition to the Stooges, others of central importance are Vicki Trickett, Quinn Redecker, George N. Neise and Samson Burke, latter as a slow-witted version of the musclemen of the title. The McKeever Twins, Mike and Marlin, of football fame, are "seen" as a Siamese twin cyclops.

Edward Bernds' capable direction is backed up by the resourceful assists of art director Don Ament, editor Edwin Bryant, composer Paul Dunlap, cameraman Charles S. Welborn and soundman James Flaster. *Tube.*

Saintly Sinners

Amiable, lower-berth item. Spiked with sentiment, making it especially suitable as support for family style attractions.

Hollywood, Jan. 18.

United Artists release of Robert E. Kent production. Stars Don Beddoe, Ellen Corby, Stanley Clements, Paul Bryar. Directed by Jean Yarbrough. Screenplay, Kevin Barry; camera, Gilbert Warrenton; editor, Robert Carlisle; music, Richard LaSalle; assistant director, Frank Mayer. Reviewed at Goldwyn Studios, Jan. 18, '62. Running time, 78 MINS.

Father Dan	Don Beddoe
Duke	Paul Bryar
Slim	Stanley Clements
Mrs. McKenzie	Ellen Corby
Joe	Ron Hagerthy
Sue	Erin O'Donnell
Idaho	Clancy Cooper
Horsefly	William Fawcett
Monsignor	Addison Richards
Uncle Clete	Earl Hodgins
Phineas	Norm Leavitt
Harrihan	Willis Bouchey
Mrs. Madigan	Marjorie Bennett
Mike	Tommy Farrell
Hank	Robert B. Williams
Sam	Max Mellinger
Tubber	David Tyrell
Attendant	Bob Watson

A pleasant departure from the customary crime melodrama and sagebrush formulas generally, "Saintly Sinners" will make an apt companion feature on twin bills directed at family audiences. Though liberally sprinkled with saccharine and given to caricature and coincidence, the Robert E. Kent production is a gentle, whimsical, good-natured little picture.

Actually, the film is a kind of minor league cross between a warmhearted, "Hoodlum Priest" and a small town, poor man's version of "Guys and Dolls." Parishful of Miracles is the general idea of Kevin Barry's quasi-Runyonesque screenplay, which describes how a kindly old priest, through a mixture of sweet naivete and uncompromising faith, generates reform among the lovably larcenous faction that flocks to his humble parish. For a picture constructed on such a modest expenditure, there is actually some pretty witty dialog in Barry's work, making up, in some part, for the scenario's contentment with two-dimensional stereotype and occasional disregard of normal behavior patterns.

Don Beddoe strikes the right note of innocent sweetness as the compassionate cleric. Ellen Corby is convincing as his skeptical housekeeper. Stanley Clements and Paul Bryar contribute fun as a pair of hapless crooks. In the chief romantic roles, Ron Hagerthy is sympathetic as a clean-cut excon and pretty Erin O'Donnell spirited as his spunky young wife. On the ball in top support are Addison Richards, Clancy Cooper and William Fawcett.

Jean Yarbrough's direction is not as taut and histrionically demanding as it might be, but, under the stringent circumstances, he has done a very satisfactory overall job. Production aid from cameraman Gil Warrenton, editor Robert Carlisle and composer Richard LaSalle is on a uniformly efficient level of skill. *Tube.*

Siege of Syracuse
(ITALIAN—DYALISCOPE— COLOR)

Overstuffed costume epic from Italy, this time centering on the exploits of Archimedes. An ornate hunk of pseudo-history hampered by clumsy editing and dubbing. Passable as a filler item for the least selective filmgoer.

Hollywood, Jan. 17.

Paramount release of Enzo Merolle production. No character names given. Stars Rossano Brazzi, Tina Louise with Enrico Maria Salerno, Gino Cervi, Alberto Farnese, Luciano Marin, Alfredo Varelli, Sylvia Koscina. Directed by Pietro Francisci. Screenplay, Francisci, Giorgio Graziosi, Ennio de Concini; camera (Eastman), Carlo Carlini; music, Francesco Lavagnino. Reviewed at the studio, Jan. 17, '62. Running time, 87 MINS.

The Italian cinema counterpart of the American hoss opera is the toga opera. In the past few years, the U.S. domestic marketplace has been crowded with such. "Siege of Syracuse" is the latest such arrival.

Haphazardly trimmed and edited and erratically post-dubbed, with

the result that performances emerge ludicrous and story senseless, the Enzo Merolle production has merit only as a means for emotional escape on the part of customers who seek nothing beyond that in their screen pursuits. The Paramount release, in its present scissored state, is serviceable as a supporting attraction and occasional filler in only the least sophisticated situations.

The screenplay welds two basic dramatic elements: the geographical vulnerability of neutral Syracuse, Sicily, wedged between the warring Roman (cowboys) and Carthaginian (Indians) legions, and the romantic travails of scientist Archimedes (Rossano Brazzi), the Greek mathematician here interpreted as a nobleman of Sicily and key political figure of the period. As an example of the esteem with which this film regards the experimental techniqques of Archimedes' science, his discovery of the utilization of solar energy is depicted as an accident in which he sets fire to Tina Louise's B.C. bikini during an experiment in heat reflection via mirrors. Fortunately, Miss Louise is not in her bikini at the time. She is swimming nearby, in the nude. Needless to say, Archimedes, renowned for his appreciation of figures and proportions, is delighted by his discovery.

Brazzi, an accomplished actor, does his career no service with this portrayal. The voice heard is not his; his lines are dubbed. Miss Louise plays mechanically, but her running parts are in good order. Physically, the production is fairly impressive, but Pietro Francisci's direction is stiff, disjointed and shallow. *Tube.*

Throne of Blood
(JAPANESE)

Hollywood, Jan. 13.
Brandon Films release of Toho production. Directed by Akira Kurosawa. Screenplay, Hideo Oguni, Shinobu Hashimoto, Akira Kurosawa; camera, Asaichi Nakai. Reviewed at Toho La Brea Theatre, Jan. 13, '62. Running time, **105 MINS.**

Taketoki Washizu ...... Toshiro Mifune
Asaji, His wife .... Isuzu Yamada
Noriyasu Odagura......Takashi Shimura
Yoshiaki Miki .... Minoru Chiaki
Yoshiteru, his son .... Akira Kubo
Kuniharu Tsuzuki .... Takamaru Sasaki
Kunimaru, his son .... Yoichi Tachikawa
Weird woman .... Chieko Naniwa

From a purely cinematic standpoint, this Japanese adaptation of Shakespeare's "Macbeth" into the historical fabric of their own culture is noteworthy for the remarkable manner in which it explores and extends the possibilities of the medium as an instrument for exciting the nerves, the senses and the emotions of an audience. It is all motion picture, an achievement of mood and photographic invention that deserves to be seen for academic purposes alone by every student of the cinema, novice through professional. Yet, admiration for the Toho production-Brandon Films release must be tempered by recognition of the enormous loss of lyric poetry suffered in translation from one culture to the other. For little but the embellished plot skeleton of Shakespeare's masterpiece survives.

In effect, what has transpired is a deemphasis of poetic language values in favor of an assault of pure sight and sound. The imagery of words is replaced by the all-seeing eye of an artistic camera. But no camera can match the suggestive beauty of language. The experience is akin to hearing a performance of Beethoven's Fifth Symphony accompanied by the lyrics of "When Johnny Comes Marching Home." Shakespearean buffs may be interested, but not necessarily pleased. Something significant is lost, for example, when Macbeth's opening remark, "So foul and fair a day I have not seen," becomes, according to the sub-titles, "What weather. I've never seen anything like it."

Nevertheless, there is no overlooking the masterful direction of Akira Kurosawa, nor the agile, energetic and explosive camerawork of Asaichi Nakai. It is a film of shattering silences and overpowering bursts of action, of moments when the attention is stimulated only by the sinister rustle of silk and others when the screen reverberates with uninhibited sound and fury. Incidentally, those who deplore violence had better come prepared. Nothing is spared for the climax, in which "Macbeth" is felled by dozens of arrows, one smack through the jugular.

Leading Japanese actor Toshiro Mifune gives a ranting, raving, rooting, tooting performance in the central role. Isuzu Yamada is calm, cool, collected and appropriately despicable as Lady M. The picture has been filmed in black-and-white. At first this seems odd, considering the Japanese reputation for color reproduction and the pageantry inherent in this play. But the element of surprise vanishes when one beholds what has been accomplished by these artisans in the two basic shades. *Tube.*

Only Two Can Play
(BRITISH)

Peter Sellers leads an accomplished team into a lighthearted wander into the land of "The Seven Year Itch." It's played mainly for laughs and they come freely

London, Jan. 16.
British Lion release through BLC of a (Leslie Gilliat) Frank Launder-Sidney Gilliat production. Stars Peter Sellers, Mai Zetterling, Virginia Maskell. Directed by Sidney Gilliat. Screenplay by Bryan Forbes, from Kingsley Amis' novel, "That Uncertain Feeling"; camera, John Wilcox; editor, Thelma Connell; music, Richard Rodney Bennett. At Columbia Theatre, London. Running time, **106 MINS.**

John Lewis .... Peter Sellers
Liz .... Mai Zetterling
Jean .... Virginia Maskell
Probert .... Richard Attenborough
Jenkins .... Kenneth Griffiths
Mrs. Davies .... Maudie Edwards
Mr. Davies .... Frederick Piper
Hyman .... Graham Stark
Bill .... John Arnatt
Mrs. Jenkins .... Sheila Manahan
Salter .... John Le Mesurier
Vernon .... Raymond Huntley
Beynon .... David Davies
Clergyman .... Meredith Edwards

Kingsley Amis' novel, "That Uncertain Feeling," has had some of its cool sting extracted for the film version, but the result is a lively, middle-class variation along the lines of "The Seven Year Itch." With Peter Sellers in nimble form, a Bryan Forbes' romp of a screenplay and the Launder - Gilliat touch in direction and production, exhibs should have little difficulty in finding cash-paying patrons for this racy piece.

Some of the humor is over-earthy and slightly lavatory, and the film never fully decides whether it is supposed to be light comedy, farce or satire. But it remains a cheerful piece of nonsense with some saucy dialog and situations capably exploited by Sellers and his colleagues. He is a member of the staff of a Welsh public library. A white collar job. He is fed up and frustrated with the eternal prospect of living in a shabby apartment with a dispirited wife, two awful kids, peeling wallpaper, erratic plumbing and a dragon of a landlady.

Into his drab life floats the bored, sexy young wife of a local bigwig and she makes a play for Sellers. The fact that she can influence her spouse to get Sellers promotion is hardly in Sellers' mind. But what is in his mind never gets a chance of jelling. Their attempts at mutual-seduction are thwarted by babysitting problem, sudden return of the husband, intrusion of a herd of inquisitive cows when attempting a nocturnal roll.

Eventually, she lands him the job, he comes to his senses and, deciding that the joys of extra-matrimonial nibbles are outweighed by the problems, turns in the job and returns to his wife, who has, herself, been indulging in a spot of come-hither with a local crackpot poet.

Bryan Forbes' screenplay has been upped with some neat dialog and some excellent situations. For instance, Sellers and his wife uncomfortably attending a smart party thrown by the sexpot hostess; and Sellers attempting to get out of her house unobserved when it is invaded by husband and friends. But it is the sidelights of characterization that provide the neatest chuckles, and Sidney Gilliat's direction makes the briskest play with these.

Sellers adds another wily characterization to his gallery. His problems as frustrated lover carry greater weight because, from the beginning, he does not exaggerate or distort the role of the humble little librarian with aspirations. Mai Zetterling and Virginia Maskell provide effective contrasts as the two women in his life. Miss Zetterling produces a piquant line in comedy sex appeal, though only in one scene is she allowed to frisk down to basics. Miss Maskell plays the wife with the slightly faded despair, but shows spirit in the closing sequences.

As a guest star, Richard Attenborough turns up sharply as a smalltime poet, Kenneth Griffiths is the worried, seedy Welch clerk to the manner born, and Maudie Edwards is a strident, credible landlady.

The decor and locations have been selected with the utmost care, John Wilcox's lensing is okay and there is an unobtrusive score by Richard Rodney Bennett. There is more subtlety is Amis' novel than is allowed to appear in this film, but hidden between the jokes, some obvious, some less so, there is a vein of truth that will not escape any married man or woman. *Rich.*

Un Coeur Gros Comme Ca!
(A Heart as Big as That!)
(FRENCH)

Paris, Jan. 16.
Films De La Pleiade release of Pierre Braunberger production. Written, directed and lensed by Francois Reichenbach. Editor, Knoute Peletier. Preemed in Paris. Running time, **90 MINS.**

Again a young filmmaker uses his camera to prod into life and catch it on the run as well as add to it by staged scenes. There are some moments of revelation, but this tale of a young African Negro boxer is more a documentary-type feature pic than an entertaining tale. It looms mainly for specialized chances.

The images are backed by the boxer's thoughts and sometimes blend to give insight and feeling to his life and needs. It shows him coming into Paris counselled by fellow passengers. His taking a little room in a worker's district, and then his wanderings and discovery of Paris and his first fight form the basis of this yarn.

Camera work is good and there are many scenes that point up the humming life. His meeting with a girl, a woman telling his fortune, and his training and talk with a blind boxer are all firstrate. But there are also many passages that seem like stuffing, such as episodes around Paris and a sudden montage of fight knockdowns from newsreels.

This gives insight into a Negro boxer's needs and attitudes, and the fact that this vocation gives him a standing in a white world. The final fight is well done. In short, another of the French essay-like films that use film to capture truth, but is an offbeater needing special handling. *Mosk.*

Chikita
(SWISS)

Zurich, Jan. 16.
Beretta-Film Zurich release of Turmus-Film Zurich (Rene Groebli) production. Directed by Karl Suter. Screenplay, Suter and Hans Gmuer; camera, H. P. Roth; music, Hans Moeckel. Stars Hanne Wieder; features Cecar Keiser, Gustav Knuth, Charles Regnier, Paul Buehlmann, Max Haufler, Ines Torelli, Franz Muxender, Margrit Laeubli. At Urban Theatre, Zurich. Running time, **100 MINS.**

(In German-Swiss dialect)

Satirical cabaret, one of the more popular forms of entertainment in the German-speaking part of Switzerland, sets the pace in this new Swiss film comedy, one of the most enjoyable local entries in some time. Its makers and players all have a cabaret background to which this film owes some of its best moments. Whether it is strong enough for the foreign market appears questionable, however, because much of its locally-slanted humor must unavoidably suffer from dubbing or subtiling.

The tongue-in-cheek story concerns an expatriate Swiss girl who owns a certain "house" somewhere in South America. Following a revolution, she comes back to her native town in Switzerland where her past soon becomes known. But instead of getting a

cold shoulder from the town's "respectable" citizens, she is discreetly cajoled into opening a "circle for cultural contacts" where tired businessmen may find peace, comfort and the rest. After a clash with the authorities, involving a teenage jazz cellar, she returns, with a new Swiss husband, to South America where, meanwhile, a counter-revolution has put her back in business.

Fastpaced direction by Karl Suter, skillful lensing by H. P. Roth (including a hilarious parody of silent movies) and a uniformly excellent cast are its best assets. There is an abundance of visual and other gags as well as an often sharply witty dialog. German stage and screen thesp Hanne Wieder as the notorious Chikita is delightful. Many of the other players, notably Cesar Keiser, Gustav Knuth and Max Haufler, offer brilliant cameos.   *Mezo.*

Walk on the Wild Side

"Mature" treatment of prostitution and girl-meets-girl situations by way of Charles K. Feldman production. Boxoffice names such as Laurence Harvey, Capucine, Jane Fonda, Anne Baxter and Barbara Stanwyck.

Columbia release of Charles K. Feldman production. Stars Laurence Harvey, Capucine, Jane Fonda, Anne Baxter; features Joanne Moore, Richard Rust, Karl Swenson, Donald Barry, Juanita Moore, John Anderson, Ken Lynch. Screenplay, John Fante and Edmund Morris, from novel by Nelson Algren; camera, Brook Benton; music, Elmer Bernstein; editor, Harry Gerstad. At Columbia homeoffice, Jan. 26, '62. Running time, 114 MINS.
Dove Linkhorn .... Laurence Harvey
Hallie .... Capucine
Kitty Twist .... Jane Fonda
Teresina Vidaverri...... Anne Baxter
Jo Courtney ....Barbara Stanwyck
Miss Precious .... Joanna Moore
Oliver .... Richard Rust
Schmidt .... Karl Swenson
Dockery .... Donald Barry
Mama .... Juanita Moore
Preacher .... John Anderson
Frank Bonito .... Ken Lynch
Lt. Omar Stroud........Todd Armstrong
Amy Gerard .... Lillian Bronson
Eva Gerard .... Adrienne Marden
Reba .... Sherry O'Neil
Spence .... John Bryant
Landlady .... Kathryn Card

It was a decade ago that producer Charles K. Feldman presented "Streetcar Named Desire," adapting this stage success to the screen. At the time of its offering it was considered a frank mirroring of perhaps imagined contemporary mores.

Producer Feldman is at it again, obviously seeking a new kind of breakthrough on the kind of material which should be, or could be, presented on the screen.

As in the case of "Streetcar," filmmaker Feldman shows good taste. Actually the difficult subject is adroitly handled although director Edward Dmytryk and screenwriters John Fante and Edmund Morris were walking on eggshells.

For it's obvious that in their treating of prostitution and lesbianism they did not want to be offensive to anyone. The result is a somewhat watered-downing of the Nelson Algren story of the Doll House in New Orleans and the madame's affection for one of the girls.

The absence of boldness in treatment renders the completed product just a little sterile. It's interesting all the way, but since the matter was decided upon in the first place, why not more deliberately?

It's in this respect that the presentation seems cagey, and, consequently, doesn't have the dramatic wallop it should have. Yet, to repeat, it's interesting. Mass audiences doubtless will go for it —for it plays out rhythmetically well—but critical kudos are not to be looked for. There's really not much of aesthetic significance to be found in the Algren adaptation.

Laurence Harvey plays a drifter in search of his lady, Capucine. He does it well but not strikingly. Capucine, it turns out, is a member of the Doll House, showing a classic. Garbo-type beauty but somehow limited as to range in emotionality via script and/or direction.

Jane Fonda cops the show (audiences will say) with her hoydenish

behavior as another member of the House and Just-Lucky-I-Guess Alumnus of the freightcar transportation circuit. Barbara Stanwyck is steely as the madame who looks to Capucine for the "affection" she cannot find in her maimed husband. Anne Baxter plays well as a cafe operator with normal affections toward Harvey.

Production is colorfully set and a song by Mack David and Elmer Bernstein offers substantial backgrounding.

Dmytryk maintains a nice pace in direction—that is, a steady pace —but more forcefulness in both his direction and the writing might have provided more dramatic impact. Musical backgrounding generally is appropriately sensitive and editing is sufficiently tight.   *Gene.*

My Geisha
(TECHNIRAMA-COLOR)

Bountiful production values and able cast must carry shallow, unstable romanticomedy-drama about an actress-wife who goes Geisha to fool her director-spouse. Okay for the average filmgoer.

Hollywood, Jan. 23.
Paramount release of Steve Parker production. Stars Shirley MacLaine, Yves Montand, Edward G. Robinson, Robert Cummings. Directed by Jack Cardiff. Screenplay, Norman Krasna; camera (Technicolor), Shunichiro Nakao; editor, Archie Marshek; music, Franz Waxman; assistant director, Harry Kratz. Reviewed at the studio, Jan. 23, '62. Running time, 119 MINS.
Lucy Dell & Yoko Mori Shirley MacLaine
Paul Farley .... Yves Montand
Sam Lewis .... Edward G. Robinson
Bob Moore .... Robert Cummings
Kazumi Ito .... Yoko Tani
Kenichi Takata .... Tatsuo Saito
Leonard Lewis .... Alex Gerry
Shig .... Nobuo Chiba
Hisako Amatsu .... Ichiro Hayakawa
George .... George Furness

Paramount should make plenty of boxoffice yen with Steve Parker's production of "My Geisha," a picture that won't be everyone's cup of orange pekoe but one that looms as slick, glamorous entertainment for the average easygoing filmgoer. Although hampered by a transparent plot, a lean and implausible one-joke premise and a tendency to fluctuate uneasily between comedy and drama, the picture has been richly and elaborately produced on location in Japan, cast with perception and a sharp eye for marquee juxtaposition.

A certain amount of elementary but traditionally evasive information on the Japanese Geisha Girl weaves helpfully through Norman Krasna's brittle screenplay about an American film actress (Shirley MacLaine) who blithely and vainly executes a monumental practical joke on her insecure director-husband (Yves Montand) by masquerading as a Geisha to win the part of "Madame Butterfly" in his arty production of same in Japan. To put it mildly, it is asking a lot of an audience to go along with such a premise.

Just as the comedy is about to peter out, there is a radical swerve into sentiment and moral significance. Montand, abruptly (and at long last) cognizant of what is transpiring, and deeply hurt, proposes B-girl monkeyshines to his

bewildered "G-girl" wife, and the marriage seems about to go to H. But honorable old Japanese proverb intervenes. All is serene at the climax.

Miss MacLaine gives her customary spirited portrayal in the title role, yet skillfully submerges her unpredictably gregarious personality into that of the dainty, tranquil Geisha for the bulk of the proceedings. Montand has his moments, but has yet to find the U.S. screen vehicle to ideally suit his special charm and personality. Edward G. Robinson does well by his role of a lovably hapless major studio producer, but his vast dramatic and comedic resources seem hemmed in by the assignment. Robert Cummings, astonishingly youthful, is a nice fit as a wolfish leading man. It's good to have him back on the theatre screen. A special impression is made in support by Yoko Tani, and there are satisfactory assists by Tatsuo Saito, Alex Gerry, Nobuo Chiba, Ichiro Hayawaka and George Furness.

Although the going thins out and slows down in spots, director Jack Cardiff keeps the picture visually stimulating, with the accomplished aid of cameraman Shunichiro Nakao and editor Archie Marshek. Interiors dominate the film, but there are one or two travelog-like interludes striking to the eye. Further credit for a glamorous production is due are director Arthur Lonergan and costume designer Edith Head. Franz Waxman's score, in keeping with plot, stresses classical and operatic strains, and does so tastefully.   *Tube.*

Twenty Plus Two

Gabby, overlong but diverting murder mystery meller.

Hollywood, Jan. 24.
Allied Artists release of Frank Gruber production. Stars David Janssen, Jeanne Crain, Dina Merrill; features Jacques Aubuchon, William Demarest, Agnes Moorehead, Brad Dexter. Directed by Joseph M. Newman. Screenplay, Gruber, from his novel; camera, Carl Guthrie; editor, George White; music, Gerald Fried; assistant director, Lindsley Parsons Jr. Reviewed at Hawaii Theatre, Jan. 24, '62. Running time, 102 MINS.
Tom Alder .... David Janssen
Linda .... Jeanne Crain
Nikki .... Dina Merrill
Pleschette .... Jacques Aubuchon
Slocum .... William Demarest
Mrs. Delaney .... Agnes Moorehead
Leroy Dane .... Brad Dexter
Honsinger .... Robert Strauss
Toomey .... Fredd Wayne
Collinson .... George N. Neise
Harbin .... Mort Mills
Bellboy .... Robert Gruber
Margue Attendant .... Will Wright
Stewardess .... Teri Janssen

In "Twenty Plus Two," Allied Artists has an overlong, but diverting, murder mystery melodrama for support or spot top placement in situations that cater to whodunit buffs. Written and produced by Frank Gruber, the film is an involved and verbose counterpart of a pulp fiction piece, with dialog that often sounds as if it was translated from a police blotter and glib-talking characters who often behave as if breaking and entering was the only way to enter a scene—in short, the standard operating procedure of this minor, though popular, story-telling form.

David Janssen, of "Richard Diamond" television fame, is in his

customary element as a remarkably composed and perceptive missing-heir tracer who methodically sniffs out the mystery of a long lost heiress who vanished after an unhealthy skirmish with a sex fiend, later film star—an uncomfortable parallel. Who should the girl turn out to be but an old flame of the hero's, whom he met in Tokyo during the Korean War. Gruber's fiction concentrates on the machinery of sleuthery, with character substance and development a poor second. But that's not apt to trouble those who prefer their whodunits straight, and not distilled by too many fancy whys and wherefores.

Janssen, an actor with star quality, gives a cocky, competent performance, somewhat mannered and tarnished by a tendency to swallow dialog, but on the whole poised and relaxed, creating a kind of "Diamond" in the rough character. Jeanne Crain is attractive as ever in a secondary femme role, a kind of afterthought part to weave another pretty girl into the pattern. Dina Merrill draws the central distaff character, and handles it with assurance. Jacques Aubuchon, William Demarest and Agnes Moorehead are especially strong, and there are other efficient portrayals by Brad Dexter, Robert Strauss, Fredd Wayne, George N. Neise, Mort Mills and Will Wright.

Joseph M. Newman's direction keeps the plot machinery humming, with stalwart aid from cameraman Carl Guthrie and editor George White. David Milton's sets occasionally seem a trifle extravagant to suit the status of the characters. Gerald Fried's score appropriately alternates between the brassy and the sexy, depending on whether the hero is moving or just plain operating.   *Tube.*

Le Tracassin
(The Busybody)
(FRENCH)

Paris, Jan. 23.
Pathe release of Raoul Ploquin-Pathe production. Stars Bourvil; features Pierrette Bruno, Armand Mestral, Maria Pacome. Directed by Alex Joffe. Screenplay, Joffe Jean-Bernard Luc; camera, Marc Fossard; editor, Eric Pluet. At Marignan, Paris. Running time, **115 MINS.**

Andre	Bourvil
Juliette	Pierrette Bruno
Clairac	Armand Mestral
Mrs. Gonzales	Maria Pacome

Satirical, slapstick comedy looks at a hectic day in the life of a busy ordinary Frenchman. It lampoons automation, city crowding, traffic problems, and manages to inject some plot via the hero's trying to get an apartment so he can marry his long-waiting fiancee. Having some bright ideas, this is somewhat stretched and overlong. It's mainly for special situations abroad.

The middleaged little man, Bourvil, decides to buy his fiancee some things and himself a new wardrobe to celebrate their second year of engagement. He also has a sister about to give birth to a baby. But all this leads to problems of parking and a bevy of tickets, a run-in with a woman who turns out to be his boss' new flame and missing out on an apartment.

Working for a tranquilizer pill firm, Bourvil gulps these down through his trials and ends in a fit of euphoria and laughing as he is

fired, almost loses his girl and gets arrested. This is an explosively funny passage helped by his perfection in clowning, timing and miming.

Being French it has him and the fiancee intimate though they need an apartment to get married. And being a comedy it has its happy ending. Main flaw is that there is no story and the gags sometimes run down. Alex Joffe has directed conscientiously and used trick work well. But it lacks the human depth and deeper comic perception and invention.

But it does garner many yocks. Cut down, this pic could be of playoff value abroad on its general good humor and spoofing of over-animated city life. Bourvil, as the ordinary man, keeps the film together on his clever portrayal and underlining of foibles. Technical qualities are good.   *Mosk.*

Deadly Duo
Meller for lower berthing in less discriminating situations.

Hollywood, Jan. 25.
United Artists release of Robert E. Kent production. Stars Craig Hill. Marcia Henderson, Robert Lowery. Directed by Reginald LeBorg. Screenplay, Owen Harris, from novel by Richard Jessup; camera, Gordon Avil; editor, Kenneth Crane; music, Richard LaSalle; assistant director, Frank Mayer. Reviewed at Goldwyn Studios, Jan. 25, '62. Running time, **70 MINS.**

Preston Morgan	Craig Hill
Sabena & Dara	Marcia Henderson
Thorne Fletcher	Dayton Lummis
Lt. Reyes	Carlos Romero
Manuel	David Renard
Jay Flagg	Robert Lowery
Lenora	Irene Tedrow
Billy	Peter Oliphant
Policeman	Manuel Lopez
Luis	Marco Antonio

"Deadly Duo" is one of the lesser efforts to roll off the assembly line of Harvard Film Corp., United Artists' small picture shop headed by Robert E. Kent. It will fill out a double bill as designed, but, except for its apt brevity, fails to smoothly perform its utility function.

The Owen Harris melodrama, from a novel by Richard Jessup, is concerned with identical twin sisters. It is the old formula: one angelic, one diabolic. The wicked one masquerades as the good one to haul in some big money that is coming to the latter, even goes so far as to attempt to rub out her sis, but the plot backfires in a hasty, ludicrous climax.

Marcia Henderson brings contrast to her dual delineation. Craig Hill is competent and appealing as a young attorney with integrity. Irene Tedrow is effective as a bitter mother-in-law who comes to see the error of her ways. Others in prominent roles are Dayton Lummis, Carlos Romero, David Renard and Robert Lowery.

Reginald LeBorg's direction is rather stiff and artificial, especially in the film's awkward, let's-get-it-over-with conclusion. Art, musical and technical production contributions are adequate.   *Tube.*

Cuanto Vale tu Hijo
(What Is Your Child Worth?)
(MEXICAN)

Mexico City, Jan. 30.
Peliculas Nacionales release of Producciones Matouk production. Stars Julio

Aldama, Lilia Prado; features Amanda del Llano, Beto el Boticario, Juan Carlos Ortiz and special role by Rosa Carmina. Directed by Mauricio de la Serna. Screenplay, Mauricio de la Serna from original by Dino Maiuri; camera, Manuel Gomez Urquiza; music, Sergio Guerrero. At Orfeon Theatre, Mexico City. Running time, **90 MINS.**

Film revolves around young Juan Carlos Ortiz, hit by a speeding car and taken to a hospital where, as doctors fight for his life, flashback theme develops a story of a humble Mexican family, with the picture striving not too successfully to put across social messages dealing with such problems as shanty towns, street peddlars, etc.

Principal merit of film, done with minimum budget and reflecting this in photography and settings, is that the public at which it is aimed obviously will identify the struggling young couple. And with this identification, their hopes, fears, and a succession of incidents in their daily routine as they seek fortune and a better life for their child in the big city. The fight for subsistence, shelter and adjustment to complexities of city life are rounded out with the fleeting moments of happiness, misery and sorrows, with all this sometimes over-melodramatically presented.

Actors do the best they can with roles assigned them. However, the picture will have a certain appeal in substandard Latin American areas with its mirroring of sordidness of life in the lower strata of south of the border society.   *Emil.*

Les Parisiennes
(FRENCH)

Paris, Jan. 30.
Cinedis release of Francos Films-INCEI production. Stars Francoise Arnoul, Francoise Brion, Catherine Daneuve, Dany Robin, Dany Saval, Christian Marquand; features Elina Labourdette, Darry Cowl, Paul Guers, Jean Poiret, Johnny Hallyday. Directed by Jacques Poitrenaud, Michel Boisrond, Claude Barma, Marc Allegret. Screenplay, Roger Vadim, Claude Brule, Annette Wademant, Jean-Loup Dabadie; camera, Henri Alegan, Armand Thirard; editor, L. Azav. At Colisee, Paris. Running time, **100 MINS.**

Francoise	Francoise Arnoul
Jacqueline	Francoise Brion
Ella	Catherine Deneuve
Sophie	Dany Robin
Antonia	Dany Saval
Christian	Christian Marquand
Jean	Jean Poiret
Parker	Barry Cowl
Mother	Elina Labourdette
Michel	Paul Guers
Jean	Johnny Hallyday

Still another sketch pic in a still lively cycle here. This one deals with four tales of zany, innocent, logically perverse or conniving Paris girls. It is sentimental, futile, puerile and smothers its freewheeling attitude toward sex in talk. But it has some sprightly misses in various stages of undress, and some zesty moments to make this a possible playoff bet, but arty theatre chances seem more limited.

In one sequence, a dizzy dancer barges in on a man's cab to take him on a whirl of Paris. He turns out to be an American impresario and she gets a role in Yank pix. Second has a faithful wife nonplussed when her husband tells her an old flame thinks she was a bad lover.

Then comes a tale of a girl who seduces her best friend's boyfriend

to show her she is not right in thinking him the perfect man. Last is an innocent who invents an affair to dazzle her friends but finally meets a young rock-and-roller for first love. The twist and r-and-r are thus dragged in to give this an up-to-date slant.

Sketches are simply mounted and do exude the old French pic myths of the easy French misses and the treating of sex as an eternal affair that should not be taken too seriously. Dany Saval, Francoise Arnoul, Francoise Brion, Dany Robin and Catherine Deneuve are all svelte lookers and come across agreeably.

Main appeal is the prowess of these girls. Men are secondary figures. Direction is adequate but sans the wit and punch to make these little interludes more pungent and graceful. Technical credits are good. Pic needs a hard sell but has the handles for possible chances abroad if well sold and promoted.   *Mosk.*

The Underwater City
(FANTASCOPE)

Exploitable, but overly-wordy, lower berth sci-fi melodrama about man's first housing colony on the ocean floor.

Hollywood, Jan. 30.
Columbia Pictures release of Alex Gordon production. Stars William Lundigan, Julie Adams. Directed by Frank McDonald. Screenplay, Owen Harris; camera, Gordon Avil; editors, Al Clark, Donald W. Starling; music, Ronald Stein; assistant director, Robert Agnew. Reviewed at the studio, Jan. 30, '62. Running time, **78 MINS.**
Bob Gage .... William Lundigan
Dr. Monica Powers .... Julie Adams
Tim Graham .... Roy Roberts
Dr. Halstead .... Carl Benton Reid
Chuck Marlow .... Chet Douglas
George Burnett .... Paul Dubov
Phyllis Gatewood .... Karen Norris
Dotty .... Kathie Browne
Lt. Wally Steele ...... Edward Mallory
Dr. Carl Wendt..... George De Normand
Meade .... Edmond Cobb
Winchell .... Roy Damron
Civilian .... Paul Power

Although filmed in Eastman Color and apparently designed for somewhat more ambitious commercial purposes, Alex Gordon's production of "The Underwater City" has been re-ticketed by Columbia for domestic release in black-and-white, a marketing revision apt to alter its programming status and resultant boxoffice destiny. Being an underwater melodrama, there is no question but that disregard of tint represents a significant loss of pictorial value. However, color alone does not make an attraction of "A" quality out of a product in which more attention has been devoted to exploitation than to dramatic flow and substance. Chances are "The Underwater City" has found a home in its natural element—the bottom half of a double bill.

Owen Harris' gabby, waterlogged screenplay amounts to a rather unfathomable fish story about man's first attempt to set up living quarters in a kind of sub-suburbia housing development on the ocean floor. The object of this curious expedition appears to be the construction of a kind of giant fall-in shelter down in Davy Jones' locker room, where folks can cool off in case things get too hot on the surface. The film drags along at an octopus pace, with more than the endurable quotient of pretentious, pseudo-high falutin' knots and what-knots about just what this escapade is all about, with the result that most customers may find themselves nearly asleep in the deep until the turbulent conclusion in which the ocean floor caves in, leaving only one "cell" (the symbolic "honeymoon cottage") erect and livable.

Caught up in the aquamire are costars William Lundigan and Julie Adams, along with featured players Roy Roberts, Carl Benton Reid, Chet Douglas, Paul Dubov, Karen Norris, Kathie Browne and Edward Mallory. These players give their all in a losing cause, as, regrettably, do director Frank McDonald and the various craftsmen, who have managed to make the physique and decor of oceanographic real estate reasonably convincing, if uninviting, through the use of Fantascope effects, miniatures and some plain old resourceful ingenuity.   *Tube.*

Brushfire

Slipshod, sluggish melodramatic account of modern guerrilla skirmishes in Southeast Asia. Slim supporting item.

Hollywood, Jan. 29.
Paramount release of Jack Warner Jr. production. Stars John Ireland, Everett Sloane, Jo Morrow. Directed by Warner. Screenplay, Irwin Blacker; camera, Ed Fitzgerald; editor, Roy Livingston; music, Irving Gertz; assistant director, Robert Farfan. Reviewed at the studio, Jan. 29, '62. Running time, **80 MINS.**
Jeff Saygure .... John Ireland
Chevern McCase .... Everett Sloane
Easter Banford .... Jo Morrow
Tony Banford .... Al Avalon
Martin .... Carl Esmond
Vlad .... Howard Caine

There is a good film story in the current small scale warfare of politically problematical Southeast Asia, but "Brushfire" isn't it. The Jack Warner Jr. production for Paramount is a talky, shallow, slipshod "B" melodrama, serviceable as a supporting item in situations where particular people do not ordinarily congregate.

The film, directed by Warner and written for the screen by Irwin Blacker, describes the efforts of a makeshift band of freedom-fighting residents of the Southeast Orient, led by two veteran soldiers who have stayed on after the war as plantation owners, to rescue a pair of young Americans who have been apprehended and held as hostages by the Communist element in the vicinity. There are several flurries of action, but the going is generally lethargic and artificial, burdened by uninspired philosophical prattle that palsies the tempo and stalls the plot machinery.

Principal roles are mechanically dispatched by John Ireland, Everett Sloane, Jo Morrow, Al Avalon, Carl Esmond and Howard Caine. Irving Gertz's music is helpful and Ted Hosopple's sets, though stringently conceived, are in an acceptable jungular vein. Balance of production credits are individually adequate, but the sum total of the production isn't.   *Tube.*

Moerderspiel
(Murder Game)
(GERMAN)

Berlin, Jan. 30.
Bavaria release of Utz Utermann and Claus Hardt production, in collaboration with Les Films Gibe (Paris) and Filmaufbau (Goettingen). With Magali Noel, Harry Meyen, Goetz George, George Riviere, Hanne Wieder. Directed by Helmuth Ashley. Screenplay, Thomas Keck, Helmuth Ashley; camera, Sven Nykvist; music, Martin Boettcher; Rolf Zehetbauer; editor, Walter Boos. At Ufa Pavillon, Berlin. Running time, **91 MINS.**
Eva Troger .... Magali Noel
Andreas Troger .... Harry Meyen
Kersten .... Goetz George
Female Journalist . ... Hanne Wieder
Dr. Rosen .... Wolfgang Reichmann
Babsy .... Anita Hoefer
Dahlberg .... George Riviere
Claudia Ahrends ...... Margot Hielscher
Hauser .... Heinz Klevenow
Margit .... Uschi Siebert

The most noteworthy thing about this German film is the great camerawork by Sven Nykvist, a Swede, whose pictorial account becomes much of the thrill in this mystery. Lensing offers fascinating scenes and remains interesting throughout. Along with the superb acting, this expertly-directed film comes close to being in the international class and recommends itself for export.

Although the villain is known right at the outset, this murder story contains suspense which never lets up. The question is here: How does he get tracked down? The villain, a pathological murderer of blonde women, has just added another victim to his list. When leaving the house in which he committed the crime, he's seen by a man who knowns him. Fearing the person could become dangerous to him, he follows him to a high-society party at which he intends to kill him. A good chance to do it occurs when the bunch of snobs play a "murder game" just for fun. By mistake, he kills another one. He manages to escape police suspicion via his cleverness yet a little carelessness finally betrays him.

Harry Meyen's portrayal of the cold-blooded killer is impressive. The lineup of top support includes the French thespians Magali Noel and George Riviere; Goetz George, Wolfgang Reichmann and Hanne Wieder comes along with a particularly memorable performance as a frivolous gossip columnist.

Helmuth Ashley, a former cameraman, directed this with much knowhow. Technically, this film makes a polished impression. In toto, one of the best German pix of the season.   *Hans.*

Les Demons De Minuit
(Midnight Folly)
(FRENCH)

Paris, Jan. 30.
Unidex release of GEF-Unidex production. Stars Charles Boyer, Pascale Petit; features Charles Belmont, Maria Mauban, Berthe Grandval. Directed by Marc Allegret, Charles Gerard. Screenplay, Bernard Revon, Serge Friedman, Pascal Jardin; camera, Gilbert Sarthre; editor, Suzanne De Troeye. At Normandie, Paris. Running time, **85 MINS.**
Pierre .... Charles Boyer
Daniele .... Pascale Petit
Katherine .... Maria Mauben
Claude .... Charles Belmont
Sophie .... Berthe Grandval

Film is a slim look at emotional disorders in the French upper classes with a peek at offbeat night life. But the characters are foggy, direction listless. This shapes mainly a dualer for offshore chances on the theme and the Charles Boyer name. Otherwise, it is mainly a local affair.

Boyer (a governmental minister) gets a call from a married woman who threatens to commit suicide because of his son. Not knowing where to find her, he goes looking for his son. He meets a young unhappy rich girl who helps. On the trip, the jaded youth of Paris is exposed in strip poker games and other pursuits. The son is found and goes to see the woman who he has jilted while Boyer finds a brief moment of love with the girl.

Boyer walks through this with his customary elegance as do the others. But this is soapy in outlook and conventional in treatment and scripting.   *Mosk.*

Jules Et Jim
(Jules and Jim)
(FRENCH-FRANSCOPE)

Paris, Feb. 6.
Cinedis release of Sedis-Films De Carrosse production. Stars Jeanne Moreau, Oscar Werner, Henri Serre; features Marie Dubois, Vanna Urbino, Boris Bassiak. Directed by Francois Truffaut. Screenplay, Truffaut, Jean Gruault from novel by H. P. Roche; camera, Raoul Coutard; editor, Claudine Bouche. At Studio Publicis, Paris. Running time, **110 MINS.**
Catherine .... Jeanne Moreau
Jules .... Oscar Werner
Jim .... Henri Serre
Therese .... Marie Dubois
Gilbert .... Vanna Urbino
Albert .... Boris Bassiak

Francois Truffaut, who made "The 400 Blows," one of the top New Wave pix, has put together a tender tale that avoids mawkishness and impropriety in treating the lives of two friends who are mixed up with a woman they share. One is a Frenchman, the other an Austrian and the girl is French. Plot covers from 1912 until about 1930.

It depends more on atmosphere, insight into characters and emotions than on story values. Thus this film appears something for foreign arty spots via its adroit, knowing handling of theme. Subsequents are somewhat more questionable for it. But with stronger fare becoming arty draws this might fill the ticket.

Truffaut has shrewdly employed the physiques and characters of his principles sans exploiting them. Jeanne Moreau is exceptional as the headstrong girl who never quite finds what she wants as she ends her life of whim, female demands in a sudden death plunge in her car with Jim, her husband's best friend. Latter is solidly limned by Henri Serre.

The husband is done in a vein of rumpled honesty and dignity by Oscar Werner. The three are shown at their first meeting in a frilly 1912 Paris, with Werner winning the girl but Serre holding aloof though attracted. The first war comes and goes, and Werner marries the girl and takes her to live in Austria.

Serre comes to visit them and finally has a love fling with Miss Moreau, now also a mother. Werner, wishing to have her somehow, accepts this new situation as he has accepted all of her desires. They then drift apart and back. The last caprice, of course, is the suicide leaving the bewildered Werner with at least a daughter.

Truffaut has a light touch for evoking moods, time, place and desires. There is nothing dank, desparing or thematic about all this. It is a successful look at life. Its very forthright attempt to grasp life sometimes makes it uneven. But, overall, this is candid entry that should be heard of on local and Yank art marts.

Truffaut uses the scope screen well. A little pruning can make this even more palatable and avoid some pranks that are not absolutely necessary. An offbeat pic with potential if well handled and placed.   *Mosk.*

The Four Horsemen of the Apocalypse
(C'SCOPE—COLOR)

Pictorially rich remake of Metro's 1921 triumph. Artificial direction and icy leading performances don't help love story updated to World War II setting. Fair prospects.

Hollywood, Feb.1.

Metro release of Julian Blaustein (in cooperation with Moctezuma Films) production. Stars Glenn Ford, Ingrid Thulin, Charles Boyer, Lee J. Cobb, Paul Henreid, Paul Lukas, Yvette Mimieux; introduces Karl Boehm. Directed by Vincente Minnelli. Screenplay, Robert Ardrey, John Gay, based on Vicente Blasco Ibanez novel; camera (Metrocolor), Milton Krasner; editors, Adrienne Fazan, Ben Lewis; music, Andre Previn; assistant director, Eric von Stroheim Jr. Reviewed at the studio, Feb. 1, '62. Running time, 153 MINS.

Julio Desnoyers .... Glenn Ford
Marguerite Laurier ...... Ingrid Thulin
Marcelo Desnoyers .... Charles Boyer
Julio Madariaga .... Lee J. Cobb
Etienne Laurier .... Paul Henreid
Karl Von Hartrott...... Paul Lukas
Chi-Chi Desnoyers .....Yvette Mimieux
Heinrich Von Latrott ...... Karl Boehm
Dona Luisa Desnoyers
Harriet MacGibbon
Elena Von Hartrott..... Kathryn Givney
Armand Dibier .... Marcel Hillaire
General Van Kleig ..... George Dolenz
Colonel Kleinsdorf.... Stephen Bekassy
Miguel .... Nestor Paiva
Francois .... Albert Remy

Out of the Vicente Blasco Ibanez novel and guided by the inspiration of Rex Ingram's monumental silent screen version for Metro in 1921, producer Julian Blaustein and director Vincente Minnelli have fashioned a remake of this epic romantic saga that is rich in cinematic invention, photographic imagery and uncompromising production values.

Curiosity among younger filmgoers unfamiliar with the story—which became a milestone in motion picture history 40 years ago—plus the natural desire of older audiences to refresh their memories and draw comparisons, should place the Metro release in a fairly comfortable moneymaking category. Although "The Four Horsemen of the Apocalypse" is a screen spectacle of dynamic artistic proportions, it gradually becomes a victim of dramatic anemia—a strapping hulk of cinematic muscle rendered invalid by a weak heart. Lamentably, the romantic nucleus of this tragic chronicle of a family divided and devoured by war fails in the adaptation by Robert Ardrey and John Gay to achieve a realistic and compassionate relationship between the lovers.

Director Minnelli and leads Glenn Ford and Ingrid Thulin must share responsibility with the writers for this fundamental weakness. Minnelli, whose artistry with celluloid produces some noteworthy passages in this film—especially several montage sequences conveying transition and/or thought processes—falters in his execution of the love story. In the central romantic passages, the actors posture and react in an artificially stagey manner, not too distant (and can this be significant?) in spirit and style from the technique of silent screen love. Indeed it is quite possible that Ford's characterization was plagued by the ghost of Valentino, whose enactment of the leading role in 1921 was his first screen triumph. There is, for instance, a tight eyeball shot of Ford's orbs reminiscent of Valentinography.

At any rate, Ford's performance is without warmth, without passion, without magnetism. Warmth is also missing in the performance of Ingrid Thulin. Part of the histrionic inadequacy stems from the distasteful nature of the hero-heroine situation. He is a procrastinator-playboy who escapes into neutrality until no longer able to live with himself; she is a woman who callously walks out on her patriot-husband while he is off at war, until no longer able to live with herself.

However, the film, as noted, shines in other areas. Frank Santillo's montages contribute touches of art and explanation to a picture that is sometimes wobbly, choppy and incomplete in the area of exposition. The device of veiling black-and-white newsreel photography in a splash of hot, vivid color registers with great emotional effect, notably in passages utilizing the novel technique of quadruple image superimposition. Further heightening the impact in this regard are the convincing A. Arnold Gillespie-Lee LeBlanc special visual effects, and the fascinating phantasmagorial figures of the Four Horsemen (Conquest, War, Pestilence and Death) masterfully designed by Tony Duquette. Milton Krasner's soft Metrocolor photography and striking compositions are a tonic for the eye.

Another major assist is that of Andre Previn, who has composed a tearing, soaring, emotionally affecting score to take up some of the slack in the love story. Time and place are accurately suggested through the art direction of George W. Davis, Urie McCleary and Elliot Scott and the set decoration of Henry Grace and Keogh Gleason. But neither the Rene Hubert-Walter Plunkett costumes nor the Sydney Guilaroff hairstyles seem especially indigenous to the period—roughly 1938-44—as updated from the book and earlier film.

There are several fine performances, though none of an unforgettable nature. Four veteran character actors carry most of the histrionic load: Charles Boyer as the hero's wishy-washy father; Paul Henreid as the heroine's idealistic, cuckolded spouse; Lee J. Cobb in a brief, but characteristically dynamic portrait of the brood's "primitive obsessed" patriarch; and Paul Lukas as the family's misguided, troubled Nazi henchman.

Of the younger players, Austrian actor Karl Boehm makes a strong and favorable impression as a dedicated Nazi (his first U.S. picture role), and Yvette Mimieux is spirited as the clan's patriotic gift to the French underground. George Dolenz scores as a Nazi general, and others of value are Harriet MacGibbon, Marcel Hillaire, Stephen Bekassy, Nestor Paiva and Albert Remy. *Tube.*

Horace 62
(FRENCH—DYALISCOPE)

Paris, Feb. 6.

Pathe release of Franco London Film production. Stars Charles Aznavour; features Raymond Pellegrin, Giovanna Ralli, Daniele Godet, Paolo Stoppa, Jean-Louis Trintignant, N. Bernardi. Written and directed by Andre Veraini; camera, Marcel Grignon; editor, Borys Lewin. At Balzac, Paris. Running time, 90 MINS.

Horace .... Charles Aznavour
Noel .... Raymond Pellegrin
Camille .... Giovanna Ralli
Monique .... Daniele Godet
Joseph .... Jean-Louis Trintignant
Umpire .... Paolo Stoppa
Napo .... N. Bernardi

An ancient Greek tragedy is transposed to present-day Paris via a Corsican vendetta that takes several lives despite its puerile reasons for being. Idea is good but this does not have the punch in direction, and the drive and precision to make it more than an acceptable gangster actioner. It looks mainly for dualer fare abroad.

Charles Aznavour is miscast as the peaceful Horace, who is unwittingly forced into the killing. Others are adequate but most characters are too one dimensional to give this the force about absurd vendettas that it needs.

Andre Versini, for his first pic, shows he can adequately put a film together but does not display the forcefulness to make this bloody tale either moving or original. It is technically good. *Mosk.*

Pokelanie
(Generation)
(POLISH)

Paris, Feb. 6.

Polski State Film release of Kadr production. With Tadeusz Lomnicki, Urszula Modrzynska, Tadeusz Janczar. Directed by Andrzej Wajda. Screenplay, Wajda, Boghdan Cachani; camera, J. Lipman; editor, R. Mann. At the Florida, Paris. Running time, 90 MINS.

Boy .... Tadeusz Lomnicki
Girl .... Urszula Modrzynska
Fighter .... Tadeusz Janczar

The first films of this Polish director made dents at film fests. But this pic is one of the most incisive of all his films despite the fact it was made in 1956 when there was more central governmental control of screen productions in Poland.

Story concerns a youth during the occupation of Poland in the last World War who comes to adulthood through love and adversity. It is true that the members of the old Polski governmental underground here are treated mainly as gangster types with the Communists more humane and active.

This has a flair for the period and its characters which makes it a telling drama.

Director Andrzej Wajda's feeling for the period and heroism weld this so well it becomes a moving tale of youth in crisis. It looms mainly a specialized bet abroad. It might play off in some arty houses if well handled. This is perfectly acted and directed, with technical credits tops. *Mosk.*

The Bashful Elephant

Supporting item about a homeless waif and her animal friends in Austria. Few refinements could still make it fairly tasty tidbit for moppet market.

Hollywood, Feb. 7.

Allied Artists release of Dorrell and Stuart E. McGowan production. Stars Molly Mack, Helmut Schmid, Kai Fischer. Directed and screenplay by Dorrell and Stuart E. McGowan; camera, George Tysen; editor, Hans Nikel; music, Ronald Stein; assistant director, Rudi Zehetgruber. Reviewed at the studio, Feb. 7, '62. Running time, 82 MINS.

Tristy .... Molly Mack
Kurt .... Helmut Schmid
Steffi .... Kai Fischer
Tavern Owner .... Buddy Baer
Father Francis............... Fritz Weiss
Police Inspector........Arnulf Schroeder
Fritz .... Hans Schumm
Constable .... Hans Posenbacher
Policeman .... Gernot Duda
Dog .... Jeffrey
Elephant .... Valle

With a few judicious snips and splices, "The Bashful Elephant" would be a far more presentable film in the exhibition category for which it is most suitable—the moppet market. Without the scissoring, it is neither a totally desirable attraction for the kiddies nor is it an especially palatable item for older audiences. Either way, the McGowan International production for Allied Artists shapes up as supporting fare, but its value and utility prospects would be strengthened by a conscientious effort to mold it specifically for children.

Written, produced and directed by Dorrell and Stuart E. McGowan, creators of "The Littlest Hobo," a like venture of several years back, this number, filmed in Austria, describes with a kind of primitive, fairy tale charm the efforts of a refugee Hungarian orphan to find some appropriate foster parents in Austria. Her hunt is complicated by the mystichemical attachments of a dog (a Red dog who turns on her pursuers and accompanies her across the Iron Curtain) and an elephant (a dog, maybe . . . but an elephant!). As anticipated, the happily-ever-after climax soon materializes.

The picture goes astray when it wanders briefly into an unsavory dark alley, a tangent not in keeping with the otherwise sweet, gentle nature of the fanciful story. It lurches the audience momentarily into a contradictory reality, and could easily be eliminated with no loss of story sense or drift. The snipping would involve a facet of the film's secondary romantic relationship in which the prospective foster mother walks out on her boy friend and tangles with a propositioning bartender. Okay for adults, but not the most desirable quality in what is primarily a film for children.

Molly Mack is sweet as the homeless waif, Helmut Schmid forceful and curvaceous Kai Fischer sincere as the foster-folks-to-be. Buddy Baer adds the note of menace as the burly barkeep. The McGowans have a keen sense of the impact and simplicity of purely visual values, and they have extracted this quality nicely from the Austrian crew. The producers also seem to be operating on another sound premise: any picture that loves dogs, children and elephants can't be all bad. *Tube.*

All Night Long
(BRITISH)

Top jazz players and leading thesps in a mood mixture of jazz and jealousy with an "Othello" angle.

London, Feb. 6.

Rank release of a Rank (Bob Roberts) production. Stars Patrick McGoohan, Keith Michell, Paul Harris, Betsy Blair, Richard Attenborough, Marti Stevens. Directed by Michael Relph, Basil Dear-

den. Original screenplay by Nel King. Peter Achilles; camera, Ted Scaife; editor, John Guthridge. At Leicester Square Theatre, London. Running time, **95 MINS.**

Johnny Cousin .... Patrick McGoohan
Delia Lane .... Marti Stevens
Emily .... Betsy Blair
Cass Michaels .... Keith Michell
Aurelius Rex .... Paul Harris
Rod Hamilton.....Richard Attenborough
Berger .... Bernard Braden
Benny .... Maria Velsaco
Phales .... Harry Towb
Themselves......Dave Brubeck, Johnny
Dankworth, Charles Mingus, Tubby
Hayes. Keith Christie, Ray Demp-
sey, Allen Gantley, Bert Courtley,
Barry Morgan, Kenny Napper, Colin
Purbrook, Johnny Scott, Geoffrey
Holder

This is a brave attempt to make a jazz pic with a difference. And though, thanks to a rather strained plot it doesn't quite come off, there are compensations in two or three interesting pieces of thesping and some very-easy-on-the-ear jazz played by topliners. Yarn is pitched on the "Othello" theme—many of the players are named to add to the illusion, thus Emilia becomes Emily, Cassio becomes Cass Michaels, Bianca becomes Benny, and so on.

Action occurs during an allnight jazz party, run by Richard Attenborough, in a luxurious, converted East End warehouse. Drummer Patrick McGoohan wants to become a bandleader, and is jealous of top jazzman (Paul Harris). He seeks to destroy Harris' marriage and persuades the wife to resume her singing career with McGoohan's outfit.

To do this, he plants the seeds of jealousy in Harris's mind, persuading him, by lies, and a faked tape recording, that the wife is having an affair with Keith Michell, Harris's sax player and business manager. The evening nearly ends in tragedy but everything is rather unsubtly ironed out.

Basil Dearden has directed with a feeling for mood but has allowed some of the acting to get out of hand with that fine actor McGoohan giving a particularly exaggerated, and at times even incongruous performance as the heavy. He does a fine job, however, in simulating the actions of a drummer and it is difficult to believe, at times, that Allan Gantley and not McGoohan is actually giving out with the music. Harris, a large Negro actor, brings a dignified presence to the Othello role, while Betsy Blair is fine in another of her inimitable portraits of the slightly fading, tolerant wife. Marti Stevens, better as a thrush than when acting, has the Desdemona role. Richard Attenborough, Maria Velasco, Bernard Braden and Keith Michell give the top support.

There are plenty of cool jazz interludes to take the audience's mind off the plot, and Dave Brubeck and Charlie Mingus, Tubby Hayes and Johnny Dankforth are always prominent. There is no background music to the film and this device is most effective, the many silences building up the dramatic atmosphere smoothly. Ted Scaife's photography is limited, in that most of the action is the warehouse interior, but he moves his camera fluidly and well. *Rich.*

Gun Street

Unsatisfactory lower berth western.

Hollywood, Feb. 8.

United Artists release of Robert E. Kent production. Stars James Brown, Jean Willes, John Clarke. Directed by Edward L. Cahn. Screenplay, Sam C. Freedle; camera, Gilbert Warrenton; editor, Kenneth Crane; music, Richard La Salle; assistant director, Herbert S. Greene. Reviewed at Goldwyn Studios, Feb. 8, '62. Running time, **67 MINS.**

Sheriff Morton .... James Brown
Joan Brady .... Jean Willes
Sam Freed .... John Clarke
Wille Driscoll .... Med Flory
Dr. Knudson .... John Pickard
Mrs. Knudson .... Peggy Stewart
Pat Bogan .... Sandra Stone
Frank Bogan ..... Warren Kemmerling
Mayor Phillips .... Nesdon Booth
Jeff Baxley .... Herb Armstrong
Operator .... Renny McEvoy

"Gun Street" is a dead-end. After a 67-minute buildup to an anticipated conclusive shoot-out, the Robert E. Kent production misfires and leaves the audience high, dry and frustrated. The lawman chases the killer all over the sagebrush scenery, finally corners him, promptly discovers his prey has just expired of gunshot wounds suffered at the beginning of the picture. Talk about letdowns.

Were there irony in this climax, it would be okay, but the only irony is that the audience has plowed through scene after scene of lethargic exposition and contrived melodramatics, patiently waiting for the moment of truth that never materializes. Possibly there was on unbalance in the budget that prevented a climactic burst of activity. Whatever the reason, the United Artists release is an unsatisfactory lower berth western.

Writer Sam C. Freedle apparently has been watching "Gunsmoke." In his cast of characters there is a Dillon-esque sheriff (James Brown), a Kitty-ish gambling hall madame (Jean Willes) with designs on the big lawman, a sidekick deputy (John Clarke) with "Chester" tendencies albeit without the limp, and even a doc (John Pickard). The acting is uniformly mechanical, with only Med Flory as a misguided bouncer setting off any characterizational sparks.

Edward L. Cahn's direction is frequently sluggish and awkward. Other contributions are satisfactory within the boundaries of budget stringency and production compromise. *Tube.*

Vie Privee

(Private Life)
(FRENCH—COLOR)

Paris, Feb. 13.

Pathe release of Progefi (Christine Gouze-Renal)-CIPRA production. Stars Brigitte Bardot, Marcello Mastroianni; features Gregor Von Rezzori, Eleonore Hirt, Dirk Sanders, Ursula Kubler. Directed by Louis Malle. Screenplay, Malle, Jean-Paul Rapponeau, Jean Ferry; camera (Eastmancolor), Henri Decae; editor, Kenout Peltier. At Paris, Paris. Running time, **105 MINS.**

Jill .... Brigitte Bardot
Fabio .... Marcello Mastroianni
Griccha .... Gregor Von Rezzori
Cecile .... Eleonore Hirt
Carla .... Ursula Kubler
Dirk .... Dirk Sanders

This is a thinly-veiled interpretative film based on the film star life of Brigitte Bardot, with Miss Bardot playing the girl in question. Main points and general theme of the pic boil down to B.B. herself. Where her pull is still big, this should be a solid entry with more hardsell needed where she is not so much of a draw.

Producer Christine Gouze-Renal and director Louis Malle have wisely not exploited the B.B. legend but rather have used it in a tasteful manner. This is elegantly produced but has a synthetic surface quality which makes it loom more a playoff item. Dubbing looks like a must.

A young, 18-year-old French miss lives with her widowed mother in high style in Switzerland. She seems to have a yen for the husband (Marcello Mastroianni) of her older friend.

Going to Paris, she leads the life of a carefree model and dancer until a pic producer spots her, and turns her into a world star. Then her renown is neatly underlined in a clever montage bit. Caught in a surging crowd one day she cracks up, and goes back to hide out in Switzerland.

Here she meets the man she previously had a yen for (separated from his wife), and true love blooms. But the ever-present press and photogs, and a predatory producer, interfere with their lives. When he is putting on a old drama in Italy, her presence almost ruins his show and life.

But they make up. Mounting a roof to see the show, flash bulbs pop in her face. She loses her footing, and the pic ends in a brilliantly conceived shot of her, in slow motion as she falls.

B.B. is one of those natural stars who zoomed into international focus. She became favorite sex symbol of the postwar years. But she does not quite have the bite of her other roles in this film.

Other characters are somewhat one dimensional though Mastroianni manages to give some weight to her last-chance lover. Director Malle has tried to catch all the child-woman characteristics of Miss Bardot, and succeeds in many spots. But Miss Bardot, as herself, seems tame compared to her other screen forays. She is stunningly lensed on the whole.

Her flock of callow first-love interests, the public adulation and hate culminating in an excellently mounted crowd riot lead into the heart of the film. Miss Bardot again shows the strides she has taken as an actress. Film hardly explains her international fame, but makes a general statement about the sad life of a poor, little rich girl and film star.

Metro reportedly put up most of the coin to get international distrib rights on this film except for Italy, France and other French-speaking countries. Pic looks to make a sizable wad world-wide, with Yank chances big if well-publicized and skillfully booked. Color is excellent and direction subtle. This is a meaty exploitation affair via her name.

Supporting cast is good and this will probably overcome that old jinx about pix concerning film stars find it hardgoing at the wickets. Sex is not overstressed, the love scenes are handled with restraint, and her undraped sequences are natural. In short, B.B. has progressed in ease and assurance but seems a bit stymied in playing herself. Yank title is "A Very Private Affair." *Mosk.*

Satan Never Sleeps
(C'SCOPE—COLOR)

Struggles of two Catholic priests in turbulent Communist climate of 1949 China. Unsatisfactory variation on "Going My Way."

Hollywood, Feb. 16.
20th-Fox release of Leo McCarey production. directed by McCarey. Stars William Holden, Clifton Webb; features France Nuyen; introduces Weaver Lee. Screenplay, Claude Binyon, McCarey, based on novel by Pearl S. Buck; camera (De Luxe), Oswald Morris; editor, Gordon Pilkington; music, Richard Rodney Bennett; assistant director, David Orton. Reviewed at Fox Wilshire Theatre, Feb. 16, '62. Running time, 133 MINS.

Father O'Banion	William Holden
Father Bovard	Clifton Webb
Siu Lan	France Nuyen
Sister Agness	Athene Seyler
Kuznietsky	Martin Benson
Sister Theresa	Edith Sharpe
Chung Ren	Robert Lee
Ho Son's Mother	Marie Yang
Ho Son's Father	Andy Ho
Ah Wang	Burt Kwouk
Ho San	Weaver Lee
Sister Mary	Lin Chen
Ho San's Driver	Anthony Chinn

With basically the same character premise he utilized to advantage in his 1944 production of "Going My Way," Leo McCarey has failed in "Satan Never Sleeps." He has failed not necessarily because, the idea of two lovably whimsical priests has lost its edge and charm through repetition, but principally because he is here dealing not with the conflicts of young love and juvenile delinquency, but with grave and complicated matters of political and social ideologies on an international scale that do not lend themselves to light, cursory treatment and cannot gracefully be translated into comedy-melodrama.

The modern film audience is not apt to accept a two-dimensional portrait of the Communist as merely a bumbling, irrational arch-villain. The 20th-Fox release is not a promising boxoffice candidate. It will have to rely heavily on the reputation of its producer-director and the marquee allure of names like William Holden and Clifton Webb.

China in its critical year of 1949 is the setting of the screenplay by Claude Binyon and McCarey, from a novel by Pearl S. Buck. Cornered in this moment of imminent national alteration to Communism are two Catholic priests, played by Webb and Holden, the latter adoringly but hopelessly pursued by a Chinese maiden (France Nuyen). The priests are soon imprisoned by the local People's Party leader (Weaver Lee), who also rapes the girl. Lee eventually sees the light when: (1) Miss Nuyen gives birth to his child, (2) his parents are murdered by the Reds, (3) he is reprimanded and demoted for personal ambition and leniency. A visiting dignitary from the Kremlin, a complete caricature of a figure, actually and literally scolds Lee for "thinking."

More occurs in the final 15 minutes of this picture than in the preceding 118, including: (1) a counter-revolutionary outbreak, (2) the defection of Lee, (2) the flight of the central foursome towards free Hong Kong, (4) several cold-blooded murders, (5) the mortal self-sacrifice of Webb, (6) the uncanny marriage of Miss Nuyen to

Lee, probably the most despicable "hero" on film record, (7) the baptism of their illegitimate child.

Holden, Webb and Miss Nuyen make the most of their characters. Holden is a kind of leather-jacketed variation (how styles change) of Bing Crosby's sweatshirted Father O'Malley, Webb a wry, caustic version of Barry Fitzgerald's Father Fitzgibbon. Miss Nuyen plays vivaciously as the sweet nuisance. The Red villains are absurdly all black, with the exception of Lee, whose ultimate whitewashing can be sensed throughout the film by any sharp, perspective viewer, at least partially a result of McCarey's rather obvious direction. Support is satisfactory, with Athene Seyler and Martin Benson in key roles.

Outdoor locations in England and Wales pass acceptably for China. Tom Morahan functioned as production designer. Sets by art directors Jim Morahan and John Hoesli (credited as associate and assistant, respectively) are attractive and colorful, especially the mission and its charming garden patio. Oswald Morris' photography is skilled and Richard Rodney Bennett's music is unobtrusively correct. Gordon Pilkington's editing is dramatically cumulative, but there could have been more of it. A routine, but listenable, title ballad by Harry Warren, Harold Adamson and McCarey is sung smoothly by Timi Yuro over the main titles. *Tube.*

Toller Hecht Auf Krummer Tour
(A Daring Chap in Crooked Tour)
(GERMAN)

Berlin, Feb. 13.
FTR-DFG release of Astra production. Features Michael Hinz, Christine Kaufmann, William Bendix, Ron Randall. Directed by Akos von Rathony. Screenplay, Milton Krims and Alexander Badal; camera, Ernest W. Kalinke; music, Herbert Jarczyk; editor, A. Schoennenbeck. At numerous West Berlin cinemas. Running time, 91 MINS.

Inge	Christine Kaufmann
Helmut	Michael Hinz
Sergeant Harrigan	William Bendix
Captain Smith	Ron Randall
Mary	Wera Frydtberg
Max	Walter Gross
Moritz	Karl Lieffen
McNulty	Gary Marshal

What was expected to be just another domestic run-of-the-mill comedy turns out to be a pleasant surprise inasmuch as this modestly budgeted film, which preemed day-date in several Berlin nabe houses, provides better taste, imagination and entertainment than so many a socalled top native production viewed here in recent months. This little and amiable film has an amusing plot. Since it revolves very much around Americans, with William Bendix in the cast, it may prove suitable in the U.S. in some spots.

Plot centers around a German boy, Michael Hinz, who never knew his parents and whose friends are Americans. All that he wants is to go to the U.S. He steals a U.S. Air Force uniform, an ID card and supplies himself with travel papers and nearly manages to get on a U.S.-bound military plane. That he's caught shortly before his departure is indirectly the fault of a German girl who's in love with him and who wants him to stay in

Germany. He's acquitted by the Court Marshal and a friendly U.S. sergeant wants to adopt the boy. But there's the girl whose indefatigable love convinces him that he's better off with her.

Excellent performances are turned in by Hinz as the young German boy, Christine Kaufmann, as the girl, and particularly, William Bendix as the U.S. sergeant who causes many chuckles. Lineup of supporting players includes Australian-born Ron Randell, as air force captain; Gary Marshal, as another American sergeant, and Walter Gross, as one of the Germans.

Akos van Rathony obviously had fun directing this picture. There are many sequences which poke fun at both German and American habits. Technically, the film is only fair. But this doesn't mar its charm. *Hans.*

Les Ennemis
(The Enemies)
(FRENCH)

Paris, Feb. 14.
CFDC release of Belles Rives Films-Sirius-Vega production. With Roger Hanin, Claude Brasseur, Pascale Audret, Dany Carrel, Michel Vitold. Directed by Edouard Molinaro. Screenplay, Molinaro, Francois Nourrissier, Andre Tabet from book by Fred Noro; camera, Louis Maille; editor, Gilbert Natol. At Ermitage, Paris. Running time, 90 MINS.

Jean	Roger Hanin
Vigo	Claude Brasseur
Christine	Pascale Audret
Lilia	Dany Carrel
Smolov	Michel Vitold
Patrick	Daniel Cauchy

Action-spy tale is slickly made but concentrates too much on flashy technique rather than building characters. Result is mainly a dualer or playoff item for abroad on its sleek technical aspects and action.

A Russian embassy attache in Paris loses some papers of high value. Then he is either kidnaped or has chosen liberty for a little salesgirl. But two stalwart French undercovermen solve it. He had been used by the girl and then kidnaped by a group of thugs who wanted the key to the code.

They even try to sell it to the Yanks, who are pictured as stereotype backslappers, gum chewers and willing to pay fabulous sums for Russian secrets. But the gang is captured.

Director Edouard Molinaro is more interested in flashy cutting and effects than in getting a sharp edge and solidify into this suspense item. It is technically okay, with thesping acceptable. But the attempt at hardboiled flippancy falls flat. *Mosk.*

Journey To The Seventh Planet
(COLOR)

Mediocre, but exploitable sci-fi adventure item.

Hollywood, Feb. 15.
American International release of Sidney Pink production. Stars John Agar, Greta Thyssen. Directed by Pink. Screenplay, Ib Melchior, Pink, from latter's original story; camera, Age Wiltrup; assistant director, Szasza Zslbery. Reviewed at Academy Theatre, Feb. 14, '62. Running time, 80 MINS.

Don	John Agar
Greta	Greta Thyssen
Ingrid	Ann Smyrner

Ursula	Mimi Heinrich
Eric	Carl Ottosen
Barry	Ove Sprogoe
Svend	Louis Miehe Renard
Karl	Peter Monch
Ellen	Annie Birgit Garde
Lise	Ulla Moritz
Colleen	Bente Juel

"Journey to the Seventh Planet" is a routine sci-fi adventure film, calculated to whet the fanciful cinematic appetites of surviving Buck Rogers buffs. Though more resourcefully mounted than written, the Sid Pink (Cinemagic) production for American International, filmed in Sweden, has sufficient thrust and a light enough payload to make the customary swift single boxoffice orbit around the saturation loop.

The Sid Pink-Ib Melchior screenplay, from the former's original yarn (which makes more fun than sense), dramatizes the astronomical predicament of a UN space exploration unit, circa 2001 A.D., on the planet Uranus. The gentlemen encounter a kind of poor man's Twilight Zone situation in which a local evil force causes their innermost desires and fears to materialize. Occasionally this takes the form of a cyclops-dragon or giant man-eating spider, but generally manifests itself in the more conventional Freudian shape of sexy women clad in wispy garments—which is a helluva commentary on the state of mankind's sub-conscious preoccupations. At any rate, the idea is to destroy the evil force, which, resides in a sub-zero cave and consists of a kind of giant, bloodshot, gooey eye. After several skirmishes in which the investigators from earth nearly write their own obituary by defying the privacy of the eye, they succeed by spraying the unholy place with liquid oxygen, snuffing out the wicked Allah's life.

Prominently implicated in this hocus-pocus opus are John Agar, Greta Thyssen, Ann Smyrner, Mimi Heinrich, Carl Ottosen, Ove Sprogoe, Louis Miehe Renard and Peter Monch, all of whom dispatch two-dimensional characters with sufficient concern. An oddity is the apparent dubbing of Miss Thyssen's voice, an unusual and distracting situation for an American actress in an English-speaking film.

Among the capable physical contributions to a film highly dependent for dramatic interest upon abstracts, miniatures, opticals and special effects are those of montage director Melchior, cameraman Age Wiltrup, production supervisor Eric Molberg and the main title-effects staff of Bent Barford Films. Pink tripled in brass as director. *Tube.*

The Couch

Another homicidal maniac. For less demanding audiences.

Hollywood, Feb. 14.
Warner Bros. release of Owen Crump production. Stars Grant Williams, Shirley Knight, Onslow Stevens. Directed by Crump. Screenplay, Robert Bloch, from a story by Blake Edwards and Crump; camera, Harold Stine; editor, Leo H. Shreve; music, Frank Perkins; assistant director, James T. Vaughn. Reviewed at the studio, Feb. 12, '62. Running time, 100 MINS.

Charles Campbell	Grant Williams
Terry	Shirley Knight
Dr. Janz	Onslow Stevens
Lindsay	William Leslie
Jean	Anne Helm
Lt. Kritzman	Simon Scott

Sgt. Bonner	Michael Bachus
Sloan	John Alvin
D.A.	Harry Holcombe
Mrs. Quimby	Hope Summers

Owen Crump's production of "The Couch" is too shabby and shopworn around the motivational and expositional edges to appeal to pick-and-choose film shoppers. But the wear and tear isn't as apt to disturb appreciably less particular consumers who, being less inclined to indulge in meticulous observation, will accept the picture as a standard piece of cinematic furniture in the psychological-suspense line. As such, the Warner Bros. release should prove a serviceable commodity in the current market, though limited in appeal and commercial value to situations in which the prestige and marquee allure of a product are secondary issues overshadowed by the beckoning image of an old-fashioned, pot-boiling, murder melodrama with new-fangled psychological overtones.

The bloody campaign of a paranoiac is traced by Robert Bloch's scenario, from a story by Blake Edwards and producer-director Crump. The killer (Grant Williams) employs the melodramatically advantageous technique of phoning in his immediate homicidal intentions to the local police authorities. Otherwise he is a singularly uninteresting lad, one for whom the audience can feel no genuine compassion. As a result, it becomes a cut and dry case of just when he'll be caught in the act by the cops, which eventually he is in spite of some slipshod work by the L.A. gendarmes. The motivations for his mental disarray are illustrated via through-the-eyeball scenes on the analyst's couch, but the history of his case never comes into dimensional focus.

Though hemmed in by rather shallow script scrutiny of the character, Williams delivers an agitated, menacing, appropriately unstable portrayal of the crazy figure. Shirley Knight is attractive as the analyst's rather gullible niece who comes to represent the killer's adored sister, just as the analyst (Onslow Stevens) represents the hated authority of a deceased father. Stevens plays with competence, as do William Leslie and Simon Scott in key-roles. Anne Helm and Hope Summers share several irrelevant passages, apparently inserted to add incidental character color, but candidates for deletion under more perceptive direction. The time might better have been devoted to more pertinent matters.

Production assists are generally capable, notably Harold Stine's camerawork, Jack Poplin's art direction ad Frank Perkins' score. *Tube.*

Sweet Bird Of Youth
(C'SCOPE—COLOR)

Cleansed translation of Tennessee Williams play, notable for a superlative performance by Geraldine Page. Should fly high at the b.o.

Hollywood, Feb. 20.

Metro release of Pandro S. Berman production. Stars Paul Newman, Geraldine Page, Shirley Knight; features Ed Begley, Rip Torn, Mildred Dunnock, Madeleine Sherwood, Philip Abbott. Directed by Richard Brooks. Screenplay, Brooks, based on the Tennessee Williams play; camera (Metrocolor), Milton Krasner; editor, Henry Berman; assistant director, Hank Moonjean. Reviewed at the studio, Feb. 20, '62. Running time, 120 MINS.

Chance Wayne	Paul Newman
Alexandra Del Lago	Geraldine Page
Heavenly Finley	Shirley Knight
"Boss" Finley	Ed Begley
Thomas J. Finley Jr.	Rip Torn
Aunt Nonnie	Mildred Dunnock
Miss Lucy	Madeleine Sherwood
Dr. George Scudder	Philip Abbott
Scotty	Corey Allen
Bud	Barry Cahill
Dan Hatcher	Dub Taylor
Leroy	James Douglas
Ben Jackson	Barry Atwater
Mayor Hendricks	Charles Arnt
Mrs. Maribelle Norris	Dorothy Konrad
Prof. Burtus Haven Smith	James Chandler

The dark, negative side of life is exposed on the screen again in Pandro S. Berman's production of "Sweet Bird of Youth," a tamer and tidied but arresting version of Tennessee Williams' Broadway play. Resourcefully directed and reconstructed by Richard Brooks, the film retains enough of the play's brute power to insure a healthy moneymaking margin for Metro. Mushrooming public reaction against unsavory themes should be counterbalanced in this instance by the strong marquee array of names, literary and histrionic, and by a rash of topflight performances, most notably one of definite Academy potential by Geraldine Page that will cause talk.

One has to pry deep to find edification or human enlightenment in the raw melodmamatic elements. But it's a glossy, engrossing hunk of motion picture entertainment, slickly produced by Berman.

In altering the playwright's Dixie climax (castration of the hero) Brooks has slightly weakened the story by damaging character consistency and emotional momentum. But he has accomplished this revision as if winking his creative eye at the "in" audience saying, "yes, we have compromised, but you get the general idea." The "general idea" is that the menace, or grisly potential, can be equally as frightening as the act.

Four members of the original Broadway cast re-create their roles: Paul Newman, Miss Page, Rip Torn and Madeleine Sherwood. Newman brings thrust and vitality to the role, but has some overly-mannered moments that distract. Paradoxically, these mannerisms, which tend to diminish his stature and versatility as an actor, serve to make him a star.

But this is Miss Page's picture. She draws the best, wittiest and most acid lines and the most colorful character and what she does with this parlay is a lesson in the art of acting. Her portrayal of the fading actress seeking substitute reality in drink, sex and what have you to offer is a histrionic classic. Shirley Knight is sympathetic and attractive as the distraught daughter of a corrupt political boss, and Ed Begley is outstanding in a perceptive portrayal of the latter. Torn tears off an intense, menacing enactment of Begley's vacuous son, although the seeming degree of menace isn't consistent with the revised ending. Solid support is generated in major roles by Miss Sherwood, Mildred Dunnock and Philip Abbott.

Milton Krasner's dexterous lenswork is an important assist to the production, as is the lived-in suggestion of sets by George W. Davis and Urie McCleary and furnishings by Henry Grace and Hugh Hunt. Henry Berman's editing brings dramatic clarity and momentum, with astute cut-screen flashback techniques of special interest. Music, rather surprisingly, is dated and corny, such as the use of "Ebb Tide" for marine scenes. Harold Gelman supervised. *Tube.*

La Fayette
(FRENCH)
(TECHNIRAMA 70—COLOR)

Paris, Feb. 20.

UFA-Comico release of Films Copernic-Cosmos Film production. With Michel Leroyer, Howard St. John, Jack Hawkins, Wolfgang Preisa, Pascale Audret, Orson Welles, Georges Riviere, Vittorio De Sica, Rossana Schiaffino, Edmond Purdom, Jacques Remy, Liselotte Pulver. Directed by Jean Dreville. Screenplay, Suzanne Arduini, Jacques Sigurd, Jean Bernard-Luc, Francois Ponthier, Maurice Jacquin; camera (Technicolor), Claude Renoir, Roger Hubert; editor, Rene Le Haneff. At Normandie, Paris. Running time, 160 MINS.

La Fayette	Michel Leroyer
Washington	Howard St. John
Cornwallis	Jack Hawkins
Baron	Wolfgang Preiss
Adrienne	Pascale Audret
Ben Franklin	Orson Welles
Bancroft	Vittorio De Sica
Minister	Georges Riviere
Simiane	Rossana Schiaffino
Dean	Edmond Purdom
Queen	Liselotte Pulver
King	Jacques Remy

With big-scale adventure actioners the big international grossers in recent years, France now gets into the act with this tale of the liberty-loving, young French 18th Century nobleman who helped the American colonists beat England. The overall $2,000,000 budget seems well spent. This emerges as fairly solid spectacle on this rarely touched on, in films, episode in French and American history.

It is somewhat overlong with some padding in the first part, such as attempts to deter La Fayette from going to America. This can easily be sheared to weld this into an okay playoff item for the U.S., with European prospects also good.

The characters are skin deep as far as motivation goes. The era is limned in a familiar way from the French elegant court intrigues to the American Revolutionary war battles. But its very simplicity helps make this tale of man's need for and fight for liberty a disarming spectacle film.

The recently, little treated American Revolution is also rated a biz peg. Film picks up the 20-year-old La Fayette in 1776 involved in barroom liberal meetings, drinking and battles with one of the minister's policemen. He gets taken up with the American cause. Then selling some of his lands he leaves his wife, buys a ship and goes off with some friends to join General Washington.

Battle scenes have okay movement, and the eye appeal as well as the Yank reconstructions are all passable. The derring-do is good being buoyed up by the sincere charging, battling and zeal of La Fayette, played with the right stalwart approach by newcomer Michel Leroyer.

Howard St. John makes Washington the schoolboy's portrait of uprightness and directness with a leavening of humanity. Jack Hawkin's British General Cornwallis has the right unruffled interpretation. English dialog seems somewhat stilted but blends well with the predominantly French speech.

Orson Welles etches a sprightly figure of Ben Franklin while Vittorio De Sica scores in a brief bit as a wily profiteer. Other noted names play small parts. There is a tendency to bog down in talk and historical quaintness at the beginning, but the pic picks up via its American war sequences.

Film may not have the veneer for arty house use or for some first runs. But this does possess a simplicity, movement and production dress for playoff chances. Director Jean Dreville does acceptable work if he lacks the breeziness and robustness to give a more dynamic tang. Color is dressy, technical credits fine, and general production dress of good order. *Mosk.*

Hitler

Der Fuehrer, through a boudoir peephole. A heavyweight, two-dimensional biopic focusing unconvincingly on subject's afflicted love life.

Hollywood, Feb. 19.

Allied Artists release of E. Charles Straus production. Stars Richard Basehart, Cordula Trantow, Maria Emo, Carl Esmond. Directed by Stuart Heisler. Screenplay, Sam Neuman; camera, Joseph Biroc; editor, Walter Hannemann; music, Hans J. Salter; assistant director, Clark Paylow. Reviewed at Directors Guild of America. Feb. 19, '62. Running time, 107 MINS.

Adolf Hitler	Richard Basehart
Geli Raubal	Cordula Trantow
Eva Braun	Marla Emo
Paul Joseph Goebbels	Martin Kosleck
Ernst Roehm	Berry Kroeger
Gregor Strasser	John Banner
Heinrich Himmler	Rick Traeger
Herman Goering	John Mitchum
Gen. Heinz Guderian	Martin Brandt
Dr. Morrell	John Wengraf
Field Marshal Edwin Rommel	Gregory Gay
Julius Streicher	Theodore Marcuse
Lt. Edmund Heines	Lester Fletcher
Emil Maurice	Albert Szabo
Schoenberg	Norbert Schiller
Lt. Col. von Stauffenberg	William Sargent
Frau Raubal	Celia Lovsky
Grell Braun	Narda Onyx
Martin Bormann	G. Stanley Jones
Major Buch	Ted Knight
Wagner	Willy Kaufman
Anna	Sirrey Steffen
Schmidt (Putzi)	John Siegfried
S.S. Officer	Otto Reichow
General Jodl	Walter Kohler
General Keitel	Carl Esmond

This E. Charles Straus production of "Hitler" gives one the odd and uncomfortable sensation of peeping in on history through the keyhole of a bedroom door. Although no doubt designed to offer a novel slant and fresh insight into the personality of the madman, scenarist Sam Neuman's Freudian eye-view fails to credibly link this shadowy, hypothetical facet of the Hitler story with the fabric of his rise and fall. Furthermore, since the film is preoccupied with the wretched and

unsavory details of his "love" life, and chooses to skim over everything else, there is never really any true penetration into the Hitler phenomenon. It is an unsatisfactory film, and will need all the exploitation impetus Allied Artists can muster if it is to make a box-office showing.

The "Hitler" of this picture could not possibly have risen to world, or even national, prominence. He is a totally unbelievable figure — almost a buffoon — as sketched and portrayed. That Hitler could rise was a disgrace to mankind, but certainly he had attributes, however evil and demagogic, that enabled him to attain his exalted position. By painting him as a figure without any dynamism, Neuman has created only a kind of Frankenstein monster from whom no lesson is to be learned.

Richard Basehart tries hard in the title role, but he remains unacceptable in the characterization and almost Chaplinesque ("The Great Dictator") in several passages. Cordula Trantow and Maria Emo enact the two women in Hitler's life, his niece Geli and Eva Braun, respectively, both victimized by the impotence and Oedipus complex with which he is here seen afflicted. Prominent stereotypes on display are Martin Kosleck in his inevitable enactment of Goebbels, Berry Kroeger as the ill-fated Ernst Roehm, John Banner as Strasser, Rick Traeger as Himmler, John Mitchum as Goering, Carl Esmond as General Keitel.

Stuart Heisler's direction is heavyhanded and obvious. Adequate assists are fashioned by cameraman Joseph Biroc, editor Walter Hannemann (who has incorporated the usual newsreel footage that goes with a film on Nazism), are director William Glasgow and composer Hans J. Salter.

But the overall effect is tantamount to spending 107 minutes with a wild bore. *Tube.*

Una Vita Difficile

(A Difficult Life)
(ITALIAN)

Rome, Feb. 20.

Dino DeLaurentiis production and release. Stars Alberto Sordi; features Lea Massari, Franco Fabrizi, Lina Volonghi, Claudio Gora, Antonio Centa, Paolo Vanni, Loredana Capelletti, Minor Doro, Daniele Vargas. Directed by Dino Risi. Story and screenplay, Rodolfo Senego; camera, Leonida Barboni; music, Carlo Savina; editor, Tatiana Casini. At Metropolitan, Rome. Running time, **115 MINS.**

Silvio Magnozzi .... Alberto Sordi
Elena .... Lea Massari
Elena's mother .... Lina Volonghi
Simonini .... Franco Fabrizi
Comm. Bracci .... Claudio Gora
Elena's friend .... Antonio Centa

Pic is heading for top figures in this country, aided by Alberto Sordi's b.o. pull and fine word-of-mouth. This is a bit special in its local nuances for wide foreign consumption, but rates attention in certain export areas where its strong human message will come across.

Silvio Magnozzi (Sordi) is a failure in almost anything he tackles, not being aided by an unshakeable pride in his principles which condemn all compromises. His refusal to be a yes-man loses him promising jobs, book sales, etc. while other less-endowed people make the grade by bowing and scraping to the powers that be. Finally, in desperation, he briefly gives in, becomes a success, even winning back his wife.

But he doesn't resist it for long and in one last, violent outburst at the facile life which surrounds him, regains the integrity which momentarily escaped him. Sordi does his usual outstanding job with the role, especially in latter phases, with a topnotch assist from Lea Massari, as his wife. Lina Volonghi, Claudio Gora and Franco Fabrizi also back colorfully.

Director Risi takes too long to establish the initial mood, but once he zeroes in on Roman highlife and all the falsity which can surround it, his camera is brutally frank and his scenes hardhitting. Leonida Barboni's lensing also deserves top mention. *Hawk.*

Un Cheval Pour Deux

(A Horse For Two)
(FRENCH)

Paris, Feb. 20.

SNC release of Horizons Films production. Stars Jean-Marc Thibault, Roger Pierre. Directed by Thibault. Screenplay, Thibault, Pierre; camera, Rene Bucaille; editor, M. Baby. At Mercury, Paris. Running time, **90 MINS.**

Maurice .... Roger Pierre
Roland .... Jean-Marc Thibault

Jean-Marc Thibault and Roger Pierre are two fine vaude and nitery comics of good humor and easy going comedics who have just missed on getting the right blend into their pix. This one finally succeeds for a bright, simple comedy that is visually witty and generally entertaining for good results here and good chances for offshore spots. It has plenty of guileless shenanigans and yockful aspects.

Director Thibault has never forced things and has allowed the comedy to develop easily with engaging results. A simple minded, petty thief (Roger Pierre), who has been in prison during the last war for stealing a bicycle, is freed during the liberation. He goes home to don an old-fashioned suit and move in on a kindly postoffice worker (Thibault) with a scheme to steal a horse and sell its meat on the black market.

The hiding of the horse in the apartment is done with maximum gag content replete with the physical and biological problems. There is the eventual refusal to kill the animal because they have fallen in love with it. A mad brawl to save the horse from being killed in a slaughterhouse ends this winning comedy.

Thibault's direction and limning of the nice guy role, Pierre's winning petty thief plus good technical aspects and supporting roles make this a solid little comedy that should have good playoff chances everywhere. *Mosk.*

Sound of Life

(RUSSIAN-COLOR)

Artkino release of Gorky Film (Mosfilm Studios) production Directed by T. Lukashevitch. Features Vasil Livenov. Screenplay by I. Manevich, based on Vladimir Korolenk's novel "Blind Musician." At Cameo Theatre, N.Y., Feb. 10, '62. Running time, **79 MINS.**

Peter .... Vasil Livanov
Uncle Maxim .... Boris Livanov
Evelina .... L. Kurdymova
Anna .... M. Strizhenova
Feodor .... A. Gribov
Young Peter .... Sergi Shestopalov

"Sound of Life" or "Sleepy Muscianto," as originally released in Europe, is one of the lesser Russian film efforts. Pic lasted only week at this bandbox cinema, now the outstanding Russian-language house in the U.S. Which gives somewhat of an idea.

This one details the rise of a wealthy, blind pianist from a child prodigy to the point where he gives his own concert. After seemingly enrolled at the Kiev Conservatory, Vasili Livanov, the musician, joins up with two blind beggars. He travels around as sort of a blind troubador or wandering minstrel. This is supposed to gear him for his great concert and reunion with his childhood sweetheart. He tells his friends on returning from his wanderings (which permit the use of typico Russian choral groups and allow him to strum his guitar while warbling) that he no longer is blind because "he has felt the pulse of life."

Earlier passages when the pianist as Peter, the child, hint some promise for a worthwhile pic. But once he becomes a grown man and goes on his meanderings, the plot likewise begins to wander. This looks like a fairly good idea, which neither the scripter nor the director could handle intelligently.

A rather excellent performance by Livanov, fairly widely known to Russo pix patrons, as the sightless musician, is seldom helped by either the direction or script. Comely L. Kurdymova, as his slight heart interest, does what she can with her role. But here again she is unable to overcome the material or the direction.

No cameramen is is given credit. It's just as well because the Sovcolor tinting still leaves plenty to be desired. *Wear.*

I Nuovi Angeli

(The New Angels)
(ITALIAN)

Rome, Feb. 20.

Titanus release of Titanus-Arco Film-Galates production by Alfredo Rini. Directed by Ugo Gregoretti. From stories by Mino Guerrini and Gregoretti; camera, Tonino delli Colli; editor, Nino Baragli; music, Piero Umiliani. Previewed in Rome. Running time, **97 MINS.**

Another unusual and stimulating film from Italy, "Nuovi Angeli" is Ugo Gregoretti's first feature pic after an apprenticeship in tele. It's a more than promising debut. Brought in at a modest cost, this should do extremely well in home territories, with word-of-mouth a useful assist. Export chances are more for curio slotting, subject matter and problems touched being primarily local in impact.

Gregoretti dissects current Italian manners and morals the length of the boot with an unusually keen and intelligent knife. The observation is more often than not tongue-in-cheek, whether its of antiquated Sicilian courting habits or brashly aggressive sex talk among north Italian youth. But it becomes understanding and analytical when dealing with the advance of mechanization in local industries and its effect on Italian man.

In a niche of its own, this vehicle is not quite a feature in the usual sense, nor a documentary in the accepted manner. Film is something in between, new and exciting. Actors, all non-pros, contribute vivid cameos. *Hawk.*

Cape Fear

Well-made shock drama with Mitchum as Mr. 100% Nasty and solid cast values. Villainy for its own sake. Should be a winner with heavy sell, albeit not for the kiddies.

Universal release of Melville-Talbot production, produced by Sy Bartlett. Stars Gregory Peck, Robert Mitchum, Polly Bergen; features Lori Martin, Jack Kruschen, Martin Balsam, Barrie Chase. Directed by J. Lee Thompson. Screenplay by James R. Webb, based on novel, "The Executioners," by John D. MacDonald; camera, Samuel Leavitt; music, Bernard Herrmann; editor, George Tomasini; asst. director, Ray Gosnel Jr. Reviewed at Universal homeoffice, March 1, '62. Running time, **105 MINS.**

Sam Bowden .... Gregory Peck
Max Cady .... Robert Mitchum
Peggy Bowden .... Polly Bergen
Nancy Bowden .... Lori Martin
Mark Dutton .... Martin Balsam
Dave Grafton .... Jack Kruschen
Charles Sievers .... Telly Savalas
Diane Taylor .... Barrie Chase
Garner .... Paul Comi
Officer Marconi .... John McKee
Deputy Kersek .... Page Slattery
Officer Brown .... Ward Ramsey
Judge .... Edward Platt
Dr. Pearsall .... Will Wright
Waitress .... Joan Staley
Ticket Clerk .... Norma Yost
Dr. Lowney .... Mack Williams
Lt. Gervasi .... Thomas Newman
Vernon .... Alan Reynolds
Waiter .... Herb Armstrong
Pianist .... Bunny Rhea
Betty .... Carol Sydes
Young Blades ... Alan Wells, Allan Ray
Police Operator .... Paul Levitt

As a forthright exercise in cumulative terror, Melville-Talbot's "Cape Fear," produced by Sy Bartlett, is a competent and visually polished entry. The Universal release, however, is essentially an amoral entertainment. It will arrest those who dote on the genre, or repel others who will peg it as a horror tale for its own sake and without any other point to make. It is definitely not for the impressionable young. While there may be some resistance to the title, the pic should still do comfortably at the wickets, although Universal will have to gun the campaign and hope for favorable word-of-mouth from there. It has, for a starter, strong marquee allure.

"Cape," in revolving around a psychopath, may incidentally rub some sensibilities with its allusions to forced sodomy, but it is the overall stark and unexplained brutality—implicit more than explicit—to no apparent intellectual purpose that is the dominant disturbance set off by the film.

Taken from John D. MacDonald's magazine-serialized novel, "The Executioner," the James R. Webb screenplay deals with the scheme of a sadistic ex-convict (Robert Mitchum) to gain revenge against a smalltown Georgia lawyer (Gregory Peck), his wife and daughter. Peck, it seems, had testified against him eight years earlier for the savage assault on a woman in a parking lot. Mitchum's menacing omnipresence causes the family much mental anguish. Their pet dog is poisoned, the daughter has a harrowing encounter with the degenerate, and there is the culminating terror in Georgia swampland where Mitchum is lured by a ruse and defeated.

Film achieves a goodly amount of suspense in the earnest but unstylish telling, yet the plot is always on the surface; anyone looking for the ironic twist or the pungent fillip is in for disappointment. What ails Mitchum obviously requires violent sexual expression

—the women he takes have to be clobbered as well as violated. But in the undiluted flow of evil, there is nothing in the script or J. Lee Thompson's direction which might provide audiences with some insight to Mitchum's behavior. The why of his attempted retribution is, of course, stated, but there are no intimations of what might have produced so warped and hardnosed a personality. This failure of insight tends to weaken the dramatics as well as giving the film an objectionable moral example.

It is disclosed that Mitchum's wife divorced him after his conviction, and that on his release he degraded her with a vengeance. This amplifies, but sheds no basic light, on his depravity. With Mitchum a single shade of black, with no cause and effect evident, there are elements of dissatisfaction for discriminating audiences.

Peck, displaying his typical guarded self, is effective, if perhaps less distraught over the prospect of personal disaster than his character might warrant. Granting the shallowness of his motivation, Mitchum has no trouble being utterly hateful. Wearing a Panama fedora and chomping a cocky cigar, the menace of his visage has the hiss of a poised snake. Polly Bergen, breaking an eight-year screen absence, turns in a sympathetic job as Peck's wife. She makes a fine suburban matron.

In support, Jack Kruschen is the most beguiling as the raunchy lawyer hired by Mitchum to check police harassment. Martin Balsam, as the local police chief, does well in a role that's no strain on his formidable talent; Lori Martin (of video's "National Velvet" series) is good as Peck's daughter; and Telly Savalas is smooth as a private eye more credible than most of his fictive profession. Perhaps the surprise stint, however, is contributed by Barrie Chase, hitherto with a hoofer identity (as Fred Astaire's tv partner), who is generally impressive as a doxy victimized by Mitchum's fists. Lesser parts are all dispatched capably.

Thompson's direction is reliable but uninspired, though the one-note story makes it hard to hold him responsible. Samuel Leavitt's camera admirably captures the dark mood; George Tomasini's editing is sharp and savvy; and Bernard Herrmann lends a workmanlike score to enhance the tension. Other credits are firstrate.
Pit.

Adorable Menteuse
(Adorable Liar)
(FRENCH)
Paris, Feb. 26.
Fernand Rivers release of Elefilm production. Stars Marina Vlady; features Macha Meryl, Michel Vitold, Jean-Marc Bory, Claude Nicot, Jean-Francois Calve. Directed by Michel Deville. Screenplay, Deville, Nina Companeez; camera, Claude Lecomte; editor, Nina Companeez. At Marignan, Paris. Running time, 110 MINS.
Juliette .... Marina Vlady
Sophie .... Macha Meryl
Martin .... Jean-Marc Bory
Tartuffe .... Michel Vitold
Sebastian .... Claude Nicot
Brevant .... Jean-Francois Calve

Film comedy deals with a pretty femme liar and her so-called rehabilitation via her love for an older man. Early part is full of young feminine caprices and rather intriguing. But yarn segues into its more serious segment a bit arbitrarily. Mainly good as an exploi-

tation pic abroad on its breezy aspects and fresh playing.

A comely 18-year-old girl (Marina Vlady) feels lying is the salt of femininity. She drags her zany sister along on her escapades. But a surly 40-year-old neighbor gets their attention, and she sets out to win him. This finally leads to love, but he will not take her seriously because he knows about the prevarications of her past. But there's a happy ending, as love wins out.

Director Michel Dreville shows an inventive flair in handling thesps and light comic touches. But he can not make the film progress solidly. Hence, this appears somewhat overstretched. Marina Vlady is pretty and the remainder of the cast adequate, with technical qualities good.
Mosk.

A Cavallo Della Tigre
(On the Tiger's Back)
(ITALIAN)
Titanus Film release of a Titanus-Film 5 (Alfredo Bini) production. Features Nino Manfredi, Mario Adorf, Valeria Moriconi, Gian Maria Volonte, Raymond Bussieres. Directed by Luigi Comencini. Story and screenplay, Comencini, Age, Scarpelli, Monicelli; camera, Aldo Scavarda; editor, Nino Baragli; music, Piero Umiliani. At Astoria, Rome. Running time, 120 MINS.
Giacinto .... Nino Manfredi
Tagliabue .... Mario Adorf
Wife .... Valeria Moriconi
Papaleo .... Gian Maria Volonte
Il sorcio .... Raymond Bussieres

Offbeat pic with a deliberately nonconformist approach to a prison-escape yarn. Will need heavy selling in all situations, with mild b.o. outlook in the offing, even though certain foreign marts beckon.

Story deals mainly with the downbeat adventures of a poverty-harassed van driver, Giacinto, whose family plight drives him to theft. Lacking the know-how, he's jailed and falls in with a group of vet hoodlums, and almost unwittingly helps them escape.

After a long chase, he decides it's all no use, allows his wife's lover to turn him in for the police cash reward, so that his family can be saved from starvation.

Film is a natural for comedian Nino Manfredi, who gets good support from Mario Adorf, his bullish cellmate and murderer, and also from Raymond Bussieres, as another thief, and Valeria Moriconi, as Giacinto's wife. Others in a colorful cast are likewise deserving.

Luigi Comencini's adroit direction nevertheless cannot overcome a certain monotony in the chase format. And audiences are too often uncertain about whether to laugh at or fell for the main characters. Technical credits fine.
Hawk.

Rencontres
(Meetings)
(FRENCH)
Paris, March 6.
Fernand Rivers release of Film Promotion production. Stars Michele Morgan, Pierre Brasseur, Gabriele Ferzetti; features Diana Gregor, Pierre Brasseur, Gabriele Ferzetti; features Diana Gregor, Monique Melinand. Directed by Philippe Agostini. Screenplay, Bertram Lonsdale, Odette Joyeux, Agostini; camera, Jacques Robin; editor, Victoria Mercanton. At Marignan, Paris. Running time, 95 MINS.
Husband .... Pierre Brasseur
Wife .... Michele Morgan
Writer .... Gabriele Ferzetti
Sister .... Diana Gregor
Maid .... Monique Melinand

Three name actors are wasted in this static tale of love and suspense. Surface characterization and lacklustre direction have this mainly a local item.

A pianist who has lost his talents after an accident decides to bring off an insurance hoax. But his wife falls for a writer which botches up everything.

Players walk through their roles, but Michele Morgan, Pierre Brasseur and Gabriele Ferzetti deserved more than this below-average pic. *Mosk.*

Challenge to Live
(JAPANESE—TOHOSCOPE—COLOR)
Hollywood, Feb. 26.
Toho release of Masumi Fujimoto production. Stars Tatsupa Mihashi, Yoko Tsugasa. Directed by Eizo Sugawa. Screenplay, Kaneto Shindo, from Shintaro Ishihara's novel. "Challenge": camera (Eastman), Fukuzo Koizumi; music, Masaru Sato. Reviewed at Toho La Brea Theatre, Feb. 26, '62. Running time, 99 MINS.
Izaki .... Tatsuya Mihashi
Saeko Sawada .... Toko Tsukasa
Keiko Takamine ...... Yumi Shirakawa
Sawada (President) ...... Masayuki Mori
Prime Minister Mesacin... V. S. Shes
Effran .... Chanty Zebery
Malt .... Schuan

"Challenge to Live" is a ponderous account of a young man's struggle to resurrect his courage and self-respect and erase the mental stigma of a traumatic wartime experience by unselfishly dedicating himself to a humanitarian cause in peacetime. The sub-titled Toho import, produced by Masumi Fujimoto, has inspirational value and romantic appeal for the Japanese market in this country, but lacks the kind of provocative approach, novel cinematic technique and universal significance and clarity that can carry an art house entry.

Several fine performances lend dramatic impetus to Kaneto Shindo's screen story of a young Japanese oilman who leads his company in a combination enterprising venture and humanitarian gesture to puncture an international carte against the purchase of oil from newly-independent Iraq. In so doing, he dissolves his romance with the daughter of the president of his company and even gives his life, but, in death, recovers the identity and conviction he lost as the corrosive result of a wartime mercy killing.

Rich underplaying by Tatsuya Mihashi brings appeal and dimension to the hero. Yako Tsukasa is interesting and attractive as the uneasy, immature daughter, who happens to be the sister of the mercy killing victim. Masayuki Mori gives a convincing delineation of the understanding, idealistic tycoon—a welcome departure from the ordinary screen depiction of the rich as shallow and selfish. Effective in support are Yumi Shirakawa, V. B. Shes, Chanty Zebery and Schuan.

After an energetic, semi-abstract start, director Eizo Sugawa slows his film down to a rather deliberate pace, only once or twice enlivened by arresting motion or action. Capable assists are those of cameraman Fukuzo Koizumi, art director Iwao Akune and composer Masaru Sato.

I Giorni Contati
(The Days Are Numbered)
(ITALIAN)
Rome, Feb. 27.
Titanus release of a Titanus-Metro production. Features Salvo Randone, Franco Sportelli, Vittorio Caprioli, Regina Bianchi, Paolo Ferrari, Angela Minervini. Directed by Elio Petri. Screenplay, Petri, Carlo Romano, Tonino Guerra from story by Petri and Guerra; camera, Ennio Guarnieri; editor, Ruggero Mastroianni. Previewed in Rome. Running time, 100 MINS.
Cesare .... Salvo Randone
Amilcare .... Franco Sportelli
Art merchant .... Vittorio Caprioli
Giulia .... Regina Bianchi
Vinicio .... Paolo Ferrari
Graziella .... Angela Minervini

One of the first pix under the recent Titanus-Metro coproduction pact, this film is a worthy entry in year's quality stakes, and a further example of Italian production's versatility and high standards. Downbeat theme will, however, have to be overcome via special promotion before the film finds its b.o. niche. Export chances likewise depend on strong sell and word-of-mouth.

Tale deals with a Roman plumber who sees a man die suddenly of a heart attack before his eyes on a tram. This shocks him into realization that same might happen to him, and what has he had out of life to date? He decides to quit working, take a long vacation, roam the city, breathe in fresh air and sunlight "before it's too late."

Full of enthusiasm, he visits museums, tries to catch up on scientific progress, culture, night life, etc. Windup, however, sees him going back to work, discouraged and realizing that "it's already too late" to catch up with life's events for which he has never had to time or the preparation. Salvo Randone does an outstanding job in the key role, with fine support from Franco Sportelli, as an old friend and counsellor; Vittorio Caprioli, as an offbeat art dealer; Regina Bianchi, cast as an old flame he nostalgically tries to befriend; Paolo Ferrari, as a one-time assistant who's become involved in some shady deals, and Angela Minervini, as a piquant but pathetic nymphette who lives next door.

Basically, however, it's Elio Petri's pic (and only his second effort to date) all the way. He gives a very personal and well-conceived tale a unity of style (his hand-held camera work is extremely effective) and a surrealistic contrast offered by the outside world to the aging hero's human and realistic approach to it. Offbeat lensing job by Ennio Guarnieri adds to pic's stylized impact, despite many from-the-hip sidewalk takes. Ruggero Mastroianni's editing is likewise rapid and in keeping with the concept of the pic. *Hawk.*

State Fair
(C'SCOPE—COLOR)

Remake of the Rodgers & Hammerstein filmusical. Too outmoded in style for jet-age audiences.

Hollywood, March 9.

Twentieth-Fox release of Charles Brackett production. Stars Pat Boone, Bobby Darin, Pamela Tiffin, Ann-Margret, Tom Ewell, Alice Faye. Directed by Jose Ferrer. Screenplay, Richard Breen, from an adaptation by Oscar Hammerstein 2d, Sonya Levien, and Paul Green of Philip Stong's novel; camera (De Luxe), William C. Mellor; editor, David Bretherton; music, Richard Rodgers; asst. director, Ad Schaumer. Reviewed at Culver Theatre, March 9, '62. Running time, 118 **MINS.**

Wayne	Pat Boone
Jerry Dundee	Bobby Darin
Margie	Pamela Tiffin
Emily	Ann-Margret
Abel Frake	Tom Ewell
Melissa Frake	Alice Faye
Hiplewaite	Wally Cox
Harry	David Brandon
Doc Cramer	Clem Harvey
Squat Judge	Robert Foulk
Betty Jean	Linda Henrich
Red Hoerter	Edward "Tap" Canutt
Lilya	Margaret Deramee
Jim	Albert Harris
Usherette	Bebe Allan
George Hoffer	George Russell

"State Fair" is still as American as mom's apple pie, but the pie is stale after 17 years in the pantry. It looks like some tough boxoffice sledding may be in store for the 20th-Fox release, which marks the third time around (1932, 1945) on the screen for this vehicle.

Mature adult moviegoers are familiar with the Rodgers & Hammerstein musical. Those who elect to take it in again may find it too familiar and tepid for their jet-age tastes. The moneymaking issue seems to hinge largely on whether younger audience will turn out to see the quartet of young stars producer Charles Brackett has assembled for the remake. But younger filmgoers, as well as older ones, are likely to grow restless and uneasy watching a picture that adheres too rigidly to old style filmusical techniques that have been superseded and antiquated by the thrust, cohesion and vigor of the modern musical. Outlook is none too promising.

To the five original R&H refrains retained in this version, five new numbers with both music and lyrics by Richard Rodgers have been added. The old songs are still charming, but the excitement they once generated is gone, partially through age and familiarity, partially because (unless memory betrays) they are not rendered with quite the zest and feeling of the 1945 cast by the current starring foursome. The new ditties by Rodgers aren't bad, but they aren't good as the old songs. Rodgers is a fair country lyricist, but he's no Hammerstein, fairest country lyricist of 'em all.

Richard Breen's updated, reset (from Iowa to Texas) scenario isn't otherwise appreciably altered from the last time out. Same three love affairs are there (involving four people and two Hampshire hogs). Same brandy-spiked mince meat episode. Fairgrounds, however, have been switched to Dallas, and there's something crass and antiseptic about the atmosphere—a significant loss. Only one heavy on the premises—a redheaded racing car bully—and he's *all* heavy.

Jose Ferrer's direction has a monotonous air about it—love scene to ferris wheel to alternate love scene to merry-go-round and back again. And his incorporation of the tunes lacks the natural in-and-out flow and dramatic meaning vital for a musical to be completely palatable to a modern audience. **Songs must be rendered as an extension of an emotion that cannot as easily be expressed in normal conversation. One should not be left with the feeling that the dramatic action has merely paused so that a vocalist can warble on cue. This is very likely the most serious shortcomings of the film.** Times and tastes have changed, but the style of "State Fair" hasn't kept pace.

None of the four young stars comes off especially well. Pat Boone and Bobby Darin emerge rather bland and unappealing. Pamela Tiffin's range of expression seems rather narrow on this occasion. Of the four, Ann-Margret makes perhaps the most vivid impression, particularly during her torrid song-dance rendition of "Isn't It Kind of Fun," the film's big production number. Tom Ewell is natural and amusing as the lovable father, Alice Faye poised, sure, and attractively maternal as the lovable mother. Wally Cox has a strong bit as the mince-meat taster, and others notable in support are Linda Henrich, David Brandon, Clem Harvey, Robert Foulk, Edward "Tap" Canutt, Margaret Deramee, Albert Harris, Bebe Allan and George Russell.

William C. Mellor's camera work, though rather standard in technique, is proficiently so, and energetic and hustling where it counts. Music supervisor-conductor Alfred Newman, with Ken Darby's assistance, has dispatched his chores capably, if without special inspiration. Art direction on interiors by Jack Martin Smith and Walter M. Simonds is adequate, but without flair or domestic personality. Ditto set decoration by Walter M. Scott and Lou Hafley. There is something almost oppressively all-American about the premises. Marjorie Best's costumes have a pleasing and apt simplicity. There is a predictable monotony—a kind of see-saw regularity — about the editing by David Bretherton. Nick Castle's choreography is flashy, but not ingenious. *Tube.*

Six Black Horses
(COLOR)

Serviceable western for pairing purposes. Dramatically unstable but photographically appealing.

Hollywood, March 8.

Universal release of Gordon Kay production. Stars Audie Murphy, Dan Duryea, Joan O'Brien. Directed by Harry Keller. Screenplay, Burt Kennedy; camera (Eastman), Maury Gertsman; editor, Aaron Stell; music, Joseph Gershenson; assistant director, Ivan Volkman. Reviewed at Wiltern Theatre, March 8, '62. Running time, **80 MINS.**

Ben Lane	Audie Murphy
Frank Jesse	Dan Duryea
Kelly	Joan O'Brien
Boone	George Wallace
Mustanger	Roy Barcroft
Puncher	Bob Steele
Indian Leader	Henry Wills
Undertaker	Phil Chambers
Mexican Girl	Charlita Regis

The relative scarcity of the big theatre screen color western since television galloped into the picture makes this modest and otherwise not especially choice Universal entry a rather handy item in the current cine-marketplace. The Audie Murphy starrer should pair off serviceably wherever moppets or buffs of the sagebrush idiom convene.

Cameraman Maury Gertsman's picturesque panoramic views of Utah compensate to some extent for the inadequacies and irregularities of Burt Kennedy's original screenplay. Those not impressed with the dramatic doings (and there will be many) can at least admire the scenery against which Gordon Kay's handsome outdoor production is framed.

The story has to do with the vendetta of a widow (Joan O'Brien) against the hired gun (Dan Duryea) responsible for the demise of her husband. Implicated in her astonishingly elaborate scheme to dispose of Duryea is Murphy, an itinerant, unemployed wrangler who happens to owe his neck to the intended victim, but loses his heart to the girl. Murphy's dilemma is solved when Duryea unaccountably but conveniently turns ornery. There is a showdown. At last count, boy and girl are riding off into yon sunset and other critter is ticketed for big movie show in sky, stylishly via "six black horses . . . with plumes . . . pulling a fancy rig," as so specified at an earlier philosophical juncture.

The three principals are appealing in spite of the unlikely dramatics with which they are forced to reckon. Supporting work is colorful, notably that of George Wallace, Roy Barcroft, Bob Steele and Henry Wills.

Harry Keller's direction keeps matters humming along at a pretty good clip, with one rather unaccountable slip-up when a morning-expired corpse is still moving around a little in the p.m. One of the more remarkable cases of reluctant rigor mortis. Competent assists to the production are those of art directors Alexander Golitzen and Robert Luthardt, soundmen Waldon O. Watson and Frank H. Wilkinson, music supervisor Joseph Gershenson and editor Aaron Stell. *Tube.*

War Hunt

Engrossing but evasive account of a war-obsessed, front-line-GI who has forgotten how to live in peace.

Hollywood, March 5.

United Artists release of Terry Sanders's production. Stars John Saxon; introduces Robert Redford. Directed by Denis Sanders. Screenplay, Stanford Whitmore; camera, Ted McCord; editor, John Hoffman; music, Bud Shank; assistant director, Jack Bohler. Reviewed at Goldwyn Studios, March 5, '62. Running time, **81 MINS.**

Private Raymond Endore	John Saxon
Private Roy Loomis	Robert Redford
Capt. Wallace Pratt	Charles Aidman
Sgt. Van Horn	Sydney Pollack
Private Crotty	Gavin MacLeod
Charlie	Tommy Matsuda
Corp. Showalter	Tom Skerritt
Private Fresno	Tony Ray

"War Hunt" is a taut, gripping, but not altogether satisfying drama. With a little more character penetration and a little less melodramatic spit and polish, it might have been a small classic of its genre. But scenarist Stanford Whitmore's tale of a demented GI who cannot contain his killer tactics when the Korean War expires lacks the necessary cohesion and clarity to register with genuine emotional impact.

Still, it's a better than average try on the part of the up-and-coming producer-director team of Terry and Denis Sanders to fashion absorbing war fiction in the moderate scale category for the screen. Though they seem to have fallen somewhat shy of their probable artistic aspirations on this occasion, the United Artists release will make a choice and beneficial companion attraction, and could even carry the meat end of a twin bill in any action situation dominated by male audiences.

The presumably fictional incident upon which Whitmore's yarn is pegged implicates three characters: a "rookie" in the front lines (Robert Redford), the relentless killer (John Saxon), and a young Korean orphan (Tommy Matsuda), who hero-worships the latter. When the cease-fire order fails to deter Saxon from continuing his nightly one-man sniper patrols behind enemy lines, and he has the further audacity to bring the boy along for a lesson in the art of intimate cut-throat warfare, Redford must act. Saxon, the incurable bird of prey, is cut down, but the boy is last seen racing off into the brush, his destiny perhaps warped by his close association with a human animal.

Saxon plays with a fierce intensity, but his efforts are blunted by the fact the character has no roots. We must accept him the way he is, without the desirable explanation. Redford, an appealing and promising newcomer to the screen, emotes with sensitivity. But he, too, is hemmed in by a not fully dimensional character. Master Matsuda is fine as the lad. **Gavin MacLeod makes a vivid impression as a weary trench jockey and others of considerable value and color are Charles Aidman, Sydney Pollack, Tom Skerritt and Tony Ray.**

Under Denis Sanders' brisk, explosive direction, there are a number of noteworthy assists. These include Ted McCord's dexterous and occasionally inventive cinematography, Ray Meadows' keen reproduction of the sounds of combat, and Bud Shank's novel music, stressing flute, guitar and tympany in a compellingly plaintive counterpoint to the naturally terrifying tone and rhythm of front-line warfare. John Hoffman's editing and Edgar Lansbury's art direction are other able assists. Vance Johnson's title design (close-ups of gently quivering reeds and weeds accompanied by a children's choir in a pastoral Korean chant) is memorable. *Tube.*

Premature Burial
(PANAVISION—COLOR)

The third in AIP's Poe cycle. Well-acted but horror film buffs may find the plot, sets and treatment too familiar to generate much shock. Okay exploitation.

American International release of Roger Corman production. Stars Ray Milland, Hazel Court, Richard Ney, Heather Angel. Directed by Corman. Screenplay, Charles Baeumont, Ray Russel, based on Edgar Allan Poe story; camera (color and Panavision), Floyd Crosby; editor, Ronald Sinclair; music, Ronald Stein. Reviewed in N.Y., March 8, '62. Running time, **81 MINS.**

Guy Carrell	Ray Milland
Emily Gault	Hazel Court
Miles Archer	Richard Ney
Kate Carrell	Heather Angel
Dr. Gideon Gault	Alan Napier
Sweeney	John Dierkes
Mole	Richard Miller
Minister	Brendan Dillon

Having earlier come up with a couple of lively boxoffice winners based on Edgar Allan Poe's "House of Usher" and "Pit and The Pendulum," producer-director Roger Corman seems to have run thin in imagination on this third trip to the same literary well. Not only is the plotting in "Premature Burial" discouragingly predictable, but its gloomy and cavernous interior setting is peculiarly similar to those in the first two pix. By this time, many film fans (and at least one reviewer) are as familiar with Corman's downstairs dungeon as they are with their own basement hobbyshops.

The picture obviously has hefty exploitation potential via its title and Poe's rep. However, it's unlikely that its appeal will reach beyond the circle of the horror film buffs to attract those patrons who were so delighted by ghoulish fustian of the "Usher" and "Pit." Ironically, it may be that the extremely competent cast, headed by Ray Milland, plays too honestly in situations which require a certain amount of unrestrained flamboyance.

While the first two pix featured living burials in subplots, "Premature" finally gives the subject closeup treatment.

Milland is cast as a 19th Century English gentleman who, with his weirdo sister, Heather Angel, has withdrawn from the world to his country house, apparently built in the middle of a swamp (or over a peat bog) from all the mist that swirls around. Because he suffers from catalepsy (whose victims appear dead when, in fact, they are very much alive), Milland is obsessed with the thought that he'll be packed away before his rightful time. Against his own better judgment, he agrees to marry Hazel Court, who promises to cure him with love.

Instead, however, Milland gets worse. He starts seeing the faces of gravediggers at the window and hearing their mournful cries from the swamp. Eventually, after his wife persuades him to destroy his lockproof crypt (from which he could always escape), he suffers what seems to be a fatal heart attack, and thus is buried alive, just as he had feared. How he gets out, and who has been responsible for the concerted campaign to drive him mad, need not be divulged here. Suffice to say, nobody lives happily ever after, which is the way these things are supposed to go.

Giving Milland nice support are Miss Angel and the lovely Miss Court, plus Richard Ney, as the doctor friend, Alan Napier as Milland's somewhat inscrutable father-in-law, and John Dierkes, as a rather fearsome gravedigger. The Charles Beaumont-Ray Russell screenplay, though short on the kind of plot surprises which create suspense and interest, is cleanly dialoged with a minimum of verbal cliches. And Floyd Crosby's camerawork (in color and Panavision) is as effective as always, though he and Corman might try eschewing those blue-and-purple dream sequences next time out.
Anby.

Rome Adventure
(COLOR)

Troy Donahue, Angie Dickinson, Suzanne Pleshette, Rossano Brazzi in a wide-eyed tour of scenic points in Italy with an unlikely young-love romance along the route. Sell values.

Warner Bros. release of Delmer Daves production, written & directed by Daves. stars Troy Donahue, Angie Dickinson, Rossano Brazzi, Suzanne Pleshette; features Constance Ford, Al Hirt. From novel by Irving Fineman; camera (Technicolor). Charles Lawton; editor, William Ziegler; music, Max Steiner. At Radio City Music Hall, N.Y., March 15, '62. Running time **118 MINS.**

Don	Troy Donahue
Lyda	Angie Dickinson
Roberto	Rossano Brazzi
Prudence	Suzanne Pleshette
Daisy	Constance Ford
Al	Al Hirt
Albert	Hampton Fancher
Contessa	Iphigenie Castiglioni
Young Man	Chad Everett
Mrs. Riggs	Gertrude Flynn
Agnes	Pamela Austin
Angelina	Lili Valenty

As producer, director and scripter Delmer Daves seems to have been uncertain as to just what he was setting out to do with "Rome Adventure." For the finished product is as much a travelog as it is a story of a couple of young Americans on the loose in Italy and engaged in off-and-on romance.

Pictorial values have their place on the screen, of course. when presented as background. But in this instance the scenic stress is such that the picture in large part comes off as a guided tour and the makebelieve story frequently gets lost.

This almost rates as a blessing, it might be said, because the script by Daves, from a novel by Irving Fineman, is an unlikely and shallow affair, played stiltedly and unimaginatively directed.

Producer Daves apparently is pitching for the teenage market, which is sizeable, via employment of relatively new and pretty faces enmeshed in romantic adventure on foreign terrain. Not a bad commercial thought.

Doubtless there will be boxoffice response as the message is gotten across that Troy Donahue is teamed with Suzanne Pleshette and Angie Dickinson. There are Donahue fans who, on the basis of the performer's work here, evidently are not overly concerned with acting. Distracting to the non-partisans (at least one male observer) is his elaborate hair-do.

Miss Pleshette is a very pretty gal and talent shows through. But she and the also highly attractive Angie Dickinson are handicapped with dialog that's apparently intended to be frisky, instead is largely banal.

Miss Pleshette is a librarian in a femme college. She's chided for recommending a hotsy book, heads for Italy "where they know all about love." Rossano Brazzi, that familiar charmer of the boot country, is on hand to prove her point.

Also encountered is Donahue, an art student who travels all over the place on a motor scooter. Miss Dickinson is an old flame Donahue eventually wants to extinguish. Constance Ford, Al Hirt, Hampton Fancher and Iphigenie Castiglioni are in featured roles.

Daves has given his production an expensive look. Many of the interiors are nicely set and the gals' wardrobes are attractive. Charles

Lawton's photography (Technicolor) is a major asset, capturing more adventure out of the Italian sightseeing than the story. Editing is fair enough and Max Steiner's music is firstclass.
Gene.

Sol en Llamas
(Flaming Sun)
(MEXICAN-EASTMANCOLOR)
Mexico City, March 6.

Peliculas Nacionales release of Rosas Films production. Stars Antonio Augilar, Maricruz Olivier, Fernando Soler; features Irma Dorantes, Domingo Soler, Beatriz Aguirre, Hector Godoy, Jose Chavez, Antonio Raxel, Manuel Arvide. Directed by Alfredo E. Crevenna. At Alameda Theatre, Mexico City. Running time, **90 MINS.**

The Mexican Revolution is a favorite theme of recent screenplays. This one covers the end of dictator Porfirio Diaz' era chronicling the instigation of the first outbreaks of rebellion.

Director Alfredo B. Crevenna has bypassed telling of another "historic episode" of the revolution, concentrates his camera on a family in the latter days of the Diaz regime; an old hacendado, stern and unyielding, a tyrant in his own domain; his peones, his children—and how all react to a social crisis through which the republic passed.

As in other films, director Crevenna has a natural setting, with action unfolding in its entirety on the La Gaviota hacienda in the State of Mexico. Fernando Soler, as the old hacendado who holds to the line of tradition in what he considers his rights, portrays an excellent character, true to type. Maricruz Olivier, as the daughter, also gives an excellent performance as a girl of the aristocracy of that era.

Antonio Aguilar, as the idealist who inspires the peones, without recourse to unnecessary violence, is also convincing.

This is a better-than-average effort because of coordinated acting, direction and realistic photography in color. Pic shows a technical maturity seen in few Mexican screen efforts although it just misses being great by over-dramatizing certain sequences which depict the widening division between the old feudal organization and enslaved peones.

In smaller roles Irma Dorantes, the late Domingo Soler, Beatriz Aguirre and Hector Godoy add to the realism.

As a film version covering an aspect of the budding Mexican revolution, this one will have interest in Spanish-speaking areas, and can even be shown effectively in English language markets because of the good technical aspects and uniformly good acting by the cast.
Emil.

Jessica
(PANAVISION—COLOR)

Hackneyed modern takeoff on "Lysistrata."

Hollywood, March 16.

United Artists release of Jean Negulesco production. Stars Maurice Chevalier, Angie Dickinson, Noel-Noel; Introduces Danielle De Metz. Directed by Negulesco. Screenplay, Edith Sommer, from Flora Sandstrom's novel, "The Midwife of Pont Clery"; camera (Technicolor), Piero Portalupi; editor, Henzo Lucidi; music, Mario Nascimbene; assistant director, Ottavio Oppo. Reviewed at Fox Wilshire

Theatre, March 16, '62. Running time, **105 MINS.**

Jessica	Angie Dickinson
Father Antonio	Maurice Chevalier
Old Crupi	Noel-Noel
Edmondo Raumo	Gabrielle Ferzetti
Nunzia Tuffi	Sylva Koscina
Maria Lombardo	Agnes Moorehead
Luigi Tuffi	Marcel Dalio
Nicolina Lombardo	Danielle De Metz
Gianni Crupi	Antonio Cifariello
Virginia Toriello	Kerima
Beppi Toriello	Carlo Croccolo
Mamma Parigi	Georgette Anys
Rosa Mesudino	Rossena Rory
Pietro Masudino	Alberto Rabagliati
Antonio Risino	Angelo Galassi
Filippella Risino	Marina Barti
Lucia Casabranca	Manuela Rinaldi
Filippo Casabranca	Gianni Musy
Rosario	Joe Pollini

Jean Negulesco's "Jessica" is a trite, frivolous variation on the oft-exploited "Lysistrata" theme. Except for the picturesque scrutiny of Sicily, there is little to recommend it to modern filmgoers save those with the most easygoing, escape-at-all-costs dispositions. An aggressive campaign, with the emphasis bluntly on sexual attractions, may generate some mild boxoffice response. But the domestic outlook is pretty dim for the United Artists release, a Franco-Italian coproduction produced and directed by Negulesco.

Angie Dickinson enacts the title role of an anatomically-streamlined midwife from America who unwittingly tips the Freudian scale in a small Sicilian village just by sheer sex appeal. As Edith Sommer's screenplay, from Flora Sandstrom's novel, "The Midwife of Pont Clery," has it, the misguided senoritas of the community Lysistrategically organize a sex strike. Objective: "no babies, no midwife." As any fool kin plainly see before the picture is a third unspooled, "Jessica" will fall for yon handsome widower Marquis, and strike will expire of natural causes.

It is no strain on Miss Dickinson's histrionic ability to wiggle through this role. Her proportions are tailored to its specifications, and that's about all that's required.

Maurice Chevalier breezes through the part of village priest with that familiar sunny countenance, and pauses occasionally to narrate or tackle one of several listenable, but undistinguished, ditties by Marguerite Monnet (music) and Dusty Negulesco (lyrics). Venerable Gallic character actor Noel-Noel chips in the most charming characterization as an aged gardener. Satisfactory featured support is dispatched by Agnes Moorehead, Marcel Dalio, Gabrielle Ferzetti, Sylva Koscina, Antonio Cifariello, Kerima and Danielle De Metz, here "introduced" to U.S. screen audiences.

Piero Portalupi's camera zeroes in on the scenic splendor of the locale. Capable production assists are made by editor Renzo Lucidi, art director Giulio Bongini, and composed-arranger Mario Nascimbene.
Tube.

Experiment in Terror

Suspense melodrama with concentration on artistic camera work, but sufficiently saleable appeal. Should be a winner, though production is overlong, overwritten and over directed.

Hollywood, March 13.

Columbia release of Blake Edwards (Don Peters) production, directed by Edwards. Stars Glenn Ford and Lee Remick; features Ross Martin and Stefanie Powers. Screenplay by Mildred and Gordon Gordon from their novel, "Opera-

tion Terror"; camera, Philip Lathrop; music, Henry Mancini; editor, Patrick McCormack; ass't. director, Sam Nelson. Reviewed at Columbia studio, March 13, '62. Running time, **123 MINS.**

John Ripley	Glenn Ford
Kelly Sherwood	Lee Remick
Toby	Stefanie Powers
Brad	Roy Poole
Popcorn	Ned Glass
Lisa	Anita Loo
Nancy	Patricia Huston
Special Agent	Gilbert Green
Captain Moreno	Clifton James
Man Who Picked Up Kelly	Al Avalon
Chuck	William Bryant
FBI Agent No. 1	Dick Crockett
Landlord	James Lanphier
Joey Soong	Warren Hsieh
Drunk	Sidney Miller
Attorney Yung	Clarence Lung
Welk	Frederic Downs
Edna	Sherry O'Neil
Penny	Mari Lynn
Dave	Harvey Evans
Raymond Burkhardt	William Sharon
Red Lunch	Ross Martin

"Experiment in Terror" is the kind of suspense melodrama that has generally been solid stock at the boxoffice. Columbia should expect similarly good reactions from this Blake Edwards production, which he also directed, though for the most part, the picture is an experiment in cinematography that emphasizes "artistic" camera technique that is cute but does little to aid the story.

Written by Mildred and Gordon Gordon from their book and Ladies' Home Journal serial, "Operation Terror," the film treatment embraces a number of unnecessary character bits that merely extend the plot and, despite their striking individual reaction, deter from the suspense buildup by drawing too much momentary attention in themselves. Picture, resultantly, is overlong as well as being overwritten and overdirected.

Edwards' particular interest seems to lay in the camera angles. He concentrates on overhead shots and unusual perspective merely for visual effect. While interesting, they tend to detract from the taut storyline, giving the picture an overly conscious directorial feeling. Only in the climactic scenes, which take place in San Francisco's Candlestick Park during an actual baseball game of capacity attendance, does the overhead filming become fully valuable. These are beautifully filmed scenes.

The "experiment" is a terrifying episode in which a bank teller is forced by a psychopathic killer into embezzling $100,000 under threat of murder. She goes to the FBI, whose participation is a vivid display of efficiency in criminology. Glenn Ford and Lee Remick play the FBI agent and bank teller, respectively. For Miss Remick it is a handsome role played with nicely-modulated control and a natural feeling that is devoid of the extreme emotional tension often exposed in such characters. Ford has solidarity, but his role is merely that of a staunch agent doing his job well.

Strongest reaction goes to the killer and to character bits. After being kept under cover throughout the filming to avoid any identity with his role, mostly a series of surprise disguises, Ross Martin should find any frustrating lack of recognition satisfied in strong reaction he is bound to garner for a fine performance. He is a frighteningly realistic psychopath.

Similarly, Patricia Huston is a standout, though her character is entirely superfluous to the plot and picture would have benefitted from the entire role being cut. Again, Edwards must have left it in because of the striking visual effects it adds. Ned Glass is bright in another supporting spot, while Al Avalon, Sidney Miller and Roy Poole contribute. Stefanie Powers looks promising as Miss Remick's sister, also threatened by the killer.

Picture was shot extensively in San Francisco, though story could be placed in any area. However, Philip Lathrop's camera took fine advantage of known Bay City landmarks, giving the film a nice visual style. Patrick McCormack's editing shows well in fast cuts for shock effect. James M. Crowe's sets add to the mood, which is amply complemented by a typical Henry Mancini score.

Gordon's original "Operation Terror" title was changed for film and new Bantam Books paperback comes out next month using film title. *Dale.*

Rheinstitut Aurora
(Matrimonial Agency Aurora)
(GERMAN)

Berlin, March 6.
Nora release of Kurt Ulrich production. Stars Eva Bartok and Carlos Thompson; features Claus Holm, Hans Nielsen, Elisabeth Flickenschildt. Directed by Wolfgang Schleif. Screenplay, Walter Forster; camera, Friedel Behn-Grund; music, Peter Sandloff. At Zoo Palast, Berlin. Running time, **102 MINS.**

Eva Horn	Eva Bartok
Christinow Tomkin	Carlos Thompson
Arnold Lewanddowski	Claus Holm
Lore Karmann	Ina Duscha
Dr. Burgmueller, lawyer	Hans Nielsen
Hortense von Padula	
	Elisabeth Flickenschildt
Friedrich, her son	Rainer Brandt
Charles, butler	Albert Bessler
Mrs. Pearl	Ljuba Welitsch
Graf Hohenperg	Rudolf Vogel
Fraeulein Stadlmeier	Ruth Nimbach
Herr Bolwieser	Werner Gross
Zenzi	Carsta Loeck

This German whodunit, which stars magyar beauty Eva Bartok and Argentine - born Carlos Thompson, has pros and cons to offer. Plot appears considerably contrived but it's skillfully directed. Nothing much rings true even if there's a good deal of suspense. Acting by the central figures isn't exciting but there's excellent support. Domestically, this is probably a sure bet; internationally, there's little to lure patrons.

Eva Bartok is accused of having murdered her husband. Before she starts her 15-year sentence, the prison grants her a respite to settle inheritance matters. Being a temporary free citizen, she and her clever lawyer set out to track down the real killer. Their paths lead them to a dubious matrimonial agency which has Carlos Thompson as a decoy for wealthy women on its payroll. Thompson appears a logical suspect for the murder and from then on the pic becomes a matter of tracking down the actual slayer.

This is a rare mixture of a mystery and love story plus comedy. Although the script leaves much to be desired, Wolfgang Schleif skillfully manages to overcome the various script deficiencies. Top acting honors go to Elisabeth Flickenschildt whose portrayal of a matrimonial agent is a fine piece of thesping; Hans Nielsen, as a

lawyer; and Rudolf Vogel and Walter Gross, two suitors, who contribute nice comedy. Eva Bartok looks very attractive while her starring partner, Carlos Thompson, appears on the wooden side. Technically, this reaches an okay standard. *Hans.*

Le Bateau D'Emile
(Emile's Boat)
(FRENCH) (DYALISCOPE)

Paris, March 13.
Cinedis release of Intermondia Films production. Stars Annie Girardot, Lino Ventura, Pierre Brasseur, Michel Simon. Directed by Denys De La Patelliere. Screenplay, Albert Valentin, Michel Audiard, De La Patelliere from novel by Georges Simenon; camera, Robert Juillard; editor, Jacqueline Thiedot. At Marignan, Paris. Running time, **105 MINS.**

Fernande	Annie Girardot
Emile	Lino Ventura
Francois	Pierre Brasseur
Charles	Michel Simon

Sleekly mounted pic touches on several themes from social satire, situation comedy and love drama. Lack of penetration in characterization makes this primarily a melodrama with playoff rather than arty theatre chances in store abroad. Its cast and pungent dialog have this a good local bet.

A cantankerous black sheep member of a rich fish canning family comes back from riotous living abroad to die. But to annoy his unctuous brother, he decides to leave his share of the business to an illegitimate son who has a small fishing boat. Latter is a loutish but sentimental type living with a vulgar girl.

Pic then delves into the machinations of the family to get the bastard son into the company as a big wig before he can find out about his inheritance. But he finally prefers his boat and the lower life.

Film is directed in a glossy style which robs it of a true feeling for place while theatrical dialog interferes with the action.

Annie Girardot is the only character that emerges from this while the remainder give skilful performances if overdone in bearing and credibility. Technical credits are good. *Mosk.*

Village Of Daughters
(BRITISH)

Light comedy that never fulfills promise of its basic idea. Presence of a tv personality, Eric Sykes, may give U.K. b.o. a life.

London, March 13.
Metro production (George H. Brown) and release. Stars Eric Sykes, Gregoire Aslan, Scilla Gabel. Directed by George Pollock. Original story and screenplay by David Pursall and Jack Seddon; editor, Tristam Cones; camera, Geoffrey Faithfull; music, Ron Goodwin. Ritz Theatre, London. Running time, **86 MINS.**

Herbert Harris	Eric Sykes
Angelina Vimercati	Scilla Gabel
Gastoni	Gregoire Aslan
Don Calogero	John Le Mesurier
Marcio	Eric Pohlmann
Puccelli	Warren Mitchell
Predati	Peter Illing
Postman	Graham Stark
Faccino	Monty Landis
Bus driver	Harold Kasket
1st Pickpocket	Martin Benson
2nd Pickpocket	George Pastell
Annunziata	Yvonne Romain
Lucie	Jill Carson
Gioia	Talitha Pol
Aliza	Bettine Le Beau
Sophia	Dalia Penn
Natasha	Carol White
Maria Gastoni	Ina De La Haye
Carlotta Passati	Golda Casimir
Gloria Balbino	Eileen Way

"Village Of Daughters" is one of the first results of the expanding production program planned by Metro for its British studio. It is a modest light comedy, set in Italy, with a neat basic idea and the stellar advantage, in Britain at least, of Eric Sykes as its leading man. Sykes is a click tv writer and performer, with an inventive if slightly zany sense of humor.

But this comedy proves again that a comedian who is a success on television in small doses is not necessarily equipped to carry a complete film. Despite many witty and amusing touches Sykes seems often to be form diving in the twists of the David Pursall-Jack Seddon screenplay. A lighter touch by director George Pollock might also have given "Daughters" a life. However, the lazy atmosphere of Italian village life has a charm that keeps the pic on a reasonably diverting plane.

Sykes is an English commercial traveler who becomes stranded in Italy and wanders into the village of Mazzento. He finds the village in a turmoil. When the local stone quarry closed down, all the eligible young men had left the village to find work, leaving the place a village of comely daughters. One of the exiles, having made his fortune, writes to the mayor and asks him to pick a bride for him. The lobbying and matchmaking becomes so fierce that the local priest hits on a solution. Let the first stranger to enter the village make the choice. It is not necessary to be an astute student of filmic affairs to guess that Sykes is the fall guy, and soon he is up to his ears in intrigue.

Nothing wrong with that as a comedy idea, but it needed a sharper touch than this one has. Sykes gives a slightly nervous but energetic performance. And such tried troupers as John Le Mesurier, Peter Illing, Gregoire Aslan, Monty Landis, Graham Stark and Eric Pohlmann turn in sound thesping.

There is also a bunch of pretty girls as the daughters who are perhaps stronger on looks than talent. But the leading lady, a Continental miss named Scilla Gabel, shows distinct personality as well as being a looker. Lensing and music are all okay, though there is a title song (by Normall Newell & Ron Goodwin) which is unlikely to make sweet musical history. *Rich.*

All Fall Down

Artful, but uneven drama of two brothers, younger of whom must see the other as he truly is to attain emotional maturity. A near-miss artistically, but top performances and other factors should insure respectable b.o.

Hollywood, March 14.

Metro release of John Houseman production. Stars Eva Marie Saint, Warren Beatty, Karl Malden, Angela Lansbury, Brandon deWilde. Directed by John Frankenheimer. Screenplay, William Inge, based on James Leo Herlihy's novel; camera, Lionel Lindon; editor, Fredric Steinkamp; music, Alex North; assistant director, Hal Polaire. Reviewed at the studio, March 14, '62. Running time, 111 MINS.

Echo O'Brien	Eva Marie Saint
Berry-Berry Willart	Warren Beatty
Ralph Willart	Karl Malden
Annabel Willart	Angela Lansbury
Clinton Willart	Brandon deWilde
Mrs. Mandel	Constance Ford
Schoolteacher	Barbara Baxley
Hedy	Evans Evans
Myra	Jennifer Howard
Bouncer	Madame Spivy
Captain Ramirez	Albert Paulson

Within John Houseman's production of "All Fall Down," there some truly memorable passages—moments and scenes of great pith, poignance, truth and sensitivity. How disheartening it is, then, that a potentially outstanding film like this be marred by unaccountable oversights and inconsistencies so incongruous to the peaks achieved. The sum total is an artfully produced, cinematically rich, histrionically noteworthy, dramatically uneven near-miss, a film that, with just a degree of less compromise at the creative core, might have been "the one to see" in 1962.

For Metro, it is a dark horse contender. Its imposing creative battery (Houseman, Frankenheimer, Inge) will attract the attention of those who take their filmgoing seriously. Warren Beatty is hot. There are several performances in it of Academy Award potential that will stimulate conversation. Many patrons, especially younger ones, will be able to identify with the characters. These factors will boost the boxoffice, and should make it a successful commercial venture. But those story lapses will exert a gravitational force on the film's ultimate moneymaking altitude.

A 16-year-old boy (Brandon deWilde) who idolizes his emotionally unstable older brother (Beatty) is the pivotal figure, the principal character of concern, in William Inge's screenplay based on James Leo Herlihy's novel. The important issue is that the adolescent matures into a decent young man. But his path to maturity is threatened by his adulation for his brother, a selfish, irrational free spirit who survives on odd jobs and loose women. When the older boy proceeds to destroy a young spinister (Eva Marie Saint) whom deWilde adores in a hopeless, adolescent fashion, the latter has his moment of reckoning. The film concludes on an optimistic note.

Unforgettable scenes arise out of the relationships between the two boys and their parents. Moments are produced that gnaw at the heart and arouse the emotions as the family gropes for communication. Angela Lansbury and Karl Malden, as the tragicomic elders, create indelible, dimensional and deeply affecting people. Two significant performances, especially Miss Lansbury's.

Yet it is a picture of dramatic contrasts, of highs and lows, towering strengths and feeble weaknesses. Seemingly minor expositional issues, yet matters of concern such as the family's means of support are completely overlooked. It is never stated just what the old man does for a living, and the audience is entitled to some explanation. Even more damaging are the far-fetched reactions of various women of at least some pride, social standing and substance who swoon prostitutionally at first sight of nogoodnik Beatty. Then, too, there are inconsistencies and unlikelihoods in the behavior of the two central characters (especially Beatty's) and at least one major mechanical goof (a key scene in which deWilde overhears a conversation in the cellar, although he obviously cannot since he's peering in through a closed window and it is pouring).

Beatty gives his best screen performance to date, although his range of emotions is not especially wide and his style incorporates distracting elements of Dean and Brando and stresses a kind of monotonous squint-scowl. Still, he's got that undeniable star quality—the animal chemistry that overpowers femme audiences and should insure his leading man status for many years. Miss Saint creates a sound and stimulating portrait of the heroine. DeWilde has one or two small lapses, but his enactment has roots in life. He executes the character growth subtly and believably. Staunch support is pitched in by Constance Ford, Barbara Baxley and Evans Evans as three women who fall under Beatty's spell. Others of value are Madame Spivy and Albert Paulson.

Cinematically, "All Fall Down" is virtually an art film. There are some masterful strokes in John Frankenheimer's design, notably the slow, poetic three-ply dissolves he has accomplished with editor Frederic Steinkamp, and the sensitive and painstaking photographic qualities, textures and compositions he has executed with cameraman Lionel Lindon.

Both art direction and set decoration exude authenticity and human personality, a tribute to the teams of George W. Davis-Preston Ames, Henry Grace-George R. Nelson, respectively. Additionally capital contributions are made by composer Alex North and soundman Franklin Milton. *Tube.*

L'Oeil Du Malin
(The Evil Eye)
(FRENCH)

Paris, March 20.

Lux release of Rome Paris Films production. Stars Jacques Charrier, Stephane Audran, Walter Reyer. Written and directed by Claude Chabrol; camera, Jean Rabier; editor, Bruno Drigo. Preemed in Paris. Running time, 80 MINS.

Mercier	Jacques Charrier
Helene	Stephane Audran
Hartman	Walter Reyer

New Waver Claude Chabrol, after some highly personalized pix that turned out to be flops, in this turns to a solidly carpentered psychological suspense pic. It has tautness and pacing but relies somewhat too much on dialog to keep this from really breaking through to the motivations of its characters.

It states its case neatly but rarely allows the pic to go deeper into the backgrounds of its characters. Thus, this looms a possible dualer or specialized item. Art theatre chances would be more dubious.

A second-rate French journalist is sent to West Germany to do a series of articles. He notices a seemingly happy couple living near him. The man is a noted writer and she is French. He manages to worm his way into their lives, and then tries subtly to win the woman. His interference leads to the man killing his wife.

Jacques Charrier has the good looks and obsequious charm that make his spiritless character acceptable, while Stephane Audran and Walter Reyer are good as the couple.

Chabrol has given this solid pacing. But, all in all, it remains a dexterous surface exercise with fine technical aspects. *Mosk.*

Los Barbaros del Norte
(Barbarians of the North)
(MEXICAN)

Mexico City, March 20.

Peliculas Nacionales release of Cinematografica Filmex, S.A. production. Stars comic "Clavillabo," Adilia Castillo, Javier Solis; features Rodolfo Landa, Roberto Meyer, Yolanda Ciani, Roy Fletcher, Jose Baviera, Fidel A. Espino, Armando Arreola, Jorge Casanova, Maria Cristina Ortiz, Adolfo Aguilar, Jose Alonso Cano. Directed by Jose Diaz Morales. Original story and screenplay, Julio Porter and Pancho Cordova.

This is another Clavillazo film with the comic catering to his public. In this one, he's Mexican equivalent of a sheriff who brings law and order to a northern village, with comic overtones. Actually, the film tries hard to be a parody of the American western although it falls short because of weak script and spotty direction.

Comic never pays too much attention to script, relying on his mugging and zany actions. In this one where he attempts playing a sort of Jesse James, Buffalo Bill and quick-on-the-draw gunslinger rolled into one, the attempt at parody falls flat. Maybe because the Mexican idea of Hollywood westerns is distorted. But mostly because Clavillazo dictates the line his scripts must follow and gag lines as well as comic situations.

Rodolfo Landa, head of the National Assn. of Actors, while turning in a good performance, is lost in this one. Other members of cast are so-so. And Javier Solis, while good over radio and on disks, somehow just doesn't project as a screen personality. *Emil.*

A Public Affair

Semidocumentary dramatization of lawmaking process. Interesting and enlightening, but too offbeat in theatrical pic style for better than lower berth status.

Hollywood, March 20.

Parade release of Bernard Girard-Robert Lewis production. Directed and screenplay by Girard; camera, Howard Schwartz; editor, Robert Seiter; music, Joe Green; assistant director, Nathan R. Garragan. Reviewed at Goldwyn Studios, March 20, '62. Running time, 75 MINS.

Sam Clavell	Myron McCormick
Senator Fred Baines	Edward Binns
Hal Green	Judson Pratt
Phyllis Baines	Jacqueline Loughery
Malcomb Hardy	Paul Birch
Bill Martin	Harry Carey Jr.
Tracey Phillips	Grace Lee Whitney
Leonard Lohman	Peter Brocco
Senator Armstrong	Mack Williams
George Babcock	Noel Drayton
Senator Hopkins	Tyler McVey
Marshall Thor	Lou Kane

"A Public Affair" is a theatrical oddity; a tidy, intelligent and worthwhile indie picture that, paradoxically, can aspire to little more than spot supporting status in filmdom's commercial pattern. A film of considerable educational value, the Bernard Girard-Robert Lewis production succeeds to some extent in providing audiences with insight into the legislative processes of state government. Had the producers aimed their project at television, their native medium, the result would have been an engrossing and edifying public service special. In the theatrical spectrum, it will have to suffice as an earnestly-produced, neatly-executed "offbeat" item shy the traditional qualifications for more than secondary commercial planting.

Resourcefully written and briskly directed by Girard, the film explores the campaign of a pair of dedicated California lawmakers to hurdle the muckraking strategy of the opposition as they propel into law a bill proposing measures for curbing unscrupulous practices in the collection agency field. As reined by Girard, the picture is instilled with the clipped, documentary style common to television—brisk, brief scenes that impart a sense of realism and momentum. But the technique bypasses the simplification and personalization processes to which filmgoers are accustomed in their cinema pursuits. The human, or intimate character, element is relegated to secondary status as the film sticks to its forthright, uncluttered design of audience enlightenment first, emotional involvement second. Commercially, it is a novel approach.

The acting is thoroughly professional, but there is little time or room for deep character penetration in the performances. Competent portrayals are etched by Myron McCormick, Edward Binns and Judson Pratt in the central roles, with generally sound work in somewhat lesser niches by pretty Jacqueline Loughery, Harry Carey Jr., Grace Lee Whitney, Peter Brocco, Mack Williams, Noel Drayton, Tyler McVey, Lou Kane and Armand Alzamora. Paul Birch is outstanding in his delineation of an unsavory collection agency bigwig.

Modest means do not seem to have hampered the craftsmen from mounting a fairly slick piece of cinematic machinery, much of it filmed on-the-spot in Sacramento and L. A. Notable among these efforts are the resourceful photography of Howard Schwartz and the taut editing of Robert Seiter. *Tube.*

Forever My Love
(COLOR)

Romy Schneider, Karl Boehm starred in elaborate costumer that's packed with action, colorful scenes and some excellent portrayals; absence of U.S. marquee names and length likely will confine most of playdates to arty theatres.

Paramount release of Ernest Marischka production. Written & directed by Marischka. Stars Romy Schneider, Karl Boehm; features Magda Schneider. Camtra (Technicolor), Bruno Mondi; editor, Alfred Srp; music, Anton Profes; song "Forever My Love," sung by Jane Morgan. Tradeshown in N.Y., March 22, '62. Running time, **147 MINS.**

Princess Elisabeth ..... Romy Schneider
Emperor Franz Josef ... Karl Boehm
Duchess Ludovika .... Magda Schneider
Archduchess Sophie .... Vilma Degischer
Duke Max of Bavaria.... Gustav Knuth
Police Major .... Jaseph Meinrad
Princess Helene .... Uta Franz

"Forever My Love" is a beautifully photographed, well directed and produced film with several magnificent performances and awe-inspiring scenes but which does not look to get far in the U.S. except at some arty theatres. Because so patently overboard in length and lacking star names that mean much at the American boxoffice, this Austrian production will find it tough crashing the usual U.S. firstruns.

It's about Franz Josef, young Emperor of Austria; his courtship and marriage to Princess Elizabeth (Sissi) of Bavaria and the tremendous influence she exerted in bringing peace with rival nations was originally released in Europe about two years ago under the original title, "Sissi." Produced in Austria, in the German language, it was dubbed into English and considerably trimmed down from original length for the present production with the new tag, "Forever My Love." Title derives from the song of same tag by Hal David and Burt Bachrach, sung for the American version by Jane Morgan. Paramount has it for distribution in the U.S. and England.

Producer-director Ernst Marischka has made an unusually fast-moving, inspired story out of what could have been a routine costumer about royal personages. He has incorporated numerous scenes of "pomp and circumstance," some sly comedy moments and several suspenseful episodes. But the pic is so overlong and devoid of marquee lustre that it never will measure up to its potential as a vivid, interesting screen vehicle. Perhaps some of its over-length stems from the fact that Marischka also did the screenplay.

Karl Boehm, who portrays the youth Kaiser, has been working recently in some American pix in Hollywood but said films have not gotten around enough yet to make his name familiar. Romy Schneider, not quite 24 yet, as Sissi, his comely wife, also is not very well-known to U.S. audiences. Yet these two make one of the most attractive couples seen on the screen in some time. Oddly enough the Duchess of Bavaria, Sissi's mother in the pic, is portrayed by Magda Schneider, Romy Schneider's real mother.

Archduchess Sophie, Josef's mother, is made a scheming character by Vilma Degischer but one of the most intriguing portrayals in the production. Gustav Knuth plays Max of Bavaria, Sissi's father, homeloving individual. Uta Franz is sufficient as Sissi's sister while Joseph Meinrad is superb as the efficient, natural police major.

Plenty of plaudits go to Bruno Mondi for his excellent color (Technicolor) photography, particularly his shots along the French Riviera and in the Alps. Film has been smartly scored by Anton Profes, with a special bow to him for the music in the ballroom scenes. Marischka deserves a better break than the one he will get on this pic. Perhaps on his next one, there will be more guidance on actual footage for a much more e[illegible]ve result. *Wear.*

La Gamberge
(The Dance)
(FRENCH—DYALISCOPE)

Paris, March 20.

Pathe release of Parc Film-CDC production. Stars Jean-Pierre Cassel; features Arletty, Jean Poiret, Francoise Dorleac, Michel Serrault, Micheline Francey. Directed by Norbert Carbonnaux. Screenplay, Francois Billetdoux, Jacques Gall, Francois Gall; camera, Pierre Petit; editor, Colette Charbonneau. At Balzac, Paris. Running time, **90 MINS.**

Albert .... Jean-Pierre Cassel
Mrs. Albert .... Arletty
Francoise .... Francoise Dorleac
Vieux .... Jean Poiret
Petrarque .... Michel Serrault
Aunt .... Micheline Francey
Antonin .... Michel Vitold

Attempt at a satirical situation comedy, in the American vein, does not quite come off in this film. Gags and pot shots at youth, yellow journalism and tele are too telegraphed to give this the ease and movement it needs. Characterizations and inventiveness are also somewhat surfacy, with too many local allusions, making this a questionable export item.

A young country girl hitches a ride to Paris where she hopes to have a career and meet a Prince Charming. The boy falls for her but she falls in with a conniving newspaper publisher who launches her as the girl who is looking for a Prince.

This looks at juve delinquents and young love plus gags at existing politics and local problems. But director Norbert Carbonnaux has not given this the pace or flair for situations and satire to take it off the ground.

Thesps try hard but can never give this comedy the brightness it needs. It is technically good, with a few fine isolated bright spots but not enough to make it a heavyweight wicket contender. *Mosk.*

Follow That Dream
(PANAVISION-COLOR-SONGS)

Elvis, sans pelvis, in a sporadically amusing romanti-comedy with songs. Good b.o. potential.

Hollywood, March 19.

United Artists release of David Weisbart production. Stars Elvis Presley, Arthur O'Connell; features Anne Helm, Joanna Moore. Directed by Gordon Douglas. Screenplay, Charles Lederer, based on Richard Powell's novel, "Pioneer, Go Home"; camera (De Luxe), Leo Tover; editor, William B. Murphy; music, Hans J. Salter; assistant director, Bert Chervin. Reviewed at Crest Theatre, March 19, '62. Running time, **109 MINS.**

Toby Kwimper .... Elvis Presley
Pop Kwimper .... Arthur O'Connell
Holly Jones .... Anna Helm
Alicia Claypoole .... Joanna Moore
Carmine .... Jack Kruschen
Nick .... Simon Oakland
Judge .... Roland Winters
H. Arthur King .... Alan Hewitt
George .... Howard McNear
Jack .... Frank de Kova
Endicott .... Herbert Rudley
Eddy and Teddy Bascombe Gavin and Robert Koon
Al .... Robert Carricart
Blackie .... John Duke

"Follow That Dream" is a kind of second cinematic cousin to "Tammy," with Elvis Presley as the hinterland's newest answer to the supposed advantages of formal booklarnin'. Presley buffs figure to take very kindly to the David Weisbart production, which displays their hero in good form in the kind of vehicle in which the record shows him to be most salable — the light romantic comedy with songs. Sardonic laughter may arise from time to time out of the literate or loge brigades, but the last laugh should be UA's, enroute to the bank. This should be an especially large ozone item.

Scenarist Charles Lederer has constructed several highly amusing scenes in tailoring Richard Powell's novel, "Pioneer, Go Home," to fit the specifications of the screen. And director Gordon Douglas has made capital of the screenplay's better moments, translating the comedy of the typewriter into amusing and fast-paced visual terms, with the aid of his star and a company of accomplished supporting players. There are lags and lapes in the picture, to be sure, but, by Presley pix standards, it's above average.

Presley portrays what amounts to a cross between "Li'l Abner" and male counterpart of "Tammy," a sort of number one son in a makeshift, itinerant brood of "Real McCoys" types who plant themselves on a strip of unclaimed Florida beach and proceed to play homesteaders whilst befuddled officials of city and state, welfare workers and thugs haplessly attempt to unsquat them from their profitable perch.

Presley conveys the right blend of horse sense and naivete in his characterization, and delivers five songs with vocal competence but nary a wiggle. The songs, four with a beat and one slow ballad, hamper the comic momentum of the story and are hardly distinguished ditties but, with EP doing the warbling, are apt to enjoy a commercial destiny on wax beyond their natural potential. They are the work of five separate composer-lyricist teams.

Arthur O'Connell scores as the big daddy of the clan, and is principal pawn in a running gag involving an overly-pressurized outhouse john. There's a heavy streak of earthy humor in the film. Anne Helm is decorative and able as the Elvis-a-vis, or Daisy Mae to his Abner. Joanna Moore, whose Georgia drawl brings a touch of lingual authenticity to the premises (Southern accents are not exactly in abundance), is effective as a welfare worker interested only in her own welfare. Especially chipper supporting work is contributed by Howard McNear and Simon Oakland. Others of value include Jack Kruschen, Roland Winters, Alan Hewitt, Frank de Kova, Herbert Rudley, Robert Carricart, John Duke and twin moppets Gavin and Robert Koon.

Filmed in Florida, the production benefits from the know-how of cameraman Leo Tover, editor William B. Murphy, art director Mal Bert and composer Hans J. Salter. *Tube.*

The Counterfeit Traitor
(COLOR)

William Holden, Lilli Palmer and Hugh Griffith engaged in World War II espionage. An exciting story skillfully told; firm "A" at the boxoffice.

Paramount release of Perlberg-Seaton production, produced by William Perlberg, directed by George Seaton. Stars William Holden and Lilli Palmer; features Hugh Griffith. Screenplay, Seaton, from Alexander Klein novel of same title; camera (Technicolor), Jean Bourgoin; editor, Hans Ebel; music, Alfred Newman. Previewed at DeMille Theatre, N.Y., March 18, '62. Running time, **140 MINS.**

Eric Erickson .... William Holden
Marianne Mollendorf ..... Lilli Palmer
Collins .... Hugh Griffith
Klara Holtz .... Erica Beer
Ingrid Erickson .... Eva Dahlbeck
Hans Holtz .... Helo Gutschwager
Max Gumpel .... Ulf Palme
Bruno Ulrich .... Werner Peters
Otto Holtz .... Carl Raddatz
Wilhelm Kortner .... Charles Regnier
Jaeger .... Stefan Schnabel
Baron Gerhard Von Oldenbourg Ernst Schroder
Hulda Windler ...... Ingrid Van Bergen

Born in New York and naturalized a Swede, Eric Erickson undertook to camouflage himself as a Nazi sympathizer during World War II, but actually functioned as an agent for the Allies. He was in the oil business, adroitly gained access to information about German refineries and passed the intelligence along to the British.

The fact-based book by Alexander Klein is the genesis of strong cinematic story-telling in the Perlberg-Seaton production of "The Counterfeit Traitor." It comes off as an espionage thriller of high order, melodramatic and adventure-laden as all getout but never forsaking an aura of genuineness.

With William Perlberg handling the production reins and George Seaton directing from his own screenplay, the feature ran into weather-locationing troubles in Germany, Sweden and Denmark—this is a matter of record—but no problems are mirrored in the finished product.

Unlike so many glorifying-some-one wartime retrospectives, this one has the ring of authenticity. Perhaps a better term would be production integrity, for the film-makers cut no corners and made no compromises in getting across the actioner. It's clear that Perlberg and Seaton ernestly set out for the best possible in their venture—and got the best out of William Holden, Lilli Palmer and Hugh Griffith.

But there's a point to be pondered over. Why is the color (Technicolor) so inferior—and it is inferior—in the first couple of reels? Even the sound at the outset is blurry.

These are flaws, without doubt. But there are hard-hitting story values, and staging, that are more than compensating.

All in all it's a work of substance, this filmization of the now living Eric Erickson who denied himself reputation among family and friends in order to surreptitiously work for the anti-Third Reich forces.

Playing the principal part with remarkable effectiveness is William Holden. He is the astute observer of human behavior who can spot a Nazi for double-cross purposes. And, although married, can go in love with a partisan named Marianne Mollendorf (Lilli Palmer) who comes to a sympathetic end in

a courtyard execution by the Germans.

Miss Palmer is an accomplished performer in this outing. She plays with sincerity the part of a woman of devotion to the anti-Nazi cause and, womanly, falling for the manly Holden.

Hugh Griffith is properly coy and cunning as the British Intelligence major domo who reasons with Holden that the latter's role is one of unrewarding sacrifice in wartime. Griffith does a top-calibre professional portrayal.

Others in the cast have names unfamiliar in the United States, but their competence cannot be questioned. Particularly standout is Helo Gutschwager, as a vicious, brainwashed 12-year-old member of the Hitler Youth Movement, wholly capable of ratting to the Gestapo on his own German but un-Nazi father.

Erica Beer, Ulf Palme, Werner Peters, Eva Dahlbeck, Carl Raddatz, Charles Regnier, Stefan Schnabel, Ernst Schroeder and Ingrid Van Bergen are other members of the competent cast.

Scripter-director Seaton has gotten into this one an abundance of nice-paced and plausible action and credible romance. It figures to be a bigtime winner with the general audiences. Jean Bourgoin's color cinematography makes it appear, in part at the beginning (as aforementioned) that someone was remiss but the early technical shortcomings become forgotten about. Alfred Newman fiddled well in providing the all-times appropriate musical score. *Gene.*

The Road To Hong Kong
(BRITISH)

Lively addition to this famous series. Sci-fi spoof laced with zany situations and sharp wisecracks; mixture, as before, should lead to boxoffice ditto.

London, April 3.

United Artists' release of Melnor (Melvin Frank) Production. Stars Bing Crosby, Bob Hope, Joan Collins; features Dorothy Lamour, Robert Morley. Directed by Norman Panama. Original screenplay, Norman Panama, Melvin Frank; camera, Jack Hildyard; editor, John Smith; Robert Farnon; songs, Jimmy Van Heusen & Sammy Cahn. Running time, **91 MINS.**

Harry Turner	Bing Crosby
Chester Babcock	Bob Hope
Diane	Joan Collins
Dorothy Lamour	Dorothy Lamour
The Leader	Robert Morley
Dr. Zorbb	Walter Gotell
Jhinnah	Roger Delgardo
Grand Lama	Felix Aylmer
First U.S. Official	Alan Gifford
Second U.S. Official	Robert Ayres
Lady at Airport	Jacqueline Jones

The seventh "Road" comedy, after a lapse of seven years, should cause a seven-year itch among tab buyers to get in an the laughs. For they come thick and fast in this genial piece of nonsense. Perhaps the old formunla creaks occasionally, but not enough to cause any disappointment while the zany situations and razor-edge wisecracks keep the whole affair bubbling happily. It has been concocted with the usual zest of Norman Panama and Melvin Frank. While one or two of the sequences are over-prolonged, enough good humor has been packed into 91 minutes to satisfy most patrons.

This one takes the boys on a haphazard trip to a planet called Plutonius, though this only happens as a climax to some hilarious adventures in Ceylon and Hong Kong. It's almost useless to outline the plot. But it involves Bing Crosby and Bob Hope as a couple of flop vaudevillians who turn con men. Somewhere along the line, Hope loses his memory and that, in a mysterious manner, leads them to involvement with a mysterious spy (Joan Collins) a secret formula and a whacky bunch of thugs called the Third Echelon, led by Robert Morley. He plans to send a rocket to the moon and from there control the destiny of the world. Naturally, Bing and Bob become the unwilling aeronauts.

With this sketchy but sufficient storyline, Panama and Frank have virtually let the two stars loose. They are chased through Hong Kong's bazaars, become involved in a vaudeville act (enter Dorothy Lamour), have cockeyed adventures in the space ship and generally wisecrack and caper energetically through a safe laughter belt. Hope ogles the gals. Crosby baits Hope and also sings a couple of pleasant numbers. Hope baits Crosby. Both bait the audience. The result is an amiable comedy which should please nostalgic customers and entice those who haven't seen any of the previous "Road" pix.

The script is spiced with a number of private jokes (golf, Hope's nose, Crosby's dough, reference to gags from previous "Road" films) but not enough to be irritating to those not in the Crosby-Hope clan. Major disappointment is Joan Collins, who though an okay looker, never seems quite abreast of the comedians. She plays the girl spy who unwittingly involves the boys in their adventures and it would have pleased many to have seen Miss Lamour play the role. As it is, Miss Lamour plays herself as a vaude artist who rescues the Crosby-Hope team from one of their jams. She still looks stunning and puts over a number well, but has nothing more to do than to mug through a routine scene.

In support, Morley, as the leader of the Third Echelon, plays Morley in his usual puffy, effective style. Walter Gotell, as a scientist, and Felix Aylmer, as a Grand Lama, crop up with useful contributions.

Panama's direction errs only in occasionally allowing scenes to milk the yocks a shade too long. Notable instance of this is a sequence in the rocket when Crosby and Hope, who have unknowingly replaced a couple of experimental apes, are fed with bananas and milk through a machine. At first view this is a sidesplitter, but it hangs around a bit too long.

Jack Hildyard has done a smooth lensing job while Wally Veevers and Ted Samuels have chipped in with some effective special effects.

As guest artists, Frank Sinatra and Dean Martin help to round off the film. David Niven appears for no good reason while the best interlude is that of Peter Sellers. He plays a native medico, examining Hope for amnesia and it is a brilliantly funny cameo.

Jimmy Van Heusen and Sammy Cahn have produced a duet for Crosby and Hope called "Teamwork" and a romantic ditty for Crosby which the performers expertly put over. *Rich.*

Harold Lloyd's World of Comedy

Boff film anthology of past Lloyd hits from 1920 to 1932; clips and longer segments edited together in showmanship which should appeal to every type of audiences. One of great novelties of the year.

Hollywood, March 30.

Continental release of Harold Lloyd production. Stars Lloyd; features Jobyna Ralston, Constance Cummings, Josephine Crowell. Narration, Art Ross; music, Walter Scharf; sound effects, Del Morris. Previewed in Hollywood, Calif., March 29, '62. Running time, **95 MINS.**

Harold Lloyd comes out of retirement with this assembly of clips and long sequences from his comedic releases down through the years. "Harold Lloyd's World of Comedy" is a return to the golden age of laughter, in a day when too many producers seemingly prefer downbeat subjects to entertainment, and in its 95-minutes' running time is embodied a surefire blockbuster which may be exploited to top returns.

The comedian who started his career in one-reelers as Lonesome Luke and progressed to the bespectacled and frantic character who packed more gags and situations in his films than any other, then or since, will be a new and delightful personality for younger theatregoers and a welcome treat for older patrons who followed him religiously. Film has been edited by Lloyd personally from considerably in excess of 100,000 feet of his comedies, and he's come up with a belly-laugh novelty which will delight every type audience. Most of the footage is silent, despite fact he cuts in some of his talking pix; it's more effective that way, for Lloyd's sight gags, which he employed to such great advantage, do not require dialog.

Lloyd builds his film around sequences from seven features, leading up to main portion with clips from half a dozen shorts. Features, which many will recall with enthusiasm, include "Hot Water," "Why Worry," "Girl Shy"—silents—and the talking "Professor Beware," "Movie Crazy," "Feet First," "Milky Way." Among the clips are footage from "The Freshman," "A Sailor Made Man," "Kid Brother," "Hunted Spooks," "An Eastern Westerner" and several others. Lloyd digs back to 1920 for start of his spread, which extends to 1932.

Unfoldment is hilarious comedy, slapstick and situation, not seen on the screen since Lloyd bowed out of his own picture-making with "Movie Crazy" in 1932. Jobyna Ralston, for many years his leading lady in silents, appears in several sequences, as do, too, Barbara Kent and Constance Cummings in his later effusions.

Feature, which Lloyd is using as a test and will pave the way to future excursions into the pact if it proves boxoffice, will be shown as a special entry at the upcoming Cannes Film Festival, with comedian slated to make a personal appearance.

Lloyd produced film, with Jack Murphy his associate producer, and special narration written by Art Ross. Harold Lloyd Jr. is listed as story consultant. Sound effects by Del Harris are inserted for showmanship effect, and Walter Scharf wrote a complete music score, with orchestration by Lew Shuken and Jack Hayes. *Whit.*

Postman's Knock
(BRITISH)

The Spike Milligan name is good marquee value in Britain, but the comedy doesn't employ his gifts adequately; fair dualer.

London, March 27.

Metro (Kinnoch) production and release. Stars Spike Milligan, Barbara Shelley; features John Wood, Wilfred Lawson, Miles Malleson, Archie Duncan, Ronald Adam. Directed by Robert Lynn. Screenplay, John Briley, Jack Trevor Story, from Story's original; additional dialog, Spike Milligan, George Barclay; music, Ron Goodwin; camera, Gerald Moss; editor, Geoffrey Foot. Previewed at Metro Private Theatre, London. Running time, **87 MINS.**

Harold Petts	Spike Milligan
Jean	Barbara Shelley
P. C. Woods	John Wood
Inspector	Archie Duncan
Postman	Wilfred Lawson
Psychiatrist	Miles Malleson
Mr. Fordyce	Ronald Adam
District Supt.	Bob Todd
Rupert	Warren Mitchell
Sam	Arthur Mullard
Pete	John Pennett
Joe	Lance Percival
Villager	Mario Frabizi

Spike Milligan, one of Metro's British contract thesps, is a big name on tele, with a zany sense of nonconformist humor which here has been labeled "goonery." But he is a funny fellow whose contributions to the gaiety of an audience must be fairly shrewdly rationed. In "Postman's Knock," he has to bear the brunt of most of the picture's action and, to do that, he needs a specialized form of comedy role. In this, he has a role which could have been played as well and, more logically, by several other comedians. The public image of Milligan is never that of a downtrodden, naive character and certainly not that of the guy who gets the girl.

With this prime fault, plus some competent but not humorously inspired direction by Robert Lynn, "Postman's Knock" emerges as an inconspicuous comedy which will serve as a modest dualer. But this and the recent "Village of Daughters" hardly add up to a boff start for Metro's expanding British production lineup.

Milligan plays a country postman who gets elevated for training at London's top mail dépot. He runs into plenty of problems on his first visit to the big city and finds simple romance with an unsuccessful art student. He has his life further complicated when the two are suspected by police and Post Office officials as being the brains behind a gang of mail robbers. All this trickles along amiably but funnier dialog would have helped while the romantic issue bogs down the entire affair.

There are some excellent moments, but not enough to get the best out of Milligan's curious form of humor. The discovery that, as a mail sorter, he can work faster than an expensively installed electric machine is a sure yock. There is also a final Mack Sennett chase through the Central Post Office in which cops and robbers get mixed up in a whirl of slapstick.

Milligan largely plays pianissimo and his supporting cast work loyally to keep the tempo of the film at

the bubbling point. John Wood has an arduous job as a cop who, in various disguises, is detailed to keep tabs on the suspected couple. Wood mugs valiantly but can do nothing to prevent the chore becoming monotonously unfunny. Warren Mitchell, Arthur Mullard, John Bennett and Lance Percival are a bunch of labored crooks. Miles Malleson, as a psychiatrist, and Wilfred Lawson, as Milligan's mentor in learning how to be a bigtime postman, chip in with useful contributions.

Only notable femme role is that of Milligan's girl friend. It's played by Barbara Shelley and she has little chance to show her undoubted ability. She is a cool goodlooker who appears to be having an uphill fight to prove to British producers that she could well be a top asset in U.K.'s femme film thesping. London location scenes are well done. The lensing of Gerald Moss and the editing of Geoffrey Foot are worthy of a far better screenplay. *Rich.*

The Horizontal Lieutenant
(C'SCOPE—COLOR)

Buck private in the service comedy genre. Meagre fun, in spite of efforts of Jim Hutton and Paula Prentiss. B.o. prospects not too promising.

Hollywood, March 21.

Metro release of Joe Pasternak production. Stars Jim Hutton, Paula Prentiss, Jack Carter. Directed by Richard Thorpe. Screenplay, George Wells, based on Gordon Cotler's novel, "The Bottletop Affair"; camera (Metrocolor), Robert Bronner; editor, Richard W. Farrell; music, George Stoll; assistant director, William Shanks. Reviewed at Beverly Theatre, March 21, '62. Running time, **90 MINS.**
Lt. Merle Wye .... Jim Hutton
Lt. Molly Blue ....Paula Prentiss
Lt. William Monck......... Jack Carter
Akiko .... Miyoshi Umeki
Commander Hammerslag .... Jim Backus
Colonel Korotny .... Charles McGraw
Yeoman Buckles .... Marty Ingels
Roy Tada .... Yoshio Yoda

"The Horizontal Lieutenant," Joe Pasternak production for Metro, never really gets off the ground. The basic premise is lean, the gags are tired and the incidental situations are shopworn and obvious. Costars Jim Hutton and Paula Prentiss, here paired for the fourth consecutive time, are a popular couple with film audiences, but at this relatively early stage in their blossoming careers it is doubtful that they can carry as tepid a concoction as this.

Based on Gordon Cotler's novel, "The Bottletop Affair," George Wells' screenplay has Hutton as an accident-prone looie assigned to the unenviable 1944 task of capturing a Japanese soldier still at large on a South Pacific island already occupied by the Americans for seven months. The capture is made after a series of contrived failures.

Neither Hutton nor Miss Prentiss has much of an opportunity to work to comic advantage, especially the latter. Most of Hutton's contribution consists of spills and cross-eyed reactions to hard knocks on the noggin. He's capable of better things. Others implicated in the plot, none with a significant amount of comedy success, are Jack Carter (nitery-tv comic in his screen debut), Jim Backus, Miyoshi Umeki and Charles McGraw. Marty

Ingels does well in a drunk bit, and Yoshio Yoda, a product of the USC cinema department in his picture bow, has a major assignment which he dispatches with a certain amount of flair. Yuki Smimoda handles some jiu-jitsu with accomplishment.

Director Richard Thorpe fails to generate the necessary momentum, but he hasn't much of a script to work with. The assists of cameraman Robert Bronner, editor Richard W. Farrell, art directors George W. Davis and Merrill Pye, and composer George Stoll are adequate, but instill no special style or excitement into the production. A routine title tune by Stoll and Stella Unger is sung by The Diamonds. *Tube.*

H. M. S. Defiant
(BRITISH-COLOR)

Drama of the old British Navy; firstrate marquee value: Alec Guinness, Dirk Bogarde and Anthony Quayle along with some tough battle scenes.

London, March 27.

BLC release of a Columbia presentation of a John Brabourne production. Stars Alec Guinness, Dirk Bogarde, Anthony Quayle; features Tom Bell, Maurice Denham, Victor Maddern, Murray Melvin. Directed by Lewis Gilbert. Screenplay, Nigel Kneale, Edmund H. North, from "Mutiny," a novel by Frank Tilsley; camera, Christopher Challis; music, Clifton Parker; editor, Peter Hunt; special effects, Howard Lydecker. At Odeon, Leicester Square, London. Running time, **101 MINS.**
Capt. Crawford .... Alec Guinness
Lieut. Scott-Paget........ Dirk Bogarde
Vizard .... Anthony Quayle
Evans .... Tom Bell
Surgeon Goss .... Maurice Denham
Admiral Jackson.......Walter Fitzgerald
Dawlish .... Victor Maddern
Wagstaffe .... Murray Melvin
Kilpatrick .... Nigel Stock
Wheatley .... Johnny Briggs
Ponsonby .... Richard Carpenter
Sgt. Kneebone .... Bryan Pringle
Mrs. Crawford .... Joy Shelton
Harvey Crawford .... David Robinson

Getting in well ahead of "Mutiny On The Bounty," with which it shares a kindred theme, "H.M.S. Defiant" is a strong naval drama about the days of the Napoleonic wars, enhanced by the strong marquee appeal of Alec Guinness, Dirk Bogarde and Anthony Quayle. There is a firstclass naval battle and some scenes of violence which are perhaps a shade overdone. But mostly it is an intriguing battle of character between two excellent actors, Guinness and Bogarde, and stacks up to a more than worthwhile booking.

Based on Frank Tilsley's novel, "Mutiny," story is of the time of old press gangs. British navy conditions were appalling and it was the mutiny depicted in this pic which did much to give the British naval men a new deal. Guinness plays the skipper of the "Defiant" which, when it sets out to help tackle the Napoleonic fleet, is ruptured by a tussle for power between Guinness and his first lieutenant (Bogarde). Guinness is a humane man, though a stern disciplinarian. Bogarde is a sadist, anxious to jockey Guinness out of position. The captain's midshipman son, who is in the crew, is the pawn between the two, with Bogarde ill-treating him unmercifully to goad Guinness.

Below deck the crew, led by Quayle and Tom Bell, is plotting mutiny against the bad food, stinking living conditions and constant floggings ordered by Bogarde. But it is to be a full scale mutiny co-

ordinated with all the ships in the fleet. However, events bubble up in the "Defiant" and the private mutiny takes place when Guinness is wounded. The film moves to a tough climax with the murder of Bogarde by Bell, but when the "Defiant" saves the British fleet by tackling a French fireship all is set for an ending which gives the men their way.

Though directed fairly slowly by Lewis Gilbert, so that the excitement never comes often enough to a head, it is good rousing stuff, with fine color photography by Christopher Challis and slick artwork and special effects.

Guinness' role does not give this actor scope for his fullest ability. It is a part that could have been played equally effectively perhaps by several other actors, which is not a usual comment about a Guinness performance. But, quietly and sincerely, he presents a figure of considerable interest, and there are at least three scenes where he flashes to his full power. Bogarde's is the more showy portrayal. Lately, his roles appear to have grown in maturity, and this one enhances his reputation.

Quayle makes an impressive appearance as the leader of the rebels, determined and tough, but realizing that there is a right and a wrong way to stage a mutiny, like anything else. Bell, as his right hand man; Maurice Denham, as a drunken ship's doctor; Nigel Stock, as a brutal petty officer; Murray Melvin, Victor Maddern, David Robinson and Walter Fitzgerald are others who stand out in a reliable cast. The women get little of a show, but Joy Shelton, as Guinness' wife, is touching in one short scene with him.

Rich.

Reprieve

Compassionate, but lethargic and mechanical biopic of artist-convict John Resko. Strong cast and exploitability will have to carry b.o. burden.

Hollywood, March 26.

Allied Artists release of A. Ronald Lubin production. Stars Ben Gazzara, Stuart Whitman, Ray Walston, Vincent Price, Rod Steiger, Broderick Crawford, Dodie Stevens, Jack Kruschen, Sammy Davis Jr. Directed by Millard Kaufman. Screenplay, Kaufman, based on John Resko's autobiography; camera, Joseph Biroc; editor, George White; music, Leonard Rosenman; assistant director, Clark Paylow. Reviewed at Academy Awards Theatre, March 26, '62. Running time, **105 MINS.**
John Resko .... Ben Gazzara
Principal Keeper ...... Stuart Whitman
Iggy .... Ray Walston
Carl Carmer .... Vincent Price
Tiptoes .... Rod Steiger
Warden .... Broderick Crawford
Resko's Sister .... Dodie Stevens
Resko's Father .... Jack Kruschen
Wino .... Sammy Davis Jr.
Resko's Mother .... Naomi Stevens
Resko's Wife .... Carmen Phillips
Resko's Daughter .... Susan Silo
Nick .... Timothy Carey
Duke .... Roland LaStarza
Lefty .... Tim Gilson
Storekeeper .... Arthur Malet
Stanley .... Lee Krieger
Gunther .... Myron Healey
Barber .... Josip Elic
Art Teacher .... Jack Albertson
Commissioner .... Robert H. Harris
Con .... Andy Albin
Gallery Man .... Burt Lange
1st Guard .... John Kellogg
2nd Guard .... Adam Williams
3rd Guard .... Robert Christopher
4th Guard .... Warren Kemmerling
5th Guard .... Kreg Martin
6th Guard .... John Close
7th Guard .... Billy Varga
Greer .... Reggie Nalder
Cell Block Guard .... John Dennis

This is Allied Artists fourth

link this year in a chain of non-fiction pictures that has ranged from Eichmann to Rothstein to Hitler. "Reprieve," the story of artist-convict John Resko, is the best of the quartet, due in no small measure to the fact that it is the first of the four to deal with a sympathetic character. However, in spite of its superiority over the preceding threesome, the Millard Kaufman-A. Ronald Lubin production, written and directed by the former and produced by the latter, is not an especially satisfying or gratifying screen work. It will have to rely on its imposing array of players and exploitable topic to make the boxoffice grade.

The quality and impact of a biographical film ordinarily depends upon the depth with which it penetrates into the personality of its subject. In this respect, "Reprieve" fails. Kaufman's portrait of Resko is skin deep and his execution mechanical, something of an oddity considering the fact that the film stems directly from Resko's autobiography, with Resko serving as technical adviser. The screen story covers the period (1931-1949) from Resko's murder of a storekeeper through his regeneration through art in prison to the ultimate commutation of his life sentence and release from the pen. It is a straightforward film treatment, seriously and compassionately drawn but shy the cinematic flair and character insight to arrest or excite an audience. There is, for example, no background provided on Resko, a bothersome shortcoming.

Ben Gazzara's delineation of the title character is firm, persuasive and sympathetic, but his success in the role is abbreviated by the lack of character focus and uncompromising honesty, as written, and dramatic thrust or variety, as directed.

A kind of sub-plot in the film, though not an especially timely one, is the metamorphosis of penal institutions over the two-decade span of the story. As Resko's tale unfolds, the sadistic old guard is seen dissolving in the background, replaced by a more enlightened prison hierarchy. Personification of the latter category, Stuart Whitman does an able job as Resko's most ardent supporter. In the former classification, Rod Steiger and Broderick Crawford etch vigorous cameos. Ray Walston adds a light, comic note as an unstable, unlucky inmate eventually befriended by the hero. Sammy Davis Jr. scores as another cell-mate aided by Resko.

Others capable in important roles are Vincent Price, Dodie Stevens, Jack Kruschen, Naomi Stevens, Carmen Phillips, Susan Silo, Roland LaStarza, Tom Gilson, Arthur Malet, Lee Krieger, Josip Elic and Jack Albertson. Timothy Carey, employing Yogi Bear-like articulation, dashes off a colorful characterization.

Leonard Rosenman's score, mostly in a semi-progressive jazz vein, adds a racy note. Adequate contributions are made by cameraman Joseph Biroc, art director Howard Richmond and editor George White. *Tube.*

The Music Man
(TECHNIRAMA—TECHNICOLOR)

High-powered screen version of long-run hit musical. An audience pleaser with warm American sentimental values.

Warner Bros. release of Morton DaCosta production. Stars Robert Preston, Shirley Jones; features Buddy Hackett, Hermione Gingold, Paul Ford, Pert Kelton, Buffalo Bills. Directed by DaCosta. Screenplay by Marlon Hargrove based on Meredith Willson-Franklin Lacey stage libretto; cameraman, Robert Burks. Editor, William Ziegler; dances, Onna White; arrangements of Willson score, Charles Henderson; conductor, Ray Heindorf. Previewed April 11 at RKO 58th St. Theatre, N.Y. Running time, **151 MINS.**

Harold Hill	Robert Prestone
Marian Paroo	Shirley Jones
Marcellus Washburn	Buddy Hackett
Eulalie Shinn	Hermione Gingold
Mayor Shinn	Paul Ford
Mrs. Paroo	Pert Kelton
Tommy Djilas	Timmy Everett
Zaneeta Shinn	Susan Luckey
Winthrop Paroo	Ronny Howard
Charlie Cowell	Harry Hickox
Constable Locke	Charles Lane
Mrs. Squires	Mary Wickes
Buffalo Bills	Jacey Squires, Olin Britt, Ewart Dunlop, Oliver Hix

Allowing something of slowness at the very start and the necessities of establishing the musical way of telling a story, plus the atmosphere of Iowa in 1912, that's about the only criticism of an otherwise building, punching, handsomely dressed and ultimately endearing super-musical in widescreen and color. "The Music Man" is superior entertainment.

Call this a triumph,' perhaps a classic, of corn, smalltown nostalgia and American love of a parade. Dreamed up in the first instance out of the Iowa memories of Meredith Willson, fashioned into his first legit offering with his long radio musicianship fully manifest therein, the transfer to the screen has been accomplished by Morton DaCosta, as producer-director, with faithful adherence to Willson's, and his own, original work.

DaCosta has some camera ideas of his own, notably the use of the "iris" wipe and split-screen vignettes, unusual in modernday color features, though once a commonplace of the silents, usually credited to D. W. Griffith in monochrome technique. These camera angles are helpful to the producing change of pace in a relatively long unreeling of two-and-a-half hours. Robert Burks' photography is brilliant, the art direction of Paul Groesse strong in Iowa feeling and the editing of William Ziegler undoubtedly a major assist to the sequencing and acceleration.

Willson's score and the musical management generally emerge with an owed debt to conductor Ray Heindorf and his arrangers, Charles Henderson, for the vocals, plus Heindorf, Frank Comstock and Gus Levene for the orchestrations.

DaCosta's use of several of the original Broadway cast players is thoroughly vindicated. Paul Ford is wonderfully fatuous as the bumptious mayor of River City. Pert Kelton shines with warmth and humanity as the heroine's earthy mother, so much so that she would seem a real bet for character development in further films. Miss Kelton shows a style that is seldom seen nowadays, the mark of professionalism from her days as a child performer on the Keith time.

Enriching the environment of the story's era are the Buffalo Bills, also from the show. Willson originally utilized old barbershop hokum as part of the running business between the townspeople and the con man who is out to promote them for band instruments and uniforms. This foursome serves the screen version well. Say the same for a number of experienced troupers in the bit parts, many of them brought west by Da Costa.

But the only choice for the title role, Robert Preston, is the big proof of showmanship in the casting. Warners might have secured bigger screen names but it is impossible to imagine any of them matching Preston's authority, backed by 883 stage performances. His know-how in this film is as close to a tour de force as is likely to be seen during the calendar year of 1962 Not only does he project verve, singing and dancing with a beguiling style of his own creation, but his acting has remarkable plausibility. His con man tactics are just from total conviction.

As scene follows scene the audience is carried along by his characterization and also the utterly charming performance of Shirley Jones, who takes another leap forward, career-wise, with "The Music Man." With the romance in capable hands, and played against the numerous side-incidents and characters the Iowa village attains an incarnation which is, of course, all-essential to audience identification.

Buddy Hackett is directed for modulation and Hermione Gingold in the same vein. This is wise, since either role could have gotten laughs at the expense of story and pace. Miss Gingold has several scoring lines and shines in antique styling. Hackett is sure to amuse the public.

The little boy with the stammer and the bashful ways is a small gem as impersonated by Ronny Howard. He stays safely away from precociousness in all his scenes. Another firstclass job af acting is to be credited the tipoff rival travelling salesman role in the hands, and the excellent rhetoric, of Harry Hickox.

The choreography of Onna White, with Tom Panko's aid, has zing and period humor. It rates along with the other component values as an imaginative contribution.

A trade reviewer will not end without speculating as to whether such a thoroughly native America tunepic as this one will go over with Europeans who have been habitually cold to Hollywood musicals, though "West Side Story" is currently reported breaking the resistance. On the whole this writer would hazard the guess that "The Music Man" can travel quite widely on its basics—pace, bounce and innocent merriment.

Land.

Samar
(COLOR)

Adventure meller filmed in Philippines. Colorful production values offset by skimpy characterizations. Sound companion with WB's "House of Women."

Hollywood, April 4.

Warner Bros. release of George Montgomery production. Stars Montgomery, Gilbert Roland, Ziva Rodann, Joan O'Brien, Nico Minardos. Directed by Montgomery. Screenplay, Ferde Grofe Jr., Montgomery; camera (Technicolor), Emmanuel Rojas; editor, Walter Thompson; music, Harry Zimmerman; assistant directors, Mario Barri, Vicente Nayve, Jairo Mullen. Reviewed at the studio, April 4, '62. Running time, **89 MINS.**

Here is a film for the vicarious he-man, a crimson-spattered adventure melodrama that is approximately as subtle as a right to the jaw. Actually, a considerable amount of production energy and ingenuity obviously went into the making of "Samar," but within its Atlasian physique lurks a 97-pound weakling of skin-deep melodramatization. The film, produced, directed and co-written by George Montgomery, is an improvement over his last Philippines-based feature, "The Steel Claw," but running mate status opposite Warner Bros.' "House of Women" should amply fulfill its commercial potential.

The exodus of the inhabitants of a colony of Filipino political prisoners to escape the tyranny of Spanish rule in 1870 is the core of the scenario by Montgomery and Ferde Grofe Jr. Leader of the movement from the penal colony on the coast of the isle of Samar to a rich, fertile valley in the interior is the warden of the colony (Gilbert Roland), assisted by a soldier of fortune and part-time medic (Montgomery). Enroute to freedom, the refugees engage in several bloody skirmishes with jungle headhunters, ultimately necessitating battlefield amputation of Roland's arm in a sequence that is not for the squeamish customer. The screenplay is weak on characterization, but the production is strong on action. Not much concern is aroused over the fate of the characters, but there are other diversions, chiefly pictorial, to keep one from worrying about the merits of the story.

Montgomery gives a masculine performance, relying mostly on biceps and bare chest for character suggestion. Roland is capable. Ziva Rodann and Joan O'Brien supply romantic interest, mostly irrelevant. Nico Minardos has a key role, which he handles with spirit, and Mario Barri is helpful in support.

More intimate passages tend to be shallow and awkward, as helmed by the busy Montgomery, but he has whipped up a pretty handsome and impressive production, lensed with a noticeable appreciation of and flair for color and composition by Emmanuel Rojas.

Tube.

The Man Who Shot Liberty Valance

Generally arresting John Ford western, though hampered by several story flaws. Has the marquee weight and engaging style for good b.o.

Hollywood, March 23.

Paramount release of Willis Goldbeck production. Stars James Stewart, John Wayne; features Vera Miles, Lee Marvin, Edmond O'Brien, Andy Devine, Ken Murray. Directed by John Ford. Screenplay, James Warner Bellah, Goldbeck, based on story by Dorothy M. Johnson; camera, William H. Clothier; editor, Otho Lovering; music, Cyril Mockridge; assistant director, Wingate Smith. Reviewed at Hollywood Paramount Theatre, March 23, '62. Running time, **123 MINS.**

Ranson Stoddard	James Stewart
Tom Doniphon	John Wayne
Hallie Stoddard	Vera Miles
Liberty Valance	Lee Marvin
Dutton Peabody	Edmond O'Brien
Link Apleyard	Andy Devine
Dr. Willoughby	Ken Murray
Starbuckle	John Carradine
Nora	Jeanette Nolan
Peter	John Qualen
Jason Tully	Willis Bouchey
Maxwell Scott	Carleton Young
Pompey	Woody Strode
Amos Carruthers	Denver Pyle
Floyd	Strother Martin
Reese	Lee Van Cleef
Handy Strong	Robert F. Simon
Ben Carruthers	O. Z. Whitehead
Mayor Winder	Paul Birch
Hasbrouck	Joseph Hoover

"The Man Who Shot Liberty Valance" is an entertaining and emotionally involving western. Fortified with the big established marquee names of James Stewart and John Wayne plus infectiously lowbrow touches that bring homey warmth and irresistibly obvious humor to a John Ford picture, the Willie Goldbeck production and Paramount entry has the earmarks for good boxoffice. Yet, while it is both an enjoyable film and a promising contender, it falls distinctly shy of its innate story potential, and this will bother the more discerning filmgoer.

There was a time when "Liberty Valance" might have been considered something of a classic of the screen western genre. But these are leaner, more demanding years for the hoss opera. The American public is both saturated with westerns (horseback heroes have been climbing out of the living room woodwork for over five years) and reasonably, though perhaps reluctantly, enlightened about what really went on in the early west. A certain amount of sophistication has set in, and "Valance," for the most part, defies this element of informed discrimination. As a result, the sharp customer may be diverted by what he sees and moved by what Ford has made him feel, but ultimately he will find the story fanciful and unconvincing.

Equally damaging to the total impact of the picture is that Ford and its writers have somewhat overplayed their hands. They have taken a disarmingly simple and affecting premise, developed it with craft and skill to a natural point of conclusion, and then have proceeded to run it into the ground, destroying the simplicity and intimacy for which they have striven.

The long screenplay by James Warner Bellah and producer Goldbeck from a short story by Dorothy M. Johnson has Stewart as a dude eastern attorney forging idealistically into lawless western territory, where he is promptly greeted by the sadistic, though sponsored, brutality of "Valance" (Lee Marvin), a killer who owes his allegiance to the vested interests of wealthy cattlemen opposed to statehood, law and order. Logic whispers that a varmint without a single redeeming virtue such as "Valance" no doubt would have been removed from scene, but in the film he is tolerated with an uncanny degree of patience until

finally he goads Stewart into the showdown.

The audience instantly senses that Stewart did not fire the fatal shot that gives him his reputation and destines him for political fame. Because the audience knows that: (1) Stewart can't hit a paint can at 15 paces, (2) Stewart has won the heart of the sweetheart of John Wayne, best shot in the territory and a man of few words but heroically alert and forthright actions. Had the body of the film (it is told in flashback) ended at this maximum point, it would have been a taut, cumulative study of the irony of heroic destiny. But the film's creators have refused to give the audience the benefit of the doubt. The picture concludes with 20 minutes of condescending, melodramatic, anti-climactic strokes. What should have been left to enthrall the imagination is spelled out until there is nothing left to savor or discuss.

Stewart and Wayne do what comes naturally in an engagingly effortless manner. Vera Miles, a first-class actress, is consistently effective. Marvin is evil as they come. Andy Devine etches a contagious portrait of a sheepish marshal. Ken Murray gets in one or two good licks as a coroner-physician.

There is a portrayal of great strength and dignity by Woody Strode, and satisfactory support by John Carradine, Jeanette Nolan, John Qualen, Willis Bouchey, Carleton Young, Denver Pyle, Strother Martin and Lee Van Cleef, among others. But the most memorable characterization in the film is that of Edmond O'Brien as a tippling newspaper editor deeply proud of his profession. When "best supporting" candidates are gleaned from this year's crop, he should be high on the list.

William H. Clothier's careful camerawork is an asset to the production; likewise the art direction by Hal Pereira and Eddie Imazu, although at times it seems a trifle confined. Editing by Otho Lovering is competent, but some 20 minutes less film, as noted, would have made this a better film. Cyril Mockridge's score instills a plaintive, wistful, cowboy flavor.

Tube.

Don't Knock The Twist

Sequel to "Twist Around the Clock." Same formula, and, with twist still hot commodity, looms satisfactory b.o. candidate for same audience.

Hollywood, April 2.

Columbia Pictures release of Sam Katzman production. Stars Chubby Checker, Gene Chandler, Vic Dana, Linda Scott, Carroll Bros., The Dovells. Directed by Oscar Rudolph. Screenplay, James B. Gordon; camera, Gordon Avil; editor, Jerome Thoms; music (supervisor), Fred Karger; assistant director, Sam Nelson. Reviewed at the studio, April 2, '62. Running time, 86 MINS.

Chubby Checker .... Himself
Duke of Earl .... Gene Chandler
Vic Dana .... Himself
Linda Scott .... Herself
Carroll Bros. .... Themselves
The Dovells .... Themselves
Ted Haver .... Lang Jeffries
Dulcie Corbin .... Mari Blanchard
Madge Albright .... Georgine Darcy
Billy Albright .... Stephen Preston
Mrs. Morrison .... Barbara Morrison
Dressmaker .... Nydia Westmna
Joe Albright .... James Chandler
Ruth Emerson .... Elizabeth Harrower
Mrs. Kay .... Hortense Petra
Herb Walcott .... Frank Albertson
Fashion Editor .... Viola Harris
Frank Emerson .... Peter Dawson
Director .... Dave Lanfield
Mr. Fullerton .... Tim Sullivan
Reporter .... Ralph Montgomery

If at first you do succeed, try, try again. That appears to be the rational method of producer Sam Katzman, filmdom's fastest man with a fad. Having parlayed the rock 'n' roll into two enterprising filmic ventures several years back when r-and-r was the rage, Katzman has now duplicated the opportunistic two-play feat for Columbia with their sequel to his successful "Twist Around the Clock."

"Don't Knock the Twist" may not be the definitive work in the Twist prism, in fact it may be to the cinema what St. Vitus Dance is to terpsichore. Still, the screen marketplace is less cluttered now with Twistianity than it was at the time of the first release, and the step is still alive and writhing. The audience that clasped "Clock" to its bosom (or pelvis girdle) should be about ripe to clasp again.

Chubby Checker, the acknowledged "King of the Twist," but something less than regal in the thespic strata, repeats his starring role for Katzman's sequel, and has more to do this time. A slim plot about preparations for a television twist spec that are almost thwarted by jealousies arising out of a romantic triangle provides the frivolous base for a series of musical specialties including some half dozen by Checker, one by Vic Dana, a pair by the frenetic Dovells, a shifty swifty by the Carroll Bros., a singleton by Linda Scott, and a showy solo by Gene "Duke of Earl" Chandler.

James B. Gordon's screenplay is appropriately skippy, being mostly a linking secondary issue. Oscar Rudolph's direction is adequate under the helter-skelter circumstances. Hal Belfer's choreography is twistably sound and hip in individual cases, but the ensemble dancefloor gyrations seem a bit disorganized and amateurish, apparently intended that way as an impression of how the general public tackles it. Gordon Avil's camera is active and observant of nuances of the performing lower anatomy, particularly on the distaff side. Jerome Thoms' editing brings the film a sensibly rapid tempo. It appears as if George Van Marter's sets for Katzman's initial twist-flick were never struck in anticipation of the follow-up. Much of Don Ament's new production design is quite similar.

Lang Jeffries, Mari Blanchard and Georgine Darcy handle the romantic issue satisfactorily. Other prominent parties are Stephen Preston, Barbara Morrison, Nydia Westman, James Chandler, Elizabeth Harrower, Hortense Petra, Frank Albertson and Viola Harris.

Tube.

House Of Women

Prison meller dealing with lovable lady cons and their walled-in sprigs. Half of serviceable WB exploitation package.

Hollywood, April 4.

Warner Bros. release of Bryan Foy production. Stars Shirley Knight, Andrew Duggan, Constance Ford; features Barbara Nichols, Margaret Hayes, Jeanne Cooper. Directed by Walter Doniger. Screenplay, Crane Wilbur; camera, Harold Stine; editor, Leo H. Shreve; music, Howard Jackson; assistant director, Russell Saunders. Reviewed at the studio, April 4, '62. Running time, 85 MINS.

Erica .... Shirley Knight
Warden Cole .... Andrew Duggan
Sophie Brice .... Constance Ford
Candy Kane .... Barbara Nichols
Zoe Stoughton ....Margaret Hayes
Helen Jennings .... Jeanne Cooper
Mrs. Hunter .... Virginia Gregg
Doris .... Patricia Huston
Doctor .... Jason Evers
Addie Gates .... Jennifer Howard
Clemens .... Caroline Richter
Jackie .... Gayla Graves
Aggie .... Colette Jackson
Mrs. Stevens .... Jacqueline Scott
Mr. Dunn .... Paul Lambert
Nan .... Carolyn Komant
Sarah .... Virginia Capers
Tommy (minor) .... Drew Vigen
Robin (minor) .... Laurie Sheridan

Warner Bros. has what shapes up as a moderately serviceable exploitation package in "House of Women" and "Camar" (see adjoining review), which will be paired in release. It's a twin bill for people who prefer emotional sensations over cerebral stimulation in their cinema pursuits. As such, the pairing should prove advantageous to both features, neither of which has sufficient merit to carry an exhibition load alone or aid, in support, the prospects of any distinguished attraction.

Troublesome matters of bosom buddies in a distaff prison are illustrated in Bryan Foy's production of Crane Wilbur's "House of Women." Only new wrinkle in a film liberally crammed with the cliches of the prison pic is the residential presence in the pen of the offsprings of the lady inmates.

The heroine (Shirley Knight) has been sentenced to five years for being accessory to an armed robbery, a pretty stiff sentence considering: (1) it's her first offense, (2) she's pregnant, (3) she claims she was an unwitting participant, (4) she's about the sweetest thing since Little Mary Sunshine. So sweet she is that she even melts the heart of a sadistic, vengeful warden (Andrew Duggan), who believes penal supervision is a numbers game. How Duggan ever got the job is one of the mysteries of a very mysterious picture in which the inmates generally seem far more sensible, likable and well-adjusted than the staff. At any rate, the unlikely romance of pen-pals Knight and Duggan soon dissolve over his selfish measures in a parole board meeting, followed by the usual riot in cell block and the ultimate release of mother and reunion with child, who can spend its first three years in the pokey with parent.

Miss Knight gives a fragile, pure-as-the-driven-snow portrayal. Duggan is a composed, distracted villain. Among the flashier inmates, or cell block-busters, are Constance Ford as an anguished mother and Barbara Nichols as an ex-stripper with heart of gold, turned contented prisoner (she doesn't want out). Jason Evers is strong as the prison medic, and other prominent parties are Margaret Hayes, Jeanne Cooper, Virginia Gregg, Patricia Huston, Jennifer Howard and Paul Lambert.

Walter Doniger's direction tends to be rather stilted and theatrical. Reliable assists are given the production by cameraman Harold Stine, are director Leo K. Kuter, editor Leo H. Shreve and composer [illegible]

The Magic Sword
(COLOR)

St. George meets dragon in razzledazzle fantasy for kiddies.

Hollywood, April 6.

United Artists release of Bert I. Gordon production. Stars Basil Rathbone, Estelle Winwood, Gary Lockwood, Anne Helm. Directed by Gordon. Screenplay, Bernard Schoenfeld, from story by Gordon; camera (Eastman), Paul Vogel; editor, Harry Gerstad; music, Richard Markowitz; assistant director, Herb Mendelson. Reviewed at Academy Awards Theatre, April 6, '62. Running time, 80 MINS.

Lodac .... Basil Rathbone
Sybil .... Estelle Winwood
Princess Helene .... Anne Helm
St. George .... Gary Lockwood
Sir Branton .... Liam Sullivan
Sir Patrick .... John Mauldin
Sir Dennis .... Jacques Gallo
Sir Ulrich .... Leroy Johnson
Sir Pedro .... David Cross
Sir James .... Angus Duncan
Sir Anthony .... Taldo Kenyon
Hag & Intruder.......... Maila Nurmi
Ogre .... Jack Kosslyn
Anne .... Lorrie Richards
Princess Laura .... Ann Graves
Princess Grace .... Marlene Callahan
King .... Merritt Stone
French Gild .... Danielle de Metz
Siamese Twins...Nick & Paul Ben Tempi
Dwarf No. 1...................Ted Finn
Dwarf No. 2 .... Angelo Rossito
Pinhead No. 1.................Dick Kiel

The fun house in Coney Island has nothing on Bert I. Gordon's production "The Magic Sword," a terror-fantasy loosely based on the legend of "St. George and the Dragon." Replete with painstaking special effects to dazzle the eyes and activate the imaginations of younger children, the United Artists release should get its biggest play as part of dual attractions aimed at the kiddie market. Adults who tag along or happen in should find the cinema effects impressive enough for them to tolerate the story, which, if one maintains the right attitude, can prove sporadically amusing and sufficiently diverting.

Actually, had producer-director Gordon and scenarist Bernard Schoenfeld so chosen, they might have cooked up a pretty ingenious tongue-in-cheek approach to the venerable tale, so that even the more sophisticated and discriminating of adults might have discovered more than the average share of screen jollies, with no significant loss of tot appeal. But Gordon and staff have chosen to remain preoccupied with cinematic technique, thus leaving their product to be inherited almost exclusively by kiddie patrons. Adults will simply have to manufacture the latent spoofery in their minds.

The acting, as it should be, is broad and exaggerated in style. Basil Rathbone, in his accomplished villainous tradition, enacts the wicked "Lodac," whose idea of daily repost for his hungry dragon is a dish of princess pie. Estelle Winwood is amiable as a cheery sorcerers. Gary Lockwood amply dashing as St. George, Anne Helm attractive as the princess in distress. Various knights, ogres, hags, dwarfs, pinheads and assorted royalty are played capably by a spirited cast, with Liam Sullivan noteworthy as a treacherous, eyebrow-cocking VIP in this bubbling fantasyland. John Mauldin and Jacques Gallo are prominent participants.

The ingenuity absent in the story is made up for in the production, which is a credit to Gordon's flair for special visual effects, his forte. Skillfully contributing to the trickery and imagery are cameraman Paul Vogel, art director Franz Bachelin, editor Harry Gerstad, set

decorator George M. Nelson and mechanical special effects expert Milt Rice, each effort an integral and vital part of the fantasy created. James Brock's wild sound effects and Richard Markowitz's score round out a colorful production. *Tube.*

Lila
(GERMAN-SWEDISH; COLOR)

Hollywood, April 4.

Parade release of Rhombus-Sandrew production (Riley Jackson-Robert Patrick presentation). With Erika Remberg, Joachim Hansen, Birger Malmsten, Edvin Adolphson. Alfred Maurstad, Ann-Marie Gylleen, Iso Quensel. Screenplay, Adolph Schutz. Rolf Husberg, based on novel by J. A. Friis; camera (Eastman), Sven Nykvist; editor, Lennard Wallen; music, Lars-Erik Larsson. Reviewed at Goldwyn Studios, March 30, '62. Running time, **90 MINS.**

Lila	Erika Remberg
Anders	Joachim Hansen
Mellet	Birger Malmsten
Aslak	Edvin Adolphson
Jompa	Alfred Maurstad
Inger	Ann-Marie Gyllen
Elli	Isa Quensel

Lapland is the novel and intriguing setting for this otherwise shopworn romantic drama of a spirited maiden torn between two cultures—the modern and the primitive. The film, a Rhombus-Sandrew production of German-Swedish origin, will have a limited art house appeal in U.S. arising [illegible] geographic [illegible] values and photographic beauty. But customers are apt to find the story rather tedious, unrewarding going. Conversely, any general market notions of a secondary, supporting nature "Lila" may be entertaining must be considered dubious owing to the picture's total lack of marquee allure or instant identification.

The experience of witnessing "Lila" is roughly tantamount to running across a National Geographic article in an issue of True Romances, or vice versa. The Adolph Schutz-Rolf Husberg screenplay, based on a novel by J. A. Friis, relates the story of a maiden who, in infancy, is discovered by a childless Lapland couple after a harrowing experience in which her settler parents are killed by marauding wolves. Raised by the Laplanders and betrothed to a wealthy member of the itinerant tribe, she ultimately falls in love with a young man of the modern world and, after many setbacks, becomes his and returns to the world to which she really belongs.

The film offers audiences a fascinating glimpse at the Lapland way of life—the primitive customs, the tight-lipped stance toward the advancing and intruding outside world and the physically trying but scenically breathtaking environment in which they live. Eastman Color bathes the screen in the brilliant hues of Lapland apparel and picturesque country. Sven Nykvist's camera catches it all appreciatively and Lars-Erik Larsson's score is fittingly pastoral.

The picture is dubbed, and performances suffer accordingly. Erika Remberg is attractive in the title role. Other agreeable participants in this slight, but nonetheless beguiling confection from abroad are Joachim Hansen, Birger Malmsten, Edvin Adolphson, Alfred Maurstad, Ann-Marie Gyllen and Isa Quensel. *Tube.*

Stork Talk
(BRITISH)

Coy comedy offers more smirks than yocks; moderate dualer.

London, April 3.

Unifilms release and production of a Lionel Clyne (Bruce Newbury) presentation. Stars Tony Britton, Anne Haywood, John Turner; features Daphne Anderson, Barie Kean, Gladys Henson, John Sharp, Nicole Perrault. Directed by Michael Forlong. Screenplay, Donald Ford from Gloria Russell's original play; extra dialog, Peter Rosser, William Hepper; camera, Norman Warwick; editor, John Jympson. Previewed at Studio One, London. Running time, **97 MINS.**

Dr. Paul Vernon	Tony Britton
Lisa Vernon	Anne Heywood
Dr. Robert Sterne	John Turner
Tina Money	Nicole Perrault
Dr. Mary Willis	Daphne Anderson
Mrs. Webster	Marie Kean
Papa Pierre	John Sharp

Though smoothly mounted and conscientiously acted, this would-be sophisticated comedy fails to get off the ground, mainly because of a limp screenplay. Director Michael Forlong has been unable to whip it into shape, and the pic comes out as coyly facetious rather than funny. The yarn takes place mainly in a maternity clinic. Hero (Tony Britton) is a gynaecologist, estranged from his wife. During her absence he gets slightly loaded at a party, picks up a French girl and finds to his dismay that she has spent the night in the other bed in his room.

He employs her as a servant in his house. Then his wife, pregnant, returns to him. Britton's problem is that both his wife and the French girl are pregnant. A scheme is cooked up whereby the two babies shall be registered as the wife's twins, but this unethical plot calls for some hasty re-thinking when both women give birth to twins. The dubious situation is ironed out when the French femme falls for one of his doctor colleagues, and they get married.

It's a distasteful idea in the first place, and it would have needed far sharper and wittier treatment to keep it alive. Britton plays the lead suavely but without much conviction. John Turner is a useful support as the gynaecologist colleague. Annie Heywood's performance as the wife does little to enchance her reputation, but Nicole Perrault, as the French girl, has definite appeal.

Among the lesser roles, Gladys Henson as a shrewish matron, Daphne Anderson and Marie Kean provide worthwhile assistance. Technically, there is some useful work by camera boss Norman Warwick. But the editing of John Jympson is erratic and the Mike Sammes Singers dutifully put over a fairly nauseating credit title [illegible]

Twice Round The Daffodils
(BRITISH)

Easygoing adaptation of a moderately successful West End play. Rather more slapstick than necessary, but still genial entertainment for understanding audiences.

London, April 3.

Anglo Amalgamated release of a Peter Rogers' production. Stars Juliet Mills, Donald Sinden, Donald Houston, Kenneth Williams, Ronald Lewis. Directed by Gerald Thomas. Screenplay, Norman Hudis, from play, "Ring for Catty," by Patrick Gargill & Jack Beale; camera, Alan Hume; editor, John Shirley; music, Bruce Montgomery. At Plaza Theatre, London. Running time, **89 MINS.**

Catty	Juliet Mills
Ian Richards	Donald Sinden
John Rhodes	Donald Houston
Bob White	Ronald Lewis
Henry Halfpenny	Kenneth Williams
Chris Walker	Andrew Ray
George Logg	Lance Percival
Harriet	Joan Sims
Janet	Jill Ireland
Joyce	Nanette Newman
Dorothy	Amanda Reiss
Dora	Sheila Hancock
Matron	Renee Houston
Mrs. Rhodes	Mary Powell

The "Carry On" team of Peter Rogers and Gerald Thomas bought the West End play, "Ring for Catty," a few years back but decided that life in a tuberculosis sanatorium was then a trick subject for a film. So they used some of its ideas in a successful film farce, "Carry On Nurse." Now they have had another go at it. "Twice Round the Daffodils" (all patients have to walk twice round a daffodil bed before they are apparently regarded as cured) still leans over heavily on "Carry On" slapstick, but does have a rather more serious and romantic undertone. Film could well stack up as a b.o. winner among undemanding patrons.

A shrewd amount of predictable situations are employed such as the dragon of a matron, a pretty nurse losing her skirt and a number of bedpan gags. The pic relies considerably on slick cameo performances from several proven farceurs. It also succeeds in making several characters more plausible than in the record "Carry On" series.

Thomas' direction and the screenplay by Norman Hudis give full scope to the cast. They are mainly stock characters. There is Donald Houston, as the grouch who does not believe he is ill; Kenneth Williams, in his usual performance as a mincing chess addict; Donald Sinden, as an RAF pilot with a roving eye for the dames, and Renee Houston as the tough matron. There are some other interesting characters, notably Lance Percival, as a not so wooden rural bumpkin; Andrew Ray, as a young orphan with poetic inclinations; and Ronald Lewis as the most balanced of all the patients who doesn't look very ill at all.

Juliet Mills plays the nurse, Catty, who falls for Lewis and does it with competence, if not inspiration. Jill Ireland and Amanda Reiss make delectable nurses.

Thomas' direction is sure and Alan Hume has done a satisfactory job with his lensing. *Rich.*

Go To Blazes
(BRITISH-COLOR)

Happy-go-lucky comedy with some slick performances; lacks pace, but still okay for amiable yockery.

London, April 3.

Warner-Pathe release of Associated British Film (Kenneth Harper) production. Stars Dave King, Robert Morley, Daniel Massey, Dennis Price. Directed by Michael Truman. Screenplay by Patrick Campbell, Vivienne Knight from original story and adaptation by Peter Myers, Ronald Cass; camera, Erwin Hillier; editor, Richard Best; music, John Addison. Previewed at Corner Theatre, London. Running time, **84 MINS.**

Bernard	Dave King
Arson Eddie	Robert Morley
Harry	Daniel Massey
Withers	Dennis Price
Colette	Coral Browne
Alfie	Norman Rossington
Chantal	Maggie Smith
Salesman	Miles Malleson
Scrap Dealer	Wilfred Lawson
Sergeant	David Lodge
Chief Fire Officer	John Welsh
Judge	Finlay Currie
Pipe Smoker	James Hayter

With less lingering on certain sequences and a few more comedy situations pumped into the screenplay, "Go To Blazes" could have set the boxoffice afire. As it is, the pic creates an amiable comedy without measuring up to its potential. There are too many implausibilities which overstep farcical license and these might have been ironed out.

An assorted trio of smalltime crooks are constantly frustrated by an inability to get away after they've grabbed. Their latest coup is foiled because their car is held up to give the right of way to a fire engine. Languishing in the cooler they hit on an idea and when they are released, they acquire a secondhand fire engine with which to launch their robberies. The stunt goes haywire at first attempt because, inevitably, they run into a real fire and are unable to carry on.

Undaunted, they hire a dedicated fire chief, who has been tossed out of the brigade for shady arson dealings, and he turns them into trained fire fighters. Then, with the help of a professional fire raiser, they stage a fire as cover at a dress salon next to a bank they plan to rob.

Of course, that goes wrong too. There is a lot of fun extracted from the rigorous training routine and from the actual disastrous bank robbery. There are also some amusing bits of by-play. But it is all too leisurely to cause anything but smiles.

However, despite its weaknesses, there is some good camerawork by Erwin Millier and sound direction by Michael Truman. Where the pic really scores is in its cast. Outstanding are Robert Morley, as the man with a passion for arson, and Dennis Price, as the ex-fireman with a record. Both are well observed comedy performances and they are aided, better than the other thesps, by the dialog writers. Dave King, previously best known as a tv comic, shows signs of possibilities as a straignt actor as the leader of the three crooks. The other are Norman Rossington and Daniel Massey and both do marvels to this yarn. The femme side is less served. Two decorative actresses, Coral Browne and Maggie Smith, have the leading distaff roles but they are sketchily written roles that offer neither actress much scope. *Rich.*

Sept. Peches Capital
(The Seven Cardinal Sins)
(FRENCH-DYALISCOPE)

Paris, April 3.

Pathe release of Films Gibe-Franco London Films-Titanus production. With Jacques Charrier, Jean-Claude Brialy, Jean-Pierre Cassel, Claude Rich, Dany Saval, Claude Brasseur, Eddie Constantine, Micheline Presle. Laurent Terzieff, Jean-Louis Trintign:nt. Jean Desailly, Marina Vlady, Sami Frey, Jean-Pierre Aumont, Marie-Jose Nat, Pierrette Pradier. Directed by Claude Chabrol, Edouard Malinaro, Jean-Luc Godard, Jacques Demy, Roger Vadim, Philippe De Broca, Sylvain Dhomme. Screenplay, "Avarice," by Felecien Marceau, "Envy," Claude Mauriac; "Sloth," God rd; "Lust," Roger

Peyrefitte,, Demy; "Pride," Marceau, "Gluttony," Daniel Boulanger; "Anger," Eugene Ionesco; camera, Jean Rabier, Louis Miaille, Henri Decae, Jean Penzer; editor, Jacques Gaillard, Jacques Feyte. At the Paris, Paris. Running time, 110 MINS.

Antoine	Jacques Charrier
Suzon	Daniele Barraud
Rosette	Dany Saval
Riri	Claude Brasseur
Eddie	Eddie Constantine
Nicole	Nicole Mirel
Bernard	Laurent Terzieff
Paul	Jean-Louis Trintignant
Valentin	Georges Wilson
Catherine	Marina Vlady
Husband	Jean-Pierre Aumont
Lover	Sami Frey
Wife	Marie-Jose Nat

After a flock of oldtime film directors worked on the sketch pic, "Frenchwoman and Love," the New Wavers get their chance with this episodic film entry. The newcomers get the nod with a more inventive group of filmic chapters full of tasteful nudity and witty, tongue-in-cheek looks at human foibles. All of which makes this an exploitable item with okay chances in the foreign field.

A number of top names are used in bit parts. Sketches are naturally short on characterization but have the unifying theme of the seven deadly sins around which to weave little illustrative fables. There is enough wit and eye-appeal to keep the vehicle from lagging. Added to this are good technical aspects and enough diversity, via the different directors, to keep it perking along.

The bit on lust, directed by Jacques Demy, emerges one of the most stylish, with two Left Bankish types discussing the same, and one seeing women around him nude. The other reminisces about his childhood. Neatly paced, with clever special effects of a lustfull hell, this is a fine interlude.

Claude Chabrol's entry on avarice spins a well-known bit about a joy girl and a student who has won a raffle for her. Chabrol has given this zest and comedic value.

Roger Vadim donates a slickly mounted sequence on an adulterous wife who leaves her lover in the lurch when she finds her supposedly faithful husband has been cheating on her. Philippe De Broca's look at gulttony, has perhaps the most bite.

Jean-Luc Godard's "sloth" has a freewheeling feel. It depicts a film star who is too lazy to take advantage of a willing starlet. Edouard Molinaro's skit about envy has a little maid winning a rich man away from a film star. This one lacks the incisiveness of the others. Weakest of the lot is possibly playwright Eugene Ionesco's anger skit which has a fly in a husband's soup leading to a fight that catches on and spreads to the blowing up of the world. The comedics seem forced in this.

In short, this has enough Rabelaisian humor and sly looks at human weaknesses to pass muster without any undue censorship problems. Most of the players acquit themselves well in their small roles, with Georges Wilson as the overeater; Daniele Barraud, as the stingy courtesan; Marina Vlady, as the adulterous wife; and Eddie Constantine, as the lazy film star, outstanding. Joe Levine already has this set for the U.S. *Mosk.*

Lemmy Pour Les Dames
(Lemmy For These Girls)
(FRENCH-DYALISCOPE)

Paris, April 3.

Prodis release of CICC production. Stars Eddie Constantine; features Francoise Brion, Claudine Coster, Eliane D'Almeida, Jacques Berthier. Directed by Bernard Borderie. Screenplay, Marc-Gilbert Sauvajon, Borderie from novel by Peter Cheney; camera, Armand Thirard; editor, Christian Gaudin. At Balazac, Paris. Running time, 90 MINS.

Lemmy	Eddie Constantine
Sophie	Eliane D'Almeida
Francoise	Claudine Coster
Nollet	Jacques Berthier
Girl	Francoise Brion

Eddie Constantine is now a staple and his pix rarely hold surprises. This Yank actor, now a star here, again essays a hard-drinking Yank G-Man who gets his way with girls, is invincible in fisticuffs, and solves all. This one is easygoing but somewhat flabby in direction and story, with mainly local chances in store via the Constantine name.

Here he is on vacation and gets mixed up in the murder of a girl. It seems five girls have been blackmailed for a youthful mistake and are forced to turn secrets (their husbands happen to be government people in various Western nations), over to some Eastern agent.

Constantine solves it all after the usual fights. He is his phlegmatic, vulgar self who is basically a sort of knight at heart. The fights are well done for a change but this slogs along with some lifts from time to time but sans the snap, edge and suspense to make it more than a routine entry. Technical credits are passable. *Mosk.*

The Sorrows of Lenka
(Trapeni)
(CZECHOSLOVAKIAN)

Mar Del Plata, April 3.

Czechoslovakian Film production. Features Uavel Bartl, M. Bradac, Vaclav Fiser, Zdenek Jarolim, Zora Jirakova, Vaclav Korn, Jorge Kotrbova, Rudolf Krulis, Zdenek Mika, D. Neumanova. Directed by Karel Kachyna. Screenplay, Kachyna, based on story by Jan Prochazka; camera, Josef Illik; editor, J. Chaloupek. At Mar Del Plata Film Fest. Running time, 140 MINS.

The Czech film industry can be proud of this charming, deceptively simple tale of a little country girl and her affection for a misunderstood (and therefore mean to everyone else) horse. In outline, "Lenka" could hardly be more corny, but as written and directed by Karel Kachyna it has a clean clarity that only talented, sophisticated filmmakers know how to bring off. The pic might be effectively shortened and easily dubbed (there is a minimum of talk) for limited Stateside release. It's devoid of propaganda and kids would love it. So would some oldsters, if they can overlook the tendency, usual in such pictures, to make the animals more intelligent than some of the humans.

The main highlight of the film is the delightfully sensitive performance of Jorge Kotrbova as the heroine of the title. Miss Kotrbova, who must just be starting her teens, is vastly affecting as a little girl whose adolescent confusions in an adult world are paralleled in those she sees faced by the horse, kept by the meantem-

---

pered farmer next door. While the relations of girl-to-horse may be over-romanticized, there is a direct and amusing honesty in the picture of family relations.

All technical credits, especially the camerawork of Josef Illik, are excellent. *Anby.*

Kermis In De Regen
(Fair In the Rain)

Amsterdam, April 3.

Polygoon-Profilti Productie 1962. Director, Kees Brusse. Script, Kees Brusse, Mieke Verstraete, Guus Verstraete, adapted from novel by Joop van den Broek. Music, Cor Lemaire. Camera, Huib de Ru. With Guido de Moor, Ko van Dijk, Mieke Varstraete, Andre Domburg, Guus Verstraete, Kees Brusse. At the City Theatre, Amsterdam. Running time, 96 MINS.

Slowly paced, incoherently told, "Fair in the Rain" is first Dutch feature film to be produced in a year. Directed by actor Kees Brusse, making his debut in that capacity, story concerns provincial bank robbery and simultaneously, killing of girl, only witness to a car robbery.

As presented tale is shy on suspense and characterization. Though actors are well cast and handled, it is a shaky debut for Brusse, who is also responsible for scenario. Prospects for home market should be o.k., with maybe export possibilities to Scandinavia and Germany. Otherwise little playoff internationally. *Saal.*

Malefices
(Sorcery)
(FRENCH-DYALISCOPE)

Paris, April 3.

Paramount release of SNEG-Marianne production. Stars Juliette Greco, Jean-Marc Bory, Liselotte Pulver; features Mathe Mansoura, Jacques Decqmine. Directed by Henri Decoin. Screenplay, Claude Accursi, Albert Husson, Decoin from novel by Boileau-Narcejac; camera, Marcel Grignon; editor, Robert Isnardon. At Elysees, Paris. Running time, 105 MINS.

Myriam	Juliette Greco
Francois	Jean-Marc Bory
Catherine	Lisalotte Pulver
Ronga	Mathe Mansoura
Vial	Jacques Dacqmine

A would-be suspense pic, with undertones of suggested supernatural aspects, this does not quite come off. Direction lags without the mood, characterization or atmosphere to make this anything but a lower-case dualer entry. Theme and the Juliette Greco name could help for playoff use.

A veterinarian is called to care for a woman's leopard in a small French town. The woman, Miss Greco, is from Africa and wants only to go back. Love blooms between her and the vet, but his wife begins to be prone to accidents. He thinks that Miss Greco is doing it and lets her drown in an auto accident.

He turns himself into the police for letting her drown. Miss Greco is haplessly used and never can suggest menace or sorcery, while the remainder of the cast is bogged down in this slow-moving affair. It is only par technically. *Mosk.*

Tres Veces Ana
(Three Times Anna)
(ARGENTINE)

Mar Del Plata, April 3.

Marcelo Simonetti production. Features Maria Vaner, Walter Vidarte, Luis Medina Castro, Alberto Argibay, Lautaro Murua, Jorge Rivera Lopez. Directed by David Jose Kohon. Screenplay, Kohon; camera, Ricardo Aronovich; editor, Antonio Ripoll; music, Modern Jazz Quartet. At Mar Del Plata Film Fest. Running time, 113 MINS.

This second film by young Argentine director-writer David Jose Kohon already has had a big commercial success in Argentina. And some judicious editing might make it a likely stateside entry for the arties. In the title role, Maria Vaner gives a beautifully varied performance. She rates international attention and probably will get it.

"Anna" is actually three different stories, connected only by their common themes of love and loneliness. In the first, Miss Vaner is seen as an innocent young girl whose first ecstatic love affair leads to pregnancy, abortion and loss of all illusions. In the second, she plays a pseudo-beatnik ((Argentine-style, which is patterned closely after the French) edging towards nymphomania, and in the third the dream girl (literally) of an introspective newspaperman.

Of the three episodes, the second is the most lively and poignant. The milieu is bizarre and the pace is swift. The first and last episodes, however, are elaborately over-directed by Kohon who never hesitates to make a good point more than once. Since he is a director and writer of substance and individual style, the film merits attention even through its patches of tedium. The contemporary Buenos Aires locales are handsomely but not artily, caught in the camerawork of Ricardo Aronovich. The physical production is excellent. *Anby.*

Artillery Sergeant Kalen
(Ogniomistrez Kalen)
(POLISH)

Mar Del Plata, April 3.

Film Polski presentation of Studio Group production. Features Wieslaw Golas, Zofia Slaboszowska, Josef Kostecki, Josef Lodynski, Leon Niemczk, Zdzuslaw Karszewski, Janusz Klosinski, Tadeusz Teodoczyk, Janus Strachocki, Sylvester Przedwojewski, Tadeusz Somogi, Henryk Hunko. Directed by Ewa and Szeslaw Petelski. Screenplay, the Petelskis, based on novel by Jan Gerhard; camera, Mieczyslaw Jahoda; editor, Felicja Rogowska. At Mar Del Plata Film Fest. Running time, 112 MINS.

It is hard to tell who was doing what and to whom in this pic. Set in the closing days of World War II, script recounts the adventures of a Polish soldier caught among what seemed like six different armies—the Communist Polish freedom fighters, the anticommunist freedom fighters, the Ukrainian fascist freedom fighters, and some other groups impossible to identify without a scorecard. Interestingly enough, there was not a Nazi in the bunch.

At the start of the film, it seems that the titular Sgt. Kalen will be a sort of Polish version of the good soldier Schweik, a natural fall guy baffled by the inconsistencies, ironies and horrors of war.

It doesn't work out that way, though. It becomes a series of

melodramatic adventures played absolutely straight. There is a certain irony in the tragic ending—wherein the sergeant is accidentally killed by his own (Soviet Polish) buddies. But it comes too late to give greater meaning to the film. "Kalen" is a far cry from such other recent Polish exports as "Kanal" and "Ashes and Diamonds" (both of which succeeded in telling remarkably complex stories), with stateside chances nil. Performances and technical credits are good.   *Anby.*

The Old Young People
(Los Jovenes Viejos)
(ARGENTINE)

Mar Del Plata, April 3.
Jorge Siri Lonchi production. Features Maria Vaner, Alberto Argibay, Emilio Alfaro, Jorge Rivera Lopez, Marcela Lopez Rey, Graciela Dufau, Beatriz Matar, Anita Larronde. Directed by Rodolfo Kuhn. Screenplay, Kuhn; camera, Ricardo Aronovich; editor, Antonio Ripoll; music, Sergio Mihanovich. At Mar Del Plata Film Fest. Running time, **98 MINS.**

That Argentina is developing some firstrate young film talent is evident in this first feature film directed by Rodolfo Kuhn. However, Kuhn, like his contemporaries, still has to develop his own style, now strongly under the influence of the new French and Italian filmmakers. He may also need a scriptwriter (other than himself). "The Old Young People" is another tale of bored, young people who discuss their boredom at boring length. There is, of course, significance in this phenomenon, which certainly is not limited to Paris, Rome or New York. But for all their talk, Kuhn's characters on only one occasion succeed in giving their situation particular meaning.

Nevertheless, "People" is a thoroughly professional, stylish job of filmmaking, undisciplined as to running time (it could be cut by 10 to 15 minutes). For an arty U.S. audience, it would offer an unique view of upper middleclass life in Buenos Aires. The one provocative point made (but never really developed) is that these young people are subjected to all the aspects of a disillusioned European culture without having been directly involved in the causes. "We can't even blame the war," says one young man. "Well," answers his friend, "we always have Peron."

Story concerns the promiscuous affairs of three young B.A. blades, one of whom eventually finds a meaningful relationship with a girl. In the two key roles, Maria Vaner and Alberto Argibay are especially good. If this film is any criterion, Argentina is loaded with goodlooking femmes who can also act. The physical production is fine.   *Anby.*

Devtchata
(Girls)
(RUSSIAN)

Mar Del Plata, Apr. 3.
Mosfilm production. Features Nadezhda Rumiantseva, Nikolay Rybnikov, Luciena Ovtchinnikova, Inna Makarova, Nina Menshikova, Svetlana Druzhinina, Stanislav Khitrov. Directed by Yuri Tschuliukin. Screenplay, Boris Bedny; camera, Timofey Lebeshev; music, A. Pakhmutova. At Mar Del Plata Film Fest. Running time, **90 MINS.**

Bright and sparkling, "Devtchata" is a comedy, simple in plot but strong in texture. It might be turned into a musical called "Les Girls (Moscow version)."

This film's greatest asset is petite Nadezhda Rumiantseva. She bounces through her role with tremendous vitality and charm.

Story concerns a snowbound lumbering settlement, where the champion woodcutter and local ladykiller makes a bet that he'll add the little cook (Rumiantseva) to his string of conquests. But she has a mind of her own and refuses to play the game of love the easy way.

Secondary characters are only sketched in, especially on the femme side. One girl's marriage has broken up and another is embittered toward life in general. The film's happy end includes changed attitudes towards life of these two.

Director Yuri Tschuliukin composes movements with the care of a choreographer. T. Lebeshev's black and white lensing is excellent.

This is a Soviet pic that should find markets in the West, including the U. S., thanks to its light touch and the impact of Rumiantseva's personality.   *Chile.*

Five Finger Exercise

Shaky translation of the London and B'way stage hit, uneven in adaptation and performance.

Hollywood, April 13.
Columbia Pictures release of Frederick Brisson production. Stars Rosalind Russell, Jack Hawkins, Maximilian Schell, Richard Beymer; features Annette Gorman. Directed by Daniel Mann. Screenplay, Frances Goodrich, Albert Hackett, based on play by Peter Shaffer; camera, Harry Stradling; editor, William A. Lyon; music, Jerome Moross; assistant director, R. Robert Rosenbaum. Reviewed at the studio, April 12, '62. Running time, **108 MINS.**

Louise Harrington ..... Rosalind Russell
Stanley Harrington.... Jack Hawkins
Walter .... Maximilian Schell
Philip Harrington ..... Richard Beymer
Pamela Harrington..... Annette Gorman
Mary .... Lana Wood
Helen .... Terry Huntingdon
Salesman .... William Quinn
Alice .... Kathy West
Girl .... Valora Noland
Woman .... Mary Benoit
Girl .... Jeannine Riley
Girl .... Karen Parker
Announcer .... Bart Conrad

Frederick Brisson, who transplanted this 1958 London stage hit to Broadway in 1959, where it met with further success, has now transplanted it into the more taxing idiom of the screen. But the popularity is not apt to be duplicated among picturegoers, the great bulk of whom presently are disenchanted with the kind of weighty, deeply psychological adult theme that is probed in Peter Shaffer's melodrama of festering, corrosive personality conflicts that destroy the togetherness of an upper middle class family.

It appears that something has been misplaced in the translation, as adapted by Frances Goodrich and Albert Hackett, and directed by Daniel Mann. For one thing, the trimming to 108 minutes of film apparently has taken its toll of both characterization and plot. Resolution of the problem is abrupt and anything but persuasive, leaving the audience suspended and unconvinced. Furthermore, although there are two solid performances by Rosalind Russell and Jack Hawkins, there are three equally weak ones by Maximilian Schell, Richard Beymer and Annette Gorman as the younger people enmeshed in the domestic warfare. All things considered, the Columbia release is not a promising contender.

The title refers to the significance of five fingers operating in coordination to create harmonious music, as in a piano study for beginners. The thoroughly uncoordinated "five fingers" in this family melodrama, reset in California from the original England, are an uncultured, intolerant, self-made businessman-father (Hawkins), a culture-obsessed, pseudo-intellectual mother (Miss Russell), a confused, educated, "mama's boy" son (Beymer), an animated, high-spirited daughter (Miss Gorman), and a young German refugee (Schell), who has been employed by the family as tutor, and yearns to become a permanent part of it though not in quite the classification the mother fancies. At any rate, the quivering quintet gropes for communication but fails dismally, until finally Schell attempts to take his own life. This traumatic

incident somehow seals the emotional dikes, although it is not made clear exactly why and how in a hasty, afterthought finish.

There are no supporting roles of any consequence, and even Miss Gorman's role appears to have been sliced to absolute essentials. Director Mann has managed to generate considerable physical activity in what is primarily a static, house-bound play, but he has his characters behaving in a somewhat overly-theatrical fashion. Harry Stradling's photography is dramatically observant; Rose Bellah's art direction aptly suggestive of social position and physical place; Jerome Moross' score expressive. William A. Lyon's editing is mechanically stable, but the film as a whole does not convey the full-circle state of family affairs apparently intended (relative harmony through discord back to harmony). There is no true beginning and no true resolution.

Miss Russell's gowns were designed by Orry-Kelly, and an unusual four-minute trailer has been filmed to demonstrate some of the decisions made in fashioning the correct wardrobe for the character. The gowns are not especially exciting and neither is the trailer, which does not particularly entice one into seeing the picture.
                                Tube.

Big Red
(COLOR)

Lesser Disney effort about a boy, a dog and a man who learns a lesson from their camaraderie. Has the ingredients for presentable b.o.

Hollywood, April 13.
Buena Vista release of Walt Disney production. Stars Walter Pidgeon; introduces Gilles Payant; features Emile Genest, Janette Bertrand. Directed by Norman Tokar. Screenplay, Louis Pelletier, from novels by Jim Kjelgaard; camera (Technicolor), Edward Colman; editor, Grant K. Smith; music, Oliver Wallace; assistant director, Arthur J. Vitarelli. Reviewed at Academy Awards Theatre, April 13, '62. Running time, **89 MINS.**

"Big Red" is not one of the choicer Walt Disney products, but the arf 'n' arf combination of the magnetic Disney banner and the appeal of a boy-and-his-dog story for the all-important family audience suggests a respectable box-office response.

"The Hound That Thought He Was a Human Being" would be an apt sub-title for the Buena Vista release, co-produced by Winston Hibler and directed by Norman Tokar from a screenplay by Louis Pelletier. Gleaned from the novels of Jim Kjelgaard, the yarn, set and shot for the most part in Canada's lush, picturesque Quebec province, is concerned with the manner in which a resourceful lad (Gilles Payant) and a frisky Irish setter team up to illustrate the advantages of togetherness to a lonely, businesslike sportsman (Walter Pidgeon). Along the way, the setter takes up with an attractive lady setter, and the two pooches carry on in a most un-doglike fashion, Mr. Red going so far as to deny himself a nice juicy bone so that the missus will have something good to sink her chops into. To children, this canine domesticity may seem perfectly natural and acceptable. But the spectacle of a dog carting home a bowser bag may be a little too much Ken-L-

Ration for the average adult to swallow.

Pidgeon plays the North Woods sportsman with his customary aplomb. Master Payant, a handsome lad from Canada, makes a likable impression in his screen bow-wow. The setter, who goes professionally by the name of Champion Red Aye Scraps and remotely resembles a Thurber dog, rates a PATSY nomination for quizzical head tilts alone. William B. Koehler trained the educated dogs who participated. Emile Genest and Janette Bertrand are amiable in support.

The outstanding quality of the film is Edward Colman's photography, for which some of the credit is due and not oft-filmed scenic splendor of the St. Lawrence River region of Quebec. Oliver Wallace's music is a dramatic asset, as is Grant K. Smith's editing, save for a bit of repetition in dog reactions, however appealing the response of a pooch befuddled by human behavior. Art direction by Carroll Clark and Marvin Aubrey Davis is accomplished. *Tube.*

Douce Violence
(Sweet Violence)
(FRENCH) (C'SCOPE)

Paris, April 10.

20th-Fox release of Paris Interproductions-Contact production. With Elke Sommer, Pitrre Brice, Vittoria Prada, Christian Pezey, Agnes Spaak, Claire Maurier. Directed by Max Pecas. Screenplay, Pecas, Jacques Aucante, Grisha Debat; camera, Marc Fossard; editor, Paul Cayatte. At Ermitage, Paris. Running time, **85 MINS.**

Elke	Elke Sommer
Maitre	Pierre Brice
Barbara	Vittoria Prada
Olivier	Christian Pezey
Claire	Claire Maurier

Tale of morally drifting students living on a rich woman during a summer vacation lacks any depth or insight into the subject for arty theatre chances abroad. It does have some nudity and violence that could slant it for grind houses, but this at best.

A disillusioned but decent youth is seduced by a German girl, Elke Sommer, who is more for sensations than love in any romantic sense. He finally wises up and goes back to an upright girl, leaving the immoralist chastened.

Miss Sommer emerges as a caricature Brigitte Bardot with pouts, sensual dancing and exposed epidermis. But the film's stilted and the lack of any feeling for the subject make her more a grostesque pinup than any sex symbol. Remainder of the cast can not do much with the characters either. Technical credits are par. *Mosk.*

Safe at Home

Lightweight, sugarcoated baseball item for moppets, with Mantle and Maris as b.o. bait.

Hollywood, April 9.

Columbia Pictures release of Tom Naud production. Stars Mickey Mantle, Roger Maris; features William Frawley, Patricia Barry, Don Collier, Eugene Iglesias, Flip Mark; introduces Bryan Russell. Directed by Walter Doniger. Screenplay, Robert Dillon, from story by Naud and Steve Ritch; camera, Irving Lippman; editor, Frank P. Keller; music, Van Alexander; assistant director, Leonard Katzman. Reviewed at the studio, April 9, '62. Running time, **84 MINS.**

Mickey Mantle	Mickey Mantle
Roger Maris	Roger Maris
Bill Turner	William Frawley
Johanna Price	Patricia Barry
Ken Lawton	Don Collier
Hutch Lawton	Bryan Russell
Mr. Torres	Eugene Iglesias
Henry	Flip Mark
Mike Torres	Scott Lane
Henry's Father	Charles G. Martin
Ralph Houk	Ralph Houk
Whitey Ford	Whitey Ford
Mrs. Torres	Desiree Sumarra
Joe	Joe Hickman
Phil	Chris Hughes
Jackie	James R. Argyras
Coach Benton	Fred A. Schwarb
Hank	Joe Morrison

Armed with junior America's two foremost matinee idols—the M&M Twins, Mantle and Maris—this lightweight confection, properly exploited, could amass a presentable batting average at the boxoffice. Designed for the moppet legions, the Naud-Hamilburg production, produced by Tom Naud and timed to coincide approximately with resumption of the annual pennant chase, should fare well as a matinee, weekend or holiday attraction. But the Columbia release is strictly kiddie fare, and should be so programmed.

Scripted by Robert Dillon from a yarn by producer Naud and Steve Ritch, "Safe at Home" is a Horatio Alger story about an impressionable Florida lad who fancies himself and his dad intimate friends of Messrs. M&M, boasts of his palsy-walsy association to the local Little League rascals, then must put up or shut up. Cornering the harassed sluggers at spring training camp, the resourceful, but overly-imaginative lad is given an honesty-is-best-policy preachment by the clean-cut heroes, who then proceed to invite the whole horde of youngsters to camp for a climax of pure, red-blooded all-American bathos. Underlying moral to moppets: but a nuisance, be aggressive, be honest and nail your man

Mantle and Maris are no thespic threats to the ranks of Hollywood leading men. William Frawley is personable as a lovably irascible coach. Patricia Barry and Don Collier supply secondary romantic interest with restraint. Bryan Russell, in his screen debut as the boy, is reminiscent of the young Dean Stockwell in manner and appearance, but something less, histrionically. Other prominent moppets are Flip Mark, Scott Lane and Chris Hughes. Eugene Iglesias is persuasive as a worried father. Yankee manager Ralph Houk and mound ace Whitey Ford contribute bits.

Walter Doniger's direction leans to sentimental stickum. It is also somewhat repetitious and tends to be confusing and not very well integrated in several sequences.

Film was shot in Florida. Production credits, including Irving Lippman's lenswork, Frank P. Keller's editing and Van Alexander's score, are satisfactory. *Tube.*

L'Assassin East Dans L'Annuaire
(FRENCH)

Paris, April 10.

Gaumont release of Marianne SNEG production. Stars Fernandel; features Marie Dea, Edith Scob, Maurice Teynac, Georges Chamarat. Directed by Leo Joannon. Screenplay, Jacques Robert, Jean Halain, Joannon from novel by Charlés Exbrayat; camera, Pierre Petit; editor, Raymond Lamy. At Ambassade-Gaumont, Paris. Running time, **90 MINS.**

Albert	Fernandel
Inspector	Robert Dalban
Edith	Marie Dea
Brother	Maurice Teynac
Leclerc	Georges Chamarat
Jenny	Edith Scob

Comic Fernandel has been pushed into a whodunit that gives him little scope for being funny. Lacklustre direction also bogs this down to make it a chancey export item even with the Fernandel name.

The comedian is a lonely man who is the butt of office jokes. But he is involved in a holdup which then turns into a series of murders that make him look guilty.

Some of the plotting is suspenseful but Fernandel hams his role and mouths things pedantically to rob his character of much comic meaning. It all goes to make the general happenings out of key with his performance. Technical credits are par. *Mosk.*

Waltz Of The Toreadors
(BRITISH—COLOR)

Handsomely produced version of Jean Anouilh's stageplay. Excellent acting vehicle for Peter Sellers, but too many conflicting moods; good b.o. marquee value.

London, April 12.

Rank release of Julian Wintle-Leslie Parkyn (Peter de Sarigny) production. Stars Peter Sellers, Danny Robin, John Fraser, Cyril Cusack, Margaret Leighton; features Jean Anderson, Raymond Huntley, John Le Mesurier. Directed by John Guillermin. Screenplay, Wolf Mankowitz from Jean Anouilh's play; camera, John Wilcox; editor, Peter Taylor; music, Richard Addinsell. At Odeon, Leicester Square, London. Running time, **104 MINS.**

General Fitzjohn	Peter Sellers
Ghislaine	Dany Robin
Emily	Margaret Leighton
Robert	John Fraser
Doctor	Cyril Cusack
Estella	Prunella Scales
Sidonia	Denise Coffey
Agnes	Jean Anderson
President of Court	Raymond Huntley
Undertaker	Cardew Robinson
Innkeeper	John Glyn-Jones
Vicar	John Le Mesurier
Mrs. Bulstrode	Vanda Godsell
Rosemary	Catherine Feller

A considerably broadened version by Wolf Mankowitz of Jean Anouilh's ironic stage comedy has resulted in a capital acting opportunity for Peter Sellers, which this standout performer gratefully accepts. But the play has lost much in spirit in its transition. Against this must be credited some wonderfully inventive situations which will satisfy all but the most discerning. With Sellers, Margaret Leighton, Cyril Cusack and Dany Robin in effective roles, there can be no doubt of the pic's marquee value and boxoffice impact.

Pic is handsomely mounted, and it's directed with zest and pace by John Guillermin. But too many moods jostle for it to be a complete success. Slapstick, farce, high comedy, drama and tragedy are all there but they don't always make easy companions. Particularly there is a scene between Sellers and Miss Leighton, fortunately towards the end of the film, which is agonizing in its tragic implications and is uncomfortably divorced from the main spirit of this lively picture.

Mankowitz has transferred the yarn from France to Sussex. Briefly, it concerns an elderly general, about to retire before the First World War. He is a man with a roving eye for the girls, trapped by a neurotic, shrewish, sham-invalid of a wife and two unprepossessing daughters. For 17 years, he has had a platonic romance with a French woman, never having a real opportunity to consummate their love. She turns up at his castle determined that this sad state of affairs should end. It is his last chance to find the happiness for which he has patiently awaited. But, of course, it never happens. She falls for a young soldier, who turns out to be Sellers' illegitimate son, and Sellers is left, still trapped with his wife. He is left too, with loneliness and broken dreams, knowing all the time that those dreams have always been adolescent escape from reality.

This is probably Sellers' most rounded film performance yet. He extracts laughs and compassionate pity with equal ease, whether he is being caught up in a drunken party at a tavern, conducting a riotous mock duel with his local doctor (Cyril Cusack), taking charge of a court martial, leching after his maids, facing up to the fact that he is a failure or in the more tragic moments, stripping his soul bare as he struggles in his hateful scenes with his wife. It is a witty performance full of subtlety as well as broad fun.

Dany Robin gives a pleasant but unexceptional performance as his would-be mistress. Margaret Leighton is remarkably striking as the wife, even though her drab role seems completely out of key with the rest of the film. Cyril Cusack contributes much of the dry wit. John Fraser is a sufficiently gauche young officer until he decides to storm the defenses of Miss Robin. Minor roles by Cardew Robinson, as an opportunistic undertaker; Raymond Huntley, in charge of a courtmartial; and Vanda Godsell, as a voluptuous shopkeeper, are all sharply played.

John Wilcox's camera provides a colorful feast for the eye. Richard Addinsell's score is bright, and there must be a benevolent nod to Peter Taylor's editing. In tagging "Waltz of the Toreadors" a near miss, it must be emphasized that this is likely to be the opinion only of those who have seen the play and appreciated its wryly pathetic atmosphere. *Rich.*

Carry On Cruising
(BRITISH—COLOR)

Potentially profitable segment of familiar yock skein. Familiar faces, familiar gags and situations and, probably a familiar click boxoffice result.

London, April 10.

Anglo Amalgamated release of a Peter Rogers' production. Stars Sidney James, Kenneth Williams, Kenneth Connor, Liz Frazer, Dilys Laye, Emma Cannon, Lance Percival; features Vincent Ball, Jimmy Thompson, Cyril Chamberlain. Directed by Gerald Thomas. Screenplay, Norman Hudis, from story by Eric Barker; music, Bruce Montgomery; camera, Alan Hume; editor, John Shirley. At New Victoria, London. Running time, **89 MINS.**

Captain Crowther	Sidney James
Leonard Marjoribanks	Kenneth Williams
Arthur Binn	Kenneth Connor
Gladys Trimble	Liz Fraser
Flo Castle	Dilys Laye
Wilfred Haines	Lance Percival
Sam Turner	Jimmy Thompson
Tom Tree	Cyril Chamberlain
Bridget Madderley	Esma Cannon
Jenkins	Vincent Ball

Latest in the "Carry On" string of boxoffice click comedies is "Carry On Cruising." There's no reason to believe that it won't "Carry On" cashing in. Main difference is that it is now launched in color. Fact is that, despite commonplace loyalty to a proven formula, there is evidence that it is beginning to wear very thin.

Maybe Norman Hudis, who has so skillfully scribed this run of comedy hits, should have a Sabbatical. Perhaps a new writer might infuse new angles into predictable situations, gags and characters. And new faces might help. These questions can only be answered by the public response, but they loom largely in watching the latest antics of the "Carry On" crew.

In this instance, Sidney James is the veteran, highly improbable, skipper of a Mediterranean cruising vessel. He is inflicted with five hamheaded substitutes for well-tried key men in his regular complement. They are all over anxious to please and so everything goes disastrously wrong. This provides opportunity for a string of good-humored, but contrived and largely irrelevant slapstick gags and situations.

Jumping, familiarly, through their well-placed circus hoops are Sidney James (he glowers), Kenneth Williams (he plays archly), Kenneth Connor (he dithers). Liz Fraser (she flaunts a shapely figure) and Esma Cannon (she twitters). They offer nothing new because they are provided with nothing new. Lance Percival, as the tyro ship's cook, has some bright moments while Jimmy Thompson, as a suave bartender, copes with little material. Dilys Laye, a comparative newcomer to this frenzied scene, works hard in some brittle comedy campaigns.

Direction by Gerald Thomas is boisterously effective, but he could probably direct one of these "Carry On" pix in his sleep. Alan Hume's camerawork takes full advantage of the bonus of color.

Major switch in this series, which, despite its record, looks to be needing a cool, severe look from its parents, is that the original story is by Eric Barker. This comedian has appeared in a couple of the series, but, somehow, he couldn't find a role for himself in this latest "Carry On."   *Rich.*

A Soldier's Prayer
(JAPANESE)
Montreal, April 9.
Cadieux Associates release of Shochiku Pictures (Shigeru Wakatsuki-Kobayashi) production. Features Tatsuya Nakadai, Michiyo Aratama, Taketoshi Naito; directed by Masaki Kobayashi; Screenplay, Zenzo Matsuyama and Kobayashi; based on the last two volumes of the six-volume novel, "The Human Condition" by Jumpei Gomikawa; camera, Yoshio Miyajima; editor, Keiichi Uraoka; music, Chuji Kinoshita. North American premiere at Orpheum Theatre, Montreal, April 9, 1962. Running time, 190 MINS.
Kaji .... Tatsuya Nakadai
Michiko .... Michiyo Aratama
Pfc. Tange .... Taketoshi Naito
Cpl. Hironaka .... Keijiro Morozumi
Private Terada .... Yusuke Kawazu
Ryuko .... Kyoko Kishida
Umeko .... Reiko Hitomi
Capt. Nagata .... Fujio Suga
Cpl. Kirihara .... Nobuo Kaneko
A girl refugee .... Tamao Nakamura
A woman in the settlers'
   village .... Hideko Takamine
Village elder .... Chishu Ryu

(In Japanese: English Subtitles)
Completed late last year, this is the final part of Kobayashi's trilogy, "The Human Condition" parts one and two being "No Greater Love" and "Road to Eternity." Opening with a summary of what happened in the two previous films, ending with Kagi wandering alone on the battlefield after being defeated by the Russians, "A Soldier's Prayer" shows the final disillusionment in the three-year agony of the simple Japanese soldier who endures much, only to end by losing everything. Sick and weary, Kagi gives himself up to the Russians, under the impression that the conquerors will surely dispense a more humane rule than the Imperial Japanese. But once again his illusions are shattered. The Russians, like the Japanese, also rape the women, are also brutalized by war. In the prison camp he finds himself under the heel of the Japanese officers who act just as they did before they lost the war. Surrounded on all sides by death and darkness, brutality and filth, Kagi is plunged into despair.

In his breaking mind he continues to cling to the belief that somewhere, goodness must exist in man. He believes that if only he could speak to his captors they would join hands with him in establishing a better society. But while men may live under different political labels, their primary patterns of behavior remain the same, and those most frequently encountered by Kagi are opportunists —made so by their systems in order to survive. It is a bleak picture, and one sure to provoke discussion and dissent.

Kagi, forced to kill once more to avenge the death of a friend, breaks out of the camp, and with failing strength attempts to continue his journey to his wife. In his hand he clutches a dumpling as a gift. He struggles on through a mounting snow storm, falling and rising, finally to fall for the last time. The snow flakes cover his dead body, alone in a wilderness of nature.

This complicated and many-sided examination of the human condition is a great triumph for Kobayashi. His control of this 9 hours and 44 minute epic of self-examination and repentence, of military evil and the power of resistance, of the crime and the punishments, of the individual against the state, is one of the finest achievements in film making.

His control of his material, his exposition of the theme, his manipulation of the cast, all reconcile the diverse elements and points of view to give clarity to the mission of Kagi, who sets out from the clear tranquility of a simple life to make a frightening descent into Hell. If there is any weakness in the writing or playing of the part of Kagi it is that he seems to lack spiritual motivation, which was so strong in his opposite number in "The Harp of Burma."

Filmed in Grandscope, all technical aspects are satisfactory. The sub-titles are frank enough to upset squeamish censors. Unlike the current crop of fashionable foreign films which require audiences to wonder what is being said, this humanitarian study will leave most audiences pondering deeply and painfully over what has been said about the state of mankind. For specialized exhibition, this latest trilogy should become as celebrated as the Pagnol, Gorki, Apu and "Quiet Flows the Don" three-part works.   *Prat.*

Geronimo
(PANAVISION—COLOR)

Toned down new screen version of the famed Apache's latter day exploits. Solid production values and good title portrayal by Chuck Connors. Adults may have reservations, but appeal to moppets should make it healthy b.o. contender.

Hollywood, April 20.
United Artists release of Arnold Laven production. Stars Chuck Connors; introduces Kamala Devi; features Ross Martin, Pat Conway, Adam West, Armando Silvestre, Lawrence Dobkin, John Anderson, Enid Jaynes. Directed by Laven. Screenplay, Pat Fielder, from story by Miss Fielder. Laven; camera (Technicolor), Alex Phillips; editor, Marsh Hendry; music, Hugo Friedhofer; assistant director, Mario Cisneros. Reviewed at Goldwyn Studios, April 20, '62. Running time, 101 MINS.
Geronimo .... Chuck Connors
Teela .... Kamala Devi
Mangus .... Ross Martin
Maynard .... Pat Conway
Delahay .... Adam West
Huera .... Enid Jaynes
General Crook ...... Larry Dobkin
Senator Conrad ...... Denver Pyle
Natchez .... Armando Silvestre
Burns .... John Anderson
Mrs. Burns .... Amanda Ames
Giantah .... Mario Navarro
Col. Morales .... Eduardo Noriega
Mrs. Marsh .... Nancy Rodman
Kincaide .... Joe Higgins
Corporal .... Robert Hughes
Cavalryman .... James Burk
Indian Scout .... Hill Hughes

They sure don't make Injun pictures the way they used to. That's apt to be the observation and reaction of most adults who take in this new film version of the life and times of the famed "Geronimo," whose name was to become a part of modern American military vernacular. The Laven-Gardner-Levy presentation, produced and directed by Arnold Laven and long in the works, continues the screen's preoccupation with the philosophical, psychological and romantic ramifications of Indian matters in the late 19th century at the expense of the straight-from-the-shoulder, uninhibited action ingredients that characterized the early indifferent-to-racial-stereotypes westerns. In some ways the modern Indian picture may be better, yet something haunting and stirring has been lost in the metamorphosis. Still, the United Artists release figures to be a popular attraction with youngsters, who find little such diversion in the current market. "Geronimo" should garner ample wampum.

Time was when Indians on the warpath were known to claim a few scalps in their pursuits. Although Geronimo's band of idealistic warriors are acknowledged to be scalpers in Pat Fielder's screenplay, from the story she penned with producer Laven, there is no evidence of such menacing behavior in this film. In fact, the Indians of Miss Fielder's scenario are unbelievably henpecked, domesticated and generally wishywashy—proud and arrogant in their war-making but meek enough to be bossed about by a frail, lone white woman in more intimate business.

Further detrimental to the desired realism is the dialog. "Geronimo" and his braves are probably the most literate and certainly the most fluent Indians ever to grace the screen, able to communicate with several nationalities simply by employing English in the most articulate, up-to-date American fashion. Gone are the days of the "how" and the "white man speak

with forked tongue." When "Geronimo" remarks, "she's a pig," referring to an eligible maiden, it seems to come right out of the corner of New York's 8th Avenue and 42d Street.

The story describes the latter, leaner days of Geronimo's career, during which, denied humanitarian treatment by white supervisors on the reservation, he escaped and fled with some 50 tribesmen to Mexico, where he waged a courageous "war" against the U.S. to focus attention on the principle of the issue—treatment of the Indian as a human being. The picture has an uplift ending that may fool youngsters into concluding that the Indian ultimately got a decent shake after all—a false note of resolution contradicted by history to this day.

Chuck Connors gives the film a decided lift with an impressive portrayal in the title role. He is a rather subdued, blue-eyed "Geronimo," but a surprisingly convincing one. Kamala Devi, in her screen bow, is glamorous—a bit too glamorous—as his squaw, but emotes capably. Ross Martin seems out of his element as the hero's sidekick. A competent actor, he tries hard, but has a tendency to approach the role as if the Apaches vs. the Cavalry is a frontier version of the Sharks vs. the Jets. The result is a kind of cigar store Indian. Pat Conway plays the chief antagonist too sadistically and too obviously—grinning constantly at the awful prospect of bloodshed. Others in prominent parts are Adam West, Enid Jaynes, Larry Dobkin, Denver Pyle, Armando Silvestre and John Anderson.

The picture was filmed in Mexico, and is a fine physical production. Cameraman Alex Phillips' sweeping panoramic views and subtle lighting are solid assets, as are Marsh Hendry's snug, cumulative editing and Hugo Friedhofer's dramatically expressive Indianesque score. Other production values are almost equally strong.
Tube.

El Pecado de Una Madre
(A Mother's Sin)
(MEXICAN)

Mexico City, April 17.
Peliculas Nacionales release of Producciones Brooks production. Stars Libertad Lamarque, Dolores del Rio; features Pedro Geraldo, Enrique Rambal, Tere Velazquez. Directed by Alfonso Corona Blake. Screenplay, Julio Alejandro from story by Fernando Galiana; camera, Jack Draper. At Roble, Americas, Orfeon, Ariel theatres, Mexico City. Running time, 90 MINS.

This is a soap opera type of tearjerker capably directed by Alfonso Corona Blake. Film has been cleverly designed to appeal to sentimental and emotional Latin fans who will suffer as they see the mother suffer for her "sin of love."

Briefly, the story has Libertad Lamarque as the femme who loves not wisely but too well, with object of her attentions, Enrique Rambal, married to Dolores del Rio. One Sunday afternoon there is a car crash, the lady's man goes on to meet his maker and Miss Lamarque is miraculously saved to give birth to a son, Pedro Geraldo. Miss del Rio, in a noble gesture, adopts the boy but only

when Miss Lamarque renounces all rights to the baby.

The false mother takes her role seriously but mamma Lamarque repents, wants to see her child again, is repudiated by the boy who seems to be following in his father's footsteps by becoming an entertainer, a singer of old ballads (formerly sung by his father Rambal and Miss Lamarque), and with an eye out for the senoritas.

There's a tremendous lot of sobbing and crying and suffering throughout the film, but the audience loves it all. Rambal has a brief appearance as the lusting lover who causes all the trouble. Miss del Rio and Lamarque suffer on an equal plane while Pedro Geraldo shows signs of maturing as an actor. Tere Velazquez is the love interest in the film.

This one, already doing boffo boxoffice in Mexico, will clean up here and throughout the entire Latin American area where both Miss Lamarque and Miss del Rio still have strong boxoffice pull.
Emil.

La Chambre Ardente
(The Ardent Room)
(FRENCH)

Paris, April 17.
UFA-Comacico release of International Production-UFA - Comacico - Taurus Film production. Stars Nadja Tiller, Jean-Claude Brialy; features Claude Rich, Pierrette Pradier, Walter Giller, Edith Scob. Directed by Julien Duvivier. Screenplay, Charles Spaak, Duvivier from novel by John Dickson Carr; camera, Roger Fellous; editor, Paul Cayatte. At Normandie, Paris. Running time, 110 MINS.
Myra .... Nadja Tiller
Marc .... Jean-Claude Brialy
Stephane .... Claude Rich
Lucie .... Pierrette Pradier
Michel .... Walter Giller
Marie .... Edith Scob

Whodunit, with a dash of supernatural flavor, spends too much time explaining things, with a neglect of acting and suspense. Makes this mainly a playoff possibility abroad.

Relatives gather in old German chateau where an old man is dying. Most want his money but one girl happens to be descended from a woman who was betrayed by the old man's ancestor. She begins to get hallucinations after the old man dies. But it seems he may have been poisoned by the nurse who was in love with one of the would-be inheritors.

Vet director Julien Duvivier has let this ramble on. Furtive goings and comings in the chateau fail to maintain interest in this overlong affair. It lacks sharpness in direction and punch in direction and acting. The technical credits are par but the acting is uneven with too much palaver obscuring the characterization.
Mosk.

A Kind Of Loving
(BRITISH)

New talent conquers in compelling, down-to-earth drama about fumbling young love in a harsh North Country setting. This has a chance to do as well as "Saturday Night and Sunday Morning."

London, April 17.
Anglo Amalgamated release of a Joseph Janni production. Stars Alan Bates; features Thora Hird, June Ritchie. Producer, Joseph Janni. Directed by John

Schlesinger. Screenplay by Willis Hall, Keith Waterhouse, from Stan Barstow's novel; camera, Denys Coop; editor, Roger Cherrill; music, Ron Grainer. At Warner Theatre, London. Running time, 112 MINS.
Vic .... Alan Bates
Ingrid .... June Ritchie
Mrs. Rothwell .... Thora Hird
Mr. Brown .... Bert Palmer
Mrs. Brown .... Gwen Nelson
Jim Brown .... Malcolm Patton
Christine .... Pat Keen
Conroy .... James Smethurst
Jeff .... James Bolam
Les .... Michael Deacon
Dorothy .... Patsy Rowlands
Registrar .... Peter Madden
Pub Pianist .... Edna Ridgway

"A Kind Of Loving" is the latest in the profitable field of British pix which feature down-to-earth yarns filmed against a harshly realistic middleclass setting. "Saturday Night And Sunday Morning" and "Taste Of Honey" helped to trigger off this trend, and have proved profitable box-office pix. This new one has all the ingredients to make it an equal draw.

This leans almost exclusively on newish talent. The director, John Schlesinger, makes his bow as a feature director. Previously he has been a top documentary man. Cameraman Denys Coop is also a comparative newcomer to the top league. The femme lead, June Ritchie, is a 20-year-old with no previous film experience. The star, Alan Bates, has made only one film before of any impact, "Whistle Down Wind." In "Loving," he fully justifies the decision of the Anglo Amalgamated toppers to buy him out of his contract when he was playing in "The Caretaker" on Broadway. Schlesinger cast most of the other roles from virtually unknown players, with the exception of one key part, that played by vet Thora Hird.

With this fresh talent, the result was a gamble, but it has come off handsomely. The censor has recognized the sincerity behind the film and has passed some surprisingly frank dialog and situations in the screenplay by Keith Waterhouse and Willis Hall. It is set in a Lancashire industrial town and tells the bittersweet yarn of a young draftsman who is attracted by a typist in the same factory. It is a physical attraction which he cannot resist. She, on the other hand, has a deeper feeling for him.

The fumbling romance proceeds, often hurtfully, often poignantly. The inevitable happens. She becomes pregnant and he grudgingly marries her. It is obvious from the start that the union is purely physical and it is not helped by the nagging of her mother. Eventually, he walks out after a stormy scene. But he finds no sympathy from his relatives. And eventually the two young people get together again and find that, despite everything, their love can develop into something deeper and more satisfying.

Schlesinger handles this film with a sharp documentary eye, but does not forget that he is unfolding a piece of fiction. The tremulous moment when the girl first gives in to the boy's physical craving, an opening wedding sequence, the desolate seashore when they go on honeymoon, the girl discussing birthcontrol hesitantly, a pub crawl, the tender scenes as the young lovers walk in the park. These and many other sequences are all handled with tact, shrewd

observation and wit by the director.

The picture captures the full flavor of the busy streets, back alleys, taverns and harsh, and grey moorlands of industrial Lancashire. There is a vivid, earthy realism about the whole project.

Miss Ritchie makes an appealing debut as the bewildered Lancashire lass and should merit careful watching in the future. Bates is a likeable hero who will hold most audience's sympathy despite his weaknesses, and without drawing too much away from Miss Ritchie. Thora Hird's role as the mother-in-law is overwritten but it is excellently played and most effectively heightens the drama. Of the large cast of unknowns Bert Palmer, Gwen Nelson, Pat Keen, James Bolam and Jack Smethurst give exceptionally able support.

Photographed in many parts of Lancashire to represent a composite town, lenser Coop has skillfully caught the peculiar grey drabness of the area. Roger Cherrill has cut with precision. Ron Grainer's music is unobtrusive but fitting. All round, here is a film that is bold, compelling and often moving, though laced with humor.
Rich.

Self-Portrait
(CANADIAN)

Toronto, April 9.
NFB release of National Film Board production, assembled and annotated by Guy Glover, assisted by David Mayerovitch. Black and white (with color). Premiere at Little Cinema, Toronto. Running time, 150 MINS.

This is an anthology of scenes from 21 years (1939-1960) of Canadian filmmaking. The text on the screen identifies the film and its makers before each excerpt is shown, and the commentator (Guy Glover) notes the significant characteristics of the film's style and subject. Some of the 41 films represented here are as short as four minutes, some as long as an hour; but enough is shown of each to give the feel of its subject, acting and direction.

Beginning with "Heritage" (1939), a film of the prairie dust bowl, "Self-Portrait" passes through two decades of Canadian life to the space age, recognized by "Universe" (1960), the concluding film. Here are scenes from "Churchill's Island," (1941), the first Canadian documentary to win an Academy Award, and 'V for Victory" (1942), one of the first hand-drawn films made by the now internationally-famous Norman McLaren. The forgotten years also bring with them the names of film-makers and artists who have since become famous outside Canada: former commentator, Lorne Green, composer Louis Applebaum, Wayne and Shuster (who wrote the lyrics for "The Proudest Girl in the World" (1944), and producer, Sydney Newman.

"Self-Portrait" opens with a montage of pictures of the NFB's first Ottawa headquarters, of the Board's staff of early days, and of production stills. It closes with a similar montage showing the new Montreal $6,000,000 studios with its present film makers. For theatre audiences an intermission is provided; for showing on televi-

sion, the whole breaks into five 30-min. periods.

To those who know little of Canada's recent history, this film will be of constant interest; to those who have heard of the Board and haven't seen its early work, this is a quick and pleasant way to catch up with the past. Production by Glover is quiet and the tone of the film is modest. Music would have taken' the documentary chill off of the linking sequences and the narration, while thankfully avoiding bombast, could perhaps have been written and spoken with a touch of poetry and drama. *Prat.*

Les Petits Matins
(Early Mornings)
(FRENCH)

Paris, April 17.
Gaumont release of Paris Elysees Film-Metzger and Woog production. With Darry Cowl, Agathe Aems, Fernand Gravey, Francis Perier, Francis Blanche, Roger Coggio. Directed by Jecqueline Audry. Screenplay, Stella Kersova, Pierre Pelegri, Pierre Laroche; camera, Robert Lefevbre; editor, J. L. Castelli. At Mercury, Paris. Running time, 100 MINS.
Sophie .... Agathe Aems
Rich Man .... Fernand Gravey
Boxer .... Roger Coggio
Manager .... Pierre Mondy
Customs Man .... Francis Blanche
Masher .... Francois Perier
Pilot .... Gilbert Becaud
Jean-Paul .... Jean-Claude Brialy

This fits in with the sketch cycle here. However, it has one character, a knowing 18-year-old g i r l hitchhiker, and her adventures on her way to the Riviera from Belgium allow for fitting a bunch of noted players into the pic. This remains a surface affair with mainly local chances because of failure to either try for characterization or more inventiveness in t h e sketches.

The girl is pert and fetching. She has many men breathing hard for her but manages to remain chaste till she finally finds love. Film ambles along fairly entertainingly with a bevy of local stars doing takeoffs on their screen and private personalities. This makes it quite chancey abroad.

Film is technically okay with the direction nimble and playing reasonable within its sketch limitatfons and the lightweight scripting. *Mosk.*

Sweet Violence
(FRENCH—C'SCOPE)

Hollywood, April 10.
Audubon Films release of Joel Lifschultz production. No stars. Directed by Max Pecas. Screenplay, Jacques Aucante; camera, Marc Fossart; editor, Paul Cayatte; music, Charles Aznavour, Georges Garvarentz. Reviewed at Sunset Theatre, April 10, '62. Running time, 75 MINS.
Elke .... Elke Sommer
Maitre .... Pierre Brice
Olivier .... Christian Pezy
Barbara .... Vittoria Prada
Claire .... Claire Maurier
Charly .... Robert Darame
Mick .... Jenny Astruc
Choutte .... Michelle Bardollet
Dominique .... Agnes Spaak

"Sweet Violence" is the French equivalent of "Rebel Without a Cause," with a little "Not Tonight Henry" thrown in for good measure. Essentially, it is an enterprise in cinematic flesh-peddling, thinly veiled under the pretense of art and social significance . . . a kind of wolf in sheep's clothing. But art house patrons will see right through it, leaving the Joel Lif-

schultz production and Audubon Films release to be inherited by sensation seekers. The customer lure is Elke Sommer, a large young lady who peeks out from behind a mop of platinum hair and little more. She has, it is said, been compared to Brigitte Bardot. The only true resemblance is that of gender.

Written by Jacques Aucante, "Sweet Violence" surveys again the shiftless youthful international set in France who live on instinct (i.e., sex), spurn any form of involvement, and loathe the "little" things like gratitude and love. Into this nest of listless, tiresome oddballs comes a latently decent young chap. After a series of traumatic incidents, he comes back to the civilized world remarkably unscathed. Among the incidents are a torrid, artless dance by Miss Sommer, a run-in with the French idea of an average American (the gum-chewing caricature variety), and a climactic showdown scene in which hero and heavy match nerves by leaping, blindfolded, at a given count onto a building ledge from a platform being pulled skyward by a crane. This latter sequence is a kind of Gallic version of what might be Harold Lloyd's version of the Yankee teenage version of that quaint and popular sport known as "chicken."

Miss Sommer towers over her leading man (Christian Pezy), and it is doubtful that he could go 10 rounds with her. The acting in general is pretty poor, and the problems of the cast are compounded by Max Pecas' direction, whose style often reminds one of the Valentino era of the screen, and by the timing of the sub-titles, which frequently precede the spoken word by one sentence. CinemaScope widens the titles on the screen, but certainly doesn't improve what they are saying. *Tube.*

The Miracle Worker

Story of the young Helen Keller, artfully reproduced on film. Within certain limitations, a promising b.o. contender.

Hollywood, April 26.
United Artists release of Fred Coe production. Stars Anne Bancroft, Patty Duke; features Victor Jory, Inga Swenson, Andrew Prine. Directed by Arthur Penn. Screenplay, William Gibson, from his play; camera, Ernest Caparros; editor, Aram Avakian; music, Laurence Rosenthal; asst. directors, Larry Sturhahn, Ulu Grossbard. Reviewed at Goldwyn Studios, April 26, '62. Running time, 106 MINS.
Annie Sullivan .... Anne Bancroft
Helen Keller .... Patty Duke
Capt. Keller .... Victor Jory
Kate Keller .... Inga Swenson
James Keller .... Andrew Prine
Aunt Ev .... Kathleen Comegys
Viney .... Beah Richards
Mr. Anagnos .... Jack Hollander
Percy (10 years) .... Michael Darden
Martha (10 years) ...... Dale Ellen Bethea
Helen (7 years) .... Peggy Burke
Percy (8 years) .... Walter Wright Jr.
Martha (7 years) ...... Donna Bryan
Helen (5 years) .... Mindy Sherwood
Martha (5 years) .... Diane Bryan
Percy (6 years) .... Keith Moore
Young Annie (10) .... Michele Farr
Young Jimmie (8) .... Allan Howard
1st Crone .... Judith Lowry
2d Crone .... Wm. F. Haddock
3d Crone .... Helen Ludlum
Belle .... Dog

Something has been lost in translation to the screen of William Gibson's "The Miracle Worker." On the other hand, something has been gained in the progression to theatrical film. But any debate over artistic profit and loss must, ultimately, conclude with the admission that this dramatization of the dawn of comprehension in the mind of Helen Keller is a powerful story and a source of profound inspiration in any medium.

A celebrated television show, later a critical, artistic and popular hit on the stage, the Fred Coe production appears destined for commercial success as a motion picture, although the magnitude of its appeal may be leveled somewhat by a curious reluctance on the part of many people to expose themselves to such a grim, emotionally devastating experience. "Miracle Worker" takes a lot out of a viewer, and there are those who shy away from anything that appears to demand total involvement, even if it is an ennobling and uplifting event.

The United Artists release was adapted from his play by Gibson, directed by Arthur Penn, who staged the legit version, and stars Anne Bancroft and Patty Duke in the roles they introduced to Broadway. Obviously, the project is in good, loving hands. Within the boundaries of cinematic resourcefulness and invention. Messrs. Coe, Penn, Gibson, staff and artists have gone about as far as they can go in conversion to films, only often it's not far enough to duplicate the overpowering flesh-and-blood simplicity of a stage production.

Gibson's screenplay relates the story of the young Helen Keller and how, through the dedication, perseverance and courage of her teacher, Annie Sullivan, she establishes a means of communication with the world she cannot see or hear. The Misses Bancroft and Duke, both of whom are renowned for their prior portrayals of Misses Sullivan and Keller, respectively, here again tackle the juicy, but enormously exhausting, roles with great artistry and conviction. It is very likely that reenacting these

roles on film posed the greatest challenge of all to their thespic resources.

Whereas, on stage, a performer can sustain and build progressively, on film one must preserve histrionic continuity in bits and pieces. In a scene such as the celebrated eight-minute skirmish between the young hellion and her tutor, this can pose tremendous problems that reverberate from player to director down through editor, all profoundly dependent on the others. And it is here that we discover, in spite of the supreme efforts of all concerned, a loss of value in the transition. This scene, performed in the flesh, has unforgettable and brutal impact, whereas in the film the cumulative effect and sense of exhausted relief at the conclusion is diminished. This highlight interlude simply does not seem as remarkable an acting achievement on film even though, ironically, it is probably far more difficult to execute.

Where the picture really excels, outside of its inherent story values, is in the realm of photographic technique. It is here that director Penn and cameraman Ernest Caparros have teamed to create artful, indelible strokes of visual storytelling and mood-molding. The measured dissolves, focal shifts and lighting and filtering effects that have been conceived and achieved enrich the production considerably. Some may quibble that "The Miracle Worker" needs no such pictorial window dressing, but there really is no disputing the value of such imagery in arousing emotional participation. In the case of Annie's recollections, the fuzzy, spotty superimposition of her thoughts provides an explanatory parallel absent on the stage. And in the silent scenes that introduce the savage, groping youngster behind the main titles, the film instantly grabs and enthralls the audience as was impossible in the play. And to these attributes the haunting, often chilling, score by Laurence Rosenthal, the authentic art direction by George Jenkins and the taut, brisk editing by Aram Avakian.

Formidable featured support is contributed by Victor Jory and Inga Swenson as Helen's well-meaning, but overly-indulgent parents. Andrew Prine is effective as the troubled half-brother. Strong in prominent roles are Kathleen Comegys, Beah Richards, Jack Hollander and Michael Darden. *Tube.*

It's Trad, Dad!
(BRITISH)

Breezy boxoffice bonanza slanted mainly towards teenagers. Packed with top pop tunes and performers, and some slick direction.

London, April 24.
BLC release of a (Milton Subotsky) Columbia Picture production. Stars Helen Shapiro. Directed by Dick Lester. Screenplay, Subotsky; camera, Gilbert Taylor; editor, Bill Lenny; incidental music, Ken Thorne. At London Pavilion, London. Running time, 73 MINS.
Helen .... Helen Shapiro
Craig .... Craig Douglas
Coffee Shop Owner..... Timothy Bateson
Mayor .... Felix Felton
TV Director .... Frank Thornton
Police Chief .... Arthur Mullard
Head Waiter .... Derek Nimmo

Customer .... Mario Fabrizi
TV Director .... Ronnie Stevens
Narrator .... Derek Guyler
With John Leyton, Temperance Seven, Kenny Ball & His Jazzmen, Terry Lightfoot & His New Orleans Jazz Band, Chris Barber & His Band, Ottilie Patterson, Chubby Checker, Mr. Acker Bilk & His Paramounet Jazz Men, Bob Wallis & His Storyville Jazz Men, Gene Vincent, Sounds Inc., Brook Bros., Gary (U.S.) Bonds, Del Shannon, Gene McDaniels, David Jacobs, Pete Murray, Alan Freeman.

Here is a gimmick film which is slanted directly at teenage fans of jazz, but should also amuse some older squares. It will certainly make sweet boxoffice music over here, and is a safe bet for any audience which likes lively, pop music. It is a simple showcase for introducing a parade of pop performers. But it is also enhanced by some very slick directorial technique by a comparative newcomer, Dick Lester, and sharp editing by Bill Lenny. Apart from the hefty salaries paid, it was probably made on a shoestring.

Milton Subotsky's storyline is as slim as a chorine's waist but it serves to introduce a batch of top bands and performers who, between them, put over some 25 numbers with skill and zest. Helen Shapiro, Britain's teenage vocal prodigy, and Craig Douglas play a couple of youngsters who resent the attitude of the pompous mayor of their small town against the jukebox and jazz activities of the youngsters in the town.

They decide to persuade some top disk jockeys to help them stage a trad jazz fiesta. By invading tele and recording studios, they achieve their objective and so does the producer, for singers and bands are thus introduced more logically than in many similar gimmick pix.

Both Miss Shapiro and Douglas prove themselves more hip with the vocalizing than the thesping, but they get by. America is represented by such as Chubby Checker and Gary (U.S.) Bonds. But this mainly is a Wave-the-Union-Jack benefit for Britain's pop musical performers, and, overall, they do themselves proud.

Felix Felton, as the mayor; Arthur Mullard, as a fumbling police chief; Derek Nimmo as a supercilious waiter; and Mario Fabrizi, playing a spaghetti eating nightclub patrons, have smart cameos, but they are all chorus to the trad performers.

Most interesting aspect of this bright little film is the direction of Dick Lester, a comparative newcomer to the feature film scene. He has worked out some witty and unexpected camera angles, smartly exploited by lensman Gilbert Taylor. And he keeps the screen alive through pace and shrewd cutting by Bill Lenny. "It's Trad, Dad!" is corn, but cheerful boxoffice corn. *Rich.*

Lonely Are the Brave

Appealing yet disconcertingly unrealized study of the misfit versus civilization. Fine portrayals help, but yarn suggests it will need plenty of trade and public sell.

Universal release of a Joel Productions picture, produced by Edward Lewis. Stars Kirk Douglas; introduces Michael Kane, and features Gena Rowlands, Walter Matthau. Directed by David Miller. Screenplay by Dalton Trumbo from the Edward Abbey novel "Brave Cowboy"; camera, Philip Lathrop; editor, Leon Barsha; music, Jerry Goldsmith; assistant directors, Tom Shaw and David Silver. Reviewed at Universal homeoffice, April 26, '62. Running time, **107 MINS.**

Jack Burns .... Kirk Douglas
Jerri Bondi .... Gena Rowlands
Sheriff Johnson .... Walter Matthau
Paul Bondi .... Michael Kane
Hinton .... Carroll O'Connor
Harry .... William Schallert
Gutierrez .... George Kennedy
Reverend Hoskins .... Karl Swenson
1st Deputy in Bar ...... Bill Mims
Old Man .... Martin Garralaga
Prisoner .... Lalo Rios

Often touching, and well served by its performances and photography, Joel Productions' "Lonely Are the Brave," produced by Edward Lewis, ultimately blurs its focus on the loner fenced in and bemused by the encroachments and paradoxes of civilization. Its makers have approached the misfit theme with a skittishness not unlike that exhibited by cowboy Kirk Douglas's horse. They have settled for surface instead of substance.

The failure of the Dalton Trumbo screenplay from an Edward Abbey novel is that it does not provide viewers with a sustained probing of the hero's perplexity. It is content only to state, rather explicitly, the dilemma, with the result that Douglas is pitiable only at a distance—audiences will doubtless sympathize, but they are not likely to "empathize." Nor are they apt to discern the larger implications of all-but-vanished individualism in a highly organized society.

As to how well the Universal release makes out, much will depend on that familiar one-two of campaign and early customer reaction. The surmise is that, with considerable nursing, it should do okay, but not exciting at the boxoffice.

The plot is sparing enough. Douglas, the footloose, arrives back at the New Mexico homestead of old friends Michael Kane and Gena Rowlands. Kane is in the Albuquerque jail on an aid-and-comfort to wetbacks rap, and good guy Douglas contrives to get himself tossed into the same pokey from where he plans to bust out with Kane. The buddy opts to stay, however — his ways are changed, and there is the wife and a son to consider—but Douglas, not one for the year's confinement he faces, makes off and takes to the hills ringing town. In a splendidly orchestrated pursuit, he eludes the cops only to be stopped when he and horse, attempting to cross a rain swept highway, are hit by a huge truck.

Good symbolism, that, having him chopped down not by fellow creatures but by technological progress. By contrast, most of the symbols (they are almost rampant) are announced with a kind of pandering clarity. At the outset, cowpoke and horse are framed by the New Mexico rock and sagebrush country. Raise sound and cut—to jets whooshing overhead, a wired fence with no trespass caveat, the zip of highway traffic, etc. Similarly, the accentuation in dialog, epitomized in the line, "Either you go by the rules or you lose." The film is too indulgent of the verbal where a gesture, expression, or quiet incident would convey better impact.

Of itself, the prolonged and climactic mountain chase is an entertaining sequence, a compelling melange of scenic sweep and tight action astutely arranged by director David Miller and excellently photographed by Philip Lathrop. It somehow, also, very nearly subordinates the message, except again for certain symbols, chiefly a military helicopter thrown into the hunt.

As the loner, Douglas is extremely likable and understands his part within its limitations, as written. Most beguiling performance, however, is turned in by Walter Matthau as the laconic and harassed sheriff, who has never faced his quarry but develops an intuitive sympathy for him. The force he heads is almost pure comic strip, making for some appealing levity. Yet, perceptive audiences may find such boobery too farcical for credibility.

Gena Rowlands, as the friend's wife (she was originally sweet on the undomesticated Douglas), is good as the voice of exasperation over what she sees merely as male obstinacy. Michael Kane, a veteran of legit making his screen debut, contributes effectively as the reformed buddy. There is polished support in lesser roles from Carroll O'Connor, George Kennedy, Karl Swenson and William Schallert, latter as a diverting boob in the sheriff's office.

Miller's direction is smooth and knowing, being particularly impressive in the mountain pursuit footage. Jerry Goldsmith has lent an enhancing score, wistful, compassionate and symbolic. Lathrop's camera, Leon Barsha's sensible editing, and the contribution of sound men Waldon O. Watson and Frank H. Wilkinson are all potent components. They furnish "Lonely" with almost enough virtues to redeem its flawed telling. *Pit.*

Le Septieme Jure
(The Seventh Jurist)
(FRENCH)

Paris, May 1.

Pathe release of Orex Films production. Stars Bernard Blier; features Maurice Biraud, Daniele Delorme, Francis Blanche, Jacques Riberolles, Francoise Giret. Directed by Georges Lautner. Screenplay, Jacques Robert, Pierre Laroche from the novel by Francis Didelot; camera, Maurice Fellous; editor, M. David. At Paris, Paris. Running time, **105 MINS.**

Gregoire .... Bernard Blier
Wife .... Daniele Delorme
Jurist .... Maurice Biraud
Catherine .... Francoise Giret
Sylvain .... Jacques Riberolles

Fairly slick psychological entry about a murderer, an ordinary man, who ends up on the jury condemning a man for the crime. But it's rather pat and flat in characterization. It remains too surfacey for irony and is a bit dated in expressionistic techniques.

A middleaged man with two grown children one Sunday wanders off for a walk while everybody is snoozing after a heavy meal. He sees the town loose girl sunbathing nude and tries to kiss her and strangles her when she screams.

Then comes his commentary about his feelings and justifications, the trial, his astuteness as a jurist acquitting the man. But town pettiness drives the man almost to suicide which is forced when the ex-jurist scuffles with him for the gun. His petty wife has him shipped off to an asylum rather than let him confess.

Bernard Blier is jowly and heavy but able to project the character of the trapped-by-own-guilt jurist while director Georges Lautner shows a good deal for atmosphere and pacing but has allowed this to be too predictable and preachy without the insight to make this gripping and a deeper look at justice, responsibility and small town meanness. It is technically neatly wrapped. *Mosk.*

La Denonciation
(The Denunciation)
(FRENCH—FRANSCOPE)

Paris, April 24.

CFDC release of Films Pleiade production. Stars Maurice Ronet, Francoise Brion, Nicole Berger; features Sacha Pitoeff, Michele Grellier, Francois Maistre. Written and directed by Jacques Doniol-Valcroze. Camera, Henri Raichi; editor, Bob Wade. Preemed in Paris. Running time, **105 MINS.**

Michel .... Maurice Ronet
Elsa .... Francoise Brion
Eleonore .... Nicole Berger
Malterner .... Sacha Pitoeff
Victoire .... Michele Grellier
Patrice .... Francois Maistre

A mixture of a suspense theme with sidelights of morality plus political skulduggery, this pic seems somewhat too overladen to have this keep up interest throughout.

Going to a nightclub one afternoon to retrieve a sweater he left there, a young film producer comes upon a body and is then knocked out by someone. It develops the cadaver was a man he once worked with in the resistance and who had become involved in some rightist political activity.

It seems the producer had cracked under Nazi torture and sold out his comrades but it had been covered up at war's end. He finally finds peace with himself only to be shot down by one of the killers.

Director-writer Jacques Doniol-Valcroze has overloaded this to bog down complete interest. But he displays a flair for potent imagery. However, he foists a striptease on the film when the producer's wife does one as a gag before they bed down one night, as well as other erotic sequences with the wife that have nothing to do with the tale. It is technically good but somewhat talky sans the pace and depth to make his final conversion dramatically sound. *Mosk.*

Lad: A Dog
(COLOR)

Adventures of Albert Payson Terhune's renowned collie, translated to screen with syrupy affection. Serviceable holiday fare for tykes and families.

Hollywood, April 26.

Warner Bros. release of Max J. Rosenberg production. Stars Peter Breck, Peggy McCay. Directed by Aram Avakian, Leslie H. Martinson. Screenplay, Lillie Hayward, Roberta O. Hodes, from novel by Albert Payson Terhune; camera (Technicolor), Bert Glennon; editor, Tom McAdoo; music, Heinz Roemheld; asst. director, Claude Binyon Jr. Reviewed at studio, April 26, '62. Running time, **98 MINS.**

Stephen Tremayne .... Peter Breck
Elizabeth Tremayne....... Peggy McCay
Hamilcar Q. Glure..... Carroll O'Connor
Angela .... Angela Cartwright
Lester .... Maurice Dallimore
Hilda .... Alice Pearce
The Poacher .... Jack Daly
Sheriff .... Charles Fredericks
Constable .... Tim Graham
Miss Woodward .... Lillian Buyeff

Warner Bros. has a marketable holiday attraction for the family

trade in "Lad: A Dog." which is poised for Memorial Day release in companionship with the studio's 22-minute cartoon featurette, "Adventures of the Road Runner." The Max J. Rosenberg production is in the tradition of "Lassie" and other such animal epics glorifying the good works of talented four-telling the good guys from the bad legged creatures with sunny dispositions and uncanny instincts for guys.

Wee moppets, for whom the cliche of the dog picture is still a fresh thrill, should take very kindly and enthusiastically to the film, based roughly on the actual adventures of Albert Payson Terhune's collie, as published 41 years ago in his book. Adults, on the other hand, will discover about a 98% quotient of predictability.

The Lillie Hayward-Roberta O. Hodes adaptation describes, with unabashed sentiment and a good degree of conversational redundancy, how Lad manages remarkably to: (1 help restore, through affection and a keen, alert sniffer, the functions of a little girl's legs, (2) win a solid gold "best in show" cup, without the aid of experience, against the most gifted show dog in the world, (3) help save the family from a fire and, in the process, bring to justice a demented neighborhood troublemaker.

Peter Breck and Peggy McCay are agreeable as Lad's devoted owners, although there are passages when they are handicapped by the rather artificial everybody-face-the-camera style of emoting engineered by the direction of Aram Avakian and/or Leslie H. Martinson, who shared helmsmanship. Otherwise the direction, though at times almost unbearably syrupy, is standard for this kind of film.

Carroll O'Connor gives a fine performance as a neighbor obsessed with material prestige who comes to see the error of his ways. Little Angela Cartwright, as the youngster who regains her ability to walk, is accomplished at expressing emotion. The rest of the cast perform well, and that goes for the canine star of the show.

Picturesque Technicolor photography by Bert Glennon, a sprightly score by Heinz Roemheld and careful art direction by Jack Poplin raise the quality of the production. The film seems rather long and has a few repetitious spots that might have been smoothed out by editor Tom McAdoo.

The companion "Road Runner" piece continues the popular cartoon adventures of the frustrated, but indestructible, coyote who tries in vain to seize, and presumably devour, the absolutely unconquerable and not at all likable road runner. ("Lad" would catch him, by gum.) The featurette directed by Chuck Jones is somewhat patchy and disjointed—at one point straying away from the central premise for at least five minutes. *Tube.*

That Touch of Mink

Conventional and thin in comedic plot, but all the chemistry is there for fancy takes at the b.o. Four deft performances are the main asset.

Universal release of a Granley-Arwin-Nob Hill picture; executive producer, Robert Arthur; produced by Stanley Shapiro and Martin Melcher. Stars Cary Grant, Doris Day. Features Gig Young, Audrey Meadows. Directed by Delbert Mann. Screenplay by Stanley Shapiro and Nate Monaster; camera (Eastman color), Russell Metty; editor, Ted Kent; assistant directors, Phil Bowles, Carl Beringer. Reviewed at Universal homeoffice, May 2, '62. Running time, **99 MINS.**

Philip Shayne	Cary Grant
Cathy Timberlake	Doris Day
Roger	Gig Young
Connie	Audrey Meadows
Young Man	Dick Sargent
Dr. Gruber	Alan Hewitt
Beasley	John Astin
Collins	John McKee
Miss Jones	Jan Burrell
Millie	Jrne Ericson
Hodges	Willard Sage
Williams	Russ Bender

The recipe is potent: Cary Grant and Doris Day in the old cat-and-mouse game. Pure gag-propelled farce, in which the commercial values tote up in a way that should handily extend the recent continuity of comedic success at the boxoffice. The gloss of "That Touch of Mink," however, doesn't obscure an essentially threadbare lining. In seeming to throw off a sparkle, credit performance and pace as the key virtues of this Universal release. The rest of it is commonplace.

The Stanley Shapiro-Nate Monaster screenplay maintains a generally good clip, all to the good, but too often there's a hampering second-hand air about situation and joke. Throughout, it seems, the determination is to keep faith with American sex mythology at any cost.

In this particular arrangement of coy he-she-nanigans, the comedy is premised on the conflict of her inexperience and his old pro suavity. He's a company-gobbling financier; she's a trim chick legging it through Manhattan canyons in search of a job. It starts when his limousine splatters her with puddle water. Fortuitous meeting and mating maneuvers follow, with the action shuttling between Gotham and Bermuda or Gotham and New Jersey suburbia.

Though short of the mark if you count sharp wit, there's still a fair amount of jollity churned out of all this for most audiences. Yet the burden for laughs is on the subsidiary humor—the neurotic syndrome of Gig Young as Grant's sauce-addicted fiscal adviser, and most especially in some wacky sequences in an Automat. Funniest of these is the no-cost method devised by payroller Audrey Meadows to keep roommate Day in groceries.

However one assesses the "innocent" fun, there's mention to be made of a regrettable lapse in the way psychiatry is kidded. Young's head-shrinker is depicted in the unethical light of capitalizing on big business tips dropped by his patient, stealing out of the seance to phone his broker while Young rambles on unawares. This isn't satire, just an offensive contribution to the mounting misinformation pertaining to an ambiguous but critical area of therapy.

Although Grant gives his tycoon the advantage of long seasoning at this sort of gamey exercise, he's clearly shaded in the laughgetting allotment. As written, Miss Day's clowning has the better of it; and she, by the way, certifies herself an adept farceur with this outing. But not surprisingly, the featured bananas make the best comedic score. Young, who may be getting typed as a wisecracking lush, affirms his claim to the characterization. And Miss Meadows seems born to the dry, caustic comedienne, which is no surprise per her tv track record. It pays her high compliment to say she reminds viewers of the Eve Arden heyday. There's strong support down the line, with particularly effective contributions from Dick Sargent, Alan Hewitt and John Astin.

Delbert Mann's direction suggests that he enjoys presiding over comedy. Giving his principals their head, he has also kept the action as lively as the script permits. The technical credits are all stalwart, from Russell Metty's camera to Ted Kent's editing.

Of some trade interest, incidentally, is the wholesale fragmenting of production covet in what's become a now-familiar maze of profit and tax maneuvering. The percentage pie carves up three ways, among Granley (Grant), Nob Hill (Shapiro), and Arwin (Doris Day-Martin Melcher), per screen credits for each. Further, Robert Arthur gets executive producer billing, with Shapiro and Melcher listed as producers, separate and additional to their corporate identities. Everybody figures to have a juicy melon to slice. *Pit.*

The World's Greatest Sinner
(WITH COLOR SEQUENCE)

Uninhibited sexploiter of limited commercial appeal, takes from Elmer Gantry. Semi-professional cast, low budget, deter from any dramatic value.

Hollywood, May 2.

Frenzy Production Inc. release of a Timothy Carey production. Stars Timothy Carey, Gil Baretto; features Betty Rowland, James Farley, Gail Griffen, Grace de Carolis, Gitta Maynard, Carolina Samario, Victor Floming. Direction and screenplay by Carey. Assistant producers, Anthony M. Lanza, George E. Nahas, George F. Carey; cameramen, Ove H. Sehested, Robert Shelfow, Frank Grande, Raymond Steckler; editor, Carl Mahakian; music, "Zappa"; assistant director, Gene Koziol. Previewed at Screen Directors Guild, May 1, '62. Running time, **82 MINS.**

Clarence Hilliard	Timothy Carey
Alonzo	Gil Baretto
Edna Hilliard	Betty Rowland
Devil	James Farley
Betty Hilliard	Gail Griffen
Mother	Grace De Carolis
Elderly Woman	Gitta Maynard
Priest	Gene Pollock
Guitar Player	Whitey Jent
Nate	Carolina Samario
Office Boss	Victor Floming
Secretary	Ann Josephs
Old Lady in Church	Jenny Sanches
Followers	Tyde Rule, Gene Koziol.

Dana Madison, Titus Moede, Betty Sturm, Marty Prisco, George F. Carey, Duana Dedda, Doris Carey, Eleanor Enderle, Jerry Mobley, George Seemer, Ben Avila, Joe Powell, Bob Divorsney, Victor Corey, Don Mozee.

The current tendency of experimental filmmakers to be as daring as they can usually results in their leaning so far for shock effect that they lose touch with realism. Timothy Carey, a character actor who has given the screen some interesting, off-beat characterizations, has ventured boldly, if unwisely, into fields of production, directing and writing with "The World's Greatest Sinner."

Granting Carey purpose in trying to convey a moral message in terms of "stark portrayal of human emotions," the result is a film of questionable value, commercial or otherwise, which cannot help but offend many groups with even the "moral" ending carrying its own repellent shock device.

Carey portrays a neurotic business man, rebelling against the mediocrity of his life, in search of a faith, a plan, or a gimmick that will bring him success and spiritual satisfaction. He becomes obsessed with the idea that he, himself, is a supreme being. Rejecting God, he sets out to convert. He first converts two by assuring them that they, too, are "supermen." Evangelist style, he draws crowds for his sermons with a flashy display: guitar, rock 'n' roll, garrish costume, suggestive body contortions. An elderly woman, flattered by his attention and impressed by his claim of divinity, agrees to finance his campaign.

As a self-styled "god" he gains national prominence and enters politics with the backing of a shady politician. His mother dies, his wife and daughter leave him, and he begins to doubt himself. He challenges God to a test of supremacy. Stealing a religious object from a church and violating it, he is shown, by a miracle, that he is human and fallible. He repents.

The black and white photography, with one exception, is a melange of bad lighting, awkward angles, and enforced company. A climactic color sequence is utilized in an apparent attempt to duplicate the horror effect used in "Jack the Ripper," but it turns out to be only ludicrous. A dance hall sequence, briefly comes closest to conveying the frenetic, fanatic drive for which Carey was obviously striving.

Carey's portrayal of the obsessed man is a masterpiece of bad acting. The supporting cast is obviously limited in experience and shows it, with only Gil Baretto, as Alohzo, standing out. Only Betty Roland, Citta Maynard, Caroline Samario, James Farley, Victor Floming, Gail Griffin and Grace De Carolis have enough screen time to create any lasting impressions. The music, as such, is notable more for its quantity than its quality and is hampered by an exceptionally poor soundtrack. *Robe.*

Merrill's Marauders
(COLOR)

Jeff Chandler's last film role. Beautifully directed and photographed, a dynamic cine-version of Merrill's Burmese exploits.

Hollywood, May 3.

Warner Bros. release of United States Productions picture, produced by Milton Sperling. Stars Jeff Chandler, Ty Hardin, Peter Brown, Andrew Duggan. Will Hutchins, Claude Akins. Directed by Samuel Fuller. Screenplay, Milton Sperling, Samuel Fuller, from book by Charlton Ogburn Jr.; camera (Technicolor), William Clothier; editor, Folmer Blangstead; music, Howard Jackson; asst. director,

William Kissel. Reviewed at Warner Bros. Studio, May 3, '62. Running time, **98 MINS.**

Brig. Gen. Merrill .... Jeff Chandler
Lt. Lee Stockton .... Ty Hardin
Bullseye .... Peter Brown
Major George Nemeny .. Andrew Duggan
Chowhound .... Will Hutchins
Sgt. Kolowicz .... Claude Akins
Burmese Girl .... Luz Valdez
Gen. Stilwell .... John Hoyt
Muley .... Charles Briggs
Officer .... Chuck Roberson
Officer .... Chuck Hayward
Medic .... Jack C. Williams
Corp. Doskis .... Chuck Hicks
Lt. Col. Bannister ...... Vaughan Wilson
Taggy .... Pancho Magolona

Director Samuel Fuller, taking a lesson from the subject of his film, leads, inspires and drives his cast and crew into giving him, in "Merrill's Marauders," a motion picture of excellent quality and a strong boxoffice prospect to boot. Jeff Chandler's last role, as Brigadier General Frank Merrill, is one of his best. The rugged, gray-thatched Chandler fits this role naturally and portrays one of World War II's most colorful personalities with a proper blend of military doggedness and personal humanity.

When Fuller—he was a G.I. in Europe—took his small cast and crew to the Philippines to shoot "Merrill's Marauders," he did plenty of preliminary screening and, down the line, he got the results he wanted. After Chandler, this film owes much of its excellence to William Clothier's Technicolor photography, both in his feeling for cinematic design and his superb use of color. He moves from beautifully framed intimate shots that dramatically progress the story to magnificent full-scale battle shots, all of which give the picture scope and grandeur.

Charlton Ogburn's book was a springboard only for the scenarists, producer Milton Sperling and Fuller. They elaborated it into a screenplay that balances battle scenes with character-establishing vignettes and gives the subject-hero a closer contact with his men through playing his story against the background of their daily activities, their fixture of personalities.

Ty Hardin's Lieutenant Stockton is a stock character—the young, still over-sensitive officer—but he conveys a tenderness, a sense of truth that keeps the role from seeming stereotyped. John Hoyt creates an amazing physical likeness of "Vinegar Joe" Stilwell in his one scene as the peppery old soldier.

In comparison to Chandler's and Hardin's roles, the rest of the cast is only supporting. But Andrew Duggan (as Doc Nemeny) and Peter Brown, Will Hutchins and Claude Akins (as enlisted men) bring effective interpretation to some colorful characters. In the almost entirely male cast, the brief introduction of a lovely Burmese maiden, played sans dialog by Filipino actress Luz Valdez, is pleasant but dramatically meaningless.

The battle sequences can compare with any seen on the screen. Considering the small number of troops available, Fuller creates an amazing impression of large scale maneuvers. He follows battle scenes with quietness, ending these with unexpected return to violent action. Here the hand of editor Folmar Blangsted is most obvious, juxtaposing these alternating moods so that even the quiet scenes build in suspense towards the next use of action. Howard Jackson's score, neither martial nor lushly melodic, is only occasionally guilty of resorting to an Oriental effect. It is pleasant and fitting but, on the whole, routine. For a war picture, "Merrill's Marauders" is refreshingly free of close-hand slaughter, too often used for shock effect. The battle scenes are outstanding examples of group movement. One scene makes a tremendous impression, visually and dramatically.

Merrill's men, invading a railroad station held by the Japanese, are forced to approach across the siding through enormous concrete forms. Fuller uses an overhead shot that gives the approach the feeling of a beautifully choreographed ballet, a labyrinth leading to unknown dangers, then they're through and the camera draws back for a full-screen shot of the entire railroad yard, littered with the dead as far as the eye can see. This is one of the best visual impressions of carnage since the Atlanta sequence in "Gone With the Wind." *Robe.*

Bon Voyage
(COLOR)

Disney does it again; boff returns expected.

Hollywood, May 5.

Buena Vista release of Walt Disney production. Stars Fred MacMurray, Jane Wyman, Michael Callan, Deborah Walley; features Jessie Royce Landis, Tommy Kirk, Georgette Anys, Kevin Corcoran, Ivan Desny. Direction by James Neilson. Screenplay, Bill Walsh, from book by Marrijane and Joseph Hayes; camera, William Snyder; music, Paul Smith; editor, Cotton Warburton; assistant director, Joseph L. McEveety. Reviewed at Academy Awards Theatre, May 4, '62. Running time, **130 MINS.**

Harry Willard .... Fred MacMurray
Katie Willard .... Jane Wyman
Nick O'Mara .... Michael Callan
Amy Willard .... Deborah Walley
Comtesse DuFresne. Jessie Royce Landis
Elliott Willard .... Tommy Kirk
Madame Clebert .... Georgette Anys
Skipper Willard .... Kevin Corcoran
Rudolph Hunschak ... Ivan Desny
The Girl .... Francoise Prevost
Horace .... Alex Gerry
Judge Henderson....... Howard I. Smith
The Tight Suit .... Casey Adams
Librarian .... James Millhollin
Sewer Guide .... Marcel Hillaire
The Englishman .... Richard Wattis
Penelope .... Carol White
Florelle .... Marie Sirago
Mrs. Henderson .... Doris Packer
Shamra .... Ana Maria Majalca
Shamra's Father .... Hassan Khayyam

Walt Disney dishes up another comedy blockbuster in this rollicking tour de force of an American family seeing Europe for the first time. Gross-wise, the Technicolor feature, sparked by surefire ingredients, conceivably could duplicate the b.o. success of Disney's two previous boffers, "Shaggy Dog" and "Absent-Minded Professor."

Based on tome by Marrijane and Joseph Hayes, film gets whimsical scripting by Bill Walsh—also credited with previous pair—and James Neilson's bright direction gives action a heady froth to which entire cast responds. Music score by Paul Smith is a potent asset that adds high polish.

As action swings from the full Paris sequences to Cannes on the Riviera there is at first a suggestion of anti-climax, but this is soon dispelled as spectator is caught up in the merriment of situations themed on a pop note.

Plotline has Fred MacMurray, a Terre Haute, Ind., plumbing contractor, and his family boarding the S.S. United States in N.Y. for Europe, after he and his wife, Jane Wyman, have planned trip for years. Their brood consists of a romance-ready daughter, Deborah Walley, and two sons, teenager Tommy Kirk, more interested in girls than the Eiffel Tower, and 12-year-old Kevin Corcoran, constantly getting lost.

MacMurray soon discovers that his holiday isn't entirely the carefree existence he had pictured. He finds his daughter falling in love with a wealthy offspring of divorced parents, Michael Callan, who doesn't believe in marriage; he's run ragged trying to play the father to his energetic younger son, who in turn is trying to be the perfect son to his father. His teenager nearly gets into a mess with a French mam'selle, and last of all he finds the most notorious playboy of Europe making a play for his wife. Disney riffles his action through the interesting and sometimes fascinating backgrounds of shipboard; Paris in all its scenic glory; the beach and casinos of the Riviera.

MacMurray continues the comic perambulations of his two prior Disney excursions in a character combining good-natured humor with warmth and understanding, even topping those two past portrayals. Miss Wyman delivers soundly as a wise mother who discovers she is in unfamiliar ground when it comes to her own experiences with a playboy. Pair's children are exceptionally well cast and turn in smart performances. Callan lends interest to the disillusioned rich boy who finally falls for the daughter, and Ivan Desny offers a brief but illuminating contribution as the playboy. Balance of cast generally disport themselves competently.

Technical credits have been particularly well handled, especially the color photography of William Snyder. Others include Carroll Clark and Marvin Aubrey Davis' art direction and set decorations by Emile Kuri and Hal Gausman; editing by Cotton Warburton; Bill Thomas' costumes. *Whit.*

Lisa
(C'SCOPE—COLOR)

Sporadically interesting romantic melodrama based on Jan De Hartog's "The Inspector." Handsomely photographed against authentic European backgrounds, but will need heavy sell to trade and public.

20th-Fox release of Mark Robson production. Stars Stephen Boyd, Dolores Hart; features Leo McKern, Hugh Griffith, Donald Pleasence. Directed by Philip Dunne. Screenplay, Nelson Gidding, based on novel by Jan De Hartog; camera (De Luxe Color), Arthur Ibbetson; editor, Ernest Walter; music, Malcolm Arnold; assistant director, Kip Gowens. Reviewed in N.Y., April 26, '62. Running time, **112 MINS.**

Peter Jongman .... Stephen Boyd
Lisa Held .... Dolores Hart
Brandt .... Leo McKern
Van der Pink .... Hugh Griffith
Sergeant Wolters ..... Donald Pleasence
Avoob .... Harry Andrews
Dickens .... Herbert Stephens
Thorens .... Marius Goring
De Kool .... Finlay Currie
Dr. Mitropoulos .... Harold Goldblatt
Browne .... Neil McCallum
Commissioner Bartels .... Geoffrey Keen
Mrs. Jongman .... Jean Anderson
Anaka Jongman .... Jane Jordan Rogers
Inspector Cobb .... Jack Gwillim
M.P. Sergeant .... Tibby Brittain
Rachel .... Ann Dickins
Barge Woman .... Vi Stevens
Detective Inspector...... Derek Francis
Agriculture Officer .... John Welsh
Sergeant Greninger .... Victor Brooks

"Lisa," based on the Jan De Hartog novel, "The Inspector" (and known by that title almost until the time of release), reflects a similar quality of indecision in its narrative. This tale of a Dutch police officer who risks life and reputation to get a pretty ex-Auschwitz inmate to Palestine (right after the war) is part mystery, part romance, part action drama, with no one element dominating to give the film the kind of sock suspense or emotional appeal needed in today's market.

It's hard to point the fault—in the script by Nelson Gidding, the direction of Philip Dunne or the playing of Stephen Boyd and Dolores Hart as the principals. Individually they all seem competent enough, but the final result is curiously unexciting. One reason may be that the two principal characters—as written, directed and played—never are very deeply perceived, for all the psychological motivations ascribed to them. Consequently, plot situations (which are not particularly inventive) and subsidiary characters must sustain audience interest.

The locales, ranging from Holland to Tangier and the shores of Palestine, offer plenty of opportunity for colorful camerawork, beautifully executed in De Luxe color and CinemaScope by Arthur Ibbetson. The story opens in Holland as Boyd, a Dutch police inspector, trails a former Nazi (Marius Goring) suspected of luring girls out of the country into white slavery in South America.

Because the girl in this case, Miss Hart, strongly reminds Boyd of his late fiancee, who he failed to save from a Nazi concentration camp, the inspector takes a more than personal interest in the case. He follows them to London, has a showdown with Goring in which the latter is accidently killed, and then sets out to grant the girl her one desire: to get to Palestine.

In the course of their flight out of Holland to France and then Tangier, where Boyd expects to make contact with someone who'll smuggle the girl into Palestine, the fugitives fall in love, a situation complicated by the policeman's guilt feelings re his late fiancee, and the fact that Miss Hart, who was used as "a living corpse" for Nazi medical experiments, is convinced she cannot have "normal relations" (that's how it's euphemized in the script) with a man.

The action episodes are, in fact, the best things in the film, especially the flight by canal barge out of Holland, with Leo McKern contributing a sharp and humorous portrait of a bristling, crochety old sea dog. Hugh Griffith, who sounds more like Sidney Greenstreet every day, is amusing if not wholly believeable as a rather bizarre Tangier smuggler, given to swilling champagne and taking a tennis racquet after the bats which invade his apartment at nightfall. Robert Stephens, Donald Pleasence and Finlay Currie also are sharply effective in lesser roles. Producer Mark Robson obviously didn't stint in the casting

of these subsidiary characters **or in the entire physical production.** *Anby.*

13 West Street

Teenage violence ignites Alan Ladd's revenge obsession. Everybody's sick, sick, sick. Slick production but limited b.o. Will need hard sell.

Hollywood, May 2.

Columbia release of Ladd Enterprises production, produced by William Bloom. Stars Alan Ladd, Rod Steiger; features Michael Callan, Dolores Dorn. Directed by Philip Leacock. Screenplay by Bernard C. Schoenfeld and Robert Presnell Jr. from the Leigh Brackett novel, "The Tiger Among Us"; camera, Charles Lawton Jr.; editor, Al Clark; music, George Duning; assistant director, Eddie Saeta. Reviewed at Columbia Studio, May 1, '62. Running time, **80 MINS.**

Walt Sherill	Alan Ladd
Det. Sgt. Koleski	Rod Steiger
Chuck	Michael Callan
Tracey Sherill	Dolores Dorn
Paul Logan	Kenneth Mac Kenna
Mrs. Landry	Margaret Hayes
Finney	Stanley Adams
Everett	Chris Robinson
Mrs. Quinn	Jeanne Cooper
Bill	Arnold Merritt
Tommy	Mark Slade
Joe Bradford	Henry Beckman
Noddy	Clegg Hoyt
Jack	Jordan Gerler
Doctor	Robert Cleaves
Negro	Bernie Hamilton
Mexican	Pepe Hern
Mr. Johnson	Frank Gerstle

Teenage delinquency, its cause and cure, continues to fascinate filmmakers. Some of the ingredients of any motion picture exploring this theme have become producer cliches: (1) display of violence as boxoffice stimulant; (2) hope that such film may bring forth another James Dean; (3) belief that to cure social ills it is necessary to portray them; and (4) denied but true, an overt wish to venture into territory, questionable in taste but bearing a strong aroma of potential profit.

"13 West Street" exemplifies all of these cliches and, of course, the tale it unfolds isn't new. Metro's "Key Witness" (1960) told a somewhat similar story with less noise and more success. For its violence, "13 West Street" begins with the brutal beating of a man by five youths, ends with another beating and an attempted drowning. When the average viewer is subjected to 75 minutes of oft-repeated violence, five minutes of climactic "repentance" won't amount to much.

Ladd, a mild-mannered space engineer, is brutally beaten by the teenagers for no apparent reason. He tries to find them, less for vengeance than curiosity as to their motivation. Police officer Rod Steiger doesn't produce results quickly enough for Ladd, who assumes the search on his own, against the advice of the police and the pleas of his wife. His curiosity changes to a revenge obsession.

The double search dovetails as the boys' identities become known; they prove to be from wealthy families, overprivileged children. Michael Callan, the paranoic leader (it's always the fault of one youth!), and the boys beat up Ladd a second time to scare him off their trail and threaten his wife. Callan drives one of the boys to suicide and is finally cornered by Ladd, who attempts to kill him but stops just short of murder.

The latest candidate for the Dean's chair, Callan is a handsome, talented actor with feeling for mood and expression, resources which are not sufficiently exploited this time by director Philip Leacock. In a part requiring a gradual psychological change, Ladd only conveys fatigue, bordering on boredom. Steiger's formula-plan detective permits him little opportunity to build but he projects warmth and concern for his client with telling conviction.

Miss Dorn's stage-acquired talent has lost some of its "heft" in her transition from the Chekhovian world of "Uncle Vanya" to a film that expects establishment of character in a few expressions. Despite this, she registers favorably, creating sympathy as Ladd's wife.

Director Leacock, working with older "children" than those who gave him his reputation, sacrifices some directorial integrity to keep the film moving, primarily with repeated scenes of violence. The script of Bernard Schoenfeld and Robert Presnell is unable to convey in 80 minutes what Leigh Brackett took an entire novel to relate, so they have kept the action and discarded most of the motivation—to wit, a slick, quick explanation of what bugs these kids.

Charles Lawton's excellent camera work, abetted by the expert editing of Al Clark, is a major asset throughout but at its best in a beautifully-staged and photographed car chase through the Hollywood Hills at night. George Duning's score never intrudes, stopping completely when needed to accent director Leacock's effective use of natural sound effects for suspense.

Callan's accomplices are convincingly portrayed by Chris Robinson, Mark Glad, Clegg Hoyt and, very fine as the suicide, Arnold Merritt. Jeanne Cooper, in a brief scene as Merritt's aunt, beautifully delivers the most telling line in the film when she says to Ladd, after the boy's death—"I hope that you sleep well tonight." The late Kenneth MacKenna, seen briefly as a high school principal, Margaret Hayes, Joe Bradford and Jordan Gerler contribute impressive bits. *Robe.*

Anni Ruggenti
(Roaring Years)
(ITALIAN)

Rome, May 1.

Incei release of a SPA (Achille Piazzi)-Incei production. Stars Nino Manfredi; features Gino Cervi, Michele Mercier, Gastone Moschin, Rosalia Maggio, Linda Sini, Angela Luce, Carla Calo, Gino Brillante, Salvo Randone. Directed by Luigi Zampa. Screenplay, Ettore Scola, Ruggero Maccari, Luigi Zampa; from story by Sergio Amidei, Vincenzo Talarico; camera, Carlini; music, Piero Piccioni. At Capranica, Rome. Running time, **106 MINS.**

Omero	Nino Manfredi
Podesta	Gino Cervi
DeVincenzi	Salvo Randone
Elvira	Michele Mercier

Nicely made pic about Fascist foibles in the prewar years of a South Italian town, but looks limited to Italo audiences who'll appreciate the satire and spoof.

Based on or inspired by Gogol's "Inspector General," plot has a smalltime insurance salesman visiting the town being mistaken for a Fascist inspector sent from Rome to give the local administration the o.o. Situation which ensues is replete with risible double-entendress.

Nino Manfredi is excellent in a measured rendering of the insurance peddler. Salvo Randone is fine as a future resistance leader while Gino Cervi is solid as the town mayor and Michele Mercier comely as his daughter.

Locations are taken proper advantage of by Carlo Carlini's camera and by director Zampa, who has always had a knack for depicting smalltown milieus. Technical credits are likewise fine. *Hawk.*

Ride the High Country
(C'SCOPE—COLOR)

Traditional western with a gimmick storyline and artistic production values. In the hard-to-sell category between an expensive "B" and a blockbuster.

Hollywood, May 4.

Metro-Goldwyn-Mayer release, produced by Richard E. Lyons. Stars Randolph Scott and Joel McCrea. Directed by Sam Peckinpah. Screenplay by N. B. Stone Jr.; camera (Metrocolor), Lucien Ballard; editor, Frank Santillo; music, George Bassman; assistant director, Hal Polaire; art direction, George W. Davis and Leroy Coleman; sound, Franklin Milton. Reviewed at Vogue Theatre, Hollywood, May 2, 1962. Running time, **94 MINS.**

Gil Westrum	Randolph Scott
Steve Judd	Joel McCrea
Elsa Knudsen	Mariette Hartley
Heck Longtree	Ron Starr
Judge Tolliver	Edgar Buchanan
Joshua Knudsen	R. G. Armstrong
Kate	Jenie Jackson
Billy Hammond	James Drury
Sylvus Hammond	L. Q. Jones
Elder Hammond	John Anderson
Jimmy Hammond	John Davis Chandler
Henry Hammond	Warren Oates

The old saying "you can't make a silk purse out of a sow's ear" rings true for Metro-Goldwyn-Mayer's artistic western "Ride the High Country." It remains a standard story, albeit with an interesting gimmick and some excellent production values, but lies in the hard-to-sell area in between an expensive "B" and a big one. It is doubtful if Randolph Scott or Joel McCrea, teamed for the first time, can draw the mainstem crowds. If so, this limits the film.

Similarly, while Scott and McCrea are each top drawing cards abroad, Metro may find the foreign grosses they are probably eyeing limited for similar reasons. This market depends essentially on action. Though "Country" has plenty of it, the important underlying theme touches on the disintegration of the old western hero. It abounds in highly-developed comedy satire that may not be appreciated abroad.

Scott and McCrea play their ages in roles that could well be extensions of characters they have each played in countless earlier films. They are quick-triggered ex-lawmen, former famed "town-tamers" whom life has passed by and who are now reduced to taking jobs as guards for a gold shipment. They engage in one last battle—over a woman and involving a youth who epitomizes their own youth—but the major battle is one Scott has with himself and the lesser the one they both have with a group of rugged young brothers whose intentions toward the young lady are less than honorable.

Cinematically, producer Richard E. Lyons has turned out a top quality film. Lucien Ballard's photography beautifully captures the scenic California locations where it was filmed and Frank Santillo's editing takes good care of well placed angle shots and mood scenes.

It is Sam Peckinpah's direction, however, that gives the film greatest artistry. He gives N. B. Stone Jr.'s script a measure beyond its adequacy, instilling bright moments of sharp humor and an overall significant empathetic flavor.

Performances throughout are excellent, Scott and McCrea better than they have ever been. Newcomers Mariette Hartley and Ron Starr show every potential for important careers and the entire supporting cast is a collection of standards—Edgar Buchanan, R. G. Armstrong, James Drury, L. Q. Jones, John Anderson, John Davis Chandler and Warren Oates—and, in an uncredited bit, that always bright face of Percy Helton. Jenie Jackson, also in her film debut, has visual flair as an obese madam, though she is allowed the only note of bad taste by costuming with extra bosom padding for flash comedy that isn't necessary.

George Bassman's score is helpful and art direction by George W. Davis and Leroy Coleman fine. *Dale.*

Night Creatures
(BRITISH-EASTMANCOLOR)

Slick costume meller from the Hammer assembly line. Good values, albeit moderately exciting. Should do well enough.

Universal release of a Hammer-Major Production, produced by John Temple-Smith. Stars Peter Cushing. Features Yvonne Romain, Patrick Allen, Oliver Reed. Directed by Peter Graham Scott. Screenplay, John Elder; camera (Eastmancolor), Arthur Grant; editor, Eric Boyd-Perkins; music, Don Banks; assistant directors, John Peverall, Peter Medak. Reviewed at Universal homeoffice, May 3, '62. Running time, **81 MINS.**

Dr. Blyss	Peter Cushing
Imogene	Yvonne Romain
Captain Collier	Patrick Allen
Harry	Oliver Reed
Mipps	Michael Ripper
Rash	Martin Benson
Bosun	David Lodge
Squire	Derek Francis
Mrs. Rash	Daphine Anderson
Mulatto	Milton Reid
Frightened Man	Jack MacGowran
Jack Pott	Peter Halliday
Dick Tate	Terry Scully
Tom Ketch	Sydney Bromley
Gerry	Rupert Osborn
Wurzel	Gordon Rollings
Peg-Leg	Bob Head
Pirate Bosun	Colin Douglas

"Night Creatures," a Hammer-Major Production, is another of those mood-crusted, fanciful costume mellers the British are generally so deft at, and which seem to find a steady market in the U.S. Pure escapism, of course, but notable is that the Hammer imprimatur has come to certify solid values in all production departments, and there's no mystery why these films rate audience allegiance. It's logical to figure, therefore, that this Universal release will follow form and do nicely as a programmer.

More impressionable minds may find some moderately chilling moments in "Creatures," but terror is much less the point or effect herein than a reasonably plausible delineation of a legend. The chief ingredients of the 18th century Britain story are swamp phantoms and smugglers. The latter are proper townsfolk by day, contraband runners by night, their operation braintrusted by a former sea pirate turned village vicar. Acting

on a tip, the Crown dispatches a band of seamen to investigate the town, and the resultant effort to uncover the illicit traffic is the preoccupation of John Elder's good screenplay. In cracking the smuggling ring the King's sailors also solve the mystery of the luminous nocturnal swamp "illusions," and the vicar's hidden identity.

The suspense contained in all this is less ominous in quality than just plain curious, but still sufficiently arresting for the trade it's designed to fetch. Visually, the pic is quite up to par, replete with stock villainy, swirling swamp mist and the rest that keynote this cinematic genre. There's the usual love interest, too, memorable in this case if only because of the femme's mammary distinction.

The histrionics are generally convincing, especially Peter Cushing as the pirate-cum-vicar, a pariah thought to have met his end years earlier by hanging. Also making stalwart contributions are Patrick Allen as the captain of the King's sailors; Oliver Reed, one of the smugglers and the young man in love; and Yvonne Romain, a woman to literally watch. Others impressing in a melange of flavorsome characterizations are Michael Ripper, Martin Benson, Derek Francis and Milton Reid.

Peter Graham Scott's direction is savvy, and the range of technical credits are all on the plus side, especially Arthur Grant's photography. Mention should also be made of Les Bowie's special effects.

Pit.

Cartouche
(FRENCH—DYALISCOPE—COLOR)

Paris, May 1.

Cinedis release of Ariane-Filmsonor-Vides Films production. Stars Jean-Paul Belmondo, Claudia Cardinale, Odile Versois; features Jess Hahn, Jean Rochefort, Noel Roquevert, Marcel Dalio. Directed by Philippe De Broca. Screenplay, Charles Spaak, Daniel Boulanger; camera (Eastmancolor), Christian Matras; editor, Laurence Mery. At Marignan, Paris. Running time, 125 MINS.

Cartouche .... Jean-Paul Belmondo
Venus .... Claudia Cardinale
Isabelle .... Odile Versois
Malichot .... Marcel Dalio
La Douceur .... Jean Rochefort
La Taupe .... Jess Hahn
Inspector .... Noel Roquevert

Familiar swashbuckler concerns a good-natured Robin Hood-type bandit of 18th Century France. But it has enough wry and tongue-in-cheek aspects, sans sacrificing the action, to make it an above average entry of the kind here, with playoff possibilities abroad on its derring-do.

Cartouche (Jean-Paul Belmondo) joins the army to escape the leading gang chief he has always fought. Here he finds two sidekicks and they run off with the regimental money to come back and take over the gang. He also garners a comely gypsy, Claudia Cardinale.

Then he robs only from the rich and all goes well till he falls for a noblewoman and gets caught in a trap to be saved via the sacrifice of his gypsy's life. Belmondo has the flair, insouciance and charm for the bandit role with enough acrobatic prowess to put it over. Miss Cardinale is decorative while Jess Hahn and Jean Rochefort are properly stalwart as the cohorts.

Color is rightly splashy. This manages to sail along with enough fights and escapes to make it a diverting costume actioner. But pic lacks a breath of dash and bombast to make it an unusual entry of this sort. It is an okay entry. Production dress and technical qualities are top grade.

Mosk.

The White Bear
(POLISH)

Toronto, May 1.

Godsinski release of Film Polski production. In charge of production, Zwonimir Feric; directed by Jerzy Zarzycki; screenplay, Jerzy Broszkiewicz, Stefan Matyszkiewicz, Konrad Nalecki, Jerzy Zarzycki, from a short story by Robert Azderbal & Roman Fister; music, Stanislaw Wislocki; camera, Stefan Matyszkiewicz; editing, Tomira Karpowicz. North American premiere at Civic Square Theatre, April 26, '62. Running time, 96 MINS.

Henryk Fogiel ...... Gustaw Holoubek
The Professor .... Stanislaw Milski
Anna .... Teresa Tuszynska
Michal .... Stanislaw Mikulski
Major von Henneberg .. Adam Pawlikowski
Lili .... Lillian Niwinska
Captain Grimm .... Emil Karewicz

This is another Polish film of unusual merit, based on a true story of a Jewish scientist who escapes from a train carrying prisoners to a concentration camp, and who manages to hide from the Nazis by assuming the disguise of a performing bear. Zarzycki (who made "The Undefeated City") is not so much interested in hide, seek and chase but in contrasting the beliefs of the Jew with those of the German general in charge of the town. In the climax, his confident, arrogant and philosophic attitude towards life vanishes and he is revealed as the beast.

The ending is apt to tail off in some confusion, otherwise this is a well-photographed, well-acted, intelligent and thoughtful story for those specialized cinemas that do not depend on movies with festival reputations and awards.

Prat.

She'll Have To Go
(BRITISH)

Periodically amusing dualler that will suit easygoing audiences.

London, May 1.

Anglo Amalgamated release of Asher Brothers' production. Stars Bob Monkhouse, Alfred Marks, Hattie Jacques; features Dennis Lotis, Anna Karina. Directed by Robert Asher. Screenplay, John Waterhouse, based on Ian Stuart Black's play, "We Must Kill Toni"; camera, Jack Asher; editor, Gerry Hamblin; music, Phil Green. At Hammer Theatre, London. Running time, 89 MINS.

Francis Oberon .... Bob Monkhouse
Douglas Oberon .... Alfred Marks
Miss Richards .... Hattie Jacques
Toni .... Anna Karina
Gilbert .... Dennis Lotis
Arnold .... Graham Stark
Chemist .... Clive Dunn
Macdonald .... Hugh Lloyd
Doctor .... Peter Butterworth

This one pretends to be nothing more than a modest dualer geared to raise a few yocks, in which it periodically succeeds. Directed briskly by Robert Asher, lensed satisfactorily by his brother Jack, the action is mainly confined to the interior of a "stately home." Phil Green has contributed some nimble music and Sonny Miller has turned in a couple of lyrics which will rate airing.

The comedy has a rather simple theme. Two penniless brothers find that their late grandmother has willed her cash to a distant unknown cousin. To get their mitts on the legacy they decide that the girl either must be murdered or married. Murder seems the best way until they meet the girl and find that she is quite a looker. But marriage raises problems.

This plot is enough to raise some laughs. Alfred Marks turns in a workmanlike performance, with the advantage of the better written part, while Bob Monkhouse, as his brother, tends to ham it too much. Hattie Jacques has a rich little role as a woman's magazine writer. A comely Danish femme named Anna Karina, in her first British film, decorates the screen delightfully without contributing anything spectacular in the way of thesping. These are the major roles but Peter Butterworth, as a shortsighted doctor; Clive Dunn, as a chemist, and Graham Stark, as a photographer, furnish some useful comedy bits.

Most interesting piece of casting is Dennis Lotis, a top pop singer, in a non-vocalizing role as the brothers' manservant. Lotis has a pleasing appearance and an easy manner which could win him further acting roles.

Rich.

Es Dach Ueberem Chopf
(A Roof Over Your Head)
(SWISS)

Zurich, May 1.

Praesens-Film A.G. Zurich release of Praesens and Gloriafilm A.G. (Max Dora) production. Features Zarli Carigiet, Valerie Steinmann, Erika Halm, Gion Janett, Micha Kasics, Willi Fueter, Fred Tanner, Heinrich Gretler, Walburga Gmuer, Alfred Schlageter, Eva Langraf, Bruno Ganz, Kurt Brunner, Elsbeth Gmuer, Paul Buehlmann, Charles F. Vaucher, Angelica Arndts, Bella Neri, Kurt Heinz Fischer, Heidy Forster. Directed by Kurt Frueh. Screenplay, Frueh and Jean-Pitre Gerwig; camera, Emil Berna; music, Walter Baumgartner; editor, Hans Heinrich Egger. At Urban Theatre, Zurich. Running time, 101 MINS.

Based on a successful radio serial, this new Swiss comedy about the problem of poor families with many children trying to find adequate housing within their means has the ingredients to become a popular on the local market. A wider distribution seems doubtful because it is too locally slanted to be of much interest beyond the Swiss border.

Judged by Swiss standards, this rates among the better pix efforts in some time. It is well made, free of any false pathos and generally enjoyable. Plot concerns a poor couple with six children living in a shack, who are one day miraculously offered a comfortable new apartment at a ridiculously low rent. It turns out that the house-owner intends to "use" this noisy eight-piece family to drive off a couple of nagging tenants. When his plan backfires, he wants to unlodge them again. But by that time, neighbors stand up in their defense, forcing him to revoke his intentions.

Direction by Kurt Frueh moves at an agreeable pace and keeps a nice balance between the many humorous scenes and the basically serious story. Lensing by vet Swiss cameraman, Emil Berna, is of his usual high quality. Performances are generally above par, but Swiss comedian Zarli Carigiet as the father dominates the cast with a true-to-life portrayal that is both hilarious and pathetic.

Mezo.

Donnez-Moi Dix Hommes Desesperes
(Give Me Ten Desperate Men)
(FRENCH-ISRAELI)

Paris, May 1.

CF release of Como Films-Cila-Films Du Chapiteau-Israel Films production. With Pascale Audret, Jacques Riberolles, Maurice Sarfati, Francis Lax, Scott Finch, Philippe Clair, Oded Theomi, Yael Elbaz. Directed by Pierre Zimmer. Screenplay, Zimmer, Antoine Tudal, Jacques Lanzmann; camera, Andre Dumaitre; editor, James Cuenet. Preemed in Paris. Running time, 110 MINS.

Daniel .... Jacques Riberolles
Sarah .... Pascale Audret
Simon .... Maurice Sarfati
Florist .... Francis Lax
Fiancee .... Yael Elbaz
Yemen .... Oded Theomi

Tale of a Palestinian khibboutz, handled by 12 young men and two girls on the Arab border just before Israel became a state, is somewhat too conventional in characters, mounting and execution to do justice to this period. It emerges mainly a playoff item abroad on its theme without the weight for arty chances.

Everything is just too schematic. The group arrives and builds its outpost. The leader is a stalwart Frenchman while the others come from most European countries and the U. S. There is the warrior, the more biblical one, the cowardly one, etc. There is a brush with the Arabs, and then the hunt for water and the fraying of nerves.

Into this setup comes a young girl who had been a concubine for the Nazis. The khibboutz survives all, gets water, and hears Israel proclaimed a state. Thus it becomes a vet center as new, young Israelis come through to begin other ones.

Dialog is also too preachy to fit this bare theme. It may be an okay Israeli item and is technically good. But the French writing, directing and thesping are not close enough to their subject. Israeli settings, where the pic was made, help as do the Israeli thespians.

Mosk.

Ihr Schoenster Tag
(Her Most Beautiful Day)
(German)

Berlin, May 1.

Nora release of Melodie-Film production. Stars Inge Meysel, Rudolf Platte and Sonja Ziemann; features Brigitte Grothum, Goetz George and Gert Guenter Hoffmann. Directed by Paul Verhoeven. Screenplay, Curth Flatow and Horst Pillau, after stageplay by Flatow and Pillau; camera, Heinz Hoelscher; music, Friedrich Schroeder; editor, Martha Duebber. At Zoo Palast, Berlin. Running time, 92 MINS.

Annie Wiesner .... Inge Meysel
Karl Wiesner .... Rudolf Platte
Helene Wiesner .... Sonja Ziemann
Inge Wiesner .... Brigitte Grothum
Herbert Wiesner .... Axel Scholtz
Adam Kowalski .... Goetz George
Erich Seidel ... Gert Guenter Hoffmann
Dan .... Rexi Hegyi

This is the film version of Curth Flatow and Horst Pillau's stageplay, "Window to the Hall," a popular piece about common Berlin people which proved a big success at West Berlin's Hebbel Theatre sometime ago. Although the film sticks close to the original, it falls somewhat short of the legit work. It has the same lovable characters but the humor, sentimentality and atmosphere is not as genuine as it was on the stage. Paul Verhoeven's direction is routine yet he doesn't seem to have the feel for this popular piece. Neverthe-

less, this pic has still sufficient ingredients to please the less demanding clientele, and is one of the better German comedies. It even may have some export chances.

Principal figures are a streetcar conductor and a femme gatekeeper of a Berlin dwelling house, portrayed by Rudolf Platte and Inge Meysel respectively, who both repeat here their successful stage performances. She wants to make "something big" of her children. Her eldest daughter (Sonja Ziemann) is married (allegedly) to an American millionaire. But she returns from the U.S. with an illegitimate child. Frau Wiesner's dream world collapses when she learns that her daughter never was married. Much to her dismay, also the younger daughter and her student son give her substantial problems.

Miss Meysel and Platte turn in the best performances and also take care of most of the laughter. A convincing performance is contributed by Guenter Hoffmann, a plumber who used to go with Miss Ziemann before her American adventure. Little Dan, the illegitimate child, is delightfully played by Rexi Hegyi, son of a Berlin-stationed American. Film's technical credits are okay. *Hans.*

Cannes Festival

Strangers in the City
(SCANOSCOPE)

Sometimes awkward in telling, but a first film on a touchy subject that has art house possibilities in the U.S., and playoff chances.

Cannes, May 8.
Embassy release of Carrier production. With Robert Gentile, Camilo Delgado, Rosita De Triana, Creta Margos, Robert Corso, Kenny Delmar. Written, directed and photographed by Rick Carrier. Editor, Stan Russell; music, Bob Prince. At Cannes Film Fest. Running time, 80 MINS.
Filipe .... Robert Gentile
Jose .... Camilo Delgado
Antonia .... Rosita De Triana
Elena .... Creta Margos
Caddy .... Robert Corso
Mr. Lou .... Kenny Delmar
Dan .... Bob O'Connell
Grocery Man .... John Roeburt
Jo .... Ruth Kuzab

A first film by a Yank newcomer, Rick Carrier, who made this on his own in New York about the disintegration of a Puerto Rican family, this bodes a future for the new, if sometimes still awkward talent. The sincerity, visual flair and drive overcome the at times overdone dramatics, to make this a film with edge that could pay off in savvy U.S. arty house placement.

European film fests possibly have done more for these completely new indie pix producers in the U.S. than Yank film people, but this one has already been picked up by Embassy Pictures for international handling. Like "The Connection," "On the Bowery," "Savage Eye," "Shadows" and "The Exiles," this underscores the growing offbeat personal production springing up in America.

This film shows a Puerto Rican family in a Manhattan slum. The father is a vain, proud man with a lack of understanding of America or his family—and he has just lost his job. His teenage son and daughter go to look for work but he orders his wife to stay home. The boy runs into local racism and general hoodlumism as a delivery boy while the girl, a beauty, is used by factory workers and then becomes a sort of call girl for a dressmaker.

The boy faces up to the foppish leader of the local gang when he thinks he has molested his sister. In a well-staged fight, finally they become friends.

The sister is found out, and the mother goes out to remonstrate with a bully who had seduced her daughter, only to kill him in a scuffle. Returning home, the enraged husband turns on her and she is accidentally electrocuted. The husband then takes poison. The son comes back with his sister after having dragged her away from her skidding life.

It may sound overly melodramatic, but this has a neat insight into N.Y. life, as this producer sees it. Though this pic shows mainly bigoted people, it also depicts how their own weaknesses help betray this family. Much of the wickedness is from plain ignorance.

This is a film with definite anger at all this waste. It manages to make its point without preaching. Too, it brings this new emigrant U.S. life into focus without distorting it too much. Some of the acting is skimpy. But Robert Gentile, as the son; Creta Margos, as his pliant comely sister; Rosita De Triana, as the anguished mother and Robert Corso, as the foppish gang leader, are standout.

Rick Carrier shows a forceful directorial hand that should improve as he learns how to handle thesps and allow his drama to build more easily. But it is an impressive start, having a ring of feeling and authentic place. Film looks at a U.S. problem s e v e r e l y but humanely. *Mosk.*

L'Ecclisse
(Eclipse)
(ITALO-FRENCH)

Cannes, May 8.
Cineriz release of an Interopa (Robert, Raymond Hakim)-Paris Film coproduction. Features Monica Vitti, Alain Delon, Francisco Rabal, Lilla Brignone. Directed by Michelangelo Antonioni. Story and Screenplay, Antonioni, Tonino Guerra; camera, Gianni di Venanzo; music, Giovanni Fusco. At Cannes Film Fest. Running time, 130 MINS.
Vittoria .... Monica Vitti
Piero .... Alain Delon
Riccardo .... Francisco Rabal
Vittorio's mother .... Lilla Brignone

Topnotch entry in the growing quality film market. "Eclipse," like Antonioni's previous "Avventura" and "La Notte," should get plenty of mileage on global cinema screens as well as reap critical plaudits.

Audiences are more likely to give "Eclipse" a split decision, as with all this controversial director's films. Because it has the same exasperating pace as well as the same delving at length and in depth into the basic lack of communication between human beings. What results is a series of long silent sequences which are meaningful and powerful to those spectators who, as Antonioni has often said, are both willing and able to "work" for their enjoyment. For those who have seen "Avventura" and "La Notte," "Eclipse" makes an apt wrapup for a telling trilogy.

Vittoria (Monica Vitti) emerges from an unhappy love affair with an intellectual, Riccardo (Francisco Rabal), and almost by accident and with infinite caution accepts the down-to-earth courtship of a young stockbroker, Alain Delon, whose designs (and conversation) are less complicated. Both fear involvement, neither is really able to get his message of life and love across to the other, and the melancholy finale signals another split.

Above this outline hovers the theory (also pointed out via repeated visual effects) that modern society and the money which commands it are turning man into an object, more and more devoid of human characteristics, unable to maintain normal relationships. The eclipse symbol may therefore be applied on various levels in this pic.

Antonioni confirms his mastery of cinema conceived as literature, and there's certainly no one who today can match his pregnant silences nor the unity of style and theme as applied to his last three films. On the other hand, it's hard to see how he can go much further in this direction. He himself seems to put the finis note to the series with a long windup sequence depicting the eclipse of sentiments, symbolized by the places, people, and objects which have witnessed Vittoria and Piero's brief and aborted affair, all veiled by a sudden darkness.

Miss Vitti once again proves an ideal performer for Antonioni's thematics in what is probably her best role to date. Delon is excellent as her would-be love. Some trenchant scenes are neatly done by Lilla Brignone, as Vittoria's mother, while Francisco Rabal makes the most of a brief appearance as her previous love. Nor should one forget the vital fingertip assistance given the director by Gianni di Venanzo's moodful camerawork and Giovanni Fusco's haunting musical scoring. Other production credits are all top drawer. This pic was invited to the festival. *Hawk.*

Zaduszki
(All Soul's Day)
(POLISH)

Cannes, May 8.
Polski State Film release of Kadr production. With Edmond Fetting, Ewa Krzywska, Jadwiga Chojnacka, Beata Tyszkiewicz. Written and directed by Tadeusz Konwicki. Camera, Kurt Weber; editor, R. Mann. At Cannes Film Fest. Running time, 93 MINS.
Michel .... Edmond Fetting
Vala .... Ewa Krzywska
Katarin .... Beata Tyszkiewicz
Landlady .... Jadwiga Chojnacka

A pair of lovers go off to a small hotel in a little town. But memories of the war intrude on their idyll. In this framework is laced a well-paced look at the war sores of Poland, its people and a glimpse of the country today. Its inside theme and treatment make this primarily a specialized entry abroad, but worth special arty spotting, too.

The boy and girl relive certain wartime experiences in flashback. She was a Communist who drove a boy who lover her to give himself up. The director-writer Tadeusz Konwicki has a good flair for character and visuals, and tells his story slowly but well.

It is a daring pic for an Eastern bloc production. It shows both sides, the Communists and reps of the old government during the war. Acting is fine throughout and technical credits have the usual Polish smartness. *Mosk.*

La Poupee
(The Doll)
(FRENCH—COLOR—FRANSCOPE)

Cannes, May 8.
Procinex release of Procinex-Ajace production. With Sonnie Teal, Zbigniew Cybulski, Catherine Millinaire, Daniel Emilfork, Laszlo Szabo, Jacques Dufilho, Max Montavon. Directed by Jacques Baratier. Screenplay, Jacques Audiberti, Baratier; camera (Eastmancolor), Raoul Coutard; editor, Leonide Azar; music, Joseph Kosma. At Cannes Film Fest. Running time, 100 MINS.
La Poupee .... Sonnie Teal
Dictator .... Zbigniew Cybulski
Catherine .... Catherine Millinaire
Pio .... Daniel Emilfork
Student .... Laszlo Szabo
Nurse .... Jacques Dufilho
Scientist .... Max Montavon

Offbeater is a sort of scifi political satire. Though it may be familiar, this has style and cleverness. Film could be a possible arty theatre entry if well exploited on its theme.

In a mythical South American country, a dictator holds sway with a flighty wife doing most of the deciding. Ferment goes on among the young leftists and even among the monied set. A scientist invents a way to reproduce objects. In showing it to the dictator's wife, he finds he can make another version of her.

Meanwhile, a young leftist, who looks like the dictator, takes up with a rich girl and goes to a party at the dictator's home. But the dictator is killed. The hapless young man has to replace him but gets to like it and becomes like the ex-leader. All sorts of themes can be read into this about power corrupting, scientists' need to take a stand, etc. But it manages to keep up interest despite its symbolism because of the adroit direction of Jacques Baratier, and clever plotting.

Yank femme impersonator Sonnie Teal makes a solid contribution as the weird double of the dictator's wife. Polish actor Zbigniew Cybulski is effective in the double role of dictator and leftist with the remainder of the cast adequate.

Though reminiscent of a silent classic, the German "Metropolis," which also had a double of a woman, this has neat technical color envelope. It emerges a political parable. This could be used as an actioner as well as for specialized art dates. Descriptive tangy songs add a good underlining to the action. *Mosk.*

Mondo Cane
(A Dog's World)
(ITALIAN)

Cannes, May 8.

Cineriz production and release. Directed by Gualtiero Jacopetti and Paolo Cavara. Franco Prosperi. Commentary and editing, Gualteiro Jacopetti; camera (Technicolor), Antonio Climati, Benito Frattari; music, Riz Ortolani, Nino Oliviero; commentary spoken by Stefano Sibaldi. At Cannes Film Fest. Running time, **105 MINS.**

Impressive, hard-hitting documentary feature whose controversial elements will help sell it both at home and in many foreign marts. Exploitable pic could gain from further editing.

Brash and provocative are only two of the adjectives which can help illustrate this truly modern documentary, modern in that it no longer merely illustrates, but also provokes thought. In the case of "Dog's World," there's no doubt that many spectators will be irked by some of content, but it's just as sure that they'll be talking about it for some time to come. Likewise, there will be those who'll be repulsed by some of the film's stronger bits (they may even strike some as lacking in taste), yet a pondered view must evoke the conclusion that we do indeed live in a dog's world and that, per some of the highlights, we have much to be ashamed of.

Various themes pop up along the way through this pic, notably the cruel treatment inflicted on animals, including the human species. Vehicle is impressive on many counts: first, the material found on a round-the-world hunt; second, the justaxposition of the various elements, sequences, and themes in order to provoke the viewer; third, the adult commentary which, in its original Italian version, manages glibness, irony and satire without overdoing it.

While nearly all bits are patently real, there are two sequences (one concerning the slow death of all life on a Bikini atoll; the other depicting children polishing human skulls and bones in a Roman catacomb) which, despite assurances to the contrary, smack of staging. They might best go or benefit from re-editing.

Yet the total effect is grimly stimulating from the visual standpoint, depressing in the conclusions drawn. Whether one sides with his views or not, Gualtiero Jacopetti deserves credit for a shattering view of the world today, just as Riz Ortolani and Nino Oliviero rate nods for their musical backdropping and Antonio Climati and Benito Frattari for their Technicolor lensing.

Hawk.

Furyo Syonen
(Bad Boys)
(JAPANESE)

Cannes, May 8.

Iwanami production and release. Written and directed by Susumu Hani. Camera, Manji Kano; editor, T. Takemithu. At Cannes Film Fest. Running time, **90 MINS.**

Tale of a delinquent boy of 17, using non-actors, bears a solid insight into his comportment, and a look at reform school life. This is a probing pic that has the spark for arty chances abroad.

Arrested for a holdup, the youth is sent to reform school. Fragments of his past life are pieced together during his questioning and in flashbacks during his prison life. Arrogant and petulant, he is not yet vicious. In the reform school, he becomes a victim of the older boys but finally gets with a group who accept him.

The on-the-spot lensing in the streets have a staccato reality while the prison scenes reveal the boy's needs swelling into a crescendo when they are allowed to yell out their feelings. Non-pro actors are all exceptional. The fine pacing, insight and cohesive direction of Susumu Hani, for his first film, mark him a director likely to be heard from.

This is a different type film from Japan and this aspect can be played up for foreign hypoing. On the surface, it may resemble other juve delinquent films but its sharpness marks it a good notch above such others. It is technically good.

Mosk.

Procesí K Panence
(Pilgrimage to the Virgin)
(CZECH)

Cannes, May 8.

Czech State Film production and release. With Vaclav Lohnisky, Martin Tapak, Josef Kemr, Anna Meliskova. Directed by Vojtech Jasny. Screenplay, Miroslav Stehlik; camera, Jaroslav Kucera; editor, J. Stupochna. At Cannes Film Fest. Running time, **85 MINS.**

Elder	Vaclav Lohnisky
Agitator	Martin Tapak
Worker	Josef Kemr
Girl	Anna Meliskova

The Czechs often are tagged the most hidebound of the Eastern Bloc smaller countries, but now comes up with a situation comedy that spoofs agitators trying to get a holdout town into a collective setup. It finally piles on the plus values for the latter, but maintains a witty look at both sides and shows a definite thaw in Czech film subject matter.

A sleepy town sets dogs on a group of agitators who try, on their own time every week, to bring these obstinate farmers into a collective arrangement. Battles rage but love blooms, too, and there is depicted even a fondness of one group for the other.

The townspeople finally decide to go on a Sunday pilgrimage to the Virgin like old times to thwart the Communist bunch who have decided to convert them even on a Sunday. The whole procession turns into a road blocking mixup. When reprimanded by their superiors the non-collectives get mad and sign up since they do not want their own agitators mocked.

Director Vojtech Jasny has given this snappy pacing and witty progression at the beginning, helped by good type casting and a clever script. It bogs down in the second part but still remains an almost successful Iron Curtain comedy.

It looms a chancy possibility abroad. Well placed and handled, it might do in special situations.

Mosk.

Mr. Hobbs Takes a Vacation
(C'SCOPE—COLOR)

Amiable, but often misguided, tour of togetherness. Still, strong family fare, therefore favorable b.o. prospect.

Hollywood, May 11.

Twentieth-Fox release of Jerry Wald production. Stars James Stewart, Maureen O'Hara; features Fabian, John Saxon, Marie Wilson, Reginald Gardiner; introduces Lauri Peters, Valerie Varda; with Lili Gentle, John McGiver, Natalie Trundy, Josh Peine, Minerva Urecal, Michael Burns, Richard Collier, Peter Oliphant, Thomas Lowell, Stephen Mines, Dennis Whitcomb, Michael Sean. Directed by Henry Koster. Screenplay, Nunnally Johnson, based on novel by Edward Streeter; camera (De Luxe), William C. Mellor; editor, Marjorie Fowler; music, Henry Mancini; assistant director, Joseph E. Rickards. Reviewed at Fox Wilshire Theatre, May 11, '62. Running time, **115 MINS.**

Mr. Hobbs	James Stewart
Peggy	Maureen O'Hara
Joe	Fabian
Byron	John Saxon
Mrs. Turner	Marie Wilson
Reggie McHugh	Reginald Gardiner
Katey	Lauri Peters
Marika	Valerie Varda
Janie	Lili Gentle
Mr. Turner	John McGiver
Susan	Natalie Trundy
Stan	Josh Peine
Brenda	Minerva Urecal
Danny Hobbs	Michael Burns
Mr. Kagle	Richard Collier
Peter Carver	Peter Oliphant
Freddie	Thomas Lowell
Carl	Stephen Mines
Dick	Dennis Whitcomb
Phil	Michael Sean

Togetherness, all-American family style, is given a gently irreverent poke in the ribs in Jerry Wald's production of "Mr. Hobbs Takes a Vacation." This is a fun picture with enough going for it on the plus side of the ledger to make it a promising boxoffice candidate for 20th-Fox, although it misfires, chiefly in the situation development department.

Nunally Johnson's screenplay, based on the novel, "Hobbs' Vacation," by Edward Streeter, is especially strong in the dialog area. The film is peppered with refreshingly sharp, sophisticated references and quips, many of a topical, up-to-date nature. But Johnson's screenplay falls down in development of its timely premise, leaving the cast and director Henry Koster heavily dependent on their own comedy resources in generating fun. Koster manages more often than not to keep the bubble bubbling but some incidents elaborately and promisingly set up fail to jell or gather momentum. A shot of a hapless, terrified motorist hemmed in by thundering, Diesel belching trucks and bus on the "freeway" is sharp pictorial commentary, yet the film, which utilizes as a story springboard a flimsy flashback ("How I spent my summer vacation" and lived to regret it), tends to rely too much on antique material for running gags. An encounter with a temperamental Rube Goldberg-type water pump is, for instance, too familiar a device to be repeated.

"Hobbs" (James Stewart) is a St. Louis banker who has the misfortune to spend his vacation at the seashore with 10 other members of his immediate family, setting up a series of situations roughly designed to illustrate the pitfalls of that grand old Yankee institution, the family reunion.

The picture has its staunchest ally in Stewart, whose acting instincts are so remarkably keen that he can instill amusement into scenes that otherwise threaten to fall flat. Some of the others in the cast, endowed with less intuitive gifts for light comedy, do not fare as well. Maureen O'Hara is decorative as Mrs. Hobbs. Fabian struggles along in an undernourished romantic role, and warbles, with considerable uncertainty, an uninspired ditty, tagged "Cream Puff," by Johnny Mercer and Henry Mancini, who has composed a satisfactory score for the film. John Saxon is mired in a stereotypical role of a pompously dense intellect. Reginald Gardiner plays Reginald Gardiner to perfection. Best support comes from Marie Wilson and John McGiver as a pair of wild house guests. Two newcomers to the screen make their mark: cutie Lauri Peters as Hobbs' teenaged daughter and shapely Valerie Varda as a friendly neighborhood sexpot. Prominent roles are dispatched reliably by Lili Gentle, Natalie Trundy, Josh Peine, Minerva Urecal and Michael Burns.

William C. Mellor's camerawork is polished, but Marjorie Fowler's editing, apparently owing to last-ditch trimming decisions, tends to contradict some of the dialog. Art directors Jack Martin Smith and Malcolm Brown have come up with a suitably pitiful beach abode for the ill-starred rendezvous of the Hobbs-nobbers.

Tube.

A Weekend With Lulu
(BRITISH)

Moderate vehicle on humor road. For tandem bookings.

Hollywood, May 8.

Columbia Pictures release of Ted Lloyd production. Stars Bob Monkhouse, Leslie Phillips, Alfred Marks, Shirley Eaton, Irene Handl; introduces Russ Conway. Directed by John Paddy Carstairs. Screenplay, Lloyd, from story by Lloyd, Val Valentine; camera, Ken Hodges; editor, Tom Simpson; music, Tony Osborne, Trevor H. Stanford; assistant director, Chris Sutton. Reviewed at the studio, May 8, '62. Running time, **91 MINS.**

Fred	Bob Monkhouse
Tim	Leslie Phillips
Comte De Grenoble	Alfred Marks
Deirdre	Shirley Eaton
Florence Proudfoot	Irene Handl
Patron	Sidney James
British Tourist	Kenneth Connor
Station Master	Sydney Tafler
French Pianist	Russ Conway
Inspector Larue	Eugene Deckers
Chiron	Graham Stark
Card Seller	Harold Berens
Postman Leon	Tutte Lemkow
Flying Corsican	Stuart Hillier
Lodge Keeper	Andreas Malandrinos
Count's Chauffeur	Ernest Walder
Madame Bon-Bon	Judith Furse
Patron	Denis Shaw
Count's Butler	Keith Pyott
Humper	Gordon Rollings
Lodgekeeper's Wife	Edie Martin
Bon Viveur	Harold Kasket
Mayor	Alexis Bobrinskoy

"A Weekend With Lulu" roughly follows the roadmap pattern of such memorable vehicular farces as "Genevieve" and "Titfield Thunderbolt," but without the comedic inspiration of its forerunners. Still, while not in the major leagues of British screen humor, the Ted Lloyd (Hammer Film) production is a diverting item bolstered by a host of accomplished performances by a number of England's seasoned character comedy players.

By accenting and ballyhooing the film's skeletal similarity to those earlier hits, Columbia might generate a mild response in the arty sphere, but "Lulu" is apt to be most useful as a companion attraction in general situations, where its misfires, irregularities and basic

mediocrity will more easily be forgiven.

Ice cream truck hauling a dilapidated trailer is the transportational prop around which producer Lloyd's screenplay rotates. At the controls of this vehicle are four Britishers in pursuit of a cozy weekend at the seashore who somehow wind up on a merry chase through France, pursued by hapless gendarmes, distracted racing cyclists and determined roues.

Making up the oddball foursome are Bob Monkhouse, Leslie Phillips, Irene Handl and Shirley Eaton. Monkhouse and Phillips are fine foils for each other as the dominant and recessive co-captains of the geographical blunder. Miss Handl is excellent as the unwelcome old crone accompanying her daughter, Miss Eaton, who shapes up at the moment as Britain's reply to the BB's of France, CC's of Italy and MM's of America. Prominent in a string of top-flight supporting performances are those of Alfred Marks, Sidney James, Sydney Tafler, Eugene Deckers and Graham Stark. Russ Conway, a matinee idol type, is inauspiciously "introduced" in a totally irrelevant passage during which he exchanges a series of smiles with Miss Eaton. Conway, if nothing else, can really smile.

Production assists are generally adequate. Highlight ingredient is the rinky tink, honky tonk score by Tony Osborne. Director John Paddy Carstairs keeps the comedy rolling amiably along, but the film lacks that one really hilarious, ingenious passage that can make the big difference in a motion picture farce. *Tube.*

The Cabinet Of Caligari
(C'SCOPE)

Capable remake of the German silent classic of 1921. Ambitiously produced, but less art than shock emerges in the revision. Salesmanship flair could pay off at the b.o.

Hollywood, May 9.

Twentieth-Fox release of Roger Kay production. Stars Glynis Johns, Dan O'Herlihy; features Dick Davalos, Lawrence Dobkin, Constance Ford, J. Pat O'Malley, Vicki Trickett, Estelle Winwood. Directed by Kay. Screenplay, Robert Bloch; camera, John Russell; editor, Archie Marshek; music, Gerald Fried; assistant directors, Lee Lukather, Harold E. Knox. Reviewed at the studio, May 9, '62. Running time, **105 MINS.**

Jane	Glynis Johns
Paul and Caligari	Dan O'Herlihy
Mark	Dick Davalos
David	Lawrence Dobkin
Christine	Constance Ford
Martin	J. Pat O'Malley
Jeanie	Vicki Trickett
Ruth	Estelle Winwood
Vivian	Dorken Lang
Bob	Charles Fredericks
Little Girl	Phyllis Teagardin

Since it stems from a classic of the silent screen, this competent reproduction of that highly regarded 1921 shocker, is apt to disappoint customers aware of the reputation of its predecessor in academic circles. The remake, produced and directed by Roger Kay under the executive aegis of Robert L. Lippert, should meet with somewhat greater approval from the multitudes unfamiliar with the celebrated source.

Stripped of the mysterious eloquence of silence and the original shock and novelty of a psychological theme, "The Cabinet of Caligari" has evolved into a fairly standard terror-melodrama and should be promoted not under the veiled pretense of cinema art, which the new, revised version is not, but as a brisk, provocative mystery-shocker with story surprises. An honest, imaginative, but unpretentious, campaign that won't raise expectations too high in more discerning circles, coupled with some flair and enthusiasm on the exhibitors' end, could pay off handsomely for the 20th-Fox release.

Robert Bloch's screenplay is interesting but far from pat. The tale of a young woman (Glynis Johns) imprisoned in the peculiar, remote household of an apparent pervert-madman (Dan O'Herlihy), the film concludes with an ironic twist that will have audiences recounting and second-guessing when they leave the theatre. Trouble is, if they stop to analyze too much, they will find themselves something less than convinced. The story does not completely come to terms with itself and, under Kay's guidance, has a slight tendency to tip off its surprises. But the slack is taken up by John Russell's stark, agile photographic techniques, editor Archie Marshek's manipulation of stills to create novelty and shock images in climactic scenes, a number of first-rate performances, and director Kay's welding of these elements into a pictorially and histrionically gratifying compound.

Miss Johns, a skillful, expressive actress, gives a spirited performance. Dan O'Herlihy is smooth and magnetic in a dual role (the evil Caligari and the kindly doctor) that tends to telegraph the surprise ending. Colorful support is supplied by Dick Davalos, Lawrence Dobkin, Constance Ford, J. Pat O'Malley, Vicki Trickett, Estelle Winwood, Doreen Lang, Charles Fredericks and Phyllis Teagardin.

A lively, variable score by Gerald Fried helpfully punctuates the alternate tension and hysteria. Production designer Serge Krizman and set decorator Howard Bristol have combined talents to shape and dress, respectively, a set that attractively fits the story's ambiguous specifications. It seems to be what it is not, and it is not what it seems to be. *Tube.*

Mothra
(JAPANESE—TOHOSCOPE—COLOR)

Crudely Managed Monster Melange Must Scrounge for U.S. Dates.

Hollywood, May 10.

Columbia Pictures release of Tomoyuki Tanaka production. With Jelly Ito, Ken Uehara, Yumi Ito, Emi, Ito, Takashi Shimura, Seizaburo Kawazu, Kenji Sahara, Akihiko Harata, Yoshio Kosugi, Yoshibumi Tajima, Yasushi Yamamoto, Haruya Kato, Ko Mishima, Tetsu Nakamura. (No character names given). Directed by Inoshiro Honda. Screenplay, Shinichi Sekizawa, from story by Shinichiro Nakamura, Takehiko Fukunaga, Yoshie Hotta; camera, Hajime Koizumi; editor, Ichiji Taira; assistant director, Masaji Nonagase. Reviewed at the studio, May 10, '62. Running time, **101 MINS.**

"Mothra" is a ludicrously written, haphazardly executed monster picture from the Toho filmmakers of Japan. Though elaborately produced in Tohoscope and color, with a large cast and plenty of production fireworks, the post-dubbed film is too awkward in dramatic construction and crude in histrionic style to score appreciably at the boxoffice. Exploitation measures are bound to lure thrill-seekers who flock indiscriminately to monster films, but even cinemutation buffs should wince at this one.

Title of the Columbia release refers to a king-sized creature that, in the course of the picture, undergoes metamorphosis from caterpillar to moth and wrecks several metropolises as it pursues, by telepathy, two foot-high maidens who have been kidnapped for commercial purposes from a remote South Sea isle in the atomic test area. Every once in awhile the action flashes back to the island where exotic natives are found singing and dancing. At any moment, one expects Hope, Crosby ad Lamour to pop into the picture.

Neither the spectacular special effects nor the adept miniature work makes up sufficiently for what otherwise is a pretty embarrassing effort on the part of the Toho people to duplicate a western screen staple. *Tube.*

Congo Vivo
(ITALO-FRENCH)

Rome, May 8.

Dino DeLaurentiis release of a R.O.T.O.R. (Carmine Bologna)- Orsay Films coproduction. Stars Gabriele Ferzetti, Jean Seberg. Featured Bachir Toure, Frederique Andrew. Directed by Giuseppe Bennati. Screenplay, Bennati, Paolo Levi, Lucia Brudi, William Denby, from story by Bennati; camera, Giuseppe Aquari; music, Piero Piccioni; editor, Franco Fanaticelli. At Barberini, Rome. Running time, **107 MINS.**

Roberto Santi	Gabriele Ferzetti
Annette	Jean Seberg
Abbe	Bachir Toure
Eleonora	Frederique Andrew

Strange blend of fact and fiction, this has obvious exploitation factors for Columbia, which has foreign distribution of the pic via the Congo controversy which is directly touched on in plot and setting. Jean Seberg name may help, but this pic will need all the push it can get even in the dubbed version.

Producers and director deserve full credit for the job turned out under trying conditions (pic was shot in the midst of the unexpected Congo upheaval). But it's obvious that difficulties encountered have compromised the ultimate result, which suffers from confusion of issues and remains a valiant try, and no more. Plot is split between a love story, with racial innuendos, between an Italian correspondent and the wife of a Belgian businessman who remains behind in Elizabethville on the eve of the known events, and the shaded-in rendering of the Congo revolution. This has newsreel shots well intergrated with on-the-spot sequences depicting the newsman's visits to Lumumba Mobutu and other Congo statesmen.

Acting, with the exception of a few scenes between Seberg and Ferzetti, is only adequate, reflecting the forced rush job on the pic. Technical credits are in keeping, with a nod to a haunting musical score by Piero Piccioni. *Hawk.*

Carillons Sans Joie
(Bells Without Joy)
(FRENCH) (DYALISCOPE)

Unidex release of Lisa Films production. Stars Paul Meurisse, Raymond Pellegrin, Dany Carrel, Roger Hanin. Directed by Charles Brabant. Screenplay, Claude Brule, Claude Barma, Denys Le La Patelliere, Brabant from novel by Charles Bourgeon; camera, Ghislain Cloquet; editor, Claude Durand. At Normandie, Paris. Running time, **100 MINS.**

Lamberieux	Paul Meurisse
Bourgeon	Raymond Pellegrin
Maurice	Roger Hanin
Lea	Dany Carrel

Based on a true incident during the last war, when a small, ill-equipped French garrison faced German might over a bridge in Algeria during Allied landings, this emerges an okay war item. But it's still somewhat conventional and surface in characterization, hence seeming to lack the fillip for arty theatre chances, and mainly a dualer or playoff item abroad.

Story has the Allied landings giving French soldiers some hope and breaking out caches of arms. A group is sent to cover a bridge with orders to let no foreign soldiers pass. A martinet captain, who lives by the book, applies this to a German company that wants to pass. Then a series of ruses keep the Germans in abeyance. Finally some drunken shooting leads to an attack and the wiping out of the French and the herding up of a little Jewish community.

Director Charles Brabant has handled this discretely, including a love affair and a look at bigotry. But he has not been able to give this a true feel of men in war.

Acting is good, within the confines of strictly familiar characters. The final battle is sharp and neatly done. So this is a conventional if solidly carpentered war film. *Mosk.*

Senilita
(When A Man Grows Old)
(ITALIAN)

Rome, May 8.

Columbia-Celad release of a Moris Ergas (Zebra) production. Stars Claudia Cardinale, Anthony Francoisa; features Betsy Blair, Philipe LeRoy, Marcella Valeri, Nando Angelini, Ersilia Di Marco, Raimondo Magni. Directed by Mauro Bolognini. Screenplay, Bolognini, Tullio Pinelli, Goffredo Parise, based on novel by Italo Svevo; camera, Armando Nannuzzi; music, Piero Piccioni; editor, Nino Baragli. At Quattro Fontane, Rome. Running time, **97 MINS.**

Emilio	Anthony Franciosa
Angiolina	Claudia Cardinale
Amalia	Betsy Blair
Balli	Philine LeRoy
Soriani	Nando Angelini

Stylishly fashioned story of an impossible love affair, with Anthony Franciosa, Claudia Cardinale, and Betsy Blair for marquee bait abroad. But this pic will need a hard sell on the part of Columbia, which has world rights via a preproduction deal.

Rapidly approaching middle age, Emilio Brentani (Anthony Franciosa) grasps in desperation for the love of Claudia Cardinale, an eternal flirt, forgetting friendship, work, and even abandoning his sister Amalia (Betsy Blair) to pursue the girl, not realizing that he means nothing to her and never will. When she abandons him for one final time, Emilio finds himself more alone than ever, with time rapidly creeping up.

What basically hurts this paten-

tially moving and engrossing picture is the casting of Franciosa as Emilio. This Yank is too handsome, too youthfully exhuberant to lend credence to his plight, his solitude, and his fear of oncoming senility. At that, his performance is a good one. Miss Cardinale is likewise good as the flirt. Two outstanding efforts are turned in by Betty Blair, as Emilio's sister, and Philipe LeRoy, as his best friend.

Direction faithfully evokes the '20s atmosphere, telling its story with elegance and intelligence, though warmth and pathos are often lacking in a tale which has all the elements of tragedy. Production credits are outstanding.

Hawk.

Information Received
(BRITISH)

Ordinary crooks' comeuppance meller with attractive performances. Okay programmer prospects.

Universal release of a United Co-Production Ltd. production. No stars. Features Sabina Sesselman, William Sylvester, Hermione Baddeley, Edward Underdown. Directed by Robert Lynn. Screenplay by Paul Ryder from story by Berkeley Mather; camera, Nicholas Roeg; editor, Lee Doig; music and song "Sabina" by Martin Slavin; assistant director, Roy Baird. Reviewed at Universal N.Y. homeoffice, April 19, '62. Running time, GG *MINS.*

Sabina Farlow	Sabina Sesselman
Rick Hogan	William Sylvester
Maudie	Hermoine Baddeley
Drake	Edward Underdown
Supt. Jeffcote	Robert Raglan
Sgt. Jarvie	Frank Hawkins
Mark	David Courtney
Patterson	Peter Allenby
Farlow	Walter Brown
Johnny Stevens	Bill Dancy
Country Policeman	Don Meadon
Prison Trusty	Ted Bushell
TV Announcer	Tim Brinton
Willis	Johnny Briggs
Librarian	David Cargill
Darnell	Larry Taylor
Warder Benham	Douglas Cameron
Judge	David Ensor
Squar Car Policeman	Tony Shepherd

Devotees of the stylish made-in-Britain crime drama are sloughed with this one. "Information Received," a Universal release in the U.S., is a small and unassuming variation on the battle of wits theme, hampered only by the fact it doesn't vary enough. Despite some pleasant performances and an admirable economy in the telling, the opus is simply too modest for more than routine outlook in a lower berth slot.

The plot is this: A safe-cracking operation hires an American expert for a big caper. He's intercepted by Scotland Yard on the ship over and jailed on an old charge. His employers, geared for such contingencies, spirit him out of prison—but unfortunately their man (unknown to them on sight) is a phony substituted by the police.

Paul Ryder screenplay from a Berkeley Mather story fails to make enough of it thereafter. With the possible exception of a spicy Germanic blond with double-crossing eyes for the impostor, there's nothing to feint audiences out of position. Potential suspense elements are herein denied, and it's to the serious detriment of the film.

Of the polished performances, William Sylvester is appealing as the bogus Yank, and Sabina Sesselman does nicely as the opportunistic blond. There's an amusing **and too short contribution from Hermione Baddeley as a faded biddy, and Edward Underdown is efficient as the kingpin crook. Others giving a good account are Robert Raglan, Frank Hawkins and Walter Brown.**

Director Robert Lynn has resisted any temptations to adorn or digress, but in this case that's not virtuous. Martin Slavin has provided a misplaced jazz score, and also a ho-hum song over the credits. Technical contributions, including Nicholas Roeg's photography and Lee Doig's editing, are always competent but seldom interesting.

Pit.

Road to Eternity

Montreal, May 8.

Cadieux Associates release of Shochiku Pictures (Tatsuo Hosoya) production. Features Tatsuya Nakadai, Michiyo Aratama, Keiji Sada. Directed by Masaki Kobayashi; screenplay, Zenzo Matsuyama and Kobayashi; based on the middle section of the six-volume novel "The Human Condition" by Jumpei Gomikawa; camera, Yoshio Miyajima; editor, Keiichi Uraoka; music, Chuji Kinoshita, North American premiere at Orpheum Theatre, Montreal, March 9, 1962. Running time 181 MINS.

(Japanese; English Subtitles)

Kaji	Tatsuya Nakadai
Michiko	Michiyo Aratama
Kageyama	Keiji Sada
Kudo	Hideo Kisho
Hino	Jun Tatara
Yoshida	Michio Minami
Shinjo	Kei Sato
Tange	Taketoshi Naito
Obara	Kunie Tanaka
Sasa	Kokinji Katsura
Tokunaga	Kaneko Iwasaki

This is the second part of Kobayashi's great and monumental trilogy concerning the dilemma of a young Japanese who is forced to play a part in war, yet is the loser whichever side he takes. (Part 1 "No Greater Love" is distributed by Brandon Films under the title of the trilogy, "The Human Condition" in a version cut from 208 minutes to 138. It was reviewed in VARIETY in December, 1959.)

Part 2 (completed early in 1960) begins with a quick summary of what took place in the preceding film, ending with the solitary figure of Kaji leaving for service in the army.

The mentality of the Imperial Army of Japan, the brutalities and stupidities of army life, the way men act when facing violent death, and the way men are reduced to bestiality by killing and primitive treatment, are the elements which make this slow-moving tragedy of the human condition so compelling and piercing.

Truly shattering, with a stark visual conception and culminating dramatic power, this second part of the trilogy is (like part two) remarkably self-contained and needs no explanations from its companion pictures to make its story-points clear.

Prat.

La Guerra Des Boutons
(The War of the Buttons)
(FRENCH)

Paris, May 8.

Warner Bros. release of Gueville production. With Jean Richard, Jacques Dufilho, Michel Galabru. Directed by Yves Robert. Screenplay, Francois Boyer, Robert from novel by Louis Pergaud; camera, Andre Bac; editor, Marie Yoyotte. At Balazac, Paris. Running time, 95 MINS.

Lebrac	Jean Richard
Lancret	Jacques Dufilho
Balatier	Michel Galabru

Tale of kid warfare between the moppets of two neighboring rural towns looms mainly for kiddie use abroad though it won one of the top film critic awards here, Le Prix Jean Vigo. It looks at kids with the distance of grownups, on how cute they are, and rarely gives insight into their actions or makes a point about it all. But it is gentle, fairly refreshing, and naturally played by a group of youngsters.

The gangs cut each other's buttons off and one even fights nude one day. A stool pigeon and a runaway make up the dramatic aspects of the pic. Grownups are properly stereotyped but, unfortunately, so are most of the kids.

All this is pleasantly concocted but lags and repeats itself to make it of little art value abroad, with mainly dualer or playoff chances in store. It is technically good but a lot of the kiddie patter is badly recorded and almost unintelligible at times.

Mosk.

It Happened in Canada
(CANADIAN)

Toronto, May 8.

Temple Films release of Luigi Petrucci production; written, directed & photographed by Luigi Petrucci; music, Carmine Rizzo; editing, Petrucci. Premiere at Christie Theatre, Toronto. Running time, 95 MINS.

Rita	Gisela Zdunek
Andrea	Nello Zordan
Maria	Dedena Morello
Carlo	Pino Ubaldo

and: Alfredo Gerard, Frank Benevenuto, Joe Maniscola, Adelino Barbati, Renee Walters, Renata Di Faveri, Antonietta Martino, Frank Picchioni, Italia Bacovich.

(In Italian; English Subtitles)

Filmed in Toronto's Italian quarter, this modest picture turns out to be a pleasant and rather winning study of the difficulties of immigrants adjusting themselves to a new way of life. A one-man film shot on the streets and in actual homes in the semi-improvisational technique, this is more an Italian than Canadian film. It is neither an art house nor commercial proposition, and will probably have to depend on income from showings in Italy and Italian communities abroad.

Story concerns Rita, a pretty young Roman girl, who faces a bleak future at home and decides to come to Canada to marry Andrea, a man she has never seen. Her romantic illusions are quickly shattered when she meets him in Toronto: aging, a common laborer, living with the memory of his dead wife. The country disappoints her, the winters are long and cold, and she remains hidden among her own people, following the old customs and way of life. In her loneliness she turns to Carlo, carefree, irresponsible nephew of Andrea. Although she falls in love with him, she cannot forget her obligation to Andrea nor the unhappiness she has brought him. When Carlo dies in a construction accident, she accepts his child by another woman and decides to make a new life with Andrea.

The truth and sincerity of this film atones for its plot deficiencies. While it lacks the art and sensitivity of Vittorio DeSica, it is in the tradition of his simple films about people in ordinary walks of life. At times the situations are annoying as in the scenes where characters talk about winter unemployment being severe, yet Andrea appears to have no difficulty changing jobs.

The players are all likeable people who look as if they came from the streets and know what life is about. The score is pleasant, the narration strikes a melancholy note, and the whole flows along with a drab, Italin eloquence. As a first film, it's a credit to the determination and feeling of Luigi Petrucci, who came to Canada in 1952 having had some experience of film making in Italy. The mother's closing appreciation of life in Canada is nice to hear.

Prat.

Il Disordine
(Disorder)
(ITALO-FRENCH)

Rome, May 8.

Titanus release of a Titanus-S.N.P.C. (Paris) coproduction. Features Samy Frey, Louis Jourdan, Curd Jurgens, Antonella Lualdi, Tomas Milian, Renato Salvatori, Jean Sorel, Susan Strasberg, Alida Valli, Georges Wilson. Directed by Franco Brusati. Screenplay, Brusati, Francesco Ghedini; from story by Brusati; camera, Leonida Barboni music, Mario Nascimbene; editor, Ruggero Mastroianni. At Metropolitan, Rome. Running time, 97 MINS.

A fascinating, disconcerting entry from Titanus, stylishly made by director Franco Brusati, but with the final returns depending principally on the proper bally approach. Proper lingual versions could result in deserved foreign interest. Names should prove marquee aids.

Episodic tale defies retelling. Suffice it to say that it points out the confusion reigning in current manners and mores via chain reaction of various characters to others. It provokes thought on many levels, though admittedly at times the director-writer is asking much in audience participation in delving under the surface of his symbolic episodes.

But even so, this is strangely gripping at times, and always equipped with a slick patina of style which makes insignificant things appear portentous. Most actors have little chance to expand their characterizations due to the restricted parts, but they too are aptly chosen and effective.

Technically, this film rates top recognition, with lensing particularly standout.

Hawk.

Cannes Festival

Boccaccio 70
(ITALO—FRENCH—COLOR)

Cannes, May 8.

Cineriz release of a Concordia (Carlo Ponti-Antonio Cervi) - Cineriz - Francinex-Gray Film coproduction. (Embassy Int'l release outside Italy, France, Belgium, Switzerland.)

"THE TEMPTATION OF DR. ANTONIO"

Stars Peppino DeFilippo, Anita Ekberg. Directed by Federico Fellini. Screenplay, Fellini, Ennio Flajano, Tullio Pinelli, Cesare Zavattini, camera (Technicolor), Otello Martelli, music, Nino Rota, editor, Leo Catozzo.

"THE JOB"

Stars Romy Schneider, Tomas Milian, Romolo Valli. Directed by Luchino Visconti. Screenplay, S. Cecchi D'Amico, Visconti, Cesare Zavattini; camera, (Technicolor), Giuseppe Rotunno. Music, Nino Rota; editor, Mario Serandrei.

"THE RAFFLE"

Stars Sophia Loren. Directed by Vittorio DeSica. Screenplay, Cesare Zavat-

tini; camera (Technicolor), Otello Martelli; music, Armando Trovajoli; editor, Adriana Novelli.

At Cannes Film Fest. Running time, **140 MINS.**

(Note: Film is being shown in Italy with the addition of another episode directed by Mario Monicelli which however will not appear in the U. S. and other non-Italian release areas for reasons of length.)

Surefire commercial entry which should easily repeat its successful Italian release in other world areas, including the U.S., where Embassy bally tactics should further insure its impact.

Pic differs from most sketch items by the fact that each segment was separately conceived and executed, making episodes pocket-sized feature pix on their own. There's nothing pocket-sized about the production values, however, all three being expensively mounted and lavishly lensed in Technicolor. Taken as a whole, "Boccaccio 70" is a varied and provocative triple bill reflecting the tastes, talent, and style of its three authors, Federico Fellini, Luchino Visconti and Vittorio DeSica.

First item, Fellini's "Temptations of Dr. Antonio," is the most disconcerting of the lot, being a searing, violent denunciation of hypocrisy with special attention to bigoted censorship. It's obvious that the sometimes violent initial reaction, especially in Italy, to "La Dolce Vita's" outspokenness, has triggered a likewise forceful reaction from that film's author. Episode deals with a Doctor Antonio who is carrying on a one-man campaign against loving couples and other external expressions of love and sex. When a giant, provocative poster of Anita Ekberg expounding the sincures of milk is set up facing his apartment, Antonio tries to fight one more battle against his concept of immorality. But he is defeated when the ebullient Miss Ekberg comes to life and drives him berserk. Director's approach is at times overloud, obvious and repetitious in his barbs, but there's no gainsaying the overall impact of the piece, which enjoys apt performances by Miss Ekberg and Peppino DeFilippo, who is the harried Dr. Antonio.

Second item, "The Job," provides a complete change of pace via Luchino Visconti's elegant styling of a modern boudoir piece, in which nuances of dialog and acting, as well as lush sets and color, help gain the total effect. In keeping with film's title, episode deals with young count who's mixed up in a call girl scandal and fears his wife will divorce him. Instead, bored by her routine life, she borrows a page from the call girls, begins charging her errant spouse mammoth fees for every intimate service. Part Two is beautifully acted by Romy Schneider, a looker in a change of pace role, and by some others.

Act Three, the most completely enjoyable of the lot, has Sophia Loren as the object of a raffle among visitors to a provincial fairground in northern Italy. The winner gets to sleep with her, and the money goes towards the dowry which will allow her marriage and an independent life. Vittorio De Sica tells the tale (which has a twist ending) with a brash and earthy humor aptly keyed to the provincial setting, plus a colorful eye for details. Dominating the proceedings is another winning performance by Miss Loren, one of

her best and one which can only add to her stature gained via "Two Women."

As indicated, production and technical values on this pic are all top-drawer, including sets, outfittings, music and editing. Only last-named could stand some tightening here and there to further heighten general impact of the triple package, which is a bit long on its current running time, and despite the removal of one whole episode (see above). All in all, there's more than enough for all tastes. Shown only out of competition. *Hawk.*

Muz Z Prvniho Stoleti
(Man of the First Century)
(CZECHOSLAVAKIAN - SCOPE)

Cannes, May 8.

Czech State Film production and release. With Milos Kopecky, Anita Kajlichova, Vit Olmer, Radovan Lukavsky. Directed by Oldrich Lipsky. Screenplay, Lipsky, Milos Fiala; camera, Vladimir Novotny; editor, Jan Kohout. At Cannes Film Fest. Running time, **100 MINS.**

Man .... Milos Kopecky
Eve .... Anita Kajlichova
Adam .... Vit Olmer
Peter .... Radovan Lukavsky

Sci-fi pic is also a morality tale which has exemplary special effects. However, this is somewhat flat and overly emphatic in its message of classlessness and the hangover of human pettiness in the future world. Film lacks the flair for untoward chances abroad. But its excellent special effects, with some cutting, could make this for dualer possibilities for foreign usage.

A griping worker accidentally is sent aloft in a space ship. He returns to earth with an advanced humanlike denizen from another planet over 500 years later. The new world is spotless, full of gadgets and free from all problems.

Well meaning, this vehicle is too heavyhanded in its moralizing, and seems more like a long vaude sketch than a film. Acting is properly expressionless except for the petty "earth man."

This is technically clever and almost holds interest on this score alone. But, even taking place in the future, it seems old fashioned. *Mosk.*

Liberte I
(SENEGALESE)

Cannes, May 15.

Pathe release of P.A.T. Films-Sora-Ucina production. Stars Maurice Ronet, Corinne Marchand; features Nanette Senghor, Iba Gueye, Assane Fall. Directed by Yves Ciampi. Screenplay, Ciampi, Jean Campistron, J. C. Tachella, R. M. Arlaud, Marcel Moussy; camera, Emile Vilerbue, Guy Susuki; editor, Georges Alepee. At Cannes Film Fest. Running time, **89 MINS.**

Michel .... Maurice Ronet
Anne .... Corinne Marchand
Malik .... Iba Gueye
Aminata .... Nanette Senghor
Adoulaye .... Assane Fall

French directed and conceived, this is really a Senegalese-French coproduction and does not yet display a new African film movement. Tale of superstition vs. progress is handled conventionally by director Yves Ciampi and it seems to have no foreign interest.

A French engineer is building a road in Senegal and runs into trouble when he finds a sacred tree must be torn down. His Negro friend is in the government but feels that tact is necessary while his fiancee just wants to go back to France.

Things come to a head when the

workers fight with the villagers over the tree. It's finally decided to cut the tree down. New modes in Africa are treated superficially and the dances, modern touches, etc. are somewhat too flimsy.

Film is technically par, but it seems too stereotyped. *Mosk.*

Joseph the Dreamer
(ISRAEL-COLOR)

Cannes, May 15.

Yoram Gross (Tel Aviv) production and release. Directed, photographed and animated by Alina and Yoram Gross. Screenplay, Natan Gross; editor, Helga Cranston; main puppets and scenery, John Pyle; music, Eddi Halpern. At Cannes Film Fest. Running time, **68 MINS.**

Inevitably Israel has turned to the Bible for a motion picture subject. And this puppet version of the story of Joseph and his brothers can best be described as a bold try and an unqualified failure. It is a difficult medium at best, even in the hands of experts, and the lack of such expert knowledge is all too evident here.

Natan Gross's screenplay, as would be expected, adheres closely to the biblical story. The narration over the action is kept down to a bare minimum, giving the plot full visual expression. Essentially, however, it's a tale that calls for human characterizations, and the use of puppets, apart from providing a dubious novelty angle, are more of a hindrance than a help. Color is passable. *Myro.*

Un Singe En Hiver
(A Monkey In Winter)
(FRENCH-TOTALSCOPE)

Cannes, May 15.

UFA-Comacico release of Cipra-Cite (Jacques Bar) production. Stars Jean Gabin, Jean-Paul Belmondo; features Suzanne Flon, Paul Frankeur, Noel Roquevert, Gabrielle Dorziat. Directed by Henri Verneuil. Screenplay, Francois Boyer, Michel Audiard from novel by Antoine Blondin; camera, Louis Page; editor, Monique and Francoise Bonnot. At Cannes Film Fest. Running time, **105 MINS.**

Albert .... Jean Gabin
Gabriel .... Jean-Paul Belmondo
Wife .... Suzanne Flon
Friend .... Paul Frankeur
Landru .... Noel Roquevert

This is a smooth vehicle for the acting talents of oldtimer Jean Gabin and newcomer Jean-Paul Belmondo. Dialog is crisp with a leavening of bite. Film is primarily an anecdote that is kept intact by the thespian knowhow of the principals. As such, it looms a solid entry on its home grounds with specialized chances abroad if well handled and spotted.

Gabin is a crusty alcoholic who takes a vow, during a bombing in the last war, that he will give up drinking if he and his wife come through intact. He does and keeps his vow. After the war, a young man moves into the hotel and goes off on a drinking bout. He awakens something in Gabin for his drinking had been his means of finding his old days in China again.

The young man has a daughter in a nearby school but is afraid to see her. Gabin finally goes on an epic binge with him, getting the man's daughter and setting off mighty fireworks.

Gabin is loud, angry but determinedly individualistic. He manages to make his role sympathetic

while Belmondo holds his own with the shrewd, grizzled veteran. The tart dialog may be somewhat too indulgent for foreign spots but it rings the bell for Continental Gabin fans.

Film has been ably directed. It is a saucy, cantankerous French entry of intransigent individualism that could find echoes abroad. *Mosk.*

Les Oliviers De La Justice
(The Olive Trees of Justice)
(FRENCH)

Cannes, May 15.

Georges Derocles production and release. With Jean Pelegri, Pierre Prothon, Marie Decaitre, Huguette Poggi. Directed by James Blue. Screenplay, Jean Pelegri, Sylvain Dhomme, Blue from novel by Pelegri; camera, Julius Rascheff; editor, Suzanne Gaveau. At Cannes Film Fest. Running time, **81 MINS.**

Jean .... Pierre Prothon
Father .... Jean Pelegri
Mother .... Marie Decaitre
Aunt .... Huguette Poggi

A young American filmmaker, James Blue, directed this first incisive French feature film look at Algeria. Apparently its merit brought an invitation at the last minute to show here with the group of promising first pix chosen by the French Film Critics for special screening. It deserves it.

Film deals with a Frenchman from Algeria who goes back when his father becomes ill. His ruminating on his past life, his father and the country make him decide to stay on there despite the Algerian struggle.

With the cease fire in Algeria, this may be able to get its censor visa soon. This vehicle is a look at the people who built and colonized that country, their rapports with the Arabs and behind it all the war and its effects.

The young Frenchman walks through Algeria and is reminded of his youth. His father is shown as a stalwart pioneer type who is good to his Arab works on but still does not quite accept them.

The simple conflicts of Arab beliefs and progress are blocked out as well as the need to understand that a new country is being born and that, though it may be difficult, perhaps the French and Algerians can live in peace with each other. Director Blue is objective with a good filmic sense. There is no preaching but he effectively depicts a man's reaching of understanding and a finding of a cause.

Acting is sober, Jean Pelegri being especially effective as the rigid but humane father.

This is well made and expertly edited. The subject could make this worth specialized handling abroad. It sometimes takes short cuts in making its points but is a fine start for filmmaker Blue. *Mosk.*

Advise and Consent
(PANAVISION)

Major production about politicians and demagogs in U.S. Senate. Dramatic strength part of the way and, with it, some dubious values.

Columbia release of Otto Preminger production. Stars Henry Fonda, Charles Laughton, Don Murray, Walter Pidgeon, Peter Lawford, Gene Tierney, Franchot Tone, Lew Ayres, Burgess Meredith, Eddie Hodges, Paul Ford, Georges Grizzard, Inga Swensen. Directed by Otto Preminger. Screenplay, Wendell Mayes from novel by Allen Drury; camera (Panavision), Sam Leavitt; editor, Louis Loeffler; music, Jerry Fielding. Previewed at New York's Criterion Theatre, May 14, '62. Running time, **140 MINS.**

Leffingwell .... Henry Fonda
Seab Cooley .... Charles Laughton
Brig Anderson .... Don Murray
Munson .... Walter Pidgeon
Dolly Harrison .... Gene Tierney
Lafe Smith .... Peter Lawford
Ellen .... Inga Swensen
Harley Hudson .... Lew Ayres
Gelman .... Burgess Meredith
Van Ackerman.......... George Grizzard
Stanley Danta .... Paul Ford
President .... Franchot Tone

Allen Drury's big-selling novel has also served as a stage play, moderately profitable, whose rights delayed the U.S. release of the Otto Preminger film version, now due in June. Meantime the film was unreeled at the Cannes Film Festival where the question arose, inevitably, of what sort of "image" it projects of the U.S. Senate. A trade reviewer must wonder, too, whether foreign audiences generally will not be somewhat puzzled by the American-style in-fighting. Not that foreign lands do not have considerable awareness of dirty doings in their own parliaments.

Preminger has worked the basic inter-play into a slick production which has a high infusion of topicality. Here are the issues of recent partisan politics in Washington. There are recognizable projections of character assassination, McCarthy-like demagoguery and use of the two hard-to-answer smears of this ill-natured generation: "*Are you now or were you once a homosexual, and/or a Communist?*"

As interpreted by producer-director Otto Preminger and scripter Wendell Mayes, "Advise and Consent" is intermittently well dialogued and too talky, and, strangely, arrested in its development and illogical.

It grips the interest of the onlooker despite an apparent off-balance in stress on story situations. In retrospect, there's an explanation for this. The words spoken by the characters are articulately strung together and have sting. Everybody is in forceful command of the English language, and the verbal clashes between and among the denizens of D. C. officialdom are exciting. But they add up to only remote meaning in the end because the story line is just too suggestive of contrivance.

Preminger took on a hot subject, with his usual publicity-value knowledge aforehand. The controversy already developed as part of a skillful campaign obviously will stir boxoffice interest. Picture itself has a fair-enough measure of commercial plusses. All in all, look for some impact in initial exposures in the States, sustained robust selling will be required for adequate results in the full domestic marketing. The trade, too, needs to be persuaded not to take the b.o. power for granted.

There's a question mark concerning international outlets and the "image" factor. There has got to be speculation as to the film's reflections on McCarthyism, deviation, physical feebleness and suicide among America's political elite—all vis-a-vis enhancement of the Stars and Stripes. Also, theatre-goers among the general public overseas might find the Pennsylvania Avenue action just too parochial and beyond their ken.

Preminger has endowed his production with wholly capable performers. Henry Fonda as the Secretary of State nominee, Charles Laughton as a Southern-smooth rebellious solon, Don Murray as the focal point of the homo-suicidal scandal and Walter Pidgeon as a Majority leader fighting in best stentorian tradion in Fonda's behalf all register firmly. The characterizations come through with fine clarity.

Gene Tierney is back on the screen, deserving a welcome with her portrayal of a Washington hostess. George Grizzard is particularly strong as the McCarthy type villain who delves into Murray's past and undertakes political blackmail re the latter's "abnormal" background. Peter Lawford, Inga Swensen, Lew Ayres, Burgess Meredith, Paul Ford and Franchot Tone (as the ailing President who wants Fonda as new Mr. Secretary) add additional strength to the unreeling.

Disturbing is lack of sufficiently clear motivation for the nub of the action. Why are Pidgeon and Laughton so pro and con about confirmation of the Presidential appointee? And isn't the Murray character too strong to kill himself? He's a stable family man, talented and respected, hardly likely to do himself in with a razor blade across the throat (as per dialog) rather than face the fact that in the years-ago War he was enamored (as strongly indicated) of another male, as now threatened by the vicious senator.

The settings are powerfully like real. A Senate hearing room, the Senate itself, a party home in immediate Washington and varying apartments plus a place in D. C. suburbia all have the look of genuineness. The camera work is on the beam all the way. The running time of 140 minutes is too much; it becomes a chore to sit through so marathon a conversational piece, albiet on and off stimulating.

Henry Mancini's musical background is a superb drama all in itself. *Gene.*

Hatari
(COLOR)

Elaborately produced if dramatically negligent and overlong African adventure for the moppet and family trade. Should be strong grosser in spite of its misfires.

Hollywood, May 12.

Paramount release of Howard Hawks production. Stars John Wayne, Hardy Kruger, Elsa Martinelli, Gerard Blain, Red Buttons. Directed by Hawks. Screenplay, Leigh Brackett, from story by Harry Kurnitz; camera (Technicolor), Russell Harlan; editor, Stuart Gilmore; music, Henry Mancini; assistant directors, Tom Connors, Russ Saunders. Reviewed at Egyptian Theatre, May 12, '62. Running time, **159 MINS.**

Sean .... John Wayne
Kurt .... Hardy Kruger
Dallas .... Elsa Martinelli
Chips .... Gerard Blain
Pockets .... Red Buttons
Indian .... Bruce Cabot
Brandy .... Michele Girardon
Luis .... Valentin de Vargas
Doctor .... Eduard Franz

Howard Hawks' expensive production of "Hatari" houses a wholesome screen adventure story, filmed on an elaborate scale mostly in the wilds of the African veldt. The picture leaves a lot to be desired in terms of story substance and dramatic approach, but that's not apt to retard it too significantly at the boxoffice. In tailoring his film precisely to the uncomplicated specifications of the vast family audience, producer-director Hawks may have alienated the affections of those who prefer nuance, depth and boldness in their screen entertainment, but the concept seems commercially sound—in losing an adult hierarchy, he has gained a young multitude. The Paramount release shapes up as a moneymaker, but it has a lot of money to make up.

"Hatari" is an ambitious undertaking. Its cast is an international one, populated by players of many countries. Its wild animals do not come charging out of dusty stock footage studio libraries but have been photographed while beating around the bush of Tanganyika, East Africa. However, in this instance, the strapping physique of the film unhappily emphasizes the anemic condition of the story streaming within and, while this may not trouble the moppets who flock to see it, it may, owing to overly extensive running time, take a heavy toll of adult patience.

Leigh Brackett's screenplay, from an original story by Harry Kurnitz, describes at exhaustive length the methods by which a group of game catchers in Tanganyika go about catching wild animals for the zoo when not occupied at catching each other for the woo. Script lacks momentum. It never really advances toward a story goal. Partially as a result of this static condition, Hawks' directorial style and Stuart Gilmore's editorial rhythm grow monotonous. The film switches tediously back and forth from love interlude to wild animal chase, rescued only by occasional outbursts of comedy which, though largely of the obvious variety, do enliven the tempo somewhat. Best sequences, though there seem to be a few too many of them, are those illustrating the captures via jeep and truck of various fender-bending beasts. The rhino passages are especially thrilling and sensationally photographed. Cameraman was Russell Harlan, his associate Joseph Brun.

John Wayne heads the colorful cast assembled for this zoological field trip. The vet star plays with his customary effortless (or so it seems) authority a role with which he is identified; the good-natured, but hard-drinking, hot-tempered, big Irishman who "thinks women are trouble" in a man's world.

Germany's Hardy Kruger and French actor Gerard Blain manage, resourcefully, to pump what vigor they can muster into a pair of undernourished roles. Red Buttons and Elsa Martinelli emerge the histrionic stickouts, Buttons with a jovial portrayal of an ex-cabbie who "just pretends it's rush hour in Brooklyn" as he jockeys his vehicle through a pack of frightened giraffe, Miss Martinelli as a sweet but spirited shutterbug and part time pachydermatologist. Bruce Cabot, Michele Girardon, Valentin de Vargas and Eduard Franz round out the cast professionally. But the animals steal the show.

Among those who merit praise for the slick outdoor production are art directors Hal Pereira and Carl Anderson, special photographic effects man John P. Fulton, soundmen John Carter and Charles Grenzbach and associate producer-second unit director Paul Helmick. However, it has remained for composer Henry Mancini to instill the outstanding and only truly noteworthy artistic ingredient into this film. His incongruously conspicuously score brings both character and humor to the picture—for example, an inspired bit of boogie to accompany an elephant bath. Mancini's melodies are contagious and they are haunting. *Tube.*

The Intruder

Desegregation in the South, intelligently confronted in resourcefully produced indie drama. Significant stride in timely sociological direction for U.S. filmdom, but will have to be marketed with care and taste to stimulate deserved b.o. reaction.

Hollywood, May 14.

Pathe America release of Roger Corman production. Stars William Shatner; features Frank Maxwell, Beverly Lunsford, Robert Emhardt. Directed by Corman. Screenplay, Charles Beaumont, from his novel; camera, Taylor Byars; editor, Ronald Sinclair; music, Herman Stein. Reviewed at Pathe Labs, May 14, '62. Running time, **84 MINS.**

Adam Cramer .... William Shatner
Tom McDaniel .... Frank Maxwell
Ella McDaniel .... Beverly Lunsford
Verne Shipman .... Robert Emhardt
Vi .... Jeanne Cooper
Sam Griffin .... Leo Gordon
Joey Green .... Charles Barnes
Mr. Paton .... Charles Beaumont
Ruth McDaniel .... Katherine Smith
Phil West.......George Clayton Johnson
Bart Carey .... William Nolan
Mrs. Lambert .... Phoebe Rowe
Sheriff .... Bo Dodd
Gramps .... Walter Kurtz
Jack Allardyce .... Ocee Ritch

Roger and Gene Corman's "The Intruder" comes to grips with a controversial contemporary issue—integration, and those who would defy the law of the land—in an adult, intelligent and arresting manner. Limited funds have not deterred these two forthright independent filmmakers from tackling this significant subject boldly, honestly and uncompromisingly. The film, a Pathe America release, is a credit to an industry that has been charged, and not entirely without cause, of playing it safe by avoiding ticklish, pertinent, up-to-date sociological matters in view of commercial realities. While "The Intruder" is obviously not going to cause any boxoffice stampede, it can, if sold as resourcefully as it was produced, emerge a profitable commercial enterprise as well as an important, worthwhile artistic effort and a boost to the prestige of U.S. filmdom in more influential, discriminating circles here and abroad.

The picture is not without one or two major story flaws, but these shortcomings are overridden by its innate overall significance. The main thing is that this is a provocative, timely matter of importance and concern to all Americans,

and this should be emphasized. The film should not be cheapened in the selling by playing up its sexual or psychological ramifications. It could be strong art house fare and might even, in the big cities, make a run for the money in the general market, if adroitly handled. An intelligent campaign, faithful to the spirit of the picture, could do the trick.

Charles Beaumont's screenplay, from his novel, dramatizes the campaign instigated in a Southern U.S. town by a slick, cocky, vain, unstable merchant of hate (from the so-called "Patrick Henry Society" in Washington) to urge the white residents to strike back against the law of integration. The man's primary incentive is actually personal ambition, but the mobs that at first rally round turn away in disgust when the true motives surface after a series of terrifying, reprehensible incidents including the murder of a colored preacher, the maiming of a courageous white editor and the near-lynching of a Negro student. Minor discrepancies (why didn't anyone attempt to notify federal authorities, who are conspicuously absent?) are overshadowed by true and telling moments and lines such as the remark of an elderly colored man as he watches the young colored students proceed toward the "white" school for the first time: "You Negroes are going to cause some of us niggers to get killed."

William Shatner, a fine young actor who deserves to be seen on the screen more frequently, masterfully plays the bigot. Especially sharp, noteworthy support is contributed by Jeanne Cooper and Leo Gordon. Others who score in prominent parts are Frank Maxwell, Beverly Lunsford, Robert Emhardt, Charles Barnes and Katherine Smith. Balance of the cast is fine.

This film is a major credit to the Cormans (producer-director Roger and exec producer Gene), to scenarist Beaumont, cameraman Taylor Byars, editor Ronald Sinclair and composer Herman Stein, as well as others responsible for its execution. It is a sign of a new maturity on the part of the U.S. motion picture industry. It must not be allowed to expire of malnutrition in its embryo stage. *Tube.*

Cannes Festival

Devi
(Goddess)
(INDIAN)
Cannes, May 15.
Satyajit Ray production and release. With Sharmila Tagore, Soumitra Chatterjee, Chhabi Biswas, Karuna Maukherjee. Directed by Satyajit Ray. Screenplay, Prabhat Kumar Mukhopadhaya, Ray; camera, Subrata Mitra; editor, Dullal Duta. At Cannes Film Fest. Running time, **98 MINS.**
Daya .... Sharmila Tagore
Uma .... Saumitra Chatterjee
Kiliknar .... Chhabi Biswas
Qiliknar .... Chhabi Biswas
Hara .... Karuna Banerjee
Tara .... Purendu Makherjee

Satyajit Ray, known for his moving trilogy, "Pather Panchali" and "World of Apu," now looks at a case of a religious miracle which is based on personal hallucination and superstition. Having the same feeling for place, people and imagery as its predecessors, it looms an arty house entry.

A young, happy married couple suddenly find their lives shattered when the boy's father, a religious man, dreams that the girl is a reincarnation of a deity and sets her up as such in the boy's absence. When he returns, he tries to stop a seeming curing of a fatally ill child. He tries to reason with her, but, being only 17 and confused, she is not quite sure if she is not really a Goddess.

Ray has told this with a luminous pattern of scenes, an insight into his characters and a subdued but never faltering pace. It has stringent allusions to Indian life and beliefs, and should find a specialized audience if well placed and handled.

Ed Harrison has this for U.S. distribution. *Mosk.*

Without Each Other
(COLOR)

Indie Yank pic in color has the technical brightness for regular release with some arty chances, too; no names, so it will need plenty of plugging.

Cannes, May 15.
Allen Klein production and release. Stars Tony Anthony; features Ann Hergira, Michael Dunn, Brud Talbot, Ann Harris. Directed by Saul Swimmer. Screenplay, Swimmer, Tony Anthony, Ted Apstein, William Herman; camera (Pathecolor), Arthur Ornitz; editor, Ralph Rosenblum; music, Dimitri Tiomkin. At Cannes Film Fest. Running time, **90 MINS.**
Boy .... Tony Anthony
Mother .... Ann Hergira
Dwarf .... Michael Dunn
Girl .... Ann Harris
Boyfriend .... Brud Talbot

Indie U.S. film arrived too late to take part in the Critic Section at this festival, reserved for promising first pix, but was underwritten by the crix for a special showing that got good response. It is a neatly turned-out tale made by a young group of filmmakers in Florida, and scored in Hollywood.

It is in the Hollywood tradition of a boy's return to a mother he has never seen, and the small town pettiness that is finally overridden by awakening feeling that have been a bit obscured by too much self-indulgence. There is an added fillip in looking at youth and loneliness could make this a possible arty entry. But best bet seems for general playoff since it lacks names.

A boy, who works in a circus, goes to his mother, whom he has not seen since a baby, to announce his father's death. She has become an eccentric recluse in a crumbling house looked after by a dwarf, expertly limned by Michael Dunn. Back taxes have decided an auction of the house with a local resident coveting the property for his son. The boy comes back to his neurotic mother and tries to pay the taxes only to be rebuffed by town intrigues. He also gets into a fight with a local bully.

A drunken approach to the house by a group of youths leads to his mother having a heart attack and dying later. The boy parades her coffin through the city and the whole town follows the circus truck back to the grounds for the burial. Then he goes off alone as he had come.

The sentimentality is restrained and shows a renewal of sincere feeling for a story that has social overtones. Color photography of Arthur Ornitz has the right lushness.

Newcomer Tony Anthony still has some Methodics that could best be forgotten, in his long pauses and eye blinking for emphasis. However, he should be heard from later. Ann Hergira is properly cast as the mother while the remainder of the cast is effective.

Dimitri Tiomkin's tinkling score is also an asset in this soundly made little drama that has the polish for programmer use. Film is fresh, and its naive qualities are a help in this story. Producer Allen Klein has given this a good production dress. *Mosk.*

Les Amants De Teruel
(The Lovers of Teruel)
(FRENCH—COLOR—TOTALSCOPE)
Cannes, May 15.
Cinedis release of Monarch production. Stars Ludmila Tcherina; features, Milenko Banovitch, Milko Sparemblek, Stephen Grebel, Roberto. Written and directed by Raymond Rouleau; camera (Technicolor), Claude Renoir; choreography, Milko Sparemblek; music. Mikis Theodorakis; editor, Marinette Cadix. At Cannes Film Fest. Running time, **93 MINS.**
Isa .... Ludmila Tcherina
Director .... Rene-Louis Lafforgue
Diego .... Milenko Banovitch
Grebilito .... Stephen Grebel
Manuel .... Milko Sparemblek
Dwarf .... Roberto
Pablo .... Antonie Marin

What started out to be a full-length dance film emerges a mixture of expressionistic filmmaking with little dance but plenty of offbeat symbolism, special effects and sombre pacing. Makes this primarily an arty entry abroad.

Pic is shot on a sound stage which is supposed to represent a shabby slum area. Here, an ambulant theatre company is giving a mime-ballet (based on an old Spanish legend) but it seems the ancient tale is being relived by members of the troupe itself.

Lead dancer, Ludmila Tcherina, had been in love with her leading man but he had disappeared on their wedding day. While she is waiting for him, another member of the troupe courts her. Finally, this leading man reappears, only to be murdered by the other suitor. She goes mad, and dies under a train.

Film starts at a snail's pace. A surrealistic group of images, special effects and some dance fill in the background before the show goes on.

Director Raymond Rouleau has piled things on with greenish faces and masks plus shifting colors. Barely does a true mood break through. Color is effective but bogged down by overdone facial colorings.

Ludmila Tcherina has the classic beauty for the doomed girl. She has some moments but is mainly a victim of this slow-moving affair.

This heavyweight film will need hardsell and special placement, but may have a chance if sold right to specialized arty audiences who go for offbeat films. But it is a chancy entry. *Mosk.*

Adorable Julia
(FRENCH-AUSTRIAN)
Cannes, May 15.
Jacques Mage release of Wisner Murdus Films-Etoile production. Stars Lili Palmer, Charles Boyer, Jean Sorel, Jeanne Valerie. Directed by Alfred Wiedenmann. Screenplay, Marc-Gilbert Sauvajon, Guy Bolton, Pascal Jardin, from play by Somerset Maugham; camera, Werner Krien; editor, A. Wilhelm. At Cannes Film Fest. Running time, **97 MINS.**
Julia .... Lili Palmer
Michel .... Charles Boyer
Tom .... Jean Sorel
Aive .... Jeanne Valerie

A real international affair is this Austrian-French pic given as an Austrian entry at the Cannes Fest in French. It is a familiar, old-fashioned tale that remains somewhat too stagey for anything but dualer or specialized playoff abroad on the Lili Palmer and Charles Boyer names.

An aging but attractive actress takes a young lover and finally realizes he is the last one and that her patient, adoring husband is the thing for her. It is full of theatrical asides, quaintness and static and telegraphed developments.

Miss Palmer has the charm for the capricious actress role, but seems to lack being the more overbearing personality the role calls for. Charles Boyer walks through his part while Jean Sorel is too wooden as the climbing lover.

It is technically acceptable but a bit of schmaltzy film material that has little place in today's film currents and tastes except perhaps in its home market. *Mosk.*

S-A Furat O Bomba
(A Bomb Has Been Stolen)
(ROUMANIAN)
Cannes, May 22.
Bucarest Studios production and release. With Darie Iurie, Liliana Tomasco, Haralambie Boros, Eugenia Balaure. Written and directed by Ion Popesco Gopo. Camera, Stephan Horvath; editor D. Capoiani. At Cannes Film Fest. Running time, **65 MINS.**
Boy .... Darie Iurie
Girl .... Liliana Tomesco
Gangster .... Haralambie Boros
Moll .... Eugenia Balaure

Ion Popesco Gopo has won several prizes at this festival for his clever animated shorts. Now he does a live pic but utilizes cartoon conceptions in movement and action to make this a naive, little comedy that comes over well. Having no talk, it could be used as a medium length item with another for offbeat spots abroad or for video.

In some unnamed land, a group of gangsters steal an atomic bomb but it falls into the unknowing hands of a young, unemployed man. He wanders about town, the bomb gets passed around, and finally the gangsters and government gang up against him. But a girl he has met and loved helps hand out pieces of the bomb which are used by people to take them scudding around without vehicles and to make things grow in the fields.

Gopo has been able to find the right rhythm in this film and built in spoofs on horror pix, gangsters, rock-n-roll and other foibles but without propaganda. It has its little preaching about the A Bomb but does it with tact and wit.

In short, a small but beguiling comedy from the East which is based mainly on visuals. A clever musical track and sound backing

also help as well as the stylized playing of the actors.   *Mosk.*

El Angel Exterminador
(The Exterminating Angel)
(MEXICAN)

Cannes, May 15.
Gustavo Alatriste production and release. With Silvia Pinal, Jacqueline Andere, Jose Baviera, Augusto Benedico, Luis Beristain, Antonio Bravo. Written and directed by Luis Bunuel from a story by Bunuel, Luis Alcoriza. Camera, Gabriel Figuesoa; editor, Carlos Savage Jr. At Cannes Film Fest. Running time. **92 MINS.**

Walkiria	Silvia Pinal
Roc	Jacqueline Andere
Leandro	Jose Baviera
Doctor	Augusto Benedico
Cristian	Luis Beristain
Russell	Antonio Bravo

Unusual offbeater could be pegged a parable, social satire as a dream film. It has power and solidity that evoke discussion, and should be in for an arty house career abroad.

Director Luis Bunuel, a Mexican of Hispano origin, copped the Grand Prix at the last Cannes Fest for his "Viridiana," and may be in for a kudo on this one. In a strange manner, it exerts a hypnotic draw via perfection in mounting and acting. Buffs may have a greater feeling for the parade of symbols and ideas, but it has enough power even to draw the uninitiated.

A group of rich people go to a friend's home for late supper after the opera. The servants leave and the group notices suddenly that they lack the will or the ability to get out of the house. They find themselves in the living room unable to leave the spot. Time seems to go on and they remain on. Problems of privacy, food, water and human association and comportment come up. People outside can't get into the house and it is put under quarantine. They finally manage to find a way of getting out and offer their thanks in a church.

Pic ends in revolts outside, the church quarantined and a group of sheep heading to the church. So symbols and ideas abound. In the living room, these people had been stripped of any social facades. A bear and some sheep wander in during their seeming imprisonment. It probably can be explained but each spectator can find his own way in this fascinating filmic maze.

Drugs, cabalistic signs, and attempts to marshall the people into action all seem to fail as they slowly sink into near violence. It may be a razor sharp look at purgatory. The symbols may have or not have any true, clear meaning, but do have shock value.

Thus one woman seems to see a human hand scuttling about (it turns out to be a hallucination), a box of drugs becomes a seemingly healing affair but arouses envy, and slowly turns into a sort of Pandora's Box.

But whatever, this is a film of depth, and is absorbing and offbeat with a brilliance in technique and observation that could have this a contender if well placed and hypoed.

Acting is of a piece and brilliantly utilized by director Bunuel while Gabriel Figueroa's crystal-like lensing is another asset.

Director Bunuel made his first surrealist films in Paris in the 1930's, then worked in the U.S. and finally settled in Mexico where he began to make pix again. He broke into world marts again when he won a prize in Cannes for his "Los Olvidados" in 1950. Since then Cannes has given him other prizes culminating in the Golden Palm last year.   *Mosk.*

Les Enfants Du Soleil
(Children of the Sun
(MOROCCAN)

Cannes, May 22.
Djinn Films production and release. With Mustapha Brick, Amina Bel Kahia, Tayeb Sadiki, Afifi. Directed by Jacques Severac. Screenplay, David Dayan, Brahim Sayah; camera, Jacques Klein; editor, Jacques Mavel. At Cannes Film Fest. Running time, **85 MINS.**

Abdou	Mustapha Brick
Yasmina	Amina Bel Kahia
Tahar	Tayeb Sadiki
Afifi	Afifi

Familiar story of poor shoeshine boys, this time in Morocco, has them getting into several situations but seemingly heading for decency and law abiding at the end. It is acceptably done but remains mainly an Arabic country bet at best.

One boy is saving money to buy his mother a sewing machine. He finally has the money for the machine only to see it broken in an accident. However, instead of rebelling, he decides to save up again.

Film is simply done but has some interest in its views of Arab child life. But this rarely has the probing quality needed to make this more than an average look at youth.

It is technically acceptable as is the acting. But the routine direction of Jacques Severac does not give this the feeling it lacks.   *Mosk.*

Le Petit Etranger
(The Little Stranger)
(LEBANESE)

Cannes, May 15.
Mario E. Eraktingi production and release. With Vasso-Gabriel, Laura Azar, Chakib Couri, Gaston Chicane. Directed by Georges M. Nasser. Screenplay, Ramez Noujaim; camera, Ibrahim Shamate; editor, Azar. At Cannes Film Fest. Running time, **95 MINS.**

Dori	Vasso Gabriel
Girl	Laura Azar
Foreman	Chakib Couri

About a 13-year-old's coming of age when he runs away from home, this is too confused and too crowded with excess violence for anything but grind chances abroad. The boy's brother is in jail for killing his girl's lover. The boy finds out the girl has become the mistress of the local boss who runs the company where all work. In his chagrin, he also finds that men and women are ruthless and selfish. After many beatings he becomes a man ready to face the world.

All of this is told too emphatically with little insight into character. George M. Nasser may emerge a director when he learns how to tell a story clearly before worrying about camera angles.   *Mosk.*

Cupola
(Dome)
(JAPANESE; SCOPE)

Cannes, May 15.
Nikkatsu production and release. With Eijiro Tono, Tokuko Sugiyama, Sayari Yoshimaga, Yoshihiro Ichikawa. Directed by Kiriro Urayama. Screenplay, Chiyo Hayafune, Shohei Imamura, Urayama; camera, Masaki Mimetsu; editor, Mutsuo Tanji. At Cannes Film Fest. Running time, **100 MINS.**

Tatsugoro	Eijiro Tono
Tomi	Tokuko Sugiyama
Jun	Sayuri Yoshinaga
Takayuni	Yoshihiro Ichikawa

This is about a family with economic problems, and does have some sentimental, preachy aspects. But the pic overcomes this via an expert handling of children, a feeling for evolving times and people plus some expert imagery. Though having a disarming flair, it appears mainly for specialized and language spots abroad.

A teen-age girl and her younger brother fight against the pettiness of an unemployed father to find their way in a changing portion of a backward section of Japan. The adventures have plenty of amplitude heightened by some fine acting.

The girl finally finds what she wants to do and the boy also shows signs of developing into a decent human being who will rise above his lower working classes. Of more meaning in Japan where these social and economic changes are current this vehicle climbs to general international level via its insight into youth. Spirited mounting and a general knowhow.

This deals with the ordinary life and its problems and looks at racism. All this adds up to a well-made film that has something to say. And it says it well, but without the fillip to keep its message and treatment balanced for more untoward foreign chances. Technically it is tops.   *Mosk.*

Dom Bez Okien
(The Impossible Goodbye)
(POLISH)

Cannes, May 15.
Polski State Film release of Rytm production. With Wieslaw Golas, Elizabieta Cryzewaka, Jan Swiderski, Danuta Szaflarska, Josef Kondrat. Directed by Stanislaw Jedryka. Screenplay, Aleksander Scibor-Rylski; camera, Czeslaw Swirta; editor, K. Lewkowicz. At Cannes Film Fest. Running time, **98 MINS.**

Robert	Wieslaw Golas
Therese	Elizbieta Cryzewska
Wife	Danuta Szaflarsko
Director	Josef Kondrat
Kieberg	Jan Swiderski

There is some polish in this pic about a smalltime circus. On the edge of failure, the tent show is further sloughed by a new mime who also almost wercks the operation by destroying the other performers' faith in their talents. But film also tries for symbols that are not quite clear or effective. Result is a vehicle with slight foreign chances except for a few language houses.

There is a good sawdust feel in this yarn about a second rate circus. The people seem to have had circus training, and this builds up good atmosphere. But the mime's background and needs are never too clear.

Direction is smooth and incisive, acting good, and technical credits fine.   *Mosk.*

Hell Is for Heroes

Arresting war drama with interesting combat procedure elements. Exploitable item for action market, but unstable in higher dramatic sphere.

Hollywood, May 22.
Paramount release of Henry Blanke production. Stars Steve McQueen, Bobby Darin, Fess Parker; features Nick Adams, Harry Guardino, James Coburn. Mike Kellin; introduces Bob Newhart. Directed by Donald Seigel. Screenplay, Robert Pirosh, Richard Carr, from story by Pirosh; camera, Harold Lipstein; editor, Howard Smith; music, Leonard Rosenman; assistant directors. William McGarry, James Rosenberger. Reviewed at the studio, May 22, '62. Running time, **90 MINS.**

Reese	Steve McQueen
Pvt. Corby	Bobby Darin
Sgt. Pike	Fess Parker
Sgt. Larkin	Harry Guardino
Cpl. Henshaw	James Coburn
Pvt. Kolinsky	Mike Kellin
Capt. Loomis	Joseph Hoover
Pvt. Cumberly	Bill Mullikin
Sgt. Frazer	L. Q. Jones
Monique	Michele Montau
Capt. Mace	Don Haggerty
Homer	Nick Adams
Pvt. Driscoll	Bob Newhart

Producer Henry Blanke has framed and mounted a gripping, fast-paced, hard-hitting dramatic portrait of an interesting World War II battlefield incident in "Hell Is for Heroes." The Paramount release should be a popular attraction with male audiences and filmgoers who prefer an emphasis on explosive, nerve-shattering action in their war dramas. Exploited as a raw, turbulent and yet intimate depiction of the ironic patterns of combat behavior, as enacted by a company of youthful, virile and reliable actors, the film might earn its stripes in the action market. However, those whose patronage of a screen war story depends on how thought-provoking its moral and how believable its tone and construction are apt to entertain reservations. There are occasional duds in the film's dramatic arsenal.

Recollections of an actual and tightly classified incident near the dragon's teeth of the Siegfried Line during the dark days of World War II inspired the story by Robert Pirosh, adapted into screenplay form by Richard Carr and Pirosh, creative activator of the film who bowed out as its producer along the way. Pivotal character of the drama is a surly, rebellious, busted NCO (Steve McQueen) whose front-line courage, leadership and keen sense of improvisation in the course of a grim and seemingly hopeless campaign to hold off a large German force in the face of incredible odds backfires into a potential court martial wrap for usurping authority.

This pregnant situation is rather conveniently (though truth may be stranger than fiction) resolved when the angry young private finishes the job interrupted with the arrival of brass by destroying both himself and the German position in an act of monumental heroism, leaving the moral-philosophical issue somewhat suspended. The point-of-view is unmistakably there, but it is up to the filmgoer to make something of it.

McQueen plays the central role with hard-bitten businesslike reserve and an almost animal intensity, permitting just the right degree of humanity to project through a war-weary-and-wise veneer. Bobby Darin has a color-

ful role of a battlefield hoarder, which he portrays with relish. Harry Guardino is excellent as an uncertain sergeant. James Coburn fine as a practical corporal. Nick Adams chips in a vivicaous account of a Polish refugee pitifully detached from society in a broken wartime world. Fess Parker, Mike Kellin, Joseph Hoover and Bill Mullikin score in key roles, L. Q. Jones and Don Haggerty in smaller ones. Michele Montau, the only femme, comes on fairly strong in a role that may remind war buffs of the Denise Darcel character in an earlier Pirosh film, "Battleground."

In general, the cast operates with ethusiasm under director Donald Siegel's adept command. But the film does not nearly come off in a league with great, lofty war films the artistic calibre of "Paths of Glory," which it roughly resembles. For example, integration of comedy elements via Bob Newhart (whom the picture introduces to screen audiences), while accomplished with considerable flair, weakens believability of the entire situation through comic exaggeration. Newhart's mock phone monolog for the benefit of Nazi eavesdroppers is funny artificially in an atmosphere of deadly serious peril. War films are fragile enterprises in which the impact of the whole is utterly dependent upon the credibility of each and every link in the dramatic machinery. One strip of the gears and the whole transmission breaks down.

As a physical production, the film is first-rate. Among the effective contributions are those of cameraman Harold Lipstein, editor Howard Smith, are directors Hal Pereira and Howard Richmond, soundman Philip Mitchell and John Wilkinson, and composer Leonard Rosenman. *Tube.*

The Spiral Road
(EASTMAN COLOR)

Plodding tale of a doctor's spiritual redemption in the jungles of Java. Tepid outlook.

Universal release of a Robert Arthur production. Stars Rock Hudson, Burl Ives, Gena Rowlands. Features Geoffrey Keen, Neva Patterson, Will Kuluva, Philip Abbott, Larry Gates. Directed by Robert Mulligan. Screenplay, Neil Patterson and John Lee Mahin (from a novel by Jan de Hartog); camera (Eastman color), Russell Harlan; editor, Russell F. Schoengarth; music, Jerry Goldsmith; assistant director, Joseph Kenny. Previewed at Universal homeoffice, May 19, '62. Running time, **145 MINS.**

Anton Drager	Rock Hudson
Brits Jansen	Burl Ives
Els	Gena Rowlands
Willem Wattereus	Geoffrey Keen
Louise Kramer	Neva Patterson
Dr. Sordjano	Will Kuluva
Frolick	Philip Abbott
Dr. Kramer	Larry Gates
Inspector Bevers	Karl Swenson
The Sultan	Edgar Stehli
Laja	Judy Dan
Dr. Martens	Robert F. Simon
Stegomyia	Ibrahim Bin Hassan
Burubi	Reggie Nalder
Dr. Hatta	Leon Lontok
Major Viormans	David Lewis
Mr. Boosmans	Parley Baer
Van Bloor	Fredd Wayne
Krasser	Leslie Bradley
Mrs. Boosmans	Barbara Morrison
Dr. Sander	Martin Brandt

Being uninspired, Robert Arthur's production of "The Spiral Road" is the uninspiring tale of an atheist's conversion to God. The picture, moreover, takes the devil's own time getting down to cases and the resolution, and of its numerous defects, prolonged length is a major infirmity of this chronicle of jungle medicine in Java as practiced by the Dutch.

The presentday Hollywood penchant for sophisticated characterization and depth story is not to be discerned here. Contrarily, the leaden plot has the aura of a throwback, being simply a naive adventure drama of skin-deep dimension. Even subjected to extensive pruning—which it sorely needs—it is hard to envision the Universal release as any but a dubious boxoffice bet, granting even the normally potent attachment of Rock Hudson's name.

A novel by Dutch author Jan de Hartog (whose output has become much-favored by filmmakers) is the source for the flabby Neil Paterson-John Lee Mahin screenplay. It concerns an opportunistic, gainsaying freshman medic (Rock Hudson) and his determination to ride to scientific fame on the research of a seasoned jungle physician (Burl Ives). Hudson's arrogance and cynicism are played against sundry goodhearts — his suffering wife (Gena Rowlands), the Salvation Army man (Geoffrey Keen), and highminded types who constitute his superiors in the government medical mission.

In much more time than it takes to tell, it becomes apparent that for all his cocksure exterior, Hudson, lacking faith in the divine, is soul-sick. Also, that he'll be tested in the crucible, in this instance a terrifying ordeal alone which pits his rationality against a witch-doctored tribe on black magic maneuvers. So much pat melodrama, albeit a reasonably enlivened windup to things.

Hudson is satisfactory as the redeemed heavy, at times even giving his role more than it rates. His devotees, however, are apt to wish he was back romping with Doris Day. Ives and Miss Rowlands are generally effective, though Ives' typical bombast does grow tiresome. Keen, the British actor, is good but wasted in this effort. There is dependable support from Neva Patterson, Will Kuluva, Philip Abbott and Larry Gates.

Direction by Robert Mulligan is as flatfooted as the scenario is diffuse. Other technical credits, including Russell Harlan's photography and Jerry Goldsmith's music, are on a par with the rest of the contributions. *Pit.*

Tales of Terror

Three macabre items presenting Price, Lorre, Rathbone. Promising bet in the goose-bump market.

American International release of Roger Corman production. Stars Vincent Price, Basil Rathbone, Peter Lorre, Debra Paget. Screenplay, Richard Matheson, based on Edgar Allen Poe stories; camera (color and Panavision), Floyd Crosby; editor, Anthony Carras; assistant director, Jack Bohrer. Reviewed in New York, May 23, '62. Running time, **90 MINS.**

Fortunato, Valdemar, Locke	Vincent Price
Montresor	Peter Lorre
Carmichael	Basil Rathbone
Helene	Debra Paget
Lenore	Maggie Pierce
Morella	Leona Gage
Dr. Elliot James	David Frankham

Now comes the fourth in American Internationals cycle of horror pix, each based on the works of Edgar Allen Poe. The fourth, "Tales of Terror," has three spine ticklers for the trade, "Morella," "The Black Cat" and "The Facts in the Case of M. Valdemar." The three tales make a heavy dose, even for thrill-prone teenage set.

It's to the credit of producer-director Roger Corman that the first two, "Morella" and "The Black Cat" trip through the horror hoops in a mad grace going beyond strictly fan appeal. Corman and scenarist Richard Matheson do get bogged down in the long-winded latter story, "The Facts in the Case of M. Valdemar." It's only the final scene in "Valdemar" which is a shocker—and a real ugly one at that.

Whether audiences will have been rendered limp by the Poe cycle is anybody's guess. Producer Corman, though, plays his latest entry for all it's worth and has assembled some tasty ghoulish acting talent which have marquee strength. Vincent Price leers, is mad, is tender—and even laughs straight. Peter Lorre has a madcap time of it and Basil Rathbone is a heavy's heavy. Price, Lorre and Rathbone have a special marquee meaning to the skull and bones trade. There's also some feminine decorative lure in Debra Paget. Supporting cast is competent, color lavish and music eerie.

The best realized nightmare and the shortest of the trio is "Morella." This has Vincent Price dying a living death since the sudden demise of his wife, Morella, played by Leona Gage. She died soon after the birth of her baby. Twenty-odd years yater, the baby grown up to a living doll revisits her mad father in his haunted mansion. The doll, whose moniker is Leonore, is portrayed by Maggie Pierce. The short piece is played for its nightmarish terror and it clicks, hitting hidden human recesses. Simulating a woman's face after 20-odd years of death is a matter of taste. This reviewer found it repulsive.

"The Black Cat" comes next. It is too long, but as a mad caper it has its moments. Peter Lorre, reeling and leering, plays a drunken husband who drives his wife into the hands of another man. (Every vice has its Vincent Price). Lorre, in revenge, murders his wife and entombs her and Price behind a brick wall in the cellar of his house. The domestic cat which he hated proved his undoing, for its yowling behind the wall informs the gendarmes. Why Lorre would leave his wife nightly for the bottle appears to be a special sort of madness. For his wife, portrayed by Joyce Jameson, seems far more fetching than the bottom of a glass.

The last of the trio and the weakest is "The Facts in the Case of M. Valdemar." The commanding performance of Basil Rathbone and the beauty of Debra Paget cannot save this long-drawn out talky tale. Price is there again and David Frankham joins in a supporting role. Only the last few moments have moments of horror, liquid putrification. Ugh. By this time the dead flesh had worn thin. *Horo.*

Il Commissario
(The Police Commissioner)
(ITALIAN)

Rome, May 22.

Dino DeLaurentiis production and release. Stars Alberto Sordi; features Franca Tamantini, Franco Scandurra, Alessandro Cutolo, Angela Portaluri. Directed by Luigi Comencini. Story and screenplay, Ago. Scarpelli; camera, Aldo Scavarda; music, Carlo Rustichelli. At Corso Cinema, Rome. Running time, **101 MINS.**

Dante Lombardozzi	Alberto Sordi
Marisa	Franca Tamantini
Police Chief	Alessandro Cutolo
Martarazzo	Franco Scandurra
Irma	Angela Portaluri

Ideal comedy-drama vehicle for Alberto Sordi, who seemingly can do no wrong for Italo audiences. Pic looks another winner on the local market for Dino DeLaurentiis, and another feather in Sordi's cap as a creator of memorable local characters. Export values are less apparent, though Italian lingual areas should prove fruitful customs.

Once more Sordi, as in his previous "The Cop" and "A Difficult Life," plays an over-zealous climber in a world over-stuffed with conformists. Here his bumbling but instinctively adroit snooping uncovers the true solution to an already "solved" crime which others have wanted to cover up.

Sordi manages to toe the fine line between comedy and pathos in pro fashion, creating an unforgettable cameo of inspector Lombardozzi. Providing valiant assists are Franca Tamantini, as a harried fiance; Alessandro Cutolo, the police chief; Franco Scandurra, as another superior of Sordis; and Angela Portaluri. as a call girl involved in the scandal-murder.

Director Luigi Comencini, lenser Aldo Scavarda, and others involved deserve top credit for a slick job turned out in record time for a topnotch production per-lira value. *Hawk.*

Ophelia
(FRENCH)

Paris, May 22.

Lux release of Boreal production. Stars Alida Valli, Juliette Meyniel; features Andre Jocelyn, Claude Cerval, Sacha Briquet. Directed by Claude Chabrol. Screenplay, Chabrol, Martial Matthieu; camera, Jacques Rabier; editor, Jacques Gaillard. Preemed in Paris. Running time, **105 MINS.**

Yvan	Andre Jocelyn
Lucie	Juliette Meyniel
Claudia	Alida Valli
Adrien	(Claude Cerval
Gravedigger	Sacha Briquet

Looking like an updated takeoff on Shakespeare's "Hamlet," or a case of Hamlet fixation, this manages to hold attention despite its seemingly split motifs. This is done via the adroit imagery and atmospheric feeling of director Claude Chabrol. It thus appears mainly an arty theatre bet abroad, at best.

An industrialist is buried in a small town. His son seems to be shattered by the situation while his mother already smiles knowingly at the dead man's brother. Soon they marry, and the son walks the streets to the snickers of the petty townsfolk. Passing a theatre showing Sir Laurence Olivier's film version of "Hamlet," he gets the idea he is in the same position.

So the Hamlet design falls into place. He upsets his mother and uncle-stepfather by morose and hysterical acting and begins to plot to show they really poisoned his father. He turns the family retainer's daughter into Ophelia and the rest of the Hamlet characters follow.

Film suffers from the obvious attempts to create coincidental patterns with the Shakespeare model

as well as from the dandified acting and character of the Hamlet figure. There is acid fun poked at the snide townspeople as well as at a professional strikebreaker hired by the uncle for protection from his striking workers.

Director Chabrol has given this some striking imagery and at times a dramatic flair. It might have been more forceful if played as an out-and-out updated version of the Hamlet tale. Characters remain mainly one dimensional. Technical credits are good while the actors do as best they can with their dual-type bits. *Mosk.*

Nuestros Odiosos Maridos
(Our Hateful Husbands)
(MEXICAN)

Mexico City, May 22.
Peliculas Nacionales release of Cinematografica Filmex production. Stars Julio Aleman, Rosita Arenas, Barbara Gil; features Miguel Corcega, Oscar Ortiz de Pinedo, Eduardo Alcaraz, Aurora Walker, Arturo Cobo, Marianela Pena, Antonio Brillas, Leon Mickel and Fernando Fernandez. Written, produced and directed by Humberto Gomez Landero. Camera, Raul Martinez Solares. At Alameda Theatre, Mexico City. Running time, **90 MINS.**

A Mexican comedy effort having agility and grace, and avoiding customary slapstick situations. Director Humberto Gomez Landero, also responsible for the screenplay, has drawn professional performances from starlets and vet actors. Dialogue is more carefully prepared and the satire is quite well defined in the war of sexes where husbands ally against wives to dominate their respective marriage problems.

There are some absurd situations and sometimes a strain for laughs. Sonia Furio has a difficult job transforming from a loving mother into a vamp. But the overall idea is not bad and this one will gross well. Rosita Arenas and Barbara Gil are easy on the eyes if a little clumsy with their lines. *Emil.*

Escape From Zahrain
(PANAVISION—COLOR)

Exploitable straight action fare marred by raggedness around romantic and idealistic edges. At core, an exciting chase drama that should attain modest speed in action market.

Hollywood, May 15.
Paramount release of Ronald Neame production. Stars Yul Brynner; features Sal Mineo, Jack Warden, Madlyn Rhue. Directed by Neame. Screenplay, Robin Estridge, based on story by Michael Barrett; camera (Technicolor), Ellsworth Fredricks; editor, Eda Warren; music, Lyn Murray; assistant director, Tom Connors Jr. Reviewed at the studio, May 15, '62. Running time, **92 MINS.**
Sharif .... Yul Brynner
Ahmed .... Sal Mineo
Huston .... Jack Warden
Laila .... Madlyn Rhue
Tahar .... Anthony Caruso
Ambulance Driver...... Leonard Strong
Hassan .... Jay Novello

Buffs of the straight action drama will have a field day with Ronald Neame's rip-roaring adventure production of "Escape From Zahrain." Since attempts to broaden its dramatic scope with idealistic overtones and romantic undercurrents are abortive and

tend to distract from the primary issue—a good old-fashioned chase —the Paramount release should not be marketed with any pretense in the direction of these negative aspects. It is essentially a film for the action market and, exploited as such, will make its best showing there.

As in last year's 20th-Fox release, "The Big Gamble," which this film resembles in structure, the star of the show is a truck—which bears a party of escaped prisoners across a desert in a journey somewhat more perilous than a typical weekday five o'clock on the Hollywood Freeway. Unlike "Gamble," and here it is superior, the party is being pursued diligently by the government police of "Zahrain," a fictitious but readily identifiable Near Eastern Arab state. Leader of the fleeing company is a rebellious patriot (Yul Brynner) determined to rid his country of imperialist western elements as well as its own decadent leadership. Aboard for the rugged ride is a Moslem lass (Madlyn Rhue), at first a hostage, later an astonishingly delighted guest who, apparently by osmosis (not even a smooch) falls in love with Brynner. In the most unlikely decision of the current filmic year, she prefers to tag along in mortal danger with the hunted convicts when given the opportunity to remain behind in safety at a remote oil pumping station. One can only conclude she has read the script.

Brynner plays with his characteristic stoicism of emotional expression. Sal Mineo, shirt carefully unbuttoned to display just enough pectoral for he-man stature, rides along as a student patriot. Miss Rhue, as is true of the average woman in such adventure rumpuses, is incongruous and unbelievable in the surroundings, palsying the action with undernourished love stuff. Anthony Caruso, Jay Novello and Leonard Strong are lively in character roles. But Jack Warden, with sensitive timing, masculinity and compassion, steals the film and injects its only humor as a resourceful Yank. James Mason puts in an unbilled cameo as an oil company maintenance man.

Neame's direction from the Robin Estridge scenario rolls matters along at a rapid tempo when action is the word. Ellsworth Fredrick's camerawork, accompanied by John Fulton's special photographic effects and Irmin Roberts' second unit photography, is dexterous and accomplished. Eda Warren's editing is taut. An Arabesque background score by Lyn Murray complements the story. *Tube.*

La Voglia Matta
(That Certain Urge)
(ITALIAN)

Rome, May 22.
Indie release of a D.D.L. Production. Features Ugo Tognazzi, Catherine Spaak. Gianni Garko, Beatrice Altariba, Jimmy Fontana, Franco Giacobini. Directed by Luciano Salce. Screenplay, Salce, Castellano, Pipolo; camera, Enrico Menzger; music, Ennio Morricone; editor, Roberto Cinquini. At Metropolitan, Rome. Running time, **120 MINS.**
Antonio Berlingheri .... Ugo Tognazzi
Francesca .... Catherine Spaak
Piero .... Gianni Garko
Silvana .... Beatrice Altariba
Fiance .... Jimmy Fontana
Alberghetti............Franco Giacobini

Delightful bitter-sweet comedy with topnotch audience appeal and

many elements for critical recognition as well. With proper lingual versions, this pic, which is already heading for high b.o. totals in this country, should prove a fine export bet as well.

Antonio Berlingheri (Ugo Tognazzi) is a middleaged businessman who becomes accidentally involved with a gang of teen-agers on a weekend by the sea. They run circles around him though he gamely tries to keep up with them in their showoff efforts at love and prowess. Subsequently, he falls for one of them, Catherine Spaak, not realizing that in her childish code, he's just another flirt for the books.

He tries to shake off the experience, but it's one he'll remember. Director Salce here has expertly explored the often unconsciously cruel world of the adolescent, set off even more by justaxposition with the shock of oncoming middle age on the part of the businessman.

There are touches of poor taste here and there, and of overemphasis, but what remains is a lively, amusing, yet stirring and a moving picture of youth today. Tognazzi, a widely known Italo comedian, has never been better than in this oft-pathetic characterization. Miss Spaak is completely charming and winning as Francesca, his two-day flirt.

Remainder of a large cast has been ably chosen and, guided in backdrop chores. Music is apt, and technical values are all in keeping. Some trimming of overweight footage, especially towards the end, would heighten the total effect. *Hawk.*

Estoy Casada, Ja Ja
(I'm Married, Ha Ha)
(MEXICAN)

Mexico City, May 22.
Columbia Pictures release of Alfa Films production. Stars Ana Luisa Pelufo, Alfredo Varela Jr. Directed by Miguel M. Delgado. At Palacio Chino, Mexico City. Running time, **90 MINS.**

This depicts a newlyweds' honeymoon without the honey as they spar off against each other, only to wind up in the inevitable clinch. Miguel M. Delgado has directed this one with verve for comedy situations. And surprisingly enough, the picture comes out as a better than the average Mexican comedy.

Ana Luisa Pelufo is a star of constantly improving technique, and she capably handles the light comedy in this one. As well as she also is adept at displaying her pleasing figure in a successive number of creations. Mauricio Garces, as the other half of the newlyweds, displays a fine sense of timing with Oscar Ortiz de Pinedo and Alfredo Varela Jr. adding to the comedy.

While this one did not preem in a frontline first run, it merited such distinction. Film will do well nationally and in the Spanish language markets, where Miss Pelufo has been building up a boxoffice name. *Emil.*

The Pot Carriers
(BRITISH)

Lively slice of life in the cooler; good popular booking.

London, May 29.
Warner-Pathe release of an Associated British (Gordon L. T. Scott) production. Stars Ronald Fraser, Paul Massie, Carole Lesley, Dennis Price; features Paul Rogers, Davy Kaye, Eddie Byrne, Alfred Burke, Vanda Godsell, Campbell Singer, Patrick McAlinney. Directed by Peter Graham Scott. Screenplay, T. J. Morrison, Mike Watts from Watts' play; camera, Edwin Hillier; editor, Richard Beatt; music, Stanley Black. At Warner Theatre, London. Running time, **84 MINS.**
Redband .... Ronald Fraser
Rainbow .... Paul Massie
Wendy .... Carole Lesley
Smooth Tongue .... Dennis Price
Governor .... Paul Rogers
Mouse .... Davy Kaye
Chief Officer Bailey...... Eddie Byrne
P. O. Mott .... Campbell Singer
Lang .... Alfred Burke
Dillon .... Patrick McAlinney
Bracket .... Neil McCarthy
Mrs. Redband .... Vanda Godsell
P. O. Tom .... David Davies
Judge .... David Ensor
Young Prisoner .... Keith Faulkner

This lively slice of life in jail is a moderately unpretentious job but it shrewdly captures the atmosphere of the locale, neatly blends comedy and drama and offers some sharp thesping. Pic should make a popular booking for most houses, though it doesn't boast much marquee value for the States and some don't find such appeal in prison yards. Screenplay has been adapted by T. J. Morrison and Mike Watts from the latters play. Pic title is used to spotlight one of the supreme indignities of prison.

Paul Massie plays a first offender sentenced to a year's jail for grievous bodily harm, after slugging another man in a jealous tiff with his girl friend. He is sickened at the thought of prison life, its degradations and the philosophical way in which old inmates accept their fate and constantly come back for further doses of imprisonment. Assigned to the Kitchen Gang, he quickly settles down to the routine and joins in the "fiddling" which is highly organized among the prisoners, which mainly consists of stealing chow from the kitchens and swapping it for luxuries which another member of the gang lifts from the officers' mess.

Climax of the film is when Massie loses his remission by taking the blame for one of his cellmates caught, innocently, with a knife. The cellmate is due to be released in a month after a long spell in the cooler. Moral of the film is Massie's final remark to the guy: "Just don't come back, otherwise it won't have been worth it."

Though the relationship between the prisoners and the staff is largely played for laughs, there is throughout the more serious underlying intent of showing the misery, the boredom, the humiliation of the prison system. Atmosphere has, seemingly, been carefully captured and the script obviously has been written by men who know their prison onions, though not from personal experience. Sometimes, in fact, the prison jargon is confusing but it adds to the authenticity.

In a large, mainly male cast, there are some notable bits of thesping, biggest impact being made by Ronald Fraser as the "trusty" who gets framed for the knife carrying and is the kingpin

among the fiddlers. Fraser, who has a rugged face, has made several appearances in pix but this is his biggest opportunity. And his performance is topflight. He is an actor of warmth, humor and has impeccable timing.

Paul Massie is a likeable, straightforward hero. There also is an excellently cast selection of prisoners, notably diminutive Davy Kaye, a perky little housebreaker; Dennis Price, suavely debonair as "Smooth-Tongue" Bertie; Alfred Burke, playing the "heavy," Patrick McAllinney, Keith Faulkner and Neil McCarthy. On the side of the law there are sympathetic portrayals by a reasonably human warder by Eddie Byrne and by Paul Rogers as the prison governor. The distaff side doesn't get much of a show, but Carole Lesley has a few moments of impact as Massie's bewildered girl friend and Vanda Godsell turns in a neat cameo as Fraser's wife.

Direction by Peter Graham Scott is deft. Erwin Hiller does his usual firstrate job with the camera. Stanley Black has contributed a score which matches the varying moods. *Rich.*

Cannes Festival

Long Day's Journey Into Night

Excellent translation of Eugene O'Neill play, with some top performances; probing theme slants this for arty spots for best results.

Cannes, May 22.

Ely Landau production and release. Stars Katherine Hepburn, Ralph Richardson, Jason Robards Jr., Dean Stockwell; features Jeanne Barr. Directed by Sidney Lumet. Screenplay from play by Eugene O'Neill; camera, Boris Kaufman; music, Andre Previn; editor, Ralph Rosenblum. At Cannes Film Fest. Running time, **176 MINS.**
Mary Tyrone .... Katherine Hepburn
James Tyrone .... Ralph Richardson
Jamie .... Jason Robards Jr.
Edmund .... Dean Stockwell
Cathleen .... Jeanne Barr

This is an excellent film adaption of the late Eugene O'Neill's lengthy stage work. It has power in its characters and their tortured introspective lives.

The O'Neill name and cast names should help, along with its Broadway legit background. Producer Ely Landau and director Sidney Lumet have wisely not tried to tamper with O'Neill's original to make it too filmic. No additional dialog has been added.

There have been a few cuts but otherwise it is as O'Neill wrote it. And his powerful language manages to overcome the limited sets and dependence on the spoken word. It takes a family through the probing of themselves, their relations and their relative reasons for acting as they do. It all develops when the mother one day begins to sink back to drug addiction.

Katherine Hepburn's beautifully boned face mirrors her anguish and needs. She makes the role of the mother breathtaking and intensely moving. There is balance, depth

and breadth in her acting. Ralph Richardson brings his authority to the part of the miserly father who has made money as a theatrical matinee idol but can't shake his skinflint habits because of a childhood of poverty. Jason Robards Jr. has flair and insight as the tortured older brother while Dean Stockwell is effective as the younger brother.

Director Lumet has allowed his camera to record as well as to observe. Gets the most from the juxtapositions of talk and pause, faces and actions. He has not given way to any untoward visual tricks but kept his work sober.

This is a lesson in filmed theatre in allowing the playwright's work to speak for itself. It works here because of O'Neill's dramatic sense, density of feeling and the searing look at his own life.

Made reportedly for $400,000, since the principals took minimum pay because of their desire to do this property, this could possibly pay off in savvy art dates. Its length, talk and weight could make this chancier generally abroad, but it has the possibilities for offshore metropolitan areas.

Boris Kaufman's knowing lensing is a notable asset, as is Andre Previn's discreet score.

This is an unusual film and a difficult one, but could pay off if well handled and placed. One of the main problems is the length. It will do as is in arty spots but could be sheared for later runs. Incidentally, the editing of Ralph Rosenblum is exemplary. *Mosk.*

Electra
(GREEK)

Cannes, May 22.

United Artists release of Finos Films production. Stars Irene Papas; features Aleka Catseli, Yannis Fertis, Theano Ioannidou, Notis Pervalis, Takis Emmanouil. Written and directed by Michael Cacoyannis from play by Euripides; camera, Walter Lassally; editor, L. Antonakis; music, Mikis Theodrakis. At Cannes Film Fest. Running time, **110 MINS.**

Chalk up a pictorially excellent and dramatically smart film rendition of this Greek tragedy. The sombre tale of vengeance has a measured but stately tread. It rises and falls in intensity but keeps up interest, emerging a film with the polish and depth for good arty house possibilities abroad.

Agamemnon, returning victoriously from war, is killed by his wife Clytemestra and her lover Egisthe in his bath while the children Electra and Orestes wait outside. The boy is rushed off by an old retainer and the girl grows up virtually as a prisoner. Her hatred and need for revenge expand.

She is married off to a poor farmer who respects her. Back comes Orestes, and the brother and sister unite to plot their vengeance. This ends with the bloody killing of their mother, and their wandering off wondering if the Gods had been right in ordering this deed.

Director Michael Cacoyannis, the Greek director, who introduced Melina Mercouri, finally has come up with a worthwhile film.

Film keeps the beauty of the text about this tragedy and both the sombre and gay Greek choruses of women. Playing is stylized

but fits into the pattern of vengeance.

Irene Papas has nobel beauty and tragic stance as Electra. There is nothing flamboyant or demonic about her but a quiet overbearing dedication that breaks out in fearful joy or searing pity as she goes through with her destiny. Others are adequate.

The visual beauty of Walter Lassally's camerawork, the excellent blending of visual and plastic aspects, make this a successful transposition of Greek tragedy to the screen. It should get plenty of art house attention on world screens. Mikis Theodrakis dramatically powerful music also is an asset.

Purportedly made for about $70,000, with United Artists putting up most of the coin for world rights except Greece, it has a solid production dress that belies this figure. UA has a fine arty pic whose dramatic values may also have this a playoff contender. *Mosk.*

Yang Kwei Fei
(FORMOSAN—COLOR)

Cannes, May 22.

Run Run Shaw production and release. Stars Li Li-Hua, Yen Chuan; features Chao Lei, Li Hsiange-Chun. Directed by Li Han-Hsiang. Screenplay, Wang Chi-Po; camera (Eastmancolor), T. Nishimoto; editor, Chiang Hsing-Ling. At Cannes Film Fest. Running time, 103 MINS.
Yang Kewi Fei .... Li Li-Hua
Emperor .... Yen Chuan
Killer .... Chao Lei
Mei .... Li Hsiang-Chun

This is a colorful, well-mounted look at an ancient Emperor and his favorite caught up in an army mutiny and court intrigue. This leads to her death to show her love for the Emperor. Though somewhat tableau-like, this film has eyefilling qualities that slant it for good lingo chances in the U.S. but without the depth for arty chances.

Yank Kewi Fei, the Emperor's new concubine, has a rapacious brother who takes advantage of her position to gain power and get the army to lead the mutiny that brings on his sister's death. There are some excellent scenes of army might and pillage plus some gentle love and court bits. But this relies too much on spectacle.

Color is fine, direction sumptuous and production opulent. This Run Run Shaw opus should find a fine career for itself in Asia. It is much the same story that the late Japanese director Kenji Mizoguchi turned into a masterpiece in a Japanese-Chinese coproduction with Shaw some years ago. This is not up to the original in mood or depth of characterization. *Mosk.*

Pleneno Yato
(Captive Flock)
(BULGARIAN)

Cannes, May 22.

Bulgar Films production and release. With Peter Slabakov, Dimiter Bouinozov, Atanas Velikov, Stefan Illier. Directed by Doutcho Mundrov. Screenplay, Emil Manov; camera, Gueorgui Alourkv; editor, G. Guenkov. At Cannes Film Fest. Running time, 84 MINS.
Teacher .... Peter Slabakov
Boris .... Dimiter Bouinozov
Friend .... Atanas Velikov

Competently made tale of a group of political prisoners during the last war, who bravely face up

to their execution and help uncover an outside informer, this is still in the old fashioned revolutionary groove with mainly local chances looming.

There is a solidity in the prison atmosphere and some okay if stereotyped characters. The Bulgarian Communist takeover is still being explored but this lacks the insight and depth. This also lacks much to attract foreign interest. *Mosk.*

Proces De Jeanne D'Arc
(Trial of Joan of Arc)
(FRENCH)

Cannes, May 22.

Pathe release of Agnes Delahaie production. With Florence Carrez, Jean-Claude Fourneau, Roger Honorat, Marc Jacquier, Jean Gillibert, Andre Reigner. Written and directed by Robert Bresson. Camera, L. H. Burel; editor, Germaine Artua. At Cannes Film Fest. Running time, 65 MINS.
Jeanne .... Florence Carrez
Cauchon .... Jean-Claude Fourneau
Interrogator .... Roger Honorat
Inquisitor .... Marc Jacquier

Joan of Arc is judged again in this new austere version of the trial and burning of the 15th Century French saint. Director-author Robert Bresson has relied on trial and rehabilitation transcripts. This sober, clean pic is both revealing and sedate in avoiding any untoward dramatics.

Vehicle relies on the play of questions and answers, done mainly in medium shots, to achieve an insight into Joan of Arc character. Using non-actors, there are no false dramatics. This unveils another side of this oft-filmed tale, and the state and church politics of that century.

She is seen as a direct, dedicated girl trying to show that her tasks were real and from the Lord. In the background are the English who want her destroyed to do away with her myth and the Church collaborating.

As each scene fades into the other, interest is built up and the ideas take some human shape. Her burning is done with a minimum of effect but with heightened feeling. Its length and the subject matter slant this primarily for specialized and arty spotting abroad. This has a simple beauty and depth that make it different from other forays into this territory.

Lensing has the right translucent quality. All the non-actors give it a deeper finish. It is a deeply personal film by director Bresson but one that needs careful handling. *Mosk.*

L'Amour A Vingt Ans
(Love is 20 Years Old)
(FRENCH-ITALO-JAPANESE)
(Totalscope)

Cannes, May 22.

20th-Fox release of Ulysse-Unitec-Cinesecolo-Toho Town Film production. With Jean-Pierre Leaud, Marie-France Pisier, Eleonora Rossi-Drago, Christina Gajoni, Geronimo Meynier, Nami Tamura, Koji Furuhata, Barbara Frey, Christian Doermer, Barbara Lass, Zbigniew Cybulski. Directed by Francois Truffaut, Renzo Rossellini, Marcel Ophuls, Shintaro Ishihara, Andrzej Wajda. Screenplays by Truffaut, Rossellini, Ishihara, Ophuls, Jerzy Stawinski; camera, Raoul Coutard, Mario Montuori, Shigeo Hayashida, Wolfgang Wirth, Jerzy Lipman; editor, Claudine Bouche; music, Georges Delerue. At Cannes Film Fest. Running time, 123 MINS.
FRANCE
Boy .... Jean-Pierre Leaud
Girl .... Marie-France Pisier

Sketch films are still extremely popular here, but this takes an international stride via five young directors contributing episodes on young love from five different countries. There is enough verve, pace, drama and intensity in these entries to make this okay for some good foreign chances. Three out of the five episodes are exceptional, a fairly good average, with one so-so and another uneven. But they add up to a diverse outlook on an evergreen subject. A little pruning on two of the sketches would make it even more palatable.

French "New Waver" Francois Truffaut donates a sort of epilog. Here the hero is 16 when he has his first crush. He meets the girl and becomes a friend of the family, but he is just a pal to her. The girl is physically older. It is pleasantly played and has wit and brightness in playing and direction that makes this a smart teeoff.

Marcell Ophuls, son of the late Max Ophuls, displays verve and tenderness that makes this tale of a young man's acceptance of paternity and love from a girl he had known only briefly in a beguiling entry. A busy newsman comes back from his travels to accept his paternity responsibility. Getting to know her he finds he loves the girl and accepts his readymade family. Acting is fresh, and Ophuls looms a new bright filmic talent.

Polski filmmaker Andrzej Wajda now looks at an ex-war hero who does a brave thing which brings him the brief love of a girl. But at a party he is kidded by boys who are tired of war tales and interested in themselves. There is a bite in this sequence, heightened by the bright beauty of Barbara Lass, the awareness of his unfitness among modern youth by Zbigniew Zybulski. There is knowing handling by director Wajra.

While the others manage to get a feeling for place and character, Renzo Rossellini's episode has the faults of sketchiness. A kept young man falls for a working girl but his hardbitten mistress makes it clear that the boy can never leave the luxury she gives him. This can be sharpened a bit by cutting.

The Japanese is the most dramatic one. An inhibited young worker suddenly turns to murdering women. There is a feeling and solid progression in the first part, but it loses balance in the sudden turn to murder.

This worldwide sketch production looms a worthwhile arty and playoff entry abroad. Joe Levine's Embassy Pictures already has taken it for the U.S. Georges Delerue has concocted a catchy tune sung in each lingo at the end of each sketch. *Mosk.*

Harry Of Kammertjener
(Harry and His Valet)
(DANISH)

Cannes, May 22.
Rialto Film release of Christensen production. With Osvald Helmuth, Ebbe Rode, Gunnar Lauring, Henning Moritzen, Lisa Ringheim. Directed by Bent Christensen. Screenplay, Christensen. Leif Panduro; camera, Kjed Arnholtz; editor, L. Mollera. At Cannes Film Fest. Running time, 106 MINS.

Harry .... Osvald Helmuth
Fabricius .... Ebbe Rode
Eveque .... Gunnar Lauring
Igor .... Henning Moritzen
Magdalena .... Lisa Ringheim

Quaint look at human foibles, with a picaresque twist, this is somewhat too heavyfooted in its comedics to come off. The idea is good and the mounting good-natured. But it tries too hard to be funny. Film looks like a likely Scandanavian and Germanic gambit, but limited for other spots except for some lingo situations.

A kindly, aging man inherits some money. Instead of allowing it to give him security, he spends the coin to hire a valet. He has always wanted one and feels only this will bring him a certain love he has lacked. It changes his life and that of his only friends, two petty thieves. At the end the valet, who wants to work, but finds the noble classes have about disappeared, gives the old man back the money paid him, and goes on working for him.

Film might have had more bite if handled properly. But all this is dished up in an academic, theatrical manner with repetitive scenes bogging down the main comedy points. In short, the idea was good. But it does not quite jell for arty chances abroad. *Mosk.*

Ket Felido A Pokolban
(Two Half Times in Hell)
(HUNGARIAN)

Cannes, May 22.
Hungarofilm release of Hunnia production. With Imre Sinkovics, Dezso Garas. Directed by Zoltan Pabri. Screenplay, Peter Bacso. Fabri; camera, Ferenc Szecsenyi; editor, R. Szecsenyi. At Cannes Film Fest. Running time, 120 MINS.

Dio .... Imre Sinkovics
Steiner .... Dezso Garas

Tale of a work camp of political and Jewish prisoners used by Germans and Hungarians for building in Russia during the last war, this is an offbeat item that packs some punch. But it also is somewhat hampered by conventional characters in this stark war film. It still has enough stuff for special spotting abroad but not quite the depth for arty chances.

The Eastern Front German soldiers need some diversion so a match between the Germans and the Hungarian prisoners in soccer is planned when it is found a former international star is interned.

Pic then shows how the team is selected by the star player, the problems involved and the game itself, which ends in tragedy. An attempted escape has them condemned but German insistence has the game go on anyway. The cheering fellow prisoners egg them on to a victory which they know will still not alter their executions. A deliriously happy group of prisoners breaks onto the grounds and prompts a touchy German to shoot one, and starts a mass slaughter.

Director Zoltan Fabri has handled this with visual strength and

framed a sort of parable on war as a sport. Film, however, has too many conventional types, even to a comedy relief bit. Plot allows too many side issues to sometimes obscure its dramatics. But this is solidly acted and technically impressive. It's a contender for offbeat slotting. *Mosk.*

Setenta Veces Siete
(Seventy Times Seven)
(ARGENTINE)

Cannes, May 22.
Araucania Films production and release. Stars Isabel Sarli, Francisco Rabal, Jardel Filho; features Blanca Lagrotta, Jacobo Finder, Nelly Prono. Directed by Leopoldo Torre Nilsson. Screenplay, Dalmiro Saenz. Beatrice Guido Nilsson; camera, Ricardo Younis; editor, Oscar Lagomarsino. At Cannes Film Fest. Running time, 89 MINS.

Cora .... Isabel Sarli
Pascual .... Francisco Rabal
Pedro .... Jardel Filho
Madre .... Blanca Lagrotta
Padre .... Jacobo Finder
Duena .... Nelly Prono

Elemental tale is treated with a knowing imagery to make for a deceptively adventurous and revealingly dramatic tale. This looms as a definite Latin language bet for the U.S. on its surface qualities.

In an almost primitive Argentine outpost a comely girl with a scarred face works in a sporting house. A growing remorse leads to her fighting off a patron. Her past is seen in flashback.

It shows her as a resigned but shapely girl, working in a run-down roadhouse, who goes off with a sheepherder. There is a fugitive she saves, and an episode by a well.

Director Leopoldo Torre Nilsson has given this a controlled visual unity and shows a solid outlook. So it emerges a sort of morality tale.

Isabel Sarli's impassive face is well used as the pliant woman. It is an offbeat affair and perhaps too divided in theme and treatment. This is a simple tale which has appeal for the homegrounds, with more chancy possibilities abroad. *Mosk.*

O Pagador De Promess
(The Given Word)
(BRAZILIAN)

Cannes, May 22.
Oswaldo Massaini production and release. With Leonardo Vilar, Gloria Menezes, Dionisio Azevedo, Gerlado D'El Rey, Roberto Ferreira, Othon Bastos. Directed by Anselmo Duarte. Screenplay, Duarte, Dias Gomes from play by Gomes; camera, Chick Fowle; editor, Carlos Coimbra. At Cannes Film Fest. Running time, 90 MINS.

Ze-a-L'Ane .... Leonardo Vilar
Rosa .... Gloria Menezes
Abbey Olavo .... Dionisio Azevedo
Beau-Gosse .... Geraldo D'El Rey
Reporter .... Roberto Ferreira

A strong theme, expert handling and successful pacing make this an unusual Brazilian film with arty theatre chances abroad. It concerns a farmer whose vow to carry a cross into a church if his wounded donkey is saved leads him into becoming a cat's paw for various groups.

The man has lugged a heavy cross 10 miles and arrives with his wife to find the church closed. He has divided his land among the poor and now awaits the church opening. His wife is seduced and he is not allowed in the church by the priest who has found he

made his vow to a group of macumba cultists.

A cynical reporter uses the story to make hints about the man being a communist, since he gave away his land. Crowds begin to collect. It grows into a sort of carnival, with dancing, and a crucible spot for Brazilians facing such problems as church disavowment of Negro sects, fanaticism among church people, minorities, etc.

Director Anselmo Duarte has given this robust rhythm and built his symbols and statements on a solid visual basis. Acting is acceptable if overdone at times. A battle with the police leads to the man's death and he is put on his cross and carried into the church. *Mosk.*

Le Caporal Epingle
(The Hard Luck Corporal)
(FRENCH)

Cannes, May 22.
Pathe release of Films Du Cyclope production. Stars Jean-Pierre Cassel; features Claude Brasseur, Claude Rich, Jean Carmet, Jacques Jouanneau, Mario David, Conny Froboess, O. E. Hasse. Directed by Jean Renoir. Screenplay, Renoir, Guy Lefranc from novel by Jacques Perret; camera, Georges Leclerc; editor, Rene Lichtig. At Cannes Film Fest. Running time, 103 MINS.

Corporal .... Jean-Pierre Cassel
Pater .... Claude Brasseur
Ballochet .... Claude Rich
Emile .... Jean Carmet
Penche .... Jacques Jouanneau
Erika .... Conny Froboess
Voyager .... O. E. Hasse

Oldtime filmmaker Jean Renoir is right in his element in this tale of an escape-prone French soldier in a prisoner of war camp during the last debacle. It has a heightened feel for human crisis and the need for action, leavened by expert observation, to make this a film with art and general playoff chances abroad.

Film is handled lightly without any undue dramatics. There are well-blocked characters, the feel for time and place, and a verve and zest in dialog, imagry and playing. After the French defeat and armistice, thousands are still kept as prisoners while the war with England goes on.

The assorted French internees gripe, protest, find easy niches or try to escape, as does the hero, Jean-Pierre Cassel. His many attempts usually end in failure except for a last try that gets him back to Paris. But then he is ready to go on and try to join the Free French Army in England.

Renoir easily breathes life into his people and situations. The corporal, appealingly played by Cassel, is disciplined severely after every escape and finally takes a sift berth with a shrewd friend who has worked out a system of comfort. But a sudden rebelling against this setup when he realizes this is a form of evasion and cowardice, keeps him trying to escape again. It also leads to a bravado attempt by his chastened, slightly cowardly friend.

The Germans are mainly depicted as simple soldiers and human. But there is no whitewash intended. Renoir's generosity and tenderness, without any false sentimentality or mawkisness, point up the idiocy of war as well as man's comportment in it. It is sustained admirably. This is a deeply compassionate film and an entertaining one.

Acting roles are expertly moulded by Renoir. The ease in style and technique give this a feel of timelessness in commenting on all wars and the men in it. It will inevitably be compared with his earlier prisoner-of-war film, "La Grande Illusion."

This rarely lets down and keeps up interest all the way. Right placement should get this plenty of art and general mileage on world screens. *Mosk.*

Das Brot Der Fruchen Jahre
(The Bread of the Young Years)
(GERMAN)
Cannes, May 22.

Atlas release of Modern Art Film (Hans-Juergen Pohland, Berlin) production. With Christian Doermer, Karen Blanguernon and Vera Tschechowa. Directed by Herbert Vesely. Screenplay, Vesely. Leo Ti and Heinrich Boell (dialogs), based on novel by Boell. Camera, Wolf Wirth; music, Attila Zoller. At Cannes Film Fest. Running time, **85 MINS.**
Walter Fendrich......Christian Doermer
Ulla Wickweber ..... Vera Tschechowa
Hedwig Muller...... Karen Blanguernon

Have the Germans lost their knack for making good, international films? This question arises after seeing "Bread of the Young Years." Herbert Vesely, former maker of successful short features, was given the chance to direct the film without any compromise. Artistic ambition was put above all. Vesely had one of Germany's top cameramen, Wolf Wirth, at his disposal. Heinrich Boell, Germany's ace novelist, helped on the script. A group of young, unconventional players was used for the cast.

But the net result must be called disappointing. Vesely is a fine technician. But he went overboard with formalisms. His handling of the players is seldom felt. The characters do not stir much interest. As a consequence, the film lacks warmth, and has a number of dull moments.

Plot concerns a young man who gives up his financially independent life. He breaks up with well-to-do society of which he has become a member, to find himself back as his former self which he finds gave him more freedom. He leaves everything behind, including his fiancee to start a new life with another girl. Film story thus depicts a rebellion against materialism.

Despite the fact that pic is neither fish nor fowl, there is no doubt that it will lead to discussion. Ordinary cinema patrons are asked to show too much patience. Reportedly, the film has been sold to nearly a dozen countries. So a financial loss doesn't seem involved, which is some consolation for the courageous filmmakers. *Hans.*

Koda Derevia Byli Bolchini
(When the Trees Were Big)
(RUSSIAN)
Cannes, May 22.

Mosfilm release of Gorki Studios production. With Inna Goulaya, Youri Nikouline, L. Kouraviev. Directed by Lev Koulidjanov. Screenplay, Nicolay Figourovsky; camera, V. Guinsbourg; editor, A. Afanassiev. At Cannes Film Fest. Running time, **95 MINS.**
Kouzma .... Youri Nikouline
Natacha .... Inna Goulaya
Boy .... L. Kouraviev
Director .... V. Choukchine

A gentle, tender tale of a Russian drone who finally has his conscience awakened and decides to take his place in society, this is somewhat too sentimental to have much chance in most of the foreign market. However, it manages to sustain its mood, and it unveils a director with temperament in Lev Koulidjanov and a disarming actress in Inna Goulaya.

A workshirker decides to pass himself off as a young pretty girl's father on collective farm. And he succeeds and lives off her only to bring her trouble.

But he finally tells her the truth, and she will not believe him. So he decides to stay on. All this is tastefully handled and it even gently pokes fun at bureaucracy. The listless worker is made to assume his responsibilities through love rather than flag-waving.

The imagery is clear and the playing fresh. It is a plus mark for the production that it manages to keep interest alive and build up the characters despite its telegraphed aspects. Another mark in the thawing Russo cinema where individuals are becoming almost as important as the collective. *Mosk.*

Alias Gardelito
(Alias Big Shot)
(ARGENTINE)
Cannes, May 29.

Rio Negro production and release. With Tonia Carrero, Walter Vidarte, Alberto Argibay, Lautaro Murua, Nora Palmer. Directed by Lautaro Murua. Screenplay, Bernardo Kordon. Augusto Roa; camera, Oscar Melly; editor, Saulo Benavente. At nCanes Film Fest. Running time, **90 MINS.**
Toribio .... Walter Vidarte
Wife .... Tonia Carrero
Boss .... Lautaro Murua
Friend .... Alberto Argibay
Girl .... Nora Palmer

The rise and fall of a petty hoodlum is given an extra dimension in this modest but effective pic. Yet there is not enough bite and originality to make for arty chances abroad even though it does possess possibilities for language situations.

Involved in petty stealing, and at odds with his family, the hero is prey to dreams of a singing career. But he rarely gets away from his lawless ways, and drifts back to his old life by getting into a big smuggling racket.

Director Lautaro Murua has been able to fill in lowlife aspects without overcharging the film. This does not preach but shows how poverty and listlessness can lead these young boys down the old criminal paths.

Film has a density in character that puts it a cut above such type films. Only drawback is a tendency to do telegraph developments. But it underlines a new director in Lautaro Murua. It is technically good. *Mosk.*

Le Crime Ne Paie Pas
(Crime Does Not Pay)
(FRENCH—'SCOPE)
Cannes, May 29.

Under release of Transworld-Cosmas Film production. Stars Edwige Feuillere, Gabriele Ferzetti, Michel Morgan, Annie Girardot, Christian Marquand, Pierre Brasseur, Danielle Darrieux, Perette Pradier, Richard Todd. Directed by Gerard Oury. Screenplay, Oury, Paul Gordeaux, Jean-Charles Tacchela, Jean Aurenche, Pittre Bost, Henri Jeanson, Rene Wheeler, Boileau-Narcejac, Jacques

Sigurd, Frederic Dard; camera, Christian Matras; editor, R. Dwyre. At Cannes Film Fest. Running time, **158 MINS.**
Lucrezia .... Edwige Feuillere
Chevalier .... Gabriele Ferzetti
Jeanne .... Michele Morgan
Gabrielle .... Annie Girardot
Martin .... Pierre Brasseur
Louis .... Christian Marquand
Lucienne .... Danielle Farrieux
Helene .... Perette Pradier
Soldier .... Richard Todd

Still another sketch pic with a clever connecting link of a man about to commit a crime seeing a film on the same subject. It has a bevy of stars and some okay stories based on famous crimes. Sketches are uneven but this production emerges a solid playoff item if seemingly not quite of arty house calibre.

A man goes to see a film called "Crime Does Not Pay." From this, three sketches are worked out. Then his machinations make up the fourth episode.

First, located in 15th Century Venice concerns the revenge of an aging mistress on her lover who deserts her. She is in turn avenged by the murdered lover's flame. Operatic and static, the main plus values are the Venice color and smart costuming.

Another is a tale of political intrigue in 19th Century France when an attempt to blackmail a progressive public figure (by trumping up a vile story about his wife) ends in her killing the blackmailer and being vindicated by courts. It is properly melodramatic.

The third shows the best inventiveness. It as a conniving wife persuading her husband to knock off her lover, then doublecrossing him by having him arrested so she can have a new romance, her doctor. But the husband had prepared poison in the wine for the lover, and the wife and doctor accidentally drink it.

Last is a plodding one about a husband's complicated attempt to murder his wife.

Players all do adequately in their short stints with comic Louis De Funes a standout in a brief bit as a doubletalking waiter. Director Gerard Oury has been unable to get the right suspenseful flair into these tales based on true stories. But there are enough twists, name actors and production values for good returns in regular situations. *Mosk.*

Konga Yo
(Unite, Congo)
(CONGO-COLOR)
Cannes, May 22.

Ekebo Films production and release. Stars Roger Pigaut, Nicole Courcel; features Jean Lefebvre, Sophie M'Bali, Guy Dikolo, Paul Kantole. Directed by Yves Allegret. Screenplay, Rene Wheeler, Jacques and Francois Gall, Allegret; camera (Eastmancolor), Henri Persin; editor, Maurice Serein. At Cannes Film Fest. Running time, **108 MINS.**
Marie .... Nicole Courcel
Georges .... Roger Pigaut
Jean .... Jean Lefebvre
Angele .... Sophie M'Bali
Sylvain .... Guy Dikolo
Timotee .... Paul Kantole

French-directed pic, with mixed French and Congo thesps, pokes around in a tale situated in the early Congo upheavals after independence to come up with a film conventional in characterization and forced in plotting. But this does have some okay action footage for possible dualer or special use abroad on its locale and theme.

Fleeing the troubles are two white men, a white woman and

two Congolese. One man feels cheated by losing all his business. The white girl seems to have lost everything and wants only to leave. They run into all sorts of tribal conflicts and talk about politics and listen to the radio to fill the confused skein of events. The man finally joins up with one side while the girl decides to go back to Europe after they have had a try at love.

Color is good and director Yves Allegret has given this some savvy imagery. But he has been unable to overcome the confused story and stereotype characters. Actors do acceptably.

This is a mixed-up affair and really more a French pic made in Africa than any example of a new African surge of filmmaking. But it does have a feel for place and manages to mirror some of the early mixups of Congo independence. *Mosk.*

Phaedra
(U.S.-GREEK)
(In English)

Wife's love affair with stepson. Powerful boxoffice with Melina Mercouri directed by Jules Dassin.

Paris, June 5.

United Artists release of Melinafilm production. Stars Melina Mercouri, Anthony Perkins, Raf Vallone; features Elisabeth Ercy, Giorgos Karoussos, Georges Sarris, Andreas Philipides, Olympia Papadouka. Directed by Jules Dassin. Screenplay, Margarita Liberaki, Dassin from original script by Miss Liberaki; camera, Jacques Natteau; editor, Roger Dwyre; music, Mikis Theodrakis. At Colisee, Paris. Running time, **115 MINS.**

Phaedra	Melina Mercouri
Alexis	Anthony Perkins
Thanos	Raf Vallone
Father	Giorgos Karoussos
Ercy	Elisabeth Ercy
Ariane	Georges Sarris
Andreas	Andreas Philipides
Anna	Olympia Papadouka

Jules Dassin unfolds another filmic bouquet for the Greek actress Melina Mercouri. After showing her as a vital, dynamic joy girl in "Never On Sunday," he now gives her a chance to play tragedy. Her histrionics are just as effective. This unabashedly romantic affair looms a solid arty theatre and playoff entry in the U.S. with plenty of worldwide mileage also indicated.

Dassin and scripter Margarita Liberaki have transposed the Greek tragedy to modern Greece among its new nobility, the rich shipbuilders and shipowners. It is more ironic than tragic because the passion-obsessed wife who falls in love with her stepson borders more on neurosis than on divine destiny.

Phaedra (Miss Mercouri) is married to one of the top shipowners in Greece, Thanos (Raf Vallone). She has a son by him while he has a 24-year-old son Alexis (Anthony Perkins) from a former English wife, who lives in London. He wants the boy to come back to teach him the trade. He begs Phaedra to try and persuade him.

It is love at first sight. They fight it but finally consummate their love in Paris. He feels remorse because he has gotten to like his father who he now feels was unjustly maligned by his mother. But he finally gives in and comes to Greece where his father presents him with a high-powered auto, and plans to have him marry a relative's daughter and join up two big companies.

But Phaedra's love brings on tragedy and destruction. She opposes the marriage. She even kisses him daringly on a floor landing of the house, and finally can't contain herself and tells her husband. He beats the son mercilessly. The latter goes off to death in his car, and she commits suicide.

There has been an attempt to hue to the tragic root of the tale. The Greek chorus is exemplified by dark-dressed women who watch the parties of the opulent and speak in many languages. They show up when a ship, called the Phaedra, is lost. Dassin himself plays an old Greek who remarks that the crate bringing in the son's car looks like a coffin. Some of this padding is just padding.

It is mainly a plush tale of passion among the rich. The first love of the mother and stepson is done before a roaring fireplace which is right in this forthrightly dramatic opus. Miss Mercouri is sometimes reminiscent of Garbo in her sacrificing of all to her emotions, but plays everything to a quivering hilt.

Miss Mercouri's face is at times ravaged or full of hungry beauty. She succeeds in making her obsessiveness gripping even in the scenes in broad daylight. Anthony Perkins is all repressed smiles and boyishness but does make the boy an attractive, emotionally trapped youth who actually loves his auto almost as much as his stepmother.

Vallone has a bull-like drive and sincerity as the ambitious but generous father. Remainder of the cast is excellent. The bright, luminous lensing of the Greek countryside, the fine editing and Dassin's decision to play this as unbridled drama combine to make this a film reminiscent of the sleek escapist fare of pre-war Hollywood. But it has a solidity of insight into the big money world to make it up to date.

Although a form of incest is committed, all pay their retribution. The love scene is done with taste and more in filmic symbolism than in downright undraping. If there is some code or censorship trouble, this should be able to override it as "Sunday" did. Pic appears to be another hit for Yank director Dassin. *Mosk.*

Zotz

Shock specialist William Castle turns to comedy-fantasy in flubber-type item about a professor and a magic coin. Exploitable pic with moppet appeal.

Hollywood, May 24.

Columbia Pictures release of William Castle production. Stars Tom Poston, Julia Meade, Jim Backus, Fred Clark, Cecil Kellaway. Directed by Castle. Screenplay, Ray Russell, based on novel by Walter Karig; camera, Gordon Avil; editor, Edwin Bryant; music, Bernard Green; assistant director, Carter De Haven Jr. Reviewed at the studio, May 24, '62. Running time, **85 MINS.**

Prof. Jonathan Jones	Tom Poston
Prof. Virginia Fenster	Julia Meade
Horatio Kellgore	Jim Backus
General Bulldiver	Fred Clark
Dean Updike	Cecil Kellaway
Cynthia Jones	Zeme North
Persephone Updike	Margaret Dumont
Dr. Kroner	James Millhollin
Josh Bates	Carl Don
Igor	Mike Mazurki
Jimmy Kellgore	Jimmy Hawkins
Mr. Crane	Bart Patton
Miss Blakiston	Judee Morton
Captain Byron	Michael Westfield
Major Folger	Russ Whiteman
Lt. John G. Stefanski	George Moorman
Secretary	Elaine Martone
Nurse	Susan Dorn

Akin in style and structure to Walt Disney's "Absent Minded Professor," William Castle's production of "Zotz" is a slight but exploitable comedy-fantasy best suited to the easygoing dispositions and vulnerable imaginations of children. Poor man's flubber it may be, and second hand at that, but kids exposed to and beguiled by the simplicity of the technique are apt, for awhile, to adopt zotzery as a do-it-yourself sport in much the same fashion as moppets of the early '40's climbed on the "pattycake" fad-bandwagon after going on the "Road" with Crosby and Hope. The Columbia release certainly lends itself to merchandising and/or gimmickry, i.e., Zotz coins for kiddie customers. Thoughtfully exploited, the film could be a successful attraction over the short haul.

"Zotz" is the three-ply power possessed by the bearer of an ancient coin, enabling its owner to: (1) inflict sudden pain by the point of his index finger, (2) create slow motion by uttering the magic word, (3) killing his chosen victim by employing both techniques at once. Ray Russell's brittle screenplay, from Walter Karig's novel, plants the coin in the possession of a somewhat absent-minded professor of ancient Eastern languages (Tom Poston), then traces his misadventures first at school, later at the Pentagon (where he is rebuffed in a semi-satirical sequence), finally in a struggle with hapless Communist agents with zotz plots of their own.

Castle's direction makes the most of the slight, er-zotz yarn, coaxing spirited performances from a cast that has appeal, but little in the way of marquee magnetism. "Zotz" will have to be its own marquee.

As the likable but harassed prof, Poston, noted for his television work, segues into the cinema personably and unaffectedly. Vidpitchwoman Julia Meade is attractive and appealing as the romantic interest. Jim Backus and Fred Clark contribute top-flight comedy characterizations. Cecil Kellaway and Margaret Dumont work with veteran skill and spirit. Zeme North makes a good impression as Poston's perturbed niece, and Carl Don and Mike Mazurki score as the heavies caught Red-handed. James Millhollin is especially amusing as a dubious psychiatrist, and Louis Nye chips in a funny cameo.

Gordon Avil's lensmanship meets the special requirements of fantasy photography. Edwin Bryant's editing is generally competent, though a bit slow on the draw in spots. An outstanding ingredient is Bernard Green's whimsical, effervescent music, brightly punctuating and highlighting comic values. *Tube.*

The Case Of Patty Smith

Dramatization of abortion problem in U.S.A. Enlightening facets blunted by weak dramatic development, but will do as spot entry.

Hollywood, May 29.

Leo A. Handel production. No release set. Directed and screenplay by Handel; camera, Howard Schwartz; editor, Stanford Tishchler; music, Ingram P. Walters; assistant directors, Nate Barragar, Bill Derwin. Reviewed at Sunset Theatre, May 29, '62. Running time, **93 MINS.**

Mary	Merry Anders
Dr. Miller	J. Edward McKinley
Patty	Dani Lynn
Allan	Carleton Crane
Top	Bob Rudelson
Sidy	Speer Martin
Reep	Sean Brian
Father O'Brien	David McMahon
Colbert	Bruno Ve Sota
Lt. Powell	Jack Haddock
Johnny	Joe Conley
Dr. Nielson	Leif Lindstrom
Myra	Mary Patton
Crawford	Sid Cane
Dr. Fridden	Sherwood Keith
Pawnbroker	Phil Clarke
Bartender	Harrison Lewis
Jean	Adrienne Hayes
Dr. Miller's Nurse	Mary Benoit
Dr. Fridden's Nurse	Sally Hughes
"Doctor"	Ralph Neff
Narrator	Barney Biro

The case against America's legal stance toward abortion is illustrated in this independent film, written-produced-directed by Leo A. Handel but as yet not firmed for general release. Although enlightening in its exposure of some appalling statistics a few not necessarily common knowledge—the picture stumbles in dramatic development and is guilty of oversimplifying its case. Its dramatized argument, while important and worthy of consideration in view of the dire consequences resulting under existing law, is weakened by the slanted nature of the story. For Handel has chosen to dramatize a provocative, but unrepresentative case that will not satisfy those who come to see his film not for shallow sensual reasons but for cerebral stimulation—the very audience that is his objective. As a result, the film is limited in appeal.

"The Case of Patty Smith" is concerned with the situation arising out of the rape and resultant pregnancy of a 21-year-old girl, who, somewhat naive and understandably agitated, drifts—at least partially owing to the nature of the law—into the wrong corrective channels. Rebuffed by law-abiding medical men for one reason or another, and verbally spanked for her intentions by a Catholic priest, she winds up in the inept, irresponsible hands of a criminal abortionist and pays with her life.

Dani Lynn, who makes her screen bow, tends to play the tragic title character somewhat monotonously, relying mostly on one expression in projecting inner turmoil. Merry Anders gives a sincere performance as her sympathetic girl friend. Others in key roles—that run to stereotype—are J. Edward McKinley, Carleton Crane, Bob Rudelson, Speer Martin, Sean Brian, David McMahon, Bruno Ve Sota, Jack Haddock, Mary Patton, Joe Conley, Sid Cane, Sherwood Keith, Phil Clarke and Harrison Lewis.

Handel leans to pontification, or sermonizing, in his dramatization, giving a number of scenes the characteristic of overly-detailed lectures. However, those details that keep seeping through—such as the fact that 8,000 U. S. abortionees die each year, or a rate of one-per-hour—alert one to the significance of the message and the intrinsic value of Handel's project.

Photography by Howard Schwartz is directed and discerning, and other able contributions are made by editor Stanford Tischler, art director Ted Holsopple, soundman Denzil Daniels and composer Ingram P. Walters. *Tube.*

Una Domenica d'Estate
(A Summer Sunday)
(ITALIAN—COLOR)

Rome, May 29.

Dino DeLaurentiis release of Emo Bistolfi-Leo Film production. Features Ugo Tognazzi, Raimondo Vianello, Jean Pierre Aumont, Anna Maria Ferrero, Karin Baal, Francoise Fabian, Gina Rivere, Angelo Zannoli, Ulla Jacobsson, Eddie Bracken, Jacques Bergarac, Dominique Boschero, Franco Fabrizi. Directed by Giulio Petroni. Screenplay, Ugo Pirro, Bruno Baratti, from story by Alberto Moravia, Ugo Pirro, Sergio Amidei; camera (Eastmancolor), Franco Villa; editor, Dolores Tamburini. At Capranica, Rome. Running time, **95 MINS.**

Milena	Anna Maria Ferrero
Armando	Eddie Bracken
Olga	Ulla Jacobsson
Silvana	Karin Baal

Valerio .... Jean Pierre Aumont
Osvaldo .... Jacques Bergerac
Benito .... Ugo Tognazzi
Adolfo .... Raimondo Vianello

Light summerweight comedy with big local comedy values in the Tognazzi-Vianello teaming, plenty of s.a. and beautiful girls, seaside frolicking, and superficial laughs for good home-market b.o. Some foreign areas might also go for the item if properly handled.

Vignette story line interweaves several episodes all taking place on beach resort near Rome, complete with mistaken identity trimmings and other plot asides equipped for laughs. Credit script and direction with being several notches above norm for this type of pic, however.

Ugo Tognazzi and Raimondo Vianello make the most of their roles as undertakers who stop by the beach on their way to work. Eddie Bracken, Jacques Bergerac, Ulla Jacobsson, Karin Baal and other foreign (non-Italian) names populate the landscape in lively fashion with little depth of characterization called for in the general fun.

Franco Villa's Eastmancolor lensing and other production credits are good assets for this entertaining feature. *Hawk.*

Strongroom
(BRITISH)

Taut, modest bank robbery thriller. No marquee value, but some excellent performances make this a worthwhile dualer.

London, May 29.

British Lion-Bryanston release through BLC) of a Theatrecraft (Guido Coen) production. Stars Darren Nesbitt, Colin Gordon, Ann Lynn, Keith Faulkner. Directed by Vernon Sewell. Screenplay, Max Marquis, Richard Harris, from idea by Richard Harris; camera, Basil Emmott; editor, John Trumper; music, Johnny Gregory. At Leicester Square Theatre, London. Running time, 80 MINS.
Mr. Spencer .... Colin Gordon
John Musgrove .... John Chappell
Rose Taylor .... Ann Lynn
Griff .... Darren Nesbitt
Len .... Keith Faulkner
Alec .... Morgan Sheppard
Charlady .... Hilda Fenemore
Charlady .... Diana Chesney
Creighton .... Ian Colin
Police Sergeant .... Kevin Stoney
Mortuary Attendant ..... Duncan Lewis
Police Inspector ...... Lockwood West

This is a modest, unpretentious supporting pic which, sans names, still measures up as a useful booking, especially if booked with a film of contrasting flavor. Vernon Sewell has done a workmanlike job of direction while the screenplay commendably restricts the tempting opportunity of a happy ending.

Three young men plan a bank robbery over the four day Easter Bank Holiday. Unexpected arrival of two scrubwomen throws their plans somewhat out of kilter, and they are forced to lock the bank manager and a girl clerk in the bank vault. Realizing that this would bring them a murder rap, the trio decides that one of the crooks should phone the police and leave the strongroom keys by the phone box.

But en route he is involved in an auto crash and killed. The problem of the other two is how to rescue their victims without risking their own necks. They decide, reluctantly, to return to the scene of their crime, and get oxygen to the trapped couple.

Meanwhile, flung together in this unexpected dilemma, the stuffy bank manager and the shy young girl clerk are drawn together as death by suffocation approaches. But there's no mushiness. The crooks are hooked by the police and they are faced with their comeuppance, for the girl dies before they can rescue her.

The edginess of the crooks is nicely portrayed by Darren Nesbitt, a burly young actor, and by Keith Faulkner, a contrasting, weaker type. Colin Gordon, usually cast in smallish, telling comedy cameos, has a bigger opportunity as the bank manager and takes it well, while Ann Lynn, though no glamor girl, presents a neatly rounded performance as the girl. There is also a string of effective performances by such as those by Kevin Stonely, John Dearth, Lockwood West and others as contrasting cops. Duncan Lewis scores briefly as a mortuary attendant. Only jarring notes are a couple of overwritten and overplayed performances by Hilda Fenemore and Diana Chesney as conventional scrubwomen.

Dialog is natural while the suspense is skilfully sustained by screenplay writers and directors. Technical credits are all satisfactory. The entire film, while obviously produced on a small budget, stands up admirably to more lavish productions. *Rich.*

Two And Two Make Six
(BRITISH)

Flimsy, but pleasant, comedy drama with a couple of engaging performances by young players which could help out satisfactorily as a dualer.

London, May 29.

British Lion-Bryanston release (through BLC) of a Bryanston presentation of a Monja Danischewsky production. Stars George Chakiris, Janette Scott, Alfred Lynch, Jackie Lane. Guest stars, Bernard Braden, Athene Seyler, Malcolm Keen. Directed by Freddie Francis. Story by Monja Danischewsky; camera, Desmond Dickinson, Ronnie Taylor; editor, Peter Taylor; music, Norrie Paramor. At Leicester Square Theatre, London. Running time, 89 MINS.
Larry Carado .... George Chakiris
Irene .... Janette Scott
Tom .... Alfred Lynch
Julie .... Jackie Lane
Aunt Phoebe .... Athene Seyler
Sergeant Sokolow .... Bernard Braden
Harry Stoneham ...... Malcolm Keen
Lady Smith-Adams..Ambrosine Philpotts
Night Porter .... Jack McGowran
Colonel Thompson........ Robert Ayres
Mack .... Edward Evans
Ted .... Harry Locke
Young Man .... Jeremy Lloyd
Hotel Receptionist.......Marianne Stone
Prudence .... Nina Parry

This is a light comedy drama of flimsy proportions which needed rather more effervescence and wit to get it off the ground. Written and produced by Monja Danichewsky, who had much to do with the success of some of the old Ealing comedies, faith has been placed in cameraman turned director Freddie Francis to helm the pic. Though he does a useful job, it doesn't quite tingle enough. However, it is an amiable dualer. One or two of the younger thesps give some fresh performances.

Idea has George Chakiris as a cheerful, undisciplined Yank Air Force corporal based in England. Constantly in trouble through his liking for fast horses and fast chicks, his latest escapade results in him (or so he fears) killing a sergeant in the course of resisting arrest. He hops camp and goes on the lam from the police. He borrows a motor bike from his girl friend (Jackie Lane) and takes her along. Object is to smuggle on to a ship for the getaway. Eventually the problem is resolved by Chakiris giving himself up. He gets lenient treatment because he shows willingness to marry and settle down.

There are some bright lines but they are sporadic. The picture's problem is that it veers in slightly wobbly style between romantic comedy and more serious drama. Chakiris gives a likeable performance as the U.S. airman. Alfred Lynch copes with a less developed role as the other young man, with one or two lively sequences with Jackie Lane, who is not in the same thesping league as her colleagues.

The real surprise comes from Janette Scott. Miss Scott, who falls for the airman, has graduated the hard way from juve stardom. She has developed into an attractive and mature young actress. In this she has neat touches of comedy. Three guest stars, Bernard Braden as the sergeant, Athene Seyler, as a middle-aged schoolmistress with up-to-date ideas, and Malcolm Keen as an alcoholic Shakespearian actor, all score heavily.

Lensing by Desmond Dickinson and Ronnie Taylor is okay. Location sequences are fine. Norrie Paramor's music is aptly gay. Craig Douglas sings the credit title song well, though it doesn't sound as if it is likely to crash the Top 10. *Rich.*

Lolita

Fitfully amusing film adaptation of Nabokov's novel, whose pubescent "nymphet" heroine has been turned into a busty bobbysoxer of indeterminate teenage. With most of the shock and much of the satire gone, pic will have to depend on lurid rep of the original. Intense public curiosity should make for boff opening dates.

MGM presentation, in association with Seven Arts, of James B. Harris production. Stars James Mason, Shelley Winters, Peter Sellers, Sue Lyon. Directed by Stanley Kubrick. Screenplay, Vladimir Nabokov, based on his novel; camera, Oswald Morris; music, Nelson Riddle; "Lolita" theme, Bob Harris; editor, Anthony Harvey; asst. directors, Rene Dupont, Roy Millichip, John Danischewsky. Reviewed in N.Y., June 7, '62. Running time, 152 MINS.
Humbert Humbert .... James Mason
Charlotte Haze .... Shelley Winters
Clare Quilty .... Peter Sellers
Lolita Haze .... Sue Lyon
Vivian Darkbloom ...... Marianne Stone
Jean Farlow .... Diana Decker
John Farlow .... Jerry Stovin
Dick .... Gary Cockrell
Mona Farlow .... Suzanna Gibbs
Lorna .... Roberta Shore
Roy .... Eric Lane
Mrs. Starch .... Shirley Douglas
Bill .... Roland Brand
Charlie .... Colin Maitland
Physician .... Cec Linder
Hospital Attendant........ Irvin Allen
Nurse Mary Lore .... Lois Maxwell
Swine .... William Greene
Potts .... C. Denier Warren
Louise .... Isobel Lucas
Receptionist at Hospital..Maxine Holden
Miss Lebone .... Marion Mathie
Rex .... Craig Sams
Tom .... John Harrison
Beale Senior .... James Dyrenforth

"Lolita," Vladimir Nabokov's witty, grotesque novel of several years back, is, in its film version, like a bee from which the stinger has been removed. It still buzzes with a sort of promising irreverence, but it lacks the power to shock and, eventually, makes very little point either as comedy or satire. The novel has been stripped of its pubescent heroine and most of its lively syntax, graphic honesty and sharp observations on people and places in a land abundant with cliches.

The result is an occasionally amusing but shapeless film about a middleaged professor who comes to no good end through his involvment with a well-developed teenager. While scenarist Nabokov and director Stanley Kubrick have followed the outline of the original closely, the cold heart and malignant blood are missing. The fact that the first third of the picture is so good, bristling, as it does, with Nabokovisms—(a gun, for example, referred to as a "tragic treasure")—underscores the final disappointment.

The moralists can rest easy, for while it seems likely that the lurid reputation of the novel, and the intense public curiosity about the film, will make for boff opening dates, its longrange business prospects are spotty. Nabokov fans, unless they feel that any Nabokov is better than none, are likely to feel cheated, and less esoteric patrons may simply be confused, if not bored.

Since producer James B. Harris and director Kubrick are men of talent, there is much about the film that is excellent. James Mason has never been better than he is as erudite Humbert Humbert, driven by a furious passion for a rather slovenly, perverse "nym-

phet" (a term, incidentally, which is used only once in the entire film). He is especially good in the early sequences as he pursues Lolita to the point where he even marries her mother, "a clumsy, trustful seal," whom Shelley Winters plays to bumptuous perfection. Matching these two performances is that of Peter Sellers who, as a preposterously smug American playwright (Mason's rival for Lolita's affections), gets a chance to run through several hilarious changes of character.

With the obvious intent of avoiding the kind of censorship problems which faced the book, Kubrick and Harris have cast in the title role a pretty real-life teenager who appears well on her way to womanhood. Under Kubrick's careful direction, Sue Lyon makes an auspicious film debut as the deceitful child-woman who'd just as soon go to a movie as romp in the hay. It's a difficult assignment and if she never quite registers as either wanton or pathetic, it may be due as much to the compromises of the script as to her inexperience.

The film takes the form of one long flashback, opening with Mason's murder of Sellers at the climax of a weird ping-pong game, then going back to detail the events leading up to the crime. Mason is shown arriving in a small New Hampshire university town where he rents a room in the home of a well-to-do widow, largely in order to be near her young daughter. As Mason maneuvers to get near Miss Lyon, her mother, Miss Winters, maneuvers to get near Mason.

The "triangle" is amusingly detailed through the marriage of Mason and Miss Winters, coming to an end finally when Miss Winters learns the truth of Mason's passion and threatens to walk out on him. The lady's untimely death, however, enables Mason to pursue conquest of the willing girl. He takes her out of "Camp Climax" (where she had been sent by her jealous mother) and the two set up housekeeping in another university town.

Shadowing this idyll all the while is the presence of the ubiquitous Sellers who, in numerous, improbable disguises, eventually gets Lolita away from the professor, paving the way for the final showdown between the two roues.

There are many brilliant touches in Kubrick's handling of this strange farce, as when the camera picks up Mason, just after his wife's death, lolling contentedly in a hot tub, sipping a scotch, listening tipsily as some drab friends try to console him over his bereavement. But there are also some inexplicable omissions — that is, considering the director's fondness for ironic visual detail. For example, he never captures (with camera) the bizarre panorama of American highway life (so beautifully done in the novel's prose) during Humbert and Lolita's mad cross-country flight. For the most part, the last two thirds of the film is strict, straight plot.

While the film is certainly "adult" in theme, it is never objectionable. In fact, it's most sensuous scene is also one of its wittiest, when Humbert is shown painting the toenails of his bored, youthful mistress.

The entire physical production is fine, especially Oswald Morris' crisp black-and-white photography. Nelson Riddle's score is lush without being obtrusive. There also is hefty exploitation item in the catchy "Lolita Ya-Ya" number which manages to suggest some of the coarse, funny appeal lacking in the character of the film Lolita herself. *Anby.*

El Caballo Blanco
(The White Horse)
(MEXICAN—EASTMANCOLOR)

Mexico City, June 5.
Peliculas Nacionales release of Cinematografica Filmex production. Stars Joselito, Antonio Aguilar, Sara Garcia, Luz Maria Aguilar; features David Reynoso, Florencio Castello, Eleazar Garcia, Emilio Garibay. Directed by Rafael Baledon. Screenplay, Adolfo Torres Portillo. At Alameda Theatre, Mexico City. Running time, 90 MINS.

Producers have taken the combination of a child singer, a charro ditto and a white horse who can dance the Veracruz huagandos as a surefire boxoffice draw, and they made no mistakes. This one shapes as a boxoffice success.

Director Baledon milks his star Joselito for all the pathos and cuteness he can. Story tells of a young Spaniard who comes to Mexico. He can sing well but falls off horses badly. And he's kidnapped by a group of bandits who are not a bad sort, even diverting in a way, although they do hold up stagecoaches.

The lad makes friends with a charro who saves him, also is in good singing form, and the pair go through a series of adventures. There is a horse quite versed in sagacity and stage tricks. The boy, the cowboy and the horse naturally break out in song between adventures. And back home a grayhaired grandma bites her nails wondering about the "lost lad," and the reason he prefers the cowboy's company instead of home with those who love him.

The direction is smooth, with an eye on mothers, the kids and grandmas, so that they leave theatre completely happy. Songs are better than average and the action is fast paced. Youngster Joselito is at least sympathetic if not a great actor, and his singing is good. Tony Aguilar also is in good voice and turns in a better performance in this one than in his last few screen appearances. Sara Garcia is the worried grandma while Luz Maria Aguilar adds some love interest. *Emil.*

Barabbas
(ITALIAN-COLOR)

Longish Bibical yarn which needs patient viewing as first half stolidly unspools narrative and characterization. Later, impressive production values steer this into the big-class boxoffice league.

London, June 7.
Columbia presentation of Dino De Laurentiis production, released through BLC. Stars Anthony Quinn, Silvana Mangano, Arthur Kennedy, Katy Jurado, Harry Andrews, Valentina Cortese, Vittorio Gassman, Jack Palance, Ernest Borgnine. Directed by Richard Fleischer. Screenplay, Christopher Fry, based on Par Lagerkvist's novel; camera, Aldo Tonti; editor, Raymond Poulton; music, Mario Nascimbene. At Odeon, Haymarket, London, June 4, '62. Running time, 144 MINS.

Barabbas	Anthony Quinn
Rachel	Silvana Mangano
Pilate	Arthur Kennedy
Sara	Katy Jurado
St. Peter	Harry Andrews
Julia	Valentina Cortese
Sahak	Vittorio Gassman
Torvald	Jack Palance
Lucius	Ernest Borgnine
Joseph of Aramathea	Arnoldo Foa
Disciple	Laurence Payne
Lazarus	Michael Gwynn
Blind Man	Tullio Tomadoni
Rufio	Norman Wooland
Emperor	Ivan Triesault
Christ	Roy Mangano
Commander of Gladiators	Bobby Hall
Gladiator	Joe Robinson

"Barabbas," long in release on home grounds (Italy) is technically a fine job of work, reflecting big thinking and infinite patience on the parts of producer Dino De Laurentiis and director Richard Fleischer. But the audiences will also need patience to cope with a longish first half in which the narrative and characterization are unveiled somewhat pompously and heavily by scripter Christopher Fry. Fortunately, there are some good performances and some standout production sequences which stamp the pic as a boxoffice project for Britain and U.S.

Anthony Quinn does a formidable job in the title role and Vittorio Gassman and Jack Palance are others who, particularly, give fine accounts of themselves. The film is often unnecessarily brutal and bloody. The opening sequence, behind the credits, which shows Christ being savagely scourged is one, for example, that is unlikely to endear "Barabbas" to many customers. But in Technirama 70 and shot in Technicolor it has many qualities that will make it click and one or two sequences which stand up to the chariot race highlight in "Ben-Hur."

Set in Jerusalem 2,000 years ago, the film tells the story of Barabbas, thief and murderer, who was released from prison by the will of the people and replaced, in jail and on the Cross, by Jesus Christ. Barabbas' conscience plagues him. In a struggling, almost bovine manner he tries to find the truth about the new wave of faith that is sweeping the country. He is baffled when Rachel, the woman he covets, insists that Christ will rise from the dead. He seeks out the disciples but can find neither peace nor explanation. Rachel is stoned to death. Barabbas returns to his old haunts and, swiftly arrested again, finds himself sentenced to a living death in the sulphur mines of Sicily. Chained to Sahak, a young Christian, he plods on, despairingly, until one day the mine collapses. Sahak and Barabbas are the only two survivors and they are transferred to the Roman gladiatorial school. There comes a struggle in Barabbas's conscience. Sahak admits his Christian faith. Barabbas denies his. But, in the end, he goes to his death on the Cross having being drawn by the words of St. Peter.

All this is quite a lot to digest, even when scribed by Fry. Characters are brought in and tossed away in infuriating fashion. But where the film hits the bell is in Fleischer's bold, dramatic handling of certain scenes, allied to some slick lensing by Aldo Tonti. The scenes in the Rome gladiatorial pit, sharply etched by Jack Palance as the top boy, have an urgent excitement, with Palance's sadism matched only by Quinn's bewildered concentration.

The scenes in the sulphur mines have also been worked out with intense care and precision. They last long enough to set the mood of the later stages, but not long enough to be depressing. The stoning of Rachel and the Christians allegedly setting fire to Rome are also big sceen boffs.

Individually, the performances are uneven. Quinn is firstclass in a role which could have become monotonous after his beefy approach to his scenes with a vital Katy Jurado following his release from jail. Palance plays the sadistic gladiator with a liplicking panache that tends to pinpoint the fact that the whole pic is a shade too violent, but certainly the thesp makes Torvald a vivid and urgent figure in the setup. Silvana Mangano does an adequate job of work as Rachel, but the part never comes to life and nor does that of Ernest Borgnine, as a Christian doing undercover work among the Romans.

Arthur Kennedy as Pilate, Harry Andrews as St. Peter, Michael Gwynn as Lazarus, Arnoldo Foa as Joseph and Ivan Triesault as the Roman Emperor all fulfil adequate stints. But though Norman Wooland copes competently with the job of playing a Governor Valentina Cortese as his wife doesn't stand a chance with a ludicrously written role which, let's face it, Miss Cortese doesn't approach with overmuch nous. Of the other main performances the most unexpectedly offbeat and successful one is by Vittorio Gassman as Sahak the determined Christian. He plays it with an obstinate and telling sincerity.

There must be cheerful nods to Maria De Matteis who created the costumes, Maurizio Chiari, who dressed the sets, and Mario Chiari for his art-direction. Mario Nascimbene's music is suitably significant at the right times. Nobody seems to get a credit for special effects. The sulphur mine sequences and the razing of Rome by fire must have taken a lot of careful thought. *Rich.*

Sinaia
(ISRAELI)

Tel Aviv, June 5.
Israel Motion Picture Studios (Mati Raz) production released by Coproduction LTD-Du-Or Films LTD and Margot Klausner. Stars Dina Doronne, Shimon Israeli and Yiftah Spektor. Directed by Ivan Longyel. Screenplay, Moshe Hadar; camera, Marko Yakovlevich; editor, Dan Shick; music, Noam Sheriff. At Armon David, Tel Aviv. Running time, 85 MINS.

This picture is named for the Sinai desert where the Jews have wandered for 40 years before they reached Canaan. The same thing is happening to Israeli pictures. They are still in the wilderness if on their way to the land of money. "Sinaia" is not a good picture. But considering that it was produced for less than $100,000 it might have been much worse.

Pic is based on a true-life story. During the Sinai campaign (that's how the Israelis call the Suez war

of 1956), an Israeli patrol found the body of a dead woman in a camp. She was clutching a white bundle in which was a baby girl. The soldiers fed the baby and saved her while the mother died.

But here the script has an Israeli Air Force pilot meeting an Israeli army officer at an abandoned Bedouin camp behind the Egyptian lines. The pilot has lost his plane while the officer is cut off from his unit. They find a young woman and her little baby. The pilot is kind to the woman; the officer is not because he hates all Arabs. The Israeli pilot repairs a small Egyptian plane and they plan to take off with the woman and child. The plane starts off but the load is too heavy, and it crashes killing the pilot and woman. Only the baby lives. The officer, who had remained behind, takes the baby on one arm and a submarine gun on the other and starts out on the desert, walking towards a better future. Or so the plot reads.

This plot is not sufficient for 85 minutes, and the pic becomes duller and duller as it progresses. Young Israeli director, Ivan Lengyel, haunted by a bad script, apparently tried to solve his problem by going primitive. The pic shows this. However, there are some inspiring shots and the film actually does not lack tension all the time.

Yiftah Spektor, in the role of the pilot, underacts. Shimon Israeli, the Army officer, overacts while Dina Doronne, as the Bedouin woman, acts well. *Lapid.*

A House Of Sand
(COLOR)

Pointless medley of sexy charades on the beach.

Hollywood, June 4.
Robert Darwin production. No stars. Directed and screenplay by Darwin; camera (Eastman) and editor, Darwin; music, Willard Jones; assistant director, Gillespie. Reviewed at Directors Guild Theatre, June 4, '62. Running time, **59 MINS.**

The Girl	Mary Staton
First Man	Donald Conley
Second Man	Roland Carey
Third Man	Vance Gillespie

Latest entry in the do-it-yourself cinema sweepstakes is this sensually provocative but pointless independent offering, written, directed and produced by Robert Darwin. It is Darwin's theory of cinematic evaluation that fashioning acceptable film entertainment for a discriminating adult audience need not depend upon a tremendous outlay of capital. Maybe so, but his stringent production of "A House of Sand" is not a very convincing argument. Under the veiled pretense of art and experimentation, Darwin has actually succeeded in creating a film commercially suitable only for off-the-beaten-path theatres that cater to sensual thrill-seekers.

Darwin's primitive storyline amounts to a kind of Freudian eye-view of "Gidget." It is simply an elaborate sex charade, or "One Million B.C." as it might have transpired on Muscle Beach. Heroine of the film is a lonely, imaginative 16-year-old would-have-been nymphet whose 59-minute daydream on the beach could be titled "From Here to Maternity." Her latently awakening libido inspires

a dream sequence in which she spies vicariously upon the impromptu affair of two lovers, is spurned by an anti-social bongo banger, attacked by an overzealous Atlasian brute and confused by a fussy fisherman.

Mary Staton, whom the picture "introduces," plays the odd young lady as a sort of cross between "Lolita" and "Little Mary Sunshine." The three thoroughly overmatched young men are Donald Conley, Roland Carey and Vance Gillespie. Conley registers in the film's best moment—a priceless portrait of a pompadorable young man tending to his educated hairdo. Jill Janssen and Ted Morgan cavort as the playful young couple.

The film embodies a gushing score by Willard Jones, extracted from the exotic melodies of Lee Baxter. Darwin shows a flair for dramatic photography, relying almost exclusively on the storytelling virtue of the lens, accompanied by an absolute minimum of dialog. There is great mobility and visual impact in some of his Eastman Color compositions, although a third of the footage seems to consist of flesh, the other two-thirds water. A "New Wave" production, in the most literal sense of the term. *Tube.*

The Last Winter
(DANISH)

Toronto, June 8.
Astral release of Rialto Film. Produced by Preben Philipsen in association with Minerva Film. Directed by Edvin Tiemroth. Stars Tony Britton, Dieter Eppler, John Wittig, Axel Strøbye. Written by P. C. Green, C. C. Vassar, Jørgen Roos, Basil Dawson; adapted by Karl Bjarnhoff; camera, Ernst W. Kalinke; editing, Tiemroth; music, Sv. Erik Tarp. North American premiere Christie Theatre. Running time, **85 MINS.**

(In English)

Denmark's entry at last summer's Moscow film festival is a well-intentioned, conscientiously-made story of the fight for freedom by the underground Danes against the occupying Germans. Unfortunately, it's also tedious and longwinded. In placing emphasis on and spending time with the wrong characters, the narrative fails to develop along the proper lines.

A doctor who has managed to remain neutral throughout the occupation finds himself, during the last winter of the war, being pressed from the other side by a British secret agent who needs the doctor's help to destroy the Germans.

The doctor's moral predicament is never fully explored or developed, the film's footage being taken up instead with small talk and byplay of an inconsequential nature. Performances are adequate and technical credits good. The whole seems dated and remote, and while the Danes' part in the resistance movement no doubt deserves to be recognized, this film does not appear to have any special application or appeal to domestic or foreign audiences. *Prat.*

Boys' Night Out

Extra-marital ineptitude of the American male. Exaggerated and only sporadically amusing romantic farce. Moneymaking possibilities linked to power of strong cast names and glamorous production image, but awkward and unrealistic preoccupation with sex apt to be b.o. deterrent.

Hollywood, June 6.
Metro release of Martin Ransohoff production. Stars Kim Novak, James Garner, Tony Randall; features Howard Duff, Janet Blair, Patti Page, Jessie Royce Landis, Oscar Homolka, Howard Morris, Anne Jeffreys; guest stars Zsa Zsa Gabor, Fred Clark, William Bendix, Jim Backus, Larry Keating, Ruth McDevitt. Directed by Michael Gordon. Screenplay, Ira Wallach, as adapted by Marion Hargrove from story by Marvin Worth, Arne Sultan; camera (Metrocolor), Arthur E. Arling; editor, Tom McAdoo; music, Frank De Vol; assistant director, Ivan Volkman. Reviewed at Egyptian Theatre, June 6, '62. Running time, **113 MINS.**

Cathy	Kim Novak
Fred Williams	James Garner
George Drayton	Tony Randall
Doug Jackson	Howard Duff
Marge Drayton	Janet Blair
Joanne McIlhenny	Patti Page
Ethel Williams	Jessie Royce Landis
Dr. Prokosch	Oscar Homolka
Howard McIlhenny	Howard Morris
Toni Jackson	Anne Jeffreys
Moss' Girlfriend	Zsa Zsa Gabor
Mr. Bohannon	Fred Clark
Slattery	William Bendix
Peter Bowers	Jim Backus
Mr. Bingham	Larry Keating
Beulah Partridge	Ruth McDevitt

In "Boys' Night Out," four grown men, genus Americus Suburbicus, rent a town pad on the co-op plan for the express purpose of sharing, one by one, an illicit evening per week with a voluptuous and accommodating blonde. Red-blooded male audiences will be astonished to discover that boy one does nothing but gab, boy two nothing but putter, boy three nothing but eat, and that boy four ups and marries the girl. This sad commentary on the American male is apparently designed as a frivolous but sophisticated romantic farce with tongue-in-cheek overtones. It turns out to be something more than that. Perhaps unintentionally, the Martin Ransohoff production transmits an image of the average Yank as a guy obsessed with extra-sexual activities, but thoroughly inept and incapable. In short, a boob. Furthermore, the film's satirical edge is blunt and obvious, its plot instantly predictable in accordance with billing specifications and Hollywood romanticomedy tradition, and its humor spotty. Marquee names, a sleek production image and glamour allure will have to do the boxoffice trick for the Metro release.

Since the element of story surprise, so vital in humor, is completely absent in the Ira Wallach screenplay, adapted by Marion Hargrove from a story by Arne Sultan and Marvin Worth, the audience is forced to seek comedy rewards in isolated doses — individual gags and situations. Through the efforts of several skilled farceurs in the cast and a few good lines in the script, there are some bright moments, but not nearly enough to compensate. What the writers have done is to draw an exaggeration of the U.S. male (and wife), but it is not an honest or representative exaggeration — and social farce-satire must have roots in fact in order to hit a responsive chord in an audience.

Kim Novak slinks and purrs through the role of the object of all this extra-martial monkeyshine, an upstanding young post-grad sociology student who is secretly compiling data for a thesis on "Adolescent Sexual Fantasies in the Adult Suburban Male." James Garner seems comfortable in the part of the number one son-of-a-gun who wins her heart. Tony Randall and Howard Morris (television funnyman in his screen bow) walk off with comedy honors, but Howard Duff appears out of place in this element. Janet Blair and Anne Jeffreys have spirit as two of the wives, but Patti Page lacks acting ease as the third. Jessie Royce Landis and Oscar Homolka are capable in key support. Outstanding in the roster of "guest stars" assembled by producer Ransohoff are Fred Clark, Jim Backus and William Bendix. The others are Zsa Zsa Gabor, Larry Keating and Ruth McDevitt.

Director Michael Gordon often settles for farce where there is somewhat greater potential, such as a Little League baseball sequence that might have had some observational merit had it not been rushed and exaggerated out of proportion and beyond the elusive realm of satire.

Photography by Arthur E. Arling is pleasing to the eye, editing by Tom McAdoo tidy, music by Frank De Vol comically and romantically helpful. Art direction by George W. Davis and Hans Peters and set decoration by Henry Grace and Jerry Wunderlich are gaudy. Miss Page sings the routine but commercially promising title tune by Sammy Cahn and James Van Heusen.

Film is a coproduction between Miss Novak's indie company, Kimco, and Ransohoff's Filmways outfit, in association with Joseph E. Levine's Embassy Pictures. *Tube.*

Le Rendez-Vous De Minuit
(Midnight Meeting)
(FRENCH)

Paris, June 12.
Lux release of Editions Cinegraphiques-Argos Films-Roger Leenhardt production. Stars Lili Palmer, Michel Auclair, Maurice Ronet. Directed by Roger Leenhardt. Screenplay, Jean-Pierre Vivet, Leenhardt; camera, Jean Badal; editor, Henri Lanoe. At Ralmu, Paris. Running time, **90 MINS.**

Anne,	
Eva	Lili Palmer
Pierre	Maurice Ronet
Jacques	Michel Auclair

Oldtime film critic Roger Leenhardt, who made a good feature pic, "The Last Vacation," back in 1947, now has come up with his second one, and he seemingly waited too long. This is a flat study of identification with screen personages. It remains surface and sketchy throughout. Small chances loom abroad in spite of the Lili Palmer name.

A film critic sees a woman crying during a pic screening. She leaves and he follows. She has seen the pic many times and identified herself with the heroine, a very rich woman who cannot find meaning in life, and kills herself. She intends to do the same. Film then shows her scenes with the critic

interspersed with scenes from the film.

She is a refugee actress, and she finally gives the man the slip. So he finds the pic about to end in a suicide from a Paris bridge. He rushes to save her. However, she is hiding and he thinks she did make the dive. His concern has her deciding against the suicide.

All the ideas rarely fuse while the dialog is fussy and platitudinous. Direction is listless and technical credits only par.

Miss Palmer can not do much with her dual roles since the characters are only skimpy ideas rather than flesh and blood. Others suffer, too. *Mosk.*

Airborne

Adequate lower berth item about the care and feeding of the potential paratrooper.

Hollywood, May 31.
Art Diamond production. Cast: Bobby Diamond, Robert Christian, Mikel Angel, Bill Hale, Carolyn Byrd, Barbara Markham. Directed and screenplayed by James Landis; camera, Larry Raimond. Reviewed at Pix Theatre, May 31, '62. Running time, **78 MINS.**

How they "separate the men from the boys" down in quaint old Fort Bragg, home of the fighting 82nd, is described in "Airborne," a sort of glorified recruiting film. The Art Diamond production has been competently filmed at on-the-spot training camp locales and is enacted with considerable skill and energy by a cast of lesser-known players under the surveillance of director James Landis, but the latter's screenplay is little more than a medley of cliche incidents, stereotype characterizations and maudlin resolutions. The picture will suffice as a supporting filler on twin-bills aimed primarily at male audiences.

Naive country boy makes good and shows up big city barracks bully when chips are down in the general idea of Landis' predictable plot. Bobby Diamond, of television "Fury" fame, plays the green farm lad with boyish enthusiasm and a few more "shucks" than are tolerable. Bill Hale dispatches with brisk authority that familiar role—"toughest sergeant in jump school." The boys in the barracks are well-played, Robert Christian and Mikel Angel in leading parts. Pretty Carolyn Byrd, a promising newcomer to the screen, supplies romantic interest.

Paratroop training procedures have been proficiently lensed by cameraman Larry Raimond.
Tube.

The Interns

Undistinguished depiction of lives and loves of five candidate medics. Youthful cast and now-popular medical topic will have to provide b.o. backbone.

Hollywood, May 25.
Columbia Pictures release of Robert Cohn production. Stars Michael Callan, Cliff Robertson, James MacArthur, Nick Adams, Suzy Parker, Haya Harareet; features Anne Helm, Stephanie Powers, Buddy Ebsen, Telly Savalas. Directed by David Swift. Screenplay, Walter Newman,

Swift, based on novel by Richard Frede; camera, Russell L. Metty; editors, Al Clark, Jerome Thoms; music, Leith Stevens; assistant director, Eddie Saeta. Reviewed at Warner Hollywood Theatre, May 25, '62. Running time, **130 MINS.**

Dr. Considine	Michael Callan
Dr. John Paul Otis	Cliff Robertson
Dr. Lew Worship	James MacArthur
Dr. Sid Lackland	Nick Adams
Lisa Cardigan	Suzy Parker
Mado	Haya Harareet
Mildred	Anne Helm
Gloria	Stephanie Powers
Dr. Sidney Wohl	Buddy Ebsen
Dr. Riccio	Telly Savalas
Nurse Flynn	Katharine Bard
Didi Loomis	Kay Stevens
Dr. Hugo Granchard	Gregory Morton
Mrs. Auer	Angela Clarke
Nurse Connie Dean	Connie Gilchrist
Loara	Ellen Davalos
Dr. Dave Simon	Charles Robinson
Olga	Carroll Harrison
Dr. Duane	John Banner
Samantha	Mari Lynn
Dr. Joe Pareilli	Brian Hutton
Dr. Bonny	J. Edward McKinley
Gwen	Bobo Lewis
1st Intern	Ira Barmak
Rosco	Bill Gunn
Dr. Apschult	William O. Douglas
Dr. Petchek	Don Edmonds
Mrs. Lawrence	Mavis Neal
Dr. Baker	Brent Sargent
Samantha's Son	Mark Kantor

An up-and-coming young cast and the current popularity of medicine men in entertainment will have to carry the boxoffice payload for Robert Cohn's production of "The Interns." For, in its apparent attempt to dramatize candidly and irreverently the process by which school-finished candidate medics manage to turn into regular doctors, the film somehow succeeds in depicting the average intern as some kind of a Hippocratic oaf. At times the Columbia release comes perilously close to earning the nickname, "Carry On, Intern."

The separate stories of five interns, four male and one female, are traced alternately in a sort of razzle-dazzle style by the Walter Newman-David Swift screenplay from Richard Frede's novel. Three of the stories are predictable from the word go and the other two are thoroughly unbelievable. In one, intern Cliff Robertson, for no plausible reason, falls madly in love with pregnant, unwed model Suzy Parker and promptly sacrifices his medical career in an abortive abortion attempt.

Intern number two, James Mac-Arthur, outspoken in his dedication to becoming a surgeon, naturally becomes an obstetrician in between wooing a young nurse (Stephanie Powers) out of a bad case of wanderlust and turning in his best buddy, Robertson, to the authorities.

Intern number three, Michael Callan, literally goes batty trying to romance his way into the good graces of a foremost medic. The fourth intern, Nick Adams, proclaims his mercenary viewpoint of the profession, then is so affected by the tragedy of his first big patient, a Eurasian girl, that he sacrifices everything and moves all the way to the remote Far East, to aid the underprivileged. Intern number five, Haya Hararect, has a running debate with her idol, chief surgeon Telly Savalas, who hates lady surgeons. She becomes his assistant.

As these personal stories unfold, a kind of cross-section of hospital life is transpiring in the background. Chief features are a rather gory childbirth sequence, a mercy killing incident and a wild party

passage imitative of the one in "Breakfast at Tiffany's," but hardly as appropriate or amusing. Supporting characters run to stereotype, i.e., the ugly; prim nurse who removes her spex, lets her hair down, gets stinko and becomes the hit of the party.

Under the circumstances, none of the players can achieve much in the way of dimension or appeal, although the cast is comprised of several promising young people and a number of reliable older ones. There is no single stickout performance.

Dramatic concept engineered by director David Swift and executed with the aid of editors Al Clark and Jerome Thoms is a whirlwind, hit-and-run series of abrupt transitional cuts in an effort to develop **and knit the five separate but related dramas. It is an advantageous technique for this kind of film, in which several characters have equal importance.** Capable contributions are made by cameraman Russell Metty, art director Don Ament and composer Leith Stevens.
Tube.

The Phantom of the Opera
(BRITISH—TECHNICOLOR)

British remake of an oldie. Provides enough moments of suspense to make a sound booking for average houses.

London, June 8.
Rank and Universal release of a Hammer production. Stars Herbert Lom, Heather Sears. Produced by Anthony Hinds. Directed by Terence Fisher. Screenplay, John Elder; camera, Arthur Grant; editors, James Needs, Alfred Cox; music, Edwin Astley. Previewed, Leicester Square Theatre, London, June 6, '62. Running time, **84 MINS.**

The Phantom	Herbert Lom
Christine	Heather Sears
Lattimer	Thorley Walters
Lord D'Arcy	Michael Gough
Harry	Edward De Souza
Rossi	Martin Miller
Cabby	Miles Malleson
Charwoman	Miriam Karlin
Vickers	John Harvey
Bill	Harold Godwin
Dwarf	Ian Wilson
Xavier	Marne Maitland
Yvonne	Sonia Cordeau
Mrs. Tucker	Renee Houston

Hammer's slick horror experts have disinterred "The Phantom of the Opera," and, in the new version, Herbert Lom somewhat precariously follows in the macabre footsteps of the late Lon Chaney and Claude Rains. Switched to a London Opera House background, lushed up in color, with a new character, a dwarf, rather confusingly brought in to supplement the sinister activities of The Phantom, it still provides a fair measure of goose pimples to combat some potential unwanted yocks. In the shadow of its predecessors the current "Phantom" seems a reasonable booking for average houses, without doing anything to erase oldtimers' memories of the earlier versions.

Basically, the story remains the same. Baleful goings on backstage at the opera which suggest that the place is invaded by evil spirits. The evil spirit is, of course, the Phantom but he turns out to be a rather more sympathetic charac-

ter than of old and much of his malignance is now switched to a new character, a dwarf, played effectively by Ian Wilson.

However, the atmosphere of brooding evil still works up to some effective highlights, with the terror of the heroine (Heather Sears) paramount, the bewilderment of the hero (Edward De Souza) and the eerie personality of the Phantom still motivating the action. Production highlights involve some shock effects, notably when the opera singing heroine is dragged backstage by the dwarf to meet the hideous Phantom, who decides to make her a great operatic star, the attack by the dwarf on the hero when, through underground sewers, he seeks to trace the Phantom and the moment when the latter rips off his mask to confront the heavy. Also, of course, the hokum, but stirring, climax when the Phantom crashes to his death on the stage to prevent Miss Sears being rubbed out by a collapsing chandelier.

Color lensing by Arthur Grant is effective and the script, though occasionally veering towards parody, manages to avoid banality. Music by Edward Astley is well in the mood.

Herbert Lom's personality manages to come through his hideous disguise as the Phantom with a chip on his shoulder, and Michael Gough as the arrogant composer and Edward De Souza as the protector of Miss Sears are competent, while Miss Sears, herself, gives a small but effective performance as the heroine, greatly helped by the singing voice of opera singer Pat Clark. Smaller contributions are tellingly swung in by Martin Miller as a temperamental conductor, Michael Ripper and Miles Malleson as differing cabdrivers and Miriam Karlin as a scrubwoman.

This present version of "The Phantom of the Opera" gets by because it makes no pretense of being a "big" pic. It may well have achieved a good effect by persuading film producers that "The Phantom" has had its chips. The first sinister impact is now lost in an aura of no surprise. *Rich.*

The Story Of The Count of Monte Cristo
(FRENCH—COLOR—DYALISCOPE)

French-made with dubbed dialog. Best U.S. market chances via child appeal.

Hollywood, June 4.
Warner Bros. release of Jean-Jacques Vital-Rene Modiano production. Stars Louis Jourdan, Yvonne Furneaux, Pierre Mondy, Franco Silva. Directed by Claude Autant-Lara. Screenplay, Jean Halain, based on novel by Alexandre Dumas; camera (Technicolor), Jacques Natteau, Jean Isnard; editor, Madeleine Gug; music, Rene Cloerec; assistant director, Ghislaine Autant-Lara. Reviewed at the studio, June 4, '62. Running time, **130 MINS.**

Edmond Dantes	Louis Jourdan
Mercedes	Yvonne Furneaux
Caderousse	Pierre Mondy
Mario	Franco Silva
Villefort	Bernard Dheran
Fernand de Mortcerf	Jean-Claude Michel
Vidocq	Jean Martinelli
Haydee	Claudine Coster
Abbe Faria	Henri Guisol
Mme. Caderousse	Marie Mergey
Albert de Mortcerf	Yves Renier
Benedetto	Alain Ferral

Some three eventful decades separate this new screen version

of "The Story of the Count of Monte Cristo" from the last one. Seemingly, then, the time would be ripe for a remake of the popular adventure-romance by Alexandre Dumas, pere. Perhaps on this assumption, coproducers Jean-Jacques Vital and Rene Modiano have spared little expense in mounting a pictorially rich and dramatically expansive reproduction of the story for the new screen generation. But one vital miscalculation strips their effort of sufficient appeal for the bulk of the modern audience. In adhering rigidly to the plodding, stilted and weighty melodramatic style reasonably fashionable in less sophisticated bygone times, the creators of this version have failed to sense, or refused to reckon with, the realistic requirements of modern screen storytelling, unwritten entertainment rules that govern even the adaptation of a courtly costume classic if it is to capture the imagination and soothe the impatient disposition of the selective 1962 picturegoer.

The fact that it was made in France, cast without much regard for the U.S. marquee (only the name of Louis Jourdan will improve its fate here), and post-dubbed via the not-easily-synchronized merger of French lip with English tongue compounds the dubious nature of the enterprise as a Yankee attraction. Warner Bros. should aim its campaign at children—suggesting to parents that here is an opportunity for their youngsters to acquaint themselves, the easy, condensed way, with an oft-referred to work of romantic fiction.

The film, adapted by Jean Halain from the novel and directed by Claude Autant-Lara, sketchily depicts the unfortunate career of Dumas' hero, Edmund Dantes (Jourdan), as he coldly pursues a campaign of vengeance against those who conspire diabolically in causing his 17-year imprisonment (1814-1831) for crimes of which he was innocent.

Possibility of perceiving superior performance is denied the U.S. recipient forced to tune in on a counterfeit sound track. Jourdan, a reliable actor, fashions an intense, somber portrait of the central figure. Others of import in the cast include Yvonne Furneaux, Pierre Mondy, Franco Silva, Bernard Dheran, Jean-Claude Michel, Henri Guisol, Yves Renier and Alain Ferral.

There is beauty in the photography, some of the scenes composed through the lens of cameramen Jacques Natteau and Jean Isnard and embellished by Technicolor and Dyaliscope conveying the rich brush-stroke quality of a 19th century painting. Luxuriant sets by Max Douy and a virile background score by Rene Cloerec are additional assets. But the histrionic style engineered by director Autant-Lara keeps the characterizations artificial, and this is the common denominator to which all efforts of those involved are reduced. *Tube.*

Birdman Of Alcatraz

Biopic of still-jailed, convict-they-won't forgive. Outstandingly done in all departments. Word-of-mouth should make it top b.o. attraction.

Hollywood, June 8.
United Artists release of Stuart Millar-Guy Trosper production and Harold Hecht presentation. Stars Burt Lancaster; features Karl Malden, Thelma Ritter, Neville Brand, Betty Field, Telly Savalas, Edmond O'Brien. Directed by John Frankenheimer. Screenplay, Guy Trosper, based on Thomas E. Gaddis' book; camera. Burnett Guffey; editor, Edward Mann; music, Elmer Bernstein; asst. director, Dave Silver. Reviewed at Goldwyn Studios, June 8, '62. Running time, **147 MINS.**

Robert Stroud ...... Burt Lancaster
Warden Shoemaker ...... Karl Malden
Elizabeth Stroud .... Thelma Ritter
Bull Ransom .... Neville Brand
Stella Johnson .... Betty Field
Feto Gomez .... Telly Savalas
Tom Gaddis .... Edmond O'Brien
Roy Comstock .... Hugh Marlow
Dr. Ellis .... Whit Bissell
Kramer .... Graham Denton
Jess Younger .... James Westerfield

"Birdman of Alcatraz" is the finest "prison" picture ever made, except that it is not really a "prison" picture in the traditional and accepted sense of the term. Heretofore, with few exceptions, the core of the "prison picture" has been prison life itself, around which has been constructed dramatizations of those who were a part of that secret sealed life on the negative side of society. Popularity of the prison film sprang from public curiosity about the shadowy penal way of life. "Birdman" reverses the formula and brings a new breadth and depth to the form. In telling, with reasonable objectivity but understandably deep compassion the true story of Robert Stroud, it achieves a human dimension way beyond its predecessors. For the core of "Birdman" is the intimate story of one unfortunate human being, and "prison life" is only the inseparable but secondary issue against which his tragic tale is drawn.

The Stuart Millar-Guy Trosper production (and Harold Hecht presentation) is certainly one of the outstanding film achievements in a thus far rather lean cinema year. Like any superior accomplishment, it will be discussed. And public discussion is the surest forerunner to the commercial success of any project. Public interest will be aroused not only because of the excellence of the film, but because it is a true story and because it contains a masterful, Oscar-calibre performance by Burt Lancaster and several noteworthy ones in support. Grimness of the story image is apt to rule out blockbuster proportions, but it's still a bright and promising contender for United Artists.

Trosper's penetrating and affecting screenplay, based on the book by Thomas E. Gaddis, delicately and artfully sketches the 53-year imprisonment of the now 72-year-old "Birdman," Stroud, illustrating the highlights and lowlights of that terrible, yet miraculously ennobling span. The screenplay's, and the film's, only real flaw is its dismissal of Stroud's background, leaving the audience to mull over psychological ramifications and expositional data by and large denied it. But this may be quibbling; the important story, with its vital sociological queries, is there for all to see in plain black and white.

There is a fascinating ironic twist in the story. Stroud spent a staggering total of 43 years in solitary confinement. The irony is that solitary appears to have been the indispensable ally that enabled him to accomplish his remarkable feats of scientific research and discovery, principally in the field of avian diseases. The film depicts his regeneration through the gentle cure of birds who share his cell after he killed two men (one of them a prison guard). The parallel between caged birds and caged men adds another note of irony to the story.

Lancaster gives a superbly natural, unaffected performance—one in which nobility and indestructibility can be seen cumulatively developing and shining from within through a weary exterior eroded by the deep scars of time and enforced privacy in a "prison within a prison." His running clash with the narrow-minded and vengeful "warden Shoemaker" is a highlight of the film, consummating in a powerful scene depicting their opposing views on penology. Karl Malden is excellent as the warden.

Four distinguished top supporting performances light up the picture. They are those of Telly Savalas as a fellow inmate and birdkeeper, Thelma Ritter (in a change of pace from her customary characterization) as Stroud's mother (whose seemingly unselfish devotion to the cause of her son ultimately grows suspect), Neville Brand as an understanding guard, and Betty Field as the woman who marries Stroud in prison, then reluctantly drifts away at his realistic request. Edmond O'Brien narrates and plays the author. Others who perform with skill are Hugh Marlow, Whit Bissell, Graham Denton and James Westerfield.

John Frankenheimer's trenchant, sensitive direction is a prime factor in the success of the production. His firm surveillance of the cast is evident in the uniform excellence of characterization, and his keen sense of visual drama keeps the picture alive for the eye in spite of the close physical quarters in which it is set. In this latter aspect, he receives the astute aid of cameraman Burnett Guffey. And production savvy is deflected in all other areas, not the least of which are Edward Mann's editing, Ferdie Carrere's art direction, Elmer Bernstein's music and George Cooper's sound, right down through Robert Schiffer's unusually adroit and realistic makeup work. *Tube.*

Sanjuro
(JAPANESE—TOHOSCOPE)

Powerful action film with human, if remarkably cerebral hero. Robin Hood Japanese style.

Hollywood, June 14.
Toho release of Ryuzo Kikushima-Tomoyuki Tanaka production. Stars Toshiro Mifune; with Tatsuya Nakadai, Reiko Dan, Yozo Kayama, Takashi Shimura. Directed by Akira Kurosawa. Screenplay, Kikushima, Hideo Oguni, Kurosawa; camera, Fukuzo Koizumi; music, Masaru Sato. Reviewed at Toho La Brea Theatre, June 14, '62. Running time. **96 MINS.**

Roughly the Japanese equivalent of an American western,

"Sanjuro" brings to the screen an epic hero far more formidable than the celebrated tall men and top guns of the 19th century Yankee frontier. The charm of this fascinating Toho production and release, stylishly directed by Akira Kurosawa, is the personality of this hero, powerfully played by Toshiro Mifune. Audiences may smile or scoff at his improbably bold feats with the sword, but this is only one facet of an otherwise compellingly human though absolutely heroic character. The film appears certain to be a big favorite with Japanese audiences, and is exciting and entertaining enough to please most art house browsers.

It is not inconceivable that, just as "Seven Samurai" led to "The Magnificent 7" "Sanjuro" would also lend itself to translation into the Yankee western idiom. At any rate, it is certainly worth the attention of enterprising Hollywood screen producers on the prowl for likely action material.

Story is set in the turbulent mid-1800's of Japan, and describes the remarkable manner in which one man, the warrior "Sanjuro," destroys the wretched machinery of a corrupt ruling faction. Although an invincible swordsman, it is not this aspect of his identity that gives him his greatest appeal. Unlike many of the mighty adventure heroes of the west, he is endowed with an incredible sense of logic—a Gestaltian way of reasoning invariably correct in drawing the simplest, most natural conclusions when others have jumped to theirs emotionally and illogically. The character is also very human—especially in his appreciation of little things such as sake, sleep and money. In short, a well-rounded figure: physically epic, mentally agile, emotionally normal—a kind of cross between Robin Hood and a typical Humphrey Bogart character.

As usual, Kurosawa doesn't compromise in the battle and brutality area. This one features a rousing climactic duel between the title roleist and his chief adversary that outdoes the average western showdown by a dramatic mile. As the two old men stand intimately face to face, toe to toe, the screen freezes for what seems an eternity. Then the swords flash and, in one horrible movement, "Sanjuro" has severed an artery in his opponent's chest. There is no question that it is an artery. The audience can tell because it gushes across the screen with the sudden furious force of Old Faithful. *Tube.*

Gigot
(COLOR)

An appealing, gently-paced comedy with Jackie Gleason as a mute Parisian janitor. Star is superb when he isn't laying the pathos on with too heavy a hand. Stylish production. Good boxoffice outlook for all audiences.

20th-Fox presentation of Kenneth Hyman (Seven Arts) production. Stars Jackie Gleason; features Katherine Kath, Diane Gardner. Directed by Gene Kelly. Screenplay, John Patrick, based on a story by Gleason; camera (DeLuxe Color), Jean Bourgoin; music, Gleason

(arranged and conducted by Michel Magne); editor, Roger Dwyre; asst. director, Paul Feyder. Reviewed in N.Y., June 12, '62. Running time, **104 MINS.**

Gigot	Jackie Gleason
Colette	Katherine Kath
Mme. Brigitte	Gabrielle Dorziat
Gaston	Jean Lefebvre
Jean	Jacques Marin
Alphonse	Albert Remy
Lucille Duval	Yvonne Constant
Mme. Greuze	Germaine Delbat
Bistro Proprietor	Albert Dinan
Nicole	Diane Gardner
Priest	Camille Guerini
Albert	Rene Havard
M. Duval	Louis Falavigna
The Gendarme	Jean Michaud
Baker	Richard-Francoeur
Baker's Wife	Paula Dehelly
Blade	Jacques Ary
Pierre	Franck Villard

With a little judicious pruning and a somewhat less obvious attempt to tug at the old heart strings, Jackie Gleason's "Gigot" might have emerged as a modern classic. As it is, the film is an immensely appealing but gently-paced comedy, full of good humor and wry observations on life. At its best, which is about 50% of the time, it has a sort of comic strip gaiety not seen on the American screen in several decades. This factor, coupled with the magic of the Gleason name, should assure it a welcome reception almost everywhere.

If anyone needed further evidance that Gleason is a superb actor, "Gigot" is it. But, like all great talents, Gleason needs a certain amount of discipline. From time to time throughout the film, he seems compelled to slip out of the title role—that of a mute, bedraggled Parisian janitor, the butt of all practical jokes, old and new—into his more famous public personality, that of the irrepressibly bumptuous character not too far removed from Broadway and the Palace. This happens, it's true, infrequently, as when he goes into a quick softshoe routine to amuse a sad-faced moppet, but it's enough to destroy an illusion which, if it had been maintained throughout, would have resulted in an unalloyed delight. This also makes it a little more difficult to accept the moments of heavy pathos as anything more than play-acting affectation.

Such, however, may seem like a trivial reservation to the vast mass audience for whom the Great One can do no wrong.

John Patrick's screenplay, based on an original story by Gleason, recounts the alternately sad-then-glad adventures of Gigot (literally, "leg of lamb"), who lives in a basement hovel in a working class quarter of Paris and scrounges for a living as a general handyman. Animals, birds, and even rodents love him. Though a mute, he is not a dunce, but his eccentricities (on his days off he goes to funerals—anybody's funeral) are a source of some amusement in the neighborhood.

Finally one night he befriends an apparently consumptive street-walker and her small daughter, whom he takes into his basement to care for. As his affection for the little girl grows, the avaricious mother threatens to walk out on Gleason unless he comes up witn some cash, compelling him to steal a wad of money from the local baker and leading to a final crisis and happy ending. The latter, incidentally, is a delightful but direct steal from "Tom Sawyer," wherein the supposedly dead Gigot watches his own magnificent funeral as he hides in a cemetery tree. Unable to restrain his tears, he carefully blows his nose in a chestnut leaf.

Gleason and director Gene Kelly have filled out Patrick's somewhat thin outline with a good deal of cinema substance. Early on, when Gigot is first seen crashing a funeral, Kelly's camera, sans expositive dialog, manages to tell the funny, knife-sharp story of three generations of a French family (including a wronged wife and a not-so-bereaved mistress) standing at graveside. Later, in what may be the highpoint of the picture to many, the jokesters of the neighborhood get Gigot tight on Pernod and Eau de Vie, setting the stage for Gleason to do a set of drunken impressions and a frenzied dance of sheer happiness that hit just the right note of high humor and pathos.

Adding tremendously to the style and authenticity of the production is the fact that Gleason has surrounded himself with some of France's best character actors. Their heavily accented English is occasionally hard to understand, but their faces and their mannerisms could not be duplicated anywhere else in the world. Among the standouts are Katherine Kath as the hard-as-rocks demimondaine; Gabrielle Dorziat, as Gigot's penny-pinching employer; Jean Lefebvre, as a rather wistfully ineffectual detective; and Yvonne Constant, as the neighborhood Bardot. Besides Gleason, the only other American in the cast is tiny Diane Gardner, a sweet-faced child who seems enchanted by Gleason.

Because the film is so gently plotted, it eventually becomes somewhat repetitious and might have been more tightly edited. There is also a tendency for Gleason's musical score, full of small but charming themes, to occasionally well up in huge, elaborate orchestrations which almost overwhelm the screen images.

In making the picture in Paris, Seven Arts producer Ken Hyman obviously spared no expense on the physical production. Jean Bourgoin's color camerawork is fine, soft and mellow in the muted pastels which always seem unique to Paris. *Anby.*

It Happened In Athens

(C'SCOPE—COLOR)

Unsatisfactory dramatization of rebirth of Olympic Games in 1896.

Hollywood, June 14.

20th-Fox release of James S. Elliott production. Stars Jayne Mansfield, Trax Colton, Nico Minardos, Bob Mathias; introduces Maria Xenia. Directed by Andrew Marton. Screenplay, Laslo Vadnay; camera (De Luxe), Curtis Courant; editor, Jodie Copelan; music, Manos Hadjidakis; asst. dicetors, Foster Phinney, Henry Yatrou. Reviewed at the studio, June 14, '62. Running time, **100 MINS.**

Eleni	Jayne Mansfield
Spiridon	Trax Colton
Vinardos	Nico Minardos
Coach Graham	Bob Mathias
Christina	Maria Xenia
Grandpa Loues	Ivan Triesault
Maria	Marion Silva
Du Bois	Roger Fradet
Connolley	Ben Bennett
Mama Loues	Lili Valenty
De Coubertin	Jean Murat
O'Toole	Denton De Gray
Burke	Todd Windsor
Drake	Bill Browne
George	Gustavo De Nordo
Announcer	George Graham
Nicos	Paris Alexander

Ill-conceived and clumsily executed, this James S. Elliott production very likely will have to be relegated to lower berth status, although its physical production values and running time obviously aspired to a better fate.

Laslo Vadnay's scenario, roughly based on an actual occurrence in Greece, circa 1896, depicts, without a semblance of story surprise or innovation, the events surrounding the Horatio Alger triumph of a young, untrained Greek shepherd lad in the marathon race of that year's Olympic games, the first held after a 2,672 year lapse.

Trax Colton essays the lad with boyish enthusiasm. Jayne Mansfield plays the Greek screen star who, as a publicity stunt, offers her hand in marriage to the winner of the marathon, but withdraws to allow the victorious Colton to marry his true love. Miss Mansfield, who does more posing than acting, spends most of her footage dressing or undressing. Sometimes the story pauses just to watch pointedly as she begins peeling. This can be viewed as diversion, and male audiences won't mind, but it does not say much for Andrew Marton's direction. Marton does appreciably better with crowd reaction shots, a skill he no doubt developed as second unit helmsman on the "Ben-Hur" chariot sequence.

Nico Minardos and Bob Mathias have important roles, as does Maria Xenia, who is "introduced" by the film. Adequate is the best that can be said of their efforts.

Curtis Courant's De Luxe Color photography is a trifle dark. Manos Hadjidakis, of "Never On Sunday" fame, has composed a score in the Greek idiom for this film. Its novelty as melodic background makes it pleasant at first, but after awhile the strains grow monotonous. Other production credits are fair, at best. *Tube.*

Adventures Of A Young Man

(C'SCOPE—COLOR)

Ernest Hemingway's Nick Adams, carefully but not altogether successfully translated to the screen. Has b.o. possibilities, but needs special selling.

Hollywood, June 5.

Twentieth-Fox release of Jerry Wald production. Stars Richard Beymer, Diane Baker, Corinne Calvet, Fred Clark, Dan Dailey, James Dunn, Juano Hernandez, Arthur Kennedy, Ricardo Montalban, Susan Strasberg, Jessica Tandy, Eli Wallach; features Paul Newman. Directed by Martin Ritt. Screenplay, A. E. Hotchner, based on stories by Ernest Hemingway; camera (De Luxe), Lee Garmes; editor, Hugh S. Fowler; music, Franz Waxman; asst. director, Eli Dunn. Reviewed at the studio, June 5, '62. Running time, **145 MINS.**

Nick Adams	Richard Beymer
Carolyn	Diane Baker
Contessa	Corinne Calvet
Mr. Turner	Fred Clark
Billy Campbell	Dan Dailey
Telegrapher	James Dunn
Bugs	Juano Hernandez
Dr. Adams	Arthur Kennedy
Major Padula	Richardo Montalban
Rosanna	Susan Strasberg
Mrs. Adams	Jessica Tandy
John	Eli Wallach
Brakeman	Edward Binns
Ludstrum	Whit Bissell
Montecito	Philip Bourneuf
Sig. Griffi	Tullio Carminati
Eddy Bolton	Marc Cavell
Mayor	Charles Fredericks
Joe Boulton	Simon Oakland
George	Michael Pollard
The Battler	Paul Newman

The formidable task of assembling the bits and pieces of Ernest Hemingway's autobiographical young hero, Nick Adams, and welding them into a single, substantial flush-and-blood screen personality has nearly been accomplished in Jerry Wald's production of "Adventures of a Young Man." The potential for this achievement appears to have existed in A. E. Hotchner's screenplay. But, while the film has been executed with concern, integrity and respect for the pen from which it flows, it has a disquieting tendency to oscillate between flashes of artistry and truth and interludes of mechanics and melodramatics. Director Martin Ritt has attained some shining moments but, by laboring several lesser passages past their emotional peaks, he has failed to regulate the picture's dramatic pulse. A penetrating and expressive performance in the central role might have carried the film over the hurdles of the basic episodic unbalance that Ritt has not corrected. But Richard Beymer's portrayal is not up to the challenge.

The artistic upshot, then, is a near-miss. Therefore, this being the sort of pretentious literary project aimed primarily at a more selective, discerning audience, it is apt to be a case of touch and go at the boxoffice. To further its wicket potential and yet remain faithful to the spirit of the enterprise, 20th-Fox would be wise to emphasize the uplifting values of the story, as a lure for the family trade prone to be less influenced by critical reservations than by the wholesome, character building, almost academic nature of the project.

Hotchner's scenario, gleaned from the prose of 10 of Hemingway's short stories, traces the path to maturity of Nick Adams. It follows him in his restless, searching pursuit of knowledge and worldly experience with which to build his character, advance his potential, shape his identity and prepare him for his destiny in the higher sphere to which he aspires. It leads him from the idyllic simplicity but domestic unrest of his rural Michigan childhood environment to trying but edifying experience with assorted lost but somehow noble personages on the open road to disappointment in the objective big-time of New York. It tags along as Nick is exposed to the passions of war and tragedy of unfulfilled first love in Italy, and follows him home for the discovery that he is a man prepared to grapple with the major challenge of life.

Beymer lacks the warmth, depth and expressiveness required for the role. The growth, the transition from boy to man, is not as gradual, as smoothly cumulative, as it should be. Since Hotchner's script employs Hemingway's patented economy of language, it is those profound feelings, thoughts and emotions that lurk beneath the spoken word. They do not surface clearly or forcibly in Beymer's delineation.

There are a host of fine performances and a few weak ones. Paul Newman, almost unrecognizable behind a masterfully gro-

tesque yet realistic makeup mask by Ben Nye, re-creates the punch-drunk "Battler" character he en ago. It's a colorful and compassionate acting cameo, and Newman merits credit not only for the performance but for the fact that, as a top star, he's not above the undertaking of a small character role when it represents an artistic challenge.

Other important standouts are Ricardo Montalban as a perceptive Italian officer, Fred Clark as a slick but sympathetic burlesque promoter, Dan Dailey as a down-and-out advance man, Juano Hernandez as the Battler's devoted watchdog "trainer," and Eli Wallach as a practical but kind Italian Army orderly. Probably the finest performance in the film is Arthur Kennedy's as Nick's peace-loving, recessive father. And Jessica Tandy is excellent as the fanatical, domineering mother who leads Kennedy to his self-destruction.

James Dunn is affecting in a small role, and others who attract favorable attention in parts of some consequence are Edward Binns, Simon Oakland and Corinne Calvet. Diane Baker and Michael Pollard are unfortunately implicated in scenes that leave something to be desired. Susan Strasberg shares with Beymer the weakest and most lethargic passage (World War One) of the picture, a lengthy romantic interlude in the latter part that stalls the film's momentum. Miss Strasberg's characterization is wooden.

The picture is beautifully mounted and photographed. De Luxe Color camerawork by Lee Garmes is extremely sensitive to the temperament of the weather and the natural splendor of the wide open country, and it seems as if, almost miraculously, he has managed to capture Hemingway's weather and Hemingway's country. Except for those deliberate passages toward the end, which could have been trimmed, Hugh S. Fowler's editing of the long 145-minute film is adroitly executed.

Truly outstanding contributions are the meticulous, meaningful art direction and set decoration by the respective teams of Jack Martin Smith-Paul Groesse and Walter M. Scott-Robert Priestly. Also excellent is Don Feld's accurate, perceptive costuming. Franz Waxman has composed a hauntingly plaintive, pastoral score, highlighting the flute. Other fine efforts are those of soundmen E. Clayton Ward and Warren B. Delaplain and special photographic effects team L. B. Abbott and Emil Kosa.   *Tube.*

Le Monte-Charge
(The Freight Elevator)
(FRENCH)
Paris, June 12.
Gaumont release of SNEG-Marianne-Galatea production. Stars Robert Hossein, Lea Massari; features Maurice Biraud, Robert Dalban. Directed by Marcel Bluwal. Screenplay, Frederic Dard, Bluwal from a novel by Dard; camera, Andre Bac; editor, G. Vaury. At Ambassade-Gaumont, Paris. Running time, **85 MINS.**
Herbin .... Robert Hossein
Marta .... Lea Massari
Ferry .... Maurice Biraud
Inspector .... Robert Dalban

Combo drama and whodunit sometimes over reaches in coincidence and narration. But it has a flair for atmopshere which keeps this fairly absorbing

throughout. So it looms a good playoff bet but does not wield the weight for likely art house chances.

Marcel Bluwal, tele director, makes a nice transposition to feature films. He uses the economy, of means in unfolding this tale of a strange murder on Christmas Eve. He also reflects a neat feeling for mood and is aided by some fine acting.

A young man comes home from prison and is not allowed into the Paris area since on probation. He picks up a richly dressed girl who is with her daughter. They go to her place, then out and back to find her husband dead on a sofa. However, he will not call the police and rushes off.

But he is drawn back and follows her as she goes out again and picks up another man. He then goes up and hears the same scene reenacted and hides in a nearby apartment. It seems she had planned this elaborate affair to kill her husband and pass it off as suicide. Somewhat over-elaborate in plotting, this still holds interest.

Robert Hossein, as the man who eventually gets trapped in the crime, and Lea Massari, as the woman, are effective with a neat assist from Maurice Biraud as the man who calls the police. Pic is expertly lensed.

This is also a solid playoff item. Paramount has the film for marts outside of France and should be able to use it effectively for some spots. Incidentally, the freight elevator of the title is the one used to go up to the woman's apartment.   *Mosk.*

The Sky Above — The Mud Below
(FRENCH DOCUMENTARY —COLOR)

Absorbing footage, at times beautiful and repellent, of an heroic French-Dutch expedition into uncharted jungle. Recent Oscar wreath and strong exploitation make it a promising b.o. contender.

Embassy Pictures release of an Ardennes Film Production, with cooperation of Michael Arthur Films. Produced by Arthur Cohn and Rene LaFuite. Written and directed by Pierre-Dominique Gaisseau. Camera (Agfacolor), Gilbert Sarthre; editor, Georges Arnstam; narration, William Peacock; asst. director Gerard Delloye. Reviewed in N.Y., June 18, '62. Running time, **90 MINS.**

An adventurous team of French documentarians set out in 1959 to make a south-to-north bisection of Dutch New Guinea, 435 miles (as the crow flies) of largely uncharted jungle, replete with such obstacles as tricky rivers and head-hunting primitives. The expedition, or rather its remnants, finally made it seven months and 1,000 circuitous miles later. "The Sky Above—the Mud Below" (originally "Le Ciel et la Boue") is the filmed record of that heroic saga, and easily one of the best such documents in cinema annals. It is being released by Embassy Pictures.

The picture, which took the Academy Award this year for best feature-length documentary, is always compelling, often lyrically beautiful, occasionally repugnant. Its dramatic force operates on two levels—as, per the soundtrack, a fascinating "leap backwards in

time," and as the chronicle of persevering explorers. The two are intertwined, and it is this that endows the film with its sustained impact.

The saga is one of statistics as much as human valor. Starting out with 60 Papuan porters and four soldiers as escort for the journey's early legs, the expedition ultimately succeeded at a cost of three dead, eight wounded, 22 felled by illness. By the end, of the seven Frenchmen who set out, only two—including Pierre-Dominique Gaisseau, the organizer-leader—had completed the journey. By rafts, dug-out canoes and by foot, the expedition traversed mountains as high as 16,400 feet, and faced a temperature range of 35 to 132 degrees.

The Agfacolor camera of Gilbert Sarthre (one of those forced back in the later stages) is remarkably observant, avidly recording the sidebar incident as well as the main event. The sense of the primeval is conveyed with impressive effect. Scenes of assorted natives—pygmies and taller specimens—performing their rituals of war and fertility, or poking about the expedition camp wide-eyed, are by turns startling and amusing. And always in focus as a prime character, the inhospitable New Guinea terrain—vaulting up, swooping down, strangling with its dense underbrush.

A few scenes—an explorer frantically hacking leeches in an emotional binge, or hordes of flies swarming around the heads of the men—are repellent, however pertinent to all the grim documentation. Regrettably, the calm English narration delivered by William Peacock gets a bit coy and patronizing in spots, but this is a decidedly minor flaw. Georges Arnstam's editing dallies in a few places, but is plenty trenchant for the most part.

Strong exploitation and the Oscar laurel should get this one off the ground nicely in most situations, and the word-of-mouth should take over from there.
     Pit.

Madame Sans-Gene
(ITALO-FRENCH-SPANISH)
(Color)
Paris, June 19.
Cinedis release of GESI-Champion-Cine Alliance-Agata Films production. Stars Sophia Loren, Robert Hossein; features Renaud Mary, Marina Berti, Carlo Giuffre, Julien Bertheau. Directed by Christian-Jaque. Screenplay, Jean Ferry, Henri Jeanson, Christian-Jaque based on play by Victorien Sardou, Emile Moreau; camera (Technicolor), Roberto Gerardi; editor, Jacques Desagneau, Eraldo Da Roma. At Gaumont-Palace, Paris. Running time, **97 MINS.**
Madame Sans-Gene ...... Sophia Loren
Lefebvre .... Robert Hossein
Napoleon .... Julian Bertheau
Fouche .... Renaud Mary

Oscar-winner for role in "Two Women," Sophia Loren now gets a chance to play an earthy laundress of the Napoleonic times. Pic is a goodnatured, operetta-like romp. On its color, names and respectable production values, this could be an okay worldwide payoff item. But this film would need good-selling tactics while arty chances appear slim.

Miss Loren has been doing a little lieutenant's laundry for some time when the French Revolution breaks out. He is Napoleon but she loses sight of him. She falls

for a professional soldier, Robert Hossein, who she follows about. He is finally made a nobleman when Napoleon comes to full power.

Napoleon decides to make him a king of a territory coveted by his sisters. But Miss Loren's frank talk at court starts an incident that almost loses her man. But Napoleon recognizes her, and all is straightened out.

Film is tongue-in-cheek all the way. As such, it is fairly diverting. History is reduced to simple terms and there is no attempt to recreate the times. It is mainly a vehicle for Miss Loren's fiery, bosomy and earthy attributes and she acquits herself well. Others are adequate but she is the mainstay.

Director Christian-Jaque has given this a disarming, hokey treatment that makes it easy on the eyes with production rated okay. Battles are kept down to a personal exploit of Miss Loren and her hubby while court scenes are properly lush.

In short, this is an oldfashioned costumer with enough inventiveness to give it the finish that could make it a good item in today's actioner marts. Color is good as are technical credits. Title literally means "Mrs. Flippant."
     Mosk.

Hermaids of Tiburon
(AQUASCOPE-COLOR)

For lower berth purposes, adequate underwater meller.

Hollywood, June 13.
Filmgroup release of John Lamb production. No stars. Directed and screenplay by Lamb; camera (Eastman), Lamb, Hal McAlpin, Brydon Baker; editor, Bert Honey; music, Richard La Salle. Reviewed at Pix Theatre, June 13, '62. Running time, **77 MINS.**
Mermaid Queen .... Diane Webber
Dr. Samuel Jamison ..... George Rowe
Milo Sangster .... Timothy Carey
Pepe Gallardo ...Jose Gonzales-Gonzales
Ernst Steinhauer .... John Mylong
Senor Barquero .... Gil Baretto
Mermaids ....Vicki Kantenwine, Nani Morrissey, Judy Edwards, Jean Carroll, Diana Cook, Karen Goodman, Nancy Burns

Dramatically it is little more than a glorified "Sea Hunt," but John Lamb's production of "The Mermaids Of Tiburon" has enough eye appeal and pure escapist value to serve usefully as a running mate on exploitation packages designed for hit-and-run saturation bookings.

Lamb's uncomplicated scenario has two men—a marine biologist and a killer—scouting the coastal waters of the remote Mexican island of Tiburon in search of "fire" pearls. The former is befriended by a local sorority of giggly mermaids who come to his aid in a mortal debate with the ruthless heavy. While all of this is transpiring, a hackneyed narration keeps intruding with pretentious mumbo jumbo about believing in mermaids, Darwin's theory, and other such unnecessarily grand observations.

Although the novelty of underwater photography has worn off, Lamb's Eastman Color-Aquascope views of marine activity are, by and large, superior to his surface views of human activity. The actors seem to take on added stature and dignity down in the bubble-up. It's the

water that makes them good. George Rowe plays the biologist, Timothy Carey the killer, Jose Gonzales-Gonzales an ill-fated Mexican skipper. The mermaid queen is played by Diane Webber, a gorgeous dish of fish.

Richard La Salle's score has an exotic Latin flavor, and adds helpful dramatic punctuation marks to the action. Other production credits on the Filmgroup release are satisfactory. *Tube.*

The Notorious Landlady

Comedy-suspense meller in which the comedy is sporadic and the suspense is contrived. But, thanks mostly to Jack Lemmon, there are some worthwhile rewards. Enough going for it to shape up as likely good moneymaker.

Hollywood, June 20.

Columbia Pictures release of Fred Kohlmar production. Stars Kim Novak, Jack Lemmon, Fred Astaire. Directed by Richard Quine. Screenplay, Larry Gelbart, Blake Edwards, based on story by Margery-Sharp; camera, Arthur Arling; editor, Charles Nelson; music, George Duning; assistant director, Carter De-Haven Jr. Reviewed at Directors Guild Theatre, June 20, '62. Running time, **127 MINS.**

Carlye Hardwicke .... Kim Novak
William Gridley .... Jack Lemmon
Franklyn Ambruster .... Fred Astaire
Inspector Oliphant...... Lionel Jeffries
Mrs. Dunhill .... Estelle Winwood
Miles Hardwicke .... Maxwell Reed
Mrs. Brown .... Philippa Bevans
Stranger .... Henry Daniell
Coroner .... Ronald Long
Lady Fallott .... Doris Lloyd
Dillings .... Richard Feel
Ambruster's Secretary Florence Wyatt
Elderly Colonel ..... Frederick Worlock
Carstairs .... Dick Crockett
Henry .... Scott Davey
Counsel .... Jack Livesey
Coroner's Officer ...... Tom Dillon
Man .... Benno Schneider
Old Man .... Carter DeHaven Sr.
Woman .... Cecil Weston

"The Notorious Landlady" is a comedy-suspense melodrama, somewhat akin in essence and style to "Arsenic and Old Lace." Unlike its distant theatrical ancestor, however, the Fred Kohlmar production is neither sound enough as a mystery nor consistently merry enough as a comedy. But Columbia need not fret too much over such disparaging comparisons. For, "Landlady" is fortunate to have in its employ Jack Lemmon, thanks to whose comic perception, the picture has some scattered moments of notable comedy. These and the potent marquee trio of Lemmon-Kim Novak-Fred Astaire insure the Columbia release of a healthy boxoffice response.

Screenplay, concocted by Larry Gelbart and Blake Edwards from a story by Margery Sharp, deals with the plight of a Yankee foreign service diplomat (Lemmon) newly-arrived in London, who becomes implicated in some confusing homicidal shenanigans involving his landlady (Miss Novak). Seems the landlady is suspected of having done in her husband, who has disappeared. In the midst of a budding Novak-Lemmon romance, the "dead" hubby shows up, only to be plugged for real by his wife in a scuffle over some gems he had pilfered and she had pawned.

In the ensuing trial, Miss Novak's neck is saved by the "witness" testimony of a neighboring nurse, who actually has designs on the jewels herself, but is apprehended in the nick of time in a furious three-ply alternating climactic sequence marked by: (1) an up-and-down helicopter ride, (2) a slugging match between Miss Novak and the bad nurse, (3) a wild chase, with Lemmon desperately pursuing a runaway wheelchair containing the nurse's intended victim, Estelle Winwood.

Although the mystery plot is completely contrived and doesn't hold together, and the comedy comes only in occasional clusters and is largely manufactured on the spot by the resourceful Lemmon, the screenplay by Gelbart and Edwards does have some bright and witty lines, and there are one or two hilarious little scenes that have been executed with savvy under the guidance of director Richard Quine. For example, there's a memorable moment when the chopper must come down to earth so that its driver can restore his geographical bearings by asking directions of a farmer.

Miss Novak's latitude of expression remains narrow, but she utilizes her emotional resources to what appears maximum advantage on this outing. Coupled with her sexy attitude and natural physical endowments, it gets her by in the role. Astaire is adequate as Lemmon's diplomat employer. Supporting cast, almost entirely British, is accomplished, with major assists coming from Lionel Jeffries, Miss Winwood, Maxwell Reed and Philippa Bevans.

George Duning's score utilizes several well-known pop tunes to advantage, and is consistently helpful in its punctuation of both suspense and comedy facets. His incorporation of Gilbert & Sullivan patter-type melodies into a band concert during the climactic chase passage is an inspired addition to the scene's humorous momentum and impact.

Arthur Arling's photography and Charles Nelson's editing are satisfactory, and art director Cary Odell has managed to capture the London flavor in his Hollywood sets. Miss Novak designed her own gowns. Some of them are both smart and flattering. But, of course, Miss Novak the actress has a way of making Miss Novak the designer look good just by being inside those gowns. *Tube.*

The Wild Westerners
(COLOR)

Routine western with production values.

Hollywood, June 21.

Columbia Pictures release of Sam Katzman production. Stars James Philbrook, Nancy Kovack, Duane Eddy, Guy Mitchell. Directed by Oscar Rudolph. Screenplay, Gerald Drayson Adams; camera (Eastman), Gordon Avil; editor, Jerome Thoms; music, Duane Eddy; asst. director, Sam Nelson. Reviewed at the studio, June 21, '62. Running time, **70 MINS.**

U.S. Marshal Jim McDowell
.... James Philbrook
Rose Sharon .... Nancy Kovack
Deputy Marshal Clint Fallon Duane Eddy
Deputy Johnny Silver .... Guy Mitchell
Chief U.S. Marshal Reuben Bernard
.... Hugh Sanders
Crystal Plummer ...... Elizabeth MacRae
Sheriff Henry Plummer....Marshall Reed
Governor John Bullard..... Nestor Paiva
Judas .... Harry Lauter
Deputy Marshal Casey Banner Bob Steele
Yellow Moon .... Ilse Burkert
Ashley Cartwright .... Terry Frost
Wasna .... Hans Wedemeyer
Hanna .... Don Harvey
Martha Bernard......Elizabeth Harrower
Lulu .... Frances Osborne
Reverend Thomas .... Tim Sullivan
Jake .... Pierce Lyden
Sam Clay .... Joe McGuinn
Moose .... Charles Horvath
Lily .... Marjorie Stapp

Assembly line western out of producer Sam Katzman's instant-movies enterprise. But compactness of length and Eastman Color embellishment bring utility value and a veneer of expense to the Columbia release, it will make an adequate companion item where cinematic doubledeaders are still welcomed in spite of flip-flops in quality from A to B halves of the program.

Written by Gerald Drayson Adams, the screenplay describes hardships encountered in the Montana Territory of 1864 by U.S. marshals attempting to transport gold to the east to aid the Union cause. Central characters in the tale are one of the marshals (James Philbrook) and his bride (Nancy Kovack) who has tricked him into wedlock but proves her mettle and earns his respect and affection in the course of several skirmishes, first with Indians, later with outlaws. The gold-hungry outlaws are led by a sneaky sheriff, giving the baddies access to inside information until he overplays his hand.

Philbrook and Miss Kovack are satisfactory central figures. Duane Eddy wins no acting awards as a mixed up deputy marshal, nor does Guy Mitchell as a heavy whose characterization is as black as his outfit. Key support comes from Hugh Sanders, Elizabeth MacRae, Marshall Reed, Bob Steele and Ilse Burkert. Oscar Rudolph's direction reflects the production haste and stringency.

Gordon Avil's photography is fine, but upper echelon decisions to edit in old footage of Indian raids apparently borrowed from fancier western productions of the past result in visual distractions, distortions and sharp color discrepancies. Otherwise, various departmental contributions to the film are acceptable. *Tube.*

The Tartars
(ITALIAN—COLOR)

Unsatisfactory exploitation meller. Dim b.o. prospect.

Hollywood, June 19.

Metro release of Lux Films production. Stars Victor Mature, Orson Welles. Directed by Richard Thorpe. Screenplay, Domenico Salvi, Sabatino Ciuffini, Oreste Palella, Mario Frattini, Ambrogio Molteni, Julian de Kassel; camera (Technicolor), Amerigo Gengarelli; editor, Maurizio Lucidi; music, Renzo Rossellini; asst. directors, Giorgio Gentili, Ambrogio Molteni. Reviewed at the studio, June 19, '62. Running time, **83 MINS.**

Oleg .... Victor Mature
Burundai .... Orson Welles
Helga .... Liana Orfei
Ciu Ling .... Arnoldo Foa
Eric .... Luciano Marin
Samia .... Bella Cortez
Sigrun .... Furio Meniconi
Togrul .... Folco Lulli

This is another of those exploitation items from Italy. It took six screenwriters to create it. Two screen warhorses, Victor Mature and Orson Welles, costar in the Lux Film production and that should supply the necessary marquee bait to bring out the usual escapist customer who attends these overstuffed extravaganzas. The Metro release, serviceable as another temporary plug in the Hollywood product breach, doesn't figure beyond that.

The story traces the clash of the wicked, barbaric Tartars and the peaceful Vikings in medieval Russia. Mature plays the Viking chieftain, Welles the Tartar chieftain. Each camp holds a beautiful hostage, and they are treated as one might expect. The film does not clearly resolve the political situation, favoring instead the romantic angle. At the finish, both Mature and Welles are dead, the Viking fortress is in flames, and Vikings and Tartars are hacking away at each other ferociously, whilst two young lovers (Romeo

Viking and Juliet Tartar) are slipping off together up the lazy Volga in the noonday sun.

Pretty crude and stilted to begin with, performances come out even poorer through the added handicap of poet-dubbing. Watching Mature and Welles, one feels the same sense of regret as that inspired by the spectacle of viewing two ex-world-heavyweight champions battling it out on the comeback trail for the Eastern Yugoslavian title. Richard Thorpe's direction is of little appreciable dramatic aid. The physcal production dwarfs the story. *Tube.*

The Webster Boy
(BRITISH)

Lower half item largely saved by a sound cast. Wobbly box-office prospects.

London, June 19.
Regal International release of Emmet Dalton production. Stars John Cassavetes, Elizabeth Sellars, David Farrar; features Niall MacGinnis, Geoffrey Bayldon, Richard O'Sullivan. Directed by Don Chaffey. Screenplay by Ted Allan from a story of Leo Marks; camera, Gerrard Gibbs; editor, John Trumper; music, Wilfred Joseph. At Plaza Theatre, London. Running time, 83 MINS.
Vance Miller .... John Cassavetes
Margaret Webster ..... Elizabeth Sellars
Paul Webster .... David Farrar
Jimmy Webster ..... Richard O'Sullivan
Headmaster .... Niall MacGinnis
Charles Jamieson ..... Geoffrey Bayldon
Michael Johnson ...... Karl Lanchbury
Alfred Baxter .... John Bull
Donald Saunders .... Norman Rodway
Grant .... Harry Brogan
Alvin Roberts .... John Geary
Vic .... Seymour Casse
Mary .... Aideen O'Kelly

This drama is an unexpectedly unimpressive affair to command the services of thesps of the calibre of John Cassavetes, Elizabeth Sellars and David Farrar. But it's as well that they are on hand for they make a conscientious and fairly successful attempts to bring conviction to the screenplay.

Yarn concerns an American gambler who, after a term in the cooler, returns to England to try and take up again with the girl he gave the air some 14 years before. But she has since married and has a 14-year-old son. The gambler's efforts to get the woman back bring jealousy and upset to the household.

It also has a bad effect on the boy, who gets to the point when he isn't sure which of the two men is his real father. Most of the action takes place in school where he is the victim of bullying by senior boys and a brutally sadistic master.

Although the dramatic premise of this idea is okay it is not worked out with sufficient intensity. And it is never made fully clear if there is any justification for believing that the youngster is illegitimate. There's some touches of naivety and psuedo psychology in the dialog while a number of lines earn unwanted laughter.

Don Chaffey's direction is not as sure of touch as usual but overall the cast acquits itself well. John Cassavetes brings charm and authority to the role of the gambler. David Farrar delivers with a soundly convincing show as the serious jealous husband. Elizabeth Sellars hasn't great opportunities as the wife torn between the two men, but turns in a nicely rounded performance.

Richard O'Sullivan handles the role of the bewildered, frightened youngster admirably. There is a brilliantly odious piece of work by Geoffrey Balydon as a sick-minded, sadistic schoolmaster.

The lensing and settings are authentic though the school itself seems a very rumly-run place. *Rich.*

Karlovy Fest

Devyat Dney Odnogo Goda
(9 Days of Year)
(RUSSIAN)

Karlovy Vary, June 19.
Mosfilm production and release. Stars Alexei Batalov, Innokenti Smoktunovsky; features Nikolay Plotnikov. Directed by Mikhail Romm. Screenplay, Romm, Danil Khrabrovitsky; camera, Gherman Lavrov; editor, D. Tatevskaya. At Karlovy Vary Film Fest. Running time, 110 MINS.
Dmitry .... Alexei Batalov
Lelya .... Innokentu Smoktunovsky
Illya .... Nikolay Plotnikov

Film deals with nine of the key days in the life of a young thurmo-nuclear scientist who has been severely injured by overexposure to radiation. It has style and does away with flag-waving or mock heroics to make this a fine drama. However, its talky aspects and theme have this mainly for some specialized spots abroad.

Though warned not to expose himself anymore, his absorption in his work lead to an inadvertent step and an intensifying of his illness. Meanwhile, he has married a girl and his sickness and involvement in his work almost ruin their marriage.

However, they are reconciled and film ends as he decides to undergo an operation that has only been performed on dogs, and then not always successfully. The scientist offers his dedication as something he has to do for humanity. However, this is handled with tact.

There is also a sheen in the characterizations and poking fun at over-indulged scientists. Alexei Batalov, as the probably doomed man, has a restraint that makes his role ring true. Innokenti Smoktunovsky is svelte, femme, being well groomed in a change from the usual Russo heroine.

Mikhail Romm's polished direction makes this an adult drama that veers more towards dealing with its characters' individual outlook. On this alone it might be worth specialized release in certain foreign spots. Film is technically excellent. *Mosk.*

Karami-Ai
(The Inheritance)
(JAPAN)

Karlovy Vary, June 19.
Schochiku production and release. Stars Keiko Kishi; features So Yamamura, Misake Watanabe, Minoru Chiaki. Directed by Masaki Kobayashi. Screenplay, Koichi Inigaki; camera, Ko Kawamata; editor, S. Miyaki. At Karlovy Vary Film Fest. Running time, 107 MINS.
Jasuko .... Keiko Kishi
Senzo .... Misake Watanabe
Clerk .... So Yamamura
Marie .... Minoru Chiaki

This pic again indulges in the Japanese penchant for probing corruption and man's actions under impending death. Clinical outlook make this reminiscent of "Ikiru"

and "Odd Obsession." This looms as an arty entry, at best, because of its unrelieved look at human pettiness.

A dying industrial magnate expresses the desire to see three illegitimate children he has never known. His young wife plots with a lawyer to discourage this and his secretary, living in his home, is dragged into things when the dying man makes her his mistress.

She finally ends up with the inheritance. But even she, seemingly decent, has lied, to win out. Most characters are fairly unsavory, but the concise visual impact and the fine acting make this a searing look at corruption.

Scope is used with an expert feeling. This harsh if absorbing pic may be somewhat too forthright for Western patrons. *Mosk.*

Slnceto I Sjankata
(Sun and Shadow)
(BULGARIAN)

Karlovy, Vary, June 10.
Bulgaro Film production and release. With Anna Prucnalova, Dimo Kolarov. Directed by Rangel Vylchanov; screenplay, Valerij Petrov; editor, R. Lindalinov. At Karlovy Vary Film Fest. Running time, 70 MINS.
Girl .... Anna Prucnalova
Boy .... Dimo Kolarov

This story of the chance meeting at a Bulgar beach resort between a local boy and a girl from some Western country is unfolded as a poetic love affair. There are overtones of fear for Atomic annihilation which overshadow their idyll. Knowing direction, fine acting and expert visual conception make this a film with arty chances abroad.

The girl is headstrong, pretty and tender while the lad is direct and solid. He has a belief in life against the fear of death emerging as their relationship grows. A series of simple scenes is used to point up their characters and feelings. The girl confides her fear of war and world destruction while the boy maintains man will never do this again. Her intensity and sensibility bring on a hallucination about the effects of the Atomic Bomb on the beach that is shattering in its intensity. They finally decide that as long as man is in danger of war they will be separated.

The director shows a flair for using symbols that help build this into a non-partisan plea against war. Anna Prucnalova is fetching as the obsessed girl while Dima Kolarov is properly strong as the boy. This is technically fine, an unusual little film that manages to mix its themes adroitly. *Mosk.*

Felmegyek A Ministerhez
(I'll Go to the Minister)
(HUNGARIAN)

Karlovy Vary, June 19.
Hungarofilm production and release. With Antal Pager, Itala Bekes, Laszlo Banhidy. Directed by Frigyes Ban. Screenplay, Zoltan Galabardi, Miklos Markos; camera, Ference Szecsenyi; editor, R. Szecsenyi. At Karlovy Vary Film Fest. Running time, 90 MINS.
Balogh .... Antal Pager
Wife .... Itala Bekes
Minister .... Laszlo Banhidy

Attempt at a lighthearted look at one farmer who holds out from

a collective, this is too heavy-footed to have the comedics take effect. Film plays it both ways, in having the man finally join up and also put in a plea for individual workers, too. Thus it appears mainly a local item. The holdout is a crafty fellow who manages to get to the Minister of Agriculture and return to his home town in triumph.

Direction and acting are conventional, this lacking the fillip to bring it off. *Mosk.*

Celebrul 702
(The Famous 702)
(ROUMANIAN)

Karlovy Vary, June 19.
Bucaresti Film production and release. With Radu Beligan, Ion Tintesteano, Sanda Toma. Directed by Mihai Iacob. Screenplay, Alexandru Mirodan, Iacob; camera, Andrei Feher; editor, D. Ionesco. At Karlovy Vary Film Fest. Running time, 90 MINS.
Kid .... Radu Beligan
Diana .... Sanda Toma
Harrison .... Ion Tintesteano

This satire on the so-called American Way of Life is reviewed mainly for the record. Its lack of true invention or snap make it dubious for export. And its attempts at poking fun at certain aspects of Yank life are done better by American filmmakers themselves.

It takes place in a prison cell. Obviously a Yank in cell 702 writes a bestseller and his execution is held up. He gets a fancy cell with all modern conveniences. He finally decides to write a book that will tell all about the corruption.

The takeoffs on tele commercials, the characterizations, the chases and the whole comedic outlook just do not jell. There is nothing wicked in this. It just simply is minus the knowhow and the insight.

Shown at the Eastern Bloc film fest, Karlovy Vary, it had Easterners as well as Western spectators ankling en masse. *Mosk.*

The Pigeon That Took Rome

Writer-producer-director Mel Shavelson provides a comedy carefully plotted for the world market. It's realistically set in World War II Italy, has some fun for all. Offers Charlton Heston in a switch from the Biblicals. Boxoffice response should be simpatico.

Paramount release of Llenroc production; produced, directed and written by Melville Shavelson. Stars Charlton Heston, Elsa Martinelli; features Harry Guardino, Salvatore Baccaloni, Marietto, Gabriella Pallotta, Debbie Price, Brian Donlevy. Camera, Daniel Papp; editor, Frank Bracht; music, Allesandra Cicognini. In New York June 20, 1962. Running time, **101 MINS.**

Capt. Paul MacDougall Charlton Heston
Antonella Massimo ...... Elsa Martinelli
Sgt. Joseph Contini .. Harry Guardino
Ciccio Massimo ..... Salvatore Baccaloni
Livio Massimo .... Marietto
Rosalba Massimo ..... Gabriella Pallotta
Luigina .... Debbie Price
Col. Sherman Harrington Brian Donlevy
Monsignor O'Toole .... Arthur Shields
The General .... Bob Gandett
Oberst Wilhelm Krafft . Rudolph Anders

On his own after the partnership splitup with Jack Rose, Melville Shavelson functions as producer, director and writer and shows good control in all three categories with "Pigeon That Took Rome." This is a good-fun comedy and there's no incongruity in the fact that the setting is authentic-looking World War II Italy. Indeed, the backgrounds are reminiscent of Italy's own "Shoe Shine," "Open City," etc., staging.

Shavelson theorized that the typical American comedy, with either highly polished dialog or out and out slapstick, too often has only intramural stateside appeal. His adaptation of "The Easter Dinner," a novel by Donald Downes, clearly is an endeavor to broaden the acceptance scope without impairing the domestic impact. He has come up with a wacky story that plays out amusingly well and is one that should be nicely received at home and abroad.

Interesting casting has to do with Charlton Heston, ex-Moses, ex-Ben-Hur, ex-El Cid, who's now an American infantry officer assigned to a cloak-and-dagger role in Rome before the Nazis decide to leave and the Yanks walk in. It comes to be that homing pigeons represent his contact with the Allies. His birds provide an Easter dinner for a local and friendly family who do not know they're partaking of a part of "the American Air Force," as stated by one of the characters. Heston becomes replenished with German pigeons, gives them ankle bracelets with false war information, and one of these messengers heads unexpectedly to the Allies, instead of the enemy. Rhyme and reason are elusive but the misinformation received by, but unintended for, the Allies makes the taking of Rome an easy conquest.

Heston plays the bewildered American officer with enough effectiveness to suggest that he can be at home with cinematic mischief and he doesn't always have to be linked with the Biblicals and/or historicals. Harry Guardino is Heston's radio man, a sort of funny fellow sidekick who becomes enamored of a local girl who happens to be pregnant by previous misfortune. He gets her, Gabriella Pallotta, to the church on time—that is, they get married.

Elsa Martinelli is Heston's romantic vis-a-vis, not one easily won over but eventually, of course, they go hand in hand. Salvatore Baccaloni, as might be expected of an oldtime opera basso buffo, takes all opportunities to upstage everybody as Papa of the local Italian family enmeshed with the Americanos.

Livio Massimo is the age 10 member of the Italian clan, capable of stealing anybody's pigeons; Brian Donlevy is a ramrod kind of American colonel from West Point, and Arthur Shields is a caricature of an Irish priest.

Rudolpf Anders plays a Nazi officer with appropriate ludicrousness.

Shavelson has gotten into the 101 minutes of running time some good, imaginative humor. He has his picture rolling without pause and endowed it with witty dialog and script situations. The performances are savvy, the editing sharp and the music, used to bridge one scene to another, correctly functional. *Gene.*

Panic In Year Zero

A family struggles for survival after nuclear attack. Skillfully made exploitation pic.

American International release of Lou Rusoff - Arnold Houghland production. Stars Ray Milland, Jean Hagen, Frankie Avalon, Mary Mitchel. Directed by Milland. Screenplay, Jay Simms, John Morton, from story by Simms; camera, Gil Warrenton; editor, William Austin; music, Les Baxter; assistant director, Jim Engle. Reviewed at Academy Awards Theatre, June 27, '62. Running time, **92 MINS.**

Harry Baldwin .... Ray Milland
Ann Baldwin .... Jean Hagen
Rick Baldwin .... Frankie Avalon
Karen Baldwin .... Mary Mitchel
Marilyn Hayes .... Joan Freeman
Mr. Johnson .... Richard Garland
Carl .... Richard Bakalyan
Mickey .... Rex Holman
Andy .... Neil Nephew
I'. Strong .... Willis Buchet
Hogan .... O. Z. Whitehead
Haenel .... Byron Morrow
Mrs. Johnson .... Shary Marshall
Harkness .... Russ Bender
Becker .... Hugh Sanders

The aftermath of a nuclear attack is the morbidly fashionable subject pursued by this serious, sobering and engrossing film. The topic is unpleasant enough to repel one kind of customer, exploitable enough to attract another kind. Through imaginative, but not frivolously sensational selling, this American International release, produced by Lou Rusoff and Arnold Houghland, might break the exploitation barrier and reach a sizeable portion of the more discriminating audience as well.

The screenplay by Jay Simms and John Morton, from a story by the former, advances the theory that, in the event of a sudden wholesale outbreak of nuclear warfare, civilization will swiftly deteriorate into a decentralized society of individual units, each necessarily hostile in relations with all others as part of a desperate struggle for self-preservation. A family unit of four—father, mother and two teenaged children—is followed here in the wake of a series of initial nuclear blasts destroying Los Angeles and four other major U.S. cities (excluding Washington—a rather astonishing oversight on the part of the unspecified enemy). The family is followed to an isolated cave in the hills where, thanks to the father's negative ingenuity, it remains until it is safe to come out and return home for the enormous task of rebuilding. The family has plenty of scars, physical and emotional, to show for its experience.

Ray Milland manages capably in the dual task of director and star (he's the resourceful father), but it's safe to observe that he'd probably have done twice as well by halving his assignment, one way or the other. Jean Hagen fashions a sincere delineation of the perturbed mother. Frankie Avalon, for the most part, does nicely as the son. Mary Mitchel (the daughter) and Joan Freeman are satisfactory in roles with one thing in common—both are raped. Richard Bakalyan, Rex Holman and Neil Nephew add menace as three young punks, and Richard Garland, Willis Buchet and O. Z. Whitehead score in key character portrayals.

General level of production skill is efficient, but Les Baxter's background score is a bit too obtrusively racy in spots. Among the sound journeyman assists are those of cameraman Gil Warrenton, editor William Austin, art director Daniel Haller and special effects men Pat Dinga and Larry Butler. *Tube.*

El Cuerpo y la Sangre
(The Body and the Blood)
(CHILEAN)

Santiago, July 3.
Catholic University Film Institute Production. Features Monica Sotomayor, Silvia Pileiro, Eva Knobel, Ines Alonzo, Nelly Meruane, Elena Moreno, Josse van der Rest. S. J. Jorge Boudon and Mario Lorca. Direction and screenplay, Rafael C. Sanchez S.J.; camera, Andres Martorell and Rene Kocher; music, Juan Lemann. Previewed, June 23. Running time, **93 MINS.**

This film's objective is to explain the meaning of the Mass. Developed on a double level it is part documentary and part fiction.

The documentary element is provided by Josse van der Rest S. J. officiating mass at the Vitacura church, a good setting thanks to its modern design and severe beauty. This is interwoven with a plot based on everyday incidents and family life, whose aim is the clarification of the lyturgical symbols.

Made at a cost of $30,000, it is the Catholic University Film Institute's first feature. The cast consists of legit actors and Monica Sotomayor, a seven year old moppet. Acting is only adequate and players' inexperience in films is evident. On the other hand, lensing and editing reach a better level than usual in local product.

Pic should do well predominantly Catholic audiences, but its chances on general release are limited. *Chili.*

El Joven Rebelde
(The Young Rebel)
(CUBAN)

Sestri Levante, June 26.
Cuban Institute of Arts and Industry production. Directed by Julio G. Espinosa. Screenplay, Cesare Zavattini; camera, Juan Marine. With Blas Mora, Reinaldo Mirevalles, Angel Espasande. At Cinema Latino Americano. Running time, **90 MINS.**

As Cuban feature films, this seems to have been made with the artistic aid of European artists. This looks more palatable than some documentaries, and to have less propaganda. In "Young Rebel" there is only a mention of Castro and he is not built into a Father of the Revolution. The anti-hero is a young boy who runs away from home to join the rebels in the mountains. He arrives with the required rifle, but is disappointed when he does not find adventure and action. It is drill and discipline, rationed food. And when there is at last a battle, the boy is neither scared nor brave.

A veteran of the pre-Castro days, director Espinosa apparently has learned that all war films run along the same line. The first part, however, thanks probably to the script by Italian Cesare Zavattini, has brilliant touches. It gives a good insight into the character of the "young rebel." Acting and technical credits are good. Film will rate only as a curiosity item for film clubs. *Saal.*

Tres Veces Ana
(Three Times Anna)
(ARGENTINE)

Sestri Levante, June 26.
A Marcello Simonetti production. Directed by David Jose Kohon. Screenplay, Kohon; camera, Ricardo Aronovich; editor, Antonio Ripoll. With Maria Vaner, Walter Vidarte, Alberto Argibay, Luis Medina Castro, Lautaro Murua. At Cinema Latino Americano. Running time, **115 MINS.**

Three times Anna means three sketches in which a character named Anna is featured. The first, called Earth, gives a down-to-earth Anna, in love with a clerk. The idyl is broken when she becomes pregnant. Second one, The Air, is located among beach beatnicks. Here Anna is an easy-going girl, unstable, and looking for kicks. The third Anna, in the sketch, The Cloud, exists only in the mind of a timid layout man on a newspaper.

Director Jose Kohon has tried to pace his film according to the mood of the different stories, quick for the second part, very slow and meditative for the third. To use the same actress in three different roles might seem a tour de force, but here it only results in forced acting. The characters of the men opposite Anna are better drawn.

The film could have some chance for distribution outside South America, but film should be cut by at bit and the order of the sequences altered so that dramatic impact is stressed. Technical credits are very good. *Saal.*

Realengo 18
(Commune 18)
Sestri Levante, June 26.
Cuban Institute of Arts and Industry production. Directed by Oscar Torres (in association with Eduardo Manet). Camera, Harry Tanner; music, Enrique Ubieta. With Tete Vergara, Rene de la Cruz, Pablo Ruiz Castellanos, Ester Guerra, Rita Limonta, Coraldo Gonzales. At Rassegna del Cinema Latino Americano, Sestri Levante, Italy. Running time, **60 MINS.**

One of the first feature films to be produced in Cuba after the revolution, this special item is remarkably restrained in its conceptions. The one American who appears may seem a little ridiculous but no extra effort seems to have been made to picture him as a villain.

Story develops in a village during the '30's when, in the Realengo 18, the workers rebelled against the government. One of the leaders, a simple coffee picker, is killed by the army, in which his son has enlisted.

It is a simple pic, interesting because of its origin, and surprisingly well acted and directed. In style, it can be best compared with Russian films of the early '20's. Plot could easily be defined as a twisted adaptation of Gorki's "The Mother." *Saal.*

Berlin Festival

The Duel
(DANISH)
Berlin, June 26.
Nordisk Films Kompagni production and release. Stars Frits Helmuth, Malene Schwartz, John Price. Directed and screenplay by Knud Leif Thomsen. Camera, Henning Kristiansen; music, Ib Glindemann. At Berlin Film Fest. Running time, **105 MINS.**

"The Duel" is currently one of Denmark's top boxoffice draws, and is well above average quality of the output from that small film-producing nation. Knud Leif Thomsen's direction and screenplay are on sure grounds when he's handling the boy-meets-girl aspect in the first half. But it is less confident when the plot switches to heavy melodramatics later.

There is an ingenious twist to the plot in which a film director is faced in real life with a mythical situation he had been developing in a picture. Frits Helmuth, as a medical student making a buck on the side by playing the piano in a strip joint, becomes wildly jealous when he discovers the girl he loves (Malene Schwartz) had previously had an affair with her film-director boss. He challenges the latter to a duel.

The appealing atmosphere of the earlier part of the yarn is not sustained, however, partly through script weaknesses. The second half is also too long, and could be improved by discreet editing.

Principal performances are okay, especially the femme role which is played with considerable charm and warmth by Malene Schwartz. Frits Helmuth makes a suitably moody medical student, though John Price tends to make the film director too much of a heavy. There is, by the way, a frank strip

scene which should provide a lively exploitation angle. *Myro.*

Las Hermanos
(The Sisters)
(ARGENTINIAN)
Berlin, June 26.
Argentina Sono Film (Buenos Aires) production. Stars Mirtha Legrand, Silvia Legrand. Directed by Daniel Tinayre. Screenplay, Silvina Bullrich from novel by Guy de Cars; camera, Alberto Etchebehero; music, Lucio Milena. At Berlin Film Fest. Running time, **125 MINS.**

Based on a French novel, this Argentinian selection for the Berlin festival is definitely a lower-case entry. It does little credit to the industry of that country. It is a melodramatic and novelettish yarn, largely predictable, with few redeeming qualities. Its length makes it something of an endurance test.

Plot unfolds in a series of prolonged flashbacks. Police call at a convent to interview a nun, whose twin sister, a mannequin of easy virtue, has been found murdered. It transpires that the girl had fallen for a pimp who had installed her in a luxury apartment. Later she meets a Spanish air attache whom she wants to marry, but cannot get out of the first man's clutches.

The denouement in which it is finally revealed that the procurer killed the twin sister, and that the mannequin had swapped her fashionable outfit for the nun's habit, lacks the element of surprise which was obviously intended. There are several continuity fluffs which do not help. Direction is generally on the slack side. The twin sisters are played by real-life twins, Mirtha and Silvia Legrand, both lookers. Other performances are just about adequate. *Myro.*

The Hands
(GREEK)
Berlin, June 29.
J. Roberts Productions release of a John G. Contes production. Stars Antouanette Rondopoulou, Alexander Mamatis, Agapi Evangellidi, Mary Vlissidi, Basil Maros, Basilis Gikas. Directed, written and edited by Contes. Camera, Fotis; music, Th. Antoniou. At Berlin Film Fest. Running time, **95 MINS.**

Opening titles explain that this is a symbolic picture, and that hands are one of God's greatest gifts to man. A final title says it is dedicated to "youth abandoned to the whirlwind of our time." In between there's 75 minutes of screen time filled in abstract style, without dialog, making it an extreme offbeater. Commercial prospects look dubious, though some film buffs may be intrigued or fascinated by its contents.

As the credit titles are being introduced, there's a background of bitter street battles, but the action which follows immediately has no relation to this intro. It is a calm sequence of young people enjoying a ball game on a beach. That's followed in turn by a number of scenes which might suggest that man's hands were really made for caressing women.

There is little attempt at characterization in the conventional sense, but there is emphasis on one man who has lived loosely, gets jailed for a killing, eventually returns to his faith, and finally dies in the war.

The continuity is by no means as concise as related in this outline. Most audiences are likely to be bewildered by it all. Technically it's okay, though some of the stock war footage does not match too well. *Myro.*

Tonny on the Wrong Road
(NORWEGIAN)
Berlin, June 29.
Ess-Film A/S (Oslo) production. Stars Per Christensen, Liv Ullmann. Directed by Nils R. Muller. Screenplay, Sverre Gran; camera, Hans Nord; music, Egil Monn-Iversen. At Berlin Film Fest. Running time, **87 MINS.**

Moderately entertaining meller from Norway, another country with limited filmmaking resources. It's mainly for local consumption, but could make the bottom half of a double bill.

In a superficial way, the script probes the mind of an unwanted child, the illegitimate son of a drunk and a prostie, who has never experienced parental love and inevitably winds up in reformatory, and then in prison. An attempt to go straight after a gaol stretch meets with predictable failure. His girl prefers an honest worker.

Direction is straightforward, camerawork is okay and principal performances are adequate for the simple needs of the story. *Myro.*

Il y a un Train Toutes les Heures
(There's a Train Every Hour)
(BELGIAN)
Berlin, June 26.
CBF (Brussels) release of a Cavens-Levie production. Stars Evelyne Axell, Stig Gerson. Directed by Andre Cavens. Screenplay, Theodore Louis. camera, Albert Le Berrurier; music, Nelly Le Berrurier. At Berlin Film Fest. Running time, **115 MINS.**

Feature production is quite a rarity for the Belgian film industry which usually confines its activities to making shorts and documentaries. This latest attempt, however, will do nothing to establish a reputation in the feature film field, for prospects outside its own territory must be regarded as negligible.

Directed in painfully slow tempo, the plot describes the emotions of a youngish wife whose married life is not all that it should be. So she takes a vacation on her own to get things sorted out, and meets a young man who offers the sort of companionship which she is denied at home. But she's determined to be a faithful wife, and insists on returning to her husband.

It's all very trite, not helped by embarrassingly poor dialog and indifferent performances. *Myro.*

The Weaver of Miracles
(MEXICAN)
Berlin, June 26.
Sagitario Films release of a Rafael Lebrija production. Stars Pedro Armendariz. Columbia Dominguez. Directed by Francisco del Villar. Screen adaptation by Julio Alejandro, Emilio Carballido, Humberto Robles from novel by Hugo Arguelles; camera, Gabriel Figueroa; music, Carlos Jimenez Mabarak. At Berlin Film Fest. Running time, **100 MINS.**

The fanaticism of ignorant peasants is the theme of Francisco del Villar's first feature film, and he has treated the subject thoughtfully and delicately. It's appeal, however, must be regarded as extremely limited. And the pic rates as only a modest arty bet, though it could play Spanish language theatres with some success.

Action takes place on Christmas Eve, and spans just a few hours. As the village is preparing for its festivities, a one-armed basket weaver seeks help and shelter for his wife who is in labor. The woman is taken in by the local midwife, who with an eye on the commercial possibilities, makes up a bed in the stable. The peasants believe they're participating in a latter-day miracle, and hysteria sweeps through the village, as they leave the church to pray outside the stable door.

Atmosphere is well established and neatly sustained. There are excellent mob scenes as the fanatical villagers sieze the new-born infant from its cot and take it to the church, to rest in the manger used earlier in the day for the nativity play. Final sequence in which the mother claims her child at the church, only to realize that it is dead, provides a vivid commentary on the effects of ignorance.

Though production qualities are okay, acting is somewhat uneven. Principal roles of midwife and her adopted son are heavily handled by Columbia Dominguez and Pedro Armendariz. Enrique Lucero gives an unrelieved study of the basket weaver. *Myro.*

Al Zouga Talattshar
(Wife No. 13)
(UNITED ARAB REPUBLIC)
Berlin, June 26.
Gamal El Leithy Films (Cairo) production. Stars Roushdi Abaza, Chadia, Hassan Fayek, Chewikar Sakkal. Directed by Fatin Abdel Wahab. Screenplay, Abul Soud El Libiary, Aly El Zorkani; camera, Kamal Kuriem. At Berlin Film Fest. Running time, **105 MINS.**

This is an unsophisticated comedy which will surely be a hit in the Arab-speaking territories, but it is unlikely to make much of an impact in Western markets.

Mourad Salem (Roushdi Abaza) is not only a very rich man, he's also a fast worker. He meets a local beauty on the beach at Alexandria, and soon he's hired her father as his manager. Within a day he's wedded.

But it takes much longer before his wife is bedded, for having learned from a jilted fiancee that she is wife No. 13, she is determined not to become divorcee No. 13. So by various subterfuges she withholds her favors from her husband.

There's not much subtlety about the plot, and the comedy is played on near-slapstick lines. It has pace and a few laugh situations. The acting, though exaggerated by Western standards, suits the mood of the production. *Myro.*

A Fulfilled Life
(JAPANESE)

Berlin, June 26.
Shochiku Company production and release. Stars Ineka Arima, Koshiro Harada. Directed by Susumu Hani. Screenplay, Hani and Kunio Shimizu; camera, Shigechei Nagano; music, Toru Takemitsu. At Berlin Film Fest.

Based on a novel by Tatsuzo Ishikawas, "A Fulfilled Life" is hampered by confused plotting and erratic cutting. The former fault may be attributable to the inadequacy of the German subtitles used for the presentation at the Berlin festival, at which it was the official Japanese entry. It's an unlikely prospect for the U. S. market.

Plot centers on a young actress, unhappily married and seeking a divorce, though her husband is still very much in love and is reluctant to let her go. Among the side issues woven into the main story line, are a demonstration against the Japanese security agreement with the U. S. Also the fate of a young widow who attempts suicide after her in-laws discover she has had an affair with a married man.

Direction appears slow and somewhat ponderous, and the performances are in the same key. Editing is most unsatisfactory with abrupt cuts from one scene to another disconcerting. *Myro.*

Pikku Pietarin Piha
(Little Presents)
(FINNISH)

Berlin, June 28.
Suomi Filmi Oy (Helsinki) presentation and release. Stars Leevi Kuuranne and Tuukka Tanner. Directed and scripted by Jack Witikka; camera, Yrjo Aaltonen; music, Simon Parmet. At Berlin Film Festival. June 27, '62. Running time, 74 MINS.

Heavily sentimental yarn about an orphan boy who yearns for maternal love, this Finnish contender at the Berlin fest is likely to have its main appeal within the Scandinavian markets, though it will have some attraction for unsophisticated audiences generally.

Though the film is kept down to 74 minutes, the story unspools leisurely against its rural background. The setting is a courtyard in a tiny village, and the action rarely moves out of that confined area. There is a warm and gentle sincerity to the plot, which gives it added appeal.

Acting is competent. There's a pleasantly restrained moppet performance by Tuukka Tanner, while Elsa Turakainen adequately portrays the mystery woman who is more like a fairy godmother than a step mother. *Myro.*

Karlovy Fest

Akee Kalimantan
(Operation Kalimantan)
(CZECH-INDONESIAN)
(Color)

Karlovy Vary, June 19.
Czech State Film-Indo Film production and release. With Bambang Hermanto, Martin Razek, Gustav Heverie. Directed by Vladimir Sis. Screenplay, Sis, S. Suryadarma; camera (Agfa), Josef Vanis; editor, H. Hejik. At Karlovy Vary Film Fest. Running time, 65 MINS.
Bitah .... Bambang Hermanto
Officer .... Martin Razek
Sutu .... Gustav Heverie

Czech technicians and a director made this pic in Indonesia to commemorate the early military operation that helped free Borneo from the Dutch. Film is artfully lensed but emerges the usual revolutionary war pic. It seems to be mainly for Asian or East-European consumption.

A patrol is parachuted from Java into Borneo. They lose their radio but fight their way through the jungles and manage to get a message into headquarters for eventual reinforcements. Dutch are conventional villians and the Indonesians properly heroic.

This is an okay actioner and its short length makes it easy to take. Some solid lensing, if too contrived, plus color, will help in its intended arts. *Mosk.*

Konigskinder
(Royal Children)
(EAST GERMAN)

Karlovy Vary, June 26.
DEFA production and release. With Annekatrin Burger, Arnin Mueller-Stahl, Ulrich Thein, Marga Legal Directed by Frank Beyer. Screenplay, E and W. Gorrish; camera, Gunter Marczinkowski; editor, Hildegarde Conrad. At Karlovy Vary Film Fest. Running time, 90 MINS.
Magdelena .... Annekatrin Burger
Michele .... Arnin Mueller-Stahl
Jugens .... Ulrich Thein
Mother .... Marga Legal

East Germany is still dealing with the fate of young communists under Nazism. But this has a disarming expressionistic look at love and war that holds its own with the propaganda content. However, it looms mainly Eastern Bloc fare.

Two boys and a girl, childhood friends, find the war leading them into a strange odyssey. One boy is in love with the girl. He is a communist and is jailed while the other one becomes a Nazi. The war brings the two men together in a disciplinary batallion on the Russian front while the girl is in Moscow learning how to eventually work with them in the takeover of Germany.

Director Frank Beyer shows a strong ability to suggest time and atmosphere simply, and has a dynamic style in battle scenes. This actually is neatly packaged propaganda that just lacks something. It is technically fine. Acting is good within the confines of the simple characterizations. *Mosk.*

Detstvo Ivana
(The Childhood of Ivan)
(RUSSIAN)

Karlovy Vary, June 26.
Mosfilm release of Gorki Studio production. With Kolia Bourliaiev, Z. Zoubkov, E. Jarikov, S. Krilov. Directed by Andrei Tarkowski. Screenplay, Vladimir Bogomolov, Mikhail Papava; camera, Vladimir Iousov; editor, L. Feiginovici. At Karlovy Vary Film Fest. Running time, 95 MINS.
Ivan .... Kolia Bourliaiev
Kolia .... Z. Zoubov
Galtsev .... E. Jarikov
Katssonov .... S. Krilov
Griasnov .... N. Griko

Earmarked by the Russians for a competing spot at the Venice Film Fest in August, this may make a mark for itself. It is a lyrical war pic like "Ballad of a Soldier" and "When the Cranes Are Flying." Its poetics, if sometimes measured, its sincere bravura and general simplicity tag this a pic with strong export chances.

The heroics are in keeping with a general look at war that destroys as well as marks men and children. Done in a flamboyant manner, it is saved by new director Andrei Tarkowski's obvious deep feeling for the subject.

A 12-year-old boy has seen his mother killed and has stayed behind to help the army by spying on th Germans. He is adopted by a captain who wants to send him off to school but the boy rebels and comes back. Pic details his happy thoughts of his early life and his mother.

Also depicted is a captain's love for a young femme medical soldier. Heroics are kept down but this has a rich use of camera editing and war's horror as well as its few acceptable features in making man more aware of himself.

Acting is smooth. The boy avoids any mawkishness while technical credits are firstrate. It is a measured but moving look at war through a marked child's eyes. *Mosk.*

Zalene Obzory
(Green Horizons)
(CZECH)

Karlovy Vary, June 26.
Czech State Film production and release. With Petr Kostka, Vaclav Lohnisky, Marie Tomasova, Jana Brejchova, Josef Patocka. Directed by Ivo Novak. Screenplay, Jan Prochazka, Novak; camera, Vaclav Hanus; editor, Karel Skvor. At Karlovy Vary Film Fest. Running time, 100 MINS.
Ondrej .... Petr Kostka
Cimler .... Vaclav Lohnisky
Marta .... Marie Tomasova
Jana .... Jana Brejchova
Musilek .... Josef Patocka

Young agronomist comes to a collective and wins over many people, but alienates others. In the end he is severely beaten by rough shirkers and drunkards, but the pic intimates he will come back as he goes off to the hospital. This appears primarily a local entry.

Film is just too corny in spite of the director's feel for the visual. It places too much emphasis on the collective and its holdouts. Hence, it is just an Eastern Bloc pic. It is technically fine. *Mosk.*

Barravento
(The Turning Wind)
(BRAZIL)

Karlovy Vary, June 26.
Iglu Films production and release. With Antonio Sampaio, Luiza Maranhao, Aldo Texeira, Lucy Carvalho. Written and directed by Glauber Rocha. Camera, Tony Rabatony; editor, Braga Neto. At Karlovy Vary Film Fest. Running time, 80 MINS.
Barravento .... Antonio Sampaio
Girl .... Luiza Maranhao
Fisherman .... Aldo Texeira
Daughter .... Lucy Carvalho

Made by a 20-year-old boy, this look at macumba religious rituals and the plight of the Negro fishermen exploited by white bosses is more well meaning than successful. It is only for a few lingo situations abroad.

Director Glauber Rocha lets the narration lag and powders it with too much macumba dance color. But he does manage to portray a little known aspect of Brazil. The cast is colored except for one girl and her father who live in the village. They all acquit themselves adequately. Technically the film is par. *Mosk.*

Dablova Past
(The Devil's Trap)
(CZECH)

Karlovy Vary, June 26.
Czech State Film production and release. With Vitezslav Vejraka, Miroslav Machacek, Vit Olmer, Karla Chadimova, Vlastimil Hasek, Cestmir Randa. Directed by Frantisek Vlecil. Screenplay, F. A. Dvorak, K. M. Kratochvil; camera, Rudolf Milic; editor, Miroslav Hajek. At Karlovy Vary Film Fest. Running time, 85 MINS.
Spaleny .... Vitezslav Vejraka
Probus .... Miroslav Machacek
Jan .... Vit Olmer
Martina .... Karla Chadimova
Filip .... Vlastimil Hasek
Regent .... Cestmir Randa

After the Ingmar Bergman's medieval, religioso pix, the Czechs now delve into a tale of 16th Century superstition and religion. It is handled with tact and flair for time, place and character. But this makes too much over about what turns out to be a slim subject. Film manages enough interest, and could be an arty entry abroad on its generally well-sustained tale.

A priest rides into a little town. He is really from the inquisition on a study about a supposed case of a pact with the Devil.

A miller's house had been burned down over 100 years ago but the family survived. Now the son of the originals and his son live in it. It has been rebuilt. The father is always looking for water and knows about the land. He even knows when a building will collapse. But his reasons are scientific and material, but the fanatic churchman pegs him a sorcerer.

The Czechs have given this a materialistic sheen and somewhat overplay it. But the fine acting, moody lensing and offkey use of sound for eerie effects plus fine production values and the well-told story make for good entertainment. *Mosk.*

Na Malenkom Ostrove
(On A Small Island)
(BULGARIAN)

Karlovy Vary, June 26.
Bulgarofilm production and release. With Ivan Kondov, Stefan Peichev. Directed by Rangel Valchanov. Screenplay, Valery Petrov; camera, Dimon Kolarov; editor, S. Peronkov. At Karlovy Vary Film Fest. Running time, 90 MINS.
Doctor .... Ivan Dondov
Kosta Rica .... Stefan Peichev
Sheko .... Konstantin Kostov
Student .... Ivan Andonov

The usual tale of men on an island penal colony, plus a flavoring of early Communist heroism, gets a positive push here via adroit direction and good pacing. It appears only for dualer chances abroad. A group of men in an aborted leftist uprising in the Bulgaria of 1923 are imprisoned on an island and controlled by a sadistic, militaristic captain. Film details a group of aborted escapes and the final uprising.

If the characters are stereotyped there is a gusto that makes this eminently worthwhile.

Rangel Valchanov's sharp direction, the cohesive acting, the solid technical values hint that little Bulgaria may be a rising film producing country in the Eastern Bloc and one to be heard once they leave the revolutionary films behind. *Mosk.*

Tlayucan
(MEXICAN)

Karlovy Vary, June 26.
Matouk production and release. With Julio Aldama, Jorge Martinez, Norma Angelica, Anita Blanch, Noe Murayama, Andres Soler. Written and directed by Luis Alcoriza. Camera, Rosalio Solano; editor, Carlos Savage. At Karlovy Vary Film Fest. Running time, **105 MINS.**
Husband .... Julio Aldama
Priest .... Jorge Martinez
Wife .... Norma Angelica
Spinster .... Anita Blanch
Blind Man .... Noe Murayama
Don Carlos .... Andres Soler

Folk saga of a little Mexican village has an added asset in the deep insight into motives and actions of this crucible pueblo which is poor, but a mecca for tourists. It looms a definite Latino language entry abroad. Pic could be an arty bet if well handled.

Local priest is hard on the poor peasants for their lateness in paying for local fetes and pilgrimages. But when a sick boy has a distraught father failing to find the needed money for medicine he steals a pearl from the local Saint's crown in the church. He is caught but the pearl is lost. However he is backed by his fellow townsmen and allowed to go free. His wife finds the lost pearl and they put it back as the town wakes up to cry miracle.

The film blends social and psychological outlooks but is never preachy. The story takes a while to get going since new director Luis Alcoriza, sometimes lacks the right visuals and direct statements. This is a fresh, impertinent look at human nature and has good humored ribbing of man's foibles. It is technically fine and thesping is okay. *Mosk.*

Pojken I Tradet
(The Boy in the Tree)
(SWEDISH)

Karlovy Vary, June 26.
Sandrews production and release. With Tomas Bolne, Anders Henrikson, Heinz Hopf, Brigitta Pettersson, Ake Liniman. Written and directed by Arne Sucksdorff. Camera, Gunnar Fischer; editor, Sucksdorff, E. Nollender. At Karlovy Vary Film Fest. Running time, **85 MINS.**
Gote .... Tomas Bolne
Cervin .... Anders Henrikson
Max .... Heinz Hopf
Manne .... Bjorne Gustafson
Marie .... Brigitta Pettersson
Sten .... Ake Liniman

Arne Sucksdorff once made a nature feature pic about a little boy and an otter, "The Great Adventure," that was successful. But in his first feature with live actors he comes-a-cropper despite the story about a nature-loving boy betrayed by family, life and friends. The story is just too loose and direction too wavering to make this jell. Hence, this is a dubious **item for foreign placing.**

Here, a teen-ager is not understood at home and takes up with two delinquent game poachers who are in it for kicks. He really loves nature and animals but goes along with them. When a local forest ranger closes in, the boys panic.

Director Sucksdorff sometimes shows a bit of his old form in the scenes of the boy living off the land. But the stilted tale, the too simple motivations and his final suicide add this up to a fairly lame, uneven melodrama.

Pic is technically good looking in well contrasted lensing but has too much of a tendency for un-necessary camera movements and erratic cutting. *Mosk.*

Na Semi Vetrach
(FOUR WINDS OF HEAVEN)
(RUSSIAN)

Karlovy Vary, June 26.
Mosfilm production and release. With Larisa Luzhina, Vyacheslav Tikhonov, Clara Luchko, Leonid Bikov. Directed by Stanislav Rostotsky. Screenplay, Alexandra Galich; camera, Vyacheslav Shumsky; editor, D. Lavorov. At Karlovy Vary Film Fest. Running time, **105 MINS.**
Svetlana .... Larisa Luzhina
Suzdalev .... Vyacheslav Tikhonov
Doctor .... Clara Luchko
Postman .... Leonid Bikov

Another Russo war pic with sentimental overtones, this is not up to its predecessors, either on detail or treatment. It is less likely to succeed abroad, looking to be mainly a local entry.

A girl arrives to marry her fiancee but she finds an empty house and her man off at the front since war has broken out. She waits in the house which serves as headquarters for a newspaper unit, a hospital and finally as a last stand for a besieged group.

This has some good passages and a beguiling heroine. But it is somewhat flat generally. It is technically fine. *Mosk.*

The Three Stooges In Orbit

With canny exploitation and proper pairing, looms another click for venerable slapstick trio.

Hollywood, July 2.
Columbia Pictures release of Norman Maurer production. Stars The Three Stooges (Moe Howard, Larry Fine, Joe De Rita). Directed by Edward Bernds. Screenplay, Elwood Ullman, from story by Maurer; camera, William F. Whitley; editor, Edwin Bryant; music, Paul Dunlap; assistant director, Eddie Saeta. Reviewed at the studio, July 2, '62. Running time, **87 MINS.**
Moe ....The
Larry .... Three
Curly-Joe .... Stooges
Carol ....Carol Christensen
Capt. Tom Andrews ... ,Edison Stroll
Professor Danforth ..... Emil Sitka
Ogg ....George N. Neise
Zogg .... Rayford Barnes
Williams .... Norman Leavitt
Chairman .... Nestor Paiva
General Bixby .... Peter Dawson
Dr. Appleby .... Peter Brocco
Colonel Smithers .... Don Lamond
George Galveston ...... Thomas Glynn
Mr. Lansing .... Maurice Manson
WAF Sergeant .... Jean Charney
Personnel Clerk .... Duane Ament
Colonel Lane .... Bill Dyer
Welby .... Roy Engel
Bathing Girl .... Jane Wald
Tooth Paste Old Maid . Cheerio Meredith

Success of their most recent vehicle, "Three Stooges Meet Hercules," looks apt to be duplicated by the venerable team's newest effort for Columbia. Exploited as aggressively as "Hercules," which the trio accompanied with fruitful personal appearances in many key city engagements, "Orbit," if paired with an attraction designed for roughly the same audience, should strike an equally responsive chord in the moppet-to-early-teen mart.

Clonk for clonk and splat for splat, "Orbit" attains more comedy mileage than "Hercules." Again the formula is slapstick farce in a fantasy frame, with Elwood Ullman's screenplay, from producer Norman Maurer's story, following the classic pattern of "Stooges" comedy: three heads are better than one, if jarred together at periodic intervals. Plot implicates Moe, Larry and Curly-Joe in a struggle for possession of an all-purpose military weapon (a three-way cross between a tank, a sub and a rocket) between its inventor and Martian agents.

Some of the topical matters kidded have lost their edge through recent comedy overexposure, but the wild "Stooge" approach manages to extract the last ounce of visual fun from creaky ideas for the young and easy going audience. Several of the sight gag routines, however, are traditionally surefire in approach, and calculated to amuse any customer. In the screen slapstick comedy spectrum, the Stooges just about stand alone now, their only real competition coming from occasional releases composed of clips from silent film archives.

Romantic interest is capably executed by pretty Carol Christensen and Edison Stroll. Emil Sitka is a standout as the inventor. Balance of support is unusually game, in view of all the pastry being hurled into kissers.

Edward Bernds' direction is properly fast and furious. Considerable ingenuity has gone into the production, with especially resourceful efforts from cameraman William F. Whitley, editor Edwin Bryant and art director Don Ament. Paul Dunlap's music is helpful. Sound effects, always important where Stooges' skullduggery is concerned, are adroitly engineered by William Bernds. *Tube.*

World By Night No. 2
(TECHNIRAMA-DOCUMENTARY-COLOR)

Followup to last year's worldwide melange of after-dark cabaret entertainments. Offbeat interest, often amusing, but protracted running time makes for tedium. Specialized handling indicated; dualer spots may resist because of length.

Warner Bros. release of Julia Film production. Features portions of Cabaret entertainment around the world. Produced by Francesco Mazzi. Directed by Gianni Proia. Script, Carlo Laurenzi; music, Piero Piccione. Reviewed July 5, '62, in New York. Running time, **118 MINS.**

This is a sequel to last year's "World By Night," feature-length global tour of cabarets, al fresco divertissements, etc., comprising the balance of footage lensed by the same team of nocturnal-prowling Italians. As with the first marathon, it can be justified for the program market, and, since it appears to represent a modest deal for Warner Bros., should compensate the distrib with enough U. S. dates.

There could be some exhibitor resistance to No. 2, however, owing to its extended running time, suggesting specialized situations may be somewhat more receptive in certain markets.

Regardless the offbeat nature and much to arrest the eye and ear, all that vicarious gay living isn't without considerable tedium after a while.

The pub-crawling is scarcely more than titillation of the senses, although the Italians have tried to invest it with some social point, notably in two sequences. In one, the camera follows a bevy of husband-shedding women on an escape-from-it-all patrol of Reno showplaces; the other, which serves to open and close the film, of vapid revelers awaiting the midnight gong in a San Francisco boite that stages a nightly New Year's Eve wingding.

Mostly film amounts to ordinary Cook's touring ranging from the western U. S. to Africa and Japan. Much of the footage is amusing, some genuinely exciting. There is also much repetition per the variations on the striptease (and not obscuring some fine sado-masochist nuances). The more lively moments exhibit Al Hirt's dixieland combo tooting for a blacktie party on a riverboat, a splashy can-can revue at the Las Vegas Tropicana, a strange (and cruel) ritual "entertainment" in Japan, and some pulse-quickening coverage of the Rio Mardi Gras.

The color is fittingly garish while other technical contributions are efficient. Lensing is solid, but in a few instances might have been more artful.

"World By Night No. 2" might

make for better impact if more scissoring is administered. *Pit.*

Swingin' Along
(C'SCOPE—COLOR)

Bantamweight comedy with songs. With disk names item serviceable for summer junior mart.

Hollywood, July 6.
Twentieth-Fox release of Jack Leewood production. Stars Tommy Noonan, Pete Marshall, Barbara Eden; guest stars Ray Charles, Roger Williams, Bobby Vee. Directed by Charles Barton. Screenplay, Jameson Brewer; camera (De Luxe), Arthur E. Arling; editor, Betty Steinberg; music, Arthur Morton; assistant director, Ad Schaumer. Reviewed at the studio, July 6, '62. Running time, **74 MINS.**

Freddy	Tommy Noonan
Duke	Pete Marshall
Carol	Barbara Eden
Aunt Sophie	Connie Gilchrist
Ginny	Carol Christensen
Officer Sullivan	Alan Carney
Bookie	Mike Mazurki
Georgie	Tommy Farrell
Willie	Lennie Bremen
Tony	Don Diamond
Priest	Ted Knight
Mrs. Crenshaw	Terry Miele
Psychiatrist	Frank Wilcox
Secretary	Sandra Warner
TV announcer	Art Baker
Himself	Ray Charles
Himself	Roger Williams
Himself	Bobby Vee

In "Swingin' Along," 20th-Fox has a frivolous farce-musical concoction of value primarily as a running mate with grade A attractions aimed at the hot weather teenage mart. It will be an especially handy companion number for the ozone emporiums, or for hardtops frequented by younger audiences.

Oddly enough, the film's hardiest commercial appeal at the moment stems from afterthought additions to the production. Once designed as a vehicle for costars Tommy Noonan and Pete Marchall, the Jack Leewood production was re-evaluated commercially upon original completion and resultantly inflated with "guest stars" from the recording field. Inclusion of these "guest" passages palsies the tempo of the film and virtually wrecks the continuity of the comedy story-line, but the guest artists do happen to be hot commodities and, if ballyhooed properly, could create an attendance stir in the teenage community.

The misadventures of a San Francisco-based schnook (Noonan) are traced in Jameson Brewer's screenplay. Plot describes how Noonan, an amateur tunesmith, and Marshall, a con man, pool resources to walk off with first prize in a songwriting contest. Most of the comedy is of the slapstick, visual variety, highlights being a downhill pursuit of a runaway piano on wheels, and a building ledge pursuit of Noonan's finished musical manuscript.

Noonan & Marshall are pretty traditional in their approach to comedy teamwork — Noonan the childish clown, Marshall the handsome straight man. Barbara Eden and Carol Christensen are strong visual assets in romantic parts. Connie Gilchrist, Alan Carney and Mike Mazurki help out considerably in comedy support. Guest stars are Ray Charles, Roger Williams and Bobby Vee. Charles' appearance is of particular note in that, despite its total irrelevance to the story, it could someday be a valuable strip of celluloid for

collectors of jazz music-a-la-cinema —a rare illustration of a formidable vocal artist in action.

Picture is lopsided, adhering to the storyline in the early going, later evolving into staccato musical comedy patchwork. Betty Steinberg's editing reflects all the production revisions and reversals, but she has managed as smoothly as possible under the circumstances. Same goes for director Charles Barton. Arthur E. Arling's photography is agile and colorful. Arthur Morton's score is tuneful. Several refrains have been composed for the occasion. "Song Of The City," a rhapsodic composition by Walter Kent and Walton Farrar, gets the biggest play, but Ray Charles' feverish rendition of his twist classic, "What'd I Say," easily steals the show, musically.
Tube.

The Nun And The Sergeant

Routine war meller with possible action market appeal, sans questionable orgy scene.

Hollywood, June 29.
United Artists release of Eastern Film Productions. Stars Robert Webber, Anna Sten; features Leo Gordon, Hari Rhodes, Robert Easton, Dale Ishimoto, Tod Windsor. Producer, Eugene Frenke; associate producer, Harold Even. Directed by Peter Adreon. Original screenplay, Don Cerveris; camera, Paul Ivano; editors, John Hoffman, Carl Mahakian; art director, Bob Kinoshita; sound, Woody Clark. Reviewed at Pix Theatre, Hollywood, June 29, '62. Running time, **73 MINS.**

A low-budget programmer for the war action market that removes itself from the family market by the inclusion of an overdone orgy bit that is comparatively meaningless, considering that nothing is consummated, but scene would have same effect on impressionable youngsters through its suggestion.

A tough Marine sergeant, Robert Webber, given a dangerous demolition assignment, takes it upon himself to avoid losing "good" Marines by forcibly enrolling "brig" inmates, including every "bad" or "oddball" type. The reluctant volunteers plot revenge and escape at first opportunity but the regeneration bit can be seen a mile off. Team is hampered by having to take along a nun (Anna Sten) and several Oriental schoolgirls they rescue. Fatalities by pic's end include one girl, one soldier (the longest holdout against regeneration) but the rest of the Marines are seen making a seemingly suicidal attempt on an enemy ammo dump while wounded nun is carted to safety and medical care by rest of girls in the hazy fadeout.

Anna Sten has nothing to do in part except murmur platitudes and get dunked in river in attempt to save girl. Webber holds pic together with aid of occasional thespic lifts from motley crew. Adreon directs with eye for action but puzzles with his insertion of a brutal, frankly disgusting scene of girls getting drunk on sake they find in abandoned house, with uninhibited Marines joining in. Much is suggested but nothing is realized except unsuccessful attempted rape of one girl. This could have been intended to inten-

sify following scene where convicts resolve to remain with sergeant but fails to do so. Technical credits are good considering obviously limited budget, especially camera work of Paul Ivano. *Robe.*

Berlin Festival

Out of Tiger's Mouth

First production by Ruggles-Whelan Enterprises filmed on location in Macao and Hong Kong on refugee problem; appealing child performances, but b.o. looks only fair.

Berlin, July 3.
Pathe-American release of a Ruggles-Whelan Enterprises production. Stars Loretta Han-Yi Hwong, David Fang. Directed by Tim Whelan, Jr. Screenplay, Wesley Ruggles, Jr. and Whelan; camera, Emmanuel I. Rojas; music, Howard Wells. At Berlin Film Fest. Running time, **83 MINS.**

Little Moon	Loretta Han-Yi Hwong
Peaceful	David Fang
Grandma Yang	Lilian Wai
Madame Pang	T'ang Juo Ch'ing
Mario	Mario Barri
Su Mei	Lolita Shek
Boatman Feng	Feng Yi
Beggar Girl	Victoria Chan

The first production of the youthful team of Wesley Ruggles, Jr. and Tim Whelan, Jr. had the distinction of being invited to this festival, and that should help in exploiting its forthcoming release in the U.S.. That help should not come amiss because this sincere attempt to put the focus on to the world refugee problem, looks only a fair contender for b.o. honors. "Out of Tiger's Mouth" is set primarily in Hong Kong (though there are some invicidental locations in Macao). It deals with the plight of two child refugees from the Chinese mainland. It could, however, just as easily have been filmed in any other part of the world that has faced a similar problem, though the choice of background gives it an air of topicality.

The story, as scripted by Ruggles and Whelan, is simple and unpretentious, with a few unnecessary screen cliches. The two youngsters are placed by their gradmother in the care of a boatman who promises to deliver them to their uncle in Hong Kong. However, he sells them to a brothel keeper in Macao instead. And it takes the inevitable prostie with the heart of gold to rescue them from the sporting house and smuggle them on to a boat for the island. There they are soon robbed of what little money they have, forced to beg and even steal. And when they finally discover that their uncle is dead, realize they have to face the future alone.

Sincerity is undoubtedly the dominating feature in the treatment. There are many pathetic little twists to the plot. But it never really tugs at the heart strings, and therein lies its main weakness. The little Chinese girl, imported from Hollywood, is cute without precocious. David Fang, as the nine-year old brother, is less confident. Some of the other locally recruited players speak their dialog in stilted style.

The slum backgrounds of Hong Kong, and the glimpses of the

modern part of the city are strikingly photographed. Howard Wells background music has the right Chinese flavor. *Myro.*

Time of the Heathen

A Yank indie pic picked up by British Lion International Films for world release. An academic look at bigotry. Sometimes sketchy, this looms as a specialized entry.

Berlin, July 3.
Lion International Films release of Calvin Floyd-W. Ronald Lerner production. With John Heffernan, Barry Collins, Orville Steward, Stewart Heller, Ethel Ayler, Nathaniel White. Written and directed by Peter Kass. Camera, Al Gramaglia; editor, Albert Tompkins. At Berlin Film Fest. Running time, **75 MINS.**

Gaunt	John Heffernan
Jesse	Barry Collins
Link	Orville Steward
Ted	Stewart Heller
Marie	Ethel Ayler
Cal	Nathaniel White

A gaunt, bible-reading man tracks aimlessly around in the backcountry region of some southern U.S. state. He gets mixed up in a racist matter and turns out to be the tortured man who dropped the A Bomb on Hiroshima during the last war. Pic tries to take on too much. But it docs have a definite outlook and a solid technical envelope to make this a specialized bet. But that seems it, at best.

The man comes upon a farm where a white youth has tried to rape a Negro maid, and she has been killed by accident. The bigoted father decides to blame it on the interloper. From there on, this becomes unbelievably involved, with the climax a lot of chase and killings.

Peter Kass, for a first production, displays good visual flair. The actors appear well typed. But they rarely take on human dimensions. It does castigate bigotry and man's inhumanity to man. But a tacked on hallucination sequence is not adequate enough to make this film transcend its chase story.

Film is technically good for an ambitious, if mainly sketchy theme. It is an okay try but still lacking in insight. *Mosk.*

Kaachan Shiguno Iyada
(Don't Ever Die, Mother)
(JAPAN)

Berlin, July 3.
Shochiku production and release. Stars Ineko Arima; features Kiyoshi Hirabayashi, Jiro Yamazaki, Tsptomu Shimomoto. Directed by Yoshio Kawazu. Screenplay, Keisuke Kinoshita; camera, Ryoichi Arano; editor, Kaname Okada. At Berlin Film Fest. Running time, **80 MINS.**

Mother	Ineko Arima
Yoshiyuki	Kiyoshi Hirabayashi
Yoshihisa	Jiro Yamazaki
Father	Tsutomu Shimomoto

Tender tale of two little boys of a poor family, this tugs at the sentiments rather than jerking at them. Film is moving but in good taste. Its well balanced aspects make this something that could playoff in regular spots on its sheer entertainment value. The pathos hint possible arty house use.

A sick father and an industrious, loving mother surround their two little boys who do not really feel their poverty. Time and seasons pass, the father dies. The boys are

good but sometimes slightly disobedient.

The mother is shown as both a tower of love and security for the little boys as well as a sorely tried but courageous woman. This role is played with warmth and strength by Ineko Arima. The boys are perfect in reactions and action.

This is a slow but telling tale. It depicts the basics in life. Film is technically excellent and shows the Japanese can handle a plot through the eyes of children.

Pic is a fragile, poetic story, managing to show the life of children without being childish. It is not afraid of sentiment but does not wallow in it. Here is that rare successful sentimental pic which, with proper handling and exploitation, could give it wide world showing.   *Mosk.*

Os Cafajestes
(The No-Good Ones)
(BRAZIL)
Berlin, July 3.
Magnus-Film (Rio de Janiero) production. Stars Jece Valadao, Daniel Filho, Norma Benguel, Lucy Carvalho. Directed by Ruy Guerra. Screenplay, Miguel Torres, Guerra; camera, Tony Rabatton; music, Luis Bonfa. At Berlin Film Fest. Running time, **92 MINS.**

Having surprisingly walked off with the grand prix at the recent Cannes Film Fest, there was particular interest in this Brazilian entry at Berlin. In some measure, it was rewarded. "The No-Good Ones," with its extensive nudity and erotic lovemaking scenes, may well face censorship trouble in many parts, but if that hurdle can be overcome it's loaded exploitation possibilities may turn it into a money-spinning production.

Script, by director Ruy Guerra and Miguel Torres, confines the action to four characters and a single day. Story line is sensitively developed, though the screenplay lapses towards the end, and some of the dialog evoked unintentional laughter.

A rich playboy, who has always lived on his allowance, finds himself in a desperate position when his father faces bankruptcy. The thought of work never enters his mind, and instead he tries his luck at blackmail. With the aid of an accomplice, who is promised a car in return for his services, he sets out to photograph his uncle's mistress in the nude, and eventually extract money from the old man. The girl is lured to a deserted beach and persuaded to bathe in the nude. The accomplice, who had been concealed in the luggage compartment of the car, photographs the girl from a variety of angles while she is cavorting in this manner.

The plan, however, goes awry when the girl breaks the news that she is no longer the uncle's mistress. But she suggests they should try the same scheme on his daughter. The second girl is lured to another beach, but plot No. 2 also goes wrong when the playboy finds he's rather fond of his cousin, and doesn't want to be a party to the blackmail photographs.

The extended nudity sequences, running for several minutes, is delicately handled and magnificently lensed. They have a sincere artistic quality, and are without erotic overtones. Same cannot be

said, however, of the frank lovemaking between the first girl and the accomplice, or the attempted rape of the second by the same man. It is these scenes that may evoke censorship problems.

Performances by the four principals are up to standard. Both girls are attractive, and Norma Benguel, who is involved in the main nudie scenes, is delightfully unashamed. Technical highlight is Tony Rabattoni's camerawork, and there is a haunting musical background.   *Myro.*

Ohne Datum
(Without Date)
(GERMAN)
Berlin, July 3.
Otto Domnick (Stuttgart) production. Directed by Otto Domnick. Screenplay, K. G. Hufnagel; camera, Ottomar Domnick; music, Habenstock Ramati. At Berlin Film Fest (outside competition). Running time, **88 MINS.**

"Without Date" is, after "Jonas" and "Gino" Otto Domnick's third offbeat opus. As usual, he dedicates himself to the extreme experiment. It's a film without action. Producer-director aims at showing the psychological situation of a man who's suffering from cancer and who is given only a short time to live.

What Domnick is driving at is clear but it's strenuous and tiresome to follow a full-length film of such calibre. There's a certain plus about the camerawork but otherwise there's nothing that could be termed interesting or essential. Films like this have no future. Dr. Domnick claims that his film only applies to an especially thin circle of interested persons.   *Hans.*

No Exit
(Stateless)
(IN ENGLISH)
Berlin, July 3.
Fernando Ayala and Hector Olivera production. Stars Viveca Lindfors, Rita Gam, Morgan Sterne, Ben Piazza. Directed by Tad Danielewski. Screenplay, George Tabori, based on play by Jean-Paul Sartre; camera, Ricardo Younis; editor, Carl Lerner; music, Vladimir Ussachevsky. At Berlin Film Fest. Running time, **85 MINS.**
Inez .... Viveca Lindfors
Estelle .... Rita Gam
Garcin .... Morgan Sterne
Bellboy .... Ben Piazza
Florence .... Susana Mayo
Gomez .... Orlando Sacha
Captain .... Manuel Roson
Carmencita .... Mirtha Miller
Robert Miguel .... A. Iriarte
Shirley .... Elsa Dorian
Albert .... Mario Horna
Roger Delaney, 3d .... Carlos Brown

Filmed in English in Buenos Aires, "No Exit" was screened without national status when shown at the Berlin festival because of the confusion of its real identity. It is claimed to be the first English language film to have been made in the Argentine.

Based on a J. P. Sartre play which probes the tortured minds of three people destined to be together for eternity in hell, the pic is sincerely made though its transference to the screen medium is by no means successful. Name value of the stars and author will be an exploitation aid, but it looks only a fair arty theatre film.

In a bid to give the story cinematic movement, scripter George

Tabori has resorted to the use of flashbacks to explain how the three principal characters wound up in hell. Morgan Sterne is shown as a journalist who betrayed his colleagues in the Resistance movement. Viveca Lindfors is the lesbo who seduces a perfectly normal girl away from her husband, while Rita Gam marries a rich old man for his money and then drives him to suicide after she has killed their son and heir.

However, most of the action is confined to the room that the three share in hell, and the script strains to maintain a tense and taut atmosphere. The lesbian unsuccessfully woos the other woman, but the latter in turn easily attracts the one man, and they frankly make love together to the complete and utter disgust of the abnormal looker-on.

Tad Danielewski's direction does not attempt to conceal the legit origins of the piece, and it is largely a static play on film. The flashbacks provide some opportunity of action, but basically it is confined to the one room, and there's not much that can be done about it.

To some extent, this is reflected in the performances, particularly as they are not cut and dried roles, but involve difficult interpretation. Miss Lindfors plays the lesbo with earnest conviction, never trying to justify her abnormality. Rita Gam has the less demanding role, and her interpretation of the sensuous woman is frank and lively. Morgan Sterne plays the traitor with an air of unrelieved gloom. Ben Piazza is also given starring status, but his role is of less significance. He's the bellboy who shows the new arrivals in hell to their allotted accommodation, and strikes an intriguing note.

Technical aspects are adequate, and there's a vivid electronic musical score by Vladimir Ussachevsky.   *Myro.*

Galapagos
(German-Color)
Berlin, July 3.
Heinz Sielmann production and release. Directed by Sielmann. Camera, Sielmann and Klaus Philipp; underwater camera, J. Eibl-Eibesfeldt and Sielmann; music, Hans Posegga; commentary, Walter Schneider. At Berlin Film Fest. Running time, **96 MINS.**

Filmed on the Archipelago of Galapagos (about 600 miles from the equator), on the islands where Charles Darwin is said to have developed his theories on the origin of man, this full-length documentary contains a wealth of fascinating material. Nevertheless, it will probably be a tough proposition to sell, because it is barely strong enough to sustain first-feature film status. Pic is on the longish side for playing as a supporting film.

There is an abundance of animal life around the islands, and Heinz Sielmann and his team have brought to the screen some intriguing scenes of the birds, fish and animals that inhabit Galapagos. The two camera teams obviously have worked patiently to capture some of the sequences, notably the head-to-head fights by toads who challenge one another for the right to a hole in the ground.

Film has been handsomely lensed in Agfacolor. And there are

some excellent underwater scenes. It's been briskly edited, with a straightforward descriptive commentary.   *Myro.*

Los Atracadores
(The Street Thieves)
(SPANISH)
Berlin, July 3.
PE Films production and release. With Pierre Brice, Manuel Gil, Julian Mateos, Agnes Spaak. Directed by Rovira-Beleta. Screenplay, Manuel Sola, Rovira-Beleta; camera, C. Aroyo; editor, A. Lurrea. At Berlin Film Fest. Running time, **102 MINS.**
Vidal .... Pierre Brice
Ramon .... Manuel Gil
Carmelo .... Julian Mateos
Isable .... Agnes Spaak

Familiar tale about a group of delinquents who go from petty violence to holdups and then to murder, with the blame on society, and parents as well as them. This looks more important on its home grounds than abroad. It is well put together but without the needed depth to make it more than a possible language entry abroad.

A young factory worker gets mixed up with a lawyer's son, who wants to form a gang as his revolt against what he thinks is the older generation's blotching of life and society, and a third lad, a young rogue. It all leads to an accidental murder.

Meanwhile, the leader is enamored of the worker's sister and when she is used by a sort of white slave ring, they avenge her and then want to break up. However, they are besieged by the police with one killed, one sent up for the life and the last executed. Last is a powerful scene.

Film is ably done but the generally pat episodes and outlooks limit it. The young thesps perform well. It all adds up to the discovery of a possible budding new director.   *Mosk.*

Die Rote
(The Redhead)
(GERMAN)
Berlin, July 3.
Europa release of Real Film (Hamburg) production (in collaboration with Magic—C. C. Champion, Italy). Stars Ruth Leuwerik, Rossano Brazzi, Giodgio Albertazzi, Gert Froebe. Directed by Helmut Kaeutner. Screenplay, Kaeutner, based on novel by Alfred Andersch; camera, Otello Martelli; music, Zanetti and Tortorella; editing, Klaus Dudenhoefer. At Berlin Film Fest. Running time, **101 MINS.**
Franziska .... Ruth Leuwerik
Fabio .... Rossano Brazzi
Patrick .... Giorgio Albertazzi
Herbert .... Harry Meyen
Joachim .... Richard Muench
Kramer .... Gert Froebe

Helmut Kaeutner's "The Redhead," Germany's entry at the 1962 Berlin festival, may be classified as an ambitious, offbeat effort. Unfortunately the outcome of this experiment is disappointing. Using as its background the bleak wintery city of Venice, seldom filmed thus, this adaptation of Alfred Andersch's bestseller fails to get below the surface of its literary equivalent. The cold intellectual quality that has dominated so many of Kaeutner's pix is also very much evident in this one. Because of lack of emotional impact, commercial prospects seem very doubtful.

Fleeing her unhappy environment, which includes an unsatisfactory marriage and an indifferent lover, the Redhead, Ruth Leu-

werik, arrives in Venice and sets out in search of a job. During her wanderings she encounters three men of varying character each involved in his battle of existence. Her emotional involvement with each of the characters leads her into a web of hatred and decadence which she's able to escape only by leaving Venice.

Film has been expertly lensed by Italian cameraman Otello ("La Dolce Vita") Martelli whose work conveys the depressing atmosphere of the winter-bound city. There's an extensive use of inner monologs. But Kaeutner somehow lacks the insight and sensitivity of these men. Result is a rather monotonous opus which retreats into vagueness.

The acting is uneven. In her first pic of international significance, Miss Leuwerik has taken on a role which seems too demanding for her. She fails to convey adequately the inner turmoil of her character. Lineup of the three men includes Rossano B r a z z i, Giorgio Albertazzi and Gert Froebe. All three parts are hampered by sketchy writing, but Albertazzi manages to make an impression as an exiled Englishman haunted by his past. There are controversial sex elements which may cause difficulties with censors but these probably won't help the film's b.o. prospects. All other technical credits are way above the German average. *Hans.*

Ham Dono
(We Two)
(INDIAN)
Berlin, July 3.
Santa Cruz release of Dev Anand production. Stars Dev Anand; features Nanda, Sadhana, Jagirdar, Liela Chitnis, Rashid Khan, Lalita Pawar, Jagdish Raj. Directed by Amar Jeet. Screenplay, Nirmal Sircar, Vijay Anand; camera, V. Ratra; editor, Ahaman Vir. At Berlin Film Fest. Running time, **95 MINS.**
Anand, Varma .... Dev Anand
Ruma .... Nanda
Mita .... Sadhana
Father .... Jagirdar
Mother .... Liela Chitnis
John .... Rashid Khan
Firned .... Jagdish Raj

Film appears mainly for home consumption on its simple moralities, melodramatic coincidences plus obvious construction and treatment.

A young man goes off to war, in India, when his future father-in-law makes it clear to him he can not support his daughter as he should. But the fiancee moves in with his mother. He meets an officer who is his exact double; he should be because the same actor plays both roles.

When he thinks the other is killed, he goes to visit the friend's home but is mistaken for him and becomes involved in playing the game.

Dev Anand plays both characters archly. The remainder of the cast makes sure they are perfectly understood by excessive underlining of sentiments. It is technically acceptable and even the split screen special effects are well done. But this lacks the charm, wit and simplicity that might have made this morality tale more entertaining.
Mosk.

San Sebastian Fest

Pueblito
(Little Village)
(MEXICAN)
San Sabastian, July 3.
Pelimex release of Bueno production. With Maria Elena Marquez, Lilian Prado, Columba Rodriguez, Fernando Soler, Jose Alonso Cano. Directed by Emilio Fernandez. Screenplay by Mauricio Magdaleno; camera, Alex Philips; music, Antonio Diaz Conde. At San Sebastian Film Fest. Running time, **94 MINS.**

Emilio (El Indio) Fernandez tries to blend lofty idealism and rural hijinks, the result being a caricature similarity to "Baker's Wife." It's a shrill, almost melodramatic plea for schools in the stix. A government architect visits a hamlet deep in the backwoods to find that his mission was provoked by the town's schoolmarm. She conducts class in a barnyard lean-to and wants to see a school building constructed.

Opposition comes from Don Cesar, leading landowner and businessman. Cesar's wife is too young and pretty for her own good and soon throws her lot in with the architect and his project. The school is built, the architect leaves, Cesar's wife returns to him and the Indian town, lost on the Mexican landscape, responds happily to social progress.

There are many deft sequences in "Pueblito" which accent the depth and beauty of primitive ways in modern Mexico. This is aided by Alex Philips' sharply-etched black and w h i t e photography. "Pueblito" will draw on its sentimental idealism with a better-than-even chance for extensive playdating in the Spanish - language market. *Hank.*

Le Soleil Dans L'Oeil
(Sun In Your Eyes)
(FRENCH)
San Sebastian, July 3.
Films Borderie-Reggane Films coproduction. With Anna Karina, Georges Descrieres, Jacques Perrin. Directed by Jacques Bourdon. Screenplay by Dominique Aury, Eric Schlumberger, Jacques Bourdon; camera, Lucien Joulin; editor, Denise Nathot At San Sebtstian Film Fest. Running time, **102 MINS.**

The first half of this Gallic entry is an achievement in itself but director Jacques Bourdon shifts from romantic purity to ultramodern, cynical brainbeating. This leaves a triangular conflict, capriciously unresolved.

A y o u n g Parisienne (Anna Karina) quits the Metropole bedside of her lover for a vacation in Corsica. In between her daily missives to Paris, she succumbs almost imperceptively to the unrestrained elan and charm of an adolescent Corsican (J a c q u e s Perin). The idyll is climaxed by a "nuit d'amor." Soap bubble bursts with the arrival of the lover from Paris. He probes like a surgeon to determine the calibre of her perfidy.

Anna Karina and Jacques Perin contribute firstrate performances. Georges Descrieres, of the Comedie Francais, has the ungrateful role of the mature, protective lover who panics indecently as the young

islander stirs responsive chords in his young mistress. *Hank.*

La Fusilacion
(The Firing Squad)
(ARGENTINE)
San Sebastian, July 3.
Araucania Films production and release. With Romualdo Quiroga, Juan Carlos Lamas, Aldo Mayo, Marcela Lopez Rey. Directed by Catrano Catrani. Screenplay by Saulo Benavente, Catrani; camera, Pedro Marzialetti; music, Ariel Ramirez. At San Sebastian Film Fest. Running time, **98 MINS.**

"Firing Squad" was adapted for the screen from Felix Luna's novel. It deals with a rebellion of mountaineers in the interior of Argentina. The event took place in 1870 when a central government was for the first time created in Buenos Aires.

It contains an epic note in the conflict between the Federals and the mountain-guards. Both are imbued with patriotic zeal. Somewhat obscurely, the rebel chief disbands his forces and is in turn speared to death by a rival marauding group. The Federals pick up the trail and bring the murderer to a dramatic death.

Though the story line is sometimes bewildering and the repetitious images of men on horseback almost exasperating, the spectator nevertheless senses the majesty and passionate honesty of Catrani's sweeping tale of a moment in Argentine history.

If the film does nothing else than call attention to Catrani as a director, to composer Ariel Ramirez for a great and unusual score, and to Marcela Lopez Rey, as a young Argentine actress with talent, then the project is worthwhile. Because the film has little or nothing else that can be exploited. *Hank.*

L'Isola di Arturo
(Arthur's Island)
(ITALIAN)
San Sebastian, July 3.
T. M.-Carlo Ponti production. With Key Meersman, Vanni de Maigret, Reginald Kernan, Luigi Giuliani. Directed by Damiano Damiani. Screenplay by Elsa Morante, D. Damiani. Cesare Zavattini; music, Carlo Rustichelli. At San Sebastian Film Fest. Running time, **106 MINS.**

In his first film two years ago Damiano Damiani demonstrated his ability to evoke the dream world of early adolescence to win the critic's jury San Sebastian prize. With "Isola de Arturo," Damiani has developed this film genre to heights previously achieved by Rene Clement and Truffaut. Put this on the list of those pix that bring excitement and audiences to arty houses and lift talented directors from obscurity to merited recognition.

Pic is the story of Arthur, a 15-year-old who worships but rarely sees his father, Reginald Kernan. Father returns from one of his frequent voyages with a 17-year-old wife, Nunziata (Key Meersman) but leaves shortly after on another of his many mysterious trips. Arthur is emotionally pried apart as his father image comes into conflict with his growing love for the abandoned childbride. Kernan's climatic return finally reveals his homosexual frailties. Collapse of Arthur's idolatry coincides with his emerging manhood.

Damiani skillfully bridges the

unknown void between childhood and adolescence with an interwoven pattern of poetic beauty and stirring dramatic narrative. Distilled from Elsa Morante's book by the same name, the novelist, director and Zavattini have fashioned an effective screenplay.

Vanni de Maigret, as the boy, and Miss Meersman, as the young bride, turn in outstanding performances. Former Boston medico Kernan can forget about operating tables for his role as the homo father is distinguished in every respect.

Talented cast of unknowns, superior camera lensing and haunting music are expertly integrated by director Damiani. "Isola" is above all a brilliant directorial achievement with fine prospects for arties.
Hank.

(Note: This pic won the Golden Sea Shell.)

El Sol En El Espejo
(The Sun in the Mirror)
(SPANISH—ARGENTINE)
San Sebastian, July 3.
Federico J. Alcardi production and release. With Yvonne Bastien, Luis Davila, Jose Isbert, Maruja Asquerino, Gracita Morales, Enzo Viena, Alberto Dalbes. Directed by Antonio Roman. Screenplay by A. Roman, J. L. Colina, A. Vich; camera, Manuel Berenguer; music, Manuel Parada. At San Sebastian Film Fest. Running time, **94 MINS.**

Antonio Roman, director of this Spanish- Argentine coproduction, took popular playwright Alfonso Paso's legit success "Los Pobrecitos" (The Unfortunates) too literally in adapting it for the screen. Consequently, the film has a staccato delivery of good lines that are weighted under by a limited, static locale.

A big and effective cast, including Jose Isbert, Maruja Asquerino, Gracita Morales and Enzo Viena, is confined to the corridors, dining room and individual lodgings of a rundown boarding house and compelled to declaim instead of act. Every pensionnaire is on the skids with no reasonable hope in sight for all the troubles they see until a finale fairy tale contrivance showers pesetas and solutions.

Jose Isbert, Spain's vet comic, who starred in "Welcome- Mr. Marshall" and "El Cochecito." scores as the poverty-ridden lodger who ignores his woes in the self-indulgent role of a retired, heavily-decorated army colonel.

"Espejo" will probably show a profit with heavy nabe support in the Spanish lingo market. *Hank.*

The Wonderful World of The Brothers Grimm

First story film in Cinerama, combining straight drama and fantasy. As result of novelty and imaginative artistry, ought to register big boxoffice.

Denver, Col., July 14.

Metro-Goldwyn-Mayer-Cinerama picture produced by George Pal. Stars Laurence Harvey, Karl Boehm, Claire Bloom, Yvette Mimieux, Russ Tamblyn. Features Walter Slezak, Barbara Eden Oscar Homolka, Arnold Stang, Jim Backus, Martita Hunt, Ian Wolfe, Betty Garde, Buddy Hackett, Terry-Thomas, Cheerio Meredith, Bryan Russell, Tammy Marihugh, Walter Rilla, Beulah Bondi, Clinton Sundberg, Sandra Gale Bettin, Robert Foulk, Otto Kruger, Robert Crawford Jr., Sydney Smith. Directed by Henry Levin and George Pal. Screenplay by David P. Harmon, Charles Beaumont and William Roberts, from screen story by Harmon based on "Die Bruder Grimm" by Hermann Gerstner; camera Paul C. Vogel; special effects Gene Warren, Wah Chang, Tim Barr and Robert R. Hoag; editor, Walter Thompson; music Leigh Harline; words and music by Bob Merrill; assistant director, Al Jennings. Reviewed at Cooper Theatre, Denver, Col., July 14, '62. Running time 135 MINS., plus intermission.

THE BOOK

Wilhelm Grimm	Laurence Harvey
Jacob Grimm	Karl Boehm
Dorothea Grimm	Claire Bloom
Stossel	Walter Slezak
Greta Heinrich	Barbara Eden
The Duke	Oscar Homolka
Rumpelstiltskin	Arnold Stang
Story Teller	Martita Hunt
Gruber	Ian Wolfe
Miss Bettenhausen	Betty Garde
Mrs. von Dittersdorf	Cheerio Meredith
Friedrich Grimm	Bryan Russell
Pauline Grimm	Tammy Marihugh
The Priest	Walter Rilla

THE DANCING PRINCESS

The Princess	Yvette Mimieux
The Woodsman	Russ Tamblyn
The King	Jim Backus
The Gypsy	Beulah Bondi
The Prime Minister	Clinton Sundberg

THE COBBLER AND THE ELVES

The Cobbler	Laurence Harvey
The Mayor	Walter Brooke
The Ballerina	Sandra Gale Bettin
The Hunter	Robert Foulk

And the PUPPETOONS

THE SINGING BONE

Ludwig	Terry-Thomas
Hans	Buddy Hackett
The King	Otto Kruger
The Shepherd	Robert Crawford, Jr.
The Spokesman	Sydney Smith

The Cinerama process has come of age as a dramatic tool with "The Wonderful World of the Brothers Grimm." Producer George Pal demonstrates beyond question that the out-sized sceen medium can open a new and exciting era in motion pictures. The novelty of seeing a story in Cinerama — 10 years after the process gave birth to five unusual, in effects, travelogue epics—should generate wide and profitable public interest in this joint MGM-Cinerama project. But there is more to "Brothers Grimm" than just its novelty and visual grandeur, and the excitement that stems from being, quite frequently, a participant in the screen action. "Grimm" is a delightful, refreshing entertainment, which takes full advantage of the ingenuity of which the film medium is capable.

Although the performers, from stars to bit players, are uniformly ingratiating—and properly nasty as occasion requires—if there is a star that shines beyond compare in this two hour and 15 minutes show (plus intermission) it is SPECIAL EFFECTS. The major Fairy Tales sequences — "The Dancing Princess," "The Cobbler and the Elves" and "The Singing Bone"—are as charming and artfully executed as anything Special Effects has created in years.

Some among the group of 400-odd newsmen and exhibitors junketed, from as far away as Japan, to Denver for the special preview Saturday morning at the Cooper Theatre (first house in the world built from the ground up and around — its a spherical shaped auditorium with 800 capacity—to accommodate Cinerama) speculated whether "Grimm" would hold as much appeal for adults as for young audiences. It would appear that the warm applause at the intermission and the fadeout title —*lived happily ever after*—should quiet such speculation. The public more than once has given evidence that it appreciates cinematic resourcefulness and vitality as much, perhaps even more on occasion, as the professionals.

While the Cinerama process now has stepped across the threshold to maturity as a story form, it still is in its 'teens technically. This is not to say that it has not progressed tremendously. It has. There are stretches of considerable length, notably in the second half of the film, when the panel lines are not noticeable at all and the three panel canvas of screen appears to be one unit. There are, however, times when the contrast in film projected from three individual booths is marked and there emerges three distinct and somewhat distracting "pictures." Moreover, the technicians have not yet licked the jiggle, notably in the right panel, and at this showing at least the center panel did its own dancing on a couple of occasions.

It appears that the key here may be in lighting and color composition. When there is uniform lighting and the background colors are in solid tones (deep green, brown, black) where the three film strips join there is no separation in the picture. No doubt that with more concentrated development than the process has received since its introduction via "This Is Cinerama" in September, 1952, these continuing technical shortcomings can be licked. But these are considerations which do not figure to loom disadvantageously (not seriously anyway) as far as public acceptance goes.

Nor is it important whether or not the biographical aspects of "Brothers Grimm" are entirely according to Hermann Gerstner's "Die Bruder Grimm" whence David P. Harmon fashioned the screen story which in turn was molded into script form by Harmon, Charles Beaumont and William Roberts. Its purpose—and director Henry Levin has accorded it appropiate visual interpretation—is simply to provide a bridge for the Fairy Tales sequences. Thankfully, it is a sturdy bridge, enabling the imaginative (some call him loony) Wilhelm and his more practical brother Jacob to emerge as engaging flesh and blood personalities. There is a deceitful simplicity about the skillful and remarkably balanced acting of the respective brothers by Laurence Harvey and Karl Boehm. And their sustained efforts are strongly complimented by Claire Bloom, as the understanding, but at times irritated, wife of the story spinner.

In this, "the book" section of the film, other important acting contributions are made by Walter Slezak, Barbara Eden, Oscar Homolka, Arnold Stang, Martita Hunt, Ian Wolfe and the Wilhelm Grimm children — Bryan Russell and Tammy Marilhugh. In lesser roles, Betty Garde, Cheerio Meredith and Walter Rilla also perform effectively.

Pal himself shares directorial credit with Levin, as the producer also is responsible for directing the Fairy Tales sequences. Let it be said as the best form of compliment that Pal and Grimm are sympatico, although, to one observer at least, he permitted Jim Backus as the King to sound too much like "Mr. Magoo" in "The Dancing Princess" sequence.

This traditional fairy tale of the princess who finds her true love in the humble woodsman has been interestingly choreographed by Alex Romero and charmingly interpreted by Yvette Mimieux (a remarkably versatile young actress) and Russ Tamblyn.

Latter also gets quite a vigorous workout as a sometimes visible, and then invisible guest, on the tail gate of a coach racing around mountain paths in a wild ride, which, for sheer visual stimulus, compares favorably with the roller-coaster thriller of "This is Cinerama." Here camera trickery is dominant and appreciation goes to cinematographer Paul C. Vogel, who, it should be added, overall does a splendid job. And those aforementioned special effects experts — quartet consists of Gene Warren, Wah Chang, Tim Barr and Robert R. Hoag—star here, too, as well as in other sections of "Bros. Grimm."

As far as acting honors go, Harvey is dominant, for in addition to playing Wilhem he also enacts, and with touching warmth offset by a trace of irrascibility, the title role in "The Cobbler and the Elves." This sequence, with its Christmas setting and assortment of orphans and puppets which performs a miracle in the cobbler's shop overnight, is entirely enchanting—even though the memorable snowscapes are somewhat victimized by the division of the panels on the huge screen. Short, but effective, performances here are made by Walter Brooke, Sandra Gale Bettin and Robert Foulk. As for the puppets — they're all loveable.

Fairy tales wouldn't have lasted through the ages, of course, if they didn't at times scare the living daylights out of tots. "The Singing Bone," dealing with a titanic encounter involving a supercilious aspiring knight and his servant with a fire-spouting dragon is full of exaggerated chills and wry humor. Buddy Hackett (who reminds of the late Lou Costello) as the humble servant who finally emerges as the shining knight over his dastardly master, is enchanting. And Terry-Thomas also is excellent as the master whose cowardice ultimately strips him of honor and glory. Otto Kruger is authoritative as the king here.

So many have contributed so much — and deserving praise is merited despite certain flaws in this film—that a critic, without meaning to, might easily slight some in proportion to contribution. Obviously, the score by Leigh Harline and the words and music by Bob Merrill to a series of songs, though not by themselves dominant factors, make very significant contributions to the total effect of "Bros. Grimm." This, it should be added, is as it should be, for when the music element predominates in other than a musical picture there is an imbalance.

Also, while Special Effects was singled out, that would not have been as effective if not appropriately complimented by the art direction contributions of George W. Davis and Edward Carfango, supplemented by the set decoration by Henry Grace and Dick Pefferle. Film editor Walter Thompson, in collaboration with directors Levin and Pal, also figured importantly in determining the pace of the film. There are scenes which could be trimmed advantageously here and there, but that's a matter of opinion. The recording, supervised by Franklin Milton, is generally of a high quality, but sometimes it seems the extreme range of the sound track is used more for effect than dramatic purpose.

Finally, one man is responsible for the attributes and the deficiencies, which in summation are minor, considering the areas explored. That man is, of course, George Pal, the producer. And he need not offer any apology. He has created an enchanting world in "The Wonderful World of the Brothers Grimm," a pictorial world which is a trailblazer in the annals of motion picture history, commercially and artistically.

Pry.

Tarzan Goes To India
(C'SCOPE-COLOR)

Further adventures of brighter, more subdued Tarzan. Impressively mounted production. Satisfactory summer b.o. for young crowd.

Hollywood, July 10.

Metro release of Sy Weintraub production. Stars Jock Mahoney; features Jai, Leo Gordon, Mark Dana, Feroz Khan, Simi. Directed by John Guillermin. Screenplay, Robert Hardy Andrews, Guillermin, based on characters created by Edgar Rice Burroughs; camera (Metrocolor), Paul Beeson; editor, Max Benedict; music, Ken Jones; assistant directors, Dennis Bertera, Chimankant Gandhi. Reviewed at the studio, July 10, '62. Running time, 88 MINS.

Tarzan	Jock Mahoney
Jai, Elephant Boy	Himself
Bryce	Leo Gordon
O'Hara	Mark Dana
Raju Kumar	Feroz Khan
Princess Kamara	Simi
The Maharaja	Murad
Raaj	Jagdish Raaj
Chakra	G. Raghaven
Drive	Aaron Joseph
Pilot	Abas Khan
Mooty	Pehelwan Ameer
Conservation Officer	K. S. Tripathi

Name's the same, but the character is counterfeit. Widespread appeal of the original primitive ape man will never be duplicated by his jet age descendant, an articulate, subdued, businesslike troubleshooter in the jungles of the world. Still, the Sy Weintraub production for Metro, 36th in the venerable screen series that began in 1918 and first to be endowed with CinemaScope, has the large-scale production sheen and exotic faraway flavor—it was filmed entirely in India—to attract the preteen audience and register satisfactorily as a hot weather program offering.

Screenplay by Robert Hardy Andrews and John Guillermin, directed by the latter, transports Edgar Rice Burroughs' loin-clothed hero to India, where he aids a young elephant boy in the rescue of a pack of pachyderms callously doomed to be submerged under the waters of a giant new jungle reservoir. To do this, Tarzan must battle, tooth, nail and tusk, the uncooperative dispositions of both elephant and man, latter in the form of inflexibly cruel construction interests.

Jock Mahoney, who had a secondary role in the last edition (Paramount's "Tarzan The Magnificent"), has graduated to the title character, a role he endows with admirable physique, dexterity and personality. A long-time film stunt man, Mahoney is the best Tarzan in years. Jai, the Elephant Boy, a pint-sized modern variation of the '30's Sabu, scores in a prominent role. Most of the other characters run to stereotype. Leo Gordon and Mark Dana essay the heavies. Feroz Khan and Simi carry off a minor romantic interest.

Although burdened with dramatic superficiality, "Tarzan Goes to India" has been impressively produced. Under Weintraub and directorial surveillance of Guillermin, all artisans and craftsmen assigned to the film have executed their tasks with skill, most notably cameraman Paul Beeson and art director George Provis, who have used the exotic picturesque locales and views of India's Mysore Province to advantage.

Other sizable assists are those of editor Max Benedict, composer Ken Jones, soundman Bill Howell and second unit photographer Ellis R. Dungan. *Tube.*

Baron Prasil
(Baron Munchausen) (CZECH) (Color)

Karlovy Vary, July 10.

Czech State Film release production and release. With Milos Kopecky, Jana Brejchova, Rudolph Jelinek, Jan Werich, Rudolf Hrusinsky, Karel Hoger. Directed by Karel Zeman. Screenplay, Zeman, Josef Kainar, Jiri Brdecka from book by G. A. Burger; special effects, Zeman; camera (Agfa), Jiri Tarantik; editor, Zdenek Rozkopal. At Karlovy Vary Film Fest. Running time, **80 MINS.**

Baron Munchuasen	Milos Kopecky
Bianca	Jana Brejchova
Tonik	Rudolf Jelinek
Cyrano	Karel Hoger
Sultan	Rudolf Hrusinsky

Karel Zeman's "Wonderful World of Jules Verne," mixing animation, special effects and live characters, played off in the U.S. as well as winning the Grand Prix at the Brussels Film Fest in 1959. This utilizes the same style with the addition of color in depicting the tall tales of the famed, voluble Baron Munchausen. Special slotting looms for this as well as arty houses.

It may not be as consistently successful as its predecessor but this film has a wealth of invention and an overall wit that keep it of interest through most of the footage. Color is strikingly used in a series of scenes that may have one tone or spots of tint.

A rocket ship lands on the moon, and the occupant finds Cyrano De Bergerac, characters from Jules Verne's books and the Baron Munchausen. The latter decides he should learn earthly things and wafts him back there.

Sly satire and straight adventure are the film's backbone. They land on earth in the 18th Century and in a Sultan's palace. Here they free a captive princess who falls for the spaceman. Then they flee and are picked up by a Dutch boat which is swallowed by a mighty fish. The fish is finally washed ashore. Then comes Munchausen's ride under the sea after being abducted by a giant bird and his flight on a cannonball to looksee the enemy.

Effects and inventiveness are tops but this sometimes belabors a point. Milos Kopecky has the right haughtiness for the spouting Baron, and the others blend well. It just does not quite have sheer action and adventure of the former pic. *Mosk.*

Eien No Hito
(Immortal Love) (JAPAN)

Berlin, July 3.

Shochiku production and release. Stars Hideko Takamine, Keiji Sada, Tatsuya Nakadai; features Yoshi Kato, Masakazu Tahmura, Yukiko Fuji. Written and directed by Keisuke Kinoshita; camera, Hiroyuki Kususa; music, Chuji Kinoshita; editor, Yoshi Shugihara. At Berlin Film Fest. Running time, **107 MINS.**

Sadako	Hideko Takamine
Takashi	Keiji Sada
Heibei	Tatsuya Nakadai
Sojiro	Yoshi Kato
Eiichi	Masakazu Tamura
Morito	Masaya Tozuka
Naoko	Yukiko Fuji

Saga of an ill assorted husband and wife over a 28 year period, this avoids melodramatics and hokum by a deep insight into motivations plus some smoothness in acting, directing, writing and technical knowhow. However, its leisurely pace makes it mostly an arty house bet.

A crippled war veteran son of a big landowner in a small town, forces himself on a sharecropper's daughter who is awaiting the return of her loved one. She is practically sold to the family by her heavyhearted father. But her fiancee comes back and they decide to run off only to have him change his mind thinking she would be better off without him.

Director-writer Keisuke Kinoshita manages to turn what seems like melodrama into a lyrical and compassionate look at man's condition. He is neither afraid of sentiment or coincidence and manages to give a good feeling for what is transpiring outside this little community though the wars are never shown.

This is expertly played, meaningfully directed, with fine production. A Hispano-type ballad connecting five episodes in the life of the couple is in key with the human comedy manner of treatment. *Mosk.*

Guns of Darkness

Escape yarn with an anti-violence moral: fairly turgid stuff despite okay marquee value.

London, July 10.

Warner-Pathe release of an Associated British presentation of a Cavalcade Concorde (Thomas Clyde) production. Stars David Niven, Leslie Caron, features James Robertson Justice, David Opatoshu, Richard Pearson, Eleanor Summerfield, Derek Godfrey. Directed by Anthony Asquith. Screenplay, John Mortimer, from Francis Clifford's novel, "Act of Mercy."; camera, Robert Krasker; editor, Frederick Wilson; music, Benjamin Frankel. At Warner Theatre, London. Running time, **102 MINS.**

Claire Jordan	Leslie Caron
Tom Jordan	David Niven
Bryant	James Robertson Justice
Rivera	David Opatoshu
Hermandez	Derek Godfrey
Bastion	Richard Pearson
Mrs. Bastian	Eleanor Summerfield
Dr. Swann	Ian Hunter
Lieutenant Gomez	Sandor Eles
Gabriel	Steven Scott
Gabriel's Cousin	Tutte Lemkow
Nightculb Singer	Dorita Sensier
Indian Boy	Ali Nagi
General Zoreno	Barry Shawzin
Sergeant	Peter Allenby

That sensitive director, Anthony Asquith, is slightly off form with this one. An advocate of anti-violence, he pursues a theme that he has explored before, that violence is sometimes necessary to achieve peace. But though he has assembled some big guns in the shape of David Niven, Leslie Caron, David Opatoshu and James Robertson Justice, which should give a hypo to the boxoffice, the result is a resounding fall between two stools. The film does not stand up satisfactorily as a psychological study. And as a pure "escape" yarn, its moments of tension are only spasmodic. However, the performances of Niven, Opatoshu and Derek Godfrey offer some reward.

John Mortimer's screenplay is not positive enough to enable Asquith to keep a firm grip on the proceedings. There are times when the film plods as laboriously as do the stars in their escape to the frontier. It opens in Tribulacion, capital of a South American republic, during a revolution. The president is deposed in a swift coup and, wounded, has to take off in a hurry. Niven, a rather boorish PRO with a British-owned plantation, elects to smuggle him across the border, for reasons which are not even clear to Niven himself. Tagging along is Niven's wife (Leslie Caron) with whom he is having an emotional upheaval.

The arduous journey, partly in an auto but mainly on foot, involves Niven in a spot when he has to kill a man despite his ideals and moral hatred of violence. But after a long, long time, it results in him being reconciled with his pregnant young wife around the president's death bed.

Film is full of glaring implausibilities but offers some well directed sequences. The opening, for instance, is full of sharp foreboding, with the uprising taking place during a wryly observed and somewhat foolish New Year's Eve party at the plantation. A highspot, which happens rather too early, is when Niven, Miss Caron and the prexy (David Opatoshu) are trapped in their auto in a river filled with quicksand. Another chill moment is when she ventures into an apparently deserted village and is menaced by a bunch of sinister youngsters.

Taken as an adventure yarn there are not enough thrills once the film gets underway. As a study of marital problems it is insufficiently developed. And taken as a peek at a man's conscience, it seems too glibly portrayed. Niven's charm seeps through his mask of boorishness but he manages skilfully to keep up an illusion of high voltage danger. Opatoshu gives an excellent show as the disillusioned, yet philosophical president. Miss Caron, however, in a bid to get away from her "Gigi" image, seems uncomfortable, with her role coming over as curiously colorless.

Casting of James Robertson Justice, that magnificent extrovert, as a mealymouthed, sycophantic plantation boss, is a crass error. But Derek Godfrey fares well as the brains behind the uprising. Richard Pearson, Sandor Eles and Eleanor Summerfield contribute useful cameos. Ian Hunter scores briefly as a cynical doctor.

Robert Krasker's camerawork, the location sequences and the studio matching are all okay. Benjamin Frankel has chipped in with an unobtrusive but sound score. "Guns" is a clear case of a lot of talent failing to jell. If blame can be laid firmly it must be at the doorstep of scriptwriter Mortimer. *Rich.*

Tiara Tahiti
(BRITISH-COLOR)

Sharp acting duel between John Mills and James Mason. Lush color locations in Tahiti plus good performances add up to more than useful boxoffice bet.

London, July 10.

Rank release of an Ivan Foxwell production. Stars James Mason, John Mills; features Rosenda Monteros, Claude Dauphin, Herbert Lom, Libby Morris, Gary Cockrell, Madge Ryan, Peter Barkworth, Roy Kinnear, Jacques Marin. Directed by William T. Kotcheff. Screenplay, Geofrey Cotterell, Ivan Foxwell, from Cotterell's novel; camera, Otto Heller; editor, Antony Gibbs; music, Philip Green. At Odeon, Leicester-Square, London. Running time, **100 MINS.**

Brett Almsley	James Mason
Lt. Col. Clifford Southey	John Mills
Henri Farengue	Claude Dauphin
Chong Sing	Herbert Lom
Belle Annie	Rosenda Monteros
Desmoulins	Jacques Marin
Adele Franklin	Libby Morris
Millie Brooks	Madge Ryan
Joey	Gary Cockrell
Lt. David Harper	Peter Barkworth
Capt. Tom Enderby	Roy Kinnear

Teaming of James Mason and John Mills in a subtle clash of personalities between two offbeat characters is a useful boxoffice stroke. It also helps the idea of the film a great deal. Add the lushness of rich Tahiti locations and throw in the nubile Rosenda Monteros for romantic measure, and this has the ingredients of a pic which has something to offer most film patrons. This one has a polish and an intriguing situation which spells success.

Action stems from Germany, just after the war. A jumped up, pompous lieutenant colonel with a king size inferiority complex (John Mills) clashes with a sophisticated, carefree junior officer (James Mason). Pre-war Mills had been a clerk in the stockbroker's office in which Mason had been a junior partner. Mason still has the effect of making Mills feel like a cheap jerk. Mills stops Mason when he tries to smuggle loot back to London, and Mason is cashiered.

He finds a life of dissolute ease and enchantment in Tahiti, with a native girl and no worries. Mills, well after the war, arrives to

negotiate a deal to build a hotel in Tahiti, comes across Mason and finds to his intense irritation that Mason still has the same effect on him, that of reducing him to fumbling ineptitude and humility.

Situation resolves when Mason is nearly murdered by a thug employed by a local shopkeeper who covets Mason's girl friend (Rosenda Monteros). Mills is accused of the crime and, from lighthearted revenge, Mason wipes off the old score by seeing that the tetchy upstart is deported in disgrace from the South Seas paradise, the hotel mission stillborn.

The two male stars in this pic have a field day. Mason is fine as the mocking wastrel while Mills is equally good in a more difficult role that could have lapsed into parody, but for the thesp's shrewd observation and professional knowhow. Every inflection, every gesture is supremely right for the cocky, affected character with a chip on his shoulder.

These two carry the main burden of the film but get affectionate alliance from a string of people. As Mason's girl friend, the newly introduced Rosenda Monteros is attractive, though it is unlikely that she will be a contender for top acting honors for quite awhile. Claude Dauphin coasts along in a minor guest role as the local boss of tourism. Jacques Marin offers some choice bits as the local police officer with a yen for writing thrillers.

Herbert Lom (skilfully made up as a Chinese) has a serio-comic role as the local tradesman who is the frustrated rival for the affections of Miss Monteros, and does it up brown. Madge Ryan and Libby Morris chip in with neat cameos as a couple of typical Yank femme tourists out to live it up. Gary Cockrell, Peter Barkworth and Roy Kinnear effectively handle the three other significant parts.

Screenplay has many moments of amusing wit, but is never egghead. In fact, the script and the direction of William A. Kotcheff, a tele director making his screen debut, both offer bonuses to Mason and Mills which are deftly grabbed. Phil Green backs the film up with a score that smacks of the lazy surfiness of Tahiti. Otto Heller's camerawork doesn't miss a trick in giving strangers to Tahiti a vicarious kick.

On the rare occasions that the script gets slightly flabby and attention may wander there are plenty of local young femmes to augment the scenery. And there is a belly dance sequence preceding the credit titles which is a dilly.
Rich.

Kohayagawake No Aki
(Late Summer)
(JAPAN—COLOR)
Berlin, July 3.
Toho production and release. Stars Ganjiro Nakamura and Setsuko Hara. Directed by Yasujiro Ozu. Screenplay, Takago Noda and Ozu; camera, Asaichi Nakai; music, Toshiro Mayuzumi. At Berlin Film Fest. Running time, **103 MINS.**
Manbei Kohayagawa ..Ganjiro Nakamura
Akiko Kohayagawa ....Setsuko Hara
Noriko Kohayagawa ......Yoko Tsukasa
Hisao Kohayagawa ......Keiju Kobayashi
Fumiko Kohayagawa ..Michiyo Aratama
Tsune Sasaki ....Chieko Naniwa
Yanouske Kitagawa ......Daisuke Kato

A sincere and sensitively made picture, "Late Summer" is a fair

example of the stylish pictures coming out of Japan. It is tastefully and artistically directed. Though it is not without merit· this pix will probably have only limited appeal to Western audiences.

It is the story of a man in the late summer of his life, who had been something of a rake in his time. He'd had his own mistress, and fondly believes that her teenage daughter is his. Now, the family brewing business is in a decline, and there are family problems to be resolved before it is too late. For instance, a new match must be made for his widowed daughter, and a husband found for another daughter.

In a gentle way, the story unfolds leisurely as the characters come vividly to life. The old man renews his association with his former mistress to the anger of his family, but their annoyance is forgotten when he suffers a heart attack. He recovers from that attack, but shortly afterwards has a fatal one. And so, the decisions concerning all the family's future, can be no longer postponed.

Film has been professionally lensed in Agfacolor, and the acting is universally good. The two stars, Ganjiro Nakamura as the man, and Setsuko Hara as the widowed daughter, make a particularly fine impression.
Myro.

La Steppa
(The Steps)
(ITALIAN—COLOR)
Berlin, July 3.
Columbia release of a Morris Ergas (Zebra) production. Stars Charles Vanel, Daniele Spellone, Marina Vlady. Directed by A. Lattuada. Screenplay, Lattuada and Pinelli Cureli; camera. Serfain; music, Turchi. At Berlin Film Fest. Running time, **110 MINS.**

A Chekhov short story has been expanded into a full-length film in this Morris Ergas production. But it has been given largely a documentary flavor· with little thought to narrative development. It can only have small playoff chances outside its native territory. And it lacks the essential qualities that give this type of film an arty flavor.

There is little substance to the tale, and therefore director Lattuada has been obliged to make this virtually into a travelog showing the hazards that were encountered when horse-drawn caravans crossed the Russian steppes. But since this was filmed on location in Yugoslavia it hasn't the authenticity that such a treatment demands.

The story, such as it is, concerns a small peasant boy who is sent away from home in the care of his uncle to go and study in the big city. And for its entire running time, the film describes his adventures on the way. Some are quite diverting, such as the folk dancing sequence, though that's a bit overlong, and another showing the male travellers harpooning fish in a stream. But by and large, it's conventional stuff, and has been better done in many Westerns.

Though Lattuada has tried to give the film some impetus, he's been handicapped by the very flimsy material put at his disposal. His direction, however, captures the period atmosphere, and the scenic effects in color and scope are attractive. Marina Vlady, an Italian

actress with good looks, is given star billing, but has nothing more than an insignificant role which calls for about two brief appearances and one line of dialog. Other principal roles are ably filled by Charles Vanel and Daniele Spellone.
Myro.

Das Leben Von Adolf Hitler
(The Life of Adolph Hitler)
(WEST GERMAN)
Karlovy Vary, July 10.
Transocean release of Walter Koppel-Real Film production. Directed and edited by Paul Rotha, assisted by Helga Koppel, Robert Neumann; commentary by Neumann, spoken by Hans Paetsch, Horst Fleck, Heinz Piper. At Karlovy Vary Film Fest. Running time, **105 MINS.**

British film historian, filmmaker and pic critic Paul Rotha has compiled a life of Adolph Hitler from old German, and other national newsreels, films and shorts. Coming after "Mein Kampf," it may seem to have some of the bloom off, but it does have enough new footage, biographical coherence and scenic and editing solidity to give it arty and general playoff possibility abroad.

Hitler's early life is sketched midway in the pic. First comes a general look at the times and then the Nazi rise to power and the horrors it left in its wake. A knowing commentary, excellent visual counterpoint, associations and thoroughness in this montage film make it an imperative look at the terrible Nazi scourge and the misery it caused.

It raises the question of why the Germans went along blindly alone on the whole, in spite of the opposition, but can not quite answer it. The reasons are there, as is the lesson.

Shots of the Hitler machine in action, war stuff, meetings with Franco and Mussolini are primarily new, at least not as familiar as those used in the many films of this type. It is a tribute to Rotha's astuteness and patience. This is a necessary and important film, and should take place in the theatre as well as video spots internationally.
Mosk.

La Bellezza Ippolita
(The Beautiful Ippolita)
(ITALIAN)
Berlin, July 3.
Cineriz (Alfred Bini) production and release. Stars Gina Lollobrigida; features Enrico Maria Salerno, Milva. Directed by Giancarlo Zagni. Screenplay, Elio Bartolini, Pasquale Festa Campanile, Massimo Franciosa, Zagni; camera, Aldo Scavarda; editor, Flavio Mogherini; music, Carlo Rustichelli. At Berlin Film Fest. Running time, **90 MINS.**
Ippolita .... Gina Lollobrigida
Luca .... Enrico Mario Salerno
Ardiana .... Milva

An invited entry to the Berlin festival, "The Beautiful Ippolita" is little more than a comedy vehicle for Gina Lollobrigida, and as such it has marquee values to help the boxoffice. That, however, is going to be the main basis of its appeal for it is thin in story values, and its humor is neither original nor very strong.

Sporting a blonde wig, the star plays a vaudeville artist who gives up her life in a secondrate troupe to marry a garage owner and look

after the pumps. Miss Lollobrigida has a twinkling eye for all the customers calling at the filling station, and that makes him jealous. When she accepts an invitation to a dance, he takes advantage of her absence to make love to her friend, but she discovers them in bed and pays him back in her own coin.

There's not much subtlety in the proceedings and it depends almost entirely on the lively, earthy performance of the star, who wears a wide range of revealing and provocative costumes to offer some obvious exploitation angles. There are a couple of amusing sequences, notably the star's performance in a tango contest when she partners one of the filling station's patrons. And another when she takes a day off to accompany a young Viennese who had come specially to take her off to Venice.

Giancarlo Zagni's direction is short on vitality and inspiration. Miss Lollobrigida infuses a certain amount of gusto into the proceedings. Enrico Mario Salerno makes a fair showing as the husband who cannot stand his wife's flirtatious nature. The other girl is nicely played by Milva while smaller roles are adequate.
Myro.

Polnocna Mse
(Midnight Mass)
(CZECH)
Karlovy Vary, July 10.
Czech State Film production and release. With Margit Bara, Josef Kroner, Ladislav Chudnik, Hanjo Hasse, Ivan Mastrik, Emilia Vasaryova. Directed by Jiri Krejcik. Screenplay, Peter Karvas, Albert Marencin; camera, Rudolf Stahl; editor, Josef Dobrichovckey. At Karlovy Vary Film Fest. Running time, **90 MINS.**
Valentin .... Josef Kroner
Marian .... Karol Machata
Palo .... Ladislav Chudnik
Angela .... Margit Bara
Brecker .... Hanjo Hasse
Durko .... Ivan Mistrik
Katka .... Emilia Vasaryova

This film recounts the terrible dilemma of a collaborationist family during the last war when a wounded partisan son comes home. It is well mounted and a taut drama despite the familiar subject matter. There could be some playoff mileage abroad in this because of the suspenseful and sleek treatment. But it lacks the penetration for many arty theatre chances.

As the Russians approach a family in a small Southern Czech village, one son is revealed as a local Nazi sympathizer, the daughter making love to a German major and one young son a partisan. The latter is wonded and hidden in the house over the Nazi son's objections.

It is Christmas Eve and a midnight mass has been allowed. The local priest is ordered to tell the people to give up the escaped partisan, for he is known to be hiding somewhere, but rather than do this informs the major where the partisan is.

Lensing is properly crisp and direction manages to get suspense into this. Acting is uniformly acceptable if some are sterotypes.
Mosk.

Kid Galahad
(COLOR)

Another likely Presley moneymaker; Elvis cast as boxer in familiar prizefight story with songs.

Hollywood, July 20.

United Artists release of David Weisbart production. Stars Elvis Presley, Gig Young, Lola Albright, Joan Blackman, Charles Bronson; features Ned Glass, Robert Emhardt, David Lewis. Directed by Phil Karlson. Screenplay, William Fay, based on story by Francis Wallace; camera, (De Luxe), Burnett Guffey; editor, Stuart Gilmore; music, Jeff Alexander; assistant director, Jerome M. Siegel. Reviewed at Academy Awards Theatre, July 20, '62. Running time, 95 MINS.

Walter Gulick	Elvis Presley
Willy Grogan	Gig Young
Dolly Fletcher	Lola Albright
Rose Grogan	Joan Blackman
Lew Nyack	Charles Bronson
Lieberman	Ned Glass
Mayn: rd	Robert Emhardt
Otto Danzig	David Lewis
Joie Shakes	Michael Dante
Zimmerman	Judson Pratt
Sperling	George Mitchell
Marvin	Richard Devon
Ralphie	Jeffrey Morris
Father Higgins	Liam Redmond

Two of the screen's most salable staples are united in David Weisbart's production of "Kid Galahad." One is Elvis Presley, whose following doesn't seem to have diminished appreciably over the years in spite of the subtle alteration of his public image from the swivel-hipped, sideburn-adorned hound dog howler into the mellowed, mannerly matinee idol that he is today. The other is one of the most hackneyed yarns in the annals of cinema fiction—the one about the wholesome, greenhorn kid who wanders into training camp (be it Stillman's Gym or the Catskills), kayoes with one mighty right the hardest belter on the premises, gets an instant nickname (usually "Babyface," occasionally "Killer" or "Sugar") and proceeds to score a string of victories enroute to the inevitable big fight in which the fix is on but the kid, who is all heart, nails his man anyway.

The story may be old, the direction not especially perceptive, the performances in several cases pretty poor, but United Artists' "Kid Galahad" is apt to be a moneymaker in spite of all this. It will be a special favorite with the youngsters who: (1) like Elvis more than most other people, (2) are that much less familiar with this workhorse plot than older audiences are.

Presley's acting resources are limited, but he has gradually established a character with which he does not have to strain too much for emotional nuance—the soft-spoken, unaffected, polite, unspoiled, forthright and ultimately two-fisted country boy. It is, however, a surprisingly paunchy Presley in this film, and the added avoirdupois, unaided by camera, is not especially becoming. Elvis sings some half a dozen songs—most commercial of which figures to be "Home Is Where The Heart Is," a sentimental ballad with juke potential.

Gig Young labors through the trite, confusing part of the mixed-up proprietor of the upstate boxing stable. Pretty Joan Blackman overacts as Presley's girl. But there are two strong principal performers. One is Lola Albright's (an accomplished actress who deserves bigger and better roles) as Young's unrequited torch-carrier, the other Charles Bronson's as an understanding trainer. Assorted supporting stereotypes are delineated adequately by the balance of the cast, chief among whom are Ned Glass, Robert Emhardt, David Lewis and Michael Dante.

William Fay's screenplay, based on a story by Francis Wallace, is notable for some brisk, up-to-date dialog, in contrast with the antiquity of its plot. Phil Karlson's direction has some unaccountable lapses of perception, although the fault may lie partially with the limitations of several of his players from whom he apparently was unable to extract the desirable reaction. Burnett Guffey's photography is sharp and colorful. Stuart Gilmore's editorial savvy shows through on prize ring sequences—in which editing makes the big difference. Cary Odell's art direction is capable. However, Idyllwild, California does not closely resemble the Catskill Mountain terrain of N.Y., locale of the story. Jeff Alexander's music is helpful and unobtrusive. *Tube.*

I Thank a Fool
(BRITISH-COLOR)

Classy cast struggle with over-pressurized, implausible meller; name stars may put it over at boxoffice.

London, July 17.

Metro release of an Anatole de Grunwald production. Stars Susan Hayward, Peter Finch; features Diane Cilento, Cyril Cusack, Kieron Moore, Athene Seyler, Richard Wattis, J. G. Devlin, Clive Morton, Miriam Karlin, Brenda De Banzie, Richard Leech. Directed by Robert Stevens. Screenplay, Karl Tunberg, from Audrey Erskine Lindop's novel; production designed by Sean Kenny; camera, Harry Waxman; editor, Frank Clarke; music, Ron Goodwin. Previewed at Metro Private Theatre, London. Running time, 100 MINS.

Christine Allison	Susan Hayward
Stephen Dane	Peter Finch
Liane Dane	Diane Cilento
Captain Ferris	Cyril Cusack
Roscoe	Kieron Moore
Aunt Heather	Athene Seyler
Ebblington	Richard Wattis
Woman in Black Maria	Mirian Karlin
O'Grady	Laurence Naismith
The Judge	Clive Morton
The Coroner	J. G. Devlin
Irish Doctor	Richard Leech
Nurse Drew	Brenda De Banzie
Irish Barmaid	Marguerite Brennan
Polly	Yolande Turner
Wardress	Judith Furse
Sleazy Doctor	Peter Sallis
Restaurant Manageress	Joan Benham
Landlady	Joan Hickson

Co-starring of Susan Hayward and Peter Finch in this has not produced the chemistry that might have been anticipated. It is not the fault of the principals, but simply that the somewhat turgid screenplay and the implausibilities of this meller are too much for the cast. Robert Stevens' direction is fussy and the editing does not help to tidy up an ambling script. However, with its cast, this pic could well get by at the wickets.

Miss Hayward plays a Canadian doctor who follows her lover to England and, at his own request, gives him an overdose of morphia when he becomes incurably ill. She is thus faced with a murder rap as well as one of unprofessional adulterous conduct with one of her patients. Finch is the prosecuting counsel and he throws the book at her, landing her in jail for two years. When she is released, Finch persuades her to work for him as nurse-companion to his young wife who earlier had been involved in an auto accident in which her father had been allegedly killed.

From that unlikely development on, she is caught up in a web of deceit, suspicion and lies, climaxing in her being suspected of yet another mercy killing when the young wife is found dead after an overdose of pills. This time Finch defends her at the inquest but, right up till the end, she is not sure whether or not he is double-crossing her.

Finch and Miss Hayward pursue their ways with admirable doggedness, but rarely has Finch looked more unhappy in a part. Miss Hayward's role is written with little variation of mood but it contrasts effectively with Diane Cilento's more fleshy character and portrayal of the nutty young wife. It is an exaggerated performance but helps to lift the pic often. Only other role of real weight is played with deft expertise by Cyril Cusack, as Miss Cilento's unscrupulous father. But even Cusack seems relieved when in the contrived finale he has to do a suicide fall.

Kieron Moore and Athene Seyler have chores that never rise to their expected significance, but they are both well handled. Several others chip in with excellent cameos though many of them seem highly irrelevant.

Sean Kenny has provided excellent production decor. The West Ireland location scenes particularly lend themselves to some snazzy lensing by Harry Waxman. Ron Goodwin's score aims to accentuate the eerie atmosphere that constantly tries to break through the screenplay, and often succeeds. With so much concerted talent on hand it is a pity that "I Thank a Fool" is not more impressive. *Rich.*

The Pirates Of Blood River
(MEGASCOPE-COLOR)

Satisfactory adventure meller for action buffs. Should be sturdy, program item.

Hollywood, July 19.

Columbia Pictures release of Anthony Nelson Keys production. Stars Kerwin Mathews, Glenn Corbett, Christopher Lee, Marla Landi. Directed by John Gilling. Screenplay, John Hunter, Gilling, from story by Jimmy Sangster; camera (Eastman), Arthur Grant; editor, Eric Boyd-Perkins; music, Gary Hughes; assistant director, John Peverall. Reviewed at the studio, July 19, '62. Running time, 87 MINS.

Jonathon	Kerwin Mathews
Henry	Glenn Corbett
La Roche	Christopher Lee
Bess	Marla Landi
Brocaire	Oliver Reed
Jason Standing	Andrew Keir
Hench	Peter Arne
Mac	Michael Ripper
Mason	Jack Stewart
Smith	David Lodge
Maggie	Marie Devereux
Margaret Blackthorne	Diane Aubrey
Commandant	Jerold Wells
Timothy	Dennis Waterman
Martha Blackthorne	Lorraine Clewes
2nd Settler	John Roden
Blackthorne	Desmond Llewelyn
Silas	Keith Pyott
Seymour	Richard Bennett
Martin	Michael Mulcaster
Silver	Dennis Shaw
Kemp	Michael Peake
Lance	John Colin
Carlos	Don Levy
Penal Colony Guard	John Bennett
Pugh	Ronald Blackman

Action aficionados will get a boot out of this British entry. Anthony Nelson Keys' production for Hammer Films wastes little time on dramatic nuance or romantic mush; instead stresses visual adventure elements all the way, which should make it a special favorite with the moppet brigade, male division. The exploitable Columbia release, filmed in Megascope and Eastman Color, should pair off neatly as a program attraction aimed at audiences that prefer to be assaulted pictorially rather than challenged psychologically.

The trying experiences of a courageous young Huguenot (Kerwin Mathews) early in the 18th century are the focal point of the screenplay by John Hunter and director John Gilling from a yarn by Jimmy Sangster. Falsely convicted of romantic misconduct, Mathews is banished to a penal colony, from which he escapes, only to fall into the hands of a band of cutthroat corsairs. Balance of the film illustrates Mathews' successful attempts to lead his group to victory over the buccaneer intruders, who haplessly try to make off with Huguenot treasure.

Mathews, rapidly becoming one of the screen's foremost adventurers, engineers another solid, swashbuckling performance. Glenn Corbett is rather rigid and mechanical as his chief ally, but Christopher Lee lends maknetic personality to the role of the cunning pirate chieftain. Support is dispatched satisfactorily.

Although dialog is stilted and unlifelike, there's nothing tame or static about action elements — as forcefully directed by Gilling, who is not one to compromise when a little gore seeps into the storyline. But, then, gore is a specialty in the Hammer Film operation. Gilling receives journeyman assists from cameraman Arthur Grant, editor Eric Boyd-Perkins, art director Don Mingaye and special effects expert Les Bowie. The film also benefits from a melodic score by Gary Hughes. *Tube.*

La Loi Des Hommes
(The Law of Men)
(FRENCH)

Paris, July 17.

CFDC release of Filmatec production. Stars Micheline Presle, Philippe Leroy-Beaulieu; features Arletty, Jose-Luis De Villalonga, Marcel Dalio, Berthe Grandval, Pierre Mondy. Directed by Charles Gerard. Screenplay, Pascal Jardin, Gerard; camera, Claude Robin; editor, Bernard Lefevre. At Marignan, Paris. Running time, 100 MINS.

Sophie	Micheline Presle
Dandieu	Philippe Leroy-Beaulien
Princess	Arletty
Lawyer	Marcel Dalio
Priest	Jose-Luis De Vallalonga
Secretary	Berthe Grandval

Aping the Yank style of hard-boiled police tales does not come off in this French film. Gallic temperament tries to explain all and forces doses of violence and offbeat characters. It remains mainly a local gambit with only possible dualer chances in other countries on its heavy-handed plotting.

A stolid young detective thinks a lovely femme reporter knows too much about a mysterious holdup. He begins tracking her and though beaten up and tricked at every turn manages to become her lover and find she had masterminded the affair just for kicks.

The overplotting, the French lack of familiarity with this type of tale and the wooden thesping all combine to foil the attempts at true adventure.

Micheline Presle does the female reporter self-consciously while Philippe Lefoy-Beaulieu is wooden rather than dedicated as the relentless policeman. Others try their best to etch portraits among the assorted policeticos, hoodlums, etc., that infest the pic but to no avail. *Mosk.*

Some People
(BRITISH-COLOR)

Offbeat pic about problems of bored youth, designed as a boost for the Duke of Edinburg's Award scheme for youngsters. Presence of Kenneth More gives British b.o. chances a boost.

London, July 17.

Anglo Amalgamated release of James Archibald production. Stars Kenneth More; features Ray Brooks, Annika Wills, Michael Gwynn, Cyril Luckham, David Andrews, Angela Douglas, Harry H. Corbett, Fanny Carby. Directed by Clive Donner. Screenplay, John Eldridge; camera (Eastman color), John Wilcox; editor, Fergus McDonnell; music, Ron Grainer. At Studio One, London. Running time, 93 MINS.
Mr. Smith .... Kenneth More
Johnnie .... Ray Brooks
Anne .... Annika Wills
Bill .... David Andrews
Terry .... Angela Douglas
Bert .... David Hemmings
Tim .... Timothy Nightingale
Jimmy .... Frankie Dymon Jr.
Johnnie's Father ...... Harry H. Corbett
Johnnie's Mother .... Fanny Carby
Vicar .... Michael Gwynn
Clerk of Court .... Fred Ferris
Magistrate .... Cyril Luckham
Harper ...?................ Richard Davis
Mike .:..................... Dean Webb

This one is something of a hybrid. It is designed as a feature entertainment film, a peek at the problems of modern youth in danger of becoming delinquents. As such it stands up as reasonable entertainment though in a lesser league than "The Wild Ones." But also planted firmly in the film, some unabashed propaganda for the Duke of Edinburgh's Award Scheme for youth. The propaganda is done with good humor and understanding and is not sticky. But its very presence will be somewhat disturbing to many, despite having Kenneth More to put over the message.

The pic is set in the industrial town of Bristol. Three lads are part of a gang of "ton-up" (100 m.p.h.) motor cyclists. Involved in an accident, they are banned from driving. Then out of sheer boredom, they become poential young hoods. Luckily, they become involved with More, playing a voluntary church choirmaster. He gives them the opportunity of rehearsing their rock 'n' roll combo. And gradually, they become interested in the new pursuits that the Duke's scheme has to offer youngsters of initiative. Only one of the trio is suspicious and his actions cause

the slight dramatic climax but, of course, everything ends up rosily.

John Eldridge's storyline is loose. Clive Donner's direction is leisurely but affectionate.

John Wilcox's color photography is sound while Ron Grainer has turned out a useful score, with Johnny Worth, two or three pop numbers are put over deftly by The Eagles combo.

More handles the role of the sympathetic choirmaster with his usual, easy charm. He obviously played the part because of his interest in the Duke's scheme and this interest is reflected in his performance. But the revelation is in the performances of some of the youngsters, full proof that there is a lot of talent around worthy of encouragement. Ray Brooks, David Andrews and David Hemmings play the three main teenagers with authority and may develop into firstclass thesps.

Angela Douglas is pertly provocative as a young blonde who can handle a song and a boy with equal assurance. There is also a standout cameo by Harry H. Corbett as Brooks' father, who finds it difficult to communicate with the boy he has sired.

"Some People" title refers to a song in the film which opines that some people think modern kids are no good but actually it's their critics who are all mixed up. Film may well need careful selling but, if it is teamed up with a strong partner, it can help to provide a rewarding program for most audiences. *Rich.*

Der Rosenkavalier
(BRITISH-COLOR)

Strictly for art houses, and opera connoisseurs. Another of Paul Czinner's praiseworthy attempts to capture art for posterity.

London, July 17.

Rank release of a Paul Czinner production. Stars Elisabeth Schwarzopf, Sena Jurinac, Anneliese Rothernberger, Otto Edelmann, Erich Kunz. Directed by Paul Czinner. Music by Richard Strauss, with Herbert Von Karajan conducting Vienna Philharmonic; libretto, Hugo von Hofmannsthal; stage production, Rudolf Hartmann; decor, Teo Otto; camera, S. D. Onions; editor, Philip Barnikel. At Odeon, Leicester-Square, London. Running time, 192 MINS.
Princess von Werdenberg ....
Elisabeth Schwarzkopf
Baron von Lerchenau .... Otto Edelmann
Octavian .... Sena Jurinac
Herr von Faninal .... Erich Kunz
Sophie .... Anneliese Rothenberger
The Duenna .... Judith Hellwig
Vienna State Opera Chorus, Mozarteum Orch, and Vienna State Opera Ballet.

The successful attempts of Dr. Paul Czinner to bring the Royal and Bolshoi Ballets to screen posterity are now followed by the full Salzburg Festival performance of Richard Strauss' opera, "Der Rosenkavalier." Done with his multi-camera technique, it is a fascinating experience. But it is, of course, strictly for opera connoisseurs. Here its performances are, so far, restricted to a showing at the Bath Festival and a short season currently at the Festival Hall.

Story of romantic intrigues in Vienna is, of course, strictly for the birds. But Strauss' music is enchanting and Cziner has nothing

but talent on his hands when it comes to his cast. The principals, the delightful Elisabeth Schwarzkopf, Otto Edelmann, Sea Juronac, Erich Kunz and Anneliese Rothenlerger are finely supported by the other singers, the Vienna State Opera chorus, the Mozrateum Orchestra and Vienna State Opera Ballet.

Color, sound, costumes and production are all lavish. They all add up to a prestige production which, while having many dull moments in its over-long 192 minutes, will satisfy all opera lovers and may well convert some of the more wary visitors. *Rich.*

Une Grosse Tete
(A Swelled Head)
(FRENCH-FRANSCOPE)
Paris, July 17.

Fernand Rivers release of Belmont Films-Paris Overseas Films production. Stars Eddie Constantine; features Georges Poujouly, Alexandra Stewart, Lihane David, Jean Galland, Christian De Tilliere, Serge Davri. Written and directed by Claude De Givray. Camera, Michel Kelber; editor, Guillenm Agnes. At Cinemonde-Opera, Paris. Running time, 90 MINS.
Napo .... Eddie Constantine
Georges .... Georges Poujouly
Francoise .... Alexandra Stewart
Marianne .... Liliane David
Uncle .... Jean Galland
Nephew .... Christian De Tilliere
Policeman .... Serge Davri

Yank actor-singer Eddie Constantine, who became a film star here playing as a Yank private eye or G-Man, now lends himself to one of the new style director's good natured odes to U.S. adventure pix. It comes off as an entertaining romp but lacking the true zest to get too far abroad.

But its general bonhommie, action and surface but pleasing characterizations may have this something for foreign playoff chances. It has the old New Wave feeling in improved bits, scant attention to academic editing and private gags. Here Constantine takes over the old house of an elderly man which some unscrupulous real estate agents are trying to gain control of.

A middle-aged adventurer, he picks up a young mechanic and they turn the land into a runway for stripped down engine-driven frames called carts. He sees to the boy's education and then a girl comes between them.

Laced with references to many old film masterpieces, and full of gag-filled fights and incidents, this manages to keep fairly entertaining. It bogs down at times but its general good nature brings it off.

If director Claude De Givray can settle down and learn to tell a story in his own way he may emerge a needed new filmmaker with a feel for comedy adventure yarns so sorely needed here. Technical aspects are par and actors have an ease and relaxed quality in keeping with the tongue-in-cheek carryings-on. Fights are well staged for a French pic. *Mosk.*

The Lion
(BRITISH—COLOR)

Name value in a telling drama about family relationship, a child's strange affection for a lion and a near tragedy; graphic jungle and animal shots add up to bright b.o. prospects.

London, July 24.

20th-Fox release of Samuel G. Engel (Cecil Ford) production. Stars William Holden, Trevor Howard, Capucine; features Pamela Franklin. Directed by Jack Cardiff. Screenplay, Irene and Louis Kamp, based on novel by Joseph Kessel; camera (De Luxe color), Ted Scaife; editor, Russell Lloyd; music, Malcolm Arnold. At Leicester Square Theatre, London. Running time, 96 MINS.
Robert Hayward ...... William Holden
John Bullit .... Trevor Howard
Christine .... Capucine
Tina .... Pamela Franklin
Bogo .... Makara Kwaltha Kamadh ni
Ol' Kalu .... Zakee
Orlunga .... Paul Oduor
Kihero .... Samuel Obiero Romboh
Elder of Masai ... Christopher Agunda

Problem with most films with a jungle background is that the animals and scenery are usually so much more fascinating than the human beings. The people and the story tend to get in the way. This does not happen unduly in "The Lion," a superior yarn of its type. A literate screenplay with easy dialog, observant direction and capital playing by the principals make this a holding, often exciting drama. The combo of William Holden and Trevor Howard (seen together before in "The Key") should draw business, yet it is the remarkable thesping of a moppet named Pamela Franklin and the wonder shots of African wild animals that likely will linger in the memory.

Director Jack Cardiff, with his lensing knowhow, was bound to have a picnic in and around the Game Reserve territories of Kenya and Yganda. But he has disciplined himself and his cameraman, Ted Scaife, so that the storyline is not constantly being held up while the camera lingers lushly in its De Luxe color.

Story opens with the arrival of Holden, a New York attorney at Kirinyaga Game Reserve in Kenya. He's there at the request of his ex-wife (Capucine), who has married Trevor Howard, a big game hunter turned warden. She is worried that their 11-year-old daughter (Pamela Franklin) is being reared in an uneasy atmosphere of jungle lore and local tribal law which could eventually spell unhappiness, even disaster for her.

Holden treads wearily, for he realizes that he is still drawn towards Capucine, and she to him and that Howard senses it. Growing tension rises between the three adults. But he, too, is worried when he sees the strange, almost witchcraft relationship between the daughter and animals, and her excitement about the primitive native life. Particularly she has an amazing relationship with "King," a full-grown jungle lion, that had been reared with her from cubdom. To Holden it has an essence of evil which convinces him that the child must be taken out of the environment. How the situation is resolved is skillfully blended into the screenplay, involving the child, the lion, a native crisis and the tense mental tug of war between the three adults over the child's future.

There are some highspot production scenes, notably a ceremonial native "coronation," and a hair-raising sequence when Howard is showing Holden around the Reserve. He drives perilously among rhinos, hippos and elephants, baiting them, in order to demonstrate his command over the situation and to scare the "city slicker."

First meeting of Holden and his daughter is touching and that between the moppetts, Holden and King the Lion, a nailbiter. The payoff when the lion goes beserk when attacked by a native leading to the climax has both excitement and tenderness. It results in Howard deciding to return to big game hunting while Holden, Capucine and the child (now cured of Africa-itis) set off to make a new life in the U.S.

And always that camera is straying around the jungle and the Reserve, picking up intimate shots of every type of animal and giving the tab-buyer a real blow by blow description of life in that colorful and awesome area of Africa.

Young Miss Franklin, whose only other pic appearance was also a hit, in "The Innocents," with Deborah Kerr, gives a wise, beyond-her-years performance. It is almost impossible to believe that her scenes with the lion are faked and that the lion is really a well trained tame animal now back in his Californian menagerie. Miss Franklin also handles her delicate scenes with the three adults with astute change of mood. This is an intelligent piece of thesping that marks the youngster as one of the better child stars.

Holden is pleasantly charming and understanding as the ex-husband. Miss Capucine looks as coolly beautiful in the jungle as in a boudoir while Howard, at times looking fiercer than any of the animals around him, gives a powerful study of a rugged no-nonsense character with a temper that, any moment, could unleash evil happenings. Native actors give colorful support.

Scaife's lensing is firstclass. Only technical problem perhaps concerns the particular print seen. Altogether, however, a superior offering, blending moments of both mental and physical intensity.
Rich.

Bonne Chance Charlie!
(Good Luck Charlie)
(FRENCH—FRANSCOPE)

Paris, July 24.
Unidex release of Belmont Films production. Stars Eddie Constantine; features Albert Prejean, Carla Marlier, Robert Moore. Directed by Jean-Louis Richard. Screenplay, Richard Jacques Houbart; camera, Michel Kelber; editor, Françoise Javet. At Elysees, Paris. Running time, 90 MINS.
Charlie .... Eddie Constantine
Cardin .... Albert Prejean
Girl .... Carla Marlier
Sophocles .... Robert Moore

Up to now Eddie Constantine, the Yank who became a Continental pic star, has been fighting gangsters, white slavers, opium and other type underworld characters in his tongue-in-cheek popular pix. But here he runs up against a non-repentent Nazi war criminal. And, if laudable, the plotting and theme do not seem to jell with his personality.

Constantine is made out as a man who has succeeded in life but goes to Athens to track down the Nazi in order to help a friend. Said friend sought his help because of the atrocities committed and because his brother was a victim.

Constantine is his phlegmatic self and manages to meet a girl and get into one solidly staged fight. But the theme makes both director Jean-Louis Richard and Constantine mute the usual zany, gag ridden goings-on.

The criminal, when cornered, spouts what sounds like Eichmann's excuses but is shot down by Constantine when he overhears him trying to convert a young man and spieling the old Nazi hate line. Pic has some nice production values in Athens and is fetchingly cut and shot. But the conflict of themes and exaggerated slotting hurt.

Constantine plows through this with his usual ease but is hard put when forced to make long speeches about his motives. Pic may have some playoff chances abroad on its theme. *Mosk.*

Jovenes y Bellas
(The Young and Beautiful Ones)
(MEXICAN—COLOR)

Mexico City, July 24.
Peliculas Nachionales release of Alameda Films and Cesar Santos Galindo production. Stars Gaston Santos, Maria Eugenia San Martin, Alfonso Mejia, Maria Duval, Erna Martha Baumann, Begoña Palacios, Fernando Lujan, Roberto Cobo; features Norma Angelica, Alvaro Ortiz, Alejandro Ciangherotti Jr., Yolanda Ciani, Arcelia Larranaga, Jose Baviera, Aurora Alvarado, Magda Ursizu, Argentina Sepulveda and Luis Aragon, with special role by Ariadne Welter plus the voice of Andy Russell. Directed by Fernando Coates. Screenplay, Julio Porter. At Alameda Theatre, Mexico City. Running time, 90 MINS.

This musical comedy effort, featuring an army of younger talent, is a pleasing Mexican effort. The young ladies in principal roles are easy to look at and there's fast paced comedy and musical numbers including latest dance rhythms.

Story line is unimportant since it treats of a group of young senoritas who are far too dedicated to "rock and roll," sent to the country by their parents to get over this "lunacy." But the country bumpkins also are hep to modern swing so the girls and boys have a grand old time in the sticks.

Fernando Cortes has given this one the pace and frivolity it needs, without overstepping bounds of good taste. The comedy situations are skillfully aimed at Spanish language audiences. Overall effect gives this enough to make it a boxoffice hit in rerun and nabe houses, and over the Spanish language circuit. *Emil.*

Madison Avenue

It isn't Madison Avenue, nor advertising, nor much of a picture. Tiresomely complicated plotting and bloodless characters; lower half item with good names.

20th Century-Fox production and release. Stars Dana Andrews, Eleanor Parker, Jeanne Crain, Howard St. John, Eddie Albert. Directed by Bruce Humberstone. Adapted by Norman Corwin from novel, "The Build-Up Boys" by Jeremy Kirk; cameraman, Charles G. Clarke; editor, Betty Steinberg; score and conducting by Harry Harris; art direction, Duncan Cramer, Leland Fuller. Reviewed at Brandt's Beacon, N.Y., July 29, '62. Running time, 93 MINS.
Clint Lorimer .... Dana Andrews
J. D. Jocelyn .... Howard St. John
Brock .... David White
Anne Temaine .... Eleanor Parker
Peggy Shannon .... Jeanne Crain
Stipe .... Henry Daniell
Miss Haley .... Kathleen Freeman
Kati Olsen .... Betti Andrews

This belated review is for the files. "Madison Avenue" was shot some years ago by 20th-Fox with a marquee-worthy cast headed by Dana Andrews, Eleanor Parker, Jeanne Crain, Eddie Albert, Howard St. John and Henry Daniell. Held back from reviewers and theatres, it is only now "sneaking" into N.Y. nabe playoff as the lower half of a summer bill with 20th's recent "Mr. Hobbs Takes a Vacation."

A look at the picture explains the un-Madison Avenueish quiet attendant upon this production, a much ado about pretty dull and pretty unbelievable business world back-stabbers. Despite the title, there is very little Madison Avenue, or even New York, in the tale. Mostly it concerns pressagentry of the kind which likes to masquerade as public relations. The locale is principally in Washington, as described, but not shown. Story derives from a novel, "The Build-Up Boys," by Jeremy Kirk. A reviewer can only guess how far off-target the film version is.

A number of curiosities pervade the 90-odd minutes. A striking credit is the script by Norman Corwin. That is hard to believe, it's so mediocre. Further puzzlement is inherent in the circumstance that Corwin spent years at CBS in Manhattan and surely has met flesh-and-bone admen. In any event, starting with the script the line of blame goes straight to producer-director Bruce Humberstone. The reviewer cannot know whether to think Betty Steinberg's editing "salvaged" a mess so that, at least, it "plays," or whether she was one of the culprits.

The characters are weirdly stock. Eddie Albert is first presented as the eccentric head of a Washington milk company. He flies toy airplanes in his office, conducts his own milk route, has never met his advertising agent, Eleanor Parker, and is offered as an amiable boob—almost a caricature of the Eddie Albert stereotype. But later in the film, he is a double-crosser, hard as nails, conceited as a presidential aspirant. True, there is an implication—in the dialog—that he and others have been contaminated by "build-up." Only none of this, as handled, is believable.

Miss Parker herself undergoes transformation from an impoverished, plain-jane adwoman to a fashion plate with a hardening character. Again there is an implication of some moral made in the novel but barely more than a throwaway in the screen script. She is one of the two women who want Dana Andrews to marry them. In the end the other gal, Jeanne Crain, gets the ring and the "I Love You" declaration—but the audience is entitled to doubt the sincerity of the proposal. The trouble is that the villainy is contrived, surface and without subtlety or dramatic power.

There is, under the generalities set forth, next to nothing to say for the players, except that they are slightly better than a bad film. The production values are so-so. Camera work is clear, art direction plausible, and the special score does not intrude.
Land.

Two Weeks In Another Town
(COLOR)

Unsatisfactory psychological meller about a fallen Hollywood star in search of himself. Dim b.o. contender.

Hollywood, Aug 1.

Metro release of John Housem n production. Stars Kirk Dougl:s. Edward G. Robinson. Cyd Charisse: fe tures George Hamilton, Dahlia L:vi. Claire Trevor, James Gregory, Rosann Schiaffino. Directed by Vincen'e Minnelli. Screenplay, Charles Schnee. based on novel by Irwin Shaw; camera (Metrocolor). Milton Krasner; editors, Adrienne Fazan, Robert J. Kern Jr.: music. David Raksin: assistant director, Erich Von Stroheim Jr. Reviewed at Academy Awards Theatre, Aug. 1, '62. Running time, 106 MINS.

Jack Andrus ...... Kirk Douglas
Maurice Kruger.... Edward G. Robinson
Carlotta .... Cyd Charisse
Davie Drew .... George Hamilton
Veronica .... Dahlia Lavi
Clara .... Claire Trevor
Brad Byrd .... James Gregory
Barzelli .... Rosanna Schiaffino
Janet Bark .... Joanna Roos
Lew Jordan .... George Macready
Tucino .... Mino Doro
Zeno .... Stefan Schnabel
Assistant Director .... Vito Scotti
Dr. Cold Eyes .... Tom Palmer
Ravinski ...... Erich von Stroheim Jr.
Chanteuse .... Leslie Uggams

Prospects are bleak for this psychological melodrama about a skidding Hollywood star and his desperate struggle for self-realization. Only widely scattered spurts and patches of incisive storytelling or cinematic flair bring any distinction to an otherwise highly disappointing effort by the fairly imposing creative team that worked on the Metro release.

United for purposes of conveying Irwin Shaw's novel to the screen were such ordinarily reliable picture shapers as producer John Houseman, director Vincente Minnelli and scenarist Charles Schnee, not to mention performers the calibre of Kirk Douglas and Edward G. Robinson. "Two Weeks In Another Town" is not an achievement about which any of these creative people are apt to boast.

Douglas stars as the unstable actor, fresh off a three-year hitch in sanitariums, who goes to Rome to rejoin the director (Edward G. Robinson) with whom, years earlier, he'd scored his greatest triumphs. In the course of a series of shattering incidents, Douglas comes to discover that it is upon himself alone that he must rely for the stability and strength of character with which he can fulfill his destiny. In making this discovery, he is able at last to shed the selfish and parasitic individuals upon whom he's always foolishly depended.

Douglas emotes with his customary zeal and passion, but labors largely in vain to illuminate an unbelievable character. Even less believable is the character of his ex-wife, a black-as-night, hard-as-nails seductress exotically overplayed by Cyd Charisse. Just what they see in each other to prolong their most unlikely, destructive relationship is quite baffling.

Only remotely lifelike characters in the story are Robinson and Claire Trevor as an ambiguous married couple whose personalities transform under the secretive cover of night. But the characters are as despicable as they are complex, and this film is desperately in need of simpler, nicer people. Robinson and Miss Trevor; two reliable performers, do all they can with the roles. George Hamilton is satisfactory as a confused young actor, as is Dahlia Lavi as the Italian girl befriended by Douglas. Rosanna Schiaffino chips in a fiery portrayal of an Italo screen star, and others prominent in support are James Gregory, Joanna Roos, George Macready, Mino Doro and Tom Palmer.

The cinematic skills of cameraman Milton Krasner, editors Adrienne Fazan and Robert J. Kern Jr., and art directors George W. Davis and Urie McCleary are evident but overshadowed by the overall dramatic mediocrity. There is a haunting score by David Raksin. A considerable amount of footage from "The Bad and the Beautiful" is cleverly incorporated into the drama. As a matter of fact, the portion of the film-within-a-film is livelier than just about anything else in the film.

A rather sad commentary, in that both pictures were produced by Houseman, directed by Minnelli, written for the screen by Schnee, and starred Douglas. *Tube.*

No Man Is An Island
(COLOR)

Biopic based on World War II experiences of Navy hero George R. Tweed on occupied Guam. Action mart best bet.

Hollywood, July 25.

Universal release of John Monks Jr.-Richard Goldstone production. Stars Jeffrey Hunter; introduces Barbara Perez. Directed and screenplay by Monks and Goldstone; camera (Eastman), Carl Kayser; editor, Basil Wrangell; music, Restie Umali. Reviewed at Westwood Village Theatre, July '62. Running time, 114 MINS.

George R. Tweed ...... Jeffrey Hunter
Sonn Sonnenberg ... Marshall Thompson
Joe Cruz .... Barbara Perez
Chico Torres .... Ronald Remy
Al Turney .... Paul Edwards Jr.
Chief Schultz .... Rolf Bayer
Vicente .... Vicente Liwanag
Roy Lund .... Fred Harris II
Mr. Shimoda .... Bert Avellana
Mrs. Nakamura .... Chichay
Florecito ..... Antonio dela Mogueis
Major Hondo .... Vic Silayan
Commander Oto Harada. Bert Laforteza
Sus Quintagua .... Eddie Infante
Tumon .... Nard Ramos
Primera Quintagua .... Rosa Mia
Santos .... Mike Anzures
Father Pangolin ..... Joseph de Cordova
Limtiago .... Mario Barri
Tommy Tanaka .... Stevie Joseph
Japanese Sgt.-Major .... Ding Tello
Antonio Cruz .... Burt Olivar
Josefa Cruz .... Veronica Palileo

Biography implies truth, not toying with fact and utilizing artificial dramatic devices to mislead and distort for purposes of heightening emotional impact. "No Man Is An Island" is second-rate depiction of the heroic World War II activities of George R. Tweed, USN. Filmed in the Philippines, the Universal release will suffice as an entry for the less demanding action mart.

The picture, written, directed and produced by John Monks Jr. and Richard Goldstone, describes Tweed's exploits on Guam between Dec. 7, 1941 and ultimate liberation of the island, an event the success of which Tweed helped insure by signaling to the U.S. fleet from the secret hilltop outpost he occupied for several years during Japanese occupation.

Jeffrey Hunter, recently seen as Jesus in "King Of Kings," a role obviously tough to follow, plays Tweed. He plays it earnestly, but the character, as written, is far from substantial, and the direction has not come to the actor's aid where he needs it most—in scene endings in which his silent outward expressions are supposed to project inner feelings and conclusions. Hunter is an extraordinarily handsome—almost pretty—actor, but such looks can be a drawback and a distraction in poorly developed roles. Adequate in prominent assignments are Marshall Thompson, Ronald Remy, Paul Edwards Jr., Rolf Bayer, Chichay, Joseph de Cordova and Burt Olivar. Unresolved romantic interest is fashioned with uncertainty by Barbara Perez.

Outstanding feature of the film is Carl Kayser's photography, which utilizes the zoom to special advantage, both dramatically and as a means of illustrating the trigonometry of island combat. Balance of credits generally attain a level of efficiency without flair. In addition to producers Monks and Goldstone, coproducer was Rolf Bayer and associate producers were Robert A. Lewis and Albert R. Joseph. *Tube.*

Vaxdockan
(The Doll)
(SWEDISH)

Flora Film release of Lorens Marmstedt production. Stars Per Oscarsson, Gio Petre. Directed by Arne Mattsson. Screenplay by Lars Forssell and Eva Seeberg; camera, Ake Dalquist; music, Ulrik Neumann; editor, Ingemar Ejve. Previewed in Stockhold. Running time, 91 MINS.

Night Watchman .... Per Oscarsson
Doll .... Gio Petre
Barber .... Tor Isedal
Landlady .... Elsa Prawitz
Concierge .... Bengt Eklund
Young Girl .... Malou

Lorens Marmstedt was one of Sweden's most prominent independents during the 1940s and early 1950s. He produced several of Ingmar Bergman's early films and most of Hasse Ekman's best films. But when additional entertainment taxes were introduced about a decade ago, Marmstedt and the other independents became inactive. "The Doll" is his first serious production in many years.

The film centers on a young night watchman, who is neurotically lonely in Stockholm. He rents a room, high up in an old shabby house, where several other tenants live, and a lonely landlady whose face is deformed by burns. On one of his nightly rounds in Stockholm's new, ultra modern shopping area, the watchman enters a storeroom filled with display dolls. A couple of thieves run out of the room as he enters and in their hurry they knock over a display doll. The watchman goes over to the fallen doll and starts uttering words of comfort. He then decides to take the nude, female doll home with him and make it look as if the thieves had stolen it.

When he gets it home, he starts talking to it and is delighted to have some company. He treats the doll more and more as if it were a real woman and eventually begins to carry on conversations, believing that it has come to life and talks, moves and loves him. He starts buying flowers, food, clothes and ornaments for it. In his mind, the dummy becomes demanding at times, wants him to introduce it to others and go out and have a good time. The film unavoidably leads to tragedy.

Per Oscarsson plays the part of the watchman intensively and convincingly. However, the doll's transitions from a thing to a living woman are not entirely convincing. The subject is not sufficiently developed to sustain attention. Furthermore, the old, shabby environment seems very out of place in prosperous Sweden, where citizens are not complaining about the shabbiness of their apartments, but the loneliness of their cubicles in suburbia.

However, "The Doll" should be of some interest to art theatre audiences. *Fred.*

The Pirates Of Blood River
(BRITISH-COLOR)

Easygoing bit of hokum for not overfussy patrons; cutlasses and all that, but little marquee appeal.

London, July 31.

BLC release of a Columbia presentation of a Hammer production. Stars Kerwin Mathews, Christopher Lee, Glenn Corbett; features Marla Landi, Oliver Reed, Andrew Keir, Peter Arne, Marie Devereux, Diane Aubrey. Produced by Anthony Nelson Kays. Directed by John Gilling. Screenplay, John Hunter & John Gilling, from story by Jimmy Sangsterl; camera (Technicolor), Arthur Grant; editor, Eric Boyd-Perkins; music, Gary Hughes. At London Pavilion. Running time, 84 MINS.

Jonathon .... Kerwin Mathews
Henry .... Glenn Corbett
LaRoche .... Christopher Lee
Bess .... Marla Landi
Brocaire .... Oliver Reed
Jason Standing .... Andrew Keir
Hench .... Peter Arne
Mac .... Michael Ripper
Mason .... Jack Stewart
Smith .... David Lodge
Maggie .... Marie Devereux
Margaret Blackthorne...... Diane Aubrey
Penal Colony Guard ..... John Bennett

This one is strictly a dualer, some hokum designed for easygoing audiences. As such, it's by no means a bad adventure yarn with plenty of action and some competent, straightforward pieces of thesping. It follows the admirable Hammer policy of playing hokey material straight. Hence, it is acceptable even if some of the situations are contrived and occasionally the dialog is unintentionally amusing.

Storyline concerns a band of religious settlers on a West Indian island. Son of the leader is falsely accused of having an affair with the wife of one of the settlers and is banished to a penal colony for life. He escapes from the cooler and falls in with a band of pirates led by LaRoche (Christopher Lee) who, in the true tradition of second feature films, has a patch over one eye and has lost a hand. Only the parrot is missing. The pirate king rightly assumes that the settlers have some secret treasure and, promising to right the settlers' wrongs, persuades the escaped con to lead them to the settlement.

What follows is allround double-crossing, the rescue of damsels in distress, plenty of flashing cutlasses and a highly implausible ending. It adds up to modest entertainment shrewdly geared to what will be a successful boxoffice haul, particularly when paired with another pic, as here.

Christopher Lee, a capable

actor who, for his own sake, has probably been playing these type of parts too long, registers as the Pirate king, playing it with the right touch of sinister aplomb. Kerwin Mathews and Glenn Corbett, inexplicably imported from Hollywood, are adequately dashing heroes. Andrew Keir is a dour leader of the settlers while Peter Arne turns in a canny performance as one of Lee's more rebellious henchmen. Femme side is limited but is suitably handled by Marla Landi, Diane Aubrey and Marie Devereux.

John Gilling directs briskly while Arthur Grant's Technicolor lensing is okay. As usual in this type of film, the music is laid on too heavily and without subtlety.
Rich.

Locarno Fest

The Reluctant Saint

Synthetic treatment of a pic version about a supposedly real Saint who could fly. This looms mainly a dualer or playoff entry with some value via the name of Oscar-winner Maximilian Schell. It is a Yank indie made abroad.

Locarno, July 31.
Columbia Films release of Dmytryk-Weiler production. Stars Maximilian Schell, Ricardo Montalban, Lea Padovani, Akim Tamiroff; features Mark Damon, Elisa Cegani, Arnoldo Foa. Directed by Edward Dmytryk. Screenplay, John Fante, Joseph Petracci; camera, Pennington Richards; editor, Manuel Del Campo; music, Nino Rota. At Locarno Film Fest. Running time, **100 MINS.**

Giuseppe .... Maximilian Schell
Don Raspi .... Ricardo Montalban
Mother .... Lea Padovani
Bishop .... Akim Tamiroff
Aldo .... Mark Damon
Carlotta .... Luciana Paluzzi
Sister .... Elisa Cegani
Felixa .... Arnoldo Foa

Purportedly based on the life of a real 17th Century Italian Catholic Saint of the Franciscan order of monks, this film is played mainly for laughs, with only a smattering of religious ritual. Though shot in real 17th Century Italo towns, b u i l d i n g s and churches, it rarely evokes the time or gives insight into the religious aspects of the story. Thus this looms mainly a playoff item with some possible arty theatre placement on its theme. But this latter looks dubious.

Schell plays a good-natured, slightly half-witted peasant youth. He is the butt of town jokes and the bane of his mother's life. She finally gets him packed off to a monastery o p e r a t e d by her brother.

Here, too, he upsets routine and is confined to the stable. But his way with animals touches a visiting Bishop who recommends him for the priesthood. He gets through hard exams by what seems providence, and actually becomes a priest. Praying one day before the head of a Madonna statue he has broken, he rises off the ground. This leads to town hysteria and an attempt to exorcise him which brings on a vision of the Madonna to all and his consequent Sainthood. Pic ends with him floating alongside his fellow monks as they wind down a country road singing.

Schell has neither the inner intensity to hint at sainthood nor the help of a more severe story treatment to make this fable of miracle either affecting or meaningful.

Writers and director seemed to take the middle road of tongue-in-cheek treatment with the lines.

Though produced in English abroad, this, paradoxically, might have been better served if made in Hollywood. There its semi-serious, self-conscious tale of a Saint might h a v e received a lighthearted entirely fictional glaze to make it palatable. But the plethora of different accents, the real locale and the different modes of playing this unacceptable as either comedy, drama or a true look at Sainthood.

Director Edward Dmytryk has staged this listlessly, and has been unable to get much from the actors. Aside from Schell's vacillating performance, Ricardo Montalban is a sort of stereotyped heavy as the monk who will not believe until he sees an apparition of the Madonna. Akim Tamiroff is hard put to play an earthy Bishop while Lea Padovani is too beautiful and fragile to ably etch the hardbitten, overworked mother.

This is technically acceptable but a miss in its mixture of approaches and playing. The production dress is acceptable. But the truly intense and incisive filmic tales of this kind that have come from foreign studios since the war make this appear a hybrid. Foreign chances also seem spotty. *Mosk.*

Et, Morte La Mort
(And, Death Is Dead)
(MOROCCAN)

Locarno, July 31.
Bennis Films production and release. With Mustapha Bennis, Mary Von Meyer, Laslo Szabo. Written and directed by Gilbert Vergnes. Camera, A. Lalli Ali; editor, F. Berganof. At Locarno Film Fest. Running time, **90 MINS.**
Faradji .... Mustapha Bennis
Laslo .... Laslo Szabo
Sandra .... Mary Von Meyer

Made on a shoestring in Morocco by a couple of Frenchmen, this emerges unwittingly a takeoff on the New Wave French films which have now run their course. There is nothing to recommend this for any untoward foreign interest. But the violence and fairly well done fight scenes may have it paying off in North Africa because of its $20,000 nut.

A seeming gangster tale is told mainly by a dry commentary in which the inner workings of the characters are analyzed or hinted at. There is flat lensing, surface characterization and the attempts at spontaneousness by concealed camera work.

There is the drifting hero and his unfeeling amoral ways and complaints until what he thinks love comes along. Tale shows him running into a Moroccan detective trying to bury a body of a friend killed by mistake by international dope runners. He goes with him to Morocco where he falls for the wife but helps the detective track down the gang.

Film has sometimes some of the early ease of silent pix. But this bogs down and falls into fairly adolescent tactics. For a first pic, there is a glimmering of filmic feel by director Gilbert Vergnes but he has a long way to go to

make an acceptable screen production. *Mosk.*

Cudna Devojka
(Strange Girl)
(YUGOSLAVIA)

Locarno, July 31.
Avala Film production and release. Stars Spela Rozin, Voja Miric, Zoran Radmilovic. Directed by Jovan Zivanovic. Screenplay, Jug Grezelj from novel by Grozdana Olujic; camera, Stevan Miskovic; editor, I. Ivanovic. At Locarno Film Fest. Running time, **95 MINS.**
Minja .... Spela Rozin
Nenad .... Voja Miric
Pedja .... Zoran Radmilovic

This tender tale of an embittered drifting young girl of 18 who finally finds love has a fine feel for character. It may seem conventional but the pic possesses that briskness of observation and concern for its people that makes it a good cut above the ordinary. Lingo chances are evident and perhaps specialized spots abroad if well handled.

There is a further peg in one of the first films from a socialist country which could have been produced anywhere. There is no propaganda but a truth in undertaking to portray a situation in the young life of a girl. And its optimism is fresh, lacking any hackneyed overtones. But this does have a tendency to get diffuse at the end.

A girl who had undergone a bad experience with an older man in her small town goes to the big city as a student. On the way she meets a journalist and spends a night with him. She is bitter, listlessly immoral and drifting till she meets a serious student. It leads to her getting married and awakening to life.

Film is in the new vein via its direct look at youthful morals, gray lensing plus a series of scenes rather than bothering with too much storyline.

This is a good step forward for Yugoslav films bogged down too much in partisan pix of late. Jovan Zivanovic's perceptive direction, Spela Rozin's looks and subtle limning of the hurt girl as well as the solid work of Voja Miric, as the steadfast boy, are all worthy of note and imply a film future for them. *Mosk.*

Congehovdingen
(The Musketeers)
(DANISH—COLOR)

Locarno, July 31.
Flamingo Film production and release. With Jens Osterholm, Dirch Passer, Birgitte Federspiel. Directed by Hannelise Hovmand. Screenplay, Carit Etlars; camera (Agfacolor), Henning Christiansen; music, Erik Fiehn. At Locarno Film Fest. Running time, **117 MINS.**
Musketeer .... Jens Osterholm
Poacher .... Dirch Passer
Wife .... Birgitte Federspiel
Danish actioner looms mainly a local item or perhaps for moppet bills abroad. It is in the Robin Hood syndrome about a daring warrior who saves Denmark from the Swedes in the 18th Century.

Production values are skimpy but there is some good natured action and involved scripting about how a musketeer gets up a group of fighters and defeats the Swedes.

Film does have some good color lensing but the playing is arch and the adventure aspects are done with a naive outlook. This outlook makes it refreshing if fairly childish. *Mosk.*

Lulu
(AUSTRIAN)

Locarno, July 31.
Gloria release of Otto Durer production. Stars Nadja Tiller, O. E. Hasse, Hildegard Knef; features Mario Adorf, Charles Regnier, Rudolf Forster, Leon Askin. Written and directed by Rolf Thiele; based on the plays of Frank Wedekind; camera, Michel Kelber; music, Carl De Groof. At Locarno Film Fest. Running time, **100 MINS.**
Lulu .... Nadja Tiller
Schon .... O. E. Hasse
Baroness .... Hildegard Knef
Trainer .... Mario Adorf
Father .... Rudolf Forster
Son .... Leon Askin
Jack the Ripper....... Georges Regnier

Made as silent films twice in Germany via Leopold Jessner's version Frank Wedekind's trilogy of plays about a nymphomaniac gets a fairly synthetic revival in this new version. Sans a feeling for the times or characters, this is an arty and curiously outmoded expressionistic pic which looks to have only specialized chances abroad at best.

Lulu (Nadja Tiller) is picked up at the age of 14 by a rich, eccentric doctor when she tries to steal his watch. He turns her into a woman of the world. He marries her off to a rich man who likes to have her dance for him half nude. This man suffers a heart attack when he finds her cavorting with an artist. She is married off to the latter who commits suicide. She finally gets her benefactor to marry her. She finally kills him in a fight over a gun.

She is freed from prison by the dead man's son, a lesbian admirer and other characters. They flee to Paris and then London where they are reduced to dire straits and she becomes an outright prostie. She is finally killed one night.

Nadja Tiller is a tall healthy looking girl who lacks the sensual temperament or projection to make anything out of Lulu's supposedly fatal appeal. Without the showing of how environment formed her, and made her both victim and femme fatale, this remains an artificial pic.

Rolf Thiele's lacklustre direction drops this between two modes of presentation. In spite of its plot, this film generates little sexy steam but it could be a hypo item on this very Hildegard Knef and O. E. Hasse bring some thespic weight to the lesbo and benefactor roles respectively.

But this version of the Wedekind plays is old hat and wooden. It appears a likely Teutonic grosser but will be hard put to find a niche in world marts. Chiaroscuro lensing is overdone but otherwise credits are good and production values acceptable. *Mosk.*

Reach For Glory
(BRITISH)

British film produced by Yanks brings up some worthwhile problems but rarely copes adequately enough with any to make this more than a good programmer; its theme could possibly mean specialized bookings, too.

Locarno, July 31.
Columbia release of John Kohn-Jud Kimberg production. With Michael Anderson Jr., Martin Tomlinson, Oliver Grimm, Harry Andrews, Kay Walsh. Directed by Philip Leacock. Screenplay,

John Kohn. Jud Kimberg from novel by John Rae: camera, G. Huke: editor, F. Wilson. At Locarno Film Fest. Running time, 80 MINS.
Lewis .... Michael Anderson Jr.
John .... Martin Tomlinson
Mark .... Oliver Grimm
Captain .... Harry Andrews
Wife .... Kay Walsh
———

In this tale about a group of adolescent boys at a military school in Britain during the last war, the themes of racism, war hate and its effect on youth, conscientious objection and the consequences of parental weakness on youth are all touched on.

Film is well meaning, tightly and economically made but still lacks the edge to make these powerful points have the necessary impact. Result is a diffuse pic which is interesting but does not emerge a heavyweight. Okay handling of youngsters and its pacifistic moral could give it good playoff possibilities abroad, with a fair chance in specialized spots if well sold.

A group of London youths chafe in a country school to which they have been evacuated. The war fills them with dreams of glory and a desire for action that is unfortunately turned to gang warfare, spartan, cabalistic rituals, anti-semitism and general unrulyness.

Into this comes a refugee Jewish boy from Germany. He becomes the friend of one of the boy's in the London gang but is twitted by the others, first as a Nazi and then as a Jew. Grudgingly accepted, he runs off during a fight with another gang is sentenced to a mock execution. To scare him, real bullets are first inserted in the guns but then removed for blanks. But one lad makes a mistake, and the boy is killed.

This produces an outcry that they have been allowed to train with real guns and thus should not be condmned when they use them. What is basically realistic in the film is watered down by series of dreams by one boy who pictures himself as a war hero.

Shame at conscientious objectors is also worked in via a brother of one of the boy's and false accusations of budding homosexuality.

Philip Leacock's matter of fact direction lacks the weight to weld this into dramatic look at war's shattering effects on adolescence.

Most of boys are good in their roles. Martin Tomlinson and Oliver Grimm are especially effective as the two friends kept apart and involved in tragedy by the fault of wars misunderstandings and human frailities. Overall this is just a good small film on a big subject. Production dress is fine. It is a sound start for two young Yank producers, John Kohn and Jud Kimberg. *Mosk.*

Kabuliwala
(INDIAN)
Locarno, July 31.
Bimal Roy production and release. With Balraj Shani, Sonnu. Directed by Hemen Gupta. Screenplay. Khalil; camera, Kamal Bose: editor, Amit Bose. At Locarno Film Fest. Running time, 95 MINS.
Kabuliwala .... Balraj Shani
Mini .... Sonnu
———

The late Indian poet Tagore's story was made once before in the Bengal section of India. Here it gets another filmic round from the Hindu filmmakers. Pic emerges a tender, sentimental opus that manages to avoid being mawkish but lacking the needed shadings of characterization to make it more than a local item or, at best, a language film in foreign spots.

An Afghanistan farmer goes to India to make enough money to save his farm. He thinks only of his little daughter and transfers this affection to a little Indian girl. At first she fears this stranger, called the Kabuliwala by the Indians, but then they become friends.

It deepens into a great mutual esteem but one day he kills a man who tries to cheat him and is sent to prison. Getting out, he finds the little girl grown up. Suddenly he realizes his own daughter may have forgotten him.

Thesps manage to give the characters enough substance to keep this from lapsing into too much pathos. In short, this is well made and tender but the story gets too sentimentalized and arch to give it the fillip for arty chances abroad. But this should make a bundle on its home grounds. *Mosk.*

Voskresenie—Part II
(Resurrection)
(RUSSIAN)
Locarno, July 31.

A rare thing in VARIETY pic reviews, but this 175-minute Russo pic calls for an added review because only its first part (90 mins.) was appraised last September during the Russian Film Week in Paris. Complete version is a detailed filming of the Leo Tolstoy novel and a work of solid dramatic structure. But it is too long and not sustained well enough by the direction to bring it off completely.

As a result this needs pruning which might punch it up and possibly make for arty chance abroad on its stout production values, fine playing and story value.

All the material is there. A middle-aged Russo nobleman is called to jury duty in turn-of-the-century Czarist Russia. He finds that he knows one of the defendants, a still beautiful woman, in a poison case. He had seduced her when she worked for his aunts and left her with child long ago.

It had led to her being fired and then drifting into prostitution. As the trial progresses he relives the times with her. She is almost acquitted except for a jury slip. Then he decides he is responsible for her sorry lot and tries to make it up to her.

But she had tried to force him out of her mind because of the pain she had suffered. He keeps going to see her and begins to help other people and political prisoners in the prison. When she is sent to Siberia he follows her, but she will not marry him and decides to throw in her lot with a political prisoner as he goes back to try to live as man.

The insight into human compassion is there but the director at times piles on too much bravura and repeats actions already made clear. However, this is done with vigor and a solid feeling for the time. Tamara Semina is an actress with force and presence who makes the early innocence, later debauchery and final redemption always true and alive.

Evgeny Matveev plays the early lecherous nobleman and later the benevolent, chastened man that is just right in this difficult role.

Film sometimes puts too much emphasis on the corruption of the times, the moralizing and emerging political aspects. But, overall, it is an exacting, well-made version of a literary classic that thus bodes foreign chances. Same story has been made twice in Hollywood. *Mosk.*

En El Balcon Vacio
(On An Empty Balcony)
(MEXICAN)
Locarno, July 31.
Ascot-Torre production and release. With Nuri Perena, Maria Luisa Elio, Conchita Genoves, Belina Garcia. Directed by Jomi Garcia Ascot. Screenplay, Maria Luisa Elio, Ascot, Emilio Garcia Riera; camera, Jose Torre; editor, J. Espegela. At Locarno Film Fest. Running time, 60 MINS.
Gabriela, as a girl ... Nuri Perena
Gabriela, as a woman Maria Luisa Elio
Mother .... Conchita Genoves
Sister .... Belina Garcia
———

Made in 16m for around $4,000 by a group of Spanish refugees in Mexico, this makes up in mood, atmosphere and feeling for what it lacks in technique. However, it looms mainly for the usage or special supporting fare. It's stream of narration and format also making this a good tele possibility.

A woman reminisces about her childhood in Spain and she is seen as a girl there. The revolution leads to the family's taking refuge in France and then going to settle in Mexico. As a grown woman, she visits her home in Spain but can not recapture the time and her old self.

Although made entirely in Mexico, there is a good feel for Spain. The little girl sees the beginning of the Spanish Revolution via scenes she witnessed there. Then comes her uprooting and her lonely life in France till she makes a friend there. Then in Mexico, she feels the call and images of Spain.

The use of newsreel footage and a feel for the imagery of memory transposed in a slightly dreamlike manner are in keeping with the new style narrative springing up in European films of late. The non-pro players do well. Director Jomi Garcia Ascot has managed to succeed in intimating character and emotion in spite of his limited budget. It is techncally uneven, but acceptable. *Mosk.*

Wyrok
(The Verdict)
(POLISH)
Locarno, July 31.
Polski Film release of ZRF production. With Wienczyslaw Glinski, Nanna Zembrzuska, Grzegorz Roman, Josef Nowak, Lidia Korsakowna. Directed by Jerzy Passendorfer. Screenplay, Jerzy Przedzzicki, Passendorfer; camera, Wladyslaw Forbert; editor, J. Sajica. At Locarno Film Fest. Running time, 75 MINS.
Editor .... Wienczyslaw Glinski
Wife .... Nanna Zembrzuska
Adas .... Grzegorz Roman
Zarebskl .... Josef Nowak
Mother .... Lidia Korsakowna
———

Problem film about a child being fought over in court by his alcoholic, negligent mother and a fairly well-to-do couple, pic manages to avert melodrama and soap opera by tasteful observation. But this lacks the weight for solid export value except possibly video usage.

A little boy of five runs off from home where his dipso mother lives with a brutal hoodlum who also makes her work. Kid is picked up by a newspaperman who takes him home. He and his wife, on the verge of divorce due to a lack of children, take to the boy. Finally his mother claims him again but the beastly boozer makes a deal with the newsman for the child without consulting the mother.

Then the mother goes to court where both sides are given. It ends there. But director Jerzy Passendorfer has wisely sketched in the child's environment and the adult comportment, concentrated on how a child looks at grownups. The moppet's naturalness make this pay off and keep this slight affair interesting. It might even make dualer fare. *Mosk.*

Moshi-Moshi, Hallo Japan
(Hello, Hello, Japan)
(GERMAN-JAPANESE-COLOR)
Locarno, July 31.
Knoop Film-Iwanami production and release. Directed and edited by Walter Knoop. Screenplay and commentary, Knoop, Hans Hermann: commentary spoken by Hans Daniels; camera (Ansco), Eikichi Uyenatsu, Shizuo Komura, Ken Akimoto, Tatsuo Watanaba, Hiroshi Murata, Knoop. At Locarno Film Fest. Running time, 80 MINS.
———

Documentary on various parts of Japan in a haphazard mixture of images that give little insight into that colorful country. Lingering too much on construction and obvious touristic gambits, this emerges a heavyhanded affair that appears limited to the countries of origin with little except programmer filler or cutdown tele usage looming in other markets.

Filmed mainly by Japanese cameramen, the color is surprisingly flat and unimaginative. The many other Japanese films have set higher standards. A series of New Year's Eve rituals are shown, then the inevitable tuna fishing, building and launching a tanker, girl shows, Kabuki, old temples and a plethora of street scenes.

Nowhere is there a seemingly concerted attitude towards the country. It remains a surface travelog. In short, German filmmaker Walter Knoop obviously went to Japan but saw nothing of pure and original note. And everyday has seemingly lost out on this overlong documentary feature.

There is one scene of the nude-to-the-waist femme pearldivers that is done with some taste even if a phoney shark scare is worked in. This could be a hypo for dualer usage. And, in spite of the limited talents involved, this still manages to exert some interest in its sheer scenic contrasts. But the sluggish commentary even gets in the way of that. *Mosk.*

Too Young, Too Immoral

Every fault and none of the merit of Manhattan's underground filmmakers. Strictly for the male insomniac trade.

Rialto International release of R. A. Phelan production. Features John Francis, Larry Healey, Raymond Phelan, Taylor Mead, Donald Ratka, Susan Ashley, Brenda deNaut. Directed, photographed and edited by Raymon Phelan. Music, Bob Vinas, Kenny Harris and Joe Boppo. At Rialto, N.Y., Aug. 10, '62. Running time, **88 MINS.**

Mr. Claude .... John Francis
Joseph .... Larry Healey
Tony Brooks .... Raymond Phelan
Scribbles .... Taylor Mead
Gene Brooks .... Donald Ratka
Mary Boyd .... Susan Ashley
Leeta .... Brenda DeNaut

Possibly, but not probably, conceived as American avant garde. "Too Young, Too Immoral" (with an exclamation mark wasted and here omitted) is more like American primitive. Shot in New York, it's an artless tale of drug addiction, artlessly photographed, directed and acted. Most of the actors, in fact, appear to be fully qualified to pass as amateurs. The pic looks and sounds like a shoestringer, without any sign of creative vitality to redress things. The distrib, Rialto International of New York, is obviously aiming for that exploitation circuit catering to male insomniacs; but for conventional theatres, this one is not even a poor bet.

The level of thesping, like the dialog (uncredited), is just plain embarrassment. Raymond Phelan, bowing his first feature, is plenty fascinated by the Manhattan concrete and asphalt, but his feel for the city is unfailingly cliche. The story is narrated by the brother of a narcotics victim. The brother is apt to elocutionize such lines as, "My God, what's happening to my brother?" The latter, having vowed to kick to habit for the sake of his love, is killed trying to elude his sources (chiefly a Mr. Big who's confined to a wheelchair and owns a Rolls Royce), who don't want him off the lucrative hook. The brother attempts to unravel his kin's mysterious death, and the pic finales with the villains meeting their own violent, melodramatic death.

There's a crude bedroom scene, apparently intended for extraneous affect. It's as dull as the rest of the yarn.

On the technical side, sound is poorly dubbed, and other contributions (including sporadic bongo-drum scoring) only assure the film's defeat. *Pit.*

Five Weeks In A Balloon
(C'SCOPE—COLOR)

Verne fantasy with laughs. Family fare. Good cast. Good b.o.

Hollywood, Aug. 7.

20th-Fox release of Irwin Allen production. Stars Red Buttons, Fabian, Barbara Eden, Cedric Hardwicke; features Peter Lorre, Richard Haydn, Barbara Luna, Billy Gilbert, Herbert Marshall. Directed by Allen. Screenplay, Charles Bennett, Allen, Albert Gail; camera (De Luxe), Winton Hoch; editor, George Boemler; music, Faul Sawtell; assistant director, Ad Schaumer. Reviewed at the studio, Aug. 7, '62. Running time, **101 MINS.**

Donald O'Shay .... Bed Buttons
Jacques .... Fabian
Susan Gale .... Barbara Eden
Fergusson .... Cedric Hardwicke
Ahmed .... Peter Lorre
Sir Henry Vining .... Richard Haydn
Makia .... Barbara Luna
Sultan-Auctioneer .... Billy Gilbert
Prime Minister .... Herbert Marshall
Consul .... Reginald Owen
Sheik Ageiba .... Henry Daniell
Slave Captain .... Mike Mazurki
Inspector .... Alan Caillou
Myanga .... Ben Astar
Randolph .... Raymond Bailey
The Duchess .... Chester the Chimp

Jules Verne's first novel is the source of this unstable but enterprising new effort by producer-director Irwin Allen. In an apparent bid to widen the potential audience range for his new fantasy (his third in three years for 20th-Fox), Allen has taken a conventional balloon-adventure and dealt with it tongue-in-cheek style—in effect approaching Verne in a kind of wild "Road" picture vein. Goal of the kidding approach seems to be to make it more palatable for adults—who might, understandably, have had their fill of both balloon stories and Verne fantasies in recent years (Verne and Edgar Allen Poe seem to be running neck-and-neck as authors most thoroughly exploited by the modern screen).

At any rate, "Five Weeks In a Balloon" has been designed with a something-for-everybody, "whole family" commercial concept: spoofery for the adults, romance and high adventure for the older youngsters, African wildlife and aerial fantasy for the tykes. There is, however, an inherent danger in the film that aims, a bit too ambitiously, to span and please all age groups. Each separate facet tends to subtract from the impact of the others. But the picture has been attractively and resourcefully mounted and colorfully and enterprisingly cast. Together with Allen's salesmanship zeal, this seems to forecast a favorable boxoffice response.

The screenplay by Allen, Charles Bennett and Albert Gail dramatizes the perilous mission of a small party of Britishers bent on crossing 4,000 miles over Africa by balloon in order to plant the English flag on unclaimed land prior to the arrival there of international slave traders.

Cedric Hardwicke plays the leader of the expedition with his customary reserve and aplomb. Red Buttons is satisfactory as the erratic young reporter forever embroiling the group in narrow scrapes. Fabian pairs off romantically with "slave girl" Barbara Luna, Buttons with "schoolteacher" Barbara Eden. Bulk of the comedy is attended to by Richard Haydn, Peter Lorre and Billy Gilbert, each in his characteristic fashion: Haydn the foppish, pompous caricature of a Britisher, Lorre in a lampoon of himself, Gilbert as a boozing, sneering sultan. Adept featured support is dispatched by Herbert Marshall, Reginald Owen, Henry Daniell and Mike Mazurki.

Stock footage of romping African veldt creatures is effectively incorporated, although of dubious necessity to the story. Photography by Winton Hoch is observant and agreeable to the eye. Among other skilled production assists are those of editor George Boemler, art directors Jack Martin Smith and Alfred Ybarra, composer Paul Sawtell and the special photographic effects team of L. B. Abbott and Emil Kosa Jr. The title song by Podi Desmond, borrowed from a familiar public domain refrain and dressed up with innocuous lyrics, is sung adequately by the Brothers Four over the main titles. *Tube.*

Kohayagawake No Aki
(Late Summer)
(JAPANESE—COLOR)

Paris, Aug. 7.

Toho production and release. With Genjiro Nakamura, Setsuko Hara, Yoko Tsukasa, Keiju Kobayashi, Michiyo Aratama, Chieko Naniwa, Disuke Kato. Directed by Yasujiro Ozu. Screenplay, Takago Noda, Ozu; camera (Agfa), Asaichi Nakai; editor, T. Mayuzu. Preemed in Paris. Running time, **100 MINS.**

Manbej .... Genjiro Nakamura
Akiko .... Setsuko Hara
Noriko .... Yoko Tsukasa
Hisao .... Keiju Kobayashi
Fumiko .... Michiyo Aratama
Tsune .... Chieko Naniwa
Yanosuke .... Daisuke Kato

Besides being the most numerically high in the world today, Japanese film production also has shown itself to be one of the most quality-laden also at many film fests. Here is a film of tender and humane insight, solid comedics and drama and a perfection in thesping, direction, technical quality and overall impact. Yet it will be a difficult film for many foreign spots.

Director Yasujio Ozu is considered one of the great Japanese pic veterans and yet the Japanese film people seemingly have shied from sending his pix abroad, considering them too Japanese in outlook, mood and treatment.

There are buff audiences developing, but the Japanese film still seems to have to find its rightful niche abroad. This pic is worth a try on its perfection and ease in depicting the human condition through a family.

It is deceptively simple which may be why the more subtle films have not caught on in the West. More dynamic pix like "Rashomon," "The Gates of Hell," and such poetic pix as "Ikuru" or "Ugetsu" have gotten some okay distrib, but the real Japanese breakthrough has yet to come.

Here, the aging hand of an institutional brewery, in financial trouble, is also a rather roguish, lovable scamp and not too ready to make necessary decisions on a needed merger, finding a husband for a widowed daughter or helping another choose between love and security.

Instead, he goes off to see an old mistress whose free living young daughter he thinks is his own. Things come to a head when he has a heart attack but there is relief when he seemingly recovers. But when he dies, all are faced with the loss and a need to act. Most take their stand and the film ends not in resignation, or revolt, but in an acceptance of life, with changes, self realization and decisions also involved.

This is told with a rare emotion that makes all the characters alive and important. Each scene is set with directness and insight. There is no camera movement, frequent headon shots of talk. But the people are living within themselves and this is made evident by the observation, the knowing and simple comment on their actions, and the solid feeling for place and action.

The film builds a hypnotic, fascinating feeling for life in movement, and there is wit, sudden shafts of almost Rabelasian comedics and, overall, a love and belief in live. There is no mawkishness or melodramatics which make this a look at life that transcends its time and place.

The stunning color, the expertise in acting, the disarmingly simple if complex underneath, direction combine to make this firstrate filmmaking.

Unfortunately, it might look like melodrama or almost conventional hokum to the mass audiences. But it is worth a chance by an enterprising distrib or exhib. The time may be ripening when these fine but difficult Japanese pix may find their audiences. This could be the one. *Mosk.*

Mix Me A Person
(BRITISH)

Heavygoing psychiatric meller which aspires to pretensions not revealed in the screenplay; Anne Baxter as a name draw may help, but this one disappoints.

London, Aug. 14.

BLC release of a Wessex-British Lion (Sergei Nolbandov) production. Stars Anne Baxter, Adam Faith, Donald Sinden; features Carole Ann Ford, Jack MacGowran, Glynn Houston, Dilys Hamlett Alfred Budge, Meredith Edwards, Ed Deveraux, Walter Brown. Directed by Leslie Norman. Screenplay, Ian Dalrymple from Jack Trevor Story's novel; camera, Ted Moore; editor, Ernie Hosler; music and lyrics, Johnny Worth. Previewed at Columbia Theatre, London. Running time, **116 MINS.**

Dr. Anne Dyson .... Anne Baxter
Philip Bellamy Q.C. ...... Donald Sinden
Harry Jukes .... Adam Faith
Socko .... David Kernan
Nobby .... Frank Jarvis
Dirty Neck .... Peter Kriss
Jenny .... Carole Ann Ford
Gravy .... Anthony Booth
Mona .... Topsy Jane
Terence .... Jack MacGowan
Max Taplow .... Walter Brown
Sam .... Glyn Houston
Doris .... Dilys Hamlett
Johnson .... Meredith Edwards
Lumley .... Alfred Burke
P. C. Jarrold .... Russell Napier
Receptionist .... Barbara Barnet
Lorna .... Julie Milton
Tough .... Tim Pearce
Supt. Malley .... Ed Devereaux
Insp. Wagstaffe .... Ray Barrett
Prison Governor .... Donald Morley
Patrol Officer .... Lawrence James
1st Prison Officer .... Gilbert Wynne
2d Prison Officer .... Norman Johns

Considering the allround talent on hand, this one is a disappointment. Direction and thesping rarely rises above a flatfooted, cliche-ridden screenplay by Ian Dalrymple, with plenty dialog evoking undesired yock reaction. However, in their various ways, the three stars, Anne Baxter, Adam Faith and Donald Sinden, have names that could draw customers. But the pic may then have to contend with possible unfavorable word-of-mouth.

Faith plays an 18-year-old who faces the big drop when he is found guilty of murdering a cop. His assigned counsel (Donald Sinden) does not believe in his innocence and nor does the jury. Only Sinden's wife, a psychiatrist (in the unlikely person of the pleasant Miss Baxter), believes in the lad after she draws his story out of him during prison visits. This the audience sees in flashback. How, showing off to his girl friend, Faith "borrows" a flashy Bentley and, in a dark country lane, has a flat. A policeman is helping the lad to change the tire and, needing a jack, the cop waves at a truck. But it doesn't stop. Instead, there's a shot from the driver's cabin and the cop is killed. Min-

utes later, dazed and holding the gun, Faith is found beside the corpse by a police car.

Patiently Miss Baxter tries to piece together evidence to prove his innocence and eventually finds that the owner of the stolen Bentley is gun-running for the Irish Republican Army under the guise of running a frozen food factory. It was, of course, the gun-runners who killed the cop. And it all comes out in a series of occasionally muddled and inconclusive happenings which, involves, among other problems, that of Miss Baxter being trapped in a giant freeze by the fanatical leader of the rebels.

She gets out, teeth only slightly chattering, to jerk Faith from hangman's grasp in, as they say, the nick of time.

Thanks largely to some very stolid and often naive dialog, the yarn rarely comes to life. Often, in fact, it makes precious little sense. There are many irritating loopholes in behavior which jar.

On the credit side, this has been directed with evident sincerity by Leslie Norman. Young Faith, who sings a banal credit song and a lively novelty number that should do well in the charts, has a very creditable stab at his first serious essay in straight acting. As yet his range is limited, but he attracts plenty of sympathy from onlookers in a tricky, downbeat role.

Sinden spends most of his time either flirting charmingly with Miss Baxter (it is never really established that she is his wife), arguing with her over legal procedure or the innocence of Faith. The latter two phases he conducts with the effort of a man severely controlling a bout of bad temper. However, in fairness to Sinden, it is a cardboard role. Miss Baxter, attractive as ever, does not convince as the East End girl who has become a celebrated doctor of psychiatry but she has to cope with some very desperate moments.

Walter Brown does nicely as the owner of the stolen car. Jack MacGowran is sound in the overwritten and melodramatic role of the Irish rebel. Young talent, in the shape of Carole Ann Ford, Peter Kriss, Topsy Jane, and Anthony Booth, chip in with useful studies as Faith's adolescent companions.

The cops are convincing and the prison atmosphere evoked with clammy authenticity. Elegant sets in the Homes of Miss Baxter and Sinden highlight effectively the drabness of the jail. Editing is sometimes a shade haphazard but other technical credits measure up.

Major complaint about the film, which presumably set out to be a serious psychiatric study, is that it is too superficial, lapses into meller and does not really know what it is seeking to say.
Rich.

Vancouver Fest

Teen Kanya
(Two Daughters)
(INDIA)
Vancouver, Aug. 7.
Edward Harrison release of Satyajit Ray production. Written and directed by Satyajit Ray. Features Anil Chatterjee, Chandana Bannerjee, Soumitra Chatterjee, Aparna das Gupta. Camera, Sundra Ray; music, Satyajit Ray. At Vancouver Film Fest. Running time, 116 MINS.
Nanda .... Anil Chatterjee
Ratan .... Chandana Bannerjee
Amulya .... Soumitra Chatterjee
Mrinmoyee (Pugle) ... Aparna das Gupta

India's ace filmmaker, Satyajit Ray, emerges from this sensitive treatment of two stories by the poet Rabindranath Tagore with his reputation for craftsmanship and understanding solidly enhanced. He has his own inspired way of interpreting the basics of human nature in a visually poetic manner. In this film, he maintains his ability to project pure humanism, without any traces of sentimentality or pious pity.

"Two Daughters" title is a misnomer since the literal translation of "Teen Kanya" is "Three Daughters." Ray was originally commissioned by the Indian government to make a composite film of three Tagore short stories in conjunction with the Tagore Centenary in 1961, commemorating the poet's birth. The third story, "Manihara," was not completed in time for the pic's scheduled release. Also Ray has reportedly refused to add it to the present 116 minutes of running time on the grounds that the length of the full three sections would be too much for Western audiences.

The two Tagore stories in this film are called "The Postmaster" and "Samapti." The first is a poignant tale about an orphaned girl's faithful devotion for the new postmaster in a remote Indian village. Chandana Bannerjee makes her role as Ratan, the lonely youngster, a rare and moving study under the sure directorial hand of Ray. Anil Chatterjee is well cast as the Calcutta poet who is horrified by the squalor in which he is forced to work, and which he leaves as soon as he can.

"The Postmaster" is the shorter of the two stories, running 46 minutes. "Samapti," the second story, lasts 70 minutes and is an Eastern version of Shakespeare's "Taming of the Shrew," in which the clash between traditional and modern ideas about marriage in India produces a generous range of emotional moods and sentiments. Tale concerns a young law student determined to marry the girl of his own choice rather than the wife selected for him by his doting mother. The girl he picks, a tomboy, is not ready for marriage. And before she accepts the awareness of love, there is plenty of scope for humor, drama, pathos and subtle tenderness.

Aparna das Gupta is impressive in her screen debut as the reluctant bride. Her transformation from tomboy to woman becomes a beautiful characterization. Soumitra Chatterjee is the young student who defies his protective mother. He plays this role with just the right blend of youthful arrogance and developing uncertainty. But it is Ray's touch that distinguishes the film and makes his work as producer - writer - director - composer a tour de force.

Technically ragged at times, Ray's immense ability to reveal every aspect of character and emo-

tion simply and warmly makes one oblivious of sub-titling defects, in-balanced exposure or muddy printing. "Teen Kanya" is a worthy successor to his "Apu" trilogy. It should prove to be a superior art entry.
Shaw.

Prapanch
(Family Life)
(INDIAN)
Vancouver, Aug. 7.
Indian National Pictures Ltd. production and release. With Sulochana, Seema, Kusum Deshpande, Amar Shaikh, and Shrikant. Directed by Madhukar Pathak. Screenplay, G. D. Madgulkar; camera, K. B. Kamat Ghanekar; music, Sudhir Phadke; editor, Bhanudas Divkar. At Vancouver Film Fest. Running time, 97 MINS.
Paru .... Sulochana
Deva .... Amar Shaikh
Shankar .... Kusum Deshpande
Champs .... Seema
Aunt .... Shrikant

Depressing, unrelieved story of grinding poverty because of India's age-old struggle with the population explosion. Tale is built around the family life of a poor village potter who carries the heavy burden of feeding a household comprising his wife, six children and an old, blind aunt. Shot mostly on location in Maharashtra region, film is a grimly realistic portrayal of rural struggle.

Pic was the 1961 winner of the all-India Certificate of Merit in the State Awards, which means it was selected by the government as best film of the year. Award is certainly not deserved on the basis of artistic merit.

Film only has been seen outside India (in Russia) prior to Vancouver showing, and first print sent here was marred by exceptionally poor sub-titling. Second print screened is untitled, and benefitted from a voice-over spoken commentary. Otherwise, technical work is good, with photography a plus. Direction is as honest as underlying theme will permit. Good acting by principals also helps.

Even the most specialized audience for Indian pix would find this heavy going, and it offers little or no exploitation possibilities for the bravest of arty houses. As an authentic treatment of Marathi life and with its pitch for family planning, film's best chance lies with distribution by such an organization as UNESCO. *Shaw.*

Farewell, Doves!
(RUSSIAN)

Vancouver, Aug. 7.
Sovexportfilm release of Yalta Film Studio production. Stars Alexei Loktev, Svetlana Savyolova. Written and directed by Yakov Segel. Camera, Yuri Ilyenko. At Vancouver Film Fest. Running time, 93 MINS.
Gena .... Alexei Loktev
Tanya .... Svetlana Savyolova
Maria Yefimovna .....Valentina Telegina
Maxim Petrovitch ..... Sergei Plotnikov

Billed as Russia's newest export, this starts out as a basic boy-meets-girl story, with romantic plot and effective, light comedy touch, but winds up a heavyhanded plug for the Young Communist League. At the opening, the young hero is not a party member, being too busy looking after his beloved pigeons. But when a new kind of love enters his life in the person of a card-carrying blonde beauty,

it's goodbye birdies as the title indicates.

Writer-director Segel's two previous pix, "The House I Live In" at the 1959 fest, and "First Day of Peace" in '60, showed promise of better things to come. In this, he gets in some good licks at the expense of petty corruption in the party, unsponsored fun and snafus. He even manages some minor leg-pulling of the party line. But all good things must come to an end, even in a "new" Russian picture, and the serious message is delivered.

The fun bits give this a chance and the early moments are well worth the leaded ending. Alexei Loktev has a Horst Buchholz-appeal as the buoyant birdman, and Svetlana Savyolova is disarmingly efficient with her big blue eyes and flaxen tresses. Technical credits are excellent. *Shaw.*

The 300 Spartans
(C'SCOPE—COLOR)

Another larger-than-life historical spectacle for the exploitation course; slightly above par in certain areas but woefully weak in others. Should be satisfactory contender over short haul.

Hollywood, Aug. 17.

Twentieth-Fox release of Rudolph Mate-George St. George production. Stars Richard Egan, Ralph Richardson, Diane Baker, Barry Coe, David Farrar, Donald Houston; introduces Anna Synodinou; with Kieron Moore, John Crawford, Robert Brown, Laurence Naismith, Anna Wakefield, Ivan Triesault, Charles Fawcett, Michael Nikolinakos, Sandro Giglio, Anna Raftopoulou, Dimos Starenios. Directed by Mate. Screenplay, St. George, based on original story material by Ugo Liberatori, Remigio Del Grosso, Giovanni D'Eramo, Gian Paolo Callegari; camera (De Luxe), Geoffrey Unsworth; editor, Jerome Webb; music, Manos Hadjidakis; assistant director, Fred R. Simpson. Reviewed at the studio, Aug. 17, '62. Running time, **108 MINS.**

Leonidas .... Richard Egan
Themistocles ...... Sir Ralph Richardson
Ellas .... Diane Baker
Phylon .... Barry Coe
Xerxes .... David Farrar
Hydarnes .... Donald Houston
Gorgo .... Anna Synodinou
Ephialtes .... Kieron Moore
Agathon .... John Crawford
Pentheus .... Robert Brown
First Delegate .... Laurence Naismith
Artemisia .... Anne Wakefield
Demaratus .... Ivan Triesault
Mogistias .... Charles Fawcett
Myron .... Michael Nikolinakos
Xenathon .... Sandro Giglio
Toris .... Anna Raftopoulou
Samos .... Dimos Starenios

Absence of dramatic finesse or characterizational nuance and dimension isn't apt to disturb appreciably the easygoing, escape-seeking audiences for whose entertainment "The 300 Spartans" is primarily designed. In some aspects, notably magnitude of physical mounting and strength of historical source material, the Rudolph Mate-George St. George production is a cut above the average for these exploitation extravaganzas filmed abroad, and this should be reflected to some extent at the boxoffice. The 20th-Fox release, filmed in Greece, offers no lure or rewards for the choosy customer, and should make no pretense in such directions, but within the limits of its commercial design, it should do quite satisfactorily as a hit-and-run saturation entry.

The hopeless but ultimately inspiring defense of their country by a band of 300 Spartan soldiers against an immense army of Persian invaders in 480 B.C.—known to history as the Battle of Thermopylae—is the nucleus around which St. George's screenplay is constructed. The inherent appeal and magnitude of the battle itself virtually dwarfs and sweeps aside all attempts at romantic byplay. In fact, the script's feeble side issues only serve to clutter the film unnecessarily and impede the progress of the main story, which provides all the drama required. Intimate scenes are stilted and characters two-dimensional, but the battle sequences are interesting and adroitly handled.

An international cast has been assembled for the enterprise, primarily populated with Britishers, Greeks and Americans. It is one time when the Yankees most decidedly do not cop first place. Richard Egan, as King Leonidas of Sparta, is physically suitable for the character, but the heroic mold of his performance is only skin deep—more muscle than corpuscle. Ralph Richardson, as might be expected, does the best acting in the picture, but no one is going to list this portrayal as one of the great achievements in his career. Diane Baker is glaringly miscast. The fragile actress has been assigned the part of a Spartan girl who knocks two large men off their feet, bodily. As written, it's a role that required an actress of at least Lorenesque proportions. Barry Coe shares the romantic plot fabric with Miss Baker. David Farrar is effective as the tyrannical Persian King Xerxes. Key portrayals are etched adequately by Donald Houston, Kieron Moore, John Crawford, Robert Brown, Anne Wakefield and Anna Synodinou, Greek actress whom the film introduces.

Outside of battle scenes, the players tend to perform and posture rather artificially, reflecting the shortcomings of Mate's direction. But battle passages he has managed ably, with the valuable assistance of a second unit headed by Richard Talmadge. Most departmental contributions are skillfully executed, notably Geoffrey Unsworth's camerawork, the second unit lensmanship of Cyril Knowles and Jerry Kalogerados, and Arrigo Equini's artwork.

Tube.

La Croix Des Vivants
(The Cross of the Living)
(FRENCH)

Paris, Aug. 14.

Warner Bros. release of Christina Film production. Stars Pascale Petit, Karl Boehm, Giani Esposito, Gabriele Ferzetti; features Roger Dumas, Marie Dubois, Madeleine Robinson, Alain Cuny. Directed by Yvan Govar. Screenplay, Maurice Clavel, Alain Cavalier, J. C. Dumoutier, Govar; camera, Andre Bac; editor, Paul Cayatte. At the Raimu, Paris. Running time, **90 MINS.**

Maria .... Pascale Petit
Gus .... Karl Boehm
Yan .... Giani Esposito
Nell .... Marie Dubois
Abbe .... Gabrielle Ferzetti
Van Dorneck ...... Madeleine Robinson
Count .... Alain Cuny

This is a stilted drama that has a flock of good thesps wasted in surface roles. It looms mainly of playoff value in Continental spots with small chance for Yank houses.

A man accused of having killed his stepfather comes back to his home town after being acquitted. But here he meets townspeople suspicion and the hatred of a man he was to have helped before the accident, as the death is classified.

He has one friend who has a concubine he is intending to marry. But the girl falls for the returned man, and it leads to tragedy all around when she is killed in an accident and the townsfolk feel that he again is the killer. To save him from a posse, the priest of the town sacrifices himself.

All this is lugubriously written, directed and played. It emerges pretentious and heavy-handed sans any feel for drama or sacrifice needed to make this tenable. Smudgy lensing and tight budget aspects do not help either.

A good group of Austrian, French and Italo actors is wasted in this. There's some Belgian, Italo and German coin in this production. If this is an example of Common Mart coproducing, it is a negative attempt. Worthy thespians can do nothing with their skin-deep characters and the flaccid direction.

Mosk.

Vainqueurs Et Vaincus
(Victors and Vanquished)
(SWEDISH—DOCUMENTARY)

Paris, Aug. 14.

Athos release of Sjoberg production. Directed and compiled by Tore Sjoberg. Editor, Erik Holm; commentary, Marcel Criozaz, spoken by Jean Michel. At the Napoleon, Paris. Running time, **80 MINS.**

This documentary uses the newsreel and documentary footage on the Nazi reign, made by both the Germans and Allies, that was used by the prosecution during the Nuremberg war criminal trials. It is another searing indictment of this infamous period and is mounted with tact and power. Though following on the heels of other pix of this type, this production has enough new aspects, insight and interest for specialized film bookings abroad or for tele usage.

Divided into three parts, it delves into the Nazi war guilts, the war crimes and the evils and criminal acts perpetuated against humanity. Close up of the war criminals in the dock, it gives a shattering rundown of the Nazi infamy.

First, comes the preparations for war and the breaking of all treaties, then the disregard of all pacts in treatment of prisoners of war as well as the terror and inhumanity of the concentration camps. It points up the evil racism and horrendous destruction carried out in its name.

A subdued, instructive commentary, expert editing and a solid collection of footage make this another worthy testimony on a terrible time of recent history and a reminder that it has to be understood so as to be able to avoid or combat any future manifestations of this kind anywhere in the world.

Mosk.

Morning Star
(RUSSIAN—COLOR)

Artkino release of Leningrad (Frunze Film Studios) production. Stars R. Chokoeva. Directed by R. Tikhomirov. Screenplay, I. Meneker; music, M. Rauverger; ballet master, N. Tugelev; music by Leningrad Philharmonic Society Orch. At Cameo Theatre, N.Y., starting Aug. 18, '62. Running time, **92 MINS.**

Cholpon .... R. Chokoeva
Nurdin .... U. Sarbaschev
Temir Khan .... N. Tugelev
Ai-Dai .... B. Beishenova
Jinn .... S. Abdushilov
With Corps de Ballet of Kirghizian State Opera Co.

Here is a highly artistic ballet screen vehicle that likely not only will attract ballet admirers but also will draw plenty of arty pic devotees. Russo ballet pix always have done well in N.Y., and this is one of the topflight ones in this category.

Billed as an exotic ballet, "Morning Star" is filled with an amazing amount of vigorous terpsing and semi-nudity. Latter is almost unheard of in a Russian picture, but it's here. There's one scene where the king, in trying to cheer up the disconsolate hero, trots out a bunch of dancers, who seldom stress the toe gymnastics but go in for more down-to-earth gyrations. In fact, they seem to outstrip a routine stripper.

Basic story is that of a young hero prince who is vamped by the typical Russo bad girl. Only here, the so-called vampire is a 100-year-old femme who is turned into a comely miss by the wave of a wand. Running true to form for this type of fable, it is the good, wholesome miss who overcomes the vamp and her demon pals.

The Prince is nicely played by U. Sarbasgev, typical youthful toe dancer. His sweetheart, the good girl, is portrayed by R. Chokoeva, who looks more like a Mongolian than a Russian. Incidentally, she is the most-honored of the ballet dancers in this pic. Her rival, the bad femme, is played by B. Beishenova, a rugged, daring type ballet stepper. N. Tugelev is well cast as the king. The whole affair is backed by the Corps de Ballet of the Kirghizian State Opera, with the Leningrad Philharmonic Society orch playing the background music.

A different Russo color system is employed and is a shade better than the more familiar Sovcolor. Camera work, as so often in the case with a Russian pic, is topflight but no credit is given.

Wear.

El Espejo de la Bruja
(The Witch's Mirror)
(MEXICAN)

Mexico City, Aug. 14.

Peliculas Nacionales release of Cinematografica, S.A. production. Stars Rosita Arenas, Armando Calvo, Isabela Corona; features Dina de Marco. Directed by Chano Urueta. Screenplay, Alfredo Ruanova; camera, Jorge Stahl; music, G. C. Carreon. At Mariscala Theatre, Mexico City. Running time, **90 MINS.**

Merit of this macabre type of horror film is its trick photography, rather well conceived and executed by cameraman Jorge Stahl. Story line is weak with a blend of witchcraft and science.

Isabela Corona, an actress deserving better things, plays the central character of a witch in the traditional setting of a bleak house. There is the love interest couple (Rosita Arenas and Armando Calvo) who seek to break down the mysterious carrying-ons of Corona.

The "bewitched" mirror of the witch aids in achieving such things as a hand having a life of its own; a piano that plays with no hands touching it, flowers wither from the breath of an evil wind; the witch turns into a cat; and so on.

None of this is original but the trick photography effects are excellent, contribute most of value to this nabe house effort which seemed to be immensely enjoyed by audience at the theatre.

Emil.

Vancouver Fest

Eroica
(POLAND)

Vancouver, Aug. 14.

Film Polski release of Kadr Film Unit production. Features Edward Dziewonski, Barbara Polomska, Leon Niemczyk, Ignacy Machowski, Kazimierz Opalinski, Jozef Nowak, Roman Klosowski, Mariusz Dmochowski, Bogumil Kobiela, Jozef Kostecki, Tadeusz Lomnicki. Directed by Andrzej Munk. Screenplay, Jerzy Stefan Stawinski; camera, Jerzy Wojcik; editors, Jadwiga Zaicek, Miroslawa Garlicka; music, Jan Krenz. At Vancouver Film Fest. Running time, **83 MINS.**

Part One: "Scherzo Alla Pollaca"
Dzidzius .... Edward Dziewonski
Zosia .... Barbara Polomska
Lt. Kolya .... Leon Niemczyk
Part Two: "Ostinato Lugubre"
Kurzawa .... Jozef Nowak

Dabecki .... Bogumil Kobiela
Zak .... Jozef Kostecki
Zawistowski .... Tadeusz Lomnicki

"Eroica" is a film made several years ago by the late Andrzej Munk, but not previously given a North American release until this fest showing. It consists of two separate stories, unrelated in themselves, but complementary in theme in that both are concerned with an aspect of the disillusionment of Poles in the calamitous days of 1944.

"Scherzo Alla Pollaca," the first vignette, treats this theme in comic form, with the hero cast as a disenchanted volunteer trying to avoid underground training for the Warsaw uprising. His drunkenness, disregard for safety and believable cowardice when sober are stated with humorous effect that often borders on the burlesque, but come out as something sane in a world gone mad. His will to survive finally becomes more acceptable than any desire for heroic death. Edward Dziewonski's portrayal of the cowardly hero is great. Andrzeij Munk's direction makes the most of the opportunities to scoff rather than stress the solemnities of war.

"Ostinato Lugubre," more assured as an episode, revolves around the grim joke in which a fictitious escapee from a German POW camp for Polish officers boosts the morale of his fellow prisoners. In point of fact, the "escapee" lies hidden from Germans and comrades alike to maintain the illusion that he did get away. The humor in this role is far more subtle than in "Scherzo."

Western release at this time of an Iron Curtain film that pokes fun at its country's own military traditions is refreshing, if not of any particular significance. For aficionados of the Polish school of filmmaking, via the later "Ashes And Diamonds," this early Munk looms as a good art house bet. Technically the film is satisfactory and music effective. Biggest plus is contained in the visual humor.

Shaw.

Am Galgen Hangt Die Liebe
(Love On The Gallows)
(WESt GERMAN)
Vancouver, Aug. 14.

Export Union Der Deutschen Filmindustrie release of Auglst Rieger production. With Carl Wery, Annie Rosar, Marisa Mell, Bart Fortell, Sieghardt Rupp, Michael Janisch, Eduard Kock, Guido Wieland, Juerg Holl, Michael Lenz. Directed by Edwin Zbonek. Screenplay, Erna Fentsch; camera, Walter Partsch; editor, Eleonore Kunze. At Vancouver Film Fest. Running time, **93 MINS.**

Nigolaos .... Carl Wery
Marulja .... Annie Rosar
Petros .... Bert Fortell
Alka .... Marisa Mell
Alexandros .... Sieghardt Rupp
German Officer......... Michael Janisch
Corporal .... Eduard Kock

West German second World War film is based on legend of Philemon and Baucis in Ovid's "Metamorphoses" in which an old couple who were the only people on earth to give hospitality to the god Jupiter were granted one wish. They asked to be allowed to die together, and Philemon was turned into an oak tree, his wife Baucis into a lime tree, and the branches of the two trees intertwined.

Parallel in this has the scene set in 1944, in the Greek mountains, with fanatical partisans fighting German occupation troops. A partisan leader is hunted down by the Germans and finds shelter in a hut inhabited by an old couple, who disapprove of the fighting but regard hospitality to all who enter their abode as a sacred duty. The partisan is hidden from the German officer and corporal who search the hut. When the situation is suddenly reversed and the two Germans seek safety, the couple give them the same sanctuary.

Conclusion between the legend and this story is not quite the same as the partisan leader comes back to claim the lives of the aged couple for giving his enemy the same break he had enjoyed.

Film holds some interest in having Germans play both sides realistically, but early moments of truth deteriorate into a clumsy attempt to draw a distinction between undisciplined fanaticism and justifiable patriotism that doesn't jell. Acting of Carl Wery and Annie Rosar as the old couple is the best thing here, as they convey the essence of the Ovid legend. Technical credits are okay, and English sub-titles adequate.

Shaw.

The Chapman Report
.(COLOR)

Filmization of controversial bestseller. Curiosity of younger audiences should be helpful wicket factor.

Hollywood, Aug. 8.

Warner release of Richard D. Zanuck (DFZ) production. Stars Efrem Zimbalist Jr., Shelley Winters, Jane Fonda, Claire Bloom, Glynis Johns, Ray Danton. Ty Hardin, Andrew Duggan, John Dehner; with Harold J. Stone, Corey Allen, Jennifer Howard, Cloris Leachman, Chad Everett, Henry Daniell, Hope Cameron, Roy Roberts, Evan Thompson. Directed by George Cukor. Screenplay, Wyatt Cooper, Don M. Mankiewicz, as adapted from Irving Wallace's novel by Grant Stuart, Gene Allen; camera (Technicolor), Harold Lipstein; editor, Robert Simpson; music, Leonard Rosenman; assistant directors, Sergei Petschnikoff. James T. Vaughn. Reviewed at Academy Awards Theatre, Aug. 8, '62. Running time, 125 MINS.

Paul .... Efrem Zimbalist Jr.
Sarah Garnell .... Shelley Winters
Kathleen Barclay .... Jane Fonda
Naomi .... Claire Bloom
Teresa .... Glynis Johns
Fred Linden .... Ray Danton
Ed Kraski .... Ty Hardin
Dr. Chapman .... Andrew Duggan
Geoffrey .... John Dehner
Frank Garnell .... Harold J. Stone
Wash Dillon .... Corey Allen
Grace Waterton .... Jennifer Howard
Miss Selby .... Cloris Leachman
Water Boy .... Chad Everett
Dr. Jonas .... Henry Daniell
Ruth .... Hope Cameron
Alan Roby .... Roy Roberts
Cass Kelly .... Evan Thompson

"The Chapman Report" is a talky melodramatization of several abnormal patterns in the sexual behavior of the upper middleclass American female. The fact that it stems from a provocative bestseller gives it a comfortable commercial head start, but ultimately its thematic pointlessness, story shallowness and dramatic disjointedness is apt to limit its money making range. The Darryl F. Zanuck production for Warner Bros., produced by Richard D. Zanuck, figures to enjoy its greatest popularity with younger audiences, principally among teenage girls for whom the topic will arouse natural curiosity.

The Wyatt Cooper-Don M. Mankiewicz scenario, from an adaptation by Grant Stuart and Gene Allen of Irving Wallace's novel, attempts the feat of dramatically threading together the stories of four sexually unstable women who become voluntary subjects for a scientific sex survey conducted by a noted psychologist and his staff.

One (Claire Bloom) is a hopeless nympho and alcoholic. Another (Jane Fonda) suffers from fears of frigidity. The third (Glynis Johns), a kind of comedy relief figure, is an intellectual who feels there may be more to sex than she has realized in her smugly satisfied marital relationship. The last (Shelley Winters) enters into a clandestine extra-marital affair with an irresponsible little theatre director.

The audience is required to continually shift gears and build to new varying emotional peaks, but none of the four episodes is plausible or substantial enough on its own merits. After elaborately developing and illustrating the four cases, the film concludes with the declaration that these are merely exceptions to the rule of happily married life in suburbia.

Miss Johns does the best acting in the film, rising above the flimsiest of the four episodes with a spirited and infectious performance. Miss Fonda seems miscast and is affected and unappealing in her role. Miss Bloom suffers up a storm. Miss Winters plays with conviction. The men are all two-dimensional pawns, seemingly left to their own resources by director George Cukor, who has kept Harold Lipstein's camera trained almost exclusively on the four ladies.

Efrem Zimbalist Jr. plays the interviewer who thaws Miss Fonda by showering her with love and affection. Zimbalist has a welcome attribute—mature masculinity—in these days of the somewhat callow and effeminate leading man—but his performance is wooden. Satisfactory featured contributions are made by Ray Danton, Ty Hardin, Andrew Duggan, John Dehner and Harold J. Stone, with adequate support by Corey Allen, Jennifer Howard, Cloris Leachman, Chad Everett, Henry Daniell, Hope Cameron, Roy Roberts and Evan Thompson.

Robert Simpson has done an able job of splicing together the four stories. Leonard Rosenman's music helps create the desired moods. Orry-Kelly's costumes have flair and accurately represent social status. *Tube.*

Billy Budd
(C'SCOPE)

Somewhat flawed screen translation of Melville's powerful allegory. Slipups will hurt b.o. pull with choosy set.

Hollywood, Aug. 20.

Allied Artists release of Peter Ustinov production. Stars Robert Ryan, Peter Ustinov, Melvyn Douglas, Terence Stamp; with Ronald Lewis, David McCallum, John Neville, Paul Rogers, Lee Montague, Thomas Heathcote, Ray McAnally, Robert Brown, John Meillon, Cyril Luckham, Niall MacGinnis. Directed by Ustinov. Screenplay, Ustinov, Robert Rossen, based on play by Louis O. Coxe and Robert H. Chapman from novel, "Billy Budd Foretopman," by Herman Melville; camera, Robert Krasker; editor, Jack Harris; music, Antony Hopkins; assistant director, Michael Birkett. Reviewed at Academy Awards Theatre, Aug. 20, '62. Running time, 123 MINS.

Master-at-Arms John Claggart
.... Robert Ryan
Capt. Edward Fairfax Vere
.... Peter Ustinov
The Dansker .... Melvyn Douglas
Billy Budd .... Terence Stamp
Jenkins .... Ronald Lewis
Lieut. Wyatt .... David McCallum
Lieut. Ratcliffe .... John Neville
Lieut. Seymour .... Paul Rogers
Squeak .... Lee Montague
Payne .... Thomas Heathcote
O'Daniel .... Ray McAnally
Talbot .... Robert Brown
Kincaid .... John Meillon
Hallam .... Cyril Luckham
Capt. Graveling .... Niall MacGinnis

Peter Ustinov's production of "Billy Budd" is a near miss, and Ustinov, alas, is the culprit. The ubiquitous Mr. U quadrupled in function as producer, director, co-scenarist and star of the Allied Artists release. As producer, he is to be commended for spearheading the noble effort to translate Herman Melville's highly-regarded, thought-provoking last story to the screen—a difficult task—and for populating its cast with respected, seasoned actors plus a fine young newcomer in the title role. As writer, he has collaborated with Robert Rossen in the construction of a workable and literate screenplay. But as director he is guilty of at least one major flaw of execution in which Ustinov, the actor,

is most prominently implicated.

Since "Billy Budd" is primarily a film for pick-and-choosers, its ultimate artistic shortcomings may have a proportionately greater negative effect at the boxoffice. Stimulation of mass audience curiosity can probably best be accomplished by an aggressive buildup campaign on behalf of tyro Terence Stamp, a goodlooking actor whose sensitive, appealing introductory performance in the title role stamps him as an important addition to the ranks of young leading men on the screen.

"Billy Budd," of course, is the allegorical tale of the clash of an incredibly good-hearted young foretopman and an inhumanly sadistic master-at-arms aboard a British fighting vessel in 1797, and the issue of moral justice vs. the wartime military code that arises when the former is condemned to hang for killing the latter, though recognized even by those who sit in judgment upon him as being spiritually innocent.

The clash between Budd and his tormentor, Claggart — archetypes of good and evil—has been carried off well by Stamp and Robert Ryan under Ustinov's guidance. Where Ustinov has slipped is in the development and delineation of the character he himself plays —the overly conscientious Captain Vere, whose judgment in favor of military over moral ramifications of the issue sends Budd to his death. Claggart is black and Budd is white, but Vere is the key role—the all-too-human middleman whose ethical dilemma and subsequent sense of guilt and remorse must be profoundly felt by the audience if the film is to be successful. As executed in his-trionic-directorial overlap by Ustinov, the character is not as sharply defined as it must be. Audience compassion is never properly aroused. As a result, the film concludes without the required emotional impact.

Melvyn Douglas is a trifle overly ominous as the expository Dansker. Lee Montague is a standout as Claggart's henchman. Ronald Lewis, David McCallum, John Neville, Paul Rogers and John Meillon perform skillfully in support.

Thematically apropos black-and-white photography sacrifices obvious color values inherent in a sea story, but is dexterously dispatched by cameraman Robert Krasker. Jack Harris' editing is adept, Peter Murton's art direction authentic, Antony Hopkins' score dramatically valuable. Don Ashton rates a bow for his production design. Exec producer of the enterprise was A. Ronald Lubin.   *Tube.*

Term of Trial
(BRITISH)

Interesting marquee lineup in an equally interesting, though downbeat straggly pic; potential b.o. with discerning audiences, with Laurence Olivier, Simone Signoret as star names.

London, Aug. 21.

Warner-Pathe release of a Romulus (James Woolf) production. Stars Laurence Olivier, Simone Signoret; features Terence Stamp, Roland Culver, Frank Pettingell, Thora Hird, Newton Blick, Hugh Griffith, Sarah Miles. Directed and written by Peter Glenville. Based on James Barlow's novel; camera, Oswald Morris; editor, James Clark; music, Jean-Michl Demase. Reviewed at Corner Theatre, London. Running time, 130 MINS.
Graham Weir .... Laurence Olivier
Anna................ Simone Signoret
Trowman .... Roland Culver
Ferguson .... Frank Pettingell
Mrs. Taylor .... Thora Hird
Det. Sgt. Keirnan........Dudley Foster
Mr. Taylor .... Norman Bird
Prosecutor .... Newton Blick
Sylvan-Jones .... Allan Cuthbertson
Magistrate .... Nicholas Hannen
Thompson .... Ray Holder
Joan .... Barbara Ferris
Constance ...... Rosamund Greenwood
Inspector Ullyat .... Lloyd Lamble
Mrs. Thompson .... Vanda Godsell
Chard .... Earl Cameron
Collins .... Clive Colin Bowler
Shirley Taylor .... Sarah Miles
O'Hara .... Hugh Griffith
Mitchell .... Terence Stamp

Those who deplore Sir Laurence Olivier playing "little," defeated men and regard him as boxoffice disaster unless he is doing a Henry V or Hamlet have another chance to appraise this fine actor's work in "Term of Trial." For here he's an idealistic, but seedily unsuccessful schoolmaster in a small mixed school in the North of England. With Olivier, are Simone Signoret and two newcomers, Terence Stamp and Sarah Miles, both rightly hailed as click new discoveries.

Such a lineup should bring in patrons who will find a holding, though somewhat untidy film. This is due, largely, to an uneven screenplay by Peter Glenville which makes his task as director rather tougher than it should have been.

Olivier's performance is gloomy, often deliberately dull, but it is minutely observed in detail and is never less than absorbing. Let it be put on record that he has one scene in the dock of a blazing theatrical intensity which, though it may be contrived, is boff thesping. His acting is always rewarding. There is another scene, a quarrel in bed with his wife, played by Simone Signoret, which is masterly work by both players. It's also written on a level which, unfortunately, Glenville doesn't always sustain.

Olivier has had to settle for this inferior teaching job because as a pacifist during the war he went to jail. He's afflicted with a sense of inferiority, a nagging scold of a wife and a taste for hard liquor. He also suffers from a suspicious headmaster and a class which, inevitably, contains the school bully, played with remarkable assurance by Terence Stamp. Olivier is delighted when he sees a desire to learn in a young 15-year-old girl (Sarah Miles) but, rather naively, fails to see that she is precociously sexually aroused by him.

The "crush" comes to a head when he takes some of the pupils on a school trip to Paris. The girl comes to his hotel room late at night and is affronted when he gently dismisses her advances with a playful wallop on her posterior. She then feeds her mother with the tale that she has been indecently assaulted and he lands in the courtroom. There, though dismissed on probation, his name is not cleared, even though the girl eventually admits her lie. There is a final, ironic twist in which his marriage is precariously saved. His wife seemingly but not very convincingly has a new feeling for him when she believes that he has actually proved himself a man and not a mouse.

There are several loose ends, which could have emerged from the writing or the editing. But overall the characters are well drawn, the situations dramatic and the thesping all round is tops. Apart from Olivier, Miss Signoret gives another of her effacing yet significant portrayals of an edgy wife. In Sarah Miles, making her debut as the young girl, there is evidence of a sharp intelligence and a flowering promise. The role played by young Stamp fades out disappointingly, but the youth seems another bright example of the current Finney-O'Toole-Courtenay school of acting.

Thora Hird, as the girl's acid tongued mother, can play this type of role on her head. In the excellent supporting cast, Hugh Griffith and Newton Blick, as opposing lawyers, Frank Pettingell, as the headmaster, Roland Culver and Allen Cuthbertson, as differing teachers, and Norman Bird, as the girl's father, all contribute fine assist, with Griffith, as usual, outstanding.

Where "Term of Trial" tends to fall down is that some of the situations are contrived with little logic, and the irony is often injected predictably. The dark atmosphere of the frowsy little school is admirably caught. Oswald Morris' lensing and Glenville's direction both try, often successfully, to get out of a rut.   *Rich.*

Almost Angels
(COLOR)

The Vienna Boys Choir faces life. To be coupled with re-released "Lady and the Tramp" for an all-Disney family confection.

Hollywood, Aug. 24.

Buena Vista release of Walt Disney production. Stars Peter Weck, Sean Scully, Vincent Winter; with Hans Holt, Bruni Lobel, Fritz Eckhardt, Gunther Philipp. Directed by Steven Previn. Screenplay, Vernon Harris, based on original idea by R. A. Stemmle; camera (Technicolor), Kurt Grigoleit; editor, Alfred Srp; assistant director, Rudolf Nussgruber. Reviewed at Academy Awards Theatre, Aug. 24, '62. Running time, 93 MINS.
Max Heller .... Peter Weck
Director Eisinger .... Hans Holt
Father Fiala .... Fritz Eckhardt
Frau Fiala .... Bruni Lobel
Radio Commentator..... Gunther Philipp
Toni Fiala .... Vincent Winter
Peter Schaefer .... Sean Scully
Friedel Schmidt .... Denis Gilmore
Ferdy .... Hennie Scott
Music Teacher .... Heinz Grohmann
Wardrobe Mistress.....Rose Renee Roth
Seamstress .... Heide Grubl
Sister-Nurse .... Ferda Maren
Woman .... Liselotte Wrede
Choirmaster I .... Hermann Furthmosek
Choirmaster II .... Hans Christian
Choirmaster III .... Walter Regelsberger
Misignore .... Oskar Willner
Mathematics Teacher .... Walter Varndel
Felix Meinl........ Bernhard Hindinger
Woman .... Anni Schoenhuber
Mother .... Elisabeth Stiepl

The Disney banner and the unprecedented demand for family product are the factors upon which this otherwise somewhat dubious offering will have to rely for respectable boxoffice returns. Filmed in and around Vienna, the Buena Vista release is an attempt to build a story around the wondrous warbling of the Vienna Boys Choir. Painless culture, one might term it.

But "Almost Angels" is almost unbearably saccharine in story style, and the singing interludes, at first a tonic for tired ears, eventually overstay their welcome. The film is basically a short subject bloated into feature length. Coupling with re-release of the 1955 Disney full-length cartoon; "Lady and the Tramp," may rule out many would-be customers unwilling to go seconds, but the all-Disney show should register with some strength in the moppet realm.

Sentiment seeps out of every dramatic pore in Vernon Harris' scenario, based on an "original idea" by R. A. Stemmle. Maybe Stemmle's idea was original, but what's been done with it would have been discarded as antique when Freddie Bartholomew was in knee pants. Story pivots around the adventures of a not especially bright lad (Vincent Winter) whose beautiful voice enables him to get into the VBC and stick, despite poor grades, schoolmate sabotage and a dubious father.

Steven Previn's direction emphasizes sentiment at every turn. There is more sweetness in this picture than in a sack of Spreckels. Master Winter, of "Little Kidnappers" fame, is still a capable young actor, and the best moppet thespian in the film. Sean Scully, as his sidekick, is a handsome lad but a rather self-conscious actor. Peter Weck plays their teacher, a character who sets some kind of a record for sweetness and understanding. Bruni Lobel and Fritz Eckhardt do the best acting in the picture as Winter's mother and father. Hans Holt and young Hennie Scott are satisfactory in key supporting roles.

Austrian exterior sites and interior sets of Warner and Isabell Schlichting will be especially interesting to U.S. audiences. Kurt Grigoleit's photography is capable, Alfred Srp's editing mechanically sound. The music of Schubert, Brahms and Strauss is featured, a treat for audiences favorably disposed to "serious" music. The Vienna Symphony, conducted by Helmuth Froschauer, performs the score. Musical director is Heinz Schreiter.   *Tube.*

If A Man Answers
(COLOR)

Lightweight romanticomedy in which the fun is widely scattered. Glamorous Ross Hunter touch and teen-pull of Dee & Darin will have to bolster b.o.

Hollywood, Aug. 24.

Universal-International release of Ross Hunter production. Stars Sandra Dee, Bobby Darin, Micheline Presle. John Lund; features Cesar Romero, Stefanie Powers; with Christopher Knight, Ted Thorpe, Roger Bacon, John Bleifer, Pamela Searle, Warrene Ott, Dani Lynn, Charlene Holt, Gloria Camacho, Edmay Van Dyke, Rosalee Calvert, Gladys Thornton. Directed by Henry Levin. Screenplay, Richard Morris, from novel by Winifred Wolfe; camera (Eastman), Russell Metty; editor, Milton Carruth; music, Hans Salter; assistant director, Phil Bowles. Reviewed at Westwood Village Theatre, July 31, '62. Running time, 102 MINS.
Chantal .... Sandra Dee
Eugene .... Bobby Darin
Maman Stacey .... Micheline Presle
John Stacey .... John Lund
Robert Swan .... Cesar Romero
Tina .... Stefanie Powers
Richard .... Christopher Knight
Florist .... Ted Thorpe
Messenger .... Roger Bacon
Tabacconist .... John Bleifer
Model .... Pamela Searle
Rita .... Warrene Ott
Bunny .... Dani Lynn
Lisa .... Charlene Holt
Models....Gloria Camacho, Edmay Van Dyke, Rosalee Calvert
Boston Maid .... Gladys Thornton

The teenage draw of Sandra Dee and Bobby Darin and the

characteristic sheen and glamour that attracts women of all ages to Ross Hunter pictures will have to carry the boxoffice burden for "If A Man Answers." Beyond these mild commercial attributes, the Universal-International release has little with which to entice or satisfy the choosy modern picturegoer.

Richard Morris' screenplay, from the novel by Winifred Wolfe, is divisible into three distinct sections as it pointlessly and with only widely scattered amusement pursues the basic topic of wifemanship—or how to win at marriage without actually cheating. First course is the capture of the mate. Second illustrates the procedure of training one's spouse as if he were a household pet (a method that might be labelled "animal husbandry"). Third describes the ritual of keeping one's husband jealous and on edge, accomplished simply by having one's mother constantly phone and hang up "if a man answers" — man, naturally, being the thoroughly irritated husband. Each of the three premises is milked to rather exhaustive lengths.

Miss Dee generally overacts when she should be natural and unassuming, and comes up blank when she ought better to be acting. Husband Bobby Darin, although affected in spots, does somewhat better in the comedy line. Micheline Presle lends her Gallic charm to the role of Miss Dee's mother, and John Lund, one of the screen's most accomplished and recently least exploited farceurs, is on hand in the bland and thankless part of Miss Dee's perturbed father. Cesar Romero is durably handsome as Darin's sex-propelled father. Stefanie Powers plays the vixen who vies with Miss Dee for Darin's postmarital attention. Supporting roles are dispatched adequately.

Director Henry Levin has kept matters light and frothy, getting about as much mileage as possible out of a script that is as weighty as a toasted marshmallow. As is typical of Hunter productions, the sets by Alexander Golitzen, decorations by Howard Bristol and gowns by Jean Louis are elaborate and elegant. Russell Metty's photography, Hans Salter's score and Milton Carruth's editing are competently performed, although at least slight acceleration of the pace would, as noted earlier, have been welcomed. Darin has penned a title tune, which he sings over the clever animated credits. It's a frisky ditty with a twist tempo, and will be a helpful selling point.
Tube.

Montreal Fest

Historia Zoltej Cizemki
("The Yellow Slippers")
(POLISH)

Film Polski production. Directed by Sylwester Checinski; screenplay, Zizislaw Skowronski, Wanda Zolkiewska from a story by Antonina Domanska. Camera (color), Zbigniew Hartwig; editor, Janina Niedzwiecka; music, Zbiegniew Turski. At Montreal Film Festival, Aug., 1962. Running time, 83 MINS.
Wit Stdosz .... Gustaw Holoubek
Rafal .... Andrzej Szczepkowski
Wawrzek .... Narek Kondrat
Gregorius .... Bronislaw Pawlik

The King....... Kazimierz Biaioszcynski
And: Bogumi Kobiela, Bohdan Niewinowski, Mieczyslaw Czechowicz, Bohdan Baer, Eugeniusz Szewczyk, Beata Barszcewska and others.

This is one of Poland's specially made features for children and was shown on a program of children's films at Montreal's festival. It tells of the adventures of a country wonder child—the little sculptor, Wawrzek—who goes to work for the great master, Wit Stwosz. The story culminates in the unveiling of Stwosz's greatest masterpiece, the Altar of the St. Mary's Church in Cracov.

The boy is pleasing played by 10-year old, Marek Kondrat, son of the actor, and the deliberately artificial studio sets give a charming air of fantasy to the whole.
Prat.

Taiyo No Hakaba
("The Sun's Burial")
(JAPANESE COLOR)

Shochiku Film release of Tomio Ikeda production. Directed by Nagaisa Ohshima. Screenplay, Ohshima & Toshiro Ishido; camera (Grandscope & Eastmancolor), Ko Kawamata; music, Riichiro Manabe. At Montreal Film Festival, August, 1962. Running time, 87 MINS.
Hanako .... Kayoko Honoo
Takeshi .... Osao Sasaki
Shin .... Masahiko Tsugawa
Tatsuo .... Koji Nakahara
Yasu .... Yusuke Kawazu
Yosematsu, Hanako's father
                       Junzaburo Ban
Yosehei .... Fumio Watanabe
Batasuke .... Kamatari Fujiwara
Chika, his wife ...... Tanie Kitabayashi
The Agitator .... Eitaro Ozawa

This film was Japan's official entry at Montreal, but after seeing it the program committee rightly gave it a morning showing and with the cooperation of Seneca International Ltd. of New York, substituted "Yojimbo" instead.

"The Sun's Burial" (accurately sub-titled by Shochiku as "the sewer of modern Japan") is nothing more than a sex and violence story more suitable for double-feature grind houses than a festival. It pretends to be concerned about delinquent youth in the slums of Tokyo and wants to show society that "unless drastic changes take place in the world surrounding them, there is nothing for these characters but ultimate destruction."

Having said his piece, director Ohshima proceeds to carry out the destruction of his "gutter rats" by murder, rape, suicide, gun fire, arson and accident. If this had been done with any skill, it might have passed, but the proceedings are tedious and confused and the characters dismal. They are lead by a provocative girl who takes blood from impoverished laborers to sell to cosmetics manufacturers. There are gang wars and love affairs, alcoholics and dope fiends, cowards and sadists. The best that can be said of the cast is that they look their parts.
Prat.

Zimlia
("Earth")
(USSR)

Produced at the Vufku Studio, Kiev, 1930. Script and direction by Alexander Dovzshenko; camera, D. Demutzky; music, L. Revutzky. Features S. Shkurat, S. Svashenko, Y. Solntzeva, E. Maksimova. At Montreal Film Festival, Aug., 1962. Running time, 63 MINS.

This famous film was shown as a retrospective at Montreal's festival together with Dovzshenko's last film "Poem of the Sea" (Poima O More). (The latter pic was reviewed from Paris by *Mosk.* in Oct. 1960.) "Earth" was the sixth of Dovzshenko's eleven productions, and it embodies the quintessence of his philosophy of life: that the tenets of the Marxist are related to the attachment of simple men to the land of their forefathers.

Showing how the machines come to help the collectivization of farms in the Ukraine, "Earth" is well-known for its simplicity, lyricism and deep-feeling for humanity and nature. This new print (specially made for last year's Moscow festival) is proof that it remains one of the finest examples of the poetic cinema of the silent period.
Prat.

Venice Films

Homenaje A La Hora De La Siesta
(Homage At Siesta Time)
(ARGENTINE-FRENCH)

Venice, Aug. 25.
Procides release of Imperial-Nestor Gaffet production. Stars Alida Valli, Paul Guers, Alexandra Stewart; features Maurice Serfati, Luigi Picci. Directed by Leopoldo Torre Nilsson. Screenplay, Beatrice Guida, Torre Nilsson; camera, Albert Eichebere; editor, Jacinto Cascales. Scheduled for Venice Film Fest; caught at studio preview. Running time, 85 MINS.
Balmont .... Paul Guers
Constance .... Alida Valli
Mariana .... Alexandra Stewart
Lombardo .... Maurice Sarfati
Alyosia .... Luigi Picci

Argentine director Leopoldo Torre Nilsson has made a name for himself at film festivals via films on upper class problems in Argentina. Here, he leaves his usual themes for a look at martyrdom and faith. Though on less sure grounds, he still manages to make a taut, sturdy study of the clash of belief and cynicism.

This seems primarily a specialized entry abroad, needing hardsell and proper placement for best results. Its characters are mainly centered in four widows of missionaries killed by primitive natives along the Amazon. They go to the site to pay their last respects and also for a special meeting to be held by church groups. Along is a quizzical journalist.

All are trapped alone for a few days because of the rain and the wait for the others. The scribe probes each one to find out what their men where like. Each reveals herself and, inadvertently, her husband. Into this comes a man who was present at the burning of the missionaries. But it seems only one man was a true martyr while he killed the fearful others at their request.

One woman gives herself to the man to hush this up and finally kills him in her fanatic desire to have her husband's name unsullied. She is slain while destroying the evidence. The newsman is left in the midst of the homage to the dead men wondering if it is better to tell the truth.

Pic ends on this ambiguous note. Though the various reasons for altruism and religious dedication are treated, and false and prideful reason castigated, this tends too much to reveal character, motivation and action in highly bravura moments and treatment. Result is that the personages sometimes remain surface.

Mixed bag of French, Italo, Argentine and Latino thesps do acceptably despite the prevalence of talk. This looms an unusual, if uneven film with enough interest in its theme to make it a definite lingo entry and an arty possibility. It is technically good. Pic is competing at the Venice Fest.
Mosk.

Vivre Sa Vie
(Live Her Life)
(FRENCH)

Venice, Aug. 28.
Films De La Pleiade release of Pierre Braunberger production. Stars Anna Karina; features Sady Rebiot, Monique Messine, Mario Botti, Gisele Hauchecorne. Written and directed by Jean-Luc Godard. Camera, Raoul Coutard; editor, Agnes Guillemot. At Venice Film Fest. Running time, 80 MINS.
Nana .... Anna Karina
Raoul .... Sady Rebiot
Yvette .... Monique Messine
Elizabeth .... Gisele Hauchecorne
Philosopher .... Brice Parain

As he looked at a young, cynical hoodlum in "Breathless," director Jean-Luc Godard brings his dispassionate outlook to a pretty girl who slips into prostitution. Nothing sentimental here but a knowing series of episodes that skillfully probe the girl's character and life.

Godard eschews his jump cutting and brittle pacing of the past to make a well sustained, non-sensational look at a girl adrift in Paris. One of the early New Wavers, he shows his deep historical knowledge of films by deft illusions to other directors, other pix, and even has some scenes from Carl Dreyer's "Passion of Joan of Arc" when the protagonist goes to a film. It probes her feelings via her reactions to some of the scenes.

Godard breaks with the old ideas of story and continuity to build a picture that goes below the surface in looking at a girl's personality. There are no moral judgments but neither is there leering or exploiting of the material. As the heroine keeps saying, "That is how it is."

She is depicted via 12 little episodes, each getting a title on the screen. First she breaks with a rather weak, self-indulgent boyfriend. The girl gets locked out of her apartment, leaves her job and finally goes into prostitution. She ends up with a procurer. When she tries to break with him for a young man she is sold to another group only to be shot down when they fight over money.

Godard mixes titles, unusual use of sound, and long scenes of dialog to finally come up with a deeply-etched picture of a decent if immoral girl whose immorality points to the general outlook of the times. The only weapon and possession she has are her looks, the story reads. She finally uses them to get along.

The first encounter, then her succeeding ones, and her talks with people are also neatly employed to show a picture of a girl who gives her body but never herself.

A few nude shots are all that are shown of her professional days. It has a sombre progression leavened with her sudden shafts of insight. Godard is brilliantly served by his wife, Anna Karina, in this film.

Miss Karina gives the girl a ring of truth and depth. She may not feel too deeply but has a pure if confused psychology that keeps her above what she falls into. There may be some censorship problem on its refusal to condemn her mode of life.

Film looms a solid arty entry and its theme and brisk treatment could also make this a playoff item if well handled. This appears to be a film that will be heard from in foreign marts.

Godard emerges as one of the most talented of the early New Wavers. He is now a definite part of the industry here with a batch of unusual pix to his credit. Technical credits and thesping, of both pro and non-pro actors, are all first-rate. Pic competes at the festival here. *Mosk.*

Mamma Roma
(ITALIAN)

Venice, Aug. 28.

Cineriz release of an Arco Film (Alfredo Bini) production. Stars Anna Magnani; features Ettore Garofalo, Franco Citti, Silvana Corsini, Luisa Loiano. Written and directed by Pier Paolo Pasolini; camera, Tonino delli Colli; music, coordinated by Carlo Rustichelli; editor, Nino Baragli. At Venice Film Fest, but caught at preview. Running time, **110 MINS.**

Mamma Roma	Anna Magnani
Ettore	Ettore Garofalo
Carmine	Franco Citti
Bruna	Silvana Corsini
Biancofiore	Luisa Loiano

Strong arty entry with Anna Magnani name and hefty word-of-mouth to help it achieve general distribution both in Italy and abroad. Sure to be one of best and most-discussed Italo-pix of the new season.

Hard-hitting item, the second directed by novelist Pier Paolo Pasolini after "Accattone," is set in Rome's seamy suburbs as was the other pic. Basically, though infinite realistic details heighten its overall impact, the pic is about a prostitute's efforts to begin a new life with her grown son. Though she settles in a new part of town, her past haunts her and she is occasionally forced to return to her former beat to gather some quick coin, hoping that the son doesn't hear about it. The latter, despite her efforts, is slowly corrupted by the city environment, eventually dying after being caught thieving.

Despite Miss Magnani's presence, it's writer-director Pasolini's film all the way. He again manages a realistic-poetic tour de force in telling his tragic tale in grimly human terms. Miss Magnani is splendid and in rare form as the mother, a return to the instinctively earthy roles which first gave her fame. Ettore Garofalo, in his first pic role, is a definite find as her pug-ugly son, a youthfully tragic figure while Franco Citti is perfectly suited to his role as Miss Magnani's ex-husband. Silvana Corsini is fine as the unglamorous neighborhood temptress. Other roles are colorfully cast.

Pic could stand a bit of trimming for pace and length. Tonino delli Colli's lensing on locations in and around the Eternal City is a further asset. Carlo Rustichelli's adaptation of classic music to backdrop the action makes for very effective dramatic device. Other credits are tops. This is being shown in competition. *Hawk.*

Jigsaw
(BRITISH)

Excellent police yarn showing the tracking down of a murderer. Has an almost documentary flavor, with plausible performances and crisp script. Sound British marquee value and a good bet all round.

London, Aug. 22.

BLC release of British Lion-Britannia presentation of a Val Guest production. Stars Jack Warner, Ronald Lewis, Yolande Donlan. Features Michael Goodliffe, John Le Mesurier, Moira Redmond, Brian Oulton, Ray Barrett, John Barron, Joan Newell, Graham Payn, Norman Chappell, John Horsley, Charles Houston, Reginald March. Produced, directed and written by Val Guest, from Hilary Waugh's novel, "Sleep Long, My Lovely"; camera, Arthur Grant: editor, Bill Lenny. Reviewed at Columbia Theatre, London, Aug. 21, '62. Running time: **107 MINS.**

Det.-Insp. Fellows	Jack Warner
Det.-Sgt. Wilks	Ronald Lewis
Jean Sherman	Yolande Donlan
Clyde Burchard	Michael Goodliffe
Mr. Simpson	John Le Mesurier
Joan Simpson	Moira Redmond
Mrs. Simpson	Christine Bocca
Frank Restlin	Brian Oulton
Sgt. Gorman	Ray Barrett
Andy Roach	Norman Chappell
Ray Tenby	John Barron
Mrs. Banks	Joan Newell
Mr. Bunnell	Peter Ashmore
Hilders	Reginald Marsh
Mr. Blake	Graham Payn
Chief Constable	Robert Raglan
Supt. Ramsey	John Horsley
Glazier	Gerald Cempion
Dr. MacFarlane	Robert Moore
Garage Foreman	Charles Houston
Porter	Timothy Bateson
Luggage Clerk	Harry Brunning

Without sensationalism Val Guest has spun a firstrate detective thriller which has the authentic stamp of a documentary in its attention to detail. Plenty of red herrings keep the audience alert and, though Guest resists the temptation to show the murderer at work and his subsequent cutting up of the body, he still provides customers with plenty of excitement as they guess "whodunit" and how. As an example of the technique of the cop, stripped of glamor, at work "Jigsaw" rates generous critical nods. Longish cast is okay for British consumption, but may be short on stellar value abroad.

What seems a routine shopbreaking job leads to discovery of an ugly crime. The police machinery slides smoothly and patiently into action. There is a surprise false lead to the identity of the victim, suspicion falls heavily on a traveling salesman but he is cleared and, once again, the cops are left without a clue as to the victim or the likely killer. When, eventually, the right man is brought in the police are unable to break his story until a slick twist at the end trips him up.

Males in the audience will identify themselves with the cops as they go about their task, and most will be pretty glad that they're not involved in a job that brings more headaches than glamor, more perspiration than sudden inspiration. It's a question of sifting resifting, asking questions, following up apparently hopeless clues, waiting for a break and being able to recognize it when it comes. Made with the full cooperation of the Brighton police "Jigsaw" should give a boost to the citizens' pride in the detective force. Guest has written a tight, smooth script in which most of the characters are completely recognizable as ordinary human beings instead of glamorized molls and crooks. The clues never lead to sleazy underground night clubs or saloons. In fact, there's not an obvious jailbird among the entire cast. He has also directed sharply, getting away to a sock start and keeping atmosphere alert by astute cutting.

Jack Warner, who on BBC-TV is the w.k. cop, P. C. Dixon of "Dixon of Dock Green," has been hiked to Detective-Inspector. He's a dedicated policeman whose theory is that "there's always a road between killer and killed. One's just got to ask enough questions. Human, workaday dialog helps Warner to sustain the role credibly. Ronald Lewis is also okay as his patient young asasistant. Michael Goodliffe has some rich moments as the suspect Lothario of a traveling salesman and he brings a nervy intensity to the role which is a neat foil to the police calm. Moira Redmond as the victim.

Yolande Donlan makes a guest appearance as the fading young spinster who has a brief, bittersweet affair with the murderer and, unsuspectingly, escapes being his second victim. Miss Donlan gives striking evidence of her own contention, that she need not be restricted to dizzy, dumb blonde roles. This is a part flecked with pathos and vouchingly played. *Rich.*

Venice Films

Lyudi Y Zvery
(The Men and the Beasts)
(RUSSIAN)

Venice, Aug. 29.

Sovexportfilm release of Maxim Gorki-DEFA coproduction. Features Nikolai Eremenko, Tamara Makarova, Jeanne Bolotova, Tatiana Gavrilova, Vitaliy Doronine, Serghei Gherasimov. Written and directed by Gherasimov. Camera, Vladimir Rappoport; music, A. Katchaturian. At Film Festival, Venice. Running time, **190 MINS.**

Pavlov	Nikolai Eremenko
Anna	Tamara Makarova
Tania	Jeanne Bolotova
Maria	Tatiana Gavrilova

Massive and lengthy Russo pic with little basic appeal to Western audiences though elaborately produced and diligently acted by a strong cast. Main interest however lies in approach to story, which deals with problems faced by a war vet who has spent 17 years outside Russia in quest of a future.

His travels have taken him from the Sudan to Canada, from Argentina to Hamburg (apparently without visa problems or work permits) where he's been able to glimpse a mainly corrupt and debauched capitalist world at work and play. Once home again, he's treated with suspicion by most because of his absence, including his brother, who hasn't the courage to openly embrace him. Story is unfolded in flashback as he hitchhikes homeward with a couple, mother and daughter, who ply him with the appropriate questions.

Good stolid performances are offered by Nikolai Eremenko, Tamara Makarova, Jeanne Bolotova, and others, while other credits are good. Director Gherasimov's script is often redundant, while his picture of western life is cliche-ridden. Two fellow-escapees from Russia are typically depicted as drunken, money-mad opportunists, and the emptyness of the free world, as a clincher, eventually drives him to near suicide. He is cured only by a hasty return to his Soviet homeland.

Film's foreign locations included East Berlin's DEFA Studios (for the Hamburg sequences) and three weeks in Cuba to film bits set in Argentina. *Hawk.*

Sarang Bang Sonnim Omoni
(My Mother and the Roomer)
(SOUTH KOREAN-SCOPE)

Venice, Aug. 29.

Shin Films release and production. With Choi Un-Hi, Kin Jin Kyu, Chun Young-Sun. Directed by Shin Sang Okk. Screenplay, Choo Yo-Sup; camera, Choi Soo Yong; editor, Shin. At Venice Film Fest. Running time, **105 MINS.**

Ok-Hee	Choi Un-Hi
Mother	Kin Jin Kyu
Han	Chun Young-Sun

Film has a nice feel for character and situation with some beguiling moppet work, but it does not possess that extra insight or dramatic plus for any art chances abroad.

A little girl, living with her widowed young mother and who had never known her father, tells the story. A boarder comes to the house and he falls for the mother and vice-versa. But the old mores in the village frown on widows remarrying and the mother-in-law, a power in the family, is also against it.

The little girl's love for the man, a scandal that is cleared up, and the mother-in-law coming around, leave things open for them. But the mother can not yet break with taboos. However, there is an inkling she will as the pic ends. The theme is probably a more pungent one in Korea but the scene setting and the feel for the place and people make it acceptable anywhere.

Technical credits are good and this may foreshadow a growing Korean pic industry of worth in the near future. *Mosk.*

Smog
(ITALIAN)

Venice, Aug. 29.

Titanus release (Metro in rest of world) of Titanus-Metro production by Goffredo Lombardo. Features Enrico Maria Salerno, Annie Girardot, Renato Salvatori, Susan Mueller, Isabella Albonico, Joan Houseman, Len Lesser, Peter Howard, Michele Guarini, Fred Catania, Casey Adams, Peter Opp, Graziella Granata, Lorendana Capelletti, M. Brigham, Billie Scheiner. Directed by Franco Rossi. Screenplay, Rossi, P. M. Pasinetti, Franco Brusati, G. D. Giagni, in collaboration with P. F. Campanile, Massimo Franciosa, Ugo Guerra; camera, Ted McCord; music, Piero Umiliani; editor, Mario Serandrei. At Film Festival, Venice. Running time, **100 MINS.**

Vittorio	Enrico Maria Salerno
Mario	Renato Salvatori
Gabriella	Annie Girardot

Another prestige item in the successful Titanus-Metro program, destined for specialized bookings outside Italy. Despite its noteworthy merits, slowish pace and diffused impact, somewhat in the manner of Michelangelo Antonioni's films, make a hard sell necessary. There's a curio angle which could help exploitation: pic was entirely shot in the Los Angeles area by the Italian company, first such case.

Story deals with brief Los Angeles visit, prompted by delayed plane connections, of a fast-rising Italian lawyer (and political climber) headed for Mexico City on business. He meets some Italians who work in L.A., tags along with them on some visits and parties. Gabriella (Annie Girardot), an Italian emigree who's found a solid niche in the US, briefly falls for the lawyer, but drops him for her more instinctive boy friend (Renato Salvatori) when she realizes the lawyer's empty ambition.

Pic development is deceptively bare, only slowly unfolding its indirect slap at current Italian social-political trends personified by the gutless, calculating, ever-compromising lawyer. By contrast, director Rossi depicts the Yank setting with tongue-in-cheek but loving care. His Americans, as contrasted to the visiting climber, are direct, sincere, spontaneous denizens of another, freer world, one which he will never understand, but which Gabriella, in her search for herself, may eventually adopt. Acting by Salerno, Annie Girardot, and Renato Salvatori is uniformly apt, ably backed by a Yank cast recruited on the spot.

Ted McCord rates an extra bow for his striking lens job of deliberately surreal Los Angeles area backdrops chosen by Rossi. Though it's planned that way, some of the long bridge sequences and linking shots of car rides through L.A. are repetitious and overlong, and some trimming could only help general audience reaction. *Hawk.*

Electra
(GREEK)
Venice, Aug. 26.
J. N. Film release and production. Stars Anna Synodinou. Thanos Cotsopoulos; features, Kakia Panayotou, Theodoros Moridis, Vassilis Canakis, Elly Vozikiadou, Pitsa Capitssinea. Directed by Ted Zarpas from the stage production by Takis Mouzenidis. Screenplay based on the tragedy by Sophocles; camera, G. Eptamenitis; editor, E. Siaskas. At Venice Film Fest. Running time 115 MINS.
Electra .... Anna Synodinou
Orestes .... Thanos Cotsopoulos
Clytemnestra .... Kakia Panayotou
Tutor .... Theodoros Moridies
Aegisthus .... Vassalis Canakis
Chrysothemis .... Elly Vozikiadou

Noted Greek director Michael Cacoyannis adapted Euripides' antique tragedy play "Electra" to film terms this year for an award at the recent Cannes Film Fest, and now comes Sophocles' "Electra" which remains a filmed play by the National Greek Theatre. Latter looms mainly a fine educational bet, a language entry, for tv use, and for specialized theatrical release with legit buffs the main target.

However this manages to can the play without losing its intrinsic values due to the expert performances primarily. A short documentary look at the ancient Epidaurus Theatre where it was filmed and an acceptable if didactic explanation of Greek theatre proceeds the play itself. Then comes the play.

Electra, daughter of Clytemnestra who slew her father with her lover after he came home triumphantly from the wars when she was a child, has waited since childhood for revenge. Though living with her mother she damns her eternally and awaits the return of

her brother Orestes to take vengeance.

He returns but is passed off as dead by a friend to allay suspicions. But he finally reveals himself to Electra and slays the infamous mother and her lover. Shot with the audience in view, at times, this relies wisely on the play which has the tautness, depth and expertise in acting to have it come through in this filmed form.

Anna Synodinou is a moving Electra devoured by the need to avenge her father's death and subordinating all reason to it. Her sister stands for reason but the destinies are worked out inexorably and this creates the state of pity and terror as it comments on the human condition. The people are trapped in mortality but can still act and try to exert a humanity no matter the horror of their actions.

The massive three-door palace front to the round stage is effective scenically. The well rehearsed troupe is expert and the Greek chorus takes on a life of its own besides commenting on the action. Sometimes shots do not match but at times the combination of the audience and play, and sudden cuts from long to close shots, give an intensity that overcomes the essential second hand photographed legit aspect of the undertaking.

It is worth putting on film and Ted Zarpas has wisely kept from trying to make it all filmic or trying to cover up its play origins. It speaks for itself with moments of dramatic intensity and the inevitable static moments. But, overall, this shapes a neat cultural gambit with enough power in its film form for arty use. *Mosk.*

Cuando Estallo La Paz
(When Peace Breaks Out)
(SPANISH)
Venice, Aug. 27.
Soraya release of Cinearte production. With Laura Valenzuela, Augustin Gonzales, Jose Isbert. Directed by Julio Diamante. Screenplay, Diamante from the book by W. Fernandez Florez; camera, Manuel Rojas; editor, Gaby Pemena. At Venice Film Fest. Running time, 95 MINS.
Aurora .... Laura Velenzuela
Javier .... Augustin Gonzales
Father .... Jose Isbert

Satire on war profiteers has a witty flair for recreating the Spain of the 1920s plus some telling hoots at human foibles. But much of its targets seem too generalized, and in specific cases too sectional, to give it the overall bounce, wit and drive for untoward foreign chances. It looms mainly a language possibility.

A small imaginary Spanish town gets shaken out of its torpor during the First World War when people take sides for the Germans or French. Friends become enemies, some take advantage of it, others brave social taboos, and it all completely upsets the life of the hero who loses his girl, goes to prison and finally ends up a lonely old man.

For a first film it displays a director, Julio Diamante, who has a nice feel for revealing comic characterization. But there is also a tendency to repeat gags and allow characters to remain sketchy and perfunctory. More firmly developed scripts, and more incisive pacing could make his

future pix more negotiable internationally.

As is, it could have some controversial aspects on its homegrounds where it looks at bureaucracy and profiteering may hit closer. It is technically good, amiably played, especially by Jose Isbert as a cantankerous Germanophile, and a seemingly freer type satirical pic from Spain. *Mosk.*

David And Lisa
A U.S. indie that treats mental derangement with tact and insight. Could be an art entry on its subject.

Venice, Aug. 27.
Peter Heller-Lisa and David Co. release and production. Stars Kier Dullea, Janet Margolin; features, Howard Da Silva, Neva Patterson. Directed by Frank Perry. Screenplay, Eleanor Perry; camera, Leonard Hirschfield; editor, Irving Oshman. At Venice Film Fest. Running time, 85 MINS.
David .... Keir Dullea
Lisa .... Janet Margolin
Doctor .... Howard Da Silva
Mother .... Neva Patterson

Tact, taste, insight and forthrightness make this one of the most incisive and original films treating mental problems to come along in some time. Its theme and combined fine thesping and mounting could slant this for specialized art chances as well as regular programming.

A young man is brought to a mental home by his doting mother. He seems intelligent, haughty and sophisticated. But he can not bear to be touched by anybody. He keeps aloof from everybody but slowly begins to accept and talk to the head psychiatrist.

He is worshipped by a younger boy and becomes interested in the case of a schizoprhenic girl called Lisa who talks backwards in rhyme and takes herself for two girls. He manages to get to her and both are aware of each other's weak spots.

But as he progresses he gets frank with his social climbing, snobbish mother and she takes him out of the home. But he relapses and comes back on his own. A crisis, which has Lisa running off, also helps him make a first move towards allowing himself to feel something for somebody and perhaps put him on the road to recovery.

Film appears clinically observant and authentic and is refreshingly free of jargon and pseudo-psycho dramatics. It does have a tendency to be too spare and make each scene a point about psychotic behavior or reactions to it by outsiders. This sometimes forces the dramatic and documentary unfoldment of the boy's and girl's reactions.

But there is no forced love affair or cliche suspense aspects. Keir Dullea has the knifelike, frigid presence that is right in his case of bottled up feelings that have made him fear death and any human emotion. A scene between himself and his father also has a poignant tug. Even some comic scenes are in keeping with the subject.

Yet the scenes between him and the doctor, and him and the girl, have the most validity and give the film its main appeal. Howard De Silva has the seeming detachment, tempered by a wary hu-

manity, to get the boy to finally reveal himself and Janet Margolin has the touching disorder and mute need for help required for the part of the girl.

For a first film Frank Perry shows a concise feel for making the telling points in each scene. A tight ordered script by Eleanor Perry also helps. It was taken from a book by a practicing psychiatrist.

Lensing has a fine snap and atmospheric feel and editing is crisp with music sometimes too insistent. In short, this is a thoughtful filmed case history with the right balance of the clinical and the human. The depiction of dreams, advance, revelation and realization are relevant and revealing throughout.
Mosk.

Los Inundados
(The Flood Area)
(ARGENTINE)
Venice, Aug. 26.
America Nuestra release and production. With Pirucho Gomez, Lola Palombo, Maria Vera, Hector Palavecino. Directed by Fernando Birri. Screenplay, Birri, Mateo Booz; camera, Adelqui Camuso; music, Ariel Ramirez. At Venice Film Fest. Running time, 85 MINS.
Gaitan .... Pirucho Gomez
Wife .... Lola Palombo
Pilar .... Maria Vera
Raoul .... Hector Palavecino

A new director displays a comedy flair, wit and observation that make this social comedy palatable. Though pleasant, it sometimes has a tendency to repeat effects which make this more a lingo entry than an art possibility. But right handling could have this a specialized entry if well placed and plugged.

A group of poor people who live in mud and straw huts on country flatlands get washed out by a flood. They are rescued by the milita and then become public charges. These good natured, simple people then are used by local politicians and finally driven off their new squatter quarters.

But some persist and one family finds itself hooked to a train after sleeping in an old car. They are shunted about as their case is trying to be solved and finally end up in their old house wondering when another flood might send them off again on a wondrous trip.

Main appeal of the pic is in its clever pacing and satiric bite. It takes its potshots at human pettiness, bureaucracy, governmental sloth and human foibles with unerring rightness but without any bitterness or cynicism. Result is an earthy pic that manages to show concern and affection for its characters without archness.

The fat, doughty mother, the fey father, the lovestruck daughter and the many kids are all well limned as are others. Reminiscent of good depression Yank comedies, this has a solid foot in today's Latino problems with the right mixture of satire and pace. When director Fernando Berri gets a firmer hold on his content, invention and outlook he should emerge a director with international potential. Technical credits are fine and this is another notch for the rapidly developing Argentine films displayed at fests this year.
Mosk.

La Commare Secca
(ITALIAN)

Venice, Aug. 29.
Cineriz release of an Antonio Cervi production. Features Francesco Ruiu, Giancarlo de Rosa, Vincenzo Ciccora, Alvaro D'Ercole, Romano Labate, Lorenza Benedetti, Emy Rocci, Erina Torelli, Renato Troiani, Marisa Solinas, Wanda Rocci, Alfredo Leggo, Carlotta Barilli, Santina Lisio, Gabriella Giogielli, Clorinda Celani, Ada Peragostini, Silvio Laurenzi, Allen Midgette. Directed by Bernardo Bertolucci. Screenplay, Bertolucci, Sergio Citti, Pier Paolo Pasolini, from story by Pasolini; camera, Gianni Narzisi; music, Carlo Rustichelli; editor, Nino Baragli. At Venice Film Festival. Running time, 94 MINS.
Canticchia .... Francesco Ruiu
Nino .... Giancarlo de Rosa
Sindaco .... Vincenzo Ciccora
Francolicchio .... Alvaro D'Ercola
Pipito .... Romano Labate
Milly .... Lorenza Benedetti
Domenica .... Emy Rocci

Impressive first effort by 21-year-old director Bernardo Bertolucci made with an entirely non-pro cast. Low-budgeter should make a strong showing on the Italian market, with export chances more limited.

Around the squalid murder of a prostitute on a Roman river bank, Bertolucci has spun the tale of several Romans directly or indirectly involved in the case. It's told in various flashbacks as each suspect is interrogated by police, his words often not matching the images which tell the true story in each case. It makes for an intriguing and suspenseful development, at the same time allowing the writer-director digressions on various aspects of Roman life, colorfully depicted and dramatically and professionally acted by a stunning cast of unknowns. Bertolucci also shows an early visual talent, his use of camera being extremely striking, while he rarely lets pace lag. Music, dramatically used as well, is another top credit in a most promising debut.
Hawk.

Kusa-O Karu Musume
(The Grass Cutters)
(JAPANESE-COLOR-SCOPE)

Venice, Aug. 28.
Nikkatsu release and production. With Sayuri Yoshinaga, Mitsuo Hamada, Yuko Mochizuki, Nijiko Kiyokawa, Shiro Osaka. Directed by Katsumi Nishikawa. Screenplay, Yojiro Ishikawa, Katsumi Miki; camera (Eastmancolor), Issen Iwasa; editor, Akira Suzuki. At Venice Film Fest. Running time, 87 MINS.
Moyoko .... Sayuri Yoshinaga
Tokizo .... Mitsuo Hamada
Sodeko .... Yuko Mochizuki
Tameko .... Nijiko Kiyokawa
Kinsaku .... Shiro Osaka

Probably geared for programmer use on its home grounds, this goodnatured, bucolic comedy-drama could do the same in language spots abroad. Though having an easy and entertaining aspect it lacks the deeper look, feel and flair for its nomadic characters for any foreign art house chances.

A group of farmers go out to cut grass every summer. They camp near another group and each is headed by an old woman. Each brings a nubile girl and a marriageable male respectively. The matchmaking is the mainstay of the pic but it also has nicely handled, if stereotyped, characters, a gentle concern for them without being stilted and a breezy pace and nice color lensing. *Mosk.*

La Bandida
(MEXICAN—COLOR)

Venice, Aug. 26.
Peliculas Rodriguex release and production. Stars Maria Felix, Pedro Armendariz, Ignazio Lopez Tarso, Emilio Fernandez, Katy Jurado. Directed by Robert Rodriguez. Screenplay, Rodriguez, Rafael Garcia Travesi; camera (Eastmancolor), Rosalio Solano; music, Raul Lavista. At Venice Film Fest. Running time, 110 MINS.
Bandida .... Maria Felix
Herrera .... Pedro Armendariz
Gomez .... Emilio Fernandez
Pedro .... Ignazio Lopez Tarso
Jarocha .... Katy Jurado

Mexican oater, taking place during the 1910 revolution, goes overboard in melodrama, hokum, songs and would-be eroticism and salty talk. Its overblown dramatics lack the tang, drive and insight to make this anything but a Latino lingo entry. Otherwise its excesses smack of parody and it stands a little chance in regular foreign pic marts.

Two robust, dynamic men and their followers are about to fight each other during the last days of the revolution since they are for different men. But they are stopped by the army and arrested. They are amnestied when the revolution is supposedly over. One goes home to find his mistress bedded down with another and kills him and the other goes to bury his wife.

The mistress of the former (Maria Felix) had been a notorious joy girl and goes back to work while her ex-lover (Pedro Armendariz) sulks. The other man (Emilio Fernandez) meets him and they both go for his discarded mistress now running a bawdy house.

Film is then laced with cock fights, songs, flagellations, scenery chewing histrionics and a suspenseful Russian roulette bit. Fernandez finally kills Armendariz over Miss Felix and rides off alone to take up the revolution again when the president is reported killed.

Color is ripe and technical dress is opulent. But the erotics fall short, the thesping is overdone, and the story misses being able to make this fable into okay general entertainment. It may be a solid grosser in the Latin American marts however. *Mosk.*

Un Uomo da Bruciare
(A Man for Burning)
(ITALIAN)

Cino Del Duca release of an Ager-Sancro-Alfa Production. Features Gian Maria Volonte, Didi Perego, Spyros Fokas, Lydia Alfonsi, Marina Malfatti, Vittorio Duse, Alessandro Soerli, Turi Ferro. Written and directed by Valentino Orsini, Paolo Taviani, Vittorio Taviani. Camera, Toni Secchi. Music, Gianfranco Intra. At Venice Film Festival. Running time, 93 MINS.
Salvatore .... Gian Maria Volonte
Barbara .... Didi Perego
Jachino .... Spyros Fokas
Francesca .... Lydia Alfonsi

Remarkable first pic effort by a team of three young writer-directors, pic is nevertheless limited in its export hopes by film's theme, too local for general acceptance.

Social approach to the subject of the Mafia and of fear in Sicily finds Salvatore the man who tries to combat the "honorable" island society almost single-handedly, overcoming century-old apathy of his fellow peasant and workers. Climax occurs when he succeeds in convincing them to strike against their bosses. One hour later, he's shot in an ambush, but presumably, the seed of revolt has been sown. Development

is steadfast and surprisingly united in style despite parallel work of three filmmakers. Gian Maria Volonte is properly brooding as the trouble-rouser while others go about their lesser roles with a sort of grim dedication. Technical credits are good. *Hawk.*

Third of a Man
Mental problems are used as basis of this pic. Lack of insight slants this mainly for playoff uses.

Venice, Aug. 28.
United Artists release of Phoenix Films production. Stars James Drury, Jan Shepard, Whit Bissell, Jimmy Gaines, Simon Oakland. Written and directed by Robert Lewin; camera, Vils Lapenieks; editor, Floyd Knudston. At Venice Film Fest. Running time, 82 MINS.
Emmet .... James Drury
Helen .... Jan Shepard
Maxwell .... Whit Bissel
Leroy .... Jimmy Gaines
Doon .... Simon Oakland

Mental aberration seems to be becoming a fashionable indie Yank pic theme. But this one, though well meaning, uses it as a gimmick rather than an incisive theme. It thus looms mainly as a bet for lessor situations.

In a small Yank town an asylum is perched on a hill above it. Its most ferocious enemy is an unbalanced, violent man who has an illegitimate son he is haphazardly bringing up. The mother lives in the town, but will not marry him due to his instability, and the little boy does not know it is his mother.

And it seems that the man's brother is in the asylum, secretly committed by him. The brother has a fear of water and cannot talk. He escapes and meets the little boy who gives him confidence and takes care of him. But the brother gets up a posse to hunt down the maniac and they find him after he has overcome his fear and saved the boy from drowning.

He is rescued from the mob and the brother is locked in with some asylum inmates by mistake and some group therapy seems to set him right with reconcilations with his son and his mother in sight. The insane brother may also be on the way to being cured.

But characters are skin deep and motivations uneven. Acting cannot give them much credence either though Simon Oakland makes a try to give pathos to the sick man, but is unfortunately made up to resemble Frankenstein. The meeting with the inmates also skirts bad taste and is just made palatable by obvious sincerity. A kindly, understanding psychiatrist fills in the plot and theme.

Director Robert Lewin obviously had some budget restrictions.

Narration is sometimes ragged and some comic and love scenes are sometimes overindulged for relief, rather than being an intrinsic part of things. Production dress is fair as are technical credits. *Mosk.*

The Time and The Touch
American indie made in English by a Mexican director in Mexico is a May-December romance that lacks the lyricism or character insight to make a strong art contender.

Venice, Aug. 29.
N. V. Productions release and production. Stars Vicki Cummins; features, Xavier Marc, Tito Guizar. Directed by Benito Alezraki. Screenplay, Alezraki, Emilio Carballido; camera, Walter Reuter; music, Carlos Mabarak, Enrico Cabiati. At Venice Film Fest. Running time, 110 MINS.
Elizabeth .... Vicki Cummins
Aristeo .... Xavier Marc
Max .... Tito Guizar

A middleaged American woman, a widow, living in Mexico, takes up amorously with a poor teenage boy. Their idyll is shattered by age differences and mainly a sinister middleaged man. But the clear insight into the relationship, a lyric quality, or even a feeling and compassion for the affair, are missing. It makes this lag over its longish length.

The women had been married to a Mexican much older than her and had led a sheltered life till then. Now with her husband dead she is drifting One day, in a cheap theatre, she is set on by a drunkard and saved by a house peanut vender, a teenage boy.

When he comes for a reward he finds her alone and makes a pass and they become lovers. But the demands of his poor, avid family almost ruin it till she brings them presents. They go off on a seaside trip where an aging male adventurer tries to lure the boy off on a world trip for adventure. His lies about the women have him leaving her and she going off alone.

Director-writer Benito Alezraki unfortunately can not convey any insight into the relationship and the thesping of vet actress Vicki Cummins is no help either. Though still attractive she plays it like a knowing, hardened woman rather than the secluded lonely widow she is supposed to be.

Xavier Marc is properly boyish but somewhat unable to project elan, while Tito Guizar limns an okay part as the adventurer. It is okay technically. *Mosk.*

Requiem for A Heavyweight

Screen translation of tv success still packs dramatic punch but added weight has slowed pace.

Hollywood, Sept. 4.

Columbia release of David Susskind production. Stars Anthony Quinn, Jackie Gleason, Mickey Rooney, Julie Harris; with Stan Adams, Madame Spivy, Val Avery, Herbie Faye, Jack Dempsey, Barney Ross, Alex Miteff, Rory Calhoun, Cassius Clay, Gus Lesnevich, Willie Pep, Steve Belloise, J. J. Ballargeon, Paoli Rossi, Michael Conrad, Abe Simon, Stan Ross, Lou Gilbert. Directed by Ralph Nelson. Screenplay by Rod Serling, as adapted from his teleplay; camera, Arthur J. Ornitz; editor, Carl Lerner; music, Laurence Rosenthal; assistant directors, Anthony La Marca, Michael Hertzberg. Reviewed at Columbia Studio, Sept. 4, '62. Running time, **85 MINS.**

Mountain Rivera	Anthony Quinn
Maish Rennick	Jackie Gleason
Army	Mickey Rooney
Grace Miller	Julie Harris
Perelli	Stan Adams
Ma Greeny	Madame Spivy
Bartender	Herbie Faye
Jack Dempsey	Himself
Ring Opponent	Cassius Clay
Hotel Desk Clerk	Steve Belloise
Ring Doctor	Lou Gilbert
Referee	Arthur Mercante

Rod Serling's poignant portrait of the sunset of a prizefighter has lost some of its dramatic weight in the transition from the very small to the very large screen. However, it still packs considerable punch as a character study, although its action has slowed to where the plot padding is often obvious.

The impact that "Requiem for a Heavyweight" made on its viewers in the shorter tv version has lost some of its strength but has not let go completely. The shift in emphasis to build up the part of the trainer has resulted in two brilliant performances. These alone should create an appeal that could put the pic into the winner class.

Director Ralph Nelson, concentrating on character analysis, has allowed the pace to falter through apparently stretched sequences. Some of the casting, no doubt done for authenticity and atmosphere, has boomeranged. Julie Harris plays her employment counselor as though she never really believed in the character. Not beautiful by any means, she is still not the plain Jane who could become attracted to this wreck of a man. Spivy, physically and vocally perfect as Ma Greeny, the gang boss, is unable to create the necessary menace. A major disappointment, as her first (he-she) appearance visually stimulates the audience into expecting a scene that never materializes. Stan Adams' unethical wrestling promoter, is properly vulgar.

Casting actual boxing personalities is atmospheric but distracting and often ludicrous, particularly an amateurish bit by Jack Dempsey. There's a superb establishing shot at the pic's start of a young fighter (Cassius Clay) giving Anthony Quinn a brutal beating. Here Arthur Ornitz's camerawork is so personal, going out of focus with every blow from the flailing fists, that he makes the viewer feel that he is taking the beating. With relief, the bell rings and the credits appear.

The performances of Quinn and Gleason are equally matched and carry the picture, no small chore. Quinn's punchy, inarticulate behemoth is so painfully natural that one winces when he feels pain, whether to his body or his feelings. He has created another portrait to add to a carefully selected gallery and is as good as the audience expects him to be. Gleason, however, still new enough at serious acting to be unpredictable, is amazingly fine and, with a flashier role, may be favored when the two performances are compared. In some of his closeups, he conveys, visually, the best interpretation of fear since Gene Lockhart in "Blackmail." He's weak, crafty, shifty and still a little pathetic.

Mickey Rooney, hampered with some bad makeup, is warm and sympathetic as Army, the trainer, but doesn't really shine except for one card-playing scene. It's the only funny bit in the pic and he steals it from under Gleason's nose. The plot contains some glaring implausibilities.

After concern of the employment counselor, played by Miss Harris, for the fighter is firmly established, one wonders why, having told him that she'd set up an appointment for the same evening with a potential employer, she then makes no attempt to get it under way, but idles away what seems to be most of the evening drinking beer with Quinn. The jukebox in the bar in which they're meeting, one frequented by broken-down prizefighters, features schmaltzy mood music that would be better-suited to a dimly-lit cocktail lounge.

A subsequent scene has Quinn stumbling about a classy hotel corridor beating on doors and shouting, but getting little response. However, when he lurches into a waiter and knocks some dishes off a tray, a door flies open and there's Miss Harris! Just then an elevator door conveniently opens and the embarrassed Quinn escapes into it. Another technical fault is in the sound track. Voices of several characters, particularly those of Miss Harris and Stan Adams, have a sibilant shrillness that is irritating.

Laurence Rosenthal's score is generally effective, used primarily for dramatic underscoring.

This requiem for a heavyweight has become a double tragedy—that of a doomed fighter and the man who caused it. *Robe.*

Pressure Point

Provocative discussion of bigotry laid in the framework of white psychopath patient-Negro doctor relationship. Film will depend on method of sale for commercial success.

Hollywood, Sept. 5.

United Artists release of Stanley Kramer production. Stars Sidney Poitier and Bobby Darin; guest star, Peter Falk; with Carl Benton Reid, Mary Munday, Howard Caine, Gilbert Green, Barry Gordon, Richard Bakalyan, Lynn Loring, Anne Barton, James Anderson, Yvette Vickers, Clegg Hoyt, Butch Patrick. Directed by Hubert Cornfield. Screenplay, Hubert Cornfield, S. Lee Pogostin, based on story by Robert Lindner; camera, Ernest Haller; music, Ernest Gold; Ass't. director, Philip Bowles; production design by Rudolph Sternad. Reviewed at Screen Directors Guild Theatre, Hollywood, Sept. 5, 1962. Running time, **87 MINS.**

Doctor	Sidney Poitier
Patient	Bobby Darin
Young Psychiatrist	Peter Falk
Chief Medical Officer	Carl Benton Reid
Bar Hostess	Mary Munday
Boy Patient	Barry Gordon
Tavern Owner	Howard Caine
Mother	Anne Barton
Father	James Anderson
Drunken Women	Yvette Vickers
Pete	Clegg Hoyt
Jimmy	Richard Bakalyan
Playmate	Butch Patrick

Stanley Kramer, in this provocative discussion of questions paramount in today's society, presents a film that has a good deal of artistic value but which will depend greatly on its method of sale for commercial success. There are qualities of subtle sensitivity that point clearly toward the art house route which could develop a word-of-mouth sendoff leading to important reception. Indiscriminate mainstem or multiple booking could give it exposure in less meaningful areas that might short-circuit long run boxoffice potential.

Story, based on a composite of case histories from the late Dr. Robert Lindner's book, "The 50-Minute Hour," is triggered by an explosive patient-doctor relationship between an American-German Bundist imprisoned for sedition and his Negro psychiatrist. Superficially, the film has considerable dramatic impact in the pressure of the relationship alone, as the prisoner contemptuously displays his "white Christian" disdain towards the doctor. However, Kramer uses this personal situation to create a framework for a much larger commentary on major issues of prejudice abroad today in this country. Notably, the film is a strong and carefully developed attack on bigotry, the underlying message fraught with evidences of the sickness of bigotry and its dangerous consequences for civilization. How the picture may go over in certain areas in the South, where racial strife is boiling, is conjectural.

There are strong moments in which the patient's development toward psychopathy are explored. His hatred for Jews, his contempt for authority or other persons' success is frequently displayed. In a major sequence, Kramer integrates newsreel clips of a wartime Nazi Bund rally in Madison Square Garden that vividly shows the extent to which the sickness of bigotry can go and be exploited by a foreign power.

There are no resolutions to the questions raised in the film, but it does become thought provoking to the degree that it opens up avenues toward such resolution.

Within the story and immediate characterizations, other sensitive hints of abnormal human behavior—homosexuality, bestiality, sadist-masochistic relationships—are also present, but these are not fully explored. The picture remains fragmentary, but it has considerable power in its initiation of the subject.

Hubert Cornfield, who collaborated on the screenplay with S. Lee Pogostin, directs in a style very much like European films. He works for visual effect, using considerable pantomime and arty camera angles for sequences depicting patient's mental disturbances. While these are handsomely executed, it could be that he has gone overboard to achieve these artistic effects. Ernest Haller's expert camera work is an asset, as are optical effects by Pacific Title Company.

Bobby Darin gives a strong performance as the patient, delivering a believable, natural characterization. He plays with a frighteningly realistic attitude of distrust and psychopathic fear. Sidney Poitier, on the other hand, is careful as on the other hand, is careful as the psychiatrist, acting with intense, planned response at all times. He is strong and clinical, perhaps too much so at times. Frequently, too, he is guilty of sloppy diction, also a characteristic Darin's performance, but believable in his character.

In small roles, Peter Falk stands out as the young psychiatrist whose problem with a young Negro patient was the reverse situation that brought out Poitier's flashback story. Moppet Barry Gordon is excellent as Darin as a child. Mary Munday, Howard Caine, Lynn Loring, Anne Barton, James Anderson and Carl Benton Reid contribute greatly.

Ernest Gold's unusual score is an asset, production design by Rudolph Sternad is fine. *Dale.*

Damon and Pythias (EASTMANCOLOR)

Above average spear-and-sandal epic should make out oke at the boxoffice.

Metro release of International Motion Picture Enterprises production. Produced by Sam Jaffe. Stars Don Burnett, Guy Williams; features Ilaria Occhini, Liana Orfei, Arnoldo Foa, Carlo Giustino, Andrea Bosic, Carla Bonavera, Osvaldo Ruggeri. Directed by Curtis Bernhardt; screenplay, Bridget Boland (from original story by Sam Marx); camera (Eastman color), Aldo Tonti; music, A. F. Lavagnino. Reviewed in New York, Sept. 5, '62. Running time, **99 MINS.**

Pythias	Don Burnett
Damon	Guy Williams
Nerissa	Ilaria Occhini
Adrianna	Liana Orfei
Dinoysius the Tyrant	Arnoldo Foa
Cariso	Carlo Giustino
Arcanos	Andrea Basic
Mereka	Carla Bonavera
Demetrios	Osvaldo Ruggeri

Although "Damon and Pythias" measures a cut or two above the run of spear-and-sandal spectacles, its virtues should not alienate the seemingly resilient audience for this kind of escapist mummery. In short, the Metro release should do nice enough in tandem on the saturation runs.

Agent - turned - producer Sam Jaffe has gone for more than the merely mindless eye-filling values with his first picture. The dialog maintains a relatively intelligent and persuasve level, the acting is good or better, and Curtis Bernhardt's direction is smooth and even rather thoughtful. Shot in Italy, the film is not diffuse with agitated scenes, and Bridget Boland's screenplay (from an original yarn by associate producer Sam Marx) evidences more than the usual concern for contemplative story.

Based on the Damon and Pythias legend, of as stout a friendship as ever there was, the film hews to its purpose, echoing the maxim that there's nothing as potent as an idea whose time has come. The idea is the Pythagorean (pre-Christ) love-thy-neighbor philosophy. As exemplified in the relationship of the two friends, it is put to the ultimate test (one life for another) and eventually triumphs.

As Damon, a sort of rascally bohemian in ancient Syracuse, Guy Williams etches a simpatico performance, while Don Burnett as

Pythias, an Athenian proponent of the love credo, contributes an okay job in a part that doesn't allow much latitude. Ilaria Occhini as the wife of Pythias, and Liana Orfei as Damon's inamorata, are both decorative and effective. Arnoldo Foa, as dictator of Syracuse, invests his characterization with a nice shading, and others in the capable cast include Carlo Giustino, Andrea Bosic, Carla Bonavera and Osvaldo Ruggeri.

Aldo Tonti's lensing is sharp and relevant, and other technical contributions rate good. **Pit.**

Venice Films

Cronaca Familiare
(A Family Chronicle)
(ITALIAN—COLOR)

Venice, Sept. 5.

Titanus release of a Titanus-Metro production. Stars Marcello Mastroianni; features Jacques Perrin, Salvo Randone, Silvie, Valeria Ciangottini, Serena Vergano. Written and directed by Valerio Zurlini. Based on the novel by Vasco Pratolini. Camera (Technicolor) Giuseppe Rotunno. Music, Goffredo Petrassi. At Venice Film Festival. Running time, **120 MINS.**

Enrico .... Marcello Mastroianni
Lorenzo .... Jacques Perrin
Grandmother .... Silvie
Salocchi .... Salvo Randone

An exquisitely fashioned film based on a bestseller by Vasco Pratolini, lovingly directed by Valerio Zurlini and beautifully acted by Marcello Mastroianni and others. Pic will nevertheless need all the breaks it can summon to insure itself a proportionate b.o. impact in non-Italian areas, where Metro is handling release, due to extremely slow pace, even-planed development, and static action.

Director boasted during shooting that he would not change a comma in his pic version of Pratolini's novel, and he obviously has not. Film, as was the book, is about two brothers: one a working journalist who has always struggled for his daily meal, the other a slightly spoiled idealist adopted and brought up by a well-to-do family when their mother dies and father disappears. Warm affection eventually arises between brothers who had rarely seen one another in their youth. Work takes the newsman to Rome while his brother remains in Florence. When they meet again, the younger brother is already very ill and the reporter desperately tries to save him by having him treated in a hospital and later in a private clinic, but it's all in vain, and he dies. Tale is told in flashback form without climaxes but with several deeply moving moments as the scribe thinks back on his life, and on his brother's seemingly inescapable tragic destiny.

Marcello Mastroianni gives one of his very best performances as the reporter who takes over a father's role vs. his brother. Jacques Perrin capably outlines the role of the doomed younger brother, while Silvie and Salvo Randone ably bring to life roles as grandmother and guardian, respectively. Other minor roles are well filled.

Director Valerio Zurlini here

has done his best work to date with material he obviously felt and loved, with great taste and restraint. His use of muted colors in tandem with Technicolor lenser Giuseppe Rotunno, is another outstanding facet of pic. He has eliminated all brights reds, blues, and other glaring hues as though blurred by time in the newsman's flashback recollections. Music by Goffredo Petrassi is appropriate if at times too loudly recorded for adverse effect. Other technical credits are tops in a film of great prestige and quality, but whose commercial probabilities outside the Italian orbit must ultimately be rated as limited.
Hawk.

Therese Desqueyroux
(FRENCH)

Venice, Sept. 6.

20th-Fox release of Filmel production. Stars Emmanuelle Riva, Philippe Noiret, Edith Scob, Sami Frey; features, Renee Devillers, Jacques Monnot, Lucien Nat. Directed by Georges Franju. Screenplay, Francois Mauriac, Claude Mauriac, Franju from the novel by Francois Mauriac; camera, Christian Matras; editor, Gabriel Natot. At Venice Film Fest. Running time, **105 MINS.**

Therese .... Emmanuelle Riva
Bernard .... Philippe Noiret
Anne .... Edith Scob
Jean .... Sami Frey
Mother .... Renee Devillers
Father .... Lucien Nat

20th-Fox has one of those rare films, a social and psychological drama that remains taut and absorbing throughout due to a rare combination of observant direction, expert thesping and an insight into the personages. It looms a solid European entry and should be heard in the world art marts.

A woman has tried to poison her husband in a provincial section of France. She is freed when he does not press charges. But on her way back to him she thinks over what led to it. She is a sensitive almost exalted girl who marries the son of a rich, landed family. But the man is direct, stuffy and incapable of awakening any feeling or love in her. She becomes frigid, dissatisfied and disenchanted.

Her decision to try to poison her husband just comes on naturally one day when he takes too much of an arsenic compound medicine. He is addicted to and gets ill. After being found out and released she is locked up by her husband and almost drifts into madness. He finally decides to let her live in Paris but is never capable of forgiving and perhaps helping to take up their life again. She thus finally feels that she is free.

Emmanuelle Riva has a way of overcoming her ordinary looks by an intense projection of internal sincerity and etches a brilliant picture of this fragile tragic woman almost destroyed by human pettiness, pride and indifference. Others all limn their parts well and the technical aspects are good. A literate script is also a help.

But it is director Georges Franju who deserves the main plaudits. He keeps this from being literary, in spite of a commentary, by a controlled feel for visual detail, sight revelation and a pace and rhythm that build this probing drama into a film of strength and originality.
Mosk.

Rakas
(Darling)
(FINNISH)

Venice, Sept. 5.

Kurkvaara-Filmi Oy release and production. With Jaakko Pakkasvirta, Sinikka Hannula, Liana Kaarina, Leena Takala. Written and directed by Maunu Kurkvaara from an idea by Soili Kotala. Dialog, Kotala; camera, Maunu Kurkvaara; music, Osmo Lindeman. At Venice Film Fest. Running time, **80 MINS.**

Jaska .... Jaakko Pakkasvirta
Sini .... Sinikka Hannula
Mirku .... Liana Kaarina
Gunvar .... Leena Takala

"Darling" is the first Finnish pic to show up in a film fest special section, since the searing, right and pacifistic war epic, "The Unknown Soldier," some years ago, with possible foreign chances. It is a fresh tale of young love.

A young artist, who believes that any serious tie with a woman will slow him down and interfere with his life, nevertheless has a two-year relationship with a young secretary. He is not above dragging her to strip parties or making passes at her best friend.

When she is pregnant some months by him he decides to marry her but a fight sends him off in a huff. They both think of their relationship and he understands he needs her and comes back. It is simple and sometimes slow but there a rightness in tone and the relationship is handled with tact. A scene when she bathes and he writes and then he tries to draw her nude, and realizes the beauty of her pregnancy, reaches a poetic balance that makes it a scene of dignity. Sometimes the direction is turgid but it manages to give an insight into youth that overcomes its boundaries.

Acting is properly restrained and the director, though sometimes too surface at times in his look at his people, displays a sense of pace and style that could have heard from in the future from this small filmmaking country. It is technically per.
technically par.
Mosk.

Black Fox

Documentary shapes an incisive filmic essay on the rise and fall of Adolf Hitler. This adds new material and a clear outlook. For specialized art spots.

Venice, Sept. 6.

Image Productions-Al Stahl-Le Vien International Productions-Animated Productions release and production. Written and directed by Louis Clyde Stoumen. Commentary spoken by Marlene Dietrich; animation supervision by Al Stahl; editor, Kenn Collins, Mark Wortreich. At Venice Film Fest. Running time **89 MINS.**

After a Swedish compilation pic, made by a German, and a German one, made by a Britisher, "Mein Kampf" and "The Life of Adolf Hitler," respectively, on the life and times of the German dictator, comes an American version which displays new material and a more unique perspective and insight to make this a definite art and specialized bet with video usage also there.

Filmmaker Louis Clyde Stoumen adds a feel for the historical process in broadening the infamous canvas via astute use of Goethe's political and human foible allegory "Reynard the Fox" and engravings

of Dore on Teutonic myths and the drawings of contemporary artists. Film sets out to show that Germany, on the whole, backed Hitler by accepting his excesses in the name of recovery even if he never got more than 30% of the votes at the poll.

Then his career, henchmen and destructive career is neatly limned via plenty of new footage, photos and other material. A clear commentary underlines the inexorable steps towards world war and the inhumanities practiced by the Nazis.

Marlene Dietrich's mellifulous, accented voice is a neat counterpart to the blending of fact and image and she also adds a note of drama and feeling without any false histrionics. It is all soberly and absorbingly executed. A final point that this sad period of mankind has to be understood, and its causes made clear before guilt about usage of the atomic bomb can be adequately debated, winds this provocative pic.
Mosk.

Dulcinea
(SPANISH)

Venice, Sept. 4.

Nivi Film release of Aspa production. Stars Millie Perkins, Cameron Mitchell, Folco Lulli; features Vittoria Prada, Walter Santesso. Written and directed by Vicante Escriva and based on Cervantes' "Don Quixote." Camera, Goffredo Pacheco; music, C. Basurko. At Venice Film Fest. Running time, **102 MINS.**

Dulcinea,
Aldonza .... Millie Perkins
Priest .... Cameron Mitchell
Sancho .... Folco Lulli
Woman .... Vittoria Prada
Diego .... Walter Santesso
(In English)

A Spanish pic made in English with two fair Yank name thesps, namely Millie Perkins and Cameron Mitchell, this is a cut above Hispano costumers in delving into the effect of the Don Quixote myth on a bar maid who is given a love note from the Knight of the Sad Countenance. But it focuses too much on ideas and leaves the true touch of legend just missed. So it looms a chancey art bet.

A bar maid, who also usually has to accommodate customers, hears about the supposedly mad knight who goes about righting wrongs and helping the oppressed. Then one night Quixote's squire appears and gives her a letter addressed to his beloved Dulcinea. The girl is so moved that she tracks down Quixote who is dying and who has confessed that there was no Dulcinea and so disavowed his cause and life.

But she comes in and claims she is Dulcinea. Then she goes off trying to do right by helping beggars, stricken people and those during a plague. She is arrested as a witch and finally burned when she refuses to abjure that she is Dulcinea.

Plenty of ideas are raised about the reality of myths, Church dogma is questioned, and pic manages to firm its point that people make their own decisions and can do good on their own and achieve grace and dignity even without the Church. Though a point made many times before, it may be more relevant on home grounds.

Production dress is adequate and location shooting in 16th century towns and edifices helps. The lensing has fine form and beauty that aid in recreating the times. But

the twangy voice of Miss Perkins, and her winsome rather than earthy qualities, detract from her supposedly robust maid who finally achieves salvation, if she is burned, by a belief in a cause. Cameron Mitchell has a small but telling cameo as a defrocked priest made to see the light by Miss Perkins' obvious dedication. He plays it in the right charged, demonic manner and Folco Lulli has the correct blend of wile and humility as Sancho Panza.

Quixote is never seen except on his death bed and only from behind. Dialog is sometimes stilted but is acceptable due to its time and place. In short, this has shortcomings but also a certain tang and offbeat quality that could make it a worthy if limited entry abroad. But it will need hard sell and personalized placement all along the line. *Mosk.*

Parigi O Cara
(Paris, My Love)
(ITALIAN-COLOR)

Euro International release of an Alessandro Jacovoni (AJACE) Production. Stars Franca Valerio; features Vittorio Caprioli, Margherita Girelli, Greta Gonda, Nunzia Fumo, Anna Maria Ubaldi, Marina Neucci, Pina Madonna, Fiorenzo Fiorentini, Elena de Merick, Antonio Batistella, Michele Bardollet, Lydia Rogier, Gisele Gallois, Walter Ball, Jacqueline Doyen, Benadeh Abdelkader, Martin Kempfer, Bernard Tiphaine, Marc Doelnitz. Directed by Vittorio Caprioli. Screenplay, Caprioli, Franca Valeri, Renato Mainardi, Silvana Ottieri, from story by Caprioli; camera, (Eastmancolor) Dario di Palma; music, Fiorenzo Capri; editor, Nino Baragli. At Venice Film Festival. Running time, **95 MINS.**

Delia .... Franca Valeri
Avallone .... Vittorio Caprioli

Highly amusing picture shot in Rome and Paris, with a good Italo-French b.o. potential aided in Italy by Franca Valeri name for marquee lure. Elsewhere some of local slants will get lost in shuffle, but some offbeat interest is warranted.

Story, an ideal vehicle for comedienne Franca Valeri, shows her as a Rome prostie with a yen for far-away Paris, where her brother works. She eventually heads for the French capital, but new milieu is variously disappointing to her, and when she finds a fellow Italian who wants to return to the Eternal City, she teams with him and heads back. Pic is all nuances, dialog jabs, and incidentals, including many solo bits by Miss Valeri, all highly risible sequences in which her character spoofing digs below the surface of pic which is mainly intended to please eye and ear. Occasionally, plot (and Miss Valeri) is repetitious, and the ending comes abruptly, but on the whole, it's all good fun cut several notches above the norm for the genre.

Technical credits, including Dario Di Palma's Eastman-color (Technicolor-processed) lensing chore in Rome and Paris locations, are high quality. Colorful cast backs up principals in pro fashion. *Hawk.*

Noz W Wodzie
(Knife in the Water)
(POLISH)

Venice, Sept. 6.

Polski State Film release of Kamera production. With Leon Niemesyk, Jolanta Umecka, Zygmunt Malanowicz. Directed by Roman Polanski. Screenplay, Polanski, Jerzy Skolimowski, Jakub Goldberg; camera, Jerzy Lipman; music, Krzystof Komeda. At Venice Film Fest. Running time, **95 MINS.**

Andjrez .... Leon Niemesyk
Kataryna .... Jolanta Umecka
Student .... Zygmunt Malanowicz

Middleaged cocksureness, arrogance and incomprehension versus teenage revolt, with a young woman as a sort of arbiter, is the theme of this lively and inventive little pic. It may stay skin-deep in characterization but has the inventiveness and style to make it a possible specialized foreign entry with dualer playoff also there. It needs smart handling but word-of-mouth and critiques could help.

A couple driving along a deserted road to the sea almost run over a young man who flags down the car too closely. The driver is a self absorbed husband, the woman his pretty, irritated young wife, and the hitchhiker a teenager.

They take him along and the husband, out of sheer patronizing good will, invites him to come sailing on their boat. Pic is then all concerned with the boat ride and the subtle battle of personalities between the men and the wife's amused onlooking.

The boy has a habit of playing with a switchblade knife which he feels is needed on shore. But he is gradually revealed as a boy whose wiseguyish defenses cover up a hurt sensibility. The husband is a self-made man and delights in showing up the boy. A final blow-up has him knocking him in the sea.

They think he has drowned and the husband goes to shore, swimming, for help. But he has hid behind a buoy and comes aboard to seduce the wife. She brings in the boat and assures the husband the boy is alive and she had cheated on him. The husband is left to choose between believing her or feeling a murderer. It is left unresolved.

For a first pic director Roman Polamski shows a flair for simple character revelation and wit. He sometimes overindulges and charges the affair with gratuitous bits but it manages to keep up interest even if it lacks the pungent insight to get deeper into character and bring off the ironic end. Its social side is soft pedaled and it has a neat technical envelope and gracious playing by a three-actor cast. A very promising first pic. *Mosk.*

Les Dimanches De Ville D'Avary
(Sundays at Ville D'Avray)
(FRENCH—FRANSCOPE)

Venice, Aug. 31.

Columbia release of Terra-Fides-Orsay-Trocadero production. Stars Hardy Kruger; features Nicole Courcel, Patricia Gozzi, Daniel Ivernel, Andre Oumansky. Directed by Serge Bourguignon. Screenplay, Antoine Tudal, Bernard Eschasseriaux Bourguignon from the novel by Eschasseriaux; camera, Henri Decae; editor, Leonid Azar. At Venice Film Fest. Running time, **110 MINS.**

Pierre .... Hardy Kruger
Madeleine .... Nicole Courcel
Francoise .... Patricia Gozzi
Friend .... Daniel Ivernel
Nurse .... Andre Oumansky

A basically dramatic tale of loneliness and mental difficulty is treated in a muted, dreamy style. This makes a slow but pictorially impressive film due to new director Serge Bourguignon's feeling for imagery and style. But it also leads to some preciosity and this remains primarily an art possibility on its visual qualities with playoff chances calling for hard sell.

An amnesic pilot, who thinks he had killed a little girl during the French-Indonesian War, has blotted it out and is living in a little town with a nurse who had fallen in love with him. One day he sees a little girl being put into a local orphan home by a father who runs off. He finds a letter the man has dropped stating he will never be back. One day he wanders into the orphanage and takes the girl for a walk.

They immediately take to each other and she passes him off as her visiting father. Every Sunday their relationship and love grow. But complications lead to tragedy. A friend of the nurse tells the police about it and they find them together and misinterpret a gesture of his towards the little girl and kill him.

Director Bourguignon manages to keep this fairly fragile film together by a good feeling for the gray atmosphere of the little town and a tender attention to he relationship between the child-like man and the child. But sometimes things are forced. Some attempts at poetic symbolism do not have depth and make some aspects stilted.

Technical qualities are fine and Hardy Kruger is good as the man while Patricia Gozzi sometimes lacks the spontaniety of childhood. But this platonic and spiritual Lolita-like pic could be an art item if well handled. In spite of a tendency to overdo effects it marks Bourguignon as a director to be heard from. *Mosk.*

Megszallottak
(The Obsessed Ones)
(HUNGARIAN)

Venice, Sept. 11.

Hungarofilm release and production. With Gyorgy Palos, Adam Szirtes, Eva Papp. Directed by Karoly Makk. Screenplay, Istvan Almasi, Gyula Kekesdi; camera, Gyorgy Illes; music, Szabolcs Fenyes. At Venice Film Fest. Running time, **103 MINS.**

Laszlo .... Gyorgy Palos
Director .... Adam Szirtes
Girl .... Eva Papp

Tale of two men struggling to do something worthwhile for themselves, plus a part of their country, and stymied by red tape, has a nice flair for character and observation. But its tale and forced happy ending make this a chancey item for foreign spots.

A hydro-engineer goes to an arid spot but does not seem too interested in getting water. He is disillusioned with all the government hindrance he has run into in the past. But the director of a collective farm becomes his friend and a local girl his mistress. He is fired when his friend taps water on his own.

Research convinces him that a part of a river is under the land. Still, governmental slackness and disinterest bog down the affair to lead to dispair. However, in steps a commissar to lend a hand for a happy ending.

In spite of this it does take pot shots at bureauocracy and talks of the corrupt previous Communist leaders. Its insidey aspects make this a curio item and shorn of the ending, which forces a collective solution rather than an individual one, it has a neat pace and feel for the evolving characters.

Thespe are warm and a literate script keeps up interest most of the way. Karoly Makk's direction manages to have his individuals and their actions telling and he is aided by competent technical values. This is the first Hungarian film in some years that manages to overcome its propagandist envelope. It has neat visual qualities too. *Mosk.*

Una Storia Milanese
(A Milanese Story)
(ITALIAN)

Lux Film release of a "22 December S.p.A." — Galatea production. Features Daniele Gaubert, Enrico Thibaut, Romolo Valli, Lucilla Morlacchi, Regina Bianchi, Giancarlo Dettori, Rosanna Armani- Ermanno Olmi. Directed by Eriprando Visconti. Story and screenplay, Visconti, Renzo Rosso, Vittorio Sermonti; music, John Lewis; camera, Lamberto Caimi; editor, Mario Serandrei. At Venice Film Festival. Running time, **93 MINS.**

Valeria ....Daniele Gaubert
Giampiero ....Enrico Thibaut
Mr. Gessner ....Romolo Valli
Francesca ....Lucilla Morlacchi
Turchi ....Ermanno Olmi
Vicki ....Rosanna Armanni
Valeria's mother ....Regina Bianchi
Dario ....Giancarlo Dettori

Sensitively treated story of a teenage love affair showing promise for neophyte director Eriprando Visconti. Needs proper sell but should do okay biz on home market and interest the foreign quality markets as well.

Story is mainly about Valeria, of how she drops her first fiance, takes up with one of his friends, becomes pregnant and almost marries him, eventually falling out of love once more and progressing to still another acquaintance — all without much regret, with the matter-of-factness which characterizes some of the youth of today. Backdropping the story is a modern and bustling Milan, a general setting dear to another Italian director, Michelangelo Antonioni, whose work this resembles. There are some slow stretches in Visconti's film and others showing his relative inexperience, yet pic has quality and has been made with taste and deep insight into the thoughts and manners, of the strata of society depicted.

Daniele Gaubert is fine as Valeria, Enrico Thibaut a bit stiff at times as her almost-spouse, Lucilla Morlacchi good as his sister, Romolo Valli expert in limning the role of his father. Others back aptly, and there's a neatly fashioned assist from director Ermanno Olmi as the suitor who finally wins Valeria.

Lensing by Lamberto Caimi against grey and foggy north Italian backdrops, is often breathtaking while other credits, especially John Lewis' mood-setting original backdrop score, are fine. *Hawk.*

Il Mare
(The Sea)
(ITALIAN)

Globe Films International release of Gianni Buffardi production. Features Umberto Orsini, Francoise Prevost, Dino Mele. Written and directed by Giuseppe Patroni Griffi. Camera, Ennio Guarnieri; music, Giovanni Fusco. At Venice Film Festival. Running time, **110 MINS.**

The Man .... Umberto Orsini
The Woman .... Francoise Prevost
The Boy .... Dino Mele

Pretentious pic on boredom and lack of communication between people inspired by Michelangelo Antonioni's films, but which doesn't come off because of inept script and handling.

In a wintertime Capri, lashed with rainstorms, three individuals meet; an actor, a woman who's had a previous experience on the island, and a youngster. Each has complex burdens and problems, each has an inexpressed desire for something, played out via an intertwined game of tag and ultimately ending in nothing. Intentions of author-director Patroni Griffi whose first pic this is may be good and valid, but he doesn't bring it off. Pic is static and generally as dull as the world it wants to portray. Dialog is at times unconsciously funny. Actors are burdened with impossible tasks with Francoise Prevost best. Pic boasts a firstrate lensing job by Ennio Guarnieri and apt music by Giovanni Fusco.   *Hawk.*

Kwiecien
(Spring)
(POLISH)
Venice, Aug. 31.

Polski Film release of Kamera production. With Piotr Pawlowski, Henryk Bak, Leszek Herdegen. Directed by Witold Lesiewicz. Screenplay, Jerzy Henj camera, Czeslaw Swirtz; music, Tadeux Baird. At Venice Film Fest. Running time, 95 MINS.
Captain .... Piotr Pawlowski
Colonel .... Henryk Bak
Szumibor .... Leszek Herdegen

Films in which Polish filmmakers have looked at soldiers in the old army, before the Communist takeover, with sympathy are not new. This one follows that line. It has a twilight feel for the end of the war and ironic excesses committed in its name. But its slow unfoldment and fairly conventional tale limit this for export except for actioners on its fairly well done war scenes.

A hot-headed colonel tries to force his men on to heroics though the war is almost over. This concerns the reformed Polski army who fought the Germans near the end of the war. A war weary adjutant tries to soft pedal the colonel but he keeps on with his men and is killed fighting in the front lines. All his men decide to get his body.

The colonel is made out to be a martinet hero whose futile heroics served some purpose in instilling his men with spirit. Politics are kept to a minimum, but this has a gray, lagging finish that may somewhat reflect the weariness of years of war. Yet it does not have the insight into character, the strength in direction, or the needed ironic bite to bring it off entirely.

It is technically good and does have a good feeling for recreating the last days of the war.   *Mosk.*

Koiya Koi Nasuna Koi
(The Mad Fox)
(JAPANESE—COLORSCOPE)

Toei production and release. Features Hashizo Okawa, Michiko Saga. Directed by Tomu Uchida. Screenplay, Yoshitaka Yoda; camera, Sadatsugu Yoshida; music, Chuji Kinoshita. At Venice Film Festival. Running time, 110 MINS.

Yasuna .... Hashizo Okawa
Shkaki.
Kuzunoha,
Fox .... Michiko Saga

Elegantly produced costumer is set in Japan during the first century. Legend is told by blending real and theatrical settings. Foreign chances, however, remain very restricted due to an intricate plot skein which makes it very hard to follow by western eyes, as well as by slow eastern pace.

Yasuna, an astronomer's assistant, is falsely accused of having stolen a precious manuscript. Tortured together with his fiance, Sakaki, he goes berserk and the girl dies. Later, in a forest, he meets and settles down with a family of white foxes who are disguised as human beings, and has a child by one of them. Eventually, his long dream ends and the desperate Yasuna is transformed into a stone.

Pic boasts the usual tasteful decor of the best Japanese films, and is diligently acted by a large cast. It is, however, too far removed from Western concepts, with main appeal remaining a visual and esthetic excitement.   *Hawk.*

Kashi To Kodomo
(The Pitfall)
(JAPANESE)
Venice, Aug. 30.

Teshigahara release and production. With Hisashi Igawa, Kazuo Miyahara, Kan-Ichi Omiya, Kunie Tanaka. Directed by Hiroshi Teshigahara. Screenplay, Kobo Abe; camera, Hiroshi Segawa; editor, Fusako Shuzul. At Venice Film Fest. Running time, 95 MINS.
Miner .... Hisashi Igawa
Son .... Kazuo Miyahara
Worker .... Kan-'chi Omiya
Murderer .... Kunie Tanaka

Social protest film is cloaked in a suspense and supernatural form. It makes it uneven, but it is saved by pungent direction, expert playing and fast pacing. It has special significance in Japan and could be a dualer or actioner item abroad.

A poor miner finds he is being followed by a mysterious man in white. He keeps fleeing with his son. One day he gets a job and is sent off to a supposed other one. It turns out to be a deserted village with only one woman living in it. He is killed by the stranger in a macabre scene. His son has seen but not been seen.

The murderer pays the woman in the town to say the man has been killed by another miner and gives his description. The dead man turns out to be a ringer for a coal miner union leader and the described assailant the head of a rival union.

Both begin to suspect each other and go to the site of the murder to find the woman dead. Each thinks the other did it and end up killing each other. The dead man and woman also get resuscitated as ghosts and watch the unfoldment and comment on it. It ends with a question as to who has hired the killer but suspicion is thrown on the mine owners.

For a first pic it benefits from snappy movement and visual knowhow and builds an aura of suspense and surprise. But its ectoplasm aspects and look at rather far fetched corrupt tactics do not quite mix well enough to bring it off entirely. But it's a neat little film and bodes a future di-

rector of worth when he gets down to telling simpler more forthright stories. And added hypo factor is an adroitly done seduction scene and the well manned fights.   *Mosk.*

Tres Cabras De Lampaio
(Three Henchmen of Lampaio)
(BRAZILIAN-COLOR)
Venice, Sept. 1.

Texeira release and production. With Milton Ribeiro, Aurelio Teixera, Gracinda Preiro, Miguel Torres. Directed by Teixeira. Screenplay, Miguel Torres; camera (Eastmancolor). Helio Silva; music, Catulo Paula. At Venice Film Fest. Running time, 95 MINS.
Gavaio .... Milton Ribeiro
Arveredo .... Aurelio Teixera
Serenata .... Miguel Torres
Girl .... Gracinda Preiro
Cowherd .... Catulo De Paula

Brazilian oater concerns a dedicated lawman hounding down three bandits who have a woman and guide in tow. It has an excess of violence, plus some good color and scenery, but lacks the true feel of adventure and narration to make this anything but a Latino lingo entry.

A group of bandits attack a town but the police have been warned by a spy and mow them down except for three. These hunt down the spy and draw and quarter him and then take off across the desert with a woman and a kidnaped guide. One bandit is a proud, haughty type who has had it in the family for generations, the other one through circumstance and one primarily a guitar playing singer.

Naturally the middle man falls for the woman and it is reciprocated. The harsh leader killer tries to get her and it leads to a knockdown brawl with the killer left tied up and the man and woman escaping together.

Thesps have a rugged air and Milton Ribeiro the right menacing air as the head man.   *Mosk.*

Cifra Impar
(Odd Number)
(ARGENTINE)
Venice, Sept. 5.

Harding-Shon release and production. With Lautaro Murua, Maria Rosa Gallo, Sergio Ronan, Milagros De La Vega. Directed by Manuel Antin. Screenplay, Julio Cortazar; camera, Ignacio Souto; music, Virtu Maragno. At Venice Film Fest. Running time, 90 MINS.
Luis .... Lautaro Murua
Laura .... Maria Rosa Gallo
Nico .... Sergio Ronar,
Mother .... Milagros De La Vega

Tale of a married couple haunted by the memory of the husband's dead brother, who had once been in love with the wife, is fairly adroitly done but remains shallow in theme and characterization. It remains a Latin circuit item.

A sickly painter introduces his robust down-to-earth brother to his fiancee. Love develops and they are kept apart by the sick man's pleading and the woman's weakness, as well as the mother's siding with the ill man.

When he dies they marry and go to Paris but the mother keeps sending letters and talking about the dead son as if he were alive. Then she says he is coming to Paris. Both know he is deceased but go to the station anyway and the man realizes they will always be haunted and kept apart by the memory of the brother.

Direction is clean and concise and uses a blend of flashbacks, memories and commentary to good effect. But once the pessimism of the wife is established, and the man's apparent health and understanding of how he was jealous of his brother, who got all the attention as a youth, it tends to repeat things and just fill out time to build a bit of suspense. It is technically good and thesping is okay.   *Mosk.*

Uzavreli Grad
(The First Fires)
(YUGOSLAVIAN—SCOPE)
Venice Aug. 30.

Avala Film release and production. With Ilija Dsuvalokovski, Bata Zivojinovic, Dragomir Felba. Directed by Voljko Bulajic. Screenplay, Bulajic, Vladimir Spindler, Banco Baratti; camera, Kresmir Groevie; music, Valdmir Kraus Raiteric. At Venice Film Fest. Running time, 120 MINS.
Siba .... Ilija Dsuvalokovski
Kozunlija .... Bata Zivojinovic
Rada .... Dragomir Felba

Pic is a sprawling epic about the building of a blast furnace. It puts a group of assorted characters into this work site and unfolds their little tales and dramas within the big one of a man's troubles in getting the work done. It has a feel for people in action and crisis, but tends to be somewhat conventional in character and unfoldment.

The foreman manages to keep his mixed and partly motley crew together and their loves, hatreds, wants and needs, and dedication to work, finally manage to allow for success even if the foreman is fired due to some human mistakes.

Director Voljko Bulajic has an insight into his skin deep characters and manages to avoid sentimentality by a right balance of taste and observation. Though familiar this crucible pic moves along briskly but is overlong. Some pruning would help. Acting is good and technical credits are par.   *Mosk.*

Sword of the Conqueror
(Eastmancolor)
(Italian-made)

Meller occasionally lifted out of scripting and acting ruts by well-handled action scenes, plus excellent color lensing.

Los Angeles, Sept. 10.

United Artists release of a Titanus Production by Gilberto Carbone. Stars Jack Palance, Eleonora Rossi Drago, Guy Madison. Features Carlo D'Angelo, Andrea Bosic. Edy Vessel. Ivan Palance and Vittorio Sanipoli. (No list of characters given.) Directed by Carlo Campogalliani; screenplay by Roberto Gianviti, Alessandoro Ferrau from story by Paola Barbara and Primo Zeglio; camera (Eastman color). Angelo Baistrocchi; editor, Mario Serandrei; music. Carlo Rustichelli. Reviewed at Goldwyn Studio, Sept. 10, '62. Running time: **95 MINS.**

(English Dubbed Dialog)

Belonging to the swordplay and blood-letting school of dramatics, "Sword of the Conqueror" packs enough battle action and demonstration of physical courage to make it a legitimate entry into what may rapidly be becoming an overcrowded field. The excellent technical values, displayed in some fine color work and well-drafted invasion scenes, frequently override the childish plot, inept acting and amateurish dubbing.

Palance, as Lombard chief Alboin, wars against the Gepidae, whose top general is Amalchi, played by Guy Madison. Treachery on part of the Gepidaean prime minister makes Amalchi a traitor in eyes of his king. Original touch here is that Rosmunda. Eleanora Rossi Drago), daughter of king, has son by Amalchi unknown to her father. Tyke is hidden up in the hills with loyal peasant family. When Alboin sends his emissary to the king to offer peace and asks for hand of Rosmunda. Her father agrees but same treacherous prime minister has emissary killed in tournament and once more fall guy Amalchi gets the blame. It just isn't his day.

Amalchi is put in prison, Alboin invades country, kills king, tries to make time with Rosmunda. Amalchi escapes but is believed dead. Thanks to indefinite period of film, touches of Roman arena, complete with lions, are blended with bits and pieces of Attila-like types, Visigaths, and some original creations who look like Hollywood comedians in fright wigs. The good guys wear blonde wigs, the bad ones black wigs. Makes it perfectly simple, in the battle scenes, to keep track of the carnage.

Amalchi returns with Marines in shape of sympathetic tribe whose aid he enlists by passing courage test (and it's a mess!). Big battle, much blood let, much reconciliation, much too much!

Palance's Benda-mask face lends credence to his role, which is generally villainous but with civilization occasionally trying to break through his savage exterior. Signorina Rossi Drago is sensationally beautiful, despite a red wig that doesn't fit too well, but walks through her scenes with all the emotional impact of a zombie. Madison's acting is almost as bad

as the costumes he's given to wear. Some of the supporting parts, played by Italians, are theatrically effective but not always compatible with the English voices they've acquired in dubbing. One unfortunate chieftain comes up sounding like the late Eugene Palette.

Director Campogalliani concentrates all his energy and talent on the quite excellent battle scenes, and is particularly well supported by the top notch color lensing of Angelo Baistrocchi. Carlo Rustichelli's martial score is more effective in the action sequences than as underscoring for the more plodding sections of the narrative. *Robe.*

Life for Ruth
(BRITISH)

Provocative probe into a man's conscience that will stimulate wicket reaction.

London, Sept. 7.

Rank release of Allied Film Makers (Michael Relph) production. Stars Michael Craig, Patrick McGoohan. Janet Munro. Directed by Basil Dearden. Screenplay, Janet Green & James McCormick; editor, John Guthridge; camera, Otto Heller; music, William Alwyn. At Leicester Square Theatre, London. Running time, **91 MINS.**

John Harris .... Michael Craig
Dr. Brown .... Patrick McGoohan
Pat Harris .... Janet Munro
Hart Jacobs .... Paul Rogers
Mrs. Gordon .... Megs Jenkins
Teddy's Mother .... Maureen Pryor
Teddy's Father .... Frank Finlay
Mr. Gordon .... John Barrie
Mapleton .... Basil Dignam
Clyde .... Leslie Sands
Duty Sister .... Ellen McIntosh
Harvard .... Michael Aldridge
John's Father .... Malcolm Keen
Ruth .... Lynn Taylor
Teddy .... Freddy Ramsey
Crown Counsel .... Norman Woolland
Defending Counsel... Michael Bryant
Vicar .... Maurice Colebourne
Marshall .... John Welsh

The team of Michael Relph and Basil Dearden are specializing in pix which, designed for entertainment, use provocative themes that compel the filmgoer to think. And Janet Green and James McCormick are scriptwriters who provide ready material for them. The latest, "Life For Ruth," must provide ammunition for tab buyers' argument or, at least, discussion.

The writers have occasionally skated over glibly through their points and, perhaps, sat over cosily on a fence. But who can say what is right or wrong about any man's tussle with his own conscience? Sufficient that the questions are posed.

First problem that confronts an honest working man (Michael Craig) occurs when his eight-year-old daughter and her next door playmate are involved in a boating accident. His daughter is clinging to the boat and is not in such immediate danger as the drowning boy. Which should he try first to save? A tough problem for any father. He rescues both, but by then his daughter is gravely ill. Only a blood transfusion can save her. Because of his strict religious principles (he is a member of the Jehovah witness sect, though it is not stated in the film) he adamantly refuses, and the child dies. That was his second distressing problem.

The doctor who urged the trans-

fusion is so irate that he gets the father tried for manslaughter. This is good telling stuff for drama and it brings up issues about religion, the law, conscience, marital relationship all posed with intelligence and conviction. The ending seems contrived, but on reflection, is perfectly valid and is the only logical way of ending a film which doesn't seek to dogmatise, but merely to ask two questions. What would you do?

Thesping is crisp all round, with Michael Craig surmounting a gloomy type of role as the dogged religionist, and Janet Munro, gaining stature with every film, as his baffled dismayed young wife. Patrick McGoohan, long established in this reviewer's mind, as one of the sharpest talents among Britain's younger actors, is excellent in a tricky role which is not so clearly defined as the other top jobs.

Michael Bryant, edgily persuasive as the defending counsel, Norman Woolland, in the more conventional part of the counsel seeking to nail Craig, Paul Rogers, as a Jewish solicitor who, briefly, but brilliantly hints at racial problems of persecution, Megs Jenkins, John Welsh, Malcolm Keen and Maurice Colebourne are others who help to etch this very worthy picture.

Otto Heller's bleak photography of the North of England setting, John Guthridge's editing and William Alwyn's unobtrusive musical score all lend aid to Dearden's adroit direction. *Rich.*

Mr. Arkadin
('Confidential Report')
(ANGLO-FRENCH)

Orson Welles long-time-no-see melodrama. One for the cine-addicts.

M. & A. Alexander release of Filmorsa (Louis Dolivet) production. Stars Orson Welles, Michael Redgrave, Akim Tamiroff, Katina Paxinou, Mischa Auer. Features Patricia Medina, Paola Mori, Robert Arden, Peter Van Eyck, Jack Watling, Gregoire Aslan, Suzanne Flon. Directed-written by Orson Welles (from original story by Welles); camera, Jean Bourgoin; editor, Renzo Lucidi; music, Paul Misraki. Reviewed in N.Y., Sept. 12, '62. Running time, **93 MINS.**

Gregory Arkadin .... Orson Welles
Burgomil Trebitsch....Michael Redgrave
Mily .... Patricia Medina
Jakob Zouk .... Akim Tamiroff
The Professor .... Mischa Auer
Raina ....Paola Mori
Guy an Stratten.......... Robert Arden
Sophie .... Katina Paxinou
Marquis of Rutleigh...... Jack Watling
Bracco .... Gregoire Aslan
Thadeus .... Peter Van Eyck
Baroness Nagel .... Suzanne Flon

Quiescent as a "personal" filmmaker since he wrote-directed "Touch of Evil" for Universal (circa '58), Orson Welles' delayed bounce-back is with the forthcoming "Trial," from the Franz Kafka classic and starring Tony Perkins, which he screenplayed and directed. (American distribution is optioned by Astor Pictures, but the deal is not finalized.

Interimly, New York audiences will have a chance to inspect—commencing Oct. 2 at the uptown New Yorker—a Welles pic completed in '55, "Mr. Arkadin," released abroad by Warners as "Confidential Report" but bypassed by distribs this side for some years until picked up by Coast vidfilm distributor M. & A. Alexander. But for reasons unspecified, no effort

was made since to put "Arkadin" into U.S. theatrical exhibition.

Chronologically, "Arkadin" is the third of Welles' "personal" pictures, falling between "Magnificent Ambersons" (1942, for RKO) and "Lady From Shanghai" (1948, for Columbia), and assertedly his most ambitious project since "Citizen Kane." There have been variously told tales of a dispute over the version handled by Warners, the substance of which is that Welles, claiming his work had been butchered, disowned the pic. It's believed his row was with "Arkadin" producer Louis Dolivet.

Since VARIETY unaccountably carried no review of the pic originally, this is to now redress the omission. Whether the print to be shown by the New Yorker is primarily the Welles conception or something of a mutation, "Arkadin" is at once a fascinating (inevitably) and dismaying effort, frequently suggestive of self-parody; and indeed, in scenario and technique, it is a 93-minute echo of "Kane" and that film's bravura style.

Instead of newspaper tycoon Charles Foster Kane, here is Gregory Arkadin, shadow figure, arch-capitalist, graduate of a Polish "white slave" ring, but whose latterday power and riches are shrouded. Instead of Kane's Xanadu, Arkadin has a castle in Spain. Instead of inanimate "Rosebud," there is a daughter (Welles' wife, Paola Mori), pretty, vital and overprotected.

The Welles imprimatur is all-pervasive, expectably in a "signature" pic. It is gray-toned, and the sharp interest is preferred to dissolve—the device employed, together with overlap dialog, to such brilliant time-telescoping effect in "Kane." His camera still angled skyward from somewhere around the knees, either for composition or stressed characterization (to suggest a powerful figure of Arkadin). The angular lensing, even at this advanced date, retains its capacity to thrall; but likewise, it often seems no more now than tiresome affect.

Welles' scenes, as is true of the whole body of his personal work, are often remarkable vignettes in themselves, playing like symbolic pasquinades. His action is kinetic, accentuated by a camera avid for crisp detail, capturing a bit of business, framing an effect to illuminate character (Arkadin's eyes straying to a bikini-clad femme as his conversation proceeds), intensifying mood almost to surrealist level. This expressing of tale and viewpoint in striking cinematic terms is, of course, the Welles metier.

The visual trickery in "Arkadin," albeit often irrelevant, is almost always fascinating—just because it's a Welles orchestration, filling the screen with arresting oddment, with delicious detail—with, in short, excitement.

Technically, the salient flaw is the sound—conspicuously post-dubbed. Except for some aphorisms that alone explain the film, the dialog is a constant impediment, notably that supplied Robert Arden in a key role as an American con artist. Arden himself passes muster physically, but his thesping is distractingly one-note and a cornball performance damaging to the total.

Welles' story is a parable, and

verbalized as such by Arkadin at one point. It concerns a scorpion and a frog, and the moral is that character is immutable and thus logical even when seemingly illogical.

Told in flashback, Arkadin is an amnesiac and hires a small-time Yank smuggler to trace his past. His ulterior purpose is to turn up, and eradicate, old nefarious associates who conceivably might disclose the truth about him to his daughter. The American goes to work, and the murders follow. He, too, is marked for extinction, but in the end manages to reach the daughter before Arkadin does, leading him to believe he has been revealed, though the truth is otherwise and this is just a ruse to save the Yank's neck. Unexpected by him is that Arkadin would commit suicide (in high Wellesian style) by leaping from a single-engine plane.

Engaging meller it may be, but missing the incisive delineation that marked "Kane." The melange of darting narrative simply gets the upper hand—a case of visual virtuosity overwhelming the Arkadin parable. Film's chief virtue is the unity of Welles' outlook—as in "Kane," he does not pass judgment on Arkadin, for again the character is shaped by divergent subjectivity from within the film. But it comes off less effectively.

Part of Welles' achievement is his delightful employment of senior cinema pros in vividly animated parts. Thus, Katina Paxinou and Michael Redgrave excel as Arkadin's estranged wife and a homosexual antique merchant. Ditto Mischa Auer—with the funniest lines— as maestro of a flea circus, and Akim Tamiroff as the comicly forlorn onetime Arkadin associate. Caricatures all, and beautiful. Paola Mori is efficient as the daughter, and others appearing to nice advantage include Patricia Medina (as the smuggler's corrupt girl), Peter Van Eyck, Suzanne Flon, Jack Watling and Gregoire Aslan.

Credited with editing is Renzo Lucidi, but his contribution would seem academic. Jean Bourgoin's camera is responsive to Welles, and Paul Misraki's score is appropriate.   *Pit.*

Tiao Medonho
(BRAZILIAN)
Venice, Sept. 8.

Farias-Richers release and production. Directed by Roberto Farias. Screenplay, Farias, Luiz Carlos Barreto; camera, Amleto Daisso; music, Remo Usai. At Venice Film Fest. Running time, 100 MINS.

Tiao	Eliezer Gomes
Grilo	Grande Otello
Tonio	Reginaldo Farias
Lino	Jorge Doria
Cachaca	Atila Orio
Wife	Ruth De Souza

Competently turned out pic, with social and race overtones, looks a natural for Latin circuits in its zesty pace and okey, if familiar, characterizations. It does not stack up for art chances in U.S. but could be actioner or dualer fare.

A group of fairly poor people from a slum area of Rio De Janeiro hold up a pay train. Then the loot is shared and all admonished not to spend much or suffer reprisals. They are a mixed white and Nergo group. A young white youth says he represents the mastermind and takes his cut accordingly.

Each begins to itch to spend the money on pain of trouble with wives etc. The so-called liaison with the chief, who is the mastermind himself, takes up with a rich girl and cars. Tiao Medenho is a Negro and the brawn and executioner of the group. He also has two families. A squealer brings things to a head and the whole group is wiped out.

Young director Roberto Farias shows a nice feel for pace and the personages are well limned if coventional. Poverty and the leader's racism also help make its modern points. But above all it is a savvily made little melodrama with obvious Yank influences but well assimilated to make this an interesting look at Brazilian lowlife.   *Mosk.*

Hero's Island
(PANAVISION—TECHNICOLOR)

Fair costumer. Action market item.

United Artists release of Daystar-Portland production, produced, written and directed by Leslie Stevens. Stars James Mason, Neville Brand, Kate Manx, Rip Torn. Camera (Technicolor), Ted McCord; editor, Richard Brockway; music, Dominic Frontiere. Reviewed at Academy Awards Theatre. Sept. 14, '62. Running time, 94 MINS.

Jacob Webber	James Mason
Devon Mainwaring	Kate Manx
Kingstree	Neville Brand
Nicholas	Rip Torn
Wayte	Warren Oates
Thomas Mainwaring	Brendan Dillon
Enoch	Robert Sampson
Dixey	Dean Stanton
Cullen	Morgan Mason
Jafar	Darby Hinton
Pound	Robert Johnson
Meggett	Bill Hart
Bullock	John Hudkins

"Hero's Island," described as the first effort of Daystar Productions to enter the "family film" field, will, despite some excellent technical values, not make much of an impression in that category due to failure on the part of the producers, either to ascertain what constitutes a "family film," or to abide by the restrictions prevailing there.

Production costs will have better chance of recovery in the straight action field where tickets are bought according to amount of gunpowder exploded and blood spilled, rather than niceties of speech and diligence of research.

A co-production with star James Mason's Portland Productions, the pic deal with a couple, former indentured servants, settling on an island off the Caroline coast in 1718, who are threatened by fishermen who's been using the island. Husband is killed by fishermen, just before Mason is washed ashore, only survivor, he says, of just before Mason is washed again attack, he intervenes and drives them away.

The attackers engage services of Neville Brand, a cutthroat, to aid them but, in interim, one of fishermen (Rip Torn) rebels against murderous intent of others and is tossed overboard. Washed ashore, he throws in his lot with settlers. During attack Mason remains aloof until the two children are captured. When he attacks, Brand recognizes Mason as former sailmaster of the pirate Blackbeard. Brand is slain and Mason returns to his life of piracy. Torn remains with widow and children, to help them settle island.

Chief asset of film is Ted McCord's brilliant, imaginative camerawork, which makes most of the restricted playing area. In all other departments, particularly in Stevens screenplay and direction and the acting, the film is frequently gawkish and inept.

Mason is impressive in his early scenes but grows overly melodramatic near picture's end. The wife, played by Kate Manx (in real life Mrs. Leslie Stevens) is never believable as a woman who "has picked cotton for seven years to earn her freedom" and had borne two children. Despite an expressive face, she reads her lines as though they were being fed by a prompter out of camera range. The collection of accents is almost as mixed as the styles of acting. Neville Brand and Rip Torn display the uncertainty of two trained soldiers who blindly obey but don't believe in their commanding officer.

Richard Brockway's editing is never really tested until Mason and Brand duel, where an excellent use of cross-cutting alternates between head-on, close-up shots of a single swordsman, bringing the flashing blades right into the camera. Dominic Frontiere's score is a moody mixture of seascape and schmaltz, accelerated during the fighting scenes.   *Robe.*

Gypsy
(MUSICAL—TECHNICOLOR —TECHNIRAMA)

Memoirs of a stripper and her stage mama. Handsomely mounted, occasionally quite funny. Good performances and production but essentially unpleasant central character. Yet should do okay.

Warner Bros. presentation of Mervyn LeRoy production directed by LeRoy. Stars Rosalind Russell, Natalie Wood, Karl Malden. Screenplay by Leonard Spigelgass based on stage libretto of Arthur Laurents, derived from Gypsy Rose Lee's autobiography. Music, Jule Styne; lyrics, Stephen Sondheim; camera (Technicolor), Harry Stradling Jr.; choreography, Robert Tucker, costumes, Orry-Kelly; editor, Philip W. Anderson; conductor, Frank Perkins. Reviewed at RKO 58th St., N.Y., Sept. 24, 1962. Running time, 149 MINS.

Rose	Rosalind Russell
Louise	Natalie Wood
Herbie Sommers	Karl Malden
Tulsa No. 2	Paul Wallace
Tessie Tura	Betty Bruce
Mr. Kringelein	Parley Baer
Grandpa	Harry Shannon
"Baby" June	Suzanne Cupito
"Dainty" June	Ann Jilliann
"Baby" Louise	Diane Pace
Mazeppa	Faith Dane
Electra	Roxanne Arlen
Betty Cratchitt	Jean Willes
George	George Petrie
Mervyn Goldstone	Ben Lessy
Pasty	Guy Raymond
Cigar	Louis Quinn

There is a wonderfully funny sequence involving three nails-hard strippers which comes when "Gypsy" has been unreeling about an hour. The sequence is thoroughly welcome and almost desperately needed to counteract a certain Jane One-Note implicit in the tale of a stage mother whose egotisms become something of a bore despite the canny skills of director-producer Mervyn LeRoy to contrive it otherwise. On a balance of these LeRoy efforts and the novelty value of Natalie Wood as Gypsy Rose Lee against the essentially disagreeable central role played by Rosalind Russell, this musical in Technicolor impresses as an okay prospect at the boxoffice.

Miss Russell's performance as the smalltime brood-hen deserves commendation. It is cleverly managed all the way, with much help from the camera angles of Harry Stradling Sr. There is almost, not quite, a victory of technique over substance. Unfortunately nothing really happens in "Gypsy" which is not predictable from the first, and extremely slow, quarter hour of the footage. There is the further audience dissatisfaction factor in that this obnoxious creature never changes or mellows and is the same hard-to-bear personality at the fadeout as 20 years earlier.

Roz Russell, having specialized in versatility and offbeat roles, is less surprising than that sometime heavy, Karl Malden, as the mother's incredibly loyal lover who finally screams when he perceives that she cares for nobody and nothing except her own ego compulsions. That he dissolves into the character, that he manages in the younger period to appear appropriately young, is a considerable tribute to the not just-discovered artistry of the man.

About Natalie Wood: it is not easy to credit her as a stripper but it is interesting to watch her, under LeRoy's guidance, go through the motions in a burlesque world that is prettied up in soft-

focus and a kind of phony innocence. Any resemblance of the art of strip, and its setting, to reality is, in this film, purely fleeting. Omitted altogether are closeups of the moron audiences.

There are some beguiling satirical touches in the re-creation of the hokey vaudeville routines starring "Baby June" Havoc, well impersonated by Ann Jilliann, whose flight from the mother turns the latter's attention upon the previously neglected sister, Louise, the Gypsy Rose of later show biz. The film, of course, is based upon the autobiography of Gypsy Rose Lee and the musical comedy in which Ethel Merman starred.

More chronicle than musical, there are advantages still in some of the music (Jule Styne) and lyrics (Stephen Sondheim) and the choreography (Robert Tucker). Taking off from the stage book of Arthur Laurents, the adaptor, Leonard Spigelgass, has probably done a pro job in making the thin plot carry the weight. It is uphill going, however, to make the characters come alive and escape from the stereotype of theatrical literature's fascination with own monsters complex.

There are numerous bit parts. One weakness probably is that all the real story focus is upon the stage mother. Miss Wood has one teenage infatuation for a will o' wisp hoofer (Paul Wallace) but in the final period of her big money success, as a strip queen, no interpersonal relationships are shown (there is now no time left if the film is to stay within manageable length).

In short, the production and the performances in "Gypsy" are superior to the story which ends with a soft-headed, rather than soft-hearted, reconciliation between mother and daughter. Fadeout arm-in-arm.   *Land.*

Secrets of the Nazi Criminals
(SWEDISH-MADE)

Strong major cinematic documentary on Nazi barbarism during World War II. Superior to its title, picture is top-caliber, organized knowledgeably by a Swedish company. Those induced to see it will not go away unmoved. It is very real.

Trans-Lux Distributing Corp. release of Minerva International (Sweden) production. Produced by Tore Sjoberg. Script by Erik Holm. Edited by Sjoberg, Holm and Ingemar Ejvel. English translated by Crawford Moller; narrated by Claude Stephenson; American prosecutor Jackson's speeches read by William Hurley. Previewed in New York, Sept. 20, '62. Running time, 84 MINS.

(Dubbed in English)

Herein is astute handling of a massive amount of footage about the Nuremberg trials and backgrounds of various of the Nazi criminals of World War II. Some of it has been seen before but unlikely with such telling effect. Other material was not familiar to this observer.

The American distributor, Trans-Lux, claims that "every foot of this picture is authentic." This appears to be so; nothing is "staged" in the usual sense. Giving distinction to "Secrets of the Nazi Criminals" is the excellent editing job

performed by the Swedes involved, Minerva International, producer Tore Sjoberg, editors Sjoberg, Ingemar Ejve Holm and scriptwriter Holm. They prove themselves a proficient group.

The import, all done in dubbed English, is by no means (or should not be) an exploitation special; it's devoid of shallowness. It is, instead, a penetrating analysis of the men brought before Nuremberg and other international courts.

Hitler's rise to power passes in review by the way of recognizable documentation. And then comes the Third Reich masterminds on trial, with good detail pictorially on each, including Himmler, Goering, Hess, Goebbels, Denitz and Keitel.

It is shown that each committed a crime against humanity. And each of them is exposed pictorially. Those who chose not to commit suicide are seen grotesquely following their execution.

They are seen with jaws ajar and clipped ropes still around their necks. But before this they are seen as living persons, powerful to the extreme and arrogant. The execution of the Jews is vivid. Bodies upon bodies are on view in the pits following gas-chamber annihilation.   *Gene.*

Two Tickets to Paris

Another Joey Dee Twister with appeal for Dee-inclined teenagers.

Columbia release of Harry Romm production. Stars Joey Dee, Gary Crosby, Kay Medford; features Jeri Lynne Fraser, Lisa James, Charles Nelson Reilly, Richard Dickens, Nina Paige. Directed by Greg Garrison. Writer, Hal Hackady; camera, William O. Steiner; music, Henry Glover; editor, Ralph Rosenblum. Previewed in New York, Sept. 13, '62. Running time, 90 MINS.

Joey	Joey Dee
Gary	Gary Crosby
Aggie	Kay Medford
Piper	Jeri Lynne Fraser
Coco	Lisa James
Claypoole	Charles Nelson Reilly
Tony	Richard Dickens
Dumb Blonde	Nina Paige
Marmaduke	Sal Lombardo
Mrs. Patten	Jeri Archer
Le Claire	Michele Moinot
Charles	Jay Burton
The Starliters	Themselves

Perhaps this might sound inviting to the teenagers but there's really not much in the way of sound values for the general public. "Two Tickets to Paris" is a musical in which Joey Dee, between his Twisting exercises, experiences the alternate torments and joys of young love. Harry Romm, who now seems to specialize in this sort of thing, has produced an apparent quickie in a very elaborate setting, latter being the ultra-luxurious French Lines' France.

Dee is simply not at home before the cameras except when gyrating. He's a twister, but is neither actor nor striking personality.

Speaking assignments are handled in inept fashion by just about all concerned. Hal Hackady's story line, focusing on two in-love youngsters who somehow are enjoined from getting married until a show business engagement is fulfilled in Paris, loses much of whatever zest it had to begin with because of the unconvincing performances.

Henry Glover's original score is fair for the course and a few standards are reprised and are a help.

Songs and dances aboard the France provide some color and

the Harry Romm production generally has some exploitation values for some market situations.

Jeri Lynne Fraser is a cutie as Dee's mate in the on-and-off romance, Kay Medford labors as a chaperone, Lisa James is on the ball as a romantic Latino whose violent kisses cause complications among all concerned. Gary Crosby is aboard ship to make a pass at Miss Fraser. The Starliters make with competent musicality. Technical credits modest.   *Gene.*

Bandits on the Wind
(JAPAN)

Action - filled 15th Century Japanese drama with considerable attention to the sociological structure of ancient Japan. Film should do well in specialized U.S. bookings.

Toho Company Ltd. release of its own production. Executive producer, Tomoyuki Tanaka; directed by Hiroshi Inagaki; screenplay by Masato Ide; photographed by Kazuo Yamada; music by Ken Ishii. Stars Yosuke Natsuki, Izumi Yukimura, Makoto Sato, Akiko Wakabayashi, Somegoro Ichikawa. American premiere Sept. 14, 1962, at Toho Labrea Theatre, L.A. Running time, 110 MINS.

Taro	Yosuke Natsuki
Kayo	Izumi Yukimura
Gale	Makoto Sato
Gen.	Somegoro Ichikawa
Yuri	Akiko Wakabayashi

Toho Co. Ltd. continues its policy of presenting American premieres of its latest films at the company's L.A. outlet. Present action-packed Samurai drama, in many respects similar to the famed "Seven Samurai," is a mixture of blood and guts banditry and warfare that ravaged in 15th Century Japan and a discussion of the sociological makeup of the Japanese people. It has sufficient interest in both areas to provide a solid program in the foreign film field .

Particularly prominent in the film are the direction of Hiroshi Inagaki and photography by Kazuo Yamada. Latter is artistic in style, concentrating greatly on dark mood shots and symbolic usage of cloud formations and windy dust scenes that are striking in their depiction of the poverty-stricken times.

Story concerns a group of bandits who seek refuge in the once prosperous village of Yaeyama after ransacking a mansion. The local priest, seeing a family standard in their midst, believes they are from the Amagasaki clan which once ruled the province. One of the younger bandits poses as the heir of the former ruler. They provide food and a new start for the village, also effecting the escape from near-slavery in the castle of the current dissolate ruler of the village's entire population of young men. In return, they are worshipped and revered by the villagers, though eventually sought and slaughtered by the great army of the Akechi clan who fear they will rise to too much power.

Performances, particularly by Yosuke Natsuki, as the bandit leader; Makoto Sato, a sex-hungry bandit, and Somegoro Ichikawa, the posing heir, are excellent. Izumi Yukimura and Akiko Wakabayashi are beautiful as the two major femme interests. Smaller roles of villagers and warriors are done by a beautiful collection of actors who form an overall strikingly effective cast.

Tomoyuki Tanaka is exec pro-

ducer. Screenplay is well constructed by Masato Ide and stirring music is by Ken Ishii. *Dale.*

Dangerous Charter
(PANAVISION—PANASOUND—COLOR)

Adequate lower berth exploitation item. Helpful support if wisely paired.

Hollywood, Sept. 19.
Crown-International release of Robert Gottschalk-John R. Moore production. Directed by Gottschalk. Screenplay, Paul Strait, from original story by Gottschalk; camera (Technicolor), Meredith M. Nicholson; editor, George White; music, Ted Dale; assistant director, Joe Boyle. Reviewed at Pix Theatre, Sept. 19, '62. Running time, 76 MINS.

Marty	Chris Warfield
June	Sally Fraser
Dick	Richard Foote
Manet	Peter Forster
Kick	Chick Chandler
Joe	Wright King

Tailored for the bottom half of dual bills, this indie exploitation item will prove handy in that capacity unless paired with too eminent an attraction, in which case its presence may irritate quality-conscious audiences. Carefully programmed and profitably exploited, the Crown-International release, produced by Robert Gottschalk and John R. Moore, can fulfill its function.

The screenplay by Paul Strait, from an original story by Gottschalk, who also served as director of the film, is concerned with the predicament of a trio of impoverished fishermen who, discovering an abandoned yacht containing a corpse who died of the mumps, are awarded the vessel by the Coast Guard in hopes that while operating it as a charter boat they will help solve the mystery of its ownership. Sure enough, the men are soon confronted by the owners and ordered at gunpoint to aid in the smuggling of half-a-million dollars of heroin into Catalina, of all places.

As the three fishermen, Chris Warfield, Chick Chandler and Wright King are amiable enough, although the latter tends to overact. Sally Fraser is decorative as Warfield's girl. Peter Forster is a colorful heavy, and Richard Foote wins some offbeat sympathy as a guitar-strumming junkie with a conscience.

Gottschalk's direction is mechanical. Although edited down to 76 minutes, there is at least one scene rendered irrelevant in the trimming process that should have been spotted and snipped to tidy up continuity. Meredith M. Nicholson's camerawork is, within budget limitations, capable. The picture was shot in Technicolor and Panavision. "The Sea Is My Woman," a trite tune by Rod Therwood, serves as main title background and occasional theme within Ted Dale's score.   *Tube.*

Hands of a Stranger

Mild suspense entry for program market.

Hollywood, Sept. 14.
Allied Artists release of Newton Arnold, Michael duPont production. Stars Paul Lukather, Joan Harvey. Features James Stapleton, Irish McCalla. Directed by Arnold. Original story-screenplay, Arnold; camera, Henry Cronjager; editor, Bert Honey; music, Richard LaSalle. Reviewed at Pantages Theatre, Holly-

wood, Cal., Sept. 14, '62. Running time, 95 MINS.

Dr. Gil Harding	Paul Lukather
Dina Paris	Joan Harvey
Vernon Paris	James Stapleton
Dr. Russ Compton	Ted Otis
Dr. Ken Fry	Michael duPont
Police Lt. Syms	Larry Haddon
George Britton	Michael Rye
Eileen Hunter	Elaine Martone
Cab Driver	George Sawaya
Skeet	Barry Gordon
Carnival Barker	David Kramer
Sue	Sally Kellerman
Holly	Irish McCalla

"Hands of a Stranger" stirs up enough mild suspense to rate as an okay entry for the program market. Its theme is sufficiently novel to attract less discriminating audiences, but much of the unfoldment is sloppy, which militates against what might have been a fairly strong melodrama. A 10 to 15-minute trim would speed up action.

Co-produced by Newton Arnold, who also scripted and directed with Michael duPont (reputedly of the Delaware family), plot revolves around a surgeon transplanting the powerful hand of an unknown murdered man onto the wrists of a brilliant young concert pianist who loses his hands in an auto accident. When the musician comes out of shock, he embarks upon a trail of vengeance against surgeon, and his assistants who participated in the successful operation.

Paul Lukather handles himself well as the surgeon and James Stapleton portrays the pianist, whose mind becomes twisted by his tragic circumstances, frequently over-directed. Joan Harvey plays his sister whom he nearly murders, and Larry Haddon enacts a police lieutenant interested in the case and whose bullet saves Lukather from being strangled by the maddened musician. Other roles are acceptably undertaken.

Producers give film suitable production values and technical credits are okay, particularly camera work of Henry Cronjager.
Whit.

Le Combat Dans L'Ile
(Island Battle)
(FRENCH)
Paris, Sept. 25.

UGC release of Nouvelles Editions De Films production. Stars Romy Schneider, Jean-Louis Trintignant, Henri Serre. Directed by Alain Cavalier (supervised by Louis Malle). Screenplay, Cavalier, Jean-Paul Rapponeau; camera, P. Lhomme; editor, P. Gilette. At Normandie, Paris. Running time, 100 MINS.

Anne	Romy Schneider
Clement	Jean-Louis Trintignant
Paul	Henri Serre

Fresh, taut direction makes this tale of love and political skullduggery a fetching item. It just misses in writing and characterization to have this an arty house bet abroad. But it has the solidity for playoff use. Film also denotes a new director with a fine narrative sense in Alain Cavalier.

A young man is a part of an extremist political group dedicated to creating chaos in Western countries. Group would take control and then fight the East. He is involved in a plot to kill an important labor leader but it is thwarted. He goes off to find the squealer, leaving his young actress wife with a liberal friend who now hates him.

Love blossoms between them and then the husband comes back for revenge and a final duel in which he is killed. Romy Schneider has a feel for the role of the emotional actress and is only betrayed by the lack of good writing of her role. Jean-Louis Trintignant is properly menacing as the fascist youth while Henri Serre solid as the other man.

It naturally has echoes here of the recent Algerian problems and the still problematical politico extremists here. It is neatly packaged and direction takes elliptical short cuts that give it a brisk, tart air. Main shortcoming is the overly melodramatic ending.

But this may be the forerunner of deeper and more forthright pix on the usually taboo subject.

Sharp lensing and dynamic editing also help make this little pic a refreshing action drama. However, the bigger significance, and dramatic insight are lacking to give this the needed arty fillip.
Mosk.

The Longest Day
(C'SCOPE)

Blockbusting boxoffice worldwide.

Paris, Sept. 27.

20th-Fox release of Darryl F. Zanuck production. With John Wayne, Robert Mitchum, Henry Fonda, Robert Ryan, Rod Steiger, Robert Wagner, Richard Beymer, Mel Ferrer, Jeffrey Hunter, Paul Anka, Sal Mineo, Roddy McDowall, Stuart Whitman, Steve Forrest, Eddie Albert, Edmund O'Brien, Fabian, Red Buttons, Tom Tryon, Alexander Knox, Tommy Sands, Ray Danton, Henry Grace, Mark Damon, Dewey Martin, Ron Randell. Directed by Ken Annakin for the British scenes; Andrew Marton for the American scenes, Bernhard Wicki (German episodes) as supervised by Darryl F. Zanuck with Elmo Williams as coordinator of battle scenes. Screenplay, Cornelius Ryan from his own book with additional episodes by Romain Gary, James Jones, David Pursell, Jack Seddon. Camera (CinemaScope), Jean Bourgoin, Henri Persin, Walter Wottitz and Guy Tabary for helicopter shots; music, Maurice Jarre with thematic music by Paul Anka and arranged by Mitch Miller; editor, Samuel Beetley; art directors, Ted Aworth, Vincent Korda; special effects, Karl Baumgartner, Karl Helmer, Augie Lohman, Robert MacDonald, Alex Weldon. Preemed at Palais de Chaillot, Paris. Running time, 180 MINS.

THE AMERICANS

Col. Vandervoort	John Wayne
Gen. Cota	Robert Mitchum
Gen. Roosevelt	Henry Fonda
Gen. Gavin	Robert Ryan
Commander	Rod Steiger
U.S. Ranger	Robert Wagner
Schultz	Richard Beymer
Gen. Haines	Mel Ferrer
Ser. Fuller	Jeffrey Hunter
Ranger	Paul Anka
Pvt. Martini	Sal Mineo
Pvt. Morris	Roddy McDowall
Lt. Sheen	Stuart Whitman
Col. Newton	Eddie Albert
Gen. Barton	Edmund O'Brien
Ranger	Fabian
Pvt. Steele	Red Buttons
Lt. Wilson	Tom Tryon
Gen. Bedell Smith	Alexander Knox
Ranger	Tommy Sands
Capt. Frank	Ray Danton
Gen. Eisenhower	Henry Grace
Pvt. Harris	Mark Damon
Pvt. Wilder	Dewey Martin
Col. Caffey	John Crawford
Williams	Ron Randell
Gen. Bradley	Nicholas Stuart
Rear Adm. Kirk	John Meillon

THE BRITISH

RAF Pilot	Richard Burton
Capt. Maud	Kenneth More
Lord Lovat	Peter Lawford
Major Howard	Richard Todd
Gen. Parker	Leo Genn
Padre	John Gregson
Pvt. Flanagan	Sean Connery
Briefing Man	Jack Hedley

THE FRENCH

Janine	Irina Demich
Mayor	Bourvil
Roulland	Jean-Louis Barrault
Kieffer	Christian Marquand
Mme. Barrault	Arletty
Mother Superior	Madeleine Renaud
Sgt. Montlaur	Georges Riviere
Adm. Jaujard	Jean Servais
Renaud	Georges Wilson

THE GERMANS

Gen. Blumentritt	Curt Jurgens
Mar. Rommel	Werner Hinz
Mar. Rundstedt	Paul Hartmann
Ser. Kaffeeklatsch	Gerd Froebe
Maj. Pluskat	Hans Christian Blech
Gen. Pemsel	Wolfgang Presis
Lt. Col. Ocker	Peter Van Eyck
Col. Priller	Heinz Reincke
Gen. Marcks	Richard Munch
Gen. Salmuth	Ernst Schroeder
Cao. During	Karl Meisel

For his last personally produced feature, the new president of 20th-Fox, Darryl F. Zanuck, has achieved a solid and stunning war epic. From personal vignettes to big battles, it details the first day of the D-Day Landings by the Allies on June 6, 1944.

The savage fury and sound of war is ably caught on film. It emerges as a sort of grand scale s e m i - fictionalized documentary concerning the overall logistics needed for this incredible invasion. It carries its three hour length by the sheer tingle of the masses of manpower in action, peppered with little ironic, sad, silly actions that all add up to war.

No moralizing here but movement. The prospect is for big box-office on world screens. The best-selling book, the expert advance ballyhoo, the who's who cast of stars and, above all, the fantastic cacophony of conflict slant this as sure blockbuster.

It begins with looks at top ranking German officers and their reactions to what they know is the impending Allied invasion. Some believe it, some do not. Marshal Rommel even leaves on June 5 to take a pair of shoes to his wife in Germany. Then the waiting Yank, French and British soldiers and officers get Gen. Dwight D. Eisenhower's decision to go ahead in spite of bad weather.

The mighty armada moves ahead and commandos and diversionary raids are launched. There is furious fighting for a bridge. Parachutists land in a town and are slaughtered. Various little incidents of unawareness on the German side, or heroism or fright or the baptism of fire on the Allied side, are ably blocked out.

One man in a bunker suddenly sees the invading fleet loom up and calls a skeptical German officer who only believes it when the fleet's guns beat a deafening tattoo on the shore. Then the landing boats. The Germans had only two planes ready and the refusal of Gen. Jodl to awaken Hitler kept reinforcements from being sent.

But a good segment of the landing forces are pinned down on the beach and suffer terrible casualties. Then there are the breakthroughs and the linking up of forces as the longest day, as Rommel called it, comes to a close. The film has one of the longest credit lists for some time and everybody on it certainly deserves the mention.

On that score the use of over 43 actual star names in bit and pivotal spots helps keep up the aura of fictionalized documentary. But since it is the action, time and place, and the actual machinery of war, that are the things, they are kept after the title in billing which removes the problem of star placements etc.

They all deliver resoundingly and one would be hard put not to name everybody. Some, however, loom larger than others in the story. Therefore, and without any intention to slight, special pats are due to John Wayne and Robert Mitchum as laconic commanders; to Red Buttons, for some welcome comedy relief as well as a shattering dramatic sequence; to Richard Todd, Richard Burton, Robert Ryan, Jeffrey Hunter, Sal Mineo, Peter Lawford, Rod Steiger, Edmond O'Brien, Henry Fonda, Eddie Albert, Alexander Knox, Leo Genn, Robert Wagner and Hans Christian Blech, as the German who first sees the Allies armada approaching the Normandy coast. Irina Demich, making her debut as a member of the French Resistance, has a sultry quality and shows promise of acting ability.

Cornelius Ryan, aided by additional scenes from Romain Gary, James Jones, David Piersell and Jack Seddon, has fashioned a canny and clever script from his own book. Zanuck himself marshalled three directors (Andre Marton, Bernhard Wicki and Ken Annakin) and a coordinator (Elmo Williams) for the battle scenes, who all deserve highest praise.

The battles ably take their places among some of the best ever put on the screen.

A German strafing the beach, Yanks scaling a treacherous cliff only to find that there was no big gun there, British commandos taking a bridge, Yanks blowing up a big bunker, the French taking a town, all are done with massive, pungent action. The black and white and CinemaScope screen help keep the focus on surge and movement.

Any flaws? A few, but it would be captious to carp too much about them. Sometimes the anecdotes come along for their own sake rather than seeming a part of this boiling bullet ballad. A comic French mayor greeting the British on the beach is one such point. And the lines about war's pointlessness are sometimes superfluous, since implicit in the situation.

Enough to say this film is a feather in Zanuck's cap and also bodes well for 20th-Fox's future. It has what looks like a b.o. bonanza in the gripping pageant of action.

Film is technically superb with all aspects rating nods. Even the three directors, who sometimes display differing personal outlooks towards war and heroics, have been merged ably as one unit showing that the last war was both hell and heroic, chance and planning, men and guns.

The international version, with Germans speaking German and the French French, was shown at its Paris preem. All these scenes were shot in English also and will serve in Anglo speaking areas. Its Yank and foreign potential at the wickets look long and profitable. (The "international" version, with appropriate subtitles, is also being used for first Yank roadshow dates.)

It should be added that though, historically, the outcome of the film is evident, it still packs suspense in its shear mechanics. Even the Germans get their just deserts as far as military knowhow is concerned. *Mosk.*

Smashing of the Reich
(DOCUMENTARY)

Well-edited, with low key narration but material familiar. Coupled with 'Kamikaze' for exploitation houses. Fair prospects.

Brigadier Film Associates release of an Irja production, produced by Perry Wolf. Writer, Wolf; music, Norman Dello Joio; narration, Jim Stephens. Reviewed in New York, Sept. 26, '62. Running time, **84 MINS.**

Here we go again—with another how-the-war-was-won recital. This one has substantial merit, but the commercial question is whether there hasn't been a surfeit of these infatuations via both theatrical and home screens.

Produced by New York television producer-scribe Perry Wolf, "Smashing of the Reich" is being paired with another Wolf project, "Kamikaze," a bit of counterpoint dualing that's obviously aimed for hit-and-run exploitation bookings. Promoted aggressively, the tandem may bail some hay in program situations.

"Reich" is an astutely composed documentary, not a hasty patchwork. In tone it is neither sensational or arty, just a story told straight and well, with sustained interest. Much of the footage seems fresh, or at least seldom glimpsed. And there is fine attention to sidebar—inspiring sequences of the French Resistance "assisting" the Germans out of Paris; the Yank-Soviet hookup at the Elbe River; and of concentration camp liberations.

Armchair military historians may carp that "Reich" seems to pack an air power accent, since the role of the fly boys is dominant for more than half the film. Reflectively, however, it must be conceded that air might did indeed account for much smashing, in fact setting up Germany for the ground blows.

The narration, written by Wolf, is economic and low-key (all to the good), and delivered by a well-modulated Jim Stephens. Norman Dello Joio's score is effective throughout, but especially for the Paris footage.

Film, incidentally, bears a very specific dedication—to a deceased chum of the producer. *Pit.*

Education Sentimentale
(FRENCH—DYALISCOPE)
Paris, Oct. 2.

UFA-Comacico release of UFA-SFC production. Stars Jean-Claude Brialy, Marie-Jose Nat, Dawn Addams. Directed by Alexandre Astruc. Screenplay, Roger Nimier, Roland Laudenbach, Astruc from book by Gustave Flaubert; camera, Jean Badal; editor, Running time, **90 MINS.**

Frederic	Jean-Claude Brialy
Anne	Marie-Jose Nat
Catherine	Dawn Addams
Didier	Michel Auclair
Barbara	Carla Marlier
Charles	Pierre Dudan

Director Alexandre Astruc now seems a flash in the pan after this lifeless look at the criss-cross loves of a young, idealistic provincial in Paris. Updated from a Gustave Flaubert novel this lacks the feel for character, place and life to make it palatable. Foreign chances are extremely chancey.

A young, good student, lives in the servant's quarters of an industrialist who employs him. He is enamored of the young wife of a climbing employee who is also friendly with the boss. But he ends up with the discarded mistress of the climber. Then he manages to get to the wife only to be left in the lurch.

Astruc rarely shows concern or insight into the cardboard characters. Hence, their emotional lives are hardly revealing. It resembles the many French and Italo pix on listless love and ironic sentimental loss. But it lacks the flair for making all this interesting. Technically it is only passable.

Thesps cannot do much with their essentially surface characters. Pic appears mainly local with even the many love scenes minus the bite, snap or sensuality for hypo purposes. *Mosk.*

Arsene Lupin Contre Arsene Lupin
(Arsene Lupin Against Arsene Lupin)
(FRENCH—DYALISCOPE)
Paris, Oct. 2.

Gaumont release of Cinephonic-DAMA-Chavane production. Stars Jean-Claude Brialy, Jean-Pierre Cassel; features Fran-

çoise Dorleac, Genevieve Grad, Jean Le Poulain. Directed by Edouard Molinaro. Screenplay, Georges Neveux, Molinaro, Francois Chavane from book by Maurice Blanc; camera, Pierre Petit; editor, Robert Isnardon. At Ambassade, Paris. Running time, **110 MINS.**

Francois	Jean-Claude Brialy
Genard	Jean-Pierre Cassel
Nathalie	Francoise Dorleac
Catherine	Genevieve Grad
Charly	Daniel Cauchy
Prefect	Jean Le Poulain

Treatment just does not have the jauntiness of serious action to bring off this story of the 1920's via the shenanigans of the two sons of the famed turn-of-the-century gentleman burglar Arsene Lupin. So it does not appear likely as an arty entry abroad, mainly having second feature pic status via its comic qualities.

Film begins with the burial of Lupin. But it develops he left two sons. They begin to commit burglaries and come into conflict as they drive the police crazy. Finally they join forces to save some jewels for a comely Princess.

Director Edouard Molinaro uses many varied and speeded up shots plus a lot of period dancing and music. But the right balance of time and pace eludes him. He sacrifices the satire for flashy camera work.

Jean-Pierre Cassel and Jean-Claude Brialy have the bounce for the roles of the two thieves but not the polish called for. This appears mainly a local item with some secondary chances offshore on its colorful carryings-on. *Mosk.*

The Loneliness of the Long Distance Runner
(BRITISH)

Another sturdy entry in wave of realistic British "angry young man" pix. Standout debut by Tom Courtenay; should click with discerning audiences.

London, Sept. 28.

British Lion-Bryanston release (through BLC) of Woodfall (Tony Richardson) production. Stars Michael Redgrave, Tom Courtenay; features Avis Bunnage, Dervis Ward, James Bolam, Topsy Jane. Directed by Tony Richardson. Screenplay by Alan Sillitoe from his original short story; music, John Addison; editor, Anthony Gibbs; camera, Walter Lassally. At Warner Theatre, London. Running time, **104 MINS.**

Colin Smith	Tom Courtenay
Mrs. Smith	Avis Bunnage
Mike	James Bolam
Brown	Alec McCowen
Detective	Dervis Ward
Mr. Jones	James Cairncross
Roach	Joe Robinson
The Governor	Michael Redgrave
Audrey	Topsy Jane
Gladys	Julia Foster
Ronalds	John Bull
Stacey	Philip Martin
Public school boy	Christopher Williams
Booking office clerk	Frank Finlay
Doctor	Peter Duguid
Tory politician	Robert Percival

This is the latest in the current trend of British down-to-earth films which aim to put over a message of social significance. It is difficult to conjure up much sympathy for the young "hero" who comes out as a disturbed young layabout (he seems thoroughly to deserve his fate of landing in Borstal the corrective establishment for British juve delinquents). Yet the performance of newcomer Tom Courtenay and the imaginative, if sometimes over-

fussy, direction of Tony Richardson, plus some standout lensing by Walter Lassally makes this a worthwhile pic. It should be appreciated by all discerning ducat buyers.

Alan Sillitoe has written a sound screenplay from his own short story. Though there are obvious signs of padding, it remains a thoroughly professional job. The flashback technique is used ingeniously, though perhaps overmuch. Courtenay, latest in the modern wave of young British actors who rely on ability rather than in conventional good looks, plays a young man from an unhappy home in the Midlands. Apparently on the grounds that the world owes him a living, he seems not interested in work and, inevitably drifts into petty crime and gets sent to Borstal.

He is resentful about "the system" and takes a strange way of getting back at it. A natural born runner ("we had plenty of practice in running away from the police in our family," he says bitterly), he is selected to represent Borstal in a long distance race against a public school team. It is the ambition of the governor (Michael Redgrave) to win the cup for Borstal. But Courtenay gets his socalled revenge on "the system" by deliberately losing the race when he has victory in his hands.

It is a dubious climax which doesn't fully make the author's point but, as Courtenay trains for the race, there are logical and excellent ways of flashbacking to the events that lead up to his sentence. He gives an impressive performance of brooding sulkiness and wry humor, and must be marked as a new actor to watch. Michael Redgrave as the rather pompous, stuffy governor who, to Courtenay's jaundiced eye, represents "the system," brings his polished touch to a role that could have become irritating.

They are supported by several other interesting performances, notably Avis Bunnage, as Courtenay's sluttish mother; James Bolam, as his fellow delinquent, and Alec McCowen, as a psychiatrist, a part which unfortunately, and inexplicably, fades out early.

Richardson's fluent, imaginative direction is helped considerably via some superb photography by Lassally. John Addison's music, while harping overmuch on the "Jerusalem" theme, is particularly impressive during the lonely scenes when the long distance runner is way out in front with his own thoughts. Borstal atmosphere appears to have been captured accurately and so are most of the drab urban scenes. Major snag is the Midlands accent which is often difficult to grasp accurately. *Rich.*

Kamikaze
(DOCUMENTARY)

Coupled with "Smashing of the Reich," and likewise well-done documentation. But a heavy dose of warfare on one bill could numb some viewers.

Brigadier Film Associates release of an Irja production, produced by Perry Wolf.

Writer, Wolf; music, Norman Dello Joio; narration, Duncan Elliot. Reviewed in New York, Oct. 1, '62. Running time, **89 MINS.**

This playmate to the same producer's "Smashing of the Reich" (see separate review) is likewise a very competent reprise, in this case the Pacific war. Either pic of itself, however, seems a sufficient quota for an audience; but pairing them, as distrib Brigadier Film Associates intends, might be overboarding the war-is-hell-stuff. After a time it gets numbing.

Producer-scripter Perry Wolf has, again, collated and edited some superb clips for a document that spans the pre-Pearl Harbor preparations (Japanese) to the Yank's A-bomb knockout blows. Again, too, much of the footage appears fresh, with considerable oddment for Occidental eyes. As for instance, scenes of the Japanese homefront, including some dilly shots of youngsters making with "war games."

"Kamikaze" (title, of course, refers to the Japanese suicide pilots) makes a strong point at the outset that plenty of evidence was available an attack on Pearl Harbor was imminent in the days just before it came off. To each sign, however (including decoded messages, the sighting of planes, etc.), U.S. inaction was the response, and the forever-dangling question is why. The Pearl Harbor debacle is preceded by alternating sequences of Japanese preparations and the good Hawaiian life of the tourists and seamen, an effective prolog to the piece.

Wolf has again scripted in deference to the eye, and Duncan Elliot's delivery is properly dispassionate. Norman Dello Joio has contributed another able score.

Of those battle shots, they're excellent but, after a time, it gets to be too much of a chilling, staggering thing. The message, one hopes, should get through: war isn't for humans. *Pit.*

Le Diable et les Dix Commandements

(The Devil and the 10 Commandments) (FRENCH—FRANSCOPE)

Paris, Oct. 2.

Cinedis release of Mondex-Filmsonor-Procinex-INCEI production. With Charles Aznavour, Jean-Claude Brialy, Danielle Darrieux, Alain Delon, Fernandel, Mel Ferrer, Madeleine Robinson, Francoise Arnoul, Claude Dauphin, Micheline Presle, Lino Ventura, Michel Simon, Georges Wilson, Louis De Funes. Directed by Julien Duvivier. Screenplay, Duvivier, Rene Barjavel, Pascal Jardin, Henri Jeanson, Michel Audiard; camera, Roger Fellous; music, Jacques Brel, Gilbert Becaud, Charles Aznavour. At Marignan, Paris. Running time, **120 MINS.**

Denis .... Charles Aznavour
Clerk .... Jean-Claude Brialy
Clarisse .... Danielle Darrieux
Son .... Alain Delon
Patient .... Fernandel
Philippe .... Mel Ferrer
Mother .... Madeleine Robinson
Mistress .... Francoise Arnoul
Husband .... Claude Dauphin
Wife .... Micheline Presle
Gangster .... Lino Ventura
Thief .... Louis De Funes
Plumber .... Michel Simon
Father .... Georges Wilson

Following up on the sketch film cycle comes another with one director interpreting the 10 Commandments in an ironic insouciant manner and with a bevy of star names at his disposal. This has a few episodes below par but with enough diverting gambits to slant it for foreign playoff and even arty spots on its names, intermittent wit and general sprightliness.

The few dramatic skeins suffer from a lack of character depth in short segments and force things to the point of hokum and melodrama. But some comic bits benefit from the right sort of wry comedics to bring them off. Episodes have the Devil himself as a commentator and demonically showing how the 10 Commandments can sometimes work against those who try to abide by them or use them as a shield rather than a way of life.

One has a plumber in a nunnery prone to prououncing the name of the Lord in vain. Taken to task, he has to learn the commandments into which act gets the Devil and the illustrative ensuing sketches on various commandments.

A wife tires of her rich husband and the wife of a friend gives in to her husband for a necklace. But in trying to smuggle it in without her husband knowing it ends up as a gift to the wife of the giver. Then a priest takes vengeance on a gangster who has been responsible for his sister's suicide by forcing him to kill him, the hitch being it is suicide for him too even if he gets the man. Another episode has a man announcing he is God. He changes things for a peasant family only to end up a mental patient.

A young man finds out his nagging mother is not his real one. He goes off to see his actual mother, a noted actress. But she almost seduces him before she finds out who he is. As a result, he decides the woman who brought him up is a better person than his real mother. A thief is shaken down by a blackmailer but they both lose out when they accidentally change the bag containing loot with that of a worker.

This segmented affair relies on trick endings rather than actual pointed insight and flair in the episodes. Some are telegraphed or forced but the one on stealing has fine comic touches because of the expert thesping of Louis De Funes. Oldtimer Julien Duvivier has given this lush, workable but uninspired mounting. Production dress is good. In short, this has some hypo points on its idea, but calls for careful selling. *Mosk.*

The Boys

(BRITISH)

Juvenile delinquency under the microscope again. A prolonged court case, enlivened, occasionally, but sometimes bogged down by flashbacks. Always holding because of Richard Todd and Robert Morley as respective counsels. Good prospects.

London, Sept. 14.

Gala Film release of a Galaworldfilm production. Stars Richard Todd, Robert Morley. Produced and directed by Sydney J. Furie; screenplay by Stuart Douglass; editor, Jack Slade; music, "The Shadows"; camera, Gerald Gibbs. Previewed at National Film Theatre, London, Sept. 12, '62. Running time, **124 MINS.**

Victor Webster .... Richard Todd
Montgomery .... Robert Morley
Judge .... Felix Aylmer
Stan Coulter .... Dudley Setton
Billy Herne .... Ronald Lacey
Ginger Thompson .... Tony Garnett
Barney Lee .... Jess Conrad
Robert Brewer .... Wilfred Bramble

Sydney J. Furie, a young energetic Canadian, established himself as a topline director with "The Young Ones," a click musical in the United Kingdom. Maybe he's a shade unwise with this effort to have saddled himself with the twin chores of director and producer. But it comes out as a workmanlike job that could have been rather better with more ruthless cutting and a bit more bite in the sturdy screenplay of Stuart Douglass.

It's another study of juvenile delinquency, but interest is kept alive because of suspense geared adroitly on the theme of whether or not the boys in the dock are guilty. There are four of them, accused of the murder of a garage nightwatchman. Richard Todd, prosecuting, relentlessly plants in the audience's mind they are guilty young thugs. Robert Morley, defending, makes the viewers wonder. Flashbacks, over-prolonged, keep the audience pondering. Then comes a final switch which upsurges interest. Real problem that is posed is whether the British law is archaic in that it insists that a murder done for pleasure or passion can still enable the murderers to escape the noose. But, if it's done for gain, then the character is doomed to execution.

In this case the loot is a mere couple of dollars, but the principle remains the same. The four boys set out on a night of high jinks which leads to tragedy. The result is trial and the court sequences, like most, offer the tension and drama that make for good cinema. But this depends entirely on good acting and this film has its full quota. Todd, an earnest, humorless prosecutor, does one of his best bits of thesping and he has an excellent foil in defending counsel Morley, who adds his own distinctive touches of comedy to his orations.

The four boys are fine, particularly Dudley Setton and Jess Conrad, a pop singer who is aspiring to dramatic roles and earning the right to have them. There are also some excellent smaller contributions by such skilled performers as Wilfred Bramble, Alan Cuthbertson, Colin Gordon, Betty Marsden, Patrick Magee, Felix Aylmer, Harold Scott and Laurence Hardy. Their parts are written so certainly that none can fail.

When the film drops it is because of several too facile flashbacks which give "The Boys" plenty of chances, but slow down the action. Some are not necessary. But Furie otherwise keeps a firm hold on the proceedings and Gerald Gibbs' lensing matches the authenticity of the courtroom and sleazy late night West End scenes.

Sound pic that puts over a point of view with sincerity. *Rich.*

The Dock Brief

(BRITISH)

Arty, bolstered-up version of a radio and stage playlet which may stimulate wicket interest via its stars, Peter Sellers and Richard Attenborough. But it will need help from the sales department.

London, Sept. 25.

Metro release of a Dimitri De Grunwald production. Stars Peter Sellers, Richard Attenborough; features Beryl Reid, David Lodge, Frank Pettingell, Audrey Nicholson, Tristram Jellinek. Directed by James Hill. Screenplay by Pierre Rouve, from John Mortimer's play; camera, Edward Scaife; editor, Ann Chegwidden; music, Ron Grainer. At Plaza Theatre, London. Running time, **88 MINS.**

Morgenhall .... Peter Sellers
Fowle .... Richard Attenborough
Doris .... Beryl Reid
Bateson .... David Lodge
Tuppy Morgan .... Frank Pettingell
Perkins .... Tristram Jellinek
Morgenhall's Girl.....Audrey Nicholson
Judge Banter .... Eric Woodburn
Clerk of Court .... John Waite
First Warder .... Patrick Newell
Second Warder .... Henry Kay
Photographer .... Frank Thornton
Examiner .... Eric Dodson

This offbeat, arty film gets away to a good start with the stellar pull of Peter Sellers and Richard Attenborough, but it will still need sturdy salesmanship to get it moving in the less discriminating houses. It is less a narrative film than a duel in thesping between two proven performers and there are some thin passages where scriptwriter Pierre Rouve obviously had to pad out the story line. Originally a radio play by John Mortimer, it is a bold attempt by Dimitri De Grunwald to present something different and, on the whole, it's a fair try.

Sellers plays an aging, unsuccessful barrister who gets the chance of a lifetime when briefed to defend Attenborough, a mild birdseed merchant who has murdered his wife because he wanted peace. He is bored with her because of her raucous sense of humor. It is the last straw when she doesn't elope with their equally raucous and boisterous lodger. Sellers plans his campaign optimistically and is quite undaunted when Attenborough admits the crime and shows the flaws in all Sellers defense arguments.

The lawyer turns Attenborough's cell into a courtroom and the two rehearse the case thoroughly. But at the trial everything goes wrong. Sellers' rhetoric crumbles and Attenborough is found guilty. But the wry, ironic twist is that he is reprieved on the grounds that his lawyer was so crassly inefficient that he didn't receive a fair trial.

The screenplay is a literate job, with a deft mixture of comedy and pathos. Sellers has the opportunity of showing many moods and much of his work is good. But there is a danger that he is being overexposed and some of the tricks are beginning to show up. He is in peril of giving a string of excellent imitations and impersonations rather than a sustained performance. Attenborough comes out of the acting duel rather better. He too, playing the mock judge, mock winesses, mock jurymen, as well as the murderer, has plenty of opportunity of showing his versatility and he gives a well thought-out, intelligent performance.

Remainder of the cast hasn't such opportunity. However, Beryl Reid, as the wife; David Lodge, as the lodger; and Tristram Jellinek, as the prosecuting counsel, have some excellent moments. James Hill's direction is smooth but the action of the yarn is uneven and some of the twists are readily predictable. Lensing by Edward

Scaife, editing by Ann Chegwidden and Ron Grainer's music are all satisfactory. *Rich.*

Le Repos Du Guerrier
(Warrior's Rest)
(FRENCH—COLOR—FRANSCOPE)
Paris, Oct. 2.

Cocinor release of FranCos Film-INCEI Film production. Stars Brigitte Bardot, Robert Hossein; features, Jacqueline Porel, Michel Serrault, Jean-Marc Bory, Robert Dalban. Directed by Roger Vadim. Screenplay, Vadim, Claude Choublier from novel by Christiane Rochefort; camera (Eastmancolor), Armand Thirard; editor, Victoria Mercanton. At Venice Film Fest. Running time, **100 MINS.**

Genevieve .... Brigitte Bardot
Renaud .... Robert Hossein
Pierre .... Jean-Marc Bory
Raphaele .... Micheyl Meril
Sculptor ...... James Robertson Justice
Mother .... Jacqueline Porel

After veteran directors Claude Autant-Lara and H. G. Clouzot, Roger Vadim now tries to make a dramatic actress of Brigitte Bardot. It still does not quite come off but Vadim, who created her in "And God Created Woman," has a shrewd eye for her capabilities and has her adequate in this tale of a prim girl who is initiated into love by a destructive alcoholic.

All of this is lushly told. It has a great deal of suggestiveness and shrewdly concealed nudity. This could have this as a specialized and playoff bet with the Bardot name and its scenes of an elegant bohemian world okay selling points. Miss Bardot's famed frank and pouting natural sex kitten aspects are throttled in this to depict the finding of physical love.

She is an inhibited, middleclass girl at the beginning, more interested in bank accounts and settling down with a boy she does not particularly love than in any adventure. She goes to collect an inheritance in a small town and by mistake enters another room in a hotel where she finds a man who has taken an overdose of sleeping pills.

He is saved and she suddenly finds herself saddled with him, and physical love blooms. She brings him back to Paris and they hole up in her apartment for lovemaking, drinking, fights and his steady attempt to drag her down with him and not to give in to a growing love for her.

He finally does in hokey scene in a ruined Church in Florence, Italy, where he shouts for her to marry him as the wind whips her unruly hair. So this has Miss Bardot playing as a redeemer, rather than a symbol of destructive sex. After her awakening she goes through hell as he reduces her to all sorts of degradations. He even picks up a joy girl and goes off with her while in her company.

But Miss Bardot wins out. Director Vadim displays a glossy flair for languid necking parties, brittle, supposedly intellectual tirades about love and society. Miss Bardot looks alternately fresh and marked as she goes through her calvary to finally find love that is both human as well as physical.

Robert Hossein has the smug, hurt arrogance for the role of the alcoholic lover. Other parts are well taken. But all this revolves about Miss Bardot's charms. Vadim cleverly tries to mask this in another character. It is Miss Bardot who has to sell this pic abroad, aided by the canny sensuality which is always masked in an effort to avoid censorship problems and still have a titillating quality that might give it a word-of-mouth plus.

Miss Bardot does speak her lines with more assurance and authority, and does have her moments when she can be her sexy childish self. It looks to be a solid grossing entry here and with the right placement, selling and programming could possibly beat the jinx that has settled on Bardot pix in the U.S. of late. Film is technically solid. *Mosk.*

Patterson-Liston Fight
Allied Artists release of Graff, Reiner & Smith production, produced by Manny Spiro. Camera director, Frank Zucker; editorial supervisor, Leonard Anderson; narration, Chris Schenkel. Reviewed in New York, Sept. 27, '62. Running time, **13 MINS.**

Except for a humbug script, Allied Artists' theatrical release of the Chicago fiasco is a fine job of sharp, well-edited footage. Producer Manny Spiro is an experienced hand at these productions, and the reel reflects his savvy. Most of it, perforce, is padding—color stuff fore and after the bout, and including the automatic slow-motion reprise of the knockout. Clearly, it was a stinging left cross that spun the champ off the ropes and decked him for the count.

Beyond that, there's some interest in the post-kayo frames, with the ring hysteria as press and broadcast contingent swarmed around. Of the fighters, only pick-up on the track is Patterson's true-blue remark that new champ Liston should have his chance for public favor.

Spiro's crew, as on previous fight pix, includes Frank Zucker as camera director and Leonard Anderson as editorial supervisor. Again, too, it's Chris Schenkel's voice over, and without phony hysterics. Photography is unusually sharp throughout. All things considered, a worthy recap that at least answers the "question" as to payoff punch. *Pit.*

Carnival of Souls

First production by Lawrence, Kans., company emerges as lightweight ghost story, capably done and technically okay but thin. For lower half of easier duals.

Lawrence, Kans., Sept. 27.

Herts-Lion International-American International release of Harcourt Productions production. Cast, Candace Hilligoss, Frances Feist, Sidney Berger, Stanley Leavitt, Art Ellison, Hark Harvey, Tom McGinnis, Forbes Caldwell. Produced and directed by Harvey. Screenplay, John Clifford from original by Clifford and Harvey. Camera, Maurice Prather. Editors, Dan Palmquist, Bill DeJarnette. Music, Gene Moore. Titles, Dan Fitzgerald. Sound, Ed Down. Assistant director, Reza Bariyi. Production manager, Larry Sneegas. Reviewed at world premiere Granada Theatre, Lawrence, Kans., Sept. 26, 1962. Running time, **80 MINS.**

Occasionally a feature film emerges from the midwest, although this is the first ever out of Lawrence, Kans., where a group of commercial film pros veered off into a try at producing theatrical entertainment. As the first from Harcourt Productions, "Carnival of Souls" is a creditable can of film, considering it was put together for less than $100,000.

The ghost story, on a format more familiar in literature, has Candace Hilligoss, a dressy blonde, and a couple of gal pals, nudged off of a bridge and a watery death in the swirling river. She surprisingly emerges from the river and lifelike enough goes on to an eerie existence as a new organist at a Salt Lake City church through the balance of the film.

An old pavilion in a sad state of disintegration peculiarly fascinates her, but pasty faces and fantasies swirl about her, and intermittently head ghost, Harvey, appears from mirrors and pools to chill her and the audience. In the end the battered car is dragged from the river and is seen to contain the bodies of the three dead girls. The audience then knows that Miss Hilligoss as Mary has been but a lovely and haunted phantom through about 75 of the film's 80 minutes.

It isn't enough story to prevail, but there is a fair share of suspense and some moments of good comedy. Veteran trouper Frances Feist is standout as the landlady who rents a room to the lithesome haunt, and Miss Hilligoss with a sort of misty quality about her does creditably as the lovely soul without a heart. Sidney Berger, University of Kansas speech instructor, does well with the role of the roomer across the hall who would like to make out with the fascinating phantom, but can't quite put his paws on her.

Capable supporting roles are handled by Stanley Leavitt as the doctor, Art Ellison as the Minister, and Harvey as the ghost menace. Pace is satisfactory, but judicious snipping could take out a rough spot or two and five minutes from the running time. Most of the technical crew have some affiliation with Centron Studios, commercial film producers, at Lawrence, and interiors were shot there.

Premiere at the Granada Theatre, Lawrence, was largely for hometown consumption. *Quin.*

We'll Bury You

Documentary on the rise of Communism. Flashy trade and consumer selling could make it "sleeper" b.o. click.

Hollywood, Oct. 4.

Columbia Pictures release of Jack Leewood-Jack W. Thomas production. Written by Thomas; narrator, William Woodson; editors, Alan Presberg, Philip R. Rosenberg; sound, Continental Sound Corp.; special effects, Ray Mercer & Co. Reviewed at the studio, Oct. 4, 1962. Running time, **77 MINS.**

Columbia's "We'll Bury You" could well be this year's boxoffice "sleeper," just as "Mein Kampf," the Swedish historical, came virtually out of nowhere last year to became a commercial click and launch a rash of imitations.

Underlying its inflammatory, bombastic title, the apparent fuse for what promises to be an explosive exploitation campaign, "We'll Bury You" is actually a kind of pocket-size illustrated history of the rise of Communism in Russia and satellite countries, beginning with its German creator, Karl Marx, and concluding with a plea for the free world to rise to the Red challenge. In between is an often fascinating and sufficiently informative study of the topic, marred only by the narrative's occasional tendency to waver from an objective, factual tone and lapse into an overly emotional disposition, particularly as the historical story advances toward the less detached, more ominous present. Facts themselves are stark and shocking enough to get the message over without such narrative embellishment.

The film clips are often altogether astonishing. Rarely seen crude footage of such figures as Lenin and Trotsky in action is priceless. There are also some extremely dramatic shots, such as that of a Russian warship sinking during the Russo-Japanese War, with hundreds of seamen pouring over the side like terrified ants. Periodic shots of mutilated corpses the result of various political purges and mass execution seem, however, almost needlessly brutal. Only twice, and then briefly, does the narration give way to the original sound-on-film—once the voice of Churchill, the other a portion of the Nixon-Khrushchev "Kitchen Debate."

Overall, it is an adroit and enterprising job of compilation and execution, from producers Jack Leewood and Jack W. Thomas on down. Thomas penned the narrative, spoken by William Woodson. Dr. Robert W. Lowe of Georgetown University served as script consultant. Especially strong credits are those of editors Alan Presberg and Philip R. Rosenberg and researchers Donald Armstrong and John Detra. *Tube.*

Le Bonheur Est Pour Demain
(Happiness Is for Tomorrow)
Paris, Oct. 9.

Prodis release of Fred Tavano production. With Jacques Higelin, Irene Chabrier, Henri Crolla, Jean Martinelli, Gina Manes. Directed by Henri Fabiani. Screenplay, Edouard Sergent, Henri Graziani, Fabiani; camera, Jean Pnezer; editor, A. Levi-Alvares; music, Henri Crolla. At Studio 43, Paris. Running time, **85 MINS.**

Alain .... Jacques Higelin
Annie .... Irene Chabrier

Jose .... Henri Crolla
De Guen .... Jean Martinelli
Woman .... Gina Manes

Somewhat schematic and surface in the treatment of story and characters, this pic is still one of the first to treat the acual worker problem here. It has a tendency towards forced poetics, but imbedded in it is a nice feel for youth coming of age and a little-seen part of French life. Film is primarily for special situations abroad.

A young man runs off from home and is helped by a shipyard worker. He gets enamored of a pretty young secretary and takes a job in the shipyard. But his unformed desires for something better, his inability to compromise, have him ready to run out on the girl and his new friend.

But she tells him off, in all of youth's brutality. So he runs off and climbs a high crane, presumably to throw himself off. But the girl's father climbs up and talks him out of jumping. He points out that study, work and his daughter are worth more than a pointless, rash act.

The late Henri Crolla, who was a guitarist and songwriter, shows a projection and humanity, as the friend, that would have probably made him a fine actor. The others also are good. Director Henri Fabiani displays a feel for the simple scenic unrolling of ordinary life.

It just lacks a more inspired, deeper insight into the characters. This remains on a literary level while the work itself has a ring of authority. When Fabiani melds his documentary flair with an ability to make real characters part of this he could emerge a new director of importance. As is, it is an okay first effort. Production aspects and technical qualities are good. *Mosk.*

La Planque
(The Hideout)
(FRENCH)

Paris, Oct. 9.
Paramount release of CAF-Hoche Films production. With Mouloudji, Louise Carletti, Francis Blanche, Robert Porte. Directed by Raoul Andre. Screenplay, Yves Jamiaque, Andre; camera, Marcel Weiss; editor, Gabriel Rongier. At Elysees, Paris. Running time, **90 MINS.**
Georges .... Mouloudji
Giselle .... Louise Carletti
Edouard .... Francis Blanche
Doctor .... Yves Vincent
Patient .... Robert Porte
Director .... Jacques Dumesnil
Mado .... Maria Vincent

A good idea for an offbeat suspense item is not quite brought off because it lacks penetrating direction and playing. If it misses the foreign art house depth, this pic could still be a playoff item or specialized entry on its fairly well sustained tale.

A partisan in France during the occupation is hidden from the Gestapo by a friend who runs an asylum. But the friend is arrested and the partisan kills an informer planted among the patients. But nobody believes his story and he is almost driven mad himself except for the help of a young doctor and a patient's daughter who has taken a liking to him.

They try to find someone who can back his tale but fail. He escapes and his picture in the newspaper leads to someone showing up to clear him.

The thin borderline between madness and sanity is invoked, as well as the irony of almost martyred heroism. But director Raoul Andre has not been able to punch this up, and the film has a way of lagging its tempo and dramatics. Thesping also does not quite give the characters the edge they need.

Hence this shapes for the most part a neat second feature just missing the solidity and treatment of its clever plotting to make it offshore art house fodder. The asylum inmates and atmosphere are the plus portion of this fine little film. It has an okay technical envelope. *Mosk.*

Cielo Rojo
(Red Sky)
(MEXICAN—COLOR—SCOPE)

Mexico City, Oct. 9.
Peliculas Nacionales release of CICSA production. Stars Rodolfo de Anda, Patricia Conde, Sonia Furlo; features Rita Nacedo, Dagoberto Rodriguez, Felix Gonzalez, Pablito Marichal, Luis Aceves Castaneda and Fanny Schiller. Directed by Gilberto Gazoon. Screenplay by Raul de Anda, from play, "Wings of the Fish," by Fernando Sanchez Mayans. Adaptation by Fernando Galiana. At Alameda Theatre, Mexico City. Running time, **90 MINS.**

This film is based on the prize-winning play "Las Alas del Pez" (Wings of the Fish), by playwright Fernando Sanchez Mayans. Action laid in Acapulco. Plot concerns one of the young Quebrada Cliff high divers. Rodolfo de Anda, youngest son of the elder de Anda, plays this role.

Rodolfo as son of a foundered marriage, which has embittered his mother (excellently interpreted by Rita Macedo), leaves home to try his wings in the world. His mother's attempts at directing him into a good, affluent citizen only irritate the lad who feels he can personally find love, maturity and the tenderness he has never known. But his impetuous youth makes him hurt the people he touches. Including a young girl (Sonia Furio), who also seeks love and understanding.

Direction by Gazcon is strong and full of realism at times. In other scenes he falters, and there is a tendency to overdo melodrama in certain sequences. There is some overacting, possibly due to the youth of the principal players. Patricia Conde is comely, but she carries off the role of a deceived girl. Standout is young de Anda, a natural actor. Sonia Furio, Luis Aceves Castaneda and others turn in satisfactory performances.

The star without credit is Acapulco itself. There are times when film has appearance of a tourist propaganda documentary. Raul de Anda Jr. produced.

A better than average Mexican effort, despite its faults, that should do well in Spanish language areas because of the stature of dramatic work on which it is based. *Emil.*

Little Humpbacked Horse
(RUSSIAN—COLOR)

Artkino release of Central Documentary Films Studio production. Stars Maya Plisetskaya and the Bolshoi Ballet. Directed by Alexander Radunsky. Music, Schedrin; conductor of Bolshoi Theatre Orch. Zhuraitis. At Cameo, N.Y., starting Oct. 6, '62. Running time, **85 MINS.**
Queen Maiden .... Maya Plisetskaya
Ivan .... Vladimir Vasilyev
Little Humpbacked Horse
.... Anya Scher Binina
The King .... Alexander Radunsky
(*English Narration*)

This ballet pic is probably the finest of its kind to come out of Russia in some time. Production should reap plenty of peace at the Cameo where a run of several weeks is in prospect. Production stars Maya Plisetskaya, new prima ballerina replacing Talina Ulanova now touring U.S. Plisetskaya is quite photogenic and is helped by some excellent camera work (lensman is not credited) in closeups.

Billed as a Fairy Tale in Magicolor, this is a filmed version of a Russo-concocted yarn, done at the Bolshoi Theatre. Many of the sets loudly proclaim that it is photographed in a theatre.

Starting quite slowly even for a Russian pic, camera and narrator attempt to explain how Ivan (Vladimir Vasilyev) obtained his humpbacked horse, which is supposed to bring him luck, and, of course, it does. The usual implausibile fairy tale has Ivan, because he's a nice guy, given three horses, including the lucky one (Anya Scherbinina). Ivan's two brothers steal two of the horses and try to sell them to the king (Alexander Radunsky).

Through Anya's guidance, Ivan circumvents the sale and becomes No. 1 stable boy, a sort of right-hand man to the king. But he winds up with the task of trying to locate the Queen Maiden because the crowned monarch falls in love with her. All of this brings plenty of dancing by Miss Plisetskaya and Vasilyev. Then there's an under-water ballet and, of course, the hero triumphs via the lucky presence of Anya, the humpbacked horse.

As long as this film sticks to dancing, it is great entertainment, despite the laborious plot. When the producers try to ring in miniatures and special effects that's exactly what they look like—minnies and arty effects. Color is a bit above par for Russian pix, being listed as Magicolor. *Wear.*

The Manchurian Candidate

Firstrate, offbeat suspense drama. One of the year's big grossers.

United Artists release of M. C. Production (Howard W. Koch executive producer; George Axelrod, John Frankenheimer, producers, directed by John Frankenheimer. Stars Frank Sinatra, Laurence Harvey, Janet Leigh; features Angela Lansbury, Henry Silva, James Gregory, Leslie Parrish. Screenplay by George Axelrod, based on novel by Richard Condon; music, David Amram; camera, Lionel Lindon; editor, Ferris Webster; asst. director, Joseph Behm. Reviewed in New York, Sept. 27, '62. Running time, **126 MINS.**
Bennett Marco .... Frank Sinatra
Raymond Shaw .... Laurence Harvey
Rosie .... Janet Leigh
Raymond's mother .....Angela Lansbury
Chunjin .... Henry Silva
Senator John Iselin...... James Gregory
Jocie Jordon .... Leslie Parrish
Senator Thomas Jordon.... John McGiver
Yen Lo ....: .... Khigh Dhiegh
Corporal Melvin .... James Edwards
Colonel .... Douglas Henderson
Zilkov .... Albert Paulsen
Secretary of Defense..... Barry Kelley
Holborn Gaines .... Lloyd Corrigan
Berezovo .... Madame Spivy

Every once in a rare while a film comes along that "works" in all departments, with story, production and performance so well blended that the end effect is one of nearly complete satisfaction. Such is "The Manchurian Candidate." George Axelrod and John Frankenheimer's jazzy, hip screen translation of Richard Condon's bestselling novel. With Frank Sinatra, Laurence Harvey, Janet Leigh and Angela Lansbury all giving top performances, the picture not only has strong built-in boxoffice values, but the controversial makings for the kind of word-of-mouth that turns a good grosser into a blockbuster.

The exact nature of "Manchurian Candidate" may be hard to define, but perhaps "suspense melodrama" is the best term. Its story of the tracking down of a brainwashed Korean war "hero," being used as the key figure in an elaborate Communist plot to take over the U.S. government, is, on the surface, one of the wildest fabrications any author has ever tried to palm off on a gullible public. But the fascinating thing is that, from uncertain premise to shattering conclusion, one does not question plausibility: the events being rooted in their own cinematic reality.

As scripted by Axelrod and directed by Frankenheimer, who also double as coproducers under exec producer Howard W. Koch, "Manchurian Candidate" gets off to an early start (before the credits) as a dilemma wrapped in an enigma; a small American patrol in Korea is captured by the Chinese Communists. Shortly thereafter, the sergeant of the group, Laurence Harvey, is seen being welcomed home to Washington as a Congressional Medal of Honor winner, having been recommended for that award by his captain, Frank Sinatra, who led the illfated patrol. But something is obviously wrong. Harvey himself admits to being the least likely of heroes, and Sinatra, though he testifies that the sergeant is "the bravest, most honorable, most loyal" man he knows, realizes this is completely untrue. But why?

The captain's subsequent pursuit of the truth comprises the bizarre plot which ranges from the halls of Congress, New York

publishing circles and an extremely unlikely Communist hideout in mid-Manhattan, to a literally stunning climax at a Madison Square Garden political convention.

Like all the best films, there probably has never been anything quite like "The Manchurian Candidate" before, though in sheer bravado of narrative and photographic styles it shares the tradition of Hitchcock, Capra, Welles and Hawks. In character and incidental comment, it displays irreverence towards hallowed cliches, be they (all-consuming) mother love, the commercialization of Christmas ("'The 12 Days of Christmas'?—one day is quite loathsome enough"), Iron Curtain spies (here the Russ agent is an apprehensive boor and the Chinese a whimsical, literate mind from outer Manchuria, if not space), to say nothing of homegrown political frauds who hide behind portraits of Abe Lincoln. A major character in the proceedings is a thinly disguised takeoff on the late Sen. Joseph McCarthy, played with farcical but devastating gusto by James Gregory. "The Manchurian Candidate" thus restores a topical excitement to American films which has been almost totally lacking since Hollywoodites started taking up residence abroad. This film could not have been made anywhere but in the U.S.

"Candidate" must inevitably come up for a bundle of Oscar nominations next spring. Most likely to succeed is Angela Lansbury, whose performance as Harvey's scheming, caustic mother ("Raymond, why do you always have to look as if your head were about to come to a point?") is one of the most poignant and diamond-hard of the ear. Equally good is Harvey, who succeeds in making appealing a character correctly described as "completely unlovable"—by far his best role since "Room at the Top." Also ripe for kudos are Frankenheimer, as director, and Axelrod, for best script from another medium.

Less showy, but no less effective, is Sinatra who, after several pix in which he appeared to be sleep-walking, is again a wide-awake pro creating a straight, quietly humorous character of some sensitivity. A pleasant surprise is Janet Leigh as a sweet, swinging N.Y. career girl. The actress only has two or three scenes, but they count. One especially, on a Washington-to-New York train in which she picks up a semi-hysterical Sinatra, registers as one of the great love scenes since Bogart and Bacall first tossed non-sequiturs at one another in "To Have and Have Not." ("Are you Arabic?" asks Miss Leigh, "Or, to put it another way, are you married?"). One of the brilliant achievements of the film is the way Axelrod and Frankenheimer have been able to blend the diverse moods, including the tender and explosively funny as well as the satiric and brutally shocking.

Supporting work, with perhaps one exception, is fine. Henry Silva is suitably sinister as a Red agent and pretty Leslie Parrish is lively and believable as Harvey's illfated romance. Only John McGiver, as a liberal senator who, presumably, should be appealing, since he's portrayed as being on the side of

right, strikes a false note. It's a mannered, pompous performance right out of summer stock.

Some mention should be made too of the form of the film. Though it includes three flashbacks (two of which are hypnotically weird dream sequences), the picture moves forward with a constantly increasing tension and momentum which never allow for audience second-guessing of the macabre plot twists or coincidences. The quick cuts and tricky juxtaposition of scenes match the flamboyance of the script. So do Lionel Lindon's slick b/w photography and Ferris Webster's editing. David Amram's music is a witty, though never obtrusive counterpoint to the action.   *Anby.*

Dr. No
(BRITISH—TECHNICOLOR)

Ian Fleming's Secret Service agent-hero, J a m e s Bond, comes to the screen for the first time in a piece of amusing, hokey action. Ought to please generally.

London, Oct. 4.

United Artists release of Harry Saltzman & Albert R. Broccoli presentation for Eon Productions. Stars Sean Connery. Directed by Terence Young. Screenplay by Richard Maibaum, Johanna Harwood & Berkely Mather; based on Ian Fleming's story, editor, Peter Hunt; camera, Ted Moore; music, Monty Norman. Previewed at Pavilion, London, Oct. 2, '62. Running time, 110 MINS.

James Bond .... Sean Connery
Honey .... Ursula Andress
Dr. No .... Joseph Wiseman
Felix Leiter .... Jack Lord
M .... Bernard Lee
Professor Dent .... Anthony Dawson
Quarrel .... John Kitzmiller
Miss Taro .... Zena Marshall
Sylvia .... Eunice Gayson
Miss Moneypenny ....Lois Maxwell
Strangways .... Tim Moxon
Girl Photographer ......Margaret LeWars

First screen adventure of Ian Fleming's hardhitting, fearless, imperturbable, girl-loving Secret Service Agent 007, James Bond, is an entertaining piece of tongue-in-cheek action hokum. It's to be the first of a series which should be both popular and profitable. Not designed for sophisticates but for those who like straightforward action laced with humor.

Picked to portray Bond is rugged Sean Connery, a stalwart, confident actor who looks as if he may have landed himself a career as Bond. He excellently puts over a cool, fearless, on-the-ball, fictional Secret Service guy. Terence Young has directed with a pace which only occasionally lags. He and script throw in plenty of conventional, but acceptable melodrama gimmicks.

The hero is exposed to pretty (and sometimes treacherous) gals, a poison tarantula spider, a sinister crook, flame throwers, gunshot, bloodhounds, beating up, near drowning and plenty of other mayhem and malarkey, and comes through it all with good humor, resourcefulness and what have you.

Connery, as Secret Service Agent 007 (the 00 means he is licensed to kill, and does) is sent to Jamaica to investigate the murder of a British confidential agent and his secretary. Since both murders happen within three or four minutes of the credit titles the pic gets away to an exhilarating start. He becomes involved with the activities of Dr. No, a sinister Chinese scientist (Joseph Wise-

man) who from an island called Crab Key is using a nuclear laboratory to divert off course the rockets being propelled from Cape Canaveral. Connery gets into plenty of trouble when he penetrates Dr. No's h.q.

Wiseman is a bland heavy, Anthony Dawson a shifty geological professor, Bernard Lee an authoritative Secret Service chief, Jack Lord a C.I.A. man, and John Kitzmiller a Jamaican aide to Connery. Sometimes Kitzmiller is compelled to revert to that now old-fashioned type of Clarence Muse colored actor mugging but, overall, comes out as a forceful personality. Among the dames with whom Connery becomes involved are easy-on-the-eye Ursula Andress, who shares his perilous adventures on Crab Key, and spends most of her time in a bikini, Zena Marshall as an Oriental charmer who nearly decoys him to doom via her boudoir and Eunice Gayson, whom he picks up in a gambling club in London and who promises to be the biggest menace of the lot. But she is an irrevelant doll who fades out of the pic when Connery is switched to Jamaica.

Ted Moore has done a swell job with his lush color photography of the West Indies and Monty Norman's music and Peter Hunt's editing are both technically okay. Production values in this pic are topclass including some polished artwork and ingenious scientific special effects. As a screen hero James Bond is clearly here to stay. He will win no Oscars but a heck of a lot of enthusiastic followers.   *Rich.*

The Password Is Courage
(BRITISH)

Real life war yarn which has been souped up beyond the realms of conviction; Dirk Bogarde's name helps and this could do useful b.o., despite its flaws.

London, Oct. 11.

Metro release of Andrew & Virginia Stone production. Stars Dirk Bogarde; features Maria Perschy, Alfred Lynch, Nigel Stock, Reginald Beckwith, Ferdy Mayne, George Mikell, Olav Pooley. Direction and screenplay by Stone, from John Castle's biography of Charles Coward. Camera, David Boulton; editor, Noreen Ackland (under supervision of Virginia Stone). Previewed at Metro Private Theatre. Running time, 116 MINS.

Charlie Coward .... Dirk Bogarde
Irena .... Maria Perschy
Pope .... Alfred Lynch
Cole .... Nigel Stock
Unterofficer .... Reginald Beckwith
Schmidt .... Richard Marner
Aussie .... Ed Devereaux
Pringle .... Lewis Flander
Necke .... George Mikell
Robinson .... Richard Carpenter
French Farmwoman....Margaret Whiting
German Doctor .... Olav Pooley
1st German Officer........Ferdy Mayne
2nd German Officer....... Olav Pooley
1st German Goon .... Colin Blakely

Based on the wartime adventures of Sergeant-Major Charles Coward, this real life yarn is another in the procession of war stories and, maybe, audiences have had the theme a shade too often. This one has been blown up as a star vehicle for Dirk Bogarde and an opportunity for Andrew and Virginia Stone to exercise their gleeful skill with special effects.

Stone's screenplay, based on a biog of Coward by John Castle, has pumped into its untidy 116

minutes an overdose of slapstick humor. Result is that what could have been a telling tribute to a character of guts and initiative, the kind that every war produces, lacks conviction. It seems too much a confected piece of fiction. Still, Bogarde's name can spell boxoffice and the pic provides easygoing entertainment for the easygoing.

Coward (Bogarde), a breezy, likeable character, becomes a prisoner of war and is dedicated to sabotaging and humiliating his German captors. As senior soldier in Stalag 8B, he rallies the other men to escape so that they can get back to fighting the Nazis. Coward's main problem is to make contact with the Polish underground to get maps, money, etc., before escaping through a 280-foot tunnel which the prisoners have laboriously built. In charge of a batch of prisoners at a lumber yard, he contrives, with his colleagues, to burn down the yard.

He convinces the German officer in charge that it was because the officer was smoking on duty, promises not to report the incident on condition that Coward gets the afternoon off in nearby Breslau, without a guard.

There he contacts a blonde optician and the escape goes through with some tension, but the ringleaders are recaptured and sent to Auschwitz. As the Allies advance, pushing the enemy to the west, Coward and his sidekick, Pope (Alfred Lynch), escape again and join the American lines by commandeering a fire engine and riding triumphantly through occupied villages.

These, and other incidents, sound like something dreamed up by an expansive, imaginative scriptwriter. In "The Password Is Courage," they seem more like reel life than real life. The whole, incredible adventure never seems to hold the feeling of having actually happened.

Bogarde gives a performance that is never less than competent, but never much more. The best male performance comes from Lynch, as Corporal Pope, a philosophical soldier devoted to Coward. He is a composite of several characters in Coward's actual story. Maria Perschy, a personable Hungarian, girl making her first appearance in a British film, brings some glamor to the film as the underground worker. Nigel Stock, Ed Devereaux, Lewis Flander, George Mikell, Ferdy Mayne, Colin Blakeley and several others give Bogarde and Lynch stout aid in support roles.

But the casting of Reginald Beckwith, a typically British character actor, as a Nazi officer pinpoints the fact that all the Germans are made to look like idiots which, again, destroys much of the realism.

The Stones have worked out some sharp technical effects with fire, train sabotage and the like, ably executed by Bill Warrington. David Boulton's lensing does justice to Metroscope and the music (uncredited) is unobtrusively okay.

As a piece of fiction, this film would satisfy the average audiences. As a slice of real life and a tribute to an offbeat character, it is hollow stuff.   *Rich.*

Le Gentleman D'Epsom
(FRENCH—TOTALSCOPE)

Paris, Oct. 9.

UFA-Comacico release of Cipra-Cite Films-CCM production. Stars Jean Gabin; features Paul Frankeur, Frank Villard, Louis De Funes, Madeleine Robinson. Directed by Gilles Grangier. Screenplay, Albert Simonin, Michel Audiard, Grangier; camera, Louis Page; editor, Jacques Desagneaux. At Balzac, Paris. Running time, **83 MINS.**

Richard	Jean Gabin
Maud	Madeleine Robinson
Arthur	Paul Frankeur
Lucien	Frank Villard
Charly	Jean Lefebvre
Ripeux	Louis De Funes

Vet actor Jean Gabin again essays a type of role that has become familiar for him of late. He is an old snob living off racetrack touting, and not above some clever underhand actions. He walks through this role with his usual aplomb, but the pic neglects to build any story or indulge in any deeper characterization. Result is a breezy series of anecdotes that rate this as more of a local than foreign entry, except for possible special situations on the Gabin name.

Gabin's meal ticket is a group of people to whom he gives a different horse in a daily race, with each putting down a bet for him. He is thus bound to win. He also considers himself a great handicapper and does make some killings at times.

One day he meets an old flame and hides his ordinary financial means. She is married to a rich American and in for clothes buying. He takes her on a big night spree, and gives a bad check.

But he gets another sucker and manages to make a great track cleanup by mistake to end this on an upbeat note. But all of this is quite surface and oversimplified. But it gives the still dynamic Gabin another chance to play a domineering role. All this is done with a general breeziness that makes this lightweight affair a good local entry.

Credits are okay and the support is fine. Louis De Funes takes a small role and with his finesse in pointed mugging and timing proves himself to be one of the best comedians around here.

Mosk.

The Quare Fellow
(BRITISH)

Grim 'entertainment,' in intelligent protest against capital punishment based on Brendan Behan's play. Sound leading performances but strength is in the excellence of the small part players all down the line.

London, Oct. 4.

British-Lion release through BLC of a Havelock-Allan production. Stars Patrick McGoohan, Sylvia Syms. Features Walter Macken, Harry Brogan, Marie Kean, Dermot Kelly, John Welsh. Produced by Anthony Havelock-Allan. Written and directed by Arthur Driefuss, from an adaptation of Brendan Behan's play by Jacqueline Sundstrom and Driefuss; camera, Peter Hennessy; editor, Ted Marshall; music, Alexander Faris. Previewed at Rialto, London, Oct. 2, '62. Running time, **90 MINS.**

Crimmin	Patrick McGoohan
Kathleen	Sylvia Syms
Regan	Walter Macken
Donelly	Dermot Kelly
Chief Warder	Jack Cunningham
Holy Healy	Hilton Edwards
Prison Governor	Philip O'Flynn
Dr. Flyn	Leo McCabe
Lavery	Norman Rodway
Mrs. O'Hara	Marie Kean
Mickser's Wife	Pauline Delaney
1st Customs Officer	Geoff Golden
2nd Customs Officer	Tom Irwin
Poet	Joe O'Donnell
Meg	Agnes Bernelle
Minna	Iris Lawler
Prison Chaplain	Dominic Roche
Himself	Arthur O'Sullivan
Silvertop	Aubrey Morris
Mickser	Robert Bernal
Clancy	Frank O'Donovan
Carroll	John Welsh

Based on Brendan Behan's play this is an allout protest against capital punishment. It is downbeat entertainment but honest and has the benefit of a sterling cast, virtually all Irish. It has also been shot entirely in a Dublin prison and on location. These two assets make for an authenticity which gives class to the production. The last days of a condemned murderer will not be everybody's idea of a gay outing. Pic will need careful selling. But it has something to say and says it well.

Patrick McGoohan is a young man from the Irish backwoods who takes up his first appointment as a jail warder with lofty ideals. Criminals must be punished for the sake of society is his inflexible theory and that also embraces capital punishment. But when he arrives he is shaken by the prison atmosphere. Two men are awaiting the noose. One is reprieved but hangs himself. That shakes McGoohan. He meets the young wife of the other murderer and his convictions totter still more when he hears precisely what caused her husband to murder his brother. Mostly, though, he is influenced by a veteran warder (Walter Macken) who believes that capital punishment is often a worse crime than the original offence.

"The Quare Fellow" (Irish prison slang for a guy due to be topped) is mostly a study of men's conscience and convictions. Such thin storyline as there is hinges on whether the murderer will be reprieved. He is not, despite the admission of last minute evidence by the wife that the reason for the murder was because she was discovered in bed with her brother-in-law. Further complication is that the wife (Sylvia Syms) is easing the strain of the waiting days with drink and the solace of McGoohan's bed. This, incidentally, was not a factor in the play and adds a touch of unnecessary artificiality to the screenplay. Viewpoint of Arthur Driefuss, who directed and wrote the screenplay, is that it helps the young warder to realize that there is guilt and fault in everybody.

The film, a mixture of grim humor and cynical starkness, brings out the clamminess and misery of prison life, and is helped by the grey lensing of Peter Hennessy. McGoohan, a powerful young actor, has a tricky task in that much of his job is done in the background. But he brings awareness and understanding to the part and has some quiet, excellent scenes with both Miss Syms and Macken. The femme star, a mixture of charm and sluttishness, has one of her best opportunities and takes it well. Too often she, like many other young British actress, has been condemned to colorless roles. Macken is authoritative as the warder with a conscience.

Other noteworthy thesping in lesser roles comes from Dermot Kelly as a warder who believes in keeping prisoners to heel, Pauline Delaney, Robert Bernal, Hilton Edwards, Frank O'Donovan, Aubrey Morris and Arthur O'Sullivan as the sadistic, cynical hangman. There is one scene, however, on the eve of the execution in which the hangman gets involved in a saloon brawl which strikes a ludicrously false note. It is doubtful, even in feckless Dublin, whether a hangman would take the tools of his trade around on a saloon jag and lose them. *Rich.*

Der Zigeunerbaron
(The Gypsy Baron)
(GERMAN—SONGS—COLOR)

Berlin, Oct. 9.

Constantin release of Berolina (Kurt Ulrich) production. Stars Carlos Thompson, Heidi Bruehl, Willi Millowitsch; features Daniele Gaubert, Peer Schmidt, Ida Ehre. Directed by Kurt Wilhelm. Screenplay, Heinz Oskar Wuttig, from operetta by Johann Strauss; camera, Willi Sohm; music, Johann Strauss; editor, Martin Duebber. At Marmorhaus, Berlin. Running time, **104 MINS.**

Sandor von Barinkay	Carlos Thompson
Arsena	Heidi Bruehl
Kalman Zsupan	Willi Millowitsch
Saffi	Daniele Gaubert
Erno	Peer Schmidt
Czipra	Ida Ehre
Pali	Pierre Parcel

In 1954, Berlin's Kurt Ulrich produced Johann Strauss' operetta, "The Gypsy Baron" for the screen. The result fell considerably short of the well remembered (1935) UFA production which saw Adolf Wohlbrueck (Anton Walbrook) playing the "Gypsy Baron." This 1962 production doesn't even reach the mediocre quality of Ulrich's 1954 venture. He probably picked "Baron" because this operetta work is in public domain.

The latest "Gypsy Baron" probably represents Germany's filmmaking at its current weakest. Omitting the music, there's practically nothing positive about this production. The acting and direction are wishy-washy, the jokes corny, and the "action" and dance sequences are of provincial calibre. This pic is only something for the less fussy patrons.

Argentine-born Carlos Thompson plays Sandor von Barinkay, the Gipsy Baron, and makes himself overly irresistible. His role's singing voice is by Fritz Wunderlich of the Munich State Opera. At times Wunderlich's voice is heard before even Thompson opens his mouth.

Heidi Bruehl makes a cute Arsena, daughter of the wealthy Zsupan, a pig dealer, but hardly more than that. Her acting abilities seem limited. Willi Millowitsch (Zsupan) tries hard to be funny but with no special results. About the only one who measures up to expectations is French actress Daniele Gaubert in the role of Saffi, the gypsy girl.

The biggest advantage about this celluloid version of "Gipsy Baron" is still the ever-appealing music. Exteriors, incidentally, were filmed in Yugoslavia as substitute for Hungary where the story actually occurs. *Hans.*

Eva
(FRENCH-ITALIAN)

Paris, Oct. 9.

Rank release of Paris Film-Interopa Film production. Stars Jeanne Moreau, Stanley Baker; features Virna Lisi, Giorgio Albertazzi. Directed by Joseph Losey. Screenplay, Hugo Butler, Evan Jones from book by James Hadley Chase; camera, Gianni Di Venanzo; music, Michel Legrand; editor, Reginald Buck. Franca Silvi. Preemed in Paris. Running time, **100 MINS.**

Eva	Jeanne Moreau
Tyvian	Stanley Baker
Francesca	Virna Lisi
Branco	Giorgio Albertazzi

(In English)

Made by an American director in Italy using English, with French producers and French, British and Italo actors, this is a sleek, mannered look at an affair between a cold, almost psychotic, call girl and a writer who is a fraught with overtones of masochism. It has the theme and treatment for good Yank playoff chances and could have some arty theatre mileage. But it needs the hardsell.

A blustering, self satisfied British writer, who has a bestseller and smash pic under his belt, has also amassed an Italian fiancee and lives in Venice and Rome. His film producer suspects him and being in love with his fiancee, is having him investigated.

He has to come up with another story, and goes off to a posh secluded house on an isle near Venice. A broken rudder had let a boat in with an enigmatic, hard-looking French girl and an older man. They had broken into the house and she was calmly in the bathtub when the writer comes in. He wants to throw them out until he ogles the femme.

He throws out the older man who had paid off the girl in paintings for a night of love. The writer tries to get next to her but she knocks him cold with an ashtray. Thus starts an obsession. She teases and tantalizes before she finally gives in but warns him not to fall in love. He does, and she begins to shun him. He drops his fiancee and spends all on her till she finally throws him out.

He marries but is haunted by the other. On his honeymoon, when his wife is away for a day, he brings the girl back to his love nest, but she refuses him. When his wife comes back and finds her, he becomes a sort of exile guide always hounding her steps.

He even tries to kill her but can't do it. She flagellates him roundly with a riding crop. It ends with her going off on a trip from which she may not return, and he is destined to become a derelict. All this is played at too high a pitch by director Joseph Losey.

Picture is reminiscent of pre-war Yank femme fatale films. But it seems somewhat oldhat today. Of course, the prostie is becoming a popular film figure these days, and this also looks at the difficulty of loving. But there is not enough character to give acceptance to the over-indulgence in re Jeanne Moreau as the cold-hearted harlot.

Miss Moreau, a French star, speaks good English but is hampered by the over-decorated, overstylized vamp she is called on to play. Stanley Baker acquits himself acceptably as the climbing ex-coal miner, and others are adequate.

This has a solid production dress from producers Robert and Raymond Hakim, and expert technical aspects. At times, director Losey does get deeper into the hopelessness of tangled loves. But he has not given it the out-and-out melodramatics to make it a rousing entry.

Picture could be a good exploitation item on circuits, with a possible art tag.

Incidentally, this production was yanked from the recent Venice Film Fest because of squabbles between the producers and director, and between the fest officials and producers who wanted a different showing date. Its arty aspects might have benefited from the festival airing. *Mosk.*

Gay Purr-ee
(COLOR)

Full-length cartoon musical. Solid values in art, music, voice and production areas, plus top offscreen "cast" names, offset story inadequacies. Good "family" attraction, but will need trade and consumer sell.

Hollywood, Oct. 11.
Warner Bros. release of UPA production. Voices of Judy Garland, Robert Goulet, Red Buttons, Hermione Gingold, Paul Frees, Morey Amsterdam, Mel Blanc, Julie Bennett, Joan Gardner. Directed by Abe Levitow. Written by Dorothy & Chuck Jones; camera (Technicolor), Roy Hutchcroft, Dan Miller, Jack Stevens, Duane Keegan: editors, Sam Horta, Earl Bennett; art director, Victor Haboush; music, Harold Arlen; lyrics, E. Y. Harburg; production designers, Robert Singer, Richard Ung, "Corny" Cole, Ray Aragon, Edward Levitt, Ernest Nordli; color stylists, Don Peters, Gloria Wood, Robert Inman, Phil Norman, Richard Kelsey; animators, Ben Washam, Phil Duncan, Hal Ambro, Ray Patterson, Grant Simmons, Irv Spence, Don Lusk, Hank Smith, Harvey Toombs, Volus Jones, Ken Harris, Art Davis, Fred Madison. Reviewed at Academy Awards Theatre, Oct. 11, '62. Running time, 85 MINS.

The artwork in "Gay Purr-ee" ranks with the finest ever manufactured in the specialized realm of the animated cartoon. This superior facet of the UPA production will be a welcome bonus for adults attracted to the film by the star-studded cast of "speaking" and "singing" voices or the urgings of their children. Essentially a "family" entertainment, the Warner Bros. release is hampered by an uninspired storyline, but its otherwise slick and meticulous production values overshadow the weaknesses with ample artistry to register favorably at the boxoffice within cartoon invitations. Furthermore, the current absence of new full-length animated Disney competition affords a choice opportunity for the UPA-Warners item to fill a programming hole. However, aggressive trade and consumer selling is necessary.

"Purr-ee" adds up to a kind of feline afterthought to Disney's "101 Dalmations," though it does **not figure to score quite as strongly at the kitty. Emphasis in the UPA effort is more on music, however, with frequent breaks in story continuity for warbling accompanied by stunning splashes of color.** Harold Arlen and Yip Harburg have penned eight numbers, one of which, a dramatic blues titled "Paris Is a Lonely Town" and sung explosively by Judy Garland, has the earmarks of a hit. The other refrains are appropriate in context, but lack the haunting quality for outside success.

The Dorothy and Chuck Jones story describes the plight of "Mewsette" (Miss Garland), a country bred Gallicat who purr-ambulates to Paris, is kit-napped by some dastardly cat-nippers, then rescued at the brink of catty-cornered

catastrophe by her forsaken lover, "Jaune Tom" (Robert Goulet) and his faithful sidekick, "Robespierre" (Red Buttons).

Voice work is A-1, with exceptional efforts by Buttons and Paul Frees (as the villain). Hermione Gingold has a key role, and there is accomplished vocal support from Morey Amsterdam, Mel Blanc, Julie Bennett and Joan Gardner. Miss Garland's singing is characterized by her patented verve, oomph and feeling, and Goulet sings clearly and robustly.

Outstanding contributions to the production, helmed by Abe Levitow for exec producer Henry G. Saperstein, are those of art director Victor Haboush and the large, talented staffs of color stylists, animators and production designers (names listed above in credits). Decision to depict provincial French exteriors in a Van Gogh motif was inspired, and a passage in which impressions of the works of 11 great artists are represented onscreen with feline principals is a memorable one.

Credit also is due such contributors as music arranger-conductor Mort Lindsay, vocal arranger Joseph J. Lilley, and the camera and editorial staffs, also listed above. John Hitesman's main titles adroitly link story characters with image of the voice behind the scenes. *Tube.*

The War Lover

Lack of sharp focus on title character strips otherwise okay filmization of John Hersey's novel of appeal for discriminating audience. But still good action market entry.

Hollywood, Oct. 10.
Columbia Pictures release of Arthur Hornblow Jr. production. Stars Steve McQueen, Robert Wagner, Shirley Anne Field. Directed by Philip Leacock. Screenplay, Howard Koch, from novel by John Hersey; camera, Bob Huke; editor, Gordon Hales; music, Richard Addinsell; asst. director, Basil Rayburn. Reviewed at studio, Oct. 10, '62. Running time, 105 MINS.

Buzz Rickson	Steve McQueen
Ed Bolland	Robert Wagner
Daphne	Shirley Anne Field
Lynch	Gary Cockrell
Junior Sailen	Michael Crawford
Brindt	Bill Edwards
Lamb	Chuck Julian
Handown	Robert Easton
Prien	Al Waxman
Farr	Bom Busby
Bragliani	George Sperdakos
Haverstraw	Bob Kanter
Emmet	Jerry Stovin
Vogt	Edward Bishop
Murika	Richard Leech
Randall	Bernard Braden
Woodman	Sean Kelly
Braddock	Charles De Temple
Sully	Neil McCallum
Singer	Viera
Street Girl	Justine Lord
Hazel	Louise Dunn
Vicar	Arthur Hewlett

Arthur Hornblow's production of John Hersey's "The War Lover" is accomplished in all respects save one. Lamentably, that one flaw happens to be a major one: lack of proper clarification of or penetration into the character referred to by the title. This single conspicuous shortcoming strips the film of its potential "prestige picture" appeal for more discerning, demanding audiences, leaving it to be claimed by less choosy buffs of the war picture. Since its action scenes have been meticulously and expertly mounted, an air of authenticity pervades the film that, coupled with its earnest, skillful performances, gives the Columbia release some promise as a contender for the action market buck.

Fuzziness of the central character drains Howard Koch's screenplay of emotional impact. The scenario seems reluctant to come to grips with the issue of this character's unique personality—a "war lover" whose exaggerated shell of heroic masculinity covers up a psychopathic inability to love or enjoy normal relationships with women. The film tends to dodge this psychological facet every time it is approached, often leaving the audience suspended and groping for clear understanding of the character. The story transpires in 1943 England and focuses on B-17 bombing raids over Germany, with the title character (Steve McQueen) a pilot of one of the planes.

That the central character emerges more of an unappealing symbol than a sympathetic flesh-and-blood portrait is no fault of McQueen, who plays with vigor and authority, although occasionally with too much eyeball emotion. Robert Wagner and Shirley Anne Field share the film's secondary, but interesting, romantic story. Wagner, a rapidly improving actor, does quite well, and the English Miss Field has a fresh, natural quality rarely found in the ranks of young leading ladies in Hollywood—where the perfect features of physical beauty tend to be over-

emphasized. Supporting work is strong, notably that of Gary Cockrell, Michael Crawford and Jerry Stovin.

Outside of his failure to focus more lucidly and attentively on the central issue, director Philip Leacock has done a sound job. Scenes of the bombing raids and accompanying aerial incidents are adroitly and authentically executed through the meshing, imaginative teamwork of Bob Huke's photography, Gordon Hales' editing, Bill Andrews' art direction, the Ron Taylor-Skeets Kelly aerial camerawork and the Norman Bolland-Red Law sound, all under Leacock's careful surveillance. Composer Richard Addinsell's theme is affecting and the film's incidental music is the music of the time. *Tube.*

Two For The Seesaw
(PANAVISION)

Good b.o. looms for this translation of the hit Broadway play in spite of film's tendency to expose its talky, listless aura.

Hollywood, Oct. 15.
United Artists release of Walter Mirisch production. Stars Robert Mitchum, Shirley MacLaine. Directed by Robert Wise. Screenplay, Isobel Lennart, based on play by William Gibson; camera, Ted McCord; editor, Stuart Gilmore; music, Andre Previn; assistant director, Jerome M. Siegel. Reviewed at Academy Awards Theatre, Oct. 15, '62. Running time, 119 MINS.

Jerry Ryan	Robert Mitchum
Gittel Mosca	Shirley MacLaine
Taubman	Edmon Ryan
Sophie	Elisabeth Fraser
Oscar	Eddie Firestone
Mr. Jacoby	Billy Gray

The multitudes who haven't yet seen William Gibson's "Two for the Seesaw" figure to respond as favorably to the screen version as playgoers did for the stage version. The play does lose something in translation, but the loss is apt to be sensed only by those able or prone to draw such comparisons. Spearheaded by Shirley MacLaine's enactment of Gittel Mosca, a portrayal that is sure to be talked about, the Walter Mirisch production for United Artists shapes up as a good boxoffice prospect.

There is a fundamental torpor about "Seesaw" that is less troublesome on stage than it is on screen, a medium of motion that exaggerates its absence, that emphasizes the slightest hint of listlessness. On film, it drags. It drags in spite of the charm, insight, with and compassion of Gibson's play, the savvy and sense of scenarist Isobel Lennart's mild revisions and additions, the infectious friskiness of Miss MacLaine's performance and the consummate care taken by those who shaped and mounted the film reproduction.

The basic flaws appear to be the play's innate talkiness and the unbalance of the two-way "Seesaw." The selection of Robert Mitchum for the role of Jerry Ryan proves not to have a been a wise one. The strong attraction "Gittel" is supposed to feel for "Jerry" becomes less plausible because of Mitchum's lethargic, droopy-eyed enactment. Something more appealing and magnetic is needed to make this love affair ring true.

Miss MacLaine's performance in the meaty role of the disarmingly candid, stupendously kindhearted Miss Mosca, is a winning one. Her

handling of the Yiddish dialect and accompanying mannerisms is sufficiently reserved so that it does not lapse into a kind of gitgat-gitterless caricature. Minor roles written into the screenplay are dispatched effectively by Edmon Ryan, Elisabeth Fraser, Eddie Firestone and Billy Gray.

Director Robert Wise has succeeded in many respects, but the several aforementioned shortcomings of "Seesaw" as a motion picture were largely his to correct. Photogrphically and artistically, it is a superior film. The compositions, textures and lighting subtleties accomplished by cameraman Ted McCord go a long way toward alerting and interesting the eye when the action flags, as it does so often. Boris Leven's production design conveys that New York character and the personality of the principals. The contributions of McCord and Leven are especially noteworthy for the atmosphere created in a bohemian Village party sequence. Stuart Gilmore's editing is smooth, and Andre Prèvin's melancholy score is moving, but neither is exactly helpful in enlivening the tempo.

"Seesaw" is pretty frank in its attitude toward adult matters such as who sleeps where, when, and with whom. But this is honest, not obnoxious. It shouldn't and won't bother anybody except those who aren't satisfied unless they are bothered. ·Tube·

The Legend Of Lobo
(COLOR)

Lesser Disney animal opus. Satisfactory contender for kiddie mart buck.

Hollywood, Oct. 19.
Buena Vista release of Walt Disney production. Screenplay, Dwight Hauser, James Algar, based on story by Ernest Thompson-Seton; camela (Technicolor), Jack Couffer, Lloyd Beebe; editor, Norman Palmer; music, Oliver Wallace. Reviewed at Academy Awards Theatre, Oct. 19, '62. Running time, 67 MINS.

"The Legend of Lobo" ranks as about the skimpiest and least effectual of Walt Disney's animal operettas. But the fact that adults in attendance will find little to ululate about doesn't figure to deter the moppet brigade from flocking to see the Buena Vista release in satisfactory, though not unusually large, numbers.

The film, coproduced by James Algar, runs only 67 minutes, yet actually drags. Aside from a smattering of information such as the fact that wolves are monogamous critters, co-scenarists Algar and Dwight Hauser, working with a story by Ernest Thompson-Seton, have done an astonishingly half-hearted and unimaginative job of translating the legend into a film story. The scenario, punctured by overly abundant musical breaks in which narrator Rex Allen and the Sons of the Pioneers chant a rather monotonous title tune by Richard M. and Robert B. Sherman, traces the career of the great legendary wolf, Lobo, who roamed New Mexico around the turn of the century. But it is never made quite clear in the film why Lobo became such a legend. Some fascinating details, such as Lobo's impressive proportions and abili-

ties, are hardly even hinted at, narratively or pictorially.

Lobo is traced from puppyhood to maturity, and observed in various skirmishes with animals and man, as well as in intramural activities with his own kind. Best interlude is his bout with a very self-sufficient badger. The narrative is written from the wolf's point-of-view, with man as the heavy. It is sprinkled with such patented Disneyesque observations as, when pup Lobo takes up with a baby antelope (his natural prey), "so an unusual friendship developed—one of those things that only happens in nature" (and, the narration might have added, inevitably happens in nature-a-la-Disney).

Film was shot entirely in Arizona mesa country by photographers Jack Couffer and Lloyd Beebe, with Couffer serving as field producer for Cangary Limited. The Technicolor camerawork is painstaking and picturesque. Norman Palmer's editing tautly binds action and reaction, such as animal response to rifle fire. Score by Oliver Wallace is often used to comic story advantage, such as its accompaniment of the Lobo-badger fracas with the strains of a square dance. Tube.

Escape From East Berlin

Suspense meller based on actual escape incident. Shy dramatic finesse, but okay suspense item for less choosy customers. Saturation programming best bet.

Hollywood, Oct. 17.
Metro release of Walter Wood production. Stars Don Murray, Christine Kaufmann; introduces Carl Schell. Directed by Robert Siodmak. Screenplay, Gabrielle Upton, Peter Berneis, Millard Lampell, from story by Miss Upton and Berneis; camera, Georg Krause; editor, Maurice Wright; music, Hans-Martin Majewski. Reviewed at the studio, Oct. 17, '62. Running time, 89 MINS.
Kurt Schroeder .... Don Murray
Erika Juergens......Christine Kaufmann
Brunner .... Werner Klemperer
Ingeborg .... Ingrid Van Bergen
Kurt's Mother...Edith Schultze-Westrum
Uncle Albert .... Bruno Fritz
Marga .... Maria Tober
Gunther .... Horst Janson
Major Schmidt .... Carl Schell

The real-life escape to the West last January of 28 East Germans via a tunnel under the "Wall" served as the basis for Walter Wood's production of "Escape From East Berlin." A suspense melodrama with political overtones, the film is timely, topical and exploitable. It lacks the insight, penetration and dramatic neatness to attract fussier filmgoers, but should prove serviceable for Metro as a short haul saturation item.

A considerable amount of suspense has been generated in the Gabrielle Upton-Peter Berneis-Millard Lampell scenario about a young East Berliner (Don Murray) who burrows a tunnel under the infamous wall and leads his family and a couple of dozen others to freedom. Accepted purely as a suspense entry, the film is sufficiently engrossing. But more careful scrutiny discloses a number of dramatic errors, oversights and cliches. Oddly enough, at times one tends to forget he is watching a depiction of a 1962 incident—it

is almost as if the time is 1939, and the Nazis are in charge.

The cast, almost entirely German, performs competently under Robert Siodmak's generally able direction, marred by a rather erratic climax. Murray and Christine Kaufmann are earnest and attractive in the leading roles. The film introduces Carl Schell, brother of Maria and Maximilian. He plays capably, but makes no especially vivid impression. Horst Janson is memorable in a small role.

Skillful assists to the production are those of cameraman Georg Krause, art directors Ted Haworth and Dieter Bartels, soundman Heinz Garbowski and composer-conductor Hans-Martin Majewski. But Maurice Wright's editing leaves several loose ends dangling from the scenario. Tube.

Two Before Zero
(DOCUMENTARY)

Anti-communist tract. A mixed exploitation prospect.

Ellis Films release of Motion Picture Corp. of America (Fred A. Niles) production. Directed by William D. Faralla. Features Basil Rathbone and Mary Murphy. Narration written by Bruce Henry; camera, Jack Whitehead; editor, Robert L. Sinise; music, Sid Siegel. Reviewed in New York, Oct. 18, '62. Running time, 78 MINS.

"Two Before Zero" is a hybrid documentary on Bolshevik behavior and the Orwellian implications of communism. It is simplified and emotional, intended to exploit boxofficewise presentday East-West tensions. It will find a presold type of spectator in selected situations.

Turned out by Motion Picture Corp. of America, a Chicago outfit, and released by Ellis Films, "Zero" employs Basil Rathbone and Mary Murphy in stagey, self-conscious symbolic roles, laced with clips parading the top communist names, past and present, and a grisly recital of Soviet atrocity over the years. Rathbone, as the figure of History, and Miss Murphy, who seems intended to symbolize American innocence, are staged somewhat like ancient Greek drama. Their duolog, which also serves to narrate the pic, is embarassingly "arty," incomplete in historical analysis, and at times inaccurate as to facts.

It has been produced with technical competence. The actors do the best they can with their lines, but the fault is not to be found in the stars. Pit.

Rififi in Amsterdam
Amsterdam, Oct. 16.
Nederlandse Filmproductie Maatschappij (P. van Moock) production. With Maxim Hafel, Els Eillenius, Johan Kaart, Rijk de Gooyer, Jan Blaaser, Ton van Duinhoven, Anton Geesink. Directed by JohnKorporaal. Screenplay, Kor-poraal and Emile Brumstede, based on book by W. H. van Eemlandt; camera. Eduard van der Enden; editor, Lien d'Oliveryra. At City Theatre, Amsterdam. Running time, 105 MINS.

This Dutch feature film is strictly for the home market because it has no aspects, storywise or artistically, that would make it a worthy item for export. Story is stereotyped, depicting a pro-

vincial gang fight over a hidden treasure, with the law likewise hunting for the briefcase containing jewels.

Plot develops slowly and story follows all kinds of side issues, few of which have to do with locating the jewels. Characters are mostly too bleak. Blame for this film to jell can be put on director John Korporaal, since he also wrote the script.

"Rififi In Amsterdam" follows a style that was popular in Dutch film producing circles in the 30's. Songs are inserted in the film that slow up the action. At the climax of the film, a popular Dutch singer, Willy Alberti, comes in to sing a song.

Technical credits are okay, but the acting is awkward and amateurish. This is the type of film that should be left to foreign directors who have proved they can do them more professionally. Saal.

The Wild And The Willing
(BRITISH)

Perceptive glimpse at the old hat "Angry Young Man" theme, enlivened by good performances by a wave of new youngsters.

London, Oct. 16.
Rank release of a Betty E. Box-Ralph Thomas production. Stars Virginia Maskell, Paul Rogers; features Ian McShane, Samantha Eggar, John Hurt, Catharine Woodville, David Sumner, John Standing, Johnny Briggs, Johnny Sekka, Charles Kay, Jeremy Brett, John Barrie, Megs Jenkins, Richard Warner, Ernest Clark, John Welsh, Harry Locke, Richard Leech. Directed by Ralph Thomas. Screenplay, Nicholas Phipps, Mordecai Richled, adapted from "The Tinker," a play by Laurence Dobie and Robert Sloman; camera, Ernest Steward; editor, Alfred Roome; music, Norrie Paramor. At Odeon, Leicester Square, London. Running time, 123 MINS.
Virginia .... Virginia Maskell
Professor Chown .... Paul Rogers
Harry .... Ian McShane
Josie .... Samantha Eggar
Phil .... John Hurt
Sarah .... Catharine Woodville
John .... David Sumner
Arthur .... John Standing
Dai .... Johnny Briggs
Reggie .... Johnny Sekka
Gilby .... Jeremy Brett
Tibbs .... Charles Kay
Mr. Corbett .... John Barrie
Fire Chief .... Victor Brooks
Vice-Chancellor........... Ernest Clark
Jane .... Denise Coffey
First Customer .... George A. Cooper
Second Customer .... Harry Locke
Mrs. Corbett .... Megs Jenkins
Police Inspector .... Richard Leech
Clara .... Marianne Stone
Coroner .... Richard Warner
Publican .... John Welsh
Policeman .... Jeremy Young

It could be that this one may be a little late in the "Angry Young Man" series but it is a wellmade and exciting picture if only because producer Betty E. Box and director Ralph Thomas have unleashed a half dozen new potentials in key roles. Britain for some years, has not been so rich in vigorous young talent. Several of those in "The Wild and the Willing," adapted from "The Tinker," a play by Laurence Dozie and Robert Sloman which didn't make the grade in the West End, seem likely entries for bigger things.

Though it has nothing much new to say on its chosen theme—youth trying to find its place in society—the screenplay is lucid and the background of a provisional university authentic. Spiced with

humor and sex, it should prove solid b.o.

It concerns a brilliant young student from a poor working class family who is acutely class-conscious and rebels against the university, its professors and the opportunities they offer. He does not know where he is going and is arrogantly content to drift along raising cain, drinking beer, playing football and pawing his girl friend, another student. He is a leading light in the university with a particular influence on his roommate, a shyer, more introspective lad. His professor recognizes the boy's ability but dislikes him for his brashness.

Things come to a head at a cocktailerie thrown by this prof. They openly insult each other and the professor's wife is attracted to the student. Her marriage is virtually on the rocks and she spends her time in drinking and dallying with selected students. Her husband knows about her indiscretions but chooses, contemptuously, to ignore them.

The wife and the student have a brief affair but when she rejects his plea for her to run off with him, he is stung into a reckless stunt in connection with the university Rag. He and his roommate climb the school's tower, and the result is tragedy. The film ends with the student being sent down in disgrace. But it seems that he may be on the treshold of a more useful, understanding life.

Some of the opening student scenes are rather too hearty but gradually the film settles down to a thoughtful pace, rising to a grim climax with the tower climb. Throughout there is a complete air of realism. The students, the professors and the townsfolk are real people about whose problems audiences will care. Ralph Thomas has directed with tact and his brought out some surprisingly sure performances from his inexperienced actors.

Ian McShane, with a broad Manchester accent, came straight from drama school to play this leading role. He is a virile, goodlooking young man with authority who is a real discovery, as is John Hurt, also a first timer, who plays his sensitive roommate. Johnny Briggs, John Standing, Johnny Sekka, Jeremy Brett and John Sumner also click as students.

On the distaff side, a couple of other newcomers, Semantha Eggar and Catharine Woodville are noteworthy new candidates for future stardom. The role of the humorless, cold professor is safe in the capable hands of Paul Rogers while Virginia Maskell, one of Britain's most improved young actresses, gives a deftly observed performance as the young, unhappy wife.

Ernest Steward's camerawork is firstclass and all other technical departments do their stuff well. Norris Paramor has provided a lively score. Johnny Sekka, as well as being provided with some shrewd lines as a Negro student, also has a distinctive singing voice. This he puts to good effect in a closing calypso, which sums up the whole film in a touching finale.

The faults of "The Willing" are largely those caused by the film covering wellworn ground and because the screenplay has rather too many interwoven themes. But it is a sturdy addition to current crop of British "down to earth" pix.
Rich.

Axel Munthe, der Arzt Von San Michele
(Axel Munthe, Doctor of San Michele)
(GERMAN-ITALIAN-FRENCH)
(COLOR)

Berlin, Oct. 16.
Gloria release of CCC (Arthur Brauner) and Divina production, in collaboration with Cine-Italia (Rome) and Criterion-Films, Paris. Stars O. W. Fischer, Rossana Schiaffino, Sonja Ziemann; features Maria Mahor, Valentina Cortese. Heinz Erhardt. Directed by Georg Marischka, Rudolf Jugert. Screenplay, Hans Jacoby, H. G. Petersson, adapted from book, "Axel Munthe, Doctor of San Michele," by Axel Munthe; camera, Richard Angst; music, Nascimbene; sets, Willy Schatz and Warner Achmann; editor, Jutta Hering. At the Marmorhaus, Berlin. Running time, 144 MINS.
Axel Munthe .... O. W. Fischer
Antonia .... Rossana Schiaffino
Princess Clementine ...... Sonja Ziemann
Ebba .... Maria Mahor
Eleonora Duse .... Valentina Cortese
Brunoni .... Heinz Erhardt
Natascha .... Ingeborg Schoener
Munthe's client .... Renate Ewert
Paulette .... Christiane Maybach
Leblanc .... Antoine Balpetre
Petit-Pierre .... Fernand Sardou

The late Axel Munthe (1856-1949), a Swede, was an unusual personality. He was a successful medico, a helper of the needy, a friend of animals, a poet and philosopher. And he had a way with women, being a handsome chap. Moreover, he wrote a book, "Axel Munthe, the Doctor of San Michele," which has been translated into more than a dozen of lanaguages. This German-Italian-French coproduction depicts the life story of this unusual man, and O. W. Fischer, Germany's top screen lover, plays the title part. There's no doubt but that he loved the role very much.

The film is disappointing, and the fault may lie with O. W. Fischer. This is no Axel Munthe story but an O. W. Fischer film. Fischer is walking and talking through the entire film, and one always feels that he's merely acting. One is convinced that he dominated the director. It's reported that he changed dialog passages extensively. True or not, one must be an ardent Fischer fan to like his portrayal of the famous Swedish doctor. Others will feel that there's too much Fischer and, besides, too much philosophical chatter.

Additionally, it's hard to decide where the direction begins and ends. Originally, Georg Marischka was named the film's director but screen credits list Rudolf Jugert (who took over) as director. This indicates the behind-the-scenes controversy between the directors and Fischer.

The cast includes some star names but few show up to advantage in this. Most of the characters remain sketchy. In addition, "Axel Munthe" is overly long. The number of dull moments is remarkably high for the 144-minute pic. Technical credits are generally adequate.
Hans.

El Extra
(The Extra)
(MEXICAN—COLOR)

Mexico City, Oct. 23.
Columbia Pictures release of Posa Films International production. Stars Cantinflas; features Alma Delia Fuentes, Carmen Molina, Guillermina Tellez Giron, Alejandro Ciangherotti, Magda Donato, Leon Barroso, Raul Meraz, Guillermo Rives and "Chabelo." Directed by Miguel M. Delgado. Screenplay by Jaime Salvador, Alfredo Varela Jr. from original story by Jose Maria Fernandez, Varela Jr.; camera, Rosalio Selano; music, Cesar Carrion. At the Roble, Mexico, Olimpia, Polanco and Opera theatres, Mexico City. Running time, 90 MINS.

In his latest Mexican film, Cantinflas plays not so much the role of an extra as a sort of jack-of-all-trades and hanger-on at studios who effectively louses up scenes being shot, causing sundry directors to froth at the mouth.

But the comic also has a "heart of gold" and lends money to those short of cash, gives counsel to would-be actors and actresses, and specifically helps one lass achieve stardom after the usual discouragements. Alma Delia Fuentes, as the gal who makes the grade and then spurns her benefactor for the more opportune company of a producer, is comely. Finale has Cantinflas, struggling off the snub, already picking up another starlet of future for fashioning into star material.

It is rather obvious that the comic enjoys himself in this one. While he is not the selfsame decrepit Cantinflas of old, he does come back nearer to the role that made him famous in his native Mexico—the average Juan Doe of the streets who fights against adversity and does all he can to help his fellow man.

Cantinflas has a chance to display his comedy bent in dream sequences where he imagines how the scene should have been shot, instead of way it was actually directed by director. Opportunities range from a French Revolution sequence where a bewigged Cantinflas contributes to the confusion to a funny take off on Camille and also a sequence where he plays an Aztec Indian with special vim and comic flair.

Cantinflas is the center of attention 90% of the screen time in this one, yet he does not pall since the pace and contrasts between bona-fide and comic-angled scenes is well timed. More than ever, Cantinflas in this one is the tramplike character who talks a lot and says nothing much, a role especially dear to his Mexican fans.

Mario Moreno as Cantinflas playing Cantinflas is in his element. Aside from which the production is luxuriously staged, the Eastmancolor good and sound faultless. Supporting cast serves as foils for the comic's style. There is a laughable scene where the actor billed as "Chabelo," in knickers, as a bully, towers over Cantinflas but is eventually brought down to size by the comic. Comic's "acting lessons" for Miss Fuentes so that she can make the grade are also not without some sly wit.

In toto, this one turns out to be an excellent Cantinflas vehicle which will enrich the comic not only in his traditional markets but possibly via worldwide release as well.
Emil.

Les Mysteres De Paris
(The Mysteries of Paris)
(FRENCH—COLOR—DYALI-SCOPE)

Paris, Oct. 23.
Unidex release of PAC-DAMA production. Stars Jean Marais, Dany Robin, Raymond Pellegrin, Jill Haworth; features Pierre Mondy, Noel Roquevert, Jean Le Poulain. Directed by Andre Hunnebelle. Screenplay, Jean Halain, Pierre Foucault, Diego Fabbri from novel by Eugene Sue; camera (Eastmancolor), Marcel Grignon; editor, Jean Feyte. At Normandie, Paris. Running time, 110 MINS.
Rodolphe .... Jean Marais
Irene .... Dany Robin
Marie .... Jill Haworth
Baron .... Raymond Pellegrin
Chourineur .... Pierre Mondy
Maitre .... Jean Le Poulain
Shoemaker .... Noel Roquevert

Remake of a novel that has been done several times already, Eugene Sue's turn-of-the-century melodrama about Paris lowlife and highlife, this looms mainly a local entry on its flashy direction and obvious posturing. Only possible foreign slotting could be for moppet shows via its moral ending.

A nobleman's carriage runs over a man, and he decides to help the man's pretty orphan daughter as he expires. He dons workers' clothing and goes into the French worker and criminal districts. Here he is struck by the squalor and decides to help these people. Also he is enamored of the girl when he finds her.

Hence, he lives in two worlds but becomes the enemy of an evil leader. Latter wants him out of the way as he won't reveal some building shenanigans. All ends happily. Production values are okay but director Andre Hunnebelle lacks the snap and drive that would make this hoary tale a more winning adventure yarn.

Lagging treatment unfortunately robs this ripe old yarn of the bounce and mock seriousness it needs. Pic has local chances on the widely known book but little for offshore spots. Acting is mechanically proper, with good and bad guys well defined.
Mosk.

What Ever Happened To Baby Jane?

Powerful acting by Bette Davis and Joan Crawford overcomes tedious beginning; word-of-mouth could make it top grosser.

Hollywood, Oct. 20.

Warner Bros. release of Seven Arts-Associates and Aldrich production. Stars Bette Davis, Joan Crawford. Features Victor Buono. Produced and directed by Robert Aldrich. Screenplay by Lukas Heller, based on novel by Henry Farrell; music, Frank DeVol; camera, Ernest Haller; editor, Michael Luciano; sound, Jack Solomon; asst. director, Tom Connors. Reviewed at Pantages Theatre, Los Angeles, Oct. 18. Running time, **132 MINS.**

Jane Hudson .... Bette Davis
Blanche Hudson .... Joan Crawford
Edwin Flagg .... Victor Buono
Marjorie Bennett .... Della Flagg
Elvira Stitt ....Maidie Norman
Mrs. Bates .... Anna Lee
Liza Bates .... Barbara Merrill
Baby Jane (child) .... Julie Allred
Blanche (child) .... Gina Gillespie
Ray Hudson .... Dave Willock
Cora Hudson .... Ann Barton

Many of the prime ingredients of a boxoffice smash—notably a suspenseful story, outstanding director, topflight technicians, and topnotch performances by two female "stars," in the truest sense of the word—are present in Seven Arts' "What Ever Happened to Baby Jane?" The potential is somewhat hampered, however, by a long introduction that creates less suspense than tedium, and needs drastic pruning. Once past the intro and credits, "Baby Jane" becomes an emotional toboggan ride, stopped only by its horribly obvious outcome.

Teaming Bette Davis and Joan Crawford now seems like a veritable prerequisite to putting Henry Farrell's slight tale of terror on the screen. Although the results heavily favor Miss Davis (and she earns the credit), it should be recognized that the plot, of necessity, allows her to run unfettered through all the stages of oncoming insanity, which the uninhibited lady proceeds to do—like a mad organist, warming up to Berlioz' "Damnation of Faust," with, eventually, every stop out.

Whisky-voiced, slovenly, wonderfully and hideously gowned and madeup throughout the film, Miss Davis quickly overcomes a viewer's earlier impatience, finally leaving one emotionally exhausted. Her slip-over into total madness is, possibly, less effective than was Gloria Swanson's in "Sunset Boulevard," but only because the viewer knows all along that it is unavoidable.

Miss Crawford gives a quiet, remarkably fine interpretation of the crippled Blanche, held in emotionally by the nature and temperament of the role. Physically confined to a wheelchair and bed throughout the picture, she has to act from the inside and has her best scenes (because she wisely underplays with Davis) with a maid and those she plays alone. In one superb bit, Miss Crawford reacting to herself on television (actually, clips from the 1934 "Sadie McKee"), makes her face fairly glow with the remembrance of fame past. A genuine heart-breaker.

The slight basic tale is of two sisters, complete opposites. As children, Jane is "Baby Jane" (a travesty on the many Mary Pickford-Shirley Temple imitators), a vaudeville star and the idol of the public. Offstage, she's a vicious brat, domineering her plain, inhibited sister and preening parents. Eventually both girls go into films, where the dark, mousey Blanche blossoms into a beauty and fine actress, and becomes Hollywood's top star. Jane, unable to grow beyond her limited child-talent, works only because Blanche forces studios to give her roles.

As the result of an accident, hazily presented, Blanche is permanently crippled. Jane, dependent on her sister for her livelihood, is forced to care for her, her hate growing with the years. So, also, does the "Baby Jane" illusion until, living it daily, she determines to get rid of Blanche and return to vaudeville (wherever that is!). Advertising for an accompaniment, the sole applicant is a huge, ungainly lout (a superb off-beat performance by Victor Buono), who sizes up the situation's opportunities and goes along, planning to get enough money to enable him to break the tarnished-silver cord binding him to a possessive mother.

The chain of circumstances grow, violence creating violence. To detail the plot beyond this point is meaningless. Director Robert Aldrich has generally made good use of Ernest Haller's camera wizardry and Michael Luciano's expert editing although the latter still has work to do. Once the inept, draggy start is passed, the film's pace builds with ever-growing force.

Occasionally, Aldrich oversteps his generally strong power of suggestion. Instance: a carefully-dropped remark by Jane about a rat, seconds after bringing the already-terrorized Blanche her luncheon tray, tells everything (and here a Hitchcock would have stopped). There is no reason for showing the rodent, and it is repulsive. Aldrich immediately recovers, however, by a brilliant overhead shot of Blanche, endlessly circling in her wheelchair, as certainly trapped as a squirrel in a cage.

Some fast takes throughout the film add much to the suspense, including a pan shot of a billboard advertising an undertaker, and one of a drunken Buono, careening about the hallway in Blanche's wheelchair, almost scaring Jane *into* her wits.

Beyond the two femme stars and their heavy-weighted male backstop, the supporting cast is merely that, Maidie Norman has some effective moments as the maid, but Anna Lee, Julie Allread, Gina Gillespie and Marjorie Bennett are limited in their roles. One fast shot that might escape many viewers is of the child Blanche's face as she utters a single vengeance-promising remark, to be recalled later during the adult Blanche's confession.

Frank DeVol's score, except for an ear-and-taste violating song, "I've Written a Letter to Daddy," which serves as Jane's leit-motif, is routine. Minor plot inconsistencies pop up, but not enough to detract the hypnotized-with-horror average viewer. A film clip, probably from the 1933 "Parachute Jumper," inserted to establish Jane's ineptness as an actress, fails to do so. Despite its shortcomings, however, "Baby Jane" gives the motion picture screen its best "shocker" since "Psycho," and two fine actress worthy roles. *Robe.*

Un Dia de Diciembre
(One Day in December)
(MEXICAN)

Mexico City, Oct. 30.

Peliculas Nicionales release of Production Cinematografica Mexicana Independiente production. Stars Jorge Martinez de Hoyos, Beatriz Aguirre, Emir Angel Dupeyron; features Luis Aragon, Jacqueline Andere. Directed by Fernando Cortez. Screenplay, Alejandro Verbintzky from original by Roberto Gomez Bolanos; camera, Jorge Sthal. At Mariscala Theatre, Mexico City. Running time, **90 MINS.**

This is one of the independently produced films, of three made under auspices of the Mexican Assn. of Independent Exhibitors. Original plan by these independents had been to turn out 30 films with accent on quality, but the project has been suspended pending reorganization of association plans.

This film is by no means a festival award product but, surprisingly enough, it is sympathetically directed by Fernando Cortes and develops a Christmas story about an average Mexican boy, full of innocence and who wishes to reaffirm the Xmas spirit within his family and in his neighborhood.

There are no monsters, giants, geni or rides on a magic carpet. Director Fernando Cortez develops a simple story intended for children and nabe patrons, with a full share of tear-jerker situations. Youngster Emir Angel Dupeyron is believable as central character. Beatriz Aguirre is effective as the mother as is Jorge Martinez de Hoyos in role of an understanding father.

This depicts a world without malice, replete with love and compassion. This one merits success in Spanish language markets.

Emil.

Atras de las Nubes
(Behind The Clouds
(MEXICAN)

Mexico City, Oct. 30.

Peliculas Nacionales release of Cinematografica Jalisco production. Stars Luis Aguilar, Marga Lopez; features Dagoberto Rodriguez, Joaguin Cordero, Ofelia Montesco, Jose Elias Moreno, Andres Soler and Arturo Martinez. Directed by Gilberto Gazcon. Screenplay, Josefina Vicens and Gilberto Gazcon from original by Jesus Mario Valentin Gazcon; camera, Ignacio Torres. At Alameda-Ariel Theatres, Mexico City. Running time, **90 MINS.**

This is yet another revolutionary tale, but with the accent on a romantic love story. Singer Luis Aguilar debuts in this as coproducer with Valentin Gazcon.

While not an extraordinary effort, story is pleasantly developed and acting is professional by all concerned. *Emil.*

Period Of Adjustment
(PANAVISION)

Tennessee Williams' serio-comedy about marital mayhem. Uneven film, but more peaks than valleys. Savvy trade and consumer selling could pay off.

Hollywood, Oct. 12.

Metro release of Lawrence Weingarten production. Stars Tony Franciosa, Jane Fonda, Jim Hutton. Directed by George Roy Hill. Screenplay, Isobel Lennart, based on Tennessee Williams' play; camera, Paul C. Vogel; editor, Fredric Steinkamp; music, Lyn Murray; assistant director, Al Jennings. Reviewed at Beverly Theatre, Oct. 12, '62. Running time, **112 MINS.**

Ralph Baitz .... Tony Franciosa
Isabel Haverstick .... Jane Fondo
George Haverstick .... Jim Hutton
Dorothea Baitz .... Lois Nettleton
Stewart P. McGill........John McGiver
Mrs. Alice McGill ...... Mabel Albertson
Desk Sergeant .... Jack Albertson

"Period of Adjustment" is lower case Tennessee Williams, but it also illustrates that lower case Williams is superior to the upper case of most modern playwrights. The lapses, inconsistencies and unlikelihoods of Williams' stage comedy-drama have not been eradicated in Isobel Lennart's screen adaptation for producer Lawrence Weingarten, but neither, happily, have the insights and substance that enable this examination of modern marriage to involve an audience emotionally with the seemingly comical but fundamentally critical experiences of two young couples on the brink of marital disaster.

"Period of Adjustment" is an uneven film, but at least when it hits its dramatic and comedic peaks, it hits them with impact. Very likely—and understandably—the Metro release will be ballyhooed as Tennessee Williams' first comedy, which could be unfortunate in the respect that many customers may be unprepared for and resultantly confused by its more serious dramatic aspects. The film, therefore, should not be described as an out-and-out, open-and-shut case of comedy. A potential audience must not be thus misled. There should be a tipoff that the picture embodies a more substantial and intimate streak. Handled with salesmanship finesse, it could evolve into a very successful attraction for Metro. The relatively youthful and attractive cast pitches in with some sound performances, and these factors will aid the commercial cause.

Jane Fonda-Jim Hutton and Lois Nettleton-Anthony Franciosa are the two teams whose emotional instability is explored. The togetherness of the first couple—newlyweds—is threatened by the insecurity of the afflicted groom, whose periodically severe outbreaks of the shakes are the manifestation of a long-standing complex wherein he feels compelled to hide behind a false he-man facade for fear of being found inadequate or below par at the supreme sexual moment.

Relations of the second pair are impaired by a more routine issue — in-law interference — coupled with the wife's accurate knowledge she was wed for money, not love—an original mercenary motive disolved, however, after six years of marriage. Doesn't sound very funny, but there are spurts and flashes of good fun, both in dialog and situation. And both stories are resolved happily, ultimately tipping the scales in favor of comedy over drama.

The promising Miss Fonda gives an animated performance and makes an impression, but there are times—particularly at the outset—when animation lapses into over-animation, stripping the character of believability. The character, however, tends to be fuzzy and inconsistent as written, and this may be the major part of Miss Fonda's problem. She does have some fine moments, though. Hutton does gen-

erally well by the part of the afflicted husband, although here again there are inconsistencies and contradictions in the character's personality, as penned. Franciosa has the meatiest part, and plays it to the hilt, creating an appealing, attractive, masculine person. Miss Nettleton is solid as the gradually more desirable wife. John McGiver is effective as the intrusive father-in-law, Mabel Albertson excellent as his troublemaking spouse. Jack Albertson has a good scene as a desk sergeant.

George Roy Hill's direction has peaks and valleys. He's coaxed and captured some perfectly timed and perceptive reactions from his players, but at other times he's settled for unnecessary exaggeration, and has failed to detect the fact that a pregnant running gag involving some progressively more intoxicated caroleers has been overworked to the point of diminishing returns. All production credits are favorable, including Paul C. Vogel's photography, Fredric Steinkamp's editing, Lyn Murray's score and the George W. Davis-Edward Carfagno art direction. *Tube.*

Tanze Mit Mir in Den Morgen

(Dance With Me Into the Morning)
(AUSTRIAN—SONGS—COLOR)

Berlin, Oct. 30.

Nora (German) release of Stadthalle Wien production. With Paul Hoerbiger, Guggi Loewinger, Rex Gildo, Oskar Sima, Lotte Lang. Guest singers: Gerhard Wendland, Camela Corren, Danny Mann, Peter Beil, Peter Hinnen, Chris Howland, Ines Taddio, Kurt Grosskurth and George Dimu. Directed by Peter Doerre. Camera, Hanns Matula; choreography, Willi Dirtl; artistic supervision, Paul Loewinger. At Roxy Palast, West Berlin. Running time, **93 MINS.**

Johann Ebeseder .... Paul Hoerbiger
Franziska, his grand-daughter .... Guggi Loewinger
Stefan Breuer .... Rex Gildo
Franz Biedermann .... Oskar Sima
Daisy, his daughter .... Evi Kent
Amalia Strassmeier .... Lotte Lang
Wenzel Kainz .... Rudolf Carl
Max, his son .... Udo Juergens

The best that can be said about this Nora release is that it will probably please large segments of the German teenage set. Production cashes in on the popularity of several German disk faves including Gerhard Wendland whose current hit, "Tanze mit mir in den Morgen" supplies the title for this thin-plotted musical. Pic will do well in the German-lingo market but there's nothing special about it to give other than limited chances elsewhere.

Film is a routine mixture of a meagre plot, some familiar situations, a bit of sentiment plus a lineup of guest singers. Story concerns a poor theatre director who struggles along to keep his pitiful enterprise alive; there are the authorities that want to tear down the shabby house; there's a young man among the authorities who falls in love with the director's twist - conscious granddaughter; and it goes more of the same. In the end, the theatre burns down but suddenly a rich American woman, a far-distant relative of the theatre director, shows up and gives him money so that he can buy himself a show-boat. There are several song and dance sequences along the line.

Of the various warblers, only a few rate adult attention. This applies in particular to two of foreign nationality: Carmela Corren, young Israeli chirp, proves that she's a win for the German disk market, and British Chris Howland, who has made himself a name via deejaying, disks, pix and tele in this country, clicks with his amusing "piggy bank" song. Of the actors, only the oldtimers such as Paul Hoerbiger (the theatre director), Josef Egger, Rudolf Carl and especially Oskar Sima give evidence that they know their trade.

Peter Doerre directed this unpretentious musical. Okay technical credits. The Blue Danube city supplies the background for this production. *Hans.*

Printemps De Jeunes Filles

(Springtime For the Girls)
(RUSSIAN-COLOR-SCOPE)

Paris, Oct. 30.

Sovexport release of Mosfilm production. With Mira Koltsova, Lev Barachkov, Lioudmilla Ovtchinnikova, Beriozka Ballet. Directed by Veniamin Dorman, Genrikh Oganissian. Screenplay, M. Dolgopolov, I. Prout, N. Nadejdina; camera (Sovcolor), Viatcheslav Choumski; music, Alexandre Fliarkovski; choreography, Nadia Nadejdina. At Kinopanorama, Paris. Running time, **85 MINS.**

Galia .... Mira Koltsova
Volodia .... Lev Barachkov
Nasstia .... Lioudmila Ovtchinnikova

One of the rare out-and-out commercial, Russo pix finds its way here, dubbed into French. It is a slight romantic story geared to the dances of the all-femme Beriozka Ballet. Somewhat stodgy and sweet, it still has some good humor with some expert dance sequences. But the film is a limited item at best.

A young optician falls for a dancer in the ballet company and gets a job on a boat to follow them on a tour of the Volga factories and countryside. After some misunderstandings the boy finally is well on the way to getting girl. All this is quite good natured. But the pace and flair for a tuner are missing.

The ballet portion is eyecatching entry as the girls seem to float above the stage. Color is acceptable but the players shape stereotyped if competent. It probably will be sock at home but somewhat too facile for untoward foreign chances in the West. *Mosk.*

Live Now—Pay Later

(BRITISH)

Somewhat uncertain combo of comedy and drama. Some neat performances, but a sprawling script which doesn't sufficiently develop the key characters.

London, Oct. 23.

Regal Films International release of a Jay Lewis (Jack Hanbury) production for Woodlands Productions. Stars John Gregson, June Ritchie, Ian Hendry; features Liz Fraser, Geoffrey Keen, Jeanette Sterke, Peter Butterworth, Nyree Dawn Porter, Ronald Howard, Harold Berens, Thelma Ruby, Monty Landis, Joan Heal, Geoffrey Hibbert, Judith Furse, Andrew Cruickshank, John Wood. Directed by Lewis. Screenplay, Jack Trevor Story from Jack Lindsay's novel, "All On the Never Never"; music, Ron Grainer; editor, Roger Cherrill; camera, Jack Hillyard. At Carlton, London. Running time, **104 MINS.**

Albert .... Ian Hendry
Treasure .... June Ritchie
Callendar .... John Gregson
Joyce Corby .... Liz Fraser
Reggie Corby .... Geoffrey Keen
Grace .... Jeanette Sterke
Fred .... Peter Butterworth
Marjorie Mason ..... Nyree Dawn Porter
Cedric Mason .... Ronald Howard
Solly Cowell .... Harold Berens
Hetty .... Thelma Ruby
Arnold .... Monty Landis
Jackson .... Kevin Brennan
Ratty .... Malcolm Knight
Gloria .... Bridget Armstrong
Mrs. Ackroyd .... Judith Furse
Mrs. Pocock .... Joan Heal
Bailiff .... Michael Brennan
Major Simpkins......... William Kendall
Lucy .... Georgina Cookson
Coral Wentworth ..... Justine Lord
Price .... Geoffrey Hibbert
Vicar .... Andrew Cruickshank
Curate .... John Wood

The pernicious influence of widespread credit buying, causing wives to get into debt, corruption, distortion of personal views and a cynical "grab what's going while you can" attitude is a valid, timely theme for a picture. But this one wavers too uncertainly between broad comedy, farce and romantic drama. There is also the jarring introduction of the death of a young wife in a road accident which is a contrived plot point but certainly doesn't fit the general atmosphere of the film.

Jack Trevor Story's screenplay has many amusing moments, but overall it is untidy and does not develop the personalities of some of the main characters sufficiently. Extraneous situations are dragged in without helping the plot development overmuch. Jay Lewis has directed with verve. Also there are some very useful performances, okay artwork, satisfactory lensing by Jack Hillyard and a lively enough score by Ron Grainer. Where the film falls down is in its sheer superficiality and that few of the characters can be taken seriously, or beget sympathy.

Ian Hendry plays a smart aleck, philandering, doublecrossing tallyman who, with two illegitimate babies to his discredit, still finds that the easiest way to bluff his femme patrons into getting hocked up to their eyebrows in installment buying is via the boudoir. The character has a certain brash, breezy assurance, but no charm. And that's the way Hendry plays it, to the point of irritation.

In most of the film he is trying to patch up a row that he has had with his steady girl friend. For the remainder, he is cheating his employer (John Gregson), a real estate agent and a string of creditors. He is also not above a little blackmail to further his progress with his boss. It is Hendry's first major film and, on this showing, judgment must be reserved as to his future.

June Ritchie, as the main girl in the case, confirms the promising impression she made in her debut in "A Kind of Loving," but she can do little in this cardboard role of wronged young mistress. Two established players, John Gregson and Geoffrey Keen, confidently handle the roles of Hendry's ambitious, conniving boss and an equally ambitious, scheming and pompous real estate man.

Playing Keen's simple, humiliated wife is Liz Fraser. This film sets up some sort of a record in that Miss Fraser, till now mostly engaged in frothy bosomy, undress roles, keeps her clothes on throughout while most of the other femmes seem to be stripping at the drop of Hendry's hat. Miss Fraser is anxious to break away from pinup roles and this small, but effective performance (she's the woman who gets bumped off) proves that she deserves more significant, worthy roles in the future.

Nyree Dawn Porter and Justine Lord, two of the salesman's willing bedroom victims, are both well equipped for their roles. Judith Furze, Joan Heal, Thelma Ruby and Bridget Armstrong chip in with some predictable, but acceptable comedy.

The interior of Gregson's credit store is well done. And it is a pity that it is put to use in only one sequence, involving Hendry and a tipsy Miss Ritchie, Ruth Batchelor and Clive Westlake have concocted a catchy title song. "Live Now—Pay Later" has a number of worthwhile points but must be rated a near miss. *Rich.*

La Lutte Finale

(The Final Battle)
(GERMAN—FRENCH)

Paris, Oct. 30.

Georges Glass-Jean Marin release of Aero Film production. Selected and mounted newsreel footage by Peter Rosinski, Raphael Nussbaum. Commentary by Jean Serge spoken by Serge. Max Megy; editor, Georges Marschack. At Studio De L'Etoile, Paris. Running time, **70 MINS.**

This a strange one. A compilation subject about the Russia of the Czar and then covering the Revolution seems to resemble the Yank "We'll Bury You," reviewed in VARIETY, Oct. 10 issue. But not completely since this runs 70 mins., not 77, and seems to have some different footage with German and French backgrounds.

"Bury," a Columbia release in the U.S., is a condemnation of Russia while this is anti-Stalin but seemingly pro-Khrushchev and Lenin. It also gives a lion's share of credit for the successful Revolution to the banished Trotsky.

This shows the Czar at play while Russians suffer and then the First World War plus the beginnings of the Revolution with the aborted German tries and flashbacks to the first 1905 anarchistic rumblings in Russia. Also shown is Russo-Japanese war footage but without the shot of the sunken Russo vessel mentioned as a highlight for the other pic.

The Lenin and Trotsky footage is sharp and unusual as are some rugged shots of executions of Red soldiers by White Army people. Pic shows various armies—Russo, Yank, British and French trying to put down the Revolution. But all is based on the commentary which is much too didactic and full of loopholes.

The images are the thing and the old footage still remains absorbing but seemingly can be bent to any outlook: This ends with Khrushchev's rise to power and the takeover of Lithuania and the anti-Stalin speech of K. There is obviously a link between the two pix but both have different viewpoints. This review is mainly for the record. *Mosk.*

The Main Attraction

(BRITISH-COLOR)

Corny yarn but some good performances, a few lilting songs and colorful circus atmosphere. For Pat Boone fans.

London, Oct. 23.

Metro release of a Seven Arts (John Patrick) production. Stars Nancy Kwan,

Pat Boone; features Mai Zetterling. Yvonne Mitchell, Keiron Moore, John Le Mesurier. Directed by Daniel Petrie. Screenplay, John Patrick; camera, Geoffrey Unsworth; editor, Geoffrey Foot; music, Andrew Adorian. Previewed at Metro Private Theatre. Running time, **90 MINS.**

Tessa	Nancy Kwan
Eddie	Pat Boone
Gina	Mai Zetterling
Elenora	Yvonne Mitchell
Ricco	Keiron Moore
Bozo	John Le Mesurier
Bus Driver	Carl Duering
Proprietor	Warren Mitchell
Burton	Lionel Murton
Clown	Lionel Blair
Band Announcer	Frank Sieman

Pat Boone's attempt to escape from his own image of the cleancut All-American youth is a good try. Playing with Nancy Kwan, Boone is a cynical, drifting young man with an eye for the gals but no desire, at first, to settle down. Performance is handicapped by John Patrick's screenplay which is neither sharp nor decisive enough. Nevertheless, Boone, in between singing four pleasant songs, smokes, drinks and h— — — tumbles with the sexy Mai Zetterling. Enough for his fans to realize that Boone is no longer in only prissy roles.

Boone gets fired from his job in an Italian cafe after a punch up with some drunks. He's picked up by Miss Zetterling, who is something of a dipso-nympho, and he becomes her stooge in her circus ventriloquist ac' He also becomes her lover. But Boone also becomes enamored with Nancy Kwan. She is a young equestrienne, part of an act run by Keiron Moore and his wife, Yvonne Mitchell, who is her crippled sister.

After complications, the hero hops the circus and catches up with Miss Kwan who has also broken away because of problems. Up in the Alps, the pair have a splendid night of bliss in a chalet, and then get involved in an avalanche. But all's well. Director D niel Petrie and scriptist Patrick steer the six main characters back into the receptive arms of their chosen.

Geoffrey Unsworth's lensing makes the most of both the circus atmosphere and the local scenery while Andrew Adorian has chipped in with a pleasing score. Petrie's direction is sometimes flabby, but highlights a few dramatic situations effectively.

Best performance comes from Miss Zetterling. She clearly realized that the role had to be overplayed and does it with abandon. Miss Kwan's part is rather too naive but there are some rewarding supporting roles by a stolid Moore, John Le Mesurier and Miss Mitchell, who suffers to good effect as the crippled elder sister.

Boone gives a pleasant performance but will have to give second thoughts about ever playing a heavy. There are four songs which he puts over persuasively. He has had a hand in writing two of them, the title song, "Main Attraction" and (the best) "Amore Baciami." The numbers are worked logically enough into action. *Rich.*

The Loves Of Salammbo
(C'SCOPE—COLOR)

Inferior exploitation item.

Hollywood, Oct. 22.

Twentieth-Fox release of Fides-Stella production. Stars Jeanne Valerie, Jacques Sernas; with Edmund Purdom, Arnoldo Foa, Riccardo Garrone, Kamala Devi, Charles Fawcett. Directed by Sergio Grieco. Screenplay, John Blamy, Barbara Sohmers, from story by Gustave Flaubert; editor, Enzo Alfonzi; music, Alexandre Derevitsky. Reviewed at the studio, Oct. 22, '62. Running time, **74 MINS.**

"The Loves of Salammbo" lasts only 74 minutes but a more inept job of filmmaking is difficult to imagine. Fides-Stella production has been gathering dust on 20th shelves for over a year.

Total confusion prevails in the Italo-filmed item, from scenario, through editing, through scoring, through dubbing. Storyline has something to do with internal strife in ancient Carthage over delayed payment of pick-up forces who were hired to defend the country against the Romans. The acting is stilted under director Sergio Grisco. Photography is erratic, editing is chaotic, scoring is obtrusive and anachronistic. Much of the film sounds as if it was dubbed one second off beat in an echo chamber. *Tube.*

Capurcita y Pulgarcito Contra Los Monstruos
(Little Red Riding Hood and Tom Thumb Against Monsters)
(MEXICAN—EASTMANCOLOR)
Mexico City, Oct. 23.

Peliculas Nocionales release of Peliculas Rodriguez production. Stars Maria Gracia, Cesarea Quezadas, Jose Elias Moreno; features Manuel "Loco" Valdez, El Enano Santanon, Ofelia Guilmain, Magda Donato, Armando Gutierrez and Quintin Bulnes. Directed by Roberto Rodriguez. Screenplay, Fernando Morales Ortiz and Adolfo Torres Portillo; camera, Rosalio Solano; music, Raul Lavista. At Alameda Theatre, Mexico City. Running time, **90 MINS.**

Director Roberto Rodriguez is an old hand in directing this series of films using characters dear to the hearts of youngsters. In this one Little Red Riding Hood and Tom Thumb fight familiar screen monsters, and naturally win.

Not much on plot but the color and photography are good and interpretation by such old favorites (of former films) as Manuel "Loco" Valeez, and Jose Elias Moreno is adequate.

The gold mine discovered by the Rodriguez brothers continues to be mined in this series, with this one likely to do good business at boxoffice here and in Spanish language markets. *Emil.*

How the West Was Won
(CINERAMA—TECHNICOLOR)

In three words: a boffo blockbuster.

London, Nov. 2.

Metro release of MGM-Cinerama (Bernard Smith) production. Stars Spencer Tracy, Carroll Baker, Lee J. Cobb, Henry Fonda, Carolyn Jones, Karl Malden, Gregory Peck, George Peppard, Robert Preston, Debbie Reynolds, James Stewart, Eli Wallach, John Wayne, Richard Widmark; features Brigid Bazlan, Walter Brennan, David Brian, Andy Devine, Raymond Massey, Agnes Moorehead, Henry (Harry) Morgan, Thelma Ritter, Mickey Shaughnessy, Russ Tamblyn. Directed by Henry Hathaway, John Ford, George Marshall. Screenplay, James Webb; camera (Technicolor), William H. Daniels, Milton Krasner, Charles Lang Jr., Joseph LaShelle; editor, Harold F. Kress; music, Alfred Newman; asst. directors, George Marshall Jr., William McGarry, Robert Saunders, William Shanks, Wingate Smith; art direction, George W. Davis, William Ferrari, Addison Hehr; set decoration, Henry Grace, Don Greenwood Jr., Jack Mills; 2d unit camera, Harold E. Wellman; costumes, Walter Plunkett; special effects, A. Arnold Gillespie, Robert R. Hoag; production supervisor for Cinerama, Thomas Conroy. Reviewed at Casino Theatre, London, Nov. 1, '62. Running time, **155 MINS.**

Narrator	Spencer Tracy
Eve Prescott	Carroll Baker
Lou Ramsey	Lee J. Cobb
Jethro Stuart	Henry Fonda
Julie Stuart	Carolyn Jones
Zebulon Prescott	Karl Malden
Cleve Van Valen	Gregory Peck
Zeb Rawlings	George Peppard
Roger Morgan	Robert Preston
Lilith Prescott	Debbie Reynolds
Linus Rawlings	James Stewart
Charlie Gant	Eli Wallach
General Sherman	John Wayne
Mike King	Richard Widmark
Dora Hawkins	Brigid Bazlen
Colonel Hawkins	Walter Brennan
Attorney	David Brian
Peterson	Andy Devine
Abraham Lincoln	Raymond Massey
Rebecca Prescott	Agnes Moorehead
General Grant	Henry (Harry) Morgan
Agatha Clegg	Thelma Ritter
Deputy Marshal	Mickey Shaughnessy
Confederate Soldier	Russ Tamblyn

There can be no element of doubt about "How the West Was Won." This, the first story-line film in Cinerama to reach Europe, is the blockbuster supreme, a magnificent and exciting spectacle which must, inevitably, dwarf the earnings of the travelogs in the three-screen process. It will, undoubtedly, run for several years, and will become one of the industry's all-time top grossers.

Backed by a substantial campaign, the spectacular opened in London with an advance of almost $450,000, including an unprecedented ticket brokers' guarantee of $280,000 for the first year of the run. That's indicative of the success to come, and Metro and Cinerama, who are 50-50 partners in the production, should be reaping lush returns.

Technically, there's a vast improvement in the process. The print joins are barely noticeable, and the wobble, which beset earlier productions, has been eliminated. And that enhances the entertainment immeasurably, for the customer can concentrate on the breathtaking backgrounds and action without any distraction.

It would be hard to imagine a subject which lends itself more strikingly to the wide-screen process than this yarn of the pioneers who opened the American West. It's a story which naturally puts the spotlight on action and adventure, and the three directors between them have turned in some memorable sequences. George Marshall, for example, has the credit for the buffalo stampede, started by the Indians when the railroad was moving out West. This

magnificently directed sequence is as vivid as anything ever put on celluloid, and has the excitement to compel an audience to sit bolt upright in their seats. Undoubtedly, the highlight of Henry Hathaway's contribution is the chase of outlaws who attempt to hold up a train with a load of bullion. This item must, inevitably, be regarded as the latter day widescreen "Great Train Robbery." The scene packs more excitement and dramatic punch in a few minutes than many motion pictures in two hours. It's unforgettable. John Ford's directorial stint is limited to the Civil War sequences, and though that part does not contain such standout incident, there is the fullest evidence of his high professional standards.

The story is far and away at its best when the emphasis is on the action, but the more intimate moments of the plot come out surprisingly well on the big screen. As the cast list indicates, more than a dozen front ranking international stars, together with top supporting names, are used to tell the story, and though the majority have smallish roles, their appearances on screen serve a two-fold purpose. Having familiar names around eases character identification in such a vast subject; and additionally, of course, they are invaluable as extra boxoffice bait.

The story-line is developed around the Prescott family, as they start on their adventurous journey out West. Karl Malden and Agnes Moorehead are the parents, and with them are their two daughters, played by Debbie Reynolds and Carroll Baker. They start their journey out West down the Erie Canal, and when James Stewart, a fur trapper, comes on the scene, it's love at first sight for Miss Baker. Although they're headed in opposite directions, he eventually gets her man. After her parents lose their lives when their raft capsizes in the rapids—and that's another of the highly vivid sequences directed by Hathaway—Miss Reynolds joins a wagon train to continue her journey and tries, in vain, to resist the charms of Gregory Peck, a professional gambler, who is first attracted to her when she's believed to have inherited a gold mine.

They are the principal people in the "intimate" part of the story, and Miss Reynolds is about the only one lasting the whole length of the picture. Her performance is a surprise even for her most devout fans. There's an unexpected quality to her acting and a wider emotional sweep than usual. She ages with delicate grace, and towards the end, when her possessions are being sold by auction, she looks back philosophically on a happy and contented life.

As always, Peck gives a suave and polished gloss to his role of the gambler, and though it's an undemanding part he gives it notable distinction. Stewart has some fine, if typical, moments in his scenes, and he gets involved in a magnificently directed fight with some unprincipled adventurers who try to rob him and his friends of their possessions. It's a noholds barred punch-up in which anything goes.

Richard Widmark makes a vital impression as the head man of the construction team building the

railroad. He's tough and uncompromising, and it's his determination to press on disregarding the human suffering he may cause, that leads to a clash with the Indians, and the previously mentioned buffalo stampede. John Wayne is another top ranking star with only a minor part as General Sherman in the Civil War episode, but he, too, makes the character stand out.

Another superb cameo comes from Eli Wallach, as the bandit who leads the gang in the train robbery, while Robert Preston plays the wagon master with great authority and sincerity. There's another excellent portrayal from Henry Fonda, who is the white man's emissary to the Indians, and he invests the part with considerable dignity. Other distinctive contributions come from Lee J. Cobb, Carolyn Jones, Karl Malden and George Peppard, and all the feature players.

The courage and tenacity of the pioneers is effectively etched in James Webb's screenplay, but the narrative is no more than a peg for the magnificent action sequences, which nightly dominate the production. The story is never intended to be more than a slender thread. That's surely the right approach, and is underlined by Bernard Smith's monumental production. The technical credits cannot be faulted, and the four cameramen contribute some of the best ever lensing seen in motion pictures. The music is another pleasing feature, and the trio of art directors have designed some impressive sets.

Spencer Tracy is heard but not seen as the narrator. In a clear, well-spoken commentary he provides the introduction to the story, and also the closing comments. And the final scene, of the present day West, with its crowded highways, is a striking salute to the adventurous pioneers. *Myro.*

Young Guns of Texas
(C'SCOPE—COLOR)

Young sons of Hollywood guns in a humdrum supporting western.

Twentieth-Fox release of Maury Dexter production. Directed by Dexter. Stars James Mitchum, Alana Ladd, Jody McCrea, Chill Wills; introduces Gary Conway. Screenplay, Henry Cross; camera (De Luxe), John Nickolaus Jr.; editor, Richard Einfeld; music, Paul Sawtell, Bert Shefter; assistant director, Clarence Eurist. Reviewed at the studio, Nov. 2, '62. Running time, 78 MINS.
Morgan Coe .... James Mitchum
Lily Glendenning .... Alana Ladd
Jeff Shelby .... Jody McCrea
Preacher Sam Shelby ...... Chill Winds
Tyler .... Gary Conway
Martha Jane Canary....Barbara Mansell
Jesse Glendenning........Robert Lowery
Luke .... Troy Melton
Pike .... Fred Krone
Red .... Alex Sharp
Sheriff .... Robert Hinkle

"Young Guns of Texas" is a grade B western with some grade A names to adorn a marquee. Grade A surnames, that is. Starring in the Maury Dexter production are James Mitchum, Alana Ladd and Jody McCrea. Although, at this embryo juncture in their careers, the resemblance to their fathers is considerably more physical than histrionic, their appearance in the 20th-Fox release gives it the kind of casting novelty that, properly ballyhooed, can enhance

its commercial value as a supporting attraction.

Beyond the offbeat casting, however, there is little in "Young Guns" to entice even the western addict. Henry Cross' undistinguished screenplay interweaves two basic stories. One concerns the illfated romance of Mitchum and Miss Ladd against the wishes of her father, who resents the fact that Mitchum has been raised by Comanches. The other is concerned with the plight of a young fellow (Gary Conway) searching for his brother, who has been accused of pilfering Union funds. The two issues are resolved in a showdown skirmish with perhaps the most tactically inept band of Apaches ever to thunder across the screen.

The three co-starring youngsters needed a firm directorial hand in this vehicle. Director Dexter didn't supply that firmness, with the result that all three seem ill-at-ease. The picture gets off to a solid start with a rousingly unbelievable fistfight, then limps along lethargically the balance of the way. Of the young people involved, screen newcomer Conway makes the most vivid and favorable impression. Chill Wills puts in a reliable appearance. Others of note are Barbara Mansell, Robert Lowery and Robert Hinkle.

Art, photographic and musical contributions to the film are adequate. Editing is uneven, however —sluggish over the long haul, yet abrupt in transition once or twice. There's a trite title tune, composed by Paul Sawtell and Bert Shefter, with lyrics by John Herring. Kenny Miller sings it over the titles. *Tube.*

Girls, Girls, Girls!

Light drama with music concentrating heavily on salability of Elvis Presley. Film is a general romantic story with handsome color photography.

Hollywood, Oct. 31.

Paramount release of Hal Wallis (Paul Nathan) production. Stars Elvis Presley; features Stella Stevens, Jeremy Slate, Laurel Goodwin. Directed by Norman Tourog. Screenplay by Edward Anhalt and Allan Weiss, based on original story by Weiss; dances staged by Charles O'Curran; scored and conducted by Joseph J. Lilley with vocal accompaniment by The Jordanieres; camera, Loyal Griggs; editor, Stanley E. Johnson; asst. director, D. Michael Moore. Reviewed Oct. 26, '62, at Village Theatre, Westwood. Running time, 101 MINS.
Ross Carpenter .... Elvis Presley
Robin Gantner .... Stella Stevens
Wesley Johnson .... Jeremy Slate
Laurel Dodge .... Laurel Goodwin
Kin Tung .... Benson Fong
Sam .... Robert Strauss
Chen Yung .... Guy Lee
Alexander Stavros .... Frank Puglia
Mama Stavros .... Lili Valenty
Madame Yung .... Beulah Quo
Mai Ling, Tai Ling and their little brother Ginny Tiu, Elizabeth Tu and Alexander Mai Ling, Tai Ling and their little
brother......Ginny Tiu, Elizabeth Tiu and Alexander Tiu

"Girls, Girls, Girls!" is just that —with Elvis Presley there as the main attraction. Apparently, from the grosses racked up by the performer's earlier pix, he remains generally a salable attraction. This new effort hinges on the popularity of the entertainer, who is given a plethora of songs regardless of whether they fit smoothly into the action.

Hal Wallis' production, directed by Norman Taurog, puts the entertainer back into the non-drama-

tic, purely escapist light musical vein. The thin plot, scripted by Edward Anhalt and Allan Weiss from an original story by Weiss, has him the romantic interest of two girls. Hackneyed tale is of poor boy fisherman who meets rich girl who doesn't tell him she is rich but who, naturally, falls in love with him.

Presley, on the other hand, is far more interested in recovering a sleek sailboat originally built by his father but then forced into other hands. All the usual elements, including a dastardly villain who turns out to be a wolf, but not in disguise, are present. Notably, Weiss also penned story for the earlier "Blue Hawaii," which Taurog also directed for Wallis.

Essentially, Presley plays himself in the breezy sea session. He handles the role capably, though one would hardly expect a hardened fisherman to be as soft, smooth and white as the one Presley depicts. The character has little depth, but he is pleasant.

Most striking thing about the picture is the introduction of new Paramount pactee Laurel Goodwin, who makes an auspicious film bow. Youngster has the cute, homespun potential of a Doris Day.

Stella Stevens, however, is wasted in a standard role as a sultry torch singer who has given up ever really nailing the guy. She does her best but, aside from singing three songs (her first singing in a film) in a style suitable for the character, there just isn't enough for her to do.

Jeremy Slate plays the villain with a combination of crass charm and broad comedy. His is a solid performance. Also fine are Benson Fong, Robert Strauss, Guy Lee, Frank Puglia, Lili Valenty and Beulah Quo. Cute scene features moppets Ginny and Elizabeth Tiu in a Chinese song.

Notably, Wallis edited out five minutes from the film previewed, taking out two songs, which quickens the pace of one drawn out section.

Production is dressed nicely by Edith Head. Musical numbers were staged by Charles O'Curran, scored and conducted by Joseph J. Lilley, with vocal accompaniment by The Jordanieres, Loyal Griggs' Technicolor photography is handsome. *Dale.*

Mutiny On The Bounty
(PANAVISION-COLOR)

Boffo boxoffice spec.

Metro release of Aaron Rosenberg (Arcola) production. Stars Marlon Brando, Trevor Howard, Richard Harris; features Hugh Griffith, Richard Haydn, Tarita. Directed by Lewis Milestone. Screenplay, Charles Lederer, based on the novel by Charles Nordhoff-James Norman Hall; camera (Technicolor), Robert L. Surtees; editor, John McSweeney Jr.; art directors, George W. Davis, J. McMillan Johnson; music, Bronislau Kaper; asst. director, Ridgeway Callow. Reviewed at the studio, Nov. 5, '62. Running time, 185 MINS.
Fletcher Christian....... Marlon Brando
Captain Bligh........ Trevor Howard
John Mills .... Richard Harris
Alexander Smith .... Hugh Griffith
William Brown .... Richard Haydn
Mathew Quintal .... Percy Herbert
Michael Byrne ....: Chips Rafferty
John Fryer .... Eddie Byrne
Edward Young .... Tim Seely
William McCoy .... Noel Purcell
Edward Birkett .... Gordon Jackson
John Williams .... Duncan Lamont
Samuel Mack .... Ashley Cowan
James Morrison ...... Keith McConnell
Maimiti .... Tarita
                    (Taritatumi Teriipaia)
Minarii .... Frank Silvera
Chief Hitihiti .... Matahaii Tama

Metro's 1962 version of "Mutiny on the Bounty," after some two years of gestation and strenuous labor pains, has emerged a physically superlative entertainment. It may be somewhat short of genuine dramatic greatness, but it is often overwhelmingly spectacular and overall has the look of a hefty boxoffice attraction.

Pictorially stunning in Technicolor and ultra Panapision 70, it's the kind of picture that will satisfy the adventurous spirits of most audiences. Moreover, there is just enough romantic dalliance and display of lustful intentions against idyllic Tahitian backgrounds to balance out the muscular action of men straining against hostile elements at sea and the cruel lash of a sadistic captain.

Although Metro's 1935 Academy Award winner "Bounty" is now beyond criticism in the minds of many and the performances of Clark Gable and Charles Laughton have become cherished memories, the new edition is generally superior. Its only handicap is that unfortunate and outlandish $18,-000,000 production cost, but even so the odds are in its favor in terms of prolonged ticket activity.

Marlon Brando as Fletcher Christian and Trevor Howard as Capt. Bligh have etched their own brilliant entries in the "Bounty's" log. Brando in many ways is giving the finest performance of his career. While Howard is always hot on his heels, the Britisher does not, as the script is developed by Charles Lederer and directed by Lewis Milestone, have the same range of character growth. Bligh comes aboard at Portsmouth the hard, intractable master. Basically he does not change. However, Howard does take full and dramatically intriguing advantages of opportunities while at sea and in Tahiti to open windows on Bligh's black and lonely soul to bring alive the image of a man of dauntless courage and fortitude, but withal a monster in navy dress.

Brando's Fletcher Christian is a many faceted character development, full of arresting subtleties in facial expression, voice inflection and gestures. He boards as a foppish aristocrat, with more arrogance than true gentlemanly breed-

ing, but underneath the veneer there is the steel of a Royal Navy officer. The struggle within Christian as he suffers humiliation by his captain before the crew, his repressed revulsion and desire to rebel against the skipper's brutalizing of the men and his contempt for Bligh's foolhardy stubborness in attempting to go round the Horn in raging winter seas is brilliantly suggested as well as projeced by Brando. He has, too, given the screen its most realistic moment of death—eyes fixed and staring, breathing suspended— even though the lead into this is a conventional buildup. There are times when one becomes conscious of a certain superficiality in Brando's performance, but those are not serious reservations.

Indeed, one might wish that the surge of action had been subordinated to permit closer ties with many members of the "Bounty's" crew. That may or may not be a deficiency of the workmanlike screenplay by Charles Lederer, but it's the spectacular action that will build the boxoffice momentum. And director Milestone has come up with some terrific scenes and sequences, from opening a man's back by laying on the whip to fighting wind, cold, snow, rain, towering seas and a murderous, runaway cask in the hold. No storm on screen has ever equalled that of the illfated assault on the Horn, and it's doubtful any ship at sea could withstand such a beating.

This is a superb blending of direction, photography and special effects artistry (One might also recognize, of course, that the actors took quite a beating). The lensmanship of Robert L. Surtees is magnificent throughout the picture and his versatility in lighting seascapes, specially at dusk, is particularly notable.

Milestone, who often shot as Lederer turned out pages of script, time and again had to reshoot scenes for one reason or another. Milestone also experienced long lapses in filming and continuity but can take pride in a job well done. So, it should be noted, can producer Aaron Rosenberg.

The 185 minutes of "Bounty" do not cause strain: in fact, they pass rather quickly because there generally always is something of interest on the screen to hold attention. Story actually divides into three chapters — the horrendous voyage from England to the South Seas in quest of specimens of a breadfruit plant for transference to Jamaica to stock Britain's larder; the five months' layover at Tahiti while awaiting the proper time to begin the transplanting operation; the mutiny and subsequent haven on Piticairn Island, mislocated on admiralty charts and discovered by accident.

Intermission comes after the visit to Tahiti, where the native gals frolic and generously entertain their fairskinned, if not always handsome, visitors. The native costumes and dances are colorful and the lush tropical scenery is enchanting after the long sea voyage. Enchanting also is Tarita. She plays the island chieftain's daughter, who invites Brando into her heart and who refuses to be cast out of his life. Tarita (Taritatumi Teriipaia) is a 19-year-old

native, whose swaying hips will find their own varying levels of audience appreciation. As for acting ability, she is adequate to the demands of the role.

The mutiny on the homeward voyage gets the film off to a rousing second start. However, the climactic sequences on Pitcairn, where Christian determines to return home and attempt to justify seizure of Bligh's command before injuries aboard the blazing Bounty end his life, having a diminishing dramatc effect. This is unfortunate, but will not seriously affect overall enjoyment of the picture.

The "Bounty's" crew includes some fine actors. Like the stars, they also provide sturdy performances, notably Richard Harris, as the seaman accused of stealing a head of cheese. He tells the crew he actually stole it for the captain and thereby sets the beast stirring in Bligh. Richard Haydn also has some good moments as the botanist in search of the breadfruit plant and Tim Seely shows confusion, sensitivity and strength as a young midshipman. Others who shape up fine as sailors are Hugh Griffith, Percy Herbert, Gordon Jackson, Noel Purcell, Chips Rafferty, Dunchan Lamont, Ashley Cowan, Eddie Byrne and Keith McConnel. A pair of colorful island headmen are portrayed by Frank Silvera and Matahiarii Tama.

Almost, but not quite, as important a figure in the story as Brando and Howard is the Bounty herself, sarcastically referred to by Brando at one point as "a 95-foot chamberpot." Dialog or no, the Bounty is a fine accomplishment for art directors George W. Davis and J. McMillan Johnson, as well as set decorators Henry Grace and Hugh Hunt and the Nova Scotia shipwrights who built her.

Others whose contributions helped turn out a lavish production are John McSweeney Jr., who had to snip and paste a lot of footage in accomplishing a good editing job; special effects experts A. Arnold Gillespie, Lee LeBlanc and Robert R. Hoag; choreographer Hamil Petroff; second unit director James C. Havens and recording supervisor Franklin Milton.

The Bronislau Kaper musical score deftly enhances the various dramatic moods. As a composition it has individual merit and should stand on its own in record release. However, there are times in the picture when the sweep and surge of the music has such distinctive force that it seems to be trying to overpower scenes. It might be wise to tune down the music in volume at least. The central theme, however, will emerge a pop diskseller.

Not all who board the "Bounty" will be completely pleased with the voyage, but the majority will get their money's worth, with interest, and will encourage others to enjoy the experience too.
Pry.

Kill Or Cure
(BRITISH)

Lowercase Terry - Thomas comedy-whodunit.

Hollywood, Nov. 8.
Metro release of George H. Brown production. Stars Terry-Thomas, Eric Sykes; features Dennis Price, Lionel Jeffries, Moira Redmond, Katya Douglas. Directed by George Pollock. Screenplay and story, David Pursall, Jack Seddon; camera, Geoffrey Faithfull; editor, Bert Rule; music, Ron Goodwin; asst. director, Jan Darnley-Smith. Reviewed at the studio, Nov. 8, '62. Running time, 88 MINS.

J. Barker-Rynde	Terry-Thomas
Rumbelow	Eric Sykes
Dr. Crossley	Dennis Price
Inspector Hook	Lionel Jeffries
Frances	Moira Redmond
Rita	Katya Douglas
Richards	David Lodge
Burton	Ronnie Barker
Mrs. Crossley	Hazel Terry
Roger	Derrin Nesbitt
Riggins	Harry Locke
Clerk	Arthur Howard
Asst. Clerk	Tristram Jellinek
Barman	Peter Butterworth
Waitress	Patricia Hayes
Mrs. Clifford	Anna Russell
"Mandy" trained by	John Holmes
"Junia" trained by	Mrs. B. Woodhouse

Not even merry Terry-Thomas could put life into this limp comedy whodunit. Both comedy and mystery are strained and obvious.. The Metro release, ground out by producer George H. Brown at Metro's British plant in Borehamwood, will make a satisfactory supporting item, but hasn't the stature to hold its own as a featured attraction.

The David Pursall-Jack Seddon original premise seems to have had possibilities, but the inspiration to realize that potential is absent in their scenario. Thanks to the clowning of Thomas, Eric Sykes and Lionel Jeffries, there is some sporadic amusement, but mostly the material lets them down and leaves them to their own comedy resources. Thomas is cast as combination photographer-private investigator (snaps and snoops) who is implicated in some foul play at a British health farm.

Support is capable, and so is George Pollock's direction, but the deft British touch with comedy is scarcely evident. Best facet is Ron Goodwin's obtrusively lighthearted musical score.
Tube.

The Swordsman of Siena
(C'SCOPE—COLOR)

Swashbuckling adventure meller in the style of the wartime programmers. Film is best suited for drive-ins or neighboorhoods. Has exploitation values that could be beneficial abroad.

Hollywood, Nov. 8.
Metro-Goldwyn-Mayer release of Jacques Bar production. Stars Stewart Granger; features Sylva Koscina, Christine Kaufmann. Directed by Etienne Perier. Screenplay by Michael & Fay Kanin and Alec Coppel based on story by Anthony Marshall; music by Mario Mascimbene; camera (Eastmancolor), Tonino Delli Colli; editors, Robert and Monique Isnardon; asst. director, Gus Agosti. Reviewed at Academy Theatre, L.A., Nov. 7, '62. Running time, 97 MINS.

Thomas Stanwood	Stewart Granger
Orietta Arconti	Sylva Koscina
Serenella Arconti	Christine Kaufmann
Don Carlos	Riccardo Garrone
Father Giacomo	Tullio Carminati
Paresi	Alberto Lupo
Hugo	Fausto Tozzi
Gino	Carlo Rizzo
Leoni	Claudio Gora
Countess of Osta	Marina Berti

During that era over a dozen years back, when swashbuckling adventure dramas were more or less standard fare, Metro-Goldwyn-Mayer might have had a chance to slip by with "Swordsman of Siena," although even then the lack of ingenuity in the Jacques Bar production would certainly have been apparent to most audiences. The title itself is pretty much a giveaway and it takes only a few minutes into the first reel to discover almost exactly what is going to take place on the screen for the remaining hour and a half.

Nonetheless, there remains a limited audience for "Swordsman," which could do sufficient business in drive-ins and neighborhoods wherein youngsters may be amused, if not immersed, in the action, color and at least superficially adventurous character of the film. It appears destined, however, for the lower half of the bill in most instances. Some heft in Stewart Granger and Christine Kaufmann names but others like Sylva Koscina and Tullio Carminati, are known in Europe and, in the light of grosses abroad, the picture could well catch on sufficiently in that area.

Bar and director Etienne Perier —same duo that made "Bridge to the Sun"— filmed it in Italy, although most of the shots are done in interiors that look just like any photoplay made in a studio.

Granger plays the title role in the Michael and Fay Kanin and Alec Coppel screenplay (based on a story by Anthony Marshall). It is a well worn tale of the dashingly handsome, fearless but mercenary adventurer who finds his morals midstream in the action and switches to the right side— and to the arms of the lovely lady. He begins a swordplay—one man against 20 and nearly gets them all until he is caught—only to find he is fighting against the man for whom he is going to work.

Absolved, he gets the job of guarding the hated Duke's betrothed, a cold and apparently-to-all - but - the - audience - heartless beauty who is promised to the Duke, who has underhandedly taken over the city once ruled by her father and who also, in effect, had her father killed. The lady, however, is actually a Saint in disguise, the leader of the underground who plot to overthrow the Duke. Granger soon is aiding them and all ends pretty much the same as most of these tired stories do.

Granger looks good and plays the role with pleasant dash. He is no Errol Flynn or Fairbanks, but he does have a certain amount of charm. Miss Kaufmann is lost as the defiant younger sister of Sylva Koscina, who plays the Duke's betrothed. She is a better actress than she has a chance to show in the role. Miss Koscina does well with her role. Carminati, Riccardo Carrone, Fausto Tozzi and Alberto Lupo are fine in standard roles.

Most impressive in the film is a section of authentic and beautiful dancing of the 1500's period in which the story takes place. Uncredited costumes, handsome throughout, are particularly complementary in this area. Similarly, Mario Nascimbene's music is pleasing throughout. On the other

hand, the Eastmancolor in review print frequently was dull and hazy.
Dale.

Et Satan Conduit Le Bal
(And Satan Calls the Turns)
(FRENCH)

Paris, Nov. 13.

Cocinor release of Cocinor-Marceau, Saphrene-Hoche-Coen production. Directed by Grisha Dabat. Screenplay, Dabat, Roger Vadim; camera, Raoul Coutard; editor, Kenout-Peltier. At Mercury, Paris. Running time, 82 MINS.

Eric .... Jacques Doniol-Valcroze
Wife .... Franciose Brion
Ivan .... Jacques Perrin
Emmanuelle .... Catherine Deneuve
Jean .... Henri-Jacques Huet
Isabelle .... Barnadette Lafont

Roger Vadim, who launched Brigitte Bardot in "And God Created Woman," and has another Bardot hit pic with "Warrior's Rest," turned part producer and part scripter for this one. It has his usual elegant sex play and shallow immorality. But it is too sketchy, fragmentary and talky for more than exploitation use abroad on its theme. It looks chancey for arties.

All the paraphernalia of the now absorbed New Wave is used by new director Grisha Debat. There is the jump cutting within a scene for emphasis, overlapping dialog and sharp elipses to join scenes. Film takes a look at youthful and middleaged love problems in some resort area, with the few older generation characters the heavies.

Three couples hole up in the villa of a rich, neurotic businessman. He is enamored of a flighty actress who carries on with a writer who has his free-thinking girl along. The latter is piqued and gives in to a young gigolo who has a pouting, simpering girl from a rich family along.

The latter's dad shows up and tries to buy off the boy and finally shoots him. Playing is acceptable but the thesps cannot do much with these by now stereotyped, tired and disenchanted people. It lacks the insight and depth to give these odd scenes some punch and drama.

Lensing is sharp if somewhat dark. Technical qualities are good. But director Debat has yet to find a more firm personal style. The sophistication is thin and complications are more whim and fancy than incisive progressions.
Mosk.

La Cuccagna
(ITALIAN)

Rome, Nov. 6.

Euro International release of a C.I.R.A.C.-Giorgio Agliani production. Features Donatella Turri, Luigi Tenco, Umberto D'Orsi. Directed by Luciano Salce. Screenplay, Salce, Luciano Vincenzoni; camera, Silvio Fraschetti; music, Ennio Moricone; editor, Roberto Cinquini. At Quattro Fontane, Rome. Running time, 97 MINS.

Rossella .... Donatella Turri
Giuliano .... Luigi Tenco
Visona .... Umberto D'Orsi

Good lightweight item with good penetration potential for Italo audiences. Has some exploitable aspects, but otherwise faces an uphill export trek.

Luciano Salce has directed (and helped write) this look at a young job-seeking girl's difficult road to success with considerable insight and adroit observation. Loose cash and even looser morals make for plenty of pitfalls and adventures, most of which girl (Donatella Turri) manages to avoid, with the aid of a moody boy friend (Luigi Tenco). Also involved is a zany, hard-driving businessmen (Umberto D'Orsi) with a weakness for starting enterprises but leaving others to fend with them. Total impression, however, is episodic, and film disperses its effects too much.

Donatella Turri has that roughhewn unpolished charm in her first film role, and may go places. But Luigi Tenco is too unsympathetic and sullen as her vis-a-vis. Umberto D'Orsi shows tongue-in-cheek satiric flair in the role of the gal's multiple employer. Technical credits are okay.
Hawk.

Le Chevalier De Pardaillan
(The Knight From Pardaillan)
(FRENCH—COLOR—FRANSCOPE)

Paris, Nov. 6.

Prodis release of Florida Films-Fonorama production. Stars Gerard Barray; features Michele Grellier, Guy Delorme, Kirk Morriss, Giana Maria Canale. Directed by Bernard Borderie. Screenplay, Andre Haguet, Borderie from noval by Michel Zevaco; camera (Eastmancolor), Henri Persin; editor, Christian Gaudin. At Miramar, Paris. Running tme, 85 MINS.

Pardaillan .... Gerard Barray
Violetta .... Michele Grellier
Maurevert .... Guy Delorme
Fausta .... Giana Maria Canale
Charles .... Philippe Lemaire
Picouic .... Claude Vega

Cloak-and-sword actioner of political skulduggery in 16th Century France is the local equivalent of a Yank western. Though some swordplay is well done, this never gets out of the rut of the usual and stereotyped. It is without the robust, satirical flair, or the serious recreation of period, to make it of much use for foreign spots. Film looks mainly like an okay local item.

A wicked, wily Duke is plotting to be king and kidnaps a gypsy, really a girl of noble blood, who is loved by a hotblooded freelance knight. The knight plays all around in getting her back and helps a rightful man to the throne, aided by a good-natured nobleman, a dim-witted but muscular giant, and a frightened little man.

Some of the action footage is okay with nice color and settings. Acting is somewhat lethargic though Gerard Barray has some dash as the superman knight. Direction is splashy but without the incisiveness to keep this type of pic interesting throughout.
Mosk.

Virginie
(FRENCH)

Paris, Nov. 6.

Valovia release of Corona-Films De La Pleiade production. Stars Jean-Marc Thibault, Roger Pierre; features Michele Girardon, Mireille Darc. Directed by Jean Boyer. Screenplay, Michel Andre, Boyer from play by Andre; camera, Christian Matras; editor, Madame Jacqueline. At Le Paris, Paris. Running time, 85 MINS.

Olivier .... Jean-Marc Thibault
Pierre .... Roger Pierre
Betty .... Michele Girardon
Brigitte .... Mireille Darc

Though practically all shot in a sailing boat, this still shows its theatrical derivation by too much talk, listless visual gags and skin-deep characters. This situation comedy looks mainly a local item.

A scientist and journalist set out to sail to Argentina and make a little pic and study fish on the way. Into this come two shipwrecked femmes. The serious one is hooked, but a misunderstanding has it revealed as a bet. But this ends happily, and the other gets the second girl.

Jean-Marc Thibault and Roger Pierre are an ingratiating comedy team but here lack the material to do much. Michele Girardon and Mireville Darc are too mannered as the girls. John Boyer's dull direction does not help either. This pic just lacks the sprightliness to come off.
Mosk.

L'Oiseau De Paradis
(The Bird of Paradise)
(FRENCH-COLOR)

Paris, Nov. 13.

Cinedis release of Speva-Cine Alliance Filmsonor production. With Narie Hem, Sam El, Nop Em, Skarine. Directed by Marcel Camus. Screenplay, Jacques Viot, Camus; camera (Eastmancolor), Raymond Lemoigne; editor, Andree Feix. At Bretagne, Paris. Running time, 92 MINS.

Dara .... Narie Hem
Sok .... Sam El
Khem .... Nop Em
Tith .... Skarine

United Artists has this for the Western world except for France, Italy, West Germany, Belgium and Switzerland. Marcel Camus, who made the prizewinning "Black Orpheus" in Brazil, brings back another exotic item from Cambodia in Asia, played mostly by nonactor natives. But it is very much the same tale of doomed love and legend sans the more penetrating, frenetic pulse of the former. Its color and locale still slant this for arty theatre chances abroad. But a hardsell is necessary.

A young knockabout worker, who had left the Buddhist priesthood, gets enamored of a beauteous dancing girl after a chance meeting. She is coveted by a brutish but successful, young businessman.

They lead parallel paths, with the two men enemies after some brushes, and the girl having only seen the young worker by accident. But in a beautiful old city of temples they are drawn together as if they had lived a love once before on this very site. Both are killed by the love crazed other man but are joined forever in a better reincarnated life.

Camus peppers this with a look at brutal Cambodian boxing in which hands and feet are used and a fighter can be hit while down, sinuous dancing, boat races and a flock of romanticized native aspects. The actors are engaging if sometimes showing their lack of thespic background. The color is lush with technical credits adequate.

But the poetic elan seems uneven and the story much too slim to keep it moving briskly. The characters are more idealized stereotypes than creatures of either flesh and blood or true transcending legend. It is gentle, tender and well meaning, and its spurts of violence and philosophizing are hot too overdone. Although comparisons are odious, it has too much of the outlook of "Orpheus," and is not quite up to it.
Mosk.

Reach For Glory
(BRITISH)

Sincere, but muddled and over-symbolic war yarn; Sympathetic treatment of kid thesps but this pic rarely stands up to its good intentions.

London, Nov. 7.

Gala release of a Blazer (John Kohn, Jud Kinberg) production. Stars Harry Andrews, Kay Walsh, Michael Anderson Jr.; features Oliver Grimm, Michael Trubshawe, Cameron Hall, Alan Jeayes, Richard Vernon, George Pravda. Directed by Philip Leacock; screenplay by Kohn, Kinberg, John Rae, from Rae's novel, "Custard Boys"; editor, Freddy Wilson; camera, Bob Huke; music, Bob Russell. Previewed at Gala-Royal, London. Running time, 86 MINS.

Capt. Curlew .... Harry Andrews
Mrs. Curlew .... Kay Walsh
Lewis Craig ...... Michael Anderson Jr.
Mark Stein .... Oliver Grimm
John Curlew .... Martin Tomlinson
Willy Aldrich .... Freddy Eldrett
Michael Freen .... James Luck
Peter Joy .... John Coker
Major Burton ...... Michael Trubshawe
Vicar .... Arthur Hewlett
Headmaster .... Cameron Hall
Crabtree .... Alan Jeayes
Dr. Aldrich .... Richard Vernon
Mr. Freeman .... Russell Waters
Mrs. Freeman .... Pat Hayess
Mr. Stein .... George Pravda
Lance Freeman .... John Rae

Latest entry in the somewhat saturated war film market is an odd item which has been held up for quite awhile. Despite its worthy intentions, this fails to hit its target cleanly. It looks at war through the eyes of a bunch of London youngsters evacuated to the country during the last World War. They team up as a gang, bitterly opposed to the local youngsters.

They are all upset that they are too young to join the services and are scared that the war will be over before they can get into it. They take it out on the locals by hooliganism. Into the gang comes a shy, sensitive local lad and, further complication, is the arrival of a refugee boy from Vienna.

These are the ingredients of a screenplay which is never quite decisive enough. Is it protesting that it's wrong for boys not old enough to join the forces to be taught the rudiments of warfare? Or is it protesting that in this case it is futile to expect the boys not to learn to hate? The two points mingle, but never sharply enough. Film also poses problems of anti-Semitism and racial hatred. It tilts for and against conscientious objectors. In fact, it has a go at so many things that it is difficult to detect the production's main target.

Philip Leacock has directed the young actors with the tact which always marks his work when dealing with children. He brings out a confidence in them which has produced some very good performances. Michael Anderson Jr., son of the director, shows sharp intelligence as the bullying leader of the London evacuees, and Martin Tomlinson is equally well cast as the sensitive lad torn between his juvenile desire to go along with the mob and his friendship for the puzzled Austrian lad whose presence builds up to a contrived but effective climax.

Oliver Grimm plays this latter role with moving sensitivity. Among the elders are Harry Andrews, a retired Army officer bedevilled by a nagging wife (Kay Walsh) and the living lie which

she has created about her elder son being a war hero when, in fact, he is a conscientious objector. There are also neat performances by Michael Trubshawe, Cameron Hall, Alan Jeayes, George Pravda and John Rae, the last as a local Victoria Cross hero.

But none of the adults really comes to life. They are puppet characters. It is the children that give this worthy, but cardboard, film any life at all.

Bob Huke's camerawork is sound and the location sequences are well portrayed. But the over-all effect is of a good idea gone wrong through too many muddled motives battling against each other. It never knows what it wants to say, and gives up on the attempt. *Rich.*

Vom Zar Bis Stalin
(From Czar to Stalin)
(GERMAN)

Berlin, Nov. 6.
Aero Film (Raphael Nussbaum) production. Directed by Nussbaum. Screenplay, Peter Rosinski, Franz Baake; commentator, Horst Niendorf; editor, Erika von Stegmann. At Titania Palast, West Berlin. Running time, **87 MINS.**

Raphael Nussbaum, young Berlin-born producer who holds both a German and Israel passport, deserves credit for having turned out the most interesting political full-length documentary of German origin in some time. His 87-minute film dedicates itself to the history of the Russian Revolution as well as the parallel developments in neighboring European countries. This depicts the revolution's cause, results and after-effects. It traces the careers of Lenin and Stalin, and ends with the Party congress in Moscow of 1961.

Although entirely political, this is not a propaganda film of conventional calibre. It must be regarded as a historical document. It has the quality to recommend itself for international release. Outside the cinema circuit, it looks good as a specialty for tele and universities.

Nussbaum collected an imposing amount of vintage footage including newsreel excerpts dating back to 1905. Much of the footage probably has never been seen before. This goes especially for private films secretly taken of the Czar family and European sovereigns of that era. One of the film's highlights is the voice of Leon Trotsky, one of the major leaders of the Bolshevistic revolution, whom the Stalinists murdered in Mexico. Trotsky is seen (reading from a manuscript) speaking about the "betrayed revolution" and the brutality of the Tcheka, the secret police, which he identified with the Nazi Gestapo.

This gives a highly informative insight into one of mankind's most important historical and political chapters. It points up that, in the light of the oppression of the Russian people by the ruthless Czar rulers, the revolution was bound to occur. However, it also makes clear that real Communism is an illusion. And that this ideology won't be able to conquer the world other than by brute force.

Films are too often carelessly called highly interesting. This one deserves the attribute in its fullest meaning. Many patrons will find

it as exciting as a detective thriller. Technically, this Aero Film production is firstrate. *Hans.*

San Francisco Fest

Sang Nok Soo
(The Evergreen)
(SOUTH KOREAN)

San Francisco, Nov. 3.
Shin Films release and production. With Choi Eun-Hi, Shin Young-Kyun, Hu Chang-Kang. Directed by Shin Sang Okk. Screenplay, Kim Yank-Kun; music, Jyung Yoon-Ju; photography, Bal Sung-Hak. At San Francisco Film Fest. Running time, **155 MINS.**
Choi Eun-Hi .... Chai Yung-Shin
Shin Young-Kyun ...... Park Tong-Tyuk
Hu Chang-Kang .... Kim Kun-Bal

Young Korean director Shin Sang Okk, whose "My Mother and the Roomer" was shown at the Venice Festival, has switched from the earthier theme of that pic to a filmic biography of a maiden, Chai Yung-Shin, who was a combination Miss Dove and Joan of Arc to the Korean people during the Japanese occupation. Her principal weapon was education of the peasants and she sacrificed her life to her cause.

Shin's tendency to dwell endlessly on a particular theme makes his film frequently draggy and many minutes overlong. While he has borrowed liberally from the Japanese and the Mexicans in pictorial composition and acting, the beginning of a personal style is discernible in this slight film. While not actually of Festival calibre, it is surprisingly good for such a young country, as far as filmmaking is concerned.

Shoi Eun-Hi dominates almost the entire picture with her patient, determined, long-suffering heroine who literally kills herself with overwork. Park Tong-hyuk, a fellow student who belatedly realizes that he loves her, is torn between the leadership needed among his own vacillating followers and the emotional need that takes him to the distant village where his sweetheart is teaching. Kim Kun-bai is excellent as the village boy who becomes her first student and later her assistant but whose love for her is never declared.

Technically, the photography is frequently dark and too imitative of the Japanese slow dissolves and blurry filtering. The large supporting cast is excellent. An interesting sidelight is the use of "Auld Lang Syne" as the melody for their substitution for a national anthem, due to the Japanese having forbidden the real one. When first sung, it is referred to as an "old Irish melody." The natives are portrayed as Christians, but of no particular denomination. *Robe.*

Orm Ok Savan
(Embrace of Fate)
(THAILAND—COLOR)

San Francisco, Nov. 6.
A Chindavan Film Productions presentation. Directed by Siri Sirichinda. Screenplay, D. Kalyamarn; photography (Kodachrome), Samarn Tongapsindr; art director, Aural Sirisonbat; narrators Rujira and Marasri Isnlangura. At San Francisco Film Fest. Running time, **90 MINS.**
Leading Lady and Mother
.... Potchara Chowraj
Leading Man .... Mitro Chaibanja

Leading Lady's Grandfather
.... Suwin Sawang Ratna
Leading Man's Brother
.... Sakarindr Punjaritre
Servant .... Dok Din Kalyaman

Not meant seriously as a competitive entry but as an exhibition of the art of narration, "Embrace of Fate" was edited down to a 20-minute synopsis for this showing to enable the live narrators to also show their versatility by "telling" part of an American film. In Thailand, films are produced in 16m and are silent. Teams of narrators, such as the Isdanguras, sit in the theatre and follow the film visually, while providing all the dialog and sound effects.

Working with recorded musical background and amplification, the husband-wife team (Rujira and Marasri Israngura), who were film stars in Thailand before they "retired" to become narrators, displayed an amazing job of enacting, vocally, not only all the characters in the films but every sound effect with perfect timing and believable realism. The film was equally interesting, from a technical slant, in its astonishingly clear camerawork and color. It was hard to believe that the sharp, clean tones and excellent depth were in kodachrome and were being projected by a 16m arc projector.

Acting, script and direction were something else again. Ostensibly a tale of mixed-up family relations, most of it derives, unadulterated, from "The Perils of Pauline," with even the bit about the hero being held on a railroad track in the path of an oncoming train. Needless to say, it ends happily.

Mr. and Mrs. Israngura also displayed their skill at sight narration by "telling" a sequence from John Ford's "My Darling Clementine," with not only voices for Henry Fonda, Walter Brennan, Ward Bond, Grant Withers, etc., but also all the accompanying sounds of gunshots, horses, cattle, wind, dance hall girls and fights. "Yipee-i-o" sounds pretty much the same in Thai and English but Fonda came out sounding like John Gilbert while Brennan was vocally conceived as a Toshiro Mifune type.

"Embrace of Fate" probably the first Thai film to be seen in the U.S., judged only on its technical merits is excellent but, as an example of film as an art form, is still in very early stages. As entertainment, it more than succeeded but utilizing the time during a serious film festival was unfortunate and might have better made way for a more serious contribution. *Robe.*

Dheuer Pare Dheu
(Waves After Waves)
(INDIA)

San Francisco, Nov. 6.
A Renaissance Films (B. K. Sanyal, M. Dutta Gupta) production. Directed by Sanyal. Screenplay by Sanyal and S. Guhathakurta from original story by S. Dey; camera, Sanyal. At San Francisco Film Fest. Running time, **100 MINS.**
Netal, the fisherman ....Shankar
Padma, a village girl..........Shampa
Loton, their friend ....Badal

"Waves After Waves," other than its music, is a first attempt at filmmaking by the entire cast and tech-

nical crew associated with the pic including producer-director B. K. Sanyal. A former photographer, he was evidently an excellent one as the only really outstanding thing about his film is the beauty of its pictorial composition. In almost every other respect, it ranges from fair to very bad.

What Sanyal apparently conceived as a tranquil, idyllic picture of life in a Bengali fishing village is so burdened with tedious, almost motionless passages that the festival audience was driven out of the theatre with boredom.

The one professional touch to which the film lays claim is the score by Ravi Shankar, who did the music for the "Apu" triology. Interesting in short passages and effective when used to underscore some scenes, the narrow range (most of the music is played on the sitar, which allows little variation) quickly becomes repetitious and eventually irritating to the western-trained ear.

Evidently some plots are universal, as "Waves" emerges as something of an Indian version of "The Way of All Flesh," complete with the returned hero watching his family, apparently adjusted to his years of absence, through the window, whereupon he abandons any idea of a reconciliation. This version, however, ends with a suicide. Two boys and a girl, of different stations in life, spend a happy childhood together. The poor boy, a fisherman, marries the girl.

Despite the poverty and hardships they have a happy life until the husband takes a job on a fishing boat which will be gone for several months. He is presumably lost at sea and, after 10 years, the widow marries the childhood friend. Fisherman returns, sees that they're presumably content, and drowns himself.

The non-pro cast displays a naturalness that might have seemed forced in a less pliable group. A former postman, Shankar, is excellent as Natai, the fisherman, combining a virility that fits his hardy profession with a sensitivity that makes his emotional scenes believable. Like others in the cast, however, he is hampered with the long sustained, plodding tempo that apparently is a requisite to Indian story-telling. Scenes that, at best, have little movement, are held interminably.

Unlike the universality of Satyajit Ray's films, which are about people with whom one can identify, "Waves" is most unlikely to find acceptance with any but Indian audiences. *Robe.*

Czas Przeszly
(The Past)
(POLISH)

San Francisco, Nov. 6.
A Film Unit KADR of Film Polski (Leonard Buczkowski) production. Directed by Buczkowski. Original story and screenplay, Andrzej Szczypierski; photography, Jerzy Wojcik; music, Adam Walacinski. At San Francisco Film Fest. Running time, **93 MINS.**

Fram .... Adam Hanuszkiewicz
Von Steinhagen ...... Gustaw Holoubek
Antoni .... Tadeusz Domnicki
Weber .... Hanryk Bak
Monika .... Alina Janowska
Judge .... Henryk Szletynski
Counselor .... Ignacy Machowski
Klara .... Barbara Horowianka
Silny .... Cezary Julski

Malyl .... Aleksander Sewruk
Anna .... Wanda Majerowna

After the brilliant Polish films made by Majda and Kawalerowicz, some of which have been seen here at previous festivals, much more was expected of this Polish entry than it was able to deliver. Unfortunately scheduled immediately after the Brazilian "The Given Word," it seemed even more ponderous than it actually was. But there is little doubt that the general impression created was out and out boredom.

Camerawork of Jerzy Wojcik, who contributed much to Wajda's "Ashes and Diamonds" and "Sampson" and Kawalerowicz's "Joan of the Angels," has given this a veneer of brilliance that compensates a bit for the torpid script. Adam Hanuszkiewicz, as the misjudged Fram, and Alina Janowska, cast as his faithful love, are excellent within the limited framework of their roles. However, the most effective character is Henryk Bak, as an unfeeling Gestapo officer.

The Poles apparently are determined to explore every facet of the last World War in which they participated before discarding the subject and going on to something else. The principle of "The Past" is a worthy one and thought-provoking but its treatment prevents it making any discernible impression on serious filmgoers. The message, boiled down to the question of "What is justice?", points out the irony in human relations that can allow an enemy (Germany) to eradicate much of its guilty conscience at the same time some individuals (such as the Polish hero of the film) spend the remainder of their lives being falsely judged by their fellow citizens. And blamed for something that occurred without their knowledge or consent. In this instance, the hero, imprisoned by the Germans, is permitted to escape with the purpose of leading the way to the partisan leaders while his fellow prisoners are executed. *Robe.*

Le Dolci Notti
(The Sweet Nights)
(ITALIAN—COLOR—SONGS)
Rome, Nov. 6.
Interfilm release of an Italcaribe production. Directed by Vinicio Marinucci. Story and screenplay, Angelo Faccenna, Giuseppe Scotee; camera (Eastman color), Fulvio Testi; commentary by Vincio Markinucci; voice of Corrado Mantoni; music, Marcello Gimbini; editor, Roberto Cinquini. At Adriano, Rome. Running time, **100 MINS.**

This pic, one of those locally popular potpourri efforts featuring various show biz aspects' around the world and liberally laced with sex, is neither the best nor the worst of its kind. All must eventually suffer from an inflation of such items. In Italy, payoff should be okay, aided by a good title.

Predictably, the film repeats previous patterns in visits to Paris, Gotham, Las Vegas, Tokyo, Rio, Haiti, Mexico City, etc. Las Vegas' Rhythemettes, seen in previous items of this genre, are in again for some precision terping, and there are the usual Harlem niteries, Japanese Geisha cliches and other oft-seen stints.

A serio-comic Mexican bullfight gives the pic a lift as do other topnotch acts and solo stints by performers in various parts of world. Occasionally, as in glimpses of a U.S. pro-football game, and barside drunks (also U.S.), commentary over-reaches for its symbolisms. But generally Vinicio Marinucci keeps tongue in cheek.

This is especially so in the finale spoof of Rome's "Dolce Vita," in which a twist backdrop highlights Via Veneto's principal vice (per this film)—eating spaghetti. Technical credits okay.
Hawk.

It's Only Money

Zany world of the oldtime Jerry Lewis is revisited, with slapstick fun sufficient to guarantee a good payoff.

Paramount release of Paul Jones production. Stars Jerry Lewis; features Zachary Scott, Joan O'Brien, Mae Questrel, Jesse White, Jack Weston. Directed by Frank Tashlin. Screenplay, John Fenton Murray; camera, W. Wallace Kelley; editor, Arthur Schmidt; music, Walter Scharf. At Paramount homeoffice projection room Nov. 16, '62. Running time, **84 MINS.**

Lester March .... Jerry Lewis
Gregory DeWitt .... Zachary Scott
Wanda Paxton .... Joan O'Brien
Cecilia Albright .... Mae Questrel
Peter Flint .... Jesse White
Leopold .... Jack Weston

Jerry Lewis is a would-be private eye undertaking to locate a missing heir who turns out to be himself in "It's Only Money." Lewis is once again the slapstickler for laughs as of old, sans imitations of Chaplin and Jolson, and when playing himself he plays best. It's nonsense of the type which brought the performer a robust following in past and doubtless will be a boxoffice click.

Lewis herein is a television repairman who has had an overdose of Mike Hammer paperback and yens to be a shamus, as is his friend, Jesse White. They hear about the quest for the missing scion of an electronics tycoon and set out to locate same. Turns out their quarry is none other than Lewis.

That's about the nub of the John Fenton Murray screenplay. It makes for a sturdy hook upon which to hang a frolicsome string of cinematic shenanigans ranging from Pearl White cliff-hanging and murderous hayhem as per Peter Lorre to the broadest burlesque on private detectiveness.

Lewis demonstrates his familiar flair for the absurdities, like when he used to cavort with erstwhile partner Dean Martin. Besides which at the end he gets the girl, she being pretty-shapely Joan O'Brien.

Mae Questrel is an amusing character, a middle-aged Betty Boop who's looking for her late brother's long-lost son and at the same time awaiting her marriage to the family's attorney. Latter is played villainously in the broadest sense by Zachary Scott. White and Jack Weston, as the butler, similarly eschew the subtleties, and the overall effect is yockville for the Lewis fans.

Producer Paul Jones and director Frank Tashlin had an apparent field day in dishing out the zanyisms on screen. Perhaps overplayed but nonetheless laughable is one scene in which Lewis comes under attack by an army of electronic lawn mowers. Tashlin has gotten an abundance of insane action in those 84 minutes of running time.

Walter Scharf's music blends nicely with the sight gags and the editing by Arthur Schmidt is tight. Camera work is in sharp focus and other technical credits all professional. *Gene.*

Everybody Go Home
(Tutti a Casa)
(ITALIAN)

Davis-Royal release of Dino de Laurentiis production. Stars Alberto Sordi; features Martin Balsam, Serge Reggiani, Carla Gravina. Directed by Luigi Comencini. Screenplay, Comencini, Age Scarpelli and Marcello Fondato; camera, Carlo Carlini; music composed by Francesco Lavagnino, directed by Franco Ferrara. At New York's Guild Theatre. Running time, **115 MINS.**

2nd Lt. Alberto Innocenzi . Alberto Sordi
Corp. Fornaciari .... Martin Balsam
Priv. Ceccarelli .... Serge Reggiani
Young Codegato .... Nino Castelnuovo
Capt. Passerin .... Mario Feliciani
"Available" girl .... Didi Perego
Silvia Modena .... Carla Gravina
Maria Fornaciari .... Jole Mauro
American Paratrooper .... Alex Nicol
Innocenzi's father ....Eduardo de Filippo

(Italian, With English Titles)

Alberto Sordi, very popular film performer in his native Italy, hasn't yet been too strong an export commodity, presumably because his pictures have been basically designed for local appeal. He was introduced to the U.S. with "Best of Enemies" and now is at hand in "Everybody Go Home," an unusual and interesting study of wartime Italy which has the air of authenticity and enough dramatic impact to indicate successful bookings in specialized situations in the American market.

Translated from "Tutti a Casa" into "Everybody Go Home," Dino de Laurentiis' production is often a skilled combination of delicate comedy and yet a provocatively graphic reproduction of a battleweary country and the soldiers and citizens who were so frustratingly caught in the state of displacement that came with Italy's armistice with the Allies. This was in 1943.

Sordi is an agreeable and persuasive player with a range of deft nuances conveying mild little satire, dramatic emotionalism and straight story-telling points. He's a second lieutenant herein, very much concerned about returning to his home, as is everybody else on view.

If there's a complaint to be offered, it is that the picture is so vivid in its staging of the confused, impoverished Italian homeland that the efforts at satire perhaps might not have been undertaken at all.

Director Luigi Comencini and cinemotographer Carlo Carlini, working on the screenplay by Comencini, Age Scarpelli and Marcello Fondato, show a keen awareness of the dramatic potency that can be drawn from real-life hardships. The Italians' lust for food, the soldiers who are being taken to Germany, a girl who is "available"—these are the elements brought in with cinematic understanding.

Martin Balsam, an American, is quite at home as the Italian corporal traveling with Sordi. Sergi Reggiani as a private, Carla Gravina as a Jewish girl seeking refuge from the Nazis and Alex Nicol as a Yank paratrooper who finds a haven with an Italian family register with uniform competence.

Francesco Lavagnino composed a serviceable musical background, editing is sound and all technical credits are good. English titles are to the point, leave no doubt as to what's going on and being said. *Gene.*

Hansuli Banker Upakatha
(Folk Tales of River Bend) (INDIAN)

San Francisco, Nov. 13.

A S. L. Jalan production. Directed and written by Tapan Sinha. From original story by Tara Shankar Banerjee; camera, Bimal Mukherjee; music, Hementa Mukherjee. At San Francisco Film Fest. Running time, 90 MINS.

Kali Banerjee	Banwari
Dilip Roy	Karali
Ranjana Banerjee	Pakhi
Anuva Gupta	Kalobau
Lily Chakraborty	Nasu Bala

What Satyajit Ray's "Apu" films said about one Indian family, "Folk Tales of River Bend" attempts to say about the village as a whole. Director Tapan Sinha, a juror at the 1961 Frisco festival, conveys an awareness of the changing India through both his story line and the use of contrasting styles in enactment. The basic earthiness of the Indian people comes over better in this film than perhaps in those of Ray, supplying a humor that is greatly needed. "The past" is portrayed in an exaggerated, flowery style and language.

Sinha's people are not as universal as Ray's but they ably present two aspects of Indian life. While not the poet with the camera that his better-known contemporary is, he keeps his story and cast moving.

Inhabitants of a small village on a bend of the Kopai River are tied to their less-than-adequate existence through a combination of circumstances—the greed and ruthlessness of their "landlord," the fears and restrictions of their religious beliefs and superstitions, and their illiteracy.

They are "led" by a chief who is a mixture of courage and amiable stupidity, aware of his people's needs and his own inadequacies. The role is excellently played by Kali Banerjee in an "old school" manner that allows the handsome, virile thespian to use virtually every known melodramatic gesture.

The break in this isolationism is made by Karali (Dilip Roy), young, restless, and intelligent lad, who eventually leads the younger men from their drab provincialism. He never loses his love for his village and people but realizes that, like the chief, some will never change. When the chief is slain, the final break is made. The film ends (the action is in 1941) when the ravages of a monsoon are followed by the outbreak of war and progress is forced upon them.

Hementa Mukherjee's score makes frequent use of folk songs that are particularly effective. printing of the subtitles is very bad, and frequently hard to read.

Sinha's combination of styles may be confusing to some filmgoers but his social comments are obvious, interesting and well-stated. And his people are heartwarming. *Robe.*

Portrait Robot
(FRENCH)

Paris, Nov. 13.

Disexi release of Pavox-Cinetel-Silver Films production. Stars Maurice Ronet, Andrea Parisy, Jacques Riberolles; features William Sabatier, Nanna Michael. Written and directed by Paul Paviot. Camera, Andre Villard; editor, Francine Grubert. At Latin, Paris. Running time, 78 MINS.

Gilbert	Maurice Ronet
Clotilde	Andrea Parisy
Pascal	Jacques Riberolles
Karin	Nanna Michael

Moderate little suspense item is not strong enough on story, personages or treatment to rank this as more than dualer abroad. A young journalist, whose love life is shaky, awakens one morning after a big drunk to find himself a murder suspect.

He gets back his girl but finally goes into hiding with a friend. He discovers that it is the latter who did the killing.

Director Paul Paviot keeps this moving but can not do much with the facile story. Thesping is acceptable and technical aspects passable. *Mosk.*

In Search Of The Castaways
(BRITISH—TECHNICOLOR)

Spectacular, lively piece of Disney hokum. A certain b.o. winner.

London, Nov. 13.

Walt Disney production and release. Stars Maurice Chevalier, Hayley Mills, George Sanders, Wilfrid Hyde White; features Michael Anderson Jr., Keith Hamshere, Wilfrid Brambell, Antonio Cifariello. Directed by Robert Stevenson. Screenplay by Lowell S. Hawley from Jules Verne's novel "Captain Grant's Children"; camera (Technicolor), Paul Beeson; special effects, Peter Ellenshaw; editor, Gordon Stone; music, William Alwyn; songs, Robert B. Sherman, Richard M. Sherman. Previewed at Studio One, London. Running time, 100 MINS.

Jacques Paganel	Maurice Chevalier
Mary Grant	Hayley Mills
Thomas Ayrton	George Sanders
Lord Glenarvon	Wilfrid Hyde White
John Glenarvon	Michael Anderson Jr.
Thalcave	Antonio Cifariello
Robert Grant	Keith Hamshere
Bill Gaye	Wilfrid Brambell
Captain Grant	Jack Gwillim
Guard	Ronald Fraser
Maori Chief	Inia Te Wiata

Walt Disney has come up with another splendid piece of spectacular hokum, lavishly colored and packed with incident and special effects. It can hardly fail to appeal to all types of audience, though apparently aimed mainly at the moppets. "Castaways" is a blend of every Disney trick, combining adventure and humor. With a cast headed by Maurice Chevalier, Hayley Mills and George Sanders, the marquee is safely taken care of.

Jules Verne's yarn concerns a French scientist who finds a bottle containing a note which reveals the whereabouts of Captain Grant who mysteriously disappeared two years before. The Frenchman and the sea captain's two children persuade a wealthy shipping owner and his son to set off for South America in search of the missing man.

The trail eventually leads successfully to Australia and New Zealand. What goes on during the 100 minutes' screenplay is nobody's business. Without giving away too much of the action, it can be revealed that the party survives giant condors, jaguars, flood, lightning, crocodiles, an avalanche, an earthquake, a huge waterspout, mutiny by Grant's former quartermaster, imprisonment by unfriendly Maoris and an erupting volcano. Apologies to Disney if anything has been omitted in this blow by blow report.

Paul Beeson's lensing does magnificent justice to some canny special effects while Robert Stevenson keeps the action moving constantly. There are a couple of lively songs and a cheerful score.

Thesping is done throughout with a tongue in the cheek exuberance which suggests that Disney and Stevenson have given the actors the go ahead to have fun. At times it almost looks as if they are making up the situations and dialog as they go along. Maurice Chevalier as the scientist and Wilfrid Hyde White, as the shipowner, particularly ham it up most engagingly. Although both look as if they are not taking their chores very seriously, the end product is a couple of very astute, pleasant performances. George Sanders is a suave heavy while Wilfrid Brambell has a riotous time as one of Captain Grant's crew who has been captive for two years. He has become a Bible punching nutcase but manages to lead the party out of Maori hands with ingenious ease and a series of fascinating cackles.

Jack Gwillim, Ronald Fraser, Antonio Cifariello and Inia Te Wiata are other adults who lend useful support. The three young people, of course, fit excellently into the adventurous scheme of things. Hayley Mills is a resourceful, charming young heroine. Keith Hamshere and Michael Anderson Jr. intrepidly face the innumerable hazards. Proof that young Miss Mills is rapidly growing up is evident in a closing sequence. There's a hand in hand scene between her and Anderson Jr. which points to romantic things to come for the teenage star.

It is easy to poke gentle fun at such a tongue-in-the-cheek pic. But not at the boxoffice where business will be both serious and highly profitable. *Rich.*

La Risa de la Ciudad
(Smiles of the City) (MEXICAN)

San Francisco, Nov. 13.

A Cinematografica Jalisco S.A. (Valentin Gazcon) production. Directed by Gilberto Gazcon. Screenplay, Gilberto Gazcon and Francisco Cordova from original story by Cordova; camera, Ignacio Torres; music, Gustavo Cesar Carrion. At San Francisco Film Fest. Running time, 110 MINS.

Beto	Joaquin Cordero
Don Tencho	Jose Elias Moreno
Leticia	Alma Delia Fuentes
El Ronson	Adalberto Martinez
Polo	Julio Aleman

Despite the disadvantages of being shown late in the festival, "Smiles of the City" displayed cinematic values of its own that made an excellent impression. Most of the contemporary Mexican films seen at pix fests have dealt with the country peasant. It was refreshing to see one that depicts a side of big-city life.

While lacking in really superb acting, scripting and choreography that have made some Mexican films cinematic works of art and far from subtle in its patriotic propaganda (to sell the worthy efforts of the country towards self-improvement), "Smiles" is superior to the run-of-mill films made purely for the local Mexican market. This is particularly noticeable in the ensemble acting and the skilled direction of Gilberto Gazcon. With his actors, he has achieved better results than with his technical crew. Actors can be inspired, a budget can't.

Plot deals with street performers living in a "squatters' village" on the edge of Mexico City. Like the other "citizens" of this area, they have no ambition, satisfied to eke out a daily existence. Their leader, Joaquin Cordero, is a clown who keeps his group together more by bluster than inspiration. Things begin to change when an old man, nicely played by Jose Elias Moreno, enters their lives. He is, of course, Cordero's grandfather although he never reveals his identity.

New problems are dealt with as they come up, old ones more slowly, but changes in integrity, self respect and moral values are gradually introduced by the old man. Tragedy continues to plague them, however, and poverty is ever present. When their "village" is destroyed by fire, the government moves them to a more remote area. They at first rebel but, led by Cordero, who has truly become a leader, they create decent quarters and new lives. End of moral.

Moreno, Cordero and, to a lesser extent, Julio Aleman, as a strolling musician-pickpocket who reforms when his younger brother begins to follow the same pattern, frequently overcome their cliche-ridden lines. Fortunately, the overall ensemble work is excellent. Strains of "La Strada" are sometimes apparent, but fleetingly.

Because of the limited budget, the poor technical aspects of the film detract from it. An original touch is used to both combine and contrast the extremes of emotions present on the "day of the dead," with fast cross-cutting between the laughter and carnival of the celebrants and the grief of a funeral party. Some of the settings are different, having the heroine work in a chicken slaughter-house or the performers working in front of a national monument or cathedral. The half-light that, used by Gabriel Figueroa, could be artistic but here only underscores the inadequate lighting facilities. Gustavo Carrion's score is adequate but inspiring.

While unlikely to make a big impression on the more discriminating international market, "Smiles" should do very well in the Spanish-language situations. Its promise is great enough, also, to make one wish to see what director Gazcon could do with an adequate budget and a first-rate script. *Robe.*

Hamlet
(WEST GERMAN)

German TV film dubbed for U.S. dates. Unorthodox approach. Some art situation appeal.

A Dmytryk-Weiler presentation of a Bavaria Atelier Gesellschaft (Hans Gottschalk) production. Stars Maximilian Schell. Adapted and directed by Franz Peter Wirth from the A. W. von Schlegel translation of play by Shakespeare. Camera, Kurt Gewissen, Hermann Gruber, Rudolf H. Jakob, Boris Geriup; music, Rolf Unkel; English dialog director, Fred Brown. English dubbing directed by Edward Dmytryk. At San Francisco Film Festival. Running time, 130 MINS.

Hamlet	Maximilian Schell
Claudius	Hans Caninberg
Gertrude	Wanda Roth
Ophelia	Dunja Movar
Polonius	Franz Schafheitlin
Laertes	Dieter Kirchlechner
Horatio	Karl Michael Vogler
Rosenkrantz	Eckard Dux
Guildenstern	Herbert Botticher
Osric	Karl Lieffen
Bernardo	Rolf Boysen
Francisco	Michael Paryla
The Ghost	Alexander Engel
First Player	Adolf Gerstung
Gravedigger	Paul Verhoeven

Produced originally in 1960 by Hans Gottschalk for television presentation on Eurovision, the Frisco Fest showing of "Hamlet" is a world preem of footage as a theatrical presentation. The film will undoubtedly have initial success in the specialized film houses because of the star and story but novelty aspect may quickly dissipate.

Film is one of considerable merit and, in its televised form, met with great success, as much for Wirth's imaginative staging within the confines of the small screen as for Schell's interpretation of the title role. It's told in the format of a chamber play. Schell's conception sees the Dane as a modern, healthy-minded, loving son whose desire to revenge the murder of his father and the usurpation of his throne lead him to feign madness. Speeches have been edited, eliminated, moved, even given to other characters to speak as backdrop to Hamlet's maunderings.

American director Edward Dmytryk, having worked with Schell on "The Reluctant Saint," convinced him that the filmed "Hamlet" could find favor in English-speaking countries. They decided to dub the film in order to permit Schell to repeat his role in English and because of the difficulty in condensing Shakespearean lines into capsuled subtitles. This decision was a mistake. A translation is no good unless, as someone said, it gives you the music of a poem along with the words in it. And this one is, at best, only an echo.

Watching actors mouth German while the ear is hearing English is distracting enough but the effort to convince one's self that the emotion depicted on the screen is exactly duplicated by another person's voice becames too taxing. Even the bilingual Schell suffers in the process. Frequently his lips move slowly while his voice ripples rapidly through the lines, making them sometimes unintelligible and having little meaning as in his "There are stranger things in heaven and earth."

Shakespearean English requires flawless diction and doubly so when the English is spoken with an accent. This is evident in the choice of voices for the dubbing cast, but it might have been better, actually, to have used accented English throughout as some of the precise, English-stage-type voices used by lesser characters sound alien against the varied accents of Hamlet, Claudius and others. Frequently the voices sound detached from the bodies. Wirth uses many closeups, particularly of the major characters, and holds them for the extended speeches. This accentuates the conflict between the visual German and the aural English.

Director Wirth's staging will certainly cause controversy but "Hamlet" has been presented in many variations and has withstood them all. His use of multi cameras to simultaneously shoot a scene is inventive and helps considerably in diminishing the confinement of the small playing area, and must have been a great help in the editing. Original without being arty in his choice of camera angles and framing, he makes the minimum of scenery and use of stylized props balance the sometimes ornate costumes. The latter, for the most part, are black with little ornamentation and an occasional touch of white or grey. The lighting is truly skillful and many of the shots have a beautiful heavy-inked lithographic effect.

Some touches in filming and adaptation are brilliant. The "To be or not to be" soliloquy is shot with only Schell's eyes showing between two steps of the cantilevered stairway. Ophelia's description of Hamlet's visit (". . . as I was sewing in my closet"), usually never shown, is glimpsed briefly without dialog so that her lines to her father bear more impact. In another scene, immediately after showing Claudius and Polonius plotting against Hamlet, the camera sweeps up to reveal him listening.

Other attempts are less effective. Polonius' beautiful advice to Laertes (" . . . and these few precepts in thy memory . . .") is ruined by having him apparently cribbing it from a book and even prompting himself from it as he speaks. Interpretation of Shakespeare's writing is such a variable thing that the meaning of a line can be lessened or destroyed by the least change. The familiar "the *play's* the thing" is altered completely by Schell speaking it as "the play *is* the thing."

Schell's interpretation of the Dane is interesting but, eventually, unconvincing. There is often a semblance of indolence, a laziness in his manner that conveys unconcern. While his general concept is revenge, he is too chameleon-like in his uncertainty of moods, contrasted with his certainty of purpose. We're never sure what this man is about and we cannot fully sympathize with people we don't understand. Ironically, his scenes in which he is pretending to be mad are some of his best. He brings out the humor of feigned madness and underscores unsympathy of his enemies by making them accept his pretended mental state as authentic. But there's no overlooking the fact that he "speaks not always with good accent and good discretion."

To speed up the action and shorten the running time the character of Fortinbras has been eliminated and, along with him, Marcellus, Reynaldo, the second gravedigger and others. Even with these cuts and the skillful editing permitted by the clever camera work, the pace frequently bogs down due to the emphasis on the single character. Many in the audience may find it too slow for their tastes, especially if, like Polonius, they're "for a jig or a tale of bawdry, or they sleep."

Hans Caninberg's Claudius is considerably younger than the usual concept and apparently younger than Wanda Roth's Queen Gertrude. It is uncertain what this is meant to convey, other than stating that their attraction to each other is primarily sexual. Dunja Mover's Ophelia lacks the supersensitiveness necessary to the role if one is to believe that a suitor's rejection could drive her into insanity and suicide. She is also guilty of bad diction, garbling such important speeches as "O, what a noble mind is here o'er thrown."

Franz Schafheitlin, a visually perfect Polonius, is guilty of fluctuating between senile uncertainty and obstinate conviction. He is aware of the humor in his lines and gives a delightful, cranky, scholarly-critical reading to Gertrude and Claudius of Hamlet's letter to Ophelia, more concerned with the correctness of the wording than the portent. Outstanding in a brief scene is Paul Verhoeven's Gravedigger. Playing beautifully against Schell, the two make the scene really come alive.

Karl Michael Voglen's Horatio, Dieter Kirchlechner's Laertes and Adolf Geratung's First Player stand out among the generally excellent supporting cast. Rolf Unkel's score, most effective in the quieter passages of the film, was probably the most traditional touch in this particular production. **The film was screened twice at the premiere, first in the English-dubbed version, then in the original German.** *Robe.*

Le Masque De Fer
(The Iron Mask)
(FRENCH—COLOR—DIALISCOPE)

Paris, Nov. 20.

Gaumont release of Ceres-SNEG-Marly-Fucha production. Stars Jean Marais; features Jean-Francois Poron, Sylva Koscina, Gisele Pascal, Jean Rochefort, Noel Roquevert. Directed by Henri Decoin. Screenplay, Cecil Saint Laurent, Gerald Devries; camera (Eastmancolor), Pierre Petit; editor, Louisette Hautecouer. At Lord Byron, Paris. Running time, **130 MINS.**

D'Artagnan	Jeas Marais
Louis XIV	Jean-Francois Poron
Isabelle	Claudine Auger
De Chaulmes	Gisele Pacal
Truand	Jean Rochefort
Marion	Sylva Koscina
Anne	Germaine Montero
Vandreuil	Philippe Lemaire
Mazarin	Enrico-Maria Salerno
Saint Marc	Noel Roquevert

A supposedly tongue-in-cheek cloak and sword opus of political skulduggery in 17th Century France and the local equilavent of the Yank oater, short circuits too much action with talk, and lacks the dash and feeling for time and characters. Hence, this is only a local exploitation or actioner item. It looks only good for dualer or moppet use in foreign spots.

An aging D'Artagnan helps the ailing king and his advisors by bringing back his twin brother, who had been kept imprisoned wearing an iron mask, to fill in for the king until rebels and usurpers are cleaned up. There is plenty of swordplay and some nice costuming.

But director Henri Decoin lacks the gusto and punch to make this a true parody. Thesps work valiantly but all this emerges as is an average costumer without the needed zest to lift it above the ordinary. *Mosk.*

The Amorous Prawn
(BRITISH)

Easygoing escapist comedy based on longrun play. Reliable British comedy cast and intriguing title make this a likely favorite despite lack of names for U.S.

London, Nov. 13.

BLC release of a British Lion (Leslie Gilliat) production. Stars Ian Carmichael, Joan Greenwood, Cecil Parker; features Dennis Price, Robert Beatty, Liz Fraser, Bridget Armstrong, Reg Lye, Harry Locke, Derek Nimmo, Sandra Dorne, Finlay Currie, Robert Nichols. Directed by Anthony Kimmins. Screenplay by Kimmins and Nicholas Phipps, from Kimmins' play; editor, Thelma Connell; camera, Wilkie Cooper; music, John Barry. At Odeon, Marble Arch, London. Running time: **89 MINS.**

Lady Fitzadam	Joan Greenwood
General Fitzadam	Cecil Parker
Corp. Sidney Green	Ian Carmichael
Larry Hoffman	Robert Beatty
Prawn	Dennis Price
Suzie Tidmarsh	Liz Fraser
Uncle Joe	Reg Lye
Biddy O'Hara	Bridget Armstrong
Willie Maltravers	Derek Nimmo
Albert Huggins	Harry Locke
Sam Goulansky	Robert Nichols
Mac	Roddy McMillan
Sergeant at Exchange	Godfrey James
Landlord	Eric Woodburn
Dusty Babs	Sandra Dorne
Lochaye	Finlay Currie

Anthony Kimmins' comedy, "The Amorous Prawn," chalked up well over 1,000 performances on the stage. Now, directed by the play's author, it shapes up as non-demanding light entertainment, cheerfully put over by a reliable cast of popular British thesps. The title, which is a contrived gimmick having virtually nothing to do with the slim plot, should intrigue ducat buyers into an evening of amiable escapism.

General Fitzadam (Cecil Parker) is on the eve of retirement but is a bit short of cash for his retirement cottage. While overseas on a military mission his wife hits on the idea of converting his military headquarters in Scotland into a guest house.

The idea occurs when she sees an advertisement by a couple of Americans looking for some good trout fishing. The general's army staff is brought into the scheme and turned into maitre d'hotel, chauffeur, maids, chef, et al. The whole bunch share the proceeds, including the lavish tips handed out by the two Yanks when they land fish.

Two major complications develop. One is the sudden, unexpected return of the general which, at first, calls for a considerable amount of repetitious camouflage by the conspirators. This works out, however, when the general finds out about the racket but decides to go along with it to revenge a peeve against the War Office. The second is when an unexpected guest turns up who is revealed as the Minister of State for War. He, too, discovers the impudent hoax but has to keep silent when it's discovered that the blonde in his bed is not his wife, but a local barmaid.

Much of the fun comes from a series of double takes, hurried changing from army clothes into civvies, some gentle sex play, the conning of the Yanks, and the feud betweene the local laird and the poacher employed to keep the anglers happy. There are some soggy spots but on the whole Kimmins' direction and the acting keeps the comedy on a fairly ebullient plane.

Cecil Parker produces one of his typical, bumbly performances, but Joan Greenwood, as his wife, is not so peppily in character as she normally is in this sort of drawing room farce. Ian Carmichael does a shrewd job as the wily corporal who becomes maitre d'hotel in the scheme while Liz Fraser and Bridget Armstrong, as a couple of members of the women's armed forces who turn maids (Miss Fraser is given an opportunity to strip to her scanties) provide some pulchritude.

Derek Nimmo, Sandra Dorne, Finley Currie, Harry Locke and Reg Lye chip in with some useful

support. Robert Beatty and Robert Nichols are the two Americans who are mostly stooges to the activities while Dennis Price, as the War Minister, once again turns up trumps with an impeccably poised, though scarcely urgent, performance.

Scottish scenes are well lensed by Wilkie Cooper and editor, music man and sound recorists all help in an unambitious picture which will speedily be forgotten, but may well earn some useful cash from audiences demanding nothing more than some sly laughs.   *Rich.*

Si Yo Fuera Millonario
(If I Were A Millionaire)
(MEXICAN)
Mexico City, Nov. 13.

Peliculas Nacionales release of Cinematografica Filmex production. Stars Amador Bendayan, Teresa Velazquez, Enrique Rambal; features Antonio Aguilar, Miguel Aceves Mejia, Chino Herrera, Cesar Costa, Lorena Velazquez, Patricia Moran and guest appearances of Maria Felix, Sonia Infante, Elvira Castillo, David Reynosa. Directed by Julian Soler. Screenplay, Fernando Josseau and Raul Zenteno. At Alameda Theatre, Mexico City. Running time: 90 MINS.

Veteran actor Julian Soler takes a hand in directing this comic interpretation of theme, with series of known and unknown players, headed by Maria Felix, giving their reactions to riches.

Soler's direction is sure and the picture turns out to be moderately diverting since the story is treated with light touch. Venezuelan comic Amador Bendayan is starred and is the link in series of episodes with some developing situations that had the audience laughing loudly.   *Emil.*

Tragodie tou Aegaeou
(Aegean Tragedy)
(GREECE—DOCUMENTARY)
San Francisco, Nov. 13.

A Basil Maros Production. Directed and edited by Maros. Screenplay, Angelos Prokopiou; music, Janni Markopoulos; narrated by Vassilis Zochos. At San Francisco Film Fest. Running time, 65 MINS.

Although producer-director Basil Maros calls his documentary "a modern Greek tragedy—with the Greek people as chorus," the film covers the period 1914-1945 better from a reporting angle than that of historical comment. Most of the material has been taken from newsreel footage and historical film records. And it is frequently fascinating in its review of a country whose comparatively modern history is less known than other parts of Europe.

Tracing the political history from the 1914 era of King Constantine through two World Wars and several types of government, Maros' carefully selected footage (some of which appears to be captured German film made during their occupation) does a good job of depicting the turmoil and unrest that swept the country time and time again, through war, civic rebellion or political dictatorships. And also even during what was considered brief peaceful eras while the Greek people failed to solidify as a nation.

His film so frequently concerns itself with important military and political figures that perhaps not enough coverage is given the Greek people as a nation. They are generally shown as masses of refugees fleeing the troops of Mustafa Kemal or in demonstrations for the various kings, dictators, prime ministers or military figures.

Some of the most effective shots are those of the aforementioned refugees moving into Piraeus from Asia Minor and the chilling demonstrations by Greek children under military dictatorship that remind one of young Nazis parading. Film also depicts the obvious affection of Maros for his country's leaders and the "scorched earth" policy of the retreating Germans that shows them dumping railroad cars, trucks and much other large equipment into the Corinth Canal to keep them from the Greeks.

As a record of a tumultous time, "Aegean Tragedy" is an important film document but as an expression on film it is more motion than emotion.   *Robe.*

Mafioso
(ITALIAN)
Rome, Nov. 13.

Dino DeLaurentiis release of a C.C.C. (Antonio Cervi) production. Stars Alberto Sordi; features Norma Bengell, Ugo Attanasio, Carmelo Oliviero, Gabriella Conti. Directed by Alberto Lattuada. Screenplay, Marco Ferreri, Rafael Azcona, Age, Scarpelli, from story by Bruno Caruso; camera, Armando Nannuzzi; music, Piero Piccioni; editor, Nino Baragli. At Adriano, Rome. Running time, 105 MINS.
Antonio Badalamenti...... Alberto Sordi
Marta .... Norma Bengell
Don Vincenzo .... Ugo Attanasio
Don Liborio .... Carmelo Oliviero
Rosalia .... Gabriella Conti

Smoothly fashioned item with big Italo grossing potential on the Alberto Sordi name linked with Sicilian subject matter and title. Foreign chances seem more limited, with the pic qualifying more for general audience tastes than arty consumption.

Sordi fans looking for his usual comic performance are also in for a standout stint. Here he's a Sicilian working in a Milan factory who returns to his hometown with his northern wife and kids, only to be sent to N.Y. by the Mafia to shoot and kill one of the society's enemies. He goes through it, albeit with qualms and fear, returns to a family, which thinks he's been away on a hunting trip, and resumes his job as though nothing had happened.

Beautifully built-up script, perceptively and skillfully brought to life by director Alberto Lattuada, however, falls down on the windup. Admittedly, it's a tricky proposition to make a straight killer out of a popular personality such as Sordi's, and authors nearly bring it off here by evading the issue. After the murder, the pic is speedily brought to a halt, with the final shot a near-repeat of opening one, showing factory official Sordi walking across his working area. But second-thought about the finale shows it basically evades most issues and cannot be said to be ultimately satisfying.

Nevertheless, the general impression of the film remains a very positive one, with Sordi amusingly delineating the returning Sicilian. He is neatly assisted by Brazilian actress Norma Bengell and a large and colorful cast. Technical credits, including Armando Nannuzzi's lensing (some of it on location in New York) and Piero Piccioni's music, are fine.   *Hawk.*

Los Valientes No Mueren
(The Brave Don't Die)
(MEXICAN)
Mexico City, Nov. 13.

Peliculas Nacionales release of Producciones Brooks production. Stars Pedro Armendariz, Miguel Aceves Mejia, Ana Bertha Lepe, Marina Camacho; features Juan Garcia, Felia Magana, Marcelo Chavez, Eric del Castillo. Directed by Gilberto Martinez Solares. Screenplay, G. M. Solares from original by G. M. Solares, O. Jason and Fernando Galiana.

A singing "charro" or cowboy epic with an eye on the export (Spanish language) market. Armendariz has a typical gunslinger role as the valiant "macho" (he man) aided and abetted by a falsetto singing and gun-carrying Miguel Aceves Mejia.

Anybody with a true knowledge of Mexico will immediately see holes in this one. The "charros" here are not the authentic gentlemen cowboys of Mexico but sombrero clad, two-gun men who attempt to emulate the counterparts of their Hollywood western gunmen.

Photography in black and white is satisfactory but there's a good deal of concentration on a bathing beauty contest in a tiny Mexican village. Girls in a small village just don't display their charms as do Ana Bertha Lepe and Marina Camacho.   *Emil.*

The L-Shaped Room
(BRITISH)

Tenderly written and directed study of loneliness; excellent performances by Leslie Caron and newcomer Tom Bell make it a good bet for intelligent audiences.

London, Nov. 13.
British Lion presentation through BLC of a Romulus (James Woolf and Richard Attenborough) production. Stars Leslie Caron; features Tom Bell, Bernard Lee, Brock Peters, Cicely Courtneidge, Patricia Phoenix, Emlyn Williams, Avis Bunnage, Harry Locke, Nanette Newman. Directed by Brian Forbes. Screenplay by Forbes from Lynne Reid Banks' novel; camera, Douglas Slocombe; editor, Anthony Harvey. At Columbia Theatre, London. Running time, 142 MINS.
Jane .... Leslie Caron
Youth in Street .... Anthony Booth
Doris .... Avis Bunnage
Sonia .... Patricia Phoenix
Jane 11 .... Verity Emmett
Toby .... Tom Bell
Mavis .... Cicely Courtneidge
Newsagent .... Harry Locke
Girl in Newsagent's...... Ellen Dryden
Dr. Weaver .... Emlyn Williams
Monica .... Jennifer White
Johnny .... Brock Peters
Bert .... Gerry Duggan
Charlie .... Bernard Lee
Girl at End .... Nanette Newman

Lynne Reid Banks' bestseller novel seemed, on the surface, to be unlikely material for a film. Largely set in the restricted area of a faded lodging house the novel had little enough glamour or strength of plot to recommend it, excellently written though it was. But Bryan Forbes' screenplay and his tactful, sensitive direction have created a tender study in loneliness and frustrated love. "The L-Shaped Room" is in the current British down-to-earth, unglamorous league but it is articulate, often moving and has a number of well observed performances. Leslie Caron's name is useful marquee bait and she turns in a sympathetic piece of thesping.

Yarn concerns a girl with a background of provincial France who, in London, has a brief affair resulting in pregnancy. Rejecting the idea of an abortion she decides to live it out on her own. And, in the loneliness of her L-shaped room in a seedy tenement, she finds a new hope and purpose in life through meeting others who, in various ways, suffer their own loneliness and frustration. Particularly, there are an unsuccessful young writer and a Negro jazz musician. Without knowing about the girl's pregnancy, the writer falls for her. The colored boy, jealous, reveals her secret. The two part and, when he tries to return to her, it is too late. There is no compromise with a happy ending. She has her baby and leaves the L-Shaped Room to a new tenant, equally lonely and puzzled.

This brief outline gives no credit to the film's many subtle undertones. Not a great deal happens but it is a thoroughly holding and intelligent film having the quality of a film like "Marty." Forbes' direction never falters and he is backed by highly competent technical assistance. The drabness of the bedsitters is well drawn. Among the standout scenes are one in a jazz cellar and one of those hearty Christmas parties where everybody is trying just a shade too hard to enjoy themselves.

Miss Caron and Tom Bell, yet another of Britain's new wave of young actors, make a strong team. Though they, plus Brock Peters, as the Negro lad, bear the brunt of such action as there is, the trio are well supported by a number of others.

Vet Cicely Courtneidge makes a sharp comeback as a retired vaude artist, living with her cat and her faded press clippings. Other notable jobs are done by Avis Bunnage. (a landlady who prides herself on the respectability of her house, despite two of her lodgers being prosties.) and Bernard Lee, as her boozey, hearty gentleman friend.

The harlots are played by Patricia Phoenix and Verity Emmett. Miss Phoenix, very much out of character from that which she plays in the tv series, "Coronation Street," is the tart with the heart of gold and gives an exremely vivid performance. Emlyn Williams, as a smooth abortionist, and Gerald Sim, as a sympathetic hospital doctor, also make keen impressions in short roles.

"The L-Shaped Room" is a striking example of the fact that, in a film, people about whom audiences can care are often more important to the film's fate than a frenetic string of happenings. Despite the fact that the action is often very slow and that its theme is fundamentally downbeat, the film can boast both warmth and humor.
            Rich.

Constantine and the Cross
(ITALIAN—DUBBED)

More spear-and-sandal. If the devotees haven't cooled, this should do okay biz.

Embassy release of Jonia Film (Italian) production, produced by Ferdinando Falicioni. Stars Cornel Wilde, Christine Kaufmann, Belinda Lee. Directed by Lionello de Felice. Screenplay, Ennio de Concini, de Felice, Ernesto Guida, Franco Rosetti, Guglielmo Santangelo; camera (Eastmancolor, Totalscope), Massimo Dallamano; music, Mario Nascimbene. Reviewed in New York, Nov. 16, '62. Running time, 120 MINS.

Constantine .... Cornel Wilde
Livia .... Christine Kaufmann
Fausta .... Belinda Lee
Helena .... Elisa Cegani
Maxientius .... Massimo Serato
Hadrian .... Fausto Tozzi
Maximianus .... Tino Carraro
Constantius Cloro .... Carlo Nichi
Apuleius .... Vittorio Sanipoli

Here's more of that old Roman swordplay, more than customarily lavish to the eye, and a fairly promising contender. At any rate, those who can't get enough of ancient history, cinema style, should dig it.

Italo pic (originally "Constantino Il Grande," unreviewed by VARIETY) concerns warrior Constantine's rise to emperor status and his simpatico disposition toward the outlawed Christians, who subsequently raised him to the altar as a saint. As history records, he promulgated the "Edict of Tolerance," and Christians have been free to worship in Rome ever since.

There's blood-letting, political intrigue, and romance, par for the spectacle course, in this Embassy release (in the U.S.). Scenes of battle, between rival imperial armies, have been well staged. But a couple of sequences, of torture and Christian-eating lions, do get somewhat graphic.

Performances are okay, or at least appropriate. Cornel Wilde as Constantine is contemplative and staunch. The late Belinda Lee is appealing as his wife, and Christine Kaufmann does well enough as an ill-fated Christian. Of the "meaty" (no pun) supporting roles, Fausto Tozzi is persuasive as Constantine's chum and Miss Kaufmann's enamored, but the real chew-'em-up opportunity goes to Massimo Serato as a scheming politico. He's fine.

There were enough chefs-descreenplay — five are credited — which may at least explain the longish unfoldment of story. Lionello de Felice's direction seems reasonably thoughtful; ditto Massimo Dallamano's photography. Other technical credits are all good. *Pit.*

The Four Days of Naples
(Le Quattro Giornate di Napoli)
(ITALIAN)
Rome, Nov. 20.

Titanus release (Metro in other countries) of Titanus-Metro Film production. With Charles Belmont, Regina Bianchi, Aldo Giuffre, Lea Massari, Jean Sorel, Franco Sportelli, Gian Maria Volonte, Georges Wilson, Frank Wolff, Luidi de Filippo, Pupella Maggio, Dominico Formato, Curt Lowens, Raffaele Barbato, and the people of Naples. Directed by Nanny Loy. Screenplay, P. F. Campanile, Massico Franciosa, Carlo Bernari and Loy; from a story by Vasco Pratolini, Campanile, Franciosa and Loy; comera, Marcello Gatti; editor, Ruggero Mastroianni; music, Carlo Rustichelli. At Supercinema, Rome. Running time, 124 MINS.

Concetta .... Regina Bianchi
Pitrella .... Aldo Giuffre
Maria .... Lea Massari
Livornese .... Jean Sorel
Prof. Rosati .... Franco Sportelli
Sailor .... Charles Belmont
Stimolo .... Gian Maria Volonte
Salvatore .... Frank Wolff
Cicillo ... . Luigi DeFilippo
Mother Arturo .... Pupella Maggio
Reformatory director... Georges Wilson
Ajello .... Raffaele Barbato
Gennarino .... Domenico Formato
Sakau .... Curt Lowens

List this as one of the major Italian achievements of the year. Pic is one of most moving, rousing epics of resistance against Nazism seen in a long time. Anti-climactically, however, some of its very qualities may limit its impact boxoffice-wise in non-Italian areas. Home-market success is assured.

Film is a fresco of four days of resistance attacks on German occupation forces in Naples on the eve of the Yank troops' arrival in the South Italian city. It is inspired by actual events in a heroic, if perforce disorganized harassing stand, said to have been the kernel of the entire Italian resistance movement in the last days of the Italian campaign. While there's no denying that the picture takes a definitely strong stand in condemning Nazi brutality, it is basically and ultimately a film which condemns all brutality—hence war.

Much has been argued about the film's tampering with history, and this only historians (and then with difficulty, due to lack of objective documentation) can determine. What is true is that it reflects the spirit of the Neapolitan rebellion via episodes which may or may not be factually accurate. There is also more than a dubious hint that it was the people of Naples who handed over the city to the latecoming Allied Forces, having by their movement forced the Germans to evacuate the city.

However, it's a rousing show which Nanny Loy directed, with few lags and some concessions to hind-sight melodramaticisms by a naturally melodramatic people such as the Neapolitan. The development is deliberately confused, as were those days, and cameos are picked up, dropped, and then taken up once more.

Acting, with a few exceptions due to exaggeration, is dedicated and able. All actors agreed (in the Italo version) to omit personal credits in tribute to the people of Naples who took part in the revolt. Marcello Gatti has done an outstandng job with his camera while Gianni Polidori (credited as art director) deserves much credit for his elaborate on-the-spot reconstruction of a shattered Naples. Carlo Rustichelli's music, inspired by local folk tunes, is likewise apt. Pic is elaborately mounted. *Hawk.*

L'Oeil Du Monocle
(The Monocled Eye)
(FRENCH)
Paris, Nov. 27.

Prodis release of Viatele-Films Borderie-Arex Films production. Stars Paul Neurisse; features Maurice Biraud, Gala Germani, Elga Andersen, Robert Dalban. Directed by Georges Lautner. Screenplay, Jacques Robert, Jacques Remy; camera, Maurice Fellous; editor, Michele David. At Balzac, Paris. Running time, 105 MINS.

Dromard .... Paul Meurisse
Martigue .... Maurice Biraud
Diana .... Gala Germani
Erika .... Elga Andersen
Poussin .... Robert Dalban

Tongue-in-cheek secret service pic is replete with many killings, gore, girls and glibness. Still it lacks the needed punch and drive in the direction to make this only a possible dualer item abroad.

During the last World War, the Germans buried a lot of secret documents that could embarrass the French, English, Russian or today's Germany, with a great treasure also involved, according to the plot. One German knows where it is and pic details how the various powers fight over him.

Main plus angle is Paul Meurisse's wry wit, elegance and dry humor as the French secret service man. He sometimes invests the obvious happenings with a sharp edge of clever satire that is mainly absent from the general writing of this. Director Georges Lautner just does not have the snap and sure footedness to imbue this comedy-actioner with the right balance and potency.

Result is a fairly lagging affair with some clever moments and solid action segs but not having the overall progression to make it too much. *Mosk.*

Die Gluecklichen Jahre Der Thorwalds
(Happy Years of the Thorwalds)
(GERMAN)
Berlin, Nov. 20.

Europa release of Allgemeine Film Produktion GmbH production. Stars Elisabeth Bergner, Hansjoery Felmy, Loni von Friedl, Robert Graf. Directed by John Olden and Wolfgang Staudte. Screenplay, Maria Matray and Answald Krueger; adapted from play, "Time and the Conways," by John B. Priestley; camera, Siegfried Hold; music, Siegfried Franz. At Gloria Palast, West Berlin. Running time, 90 MINS.

Frau Thorwald .... Elsabeth Bergner
Peter .... Hansjoerg Felmy
Maria .... Johanna Matz
Martin .... Dietmar Schoenherr
Helga .... Brigitte Grothum
Erika .... Elfriede Irrall
Katrin .... Wega Jahnke
Brigitte v. Tienitz......Loni von Friedl
Ernst Bieber .... Robert Graf
Dr. Schaub .... Dieter Borsche

This one marks the return of Elisabeth Bergner to the German screen after an absence of three decades. Her comeback performance is the best thing about this film. It should have the German critics raving. There's a possibility that this will mark the beginning of "a new Bergner era" here. But despite remarkably good acting, this is not a very convincing film. However, the pic should do very well in this country.

Directed by John Olden and Wolfgang Staudte (the latter took over when the former was taken ill), this is an adaptation from John B. Priestley's play, "Time and the Conways." The Germanized version centers around a well-to-do German bourgeoisie family with the father killed in an accident. Central figure is Frau Thorwald (Elisabeth Bergner), mother of six children, two boys and four girls, ranging from 15 to 26 when the film begins. All that mother has on her mind is her children and she spoils them.

The years roll by and after World War I, the postwar misery, inflation and other factors make the Thorwald fortune shrink. Frau Thorwald realizes too late that she's been living in a dream world. She also realizes that all her children have become failures in adult life. And there is nothing left for the Thorwalds but to realize that the happy years are definitely over.

The cast includes exceptionally good players. The two sons, Hansjoerg Felmy and Dietmar Schoenherr, are in this category. The four daughters are Johanna Matz, Brigitte Grothum, Elfriede Irrall and Wega Jahnke. Fine support is given by lovely Loni von Friedl, Robert Graf and Dieter Borscher.

The picture's prime deficiencies stem from directorial mishandling. Direction lacks smoothness or a clear concentration. And there's too much cliche as to situations and character motivations.

Again, the best thing about this is Elisabeth Bergner. Her portrayal of a happy, later illusioned mother is superb. Pic's technical credits are average. *Hans.*

Comment Reussir En Amour
(How to Succeed in Love)
(FRENCH)
Paris, Nov. 27.

Cinedis release of France-Cinema, Mannic Films, PCM production, Stars Dany Saval; features Jean Poiret, Michel Serrault, Jacqueline Maillan, Noel Roquevert, Andre Luguet, Roger Pierre, Dominique Davray. Directed by Michel Boisrond. Screenplay, Annette Wademant; camera, Robert Lefbvre; editor, Claudine Bouche. At Normandie, Paris. Running time, 90 MINS.

Sophie .... Dany Saval
Bernard .... Jean Poiret
Inspector .... Michel Serrault
Edmee .... Jacqueline Maillan
Director .... Noel Roquevert

Attempt at a frothy situation comedy, in the Yank manner leavened with franker French in insouciance, does not come off because of obvious plotting and the lack of witty thesping and perceptive direction. It looms mainly a home item.

A young publisher is enamored of a flighty, frivolous girl whom he finally marries after a wild courtship. Then her zany petulance almost costs him his job and leads to various little situations. But the snap needed to have these familiar happenings become witty and intriguing are just not there.

Dany Saval is much too brittle to make her dim-witted character beguiling. Jean Poiret has more comic feel but is somewhat defeated by his role. It is technically only par. *Mosk.*

Billy Rose's Jumbo
(MUSICAL COMEDY—PANAVISION—METROCOLOR)

Musical circus spec looks like potential goldmine.

Hollywood, Nov. 28.

Metro release of Euterpe-Arwin picture, produced by Joe Pasternak and Martin Melcher. Assoc. producer, Roger Edens. Stars Doris Day, Stephen Boyd, Jimmy Durante, Martha Raye. Dean Jagger. Directed by Charles Walters. Screenplay, Sidney Sheldon, based on musical play by Ben Hecht and Charles MacArthur, produced by Billy Rose. Music and lyrics by Richard Rodgers and Lorenz Hart. Camera, William H. Daniels; editor, Richard W. Farrell; art directors, George W. Davis, Preston Ames; set directors, Henry Grace, Hugh Hunt; sound, Franklin Milton; 2nd unit director, Busby Berkeley; asst. director, William Shanks. Circus acts coordinated by Al Dobritch. Reviewed at Hollywood Paramount, Nov. 28, '62. Running time, 123 MINS.

Kitty Wonder	Doris Day
Sam Rawlins	Stephen Boyd
Pop Wonder	Jimmy Durante
Lulu	Martha Raye
John Noble	Dean Jagger
Harry	Joseph Waring
Tina	Lynn Wood
Ellis	Charles Watts
Parsons	James Chandler
Madison	Robert Burton
Hank	Wilson Wood
Eddie	Norman Leavitt

One of the final productions ever seen in the old N.Y. Hippodrome, "Jumbo" was a dull book musical of the 1935 season, with a curious mid-depression tie-in with Texaco Gas. Now, some 27 years later, the showmanship of Metro has turned the combo musical and circus into a great film entertainment with every prospect of big boxoffice.

Here is Doris Day back as a songstress, and Jimmy Durante encoring from the original Hipp live version. The music of Richard Rodgers and the lyrics of the late great Lorenz Hart are assets and the film contains a wonderful elephant, Sydney, a mountain of effective ham.

Joe Pasternak and Martin Melcher have taken the work out of the dusty files of the past and stuck it right up there among the all-time great screen musicals. "Jumbo," obviously slanted for the Christmas-New Year trade, will probably be around for the Fourth of July traffic also, and will be remembered long after it has paid off initial production costs.

It's a toss-up whether the music, comedy, or sawdust-and-tinsel of "Jumbo" makes the greatest impression. Much of the Rodgers and Hart score for the 1935 legit version has been retained, some of it necessarily being used only as background. The big hits, however —"Little Girl Blue," "My Romance," and "Most Beautiful Girl in the World"—are given full-scale production.

The latter, reprised beautifully by Durante in a touching sequence, first serves Miss Day and Boyd as a merry-go-roundelay. "This Can't Be Love," from Rodgers and Hart's 1938 "Boys From Syracuse" and "Why Can't I?" from their 1929 "Spring Is Here," have been added to the score, the latter as a delightful duet by the two femme leads.

The overall excellent, professional handling of director Charles Walters, is greatly responsible, though never obvious, for the 123 minutes going by in a hurry. He adds to his past prowess as a musical and comedy director the talent of a great ringmaster.

Doris Day may never have sung better than she does in "Jumbo." While the story is no challenge to her thespic talents, her return to the thing she does so well, could (and should) persuade her to make more musicals, even if she is given some of the male lead's numbers to perform.

In the legit version Durante was Claudius B. Bowers, a circus press agent. He is now the circus-owner, with Doris Day as his daughter, and Martha Raye as his 14-year-awaiting fiancee. Durante plays the role as Durante. Who'd have it otherwise?

Stephen Boyd, handsome, virile, excellent within the limits of his role, has star billing but his part is strictly in support of his leading lady. It's doubtful that singing is his own, but he handles his musical sequences well, especially the "What Is a Circus" number where he can do his own lines as a diseur, rather than trying to sing.

Martha Raye, too long absent from the screen, only has room to swing a couple of times but she makes them big—especially a wonderful lion-costume bit in the parade and her duet with Miss Day —as well as all of her encounters with Durante in their endless wedding-date-decision routine.

Some of the greatest acting in the film is contributed by Sydney, who plays the title role. A flamboyant performer in the best Victor Buono style, Sydney's "Jumbo" flirts, emotes, dances, almost sings, and breaks your heart in his farewell scene with Doris Day. Then, "ham" to the end, he reappears in the finale, all in white and bigger than Sinatra in "Till the Clouds Roll By."

Joseph Waring, Lynn Wood, Charles Watts, James Chandler, Robert Burton, Wilson Wood, Norman Leavitt and Grady Sutton make brief but telling appearances.

Dean Jagger, despite co-star billing, has only a few scenes as Boyd's father and the owner of the rival circus. Though brief, they're important to the plot as he's the heavy. Jagger makes him a colorful villain, ironically named John Noble, and rotten to the core.

Sidney Sheldon's screenplay (he receives full credit although report has it that several scripters have had a go at it) retains only the basic circus-boy-meets-circus-girl format of Ben Hecht and Charles MacArthur's original book, with the ending the most important switch. Instead of the originally-conceived merger of the two circuses then the wedding of the boy and girl, Jagger's villainy drives Boyd into leaving and, with Jumbo rejoining Day, Durante and Raye. The old version would have made Jagger's deeds more understandable, if not completely forgivable.

William H. Daniels' color photography (Metrocolor) recaptures the gaudy, tinselly colors of the circus, blending them skillfully with the less-theatrical but more restive hues of every-day life. The many circus and/or musical sequences give Morton Haack's costumes, as well as the combined artistry of art directors George W. Davis and Preston Ames and set decorators Henry Grace and Hugh Hunt major exposure. Sets and costumes are beautifully coordinated and are as festive as pink lemonade and cotton candy.

Richard W. Farrell's excellent editing stands out particularly in the circus act presentations and creates a real nerve-tingler in one sequence where spectators are torn between attention to a beautifully-filmed Butterfly Girl act and tension caused by a quickly-brewing storm.

A major contribution is Busby Berkeley's directing of the circus-act sequences, coordinated by Al Dobritch. The two have somehow managed to present most of a circus within the time space of the film, without interfering with the story's advance or the presentation of non-circus musical numbers.

The list of circus artists include current versions of at least two acts—The Hannefords and The Barbettes — that, like Durante, played in the 1935 Hippodrome production. Seen as themselves (and, in some cases, doubling, almost imperceptibly, for the stars) are Ron Henon, The Pedrolas, The Wazzans, Billy Barton, Corky Cristiani, Victor Julian, Richard Berg, Joe Monahan, Miss Lani, Adolph Dubsky, Pat Anthony, and Janos Prohaska. *Robe.*

Sodom and Gomorrah
(ITALIAN—COLOR—ENGLISH DIALOG)

Another long Biblical epic with good sound performances and some striking special effects. Title and leads should insure brisk business.

London, Nov. 29.

Rank release of Goffredo Lombardo & Joseph E. Levine presentation of Titanus (Lombardo) production. Stars Stewart Granger, Stanley Baker, Pier Angeli, Rosanna Podesta, Anouk Aimee. Features Rik Battaglia, Giacomo Rossi Stuart, Claudia Mori, Feodor Chaliapin. Directed by Robert Aldrich. Screenplay, Hugo Butler and Giorgio Prosperi; camera, Silvano Ippoliti, Mario Montuori, Cyril Knowles; editor, Peter Tanner; music, Miklos Rozsa. At Odeon, Marble Arch, London. Running time, 153 MINS.

Lot	Stewart Granger
Ildith	Pier Angeli
Astaroth	Stanley Baker
Bera	Anouk Aimee
Shuch	Rossana Podesta
Maleb	Claudia Mori
Melchir	Rik Battaglia
Ishmael	Giacomo Rossi Stuart
Alabias	Fedor Chaliapin
Eber	Enzo Fiermonte
Tamar	Soilla Gabel
Malik	Giovanna Galletti
Nacor	Aldo Silvani
The Captain	Antonio De Teffe

Director Robert Aldrich has said, "Every director ought to get one Biblical film out of his system, but there's not very much that you can do about this sort of picture." Too true, and Aldrich has done everything possible to insure brisk wicket biz. The title is provocative, the steller names attractive, and Aldrich has flung in plenty of incident and some stirring special effects. Net: "Sodom and Gomorrah" has many of the faults of the Biblical epic, but many good qualities. It is too long, inevitably. It starts slowly and has many static passages in between the highspot events. And some of the dubbed voices clash uneasily with the accents of Stewart Granger, Stanley Baker, Pier Angeli and the other stars. Yet its 153 minutes do not hang too heavily because the intriguing background and clash of characters always make for dramatic interest.

Storyline concerns Lot's pilgrimage to the Valley of Jordan with the Hebrews. They set up camp in the Valley but are almost immediately involved in a bitter clash between the Helamites, who covet the wealth of Sodom and Gomorrah, two cesspools of depravity, ruled over by the cold, beautiful, unscrupulous Queen Bera who, incidentally, is being doublecrossed for power by her scheming brother. Bera decides to use the Hebrews as a buffer between her and her enemies and makes a deal with Lot that the Hebrews should work the Valley and defend it. The seal is put on the pact when Bera presents Lot with her favorite slave girl, Ildith, who becomes Lot's wife.

From then on there is endless complicated incident. Lot and Astaroth, Prince of Sodom, fight to the death. Lot's daughter Shuch falls in love with Astaroth who rapes both her and her sister and the Halamites are stopped in battle by the combined forces of the Sodomites and Hebrews. Big production value comes from this scrap which involves rivers of flaming fire and the drowning of the marauders by the breaking of a great dam. The Hebrews are forced to live in Sodom and gradually Lot finds that he and his people are being corrupted by the Sodomites. There is rape, double-crossing, duels, torture, before Lot gets another vision, and leads his people away from Sodom just before the two cities are destroyed by the wrath of God. The crumbling cities make another mighty piece of special effects, and is impressive screen fare. And, of course, Lot's wife does look back and is turned into a pillar of salt in an accurate lift from the Bible which, nevertheless, looks to be a phoney climax.

Stewart Granger makes a distinguished, solemn and sincere figure of Lot and Stanley Baker, as the treacherous Prince of Sodom, is sufficiently sneaky though he has only a couple of highspots in his role. Aimee Anouk is an impressively sinister Queen, Pier Angeli has some moments of genuine emotion as Lot's wife and Rosanna Podesta and Claudia Mori play the shadowy roles of Lot's daughters adequately. Rik Battaglia, Feodor Chaliapin, Scilla Gabel and Giacomo Rossi Stuart are others who stand out in a longish cast. The artwork, special effects and location work (giving evidence of a second unit at work) give Aldrich's sure direction valuable assistance, though Miklos Rosza's musical score, with its heavy leaning on celestial music, tends to be obtrusive and makes some of the dialog hard to follow.

There will be a number of occasions, particularly early, when patience will be strained but there are also many rewarding situations, some genuine thrills and, at least, the screenplay is not overloaded with the kind of anachronistic dialog that too often creeps into these religious sagas. "Sodom" is a likely big money spinner. *Rich.*

Volga, Volga
(RUSSIAN—COLOR—KINO-PANORAMA)

Paris, Dec. 4.

Jacques Mauleair release of Gorki Studio production. With N. Sergeev, V. Tielegina, G. Ipifantsev, N. Ghoudrakova. Directed by Iakov Segel. Screenplay, V. lejov, Segel; camera (Sovcolor), B. Mona-

stirski. I. Zarafran; editor, X. Blinova. At Kinopanorama, Paris. Running time, 80 MINS.

Stepan .... N. Sergeev
Alexei .... V. Tielegina
Natahsa .... G. Ipifantsev
Nastia .... N. Ghoudrakova

The first Russian film in its Cinerama-type process, Kinopanorama, is a simple tale of an aging and retiring captain's last trip down the Volga. He is on his old tug boat, as old as he is, and is about to scrap it. No untoward bits of bravura here, but it is a fresh film which proves that an unassuming tale can be told in this triple screen process without drowning it.

The lines are less noticeable than heretofore while the color and panels are fairly well balanced if off at times. No pushy propaganda either except for a musically crashing and visually stirring tribute to the defenders of Stalingrad. This is justified by the man's going to lay a wreath on the tomb of his only son who fell in battle there.

For the remainder, it spins the old man's reminiscences at various stops, uses adroit flashbacks to his early life, and has a side tale about his new assistant who is a girl chaser.

Color shots of the Volga are tasteful and sometimes stunning. The cabin boy going on a swing or the assistant catching up with his ship when a girl crane operator puts him out to it on a hoisted car are a few moments that utilize the tremendous screen for eye-catching effect. Otherwise, this tender tale could have been made in small screen and black and white. Director Iakov Segel is good at tugging at the emotions.

Acting is effective. This entry may not have the scope for the U.S. as yet. But it might be useful when the big scale sheen of this process wears off. Color is fine as are technical credits. *Mosk.*

We Joined The Navy
(BRITISH—COLOR)

Kenneth More's breezy personality keeps a tenuous spree simmering, though sometimes precariously, through some lighthearted fun. Joan O'Brien, Lloyd Nolan, Mischa Auer add Yank support.

London, Nov. 27.

Warner-Pathe release of an Associated British (Daniel M. Angel) production. Stars Kenneth More, Lloyd Nolan, Joan O'Brien, Mischa Auer; features Jeremy Lloyd, Dinsdale Landen, Derek Fowlds, Denise Warren. Directed by Wendy Toye. Screenplay by Arthur Dales, based on John Winter's novel; camera (Eastmancolor), Otto Heller; editor, Richard Best; music, Ron Grainer. Previewed at Corner Theatre, London. Running time, 109 MINS.

Bodger .... Kenneth More
Ryan .... Lloyd Nolan
Carol .... Joan O'Brien
Colonel & President .... Mischa Auer
Dewberry .... Jeremy Lloyd
Bowles .... Dinsdale Landen
Carson .... Derek Fowlds
Collette .... Denise Warren
Dewberry Sr. .... John Le Mesurier
Mrs. Dewberry .... Lally Bowers
Admiral Blake .... Laurence Naismith
Admiral Filmer .... Andrew Cruickshank
Admiral Thomas .... Walter Fitzgerald
Rear Admiral .... John Phillips
Commander R.N. .... Ronald Leigh-Hunt
C.P.O. Froud .... Arthur Lovegrove
P.O. Gibbons .... Brian Wilde
Commander Spelling U.S.N Paul Maxwell
Commander Hurley U.S.N. .... Nicholas Stuart
Consul .... John Barrard
Consul's Wife .... Esma Cannon
Orator .... Kenneth Griffith
Albert .... Hank

As inconsequential as its title, this lighthearted frolic provides an easygoing vehicle for the charm and comedy knowhow of Kenneth More. His popularity alone should insure ready patrons for a piece of pleasantly mounted frivol which makes the minimum assault on the brain. Casting of dependable Lloyd Nolan, Joan O'Brien and vet Mischa Auer (in a dual role) plus three new young male faces, adds useful support to More's smooth endeavors.

Wendy Toye, one of Britain's few women directors, has helmed the pic with brisk gaiety but Arthur Dales' screenplay never adds up to a really cohesive yarn. It's mainly a string of gag situations and it is a matter of hit-and-miss which one of these will make ticket buyers yock. None of them is particularly new, but the ebullient cast usually gives them a fresh look.

Lientenant Commander Badger R.N. (Kenneth More) is a likable guy whose habit of tactlessly saying the right thing at the wrong time gets in the hair of the Admiralty top brass. He's sent to Dartmouth to train naval cadets, but even there he runs into trouble.

So he's posted to liaison duties with the American Sixth Fleet in the Mediterranean, where everyone hopes he'll be harmless. Unfortunately, with him go three irrepressible midshipmen. They run afoul of the Yank Vice-Admiral in charge. From then on, it's a series of irrelevant mishaps and clashes leading up to More and his midshipmen clearing up a revolution in a local republic practically singlehanded, through a string of blunders. It's when the revolution scenes start that the film becomes overly shapeless, though a number of laughs keep the comedy afloat to its climax.

More sails through his role with disarming ease while Nolan, as the testy Top Tar, brings needed weight to his role. Pretty Miss O'Brien provides the scanty, but pleasant, light romantic relief with More. Auer mugs cheerfully through a couple of brother roles, playing both the prexy of Moronia and the rebel-leading colonel.

Three newish young actors, Jeremy Lloyd, Dinsdale Landen and Derek Fowlds, play the scatty midshipmen jovially. Lloyd is a particularly droll character of the silly ass type. A Windmill soubrette Denise Warren, also scores with an appearance as a risque cabaret singer-dancer, as does an educated pooch, "Albert."

Production credits are mainly high, with some easy on the eye color camerawork by Otto Heller, authentic sets, and a tuneful score by Ron Grainer which leans heavily on the nautical motif. Richard Best's editing is occasionally jerky, *Rich.*

A Girl Named Tamiko
(PANAVISION—COLOR)

Laurence Harvey, France Nuyen in Tokyo for flamboyant affairs of love, colorfully backgrounded and engagingly performed. Major bookings are in order.

Paramount release of Hal Wallis production. Stars Laurence Harvey, France Nuyen, Martha Hyer; features Gary Merrill, Michael Wilding, Miyoshi Umeki. Directed by John Sturges. Screenplay, Edward Anhala, based on novel by Ronald Kirkbride; camera (Technicolor), Charles Lang Jr.; editor, Warren Low; music, Elmer Bernstein; assistant director, D. Michael Moore. Reviewed in N.Y., Dec. 3, '62. Running time, 110 MINS.

Ivan Kalin .... Laurence Harvey
Tamiko .... France Nuyen
Fay Wilson .... Martha Hyer
Max Wilson .... Gary Merrill
Nigel Costairs .... Michael Wilding
Eiko .... Miyoshi Umeki
James Hatten .... Steve Brodie
Mary Hatten .... Lee Patrick
Minya .... John Mamo
Kimitaka .... Bob Okazaki
Otani .... Richard Loo
Akiba .... Philip Ahn

This newest from producer Hal Wallis has its share of shortcomings; there's now and again a bit of fuzziness in character development and plot detail. But these may well be overlooked for the story of emotional conflicts in modern-day Japan is a fairly arresting work. It is colorful, provocative and measures up nicely in "A"-class salability. Very good are the scenic values; as a matter of fact, some of the Technicolor-Panavision photography of the Oriental customs and rituals and the exotic backgrounds is strikingly effective.

Laurence Harvey's character is not one immediately easy to accept and this is one of the flaws. As Ivan Kalin, he's a Chinese-Russian photographer and looks, speaks and romances like a British matinee idol. Thus there's a certain lack of conviction but this is not too severe a drawback as the story unwinds and the interest mounts.

The girl of the title is France Nuyen, thoroughly enchanting as the librarian whose family adheres to the Japanese traditions while she breaks away to engage in the romance with Harvey. Martha Hyer, as an American girl, very much on the loose in flitting from man to man, handles the part fittingly. There are some bold dramatics as Miss Hyer is either loving or posing as she takes a fling at being a photographer's model.

Gary Merrill fits in as a brooding business man who cares and yearns for Miss Hyer only to have her walk out on him. Michael Wilding is a British art dealer with a distaste for the devious measures taken by Harvey in order to get his much-wanted visa to go to the United States. Miyoshi Umeki is a slant-eyed cutie who does the cohabitat bit with Wilding. These two make for a colorful pair and their East-West mating game is rendered plausibly.

Steve Brodie, Lee Patrick, John Mamo and Bob Okazaki, in lesser roles, contribute uniformly good performances.

John Sturges has directed the Edward Anhalt screenplay with an old pro's sense of how to get strong material on the screen without being offensive. One particularly provocative scene, done in good taste, has Miss Nupen and Harvey sharing their bath with a Japanese family. It's an old custom.

The music is appealing all the way, probably could do well on its own as an LP. As aforementioned, Charles Lang's photography is firstrate. And a major nod to Edith Head for her Oriental and Occidental clothes designing. Editing might have been a little tighter. Technical credits all fine. *Gene.*

Days Of Wine And Roses

Fine filmization of the "Playhouse 90" drama of a love and marriage shattered by booze. Jack Lemmon and Lee Remick performances strong. Very depressing tale.

Hollywood, Nov. 28.

Warner Bros. release of Martin Manulis production. Stars Jack Lemmon, Lee Remick; features Charles Bickford, Jack Klugman. Directed by Blake Edwards. Screenplay, J. P. Miller, from his teleplay; camera, Phil Lathrop; editor, Patrick McCormack; music, Henry Mancini; asst. director, Carter DeHaven Jr. Reviewed at the studio, Nov. 28, '62. Running time, 117 MINS.

Joe .... Jack Lemmon
Kirsten .... Lee Remick
Arnesen .... Charles Bickford
Hungerford .... Jack Klugman
Leland .... Alan Hewitt
Ballefoy .... Tom Palmer
Debbie .... Debbie Megowan
Dottie .... Maxine Stuart
Trayner .... Jack Albertson
Proprietor .... Ken Lynch

In "Days of Wine and Roses," Warner Bros. has a film of emotional impact but basically limited appeal. It hails from television's former "Playhouse 90" series, and has been faithfully and painstakingly translated to the screen by two of the men responsible for the praised tv version—producer Martin Manulis and writer J. P. Miller.

An intimate and cold sober study of the corrosive effect of alcoholism on the lives of a young married couple, it requires maximum involvement and profound compassion from an audience to be appreciated. Since not everyone will be willing to participate fully in the emotional give and take, some may find it an almost intolerably depressing 117 minutes—a limitation of appeal certain to have some adverse effect on the film's moneymaking destiny. But shrewd, effective selling—with emphasis on the right values, not on superficial sordidness for its own sake—could attract customers who might otherwise keep their distance, and lift the film into the successful boxoffice sphere.

A noteworthy achievement is Jack Lemmon's powerful enactment. Another facet that will be of great advantage is the lovely and haunting title refrain by Johnny Mercer and Henry Mancini, and also the latter's generally fine background score. The song should be a good seller and is of definite Oscar potential.

Miller's gruelling drama illustrates how the unquenchable lure of alcohol can supersede even love, and how marital communication cannot exist in a house divided by one-sided boozing. The wife (Lee Remick), originally a non-drinker with a yen for chocolates that is a tip-off of her vulnerability to the habit pattern, begins to drink when her husband (Lemmon), a p.r. man and two-fisted belter whose career is floundering, is dismayed by a gap in their togetherness. Upshot is the disastrous compatibility of mutual alcoholism. The husband turns sensibly to Alcoholics Anonymous, but the irony is that the wife cannot abstain, even though it means abandoning her mate, their daughter, and everything dear, normal, respectable and useful in life. Her stubborn decision is horrible and odd, and sure to baffle most filmgoers. It appears to be a matter of abso-

lutely illogical and inflexible pride, a choice that Miller's drama does not fully clarify.

Lemmon gives a dynamic and chilling performance. Scenes of his collapse, particularly in the violent ward, are brutally realistic and terrifying. Miss Remick, too, is effective, and there is solid featured work from Charles Bickford and Jack Klugman and a number of fine supporting performances.

Director Blake Edwards has realized and fulfilled the screen potential of Miller's endeavor, utilizing and synthesizing the cinematic savvy and resourcefulness of such craftsmen as cameraman Phil Lathrop, editor Patrick McCormack, art director Joseph Wright and soundman Jack Solomon. *Tube.*

To Kill A Mockingbird

Artful starring filmization of the Harper Lee novel. One of the year's best. Should be formidable b.o. contender.

Hollywood, Dec. 4.
Universal release of Alan J. Pakula production. Stars Gregory Peck; introduces Mary Badham, Phillip Alford. Directed by Robert Mulligan. Screenplay, Horton Foote, based on Harper Lee's novel; camera, Russell Harlan; editor, Aaron Stell; music, Elmer Bernstein; asst. director, Joseph Kenny. Reviewed at Westwood Village Theatre, Dec. 4, '62. Running time, **129 MINS.**

Atticus	Gregory Peck
Scout	Mary Badham
Jem	Phillip Alford
Dill	John Megna
Sheriff Heck Tate	Frank Overton
Miss Maudie	Rosemary Murphy
Mrs. Dubose	Ruth White
Tom Robinson	Brock Peters
Calpurnia	Estelle Evans
Judge Taylor	Paul Fix
Mayella	Collin Wilcox
Ewell	James Anderson
Aunt Stephanie	Alice Ghostley
Boo Radley	Robert Duvall
Gilmer	William Windom
Walter Cunningham	Crahan Denton
Mr. Radley	Richard Hale

Harper Lee's highly regarded and eminently successful first novel has been artfully and delicately translated to the screen. Universal's "To Kill a Mockingbird" is a major film achievement, a significant, captivating and memorable picture that ranks with the best of recent years. Its success in the literary world seems certain to be repeated in the theatrical sphere.

All hands involved are to be congratulated for a job well done. Obviously loving care went into the process by which it was converted from the comprehensive prose of the printed page to the visual and dramatic storytelling essence of the screen. Horton Foote's trenchant screenplay, Robert Mulligan's sensitive and instinctively observant direction and a host of exceptional performances are all essential threads in the rich, provocative fabric and skillfully synthesized workmanship of Alan J. Pakula's production.

As it unfolds on the screen, "To Kill a Mockingbird" bears with it, oddly enough, alternating overtones of Faulkner, Twain, Steinbeck, Hitchcock and an Our Gang Comedy. The power and fascination of the story lies in the disarming and enthralling contrast of its two basic plot components. A telling indictment of racial prejudice in the deep South, it is also a charming tale of the emergence of two youngsters from the realm of wild childhood fantasy to the horizon of maturity, responsibility, compassion and social insight. It is the story of a wise, gentle, softspoken Alabama lawyer (Gregory Peck) entrusted with the formidable dual chore of defending a Negro falsely accused of rape while raising his own impressionable, imaginative, motherless children in a hostile, terrifying environment of bigotry and economic depression.

For Peck, it is an especially challenging role, requiring him to conceal his natural physical attractiveness yet project through a veneer of civilized restraint and resigned, rational compromise the fires of social indignation and humanitarian concern that burn within the character. He not only succeeds, but makes it appear effortless, etching a portrayal of strength, dignity, intelligence. An-

other distinguished achievement for an actor whose taste and high standards of role selectivity is attested to by the calibre of his films and performances throughout his career.

But by no means is this entirely, or even substantially, Peck's film. Two youngsters just about steal it away, although the picture marks their screen bows. Both nine-year-old Mary Badham and 13-year-old Phillip Alford, each of whom hails from the South, make striking debuts as Peck's two irrepressible, mischievous, ubiquitous, irresistably childish children. More than one filmgoer will be haunted by sweet, misty recollections of his own childhood while observing their capers and curiosities. Both are handsome, talented, expressive youngsters who seem destined to enjoy rewarding careers. They are joined in their activities by little John Megna, an unusuallooking tyke who also makes a vivid and infectious impression.

The merit and restraint of these three junior performances reflects great credit on the direction of Mulligan. But, paradoxically, the value of the spontaneous combustion that he has achieved with his young threesome has produced the picture's main flaw. For half the time the children, in their verbal zeal, cannot be heard clearly. This ragged articulation of youth is a definite irritant. But it is overshadowed by the overall excellence of their enactments.

Mulligan's ability to coax such fine portrayals out of pint-sized tyros is only one facet of his superlative contribution to the film. Most noteworthy is the manner in which he instills and heightens tension and terror where they are absolutely essential. Recognizing that menace cannot be expressed with more shock or impact than as seen in the eyes of the beholder, especially when the beholder is a child, he has done a masterful job of determining points-of-view from which Russell Harlan's camera witnesses the story's more frightening incidents. And again, in the long courtroom scene, Mulligan and Harlan have teamed to create a significant moment by inventive employment of the camera. When Peck, in defending his client and making his impassioned plea for justice, addresses his remarks to the bigoted jury, he is actually leaning over and speaking not to 12 people, but directly to the entire audience in the theatre.

(This is a film that should play well in the American South. The artful, intimate manner in which the scene is thus mounted and executed will be hitting home where it counts the most.)

There are some top-notch supporting performances. Especially sharp and effective are Frank Overton, Estelle Evans, James Anderson and Robert Duvall. Brock Peters has an outstanding scene as the innocent, ill-fated Negro on trial for his life. Likewise Collin Wilcox as his Tobacco Roadish "victim." Others of value are Rosemary Murphy, Ruth White, Paul Fix, Alice Ghostley, William Windom, Crahan Denton and Richard Hale. Pakula rates credit for his careful-unorthodox casting measures. It is a pleasure to see so many fresh faces on the screen.

The physical appearance and

other production facets of the film merit high praise. Harlan's photographic textures and compositions create a number of indelible images. Aaron Stell's editing is stable and snug, in spite of the long running time and the fact that the story virtually cuts its main continuity in half with the central courtroom passage. Art directors Alexander Golitzen and Henry Bumstead have created sets in Hollywood that authentically convey the physique and characteristic of 1932 Alabama. Last, but not least, there is Elmer Bernstein's haunting score—fundamentally wistful, sweet and childlike in the nature of its themes, but behind which there seems to lurk something morbidly chilling, something imminently eerie. *Tube.*

Secret of Outer Space Island

(FRENCH—COLOR)

Milgud (William S. Miller, George Gudis) production. Directed by Jean Tourane. Screenplay, Jean Tourane, Frank Scully, Richard Lavigne, Jack Dunn Trop; music, Richard Cornus, Warren Baker; narrated by Phil Tonken. American version of original French pic, adapted and produced by Trop. Previewed in N.Y., Dec. 1, '62. Running time, **66 MINS.**

(*English Narration*)

This is an American adaptation of the French pic, "Once Upon a Time," produced in France about five years ago. Fundamentally, it appears to be much the same film excepting for the English narration, but not in VARIETY files. The idea of having animals and birds carry out the story of the "happiness island" where everybody loves their neighbors perhaps has some appeal for youngsters and younger students in classrooms but as adult fare it is difficult to stomach. Hence, the film may do for kiddie matinees or perhaps as an educational subject. But that's all.

Color and sound effects are fine, and the trainer of the various domestic animals and birds who carry out the thin plot deserves praise. But even linking the dumb creatures up with the thesis of a villainous chimp that is determined to wreck aftermentioned island with an atom-like explosion wears thin early for the average viewer.

One wonders why any American producer would go to the trouble of making a Yank version of the French original. The film made in France seemingly failed to make much stir in the European market. The same applies to the U.S. production. *Wear.*

Taras Bulba

PANAVISION —EASTMANCOLOR)

Accent on action makes for boxoffice but with no help from story. Cornball plot only gets in way of rousing, thrillpacked spectacle.

Hollywood, Dec. 8.
United Artists release of Harold Hecht production. Stars Tony Curtis, Yul Brynner, Christine Kaufmann. Features Sam Wanamaker. Directed by J. Lee Thompson. 2d unit director, Cliff Lyons. Screenplay, Waldo Salt and Karl Tunberg, from book by Nikolai Gogol. Music by Franz Waxman; lyrics, Mack David; or-

chestration, Leonid Raab. Camera, Joseph MacDonald; editors, William Reynolds, Gene Milford, Eda Warren, Ace & Folmar Blanksted; art director, Edward Carrere; set director, William Calvert; sound, Stan Cooley, asst. director, Tom Shaw; 2d unit asst. director, Dave Silver. Reviewed at Academy Awards ',' eatre, Dec. 7, 1962. Running time, **123 MINS.**

Andrei Bulba	Tony Curtis
Taras Bulba	Yul Brynner
Natalia Dubrov	Christine Kaufmann
Filipenko	Sam Wanamaker
Shilo	Brad Dexter
Prince Grigory	Guy Rolfe
Ostap Bulba	Perry Lopez
Governor	George Macready
Sofia Bulba	Ilka Windish
Old Stepan	Vladimir Sokoloff
Grisha Kubenko	Vladimir Irman
Ivan Mykola	Daniel Ocko
Abbot	Abraham Sofaer
Korzh	Mickey Finn
Captain Alex	Richard Rust
Tymoshevsky	Ron Weyand
Gypsy Princess	Vitina Marcus
Redheaded Girl	Martine Milner
Dolotov	Chuck Hayward
Kimon Kandor	Syl Lamont
Zina	Ellen Davalos
Bro. Bartholomew	Marvin Goux
Mayor	Jack Raine

If producer Harold Hecht's audience goal is the same action-happy escapists who sailed "The Vikings" to boxoffice, he should capture a sizeable portion of that powerful audience with "Taras Bulba." His try at making a "Vikings"-on-horse-back is almost successful enough to compensate for the incredulous saga the scripters have woven to accompany it.

For many minutes of the two hours it takes director J. Lee Thompson to put Gogol's tale of the legendary Cossack hero on the screen, the panorama of fighting men, and horses sweeping across the wide steppes (actually the plains of Argentina) provides a compelling sense of pageantry and grandeur. But considering he directed the epic "Guns of Navarone," the only excuse one can make for his plot-handling is that he forgot to reload.

As powerful as they are, the spectacular features of "Taras Bulba" do not quite render palatable the wishy-washy subplot, seemingly devised to give Tony Curtis as much screen time as the far more colorful title-role of Yul Brynner. Even avid action-seekers are likely to find hard swallowing a hoary love story of an uncivilized Cossack lad and a polished Polish maiden. Their adventures, made up of the same mixture, as before, are modified only when the scripters, not conforming to customary plotting, have Curtis slain by Brynner, a rather too-neat plot ending.

Tony Curtis, an excellent actor when properly supervised or motivated, was seemingly neither inspired nor irritated sufficiently by his talented credits-sharer to do more than kiss and kill on cue. A running gag which has him physically challenging his father's authority leaves him the loser on all counts. Only when he's asked to use his unquestioned gift for comedy does he impress the viewer. When he can play it lightly (or in the obviously enjoyable bussing bits with his leading lady) he is effective, but these scenes are too infrequent.

Yul Brynner's Taras Bulba is an arrogant, proud, physically powerful Cossack chief. Even though the actor follows the habit of running his lines together, his actions are always unmistakably clear. He's allowed plenty of space in which to chew the scenery and there's precious little of it in which he doesn't leave teethmarks.

Christine Kaufman's delicate, always unsoiled Polish noblewoman is still another of those beautiful-but-don't-dirty visions of feminity. She never makes credible her wholesale and immediate capitulation to Curtis's charms and, during a siege, never shows the least sign of starvation, disease or dirt.

The rest of the huge supporting cast is divided between Poles and Cossacks, with the latter coming off best in both acting and action. Sam Wanamaker, Perry Lopez (as Brynner's 2nd son), Ilka Windish, and the late Vladimir Sokoloff are the more colorful of the Brynner-Curtis retinue, none of whom could be called dull or quiet.

On the other side of the steppes, Guy Rolfe (delightfully villainous as a Polish prince who doesn't pull his hand back quickly enough when pointing out one of Brynner's errors—the latter having his sword in hand), George MacReady, and Abraham Sofaer pace the action for the Poles.

The battle sequences and, to a lesser extent, the Cossack camp scenes, are the picture's greatest assets. Some of cameraman Joseph MacDonald's long shots of hordes of horsemen sweeping across the plains, as countless others pour over every hillside, are breathtakingly grand and fully utilize the wide screen. The work of the many stuntsmen is brilliant, providing thrills and spills in sufficient amount to satisfy the most bloodthirsty.

Franz Waxman's score, beautifully underscoring the changes of mood, has a love theme that should achieve popularity on its own merits. His scoring, Russian derived, for the battles and his czardas-like themes for the Cossacks are among his best work.

Robe.

Who's Got the Action?
(PANAVISION—COLOR)

Dean Martin and Lana Turner are an attractive combo in handsome settings but story and characters are derivative of (but wouldn't flatter) Damon Runyon. Fair comedy, with good exploitation pegs to help the sell.

Paramount release of Jack Rose production. Stars Dean Martin, Lana Turner; features Eddie Albert, Nita Talbot, Margo, Paul Ford, Walter Matthau, Lewis Charles, John McGiver. Directed by Daniel Mann. Script, Rose, from original novel by Alexander Rose (no relation); camera (Panavision-Technicolor), Joseph Ruttenberg; editor, Howard Smith; music, George Duning. Previewed at New York's Forum Theatre, Dec. 1, '62. Running time, **93 MINS.**

Steve Flood	Dean Martin
Melanie Flood	Lana Turner
Clint Morgan	Eddie Albert
Saturday Knight	Nita Talbot
Tony Gagoots	Walter Matthau
Roza	Margo
Judge Boatwright	Paul Ford
Clutch	Lewis Charles
Judge Fogel	John McGiver

Dean Martin loses his money on the horses, wife Lana Turner becomes his anonymous bookmaker. Other characters in a betting room show up in "Who's Got the Action?" It's a handsomely laid out production but producer-scripter Jack Rose, in taking his cues from Damon Runyon, via an original novel by Alexander Rose, didn't chalk up enough.

There's enough here to make a sale, but within limits. Martin and Miss Turner, latter looking lovely, make for a likely and agreeable couple and obviously an interesting boxoffice lure.

The story basics, along with the inhabitants of this Runyon-like world, are picturesque, as are the backgrounds of night clubs, the Hollywood Park Race Track, high-living apartments and even a courtroom. Edith Head's wardrobe for Lana Turner and others in the cast doubtless will be provocative for the femme onlooker.

Subsidiary spots are taken by Eddie Albert, who's Martin's law partner with a continuing crush on Miss Turner; Nita Talbot, who looks very much at home as a nightclub singer and intimate of the gambling boss; Walter Matthau, astutely humorous as the kingpin bookie; Margo (in real life Albert's wife), as maid to Martin and Miss Turner; Lewis Charles, as a kind-hearted bookie, and the two judges, Paul Ford and John McGiver.

Martin plays with characteristic casualness and comes just about right in this kind of situation farce. Miss Turner is appropriate all the way, particularly for dress-up-the-production purposes. All the others are in the swing of things, with aforementioned jurists Ford and McGiver standout and always refreshing.

A small part is played by Alexander Rose, author of the original novel titled "Four Horseplayers Are Missing," and he makes a cameo zany contribution.

Produces Rose has gotten across some visually interesting sets and backgrounds but scripter Rose and director Daniel Mann missed out **on story-telling clarity in a few instances. The plot seems to be out of focus once in a while and this detracts from the boff returns that might have been.**

Photography in Panavision and Technicolor is all the while in focus, George Duning's music makes for apt background; the title song done by Miss Talbot registers nicely, editing and technical credits in general smart.

Gene.

40 Pounds Of Trouble
(PANAVISION-COLOR)

Gambling casino manager meets nitery thrush and orphan girl. Entertaining concoction with family appeal. Spells good b.o.

Hollywood, Nov. 23.

Universal release of Stan Margulies production. Stars Tony Curtis, Suzanne Pleshette, Phil Silvers; introduces Claire Wilcox. Directed by Norman Jewison. Screenplay, Marion Hargrove; camera (Eastman), Joe MacDonald; editor, Marjorie Fowler; music, More Lindsey; assistant director, Tom Shaw. Reviewed at Westwood Village Theatre, Nov. 23, '62. Running time, **106 MINS.**

Steve McCluskey	Tony Curtis
Bernie	Phil Silvers
Chris	Suzanne Pleshette
Penny	Claire Wilcox
Floyd	Larry Storch
Julius	Howard Morris
Herman	Edward Andrews
Cranston	Stubby Kaye
Swing	Warren Stevens
Liz	Mary Murphy
Blanchard	Kevin McCarthy
Bambi	Karen Steele
Bassett	Tom Reese
Daytime	Steve Gravers
Cavanaugh	Paul Comi
Judge	Ford Rainey
Piper	Gregg Palmer
Dolores	Sharon Farrell
Singer	David Allen

Universal has a good boxoffice prospect in "40 Pounds Of Trouble," a slickly produced romantic comedy with a wholesome character that places it in the ideal family fare category. Witty writing by scenarist Marion Hargrove, enhanced by Norman Jewison's deft, catalytic direction and a number of vivacious performances make the Stan Margulies production and Curtis Enterprises presentation an attractive and engaging romp. Pickier patrons may have some minor reservations, but the bulk of the modern filmgoing public should find it a thoroughly palatable 106 minutes of light-hearted, effervescent entertainment.

Hargrove's "original" screenplay actually owes a little something to the Little Miss Marker-Sorrowful Jones school of screen comedy, but it's a precocious and likeable offspring. The troublesome 40-pounder of the title is moppet Claire Wilcox, who makes her screen debut as an orphaned youngster who gradually melt the heart of the businesslike, efficient manager of a Lake Tahoe, Nevada gambling resort (Tony Curtis). In the course of her conquest, she also aids the cause of husband-hunting nitery canary Suzanne Pleshette, whose romance with Curtis is complicated by the latter's relationship with his ex-wife, to whom he refuses to pay alimony, a stubborn stance that places him in jeopardy every time he leaves his Nevada legal sanctuary and crosses the border to California. The entire circumstance is resolved when Curtis is finally apprehended after a frenetic Keystone Koppish chase sequence through Disneyland that is the film's principal comedy caper.

Curtis dispatches his role with comic savvy. Miss Pleshette, whose manner is reminiscent of Joan Bennett's, handle her romantic assignment with finesse. Little Miss Wilcox is an appealing youngster, although director Jewison (in his first screen assignment after tv credits) might have obtained even better results from her by striving for more spontaneous, less practiced, childish reactions. The more takes, the more inclined children are to be self consciously and unnaturally cute. Phil Silvers has some memorable moments as the owner of the gambling establishment, notably one sequence in which he grandly strides into his domain, gruffly urging his customers to "play, play." Support is solid, with noteworthy contributions from Larry Storch, Howard Morris, Edward Andrews, Stubby Kaye, Warren Stevens, Mary Murphy, Kevin McCarthy, Karen Steele and Tom Reese.

Disneyland, which hardly needs it, gets an especially hefty plug and shows to tremendous advantage. Parts of the film were also shot in the picturesque Tahoe region with interiors at Harrah's Club. Joe MacDonald's cinematograpy is expert, as is Marjorie Fowler's editing, highlighted by a flowingly punctuated montage of **casino impressions and some accelerated hi-jinx at Disneyland. Other top-notch credits are those of composer Mort Lindsey, art directors Alex Golitzen and Robert Clatworthy, set decorator Ruby**

Levitt and soundmen Waldon O. Watson and Frank McWhorter. *Tube.*

Lawrence of Arabia
(BRITISH—COLOR)

Sweeping production. Stellar casting. Intriguing adventure subject. Must prove a hefty moneyspinner.

London, Dec. 10.
Columbia release and presentation of Sam Spiegel-David Lean (Horizon (G.B.) Pictures) production. Features Peter O'Toole, Alec Guinness, Anthony Quinn, Jack Hawkins, Jose Ferrer, Anthony Quayle, Claude Rains, Arthur Kennedy. Produced by Sam Spiegel. Directed by David Lean. Screenplay by Robert Bolt; camera (Technicolor), F. A. Young; editor, Anne V. Coates; music, Maurice Jarre. At Odeon, Leicester Square, London, Dec 9, '62. Running time, 222 MINS.

Lawrence	Peter O'Toole
Prince Feisal	Alec Guinness
Auda Abu Tayi	Anthony Quinn
General Allenby	Jack Hawkins
Sherif Ali	Omar Sharif
Turkish Bey	Jose Ferrer
Colonel Brighton	Anthony Quayle
Mr. Dryden	Claude Rains
Jackson Bentley	Arthur Kennedy
General Murray	Donald Wolfit
Gasim	I. S. Johar
Majd	Gamil Ratib
Farraj	Michel Ray
Daud	John Dimech
Tafas	Zia Moyheddin
Medical Officer	Howard Marion Crawford
Club Secretary	Jack Gwillim
R.A.M.C. Colonel	Hugh Miller

Some $15,000,000, around three years in time, much hardship, and incredible logistics have been poured into this kingsize adventure yarn. It is the first film from Sam Spiegel-David Lean since they launched the Oscar-winning "Bridge On the River Kwai" five years ago. Shapes as an equally vivid, smash b.o. success. Made in Technicolor and Super Panavision 70 it is a sweepingly produced, directed and lensed job. Authentic desert locations, a stellar cast and an intriguing subject combine to put this into the blockbuster league.

It had best be regarded as an adventure story rather than a biopic, because Robert Bolt's well written screenplay does not tell the audience anything much new about Lawrence of Arabia, nor does it offer any opinion or theory about the character of this man or the motivation for his actions. So he remains a legendary figure ("I deem him one of the greatest beings alive in our time. I do not see his like elsewhere," said Sir Winston Churchill) and a shadowy one. Was he a mystic or charlatan, a brave one, an exhibitionist, fanatic, opportunist or simply a half-nut case? Many people have a theory. Nobody has been able to do more than guess. And one of the film's faults is that cinemagoers who don't know about the Lawrence legend may be confused. The pic starts, for instance, with his fatal motor cycle crash in England. This could seem a puzzling, irrelevant scene for those who do not know how this strange soldier met his end. Another cavil is that clearly so much footage has had to be tossed away that certain scenes are not developed as well as they might have been, particularly the ending. But to turn to the many credits.

The David Lean touch gilds everything. It has clearly helped with Bolt's screenplay, which deftly pinpoints part of Lawrence's amazing lifestory, and is marked by telling dialog. It shows in the cutting, where Lean has obviously worked closely with Anne V. Coates. And he has helped to bring out some superb photography by F. A. Young. The film has every evidence of dedication by Lean, Spiegel and their entire technical crew.

Storyline concerns Lawrence as a young intelligence officer in Cairo in 1916. British Intelligence is watching the Arab revolt against the Turks with interest as a possible buffer between Turkey and her German allies. Lawrence (Peter O'Toole) is grudgingly seconded to observe the revolt at the request of the civilian head of the Arab bureau. Lawrence sets out to find Prince Feisal, top man of the revolt. From then on his incredible adventures begin. He persuades Feisal to let him lead his troops as guerrilla warriors. He tackles inter-tribal warfare but still they arduosly take the Turkish port of Aquaba. Lawrence is given the task of helping the Arabs to achieve independence and he becomes a kind of desert Scarlet Pimpernel. He reaches Deraa before the British Army is in Jerusalem, he is captured by the Turks, tortured and emerges a shaken, broken and disillusioned man. Yet still he takes on the job of leading a force to Damascus. But, though he takes Damascus and sets up a United Arab Council, the natives are already at each other's throats. He finishes a beaten man, unwanted by Arabs or the British Army. All his idealistic dreams have crumbled in the pitiless desert sands.

Subtle clashes between individuals mark the events but, from the filmgoer's viewpoint it will probably be the scenic and dramatic highlights that will impress most. A ferocious attack by Lawrence and his Arabs on a scattered bunch of retreating Turks, during which Lawrence suddenly becomes fanatically smitten with the desire to shed blood; a sweeping sandstorm; a moment when Lawrence has to become executioner and shoot a native whose life he has saved; the surging, frightening camel attack on Akabra; the slow, lonely drag through the snowy desert in winter. These are interwoven with wily scenes of politics in high places.

Lean and cameraman Young have brought out the loneliness and pitiless torment of the desert with an artistic use of color and with almost every frame superbly mounted. Michael Warre's musical score is often overlooked but is always contributory to the mood of the film, and artwork, second unit lensing, costumes and locales seem always completely right.

Peter O'Toole, after three or four smallish, but effective, appearances in films, makes a striking job of the complicated and heavy role of Lawrence. This young Irishman, as and when the screenplay demands, skillfully handles Lawrence's many moods. His veiled insolence and contempt of high authority, his keen intelligence and insight his gradual simpatico with the Arabs and their way of life, his independence, courage flashy vanity, withdrawn moments, pain, loneliness, fanaticism, idealism and occasional foolishness. O'Toole has a presence which will attract women tab buyers and convincingly builds up a picture of the Mystery Man. Spiegel's gamble with this newish British screen actor has rousingly come off.

The title of the film is its star, but O'Toole has been surrounded by thesps of top calibre. Jack Hawkins plays General Allenby with confidence and understanding and Arthur Kennedy provides a sharp portrayal of a cynical, tough American newspaperman. The two top support performances come from Alec Guinness as Prince Feisal and Anthony Quayle as a stereotyped, honest, bewildered staff officer. Guinness has a particularly well written role and plays it with shrewd, witty intuition. Jose Ferrer as a sadistic, homosexual Turkish Bey, Omar Sharif as an Arab chief and Claude Rains, playing the civilian boss of the Arab bureau, a curiously inexplicable role, also lend valuable assist. Only Anthony Quinn, as a larger-than-life, proud, intolerant Arab chief seems to obtrude overmuch and tends to turn the performance into something out of the Arabian Nights. Michel Ray, Donald Wolfit, I. S. Jofar and Howard Marion Crawford also chip in with strong support.

But, all in all, this is predominantly a Sam Spiegel and David Lean achievement. It was a big bold project and has turned out a big bold film. The occasional sluggishness in action and looseness in the screenplay are blemishes that can be forgiven in the sort of eye-taking motion picture that is designed to bring people back to the cinema and certainly deserves to. *Rich.*

Freud

Artful and provocative attempt to translate five years of Freud's life into screen drama. But bulk of filmgoers may find it too academic.

Hollywood, Dec. 11.
Universal release of Wolfgang Reinhardt production. Stars Montgomery Clift, Susannah York, Larry Parks, Susan Kohrer; features Eric Portman. Directed by John Huston. Screenplay, Charles Kaufman, Reinhardt, from Kaufman's story; camera, Douglas Slocombe; editor, Ralph Kemplen; music, Jerry Goldsmith; assistant directors, Ray Gosnell Jr., Laci von Ronay. Reviewed at Directors Guild of America, Dec. 11, '62. Running time, 140 MINS.

Sigmund Freud	Montgomery Clift
Cecily Koertner	Susannah York
Dr. Joseph Breuer	Larry Parks
Martha Freud	Susan Kohner
Frau Ida Koertner	Eileen Herlie
Professor Charcot	Fernand Ledoux
Carl von Schlosser	David McCallum
Frau Freud	Rosalie Crutchley
Jacob Freud	David Kossoff
Jacob Koertner	Joseph Furst
Babinsky	Alexander Mango
Brouhardier	Leonard Sachs
Dr. Theodore Meynert	Eric Portman

A period of five significant early years in the career of the founding father of psychoanalysis is dramatized in "Freud." The film is obviously a labor of love; the intense concern of those creatively involved is reflected in the cinematic artistry with which it has been amply endowed. Yet, alas, not even the keen and fruitful imagination of a John Huston, its director and prime creative force, can quite isolate the stirring personal drama of the man and his story from the dry, impersonal, somewhat stuffy and pretentious characteristic of a text, the academic shell from which the dramatic seed never quite escapes. As a result, the Wolfgang Reinhardt production and Universal release, for all of its integrity and artistic merit, is a film limited in appeal and acceptance. It appears des-

tined to be appreciated and perhaps even cherished by the few, but dismissed and perhaps even ignored by the many.

"Freud," nevertheless, is a worthwhile, enriching picture, one from which all who attend ought to benefit. It is informative. It is thought-provoking. From a commercial standpoint, its chief ally is likely to be the name it bears as its title. But many may respond to that name for its associated sexual connotations, and some expecting to experience vicarious sensual thrills. This is not the audience for which "Freud" is designed and at which it is aimed. There is, therefore, likely to be a disappointment factor with which it will have to contend, so attendance for the wrong reasons should not be encouraged in advertising. It is important to appeal to the right audience for the right reasons.

Intricate scenario by Charles Kaufman and producer Reinhardt, from the former's story, translates into dramatic, not biographical, terms the events of five key years (1885-1890) in Freud's life, the years during which he formulated his principal theory—that sexual instinct is the basic one in the human personality—and led him to discover and describe the presence of sexual behavior even in infancy. The drama revolves around Freud's (Montgomery Clift) treatment of a young patient (Susannah York) who has broken down mentally and physically upon the death of her father. In treating her, and relating her neuroses to his own, he is able not only to cure her, but to formulate the Oedipus Complex theory—the child's fixation on the parent of the opposite sex. This is the dramatic nucleus of the film. Around it materialize other significant facets of Freud's budding career—his battle to attain acceptance of his radical concepts, his abandonment of hypnosis as a method for the cure of hysteria and replacement of it with the "free association" technique.

The appropriately bewhiskered Clift delivers an intense, compassionate and convincing personification of "Freud." Miss York, the fast-rising young English actress, is vivid and true as his agitated patient, although the character is not always in sharp focus. Larry Parke, in his return to the screen, etches a warm and appealing portrait of Freud's friend, colleague and associate. Susan Kohner is fine as Freud's understanding wife. Among the supporting players, Eric Portman stands out with a crisp, biting enactment of Freud's orthodox superior who reveals the contradictory nature of his inner personality only when he is dying. Others who make strong impressions are Fernand Ledoux, Eileen Herlie, David McCallum, Rosalie Crutchley, David Kossoff and Joseph Furst.

Director Huston has pumped the maximum of visual vigor into a screen story basically static and clinical in nature. His mounting and execution of a number of dream sequences are especially electrifying and chilling. In these interludes, he has been masterfully aided by Douglas Slocombe's stark camera images, in contrast to the photographic realism of "normal" passages and the fuzzy, misty characteristic of "memory" sequences.

In sum, highly effective dramatic employment of the lens.

Stephen B. Grimes' sets are authentic in period and locale. Sound by Basil Fenton-Smith and Renato Caduelri is extremely sensitive, capturing every significant rustle of textile, draw or release of breath. A sombre, introspective and often melancholy musical score by Jerry Goldsmith is an asset, as are Henk Bading's eerie electronic notes. It is a long film —perhaps too long—but Ralph Kamplen's editing keeps it reasonably tidy and dramatically orderly. *Tube.*

Dilemma
(DANISH-SOUTH AFRICAN)
Paris, Dec. 11.

Produced, released, written, directed and lensed by Henning Carlsen. At La Cinematheque Francaise, Paris. Running time, 85 MINS.

Light credits for this pic stem from the fact that it was made clandestinely in South Africa, and producer-director Henning Carlsen wants to try to avoid any repercussions that could accrue there for people who helped him. It was done very much the way Yank indie Lionel Rogosin made his "Come Back Africa," and also looks at the problem of apartheid.

Carlsen goes in more for looking at it via whites, essentially, rather than the deeper penetration into the Negro mind and outlook that Rogosin attempted. Considering that it was made under the guise of a documentary on music, it is technically sound if some story points necessarily have to be telescoped at times.

It concerns a non-committed young Englishman who comes to South Africa to run a publishing company. Here he meets a spoiled young upper class girl and another dedicated young lady trying to help the Negroes in this strictly segregated country. He winds up having love affairs with both girls and also befriends a sensitive young Negro.

He finds the people on both sides a decent sort. But he is finally forced into taking sides when his Negro friend is ironically killed by some hoodlum thieves and the more liberal girl is arrested. Film ends on this note.

Director Carlsen shows a good eye for quick montage looks at both worlds and also manages to keep his characters believable if they are mainly shown on a fairly surface level. This is a telling look at this troubled country.

This looms mainly for specialized or arty spots abroad, with tele and specialized school showings indicated. Blindness on the part of the whites to the injustices, and the Negro's growing need for more rights are graphically evident.

Carlsen can make a subtle point visually, especially when it is just a neatly observed bit like a white girl's slight hesitation before accepting a cigarette lit for her by a native friend. Or the hate and hysteria evidenced by the young Englishman's secretary when he invites his native friend into the office.

The undercover making of this subject sometimes limits a more direct blending of the story with

the life and place around it. Hence, some of the liaisons and complications are sketchy.

Picture is technically excellent in spite of how made. With South Africa very much in the news these days, it also has a timely appeal. It is in English. Actors are adequate and some, like the native friend, have a spontaniety that helps keep the film above average. Side look at a Negro musical in rehearsal, and a percussive musical score are also assets.

This one has value and exploitation possibilities. *Mosk.*

On The Beat
(BRITISH)

Energetic double role is played by Norman Wisdom in a typical caper; plenty of yocks for easygoing audiences.

London, Dec. 11.

Rank release of a Rank (Hugh Stewart) production. Stars Norman Wisdom; features Jennifer Jayne, David Lodge, Raymond Huntley, Terence Alexander, Eleanor Summerfield, Esma Cannon, Eric Barker, Dilys Laye. Directed by Robert Asher. Screenplay by Jack Davies, Norman Wisdom, Eddie Leslie; camera, Geoffrey Faithfull; editor, Bill Lewthwaite; music, Philip Green. Previewed at RFD House, London. Running time, 105 MINS.
Norman Pitkin } ....Norman Wisdom
Giulio Napolitani }
Rosanna .... Jennifer Jayne
Sir Ronald Ackroyd....Raymond Huntley
Inspector Hobson .... David Lodge
Mrs. Stammers .... Esma Cannon
Doctor .... Eric Barker
Sgt. Wilkins .... Eleanor Summerfield
Oberon .... Ronnie Stevens
Chief Supt. Belcher..Terence Alexander
Vince .... Maurice Kaufmann
American Lady .... Dilys Laye
Manzini .... George Pastell
Police Sergeant .... Jack Watson
Bollington .... Campbell Singer
Man in Train .... Lionel Murton
Italian Lawyer .... Robert Rietty
Crying Lady .... Marjie Lawrence
Guillo's Mother ..... Peggy Ann Clifford
Chauffeur .... John Blythe
Newspaper Seller .... Mario Fabrizi
Mr. Bassett .... Monty Landis
Trigger O'Flynn .... Alfred Burke
Cafe Proprietor ......Cyril Chamberlain
Lady Hinchingford..........Jean Aubrey

All that Norman Wisdom requires is a vehicle that will provide him with several slapstick situations, a touch of stammering romance, a song and dance, a few chances to show pathos and some solid character actors as stooges, and he has himself a successful film. "On the Beat" provided virtually all these, and it is probably the best thing Wisdom has done.

Hugh Stewart, who has produced many Wisdom films, sticks sensibly to the formula. Jack Davies, a vet Wisdom scriptwriter (aided in this instance by Wisdom himself and gagwriter Eddie Leslie), has dreamed up a thin storyline which is easily boosted by irrelevant situations that create yocks. Robert Asher has directed breezily and, in a couple of sequences, brilliantly. The supporting cast of character actors go through their chores with dedication. Result is a commercial probability.

Wisdom, the little man always against odds, dreams of being a policeman like his dead father. He is only a parking attendant at Scotland Yard, being too short to be a cop.

All his efforts to get on the Force are foiled until his great moment. A master criminal is at work. A ruthless gangster mas-

querading as a mincing fashionable hairdresser is suspected. Wisdom looks remarkably like this man (played by Wisdom, of course) and he is planted in the salon to pick up vital evidence. Wrapping up the whole thing, Wisdom triumphs, gets his man, his girl and his copper's badge.

It would be useless to involve readers with the twists and turns of this farce, but they all add up to laughs. Wisdom beserk in the West End ladies' hairdresser has himself a ball. But perhaps the best sequence is when Wisdom dons his old man's policeman's uniform and ventures into the street.

He becomes involved in refereeing a kids' street football match, blows his whistle and has what looks like half the London police on a wild chase which has superb Keystone Cop intonations. Asher directs this scene with witty skill. Philip Green, whose lively score is a feature of the film, has provided a few moments in which this daft scamper takes on all the rhythm of a ballet sequence.

Wisdom plays the little would-be cop and the tough little Italian gangster with verve. Of the big cast around him, standout moments are provided by Eric Barker, as an eccentric police doctor and music lover, giving Wisdom a medical examination: Jennifer Jayne, as Wisdom's Italian doll, is a delectable dish. Raymond Huntley provides one of his familiar irascible performances as the police chief. Honorable mention goes to David Lodge, Terence Alexander, Eleanor Summerfield, Ronnie Stevens, John Blythe, Dilys Laye, Esma Cannon, Monty Landis and Campbell Singer for lesser roles.

Technically, the film is okay in all departments. Wisdom as a screen comedian is an acquired taste. But the person who does not get a lot of chuckles out of "Beat" must be rather intolerant. *Rich.*

The Seducers

Weak meller for the sexploitation market.

Joseph Brenner release of Wilson Ashley production. Features Nuella Dierking, Mark Saegers. Directed by Graeme Ferguson. Screenplay, Ashley; camera, Baird Bryant; editor, Bernard Leslie; music, Mort Lindsay. Previewed in N.Y., Dec. 6, '62. Running time, 90 MINS.
Jean Wells .... Nuella Dierking
Joe .... Mark Saegers
Robert Wells .... Robert Milli
Wilma .... Sheila Britt
Hank .... John Coe

A modest indie entry, "The Seducers" is a weak and involved melodrama that's been sexed up with some suggestive scenes. As a meller, the film is too illogical to generate much boxoffice spark. But the lurid sequences, along with the title, likely will enhance the picture's prospects in the sexploitation market.

Picture was shot on location in Westchester County, N.Y., on a reported budget of $65,000 provided by some 50 investors. It's the initial feature effort of Boar's Head Film Productions Inc. in association with Quest Productions. The small cast has no marquee names.

Producer-writer Wilson Ashley's

screenplay unreels a sordid yarn woven around a suburban couple. The wife, Nuella Dierking, is reasonably attractive and has an independent income. But husband Robert Milli prefers the romantic values of shapely Sheila Britt, the daughter of local junkman, John Coe.

Also rambling through the footage are a blackmailer, three killings and an anti-climactic chase up the face of Westchester's Kensico Reservoir dam. In pauses between the mayhem, Milli pitches woo to Miss Britt while the blackmailer, a shiftless itinerant portrayed by Mark Saegers, lustily eyes Miss Dierking. The two femmes also display some of their physical assets in scenes that appear to have been tossed in as an afterthought.

The cast, which labors heroically, can charge this off to experience. Ashley obviously has some talent but he needs a better frame for it than "The Seducers." Graeme Ferguson's direction is erratic—probably because it's uncertain whether to emphasize melodrama or sex on the rocks.

Baird Bryant's camerawork is fairly good under the circumstances while Bernard Leslie's editing is inclined to be choppy. The Mort Lindsay score fits the film's uneven mood. *Gilb.*

A Prize of Arms
(BRITISH)

London, Dec. 11.
BLC release of Bryanston (George Maynard) production. Stars Stanley Baker, Helmut Schmid, Tom Bell; features Douglas Blackwell, Michael Ripper, Anthony Bate, Patrick Magee, Barry Keegan, Roddy McMillan, John Westbrook. Directed by Cliff Owen. Screenplay, Paul Ryder, from original story by Nicholas Roeg, Kevin Kavanagh; music, Robert Sharples; editor, John Jympson; camera, Gilbert Taylor, Gerald Gibbs. At Plaza, London. Running time, 105 MINS.
Turpin .... Stanley Baker
Swavek .... Helmut Schmid
Fenner .... Tom Bell
Cpl. Glenn .... Tom Adams
Sgt. Reeves .... Anthony Bate
Pte. Maynard .... Rodney Bewes
Lt. Waddington .... Richard Bidlake
Day .... Douglas Blackwell
Lt. Ellison .... Mark Burns
Brodie .... Frank Coda
Leigh .... Michael Collins
Capt. James .... David Comville
Lt. Davies .... David Courtenay
RASC Sergeant Major ..... Clifford Cox
Supt. Cooper .... Barry Keegan
Colonel Bates .... Stephen Lewis
Cpl. Henderson .... Fulton Mackay
R.S.M. Hicks .... Patrick Magee
M.O. .... Jack May
Sgt. McVie .... Roddy McMillan
Col. Fowler .... John Phillips
Cpl, Freeman .... Michael Ripper
Capt. Stafford .... John Westbrook

The holdup that doesn't come off is one of the cinema's prime if oldest plots. Since crime mustn't pay on the screen, it is always a surefire thing that the crooks will get their comeuppance. Hence, the entertainment value of these pix depends on characterization, the building up of tension and the element of surprise as to how the plan will go wrong. Along these lines, "A Prize Of Arms" comes off. Tension mounts slowly but surely. The payoff, while not entirely unexpected, has a sufficiently taut impact to leave patrons satisfied. Most average audiences will go for this crisply directed and edited thriller.

Stanley Baker's carefully laid scheme for knocking off a $700,-000 army payroll seems unnecessarily complicated. This seems to shriek out for mishaps. But Paul Ryder's screenplay is smoothly efficient even though audiences are too often left in the dark about detail. Baker plays an ex-army captain who has been cashiered for Black Market activities in Hamburg. While in the army he has dreamed up a perfect plan for revenge (and to get rich). He has enlisted the help of Helmut Schmid, an explosives expert, and Tom Bell, a daring but edgy young man.

Baker learns that an army is preparing to go abroad at the time of the Suez crisis. He realizes that when troops are on the move abroad they have to take money with them. The trio plan to hijack the dough while the forces are moving towards the docks.

His carefully rehearsed plan involves the three moving into camp in army uniform and with phoney paybooks and to merge unspotted into the khaki background while they rob the till. With 12 hours to kill there are many chances of their timing going wrong and, of course, it does. One gets ill following an unavoidable inoculation. The timetable goes haywire when another gets caught up in cookhouse duty.

But by the use of a flamethrower which sets the camp in panic they get out with their loot stowed away in a spare tire. Then their plans begin to crumble. The military police get on their track. Bell's nerve falters and Baker defies the army with his flamethrower. Result is that all that is left are the charred remains of the banknotes.

Baker, Schmid and Bell play the three leads confidently, with Baker particularly on the ball in the type of harsh tough part that he plays so often and so well. But the thesping of the three stars is given greater impact by the strength of a long list of character and feature actors as officers, other ranks, detectives, etc. The cast, all male except for a brief appearance by Lynn Furlong as a canteen girl, eagerly grabs the opportunities given them by some thoroughly credible army roles. It's invidious to pick any of them out as they simply leave the impression of a complete army unit, in a typical barracks.

Camera and artwork are okay and Cliff Owen's direction punchy and sure. Holes could be picked in the screenplay and credulity is strained by the intricacies of the plot. But, overall, "Prize" adds up to a deft, commercial thriller. *Rich.*

Der 42 Himmel
(The 42d Heaven)
(SWISS; SONGS)

Zurich, Dec. 11.
Praesens—Film A. G. Zurich release of Gloriafilm A. G. (Max Dora)—Praesens production. directed by Kurt Frueh. Screenplay, Frueh, Hans Hausmann; music, Werner Kruse, Hans Moeckel; camera, Emil Berna; sound, Alfred Braun; editor, Rene Martinet. Stars Walter Roderer; features Ruedi Walter, Heinrich Gretler, Elvira Schalcher, Verena Hallau, Margrit Rainer, Peter W. Staub, Ernst Stankovski, Ruth Gutzwiller, Virginia Zango, Ulrich Beck, Joerg Schneider, Doris Ebner, Paul Buehlmann, Willy Fueter, Trudy Roth. Opened Nov. 30, '62. at the Urban Theatre, Zurich. Running time, 103 MINS.

(In Swiss Dialect)
This latest Swiss comedy-with-music is primarily a starring vehicle for local comedian Walter Roderer, a prototype of the shy, softspoken "little man" at odds with his more robust surroundings. Here, he plays a subordinate information desk clerk at City Hall whose lifelong dream is fulfilled when he is promoted to marriage official. He falls in love with a young bride whose groom come up with a sudden "No" at the civil ceremony for reasons of jealousy, but ends up with her girl-friend instead who has had a yen for him from the start.

Feature has been shot simultaneously in two versions, one with Swiss actors in Swiss dialect (reviewed here) for local consumption, the other with a German cast for Germany and Austria. The Swiss version, of course, is strictly a local item, but looks to rack up promising grosses here. It's a skillful blend of locally slanted humor, pleasant songs and generally good performances from which Roderer stands out with an enjoyable portrayal.

Direction by Kurt Frueh holds a nice pace, and the songs, interspersed generously throughout the action, are all listenable, though presumably not of hit potential. *Mezo.*

First Spaceship On Venus
(TOTALVISION—COLOR)

Colorful, but shopworn sci-fi meller, suitable for saturation bookings.

Hollywood, Dec. 12.
Crown-International release of Centrala production. Directed by Kurt Maetzig. Screenplay, J. Fathke, W. Kohlhaase, G. Reisch, G. Rucker, A. Stenbock-Fermor, Maetzig, from novel, "Planet of Death," by Stan Lem; camera (Technicolor), Joachim Hasler; music, Gordon Zahler; special photographic effects, Martin Sonnabend. Reviewed at Pix Theatre, Dec. 12, '62. Running time, 80 MINS.
Sumiko Ogimura .... Yoko Tani
Harringway .... Oldrich Lukes
Orloff .... Ignacy Machowski
Talua .... Julius Ongewe
Durand .... Michail Postnikow
Sikarna .... Kurt Rockelmann
Brinkman .... Gunther Simon
Tchen Yu .... Tang-Hua-Ta
Joan Moran .... Lucina Winnicka

All of the familiar crises of the cinematic journey into space are crammed into "First Spaceship On Venus." Appreciation is restricted to buffs of the sci-fi melodrama who are content to wade through an 80-minute barrage of post-dubbed, pseudo-scientific gobbledegook to enjoy the splashy special photographic effects, bolstered by Totalvision and Technicolor. The Crown-International release should generate satisfactory box-office response via the hasty saturation method.

Scenario is concerned with the efforts of a team of space researchers to find out what's up on Venus. It develops that the planet is in an awful mess—even worse than earth—its hostile populace having destroyed itself in the process of planning an atomic invasion of earth. The exploring party undergoes the fashionable events of space travel, including weightlessness and meteorite swarms prior to landing on Venus and contending with such phenomena as vitrified forests, goo eruptions and metallic insects. For comedy relief, as if it was needed, the party hauls along a chess-playing robot but, as the old joke goes, the critter isn't so danged smart—it's only able to beat its human opponent four games out of five.

The artisans have had a field day mounting their version of Venus. It's quite a planet, but no place to spend a summer vacation. The actors are appropriately overwhelmed. Handiest line of dialog, repeated at periodic intervals: "why, it's incredible!" It is. *Tube.*

Private Pooley
(ANGLO-EAST GERMANY)

London, Dec. 11.
Contemporary Films release of a DEFA Studios Berlin (Werner Daw-Contemporary Films production. Stars Garfield Morgan, John Rees, Cecile Cehvreau, Ferdy Mayne, Alfred Muller; features Jennifer Wilson, Andrew Ray, Ronald Leigh-Hunt, Charles Houston. Directed by Kurt Jung-Alsen. Screenplay, Franz Fuchmann, based on Cyril Jilly's book, "Vengeance of Private Pooley"; camera, Rolf Sohre; music, Andre Asriel; commentary written and spoken by Lindsay Anderson. Previewed at Berkeley Theatre, London. Running time, 70 MINS.
Albert Pooley .... Garfield Morgan
Bill Carter .... John Rees
Madame Creton .... Cecile Chevreau
Intelligence Officer .... Ferdy Mayne
Hauptsturmerfuehrer...... Alfred Muller
Ginger .... Andrew Ray
Mrs. Pooley .... Jennifer Wilson

(English Dialog)
Though one or two important facts have been distorted, this film emerges as virtually a documentary of a war incident. It is unlikely to have wide appeal, but direction, screenplay and thesping have quality. It may be a useful booking for arty houses. Story concerns a private soldier who, in 1940, was captured with a battalion gallantly holding out against the Germans near Dunkirk. They were taken to a field and massacred by the order of a German officer. Two escaped but were eventually recaptured. Private Pooley (Garfield Morgan) swears that if he gets out of the war alive, he will track down the responsible officer and bring him to justice.

Pooley is eventually repatriated but cannot persuade the British authorities to take his story seriously. With the war over, he returns to the scene of the crime and got witnesses statements concerning the massacre. And by trudging through prisoner of war camps, eventually he discovers the guilty German officer. The story is told without frills or over-dramatization. The early scenes are particularly effective and quickly put over the stench of war.

Morgan, as Pooley, and John Rees, as Bill Carter, his mate, give sound, rewarding performances. Andrew Ray, Cecile Chevreau and Ferdy Mayne perform useful service in lesser roles. The part of the German officer responsible for the crime is played with icy insolence by Alfred Muller.

Direction and camerawork are sharp and there is some effective editing. The film was shot near Pottsdam with a British, French and German cast and German technicians. Dialog is mainly in English. Lindsay Anderson fills in some background with a sober commentary which he wrote himself. *Rich.*

Ti-Koyo And His Shark
(Tikoyo e il Suo Pescecane)
(ITALO—FRENCH—COLOR)

Rome, Dec. 11.
Titanus release of a Titanus-Metro Film produced as an Italo-French coproduction by Titanus-S.N.P.C.-S.G.C. With Marlene Among, Al Kauwe, Denis Pouira, Diane Samsoi, Cocoyo. Directed by Folco Quilici. Screenplay, Quilici, Ottavio Alessi, A. Frassinet; from story by Italo Calvino; dialog, Franco Prosperi; comert (Eastmancolor), Pier Ludovico Pavoni; music, Francesco De Masi; editor, Mario Serandrei. At the Fiamma, Rome. Running time, 100 MINS.
Diana .... Marlene Among
Ti-koyo .... Al Kauwe
Ti-koyo as child........... Denis Pouira
Diana as child .... Diane Samsoi
Roau .... Cocoyo

This modern fable about a boy and his pet shark, set against a romantic Polynesian setting, should find a wide audience in most areas, with appeal for both moppet and adult viewers. For the U.S. (Metro has Yank and other non-Italian release rights via its Titanus-Metro coproduction status, pic looks like a good filler entry if proper English version can be prepped. Some trimming also might give it better pace.

Story deals with an island youth who finds and raises a baby shark. They are separated, but many years later, when both boy and shark have grown up, they meet again and resume their onetime friendship. But around them, island life has changed, the primitive life is being submerged by organized fisheries, etc. Ti-koyo and his shark vote for the good old times, and take off for a more secluded island, taking along Ti-koyo's girl friend, Marlene Among, who has made the same choice.

Pic is at its best in scenes involving the boy and shark, almost always credible thanks also to some spectacular underwater lensing credited to Masino Manunza. It's when film makes a pitch for the primitive against civilized that it sometimes becomes stilted. Then it indulges in some obvious cliches, forcing certain situations to prove a point, as well as giving it a gloss which clashes with rustic isle settings. But generally, it's a very likable subject.

Players are aptly chosen and for the most part go through their paces in pro fashion, despite occasional stiffness. Denis Pouira is winning without being over-cute as Ti-koyo the child while Hawaiian thesp Al Kauwe is good as the grownup Ti-koyo. Cocoyo, as a rustic island relic, gives the pic color. Miss Among is a looker as the grownup girl friend of Ti-koyo, while Diane Samsoi is Diana as a child.

Technical credits, entirely earned on South Sea Island locales, are fine, with Pier Ludovico Pavoni contributing an outstanding color lensing job. *Hawk.*

Varan The Unbelievable

Uninspired monster meller for saturation supporting niches.

Hollywood, Dec. 12.
Crown-International release of Jerry Baerwitz production. Directed by Baerwitz. Screenplay, Sid Harris; camera, Jack Marquette; editor, Ralph Cushman; asst. director, Leonard Kunody. Reviewed at Pix Theatre, Dec. 12, '62. Running time, 70 MINS.
Commander James Bradley Myron Healy
Anna .... Tsuruko Kobayashi
Captain Kishi .... Clifford Kawada
Matsu .... Derick Simatsu

Another in a long line of looney leviathans to emerge from sleep in the deep and indulge in some 20th-century style devastation is "Varan the Unbelievable," Crown International's Christmas season bonus for monster aficionados. The Jerry Baerwitz (Dallas) production follows in the prodigious footsteps of such formidable beasts as "Godzilla," "Gorgo" and "Dinosaurus," but adds nothing new to the genre. It is a hackneyed, uninspired carbon copy, serviceable only as a supporting filler.

Sid Harris' screenplay awakens the impregnable water dragon as a result of scientific experiments to turn the salt agua of a lake into fresh water. Disturbed from his prehistoric-originated nap, the big beast is understandably annoyed and, sensing that he just doesn't quite fit into the 1962 scheme of things, vents his rage on the Japanese countryside. After interminable and repetitious scenes of the monster bobbing up and getting bombarded by a barrage of ineffectual explosives, they finally discourage the poor fellow by detonating some chemical explosives into his one weak spot—a soft underbelly. Like all of his predecessors, he retires to his aquatic resting place. To return again? Let's hope not.

Humans prominently involved in the mayhem are Myron Healy, Tsuruko Kobayashi, Clifford Kawada and Derick Shimatsu. Production contributions are not especially satisfactory. Photography is too dark, editing is jagged. Neither Harris' scenario nor Baerwitz's direction of it can sustain interest. *Tube.*

The Savage Guns
(ANGLO-SPANISH-COLOR)

Worthwhile but overly wordy western; sharp star performances

London, Dec. 11.
Metro release of a Capricorn (Michael Carreras) production (in association with Tecisa). Stars Richard Basehart, Don Taylor, Alex Nicol, Pasquita Rico. Directed by Michael Carreras. Screenplay, Edmund Morris; camera (Metrocolor), Alfredo Fraille; music, Anton Garcia Abril; editors, David Hawkins, Pedro Del Rey. Previewed at Metro Private Theatre, London. Running Time, 83 MINS.
Steve Fallon .... Richard Basehart
Mike Summers .... Don Taylor
Danny Pose .... Alex Nicol
Fanchea .... Pacquita Rico
Juana .... Maria Granada
Ortega .... Jose Nieto
Don Hernan .... Fernando Rey
Paco .... Felix Fernandez

Michael Carreras, building up a reputation for himself as producer and director with UK's Hammer Films, broke away to make this co-production at Madrid's C.E.A. studios. He has turned out a solid Western, with some good characterization and okay production values. But it doesn't add much to the Western film legend. However, despite being over-wordy, it holds interest and may be a safe booking for many houses.

Story is just another variation of the theme of the bad man who is quelled by a peaceloving citizen and an itinerant gunman who hates to see ordinary guys kicked around. Set in a Mexican valley near Arizona, it has Don Taylor as an ex-Confederate officer who, having seen enough bloodshed in war, merely wants to go it alone in peace. But there is terrorization by a local gang with Alex Nicol as a vicious sadistic gunman. Richard Basehart, a professional gun-slinger, is drawn unwittingly into the affair when he wanders along and sees what's happening.

The screenplay follows fairly predictable lines but the leading characters are well drawn. Nicol shows an unexpectedly vicious streak as the heavy, Basehart is dependable as the visiting gunman. Taylor copes well with a rather wooden character who only comes into his own spasmodically. A most interesting performance is given by Pacquita Rico, as Taylor's wife

Supporting cast is entirely made up of Spanish feature players who in looks and performance contribute much to the film's authenticity. Alfred Fraille has done a competent task in his Metrocolor lensing and the editing is unobtrusive. *Rich.*

Diamond Head
(PANAVISION—COLOR)

Prejudice under the Hawaiian palms. Slickly produced, but heavyhanded race melodrama with punch resting with marquee names and 50th State visual allure.

Hollywood, Dec. 13.
Columbia Pictures release of Jerry Bresler production. Stars Charlton Heston, Yvette Mimieux, George Chakaris, France Nuyen, James Darren; features Aline MacMahon, Elizabeth Allen. Directed by Guy Green. Screenplay, Marguerite Roberts, based on Peter Gilman's novel; camera (Eastman), Sam Leavitt; editor, William A. Lyon; music, Johnny Williams; assistant directors, Herb Mendelson, Sam Nelson. Reviewed at the studio, Dec. 13, '62. Running time, 107 MINS.
Richard Howland.......Charlton Heston
Sloan Howland .... Yvette Mimieux
Dr. Dean Kahana......George Chakaris
Mei Chen .... France Nuyen
Paul Kahana .... James Darren
Kapiolani Kahana.....Aline MacMahon
Laura Beckett .... Elizabeth Allen
Judge James Blanding....Vaughn Taylor
Bobbie Chen .... Marc Marno
Emekona .... Philip Ahn
Coyama .... Harold Fong
Robert Parsons .... Edward Mallory
Mario .... Lou Gonsalves
Felipe .... Frank Morris
Sammy .... Clarence Kim
Photographer .... Jack Matsumoto
Newspaperman .... Yankee Chang
Loe Kim Lee .... Kam Fong Chun
Pianist .... Leo Ezell
Heckler .... Al Lebuse
Nurse .... R. Ramos

A salably glamorous cast and glossy production physique are the sugarcoated merits upon the boxoffice density of "Diamond Head" hinges. For beneath this alluring veneer lurks a contrived and banal melodrama of bigotry and bloodlines in modern, heterogeneous Hawaii. The Jerry Bresler production for Columbia amounts to a kind of thawed-out "Ice Palace," or "Giant Goes Hawaiian."

Improbabilities and inconsistencies galore reside in Marguerite Roberts' heavyhanded screenplay, from Peter Gilman's novel, about a Hawaiian agricultural tycoon, or King Bwana of Pineappleville, hellbent on holding-that-bloodline. When the baron's (Charlton Heston) baby sister (Yvette Mimieux) defiantly announces her engagement to a full-blooded Hawaiian lad (James Darren), the battle lines are drawn. This threat to inbreeding and Heston's senatorial aspirations is abruptly erased when Heston accidentally stabs Darren to death. But further complications arise when Miss Mimieux takes up with Darren's half-brother (George Chakaris) and Heston's Chinese mistress (France Nuyen) becomes pregnant. When the latter conveniently expires in childbirth (the writers have managed, thus, to evade the most ticklish issues) and Miss Mimieux and Chakiris run off together with the heir apparent, it finally seems to dawn on Heston that he's one bad guy. At the fadeout, he's mellowed enough to go after his son.

It is only one of the oddities of "Diamond Head" that no one, from conception on, ever seems to consider the possibility that the unborn child might turn out female.

Heston etches a swaggering portrait of the bullying bigot. Miss Mimieux is spirited as the liberalminded sister. Chakiris, in his first screen effort since his Oscar-winning portrayal in "West Side Story," is glum and inexpressive as the half-breed medic who captures the fair sister's heart. He also seems to be the only doctor on the

Islands. Miss Nuyen is sweet as Heston's unlikely heartthrob. Darren, despite a rich tan, seems about as 100% Hawaiian as Paul Revere. Featured support is adequately dispatched by Aline MacMahon, Elizabeth Allen and Marc Marno.

Guy Green's direction, at any rate, is high-spirited, and production ingredients are slickly eye-appealing. Sam Leavitt's photography is Eastman colorful and dramatically calculating and alert. William A. Lyon's editing is taut and Malcolm Brown's production design visually luxurious. Johnny Williams' unobtrusive score is backed up by the Hugo Winterhalter's lurching, excitable theme. *Tube.*

The Iron Maiden
(BRITISH—COLOR)

Amiable, uneven lightweight comedy. Typical Anglo-American gags but a fairly novel background theme gives it a shot in arm.

London, Dec. 18.
Anglo-Amalgamated release of a Peter Rogers production. Stars Michael Craig, Anne Helm, Jeff Donnell, Alan Hale, Noel Purcell, Cecil Parker; features Roland Culver, Joan Sims, John Standing, Sam Kydd, Brian Oulton. Directed by Gerald Thomas. Screenplay, Vivian Cox, Leslie Bricusse from original story by Harold Brooks & Kay Bannerman; camera (Eastmancolor), Alan Hume; music, Eric Rogers; editor, Archie Ludski. Previewed at Corner Theatre. Running time, **98 MINS.**
Jack Hopkins .... Michael Craig
Kathy Fisher .... Anne Helm
Mrs. Fisher .... Jeff Donnelly
Paul Fisher .... Alan Hale
Admiral Sir Digby Trevelyan
.... Noel Purcell
Sir Giles Trent .... Cecil Parker
Lord Upshott .... Roland Culver
Mrs. Fred .... Joan Sims
Humphrey .... John Standing
Vicar ... . Brian Oulton
Fred ... . Sam Kydd
Mrs. Webb .... Judith Furse
Harry Markham .... Richard Thorp
Village Policeman....... Brian Rawlinson
Rally Official .... Tom Kill
Duke of Bedford ...... Duke of Bedford

Team of producer Peter Rogers and director Gerald Thomas has come up with an amusing comedy which would have benefited from a wittier script and; perhaps, a more carefree comedian in the lead. Michael Craig is one of Britain's most dependable and capable actors but it is a moot point whether lightweight comedy is his best medium. The theme of "The Iron Maiden" is fairly old-hat, coming from the "Genevieve" school, but its setting has a refreshingly novel touch, being concerned with the passion of a certain section of Britishers with vintage traction engines.

Traction engine rallies are an offbeat way of British life and this film combines that with some functionally tourist glimpses of Woburn Abbey, the Duke of Bedford's stately home, Henley regatta and the British countryside. Michael Craig is a top aircraft designer, working for Cecil Parker, but whose main hobby is traction engines. Parker is anxious to complete a deal for a new jet plain with a visiting American aircraft tycoon (Alan Hale) but a series of misadventures in which Craig clashes with Hale and his family endanger the deal.

Eventually all is well when Craig

and his "Iron Maiden" win the National Rally. Hale is intrigued with the rally and offers to become Craig's stoker when his regular man breaks a leg. Eventually it is Hale's daughter (Anne Helm) who takes over at the critical moment. Craig lands the first prize in the rally, the contract and the girl.

Vivian Cox and Leslie Bricusse have provided some fairly predictable characters. There's the "typical" henpecked American rich man and his Cadillac, his status seeking wife and his charming but brash daughter. On the Anglo side, there's the comic vicar, the rustic policeman, the bumbling aristocrats and so on. However, though there's not much subtlety or novelty in the character drawing, the performers all jump through the comedy hoops satisfactorily.

The three Americans are newish and welcome faces to British audiences and Hale, Jeff Donnelly and cute Anne Helm as the romantic interest fit snugly into this typical British comedy. Craig gives a likeable performance as the aircraft designer, though, as previously noted, a more lighthearted touch might have helped. Cecil Parker and Roland Culver are useful foils as the two British aircraft tycoon rivals. John Standing, as stuffy, correct young Englishman; Brian Oulton as the vicar; Sam Kydd, as Craig's stoker and Noel Purcell, as a belligerent retired admiral, who is Craig's deadly rival in the traction engine race, all add to the fun. The Duke of Bedford makes an appearance as himself and proves that if ever the Stately Home of Woburn Abbey becomes too much of a burden for him he might turn out to be a useful actor.

Gerald Thomas has directed briskly and with an apt blend of slapstick and quieter comedy, and has made good use of Alan Hume's Eastmancolor lensing. Carmen Dillon's artwork is okay and several scenes of the Dorchester Hotel give the film a lushness which is a pleasant change. "Iron Maiden" should prove profitable entertainment in popular houses. *Rich.*

Agostino
(ITALIAN)

Rome, Dec. 18.
Dino DeLaurentiis release of a Baltea (Luigi Rovere) production. Features Ingrid Thulin, John Saxon, Paolo Colombo. Directed by Mauro Bolognini. Screenplay, Goffredo Parise from story by Alberto Moravia; music, Carlo Rustichelli; camera, Aldo Tonti; editor, Nino Baragli. At Fiamma, Rome. Running time, **90 MINS.**
Agostino .... Paolo Colombo
His motheer .... Ingrid Thulin
Renzo .... John Saxon

A smoothly fashioned, sometimes moving and appealing, but ultimately superficial glimpse at a child's first exposure to love, sex and life, this is based on one of Alberto Moravia's best short stories. Basically an artie, where the Ingmar Bergman recruit Ingrid Thulin's name is a help, the pic has intrinsically exploitable angles and aspects, though tastefully handled at all times.

Agostino and his widowed but still appealing mother enjoy their summer stay at a Lido Venice Hotel until a male suitor enters their life and takes the mother away from the child. The latter, puzzled, jealous and disturbed, runs off with a gang of kids who very brutally

expose him to all the facts in life. He's intrigued but basically still immature and puzzled by it all, having "lost" his mother love and not yet gained what will replace it, whatever it may be.

Story has its moments, but Bolognini's handling of it is usually too cold and often too calculating.

Another negative point is reliance on spoken commentary to explain the moppet's feelings in crucial bridges, even though Paolo Colombo as the boy is a winning find. Ingrid Thulin is excellent as the mother, and one wishes the pic allowed for more of her. John Saxon has an ungrateful part as the suitor, but does a workmanlike job of it.

Aldo Tonti's lensing of Venice lagoon locales is an outstanding asset of an intriguing pic on a vastly difficult subject. This just misses coming to life and becoming an outstanding human experience instead of the intelligent, classy and formal achievement it is. *Hawk.*

Il Sorpasso
(ITALIAN)
(Songs)

Rome, Dec. 18.
Incei release of a Fairfilm Mario (Cecchi Gori)-Incei-Sancro Film production. Features Vittorio Gassmann, Catherine Spaak, Jean-Louis Trintignant, Claudio Gora, Luciana Angiolillo, Linda Sini, Corrado Olmi. Directed by Dino Risi. Screenplay, Risi, Ettore Scola, Ruggero Maccari; camera, Alfio Contini; music, Riz Ortolani; editor, Maurizio Lucidi. At Corso Cinema, Rome. Running time, **105 MINS.**
Bruno .... Vittorio Gassmann
Roberto .... Jean-Louis Trintignant
Daughter .... Catherine Spaak
Wife .... Luciana Angiolillo
Aunt Lidia .... Linda Sini
Alfredo .... Corrado Olmi
Bibi .... Claudio Gora

Well-made pic with entertainment factors for all audience levels, this shapes as a winner on the Italian market, thanks to names and word-of-mouth. Cut several notches above the norm, film should also cop plenty of foreign attention in appropriate slots.

Story deals with the casual summertime acquaintance of an uninhibited playboy type (Vittorio Gassmann) with a young student, Roberto, whose approach to life has to the contrary always been on the staid and serious side. The two take off on a rousing two-day race along the Riviera visiting friends, picking up girls and chasing thrills in general.

A visit to Corrado Olmi's relatives and Gassmann's (long-separated) wife and daughter only briefly slow them down until a predictable tragedy sobers up the playboy at the finale. While viewable on purely risible entertainment level, pic also provides some trenchant for thought in its character delineation (the old vs. the new) and its biting barbs thrown at present-day manners and mores.

Gassmann turns in an outstanding and well-modulated performance as the lovable lout who realizes too late the damage he's done. Jean-Louis Trintignant is neatly cast as his (very) opposite number, Roberto, and makes the most of his sympathetic role.

Remainder of cast is filled with topnotch cameos, especially Luciana Angiolillo's human ex-wife bit. Catherine Spaak makes a captivating daughter, and there is plenty of other eye-appeal for the male ticket buyer.

Riz Ortolani's score includes a large number of current pop tunes to good effect, while other credits measure up. Editing job is tight at 105 minutes. *Hawk.*

1963

The Trial
(FRENCH-ITALIAN-WEST GERMAN)
Paris, Jan. 1.

UFA-Comacico release of Paris Europa-Ficit-Hisa Films production. Stars Anthony Perkins, Jeanne Moreau, Romy Schneider, Elsa Martinelli; features, Suzann Flon, Madeleine Robinson, Arnoldo Foa, Orson Welles. Written and directed by Orson Welles from the book by Franz Kafka. Camera, E. Richard; editor, Yvonne Martin. At Paris. Running time, 115 MINS.

Joseph K.	Anthony Perkins
Burstner	Jeanne Moreau
Leni	Romy Schneider
Hilda	Elsa Martinelli
Pittle	Suzanne Flon
Grubach	Madeleine Robinson
Inspector	Arnoldo Foa
Clerk	Fernand Ledoux
Lawyer	Michel Lonsdale
Priest	Orson Welles
Bloch	Akim Tamiroff

(In English)

Pic profligate and putterer, genius, flash-in-the-pan, are some of the epithets that have been applied to the peripatetic Orson Welles. Now, after five lean years, he comes up with a new pic written and directed by himself from the "nightmare" novel by Franz Kafka. Welles shows plenty still on the ball and brings in one of the most offbeat pix in years.

Film may well delight film buffs and startle or irritate many others. But with ever more difficult fare (per "Last Year At Marienbad") proving box-office in arties, this could become an international specialized entry of value. Name of Anthony Perkins and others must help. Against these pluses is the nature of the story — allegory, parable or eyes-open nightmare.

A young white-collar worker wakes up one morning to find a sinister police inspector and two seedy detectives in his room. He is technically under arrest but he is not told why. He accepts the fact after various attempts at rationalizing. This is done with the right balance of strangeness within real surroundings with just a slight sharpening of film contrast and untoward angles.

Then the film gets progressively more expressionistic and surreal as he is caught up completely in his impending trial and neglects work, one woman next door who promised adventure, and gets deeper into the complex setup of the law. The geography of the film becomes inextricably bound up with dusty file rooms, waiting rooms full of supposedly guilty men not knowing why they are there and K's final attempt to revolt against this trial for an unnamed crime which ends in his execution.

There is a conflict of styles and Welles can not resist bravura scenes that seem put into exploit personalized film bent rather than comment on, underline, or build up progression. K hounded by giggling little girls who spy on him in a slatted room and then chase him through a weirdly lit maze is a case of this type.

And actor Welles expounding on guilt, and having Akim Tamiroff fawn on him as another accused man waiting for trial news for years, are also repetitive, if well done, scenes. Tamiroff etches a meaty profile and Welles is effective as a suety, sickly lawyer holding court in a bed that

seems to have come from "Citizen Kane's" Xanadu.

Perkins as K is on screen practically all the time. His boyishness is oft pedaled to turn him into a timid but priggish type who faces up to an impersonal court, brings punishment to the two detectives who tried to steal his belongings, and finally ends up being blown up shouting that he will not destroy himself and only the executioners will have to do it. It shapes as his most knowing, incisive screen performance to date.

Jeanne Moreau, Elsa Martinelli and others have fleeting parts that are adequately done. Most outstanding is Romy Schneider as the lawyer's nurse who is irresistibly drawn to accused men. She has a shrewd insight into abandon that illuminates K's loss of ties with life, sensuality and routine.

Welles has given slight intimations that this could be a totalitarian nation or one of over-automation. K's office, with its hundred of desks, the tons of dusty files etc. attest to this. And it also may be a man's awakening to consciousness and finding himself alienated in the world and rejecting its aspects one by one.

So it is uneven and sometimes filled with arid talk but has enough visual vitality to keep it engrossing in its first part. It then gets bogged down to pick up again as K's end approaches. An arty pic, showing Welles's good and had sdes, but one that could be a solid art entry if well placed and sold.

Purists may not agree with Welles's look at Kafka, the tubercular, neurotic Czech genius, and his ending it with K's defiance, and an intimation of Atomic end, rather than leaving him a victim of society and himself. *Mosk.*

ICH Bin Auch Nur Eine Frau
(I, Too, Am Only a Woman)
(GERMAN—COLOR)
Berlin, Dec. 24.

Gloria release of Rialto (Preben Philipsen) production. Stars Maria Schell and Paul Hubschmid; features Hans Nielsen, Agnes Windeck, Anita Hoefer, Ingrid van Bergen. Directed by Alfred Weidenmann. Screenplay, Johanna Sibelius and Eberhard Keindorff; camera, Heinz Hoelscher; music, Peter Thomas; editor, Walter Wischniewsky. At UFA Pavillon, West Berlin. Running time, 89 MINS.

Lilli Koenig	Maria Schell
Martin Bohlen	Paul Hubschmid
Dr. Katz	Hans Nielsen
Housekeeper	Agnes Windeck
Pauline	Anita Hoefer
Annabella	Ongrid van Bergen
Gerda	Hannelore Auer
Mrs. Starke	Tilly Lauenstein

Alfred Weidenmann, one of Germany's better known directors, landed with the Austrian-French sex comedy, "Julia, You're Wonderful," a stout success in Germany last year. Pic proved a big audience success and also pleased most of this country's crix. His latest, "I, Too, Am Only a Woman," also a comedy, may please large segments of the playing public but hardly the professional reviewers.

Pic has a rather mediocre script, its deficiencies including corny dialog sequences and overly-familiar jokes and situations. As a result, the more fastidious patron will find the story rather stretched. Also, there's little to laugh about

this comedy. Commercially, pic will have to rely on its marquee names (Maria Schell, Paul Hubschmid) and on the new comedy reputation Weidenmann gained with his "Julia." Foreign prospects appear dubious.

It is to Weidenmann's credit that the pic also has assets to offer despite the considerable drawbacks. The director shows again his fine sense for visual impact and he knows how to handle the players.

Miss Schell may owe something to him. She's at last "different" in this one. Not only is she a refreshing departure from her crying-woman cliche but also pleasantly natural. A special word of praise should go to Hubschmid. This Swiss-born actor who once, under the name of Paul Christian, filmed in Hollywood and whose local popularity has been on a steady upbeat since he started playing (he still does) the role of Henry Higgins in the Berlin production of "My Fair Lady," gives evidence here of the fact that he's one of the most handsome and convincing middleaged German screen lovers. It's a great pity that he's being offered such inadequate material.

The thin plot concerns a female psychiatrist (Maria Schell) who knows to cure her clients, mostly rich ladies, from their various complexes. There's the handsome fashion photographer (Hubschmid) who has his own way with women. He also wants to conquer the heart of the attractive femme doctor. He pretends suffering from complexes and becomes her client. The happy ending soon becomes obvious. Film was shot in Berlin and there are some fine color camera shots of the city's streets. *Hans.*

Wild Guitar
For indiscriminate teeners.
Hollywood, Dec. 20.

Fairway International release. Cast includes Arch Hall Jr., William Watters, Cash Flagg, Nancy Czar, Marie Denn, Bob Crumb, Bill Lloyd, Mike Kannon, Jonathan Karle, Al Scott, Virginia Broderick, Paul Voorhees, Rick Dennis, Tony Flynn, Carol Flynn. Written and produced by Nicholas Merriwether. Directed by Ray Dennis Steckler; music, Alan O'Day; camera, Joseph V. Mascelli; editor, Anthony M. Lanza; sound, Samuel Kapezky. Preview in Hollywood, Dec. 17, '62. Running time, 80 MINS.

"Wild Guitar" is currently playing several Southern dates, is in San Diego and hopes to open in Los Angeles during January. Made for a reported $35,000, tale of rock 'n' roller's rise to top of Hollywood heap is interesting as an amateur effort but a professional entry for general release on the open theatrical market it most decidedly is not.

Arch Hall Jr. motorcylses into town with a guitar and an innocence which makes Joe Palooka look like a libertine. Literally minutes later he has subbed for an ailing singer on a tv show. Then a cigar puffing music czar (William Watters) has seen, signed and has started to exploit him.

Among ensuing misdeeds perpetrated by arch-villain Watters is a payola system he organizes among high school student leaders to implement Hall's campus popularity. "Why must everything be so phony?" wails Hall upon discovery of practices. To this Wat-

ters counters "that's the way life is," asking the bewildered youth to recall his own h.s. time. "Remember that popular kid everybody followed no matter what he did? The kids drank malts where he did, right? What makes you think he wasn't getting PAID to drinks his malts there?"

Hall's baby blues are ultimately opened when a former Watters protege (Bob Crumb) drunkenly spills story of way in which he was bilked and finally abandoned.

Cast is mainly non-pro, only three having faced cameras before, one of whom is Watters who is only member of cast to display professional finesse. Hall's songs, which he wrote with Alan O'Day serve as a pleasantly refreshing interludes. His acting, however, is negligible.

Direction by 22 year old Ray Dennis Steckler succeeds in giving film a certain mobility but it couldn't possibly move fast enough to get away from the Nicholas Merriwether script. Editing is professional, other technical credits ok. *Fess.*

Private Potter
(BRITISH)

Often absorbing but rather untidy, inconclusive glimpse of a man under war stress; little stellar appeal and will need hefty sales effort.

London, Dec. 18.

Metro release of a Ben Arbeid production. Stars Tim Courtenay; features Mogens Wieth, James Maxwell, Ronald Fraser, Ralph Michael. Directed by Caspar Wrede. Screenplay, Ronald Harwood and Wrede; music, George Hall; editor, John Pomeroy; camera, Arthur Lavis. Previewed at Metro Private Theatre. Running time, 89 MINS.

Private Potter	Tom Courtenay
Yannis	Mogens Wieth
Doctor	Ronald Fraser
Lt. Col. Gunyon	James Maxwell
Padre	Ralph Michael
Brigadier	Brewster Mason
Captain Knowles	Eric Thompson
Major Sims	John Graham
Captain Patterson	Frank Finlay
Cpl. Lamb	Harry Landis
Private Robertson	Michael Coles
Major Reid	Jeremy Geldt

Following his debut in "Loneliness of the Long Distance Runner," Tom Courtenay makes further impact in this film. But it is an egghead pic that doesn't quite come off. Hence, it will need some shrewd selling to get it off the pad. Yarn has a strong, imaginative idea but tails away inconclusively and falls between two stools, not quite arty, not quite commercial.

Courtenay plays an inexperienced young soldier who screams in terror while on patrol that is tracking down a terrorist leader on a Mediterranean island. As a result, the mission misfires and a colleague which is killed. The young soldier excuses himself with the plea that he saw a vision of God. Question that arises is whether he is to be court-martialled for cowardice or whether, in fact, he did have this religious experience. And, if so, whether or not he should be punished.

Reactions of his commanding officer, the medical officer and the padre form the basis of this parable. It is the conflicting clash of Army regulations and men's consciences which intrigue. But the young soldier's character is never clearly defined and the film eventually flounders in speculation and conjecture. The screen-

play writers, Ronald Harwood and Caspar Wrede (Wrede has also directed with sensitivity but little compulsion) midway lost the courage of any convictions they may have had when sitting down to their typewriters.

Courtenay acts with some imagination but it is to be hoped that he is not going to be typed in these psychological roles. Best performance comes from James Maxwell, as his commanding officer.

But gradually he begins to believe in the lad's story and then his own conscience starts to interfere. Ralph Michael, as the padre; Brewster Mason, as the brigadier, who lives by Army regulations; and Ronald Fraser, as a cheery doctor, also give vivid performances. John Graham on the side of psychiatry, Eric Thompson, Michael Coles and Harry Landis lend useful support. Mogens Wieth is burdened with an overwritten, unconvincing role as a wounded terrorist.

Camerawork by Arthur Lavis is okay but John Pomeroy's editing is too leisurely. The film starts off very sharply but never fulfills its early tension. George Hall's score is helpful but is far too obtrusive at times, especially in its blatant loudness of scenes in which complete quiet would be more effective. This is especially so during the patrol sequence when the corporal in charge, rightly, is pleading for silence from his men. The music destroys the atmosphere lamentably.   *Rich.*

La Citta' Prigioniera
(The Captive City)
(ITALIAN)

Rome, Dec. 18.

Paramount Films of Italy release of a Maxima-Lux-Galatea production. Stars David Niven, Lea Massari, Ben Gazzara; features Daniela Rocca, Martin Balsam, Michael Craig, Clelia Matania, Giulio Bosetti, Percy Herbert, Ivo Garrani, Odoardo Spadaro, Roberto Risso, Venantino Venantini, Carlo Hinterman, Adelmo di Fraia. Directed by Joseph Anthony. Screenplay, Guy Elmes, Eric Bercovici, Marc Brandel; from novel by John Appleby; camera, Leonida Barboui; music, Piero Piccioni; editor, Mario Bonitti, Raymond Poulton. Michael Billingsley. At Barberni, Rome. Running time, **110 MINS.**
Major Peter Whitfield......David Niven
Lelia .... Lea Massari
Captain Stubbs .... Ben Gazzara
Doushka .... Daniela Rocca
Feinberg .... Martin Balsam
Captain Elliot .... Michael Craig
Climedes .... Clelia Matania
Narriman .... Giulio Bosetti
Sergeant Reed .... Percy Herbert
Mavroti .... Ivo Garrani
Janny Mendoris ...... Odoardo Spadaro
Loveday .... Roberto Risso

(In English)

Okay general fare with enough suspense ingredients, marquee names and accessory values to mark it for support slotting in most export areas, including the U.S.

Pic misses being an outstanding entry of its genre in overexposure, and a lack of incisiveness in its character delineation, vital in an "intimate" suspenser such as it tries to be. It succeeds only in part. Story has mixed group of people led by a British officer holed up in an Athens Hotel surrounded by fighters of a (unidentified, but presumably leftwing) rebel party. Under the hotel, in a subcellar, is a giant arms cache, which the rebels must capture intact in order to survive. One of the surrounded group is a traitor, and audience is kept guessing, until the final scene, regarding his or her identity.

Along the way, true and false clues are thrown right and left, yet perhaps because there are too many key characters, none is sufficiently explored to enable audience to develop sympathy or even interest. Many, such as the prostitute, or even the eventual traitor, are merely superficial fragments of the whole. Only Lea Massari, as a femme resistance leader with a past, is allowed some depth as, to a degree, is Ben Gazzara's American officer, though here again his presence is unclearly motivated.

Niven gives a good straightforward performance in a role for which he is ideally suited. Daniela Rocca hasn't a chance to follow up her "Divorce, Italian Style" portrayal as the prostie. With the noted exception of Lea Massari, the remainder of the cast including such able thespers as Martin Balsam, Gazzara, Michael Craig and Giulio Bosetti haven't much chance for range.

Mario Chiari deserves credit for an impressive "outdoor" set of his wartime Athens hotel and square. Leonoda Barboni's chiaroscuro lighting and Piero Piccioni's music are in the proper sombre key.
Hawk.

Les Quatres Verites
(The Four Truths)
(FRENCH)

Paris, Dec. 24.

UGC-CFDU-Sirius release of Madeleine Films - Franco - London Films - Hispamer-Ajace production. Stars Leslie Caron, Anna Karina, Sylva Koscina, Monica Vitti, Charles Aznavour, Rossano Brazzi, Hardy Kruger, Jean Poiret, Michel Serrault. Directed by Rene Clair, Allesandro Blasetti, Luis Berlanga, Herve Bromberger. Screenplay, Frederic Grendel, Bromberger, Berlanger; camera, Armand Thirard, Jacques Mercanton; editor, Denise Natot. At Normandie, Paris. Running time, **105 MINS.**
Any .... Leslie Caron
Charles .... Charles Aznavour
Husband .... Michel Serrault
Wife .... Anna Karina
Man .... Jean Poiret
El Rubio .... Hardy Kruger
Girl .... Anna Casares
Mia .... Monica Vitti
Madeleine .... Sylva Koscina
Baron .... Rossano Brazzi

This is another sketch pic, this time with La Fontaine's Fables, four of them, transposed to human terms from their original animal aspects. This makes for moralizing. One fable is exceptional but the others are ordinary. With the Continental names in the various roles, it might be an okay local entry with foreign possibilities skimpier. Offshore possible playoff chances are there on some juicy aspects. Art chances seem thin.

Two French directors, one Italian and one Spanish reined the four segments. Spain's Luis Berlanga runs away with the quality nod. He deals with a contented organ grinder almost driven to suicide by bureaucracy and ordinary human unawareness. This has a pointed picturesque flair.

The vaude team of Michel Serrault and Jean Poiret, with their fine timing and wit, save the one about a jealous husband who loses his wife, usually kept locked up, to a foxy character who gets to him via his vanity before making a play for the wife. This is the paraphrase of the crow and the fox fable.

The Italo bit is the hare and the tortoise fable, dealing with a wife who gets her man back from an opulent mistress. Miscasting and labored plotting make this seem overlong in spite of its 25 minutes. But it has a voluptuous actress lolling about in various aspects of undress for hypo values.

And French director Rene Clair wraps up this film, with a tale of two ill-assorted people locked in an apartment over the Easter holidays—and how they fall in love. Leslie Caron is piquant as a fashion model while Charles Aznavour is sympathetic as a worker who comes to help her open a stuck door. He gets locked in, too.

But the Clair timing and wit seems off, and he can't get the spark from the two thesps. It is a controlled but lifeless bit of situation comedy which fails to pay off as a sketch.

Hardy Kruger etches a neat performance as the organ man in the bittersweet Hispano sketch. Monica Vitti cannot cope with the silly tactics she is forced to do as the wife trying to get back her husband. Sylva Koscina unblushingly adds a nice patina of undraped flesh as the meaty mistress.

Pic is generally well mounted and has some flashes of comedics. But it will have to be sold primarily on its names and hypo factors due to the uneven quality of the various roles.   *Mosk.*

Son Of Flubber

Further adventures of "The Absent-Minded Professor." Sequel doesn't match comic quotient of original, but should be another moneymaker for Disney.

Hollywood, Jan. 4.

Buena Vista release of Walt Disney production. Stars Fred MacMurray, Nancy Olson, Keenan Wynn; features Tommy Kirk, Ed Wynn, Leon Ames, William Demarest, Charlie Ruggles, Ken Murray, Paul Lynde, Elliott Reid. Bob Sweeney, Joanna Moore. Coproducer, Bill Walsh. Directed by Robert Stevenson. Screenplay, Walsh, Don DaGradi, based on story by Samuel W. Taylor and Danny Dun books; camera, Edward Colman; editor, Cotton Warburton; music, George Bruns; assistant director, Joseph L. McEveety. Reviewed at the studio, Jan. 4. Running time, **102 MINS.**
Prof. Ned Brainard......Fred MacMurray
Betsy Brainard .... Nancy Olson
Alonzo Hawk .... Keenan Wynn
Biff Hawk .... Tommy Kirk
A. J. Allen .... Ed Wynn
Judge Murdock ....Charlie Ruggles
Pres. Rufus Daggett........ Leon Ames
Mr. Hurley .... Ken Murray
Mr. Hummel ....William Demarest
Sportscaster .... Paul Lynde
Shelby Ashton .... Elliott Reid
Mr. Harker .... Bob Sweeney
Desiree de la Roche ... Joanna Moore
Defense Sec. .... Edward Andrews
Officer Hanson........James Westerfield
1st Referee .... Alan Carney
Coach .... Stuart Erwin
Officer Kelly ....Forrest Lewis
Prosecutor .... Alan Hewitt
Humphrey .... Leon Tyler
Mr. Barley .... Jack Albertson
Mr. Osborne .... Eddie Ryder
Mrs. Daggett ....Harriet MacGibbon
Mother .... Beverly Wills
Father .... Wally Boag
Baby Walter .... Wed Miller

Like most offspring of celebrated parents, "Son Of Flubber" doesn't fill its father's footprints. Father Flubber, better known as Walt Disney's "Absent - Minded Professor," had lots more bounce to the comedy ounce. "Son" is an extension of the same basic scientific formula, with minor variations, but it lacks the ingenuity, clarity and neatness of its memorable progenitor. Fortunately, though, individual scenes within the less effective whole have the same uproarious, bellylaugh quality that characterized the original, and these, coupled with the traditional magnetism of the Disney banner and leftover lure of flubber, should make the Buena Vista release a solid moneymaker.

Fred MacMurray rides again in his airborne Model T as lovable Professor Brainard atop virtually the same spirited cast that cut up in the first film, which was molded by approximately the same creative and cinematic staff headed by coproducer Bill Walsh and director Robert Stevenson. The sequel, concocted by Walsh and Don DaGradi from a story by Samuel W. Taylor and the Danny Dunn books, picks up where the original left off.

Failure of the red-taped government to shell out ready cash for his anti-gravity goo sends MacMurray back to the lab, where he promptly invents a new gaseous substance that can produce "dry rain."

MacMurray, with his knack for perfect reactions, repeats his winning performance as the flubbergasted prof. Nancy Olson, a fine actress not seen often enough in recent years, is excellent as his wife. Keenan Wynn is solid in his reenactment of a greedy loan shark, and Tommy Kirk, a young comic actor with a bright future,

scores big as his practical-minded son. There are a host of fine featured portrayals, noteworthy among which are those of Elliott Reid, Joanna Moore, Bob Sweeney, Ken Murray, Leon Ames, Ed Wynn, William Demarest and Charlie Ruggles. Paul Lynde is outstanding in his delineation of an overly partial sportscaster, as is Leon Tyler as the inflated flubberized hero of that gridiron rumpus. Strong momentary comedy impressions are made by Edward Andrews, Alan Carney, James Westerfield and many others too numerous to specify individually in a large and highly adaptable cast.

Stevenson's direction is sound and resourceful, but the material, though wittily satirical in spots and farcically robust in others, just never quite measures up in its entirety to the freshness of its forerunner. Invaluable work by the special effects unit of Eustace Lycett, Robert A. Mattey, Jack Boyd and Jim Fetherolf is a source of constant visual delight. Other tiptop contributions to the production have been made by cameraman Edward Colman, composer George Burns, editor Cotton Warburton, soundman Dean Thomas, art directors Carroll Clark and William H. Tuntke and second unit director Arthur J. Vitarelli. But "Son Of Flubber," alas, is a synthetic. As we follow the bouncing ball, we seem to be bouncing on the same old lyrics. *Tube.*

The Hook
(PANAVISION)

Lively, engrossing but not altogether successful war drama. Best suited to tastes of action buffs, should rake in that coin.

Hollywood, Jan. 9.

Metro release of William Perlberg production. Stars Kirk Douglas, Robert Walker, Nick Adams. Directed by George Seaton. Screenplay, Henry Denker, based on Vahe Katcha's novel, "L'Hamecon"; camera, Joseph Ruttenberg; editor, Robert J. Kern Jr.; music, Larry Adler; asst. director, Donald Roberts. Reviewed at the studio, Jan. 9, '63. Running time, **98 MINS.**

Sgt. P. J. Briscoe	Kirk Douglas
Pvt. O. A. Dennison	Robert Walker
Pvt. V. R. Hackett	Nick Adams
"Gook"	Enrique Magalona
Capt. Van Ryn	Nehemiah Persoff
Lt. D. D. Troy	Mark Miller
Steward	John Bleifer

Filmgoers willing to receive "The Hook" at uncomplicated face value is apt to find the Perlberg-Seaton production for Metro a gripping drama of men at war, a picture fraught with action and suspense and laced with significant questions of morality in wartime. Conversely, those for whom dramatic neatness counts are likely to be bothered by its story and character irregularities and a tendency to stray beyond pertinent, basic issues into tangents and melodramatic posture. The upshot is a film ideally suited to the cinematic tastes of war action buffs, but disappointing for the more discerning customer. Satisfactory boxoffice looms, but it is apt to reflect these basics.

Henry Denker's screenplay, based on Vahe Katcha's novel, "L'Hamecon," reduces the broad panorama of wartime conflict to its simplest, most fundamental terms. By such reduction of scope to the scale of individuals, it attempts to point out that the ordinarily impersonal machinery of combat can cease to apply rationally under intimate, calculating man-to-man circumstances. Uncompromising allegiance to "the order," that hallmark of military structure, takes on a new and frightening significance when it hinges on a pointblank and pointless kill of convenience.

The dramatic means by which this point is illustrated in "The Hook" involves the problem of how three American soldiers in the Korean War are to deal with a prisoner. Orders from headquarters are to do in the man but, after much haggling and stormy procrastinating, none of the three Yanks find themselves able to execute the senseless assignment until the prisoner, in the confusion of a sudden truce, ironically provokes the fatal action in the course of a somewhat unstable, unnecessary conclusive passage. Most of the story transpires aboard a neutral ship steaming through perilous wartime waters.

Kirk Douglas gives a characteristically virile and authoritative performance as a veteran sergeant unable, ultimately, to reconcile 19 years of hard, unemotional soldiering principles with the act of following an order to kill a man while out of actual combat circumstances. Nick Adams has some telling moments as a PFC voluntarily at the mercy of Douglas' whims, owing to an incident in which the latter had concealed evidence that would have led to Adams' court martial. There is, however, a glaring inconsistency in this relationship. For had Douglas withheld such vital evidence, it follows that he would be at least equally guilty of military misconduct as Adams. At any rate, the nature of their association is highly improbable.

Robert Walker, in his first screen assignment, is uncertain in his delineation of the third member of the party, a sensitive, learned private. Filipino actor Endique Magalona, as the prisoner, is called upon to spend most of his time staring helplessly at his hapless captors. Nehemiah Persoff is fine as the philosophical skipper of the Finnish vessel. Support is satisfactory.

Director George Seaton has failed to clarify the exact nature of establishing events at the outset, but he has brought in most of the key scenes with impact. Joseph Rutterberg's lenswork is clear and straightforward, Robert J. Kern Jr.'s editing crisp and tight where it counts. Larry Adler, the noted harmonica player, has composed the score and rendered it expressively on his instrument.

Tube.

Les Culottes Rouges
(The Red Pants)
(FRENCH)

Paris, Jan. 8.

Columbia release of Cinetel-Silver Films production. Stars Laurent Terzieff, Bourvil; features Etienne Bierry, Antoine Bourseiller. Directed by Alex Joffe. Screenplay, Joffe, Pierre Corti, Etienne Bierry; camera, Jean Penzer; editor, Eric Pluet. At Paris, Paris. Running time, **100 MINS.**

Antoine	Laurent Terzieff
Fendard	Bourvil
Schmidt	Etienne Bierry

Film is another in a cycle about escapee prisoners of war during the last debacle. It has some neat thesping and some good ideas but just does not have the depth or originality for art theatre chances abroad, with only dualer possibilities on its fairly entertaining qualities.

An adventurous type holes up with a timed fellow on one of his escapes. He uses the rather unassuming but selfish one until they are forced to flee together. Then the supposed daring soldier turns out to be the most selfish of the two and ironically is caught while the other gets away.

Bourvil is a clever comedian who manages to make the frightened little man, who won't take chances for anybody or anything, an engaging character. This is a tribute to his comic range and character building.

Laurent Terzieff is rightfully sullen and overdemanding as the dynamic but cruel would-be military hero. Director Alex Joffe has strewn this with too many gratuitous bits to detract from the basic battle of character which is the main framework of the film. All other complications are fragmentary.

Production is neatly done technically but does not have the true feel for the time. Hence, this seems mainly a local item on its name values. *Mosk.*

A Child Is Waiting

Affecting study of mentally retarded children. Grimness of dramatic topic may limit b.o. appeal, but intelligent treatment and good marquee names will help.

Hollywood, Jan. 7.

United Artists release of Stanley Kramer production. Stars Burt Lancaster, Judy Garland; features Gena Rowlands, Steven Hill; introduces Bruce Ritchey. Directed by John Cassavetes. Screenplay, Abby Mann, based on his story; camera, Joseph LaShelle; editor, Gene Fowler Jr.; music, Ernest Gold; assistant director, Lindsley Parsons Jr. Reviewed at Directors Guild of America, Jan. 7, '63. Running time, **104 MINS.**

Dr. Matthew Clark	Burt Lancaster
Jean Hansen	Judy Garland
Sophie Widdicombe	Gena Rowlands
Ted Widdicombe	Steven Hill
Reuben Widdicombe	Bruce Ritchey
Mattie	Gloria McGehee
Goodman	Paul Stewart
Douglas Benham	Lawrence Tierney
Miss Fogarty	Elizabeth Wilson
Miss Brown	Barbara Pepper
Holland	John Morley
Mrs. McDonald	June Walker
Dr. Lombardi	Mario Gallo
Dr. Sack	Frederick Draper

Again, as in "Judgment at Nuremberg," producer Stanley Kramer has dipped into productive source of live television drama and come up with a poignant, provocative, revealing dramatization of a topic that merits attention and concern. And again it is writer Abby Mann whose original work has spawned the effort. This time it is the subject of mentally retarded children upon which light is shed and, thanks to Mann's knowledgeable, penetrating and compassionate scenario and John Cassavetes' artful, arresting and sensitive direction, the result is a deeply moving and beneficial motion picture achievement.

Skillfully executed and tastefully performed though the film is, there are, nevertheless, bound to be those who sense an almost intolerably depressing experience in store and will tend to shy away from such an emotionally demanding visit to the cinema. But "A Child Is Waiting" is the sort of distinguished attraction that could, if vigorously and intelligently, sold to trade and public, override such commercial limitations. The names of Burt Lancaster and Judy Garland are certain to aid in this regard.

The film focuses intimately on one profoundly touching case, around which are woven heartrending and often shocking illustrations of behavior and activity in institutions for the mentally retarded as well as academic discussions of the role in society to be played by the afflicted, and society's responsibility to them. There is no hokiness in the dramatization. It has been done honestly, directly and informatively, and succeeds in erasing certain misconceptions.

Lancaster delivers another firm, sincere, persuasive and unaffected performance as the professionally objective but understanding psychologist who heads the institution. Judy Garland gives a sympathetic portrayal of an overly involved teacher who comes to see the error of her obsession with the plight of one child. That child, a deeply touching "borderline case," is played superbly by young Bruce Ritchey, a professional actor who manages to fit believably into a youthful cast that consists, for the most part, of actual retarded children who are patients of Pacific State Hospital in Pomona. As the lad's two troubled parents, Gena Rowlands (the director's wife) and Steven Hill pitch in with two exceptionally vivid and convincing performances. Miss Rowlands has one especially memorable scene. Others who register soundly are Paul Stewart, Gloria McGehee, Elizabeth Wilson, Barbara Pepper, John Morley, June Walker, Mario Gallo and Frederick Draper.

Joe LaShelle's camera is an agile, alert, adaptable and ever-inquisitive observer. Gene Fowler Jr.'s editing puts the right scenes in the right places, manipulating and molding the drama to maximum emotional advantage. Rudolph Sternad's production design has both character and natural simplicity. In James L. Speak's sound reproduction, there is clarity and sensitivity. An expressive and deeply affecting musical score by Ernest Gold is a vital factor.

Tube.

Les Abysses
(The Depths)
(FRENCH)

Lenox Films production and release. With Francine Berge, Colette Berge, Pascale De Boysson, Colette Regis, Paul Bonifas, Jean Legoff. Directed by Nico Papatakis. Screenplay, Jean Vauthier; camera, Jean-Michel Boussaguet; editor, Denise De Casablanca. Preemed in Paris. Running time, **96 MINS.**

Michele	Francine Berge
Marie	Colette Berge
Mademoiselle	Pascale De Boysson
Madame	Colette Regis
Monsieur	Paul Bonifas
Philippe	Jean Legoff

For a first film, director Nico Papatakis has tackled a difficult subject, a sort of satiric and surrealist look at servant-master relationships on a crumbling farm. If it does not quite transcend its

locale to make a bigger statement on this subject, this does take a searing swipe at human pettiness and looms mainly an arty bet abroad.

The pic might be worth arty theatre placement. But it calls for a personalized sell. If this does not not quite come off because of repetitiveness and overwriting, it does have a jarring and penetrating quality which is hard to overlook.

Two bedraggled maids, with a better background than their situation promises, are shown flitting about a rundown farm house. They talk, destroy, have fits of elation or fear, and bring out that they dread the return of the owners, have not been paid for three years, and seem on the verge of insanity, compounded by a more than sisterly affection.

In come the owners, a vague man, his dominating second wife and his dreamy daughter whose husband has left her. Dissension immediately breaks out and the maids are alternately out of control or obsequious. They get out of hand when they hear the house will be sold. When it's finally sold, they kill the woman and the daughter as the film ends on a look of horror.

Jean Vauthier's script is too cluttered up with verbal fireworks. Its protest, satire and insight are only intermittently effective.

But director Papatakis has charged this with some biting visuals and has obtained strange but evocative performances from the cast. Francine Berge and her real sister, Colette, play the deranged sisters and go from hystria to cowering servility to make their characters provocative if not always clear.

The others are also figures of weight in this uneven but unusual film. It is technically good for a production shot entirely on location. But the absence of some tie with reality, and the constant shifting of character, ultimately water down its forcefulness.

Mosk.

La Marcia Su Roma
(The March On Rome)
(ITALIAN-FRENCH)

Rome, Jan. 8.

Dino DeLaurentiis release of a Fairfilm-Orsay Film (Paris) production. Features Ugo Tognazzi, Vittorio Gassmann, Roger Hanin, others. Directed by Dino Risi. Story and screenplay, Risi, Gigo de Chiara, Sandro Continenza, Age, Scappelli, Scala, Maccari. Camera, Alfio Contini; music, Piero Piccioni; edtor, Alberto Galletti. At Roxy Cinema, Rome. Running time, 95 MINS.

Domenico .... Vittorio Gassmann
Umberto .... Ugo Tognazzi
Capt. Paolinelli .... Roger Hanin

Resolved for laughs, this item makes for entertaining and amusing viewing despite its grim historic original. Tognassi and Gassmann are good Italo marquee bait, as is the title, and homemarket impact is assured. Foreign chances are more limited, with many local nuances lost yet it rates some export interest.

Basic plot scheme follows Domenico (Vittorio Gassmann) and Umberto (Ugo Tognazzi) on their trek to Rome during the 1920 march which helped give Fascism its birth. As noted, most of situations are played for laughs or chuckles, but there's more than a hint of the irony that pervaded "All Go Home" and "The Great War," two pix from which this one derives more or less directly.

Local jokes abound, and the principals play to the hilt, aided by a large and colorful supporting cast. Technical credits are good, with a special nod to apt period recreation in sets and costumes.

Hawk.

The Fast Lady
(BRITISH—COLOR)

A slight joke is somewhat prolonged in this, but brisk direction and amiable comedy acting keeps the fun alive; useful b.o. for pop houses.

London, Jan. 8.

Rank release of a Julian Wintle-Leslie Parkyn production. Stars James Robertson Justice, Leslie Phillips, Stanley Baxter, Kathleen Harrison; features Julie Christie, Eric Barker, Oliver Johnston, Allan Cuthbertson, Esma Cannon, Dick Emery, Deryck Guyler, Victor Brooks, Terence Alexander, Michael Balfour, Danny Green, Eddie Leslie, Clive Dunn, Campbell Singer, Heidi Erich, Trevir Reid. Guest appearances: "Monsewer" Eddie Gray, Bill Fraser, Fred Emney, Raymond Baxter, Graham Hill, John Bolster, John Surtees, Frankie Howerd. Directed by Ken Annakin. Screenplay, Jack Davies & Henry Blyth; second unit director, Don Sharp; camera, Reg Wyer; music, Norrie Paramor; editor, Ralph Sheldon. Previewed at RFD Private Theatre, London. Running time, 95 MINS.

Charles Chingford .... James Robertson Justice
Murdoch Troon .... Stanley Baxter
Freddy Fox .... Leslie Phillips
Mrs. Staggers ....Kathleen Harrison
Claire Chingford .... Julie Christie
Wentworth .... Eric Barker
Bulmer .... Oliver Johnston
Bodley .... Allan Cuthbertson
Lady on Road Crossing..... Esma Cannon
Shingler .... Dick Emery
Dr. Blake .... Deryck Guyler
Policeman .... Victor Brooks
Police Motor Cyclist..Terence Alexander
First Bandit .... Danny Green
Second Bandit .... Michael Balfour
Third Bandit .... Eddie Leslie
Old Gentleman .... Clive Dunn
Kingscombe .... Campbell Singer
Examiner .... Trevor Reid
Guest Appearances....Eddie Gray, Fred Emney, Frankie Howerd, John Surtees, Raymond Baxter, Graham Hill, John Bolster, Bill Fraser

A thin idea has been pumped up into a reasonably brisk, amusing situation comedy, which is helped by a cast of experienced farceurs. In dialog, the pic is short on wit but there is enough slapstick fun to keep the average house audience agreeably amused. Star of the film is an impressive vintage Bentley auto while James Robertson Justice, Leslie Phillips, Kathleen Harrison, Stanley Baxter and a newish young actress, Julie Christie, carry the brunt of the thesping. There also are a number of surefire character actors giving smart comic impact.

Film conerns the efforts of an obstinate, over patriotic and gauche young Scottish civil servant to learn to drive the Bentley sports car and and thus ingratiate himself with the tycoon father of a girl for whom he has fallen. Much of the humor is of the prattfall variety but it provides predictable, easy yocks. The hero taking a driving test, for instance, and the climax, when "The Fast Lady" goes all out in pursuit of some bank bandits, provide extended sequences of crazy misadventure on the highways which echo the good, old Mack Sennett days.

Mainly, however, the comedy situations are short and often fairly unrelated. Most hilarious, thanks to a gem of a performance by Eric Barker, is the first driving test taken by the wouldbe driver (Stanley Baxter). Barker, whose brief appearance in pix are now guarantees of yocks, is superb as the nerve-wracked instructor. Allan Cuthbertson also plays, extremely well, a confident instructor who works strictly from the book.

Justice, as the gruff tycoon, who is not as tough as he makes out, has a custommade part while Baxter, as the shy Scot, Phillips, playing a typical role as a wolfish car salesman, is good. Miss Harrison as a landlady has little difficulty in projecting her personality. Miss Christie, for whom big things are promised, looks cute, but lacks the experience to build up a frail role as the love interest.

Oliver Johnston, Esma Cannon, Dick Emery, Deryck Guyler (as a tipsy police doctor testing Baxter for inebriation), Terence Alexander, Clive Dunn and Heidi Erich all chip in with telling bits. The cast list is also boosted by some guest appearances including racing champs Graham Hill and John Surtees and tv auto racing commentator Raymond Baxter, appearing as themselves in a dream motor racing sequence.

Technical departments are all okay, with a particularly bright score by Norrie Paramor. "Fast Lady" makes no pretense at sophistication or sharpness but does offer some genial escapist laughs.

Rich.

L'Amore Difficile
(Difficult Love)
(ITALIAN)

Rome, Jan. 8.

Eichberg release of an Achille Piazzi production for Spa Cinematografica (Rome) Eichberg Film (Munich). Features Nino Manfredi, Fulvia Franco, Vittorio Gassmann, Nadia Tiller, E. M. Salerno, Catherine Spaak, Claudia Mori, Lilli Palmer, Bernard Wicki.

(First Episode)
"LE DONNE"
(THE WOMEN)

Directed by Sergio Sollima. Screenplay, Alessandro Continenza, Ettore Scola, from story by Ercole Patti; camera, Carlo Carlini.

Antonio .... E. M. Salerno
Bruna .... Claudia Mori
Valeria .... Catherine Spaak

(Second Episode)
"L'AVARO"
(THE MISER)

Directed by Luciano Lucignani. Screenplay, Alessandro Continenza, Ettore Scola, from story by Alberto Moravia; camera, Carlo Carlini.

Tullio .... Vittorio Gassmann
Mr. DeGasperis .... Adriano Rimoldi
Elena .... Nadia Tiller

(Third Episode)
"L'AVVENTURA DI UN SOLDATO"
(ADVENTURE OF A SOLDIER)

Directed by Nino Manfredi. Screenplay, Manfredi, Fabio Carpi, Giuseppe Orlandini, Ettore Scola, from story by Italo Calvino; camera, Carlo Carlini.

Tomagra .... Nino Manfredi
Widow .... Fulvia Franco

(Fourth Episode)
"IL SERPENTE"
(THE SNAKE)

Directed by Alberto Bonucci. Screenplay, Fabio Carpi, Guglielmo Santangelo, Renato Mainardi, from story by Mario Soldati; camera, Enrico Menczer.

Hilde .... Lilli Palmer
Bern .... Bernard Wicki
Marshal .... Gastone Moschin

At Cinema Fiamma, Rome. Running time, 125 MINS.

Four new Italian directors do a neat job in their initial film efforts in this four-episode item which should find plenty of foreign appeal thanks to amusing and piquant treatment of often-provocative themes. It's a good value for the money spent, and augurs well for tyro talent involved.

First episode finds E. M. Salerno puzzled as to how to handle two weekend flirts, one a just-married ex-mistress, the other a would-be teenage successor to the former. Claudia Mori makes a voluptuous ex while Catherine Spaak is her usual winning self as the new prospect.

Second segment once again proves Vittorio Gassmann to be the actor of the year in an amusing cameo of the miserly suitor who narrowly avoids financial involvement when he falls for Nadia Tiller, a gambler's neglected wife.

Third story, played mute by both principals, depicts a soldier's efforts to make time with a widow on a train, harassed by his fellow passengers. Nino Manfredi, often reminding of Buster Keaton, acts and directs in risible and promising fashion.

Fourth item depicts a German couple's falling in love again under the warm Sicilian sun, spurred by an incident with two island truckdrivers. Lilli Palmer and Bernard Wicki lend acting savvy to this one, which develops slowly but reserves its punch for the climax.

All in all, this has been intelligently and tastefully directed by its four directors within the limits of each segment's short running span. Film manages to entertain while directing some pointed barbs at certain modern conventions. Technical credits are uniformly good.

Hawk.

L'Empire De La Nuit
(The Empire of Night)
(FRENCH) (TOTALSCOPE)

Paris, Jan. 8.

UFA-Comacico release of Belmont-Jacques Roitfeld production. Stars Eddie Constantine; features Elga Andersen, Genevieve Grad, Harold Nicholas, Michel De Re, Claude Cerval, Tania Constantine. Directed by Pierre Grimblat. Screenplay, Ferederic Dard, Grimblat; camera, Michel Kelber; editor, Albert Jurgenson. At Aubert, Paris. Running time, 90 MINS.

Eddie .... Eddie Constantine
Widow .... Elga Andersen
Girl .... Genevieve Grad
Sidekick .... Harold Nicholas
Melchior .... Michel De Re

Switching from the perennial G-Man role to a rough and tumble nightclub revue stager, Yank French film star Eddie Constantine goes through much the same paces as heretofore in this new pic. But this has a measure of more offbeat humor that could slant it for use abroad.

Constantine comes to Paris with a contract only to find the boss of the nitery where he was to produce the show has supposedly died. But a comely widow and sinister brothers-in-law, trying to take over the nitery empire of the deceased, has him tangling with the usurpers. The fact that Constantine had fraudulently been passed off as the widow's vis-a-vis (to get him to leave the business to the brothers) makes for a series of fairly distracting fisticuffs, complications and plotting.

Old castles, a fight during a cabaret show and willing women keep this moving along. It just lacks a certain punch to make its farfetched story easier to take. Director Pierre Grimblat has mistaken parody and surrealist touches for the logic and brashness needed to keep these type pix boiling along.

Result is a tendency to telegraph gags. But Constantine is his easygoing self helped by lookers Elga Anderson and Genevieve Grad and bouncy sidekick Harold Nicholas. It should do well locally with European spots, due to his popularity

also indicated. But it still is dubious for the Yank arty or playoff circuits. *Mosk.*

Mandrin
(FRENCH-COLOR-DYALISCOPE)

Paris, Jan. 8.

Pathe release of Franco-London Film-Films Gibe Titanus production. Stars Georges Riviere, Jeanne Valerie, Dany Robin; features Sylvia Monfort, Georges Wilson, Armand Mestral, Jess Hahn, Albert Remy. Directed by Jean-Paul Le Chanois. Screenplay, Rene Havard, Claude Desailly, Louis Martin, Le Chanois; camera (Eastmancolor), Marc Fossard; editor, Boris Levine. At Balzac, Paris. Running time, **135 MINS.**

Mandrin	Georges Riviere
Antoinette	Jeanne Valerie
Baronne	Dany Robin
Myrtille	Sylvia Monfort
Belissard	Georges Wilson
Braconnier	Jess Hahn
Cours-Toujours	Albert Remy

"Mandrin" is a combination of Robin Hood and Jesse James in 18th Century France as he takes the side of the oppressed and overtaxed poor against the nobility. This has some well-regulated action scenes, but the usual plotting. However, this is not too wordy and could be a moppet or actioner foreign entry if pruned.

This film lacks the true tongue-in-cheek zest, the robust excesses and feel for time and place needed to make these type pix of arty cinema or firstrun possibilities abroad. Mandrin (Georges Riviere) takes to the hills when he has a run-in with royal tax collectors. There he gathers up a group which assails and finally defeats the national troops.

There are the usual women in his life, the gruff and bluff sidekicks, etc. Director Jean-Paul Le Chanois has given this a nice, color mounting. Riviere has dash as the well-intentioned outlaw. It is a conventional entry in this line, with more movement than usual. It looks in for an okay career here. *Mosk.*

La Creation Du Monde
(The Creation of the World)
(FRENCH—CZECH—COLOR)

Paris, Jan. 8.

SNA release of Czech State Film production. Design, story, commentary by Jean Effel. Directed by Edouard Hofman. Commentary, Francois Perier, Martine Sarcey, Georges Aminel; music, Jean Wiener, Jean Rychlik. At Monte-Carlo, Paris. Running time, **85 MINS.**

(*Animation*)

Made in Czechoslovakia and on the cartoons of a Frenchman, this is a witty interpretation in animated form of the creation of the world. But its few gags become repetitious and the film does not have the stamina, invention or breadth for a full-length animated pic. With pruning, it might serve as an okay medium-length art entry or a possible vidpic.

God is depicted as a genial, bald and bewhiskered man busily creating the world. The Devil tries to hamper him for the main complications of the pic. Animation has the right preciseness and old fashioned air for this Biblical romp. Generally good taste keeps it from being offensive.

Anachronistic humor is the keystone, with God using a cigarette lighter when it is time for it to be lighted, sewing a hem for the sea, etc. All this is tempered by the Devil and leads up to the creation of Adam and Eve and their temptations by Satan.

A fairly clever commentary adequately describes the action. Color and workmanship is good but this is somewhat too arch and overlong to amount to much. *Mosk.*

Le Conteau Dans La Plaie
(The Knife in the Wound)
(FRENCH-ITALIAN-U.S.)

Paris, Jan. 8.

Cinedis release of Filmsonor-Dear Film-United Artists production. Stars Sophia Loren, Anthony Perkins; features Gig Young, Jean-Pierre Aumont. Jacques Marin. Directed by Anatole Litvak. Screenplay, Peter Viertel, Hugh Wheeler, Maurice Druon from an idea by Andre Versini; camera, Henri Alekan; music, Mikis Theodrakis; editor, Bert Bates. At Colisee, Paris. Running time, **110 MINS.**

Bob	Anthony Perkins
Lisa	Sophia Loren
David	Gig Young
Alain	Jean-Pierre Aumont

(*In English*)

United Artists has this suspense item for the U.S. where it will be called "Five Miles to Midnight." Though somewhat short in character projection, and with much of the pic more plot than deeper development, this has a few punchy, grisly moments as well as the star names of Sophia Loren and Anthony Perkins. It also boasts a sleek envelope, to make it a saleable playoff item.

Perkins is presented as an irresponsible young man, drifting from job to job, who has managed to marry the ripe Miss Loren. It seems he has met her in Naples when he was a GI and she was a poor girl. Now she has a job in Paris but he is always trying for new jobs. And he is not above being nasty and slapping Miss Loren around in spite of the fact that she measures up to him in weight and size.

As the story begins, Perkins is going off to try to carry on with a job he is to lose compounded by his having missed a plane. As she sees him off, she tells him she wants out from their hopeless marriage. But off he goes, and the plane crashes.

Perkins has managed to be the only escapee and comes back to force her to get his insurance money. His promises to let her go changes as he realizes he can send her up for having gotten the money under false pretense. While forcing her to drive him out of the country, she finally runs him down on the road. She slips into madness as the film winds.

Perkins at first seems to be played as a neurotic and then appears more a sort of arrested, feckless adolescent than a would-be psychotic. Miss Loren, though seemingly fun-loving if saddled with an irritable, cloying spouse, is the one that cracks up finally. Too many complications seem dragged in to make plot points. This robs the film of a dramatic, ironic edge at times. But Perkins, hiding out in their little apartment and seen only by a neighboring boy, or managing to escape detection when people barge in on Miss Loren, give some moments of welcome suspense.

Gig Young emerges as a would-be romantic entanglement but cannot do much with lacklustre lines and conventional character. Jean-Pierre Aumont has only a walk-on. Miss Loren suffers in beauty but does make the most of a few

---

dramatic scenes. Perkins turns his boyish smiles, vague intensity and sudden changes of mood into an acceptable pattern for his role of a worthless adventurer.

Anatole Litvak handles the tale in a pro manner but his direction cannot gloss over the lack of true character portrayal or the contrived scripting. It is technically good. *Mosk.*

Das Schwarz-Weiss-Rote Himmelbett
(Black-White-Red Four Poster
(GERMAN)

Berlin, Jan. 8.

Schorcht release of Franz Seitz production. Directed by Rolf Thiele. Screenplay, Ilse Lotz-Dupont, George Laforet; camera, Heinz Schnackertz, Friedl Behn-Grund; music, Rolf Wilhelm. At Marmorhaus, West Berlin. Running time, **100 MINS.**

Germaine	Daliah Lavi
Friedrich de Wehrt	Martin Held
Hortense, his wife	Margot Hielscher
Their son	Thomas Fritsch
Aunt Arabelle	Elisabeth Flickenschildt
French girl	Marie Versini
Jules Rochberg	Karl Schoenboeck
Cornelia, a maid	Monika Dahlberg

Rolf Thiele, the German director who has a special predilection for "sex-loaded" pix, has another one with this pic. He did well with "The Girl Rosemarie" some years ago but was not successful with "Lulu." "The Black-White-Red Four Poster" his latest, is not as strong as his "Rosemarie" but is better than "Lulu." The trouble with many German sex pic is self-evident in this one—they often go too far and leave too little to the imagination. This film especially goes in for bed sequences and some of them will have trouble with the censors. Domestically, this is shaped good but foreign prospects look limited.

"The Black-White-Red Four Poster" (black-white-red were the colors of the German national flag during imperial times) plays somewhere on the Rhine before the first world war. It centers on a young lad (17), son of socially prominent parents, who early discovers his taste for erotic escapades. He falls for a sexy actress who has also a romance with the boy's uncle. The boy's father ends the affair by sending him to another school somewhere in the province. But the boy continues his love affairs there. His romantic interests include his landlady and a young French girl. The outbreak of the war breaks up the latter affair.

The best thing about this pic is the thesping. Little acting masterpieces are turned in by Martin Held (the boy's father), Elisabeth Flickenschildt (the boy's aunt) and Fritz Tillmann, a school director. Daliah Lavi, the actress and Marie Versini, the French girl, are the most active females.

Thomas Fritsch, son of former German filmstar Willy Fritsch, portrays the love-mad boy. It's a promising beginning. Camera work is very good. Other technical credits are fine. Film may be described as one of the better 1962 German productions. If handled with more delicacy, it might have been able to compete internationally. *Hans.*

Kohlhiesels Toechter
(Kohlhiesel's Daughters)
(GERMAN—COLOR)

Berlin, Jan. 8.

Nora release of Kurt Ulrich produc-

---

tion. Stars Liselotte Pulver (dual role), Helmut Schmid, Dietmar Schoenherr, Peter Vogel; features Heinrich Gretler, Renate Kasche, Adelin Wagner, Gudrun Genest, Heinz Holl. Directed by Axel von Ambesser. Screenplay, Eckart Hachfeld, after an idea by Hans Kraely; camera (Agfacolor), Willy Winterstein; music, Heino Gaze; editor, Herbert Taschner. At the Hahnentor, Cologne. Running time, **97 MINS.**

"Kohlhiesel's Daughters" has probably one of the most popular German screen plots. First filmization was by the late Ernst Lubitsch more than 30 years ago. There were remakes in 1930 and 1943. There's hardly any doubt that the 1962 version will lure many German filmgoers. It qualifies for the whole German-language market.

This is the story of two peasant daughters, Liesel and Susi, who are twins and are virtually identical in appearance. The former is pretty and witty while the latter is just the opposite. A handsome peasant boy comes along and, of course, wants to walk off with the pretty one. Trouble, however, stems from mother's will according to which the ugly daughter must get married first. In order to avoid this complication, the young man marries (temporarily) the one that nature has treated so badly. But one day after the wedding, she's feautiful, too.

Axel von Ambesser, one of Germany's most capable directors, has given this the kind of amiable touch which German patrons go for. Also, he has added the sort of robust humor called for by the plot. There are plenty of laughs for the average domestic patron. Even the more demanding viewer will admit that Liselotte Pulver is ideally cast for the double role.

Helmut Schmid's portrayal of the young lover also is of high standard. The couple's appearance in this film is certainly exploitable in this country. Cameraman Willi Winterstein skillfully handled the technical difficulties of the dual role. Heino Gaze contributed the adequate score. Other credits come up to standard. *Hans.*

I Due Colonelli
(The Two Colonels)
(ITALIAN)

Rome, Jan. 8.

Titanus release of a Gianni Buffardi production for Titanus Films. Stars Walter Pidgeon, Toto; features Scilla Gabel, Adriana Facchetti, Francis Lane, Nino Taranto, Tony Ucci, Roland Barstop, Gerard Haerter. Directed by Steno. Story and screenplay, Giovanni Grimaldi, Bruno Corbucci; camera, Tino Santoni. At Barberini, Rome. Running time, **103 MINS.**

Col. Di Maggio	Toto
Col. Henderson	Walter Pidgeon
Iride	Scilla Gabel
Penelope	Adriana Facchetti
Sergeant Quaglia	Nino Taranto
Sgt. McIntyre	Francis Lane
Mazzetta	Tony Ucci
Major Kruger	Roland Bartrop
German General	Gerard Haerter

Amusing lightweight spoof on war pix, topped by chuckleful performances from Walter Pidgeon and Italo comedian Toto as rival colonels, caught up in a Greek war incident. Top Italo value, especially in depth, with some export interest thanks to the subject and the Pidgeon name.

Story deals with a small Grecian village which is alternately captured by Italian and British troops, each headed by a colonel. Each occupation also leads to a fraternizing bit with Greek beauty Iride (Scilla Gabel), the object of both officers' attention. In turn also,

each colonel captures the other, until German troops spoil the "best of enemies" relationship by bringing the impasse to a head.

All ends well, however, with Nazi troops once again the heavies. Tale is told in a fairly stereotyped manner, and directed in obvious, heavy-handedly humorous fashion by Steno. Yet this manages to entertain a general audience in consummate style.

Toto is his usual risible self, while Walter Pidgeon manages a fine etching of the British officer (including an excellent and effective job of dubbing himself onto an Italo soundtrack). Scilla Gabel and Adriana Facchetti are good as the femme interests while Francis Lane neatly shapes a tongue-in-cheek version of the duty-bound British sergeant, with Nino Taranto okay as his Italo opposite number.

Others, including well-done if standard portrayals of Nazi officers by Gerard Haerter and Roland Bartrop, provide backing aptly. Technical credits are fair, inkeeping with this moderate-budgeted production. *Hawk.*

Summer Holiday
(BRITISH—COLOR)

Lively b.o. potential. Cheerful tuner, bubbling with youthful spirits and local pop idol Cliff Richard plus bright songs, and dancing boys and gals.

London, Jan. 15.

Warner-Pathe release of an Elstree Distributors (Kenneth Harper) production. Stars Cliff Richard, Lauri Peters; features David Kossoff, Ron Moody, The Shadows, Lionel Murton, Madge Ryan, Melvyn Hayes, Una Stubbs, Teddy Green, Pamela Hart, Wendy Barry, Nicholas Phipps. Directed by Peter Yates. Choreography, musical numbers directed by Herbert Ross. Original story and screenplay, Peter Myers, Ronald Cass; editor, Jack Slade; camera, John Wilcox; music, Stanley Black; songs, Myers, Cass, Cliff Richard, Bruce Welch, Brian Bennett, Hank Marvin, Philip Springer, Buddy Kaye, Mike Conlin. At Warner Theatre, London. Running time, **109 MINS.**

Don	Cliff Richard
Barbara	Lauri Peters
Cyril	Melvyn Hayes
Sandy	Una Stubbs
Steve	Teddy Green
Angie	Pamela Hart
Edwin	Jeremy Bulloch
Mimsi	Jacqueline Daryl
Stella	Madge Ryan
Jerry	Lionel Murton
Annie	Christian Lawson
Orlando	Ron Moody
Magistrate	David Kossoff
Shepherdess	Wendy Barry
Wrightmore	Nicholas Phipps
Themselves	The Shadows

As of now Cliff Richard, Britain's leading pop singer, is a hot property on tv, stage and disks. His first starring pic, "The Young Ones," hit the boxoffice jackpot here. Now the followup promises to clean up just as much. It is custom-made for the likeable personality of Richard, offers him good scope in song and dance and does not tax his still-limited acting powers overmuch. In CinemaScope and Technicolor, producer Kenneth Harper, valuably aided by director Peter Yates, choreographer Herbert Ross and a varied array of firstleague musicians, tunesmiths and orchestrators, has come up with a lively, cheerful tuner. It shows that Richard is no flash in the pan. Also it proves that Britain has at last overcome its diffidence in tackling musical pix. It can safely be recommended to anybody except those to whom the sight of zestful youth enjoying itself is a pain in the neck.

Peter Myers and Ronald Cass have provided a screenplay which is short on wit but anyway is simply a valid excuse for a light-hearted jaunt through sunny Europe. Richard and three mechanic buddies set out for a European holiday in a borrowed double-decker London bus. They pick up (in quite the nicest way) three stranded girls, a cabaret act enroute to Athens. The boys decide to make Athens their objective. They also encounter a troupe of wandering entertainers and a stowaway in the shape of a young boy. "He" turns out to be an American girl tele singer, fleeing from the professional demands of her dragon of a mother and her agent. These two conspire to upset the youngsters' trip and try to turn the whole thing into a publicity racket.

From this thin thread of yarn, songs, situations and dance routines arise fairly naturally. Even when dragged in, they add a lot to the excitement. Richard has a warm presence and sings and dances more than adequately. He is surrounded, not only by the inevitable Shadows Group, but by a bunch of equally likeable youngsters.

Lauri Peters is pleasant as the young Yank heroine and romantic interest and Melvyn Hayes, who has a sharp comic talent; Una Stubbs, Teddy Green, Pamela Hart, Jeremy Bulloch and Jacqueline Daryl hop on the bus with Richard to lend him spirited support. David Kossoff, Madge Ryan, as the formidable stage mother Lionel Murton and Nicholas Phipps add a touch of amusing maturity to the proceedings.

Highlighted throughout are production sequences which are put over shrewdly by director Yates and into which choreographer Ross pumps an exuberant American expertise. There is a press conference, a zany barber saloon and an offbeat romp when Richard and his chums get involved with a Yugoslav shepherdess. All these add up to production and entertainment value.

Myers and Cass have written seven numbers and others including Richard have contributed another nine. "The Next Time," a lovelorn solo sung by Richard, already leads U.K.'s Top 10. Others which promise well are "Swinging Affair," "Bachelor Boy," "Let Us Take You for a Ride" and "All at Once." The tenuous romance between Clifford and Miss Peters does not turn the song catalog into a string of injected love songs. There are just enough to blend nicely. The musical side is in good hands, what with Stanley Black doing the baton waving and orchestrations.

Filmed largely in France and Greece, the editing and backgrounds give an impression of a continuous trip across Europe. John Wilcox clearly enjoyed lensing some colorful location backgrounds. "Summer Holiday" is by no means the greatest of musicals. There are evidences of inexperience and the fact that some of the young thesps have much to learn. But it is one of the best British film musicals for some time. *Rich.*

Le Massaggiatrici
(The Masseuses)
(ITALO-FRENCH)
Rome, Jan. 15.

Warner Brothers release of a Panda (Ermanno Donati-Luigi Carpentieri)-Gallus Film (Paris) coproduction. Features Sylva Koscina, Cristina Gajoni, Valeria Fabrizi, Marisa Merlini, Philipe Noiret, Ernesto Calindri, Louis Seigner, Laura Adani, Luigi Pavese, Nino Taranto, Franchi and Ingrassia. Directed by Lucio Fulci. Story and screenplay, Oreste Biancoli, Vittorio Metz, Antonio DeTuddo, Antoinette Pelevant; camera, Guglielmo Mancori; editor, Ornella Micheli; music, Lallo Gori. At Galleria, Rome. Running time, **90 MINS.**

Marisa	Sylva Koscina
Iris	Cristina Gajoni
Milena	Valeria Fabrizi
Manzini	Luigi Pavese
Bellini	Philip Noiret
President	Louis Seigner
Parodi	Ernesto Calindri
Mrs. Parodi	Laura Adani
Bice	Marisa Merlini
Professor	Nino Taranto
Ushers	Franchi and Ingrassia

Fast-paced and exploitable comedy with strong prospects in depth. Surefire title for Italy, where the scandal of call girls disguising themselves as masseuses made recent headlines, should help. Abroad, it should play well on the strength of broad comedy, strongly laced with double entendres. This is not one for the kiddies.

Plot, as dreamed up by four writers, is the familiar one about the biz exec who comes to the big city to set a deal. Then he becomes involved in a call girl affair which nearly prejudices the deal until it turns out that the people he's dealing with are likewise involved. It's all replete with mistaken identity scenes, closet caches, and the like. But director Lucio Fulci keeps the pace spinning and the gags rolling.

Some of footage may attract censor attention, but with some exceptions, it's all played lightly and for laughs rather than leers. Large cast performs capably in the required broad style, and there are some neat cameos by some of the lesser names. Technical credits are okay. *Hawk.*

Der Schatz Im Silbersee
(The Treasure of Silver Lake)
(GERMAN-YUGOSLAV- C'SCOPE)
(Color)
Berlin, Jan. 8.

Constantin release of Rialto-Film (Berlin) production, in collaboration with Jadran-Film, Belgrade. Stars Lex Barker, Herbert Lom, Pierre Brice, Goetz George; features Karin Dor, Mirko Bauman, Marianne Hoppe, Eddi Arent. Directed by Dr. Harald Reinl. Screenplay, Harald G. Petersson, adapted from novel of same name by Karl May; camera (Eastmancolor), Ernst Kalinke; music, Martin Boettcher; editor, Hermann Haller. Preemed in numerous West German cities. Running time, **102 MINS.**

Old Shatterhand	Lex Barker
Fred Engel	Goetz George
Cornel Brinkley	Herbert Lom
Ellen Patterson	Karin Dor
Castlepool	Eddi Arent
Mrs. Butler	Marianne Hoppe
Winnetou	Pierre Brice
Patterson	Jan Sid
Sam Hawkins	Ralf Wolter
Gunstick Uncle	Mirko Bauman

"Silver Lake," produced by Berlin's Rialto-Film in Collaboration with Jadran-Wilm, Yugoslavia's top producing outfit, commands attention for three reasons. It is the first big-scale CinemaScope German western. It is the most expensive (about $875,000) film made by a Teutonic company in 1962. It is, within its special scope, a remarkably well made film. This contains the ingredients for a stout moneymaker within and outside its home grounds. There's a strong demand for such big-screen outdoor pix and this one qualifies especially for patrons between 12 and 25.

"Lake" admittedly doesn't reach the overall quality of Hollywood's top westerns, yet it can compete with bulk of the stateside average outdoor epics. In fact, it's better than quite a few of them. Also, it doesn't copy the Hollywood format while there are the usual fisticuffs and gunfire, but it has a more contemplative (European) touch.

Like the big U.S. westerns, this German-Yugoslav venture benefits from the great outdoors. The picturesque Karst region of the Titoland where the film was shot is hardly less impressive than the Arkansas region where the action occurs. The Eastmancolor photography enhances this production. The competent musical score adds to the mood. And, there are the usual lovable and malicious western characters.

Plot has the unscrupulous Cornel Brinkley (Herbert Lom) trying to get hold of a secret map that will lead him and his gang to the famed treasure of the silver lake. The villains would have reached their goal had there not been Old

Shatterhand (Lex Barker) and his faithful friend, Winnetou (Pierre Brice), chief of the Apaches. The two join Fred Engel (Goetz George), who's out to track down Brinkley, and murderer of his father. Until justice triumphs, there are the familiar dangers to overcome. But Old Shatterhand and Winnetou manage to win out via their experienced western skill.

Barker, once an American Tarzan, is physically and ideally cast in the role of Old Shatterhand. He is always nice and sympathetic, and the Germans go for him. Barker is one of the few Yank screenplayers to click in German films. This is his fourth German-made film. And more are to follow.

Britain's Herbert Lom is right at home as Cornel Brinkley, the chief villain. Lom does a fine acting job. Pierre Brice, a French actor, is cast as the Indian chief Winnetou, but he seems overly mild in this. Goetz George, promising young German actor, Ralf Wolter and Yugoslav Mirko Bauman round out the cast. The latter two take care of the "comedy relief" which occasionally appears far-fetched. Yet few of the young patrons will find fault with this.

Dr. Harald Reinl deserves credit for expert handling of the Karl May filmization. He has directed a film that has many assets. Taking into consideration that this is Germany's first big-scale western drama, he did a highly praiseworthy job. There's good reason to believe that "Silver Lake" will become one of Germany's most substantial postwar boxoffice contenders. *Hans.*

Cairo

Weak grade B crime-suspense meller.

Hollywood, Jan. 23.

Metro release of Ronald Kinnoch production. Stars George Sanders, Richard Johnson. Directed by Wolf Rilla. Screenplay, Joanne Court, based on novel by W. R. Burnett; camera, Desmond Dickinson; editor, Bernard Gribble; music, Kenneth V. Jones; assistant directors, George Pollard. Reviewed at the studio, Jan. 23, '63. Running time, **92 MINS.**

Major	George Sanders
Ali	Richard Johnson
Amina	Faten Hamama
Nicodemos	Eric Pohlmann
Kerim	Ahmed Mazhar
Kuchuk	Walter Rilla
Willy	John Meillon
Ghattas	Kamal El Shennawy
Marie	Chewikar
Commandant	Salah Nazmi
Mamba	Mona
Osman	Said Abu Bakr
Doctor	Salah Mansour
Assistant Minister	Abdel Khalek Saleh
2nd Officer	Youssef Shaaban
4th Officer	Capt. Mohamed Abdel Rahman

"Cairo" is a conventional cross between two staples of the cinema: the hashish opera and the safecracking escapade. Unfortunately for the actors and artisans, who have toiled with a highly presentable degree of skill and savvy, the story in which they are implicated is laden with cliches and riddled with holes. What emerges is a film that will be passable as a supporting attraction.

A further letdown is the fact that the British-originated Metro release reunites the producer-director-star team that two years ago carved out a fine little "sleeper" thriller titled "Village of the Damned." A graphic example of the overwhelming importance of the basic written material in determining the ultimate screen potential of a project.

Joanne Court's screenplay, drummed up from a novel by W. R. Burnett, relates the story of a supposed criminal mastermind (George Sanders) who arrives in Cairo to execute a foolproof jewel robbery job he has devised in prison, organizes a gang, successfully accomplishes the dirty work and then fails to realize any of the rewards for his painstaking efforts owing to an epidemic of little oversights, accidents and character miscalculations.

For a supposedly brilliantly blueprinted jewel theft, the robbery is a dud that might just as easily have been devised by a little old lady from Pasadena. What's more, the museum containing the art treasures is absurdly accessible to thieves and so poorly guarded that Egypt might just as well give its priceless Tut-ankh-Amum jewels away. And the characters of Sanders' hand-picked gang would have been rejected as shopworn types back in filmdom's late 1930s.

What merit there is in the picture is owed to the actors and director Wolf Rilla and his crew, who have done a commendable job with sparse material. That highly seasoned pro, Sanders, does an expert job, spiced by some classic takes as he lecherously admires a belly dancer at the outset. The device of having lechery serve as the undoing of this character is hackneyed (the same device was used in "Asphalt Jungle" 13 years ago), preposterous and inconsistent. Richard Johnson, an actor with a bright future, makes a vivid impression as one of the ill-fated gem thieves. Others who come on strong are Eric Pohlmann, John Meillon, Ahmed Mazhar, Walter Rilla, Kamal El Shennawy and Salah Nazmi, with distaff support from Faten Hamama, Chewikar and Mona.

Physical values of Cairo and vicinity, rarely seen on the screen, are a substantial asset. Art, musical and technical contributions to Ronald Kinnoch's production are thoroughly competent. *Tube.*

L'Ape Regina
(The Queen Bee)
(ITALO-FRENCH)

Rome, Jan. 22.

Incei release of a Sancrofilm-Fairfilm-Les Films Marceaux-Cocinor (Paris) co-production. Stars Ugo Tognazzi, Marina Vlady; features Walter Giller, Linda Sini, Riccardo Fellini, Igi Polidoro, Achille Maieroni, Nino Vingelli. Directed by Marco Ferreri. Story and screenplay, Ferreri, Rafael Azcona, Diego Fabbri, Massimo Franciosa, P. F. Campanile; camera, Ennio Guarnieri; editor, Lionello Massobrio; music, Teo Usuelli. Previewed in Rome. Running time, **95 MINS.**

Alfonso	Ugo Tognazzi
Regina	Marina Vlady
Riccardo	Riccardo Fellini
Frate Mariano	Waltêr Giller
Igi	Igi Polidoro

Neatly fashioned arter with an intriguing, grimly humorous and thought-provoking theme. Has Vlady and Tognazzi names for added Italo lure, but its most saleable factor should be word-of-mouth, both here and abroad. In its special offbeat slot, pic rates definite foreign attention.

If told in straightforward fashion, plot about middleaged man who marries a young girl and dies when he is finally able to father a child by her, is routine. But writer-director Ferreri and his collaborators have imbued the film with sharp innuendoes and grotesquely handled symbolisms. One main theme, for example, grimly comments and spoofs man's growingly secondary station in life and the increasingly dominant place being won in business, social life and sex by woman.

Despite the symbolic trappings which might have bogged down a lesser effort, Ferreri has kept the pace moving without lags. Script occasionally over-indulges in more or less barbed comments about church conventions. This production is likely to arouse censorship attention in some areas.

Ugo Tognazzi is excellent as the harassed man who succumbs to "Queen Bee" Marina Vlady, strikingly beautiful as his demanding wife. Riccardo Fellini (the director's brother) is aptly "normal" as Tognazzi's friend while a large cast gives fine backing. A special nod goes to Igi Polidoro as another member of a colorful household.

Music by Teo Usuelli is effectively used to counterpoint grotesque action, and makes for catchy listening. Technical credits are top-drawer. *Hawk.*

Les Hommes Veulent Vivre
(Man Wants to Live)
(French; English sub-titles)

Anti-nuclear research drama. Producers ignore Russian co-leadership in A-Bombs and make Uncle Sam alone the heavy. Unlikely to reach commercial market. Too crudely anti-U.S. propaganda.

Hollywood, Jan. 20.

Rene Pigneres and Gerard Beyout presentation of Leonide Moguy production. Stars Claudio Gora, John Justin, Jacqueline Huet, Yves Massard. (No character credits). Production and directed by Leonide Moguy; script by Moguy in collaboration with Henri Torres; music, Joseph Kosma. No distributor. Reviewed at Lytton Center of he Visual Ars, L.A., Jan. 17, 1963. Running time, **110 MINS.**

Reviewed for record only, this pic by Russian-born filmaker Leonide Moguy has been seen in U.S. only by United Nations' U Thant. It was screened here for the Hollywood Foreign Press Assn. as part of series for Golden Globe Award consideration.

Moguy, an international film figure who has worked primarily in French pix, spent a few years in the early '40's in Hollywood, working for Metro and Fox as director, screenwriter and co-producer.

He has attempted to create here a wide-screen view of the dangers, real and potential, of results of nuclear research to the world. It starts off as a taut, promising suspense in the "Seven Days to Noon" class but soon gets involved so deeply in its own propaganda that confusion takes over in writing, directing and acting. Making American nuclear research the heavy might be more acceptable if some mention had been made of Russia, whose interest in the field is hardly a secret. But other than a couple of vague, general remarks that could apply to any country other than the U.S. or France, no direct mention of Russia is made. Nor is any answer, other than the actions of the principals, offered for the problem.

The story, told in flashbacks, has a famous French physicist accepting a research post in America with the same team he had worked with during the war (supposedly the Manhattan Project). Engrossed in his work, he neglects his wife and child. When his American scientist-friend abandons the project because of his fear of the outcome, he stays on, even while his child dies of leukemia and his wife leaves him.

He finally quits himself after discovering the secret of a death ray. An associate steals the death ray formula but can't make it work and tries involving scientist with international group (whose rep has a Spanish-sounding name!)- interested in ray. Scientist kills him, destroys notes and calls police, which is point at which pic begins and ends.

Claudio Gora and Yves Massard as the "good" and "bad" scientists and Jacqueline Huet as the wife try but are never able to overcome the heavy, propaganda-ridden lines with which they're saddled. Justin, a Britisher, makes an unconvincing American but is otherwise plausible as the conscience-stricken researcher. Film has English soundtrack when conversations are between people speaking that tongue, otherwise subtitles are used.

Pic has some fascinating inside shots of nuclear plants, where much of action takes place, though no technical credits are given. Print shown was hampered by being exceptionally dark but indicated that general photography was above average. Newsreel foot-

age of ex-President Eisenhower, the late Pope Pius XII and scientist Albert Einstein are inserted to underscore pacifistic message.

Picture has limited appeal as commercial entry, even outside U.S., unless anti-war phase is exploited, but will find no market in America. *Robe.*

Venere Imperiale
(Imperial Venus)
(ITALO-FRENCH)
(Color)

Rome, Jan. 22.
Cineriz release of a Royal Film (Guido Giambartolomei)-Cineriz (Rome)-S. N. E. Gaumont-France Cinema Productions (Paris) coproduction. Stars Gina Lollobrigida, Stephen Boyd; features Raymond Pellegrin, Micheline Presle, Gabriele Ferzetti, Giulio Rosetti, Massimo Girotti, Gianni Santuccio. Directed by Jean Delannoy. Screenplay, Delannoy, Jean Aurenche, R. M. Arlaud, Leonardo Benvenut, Piero de Bernardi; English dialog, John Michael Hayes; Clarke Reynolds; French dialog, Jean Aurenche, Philipe Heriat; camera (Technicolor), Gabor Pogany; music, Angelo Lavagnino. At Corso Cinema. Rome. Running time, **140 MINS.**

Paolina	Gina Lollobrigida
Jules de Canouville	Stephen Boyd
Freron	Gabrielle Ferzetti
Napoleon	Raymond Pellegrin
Josephine	Micheline Presle
Leclerc	Massimo Girotti
Camillo Borghese	Giulio Bosetti
Canova	Gianni Santuccio

(*'In English'*)

Jean Delannoy has fashioned a quality spectacle with the important assist of a script cut several notches above the norm for this type of film. Lollobrigida and Boyd names, coupled with title and a strong bally effort, should see this expensively-outfitted and lavishly-produced item off to strong grosses in general situations around the globe.

Payoff in English-language areas could be given a healthy boost. But it will in any case be conditioned by the original English language version which was shot side-by-side with French-Italian. So far it has been unavailable for reviewing. (These comments are based on final Italo print, as locally released).

This details the various amorous adventures, gleaned from historical hints and facts, of Napoleon's man-chasing sister, Paolina, from her first flirts with Freron, to an early affair with de Canouville and then to marriage with general Leclerc interspersed with various escapades until Leclerc's death in the colonies. Marriage with the Roman Prince Borghese follows and then a renewed and now scandalous affair with de Canouville ending in his death in the Russian campaign. Through it all, the pic plays up the almost morbidly jealous loyalty between Napoleon and his errant sister.

The script is literate, intelligent, almost consistently tongue-in-cheek in the best French tradition, at least in the version seen. Though there's a tendency towards scenes resolved in dialog, there's' more than enough spectacle to satisfy lovers of the grandiose. Gabor Pogany has done an outstanding job in capturing the settings of the era with his Technicolor camera.

Gina Lollobrigida has seldom looked lovelier than in this tailor-made part. And she vivaciously goes through her paces in a thoroughly pro performance. Stephen Boyd likewise comes through with a strong and ingratiating performance as her favorite lover. In other roles, Raymond Pellegrin is excellent as Napoleon, Giulio Bosetti properly dull as Borghese and Massimo Girotti puzzled as General Leclerc. Hosts of minor players fill other roles. As noted lensing is top-notch, and Angelo Lavagnino's musical score registers aptly. Editing could be somewhat tighter. Other production values are outstanding. *Hawk.*

Papa's Delicate Condition
(TECHNICOLOR)

Broad treatment of life with Corinne Griffith's father depends heavily on clowning of Jackie Gleason; could make it with inspired promotion.

Los Angeles, Jan. 29.
Paramount Pictures release of Amro Production (Jack Rose). Stars Jackie Gleason. Features Glynis Johns, Charlie Ruggles, Laurel Goodwin, Linda Bruhl. Directed by George Marshall. Screenplay by Rose, based on book by Corinne Griffith; camera (Technicolor), Loyal Griggs; editor, Frank Keller; art directors, Hal Pereira, Arthur Lonergan; music, Joseph J. Lilley (song "Call Me Irresponsible," Sammy Cahn, James Van Heusen); sound, Gene Merritt, Charles Grenzbach; asst. director, Arthur Jacobson. Reviewed at studio, Jan. 28, '63. Running time, **98 MINS.**

Jack "Papa" Griffith	Jackie Gleason
Ambolyn Griffith	Glynis Johns
Grandpa Anthony Ghio	Charlie Ruggles
Augusta Griffith	Laurel Goodwin
Corrie	Linda Bruhl
"Sparrow" Wildman	Ned Glass
Mister Harvey	Murray Hamilton
Mister Keith	Elisha Cook
Hiram Cosgrove	Charles Lane
Norman	Claude Johnson
Mr. Looby	Don Beddoe
Ellie	Juanita Moore
Stanley Henderson II	Trevor Bardette
Walter	Ken Reynard
Douglas	Benny Baker

This cinematic treatment of screen star Corinne Griffith's book about her father breaks through a heavy coating of synthetic "charm" to leave a generally pleasant aftertaste. Most of this success, however, is due to the flickers of rebellion on the part of its script-manacled star than to the Polly-andrewish plot.

The current interest in the multiple activities of Gleason and some smart selling by Paramount could give the treacly effort the needed spurt to carry it to success. As general family fare, it's a borderline vehicle because of the "condition" involved.

In pre-WW I Grangeville, Texas, the Griffith household is a happy one. There's one fly in the ointment—Papa (Jackie Gleason) has a yen for joy juice that, while never resulting in a lost weekend, is responsible for his erratic behavior while in that "delicate condition." With a loving but unsympathetic wife (Glynis Johns) and older daughter (Laurel Goodwin), his one unfailing source of sympathy and understanding is his doting six-year-old, Corinne (Linda Bruhl).

Papa blows the works, however, when, in an effort to buy a pony and cart for Corinne from a flea-bitten circus, he's conned into taking on the whole works (and its previously unmentioned debts). Mama takes off for Texarkana where her Papa (Charlie Ruggles) is mayor, and takes the kids with her. Oh, yes, Virginia, there is a happy ending and it includes the circus, so just sit still and eat your popcorn.

Somewhere along the way, but near the beginning, Jack Rose—as producer or writer, possibly both—got sidetracked into loading a slight but colorful story with classic cliches and antique situations. His script is guilty of a certain lack of honesty inasmuch as Papa, a known tippler, is never actually shown in his cups, thereby failing to create the indicated sympathy for the family. There's one exception—played for comedy —a recrimination solo scene in which the rotund rounder admits his irresponsibility to his skipped-out mate's dressmaker's dummy.

Gleason, within the tightly-drawn confines of his role, makes a valiant effort to inject some variety into it. A blown-up variation of a character he might have conceived for a tv skit, the general impression is that he's been on too long, and knows it. It is frequently a puzzle as to whether it is George Marshall or Gleason directing, but there's no doubt that it is when he's forced (or allowed) to interpolate bits of his tv characters that the film comes alive.

Often enough to hold the interest of the viewer, he overrides the plot for a brief scene of hilarity: visually mimicking a croaky vocalist; amiably blackmailing his friends into becoming partners in a drugstore; a wonderful double-take with a glass of milk; some delightful byplay with an apple-polishing chimp. He and Miss Johns make a close-to-mawkish farewell scene poignant and heartwarming.

Although they're credited with "co-star" billing, whatever that means, Miss Johns, Ruggles, and the Misses Goodwin and Bruhl have little to do but feed lines to Gleason and fill in his brief absences from the screen. Miss Goodwin, particularly, has the least role for the most billing of any actress in years. Miss Johns comes over best in her scenes with the diminutive Miss Bruhl — a delightful child, with a sandpapery voice and a button-nose, tomboyish face, she seems uncomfortable in her frilled and furbelowed costumes. But, no doubt, so were all the over-dressed little girls of that era. Ruggles is generally lost in an unbelievable part and a maze of silly dialogue.

Murray Hamilton and Elisha Cook as the circus owners; Don Beddoe as a neighbor with horrendous tastes in housepaint; Ken Reynard and Juanita Moore as the Griffith house servants; Benny Baker, Ned Glass, Charles Lane and Claude Johnson make up the types who wander in and out of the lives of the Griffiths.

Loyal Griggs' circus-y Technicolor camerawork does much to underscore the comic effect with a major assist from Edith Head's costumes. Pretty, if fussy, for the ladies, and some of the gaudiest (for Gleason) since "Jumbo." He wears them with aplomb. Frank Keller's attempt to pick up the pic's pace with some effective cutting is more valiant effort than marked success.

Robe.

The Raven
(PANAVISION—COLOR)

Prospective highgrossing comedy horror melodrama taking off from Edgar Allan Poe's poem.

Hollywood, Jan. 31.
American International Pictures release of Rober Corman production. Stars Vincent Price, Peter Lorre, Boris Karloff; features Hazel Court, Olive Burgess, Jack Nicholson. Directed by Corman. Screenplay, Richard Matheson, based on Edgar Allan Poe's "The Raven"; camera (Pathe-Color), Floyd Crosby; editor, Ronald Sinclair; music, Les Baxter; production designer, Daniel Haller; sound, John Bury; assistant director, Jack Bohrer. Reviewed at Pix Theatre, Jan. 30, '63. Running time, **85 MINS.**

Dr. Erasmus Craven	Vincent Price
Dr. Bedlo	Peter Lorre

Dr. Scarabus .... Boris Karloff
Lenore Craven .... Hazel Court
Estelle Craven .... Olive Sturgess
Rexford Bedlo .... Jack Nicholson
Maidservant .... Connie Wallace
Grimes .... William Baskin
Gort .... Aaron Saxon

Edgar Allan Poe might turn over in his crypt at this nonsensical adaptation of his immortal poem, but audiences will find the spooky going's-on of a flock of 15th Century English sorcerors as envisioned in this Roger Corman production, who handled for AIP's exec producers James H. Nicholson and Samuel Z. Arkoff, a corn-pop of considerable comedic dimensions. With a smart campaign to back it and following the success of past Poe picturizations at AIP, latest entry in what is to be a long series based on author's masterpieces should chalk up impressive grosses.

The Richard Matheson screenplay is a skillful, imaginative narrative of what comes to pass when there comes a rapping at magician Vincent Price's chamber-door by a raven—who else but Peter Lorre, a fellow magician, transformed by another sorceror, Boris Karloff.

Corman as producer-director takes this premise and develops it expertly as a horror-comedy climaxing with Price and Karloff engaging in a duel to the death in the black arts, each a master of the craft. Special effects figure prominently to add sometimes spectacular interest when the two hurl their talents at each other and Les Baxter's musical score is another assist in adding an eerie touch.

Characterizations are played straight for greater comedy value, sparked by sometimes ridiculous lines and situations. Price makes his theatricalism pay off as a sorceror who has been inactive since the apparent death of his wife, who, surprisingly, turns up at Karloff's castle, and latter plays it smooth as another of the brotherhood scheming to learn the secrets of Price's special magical powers. Lorre, whom Price helps to regain human form, is almost cute as a drunk who thinks he's a peer of the other two in their art.

Hazel Court as Price's sexy and conniving spouse; Olive Sturgess, his daughter, and Jack Nicholson, Lorre's son, lend effective support. William Baskin is in as a manservant who is bewitched by Karloff. Not the least convincing is Jim, Jr., the Raven, well trained by Moe Disesso.

Technical credits generally are superlative, particularly Pat Dinga's special effects, Floyd Crosby's color photography and Daniel Haller's lush production designing, paired with Harry Reif's set decorations. Ronald Sinclair's editing also is sharp. *Whit.*

Wild Is My Love

Haphazard exploitation item. Of interest, however, as a showcase for several promising young performers.

William Mishkin release of a General Films (Richard Hilliard) production. Features Elzabeth MacRae, Paul Hampton, Ray Fulmer, Bob Alexander. Directed by Richard Hilliard. Screenplay, Otto Lemming, with additional material by Hilliard; editor, Ray Pierce; music, Wilford Holcombe; camera, Emil Knebel, Louis MacMahon. Reviewed in N.Y., Jan. 28, '63. Running time, 74 MINS.

Queenie .... Elizabeth MacRae
Ben .... Paul Hampton
Aga .... Ray Fulmer
Zero .... Bob Alexander
Ralph Stanley, Gene Courtney, Carl Low, Mary Harrigan, Mick O'Dowd, Richard Forstmann, Victoria Ardiss, Jane Ross, Marge Randolph, Jezebel.

Somewhere within this 74-minute, lowbudget exploitation item, there is, perhaps, a funny, 25-minute featurette about three bored college boys, one of whom has a brief affair with a cornfed stripper who aspires—but not too consistently—to gentility. Producer-director Richard Hilliard and scenarist Otto Lemming, however, have padded the slight tale out to feature length by the inclusion of a silly, melodramatic subplot and some candidly photographed bump-and-grind footage. The picture also contains an unintentionally hilarious parody of the lovemaking sequence in that critically acclaimed French import of several seasons back: "Wild Is My Love" might be subtitled "Rutgers, Mon Amour."

The film does, however, serve as a showcase for some attractive young players, particularly Elizabeth MacRae, a real looker who plays the sweet but dumb stripper with a nice sense of sincerity and humor. Also good is Paul Hampton, as the college boy whose devotion to Miss MacRae convinces her that she ought to act like a lady (his disappointed reaction: "Why do you have to change now?"). Ray Fulmer and Bob Alexander, as Hampton's roommates, perform well in subsidiary roles. The other, older members of the cast simply look embarrassed at finding themselves in such a technically inept production.

Occasionally, when the script offers a scene of some real dramatic value, Hilliard's direction looks pretty good, as shown by a hair-raising sequence in which the roommates become involved in a game of Russian roulette. For the most part, however, the picture just stumbles along from inconclusive scene to inconclusive scene, the continuity hindered by choppy editing and eclectic camerawork in a wide range of styles. *Anby.*

Landru
(FRENCH—COLOR)
Paris, Feb. 5.

Lux release of Rome-Paris Film production. With Michele Morgan, Danielle Darrieux, Hildegarde Kneff, Charles Denner, Juliette Meyniel, Catherine Rouvel, Stephane Audran, Mary Marquet. Directed by Claude Chabrol. Screenplay, Francoise Sagan; camera (Eastmancolor), Jean Rabier; editor, Jacques Gaillard. At Bretagne, Paris. Running time, 110 MINS.
Celemine .... Michele Morgan
Berthe .... Danielle Darrieux
Landru .... Charles Denner
German .... Hildegarde Kneff
Flirt .... Juliette Meyniel
Fernande .... Stephane Audran
Old Woman .... Mary Marquet

A satiric, macabre comedy here is wound around the notorious French Bluebeard, Landru, who killed 11 women for their money to support his family. This is a spirited if uneven pic. It looms as having high biz potential here and could be a weighty foreign entry if well placed and sold.

The bald, bearded slayer is presented as a good family type against the bloodshed of the first World War, then going on. Personal newspaper ads get him meetings with lonely women, since there is a scarcity of men. He usually woos, wins them and then lures them to a country house where he finally does away with them. He does it for their money.

Eleven women pass in series of sketch-like scenes, done with a surefooted assurance and comedy flair that makes them acceptable rather than eerie. An aged English couple, Landru's strange but taking charm, and crafty female caricatures manage to keep it moving despite some repetitiveness of gags.

But Landru's capture, when recognized by the sister of a victim, and his subsequent trial attempt to give this a deeper significance not quite in keeping with its Grand Guignol early comedics.

The sop that war was killing far greater numbers than Landru, that he did it for his family, and that most of the women were simpering victims never quite comes off.

But this film's irreverence and balance in keeping it visually stimulating and bearable, stamp this an offbeater with potential.

Joe Levine's Embassy Pictures already has this for the U.S.

Charles Denner, in his first big screen role, develops a solid character of the engaging if sinister ladykiller. Michele Morgan, Danielle Darrieux, Hildegarde Kneff and others make good foils for this diabolical Don Juan.

Francoise Sagan has penned a deft, if sometimes repetitive, screenplay. Director Claude Chabrol has managed to walk the tightrope of taste, except for a few lapses, to make this an unusual offbeater. It will need a smart sell but could stack up as solid box-office fodder abroad. It is technically fine. *Mosk.*

30 Years Of Fun

New kix from the old flix. Entertaining and marketable compilation.

Hollywood, Feb. 8.
Twentieth-Fox release of Robert Youngson production. Includes Charlie Chaplin, Buster Keaton, Laurel & Hardy, Harry Langdon, Syd Chaplin, Charlie Chase, Snub Pollard, Billy Bevan, Phyllis Haver, Vernon Dent, Carter De Haven, Edna Purviance, Eric Campbell, Andy Clyde. Written by Youngson; music, Bernard Green, Jack Shaindlin. Reviewed at the studio, Feb. 8, '63. Running time, 85 MINS.

In this pressurized era of events and discoveries unfathomable to the average human intellect, how soothing and wistful to escape into the vacuum packed vitality of the realm of silent flickers. Courtesy of writer-producer Robert Youngson, 20th-Fox has come forth with a peek into a past as remote from 1963 as the banana peel to the neutron bomb. As in all compilations, there are ups and downs in "30 Years of Fun," but audiences young and old should find the total experience hearty and fascinating, and the picture should fit into a profitable niche in the current market, particularly in playoff dates.

The film spans a period from the Gay 90's through the frenetic 20's. Choice comedy shorties of those 30 years are linked by newsreel clips, providing a sense of historical continuity to the festivities. Thus the pratfalls of Chaplin, Keaton and others of their stature are roughly related to the current events of the years in which they worked.

Again it is Chaplin's genius that towers above his colleagues in cinematic comedy. No fewer than four separate demonstrations of Charlie's remarkable comic invention and cinema craftsmanship are woven into the fabric of Youngson's newest anthology. Others of note who cavort in and out of the film are Buster Keaton (who is seen in a memorable sequence in which he is trapped in a revolving water wheel), Harry Langdon, Syd Chaplin, the aptly-surnamed Charlie Chase, Billy Bevan, Snub Pollard, Phyllis Haver, Carter De Haven, and Stan Laurel and Oliver Hardy, seen on the occasion of their first appearance together on film ("Lucky Dog"), a partnership destined not to be resumed until a period of eight years had elapsed.

The linking footage is rewarding, too, ranging from the early efforts of the pioneering Lumiere Bros. through demonstrations of the character of the 20's, highlighted by a shot of an enterprising fellow sopping up with a sponge a stream of alcohol coursing down the gutter after it has poured out of a barrel punctured by a conscientious prohibitionist, and wringing the joyously soaked sponge into a container until he is confronted by an unappreciative cop.

Music complimentary in tempo and character to the spirit of the silent action has been composed and integrated by Bernard Green and Jack Shaindlin. Narration of Youngson's informative script is spoken by Jay Jackson. Associate producers were Alfred Dahlen and John E. Allen. A wistful song, "Bring Back the Laughter," composed by Youngson and sung by Bernie Knee, opens and closes the picture. "30 Years of Fun" was, and is. *Tube.*

This Sporting Life
(BRITISH)

Highly charged, impressive performance by Richard Harris in the latest of Britain's down-to-earth dramas. Pic tingles with vitality, and should prove strong b.o. contender.

London, Feb. 5.

Rank release of a Julian Wintle-Leslie Parkyn (Karel Reisz) production for Independent Artists. Stars Richard Harris, Rachel Roberts; features Alan Badel, William Hartnell, Colin Blakely, Vanda Godsell, Jack Watson, Arthur Lowe. Directed by Lindsay Anderson. Screenplay by David Storey from his own novel; camera, Denys Coop; editor, Peter Taylor; music, Robert Gerhard. Previewed at R.F.D. Private Theatre, London. Running time, **134 MINS.**

Frank Machin .... Richard Harris
Mrs. Hammond .... Rachel Roberts
Weaver .... Alan Badel
Johnson .... William Hartnell
Maurice Braithwaite ...... Colin Blakely
Mrs. Weaver .... Vanda Godsell
Judith .... Anne Cunningham
Len Miller .... Jack Watson
Slomer .... Arthur Lowe
Mrs. Farrer .... Katharine Parr
Lynda .... Bernadctte Benson
Ian .... Andrew Nolan
Doctor .... Peter Duguid
Waiter .... Wallas Eaton
Head Waiter .... Anthony Woodruff
Gower .... Tom Clegg
Trainer .... Ken Traill
Dentist .... Frank Windsor
Cameron .... John Gill

Set in the raw, earthy mood of such British pix as "Saturday Night and Sunday Morning," "Taste of Honey" and "Room At Top" this latest entry **is a** powerful newcomer. It has a gutsy vitality that should catch the masses. But the pic also has enough classiness in its direction, writing and acting to make it a superior contender for most boxoffice stakes. The North Country accents should not harm the production's prospects anymore than the Midland burr of "Saturday Night" did.

Two highlight performances by Richard Harris and Rachel Roberts (Rex Harrison's wife) are supported by a fairly unknown if handpicked cast. Karel Reisz, who directed "Saturday Night," produced this one and his influence can clearly be seen. Lindsay Anderson, a top documentary director, making his debut as a feature director, has brought the keen, observant eye of a documentary man to many vivid episodes without sacrificing the story line. Based on a click novel by David Storey, who also scribed the screenplay, the yarn has a sporting background in that it concerns professional rugby football. But those exhibitors, to whom a film concerning sport sniffs of death and disaster at the wickets, can relax. Though there's a strong and well portrayed sports atmosphere in action and locale this is really the study of a confused young man and his blundering attempts to find his own little farmyard where he can crow more loudly than the other cocks around him. The story of Frank Machin (Richard Harris) would have been just as holding if he had chosen some other field but rugby into which to strut and bolster his own ego.

Harris plays a miner who, at first, resents the hero - worship heaped on players of the local football team. But he has second thoughts. He gets a trial and soon becomes the skillful, ruthless star of his team. He revels in his new prosperity, and preens at the adulation that's showered on his bullet head. He doesn't realize that he is being used by local businessmen opportunists. He refuses to believe that most of the hangerson regard him as an "ape performing on the football field."

He learns the lesson too late when he hears the cheers turning to jeers. Meanwhile, he's also lost, by his oafish behavior, the one thing for which he is blindly clutching, the chance to love and be loved. He lodges with a repressed widow nursing a kingsize chip on her shoulder. She becomes his mistress but cannot give him the complete affection he needs. Not till she lies on her death bed does he realize, again too late, that his pigheaded, unimaginative lack of tact and real feeling has been the reason for her fate.

Some of the early continuity and flashbacks are slightly confusing while the ending is a shade oversentimental. But Anderson has directed with fluid skill and sharp editing keeps the film moving, even at its more leisurely moments. Denys Coop's lensing is graphic and the atmosphere of a Northern town is captured soundly.

Among the varied sequences which impress are a horrifying quarrel between Harris and Miss Roberts, a hospital death scene, a poignant interlude at a wedding when Harris first approaches the moment of truth, a rowdy Christmas party and a countryside excursion when Harris plays with the widow's two youngsters. The football scenes have a live authenticity.

Harris, last seen in "Mutiny On The Bounty," gives a dominating, intelligent performance as the arrogant, blustering, fundamentally simple and insecure footballer. His acting has a fierce allout tempo. Yet on two or three occasions, he shows a quiet tenderness and warmth. He is clearly a standout screen personality as well as an impressive actor. Miss Roberts brings commendable light and shade as well as poignance to a role that might have been shadowy and overly downbeat. Of the remainder of a stalwart cast, William Hartnell, Colin Blakely, Arthur Lowe, Vanda Godsell and, particularly, Alan Badel, as the conniving football director who, for his own ends, builds up Harris and then tries to destroy him, all give valiant support.

"Sporting Life" may well be one of the last hits of the recent cult of films of the "Saturday Night" genre, though several are still on the way. But this will be remembered as one of the more satisfying ones. ***Rich.***

La Glaive Et La Balance
(The Sword and the Balance)
(FRENCH-FRANSCOPE)

Paris, Feb. 5.

Gaumont release of Gaumont-Trianon-Ultra production. Stars Anthony Perkins, Jean-Claude Brialy, Renato Salvatori; features Pascale Audret, Marie Dea. Directed by Andre Cayatte. Screenplay, Charles Spaak, Henri Jeanson, Cayatte; camera, Roger Fellous; editor, Paul Cayatte. At Colisee, Paris. Running time, **140 MINS.**

Johnny .... Anthony Perkins
Jean .... Jean-Claude Brialy
Francois .... Renato Salvatori
Agnes .... Pascale Audret
Winters .... Marie Dea

As the title indicates, Andre Cayatte, who made "Justice is Done" and "We Are All Murderers," again takes a look at the injustice that might be inherent in meting out punishment. He stacks the cards in this one and lays it on too thick didactically. But the yarn is well spun, if sketchy, and with enough provocation to insure okay international playoff as well as specialized spots abroad.

Three young men, one an American drifter trying to paint sans talent, one a farm boy who has become a gigolo, and a crafty real estate man not above using his nubile sister to bate Americans, are captured after a kidnaping. But only two men had been chased and one might be innocent.

On this peg Cayatte builds his look at justice. He craftily fills in character aspects on the three via flashbacks and then shows the baffled police and court people plus the hung jury which finally acquits them. But an enraged mob does away with them as a voice intones about justice.

Film touches on too many things to make its point effectively, but it does build up some good looks at wild Riviera youth, court procedure and jury haggling. If it is about wayward youth it is cursory, its slaps at human pettiness are obvious and its characters petty drifters till they suddenly, either two of them or the three in cahoots, kidnap and coldbloodedly kill the child when they think themselves betrayed.

Comic scenes are dragged in to break the mood. This tries to have it both ways in being a serious look at justice, a suspense pic and a more general look at the sorrier aspects of society.

Anthony Perkins uses his petulant boyishness well and is amply backed by Renato Salvatori, as the gigolo, and Jean-Claude Brialy, as the salesman-panderer. Cayatte has a feel for recounting a story but hammers away at too many points.

Metro - Goldwyn - Mayer backed this through their local outfit, Gaumont-International, and has what looks like a fine bet for the Continent. *Mosk.*

Transport Z Raje
(Transport From Paradise)
(CZECH)

Berlin, Feb. 5.

Czech State Film Barrandov production and release. Directed by Zbyniz Brynych. With Zdenek Stepanek, Cestmir Randa, Jiri Vrstala, Ilju Prachar. Screenplay, Arnost Lustig, from novel, "Night and Hope" by Lustig; camera, Jan Curik; music, Jiri Sternwald; editor, Jiri Hajek. Previewed at Czech Film Studio, West Berln. Running time, **100 MINS.**

This Czech production revolves around twenty-four hours in the Nazi concentration camp of Theresienstadt. More precisely, it depicts the time and procedures before another transport goes off to the brutal destination of the gas chambers. The action centers on various Jewish individuals and SS beasts. Yet this isn't just another concentration camp feature pic.

Director Brynych tells the gruesome tale in a more epic than dramatic manner. As per its demanding style, film is primarily an item for festivals and the arty cinemas. It has several assets to its credit but there are also some drawbacks. In all, however, it remains a highly interesting, ambitious and quite depressing film.

Theresienstadt was a "model camp" of the Nazis who cynically referred to it as a "town which the Fuehrer donated to the Jews" Here the Jews had "a relatively good time." There were no gas chambers and the Jews even had their own administration, banks, stores, etc. It was a camp that was open to neutral inspection. In this film the arrival of representatives of the Danish Red Cross is expected momentarily. **But, of course, the infamous SS leaders didn't reveal that Theresienstadt was only a "waiting camp" or a transit camp for Auschwitz which meant death by gas.**

The film has a strong documentary flavor because of the fact that nearly all of it has been shot in authentic Theresienstadt **and** all the different nationals (the Jewish victims) speak their own language. Director Brynych has caught the depressing monotony of the camp life with great skill and has been helped by outstanding camerawork by Jan Curik. Militating against the good overall impression is his tendency to exaggerate symbolisms and some jerkiness in storytelling.

Cast is well chosen. There are several bits of outstanding acting but, unfortunately, also some overly cliche portrayals of the SS henchmen. Nevertheless this is a gripping piece of cinema art. *Hanz.*

The Wrong Arm Of The Law
(BRITISH)

Lively cops-and-robbers farce with Peter Sellers as top comedy name keeping up fairly constant yock production. Breezy boxoffice prospects.

London, Feb. 5.

British Lion release, through BLC, of a Romulus (Robert Velaise-Aubrey Baring), production. Stars Peter Sellers, Lionel Jeffries, Bernard Cribbins; features Davy Kaye, Nanette Newman, Bill Kerr, John Le Mesurier, Graham Stark, Ed Devereaux, Martin Boddey, Irene Browne, Vanda Godsell, Tutte Lemkov, Dennis Price, John Junkin. Directed by Cliff Owen. Written by Ray Galton, Alan Simpson, John Antrobus from screenplay by John Warren, Len Heath based on an original story by Ivor Jay, William Winstance Smith; camera, Ernest Stewart; music, Richard Rodney Bennett; editor, Tristam Cones. Previewed at Columbia Theatres, London. Running time, **94 MINS.**

Pearly Gates .... Peter Sellers
Inspector Parker .... Leslie Jeffries
Nervous O'Toole ...... Bernard Cribbins
Trainer King .... Davy Kaye
Valerie .... Nanette Newman
Jack Coombes .... Bill Kerr
Bluey May .... Ed Devereaux
Reg Denton .... Reg Lye
Assnt. Commissioner....John Le Mesurier
Sid Cooper .... Graham Stark
Supt. Forest .... Martin Boddey
Educated Ernie .... Dennis Price
Maurice .... John Junkin
Man in Apartment......... Dick Emery
Dowager .... Irene Browne
Brassknuckles .. .. Arthur Mullard
Misery Martin .... Dermot Kelly
Annette .... Vanda Godsell
Alf .... Barry Keegan
Siggy Schmultz .... Tutte Lemkov

A slightweight cops and robbers idea has been pepped up into a briskly amusing farce thanks to a combo of deft direction, thesping and writing. Presence of Peter Sellers and other such expert farceurs as Lionel Jeffries, John Le Mesurier and Bernard Cribbins should insure sweet boxoffice. Written by the authors of Tony Hancock's original tv series, Ray Galton and Alan Simpson, with the assistance of "Goon" writer John Antrobus, the screenplay has a fair turn of wit and a number of excellent whacky situations.

Sellers runs a top league West End dress salon as Monsieur Jules. But that's only a front. As Pearly Gates, he is the Cockney King of the Underworld. He has organized things so that no two gangs work the same territory. His own gang he runs on Welfare State lines, with free luncheon vouchers, bubbly on Sundays, holidays with pay on the Costa Brava.

Everything's going fine until the police swoop on the gang job after job, though they never make arrests, but simply confiscate the loot. Sellers realizes that an I.P.O. (Impersonating Police Officers) mob is in town. He calls an extraordinary general meeting of London's crime syndicates, negotiates with Scotland Yard and arranges for a 24-hour crime truce so that the police can concentrate on running in the I.P.O. gang. The Yard sets a trap, faking a bullion robberty for Sellers with one of their own men (Lionel Jeffries) assigned to the gang as liaison officer. Things work up to a hilarious climax as everything goes predictably wrong. Sellers makes a getaway with the loot but, of course, it is fake currency to justify the old cliche that crime mustn't pay.

Sellers has a fat part as the gangster with modern methods (for instance, he makes his gang attend evenings of educational films such as "Rififi"). And he brings his usual alert intelligence to the role. He is surrounded with some sharp talent. Jeffries amusingly plays another of his well-meaning, blundering police officers while John Le Mesurier brings dry gravity to the role of a commissioner of the police. Among the assorted gangsters, Bernard Cribbins, Bill Kerr, Davy Kaye and Graham Stark have some bright opportunities.

Nanette Newman has the only considerable femme role, as Sellers' girl friend who is also informing on him to the gang of Australian bogus police officers. Miss Newman looks ready now for meatier roles. The writers have provided some firstclass situations. There is a provocative bedroom scene between Sellers and Miss Newman, a standout sequence when the crime syndicate calls its extraordinary general meeting and also a pleasant idea when the meeting between the plain clothes police officers and the leaders of the gangs is scheduled for neutral territory and actually takes place on a carousel.

Cliff Owen has directed with verve. Locations and all technical credits help to give polish to a breezy, likeable comedy. *Rich.*

Nine Hours to Rama
(C'SCOPE—COLOR)

Incisive and intriguing historical drama concerned with nine hours leading up to assassination of Mahatma Gandhi by a bitter and confused young fanatic. Flaws around the edges but overall strength. If stylishly sold, could score at b.o.

Hollywood, Feb. 13.
Twentieth-Fox release of Mark Robson production. Stars Horst Buchholz, Jose Ferrer, Valerie Gearon, Don Borisenko, Robert Morley, Diane Baker. Directed by Robson. Screenplay, Nelson Gidding, based on novel by Stanley Wolpert: camera (De Luxe), Arthur Ibbetson; editor, Ernest Walter; music, Malcolm Arnold; assistant director, Kip Gowans. Reviewed at the studio, Feb. 13, '63. Running time, 125 MINS.

Nathuram Godse	Horst Buchholz
Superintendent Das	Jose Ferrer
Rani Mehta	Valerie Gearon
Narayan Apte	Don Borisenko
P. K. Mussadi	Robert Morley
Shiela	Diane Baker
General Singh	Harry Andrews
G. D. Birla	Jairaj
Detective Munda	David Abraham
Mother	Achla Sachdev
Karnick	Marne Maitland
Selvraj Prahlad	Harold Goldblatt
Detective Bose	Wolfe Morris
Ram Pure	Francis Matthews
Fagin Mehta	Narendra Nath
Pilpatrick	Jack Hedley
Mahatma Gandhi	J. S. Casshyap

At the core, this dramatization of circumstances surrounding the assassination of Mahatma Gandhi is an achievement of insight and impact. Close inspection by fussier customers will reveal plenty of wear and tear around the edges, but the film's weaknesses are overshadowed by its strengths. So although the Mark Robson production for 20th-Fox is limited in marquee appeal, its historical significance, rich cultural values and basic dramatic voltage should attract filmgoers. Original and dynamic selling will have to lure audiences less influenced by artistic merit than by the glamour of star names and other such commercial salad dressing.

The success of a drama focusing its attention on the assassinator of a great man is to make the character of the killer dimensional and clearly motivated. This insight and clarity are achieved in Nelson Gidding's screenplay from Stanley Wolpert's novel and bolstered by Horst Buchholz's virile portrayal of the perpetrator of one of the most reprehensible acts in the history of mankind.

For those who may have forgotten, Gandhi's assassination was devised and executed by a fanatic secret faction of his own Hindu followers who blamed his doctrine of passive resistance for their misfortunes in the internal struggle against the Moslems. The complex passions that motivated this misguided faction have been expertly synthesized into this one character so that, although the outcome is known, enough concern and sympathy has been aroused for the killer to keep the viewer on the edge of his seat right down to the foregone conclusion. Action of the drama takes place in the nine-hour span culminating with the fatal measure, with several flashback passages to illustrate the incidents of the past that contributed to the unstable frame of mind of a young man who would murder a person of Gandhi's stature.

The story falls down in its development and clarification of certain key secondary characters implicated in the deadly issue. A married woman (Valerie Gearon) for whom the killer-to-be has fallen does not make very much sense. Her love for him seems to have no real foundation other than one of instant chemistry. They are utterly incompatible from the word go, and the explanation that "opposites attract" is hardly sufficient or convincing. And her abrupt metamorphosis from sophisticated lady of the world to devout doman of India in the final scene is both superfluous and dramatically awkward. Several other important characters, too, are poorly defined, among them the assassin's unwilling accomplice (Don Borisenko), a baffling Indian politico (Robert Morley) and an impulsive prostitute (Diane Baker). But, stacked up against the force of the heart of the matter, these are relatively minor capillary breaks in a fundamentally healthy specimen.

Buchholz, as noted, delivers a performance of intensity and conviction. He's now one of the screen's finest young actors. Jose Ferrer is excellent as a desperately concerned and conscientious police superintendent guarding Gandhi against disheartening odds. An astonishingly accurate personification of the latter is etched by J. S. Casshyap. Miss Gearon, a beautiful woman, plays Buchholz's lady love with grace, delicacy and sincerity. Borisenko is appealing as the killer's uncertain sidekick, Miss Baker capable as the prostie, and Morley his reliable self as the politician. Among those in support who merit praise are Harry Andrews, Jairaj, David Abraham, Achla Sachdev, Marne Maitland and Harold Goldblatt.

Film is an outstanding effort, on both counts by producer-director Robson. It has been accomplished with scope, style, taste and intelligence. De Luxe colored views of India captured artfully through Arthur Ibbetson's lens are fascinating. Expert celluloidal knitting by editor Ernest Walter, particularly in management of flashback transitions, keeps the story moving smoothly and with momentum. Artwork by Elliot Scott is careful and attentive to detail and locale. An exotic Indianesque score has been composed by Malcolm Arnold. It is especially effective behind the imaginative main titles by Saul Bass. *Tube.*

Tempo Di Roma
(Roman Rhythm)
(FRENCH—FRANSCOPE)

Paris, Feb. 12.
Pathe release of Cyclops production. Stars Charles Aznavour; features Arletty, Gregor Von Ressori, Marisa Merlini, Serena Vergano. Directed by Denys De La Patelliere. Screenplay, Pascal Jardin, De La Patelliere from novel by Alexis Curvers; camera, Marcel Grignon; editor, Renee Lichtig. At Avenue, Paris. Running time, 90 MINS.

Marcello	Charles Abnavour
Marquise	Arletty
Sir Craven	Gregor Von Rezzori
Pia	Marisa Merlini
Geronima	Serena Vergano

This unassuming pic is a rambling account of a stranded little Frenchman in Rome who ends up finding friendship and love. But a dearth of plot structure, much inventiveness or characterization have this primarily a local item on the name pull of Charles Aznavour.

Aznavour plays a gentle little man with feeling, but the complacent sentimentality of the film strains even this talented thesp's credulity. He becomes a guide, though not knowing the city, is helped by an eccentric noblewoman and coveted by a strange rich man for some unnamed reason. He also finds love with a pretty Italian girl.

Aznavour sometimes gives this a measure of bright situation comedy in his scenes as guide, taking a test or studying for it. But all this relies on a touristic look at Italy. If this is the result of greater Common Market collaboration, it is not the right route.

Fresher scripting and insight are called for. Director Denys De La Patelliere rarely pulls this uneven production. It is only intermittently amusing and technically par. *Mosk.*

Le Meurtrier
(The Murderer)
(FRENCH—FRANSCOPE)

Paris, Feb. 12.
Cocinor release of Cocinor Marceau-International-Sancro-Corona Film production. Stars Marina Vlady, Maurice Ronet; features Robert Hossein, Gert Froebe, Yvonne Furneaux. Directed by Claude Autant-Lara. Screenplay, Jean Aurenche, Pierre Bost from novel by Patricia Highsmith; camera, Jacques Natteau; editor, Madeleine Gug. At Ermitage, Paris. Running time, 115 MINS.

Saccard	Maurice Ronet
Ellie	Marina Vlady
Corbi	Robert Hossein
Kimmel	Gert Froebe
Clara	Yvonne Furneaux

Attempt at a psychological-suspense murder film comes a cropper because of skimpy characterizations, overplaying and lacklustre direction. It appears primarily a local item with foreign spots mainly for dualer use on its theme.

A man with a neurotic wife, who will not give him a divorce, is arrested for a crime in which a husband is declared innocent. He thinks of killing his own wife but can not do it. When she commits suicide, he is blamed.

But a wily, violent police inspector links the two crimes and the two men become opposed to each other. It seems the first really did kill his wife.

Idea of paralleling two crimes may work on paper but it does not get the film treatment here to make it arresting. Gert Froebe overdoes his part of the real killer in an outmoded Teutonic manner. Robert Hossein is an unbelievable policeman.

Maurice Ronet and Marina Vlady are acceptable as the lovers but can not do much to give this film the dash and the drive it needs. Claude Autant-Lara has directed unevenly. Technical credits are okay. *Mosk.*

The Barber of Stanford Hill
(BRITISH)

Good quality dualer, though rather slight for general presentation.

London, Feb. 12.
British Lion release, through BLC, of a Ben Arbeid production. Stars John Bennett, Megs Jenkins, Maxwell Shaw. Directed by Casper Wrede. Written by Ronald Harwood; camera, Arthur Lavis; editor, Thelma Connell; music, George Hall. Reviewed at Hammer Theatre, London. Running time, 64 MINS.

Mrs. Werner	Megs Jenkins
Mr. Figg	John Bennett
Dober	Maxwell Shaw
Mr. Luster	John Graham
Willy	Trevor Peacock
Lennie	David Franks
Marilyn	Judi Bloom
Mother	Dilys Hamlett
First Customer	Eric Thompson
Mr. O	Wensley Pithey
Second Customer	Barry Keegan
Boy	Matthew Peters

This is a wellmade, well written, well conceived picture but, at 64 minutes, it has the air of a blown-up tele screenplay which is not quite strong enough to be anything but a useful dualer. It is a fantasy of a barber who is a bachelor and invents a dream world for his patrons in which he is a married man with two children. The lonely bachelor spends his Friday nights playing chess with a dumb friend under the glow of two candles lit in the Jewish tradition.

Tired of bachelordom, he decides to propose to a widow with two children. Here, he thinks, he will find all the joys of married life. But she disillusions him. He realizes that there are many drawbacks to marriage and he returns to his chess playing and his fantastic dream life with his customers.

Casper Wrede has directed with a sensitive feeling for this slight but poignant anecdote. Productionwise the film has been produced unextravagantly but effectively.

Megs Jenkins is convincing as the widow while John Bennett, as the bachelor-barber, and Maxwell Shaw, as his dumb, chess-playing friend, strike up an impressive accord. Barry Keegan Trevor Peacock, John Graham and Dilys Hamlett also chip in with useful contributions.

The team of producer Ben Arbeid, director Casper Wrede, writer Ronald Harwood, cameraman Arthur Lavis and music writer George Hall were responsible recently for the interesting offbeat picture, "Private Potter." And as a combo, they are one to be watched with interest. *Rich.*

The Winter Light
(SWEDISH)

Latest Ingmar Bergman film. Metaphysical puzzleplay for intellectuals. Heavy on introspection, shy on action.

Goteborg, Feb. 7.

A Svensk Film Industri product. Screenplay and directed by Ingmar Bergman. Stars Gunnar Bjornstrand and Ingrid Thulin; features Gunnel Lindblom, Max von Sydow, Allan Edwall. Previewed at Coshorama, Goteborg. Running Time, **83 MINS.**

Pastor	Gunnar Bjornstrand
Miss Lundberg	Ingrid Thulin
Fisherman	Max von Sydow
His Wife	Gunnel Lindblom
Sacristan	Tilan Edwall

Ingmar Bergman is apparently determined to explore every possible facet of the human soul. In this latest picture, "The Winter Light," he tackles faith, God, knowledge, loneliness, love and hate. meaning of life and suicide. All this through five actors and a church background.

A widowed village pastor fails to counsel a suicide-minded fisherman, a member of his parish, because he himself is not aware of the presence of faith in his mind. Neither is the pastor sure if he loves a middle-aged, desperately infatuated schoolteacher. Nor can he answer the obtrusive questions of his own sacristan, an invalid, who compares his own suffering with Jesus's agony on the cross.

When the depressed fisherman kills himself, the clergyman is still deep in doubts about God and Faith but he becomes certain that he does not want the love of the boring teacher. Everything is a problem. No solutions are apparent. The human mind has its limits. Before the empty church the pastor prepares the routine of worship.

Working with modest-seeming devices, this Bergman feature is without elements of sex, is lacking completely in physical violence. It adds up as a sort of philosophical puzzleplay meant for intellectuals. Still it has challenge and provocation. There is a scene when the disenchanted pastor reveals to his mistress how much disgusted he is with her love. It is a scene so brutal and ruthless as to be almost without remembered parallel on the screen.

As is his habit the director, who is practically synonymous with Sweden's film industry outside Sweden, uses his regular "stock company" of players, including Max von Sydow as the self-destroying fisherman, the same actor chosen for Jesus Christ in George Stevens' "Greatest Story Ever Told," now shooting in Utah.

Camera work is lowkey, another trademark of this unique creator. Sound and technical credits seem professional, although some film buffs combine their admiration of Bergman with charges that his technical work is sometimes careless, as if he were too preoccupied with metaphysics to be bothered with studio details.

Le Petit Soldat
(The Little Soldier)
(FRENCH)

Paris, Feb. 12.

SNC release of Georges De Beauregard production. With Michel Subor, Anna Karina Henri-Jacques Huet, Laszlo Szabo. Written and directed by Jean-Luc Godard. Camera. Raoul Coutard; editor, M. Yoyotte. At Marbeuf, Paris. Running time, **86 MINS.**

Bruno	Michel Subor
Veronika	Anna Karina
Jacques	Henri-Jacques Huet
Arab	Laszlo Szabo

Held up for three years because of mentions of torture in neutral territory by both sides during the recent Algerian War, this emerges more an espionage and love tale than a political gambit. Its talky aspects, jagged techniques and improvisation have this dated somewhat by now. But there is a crispness and dash that could have this an okay specialized item abroad if arty spots are limited while dualers may be in on its action aspects.

Jean-Luc Godard made this in Switzerland after his successful "Breathless." This too is full of jump cuts, ragged progression and impromptu performances. But Godard has a visual flair that keeps it bouncing along. He again paints a portrait of a tired, disillusioned youth who here turns to political killing and desertion rather than taking pictures of his girl, sharp and plotting uneven. But the scenes of love told via the so-called hero chase scenes, and a vividly-made gangsterism.

Characterizations are skin deep torture sequence give this some interest in spite of its uneven envelope.

Michel Subor has the right ingenuousness as the selfish youth who mixes in politics and kills and resists torture out of whim more than belief. Anna Karina, in her first screen vehicle, shows her bright film presence and budding thesp talents that were proved in later pix by Godard.

Fast film and on-the-spot shooting help give this some briskness. But it remains an uneven offering. *Mosk.*

Un Chileno En Espana
(CHILEAN)

Santiago, Feb. 12.

Produccioels Jose Bohr, released by Compania Cinematografica Nacional. Starring Manolo Gonzalez. Featuring Roberto Parada, Jose Guixe, Rosario Liansol, Salvador Cicero and Sergio Feito. Directed by Jose Bohr. Screenplay by Ricardo Montenegro (based on an idea by Jose Bohr). Camera, Jorge Morgado and Alex Phillips Jr. At Teatro Central. Running time, **106 MINS.**

The main asset of this Chilean feature is local funnyman Manolo Gonzalez, longtime star of the Teatro Opera revues. It concerns a waiter at Santiago's aristocratic Club de La Union, who plays court jester to the businessmen convening there and is given a winning lottery ticket by one of them. He then goes on a spending spree including a trip to Spain and finally returns home to the girl who all along has loved him in science. The plot is even thinner than it sounds. Supporting cast is poor and Jose Bohr's direction, haphazard and inadequate. Technical credits are also far from satisfactory.

What matters however is Manol Gonzalez, whose first pic this is. Though he does not create a character, his verbal and visual gags bring out the laughs. This, in spite of all round lack of quality has kept the B.O. moving at a pace that promises to set records for Chilean product. The film cost approximately $30,000 and is expected to bring in twice that amount in latin markets. *Chili.*

Spencer's Mountain
(PANAVISION—COLOR)

Tepid tale of a poor but noble quarry worker in Wyoming and his attempts to raise a large family.

Hollywood, Feb. 13.

Warner Bros. release of Delmer Daves production. Stars Henry Fonda, Maureen O'Hara, James MacArthur, Donald Crisp, Wally Cox; introduces Mimsy Farmer. Directed and screenplay by Daves; camera (Technicolor), Charles Lawton; editor, David Wages; music, Max Steiner; assistant director, Gil Kissel. Reviewed at the studio, Feb. 13, '63. Running time, **121 MINS.**

Clay Spencer	Henry Fonda
Olivia	Maureen O'Hara
Clayboy	James MacArthur
Grandpa	Donald Crisp
Preacher Goodson	Wally Cox
Claris	Mimsy Farmer
Miss Parker	Virginia Gregg
Grandma	Lillian Bronson
Dr. Campbell	Whit Bissell
Col. Coleman	Hayden Rorke
Minnie-Cora	Kathy Bennett
Percy Cook	Dub Taylor
Mother Ida	Mother Ida
Mr. John	Ken Mayer

In the vast expanse that constitutes the continental United States there are as many different types of people and ways of life as there are topographical varieties. In filming "Spencer's Mountain" for Warner Bros., scenarist-director-producer Delmer Daves has chosen one of the country's majestic scenic locales, the Grand Teton's, to background a quite ordinary, but generally enjoyable and often emotionally moving comedy-drama about a large, simple, hardworking family and its joys and disappointments from the cradle to the grave.

That's quite a slice of living, considering that three generations of Spencers move in and out of the story, not to overlook a wide assortment of townspeople with whom their lives are entwined to greater or lesser degree. In short, "Spencer's Mountain" is that modern-day American cinematic oddity, a story about family and small community life. To many the Spencers may seem more atypical than typical, since even country life—the kind a city-born one read or dreamed about as a child—isn't quite the same today, not in terms of externals, anyway, as of yore.

Delmer Daves, working from a novel (laid in Blue Ridge Mountain Country) by Earl Hamner Jr., has chosen to view the Spencers idealistically. This is an approach which suggests (to one viewer, in any event) that the Spencers are more symbolical than anything else of the basis of American heritage—the family that pulls together and walks straight with dignity and strength, which, after all, is more meaningful than the attainment of personal financial wealth—although, of course, that is not to be sneezed at either.

Anyway, Daves, with meaningful assistance by Henry Fonda and Maureen O'Hara and James MacArthur as their son standing on the threshold of adulthood, has produced a motion picture which, with only slight reservation, can be recommended to the family trade. A couple of romantic interludes, more through suggestion than deed, between MacArthur and Mimsy Farmer may be a little on the lusty side for the early teenagers.

But there is a tremendously good lesson for all in the relationship between Fonda and his parents, played with warmth by Donald Crisp and Lillian Bronson, as there is inspiration for the young who are plagued with uncertainties in the motto MacArthur's high-school teacher gives to him as a graduation present," The world will step aside for a man who knows where he is going."

Sophisticates may find "Spencer's Mountain" dramatically corny, but there are enough juicy kernels here to make this a satisfying and frequently delectable entertainment for the vast cross-section of film audiences. Hence, exhibs who take advantage of the inherent dramatic qualities as well as the more obviously exploitable elements should be rewarded with good to big boxoffice. In Panavision and Technicolor the picture is scenically superb. This isn't to surprising, however, since Daves, both as scenarist and director, has long demonstrated a truly cinematic perceptiveness in his work. And, of course, he is fortunate in having a cameraman with the talent of Charles Lawton at his side.

Actually Daves' script plays better than it sounds in synopsis for it is the interplay and incidents that spark humor and warmth, sentiment and a bit of boisterousness in the story which is motivated by the desire of uneducated parents to fulfill their son's desire for a college education when all that the father earns is required to keep food on the table for a brood of nine youngsters, plus husband-wife and grandparents. With less ingratiating and expert performers than Fonda and Miss O'Hara as the central characters the chances are Daves might have found himself in trouble. Fonda, in particular, can take what easily could have been an ordinary hayseed and invest such a role with depth, purposefulness and dignity

Wally Cox shines brightly, too, in the role of a minister who on his first day in town unwittingly gets stoned in the company of Fonda, who shuns the church like the plague but, in other respects, is a God-fearing citizen. Mimsy Farmer, making her screen debut, is an attractive blonde, but still needs seasoning as an actress. MacArthur handles with ease a role which does not actually make any special demands upon him and there are nice contributions as well by Virginia Gregg as the teacher; Whit Bissell, Hayden Rorke. Kathy Bennett, Dub Taylor, Hope Summers and Ken Mayer.

A lively group of child performers do what they were directed to do, and quite well, as the Fonda-O'Hara brood, but in several of these kiddie sequences Daves allows them to be almost too cute for words, and having a tot talk about "going on the toidy" once is enough. Indeed there are some scenes in this context which Daves and editor David Wages could yet trim to advantage. And they should catch a sequence in the library where Miss Farmer tells MacArthur to turn the key in the door from the inside, later tells him to unlock it, which he doesn't do,

and then she just turns the knob and walks out. Why give the boner-seekers the chance to point a finger at a picture which makes one feel there still is wondrous solidity in that great institution, the American family? *Pryr.*

Follow The Boys
(PANAVISION—COLOR)

Undernourished romanticomedy about Navy men and their ever-present wives and sweethearts.

Hollywood, Feb. 19.
Metro release of Lawrence P. Hachmann production. Stars Connie Francis, Paula Prentiss, Dany Robin, Janis Paige, Russ Tamblyn, Richard Lony; features Ron Randell, Roger Perry. Directed by Richard Thorpe. Screenplay, David T. Chantler, David Osborn, from original story by Bachmann; camera (Metrocolor), Ted Scaife; editor, John Victor Smith; music, Ron Goodwin, songs, Miss Francis, Dramsto Palumbo, Benny Davis & Ted Murray. Alexander Courage; asst. director. Jack Causey. Reviewed at studio, Feb. 19, '63. Running time, 96 MINS.

Bonnie	Connie Francis
Toni	Paula Prentiss
Michele	Dany Robin
Liz	Janis Paige
Smitty	Russ Tamblyn
Pete	Richard Long
Ben	Ron Randell
Billy	Roger Perry
Hulldown	Robert Nichols
C.M.A.A.	Paul Maxwell
Italian Farmer	Eric Pohlmann
Vittorio	David Sumner
Duty Officer	Sean Kelly
Commentator	John McLaren
Italian Barman	Roger Snowdon

Youth must be served, but the service isn't very good in this lacklustre romantic comedy about a group of gobs who find the same girls in every port—their faithfully itinerant wives or fiancees. Presumably aimed at the same largely teenage or young adult audience that embraced "Where The Boys Are," of which it is roughly —very roughly—a sequel, this Metro follow-up chugs along at a deliberate tempo and is propelled by a discouragingly flat script. The Lawrence P. Bachmann production decked out in Panavision and Metrocolor and manned by a youthful cast.

The David T. Chantler-David Osborn screenplay springs from a sufficiently pregnant premise by Bachmann, but is the victim of unimaginative comedy development. Heroines of the story are a group of girls dubbed "seagulls" because, like their namesake, they are perpetually following ships. The story dwells on four such couples and illustrates, haphazardly, their togetherness difficulties.

Problems of couple number one, a guileless singer (Connie Francis) and a radarman (Roger Perry) practicing to be a good husband by watching a blank radar screen and pretending it's a television set, is the fact they've never consummated their marriage (the groom got called to duty during their wedding breakfast). The marital relationship of couple number two (Janis Paige and Ron Randell) is in jeopardy because he prefers the seafaring life and she wants him on dry land. So, in the best husband-wife tradition, they come to a compromise. He agrees to get a land assignment and she agrees to the agreement.

Couples number three and four are all mixed up. The two guys (Russ Tamblyn and Richard Long) are wolfish swabbies of the breed

who seek a girl in every port and some port in every girl. But the lads get their signals crossed and Tamblyn winds up with the lass (Paula Prentiss) loosely affianced to Long, while Long gets collared by the gal (Dany Robin) intended for Tamblyn.

All of the performers labor under the handicap of an uninspired script and sluggish, slipshod direction—or lack of it—by Richard Thorpe. A lot of talent has been wasted in this enterprise. Miss Francis at least has the opportunity to croon several songs, which she does sweetly. Most of the tunes in the pic, including the title song were written by Benny Davis & Ted Murray. It marks Davis' return to cleffing after a long absence. Miss Franes' disking of title tune on MGM should help promote pic.

Adequate assists to the production have been made by cameraman Ted Scaife, editor John Victor Smith, art director Bill Andrews and score composers Ron Godwin and Alexander Courage. Filming took place in Nice, France. Was this trip necessary? *Tube.*

The Mind Benders

Offbeat British meller with exploitable values; primarily an art house entry.

American International release of a Michael Relph production. Stars Dirk Bogarde, Mary Ure; features John Clements, Michael Bryant, Wendy Craig. Directed by Basil Dearden. Screenplay, James Kennaway; music, Georges Auric; camera, Denys Coop; editor, John D. Guthridge. Previewed in N.Y., Feb. 1, '63. Running time, 101 MINS.

Dr. Henry Longman	Dirk Bogarde
Oonagh Longman	Mary Ure
Major Hall	John Clements
Dr. Tate	Michael Bryant
Annabelle	Wendy Craig
Professor Sharpey	Harold Goldblatt
Calder	Geoffrey Keen
Norman	Terry Palmer
Aubrey	Norman Bird
Dr. Jean Bonvoulois	Roger Delgado
Stewart	Edward Fox
Coach	Terence Alexander
Persephone	Georgina Moon
Penny	Teresa Van Hoorn
Paul	Timothy Beaton
Peers	Christopher Ellis
Porter	Edward Palmer

A British import, "The Mind Benders" is a sharp contrast to the "mass market" product usually associated with American International. For this Michael Relph production takes a novel and adult approach to sci-fi that makes the film more suitable as an art house candidate than for general release.

James Kennaway's original screenplay finds the peg for its bizarre plot in "reduction of sensation" experiments reportedly done both in the U.S. and Britain. By eliminating a subject's various senses by submerging him in an isolation tank a shortcut to brainwashing is achieved.

Film's introductory sequences follow conventional meller lines. But once the basic story pattern has been established, it moves into a fascinating study of how a man's mind can be twisted by a laboratory technique.

Suicide of elderly scientist Harold Goldblatt prompts an investigation by secret agent John Clements to determine whether military security has been violated. Clements suspects Goldblatt has turned traitor. But the scientist's associate, Dirk Bogarde, denies any treason has been committed and

blames Goldblatt's death as a result of the experiments.

Bogarde voluntarily submits to isolation to prove his theory. As part of the test Clements and another scientist, Michael Bryant, convince Bogarde that he does not love his wife, Mary Ure. Final reels wind up with a starkly dramatic childbirth scene whose shock helps Bogarde shake off the brainwashing. Realism of the delivery makes this import hardly ideal for the Saturday matinee trade.

Under Basil Dearden's firm direction, the cast absorbingly captures suspense and gruesome space age qualities frequently generated by Kennaway's script. Bogarde emerges as a dedicated scientist who shades his role with lotsa realism. Mary Ure's portrayal of the spurned wife is a touching piece of thesping.

Clements is the epitome of a secret investigator — relentless, suave and always sure of himself. Bryant turns in an emotional cameo as a scientist who has some misgivings about "mind bending" when it involves husband and wife. Wendy Craig is largely ornamental as a strumpet in whom Bogarde finds some momentary interest.

Goldblatt, Geoffrey Keen and Terry Palmer, among other players, provide good support. Denys Coop's camerawork adds to the dramatic impact as do Georges Auric's score, John D. Guthridge's editing and other technical credits.
Gilb.

The John Glenn Story
(COLOR)

Thirty-minute account of the famed astronaut's career that should find a profitable niche in more than one medium.

Hollywood, Feb. 14.
Warner Bros. release of William L. Hendricks production. Written by Hendricks; narrator, Jack Webb; camera, MSgt Walter W. Frank, GySgt Uel O. Graham; editor, J. Russell Graziano; production coordinator, Lt. Col. James R. Stockman; technical advisor, Col. A. D. Cereghino; production manager, WO James E. Carpenter. Reviewed at studio, Feb. 14, '63. Running time, 30 MINS.

"The John Glenn Story" is a straightforward biographical account of the background and achievements of the renowned U. S. astronaut. It is a 30-minute short subject sure to stir patriotic fervor. The Warner Bros. release, written and produced by William L. Hendricks, can be exhibited to advantage in theatres and on television, and will later be an especially handy and appropriate item for screening by schools, churches and other such institutions.

The film, which opens with a brief statement by President Kennedy, traces Glenn's career from his boyhood environment in New Concord, Ohio through his three-orbital space journey around the planet and subsequent fanfare. A bit slow-starting, what with much speechifying by citizens of his birthplace who played a role in his formative years, the picture comes to life and gains momentum when Glenn himself finally arrives on the scene in preparations for his significant attainment. Best scenes by far are those shot by a camera aboard the capsule Friendship 7 which record his reactions

during the eventful flight three times around the globe, accompanied by Glenn's own key observations. Even knowing the outcome, the element of suspense and concern is still remarkably keen in retrospect.

Aerial photography is breathtaking and J. Russell Graziano's editing is astute. The narrative, spoken with style by Jack Webb, runs to cliche in many instances, but they are cliches of a lofty inspirational level and, considering the subject, fairly inevitable and forgiveable. Personal insight into the man is lacking, but perspective linked with his achievement is there. For those who contributed their knowledgeable services to this praiseworthy effort, see the roster above. *Tube.*

Le Soupirant
(The Suitor)
(FRENCH)
Paris, Feb. 26.

Films Marceau release of CAPAC-Cocinor production. With Pierre Etaix, France Arnel, Laurence Ligneres, Karin Vesely. Directed by Pierre Etaix. Screenplay J. C. Carriere, Etaix; camera, Pierre Levent; editor, Pierre Gillette. At Balzac, Paris. Running time, **85 MINS.**

Man	Pierre Etaix
Laurence	Laurence Ligneres
Stella	France Arnel
Mother	Denise Peronne
Father	Claude Massot
Elka	Karin Vesely

A fine new comic film talent is unveiled in this first feature by Pierre Etaix who has two prize-winning shorts and vaude work as background. Characterization may be skimped, and some gags either underworked or familiar. But there is a timing, comedic flair and inventiveness about this that could make it a worthy art and specialized entry overseas. But it needs hard trade and public selling.

Etaix sets up his premise in a few knowing strokes. He himself is a bookish young man with well-to-do parents. His mother is slightly shrewish but absentminded while his father is timid and taken to smoking and drinking on the sly. There is a good looking Swedish girl working in the house to learn French.

The mother decides it is time for him to marry and he puts away his books, but the thought of going out, and the handy Swedish girl, has him asking for her hand. She does not understand. So out he goes into the world to find a mate.

Follow a series of sketches as his eavesdropping on pickups, and his fumbling attempts at emulation lead to risible events and then his embroilment with a silly neighbor and his infatuation with a sexy singer. He manages to get out of both to finally get the Swedish girl.

Etaix builds the character of a seemingly simpleminded average looking man who has to be put into situations by some special force. Here it is parental demands and growing libidinousness. He constantly comes into disastrous contact with inanimate objects, drunken women or the everyday world.

He gets his effects by carefully worked out scenes that revolve around one object or motif and at times brushes a poignant note. But last-named is rare and often a scene is an entirety in itself and

just worked into it for effect. Yet Etaix has the right phlegm, general aplomb and filmic visual comedy knowhow to keep this entertaining throughout, if rarely leading to explosive laughter.

More integrated action, less surface characterization, and more ambition may well turn Etaix into a valuable new comic director here. As an actor he has a delicate deadpan style that jibes with his predicaments, and there are many memorable bits in this promising first pic.

Etaix once worked for Jacques Tati but does not as yet have the more robust overall framework and personalized world that makes Tati's work richer. But he stacks up highly against most other comic directors here. It is an auspicious, if not triumphal, beginning, and he has managed to create a solid comic type if not his own world as yet. It is technically good. *Mosk.*

Fort Du Fou
(Fort of the Mad)
(FRENCH—DYALISCOPE)
Paris, Feb. 19.

Prodis release of Borderie Films-Adelphia production. With Jacques Harden, Alain Saury, Jean Rochefort, Robert Maurice, Jean-Loup Reynold. Directed by Leo Joannon. Screenplay, Georges Kessel, Jean Larteguy, Joannon; camera, Pierre Petit; editor, Christian Gaudin. At Balzac, Paris. Running time, **86 MINS.**

Noyelles	Jacques Harden
Veyrac	Alain Saury
Pretot	S. Dyuk

The French War in Indochina some years ago is the setting for this action pic. Its overplotting makes this only of dualer value abroad. The flagwaving also limits this mainly to local areas.

A captain is holed up in a fort under Communist Viet fire with a group of native Catholics he is to escort to safety. The Communist loudspeakers harass the cooped up men. All this is resolved and the captain dies happy while reinforcements come in to save the men left in the fort.

This piles on too much forced drama to allow the effects of war, personal ties and social pressures to emerge satisfactorily. *Mosk.*

Du Mouron Pour Les Petits Oiseaux
(Chicken Feed For Little Birds)
(FRENCH)
Paris, Feb. 25.

Prodis release of Champs-Elysses Prod.-CICC-Films Borderie-Variety Films production. With Dany Saval, Paul Meurisse, Suzy Delair, Jean Richard, Roland Lesaffre, Franco Citti. Directed by Marcel Carne. Screenplay, Jacques Sigurd, Carne from a book by Albert Simonin; camera, Jacques Natteau; editor, Albert Jurgenson. At Mercury, Paris. Running time, **105 MINS.**

Lucie	Dany Saval
Renato	Franco Citti
Armand	Paul Maurisse
Antoinette	Suzy Delair
Louis	Jean Richard

Made as a ribald comedy about a group of assorted scabrous characters, this leans too much on exploiting situations, rather than treating them in depth, and emerges somewhat unpleasant and coarse rather than racy and witty. It may rate as a solid French market entry on its no-holds-barred aspects but is mainly a specialized item for elsewhere.

An ex-panderer has gone straight

via buying an apartment house in a bohemian section of Paris. However, he is holding out his loot from a last job to retire with. In his house live a bubble-brained girl selling her body to a rowdy butcher to care for her parisitic Italo lover. Butcher's wife is carrying on with the butcher's assistant, an addict of rock and roll singing. There is a selfish old woman feigning herself an invalid to be helped by a loud-mouthed young janitress who covets her supposed money hoard. Add also one seedy homosexual who preys on delivery boys and, finally, a half-mad religious fanatic.

Characters romp through seedy bars, fancy brothels. The old lady finally dies of over eating. An inspector discovers the ex-crook but he manages to get away with his loot with the harebrained girl who then runs off with his car. But he has transferred his money to a case which she dumps into a river as she speeds back to her Italo lover who has meanwhile become the kept man of a prostitute.

Director Marcel Carne has bundled a lot of his pre-war pic situations, but this time it does not quite jell. It lacks feeling for character to excuse degradation as comic. It just becomes distasteful.

Dany Saval is vulgar rather than fetching as the easygoing sentimental tart. Paul Meurisee is properly suave as the ex-gangster who raises birds and only wants to retire to nature.

The tie-up retribution ending does not quite give this the right wry fillip to go with rather patronizing, glib proceedings. But it is the kind of ruthless comedy that could get some foreign play where properly booked and publicized. It is technically excellent. *Mosk.*

La Donna Nel Mondo
(The Women of the World)
(ITALIAN-COLOR)
Rome, Feb. 19.

Cineriz release of a Cineriz production. Written, edited, and directed by Gualtiero Jacopetti, in collaboration with Paolo Cavara and Franco Prosperi. Camera (Technicolor), Antonio Climati, Benito Frattari; music, Nino Oliviero, Riz Ortolani; foreign production arrangements, Stanis Nievo. At Majestic, Rome. Running time, **100 MINS.**

Gualtiero Jacopetti has come up with a highly saleable followup to his successful "Mondo Cane." Less bitter and hard-hitting than its predecessor, it is nevertheless more than able to stand up and be counted on its own. With and-or without the aid of its obvious exploitable angles, it looms as a top export value for all areas.

In his contrastful globe-spanning pursuit of world manners and mores, Jacopetti confirms his notable talent for shaping a colorful, adult travel documentary of people rather than places, again, as in his preceding pic, digging below the surface to turn up the sometimes distasteful but nonetheless significant things there.

Here, he deals mainly with the female of the species, and a colorful and fascinating jaunt it is. Once more, he's dealing with paradoxes, with deliberately shocking contrasts and effective juxtapositions. The tongue is generally in cheek, and there are fewer of the

bitter and sometimes overblown symbolisms of "Mondo Cane."

True that on the debit side there are some repetitions, and that some of the material—though approached differently — has been seen (but to be remembered also that this was shot at the same time as "Mondo Cane," which sent hordes of lensers scampering for similar material for their imitative pix) in other recently-released feature documentaries. Yet with all its faults, and with the same reservations about contrived approaches, audience-shocking tactics, etc., this pic is a trenchant, sarcastic, irreverent but significant glimpse at certain aspects of the world today, with its loneliness, its hypocrisy, its justice and injustice.

Amazing too, apart from the vast amount of unusual and original material, is the quality of its lensing, in color and in oft-prohibitive conditions, by two ex - newsreel cameramen who accompanied Jacopetti on his fruitful journey around the globe. Cutting, music, commentary and other credits all tops, and excellently blended. *Hawk.*

Jusqu'au Bout Du Monde
(Till the End of the World)
(FRENCH—FRANSCOPE)
Paris, Feb. 19.

Gaumont release of Gaumont-Caravelle-Ultra-Rumor production. With Pierre Mondy, Marietto, Didi Perego, Marie Dubois. Directed by Francois Villiers. Screenplay, Ellio Vittorini, Remo Forlani, Villiers; camera, Paul Soultynez; editor, Edouard Berne. At Aubert, Paris. Running time, **80 MINS.**

Pierre	Pierre Mondy
Pietro	Marietto
La Veuve	Didi Perego
Palma	Marie Dubois

Simple tale, of a father accepting a bastard son he has never seen until grown and then learning to love him rather than placing him in an institution, lacks observation and compassion. This makes it only an ordinary feature pic with scant export chances.

A worker goes to Corsica when an old girl friend, before dying, names him the father of her nine-year-old boy. He at first denies being the father but accepts the boy and begins to travel about the island trying to find him a home as an apprentice so he can get back to his job.

Plotting tries too hard to wring pathos and falls into rote. There is just not the right understanding to make this frail anecdote transcend its level. It is thus only an acceptable little item, well played.

Technical credits are also okay but it appears mainly a local bet. Pierre Mondy is good as the brash father and Marietto plays the moppet with some spontaneity. *Mosk.*

Schneewittchen und die sieben Gaukler
(Snow White and the Seven Jugglers)
(SWISS-GERMAN)
(Color, Songs)
Zurich, Feb. 19.

Praesens-Film A.G. Zurich release of Praesens-Independent (Max Dora) co-production. Directed by Kurt Hoffmann. Book by Guenter Neumann; music, Heino Gaze; camera, Sven Nykvist; art directors, Otto and Herta Pischinger; choreography, Don Lurio; editor, Hermann Haller. Stars Caterina Valente; features Walter Giller,

Hanne Wieder, Georg Thomalla. At Rex Theatre, Zurich. Running time, 103 MINS.

Dr. Anita Rossi .... Caterina Valente
Ines del Mar .... Hanne Wieder
Norbert Lang .... Walter Giller
Saeuberlich .... Ernst Waldow
Marcel .... Guenther Schramm
Simson .... Rudolf Rhomberg
Lukas .... Georg Thomalla
Roderich .... Gaston Palmer
Wenzel .... Otto Storr
Vitali .... Aladar Hudi
Toni .... Helmut Brasch
Burghalter ..:............. Peter W. Staub
Stauffinger .... Zarli Cariglet
Petersen .... Henry Vahl
Kampfli .... Klaus Havenstein
Hugentobler .... Horst Tappert

(In German)

Kurt Hoffman, whose previous efforts "Aren't We Wonderful?", "Spook Castle in the Spessart" and "Marriage of Mr. Mississippi," have proved big grossers in the German-lingo market, has fallen considerably below his usual high standard in this Swiss-German co-production. The color musical, filmed at Swiss winter resort of St. Moritz as well as in Zurich and Munich, was reportedly brought in at for a stiff (by local standards) $500,000. Judging by initial b.o. reaction, it will have some difficulty recouping this investment, despite the Caterina Valente name plus other known German players.

The trouble lies with a poor script, run-of-the-mill music and lyrics and lacklustre performances, apart from a few comedy highlights. Basic story idea must have looked promising on paper, but somehow went to pieces along the way. Title, which indicates kiddie fodder, also hurts.

The plot, intended as a modern variation on the Snow White tale, sees a young heating engineeress (Valente) coming to the rescue of a rundown mountain resort hotel by getting seven jobless circus artists to sub as waiters, hall porter, cook, etc. to replace the departing staff, which left because underpaid. Falling in love with the young hotel owner, she is almost nosed out by a shapely stripper, but succeeds in landing her Prince Charming.

Color photography by Sweden's Sven Nykvist (one of Ingmar Bergman's cameramen) is a definite asset. Some of the seven jugglers offer acceptable performances, but Miss Valente is too subdued to make much impact while Walter Giller as her leading man is colorless. Hanne Wieder as the would-be seductress hams it up and almost borders on bad taste at times. Beside the undistinguished music, the choreography is way below par for present-day musical comedy standards.   Mezo.

Love and Larceny
(Il Mattatore)

Major Film Distributing Corp. release of a Maxima Film and Cei-Incom-S.G.C. production. Stars Vittorio Gassman, Anna Maria Ferrero, Dorian Gray. Directed by Dino Risi. Screenplay, Sandro Continenza; adaptation, Sergio Pugliese, based on story by Agee Scarpelli; music, Pippo Barzizza; camera, Massimo Dallamano. Reviewed at Coronet Theatre, N.Y., Feb. 20, '63. Running time, 94 MINS.

Gerardo .... Vittorio Gassman
Annalise .... Anna Maria Ferrero
Elena .... Dorian Gray
Lallo Cortina .... Mario Carotenuto
Chinotto .... Peppino De Filippo
Gloria Patri .... Alberto Bonucci
The General .... Fosco Giachetti
  Others: Luigi Pavese, Linda Sini, Aldo Bufi Landi, Nando Bruni, Piera Arico, Enrico Gloria, Salvatore Cafiero, Mario Scaccis, Fanfulla, Mario Frera, Armando Bandini.

(Italian & English Subtitles)

A slight but charming comedy, "Love and Larceny" (original Italian title: "Il Mattatore") has at its center a superior performance by Vittorio Gassman as an incredibly self-assured and (usually) successful petty con artist. It's now obvious that Gassman's talents were never fully utilized by his former Hollywood employers. He is a gifted comic actor, bouyant and light of touch, who makes "Love and Larceny" a particularly attractive item for those U. S. arties which can make capital from imports of less than blockbuster proportions.

In tracing con man's rise from his position as a third-rate vaudevillian to his success as a practioner in grand larceny, the picture almost serves as a how-to handbook in the art of fraud. Moralists, however, need not be alarmed. The schemes which the intrepid hero fabricates, whether they be for obtaining a free pair of shoes or bilking the papparizi (he masquerades as Greta Garbo seeking seclusion on a lonely beach), are so wildly complex or ingenuously simple as to be of little practical value.

Gassman has a ball in the key role, donning a variety of disguises and accents to implement his escapades. He gets good support from the rest of the cast headed by Anna Maria Ferrero, his patient girlfriend who finally traps him in marriage in the course of one of his capers; Dorian Gray, a sinuously beautiful blonde accomplice, and Peppino De Filippo, Gassman's former jailmate who teaches his friend the finer arts of civilized thievery.

Dino Risi's direction is brisk and never overstated. If the film is more often wryly amusing than hilarious, it may be because some of the quality of the comic dialog is inevitably lost via the functional subtitles. All technical credits are good.   Anby.

Fietsen Naar De Maan
(Bicycling to the Moon)
(DUTCH)

Amsterdam, Feb. 19.

Filmtrust release of Pan Film (P. Hans Frankfurther) production. Features Ton Lensink, Johan Walhain, Bernhard Droog, Diny Sprock, Ingeborg Elzevier, Betsie Smeets, Simon Carmiggelt, Hedda van der Linden. Directed by Jef van der Heyden. Story and screenplay by Van der Heyden; camera, Didier van Koekenberg; editor, Rolf Orthel; music, Enrico Neckheim. At Plaza and Rialto, Amsterdam. Running time, 95 MINS.

Initial film by the new production outfit, Pan Film proves a dud because of inexperience. Lack of experience on the part of the director-scriptwriter, Jef van der Heyden, the cameraman and editor is plainly evident.

Story concerns three brothers, one a failure as a painter, the other a timid policeman, and the third a tramp who at night throws stolen bicycles into the Amsterdam canals in order to retrieve them next day. They all look for happiness, and the fulfillment of their lives, are in the words of the writer, try to "bicycle to the moon." But it is a muddled film.

Acting is okay but the camerawork is below par. Director Jef van der Heyden, who provided

scripts for television plays and one Bert Haanstra film, has written a loose script, which is not improved by the editing. "Bicycling" starts slowly and then loses pace.   Saal.

Resistance
(De Overval)
(DUTCH)

A Rudolph Meyer production of Sapphire Film, Amsterdam. With Rob de Vries, Kees Brusse, Hans Culeman, Yoka Berretty, Piet Romer. Directed by Paul Rotha. Script, L. de Jong. Costumes, Nea Roeterdink. Camera, Prosper Dekeukeleire. At the Roxy Cinema, Amsterdam. Running time, 98 MINS.

Seven years after World War II, the first Dutch film is presented that is both a tribute to the Resistance movement and a good film. Though script and talent is Dutch, the director is English, Paul Rotha, whose documentary background assured a dignified treatment of the subject. Originally, "De Overval" (meaning literally "The Raid" but for its English title "Resistance" has been chosen) was going to be directed by documentarist Bert Haanstra, but pre-production preparations took so long that Haanstra was no longer available, so that producer Rudy Meyer had to look elsewhere.

"De Overval" depicts an episode from the Dutch resistance, when in the city of Leeuwarden a group of underground workers planned and executed a raid upon the local prison in order to release a resistance fighter who knew too much so that no risks could be taken in case he would talk to the Germans. It was decided that in the same coup another 50 prisoners, all arrested by the Gestapo, would be freed. Without any bloodshed, the raid took place and the released men and women went into prearranged hiding.

This episode is reconstructed faithfully. Where the script fails is in the motivation of the characters; starting with the preparations for the raid, the spectator has to take for granted the why of the resistance movement, and though this may not be a drawback for the Dutch audience who has lived this facet of World War II history, it may be a puzzle to a foreign public, not acquainted with the subtle nuances of the resistance. It can be argued that the analysis of the resistance fighter is out of place for a film, but nevertheless it is part of the story, and it is not enough to see a baker fighting at night for freedom, or a man putting his task to free a comrade in arms before his own safety and choosing danger and maybe death while his wife is expecting a baby and wants him to stay home.

Paul Rotha has made a fast-moving picture, to which the semi-documentary technique is well suited. He ignored Dutch star system, to choose actors on type rather than professional importance. Most of "De Overval" was filmed on location, in the actual settings, and Prosper Dekeukeleire's camera work takes advantage keeping the lighting in tone with the documentary values of the film, avoiding pretty lighting that divert by its artificiality.

"De Overval" was the third Dutch film made in 1962, and while the others were directed by

Dutchmen, (one by the dialogue director of "De Overval," Kees Brusse), it took a foreigner to make the first film that promises financial and critical success.   Saal.

La Memoire Courte
(The Short Memory)
(FRENCH)

Paris, Feb. 19.

Francinor release of Rene Thevenet production. Montage pix compiled by Henri Torrent; editor, Paul Cayatte; commentary, Torrent. At the Bonaparte, Paris. Running time, 95 MINS.

Compilation film looks clearly at life in France during the occupation during the last World War as well as tracing the progress of the conflicts. Though mainly of local appeal, it is still rich enough in rarely seen material to make it something for special situations or tele usage abroad.

This details both the collaborationist and resistance aspects in France, plus the same things in other countries. Commentary is sparse and incisive. Editing is good.   Mosk.

Une Blonde Comme Ca!
(A Blonde Like That!)
(FRENCH—COLOR)

Paris, Feb. 19.

Cocinor release of Metzger & Woog-Film Monroe production. With Taina Beryll, Harold Kay, Jess Hahn Rene Lefevre. Directed by Jean Jabely. Screenplay, Jacques Robert, Felecien Marceau from book by James Hadley Chase; camera (Eastmancolor), Marcel Grignon; editor, Henri Taverna. At Mercury, Paris. Running time, 90 MINS.

Myra .... Taina Beryll
Millan .... Harold Kay
Sam .... Jess Hahn
Doc .... Rene Lefevre

Easygoing adventure tale, with supernatural effects, is aimed mainly at the moppet market. That is about where it would stand its best chances abroad. There is not enough imagination and perfection to slant it for more important chances. It appears mainly for the local market.

A girl is adopted as a Goddess by a Latin American tribe and gets magic powers as well as a split personality, one good and the other bad.

The gauche playing of Taina Beryll as the split girl, the routine direction and labored plotting have this a real miss. It is technically par. For the record, the title of this pic until release was "Miss Shumway Jette Un Sort" (Miss Shumway Casts a Spell).   Mosk.

Love Is A Ball
(PANAVISION—COLOR)

Appealing lightweight romanti-comedy. Satisfactory b.o. potential.

Hollywood, Feb. 25.

United Artists release of Martin H. Poll production. Stars Glenn Ford, Hope Lange, Charles Boyer; features Ricardo Montalban, Telly Savalas, Ruth McDevitt; Ulla Jacobsson. Directed by David Swift. Screenplay, Swift, Tom and Frank Waldman, from Lindsay Hardy's novel, "The Grand Duke and Mr. Pimm"; camera (Technicolor), Edmond Sechan; editor, Tom McAdoo, Cathy Kelber; music, Michel Legrand; asst. directors, Danny McCauley, Patrice Dally. Reviewed at Beverly Theatre, Feb. 25, '63. Running time, **113 MINS.**

Davis	Glenn Ford
Millie	Hope Lange
Pimm	Charles Boyer
Gaspard	Ricardo Montalban
Dr. Gump	Telly Savalas
Mathilda	Ruth McDevitt
Janine	Ulla Jacobsson
Mme. Gallou	Georgette Anys
Milkman	Robert Bettoni
Mme. Fernier	Mony Dalmes
Priory	Laurence Hardy
Carlo	Jean Lemaitre
Zoltan	Andre Luguet
Freddie	Jean Paredes
Stacy	Redmond Philipps
Gallou	Arom Stephan
Gretl	Erika Soucy
Mme. Girardin	Olga Valery
Soames	John Wood
Mueller	Jean Pierre Zola

Here's a perfect tranquilizer for the bruised and battered 20th century nerve, an amiable and diverting romp. Slide it under a hypercritical microscope and one can detect all sorts of flaws and ailments in the specimen but the lifesize version is sufficiently hale and hearty to charm an easygoing audience and dodge the querulous qualms of customers given to close analysis. In short, it gets by in spite of itself. Although the Martin H. Poll production lacks the heavy commercial artillery to be a world beater at the boxoffice, it has the attributes to rack up some respectable mileage for United Artists.

"Love Is a Ball" is an airy fairy tale thrust into cinematicomedic orbit by the devious new campaign of a mercenary cupid, or matrimoneymaker, who designs for fun and profit, with an emphasis on the latter, carefully tailored love affairs between his prefabricated "clients" and the most eligible heiresses of the world. As promoter and agent, he is then entitled to his cut when the desired wedlock materializes.

But, as any fool kin plainly see simply by matching characters with cast juxtaposition or marquee prominence, the blueprinted wedlock is not destined to materialize in "Love Is a Ball." Heiress Hope Lange is a shoo-in to fall not for Ricardo Montalban, who is the scrubbed, polished, though not quite grooma-cum-laude graduate of fearless Eros Charles Boyer's male-order school for candidate instant millionaire husbands, but for Glenn Ford, who has been planted by Boyer as chauffeur in Hope's household, the better to drive her swiftly into the clutches of his prized pupil. Needless to say, there's a Ford in Miss Lange's future, which leaves Montalban free to wed his true love, Ulla Jacobsson, who is Boyer's secretary. And what of Boyer? Fret not, there's always the obit section with its surviving heiresses as easy prey for the enterprising matchmaker.

The engaging screenplay was written by David Swift and Tom and Frank Waldman from Lindsay Hardy's novel, "The Grand Duke and Mr. Pimm," which was to have been the title of the picture, too, until someone started the insipid "Ball" bouncing. The scenario misfires in many places, particularly in the latter stages when all semblance of credulity abruptly crumbles, but on the whole it plays to advantage, and Swift as director has made the most of it. To this end he has knowingly synthesized the services of such contributors as cameraman Edmond Sechan, whose picturesque background views of the French Riviera are intoxicating (although his poretight closeups of the players are not very flattering to the complexion), editors Tom McAdoo and Cathy Kelber who have knit the story adeptly save for an abrupt transition or two, art director Jean D'Eaubonne whose sets have character and elegance and, in the case of a den of amour supposedly nestled in idyllic Switzerland, an imagination embellished with a sense of humor by set decorator Fernand Bernardi's erotic statues, composer Michel Legrand who has penned a gregarious score, and costume designer Frank L. Thompson whose wardrobe for Miss Lange is outrageously but appropriately wild and bizarre.

The actors bat it out expertly. Ford does what comes naturally. Miss Lange strikes most of the right notes and postures as a sexy all-American kook with 40 million clams in the kitty. Who else to play the master tutor of romance than Boyer? Montalban is a delight as the inept and unwilling suitor, and Telly Savalas just about steals the show as Miss Lange's gourmet-uncle. Ruth McDevitt does some accomplished reacting as the grandmother of the heiress. Miss Jacobsson, the pretty star of Swedish film here making her American picture debut, seems a trifle uncertain in spots, but shapes up as a find.

Supporting work is spirited, top to bottom. *Tube.*

Seven Seas To Calais
(C'SCOPE—COLOR)

Adventures of Sir Francis Drake. Marketable exploitation meller for action buffs. Saturation entry.

Hollywood, Feb. 26.

Metro release of Paolo Moffa production. Stars Rod Taylor, Keith Michell, Irene Worth. Directed by Rudolph Mate. Screenplay and story, Filippo Sanjust, George St. George, Lindsay Galloway; camera (Eastman), Giulio Gianini; editor, Franco Franticelli; music, Frabco Mannino; assistant director, Rinaldo Ricci. Revewed at the studio, Feb. 26, '63. Running time, **99 MINS.**

Sir Francis Drake	Rod Taylor
Malcolm Marsh	Keith Michell
Queen Elizabeth	Irene Worth
Burleigh	Antony Dawson
Walsingham	Basil Dignam
Arabella	Hedy Vessel
Babington	Mario Girotti
Tom Moone	Gianni Cajafi
Queen of Scots	Esmeralda Ruspoli
Fletcher	Marco Guglielmi
Mendoza	Arturo Dominici
Medina Sidonie	Gianni Solaro
Recalde	Adriano Vitale
Emmanuel	Bruno Ukmar
Francisco	Franco Ukmar
Vigeois	Aldo Buffo Landi
King Philip of Spain	Umberto Raho
Winter	Luciano Melani
Garcia	Jacopo Tecchi
Chester	Giuseppe Abbrescia
Potato	Rossella D'Aquino
Other Indian Wives	Anna Santarsiero, Luciana Gilli

The exploits of Sir Francis Drake are illustrated in this sketchy but frisky exploitation item. Filmed in Italy and decked out in CinemaScope and handsome Eastman Color, the Adelphia production will serve adequately as escapist fare, with primary appeal to children and males with a taste for uncomplicated screen adventure. Metro should find a marketable niche for "Seven Seas to Calais," principally as a saturation entry in the bigger burgs.

Written by Filippo Sanjust with the aid of George St. George and Lindsay Galloway, the film loosely traces the highlights in the career of Drake, foremost naval adventurer of Elizabethan England during its sustained gold war with Spain. Events depicted are his daring pirate-like raids on Spanish treasure arsenals in the New World, his role in foiling a Spanish-spawned assassination of the Queen, and his naval victory over the mighty Spanish armada. In between the action, he is generally found participating in Elizabeth's cat-and-mouse game with the gullible Spanish ambassadors, or kissing the Queen's hand in the best Essex-ual tradition.

As Drake, Rod Taylor emotes with the swashbuckling ardor and assurance of an embryo Errol Flynn, Keith Michell is likable as his right-hand man. Irene Worth offers an interesting interpretation of Elizabeth, a role in which she has had some illustrious predecessors. Italian actress Hedy Vessel is uncertain in her portrayal of Michell's maiden, and has been burdened with eye makeup that is about as 16th century as Max Factor. Balance of supporting work is, at best, adequate.

Director Rudolph Mate has succeeded in keeping his film moving along at a perky pace, but there are times, notably during an American Indian sequence, when the action seems on the verge of taking on the aspect of a musical comedy western. Cameraman Giulio Gianini has composed some striking seascape views. Some of Franco Mannino's score sounds suspiciously like a warmup for a Nelson Eddy solo, but at other times it is quite helpful and melodic, and plays an integral story role. Editing and sound are capably dispatched, and Nicola Cantatore's artwork is impressive. Writer Sanjust has doubled in brass as costume designer. His flair seems to lie in the latter department.

Bicycling To The Moon
(Fietsen Naar De Maan)
(DUTCH)

Amsterdam, March 1.

Filmtrust release of Pan Film (P. Hans Frankfurther) production. With Ton Lensing, Johan Walhain, Bernard Droog, Diny Sprock, Ingeborg Elzevier, Hedda van der Linden. Directed by Jef van der Hayden. Script and story, Van der Heyden; camera, Didier van Koskenberg; editor, Rolf Orthel; music, Enrico Neckheim. At the Plaza and Rialto Cinemas, Amsterdam. Running time, **95 MINS.**

Initial film by new production outfit Pan Film has proved to be a dud, due to inexperience and lack of self-criticism. In first instance there is a home market for Dutch feature films, however so-so; most films do need the financial partial backing of a subsidy in the form of a guarantee put up by cinema exhibitors and the government. But on this film it is wasted. It can be said that technicians have gained experience, but in the film itself the lack of experience on the part of director-scriptwriter Jef van der Heyden, the camera man and the cutter is utterly evident.

Story of "Bicycling to the Moon" concerns three brothers, one a failed painter, the other a sensitive and timid policeman, the third a rag-and-bone man who at night throws stolen bicycles into the Amsterdam canals, in order to retrieve them next day. They all look for happiness, and the fulfillment of their lives, in the word of the writer, try to "bicycle to the moon." It becomes a muddled film which could be retitled "Bicycle Thieves Along The Amstel," without any bite or sense for observation or characterization, false in its poetry and pathos.

Acting is alright. The camera work is below par, specially in the night scenes along the Amsterdam streets and canals. Director Jef van der Heyden, who provided scripts for television plays and one Bert Haanstra film ("The Case M.P."), has written a loose script, that has not improved by the editing; "Bicycling" starts slow and loses pace, never building the action up to a climax and has too many scenes (the intro) and details that are of no avail to the story line. Enrico Neckheim has written a pleasant score that is kind of wasted. *Saal.*

The Quick And The Dead

Adroitly executed low budget war drama, but weak in characterization. Should make okay supporting item.

Hollywood, March 1.

Beckman Film Corp. release of Sam Altonian production. No star credits. Directed by Robert Totten. Screenplay, Sheila Lynch, Totten; camera, John Morrill; editor Welles Ford; music, Jaime Mendoza. Reviewed at National Theatres screening room, March 1, '63. Running time, **92 MINS.**

Parker	Larry Mann
Riley	Victor French
Rogers	Jon Cedar
Georgio	James Almanzar
Donatelli	Louis Massad
Teresa	Majel Barret
Maria	Sandy Donigan

"The Quick and the Dead" is a lot of "little picture" for $100,000. In other words, the currency has been translated resourcefully into cinematic values that show up vividly on the screen. Yet, while this low budget indie reflects physical production savvy on the part of its makers, it falls down in story development. Depth and definition of characterization are missing, and these are the elements that ultimately separate motion picture art from mechanics, creative substance from good bookkeeping. Still, it's an impressive "college try" by all concerned that, while a trifle lengthy for secondary slotting, should nevertheless make a marketable supporting entry.

A squad of Yanks and a band of Italian partisans caught up in the see-saw struggle for occupation of Northern Italy during World War

II are the heroes of the action-packed Robert Totten-Sheila Lynch scenario. The story follows the deteriorating patrol of American dogfaces as it battles the Nazis tooth and nail, then joins up with the partisans for a successful goal-line stand at the mouth of a cave, following which the Germans flee.

Action has been exceptionally well mounted and executed by the game and spirited young company under the vigorous generalship of director Totten. But, because of the rather superficial and haphazard character development overwhelmed by the emphasis on open conflict, the audience never truly experiences the intimate and personal sense of loss that should accompany the deaths in combat of some of the principal participants. Without establishment of this keen sense of concern, the film does not come across with genuine impact. All the blood and thunder in the world cannot substitute for the arousal of empathy in the spectator for the story of one clearly-defined character.

Fine histrionic contributions are made by Victor French, James Almanzar and Louis Massad. Also able are Larry Mann and Jon Cedar. Majel Barret and Sandy Donigan have some strong moments as the distaff members of the war party.

Sam Altonian produced this brisk enterprise for Manson Film Productions, which is to be distributed next month by Beckman Film Corp. Some solid production credits have been racked up on limited means by such craftsmen as cameraman John Morrill, editor Welles Ford and art director O.R.C. Totten. Composer Jaime Mendoza's score is martial in character.

Tube.

My Six Loves
(VISTAVISION—COLOR)

Lack - lustre romanticomedy about a tired screen star who "adopts" six waifs during a sabbatical from show biz. Aimed at family trade.

Hollywood, Feb. 14, '63.

Paramount release of Gant Gaither production. Stars Debbie Reynolds, Cliff Robertson, David Janssen; features Eileen Heckart, Jim Backus, Hans Conreid, Mary McCarty. Directed by Gower Champion. Screenplay, John Fante, Joseph Calvelli, William Wood, based on story by Peter V. K. Funk; camera (Technicolor) Arthur E. Arling; editor, John Woodcock; music, Walter Scharf; assistant director, Michael Caffey. Reviewed at the studio, Feb. 14, '63. Running time, **105 MINS.**

Janice Courtney	Debbie Reynolds
Rev. Jim Larkin	Cliff Robertson
Martin Bliss	David Janssen
Ethel Swenson	Eileen Heckart
Kingsley Cross	Hans Conreid
Doreen Smith	Mary McCarty
Judge Harris	John McGiver
B. J. Smith	Max Showalter
Selina	Alice Ghostley
Bus Driver	Alice Pearce
Diane Soper	Pippa Scott
Doctor	Claude Stroud
Ava	Darlene Tompkins
Mario	Leon Belasco
Leo Smith	Billy Hughes
Sheriff	Jim Backus

Until a swarm of "adorable" moppets arrives and takes over, "My Six Loves" shapes up as a diverting romantic comedy. Unfortunately, the half-dozen urchins arrive about 15 minutes into the film and never leave. At one point, "villain" Jim Backus offers the unspeakable suggestion of "driving 'em over the state line and dumping 'em on the other side." A certain faction in every audience will be with Backus, all the way.

Prospects for the Paramount release aren't too bright. True, it is the kind of picture parents will feel safe sending their children to see, and that, if one is to judge by the recent clamor over bold, unsavory themes, is the exception to the rule these days. But, except for tinier tykes, most children aren't apt to appreciate being "saved" in this manner.

The Gant Gaither production, written by John Fante, Joseph Calvelli and William Wood from a story by Peter V. K. Funk, is concerned with the experience of a glamorous stage and screen actress (Debbie Reynolds) who, on the verge of a nervous breakdown from the publicity hubbub that engulfs her, is ordered to rest up for awhile in the Connecticut suburbs. Enter six homeless waifs abandoned by their drunken guardians. Miss Reynolds, bullied around by the local preacher (Cliff Robertson), sort of adopts them for a spell, soon learns to adore them and, in the process, Robertson too.

Only redeeming sequence in the picture is the opening one, a take-off on a publicity cocktail party spiced by the spectacle of a freeloader surreptitiously emptying sleepers into a thermos. Best line in the film: personal manager to star as he shoos her away from an eager fourth-estater — "He isn't even syndicated." The opening momentum is sustained for awhile with the advent of an insolent servant (Alice Ghostley) and her snivelling, would-be-actress daughter (Darlene Tompkins), but when the kids arrive, the whole show goes poof.

A castful of talented adults is wasted. Miss Reynolds is attractive. Robertson is mired in the role of the starchy minister. David Janssen, although Cary Grant mannerisms hamper his individuality, comes off best as the manager, mainly because of his sane attitude towards the kids—they bother him. Eileen Heckart has some good moments as the star's secretary-companion. Hans Conreid is engaging as a pseudo-intellectual playwright. Also effective in spots are Mary McCarty, John McGiver, Max Showalter, Alice Pearce, Pippa Scott and Backus.

For Gower Champion, making his feature film directorial debut, a most inauspicious start. Arthur E. Arling's cinematography is competent. John Woodcock's editing a little sluggish at times. Artificially such as rubbery vegetation shows through in the Hal Pereira-Roland Anderson sets. Walter Scharf's music is okay. "It's A Darn Good Thing," a song by Sammy Cahn and James Van Heusen, is sung by Miss Reynolds. *Tube.*

The Courtship Of Eddie's Father
(PANAVISION—COLOR)

Disarming romanticomedy on a dramatic base. Bright writing, lavish production and lively acting make it a hot b.o. bet in the family sphere.

Hollywood, March 6.

Metro release of Joe Pasternak production. Stars Glenn Ford, Shirley Jones; features Stella Stevens, Dina Merrill, Ronny Howard; introduces Roberta Sherwood, Jerry Van Dyke. Directed by Vincente Minnelli. Screenplay, John Gay, based on novel by Mark Toby; camera (Metrocolor), Milton Krasner; editor, Adrienne Fazan; music, George Stoll; asst. director, William McGarry. Reviewed at Westwood Village Theatre, March 6, '63. Running time, **118 MINS.**

Tom Corbett	Glenn Ford
Elizabeth Marten	Shirley Jones
Dollye Daly	Stella Stevens
Rita Behrens	Dina Merrill
Mrs. Livingston	Roberta Sherwood
Eddie	Ronny Howard
Norman Jones	Jerry Van Dyke

Metro has a solid boxoffice contender in "The Courtship Of Eddie's Father," a wholesome blend of comedy and sentiment aimed at the family trade, to which Hollywood picturemakers have been pointedly catering this year with a steady stream of nourishing product. The story of a dad and a lad and their divergent views on what constitutes desirable stepmotherhood, the Joe Pasternak production is richly mounted, wittily written and engagingly played by an expert, spirited and attractive cast. To be sure, once or twice along the way there are bothersome exchanges which have been sweetened or exaggerated far out of proportion with reality, and the storyline itself is about as unpredictable as an election in Russia, but the overall effect is nevertheless charming and entertaining.

In adapting the novel by Mark Toby, John Gay has penned an aware, clever and generally well-constructed scenario that stalls only during those few errant and widely scattered interludes when it slips into artificial postures of miscalculated cuteness. Glenn Ford portrays a widower who, in rearing his precocious six-and-a-half year old son (Ronny Howard) must, in the course of his romantic pursuits, take into account the future maternal preferences of the boy, whose comic-book-eye-view of candidate wives is inclined to judge statistically on the basis of bustlines and eyesockets (malevolent females in the funnies invariably have "skinny eyes" and big bosoms). It so happens that papa's choice (Dina Merrill) has rather slanty orbs compared with those of next-door-neighbor Shirley Jones, who is little Ronny's idea of an ideal mommy. There's never really any doubt about the outcome of this contest.

Ford handles his assignment with finesse. He creates a warm, likable personality and is especially smooth in his reaction takes in scenes with his charge, although it is in one or two of these exchanges that writer Gay has gotten carried away and allowed the frankness of childhood observation (which is fine, if depicted naturally) to lapse into overly-adorable precocity simply to get a rise and a gasp out of the audience. This portrayal further establishes Master Howard, who was so delightful as lisping Winthrop in "Music Man," as the outstanding moppet actor extant in Hollywood filmdom. He does wee wonders, even when the script is contriving to rate him a candidate for a good spanking.

Never any question about Miss Jones' credentials as the kind of woman any red-blooded American type would love to call mommy, bustline nothwithstanding. Dina Merrill, more glamorous than ever with locks gone brunette, is an attractive loser. The darker tresses make her a natural for a lucrative career of Gail Patrick-type sophisticated "other woman" roles. Stella Stevens, also altered from blonde to redhead, comes on like gangbusters in her enactment of a brainy but inhibited doll from Montana. It's a sizzling comedy performance of a kook, one that out-MacLaine's MacLaine.

Some unusual casting ingenuity went into the making of this picture, for which producer Pasternak is to be congratulated. Both Roberta Sherwood and Jerry Van Dyke, for example, make their film debuts and each makes a strong, vivid impression. Miss Sherwood scores as a housekeeper boning up on Spanish for an unaware trip to Portugalized Brazil, and rates a threat to the domestic domain heretofore the almost exclusive casting property of Thelma Ritter. Van Dyke chips in with a gregarious and disarming performance as a morning deejay who likes to get a rise out of his distaff listeners.

Vincente Minnelli's direction tends toward melodramatic heaviness in some of the early "serious" going and some exaggeration in several comic passages, but overall he has managed well enough, coaxed some bright performances from his cast and concluded his film with an inventive and winning fadeout scene.

The production is slick and attractive in appearance, thanks in no small measure to Milton Krasner's eye-appealing photography, Adrienne Fazan's smooth editing, Helen Rose's chic costumes, Sydney Guilaroff's color-conscious hair-styling, the rich and sturdy sets by George W. Davis and Urie McCleary and the observant set decoration of Henry Grace and Keogh Gleason. George Stoll's music is obtrusively ominous in spots, but on the whole helpfully in sync with the action of the story.

Tube.

Vice and Virtue
(Le Vice Et La Vertu)
(FRENCH—FRANSCOPE)

Paris, March 12.

Metro release of Gaumont-International, Trianon, Ultra Films production. Stars Annie Girardot, Robert Hossein, Catherine Deneuve, Otto Hasse; features Philippe Lemaire, Serge Marquand, Michel De Re. Directed by Roger Vadim. Screenplay, Roger Vailland, Vadim from the novel, "Justine," by the Marquis De Sade; camera, Marcel Grignon; editor, Victoria Mercanton. At Marignan, Paris. Running time, **100 MINS.**

Juliette	Annie Girardot
Justine	Catherine Deneuve
Schondorff	Robert Hossein
Von Bamberg	Otto Hasse
Hans	Philippe Lemaire
Ivan	Serge Marquand
Helena	Luciana Paluzzi

This film is a hoked-up look at Nazism, laced with symbolic studies of vice and virtue, as exemplified by the two heroines. There is canny and veiled eroticism in this, too. It shapes a probable exploitation bet on its tale, theme and treatment.

Vaguely based on two works of the Marquis De Sade, "Justine" and "Juliette," this traces the fate of two sisters caught up in the Nazi stream near the end of the last war. One sister has thrown in her lot with the Nazis and the other with the resistance movement. Latter's future husband is arrested on her wedding day and she goes to her sister for help.

This gets her embroiled because a Gestapo man, who wipes out the sister's protector, has her arrested so as to have no witnesses, and takes the vice-ridden sister as a mistress.

The virtuous one is sent to a brothel run for Nazi officers. The girls there are dressed as vestal virgins, given numbers and are at the pick and whim of a rather addled-looking, semi-comic bunch of degenerates.

Director Roger Vadim has tried to give the film a heavy Teutonic tang via overdressed, baroque sets, pseudo-type Wagnerian music and scenes of torture, Nazi decadence, cowardice, hysteria and elegant sensuality.

But its symbolical, rather than real characters, its lack of depth and its naive plotting and emoting make it a chancier arty house item. Like his updating of another controversial 18th Century book, "Les Liaisons Dangereuses," Vadim and scripter Roger Vailland have tried to make a statement on modern times.

Imagery is slick and the playing one - dimensional. Annie Girardot, as the symbol of vice, manages to retain some human outlooks if she is ready to sacrifice all to live. Passing a group of hanged people she is moved as much as when she is made to witness torture. She asks her fanatic Nazi lover whether he ever has any feeling and whether he ever was a child.

Catherine Deneuve, Vadim's present fiancee, and a girl he apparently trying to mold as he did Brigitte Bardot, has a pouting gaucheness and almost complete lack of thespic ability. She is comely but without the more earthy spark that ignited Miss Bardot into stardom.

A massive use of stock war footage makes the synthetic tale seem even more unreal. This may have been deliberate but Vadim's calculated direction rarely manages to make a universal comment on Fascism or give insight into its characters and actions.

Film has some cannily concocted debauchery, such as a party alongside a swimming pool with fighting, necking, etc., and suggested but practically concealed nudity.

Mosk.

Three-Penny Opera
(GERMAN—MUSICAL)

German remake of long-run legiter. Sammy Davis Jr. adds potency for U.S. market. Mixed values but more pluses than minuses.

Munich, March 6.

Gloria release of Kurt Ulrich production; U.S. distribution; Embassy Pictures. Stars Sammy Davis Jr., Curt Jurgens, June Ritchie, Hildegard Neff, Gert Froebe, Lino Ventura; features Marlene Warrlich, Walter Giller, Hilde Hildebrand. Screenplay, based on the adaptation by Bertold Brecht with music by Kurt Weill, Wolfgang Staudte and Guenther Weisenborn; directed by Staudte; camera (Cinemascope-color), Roger Fellous; music adaptation, Peter Sandloff. At Gloria Palast, Munich. Running time, **124 MINS.**

Ballad Singer	Sammy Davis Jr.
Mac, the Knife	Curt Jurgens
Polly Peachum	June Ritchie
Pirate Jenny	Hildegard Neff
Lucy Brown	Marlene Warrlich
Tiger Brown	Lino Ventura
Peachum	Gert Froebe
Mrs. Peachum	Hilde Hildebrand
Filch	Walter Giller

This picture may count on an immense "presold audience." The Brecht-Weill adaptation of John Gay's 17th Century "Beggar's Opera" has enjoyed long runs all over Europe and U.S. since its world premiere in 1928. It was often publicized as "seven different shows for one admission price: a period crime thriller, a political satire, a folklore ballad, a social-message play, a sex show, a tuneful opera, and a hilarious parody of opera."

This second picturization (the first was G. W. Pabst's version of the early 1930s) tries to fill those many protean forms. Where it succeeds, it goes up like a rocket. At other points it falls down like a stick. To cite a couple of such mishaps, the impact of the play's songs is never duplicated on the screen. There are some notably awful slips in the casting throwing otherwise effective acting occasionally out of kilter.

There is a peculiar problem about those which possibly could not be solved in the cinematic medium at all. Large legit houses were up against it, too. Those vocal solos score with all their innate power only in small theatres where they can be thrust into the spectator's face at close range.

Makers of this film attempted to reconstruct person-to-person approach by having those numbers delivered in sharp close-ups. It came off like a string of photomaton pictures or at best a filmed song recital. Suffering most under this technique is Hildegard Neff's Pirate Jenny. She has undeniable gifts as a chansonniere but suffers as handled "Three Penny Opera." Perhaps no fault of hers.

Sammy Davis Jr.'s was a last minute assignment. He scores big. In a few brief appearances as organ-grinding ballad bard, Mr. Wonderful, and in his rendition of the famous "Mac-the-Knife" song, Davis brings force and fire. He dominates Curd Jurgens, another name. Latter, a competent actor on occasions that suit his style better, Jurgens can still draw sparks here and there, but there are dull intervals in between. On the whole, it becomes sadly evident that his talents and present age will barely qualify him for the gentleman ladykiller and cutthroat.

Beggar Queen Mrs. Peachum, a figure unforgettable on the stage, emerges here without royal endowments or any other but those of a distasteful old witch. Gert Froebe, German character actor, is divided and inconsistent as Mr. Peachum. Judgment on June Ritchie's Polly may be reserved until the original voice of this visually agreeable British actress can be heard in the Anglo-Saxon soundtrack. Teutonic dubbing seemed to mar her performance.

To switch to the assets side of the ledger, a young talented looker by name of Marlene Warrlich made a very promising debut as Lucy. France's "heavy," Lino Ventura, intrigued once more as "Tiger Brown" (minus the homosexual touch of this police chief in the play). Small parts like Walter Giller's and Martin Berliner's, made themselves rather perceivable by striking some flashes.

Credit, and rather massive one, has to go to Wolfgang Staudte's direction. He displayed great know-how in handling excited masses not only when it comes to the beggars' upheaval but also when crowds are dancing and singing in the streets for merely operatic or comedic effects.

Where film moves out of the stage play's close quarters, dives, brothels, gang hide-outs, into the open of a teeming Soho area and individual action is replaced by collective one, the highlights of this film are attained. Moreover, there and then it really turns from a play to a film.

Production is lavish. Expensive, too, by German standards English language version, taken over by Joseph E. Levine's Embassy Pictures will hit the U.S. screens in early summer. "Pre-sold audience," Sammy Davis Jr., and a few of the directorial feats should prevail over the shortcomings and make the b.o. outlook rather favorable.

Jok.

Diary Of A Madman
(COLOR)

Exploitable programmer.

Hollywood, March 5.

United Artists release of Robert E. Kent production. Stars Vincent Price, Nancy Kovack. Directed by Reginald Le Borg. Screenplay, Kent based on stories by Guy de Maupassant; camera (Technicolor), Ellis W. Carter; editor, Grant Whytock; music, Richard La Salle; asst. director, Al Westen. Reviewed at 20th-Fox Theatre, March 5, '63. Running time, **96 MINS.**

Simon	Vincent Price
Odette	Nancy Kovack
Paul	Chris Warfield
Jeanne	Blaine Devry
Rennedon	Stephen Roberts
Priest	Lewis Martin
Pierre	Ian Wolfe
Andre	Edward Colmans
Louise	Mary Adams
Girot	Harvey Stephens
Dr. Borman	Nelson Olmstead
"The Horla"	Joseph Ruskin

"Diary of a Madman" is an exploitable but artless attempt to make cinema out of the works of Guy de Maupassant. It's a stylistically uninspired collaborative effort by writer-producer Robert E. Kent and director Reginald Le Borg. As noted, the United Artists release has some exploitation potential, in approximately the same vein as have the Poe-pourri of horror items out of American International Poe-ductions in the past few years.

Creative flair is the missing ingredient in this cinematic synthesis of de Maupassant stories, nucleus and only apparent source of which is his vivid ghost tale. "The Horla." Lack of imagination and recourse to shopworn visual effects waters down the impact of the horror. The mind's eye is a master cameraman when it comes to creating images of psychological horror. Seeing such essentially chilling images materialize on the screen in the form of fluorescent light rays accompanied by an articulate, matter of fact, and thoroughly human "ghost" voice significantly reduces the terror of an unseen but ominous presence that should be implied without access to photographic gimmickry lest it deteriorate into an experience tantamount to a trip through the chamber of horrors at the local amusement park.

Vincent Price undertakes the starring role of a magistrate who, after strangling a convicted murderer in self defense, has the misfortune to inherit the evil spirit, or "horla," that has possessed his victim. The residence in his mind of this parasitic ghost transforms Price into a cold-blooded murderer, but eventually he senses the spirit's peculiar inability to cope with fire and destroys both it and himself in a blaze. Since the "horla" is accredited with being simply the product of manifestation of the character's own latent evil, there remains some confusion in the viewer's mind over the exact nature of the person portrayed by Price, whose crimes seem to stem not from the evil in his heart but from momentary lapses of reason in his mind.

Price, that master of the wickedly arched eyebrow, handles his role with the ease acquired through a career of myriad villainous personifications, although there are times when he seems a man more in need of an aspirin than a psychiatrist. Nancy Kovack is attractive as the unfaithful and ring-less wife who becomes his victim. Others of prominence and adequate histrionic persuasion are Chris Warfield, Elaine Devry and Stephen Roberts. The words of the "horla" are spoken by Joseph Ruskin.

The physical production is workmanlike and colorful. Among the key assists are those of cameraman Ellis W. Carter, art director Daniel Haller, special effectsman Norman Breedlove, composer Richard La Salle, editor Grant Whytock and costume designer Marjorie Corso.

I Could Go On Singing
(PANAVISION—COLOR)

A femme 'Jolson Story.' Prospects hinge on Judy Garland appeal.

Hollywood, March 8.

United Artists release of Stuart Millar-Lawrence Turman production. Stars Judy Garland, Dirk Bogarde; features Jack Klugman. Directed by Ronald Neame. Screenplay, Mayo Simon, from story by Robert Dozier; camera (Eastman), Arthur Ibbetson; editor, Pamela Davies; music, Mort Lindsey; asst. director, Colin Brewer. Reviewed at Director's Guild Theatre, March 8, '63. Running time, **99 MINS.**

Jenny Bowman	Judy Garland
David Donne	Dirk Bogarde
George Kogan	Jack Klugman
Ida	Aline MacMahon
Matt	Gregory Phillips
Miss Plimpton	Pauline Jameson
Young Hospital Doctor	Jeremy Burnham
Reynolds	Russell Waters
Asst. Mgr. at Palladium	Gerald Sim
The Busker	Leon Cortez

The magnetism of the Judy Garland name will have to carry "I Could Go On Singing." Stuart Millar-Lawrence Turman production is pretty weighty cargo. Althought handsomely mounted and endowed with the distinctive presence of the dynamic singer, one of the great stylists of her generation,

the United Artists release is constructed on a frail and fuzzy story foundation.

Originally titled "The Lonely Stage," the picture is a blend of two primary elements. Musically, it is a kind of femme "Jolson Story." Dramatically, it is a switch on the old yarn about the child who one day discovers his parents had adopted him.

Mayo Simon's screenplay, from a story by Robert Dozier, has Miss Garland as a celebrated Yank singer who, after her second divorce, decides while in London to look up the medic with whom years before she'd had an affair that culminated with the birth of a son. It had been agreed upon at the time that the doctor (Dirk Bogarde) would raise the son, together with his wife (now rather conveniently deceased), as an adopted child, and that Miss Garland would butt out of her domestic picture. She now persuades Bogarde to let her see the lad, and it isn't long before the true parental beans are spilled. But, for some rather foggy reason (which appears to have wound up on the cutting room floor), the boy elects to play it cool and keep his distance from his new-found mater. Bogarde, who is still in love with the woman, drives her to the theatre for her performance and, while observing from the wings, realizes that she belongs on the lonely stage and not in the kitchen. He vanishes and Miss Garland goes on singing.

A soulful performance is etched by Miss Garland, who gives more than she gets from the script. She also belts over four numbers as only she can belt them, yet the impact of a live Garland stage performance is not duplicated on the screen on this occasion. The camera tends to remain in too tight, at the significant loss of that sense of audience chemistry, of the small, solitary figure onstage electrifying a throng with a passionate voice, that distinguishes Miss Garland from most of her contemporaries. Had the story been stronger, the interruption of four lengthy vocals might have seemed overly abundant and intrusive. As it is, they are a relief, and at least to some extent compensate for the absence of a sub-plot to change the pace and provide contrast.

Bogarde seems somewhat ill-at-ease in his role, employing two basic expressions—pain and a kind of confused "what am I doing here?" or "somebody must be kidding." Young Gregory Phillips does a commendable job as the boy. Jack Klugman and Aline MacMahon are helpful in featured support.

Director Ronald Neame, on the whole, has done a fair, if not especially inspired, job with flimsy material, although the continuity of the drama is choppy, a fault for which editor Pamela Davies must at least share responsibility. Arthur Ibbetson's camerawork is skillful, creating some striking and always colorful images on the screen. John Shirley's sets are tasteful, and Mort Lindsey's music a plus factor throughout. The title song, written by Harold Arlen and Yip Harburg and sung forcefully by the star, is a spirited refrain that could be a seller and certainly will help exploit the picture.

Miss Garland was rather on the plumpish side when this film was shot, and neither Edith Head's costumes nor Pearl Tipaldi's hair styles are very becoming to her.
Tube.

PT 109

Hollywood, March 12.
Young JFK in the South Pacific. Crisp combat drama that doesn't penetrate much into the Kennedy personality but keeps the action coming. Strong b.o. entry.

Warner Bros. release of Bryan Foy production. Sttars Cliff Robertson, Ty Hardin, James Gregory, Robert Culp, Grant Williams. Directed by Leslie H. Martinson. Screenplay, Richard L. Breen, from adaptation by Howard Sheehan and Vincent X. Flaherty of book by Robert J. Donovan; camera (Technicolor), Robert L. Surtees; editor, Folmar Blangsted; music, William Lava, David Buttolph; asst. director, William Kissel. Reviewed at he studio, March 12, '63. Running time, 140 MINS.
Lt. (j.g.) John F. Kennedy .... Cliff Robertson
Ensign Leonard J. Thom..... Ty Hardin
Commander Ritchie ..... James Gregory
Ensign "Barney" Ross.... Robert Culp
Lt. Alvin Cluster........Grant Williams
Yeoman Rogers .... Lew Gallo
Benjamin Kevu .... Errol John
Lt. Reginald Evans........ Michael Pate
"Bucky" Harris .... Robert Blake
Gerard Zinser .... William Douglas
Edgar E. Mauer .... Biff Elliott
Ed Drewitch .... Norman Fell
Ray Starkey .... Sam Gilyman
Leon Drawdy .... Clyde Howdy
Maurice Koway .... Buzz Martin
Pat McMahon .... James McCallion
Harold Marney .... Evan McCord
Andrew Kirksey .... Sammy Reese
William Johnson .... Glenn Sipes
John Maguire .... John Ward
Raymond Alber .... David Whorf

A film based on the younger years of an incumbent President of the United States has built-in values of a unique sort.

"PT 109" is see-worthy. Its translation from the written account by Robert J. Donovan to the dramatic dimensions of the screen has been accomplished with efficiency and vigor by producer Bryan Foy, staff, crew and cast. Although not so deep as a well (in terms of human insight) nor so wide as a churchdoor (in terms of historical perspective), 'tis enough, 'twill serve. And, owing to the worldwide interest in its central figure, this portrait of John F. Kennedy as a young hero could, if tastefully and resourcefully handled, go on to become a hot commodity for Warner Bros. It should be an especially big item with the little league set and male action buffs.

Richard L. Breen's pungent scenario, endowed with a ripe sense of humor and a keen taste for action, stems from an adaptation by Howard Sheehan and Vincent X. Flaherty of Donovan's popular tome. It plants Lt. (j.g.) John F. Kennedy on the South Pacific isle of Tulagi in Aug. 7, 1962 and follows him and crew from preparatory efforts to make the "plywood coffin" yar' for combat through their misadventure when the vessel is sliced in half by a Japanese destroyer, marooning them on the uninhabited and unlivable islands of Plum Pudding and Olasana until the historical rescue in hostile waters.

The picture does not attempt to penetrate deeply or sharply into the character of the president-to-be, nor does it offer any especially striking or unexpected slants on the young JFK's personality. Rather, the emphasis is on straight dramatic storytelling of incidents in which Kennedy happens to be the pivotal and dominating figure.

But, by thus focusing on the story and avoiding over-glamorization of a hero, it enables the Kennedy character to emerge a man with a job to do rather than a larger-than-life personage who has a date with destiny. Since there is a good deal of story to tell, it is a sound and sensible concept.

Bypassing any attempts at imitation or caricature, Cliff Robertson, as Lt. Kennedy, offers instead a warm and straightforward portrait of a dedicated, courageous patriot who is all business and determination in a crisis but has a playful streak in lighter moments. Robertson's resemblance to the President is superficial, but he manages to convey the suggestion of him without being obvious.

The all-male cast assembled by Foy performs with spirit and finesse. James Gregory attracts the most attention in a somewhat cliche but nonetheless appealing character of a commander who is a nail-hard disciplinarian of the old school, but has an underlying soft streak for his men. Gregory gives an expert delineation. Ty Hardin, Robert Culp and Grant Williams score in essentially surface characterizations of young naval officers. Lew Gallo, Errol John and Michael Pate (whose Australian inflection is keen) are effective in prominent roles. Standouts among those cast in the 109 crew are Robert Blake and Biff Elliott, both of whom draw the funniest lines and bits and handle them infectiously, Blake as a gunner's mate of the classic "Insigna" mold and Elliott as a makeshift cook whose idea of a hot meal is peanut butter sandwiches on toast and whose fishing implements are net and hand grenade. Others who merit more than passing attention are William Douglas, Sammy Reese, John Ward and David Whorf.

Leslie H. Martinson has directed with punch and pace and his helmsmanship of combat passages is realistic and explosive. It is a long picture, but it moves along at a pretty good clip, although the first 35 minutes are devoted essentially to preparatory fun and it is an hour and 40 minutes before the basic incident materializes.

Some striking Technicolor seascapes have been composed by cameraman Robert L. Surtees, whose lensing of battle action is equally adroit. Folmar Blangsted's editing is thoroughly efficient, and his knitting of complicated action patterns during combat maneuvers is particularly observant. Art director Leo K. Kuter has made an acceptable South Pacific out of Munson Island, 25 miles from Key West, Florida. Additionally important and helpful contributions have been made by composers William Lava and David Buttolph, set decorator John P. Austin, soundman Francis M. Stahl, second unit director Russ Saunders and second unit cameraman Mark Davis. The entire project was filmed under the personal supervision of Jack L. Warner.

In sum, "PT 109" may lack the "human element" artistry and sensitivity of, say, a "Mister Roberts," but nevertheless it is an exciting dramatic biography of an embryo giant at war.
Tube.

Nattvardsgaesterna
(The Winter Light) (SWEDISH)

Stockholm, March 12.

Svensk Filmindustri production and release. Stars Ingrid Thulin, Gunnar Bjornstrand, Max von Sydow, Gunnel Lindblom. Directed by Ingmar Bergman. Screenplay by Bergman; camera, Sven Nykvist; editor, Ulla Ryghe. At Roda Kvarn, Stockholm. Running time, 79 MINS.

Marta Lundberg	Ingrid Thulin
Tomas Ericsson	Gunnar Bjornstrand
Jonas Persson	Max von Sydow
Karin Persson	Gunnel Lindblom
Algot Frovik	Allan Edwall
Knut Aronsson	Kolbjorn Knudsen
Fredrik Blom	Olof Thunberg

The Swedish title of Ingmar Bergman's new film is "The Communicants," which clearly reveals the mood of the film. The English title, "The Winter Light," is more vague. This film deals more with religious doubting and searching than any of Bergman's earlier works. It opens at noon on a late November Sunday in a medieval church in the Swedish countryside and ends three-hours later in another country church. It opens when Pastor Tomas Ericsson is concluding his sermon.

After communion, Karin Persson brings her husband, a fisherman, to the pastor for guidance. Several months earlier fisherman Jonas Persson had read that the Communist Chinese were brought up to hate other people, and it was only a question of time before they got atomic bombs that would enable them to destroy humanity. These reports have made him contemplate suicide. Rather than giving guidance, the Lutheran pastor talks about his own religious doubts and personal weaknesses.

Marta Lundberg, a homely school teacher, is in love with Pastor Ericsson, who finds her attention and affection irritating. He flees to his memories of his beloved wife who died four years ago. He tries to convince himself that he died emotionally and spiritually when she died. Through Marta Lundberg's love and the sexton, who believes that Christ's greatest suffering came from the thought that God had forsaken him, Pastor Ericsson gains a new understanding of religion and the importance of love. The film illustrates that God is probably love.

Bergman, has carefully fitted together the pieces of his structure. The foundation is solid. There is nothing flashy, showy or unnecessary. He uses no tricks to awakening the attention of those who are not interested. The result is an extremely moving and fascinating film for the religiously aware and a somewhat boring one for the religiously indifferent.

Fred.

Dime With A Halo

Hollywood, Feb. 27.

Sentimental tale of five Tijuana lads who win a pile at the racetrack. Hampered by lack of natural setting and artificial approach, pic misfires. A low budgeter, can be bailed out by inventivt ad-pub treatment.

Metro release of Laslo Vadnay-Hans Wilhelm production (coproduced by Anthony Barr and Pat B. Rooney). Directed by Boris Sagal. Screenplay, Vadnay, Wilhelm; camera, Philip H. Lahrop; editor, Ralph E. Winters; music, Ronald Stein; asst. directors, Jack Gertsman, Harold H. Herman. Reviewed at the studio, Feb. 27, '63. Running time, 94 MINS.

Juania	Barbara Luna
Jose	Roger Mobley
Chuy Perez	Rafael Lopez
Mr. Jones	Paul Langton
Cashier	Robert Carrcart
Rafael	Manuel Padilla
Cesar	Larry Domasin
Domingo	Tony Maxwell
Doorman	Vito Scottti
Mr. Lewis	Jay Adler
Consul Glenson	Theodore Newton
Priest	Steven Geray
Mr. Gonzales	Jeno Mate
Stripper	Joan Connors
Mexican Woman	Tina Menard
Newsboy	Raymond Sanchez

Thus far, it's been a banner year for ragamuffins on the screen. "Spencer's Mountain" had a horde of nine, "My Six Loves" offered a sextet, and here we have a crop of five calculated to "steal your heart away." Basically, it all represents a reactionary movement on the part of Hollywood filmmakers responding to the clamor in certain circles over what seems to be a disproportionate amount of modern film fare given to adult or unsavory themes. The movement has merit and there will be those who embrace "Dime With A Halo" as the bittersweet and heartwarming little picture it was designed to be.

Had it been more realistically constructed and executed the Metro release might have evolved into one of those junior-sized gems that become box office sleepers. But, as is the custom in the great majority of films focusing on the activities of children, "Dime With A Halo" steers off the desired course and adopts a self-conscious, affectedly cute and thoroughly artificial style that betrays the potential of its premise.

Commercially, the Laslo Vadnay-Hans Wilhelm production, written by them and coproduced by Anthony Barr and Pat B. Rooney, is on unsure footing. Fundamentally, it is an entertainment aimed at the family audience. Yet it contains material not exactly conducive to acceptance by such an audience. Strippers, for example, play a key role in the proceedings and are witnessed in action. Since more sophisticated filmgoers are apt to find the going a bit tedious, it is difficult to see just where the surefire boxoffice appeal of this film lies. Fortunately, it has been produced on a modest expenditure and can, if cleverly and robustly promoted and presented, make its presence felt to a sufficient degree.

The story deals with a quintet of Tijuana urchins who, each week, pool the resources of their street hawking and place a wager, through a friendly gambler from the states, on the 5-10 pool at Caliente. As might be expected, one Sunday, after cutting in the Christ child for a slice of the action by lifting a dime from the church poor box, the six nags of their choice all come in. But the gambler friend, for some mysterious reason, has left the premises, leaving the little band of moppets without a trustworthy adult to visit the cashier for the payoff (and, although it is glided over, without transportation from Caliente back to Tijuana). After a series of misadventures, the kids finally track down the kind gambler but, as fate would have it, he dies of a coronary at the cashier's window and the cashier, in coming to his aid, steps on the winning ticket which attaches itself to a sticky morsel on his shoe and is lost forever.

Three of the five youngsters make favorable impressions, especially tiny Manuel Padilla, who draws the meatiest comedy material and rises to the occasion as a bootblack given to hiccoughs whenever circumstances look bleak. Rafael Lopez registers as the leader of the moppet party, and Roger Mobley is appealing in the pivotal role of a lad just arrived from north of the border with his older sister (Barbara Luna) who has had to resort to Tijuana stripping to support him and keep him out of a foster home. The pretty Miss Luna does a commendable job. Paul Langton is competent as the ill-fated gambler, and the balance of support is satisfactory.

Boris Sagal has handled directorial reins quite respectably on the whole, but the generally lame-sounding dialog and the basic artificiality of the story design prove more than can be compensated for in execution. Ronald Stein has composed a catchy theme, but guitar punctuation of much of the action is somewhat heavyhanded. Capable assists have been contributed by cameraman Philip H. Lathrop, editor Ralph E. Winters and art director Charles Myall.

The film should have been shot in Tijuana and not on a studio sound stage. This is one case where the physical authenticity would have made a big difference in spawning the essence of reality without which the picture flounders in a morass of artificial sentiment.

Tube.

Schaut Auf Diese Stadt
(Look At This City) (EAST GERMAN)

Berlin, March 12.

Progress release of Defa production. Directed by Karl Gass. Written by Karl Eduard von Schnitzler. Editor, Christel Hemmerling. Screened at Ratskeller, Schoenerberg, West Berlin. Running time, 82 MINS.

"Look At This City," says the late (1953) West Berlin Mayor, Ernst Reuter, several times in this East German propaganda film. It's an excerpt from a West Berlin newsreel. The East German commentator then continues this bit via ironically referring to West Berlin as a front city, a city of cold war, a NATO bastion, a city that teems with spies and fascists, imperialists, monopoly capitalists, militarists, revengists. In brief, it's dubbed a city that endangers world peace. It's repeatedly pointed out that the East German government is composed of nothing but freedom-abiding people while the West Berlin administration headed by Willy Brandt is a bunch of war mongers.

Karl Eduard von Schnitzler, the star among the East German political commentators, is the mental creator of this East German documentary film on West Berlin. The Commies have often proved that they are masters when it comes to exploiting "facts" for their propaganda purposes. While the film can't convince those who are familiar with the real West-East Berlin situation, it's certainly within the bounds of possibility that a faraway neutral viewer (the film reportedly will be shown in African and Asiatic countries too) won't be able to distinguish where the truth begins and ends. Because this is a skillful mixture of exaggerations, distortions of historical facts, some half-way truths and just pure slander.

This film's anti-American attitude is very strong. Gen. Lucius D. Clay and the late John Foster Dulles are heavily attacked. A main target is RIAS, the U.S. sponsored radio station in West Berlin. Marching U.S. soldiers are accompanied by rock-n-roll rhythms (taken from AFN). The "unholy U.S. influence" is mainly made responsible for the high suicide rate, juve delinquency and vices of all calibres in West Berlin. On the other hand, the late President Roosevelt (his funeral is inserted in the film) gets praise.

What West Berliners think of the whole situation was evidenced at the last elections (Feb. 17): The Commies got only 1.4% of the votes. And that in a city which once, before Hitler, was a stronghold of Communism.

Hans.

The Balcony

Expert film adaptation of Genet's avant garde drama. A sure "artie" hit. Will fascinate, annoy, trouble and outrage.

Continental Distributing presentation of Walter Reade-Sterling, Allen Hodgdon Productions and City Film Corp. (Ben Maddow and Joseph Strick) production. Stars Shelley Winters, Peter Falk and Lee Grant. Directed by Joseph Strick. Screenplay, Ben Maddow, based on play by Jean Genet as translated by Bernard Frechtman; camera, George Folsey; editor, Chester W. Schaeffer; music, Igor Stravinsky; asst. director, Helen Levitt. Reviewed at Coronet Theatre, N.Y., March 6, '63. Running time, 84 MINS.

Madame Irma	Shelley Winters
Police Chief	Peter Falk
Carmen	Lee Grant
Judge	Peter Brocco
Bishop	Jeff Corey
Thief	Ruby Dee
Penitent	Joyce Jameson
Horse	Arnette Jens
Roger	Leonard Nimoy
General	Kent Smith

To those who remember the Off-Broadway production of Jean Genet's "The Balcony" a couple of seasons back, a film adaptation of that uncompromisingly shocking play might seem totally unlikely—at least, for successful screen adaptation. However, Joe Strick and Ben Maddow, whose initial collaboration, "The Savage Eye," remains a classic example of realistic (some say nihilistic) cinematic reportage, have done the job superbly. With Genet's apparent approval, they have eliminated the play's obscene language (though it's still plenty rough) and clarified some of its obscurations. The result is a tough, vivid and dispassionate fantasy—one of the most original and "adult" American films in years. Needless to say, it's strictly an art entry, and attempts to sell it beyond that audience may trigger a certain amount of outrage.

This is never an easy film to watch, but also it is never boring or pretentious, and often it is acidly funny. Most of the action of the film, localed in an unnamed city in the throes of a bloody revolution, takes place in a highly special kind of brothel, equipped like a movie studio with sets, costumes, rear projection devices, etc., which permit the patrons to enact their darkest fantasies (they

can also pay with credit cards). Thus a gas company employee visits The Balcony (name of the brothel) to play out his dream of being a bishop; a milkman sees himself as a heroic general, and a mousy accountant a chief justice. The film is one of bitter ironies and disastrous self-deceptions, including the contrast between the savage and seemingly pointless war outside and the opiate peace of the brothel.

Presiding over the macabre revels is Shelley Winters, the madame who designs the illusions and is all the more ominous for her complete, almost tender detachment. The peace of the brothel is shattered with the arrival of the police chief, Peter Falk, the madame's occasional lover who is fighting a last ditch stand outside to destroy the revolution. To this end, he sends the ersatz bishop, general and chief justice in a motorcade through the city to convince the rebels that their cause is lost. The fraud works, except that the bogus officials start taking themselves seriously.

A final irony is provided when the defeated rebel leader comes to The Balcony to enact his dream —that of being the all-powerful police chief. When the real chief and his opponent wind up in a brawl, the madame has them both stripped to the skin, shorn of their physical and psychological disguises, and thrown out into the ruins of the city which no longer remembers—or cares—what all the shooting was about.

In this latter instance, Strick and Maddow seem to have considerably simplified Genet's original text, but enough of his cold view of life remains to provoke countless arguments. Most importantly, Strick and Maddow have provided this fantastic film with its own reality. It is never capricious nor purposefully obscure, proceeding always with a recognizable logic. It is full of chilling detail and knife-sharp scenes, as when the police chief harangues the populace via radio from the brothel, speaking a furious jargon of nonsensical political and tv commercial cliches. Or, a comparatively gentle moment when the madame restrains her young office assistant, Lee Grant, (for whom she has a lesbian lech), from returning to her original job with the rest of the girls: "There are plenty of good whores but not enough good bookkeepers."

The performances are excellent, beginning with those of Miss Winters, Falk and Miss Grant, and including the entire supporting cast, particularly Peter Brocco as the judge, Jeff Corey as the bishop and Ruby Dee, as the prostie who plays "thief" to Brocco's judge. George Folsey's photography is fine, as is the editing of Chester W. Shaeffer, which neatly splices actual newsreel footage with studio material to set the chaotic scene. Igor Stravinsky's music also contributes to the firstrate production.

Most notable, however, is the work of Strick as director and Maddow as scripter, both of whom have carefully avoided the temptation to festoon an already bizarre property (the mind reels to think how Orson Welles would have tricked this up!). They also have made a notable contribution

to indie lowbudget American filmmaking.   *Anby.*

Mathias Sandorf
(FRENCH-COLOR-SCOPE)
Paris, March 12.

UGC release of SFC-DIC-Procusa production. Stars Louis Jourdan; features Serena Vergano, Bernard Blier, Renaud Mary, Francisco Rabal. Directed by Georges Lampin. Screenplay, Gerard Cartier, Charles Spaak, Lampin from novel by Jules Verne; camera (Eastmancolor), C. Paniagua; editor, Henri Taverna. At Gaumont Palace. Running time, 105 MINS.
Mathias .... Louis Jourdan
Elizabeth .... Serena Vergano
Sarcany .... Renaud Mary
Torenthal .... Bernard Blier
Rotenborg .... Francisco Rabal

One of the few Jules Verne books not filmed by Americans gets a screen airing on its own grounds. It is a tale of revolution against tyranny in a mythical 19th Century country. Simplified characters, too much talk and only intermittent, but well done, action slant this primarily for playoff spots abroad.

A nobleman, siding with the revolutionary intellectuals and grounddown people, has a daughter in love with the head of the army in power. He is turned in by supposed friends but escapes as the people rise up.

There is a lot of hoary melodrama, rhetoric and sharp division between good and evil. Director Georges Lampin can not give this the more robust elan needed to make it a sparkling actioner or a crackling hokey look at revolution.

The result is a fairly well mounted but disjointed affair with a quaint if oldfashioned air. The Louis Jourdan name could help in the U.S. plus its well meaning theme, fetching color and simple one dimensional storyline. The few moments of fight, revolt and dynamics are welcome. Supporting cast is adequate with Renaud Mary etching a knowing scenery-chewing portrait of a caddish climber.
         Mosk.

Rififi In Tokyo

Hackneyed crime meller for double billing.

Hollywood, March 13.

Metro release of Jacques Bar production. With Karl Boehm, Keiko Kishi, Barbara Lass, Charles Vanel, Michel Vitold, Dante Maggio. No character name credits. Directed by Jacques Deray. Screenplay, Auguste Le Breton, adapted by Jose Giovanni, Deray, R. M. Arlaud; camera, Tadashi Aramaki; editor, Albert Jurgenson; music, George Delerue. Reviewed at Pix Theatre, March 13, '63. Running time, 89 MINS.

Except for occasional hot flashes of cinematic imagination, this Japanese-based, internationally-bred crime melodrama is little more than a routine and shopworn study of the campaign of a ring of jewel thieves. The only noteworthy plot variation is a technical one designed to illustrate that bank protection of valuables has moved into the electronic age, with all sorts of radar and video devices utilized to foil the enterprising modern thief. But the human element in this Jacques Bar production is poorly defined and constructed, a shortcoming further complicated by dubbing and choppy last-ditch editing to make the Metro release serviceable for second slotting.

The Auguste Le Breton scenario has the thieves gathering and mapping an attempt to pilfer the large, flawless diamond of a Japanese tycoon which is locked in a vault in the Bank of Tokyo. After difficulties with a gang of local thugs, as well as intra-organization romantic traumas, the three principals successfully worm their way into the modernized vault, only to have an old-fashioned door of iron bars drop out of the ceiling and sink itself into the floor, trapping the mastermind in the vault and sealing him in an ironic prison with only his treasure for company.

Basic error is the fact that Le Breton's scenario waits too long before revealing the motivations, aims and desires of the principals, with the result that audience concern for the thieves is never aroused. And, in this kind of picture, it is virtually mandatory that one feels some sense of empathy for the crooks. There's no one else to root for. Certainly not those damned electronic contraptions.

The cast, led by Karl Boehm, plays it out competently. Significantly implicated are Keiko Kishi, pretty Barbara Lass, Charles Vanel, Michel Vitold and Dante Maggio. The maze of Tokyo back alleys is the interesting setting for much of the picture, and it has been employed to dramatic advantage by director Jacques Deray and cameraman Tadashi Aramaki, both of whom display scattered cinematic flair.   *Tube.*

Mourir A Madrid
(Die In Madrid)
(FRENCH)
Paris, March 19.

Athos release of Ancinex production. Directed and compiled by Frederic Rossif; commentary, Madeleine Chapsal, Rossif; camera, Georges Basky; editor, Suzanne Baron. At Studio-Publicis, Paris. Running time, 85 MINS.

A montage of newsreel and documentary footage on the Spanish Civil War from 1936 to 1939 emerges an absorbing and incisive summing up of that sad debacle which was a proving ground for second World War. Its intense and knowing filmic mounting makes this something for arty and specialized use abroad as well as for tv.

Frederic Rossif shows a flair for welding his well-picked footage into a concise, objective look at the war. Its condemnations are in its footage. Some extra specially shot scenes on eternal aspects of Spain are also expertly used to give an ironic counterpoint to or underlining of the main theme.

Spain's feudal look in the 1930's is first blocked in and then the Popular Front vote win and the abdication of the King. A spate of anarchy sets up the Army and Church against the government which then leads on to the Civil War.

The terrible bloodletting, the rise of General Franco and the siding of Hitler and Mussolini with Franco as other countries sent only personal volunteers are aptly pictorialized. Then the sombre seesawing of the war till the victory of Franco.

The first use of civilian bombing is also shown. It ends on a mute note as Hitler reviews and praises his special division that got its first taste of war in Spain before it

started out in World War Two.

A solid, probing commentary, good music and sharp editing tie this into one of the better historical compilation pix that are still popular here and should be in foreign spots.

The contemporary history, the renewed interest in this war via books of late, and its own intrinsic visual power should make this something for offshore marts. But it calls for good personalized sell.
         Mosk.

A Face in the Rain

Intriguing meller of wartime Italy, with Rory Calhoun as only name for U.S. audiences; needs hardsell for much b.o. action in America.

Embassy Pictures (Joseph E. Levine) release of Embassy-Filmways-Calvic production. Stars Rory Calhoun, Marina Berti; features Niall McGinnis, Massimo Giuliani. Directed by Irving Kershner. Screenplay by Hugo Butler, Jean Rouverol, based on story by Guy Elmes; camera, Haskell Wexley. Previewed in N.Y. projection room, March 14, '63. Running time, 81 MINS.
Rand .... Rory Calhoun
Anna .... Marina Berti
Klaus .... Niall McGinnis
Paolo .... Massimo Giuliani

This rather intriguing meller about the Nazis in Italy during the war will require plenty of hardsell if it gets far in the American market. Film has only the Rory Calhoun name as marquee lustre for U.S. audiences even though several Italo players do yeoman work in putting across a familiar, well-worn plot. Marching Nazi helmeted troops, snooping of the Gestapo and the familiar dastardly tricks of the SS troopers have been incorporated in any number of war yarns all of which were done more effectively and with more, and better known, Yank stars.

Despite these failings, "A Face in the Rain" likely will make money in the American market because it looks like a moderately budgeted pic.

Story has Calhoun as an American spy who has been parachuted behind the German lines in Italy. He is ready to set up shop with the Italo Underground when the Gestapo rush in, and he's forced to flee. Taking refuge in the home of a language professor (one of his contacts), he is about to be turned out by the wife, Marina Berti. But the young son hides him in the attic.

It seems that Anna (Berti) is in love with Niall McGinnis, high-ranking German officer, who's trying to grab Calhoun, as apparently are some 50 other Nazi troops. It's soon evident that Anna and this German officer have been intimate. The real excitement is caused by Calhoun's many and sundry efforts to escape over the slippery tile rooftops while the rain comes down in torrents.

However, only when Anna leaves the apartment soon after her officer lover departs does he feel safe in the apartment proper and able to eat. When a Gestapo agent comes back to search the supposed empty apartment, Calhoun escapes and the Nazis scramble after Anna. She is shot down in cold blood by her German officer sweetheart because he fears being suspected of harboring a spy.

Plot has too much marching feet,

clambering over rooftops and climbing spiral stairs, with amazing lack of real action. Calhoun turns in one of his best performances as the spy while Miss Berti proves highly effective as the professor's wife who makes a play for the Nazi officer to protect her husband's life. Niall McGinnis, as the officer, is excellent. But the real scene-thefter is young Massimo Giuliani, who plays Anna's son. Support is unusually good.

Irving Kershner's direction is inclined to be uneven while, as noted, the screenplay is not the most original on this theme. Haskell Wexley's lense work is firstrate. While this is described as an Embassy-Filmways-Calvic production, John Calley is also listed as producer.   *Wear.*

La Baie Des Anges
(Bay of Angels)
(FRENCH-CINEMASCOPE)
Paris. March 12.

Pathe release of Sud Pacifique production. Stars Jeanne Moreau; features Claude Mann. Paul Guers. Written and directed by Jacques Demy. Camera. Jean Rabier; editor, Anne-Marie Cotret. At Studio Publicis, Paris. Running time, **85 MINS.**

Jackie .... Jean Moreau
Jean .... Claude Mann
Caron .... Paul Guers
Father .... Henri Nassiet

Study of gambling mania is closely observed via a couple thrown together at the gaming tables. It has some insights into the causes and effects but does not mix its documentary and human elements deeply enough. Ending is too vague. Its uneven quality, if knowing look at gambling, slant this primarily for specialized or arty houses abroad.

A young man, who has a good if small job, has not married because of the fear of being tied down to a lacklustre life. He is initiated to casino roulette via a fellow worker. He wins his first time and after an argument with his father goes off on vacation to the Riviera town of Nice.

This is done in strict exposition as well as an explanation of the game. Then he meets a tense girl to whom he brings luck. They win a lot but lose it the same night. Out of money, she stays with him and love develops, at least on his side.

She has left a child and husband because of her yen to gamble. She also admits to the boy, in a stormy scene, that she desires him mainly because he brings her luck. She leaves him but finally runs after him when she realizes that her life is empty and drifting. Film ends on this note, not making it clear whether he will cure her or she will leave eventually. Casino scenes have an intriguing air. Jeanne Moreau builds an eloquent type of the gambling dame who is essentially a .kind and amoral girl. Claude Mann is a fitting foil as a boyish. vaguely unsatisfied but more moral type.

Jacques Demy has given this a stark black and white lensing and directorial flair that is mainly concerned in stripping bare the reasons and causes of this kind of vice. But a cutting off from the background, reasons and motives, sometimes makes this too one dimensional.

But there is enough different

observation, fine playing and pictorial finesse to keep this fairly absorbing. Pic is technically fine. Here is another offbeater that would need a hard sell to make its way in foreign markets.   *Mosk.*

Ballade Pour Un Voyou
(Ballad for a Hoodlum)
(FRENCH)
Paris, March 12.

Rank release of Editions Cinegraphiques-Camera production. Stars Laurent Terzieff, Hildegarde Neff; features Michel Vitold. Philippe Noiret, Michel De Re, Etienne Bierry. Directed by Jean-Claude Bonnardot. Screenplay. Bonnardot, Jacqueline Sundstrom. Alexandre Tabor, Marcel Moussy; camera. Jean Bodal; editor, Ginette Boudet. Preemed in Paris. Running time, **85 MINS.**

Vincent .... Laurent Terzieff
Martha .... Hildegarde Neff
Chief .... Michel Vitold
Fabien .... Philippe Noiret
Max .... Etienne Bierry

Neatly-made suspense item about international skulduggery over the contents of a secret suitcase generates enough holding interest and tautness to qualify for good playoff chances abroad. Even though there are some loose ends and surface characterizations, the pic moves along firmly and is generally gripping.

A reformed ex-con. somewhat bored with life, is asked to deliver a suitcase. He is followed by a mysterious gunman and he goes from place to place as he gets notes for further meetings. He gets mad, overcomes his shadower and runs off with the suitcase. Gangsters and police close in on him and the former capture his girl to force him to come along with the suitcase.

A final meeting has him blowing up the suitcase, since it had a bomb mechanism inside to prevent opening, and finally is mowed down by the police. There is a little too much elaborate plotting at the beginning which gives it a confused air. But it then settles down when the plot swings into action.

For a first pic, Jean-Claude Bonnardot shows a fine, precise feel for mood and interest. Too many illusions to foreign and local political hands in the affair, and some forced talk pointing up man's hapless state politically are a bit superfluous.

More clarity and directness might have helped. But the expert technical aspects, a rigorous progression and neat thesping, make this an engaging actioner with enough to mark Bonnardot as a director to be heard from in the future.   *Mosk.*

The Birds
(COLOR)

Skillfully produced Hitch-shocker, mounted on rickety story. Big b.o. looms.

Hollywood, March 19.
Universal release of Alfred Hitchcock production. Stars Rod Taylor, Jessica Tandy, Suzanne Pleshette; introduces 'Tippi' Hedren. Directed by Hitchcock. Screenplay, Evan Hunter, from story by Daphne du Maurier; camera (Technicolor), Robert Burks; editor, George Tomasini; assistant director, James H. Brown. Reviewed at Directors Guild of America, March 19, '63. Running time, **120 MINS.**

Mitch Brenner .... Rod Taylor
Lydia Brenner .... Jessica Tandy
Annie Hayworth ..... Suzanne Pleshette
Cathy Brenner .... Veronica Cartwright
Mrs. Bundy .... Ethel Griffies
Sebastian Sholes ....Charles McGraw
Mrs. MacGruder .... Ruth McDevitt
Salesman .... Joe Mantell
Deputy Al Malone....Malcolm Atterbury
Drunk .... Karl Swenson
Helen Carter .... Elizabeth Wilson
Deke Carter ....Lonny Chapman
Fisherman No. 1........Doodles Weaver
Postal Clerk ....John McGovern
Man in Elevator ......Richard Deacon
Woman .... Doreen Lang
Melanie Daniels ....Tippi Hedren

The Birds is came. Sheer novelty value and the Hitchcock label no doubt will make people flock to see it and turn the Universal release into a big moneymaker, but beneath all of this elaborate featherbedlam lies a Hitch cock-and-bull story that's essentially a fowl ball.

The premise is fascinating. The idea of billions of bird-brains refusing to eat crow any longer and adopting the hunt-and-peck system, with homo sapiens as their ornithological target, is fraught with potential. Cinematically, Hitchcock & Co. have done a masterful job of meeting this formidable challenge. But dramatically, "The Birds" is little more than a shocker-for shock's-sake. It is a parody of Hitchcock by Hitchcock.

Though slickly executed and fortified with his characteristic tongue-in-cheek touches, the Sultan of shocks and suspense has settled for a featherweight scenario that is little more than a serviceable vehicle into which he is able to inject periodic shots and spurts of sanguinary horror. But Hitchcock deals more provocatively and effectively in human menace. A fantasy framework dilutes the toxic content of his patented terror-tension formula, and gives the picture a kind of sci-fi exploitation feel, albeit with a touch of production gloss.

Still, it's an experience in a theatre, and this is the special magic of an Alfred Hitchcock attraction. A kind of community chemistry runs through an audience witnessing one of his films, a delicious and infectious state of constant group expectancy that threatens, in any given frame, to send an electric charge through the entire audience and make it react as a single entity. It's like attending a block party. To a degree, "The Birds" has this unique quality.

Evan Hunter's screenplay, from Daphne du Maurier's story, has it that a colony of our feathered "friends" over California's Bodega Bay (it's never clear how far-reaching this avian mafia extends) suddenly decides, for no apparent reason other than just plain orneriness, to swoop down enmasse on the human population, beaks first. These bird raids are captivatingly bizarre and terrifying.

Where the scenario and picture slip is in the sphere of the human element. An unnecessary elaborate romantic plot has been cooked up and then left suspended. It involves a young bachelor attorney (Rod Taylor), his sister (Veronica Cartwright) whose dread of loneliness manifests itself in possessiveness, and a plucky, mysterious playgirl ('Tippi' Hedren) whose arrival from San Francisco with a pair of caged lovebirds for Taylor coincides with the outbreak of avian hostility in and around Bodega, causing some of the townfolk to suspect she may be the source of the sudden evil. Is she? Is there more here than meets a birdwatcher's eye? Hitch isn't telling. The picture ends with a long drawn-out shot of the principals motoring away, leaving Bodega Bay (and tomorrow the world?) the exclusive property of the airborne invaders—a self-styled bird sanctuary.

Aside from the birds, the film belongs to Miss Hedren, who makes an auspicious screen bow. She virtually has to carry the picture alone for the first 45-minute stretch, prior to the advent of the first wave of organized attackers from the sky. The actress' efforts notwithstanding, this early portion of the film is much too draggy. Endowed with a distinctive voice, sensitivity and a subtle sparkle, Miss Hedren has a star quality, and Hitchcock has provided her with a potent vehicle to launch her career. Of the others, Miss Tandy, a first-class actress, makes the most vivid impression. Taylor emotes with strength and attractiveness. Miss Pleshette is stuck with a character that is poorly defined. The rest of the cast, Veronica Cartwright prominent, is satisfactory.

It's a wing ding of a production, characterized by several unusual aspects. One, of course, is the obvious necessity of getting the birds to cooperate, a feat accomplished by Hitchcock with the no doubt invaluable aid of trainer Ray Berwick. Another novelty is the absence of music. Instead, Hitchcock has utilized for background mood an electronic sound device (a trautonium) upon which a tone-less composition by Remi Gassman and Oskar Sala is rendered. The effect achieved is appropriate and arresting. Other salient and resourceful contributions to an unorthodox film are Robert Burks' adaptable and subtly-Technicolored photography, George Tomasini's careful editing rhythms, Robert Boyle's observant production design.

Credit is also due such craftsmen as special photographic advisor Ub Iwerks, special effects man Lawrence A. Hampton and soundmen Waldon O. Watson and William Russell.   *Tube.*

Duel Of The Titans

Brawny but dull exploitation item for the beefcake fanciers.

Hollywood, March 21.
Paramount release of Alessandro Jacovoni production. Stars Steve Reeves, Gordon Scott. Directed by Sergio Corbucci. Ecreenplay, Corbucci, Martino, Sergio Leone, Franco Rossetti, Tessari; camera (Technicolor), Enzo Barboni, Dario

Di Palma; assistant directors, Guido Zurli, Mimmola Girosi. Reviewed at the studio, March 21, '63. Running time, **91 MINS.**

Romulus	Steve Reeves
Remus	Gordon Scott
Julia	Virna Lisi
Tarpeja	Arnella Vanoni
Curzio	Jacques Sernas
Tazio	Massimo Girotti
Amulio	Franco Volpi
Faustolo	Andrea Bosic
Rea Silvia	Laura Solari
Numa	Enzo Cerusico
Publio	Giuliano Dell-ovo
Servio	Germano Longo
Acilio	Franco Balducci
Sulpicio	Piero Lulli
Celere	Gianni Musy
Priest	Enrico Glori
Estria	Jose Greci
Sira	Inge Nystrom

Musclebound is the word for this Italo-manufactured exploitation item in which Steve "Hercules" Reeves pits his colossal biceps against the equally prodigious brawn of Gordon "Tarzan" Scott in what is apt to be ballyhooed as the beefcake battle of the century. To some it may also serve to determine once and for all just which of the two is more dependent on muscle tissue as the major source of acting ability, although in this respect it rates a dead heat.

The Paramount release is dramatically primitive, technically crude and generally dull, but, thanks to that battle of the bulge, should reap some dividends as a saturation quickie. Ninety-seven pound weaklings ought not to be admitted unless accompanied by an accredited Vic Tanny alumnus.

The story of Romulus and Remus is the basis of the Alessandro Jacovoni production, directed by Sergio Corbucci and written by him with the aid of four other scribblers. Reeves is Romulus and Scott is Remus. The film depicts their adventures from the time they are abandoned as babes at the banks of the Tiber and reared by a she-wolf to the moment when Romulus slays his power-hungry brother and goes on to found the city that was to become Rome. In between there are several battles and such other diversions as a fight between man (Reeves) and bear in an arena and an erupting volcano or, as described here in typical spectaclese, "holy mountain that vomits fire."

Actually the titanic duel between Reeves and Scott will be something of a letdown for those impressionable diehards who trust ballyhoo. A few grunts and groans, thrusts and parries, and it's all over. Pretty tame for a fourth of a ton of talent. The acting is stiff, and post-dubbing doesn't help. Production values are pretentious and unimpressive. *Tube.*

Miracle Of The White Stallions
(COLOR)

Inept dramatization of World War II rescue of Lipizzan horses of Vienna. Little b.o. pull outside of Disney label.

Hollywood, March 22.

Buena Vista release of Walt Disney production; Peter V. Herald, associate producer. Stars Robert Taylor, Lilli Palmer, Curt Jurgens; features Eddie Albert, James Franciscus. Directed by Arthur Hiller. Screenplay, A. J. Carothers, based on Col. Alois Podhajsky's book, "The Dancing White Horses of Vienna"; camera (Technicolor), Gunther Anders; editors, Alfred Srp, Cotton Warburton; music, Paul Smith; asst. director, Laci Ronay. Reviewed at studio, March 22, '63. Running time, **117 MINS.**

Col. Podhajsky	Robert Taylor
Vedena Podhajsky	Lilli Palmer
Gen. Tellheim	Curt Jurgens
Rider Otto	Eddie Albert
Maj. Hoffman	James Franciscus
Gen. Patton	John Larch
Countess Arco-Valley	Brigitte Horney
Col. Reed	Philip Abbott
U.S. Gen.	Douglas Fowley
Gen. Stryker	Charles Regnier
Rider Hans	Fritz Wepper
Groom Sascha	Gunther Haenel
Innkeeper Hager	Hans Habietinek
Dispatcher	Philo Hauser
Refugee Leader	Michael Janisch
Woman Railroad Official	Margarethe Dux
Engineer	Max Hautler
German M.P. Capt.	Robert Dietl
Att. Carl	Josef Krastl
Kreisleiter	Peter Jost
2nd Rider	Kurt Jager
3rd Rider	Olaf Tschierschke
Orderly Tellheim	Herbert Prikopa
German Capt. Ranhoff	Erik Schumann
Intruder	Helmut Janatsch
Stryker's Adjutant	Michael Tellering
Brooklyn G.I.	Hal Galilli
1st Rider	Harry Hornisch

Very likely there was a deeply moving story in the rescue of Austria's renowned Lipizzan horses during World War II, but it doesn't materialize in "Miracle Of The White Stallions," a fuzzy, laborious and generally undistinguished dramatization of that story in a confusing and insensitive scenario by A. J. Carothers plus turtle-tempoed direction by Arthur Hiller.

Robert Taylor stars as Col. Alois Podhajsky, director of the Spanish Riding School of Vienna. It is this personage's autobiography which served as the film's source material. The picture dramatizes his efforts, in the seesaw latter days of the second world war, to keep his prized stallions safe and to reunite them with the enemy-held Lipizzan mares, thus preserving the breed. This involves some tricky political and military moves that, in the film, are confusing and ill-explained.

Characters are hazily defined and genuine audience concern for man or beast is never aroused, although there is evidence in the source material of touching aspects to the tale. As for the combat scenes, this is strictly a Disneyland-eye-view of World War II.

The characters are skin-deep, limiting the actors to superficial delineations. Top roles are essayed with competence by Taylor, Lilli Palmer, Curt Jurgens, Eddie Albert and James Franciscus, with John Larch, Brigitte Horney and Philip Abbott in key support. Filmed in Austria, with Peter V. Herald in the associate producer niche, the picture sports capable camerawork by Gunther Anders, art direction by Werner and Isabell Schlicting and music by Paul Smith. Sluggish editing by Alfred Srp and Cotton Warburton doesn't help matters any. Some judicious pruning is in order. *Tube.*

Sammy Going South
(BRITISH-COLOR)

The Royal film show pic is a rather turgid one, being a disappointment from Alexander MacKendrick; little marquee appeal except for Edward G. Robinson.

London, March 26.

British Lion-Bryanston Seven Arts release, through BLC, of a Michael Balcon (Hal Mason) production. Stars Edward G. Robinson; features Constance Cummings, Harry H. Corbett, Paul Stassino, Fergus McClelland. Directed by Alexander MacKendrick. Screenplay, Denis Cannan from W. H. Canaway's novel; camera, Eastmansolor, Edwin Hillier; editor, Jack Harris; music, Tristram Cary. At Odeon, Leicester-square, London. Running time, **128 MINS.**

Cocky Wainwright	Edward G. Robinson
Sammy	Fergus McClelland
Gloria van Imhoff	Constance Cummings
Lem	Harry H. Corbett
Spyros Dracondopolous	Paul Stassino
The Syrian	Zia Moyheddin
Abu Lubaba	Orlando Martins
Heneker	John Turner
Aunt Jane	Zena Walker
Dist. Com.	Jack Gwillim
Doctor	Guy Deghy

Many of the pix selected for the Royal Film Show have come under critical fire for being worthy but dull, sincere but shoddy. "Sammy Going South" also looms as a grave disappointment as a Royal Film Show choice, coming as it does from the distinguished stable of Sir Michael Balcon and being directed by Alexander MacKendrick. It's been a long wait for a film by the alert, intelligent MacKendrick. The sense of anti-climax is therefore all the greater. Without much boost from stellar appeal, except enjoyment always in welcoming Edward G. Robinson, this turgid drama faces a difficult time at the wickets.

It is based on an uneasy, incredible idea. A 10-year-old youngster (Fergus McClelland) is orphaned when his parents are killed in an air raid during the Suez crisis. In a blur he remembers that he has an Aunt Jane in Durban and that Durban is in the South. So he sets out, armed only with a toy compass. This seems a mighty unlikely proposition. Was there no neighbor who was around to help the child?

Anyway, he sets off on the long, arduous journey and, surprisingly, despite some contrived situations, very little excitement happens. He meets a Syrian peddler who sees in the kid a chance of a reward from Aunt Jane. Then the peddler comes to a sticky end and the boy helps himself to his wallet and moves on. He meets a rich American tourist but escapes her greedy clutches.

Not until he meets up with a grizzled old diamond smuggler (Robinson) does the film flicker into some spark of human interest. The old man and the moppet strike up a splendid friendship. The boy shoots a leopard—again an unlikely happening—and saves the old man's life. And so it goes on until, at last, he gets to Durban, footsore, dirty, but still full of youthful pep.

MacKendrick's films usually strike an attitude and have intuition on points of views. Relationship between his key characters are usually more clearly defined and worked on than in this. With the exception of Robinson, looking like a slightly junior Ernest Hemingway, and Paul Stassino, as a glib crook of a guide, the others are cardboard. Fergus McClelland is no more than adequate as the young adventurer, rarely touching the heart. Adequacy is now not enough in kid performers, for there are too many stars in the junior league. Constance Cummings, Harry H. Corbett, Orlando Martins, Zia Moyheddin and Guy Deghy tackle routine chores without signs of overstrain.

MacKendrick's direction is curiously floundering and flat, with the editing haphazard. Perhaps it all stems from Denis Cannan having to tackle the screenplay from a story that never sounds remotely credible but which is played and written solidly and not with a touch of imaginative fantasy. Honorable mention to the production manager, Philip Shipway, for some interesting locations and to Erwin Hillier on camera. Some of his shots are run of mill. Others, in Eastmancolor, are most exciting. *Rich.*

Le Ore dell'Amore
(The Hours of Love)
(ITALIAN)

Rome, March 19.

Astoria release of D.D.L.S.p.A. production. Stars Ugo Tognazzi, Emanuele Riva; features Barbara Steele, Mara Berni, Umberto D'Orsi, Diletta D'Andrea, Brunello Rondi, Irene D'Aloisi. Directed by Luciano Salce. Screenplay, Salace, Castellano, Pipolo, from story by Castellano and Pipolo; camera, Erico Menczer; editor, Roberto Cinquini; music, Ennio Moricone. At Barberini, Rome. Running time, **100 MINS.**

Gianni	Ugo Tognazzi
Maretta	Emanuele Riva
Ottavio	Umberto D'Orsi
Leila	Barbara Steele

Amusing, often bitingly realistic film on a couple's marital troubles, boasting good performances by Emanuele Riva and Ugo Tognazzi. Good outlook for this at home and certain other territories.

Two longtime fiancees finally get married, and pic shows their gradual chilling to one another, until the windup finds them returning to their previous (and happy) separate quarters status as after-dark lovers. Bitter-sweet plot is given savvy, perceptive handling by director Luciano Salce, but more could have been obtained with more care.

Film seems to have been rushed in the making, and final result is uneven, making one regret it's not all up to its best moments. As noted, both Tognazzi and Miss Riva are standout as the couple while Umberto D'Orsi and Barbara Steele emerge via keen supporting characterizations. As usual in Salce's films, both settings and fringe performances are colorfully rendered and sharply observed. Technical credits are all good. *Hawk.*

Le Jour Et L'Heure
(The Day and the Hour)
(FRENCH-FRANSCOPE)

Paris March 26.

Metro release of Cipra-Terra Film-CCM-Monica Film production. Stars Simone Signoret, Stuart Whitman; features Genevieve Page, Michel Piccoli, Reggie Nalder, Billy Kearns, Henri Virlojeux. Directed by Rene Clement. Screenplay, Andre Barret, Roger Vailland, Clement; camera, Henri Decae; editor, Fedora Zincone. At Colisee, Paris. Running time, **110 MINS.**

Therese	Simone Signoret
Alan	Stuart Whitman
Agathe	Genevieve Page
Antoine	Marcel Piccoli
German	Reggie Nalder
Marboz	Pierre Dux
Pat	Billy Kearns
Druggist	Henri Virlojeux

(French Version)

MGM, through its locally-backed French company Cipra, has a stylish, well-acted entry in this tale of a French woman awakened to life and national commitment by the advent of a downed American flyer during the occupation of France in the last World War. The

extra plus of the names of Simone Signoret, the '59 Oscar winner, and Stuart Whitman should also help to make this a solid playoff item abroad, with arty spots also indicated.

Director Rene Clement, noted for such works as "Forbidden Games," "Gervaise" and "Purple Noon," again proves he is one of the best pic craftsmen practicing in French films today. He nimbly sketches in occupied France and neatly observes his characters embroiled in war, with conflicting loyalties as the war nears its end, and growing love.

Miss Signoret is a married woman with two children whose husband is a prisoner of war. She lives in a rich home and one day meets an old friend while coming home from a food foray in the country. He is transporting some Allied flyers downed behind the lines.

Some difficulty has her relenting and taking in one American till they can smuggle him out. A feeling develops between the two and she is even involved further when she is seeing him off on a train and a shadowing Gestapo man has her going along.

Production then goes through a series of adventures culminating in a solid bravura item on a crowded train when the American is caught by the Gestapo man. But he is helped by a sudden collective surge of the French as they manage to force the man out of a door. The camera seems to be amid the crowd in the narrow confines of the train corridors. It is an arresting piece of solid technical flair and knowhow.

Only drawback is a lack of warmth or feeling for the characters. Their backgrounds are sketched in via bits of dialog and action. Also there is a fine recreation of the times. But they rarely take on enough fibre and depth to make them more than stereotyped figures.

However, Miss Signoret gives a fine performance as the listless, disenchanted woman who is finally awakened by growing love. Whitman has a spontaneous charm to give a warmth and dash to his figure of the American pilot.

Camerawork is sharp and delicate as emotions and action call for it while editing is flawless. But the progression seems more embedded in general technique than in the actual self realization and change in the characters. But a soft pedaling of the love, solid chunks of techniques and overall acting excellence knit this into a neatly made vehicle that still is missing the spark to have its characters more lifelike.

But the mixed motive grabbag of Occupation hazards and shifting loyalties does help make a comment on war even if it stays mainly in the background. So chalk up a solidly carpentered film with probable international outlook, if staying resolutely French.

A good part of the production is in English via the scenes between Miss Signoret and Whitman.

The lines are good. These segs are subtitled in this version while the French bits will be likewise in the English version. Lingos shape about 50-50. Probable English title is "The Day and the Hour," literal translation.   *Mosk.*

The Man From The Diners' Club

Danny Kaye in fine fettle. Okay b.o. looms, although absence of color may limit overall potential.

Hollywood, March 6.
Columbia Pictures release of Bill Bloom production. Stars Danny Kaye; features Cara Williams. Martha Hyer, Telly Savalas. Everett Sloane. Directed by Frank Tashlin. Screenplay, Bill Blatty, from story by Blatty and John Fenton Murray; camera, Hal Mohr; editor, William A. Lyon; music, Stu Phillips; asst. director, Sam Nelson. Reviewed at Hollywood Paramount Theatre, Feb. 28, '63. Running time, **96 MINS.**
Ernie Klenk .... Danny Kaye
Sugar Pye .... Cara Williams
Lucy .... Martha Hyer
Foots Pulardos .... Telly Savalas
Martindale .... Everett Sloane
Bea Frampton .... Kay Stevens
Bassanio .... Howard Caine
George .... George Kennedy
Mooseghian .... Jay Novello
Ella Trask ...... Ann Morgan Guilbert
Minister .... Ronald Long
Quas .... Mark Tobin
Buzzy .... Cliff Carnell
Jerry Markus .... Edmund Williams
1st Beatnik .... Dean Stanton
Little Girl .... Carol Dixon
Father .... John Newton
Spinster .... Dorothy Neumann

The slapstick overwhelms the satire in "The Man From the Diners' Club," a cinematic design that may meet with the approval of advocates of wild visual comedy but is apt to disappoint those who prefer the composition of their humor the other way around. Considering the essentially topical nature of the story premise, and the pregnant possibilities inherent in a subject that lends itself so readily to more substantial and provocative treatment, this decision to pursue a frivolously farcical concept may strike some as tantamount to letting a frail tail wag a robust dog. Yet, thanks to the fine comedic abilities of Danny Kaye, who manages to wade through a hackneyed plot and usually overextended sight situations, there are sporadic bursts of merriment in the Bill Bloom production that even an occasional sophisticate may find irresistible.

Being a dandy item for moppet audiences, the Kaye enterprise would appear to be constructed on a firm commercial foundation. But, because most of the star's devout fans actually are not in the moppet realm, it may take the added impetus of attendance by Kaye's confirmed adult admirers to push the Columbia release into a respectable moneymaking category. An extra plus factor could be the stimulus of ad-pub gimmickry and promotion, an imaginative campaign geared to institutional tie-ins (a number of Diners' Club clients get hefty plugs in the film).

Bill Blatty's scenario, from a rather shopworn story he concocted in creative partnership with John Fenton Murray, casts Kaye as a nervous, browbeaten employee of the Diners' Club empire whose job it is to approve desirable applicants who wish to be card-carriers. Early scenes, the best in the film, depict his inability to endure or cope with the complex machinery of the modern business world. His tangles with the computers and filing systems that dominate his office provide some choice opportunities for Kaye to exploit his great gifts as a nimble, versatile and expressive clown, as

the little man in an impersonal bullying world.

When Kaye puts his okay on the application of a financially-ruined mobster (Telly Savalas) out on bail pending trial for tax evasion, the plot thickens, implicating the hero in a diabolical scheme whereby Savalas intends to hightail it out of the country after cremating Kaye from the ankles up so that his corpse will be mistaken for that of the mobster. The reason for this bizarre plot and the choice of Kaye as victim is simple: both men have left feet an inch longer than their right feet. The plan, needless to say, backfires in the course of a wild climactic sequence during which Savalas utilizes his D.C. card to exaggerated advantage.

The picture is liberally stuffed with situations of the sight gag variety, some of them resourcefully exploited by Kaye and director Frank Tashlin. On a number of occasions, however, notably in a rubbing table passage, they have exceeded the limits within which a gag remains effective. Savalas, an actor of enormous range and vivid presence, is outstanding in his comic enactment of the dastardly racketeer. Cara Williams has her moments as the mobster's tippling moll and Everett Sloane contributes some fine bits of nonsense as Kaye's superior, best of which is his outrage when he discovers Kaye in a restaurant about to commit the unspeakable act of paying for his check with cash. The startled Kaye responds by impulsively tearing up the money and flashing his card.

Martha Hyer dispatches the colorless role of Kaye's patient fiancee. Howard Caine gamely takes a lot of punishment in that overextended and uninspired scene on the rubbing table. Support is generally gregarious, with Kay Stevens, George Kennedy, Jay Novello and Ann Morgan Guilbert in prominent assignments.

A basically efficient level of production performance is attained by such accomplished craftsmen as cameraman Hal Mohr, editor William A. Lyon, art director Don Ament, soundman Lambert Day and composer Stu Phillips. But the absence of the traditionally glamorous color production surrounding Kaye will startle his fans and may be reflected by something of a slump in world-wide boxoffice returns. There is an adequate title song, warbled stylishly over the credits by Steve Lawrence. Last but not least a nod to special effects man Dick Albain, whose cleverly-devised props and convincing manipulation of them generally realize the comedy's potential and heighten its impact.
Tube.

Dal Sabato al Lunedi
(From Saturday to Monday)
(ITALIAN—COLOR)

Rome, March 26.
Cineriz release of a Cineriz-Castello Film (Milan) production. Features Marianne Hold, Geronimo Meynier, Sandro Panseri, Hilda Barry, Joe Laurel. Andreina Pezzi. Directed by Guido Guerrasio. Screenplay, Guerrasio, Leo Benvenuti, Piero de Bernardi from story by Guerrasio; camera (Technicolor), Giuseppe Aquari; music, Francesco Lavagnino. At Corso Cinema. Rome. Running time, **105 MINS.**
Enrico .... Geronimo Meynier
Sandrino .... Sandro Panseri
Joan .... Marianne Hold

Old lady .... Hilda Barry
Pinuccia .... Andreina Pezzi

Frail but sometimes charming little item made with a naivete which tips the fact that this is director Guido Guerrasio's first feature films effort after a warmup stint as one of Italy's foremost documentarists. Has elements for an okay payoff in depth, especially for Germany and north European areas for which it seems perhaps unconsciously keyed. Overseas chances are limited, but pic has some general appeal.

Two Milan youths go off to the North Italian lakes looking for weekend adventures. There they meet a chaperoned Dutch girl, fall for her, and follow her around. She briefly falls for one of the two, but Monday morning sees them back at work in the big city.

Marianne Hold makes a striking object for their attentions while Geronimo Meynier and Sandro Panseri act properly naive as her suitors. Hilda Barry turns in a colorful performance as the chaperone.

Color lensing, especially of countryside exteriors, is excellent. Other credits are standard. Strong contribution comes from Angelo Lavagnino's score. *Hawk.*

Paradiso Dell'Uomo

(Man's Paradise)
(ITALIAN—COLOR)

Rome, March 26.

Dino DeLaurentiis release of a Rotor Film (Carmine Bologna) production in association with Tokyo Theatres K.K. Directed by Giuliano Tomei. Second Unit director: Susumu Huni. Story and screenplay, Ivo Perilli. Camera (Technicolor), Jugyo Yoshida, Cesare Allione, Juichi Nagano; dances, Gino Landi; music, Piero Umiliani; editor, Franco Fraticelli. At Barberini, Rome. Running time, **100 MINS.**

Dino DeLaurentiis has himself a fine, generally exploitable property in this modern travelogue of Japan. Visual curio, and entertainment values make this a likely export item for most areas.

"Paradiso" follows the general pattern of many recent Italian travel documents, but is cut some notches above the norm. True, it has its purely sensational angles, such as the detailed looks at operations designed to give oriental eyes a "western" slant, and the usual fillip of near-nude females. But beyond this, it manages some intriguing footage showing the male's continued dominance of Japanese society, etc.

Major assist for director Giuliano Tomei comes from striking Technicolor hues assembled by two Japanese and on Italian cameramen, and from Piero Umiliani's apt musical backdropping. Other technical credits are equally topflight. *Hawk.*

"8 1/2"

(ITALIAN)

Rome, March 26.

Cineriz release of Angelo Rizzoli production. Stars Marcello Mastroianni, Claudia Cardinale, Anouk Aimee, Sandra Milo. Directed by Federico Fellini. Screenplay, Fellini, Tullio Pinelli, Ennio Flaiano, Brunello Rondi from story by Fellini and Flaiano; camera, Gianni di Venanzo; music, Nino Rota; editor, Leo Catozzo. At the Fiamma, Rome. Running time, **140 MINS.**

Guido .... Marcello Mastrianni
Claudia .... Claudia Cardinale
Luisa .... Anouk Aimee
Carla .... Sandra Milo
French actress .... Madeleine Lebeau
Mezzabotta .... Mario Pisu
Gloria .... Barbara Steele
Agent for French actor... Neil Robinson
Claudia's agent .... Mino Doro
Claudia's press agent——Mario Tarchetti
American reporter ...... Eugene Walter
His wife .... Gilda Dahlberg
Mysterious lady .... Caterina Boratto
Producers friend ...... Annie Gorassini
Magician friend .... Ian Dallas
Magician's partner....... Mary Indovino
Producer .... Guido Alberti
Director .... Mario Conocchia
Inspector........Cesarino Miceli Picardi
Secretary .... Bruno Agostini
Cashier .... John Stacy
Luisa's friend .... Rossella Falk
Timid admirer .... Mark Herron
Luisa's sister .... Elisabettha Catalano
Friends..... Rossella Como, Francesco Rigamonti, Matilde Calnam
Cardinal .... Tito Masini
His secretary ..... Alfredo de Lafeld
Secretary ...... Sebastiano de Leandro
Secretary .... Frazier Rippy
College Dean .... Maria Tedeschi
Saraghina .... Edra Gale
Grandmother .... Georgia Simmons
Aunts Marisa Colomber, Maria Raimondi
Dancer .... Yvonne Casadei
Hostess .... Nadine Sanders
Negro .... Hazel Rogers
Model .... Hedy Vessel
Father .... Annibale Ninchi
Mother .... Giuditta Rissone
Guido as child ...... Riccardo Guglielmi
Guido at school .... Marco Gemini

With "8½," Federico Fellini tops even his trendsetting "La Dolce Vita" in artistry. And he confirms himself one of the few undisputed masters of the visual-dramatic medium. For here is the author-director picture par excellence, an exciting, stimulating, monumental creation which i s likely to unleash almost as many controversies and discussions as "Dolce Vita" did some time back. It will similarly divide its viewers into rabid partisans and "I-don't-get-it" detractors.

Commercially, Fellini's new film should fare royally almost wherever it is shown. Less exploitable and explosive in content—at least on the surface—it cannot, however, hope to top the figures set by "Dolce Vita," a pic which admittedly also profited generously from censorship squabbles and Catholic Church opposition. "8½" should run into little or none of this harassment. Hence, it can use some savvy salesmanship of its own.

In style and cut, "8½" once again shows Fellini well in advance of his times. It is one of the most visually striking of all films, yet it has heart and an inner impact as well as an outside identification which distinguished its author's previous film as well. Like "Dolce Vita," this can (or must) be taken on several levels.

Basically, it is the story of a 43-year old director's crucial visit to a health resort to cure an undetermined illness. At the spa, he is confronted with a series of crises of a personal as well as professional nature. He is about to start a major film production, but totally lacks the inspiration for it. At the same time, he is worried about his physical condition, is becoming bored by the voluptuous mistress he has brought along with him, and disappointed by his wife's continued inability to understand him. All the while, he is hounded by production managers, would-be stars, scriptwriters, and the opportunist satellites which surround recognized film creators with false flattery and real pressure.

Flashbacks to his youth and flash-forwards in the form of daydreams illustrate the director's inner qualms and worries, resolved at the finale by his realization that, after all: "life is a feast; let's live it together," taking the good with the bad. The resulting catharsis is likely to spread to the audience as well in what is ultimately an optimistic film, and, as such, a far cry from "Dolce Vita."

But the plot should not—or cannot—be told. Fellini was right in keeping it a secret until the film's opening. For "8½" defies telling or description. It is a 140-minute seance on the psychiatrist's couch, in which the author, though the director-star in the film, turns himself inside out, confessing his innermost thoughts and problems, and finally reaching his apt conclusions. And all with the irreplaceable aid of the camera, here adroitly, inventively, dramatically used as it rarely has before. During his long seance, Fellini misses no trick in lashing out savagely at hypocrisy in every walk of life, while building up a significant, believable picture of crisis in a creative man.

Once again, Fellini gets top assistance from his large and colorful cast. Marcello Mastroianni is excellent as the middle-aged director, often deliberately bearing an uncanny resemblance to Fellini himself (as the film itself shapes as Fellini's most autobiographic work to date). Sandra Milo and Anouk Aimee fight it out for second honors, respectively as mistress and wife of the director, in two diametrically opposed but equally fine delineations.

Claudia Cardinale makes several strikingly effective appearances as Mastroianni's symbol of pure creation, while Barbara Steele, Madeleine Lebeau, Guido Alberti, Giuditta Rissone, Rossella Falk, Annibale Ninchi, Cesarino Miceli Picardi, and many many others help fill out one of the most colorful cast rosters ever put together. Ian Dallas, as a magician, and Edra Gale, as a childhood apparition, are probably the most memorable in this supporting cast.

A final nod must go to Tullio Pinelli, Ennio Flajano, and Brunello Rondi, whose assistance on the script has served Fellini well, as well as to Piero Gherardi whose sets and costumes are again in the prize-winning class, and to Nino Rota, who has penned a haunting score for the picture.

Further praise goes for Gianni di Venanzo whose highly functional lighting camerawork is also the best ever in a Fellini film. Assistant director Guidarino Guidi deserves a further nod for his help in helping assemble so colorful a list of players. *Hawk.*

14 - 18

(FRENCH)

Paris, March 26.

Rank release of Zodiac production. Compiled and directed by Jean Aurel; commentary, Cecil Saint Laurent; editor, Anne-Marie Cotret. At Marbeuf, Paris. Running time, **90 MINS.**

With the First World War getting another big round via books and public interest, an enterprising filmmaker now takes a look at it via a well-selected and compiled mounting of old newsreel footage on it from all over the world. The little seen scenes, the fine composing and simple commentary slant this for arty chances abroad, but needing the hardsell. It seems a natural for tv airing.

The causes of the conflict are neatly sketched in as the German Kaiser's muscle-flexing and the intricate alliances in Europe allow the execution of the Archduke Ferdinand of Austria swell into a war.

It seemed the last of the romantic wars as people rallied and marched off joyously. The German march through Beligium is well depicted and the feeling that it would soon be over. But then comes the slowing down at the Marne, the Somme and Verdun and the deterioration into the slogging, useless trench warfare that drags on for four hapless years.

The home bustle is contrasted to the growing waste and horror of the war as men begin to lose sight of why they are fighting. The Russian Revolution that turns German troops West and the American entry that helps stops it, along with the Alies, bring the war to supposedly end wars to a close. It ends ironically on the Versailles treaty, the German putting down of home revolution and the German army's regrouping and admonition that they were betrayed with intimations of budding Nazism on its way.

Sagely orchestrated, this has some brilliant newsreel scenes almost worthy of noted fiction films such as mass meetings in Paris, trench charges, a Russian cavalry affair and the revolution. It makes its point about war's waste as well as giving a good picture of its causes and effects.

Jean Aurel reportedly viewed miles of film from all over the world and was helped by the pointed commentary of Cecil Saint Laurent as well as the expert editing of Anne-Marie Cotret. Sometimes there is repetition in this, as was the warfare at the time, and many things, lacking images, have to be inserted via talk. There have been a lot of these sort of films recently but this has the depth and finish that could make it specialized fodder abroad. It has been well received critically here. Film is in quite good shape. *Mosk.*

Critic's Choice

(PANAVISION-COLOR)

Hope-Ball star combo should be able to bail it out at the b.o.

Hollywood, March 26.

Warner Bros. release of Frank P. Rosenberg production. Stars Bob Hope, Lucille Ball; features Marilyn Maxwell, Rip Torn, Jessie Royce Landis, John Dehner, Jim Backus. Directed by Don Weis. Screenplay, Jack Sher, from play by Ira Levin; camera (Technicolor), Charles Lang; editor, William Ziegler; music, George Duning; asst. director, Russell Llewellyn. Reviewed at studio, March 26, '63. Running time, **100 MINS.**

Parker Ballantine .... Bob Hope
Angela Ballantine .... Lucille Ball
Ivy London .... Marilyn Maxwell
Dion Kapakos .... Rip Torn
Charlotte Orr ...... Jessie Royce Landis
S. P. Champlain .... John Dehner
Dr. von Hagedorn .... Jim Backus
John Ballantine .... Ricky Kelman
Mrs. Champlain .... Dorothy Green
Sally Orr .... Marie Windsor
Phil Yardley .... Evan McCord
Harvey Rittenhouse .... Richard Deacon
Marge Orr .... Joan Shawlee
Joe Rosenfield .... Jerome Cowan
Godfrey .... Donald Losby
Mother .... Lurene Tuttle
Thelma .... Ernestine Wade
Bartender .... Stanley Adams

Possibilities are strong that the Frank P. Rosenberg production can

succeed commercially in spite of itself. It may take all the marquee might and magnetism of Bob Hope and Lucille Ball to turn the trick, but the Warner Bros. release has the earmarks of a respectable boxoffice number, though considerably less surefire than the star pair's last offering, "The Facts of Life," which, for them, was a vastly superior vehicle.

What was transparent and implausible to begin with in Ira Levin's stage play has been blown up and distorted beyond even remote resemblance to life in Jack Sher's scenario and director Don Weis' approach to it. And, incredibly enough, owing to this tendency to reach for extra laughs at the expense of believability of situation, the very crux of the drama weaving within the comedy has been sacrificed and shattered, rendering the story pointless. More has been lost thaan gained by this striving for the bellylaugh where the grin would have served.

A Broadway stage critic (Hope) whose wife (Miss Ball) writes a play is the pivotal character in this comedy. The "Critic's Choice" is whether to retain his personal self-respect and professional integrity by reviewing his wife's play or choose to bow out of the tack in order to preserve the domestic tranquility. Unfortunately, and unaccountably, the Sher-Weis version depicts this noted reviewer arriving at the theatre for the opening of his wife's effort late and in a state of third-degree inebriation, determined to review, whatever the marital consequences. After causing a complete disturbance in the theatre (including two precarious incidents during which he hangs from his heels off the balcony ledge), this renowned critic proceeds to compose a merciless pan of a play he never really saw. The off-stage suggestion of such unprofessional behavior was hard enough to swallow in the original version, but this witnessed depiction of how a man goes about preserving his "self respect" is utterly preposterous. Restraint would have made it funnier.

There are sporadic flashes of merriment in the film, the result primarily of the cheerful, reassuring of Hope and Miss Ball and occasionally chipper lines of dialog. Hope manages to be affable as the kind of Broadway stage critic who could only really exist in a Lambs Club gag. The vehicle provides Miss Ball with little opportunity to cut up in her accustomed manner, but her warm, sincere portrayal of the rather shallow-sighted unappealing wife is quite an achievement. None of the other players attains any special distinction. Caricatures of theatrical types abound. Prominent among the supporting performers are Marilyn Maxwell, Rip Torn, Jessie Royce Landis, John Dehner, Jim Backus and Ricky Kelman.

Level of cinematic craftmanship is generally a cut above the vehicle. This includes Charles Lang's photography, William Ziegler's editing and Edward Carrere's art direction. Edith Head's costumes are attractive in and becoming to the performers who wear them. George Duning's score runs to musical cliche in certain passages, but his accompaniment of the clever main titles by Pacific Title is gay, effervescent and inviting. Both titles and music theme employ a typewriter effect to introductory advantage *Tube.*

Showdown

Routine oater with oke slotting potential as second feature and subsequent run fare. Lack of color is no help.

Universal release of Gordon Kay production. Stars Audie Murphy, Kathleen Crowley, Charles Drake; features Harold J. Stone, L. Q. Jones, Skip Homier, Henry Wills, Charles Horvath. Directed by R. G. Springsteen. Screenplay, Bronson Howitzer; camera, Ellis W. Carter; editor, Jerome Thoms; music, Hans J. Salter; assistant directors, Terence Nelson, Carl Beringer. Reviewed at Universal screening room, March 29, '63. Running time, **79 MINS.**

Chris Foster .... Audie Murphy
Estelle .... Kathleen Crowley
Bert Pickett .... Charles Drake
Lavalle .... Harold J. Stone
Caslon .... Skip Homier
Foray .... L. Q. Jones
Charlie Reeder .... Strother Martin
Hebron .... Charles Horvath
Marshal .... John McKee
Chaca .... Henry Wills
Guard .... Joe Haworth
Buster .... Kevin Brodie
Smithy's Wife .... Carol Thurston
Express Man .... Dabbs Greer

This latest Audie Murphy oater out of the Universal stable is a routine affair, okay for second feature billing and slotting as drive-in and subsequent run fare. Filled out with the usual in gun and horse play, good guy-bad guy relations and the inevitable femme complications, "Showdown" moves through its paces with generally-effective thesping and adequate direction with enough impact to entertain the legions of tv-bred sagebrush fans.

Plot of the Gordon Kay production follows a pair of ranch hands, Murphy and Charles Drake, as they get mixed with a gang of desperados and then attempt to get unmixed. It seems that Drake is basically a nogoodnik but Murphy sticks by his old pal despite the buddy's weakness for booze and gambling. It is, in fact, these two frailties that put the boys into their mess with the outlaws when Drake gets into a fight which lands them shackled by their necks to a pole along with the bad guys who have recently been captured.

Under the enforced guidance of the gang's leader, Harold J. Stone, the outlaws and Murphy and Drake dig up the post to which they're chained and escape, in the process of which Drake gets his hands on $12,000 worth of bonds which he later claims he can cash as ransom for their lives. Stone, keeping Murphy prisoner, lets Drake go into town but he has to be dragged back by some of the boys after he sends the bonds to a femme acquaintance to whom he's indebted. Murphy is later allowed to go after the girl to get back the dough and eventually ends up with the girl, the money and a trail of dead outlaws he manages to knock off after they kill his buddy.

Bronson Howitzer penned the screenplay which proves sufficient to its task. Murphy performs with heroic valor and Drake plays his weakling pal with sufficient frailty. As the girl with a history of maltreatment by the less heroic partner, Kathleen Crowley emotes to excess in spots but looks well and does an adequate job. Stone makes a strong heavy without overplaying and turns in a solid job while Skip Homier, L. Q. Jones, Charles Horvath and Henry Wills support effectively.

R. G. Springsteen's direction is paced smoothly and Ellis W. Carteer's camerawork catches the settings nicely. Unlike previous Murphy oaters, this one is in black and white and could have used the color dress up for stronger impact. Hans J. Salter has set some appropriate scoring to the film which Jerome Thoms has edited with continuity. Other technical elements are also right. "Showdown" is slated for May release, although it is currently doubling with "To Kill a Mockingbird" in its Brooklyn showing. *Kali.*

Get On With It
(BRITISH)

More British carryings-on. Kids advertising and dentrifices.

Hollywood, March 29.

Governor Films release of Bertram Ostrer production. Stars Bob Monkhouse, Kenneth Connor, Shirley Eaton, Eric Barker. Directed by C. M. Pennington-Richards. Screenplay, Hazel Adair, Hugh Woodhouse; camera, Stephen Dade; music, Ken Jones. Reviewed at Crest Theatre, Westwood, March 29, '63. Running time, **86 MINS.**

David Cookson .... Bob Monkhouse
Sam Field .... Kenneth Connor
Brian Dexter .... Ronnie Stevens
Jill Venner .... Shirley Eaton
Proudfoot .... Eric Barker
Macreedy .... Richard Wattis
Duff .... Reginald Beckwith
Pharmacist .... Charles Hawtrey

In the British "Carry On" style comedies, "Get On With It" is the latest. This time it's the advertising and dental professions that get the needle, but the fun is fitful and widely scattered. The point of diminishing returns may well be imminent for these once highly lucrative travellers on the U.S. arty circuit, although the formula of one part farcicality, one part scatology and one part double-entendre dialog keeps a certain easygoing faction in every audience quite satisfied.

Mentality of the human characters in this Bertram Ostrer production is quite comparable to the IQ of the average animal in, say, a Looney Tunes cartoon. For example, a character in "Get On With It" who is sneaking into a missile site and is suddenly confronted with an electrified fence asks his companion which wire is charged with current and, upon being advised to try the top one, does so and receives an electric shock that the special effects department makes plainly visible. That is the same kind of thing that is apt to be found happening to some haplessly injury-prone creature in the "oo,oo,ow,ow,ouch" school of cartoon.

The Hazel Adair-Hugh Woodhouse screenplay is concerned with the efforts of a team of advertising men to publicize a product known as Dreem, the toothpaste with the built-in beam. It is a sort of berserk British version of Madison Avenue.

The increasingly familiar English players, most of whom crop up in all of these many exercises, do virtually all that is required of them. Main parts are essayed with gusto by Bob Monkhouse, Kenneth Connor, Ronnie Stevens, the voluptuous Shirley Eaton, Eric Barker, Richard Wattis, Reginald Beckwith and Charles Hawtrey, all experts at the comedy craft. The film has been helmed at a delirious staccato clip by C. M. Pennington-Richards. *Tube.*

It Happened At The World's Fair
(PANAVISION—COLOR)

Presley's newest, a tedious romp through Seattle Fair of '62. B.o. punch depends on extent and degree of star's staying power in junior ranks.

Hollywood, March 27.

Metro release of Ted Richmond production. Stars Elvis Presley; features Joan O'Brien, Gary Lockwood, Vicky Tiu. Directed by Norman Taurog. Screenplay, Si Rose, Seaman Jacobs; camera (Metrocolor), Joseph Ruttenberg; editor, Fredric Steinkamp; music, Leith Stevens; asst. director, Al Jennings. Reviewed at Hawaii Theatre, March 27, '63. Running time, **105 MINS.**

Mike Edwards .... Elvis Presley
Diana Warren .... Joan O'Brien
Danny Burke .... Gary Lockwood
Sue-Lin .... Vicky Tiu
Vince Bradley .... H. M. Wynant
Miss Steuben .... Edith Atwater
Barney Thatcher .... Guy Raymond
Miss Ettinger .... Dorothy Green
Walter Ling .... Kam Tong
Dorothy Johnson .... Yvonne Craig

Those for whom hippiness is just a thing called Elvis figure to welcome this Metro morsel with almost the same boxoffice ardor with which they have greeted the more recent of Presley's musicalized films. The fact that the Seattle World's Fair of 1962 is long gone won't help any at the gate, but the Ted Richmond production probably has enough salable ammunition to survive its title and make a fairly satisfactory showing.

However, this is apt to be tedious going for all but the most confirmed of Presley's young admirers. The 10-count 'em-10 tunes he sings may be cause for rejoicing among his more ardent followers but, stacked up proportionately against the skinny story in between, it seems at least three too many. Admitting the slim scenario by Si Rose and Seaman Jacobs, so many warbling interruptions upset the tempo of the yarn and prevent plot and picture from gathering momentum.

Screenplay springs off to a fairly bright start, thrusting "bush pilot" Presley and sidekick Gary Lockwood into several situations, airborne and earthbound, that have a fair humor content. But it isn't long before the plot begins to be brushed aside for one vocal after another, until the story has taken a back seat to the songs. Most of the action takes place at the Seattle Fair and vicinity, the yarn implicating Elvis with a temporarily abandoned type (Vicky Tiu) and a nifty nurse (Joan O'Brien).

Presley effortlessly executes his customary character—red-blooded wolf on the crust, clean-cut nice guy at the core. Lockwood, as his gambling chum, makes a good impression. Miss O'Brien is easy to look at. Little Miss Tiu is tiu precious for words. Everyone else involved does about as well as can be expected.

Norman Taurog's direction is capable, especially in his staging of a couple of elaborately spirited and implausible fistfights. The sights of the Seattle Fair have been expansively and apprecia-

tively photographed by Joseph Ruttenberg. Except for the monotonous see-saw alternation between song and story in the middle and latter stages, Fredric Steinkamp's editing is competent. Other skills incorporated to advantage are the art direction prowess of George W. Davis and Preston Ames and the music score of Leith Stevens. None of the 10 songs are very memorable, but they're a good bet to sell a lot of wax for Presley and RCA Victor. Musical numbers have been staged by Jack Baker, with vocal backgrounds supplied by the Jordanaires and the Mello Men. *Tube.*

Af Mila LeMorgenstein
(Not a Word to Morgenstein)
(ISRAELI)

Tel Aviv, March 16.
Produced by Joseph Zubeida in Israeli Film Studios, Herzlia. Stars Avraham Ben-Yosef, Gila Almagor, Joseph Banai, Yakov Bodo. Directors, Benjamin Koretzsky, Ben Ozerman, Arie Elias. Screenplay, Erika Ozerman, Gavriel Dagan, Benjamin Koretzky, Arie Elias; camera, Benjamin Koretzky; music, Moshe Wilensky. At Ben Yehuda Theatre, Tel Aviv. Running time, **77 MINS.**

Humorist Ephraim Eishon, on whose musical comedy this film was supposedly based, has disavowed the film version. He may be right. The play, an unpretentious but amusing b.o. success, is an amateurish, silly little film.

Three students decide to steal the exams from their professor of archaeology. In order to do so, they approach three women connected with professor's home: his daughter, her friend and the professor's old maid neighbor. The plot is discovered by a telephone technician, who listens in on various phone calls. The technician is in love with the professor's beautiful daughter, and vice versa, so the happy ending and students back to books.

Pic, cheap as it is, cost twice as much as planned (about $150,000) and the producer went into bankruptcy before opening. Meanwhile directors and scriptwriters were freely exchanged and shows in this inept final product. Only exception is the lively music by Moshe Wilensky, as long as nobody sings. *Lapid.*

Le Doulos
(The Stoolie)
(FRENCH)

Paris, April 2.
Lux release of Rome-Paris Film Champion production. Stars Jean-Paul Belmondo, Serge Reggiani; features Jean Desailly, Fabienne Dali, Michel Piccoli, Rene Lefevre, Monique Hennessy. Written and directed by Jean-Pierre Melville from novel by Pierre Lesou. Camera, Nic Kas Hayer; editor, Monique Bonnot. At the Ermitage, Paris. Running time, **108 MINS.**
Silien ....Jean-Paul Belmondo
Maurice .... Serge Reggiani
Therese .... Monique Hennessy
Gilbert .... Rene Lefevre
Inspector .... Jean Desailly
Leader .... Michel Piccoli
Kern .... Carl Studer

Director Jean-Pierre Melville has concocted a solidly paced gangster opus with a tale of friendship imbedded in plenty of gunplay, violence and subtle plotting. But the rigor, depth of character and sheer dynamics of its Yank counterparts are not quite apparent in this. Melville has called it an homage to U.S. pix of this type.

If it is not up to the standards of the better American pix of this kind, it still has a solidity in thesping, conception and direction to make it a possible foreign playoff or dualer item with some specialized handling also intimated. Latter would call for hardsell.

An ex-con, Serge Reggiani, kills a fence to avenge the murder of a friend and walks off with a flock of jewelry. His best friend, Jean-Paul Belmondo, is made out at first to be in cahoots with the police as a stool pigeon. Pic is so constructed as to make it appear that he is in fact one until a sudden explanation shows he's no stool and had made sacrifices for his friend.

It ends in a blood bath as both are killed when Reggiani tries to stop a trap laid for his friend on the assumption he was a squealer. Director Melville has handled this with too much complacency and slowness instead of letting the action speak for itself.

The contrived suspense also sometimes slows things down as well as a lack of drive. But Reggiani etches a neat portrait of a driven killer and Belmondo supplies his solid presence as the suspected stoolie who turns out to be an unselfish friend and a man waiting to quit the rackets.

This has a fine technical assurance with firstrate gun play. It looms a solid entry for the Continent if its U.S. chances appear more limited. *Mosk.*

Mar Del Plata Fest

Land of Angels
(Az Angyalek Foldje)
(HUNGARIAN)

Mar del Plata, March 26.
Hunnia Filmstudios production. Features Klari Tolnay. Directed by Gyorgy Revesz. Screenplay by Miklos Hubay, based on novel by Lajos Kassak; camera, Ferenc Szecsenyi; music, Andras Mihaly. Reviewed at Mar del Plata Film Fest. Running time, **98 MINS.**

This story of a Budapest tenement named "Land of Angels" and inhabited by workers of nearby factories takes place in 1913. It is based on a Lajos Kassak novel written in 1923. There is no straight story line, but a cleverly interwoven view of different characters and incidents, each of which contributes to the general picture. It won the "best picture" award at the festival here.

Director Gyorgy Revesz works in a manner far removed from the flat realism so often found in Russian pix of lower class life. He has deep feeling and understanding for his characters and the film reaches moments of considerable poetic intensity.

Incidents showing everyday life are punctuated by stronger events, such as murder, a strike, a railway accident and the struggle against an unscrupulous landlord. These also form the background to the love story of a young couple and the basic theme of the workers' solidarity and the birth of social consciousness in their midst.

Acting reaches a high all-round level. Ferenc Szecseny's beautiful black and white photography is another plus.

Subject matter was considered controversial in some circles at this fest, but it is worth noting that, 50 years later, conditions in many Latin American slums are by no means better than those of the Hungarian tenement.

This pic deserves to find a spot in the arties. *Chili.*

Glos Z Tamtego Swiata
(The Voice from Beyond)
(POLISH)

Mar del Plata, March 26.
ZRF "Rytm" production. Features Kasmierz Rudzki, Wanda Luczycka, Tatiana Czechowska, Danuta Szaflarska, K. Feldman, Z. Mrozewski, Maria Homerska, Marta Lipinska. Directed by Tadeusz Rozewicz. Screenplay, T. Rozewicz and K. Filipowicz; camera, Wladyslaw Forbert; music, Wojciech Kilar. Reviewed at Mar del Plata Film Fest. Running time, **86 MINS.**

Four or five victims of a quack and a medium move in and out of this story of people who, finding life on this planet unsatisfactory in one way or another, try to find consolation in patent medicines or the voices from another world, kindly provided by the medium.

This Polish film boasts some good acting, but the different stories are not knit together tightly enough. Inter-cutting lacks sharpness and the pic does not have a sufficiently strong center of gravity. Basic idea appears to be that while people lack a clearly defined attitude towards life, they will easily become victims of practices like those of "Doctor" Aksamitowski (Kasimierz Rudzki) and his medium (Wanda Luczycka).

Best performance, in the top bracket by any standard, belonged to Tatiana Czechowska as an old widow. Unfortunately the film did not show enough of her.

Film's chances on the international market are very limited. *Chili.*

El Perseguidor
(The Pursuer)
(ARGENTINE)

Mar Del Plata, April 2.
Osias Wilenski production. Features Inda Ledesma, Maria Rosa Gallo, Sergio Renan, Anadela Arzon, Zelmar Guenol. Directed by Osias Wilenski. Screenplay, Julio Cortazar, based on story by Ulises Petit de Murat; camera, Roberto Matarrese; music, Ruben Barbieri. At Mar Del Plata, March 19, '63. Running time, **75 MINS.**

This is an odd and ambitious film, based on the life of the late, great U.S. Negro jazzman Charlie Parker, told completely in white Argentine terms. It is also the first feature by young (29) Argentine director Osias Wilenski, who shows signs of a markedly original talent.

The picture flows forward and backward in time with sometimes confusing results. However, this artfully contrived juxtoposition of past and future manages to suggest a good deal of the chaos that exists in a mind teetering between ecstacy and madness. Its jazzman hero, intensely played by Sergio Renan, is by reason of his talent, a man holding on to the tail of a tiger. When he lets go he dies. Tale is told with a lot of music and, perhaps, just a few too many moody closeups of the agonized saxophonist. There is also a minimum of dialog, which is all to the good to judge from the sampling

of what is heard ("What is life?," "I am empty inside!").

These are minor reservations, however, for a film of such real pictorial style. It could have an overseas interest for very specialized houses and film societies interested in seeing what's new from Argentina. *Anby.*

Las Ratas
(The Rats)
(ARGENTINE)

Mar del Plata, April 2.
Argentine Sono Film release of Luis Saslavsky production. Stars Aurora Batista, Alfredo Alcon, Barbara Mujica; features Juan Jose Miguez, Antonio Herrero, Fernando Marin. Directed by Luis Saslavsky. Screenplay, Emilio Villalba Welsh and Saslavsky, adapted by Simon Fourcade from a novel by Jose Bianco; camera, Antonio Merayo; music, Rodolfo Arizaga. At Mar Del Plata Film Fest, March 16, '63. Running time, **80 MINS.**
Maria .... Aurora Batista
Julio .... Alfredo Alcon
Cristina .... Barbara Mujica
Antonio .... Juan Jose Miguez

Competent performances by the principals and a technically superior physical production cannot obscure the fact that this is old-fashioned soap opera. And it's not jazzed up one bit by the fact that its central theme of adultery is supplemented by a suggestion of a young boy's homosexual attachment for his older half-brother. It's still corn.

The story, told in flashback, traces the reasons for the supposed suicide of a promising young Argentine research scientist (he experiments with the rats of the title). Revealed in the curse of the plodding drama is the fact that the researcher, Alfredo Alcon, had been carrying on an affair with his step-mother, Aurora Batista. When the liaison is discovered by the researcher's teenage brother, a musical prodigy, the kid, for reasons never too clearly defined pours poison into his brother's milkshake and resolves never to play the piano again.

Despite the fact that it's all as silly as it sounds, picture was chosen as the official Argentine entry at the Mar Del Plata film fest. Expectations outside the Spanish-speaking markets are nil. *Anby.*

Colleagues
(RUSSIAN)

Mar del Plata, March 26.
Sovexport production and release. Features B. Livanov, V. Lanovoi, O. Anogriev, N. Shatskaia, T. Siomina, R. Pliat. Directed by I. Bitiukov. Screenplay, Alexei Sajarov; camera, V. Nikolaev; music, Yu. Levitin. Reviewed at Mar del Plata Film Fest. Running time, **110 MINS.**

Thesis, thesis burning bright, in the middle of the night!

This Russian pic shows three medical school graduates at the beginning of their professional life. One is simply an amusing character, another a rebel. The third is a young man full of civic spirit and sense of responsibility who, unflinchingly, accepts a post at a hospital so far away from Leningrad that its name is nearly unprouncable.

The basic idea, that one must do what is best for society as a whole rather than egotistically pursue one's own private advantage, is certainly not one to quar-

rel with. But the script fails because it constantly tries to turn curves into straight lines. The rebel against society is regenerated, sidestepping the causes (social and psychological) that have made him into what he is and the naive love story of young man No. 3 torn between two gals also avoids depth of feeling and inner conflict, remaining well within the realm of cliche. The film also has one of the most ridiculous heavies seen for quite a time. The dice are loaded to get the message over plain and clear. But quite unnecessarily human verisimilitude is sacrificed in the process.

Acting is good and there is some flashy work. However, the film as a whole does not come off and would appear to be of no particular interest for Western markets.

Chili.

La Isla
(BRAZILIAN)

Mar del Plata, March 26.

Kamera Filmes Limitada production. Features Luigi Picchi, Eva Wilma, Lyris Castellani, Jose Mauro de Vasconcelos, Francisco Negrao, Mario Benvenutti, Ruy Affonso, Mauricio Nabuco, Elizabeth Hartmann, Laura Verney. Direction, book and script by Walter Hugo Khouri. Camera, Rudolf Icsey, George Pfister, and Eugenio Owintschenko; music, Rogerio Duprat. Reviewed at Mar del Plata Film Fest. Running time, **113 MINS.**

Brazilian director Walter Hugo Khouri grazes on Michelangelo Antonioni pastures, sometimes even literally with scenery highly reminiscent of "L'Avventura." An idle millionaire and his entourage go saling and get stranded on an island where they had planned to look for a hidden (and perhaps symbolic) treasure. Tensions grow in this isolated environment and the director's intention, according to his own statement, is to show man's impossibility to escape from the very circumstances created by his own behavour.

After a slow beginning, the films quickens its rhythm but never really gets into its stride. Khouri potentially has the knack of telling a story, but his work is still too derivative to be of particular interest, either artistically or commercially.

Acting and camera work are only fair.

Chili.

The Ugly American

Successful, in part, loose translation of a hit novel with fine work by Marlon Brando, et al. But perhaps a problem in getting audiences to warm up to cold war.

Universal release of George Englund production, directed by Englund. Stars Marlon Brando; features Eiji Okada, Pat Hingle, Arthur Hill, Jocelyn Brando, Jukrit Pramoj, Kukrit Pramoj, Judson Pratt. Screenplay, Stewart Stern, from novel by William J. Lederer and Eugene Burdick; camera, Clifford Stine; editor, Ted J. Kent; music, Frank Skinner. Reviewed in Hollywood, April 26, '63. Running time, **120 MINS.**

Harrison Carter MacWhite .... Marlon Brando
Deong .... Eiji Okada
Marion MacWhite .... Sandra Church
Homer Atkins .... Pat Hingle
Grainger .... Arthur Hill
Emma Atkins .... Jocelyn Brando
Prime Minister Kwen Sai .... Kukrit Pramoj
Joe Bing .... Judson Pratt
Rachani .... Reiko Sato
Munsang .... George Shibata
Senator Brenner .... Judson Laire
Sears .... Philip Ober
Sawad .... Yee Tak Yip
Andrei Krupitzyn .... Stefan Schnabel
Col. Chee .... Pock Rock Ahn

Some of the ambiguities, hypocrisies and perplexities of cold war politics are observed, dramatized and, to a degree, analyzed in "The Ugly American." It is a thought-provoking but uneven screen translation taken from, but not in a literal sense based upon the popular novel by William J. Lederer and Eugene Burdick. Producer-director George Englund and scenarist Stewart Stern merit at least an E for effort, but the results of their difficult, earnest and well-intentioned endeavor are only partially successful, at best.

It is certainly not an attraction for that happy-go-lucky breed of filmgoer who ordinarily visits the cinema to escape from, not confront, the pressures and almost unfathomable political mysteries of the modern world around him. Outside of the presence of Marlon Brando atop the cast, and possible word-of-mouth about his fine performance, there is really little of boxoffice allure in "The Ugly American."

Focal figure of the story is an American ambassador (Brando) to a southeast Asian nation who, after jumping to conclusions in the course of dealing with an uprising of the natives of that country against the existing regime and what they interpret as Yankee imperialism comes to understand that there is more to modern political revolution than meets the casual or jaundiced bystander's eye. As a result of his experience, he senses that Americans "can't hope to win the cold war unless we remember what we're for as well as what we're against," ends up by condemning his U.S. countrymen for their complacency and indifference to the serious political issues of the day.

As an ironical footnote, the picture concludes with the scolding, imploring Brando being flicked off in the middle of a key remark in a television address by an unconcerned viewer who has been scanning a tv log.

Although skillfully and often explosively directed by Englund and well played by Brando and others in the cast, the film tends to be overly talkative and lethargic in certain areas, vague and confusing in others. Probably the most jarring single flaw is the failure to clarify the exact nature of events during the ultimate upheaval. The teeter-totter balance of power that accompanies this political transition is fuzzily defined. Heartening as it is to see American interests prevail, it is not at all clear why the Communists, who seem to have won the day, suddenly fall by the wayside in the struggle for control.

Brando's performance is a towering one; restrained, intelligent and always masculine. Japanese actor Eiji Okada of "Hiroshima, Mon Amour" renown, makes a strong impression in his U. S. film bow as Brando's old wartime buddy now popular (and seemingly Communist-motivated) leader of the strife-torn country to which Brando has been dispatched as American emissary. Sandra Church, in her screen debut, is competent as Brando's wife. Pat Hingle and Jocelyn Brando are effective as a pair of anything-but-ugly Americans and Arthur Hill seems most authentic in support as Brando's chief aide. Balance of supporting work is reliable.

Mass riot scene near the outset of the picture is frighteningly realistic; a chilling demonstration of mob fury masterfully mounted and directed by Englund. Clifford Stine's employment of the lens is dexterous and observant. Ted J. Kent's editing is dramatically taut and progressive. Art direction by Alexander Golitzen and Alfred Sweeney is outstanding. They have constructed a convincing replica of a southeast Asian village on the Universal backlot. An unobstrusive but mood-enhancing score by Frank Skinne is another asset to the production.

Tube.

Come Fly With Me
(PANAVISION—COLOR)

Frail craft kept aloft by Pamela Tiffin's sparkling performance. Has b.o. possibilities.

Hollywood, March 15.

Metro release of Anatole de Grunwald production. Stars Dolores Hart, Hugh O'Brian, Karl Boehm, Pamela Tiffin, Karl Malden, Lois Nettleton. Directed by Henry Levin. Screenplay and story, William Roberts, from Bernard Glemser's "Girl On a Wing"; camera (Metrocolor), Oswald Morris; editor, Frank Clarke; music, Lyn Murray; assistant director, Jimmy Komisarjevsky. Reviewed at Picwood Theatre, March 15, '63. Running time, **107 MINS.**

Donna Stuart .... Dolores Hart
First Officer Ray Winsley .... Hugh O'Brian
Baron Franz Von Elzingen .... Karl Boehm
Carol Brewster .... Pamela Tiffin
Walter Lucas .... Karl Malden
Hilda Bergstrom .... Lois Nettleton
Katie .... Dawn Addams
Oliver Garson .... Richard Wattis
Cardwell .... Andrew Cruickshank
Flight Engineer Teddy Shepherd .... James Dobson
Gwen .... Lois Maxwell
Co-Pilot .... John Crawford
Navigator .... Robert Easton
Armand .... Guilo Wieland
M. Rinard .... Maurice Marsac

Sometimes one performance can save a picture, and in "Come Fly With Me" it's an engaging and infectious one by Pamela Tiffin that helps spell the all-important difference between boxoffice cash or crash. The Anatole de Grunwald production has other things going for it like an attractive cast, slick pictorial values and smart, stylish direction by Henry Levin, but at the base of all this sheer sheen lies a frail, frivolous and featherweight storyline that, in trying to take itself too seriously, flies into dramatic air pockets and cross-currents that threaten to send the entire aircraft into a tailspin.

Fortunately for the Metro release, Miss Tiffin is around to bail it out almost every time the going gets too bumpy for passenger comfort. It's a performance that will generate word of mouth, particularly among teenage girls always on the prowl for screen stars to emulate. And therein lies the difference between moneymaking mediocrity and a respectable commercial click.

Airline hostesses and their romantic pursuits provide the peg upon which William Roberts has constructed his ultra-modern but erratic screenplay from a screen story he concocted out of Bernard Glemser's "Girl On a Wing." The affairs of three hostesses are described.

One (Dolores Hart) is looking for a wealthy husband and thinks she's found the fellow in a young Continental baron (Karl Boehm) until she discovers that he's been using her as a dupe to smuggle gems through customs. Another (Lois Nettleton) is a "nice girl" type, the exact opposite of her gold digger colleague, who succeeds in winning the heart and hand of yon multi-millionaire Texas businessman (Karl Malden) without really trying. The third (Miss Tiffin), after a series of cockpitfalls and hotelroominations, decides that flying so high with some guy in the sky is her idea of something to do. The "some guy" is first flight officer Hugh O'Brian.

Misses Hart and Nettleton, Boehm and Malden have the misfortune to be implicated in affairs one and two, which are utterly absurd. The four characters are all stereotypes. O'Brian has the good fortune to be bouncing his characterization off Miss Tiffin, and gets by. Richard Wattis stands out in support. Dawn Addams appears in several scenes in stylish gowns by Pierre Balmain, which make the other girls look positively shabby by contrast.

Much of the film was shot in Paris and Vienna, allowing it a scenic extravagance richly exploited by Oswald Morris' lenses. Other assets to the production are Frank Clarke's editing, William Kellner's art direction and Lyn Murray's score. In addition to the title song by Sammy Cahn and James Van Heusen, which is an already established ditty borrowed for the occasion and warbled over the titles by Frankie Avalon, there's a catchy Gallic tune, "La Chansonnette," which is utilized to advantage.

Tube.

Sparrows Can't Sing
(BRITISH)

Lively, though undisciplined cockney film. First pic effort by the controversial theatre director, Joan Littlewood. May bewilder U.S. audiences but its cheeky ebullience should whip up curiosity trade.

London, March 26.

Warner-Pathe release of Carthage (Donald Taylor) production presented by Elstree Distributors. Features James Booth, Barbara Windsor, Barbara Ferris, Roy Kinnear, Avis Bunnage, George Sewell, Murray Melvin, Stephen Lewis. Directed by Joan Littlewood. Screenplay by Miss Littlewood and Lewis, based on his play; camera, Max Greene, Desmond Dickinson; editor, Oswald Hafenrichter; music, Stanley Black; title song, Lionel Bart, sung by Miss Windsor. At Rialto, London. Running time, **94 MINS.**

Charlie .... James Booth
Maggie .... Barbara Windsor
Fred .... Roy Kinnear
Bridgie .... Avis Bunnage
Jack .... Brian Murphy
Bert .... George Sewell
Nellie .... Barbara Ferris
Chunky .... Griffith Davies
Georgie .... Murray Melvin
Ted .... Arthur Mullard
Ted's Wife .... Peggy Ann Clifford
Watchman .... Wally Patch
Perce .... Bob Grant
Caretaker .... Stephen Lewis
Arnold .... Vincent Spinetti
Momma .... Jenny Sontag
Gran .... May Scagnelli
Lil .... Fanny Carby
Yootha .... Yootha Joyce
Janet .... Janet Howse
Queenie .... Queenie Watts

Joan Littlewood, who at the theatre Workshop in London's East End, thumbed her nose cockily at most legit convention and brought

a breath of fresh air into the general stuffiness, has now tackled her first film. Her lack of experience stands out like Jimmy Durante's schnozz. At times it irritates. But "Sparrows Can't Sing" also gains by the sheer ebullience of Miss Littlewood's "don't give a heck" attitude, at least in certain scenes. For her first essay in pix, Miss Littlewood has played fairly safe. The film is based on a play that she staged at the Theatre Workshop. She and the author of the play (Stephen Lewis) collaborated on the loose screenplay and Miss Littlewood has surrounded herself with most of the Workshop cast. She also operated almost entirely on location in the East End that she knows and clearly loves so well.

So the die was cast in her favor. But still a film had to be made. Though the result may cause some furrowed brows in the States, it has a cheeky impertinence that could well break down possible resistance.

The storyline is disarmingly slight. James Booth plays a tearaway merchant seaman who comes back to his East End home after two years afloat to find that his home had been torn down during replanning and his wife (Barbara Windsor) has found herself another nest with a local bus driver. His arrival strikes uneasiness in the hearts of the locals, who know his uncertain temper. But Booth sets out to find his wife and collect his conjugal rights. He wants her back, even when he realizes that there is some doubt as to the parenthood of her new baby. There's eventually a showdown and a bonanza rough and tumble at a local saloon. Booth and Miss Windsor eventually patch things up, but the film ends with the thought that there will be another voyage, another affair and eventually another black night in the East End.

This could have been played for drama or even tragedy. The screenplay writers and Miss Littlewood's direction beckon to the brighter and breezier slant and, though there is a sober side to the film, this is mostly played for yocks. Much of the dialog, which is rather salty, appears to have been made up off the cuff of the players. This shows up dangerously in the intimate scenes, but gives gusto to others, notably the tavern sequence. Booth is a striking newish personality, a punchy blend of toughness, potential evil and irresistible charm. Miss Ferris (who also chants the Lionel Bart credit title song) is a cute young blonde who teeters delightfully through her role, on stiletto heels and with a devastating sense of logic. As, for instance, when she explains to the man with whom she's living that her husband treated her very well "apart from the booze and the birds."

A longish cast also chips in with some gay assistance. Roy Kinnear, Arthur Mullard, Wally Patch, Murray Melvin, Avis Bunnage, George Sewell, Barbara Ferris, Victor Spinetti and Stephen Lewis particularly make great impact in showcase roles. There are one or two local characters who have been given parts and who score. Notably, Queenie Watts who plays the cabaret singing boss of a saloon which, in fact, she owns and in which the scene was shot.

This is a highly colored and exaggerated version of the Cockney in which everybody is a larger than l i f e character. But the camerawork, straying carelessly around the actual East End streets, is vital and vivid. And the whole effect is one of sheer exuberance.

Miss Littlewood will make other films, it's hoped. Whether or not her natural talents should be harnessed to a more disciplined approach is a tricky point. It will probably depend on the b.o. results of "Sparrows." In England the film's prospects seem bright.

Rich.

Bye Bye Birdie
(PANAVISION-COLOR)

Colorful, imaginative, amusing musical comedy. A click.

Columbia release of Kohlmar-Sidney production, produced by Fred Kohlmar, directed by George Sidney. Stars Janet Leigh, Dick Van Dyke, Ann-Margret, Maureen Stapleton, Bobby Rydell, Jesse Pearson; features Paul Lynde, Mary LaRoche, Michael Evans, Robert Paige, Gregory Morton, Bryan Russell, Milton Frome. Screenplay, Irving Brecher; from the legiter with book by Michael Stewart,. music and lyrics by Charles Strouse and Lee Adams; camera, Joseph Biroc; choreographer, Onna White; music, Johnny Green. Previewed in N.Y., March 19, '63. Running time, 120 MINS.
Rosie DeLeon .... Janet Leigh
Albert Peterson .... Dick Van Dyke
Kim McAfee .... Ann Margret
Mama .... Maureen Stapleton
Hugo Peabody .... Bobby Rydell
Conrad Birdie .... Jesse Pearson
Ed Sullivan .... Ed Sullivan
Mr. McAfee .... Paul Lynde
Mrs. McAfee .... Mary LaRoche
Claude Paisley .... Michael Evans
Bob Precht .... Robert Paige
Borov .... Gregory Morton
Randolph .... Bryan Russell
Mr. Maude .... Milton Frome
Ballet Manager .... Ben Astar
Ursula .... Trudy Ames
Mr. Nebbitt .... Cyril Delevanti
Mayor .... Frank Albertson
Mayor's Wife .... Beverly Yates
Bartender .... Frank Sully
Ursula's Mother .... Bo Peep Karlin

"Birdie" are coming into hitsville. Credit George Sidney with directing one of the better fun and frolic tune packages. The adaptation of the successful legit musical comedy of a couple of seasons back has got to be a box-office joy domestically. And the Made-in-Yankceland label on a tuner, so frequently a deterrent overseas, needn't be masked; No matter whether they're watching on the Rhine or ogling in Ogden (Mandel, that's in Utah) the broad comedic strokes, as herein, add up to a laugh's a laugh in anybody's backyard.

Director Sidney is up-front mentioned because his is a highly creditable job. Irving Brecher's script clearly called for lots of visuals, rather than just dialog and straight story-telling, and the staging of the farcical situations is all the way adept. Additionally, there's apparently more emphasis on the dance (interesting choreography by Onna White)—more so perhaps than in the original—and the point of this is that terping knows no international language barriers. Sidney has his story and musicalities (song and dance) segueing into each other just fine.

Strikingly important in "Bye Bye Birdie" is Ann-Margret. Singer, hoofer and cutie-pie, all wrapped up into one, with okay histrionic talent to boot, this is one of the most exciting fresh personalities to take the cinematic stage in some time. The magnetism of early-vintage Judy Garland is here.

Janet Leigh, Dick Van Dyke, Maureen Stapleton, Bobby Rydell and Jesse Pearson also share in the star billing, each with proper place in the sun. That is, writer Brecher and director Sidney give them all a turn at onstage front and centre, whether for a clowning bit, song or dance. Featured but deserving of star billing is Paul Lynde, comedian powerhouse.

Story is the wacky thing about an Elvis Presley type (Pearson) who's subject to immediate Army call. Goes by the name of Conrad Birdie and he swoons the girls no end, what with all that guitar and hip-notism. Songwriter Van Dyke, trying to make time with Miss Leigh, while his mother, Miss Stapleton, interferes, also is engaged in having Presley-type appear on the Ed Sullivan tv show while doing his farewell song in Sweet Apple, Iowa. Sullivan is on view, playing the part of Ed Sullivan with remarkable authenticity.

Producer Fred Kohlmar has put together an engaging catalog of commercial entertainment. There's lots of talent involved. The songs probably won't reach "standard" proportions but, as penned by Charles Strouse and Lee Adams, doing the music and lyrics, respectively, fit in nicely. Van Dyke displays a show biz knowhow far more extensive that his current television outings would communicate. Miss Leigh is called upon to play it straight, and does so attractively. Miss Stapleton is a comedienne of the first order. Young songster Rydell gets the right kind of chance to warble. Ann-Margret, to repeat, is a wow. Presley-type Pearson is a funny take-off. And so on.

There's a particularly funny piece of business which will draw laughs in anybody's country. It's a Russian ballet on the Sullivan show wherein the conductor, purposely fed a drug to speed things up to make time for Pearson to sing Van Dyke's song, graduates the tempo to breakneck tour-jete tempo.

Johnny Green's musical interpretations are first-flight, the color camera work by Joseph Biroc is zeroed in with no room for complaints and all technical credits are strictly pro. *Gene.*

Call Me Bwana
(BRITISH—COLOR)

Amiable joke with a nice line of wisecracks for Bob Hope and some lively gags stemming from a typical Hope situation; useful marquee support will aid a potentially sock comedy.

London, April 9.

Rank release (United Artists in U.S.) of Eon (Harry Saltzman & Albert R. Broccoli) production. Stars Bob Hope, Anita Ekberg; features Edie Adams, Lionel Jeffries. Directed by Gordon Douglas. Screenplay, Nate Monaster, Johanna Harwood; camera, Ted Moore; editor, Peter Hunt; music, Monty Norman. At Odeon, Leicester Square, London. Running time, 93 MINS.
Matt Merriwether .... Bob Hope
Luba .... Anita Ekberg
Frederica Larsen .... Edie Adams
Dr. Ezra Mungo .... Lionel Jeffries
First Henchman .... Percy Herbert
Col. Spencer .... Paul Carpenter
Tribal Chief .... Orlando Martins
Second Henchman .... Al Mulock
Uta .... Bari Johnsonn
Williams .... Peter Dynley
American Major .... Robert Nichols
1st C.I.A. man .... Robert Arden
2nd C.I.A. man .... Kevin Scott

Given a good, basic comedy idea, on-the-ball service from his expert assembly line of wisecracks and a reasonable quota of gag situations, there are few like Bob Hope for jollying along a film to the taste of audiences. "Call Me Bwana" provides that material and Hope, Anita Ekberg, Edie Adams, Lionel Jeffries and a supporting workmanlike cast insure an evening's amiable fun. The Hope-Ekberg chemistry makes good stellar reading and "Bwana" should ride its faults and come in as a more than useful boxoffice project both in U.K. and the States.

Hope's gags are tossed off in his usual slick fashion. And since a great number of them are slyly but pointedly directed at Miss Ek-

berg's stimulating sculpture, thus spelling s-e-x, that department is taken care of. The visual situations and incidents seem to need spacing out a little more but they invariably crop up just in time to disguise the occasional repetition of plot.

Hope has built up a phoney reputation as an intrepid explorer of the jungles of Darkest Africa, by writing successful books based on old, secret diaries of his uncle. Actually, the nearest the timid character has ever been to Africa is to visit his aunt in Cape Cod. When an American moon-probe capsule is lost in the jungle and it's necessary to locate it before foreign powers get their thieving mitts on it, Hope is detailed for the task because of his supposed expert knowledge of the locale.

So he reluctantly lands in the unknown territory, accompanied by a Do-It-Yourself suicide kit and an agent detailed to wetnurse him (Edie Adams). Meanwhile, the sinister foreign power is on the trail, in the shapely person of agent Anita Ekberg. There she joins Jeffries, who is a fellow agent, posing as a medical missionary. The four join up on the safari, and from then on Hope is faced with the perils of wild animals, hostile natives and Miss Ekberg. From this situation Hope evokes the kind of zany humor which put the "Road" series on the map.

Overall, there's enough fun to keep this bubbling along merrily. There is Hope going through bravery tests to escape the native tribe, getting mixed up with a rouge elephant, a lion in his tub, having his pants repaired by Miss Ekberg while he's wearing 'em (and with the poisoned needle from his suicide kit), and eventually becoming airborne in the moon-capsule. All these gag situations and others, add up to a breezy, understanding comedy.

Though most of the responsibility falls on Hope and his personality, Miss Adams gives a pleasantly unobtrusive performance and La Ekberg, though an unlikely Mata Hari, is a sound and decorative foil for Hope. Jeffries brings some good grotesque comedy to his role of the missionary with a church harmonium that contains a build-in transmission set to his home-based political bosses.

Percy Herbert, Paul Carpenter, Orlando Martins, Robert Arden and Al Mulock render useful contributions in stooge roles. With ample use of back projection and the actual second unit photography directed by Henry Geddes and Bluey Hill, the suggestion of Darkest Africa gets by. Only the most fastidious carper will protest that the jungle often reeks of Pinewood Studio surroundings. *Rich.*

Paranoiac

Crisply-paced, well acted and directed mystery-horror opus which, if exploited carefully, could stand on its own substantially. Fine second feature and subsequent run fare. Absence of names.

Universal release of Hammer Film Production, produced by Anthony Hinds. Stars Janette Scott, Oliver Reed; features Sheila Burrell, Maurice Denham, Alexander Davion, Liliane Brousse, Harold Lang, John Bonney, John Stuart. Directed by Freddie Francis. Screenplay, Jimmy Sangster; camera, Arthur Grant; editor James Needs; music, Elizabeth Lutyens; asst. director, Ross Mackenzie. Reviewed at Universal screening room, March 28, '63. Running time, **80 MINS.**

Eleanor Ashby .... Janette Scott
Simon Ashby .... Oliver Reed
Francoise .... Liliane Brousse
Tony .... Alexander Davion
Harriet .... Sheila Burrell
John Kossett .... Maurice Denham
Keith Kossett .... John Bonney
Williams .... John Stuart
Vicar .... Colin Tapley
RAF Type .... Harold Lang
1st Woman .... Laurie Leigh
2d Woman .... Marianne Stone
Tramp .... Sydney Bromley
Sailor .... Jack Taylor

Latest chiller-diller out of England's Hammer Film shop, "Paranoiac" is a tidy mystery-horror pic with solid exploitation values and definite double bill and subsequent run chances. Hurting its potential as a first run gamble is the lack of name power but, with a good effort behind it, the film could make it.

"Paranoiac" marks the directorial debut of Freddie Francis, British cameraman who has done considerable work in this latter capacity but never handled directing before. Lack of experience proves no handicap for Francis, however, as he has sculpted a suspenseful and smartly-paced opus out of Jimmy Sangster's effective screenplay. His scenic plotting and the camera work of Arthur Grant, work slickly to bring the scenes off with directness and good shock values when called for.

Craftsmanlike performances are contributed by stars Janette Scott and Oliver Reed and supporters Sheila Burrell, Alexander Davion, Liliane Brousse and Maurice Denham. Plot is a reworking of the imposter-heir swindle bit in which someone poses as a long lost member of a family who just happens to turn up in time to claim a tidy inheritance. In this film, however, the imposter is revealed to the audience as such after only a little while and so there's not much made of this point as far as the audience is concerned.

It is important to the plot, however, as the phoney is impersonating a young man believed by members of his family to have committed suicide when a boy, following the death of his parents. His sister deeply misses him but his brother wouldn't mind it at all if the sister vanished too so he could have all the loot for himself. In fact he tries to convince his sister and their aunt that she's nuts so they'll pack her off and leave him with the inheritance all to himself.

No such luck. Up turns the "brother" and sister, who had begun to believe the scheming other brother, is all well again, fully accepting the imposter. A slight hitch develops though when she finds that she maybe has gone a little overboard in her feelings for the boy as she has developed incestuous feelings for him. But he digs her too and confesses which relieves her greatly.

Trouble is that the nasty brother knew all along because he had actually killed the real brother and had been holding a sort of death rite with the skeleton in the family monsion's chapel. He's discovered by the faker and its revealed that actually its the bad brother that's a little nutty. In the end, the reformed imposter gets the girl, the bad brother gets killed in a fire he set to kill the other guy off after the truth was out and the girl presumably gets the dough.

Reed plays the scheming brother with demonic skill, blending bits of spoiled brat and sneaky madman for a menacing portrayal. Miss Scott is pretty and disarming as the sister and emotes credibly. Davion makes a fine badie-turned-hero, thesping with ease and believeability. Miss Brousse is a shapely French femme who does an effective job as a phony nurse who has actually been brought to the house as bad brother's mistress instead of sister's helper and who is eventually killed by bad brother when she decides to split.

Denham is oke as the family legal counselor and John Bonney does well as his plotting son whose idea the impersonation was in the first place. Miss Burrell is effectively cold and tortured as the family aunt who knows had brother's secret and even participates in his nightly ceremony in the chapel.

Anthony Hinds produced "Paranoiac" which was nicely designed by Bernard Robinson. Other technical credits are also slick and sure, as the film comes off a polished and effective horror-meller which should tittilate fans of this ilk for sure. *Kali.*

Operation Bikini

War meller about submarine, underwater demolition work in South Pacific (last World War); Tab Hunter, Frankie Avalon, Gary Crosby, Scott Brady names may help this to moderate grosses.

American International release of James H. Nicholson-(Samuel Z. Arkoff)-Lou Rusoff production. Stars Tab Tunter, Frankie Avalon, Scott Brady, Jim Backus, Gary Crosby, Michael Dante, Jody McCrea, Eva Six. Directed by Anthony Carras. Screenplay, John Tomerlin; editor, Homer Powell; camera, Gil Warrenton; music, Les Baxter. Tradeshown in N.Y., April 4, '63. Running time, **84 MINS.**

Lt. Morgan Hayes .... Tab Hunter
Seaman Malzone .... Frankie Avalon
Capt. Carey .... Scott Brady
Chief Bosun's Mate .... Jim Backus
Seaman Givens .... Gary Crosby
Lt. Bill Fourtney.........Michael Dante
Seaman Sherman .... Jody McCrea
Reiko .... Eva Six
Seaman Davayo .... Aki Aleong
Lt. Cale .... David Lanfield
Seaman Hiller .... Richard Bakalyan
Seaman Morris .... Joseph Finnigan
Seaman Fowler .... Vernon Scott
Seaman Rich .... Raymond Guth
Perez .... Tony Scott
Dream Siren .... Judy Lewis
Other Seamen .... Steve Mitchell, M. McDermott, Wayne Winton, Duane Ament, Jody Daniels

With some names that will help in selling it, "Operation Bikini" should prove a nice little moneymaker for American International without causing much excitement at the boxoffice or winning palms, bears or seashells. The operation concerned is that of an underwater demolition team of the U.S. Navy during the last World War—and the Bikini is an island in the South Pacific. Hence, if the prospective patron has the other type bikini in mind, he's sure to be disappointed.

Main trouble with this vehicle is that the producer and his director-writer team could not make up their minds as to whether this film was going to be a comedy-drama, a sexy South Sea Islands whodunit or just a straight war meller. For a time, it looks like it might develop into a comedy aboard a Yank submarine—somewhat like "Operation Petticoat." This is especially true when Frankie Avalon sings (during his nightmare), first to his hometown sweetheart and then to an exotic dancer. But the few attempts at comedy are feeble ones on board the sub.

Then the plot centers on the operations of the UDT crew as they attempt to wipe out a recently-sunk U.S. submarine and thereby prevent new, secret radar equipment from falling into Japanese naval hands. This is the most exciting portion of the pic although unfolded in a rather disjointed manner. Just when operations are reaching their highest pitch, Tab Hunter (Lt. Hayes), becomes involved in a highly romantic affair with Eva Six. Latter plays the full-bosomed gal, who makes for plenty of diversion. Looks as if the editor used his shears at the right time as this affair becomes vividly torrid.

From then on, it's a race to see whether the Nipponese or Yank naval men will blow up opposition ships. It seems superfluous to add that the Japanese forces finish second as ship after ship is sent to the bottom by the dauntless American planes and subs.

Hunter is his usual stalwart self as lieutenant in charge of the UDT team. Frankie Avalon does well enough with his song, "Girl Back Home," although the refrain seems employed mainly to bring in the dancing siren (Judy Lewis). He does nicely with his semi-comic role. Scott Brady makes an adequate submarine captain. Gary Crosby is splendid as the tobacco-chewing daredevil seaman of the UDT outfit. Michael Dante is fine in the role of chief officer on the sub. Jim Backus plays a typical husky chief bosun's mate.

Anthony Carras directs with a certain flair for actionful scenes but bogs down in other episodes. Perhaps the John Tomerlin screenplay is as much to blame as the direction. *Wear.*

Island of Love
(PANAVISION—COLOR)

Greek-flavored farce that doesn't quite come off.

Hollywood, April 2.

Warner Bros. release of Morton DaCosta production. Stars Robert Preston, Tony Randall; features Georgia Moll, Walter Matthau. Directed by DaCosta. Screenplay, David R. Schwartz, from story by Leo Katcher; camera (Technicolor), Harry Stradling Sr.; editor, William Ziegler; music, George Duning; asst. director, Floyd Joyer. Reviewed at the studio, April 2, '63. Running time, **101 MINS.**

Steve Blair .... Robert Preston
Paul Ferris .... Tony Randall
Elena Harakas .... Georgia Moll
Tony Dallas .... Walter Matthau
Cha Cha Miller .... Betty Bruce
Prof. Pappas .... Vassili Lambrinos
Andy .... Michael Constantine
Father Anaxagoras ...... Titos Vandis
Mama Harakas .... Miranda Murat
Louie .... Lewis Charles
Nick .... Peter Mamakos
Hoods.......Nick Dimitri, Tony Rollins, Vic Lundin, Greg Benedict

Morton DaCosta is now batting .667 as a screen producer, which is a pretty fancy batting average in any book, but it takes him out of the superman category. Having slammed out two straight hits

("Auntie Mame" and "Music Man") in only two times at bat as a film-maker, he has gone down swinging with this effort, a lacklustre, Hellenically-oriented farce.

"Island of Love" appears to be one of those frustrating affairs that looked good on paper, but just doesn't reproduce right on celluloid. Certainly it is no fault of the cast, for, in co-stars Robert Preston and Tony Randall, DaCosta has populated his picture with two skillful, engaging performers who snugly fit into their roles, as do all of the supporting players. The trouble seems to be in the approach to the yarn. What crosses the screen is a kind of musical comedy without songs, a "Guys and Dolls" on the Aegean, or "Music Man" goes for Greece job. All the elements for a dandy musical are there, but someone forgot the R&H factor. What's left is a skeleton, but no one quite knows how to play the bones.

David R. Schwartz's scenario, from a story by Leo Katcher, has Preston as an ace conman who employs Randall, a 100-proof writer who is at the moment penning a "Bugs Bunny" cartoon, to compose a film version of Genesis for which hoodlum Walter Matthau will be willing to invest two million clams for production. When the film flops (Matthau has insisted his ex-stripper friend Betty Bruce play "Eve"), the hood is out two mil and gunning for our heroes, who sail to Greece. There, the enterprising Preston takes advantage of an old myth about the island of Paradeisos being an "Island of Love," promptly plants evidence that the myth was for real, turns the place into a tourist mecca and obtains exclusive rights to all commercial tie-ins. Matthau's unscheduled arrival and a love triangle round out the story.

Preston, for the most part, is still playing Prof. Harold Hill, but Hill, for the most part, is Preston —an appealing character. There's no better second leading man-comedy relief pitcher on the contemporary screen than Randall. His "drunk" is a classic drunk—the fixed eyes and unwavering determination to arrive at a set goal or destination. Femme romantic lead Georgia Moll is a fine architectural specimen. Matthau is superb as the gangster, just about walks off with the picture when he's on. Also a standout is Betty Bruce, of "Gypsy" fame, as his moll. There are other slick supporting performances by Michael Constantine, Titos Vandis, Miranda Murat, Lewis Charles, Peter Mamakos and Vassili Lambrinos.

Under DaCosta's free-wheeling direction, there are spurts of fun, but the picture fails to gain momentum and just doesn't register in concert. Partially filmed on location in Athens and on the Aegean islands of Hydra and Spetse, the film is divertingly picturesque and richly mounted in Panavision and Technicolor. But, pleasing as the tinted views of Greece are, the production tends to outweigh and engulf the story, giving it a pretentious look that makes one expect more from the story than one receives.

Harry Stradling Sr.'s photography is pretty, William Ziegler's editing tempo smooth. Edward Carrere's art direction keeps appearances appropriate to locale and character taste, particularly helpful, as is George James Hopkins' set decoration, in design of the racy, vulgar abode belonging to Matthau. *Tube.*

The Great Escape
(PANAVISION—COLOR)

Mass breakout of Allied POW's from Nazi compound. First-class film. Potential blockbuster.

Hollywood, April 11.
United Artists release of John Sturges production. Stars Steve McQueen, James Garner, Richard Attenborough; features James Donald, Charles Bronson, Donald Pleasence, James Coburn. Directed by Sturges. Screenplay, James Clavell, W. R. Burnett, based on book by Paul Brickhill; camera (De Luxe), Daniel Fapp; editor, Ferris Webster; music, Elmer Bernstein; asst. director, Jack Reddish. Reviewed at Directors Guild of America, April 11, '63. Running time, **169 MINS.**

Hilts	Steve McQueen
Hendley	James Garner
Bartlett	Richard Attenborough
Ramsey	James Donald
Danny Velinski	Charles Bronson
Blythe	Donald Pleasence
Sedgwick	James Coburn
Ashley-Pitt	David McCallum
MacDonald	Gordon Jackson
Willie	John Leyton
Ives	Angus Lennie
Cavendish	Nigel Stock
Goff	Jud Taylor
Sorren	William Russell
Griffith	Robert Desmond
Nimmo	Tom Adams
Haynes	Lawrence Montaigne
Von Luger	Hannes Messemer
Werner	Robert Graf
Strachwitz	Harry Riebauer
Kuhn	Hans Reiser
Posen	Robert Freitag
Kramer	Heinz Weiss
Frick	Til Kiwe
Preissen	Uurich Beiger
Dietrich	George Mikell
Steinach	Karl Otto Alberty

Mirisch Co. and United Artists have hit the jackpot with "The Great Escape," a film of blockbuster potential in the recent screen tradition of "Kwai" and "Navarone." From Paul Brickhill's true story of a remarkable mass breakout by Allied POW's during World War II, producer-director John Sturges and scenarists James Clavell and W. R. Burnett, with the aid of a gifted staff and spirited cast, have fashioned a motion picture that entertains, captivates, thrills and stirs, an experience rich in cinematic expression as well as dramatic impact. Since there are no marquee "naturals" in the cast, this picture will illustrate how superior story and production values can carry a project to great success without the aid of prohibitively expensive, souped-up stellar names. Its still the picture that counts, not necessarily who's in it.

The film is an account of the bold, meticulous plotting that led to the escape of 76 prisoners from a Nazi detention camp, and subsequent developments that resulted in the demise of 50, recapture of a dozen. It is a tribute to the ingenuity and improvisational flexibility under stress of an indomitable band of courageous men, an example of the remarkable feats that can be achieved when specialists instilled with singleness of purpose synthesize their skills toward a common goal against a common enemy.

The result is a miracle that is the product exclusively of war—the time of the hero. Some may see in "The Great Escape" another glorification of war, a kind of "Prison Can Be Fun" in retrospect. But this sort of negative appraisal is apt to be formulated only by the most finicky and intellectually aloof of filmgoers, and even they may find it almost impossible not to enjoy "The Great Escape" while they are seeing it. For the mass, it's a gas.

"The Great Escape" was accomplished in a compound into which only the most persistent escape artists were placed by the Nazis, whose plan was to "put all our rotten eggs in one basket, then watch this basket carefully." Early scenes depict the formulation of the mass break design. These are played largely for laughs, at the occasional expense of reality, and there are times when authority seems so lenient (unlike what one has come to imagine of Nazi methods) that the inmates almost appear to be running the asylum. At any rate, the 76 out of an intended 250 manage to burrow their way to freedom in the course of the film's suspenseful midsection, and Act III, or the balance of the show, depicts their attempts to flee Nazi-occupied territory. These final scenes are the most spectacular, and not at all anti-climactic.

There are some exceptional performances—histrionic and cinematic. Probably the most provocative single impression is made by Steve McQueen as a dauntless Yank pilot whose "pen"-manship record shows 18 blots, or escape attempts. McQueen has a style, an individuality, that is rare in the contemporary scene. He is a throwback to the personalities of earlier screen eras. He is the possessor of the kind of unique star quality with which such performers as Cagney and Bogart captured the public imagination. And he is further endowed with the agility and daring spirit of the athlete, as attested to by his motorcycling maneuvers on this occasion.

James Garner does his best screen work to date as the compound's "scrounger," a traditional type in the "Stalag 17" breed of war-prison film. Incidentally, in case any such plans are afoot, UA might be wise to avoid the hackneyed method of referring to the characters as "the scrounger," "the forger," "the mole," et. al. in their ads. There is something tired about this kind of ballyhoo, something that smacks of the cheap exploitation war film, which "Great Escape" most decidedly is not.

Charles Bronson and James Coburn do solid work, although the latter's character is anything but clearly defined. A big thing is made of a heavy suitcase he lugs around, yet its contents are never properly clarified, leading one to suspect the exposition may be lying somewhere on a cutting room floor. James Donald is a stickout as the senior British officer in the compound.

British thespians weigh in with some of the finest performances in the picture. Richard Attenborough is especially convincing in a stellar role, that of the man who devises the break. A moving portrayal of a prisoner losing his eyesight is given by Donald Pleasence. It is the film's most touching character.

Others who rate being singled out in the supporting cast are Robert Graf, especially fine as a troubled German guard, David McCallum, Gordon Jackson, John Leyton, Angus Lennie, Nigel Stock, Jud Taylor and Hannes Messemer.

Some noteworthy artistic contributions have been made by the talented staff assembled under Sturges' astute, selective surveillance. Two of the chief ones are

Daniel Fapp's cinematography and Elmer Bernstein's score. Fapp's camerawork, fine throughout, really blossoms in the final phase of the picture when the action moves out of its confined shell. His picturesque views of the German countryside are truly breathtaking —scenes of poetic pastoral splendor softly and delicately witnessed, filtered and reproduced. Bernstein's rich, expressive score is consistently helpful. His martial, Prussianistic theme is particularly stirring and memorable, and has the sound of a possible hit record.

Except for one or two apparent errors of omission, Ferris Webster has done an expert job of knitting this long film with a keen sense of dramatic perspective and momentum. Fernando Carrere's art direction is more than satisfactory. Compound and tunnel have the look and feel of reality. Other top credits are Harold Lewis' sound and Bert Henrikson's wardrobe.

Tube.

La Prostitution
(FRENCH-C'SCOPE)

Paris, April 9.

20th-Fox release of Cocifrance production. With Etchika Choureau, Alain Lionel, Evelyne Dassas, Robert Dalban, Rita Cadillac. Written and directed by Maurice Boutel under supervision of Marcel Sicot of Interpol. Camera, Quintas Albicocco; editor, E. Muse. At La Royale, Paris. Running time, 115 MINS.

Olga	Ethcika Choureau
Mario	Alain Lionel
Girl	Evelyne Dassas
Chief	Robert Dalban
Streetwalker	Rita Cadillac

Trite scripting, turgid direction and lacklustre acting make this supposed expose of prostitution only grind fodder abroad, at best. Otherwise it's old-hat hokum.

An incredibly stupid hefty but pretty provincial lass is picked up at a station when she lands in Paris. Love develops but he is a pimp and she is soon pushed into prostitution to help him. The man's wife is in on the job of breaking her in. She is also a streetwalker.

Film then details the life of prosties the final comeuppance of the group. Direction is sloppy and full of unintentional jump cuts. Despite its subject matter, all this is tame and unwittingly facetious. A misfired exploitation item is the tag for this. *Mosk.*

Grown-Up Children
(RUSSIAN)

Russians try family comedy and results very good for global playoff.

Artkino Pictures release of Mosfilm Studios production. Stars Alexei Gribov, Zoya Fedorova. Directed by Villen Azarov. Screenplay, Valentina Spirina; camera, Sergei Zaitsev, Vladimir Melbohm. At Cameo, N.Y., starting April 13, '63. Running time, 75 MINS.

Anatoly	Alexei Gribov
Zoya	Zoya Fedorova
Lucy	Lily Aloshnikova
Peter	Alex Demyanko

(With English Titles)

This Russian comedy about the younger generation and what to do about the youngsters when they grow up and marry looks as if it was made for the world market. For all of the angles and humor that make for laughable situations in any country are neatly packed into this remarkably strong Russo pic. It's the best comedy effort to come from the Mosfilm Studios to date. As such it should find plenty of dates in foreign language theatres and even some arty spots.

The day on which Alexei Gribov retires from working in his factory he comes home to find that his daughter has eloped and brought her hubby home to meet her parents. Said husband is an architect but has some of the impractical ideas of a youthful artist. When the newly-weds move into the three-room flat where Gribov and his wife Zoya Fedorova have lived for years, the conflict between the older generation and the youthful pair naturally develops. Climax is when some co-workers, all artists, come in for a jam session, and the parents are driven to distraction.

Humorous episodes are developed along broad, almost slapstick, lines, but with hilarious results. Then when the first-born arrives, the grandparents take over as if it was their own child with the inevitable results. But after months of argument, the young couple finally decides everybody will be happier if they find their own apartment.

The screen play by Valentina Spirina has been done many times, but Villen Azarov directs with such skill it comes out like something new. In fact, he directs as though he had been doing such comedies in Hollywood for some time. The camera team of Sergei Zaitsev and Vladimir Menbohm have lensed a slick film.

Gribov, of the Moscow Art Theatre, as the father who's just retiring from his factory, and Miss Fedorova, as his wife, go far in making this vehicle click. Both provide excellent portrayals. Lily Aloshnikova, the daughter who elopes, not only does well as a thespian but also is one of the comeliest Russian femmes seen in pix. Alex Demyanko makes a typical irresponsible youth as the new son-in-law. *Wear.*

The Yellow Canary
(C'SCOPE)

Serviceable Pat Boone suspense meller.

Hollywood, April 12.

Twentieth-Fox release of Maury Dexter production. Stars Pat Boone, Barbara Eden, Steve Forrest; features Jack Glugman, Jesse White, Steve Harris. Directed by Buzz Kulik. Screenplay, Rod Serling, based on Whit Masterson's novel, "Evil Come, Evil Go"; camera, Floyd Crosby; editor, Jodie Copelan; music, Kenyon Hopkins; asst. director, Clarence Eurist. Reviewed at the studio, April 12, '63. Running time, 93 MINS.

Andy Paxton	Pat Boone
Lissa	Barbara Eden
Hub Wiley	Steve Forrest
Lt. Bonner	Jack Klugman
Ed Thornburg	Jesse White
Bake	Steve Harris
Vecchio	Milton Selzer
Sam Skolman	John Banner
Joe	Jeff Corey
Rene Pyle	Jo Helton
Crystal Towers	Vici Raaf
Ponelli	Harold Gould
Policeman	Joe Turkel
Reporter	Charles Keane

"The Yellow Canary" is from Robert L. Lippert's highly efficient budget picture unit, but has been produced on a more elaborate scale than most of the product spawned and developed in that busy little "B" hive of the 20th-Fox operation. The extra expense and effort can be traced to the presence of Pat Boone as star and, to a lesser degree, the creative participation of such personnel as Rod Serling. But, alas, the increased expenditure and utilization of "name" talents have not resulted in an appreciably better film.

In fact, the added technical sheen tends to make the picture topheavy with a production slickness and savvy that the weakly defined and developed story is unable to support. Still, the Googa Mooga production should fit into a serviceable program groove—as a featured attraction in less demanding situations and as a relatively classy supporting item for major product.

Serling's screenplay, from Whit Masterson's novel, "Evil Come, Evil Go," is reasonably strong in dramatic anatomy, but limp and fuzzy in character definition. The characters are thrust at the audience, with little or no attempt to illustrate the nature of their odd dispositions toward society and each other. It is difficult for the audience to accept these personalities merely on hearsay, and the film never recovers from this initial expository weakness, not that it gets better as it goes along.

Hero of the piece is Boone, a surly singing idol whose apparently loose ways have him on the brink of divorce with his wife (Barbara Eden), who remains only for the sake of their infant. The baby is suddenly kidnapped and three people are needlessly murdered by the kidnapper, who turns out to be one of Boone's sycophants, his psychotic bodyguard (Steve Forrest). Why Forrest is doing all this is never at all clear, nor is the behavior or activities of the other characters. Boone eventually has it out with the killer in a most dubious climax. Jack Klugman plays a singularly inept cop.

It's another change of pace for Boone, who does what he can with the poorly delineated character, as written. He also warbles several old standards pleasantly in the course of his characterization. Miss Eden is her usual curvaceous self, and gets off a number of very convincing screams and shrieks. Forrest is an okay heavy, Klugman likable as the frustrated gendarme. Steve Harris makes a strong impression, and others of occasional prominence are Jesse White, Milton Selzer, John Banner, Jeff Crosby's lenswork is adequate.

Maury Dexter's production has been directed by Buzz Kulik at a brisk, businesslike clip. Floyd Crocby's lenswork is adequate, and the film is crisply punctuated by Jodie Copeland's editing. Walter Simonds' art direction is capable and Kenyon Hopkins has composed a racy, pulsating score to underline the action. *Tube.*

Gogo
(79 av Stodinni)
(ICELANDIC)

Goteborg, April 1.

Stivellproduction release of Edda production. With Kristbjorg Kjeld, Gunnar Eyjolfsson, Robert Arnfinnsson. Directed by Erik Balling. Screenplay, Gudlaur Rosinkrentz from book by I. G. Thorsteneisson; camera, Jorgen Skov. At Aveny Goteborg, Sweden. Running time, 81 MINS.

Gogo	Kristbjorg Kjeld
Ragnar	Gunnar Ekjolfsson
Gudmundur	Robert Arfinnsson
Bob	John Teasy
US drunkard	Lawrence W. Schneph

This first picture ever produced on the tiny island of Iceland is a typical beginners work. There is an awful lot of pathetic acting, moralising, car driving, boring landscapes and much too much cigarets smoking and whiskey drinking as "business" performed by stage actors working before cameras.

It is a simple "boy meets girl" plot from a local bestseller book. It is all about a beautiful widow-turned-prostitute who meets a local taxi driver and a romance starts but there is no happy end. When the driver realises that his prospective bride is a girl who entertains U.S. officers from a nearby base he gets mad also sad and performs a clumsy car-suicide.

In the second part of "Gogo" there are some short scenes of real dramatic value, but on the whole this is a picture of very slim export chances.

Almost unbelievable is the participation in this feature of actual U.S. military personnel stationed at the Keflavik base but pictured as souses and girl-corrupters.

The unknown director of an insignificant picture managed to get two high officers from the local U.S. base Keflavik on Iceland to play roles of drunkards. One, John Teasy, is believed a U.S. actor who is in charge of the U.S. Army TV network of the Keflavik base. Another officer is Lawrence W. Schneph. Both are directed to act out the curse of America's "always present sun" on the nordic island and behave in a way the local population clearly despises.

The best thing said about Americans is a remark by a local taxi driver: "He is not like the other Americans."

The disclosure has already made front page news in Swedish press.

Denk.

The Punch and Judy Man
(BRITISH)

Second attempt to project top UK tv comic, Tony Hancock. But again, despite many funny moments, the venture misfires; star's name may stir interest in Britain.

London, April 9.

Warner-Pathe release of a Macconkey (Gordon L. T. Scott) production. Stars Tony Hancock, Sylvia Syms, Ronald Fraser, Barbara Murray. Directed by Jeremy Summers. Screenplay, Philip Oakes, Tony Hancock, from Hancock's original idea; camera, Gilbert Taylor; editor, Gordon Pilkington; music, Derek Acott, Don Banks. Previewed at Rialto Cinema, London. Running time, 96 MINS.

Wally	Tony Hancock
Delia	Sylvia Syms
Mayor	Ronald Fraser
Lady Jane	Barbara Murray
Sandman	John Le Mesurier
Edward	Hugh Lloyd
Nevil	Mario Fabrizi
Mayoress	Pauline Jameson
Committee Men	Norman Bird, Peter Vaughan, John Dunbar
Clergyman	Walter Hudd
1st Escort	Brian Bedford
2nd Escort	Peter Myers
Ice Cream Assistant	Eddie Byrne
Bobby Bachelor	Russell Waters
Landlord	Kevin Brennan
1st Drunk	Gerald Harper
2nd Drunk	Laurie Main
Waiter	Michael Ripper
Master of Ceremonies	Fred Berman

Tony Hancock, one of Britain's funniest tv comedians, is proving

something of a problem child on the cinema screen. His first film, "The Rebel," had much to commend it but failed to click generally. His second, "The Punch and Judy Man," again produces many amusing sequences, but as a completely successful film it fails to jell.

Story line is too slight. Result is a series of spasmodic incidents which Hancock has, largely, to carry on his own personality, despite being surrounded by some firstclass character actors. His popularity in Britain will get this film by,but his talent is such that there should not be the misgivings which this comedy prompts.

Idea of the film was sparked by Hancock himself. And he and a comparative newcomer, Philip Oakes, collaborated on the screenplay. It might have been better if a more experienced screen scribe had helped him. Hancock plays a Punch and Judy man at a seaside resort which is ruled over by a snobbish mayor. Hancock's marriage is foundering, since he fights the snobbery while his social climbing wife (Sylvia Syms), is anxious for him to mend his ways so that she can move into the local big league.

Climax is the gala held to celebrate the 60th anni of the resort. Everything goes disastrously wrong, a free-for-all ensues and yet, out of the debacle, Hancock's wife learns that she is aspiring to a fluffy world and their marriage is patched up.

This flimsy idea had to be padded with over-many contrived sequences. The opening, with Hancock reacting to radio programs while dressing is vintage Hancock. There is a scene in which he and a small boy tackle ice cream sundaes. This sequence too long, but a neat piece of miming. And there is also a wry breakfast table sequence between Hancock and his bored wife. But the remainder, in the main, is somewhat straggly.

Director Jeremy Summers makes good use of the closeup to put over Hancock's expressive mug, and devotees of the comic will get a generous quota of giggles. But either Summers or the editor, or maybe both, have failed to keep the film on a taut and even keel. Sylvia Syms, as Hancock's disgruntled wife, takes her few opportunities avidly. Ronald Fraser shines as the officious mayor. But though designed as a Hancock vehicle, a lot of the film's uneven strength is contributed by minor characters played by British stalwarts. Eddie Byrne chips in with a neat cameo as the ice cream assistant and Barbara Murray, as a socialite and guest of honor at the gala, pinpoints once more that she is a sadly underrated femme in pix here.

Filmed mostly at a south coast Gilbert Taylor's lensing is alert and the music unobtrusive.

But the film needs a sharper script and far more punch to make it anything but a near-miss.

Rich.

The Leopard
(Il Gattopardo)
(ITALIAN—COLOR)

Rome, April 9.

Titanus release of a Goffredo Lombardo production for Titanus. Stars Burt Lancaster, Claudia Cardinale, Alain Delon; features Paolo Stoppa, Rina Morelli, Romolo Valli, Lucilla Morlacchi, Serge Reggiani, Ida Galli, Ottavia Liccolo, Pierre Clementi, Carlo Valenzano, Annamaria Bottini, Mario Girotti, Leslie French. Directed by Luchino Visconti. Screenplay, Visconti, Suso Cecchi D'Amico, P. F. Campanile, Massimo Franciosa, Enrico Medioli; based on novel by Giuseppe Tommasi di Lampedusa; camera (Technicolor), Giuseppe Rotunno; music, Nino Rota. At the Barberini, Rome. Running time, 205 MINS.

Don Fabrizio Salina ..... Burt Lancaster
Angelica Sedara .... Claudie Cardinale
Tancredi .... Alain Delon
Don Calogero Sedara ...... Paolo Stoppa
Maria Stella .... Rina Morelli
Father Pirrone .... Romolo Valli
Concetta .... Lucilla Morlacchi
Don Ciccio Tumeo ...... Serge Reggiani
Carolina .... Ida Galli
Caterina .... Ottacia Piccolo
Francesco Paolo .... Pierre Clementi
Paolo .... Carlo Valenzano
Mlle. Dombreuil ..... Annamaria Bottini
Count Cavriaghi .... Mario Girotti
Chevally .... Leslie French
Mariannina .... Olimpia Cavallo
Tutor .... Marino Mase
Youngest daughter .... Sandra Chistolini
The little prince .... Brook Fuller
Garibaldino general.... Giuliano Gemma
Bertiana .... Claudia Cardinale
Don Onofrio Rotolo ... Giovanni Mesendi
Don Diego ..... Howard Nelson-Rubien
Donna Margherita...... Lola Braccianni
Col. Pallavicino .... Ivo Carrani

Italy's top bestseller of recent literary history, Tommasi di Lampedusa's "The Leopard," comes to the screen in a magnificent film munificently outfitted and splendidly acted by a large cast dominated by Burt Lancaster's standout stint in the title role.

That said, it must also be added that, at nearly 3½ hours running time, the film is way overlong. Despite their per-se beauty, several sequences fail to trenchantly move forward the story. A judicious scissor job could only enhance the film's impact on general audiences as well as help bridge certain abrupt gaps in the film's continuity.

Otherwise, this pic looks a sure winner both here and abroad, thanks also to such built-in values as the title, the Lancaster name and its lavish trimmings. Stateside impact will also depend heavily on quality of English-language print now being readied, and which is to be considered the "original" one as most thesps spoke English dialog. (These comments are based on Italo-dubbed print screened locally.)

Judging by its ravorable local reception, it's more than likely that aficionados of the Lampedusa original will not be let down by the painstaking and expensive period reconstruction by director Luchino Visconti and his collaborators. Visconti has faithfully followed the book's main outlines, from Prince Salina's city palazzo to the country estate, the Garibaldi interludes, and Tancredi's gradual involvement with Angelica, the pawn in her father's social ascent, symbolizing the changing times, society structure and manners which form the core of Lampedusa's theme. The film story, however, ends before the Prince's death, culminating instead with the lavish Grand Ball sequence as a symbol of an era coming to its end.

As noted, Burt Lancaster's Salina is an outstanding achievement, one which almost alone brings together the film's various threads, giving it body and provoking thought. And in the final reels, when the prince sees the writing on the wall, it is again Lancaster who gives the picture some of its few deeply moving moments as he moves, a sad, lonely and aging figure in a world no longer his own through the crowded salons of the Palermo palace.

Claudia Cardinale and Alain Delon appear ideally cast as Angelica and Tancredi. Both make the most of their roles despite a certain lack of warmth perhaps dictated by the director's approach to their development. Miss Cardinale also makes a brief (veiled) appearance as her own mother. Paolo Stoppa is excellent as Don Calogero, another tailor-made part, while Rina Morelli has some fine moments as Maria Stella, the princess, as does Romolo Valli, as Father Pirrone. Lucilla Morlacchi plays the homely Concetta with apt detachment. Serge Reggiani, as Don Ciccio Tumeo, is strangely opaque in his scenes with Lancaster. One role stands out among the many colorful supporting performances: that of Leslie French as Chevally, the north Italian emissary who discusses the country's future with Prince Salina.

There's no denying that production-wise, "The Leopard" has been spared no expense. And its authentic Sicilian settings show, almost to a fault, plenty of spending. The several intimate passages vital to the story are nearly lost in the shuffle.

Likewise, for example, there is little to show Tancredi's passion—or love for Angelica while the long sequence showing the youth chasing Angelica throughout the many rooms of the palace is primarily resolved as an (excellent) stylistic exercise. For this, director Visconti must be blamed, just as he is to be praised for his tasteful coordination of the whole. Physically, this is a rich experience, thanks to Giuseppe Rotunno's outstanding Technicolor lensing job, to Mario Garbuglia's art direction, down to other aspects of a sumptuous production made with great dedication and taste. Nino Rota's musical scoring, though sometimes over-emphatic, is generally apt. 20th-Fox releases outside of Italy.

Hawk.

Il Processo di Verona
(The Verona Trial)
(ITALIAN)

Rome, April 9.

Dino DeLaurentiis release of a Duillo Cinematografica production. Features Silvana Mangano, Frank Wolf, Francoise Prevost, Salvo Randone, Ivo Garrani, Henri Serre, Giorgio De Lullo, Vivi Gioi. Directed by Carlo Lizzani. Story and screenplay, Ugo Pirro; camera, Leonida Barboni; music, Mario Nascimbene; editor, Franco Fraticelli. At the Adriano, Rome. Running time, 120 MINS.

Edda Ciano .... Silvana Mangano
Galeazzo Ciano .... Frank Wolf
Donna Rachele .... Vivi Gioi
Frau Betz .... Francoise Prevost
Judge .... Salvo Randone
Pavolini .... Giorgio DeLullo
Farinacci .... Ivo Garrani
Dino Grandi .... Andrea Checchi
Pucci .... Henri Serre
Cerosimo .... Claudio Gora

Elaborate, ostensibly faithful, and frequently gripping reconstruction of last controversial days of Count Ciano, Mussolini's son-in-law and onetime Fascist Foreign Minister. Mostly for the Italian trade which can catch intricate shadings of political intrigue in Fascism's dying days, but rates certain foreign attention because of the affair's notoriety.

Pic covers the final days of Ciano's life, in which he and his wife first count on Mussolini's intervention to save him from the firing squad, then in desperation try to buy off the Nazis by using the famed Ciano Diaries as bait. But nothing works, and Ciano is tried, found guilty, and executed, along with a group of would-be traitors to the Fascist cause. There is a serious attempt to re-create the atmosphere of the times and events (though Ciano's widow has gone to court to dispute pic's ultimate authenticity). Most of the time, director Carlo Lizzani succeeds. Where the film fails is in not turning a very human local drama into a universal one. This is likely to leave the non-initiated foreign viewer out in the cold as far as participation in described events is concerned.

There's an excellent acting job by Silvana Mangano as Ciano's wife (by far the best she's done in years) and a strikingly resemblant and forceful delineation of Ciano by of all things a Yank actor, Frank Wolf. Others who lend apt support are Ivo Garrani and Giorgio DeLullo, as Fascist bigwigs; Salvo Randone, as a trial judge, and a neat bit by Francoise Prevost, as Frau Betz, a mysterious figure who tries desperately to save Ciano in jail. Period setting, lensing, and other credits are all good. There's a haunting musical score ominously interspersed with machine-gun fire by Mario Nascimbene.

Hawk.

Pillar of Fire
(ISRAELI)

Geva Film release of Larry Frisch-Geva Films Ltd. (Izhak Agadati-Mordehay Navon) production. Features Michael Shillo, Lawrence Montaigne, Nehama Hendel, Moshe Yaari. Directed by Frisch. Screenplay, Hugh Nissenson; camera, Haim Shreiber; editor, Nelly Bogor; music, Moshe Willensky. At Cameo, N. Y., starting April 6, '63. Running time, 75 MINS.

Uri .... Michael Shillo
David .... Lawrence Montaigne
Rachel .... Nehama Hendel
Moshe .... Moshe Yaari
Kantrowitz .... Amos Mocadi
Yossi .... Uri Zohar

(English Dialog)

Here is a little documentary which contains much more suspense and excitement than many comparable foreign-made pix, having no name stars. Yarn covers an episode in Israel's War of Independence, and as such has natural appeal to a segment of the population in bigger American cities. Film should do well in foreign-language houses in a number of major U. S. spots. "Pillar of Fire" should return a tidy profit to its producers since brought in purportedly for less than $50,000.

Film is mostly a Larry Frisch effort since he's director and one of the producers. And that's to the good since he has succeeded in developing the commercial appeal in an obvious documentary-type pic. Frisch has one tough handicap—the background because long stretches of sandy desert and rolling hills are not the most romantic spots in the world. He has overcome this to a degree by keeping the action rolling.

Action is supposed to cover a single day. But the isolated Jewish settlement in the Negev desert seems to be under fire or different groups from it are out fighting from the opening scene until a rather lacklustre finale. Unfortunately, the futility of the efforts by six citizen-soldiers to ward off a tank attack seem stressed too heavily, as one after the other is bumped off in one skirmish after the other. There is no heroic finish nor any plausible end shown.

Cast of unknows appears to have been recruited mainly from the Tel Aviv stage and does nicely with the documentary-type plot. Besides Frisch's yeoman work, the original musical score by Moshe Willensky is standout. It is played for this production by members of the Israeli Symphony under his direction. *Wear.*

La Parmigiana
(The Girl from Parma)
(ITALIAN)
Rome, April 9.
Di-o DeLaurentiis release of a Documentry Films (Gianni Hecht Lucari) production. Stars Nino Manfredi, Catherine Spaak: features Didi Perego, Salvo Randone, Lando Buzzanca, Vanni de Maigret, Rosalia Maggio, Umberto D'Orsi, Mario Brega. Dorected by Antonio Pietrangelli. Screenplay, Pietrangelli, Ruggero Maccarl, Bruna Piatti, Ettore Scola, Stefano Strucchi from novel by Bruna Piatti; editor, Eraldo da Roma; camera, Armando Nannuzzi. At Metropolitan, Rome. **Running time, 120 MINS.**

Dora	Catherine Spaak
Nino	Nino Manfredi
Scipio	Salvo Randone
Amneris	Didi Perego
Michele	Lando Buzzanca
Giacomo	Vanni de Maigret
Iris	Rosalia Maggio
Ingegnere	Umberto D'Orsi
Policeman	Mario Brega

Neatly turned-out comedy-drama with both quality and general appeal. Manfredi and Spaak names will help also on home market, where outlook is good. Abroad, pic is iffier due to local connotations, but definitely rates a look-see.

Told via ironically placed flashbacks, story tells of provincial gal rapidly initiated to big city virtues and (mostly) vices, all unbeknownst to her last remaining in-laws. Her downfall is taken gracefully and candidly by Dora (Catherine Spaak) as she effortlessly journeys from man to man taking each in youthful stride and with nymphetish innocence until one final disappointment jolts her at the fadeout. Catherine Spaak is excellent as Dora, showing more maturity and versatility than before to add to her piquant charm, while standout supporting stints are turned in by Salvo Randone and Didi Perego, a middle-aged couple with which she puts up for a while. Nino Manfredi is likewise fine as her sometime steady, while Vanni de Maigret and Lando Buzzanca—t h e latter a young character actor to watch — join in with others to give able backing to rest.

Antonio Pietrangeli's direction is uneven, but when at best in certain country scenes shows a mature talent and a fine hand with actors in touching up scenes with keen atmospheric notations. Elsewhere, notably towards end of pic, he lets action wander and get slightly confused. Armando Nannuzzi's lensing is his usual standout job, while other credits measure up. Several pop songs are effectively used by uncredited cleffer to highlight action. *Hawk.*

Melodie En Sous-Sol
(Basement Melody)
(FRENCH—DYALISCOPE)
Paris, April 9.
MGM release of Cipra-CCM-Cite Films production. Stars Jean Gabin, Alain Delon; features Viviane Romance, Carla Marlier, Maurice Biraud, Claude Cerval, Dora Doll. Directed by Henri Verneuil. Screenplay, Albert Siminon, Michel Audiard, Verneuil from novel by John Trinian; camera, Louis Page; editor, Francoise Verneuil. Preemed in Paris. **Running time, 118 MINS.**

Charles	Jean Gabin
Francis	Alain Delon
Wife	Viviane Romance
Brigitte	Carla Marlier
Louis	Maurice Biraud
Inspector	Claude Cerval
Countess	Dora Doll

Perennial theme of the aging gangster and a last heist at a gambling casino gets another going over in this sleekly-made pic. A lot of excess talk for its own flowery, lowlife slang sake, and some primary characterization, do not make this different enough to give its familiar envelope a new shape. But a neat chunk of end-suspense should have it an okay local bet with foregn playoffs indicated if discreetly sheared. Arty chances are slim.

An old ex-con, Jean Gabin, sets up one last job and enlists a young ex-con, Alain Delon, to help him. It consists of robbing the bank at a casino on the Riviera. It is intricately worked out and they get the loot only to have an ironic twist losing it for them.

If crime does not pay, at least the two are not caught even if all their work has gone for naught. Gabin is his usual stolid self. Delon has bounce, edginess and ambition as the young punk who does all the leg work while Gabin does the masterminding.

Director Henri Verneuil finally gets a good half hour of suspense at the end during the mechanics of the complicated holdup and the final losing of the swag. But prelims are bogged down by would-be sharp dialog that rarely has anything to do with the characters. Their personal aspects are also delineated in too conventional a mode to lift this out of the ordinary.

In short, MGM has a fine European bet in this film produced by their local bankrolled company. Cipra, with a probable Yank playoff or dualer entry also indicated. The Gabin monicker will help. It is technically expert. U.S. title will be "The Big Grab" *Mosk.*

In Parterre Links
(Ground Floor to the Left)
(SWISS)
Zurich, April 7.
Praesens-Film A.G. Zurich release of Gloriafilm Zurich (Max Dora)-Praesens production. Directed by Kurt Frueh. Screenplay, Fritz Bruder, Frueh, Alex Freihart, based on stage play "Das Fenster zum Flur" (Window to the Hall) by Curth Flatow and Horst Pillau; camera, Emil Berna; sound, Bruno Kohler, Klaus Bietenholz; editors, Rene Martintt, Anne Demmer; music, Walter Baumgartner. At Apollo Theatre, Zurich. **Running time, 94 MINS.**

Karl Wieser	Paul Buehlmann
Annie Wieser	Valerie Steinmann
Herbert	Rene Scheibli
Helen	Ursula Kopp
Evi	Bella Neri
Danny	Gaby Froesch
Erich	Joseph Scheidegger
Sandro Jovanovic	Peter Brogle

(Swiss Dialect)
Latest Swiss family comedy-drama seems strictly a local item,

with below-par boxoffice prospects even on the home market. This type of homely middleclass family stories has been overdone in Switzerland in recent years, with initially fine financial results due to low budget, but the pulp has now apparently been squeezed to the last drop. This film, seemingly was made as a sort of test case to see if there's any money left in this type of picture. First boxoffice response plus critical reaction provide the answer: it's dead.

Yarn concerns a Zurich streetcar driver and his family, with the busybody mother trying to run their three grownup children's lives. She is finally forced to face reality when the children turn against her and insist at last upon leading their own lives.

Superficiality of characters, who are mostly run-of-the-mill stereotypes, plus same glaring implausibilities contribute to write this off as a soon to be forgotten routine entry. Direction and lensing are conventional, and acting by a cast of potentially able local players, in Swiss dialect, runs from acceptable (within script limits) to unbelevable. *Mezo.*

The Small World of Sammy Lee
(BRITISH)

Sharp, snide peep at the seamy side of Soho's stripperies. Anthony Newley, though giving virtually a one - man performance, gets some shrewd support.

London, April 9.
BLC release of a British Lion-Bryanston Seven Arts (Frank Godwin) production. Stars Anthony Newley; features Dobert Stephens, Wilfrid Brambell, Miriam Karlin, Kenneth J. Warren, Julia Foster, Toni Palmer, Harry Locke, Al Mulock, Alfred Burke, Roy Kinnear, June Cunningham. Written and directed by Ken Hughes; camera, Wolfgang Suschitzky; editor, Henry Richardson; music. Kenny Graham. Previewed at Hammer Theatre, London. **Running time, 107 MINS.**

Sammy	Anthony Newley
Patsy	Julia Foster
Gerry	Robert Stephens
Harry	Wilfrid Brambell
Lou	Warren Mitchell
Milly	Miriam Karlin
Fred	Kenneth J. Warren
Johnny	Clive Colin Bowler
Joan	Toni Palmer
Stage Manager	Harry Locke
Dealer	Al Mulock
Morrie	Cyril Shaps
Lucky Dave	Roy Kinnear
Buddy Shine	Harry Baird
Big Eddie	Alfred Burke
Rita	June Cunningham
Big Alf	Ronald Radd

Originally an award winning tele play by Ken Hughes ("Sammy" in Britain, "Eddie" in U.S.), this film has been pumped up to feature length, perhaps at overlength. Though highly overcolored, it remains a sharp, snide commentary on the sleazy side of Soho, and emerges as a firstclass vehicle for the taut talents of Anthony Newley. "Stop the World" gave Newley a bright showcase both in U.K. and on Broadway, and his current shiny rep could make this pix a possible sleeper. It will depend largely on Newley's pull, yet he is surrounded by some admirable support.

Newley, a fugitive from the East End, is the smart aleck emcee of one of the shabby stripperies which grind through the day for the benefit of jaded business men and alcoholic layabouts. Newley,

between churning out tired, near-blue gags and introducing the peelers, is an inveterate poker and horse player. The story consists entirely of his efforts to raise $840 in five hours to pay off a gangster-bookie who is threatening to cut him up if he doesn't deliver the loot on time.

Newley's attempts to meet the deadline by sundry dubious, devious deals are at once funny and pathetic. The payoff is ironic. The moral is all too simple. Stay out of the bright lights if you don't want to develop an ulcer.

Hughes' uninhibited screenplay is incisive and tart while his direction has the deft assurance of a man who is reaiing with his own idea and knows what he wants as the end product. His cameras stray restlessly around the seamier parts of Soho and the East End. Obviously he has done a lot of research on these afternoon flesh salons that still flourish in this allegedly civilized city of London.

Newley gives a restless, intelligent and perceptive performance as the little fish floundering in a pond that is too deep for him. His anxiety neurosis, as he faces his financial crisis, is superbly blended with his wisecracking apparently carefree personality as the shabby little comedian linking the weary striptease acts.

Few of the supporting actors have much opportunity to make great impact but some register brilliantly. Notably, Warren Mitchell as Newley's East End delicatessen store-owner brother. When Newley visits him to try and raise the cash there is a scene that is directed, written and acted with a sure touch. Miriam Karlin turns up in this sequence but all too briefly.

Robert Stephens provides a sly picture of the odious clubowner. Kenneth J. Warren as the gangster muscle man has several effective scenes. Julia Foster adequately provides the slight romantic interest as a North country girl, tempted down to the West End by Newley, who finds that Soho is not quite the step to stardom that she anticipates. Wilfrid Brambell, Harry Locke, Clive Colin Bowler, as Warren's sadistic young henchman, and Toni Palmer, as a goodhearted tart, also score.

The club sequences are suitably tawdry with the strippers providing a keen sense of satire. Wolfgang Suschitzky's lensing has caught perfectly the feel of the locale. In short, "The Small World of Sammy" has come up surprisingly well for an idea which, basically, is so slim and not particularly original. *Rich.*

The Sadist

Violence-laden horror pic aimed at the sadist market. Bad acting by femme leads mars "sleeper" chances.

Fairway-International Films release of Chips' Nicholas Merriweather-L. Steven Snyder production. Stars Arch Hall Jr., Richard Alden, Marilyn Manning, Don Russell, Helen Hovey. Written and directed by James Landis. Camera, William Zsigmond; editor, Anthony M. Lanza; musical director, Rod Moss. Reviewed at Toho La Brea Theatre, L.A., April 16, 1963. Running time, **95 MINS.**

Charley Tibbs .... Arch Hall Jr.
Doris Page .... Helen Hovey
Ed Stiles .... Richard Alden
Judy Bradshaw .... Marilyn Manning
Carl Oliver .... Don Russell

Although made on a shoestring, this treatise on "killing for fun" tries hard to get out of the "horror film" fare rut. Its draggy beginning, too many loose ends, and the two inept female performances must be marked against it, but it should still find success in the market at which it's aimed. There's a surfeit of killing, shown and implied.

Three schoolteachers (Richard Alden, Don Russell and Helen Hovey), on their way to a ball game, have engine trouble which forces them to stop at an out-of-the-way gas station. Finding it deserted, Alden begins his own repairs when the trio is confronted by a gun-wielding terrorist and his female companion (Arch Hall Jr. and Marilyn Manning). They're a pair of thrill killers being sought by the police and they need the teachers' car to escape.

The three victims are held at bay while Alden is forced to continue work on the stalled auto. Hall kills Russell in cold blood when he finds out he's a teacher—seems his girl friend was kicked out of a school. After many minutes of what is supposed to be suspense but threatens to turn into tedium, two motorcycle policemen show up, only to be slain by Hall. In a last-ditch attempt to escape, at which point the picture really beings to roll, Hall mistakenly shoots Miss Manning and, after a chase, kills Alden. Miss Hovey gets away only when Hall, in pursuit, meets his end in a manner which will not be revealed here.

Hall, a large, gross, figure, is ideally cast for the role but is too often guilty of "attitudes" which border on the ridiculous. Alden comes off best as the terror-confronted teacher, and Russell is quite impressive in his short-lived role. Miss Manning's contribution is, for the most part, an exhibition of gum chewing and giggling. With the plot's most demanding role, a semi-prudish schoolteacher confronted for the first time in her life with inhuman cruelty and violence, Miss Hovey, unable to register more than one or two expressions, is never convincing.

William Zsigmond's black and white photography is excellent, considering his having to show a time passage of one hot, summer afternoon, with the lighting problems entailed, while forced to shoot over a period of several months. Anthony M. Lanza's editing, too slow in the first half of the film, lingering far too long on mood-establishing scenes, picks up in the fast, final phases of the picture, however, particularly in Hall's macabre end. *Robe.*

The Stripper

Jerry Wald's last film. Unsuccessful attempt to rejuvenate an Inge flop.

Hollywood, April 19.

Twentieth-Fox release of Jerry Wald production. Stars Joanne Woodward, Richard Beymer, Claire Trevor, Carol Lynley; features Robert Webber, Louis Nye, Gypsy Rose Lee. Directed by Franklin Schaffner. Screenplay, Meade Roberts, based on William Inge's play, "A Loss of Roses"; camera, Ellsworth Fredericks; editor, Robert Simpson; music, Jerry Goldsmith; asst. director, Eli Dunn. Reviewed at the studio, April 19, '63. Running time, **95 MINS.**

Lila .... Joanne Woodward
Kenny .... Richard Beymer
Helen .... Claire Trevor
Miriam .... Carol Lynley
Ricky .... Robert Webber
Ronnie .... Louis Nye
Madame Olga .... Gypsy Rose Lee
Jelly .... Michael J. Pollard
Edwina .... Sondra Kerr
Mrs. Mulvaney .... Susan Brown
Sandra Mulvaney ... Marlene De Lamater
Dizzy .... Gary Pagett
Sonny .... Ralph Lee
Mr. Mulvaney .... Bing Russell

This final film by the late Jerry Wald is an unsuccessful attempt to convert William Inge's 1959 Broadway flop, "A Loss of Roses," into a substantial and appealing motion picture. Truth of the matter is, it had more substance, solidity and sensitivity as a play.

Like the play, the film has its merits, but they are only flashes of magic in a lacklustre package. Joanne Woodward's performance in a role expanded to focal prominence in the film is one of them. And occasionally there are moments or even scenes of poetic fragility and insight, and some scattered lines of cogent dialog ("never trust a man who shaves twice a day"). These can help the commercial cause to a slight degree, but not significantly enough. And then there is that misleading title, the last of several feeble attempts to erase the stigma of Inge's wilted "Roses," to reckon with.

Miss Woodward is the pathetic heroine of Meade Roberts' scenario based on the Inge drama. The story is set in traditional Inge country —a small town in Kansas—more specifically the modest residence of two characters into whose humdrum lives comes Miss Woodward stranded by the abrupt deterioration of the little magician's unit of which she is a part.

She is taken in by an old friend (Claire Trevor) now a widow who lives with her son (Richard Beymer), an ardent but inexperienced lad. There are attempts to make something of the mother-son relationship, but the two characters are never properly clarified, and remain two-dimensional. At any rate, Beymer fancies himself in love with the visitor and has a one-night affair with the fading, desperately accommodating and romantically vulnerable would-be actress, but finds himself unable and unprepared to follow through.

On the rebound Miss Woodward agrees to the proposition of her singularly wicked boy friend-manager (Robert Webber) to indulge in some lucrative convention stripping, although it is not precisely the breed of "show" biz she's had in mind for a career. There is an upbeat ending, however, as Miss Woodward, under urging by the newly mature, self-reliant Beymer, frees herself from this unsavory occupation and sets out solo in search of better things.

Histrionic honors go hands down to the animated Miss Woodward, who rivets attention and compassion to herself throughout with a farceful and vivacious portrayal of the goodhearted but gullible girl. Beymer is adequate, little more, in the rather baffling role of the lad, and Miss Trevor puts in one of her now rare screen appearances as the mother, a character too opaque for the kind of thespic vigor she can ordinarily invest. Lovely Carol Lynley is wasted in a thankless role which requires mostly a photogenic rear anatomy for walking away shots, a talent Miss Lynley sports and cameraman Ellsworth Fredericks appreciates. Miss Woodward's rear gets a big photographic play, too. Webber is hateful as the unredeemably nasty promoter, and is mired in the film's most artificial melodramatic moments. Louis Nye and Gypsy Rose Lee breeze through a couple of flashy character parts. Michael J. Pollard is colorful in a prominent supporting role.

Franklin Schaffner's direction tends to be a bit choppy, uneven and, in spots, heavyhanded or unobservant. There is a rather staccato tempo and a definite lack of geographic clarity about the film that indicates some editing stress and strain. Robert Simpson was the cutter. Artwork by Jack Martin Smith and Walter M. Simonds is praiseworthy. Jerry Goldsmith's score has sparkle and character, and is obtrusive in a constructive manner—when a musical lift is needed to enliven the going. *Tube.*

Drums of Africa
(COLOR)

Lacklustre blend of old African pic footage and dull new story. Slim b.o. prospect.

Hollywood, April 17.

Metro release of Al Zimbalist-Philip N. Krasne production. Stars Frankie Avalon, Mariette Hartley, Lloyd Bochner, Torin Thatcher. Directed by James B. Clark. Screenplay, Robin Estridge, from story by Arthur Hoerl. Estridge; camera (Metrocolor), Paul C. Vogel; editor, Ben Lewis; music, Johnny Mandel; asst. director, Hank Moonjean. Reviewed at the studio, April 17, '63. Running time, **92 MINS.**

Brian Ferrers .... Frankie Avalon
Ruth Knight .... Mariette Hartley
David Moore .... Lloyd Bochner
Jack Cuortemayn ..... Torin Thatcher
Kasongo .... Hari Rhodes
Arab .... George Sawaya
Viledo .... Michael Pate
Ship Captain .... Ron Whelan
Chavera .... Peter Mamakos

There are two ways of looking at Metro's "Drums of Africa." From a bookkeeper's-eye-view, it can be regarded as an example of studio resourcefulness and enterprise in taking reams of old African film footage, principally "King Solomon's Mines" variety, and pasting new dramatic meat on the old celluloidal bones. The splice of life, one might say. Or editing for fun and profit.

On the other hand, it can be regarded as counterfeit picturemaking—an attempt to succeed in business without really trying. For the only achievements of cinematic artistry on display in this film are views borrowed from the artisans of the past, who rate at least a residual or two for their efforts. The new story construction on this skeletal foundation is singularly uninspired and stumbles along awkwardly trying to gear itself to the filmic forgery holding it together. The result is a mish-mosh. Moreover, the old footage has faded a bit and doesn't match. Since the public isn't exactly deceived, the Al Zimbalist-Philip N. Krasne production is a dim box-office prospect. Fortunately, its budget-minded, exploitation-oriented design doesn't require a huge return to bail it out.

The Robin Estridge screenplay, from a story written in collaboration with Arthur Hoerl, is set in the Equatorial East Africa of 1897 and begins with a debate over whether civilized progress (the railroad and such) will tarnish the simple joys of primitivity that then reigned over the Dark Continent. Before long, however, the film has settled into a shopworn groove as, beating around the bush, the rougish railroad engineer and unspoiled bwana girl of Africa find love on a safari and ward off the threat of slave traders out for a Damascus steal.

Frankie Avalon capably essays the role of a lad on his first trip to Africa. Mariette Hartley and Lloyd Bochner are satisfactory as the romantic leads and are a good match for Deborah Kerr and Stewart Granger of the "Solomon's" footage. Torin Thatcher provides the theoretical conflict as the reactionary guide, or Barry Goldwater of the veldt. Hari Rhodes stands out as an educated native, and Michael Pate scores as an unreliable Portuguese guide who vanishes prematurely and unaccountably.

James B. Clark has done a creditable job of matching new action to the snips from the film library. But the faded scenes from the vaults show a different Africa than the fresh Metrocolored views of cameraman Paul C. Vogel which are about as Tarzanesque as Tarzana (Calif.). On the whole, editor Ben Lewis has demonstrated great resourcefulness, although there are one or two irrelevantly horrid scenes presumably incorporated for the pure sake of shock. Johnny Mandel's music and the George W. Davis-Addison Hehr art direction are adequate assists.

"The River Love," a tender romantic ballad by Russell Faith and Robert Marcucci, is warbled gently and pleasantly by Avalon. As he sings it, the screen reveals zebra and other wildlife in sweet caress. Those animals really do go ape over Yankee crooners. *Tube.*

Klaun Ferdinand A Raketa
(Clown Ferdinand and the Rocket)
(CZECH)

Berlin, April 16.

Czech State Film Barrandov production and release. Stars Jiri Vrstala. Directed by Jindrich Polak. Screenplay, Ota Hofman; camera, Jan Kalis; music, Illin Eugen. Previewed at Sovexport film studio, West Berlin. Running time, **80 MINS.**

Clown Ferdinand is a prominent figure with Czech moppets. He's said to be as popular in this Commie country as Popeye the Sailor was in the U.S. This Czech production has been tailored for the youngsters and may be shown everywhere. It even may have some limited foreign chances.

Plot is simple: A rocket ship of unknown origin is approaching a Czech city. Except for Ferdinand, a vaude clown who lives in a trailer, and three moppets who join him, the inhabitants desert the city. The giant rocket lands on an open field. Somehow Ferdinand and the kids find themselves in the rocket which eventually returns to the air.

Pic has a flavor of naivety but it's pleasant. One feels that its creators have a devotion for kids and human weaknesses, and this is what counts in this one. Jiri Vrstala, who plays Ferdinand, is the star. Director Polak led the three moppets through amiable performances. Outstanding is Illin Eugen's catchy score with the music played by the Karel Vlach handling behind the scenes and orch, incidentally, the CSSR's best and its most popular band. Technical credits are up to par. *Hans.*

Lancelot and Guinevere
(Panavision-Color)

Cornel Wilde, Jean Wallace, Brian Aherne in a visit to Camelot, sans musicality, but with horse soldiers galore. Lots of King Arthur legendary action in a clearly expensive, sometimes exciting but not too skillfully controlled large-screen, Eastman Color production. Needs heavy "sell."

Universal release of Emblem Production, produced by Cornel Wilde and Bernard Luber. Stars Wilde, Jean Wallace, Brian Aherne; features George Baker, Archie Duncan, Adrienne Corri, Michael Meacham, Iain Gregory, Mark Dignam. Directed by Wilde. Screenplay, Richard Schayer and Jefferson Pascal; music, Ron Goodwin; camera (Eastman Color—Panavision), Harry Waxman; editor, Frederick Wilson. Previewed at U homeoffice, April 25, '63. Running time, **116 MINS.**

Lancelot	Cornel Wilde
Guinevere	Jean Wallace
King Arthur	Brian Aherne
Sir Gawaine	George Bakr
Sir Lamorak	Archie Duncan
Lady Vivian	Adrienne Corri
Sir Modred	Michael Meacham
Sir Tors	Iain Gregory
Merlin	Mark Dignam
Sir Dagonet	Reginald Beckwith
Sir Bedivere	John Barrie
Sir Gareth	Richard Thorp
Sir Kaye	Joseph Tomelty
Rian	Graham Stark
Edric	Geoffrey Dunn
Sir Cedric	Walter Gotell
Brandagorus	Peter Prowse
Ulfus	Christopher Rhodes
King Leodogran	John Longden
Sir Dorjak	Bob Bryan
French Maid	Violetta Farjeon

King Arthur's beloved wife, Lady Guinevere, smooches up with his favorite knight, Sir Lancelot, and as a result the lady was almost for burning at the stake. This is a key point in this latest version of the much told (with many variations via various media) tale of King Arthur and the Knights of the Round Table. It's an elaborately mounted production that generates fair amounts of interest and excitement when the fighting's going on but barely rises above the routine in story-telling the legend.

The Richard Schayer-Jefferson Pascal screenplay is based on Sir Thomas Mallory's "Morte d'Arthur" of the 16th century. It's Cornel Wilde most of the way, he having coproduced with Bernard Luber, directed and costarred with his wife, Jean Wallace, latter making a beautiful Guinevere.

This outing smacks of modernization in terms of plot situation. But not filmmaking technique. King Arthur eagerly awaits his Guinevere at the altar in his Camelot and she's escorted by the gallant Lancelot, Wilde. The marriage takes place, but despite the affection Lancelot feels for his king, he he shares a bed with the lady whose name he reduces in the dialog to just plain Guin.

Jousting and open field battling are abundant. There's many a blood-drenched closeup provided by director Wilde and cameraman Harry Waxman. The outdoor scenes, which were filmed in Yugoslavia with native cavalrymen, are in some measure pictorially effective but at times director Wilde is just focusing on so much confused action.

It appears that a bit of the massive battle maneuvers got out of hand. A lack of production discipline also is suggested on several occasions via inadequate bridging, as with one scene going to another without the right kind of segue. No telling how much footage was left on the plains of Titoland or the cutting-room floor of Pinewood Studios, London, where the interiors were lensed. Perhaps there was a post-camerawork decision to drop some gore but in any case the production control was not complete.

But despite the shortcomings, the basic fiction is gotten across all right and this makes for interest, particularly as enhanced by the Panavision and color values. The "modernization," meaning the sex, so far as the conscientious objectors might be concerned, comes out all right, too. For, the scripters have written in a cinematic act of contrition whereby the adulterous Guin winds up in a nunnery.

An accomplished job is turned in by Brian Aherne, as King Arthur, who's able to give a good reading even when dialog is stilted. Wilde and Miss Wallace are believable, John Longden is properly sinister as Arthur's rival for the crown and Iain Gregory is appealing as a young knight fighting side by side with Lancelot.

Bob Bryan, Andrienne Corri, Michael Meacham and Mark Dignam, in support, lend adequate aid.

Ron Goodwin's music backgrounding serves nicely and other technical credits all treasure up okay. *Gene.*

Flipper
(COLOR)

Modest but marketable family-style entry about a boy on a dolphin.

Hollywood, April 16.

Metro release of Ivan Tors production. Stars Chuck Connors; introduces Luke Halpin. Directed by James B. Clark. Screenplay, Arthur Weiss, from story by Ricou Browning, Jack Cowden; camera (Metrocolor), Lamar Bowen, Joseph Brun; editor, Warren Adams; music, Henry Vars. Reviewed at the studio, April 16, '63. Running time, **87 MINS.**

Porter Ricks	Chuck Connors
Sandy Ricks	Luke Halpin
Kim Parker	Connie Scott
Hettie White	Jane Rose
Mr. L. C. Porett	Joe Higgins
Mr. Abrams	Robertson white
Sheriff Rogers	George Applewhite
Martha Ricks	Kathleen Maguire

Boy meets dolphin, boy loses dolphin, boy wins dolphin. Thus substituting gill for gal, producer Ivan Tors, television's erstwhile answer to Davy Jones, has fashioned a serviceable little "family" picture for Metro that to all intents and porpoises, should satisfy aquabrats everywhere, although any grown-up who has made the Marineland scene more than once may occasionally be hard put to keep from dropping asleep in the deep.

Actually this little fish story, or Tors opera, amounts to a kind of bubbly variation on "Androcles and the Lion." Arthur Weiss' screenplay, from a story by Ricou Browning and Jack Cowden, has a boy (Luke Halpin) rescuing an eight-foot dolphin from permanent residence in that big fish tank in the sky by removing a skin diver's spear from its torso and nursing it back to health at his dad's Florida Keys fish pen. When dad (Chuck Connors) rationally and porpoisefully suggests that a fish pen is no place for a mammal, the boy reluctantly stands by as "Flipper" is released into the open sea. But when the loyal, adhesive dolphin saves the lad from a shark, dad relents and "Flipper" becomes a member of the family.

Connors limns the father firmly but agreeably, and young Halpin, in his screen bow, demonstrates keen acting instincts as the boy on a dolphin. Connie Scott and Kathleen Maguire dispatch important roles capably, and the balance of the cast is reliable.

James B. Clark's resourceful direction is backed up by generally sound production values. Photography by Lamar Boren and Joseph Brun is skillfully performed both above and below sea level, although hurricane footage at the outset has irregularities of color and element. Still, the sequence has good cumulative effect. Warren Adams' editing is taut and trim. Music, always vital in an underwater subject, where bubbles generally are the only sound, has been well handled by composer-conductor Henry Vars. There's also a title song by Vars and Dunham. *Tube.*

Les Femmes D'Abord
(Ladies First)
(FRENCH)

Paris, April 23.

CCFC release of Vega-CFC production. Stars Eddie Constantine; features Christiane Minazzoli, Robert Manuel, Bernadette Lafont, Misha Auer. Directed by Raoul Andre. Screenplay, Michel Lebrun from book by Paul Gerrard; camera, Pierre Petit; editor, Gabriel Roncier. At Mercury, Paris. Running time, **90 MINS.**

Bobby	Eddie Constantine
Juliette	Christiane Minazzoli
Inspector	Robert Manuel
Stripper	Bernadette Lefont
Count	Misha Auer
Bobby	Jacques Harden

Eddie Constantine again walks through a gangland adventure as a Yank FBI man. Plenty of fisticuffs, a simple tale and girls make it an acceptable one in its genre with mainly local changes, on the Constantine monicker. It looks to have only dualer chances abroad.

Here Constantine saves a woman in distress and breaks up a dope ring. There are some clever gags and the fights are okay if too openhanded to stand up to the more knuckled Yank counterparts. Direction is competent if lacking punch. Constantine is his usual good-natured, wisecracking superman type. *Mosk.*

The Day Of The Triffids
(C'SCOPE—COLOR)

Exploitable sci-fi meller about a people-eating vegetable.

Hollywood, April 26.

Allied Artists release of George Pitcher production. Stars Howard Keel, Nicole Maurey. Directed by Steve Sekely. Screenplay, Philip Yordan, from the novel by John Wyndham; camera (Eastman), Ted Moore; editor, Spencer Reeve; music, Ron Goodwin; asst. director, Douglas Hermes. Reviewed at the studio, April 26, '63. Running time, **93 MINS.**

Bill Masen	Howard Keel
Christine Durrant	Nicole Maurey
Karen Goodwin	Janette Scott
Tom Goodwin	Kieron Moore
Professor Coker	Mervyn Johns
Susan	Janina Faye
Miss Coker	Alison Leggatt
Doctor Soames	Ewan Roberts
Nurse Jamieson	Colette Wilde
Bettina	Carole Ann Ford
Luis	Geoffrey Matthews
Teresa	Gilgi Hauser
Mary	Katya Douglas
Poiret	Victor Brooks
Burly Man	Thomas Gallagher
Ticket Agent	Sidney Vivian
Pilot	Gary Hope
Blind Man	John Simpson

The triffid is coming. Basically, the George Pitcher production out of England is a vegetarian's version of "The Birds," a science-fiction-horror melodrama about a vile people-eater of the plant kingdom with a voracious appetite. Although riddled with script inconsistencies and irregularities, the Allied Artists release is a more-than-adequate film of its genre and should make a healthy showing in the exploitation-saturation sphere for which it was designed.

John Wyndham's novel, "The Day of the Triffids," served as the source for exec producer Philip Yordan's screenplay. The proceedings begin with a spectacular display of celestial fireworks, a meteorite shower that leaves the earth's population heir to two maladies: blindness and the sinister company of a fast-multiplying plant aptly called Triffidus Celestus that looks like a Walt Disney nightmare and sounds like a cauldron of broccoli cooking in Margaret Hamilton's witchin' kitchen.

Hero of the piece is Howard Keel as a Yank seaman who, ironi-

cally spared the ordeal of blindness by having had his ill optics bandaged during the meteorite invasion, makes his way through a world haplessly engaged in a universal game of blind man's buff while under mortal threat of the carnivorous chlorophvll. Ultimately a marine biologist (Kieron Moore) stranded in a lighthouse with his wife (Janette Scott) discovers the means to dissolve and destroy the triffid: simple sea water. Mass blindness, however, persists at the end, leaving the picture somewhat inconclusive.

The acting is generally capable. In addition to Keel, Moore and Miss Scott, those playing prominent roles are Nicole Maurey, Mervyn Johns and young Janina Faye.

Steve Sekely's otherwise able direction has a bothersome flaw in the contradictory manner in which the triffids seem to approach and assault their victims. Ted Moore's came-awork is effective, and Wally Veever's special effects photography is a vital and skillfully - executed contribution The drama tends to lurch here and there, but on the whole Spencer Reeves has done a trim and tidy job of editing. Sound by Bert Ross and Maurice Askew is acutely sensitive in capturing the oddly alternating creak, crawl, hiss, snap, crackle and pop of the triffids. Ron Goodwin's music adheres to generally standard horror moods and patterns. *Tube.*

55 Days at Peking
(PANAVISION—COLOR)

A substantial entry for the world market although story development short of commensurate with the intense, vivid Peking siege.

Allied Artists release of Samuel Bronston production. Stars Charlton Heston, Ava Gardner, David Niven; features Flora Robson, John Ireland, Harry Andrews, Leo Genn, Kurt Kasznar, Paul Lukas, Lynne Sue Moon. Directed by Nicholas Ray. Second unit director, Andrew Marton. Original screenplay, Philip Yordan and Bernard Gordon; music, Dimitri Tiomkin; editor, Robert Lawrence. Reviewed April 16 at RKO 23d St. Theatre, N.Y. Running time, 150 MINS.
Major Matt Lewis .... Charlton Heston
Baroness Natalie Ivanoff .. Ava Gardner
Sir Arthur Robertson ... David Niven
Dowager Empress Tzu Hsi. Flora Robson
Sergeant Harry .... John Ireland
Father de Bearn .... Harry Andrews
General Jung-Lu ...... Leo Genn
Prince Tuan ...... Robert Helpmann
Colonel Shiba .... Icchizo Itami
Baron Sergei Ivanoff .. Kurt Kasznar
Julliard } .... Philippe Leroy
Dr. Steinfeldt .... Paul Lukas
Teresa .... Lynne Sue Moon
Lady Sarah Robertson. Elizabeth Sellars
Garibaldi .... Massimo Serato
Major Bobrinski .... Jacques Sernas
Lieut. Andy Marshall .. Jerome Thor
Smythe ...... Geoffrey Bayldon
Capt. Hanselman.......... Joseph Furst
Capt. Hoffman .... Walter Gotell
Gerald .... Alfred Lynch
Spanish Minister .... Alfredo Mayo
Hugo Bergmann .... Martin Miller
Mme. Baumaire ....Conchita Montes
Italian Minister .... Jose Nieto
Baron Von Meck .... Eric Pohlmann
Gaumaire .... Aram Stepham
Capt. Hanley .... Robert Urquhart
Sergeant Britten.... Ex. R.S.M. Brittain
Dutch Minister .... Felix Defauce
Austrian Minister ..... Andre Esterhazy
Japanese Minister .... Carlos Casaravilla
Belgium Minister ...... Fernando Sancho
Chiang .... Michael Chow
U. S. Marine .... Mitchell Kowal

Samuel Bronston has a very large production of uncommon visual excitement in "55 Days at Peking." Filmed in 70m Panavision and Technicolor, with director Nicholas Ray uninhibited in his framing of bloody battle, this recounting of a dramatic page in

history is another epic in the present run of epics and one that should rate on the list of worldwide commercial successes.

Bronston shows characteristic lavishness in the pictorial scope, the vivid and realistic sets and extras by the thousands in his reproduction of the capital of Imperial China in 1900. The lensing was in Spain where the company built an entire city. Set and costume designers Veniero Colasanti and John Moore did an exquisite job.

The original screenplay by Philip Yordan and Bernard Gordon presumably adheres in its description of the violent rebellion of the "Boxers" against the major powers of the period — Great Britain, Russia, France, Germany, Italy, Japan, and the United States — because of their commercial exploitation of the tradition-bound and unmodern (backward) China.

These market-seeking nations have in their Peking outpost gallant fighting men who, although only a few hundred in number, withstand the merciless 55-day siege but historic facts must stir some sympathy for the outlaw rebels. They fight encroachment by diplomats and soldiers from foreign lands. In short, this was the heyday of the "colonialism" now an issue of sensitivity with Asiatic and African nationals. "55 Days at Peking" takes sides with imperialism and this aspect may prove just a little disconcerting in some playoff markets.

The Yordan-Gordon script, as directed by Ray, succeeds fairly well in incorporating a personalized story within the framework of the vast depiction of primitive, fiery warfare. With Charlton Heston, Ava Gardner and David Niven it plays interestingly but somehow lacks appropriate power. The characterizations don't have the intensity of the struggle.

At the outset film is slow in explaining who's who and motivations for the action. It's not clear as to why an old oriental Christian missionary is brutally pinned to a water wheel and drowned. Filmgoers of today unfamiliar with the Boxer Rebellion might wonder what all those diplomats from around the world are doing under the same roof.

But explanation comes in due time and Ray moves into action. And action it is, including some of the most furious war scenes seen in anybody's picture. Housed in a relatively small compound within Peking are the military men and the ambassadors and their families. They are threatened with extermination by the Boxers in an early instance of *Foreigners, go home*.

While Nicholas Ray is identified as director of "55 Days of Peking" in the credits sheet, some of the battle scenes actually were directed by Andrew Marton. This came to be in a period when Ray was ill, and necessarily out of action. Thus, an important credit for Marton, which should not be overlooked.

Niven is the British embassy head who stubbornly refuses to surrender, risking the safety of all about him, including his wife and two children. He forces the others to join him as a "matter of principle," meaning economic self-interest.

Both Niven and Heston perform with conviction, Heston as the American Marine major who com-

mands the defense. Miss Gardner's role is not too well conceived. Hers is the part of the widow of a Russian bigshot who, it's conveyed by the dialog, killed himself upon learning of his wife's infidelity with a Chinese official.

Heston and Miss Gardner provide the romance, which develops nicely. In a heroic maneuver, Miss Gardner gets food and supplies into the legation but is wounded in so doing and dies.

Lynne Sue Moon gives a poignant performance as an Oriental 12-year-old whose American father, an Army captain, is killed in battle. Flora Robson appears strikingly authentic as the Dowager Empress Tzu Hsi whose sympathies lie with the outlaws. John Ireland is an impressive Yank sergeant. Kurt Kasznar comes off realistically as Miss Gardner's Russian brother-in-law.

Harry Andrews as the French padre, Leo Genn as a Chinese general, Paul Lukas as a German doctor, and Robert Helpmann, Ichizo Itami, Philip Leroy and Elizabeth Sellars, along with those in lesser parts, are competent contributors.

Jack Hildyard's photography is excellent, particularly in getting on the bigscreen the savage attack scenes which take up the major part of the picture. Remarkable effects are achieved such as when the attackers bring up a primitive rocket launcher and send balls of fire into the legation, and when Niven and Heston head a small group which blows up a Chinese arsenal. What a display of fireworks!

Dimitri Tiomkin provides engaging music, mainly noteworthy being the outbursts of the military bands of the various nations, at times playing simultaneously and, amusingly, clashing. The general backgrounding and "So Little Time" (lyrics by Paul Francis Webster) make for solid commodities on their own.

Dong Kingman's water colors, used with the titles, are novel and interesting. Editing for the most part is expert, one reservation being that some tightening in the early reels might have been in order.

"Peking" has a rousing finis, in which the bloodied and near-hopeless Allies are rescued by a long-delayed relief column of warriors and the Boxers are routed. It's a stirring windup, even though suggestive of Cavalry's nick-of-time routing of the Indians in wild west flickers. *Gene.*

Hud

Meaningful, often artful, contemporary western, but underlying themes apt to elude bulk of audience. Provocative elements will control b.o. destiny.

Hollywood, April 30.
Paramount release of Martin Ritt-Irving Ravetch production. Stars Paul Newman, Melvyn Douglas, Patricia Neal, Brandon de Wilde. Directed by Ritt. Screenplay, Ravetch, Harriet Frank Jr., adapted from novel by Larry McMurty; camera, James Wong Howe; editor, Frank Bracht; music, Elmer Bernstein; assistant director, C. C. Coleman Jr. Reviewed at the studio, April 29, '63. Running time, 111 MINS.
Hud Bannon .... Paul Newman
Homer Bannon .... Melvyn Douglas
Alma .... Patricia Neal
Lon Bannon .... Brandon de Wilde
Hermy .... John Ashley
Burris .... Whit Bissell
Jesse .... Crahan Denton
Jose .... Val Avery
Thompson .... Sheldon Allman
Larker .... Pitt Herbert
George .... Peter Brooks
Truman Peters .... Curt Conway
Lily Peters .... Yvette Vickers
Joe Scanlon .... George Petrie
Donald .... David Kent
Dumb Billy .... Frank Killmond

"Hud" is a near miss. A shame, since the Martin Ritt-Irving Ravetch production, piquantly directed by the former, is a film of considerable merit, with flashes of brilliance in both cinematic and histrionic execution.

Where "Hud" misfires and falls short of the mark is in its failure to filter its meaning and theme lucidly through its characters and story. This lack of clarity and dramatic neatness is likely to leave the bulk of the filmgoing audience somewhat bewildered. Many may leave the theatre with little more than a bitter aftertaste at apparently having spent almost two hours in the company of an unpleasant pivotal figure, instead of with the fresh philosophical slant on the changing patterns and values of the contemporary American West that lurks just beneath the surface and is the elusive prize that only the more analytical customer will take away as a reward. Stripped of this bonus of insight and perception, the picture loses its taste, flavor and significance and rests on the naked values of its plot, and that, alas, is liable to be the superficial way it is received by too many people.

From a commercial standpoint, then, it is the provocative, rather than the artful, values of the Paramount release that figure to shape its boxoffice destiny. Word will probably get around of its earthy, uncompromising dialog and of the unorthodox nature of its "hero" and his unsavory disposition and relationships. Much less will be made of its richer underlying substance and technical attainments. A clever ad image that hints of intended artistic stature rather than mere racy melodrama could boost its fortunes somewhat by encouraging the audience-to-be to be prepared to probe a little, not just come for pure escape and sensual stimulus.

The screenplay by Ravetch and Harriet Frank Jr., adapted from a novel by Larry McMurty, tells a tale of the modern American West, of its evolution from the land of pioneer ethics, of simple human gratifications unmotivated by greed, to the rangy real estate of

shallow, mercenary creatures who have inherited the rugged individualism of the early settlers, but not their souls, their morals or their principles. The new westerner is Hud (Paul Newman), noxious son of old Homer Bannon (Melvyn Douglas), pioneer Texas Panhandler who detests his offspring with a passion that persists to his bitter end, after he has just witnessed the liquidation of his entire herd of cattle (hoof and mouth disease) and the attempt of his son to have him declared incompetent to run his ranch. In the end, Hud is left defiantly alone with his land, abandoned by his nephew (Brandon de Wilde), who finds himself unable to share or stomach any longer the selfish excesses of his uncle and sets out, a 20th century personification of the pioneer spirit, in pursuit of better things.

It is in the relationship of father and son that the film slips. It is never clear exactly why the old man harbors such a deep-rooted, irrevocable grudge against his lad. True, the young man's character is shady and he is held responsible by his father for the accidental death of his older brother 15 years before, but it appears that "Hud" never received the fatherly compassion and understanding that a boy would desperately have needed after such an incident. It is not enough to let it rest that he is, and always was, a no-good young punk. Audience sympathy thus tends at times to gravitate to Newman, not Douglas, contrary to the creative design.

But the picture has a number of elements of distinction and reward. The four leading performances are excellent. Newman creates a virile, pernicious figure as that ornery title critter. The characteristics of old age are marvelously captured and employed by Douglas. Another fine performance is turned in by de Wilde, who seems, however, to be in a "decent younger brother" (or nephew) casting rut. Patricia Neal comes through with a rich and powerful performance as the housekeeper assaulted by Newman. Supporting work is quite competent.

Though its relative scarcity of plot or direct story thrust may bother more impatient filmgoers, the scenario is crammed with frank, pungent dialog and colorfully stated observation. Director Ritt has gotten the most out of both script and cast. The scene of the mass extermination of the diseased cattle is especially provocative and unforgettable.

The textures, compositions and points-of-view of James Wong Howe's cinematography are often striking, and responsible for a number of indelible images. Art direction by Hal Pereira and Tambi Larsen, editing by Frank Bracht and sound by John Carter and John Wilkinson are all vital and noteworthy contributions, as is Elmer Bernstein's sombre, plaintive and foreboding musical theme.

Tube.

The Slave
(C'SCOPE-COLOR)

Latest of the bulky Steve Reeves capers from Italy. Usual saturation entry.

Hollywood, April 24.

Metro release of Titanus production. Stars Steve Reeves; with Jacques Sernas, Gianna Maria Canale, Claudio Gora, Ivo Garrani, Enzo Fiermonte. Directed by Sergio Corbucci. Screenplay, Adriano Bolzoni, Bruno Corbucci, Giovanni Grimaldi, from original story by Bolzoni; camera (Eastman), Enzo Barboni; editor, Ruggero Mastroianni; music, Piero Piccioni; asst. directors, Frabco Rossellini, Mimmola Girosi. Reviewed at the studio, April 24, '63. Running time, 90 MINS.

Randus .... Steve Reeves
Vezio .... Jacques Sernas
Clodia .... Gianna Maria Canale
Cesare Grassus .... Claudio Gora
Julius Caesar .... Ivo Garrani
Gular .... Enzo Fiermonte

"The Slave" is another muscle spasm from Titanus, Italy's cinematic answer to Vic Tanny. With Steve Reeves in the title role as the son of Spartacus, the Metro release should make its presence felt briefly in the multiple-booking sphere into which these extravagantly produced escape-exploitation epics invariably fall.

"The Slave," or son of Spartacus, as created by scenarists Adriano Bolzoni, Bruno Corbucci and Giovanni Grimaldi, turns out, lo and behold, to be a composite of three formerly serialized heroes of the American screen: Zorro, the Lone Ranger and Superman. The character is a Roman centurion of Caesar's Egyptian legions who, circa 48 B.C., abruptly discovers who he really is (the son of Kirk Douglas) and instigates a campaign to free the slaves.

On the one hand he plays the role of the loyal Roman, or Clark Kent in a toga. On the other, he slips out of uniform, into an iron mask (presto, the Lone Ranger) and, with Superman-like indestructibility, bruises and batters the hapless forces of the ambitious, treacherous Grassus (Claudio Gora) and his scheming henchman Vezio (Jacques Sernas). After each skirmish, a sword-inscribed letter S (read backwards, Z for Zorro) keeps turning up in the palace of Grassus. Eventually, Stevedoreable Reeves is pardoned by Caesar and falls into a climactic clinch with Lois Lane (Gianna Maria Canale) as a narrator's voice pretentiously concludes something about all of those who have fought for the rights of the oppressed being sons of Spartacus. Oh, yeah?

Gore galore bathes this production, particularly filmed in Egypt which about makes it the Italian equivalent of the Hollywood runaway. The acting is mostly athletic or mechanical, but that matches the concept, which is more popular mechanics and sports illustrated than art. The large scale production was directed by Sergio Corbucci and sports some dexterous photography by Enzo Barboni, lavish art direction by Ottavio Scotti and a serpentine score by Piero Piccioni.

Tube.

Tammy And The Doctor
(COLOR)

Uninspired No. 3 in the cycle.

Hollywood, April 29.

Universal release of Ross Hunter production. Stars Sandra Dee, Peter Fonda; features Macdonald Carey, Beulah Bondi, Margaret Lindsay. Directed by Harry Keller. Screenplay, Oscar Broney; camera (Eastman), Russell Metty; editor, Milton Carruth; music, Frank Skinner; assistant director, Phil Bowles. Reviewed at Fox Wilshire Theatre, April 30, '63. Running time, 88 MINS.

Tammy .... Sandra Dee
Dr. Mark Cheswick .... Peter Fonda
Dr. Wayne Bentley .. MacDonald Carey
Mrs. Call .... Beulah Bondi
Rachel Coleman .... Margaret Lindsay
Jason Tripp .... Reginald Owen
Millie .... Alice Pearce
Dr. Eric Hassler .... Adam West
Vera .... Joan Marshall
Wally Day .... Stanley Clements
Traction Patient .... Doodles Weaver
Pamela .... Mitzi Hoag
Chief of Staff .... Alex Gerry
Surgeon .... Robert Foulk
Assistant Surgeon .... Jill Jackson
Dr. Crandall .... Forrest Lewis
1st Nurse .... Sondra Rodgers
Dr. Smithers .... Charles Seel
Dora .... Susie Kaye
David .... Paul Nesbitt

Only those most uncritically and chronically smitten with the "Tammy" whammy are apt to appreciate this flimsy third installment in producer Ross Hunter's six-year-old comichronicle. Two years have passed since the last edition. Now talkative "Tammy" is in her anecdotage, and it appears that it will take more than Hunter's patented glamour elixir to rejuvenate her and delay, for Universal, the inevitable point of diminishing returns.

Oscar Brodney's screenplay is little more than a slight and limp variation of what has gone before. This time "Tammy" (Sandra Dee) ankles her bayou shantyboat digs and wings to L.A., where she hires on as nurse's aide to maintain vigil over her rich companion, Beulah Bondi, who's to undergo a serious operation. There she falls for handsome intern Peter Fonda and solves the problems of everyone in sight.

Miss Dee seems a bit too chic for a hick chick from Mississipp, but she carries on gamely, considering the pitfalls that confront her in the script. For example, asked if she'd like "to go to the Bowl?" Miss Dee must reply, "Bowl? I never heard it called that! But don't you worry. I'll go before I leave."

Peter Fonda, sprig of Henry who resembles a cross betwen his dad and Fred Astaire, makes his screen bow. It's an unfortunately inane role for a debut, and young Fonda responds, said to relate, with a self-conscious, artificial performance. Others implicated prominently in the drab proceedings, none much better than adequate, are Macdonald Carey, Miss Bondi, Margaret Lindsay, Reginald Owen and Adam West. Alice Pearce has a funny moment or two.

Harry Keller's direction doesn't aid matters much. Russell Metty's photography has that glamorous Hunter sheen about it, but often it's a bit too dark to see the lack of expression on some of the actor's faces. At least one scene seems incompletely suspended by Milton Carruth's editing, but on the whole he's done a workmanlike job, as have art directors Alexander Golitzen and George Webb and composer Frank Skinner, among others who labored on the production. The original "Tammy" song by Jay Livingston and Ray Evans is revived, for no apparent reason. Debbie Reynolds, the original "Tammy," sang it better than her successor does.

Tube.

The Very Edge
(BRITISH)

Some implausibilities in this—but it's mainly a smooth meller about the effect on the married life of a young matron twice assaulted by a sex maniac. Reasonable b.o. prospect.

London, April 30.

British Lion-Garrick release (through BLC) of a Raymond Stross production. Stars Richard Todd, Anne Heywood; features Nicole Maurey, Jack Hedley, Barbara Mullen, Jeremy Brett, Maurice Denham. Directed by Cyril Frankel. Screenplay, Elizabeth Jane Howard, based on original material by Vivian Cox, Leslie Bricusse, Stross; camera, Bob Huke; editor, Max Benedica; music, David Lee. Previewed at Columbia Theatre, London. Running time, 82 MINS.

Tracey Lawrence .... Anne Heywood
Geoffrey Lawrence .... Richard Todd
McInnes .... Jack Hedley
Helen .... Nicole Maurey
Mullen .... Jeremy Brett
Dr. Shaw .... Barbara Mullen
Crawford .... Maurice Denham
Inspector Davies .... William Lucas
Sister Holden .... Gwen Watford
Simmonds .... Patrick Magee
Selina .... Verina Greenlaw

Maybe "The Very Edge" would have benefited by some sharper direction than the capable Cyril Frankel has given it. It emerges an interesting meller but it lacks the very edge of its title. Some flabby moments of scriptwriting, both in dialog and action, show up at different times. Still, it should be a worthwhile b.o. prospect and the climax, though trite, offers some worthwhile nail-biting minutes for patrons. For Britain, the marquee value is okay, but the stars may need some hardsell in the States.

Story has Anne Heywood, as an ex-model and happily married young wife of architect Richard Todd, pleasurably awaiting her first child. One day, in Todd's absence, a young sex maniac breaks into the house and assaults her. On the verge of a nervous breakdown she finds that she has lost her child and she bitterly turns against men, even rejecting her husband.

Understandably, though somewhat hurriedly, he turns to the warmth and understanding of his secretary (Nicole Maurey). Now the problem is, "Will the criminal strike again?" and life for Miss Heywood, sans her husband's affection, is a wretched affair. The man is caught, but escapes and the terror starts up all over again. Climax is a corny but tense cliffhanger. Needless to say, it brings Miss Heywood and Todd together again.

Acting throughout is sound, with the main burden falling on Miss Heywood who assumes the required emotions without overmuch strain. Todd's role is fairly colorless but well within the range of this actor. Miss Maurey also makes impact in a role which is always threatening to be more important than it is.

Among the supporting cast, Jack Hedley is a believable Scotland Yard man. The maniac is played by Jeremy Brett. It's a difficult role and Brett scores a near miss. At moments the performance loses the sinister menace that is essential.

Cyril Frankel's direction is assured though not over imaginative. Other technical credits are okay. Film stands up as a very useful entry at the wickets.

Rich.

Il Diavolo
(The Devil)
(ITALIAN)

Rome, April 30.

Dino DeLaurentiis production and release. Stars Alberto Sordi; features Gunilla Elm-Tornqvist, Anne Charlotte Sjoberg, Barbro Wastenson, Monica Wastenson, Ulla Smidje, Ulf Palme, Lauritz Falk. Directed by Gian Luigi Polidoro. Screenplay Rodolfo Sonego; camera, Aldo

Tonti; editor, Tatiana Casini. At the Metropolitan, Rome. Running time, 107 MINS.

Amedeo Ferretti .... Alberto Sordi
Corinne .... Gunilla Elm-Tornqvist
Karina .... Anne Charlotte Sjoberg
Barbro .... Barbro Wastenson
Monica .... Monica Wastenson
Priest .... Ulf Palme
Priest's wife .... Ulla Smidje
Falkman .... Lauritz Falk

Vastly amusing and intelligently made pic with the Alberto Sordi name a surefire marquee value in Italy. Film has export value as well as some exploitable aspects for certain special foreign situations. As bitter-sweet spoof of certain Italian and/or Latin charcateristics, it plays best in those areas. But others deserve a looksee as well on pic's quality and Sordi's amusing antics.

Practically an improvised and imaginatively elaborated chronicle of Sordi's recent trip to Sweden, he and his usual scripter Rodolfo Sonego, as well as director Gian Luig Polidoro, have come up with an almost consistently risible picture of various adventures lived by an Italian businessman on a Scandinavian trek. Accent, as in most Italian males' dreams of the north, is on the female of the species.

Sordi and his collaborators register in the more superficial and obvious aspects of pic, but manage as well to make some trenchant observations on the abyss which separates Northern from Latin character and morality. As such, it is one of the more intelligent studies of the Italian male seen here in a long while.

To be sure, the haste with which pic was made shows in certain spots where improvisation and over-simplification lower the quality. However, all things considered, it's a remarkable effort. Location lensing by Aldo Tonti captures Nordic local color while a large and animated as well as pretty and able cast recruited on the spot gives Sordi apt backing.
Hawk.

Black Zoo
(PANAVISION—COLOR)

Exploitable horror meller.

Hollywood, May 3.

Allied Artists release of Herman Cohen production. Stars Michael Gough, Jeanne Cooper, Rod Lauren, Virginia Grey; with Jerome Cowan, Elisha Cook, Warene Ott, Marianna Hill, Oren Curtis, Eilene Janssen, Eric Stone, Dani Lynn, Susan Slavin, Edward Platt, Douglas Henderson, Jerry Douglas, Claudia Brack, Daniel Kurlick, Byron Morrow, Michael St. Angel. Directed by Robert Gordon; screenplay, Aben Kandel, Cohen; camera (Eastman), Floyd Crosby; editor, Michael Luciano; music, Paul Dunlap; asst. director, William McGarry. Reviewed at studio, May 3, '63. Running time, 88 MINS.

Michael Conrad .... Michael Gough
Edna Conrad .... Jeanne Cooper
Carl .... Rod Lauren
Jenny .... Virginia Grey
Jeffrey Stengel .... Jerome Cowan
Joe .... Elisha Cook
Mary Hogan .... Warene Ott
Audrey .... Marianna Hill
Radu .... Oren Curtis
Bride .... Eilene Janssen
Groom .... Eric Stone
Art Student .... Dani Lynn
Art Student .... Susan Slavin
Detective Rivers .... Edward Platt
Lt. Duggan .... Douglas Henderson
Lab Technician .... Jerry Douglas
Carl's Mother .... Claudia Brack
Carl as Child .... Daniel Kurlick
Coroner .... Byron Morrow
Officer Donovan ...... Michael St. Angel

Herman Cohen's production of "Black Zoo" is a resourcefully executed and highly exploitable claw-and-fang opera that figures to make its presence felt briefly but profitably in the cinemarketplace as a saturation-booking attraction. However, outside of its commercial value and cinematic know-how, there is little to recommend in the Allied Artists release for anyone but the indiscriminate sensation-seeker.

Elaborately violent and gory, the film is constructed on a thoroughly zoo-illogical story foundation. Pivotal figure of the scenario by Cohen and Aben Kandel is the deranged proprietor (Michael Gough) of a private zoo who uses his big cats and gorillas to destroy those whom he deems his enemies. Gough belongs to a cult of animal worshippers who believe in soul transference, or continuity of animal life beyond death. He has little use for people other than an occasional munchkins for his caged beasts. When anyone comes a'prying into his affairs, Gough plays rough, promptly feeds him to the lions. Eventually he is destroyed by his own son, a mute (Rod Lauren), while his wife (Jeanne Cooper) and his beloved animal friends look on.

Gough is singularly unpleasant as the organ-playing madman. Competent histrionics are chipped in by Miss Cooper and Lauren in key roles, Virginia Grey, Jerome Cowan, Elisha Cook and Warene Ott in smaller ones. Balance of human support is adequate, and the animals are extraordinarily cooperative under Robert Gordon's skillful direction. Number among the odder spectables of the modern screen the scene in which Gough ushers a tiger, two lions, a black panther and a cougar into his parlor, seats them comfortably in easy chairs and proceeds to bat out a dreamy, sleep-inducing dirge on the organ for their listening enjoyment. It's the cats' pajamas.

Among valuable assists to the production are those of cameraman Floyd Crosby, editor Michael Luciano, art director William Glasgow and composer Paul Dunlap. Equally vital are the efforts of animal supervisor Ralph Helfer, special effects man Pat Dinga and the optical effects of the Howard Anderson Co.
Tube.

Murder at the Gallop
(BRITISH)

Miss Marple, Agatha Christie's eccentric amateur sleuth, clears up another mystery. Margaret Rutherford and smooth cast.

London, May 3.

Metro reltase of a George H. Brown production. Stars Margaret Rutherford, Robert Morley, Flora Robson. Screenplay, David Pursall, Jack Seddon & James P. Cavanagh, from Agatha Christie's "After The Funeral"; camera, Arthur Ibbetson; music, Ron Goodwin; editor, Bert Rule. at Metro Private Theatre, London, May 1, "63. Running time; 81 MINS.

Miss Marple ..... Margaret Rutherford
Hector Enderby .... Robert Morley
Miss Gilchrist .... Flora Robson
Det. Ins. Craddock .... Charles Tingwell
Mr. Stringer .... Stringer Davis
Hillman .... Duncan Lamont
Michael Shane .... James Villiers
George Crossfield .... Robert Urquhart
Rosamund Shane ...... Katya Douglas
Sgt. Bacon .... Gordon Harris

Agatha Christie's creation, Miss Marple, the indefatigable amateur sleuth, provides another unpretentious whodunit skillfully tailored to talents of Margaret Rutherford. The result is easygoing, undemanding entertainment that could produce healthy boxoffice returns.

Adapted from Miss Christie's "After The Funeral" David Pursall, Jack Seddon and James P. Cavanagh have concocted a yarn with just about the right number of red herrings and a climax which, while fairly predictable, rounds the proceedings off satisfactorily. The crime is set in a horsey atmosphere in a small village. An old recluse is discovered by Miss Marple. The police think he's had a heart attack, but Miss Marple doesn't. She suspects all four members of the old man's family, all of whom stand to benefit by his will. So Miss Marple starts to follow up her hunch. She finds that a valuable picture is probably the best clue. Two other murders and by a process of elimination she is beginning to solve the puzzle. But she has to risk being murdered herself to get the proof.

Miss Rutherford, waddling around with sagging jaws, behaving and looking rather like an impatient bloodhound, gives a joyous, energetic performance. Robert Morley performs fittingly as one of the suspects. Charles Tingwell as the patient detective, and Flora Robson, Duncan Lamont, James Villiers, Robert Urquhart and comely Katya Douglas as other suspects fill the bill admirably, and Stringer Davis makes two or three effectively fussy appearances with Miss Rutherford, his real-life spouse.

George H. Brown's production and George Pollock's direction is smooth and the film is just about the right length to fit the story. Art and camera work are both satisfactory.
Rich.

Als Twee Druppels Water
(The Dark Room Of Damocles)
(DUTCH)

Amsterdam, April 30.

A Hafbo (Paul Kijzer) release of Cineurope production. Stars Lex Schoorel, Nan Los; features Mia Goossen, Guus Verstraete. Directed by Fons Rademakers. Screenplay, Rademakers, Lili Veenman, from novel by W. F. Hermans; camera (Franscope), Raoul Coutard; music, Jurriaan Andriessen. At Calypso and Cineac cinemas, Amsterdam. Running time, 115 MINS.

Ducker-Dorbeck .... Lex Schoorel
Ria, his wife .... Mia Goossen
Marianne .... Nan Los
Ebernuss .... Guus Verstraete

In the field of feature films, Fons Rademakers is one of Holland's foremost and most prolific film director. His first film, "Village On The River," was nominated for the Oscar. Now his fourth, "Dark Room Of Damocles," is officially singled out to represent The Netherlands at the Cannes Film Fest. "Dark Room," based on the novel by W. F. Hermans (published by Grove Press in the U.S.) Rademakers points up the fact that people under pressure of suddenly altered circumstances, like war, rise above their own trivialities and develop beyond their usual limitations.

Against the background of the second World War and the German occupation, this shows the character of Ducker, a young man, married to an older woman who cuckolds him with a Quisling. Not able to make contact with other people, Ducker does not care, only loving his insane mother. One night, he sees a parachutist drop in his garden. He is a secret agent by the name of Dorbeck, who looks like Ducker except for his black hair and tough character.

Through him Ducker becomes active in the underground movement, carrying out Dorbeck's orders. He kills provocative agents, becomes a bold Don Juan. When the Germans put out a search warrants for him, a girl friend of his paints his hair black so as to disguise him, but making him look more than ever like Dorbeck, his super ego. The war over, Ducker is arrested for collaboration with the Germans. He cannot prove the existence of Dorbeck since all evidence of Dorbeck is lost. Hence, Ducker must take the responsibility.

Rademakers has made an intelligent film that can be interpreted in two ways. First is that Dorbeck really existed; second that he is only a part of Ducker's personality (through circumstances the unimaginative little man becomes a hero, but when the times become normal again, the little man must take responsibility for the actions, good or bad, of the hero).

Like Rademakers' previous pix, "Dark Room" is a cool film, observing characters, changing in acting style from one moment to the other when a scene requires it. The overall effect of this vehicle may seem bewildering. But in retrospect, the viewer is apt to rate the script well written.

Even for Holland, "Dark Room" has no name actors, the director preferring to chose the actors for suitability. Lex Schoorel, as Ducker-Dorbeck, and Nan Los in the role of Marrianne, under Rademakers' direction make the film very real. From these actors as well as the other local talent in cameo parts, the director has extracted good performances. French cameraman Raoul Coutard is responsible for the excellent camera work. This is more a broad drama than a war film, which may help sell it abroad. An English version is being prepared.
Saal.

La Punition
(The Punishment)
(FRENCH)

Paris, April 30.

Film Pleiade release of Pierre Braunberger production. With Nadine Ballot, Jean-Claude Darnal, Modeste Landry, Jean Claude. Written and directed by Jean Rouch. Camera, Michel Brault, Roger Morillere; editor, Annie Tresgot. Preemed in Paris. Running time, 60 MINS.

Nadine .... Nadine Ballot
Jean-Claude .... Jean-Claude Darnal
Landry .... Modeste Landry
Engineer .... Jean Claude

Jean Rouch again experiments with his so-called "Truth Cinema" in this hour-long pic in which a situation is set up and spontaneously played out and improvised by non-actors. Film has flashes of insight and depth but its length, anecdote rather than story aspect, as well as its offbeat qualities make this primarily an arty house supporting film abroad in some few spots.

Pic was first shown on tv here

before being released in theatres. A 17-year-old girl is late for class and is banished by an irate teacher. She has a whole day before her and decides to float around Paris in search of adventure. This comes via meetings with three different men who all prove disappointing. She finally wends her way home fending off besieging males.

Rouch has a deft and mobile camera that follows the characters every place, in buses, parks, museums, streets, etc. Format is to give characters an idea of the theme and then let them act it out on their own. If they sometimes identify and allow for revealing, punchy scenes, the fact that they are called on to explain endlessly what they feel gives this a garrulous quality not always put across by the visuals for many listless bits.

But Nadine Ballot has the youthful, naive characteristics as well as a promise of more than her fairly silly quest for adventure indicates. The men in this are mostly on the defensive against this amoral, searching, pretty little girl.

Camerawork is good. It shapes an interesting experiment that sometimes begs the question by setting up a theme, exploiting it but not always being able to make it truly telling by one controlled point of view.

This shapes as an offbeater with some fresh insights, but looks like only for specialized theatrical use. It is technically good. *Mosk.*

L'Immortelle
(The Immortal)
(FRENCH)

Paris, April 30.

Cocinor release of Como-Tamara-Hamle Film production. With Francoise Brion, Jacques Doniol-Valcroze, Catherine Blisson. Written and directed by Alain Robbe-Grillet. Camera, Maurice Barry; editor, Robert Wade. At Lord Byron, Paris. Running time, **100 MINS.**

Woman .... Francoise Brion
Man .... Jacques Doniol-Valcroze

The scriptwriter of that hermetic offbeater "Last Year In Marienbad," Alain Robbe-Grillet, now turns director-writer for this followup effort. Again there is a vague triangle, a mixture of past and present, plus intimations of the future, with a little more clarity than its predecessor. Its repetitive aspects slant this primarily for arties abroad, and calling for a hardsell.

A meek-looking French teacher meets a girl in Istanbul who speaks perfect French but says she is not French. She seems to be followed by or is sometimes with a sinister fat man with dark glasses and accompanied by two enormous dogs.

Love and meetings take place between the teacher and the girl but he can never find out much about her. One day one of the dogs appears on the road while they are driving and a crash has her killed. He still can find nothing out about her and ends up also being killed in a similar accident.

Call it obsession, dream, the difficulty of memory, this has a series of repeated scenes and intimations of mystery that are sometimes stultifying.

But here at least it is evident these two people did meet and he is a teacher if her background remains unknown. A belly dance scene in a night club is repeated with the girl doing the same thing when they are alone plus intimated bouts of love on their interminable walks about the city.

Istanbul's colorful streets, buildings and countryside add to the unreality of this arty pic. There can be little acting in a posed pic of this kind. Jacques Doniol-Valcroze has the puzzled, pained—one expression that the adventure seems to call for and Francoise Brion is a well-built young lady with a good boned face but not able to exude the mysterious femme fatale lure it demands.

Writer-director Robbe-Grillet does not have the glacial perfection in technique of Alain Resnais, who helmed "Marienbad."

This manages to hold interest and should find a niche in the growing specialized art outlets in keys if depth distrib seems extremely limited. *Mosk.*

Le Marriage de Figaro
(The Marriage of Figaro)
(COLOR)
(FRENCH)

Union Films release of Pathe Cinema presentation of a Productions Cinematographiques film (Pierre Gerin) in association with the Comedie Francaise. With members of the Comedie Francaise. Directed by Jean Meyer. Screenplay based on play by Pierre Augustin Caron de Beaumarchais; camera (Eastmancolor), Henri Alekan; music, Wolfgang Mozart, orchestrated and adapted by Andre Cadou; editor, Claude Durand. Reviewed at Normandie Theatre, N.Y., April 29, '63. Running time, **105 MINS.**

Count Almaviva .... Georges Descrieres
Countess Almaviva .... Yvonne Gaudeau
Figaro .... Jean Piat
Suzanne .... Micheline Boudet
Bartholo .... Louis Seigner
Marceline .... Denise Gence
Bazile .... Jean Meyer
Cherubin .... Michele Grellier
Antonio .... Georges Chamarat
Doubltmain .... Maurice Porterat
Brid'oison .... Georges Baconnet
Franchette .... Mme. Bonnefoux
Grippe-Soleil .... Jean-Paul Roussillon
Pedrille .... Henri Tisot

(English Subtitles)

Comedie Francaise's second film translation of one of the works in its repertory ("The Would-Be Gentleman" was the first several years ago) is a handsome, impeccably performed production with a life expectancy that should roughly correspond with the Comedie itself. Because it is a unique screen recording of an equally unique theatrical experience, this "Marriage of Figaro" may have, at the onset, a comparatively limited U.S. market, and that, of course, in the arties, but it should go on forever in the 16m, educational and film society fields.

This is not to faint-praise the film. Although it is almost a literal transcription of the theatrical experience, it subtly manages to recreate on screen the excitement of the theatre without being a flatly filmed play. It unreels with a bouyant, *opera comique* pace, and the camera moves with the action without ever self-consciously zooming in, out and around in an attempt to "open up" the Beaumarchais original. The Comedie Francaise intention was to preserve, on film, a classic heritage, and this has been done without fear or condescension.

Because the credits don't list an adaptor, it must be assumed the screenplay is the stage prompt copy. Thus, director Jean Meyer, who also performs in the film, must be credited for the film's unusual, as well as faithful, cinematic grace. While much of Beaumarchais' satire is inevitably lost in this hydrogen age, the tale of tangled seductions, revolving around the irrepressible title character, still retains a lot of mischevious fun and, to one jaded reviewer, a surprising number of real laughs. Key roles are beautifully played by Jean Piat, as Figaro; Micheline Boudet, as his fiancee; Georges Descrieres, as their bored employer, who intends to exercise his *droit du seigneur* with Miss Boudet; and Yvonne Gaudeau, as Descrieres' unhappy wife.

Adding to the purely sensual enjoyment of the film are the lovely Eastmancolor photography, Suzanne Lalique's eyefilling sets and costumes, to say nothing of the music provided by a cinematic unknown by the name of Wolfgang Mozart. *Anby.*

Les Bonnes Causes
(The Good Causes)
(FRENCH-FRANSCOPE)

Paris, April 30.

Unidex release of Georges Cheyko-Mediterranee-Flora Films-Mizar Films production. Stars Marina Vlady, Bourvil, Virna Lisi, Pierre Brasseur; features Umberto Orsini, Mony Dalmes, Jacques Monod, Jacques Mauclair, Jose Luis De Vilallonga. Directed by Christian-Jaque. Screenplay, Paul Andreota, Henri Jeanson, Christian-Jaque from novel, "The Falcon and the Dove," by Jean Laborde; camera, Armand Thirard; editor, Jacques Desagneaux. At the Normandie, Paris. Running time, **120 MINS.**

Godet .... Bourvil
Catherine .... Marina Vlady
Cassidi .... Pierre Brasseur
Gina .... Virna Lisi
Detective .... Umberto Orsini
Madame .... Mony Dalmes
Judge .... Jacques Monod
Witness .... Jacques Maulcair

Film uses a look at the inside workings of French justice on which to hang a cynical, insouciant tale of shabby characters that use justice for their own ends and the few honorable ones beaten by it. But it refrains from true comment or attitude towards the subject. This is mainly a slick playoff item with arty chances abroad possible.

A venal woman dispatches her husband by subbing a fatal content to a vial being injected into him. It seems that the young nurse has become his mistress. She then beds down with a theatrical but successful lawyer with whom she had a prior affair. When he wins the case for her she leaves him.

Larded into this is a simple, honest magistrate who gives up examining the case when he finds himself beaten by the devious lawyer. A plea in court does no good either. The moral seems to be that life is mealy, dishonest, and it is no use fighting it—so get what you can out of it. This would be acceptable if the satire were pungent and the outlook angry.

But this surefootedly exploits the affair for macabre humor and unsavory plumbing of the character's lives, motivations and actions. Marina Vlady has the right blase, dimwitted cruelty for her lovely double crossing wife role. Pierre Brasseur is the hammy, larger than life mouthpiece.

Bourvil and Virna Lisi do not fare so well as the decent people overwhelmed by their Machiavellian adversaries. Director Christian-Jaque has given this a brittle, sharp envelope with technical credits controlled and brisk. There is a ruthlessly wry aspect to this tale that might have it as exploitation item abroad.

This has a bit too much talk to bring it off properly. Some pruning could give this glossy item better offshore playoff chances. *Mosk.*

Mystery Submarine
(BRITISH)

Routine war drama, with spasmodic thrills; looks okay dualer.

London, April 30.

British Lion releast (in association with Britannia and BLC) of a Bertram Ostrer production. Stars Edward Judd, James Robertson Justice, Laurence Payne; features Robert Flemyng, Albert Lieven, Jeremy Hawk, Frederick Jaeger, Leslie Randall, Arthur O'Sullivan. Directed by C. M. Pennington-Richards. Screenplay by Hugh Woodhouse, Ostrer and Jon Manchip White from White's play; camera, Stan Pavey; editor, Bill Lewthwaite; music, Clifton Parker. Prtviewed at Columbia Theatre, London. Running time, **92 MINS.**

Lt. Commander Tarlton ... Edward Judd
Rear-Admiral Rainbird ... James Robertson Justice
Lt. Seaton .... Laurence Payne
Commander Scheffler ... Joachim Fuchs-Berger
Mike Fitzgerald .. Arthur O'Sullivan
Capt. Von Neymarck . Albert Lieven
Vice-Admiral Sir James Carver ... Robert Flemyng
Lt. Hoskins .... Richard Carpenter
Admiral Saintsbury .... Jeremy Hawk
Lt. Henze .... Frederick Jaeger
Coxswain Drage ...... Robert Brown
Telegraphist Packshaw ... Peter Myers
Donnithorne .... Leslie Randall
German Admiral .... Gerald Heinz

Yet another of the interminable permutations of pix that will be dug up from the last World War. It adds up to a reasonably sound dualer but it lacks the drive that more incisive direction and writing could have given to an interesting situation.

A Nazi U-Boat, one of a wolf pack all set to attack a British convoy, is captured by the British. A British admiral (James Robertson Justice) hits on an idea which it's hoped will reveal the location of the pack. He orders Edward Judd, a fearless, unconventional submarine commander, to take over the German U-Boat; man it with a British crew and then join the wolf pack and signal its locality. Judd takes over the suicide assignment with stiff upper lip and tidies everything up despite attacks by the Germans, the unsuspecting RAF bombers and a British frigate.

Film has been made with more competence than inspiration, for C. Pennington-Richards' direction lacks a sense of urgency. Stock shots have been welded into the narrative fluidly while art and camera work are both creditable. The thesps have little chance to be anything more than stock characters but several of them make the most of limited opportunity.

Judd tackles his chore doggedly and provides one of the two most interesting performances. The other is Arthur O'Sullivan's lively, zestful interpretation of a cantankerous civilian engineer from "neutral" Ireland.

James Robertson Justice, Robert

Flemyng, Albert Lieven, Robert Brown, Peter Myers, Leslie Randall and Gerald Heinz are among the long, virtually all-male cast which, professionally, contrives to prevent the proceedings from becoming too sluggish. *Rich.*

Waehle das Leben
(You Must Choose Life)
(SWISS)

Zurich, April 30.

Beretta-Film A.G. Zurich release of Hans Deutsch-Erwin Leiser production. Directed by Leiser. Camera, Jean-Marc Ripert, Tadashi Ohno, Hiroshi Segawa, Otto Ritter; technical director and editor, Hans Heinrich Egger; music, Robert Blum; scientific advisor, Gerhart Wagner. At Studio 4 Theatre, Zurich. Running time,100 MINS.

(With German Commentary)

Swedish filmmaker Erwin Leiser follows his initial two full-length documentaries on the atrocities of the Nazi regime, "Mein Kampf" and "Eichman and the Third Reich" ("Murder Through Signature" in Britain), with a third pic called the "first feature-length documentary on the situation of man in the atomic age." Leiser says he wants this film to be understood as a human, not a political document.

"Waehle das Leben" is an indie production by Leiser, with Swiss lawyer and publisher, Hans Deutsch, who provided much of the financing. The 18 months of filming and editing took place in Japan, Mexico, U.S. and Switzerland, complemented by material from US archives plus American, Japanese, French, British and German sources, most of it new.

The film opens with a short Mexican sequence depicting the people's completely natural and basically fearless acceptance of life and death, blends into a fleeting reminiscence of Nazi horrors as history's most gruesome example of mass destruction. Film then settles down for the remaining footage to a visualization, underlined by spoken commentary, of what remains today of the survivors of Hiroshima. The fate of these people, according to Leiser, has been practically ignored by films or books so far, which explains his desire to show authentically what it means to survive an A-bomb.

The possibilities, still largely untapped, of atomic energy for peaceful purposes are also brought into focus. But as a whole the film's message boils down to an urgent and obviously sincere plea to whom it may concern, i.e. every man and woman of any nationality, to avoid another Hiroshima. Included in the commentary are such statements as "The whole world is a Hiroshima that the bomb has not hit yet," or, at the film's conclusion, "It is for all of us to decide whether mankind must die together or can live together."

Leiser deserves credit for having kept this film free of deliberate shock values or polemic tendencies. It has the ring of truth and honesty as it restricts itself to authentic shots alone (not a single staged scene is included) and can be termed politically impartial. Nevertheless, it should come as no surprise that, due to its grim and downbeat theme, its final effect upon a paying audience is so shattering that boxoffice prospects look dubious at best. For, neces-

sary as such a film may be, few filmgoers in today's market may be expected to put their good money to be exposed to an evening's depiction of death, destruction and invalidity.

Major assets, in cinematic terms, are Swiss Han Heinrich Egger's intelligent editing and the topnotch black-and-white lensing by France's Jean-Marc Ripert, Tadashi Ohno and Hiroshi Segawa for the Japanese location sequences and Swiss vet cameraman Otto Ritter. Music by Robert Blum is both haunting and evocative. *Mezo.*

L'Attico
(The Penthouse)
(ITALIAN)

Rome, April 30.

Warner Bros. release of a Galatea production. Features Daniela Rocca, Tomas Milian, Philipe Leroy, Jean Jacques Delbo, Lilla Brignone, Mary Arden, Gino Pernice, Walter Chiari. Directed by Gianni Puccini. Screenplay, Puccini, Ennio DeConcini, Bruno Baratti, Mino Guerrini, Eliana de Sabata; camera, Marcello Gatti; editor, Mario Serandrei. At Fiamma, Rome. Running time, 98 MINS.
Daniela .... Daniela Rocca
Claudio .... Tomas Milian
Gunilla .... Mary Arden
Gabriele .... Walter Chiari
Ughetto .... Gino Pernice
Baroness .... Lilla Brignone
Gabriele's father ... Jean Jacques Delbo

Commerciable item with some deeper attempts at social criticism, not all of them successful. Cast helps locally, but this is no blockbuster. Export chances must bank on exploitable aspects.

A sort of "Dolce Vita" in reverse, pic shows the slow corruption exerted on a country gal by the big city, as she goes from one man to the next in search of one who can furnish her dream—the penthouse which symbolizes success, at least in her estimation. Much of film is played for laughs, but there are some sharp barbs thrown here and there. Result is a certain confusion in approach which added to conventional aspects of plotting are among pic's demerits.

Also, Daniela Rocca, who was so apt as the wife in "Divorce, Italian Style," is here out of her range, and since she's on screen almost throughout, film suffers, even though she has some good moments.

Though badly dubbed in local version, Tomas Milian sketches a good opportunist type while Walter Chiari appears strangely opaque in his do-gooder role and lacks conviction. Mary Arden, Lilla Brignone, and others are good in support, but best turn belongs to Jean Jacques Delbo, as Chiari's father. Director Puccini has dressed this one up with some fancy lensing and pacing, but it's a disappointing entry just the same. Technical credits are good. *Hawk.*

Le Voyage A Biarritz
(The Trip to Biarritz)
(FRENCH)

Paris, April 30.

Cinedis release of Millimax - Massimo Uleri-PCM production. Stars Fernandel; features Arletty, Michel Galabru, Catherine Sola, Helene Tossy, Rellys. Directed by Gilles Grangier. Screenplay, Raymond Castans, Jean Manse, Massimo Uleri and Grangier from a play by Jean Sarment; camera, Roger Hubert; editor, Madeleine Gug. At the Normandie, Paris. Running time, 95 MINS.
Guillaume .... Fernandel
Fernande .... Arletty
Touffanel .... Michel Galabru

Therese .... Catherine Sola
Charles .... Jacques Chabassol

Homey little pic gives comic Fernandel a chance to run his gamut of rustic charm and anger, with a dash of pathos. Simple plotting and obvious characters, with a pleasant unspooling, makes this a probable local bet with foreign chances limited except for possible playoff use on the Fernandel name.

Fernandel is a station master in a little town with the one train that comes through about to be deleted. A homecoming son and a cherished hope of a trip to Biarritz make up the core of the pic plus a quick trip to London when the station master wins a free voyage in a lottery.

The son is at first ashamed of his lower class dad but comes around and decides to marry a comely local miss after almost marrying a rich girl while on a London job. Pic is amiably directed and does not try to cover up its one-dimensional, sentimental tale. It is technically polished.

There is just the lack of character perception or dramatic fillip to bring this out of the rut of the okay programmer. Production dress is good. *Mosk.*

The Mouse on The Moon
(BRITISH—COLOR)

Erratic space travel sequel to "Mouse That Roared." Some witty, amusing sequences and performances but some too prolonged; popular British cast could whip up wicket biz.

London, May 7.

United Artists release of a Walter Shenson production. Stars Margaret Rutherford, Bernard Cribbins, David Lossoff, Ron Moody, Terry-Thomas; features June Ritchie, John Le Mesurier, Peter Sallis, Roddy McMillan, Allan Cuthbertson, John Phillips. Directed by Richard Lester. Screenplay, Michael Pertwee, from Leonard Wibberley's novel; camera, Wilkie Cooper; editor, Bill Lenny; music, Ron Grainer. Opened at London Pavilion, London. Running time, 85 MINS.
Gloriana .... Margaret Rutherford
Vincent .... Bernard Cribbins
Mountjoy .... Ron Moody
Kokintz .... David Kossoff
Spender .... Terry-Thomas
Cynthia .... June Ritchie
Benter .... Roddy McMillan
British Delegate....... John Le Mesurier
British Aide .... Michael Trubshawe
Bracewell .... John Phillips
Wendover .... Tom Aldredge
Russian Delegate .... Peter Sallis
Russian Aide .... Jan Conrad
Plumber .... Hugh Lloyd
Valet .... Mario Fabrizi
U.S. Air Force General.. Archie Duncan
Russian Air Force General
                        Richard Marner
Von Neidel .... John Bluthal
Bandleader .... Clive Dunn
American Journalist........ Kevin Scott
German Scientist .... Guy Deghy
First Member .... Eric Barker
Second Member .... Allan Cuthbertson
Fenwichian .... Frankie Howerd
Fourth Member .... Gerald Anderson
5th Member .... Robin Bailey
1st U.S. Astronaut........Edward Bishop
2nd U.S. Astronaut....... Bill Edwards
1st Russian Astronaut...Laurence Herder
2nd Russian Astronaut..... Harvey Hall

On paper the idea for this second trip to the mythical Duchy of Grand Fenwick (the first was in "Mouse That Roared") sounded a likely gag. An up-to-the-minute joshing of space travel, the Big Powers and unscrupulous politics. But though a long and able cast work hard, the proceedings rarely become as funny as they are usually threatening to do and the joke often falls erratically flat. Whereas the first pic was treated largely as satire, in this one some of the satirical touches are blunted by overplaying and for farcical effect. For this director Richard Lester must take much of the responsibility. Michael Pertwee's play is not sufficiently integrated, and the gag situations often having the appearance of being tossed hopefully into the arena.

That's not to say the pic won't do well and make a lot of new friends as well as retaining most of those who enjoyed its predecessor. But the previous one had Peter Sellers playing three very varying characters which was a considerable assist to the fun.

The Duchy of Grand Fenwick, smallest country in the world, is still badly in the red. The wily Prime Minister (Ron Moody) is worried. Disastrous explosions are happening in the local wine which is Grand Fenwick's main export. And Moody is anxious to get some greenbacks to put plumbing into the castle. He decides to seek a loan from America kidding them his Duchy wants to develop space travel research.

Washington comes through with a million bucks as a gift. The politicos argue that it will develop

the image of Yank goodwill, but not be enough for Grand Fenwick to proceed seriously as a science menace. Russia climbs on the bandwagon with the gift of a reject Russian rocket. Britain characteristically sits on the fence, apart from sending over a secret agent to find out what's really going on.

From then on it's doublecross and counter doublecross, bluffing in high places and in Grand Fenwick's gimcrack Parliament House. Eventually the Prime Minister's plans are wrecked when scientist David Kossoff hits on the discovery that the local wine makes champion nuclear fuel. Grand Fenwick gets its rocket into space and is by accident first to get astronauts on to the moon. The machination that arise from the plotting of ambitious politicians provide fair fun but some of the points needed more sting and less facetiousness.

Ron Moody (the original Fagin in "Oliver") hams up his role of the Prime Minister for all that it is worth. But he certainly makes a striking larger than life figure of the ambitious cunning but foolish "dictator" of Grand Fenwick. Margaret Rutherford as the Duchess Gloriana not unnaturally offers a different interpretation from Sellers in the original. It's a role that doesn't extend Miss Rutherford overmuch. Bernard Cribbins as the P.M.'s son with ambitions to be an astronaut is badly cast and can extract little from a role which he appears uncertain to play straight or for yocks. Terry-Thomas has some typical silly-ass scenes as the fatuous "bird watching" British spy and David Kossoff provides his own gentle brand of charm and philosophical comedy to the role of the idealistic scientist.

June Ritchie the flimsy love interest gets lost in the proceedings. But in a long list of supporting players John Phillips the inevitable John Le Mesurier as a British politician; Eric Barker Roddy McMillan Peter Sallis and Hugh Lloyd score effectively. There is also a one-minute guest appearance by Frankie Howerd as a Fenwickian trying to go to public lavatory which is monumental in its lack of point.

Special effects, Ron Grainer's lively score Wilkie Cooper's Eastmancolor camerawork and the general atmosphere of oldie-worldie charm provided by the backwater Duchy are all aids in a pic that will probably sell well on title and cast. But it could have been so much more of a comedy lark.

Rich.

In The Cool Of The Day
(PANAVISION—COLOR)

Heavyhanded romantic meller. Dim b.o. prospect.

Hollywood, May 1.

Metro release of John Houseman production. Stars Jane Fonda, Peter Finch, Angela Lansbury. Directed by Robert Stevens. Screenplay, Meade Roberts, from novel by Susan Ertz; camera (Metrocolor), Peter Newbrook; editor, Thomas Stanford; music, Francis Chagrin; asst. director, Jake Wright. Reviewed at Academy Awards Theatre, May 1, '63. Running time, 91 MINS.

Murray Logan	Peter Finch
Christine Bonner	Jane Fonda
Sibyl Logan	Angela Lansbury
Sam Bonner	Arthur Hill
Mrs. Gellert	Constance Cummings
Frederick Bonner	Alexander Knox
Leonard	Nigel Davenport
Dr. Arraman	John Le Mesurier
Dickie Bayliss	Alec McCowen
Lily	Valerie Taylor
Andreas	Andreas Markos

Feeble, ill-conceived attempt to revive a style that is an anachronism in this highly-selective, neo-realistic era. John Houseman production was written for the screen by Meade Roberts from the novel by Susan Ertz. It concerns the romantic encounter that is briefly consummated during a mutual visit to Greece by an English book publisher (Peter Finch) who is taunted and tormented by a grudging, embittered, anti-social wife (Angela Lansbury), and a fragile American girl (Jane Fonda) who has been sheltered and protected to the point of absurdity by her adoring, but overly-finicky husband (Arthur Hill). Ultimately the girl, a latter-day "Camille," falls ill, for some mysterious reason loses her will to live, and perishes, leaving her husband angry and her boy friend with a sweet memory and solitude (his wife has run off.)

Most of this romantic schmaltz is set against some interesting Greek scenery such as the Parthenon and the Acropolis, lensed in Panavision and Metrocolor by Peter Newbrook. Newbrook photographs ruins well, but is less effective with people. For example, he manages to disregard the dancers' legs in the course of a Grecian folk dance scene, which must be regarded as singular lack of photographic observance. Thomas Stanford's editing is competent, but Francis Chagrin's musical score is far too obvious, obtrusive and overbearing. A crashing crescendo to accompany the sudden appearance of the Parthenon onscreen seems a trifle unnecessary. A trite, but commercial, title ditty by Manos Hadjidakis and Liam Sullivan is sung smoothly over the titles by Nat Cole. It seems incredible, but one of the Orry-Kelly dresses worn by Miss Fonda features unaccountable tears at both armpits. The holes, spotted more than once by the camera, don't appear to have been designed by O-K.

Miss Lansbury gets off the best acting in the film as Finch's sour, scarfaced wife. She stirs up the only fun in the generally sour proceedings. Miss Fonda, sporting a Cleopatra haircut, is all passion and intensity. When she loves, boy, she really loves. Finch wears one expression. It appears to be boredom, which is understandable.

This drab film was directed by Robert Stevens. *Tube.*

The Young And The Brave

War drama with boy-and-his-dog approach. Too weak for top slots, will do as lower berther.

Hollywood, May 8.

Metro release of A. C. Lyles production. Stars Rory Calhoun, William Bendix, Richard Jaeckel. Directed by Francis D. Lyon. Screenplay, Beirne Lay Jr., from story by Ronald Davidson, Harry M. Slott; camera, Emmett Bergholz; editor, Robert Leo; music, Ronald Stein; asst. director, Harry F. Hogan. Reviewed at the studio, May 8, '63. Running time, 84 MINS.

Sgt. Ed Brent	Rory Calhoun
Staff Sgt. Peter L. Kane	William Bendix
Cpl. John Estway	Richard Jaeckel
Col. Ralph Holbein	Richard Arlen
Intelligence Officer	John Agar
Han	Manuel Padilla
Pvt. Kirk Wilson	Robert Ivers
Communist Soldier	Weaver Levy
Stretcher Bearer	Dennis Richards
Lt. Ulysses Nero	Robert Goshen
Han's Father	Willard Lee
Army Major	Beirne Lay Jr.

"The Young and the Brave" is a cross between two staples of the budget picture field—the small-scale war drama and the waif-and-dog opera. But A. C. Lyles' soldiers-and schmaltz lacks the proper seasoning to make it a palatable main course attraction. It will have to serve Metro as a supporting item.

A trite, listless scenario by Beirne Lay Jr., from a story by Ronald Davidson and Harry M. Slott, describes the efforts of several GI's who have escaped their Communist captors at about the time of the outbreak of the Korean War to get back to their own lines. Their cause is aided by a Korean tyke (Manuel Padilla), whose parents have been murdered for sheltering them, and an abandoned K-9 Corps police dog who has been rescued and befriended by the boy. They are pursued above the 38th parallel by a singularly inept squad of North Korean troops.

Some fairly respectable cast names have been assembled by Lyles for the enterprise, but these experienced actors have very little dramatic meat to sink their veteran teeth into. The three leading roles are dispatched mechanically by Rory Calhoun, William Bendix and Richard Jaeckel, and main supporting roles are handled satisfactorily but without flair by Robert Ivers, Richard Arlen and John Agar, none of whom have much to do. Padilla shows great restraint for a moppet, but his line delivery is generally unintelligible. The dog is excellent, but looks understandably scared to death in the combat sequence.

Francis D. Lyon's direction is uneven, a condition arising out of the nature of the script, which alternates between patches notable for economy of dialog and other lethargically talky passages in which the film bogs down. Emmett Bergholz's photography is very helpful in the topographical manner in which it surveys and telescopes the movements of those involved, generally from an altitudinous perch. Other staff contributions are reliable, if routine.

Tube.

Das Feuerschiff
(The Lightship)
(GERMAN)

Berlin, May 14.

Columbia release of Fono (Dr. Hermann Schwerin) production. Stars James Robertson Justice; features Helmut Wildt, Dieter Borsche, Michael Hinz. Directed by Ladislao Vajda. Screenplay, Curt Siodmak, based on tale by Siegfried Lenz; camera, Heinz Pehlke. At UFA Pavillon, West Berlin. Running time, 84 MINS.

Captain Freytag	James Robertson-Justice
Dr. Caspary	Helmut Wildt
Rethorn, steersman	Dieter Borsche
Philippi, radio man	Pinkas Braun
Fred Freytag	Michael Hinz
Gombert	George Lehn
Zumpe	Guenther Mack
Martin	Simon Martin
Trittel	Werner Peters
Eugen	Sieghardt Rupp

"Lightship" looms as one of the better German pix of the season. Adapted from a tale by the German writer Siegfried Lenz, the philosophical ingredients of the original remain on the surface. But the outcome, nevertheless, is an exciting, technically well-made and well-acted film. This one will please the domestic action trade. Also it has the depth to appeal to the more demanding patron.

Story has three bank robbers capturing a lightship with which they want to escape to Denmark. But the ship's captain isn't willing to weigh anchor for the ship's duty is to stay to warn ships of sands along the coast. The gangsters terrorize the crew but the captain doesn't give in and pays his courageous sense of duty for his life.

The film very much benefits from outstanding acting performances. James Robertson Justice, a British actor, turns in a memorable performance as the captain who sticks to his duty. Helmut Wildt portrays the intellectual gangster boss in an impressive manner. Members of the crew are well chosen as to type.

Hungarian-born Spanish director Ladislao Vajda, who's been making mostly comedies and family-type pix in recent years, proves that he's able to create hard-hitting stuff, too. This one is often remarkably brutal but the brutality is never out of place. The womanless pic keeps one spellbound. This German pic may easily sled into foreign markets, the more so as the Columbia has it for release.

Hans.

Venusberg
(GERMAN)

Berlin, May 7.

Nora release of Franz Seitz production. With Nicole Badal, Marisa Mell, Monica Flodquist, Christine Granberg, Ina Duscha, Claudia Marus and Jane Axell. Directed and written by Rolf Thiele. Camera, Wolf Wirth; music, Rolf Wilhelm. At Filmbuehne Wien, Berlin. Running time, 85 MINS.

Florentine	Marisa Mell
Pony	Nicole Badal
Christine	Monica Flodquist
Lola	Christine Granberg
Inge	Ina Duscha
Vera	Claudia Marus
Ruth	Jane Axell

This one may be given a number of superlatives: It's the most unusual but also most confusing and —more or less—most ridiculous German film of the season. Film is unusual inasmuch as no man appears in it. It's also unusual, subjectwise. The seven pretty girls that get together in a lonely holiday house up in the snowy mountains talk about what they think of love and men and whether they are happy. The talks are remarkably frank and very intimate, and often very suggestive.

The pic is confusing inasmuch as the viewer is never quite certain whether Rolf Thiele, the director, means it all seriously or is just trying to pull his (the viewer's) leg. Both is possible and much is involuntarily funny. Thiele has definitely gone overboard with his predilection for erotical themes. Most of the cinemagoers will find his latest creation ridiculous. Moreover, it's a rather dull picture.

Although "Venusberg" has received "valuable publicity" via the trouble it had with the domestic Censorship Board (many suggestive dialog scenes and nude sequences had to be cut before it was given the greenlight), its commercial prospects appear rather doubtful. Pic is too blase to make an im-

pression and may only interest the curio-seekers. Some export chances may be granted.

What goes for Thiele applies to his cameraman, Wolf Wirth. He too went overboard and lost control. Too much fancy work along the lensing line.

It may be interesting to add that none of the seven girls are of German nationality. Thiele picked Jane Axel, Monica Flodquist and Christina Granberg in Sweden. Marisa Mell and Ina Duscha are Austrians. Claudia Marus hails from Italy while Nicole Badal, who has already appeared in some Thiele films, comes from Holland. All seven girls, incidentally, are lookers. And that's one of the few assets about this film. *Hans.*

Violenza Segreta
(Secret Violence)
(ITALIAN)

Rome, May 7.
Globe Films International release of Filmstudio SpA production. Features Giorgio Albertazzi, Alexandra Stewart, Enrico Maria Salerno, Maryam, Vittorio Sanipoli, David Abramo, Sergio Ricciardi, Rosie Zichel. Directed by Giorgio Moser. Screenplay, Marco Leto, Silvio Maestranzi Berto Pelosso, in collaboration with Giorgio Moser, Tullio Pinelli. Based on novel by Enrico Emanuelli; dialogue, Emanuelli; camera, Aldo Scavarda; music, Giovanni Fusco; editor, Mario Serandrei. At the Ariston, Rome. Running time, 100 MINS.

Enrico Maraini	Giorgio Albertazzi
Elisabetta	Alexandra Stewart
Contardi	Enrico Maria Salerno
Regina	Maryam
Farnenti	Vittorio Sanipoli
Abdi	David Abramo
Tarantini	Sergio Ricciardi
Haua	Rosie Zichel

Ambitious but only sometimes intriguing psychological study set in African Somaliland. Exotic setting and some exploitable angles are a help, but pic will need plenty of sales assistance for interesting returns. Chancy export quantity.

A successful monkey trader, Enrico Mainardi, becomes involved with two women, a frigid black beauty and an equally unresponding white girl while being equally thrown off balance by the behavior of two male pals, both abnormal in different ways. The resultant clash in standards and thoughts throws the hero off his path until a final shock throws some sense into him. This seems to define a new hope in life.

Saddled with a very literary script and uninventive direction, even such able thesps as Salerno and Albertazzi fail to give their best. But one senses intelligent dedication on the part of all involved, working as they did under trying on-the-spot African conditions. There is also too much off-screen commentary by the brooding hero. Technical credits are excellent. *Hawk.*

Cannes Festival

Pour La Suite Du Monde
(For the Continuance of the World)
(CANADIAN)

Cannes, May 14.
Office National Du Film Et Radio Canada production and release. Written and directed by Pierre Perrault, Michel Brault, Marcel Carriere. Camera, Michel Brault; editor, Werner Nold. In Critics Section, Cannes Film Fest. Running time, 105 MINS.

Combo reenacted and direct documentary pic, on a French-Canadian island that goes back to old fishing methods out of years ago, is in competition in the main Cannes Film Fest.

Pic, with its on-the-spot rough qualities and directness, has a revealing directness and knowing progression that keeps this of interest throughout.

The bucolic people are shown discussing the fishing bit, and are expertly caught in their simple characters and old fashioned outlook. Multiple directors show a flair for catching these people in revealing talks and actions. The final capture of a big white porpoise, sold to a Yank aquarium, is a fitting culmination to this ruminating production.

It does not condone this inbred life of the island but does display an observation that shows it is not spoiling for the good old times but does have respect for them and their people. Its commercial chances seem limited to some specialized houses, with tv also indicated.

This is another in the so-called "Cinema Truth" school which tries to catch reality on the move so as to capture an interpretation of the same. Be that as it may, this has a fluidity in editing, lensing and movement plus a keen feel for its characters that makes it of interest. But this film lacks the fillip that could have made it more than an observant screen look at old Canadian fishing and those engaged in it.

It is technically acceptable, if there are some grainy patches. Canadian-French accents have had it subtitled in French. *Mosk.*

Hallelujah The Hills

Witty, comic offbeat non-Hollywood pic that could make for arty runs; will need careful sell but could be worth it.

Cannes, May 14.
Vermont Production release of David C. Stone production. With Peter H. Beard, Sheila Finn, Martin Greenbaum, Peggy Steffans, Jerome Raphel, Blanche Dee. Written, directed and edited by Adolfas Mekas. Camera, Ed Emshwiller; music, Meyer Kupferman. In Critics Section, Cannes Film Fest. Running time, 88 MINS.

Jack	Peter H. Beard
Leo	Martin Greenbaum
Vera (Winter)	Sheila Finn
Vera (Summer)	Peggy Steffans
Father	Jerome Raphel
Mother	Blanche Dee
Convict 1	Jerome Hill
Convict 2	Taylor Mead
Gideon	Emsh

Formerly this offbeat N.Y. filmmaking group mainly has made dramas. Now comes a zesty unusual romp that twits its subject with knowing insight and also packs in some inside film buff gags and illusions. This emerges a film that will need careful handling but could be a specialized arty house. pic.

There is not much of a story. It is mainly a joyous rush of images by a new director who has assimilated his classics and regular run of films. Two clean-cut, adventurous young American stalwarts vie for the hand of a beauteous young girl only to have her snapped up by a bearded character.

Small town life, the seasons pass in review as the two men camp out and take their turns at wooing the girl or trying to cope with outdoor life in the snow and sun. The girl's father passes his time making cracks and the mother in sassing the wooed girl or in family chores.

Time and continuity are broken with ease, but this always has fresh scenes and sly comic touches that take potshots at American cliches but with an ingratiating bonhommie reminiscent of the headier days of pre-war U.S. American comedies.

So the nice boys do not get the girl. They are not at ease in outdoor life, and their courting of the girl is sometimes tender, childishly beguiling or just plain inept. The free-wheeling breaks in time, continuity and cutting may make this reminiscent of the French New Wave tactics, but it has a bright cohesion of its own supplied by writer - director - editor A d o l f a s Mekas.

He displays a flair for visual revelation, gags and shenanigans that manage to keep this stimulating throughout. It might throw off some critics or audiences or irritate others in its seeming repetition of scenes of inside horseplay. The intimations of noted pix culminates with a bow to D. W. Griffith in showing the great ice flow rescue of Lillian Gish by Richard Barthlemess in "Way Down East."

Mekas assimilates rather than imitates. The actors are all fresh, and cavort with grace and a lack of self-consciousness. Peter H. Beard's scenes of bathing in icy waters plus a race to a river, show a possibly new Douglas Fairbanks in his bravado and derring-do.

Camerawork is clear with editing sharp and the music a counterpoint help. There are glimpses and incisive satiric shafts against war, courting habits, youthful shyness and self absorption in this madcap, bright pic.

Film is different, but it shows that Americans, working on their own, can also turn out personalized films that can comment simply on human foibles and actions. Above all, this has an inventive visual comic flair. But its very abandon will make this a touchy pic and it will need careful placement.

After such films as "David And Lisa," "The Little Fugitive," "On The Bowery," "Shadows," "The Connection" and "The Savage Eye," this shows that the N.Y. group has something to say and a talent with which to say it. Proper exposure and the growing specialized audiences may give them, finally, the place on their own home grounds they have won in many foreign spots. *Mosk.*

Deja S'Envole La Fleur Maigre
(The Frail Flowers Are Disappearing)
(BELGIAN)

Cannes, May 14.
Meyer and Tarzman production and release. With Domenico Mescolini, Valentino Gentili, Luigi Favotto, Gettino Cerqua. Written, directed and edited by Paul Meyer. Camera, Freddy Rents. In Critics Section, Cannes Film Fest. Running time, 90 MINS.

Film takes a look at various nationalities in a coal mining section of Belgium during lean times. There is no preaching here but a well-observed look at the people with poetic shafts of themselves by those involved. This makes for a good film of its kind. Only specialized chances seem in store abroad. But its theme and playing could have this of art fodder if well placed and handled.

An Italian worker sends for his family and the film details their coming and attempts to fit in. Director-writer Paul Meyer displays a good feeling for revealing scenes and handles the non-actors with sensitivity. A mature boy has a slight fling with a local girl. A younger one discovers the school, land and inhabitants of this mine-scarred section. In the background is lurking unemployment as the mines are abandoned.

Camerawork is sharp and sensitive to the moods and landscape. Simple incidents build into an absorbing unsentimental look at the workers and their lot. Knowing characterizations give a rounded feel to the enacted documentary-like tale. For a first film, it bodes well for a director of visual skill —Paul Meyer. It is technically tops. *Mosk.*

Barnvagnen
(The Baby Carriage)
(SWEDISH)

Cannes, May 14.
Europa Films production and release. With Inger Taube, Tommy Berggren, Lars Passgaard. Written and directed by Bo Widerberg. Camera, Jan Troell; editor, Wic Kjellen. In Critics Section, Cannes Film Fest. Running time, 92 MINS.

Britt	Inger Taube
Bjoern	Tommy Berggren
Robber	Lars Passgaard

Pungent tale of an unwed mother and the men in her life manages to make a statement about youth that is neither preachy, didactic or sanctimonious. It is a film with a flair for etching the characters and pinpointing their actions. For a first film, this shows promise and could be an item for specialized or arty spots abroad. However, it will need hardsell for best results.

A young girl drifts through a series of affairs until she becomes pregnant. She decides to have the baby but not the father, a young gentle but callow rock-and-roll singer.

Into her life comes a more complicated boy who ruins a growing idyll by his own problems. The girl is somewhat naive but grows in stature as she follows her emotions which allow her to break with her unheeding family and go on her own.

Thesping of the young players is light and unaffected. Inger Taube has beauty, grace and presence as the girl while Tommy Berggren displays a depth and charm as the mixed-up boy. Lars Passgaard is right as the more direct, instinctive lad. Lensing has crystal sharpness while the editing keeps these series of incidents coherent and progressive.

Director Bo Widerberg has a knowing control of the symbols and unfoldment plus an insight into youthful mores. In just outlining the emotional problems and escapades of these three people the pic gives a discerning look at Swedish youth in particular and young people in general. Last-minute arrival for the Cannes Critic's Section was put in as a double feature because of its value. *Mosk.*

Yksityisalue
(Open Secret)
(FINNISH)

Cannes, May 14.
Adams Filmi Oy release of Kurkvaara Film Oy production. With Jarno Hiiloskorpi, Sointu Angervo, Sinikka Hannula, Kalervo Missila. Written, directed and photographed by Maunu Kurkvaara. Editor, Tuomo Kattilakoski. In Critics Section, Cannes Film Fest. Running time, 75 MINS.
Boy .... Jarno Hiiloskorpi
Architect .... Sointu Angervo
Secretary .... Sinikka Hennula
Girl .... Kalervo Nissila

Film is a simple, well-told tale of a young man's first dramatic coping with life when he investigates the suicide of his boss, a noted architect and a man he had admired. Told with insight, this still lacks the size and dramatic pitch to make it more than a lingo item abroad. Pic has a worthy intensity in the unfolding.

A middle-aged architect is found dead by his assistant who then unravels what happened via meetings the several people in his life. It seems the man's selling out for commercial purposes, an unfeeling wife, and a general dissatisfaction and melancholy have all combined to cause him to take his own life.

It shows a flair for visual storytelling by young Finnish director Maunu Kurkvaara, plus a sure hand with actors. This is an intimate, personal pic, with familiar ingredients. It is technically good, and Kurkvaara should be heard from with more emphasis soon.

The Finnish cinema has made rare dents on the international scene (notably with Edvin Laine's "The Unknown Soldier" some years ago) so this could mean that more knowing filmmakers are now beginning to practice in that country.
Mosk.

Le Joli Mai
(Pretty May)
(FRENCH)

Cannes, May 14.
Ursulines release of Sofracima production. Directed by Chris Marker. Screenplay, Marker, Catherine Varlin; commentary spoken by Yves Montand; camera, Pierre Lhomme; editor, Eva Zora. In Critics Section, Cannes Film Fest. Running time, 180 MINS.

This film combines essay techniques and the current interest in the so-called "Cinema Truth" movement which looks at life on-the-spot so to speak. Film details a series of happenings, street and home interviews plus a general panorama of Paris in May last year. It gives this oo-la-la capital a new look and brings it down out of the frou-frou to reality. On this alone, it might be arty and specialized fodder abroad as well as heady telefare.

Chris Marker has taken his camera out into the streets and also has interviewed people at length indoors. It seems he had several cameras in operation to take interest away from those queried so they finally wound up talking freely.

Via intensive editing, people reveal themselves. Pettiness, common sense, posturing, guile, generosity, wit and meanness all come floating out to give a neat look at human foibles. There are shots of riots during the recent Algerian fracas, an African's attitudes towards the French, stock market worker outlooks and many others.

There is also an intensive searching out of the underside of the city, housing problems, displaced persons, a worker priest who has turned leftist, and a fine envelope of well-shot scenes of the city and terse statistics on its overcrowding, arts, etc.

None of the usual Paris cliches are here. It is an absorbing piece of filming and does not seem as long as its three hours. It can be cut if needed which is likely for many playdates. In fact there is already a two hour version. Marker, besides his wry wit and insight in the commentary, well delivered by Yves Montand, also has a flair for getting fine visual setups despite the heat of improvisation.

The lensing is also of top quality while the editing helps keep the film's motives always crisp. In short, a revealing look at Paris, and the Parisians and Parisiennes.

Film naturally would need specialized handling abroad but could pay off on the Paris tag, its unique outlook and probing, combined with good technical qualities. It appears one of the most interesting and inspired of these "Cinema Truth" pix that are springing up.
Mosk.

Seul Ou Avec Des Autres
(Alone or With Others)
(CANADIAN)

Cannes, May 14.
Association General Des Etudiants De Montreal production and release. With Nicole Bradn, Pierre Letourneau, Marie-Jose Raymond, Michell Boulizon. Written and directed by Denys Arcand and Stephen Venne. Camera, Michel Brault; editor, Gilles Groulx. In Critics Section, Cannes Film Fest. Running time, 65 MINS.

Made in French by a group of university students in Montreal, this pic combines the mood and techniques of the French New Wave and Cinema Truth schools of filmmaking. Because of its length, it looks mainly good as part of a medium length cinema program abroad or for use on tv.

A girl meets a boy and their talks and outings are pictured in improvised scenes or via monologs. Long focal lenses spy on them in various situations. At times, a deep insight into youthful relations is caught. Sometimes a speaker telling about an incident is shown to be rebuilding things via the real happenings on the screen as he or she talks.

There is the jump cutting, free swinging improvising and jangly rhythms dear to the French Wavers as well as long talk sequences stemming from the Gallic Cinema Truth methods. But this film has an individual youthful robustness and directness that gives it a tone of its own.

If it sometimes slips into preciosity, this has a personal note and fetching performances by students playing out little incidents. Pic could make it as an okay supporting entry in foreign arty spots. Blown up from 16m, this still has good definition and snap in 35m.
Mosk.

Porto Das Caixas
(BRAZILIAN)

Cannes, May 14.
Sarcent production and release. With Irma Alvarez, Paulo Padilha, Reginado Farias, Sergio Sanz, Joseph Guerreira, Margarida Rey. Directed and written by Paulo Cesar Saraceni from an idea by Lucio Cardoso. Camera, Mario Carneiro; editor, Mello Nelli. In Critics Section, Cannes Film Fest. Running time, 75 MINS.
Wife .... Irma Alvarez
Husband .... Paulo Padilha
Lover .... Reginado Farias
Soldier .... Sergio Sanz
Barber .... Joseph Guerreira
Woman .... Margaida Rey

Obviously made on a shoestring (around $7,000), this drama of poverty and an eering wife has enough atmospheric feel and dramatic intensity to emerge a biting offbeater. However, it appears limited for foreign chances except in language spots or for specialized use.

The woman in question is married to a cruel, petty railroad worker in a grimy little town. She allows men to get her. Then she tries to goad them into killing her husband and then getting her out of town.

One finally agrees only to renege. She finally does it herself with an axe. She wanders off alone as her accomplice refuses to go with her. Reminiscent of "Double Indemnity," this has an inexorable, tragic quality about it that makes its uneven acting, ordinary technical credits and, familiar story acceptable.

Film's length has it lacking a broader scope. But it does create a claustrophobic feeling and manages to make a statement about the defiling aspects of poverty. Irma Alvarez gives the wife a spontaneous sensuality and childish innocence.

In short, a promising first effort by Paulo Cesar Saraceni but without the depth good enough for anything but specialized possibilities, outside of its home grounds.
Mosk.

La Pelle Viva
(Scorched Skin)
(ITALIAN)

Cannes, May 14.
Cinematografica 61 production and release. Stars Elsa Martinelli, Raoul Grassili; features Franco Sportelli, Lia Rainer, Anna Develo. Directed by Giuseppe Fina. Screenplay, Carlo Castellaneta, Fina; camera, Antonio Macasoli; editor, Gabriele Varriale. In Critics Section, Cannes Film Fest. Running time, 90 MINS.

Film deals with the working class in Milano. There is a rightness in characterization and a depiction of the worker's lot. This is somewhat sketchy but with enough solidity for foreign language houses and specialized bookings abroad.

There is an expert feel here for a group of workers who have to travel a good 20 miles each way to and fro from work every day. The gray morning groggy trips and returns are visually effective. The intrigues also have an incisive flair for the life of one of the young workers and an unwed mother he marries.

The tenderness of their first meeting and the love affair is expertly blocked out. The man's concern with problems of his fellows is also forceful but there is a tendency to be too descriptive about his unwitting troubles with the police and his final loss of nerve.

If some of the points are academic and the pic sometimes lacks the needed deeper insight, film still is one of those rare ones with a good dramatic look at Milan's industrial life.

Elsa Martinelli eschews her usual glamor roles to cut a telling portrait of the girl-mother. Raoul Grassili has the proper acceptance of her man. It has the right gray hues photographically and expert work by both real actors and nonpros.
Mosk.

Slunce V Siti
(The Sun in the Net)
(CZECHOSLAVAKIA)

Cannes, May 14.
Czech State Film production and release. With Marian Bielik, Sana Belakova, Olga Salagova, Eliska Danova. Directed by Stefan Uher. Screenplay, Alfons Bednar, Uher; camera, Stanislav Szomolanyi; editor, Bedrich Voderka. At Cannes Film Fest. Running time, 90 MINS.
Fajolo .... Barian Bielik
Bela .... Sana Belkova
Jana .... Olga Salagova
Mother .... Eliska Danova

Extremely artily lensed film takes a look at youthful self orientation in Czechoslavakia today within a simple, almost soapy tale. If mannered, it has a visual flair and intensity that keeps this viewable. Film also points up an individualistic stand for people solving their own emotional problems. However, it looms a very specialized item abroad, at best.

A girl, with a blind mother, drifts uneasily between no comprehension of her family and an inability to find a way with a young boyfriend. Addicted to photography, he also gropes about finding a way in a socialist society.

Direction manages to make its characters fairly full bodied despite doing it as a series of vignettes and types rather than as a narrative. The actors are fresh, and youthful lovemaking is approached without any evasion. In short, this promises well in its direction and conception for a first pic for all concerned. Crisp editing also helps.

Come Blow Your Horn
(PANAVISION-COLOR)

Engaging translation of the lightweight Broadway legiter. Bright b.o. prospect.

Hollywood, May 14.

Paramount release of Norman Lear-Bud Yorkin production. Stars Frank Sinatra; features Lee J. Cobb, Molly Picon, Barbara Rush, Jill St. John; guest stars Dan Blocker, Phyllis McGuire; introduces Tony Bill. Directed by Yorkin. Screenplay, Lear, from Neil Simon's play; camera (Technicolor), William H. Daniels; editor, Frank P. Keller; music, Nelson Riddle; assistant director, Daniel J. McCauley. Reviewed at Hollywood Paramount Theatre, May 14, '63. Running time, **112 MINS.**

Alan	Frank Sinatra
Mr. Baker	Lee J. Cobb
Mrs. Baker	Molly Picon
Connie	Barbara Rush
Peggy	Jill St. John
Buddy	Tony Bill
Mr. Eckman	Dan Blocker
Mrs. Eckman	Phyllis McGuire
Waiter	Herbie Fay
Barber	Romo Vincent
Manicurist	Charlotte Fletcher
Tall Girl	Greta Randall

Art it ain't, fun it is. That about sums up "Come Blow Your Horn." Like its legit parent, the screen version of Neil Simon's Jewish-oriented family comedy is a superficial but diverting romp. For the average escape-and-relaxation filmgoer, the Essex-Tandem production should prove a pleasant, entertaining experience uncomplicated by shades of characterization or substance and dimension. In the vernacular of its star, it's a gas for the mass, shopworn and predictable along the edges but crammed with gags, spiced with sex and played with style and gusto by an attractive cast. For exhibs and Paramount, a promising "Horn" of plenty.

The streamlined picture version is a product of Norman Lear and Bud Yorkin, produced by both, directed by Yorkin, written by Lear. They have done their job well in all three departments. The simple yarn is concerned with two brothers at opposite extremities of bachelorhood, the older one (Frank Sinatra) ultimately passing into a more mature, responsible phase of life when he sees in his younger brother's (Tony Bill) sensual excesses the reflection of a ferocious personality no longer especially becoming or appealing to him. This is mighty good news to his long-suffering father, a wax fruit manufacturer from Yonkers for whom any unmarried man over 30 is a bum.

Sinatra's jaunty performance is his best in some time. The role is perfectly suited to his rakish image. It also affords him an opportunity to manifest his most consumate talent—that of singer. He warbles the lilting title tune, which has been cleverly integrated into the story fabric in accompaniment of a transitional series of fast cuts. The song, by Sammy Cahn and James Van Heusen, has all the earmarks of a hit, and will probably get an airing on the next Oscarcast.

But it's Lee J. Cobb who steals the show (albeit in the juciest part) with what might be described as a "bum" bastic portrayal of the explosively irascible old man who is forever appearing at the front door of his son's apartment when more glamorous company is expected. As a matter of fact, a major share of the film's comedy is of the "knock-knock, who's there?" variety, a rather ancient fun device. Molly Picon, one of the foremost stars of the Yiddish stage, manages to wade through the absurdities of her role—Cobb's harassed wife—with comic finesse and shines brilliantly in a bout with a battery of ringing telephones.

Tony Bill makes a fairly auspicious screen bow as the younger brother. A dark, handsome, boyish type, he should become a favorite in the fan mag sphere. Barbara Rush is attractive as the girl who eventually gets Sinatra, and Jill St. John is flashy as a guilelessly accomodating sexpot. Dan Blocker packs the appropriate wallop as an understandably jealous Texan and Phyllis McGuire is glamorously racy as his wife. Dean Martin adds a little bonus fun in an unbilled cameo bit as a bum who gets—literally—what he begs for, to his chagrin.

Cinematic ingenuity by Yorkin and staff adds lustre and novelty to the proceedings, which need the boost. For example, a refrigerator-eye-view, or open-and-shut case, of a hungry husband is the kind of photographic imagination with which Yorkin and cameraman William H. Daniels have added an unorthodox visual element to make a joke play better. Frank P. Keller's editing is astute, Edith Head's costumes observantly suited to character. Nelson Riddle's score is noteworthy for the manner in which characters are identified and accompanied by individual themes, along the order of "Peter and the Wolf." The gaudy set for Sinatra's opulent apartment is the highlight of contribution in this film of the teams of Hal Pereira-Roland Anderson (art direction) and Sam Comer-James Payne (set decoration). *Tube.*

The Nutty Professor
(COLOR)

Jerry Lewis in a slickly-mounted Jekyll-Hyde style farce.

Hollywood, May 10.

Paramount release of Ernest D. Glucksman production. Stars Jerry Lewis, Stella Stevens. Directed by Lewis. Screenplay, Lewis, Bill Richmond, from story by Lewis; camera (Technicolor), W. Wallace Kelley; editor, John Woodcock; music Walter Scharf; asst. director, Ralph Axness. Reviewed at Picwood Theatre, May 10, '63. Running time, **107 MINS.**

Prof. Julius F. Kelp and Buddy Love	Jerry Lewis
Stella Purdy	Stella Stevens
Dr. Hamius R. Warfield	Del Moore
Millie Lemmon	Kathleen Freeman
Football Player	Ned Flory
Football Player	Norman Alden
Father Kelp	Howard Morris
Mother Kelp	Elvia Allman
Dr. Leevee	Milton Frome
Bartender	Buddy Lester
English Boy	Marvin Kaplan
College Student	David Landfield
Football Player	Skip Ward
College Student	Julie Parrish
College Student	Henry Gibson
Themselves	Les Brown & Band

"The Nutty Professor" is apt to be another moneymaker for Jerry Lewis and Paramount, but it is not one of the comedian's better films. Although attractively mounted and performed with flair by a talented cast, the Ernest D. Gluckman production is only fitfully funny. What it seems to need most of all at the moment is a good trimming job by the editing department. Too often the film bogs down in pointless, irrelevant or repetitious business, nullifying the flavor of the occasionally choice comic capers and palsying the tempo and continuity of the story.

The picture was directed by Lewis and written by him in partnership with Bill Richmond. The star is cast as a meek, homely, accident-prone chemistry prof who concocts a potion that transforms him into a handsome, cocky, obnoxiously vein "cool cat" type. But the transfiguration is of the Jekyll-Hyde variety in that it wears off, restoring Lewis to the original mold, invariably at critical, embarrassing moments. Eventually, the return to character occurs in full view of an audience of admirers of model B, prompting Lewis to deliver a rather maudlin sermon with the moral that "if you don't think too much of yourself, how do you expect others to?" This touch of climactic sentiment is a characteristic of Lewis' pictures but, while a dash of "heart" can be a valuable ingredient in comedy, it doesn't register in this one, coming off flat and pretentious.

Another standard characteristic of the Lewis film is its similarity to an animated cartoon, especially noticeable on this occasion in that the professor played by Lewis is a kind of live-action version of the nearsighted Mr. Magoo who suffers typically cartoon-like mishaps such as getting flattened by a heavy falling door or having his arms stretched to floor-touching length by dropping a barbell—with miraculous "recoveries" in subsequent scenes.

Lewis handles his dual role with skill, although it is stretching the imagination a bit to accept him as the irresistibly attractive campus heart-throb, especially when he sets himself at the keyboard and croons "That Old Black Magic" to a bevy of swooning females. Somebody has got to be kidding. The voice that comes out, after all, belongs to Jerry Lewis, and that ain't Nat King Cole, brother.

Musical theme of the picture is the beautiful refrain, "Stella By Starlight." By starlight or any other light, Stella is beautiful—Stella Stevens (that is, who portrays the professor's student admirer. Miss Stevens is not only gorgeous, she is a very gifted actress. Top stardom is a meaty role away. This was an exceptionally tough assignment, requiring of her almost exclusively silent reaction takes, and Miss Stevens has managed almost invariably to produce the correct responsive expression. On her, even the incorrect one would look good. Somebody, however, should clue in the make-up department to skip all that facial goo and stop over-torturing her tresses. Naturally classic looks such as hers need no such embellishment.

Of considerable comic value in key support are Del Moore and Howard Morris, with additional contributions of prominence by Kathleen Freeman, Med Flory, Norman Alden, Milton Frome and Buddy Lester.

Dexterous, glamorous photography by W. Wallace Kelley is a big asset, and other noteworthy production aids include the Hal Pereira-Walter Tyler art direction, Walter Scharf's music and the Hugo & Charles Grenzbach sound. Much of the film was shot on the Arizona State U. campus. Editor was John Woodcock, and he should get the green light for more. *Tube.*

Savage Sam
(COLOR)

Unsatisfactory Disney western.

Hollywood, May 17.

Buena Vista release of Walt Disney production. Stars Brian Keith, Tommy Kirk, Kevin Corcoran; features Dewey Martin, Jeff York, Marta Kresten; no character-name credits. Cast also includes Rafael Campos, Slim Pickens, Rodolfo Acosta, Pat Hogan, Dean Fredericks, Brad Weston. Directed by Norman Tokar. Screenplay, Fred Gipson, William Tunberg, based on book by Gipson; camera (Technicolor), Edward Colman; editor, Grant K. Smith; music, Oliver Wallace; asst. director, Joseph L. McEveety. Reviewed at Academy Awards Theatre, May 17, '63. Running time, **103 MINS.**

It will take all the intrinsic drawing power of the Walt Disney banner to counteract the inadequacies of this undernourished western and bail it out at the box-office. "Savage Sam" is one of the least satisfactory items to emerge from the Buena Vista hopper in years.

With a screenplay by Fred Gipson and William Tunberg, based on the former's tome, the film is a depiction of the efforts of half-a-dozen Texans led by a hound named "Savage Sam" to catch up with a band of Apaches who have taken prisoner a couple of children. At the root of the picture's problem is the incongruous air of levity with which the scenarists and director Norman Tokar have approached what is obviously a dead-serious situation. This clash confuses the audience throughout and makes it impossible to take the story seriously. As a result, there is never any genuine concern for the characters, nor is there ever any doubt as to the outsome.

Brian Keith underplays, as always, his role of the posse leader. Tommy Kirk gives an appealing delineation but Kevin Corcoran, as his unmanageable younger brother, gives a harsh, irritating performance. Pretty Marta Kristen, the only female in the film, is satisfactory, as are Dewey Martin, Jeff York, Slim Pickens, Royal Dano and Brad Weston in other key assignments. Prominent in the hapless band of Indians whose intentions are never really clear and whose behavior is extremely confusing are Rodolfo Acosta, Dean Fredericks, Pat Hogan and Rafael Campos.

Satisfactory contributions to the production have been made by cameraman Edward Colman, editor Grant K. Smith, art directors Carroll Clark and Marvin Aubrey Davis and composer Oliver Wallace, but none of any special distinction. An engaging tune, "Savage Sam and Me," was written by Terry Gilkyson for the occasion. Bill Anderson was co-producer. *Tube.*

Black Gold

New-talent project and worth program slotting. Boy-wins-girl-and-gusher.

Warner release of Jim Barnet production. Stars Philip Carey, Diane McBain, James Best, Claude Akins, Fay Spain; features William Phipps, Dub Taylor, Ken Mayer, Iron-Eyes Cody, Vincent Barbi, Rusty Wescoatt. Directed by Les-

lie H. Martinson. Screenplay, Bob and Wanda Duncan, from story by Harry Whittington; camera, Harold Stine; editor, Leo H. Shreve; music, Howard Jackson. At WB homeoffice May 15, '63. Running time, **98 MINS.**

Frank McCandless	Philip Carey
Ann Evans	Diane McBain
Jericho Larkin	James Best
Julie	Fay Spain
Chick Carrington	Claude Akins
Albert Mailer	William Phipps
Doc	Dub Taylor
Felker	Ken Mayer
Charlie Two-Bits	Iron-Eyes Cody
Klein	Vincent Barbi
Wilkins	Rusty Wescoatt

"Black Gold" does offer an array of interesting, relatively new faces. It's an actioner for bottom-rung bookings, but calls desperately for tighter editing.

Jim Barnett production seems mainly assembled as a showcase for Philip Carey, Diane McBain, James Best, Fay Spain and Claude Akins, none of whom has seen the light of marquee billing but have had some experience, theatrical and/or television. This kind of vehicle will not catapult them to stardom but nonetheless they suggest promise.

Story line and production technique are plain old-fashioned, being another one about wildcatters versus the oil baron in Oklahoma a few decades back, and it's not difficult to guess who gets both girl and gusher at the end.

Screenplay by Bob and Wanda Duncan springs no surprises and and Leslie H. Martinson's direction might have gotten it on screen in less time. The 98 minutes of celluloid allows for too much lull between lusty action. Martinson does handily with barroom roughhouse and melodramatic catastrophe at the well; dull stretches in between are damaging to pace and impact.

Philip Carey, James Best and Claude Akins are the virile men of the southwest, and the ladies who wind up properly with the right men are Miss McBain and Miss Spain. Akins, the heavy, a robust, handsome personality, finales in the arms of the sheriff.

William Phipps, Dub Taylor, Ken Mayer, Iron-Eyes Cody, Vincent Barbi and Rusty Wescoatt manage to get by in supporting roles. Harold Stine's black-&-white photography and Howard Jackson's music measure up adequately. *Gene.*

A Cause, A Cause D'Une Femme
(Because, Because of a Woman)
(FRENCH)
Paris, May 14.

Fernand Rivers release of Elefilm production. Stars Jacques Charrier. Marie Laforet, Jill Haworth, Juliette Mayniel, Mylene Demongeot, Odile Versois. Directed by Michel Deville. Screenplay, Nina Companeez Deville; camera, Claude Lecomte; editor, Nina Companeez. At Balzac, Paris. Running time, **105 MINS.**

Remy	Jacques Charrier
Agathe	Marie Laforet
Cecilia	Jill Haworth
Chloe	Juliette Mayniel
Lisette	Mylene Demongeot
Nathalie	Odile Versois
Johann	Helmut Griem
Maid	Yvonne Monlaur

Situation comedy deals with a ladies' man caught up on a murder charge and on the run. It has a neat style, pleasant characters and plotting. But it is somewhat overlong with the overactive desire to please by all concerned watering down its impact. But some foreign playoff aspects are there if pruned a bit, plus specialized situations on its general grace.

Accused of murder the hero, Jacques Charrier, takes it on the lam. A host of pretty girls help him clear himself. In the interim he really falls in love. However, there is no comeuppance involved and he goes merrily on his way. Comedy is padded out with love scenes and okay light characterizations.

Charrier is personable but does not quite have the lightness and charm to make his central role airy enough to accept all the women falling at his feet. He is somewhat too plodding to give the role the drive it needs.

Mylene Demongeot cuts a diverting bit as the light-headed, big-hearted girl. Jill Haworth has the proper porcelain childish quality as the doll wife the hero loves. Others are good. Director Michel Deville displays a neat personal touch but has yet to find the right tone of situation comedy, with the right blend of personage insight and sustained narrative.

The pic is sometimes taking but without the firm handling to keep it diverting throughout. Some punch and timing should have Deville emerging one of the staple comedy directors here. *Mosk.*

Die Endlose Nacht
(The Endless Night)
(GERMAN)
Berlin, May 14.

Atlas-Film (Hanns Eckelkamp) release of Will Tremper production, in collaboration with Inter West Film (Wenzel Luedecke) and Hanns Eckelkamp. Features Karin Huebner, Harald Leipnitz, Louise Martini, Paul Esser, Wolfgang Spier. Directed and written by Will Tremper. Camera, Hans Jura; music, Peter Thomas; editor, Susanne Paschen. Preemed at Airport Tempelhof, West Berlin. Running time, **84 MINS.**

Lisa	Karin Huebner
Wolfgang Spitz	Harald Leipnitz
J. M. Schreiber	Paul Esser
Mascha	Louise Martini
Dr. Achtel	Wolfgang Spier
Herbert	Werner Peters
Silvia Stoessl	Hannelore Elsner

Will Tremper rates as one of the few outsiders among German filmmakers. Although he doesn't classify himself "a new waver," he picks unconventional subjects and his films usually have no big stars or big budgets. Two years ago, he directed "Flight to Berlin," which tackled a "boxoffice poison" subject—the divided Germany. Film received kudos but flopped at the b.o. His new film, "The Endless Night," also a rather unconventional (made without prepared script and shot nearly entirely in the huge despatching room of West Berlin airport Tempelhof), may face the same fate.

"Night," which Tremper wrote, directed and produced in collab with Berlin's Wenzel Luedecke and Hanns Eckelkamp of Atlas-Film distributing company (Duisburg), departs from the ordinary feature-type of film. It's just a series of episodes of people stranded at Berlin's airport Tempelhof because of bad weather conditions.

Tremper shows his ability in regard to dialog and brief realistic sequences and that he has an observing eye. What goes against the film's general impression is that he concentrates too much on sex. Nearly all the episodes told here, directly or indirectly, have too much of it, be it unfaithfulness, seduction or flirt. Film, for German standards, has its true merits.

But for the foreign market, it appears too talky and also perhaps too sketchy. *Hans.*

The Sex Criminal
(SWISS)
Zurich, May 12.

Praesens-Film A.G. Zurich release of Praesens (Lazar Wechsler) production. Executive producer, Max Dora. Directed by Franz Schnyder; screenplay, Richard Schweizer, Wolfgang Menge, based on an idea by Schnyder; camera, Emil Berna; music, Walter Baumgartner; editor, Rene Martinet. Features Peter Arens, Franz Matter, Fred Tanner, Mathias Wieman, Walter Kiesler, Margrit Winter, Edwin Maechler, Eva Kotthaus, Pierre Tagmann, Ellen Widmann, Kurt Heintel, Wolfgang Reichmann, Peter Ehrlich, Megge Lehmann, Maximilian Wolters, Olivia Oettli, Eva Mueller, Andrea Teuwen, Gaby Kaufmann, Beat Meyer. At Urban Theatre, Zurich. Running time, **84 MINS.**

(In German and Swiss dialect)

A universal theme, that of sex aberration, adults preying on children and under-age adolescents of both sexes, is the basis of this latest Swiss release. Assertedly based on actual cases from the files of the Zurich police, it is, in all, a commendable effort with an air of authenticity and lack of melodramatic histrionics as assets. However, lack of punch and artistic finesse limits playoff. There are four episodes illustrating different aspects of psychopatic passions. Treatment often appears wooden and contrived. Flat German and Swiss dialog and uneven performances contribute to the lacklustre overall impression.

Opening sequence shows a five-year-old girl being abused by an unknown who is brought to justice thanks to an immediate police report leading to a painstaking tracking-down of the culprit via fingerprints and other clues. Done in semi-documentary style, it offers interesting insights into criminal police methods. However, flashes from an operation of voluntary castration are in bad taste and add an unnecessary shock element. Second episode concerns a sexually frustrated young peasant whose abusal of a little girl remains unreported due to the family's "influence" in the village. A repeat of the crime is prevented at the last minute when the people finally speak up.

Third sequence is about a homosexual's seduction of a teenage boy. He is acquitted at first since denying the guilt and having had no witnesses. The boy is thus stamped a liar until the prosecutor, convinced of his truthfulness, brings the case back to court and manages to have the pervert convicted. Case four shows the seduction of a 14-year-old girl by her stepfather who threatens her not to betray him. The truth is brought to light via contrived coincidences, and the whole sequence appears the most implausible and least convincing in spite of the basic premise's plausibility.

A firmer directorial hand would have been needed to make this entry come off. As it is, it stands little chance for international consumption. Camera work, in black-and-white, is conventional, and editing is okay. *Mezo.*

Cannes Festival

Lord of the Flies
(BRITISH)

Fairly provocative tale about a group of young boys going savage on a desert island. This is of art calibre only if sold smartly.

Cannes, May 14.
Louis Allen-Dana Hodgdon-Two Arts production and release. With James Aubrey, Tom Chapin, Hugh Emwards, Roger Elwin, Tom Gaman. Written and directed by Peter Brook from the book by William Golding. Camera, Tom Hollyman; editor, Brook, J. C. Griel, M. Lubtchansky. At Cannes Film Fest. Running time, **90 MINS.**

Ralph	James Aubrey
Jack	Tom Chapin
Piggy	Hugh Emwards
Roger	Roger Elwin
Simon	Tom Gaman

There were all the elements for a firstrate offbeater here with handles for depth distrib via Goling's best-selling novel from which it was taken. Its theme of young boys reverting to savagery when marooned on a deserted island has its moments of turth, but this pic rates as a near-miss on many counts.

Titles adequately indicate that evacuation in some future war has a group of youngsters surviving an air crash on a tropical island. They meet, and one boy is elected chief, but with dissent from another. Latter says his group will become hunters and they are soon drawing blood from some wild pigs and evolving tales of a monster on the island. The last-named is a dead paratrooper swaying on a ledge.

But soon the hunting group goes completely native and persecutes and even exterminates those of the other group till a final bloody chase of the ex-leader finds them at the feet of some adults. Then they revert to weeping children again.

Peter Brook has coaxed fairly natural performances from his group of English youths. But he has drawn out his tale on a seemingly too schematic level to emerge more than illustration of the book than a film version standing on its own. Thus the savagery versus reason comes on quickly and does not get the more penetrating treatment.

Of course, children have their own canabalistic ways, secrets, cruelty and emotional trusts all mixed up. But the film's handling rarely sorts them out or gives them the dramatic touch to make this either a clear social parable, political allegory or study of instincts.

Lensing is curiously metallic but the on-the-spot shooting in the Puerto Rican jungles and beaches helps. Summing up, the film could find its commercial way on its provocative aspects of child mayhem. Pic was made with U.S. and Puerto Rican funds but with a British director and thesps. Shown at the Cannes Fest as a British pic, it may get British quota standing. *Mosk.*

Hitler? Connais Pas!
(Hitler? Never Heard of Him!)
(FRENCH)

Cannes, May 14.
Chaumiane production and release.
Written and directed by Bertrand Blier.
Camera, Jean-Louis Picavet; editor,
Michele David. At Cannes Film Fest.
Running time, **95 MINS.**

Film goes a good step beyond the current Cinema Truth movement. It orchestrates a series of interviews with 12 young French people into a particular and general reflection of young people today. But there are no teaching or forced outlooks here. This shows that basically man is primarily interested in man, and this type of film can reveal and absorb even if it is practically one long series of closeups, with people talking.

. Writer-director Bertrand Blier picked types that interested him and also mirrored certain attitudes and human aspects present not only in the French but generally in humanity. After months of talks, he filmed each for one day answering questions on the same topics. None ever met except in the editing of the film and on celluloid.

So what does this give? It gives out with some entertaining, poignant, unsettling, reassuring as well as ambiguous and clear, as is life, aspects of these people and people in general. The faces eventually become a familiar terrain as the editing cuts back and forth between them on the various subjects such as sex, jobs, parents, habits, outlooks and desires. They range in age from about 16 to 23.

There is the amoral pretty little girl with countless adventures to her credit as a seeming form of revolt against boredom. She also crassly feels an atomic war might serve to save the best of people and get rid of the others. Besides her, there is a whining wide-eyed mother who almost seems to caress victimization, a wide-eyed inarticulate 16-year-old and an aggressive, self-assured model.

The men run from the self-absorbed type to the drifter with some pocket money, to the breathless, wide-eyed mother's boy and others. If they may emerge types, they are never ridiculous or exploited but an aspect of the multifaceted sides of youth today.

Title may infer that there was hardly any interest in society, politics or anything that did not directly affect their own needs or personal desires. Perhaps the director can be scored for not bringing up politics but it is evident from the film that there would have been no true coherent response. It could be said he might have picked others, so inclined, but those shown seem a good representative choice.

The director also intercuts reactions of several to what others are saying, though they had never met. But this is not cheating either since it uses the essence of filmic montage and these reactions are on the subject in view at the moment. Though practically all in closeups, it was shot in a studio for fine highlighting of the faces. Blier displays a flair for rhythm and building-up drama, comedy and interest mainly by words but with the right balance of the angle of the faces and the intercutting.

This might be the furthest this type of interview material can go. Film may remain a milestone in this type of pix making. Extensive subtitling would make this a difficult item for abroad and strictly for specialized slotting, with tv also a good outlet. It might also be a good example of an approach towards a look at American youth today. *Mosk.*

Az Prijde Kocour
(One Day, A Cat . . .)
(CZECH-COLOR-SCOPE)

Cannes, May 14.
Czech State Film production and release. With Jan Werich, Vlastimil Bordsky, Jiri Sovak, Emilie Vasaryova. Directed by Vojtech Jasny. Screenplay, Jiri Bdrecka, Jan Werich, Jasny; camera (Agfacolor), Jaroslav Kučera; editor, Jan Chaloupek. At Cannes Film Fest, Running time, **110 MINS.**
Oliva .... Jan Werich
Robert .... Vlastimil Bordsky
Director .... Jiri Sovak
Diana .... Emilie Vasaryova

Czech fantasy shows a growing lightness in touch, growing budgets, expert color handling and a sense of humor which butters up the message in this amiable pic. Deft musical numbers are also worked into this. But its sentimentalism, if acceptable, and its repetitive aspects, peg this mainly for moppet situations abroad, if adroitly cut. It would find harder going in regular spots with arty theatre chances slim.

In a small town abound a bunch of stylized but recognizable human types. The advent of a magician with a cat that wears glasses develops the angle that if the cat removes its glasses, people take on the color fitting their personalities. Red, of course, is love, gray, is for cheats, yellow for adulterous ones and purple stands for the unstable.

Normal people remain the same. An inventive ballet sequence, with a mixture of the multicolored people, is a highspot but it gets encored a bit too much. In this a good-natured teacher, hounded by a petty, hypocritical director, falls in love with a girl in the magician's troupe but finally loses her. All the townspeople are chastened and some even change.

Into this can be read a slap at complacency in high socialist bureaucratic circles and a need for sincere self-criticism. But it is done with the influence of the Western cinema. Its clever feel for fantasy, bright progression and general grace are Middle European. Jan Werich brings his forceful presence and charm to the fore to play the revealing magician.

Acting is uniformly right in style and direction, managing to keep this from being maudlin. But its preciosity at times, and length, limit this for foreign marts even though is should emerge a highly popular item in the East both on its content and general entertainment level. *Mosk.*

El Buen Amor
(The Good Love)
(SPANISH)

Cannes, May 14.
Alfredo Matas-Jet Films production and release. With Simon Andreu. Marta Del Val, Enriqueta Carballeira, Sergio Mendizabal, Maria Sanchez. Written and directed by Francisco Regueiri. Camera, Juan Julio Baena; editor, Pablo G. Del Amo. At Cannes Film Fest. Running time, **86 MINS.**

Jose .... Simon Andreu
Carmen .... Marta Del Val
Juanita .... Enriquetq Carballeira
Fralle .... Sergio Mendiazabal
Chica .... Maria Sanchez

A gentle, observant pic is chalked up by Francisco Regueiro for his first film. It concerns a pair of adolescent would-be lovers off on a Sunday trek to another town. An X-ray of them, their desires and the effects of their backgrounds and the country on their idyll constantly perk this up when it lags. Thus, its fragile qualities slant this for Spanish-language spots abroad or some specialized situations if well handled.

The couple goes off on a rickety train. The trip is well documented as they neck, have moments of remorse or shame at being watched, or separate if a familiar face is seen. The two finally arrive in the town of Toledo. Here they see the sights as well as slowly divulge themselves.

A playful fight has them apart till they meet up before the train and eventually reveal their true feelings. Pic shows the French New Wave and Cinema Truth influences in seemingly improvised scenes, jump cutting and its statement about the times through youth.

The oppressive church, overdone prudishness, omni-present police and the shadow of the Revolution, though they were children then, looms as they go about their innocent escapade. Marta Del Val has the spontaneous freshness and emotional strength needed for her role while Simon Andreu has forthrightness as the boy if he tends towards mannerims.

Highly mobile camerawork is effective as is the editing. A first film of promise, if still lacking the means to make a more dramatic impact. It could herald a freer, fresher film movement from the Iberian peninsula. *Mosk.*

Los Venerables Todos
(The Venerable Ones)
(ARGENTINIAN)

Cannes, May 14.
NIC release of Jorge Alberto Garber production. With Lautaro Murua, Walter Vidarte, Fernanda Mistral, Maurice Jouvet, Betto Gianola, Paul Parini. Written and directed by Manuel Antin. Camera, Ricardo Aronovich; editor, Jose Serra. At Cannes Film Fest. Running time, **75 MINS.**
Ismael .... Walter Vidarte
Lucas .... Lautaro Murua
Dora .... Fernanda Mistral
Quesada .... Maurice Jouvet
Ruiz .... Betto Gianola
Efraim .... Paul Parini

This Argentine pic appears too consciously trying to obscure a tale and theme that could have been told straight-forwardly to have it come off. It may be the bad worldwide effects of that French pic, "Last Year In Marienbad." Present emulation remains mainly a lingo item, at best, for the foreign market.

A group of supposed buddies working together in an office systematically make a cruel butt of the most reserved member of the group. Latter is loved by a girl who realizes what is happening and even gives herself to the ringleader to have him let up. It ends in tragedy when the victim kills his tormentor in a fight with the implication that maybe the latter willed it.

And there are intimations that the lonely but cruel leader, followed by his henchmen in everything to escape the boredom of pettiness of their lives, could be a study of Peronism—also why it existed. Or maybe it's a look at how evil can easily overcome good.

Time is shuffled and people think about the past or near-present within the same scene a la "Marienbad." Pacing is slow and measured as is the acting trying to give a dimension to something that is mainly social and psychological. So this emerges an experimental miss. *Mosk.*

Tutune
(Tobacco)
(BULGARIAN)

Cannes, May 14.
Bulgarofilm production and release. With Nevena Kokanova, Yurdan Matev, Miroslava Stoyanova, Ivan Kassabov. Directed by Nicolas Korabov. Screenplay, Dimitri Dimov, Korabov; camera, Valo Radev; music, Vassil Kassandjiev. At Cannes Film Fest. Running time, **145 MINS.**
Irene .... Nevena Kokanova
Boris .... Yurdan Matev
Girl .... Misoslava Stoyanova
Dinko .... Ivan Kassabov

Chunky, overlong melodrama reaches back to the pre-war Russian-type film in its look at a period of Bulgar history that preceded the Communist takeover as well as castigating the grasping capitalist element and filling the tale with moments of crowd action and technical bravura. However, it does have same telling visual moments and some good acting. But this looms mainly a home product.

A climber, really in love with a young student, marries the daughter of a tobacco-curing factory owner. His wife goes mad and he takes over the business and the other girl who is loved by a communist. He slowly degrades her into using both her charm and bodily wiles to get ahead.

During the war all the characters are again brought into coincidental contact in this sprawling, epic affair. The girl ends up killing herself at the end after the death of her husband, the communist who loved her and others. This is a departure since it seems to intimate that she could not have changed even if conditions had.

The director displays obvious means at his disposal and a solid sense for movement and composition. In spite of the one-sided aspect of it all, there is a lyrical note at times and a continuity of interest mainly because of its pictorial flair. It again may indicate that the Eastern Bloc is falling back to social realism. *Mosk.*

Codine
(RUMANIAN—FRENCH—COLOR)

Cannes, May 14.
Como Films - Tamara-Unifilm-Romfilm production and release. With Alexandru Virgil Platon, Nelly Borgeaud, Francoise Brion, Maurice Sarfati, Germaine Kerjean. Directed by Henri Colpi. Screenplay, Yves Jamiaque, Dumitru Carabat, Colpi from book by Panait Istrati; camera (Eastmancolor), Marcel Weiss; editor, Jasmine Chasney. At Cannes Film Fest. Running time, **97 MINS.**
Codine .... Alexandre Virgil Platon
Zoitza .... Nelly Borgeaud
Irene .... Francoise Brion
Alexis .... Maurice Sarfati
Anastasie .... Germaine Kerjean

A gently nostalgic tale of life in the Bucharest slums of 1900 also embodies a nice flair for narration. It's really a portrait of the friendship between a little boy and a tortured giant of a man. This is a bit conventional but has the visual solidity and familiar if taking story for general distribution chances in various markets as well as specialized possibilities if given a personalized selling campaign.

"Codine" is a fiery man who believes in complete honesty among friends. He has killed a friend once for betrayal and served 10 years in prison. His miserly mother is also something he hates. Into his life comes a little boy who becomes his friend and admirer. The boy is innocent and learns about life from Codine. He sees the brutality, unemployment and human pettiness of the times as well as a certain nobility in the man himself, who manages to keep alive by sheer brute strength.

Codine finally kills another man who has betrayed him and is killed by his rapacious mother who fears losing some hoarded money to him. Color is nicely hued and acting is uneven but is good by the boy and giant. A cholera epidemic is the strong dramatic base of the pic.

French director Henri Colpi helmed this coproduction. He has taken a Rumanian classic and given it reverent filming. It just lacks the lyric sweep that a western filmmaker might have given it. But this is a more than honorable **work and one of the few East-West coproductions that shows positive results.** *Mosk.*

Carambolages
(Carom Shots)
(FRENCH)
Cannes, May 14.
Gaumont release of Gaumont International-Trianon production. Stars Jean-Claude Brialy, Louis De Funes; features Sophie Daumier, Alfred Adam, Anne Tonietti, Michel Serrault. Directed by Marcel Bluwal. Screenplay, Pierre Tcherina, Michel Audiard, Fred Kassak, Bluwal from book by Bluwal; camera, Andre Bac; editor, Genevieve Vaury. At Cannes Film Fest. Running time, **90 MINS.**
Martin .... Jean-Claude Brialy
Charolais .... Louis De Funes
Danielle .... Ann Tonietti
Solange .... Sophie Daumier
Beaumanoir .... Alfred Adam
Baudu .... Michel Serrault

This comedy is a bit reminiscent of the hit Broadway play, "How to Succeed in Business," with the climber trying murder rather than shrewd manipulations. However the lightness of touch is lacking and an attempt to make it all logical, instead of creating its own mood, has this only intermittently funny or entertaining.

Film has some chances on the home grounds with foreign placement more doubtful. It lacks the robustness and originality for arty houses and remains mainly a dualer item for the U.S. Direction is too heavyhanded to give it the ease and visual comedic flair it needs.

An ambitious young man gets the vain ear of the boss of a French equivalent of a Madison Avenue outfit. However, he sees advancement eluding him. He then suddenly begins to resort to mayhem. His plans misfire but the boss is killed accidently. And a series of unintended accidents and mistakes have each boss killed off till he reaches the top.

Louis De Funes, as the high pressure, fuming, perfectly double-taking boss, is the comic highspot of this uneven satire. Jean-Claude Brialy is acceptable as the pusher if he lacks a certain verve to help push the film on to a deeper plane of comic nonchalance. It will need plenty of selling to get it anywhere abroad.

Pic was selected as a competing film at the Cannes Film Fest.
Mosk.

The Diabolic Empress
(FORMOSAN-COLOR-SCOPE)
Cannes, May 21.
Run-Run Shaw production and release. Stars Li Ii-Hua; features Chao Lei, Chang Chung-Wen, Chen Yun-Hua, Lo Chi. Directed by Li Han-Hsiang. Screenplay, Chen Chi-Jui; camera (Eastmancolor), K. Nishimoto; Wang Shun. At Cannes Film Fest. Running time, **129 MINS.**
Wu Tse-Tien .... Li Li-Hua
Emperor .... Chao Lei
Hsuan .... Chang Chung-Wen
Ho Lan .... Lo Chi

Court intrigues in 17th Century China are the center of this elegantly made pic. Rich in hues, court ceremony and intrigues, it lacks the vigor and deeper penetration. Film looks good for nothing but language spots abroad.

A concubine, who has taken the veil, is brought back to the court of the son of her ex-lover. She has had two sons by the latter. She takes over the Emperor's court, has her two sons killed and becomes the head of a new dynasty.

All of this unfolds regally but a bit too slowly. Hence, this remains more a feast for the eye than the intellect. Direction is solid and acting pleasant, but it all remains too one-dimensional.
Mosk.

Kertes Hazak Uteaja
(A Cosy Cottage)
(HUNGARIAN)
Cannes, May 21.
Hungaro Film production and release. With Margit Bara, Gyorgy Palos, Miklos Gabor. Directed by Tamas Fejer. Screenplay, Istvan Csurka; camera, Istvan Mildebrand; editor, Zoltan Farkas. At Cannes Film Fest. Running time, **80 MINS.**
Palotas .... Miklos Gabor
Wife .... Margit Bara
Husband .... Gyorgy Palos

It seems that there are emotional troubles in Magyar suburbia also. But this skimpy pic does not have the needed observation or pacing to make it any more than a local item. If it has some good patches, this also does not emerge a pic worth film fest attention.

An engineer goes to a small town as part of his job. He meets the wife of a colleague who seems dissatisfied. She feels she is growing old and has not found what she wants in her home life despite good material means. An affair develops between her and the visitor. But it turns out to be a passing fancy, and he goes back to his wife and kids while she decides to leave her husband and go on her own.

Film unfortunately plods along **instead of delving more deeply into the woman's problems. However, it does denote a tendency to treat contemporary problems. Pic** may mean more in Hungary, in its depiction of unrest and disorientation among the more well-off bureaucrats.

Its export chances seem slim except for possible language spots in the foreign market. If compe-

tent acting and simple, the theme is not resolved. The director just lacks the needed punch. Also, he is not helped enough by a routine script. It is technically competent.
Mosk.

Seppuku
(Hara-Kiri)
(JAPANESE-GRANDSCOPE)
Cannes, May 21.
Shochiku production and release. With Tatsuya Nakadai, Shima Iwashita, Akira Ishihama, Yoshio Inaba. Directed by Masaki Kobayashi. Screenplay, Shinobu Hashimoto; camera, Yoshio Miyajima; editor, Hisashi Sagara. At Cannes Film Fest. Running time, **135 MINS.**
Hanshiro .... Tatsuya Nakadai
Miho .... Shima Iwashita
Motome .... Akira Ishihama
Jinnai .... Yoshio Inaba
Kageyu .... Rentaro Mikuni
Tango .... Masao Mishima
Hikokuro .... Tetsuro Tamba

A sombre tragedy giving off deep rage against militarism, political systems and beliefs that do not allow for a rational human outlook or future change is brought off in this stunning film. Its very lack of concessions make this one of those brilliant Japanese films that find hardgoing abroad. However, with more hardy U.S. distribs this could well emerge an important arty house item.

In spite of its mayhem and fancy swordplay, the film's measured pace and relentless look at violence, without exploiting it, may disconcert regular audiences. So it calls for specialized bookings and handling but could well be worth it.

In 17th Century Japan, the powerful centralizing Shogun breaks up various self-sufficient clans and creates a flock of rootless ronins, samurai sans masters, who roam the countryside. Some threaten to commit hara-kiri. One clan feels this is against the idealistic military shield of the samurai. Hence, when a young man comes begging they decide to force him to perform it. They make him do it with a wooden blade. This scene is shown unsparingly to underline the senselessness of this sacrifice of life.

In comes an older samurai later and he, too, is to be allowed to commit hara-kiri. But he tells a tale of how he knew the other man who died atrociously. It turns out to be his son-in-law and the man only tried to beg to save his sick son. He had beseeched a delay but it's not handed to him by the clan.

Director Masaki Kobayashi shows a sure sustained hand in building the past and present in a coherent pattern that reveals and moves as it shows men being destroyed in a tragic setup that will eventually be changed but is still one that creates these destinies. It ends in carnage as the would-be hara-kiri victim takes on the whole house, and is finally killed.

But the head of the clan covers up the deed and tries to make him out a hero who died quietly by his own hand within the code. It shows up the hypocrisy in this militaristic philosophy.

If the film probably has deeper connotations on its home grounds, it still has a universal ring to it.

Definitely this is not for the squeamish. Pic is technically audacious in its spacial scenes and cutting on various levels of past and present. Its acting has the right stern bigger-than-life quality that still keeps its people within bounds. Pic depicts their good, petty, great

and aspiring qualities without making them cyphers. Its violence is cathartic rather than exploited.
Long.

I Fidanzati
(The Fiancees)
(ITALIAN)
Cannes, May 21.

Titanus release of Titanus-Sicilia Spa 22 Decembre production. With Carlo Cabrini, Anna Canzi. Written and directed by Ermanno Olmi. Camera, Lamberto Caimi; editor, Carla Colombo. At Cannes Film Fest. Iunning time, **84 MINS.**
Giovanni .... Carlo Cabrini
Liliana .... Anna Canzi

In his second film Ermanno Olmi displays a feeling for style and visual insight that makes him one of the best young directors practicing in Italy today and adds another notch for the Italo film upbeat. It's very subtlety and assurance m i g h t make this primarily for arty theatres abroad. It has the deeper themes and newness in style and outlook for arty audiences. But depth distrib looks limited.

A young worker has a chance for advancement in going to work in a factory in southern Italy. A long engagement with a girl is going a bit sour and he leaves her. The perking industrialization in southern Italy is blocked out as well as the man's solitude at first and his acceptance of conditions and a renewal of a feeling with his fiancee through letters.

They finally express themselves and find a way towards final marriage. It seems one-dimensional but director Olmi keeps attention on his almost inarticulate characters by k n o w i n g observation, a flawless grasp of scene juxtaposition and a fluid break in time and space to show m e m o r i e s and the present mingling freely.

The personages are always interesting and made absorbing by Olmi's obvious concern for them. The boredom suffered by the new and displaced workers is not the theme of the film. This treats both the need for individual change in a developing world as well as an altering of conditions. Sharp little incidents to underline the financee's feelings plus the silent flashbacks and daydreams, and the feel of work blend all into a gentle look at a certain aspect of Italian life today.

It has the incisiveness to raise it to make this international in scope. The non-actors fit into the technique and scope of the film. An offbeater but with a newness and clarity in style to underline the changing narrative sense of filmmaking today. It is technically excellent. *Mosk.*

Le Rat D'Amerique
(American Adventurer)
(FRENCH-COLOR-
(TOTALVISION)
Cannes, May 21.

Pathe release of Franco London Film-Madeleine Films-Zebra Films production. Stars Charles Aznavour, Marie Laforet; features Franco Fabrizi. Directed by Jean - Gabriel Albicocco. Screenplay. Jacques Lanzmann, Albicocco from book by Lanzmann; camera (Eastmancolor), Quinto, Albicocco; editor, Boris Lewin. At Cannes Film Fest. Running time, **95 MINS.**
Charles .... Charles Aznavour
Maria .... Marie Laforet
Paul .... Franco Fabrizi

Vague story allows for roaming around a good part of South America in this adventure opus. Coincidence is stretched, narrative is curt and characterization is thrown to the four winds. Also. the action is either forced or sporadic and underlined by one of the most intrusive, overripe music scores in

years. So this looks mainly a possible playoff item abroad on its locales, color and large screen.

A young Frenchman disembarks in Paraguay to see a rich uncle, and remake his life. But the relatives turn out to be petty, cheap and lacking in any generosity. Scene is false and fabricated to have him on his uppers in the teeming lowlife aspects of the country. He gets involved with a girl and in gun running which leads to a flight across the border when federal troops attack.

He and the girl manage to be saved by an old railroad guard. Then comes a meeting with a shifty Frenchman, prison for the man and concubinage for the girl and murder of her forced lover after the prison release. He hides out in a copper mine where she manages to find him. They finally amass enough money for a trip back to Europe.

Charles Aznavour has a timid presence but not the robustness needed for the role of the wanderer. Marie Laforet displays an expressive face as the girl in his life, who is the only loyal thing in the pic.

There is some excellent imagery but this falls between the stools of an adventure pic, a look at man in elemental episodes and the so-called "cinema truth" aspects of recreated actions with real people. None are adequately assimilated. So this turns out to be an erratic adventure pic with some good imagery, forced progression and okay acting. It looms as a fair bet at home, but with harder going abroad. *Mosk.*

Jak Bye Kochana
(The Art of Loving)
(POLISH)
Cannes, May 21.

Polski State Film release of Kamera production. Stars Barbara Krafftowna, Zbigniew Cybulski; features Artur Mlodnicki, Wienczyslaw Glinski, Wieslaw Golas. Directed by Wojciech J. Has. Screenplay, Kazmierz Brandys from his own novel; camera, Stefan Matyjaskiewicz; editor, Sofia Zwornick. At Cannes Film Fest. Running time, **100 MINS.**
Felicja .... Barbara Krafftowna
Wiktor .... Zbigniew Cybulski
Tomasz .... Artur Mlodnicki
Traveler .... Wienczyslaw Glinski
Officer .... Wieslaw Golas

A tale of memory and its continual presence in life is adroitly fashioned in this film. The flashbacks are supple and direct and the film is clear if somewhat talky. It perhaps has too many subtle allusions to recent history for general foreign audiences. It remains a specialized export item.

An actress is on a trip to Paris from Warsaw and reflects on the last few years of her life. It goes back to the occupation and her hiding of a fellow actor who has supposedly killed a collaborator. He is weak and a bit cowardly, but suffers most from not having an audience for his vanity, ego and supposed bravery.

After the war, he leaves her but finds that he has been accused of cowardice. He finally commits suicide as she clears herself of a collaboration charge and becomes a popular actress. But on her trip she finds a simple communion with another passenger and a realization of her life through reliving her past.

This also has solid feeling for the recent past as well as telling notations on the Polish flamboyant character and thirst for needless heroism. The director gives this a solid mounting to bring out its theme clearly in showing the effects of war on a personal rather than collective level.

Acting carries the brunt of this subtle film with a finely measured, revealing performance of the woman by Barbara Krafftowna and the empty actor by Zbigniew Cybulski. It has a neat narrative style that is literary but still well sustained via its images. In short, a difficult offbeater. *Mosk.*

El Otro Cristobal
(The Other Christopher)
(CUBAN)
Cannes, May 21.

Empresa-ICAIC-Test Films-Adam Ulrych production and release. With Jean Bouise, Alden Knight, Bertina Acevedo, Pierre Chousset, Marc Dudicourt. Written and directed by Armand Gatti. Camera, Henri Alekan; music, Gilberto Valdes. At Cannes Film Fest. Running time, **115 MINS.**
Cristobal .... Jean Bouise
Anastasio .... Alden Knight
Virgin .... Bertina Acevedo

A French filmmaker is responsible for Cuba's first bow at a major film fest. Film obviously has had great means at its disposal and is a mixture of surrealism, satire and cosmic comedy. Though having some brilliant spots, this is somewhat too sketchy and confused overall to have many foreign possibilities except for Eastern Bloc countries and possibly some Latino circuits.

Film begins in heaven with the angels singling out a dictator in some mythical Latin American country whose main concern is building a canal with money from its big, rich neighbor. He is killed in an uprising and in purgatory hatches a plot to take over heaven which he does. He changes the name to hell but is finally defeated by a sailor who also has been giving the dictatorial reps trouble on earth.

So its little potshots at the U.S. and its hand in imposing its standards of living on its Latin neighbors are rather familiar and not even biting. It appears to be mainly interested in satirizing Latin strongman governments.

Snatches of the film, such as chases and crowd uprisings, have comic and mixed dramatic flair. The feeling for plastic lensing values, unusual filmic language and inventiveness are sometimes effective. But it is just too top-heavy with too many themes and effects. Eventually this bogs down in its own abandon, intellectualism and symbolism.

A Virgin Mary who joins the revolutionaries on earth, the main character symbolizing a sort of new Christopher Columbus coming back to get embroiled with the lands he discovered, simple human goodness vs. exploitation, and other aspects, make up this unusual but overloaded film that marks Cuba's first international airing. It is not a success. Music is racy and tops. *Mosk.*

Ouranos
(Glory Sky)
(GREEK)
Cannes, May 21.

Vassili Drakaki production and release. With Emilie Pitta, Phedon Georgitsis, Takis Emmanouil, Nikos Tsahirisis. Directed by Takis Kanellopoulos. Screenplay, Georges Kitopoulos, Kanellopoulos; camera, Gregoire Danilis, Giovanni Veriana; music, Argyris Kounadis. At Cannes Film Fest. Running time, **90 MINS.**
Sophie .... Emilie Pitta
Stratos .... Phedon Georgitsis
Prof. .... Takis Emmanouil
Yango .... Nikos Tsahirisis

An insistence on overlong, posed shots, a too slow tempo and self-indulgent direction make this film pretentious rather than dramatically valid and humanly taking. A platoon during the early part of Greece's losing fight against Italy in the last war is the pretext of this sombre pic. However, with all its faults, the film unveils a definite production talent as soon as attention is paid to the subject rather than in trying to achieve an arty pic at any cost.

This remains a film with slight arty chances abroad on its intermittent shafts of poetry too often obscured by too measured, heavy-handed direction. A group of soldiers come dumbly up against a stronger enemy. Their life seems to be mainly waiting, and brief periods of battles. Then it is over, and they go home defeated to undergo occupation.

The director has relied on long held closeups and artily staged group shots to try to get a tragic significance and stylized purity. But this begins to wear. And the lack of character and true dramatic insight soon make this a group of fine shots rather than a progressive tale.

Actors do have a slight human dimension in spite of the directorial static approach with technical credits of a good order. It does show a budding Greek talent that will have to set its sights lower to achieve the best results. *Mosk.*

Alvorada
(Alvorada)
(GERMAN—COLOR)
Cannes, May 28.

Constantin release of Mannesmann production. Directed and written by Hugo Niebeling. Camera (Eastmancolor), Antonio Estervao, Anders Lembcke, Herbert Mueller; music, Oskar Sala; editor, Gerfrud Petermann. At Cannes Film Fest. Running time, **75 MINS.**

This full-length documentary pic was West Germany's official entry at the 1963 Cannes Fest. Directed and written by 32-year-old Hugo Niebeling. "Alvorada" already has stirred international attention for it nearly walked off with the Oscar last April. Losing then to "The Black Fox," an American production, the film, after all, qualified itself as the best non-American documentary in the Oscar derby.

"Alvorada" dedicates itself to Brazil. It gives a substantial survey of the Brazilian people, the country's different landscapes, modern cities and old towns, and her arts and culture. It especially shows this South American state's rising industry. All this isn't done in a reporter's style. There's little narration. Niebeling's aim was to give impressions beyond information. In fact, he aimed at letting the foreign viewer personally "discover" Brazil.

Film mainly benefits from its

outstanding color photography. Some of the Eastmancolor shots are indeed breathtakingly beautiful. The editing is superb and there's also a certain plus about Oskar Sala's electronic music.

Film, all in all, is very pretentious and both technically and artistically it's above the current German average. Pic has its weaknesses, too. Some may find the film overly pretentious and too jerky at times. For the screening there, the running time was cut from 83 to 75 minutes. "Alvorada," incidentally, was financed by the German steel factories of Mannesmann.

Sheherazade
(FRENCH-SUPERPANORAMA 70)
(Color)

Cannes, May 21.
Cinedis release of Speva Film-Cine Alliance-Filmsonor-Tecisa-Dear Film production. Stars Anna Karina, Gerard Barray; features Antonio Vilar, Marilu Tolo. Directed by Pierre Gaspard-Huit. Screenplay, Marc-Gilbert Sauvajon, Gaspard-Huit; camera (Eastmancolor), Christian Matras; editor, Louisette Hautecoeur. At Cannes Film Fest. Running time, 120 MINS.
Sheherazade .... Anna Karina
Renaud .... Gerard Barray
Haroun .... Antonio Vilar
Shirin .... Marilu Tolo

First French pic in 70m has some colorful and sharp lensing but too simple a storyline and treatment for anything but playoff chances abroad on its process and exotic qualities. Despite the screen size, there is only intermittent action and it looks probably a better bet at home.

Long ago a European emissary to a Moorish Sultan, to insure free roads to the Holy Land, saves a girl called Sheherazade and falls madly in love with her. But she is promised to the Sultan. Conspirators have them banished but it is through them the Sultan is saved, though mortally wounded, and they are reunited.

There is good color and the usual lush and fantasy-like court scenes. But actress Anna Karina seems too frisky and coltish for this sort of old-fashioned adventure film that needed an exotic type. Desert scenes, when the lovers are banished, fit the big screen well as do some court dance scenes. But there is not enough true adventure or bombastic action segments to give it a blockbuster flair.

This picks up Sheherazade after her Thousand and One Nights stories. It is a one-dimensional, lush love and adventure tale rather than a true fantasy as its title seems to imply. Film has all the tongue-in-cheek dramatics of yore but without a true dynamic dash either in direction and acting to make it a cut above the usual sand and spear epics of this genre. But the 70m process and color are good. *Mosk.*

Optimistitcheskaia Traguedia
(Optimistic Tragedy)
(RUSSIAN)

Cannes, May 28.
Mosfilm production and release. With Margarita Volodina, Viatcheslav Tikhonov, Boris Andreev, Vsevelod Sanaev. Directed by Samson Samsonov. Screenplay, Sophie Vichnievskaia, Samsonov from play by Vsevelod Vichnievsky; camera, Vladimir Monakhov; music, Vassill Dekhterev. At Cannes Film Fest. Running time, 112 MINS.

Commissar .... Margarita Volodina
Alexel .... Viatcheslav Tikhonov
Presenter .... Boris Andreev
Dumb One .... Vsevelod Sanaev

Main plus in this look at the Russian Revolution is its black and white 70m format which gives it a true snap and size. But otherwise, it is an overdone and propagandistic look at the revoluton sans the true lyric collective sweep inherent in pre-war pix of this kind after which it is fashioned. It appears mainly for the home market.

A female commissar is sent among a bunch of anarchistic sailors in 1918 to weld them into a fighting unit and help save the revolution. She first shoots a would-be rapist in defense and then goes out to battle with the men to slowly win their respect.

Film resolutely is set against any individuality and the anarchists, without any chance of conversion, are wiped out. The commissar finally dies in combat against foreign anti-revolutionary troops to be hoisted up before the men to a heavenly chorus background.

Taken from a play, this film shows it via its prolonged talk scenes and lack of visual flair (despite its size) until the battle scenes. Acting is the usual overstated kind. Also, there is an attempt to mix music, heroic posing and epic events in a try for a poetic, romantic look at history.

But it just does not quite come off because of a lack of true filmic dash plus the mannered acting. *Mosk.*

The List of Adrian Messinger

Bizarre murder mystery with offbeat exploitation gimmicks and names. Profitable b.o. angles at expense of story values. Prospects good.

Hollywood, May 21.
Universal release of Edward Lewis production. Stars Tony Curtis, Kirk Douglas, Burt Lancaster, Robert Mitchum, Frank Sinatra, George C. Scott, Dana Wynter, Clive Brook; features Herbert Marshall, Gladys Cooper. Directed by John Huston. Screenplay, Anthony Veiller, based on story by Philip MacDonald; camera, Joe MacDonald; editor, Terry O. Morse; music, Jerry Goldsmith; asst. director, Tom Shaw. Reviewed at Screen Directors Guild Theatre, May 21, '63. Running time, 98 MINS.
Gethrin .... George C. Scott
Jocelyn .... Dana Wynter
Marquis of Gleneyre ...... Clive Brook
Mrs. Karoudjian .... Gladys Cooper
Sir Wilfred Lucas ..... Herbert Marshall
Raoul Le Borg .... Jaccques Roux
Adrian Messenger .... John Merivale
Mr. Karoudjian .... Marcel Dalio
Inspector Pike .... Bernard Archard
Derek .... Walter Anthony Huston
Carstairs .... Roland D. Long
Character delineations by Tony Curtis, Kirk Douglas, Burt Lancaster Robert Mitchum, Frank Sinatra

The novelty devices designed to ignite "The List of Adrian Messenger" commercially backfire against it artistically. The result is a bizarre, but curiously irritating film experience. Discerning picturegoers will be annoyed to see distracting casting excesses mar a basically enthralling murder msytery otherwise executed with considerable cinematic vitality by director John Huston and staff. Yet, in spite of its major shortcomings, the Edward Lewis production and Universal release has the marquee might and offbeat allure to score favorably at the wicket windows.

Anthony Veiller's screenplay, based on a story by Philip MacDonald, is a kind of straight-laced version of "Kind Hearts and Coronets." It is the story of a retired British Intelligence officer's efforts to nab a killer who has ingeniously murdered 11 men who represent obstacles to his goal—the acquisition of a huge fortune to which he will become heir as soon as he eliminates the 12th obstacle, the 12-year-old grandson of his aged uncle, the wealthy Marquis of Gleneyre. The crimes have been accepted by the authorities as accidents until victim-to-be number 10, prior to his own "accidental" death, gets suspicious and activates the sleuthing machinery.

The film hums along smoothly and captivatingly until the killer, having disposed of number 11, shows up at the estate of the Marquis, where he plans to dispose of the lad from the inside. Here the story begins to fall apart. Since both Scotland Yard and our principal investigator (George C. Scott) are at this time fully aware of who and where their man is, and what he is up to, it is an incredibly contrived story distortion to suppose that they would let him roam about freely for several days—seriously jeopardizing the lives of several parties. The picture thus collapses in the final third of its course.

An even mare damaging miscue, in view of the fact that it seems to have been commercially motivated and unnecessarily leads the audience into a guessing game that not only distracts from the progress of the storyline but hinders believability, is the utilization of four stars who are hidden behind facial disguises in fundamentally inconsequential roles. In the first place, the artificiality of these putty faces is instantly apparent and, since there is no reason for these minor characters to be hiding behind grotesque masks, it makes no sense to the audience from a story viewpoint. Secondly, there is no reason for anyone but the killer to be disguising himself, and the fact that there seem to be disguises all over the place makes the murderer's use of it less provocative or effective. Thirdly, all this putty peeling begins to get downright monotonous towards the end. This casting brainstorm regretably turns out to be an artistic nuisance.

Some of the acting is first rate. Scott is especially convincing. Dana Wynter is marvelous to look at as the young heir's widowed mother. Clive Brook comes out of a 26-year retirement to portray the Marquis, and he does a sound job of it. The director's son, Walter Anthony, makes it a third generation on the screen for the gifted Huston family, and performs commendably. Others of prominence and value are Jacques Roux, Gladys Cooper, Herbert Marshall and John Merivale.

Of the five stars who "guest," Kirk Douglas has the major assignment and carries it off colorfully and credibly. The others are Tony Curtis, Burt Lancaster, Robert Mitchum and Frank Sinatra. Only Mitchum is easily recognizable beneath the facial stickum.

Huston has directed the film with style and flair, and has benefitted enormously from Joe MacDonald's agile and artistic lens employment. Valuable contribu-

tions have also been made by Editor Terry O. Morse, the art directing battery of Alexander Golitzen, Stephen Grimes and George Webb, European pohtographer Ted Scaife, and composer Jerry Goldsmith, whose eerie musical theme is provocative and haunting and could become an immensely popular item in the record market. Last, but not least, credit is due makeupman Bud Westmore for his concealment of several of the most familiar faces of the twentieth century. *Tube.*

Irma La Douce
(PANAVISION—COLOR)

Engaging non-musical farce from the French legit musicomedy. Good b.o. contender but not Wilder's best form.

United Artists release of Billy Wilder production. Stars Jack Lemmon, Shirley MacLaine; features Lou Jacobi, Bruce Yarnell, Herschel Bernardi, Hope Holiday, Joan Shawlee. Directed by Wilder. Screenplay, Wilder, I.A.L. Diamond, based on play by Alexandre Breffort; camera (Technicolor), Joseph L Shelle; editor, Daniel Mandell; music, Andre Previn; asst. director, Hal Polaire. Reviewed at Directors Guild of America, May 31, '63. Running time, **147 MINS.**

Nestor .... Jack Lemmon
Irma La Douce .... Shirley MacLaine
Moustache .... Lou Jacobi
Hippolyte .... Bruce Yarnell
Inspector LeFevre .... Herschel Bernardi
Lolita .... Hope Holiday
Amazon Annie .... Joan Shawlee
Kiki The Cossack .... Grace Lee Whitney
Andre .... Paul Dubov
Concierge .... Howard McNear
Police Sergeant .... Cliff Osmond
Jojo .... Diki Lerner
Casablanche Charlie .... Herb Jones
Zebra Twins .... Ruth & Jane Earl
Suzette Wong .... Tura Satana
First Customer .... Lou Krugman
Second Customer .... John Alvin
Customer From Texas .... James Brown
Tatooed Sailor .... Bill Bixby
Poule with Balcony .... Susan Woods
Mimi the Maumau .... Harriette Young
Carmen .... Sheryl Deauville
Officer Dupont .... Billy Beck
Jack .... Jack Sahakian
Man with Samples .... Don Diamond
Gen Lafayette (Ret.) .... Edgar Barrier
Englishman .... Richard Peel
Prison Guard .... Joe Palma
Coquette .... Shorty

Billy Wilder's screen version of "Irma La Douche" is a diverting romp and a healthy boxoffice prospect. It is not, however, Wilder at his best, nor does it figure to attain the blockbuster category of some of his other films. On the plus side of the "Irma" ledger, there are scintillating performances by two stars of the first magnitude, Jack Lemmon and Shirley MacLaine, a batch of jovial supporting portrayals, a striking physical production and a number of infectious comedy scenes. These positive factors, along with the Wilder brand name and a liberal dosage of sex, should combine to insure a robust and highly profitable public response to the Mirisch Co.-Edward L. Alperson presentation and United Artists release.

But "Irma" also misses on several important counts, and the fact that it does illustrate the sizable problems inherent in an attempt to convert a legit musical into a tuneless motion picture farce. In the first place, taking the music out of a bee; it loses a part of its identity. Transplanting it in this revised form to the screen poses an even greater problem, since film is a medium of far greater realism than the stage, and many picturegoers, responding with natural concern to the "sentimental" love story, may try to take the demusicalized "Irma" too seriously instead of receiving it as pure, unadulterated farce.

But what hurts the film the most is its length. Two hours and 27 minutes is an awfully long haul for a frivolous farce. There are several draggy letdowns, one of which, a bedroom scene wherein Lemmon is induced to revive his lost male virility via sensual use of his imagination, should be sliced to absolute essentials. Other scenes could be tightened, too. Half-an-hour less film could make it a better film.

The hot-and-cold scenario by Wilder and I.A.L. Diamond, based on the play by Alexandre Breffort, traces the love affair of "Irma" (Miss MacLaine), a proud and profitable practitioner of the oldest profession, and a young gendarme (Lemmon) who gets bounced off the force when he makes the mistake of taking his job seriously. Lemmon becomes number one mec, or pimp, on the block when he knocks his predecessor's block off, thereby inheriting Irma and the rights to her estate. Complications set in when Lemmon begins to resent the nature of her profession, invents an alter ego with which he masquerades as her rich and exclusive client, grows jealous of his creation, pretends to have killed him and winds up with a long jail term for the "crime." Everything comes up roses, however, in a rather saccharine conclusion.

The film lacks the originality of some of Wilder's recent efforts. Runyonesque elements abound and there is even a touch of Saroyan. But the tipoff is a scene in which Lemmon is crammed into a paddy wagon with a crowd of flashy, fleshy streetwalkers, which had its inspirational origin in the famous Pullman berth sequence in "Some Like It Hot." So Wilder here has resorted to imitating himself, which may be the sincerest form of flattery but is not a very healthy creative sign.

Lemmon plays his juicy role to the hilt, and there are moments when his performance brings to mind some of the great visual comedy of the classic silent film clowns. His portrayal of his British alter ego is a kind of cross between Jose Ferrer's characterization of Toulouse - Lautrec and Richard Haydn's caricature of an Englishman. Miss MacLaine delivers a winning performance in the title role, and has never looked better. There's a whale of a comedy portrayal by Lou Jacobi as the versatile bistro boss-barkeep, "Moustache." Jacobi plays it pretty straight and just lets the comedy ooze out of the character, which is the perfect approach to the role. Prominent figures in the large and spirited supporting cast are Bruce Yarnell, Herschel Bernardi, and Hope Holiday.

Joseph La Shelle's photography is striking and colorful. A little more snipping and splicing by editor Daniel Mandell and the film's occasional sluggishness, particularly in the latter stages, could be reduced considerably. Alexander Trauner's art direction is outstanding, providing in his sets the necessary backdrop of authenticity to reinforce the fanciful events of the story. A frisky musical score by Andre Previn is another valuable contribution. Orry-Kelly's costumes are appropriately racy and revealing. *Tube.*

Jason And The Argonauts
(DYNAMATION 90—COLOR)

Diverting and ingeniously executed romp through Greek mythology. Solid moppet appeal makes it good summertime prospect.

Hollywood, May 27.

Columbia Pictures release of Charles H. Schneer production. Stars Todd Armstrong, Nancy Kovack; features Gary Raymond, Laurence Naismith. Directed by Don Chaffey. Screenplay, Jan Read, Beverley Cross; camera (Eastman) Wilkie Cooper; editor, Maurice Rootes; music, Bernard Herrman; asst. director, Dennis Bertera. Reviewed at the studio, May 27, '63. Running time, **104 MINS.**

Jason .... Todd Armstrong
Medea .... Nancy Kovack
Acastus .... Gary Raymond
Argus .... Laurence Naismith
Zeus .... Niall Mac Ginnis
Hermes .... Michael Gwynn
Pelias .... Douglas Wilmer
King Aeetes .... Jack Gwillim
Hera .... Honor Blackman
Hylas .... John Cairney
Phineas .... Patrick Troughton
Phalerus .... Andrew Faulds
Hercules .... Nigel Green
Polydeuces .... John Crawford
Euphemus .... Douglas Robinson
Castor .... Gernando Poggi

Here's a choice hot weather attraction for the family trade—a sure delight for the kiddies and a diverting spectacle for adults with a taste for fantasy and adventure. The Charles H. Schneer production is, most of all, an impressive display of cinematic verisimilitude for which associate producer and special visual effects expert Ray Harryhausen rates at least the motion picture equivalent of two ears and a tail. Thanks mostly to his know-how, the Columbia release seems to have the technical sheen and production magnitude to captivate an audience and surmount such commercial challenges as the absence of any appreciable marquee name bait and a sizable expenditure that the studio tabulates to be $3,000,000. The money, at any rate, is on the screen.

"Jason and the Argonauts" stems from the Greek mythological legend of Jason and his voyage at the helm of the Argo in search of the Golden Fleece. The film has a workable scenario by Jan Read and Beverley Cross and has been directed resourcefully and spiritedly by Don Chaffey, under whose leadership a colorful cast performs with zeal.

Among the spectacular mythological landscape and characters brought to life through the ingenuity of illusionist Harryhausen and the other skilled artisans on Schneer's staff are a remarkably lifelike mobile version of the colossal bronze god, Talos; fluttery personifications of the bat-winged Harpies; a miniature representation of the "crashing rocks" through which Jason's vessel must cruise; a menacing version of the seven-headed Hydra; a batch of some astonishingly active skeletons who materialize out of the teeth of Hydra; ad a yare replica of the Argo itself. In addition to Harryhausen, others whose skill played prominent roles in the success of this production are production designer Geoffrey Drake, cameraman Wilkie Cooper, editor Maurice Rootes, art directors Herbert Smith, Jack Maxsted and Tony Sarzi Braga, soundmen Cyril Collick and Red Law and composer Bernard Herrman.

Handsome Todd Armstrong does a commendable job as Jason and Nancy Kovak is beautiful as his Medea, although the studio publicity boys have come up with one of the last of the great overstatements when, in their production notes, they state that, with this role, she "is following in he illustrious footsteps of Judith Anderson and Maria Callas." That's like saying Helen Gurley Brown is following in the footsteps of Mark Twain.

Other roles of more than routine interest are dispatched ably by Gary Raymond, Laurence Naismith, Niall MacGinnis, Michael Gwynn, Douglas Wilmer, Jack Gwillim, Honor Blackman, John Cairney, Patrick Troughton, Andrew Faulds, Nigel Green, John Crawford, Douglas Robinson and Gernando Poggi. *Tube.*

A Gathering Of Eagles
(COLOR)

Familiar air force drama triangle: man, wife and duty to country. Within boundaries of concept, a commendable job, but b.o. range limited.

Hollywood, May 20.

Universal release of Sy Bartlett production. Stars Rock Hudson; features Rod Taylor, Mary Peach, Barry Sullivan. Directed by Delbert Mann. Screenplay, Robert Pirosh, from story by Bartlett; camera (Eastman), Russell Harlan; editor, Russell F. Schoengarth; music, Jerry Goldsmith; asst. director, Joseph C. Behm. Reviewed at Grauman's Chinese Theatre, May 20, '63. Running time, **115 MINS.**

Jim Caldwell .... Rock Hudson
Hollis Farr .... Rod Taylor
Victoria Caldwell .... Mary Peach
Colonel Fowler .... Barry Sullivan
General Kirby .... Kevin McCarthy
Colonel Garcia .... Henry Silva
Mrs. Fowler .... Leora Dana
Sgt. Banning .... Robert Lansing
Colonel Josten .... Richard Anderson
Sgt. Kemler .... Dichard LePore
Lt. Col. Gales .... Robert Bray
Colonel Morse .... Jim Bannon
General Aymes .... Nelson Leigh
Colonel Torrance .... Russ Bender
Major Jarvis .... John McKee
Leighton .... Ben Wright
Mrs. Josten .... Dorothy Abbott
Beresford .... John Holland
Controller .... John Pickard
Duty Controller .... Ed Prentiss
Captain Linc .... Ray Montgomery
Captain Hutchens .... R. Wayland Williams
General Hewitt .... Leif Erickson

There has been a fundamental sameness about most film dramas concerned with the post-war Air Force. The basic story conflict in virtually all of these films has been whether a man must place allegiance to his job and his country over personal friendships and simple everyday comforts and whether his wife can put up with him under the challenge of these conditions. Sy Bartlett's production of "A Gathering of Eagles" adheres closely to this formula and, although it is a highly efficient and, to some extent, edifying job of filmmaking, it will take more than smooth and straightforward execution and a smattering of technical information to capture the imagination of the selective modern filmgoing public. The Universal release is limited in appeal by the story groove it fits so neatly into, a groove that John Q. Filmgoer is likely to detect in the process of choosing an attraction to see.

Though scenarist Robert Pirosh and the director Delbert Mann have been hemmed in by "formula," within the narrow dramatic horizons of the story design, they have performed their tasks quite commendably. The familiar situations have been dramatized on paper by Pirosh about as well as could be expected and the tenor of performance, histrionic and production, is skilled and steady under the artistic surveillance of Mann and spur of producer Bartlett from

whose original story the project springs.

"Eagles" is a story of the men of the Strategic Air Command, more specifically that of a wing commander (Rock Hudson) whose dedication to the task of shaping up the somewhat negligent outfit to which he is newly assigned forces him, in he course of attempting to analyze and pinpoint what is ailing the unit, to make several unpleasant decisions that almost strain marital relations with his wife (Mary Peach) to the breaking point. Essentially, then, it is a triangle—a man, his wife and his job, the latter symbolized by the red telephone from which Hudson, even at home, must never be more than six rings away.

Hudson invests his role with the right blend of authority and warmth. Rod Taylor creates a colorful figure as the undesirably easygoing vice-commander who shapes up when the chips are down. Miss Peach, a British actress brought over for the occasion, manages to be appealing in a role that was shopworn a decade ago. Barry Sullivan capably handles the somewhat obvious role of a veteran base commander whose alcoholic intake gets him the heave-ho from Hudson. Competence in top supporting roles is achieved by Kevin McCarthy, Henry Silva, Leora Dana, Robert Lansing, Richard Anderson and Leif Erickson.

Filmed primarily on location at several SAC installations, the picture benefits from the astute Eastman Color photography of Russell Harlan, taut editing of Russell F. Schoengarth, lifelike art direction of Alexander Golitzen and Henry Bumstead and unobtrusively helpful score by Jerry Goldsmith. "The SAC Song," written by Tom Lehrer and sung by Taylor, is woven appropriately into the story to provide a melodic note of levity. Most interesting sequence in the film is the climactic one, which illustrates in dramatic fashion the fast and foolproof accuracy required of a SAC wing unit for an operational readiness inspection—or surprise alert test—designed to keep the SAC bases in razor-sharp preparedness for emergency at all times.   *Tube.*

The Thrill Of It All
(COLOR)

Latest in Universal's string of glamorous romanticomedies with Doris Day. Best of the lot —should be one of year's top grossers.

Hollywood, June 4.
Universal release of Ross Hunter-Martin Melcher production. Stars Doris Day, James Garner; features Arlene Francis, Zazu Pitts, Elliott Reed, Reginald Owen, Edward Andrews. Directed by Norman Jewison. Screenplay, Carl Reiner, based on story by Larry Gelbart, Reiner; camera (Eastman), Russell Metty; editor, Milton Carruth; music, De Vol; asst. Director, Phil Bowles. Reviewed at Westwood Village Theatre, June 4, '63. Running time, 108 MINS.
Beverly Boyer .... Doris Day
Dr. Gerald Boyer .... James Garner
Mrs. Fraleigh .... Arlene Francis
Gardiner Fraleigh ..... Edward Andrews
Old Tom .... Reginald Owen
Olivia .... Zazu Pitts
Mike Palmer .... Elliott Reid
Woman .... Alice Pearce
Maggie .... Kym Karath
Andy .... Brian Nash
Mrs. Goethe .... Lucy Landau
Dr. Taylor .... Paul Hartman
Billings .... Hayden Rorke
Stokely .... Alex Gerry
Van Camp .... Robert Gallagher
Miss Thompson .... Anne Newman
Butler .... Burt Mustin
Chauffeur .... Hedley Mattingly
1st Truck Driver ...... Robert Strauss
2nd Truck Driver ..... Maurice Gosfield
Driver .... William Bramley
Starlet .... Pamela Curran
Man .... Herbie Faye
Cabbie .... Lenny Kent
Mr. Caputo .... John Alderman
3rd Truck Driver ...... Len Feinrib

In "The Thrill of It All," Universal has another entry in the light comedy vein of such moneymaking champs as "Pillow Talk," "Lover Come Back" and "That Touch of Mink." What's more, this is the best of the four in terms of having something more to say about contemporary life than "gosh, ain't love wonderful." For every now and then, in the midst of the domestic absurdity that serves as Carl Reiner's basic plot, he has slipped in some sharp and substantial observations that American film audiences are sure to sense and appreciate. True, the Ross Hunter-Arwin production has its flaws but the combination of glamour, visual comedy gusto, the Doris Day name and the smattering of satire for the more discerning customer all add up to the promise of a smash grosser, very likely one of the top moneymakers of the year.

Reiner's scenario, from a story he wrote in collaboration with Larry Gelbart, is peppered with digs at various institutions of modern American life. Among the targets of his fairly subtle but telling assault with the needle are television, Madison Avenue, the servant problem and such specific matters as the sharp points at the rear extremities of the modern Cadillac and the maitre d' who has immediate seating for celebrities only.

Much of the dialog, too, is acid and sly and witty, such as when the potential tv sponsor tells his henchmen to "get me one of those shows where everybody in the family is smarter than the father."

But these nuggets and pinpricks of satiric substance are primarily bonuses for the more demanding filmgoer. Ultimately it is in the design and engineering of cumulative sight gag situations that comedies such as this rise or fall insofar as the mass audience is concerned, and it is precisely in this area that "Thrill of It All" excels. In addition to a running gag about a suspiciously similar weekly series of live tv dramas, there is a scene in which a swimming pool saturated with soap gives birth to a two-story-high mountain of suds and another in which James Garner, coming home from work one evening, drives his convertible into his back yard and straight into a pool that wasn't there in the morning. This latter sequence, and Garner's patiently pained expression as he slowly sinks out of sight at the steering wheel, is the choice moment of the picture.

In the "miss" department, there are several situations that sputter, including the climactic one, an unscheduled birth scene in the midst of a traffic jam on East River Drive. This scene, literally, is labored too much. And the central characters themselves are quite artificial in their distortedly lovey-dovey attitude toward each other. Sure, there are husbands and wives who get along just fine and kiss and everything, but most audiences will detect a distinctly single person's approach in the smoochy-coochy way Day and Garner display affection. It is director Norman Jewison's one big slip-up not to have toned this down to something a bit more convincing. Otherwise, he has done an expert job, and demonstrated an imaginative flair for executing comedy.

Miss Day scores again as the housewife with two children who is suddenly thrust into an irresistible position as an $80,000-a-year pitch-woman for an eccentric soap tycoon who is impressed by her unaffected quality. Bearing the brunt of these soap operatics is Garner as the gynecologist whose domestic tranquillity is shattered by his wife's sudden transition to career girl. For Garner, improving with every screen outing, this role is right up his alley. He handles it with verve and finesse. Reiner, incidentally, has resolved his plot acceptably but may have overlooked the most natural conclusion to be drawn—that becoming a career girl is precisely what destroys the desirable original image of unaffectedness that enabled Miss Day to sell soap.

Arlene Francis and Edward Andrews are spirited in the key roles of a middle-aged couple suddenly expectant parents. Zasu Pitts, since deceased, does all she can with some ridiculous shenanigans as a fretful maid. Registering well in prominent parts are Reginald Owen and Elliott Reid, and others who stick in the memory for assorted reasons are Lucy Landau, Alice Pearce, Robert Strauss and Pamela Curran. Kym Karath and Brian Nash are painless as the Day-Gardner children, thanks mostly to Reiner's perceptive mop-petalk. Sample: (upon overhearing parental conversation) "Daddy's

not planning for us to stay young." "Can he do that?"

The Hunter-Martin Melcher production, as customary, features an expensive, glamorous sheen. Contributing to this aura and image are the opulent and authentic artwork of Alexander Golitzen and Robert Boyle, flattering photography of Russell Metty, trim editing of Milton Carruth, expressive score of De Val and the stylish, becoming gowns designed by Jean Louis. There's also a breezy title song by Arnold Schwarzwald and Frederick Herbert.   *Tube.*

La Cage
(The Cage)
(FRENCH)

Cannes, June 4.
EDIC release of Lions Films-EDIC-CCDG production. Stars Marina Vlady; features Jean Servais, Philippe Maury, Colette Duval, Myriel David, Alain Bouvette. Directed by Robert Darene. Screenplay, Christine Garnier, Alain Bouvette, Pierre Tristan, Marc Boureau, Philippe Maury, Jean Servais, Georges De La Grandiere, Darene; camera, Jacques Lang; editor, Georges Arnstam. At Cannes Film Fest. Running time, 85 MINS.
Isabelle .... Marina Vlady
Michel .... Jean Servais
Philippe .... Philippe Maury
Oyane .... Myriel David
Colette .... Colette Duval
Contrematire .... Alain Bouvette

Another example of a French director doing a film on progress vs. superstition in Africa. There are a few switches but this still remains the hybrid adventure pic with intimations of African tribal magic even if neatly explained. It is fairly well mounted with some okay exotic locales for possible dualer use abroad. It lacks the scope for arties.

An African doctor comes back to his own country after studying in France. He marries and then goes into the hinterlands. Here, he crosses a white man running a plantation and the latter throws a hex on him, causing him to see his ex-wife who had died many years ago. The obsession is finally wiped out.

Marina Vlady is somewhat too blank and one-dimensionally pretty to give much force to the apparition. Jean Servais is properly menacing as the white man gone native. Others are adequate. Direction is just too flat to give this the suspense or depth to either emerge a good offbeater or a deeper look at African life today.

This looks like Africans will have to start making their own pix to eventually give a true face of themselves at film fests. This is a traditional if acceptably-made pic that may have some pull on African marts with chancier export status. It is technically passable.   *Mosk.*

The Girl Hunters
(BRITISH-MADE)

Author as his own hero. Tough private eye melodrama with effective treatment. Mickey Spillane's screen debut as Hammer.

Colorama release of Fellane (Robert Fellows) Production. Stars Mickey Spillane; features Shirley Eaton, Scott Peters, Hy Gardner, Lloyd Nolan. Directed by Roy Rowland. Screenplay by Spillane, Rowland and Robert Fellows from Spillane's novel of same title; camera, Ken Talbot; editor, Sidney Stone; music, Phil Green; asst. director, George Pollard;

assoc. producer, Charles Reynolds. Reviewed at Preview Theatre, June 7, '63. Running time, **103 MINS.**

Mike Hammer	Mickey Spillane
Laura Knapp	Shirley Eaton
Art Rickerby	Lloyd Nolan
Hy Gardner	Hy Gardner
Pat Chambers	Scott Peters
Dr. Larry Snyder	Guy Kingsley Poynter
Bayliss Henry	James Dyrenforth
Joe Grissi	Charles Farrell
The Nurse	Kim Tracy
Nat Drutman	Benny Lee
Richie Cole	Murray Kash
Georgie	Bill Nagy
Duck-Duck	Clive Endersby
Skinny Guy	Richard Montez
Red Markham	Larry Cross
Cab Driver	Tony Arpino
Bouncer	Hal Galili
Landlady	Nelly Hanham
Dr. Leo Daniels	Bob Gallico
Police	Michael Brennan, Howard Greene, Grant Holden
Detective	Francis Napier
The "Dragon"	Larry Taylor

Mickey Spillane's hardnosed private eye Mike Hammer is back in print after a few-years hiatus. Adapted to the screen his latest exploits make for a slick and entertaining adventure meller. "The Girl Hunters" also debuts author Spillane portraying his rough 'n' tumble hero for the first time on the screen. He turns in a credible job in the role.

The Colorama Features release, scripted by Spillane, director Roy Rowland and producer Robert Fellows from the author's book of the same title, has been slotted as a multiple break entry and is solid fare for this market. There's plenty of action, romance and movement in the tidy feature, with an occasional dash of rakish comedy and Spillane gruesomeness to please his fans and crime-action filmgoers.

Plot finds the private eye in the gutter from seven years of boozing and fretting because he believes that he sent his secretary and best gal to her doom when he gave her an assignment to do for him. It develops, however, that she may still be alive and Hammer straightens out and goes in search of her "just like the old days," as one of the characters comments.

Along the line he finds himself in a romantic entanglement, never forgetting the long-lost Velda, with one of his prime info sources, played cooly and with seductive restraint by Shirley Eaton. This vet of English lightweight comedies, is a very pretty blonde who spends much of her time in the film wearing just a bikini, a happenstance which intrigues Hammer and will not revolt male audience members. It's her first dramatic film role and she handles it with savvy.

Scott Peters is police captain Pat Chambers, known to Spillane fans as one of Hammer's bosom buddies. In this plot he's anything but, however, he, too, seemingly having been in love with the elusive Velda and more than put out with the private eye for her disappearance and presumed death. The actor puts plenty of bite into the role but sometimes tends to overplay his obvious distaste for his ex-chum.

As a federal agent who's also interested in the case which has the foreign intrigue element of the murder of a U.S. Senator which is linked to an international Commie plot, Lloyd Nolan turns in a pro and reliable job. N.Y. Herald Tribune and syndicated columnist Hy Gardner also does well playing himself and a pal of Hammer's (as off-screen he's a chum of Spillane's).

Pic was lensed in London at Metro but considerable care has been taken to preserve Gotham locales where the action takes place. Several fave watering spots around town like Al & Dicks and the Blue Ribbon have been faithfully reproduced by art director Tony Inglis. Gardner's office, too, has been carboned for the pic. These and some other touches too tend to lift the film somewhat over run-of-the-mill cop 'n' robbers fare.

Director Rowland has gotten effective performances out of his principal cast, which gets solid support from a host of the inevitable Spillane plot-feeding secondary characters. His pace is easy and, with cameraman Ken Talbot and operator Alan McCabe, he has gotten some good lensing. Sidney Stone has edited smoothly and Phil Green has written a musical background that is both well-fitted and nice sounding.

In all, "Girl Hunters" has been effectively translated to pix, making for good action on the screen which should do the same for the boxoffice. And, after all, who's James Bond anyway. *Kali.*

The Young Racers
(COLOR)

Trite auto racing meller. B.o. range limited.

Hollywood, June 5.

American International release of Roger Corman production. Stars Mark Damon, William Campbell, Luana Anders. Directed by Corman. Screenplay, R. Wright Campbell; camera (Pathe), Floyd Crosby; editor, Ronald Sinclair; music, Les Baxter; asst. director, Charles Griffith. Reviewed at Lytton Center, June 5, '63. Running time, **82 MINS.**

Stephen Children	Mark Damon
Joe Machin	William Campbell
Henny	Luana Anders
Robert Machin	Robert Campbell
Sir William Dragonet	Patrick Magee
Lotus Team Manager	John McLaren
Italian Driver	Miol Quesada
Announcer	Anthony Marsh
Sesia Machin	Marie Versini
Monique	Beatrice Altariba
Lea	Margreta Robsahn
Daphne	Christina Gregg

People don't talk or behave the way they do in "The Young Racers." Not even young racers, for that matter. So, on the fair assumption that people come to see people when they go to see a film, the Roger Corman production is a limited boxoffice entry in spite of its youthful cast and exploitable topic, which ordinarily might have some solid value for ozone or saturation bookings. The American International release simply doesn't have what it takes.

The picture's serious ailments can be traced directly to R. Wright Campbell's contrived, affected, pretentious scenario. The dialog is incredibly stilted and artificial, and there is too much of it. Folks just don't go around calling each other "posturing dilettantes," at least not if they expect to avoid getting a knuckle sandwich straight in the kisser. And girls, just don't say things to their boy friends like "I don't want to be your inner ear anymore."

The hackneyed story has to do with a grand prix champion (William Campbell) who, on the surface, appears to be one of those don't-give-a-damn-how-I-win-this-race-as-long-as-I-win-it chaps with a chip on his shoulder and a girl in every pit stop. He incurs the disfavor of an ex-racer turned writer (Mark Ramon) when he makes time with the latter's fiancee, then sheds her. The writer decides to get even by penning a nasty book about the racer but, in the process of getting to know him better, discovers a heart of gold beating beneath the grease and goggles.

Campbell does the best acting in the film, overcoming to some extent the trite role he is playing. Damon is rather wooden. Luana Anders plays his traveling secretary. And since when, pray tell, do young writers cart secretaries all over Europe with them? It is one of the many mysteries in Campbell's script. There are some very pretty girls in this film, which helps immeasurably. In addition to Miss Anders, there are Marie Versini, Beatrice Altariba, Margreta Robsahn and Christina Gregg. Producer-director Corman certainly has an eye for beauty. Too bad he doesn't in this instance have as good an eye for script.

Much of the film was shot at actual European grand prix sites. Floyd Crosby's photography is largely of the here-it-comes, whooosh, there-it-goes variety. Les Baxter has chipped in a racy score. It's a winner for the inner ear. *Tube.*

Marilyn

Documentary compilation of Marilyn Monroe cinematurgy, narrated by Rock Hudson. Reviewed at studio. Running time, 83 MINS.

Hollywood, June 7.

In "Marilyn," 20th-Fox conducts filmgoers on a sentimental journey through those milestones of Miss Monroe's career in which she starred in the studio's productions. It is a direct and unpretentious compilation of film clips. No attempt is made to sleuth the personal mystery of Marilyn, to analyze the emotional factors that led to her self-destruction. And although this documentary is neither penetrating nor thorough (only her films for 20th are covered), it is engrossing and affecting, and has the curiosity value to attract those picturegoers whose imaginations have been captured by the complex personality who reigned as the glamour queen of the screen for a decade. That covers a lot of potential boxoffice territory.

"Marilyn" spans 13 years of celluloid, beginning with her appearance as one of a quartet of chorines in the 1949 production of "A Ticket To Tomahawk" and concluding with shots from the unfinished "Something's Got To Give." Along the way, viewers are treated to juicy MM tidbits from such other attractions as "All About Eve," "Love Nest," "We're Not Married," "Don't Bother To Knock," "O. Henry's Full House," "Monkey Business," "Niagara," "Gentlemen Prefer Blondes," "How To Marry A Millionaire," "There's No Business Like Show Business," "The Seven Year Itch" and "Bus Stop." In all of them the camera focuses lovingly, endearingly and revealingly on the changing Marilyn, enabling the audience to sit back and study intimately the evolution of a star and the peculiar characteristics that became her trademarks. And the overtone of tragedy flavors these merry glimpses with a bittersweet tang, all the more so when we view Marilyn posing for a hair test on "Something's Got To Give," at the absolute apex of her beauty yet so near the end.

The film is revealing in other ways, too. For example, brief as these recollective passages are, they recall how rather shallow the roles handed Miss Monroe and how rather limited her histrionic abilities. A star of the first magnitude, but never truly a gifted actress. And yet capable of the fine performance in the right role, as in "Bus Stop."

There is an unfortunate gap in the story, the film skipping from 1956 ("Bus Stop") to 1962 ("Give"), thus ignoring all the non-20th milestones of her career in-between. But what is included has been assembled and edited with perception and imagination. Though the clips are brief, they manage to provide the audience with a fairly good idea of the plots and the natures of the characters being played by Marilyn.

Rock Hudson serves as narrator, and appears at the beginning and near the end for a few appreciative words about the star. There is something rather corny and shopworn about the soundstage problem with his sincere, soft-setting and a few of the observations, but Hudson minimizes the spoken approach. *Tube.*

King Kong Vs. Godzilla
(COLOR)

From Japan, comically-oriented clash between two top bananas of beast kingdom. Strong potential in saturation sphere.

Hollywood, June 3.

Universal release of Toho production. With Michael Keith, James Yagi, Tadao Takashima, Mie Hama, Yu Fujiki, Kenji Sahara, Ichiro Arishima, Harry Holcombe, Tatsuo Matsumura, Akihiko Hirata, Eiko Wakabayshi, Senkichi Omura. Directed by Inoshiro Honda. English version produced by John Beck, directed by Thomas Montgomery, written by Paul Mason, Bruce Howard: editor and music, Peter Zinner. No camera credit. Reviewed at the studio, June 3, '63. Running time, **91 MINS.**

Eric Carter	Michael Keith
Yataka Omura	James Yagi
O. Sakurai	Tadao Takashima
Fumiko Sakurai	Mie Hama
Kinzaburo Furuo	Yu Fujiki
Kazuo Fujita	Kenji Sahara
Mr. Tako	Ichiro Arishima
Dr. Arnold Johnson	Harry Holocmbe
Dr. Markino	Tatsuo Matsumura
Premier Shigezawa	Akihiko Hirata
Tamiye	Eiko Wakabayshi
Konno	Senkichi Omura

To the list of the century's great preliminary bouts — Dempsey-Firpo, Sullivan-Paar, Nixon-Kennedy, Patterson-Liston, Steve Reeves-Gordon Scott — and the main event, "King Kong Vs. Godzilla." From the mysterious East comes this monstrosity to end all monstrosities, the epic clash between the 30-year-old breast-beating, Hollywood born-and-bred gorilla with the overactive pituitary and the seven-year-old pea-brained, flame-throated, tail-wagging cross between a stegosaurus and a tyrannosaurus rex who fights out of Tokyo, Japan. Onward and upward with the arts.

The second coming of these two titans of the monster kingdom, along with public speculation over who wins this giant economy sized argument, should enable the two-for-the-price-of-one Toho production and Universal release make a quick but formidable splash in the saturation sphere. And, although not entirely played for laughs, many a filmgoer will find it comically irresistible.

The picture was filmed in Japan, and has been reinforced with added U.S. footage by producer John Beck the better to cover expository ground for English-speaking audiences without having to labor over an excess of post-dubbed explanatory passages. Actually, the exposition is hardly necessary. Kong and Pancho Godzilla just about speak for themselves.

The story, credited to Paul Mason and Bruce Howard, follows familiar trails, with a few surprises. One of these is the personality of KK. Now, all these years filmgoers have recalled this granddaddy of the skyscraper-chewing fraternity as a most impregnable, anti-social critter. Well, in this sequel, he turns out to be: (1) mentally superior to his colleagues-in-destruction, (2) benevolent, (3) chicken. True, he still has an eye for the ladies and likes to play with thains ,or room-shaped "el's"), but the new Kong runs and hides when he takes his first whiff of Godzilla's hot breath. Fortunately, he is given a chance to redeem himself for this shameful first round by the good citizens of Tokyo, who spray him with knockout gas, haul him off through the air by helium balloon (are you picturing this?) to the foot of Mt. Fuji and dump him unceremoniously, in order that he might stop Big G, who came out of an iceberg, from turning the Japanese capital into a rockpile.

The battle that ensues could only be described by Don Dunphy. For the record, let it be noted that poor Kong takes one helluva beating until he gets what for him is the equivalent of Popeye's spinach —an electric charge. Fortunately, Godzilla hates the Japanese current. The bout ends in a virtual draw. Godzy vanishes in order that his option may, at some future date, be picked up by the studio. King swims south in the direction of his home, exotic Faroe Island, which resembles a kind of Japanese setting for a Crosby-Hope-Lamour "Road" rumpus.

The miniature work of the Japanese artisans under the direction of Inoshiro Honda is first-rate. Other production credits are fine. In addition to their own Godzilla, the Toho staff, exhibiting the well-known Japanese flair for duplication, has mounted a convincing facsimile of Hollywood's Kong. The human actors are thoroughly overshadowed by these larger-than-life creatures, even the pretty Japanese girl who does the Fay Wray bit in Freudian Kong's clammy claw.

One rather ironical sidelight. The Japanese characters, in discussing the means by which they might destroy or divert Godzilla, dismiss the atom bomb as a last resort, and never resort to it.

Tube.

Cleopatra
(DELUXE COLOR—TODD-AO)

Super-colossal spectacle, with something for the mind as well as eye. Already a blockbuster.

Twentieth-Fox release of Walter Wanger production. Stars Elizabeth Taylor; features Richard Burton, Rex Harrison. Directed by Joseph L. Mankiewicz. Screenplay, Mankiewicz, Ranald MacDougall, Sidney Buchman, based on histories by Plutarch, Suetonius, Appian and "The Life and Times of Cleopatra" by C. M. Franzero; camera (Todd-AO, Deluxe color), Leon Shamroy; editor, Dorothy Spencer; music, Alex North; asst. director, Fred R. Simpson; second unit directors, Ray Kellogg, Andrew Marton. Reviewed at Rivoli Theatre, N.Y., June 11, '63. Running time, **243 MINS**, without intermission.

Cleopatra	Elizabeth Taylor
Mark Antony	Richard Burton
Julius Caesar	Rex Harrison
High Priestess	Pamela Brown
Flavius	George Cole
Sosigenes	Hume Cronyn
Apollodorus	Cesare Danova
Brutus	Kenneth Haigh
Agrippa	Andrew Keir
Rufio	Martin Landau
Octavian	Roddy McDowall
Germanicus	Robert Stephens
Eiras	Francesca Annis
Pothinos	Gregoire Aslan
Ramos	Martin Benson
Theodotos	Herbert Berghof
Phoebus	John Cairney
Lotos	Jacqui Chan
Charmian	Isabelle Cooley
Achillas	John Doucette
Canidius	Andrew Faulds
Cimber	Michael Gwynn
Cicero	Michael Hordern
Cassius	John Hoyt
Euphranor	Marne Maitland
Casca	Carroll O'Connor
Ptolemy	Richard O'Sullivan
Calpurnia	Gwen Watford
Decimus	Douglas Wilmer
Queen at Tarsus	Marina Berti
High Priest	John Karlsen
Caesarion (age 4)	Loris Loddi
Octavia	Jean Marsh
Marcellus	Gin Mart
Mithridates	Furio Meniconi
Caesarion (age 12)	Kenneth Nash
Caesarion (age 7)	Dee Russell
Valvus	John Valva

When, early in 20th-Fox's "Cleopatra," the Queen of Egypt who has been arguing with Caesar about their respective godly origins, cuts him off with an abrupt: *"You Roman generals become divine so quickly!"* It is a signal to the film industry that something new in bright dialog values has been added to the historic romance. Throughout the film there are samples of smart dialog, though it is necessary to testify that some of it does not come off and is occasionally out of place.

"Cleopatra," with an estimated $14,000,000-plus already in the till as cash guarantees from U.S. and Canadian theatres (and thus the ninth biggest money making picture of all time in the domestic market before its premiere), would rate a blockbuster even without all that advance dough. It's not only a supercolossal eye-filler (the unprecedented budget shows in the physical opulance throughout), but it is also a remarkably literate cinematic recreation of an historic epoch. Whether or not the film will eventually rack up receipts enough to go into the black ($62,000,000 in rentals) is impossible to predict. It is certain, however, to be a major moneyearner for a long time to come.

"Cleopatra" was experimentally cut 21 minutes and so unreeled for two performances Monday (17) only, thus bringing running time down to 222 minutes from the original 243. No scenes were eliminated in their entirety, but cuts were made to shorten scenes and bridges.

Director and coauthor Mankiewicz and producer Walter Wanger have not extended the frontiers of cinema art, but they have completed under harrowing conditions, a very respectable job of spectacle-making. Their most stunning achievement is not that they have made the longest film in history (4 hours and 3 mins.), but that they have managed to tell a story of such scope and complexity in such comparatively brief terms. The film covers the 18 turbulent years leading to the foundation of the Roman Empire, from Cleopatra's first meeting with Julius Caesar until her death in defeat with Mark Antony. The result is a giant panorama, unequalled in the splendor of its spectacle scenes and, at the same time, suprisingly acute in its more personal story. This is one spectacle in which the leading characters—rulers of the world, if not gods—dominate the decor and special affects.

This is due not only to the quality and focus of the screenplay, but to the talents of the three leading players. In the title role, one of the most difficult ever written, Elizabeth Taylor is a woman of continuous fascination. Though not fully at ease as the child-queen of the film's first part, she grows as the story progresses to become the mature queen who matches the star's own voluptuous assurance.

Rex Harrison is superb as Caesar, shrewd, vain and wise, formed somewhat in the image of the G.B. Shaw conception, but also unexpectedly ruthless and ambitious. His are the film's most brilliant lines, and something is lost with his assassination, which closes the film's first half.

Richard Burton then comes to the fore in the second half. Oddly he does not seem the romantic figure expected and plot-implied, partly perhaps because as a lover he is visibly overweight. The role is of a man of military competence consumed by envy of Caesar's genius and exposed in the end as self-pitying and drunken by the demands of Cleopatra's needs for a man in a larger sense than boudoir. Ironically some of the weakest moments in the film are the anticipated love scenes between Liz and Dickie. Several times these come close to bathos. The very dialog which sharpens the political and social aspects endangers the intimacy of Mark and Cleo. Says Cleopatra to Antony, after the Battle of Actium: "Without you, this isn't a world I want to live in—much less conquer." The line has the ring of a suburban housewife's lament—not a goddess.'

Happily, however, such moments are few, and the film sweeps along with a very real sense of time and place, building to a climax that is one of inevitable, tragic relief. Responsible to no little extent is the quality of the "big" scenes — Cleopatra's triumphant entry into Rome, a dazzling display of color and sound and ancient pagaentry; the grandeur of Cleopatra's barge, sailing into Tarsus; the crucial Battle of Actium, recreated on a scale perhaps unmatched in any spectacle film.

Leon Shamroy's Todd-AO, DeLuxe color photography, the special effects of L. B. Abbott and Emil Koss Jr., and second unit directors Andrew Marton and Ray Kellogg, all rate particular praise. Since Miss Taylor's hair stylist gets screen credit, it might be noted that the hairdos are not always becoming. On the other hand, Irene Sharaff's costumes are appropriately sensational, though for the naval battle of Actium she ran up a little leopard-lined parka for the star which might look more appropriate for following an America Cup race at Newport. Alex North's score is often thundrous, but only occasionally intrusive.

A few incongruities in the production draw notice. Is that not a modern drugstore plastic sponge floating in Cleo's bath? It looks like one. Is the litter borne on rolled steel rods thousands of years before their invention? But such details will not bother average viewers. Another question that could be raised is the uneven quality of Miss Taylor's voice, often more shrill than regal in big scenes. The long windup of the story has Cleopatra taking longer to die than Camille. That 20th may still excise more footage is likely and the second half is the place to do it. [Reportedly 20 minutes will be cut pronto].

An arresting scene of Cleo's fury upon hearing that Mark Antony has married in Rome calls for her to slash with a knife at his hanging garments and later at the bed they had occupied together. The subtle point seems to have been blurred by using the garments first so that the symbolism of the bed is somewhat lost.

The huge supporting cast is uniformly excellent, but especially noteworthy are Roddy McDowell as Octavian; Martin Landau as Rufioo; Hume Cronyn as Sosigenes; Kenneth Haigh as Brutus; Robert Stephens as Germanicus, and Herbert Berghof, as Theodotus.

The real star of "Cleopatra," however, is Mankiewicz, who with Ranald MacDougall and Sidney Buchman, wrote the script, after his own crystal clear conception, thus bringing order out of what had been production chaos, and also breathing new life into a genre many might have thought to be beyond revival. As Caesar observes to Cleopatra, early on: "You have a way of mixing politics and passion." So does Mankiewicz.

Anby.

Werewolf In A Girl's Dormitory

Title may give it some exploitation value as running mate on a dual horror ticket. Mediocre quality.

Hollywood, June 12.

Metro release of Jack Forrest production. No stars. Directed by Richard Benson. Screenplay and story, Julian Berry; camera, George Patrick; music, Francis Herman. Reviewed at the studio, June 12, '63. Running time, **82 MINS.**

Brunhilde	Barbara Lass
Julian Olcott	Carl Schell
Mr. Swift	Curt Lowens
Sir Alfred Whiteman	Maurice Marsac
Leonor McDonald	Maureen O'Connor
Mary Smith	Mary McNeeran

As lycanthroperas go, this one doesn't go anywhere. Apparently of German or central European origin—the screen credits discreetly omit reference to source—the Jack Forrest production is an inept entry in the horror melodrama genre. Whatever minor merit it may have had in its original tongue and state has been obliterated by post-dubbing. Still, werewolves and girls' dormitories are proven exploitation bait, and that title, with accompanying art layout, should give the Metro release some minor market value as half of a horrid horror doubleheader.

Julian Berry's screenplay is essentially a mystery. "Will the real werewolf please stand up" is the general idea. The yarn is set in a school for wayward girls situated near an eerie forest into which the maidens are stupidly prone to wander alone every time the story gets empty and the moon gets full. There are all sorts of suspects skulking around in the shadows, including a creepy young fellow named Tom whose only line, delivered at corpse-side, is "was he the monster?" There are plenty of corpses: three men, one woman, one wolf and, ultimately, one werewolf. Is Tom the werewolf? No. It turns out to be none other than Mr. Swift, the schoolmaster ("Why, it's Mr. Swift," said Tom, wolfishly).

Horror melodramas like this depend on mood for most of their impact. Unfortunately, the mood of this film is completely shattered by the dubbing. So are the performances of the actors involved. Pretty Barbara Lass is the girl we worry most about, Carl Schell her protector, Curt Lowens the werewolf. Richard Benson directed, and his best work occurs in that forest. Camerawork by George Patrick is crude and music by Francis Berman is obtrusively ominous and generally irritating or irrelevant to what's going on. There's also a rock 'n' roll song by Marilyn Stewart and Frank Owens. It's called "The Ghoul In School." Onward and upward.
Tube.

Donovan's Reef
(TECHNICOLOR)

Boisterous comedy, action-packed, never slows down enough to take survey of shortcomings; surefire ingredients for healthy, non-critical b.o.

Hollywood, June 13.

"Donovan's Reef," for a director of John Ford's stature, is a potboiler. However, the ingredients and formula are strong and too well-proven to leave much doubt as to the film's ticket-selling ability. From "North To Alaska" to the South Pacific, with plenty of beautifully photographed scenery, rousing romance, boisterous comedy, frequent fights, all mixed up with kids, Christmas, dedicated doctors, and patriotism — that's "Donovan's Reef." And it would take a pretty dour type not to enjoy it!

Where Ford aficionados will squirm is during that occasional scene that reminds them, this effort-less effort is the handiwork of the men who made "Stagecoach" and "The Informer."

John Wayne, sailing along like a dreadnaught mothering a convoy of rowboats, conveys an exuberance to match the mayhem, moving from fracas to fracas, facing up to a gang of toughs or a belligerent Boston beauty with equal courage. The only demand made is on his muscles.

Lee Marvin, since their last excursion, has had his reins tightened by Ford. This is only a comic menace where once the malevolent terror of "Bad Day At Black Rock" smouldered. Jack Warden's role hints at earlier greater prominence, edited down to harmless support and irritating in its omissions.

Ford, best when he's faced with an unknown talent, brings out the ability of Elizabeth Allen, a darkling beauty, that has been hidden in previous roles. She's delightful as a Boston ice cube whose melting point is Wayne, and it's a pleasure to see her wrappings melt. Cesar Romero and Dorothy Lamour are the victims of acute scriptitis although Dick Foran is briefly impressive as an Australian naval officer.

Marcel Dalio, Mike Mazurki, and Jacqueline Malouf, Cherylene Lee, and Tim Stafford, as the tykes about whom the plot wobbles, lend capable support when necessary. The visual beauty of Kauai, in northern Hawaii, is captured by William Clothier's Technicolor photography. Frank Nugent (an old Ford hand) and James Edward Grant's script has more holes in it than Liberty Valance. They've created a paradisical setting, "somewhere in the South Pacific," ruled by a native princess; governed by the French; protected by the Australian navy; "run" by expatriate Americans; and peopled by a league of national types.

The music, scored by Cyril Mockridge, is ersatz Mannakoora moonlight and shadows. Otho Lovering's editing, while sometimes jumpy, aims purely for action and gets it. The effect is that this Ford is a handsome, smoothly riding vehicle but no replacement for some of those Fords of the past.
Robe.

Kriss Romani
(Gypsy Law)
(FRENCH)

Paris, June 11.

This film tries to mix a documentary look at gypsy life, a romantic love tale and moppet antics. It cannot integrate them all. New director Jean Schmidt displays an obvious sympathy for the gypsies, with a strong pitch against racism, but waters it all down by too many mannered, diffuse aspects. Pic appears mainly a dualer or programmer entry abroad on its theme, with art possibilities chancier.

A robust, pretty gypsy girl rebels against being forced to marry someone in the tribe through family agreements. She runs off to go up against bigotry and finally comes back to the chosen man. Against this are scenes of gypsy ritual, courts, etc., and a tale of a little girl who sets out to find a legendary magic root to help the older girl.

Quaint scenes intermingle with gypsy revels and drama. The little girl is quite hammy in mannerisms, if charming, while real actors mingle acceptably with the true nomads. Director Schmidt has just tried to mix too many elements without a firm grasp of place, milieu and drama to have this come off solidly.

But the pic has an eye-catching photographic sheen from Jean Badal, some interesting looks at the life of Europe's wanderers and nice musical strains. When Schmidt settles down to more forceful and straightforward documentary or fictional film work, he could possibly be a needed addition to filmmaking ranks here.
Mosk.

Les Carabiniers
(The Riflemen)
(FRENCH)

Paris, June 11.

Film is a way out anti-war fable by unorthodox ex-New Waver Jean-Luc Godard who made the tale of a modern hoodlum, "Breathless." It mixes stock footage, inside gags, knowingly-fashioned silent film styles, and manages to make its point at times, if it does get repetitious.

Thus appears primarily an extremely specialized arty item for abroad but could be worthwhile if well handled and farcefully sold for buffs.

A mother with two grown sons and a daughter lives in a rundown shack. Into this come two riflemen to requisition the boys for the war of the King. They are promised all rights they want, no matter how much against human laws or decency, and go off to make their fortunes. Stock footage of war is intercut with their odyssee as the titles and asides. The brutality and uselessness of war is made apparent countless times but this finally begins to repeat itself, and in the final twists of defeat no longer has the ironic bite and verve of the earlier scenes.

But there is no denying director Godard's natural flair for getting freshness, visual knowhow and interest into his films. A scene of the arrest and execution of long haired beautiful Marxist dogma spouting girl is a pungent scene as well as the free wheeling mayhem and looting committed by the simple minded anti-heroes.

Some personal asides, such as one's visit to a film house where he is frightened by a scene of a train and tries to get into a screen during a bathing scene by a beauteous girl, adequately comment on the early film days of Mack Sennett, Lumiere Bros., etc. plus still bringing a fresh inventive gloss to the pic.

Bee stung lips on the women, the stolid one-dimensional characters of the men, the highly contrasted, dense lensing of Raoul Coutard all bring to life the early feel of silent films with their larger-than-life aspects and comments on humanity in its simplest aspects.

Marino Mase has the right brutish outlook, tempered by some gentle outbursts, for one of the brothers and the others have the right silhouettes and characters for the other figures in this sardonic, biting look at human foibles.

If going back to seemingly lost filmic modes, this still has the brash inventiveness, progression, and continuity of the growing changes in film narrative methods. If limited to specialized outlets as, yet, more selective filmgoers are giving these type pix greater adhesion. The selling will be telling for this in offshore placement. Crix approval could help plus word-of-mouth.
Mosk.

It's All Happening
(BRITISH—COLOR—MUSICAL)

Conventional, oldfashioned musical format enhanced by warm performance of star Tommy Steele, sharp contributions from top pop talent and pleasant color. Good breezy bet for the teenagers.

London, June 13.

Guest Artists appearing as themselves: John Barry, The Clyde Valley Stompers, Russ Conway, Johnny De Dittle, Carol Deene, Shane, Fenton & The Fentones, Dick Kallman, Geoff Love, Marion Ryan, Danny Williams, The George Mitchell Show with Tony Mercer, John Boulter, Dai Francis.

The warmly exuberant personality of Tommy Steele, plus some polished, slick performances by guest top pop United Kingdom artists, solidly jacks up a lazy, old-fashioned and flabby screenplay by Leigh Vance. Obviously, Vance's brief was to provide a showcase for a pop fest, but he returned to the oldest cliche in the British film musical book. Not that this should deter the teenagers, who are likely to enjoy the entire affair heartily.

Director Don Sharp has brought the whole thing to screen in under six weeks shooting at a cost of around $430,000, most of which has clearly gone to artists' fees. It is well mounted with easy-on-the-eye Eastmancolor and the cast is on the ball. Nevertheless, Steele deserves a more solid and calculated screenplay to project him to the top level of British films which he has now well earned.

He plays an a&r man who was brought up in an orphange, spends every afternoon playing uncle to the kids at the home and eventually mounts a benefit show for them. Other muzzy sidelines, such as a slight romance, get lost. Situation allows a number of guest artists to do their warbling stuff, both in recording studio and on "The Night." The final concert strays into the old never-never land of British pop music pix. The artists turn up at the last moment and, without any apparent rehearsal, give a show which would need Madison Square Garden as an adequate venue.

Steele projects a warmth which communicates itself to the audience and he has one scene when, in the orphanage, he acts and puts over a number called "The Dream Maker" with the moppets, which is splendidly disarming. His chirpy personality carries the film along cheerfully. Bernard Bresslaw as a dim private, Walter Hudd as an absent minded boss of a disk firm, Michael Medwin, somewhat unconvincing as his heel of a boss, and John Tate as his girl friend's suspicious father grapple adequately with ill defined roles. On the distaff side Angela Douglas as Steele's girl friend, Jean Harvey as a tart secretary and Janet Henfrey as an unattractive, would-be singer score whenever opportunity allows.

But, apart from Steele, the credits on this film must go to the guests who appear as themselves. Philip Green has provided them with lively songs, though with lyrics of occasional lesser distinction by Norman Newell.

Among a long list, outstanding contributions are made by Danny Williams, a stylish negro singer with a hint of Harry Belafonte about him, singing "Day Without You," Marion Ryan, singing and dancing with Steele, a sharp number called "Maximum Plus," Dick Kalmann and the George Mitchell singers and dancers putting over a production number called "Summertime." Others on hand to help considerably are Geoff Love, Russ Conway, Shane Fenton and the Fentones, Johnny De Little, John Barry, the Clyde Valley Stompers and Carol Deene, all w.k. local favorites.

Newell-Green score is the greatest aid to Steele, though it is doubtful if many of the songs will hit the Top 10 bracket. John **Jympson's editing is jerky, but obviously by the disjointed yarn. Ken Hodges has produced some pleasant Eastmancolor lensing and director Don Sharp has done a professional job, though the limping story cannot have excited him overmuch. Result is a useful booking which will neither harm nor enhance Steele's worthwhile showbiz career.** *Rich.*

13 Frightened Girls
(COLOR)

Teenage hanky-panky in diplomatic circles. Flimsy suspense meller and dubious b.o. entry.

Hollywood, June 6.

Columbia Pictures release of William Castle production. No stars. Introduces Kathy Dunn. Directer by Castle. Screenplay, Robert Dillon, from story by Otis L. Guernsey Jr.; camera (Eastman), Gordon Avil; editor, Edwin Bryant; music, Van Alexander; asst. director, Sam Nelson. Reviewed at the studio, June 6, '63. Running time, **89 MINS.**

Candace Hull	Kathy Dunn
Wally	Murray Hamilton
Soldier	Joyce Taylor
John Hull	Hugh Marlowe
Kang	Khigh Dhiegh
Mike	Charlie Briggs
Miss Pittford	Norma Varden
Peter Van Hagen	Garth Benton
Mai-Ling	Lynne Sue Moon
Argentina	Maria Cristina Servera
Australia	Janet Mary Prance
Canada	Penny Anne Mills
England	Alexandra Lendon Bastedo
France	Ariane Glaser
Germany	Ilona Schutze
Italy	Anna Baj
Japan	Aiko Sakamoto
Liberia	Judy Pace
Mexico	Luz Gloria Hervias
Sweden	Marie-Louise Bielke
Venezuela	Ignacia Farias Luque
Ludwig	Emil Sitka
Fernando	Jon Alvar
Kagenescu	Walter Rode
Russia	Gina Trikonis

The fact that it is designed for exploitation purposes does not really serve as a sufficient excuse for the incredibly contrived goings-on that occur in "13 Frightened Girls." The dramatic absurdities of the William Castle production are more than can be tolerated by any but the most puerile audiences. It will take a lot of ballyhoo and educated exploitation to overcome the dramatic deficiencies of the Columbia release and scare up a decent wicket response. But if anyone can do it, Castle can.

Somewhere near the conception of this film, there appear to have been some reasonably sound exploitation ideas, such as conducting contests in various countries to locate the proper girls for the international-flavored yarn, thus supplying a nice commercial hook in each nation. And, at the root of the screenplay, there apparently existed a story notion with some development potential—namely a premise whereby the teenage daughter of a high-ranking diplomat, by her very age, sex and unobtrusive physique, is able to obtain access to highly explosive secret information that the professionals couldn't possibly uncover. But an unfunny thing happened to this notion on the way to the finished product. It didn't work.

Almost total absence of credibility in Robert Dillon's scenario from a story by Otis L. Guernsey Jr. wrecks the possibility of audience involvement or suspense. The picture fluctuates between comedy and suspense melodrama, each devastating to the mood of the other so that the upshot is chaotic. Incidents are built up, then dropped like hot political potatoes whenever explanations and resolutions are in order.

Castle's direction is shallow and awkward, as reflected in performances. The adults manage a kind of mechanical restraint, but the children, needing firmer guidance, do not fare as well. Sixteen-year-old Kathy Dunn, an uncommonly pretty girl, is guilty of the most flagrant overemoting. There is a point at which cuteness spills over into wholesale affectedness. Miss Dunn reaches this point several times. Lynne Sue Moon is uncertain as her Red Chinese playmate. Both youngsters appear to have a screen future, but it will take more direction than this to insure it. The other dozen girls, or "Teenage Diplomats," come out as caricatures of the people of their respective nations. Adult principals are Murray Hamilton, Joyce Taylor, Hugh Marlowe and Khigh Dhiegh.

Production assists are uniformly capable, among them Gordon Avil's camerawork, Edwin Bryant's editing, Don Ament's art direction. Van Alexander's music score whimsically accompanies the action. *Tube.*

Just For Fun

British variation of Yankee teen-twist tunefilm. Too little and too late.

Hollwood, June 13.

Columbia Pictures release of Milton Subotsky production. Cast: Mark Wynter, Cherry Roland, Bobby Vee, The Crickets, Freddy Cannon, Johnny Tillotson, Ketty Lester, Joe Brown, Karl Denver, Kenny Lynch, Jet Harris, Tony Meehan, Cloda Rodgers, Louise Cordet, Lyn Cornell, The Tornados, The Springfields, The Spotnicks, Jimmy Powell, The Vernon Girls, The Breakaways, Brian Poole and the Tremeloes, Sounds, Incorporated, David Jacobs, Alan Freeman, Jimmy Savile, Irene Handl, Hugh Lloyd, Dick Emery, Mario Fabrizi, Richard Vernon, Reginald Beckwith, Jeremy Lloyd, Edwin Richfield, Harry Fowler, John Wood, Frank Williams, Gordon Rollings, Douglas Ives, Ken Parry, Gary Hope, Ian Gray, John Martin, Jack Bentley. Directed by Gordon Fleming. Screenplay, Subotsky; camera, Nicolas Roeg; editor, Raymond Poulton; asst. director, Ross MacKenzie. Reviewed at the studio, June 13, '63. Running time, **84 MINS.**

"Twist Around Big Ben" or "Carry On, Teenager" could have served as alternate titles for this British equivalent of a Yankee teen musical of the Sam Katzman variety. This is the picture that caused the "we want our money back" commotion when it was previewed recently by Columbia at the Rivoli in New York. No wonder. It's not the kind of film that ought to be sprung upon people with no warning. Anyone beyond the age of puberty has to work up a preparatory immunity to this sort of experience.

Where "Just for Fun" might have commercial value of a sort in England, it doesn't on this side of the Atlantic. In the first place, even the star names are rather obscure over here. Secondly, while the twist, holly golly and such may still be the teenage rage over there, the wave has definitely receded over here and, in addition, was thoroughly exploited by U.S. filmmakers about a year ago.

There are, however, minor merits to the Milton Subotsky production that are detectable in any market. Some of the stuff Subotsky has written to fit between the monotonous bombardment of teen musical acts and serve as comedy relief enables some accomplished adult farceurs to get in a few good slapstick licks. The loosely strung plot has to do with teenagers getting the vote and rejecting Tory and Labor parties for their own ticket—fun! Along the way, the satiric needle is administered bluntly to both parties and other likely targets. Otherwise, it's just one musical specialty after another, and there's nothing very special about these specialties.

Gordon Flemyng directed, Alan Freeman narrates and teenagers Mark Wynter and Cherry Roland serve as co-hosts for the guided tour through British teenville. Except for the accent, it's no different than Yankee teenville. *Tube.*

The Checkered Flag
(EASTMANCOLOR)

So-so indie of evil characters against sports car racing background.

Motion Picture Investors Inc. release through Mercury Pictures, of Herb Vendig production. Cast: Joe Morrison, Evelyn King, Charles G. Martin, Peggy Vendig, others. Written-directed by William Grefe. Original music by Alice Simms. Reviewed at Fairway Theatre, Johnson County, Kansas (Kansas City, Mo.), June 1, '63. Running time, **110 MINS.**

Release of "The Checkered Flag" culminates a longterm project by Motion Picture Investors Inc., originally intended to add exhibitor-backed product to the shortage of feature product for theatres. When originally conceived 4-5 years ago, the idea had much merit and the feature shortage was perhaps worse than now. Even yet, however, an independnt production with new backing is a good idea, although this one falls somewhat short in the realization.

MPI is coupling "Flag" with "Trigger Happy," a reissue of the former Pathe release, "The Deadly Companions." Latter has been shortened, provided with new advertising and exploitation, and has marquee value in the names of Maureen O'Hara, Brian Keith, Steve Cochran and Chill Wills. It is longer on production values of which "Flag" is short, has some excellent photography of Arizona landscapes and sunsets, is in Panavision and Pathe Color. Although nothing compelling, characterizations and story are a few jumps ahead of those in "Flag," and con**sequently "Trigger Happy" aids the coupling.**

The pluses for "Checkered

Flag" are the facts of its shooting in and around Sebring, Florida, and the sports car endurance race annually held there. Footage credited to J. R. Remy of the race itself is quite good and makes for fine screen interest when it is running (much of it apparently shot from a helicopter). Another plus is the exploitation possibilities, especially in drive-ins and in tie-ups with sports car clubs, etc., and the coupling with "Trigger Happy" to complete the bill.

When the story takes over, however, it becomes pretty elemental and things lag until the sports cars come racing back. Yarn of a millionaire-playboy-race driver and an alcoholic, cheating wife, both of whom are enmeshed with a poor boy-makes good race driver, has little motivation, lightweight direction and acting and episodic development. When it's all over the principals have all come to horrible, gruesome ends, and the witless connivers have proven the simple truth that cheaters never prosper.

On the profit side MPI stands to get its money back in good shape. In area saturation bookings in the midwest, the film pair is grossing above average in drive-ins and should get reasonably good play through the summer. The nut on the two is estimated at something under $150,000, which may let MPI out with samething to spare.

Quin.

Les Vierges
(The Virgins
(FRENCH)

Paris, June 11.

SNC release of Boreal production. Stars Charles Aznavour, Gerard Blain, Francis Blanche, Jean Poiret, Charles Belmont, Stefania Sandrelli; features Catherine Dorleac, Catherine Diamant. Directed by Jean-Pierre Mocky. Screenplay, Alain Moury, Catherine Claude, Mocky, Genevieve Dormann, Monique Lange: camera, Eugene Shuftan; music, Paul Mauriat, Raymond Lefevre. At Balzac, Paris. Running time, **88 MINS.**

Boss .... Charles Aznavour
Xavier .... Gerard Blain
Father .... Francis Blanche
Banker .... Jean Poiret
Francois .... Charles Belmont
Marie .... Stefania Sandrelli
Nora .... Catherine Dorleac
Genevieve .... Catherine Diamant

The loss of virginity is the theme of this sketch pic which deals with four cases of the same. Though characters are intermingled to lead from one episode to another, each is self sufficient. Theme obviously has exploitation aspects but is dealt with via the right ironic insight to make it okay for special situations abroad but somewhat skimpy for arties.

Young director Jean - Pierre Mocky is primarily a satirist but up until now, his pix have been somewhat too gritty, overstated and ponderous to make their points. But here there is a muted feel for lost innocence and less of an insistence on ugliness and sordidness for its own sake.

Film is thus more palatable but still a bit flimsy in characterization. However, the comic shafts are brighter, the looks at human foibles sharper, and the scene setting brisker. Mocky looks to emerge a heavyweight contender soon.

One teen-ager has decided to give herself to her boyfriend but he gets drunk and she ends up becoming a pickup. Another marries a stolid man she does not love and is practically raped on her wedding nite. One conniver uses her state to get a rich husband but also the man she really wants by utilizing her wiles.

Still another thinks an older man who loves her is holding back due to her virginity and she gives it away to another for him but loses him in the bargain. And one young pair can just not find a place in their desire to be modern and make love before mariage.

Lensing is crisp, editing sharp and music the right counterpoint to the serio-comic segments. Playing has the needed wile by a group of pretty new actresses while Gerard Blain brings off a prig character adequately and Charles Aznavour has the true ring of a fortyish man searching for purity in love again.

This has a bright surface polish, some telling notations on fleshly foibles and the saving grace of taste to make it acceptable if, overall, it still remains a surface look at skittish maidens.

Mosk.

Heavens Above!
(BRITISH)

Sharp, satirical dig at the Church by the Boulting Brothers. Humor uneven but almost non-stop, yet with pensive undertones; Peter Sellers and tailormade cast. Big b.o. likely.

London, June 11.

British Lion Romulus presentation through BLC of a Boulting Brothers production. Stars Peter Sellers, Cecil Parker, Isabel Jeans, Eric Sykes, Bernard Miles; features Ian Carmichael, Irene Handl, Brock Peters, Miriam Karlin, Roy Kinnear. Directed by John Boulting. Original screenplay, Frank Harvey, John Boulting, from an idea by Malcolm Muggeridge; camera, Max Green; editor, Teddy Farvas; music, Richard Rodney Bennett. At Columbia Theatre, London. Running time, **118 MINS.**

Rev. John Smallwood....... Peter Sellers
Archdeacon Aspinall ...... Cecil Parker
Lady Despard .... Isabel Jeans
Harry Smith .... Eric Sykes
Simpson .... Bernard Miles
Matthew .... Brock Peters
The Other Smallwood..... Ian Carmichael
Rene Smith .... Irene Handl
Winnie Smith .... Miriam Karlin
Mrs. Smith-Gould .... Joan Miller
Bank Manager .... Eric Barker
Fred Smith .... Roy Kinnear
Rev. Owen Smith....... Kenneth Griffith
Rockerby .... Miles Malleson
Major Fowler .... William Hartnell
Garrulous Housewife....... Joan Hickson
Shop Steward .... Harry Locke
Director General .... Nicholas Phipps
Tranquilax Executive .. Thorley Walters
Bishop .... George Woodbridge
Prisoner Governor .... Basil Dignam
Prime Minister .... Colin Gordon
Disgruntled Housewife ...... Joan Heal
Cleric .... Malcolm Muggeridge
P.R.O. .... Conrad Phillips
Tramp .... Cardew Robinson
Fellowes .... Billy Milton
Astronaut .... Howard Pays

The Boulting Brothers have tossed many irreverent jabs at many of Britain's sacred cows. They've joshed devastatingly trade unions, the Foreign Office, the army and the law. Now they've turned their guns on the Church. True, their artillery is not particularly heavy, but it is constantly on target and the result is a very funny film which will probably be enjoyed heartily by the clergy. Yet interwoven among the fun is some very shrewd and tart observation. The film pricks much of the pomposity of the church and its hangers-on. Some are going to interpret it as an attack on religion or Christianity, but that's obviously not so. It is an attack on some of the cant, bigotry and smug hypocrisy that helps to destroy true Christianity.

A measure of the merit of "Heavens Above!" is that its theme could have been just as acceptably used as a straight drama. But the Boulting Brothers have effectively employed their favorite weapon, the rapier of ridicule. The screenplay by Frank Harvey and John Boulting is full of choice jokes, but the humor is often uneven. Sometimes it is sophisticated and witty; at other times it relies on fairly predictable gags and down-to-earth, even naive humor, and the mixture often clashes uncomfortably.

But with a long, impeccable cast headed by Peter Sellers there seems no doubt about this clicking all over. It has already got away to a good start in Britain and New York.

Story concerns the appointment, by a clerical error, of the Reverend John Smallwood (Peter Sellers) to the parish of Orbiston Parva, a prosperous neighborhood ruled by the Despard family, makers of Tranquilax, the three-in-one restorative (Sedative! Stimulant! Laxative!). Whatever Sellers' qualifications, they are clearly not right for this snooty district. For he's a quiet, down-to-earth chap who happens to believe in the scriptures and lives by them.

From the moment he gives his first sermon all hell breaks out, so to speak. He shocks the district by making a Negro trashman his warden and takes a bunch of disreputable evicted gypsies into the vicarage. Soon he makes his first convert, Lady Despard. He confronts her with the Bible and she is so ashamed of her own wealth that she decides to be a do-gooder. She turns over her mansion to stray hoboes and sets up a free-for-all food service for the locals.

With these handouts, religion becomes popular among the natives, except the shopkeepers, who are put out of business. But when Sellers attacks tranquilax from the pulpit, the rot begins. The Stock Exchange trembles and a near broke Lady Despard has to stop her Lady Bountiful act. Whereupon the townsfolk turn angrily on Sellers, abuse him and run him out of town. The situation calls for top level conferences between the State and Church and the embarrassment is only ended when Sellers is appointed Bishop of Outer Space and finds himself rocketing to the moon.

Within this framework there are some very amusing verbal and visual jokes, and both are largely aided by some deft acting. Sellers adds yet another gem to his showcase. He does not miss a trick when it comes to a laugh or a wry smile. But he is no mere figure of fun. Here, the audience will believe, is a man with a message and one in whom the light of true Christianity really glows. It is a guileful portrayal of genuine simplicity.

Bernard Miles, as an acquisitive butler; Eric Sykes, Irene Handl, Miriam Karlin and Roy Kinnear (leader of the gypsies), and Isabel Jeans, a regal Lady Despard, all contribute heftily. Cecil Parker bumbles effectively as an archdeacon and George Woodbridge looks as if he had been born in Bishop's gaiters.

Kenneth Griffith is the fieriest of Welsh parsons, Miles Malleson, a grotesque psychiatrist who is clearly heading for the couch himself, and William Hartnell, Ian Carmichael, Joan Hickson, Eric Barker, Thorley Walters and others give a lift to the proceedings.

John Boulting has directed with a clear idea of what he and his brother are getting at. They've surrounded themselves with a good technical gang, including the camera of Max Greene, the sharp editing of Teddy Darvas and a neat, witty score by Richard Rodney Bennett.

Those who expect to see church steeples crumble under a blistering attack will be unlucky. But there is enough amusement to satisfy even those who want to duck the film's unmistakable and uncomfortable conclusion: "That in this material world anyone who tries to lead a truly Christian life is weighing himself down with socko odds."

Rich.

Cattle King
(COLOR)

Routine sagebrusher.

Hollywood, May 29.

Metro release of Nat Holt production. Stars Robert Taylor; features Joan Caulfield, Robert Loggia, Robert Middleton, Larry Gates. Directed by Tay Garnett. Screenplay, Thomas Thompson; camera (Eastman), William Snyder; editor, George White; music, Paul Sawtell, Bert Shefter; asstfl director, Henry E. Brill. Reviewed at the studio, May 29, '63. Running time, **88 MINS.**

Sam Brassfield .... Robert Taylor
Sharleen .... Joan Caulfield
Johnny Quatro .... Robert Loggia
Clay Mathews .... Robert Middleton
President Chester A. Arthur Larry Gates
Clevenger .... Malcolm Atterbury
Harry Travers .... William Windom
Ruth Winters .... Virginia Christine
Ed Winters .... Ray Teal
Vince Bodine .... Richard Devon
Webb Carter .... Robert Ivers
June Carter .... Maggie Pierce
Stafford .... Woodrow Palfrey
Hobie .... Richard Tretter
Tex .... John Mitchum

Even the most ardent buffs of the western idiom will find little in "Cattle King" to enthuse over. The names of Robert Taylor and, to some degree, Joan Caulfield do lend the Metro release a kind of remembrance-of-things-past quasi-glamour, but it's asking a lot of them—perhaps too much—to override the story inadequacies of the Nat Holt production and give it "A" picture stature. Except in isolated situations where westerns are accepted indiscriminately, "Cattle King" will probably have to settle for the lower half of a program.

Thomas Thompson's scenario is laid in the Wyoming Territory of 1883 and has to do with a wealthy rancher (Taylor) who fights for fenced-in, controlled grazing against the open range advocates who turn out to be singularly bad types. The story is hackneyed and the characters are trite and poorly-defined. Moreover, Thompson's screenplay contains several long, talky passages in which the prog-

ress of the plot is delayed for a lot of poorly-placed exposition about characters the audience has not yet been introduced to visually and therefore has no interest in. The dialog is as old as them thar hills. Sample: "There's sump'n in the wind—I heard it in the coyote's howl last night."

Taylor gives a straight delineation of the heroic pivotal figure. It's not much of a part for Miss Caulfield, who gets shot dead two-thirds of the way through the film. Prior to her abrupt and unexpected demise, she supplies romantic interest opposite Taylor. Robert Loggia is colorful as a loyal, but fun-loving Mexican. Robert Middleton and Richard Devon generate venom as the heavies and Larry Gates dispatches the most unusual characterization in the film, that of President Chester A. Arthur, who turns out to be a lovable old codger. Others of some import are Malcolm Atterbury as a not-so-sheepish sheepman and Robert Ivers, Maggie Pierce, Virginia Christine and Ray Teal as folks who live on Taylor's ranch.

William Snyder has captured some pretty autumn landscapes in his Eastman colored lens. Otherwise, production values are strictly of a conventional nature—all the way down the line. *Tube.*

Hamarfef
(The Cellar)
(ISRAELI)

Tel Aviv, June 4.

A Shay Film (Nachum Slonin) production. Stars Shimon Yisraeli. Directed by Nathan Gross. Story and screenplay, Shimon Yisraeli; music, Yisraeli; adapted by Eddie Halpern; camera, Yasha Yosilovitch; editor, Danny Schick. At Ben Yehuda Theatre, Tel Aviv. Running time, **65 MINS.**

This is a one-man tour de force and probably the best Israeli film made to date.

Hitler is kaput and a young German Jew returns from Dachau to his former home. The house is occupied by Hans, his former schoolmate, an ex-Nazi responsible for the death of the Jewish boy's father. Hans lives in the house with Lotte, who was the Jewish boy's sweetheart.

The Jew slips into the house and descends to the cellar, where objects, like a doll, a snapshot and a watch, raise, one by one childhood memories in flashbacks. At the end, he recalls the place where Lotte's love-letters are hidden. He finds, instead, the secret treasury of Hans, a swastika, a Nazi badge, a knife and a revolver. With the revolver he kills Hans, and leaves behind Lotte and Germany forever. The memories haunt him when he goes to Israel.

Shimon Yisraeli, a young Israeli actor, has written the story and the music of the film. Also he plays the hero, as a boy, a young man and an adult. He also portrays in flashbacks, his own father and an old schoolteacher. No other actor is seen on the screen. Hans is only a silhouette and Lotte a beautiful, faceless body with long, blond hair.

The self-imposed imprisonment in the cellar is boring rather than haunting. Somebody else might transform such a cellar into a microcosm of things past. Yisraeli's failure to accomplish this reduces the film to a static melodrama. But it has latent power and something to say.

Interestingly enough, "The Cellar" is not basically anti-German. Hans was a Nazi, but Lotte was a good girl and the old teacher represented the last vestiges of humanism in a crazy era.

Camerawork is sometimes good. *Lapid.*

Toys In The Attic
(PANAVISION)

Slightly diluted, but still toxic version of Lillian Hellman's legiter. Heavy, unsavory. But commercial lure. Needs trade and consumer sell.

Hollywood, June 2.
United Artists release of Walter Mirisch production. Stars Dean Martin, Geraldine Page, Yvette Mimieux, Wendy Hiller, Gene Tierney. Directed by George Roy Hill. Screenplay, James Poe, based on Lillian Hellman's play; camera, Joseph F. Biroc; editor, Stuart Gilmore; music, George Duning; asst. director, Emmett Emerson. Reviewed at Goldwyn Studios, May 31, '63. Running time, **88 MINS.**

Julian Berniers	Dean Martin
Carrie Berniers	Geraldine Page
Lily Prine Berniers	Yvette Mimieux
Anna Berniers	Wendy Hiller
Albertine Prine	Gene Tierney
Charlotte Warkins	Nan Martin
Cyrus Warkins	Larry Gates
Henry	Frank Silvera
Gus	Charles Lampkin

Walter Mirisch's production of "Toys in the Attic" is a somewhat watered-down version of Lillian Hellman's play, but enough of the original's emotional savagery has been retained to satisfy those film-goers who prefer their melodramatic meat raw and chewy. It is, however, not an attraction for the "I've got problems enough of my own" school of customer.

Could be that the public is tiring, plausibly, of Southern-fried neurosis operas. If so, "Toys" is laid in the deep South and liberally crammed with such sick-sick cargo as incest, adultery, imbecility, lust an a few other popular folk pleasantries. It will take all of Miss Hellman's reputation plus the power and lure of well-bally-hoed all-stops-out histrionics by some renowned performers to bail out the United Artists release.

Principal tampering scenarist James Poe has done with Miss Hellman's neatly constructed, momentum-gathering play about a New Orleans household shattered by latent incest and corrosive possessiveness is in altering the ending, apparently to suit the less sophisticated needs of the mass audience. Miss Hellman's heavyweight drama examines the tragedy that transpires as a result of a spinster sister's secret lust for her younger brother, whose monetarily-motivated marriage to a simple-minded girl sets in operation the mechanism for his ultimate disaster, which occurs after his bride is deceived by his sister into betraying him just as he is on the brink of consummating a business deal with humanitarian overtones.

Lamentably, the new ending is thoroughly artificial. It is one of those now shopworn climaxes in which everyone is seen taking off, leaving the individual who is the source of all their emotional ailments alone to rot in the house of evil she has created, as the camera pulls away to observe her wretched solitude. Aside from being hackneyed, it is a thoroughly unlifelike denouement. Otherwise, Poe's additions and subtractions are sound.

George Roy Hill has made an error or two along the way, but generally his direction is taut, progressive and fastpaced considering this is a very talky, confined piece. The performances are fine. Geraldine Page, an actress of enormous range and vitality, gives a powerful portrayal in the difficult and unappealing role of the venomous sister. Wendy Hiller, in the less provocative, unspectacular part of the perceptive, more rational older sister, holds her own in the emotional give and take with a very sensitive portrayal.

Dean Martin, in his most demanding role to date, is ingratiating as the ne'er-do-well brother who almost does well. Yvette Mimieux gives another of her misty, innocent, childlike characterizations. Gene Tierney is satisfactory as the child bride's aristocratic mother, who's having an affair with a Negro, played adequately by Frank Silvera. Nan Martin and Charles Lampkin round out the small cast competently.

Joseph F. Biroc's photography is capable, save for a scene or two dark and shadowy. Stuart Gilmore's editing is expert. The film runs a trim 88 minutes, short for a transplanted stage play. Cary Odell's art direction captures the New Orleans flavor and George Duning's music underlines the gathering menace with a sombre strain. *Tube.*

For Love Or Money
(COLOR)

Another glossy romanticomedy from Universal. better in some ways, though shy of mass appeal in some of the others.

Hollywood, June 18.
Universal release of Robert Arthur production. Stars Kirk Douglas, Mitzi Gaynor, Gig Young; features Thelma Ritter, Leslie Parrish, Julie Newmar, William Bendix. Directed by Michael Gordon. Screenplay, Larry Markes, Michael Morris; camera (Eastman), Clifford Stine; editor, Alma Macrorie; music, De Vol; asst. director, Joseph Kenny. Reviewed at Westwood Village Theatre, June 18, '63. Running time **108 MINS.**

Deke Gentry	Kirk Douglas
Kate	Mitzi Gaynor
Sonny Smith	Gig Young
Chloe Brasher	Thelma Ritter
Bonnie	Julie Newmar
Fogel	William Bendix
Jan	Leslie Parrish
Harvey Wofford	Richard Sargent
Marsha	Elizabeth MacRae
Sam Travis	William Windom
Orson Roark	Willard Sage
Nurse	Ina Victor
George	Alvy Moore
Jaime	Jose Gonzales Gonzales
Gregor	Don Megowan
Elevator Operator	Billy Halop
Male Shopper	Joey Faye
Artist	Theodore Marcuse
Red Beard	Frank Mahony

Universal's cycle of slick romantic comedies continues with this witty and engaging sophisticated farce. Crammed with attractive players, elegant sets, glamorous costumes, sharp dialog and amusingly contrived situations, the Robert Arthur production has the ingredients for boxoffice success. However, favorable as its prospects are, comedy is not quite as homespun or mass-oriented as other Universal entries of this genre, so the commercial results do not figure to be as lucrative. Yet "For Love or Money" is at least the match of any of them in terms of humor and social commentary.

The glib, sharp scenario by Larry Markes and Michael Morris is seasoned with spicy spoofery of three worthy contemporary tar-

gets: motivational research, physical fitness and modern art—and the people who practice these fads and/or professions. The wild plot has to do with a wealthy and eccentric widow's scheme to marry her three daughters off to the candidates of her choice, a goal for which she assigns her attorney the additional duties of matchmaker. All of this is engineered at a bright, effervescent clip by director Michael Gordon. In its field—romantic farce bolstered with shots of satire—the film equals anything out of Hollywood this year. Only when scrutinized from a more finicky, elevated plane do shortcomings zero into focus—deficiencies such as the somewhat hackneyed nature of events like a beatnik party or the foregone conclusions of the romantic interplay.

Kirk Douglas uncorks a flair for zany comedics as the pivotal figure in the proceedings. He plays the attorney-matchmaker who falls for the eldest daughter, a consumer research bug with Madison Avenue phraseology vivaciously played by Mitzi Gaynor. The other daughters are Julie Newmar, a delectable blonde amazon as the health addict, and Leslie Parrish, slightly miscast (but not without visual advantages) as the pretty beatnik. Even Thelma Ritter, as the screwball widow, gets the glamor treatment. She neved looked better and her reliable way with a wisecrack is a big asset to the picture.

Gig Young delivers another of his amiable boozing wolf-playboy characterizations. William Bendix comes through nicely as a good-naturedly hapless Pinkerton. An additional dash of sex is contributed solidly by Elizabeth MacRae, and two of the husbands-to-be are enacted capably by Richard Sargent and William Windom. Supporting performances are infectious right down the line.

Clifford Stine's photography is flattering and colorful. The interior sets and furnishings are especially tasteful and inviting, reflecting great credit on art directors Alexander Golitzen and Malcolm Brown and set decorator Ruby Levitt. The Jean Louis gowns are stunning. Audiences will gasp in appreciation of several of them. Alma Macrorie's editing is trim and crisp, Frank De Vol's music helpful in an unobtrusive way.

Tube.

Captain Sindbad
(COLOR)

Adventure fantasy aimed at hot weather moppet buck. Filmed on fairly lavish scale. Should do well at summer b.o.

Hollywood, June 19.

Metro release of Frank & Herman King production. Stars Guy Williams, Heidi Bruhl, Pedro Armendariz, Abraham Sofaer. Directed by Byron Haskin. Screenplay, Samuel B. West, Harry Relis; camera (Technicolor), Gunter Senftleben; editor, Robert Swink; music, Michel Michelet; asst. director, Leon Chooluck. Reviewed at the studio, June 19, '63. Running time, **85 MINS.**

Captain Sindbad .... Guy Williams
Princess Jana .... Heidi Bruhl
El Kerim .... Pedro Armendariz
Calgo .... Abraham Sofaer
Quintus .... Bernie Hamilton
Bendar .... Helmut Schneider
Lady-in-waiting .... Margaret Jahnen
The King .... Rolf Wanka
Rolf .... Walter Barnes
Iffritch .... James Dobson
Ahmed .... Maurice Marsac
Colonel Kabar .... Henry Brandon
Aram .... John Crawford
Mohar .... Geoffrey Toone

Those perennial perpetrators of cinematic tricks the Brothers King, are at it again in this fairy tale frolic for the vacationing moppet trade. The rather lavish spectacle they have mounted is based on a pretty fragile story foundation, but that isn't apt to interfere with the glee of the urchins, who are bound to be delighted with the feats of celluloidal sorcery performed by the Kings and their staff.

Apparently a costly enterprise of its genre, the Metro release will need to rack up a lot of kiddie coin to recoup but moneymaking prospects are bright for the current hot weather season The only direct competition in its class at the moment is Columbia's "Jason and the Argonauts" which, though superior to "Captain Sindbad," shouldn't cut that much of the pie so that there won't be a sizable cunk left over

The tale concocted by writers Samuel B. West and Harry Relis is elementary enough. Elementary for the uncluttered mind of a tyke, that is Sindbad's mission is simply to get to scale yon white tower of terror wherein is sealed the heart of the villainous El Kerim, a literally heartless fellow who not only is indestructible thanks to the proxy pumpmanship he has arranged with his friendly neighborhood prestidigitator, but is an absolute scoundrel whose idea of sport is having an elephant step on the head of a maiden. Since the maiden he has chosen for this game of sqoosh is Sindbad's beloved princess, it is imperative that the hero get to the heart of the matter quickly. To attain his target, he must overcome such obstacles as an invisible monster, whirlpool sucks, avalanches, bull crocidiles, a 12-headed scylla, cannibal fish and a giant hand that guards the bum's ticker

All of these pitfalls and many other visual oddities have been engineered skillfully by the staff artisans, with special credit due special photographic effects man Tom Howard and the special effects team of Lee Zavitz and Augie Lohman. Others who rate prominent recognition for their efforts on the enterprise, filmed in Germany, are art directors Werner & Isabelle Schlichting, editor Robert Swink and cameraman Gunter Senftleben, although some of the latter's process work is rather crude—with some jarring transparencies. Michel Michelet's music makes use of some pretty Borodin-like themes.

Under Byron Haskin's spirited direction, the cast performs capably. Guy Williams breezes through the title role. German actress Heidi Bruhl is a fetching princess. Abraham Sofaer has himself an uninhibited ball as the merry magician. That fine actor, the late Pedro Armendariz, is a convincing figure as the dastardly El Kerim.

Tube.

Summer Magic
(COLOR—SONGS)

A Disney delight for the youngsters; good all around boxoffice in sight.

Buena Vista release of Walt Disney production. Stars Hayley Mills, Burl Ives, Dorothy McGuire, Deborah Walley; features Una Markel, Eddie Hodges, Michael J. Pollard, Peter Brown. Directed by James Neilson. Screenplay, Sally Benson, based on the novel, "Mother Carey's Chickens" by Kate Douglas Wiggins; camert (Technicolor), William Snyder; editor, Robert Stafford; music, Buddy Baker; songs, Robert and Richard Sherman. At Radio City Music Hall screening room June 20, '63. Running time, **109 MINS.**

Nancy Carey .... Hayley Mills
Osh Popham .... Burl Ives
Margaret Carey .... Dorothy McGuire
Cousin Julia .... Deborah Walley
Gilly Carey .... Eddie Hodges
Peter Carey .... Jimmy Mathers
Digby Popham .... Michael Pollard
Lallie Joy .... Wendy Turner
Maria Popham .... Una Merkel
Tom Hamilton .... Peter Brown
Charles Bryant .... Jim Stacy
Mr. Perkins .... O. Z. Whitehead

The pre-World War I novel of Kate Douglas Wiggins' "Mother Carey's Chickens," has been fashioned into an easy-to-take entertainment that promises to be of particular delight to the younger element. The Disney trademark shows through all the way, meaning devotees of Tennessee Williams had better not be invited.

But do bid come the scads of millions, including the school vacationers, along with Mom & Dad, who doubtless will enjoy a pleasant little story about a Boston widow who takes her two children to a small town in Maine and has a ball. Of particular significance are the songs by Robert and Richard Sherman which ought to make a highly saleable album on their own and endow the picture with additional charm.

Indeed, there are enough tunes herein to make a musical but they're subordinated to the story—and properly. As a matter of fact the musical numbers figure as an integral part of the tale and are fitted in just right under James Neilson's competent direction.

Clocked at 109 minutes, "Summer Magic" could be tightened a bit, but nonetheless it has all the earmarks of a spellbinder for the kids and boxoffice enchantment for exhibitors.

Producer Disney has dressed his picture handsomely, and William Snyder's camerawork (Technicolor) gets full value out of the picturesque sets and settings.

Dorothy McGuire is the widow who has two teenage children and little cash. She comes upon a house in a town called Beulah thanks to a good-natured benefactor, Burl Ives. Offspring are Hayley Mills (who has grown to be a very pretty and appealing teenager) and Eddie Hodges.

Deborah Walley is a high-falutin' cousin (and an attractive dish) who comes to stay, Una Merkel is Ives' terribly practical wife, Michael J. Pollard is a newly-arrived, handsome school teacher who has a romantic go with Miss Walley, and Peter Brown, who shows up late at the owner of the house occupied by Mother Carey and her brood, is soon to become enamored of Miss Mills. Works out good as a Disney pic should.

Sally Benson's script plays out well. The players are an able group, whether reading a line or vocalizing the Shermans' contributions. Ives does especially well with "The Ugly Bug Ball," a novelty number pictorially enhanced by the insertion of a few Disney nature-study clips. Done engagingly by the Misses Mills, Walley and Wendy Turner is bright item titled "Femininity." Hodges also helps with the vocals.

Count on "Summer Magic" as summer click.

Gene.

My Name Is Ivan
(RUSSIAN)

Sig Shore release of Mosfilm production. Stars Kolya Burlaiev. Directed by Andrei Tarkovsky. Screenplay, Vladimir Bogomolov, Mikhail Papava from Bogomolov's short story, "Ivan"; camera, Vadim Yusov. Previewed in N.Y. projection room, June 21, '63. Running time, **97 MINS.**

Ivan .... Kolya Burlaiev
Capt. Kholin .... Valentin Zubkov
Lt. Galtsev .... Ye. Zharikov
Corp. Katasonych .... S. Krylov
Col. Gryaznov .... N. Grinko
Old Man .... D. Milyutenko
Masha .... V. Malyavina
Ivan's Mother .... I. Tarkovsky

(In Russian; English subtitles)

Basic idea of "My Name Is Ivan," also called "Ivan's Childhood," was an interesting one. But some place along the line, the whole thing was sidetracked and muddled so badly that the climax is about as exciting as a lullaby. Bogomolov's short story, originally publicized more than four years ago, by this second World War veteran was tagged "Ivan," and related the adventures of a 12-year-old Russo boy who became an intelligence scout for the Russian army.

Ivan ranges far behind enemy lines, gathering valuable information for his Russian army and reporting to his commanding officer. But as translated to the screen this basic idea is nearly 100% lost, either from inferior cutting or sloppy titling in English. Or a bit of both. Because the average patron will not realize, if ever, that this frail youth had been trained to slip in and out of enemy territory, right under the noses of all guards. Nor is the angle that his one burning desire is to defeat the invader and avenge the death of his mother and sister made clear until the film is nearly over.

The final hazardous venture behind the lines is not pointed up clearly enough for the average viewer to realize what Ivan is trying to do. This episode, on the edge of the Pripet Marshes, is well staged but the significance of it—that it is the lad's final mission and that he has been captured by the Germans—is almost completely lost. Reason for this is the director's yen to make it all symbolical, and photographically perfect.

All of which is understandable when realized that this is the first feature pic by director Andrei Tarkovsky. "Ivan" is portrayed by Kolya Burlaiev, blond-haired lad, who virtually thefts the film. Other Russians, both in the army and civilians, are well cast from a typical group of sterling Russo film players

The director has worked in every little sound effect he has ever heard of but sometimes the symbolisms are lost by mere prolongation and insistency, Vadim Yusov has done yeoman work as cameraman but one wonders about the full import of having a forest of trees wave about until the auditors are dizzy

"My Name Is Ivan" is supposed to have won three awards at the 1962 Venice Film Fest (best pic, best director best actor), which makes one wonder. Film opens at the Murray Hill Theatre June 27 after an invitational preem the night of June 26. Pic is the most recent acquisition via the cultural exchange agreement between the U.S. and Russia. *Wear.*

Buddha
(JAPANESE—COLOR)

Epic-dimension, finely made biopic of life of Asia's great religious figure. May be hardgoing as straight sell in U.S. Best bet via schools, liberal churches.

Lopert Pictures Corp. release of Daiei Picture Co. (Masaichi Nagata) production. Stars Kojiro Hongo, Charito Solis, Shintaro Katsu, Machiko Kyo, Raizo Ichikawa. Fujiko Yamamoto. Directed by Kenji Misumi. Screenplay, Fuji Yahiro; camera, (Technicolor), Hiroshi Imai; editor, Kanji Suganuma; special effects. Tatsuyuki Yokota, Soh-Ichi Aisaka. Tradeshown in N.Y., June 26, '63. Running time, **139 MINS.**

Siddhartha	Kojiro Hongo
Yashodhara	Charito Solis
Devadatta	Shintaro Katsu
Nandabala	Machiko Kyo
Kunala	Raizo Ichikawa
Usha	Fujiko Yamamoto
Ajatashatru	Hiroshi Kawaguchi
Ananda	Katsuhiko Kobayashi
Auttami	Tamao Nakamura
Matangi	Junko Kano
Amana	Mieko Kondo
Sari	Tokiko Mita
Neecha	Hiromi Ichida
Kilika	Michiko Ai
Sonna	Matasaburo
Upali	Keizo Kawasaki
Child's Mother	Reiko Fujiwara
Shariputra	Gen Mitsumura
Bhutika	Ryuzo Shimada
Arama	Joji Tsurumi
Kalodayi	Shiro Otsuji
Kaundinya	Yoshiro Kitahara
Mahakashyapa	Jun Negami
Ashoka	Ganjiro Nakamura
Griha	Toshio Chiba
Bandhu	Ryuichi Ishii
Maudgaliputra	Yoichi Funaki
Rayana	Sanemon Arashi
Jivaka	Osamu Maruyama

(In Japanese; English Titles)

"Buddha" is a colorful spectacle, a cinematic story of Gautama Buddha's life from his birth in northern India some 3,000 years ago until his passing. It is skillfully directed, generally well acted and a different, if at times gruesome, artistic story. Boxoffice prospects in the U.S.-Canada market must carry a question-mark. The film needs more trade and consumer selling than it will probably get. There is some latent educational, curiosity and even religious interest since Buddha was one of the great spiritual leaders of history, a figure often mentioned with Jesus, Mohammad and others.

For U.S. audiences, this pic has the added handicap of being subtitled and having two hours and 19 minutes running time. Obviously, this plays better for those understanding the Japanese language, the translation to wooden English phrases losing much. The film's length would hurt its turnover in arty theatres where it will find most of its American bookings.

An excellent all-star cast of Japanese actors means very little to U.S. patrons excepting for Machiko Kyo, who was in "Teahouse of August Moon" film some years back. Basic plot idea has a youthful prince, Siddhartha (Kojiro Hongo) irked at the conditions of the common people, many of them dying from starvation and untreated disease. He also is perturbed by the old religions, and turns away in horror from some of the rites including that of human sacrifice. So one night he deserts his princess wife and goes away for six years of meditations.

He resists demons, sensual dancing girls and semi-nude femmes to attain spiritual enlightenment, being reborn as the Buddha. He gathers many disciples, who carry on his work as word spreads of his miracles and good deeds. The miracle of bringing torrents of rain to a thirst-parched village,

and later of halting a huge elephant just as he was about to trample one of his priests bring him thousands of converts.

But there is too much stress on people being killed, dying of disease or being brutally punished. Opening sequences are tediously patterned, to the extent that they become boring. The period in India's history, as depicted, had sexy episodes in the royal palaces. In one of these, the king's wife is shown making a play for the younger son. Rebuffed, she wins over the captain of the guard in order to see that this son is punished—by having his eyes burned out.

Kojiro Hongo gives a superb performance as Prince Siddhartha, who later becomes the Buddha. Shintaro Katsu is his ruthless cousin and makes a vioid, villainous rival in trying to sway the populace. Charito Solis is charming as Siddhartha's wife in the earlier episodes. Miss Kyo, listed as a star, has a more or less lesser role as the sacred Nandabala who brings food to Buddha.

Kenji Misumi's direction is topflight while the lensing by Hiroshi Imai is a highlight of this pic. Screenplay by Fuji Yahiro is good enough considering how much territory he had to cover. *Wear.*

A Ticklish Affair
(PANAVISION-COLOR)
Flimsy romanticomedy.

Hollywood, June 28.
Metro release of Joe Pasternak production. Stars Shirley Jones, Gig Young, Red Buttons, Carolyn Jones. Directed by George Sidney. Screenplay, Ruth Brooks Flippen, based on story, "Moon Walk," by Barbara Luther; camera (Metrocolor), Milton Krasner; editor, John McSweeney Jr.; music, George Stoll; assistant director, William Shanks. Reviewed at Picwood Theatre, June 28, '63. Running time, **88 MINS.**

Amy Martin	Shirley Jones
Com'd'r. Key Weedon	Gig Young
Fliht Of'c'r Simon Shelley	Red Buttons
Tandy Martin	Carolyn Jones
"Gramps" Martin	Edgar Buchanan
Yeoman Corker Bel	Eddie Applegate
Capt. Haven Hitchcock	Edward Platt
Alex Martin	Billy Mumy
Luke Martin	Bryan Russell
Policeman	Robert Foulk
Fireman	Milton Frome
Grover Martin	Peter Robbins

Boxoffice prospects look mild to weak for this trite romantic comedy out of Metro. The Joe Pasternak production, was incepted in '62, when a story titled "Moon Walk" by Barbara Luther appeared in the Ladies Home Journal. Ruth Brooks Flippen's scenario, which evolved from that yarn and into "A Ticklish Affair," has a naval commander (Gig Young) falling in love with the widowed mother (Shirley Jones) of three male moppets. He meets her when, armed and accompanied by several of his men, he turns up at her house to investigate blinking Morse Code distress signals coming from the upstairs window that have been sighted by the worried fleet in San Diego harbor. As any filmgoer knows at first blink, the signals are being flashed by some fool kid. But does the U.S. Navy suspect? With this kind of fleet, there'd *better* not be a World War III.

At any rate, Miss Jones enjoys

her gigs with Gig but nixes his marriage proposal because she doesn't want her kids to have to live out of a suitcase. The youngest boy resolves the knotty situation by floating up over San Diego attached to some helium balloons so that he can be rescued by the commander. Gratefully, Miss Jones agrees to tie the knot. It isn't clear how Hotel Cluver City got down to San Diego, but it's there, clear as day, as the boy floats over the city.

Miss Jones is peachy keen as the young widder, and Young, a natural born second lead, seems out of his element at the casting summit. Red Buttons and Carolyn Jones adequately pair up as the second romantic team. The three moppets are Peter Robbins, Billy Mumy and Bryan Russell. They strengthen the case in favor of corporal punishment, especially when they occupy the screen together. Edgar Buchanan puts in a few brief, insignificant appearances.

For director George Sidney, a decidedly lowercase effort. Milton Krasner's photography is satisfactory, as are the George W. Davis-Edward Carfagno sets and George Stoll's music. John McSweeney Jr.'s editing is helpfully snug, although that sudden Culver City locale is editorially expendable. A conventional title song by Stoll and Harold Adamson is sung by Jack Jones. *Tube.*

Tarzan's Three Challenges
(DYALSCOPE-COLOR)

Latest and, in some ways, one of best in the long series. Okay b.o. prospect. Title character ain't what he used to be.

Holywood, June 20.
Metro release of Sy Weintraub production. Stars Jock Mahoney, Woody Strode; with Tsuruko Kobayashi, Earl Cameron, Salah Jamal, Anthony Chinn, Robert Hu, Christopher Carlos, Ricky Der. Directed by Robert Day. Screenplay, Berne Giler, Day, based on Edgar Rice Burroughs' characters; camera (Metrocolor), Ted Scaife; editor, Fred Burnley; music, Joseph Horovitz; assistant director, Clive Reed. Reviewed at the studio, June 20, '63. Running time, **92 MINS.**

Tarzan	Jock Mahoney
Kahn Tarim	Woody Strode
Cho San	Tsu Kobayashi
Mang	Earl Cameron
Hani	Salah Jamal
Tor	Anthony Chinn
Nari	Robert Hu
Sechung	Christopher Carlos
Kashi	Ricky Der

Just as the remote and exotic places on this planet have lost some of their original charm and appeal since becoming more accessible with the advent of the jet age, so, too, have the characters of fiction who populated those places. Even the once pristine real estate of Tarzan, darkest Africa, is now known more for its political upheavals than its primeval splendors.

In an effort, then, to prevent Tarzan from becoming a ludicrous anachronism in a world looking to space geography for its new mysteries and exotic characters of fantasy, producer Sy Weintraub and his creative unit have gradually converted the Edgar Rice Burroughs character from the simple ape man to a globetrotting troubleshooter, a kind of one-man Peace Corps in loin cloth. But, in

thus broadening the scope, they have stripped the character of much of its distinguishing identity.

In "Tarzan's Three Challenges," he has been transplanted to Thailand. Filmed there in its entirety, it is, by modern story and production standards, probably one of the best installments in the 44-year-old, 34-chapter-old screen series, and, thanks to the inevitable moppet support, very likely will show a boxoffice profit. Yet the new Tarzan lacks the imagination-stimulating qualities that made this series so successful. Much of the romance has gone out of the marriage between character and audience. The series may be hanging on the thread of tradition, living on borrowed time. Today's Tarzan is a man without a country and with only a shred of his former personality.

In this Berne Giler-Robert Day screenplay, directed skillfully by the latter, Tarzan (Jock Mahoney) is summoned to Thailand to escort a young spiritual heir from a monastery to his rightful throne at the head of an ancient land. To protect his charge, Tarzan must ward off the challenge of the brother (Woody Strode) of the dying ruler, whom he defeats in an impressive two-man tournament of strength and courage. Some interesting socio-political ramifications of the power struggle between Strode, who represents the radical younger faction of the tribe, and the young heir-apparent, who represents tradition, are touched upon but eventually submerged by the requirements of physical action.

For the purists and the kiddies, there are vines in the Thailand jungle for Tarzan to go tree-hopping on. And Mahoney, with his natural athletic prowess, is able to make a gymnasium out of the jungle in the best Tarzan tradition. Strode is a most impressive figure as the antagonist, and also briefly enacts the role of the dying chieftain. Ricki Der does capably as the young ruler and Tsuruko Kobayashi contributes the right note of concern as his devoted nursemaid.

The production is notable for a smattering of culture. In addition to this ethnic flavoring, there are also impressive action sequences, among them a roaring forest fire. Ted Scaife's photography is expert, as is Fred Burnley's editing. Among other outstanding staff efforts, Joseph Horovitz's music plays a vital role in the production with its exotic strains and explanatory emphasis of key dramatic points. *Tube.*

Berlin Festival

Lilies of the Field

Sidney Poitier in charming low-budgeter.

Berlin, June 25.

United Artists release of a Ralph Nelson Rainbow production. Stars Sidney Poitier; features Lilia Skala, Lisa Mann. Directed by Ralph Nelson. Screenplay, James Poe, based on a novel by William E. Barrett; camera, Ernest Heller; editor, John McCafferty; music, Jerry Goldsmith. At Berlin Film Fest. Running time; **94 MINS.**

Homer Smith .... Sidney Poitier
Mother Maria .... Lilia Skala
Sister Gertrude .... Lisa Mann
Sister Agnes .... Isa Crino
Sister Albertine ...... Francesca Jarvis
Sister Elizabeth ...... Pamela Branch
Juan .... Stanley Adams
Father Murphy .... Dan Frazer

It is easy to appreciate why the Berlin festival authorities invited "Lilies of the Field." Not only is there a German background to the story, but it is essentially a film which is loaded with charm and which is full of good, clean honest fun. Boxoffice chances should be brisk, even thought it may not qualify for saturation showing.

Made on a modest budget and filmed entirely on location in Arizona, "Lilies" reveals Sidney Poitier as an actor with a sharp sense of humor. His performance is in striking contrast to many of his earlier roles. He is a journeyman laborer, touring the countryside in his station wagon, working when the fancy moves him, and traveling on when he feels the need for a change. That was his philosophy until he stopped one day at a lonely farm to refill his radiator, but he met his match in the five women who ran the place.

They were all members of a holy order from East Germany, and were working arid land that had been bequeathed them. As the Mother Superior sets eyes on Poitier she is convinced that God had answered her prayers and sent a strong, healthy man, to fix the roof of their farmhouse. That was it. From then on, spellbound by the Mother's persuasive powers, he stayed on without payment, and eventually took a part time job so that he would have funds to build a chapel for the community.

Many factors combine in the overall success of the film, notably the restrained direction by Ralph Nelson, a thoroughly competent screenplay by James Poe, and, of course Poitier's own standout performance. There are a number of diverting scenes that remain in the memory, such as Poitier giving the Sisters an English lesson, with gestures to demonstrate the meaning of the phrases, and later leading them in the singing of "Aymen."

To add to the general credibility of the treatment, the Sisters frequently talk in German among themselves, particularly in the earlier sequences, but that shouldn't hurt acceptance of the film. In any event, it could easily be remedied with the aid of a few sub-titles, though that shouldn't be necessary.

Ralph Nelson, who also produced, has got some fine performances from his cast. Lilia Skala as the inspired Mother Superior, and Lisa Mann, as Sister Gertrude lead the firstrate support. This also includes fine performances by Stanley Adams and Dan Frazer.

Though not necessarily a big moneymaker, "Lilies of the Field" is a worthy festival contender, and a credit to United Artists who had the confidence to back such an offbeat subject. *Myro.*

The Caretaker
(BRITISH)

Berlin, July 2.

Caretaker Films—Lord (Michael) Birkett production (no distrib set). Stars Alan Bates, Donald Pleasance, Robert Shaw. Directed by Clive Donner. Screnplay, Harold Pinter from his own play of same name: Camera, Nicolas Roeg: editor, Fergus McDonell. At Berlin Film Fest. Running time, **105 MINS.**

Mick .... Alan Bates
Davies .... Donald Pleasance
Aston .... Robert Shaw

Harold Pinter has adapted his own three character play for the screen, but has made little attempt to broaden the canvas and its stage origins are barely disguised. Presumably he took the view that it would be folly to interfere with a hit, as the play was a commercial success in London, and was artistically acclaimed across the Atlantic.

This production of "The Caretaker," was financed by 10 prominent show biz personalities, each of whom has a $14,000 stake in it, while the author, producer, director and three stars are all on deferment. Among its backers are stars, film producers and legit impresarios, including Elizabeth Taylor, Richard Burton, Peter Sellers, Noel Coward, Harry Saltzman and Peter Bridge. It was made without a distribution deal, and was the official British selection for the Berlin festival.

The combined and dedicated efforts of the production team have resulted in a highly literate though wordy film, which will have its biggest appeal to arty theatre audiences. With intelligent promotion, it should wind up as a profitable undertaking, yielding fair returns to its backers. But it will need the careful sell, and a thoughful campaign. (The title will inevitably have to be changed in the U.S. to avoid a clash with United Artist's "The Caretakers.")

Instead of using a conventional studio, the unit took over a house in a northeast London suburb, and that provides an ideal, shabby setting for Pinter's offbeat theme. It also must have helped to keep production costs down, but that's by the way. Basically, it's a one-set play, and more or less remains as such in the film, and that made it a tough assignment for director Clive Donner. His fluent treatment, however, makes the most of the macabre verbal exchanges, and overcomes many of the static handicaps of the subject.

The three characters are two brothers and a tramp. One of the brothers, a building worker, owns a house, but it is his brother who lives in it, though just in one room, cluttered with furniture from the remainder of the house. The tramp, homeless and unemployed, is invited to stay the night, and finds himself being tossed around like a shuttlecock, in favor with one brother, and out of favor with the other. It had been suggested that he should remain as caretaker, but he is eventually thrown out, unwanted by either.

Pinter's highly personalized style of dialog is at its best and the three stars, all of whom were in the Broadway production, serve him with distinction. Donald Pleasance's standout performance as the tramp is the acting highlight, but he easily has the choicest role. It is a perceptive and subtle interpretation of a difficult part, brilliantly shaded to reflect the changing attitudes of the two brothers. Robert Shaw gives an intelligent study as the brother who offers the tramp shelter, and in one scene vividly reveals his history of mental illness, while Alan Bates completes the stellar trio with another forceful portrayal. *Myro.*

The Country Doctor
(PORTUGUESE)

Berlin, June 25.

Filipe de Solms production and release. Stars Jorge Sousa Costa. Directed by Jorge Brum do Canto. Screenplay, Fernando Namora, Jorge Brum do Canto; camera, Mario Moreira; music, Shegundo Calarza. At Berlin Film Fest. Running time, **93 MINS.**

Doctor .... Jorge Sousa Costa
Dr. Valenca .... Joao Guedes
Pharmacist .... Emilio Guimaraes
Luisa .... Irene Cruz

Portugal is in the minor league of European film-producing nations with a minute annual output, and the lack of experience is reflected in this naive feature pic. It's the country's first ever competitive entry at a major international festival, but it won't do much to boost its native film industry. Not likely to be seen outside a few Portugese and possibly a few Spanish-speaking territories.

It's a simple tale of a young doctor who takes over a rural practice from a retiring medico, and meets with opposition from the prejudiced and ignorant peasantry, mainly on account of his youth. Matters are complicated by the weekly visit of the retired doctor who has retained the confidence of the locals although has none of the idealism of his successor.

The yarn unspools leisurely and predictably. And there's no hint of subtlety either in the writing, direction or acting. The young doctor's sincere but amorous glan**ces at a young blonde visitor to the village emphasize the naivety of the treatment. Jorge Sousa Costa is personable young man, and Irene Cruz overdoes the glamour-puss character.** *Myro.*

Bushido
(Oath of Obedience)
(JAPANESE)

Berlin, June 25.

Toei Co. (Tokyo) release of a Hiroshi Okawa production. Stars Kinnosuke Nakamura, Yoshiko Mita, Masayuki Mori, Kyoko Kishida, Ineko Arima, Shinjiro Ebara. Directed by Tadashi Imai. Screenplay, Naoyuki Suzuki, based on an original story by Norio Nanjo; camera, Makoto Tsuboi; music, Toshiro Mayuzumi. At Berlin Film Fest. Running time, **119 MINS.**

Described as a saga of Samurai cruelty, "Oath of Obedience" features nearly all the unpleasant practices known to man, including brutal murder, homosexuality, rape, cruelty and torture, and, of course, hari-kari. And as it is a story of one family though three centuries, there is a repetitive overdose of all these elements. At best, it has limited arty prospects, though some judicious editing would hypo its chances.

The credo of the Samurai is that honor comes before all else. So when at the turn of the 17th Century a man obtains employment with a feudal lord, and signs an oath of allegiance which pledges his descendants for all time, it is an inevitable consequence that there should be a succession of horrors perpetrated in the name of honor. And they follow in monotonous sequence.

The original signatory commits hari-kari when he believes he has let his master down. So does his son. The next descendant is a victim of his master's homosexuality, but is caught in the act with one of the ladies of the court, castrated, and then forced to marry her. It so happens that she was already pregnant, so the succession

is maintained and thus the story of torture and cruelty continues, ending with a vaguely analogous present-day situation.

With such emphasis on cruelty, much of it downright unpleasant to watch, the film will only have limited appeal in the West. Nevertheless, it has some commendable qualities, including some fine camerawork, moving and convincing portrayals, and the right sombre note in direction. *Myro.*

Delay in Marienborn
(GERMAN)
Berlin, June 25.
Gloria release of a Hans Oppenheimer (Berlin), Hoche (Paris) and Cinematografiche Mediteranee (Rome) production. Stars Jose Ferrer, Sean Flynn, Nicole Courcel. Directed by Rolf Haedrich. Screenplay, Will Tremper; camera, Roger Fellous; editor, Margot Jahn; music, Peter Thomas. At Berlin Film Fest. Running time, **94 MINS.**

Cowan	Jose Ferrer
Lt. Novak	Sean Flynn
Nurse Kathy	Nicole Courcel
Major Menschikow	Joseph Yadin
Refugee	Hans Jochim Schmiedel

Selected to open the Berlin film festival under the German flag, "Delay in Marienborn" is a German-Franco-Italian coproduction, which was shown in the English language version. Although the film deals with the overworked theme of conflict between East and West Germany, it looks at the subject from a new angle and makes a bid to give both sides a fair hearing. It has an international cast to help it at the wickets, and had a good chance to get by as a dualer in the U.S.

One main weakness in the plot is that there are too many unexplained incidents, which may be the fault of the script, but more likely is due to erratic editing. There are also several irrelevant characters which do not help the story and tend to impede the action.

Most of the action is confined to the interior of an American military train which makes the daily journey from Berlin to Frankfurt, passing through the Eastern zone with the approval and co-operation of the East German and Soviet authorities, but which may only carry American nationals.

An East German youth, whose parents already had escaped to the West, had noticed that it is frequently held up to make way for a local train; he waits for his chance and eventually makes his bid for freedom. All doors are sealed, but a nurse spots the refugee and hides him in an empty compartment. At the border town of Marienborn, however, the Russians have been tipped that there is an escapee aboard, and refuse to allow the train to move on until he's handed over. It looks like developing into an international incident, until the Yank train commander, under the orders of higher military brass, is obliged to let the Russians have their way.

One of the unusual features of the production is that the Russians are not made the heavies they usually are in such subjects. Admittedly, they put on a show of force and call out the troops to halt the train, but they behave calmly and reasonably, knowing they have some right on their side. And there is a forceful outburst from Jose Ferrer, a newsman riding on the train, who declares he has little sympathy for the refugee as it was the Germans who started the whole unhappy

business, though he later relents when the lad has to be handed over.

Unfortunately, the direction does not take full advantage of the subject matter, and fails to build up either a claustrophobic atmosphere or adequate suspense. The verbal duels between the train commander, Sean Flynn, and the Russians lack the necessary dramatic punch.

The director also has made Ferrer an unnecessarily agressive character, thus diverting much sympathy from his role. Flynn, however, makes a convincing showing. Nicole Courcel is colorless as the nurse while Joseph Yadin (an Israeli) makes a lively Russian officer. Hans Joachim Schmiedel is a typically pathetic refugee. Technical credits are average, and there is a tuneful song over the credit tiles. *Myro.*

La Rimpatriata
(The Reunion)
(ITALIAN)
Berlin, July 2.
Galatea production and release. Stars Walter Chiari. Directed by Damiano Damiani. Screenplay, Damiani; script collaborators, Vittorio Petrilli, Enrico Ribulsi, Ugo Liberatore; camera, Alessandro D'Eva; music, Roberto Nicolosi. At Berlin Film Fest. Running time, **108 MINS.**

Cesare	Walter Chiari
Alberto	Francisco Rabal
Carla	Leticia Roman
Sergio	Riccardo Garrone
La Triste	Dominique Boshero
Nino	Mino Guerrini
Toro	Gastone Moschin
Larone	Jacqueline Pierreaux
Livio	Paul Guers

A tragi-comedy, revealing perceptive understanding of human behavior, "The Reunion" is distinguished by a fine stellar performance by Walter Chiari which gives the picture its real character and quality. Film has strong b.o. possibilities which could be hypoed by tightening of a few overdrawn sequences.

Having its world preem as the official Italian selection for the Berlin festival, the pic portrays the reactions of five men, all of whom were youthful friends, who plan a night out on the town. All have done well, with the exception of one who has a job in a picture theatre. But he was the one who was always the life and soul of the party when they were younger. And the others soon discover that he still has a way of charming women, even total strangers, over the telephone.

What starts out as a high spirited spree with girls picked up on the way, gradually imperceptibly but inevitably develops into a disaster. Walter Chiari, as the less affluent member of the group, has his fill of trouble: he's married, but has a mistress on the side, and the latter has decided to accept an offer of marriage to give their child a name and a home. As the night goes on, they move from one escapade to another, ending with a brutal beating up of Chiari after he's been cold-shouldered by a former flame.

The film is at its best when the story is pursuing a gay and lighthearted course, but the more serious incidents are credibly dovetailed into the general theme. There is one diverting scene when a blonde pickup is stretched out horizontally on a billiards table, and one of the men tees off a shot

from her breast; and another, when all are driving along a highway, and a handsome negress puts her hand out of the window of a parallel car to flick the ash from her cigaret, only to have it caressed by another of the high-spirited gang.

Aside from Chiari's dominating performance, there is also first rate work from the other members of the cast. Leticia Roman is warmly appealing as one of the girls whose night out for fun ends on a note of sadness. Dominique Boschero is an attractive specimen of female sensuousness while Jacqueline Pierreux gives a forceful display of embittered womanhood. Francisco Rabal, Ricardo Garrone, Mino Guerrini and Gaston Moschin are the other men on the spree, and offer lively and polished aid.

Damiano Damiani has smoothly directed his own screenplay, and has shown a keen appreciation for clearcut characterization. Other credits are up to par. *Myro.*

Sahib, Bibi aur Ghulam
(King, Queen and Slave)
(INDIAN)
Berlin, July 2.
Guru Dutt Films (Bombay) production and release. Stars Meena Kumari, Guru Dutt, Rehman, Waheda Rehman. Directed by Abrar Alvi. Based on novel by Bimal Mitra; camera, V. K. Murthy; music, Hemant Kumar. At Berlin Film Fest. Running time, **120 MINS.**

This Indian entry at the Berlin festival is a strange, uneasy mixture of moods and styles, which just don't blend into a complete whole. It starts off as a disarmingly naive comedy, played with charm and good humor. Then suddenly it changes to heavy and ponderous melodrama. This is extremely overlong, too, at two hours of running time, so it can only have very slight artie chances in the West.

The period is the turn of the 19th Century. There is an undercurrent of unrest as the peasants lose their land, and the British troops roam through the city looting the shops in the local market. But that aspect is hardly developed. For the first part, the emphasis is on a young country bumpkin who comes to the big city, locates a friend who works in the "big mansion," gets a job and is soon romantically entangled with his employer's daughter, but is too shy and fumbling to make much headway.

Running parallel with that theme is the despair of the lady of the manor who cannot prevail upon her husband to stay home at night, as he seems to prefer orgies with dancing girls and plenty of booze.

In a desperate bid to hold her man, she agrees to take a drink with him, and acts like she is making the ultimate sacrifice. In no time at all, she's acquired a taste for the hard stuff, becomes a confirmed alcoholic and drinks away the family fortune, while, ironically, her husband has become a teetotaller. Inevitably, she comes to a tragic end.

The naive style of the earlier part proves most appealing, and had it kept on that note, the pic might have been more palatable. But the transition to meller throws it off-key, though not, apparently,

for local audiences. In India, it is rated among the top 10 films of the last 50 years.

Production is mounted on an ambitious scale, with several lavish sets and a wide range of attractive costumes. The two main femme roles are played by striking-looking actresses, and the male leads by handsome men. Unusual score by Hemant Kumar is mainly fascinating. *Myro.*

Young Aphrodites
(GREECE)
Berlin, July 2.
Minos Film and Anzervos Studios (Athens) release of a George Zervos and Nikos Kondouros production. Features Helen Prokopiou, Takis Emmanouel, Kleopatra Rota, Vangelis Joanides. Directed by Kondouros. Screenplay, Kostas Sfikas and Vassilis Vassilikos; camera, Giovanni Variano; music. Yian Markopoulos. At Berlin Film Fest. Running time, **89 MINS.**

Apparently the passing of more than 2,000 years has made little change in the pattern of sexual behaviour of the human male or female, according to this Greek picture which based on an ancient myth and is set in the year 200 B.C. A dull, slow but exploitable item.

There's not much in the way of a plot, and what little story there is unspools at a leisurely and monotonous pace. A shepherd meets a married woman (whose husband is away fishing) and a 10-year old boy meets a 12-year old girl. Passion pursues its natural course, though in the case of the youngsters they appear to be groping until they spy the elder couple in the act.

Exploitation comes via the seminudity of both females, but some audiences may resent the continuous upper exposure by a mere child in what, is after all, a commercial pic with little art pretensions. According to a press handout, the cast is composed of nonpros. Their performances will do little to upset their amateur status. Technical credits are adequate. *Myro.*

Leven En Dood Of Het Land
(Life and Death in Flanders)
(BELGIAN)
Emile Degelin (Brussels) production. Directed by Degelin. Screenplay, Degelin, based on original stories by Karel van de Woestijne and Stijn Streuvels; camera, Paul Defru, Dirk Roelofs; music, Jos Mertens. At Berlin Film Fest. Running time, **82 MINS.**

This Belgian production calls itself a documentary feature. It is divided into two parts and utilizes exceptional amateur players. The first part (based on novelette by Woestijne) concerns a dying farmer, the second one (based on story by Streuvels) has to do with a young worker who's forced to marry an ugly girl because the latter has a child with him.

While the first episode appears overly slow, often not exactly tasteful and neither fish nor fowl, the second one reveals Emile Degelin's directorial talents in several situations. He seems to have well caught the feel of life in the Flemish country and the nature of the people there.

There is some impressive genu-

Ineness about this part. Film, however, will have a tough time obtaining many dates. It's too much of an offbeater for any situation. This can be registered as an interesting effort of writer-producer-director Emil Degelin. *Hans.*

Garrincha — Allegria Do Povo
(Garrincha—Hero Of the People)
(BRAZIL)

Berlin, July 2.
Luiz Carlos Barreto production. Directed by Joanquim Pedro. Camera, Mario Carneiro. At Berlin Film Fest. Running time, 66 MINS.

This documentary on Garrincha, idolized Brazilian football player, right winger of the Brazilian teams that won the 1958 and 1962 World Cups, primarily is an item for the soccer fan. But it may also please other segments for it gives an interesting insight into Latin American sports enthusiasm. Taking into account that there are millions of football fans all over the world, film may qualify for some special situations, possibly if cut down also for dual programs.

Pic tells how Garrincha climbed up from a poor factory worker to a football (soccer) professional and star of his team, Botafogo, with a monthly income of half a million Cruzeiros. The soccer artist Garrincha is a simple but colorful, likeable fellow who has remained modest despite all the idolization.

Amusing thing about his life is that fate has pulled his leg seven times when it gave him (who wants so badly a son) seven daughters to date. There are some excellent shots which show Garrincha in action and, in all, the fascinating sports atmosphere is well caught. On the negative side, film is not always technically firstrate. Also, it could have shown more footwork of Garrincha. The commentary (in German at the Berlin Fest) bordered sometimes on the silly. *Hans.*

La Terraza
(The Roof Garden)
(ARGENTINA)

Berlin, June 25.
Internacional Films (Buenos Aires) release of a German Szulem production. Stars Graciela Borges, Leonardo Favio. Directed by Leopoldo Torre Nilsson. Screenplay, Beatriz Guido; camera, Ignacio Souto; editor, J. M. Paleo; music, Jorge Lopez Ruiz. At Berlin Film Fest. Running time, 88 MINS.

Claudia .... Graciela Borges
Rodolfo .... Leonardo Favio
Vicky .... Marcela Lopez Rey
Alberto .... Hector Pellegrini
Valeria .... Dora Baret
Luis .... Norberto Suarez
Horacio .... Enrique Leporace
Pablo .... Luis Walmo
Mercedes .... Mirtha Dubner
Guille .... Oscar Caballero
Belita .... Belita

Leopoldo Torre Nilsson, one of Argentine's best known directors, takes a long and perceptive look at youth in revolt—against convention, authority and parental control. It is, in fact, a kind of "dolce vita" treatment of the smart young set of Buenos Aires. While it does not make a wholly satisfying picture, it has several intriguing and stimulating elements which should give it fair arty chances overseas.

The roof garden in which virtually the entire story is played out is at the top of a fashionable B.A. apartment house, complete with swimming pool. A dozen or so teenagers, all in bathing suits, have shut themselves off from the outside world and their only contact with their families is through the grandchild of the caretaker, a precocious girl who runs errands and delivers messages. Each time the adults attempt to break into the youngster's privacy, they threaten to toss the child over the rooftops, and one such warning to the elders almost ends in disaster.

The teenagers spend most of their time cavorting in the pool, swilling whisky, pairing off and making love, but their rebellion seems to have little point. It is more in the nature of an escapade in which high-spirited youth is determined to have its fling and defy the conventions, rather than making a stand on any stated principle.

The characters are mainly casually drawn, but Torre Nilsson's perceptive direction keeps them in focus and gives the story some meaning. The youthful rebellion comes to its inevitable end one dawn. And there is a neat touch of symbolism in the final sequences —some months after the spree—as the little girl, now lame from the escapade, plays in the empty pool, with the autumn leaves dropping on the roof garden.

The mainly young cast perform with an appropriate display of high spirits, and there are some interesting cameos, notably from a priest who appeals to the rebellious youth from a helicopter hovering over the roof garden. The two principal roles are played in lively style by Graciela Borges and Leonardo Favio. Belita is suitably precocious as the child while the priest is effectively portrayed by Fernando Vegal. As in all Torre Nilsson's pix, technical standards are okay. *Myro.*

Strange Lovers

Three tales concerned with facets of homosexuality. Minor entry dependent on sexsensational values.

Hollywood, July 3.
Robert Stambler-William Mahan (Mast) production. Cast includes: Walter Koenig, Joe d'Agosta, Jennifer Boles, Arlene Hedrick, Sylvia Brenner. (No character names given). Directed by Stambler. Screenplay, Stambler, Mahan, Nick Boretz, Alex Beaton; camera, F. Said; assistant director, Kamzi Thomas. Reviewed at Apollo Arts Theatre, July 3,'63. Running time, 73 Mins.

Homosexuality is the topic of this shallow and inconclusive trilogy. Had the creators of the independent production focused and concentrated whatever knowledge they have of this subject on a single set of characters in one story, perhaps promising boxoffice might have come of it. Instead they have chosen to squander their efforts on three separate-though-related dramatic vignettes, none of which is developed with sufficient finesse, clarity or penetration to be meaningful or convincing. Provocative and exploitable though the topic obviously is, the film lacks the substance or insight to rise out of that shadowy exhibition sphere dominated by sex-oriented attractions.

The first of the three yarns, entitled "End Of The Path," deals with a young man who was attacked in his early childhood by a homosexual and has been left with an emotional scar that ultimately prompts him to murder an older woman who is playing up to him. The middle piece, labeled "Homo Means Man," dramatizes the plight of a somewhat older young man who, after separating from his wife, makes a seeming homosexual contact and is beaten up and rolled by his companion, then nursed by a woman who, repulsed for her suggestion that they hit the hay together, returns her reluctant "date" to his spouse. In the third tale, called "Segue," a teenage girl who has never been able to hit it off with the boys is tricked into a Lesbian relationship by her employer, a woman with a more-than-businesslike eye for her models.

It is an oddity of all three of these stories that most of the "healthy" people implicated are obsessed with sex. In their zeal to pinch bottoms, unzip zippers or lure others into the sack, they provide a counterpoint to the three troubled principal characters, none of whom seem much inclined to engage in sexual activity.

Although the directorial tempo is extremely sluggish, the performances are generally capable, which reflects some credit on director Robert Stambler, who also co-produced with William Mahan and penned the script together with Mahan, Nick Boretz and Alex Beaton. The principal players, all of whom emote rather well under the circumstances, are Walter Koenig, Joe d'Agosta, Arlene Hedrick, Jennifer Boles and Sylvia Brenner. *Tube.*

Shock Corridor

Shoddy, shallow shocker with exploitation facets.

Hollywood, June 24.
Allied Artists release of Samuel Fuller production. Stars Peter Breck, Constance Towers; features Gene Evans, James Best. Directed and screenplay by Fuller; camera, Stanley Cortez; editor, Jerome Thoms; music, Paul Dunlap; assistant director, Floyd Toyer. Reviewed at Directors Guild of America, June 24, '63. Running time, 101 MINS.

Johnny .... Peter Breck
Cathy .... Constance Towers
Boden .... Gene Evans
Stuart .... James Best
Trent .... Hari Rhodes
Pagliacci .... Larry Tucker
Swanee .... William Zuckert
Dr. Fong .... Philip Ahn
Psycho .... Meyle Morrow
Dr. Cristo .... John Mathews
Wilkes .... Chuck Roberson
Lloyd .... John Craig
Police Lieut. .... Frankie Gerstle
Dr. Menkin .... Paul Dubov
Singing Nympho .... Rachel Romen
Dance Teacher .... Linda Randolph

In "Shock Corridor," writer-producer-director Samuel Fuller apparently is trying to say something significant about certain contemporary American values. The points are sound and have merit. But the melodrama in which he has chosen to house these ideas is so grotesque, so gruelling, so shallow and so shoddily sensational-istic that his message is devastated. For all of its innate exploitability, it is difficult to see where the Allied Artists release can have any really appreciable boxoffice impact.

Fuller's thin plot has a newspaperman (Peter Breck) contriving, with the aid of a psychiatrist no less, to get himself committed to a mental ward in order to identify a murderer known only to the inmates and whom the police have been unable to detect. The newsman gets his scoop, but winds up a catatonic schizophrenic, or the only Pulitzer Prizewinner in the psycho ward.

Within all this lurks three points about Americana, each embodied in characters the fourth-estater encounters in the hospital. A Communist-brainwashed and subsequently disgraced Korean war vet (James Best) is the mouthpiece through which Fuller pleads for greater understanding of such unfortunate individuals. Likewise, a Negro (Hari Rhodes) supposed to have been the first to attend an all-white Southern university serves to make the point that it takes enormous emotional stamina to play the role of the martyr in social progress. And the character of a renowned physicist (Gene Evans) whose mind has deteriorated into that of a six-year-old enables Fuller to get in some digs against bomb shelters and America's participation in the space race.

But all these points go for naught because the film is dominated by sex and shock superficialities. Among the gruelling passages audiences must endure, for no reason other than sheer sensationalism, are a striptease and an attack on the hero in a locked room by half-a-dozen nymphos. There's also levity in the wrong places. The audience tends to laugh at the inmates. It's not really funny business.

The dialog is unreal and pretentious, and the direction is heavyhanded, often mistaking sordidness for realism. The per-

formers labor valiantly, but in vain. Those most prominent are Breck, who really gets his lumps and earns his pay, Constance Towers as his stripper-girl friend (making her a stripper distorts and weakens the whole story—simply for an extra dash of sordid sensuality), Larry Tucker as an inmate obsessed with the Pagliacci aria, William Zuckert as a misguided editor, Philip Ahn as that misguided psychiatrist who okays Breck's absurd idea, chuck Roberson and John Crang as attendants, and Evans, Best and Rhodes as the three messagebearers.

Chief among the generally adequate production credits are photography by Stanley Cortez, Paul Dunlap's music and Eugene Lourie's sets. Jerome Thoms didn't edit out nearly e n o u g h footage. *Tube.*

Berlin Festival

Los Innocents
(The Innocents)
(SPANISH-ARGENTINIAN)
Berlin, July 2.

Sueva Films (Madrid) release of a Cesareo Gonzalez Spanish-Argentinian coproduction. Stars Alfred Alcon, Paloma Valdes, Fernando Mistral. Directed by Juan Antonio Bardem. Screenplay, Bardem, Eceiza and Quejereta; camera, Albert Curchi; music, Isidro Maizteugui. At Berlin Film Fest. Running time, 110 MINS.
Guido .... Alfredo Alcon
Elena Errazquin .... Paloma Valdes
Laura Errazquin ...... Fernanda Mistral

Juan Antonio Bardem is undoubtedly Spain's most distinguished director and his skill and authority s t a n d out in this Spanish-Argentinian coproduction, which was the official Spanish entry at the Berlin festival. Pic has obvious art qualities, with additional appeal to the Spanish lingo houses.

Under the director's assured and sympathetic guidance, there unfolds a semi-tragic love story doomed to an inevitable unhappy ending. Social differences, Bardem emphasizes, cannot transcend human emotions, and thus the romance between a poor bank clerk and a rich girl is brought to an abrupt end after the intervention of her family.

The two principal characters are brought together after her father and his wife were killed together in a car accident. That was the first clue either family had to the illicit relationship. The dead man was a powerful industrialist, and his family still wields enough authority to keep photos and reports of the incident out of the press, and to have the bank clerk transferred to an out of the way town when they become disturbed at the blossoming romance.

Though the story hardly breaks new ground, it is noted for its excellent characterizations, not only of the major roles, but the small cameos.

The film was lensed in the Argentine, and the action takes place mainly in Mar del Plata, with fine camerawork highlighting the scenic effects. Paloma Valdes, imported from Spain, plays the young girl with an appealing warmth while

Alfredo Alcon (a native Argentinian) gives a carefully observed study of a man who realizes the embarrassment of being out of one's social depth. Fernanda Mistral is the eccentric grandmother, and plays her few scenes with great aplomb. *Myro.*

Mensch und Bestie
(Man and Beast)
(GERMAN)
Berlin, July 2.

CCC Filmkunst (Berlin) and Avala Film (Belgrade) release of an Artur Brauner production. Stars Gotz George. Directed by Edwin Zbonek. Screenplay, Sigmund Bendkower, Al Bronsowy, based on idea by Robert Azderball; camera, Nenad Jovicic. At Berlin Film Fest. Running time, 84 MINS.
Franz Kohler .... Gotz George
Willy Kohler ...... Gunther Ungeheuer
Nurse .... Katinka Hoffman

One of oddest features of concentration camp life in wartime Nazi Germany was that two brothers were in one camp—one as an inmate, the other as commandant. That strange fact is the basis of an otherwise fictional story, and there are obvious possibilities for developing this situation into a powerful celluloid drama. Though producer Artur Brauner h a s made a bold try, he has been sorely let down by a script which is riddled with implausibilities.

Basic situation is expanded by having the inmate escape and his brother as pursuer-in-chief, harassed because the authorities are aware of the relationship and suspect that he may deliberately fail in his duty. But there's not much fear of that as the commandant is a dedicated Nazi and out for blood —even if it is his brother's.

Where the plot falls down is in the string of unlikely adventures of the man on the run. The first is when he is given food and shelter by a military nurse, who readily hops into bed with him after a acquaintance lasting just a few minutes. Then there is the Alsatian tracker dog who, after severely mauling the escaped prisoner, suddenly befriends him and they become inseparable companions. And finally the man, who finds him in a state of delirium, takes him home where he is breast-fed by his young wife. All these improbabilities—and others hurt this picture and could have been avoided if more attention had been given to plot construction.

Gotz George gives an adequate study of the man on the run, though his acting chances are restricted by the script. Gunther Ungenheuer makes a conventionally brutal commandant while Katinka Hoffman is attractive as the nurse. Direction looks leisurely, even though the pic has been trimmed to a convenient 84 minutes. The black and white lensing, particularly of the wintry countryside, is okay.

Only the opening sequences show camp life, and there are the familiar scenes of savage brutality, but once the escape alarm has sounded, the action folows the man on the run, making for the Russian lines, until shot by his brother as he is within earshot of his destination. A modern Cain and Abel situation which lacks the literary qualities of the original. *Myro.*

Yollymoon
(The Red Gate)
(KOREAN)
Berlin, July 2.

Sang-Ok Shin (Seoul) production. With Kim Dong Won, Han Un Jin and Chae Un Hee. Directed by Shin Sang Ok. Screenplay Kim Kwang Yoon; camera, Jeong Hae Joon; music, Jeong Yoon Joo. At Berlin Film Fest. Running time, 105 MINS.

This Korean feature pic is qualitywise, better than many Japanese productions. It's well acted and even very well photographed and not as brutal as similar Japanese productions. For a Korean pic, it has the flavor of a surprise entry. It's, of course, chiefly an item for the native market.

To keep "the red gate," the sign of purity, a young widow is forced to renounce her personal prosperity to her relatives. It takes her many years until she's able to leave the house of unhappiness. Film makes one familiar with problems of different calibre but there's something about the film which makes it quite interesting. *Hans.*

El Less Wal Kilab
(Chased By the Dogs)
(UNITED ARAB REPUBLIC)
Berlin, July 2.

Gamel el Leissi Films (Cairo) production. Stars Shokry Sarhan and Shadia. Directed by Kamal el Sheikh. Screenplay, Nageeb Mahfuz, Sabry Ezzat; camera, Kamal Kurayem; music, Andre Ryder. At Berlin Film Fest. Running time, 120 MINS.

This Arabian production, which reportedly has walked off with several honors in its native country, reveals considerable western influence but can't stand comparison with what filmites are doing in the western world. Apart from an overly-long running time of two hours, there are deficiencies with regard to cliche scripting, acting and directing. Pic stands small chance in the western market.

This concerns a man who was sentenced to five years in prison because of alleged theft. After his release, he seeks revenge on his wife who had accused him of theft and on society which he makes responsible for his ruined life. He becomes a killer and is eventually shot. It's the simple story of an unfortunate human being whom fate made a criminal.

Pic makes an attempt to criticize modern society but the outcome isn't very convincing. Everything remains too much on the surface while for western patrons the various players tend to overact considerably. *Hans.*

Alskarinnan
(The Mistress)
(SWEDISH)
Berlin, July 2.

AB Svensk Filmindustri production and release. Stars Bibi Andersson. Direction and screenplay, Vilgot Sjoman; camera, Lars-Goran Bjorne. At Berlin Film Fest. Running timee, 76 MINS.
The Girl .... Bibi Andersson
The Boy .... Per Myrberg
The Man .... Max von Sydow
The Wife .... Ollegard Wellten

One of Sweden's most successful commercial films this year, "The Mistress" is also notable for the fact that it is the first directorial effort of Vilgot Sjoman, who learned filmmaking under the guid-

ance of Ingmar Bergman. He has certainly proved an apt pupil, and has written and directed a picture which should go a long way towards establishing his reputation. Pic has definite chances in the foreign markets, including U.S. arty possibilities.

As if taking a leaf out of his master's textbook, Sjoman has given this story of a young girl's passion for a married man an unhappy ending. But that was the logical thing to do, and the more conventional type fadeout would have obviously been contrived.

Bibi Andersson is the title character, and she is torn between a young student who genuinely loves her, and a married man who has a passionate attraction for her, and who takes every advantage of that fact. She knows she is not being too logical, and is aware that her emotions always get the better of her mind. In the end, when she is determined to make a temporary break from both men in her life, the married man follows her, persuades her to spend the night with him in his sleeping car compartment. But in the clear light of day she determinedly sails off on her own.

Typical of the structure of the film, there is one incident in the plot which puts the two principal characters into focus. The married man had promised to spend a whole day with her, but then starts making one excuse after another to delay his arrival. Eventually he shows up late in the evening, there's a quick tumble in bed, and he's away again.

Miss Andersson, a polished, attractive actress, plays the girl with a passionate intensity, but without overdoing the histrionics. Max von Sydow is credible as the married man and lover, and there are okay studies by Per Myrberg, as the student, and Ollegard Wellten, as the wife. *Myro.*

Choose Life
(SWISS-SWEDISH)
Berlin, July 2.

Beretta Film (Zurich) release of an Erwin Leiser-Hans Deutsch production. Written and directed by Leiser. Camera, Jean-Marc Ripert, Hiroshi Segawa, Otto Ritter; editor, Hans Heinrich Egger; music, Robert Blum. At Berlin film fest (out of competition). Running time, 100 MINS.

Erwin Leiser, creator of the successful "Mein Kampf," and who later made the Eichmann documentary, now has completed a trilogy "dedicated to the defense of man" by his production of "Choose Life," which puts the spotlight on the dangers of this atom age. It is an extremely well-planned treatment of a complex subject, containing large hunks of original celluloid in addition to some apposite, though partly familiar, library material. In its present form, this is too long, but it is to be edited down 20 minutes. That should hypo its c o m m e r c i a l chances in many areas.

The title comes from an Old Testament quotation: "I have set before you life and death, blessing and cursing; therefore, choose life, that both thou and thy seed may live." Inspired by that text, Leiser presents atomic science as both a blessing and curse, but leaving man to make the decision between life and death. The title leaves no

doubt where the film stands on this issue.

In a neat touch of symbolism, the opening sequence shows rural Mexico where simple folk happily accept the inevitability of death, just as they enjoy the simple pleasures of life. Then a dramatic switch to the brutal realities of life, with a few quick horrific shots of concentration camp victims, and then over to Hiroshima for the aftermath of the atomic explosion, with many unpleasant (though timely) reminders of the horror effects produced by that one bomb. But there is the implicit warning that today's atomic blasts would be many times greater.

There is a convincing note of optimism permeating the film. Hiroshima has been rebuilt, but does not forget. Young people all over the world demonstrate against the bomb and plead for an end to tests; science is using atomic discoveries for peaceful purposes, including medicine. But the threat continues, and the dangers from fallout remain a constant menace.

Understandably, the largest slice of the film is focussed on Japan, limiting the amount of time devoted to other countries. There are, however, shots of Kennedy and Khrushchev, and a substantial American sequence which contrasts the shelter facilities available for the rich and poor. There is also an eerie scene of a U.S. air-raid alarm exercise in which life on the surface comes to a dramatic standstill.

Once its running time is reduced, "Choose Life" should prove an exploitable item, with the "Mein Kampf" credit an aid to promotion. An English language track is available, though this review is based on the German-speaking version which was shown at the Berlin festival. *Myro.*

Deo Gratias
(FRANCE)

Berlin, July 2.
Le Film D'Art-A.T.I.L.A. production. Stars A. Bourvil. Directed by Jean-Pierre Mocky. Screenplay, Michael Servin; camera, L. H. Burel. At Berlin Film Fest. Running time, **82 MINS.**
Georges Lachaunaye .... A. Bourvil
Cucherat ....Francis Blanche
Raoul .... Jean Poiret
The Father .... Jean Yonnel

A lightweight but amusing comedy, with near-farcical style, "Deo Gratias" has a host of amusing situations. But it is essentially a one-joke theme which shows occasional signs of being overdone. Nevertheless, it should rack up useful returns with fair playoff chances.

Michael Servin's adroit screenplay quickly establishes the point that for four generations no member of the Lachaunaye family has sought employment, and that the present bearers of that name see no reason to change that state of affairs.

Unfortunately, however, money is running out, furniture has been sold, there's no fuel on a cold winter's night, and meals have to be scrounged from friends and relatives. Desperate measures for a desperate situation: the elder son, a devout man, prays for guidance, and as he is waiting for the sign

from the Lord, he hears the sound of a coin dropping in the poor box. His prayers are thus answered, and the family fortunes are rapidly restored by a systematically planned campaign of robbing the offertory boxes in a circuit of churches.

Most of the fun derives from the planning of the operation, and the cat-and-mouse game with the church police, who quickly identify the man they are after, but are constantly outwitted by him. There are also a few amusing scenes indicating the constant improvement in the technique of extracting money from the poor boxes, culminating with a sort of vacuum attachment which clears most of the boxes with the minimum of effort.

Jean-Pierre Mocky's racy direction is just right for this featherweight piece, moving rapidly from one situation to another with hardly a letup in the action. Performances, too, are consistently good, with A. Bourvil in fine form as the thief, Jean Poiret getting plenty of laughs as his partner in crime and Francis Blanche making a suitably harassed cop. Jean Yonnel does okay in a lesser role as the father. The support is always competent. *Myro.*

Der Grosse Atlantik
(River of the Ocean)
(GERMAN-COLOR)

Berlin, July 2.
Sirius Film (Munich) production. Directed and written by Peter Baylis. Camera (Eastmancolor), Jacques Letellier; music, Jean de Rohanzinsky; narrator, Orson Welles. At Berlin Film Fest. Running Time, **76 MINS.**

This full-length documentary film, written and directed by Peter Baylis (a Britisher for Sirius-Film, a German producing outfit) was shown in English language (American Orsen Welles narrator) as a German entry at the Berlin festival. The NATO-supported pic had it easy to capture the prize for the fest's best full-length documentary if only because there were only two other documentaries competing. Except for the beautiful Eastmancolor and a number of fine but not exceptional shots taken from the air, there's nothing special about this offering. Taking into account that some full-length documentaries proved commercial clicks with domestic cinemagoers, this one stands a solid b.o. chance as well.

This picture tells the story of the Atlantic Ocean. It shows the countries tied to it by destiny, the cities who owe their wealth and power to it. The city of New York is given particularly substantial footage. The viewer follows the coast dwellers' struggle against the big sea, he sees the ships and airplanes that cross the ocean. The commentary is a mixture of matter-of-fact reporting and big pathos. It also tells of the people whose task it is to keep a constant watch over the turbulent Atlantic. *Hans.*

Beach Party
(COLOR—SONGS)

Bouncy if simple teenage musical with sand-and-surf locale. Attractive cast, slick production values, assure nice b.o. with young set.

American International Pictures presentation of a James H. Nicholson-Lou Rusoff production (Samuel Z. Arkoff executive producer). Stars Robert Cummings, Dorothy Malone, Frankie Avalon, Annette Funicello; features Harvey Lembeck, Jody McCrea, John Ashley, Morey Amsterdam, Eva Six. Directed by William Asher. Screenplay, Lou Rusoff; camera (Pathe Color), Kay Norton; music, Lex Baxter; editor, Homer Powell; asst. director, Clark Paylow. Reviewed in New York, July 10, '63. Running time, **104 MINS.**
Professor Jason Sutwell
                    Robert Cummings
Marianne .... Dorothy Malone
Frankie .... Frankie Avalon
Dolores .... Annette Funicello
Eric Von Zipper .... Harvey Lembeck
Deadhead .... Jody McCrea
Ken .... John Ashley
Cappy .... Morey Amsterdam
Ava .... Eva Six
Musicians......Dick Dale and Del-Tones
Ed .... David Landfield
Sue .... Dolores Wells
Rhonda .... Valora Noland
Tom .... Bobby Payne
Big Boy .... Duane Ament
Motorcycle Rats .... Andy Romano,
        John Macchia, Jerry Brutsche,
        Bob Harvey
Motorcycle Mice.........Linda Rogers,
                    Alberta Nelson
Perpetual Motion Dancer..Candy Johnson
Tour Guide .... Roger Bacon
Yogi Girls .... Yvette Vickers,
                    Sharon Garrett

Producers Jim Nicholson and Lou Rusoff may have put together the perfect summer attraction for the teenage set in "Beach Party." It's a bouncy bit of lightweight fluff, attractively cast (Arnette Funicello, Frankie Avalon, et. al.), beautifully set (Malibu Beach), and scored throughout (by Lex Baxter) with a big twist beat. While many adults might find it a frightening manifestation of the culture of our age, "Beach Party" has the kind of direct, simple-minded cheeriness which should prove well nigh irresistible to those teenagers who have no desire to escape the emptiness of their lives. Thus it should swing at the boxoffice.

The comparatively "elderly" Robert Cummings toplines the cast (with Dorothy Malone) and provides the picture with what real comic substance it has. Plot of Rusoff's screenplay is pegged on a study of teenage sex habits undertaken by anthropologist Cummings on the beach at Malibu. As the square professor, Cummings shows himself to be an able farceur and notably at ease in surroundings which might embarass a less professional star. Miss Malone, still lovely, is along just for the ride in a small role as the prof's long-suffering secretary. It's a waste of her talent.

Focus of the picture is on the kids throughout. What plot complications there are centre around the romantic problems of a group of young surfers, principally Avalon and Miss Funicello, each of whom undertakes a campaign to make the other jealous—he with buxom Eva Six, she with the erudite professor. Story is padded out with some lovely surf-riding sequences and a whole string of Les Baxter songs, sung variously by Avalon, Miss Funicello and the combo of Dick Dale and the Del-Tones.

Principal supporting work is handled by Harvey Lembeck, who is responsible for a grin or two

as the nitwit head of a motorcycle gang (a la "The Wild Ones"); Jody McCrea, as a not-too-bright surfer, and Morey Amsterdam, the proprietor of a sort of pseudo-beatnik Sugar Bowl, frequented by the kids.

William Asher has carefully directed the picture with an eye on his potential market. It moves quickly and easily and has been dressed with handsome production values, including spankingly clean and crisp (Pathe color and Panavision) camera work by Kay Norton. *Anby.*

Moscow Film Fest

Meet Balujev
(RUSSIAN)
Moscow, July 16.

A Lenfilm Studio production. Directed by V. Komissarzhevsky. Screenplay, V. Kozhevnikov and Komissarzhevsky; camera, V. Levitin, D. Meschiev; music, V. Christjakov. At Moscow Film Fest. Running time, **120 MINS.**

Balujev	J. Pereverzev
Dusja	N. Urgant
Zaitsev	S. Sololov
Zina Penochkina	S. Dick
Marchenko	P. Morozenka
Kapa Podgornaja	Z. Kirienko
Shpakovsky	A. Romashin
Isolda Besuglova	N. Korneva
Fokin	A. Pankov
Bubnov	S. Plotnikov
Firsov	S. Blinnikov
Petukhov	P. Krimov
Krochalev	J. Kosuchin

Balujev is a senior engineer working on a pipe laying project carrying natural gas through a remote part of the country. At first, it looks as though the problems of construction will provide the film with its drama. But the difficulties of going through a bog are dropped, and the narrative concerns itself instead with the problems of other individuals at the camp. These incidents are of little point or interest, and the characters artificial. The film meanders along talking all the time, and uncertain of what it is supposed to be saying or doing.

Film is timidly modern in that the rights of a worker as an individual are stressed, an affair is suggested, an abortion hinted and official attitudes held to be restrictive. But it's all very dull.

J. Pereverzev makes a hearty Balujev, the girls are certainly not camp workers, the score is inappropriate, the direction labored. How unfortunate that one of the few Russian films dealing with the present rather than the last war should be so confined in outlook and lacking even the elementary principles of cinema art. *Prat.*

Each Day I Cry
(Hiko Shojo)
(JAPANESE)
Moscow, July 16.

Nikkatsu Corp. production. Directed by Kei Urayama. Screenplay, Grayama & Yoshio Ishido from original story by Kei Moriyama; camera, Kurataro Takamura; music, Toshiro Mayuzumi. At Moscow Film Fest. Running time, **114 MINS.**

Saburo Sawata	Mitsuo Hamada
Taro	Asao Koike
Yumiko	Minako Kazuki
Chikako	Fukuko Sayo
Wakae Kita	Masako Izumi
Chokichi	Jun Hamamura

This is a sympathetic, well-acted study of a wilful, high-spirited young slum girl neglected by her drunken parents, who finds a companion in a boy her own age. He leaves her because she cannot seem to avoid misadventures which cast her in a dubious light and eventually take her to a reform school. Boy and girl are finally reunited and here the film should end with the hope of a better life.

Unfortunately, the director drags on to reach the same conclusion after introducing other issues of little consequence and which are under-developed.

The main part of the narrative takes a realistic view of life, in a fire in which a chicken house is burned down and the birds fly around in agony against the night sky with their feathers aflame. *Prat.*

Lupeni 29
(RUMANIAN)
Moscow, July 16.

Romfilm (Bucharest) production and release. Stars Lica Gheorghiu, Colea Rautu. Directed by Mircea Dragan. Screenplay, Nicolael Tic, Eugen Mandric, Dragan; camera, Aurel Samson; music, Theodor Grigoriu. At Moscow Film Fest. Running time, **118 MINS.**

Iona	Lica Gheorghiu
Petre Letean	Colea Rautu
Todor Baci	George Calboreanu
Varga	Stefan Ciobotarasu
Mateianu	Costel Constantinescu

Lupeni is a mining town in Rumania which was hit by industrial unrest in the '20s, and this film spotlights the culminating struggles of 1929 when workers were mown down by the military before their strikes succeeded. The subject is probably more inspiring than the resultant film, which has been directed with a heavy hand. An unlikely starter for Western territories.

At the beginning, the subject is treated as a personalized story, showing a young husband going off to work, leaving his wife and child behind at home. But there's a mine disaster that day, and he never returns. Some years later the wife gets work at the pit, but at that point, the individual narrative is submerged. And the focus is on the mass movement struggling for existence.

There are some impressive crowd scenes, but these are often too loosely edited. However, a negative nightmare sequence of a mine disaster comes across with stark realism. Much of the dialog sounds as if it come straight out of the text book. The subject provides few chances for individual performances. An overpowering score in stereophonic sound is no help, but other credits are up to average. *Myro.*

Toha-Hero of Southern Bandung
(INDONESIAN)
Moscow, July 16.

Perfini Film Studio (Usmar Ismail) production. Directed and written by Ismail. Camera, Max Tera Kusnen; music, Saiful Bachri. At Moscow Film Fest. Running time, **160 MINS.**

This Indonesian film is a worthy and sincere try by a nation that has had little experience in production. The lack of professional know-how is all too evident. Pic can only be rated a possibility for the Asian market.

It's a story of the country's war of liberation against the Dutch, culminating in an exploit of individual heroism when a soldier sacrifices his own life to blow up an enemy ammunition dump. Running through the yarn is a charming and tender romantic theme, though the treatment is always on the naive side. Despite its deficiencies, the film shows promise of technical skill, and the acting is sincere. *Myro.*

Cold Tracks
(NORWEGIAN)
Moscow, July 16.

Directed by Arne Skouen. Screenplay, Skouen and Johan Borgen; camera, Ragnar Sorenson; editor, Byern Breigutul; music, Gunnar Sonstevold. At Moscow Film Fest. Running time, **91 MINS.**

Odmund	Toralv Maurstad
Ragnhild	Henni Moan
Tormod	Alf Mailand

Norway is in the minor league among the European filmmaking countries, and that is all to clearly reflected in this festival entry. It is a slow, mainly dull wartime story, with little prospects outside the Scandinavian territories.

Twelve fugitives from Fascism are crossing the mountains towards the sea and, they hope freedom. But their departure is delayed when the guide decides to pick up his sweetheart. Bad weather interrupts the journey, and the fugitives are buried in the snow. Fifteen years later, the guide returns to the scene, only to find that his former sweetheart is now married to someone else on the expedition.

The trek across the snowy mountains lacks excitement, and the direction and action is on the heavyhanded side. *Myro.*

Naked Among The Wolves
(EAST GERMAN)
Moscow, July 16.

DEFA (East Berlin) production and release. Features Erwin Geschonnek, Fred Delmare, Armin Muller-Stahl, Gerry Wolf, Eric S. Klein. Directed by Frank Beye. Screenplay, Bruno Apitz, based on his own novel; camera, Guenther Marczinkowsky. At Moscow Film Fest. Running time, **121 MINS.**

Although there has been an abundance of films from the Eastern European bloc on the subject of concentration camps, there are few to match this East German production for sincerity and production quality. It is a powerful narrative of the last weeks at Buchenwald, before its liberation by the Yanks, and it is a moving experience. As always, this type of yarn is hard going for Western audiences, but it merits some playing time in the West.

The author had the misfortune to have had first hand experience of Buchenwald, so presumably there is an authentic background. And apart from the fact that the camp guards and the Gestapo are shown as bullies and thugs, there is little of the conventional propaganda tract in the story.

As a novel approach to the plot, the main incident revolves around a young Jewish boy, rescued from the Polish ghetto, who is secreted into the camp by a Pole. The commandant gets word that the boy is there, and starts a reign of terror, but the camp underground gets to work, moving the child from one hiding place to another, outwitting the guards until the end. By the time the boy is found, it is too late as the noise of American artillery penetrates the camp, and the guards prefer to run for it.

The climatic scenes in which the thousands of inmates realize that they are free at last is magnificently photographed. They are caught running towards the camera lens, gradually filling the screen and showing natural signs of joy and hysteria. There are, on the other hand, some incidents which strain credibility somewhat, but they are of relatively minor significance.

As it is always easier to portray heavies on the screen, it is the camp guards and the gestapo bullies who emerge as clearcut characters. But there is a high all-round standard of acting by a cast unknown in the West. Technically, the pic measures up to present day standards. *Myro.*

The Dear Family
(DANISH)
Moscow, July 16.

A/S Nordisk Films Kompagni Production. Directed by Erik Balling. Screenplay, Arvid Muller based on play by Gustav Esmann; camera (Eastmancolor), Jorgen Skov; music, Kai Normann Andersen. At Moscow Film Fest. Running time, **100 MINS.**

Friis	Gunnar Lauring
Elise	Lise Ringheim
Emily	Belle Virkner
Ida	Ghita Norby
Jacob	Ole Soltoft
William Randall	Bjorn Watt Boolsen
Claes of Lejonstam	Jarl Kulle
Valdemar Nystrom	Ebbe Langberg
Count Maagenhjelm	Henning Moritzen
Von Schldpadde	Keld Markuslund
Ludwig	Buster Larsen
Julie Hansen	Lily Broberg
Irmelin	Susse Wold

The scene is Copenhagen at the turn of the Century, and against a rich background. Story covers the misadventures of a wealthy widower, his three lovely daughters, their husbands and suitors. There are the usual incidents with early cars, lively dances, amorous dallyings and family scandals.

Dialog is occasionally witty, but the events are stagebound if nicely photographed. Acting generally is deft.

Most of this is however, of no consequence. One of the best scenes involves an Englishman who is delegated to tell a neice of "the birds and the bees." *Prat.*

Marriage Circle
(INDIAN)
Moscow, July 16.

R. D. B. production. Calcutta. With Suchitra Sen. and Soumittra Chatterjee. Directed by Ajoy Kar. Screenplay, Nripendra Krishna Chatterjee; story Ashutosh Mukherjee; camera, Bisu Chakravarty; editor, Baidvanath Chatterjee; music, Hemanta Mukherjee. At Moscow Film Fest. Running time, **120 MINS.**

The theme of racial inequality is the purpose of this drab Indian film. Unfortunately, in telling the story of a rich man's daughter who marries a poor professor, it trails off into a tedious collection of silly misunderstandings. The couple part, and when the wife later finds a new significance in the holy words from the Veda (spoken at the Hindu marriage ceremony), she goes back to her husband only to find he has disappeared.

The conflicts are slight and hardly justified, reality is barely suggested, and the emotions seldom touched by this slow film. *Prat.*

Saladin
(EGYPTIAN)
Moscow, July 16.

A Lotus Film production for the Egyptian State Cinema Commission. Directed by Youssef Chanine. Screenplay, Youssef Al Sebai; camera, Eastmancolor), Wadid Serry; music Francesco Lavagnino. At Moscow Film Fest. Running time, **180 MINS.**

Saladin	Ahmed Mazhar

Virginia .... Nadia Loufti
Richard of England ...... Salah Zulficar

Here we see the Crusades from the Arab point of view. They are the heroes—the English, French and Spanish are the villains—and they justify this attitude. This three-hour, costly Egyptian epic is a revealing production in many ways. Judged on the same level as the average Hollywood and Italian "spear and sandal" epic, it's superior in technique, story, authenticity and vigorous acting. Its makers, having learned from Hollywood, naturally follow a melodramatic and often absurd course. But their firm belief in the power of love, the uselessness of war and the dignity of the Arab people cannot be denied.

The narrative forcefully reminds Christians of the horrors they have committed in the name of Jesus Christ, who himself preached the doctrines of non-violence, of their intolerance in assuming that all Arabs were "infidels" not fit to be trusted with Jerusalem. However, the film is never disrespectful of Christianity.

Its characters are clearly cut according to conventions, yet take on a depth of feeling and an understanding of humanity. Saladin, played by Ahmed Mazhar, is noble and wise. King Richard is mighty, vain and ambitious. He wants Jerusalem not so much for the good of the Christian people but to bring glory to himself. Oddly enough, considering the Suez affair, the French and the Spanish get the back-of-the-hand treatment while Richard is portrayed with sympathy and intelligence as a man with some doubts as to the justice of his mission. but overcome by his pride. He is excellently played by Salah Zulficar.

There is not an excessive amount of dialogue and what there is does not mince words or waste time. All is fire and movement, swords clash, and blood flows over the screen as the battles move from sea to desert and into castles. And the love affair? Like everything else in this picture, it's the opposite to Hollywood: an Arab Christian is in love with an English maid!

There is not much style to the direction, being a mixture of influence, but it has many clever effects and good moments. Lavagnino's score is always part of the action, expressive and lyrical. The camera work is fluent and alive. The whole is an interesting indication of things to come from other "independent countries" making films about history and their own past.   *Prat.*

Those Who Take Risks
(AUSTRIAN)

Moscow, July 16.

A Schonbrunn Film production. Vienna. With Karl Schonbock, Sieghard Rupp, Paul Dahlke, Ewa Kerbler, Marienne Rahn. Alvy Becker, Ingeborg Gruber. Directed by Edwin Zbonck. Screenplay, Helmut Andios. Zbonck. At Moscow Film Fest. Running time, 96 MINS.

Here is an Austrian film which criticizes the West German film industry. Young girls are lured into pix, and deliberately involved in scandalous goings on for the sake of publicity.

The story appears to want to say stern and meaningful things about moral standards, about newspapers which print sensational stories and the public which wallows in such yarns. But it seems to get lost in a peep show, emerging with a final statement that if girls didn't do this sort of thing the situation wouldn't exist..

The girls are all beautiful in face and figure. And the film, if it is to be believed, is likely to raise the question: what did they do to get into the picture?   *Prat.*

Death Called Engelchen
(CZECH)

Moscow, July 16.

Czescoslovensky Film Export production and release. With Jan Kacer, Eva Polagova, Martin Ruzek, Blazena Holisova. Directed by Jan Kada, Elmar Klos. Screenplay, Milos Faber; camera, Rudolf Milic. At Moscow Film Fest. Running time, 160 MINS.

The obsession of the occupied countries with war films is understandable, and this Czech entry at the Moscow festival is one of the better kind. It is intelligently made, has several powerful situations, and a number of interesting characters. But this needs more editing if it is to make the grade in the West. It rates as a possible artie presentation.

The film, which is also known as "For We, Too, Do Not Forgive," is a story of the partisans fighting the Nazi occupationists, and is told in a series of flashbacks. Pic begins on the last day of the war when one of the most active and determined partisans is shot in the spine, and ends up paralyzed in hospital.

The hero's dreams and nightmares are the instrument for introducing the flashbacks, which vividly recall their more exciting and perilous experiences. There is one flashback, for example, when the partisans prepare to ambush Nazis who are accompanied by tracker dogs. First, they have to shoot the dogs, and then they annihilate the enemy.

There's another in which two Nazi deserters are picked up by the Partisans, and then voluntarily take up arms against their former comrades. In another, a female Partisan, who had been forced into prostitution by the Nazis, shoots one of the German officers in cold blood. There are many more, indeed far too many, particularly in the latter half. And this makes for some needless repetitive action.

The Engelchen of the title is the Nazi commandant, and the most hated of all the Germans. It is the thought that this officer is still alive that inspires the hero to recovery, and he leaves the hospital with only one thought in his mind —revenge.

The film is technically first-rate and the cast sustains a high all-round standard of acting. There is more shading than usual in the characterizations, which adds enormously to the acceptability of the subject.   *Myro.*

Signs of the Zodiac
(MEXICAN)

Moscow, July 16,

A Section De Technicos del STPC production. With Kitty de Hoyos, Angelica Maria, Pilar Souza, Blanca de Castejon, Mario Garcia, Luis Bayardo, Enrique Aquilar, Eugenia Rios, Martha Zamora. Directed by Sergio Vejar. Written by Sergio Magana; camera, Augustin Jimenez; music, Carlos Jimenez. At Moscow Film Fest. Running time, 96 MINS.

A nasty piece of "social realism" from a union which talks of making better films for Mexico. Pretentious, cliche-ridden, boring and badly acted, it concerns three families in a slum all of whom come to a dismal end. The story serves no useful purpose no matter in what light it is considered.   *Prat.*

The Boys
(FINNISH)

Moscow, July 9.

Finnish State Film Studios production. With Pentti Torkiainen, Matti Louri, Um Saurio, Liisa Nevalainen. Directed, written by Mikko Niskanen. Camera (b&w) Olavi Tuomi; music, Einar Englund. At Moscow Film Fest. Running time, 98 MINS.

Niskanen's first film is a war story that is different in that it shows a country (Finland) which was occupied by the Germans as allies. The point the story tries to make, none too clearly or quickly, is that war is degrading. This is illustrated by the effect that wartime life — without discipline and guidance — has on a group of boys neglected by their parents.

Film is well photographed and naturally acted, but is only a collection of simple incidents rather than a well-told story.   *Prat.*

The Shore of Waiting
(IRANIAN)

Moscow, July 16.

A Missiquiei production. With Dzafare, Foruzan, Fardin, Tahmine. Directed and written by Siamek Yasami. Camera, Enayatolla Famin; music, Morteza Hannane. At Moscow Film Fest. Running time, 100 MINS.

This primitive melodrama from a new filmmaking country concerns a teacher whose rich father has driven the fishermen from their beaches. He has 'bought' the sea. The son leaves his father to build a school and educate the much put-upon peasants. At the same time he saves his beloved from degradation and beatings at the hands of a violent suitor.

Artificial and familiar, the best to be said is that it is a start for Iran. Perhaps the villagers will enjoy it.   *Prat.*

Twelve Chairs
(CUBAN)

Moscow, July 16.

Margarita Alexandre production for National Institute of Cinematography. Directed by Tomas Gutierrez Alea. Screenplay, Ugo Ulive, Tomas based on novel by Ilya Ilf and Eugene Petrov; camera, Ramon F. Suarez; editor, Mario Gonzalez; music, Juan Blanco. At Moscow Film Fest. Running time, 91 MINS.
Hippolyte .... Enrique Santisteban
Oscar .... Reinaldo Miravalles
Le Cure .... Rene Sanchez
Gertrude .... Pillin Vallejo
Ernesto .... Idalberto Delgado

Here is a not unsuccessful attempt by Cubans to transpose the popular post-revolutionary Russian novel by Ilf and Petrov to the immediate aftermath of their own revolution. The story is a satirical study of the revolutionaries and aristocrats and how greed affects them both. To some extent it's surprising that it goes so far regarding wealthy people. In one scene the man deprived of his wealth says that he wants

to get to the U. S. because "it has a truly responsible democratic government."

The story follows a greedy merchant, an artful revolutionary and a shifty priest in their desperate efforts to find an English chair in which a wealthy old woman had hidden her jewels shortly before she expired. The director uses silent comedy techniques to add to the humor of the whole, while the actors give genuine comic interpretations.   *Prat.*

The Young Woman of Bai-Sao
(VIET-NAM)

Moscow, July 16.

Hanoi Feature Film Studio production. With Tra Giang, Tran Phuong, Ba Du, Minh Tri, Le Van Phuc, Minh Dang. Directed by Phan Ky Nam. Screenplay, Bui Duc Al; camera, Nguyen Khanh Dzu; music. Tran Ngoc Xuong. At Moscow Film Fest. Running time, 120 MINS.

In Indonesia's "Toha, Hero of Bandung," it was the Dutch oppressors who were getting all the hate. In this similar but better made film from Viet-Nam, a young widow changes from a shy girl into an important political figure, and it is the French who are the vile ones. These "aggressors" raped her, killed her husband, took her child and burned her village.

Although all this took place 10 years ago and the French have since gone, the film is said to be still up-to-date as U.S. Imperialists are following in the steps of the French colonialists, "turning our beautiful country into a hot-bed of war."

The events are simply told and acted with a naive charm and undeniable sincerity.   *Prat.*

A Stranger In the City
(TURKISH)

Moscow, July 16.

A Be-Ya production. With Goksel Arsoy, Nufufer Aydan. Directed by Halit Refig. Screenplay, Vedat Turkali; camera, Cetin Gurtop. At Moscow Film Fest. Running time, 110 MINS.

An old emotional melodrama, the unbelievable plot tells of a mining engineer who returns to Turkey to work in the coal mine of his native town, and also marry his childhood sweetheart. On her parent's insistence, she has married a wealthy but black-hearted fellow who throws her dog over the cliff. Local politicos spread false rumors about the engineer and the wife having a scandalous liasion.

What with the mine caving in, the birth of a baby, a boy being run over, a few brothel scenes and the hero getting beaten, there's never a dull moment. Husband finally gets biffed on the head and thrown over the cliff, leaving loving couple to spend a more restful future together.

Quickly and poorly made, confusing and unreal, this preachment against intolerance has a gusto which sees it through. It is reported to be rather daring in subject matter for Turkish films.   *Prat.*

Stories On A Train
(HUNGARIAN)

Moscow, July 16.

A Hunnia Film Studio producton. With

Ildiko Pecsi, Adam Siptes, Imre Sinke-vics, Laslo Banidi, Josef Madares, Istvan Stankos, Attila Lere, Josef Kauuki. Directed by Tomas Reni, camera, Otto Forgacs; music. Geza Berki. At Moscow Film Fest. Running time, **102 MINS.**

This train takes a familiar track. Six workers are travelling together and they begin to tell stories about an unusual companion they once worked with on different construction projects. The narrative then flashes back to the actual events in factory life. At the end, one man doubts the existence of such a worker. He happens to be on the train and reveals himself to much rugged laughter.

Apart from being an interesting glimpse into construction work going on in Hungary, all of these anecdotes are far too long and hardly worth the telling. The players seldom emerge as definite characters; the whole is unimaginative.   *Prat.*

Sci-Fi Fest

"X"-The Man With X-Ray Eyes
(COLOR)

Slick programmer with science fiction mixed with chase scenes; treats too many aspects skimpily but has exploitation handles.

Trieste, July 16.

American International release of James H. Nicholson-Samuel Z. Arkoff production. Stars Ray Milland; features Diana Van Der Vlis, Don Rickles, Harold J. Stone, John Hoyt. Directed by Roger Corman. Screenplay by Robert Dillon from original screenplay by Ray Russell; camera (Eastmancolor), Floyd Crosby; editor, Anthony Carras. At Trieste Science-Fiction Film Fest. Running time, **80 MINS.**
Dr. Xavier .... Ray Milland
Diane .... Diana Van De Vlis
Sam .... Harold J. Stone
Crane .... Don Rickles
Dr. Benson .... John Hoyt

American International has enough exploitation handles in this sci-fi thriller, with some philosophic aspects and more suggestive and justified nudy-comico scenes to have this shaping a good programmer. Film has fine technical assets, color and Ray Milland as a name.

Basically its the plot where the scientist tampers with the unknown and is severely punished in the end. Ray Milland is a doctor who has devised a drug that he thinks will allow men's eyes to see infinitely more.

He tries it on himself when he is refused a grant to continue experiments on animals. He at first is put out of commission by a blinding light but then can see inside human tissue and through clothes. This permits him to visit a party where the women are nude to him (but this is kept to bare limbs and shoulders). But it also has enough suggestiveness for those wanting kicks rather than story.

Things get worse as he kills a friend inadvertently, forcing the doctor to hide out in a carnival as a mindreader. A girl who believes in him tries to help and they go off to work on some antidote. But winning money via seeing through

cards at Las Vegas has a well-done police chase and his ending up at a revivalist meeting.

There are many interesting comic, dramatic and philosopical ideas are touched on but treated only on the surface. However, director Roger Corman keeps this moving and Ray Milland is competent as the doomed man while others are adequate if only stereotype figures. Special effects on his prism-eye world, called Spectarama, are good if sometimes repetitive.

In short, an above average sci-fi thriller with a better technical envelope to pay off commensurately.   *Mosk.*

The Amphibious Man
(RUSSIAN-COLOR)

Trieste, July 16.

Sovexport release of Lenfilm production. With K. Korieniev, M. Virzinskaya. Directed by Y. Kasancki. Screenplay, A. Blajaev, Kasancki from book by Blajaev; music, Tirentev. At Trieste Film Fest. Running time, **100 MINS.**
Sea Devil .... K. Korieniev
Alicia .... M. Virzinskaya

Legend, romaitic love, melodrama, adventure, folklore and science fiction are adroitly mixed in this Russo Sovcolor opus. It's naivite is okay via its folksy feeling. This could well be a specialized dualer abroad if its deceptive simplicity may make it more difficult for arty houses.

In some mythical Latino country, a scientist has turned his only son into an amphibious man who lurks in the waters near a little town and frightens pearl divers who dub him the Sea Devil. One day, he saves the comely daughter of an old fisherman from a shark and falls in love. But she is promised to an evil overseer of the divers by the father. And she marries the evil one. It seems the amphibious man also can walk about on land as a seemingly ordinary mortal.

Direction has a romantic flair and displays fine work with the cavorting scenes under the sea, and the Devil's trip into town which is strange and new to him. This basically is good moppet item, too, as well as entertaining for adults.

The scientist had hoped to found a brace of new people who would be completely free but realizes that the world is not ready for this yet.

Color is good, the underwater scenes are expertly done and the story fine except for too much forced plotting at the end. A successful adventure opus is the tag for this.   *Mosk.*

The Celestial Brothers
(RUSSIAN-COLOR)

Trieste, July 16.

Mosfilm production and release. Direction, editing, lensing and compilation by A. Gostiev in Sovcolor. At Trieste Sci-Fi Film Fest. Running time, **70 MINS.**

Documentary depicts the training, space flights and reception of the two Soviet cosmonauts, Nikolaiev and Popivic, who orbited together in space last year. It is of interest in its look at the preparation and the footing within the capsules in the space conscious age.

But this needs shearing of its

excess propaganda aspects and the repetitive footage of the two men at play. In this form, it could be an okay supporting film for special use abroad as well as possibly for tele.   •

Both are shown under the severe duress of space tests of noisy lights and sounds, weightlessness, parachute jumps and physical training. Then the blast off, with rockets concealed for military purposes, shots of them in the capsule and the mighty welcome of the Russo people and Premier Khrushchev's kisses. Color is good and the men come over well in their simplicity and dedication.

Shots of Lenin worked in for extra patriotic note, their visit to his mausoleum, and some speeches can be cut. It is technically good in spite of the mixture of news footage, handheld camera work and improvised aspects.   *Mosk.*

Ikarie XB I
(CZECHOSLOVAKIAN)

Trieste, July 16.

Czech State Film production and release. With Zdenek Stepanek, Radovan Lukavsky, Dana Medricka, Miroslav Machacek, Frantisek Smolik, Jiri Vrstala, Marcella Martinkova. Directed by Jindrich Polak. Screenplay, Pavel Juracek, Polak; camera, Jan Kalis; editor, Josef Dobrichovsky. At Trieste Sci-Fi Film Fest. Running time, **90 MINS.**
Vladimir .... Zdenek Stepanek
Mac Donald .... Radovan Lukavsky
Nina .... Dana Medricka
Marcel .... Miroslav Machacek
Anthony .... Frantisek Smolik
Erik .... Jiri Vrstala

This rates as a finely made futuristic look at space travel. If it has a few shafts of propaganda, this Eastern Bloc pic is otherwise refreshingly free of dogma. In these days of space travel it bodes something of dualer or specialized use abroad. Its close quarter work and solid special effects and theme also make this loom a video bet in foreign spots.

A space ship is on its way to explore a new planet in some future time when there is evidently a one-world government judging from the many differing nationality names on board. But all, of course, speaks only Czech. There is space fatigue and adventures as a radiating star induces sleep in the crew and a discovered derelict space ship is found to have live atom bombs on board.

This last is explored by two men on the space ship and it is revealed as probably American, due to dice and money clasped in the hands of a dead man. Talk has it that the 20th Century had the Hiroshima bombing but also some great men and things.

But the main appeal is the inventive interiors of the ship, Ikarie XBI, the method of eating, a comical robot and the one man who goes mad from space claustrophobia. Direction keeps the human relations on a simple almost schematic plane and the mixed female and male crew do not have any jealousy trouble.

But aside from this, the impeccable ship interiors, the space efforts on leaving the ship to examine the derelict and the gleaming workings keep this interesting despite the shallow personages. It is technically firstrate. Acting is good within its conventionally geared people. A grain more of inventiveness would have made this one of the better sci-fi pix.   *Mosk.*

Wives And Lovers

Sophisticated romanticomedy that chickens out in clutch. Fair b.o. contender.

Hollywood, July 19.

Paramount release of Hal Wallis production. Stars Janet Leigh, Van Johnson, Shelley Winters, Martha Hyer; features Ray Walston, Jeremy Slate, Claire Wilcox. Directed by John Rich. Screenplay, Edward Anhalt, based on Jay Presson's play, "The First Wife"; camera, Lucien Ballard; editor, Warren Low; music, Lyn Murray; assistant directors, Danny McCauley, Bill Poole. Reviewed at Picwood Theatre, July 19, '63. Running time, **102 MINS.**
Bertie Austin .... Janet Leigh
Bill Austin .... Van Johnson
Fran Cabrell .... Shelley Winters
Lucinda Ford .... Martha Hyer
Wylie Driberg .... Ray Walston
Gar Aldrich .... Jeremy Slate
Julie Austin .... Claire Wilcox
Mrs. Swanson .... Lee Patrick
Mr. Liberti .... Dick Wessel
Dr. Patridge .... Dave Willock

An adult comedy about adult matters should respect its adult audience enough to face facts squarely and honestly, not hedge when the going gets touchy. Failure to be consistent with itself mars "Wives And Lovers" an otherwise highly polished and pleasurable sophisticated comedy about a couple whose happy marriage is nearly shattered in the wake of the husband's sudden professional success. Had it maintained the courage of its convictions, the Hal Wallis production for Paramount might have ranked as the comedy find of the year among more discerning filmgoers.

The film excels in one area. Edward Anhalt's scenario, from Jay Presson's stage play, "The First Wife," contains some of the sharpest, wittiest, most perceptive comedy dialog to pop out of a sound track in some time. Story relates the marital misadventure that materializes when an unsuccessful writer (Van Johnson), who for three years has been lovingly and uncomplainingly supported by his wife (Janet Leigh) while he pens a novel, suddenly hits the book-of-the-month jackpot. In a flash, the couple and their precocious tot have moved from a cramped Gotham cold-water flat to the luxury living of the fashionable Connecticut suburbs.

In the process of converting his prose into a Broadway play, Johnson becomes entangled in an affair with his glamorous agent (Martha Hyer), in retaliation for which Miss Leigh apparently gets herself voluntarily seduced by the star (Jeremy Slate) of her husband's play. This leads to a separation.

But it is here that the script pulls its punches and lapses into apologetic artificiality. Did Johnson sleep with Miss Hyer? Nosiree. Did Miss Leigh succumb to Slate? Not on your life. Having thus exonerated its romantic principals, the film can thus conclude on a note of reconciliatory sentiment in which nothing has been lost but the responsive enthusiasm of its deceived audience.

Here is the issue. When a motion picture delves into matters as frank and adult as who-slept-with-whom-last-night-and-why, it owes it to its audience to be honest to the end. Unless prepared to resolve them

intelligently, why introduce matters as bold and unsavory as these in the first place?

The acting in "Wives And Lovers" is pleasing and skillful. Miss Leigh delivers her smoothest performance in some time. Equally slick is Johnson who, in his return to the screen after a three-year absence, proves himself still a valuable leading man in the sophisticated comedy sphere. Miss Hyer, along with Shelley Winters and Ray Walston, performs professionally. Slate's solid portrayal should put his budding screen career in high gear. Lee Patrick is a stickout as an officious, independent maid.

Seven-year-old Claire Wilcox, who weighed in late last year as the moppet star of "Forty Pounds Of Trouble," draws some of the best lines and business in this, her second film, and comes through with flying colors. She's one of the best child actresses around.

Occasional mechanical inconsistencies tarnish John Rich's otherwise bright and breezy direction in his first major feature assignment. Assets to the production are Lucien Ballard's smooth lensmanship, Warren Low's brisk editing. Lyn Murray's lively background score and the expressive art direction of Hal Pereira and Walter Tyler. *Tube.*

Gidget Goes To Rome
(COLOR)

Third, and poorest, in the teen series.

Hollywood, July 11.

Columbia release of Jerry Bresler production. Stars James Darren, Jessie Royce Landis, Cesare Danova, Danielle de Metz; introduces Cindy Carol. Directed by Paul Wendkos. Screenplay, Ruth Brooks Flippen, Katherine & Dale Eunson, from story by Mrs. Flippen based on Frederick Kohner's characters; camera (Eastman), Enzo Barboni, Robert J. Bronner; editor, William A. Lyon; music, Johnny Williams; assistant directors, Tony Brandt, Milton Feldman. Reviewed at the studio, July 11, '63. Running time, 103 MINS.

Gidget	Cindy Carol
Jeff	James Darren
Aunt Albertina	Jessie Royce Landis
Paolo Cellini	Cesare Danova
Daniela Serrini	Danielle de Metz
Judge	Joby Baker
Libby	Trudi Ames
Lucy	Noreen Corcoran
Clay	Peter Brooks
Anna Cellini	Lisa Gastoni
Alberto	Claudio Gora
Russ Lawrence	Don Porter
Dorothy Lawrence	Jeff Donnell
Pinchman	Joe Kamel
1st Italian Boy	Antonio Segurini
2nd Italian Boy	Leonardo Botta
Mario	Umberto Raho
Contessa	Audrey Fairfax
Prince Bianchi	Vadim Wolkowsky
Fat Woman	Edra Gale
Lean Woman	Irina Vasailchikoff
White-Faced Poet	Charles Borromel
1st Listener	David Munsell
2nd Listener	Jan Coomer
East Indian Yoga	Leon Auerbach
Normal Woman	Norma Nedici
Old Woman	Matilda Calnan
1st Caviar Woman	Carmen Scarpita
Drunk Butler	John Stacy
2nd Caviar Woman	Melina Vukotic
Receptionist	Eva Marandi
Fontana Doorman	Mimo Billi
Henrietta	Milly Monti
Major Domo Dresser	Veronica Wells

If this is the best that can be done with "Gidget," then the time has come to discontinue the series. Even the young people for whom this third and skimpiest installment presumably is designed will find little in the Columbia release of even remote interest or stimulation.

The Jerry Bresler production introduces Cindy Carol as the new "Gidget," making three actresses who have tackled the title role in as many films. The assigned task of having made love to all three belongs to James Darren.

Ruth Brooks Flippen and Katherine and Dale Eunson are responsible for the limp screenplay that arose from Miss Flippen's yarn based on the original Frederick Kohner characters. While on vacation in Rome, "Gidget" and her steady beau, "Moondoggie," become romantically involved with others, then reunite when the "affairs" expire. Sandwiched in between these drab and predictable amorous doings is the inevitable guided tour of Rome, a site thoroughly exploited in previous films and generally with more flavor.

Miss Carol is a pretty "Gidget," but lacks the charm or spirit brought to the character by Sandra Dee, its originator. Darren has his role down to mechanical perfection. At this stage, its more of a science than an art. His singing is good. He warbles the exuberant, Italo-flavored title ditty and another refrain called "Big Italian Moon," both by George Davis Weiss and Al Kasha. Others of prominence in the cast, in addition to Danova, are Jessie Royce Landis, Danielle de Metz, Joby Baker, Trudi Ames, Noreen Corcoran, Peter Brooks, Lisa Gastoni, Claudio Gora, Don Porter and Jeff Donnell. A degree of efficiency is about all that can be achieved by these players. It is Paul Wendkos third "Gidget" directorial task. If he is lucky, it may be his last.

Among those who contributed their skills to this losing cause, filmed in Rome and California, were cameramen Enzo Barboni and Robert J. Bronner, art directors Antonio Sarzi-Braga and Robert Peterson, editor William A. Lyon and composer Johnny Williams. *Tube.*

Ballad of a Hussar
(RUSSIAN-MUSIC-COLOR)

Artkino release of Mosfilm Studios production. Stars Larissa Golubkina. Directed by Edgar Ryazanov. Ryazanov and Alexander Gladkov; camera, Leonid Krainekov. At Cameo, N.Y., starting July 13, '63. Running time, 94 MINS.

Shura	Larissa Golubkina
Rzhevsky	Yuri Yakoviev
Kutuzov	Igor Ilvinsky
Masha	Tatyana Shmyga

(In Russian; English Subtitles)

"The Ballad of a Hussar," also known originally as "The Hussar Ballad," is apparently the best operetta-type feature to come out of Russia. Also it is the strongest musical meller to be done by the Russians in many years. Booked into this West Side home of Russian films for a week or 10 days, it looks to run for several weeks. It's a sure bet for language houses and could thrive in some arty spots.

It's the deft direction of Edgar Ryazanov and sterling acting of Miss Larissa Golubkina that's responsible for 75% of the way this one jells. Perhaps an added plus factor is the well-picked cast which turns in many excellent character portrayals.

Basic plot is that Shura (Miss Golubkina), who's pledged to wed a pompous, professional Army lieutenant, sets out to deflate him. In doing so, she becomes the

heroine and medal winner in actual battle skirmishes. It all takes place during the Napoleonic invasion of Russia. While the operetta motif is obvious from the outset, the director has never let the outlandish overtones interfere with his actional story development. Result is at times reminiscent of some Hollywood western musicals, and it's all to the good.

Miss Shura emulates a Hussar (her identity as a femme is retained until the final reel) and get attached to headquarters with the Russian forces trying to stem Napoleon's advance. Her heroism finally wins her recognition and medals. Through all this fighting and bloodshed, per opera bouffe technique, there is little actual battle shooting or suffering. There is one priceless sequence when the marching Russian forces start out with their typical marching song on a spring day but before the tune is completed they are in snowbound territory around Moscow.

Miss Golubkina is quite effective with several ballads but scores best with her bright acting and cute looks. She is seen riding in several sequences like the Lone Ranger himself. Tatyana Shmyga, as the singer from Paris, also chips in with a coloratura tune that goes across nicely. Yuri Yakoviev is realistic as the blustering army officer who doesn't want to be bothered with marriage.

Besides Ryazanov's strong direction (he also helped with the script), Leonid Krainekov has contributed amazingly fine color (Sovcolor) photography, both on the colorful countryside and on the ornate interior scenes. *Wear.*

Kiss of the Vampire
(COLOR)

From the Hammer Horror Mill, another well-made goblet of blood. Shriek trade will love it.

Universal release of a Hammer Films production. Produced by Anthony Hinds. Stars Clifford Evans and Noel William. Directed by Don Sharp. Screenplay by John Elder; camera, Alan Hume; music, James Bernard; editor, James Needs; assistant directors, Douglas Hermes, Hugh Harlow. At Universal, July 22. Running time, 88 MINS.

Professor Zimmer	Clifford Evans
Ravna	Noel Willman
Gerald Harcourt	Edward De Souza
Marianne	Jennifer Daniel
Carl	Barry Warren
Sabena	Jacquie Wallis
Tania	Isobel Black
Bruno	Peter Madden
Anna	Vera Cook
Disciple	Brian Oulton
Father Xavier	Noel Howlett
Police Sergeant	John Harvey
Servant	Stan Simmons
Woman at Graveyard	Olga Dickie
Girl Disciple	Margaret Read
Girl Disciple	Elizabeth Valentine

Horror pic fans will dig this latest effort from the Hammer Film shop in Britain. It is a slickly-produced color story of evil doings in Bavaria, circa 1910, replete with suspense, demonism and mystery, tightly wrapped in a skillful package of effective performance and well-paced direction.

Director Don Sharp gets the film off to a solid start as a young honeymoon couple who have run out of gas on a lonely road are eyed mysteriously from a spired

villa by a severe-looking figure and an equally-mysterious stranger warns of undefined danger in the area. This eerie mood is sustained as the couple stay the night at a strangely deserted inn and later dine at the home of the figure who, unknown to them, had been watching them on the road.

This menacing host turns out to have a whole family of wierdies and, as it develops, is the high priest of a cult of human vampires who eventually mesmerize the young bride over to their group during a bazaar masquerade party. With the help of the man who had first warned of danger, the husband manages to save wifie and kill off the blood lusters. This is all unraveled amid colorful settings which effectively evoke the eerie mood of John Elder's well-constructed screenplay.

Edward De Souza is properly dazzled and horrified at what takes place in the role of the newlywed husband and Jennifer Daniel makes a pretty victim of the sorcery. Noel William turns in a strong effort as the evil leader of the vampire cult and carries off the job in demonic effectiveness. Also turning in a competent job is Clifford Evans as the profit of doom who turns out to be the girl's saviour, he being an expert on the subject of vampires after their attempt to claim his daughter failed when he himself killed her with that ever-faithful spike in the heart. This sequence, incidentally, makes for an evocative prologue before the credits.

Also adding to the demonic flavor of the tale are performances by Barry Warren and Jacquie Wallis as Willman's disciple son and daughter. Peter Madden is effective as the retiring innkeeper of the hotel the couple stays at and Vera Cook is credible as his wife and the bereaved mother of their daughter who has been claimed by the vampires. Isobel Black is oke as the fang-toothed offspring, who eventually meets her end with the rest in a finale which resembles a Transylvannia version of "The Birds," with an attack by bats substituted for blackbirds.

Alan Hume's camera has nicely captured the colorful and eerie quality of the proceedings and Bernard Robinson and Don Mingaye have artfully designed and dressed the production. James Bernard's music lends nice emphasis in underscoring the action and "Vampire" has been crisply edited under the supervision of James Needs.

The Universal release is a solid entry in the exploitation pic sweepstakes and is a good bet to capture some of the escapist late summer biz. It also again demonstrates that consistently effective touch of producer Anthony Hinds and the Hammer Film company in turning out these slick chillers. *Kali.*

Locarno Fest

I Basilischi
(The Lizards)
(ITALIAN)

Locarno, July 23.

Galatea release of 22 Dicembre production. With Toni Petruzzi, Stefano Sattaflores, Sergio Ferrannino, Luigi Barbieri, Flora Carabella, Mimmina Quirico. Written and directed by Lina Wertmuller. Camera, Gianni Di Venanzo; music, Ennio Morricone. At Locarno Film Fest. Running time, **80 MINS.**

Antonio .... Toni Petruzzi
Francesco .... Stefano Sattaflores
Sergio .... Sergio Ferrannino
Padre .... Luigi Barbieri
Amico .... Enze Di Vecchia
Luciana .... Flora Carabella
Zia .... Mimmina Quirico

Italian films have shown an extraordinary rise via talented new filmmakers in the last few years. They now unveil a promising femme director in Lina Wertmuller. Pic looks at sleepy southern, smalltown life but neither sentimentalizes, melodramatizes or jibes at it. It may have many angles peculiarly Italian. But this has enough general scope, observation and insight to slant it for specialized and arty spotting abroad but will need the hard sell.

There is no story here for not much happens in this hilltop town located in the heel of the boot country. It mainly follows three young men around in aimless walks and musings, which deal primarily with women and sex. Also noted is the insularity, class consciousness and the rigid surface propriety of the town.

One boy suddenly gets taken to Rome by an aunt and comes back sleek and full of tall tales about the marvelous life, gadgets and women. He is to go back but somehow never does and falls back into the routine or ogling girls, walks and talks, with a new angle in his probably faked stories of his Rome adventures.

Film's only point states that maybe there is something lacking in these people that keeps them drifting and seemingly oblivious of any true contact and stand on life, progress or even the past. Perhaps there is sometimes guile in showing mainly the dreary side of smalltown life, but there is sharp observation and tender if devastating points made about the townspeople and the so-called Italo economic miracle.

Miss Wertmuller allows little, sharp incidents to suddenly break the turgid life flow as an old woman commits suicide when she finds her authority absorbed by her daughter-in-law, a hapless man floats about to finally go to the one joy girl where he passes another customer shamefacedly, and a city woman leaves a husband in a big fracas and telling off of the ogling townspeople.

Direction keeps this atmospheric anecdotal affair from lapsing into tedium. It shrewdly points up the languid lack of human direction, if there is a clinging to old hierarchal values and a definite looking down on peasants by villagers.

Lensing is properly lush because of the sunbaked quality of this beautiful but listless town. Roguish music, bright editing and good ensemble playing keep this constantly amusing and incisive with the sudden dramatic shafts convincing rather than jarring.

Perhaps a little more of a point of view, less slyness and more forthrightness should have Miss Wertmuller emerging a solid asset to Italo film ranks. And the femme manner of looking at things as a whole, and being more prone to accept instead of dissect and accuse, jives with this theme.

Its colorful accents and characters may be more difficult for general audiences abroad, if it has the handles for more specialized spots. This looms a possible sleeper on its home grounds and could coin an expression in its title, "The Lizards," referring to these youths who seem to lie vegetating in the sun. *Mosk.*

Les Grands Chemins
(The Big Roads)
(FRENCH--FRANSCOPE—COLOR)

Locarno, July 23.

Comacico release of Saphrene-Copernic-Dear Film production. Stars Robert Hossein, Renato Salvatori, Anouk Aimee. Directed by Christian Marquand. Screenplay, Pierre De La Salle, Paul Gegauff, Marquand from novel by Jean Giono; camera (Eastmancolor), Andres Winding; editor, Nadine Trintignant. At Locarno Film Fest. Running time, **95 MINS.**

Samuel .... Robert Hossein
Francis .... Renato Salvatori
Anna .... Anouk Aimee

France now has its own rock-'n-roll stars and seems to want to make its own American films too, judging from this entry. Pic collects a flock of Yank Western themes and tries to transplant them to present day provincial France, with a dash of gangsterism. It emerges a naive if sincere emulation of its American counterparts. Pic looms mainly for local use on its star names and some exorbitant mayhem, sadism and sex. But it's mainly for grind or lower case duaier usage abroad.

Remember Paul Newman getting his thumbs broken in "The Hustler" for cheating at pool? Here anti-hero Robert Hossein gets his hands broken for cheating at cards. Oater heroes and anti-heroes, drawn together by some virile feeling, are also in evidence via psychotic Hossein, and the drifting but loyal Renato Salvatori who befriends him only to kill him later.

Salvatori also has a wordless love scene as he looks deep into Anouk Aimee's eyes, follows her to a hotel and makes deep love, quite unsparingly shown. When she says something he is morose because he feels their relationship should have gone on wordlessly.

Dialog might have been better off also if wordless also, for it is slick he-man stuff that is more parody than precise prose. The destructive psychotic seemingly lets himself be caught cheating and is horribly beaten and dumped on the doorstep of his friend. But the cheated-on characters are prototypes of brutish kind also seen in Yank pix of this ilk.

Actor Christian Marquand, for his first pic, shows a definite love and knowledge of American films of this sort. Some of the fights are well staged and the relationship between the men is adequate, if forced. But the true feel for the inventive is scrappy in this. Color is good, especially some of the landscapes. Violent sentimentality is not a French forte, and this is nothing more than a hybrid psycho adventure pic.

Hossein is hammy as the sick gambler. Salvatori has the earthy simpleton projection for the victimized friend. Miss Aimee, reduced to an object, cannot do much with her role as a sexy dame. This pic remains uneven for all its good intentions and workmanship.

Marquand also overdoes closeups for making points. But this does display some fluidity, and Marquand could possibly develop into a solid commercial director if he went to things he knew instead of only reflecting film forms he likes. It remains to be seen if this will be as popular here as the better American outdoor and gangster pix are. *Mosk.*

Tiburoneros
(The Shark Hunters)
(MEXICAN)

Locarno, July 30.

Antonio Matouk production and release. Stars Julio Aldama, Dacia Gonzalez; features Tito Junco, Alfredo Varela, Amanda Del Llano, Noe Murayama. Written and directed by Luis Alcoriza. Camera, Raul Martinez Solares; music, Sergio Guerrero. At Locarno Film Fest. Running time, **95 MINS.**

Aurelio .... Julio Aldama
Manela .... Dacia Gonzalez
Manuel .... Tito Junco
Chilo .... Alfredo Varela
Adela .... Amanda Del Llano
Ramon .... Noe Murayama

Film takes a familiar situation of a middle-aged man's choosing of adventure over family life but gets over any pitfalls of sentimentality, false moralizing or melodrama. By knowing, sharp delineation of two milieus, this makes its points refreshingly and entertainly, with enough depth to have it a possible general playoff pic or for specialized chances abroad if well handled. Its Latin lingo earmarks are tops.

For his second pic, Luis Alcoriza, who worked on scripts for noted director Luis Bunuel, shows he has learned how to tell a story economically and unveil character deftly. A man hunts sharks on a little island which gives him money to send to his wife and family in the big city. He has built up respect for himself, is loved by a hoydenish but appealing 18-year-old girl and feels he has earned his name and place on his own.

But one day his wife's supplications, and his feeling that his children need him, have him going home. He finds they do not truly need him and that he actually belongs in the more primitive, poorer but humanly satisfying shark hunting grounds. So back he goes.

What Alcoriza has done is paint the poor section without patronizing. Its rough, harsh aspects are outlined but not in a reformist way. This is how it is and the pic implies that man may or can change it. The camaraderie is neatly felt as is the hurt and even fury of these people when this man they have accepted and looked up to leaves.

Knowing character insights keep this from slipping into false he-man aspects or escapism palaver. It is technically fine with a fine flair for depicting love and action sans the usual cliches or overindulged eroticism. In short, a Mexican film that may resemble others on the surface but is a great cut above them in depth, treatment and theme. It needs careful sell. It is technically fine with expert performances. *Mosk.*

Manlohua
(Manlo, The Flower)
(RED CHINESE-COLOR-DANCE)

Locarno, July 23.

Studios Halyen production and release. With Luo Hsing-Fang, Luo Che-Long, Lieou King, Li Yu-Lin, Ahliue, Tchen Yi-Kouen. Directed by Fan Lai, Tchou Chou-Houa. Camera (Sovcolor), Hsiu Ki, Tchang Kouei-Fou; choreography, Wou Pao-An, Hsiao Lien-Ming; music, Ki Tcheou, Tchou Chou-Houa. At Locarno Film Fest. Running time, **80 MINS.**

Manlo .... Luo Hsing-Fang
Adoyue .... Luo Che-Long
Hunter .... Lieou King
Heidayang .... Li Yu-Lin
Ounces .... Ahliue
Lackey .... Tchen Yi-Kouen

All-ballet pic deals with an old legend of a despot who kidnaps a young bride from a little village but faces the wrath of the people and husband to have it all end in tragedy. Dancing is lithe and dramatic, mime expert, but it is repetitious, with garish color, and mainly for Cantonese circuits or specialized dance or school showings abroad.

Sets are acceptable since it is primarily canned ballet. But dancers manage to give some depth to their characters and and bring alive the feel of legend. Music is a composite of Chinese themes with Western sound arrangements.

Dancers use mainly low-level, clean fluttering but get into sharp elevation and darting energy in fight sequences. Folk, Russian dance influences and classic ballet mingle in the terps forms. It has a certain beguilling, eye-catching quality that makes it "seeable" in spite of its head-on lensing. No "East Side Story" this, but an okay packaging of dance on film. Production values and costumes are fine. *Mosk.*

Zloto
(POLISH) (C'SCOPE)

Locarno, July 23.

Polski Film release of Kamera production. With Wladyslaw Kowalski, Krzysztof Chamiec, Barbara Krafft, Adam Pawlikowski. Directed by Wojciech Has. Screenplay, Bohdan Czeszko; camera, Stefan Matyjaszewicz; music, Lucjan Kaszycki. At Locarno Film Fest. Running time, **90 MINS.**

Boy .... Wladyslaw Kowalski
Pierre .... Krzystof Chamiec
Barmaid .... Barbara Krafft
Engineer .... Adam Pawlikowski
Edouard .... Tadeuz Fijewski
Dorothee .... Elzbieta Czyzewska

Polish pix seem still free in individual creative outlook, in spite of the Russian pull-back to more orthodox social realism. This is a pessimistic, revealing look at some aspects of Poland today. If this sometimes is too symbolic, literary and talky, this pic has depth in character and sustained visual flair, and might make a specialized arty bet abroad. Pic takes its own time, rhythm and pace to spin its heavily symbolic yarn, but it's still absorbing.

A youth is on the run because he thinks he killed a man in an auto accident. He ends up at a big power plant works near the Polski border. Here he gets involved with a group of types who seem to stand for certain aspects of the country today.

Director Wojciech Has displays a subtle feeling for revealing character associations which manages to give them depth. Here the boy seems a groping type who finds too much adult lying, evasion and pettiness about him.

A dying tubercular man who, befriends him for selfish and philosophical reasons, a group of brutish workers who use old war experiences as excuses for pettiness, some roaming girls (calling themselves dancers) who are really on

the make for more heeled men and a wily barmaid, make up his initiation into life

This is technically expert, with the actors managing to make their highly literary figures acceptable and giving it a sweep and knowing insight into human aspirations. Pic is a definite offbeater from the Eastern bloc. *Mosk.*

Passaros De Asas Cartadas
(Birds With Clipped Wings)
(PORTUGUESE)

Locarno, July 23.

Cinedex production and release. With Paulo Renato, Leonia Mendes, Rui De Carvalho, Lucia Amram, Hugo Casais. Directed by Artur Ramos. Screenplay, Luis Rebelo, Ramos, Alexandre O'Neill, Sttau Monteiro; camera, Joao Moreira; editor, Artur Ramos. At Locarno Film Fest. Running time, **85 MINS.**

Edouard .... Paulo Renato
Rosa .... Leonia Mendes
Francisco .... Rui De Carvalho
Elsa .... Lucia Amram
Frederico .... Hugo Casais

Litle Portugal rarely has pix at fests. This one shows new trends have seeped in and, more importantly, films are beginning to look at their own country more severely. Social drama may have more value for its own markets. But this displays enough character and narrative flair for Latino lingo situations and specialized booking abroad.

It concerns a drifting young crowd who spend time in listless talk, liaisons without passion and finally bring on tragedy when an irresponsible youth inadvertently leads to the accidental death of the daughter of his father's chauffeur. But the chauffeur, to insure a better life for his son, helps hush up the affair. It does make a rich girl break away from a married man she thought was different.

Director Artur Ramos shows he has seen other pix depicting the aimlessness of rich life. He gets good work from his thesps, if most of the roles are stereotyped and the plot telegraphed.

This emerges a social tract on the lack of communication and vaporous outlooks of the world today. It is technically good. This just misses being an exceptional film. *Mosk.*

Tuulinen Paiva
(Day of Wind)
(FINNISH)

Locarno, July 22.

Ruutsalo release and production. With Raili Metsa, Yrjo Tahtela. Written and directed by Eino Ruusalo. Camera, Matti Xlinin; editor, M. Letinen; music, Otto Donner. At Locarno Film Fest. Running time, **70 MINS.**

Girl .... Raili Metsa
Boy .... Yrjo Tahtela

Arty intention without invention leads to pretention. Except for an overdone love scene and nude shots, which could provide exploitation and grind use abroad, this one looms mainly for Finland.

A boy and a girl snuggle, breathe hard and finally take their clothes off on a beach. Then he tells her he must go to the city to make his way. They are on some outlying islands. Next she is seen roaming around the city looking for the boy.

What she runs into are some more quick adventures ending the pic in a sort of dream sequence of all the characters on the island beach. Acting is a series of poses and director Eino Ruutsalo uses too many aimless symbolic shots that mean nothing since no true atmosphere or mood are created.

A forced sound and music track is also of little use. In short, this seems to be a badly assimilated attempt to adopt some of the methods of Michelangelo Antonioni and Alain Resnais, but without the control, meaning and depth these men have been able to give their work. Result is aping rather than assimilation. *Mosk.*

Luciano
(ITALIAN)

Locarno, July 26.

Vorona release of Mario Lanfranchi production. With Luciano Morelli, Valentine Piacente, Anna Bragaglia, Franco Ciuffi, Paolo Carlini. Written and directed by Luigi Baldi with script aid by M. Jemma; camera, Ennio Guarnieri; music, Luciano Chailly. At Locarno Film Fest. Running time, **80 MINS.**

Luciano .... Luciano Morelli
Wife .... Valentina Piacente
Mother .... Anna Bragaglia
Father .... Franco Ciuffi
Rich Man .... Paolo Carlini

For his first feature film documentary maker Luigi Baldi has stretched a short he made on the general life and background of a real delinquent into a feature entry. It lacks the taut insight of its predecessor and sometimes does not find the right blend between realism, social statement and characterization. So it seems a chancy item for the U.S. except for specialized bookings, with depth possibilities also flimsy.

Played by the same young man who essayed role in the short, Luciano comes home from prison to find his mother gone and his father feigning illness and carrying on with another woman. He rages against the poverty and runs off to get mixed up with a man married to a rich woman who takes him home.

Here the rich are painted neurotically, incapable of love and as miserable, in their way, as the poor. Luciano leaves and goes towards home. Director Baldi shows a mobile camera and a flair for atmosphere and sudden revealing insights into human troubles. But there is a tendency to touch on too many things which make its impact light and seemingly forced in its dramatics.

But Baldi looms a possible worthy addition to the high standards of Italo filmmaking newcomers when he finds the right way of channeling his documentary talents into the needed wider social and human frames for feature pix. It is technically good and the non-actors are acceptable and at times more effective than the few pro players in the cast. *Mosk.*

Im Pokoriaetsa Nebo
(Conquerors of the Sky)
(RUSSIAN)

Locarno, July 23.

Mosfilm release of Gorki Studio production. With Nicolas Rybnikov, Vladimir Sedov, Svetlana Svetlitchnaia, Evgueni Evstigniev, Oleg Jakov. Directed by Tatiana Liosnova. Screenplay, Anatole Agranovsky, Leonide Agranovitch; camera, Valery Guinsbourg; music, Andre Echpai. At Locarno Film Fest. Running time, **100 MINS.**

Koltchine .... Nicolas Rybnikov
Charov .... Vladimir Sedov
Nina .... Svetlana Svetlitchnaia
Chief .... Evgueni Evstigniev
Bassarguine .... Oleg Jakov

Pic shapes a competent, if conventional, tale of a test pilot who pioneered the first Soviet jet plane. It sometimes gets a bit too grandiloquent and starry-eyed in outlook and characters, but has the saving grace of subdued dramatics and tasteful pacing. Made by a woman, it could have been made by a man. Another aspect of the equality of the sexes in Russia.

This does not have the deeper personage insight and flair for much arty chances abroad. Film appears mainly a possible dualer on its okay tale and well-done flying scenes. The making of the plane is taken from drawing board to testing.

But then a pitch is made about how much he did and how he helped the cause of Russia. All this was already intrinsic in the pic and did not need the final aria. But director Tatiana Liosnova, displays a puckish, tomboyish humor, an interest and ability to put technical data on screen without too much dullness. She has a firm hand in putting a tale together.

Perhaps a less didactic tale and more individual outlooks and characters could have her making worthy pix and taking her place in the Soviet scheme of picmaking. It is technically good. *Mosk.*

Tom Jones
(BRITISH—COLOR)

Lusty, boisterous 18th Century frolic based on Henry Fielding classic; star-studded cast should steer this to big league boxoffice ratings, despite occasional arty touches.

London, July 23.

United Artists release of a (Tony Richardson) Woodfall production. Stars Albert Finney, Susannah York, Hugh Griffith, Edith Evans, Joan Greenwood; features George Devine, Wilfrid Lawson, Jack MacGowran, Freda Jackson, Joyce Redman, Rachael Kempson, Angela Baddeley. Directed by Tony Richardson. Screenplay, John Osborne, based on Henry Fielding's novel: narrator, Michael MacLiammoir; camera, Walter Lassally; editor, Antony Gibbs; music, John Addison. At London Pavilion. Running time, **128 MINS.**

Tom Jones .... Albert Finney
Sophie Western .... Susannah York
Squire Western .... Hugh Griffith
Miss Western .... Edith Evans
Lady Bellaston .... Joan Greenwood
Molly Seagrim .... Diane Cilento
Squire Allworthy .... George Devine
Lord Fellamar .... David Tomlinson
Mrs. Miller .... Rosalind Atkinson
Black George .... Wilfrid Lawson
Mrs. Fitzpatrick .... Rosalind Knight
Partridge .... Jack MacGowran
Mrs. Seagrim .... Freda Jackson
Blifil .... David Warner
Mrs. Waters (Jenny Jones) Joyce Redman
Parson Supple .... James Cairnososs
Bridget Allworthy ..... Rachel Kempson
Thwackum .... Peter Bull
Mrs. Wilkins .... Angela Baddeley
Mrs. Fitzpatrick .... George A. Cooper

It's been a long wait for Albert Finney's film follow-up to "Saturday Night and Sunday Morning." And though "Tom Jones" is a period piece and very different it has the same lustiness and boisterous content with which to project the star. It should breeze its way cheerfully through the boxoffice figures. It has sex, Eastmancolor, some prime performers and plenty of action. Tony Richardson has directed John Osborne's screenplay with verve, though, occasionally, he falls back on camera tricks and and editing which are disconcerting.

Based on Henry Fielding's enduring novel, story is set in Somerset, a West Country lush county, and in London during the 18th Century. Hero is Tom Jones (Albert Finney), born in suspicious circumstances, with a maidservant dismissed because she is suspected of being his unwed mother. He is brought up by Squire Allworthy (George Devine) and leads a rollicking life in which women play a prominent part before he finally escapes the gallows after a frame-up. He finds a presumably happy ending in the arms of a neighboring daughter, Sophie, played in rather over-genteel style by Susannah York.

Ramifications of the plot, which enables Finney to indulge in considerable sexual activity with a variety of delectable dames, are too complicated to need discussion. But the somewhat sprawling, bawdy and vivid screenplay of Osborne's provides some meaty acting opportunities and the thesps grasp their chances with vigorous zest.

Finney is big league. He slips through his adventures with an ebullient gusto that keeps the overlong film on its toes for most of the time. Hugh Griffith and Edith Evans as Squire Western and his sister ham disarmingly. Miss Evans has some of the choicer cameos in the film. Joan Greenwood, George Devine and Wilfrid Lawson are others who get top credits for their work. Angela Baddeley, Rosalind Knight, Rachel Kampson, Jack MacGowran, Freda Jackson and Joyce Redman are others and rate benevolent nods. David Tomlinson with a brief but effective comedy appearance in a guest role as an aristocratic heel, and Diana Cilanto have limited roles but nevertheless prove that it makes sense to bring stars with knowhow to do brief jobs.

Eastmancolor captures some good location and period stuff, lensed well by Walter Lassally, particularly in the Newgate Prison sequence as well as a fox hunting episode.

Director Richardson has occasionally pressed his luck with some over-deliberate arty camera bits. The music of John Addison is a trifle obtrusive and lacking in period style. However, "Tom Jones" measures up as a genial energetic comedy, with an added bonus of Michael MacLiammoir putting over occasional narration with his usual smooth wit and perception. *Rich.*

The Great Dream

Drab indie meller.

Hollywood, July 16.

Gary Graver production. Directed and written by Graver; cofeaturing Graver; camera, John Willhem; music, Les McCann Ltd. Reviewed at Lytton Center, July 16, '63. Running time, **67 MINS.**

The Girl .... Lois Adams
The Boy .... Gary Graver
The Drunken Man .... Billy Rhodes
The Strange Man .... R. J. Gristak
Leader of the Toughs .... Bert Byers
The Toughs Robert Parr, Tony Tsavidis, Robert Huard

It might help if the young writer-producer-director-star of this low-budget independent film abandoned the Orson Welles bit and

delegated some authority to persons better equipped to handle certain creative phases of the work. Much of his writing, for example, is painfully pretentious mumbojumbo.

Most of Graver's skill appears to lie in the directorial and production area. It obviously took a good deal of resourcefulness and ingenuity to mount and execute this picture on a shoestring budget. And there is evidence of some cinematic flair in the new wavish manner in which Graver and his cameraman, John Willheim, have set up and photographed several sequences. On the one hand, what story there is transpires at a pace even a snail would deem lethargic. And the story itself, no doubt lofty in intent, emerges opaque and choppy and childish.

The David-and-Lisa-like yarn relates some of the hard knocks encountered by two young aspirants to Hollywood fame and fortune, a boy (Graver) and a girl (Lois Adams) who meet, sleep together and go their separate ways. In addition to those played by Miss Adams and Graver, other characters encountered along the primrose Hollywood path include a drunken midget (Billy Rhodes), a pervert (R. J. Gristak) and four youthful hoods (Bert Byers, Robert Parr, Tony Tsavidis and Robert Huard) who beat Graver up on the corner of Hollywood and Vine. There are plenty of witnesses, but nobody raises a finger in his defense. Hollywood may be a blase, callous burg, but such atrocities are not that readily acceptable to the inhabitants.

The 67-minute Yucca production sports a racy jazz score by Les McCann Ltd. Among the Graver's represented are associate producer Frances and production coordinator Jeff. *Tube.*

Chouchou and the Million
(LEBANESE)
Moscow, July 23.

Les Fils de Georges Haddad (Beirut) release of an Issam Hamaoui and Antone S. Remy production. Stars Chouchou and Chamel. Directed by Antoine S. Remy. Screenplay, Mohamed Chamel; camera, Bruno Salvi. At Moscow Film Fest. Running time, **85 MINS.**

Just for the record, this Lebanese film stars two local tele artists in a trite little comedy about an errand boy, who behaves like a congenital idiot and walks like an ape, until he inherits a million. Then he sets out to prove the old proverb about fools and their money.

The film, it is reported, is a fabulous success locally, and may possibly do well in other middle-east areas. But this can be readily discounted for most other markets. *Myro.*

The Running Man
(BRITISH—COLOR)

Carol Reed gives some lively touches to an oldhat theme. Colorful Spanish sequences and slick performances by Laurence Harvey, Lee Remick, Alan Bates.

London, Aug. 6.
BLC release of a Columbia presentation of a Carol Reed production. Stars Laurence Harvey, Lee Remick, Alan Bates; features Eleanor Summerfield, Eddie Byrne, Felix Aylmer, Alan Cuthbertson, Noel Purcell, Colin Gordon, John Meillon, Ramsay Ames, Fernando Roy. Directed by Carol Reed. Screenplay by John Mortimer, from Shelley Smith's novel; editor, Bert Bates; camera, Robert Krasker; music, William Alwyn. At Odeon, Leicester Square, London. Running time, 103 **MINS.**

Rex	Laurence Harvey
Stella	Lee Remick
Stephen	Alan Bates
Parson	Felix Aylmer
Hilda Tanner	Eleanor Summerfield
Jenkins	Alan Cuthbertson
Tom Webster	Harold Goldblatt
Miles Bleeker	Noel Purcell
Madge Penderby	Ramsay Ames
Police Official	Fernando Roy
Roberto	Juan Jose Menendez
Sam Croudson	Eddie Byrne
Solicitor	Colin Gordon
Jim Jerome	John Meillon
Spanish Doctor	Roger Delgado

The story of the man who poses as dead in order that his "widow" can pick up the insurance money is not exactly new. But a director of Carol Reed's skill can always give the yarn a lift and make it holding entertainment. "The Running Man" is just that, and with the names of Reed, Laurence Harvey, Lee Remick and Alan Bates as stellar bait this should attract patrons of all classes.

Based on Shelley Smith's novel, "Ballad of a Running Man," John Mortimer has written a smart script, with the three principal characters (they're the only ones of any importance) well delineated. Interiors were shot at Ardmore Studios, in Ireland, but main locations were lensed in Spain. There is an extra bonus of Robert Krasker's lush Technicolor camerawork.

Film opens with a memorial service for Harvey, believed drowned following a glider accident. Solemnly his wife, Miss Remick, accepts the sympathy of friends. But soon Harvey turns up, larger than life, and sets in motion their plan to collect $140,000. The wife is not happy about the plan but he persuades her that the insurance company owes them the cash because it had refused to pay up on a previous claim. The claim goes through and the wife joins Harvey in Spain where she finds that he has assumed the identity of an Australian millionaire and is already plotting to pull off another insurance swindle. She is perturbed that his new wealth is changing her husband's character.

However, all's well until they run into a representative of the insurance company on holiday. Their guilty consciences convince them that he is suspicious, and then begins the shrewdly written and directed game of cat-and-mouse which is the most satisfying part of the pic. Needless to say there's an unexpected twist and a climax which leads up to a tingling

car sequence on a perilous Spanish road. And, proving that crime doesn't pay, comes Harvey's death in a crashed plane.

Harvey has a role that suits him admirably, allowing him to run the gamut of many moods, charm, humor, brashness, harshness and fear. It is a meaty role which he plays with confidence and evident relish. Miss Remick is also admirable as the young, pretty wife, adoring Harvey but yet beset by conscience and a growing dislike of his behavior and avarice. Hers is a difficult part suggesting acute tension as she wavers between Harvey and Alan Bates, who has fallen for her and to whom she gives in one afternoon.

Bates, in the less flashy role of the insurance agent, ostensibly playing detective, is firstclass. He plays on a quiet, yet strong, note and is a most effective contrast to the flamboyance of Harvey. Harvey and Bates handle the dialog and the situations as a perfect duet.

Eddie Byrne, Colin Gordon, Noel Purcell, John Meillon, Alan Cuthbertson, Eleanor Summerfield, Eddie Byrne and Ramsay Ames are among those who have minor roles but bring professionalism to them.

My Hobo
(JAPANESE-COLOR)

Delightful, finely-directed and acted comedy from Japan. Should score with U.S. audiences.

Toho release of Tokyo Eiga production. Stars Keiji Kobayashi. Directed by Zenso Matsuyama. Screenplay, Matsuyama; camera, Hiroshi Murai; music, Hikaru Hayashi. At Toho Cinema, N. Y., starting July 23, '63. Running time, **98 MINS.**

Jumpei	Keiji Kobayashi
Komako	Hideko Takamine
Takeo	Noribei Miki
Mariko	Reiko Dan

(In Japanese; English Subtitles)

"My Hobo" turns out to be a frothy little comedy with fine direction and a stalwart performance by Keiji Kobayashi. This delightful bit of screen fun seems to firmly establish the fact that the Japanese are as skillful at making a laugh pic as a stern drama, for which they are best known in this country.

Kobayashi makes the hobo character as realistic as any like figure turned out in Hollywood. He is the loquacious beggar who adopts two waifs largely because they attach themselves to the wandering hobo despite his urgings that they return home or dig up some relative. The tramp's plight is further burdened by a designing woman who steals his hidden money, accumulated from months of begging or petty thievery. And the climax is when said girl proposes marriage in distant Tokyo when and if he agrees to steady employment.

The hobo's wanderings in search of food takes him on a sort of travelogue of some of Japan's most colorful spots. One of the more humorous sequences finds Kobayashi, disguised as an alms-seeking beggar, then a a cripple from the war begging on the streets and finally seeking money as a down-and-outer who is unable to walk.

Director Zenzo Matsuyama has made such routine scenes vivid comedy romps. Even a Keystone Cops chase becomes something worthwhile in his hands.

Besides Kobayashi, the two waifs, Hideko Takamine and Norihei Miki, often come close to thefting the pic. Reiko Dan is the girl companion who robs him and then decides to marry him if he will reform. The music by Hikaru Hayashi is a highlight for its unusualness. The lens job by Hiroshi Murai is topflight. It's in Eastmancolor. *Wear.*

Raices De Piedra
(Roots of Stone)
COLOMBIAN-DYALISCOPE)
Locarno, July 30.

Julio Roberto Pena production and release. With Max Castillo, Luis Pachon, Cecilia Rueda, Lilia Cardeno. Directed by Jose Maria Arzuaga. Screenplay, Julio Roberto Pena, Arzuaga; camera, Abdu Eljaiek, Felipe Frias; music, Javier Jaramillo. At Locarno Film Fest. Running time, **70 MINS.**

Clementi	Max Castillo
Firulais	Luis Pachon
Wife	Cecilia Rueda
Daughter	Lilia Cardeno

The sad, pungent smell of poverty is evident in this pic from South America. Rarely seen at recognized film fests, this nation shows a preoccupation with social issues and some good, if sometimes confused, filmmaking talents. Though intermittently effective, pic is mainly a Latino and lingo entry for foreign chances.

The beginning is alive with many shots of construction, with men dwarfed by it. But it only takes shape after one third of the pic is gone with the introing of a sick worker whose fainting spells and pain have little effect on others.

A pickpocket tries to get money for needed medicine but comes back too late after having been beaten and imprisoned in his both legal and illegal attempts to raise money to help the suffering sick man.

This obviously has a deep feeling and hurt about poverty, but has a tendency to bog down its important issues in too much unformed story. Director Jose Maria Arzuaga does display a good visual sense and makes his points in some scenes.

But more coherence, besides the already important content, could possibly have him contributing worthy features pix to other film fests. As is, this appears a good beginning. The on-the-spot lensing is effective as is a throbbing, jangly guitar musical background. Actors are fair if they are sometimes lost in the mass of side footage. *Mosk.*

Black Wings
(POLAND)
Moscow, July 30.

Film Polski release of a Lodz Film Studio production. Directed by Ewa and Czeslaw Petelsey. Screenplay, Aleksander Scibor-Rylski, and Petelsey; camera, Kurt Weber; music, Jerzy Makaymiuk. At Moscow Film Fest. Running time, **107 MINS.**

Kostryn	Kazimierz Opalinsky
Kjor	Czeslaw Wollejko
Miglewski	Zdislaw Karczewski
Taduesh	Stanislaw Niwinski
Zuza	Beata Tyszkiewicz

The industrial strife in the im-

mediate post World War I era is the subject of this latest Polish film, which portrays the class struggle between Silesian miners and foreign capitalists in strictly conventional terms. Not for the West.

The action takes place in Silesia in 1923, at a time when thousands of miners have been declared redundant. Ignoring a warning from the company surveyor that there is an escape of natural gas, the French and Polish mine owners insist on sending the men into the pit, with the inevitable catastrophe.

All the characters seem to have been taken straight out of a Marxist stock company, among them the wicked capitalists, the demagogic trade union leader and deputy plus the ardent communist who leads the workers in the class struggle. They are portrayed strictly according to the book, without a sign of subtlety. Camera work is mainly okay, but direction and acting is largely ponderous.

Myro.

The Cicada Is Not An Insect

(ARGENTINA)

Moscow, July 30.

Tinayre-Borras S.R.L. (Aoolfo Cabrera) production. Directed by Daniel Tinayre. Screenplay, Gori Munoz; adapted by Eduardo Borras from book by Dante Sierra; camera, Alberto Etchebehere; music, Lucio Milena. At Moscow Film Fest. Running time, **100 MIN.**

The Wife	Maria Antinea
The Prostitute	Amelia Bence
The Bride	Elsa Daniel
Intellectual Girl	Mirtha Legrand
Teacher	Malvina Pastorino
Industrialist	Jose Cibrian
Ventriloquist	Narciso Ibanez Menta
Journalist	Angel Magana
Taxi Driver	Luis Sandrini
Musician	Enrique Serrano
Maid	Tesesa Blasco
Bridegroom	Guillermon Bredeston
Model	Diana Ingro
Lady	Miryan de Urquijo
Nurse	Leda Zanda
Dostor	Guillermo Battaglia
Police Commissaire	Hector Calcano
Manager	Hermo Carpena

This stylish, outwardly sophisticated comedy-drama opens to a promising start. Six assorted couples find themselves in quarantine for 40 days in a dubious hotel for "clandestine love appointments." A French sailor with the prostitute is stricken with bubonic plague and in the headlines which follow the couples find themselves exposed—to the outer world and to themselves.

Once the situation is established and the closed world created, the author runs out of ideas and the forthcoming examination of personal motives and relationships is hardly new or interesting. There are many familiar comedy moments. Photography and direction are lively and the large cast is generally bright and amusing. The whole, however, is superficial.

Prat.

The Right Hand Of The Devil

Slickly photographed, sloppily produced attempt at suspense by one-man talent gang.

Hollywood, July 31.

A Cinema-Video International Corp. release of an Aram Katcher production. Produced and directed by and starring Katcher, plus Lisa McDonald and Brad Trumbull, based on original story by Katcher. Screenplay, Ralph Brooke; camera, Fouad Said; musical director, John Bath; supervising editor, Katcher. Reviewed at Lytton Center, July 30, 1963. Running time, **75 MINS.**

Pepe Lusara	Aram Katcher
Miss Sutherland	Lisa McDonald
Williams	Brad Trumbull
Sammy	James V. Christy
Spooky	Chris Randall
Carter	Monte Lee
Dino's Bartender	Luigi Gardneri
The Dancer	Georgia Holden

Many interesting stories have been lost during transference to the screen medium, and for many reasons. "Right Hand of the Devil," with the germ of another "Killing" evident in its basic tale, gets lost on most counts—distortion of original concept, weak attempts at artiness, limited budget, uncertain acting by a largely inept cast, but, most of all, by the domination throughout of one person.

The result is a short film that seems too long and is certain for slotting in the lesser half of the exploitation houses and drive-ins. The pic's plus values are the slight suggestions of suspense, some excellent black and white photography, and an exploitable title.

Aram Katcher is given screen credit as star, producer, director, writer of the original story, supervising editor, title designer, and makeup supervisor. Almost all of these duties should have been turned over to more professional filmmakers. In none of them is he a success.

Evidently an avid film fan, Katcher has incorporated memories of several of his favorites into his tour-de-force. His ultimate goal is uncertain—suspense, horror, sexcitement—they're all introduced but not allowed to stick around long enough to establish an identity. An actor of the Peter Lorre genre, he underplays for menace but lacks his prototype's eerie voice and demeanor. As a lover (or lecher), he's laughable.

The tale takes the viewer, literally or by suggestion, into many local night spots, with Dino's Lodge figuring prominently in the plot. In fact, the most professional performance, uncredited, is that of Jack Elton as a pianist there. Come to think of it, Elton is a pianist at Dino's. Settings range from the Sports Arena, also prominent in the plot, to a Laurel Canyon deserted mansion which serves as the center of operations.

Katcher arrives in town, rents the mansion, hires some hoods, and sets up plans to pull a multi-dollar stickup at the Sports Arena. To make it work, he romances the Arena's head cashier (Lisa McDonald), a middle-aged lonely type, pulls the job, knocks off his accomplices (he thinks), and heads for Rio. Much wine and women later, misfortune strikes and he returns to 77 Sunset Strip to work the gig again. There's a surprise ending that even "Frankenstein" fans won't swallow.

Katcher monopolizes the picture throughout and, misguided as to his own range of talents, allows supposedly suspenseful or erotic moments to turn into unintentional slapstick. Miss McDonald's successful but lonely cashier, although beautifully made up and lighted, is most unconvincing. With those looks and such a job, she'd have been anything but lonely. The rest of the cast appear to be on screen merely to run errands.

Fouad Said's excellent photography gives a professional sheen to the film that might have been better used on a more capably designed work. Ralph Brooke's script is flaw-ridden, possibly the result of erratic editing of budget limitations. Acceptance, by Cinema-Video, of the pic's limited appeal and some clever exploitation could salvage their investment but it may be that television is its true destiny.

Robe.

Promises, Promises

Tasteless sex farce.

Hollywood, Aug. 2.

Tommy Noonan & Donald F. Taylor production. Stars Jayne Mansfield, Marie McDonald, Mickey Hargitay, Tommy Noonan. Directed by King Donovan. Screenplay, William Welch, Noonan, from play by Edna Sheklow; camera, Joseph Biroc; editor, Edward Dutko; music, Hal Borne. Reviewed at Monica Theatre, Aug. 2, '63. Running time, **75 MINS.**

Sandy Brooks	Jayne Mansfield
Claire Banner	Marie McDonald
King Banner	Mickey Hargitay
Jeff Brooks	Tommy Noonan
Ship's Doctor	Fritz Feld
Babbette	T. C. Jones
Steward	Claude Stroud
Mrs. Snavely	Marjorie Bennett
Bartender	Eddie Quillan
Gigolo	Vic Lundin
Girl in Doctor's Office	Eileen Barton
Ship's Captain	Pat O'Moore

The only excuse for this shabby, sex-propelled contrivance is that obviously there is an audience waiting to devour it. If nothing else, it gets the voyeur off the streets and away from the magazine stands for awhile. Several glimpses of a bare-breasted Jayne Mansfield and one of her derierre-in-the-buff figure to satisfy the peeping Toms, Dicks and Harrys who frequent those offbeat, anatomical "art" houses where this attraction is apt to be exhibited. But beyond the occasional vicarious sensual thrill it affords the ogle-happy denizen of these cinematic flesh palaces, there is nothing in "Promises, Promises!" for anyone whose mentality surpasses that of a five-year-old.

The Tommy Noonan & Donald F. Taylor production was written by Noonan and William Welch from a play by Edna Sheklow and directed by King Donovan. The story, set on an ocean liner, describes the marital complications that arise when two wives, each of whose spouses purportedly are unable to sire an offspring, become pregnant shortly after a visit to the ship's medic by one of the husbands. Who-was-with-whom-alone-and-when is the general idea.

Noonan is gregarious as the pill-happy mate of Miss Mansfield. The latter's acting ability consists chiefly of educated body English. Marie McDonald and Mickey Hargitay limn the other couple, and others implicated prominently are Fritz Feld, an adept farceur, and T. C. Jones, of female impersonating fame, who does what comes unnaturally.

Art, music, photographic and other technical credits are routine.

Tube.

Tamahine

(BRITISH-COLOR)

Insufficiently sharp satire on the effect of a nubile Polynesian girl on a British public school. Neat performances but not, it would seem, potential boxoffice gold.

London, July 30.

Warner-Pathe release of Associated British presentation of a John Bryan-Philip Leacock production. Stars Dennis Price, Nancy Kwan, John Fraser; features Derek Nimmo, Coral Browne, Dick Bentley, Justine Lord, Allan Cuthbertson. Directed by Philip Leacock. Screenplay, Denis Cannan, based on Thelma Niklaus's novel; camera, Geoffrey Unsworth; music, Malcolm Arnold editor, Peter Tanner. At Warner Theatre, London. Running time, **95 MINS.**

Tamahine	Nancy Kwan
Richard	John Fraser
Poole	Dennis Price
Madame Becque	Coral Browne
Storekeeper	Dick Bentley
Clove	Derek Nimmo
Diana	Justine Lord
Cartwright	Michael Gough
Housemaster	Allan Cuthbertson
Oliver	James Fox
Mrs. MacFarlane	Noel Hood
Bash	Derek Fowlds
Mrs. Spruce	Viola Keats
Major Spruce	Howard Marion Crawford
Mrs. Cartwright	Lally Bowers
Lord Birchester	William Mervyn

Whether "Tamahine" is intended as a sharp, sophisticated sex comedy or a satirical joshing of the British public school system (which is as near as possible to the U.S. high school regime) is a perplexing thought. But it turns out to be an uneasy blend of both and does not quite come off. Some pleasant, bland performances help to pass the time agreeably but it seems unlikely that this film will produce congestion at the wickets.

Film concerns a Polynesian girl who, on the death of her father in the South Seas, is sent to England as the ward of his cousin, a public school headmaster. The pic is devoted mainly to the devastating effect that Tamahine has on every male in sight, and the idea quickly cloys. There are some predictable situations.

She poses nude for the art master and causes a scandal. She gets involved in a typically British public school prank. She gets her headmaster guardian feeling young again and eventually he pushes off to the South Seas. She gives goose pimples to the headmaster's son and eventually falls in love with him. A refreshing moment is during the school sports. All stiff formality goes when Tamahine, with athletic grace, that comes from being reared in nonurban surroundings, joins in and wins most of the events.

But too much of the time, this consists of a naive attitude towards sex, not over scintillating dialog in Denis Cannan's screenplay and some fairly stolid but helpful performances by reliable thesps. There are a few, however, who have helped considerably. Dennis Price, for instance. This time he is allowed to play a character which goes throughout the film. Price, as the headmaster, gives one of the best performances of his career and looks back to his peak.

Nancy Kwan frolics cheerfully in the title role. She is neat, nimble, nubile, nice but negligible, personality wise. John Fraser plays Price's schoolboy son and does it ably, though it is ridiculous to consider him as a teenage schoolboy, even if the knowhow that he left his teenage days several years ago is not general.

Derek Nimmo, as an eccentric artmaster; Justine Lord, Allan Cuthbertson, Michael Gough, Dick

Bentley Howard Marion Crawford and Lally Bowers are among those who assure that the acting helps to prop up the events. And there is that superbly poised actress, Coral Browne, in a sparkling cameo as a French courturier.

Geoffrey Unsworth has done some smooth Technicolor lensing and there is a pleasant score by Malcolm Arnold. Use of a genuine public school, for much of the shooting (the students were used as extras during their vacation) give a validity to the background. If only the screenplay had been wittier and more decisive, "Tamahine" would not have to be tagged as a near miss. It seems that those very competent characters, producer John Bryan and director Philip Leacock were, on this occasion, in two minds. *Rich.*

The Cracksman
(BRITISH-COLOR)

Fairly lively slapstick with comedian Charlie Drake getting nearer to his comic potential. Useful boxoffice contender.

London, July 30.

Warner-Pathe release of an Associated British (W. A. Whittaker) production. Stars Charlie Drake, Dennis Price, George Sanders; features Nyree Dawn Porter, Finlay Currie, Eddie Byrne, Percy Herbert, Geoffrey Keen. Directed by Peter Graham Scott. Screenplay by Lew Schwarz, Charlie Drake from an original story by Schwarz. Extra dialog by Mike Watts; camera, Harry Waxman; editor Richard Best; music, Ron Goodwin. At Warner Theatre, London. Running time, **112 MINS.**

Ernest Wright .... Charlie Drake
The Guv'nor .... George Sanders
Grantley .... Dennis Price
Muriel .... Nyree Dawn Porter
Domino .... Eddie Byrne
Feathers .... Finlay Currie
Nosher .... Percy Herbert
Magistrate .... Geoffrey Keen
Fred .... George A. Cooper
Mr. King .... Christopher Rhodes
Policeman .... Norman Bird
Sandra .... Wanda Ventham
Moke .... Richard Shaw
Choreographer .... Tutte Lemkow
Apache Dancers . Sheila Holt, Tom Gillis

Charlie Drake, the half-pint slapstick comedian from tele, has found his first essays in filming tough going. "The Cracksman" is a distinct improvement on his previous efforts. Two possible reasons are that, in this comedy, he has not "gone it alone" but has surrounded himself with some seasoned talents. Also he is for once playing a character instead of himself. This character, Ernie Wright, a dedicated locksmith, is able to raise yocks but also gain audience sympathy for his problems. The film is a lively piece of slapstick that should keep customers happy in most situations.

Drake plays an honest, little man who is the victim of fate. His problem is that he cannot resist the challenge of a lock. That's okay when he is dealing with honest folk, like the time they couldn't open the Tower of London. But he gets smoothtalked by a debonair con man into opening a locked car and a safe, and lands in jail for a year.

Later he gets trapped again, in his innocence, and this time gets three years and a reputation in the cooler for being the top cracksman in the business. When he gets out he finds himself a pawn being tossed between two rival gangs. Eventually the gangs get together to pull off a big job, the Stamford Collection of Fine Gems, with Duke to do the safe cracking. Naturally he and Nyree Dawn Porter, who turns out to be an undercover policewoman, turn the tables on the gangs.

Drake, who recently decided that he was going to take it easy after injuring himself doing his own stunts, falls back into slapstick literally in this film. He is swept down a sewer, crashed through a door, bodily flung into the boot of a car and he endures several other physical indignities for the sake of laughs. Trouble is that most of the comedy situations are stretched too long. Some more astute cutting by editor Richard Best would have added a tang to the screenplay and Peter Graham Scott's lively direction.

George Sanders and Eddie Byrne enjoy smallish but meaty roles as the rival gangsters and Dennis Price crops up occasionally in an ingratiating manner. Nyree Dawn Porter is a dainty heroine and Norman Bird and Geoffrey Keen as a magistrate score heavily in one of the funniest sequences, when Drake is in the dock. Other sock comedy sequences are an attempted mass breakout from jail and Drake, in a night club, getting entangled with some balloons and a couple of Apache dancers.

Harry Waxman's lensing is fine and Ron Goodwin has contributed a lively score. "The Cracksman" is the first indication that Drake has broken through a barrier which, somehow, has invariably prevented tv comedians in this country clicking on the big screen. *Rich.*

Doctor In Distress
(BRITISH-COLOR)

Not too hot exhibit in the successful "Doctor" series; interesting return of Dirk Bogarde to commercial stuff after a longish stint in longhair material.

London, July 30.

Rank distribution of a Betty E. Box-Ralph Thomas production. Stars Dirk Bogarde, Samantha Eggar, James Robertson Justice; features Donald Houston, Barbara Murray, Dennis Price, Mylene Demongeot. Directed by Ralph Thomas. Screenplay by Nicholas Phipps, Ronald Scott Thorn, by arrangement with Richard Gordon; editor, Alfred Roome; camera, Ernest Steward; music, Norrie Paramor. At Odeon, Marble Arch, London. Running time, **102 MINS.**

Simon Sparrow .... Dirk Bogarde
Sir Lancelot Spratt
James Robertson Justice
Delia .... Samantha Eggar
Iris .... Barbara Murray
Sonja .... Mylene Demongeot
Major French .... Donald Houston
Mrs. Parry .... Jessie Evans
Mrs. Whittaker .... Ann Lynn
Blacker .... Dennis Price
Heilbronn .... Leo McKern
Bradby .... Michael Flanders
Mrs. Clapper .... Madge Ryan
Rona .... Amanda Barrie
Woman Passenger .... Fenella Fielding
Meyer .... Reginald Beckwith
Corsetier .... Frank Finlay
Australian Sailor .... Bill Kerr

It could be that this successful "Doctor" series is beginning to show signs of wear and tear through constant competition with such tv programs as "Emergency Ward 10" and "Dr. Kildare." Anyway, it occasionally creaks. Situations and gags are often heavy-handed and the cast tends to go through its paces without overmuch animation. Its value as a N.Y. boxoffice draw is iffy. In Britain this should collect some business because of its cast.

Dirk Bogarde, who has lately been engaged in slightly more intelligent film operations, returns as a rather more mature Doctor Simon Sparrow than when he first played the role as a student. He plays the lightweight role with charm and humor. James Robertson Justice wallops his way through the familiar characterization of Sir Lancelot Spratt, the pesty surgeon. But the storyline calls for him to be far less irascable than of old, and this lessens his impact. There are some delectable girls around, notably Samantha Eggar, Mylene Demengeot and Barbara Murray. The last-named gives a bright reminder that she is a British actress who has not always been given full scope for her undoubted talent.

Donald Houston, Ann Lynn, Leo McKern, Dennis Price, Madge Ryan and particularly, Fenella Fielding, as an eccentric train passenger, give neat definitions of their respective roles. But, this time, Betty E. Box and Ralph Thomas have not been helped by a screenplay from Nicholas Phipps and Ronald Scott Thorn which does not effervesce as much as earlier ones. Perhaps it is the element of surprise which is now lacking.

The simple story concerns Justice, falling in love with a physiotherapist (Miss Murray), and Bogarde, also up to his eyes in romantic heartfluttering with Miss Eggar, a model with film aspirations, with Miss Demongeot, a Scandinavian charmer, working hard to sort out Justice's amorous problems.

Ernest Steward's color lensing is admirable and Norrie Paramor has come up with a chirpy score. This is a reasonable evening's entertainment but is a clear indication that it is time that the sponsors of the "Doctor" series should take a long, dispassionate peek at its future potentiality. *Rich.*

Running Empty
(RUSSIAN)

Moscow, July 30.

Sovexport Films release of a Lenfilm Studio production. Stars G. Yumatov. Directed by Vladimir Vengerov. Screenplay, Sergei Antonov; camera, G. Maranjyan; music, I. Shvartz. At Moscow Film Fest. Running time, **96 MINS.**

Nikolai .... G. Yumatov
Sirotkin .... A. Demyanenko
Arina .... T. Syomina
Victor .... G. Kachin
Tonya .... S. Kharitonova
Grandpa .... B. Chirkov
Akim .... A. Papanov

Snow and ice is a difficult background for a motion picture, but director Vladimir Vengerov has overcome this hurdle in this Lenfilm Studios production by adroit handling of a somewhat unusual plot. Apart from one or two obscurities towards the end, it is a competently made pic which could have limited chances in some overseas territories.

A reporter from Moscow is sent to a Siberian lumber camp to get the background for a story about a truck driver with a remarkable record. He can cover thousands of miles of the wintery countryside without repairs, whereas other drivers are always having breakdowns. Investigation, however, reveals that the driver does not follow the conventional route, but takes a dangerous short cut. This is kept secret from his employers by the simple device of entering the full mileage in his log book.

Just as the reporter has got all the facts and the driver is relieved to have got the lie off his chest, the two leave by truck for the railroad station. On the way, the gas tank develops a leak and they are stranded in the middle of the frozen wastes, helpless until the mail van comes along the next day.

It is the exploit after the breakdown that is the highlight of the film. The determination of the driver not to let the newsman fall asleep—and freeze to death—is conveyed with a rugged sincerity. A dream sequence, immediately followed by their rescue, is confusing, and this would seem to be due to careless editing. A side issue in the earlier part of the film in which there is general criticism of the driver's boss, is not clearly developed either.

The two principal performers, G. Yumatov, as the driver, and A. Demyanenko, as the reporter, give admirable performances. One is tough and rugged, the other mild and gentle. There is also an agreeable study by T. Syomina as the truck driver's girl. *Myro.*

Adventures of Nils Holgerssons
(Color)
(SWEDISH)

Moscow, July 30.

Nordisk Tonefilm release of Kenne Fant production. Stars Sven Lundberg. Directed by Fant. Screenplay, Tage and Katherine Aurell; camera, Max Willen; music, Tobjorn Lindquist. At Moscow Film Fest. Running time, **96 MINS.**

Nils Holgersson .... Sven Lundberg
Father .... Max von Sydow
Mother .... Annika Tretow

This is a fairy-tale type of adventure yarn which needs the lightest possible touch if it is to succeed. But Kenne Fant's handling of the theme is surprisingly clumsy, and all the potential charm seems to have gotten lost on the way. Only limited b.o. hopes can be expected.

It is a story of a 10-year-old boy who is disobedient to his parents and is cruel to animals. One day he is transformed by a gnome into a dwarf and carried off by a flock of wild geese from south to north Sweden, having many adventures en route. He's eventually returned to his home, restored in size and reformed in character.

The most effective of the special effects is the transition of the boy, but his reduction in size is accompanied by obvious gimmicks. On the other hand, the least convincing is the model giant goose on whose back the boy is carried. The color is good, and the aerial photography excellent. Sven Lundberg plays the title role with an appealing charm. But Max von Sydow and Annika Tretow have only slight opportunities as his parents. *Mosk.*

Gam-Peralia
(CEYLONESE)

Moscow, July 30.

Cinelanka Ltd. (Anton Wickremasinghe) production and release. Directed by Lester James Pieris. Camera, Willy Blake;

screenplay, Reggie Siriwardene; editor, Sumithra. Stars Puniya Heendeniya. At Moscow Film Fest. Running time, **79 MINS.**
Jinadasha .... Gamini Fonseke
Nanda .... Puniya Heendeniya
Piyal .... Henry Jayasene

Ceylon is one of the newest recruits to the film producing nations, and this modest picture gives a portrait of life in that country. It is a simple tale, simply told by craftsmen who still have a lot to learn about the art of picture making.

The story describes the life of a girl forced into a loveless marriage by her family. It is completely unpretentious, and the plot unspools at a leisurely pace, possibly reflecting the tempo of life in that country. Direction, writing and acting all display evidence of immaturity. But there is a measure of sincerity in the production which may augur well for the future. *Myro.*

The Beggars
(BRAZILIAN)
Moscow, July 30.
Satelites Films production and release. Stars Vanja Orjco, Osvaldo Loureiro, Rui Guerre, and Fabio Sabag. Direction and screenplay, Flavio Migliaccio. At Moscow Film Fest. Running time, **82 MINS.**

"The Beggars" is a tame farcical comedy, with contrived situations added to get a laugh at any price. It doesn't come off, and therefore looks mainly destined for local audiences which may find amusement in its forced humor.

The story concerns a girl who escapes from an approved school, but can only hope to stay free if she can get married. The only person prepared to tie the nuptial knot is a beggar, living on his wits with some friends on wasteland. From then on, the plot describes the attempts of the beggars to raise the money necessary for a marriage license, and one contrived situation follows another in steady succession.

The humor is of a very naive quality, like smearing a car with black paint, or a beggar pretending to be blind and ending up on top of a national monument. All such incidents are basically unrelated to the theme, and do not affect the progression of the plot. Direction, within the narrow limitations of the script, is acceptable while the principal players performs with gusto. *Myro.*

Kozara
(YUGOSLAV)
Moscow, July 30.
Yugoslav Film (Belgrade) production and release. Features Bert Sotlar, Mihaljo Kostic, Davor Natolic, Olivera Markovic. Directed by Veljko Bulajic. Screenplay, Ratko Durovik, Stevan and Veljko Bulajic; camera, Aleksander Sekulovic; music, Vladimir Kraus. At Moscow Film Fest. Running time, **130 MINS.**

The partisans' grim struggle against the Nazis is once more illustrated in this Yugoslav film. Although the subject could have assumed near epic proportions, it flounders rather aimlessly with an unnecessary amount of repetitive action, and without a positive story line to sustain audience interest. The pic has nothing new to say on a theme that has suffered from a surfeit of filmic treatments.

On the plus side, there are a few sweeping battle scenes which are recreated with a terrifying realism, but once that has been noted, all that is left is the more or less conventional presentation of guerilla warfare. There are moments of sentiment and bathos, and also a few which attain a high degree of suspense.

The title refers to a village which has to be evacuated on the arrival of the Germans. The partisans, fighting against great odds, find they also have to feed and move the entire civilian population. Most of the action shows their grim determination to break out of the German encirclement.

Familiar scenes of Nazi brutality, including cold-blooded murder, rape, etc., play a big part in the development, in contrast to the heroics of the partisans. This would have been far more effective if characters in the story had been properly developed. Not one emerges as an individual in his own right, and that militates against the finished pic.

Technically, the film is adequate, and the performances are competent. Further editing would be a help. *Mosk.*

The V.I.P.s
(BRITISH—COLOR)

Liz Taylor-Dick Burton names and skillfully contrived story add up to a Very Important Picture for the boxoffice.

London, Aug. 8.
Metro release of Anatole de Grunwald production. Stars Elizabeth Taylor, Richard Burton; features Elsa Martinelli, Louis Jourdan, Orson Welles, Margaret Rutherford, Maggie Smith, Rod Taylor, Linda Christian. Directed by Anthony Asquith. Original story & screenplay by Terence Rattigan; camera (Metrocolor), Jack Hildyard; music, Miklos Rozsa; editor, Frank Clarke. Previewed at Empire Theatre. London, Aug. 7, '63. Running time, **119 MINS.**
Frances Andros .... Elizabeth Taylor
Paul Andros .... Richard Burton
Marc Champselle .... Louis Jourdan
Gloria Gritti .... Elsa Martinelli
Duchess of Brighton
　　　　　　　Margaret Rutherford
Miss Mead .... Maggie Smith
Les Mangrum .... Rod Taylor
Max Buda .... Orson Welles
Miriam Marshall ...... Linda Christian
Commander Millbank .... Dennis Price
Sanders .... Richard Wattis
Joslin .... Ronald Fraser
Reporter .... David Frost
John Coburn .... Robert Coote
Miss Potter .... Joan Benham
Airport Director ..... Michael Hordern
BOAC Official .... Lance Percival
Dr. Schwutzbacher ..... Martin Miller
Doctor .... Peter Sallis
Hotel Waiter .... Stringer Davis
Jamaican Passenger ... Clifton Jones
Air Hostess .... Moyra Fraser

Producer Anatole de Grunwald, director Anthony Asquith and scripter Terence Rattigan have concocted a smooth and cunning brew with most of the ingredients demanded of popular screen entertainment. It has suspense, conflict, romance, comedy and drama. "The V.I.P.'s" looks certain to be a firm contender for top boxoffice honors.

Its main fault is that some of the characters and the by-plots are not developed enough though they and their problems are interesting enough to warrant separate pix. But that is a risk inevitable in any film in which a number of strangers are flung together, each with problems and linked by a single circumstance.

In this case the setting is London Airport and the basic problem is the necessity for at least four of the Very Important Passengers bound for the States to get out of the country pronto. Their plans go haywire when a thick fog grounds all planes overnight. Principal characters are a tycoon who is seeing his wife off to America and discovers that she is eloping with a debonair, Gallic playboy. Problem: will the plane get away before the husband can return to the airport and cut up rough? Then there is a minor tycoon whose business is in danger of being swallowed up. He has to get to Manhattan to cover a check which he has signed with insufficient funds. A film magnate has to get away by midnight or be liable for hefty income tax in Britain. Then there is an eccentric Duchess who is going to Miami, has never flown before and her main problem is how she ever found herself in such an uncomfortable situation.

Rattigan's screenplay juggles these situations and does not neglect many of the star performers. The script has literate, witty and sometimes touching dialog and Asquith has directed skillfully, in that though there is the sense of bustle inseparable from any international airport he has retained a sympathetic feeling of intimacy for all his characters.

Principal story, that of the business tycoon who has taken his wife for granted and now looks set to lose her, is played out by Elizabeth Taylor, Richard Burton and Louis Jourdan as the lover. Maybe Miss Taylor needs a sabbatical but there is a feeling of ordinariness about her thesping these days which is disconcerting. In "V.I.P.'s" she looks attractive, of course, and shows some moments of fun, fire and emotion. But it never seems likely that two such different characters as the tycoon and the gigolo would care deeply enough to play tug-o'-war over her.

Burton, however, gives a top-league performance as the business chief who eventually regains his wife but only after a few hours of taut misery, humiliating and self-enlightenment. Jourdan is also excellent as the would-be lover and he has one scene with Burton which is a little masterpiece of dual virtuosity.

Rod Taylor is energetic, forceful and very likeable as the Australian tractor-boss in a jam, but even he has to concede to one of the pic's outstanding pieces of thesping, that of Maggie Smith as his adoring secretary who eventually gets him home and dried financially as the result of an engaging piece of feminine chicanery with millionaire Burton. Miss Smith, fast establishing herself as one of England's leading young thesps, provides here an astute and sensitive portrayal of a mouse of a self-effacing secretary who dreams dreams.

The other two subplots are in strictly for giggles and get them effortlessly. There's Orson Welles, joshing every mittel-European film producer in the business, hamming it up riotously as he and his accountant (Martin Miller) try to sort out his tax problem. Elsa Martinelli, as the dumb film star protegee of Welles, has a surprisingly unrewarding role as, incidentally, does Linda Christian as Rod Taylor's expensive girl friend. Both perform adequately but the roles could have been played by lesser names just as effectively.

Finally, Margaret Rutherford as the dithering Duchess of Brighton is again likely to find herself arraigned on a charge of grand larceny for scene stealing. She is a sheer joy as the plane-scared eccentric, forever pepping herself up with pills ("they are supposed to pep me up, but they seem to pep me in all directions"), handing harassed airport officials a 1943 ration book instead of a smallpox certificate and, of course, having an endless struggle with her luggage and her seat belt.

Producer de Grunwald has cast his smaller roles with scrupulous care and the value comes out on the screen. In a long list some deserve special mention. For instance, Martin Millers comeo as the accountant, Dennis Price as Burton's urbane master-domo, Richard Wattis all a'twitter as the sycophantic, harassed airport official in charge of Very Important Persons, Ronald Fraser as a minor official, Robert Coote playing a hearty card player, Moyra Fraser as a snooty air hostess, Stringer Davis as a courteous old-world

waiter, David Frost, the "TW TW-TW" television emcee, making his screen debut as a reporter, and Lance Percival as an airport clerk.

London Airport interiors have been faithfully reconstructed in Metro's British studio and excellently lensed in Panavision and Metrocolor by Jack Hildyard. Miklos Rozsa's music is a dubious credit to the film. *Rich.*

Symphonie Pour Un Massacre
(Symphony for a Massacre)
(FRENCH)

Paris, Aug. 13.
CICC release of CICC-Ultra Films-Dear Films production. Stars Michel Auclair, Claude Dauphin; features Jose Giovinni, Jean Rochefort, Daniela Rocca, Charles Vanel, Michele Mercier. Directed by Jacques Deray; Screenplay, Claude Sautet, Jose Giovinni, Deray from novel by Alain Reynaud- Fourton; camera, Claude Renoir; editor, Paul Cavatte. At Colisee, Paris. Running time, **110 MINS.**

Georges	Michel Auclair
Maurice	Claude Dauphin
Moro	Jose Giovinni
Christian	Jean Rochefort
Helene	Daniela Rocca
Paoli	Charles Vanel
Catherine	Michele Mercier

Patly plotted pic details how one double dealer in a crime syndicate, with a good front, leads to the destruction of the whole group. Plenty of irony also creep into it. But film telegraphs too much to fit into the careful, overlong construction. This lacks the more robust outlook to put it over completely.

This does have some good acting, technical knowhow and a fine production dress. But the makers seemed to think they were doing Shakespearean or Greek tragedy rather than a "crime does not pay" opus. Result is a somewhat leisurely if still taking tale. Too many incidents are worked in just to make a plot point rather than allow it to flow.

Five men each chip in a wad to buy a big load of dope. But one intercepts the deliverer and highjacks the money. Then he has to kill another who is wise to him. Misunderstanding throws suspicion on another as all are finally wiped out because of one mistake after another.

Director Jacques Deray displays an ability to keep things moving crisply the first part of the vehicle via sharp cutting and economical patter. But then the pic goes on too long as the obvious gimmicks appear and the cumulative effect does not carry them along. But on its general solidity this could well be a solid dualer for foreign spots or even for specialized situations where its cleverness might get it some attention. *Mosk.*

Rampage
(COLOR)

Shopworn safari meller with Mitchum and Hawkins.

Hollywood, Aug. 8.
Warner Bros. release of William Fadlman production. Stars Robert Mitchum, Elsa Martinelli, Jack Hawkins. Directed by Phil Karlson. Screenplay, Robert I. Holt, Marguerite Roberts, based on novel by Alan Caillou; camera (Technicolor), Harold Lipstein; editor, Gene Milford; music, Elmer Bernstein; asst. director, Clark Paylow. Reviewed at studio, Aug. 8, '63. Running time, **99 MINS.**

Harry Stanton	Robert Mitchum
Anna	Elsa Martinelli
Otto Abbot	Jack Hawkins

Talib	Sabu
Chep	Cely Carrillo
Schelling	Emile Genest
Sakai Chief	Stefan Schnabel
Baka	David Cadiente

Here's one for the fellow who claims, "they just don't make movies like they used to, anymore." This one is almost like they used to make them. "Rampage" is an inept blend of cliche and prurience.

Robert Mitchum, Elsa Martinelli and Jack Hawkins star in the Warner Bros. release, produced by William Fadiman. The scenario by Robert I. Holt and Marguerite Roberts, from a novel by Alan Caillou, is crammed with contrived situations and hollow, pretentious dialog. Commissioned by a West German zoo, a noted trapper (Mitchum) teams up with a renowned but aging big-game hunter (Hawkins) and his mistress (Miss Martinelli) on an expedition into the Malay jungle in quest of the "enchantress," an elusive member of the big cat family. Mitchum gets his enchantress, but Hawkins loses his (Miss Martinelli) and his mind in the process.

Inserted into the preposterous plot are stuffy academic debates about trapping vs .hunting (the sheepmen vs. the cattlemen, eastern hemisphere version) and several attempts by a Malay guide (Sabu) to persuade Mitchum to sleep with his (Hawaii and the assistant (Sabu's, that is) woman. Seems it's an old Malay custom. Mitchum, by the way, refuses.

The acting is rigid and Phil Karlson's direction is heavyhanded. A title song of the calpso genre by Mack David and Elmer Bernstein has commercial possibilities. Some of the scenery (Hawaii and the San Diego Zoo) is pretty, as lensed by Harold Lipstein, and Bernstein's music theme, somewhat in the fashion of Henry Mancini's "Hatari!" score, keeps the soundtrack more interesting than the sight track. *Tube.*

Wall Of Noise

Overly glum but commercially serviceable racetrack meller.

Hollywood, Aug. 1.
Warner Bros. release of Joseph Landon production. Stars Suzane Pleshette. Ty Hardin, Dorothy Provine, Ralph Meeker; features Simon Oakland. Directed by Richard Wilson. Screenplay, Landon, based on novel by Daniel Michael Stein; camera, Lucien Ballard; editor, William Ziegler; music, William Lava; assistant director, Sergei Petschnikoff. Reviewed at the studio, Aug. 1, '63. Running time, **112 MINS.**

Laura Rubio	Suzanne Pleshette
Joel Tarrant	Ty Hardin
Anne Conroy	Dorothy Provine
Matt Rubio	Ralph Meeker
Johnny Papadakis	Simon Oakland
Bud Kelsey	Jimmy Murphy
Jack Matlock	Murray Matheson
Dave McRaab	Robert F. Simon
Mr. Harrington	George Petrie
Mrs. Harrington	Jean Byron
Adam Kasper	Fred Carson
Money	Bill Walker
Preacher	Napoleon Whiting

Some of the colts and fillies in the Warner Bros. stable are given an opportunity to clock their histrionic gifts in this racetrack melodrama, and their presence adds some interest and embryo glamor to a professionally constructed but almost oppressively sombre film. The Joseph Landon production, obviously mounted and executed on a fairly modest Bur-

bankroll, should prove a salable programmer for the studio and a serviceable hole-filler for Hollywood-product-shy exhibitors.

Since the emphasis in "Wall Of Noise" is on characterization, it is rather unfortunate that the characters chosen for close scrutiny in Daniel Michael Stein's tome, as written for the screen by Landon, are pretty unappealing types with uncommonly glum and confused dispositions. If they are truly representative of the racetrack breed, then things must be pretty morose behind the scenes from Hialeah to Hollypark. Hardly a smile is cracked by the people dramatized in this picture, and it's not always clear what's eating them or motivating them into the unsavory activity they seem so prone to pursue.

"Wall Of Noise" does, however, avoid most of the traditional pitfalls of the horserace picture in its attempt to sidestep the artificially glamorous cliches and depict the more realistic, if seamier, side of life in the nag parks. The story is concerned with the conflicts that arise when a young trainer (Ty Hardin) precariously balances himself between an illicit love life and a passionate desire to crash the winner's circle as a thoroughbred owner.

The careers of Hardin and Suzanne Pleshette, the principals in the story advance a notch via this vehicle, although neither has an especially dimensional character to portray. Hardin is sturdy and businesslike in his enactment, and Miss Pleshette displays a subtle sensuality that rivets attention when she's on the screen. Dorothy Provine, generally a very animated performer, is stuck in a rather drab, one-note role which, however, she dispatches professionally. Ralph Meeker, Simon Oakland, Jimmy Murphy and Murray Matheson are satisfactory in key characterizations. L.A. Times sports columnist Jim Murray puts in a "cameo" appearance as a sportswriter. There doesn't appear to be any danger that Murray's acting career will extend beyond playing sportswriters.

Others of brief histrionic value in the film are Robert F. Simon, George Petrie. Jean Byron, Fred Carson, Bill Walker and Napoleon Whiting. Richard Wilson's direction does little to relieve the heavy emotional air that hangs over the film, but his helmsmanship is competent in other respects. Lucien Ballard's photography is especially good in the race sequences. The picture runs a trifle long; otherwise William Ziegler's editing is fine. Other effective contributions have been made by production designer Hilyard Brown, composer William Lava and soundman Francis E. Stahl. *Tube.*

Abismos De Pasion
(Depths of Passion)
(MEXICAN)

Paris, Aug. 6.
Tepeyac release of Oscar Danciger's production. With Irasema Dilian, Jorge Mistral, Lilia Prado, Ernesto Alonso. Written and directed by Luis Bunuel from novel "Wuthering Heights," by Emily Bronte. Camera, Augustin Jiminez; music, Raoul Lavista. At Studio De L'Etoile, Paris. Running time, **90 MINS.**

Cataline	Irasema Dilian
Alexandro	Jorge Mistral

Isabelle	Lilia Prado
Eduardo	Ernesto Alonso

Based on the Emily Bronte novel, "Wuthering Heights," this was made by director Luis Bunuel about 10 years ago, but gets its first foreign airing now on the accumulated Bunuel renown. It strips down this tale of sentiment and presents a bare, unembellished but canny look at people caught. It may look like melodrama but has a deeper core and looms a solid language theatre item abroad.

The storyline is basically there. The Heathcliffe character, now Alexandro, comes home after making his fortune to a stony, rural land that could be almost anywhere especially set in the 18th century. A former orphan servant, adopted by his master, he had grown up in an almost mystical communion with his ex-master's daughter. She is now married but they flount their nearness to her husband's face.

The husband's sister falls in love with him and he whisks her off to marry her out of spite. Illness has his true love dying and he is killed by her drunken brother who had been a victim of Alexandro's new affluence by losing his home, face and self-respect.

Bunuel uses stony-faced, posing actors but he welds them neatly, because of their one-dimensional facets, into this elemental tale that makes a comment on instinctive love thwarted by social outlooks and economics.

Alexandro shown as utterly ruthless in spite of his love, and is not a victim but only a primal force, while the women are both passionate and conniving.

The sharp lensing and the brisk editing plus Bunuel's adroit direction, all blend to make this a drama that seems hoary and old fashioned on the surface but is actually meaty and deeply cognizant of human passions, for more discerning filmgoers or pic buffs. *Mosk.*

The Yellow Teddybears
(BRITISH)

Little impact emerges from this "message" pic about juve sex problems and who is responsible; one or two neat performances.

London, Aug. 6.
Compton Cameo Films release of Michael Klinger and Tony Tenser's Tekli Film (Robert Hartford-Davis) production. Stars Jacqueline Ellis, Annette Whiteley, Iain Gregory, Doug Sheldon, Georgina Patterson; features Raymond Huntley, Victor Brooks, John Bonney, John Glyn Jones. Directed by Robert Hartford-Davis. Screenplay, Donald and Derek Ford; camera, Peter Newbrook; editor, Terry Darvas; music, Malcolm Mitchell. At Cinephone, London. Running time, **85 MINS.**

Anne Mason	Jacqueline Ellis
Linda	Annette Whiteley
Pat	Georgina Patterson
Sally	Anne Kettle
Muriel Donaghue	Noel Dyson
George Donaghue	Victor Brooks
Frank Lang	Richard Bebb
Eileen Lang	Ann Castle
Mike Griffin	Douglas Sheldon
Kinky	Iain Gregory
June Wilson	Jill Adams
Paul	John Bonney
Lady Gregg	Harriette Johns
Harry Halburton	Raymond Huntley
Benny Wintle	John Glyn Jones
Musical Group	The Embers

This probe into juvenile delinquency is clearly inspired by a case reported some time ago of a school where some of the girl pupils wore yellow gollywogs as a sign that they'd surrendered their virginity. The teddybears in this film are the same flaunting symbols. It is a competently made film, with several good performances, and directed tactfully by Robert Hartford-Davis. But the screenplay is too superficial and too full of cliches for this not overly original subject to make much impact.

It is the old problem of fixing the responsibility when teenagers go wrong. The youngsters themselves, the parents, the teachers or what is nebulously described as "society"? But Donald and Derek Ford have not come up with anything very striking in the way of comment or a solution.

Annette Whiteley plays a youngster whose parents are indifferent to her. As a result she has several lovers and becomes pregnant. She is the founder of the Yellow Teddybear club. She seeks an abortion but her father discovers in time to prevent it. Outraged, he accuses the school teachers of neglect. Chief one to get the blame is the biology mistress (Jacqueline Ellis), who has discovered what the Yellow Teddybear stands for and, though horrified, has made a deal. If the club is disbanded and the girls don't misbehave in future she won't spill to the headmistress or their parents.

Some of the pupils resent her intrusion, she is framed and brought before the schoolboard. An impassioned outburst (and here's the pulpit, here's the palatable "message") fails to impress and she resigns. Meanwhile, the pregnant child has run away to London and her future is rather well defined. And then the film fades out with very little searchlight on a pressing problem.

Miss Ellis gives a spirited performance as the biology mistress. Miss Whiteley, as the goodtime girl, and Georgina Patterson as her innocent friend, are convincing though both lack experience. John Bonney, Harriette Johns, Iain Gregory, Raymond Huntley, Douglas Sheldon and Noel Dyson offer useful assistance. Victor Brooks, as Miss Whiteley's father, has an important part but he is the victim of one or two scenes that lapse into Victorian melodrama that verges on the ridiculous.

Art and location work are smooth and Peter Newbrook's camerawork satisfactory. "Yellow Teddybears" may have difficulty in surviving except in houses that specialize in allegedly sensational sex subjects. *Rich.*

The Caretakers

Superficial, ineptly - plotted drama about treatment of mental illness. Will need strong sell to hypo boxoffice.

United Artists release of Hall Bartlett production. Stars Robert Stack, Polly Bergen, Joan Crawford, Janis Paige, Diane McBain. Directed by Hall Bartlett. Screenplay, Henry F. Greenberg, from screen story by Bartlett and Jerry Paris, based on book by Dariel Telfer; camera, Lucien Ballard; editor, William B. Murphy; music, Elmer Bernstein. Reviewed at Astor Theatre, N.Y., Aug. 6, '63. Running time, 97 MINS.

Dr. Donovan MacLeod ..... Robert Stack
Lorna Melford .... Polly Bergen
Lucretia Terry .... Joan Crawford
Marion .... Janis Paige
Alison Horne .... Diane McBain
Dr. Larry Denning .... Van Williams
Nurse Bracker .... Constance Ford
Connie .... Sharon Hugueny
Dr. Jubal Harrington... Herbert Marshall
Anna .... Ana St. Clair
Edna ....,..... Barbara Barrie
Jim Melford .... Robert Vaughn
Cathy Clark .... Susan Oliver
Irene .... Ellen Corby

Indie producer-director Hall Bartlett, who, in the past, has made some entertaining, unpretentious dramas ("Crazylegs," "Unchained," etc.) has, in "The Caretakers," succeeded in doing what should be impossible: he's made a dull picture about a bunch of neurotics. With apparently the best of intentions, he has attempted to dramatize one of modern medicine's most interesting innovations—the use of group therapy for the rehabilitation of "borderline" mental cases.

The result, however, is superficial drama, plotted with an old-fashioned simplicity which cannot be disguised by an occasionally vivid scene or colorful performance. It's a weak story about a strong subject, which will need hard sell to create attention at the boxoffice..

Picture has a good cast, headed by Robert Stack, Polly Bergen, Joan Crawford and Janis Paige, with a number of attractive youngsters in support. But all, with the possible exceptions of Miss Paige and Miss Bergen, are severely limited by their one-dimensional material.

The Henry F. Greenberg screenplay basically concerns the efforts of a crusading doctor, Stack, to prove his theory that many borderline mental patients can be rehabilitated via group therapy, in surroundings that duplicate those in which the patient will later be living. The goal of the good doctor is establishment of "day clinics," where patients can come for treatment by day while continuing to live at home.

Fighting Stack's original experiment in group therapy is the hospital's head nurse, Miss Crawford, who is of a conventional frame of mind. Overseeing the conflict is the hospital head, played with a sort of Olympian weariness by yesteryear star Herbert Marshall.

Conflict comes to be centered on one patient, Miss Bergen, a housewife who shows homicidal tendencies and blames herself for the accidental death of her child. Before patience, love and understanding win out over the padded cell-and - strait - jacket theorists, the audience has been treated to a number of group "talk" sessions which are the most effective scenes in the film, largely because the patients, the only mildly interest-

ing people in the picture, take front-and-center.

Film has a couple of high voltage scenes, including one showing Miss Bergen undergoing shock treatment, and another, which is a hair-raising phony in terms of the story as told. This has a distraught Miss Bergen, blundering freely around the hospital corridors in the middle of the night, suddenly finding herself in a men's ward where rape is attempted.

Miss Bergen is effective in the key role, though it's difficult to judge a performance which is the upper register of hysteria. Janis Paige is fine—funny and appealing — as a troubled doxy. Stack is stoic and sincere in a bland role. As his bitchy opponent, a comparatively small part, Miss Crawford doesn't so much play her handful of scenes, as she dresses for them, looking as if she were en route to a Pepsi board meeting. Several lovely newcomers, Diane McBain and Susan Olivery as nurses, and Sharon Hugueny, as a young patient, do nicely. Miss Hugueny, especially, is a real screen looker.

Bartlett's direction seems to have added no dimension to the raw material, but Lucien Ballard's black - and - white photography is slick and Elmer Bernstein's score jazzes up interest in otherwise dull passages. As is so often the case these days, the opening title drawings (by Irving Block) create a mood of excitement and anticipation never realized in the film itself. *Anby.*

Stakeout!

Low budget meller adequate for lower berthing on exploitation bills.

Hollywood, Aug. 13.
Crown-International release of Robert Hughes-William Hughes-Joe R. Gentile production. Stars Bing Russell; features Billy Hughes, Bill Hale, Jack Harris, Bernie Thomas, William Foster, Eve Brent, Chris Wayne, Whitey Hughes. Directed and screenplay by James Landis; camera, Jack Specht; music, Tom Downing; asst. director, C. M. Florence. Reviewed at Nosseck Studios, Aug. 13, '63. Running time, 81 MINS.

Joe .... Bing Russell
Joey .... Billy Hughes
Stoddard .... Bill Hale
Gus .... Jack Harris
Greer .... Bernie Thomas
Henny .... William Foster
Susie .... Eve Brent
Jimmy .... Chris Wayne
Sautu .... Whitey Hughes

There is evidence in "Stakeout!" of an attempt to penetrate a little beyond the narrow exploitation sphere and create focal characters of a bit more substance and compassion than is customary in this highly commercialized field. The attempt fails decidedly short, but the remnants are acceptable enough to get by as running mate in twin bills aimed at less discriminating audiences. A good 10-15 minute trimming job on the oft-lethargic, Texas-made Crown-International release would make it a more presentable "B" than it now is.

The film, produced by the triumvirate of Robert and William Hughes and Joe R. Gentile, hums along slowly, sentimentally but engrossingly, for the first third of its route, then begins to sputter, labor and telegraph itself, and finally lapses into pure bathos. The early effort to build compassion for

the tainted hero never really pays off.

Bing Russell stars in the trite tale of an ex-con who, unable to secure steady employment because of his record, is forced to resort anew to crime and pays with his life. The attempt at character dimension is made in the development of the affectionate relationship between the ex-con and his motherless son, but too many of the scenes between this pair lapse into sentimental stickum.

It is Russell's alternately warm and embittered portrayal that gives the film what strength it has. Others of importance are Billy Hughes (as the son,) Bill Hale, Jack Harris, Bernie Thomas, William Foster, Eve Brent and Chris Wayne. James Landis directed from his own screenplay. Bits and pieces of his work have merit, but the whole is artistically unsuccessful. *Tube.*

Billy Liar
(BRITISH)

Absorbing offbeat film which may need shrewd selling as a latecomer in the British "realistic" school of pix. Top performances and direction.

London, Aug. 16.

Warner-Pathe release of Vic Films Production, for Anglo-Amalgamated. Stars Tom Courtenay, Julie Christie. Features Wilfred Pickles, Mona Washbourne, Finlay Currie, Gwendolyn Watts, Patrick Barr, Leonard Rossiter, Godfrey Winn, Leslie Randall, Ethel Griffies, Ernest Clark, Helen Fraser. Produced by John Janni. Directed by John Schlesinger. Screenplay, Keith Waterhouse and Willis Hall, from their play; camera, Denys Coop; editor, Roger Cherrill; music, Richard Rodney Bennett. Previewed at Warner Theatre, London, Aug. 14, '63. Running time, 98 MINS.

Billy Fisher .... Tom Courtenay
Liz .... Julie Christie
Geoffrey Fisher .... Wilfred Pickles
Alice Fisher .... Mona Washbourne
Florence .... Ethel Griffies
Duxbury .... Finlay Currie
Arthur Crabtree .... Rodney Bewes
Barbara .... Helen Fraser
Eric Stamp .... George Innes
Shadrack .... Leonard Rossiter
Disk Jockey .... Godfrey Winn
Prison Governor .... Ernest Clark
Danny Boone .... Leslie Randall
Rita .... Gwendolyn Watts

Based on a West End hit play by Keith Waterhouse (who wrote the novel) and Willis Hall, "Billy Liar" is an imaginative, fascinating film. It may need some shrewd selling as a late entry in a series of British realistic pix, which started with "Room at the Top." But some impressive acting and direction should make this Warner-Pathe release a click entry.

It is perhaps unfair to label the film as entirely realistic, since it moves into a world of Walter Mitty-like fantasy, and that is its only weakness. These scenes lack impact. They are pushed in and fail to develop the drama, though presenting sharp glimpses of the hero's characteristics.

Billy Liar (Tom Courtenay) is a day-dreaming young man who leads an irresponsible life as a funeral director's clerk. He fiddles the petty cash, he is at war with his parents, he has become involved with two young women who share an engagement ring. Above all, he is an incorrigible liar, dreaming dreams and, whenever possible, retreating into an invented world where he is the dic-

tator of an imagined slice of Ruritania.

Courtenay, who is probably the best of Britain's new wave of young actors, has a hefty part and is rarely off the screen. The role provides him with a large range of cameo characterizations. But he is always, apparently, happier when playing Billy Fisher, the young clerk who is striving to find the courage to break away from his surroundings. He wants to be a script writer for a tv comic and nearly persuades himself that he has landed the job.

Of the three girls with whom he is involved, Julie Christie is the only one who really understands him. Miss Christie turns in a glowing performance that will ultimately signpost a very successful career. Helen Fraser and Gwendolyn Watts provide sharply contrasting performances as the other young women in Billy Liar's complicated, muddled existence.

Mona Washbourne as his dim mother, Wilfred Pickles, playing a hectoring, stupid father, and grandmother Ethel Griffies also lend considerable color. Finlay Currie, Leslie Randall, George Innes, Rodney Bewes and, particularly, Leonard Rossiter as Billy's insufferable, unctuous boss, also supply worthy support.

Credit titles are wittily and provocatively put over in the form of Godfrey Winn, joshing himself and other disk jockeys as he does a gag sequence of BBC's longrunning and highly successful "Housewives' Choice" program.

Location sequences are blandly lensed by Denys Coop and the music of Richard Rodney Bennett is unobtrusive. Tom Courtenay, who took over from Albert Finney in the legit version of "Billy Liar," is firmly established with this picture. Its other values also assist in making it a likely success.

Rich.

80,000 Suspects
(BRITISH)

Val Guest following his recent technique of documentary with emotional undertones. Interesting, but uneasy mixture. Sharp performances could make this a boxoffice potential.

London, Aug. 15.

Rank release of Val Guest production. Stars Claire Bloom, Richard Johnson, Yolande Donlan, Cyril Cusack. Features Michael Goodliffe, Mervyn Johns, Kay Walsh, Norman Bird, Arthur Christiansen, Basil Dignam, Ray Barrttt. Direction and screenplay by Guest, from Elleston Trevor's novel; camera, Arthur Grant; editor, Bill Lenny; music, Stanley Black. At Odeon, Marble Arch, London, Aug. 15, '63. Running time, **113 MINS.**

Julie Monks	Claire Bloom
Dr. Steven Monks	Richard Johnson
Ruth Preston	Yolande Donlan
Father Maguirt	Cyril Cusack
Clifford Preston	Michael Goodliffe
Buckridge	Mervyn Johns
Matron	Kay Walsh
Mr. Davis	Norman Bird
Medical Officer	Basil Dignam
Mr. Gracey	Arthus Christiansen
Health Inspector	Ray Barrett
Dr. Rudding	Andrew Crawford
Nurse Jill	Jill Curzon
Mrs. Davis	Vanda Godsell
Joanna Druten	Ursula Howells
TV Reporter	Bruce Lewis

Val Guest is successfully following his method of making pix that combine a documentary flavor with a fictional, human interest. This time the combo doesn't quite jell, yet "80,000 Suspects" has a holding interest and is screened with a professional knowhow that rarely flags. It hasn't the impact of his film, "The Day The Earth Caught Fire," but nevertheless emerges as a worthy boxoffice entrant.

Based on the novel by Elleston Trevor, the drama concerns a city supposedly gripped by an epidemic of smallpox. Guest chose the city of Bath and, with complete cooperation from local authorities, the film has a vital authenticity which gives a fine assist to the production.

A wintry Bath is alertly screened, and audiences will capture the feeling of being involved. Apart from Guest's shrewd direction, the art work of Geoffrey Tozer and Arthur Grant's photography help considerably.

The killer epidemic sparks intense activity by local health authorities as they try to trace potential smallpox carriers. It's a painstaking process, carefully reproduced by Guest.

For b.o. hypo, producer-director-screenplay writer Guest has also played up some human emotional angles. Dedicated doctor (Richard Johnson) is trying to keep together his marriage with an equally dedicated nurse (Claire Bloom). Another medico (Michael Goodliffe) despairs of saving his own marriage to a nympho-dipso who has had an affair with Johnson, and eventually becomes a key figure in the search for the ultimate germ carrier.

The documentary and the fictional elements do not entirely jell. But Guest juggles adroitly enough with the problems to keep interest alert. The thesping is okay. Richard Johnson provides a brooding, sagacious study as the hero who is battling both to do his job and also retain the matrimonial interest of his understanding wife, played with sensitivity by an unusually warm Claire Bloom.

Yolande Donlan gives verve to the role of the promiscuous wife of Michael Goodliffe and, though her part peters out early, she makes considerable impact.

Cyril Cusack has a choice role as an understanding priest and shares one particularly sharp scene in a disinfection room with Johnson. Other roles are played with distinction by Arthur Christiansen (ex-editor of the Daily Express, who again portrays an editor, though his role is cut with some obviousness), Mervyn Johns, Kay Walsh, Norman Bird and Ray Barrett.

Credits for the film include its authenticity and literate script. Discredit is the way that the action is sometimes held up with a spot of pseudo matrimonial sentiment. Johnson and Miss Bloom cope admirably with the situation but there is a feeling that the major job of solving the smallpox problem is being shelved a little irritatingly.

Rich.

The Haunting
(PANAVISION)

Slim shocker fortified with cinematic savvy.

Hollywood, Aug. 14.

Metro release of Robert Wise production, directed by Wise. Stars Julie Harris, Claire Bloom; features Richard Johnson, Russ Tamblyn, with Lois Maxwell. Screenplay, Nelson Gidding, based on Shirley Jackson's rovel, "The Haunting of Hill House"; camera, Davis Boulton; editor, Ernest Walter; music, Humphrey Searle; asst. director, David Tomblin. Reviewed at the studio, Aug. 14, '63. Running time, **112 MINS.**

Eleanor Vance	Julie Harris
Theodora	Clairt Bloom
Dr John Markway	Richard Johnson
Luke Sanderson	Russ Tamblyn
Grace Markway	Lois Maxwell

The artful cinematic strokes of director Robert Wise and staff are not quite enough to override the major shortcomings of Nelson Gidding's screenplay from the Shirley Jackson novel upon which "The Haunting" is based. Audiences will respond to the film's intermittent terror passages, thanks to the skill of Wise, his cast and his crew, but are apt to find the whole unsatisfactory. Boxoffice prospects shape up as mild for the Metro release.

Gidding's scenario is opaque in spots, but its cardinal flaw is one of inconsistency, of failure to follow through on its thematic motivation. After elaborately setting the audience up in anticipation of drawing some scientific conclusions about the psychic phenomena field, the film completely dodges the issue in settling for a half-hearted melodramatic climax that is a distinct letdown.

The story has to do with the efforts of a small psychic research team led by an anthropology professor (Richard Johnson) to study and perhaps come to some conclusions about the supernatural powers that seem to inhabit a 90-year-old New England house with a reputation for evil. The group that convenes there for the purpose includes an unhappy spinster (Julie Harris) obsessed with guilt feelings over the recent death of her mother; a young woman (Claire Bloom) of unnatural instincts, both sexually and mentally (more explicitly, she has Lesbian tendencies coupled with an extraordinary sense of ESP); and a young man (Russ Tamblyn) who is to inherit the house and, for some preposterous reason, actually expects to make a tidy sum on it. It's not clear just why he anticipates such profit. One can plainly see that this house is not a home, except maybe as an inspirational studio for Charles Addams. The evil spirit, at any rate, eventually claims the life of one of the researchers, and the only immediate conclusion that the others can really draw is, "Let's split, cats, before them crazy poltergeists get fresh ideas."

The acting is effective all around. Miss Harris delivers an expertly agitated portrayal, although the character she is playing is the victim of expository fuziness. The lovely Miss Bloom subtly conveys the unnatural forces at play within her character. Johnson is softly reassuring as the head man and Tamblyn amusing as the skeptical heir who gets moved by the spirit. Lois Maxwell gets in a few good licks as Johnson's dubious wife.

The picture excels in the purely cinematic departments, principally in the photographic area. Under the artful surveillance of producer-director Wise, Davis Boulton has employed his camera with extraordinary dexterity in fashioning a visual excitement that keeps the picture alive with images of impending shock. Never once does a spirit materialize on the screen, yet the vile force can be sensed throughout, ever lurking behind a wall, down a corridor, in a window, waiting to strike. As photographed by Boulton, the house itself is a monstrous personality, most decidedly the star of the film.

J. B. Smith's acutely sensitive and fluid sound is of enormous value to the mood, as is Humphrey Searle's chilling, tantalizing music score. Ernest Walter's editing is dramatically taut and expressive, and Tom Howard's special effects are another asset. Elliot Scott's production design and John Jarvis' set decoration may not qualify for Better Homes & Gardens or House Beautiful but both efforts are masterpieces of eerie atmosphere. The pity is that all this production savvy has been squandered on a screen yarn that hardly merits and cannot support such artistic bulk.

Tube.

Dr. Crippen
(BRITISH)

Modest reconstruction of a familiar murder case. Sound performances but minor boxoffice potential.

London, Aug. 9.

Warner-Pathe release of a John Clein Production. Stars Donald Pleasence, Coral Browne, Samantha Eggar, James Robertson Justice, Donald Wolfit. Features Geoffrey Toone, Oliver Johnston, Elspeth March, Olga Lindo, Paul Carpenter, John Arnatt, Edward Underdown. Directed by Robert Lynn. Screenplay, Leigh Vance; editor, Lee Goig; camera, Nicholas Roeg; music, Kenneth Jones. Previtwed at Corner Cinema, London, Aug. 7,'63. Running time, **98 MINS.**

Doctor Crippen	Donald Pleasence
Belle Crippen	Coral Browne
Ethel Le Neve	SamanthaEggar
Captain Kendall	James Robertson Justice
Mr. Tobin	Geoffrey Toone
Lord Chief Justice	Oliver Johnston
Clerk of the Court	Edward Ogden
Mrs. Jackson	Elspeth March
Dr. Pepper	Douglas Bradley-Smith
Chief Inspector Dew	John Arnatt
Clara Arditti	Olga Lindo
Bruce Martin	Paul Carpenter
Paul Ardatti	Basil Henson
Mrs. Stratton	Betty Bascombe
Sgt. Mitchell	Basil Beale
Prison Govenor	Edward Underdown
Warder Harding	Ted Cast
Howlett	Ian Whittaker

It could be that the celebrated case of Dr. Crippen, who was hanged in 1910 for the alleged murder of his spouse, is a bit too familiar to arouse much boxoffice. This modest reconstruction by Leigh Vance, which presents the facts, as known, and leaves the audience to decide pro or con the doctor's guilt is a competent but hardly sparkling work.

Robert Lynn's direction is capable but unlikely to exhilarate patrons. But, with some very sound performances in certain instances, "Dr. Crippen" adds up to a modest dualler.

Whether Crippen was misunderstood, or a monster, whether he killed his wife deliberately or by accident, as he insisted to the last, are moot points. But they have been mulled over too often and for too long to create much concern. For this was a far from glamorous case and its essential suburban drabness failed recently to steer a stage musical, "Belle," to any success.

Value of the film is principally

in some sharp thesping. Donald Pleasence, as the mild-mannered medico, offers a subtle portrayal which gains involuntary sympathy because of Coral Browne's ostentatious, larger-than-life and vulgarly robust performance as his wife. As Belle, the ex-music hall singer, who nags and humiliates Crippen to a point of loathing, Miss Browne helps give the film most of its vitality.

Story starts in London's Central Criminal Ciurt, with Crippen on trial for murder and Edith Le Neve (Samantha Eggar) arraigned as an accessory. He's found guilty; she's acquitted. The film goes into flashback as incidents leading up to the death of the wife are faithfully and, often laboriously, unwound. Miss Eggar, as the pretty, wholesome young typist with whom Crippen becomes emotionally involved, has an uneven role but takes her limited opportunities avidly.

It's difficult to believe that such an attractive young woman could be drawn sexually to the faded, nondescript, middle-aged Crippen. Even more difficult to accept is that he could have expected to make his attempted getaway to Canada with Miss Eggar posing as his teenage son. But that, history has it, is what happened.

Donald Wolfit booms effectively as the prosecuting counsel. John Arnatt is a bluff, stolid Edwardian detective. Oliver Johnston, Paul Carpenter, Elspeth March, Basil Henson, Geoffrey Toone, Betty Bascombe and Edward Underdown provide useful contributions. James Robertson Justice makes a brief guest star appearance as the skipper of the ship whose suspicion of his two fleeing passengers leads to Crippen's trial.

Settings are unostentatious but adequate. Such technical credits as lensing, editing and music are okay. In short, a workmanlike job which seems unlikely to conjure up much biz. *Rich.*

L'Inconnue D'Hong Kong
(The Unknown of Hong-Kong)
(FRENCH-DYALISCOPE)

Paris, Aug. 19.

Cocinor release of Marceau-Cocinor production. Stars Dalida, Tania Beryll, Philippe Nicaud; features Serge Gainsbourg. Directed by Jacques Poitrenaud. Screenplay, Andre and Georges Tabet from an original by Andre Versini; camera, Marcel Grignon; music, Daniel Gerard. At Marbeuf, Paris. Running time, 85 MINS.

Georgia	Dalida
Mitzi	Tania Beryll
Inspector	Phillippe Nicaud
Jean	Serge Gainsbourg

Programmer fails to raise its ordinary story to above average heights. Dull direction, playing and trite tale make this entry mainly for domestic use with only grind dualer chances abroad on its exotic Hong Kong setting.

Two so-so femme singers go from Paris to a club date in Hong Kong. They score there, but one is homesick for a Paris lover and tries to blackmail a notorious Chinese gangster to get money for the home trip. She is almost killed. However, the gangster is captured thanks to her friend and her policeman boyfriend.

Though made on the spot, the film rarely gets a feel for Hong Kong's exotic aspects or acquires any added production aspects from it. Girls sing a few nondescript songs as the yarn plods to its telegraphed end.

Dalida, a pop singer, cannot do much with the ordinary ballads she chirps and is inadequate in thesping. Other players run her a close second.

This story could have been an okay filler with the right directorial snap, smart playing and flair for place, all of which it sadly lacks. Film also reflects tight pursestrings in its generally ordinary production gloss *Mosk.*

Siege of the Saxons
(BRITISH—COLOR)

Hollywood, Aug. 8.

Columbia release of Charles H. Schneer production. Produced by Jud Kinberg. Stars Janette Scott, Ronald Lewis; features Ronald Howard, John Laurie, Mark Dignam, Jerome Willis, Francis De Wolfe, Charles Lloyd Pack, Peter Mason. Directed by Nathan Juran. Screenplay, John Kohn, Jud Kinberg; camera (Technicolor), Wilkie Cooper, Jack Mills; editor, Maurice Rootes; music, Laurie Johnson; assistant director, George Pollard. Reviewed at Columbia Studio, Aug. 5, '63. Running time, 85 MINS.

People and events were quite remarkable in the days of King Arthur to judge from the goings on depicted in Charles H. Schneer's modest "epic" of that period, "Siege of the Saxons." Heroes, galloping at full tilt with bow and arrow to pick off enemy pursuers with a smile, feminine females unquestionably accepted while masquerading as boys, and kingdoms won and lost with some of the sloppiest treachery since the Cuban invasion. All these are present.

Presented as straight action adventure film is not intended to be quite as comic as it often turns out to be. The hero, a Robin Hood type played courageously by Ronald Lewis, spends a large part of his time creeping about dark castle passages or popping up at just the right moment to save the day for heroine Janette Scott. Miss Scott plays King Arthur's daughter Kate, who is being robbed of her throne by a usurper.

The siege promised in the title is a short-lived affair at the end of the film in which the English come from behind to down the invading Saxons, thus putting Kate on the throne and, in the bargain, making a nobleman of hero Lewis so he can be a peer and fit consort to the Queen. In events leading up to this victory, Miss Scott is spirited through various woodland adventures by Lewis in the somewhat unconvincing guise of his "brother."

Producer Jud Kinberg wrote the screenplay with John Kohn and the team has come up with about every cliche invented for this type of film. Nathan Juran directed serviceably but with little imagination. Wilkie Cooper and Jack Mills photographed the pic with general effectiveness, although their color lensing is often uneven and sometimes dark. Laurie Johnson has provided some adequate scoring.

"Siege" is playing in New York on a bill with Schneer's epic of another period, "Jason and the Argonauts." Junion members of the family will doubtless dig its period antics but accompanying adults may have trouble controlling an occasional giggle. *Tube.*

A New Kind Of Love
(COLOR)

Romantic farce augurs mediocre b.o. despite marquee names.

Hollywood, Aug. 22.

Paramount release of Melville Shavelson production, directed and screenplay by Shavelson. Stars Paul Newman, Joanne Woodward; features Thelma Ritter, Eva Gabor, George Tobias; guest star, Maurice Chevalier. Camera (Technicolor), Daniel Fapp; editor, Frank Bracht; music, Leith Stevens; asst. director, Arthur Jacobson. Reviewed at Westwood Village Theatre, Aug. 22, '63. Running time, 110 MINS.

Steve Sherman	Paul Newman
Samantha Blake	Joanne Woodward
Lena O'Connor	Thelma Ritter
Felicienne Courbeau	Eva Gabor
Joseph Bergner	George Tobias
Harry Gorman	Marvin Kaplan
Albert Sardou	Robert Clary
Suzanne	Jan Moriarty
Mrs. Chalmers	Valerie Varda
Bertram Chalmers	Robert Simon
Stewardess	Joan Staley
Guest Star	Maurice Chevalier

About the best that can be said of this farce is that it has been engineered with a certain amount of cinematic slickness and ingenuity. Writer-productor Melville Shavelson has proven in the past that he is capable of better things. This one is the one that got away.

Paris is the glamorous se[illegible] for the romantic romp in which, after several misunderstandings, a wolfish journalist (Newman) and a sexually-retarded career girl (Miss Woodward) fall in love. A decided lack of comic restraint and subtlety and a tendency to be tricky for the sake of trickery mark the progress of what story there is. The situations are only fitfully funny, and the good conversational gags are widely scattered.

Mr. and Mrs. Paul (Joanne Woodward) Newman, costarred, are better at dramatic assignments than comedy, particularly the former. Others prominently involved, none with a great deal of success, are Thelma Ritter, Eva Gabor, George Tobias, Marvin Kaplan and Robert Clary. Maurice Chevalier, playing himself, sings tidbits from songs with which he is identified.

Some interesting transitions and Technicolor effects highlight Daniel Fapp's camera work, but even this photographic flair begins to wear after awhile. Competent contributions have been made by such craftsmen as editor Frank Bracht, art directors Hal Pereira and Arthur Longergan and composer Leith Stevens. Costumes play a key role in the fashion-oriented storyline, and there are a number of interesting creations for the femmes to inspect, by Hollywood's Edith Head and such Paris couturiers as Christian Dior, Lanvin-Castillo and Pierre Carden. Frank Sinatra sings the more than three-decade-old "title song." *Tube.*

Hootenanny Hoot

Highly commercial folkmusical entry from Hollywood's fastest man with a fad.

Hollywood, Aug. 21.

Metro release of Sam Katzman production. With Peter Breck, Ruta Lee, Joby Baker, Pam Austin, Bobo Lewis, Loren Gilbert, Nick Novarro, Vikki Dougan; guest stars, The Brothers Four, Sheb Wooley, Johnny Cash, The Gateway Trio, Judy Henske, George Hamilton IV, Joe and Eddie, Cathie Taylor, Chris Crosby. Directed by Gene Nelson. Screenplay, James B. Gordon; camera, Ellis W. Carter; editor, Al Clark; asst. director, Milton Feldman. Reviewed at Hollywood Paramount Theatre, Aug. 21, '63. Running time, 91 MINS.

Ted Grover	Peter Breck
A. G. Bannister	Ruta Lee
Steve Laughlin	Joby Baker
Billy-Jo Henley	Pam Austin
Claudia Hoffer	Bobo Lewis
Howard Stauton	Loren Gilbert
Jed Morse	Nick Novarro
Vikki	Vikki Dougan

Following roughly the same formula utilized for his rock 'n' roll and twist concoctions, producer Sam Katzman, Hollywood's foremost trend-vendor, appears to have come up with a minor box-office bonanza in "Hootenanny Hoot," his first for Metro after a 15-year hitch with Columbia.

Again he has taken a related group of musical acts and strung them together via a featherweight romantic plot. In this case, the musical form pursued—folk music of the strictly commercial variety—has a somewhat more widespread appeal, particularly in that real estate between N.Y. and L.A. known as the rest of the country. It is also likely to be less offensive to some than the twist and the r 'n' r and, at any rate, it should do well enough to justify one of Katzman's sequels, say something along the order of "Don't Refute the Hoot."

James B. Gordon's screenplay has a familiar ring to it, relating the tale of the fellow with career and romantic problems who, while traveling across the country, discovers a musical craze budding in a small mid-western burg and promotes it into big network business, patching up his love life in the process.

Pipe-puffing Peter Breck and Ruta Lee are attractive as the feuding romantic leads. A secondary romance involves Joby Baker and Pam Austin. Baker is a rising young second lead-funnyman type. He does one of the best sneezes since Billy Gilbert. Miss Austin's fresh and wholesome good looks, coupled with her hoofing ability, stamp her as a young actress on the ascendancy. Bobo Lewis, a cross between Thelma Ritter and Imogene Coca, makes the most of a maid role. The musical acts include The Brothers Four, Sheb Wooley, Johnny Cash, The Gateway Trio, Judy Henske, George Hamilton IV, Joe & Eddie, and Cathie Taylor.

The production is engineered at a snappy clip by director Gene Nelson, with the accomplished aid of cameraman Ellis W. Carter, editor Al Clark, art directors George W. Davis and Merrill Pye, soundman Franklin Milton, musical supervisor Fred Karger and choreographer Hal Belfer, whose best dance number is the acrobatic hayseed finale. The catchy title song is by Wooley and Karger. *Tube.*

Raiders of Leyte Gulf

Philippine-localed war drama sans names. Obviously low-budget, but nicely tailored for the action program.

Hemisphere Films release of a Lynro production (executive producer Kane Lynn, producer, E. F. Romero). Features Jennings Sturgeon, Michael Parsons, Efren Reyes. Directed by E. F. Romero. Screenplay, Romero and Carl Kuntze; camera, Arsenia Dona; editor, Romero; music, Tito Aravelo. Reviewed

at the Anco Theatre, N.Y., Aug. 19, '63. Running time, **90 MINS.**

Emmett Wilson ...... Jennings Sturgeon
Lt. Robert Grimm ...... Michael Parsons
Capt. Shirai Akira .... Efren Reyes
Angel Zabala .... Eddie Mesa
Col. Lino Sebastian...... Leopold Salcedo
Aida Rivas .... Liza Moreno
Leon Magpayo .... Oscar Keesee

Though obviously budgeted on a comparative shoestring, this made-in-the Philippines World War II drama has the kind of narrative simplicity and dearth of unnecessary exposition which allows the unabashed action film to move. And this "Raiders of Leyte Gulf" does, as it details the forays and skirmishes of a small group of Yank and Filipino guerillas prepping Gen. MacArthur's 1944 return. It's a nice little program entry which delivers just what is promised.

The screenplay, by director E. F. Romero and Carl Kuntze, follows the efforts of U. S. Army officer, Michael Parsons, and his Filipino comrades to free an American intelligence officer, Jennings Sturgeon, held prisoner by a small Japanese garrison on the island of Leyte. Their efforts are complicated not only by dissension in the guerilla ranks, but also by the size and force of the Japanese garrison, headed by Efren Reyes, a loyal Japanese officer who is not without some humanity.

In a series of scenes liberally punctuated with hand-to-hand combat, gunfighting, and the like, film builds to a neat climax wherein the villagers of the captive town rise up against the Japanese to assure the success of the guerilla raiders.

The non-pro Americans in the cast, Parsons and Sturgeon, won't win any Oscars, but are made acceptable by the authentic locales and the able support by the Philippine performers, especially Efren Reyes as the troubled Japanese colonel, Leopold Salcedo as a guerilla leader, and Liza Moreno as a nurse who gives her heart to Parsons. Physical production, including camerawork, is okay, but the accents of some of the cast are occasionally a little thick. Romero's direction is swift and sure and surprisingly devoid of the usual war drama cliches. *Anby.*

Of Love And Desire
(COLOR)

Heavy drama of passion notable for return to screen of Merle Oberon and lavish, novel settings. Dubious b.o. item.

Hollywood, Aug. 21.

Twentieth-Fox release of Victor Stoloff production. Stars Merle Oberon, Steve Cochran, Curt Judgens; with John Agar, Steve Brodie, Edward Noriega, Rebecca Iturbide, Elsa Cardenas, Tony Carbajal, Aurora Munoz, Felix Gonzalez, Felipe Flores. Directed by Richard Rush. Screenplay, Laslo Gorog and Rush, from story by Stoloff and Jacquine Delessert; camera (De Luxe), Alex Phillips; editor, Harry Gerstad; music, Ronald Stein; asst. directors, Henry Spitz, Mario Cisneros. Reviewed at studio, Aug. 21, '63. Running time, **97 MINS.**

Katherine Beckman .... Merle Oberon
Steve Corey .... Steve Cochran
Paul Beckman .... Curt Jurgens
Gus Cole .... John Agar
Bill Maxton .... Steve Brodie
Mr. Dominguez .... Edward Noriega
Mrs. Renard .... Rebecca Iturbide
Mrs. Dominguez .... Elsa Cardenas
Dr. Renard .... Tony Carbajal
Maria .... Aurora Munoz
Engineer .... Felix Gonzalez
Julio .... Felipe Flores

Merle Oberon returns to the screen in this old-fashioned drama of passion laid in Mexico. Her presence may generate some sentimentally-motivated boxoffice activity, but the vehicle in which she has chosen to make a comeback is not sturdy enough.

Nymphomania and incest are two of the sweet everyday passions pursued in Victor Stoloff's production of the Laslo Gorog-Richard Rush scenario from a story by the producer and acquine Delessert. These once provocative passions are by now second nature to any active filmgoer, as familiar to this movie generation as the "big kiss" was to the '30's and '40's. At any rate, the heroine's surprise when she discovers, at the climax, that her half-brother's secret lust for her is at the psychological root of her long numphomaniacal history is no surprise to the audience, which has known all along what was ailing everybody. The audience is thus ahead of the characters throughout.

Hero of the story is the American engineer (Steve Cochran) who comes to Mexico City, falls in love with the numpho (Miss Oberon) and eventually frees her from the sordid web in which she has been held psychological captive by her half-brother (Curt Jurgens).

Miss Oberon, durably lovely, is a fine histrionic technician, and holds her own well in the heavy emotional give and take, contributing the most skillful performance in the film. Cochran goes through the paces reliably, although he never gets especially deep into his character. Jurgens, John Agar and Steve Brodie are capable, as are the balance of the supporting players.

As a bonus for filmgoers with an eye for the aesthetic and the historic, much of the 20th-Fox release transpires in the lavish, elegant homes owned by Miss Oberon and her real-life industrialist-husband, Bruno Paglai, one of which was erected almost 400 years ago by Cortez.

The editorial tempo could have been maintained at a quicker clip by Harry Gerstad and the picture can stand some trimming, especially if it tapers commercially to a supporting attraction, which it figures to. Manuel Topete's sound is rather crude, a by-product, no doubt, of the largely non-studio filming. A lot of dialog is missed. Ronald Stein's music is lushly romantic, including his "Katherine's Theme," which is crooned warmly over the titles by Sammy Davis Jr. The tune has good disk possibilities.

Director Richard Rush shows a nice flair for cinematic expression. He and lensman Alex Phillips have designed some unorthodox shots to alert the eye, including one exciting 180-degree tilt. *Tube.*

Life of the Country Doctor
(JAPANESE)

Toho production and release. Stars Hisaya Morishege, Setsuko Hara; features Chiemi Eri, Yosuke Natsuki. Directed by Kazuo Yamada. Screenplay, Ryuzo Kikushima; English adaptation, Victor Suzuki. At Toho Cinema, N.Y. Running time, **104 MINS.**

Keisai Koyama ...... Hisaya Morishege
Iku, his wife .... Setsuko Hara
Hangoro .... Yosuke Natsuki
Osaki .... Chiemi Eri
Meikai Ikeda .... So Yamamura

Practice of medicine in Japan a century ago was replete with drama which "Life of the Country Doctor" makes more than evident. For this Toho production is an absorbing study of a physician who devoted his career to the welfare of farmer patients only to discover that he's been left behind by advances in his profession.

Hisaya Morishege, who portrays the title role, pursues a leisurely—often informal existence in caring for the community. His daily routines are frequently tinged with irony, frustrations and sorrow. These add up to strong dramatic impact, but not powerful enough to propel the film into wide exposure on the art house circuit.

Setsuko Hara turns in a moving performance as the doctor's wife. The role calls for exceptional loyalty to her mate and she responds with a striking cameo. Yosuke Natsuki, as Morishege's pupil, provides the classic illustration of how the student has topped his master. Chiemi Eri is suitably wistful as Natsuqi's patient wife while So Yamamura is ably cast as onetime classmate of Morishege who went on to better things in the big city.

The rugged 19th century life in Japan is sharply mirrored by the brisk direction of Kazuo Yamada. Whether it's a scene in which travellers are fording a stream on coolies' backs or a sequence where the ignorance of the peasants is tragically revealed during a typhus epidemic the end results reflect his sure hand.

Victor Suzuki's English titles are adequate as are the camerawork and other unbilled technical credits. *Gilb.*

The Three Stooges Go Around The World In A Daze

Another healthy b.o. entry from the durable slapstick comedy team.

Hollywood, Aug. 19.

Columbia Pictures release of Norman Maurer production. Stars The Three Stooges; with Jay Sheffield, Joan Freeman, Walter Burke, Peter Forster, Maurice Dallimore, Richard Devon, Antony Eustrel, Iau Kea, Bob Kino, Phil Arnold, Murray Alper, Don Lamond, Jack Greening. Directed by Maurer. Screenplay, Elwood Ullman, from story by Maurer; camera, Irving Lippman; editor, Edwin Bryant; music, Paul Dunlap; asst. director, Eddie Saeta. Reviewed at the studio, Aug. 19, '63. Running time, **93 MINS.**

Moe Howard .... The
Larry Fine .... Three
Joe De Rita .... Stooges
Phileas Fogg .... Jay Sheffield
Amelia .... Joan Freeman
Filch .... Walter Burke
Vickers Cavendish .... Peter Forster
Crotchet .... Maurice Dallimore
Maharajah .... Richard Devon
Kandu .... Antony Eustrel
Itchi Kitchi .... Iau Kea
Charlie Okuma .... Bob Kino
Referee .... Phil Arnold
Gus .... Murray Alper
Bill .... Don Lamond
McPherson .... Jack Greening
Butler .... Emil Sitka
Timmy .... Geoffrey A. Maurer
Gatesby .... Ramsey Hill
Willoughby .... Colin Campbell
1st Mate .... Michael St. Clair
Harry .... Ron Whelan

The boxoffice success of their most recent feature-length comedies looks almost certain to be matched by this latest "Three Stooges" caper. Cooked up by producer-director Norman Maurer and seasoned by scenarist Elwood Ullman, the Columbia release, technically a satire on the Jules Verne classic, provides the durable threesome with the kind of outlandish situations that should be enthusiastically received by the kiddie brigade and the scattered adult following that finds Stooge-Style slapstick irresistible. The title may not fit on a marquee, but it conveys the point of the picture enticingly enough.

The essence of the Stooges approach follows a formula that has clicked with audiences since the days of the silent screen comedies. The concept is having adults behaving like children, or at least as children might behave in the wildest, zaniest recesses of their imagination. As for the style with which this concept is conveyed, it amounts to a flesh-and-blood version of antics ordinarily found in animated cartoons, where physical punishment meted out in one frame is so miraculously ineffectual that there is no evidence of it in the next frame.

The Maurer-Ullman version of "80 Days" has Phileas Fogg's great grandson (Jay Sheffield) attempting to duplicate his ancestor's journey on the wagered condition that he accomplish the feat without the benefit of a farthing. Fogg's sidekicks on the globe-girdling trip are his three faithful servants (Larry, Moe and Curly), and along the way he picks up a girl friend (Joan Freeman). Best sequence on the junket is a wrestling match involving Curly and a Sumo giant which concludes with the film's best sight gag, the collapse of the entire ring supporting these two heavyweights.

Considering the fact that 33 years have elapsed since their first film, Moe Howard and Larry Fine, who rate back to the original, demonstrate remarkable physical endurance. Relative newcomer Joe De Rita is a fine foil and effective replacement for the late Shemp Howard, the original "Curly." Sheffield, in his screen bow, and Miss Freeman supply satisfactory romantic interest. Walter Burke, Peter Forster and Richard Devon score as assorted villainous characters, and the balance of support is game, especially Iau Kea as the maltreated Sumo.

Backing up the specialized savvy of Maurer and Ullman are the resourceful efforts of their staff, notably those of cameraman Irving Lippman, editor Edwin Bryant, composer Paul Dunlap, are director Don Ament, special effects man Richard Albain and last but certainly not least in a Stooges caper, soundman William Bernds, who has created a kind of symphony of the human skull. *Tube.*

Carry On Cabby
(BRITISH)

Rollicking entry in the golden "Carry On" series which should hit the boxoffice jackpot with a wham.

London, Aug. 22.

Warner-Pathe release of Peter Rogers Production for Angelo Amalgamated. Stars Sidney James, Kenneth Connor,

Hattie Jacques, Liz Fraser, Esma Cannon, Charles Hewtrey. Features Bill Owen, Milo O'Shea, Judith Furse, Renee Houston, Amanda Barrie, Cyril Chamberlain, Peter Gilmore. Directed by Gerald Thomas. Screenplay by Talbot Rothwell from an idea by S. C. Green & R. M. Hills; camera, Alan Hume; editor, Archie Ludski; music, Eric Rogers. Previewed at Studio One, London, Aug. 22, '63. Running time, **91 MINS.**

Charlie	Sidney James
Peggy	Hattie Jacques
Ted	Kenneth Connor
Pintpot	Charles Hawtrey
Elo	Esma Cannon
Sally	Liz Fraser
Smiley	Bill Owen
Len	Milo O'Shea
"Battleaxe"	Judith Furse
Aristocratic Lady	Ambrosine Philpotts
Molly	Renee Houston
Small Man	Jim Dale
Anthea	Amanda Barrie
Dumb Girl	Carole Shelley
Sarge	Cyril Chamberlain
Allbright	Norman Chappell
District Nurse	Noel Dyson
Dancy	Peter Gilmore

The golden formula of the "Carry On" series which, at times, has started to look repetitious and a bit forced is back with a bang with "Carry On Cabby," and it should fairly crackle at boxoffice. For only the most longhaired will look down their noses at the lark.

"Carry On Cabby" was not, at first intended to be one of the series. Hence the film has a rather stronger storyline than usual. Also it has a different screenplay writer, Talbot Rothwell, giving Norman-Hudis who has written most of the others, a deserved chance to recharge his "Carry On" batteries.

However, the usual emphasis on parade situations, dialog and gags has brought the film inevitably back into the "Carry 'On" fold. Gerald Thomas directed with brisk knowhow and Rothwell tailored his screenplay to the familar talents of the team.

Sidney James is the cabby-owner of a prosperous fleet of taxicabs, but his domestic life is edgy because his wife claims he spends too much time with his beloved cabs. When, through a series of unfortunate but hilarious mishaps, he arrived home too late to take her out on a promised wedding anni spree, she decided to teach him a lesson by going into competition with him. She sets up a rival garage called "Glamcabs" and decks out some shapely young women in revealing uniforms as her drivers. Added insult is that she is using her husband's cash since all his money is in his wife's name.

Effect on the local populace of these gorgeous lovelies can be imagined. James, still not knowing that his wife is behind the rival firm, sets out to sabotage her business. But Glamcabs have a spy in the other camp and the girls have no difficulty in foiling the men by counter-sabotage. Eventually, there's a showdown and James and wife are estranged. Of course, there's also the inevitable reconciliation.

Slapstick and audacious dialog of vulgar but honest type of innuendo, especially along sexy lines is generously laced throughout the film. The pace is such that there is rarely time to consider a number of acute improbabilities. James has a great frolic with his role and he might have been a cabdriver all his career so autnentic is he.

Hattie Jacques extracts fun

from the role of James' wife and Kenneth Connon, Esma Cannon; Charles Hawtrey, as an accident prone nitwit; and Liz Fraser, as Sally the glamorous waitress-Mati Hari, are old students of the "Carry On" technique. and effortlessly milk the laughter. So, too, are some of the cameo players often used for one gag. The junior misses are all highly decorative.

Location scenes, particularly the climax with the rounding up by the taxi fleet of the bandits, must have been a headache but provide non stop yocks. A night attack by the men on the femme premises, Connor adrift in the chauffeuses' changing room and the girls using their feminine wiles to scout up business from susceptible male fares are all highspots. Lensing, artwork and music are all okay and the whole setup adds up to a amusing entertainment. *Rich.*

Les Saintes Nitouches
(The Zany Innocents)
(FRENCH—FRANSCOPE)

Paris, Aug. 17.
Columbia release of TransWorld-Cosmos Film production. With Marie-France Pisier, Perrette Pradier, Gisele Sandre, Bernard Blier, Lilo, Michel Subor, Christian Marquand, Darry Cowl, Birgitt Bergen. Directed by Pierre Montazel. Screenplay, Jean Marthin, Mario Bdun, Montazel from an idea by Richard Balducci; camera, Gilbert Sarthre; editor, Raymond Lamy. At Lord Byron, Paris. Running time, **90 MINS.**

Angelica	Marie-France Pisier
Catherine	Perrette Pradier
Odile	Gisele Sandre
Bibols	Bernard Blier
Mrs. Bibois	Lilo
Gerard	Michel Subor
Steve	Christian Marquand
Ingrid	Birgitt Bergen
Thief	Darry Cowl

Would-be situation comedy with Dolce Vitaish ivertones and some frilly oo-la-la love scenes falls short on most counts. It looms primarily as an exploitation item abroad.

A pretty teen-ager from a climbing, fairly well off family, steals jewelry which takes the place of her lack of interest in men. But during a sojourn with her family at a rich American's villa on the Riviera she is apprehended by insurance agents and returns all the jewelry to get a job finally with the insurance company. At the end a look at a boy makes her realize she will finally prefer men to jewelry.

Pic has an excuse to get in some Riviera frolics of rich women midnight bathing with only their jewelry, young twist parties at Saint Tropez, and a few stripped down bedroom scenes. But they are done with the proper revealment to buck censorship.

Attempts at comedy are only intermittently effective due to a lack of inventive direction, pacing and scripting. Marie-France Pisier is a pert thief, but as yet sans the timing, projection and presence for such demanding roles. Supporting cast is all right.

Pic was originally called "Jeunes Filles Des Bonnes Familles" (Girls of Good Families), but growing French self-consciousness about offshore prestige changed the title so as not to cast shy asperations on the top families. Some more daring love scene footage was also purportedly excised. Joe Levine's Embassy Films had an investment for the U.S., Canada, and Latin

American rights. It is technically good and has exploitation possibilities if art chances are slimmer. *Mosk.*

A Tout Prendre
(When All Is Said . . .)
(CANADIAN)

Montreal, Aug. 11.
Les Films Cassiopee-Orion Films Production. Directed by Claude Jutra; script, editing, Jutra; camera, Michel Brault, Jean-Claude Labrecque; music, Jean Cousineau, Maurice Blackburn, Serge Garant. Cast: Johanne, Claude Jutra, Victor Desy. At Montreal Film Festival 1963. Running time, **90 MINS.**

(In French)

Before directing this first feature, young Claude Jutra fell in love with Johanne, a colored girl who lives and works in Montreal as a singer and model. Their resulting liasion is the subject of this adolescent, egotistical absurdity and a dreary business it turns out to be. With both of them playing themselves and re-enacting their short life together the result is one of those "personal" films which is so personal it speaks only to those who made it or who know the principals.

Jutra presents himself quite candidly as a vain, selfish and unpleasant young man who leaves Johanne once she expects a child. Johanne is the only natural thing in the picture.

The narrative is seldom told in direct terms. Although the pace is lively the slapdash "new wave" techniques, free camera, photographing into light sources, rough sound effects, snatches of dialogue, interpolated scenes, superimposed thoughts and commentary, all add up to an uneven, undisciplined, overlong and fragmentary "artistic" statement in which the characters are neither whole nor interesting. In their French way they talk continuously to themselves and resolve nothing. One or two scenes have genuine merit.

Jutra has no acting ability, little imagination and no style of his own, but copies Truffaut, Godard and others with often silly results. He scorns conventional story telling methods but offers nothing of value in their stead. He has been described as courageous for putting himself and his story on the screen. Foolhardy would be a better term. We learn nothing from and are seldom touched by his experience. When all is said... his love is a bore.

Picture is "dedicated" to Norman McLaren and Jean Rouch. This may well turn out to be an embarrassment to both of them. *Prat.*

Mary, Mary
(COLOR)

Jean Kerr comedy hit loses few laughs in trip to screen; Warners-LeRoy team does it again.

Warner Bros. release of Mervyn LeRoy production. Stars Debbie Reynolds, Barry Nelson, Diane McBain, Hiram Sherman, Michael Rennie. Directed by LeRoy. Screenplay by Richard L. Breen, based on play by Jean Kerr; camera (Technicolor), Harry Stradling Sr.; editor, David Wages; music, Frank Perkins; asst. director, Gil Kissel. Reviewed at Academy Awards Theatre, Aug. 27, '63. Running time, **125 MINS.**

Mary	Debbie Reynolds
Bob	Barry Nelson
Tiffany	Diane McBain
Oscar	Hiram Sherman
Dirk	Michael Rennie

"Mary, Mary," quite contrary to the legend that stage comedies lose something in translation to the screen, is almost as comic a bit as Jean Kerr's witty play on which Richard L. Breen's screenplay is based. Even without the insurance cushion provided by the play's popularity (still on Broadway and touring!), Warners, which acquired film rights in a pre-production deal, has a funny picture that could well become one of the season's top-grossers.

That the film version, directed and produced by Mervyn LeRoy, is not as surefire a laugh hit as the play can be blamed for the most part on too much consideration for the original source and, at least a little, on the not-completely successful casting of the title role. The result is a filmed version of a play, somewhat padded, adding up to 125 minutes, of which only the last three-quarters is truly outstanding.

Except for a few bit parts, LeRoy has limited his cast to the play's five characters, one of the rare times an entire cast gets star billing. He also wisely chose to have two members of the original cast (Barry Nelson and Michael Rennie) repeat their roles in the film. The comparatively restricted playing area and small cast concentrate the viewer's attention on the dialog, heavily laden with bitingly funny observations on the foibles of mankind, with emphasis on man, the target for most of Mrs. Kerr's missiles.

A major reason for the play's lasting success, and one carried over into Breen's script, is that the good lines are pretty well distributed among all the principals. Some of the heartiest yocks are inspired by Hiram Sherman's antics as a lawyer playing Cupid.

Debbie Reynolds, as the witty wife who can't resist a well-turned phrase even at the expense of her marriage, is inconsistent in the role despite a generally attractive performance. Uncertainty as to interpretation, possibly due to an inability to combine feeling with flippancy (the basic character of Mary), mars her portrayal. While she voices serious lines with genuine feeling, she ends too many witticisms with a note of hesitancy (whereas with Mary, it's a compulsion), or heavily coats lines with a "cuteness" alien to the role.

However, Miss Reynolds still manages to interpret the sincere and sympathetic side of the role, making credible husband Barry Nelson's decision to bypass a dish like Diane McBain (who has nothing, anyhow, but beauty,

health, devotion and beaucoup bank accounts). Both Nelson and Michael Rennie, as his movie-star friend-rival, sail through their parts with professional assurance and long familiarity. Nelson gets plenty of competition for audience sympathy from Rennie's smooth pitch to the heroine. Most viewers will figure she'd make out okay with either male.

Ralph S. Hurst's design for Nelson's apartment, in which almost all of the action is contained, makes it a comfortably casual abode. The trend to inside jokes via dropping of "trade names" in films gets a particularly heavy workout, and some regional references may puzzle the general public. Harry Stradling's Technicolor camerawork is excellent although he is not allowed much room for imagination due to the restricted filming area. David Wages' editing, generally competent, would have been more effective had he exercised his scissors more judiciously, even a bit viciously, in the stodgy opening sequence.

Frank Perkins' score, aptly commercial, is not unpleasant, being mostly brass and brashness like a musical comedy overture, with sneaky violins poppinig up whenever one of the frequent romantic scenes threatens.   *Robe.*

Venice Films

En Sondag I Septembre
(A Sunday in September)
(SWEDISH)

Venice, Aug. 30.
AB Europa Film release and production. Stars Harriet Andersson, Thommy Berggren; features, Barbro Kollberg, Harry Ahlin, Axel Duberg, Jan-Erik Lindqvist, Ellika Mann. Written and directed by John Donner. Camera, Tony Forsberg; art director, Erik Aaes; music, Bo Nilsson; editor, Wic Kjellin. At Venice Film Fest. Running time, **115 MINS.**
Birgitta .... Harriet Andersson
Stig .... Thommy Berggren
Mother .... Barbro Kollberg
Father .... Harry Ahlin
Brother .... Axel Duberg
Karlsson .... Jan-Erik Lindqvist
Wife .... Ellika Mann

The tale of a married couple breaking up has become familiar in European pix of late. But young Swedish director Jorn Donner brings a sureness of character insight, visual flair and knowing thesp handling to bring fresh outlook to this theme. If it takes its time unfolding, and eschews any concessions, it still looms a solid art bet abroad.

Film is divided into three sections that display the growing of love of a couple and their decision to marry, the marriage ceremony and early days, the beginning of a breakup and the final divorce. It all takes place in a year. Each segment is introduced by a montage section that embodies the mood and feeling of the episode.

The boy and girl are in their late 20s and the marriage seems to come from a need to be alone with each other rather than any planned affair. She is already pregnant when they marry. Then a disappointment with each other sets in and they separate while a last attempt to make up ends in failure and a couple is dissolved.

It is extremely modern in concept as it displays a series of small incidents that build into a statement on marital and human relations. The dialog is sparse and literary but backed by a sharp visual counterpoint that makes it revealing of changing moods, needs, disappointments and readjustments.

Film makes its statement on youthful disengagement with an older generation that pays lip service to one form of ethics and uses another, and incisively lays bare the intricate life of a couple and the needs on both sides. This one fails and it is the fault of many complex and simple social, human and general faults. But both can go on and try again.

Early scenes have them loving and going about together and pic avoids any conventional having-fun-together montages. It does etch each one's need for the other and their final partly confused decision to marry. The marriage is also neatly etched with family outlooks and a detailed study of the ceremony itself to give it the great social, religious and moral weight it has in society. There is no irony intended but only a reflection that it should apply to those compatible enough and adjusted enough to give it its true worth.

Her pregnancy is difficult, and when on one drunken night he forces his attentions this leads to a miscarriage. But here, too, the director's meticulous taste keeps this from being a false or needlessly sensational note. It makes its statement on love without true desire, depth and need. The final scene of the attempted reconciliation delves soundly into their mutual failures.

So director Donner seems to sum up the new trends in film outlook today. It reflects a certain lack of communication and changing mores but there is no dispair here. There may be a lack of compassion which will make this difficult to book "popular" houses abroad, but its lucidity, truth and flair for detailing human actions should fit this for art situations where more discerning audiences could savor it.

Donner has also been well served in his first effort with sharp lensing by Tony Forsberg, notable sets by Erik Aaes, cogent editing by Wic Kjellin, and a solid musical backgrounding by Bo Nilsson. Donner, of Finnish origin, was a film critic, reporter and novelist and has written a book on the noted Swedish film director Ingmar Bergman.

But Donner does not deal in the problems of guilt, inhibition and divine questioning that are the driving forces of Bergman. In fact, Bergman helped him set up his production but they broke on conception and Donner brought in his film as he wanted it.

It now looks like a new name is to be reckoned with from Sweden besides Bergman. Donner's first effort may sometimes be too measured and personal, and perhaps needs a little warmth and more graphic illustration, but he shows a know-how, maturity and technical mastery that bely the fact that this is his first feature.

Harriet Andersson, who was discovered by Bergman, is faultlessly handled and reflects all the facets of the woman's desires, demands and outlooks. Whether she is suddenly twisting to show her sensuality and at the same time flaunt her husband's shortcomings, talking to her mother, or reflecting on their life together she is always admirabiy controlled, telling and right. Thommy Berggren is effective as the weak husband and others fill lesser roles adequately. In short, a most promising first pic.   *Mosk.*

Greenwich Village Story

Mainly for the record for this pic has already had a Gotham art house engagement. Beatnik milieu could slant it for depth dualer use, but its conventional frame makes top billing dubious.

Venice, Aug. 28.
Lion International Films release of Shawn International production. With Robert Hogan, Melinda Plank, Tani Seitz, Sunja Svendsen, Aaron Banks, James Frawley. Written and directed by Jack O'Connell. Camera, Baird Bryant; editor, Jean Begley, Carl Lerner. At Venice Film Fest. Running time, **95 MINS.**
Brian .... Robert Hogan
Genie .... Melirda Plank
Anne .... Taini Seitz
Claudine .... Sunja Svendsen
Painter .... Aaron Banks

Film has already has a fair Gotham art house run but has yet to be reviewed in VARIETY. This is for the record from the Venice Fest where the pic is in the running for the best first film prize. Conventional handling, in spite of its unconventional beatnik mileu, make this mainly of dualer fare for depth use.

The film does not have the sharp insights, spontaniety and forcefulness that other Gotham-based pix on the hip and beat worlds, "Shadows" and "The Connection," displayed before it. Hero and heroine are an intense youth thinking he can write the great American protest novel, and a pretty young dancer. Though living together out of wedlock she yearns for marriage and he also really does in spite of his exhortations to the contrary.

When his book turns out to be pretentious and immature, obvious by his talk and actions, he drives her out and runs off with a rich girl who loves him. Unknown to him she is pregnant and an attempted abortion has her dying as he sobs alone on finding out the news.

Director Jack O'Connell, for a first pic, does have a knack for getting some good color from the fauna of Greenwich Village, but his story does not develop a true pulse of love and need and only pays lip service to beat propensities, needs and revolts without any illuminating insight.

Robert Hogan is somewhat stiff as the writer while Melinda Plank is fetching as the girl if completely out of her depth in the few beat cabaret scenes. It is technically good on all levels with some fine-side filler scenes of Village life and types. It is just that the pic seems to want the freedom of indie outlook in outspoken theme, but treats it with the evasions and retributions that seem to also denote a desire to try to please mass audiences as well as art houses. It falls short on both counts. *Mosk.*

Storie Sulla Sabbia
(Stories on the Sand)
(ITALIAN, COLOR)

Venice, Aug. 29.
Cineriz release of Romor Film production. Features Francesca de Seta, Anna D'Orso, Guerino Banzato, others. Directed by Riccardo Fellini. Screenplay, Fellini, G. Franco Ferrara, from story by Fellini. Camera (Eastmancolor) Giuseppe Acquarl, Sandro D'Eva, Mario Vulpiani. Music, Giovanni Fusco. At Venice Film Festival. Running time, **95 MINS.**

First film by Federico Fellini's younger brother Riccardo is a three-parter which shows much promise for its maker as well as providing a neat hour and half of entertainment. It should fare okay in Italy and rates an outside looksee as well.

Plot is admittedly fragile. First episode merely shows a day in the life of a small girl living in a seaside fisherman's shack. Second details a wedding by the sea, with subsequent party. Third, a visit to cottage by three teen couples bent on some midnight fun but who accidentally are forced to witness a birth and a death during the same span.

But Fellini has, especially in the first two episodes — head and shoulders over the third — portrayed his subjects with such loving care, eye for detail, and sense of the genuine in human, relations, that they become small gems. While these first two episodes are winning in more ways than one, the third is by contrast more articifial and constructed. It is also less well performed by another group of unknowns, while players in earlier segments comprise as colorful a gathering as could be imagined. Reshaping the third episode might help the pic.

Color (Eastman) by three different cameramen (pic was shot at intervals over a longish period of time) is uniformly outstanding. Giovanni Fusco's music is apt.
           Hawk.

Un Tenttativo Sentimentale
(A Sentimental Attempt)
(ITALO-FRENCH)

Well-intentioned small - budgeter is first feature by onetime scriptwriter Franciosa Campanile. Despite a good performance by Francoise Prevost, will take hard selling due to its slow, talky and introspective and only rarely convincing analysis of an albeit topical subject.

Venice, Aug. 30.
Cineriz release of Franca Film-France Cinema Prod. coproduction. Features Francoise Prevost, Jean Marc Bory, Leticia Roman, Gabriele Ferzetti, Barbara Steele, Giulio Bosetti. Directed by Pasquale Festa Campanile and Massimo Franciosa. Screenplay, Franciosa, Campanile, Luigi Magni, Elio Bartolini. Camera, Ennio Guarnieri. Music, Piero Piccioni. At Venice Film Festival. Running time, **100 MINS.**
Carla .... Francoise Prevost
Dino .... Jean Marc Bory
Luciana .... Leticia Roman
Giulio ., ... Gabriele Ferzetti
Silvia .... Barbara Steele
Alberto .... Giulio Bosetti

Basic idea, of depicting the inner conflicts of people desiring but unable to escape from social and religious conformity in a country such as Italy which does not rec-

ognize divorce, is a good one, and to a degree, pic comes across with its points as it tells of an extra-marital affair by two married people which ostensibly fails (though ending is left open) when neither has courage to openly break away from their respective spouse and face a new life and its heightened responsibilities.

But surprisingly, the film is at its weakest where it could or should be strongest: dialog. It is here that it rarely rings true, banal lines spoiling many a scene, and generally failing to convince the spectator. Francoise Prevost, as noted, is excellent as the errant wife, while Gabriele Ferzetti is properly wooden as her habit-bound husband. Leticia Roman also effectively renders her role as the somewhat glacial wife whose opposite number, Jean Marc Bory, starts the proceedings off by chasing Miss Prevost. Bory gives the weakest performance, and is rarely believable.

Piero Piccioni's music is apt and moody, and lensing by Ennio Guarniedi—in strikingly offbeat settings in and near Rome—is slick. Other credits good. *Hawk.*

La Belle Vie
(The Good Life)
(FRENCH)

Venice, Aug. 25.

Films Du Centaure release and production. With Frederic De Pasquale, Josee Steiner, Lucienne Hamon, Francoise Giret, Gregory Chmara. Directed by Robert Enrico. Screenplay, Enrico, Maurice Pons; camera, Jean Boffety; editor, Denise De Casabianca. At Venice Film Festival. Running time, **110 MINS.**

Frederic .... Frederic De Pasquale
Sylvie .... Josee Steiner
Kiki .... Lucienne Hanon

Film deals with a young married couple and their attempts to find a way of life during the troubled Algerian War. But it lacks an insight into the characters to make their plight engrossing, real or intense. Result is a plodding pic with chancey art house prospects.

A young man is discharged from the army after serving in Algeria. He marries and later is invited to Monte Carlo by a rich uncle. However, this never-never land gives way to difficulties in finding a job, the first baby and cramped quarters, the first unfaithfulness and finally a good job.

When clear financial sailing emerges, he is called back to the army. Director Robert Enrico showed a talented hand in a prize-winning short he made last year. But here he surprisingly gives the film a pedestrian mounting and fails to breathe life into these prosaic characters.

About a third of the film is composed of newsreel footage backgrounding the story' to display man's inhumanity to man and hint at dangers of future war. This atmosphere is too strong for the picture's stereotyped characters.

The grim days of plastic bombings and police requisitions during the Algerian affair are hinted at. But the stilted acting cannot make the young couple and their universal and personal plight interesting or incisive enough to give this film sufficient weight, depth and challenge. For a first feature it has fair technical knowledge but lacks the filmic knowhow. *Mosk.*

Il Terrorista
(The Terrorist)
(ITALIAN-FRENCH)

Venice, Aug. 27.

Galatea release of a Galatea-22 December-Lyre production by Tullio Kezich and Alberto Soffientini. With Gian Maria Volonte, Philipe LeRoy, Giulio Bosetti, Jose Quaglio, Raffaella Carra, Cesare Miceli Picardi, and with Tino Carraro and Anouk Aimee. Directed by Gianfranco DeBosio. Story and screenplay, DeBosio and Luigi Squarzina; camera, Alfio Contini; Lamberto Caimi; music, Piero Piccioni. At Venice Film Festival. Running time, **95 MINS.**

Ingegnere .... Gian Maria Volonte
Rodolfo .... Philippe LeRoy
Smith .... Tino Carraro
Piero .... Jose Quaglio
Ugo .... Giulio Bosetti
Anna .... Anouk Aimee

A political tale of wartime Italian resistance in Venice, "The Terrorist" looks only a fair entry for local market, with slim export possibilities although it's well made and solidly constructed.

Film details various underground activities in Venice with focus on those of a resistance leader (Gian Maria Volonte) who spurns suggestions of moderation in his terrorist work though he knows they lead to reprisals against civilians. After various "jobs," he is spied on and caught in an ambush.

Too much of footage, however, is taken over by long talky sequences in which fine political points are made but little action is carried forward. Action stretches have some suspense, and there's an effective sequence in which a group of Fascist gendarmes execute some partisans.

But generally speaking, it's all been seen before to better effect. Director Gianfranco DeBosio nevertheless deserves credit for a solid job in his first feature film attempt. *Hawk.*

Nunca Pasa Nada
(Nothing Ever Happens)
(SPANISH-FRENCH)

Venice, Aug. 27.

Cesareo Gonzales-Cocinor Les Films Marceau (Paris) coproduction. Features Corinne Marchand, Antonio Casas, Jean Pierre Cassel, Julia Gutierrez Caba, Pilar Gomez Ferrer. Written and directed by J. A. Bardem Munoz. Additional dialog, Juan Sastre, Henry Francoise Rey; camera, Juan Julio Baena Alvarez; music, Georges Delerne; editor, Margarita Lauvergeon de Ochoa. At Venice Film Festival. Running time, **97 MINS.**

Giacomina .... Corinee Marchand
Enrico .... Antonio Casas
Giovanni .... Jean Pierre Cassel
Giulia .... Julia Gutierrez Caba
Dona Eulalia .... Pilar Gomez Ferrer
Dona Assunta ...... Ana Maria Ventura
Dona Obdulia .. Matilde Munoz Sampedro
Peppe .... Alfonso Goda
Don Marcelino .... Rafael Bardem
Geronimo .... Jose Franco
Nurse .... Tota Alba
Emanuele .... Gregorio Alonso

J. A. Bardem, one of Spain's pace-setting directors, is back with his best film in years, a penetrating study of Spanish small'town life, against which a multiple love story is played. Slick and well-constructed, it should get the nod in various European areas and rates overseas attention, albeit more specialized, as well.

A small Hiberic town in which, per the title, nothing ever happens, is set on its ear by the unexpected arrival and stay, for an emergency appendix operation, of a French stripper (Corinne Marchand). The middle-aged doctor falls for her first, prolonging her convalescence to keep her with him. They become the talk of the town.

His wife hears of the situation and walks out on him while throughout her stay the French visitor wants out herself, seeking consolation with the town's young French teacher until she finally rejoins her traveling troupe. The town then returns to its previous torpor, and the wife to the husband.

As in his best previous films, Bardem again uses his story to concentrate on the setting which conditions it. It's a grey and dismal existence, burdened by ageless traditions of conformity and honor, which he juxtaposes to the careless freedom and abandom of the town's visitor.

The resulting picture is a powerful one which those savvying the idiom will appreciate even more. Director has chosen his cast well: Corinne Marchand makes a delightful and pretty visitor, Antonio Casas gives a vigorous and deep-felt picture of the doctor, Jean Pierre Cassel is fine as the teacher who befriends the medic's wife, while latter is playel by Julia Gutierrez Caba with great feeling. Others in large cast give able backing.

Extra nods should go to Henry Francoise Rey for his fine ratio lensing of the Spanish country-side, and to Georges Delerne for his appropriately moodful musical score. *Hawk.*

In Capo al Mondo
(To the Ends of the Earth)
(ITALO-FRENCH)

Venice, Aug. 26.

Dear Release of a Zebra (Moris Ergas)-Franco-London Film coproduction. Features Sady Rebbot, Pascale Audret, Tino Buazzelli, Franco Arcalli, Piero Vida, Gino Cavalieri. Written, directed and edited by Tinto Brass. Additional dialog, Giancarlo Fusco; camera, Bruno, Barcarol; music, Piero Piccioni. At Venice Film Festival. Running time, **98 MINS.**

Bonifacio B. .... Sady Rebbot
Gabriella .... Pascale Audret
Claudio .... Tino Buazzelli
Kim .... Franco Arcalli
Gianni .... Piero Vida
Father .... Gino Cavalieri
General .... Giuseppe Cosentino
Sergeant .... Sartorelli
Marietto .... Enzo Nigro
Model .... Monique Messine
Bonifacio (as child)........ Carletto Chia

Tinto Brass has made his first feature effort an impressive statement against conformism in modern society and the hypocrisy which it furthers. Film also has exploitable angles which should help it along its way in Italy, but for export in most areas, it needs a specialized sell.

Story is a trend-of-thought exposition of a man's memories as he wanders around Venice trying to decide whether to take just any job or fight for what he wants, even though it means he'll have a hard time of it. En route, he muses about his soldier days, his friends, his political involvements, religious upbringing, and especially about his love affair with Gabriella (Pascale Audret) whom he loved but would not marry. In finale, he abandons his "easy" job offer to resume his search.

Sady Rebbot gives the hero the proper physical rendering, though much actual acting is not called for—this comes mainly from voice speaking his thoughts, while Pascale Audret makes a comely girl friend. Franco Arcalli has a good scene as Kim, an ex-partisan locked up in an asylum, Tino Buazzelli has an effective bit as another pal, and others give colorful backing.

Apart from conception, editing, and strong visual flair displayed by director Brass throughout pic, which make him a promising addition to the growing roster of valid Italo filmmakers, it is his dialog, penned in collaboration with Giancarlo Fusco, which is the film's outstanding feature.

Insouciant and outspoken, biting and humorous, this entry is one of the outstanding jobs of its kind seen here for some time, even though conversely, it will be the most difficult to properly adapt to foreign ears. Bruno Barcarol's lensing, in black-and-white and color, and Piero Piccioni's music are further assets. *Hawk.*

Il Demonio
(The Demon)
(ITALO-FRENCH)

Venice, Aug. 28.

Titanus release of a Titanus-Vox-Les Films Marceau-Cocinor co-production. Features Daliah Lavi, Frank Wolff, G. Cristofanelli, N. Tagliacozzo, Lea Russo, Francesca Marinaccio, Luca Pascarella, Maria Ciriello, Giuseppe Maccaluso, Calogero de Pascalis, Emma Canafoghi, Tommaso Sanna. Directed by Brunello Rondi. Screenplay, Rondi, Giuseppe Guerra, E. DeMartino. Camera, Carlo Bellero. Music, Piero Piccioni. At Venice Festival. Running time, **105 MINS.**

Mira .... Daliah Lavi
Antonio .... Frank Wolff
Padre Tommaso .... G. Cristofanelli
Zio Giuseppe .... N. Tagliacozzo

Brunello Rondi's first feature shows the promise, but also the pitfalls, of the neophite filmmaker. It has, however, a sensational and to a degree exploitable subject matter which, with other factors, could help it along to okay returns in some areas.

Pic is about a woman apparently possessed by the Demon who decides to wreck the marriage of her onetime lover and eventually win him back. Her major weapon is witchcraft as still practised by peasants in some backward areas of Southern Italy. She becomes a marked woman, with the entire village against her including her ex, who suffers from a love-hate conflict. In the finale, he makes love to her then stabs her to death. It's a gruesome tale made even more frightening by fact that it's loosely based on recent actual happenings.

The director is obviously well-documented on the background which is well recreated though at times he overindulges in lensing of superstitious rites, losing his main tale along the way and straining credibility. The film therefore results in an odd blend somewhere between a documentary and drama. Daliah Lavi is a striking beauty who here gives her effective utmost in a physically trying role. Frank Wolff, as her ex-fiance, has relatively little to do, but does this capably, while the rest of the colorful cast was picked up on the spot by director.

Carlo Bellero's camerawork is occasionally murky, but generally has caught the rustic setting with proper strength. *Hawk.*

Tengoku To-Jogoku
(High and Low)
(JAPANESE)

Overlong, but nevertheless engrossing, and neatly directed by Akira Kurosawa in the Alfred Hitchcock tradition. For crime pic aficionados.

Venice. Aug. 28.
Toho release of Toho-Akira Kurosawa production. Stars Toshiro Mifune; features Tatsuya Nakadai, Kyoko Kagawa, Tsutomu Yamasaki, Tatsuya Mihashi, Kenjiro Ishijama, Yutaka Sada. Directed by Akira Kurosawa. Screenplay, Kurosawa, Ryuzo Kikushima, Eijiro Hisaita. Based on Ed McBain's novel, "King's Ransom." Camera (Toho-scope), Choichi Nakai, Takao Saito. Music, Masaru Sato. At Venice Film Festival. Running time, 143 MINS.
Gondo .... Toshiro Mifune
Wife .... Kyoko Kagawa
Tokura .... Tatsuya Nakadai
Kawanishi .... Tatsuya Nihashi
Criminal .... Tsutomu Yamasaki
Aoki .... Yutaka Sada
Taguchi .... Kenjiro Ishiyama

Kurosawa has taken Ed Mc-Baine's "King's Ransom" and adapted it to a Japanese setting, with the probable addition of a social angle which, in its best moments, gives the film an added fillip transcending its meller aspects for a straight dramatic treatment.

Gondo (Toshiro Mifune), a wealthy shoe manufacturer, is faced with a decision when his chauffeur's son is mistakenly kidnapped by a man after his own son: should he put up ransom coin anyway, though this will cost him his career, or use the coin to take over the company via stock action? He finally chooses the former course, and the pic then concentrates on tracking down of kidnapper. Its a painstakingly detailed operation conducted by Tokura (Tatsuya Nakadai) and a police force sympathetic to the industrialist who has lost all. Eventually, the man is caught, with motive suspected by police all along turning out to be envy and hate by the relatively poor kidnapper for the rich man who lived on the hill in full view from his window. A tighter film, concentrating and balancing police activity and human conflicts would have given this added distinction in arty circles. As is, it's a finely tooled item, made by a master craftsman.

Acting by all hands, but especially by three principals, is able, camerawork is tops as are all other technical details. *Hawk.*

Zlate Kapradi
(Golden Fern)
(CZECHOSLOVAKIAN)

Downbeat fairytale, elegantly executed but overlong and slightly old-hat for western eyes. Looks doubtful for export overseas.

Venice, Aug. 29.
Czechoslovenski Film release and production. Features Vit Olmer, Karla Chadimova, Frantisek Smolik, Dana Smutna, Otomar Krejka, Cestmir Randa, Josef Bek, Bohumil Swarc, Radoslav Brzobohaty, Zdenek Braunschlager, Alena Bradacova, Jorga Kotrbova, Jaroslav Vojta, Marie Waltrova, Karel Postranecky. Directed by Jiri Weiss. Screenplay, Weiss, Jiri Brdecka, from fable by Jan Drda. Camera, Bearich Batkt. Music, Jiri Srnka. Editor, Antonin Selenke. At Venice Film Festival. Running time, 115 MINS.

Jura .... Vit Olmer
Lesanka .... Karla Chadimova
General .... Frantisck Smolik
General's daughter ...... Dana Smutna
Vizier .... Otomar Krejka

Jura, a shepherd, finds a magic golden fern and falls for the wood nymph designated to guard it. She reciprocates and they live together until he goes to war against the Turks, protected from harm by a magic shirt she has made for him. To win permission to go home between battles, he successfully raids the enemy camp, but the general's daughter goes back on her promises and instead tries to seduce him. More and more infatuated, he finally burns the magic to please her and is nearly killed. Back home, he finds the fern and the nymph gone.

Jiri Weiss, working hand in hand with his cameraman, has produced a very beautiful picture, in which each can draw his own present-day parallels. But it moves slowly in stretches, indulging in filigree lensing details, pretty but unfunctional. The acting is fine in all sectors, with two leading femmes striking in their beauty. Remaining credits are good.
Hawk.

Vstuplenjie
(Introduction to Life)
(RUSSIAN)

Pleasant, often poetic account of a couple of Soviet youths in the last days of the war. A specialized entry at best, but finely tooled and appealingly acted.

Venice, Aug. 31.
Mosfilm production and release. Features Boria Tokarev, Natacha Bougonova, N. Ourgant, Y. Volkov, Kolia Bourdlaev. Directed by Igor Talankin. Story based on Vera Panova' short stories, "Valia" & "Volodia." Camera, V. Vladimirov, V. Minaiev. Music, A. Schnitke. At Venice Film Festival. Running time, 105 MINS.

Mostly told in flashback form, the storyteller of the trying wartime days around Leningrad through children's eyes, watching them slowly mature with experience and exposure to hard knocks.

The boy, Volodia, for example, is evacuated from Leningrad where his parents have split, each seeking other companions. On his return to the city, he eventually meets his step-brother, of whom he was once jealous, and a new friendship is born. Pic is somewhat loosely tied, and there's a split between this and tale of girl which is handled more superficially and which the director doesn't always link sufficiently. Acting by photogenic principals is uniformly good, and camerawork is outstanding in clarity and lighting details. A further nod to A. Schnitke's fine musical scoring. *Hawk.*

Milczenie
(Silence)
(POLISH)

Venice, Aug. 26.
Kadr production and release. Features Kazimierz Fabisiak, Miroslaw Kobierzycki, Elzbieta Czyzewska, Maria Zbyszewka, Zbigniew Czybulski, Tadeusz Kalinowski, Edward Raczkowski, Stefan Wronki, Zygmund Zyntel. Directed by Kazimierz Kutz. Screenplay, Kutz and Jerzy Szczygiel, from novel by Szczygiel; camera, Wieslaw Ziort; music, Wojcheck Kilar. At Venice Film Festival. Running time, 100 MINS.

Slow-paced, moody and brooding item which despite certain artistic values is strictly for the aficionado art trade with slim export chances.

Set in 1945 Poland, film shows the inner torment of a boy accused unjustly of wanting to blow up a priest with a bomb and who is blinded in an explosion. Suffering the same torment is the priest who knows the boy to be innocent but fears that he'll lose stature and a certain hero-worship he has received since the incident if he tells what actually happened.

Boy eventually gropes his way back to life and the will to work. However, the situation remains unresolved because of the priest's continued silence, from which the picture gets its title.

Pic is an implied slap at those who try to duck decisions and refuse to meet their moral responsibilities. But slow pace makes the film's point murky in spots as plot runs off on tangents.

Cast is strong. Lensing is a bit too low-key. Wojcheck Kilar's music gives good assist. Other credits are good. *Hawk.*

The Condemned of Altona
(CINEMASCOPE)

Italian-filmed version of Sartre's controversial observations on postwar Germany. Technically and dramatically brilliant work, with several Oscar-worthy contributions, should bring them in.

A 20th-Century Fox release of Titanus production. Produced by Carlo Ponti. Stars Sophia Loren, Maximilian Schell, Fredric March, Robert Wagner; features Francoise Prevost. Directed by Vittorio De Sica. Screenplay by Abby Mann, Cesare Zavattini, based on Jean Paul Sartre's play, "Les Sequestres d'Altona"; camera, Roberto Gerardi; editor, Adriana Novelli; musical comment, Nino Rota; sound, Ennio Sensi; asst. directors, Luisa Alessandri, Giuseppe Menegatti. Reviewed at the studio, Sept. 5, 1963. Running time, 112 MINS.
Johanna .... Sophia Loren
Franz .... Maximilian Schell
Gerlach .... Fredric March
Werner .... Robert Wagner
Leni .... Francoise Prevost
Grounds-keeper .... Alfredo Franchi
Wife of Grounds-keeper .. Lucia Pelella
Driver .... Roberto Massa
Maid .... Antonio Cianci
Police Official .... Carlo Antonini
Policeman .... Armando Sifo
Cook .... Aldo Pecchioli

Considering the number of international Academy Award winners connected with the filming of "The Condemned of Altona," it's not surprising that the result is a motion picture of major importance. The work of all concerned ranges from worthy to brilliant in the case of Sophia Loren and director Vittorio De Sica.

20th-Century Fox should have excellent boxoffice results with "Altona," despite the absence of any so-called Hollywood touch. Smart selling and exploitation of the award-heavy principals will undoubtedly increase those results immeasurably. The controversial theme will undoubtedly stir some arguments which should prove less a hindrance than stimulant.

The Italian team of Carlo Ponti, De Sica, Miss Loren and Cesare Zavattini has come close to duplicating the emotional impact of "Two Women." Only the wider visual scope of "Altona" prevents the concentrated and overpowering involvement of the viewer which that film created. In a way the complete opposite of "Hud," the picture creates similar feelings in the unfolding. However, where "Hud" showed the effect of one evil person on a group of good people, "Altona" reverses to show the effect on one good person of an evil group.

The title refers to the Gerlachs, a wealthy Hamburg shipbuilding family, or what is left of it, and Altona, the Hamburg suburb in which they live. De Sica spins the tale as a series of disclosures about the family and the resultant emotional effect on Johanna (Sophia Loren), the actress-wife of the younger son (Robert Wagner). This throws the major dramatic responsibility on Miss Loren, who creates a shudderingly magnificent portrait of a beautiful, intelligent woman (nothing like the earthy peasant of "Two Women"), just beginning to recover her dignity and self-respect from the shambles of her country's militaristic past, only to have them threatened by "secrets" of her husband's family.

The massed dramatic opposition presented by "the condemned" would have overwhelmed a lesser actress. Striking flames, occasionally as brilliant if not as lasting as his leading lady, is Maximilian Schell as Franz, the eldest son whose personal war guilt has kept him a self-imposed prisoner in the attic of the Gerlach manor for 15 years until, bordering on insanity, he is roused from his self-delusion by Johanna, at first sympathetic. Reported as dead by his family, even to Johanna, Franz' self-delusion has been supported by his family, particularly his tycoon father (Fredric March), whose own war guilt has been kept subservient to his indomitable will and industrial genius, allowing him to recover and build his pre-war industrial combine.

March, whose impending death of cancer, brings the family together, creates Gerlach as much through visualization as through dialog. It is he, however, who voices the German political philosophy as imagined by Sartre (and retained by Abby Mann and Cesare Zavattini). An added coal to the flames of controversy are his self-defensive accusations that **Germany is no more war-conscious than other countries, citing the French in Algeria, the Russians, and the U.S. (via McCarthyism).** But no mention of Italy.

Robert Wagner, in the finest acting performance he has yet turned in despite an awkward introductory courtroom scene, plays Werner, Johanna's husband and the younger Gerlach. Although having earlier rebelled against his second-son status and, to lessen his own share of the Gerlach guilt, having become an idealistic lawyer dedicated to fight injustice, he quickly abandons such lipserviced ideals when it becomes apparent that he will take over the industrial empire. On the screen a comparatively short time and dropped entirely after an important self-revealing speech, Wagner makes one weak member of a strong family a memorable character. The family resemblance between March, Schell and Wagner is amazingly good, particularly the two brothers.

Francoise Prevost, one of France's best actresses, doesn't let a single-faceted, unattractive role as Leni, the daughter, prevent her from creating a dramatic image that could well be used as an example of how to brilliantly play a supporting role.

Filmed on location in Hamburg, with interiors in Italy, the tale of post-war Germany, as symbolized by the members of one family, is undoubtedly anti-German. Where Sartre's play was written from the point of view of a French writer, Mann and Zavattini have changed these observations to Italian orientation. An attempt to correlate the political theories of the characters with those who made the film will be tried by some viewers.

Roberto Gerardi's black-and-white photography, always excellent, does an exceptional job of visually carrying out De Sica's thoughts. From an intimate close-up of Miss Loren, flinging a question to her in-laws, he pulls back sharply to catch, simultaneously, the fast visual reactions of everyone. He quickly and effectively establishes Gerlach's empire with

a long, tracking shot of March riding a tug down the Hamburg waterways, surrounded by his vast holdings and acknowledging, with a curt nod, the obeisances of his many workers. Some drawings suggestive of Schell's war crimes are used behind the titles; others, shown as huge self-purging caricatures done by Schell on the walls of his attic prison, give an emotional boost.

Adriana Novelli's editing makes use of some of the fast cuts so dear to European editors, giving a dramatic pace that eliminates any static quality and adds movement to an emotionally exhausting film.

Although Mann gets sole screen credit in the U.S., he collaborated with Zavattini, a long-time collaborator of De Sica. They have retained most of Sartre's diatribes, but skirt any involvement of Italy in either judgment or guilt. Here lies the film's chief controversy; that Germany is painted black, while her collaborators (which did include Italy) are not painted, period. Much of the dialog; slanted or not, is noteworthy, such as Miss Loren's, to Schell, "Those who do not understand the past are doomed to relive it."

To establish Miss Loren's being an actress, De Sica has included two theatre scenes of her performing in Bertolt Brecht plays—one, a lengthy sequence from "The Rise and Fall of Arturo Ui," Brecht's treatment of the Hitler legend, also plays an important part in the plot. Although supposedly performed in Hamburg, the scenes were shot with members of the Berliner Ensemble in East Berlin's Bertholt Brecht Theatre.

Nino Rota is credited with musical comment, an apt description as his contributions are primarily brief underscorings for bridging shots. Although De Sica uses several sequences with no musical background at all, he brings in Dimitri Shostakovich's 11th Symphony to enhance the film's climactic and powerful end.   *Robe.*

Venice Films

La Mani Sulla Citta
(Hands on the City)
(ITALIAN)
Hard-hitting, finely made pic against corruption, graft and real estate speculation in an Italian city. Topical aspects should help this to good grosses in Italy and Rod Steiger name will help it in more limited specialized bookings elsewhere.

Venice, Sept. 5.
Warners release of Galatea production. Stars Rod Steiger; features Salvo Randone, Guido Alberti, Marcello Cannavale, Alberto Conocchia, Terenzio Cordova, Angelo D'Alessandro, Dante di Pinto, Carlo Fermariello, Gaetano Grimaldi Filioli, Vincenzo Metafora. Directed by Francesco Rosi. Screenplay, Rosi, Canevari. Camera, Gianni di Venanzo; music, Piero Piccioni; editor, Mario Serandrei. At Venice Film Festival. Running time, 105 MINS.
Edoardo Nottola .... Rod Steiger
Maglione .... Guido Alberti
Balsamo .... Salvo Randone
DeVita .... Marallo Cannavale

Rod Steiger, as city councilman Nottola, is out for a 5,000% profit on a remote suburban area which

he's just bought. Pic shows how he and his party colleagues maneuver the deal by secret alliances and other crooked methods, against the opposition of leftwing elements in the city council. Pic subtly, but clearly, shows the ease with which such tactics come off, and ends with city and government sanction — in a formal inauguration scene—of future housing projects. Film contains a very direct criticism of Italian government laissez-faire in recent real-life scandals of a similar nature, and beyond that, there's more than a hint that left wing, but especially Communist, leaders offer the only hope of saving the people and city (or nation) from such shenanigans. Tip-off is in the development of the character of the commie rep in the city government, the only one who comes out lily-white and uncorruptible, the true hero of the film.

Rosi's screenplay is as linear as is his direction in relentlessly pursuing his objectives. He deliberately concentrates on his men in their political lives and functions only, thus skipping their private existences entirely. Also, his characters have little human depth, but are almost purely symbolic pawns repping various political tendencies, in the hands of the director.

Steiger gives a powerful performance as the real estate czar, but again, neither he nor others dominate picture. Salvo Randone is good as usual as the wavering politician who helps in the deal, and Guido Alberti gives a neat picture of another top local politico. Others called in by Rosi all measure up.

Had Rosi given this film more of a universal slant against corruption everywhere, rather than the more limited localized attack with topical and politically slanted overtones, he would have made a great film. As it is, it's merely a very good one, worthy of one of today's best filmmakers.

Technical credits are all excellent, with a special bow to Gianni di Venanzo's location lensing (in Naples). thought Piero Piccioni's music is at time too important and pompous.   *Hawk.*

The Cool World

A sharp look at life in Harlem, that combines documentary insight and story values. It looms as an art and general release bet. Both timely and timeless.

Venice, Sept. 2.
Wiseman Film Productions release and production. With Hampton Clayton, Yolanda Rodriguez, Bostic Felton, Gary Bolling, Carl Lee. Directed by Shirley Clarke. Screenplay, Miss Clarke, Carl Lee from the novel by Warren Miller; camera, Baird Bryant; music, Mal Waldron; editor, Shirley Clarke. At Venice Film Fest. Running time, 125 MINS.
Duke .... Hampton Clayton
LuAnne .... Yolanda Rodriguez
Rod .... Bostic Felton
Littleman .... Gary Bolling
Priest .... Carl Lee
Blood .... Clarence Williams
Mrs. Custis .... Gloria Foster
Grandma .... Georgia Burke

"The Cool World" is the world of Harlem. Film deals generally with its physical and human aspects and also comment on the

personal feel and outlook of its characters. Both elements are well blended to make this a telling look at Harlem and probably one of the least patronizing films ever made on Negro life in New York. Good sell and careful handling should make this an art house bet and it should show some depths on its theme and treatment values.

A sharp, restless, whiplike camera picks up a Black Muslim spouting hate against the white man and claiming supremacy. Then the Harlem streets and the people listening, or letting the fanatic words float by, come to life and out of the crowd is picked a young teenager, Duke, whose one desire seems to be to own a gun that would give him standing in his own gang.

Film alternates Duke's story with general scenes of Harlem life. He tries to raise money for the gun. An attempt at stealing results in his money being snatched by a rival gang. But Duke becomes the leader of his gang and in a rumble with the rival group a boy is killed. It ends with Duke being dragged off and beaten by the police as his daydream voice, which has bolstered him during the film, comments sympathetically on the new cold killer as he passes his mother and her new lover on the street unknown to her.

The film is mainly concerned with the ghetto aspect of Harlem and the boredom of the young who mainly see violence as a way out. The gang is a way of belonging to something. Preachiness is wisely held in check. The problems of segregation and civil rights are implicit in their lives, however, and come up naturally.

Duke's mother's soliloquy about the difficulty of a normal life with jobs hard to find, bad housing etc., is revealing rather than soap boxy as is an encounter with a brother who has gone on to good education by peacefully accepting and working.

A counterpoint jazz background is an asset as is the well textured lensing, cogent editing and the natural thesping by a mainly nonpro cast. But it is chiefly the virile, well observed direction of Shirley Clarke that keeps this long film engrossing and revealing most of the way.

She creates a tenseness around the familiar characters by a knowing look at Harlem rhythms, gaiety, lurking desperation, boredom tempered with joviality, and the general oppressiveness of bad housing and employment conditions. Sometimes the characters get a bit lost in the general schematics of the pic, which at times, waters down its underlying irony.

But, overall, Miss Clarke, who also made the controversial pic "The Connection," has a firm hold on her characters and story. The jangle, bite and movement of city life is there and certain mosaic scenes reveal character and dramatic needs. Especially effective to Duke's budding love with a 15 year old prostitute and his showing her the sea for the first time at Coney Island.

A gangster hero is well etched by Carl Lee and Hampton Clayton displays presence and authority as the 14 year old Duke who, from delinquency, is now on his way to

being a hardened criminal after his arrest following the gang fight.

One weakness of the film is in using a character to state some truth on Negro life and then having him disappear. But they do fit the film's structure and are never forced. They are acceptable since they are usually within the experience of the main character, Duke, if much of what they say is already implicit in the film.

At the time of Civil Rights demonstrations, the pic may have an added exploitation value. If it shows a somewhat conventional view of tenament life, it does have a new depth and insight to add to it. In this "Cool World" the outside strivings of the Negroes and the betterment of conditions by Federal laws are still a long way off.

Miss Clarke's previous pic "Connection" had censor troubles due to a certain four letter word. "World" also has this word in the casual speech of the characters. It is used about five or six times. But again it is not used to shock or titillate, but seems natural and offhand in this milieu. Dialog is hip but understandable. *Mosk.*

El Verdugo
(The Executioner)
(SPANISH-ITALIAN)

Bitter yet often highly amusing pic about man who becomes executioner against his will. Bright chances in Latino market, and good possibilities in other world areas as well though limited in some countries to more specialized outlets.

Venice, Sept. 1.
Dear Film release of Naga Film (Madrid)—Zebra Film (Rome) coproduction. Features Nino Manfredi, Emma Penella, Jose Isbert, Jose Luis Lopez Vasquez, Angel Alvarez, Guido Alberti, Maria Luisa Ponte, Maruja Isbert, Julia Caba Alba, Xan D'As Bolas, Jose Sezatornil, Lola Gaos, Chus Lampreable, Felix Fernandez, Alfredo Landa, Jose Luis Coll. Directed by Luis Barcia Berlanga. Screenplay, Berlanga, Rafael Azcona, Ennio Flaiano, from story by Berlanga. Camera, Tonino delli Colli. Music, Miguel Asis Arbo. Editor, Alfonso Santacana. At Venice Film Festival. Running time, **95 MINS.**

Jose Luis .... Nino Manfredi
Carmen .... Emma Penella
Amadeo .... Jose Isbert

Jose Luis (Nino Manfredi) an undertaker, falls in love with Carmen (Emma Penella), daughter of an ageing executioner. He is more or less forced into proposing marriage, and in order not to lose a vitally needed new apartment under a pension plan, he has to apply to replace the old man (Jose Isbert) in his grim profession. After avoiding his duties at length, he is finally called to Mallorca for his first "job," taking the whole family with him on a tourist romp which he hopes will never end in execution.

The pardon never comes for the doomed man, however, and the physically sick executioner goes through his grim duty vowing he'll never do it again. It's a story which must be seen, however, and not told, to catch the "black humor" which pervades the whole pic making it grimly risible at all times. To carry out his neatly written film, director Berlanga has a superlative cast topped by an-

other winning performance from vet Spanish thesp Jose Isbert as the ageing executioner. Nino Manfredi and Emma Penella are likewise good as the couple, and Guido Alberti, Angel Alvarez, and others give colorful support in nicely photographed film entirely shot in Madrid and on Spanish locations. One of the best Spanish pic's in some time. *Hawk.*

Muriel, Ou Le Temps D'Un Retour
(Muriel, Or the Time of a Return)
(FRENCH—COLOR)

From the man who made that obtuse but hypnotic offbeater "Last Year In Marienbad," Alain Resnais comes another film of technical virtuosity. But this time it is a bit clearer and sometimes the tale of coping with memory seems overinflated and technically abused.

Venice, Aug. 31.
United Artists release of Dear Film-Argos Films-Alpha Productions-Films De La Pleiade production. With Delphine Seyrig, Jean-Pierre Kerien, Nita Klein, Jean-Baptiste Thierre, Claude Sainval. Directed by Alain Resnais. Screenplay, Jean Cayrol; camera (Eastmancolor), Sacha Vierny; editor, Kenout Peitier. At Venice Film Fest. Running time, **120 MINS.**

Helene .... Delphine Seyrig
Alphonse .... Jean-Pierre Kerien
Francoise .... Nita Klein
Bernard .... Jean-Baptiste Thierre
Smoke .... Claude Sainval

As in his previous pix, "Hiroshima Mon Amour" and "Last Year in Marienbad," memory and the weighing of an important past event on the characters seems to be the keystone of the film. A fortyish woman, living in a small town with her stepson, invites an old lover, whom she has not seen in 20 years, to come to see her. He appears accompanied by a 20 year old mistress whom he passes off as his niece. The stepson is suffering from an experience during the recent Algerian war when a fellow soldier tortured an Arab girl called Muriel.

He has accepted the memory as that of an old girl friend and to appease himself he finally shoots the man who raped her and goes off. The old boy friend almost insinuates himself back into the woman's graces only to have it all blow up when it is revealed that he's married.

Like "Hiroshima" and "Marienbad" the characters are basically ordinary, but pumped up in size by the film treatment. Here the platitudes and dreariness of the lives of these basically frustrated people except, for two young girls, at first give a sharp satiric look at the evasion, emptiness and lack of communication, so much a part of the so-called modern film outlook. But all this is cloaked in sudden montages to give an idea of memory at work, such as day and night shots alternating at the came time, and with overlapping dialog, spoof-type classic songs of memory on the sound track.

There can be no denying Resnals' brilliance in his rapid cutting, which replaces camera movement, plus maintenance of a mood and the knowing use of color. But an attempt to add mystery to the pic by the man's being tracked

down by his abandoned wife's brother, the boy's Algerian hurt, and the woman's vascillating quest for allaying a past love that was lost in the war, in the end makes this tale a pretentious one.

The characters are forced to stand for things that are above their abilities. It does not allow them to grow, unfold and perhaps display the propensity to change or not. This cold, glossy method finally leads up blind alleys and seems an impasse in this school of bravura cinema which practically destroys content in an insistence on technical virtuosity almost for its own sake.

Delphine Seyrig etches a mannered but acceptable, due to the film's directorial pyrotechnics, portrait of the almost spinsterish widow who basically cannot cope with herself or her memories. Her tics and needs finally almost destroy the attempt to renew this old love. Others are adequate in their both simple and complex roles. No doubt this will create word-of-mouth and some critical controversy which could help it at the wickets in specialized spots. But it appears that the overdose of brilliant editing, lensing and ambiguity in the long run will lead to a dead end in this kind of film-making. The trends seems to be developing into more of a personal affection than a new means of conveying a theme, story and outlook.

A song sung at the end by one of the characters, about age being inevitable, does have a revealing bite, insight and point, that is obscured and overdone in the film. Characters become automatons whose actions have to be pieced out rather than growing in intensity and meaning.

In "Hiroshima" the girl was reliving a tragic love with a French soldier during the occupation of France, in "Marienbad" she was a sort of sleeping princess who may or may not have had a tryst with a man a year ago, while in this film she is trying to return to a lost love without any clear idea of why. This film may get to those evolving audiences who are willing to read things into pix or are taken by its ambiguities. This will be the art pitch, but mass distribution appears severly limited for this kind of film. *Mosk.*

Bolshaia Doroga
(RUSSIAN)

Pleasant, frequently tongue-in cheek item. A lingual entry with some arty chances as well.

Venice, Sept. 5.
Sovexportfilm release of a Mosfilm production. Features Inna Goulaja, Iozeph Abraham, Roudolph Grouchinski, Youri Yakolev, others. Directed by Youri Ozerov. Story and screenplay, Guergiu Mdivani. Camera, Igor Thernikh; music, Katchaturian. At Venice Film Festival. Running time, **102 MINS.**

Hazek, per this admittedly "adapted" scenario, reluctantly serves Archduke Franz Ferdinand in the Czech army, but is later dispatched to Russia to fight in the Red Army during the October revolution. Peace finds Hasek in Moscow with the girl he has met dur-

ing a pause in battle, and later, he and his friends return to Prague where his book is headed for success.

Pic is replete with leftwing propaganda, though the pill is sweetened here and there with irony and humor, (much of it broad). Pace occasionally lags, many situations are predictable but on the whole, Youri Ozerov has directed his film ably, with fine support from his cast and a special assist from cameraman Igor Thernik and musical scorer Katchaturian. *Hawk.*

The Servant
(BRITISH)

Powerful offbeater with strong prospects on the artie circuit.

Venice, Sept. 4.
Elstree Film Distributors presentation of Springbok production. Stars Dirk Bogarde, Sarah Miles, Wendy Craig, features James Fox. Produced by Joseph Losey, Norman Priggen; directed by Losey; screenplay, Harold Pinter, from a novel by Robin Maugham; camera, Douglas Slocombe; editor, Reginald Mills; settings, Ted Clements; music, John Dankworth. At Venice Film Festival, Sept. 3, '63. Running time, **117 MINS.**

Barrett .... Dirk Bogarde
Vera .... Sarah Miles
Susan .... Wendy Craig
Tony .... James Fox
Lady Mountset .... Catherine Lacey
Lord Mountset .... Richard Vernon
Society Woman .... Ann Firbank
Other Woman .... Doris Knox
Bishop .... Patric Magee
Younger Woman .... Jill Melford
Curate .... Alun Owen
Society Man .... Harold Pinter

Invited to Venice, and selected to represent Britain at this month's Lincoln Center fest in New York, "The Servant" is for the most part strong dramatic fare, though the atmosphere and tension is not fully sustained to the end. Nevertheless, it has essential b.o. ingredients to make it an offbeat contender, particularly on the artie circuits in the U.S.

Harold Pinter's screenplay based on the Robin Maugham novel is distinguished by its literacy and sharp incisive dialog, and a difficult and unusual plot is developed thoughtfully and provocatively. There are also topical overtones, though the script was in fact written long before the recent scandals that rocked the world.

Although there is a cast of impressive length, there are only four roles of any significance, and each of these is impeccably filled. Dirk Bogarde plays a manservant who is hired by a young and elegant man about town to run a house he has just bought in a fashionable part of London, and who, almost imperceptibly, begins to dominate his master. The servant is a crafty and obnoxious character, cunningly determined to get the better of his own way and to get the better of his employer, yet at first giving the impression of total servility.

As he gains confidence, Bogarde brings his mistress into the house as a maid, telling his employer that she is his sister, and before long the girl's blatant and provocative advances have the desired result. Dominance of servant over master is now virtually complete, and the reversal of roles is the next stage to be effected.

Up to the point where the servant gains supremacy, Joseph Losey's direction is first class, despite a few conventional shots

which are used to gain effect. The last segment of the story, which puts some strain on credibility, is less convincing and, therefore, less satisfying. But the relationship of master and servant, with its underlying suggestion of homosexuality is sensitively handled. So is the relationship between the master and his fiancee, the latter always being conscious of the evil influence of the servant.

One of the most impressive features of the production is the standout performance by Bogarde, for whom the role of the servant is offbeat casting. His interpretation of the evil and menacing character goes a long way towards giving the plot conviction. He not only looks the part, but plays it with natural assurance. There is also a noteworthy performance from James Fox, a newcomer with a confident flair, who assuredly suggests the indolent young man about town. The two main femme roles are also expertly played, Sarah Miles making a highly provocative and sensuous maid, and Wendy Craig giving a contrasting study as the fiancee who is overwhelmed by events she cannot control. None of the other players has anything but a bit part, without any opportunity of adding to the production.

John Dankworth's heavy, brooding music, matched the mood of the picture, and Cleo Laine's singing of "All Gone," which is reprised on several occasions, is in the same groove. Technical credits are mainly okay, though tighter editing in the final sequence could be a help. *Myro.*

Ningen
(The Man)
(JAPANESE)

A specialized item, this picture just fails to achieve greatness, but it is nevertheless a noteworthy entry for discriminating filmgoers able to take some of the harrowing events it portrays.

Venice, Sept. 1.
Kinday-Eigakyokai production - release. Features Nobuko Otowa, Taiji Tonoyama, Keu Yamamoto. Written and directed by Kaneto Shindo. Based on story by Yayoko Nogami. Camera, Kijimomi Kuroda. Music, Hikaru Hayashi. At Venice Film Festival. Running time, 120 MINS.

Four people, three men and a woman, take off in a fishing sloop to haul a cargo of stones from a near-by island. The boat is wrecked in a storm, and the four are left without fuel and little food and water. Slowly, day by day, their resistance lowers and animal instincts begin to emerge in hate and suspicion of one another.

Eventually, two of the shipbound navigators display cannibalistic intent and murder a third, stopping in horror, however, before going through with their plan. After two months, a liner finally sights them, but safe on board at last, the woman goes crazy and dies in a fall, while the murderer commits suicide, leaving a lone survivor. It's a labor of love by director Kaneto Shindo, but like his previous tour-de-force, the dialog-less "Naked Island," it at times strains credibility while a "happy" ending here also comes

on a strained note. But all in all, and given the almost prohibitively difficult subject, Shindo has done a magnificent job in pacing, directing his faultless cast, and using his camera within the confines of the sloop.

There's an oddly apt modern musical score by Hikaru Hayashi to counterpoint the grimmer moments. *Hawk.*

En Compagnie De Max Linder
(With Max Linder)
(FRENCH)

Venice, Aug. 31.
Films Max Linder release and production. Compiled and conceived by Maud Linder. Editing, Albert Jurgensen, Yannick Bellon, Maud Linder; commentary, Rene Clair; music, Gerard Calvi. At Venice Film Fest. Running time, 90 MINS.

Charles Chaplin, Buster Keaton, Harold Lloyd, Mack Sennett and other early silent film comedy greats have been kept in the public eye by hardtop reissues and tv. But one of the greatest of them all, French film comic Max Linder, has fallen into limbo except for film buffs and oldsters. Now his daughter has compiled a film from three of his best works that shows his genius and emerges as a yock-filled affair that has art and general release chances on its entertainment values alone.

Chaplin himself has gone on record pegging Linder as his true teacher. Linder made hundreds of one-reelers in France from 1905 to about 1915. He made his best medium length pix in Hollywood and the excerpts are taken from these; "Be My Wife" (1921), "Seven Years Hard Luck" (1923) and "The Three Must-Get-Theirs" (1922).

His daughter compiled this pic as a work of love. Unfortunately she could get no short footage as a French company will not release it, but Linder is deftly introed by Rene Clair and then the almost full length pix are run off. It adequately displays the screen character of Linder, his feeling for a sustained gag and his gusto and comic brilliance.

In the first part he plays a dandyish, but charming figure, who is forever getting embroiled with his fiancee. But he gets rid of a suitor by staging a mock fight in another room with an imaginary intruder he has dreamed up. Then a supposed friend tells his girl he is carrying on with another and she jilts him as he goes off on a trip in despair. Here he loses his wallet and goes through a lot of adventures before finding her again. Then in a parody of "The Three Musketeers," done soon after the Douglas Fairbanks version, he shows his true talent by making it an excellent pic in its own right. Anachronisms, dynamic duel scenes, expert comic touches make this a ribtickling affair.

Linder appears to have had the acrobatic elan, charm and innocent brashness of Douglas Fairbanks, the ingenious building of gags a la Buster Keaton, Chaplin's mime, Harold Lloyd's aggressive innocence tempered by unconscious bravery and tenderness with all tied up in a Mack Sennett flair for zany pacing and social satire.

In short, Max Linder was a great comedian of the early screen. He

died tragically in 1925 and has practically disappeared from the public ken. The film will have to be well sold with a play on his past and meaning, but word-of-mouth should help.

Besides its historical values the film has enough laughs to please both popular and selective audiences. His was a true visual approach without vulgarity, and he was also one of the first complete comic personalities of the screen. Max Linder deserves both belated recognition and commercial interest. Pic will be called "Laugh Awhile With Max Linder" in its English version. *Mosk.*

Dragees Au Poivre
(Sweet and Sour)
(FRENCH)

Venice, Sept. 4.
Diclfilm release of Cervi Film-Number One Films production. With Guy Bedos, Jean-Paul Belmondo, Francis Blanche, Claude Brasseur, Sophie Daumier, Sophie Desmarets, Jacques Dufilho, Anna Karina, Jean-Pierre Marielle, Francois Perier, Simone Signoret. Directed by Jacques Baratier. Screenplay, Guy Bedos, Eric Ollivier, Baratier; camera, Henri Becae; editor, Nena Baratier. At Venice Film Fest. Running time, 98 MINS.

Gerard	Guy Bedos
Rakanowski	Jean-Pierre Marielle
Jackie	Sophie Daumier
Franz	Francis Blanche
Anna	Alexandra Stewart
Stripper	Rita Renoir
Call Girl	Marina Vlady
Alfonso	Jacques Dufilho
Father	Francois Perier
She	Monica Vitti
He	Roger Vadim
Giselle	Anna Karina
Genevieve	Simone Signoret
Raymond	Jean-Paul Belmondo

This film mixes a lampoon of the "Cinema Truth" type of filmmaking, takeoffs on the personal pix of Alain Resnais and Michelangelo Antonioni, some songs and dance numbers, skits, sketches and some stars in bit roles. It emerges as only intermittently witty and not up to the things it is trying to parody.

There is an occasional breezy facility, but pic drags in too many revue-type sketches and has too many inside allusions and gags for much of a chance abroad. Its satirical aspects are also blunted by burlesque, rather than knowing insight or feeling for the subjects and themes it is trying to get across. Art chances also look chancey.

"Cinema Truth" pix have gained impetus in France and the producers go out into the streets to try to catch people on the run, or have some people sit around and talk, or have them act out things to try to reach some sort of truth etc. It has not yet produced any film that's made a big box office dent although some did okay specialized biz.

The pretext of spying works in some scenes that have something to do with the principle and sometimes not.

A striptease is worked in and there is a lame try at a "West Side Story" dance scene. Songs are easily forgettable and rarely comment on the action, spring from it, or move it along. Only Francis Blanche's happy chortling as a German ogling Paris high life aspects has some semblance of brio. Choreography is also extremely lame and limited.

Monica Vitti parodies herself in a takeoff on the art school of films as a man and woman prattle on

and people around them seem frozen in a dream. This is for insiders mainly and it is a bad imitation rather than truly knowing or witty.

This pic lacks the brio, brightness and insight to bring it off. It does have enough yeasty and zesty episodes for good chances in its home market, but would need a hard sell for foreign spots. Simone Signoret, in a small bit, is one of the few names that has some meaning abroad. It is technically fair with acceptable production values. *Mosk.*

Omicron
(Omicron)
(ITALIAN)

Venice, Sept. 3.
Paramount release of Lux-Ultra-Video production by Franco Cristaldi. Stars Renato Salvatori; features Rosemary Dexter, Gaetano Quartaro, Mara Carisi, Ida Serasini, Calisto Calisti, Dante de Pinto. Written and directed by Ugo Gregoretti. Camera, Carlo Di Palma; music, Piero Umiliani; editor, Nino Baragli. At Venice Film Festival. Running time, 102 MINS.

Omicron	Renato Salvatori
Angelo	Renato Salvatori
Lucia	Rosemary Dexter
Midollo	Gaetano Quartaro
Mrs. Midollo	Mara Carisi
Widow Piattino	Ida Serasini
Torchio	Calisto Calisti
Police Inspector	Dante di Pinto

First half of "Omicron" is a hilarious laugh-getter which would have made a surefire hit almost everywhere, but the film as currently presented, can only look to okay business if changes and cuts are made on the comparatively lacking and much too confused second stanza. Ostensibly, pic was rushed into completion for the Venice Fest, and this has hurt it, but amends can surely be made to keep this a good international property with U.S. chances as well.

Story concerns an invisible Omicron, a creature from another planet, who enters the body of apparently dead Italian plant worker to spy on earthly things and report back to his chief in outer space. Coming to life (in the worker's body) in slow stages and having to learn body movements and habits by instinct, he soon becomes a national medical phenomenon as well as a plant pet because of his ability to work machines in rapid-fire order and never tire. Eventually, however, he gets involved with a girl and with a group of strikers, developing a conscience along the way. The conscience makes him unfit for spy duty, and he is recalled.

All sequences of Omicron's arrival in his earthly body, and his attempts to learn the ways of man, are extremely funny, with much of the humor of the earthy variety, and Renato Salvatori is excellent as the "inhabited" man. It's when he learns to move and "live" when he begins to worry about local politics etc. that the pic loses its entertainment punch and becomes a garbled message vehicle. Later part should and could be trimmed and re-edited for maximum clarity as well as to sustain the initial pace. The effort would be worth it, for Ugo Gregoretti's direction of his own script is intelligent, tongue-in-cheek spoofing which makes him a young talent of considerable promise.

Salvatori gets good backing in the acting department from a large

cast in which Rosemary Dexter as his girl and Gaetano Midollo as a plant supervisor deserve a nod. Music, by Piero Umiliani, Carlo di Palma's lensing, and other production credits are all good.

Hawk.

Le Feu Follet
(The Maddening Flame)
(FRENCH)

Venice, Sept. 1.
Nouvelles editions de Films release and prod., directed by Louis Malle. Stars Maurice Ronet; features Lena Skerla, Yvonne Clech, Mona Dol, Bernard Noel, Alain Mottet, Henri Serre, Alexandra Stewart, Jeanne Moreau, Ursula Kubler. Written and directed by Louis Malle from book by Drieu De La Rochelle. Camera, Ghislain Cloquet; editor, Suzanne Baron. At Venice Film Fest. Running time, 110 MINS.
Alain .... Maurice Ronet
Lydia .... Lena Skerla
Farnoux .... Yvonne Clech
La Barbinais .... Mona Dol
Dubourg .... Bernard Noel
Fanny .... Ursula Kubler
Urecei .... Alain Mottet
Jeanne .... Jeanne Moreau
Solange .... Alexandra Stewart
Frederic .... Henri Serre

This film deals with a suicide, but it is a measure of the talents and taste behind it that it avoids being grim, morbid or too-self indulgent. It is still fairly offbeat fare, however, and looms mainly as an art bet abroad where it will call for a personal and inventive sell due to its fragile if tragic structure.

A young man in his 30's has just taken a cure for alcoholism and is better if still hanging on at the clinic. He does not want to leave yet, the head doctor feels he should. He goes into nearby Paris one evening and the film recounts his meetings with former friends, none of whom can help him resolve or change a decision made, at least intimated, at the beginning of the film to kill himself. He returns, packs his bags, finishes a book he is reading and shoots himself.

But the basis of the film lies in its excellent observation, notations, dialog, commentary and acting. It takes an essentially literary situation and adequately, at times superlatively, translates it to visual status. The first shots of the man in bed with a friend of his wife, subtly displays the seeming inability to truly love or possess that plagues him.

His visits to an old bar, war, where he had spent many drunken days, to a friend now married and accepting a possibly boring if cozy relationship, with some other indulging in vague revolutionary activities, to some upper class people lost in vapid talk and living, to a den of far out poets and narcotics users, are all used to constantly remind him of the shallowness of his life and what he has been.

Pic can't generate much emotional drive since it is about a man who has already made up his mind to die and will not take a stand and change his life. But it does deal with a palpable human theme and keeps interest in the character alive throughout, in spite of his one-track outlook.

Director Louis Malle, who did "The Lovers," "Zazie," and "A Very Private Affair," makes this his most mature and accomplished film to date. The first part sustains a melancholy, moving atmosphere as it shows the man's detachment, resignation and decision to finally end it all. Maurice Ronet has his best role to date. His sickly, weary, good natured, but lost air, is kept on the right level throughout the film.

His is a performance of insight, flair and feeling that is the keynote of the film's ability to depict desperation without complete despair, intellectualism for its own sake without being pedantic, and lack of communication without losing clarity. Others are well chosen and the direction makes this journey into the recent past, through people, always meticulously revealing if its one-note theme sometimes almost lapses into preciosity.

That this is avoided is also a testimony to the knowing scripting and direction of Malle. French star Jeanne Moreau, who became a topliner in Malle's "Lovers," does a bit part unostentatiously. The lensing has the right density of contrast to fit the mood and music borrowed from the late Erik Satie is right in underlining the film's action.

English title decided on is "The Will-o'-The-Wisp." *Mosk.*

Mare Matto
(Crazy Sea)
(ITALO-FRENCH)

Disappointing, overlong entry which nevertheless has its moments. Must be sold on the Lollobrigida-Belmondo names for maximum penetration in various markets.

Venice, Sept. 1.
Paramount release of a Lux-Vides-Les Films Ariane production by Franco Cristaldi. Stars Gina Lollobrigida, Jean Paul Belmondo; features Odoardo Spadaro, Tomas Milian, Noel Roquevert, Piero Morgia, Vincenzo Musolino, Anita Durante, Rossana di Rocco, Michele Abruzzo. Directed by Renato Castellani. Screenplay, Castellani, Benvenuti, DeBernardi. Camera, Toni Secchi. Music, Nino Rota. At Film Festival, Venice. Running time, 120 MINS.
Margherita .... Gina Lollobrigida
Livornese .... Jean Paul Belmondo
Efisio .... Tomas Milian
Drudo Parenti .... Odoardo Spadaro

Various story lines are intertwined, but the film deals principally with Margherita (Gina Lollobrigida), a stingy old maid who falls for a young boarder (J. P. Belmondo) in her Genoese rooming house; Drudo Parenti (Odoardo Spandro) an aging seaman who too often forgets the years he carries in pursuit of impossible dreams and women; and Efisio (Tomas Milian) another, younger dreamer (but whose part has been sizably trimmed in the version screened); and others.
The Lollobrigida-Belmondo sequence has some effective passages; another detailing a disastrous trip from Messina to Naples on a tramp steamer with a cargo of wine is predictable and overstretched but often funny; but the best segment concerns a sailor's Sunday visit to his Sicilian home during which he has to settle accounts with his several sisters' fiances, getting the worst of most of the encounters.

Acting is uneven. Miss Lollobrigida is good in an offbeat role; J. P. Belmondo at home in the role of the likeable ne'er-do-well; Tomas Milian rarely seen in what must have been a much more siz-

able role; Odoardo Spadaro, who has to carry much of weight on his shoulders, is effective at times, but in the long run appears miscast.

Too much of the pic, which was Italy's official entry at the Venice Festival, is acted at the top of actors' lungs, and director Renato Castellani accentuates the farcical angles by stepping up the pace and forcing scenes to their conclusion —not always with success. Pic could stand some trimming to enhance its audience chances immeasurably. Lensing, Nino Rota's music, and other credits are good.

Hawk.

I Misteri Di Roma
(Mysteries of Rome)
(ITALIAN)

A feature documentary, a sort of mammoth peek behind the scenes of Roman life, with a few points of interest and a few exploitable angles which could pay off in minor b.o. domestically.

Venice, Sept. 5.
Unset release of an SPA production. With non-professional actors, and the people of Rome. Directed by Gianni Bisiach, Libero Bozzarri, Mario Carbone, Angelo D'Alessandro, Nino del Fra, Luigi di Gianni, Giuseppe Ferrara, Ansano Giannarelli, Giulio Macchi, Lori Mazzetti, Massimo Mida, Enzo Muzzi, Piero Nelli, Paolo Nuzzi, Dino Partesano, Giovanni Vento. From an idea by Cesare Zavattini. At Venice Film Festival. Running time, 100 MINS.

Made by a score of young neophite directors under the guidance of vet scripter Cesare Zavattini, pic is an uneven, often cheap and vulgar expose of all that is tawdry in the Eternal City. It is a shame that Zavattini's name should be associated with this effort which, though it has its moments, is basically a politically biased anti-church and anti-government pamphlet which shows only one side of things to (ostensibly) prove its case.

Thus the various shots of religious rites pointed out to ridicule, the recorded protests of employees against their employers (usually the city and/or state), the not-so-subtle suggestion that certain real-estate coups were brought off with the assistance of higher-ups. etc. Also, some episodes, colorful though they may be, smack of provocation; notably the interview of some prosties on their nighttime beat in which the interviewer, smelling pathos, appears to have deliberately pushed to draw tears from his interviewee.

Some other episodes are similarly geared to get a shock reaction from audiences, while others are either repetitive of many seen previously, or simply puerile and devoid of any creative intervention by (unspecified) authors.
Technical credits are uneven.

Hawk.

Twilight of Honor
(PANAVISION)

Strong courtroom drama with tv's Richard Chamberlain making theatrical film star bow to boost chances of excellent re-returns.

Hollywood, Sept. 12.
Metro release of William Perlberg-George Seaton production. Stars Richard Chamberlain, Nick Adams, Claude Rains, Joan Blackman, James Gregory; features Pat Buttram, Joey Heatherton, Donald Barry. Directed by Boris Sagal. Screenplay, Henry Denker, based on novel by Al Dewlen; camera, Philip Lathrop; editor, Hugh S. Fowler; music, John Green; asst. director, Donald Roberts. Reviewed at studio, Sept. 11, '63. Running time, 105 MINS.
David Mitchell .... Richard Chamberlain
Laura Mae Brown ..... Joey Heatherton
Ben Brown .... Nick Adams
Art Harper .... Claude Rains
Susan Harper .... Joan Blackman
Norris Bixby .... James Gregory
Cole Clinton .... Pat Buttram
Amy Clinton .... Jeanette Nolan
Judge James Tucker....... Edgar Stehli
Charles Crispin .... James Bell
Paul Farish .... George Mitchell
Judson Elliott .... Donald Barry
Sheriff "Buck" Wheeler .. Bert Freed
Theresa "Tess" Braden..Robin Raymond
Vera Driscoll .... June Dayton
Mr. McWade .... Arch Johnson
Alice Clinton .... Linda Evans

Metro has a winning parlay in Richard Chamberlain undertaking his first theatrical motion picture starring role and a strongly suspenseful courtroom drama with shock appeal. Actor makes the transition effectively from young Dr. Kildare of tv to young Attorney David Mitchell in this slickly-executed Perlberg-Seaton production embodying all the elements of a hit. Result, certain to be backed by a sock exploitation campaign to cash in on Chamberlain's terrific popularity in his teleseries, should be one of studio's most profitable pix of the season.

Plans hereafter call for studio to put Chamberlain in a feature between tv seasons, while hopefully looking forward to continuing his "Dr. Kildare" series possibly for as long as five years. Build-up he's had in "Kildare" for past two seasons and now the beginning of the third assures a powerful ready-made audience for "Twilight of Honor," which casts him as a court-appointed defense attorney who takes on an entire New Mexico town, at the risk of his career, to save his client from the gas chamber.

Frank and often startling treatment is made by producers of a section in New Mexico's criminal code—No. 12-24—which provides that a husband is innocent if he kills another man whom he discovers in the act of adultery with his wife, a case of the "unwritten law" being written. Henry Denker's polished script, based upon the novel by Al Dewlen, frequently makes use of such words as "co-habitation," "adultery" and even "prostitute" as Chamberlain's line of defense brings out that his client killed the town's most respected citizen after he found him in bed with his trampish teenage spouse.

Dexterity which writer displays is matched by the shrewd, moving direction of Boris Sagal, who is particularly proficient in his realistic courtroom sequences. Chamberlain, who takes his defense assignment by court against his will, is faced by courtroom intrigue and powerful political pressure which would railroad his client to his death, to cover, as he learns, the truth behind the slaying and save the reputation of the murdered

man. Defense attorney receives his only encouragement and assistance from Claude Rains, an elderly, former trial lawyer now semi-paralyzed who gives him the benefit of his years in combatting wily legal maneuvres of the opposition, and finally wins acquittal through the state's own witnesses.

• Chamberlain in his change of pace and character further demonstrates his ability to hold his audience, turning in a smooth and persuasive performance. He is surrounded by a thoroughly experienced cast to help him over the rough spots. One of highlights of pic is introduction of Joey Heatherton, a new sexpot from the eastern stage and television making her film bow and slated to go places. In the part of the twotiming wife of the man up for murder she registers impressively.

Nick Adams, whom Chamberlain defends, also is in for a change of pace from the character audiences know him in tv, portraying a mentally disturbed ex-soldier. Role is somewhat overdone, but generally Adams rates a hand. Joan Blackman scores decisively as distaff lead, daughter of Claude Rains in love with Chamberlain. Rains comes through with his customary brilliance, responsible for Chamberlain being appointed to handle the defense to spark his career.

Pat Buttram, as the town's most distinguished citizen who meets his death in going on the make for Adams' wife, goes dramatic here with highly satisfactory results. James Gregory, the skilled special prosecutor set to try case—and politically ambitious, delivers strongly. Other standouts in cast are Edgar Stehli, presiding judge who conducts his court in his own way; Linda Evans, murdered man's widow. There are also a multitude of excellent smaller characters.

On technical side, Philip Lathrop's camera work is particularly fluid and Hugh S. Fowler's editing sharp and dramatic. John Green's music score lends appropriate mood, as does art direction by George W. Davis and Paul Groesse.

Whit.

In The French Style

Romantic drama starring Jean Seberg with strong femme appeal; lensed in Paris for atmospheric values.

Hollywood, Sept. 6.
Columbia Pictures release of Irwin Shaw-Robert Parrish production. Stars Jean Seberg, Stanley Baker. Directed by Robert Parrish. Screenplay, Irwin Shaw, from two of his stories; camera, Michel Kelber; art director, Rino Mondellini; editor, Renee Lichtig; music, Joseph Kosma; asst. director, Michel Wyn. Reviewed at Music Hall, Beverly Hills, Cal., Sept. 5, '63. Running time, **104 MINS.**

Christina James .... Jean Seberg
Walter Beddoes .... Stanley Baker
Mr. James .... Addison Powell
Bill .... Jack Hedley
Baron .... Maurice Teynac
Dr. John Haislip......James Leo Herlihy
Guy's Fiancee .... Ann Lewis
Guy .... Philippe Forquet
Patrini .... Jacques Charon
Clio .... Claudine Auger

Irwin Shaw and Robert Parrish have fashioned a sophisticated love story of Paris, of an American girl in love with the life not quite for her, in their indie based upon two of Shaw's stories, "In the French Style" and "A Year to Learn the Language." It is a drama with strong femme appeal, lensed in the French capital to capture its flavor,

articulate and adult. A strong exploitation campaign can cash in heavily upon the title and theme.

Jean Seberg stars as the 19-year-old Chicago girl, a would-be painter who dreams of conquering the capital of art, naive, ambitious, impressionable, who has her father's financial backing for one year to prove herself. She meets early romantic disillusionment, when she becomes involved with a young French engineering student whom she believes older than she, but who turns out to be only a 16-year-old boy when the crucial moment comes and she goes to bed with him in a cheap hotel room.

The subject of les affaires is delicately and tactfully treated by Shaw in his screenplay and Parrish in direction to keep the unfoldment always within the bounds of taste. Sequence in which the girl suggests to Philippe Forquet, the boy, that she is ready for seduction and they finally unclothe in the cold, unheated room requires nearly a reel but has been handled skillfully, with sometimes humorous overtones. The technique of suggestion is followed as the femme flits from one romance to another, a French count, an Irish photographer, a newspaper correspondent always leaving her for foreign assignments. This episodic technique occasionally tends to detract but picks up strongly once the immediate story progresses.

Disenchantment for femme comes after three years of love and disappointment, hiding her wounds when she realizes the French style isn't hers, when her lack of direction and failure force her to renounce the way of life she wanted so desperately to embrace and she promises to wed a San Francisco doctor who can overlook her by now sordid past. Parrish handles his assignment with artistry and with fluid camera, draining situations of their dramatic possibilities and drawing fine performances from a cast mostly unknown to American audiences.

Miss Seberg brings life and brilliance to her portrayal, registering strongly both in the more dramatic and lighter moments. In Stanley Baker, the correspondent with whom she has a lingering affair and finally leaves for her doctor, she has a firstrate costar who makes a good impression. Forquet, the youth, is brash and talented, a welcome addition to cast. Addison Powell as the girl's father, visiting her from Chicago and who tries to persuade her to return home after he sees the disjointed pattern of her life, scores soundly, and James Leo Herlihy likewise is briefly impressive as the doctor. Jack Hedley and Maurice Teynac lend staunch support.

Technical credits are effectively executed, including Michel Kelber's artistic photography, Rino Mondellini's tasteful art direction, Renee Lichtig's tight editing and Joseph Kosma's suitable music score.

Whit.

My Son, The Hero
(ITALIAN-FRENCH)

An Italo beefcaker with added spoof values originated by U.S. distrib. Satire falters. For easy-to-please patrons only.

United Artists release of Vides-Les Films Ariane production. Produced by Alexander Mnouchkine. Features Pedro Armendariz, Jacqueline Sassard, Antonella Lualdi, Giuliano Gemma, Gerard Setty. Directed by Duccio Tessari. Screenplay by Ennio de Concini. Reviewed at United Artists, Sept. 12, '63. Running time, **111 MINS.**

Cadmus .... Pedro Armendariz
Antiope .... Jacqueline Sassard
Hermione .... Antonella Lualdi
Crios .... Giuliano Gemma
Hippolytos .... Gerard Setty
Rator .... Serge Nubret
Licina .... Tanya Lopert
Emerate .... Ingrid Schoeller

This Italian-French coproduction started out as a straight beefcake action epic under the title "The Titans" but has been changed by United Artists for release in the U.S., the distrib deciding that it might be interesting to make the English-dubbed version into a spoof of this type of film. To this end, special English dialog was put into the mouths of the cast, designed for satirical effect. UA devised a sales campaign which is itself a parody of the usual ideas used to sell such Herculean adventure pix.

The pic has been renamed "My Son, the Hero" and it is plain from the start why UA figured the picture would need something "special" to put it across. The antics of its hero, played campily by Guiliano Gemma, often defy credence, even for this type of escapism. But the new dialog, written by T. Rowe, proves unsuccessful to its task.

A saving grace may lie in the slick production values (uncredited) which offer very effective scenic values which are nicely photographed in color. Sets and exteriors are lavishly designed and have been captured for maximum scenic strength. This, however, does not alter the basic failing of the project which is that it is now neither effective as drama or comedy.

The campaign for "Hero" is highlighted by trailers and tv spots showing scenes from the film with special narration written and enacted by comedian-writer Mel Brooks. This material is quite effective for the spoof concept, it having unspooled for reviewers along with the pic. UA used this type of running narration, which gives comic emphasis to some of the more bizarre antics with Brooklynese inflections, to the dubbed track, the stunt could conceivably have come off. But the few cracks which have been added to the dialog are witless and there is no commentary to tie things together and so the idea doesn't come across.

To be sure, there's plenty of action and even a dose of romance as the hero triumphs over evil to reinstate his imprisoned brother Titans, do away with the demonic king Cadmus and win his lady fair. Late Pedro Armendariz sternly portrays the evil king and Jacqueline Sassard is attractive as the hero's lady. Duccio Tessari directed with sometimes excessive flamboyance and hero Gemma is often just too much to take with his boyish cleverness and physical progess.

The UA campaign for "Hero" is a solid one and it could possibly put the film across. But, all things considered, audiences will be better entertained by the trailers and spots than by the picture itself.

Kali.

New York Fest

All the Way Home

Late James Agee's autobiographical novel, "A Death in the Family," filmed skillfully and with remarkable sensitivity. A three-handkerchief film. Unrelenting somberness of theme suggests an abundance of careful "sell" required to gain general audience response.

Paramount release of David Susskind production. Directed by Alex Segal. Stars Jean Simmons, Robert Preston; features Pat Hingle, Aline MacMahon. Screenplay, Philip Reisman Jr.; camera, Boris Kaufman; editor, Carl Lerner; music, Bernard Green. At Philharmonic Hall, Lincoln Center, N., Sept. 14, '63. Running time, **107 MINS.**

Mary .... Jean Simmons
Jay .... Robert Preston
Ralph .... Pat Hingle
Aunt Hannah .... Alice MacMahon
Joel .... Thomas Chalmers
Andrew .... John Cullum
Sally .... Ronnie Claire Edwards
Rufus .... Michael Kearney
Walter Starr .... John Henry Faulk
Great-Great-Granmaw......Lylah Tiffany
Great-Aunt Sadie .... Mary Perry
Jessie .... Georgia Simmons
John Henry .... Edwin Wolfe
Father Jackson .... Ferdie Hoffman

The late James Agee's Pulitzer Prize-winning autobiographical novel, which had been dramatized for the stage by Tad Mosel, is now in screen form by way of a tastefully mounted and executed David Susskind production. It's a fine work artistically, devoid of artificiality. It is, too, slow and unrewarding for those who would prefer at least a little joyousness intermingled with such an unrelenting spate of cinematic somberness.

This is not to be construed as fault-finding in the usual sense. For Susskind, scripter Philip Reisman Jr. and director Alex Segal obviously undertook to translate the original faithfully. And this they did, Segal particularly capturing the sensitivity so manifest in Agee's writing.

It is a sad story, this account of "A Death in the Family," and there's just no room for glee although there are some humorous bits early in the footage.

The initial public exposure at the New York Film Festival was appropriate showcasing of the first order. The dignified aura of the Lincoln Center coincides with the dignity of the picture and a full-house audience if 2,300 seemed genuinely attentive and applauded appreciatively at the end.

But this was a class audience, perhaps appreciative of the film-making skills evidenced in "All the Way Home" more so than the general public. Thus it is that Paramount likely will have a time of it in its effort to score with mass acceptance. This is the kind of "arty" outing that demands

careful, even delicate, marketing approach. It may get by, but is not to be counted on a major box-office contender.

The story, largely as seen through te eyes of a little boy, is that of family happiness halted when the father, an amiable man, is killed in an automobile accident. Ensue the incredulity, the shock and then the grief as experienced by the man's wife, his and her other relatives, and the undisciplined, mixed-up emotions of his seven-year-old son.

Segal has drawn fine, convincing performances all around. Jean Simmons comes through with remarkable effectiveness as the widow who at first tries to close her mind to the fact that her husband is dead, and subsequently, tenderly, manages to live with the harsh reality.

Robert Preston, in a role which is not particularly demanding, is nonetheless fitting as the husband, an easy-to-get-along-with chap whose presence had brightened the household. Aline MacMahon is Aunt Hannah, compassionate and comforting. Pat Hingle's job calls for portrayal of the undertaker-brother of the victim, a disagreeable souse and he properly sees to it that no one will like this character. The part was much fatter on the stage.

Standout is Michael Kearney, the boy. This youngster never worked professionally before but his on-camera behavior appears to be that of a veteran, attesting to Segal's skill in calling the turns. There's none of the usual precocity, Kearney is a normal child alternately bewildered and saddened by the loss of his father, and now and then wandering into the carefree world of boys.

Thomas Chalmers, John Cullum, Ronnie Claire Edwards, John Henry Faulk and Lylah Tiffany are among the others contributing competent performances.

The reproduction of 1915 Knoxville, Tenn., where Agee was raised, is superb. Sets and backgrounds have all the appearances of authenticity, reflecting a good deal of care in location shooting of the picture.

Reportedly a full hour of footage was cut by Susskind from the finished product. Even so, the resultant 107 minutes of running time seems long, due to the absence of relief from the thermatic sadness.

Bernard Green's music is correctly faint and yet dramatically meaningful.

Overall, a three-handkerchief film. *Gene.*

Ikimono No Kiroku
(I Live In Fear)
(JAPANESE—ENGLISH SUBTITLES)

Brandon Films release of Toho (Sojiro Motoki) production. Stars Toshiro Mifune. Directed by Akira Kurosawa. Screenplay, Shinobu Hashimoto, Hideo Oguni, Kurosawa; camera, Asaichi Nakai. At Museum of Modern Art (in conjunction with N.Y. film festival). Running time, **105 MINS.**

Klichi Nakajima .... Toshiro Mifune
Toyo .... Kiko Miyoshi
Yoshi .... Togo Haruko
Takso Yamasaki .... Masao Shimizu
Ichiro .... Yutaka Sada
Kimie .... Noriko Senooku
Jiro .... Minoru Chiaki
Sue .... Kyoko Aoyama
Asako Kuribayashi....... Akemi Negishi
Kuribayashi .... Kichijiro Ueda
Ryoichi Suyama ...... Yoichi Tachikawa
Harada .... Takashi Shimura
Araki .... Ken Mitsuda
Hori .... Toranuosuke Ogawa
Old Man From Brazil ..... Ejiro Tono
Okamoto .... Kamatari Fujiwara
Psychiatrist .... Mobuo Nakamura

Like Federico Fellini, Japanese film director Akira Kurosawa is too talented a filmmaker to turn out a dull film even when his ideas seem a bit fuzzy. "I Live in Fear," made in 1955 and not yet released commercially in this country, is Kurosawa's blazing attack on the world's complacency in the face of total anihilation. Told in the terms of a wealthy old industrialist's monomaniacal campaign to persuade his self-satisfied family to move to the safety of Brazil, Kurosawa's message seems to be that anyone who doesn't fear the destruction of mankind must be mad. The kicker of the film is that the old man finally loses his mind and, when last seen, is staring at the setting sun, seeing in it the earth at its incinerated end.

Major flaw of the film is that one never quite believes—or understands—the sincerity of the old man, played in his familiar grunt-and-groan style by Toshiro Mifune, the ruggedly handsome hero of Kurosawa's samurai tales and here caked over with a lot of not very effective makeup. One might understand the old man's fears on a more personal and petty level, but, as written anyway, one suspects he is incapable of such God-like vision which makes him weep for all the world. He's a self-made, hard-driving old martinent who has indulged himself throughout his life to the extent that his family includes not only a long-suffering wife and several legitimate children, but also three illegitimate children and a couple of mistresses.

While the old man's obsession is never fully felt, his relations with his family are beautifully and touchingly realized. Kurosawa's grasp of such human relations is always sure and detailed in scenes both funny and sad. They are so vivid, in fact, that one keeps wanting to believe the old man, only to be brought up short with the realization, from time to time, that Kurosawa really isn't as interested in his characters as in the editorial comment he wants to make. That comment is valid and important but it is imperfectly articulated, at least by these characters.

The black and white camera work is excellent, as are all technical credits, with the possible exception of the makeup department. The English subtitles are barely acceptable. *Anby.*

Point of Order

Fascinating, skillfully edited "non-film," made up entirely of kinescope footage of the Army-McCarthy hearings. Should create hefty b.o. interest at selective theatres.

Point Films (Daniel Talbot and Emile de Antonio) production. Editorial direction, de Antonio; editorial consultants, David Bazelon, Richard Rovere; editor, Robert Duncan. At Museum of Modern Art (in conjunction with N.Y. film festival). Running time, **95 MINS.**

Even if, as a Museum of Modern Art publication suggests, "Point of Order" may not be strictly defined as a film, it will stand as one of the most fascinating presentations made during the first New York International Film Festival. Produced by Emile de Antonio and Daniel Talbot (owner of the local New Yorker Theatre, west side artie), the picture is an in-depth recap of the 1954 Army-McCarthy hearings, composed entirely of footage taken from television's kinescopes.

With the exception of a short, spoken prolog which sets the time and the issues, the picture sticks strictly to the record—and, what a record it is! It is one of those unbelievable - but - true American phenomena. The film not only tells the story of those hearings, and brings back such cherished characters as Joe Welch, Ray Jenkins and Sen. John McClellan—to say nothing of Sen. Joseph McCarthy and Roy Cohn, but also spotlights that era when panic and fraud very nearly overwhelmed this nation's constitutional heritage.

When seen now, nearly 10 years after the event, it's easy to understand why the 36 days of hearings so hypnotized the television public. Welch was certainly one of the great performers ever to appear on the small screen, whether coaxing Cohn to expose those 30 security risks (in the nation's defense plants) "before the sundown of this very day" or accepting a heavily insincere compliment from Cohn in a manner which, peculiarly, demolished Cohn. Opposite Welch, throughout, of course, is the figure of McCarthy, menacing and ambiguous and, at the very end, almost pathetic as his voice rants on in the packed hearing room which is no longer listening.

In a film of this kind, it's difficult to know where the praise should go, but certainly, in addition to de Antonio and Talbot, to editor Robert Duncan and editorial consultants David Bazelon and Richard Rovere. Most importantly, perhaps it should go to the anonymous tv cameramen and directors who took down all this material firsthand. Despite the fact that the material is blown up to 35m from the original 16m kinescopes, the quality of the photography is excellent—the occasional graininess or lighting uncertainties only adding to the overall historical impact. Picture should do very well in the selective theatres. *Anby.*

Samma No Aji
(An Autumn Afternoon)
(JAPANESE—COLOR)

Shochiku Co. presentation of a Shizuo Yamanouchi production. Features Shima Iwashita, Shin-ichiro Mikami, Keiji Sada, Mariko Okada, Chishu Ryu. Directed by Yasujiro Ozu. Screenplay, Kogo Noda and Ozu; camera (Agfacolor), Yushun Atsuta; editor, Yoshiyashu Hamamura; music, Takanobu Saito. At N.Y. film fest. Running time **113 MINS.**

Michiko Hirayama .. Shima Iwashita
Kazuo Hirayama..... Shin-ichiro Mikami
Koichi Hirayama .... Keiji Sada
Akiko Hirayama .... Mariko Okada
Shuhei Hirayama ..... Chishu Ryu
Shuzo Kawai .... Nobuo Nakamura
Mobuko Kawai .... Kuniko Miyake
Sasumu Horie .... Ryuji Kita
Sakuma .... Eijiro Tohko
Miura .... Teruo Yoshida

(English Titles)

As a view of contemporary middle class life in Japan, "An Autumn Afternoon" is unique among the Japanese imports to reach these shores, but it's highly unlikely that such would be enough to give it commercial interest here. Directed by Yasujiro Ozu, who enjoys a big reputation at home, the picture is too leisurely paced, too sentimental in design and its humorous social comments too infrequent, to cause much of a stir among U.S. artie audiences.

Screenplay, by Ozu and Kogo Noda, tells the story of a bourgeois widower's adjustment to coming old age, the departure of his children into marriage and the changes in a society which has apparently been very good to him. It's a gentle, nostalgic view of life which Ozu draws with some intrusively stark, abrupt camera techniques which are almost always inappropriate. Director intercuts between characters in a single scene, and between scenes, with the same tempo, totally eshewing anything that resembles a dissolve or slow fade. This might be effective depicting tension or violence but interrupts the flow of "Autumn Afternoon." Also intrusive are a schmaltzy musical score and the vivid Agfacolor.

The picture is nicely acted throughout, and does have its comic and affecting moments. There is one extremely funny scene in which the widower, who had been a captain of a destroyer during the war, meets an old shipmate who speculates on which might have happened if Japan had won the war: "We'd be sitting in New York right now, listening to the real thing (jazz). They'd all be wearing wigs and playing hot tunes on the samisen." *Anby.*

Au Coeur De La Vie
(In The Midst of Life)
(FRENCH—WITH ENGLISH DIALOG)

Franco London Sinfonia-Films du Centaure presentation of Rene Aulois production. Features Francois Frankiel, Eric Frankiel, Edwin Moatti, Roger Jacquet, Anne Cornaly. Directed by Robert Enrico. Screenplay, Enrico, based on three stories by Ambrose Bierce; camera, Jean Boffety; editor, Denise de Casablanca; music, Henri Lanoe. At New York film festival. Running time, **94 MINS.**

"The Mockingbird"
William Grayrock.....Francois Frankiel
John Grayrock .... Eric Frankiel
"Chickamauga"
Pilou .... Edwin Moatti
"Incident at Owl Creek"
Peyton Farquahar .... Roger Jacquet
Abby .... Anne Cornaly

Young French director Robert Enrico has here an interesting but not totally successful three-part feature based on three completely separate American Civil War short stories by Ambrose Bierce. Actually, the film started out as a featurette, based on the "Incident at Owl Creek" story, and was subsequently expanded into feature length by the addition of two more segs. As a curiosity, pic rates high, for Enrico has done an amazingly successful job catching the flavor of the American scene, both visually and in the original all-English soundtrack. Film's biz chances this side, however, would seem to be limited to a select group of artie houses and the film society circuit.

Most successful of the three segs is "Chickamauga," a macabre and terrifying view of war as seen by

a little boy, a deaf mute, to whom the carnage at Chickamauga Creek is no more than a wondrous nightmare. But here, as in "Mockingbird" and "Owl Creek," Enrico has tended to let his penchant for vivid imagery get out of control so that—ironically—any ideas are obscured. Also distracting and intrusive is his addiction to the tracking camera which makes every scene a bit of a rollercoaster ride for no particular purpose.

Such self-conscious techniques eventually overwhelm the cleanly simple Bierce tales and point up their lack of much below-surface substance. Technical credits are all good. *Anby.*

Charade
(TECHNICOLOR)

Melodrama, with heavy help-ing of comedy, brought off successfully. Cary Grant-Au-drey Hepburn and top produc-tion mean money in the bank. Excellent holiday fare.

Hollywood, Sept. 20.
Universal release of a Stanley Donen Production. Stars Cary Grant, Audrey Hepburn; features Walter Matthau; James Coburn. Produced and directed by Stanley Donen. Screenplay by Peter Stone; story by Stone and Marc Behm; camera (Technicolor), Charles Lang Jr.; editor, James Clark; music, Henry Mancini; asst. director, Marc Maurette. Reviewed at Grauman's Chinese, Hollywood, Sept. 17, '63. Running time, 113 MINS.
Peter Joshua .... Cary Grant
Reggie .... Audrey Hepburn
Bartholomew .... Walter Matthau
Tex .... James Coburn
Scobie .... George Kennedy
Gideon .... Ned Glass
Grandpierre .... Jacques Marin
Felix .... Paul Bonifas
Sylvie .... Dominique Minot
Jean-Louis .... Thomas Chelimsky

The guessing game suggested by the title refers to the many plot twists in Stanley Donen's "black comedy," not to its boxoffice prospects. "Charade," as the saying goes, has it made.

Completed some months ago, Universal wisely sat on this deluxe package until releasing time and temper were ideal. Already strong in the comedy market, studio reasoned delayed exposure could enhance its potential, indicating pic's strength by booking it as Christmas film in Radio City Music Hall. "Charade" has all the ingredients of success, some in spades, blended into a tasty dish that spells ticket-selling ambrosia.

Firsttime teaming of Cary Grant and Audrey Hepburn, a natural, gives the sophisticated romantic caper an international appeal, plus the selling points of adventure, suspense and superb comedy.

Director Donen and scripter Peter Stone, obviously "inspired" by the handiwork of other filmakers who have worked successfully in this genre, may not have the most original of plots or even treatments, but they can be proud of their final handiwork.

Basically a suspenser or "chase" film, "Charade" has several moments of violence but they are leavened with a generous helping of spoofery. Donen plays the taut tale against a colorful background of witty dialogue, humorous situations and scenic beauty—a style that has become known as "black comedy." Stone sometimes changes a plot situation with a single line of dialogue (as in some of Grant's exposures), which necessitates concentration on part of viewers.

While vacationing at a French Alps ski resort, Audrey Hepburn meets Cary Grant casually. Returning to Paris, she finds herself a widow, her husband having been murdered. Aware that her own life may be in danger, she appeals for help to the U.S. Embassy. There she learns that former World War II associates of her husband (about whom she knows amazingly little, one of the plot's weaker points), and his accomplices in the theft of $250,000 in gold, believe that she knows the money's whereabouts. Walter Matthau, her informant, advises her, for her own safety, to find the money (property of the U.S. government) and turn it over to him. He also tells her to contact him, day or night, should she be further threatened.

Grant, who has followed her to Paris, offers to help but turns out to be a member of the gang, albeit as much of a mystery to them as to her. Each time Miss Hepburn confronts him; with irregularities in his story, he diverts, but never completely allays, her suspicions with another "charade," or change of identity. This, plus growing romantic appeal he has for her, both attracts and confuses her.

The associates, one by one, come to grisly ends and the search narrows down to her and Grant. One plot twist is the early disclosure of an important clue to the money but one that will probably elude most viewers.

The ending, as in every self-respecting suspenser, is a dramatic surprise, with the real villain's denouement (it is *not* the butler), and continues to a trick comedy fadeout. Grant, suave master of romantic banter, makes a choice mate for the always delightful Miss Hepburn. The two two stars carry the film effortlessly, with the only acting competition coming from the versatile Matthau. James Coburn, Ned Glass and George Kennedy make an effective trio of villainous cutthroats. Kennedy's fight with Grant on a slippery rooftop is a real gasper.

Fast-paced, from the pre-title shot of a body tossed from a train to the finale under a theatre stage, "Charade" seldom falters (amazing, considering its almost two-hour running time). Violent incidents used are necessary to the plot, not merely inserted to accent the action. In the same manner, humor, while abundant, is never forced. Repartee between the two stars is sometimes subtle, sometimes suggestive, sometimes satirical but always witty. The occasional use of broader comedy includes one hilarious bit when the heroine tries to disrobe the hero so that she can search his suit.

Charles Lang Jr.'s Technicolor photography captures the charm of photogenic Paris (and some beautiful opening shots of Megeve, in the French Alps). He keeps the camerawork generally low-keyed as much of the action is interiors or occurs at night. James Clark's editing, brisk and economical, is responsible for much of the excellent pace.

Biggest disappointment for femme viewers, used to the fabulous costumes Givenchy usually provides for Miss Hepburn, is the wardrobe he has provided for "Charade." Other than the "haut couture" promise of her opening-sequence ski suit, there's little evidence of the high style so suitable to the star. Her gowns are attractive but . . .

Henry Mancini's score, as tunefully brittle as the dialog (he uses a combination of an English "jangle-box", an accordion and guitar for some of the offbeat effects), helps. *Robe.*

Makuchi
(The Idiot)
(JAPANESE)

Paris, Sept. 23.
Daiei production and release. With Masaykui Mori, Toshiro Mifune, Setsuko Hara, Yoshiko Kuga. Written and directed by Akira Kurosawa from novel by Feodor Dostoyevsky. Camera, Chochici Nakai; editor, T. Saito. At Cinematheque Francaise, Paris. Running time, 170 MINS.
Idiot .... Masayuki Mori
Friend .... Toshiro Mifune
Woman .... Setsuko Hara
Girl .... Yoshiko Kuga

Japanese director Akira Kurosawa's pic version of Dostoyevsky's "The Idiot" denotes it might have limited art chances but a personalized sell is necessary. It is okay for film buffs.

The growing audiences, if limited, for more difficult film fare, plus the recent accent on film art at the Lincoln Centre Film Fest in N.Y., could also raise interest for this pic helped by the Dostoyevsky tag. Though pic takes place in Japan soon after the last war, it is a faithful attempt to put the book on film.

Kurosawa has managed to keep the dense characterizations of the book if he has had to sacrifice too much time to filling out the narrative between some superlative moments of tense drama. The so-called idiot is a soldier who had narrowly escaped death and has been marked by this in the form of attacks of epilepsy and an ability to show complete compassion, not pity, for his fellow mortals. This has him labelled an idiot by most people. He moves in with a friend of the family and becomes embroiled with the seething needs, drama and tragedy of a group of people.

His attempt to help a desperate woman, coveted by a rich brutal man and a ruined, young man, ends in his own madness and the murder of the woman. In certain scenes, Kurosawa is able to actually shed light on conflicting inner turmoil by his expressive actors. Also a sensitive camera mixes this with subtle but telling symbols.

Masayuki Mori has the right blend of gentleness and goodness as the "idiot," while Toshiro Mifune has the rage for the hard-bitten, frustrated rich man. Setsuko Hara poignantly depicts the lost, desperate woman who brings on tragedy and madness for the two men.

It is visually excellent with its snow country backing and emotional probing giving it a mood that is in keeping with the original 19th Century St. Petersburg background. *Mosk.*

Twice Told Tales
(COLOR)

Promising horror trade item. Literary sources brutalized and details vulnerable to fault-ing, but those who go for Poe should like this bowdlerized Hawthorne.

Kansas City, Sept. 18.
United Artists release of Robert E. Kent's Admiral Pictures production. Stars Vincent Price; features Sebastian Cabot, Brett Halsey, Beverly Garland, Richard Denning, Joyce Taylor. Directed by Sidney Salkow. Screenplays, Robert E. Kent, based on stories by Nathaniel Hawthorne; camera (Technicolor), Ellis W. Carter; supervising editor, Grant Whytock; special effects, Milton Olsen; sound, Lambert Day. Reviewed at Englewood, Independence, Mo., Sept. 18, '63. Running time, 119 MINS.
(1) Dr. Heidegger's Experiment
Alex Medbourne .... Vincent Price
Dr. Carl Heidegger ..... Sebastian Cabot
Sylvia Ward .... Mari Blanchard
(2) Rappaccini's Daughter
Rr. Rappaccini .... Vincent Price
Giovanni Guasconti .... Brett Halsey
Prof. Pietro Baglioni ...Abraham Sofaer
Beatrice Rappaccini ...... Joyce Taylor
(3) The House of the Seven Gables
Gerald Pyncheon .... Vincent Price
Alice ... . Beverly Garland
Jonathan Maulle ...... Richard Denning
Hannah .... Jacqueline de Wit

A moral may lurk somewhere in the fact that of the three Nathaniel Hawthorne tales rounded

up and hacked to fit Robert E. Kent's Procrustian bed of horrors, the yarn least molested ("Rappaccini's Daughter") emerges most genuinely shuddery. Package is highly exploitable and any goose-pimple merchant can proceed on promotion on premise that this is as one of the season's better scarers.

Kent, under whose Admiral aegis film is released through United Artists, has used strong cast values in the three separate segments. His optical effects and mountings are solid, except in the last item, "House of the Seven Gables," in which the miniature exterior looks very miniature indeed. Interiors in "Gables" are okay until portraits and walls start oozing "blood," the orange-ish shade of which is more reminiscent of priming paint than the stuff quested by vampires.

In "Dr. Heidegger's Experiment" Sebastian Cabot is sympathetic and believable in the title role, although anyone recalling the original tale, done with gentle humor, of an old codger who tampers briefly with the geriatric progression of four even more elderly friends, will be nonplussed at producer-scripter Kent's introduction of such Poe-relation elements as a corpse in a wedding gown and hints of a 40-year-old triangle. In this, as in the stories which follow, Vincent Price has a chance to display the virtuosity which has made him master of the hounds of hell. He is particularly "colorful" as the demented genius, Dr. Rappaccini, who tries to protect his daughter by rearing her in a garden filled with poisonous plants and inoculating her with their juices until he himself must handle her, literally, with kid gloves. Joyce Taylor is a vivid and tragic figure in this tale, lifting it out of the "terror" stereotype into genuine drama.

Altogether, film looks to "promote" Hawthorne to the lonely heights of cinematic horror heretofore preempted by Poe. In using the title, "Twice Told Tales," the filmmakers did some more juggling, since only "Dr. Heidegger's Experiment" actually is in that collection. "Rappaccini's Daughter" is, to be scholarly, from "Mosses From an Old Manse." "Seven Gables" was a full length book.
Quin.

Rogopag
(ITALIAN—ENGLISH SUBTITLES)

Arco Film-Cineriz-Lyre Film presentation of Alfred Bini production. Music, Carlo Rustichelli. At N.Y. film festival. Running time, 125 MINS.
(1) "Illibatezza" (Virginity). Stars Rosanna Schiaffino, Bruce Balaban, Maria Pia Schiaffino, Carol Zappavigna. Directed and written by Roberto Rossellini; camera, Luciano Trasatti.
(2) "Il Pollo Ruspante" (The Range-Grown Chicken). Stars Ugo Tognazzi, Lisa Gastoni, Riky Tognazzi, Antonella Taito. Directed and written by Ugo Gregoretti; camera, Mario Bernardo.
(3) "Il Nuovo Mondo" (The New World). Stars Jean Marc Bory, Alexandra Stewart. Directed and written by Jean-Luc Godard; camera, Jean Robier.
(4) "La Ricotta" (Cream Cheese). Stars Orson Welles, Mario Cipriani, Laura Betti, Edmonda Aldini, Ettore Garofolo. Directed and written by Pier Paolo Pasolini; camera, Tonino Delli Colli.

All the furor that attended the hastily shutdown scheduled Italo preem of this film seems rather absurd—at least to a not-too-jaded U. S. reviewer. "Rogopag," a four-

part pic with episodes contributed by Roberto Rossellini, Ugo Gregoretti, Jean-Luc Godard and Pier Paolo Pasolini, is a sometimes amusing, but more often overblown, film anthology which, like a chain, is only as strong as its weakest link.

No one of the episodes is actually bad, but none is totally successful. Overall it's an uneven film, full of righteous indignation—both comic and sad—striking occasional sparks but never catching fire. With some judicious editing of each of the segs, to eliminate redundancies, it might be shaped into an acceptable artie offering for the U. S.

Most interesting episode—and the one which shocked the Italo censors — is Pasolini's "Cream Cheese," concerning an Italian film company shooting the Passion of Christ. The contrast between the story being filmed, and the characters filming it, is obviously meant to shock, especially when a poor, underpaid player, who portrays one of the two thieves crucified with Christ, dies on the cross as a result of stuffing himself on victuals from the portable commissary.

Pasolini tells his story in a series of scathing images: "angel" extras, during their lunch break, twist (boy-boy-style) to raucous rock-and-roll music next to the Last Supper table; the star playing the Virgin Mary feeds her pet pooch caviar, and the director, played by Orson Welles, views all with weary, detached cynicism. The images are made more disturbing by Pasolini's arbitrarily switching his camera throughout from black-and-white, to vivid color, to a sort of violet monochrome, and back to b-w.

The seg, which the censors found "sacrilegious," could instead, be interpreted as a sincere, if diffuse and unsubtle, attack on social hypocrisy, made particularly disturbing by the Passion background.

The other segs are equally well-intentioned—and equally overdone. Godard's contribution, "The New World," is a cold, cryptic look at the post-Bomb era, an austerly comic view of an upside-down world told in terms of an unsatisfactory love affair. Gregoretti's "The Range-Grown Chicken" is a funny, ultimately tragic broadside aimed at Mad Ave. huckstering techniques which hardly make this the best of all possible worlds. Rossellini contributes the lead-off seg, "Virginity," a slight but amusing tale of how an Italian airline hostess in Bangkok puts off an amorous American businessman who is really searching for a mother. It's good for a few laughs, but Rossellini doesn't possess the comic vision or invention of a director such as Vittorio De Sica. The fadeout is anticipated long before it's reached.

With the exception of the Rossellini seg, which looks like it was filmed on a miniscale budget, the physical production is good. Performances are more than okay, though Orson Welles, dubbed into Italian, has been given a voice sounding like Dennis Day's—if that can be imagined. Pic's title, "Rogopag," a conjunction of the first letters in the names of the four directors, obviously doesn't

mean a thing, and could very well have been "Paggoro." *Anby.*

The Wheeler Dealers
(PANAVISION—METROCOLOR)

Blue-chip farce takes stock of Wall Street doings. Garner tops in broad piece of silliness that should please everyone.

Metro release of Filmways Pictures (Martin Ransohoff) production. Stars James Garner, Lee Remick; features Phil Harris, Chill Wills, Jim Backus, Louis Nye, John Astin, Elliott Reid, Patricia Crowley, Pat Harrington Jr., Joey Forman, Charles Watts. Directed by Arthur Hiller. Screenplay by George J. W. Goodman and Ira Wallach, based on novel by Goodman; camera (Metrocolor), Charles Lang; editor, Tom McAdoo; music, De Vol; asst. director, Al Westen. Reviewed at Fox Wilshire, Beverly Hills, Sept. 18, '63. Running time, 106 MINS.

Henry Tyroon	James Garner
Molly Thatcher	Lee Remick
Ray Jay	Phil Harris
Jay Ray	Chill Wills
Bullard Bear	Jim Backus
Stanislas	Louis Nye
Hector Vanson	John Astin
Leonard	Elliott Reid
Eloise	Patricia Crowley
Buddy Zack	Pat Harrington Jr.
Buster Yarrow	Joey Forman
J. R.	Charles Watts
Mr. Wilson	Howard McNear
Giuseppe	Marcel Hillaire
Len Flink	Don Briggs
Thaddeus Whipple	Vaughn Taylor
Fineberg	Robert Strauss
Achilles Dimitros	John Marley
Arthur Watkins	Peter Leeds

Hollywood, Sept. 20.

This wild and woolly comedy isn't likely to upset the stock market, although the world of Wall Street is its scene. On the other hand, it should boost the growing career of James Garner. A comedy player of promise, he proves that he's no "maverick," even when surrounded by a small army of older and wiser zanies. The pic's blue-chip appeal should be general and wide, in proportion to its exploitation.

Martin Ransohoff's screen approach to George J. W. Goodman's novel is a matter of "there's nothing sacred in big business, kid them all!" As a result, director Arthur Hiller, whose background has been primarily the more restricted playing field of tv, has picked out too many targets for his arrows of outrageous farce, but he hits the bull's eye an admirable number of times.

The wheeling and dealing of stock manipulators, a sitting duck whose feathers were born for plucking, is the base of Goodman and Ira Wallach's nutty script. However, they also take on the wonderful worlds of colorful Texans, New Englanders, modern art, government investigations, publicity, New York taxis, even snobbish headwaiters. About the only thing played straight is the romance, and even that gets a ribbing.

"Wheeler Dealer" is an impossible character, but James Garner makes him as credible as possible—a slayer of giants. A breezy opportunist, with a quick-change set of ethics, he's equally a Texas-style Cash McCall, Speedy Gonzales and Robin Hood.

Lee Remick is nobody's idea of a stock analyst. Athough at times suggesting an abecedarian Hetty Green, bogged down in a man's world of stocks, only the romantic moments give her much on which to concentrate, the part being generally a pretty project for Garner to tackle along his merry way. She's wasted on a part in which a

promising starlet might better have been used.

The multiple characters who help the plot in and out of hot water include Jim Backus (appropriately named Bullard Bear), as Miss Remick's slippery Wall-Streeter boss; Phil Harris, Chill Wills and Charles Watts as an unbelievably rich trio who make Edna Ferber's Texans look like midgets; Elliott Reid as the heroine's art-critic boyfriend, too involved with his analyst to take advantage of "passing" opportunities; and Louis Nye, as an abstract painter whose style is less interesting in the result than in the doing.

Of the other types flitting about in the plot's background, John Astin's blood-sucking government investigator, Vaugh Taylor's bloodless New England type, and Joey Forman and Pat Harrington, Jr.'s cracked flacks stand out.

Charles Lang's color camera paints the surroundings bright and cheerful, making the most of the handiwork of art directors George W. Davis and Addison Hehn and set decorators Henry Grace and Keogh Gleason, who haven't stinted on the opulent sets, properly overdone in the best of Hollywood escapist tradition.

Tom McAdoo has edited proceedings to a fast gallop, matched musically by De Vol's sprightly score. Randy Sparks' title tune, chirped by his New Christy Minstrels, is as non-serious as the rest of the film.
Robe.

Stolen Hours

Susan Hayward remake of old 'Dark Victory.' Should give women good cry and do well at boxoffice. Love in the face of certain death.

United Artists release of Mirisch Co. & Barbican Films production. Stars Susan Hayward; features Michael Craig, Diane Baker, Edward Judd. Directed by Daniel M. Petrie. Screenplay by Jessamyn West; camera (color), Harry Waxman; editor, Geoffrey Foote; music, Mort Lindsey; asst. director, Colin Brewer. Reviewed at United Artists, Sept. 23, '63. Running time, 100 MINS.
Laura Pember .... Susan Hayward
John Carmody .... Michael Craig
Ellen Pember .... Diane Baker
Mike Bannerman .... Edward Judd
Eric McKenzie .... Paul Rogers
Peter .... Robert Bacon
Dalporto .... Paul Stassino
The Colonel .... Jerry Desmonde
Miss Kendall .... Ellen McIntosh
Hospital Sister .... Gwen Nelson
Reynolds .... Peter Madden
Mrs. Hewitt .... Joan Newell
Chet Baker .... Himself

Female audiences haven't had a good cry for a while, which will be remedied by "Stolen Hours." A remake of the 1939 Bette Davis starrer "Dark Victory," this affords Susan Hayward a performance which will surely arouse the sympathies of her femme viewers. Husbands should perhaps take that night for poker.

Director Daniel M. Petrie has shaped a smooth and slick production out of the story of a woman facing death as the result of brain disease. The film moves easily from discovery to pre-determined conclusion and gives Miss Hayward a chance to do some effective emoting, supported by a cast headed by Michael Craig, Diane Baker and Edward Judd.

Jessamyn West has written the screenplay for "Hours" and has fortunately chosen not to go overboard on the bathos. The result is a picture which moves well, with fine photography and credible performances, all of which amounts to a potentially strong b.o. contender. Although the supporting cast of this made-in-Britain effort means nothing to Yank viewers, Miss Hayward most likely remains a solid lure and the product itself is produced with the proper values to attract its audience effectively.

Miss Hayward's performance should arouse audience compassion via her deft handling of the role, which she essays with latterday restraint. As her doctor, who she eventually marries despite their mutual knowledge of her fate, Michael Craig does a solid job. Diane Baker is attractive and proves a capable actress as Miss Hayward's sister and Edward Judd is also strong as an ex-beau but still chum of the ailing socialite. Supporting players all handle their chores well also.

Photography, under the direction of Harry Waxman, is colorful and scenically often quite beautiful, a factor which adds considerably to the picture's overall effectiveness. Mort Lindsey's music also adds to the impact and other credits like Wilfred Shingleton's production designs, Beatrice Dawson's costuming and Geoffrey Foote's editing are all strong.

"Hours" is a stylish picture in design and follows the hanky formula to perfection without overdoing, as must often be the temptation. It has all the ingredients of b.o. success and should turn a winning trick for UA and the Mirisch Co. *Kali.*

Gone Are the Days

Hammer Bros. release of Nicholas Webster production. Stars Ossie Davis, Ruby Dee. Director by Webster. Original play and screenplay by Davis; camera, Boris Kaufman; editor, Ralph Rosenblom; music, Henry Cowen. At Trans-Lux East, N.Y., starting Sept. 23, '63. Running time, 100 MINS.
Lutiebelle .... Ruby Dee
Purlie Victorious .... Ossie Davis
Captain Cotchipee ... Sorrell Booke
Gitlow .... Godfrey Cambridge
Missy .... Hilda Haynes
Charlie Cotchipee .... Alan Alda
Idella .... Beah Richards
Sheriff .... Charles Welch
Deputy .... Ralph Roberts

Ossie Davis' "Purlie Victorious," legiter, which he has rewritten for the screen, follows the same pattern as the stageshow even down to many of the main actors being transplanted to the screen, though the title was changed. Hence, in many respects this is merely a screen version of the legiter. And as such it has most of the highlights and weaknesses of the original.

"Gone Are the Days" might even be called "Amos 'n' Andy with a message." The message passages seen dragged in and are the weakest part of this pic. It will require a hard and intelligent sell to do well in this country. It follows that the film is a dubious piece of merchandise for Dixie states. How much humor do white audience there manifest when a Negro kids white plantation owner and the minions of the law?

This modern fable concerns the Rev. Purlie Victorious, self-ordained preacher who returns to Georgia with Lutiebelle, his wife, for the avowed purpose of obtaining a barn and turning it into a church. He plans to secure the $500 for the purchase of said barn from Ol' Cap'n Cotchipee (Sorell Booke) who's holding this amount as a legacy from Purlie's cousin Bea (since diad). Lutibelle is to pose as the cousin who has come to claim her reward. This scheme goes awry so Purlie decides to beat the money out of Cotchipee, owner of the cotton plantation. Actually he gets his hands on the coin through the help of the captain's son (Alan Alda), who had grown up with Purlie. But Purlie tells a fanciful tale of making the captain beg for mercy and taking his bullwhip away along with the money.

Obtaining the barn, Purlie fashions it into a church, the first integrated meeting being the funeral of Ol' Cap'n Cotchipee, who has died of a stroke in the contest to obtain the old barn.

The original stageplay has been brought up to to date with references to the Supreme Court, integration, etc. Main weakness of the pic is that it still is a mixture (as was the legiter) or farce, fantasy, meller comedy and a sermon on tolerance.

Davis still is Purlie, as he was in he stage play, and the principal strength of the production because of his acting, either in farcical episodes or straight dramatics. His wife, Ruby Dee, again is Lutibelle and again is excellent. Booke is superb in the exaggerated characterization of an old plantation owner. He also was in the legiter. Alda makes a likely son of the old captain. Godfrey Cambridge contributes an amusing character as the boss Negro leader on the plan-

tation. Last two named also were in the stage production.

Nicholas Webster contributes an intelligent job as director, and also producer. He has been aided by the fine lensing of Boris Kaufman. *Wear.*

Lonely Lane
(Horoki)
(JAPANESE-TOHOSCOPE)

Hollywood, Sept. 24.
Toho Co. Ltd. production and release. Stars Hideko Takamine; with Kinuyo Tanaka, Daisuke Kato, Noboru Nakaya, Akira Takarada, Mitsuko Kusabue. Directed by Mikio Naruse. (No character names provided). Screenplay, Toshiro Ide, Sumie Tanaka, based on novel by Fumiko Hayashi and play by Kazuo Kikuta: camera, June Yasumoto; music, Yuji Koseki. Reviewed at Toho La Brea Theatre, Sept. 18, '63. Running time, 124 MINS.

Although probably too sombre in mood and deliberate in tempo for the taste of the average western cinema buff who leans to the arties for film entertainment, "Lonely Lane" is a touching and rewarding autobiographical account of the life and hard times of Fumiko Hayashi, who rose from poverty, squalor and constant humiliation to become a celebrated Japanese novelist.

Enriched by Hideko Takamine's luminous performance in the central role, the Toho production and release should be a popular item with Japanese audiences, particularly distaff customers and even more so those of Miss Hayashi's generation who will relate more vividly with the hardships she had to endure in the male-dominated Nippon of the first half of the twentieth century.

The screenplay by Toshiro Ide and Sumie Tanaki is based on the play by Kazuo Kituta from Hayashi's novel. It traces the heroine's artistic perseverance through various ill-fated romances with handsome but shallow men and meagre attempts at earning a living in occupations ranging from peddler to bar-maid. Starvation, degradation and betrayal, however, never manage to dim the underlying artistic spirit that enables her to endure these hardships and continue to write.

Miss Takamine's portrayal is a haunting one, a combination of sweetness, fragility, sensitivity and underlying intellectual spark. Excellent in support of her are Kinuyo Tanaka, Daisuke Kato, Noboru Nakaya, Akira Takarada and Mitsuko Kusabue. Under Mikio Naruse's measured but straightforward and compassionate direction, the story unfolds honestly and communicatively on the screen, although it does have a "Portia Faces Life" tone and flavor. *Tube.*

The Silence

Turning from his quest of God, Swedish writer-director Ingmar Bergman creates a film of sheer animal lust. It may be a cinematic masterpiece and it may never be licensed for exhibition in most countries.

Goteborg, Sept. 24.
Svensko Film production. Stars Ingrid Thulin and Gunnel Lindblom; features Jorgen Lingstrom. Birger Malmsten and Hakan Jahnberg. Written and directed by Ingmar Bergman. Camera, Sven Nykvist.

At Spegeln Goteborg. Running time, 105 MINS.

Unlike previous pictures in which he is investigating the human mind and looking for God, Ingmar Bergman is turning his attention in "The Silence" exclusively to the body and its passions; this is a film without God. Rather say, full of the devil.

The story is simple: Two lonely sisters—Ann and Ester ·traveling home to Sweden, make a stay in a strange town of· Timuku in a fictitious country. Everything seems a bit morbid—the town is full of soldiers, tanks, crowded cafe halls. There is a sort of prewar feeling on the streets. The sisters, together with Ann's seven-year old son Johan, are installed in an old hotel which looks like an ancient feudal mansion with stuffy majestic rooms, deep beds and mile-long corridors.

There is a strange relation between the two sisters. The older, Ester (Ingrid Thulin), is a masculine type, intellectual with a lesbian fixation to Ann (Gunnel Lindblom), a seductive, sexhungry animal. Instead of caring for her son, Ann is more interested in adventures in the town. But when she comes home she insists upon rendering a full report to her sister who listens eagerly about the love scene in a theatre. Ann spares no details.

Distressed by the adventures of her amorous sister, Ester despairs, undertakes to forget her love in alcohol and degradation.

Ester takes sick. It seems she is going to die, but Ann does not care. She leaves her sister and returns home with her son.

That is all. It is not much of a story. There is not much dialogue, almost no music but a tremendous dramatic force radiating from the screen leaves a strong impact on the audience. The sex scenes have vigor and primitive power to say the least.

The symbolism is for each viewer to determine. The film deals with animalistic humanity — in cages, quarreling, biting, dying. There is nothing pretentious and yet it may be a masterpiece destined to be mentioned years afterwards as a milestone in cinema.

Technical credits are all excellent with a special mention of the camera work and a birth of the new star: Gunnel Lindblom. She has the fury of an Anna Magnani and the beauty of a Sophia Loren; actually she is a veteran of many previous Bergman pictures. For the first time she has a big role, and has acted her part in a manner that should establish her as a new international star.

But can "The Silence," loaded as it is with daring excursions into sex, pass international censorship outside Scandinavia? Bergman would probably not permit cuts. "Silence" may remain an exclusive item for Swedes and in Sweden. *Denk.*

The Sword in the Stone
(CARTOON—COLOR)

King Arthur's boyhood in excellent animation feature. One of Disney's best but essentially limited to kid trade.

Buena Vista release of Walt Disney production. Directed by Wolfgang Reitherman. Story, Bill Peet, based on book by T. H. White; art direction, Ken Anderson; character design, Peet and Milt Kahl; music, George Bruns; songs, Richard M. Sherman and Robert B. Sherman; editor, Donald Halliday. Previewed at Radio City Music Hall screening room Sept. 27, '63. Running time, **XX MINS.**

Bill Peet, artist-writer and longtime member of the Walt Disney production company, has chosen a highly appropriate fable, the T. H. White book of the same title, for screen adaptation for the youngsters. It emerges as a tasty confection but, it must be emphasized, primarily for the moppet market.

The feature-length cartoon demonstrates anew the magic of the Disney animators and imagination in character creation. "Sword in the Stone" is in color by Technicolor and it's colorful and amusing all the way. But one might wish for a script which stayed more with the basic story line rather than taking so many twists and turns which have little bearning on the tale about King Arthur as a lad.

Key figures are the boy who is to become king of England because he alone has the strength to remove the sword embedded in a stone in a London churchyard (he goes by the name of Wart), and Merlin, a magician and prophet, who's alternately wise and somewhat nutty.

Others include the villainess Mad Madam Mim, who turns out to be a nice old dame; an English nobleman, a kind-hearted owl, flora & fauna, etc.

Wart finds himself in all kinds of trouble by way of Merlin's wizardry. He's turned into a little fish and is forced to flee from a giant denizen of the sea. Merlin then turns himself and Wart into squirrels. A little girl squirrel cozies up to Wart romantically, but latter will have no part of her.

And so the fable rambles with other transformations, finally leading to the day of the big tournament to determine who's to be king and, of course, it's 12-year-old King Arthur.

The songs by Richard M. and Robert B. Sherman are in the familiar Disney cartoon groove with such titles as "Higitus-Figitis," "Mad Madam Mim" and "The Legend of the Sword in the Stone." They're agreeable tunes and go along nicely with the animated action.

The White book, first published in 1938, has had a vast circulation. This, coupled with the public's know-about concerning high production caliber of any Disney cartoon, dountless will help the "sell."

Gene.

Chusingura

This may be Toho's most promising b.o. prospect for U.S. playoff. Powerful story with plenty of action. Exciting to watch.

Toho Co. Ltd. production and release. Stars Koshiro Matsumoto, Yuzo Kayama, Chusha Ichikawa, Yoko Tsukasa, Kumi Mizumo, Toshiro Mifune, Takashi Shimura. Directed by Hiroshi Inagaki. Screenplay, Toshio Yasumi; camera, Kazuo Yamada; music, Akira Ifukube. Previewed at Toho Cinema, N.Y., Sept. 26, '63. Running time, **115 MINS.**

Kuranosuke Oishi . Koushiro Matsumoto
Takuminokami Asano ... Yuzo Kayama
Kouzuke Kira .... Chusha Ichikawa
Genba Tawarabeshi .... Toshiro Mifune
Yozenin .... Yoko Tsukasa
Riku .... Setsuko Hara
Yasubei Horibe .... Tatsuya Mihashi
Kinemon Okano .... Yousuke Natsuki
Denpachiro Tamen ...... Ichiro Arishima
Gayboy Geisha .... Norihei Miki
Carpenter Goro .... Frankie Sakai
Lord Awaji .... Keiju Kobayashi
Otsuya .... Yuriko Hoshi
Ume .... Yumi Shirakawa
Saho .... Kumi Mizumo
Gunpei Takada .... Akira Takarada
Hyobe Chishaka .... Takashi Shimura

Toho Co., observing its 30th anni as a major film producing company, has turned out a powerful, attention-holding drama with "Chushingura," which may attract more patrons than either "Rashomon" or "Samurai." This vehicle has been so deftly subtitled that it no longer is handicapped by having all the dialog in a foreign tongue. Anyway, this is one of those rarity among foreign pictures—a production where the action speaks louder than words. Pic seems assured of being the most profitable Toho release to be distributed in the U.S.

Based on the Kabuki play, Toshio Yasumi has translated it to the screen with a swiftly-moving screenplay. And Hiroshi Inagaki ("Samurai" and "Rickshawman") has directed this excellent story with an eye always for action. He has expertly developed all details of the intrigue by the samurais as they secretly plan to avenge the death of their master, Lord Asano.

Perhaps this screen production makes the impact it does because the producers have concentrated on moving the story forward, neglecting or at least submerging the customs and extraneous details of Japanese court life in the 18th Century. This is done without overlooking the reason for Lord Asano's attack on Lord Kira and the subsequent edict that the former must kill himself.

Much of the picture is devoted to details of how Asano's loyal followers break up into small groups, seemingly peacefully accepting the wrong to the honest lord. But, all the while they are adroitly building an elaborate plan to slay the venerable Lord Kira.

The actual attack on Lord Kira's mansion takes this villainous leader and his guards by surprise. Of course, it is successful and Kira is slain exactly 21 months after Lord Asano's death.

The cast has a liberal sprinkling of Kabuki stars and stellar Toho players. Some of the standout performers are contributed by Koushiro Matsumoto, as leader of the avenging group; Yuzo Kayama, as Lord Asano; Chusha Ichikawa, as the villainous Lord Kira; Yoko Tsukase, Lord Asano's wife; Kumi Mizumo, as undercover femme operator for Asano's followers; Frankie Sakai, as the amusing corpenter; Yuriko Hoshi, as his sister; and Toshiro Mifune.

Besides Inagaki's magnificent direction, Kasuo Yamada grabs some laurels for his excellent color photography. Akira Ifukube has contributed a superior score.

Wear.

L'Aine des Ferchaux
(Magnet of Doom)
(FRENCH—COLOR—ENGLISH SUBTITLES)

Les Spectacles Lumbroso-Ultra Film production. Stars Jean-Paul Belmondo, Charles Vanel. Directed by Jean-Pierre Melville. Screenplay, Melville, based on novel by Georges Simenon; camera (Eastmancolor-Franscope), Henri Decae; editors, Monique Bonnot, Claude Durand; music, Georges Delerue. At Philharmonic Hall, N.Y. Film Festival. Running time, **104 MINS.**

Michel Maudet ..... Jean-Paul Belmondo
Dieudonne Ferchaux ... Charles Vanel
Lou .... Michele Mercier
Lina .... Malvina Silberberg
Hitch-hiker .... Stefania Sandrelli
Lou's friend .... Barbara Somers
Suska .... E. F. Medard
Jeff :......................... Todd Martin

On the basis of this production, American audiences may be hardput to understand the formidable reputation which director Jean-Pierre Melville enjoys in his native France. "L'Aine des Ferchaux" (literally, "The Eldest of the Ferchaux" but titled "Magnet of Doom" here), based on a novel by Georges Simenon, is an ordinary melodrama, unconventional only in the fact that most of it is set in the U.S. and a portion of it was actually filmed here. Name of star Jean-Paul Belmondo should assure it okay returns in the French market, but it has neither the narrative zip required by general American audiences, nor the kind of offbeat, unusual aspects which sell in the arties.

Story concerns an unprincipled old Parisian banker, Charles Vanel, who must flee France during an investigation into some of his shadier operations, and the young male secretary, Belmondo, an ex-pug just as opportunistic as his boss, who accompanies him into exile. Their flight takes them first to New York and then on an automobile trip south, ending near New Orleans where, ultimately, Belmondo is unable to carry out his original plan of stealing the old man's dough.

Characters played by Belmondo and Vanel are familiar scalawags, hard and uncompromising on the outside but predictably possessed of a certain inner nobility when the chips are down. Melville, in his direction and in his writing of the script, has not added dimension to the relationship between old and young. And when, finally, Belmondo acknowledges (too late) his obligations to the old man, the audience is likely to shrug and ask: "Is this all there is?"

Just about.

Film generates a little interest in Melville's handling of the contemporary American scene—motels, diners, Frank Sinatra's Hoboken birthplace, segregation, New Orleans nightlife—but none of it is revealing or pertinent. The locale, in fact, could just as well have been Canada or Brazil. A good deal of unintentional hilarity was provided the New York film festival audience by those passages in which Belmondo is required to speak English. It was apparently learned by rote and comes out sounding like a musical comedy dialect, successfully reducing the dead-earnest character to the status of a burlesque comedian. That's a flaw which can be corrected by redubbing, but it might not be worth the trouble, for the U.S. market anyway.

Belmondo, otherwise is okay, as is Vanel. Supporting performers, most of them femmes with whom Belmondo gets casually involved, are all good. The Eastmancolor-Franscope photography is generally fine. If the picture seems to ramble along, building little or no suspense, it would seem to be the fault of the director-scenarist, not of the editors.

Anby.

Un Roi Sans Divertissement
(A King Without Distractions)
(FRENCH-COLOR-SCOPE)

Paris, Sept. 24.

Gaumont release of films Jean, Giono production. With Claude Giraud, Colette Renard, Charles Vanel. Directed by Francois Letterier. Screenplay, Jean Giono from his own novel; camera (Eastmancolor), Jean Badal; editor, Francoise Javet. At Biarritz, Paris. Running time, **85 MINS.**

Langlois .... Claude Giraud
Precureur .... Charles Vanel
Clara .... Colette Renard

Film is a moody, literary affair with some excellent color lensing. Its penchant for talking things out, rather than being able to make it an intrinsic part of the action, makes this mainly an arty possibility abroad.

Pic takes place in a snowbound Southern French town in the early 19th Century. A gendarme comes in to investigate a series of disappearances of young girls. A crafty retired government man instills in the policeman the fact that the murderer is probably someone just like him rebelling against the dullness, smallness and grayness of this hamlet life.

The policeman finally tracks him down and kills him only to have the need to kill transferred to himself. He manages not to do so but ends up killing himself as a plaintive song scores the boredom that exists in life. On paper this tale probably had taking powers and its symbols were more easily acceptable. But on the screen this does not come across.

Director Francois Letterier shows a feel for well composed shots, helped by the expert color renditions of lenser Jean Badal who uses the snowy, foggy settings for eye-filling splashes of color or subdued groupings. But the film rarely can lay bare the intricate psychological aspects talked about.

Players are uneasy in their symbolical roles. Technical aspects are tops, however. There is a certain misty atmosphere of stifling small-town life and the dizzying effects of seemingly eternal snow. But a plodding, overblown air finally makes this more pretentious than profound.

Yank westerns have managed to make the points of outlaw and law enforcer similarities and interdependence without sacrificing revealing action to talk or forced symbolism. This pic does not have the movement of these pix or the depth to make it effective. This appears primarily a local bet.

Mosk.

Elf Jahre Und Ein Tag
(Eleven Years And One Day)
(GERMAN)

Berlin, Sept. 24.

Nora release of Roxy (Luggi Waldleitner) production. Stars Ruth Leuwerik, Bernhard Wicki, Paul Hubschmid. Directed by Gottfried Reinhardt. Screenplay, Jan Lustig, based on novel by Nigel Balchin; camera, Klaus von Rautenfeld; music, Hans Martin Majewski; editor, Lisebeth Neumann-Kleinert. At Marmor-

haus, Berlin. Running time, **106 MINS.**
Tina Rodenbach .... Ruth Leuwerik
Karl Rodenbach .... Bernhard Wicki
Tony Cameron ....• Paul Hubschmid
Fanni Gruber .... Margot Trooger
Pichler .... Wolfgang Doerich
Stumphf .... Heinrich Schweiger
Wotawa .... Georg Corten

This German film, which the American Gottfried Reinhardt directed, offers a plot that is so more or less the most oldfashioned one can ask for. The cast headed by Germany's leading film lady, Ruth Leuwerik, may lure large segments of native cinemagoers but it hardly contributes to prestige for German filmmaking abroad.

It's the old triangle of two men and one woman. The latter, Miss Leuwerik, finds life rather dull beside her overly patient and pedantic lawyer-husband (Bernhard Wicki). Eventually she lands in the arms of a handsome novelist (Paul Hubschmid) who's a friend of the couple. Her unfaithfulness becomes known to the husband when she gets involved in a hit-and-run accident. The generous husband not only shows understanding for his wife's side-leap but also protects her from the police by giving false information because he still loves her. Finally she goes to the police herself and the viewer learns that the couple, married for 11 years and one day, will stick together.

Ruth Leuwerik is a beautiful woman and a personality but her acting abilities seem limited. Her role in this film makes it again rather obvious. Wicki is nice as the overly tolerant mate while Paul Hubschmid is overly irresistible in this. The police are overly naive, and the script overly corny. Direction and camerawork appear overly conventional.

Pic was shot against the beautiful background of Salzburg, Austria. The interior scenes were partly shot in the houses of director Reinhardt and his star, Miss Leuwerik, both located in that area. There's not a bit imagination or originality about these "Eleven Years." *Hans.*

Drylanders
(CANADIAN)

Canada's National Film Board's first feature. Commendable in general though marred by surviving flavor of video for which first intended. Nature takes revenge on greedy wheat farmers.

Swift Current, Sask., Sept. 26.

Columbia Pictures release of National Film Board of Canada (Peter Jones) production. Stars Frances Hyland and James Douglas. Directed by Donald Haldane. Story and screenplay, M. Charles Cohen. Narration, William Weintraub; camera (Superscope b&w), Reginald Morris; editing, John Kemeny, Kirk Jones; music, Eldon Rathburn. Premiere at Cinema Theatre, Swift Current, Sept. 25, '63. Running time, **70 MINS.**
Liza Greer .... Frances Hyland
Dan Greer .... James Douglas
Bob MacPherson .... Lester Nixon
Ada MacPherson .... Mary Savage
Colin .... William Fruete
Russel .... Don Francks
Thora .... Irena Mayeska

National Film Board of Canada, long famous for its artistic shorts and functional documentaries, has at last moved into feature film production with this commendable second feature made entirely by and with Canadians, and filmed on location at Swift Current in Saskatchewan.

A good, clean, simple film made with professional care it tells the story of Dan Greer, a Boer war soldier who, despising his city life as a lowly clerk, moves with his family into the wide open-air freedom of the praries in 1907. After the usual setbacks in wheat growing and the hardships of building a home, the Greers eventually prosper as do the other wheat farmers in the growing community.

But greed and the misuse of the land bring about the revenge of nature. Years of drought follow, with choking dust, financial ruin, and near starvation. Families leave, a son goes to the city only to find mass unemployment, and Dan Greer dies a broken man. Soon after the rains begin and his widow resolves to start again.

This film was first thought of as a 90 minute three part television production for the Canadian Broadcasting Co. When it showed little interest the National Board decided to make it into its first story feature with actors.

Unfortunately, Charles Cohen's script still retains the earmarks of television. The result is a somewhat superficial review of the passing years in documentary fashion rather than a consistantly living and detailed portrait of the life of the Greers.

There is too much off-screen narration by the wife providing links which should have been dramatized and shown; the ending is good enough for television but too flat for the cinema; too many scenes of family life are merely set pieces rather than part of a well-developed story, and it was quite unnecessary in such a short film to bring in flashbacks on the death of Greer of scenes of his first years on the prairies.

However, Cohen's dialog rings true in most scenes, but Weintraub's commentary is hearts and flowers stuff. Certain scenes fail dramatically—such as the father slapping his son at the dinner table—because they happen too quickly. There is no indication of strain and tension, the characters move against a background of passing years but only rarely become a part of them.

The players bring considerable conviction to their parts: Frances Hyland has a distinctive voice and the right face for the role of the wife. She conveys intensity and emotional feeling in spite of the screenplay's lack of depth in drawing the characters. James Douglas gives a quiet performance as a simple man seeking an independent life, but the audience should have been closer to him during the depression years. Instead, he becomes a shadow and we feel nothing when he dies. Don Francks, Mary Savage, Lester Nixon and Irena Mayeska register effectively in small parts.

Don Haldane's direction is straightforward and lively and his use of the wide screen, mainly in closeups, is imaginative. The groupings and composition make this film better to look at than to hear. The location photography by Reginald Morris, carried out in windy exteriors and cramped interiors, is extremely good with pleasing black and white contrasts.

Special effects by Wally Gentleman are excellent—particularly the transition from burning sun to cracked earth, and Eldon Rathburn's music is always a part of the narrative and never obtrusive.

Peter Jones produced this picture at a cost of $200,000 which is reasonable for a costume picture made on location, and many of the residents of Swift Current appear as extras. Judged as a second feature it's worthy of being shown in any theatre. *Prat.*

Maigret Voit Rouge
(Maigret Sees Red)
(FRENCH)

Paris, Oct. 1.

Comacico release of Films Copernic, Titanus production. Stars Jean Gabin; features Francoise Fabian, Vittorio Saniploi, Guy Decomble, Brad Harris, Ricky Cooper. Directed by Gilles Grangier. Screenplay, Jacques Robert, Grangier from book by Georges Simenon; camera, Louis Page; editor, Sophie Dubus. At Colisee, Paris. Running time, **90 MINS.**
Maigret .... Jean Gabin
Lilli .... Francoise Fabian
Lognon .... Guy Decomble
Pozzo .... Vittorio Sanipoli
Charlie .... Brad Harris
Cicero .... Ricky Cooper

Vet actor Jean Gabin lends his inplacable presence to another Maigret pic based on Georges Simenon's literary character. Pic is solidly plotted if somewhat too stolidly directed. It looks like an okay local bet with lesser chances for foreign spots.

Here Maigret comes up against a couple of American gangsters out to knock off a witness who may send up their boss back in U.S. The FBI also gets into it. But Maigret's infallible logic and shrewdness end up setting things right.

There are some okay fights and a series of characters from upper and underworld haunts. But none can take on much life. Gabin himself has taken away some of the humanity of Maigret and made him a sort of unctuous law enforcer who patronizes rather than accepts his inferiors.

It is technically all right. But director Gilles Grangier lacks the punch to make this neatly dovetailed tale other than an ordinary one. *Mosk.*

Thunder Island
(C'SCOPE)

Crisp suspense meller filmed in Puerto Rico. Better than the average "B."

Hollywood, Sept. 25.

Twentieth-Fox release of Jack Leewood production. Stars Gene Nelson, Fay Spain, Brian Kelly, Miriam Colon. Directed by Leewood. Screenplay, Don Devlin, Jack Nicholson; camera, John Nickolaus Jr.; editor, Jodie Copelan; music, Paul Sawtell, Bert Shefter; asst. director, Frank Parmenter. Reviewed at the studio, Sept. 25, '63. Running time, **65 MINS.**
Billy Poole .... Gene Nelson
Helen Dodge .... Fay Spain
Vincent .... Brian Kelly
Anita Chavez .... Miriam Colon
Ramon Alou .... Art Bedard
Col. Cepeda......Antonio Torres Martino
Rena .... Esther Sandoval
Antonio Perez ...... Jose De San Anton
Jo .... Evelyn Kaufman
Linda Perez .... Stephanie Rifkinson

Skillfully designed and executed within the limited possibilities of an extremely modest expenditure, "Thunder Island" is a commendable example of frankly "B" picture craftsmanship — unpretentiously tailored to a supporting function but pound-for-pound, dollar-for-dollar a cut above average for its diminutive size. Filmed in Puerto Rico in relative haste, the Jack Leewood production for 20th-Fox's API wing will make an attractive and serviceable running mate, painlessly augmenting whichever of the studio's major releases it accompanies into the open marketplace.

While the picture leaves certain elements to be desired, principally in the area of emotional involvement with its characters, these lapses and unfulfillments are to a large degree understandable in view of the stringent specifications. The Don Devlin-Jack Nicholson scenario, a workmanlike original, deals with a plot to assassinate an exiled dictator. A callous assassin is hired by a small band of idealists who fear the dictator's possible return to power. In the process of botching the job, he inadvertently helps heal the marital wound of an estranged couple dueling over a way-of-life to pursue.

The film is briskly paced, wisely geared to action essentials and the accumulation of suspense. Where it fails is in the establishment of audience involvement—in the development of a rooting interest in the contest between the supposedly idealistic band of assassins and their target. The dictator is too nebulous a figure. Since the nature or motives of this debate-to-the-death remain somewhat obscure, it is difficult to become emotionally concerned for the participants. It's like going to a ball game in a strange town and not caring whether the visiting team or the home team emerges victorious because one doesn't know the players.

By far the most convincing and colorful portrayal is that of Gene Nelson as the sadistic, health-conscious, raisin-eating hired killer. Miriam Colon is well cast as liaison woman for the job, and Fay Spain and Brian Kelly are adequate as the troubled married couple. Art Bedard and Antonio Torres Martino capably head the supporting cast, mostly contrasted on location in Puerto Rico.

Producer-director Leewood has engineered a taut tempo and his climactic chase scene, executed in colorful El Morro Castle, is excitingly mounted and filmed—the highlight of the picture, icing on the cake. Resourceful photography by John Nickolaus Jr. and an expressive score by Paul Sawtell and Bert Shefter are key assists to the production. *Tube.*

Frau Cheney's Endo
(The End of Mrs. Cheney)
(GERMAN)

Cork, Sept. 24.

Europa release of Roxy (Luggi Waldleitner) production. Stars Lilli Palmer, Carlos Thompson, Martin Held, Francoise Rosay. Directed by Franz Joself Wild. Camera, Guenther Anders; screenplay, Johanna Sibelius, Eberhard Keindorff, based on comedy by Frederick Lonsdale; music, Hans-Martin Majewski. At Cork Film Fest. Running time, **96 MINS.**
Mrs. Cheney .... Lilli Palmer
Artur Dilling .... Carlos Thompson
Charles .... Martin Held
Madame Ebley .... Francoise Rosay
Helene .... Maria Sebaldt
Dimanche .... Wolfgang Kieling

"Mrs. Cheney," West Germany's feature film entry at the recent Cork Film Fest, can be described as a pic beyond the German average. But it offers little if anything

to make it an item of foreign interest. The more demanding international audience will find it rather dull.

Mrs. Cheney, the principal figure, is both an attractive and intelligent widow who seems to be perfect lady. But this, in fact, is only on the outside for her real "profession" is that of a thief. With the help of her butler, she aims at stealing the valuable diamonds of a rich old lady on the Cote d'Azur. But then she gets involved with amore, and the latter changes her. She becomes a loving woman and forgets all about stealing.

The best about the film is Lilli Palmer whose portrayal of "Mrs. Cheney" is not exactly a masterpiece yet something that also the more fastidious patron will enjoy. Her personality actually saves the film which otherwise would have been rather banal. Acting honors are also due for Martin Held as Miss Palmer's butler. Argentinian-born Carlos Thompson, husband of Lilli Palmer in real life, is a smart playboy with whom Miss Palmer falls in love. He's not at all impressive.

Direction by Franz Josef Wild has its witty moments but, in all, lacks the imagination and charm needed for such a boulevard comedy. Yet the main fault for these deficiencies lies with the script which is too routine. On the plus side is the good camera work and a fine score. Other credits are up to par. *Hans.*

Aarti
(INDIA)

Cork, Sept. 24.
Rajshri production, Bombay. With Meena Kumari, Ashok Kumar, Pradeep Kumar, Shashikala. Directed by Phani Majumdar. Screenplay, Vishwamitra Adil; music, Roshan; camera, Pandurang Naik. At Cork Film Fest. Running time, 120 MINS.

India has occasionally proved that it's able to produce worthwhile pix, too. Hence, "Aarti" proves a considerable disappointment for those who expected something in the Satyajit Ray class. While the story can be called of general interest, this production is just too oldfashioned on direction and general treatment to go far.

The oldhat fable of one woman and two men has one man, a poet, who is rather poor. The other is a medico, who is very rich but not as nice as the poet. The girl takes the former but the latter is so madly in love with her that he just doesn't give up until he realizes finally that he'll never get her.

Pic makes the impression as though it was made in the 1930's. For a slight compensation, there's s o m e interesting background music. *Hans.*

El Hombre De Papel
(The Paper Man)
(MEXICO)

Cork, Sept. 24.
Ismael Rodriguez production, Mexico City. Stars Ignacio Lopez Tarso, Alida Valli. Directed by Ismael Rodriguez. Screenplay, Ismael Rodriguez; music, Raul Lavista; camera, Gabriel Figueroa. At Cork Film Fest. Running time, 110 MINS.

This Mexican film topped the just-terminated Cork festival. If there had been a feature pic award at this festival, "Paper Man"

would probably have walked off with it. It's in many ways an extraordinary pic which Ismael Rodriguez directed, produced and scripted. The plot has charm and depth, the direction is highly imaginative and there's fine camerawork. And in particular, there is a piece of excellent acting on the part of Ignacio Lopez Tarso, the central figure, a mute, who was given the Waterford Glass Trophy for the best acting at this festival.

This film should find its way into many cinemas around the world. It's the kind of charming picture that many people will like, be it the ordinary or the more demanding cinema patron. Pic will be remembered for quite a while.

This is the tale of a poor and lonely mute. He suddenly becomes very rich and with his new wealth he seeks a companion in order to breach the dread walls of his isolation. His attempt is a hopeless enterprise because the people he gets in touch are only interested in his money. Pic tells of human thoughtlessness and the perfidy of men.

Tarso's portrayal of the mute and the latter's desperate efforts to break his solitute meant hard work. The actor had to mime everything he wanted to get across. He has turned in a splendid job. The femme lead is played by Italian actress Alida Vali. "Paper Man" was made by the director and team which made "The Important Man," also Mexican, shown at the festival here last year. *Hans.*

Nevesinjska Puska
(Thundering Mountains)
(YUGOSLAV)

Cork, Sept. 24.
Jadran Film (Zagreb) production. With Miha Baloh, Tatjana Beljakova, Jovan Milicevic, Petre Prlicko. Directed by Zika Mitrovic. Screenplay, Mitrovic and Slavko Goldstajn; music, Vasilije Mokranjac; camera, Ljube Denic. At Cork Film Fest. Running time, 92 MINS.

The Yugoslavs are not bad when it comes to war pix. This one has its plus points and has proved a big hit at home. Western viewers, however, will find it somewhat slow moving and naive. It's hardly something for export.

This concerns the famous hero of the Herzegovina, Micha Ljubibratic, who set out to free his country from the Turks. The film teems with battle sequences of all calibre, and near end it becomes obvious that the Turks are losing out. The final victory can't be long delayed. This tale occurs in the 19th Century, and the signs of the era seem well carried out.

Direction is adequate, and there is some good acting, especially by Miha Baloh, who is the hero. He seems suited for West European pix, too. *Hans.*

Under The Yum Yum Tree
(COLOR)

Jack Lemmon's tour-de-farce highlights one-joke sex story. Content meagre but has enough bait to insure b.o. success.

Hollywood, Sept. 26.
Columbia Pictures release of Frederick Brisson production. Stars Jack Lemmon, Carol Lynley, Dean Jones, Edie Adams; features Imogene Coca, Paul Lynde, Robert Lansing. Directed by David Swift. Screenplay, Lawrence Roman, Swift, based on Roman's play; camera (Eastman), Joseph Biroc; editor, Charles Nelson; music, Frank DeVol; asst. director, Carter De Haven. Reviewed at Westwood Village Theatre, Sept. 26, '63. Running time, 110 MINS.
Hogan .... Jack Lemmon
Robin .... Carol Lynley
David .... Dean Jones
Irene .... Edie Adams
Dorkus .... Imogene Coca
Murphy .... Paul Lynde
Charles .... Robert Lansing
Thin Man .... James Millhollin
Dolores .... Pamela Curran
Cheryl .... Asa Maynor
Liz .... Jane Wald
Boy Track Team .... Bill Bixby
Girl in class .... Vera Stough
Teacher .... Bill Edwin
Woman in Bus ...... Maryesther Denver

There are apt to be two basic types of reaction to Columbia's screen version of "Under the Yum Yum Tree." To the filmgoer who approaches the theatre as an emotional escape valve, it shou'd seem an easy to enjoy and comfortably glamorous diversion. Sophisticated pick-and-choosers, on the other hand, are likely to regard it as an overextended and exaggerated one-joke farce obsessed with sex not as it is but in its ersatz screen state—where everyone talks about it and frets over it but no one is ever grown-up enough to do anything about it.

Although this mixed response won't benefit, the Frederick Brisson production appears to be endowed with sufficient commercial horsepower to survive any negative onslaught and emerge a successful enterprise.

The Lawrence Roman-David Swift screen version of Roman's hit stage play is concerned with an experiment wherein two young people in love (Carol Lynley and Dean Jones) agree to determine their "character compatibility" prior to marriage by living together platonically. The project is complicated by the intrusion of the lecherous landlord (Jack Lemmon) of the apartment building in which they have chosen to reside. Virtue triumphs after a rather repetitious series of incidents in which the landlord, in hopes of eventually seducing his new female tenant just as he has her predecessors, pretends to aid her boy friend in his feverish attempts to keep the intimate relationship platonic.

As engineered by director Swift, the film's cardinal error is its lack of restraint. There is a tendency to embellish, out of all proportion, devices and situations that, kept simple, would have served the comic purposes far more effectively. For example, having every apartment in the building occupied by sexpots taxes the plausibility of Lemmon's preoccupation with his conquest of Miss Lynley.

Exaggeration has also spilled over into the areas of production design (Dale Hennesy) and set decoration (William Kiernan). Having Lemmon's apartment fully equipped for romantic pursuits is

one thing, but some of the props, notably a pair of pop-up, mechanical violins, strain credulity more than the sight gags are worth, and are resorted to too frequently.

For Lemmon, the role of the amorous landlord is a tour-de-farce, and he plays it to the hilt, but after awhile the character begins to get a bit tedious in spite of Lemmon's comic exuberance. Miss Lynley is a visual asset and does a satisfactory job as the somewhat ingenuous ingenue. Jones, who played the rather gullible boy friend on Broadway, effectively repeats his characterization on screen.

Imogene Coca and Paul Lynde register in comedy support, and Edie Adams and Robert Lansing in straighter assignments. Balance of support is adequate. Perhaps the best performance in the film is contributed by the curious and acrobatic feline that follows Lemmon around. This cat should win the PATSY, paws down.

Joseph Biroc's camera work is proficient, as is Charles Nelson's editing. There is a sprightly score by Frank DeVol and a rather conventional but serviceable title ditty by Sammy Cahn and James Van Heusen that, sung by James Darren over the main titles, has to vie for the audience's attention with a bit of sexy choreography conceived by Robert Tucker. *Tube.*

Johnny Cool

Gang butcher drama. Killing in variety of styles. Should get heavy play in action situations. Not for kids.

A United Artists release of a Chrislaw Production (Peter Lawford). Produced and directed by William Asher. Stars Henry Silva, Elizabeth Montgomery; guest stars Jim Backus, Joey Bishop, Brad Dexter, Hank Henry, Marc Lawrence, John McGiver, Gregory Morton, Mort Sahl, Telly Savalas, Sammy Davis Jr.; Screenplay by Joseph Landon, based on John McPartland's book, "The Kingdom of Johnny Cool"; camera, Sam Levitt; editor, Otto Ludwig; music, Billy May; asst. directors, Maxwell O'Henry, John Gaudioso. Reviewed at Samuel Goldwyn Studio, Sept. 24, '63. Running time, 103 MINS.
Johnny Cool .... Henry Silva
Dare Guiness .... Elizabeth Montgomery
Correspondent ...... Richard Anderson
Louis Murphy .... Jim Backus
Used Car Salesman .... Joey Bishop
Lennart Crandall .... Brad Dexter
Miss Connolly .... Wanda Hendrix
Bus Driver .... Hank Henry
Johnny Colini .... Marc Lawrence
Oby Hinds .... John McGiver
Jerry March .... Gregory Morton
Ben Morro .... Mort Sahl
Mr. Santangelo .... Telly Savalas
Suzy .... Joan Staley
"Educated" .... Sammy Davis Jr.
Mrs. Crandall .... Katherine Bard
Kromlein .... Steve Peck
F.B.I. Man .... Douglas Henderson
Bill .... Frank Albertson
Margaret Huntington .... Mary Scott
Undertaker .... Elisha Cook Jr.
"Cripple" .... John Dierkes

"Johnny Cool" should be a hot property in the "butcher" market, where zippy action and beaucoup mayhem are the first requirements. Peter Lawford's indie production has enough of both to give UA an exploitable natural.

The heavy accent on violence and murder—and the only "way out" this one overlooks is old age —should please those filmgoers who dote on destruction, whereas more critical viewers may wish that a bit more care had been

exercised in casting and writing. "Johnny Cool" is not the type of man that children (and a lot of adults) should meet—but they probably will.

Henry Silva, as a Sicilian-born assassin, is at home as the "delivery boy of death" for deported underworld kingpin Marc Lawrence. While his escapades would probably fall apart if analyzed, he puts such driving force into them that the viewer becomes too involved to dispute his actions. It's a pleasure to watch this actor move.

Elizabeth Montgomery, however, plays the emotionally and morally mixed-up heroine like a high school drama teacher demonstrating to her class how to play a nymphomaniac—10% sex, 90% self-consciousness.

Joseph Landon's script has more holes in it than a Swiss cheese but he stuffs most of them with action and director William Asher cuts the action in thick slices. Plot centers on Silva's doing a job for Lawrence which takes him from Sicily to Rome, then to N. Y., L. A. and Las Vegas before he's finished. When a doll comes into his life and gets worked over by some hoods, he adds revenge to his baser reasons for wiping out his assorted victims. They include Jim Backus, John McGiver, Mort Sahl, Brad Dexter and Telly Savalas, plus a pair of hoods who raped Miss Montgomery. Ironically, she's the one who puts the finger on him and pic ends with Savalas' gang making plans for Silva's future. But that's another story.

Excellent performances a r e turned in by Savalas, Gregory Morton, Lawrence and Backus. Sammy Davis Jr. has a first-rate vignette during a crap game sequence in which he throws some remarkable points with Silva's gun against his head. Joey Bishop eases the tension in a quick scene as a used-car salesman.

Sam Levitt's b & w photography does a good job of catching the many story backgrounds and unifying them. Otto Ludwig's intelligent editing is a big help in keeping the tale of vendetta sharp and exciting. The one big drawback in attracting the general market is the pic's high mortality rate and gruesome detailed violence.

Billy May's music has a pleasant, urbane style. Jimmy Van Heusen and Sammy Cahn's title tune, sung by Davis, is a swinging narrative of the "High Noon" school. *Robe.*

The Cardinal
(TECHNICOLOR)

Dramatic, fictional story of a Bostonian who becomes a Cardinal. Boxoffice prospects solid, might even become a blockbuster.

Hollywood, Oct. 15.

Columbia release of Otto Preminger production, directed by Preminger. Stars Tom Tryon, Romy Schneider, Carol Lynley; features Jill Haworth, John Huston, Burgess Meredith, Ossie Davis. John Saxon, Dorothy Gish, Maggie McNamara, Bill Hayes, Cecil Kellaway, Josef Meinard, Tullio Carminati, Robert Morse. Screenplay, Robert Dozier, from novel by Henry Morton Robinson; camera (Technicolor), Leon Shamroy; editor, Louis R. Loeffler; music, Jerome Moross; asst. directors, Gerry O'Hara, Bob Vietro, Bryan Coates. Hermann Leitner, Erich Fiz, Eric von Stroheim Jr. Reviewed at Directors Guild, Hollywood, Sept. 19, '63. Running time, 175 MINS.

Stephen Fermoyle	Tom Tryon
Mona Fermoyle	Carol Lynley
Celia Fermoyle	Dorothy Gish
Florrie Fermoyle	Maggie McNamara
Frank Fermoyle	Bill Hayes
Din Fermoyle	Cameron Prud'Homme
Monsignor Monaghan	Cecil Kellaway
Cornelius J. Deegan	Loring Smith
Benny Rampell	John Saxon
Cardinal Glennon	John Huston
Ramon Gongaro	Jose Duval
Father Callahan	Peter MacLean
Bobby & His Adora-Belles	Robert Morse
Father Lyons	James Hickman
Master of Ceremonies	Billy Reed
Hercule Menton	Pat Henning
Father Ned Halley	Burgess Meredith
Lalage Menton	Jill Haworth
Dr. Heller	Russ Brown
Cardinal Quarenghi	Raf Vallone
Cardinal Giacobbi	Tullio Carminati
Father Gillis	Ossie Davis
Regina Fermoyle	Carol Lynley
Father Eberling	Donald Hayne
Monsignor Whittle	Chill Wills
Sheriff Dubrow	Arthur Hunnicut
Woman Picket	Doro Merande
Cecil Turner	Patrick O'Neal
Jafe	Murray Hamilton
Anne Marie	Romy Schneider
Kurt Von Hartman	Peter Weck
Drinking Man (at Ball)	Rudolph Forster
Cardinal Innitzer	Josef Meinard

Otto Preminger's "The Cardinal" is a long motion picture—almost three hours—but for most of the way it is superlative drama, being emotionally stirring, intellectually stimulating and scenically magnificent. It is without question the director-producer's finest work.

Aside from being an artistic achievent—there are some minor flaws, unfortunately—"The Cardinal" should be a solid boxoffice contender for Columbia. It might even enjoy what the trade calls b'ockbuster business in view of the fortituous "pre-sell," so to speak, coming out of Rome as a consequence of the Ecumenical Council and the curiosity it has engendered about the Catholic Church and its hierarchy among people of all faiths.

This picture, like the Henry Morton Robinson novel that it lives up to more in spirit than plotwise, is a skillful, fascinating blend of fact and fiction. It has the ring of authority and inside atmosphere of the Catholic Church from the parish level to the Vatican on both the material and the spiritual plane. Yet, it is not (and it would take more than a three-hour film to touch upon it) so much a story of the Church as it is the saga of a man of humble Boston Irish-American origin who becomes an ecclesiastical prince.

Robert Dozier's remarkably fine screenplay overcomes for the most part the pitfalls inherent in the flashback, episodic dramatic technique. And, with Preminger's often acutely sensitive guidance of the performers, the film succeeds admirably in humanizing the clergy, from priest to Cardinal, without tarnishing their spiritual dedication.

No synopsis—unless it moved extensively and on many levels, material and spiritual in relation to family ties; politically and philosophically in the international context, and, finally, introspectively as regards a particular individual on the pastoral and personal plane—could hope to do justice to the overall story of "The Cardinal," not to mention a multitude of nuances of characters that encompass weakness, strength and guile.

Reduced to bare fundamentals, the story concerns the development of a Rome-educated American priest who has aspirations of clerical high office. However, he experiences shattering doubt of his ability to be a good priest and, indeed, if he ever had a true "call," having from his earliest memory been destined, according to his parents, for the priesthood.

Father Stephen Fermoyle's spiritual turmoil begins in the confessional, a sequence of intimate revelation which may disturb both Catholic and non-Catholic but which nevertheless is dramatically valid and conveys the awesome responsibility that goes with the authority (for those that submit) **to bind or remit sins in the eyes of God. He is confronted by his** sister, unrepentant for having slept with her Jewish fiance, in a desperate attempt to prove her love, after he was subjected at their engagement party to Irish-American religious bigotry even though he was about to embrace the "faith."

Father Fermoyle's torment—unswerving devotion to God and human agony over not having been able to ease the spiritual pain of a loved one—is further heightened when his sister hits the skids and by a party unknown is about to become an unwed mother. It's her life or the baby's, the doctor says in advising a craniotomy. This the priest has to deny on religious principles, thereby causing the death of his sister.

There are many other stages in Father Fermoyle's development as man and priest that deserve considered recounting as well. But these two incidents are his purgatory on earth, thus cannot be passed over lightly. They cause him to take a leave of absence from clerical duties for a period of two years, at a time when he is about to begin a career as a junior Vatican diplomatic functionary which would ensure the princely red hat he eventually obtains. This was the test of faith that would triumph, after much soul-searching including involvement in Austria with a girl who tries unsuccessfully to contest with the Church for his love.

At times the thought went through at least this observer's mind — how many extraordinary experiences can one man have in a life-time? However, the thought was fleeting. While it might be argued that Dozier and Preminger have come close to taxing an audience with all the unique experiences visited upon one man, it can be acknowledged that they have not taken that last fatal step into the implausible, which, of course, is the discipline of good dramatists.

As first a Vatican staffer with the title of monsignor, later Bishop, Father Fermoyle becomes involved with racism in Georgia and then the Nazi occupation of Austria, as an envoy of the Pope. In the Georgia sequence, Preminger attacks racism with brute dramatic force and in his brutalizing by the Klu Klux Klan of a Negro priest and Father Fermoyle (not officially representing the Vatican diplomatically but spiritually conveying brotherhood to a priest who had sought aid in Rome but was up against the barrier of foreign interference in United States church-state separation).

The scourging of the priest, especially Fermoyle, by the KKK, apparently is intended by Preminger to have allegorical significance and as such it serves a definite purpose. This, however, might be regarded as an arbitrary turn in the picture, depending upon what some members of an audience are willing to accept because of the volatile exposition of the sequence. The violence is deftly counterpointed by the Vatican's equation of the political and moral aspects of the situation.

The matter of nationalism and spiritual loyalty is exquisitely examined when Bishop Fermoyle is sent by the Vatican to Austria to censure Cardinal Innitzer for extending his benediction to the invading Nazis. In the delicate interplay between the junior and ranking prince of the church, excellently manifested in the dialog and acting, Preminger's direction reflects the consummate artist.

Emotionally and intellectually this interlude represents high drama in the purest form, for what greater dual purpose can a man hope to justify, as in the case of Innitzer (masterfully played by Josef Meinrad) than devotion to country and God. Circumstance, of course, completely disillusion Innitzer about uniting Austria with its Germanic heritage, but while he is honoring the letter, if not the spirit, of the message conveyed by the Vatican emissary the screen is electric.

Without faulting scenarist Dozier, "The Cardinal" is Preminger's picture for it moves on such a vast canvas—Rome, Boston and environs, New York (dockside scene only), Georgia, Vienna and back to Rome—with all the richly pictorial ritual of the ordination of a priest, the consecration of a Bishop, later a Cardinal, and the vast public excitement in St. Peter's Square for the election of a Pope. With all the vast canvas and the many individauls who appear upon it, the script might easily have been negated or lost, no matter how good, but it isn't.

Preminger also selected his cast wisely. Tom Tryon, who has the title role, plays it very well indeed, although there are shadings to the character which do not surface as might be desired. Romy Schneider is captivating as the Viennese girl who cannot disguise her feelings toward Tryon. Carol Lynley is effective as his troubled sister and also in a subsequent role as the latter's illegitimate daughter; Dorothy Gish and Cameron Prud'Homme, as the parents, Bill Hayes as a brother, Maggie McNamara as another sister, and

John Saxon, as the ill-fated fiance, take care of the intimate family circle nicely indeed. They're all natural.

There are, however, two who steal the picture as far as acting goes, and Academy members should be hard put to decide between them for supporting performance honors. They are John Huston and Raf Vallone. Seldom has any film been blessed with two such towering giants, and both play the roles of Cardinals on distinctive, captivating levels.

Huston can give up directing any day—though that would be a great loss—to pursue acting. As the American Cardinal Glennon, primate of Boston, he etches a vigorous, warmly human portrait of a man who is direct, authoritarian and one feels, deep down dedicated but obviously annoyed by Roman exclusion (circa 1917) of U.S. hierarchy in Vatican affairs. Vallone, mentor of Fermoyle, is the complete opposite an outwardly gentle, but basically resolute individual; a philosopher, teacher and diplomat, who is affectionately outgoing. His is a beautifully balanced performance.

Tullio Carminati contributes importantly, too, as a Cardinal close to the Pope. Ossie Davis, as the Negro priest from Georgia, is effective as are Burgess Meredith, Cecil Kellaway, Jill Haworth, Chill Wills, Arthur Hunnicutt, Peter Weck and Murray Hamilton.

Responsible for the exquisite photography mentioned earlier is Leon Shamroy. His scenes of Rome and Vienna, not to overlook snowscapes in Stowe, are among the finest, if indeed not the finest, the screen has offered. The combination of Panavision and Technicolor makes for truly outstanding pictorial satisfaction. For its so-far limited roadshow runs "The Cardinal" will be shown in 70m, with 35m to be used for other engagements.

Also top drawer is the work of composer Jerome Moross and music editor Leon Birnbaum and such technical contributions as those of editor Louis R. Loeffler, sound effects editor Peter Thornton, and production designer Lyle Wheeler. *Pry.*

From Russia With Love
(BRITISH-TECHNICOLOR)

Big boxoffice. James Bond involved in a ripe blend of dames and disaster. Highly recommended hokum.

London, Oct. 9.

United Artists release of Eon Production by Harry Saltzman and Albert R. Broccoli. Stars Sean Connery, Pedro Armendariz, Lotte Lenya, Robert Shaw. Features Bernard Lee, Daniela Bianchi, Francis de Wolff, Eunice Gayson, Peter Bayliss, Lois Maxwell, Walter Gotell, Nadja Regin. Directed by Terence Young. Screenplay by Richard Maibaum from Ian Fleming's novel; camera, Ted Moore; editor, Peter Hunt; music, John Barry; title song, Lionel Bart, sung by Matt Munro. Reviewed at Odeon, Leicester Square, London, Oct. 8, '63. Running time, **110 MINS.**

James Bond .... Sean Connery
Tatiana Romanova..... Daniela Bianchi
Kerim Bey .... Pedro Armendariz
Rose Klebb .... Lotte Lenya
Red Grant .... Robert Shaw
"M" .... Bernard Lee
Sylvia .... Eunice Gayson
Morzeny .... Walter Gotell
Vavra .... Francis de Wolff
Train Conductor .... George Pastell
Kerim's Girl .... Nadja Regin
Miss Moneypenny.......... Lois Maxwell
Belly Dancer .... Lella
Masseuse .... Jan Williams
Rolls Chauffeur .... Neville Jason

Ian Fleming's British Secret Service Agent No. C07—licensed to kill—better known as James Bond, cannot miss at the boxoffice in "From Russia With Love." It's a preposterous, skilful slab of hardhitting, sexy hokum. After a slowish start, it is directed by Terence Young at zingy pace. The cast perform with an amusing combo of tongue-in-cheek and seriousness and the Istanbul location is an added bonus. So, incidentally, is the peek at the Scottish Highlands where the climax is played out, and which matches up very well with the foreign locations.

Bond, the resourceful, dame-loving, debeonair, cynical creation of novelist Fleming is, again played by the tall, virile Sean Connery. He makes a pretty impressive figure as a shrewd, courageous Secret Service agent. If, in fact, that's the way they have to or do behave.

This action-packed motion picture has to do with Connery being detailed to go to Istanbul and lift a top secret Russian decoding machine from the Embassy. British Intelligence senses that this may be a trap, but getting the machine is important. Connery can pull it off if he will help a young Russian cipher clerk (Daniela Bianchi) to escape to the West. She thinks she is working for her Russian Government, but actually she is a pawn of Spectre, an international crime syndicate. Complicated? You bet. The plot is just a flimsy excuse for some topnotch escapism. All very cozy, irresistible and unbelievable.

Bond has a glorious slapup fight to the death with Robert Shaw, the killer detailed to bump him off. Guess who wins? He is hounded by a helicopter as he runs across moorland clutching the decoding machine. He beats off his pursuers in a motor boat by setting fire to the sea. He referees a fight between two jealous gypsy girls just before the encampment is invaded by the crime gang. Even in the last reel, when the audience is thinking it's all over he gets held up by a chambermaid who turns out to be one of syndicate's top agents. But he is never at a loss. And, despite all his problems, he always has time to risk the hazards of the bedchamber.

With these two pix Connery has made quite a name for himself and his only problem now is to avoid not being identified entirely with James Bond, whom he has created so well. He is well served, not only actionwise, but by some crisp wisecracking dialog by Richard Maibaum. Robert Shaw is an impressive, icy, impacable killer and the late Pedro Armendariz weighs in with a formidable, yet lightly played, performance as the man who knows the sinister secrets of Istanbul. The distaff side is less well served. Newcomer Daniela Bianchi is a goodlooking Italian girl with shapely legs and promising smile. But only in one bedroom sequence is she able to give evidence that she has some thesping talent.

Lotte Lenya has been lumbered with a part that doesn't fully come off. Instead of being sinister the character may be too grotesque even for this espionage pantomime. She plays the woman who defects from the Russian Secret Service to join Spectre. Disguised with an Eaton Crop and heavy pebble spectacles, she stands out as somebody up to no good from the first glimpse. Bernard Lee, George Pastell, Lois Maxwell, Walter Gotell and Peter Bayliss play smallish routine parts with their customary flair.

Special effects boys John Stears and Frank George, the stunt specialists Peter Perkins, John W. Mitchell and C. Le Messurier, cameraman Ted Moore and editor Peter Hunt can all take a bow for a picture which is going to make exhibitors buy new automobiles to go to the bank. Lionel Bart's title song is apt. John Barry's background music is pleasantly unobtrusive. Credits are disturbingly smart, clever, jazzy and crazy—even though the audence doesn't get around to the object of the exercise—knowing who did what? *Rich.*

The Incredible Journey
(COLOR)

Ideal picture for children from Walt Disney. Tale of two dogs and a cat who are so humanized-rendered that the humans on view are just subordinates. Even sophisticated adults ought to be impressed.

Buena Vista release of Walt Disney (James Algar) production. Directed by Fletcher Markle. Features Emile Genest, John Drainie, Tommy Tweed, Sandra Scott, Syme Jago, Marion Finlayson, Ronald Cohoon. Screenplay, Algar, based on book by Sheila Burnford; editor, Norman Palmer; camera (Technicolor), Jack Couffer and Lloyd Beebe; director of photography, Kenneth Peach; music, Oliver Wallace. Previewed at N.Y.'s Radio City Music Hall screening room Oct. 10, '63. Running time, **86 MINS.**

John Longridge ...... Emile Genest
Professor Jim Hunter..... John Drainie
The Hermit .... Tommy Tweed
Mrs. Hunter .... Sandra Scott
Helvi Nurmi .... Syme Jago
Elizabeth Hunter.......Marion Finlayson
Peter Hunter .... Ronald Cohoon
James MacKenzie .... Robert Christie
Nell MacKenzie .... Beth Lockerbie
Carl Nurmi .... Jan Rubes
Mrs. Nurmi .... Irena Mayeska
Mrs. Oakes .... Beth Amos
Bert Oakes .... Eric Clavering

Sheila Burnford's book of the same title has been given a vivid translation in "The Incredible Journey." The Walt Disney presentation is an exceptionally good, colorful adventurous tale for the younger element.

And while the kids doubtless will be enraptured with this recounting of what is indeed an incredible journey for two dogs and a cat, the live actioner, exquisitely photographed in the Canadian outdoors, has its moments of excitement for adults as well.

A bull terrier, Siamese cat and Labrador retriever comprise the unlikely trio of pals who, farmed out to a friend of their owners, embark on the journey—over 200 miles of treacherous terrain. They encounter crisis after crisis in what is a remarkable, nay incredible, fight to survive all sorts of adversities in their trip all the way home.

Kenneth Peach as director of photography has on display a wide range of camera assets, most importantly the scenic values of the Canadian high country, and with photographers Jack Couffer and Lloyd Beebe, the Technicolored widescreened diary of what alledgedly actually happened is a pictorial delight.

Director Fletcher Markle, with the assist of an animal trainer, has gotten an abundance of child-appealing excitement on the screen. And he sees to it that the story is told simply and directly, what with the humans on view exchanging dialog in honest fashion and an offscreen commentary by Rex Allen.

Emile Genest, John Finlayson and Ronald Cohoon are among the cast members. They all reflect professional knowhow. But the astutely-guided animals steal the show, thanks largely to an appealing screenplay by coproducer James Algar and Markle's success in getting the thrills on the screen.

Music by Oliver Wallace takes many symphonic twists and turns and on the overall is a top-drawer contributiton. *Gene.*

Take Her, She's Mine
(C'SCOPE-COLOR)

Diverting comedy for easygoing family trade. Satisfactory b.o. looms.

Hollywood, Oct. 9.

Twentieth-Fox release of Henry Koster production. Stars James Stewart, Sandra Dee; features Audrey Meadows, Robert Morley, Philippe Forquet, John McGiver. Directed by Koster. Screenplay, Nunnally Johnson, based on play by Phoebe and Henry Ephron; camera (De Luxe), Lucien Ballard; editor, Marjorie Fowler; music, Jerry Goldsmith; asst. director, Joseph E. Rickards. Reviewed at studio, Oct. 9, '63. Running time, **98 MINS.**

Frank Michaelson .... James Stewart
Mollie .... Sandra Dee
Anne Michaelson.......Audrey Meadows
Pope-Jones .... Robert Morley
Henri .... Philippe Forquet
Mr. Ivor .... John McGiver
Alex .... Robert Denver
Linda .... Monica Moran
Adele .... Cynthia Pepper
Sarah .... Jenny Maxwell
M. Bonnet .... Maurice Marsac
Miss Wu .... Irene Tsu
Liz .... Charla Doherty
Policeman .... Marcel Hillaire
Stanley Bowdry .... Charles Robinson
Mme. Bonnet .... Janine Grandel

The screen version of "Take Her She's Mine" is an improvement over the Phoebe and Henry Ephron stage play from which it springs, even though several of the revisions and additions dreamed up by scenarist Nunnaly Johnson are quite contrived and far from fresh. The visual advantages of film—its ability to divert an audience with colorful settings, glamorous people observed intimately, and action that is witnessed rather than referred to—are shrewdly exploited by director-producer Henry Koster in the case of "Take Her, She's Mine." These diversionary factors save the day.

The difficulty encountered by an older generation in comprehending the behavior of a younger generation is the business explored in this comedy. More specifically, one father's trials and tribulations when he packs his precious daughter off to college and observes, in long distance dismay with an occasional globe-trot for closer inspection, her transition from adolescent to young woman.

Unfortunately, both the collegiate audience and the sharper, more sophisticated customer will

take one look at sweet little Sandra Dee and the character she is playing and fail to appreciate "dad" James Stewart's constant misgivings. Obviously she is not *that* kind of girl, a fact of which only her father seems unaware. This, plus the tendency to distort characterization and strain credulity for the sake of a quick gag, plus the shopworn, predictable nature of the chief comedy situations are apt to scare off these more discriminating patrons.

On the other hand, the film should attract the easygoing "family" trade. Middle-aged and more elderly filmgoers figure to relate to the character played so infectiously by their old favorite, Stewart. And they will be inclined to overlook the character distortions and inconsistencies, and settle for the sheer diversion of it all. The picture won't burn up the boxoffice, but it should do all right.

An occasional dash of the "Tammy" whammy seeps into Miss Dee's characterization, but on the whole she's effective. Travilla's gowns ,however, are not always becoming to her. Audrey Meadows, a gifted comedienne, is wasted in the bland and barren role of Stewart's wife. Robert Morley, though in the somewhat irrelevant role of a jaded Britisher, has some of the best lines in the film (scenarist Johnson's dialog is sporadically sharp and funny) and delivers them as only he can.

Young Philippe Forquet is a handsome Gallic newcomer to Hollywood filmdom, but his emoting range at the moment is not exactly extensive, at least in this vehicle. However, his looks should pave the way for new opportunities. John. McGiver is especially valuable in support, and others of momentary import are Robert Denver, Monica Moran, Cynthia Pepper, Jenny Maxwell, Maurice Marsac, Irene Tsu, Charla Doherty, Marcel Hillaire, Charles Robinson and Janine Grandel.

Koster keeps the action hopping along even when the script is less than inspired, and consistently exploits cinematic possibilities. He has been stalwartly aided in this regard by cameraman Lucien Ballard and editor Marjorie Fowler. Art direction by Jack Martin Smith and Malcolm Brown is generally tasteful and functional, without any special flair. Jerry Goldsmith has contributed a whimsical score ,especially helpful in a costume party sequence that needs all the help it can get. *Tube.*

Germinal
(FRENCH-DYALIŞCOPE)

Paris, Oct.8.

Cocinor release of Marceau-Cocinor, Metzger & Woog, Laetitia production. With Jean Sorel, Claude Brasseur, Berthe Grandval, Bernard Blier, Lea Padovani, Simone Valere, Philippe Lemaire, Claude Cerval. Directed by Yves Allegret. Screenplay, Charles Spaak from novel by Emile Zola; camera, Jean Bourgoin; editor, Henri Rust. At Paris, Paris. Running time, **110 MINS.**

Etienne	Jean Sorel
Catherine	Berthe Grandval
Chaval	Claude Brasseur
Director	Bernard Blier
Mother	Lea Padovani
Clotilde	Simone Valere
Engineer	Philippe Lemaire
Grocer	Claude Cerval

Emile Zola's classic tale of a strike in a coal mine in Ninteenth Century France was made by local producers and filmmakers in Hungary. The Hungarians supplied extras, some actors and the technical facilities. French gave the classical story as well lead actors, the writer and director. The Hungarian contribution came out best because this is an academic filming of the novel, and looms mainly a local entry.

The settings of a small coal mine town back in 1863 have a good period flair and there is an impressive use of extras in the strike scenes. But director Yves Allegret has rarely been able to get the intensity in projecting this tale to make it more than a period social melodrama. He is also hampered by an ordinary script which removes much of the fire and depth of the original Zola tome.

Main actors are somewhat flat, interpreting their roles in methodical manner. A young man (Jean Sorel) comes to town and gets a job in a coal mine. He tries to have the exploited miners strike for their rights. They do and lose out, but film ends by pointing up that this was the first germinating step (this explains the title) for later strides.

And in this, the hero falls for a coal miner's daughter, the director of the mine is beset by a cheating wife and the town's women finally raid the grocery store of a lecherous owner. There is also a look at the overcrowding and the work drudgery of the time.

But all this lacks the drive to keep it from seeming old fashioned. Sorel lacks the fervor for his role as the strike leader. Berthe Grandval has sufficient beauty if a bovine appearance as the girl who cannot break tradition for love until impending death forces her to it.

Other roles are well done if they are more largely stereotypes. So this fresco may appeal to locals on the Zola name. But there is a dearth of true dramatic flair and comment on this period to make it more than a dualer item for the U. S. It is technically fine. *Mosk.*

Cry Of Battle

Plodding war meller with Philippine setting. Needs trimming for action market suitability.

Hollywood, Oct. 7.

Allied Artists release of Joe Steinberg production. Stars Van Heflin, Rita Moreno, James MacArthur. Directed by Irving Lerner. Screenplay, Bernard Gordon, from Benjamin Appel's novel, "Fortress in the Rice"; camera, Felipe Sacdalan; editor, Verna Fields; music, Richard Markowitz; asst. director, Jose Dagumboy. Reviewed at the studio, Oct. 7, '63. Running time, **99 MINS.**

Joe Trent	Van Heflin
Sisa	Rita Moreno
David McVey	James MacArthur
Manuel Careo	Leopoldo Salcedo
Col. Ryker	Sidney Clute
Pinang	Marilou Munoz
Atong	Oscar Roncal
Vera	Liza Moreno
Capt. Davis	Michael Parsons
Matchek	Claude Wilson
Capt.. Garcia	Vic Solynn

Best bet would be to trim this one down to absolute story essentials, thus sharpening the pace and making it more fit for the action market, where the customers are inclined to grow impatient if there is too much gab and romantic mush between the bursts of combat.

An earthy, colorful "heavy" performance by Van Heflin is about the only thing that distinguishes this opaque, bulky and confusing war melodrama produced by Joe Steinberg and directed rather disjointedly by Irving Lerner from B e r n a r d Gordon's haphazard screenplay. Source of it all is Benjamin Appel's novel, "Fortress In The Rice."

The picture, originally titled "To Be A Man," concerns the plight of a naive, inexperienced lad (James MacArthur) who has the misfortune to arrive in the Philippines on Dec. 8, 1941, the same day the Japanese arrive. Balance of the film describes his running misadventure with an uncouth, unsavory brute (Heflin) whose philosophy is simple enough—"you fight when you got to, you get a dame when you can, that's about it." The "dame" is Rita Moreno, and to get her he has to fight with MacArthur. Since he's already fighting the Japanese, the Filipino guerrillas and himself, it doesn't take a spectator long to figure Heflin's destiny.

MacArthur seems to be stuck in a "sensitive, green lad" casting groove. He's got it down pretty good, but merits a change of pace. For Miss Moreno, this is a steep dip in class from her superlative 'Anita' of "West Side Story." She, too, deserves better roles than Latin-flavored Filipinoritas.

The supporting cast is adequate and so, in general, are the production contributions, chief among which are Felipe Sacdalan's able lensmanship and Richard Markowitz's music, heavy on the plaintive flute and guitar. Editor Verna Fields could excise another 20-25 minutes and make "Cry of Battle" a better film. *Tube.*

Le Magot De Josefa
(Josefa's Loot)
(FRENCH-FRANSCOPE)

Paris, Oct. 15.

Valoria release of SOPAC-Productions Raimbourg-Star Presse-Arco Film production. Stars Anna Magnani, Bourvil, Pierre Brasseur; features Christian Marin, Maryse Martin, Gil Vidal. Directed by Claude Autant-Lara. Screenplay, Jean Aurenche, Pierre Bost, Bernard Dimey from novel by Catherine Claude; camera, Jacques Natteau; editor, Madeleine Gug. At Balzac, Paris. Running time, **90 MINS.**

Josefa	Anna Magnani
Corneille	Bourvil
Mayor	Pierre Brasseur
Cure	Gil Vidal

Anna Magnani is allowed to run her gamut of passionate anger, open desire and gurgling laughter in this one. But the rather arch satire on provincial life and human foibles is not up to her antics and starred presence here. In spite of a leading local comic alongside her, Bourvil, Miss Magnani's first French film appears mainly a local, item with only possibly dualer or specia situations abroad via her name.

Miss Magnani is a grocery store owner in a little French provincial town. She's from a poor family that migratede from Italy. In her poor girlhood she had spawned a son with the local mayor who now disowns her. A supposed great sum of money from an American gangster relative has the whole town suddeenly respecting her.

Petty, gossipy village types are rather overly blocked out in stereotype with general direction, playing and use not able to give them much weight. Miss Magnani is set upon by a city man who claims her son, long gone from her, will go to prison if she does not honor a bad check.

She then admits her lack of money, and turns on the fawning townspeople and the selfish mayor. All leads to her losing her shop, burned down by the enraged villagers, and her going off with the would-be check collector who is really her son's partner.

Production paints everything broadly and makes for caricature rather than poignance or satiric depth from its accomplished cast. Mark this as an unsavory bucolic affair. Technically it is okay. Bourvil is a comic help and Pierre Brasseur hams it up rightly as the egotistic mayor. *Mosk.*

West 11
(BRITISH)

Exploration of seamy side of London life. Directed with little depth, it has probably come too late in the cycle and with slight marquee value. Tentative boxoffice prospect.

London, Oct. 9.

Warner-Pathe release of Associated-British's presentation of a Daniel M. Angel production. Stars Alfred Lynch, Kathleen Breck, Eric Portman, Diana Dors. Directed by Michael Winner. Screenplay by Keith Waterhouse & Willis Hall, based on the novel, "The Furnished Room," by Laura Del Rivo; camera, Otto Heller; music, Stanley Black; title theme by Black & Acker Bilk, played by Bilk; editor, Bernard Gribble. Viewed at Century Theatre, London, Oct. 8, '63. Running time, **93 MINS.**

Joe Beckett	Alfred Lynch
Ilsa Barnes	Kathleen Breck
Richard Dyce	Eric Portman
Georgia	Diana Dors
Mrs. Beckett	Kathleen Harrison
Mrs. Hartley	Freda Jackson
Mr. Gash	Finlay Currie
Silent	Harold Lang
Jacko	Peter Reynolds
Larry	Sean Kelly
Mr. Royce	Alan McClennard

Maybe it's time that the success ful writing team of Keith Waterhouse and Willis Hall should take stock. This most prolific and usually creative duo did little to uplift this film, "West 11," an adaptation of a novel called "The Furnished Room." The London district "West 11" has been involved, in the racial problem. Though not an original theme, the undoubted talent of Messrs. Waterhouse and Hall might well have brought a little more insight light on that social problem

This is only hackneyed drama about a young man who is a layabout, a misfit, a self-pitier ("I'm an emotional leer," he says, profoundly). He gets involved with chicks, can't keep a job and gets mixed up with jazz clubs and seedy parties. Turning point in his life is when he meets up with Richard Dyce (Eric Portman), an ex-Army con-man, in his way as obviously spurious as the character Portman played in "Separate Tables." The young man, played with a mournful gloom by Alfred Lynch, thinks that he can only get back to a reasonable life by getting a violent emotional shock. So he is talked into an association with Portman, who wants his aunt bumped off. Perfect murder. Stranger to shoot stranger. No connections. Lynch falls for the complicated setup, goes to the South Coast, loses his nerve, fails to shoot the victim, but accidentally pushes her down the stairs. Death.

He just happened to have his

miniature chessboard with him and it just happens to have fallen next to the corpse as he scurries away. A police squealer is in action so he gives himself up and frankly the audience won't care a bit.

It has its merits. The sleazy locations are very authentically shown. Perhaps too authentically. They have also been photographed impeccably, as usual, by Otto Heller. Lynch is an intelligent actor but, in this instance, he fails to induce any pity. Probably the fault of the script. Kathleen Breck, his girl friend, copes reasonably. It's her first film part after a small experience in stock, but her minor talent will certainly flower. Portman, Kathleen Harrison, as Lynch's mother, Freda Jackson, Marie Ney, Finlay Currie, Peter Reynolds and a maturing, but much more capable Diana Dors, all give their professional stamp to parts that are mostly hollow. But Harold Lang as Silent, the police squealer, steals the honors. In his brief appearances he really does make an oily, impressive impact.

Director Michael Winner, a young man, making his third film, uses Ken Colyer's band and the Tony Kinsey Quartet to rollicking effect. *Rich.*

Three Plus Two
(RUSSIAN)

Cork, Oct. 8.
Gorky and Riga Studios production. With Natalia Fateyeva, Natalia Kustinskaya, Andrei Mironov, Yevgeny Zharkov. Directed by N. Nikolaevich. Camera, U. Postnikov; music, A. Volkonsky; screenplay, S. Mihhalkov. At Cork Film Fest. Running time, **98 MINS.**

As per its amusing plot and gay atmosphere, this Russian film reminds of the same country's "Girls" which, incidentally, was a Soviet entry at last year's Cork festival. It's a simple, light-plotted pic which is seen and forgotten, but which is enjoyable at the time. Bulk of average patrons will find it excellent entertainment. Nothing special for export on a broad basis, yet chances are given it to sled into western markets.

Screenplay leads the viewer to the shores of the Black Sea. There are three young men who have pitched their camp at a beautiful spot. Then come two girls who want to settle on the same location, claiming they have priority because they have been camping there before. The boys show a natural dislike for such anti-social behavior, and don't give in. After a period of hostility and some amusing episodes resulting from the fact that the two parties settle down with an iron curtain of empty cans between the two "lands," there's the conventional happy ending in the form of love.

Direction is refreshingly unpretentious if perhaps somewhat slow. Acting is pleasing while technical credits are good. *Hans.*

Il Boom
(The Boom)
(ITALIAN)

Rome, Oct. 8.
Dino DeLaurentiis production and release. Stars Alberto Sordi; features Gianna Maria Canale, Elena Nicolai, Ettore Ceri, Mariolina Bovo, Gloria Cervi. Directed by Vittorio DeSica. Story and screenplay, Cesare Zavattini; camera, Armando Nannuzzi; editor, Adriana Novelli. At Adriano, Rome. Running time, **97 MINS.**

Giovanni Alberti .... Alberto Sordi
Silvia Alberti ...... Gianna Maria Canale
Mrs. Bausetti .... Elena Nicolai
Mr. Bausetti .... Ettore Ceri
Mrs. Faravalli .... Mariolina Bovo
Mrs. Baratti .... Gloria Cervi
Mrs. Dronazzi .... Sandra Verani
Mr. Baratti .... Sandro Merli
Mr. Dronazzi .... Alceo Barnabei
Faravalli .... Antonio Mabratti

Vittorio DeSica's latest pic is a primarily commercial entry (especially on home territory) which should bring in handsome returns for producer Dino DeLaurentiis. The Alberto Sordi name remains the major lure, and since he's currently riding the crest of the wave, this factor is strong enough to overcome the film's obvious faults.

Viewed more specifically, the film's weakness is basic—an anecdote has been blown up out of proportion. Cesare Zavattini's grotesque but potentially valid story of a man who sells one eye to cover his business debts and deficits—and so that his wife won't know he's a failure—loses its impact as well as its beliveability where extended over 90 minutes playing time.

In less capable hands, the anecdote would have shattered miserably. DeSica and Sordi manage most of the time to keep it going with neat touches or trade tricks. Sordi's role is tailormade, and though he rarely touches the human aspects of his plight, his savvy gets him through most situations. He has good assistance from Gianna Maria Canale, a beauty usually wasted on lesser epic roles, as his wife, from Elena Nicolai and Ettore Ceri, as the couple who buy the eye, and by others in a large cast. Technical credits are all good.

Topical aspects implied in title —the Italo economic boom are likewise used to good ironic effect in this grotesque, serio-comic production. *Hawk.*

The Gun Hawk
(COLOR)

Routine western.

Hollywood, Oct. 8.
Allied Artists release of Richard Bernstein production. Stars Rory Calhoun, Rod Cameron, Ruta Lee, Rod Lauren. Directed by Edward Ludwig. Screenplay, Jo Heims, from story by Bernstein and Max Steeber; camera (De Luxe), Paul Vogel; editor, Rex Lipton; music, Jimmy Haskell; asst. directors, Ralph Slosser, Arthur Broidy. Reviewed at studio, Oct. 8, '63. Running time, **92 MINS.**
Madden .... Rory Calhoun
Corey .... Rod Cameron
Marleen .... Ruta Lee
Roan .... Rod Lauren
Mitchell .... Morgan Woodward
Johnny Flanders .... Robert J. Wilke
Drunk .... John Litel
Miguel .... Rodolfo Hoyos
Joe Sully .... Lane Bradford
Luke Sully .... Glenn Stensel
Roan's Woman .... Joan Connors
Blackjack .... Ron Whelan
Pancho .... Lee Bradley

Although the market for theatrical westerns seems to have dwindled considerably since the plethora of television oaters several seasons back, there's always a hard core of diehards eager to receive a color sagebrusher on the big screen. But even the most ardent buffs are apt to find this one gruelling and contrived. Richard Bernstein production for Allied Artists drags to a hokey, predictable conclusion. Several reliable actors labor in vain to bring it to life.

Rory Calhoun stars in the Jo Heims screenplay, from a story by Bernstein and Max Steeber, as an outlaw with a streak of decency. Early in the film he crosses paths with a wild young gunslinger (Rod Lauren). and it doesn't take an experienced filmgoer to foresee that Calhoun will "see himself 10 years ago" in the younger man and ultimately attempt to reform him. After slaying a couple of desperadoes, Calhoun is winged in the arm, by a pursuing sheriff (Ron Cameron) and returns to the town of Sanctuary, a haven for lawbreakers which he controls. In the final half of the film, Calhoun slowly dies of an infection from the wound. Finally, unwilling to perish in bed, he forces his young friend, Lauren, to engage him in a fast draw showdown. The reluctant Lauren, bullied into it, drills him dead. As sheriff Cameron slowly rides away with Lauren, he explains to the shaken lad that, "it meant a great deal to him (Calhoun) to die with his own kind of dignity."

Calhoun plays with his usual soft-spoken authority and is a fairly appealing figure in the first half, but is plastered with ghastly makeup and snowed under by the script in the latter half. Lauren has his moments as the confused lad. Cameron, as the sheriff, and Morgan Woodward, as a deputy on a vendetta, are stuck in two-dimensional and ineffectual roles. Ruta Lee supplies romantic interest. John Litel has a telling scene as a drunk, and Robert J. Wilke registers as a villain.

Neither Edward Ludwig's direction nor Rex Lipton's editing has corrected the lethargy of the latter portions. Tauter splicing might still help. Paul Vogel's lenswork is generally competent, although vantage points and distances are not always clear. Jimmy Haskell's musical score has occasional flair and novelty, but a humdrum heartbeat-like sound begins to grow oppressive. "A Searcher for Love," a tune by Robert P. Marcucci and Russ Faith sunk over the titles, has an exploitable teenage-appeal sound to it. *Tube.*

Captain Newman, M.D.
(COLOR)

Sugarcoated army hospital drama. Doses of comedy and sentiment should broaden b.o. range, but tend to dilute overall dramatic impact. Still, pic looms as solid moneymaker.

Hollywood, Oct. 15.
Universal release of Robert Arthur production. Stars Gregory Peck, Tony Curtis; features Angie Dickinson, Bobby Darin. Directed by David Miller. Screenplay, Richard L. Breen. Phoebe and Henry Ephron, from Leo Rosten's novel; camera (Eastman), Russell Metty; editor, Alma Macrorie; music, Frank Skinner; assistant director, Phil Bowles. Reviewed at Hollywood Paramount Theatre, Oct. 15, '63. Running time, **126 MINS.**
Capt. Josiah Newman .. Gregory Peck
Corp. Jackson Laibowitz ... Tony Curtis
Lt. Francie Corum .... Angie Dickinson
Col. Bliss .... Eddie Albert
Col. Pyser .... James Gregory
Helene Winston .... Bethel Leslie
Capt. Winston .... Robert Duvall
Lt. Grace Blodgett .... Jane Withers
Lt. Anderson .... Dick Sargent
Gavoni .... Larry Storch
Lt. Col. Larrabee ...... Robert F. Simon
Sgt. Kopp .... Syl Lamont
Werbel .... Paul Carr
Maj. Alfredo Fortuno..... Vito Scotti
Maj. Gen. Snowden ... Crahan Denton
Capt. Howard .... Gregory Walcott
Gorkow .... Charles Briggs
Cpt. Tomkins .... Bobby Darin

Universal has a potent boxoffice contender in "Captain Newman, M.D." The Robert Arthur production is certain to be popular with the filmgoer who seeks escape and diversion. More discerning audiences, however, may be less receptive to the picture's glamorized eye-view of heroics at an army base hospital in 1944.

"Captain Newman, M.D." oscillates between scenes of great dramatic impact and somewhat strained and contrived comedy of the "heartwarming" variety. Thus, what might have been a provocatively realistic dramatization of a dedicated psychiatric doctor's attempts to heal the emotional injuries of servicemen scarred by war is reduced to the common denominator of lukewarm popular entertainment. Commercially, the decision appears sound. Yet there is no telling whether the economic results might have been even more impressive had a more honest artistic course been pursued. The foundations were there.

Leo Rosten's novel was the source of the hot-and-cold scenario by Richard L. Breen and Henry Ephron. Hero of the story is Capt. Newman (Gregory Peck), chief of the neuro-psychiatric ward of a wartime army hospital who places his medical obligations above military duty, to the sometimes consternation of his superiors who would prefer to see his patients returned to combat areas at a brisker clip. Newman's treatment of three cases is illustrated. One involves a decorated corporal (Bobby Darin) who believes himself a coward for having deserted a buddy in a burning aircraft. Another concerns a colonel (Eddie Albert) who has gone beserk with a sense of guilt at having sent so many men to their deaths in aerial

combat. The third (Robert Duvall) feels shame over having hidden alone in a cellar for over a year in Nazi-occupied territory. In between all of this, Newman gets his kicks in a romance with his nurse (Angie Dickinson) and by observing the antics of his number one orderly (Tony Curtis) a glib, resourceful operator from Jersey City with a streak of Bergen County larceny.

Peck's portrayal of the title figure is characteristically restrained and intelligent. Perhaps his best scene, oddly enough, is the one in which he is quietly but expressively reacting to Darin's high-powered histrionics. It is also the film's most deeply moving passage and, in addition to serving as a boxoffice stimulant via word-of-mouth, may earn for Darin a supporting nomination in the Oscar derby. In it, Darin, under the influence of truth serum, convulsively re-creates the incident for which he brands himself a coward.

Curtis has some good moments, but essentially he is the pivotal figure in the film's secondary comic shenanigans, the portions that, being somewhat contrived and excessively sentimental, subtract from the potential of the whole—for instance, a Christmas party sequence that concludes the picture on a near-maudlin note. Basically, Curtis is playing a kind of Ensign Pulver to Peck's Mister Roberts—in addition to faint overtones of Fred Demara that seep into his characterization.

Miss Dickinson is sweet, sometimes too darned sweet, as the nurse. Russell Metty's inquisitive, never-miss-a-trick lens seizes every opportunity to pick up the Dickinson gam action, which males in the audience won't mind. The hysterical character essayed by Albert doesn' completely add up. Duvall, of "Boo Radley" fame in "Mockingbird," has a role of similar specifications. Bethel Leslie is adequate in the hastily-resolved role of his pride-smitten wife. Jane Withers has come out of retirement to enact the inconsequential part of a nurse—a character that might have some significance on the cutting room floor. Noteworthy comic support is provided by Larry Storch. The rest of the cast performs capably.

Give or take some dubious behavior here and there that could have been sensed and deleted, director David Miller has handled his assignment skillfully. Entertainment is the cardinal aim, and entertainment is what he has executed. The film could still be improved with some judicious trimming, but editor Alma Macrorie has done a nimble job of meshing comic and dramatic elements. Art directors Alexander Golitzen and Alfred Sweeney have mounted a convincing replica of a base hospital, circa 1944. Frank Skinner's musical score is unobtrusively atmospheric. *Tube.*

Il Successo
(Success)
(ITALO-FRENCH—SONGS)

Rome, Oct. 15.

Titanus release of a Fairfilm (Mario Cecchi Gori)-Incei-Montflour (Paris)-Cinetel (Paris) coproduction. Stars Vittorio Gassmann, Anouk Aimee, Jean Louis Trintignant; features Cristina Gajoni, Filippo Scelzo, Umberto D'Orsi, Grazia Maria Spina, Annie Gorassini, Franca Polesello. Directed by Mauro Morassi. Story and screenplay, Ettore Scola, Ruggero Maccari; comera, Sandro D'Eva; music, Ennio Moricone; editor, Maurizio Lucidi. At Metropolitan, Rome. Running time, **105 MINS.**

Giulio Ceriani .... Vittorio Gassmann
Laura .... Anouk Aimee
Sergio .... Jean Louis Trintignant
Diana .... Grazia Maria Spina
Francesco .... Filippo Scelzo
Marisa .... Annie Gorassini
Carla .... Franca Polesiello

Neat followup to last season's sleeper, "Il Sorpasso," with another effective performance by Vittorio Gassmann and a resultingly high commercial rating in this country. Lacks strength in depth for widespread export impact, but could fare okay in certain foreign areas.

A bitter commentary on certain ruthless climbers behind the recent Italo economic boom, "Successo" deals mainly with the relentless pursuit of money on the part of the "hero," money with which to finance a real estate speculation. To eventually bring this off, Giulio (Vittorio Gassmann) debases himself more and more in growing compromises with friends and even his wife. When he eventually succeeds in bringing off his coup, he finds himself a rich but lonely man.

Gassmann is by now unerring in playing the likeable heel (though here the accent is more on his unlikeable aspects), and it's his picture all the way. Anouk Aimee and Jean Louis Trintignant ably fill their sideline roles as wife and friend, respectively. Grazia Maria Spina is good as Trintignant's girl while Cristina Gajoni gives an amusing portrait of a demanding maid. Film has an impressive array of supporting players, all of them contributing strongly to general impact, especially Umberto D'Orsi, as a friend whose money Gassmann needs and to whom he kowtows.

Pic might have been more commercial if the main character (as in preceding "Sorpasso") had been given some human tendencies. Also more critically trenchant had it not been spiced up with four-letter gags at too many strategic points. But these comments are relative, and film's local success is assured.

Soundtrack is similarly flashy, with Ennio Moricone assembling a likeable array of current pop songs, as is Sandro D'Eva's lensing, mostly on modern Roman settings mirroring the film's "success" story. Other credits good. *Hawk.*

The Old Dark House

Comic approach to suspense chiller. Doesn't come off.

Hollywood, Oct. 14.

Columbia Pictures release of William Castle production. Stars Tom Poston, Robert Morley, Janette Scott, Joyce Grenfell. Directed by Castle. Screenplay, Robert Dillon, based on novel by J. B. Priestley; camera, Arthur Grant; editor, James Needs; music, Benjamin Frankel; assistant director, Douglas Hermes. Reviewed at the studio, Oct. 14, '63. Running time, **86 MINS.**

Tom Penderel .... Tom Poston
Roderick Femm .... Robert Morley
Cecily .... Janette Scott
Agatha Femm .... Joyce Grenfell
Casper Femm,
Jasper Femm .... Peter Bull
Potiphar .... Marvyn Johns
Morgana .... Fanella Fielding
Morgan Femm .... Danny Green

An attempt to approach a spooky suspense melodrama in a humorous vain, "The Old Dark House" succeeds only in neutralizing itself and emerges neither a satisfactory horror entry nor a sufficiently amusing spoof. A capable cast has been assembled for the Anglo-American coproduction, but even such seasoned comedy talents as Tom Poston, Robert Morley and Joyce Grenfell are hard-pressed to deliver scattered moments of mirth out of the uninspired material provided them. The Columbia release, produced and directed by William Castle, one of Hollywood's top chiller picturemakers, in association with Hammer Films, England's leading horror film firm, might generate some mild wicket response as half of a horror exploitation package.

Originally done as a straight shocker back in 1932, the new kidding version was scripted by Robert Dillon from a novel by J. B. Priestley. Poston essays the pivotal role of a Yankee car salesman in London who delivers an auto to a purchaser who resides in a spooky, secluded mansion and become embroiled in a series of fatal mishaps to members of the family residing in that establishment in order that they may share a legacy. The murders are the result of the greed of one of these individuals and, as usual, it turns out to be the least likely of the lot.

Poston is a likable leading man with sound instincts for comic reaction. Morley, for the most part, is hemmed in by Dillon's scenario, which is weak in the area of character development and takes matters for granted that need proper explanation, comedy or no. Miss Grenfell draws the funniest business as an eccentric dowager who knits non-stop by the mile with no material aim in mind. Janette Scott and Fenella Fielding share the romantic spotlight opposite Poston, the former deceptively demure, the latter a sexy-voiced siren. Peter Bull, Mervyn Johns and Danny Green round out the cast as assorted screwballs.

Adequately directed by Castle, the production, filmed in England, sports capable contributions from cameraman Arthur Grant, editor James Needs, composer Benjamin Frankel, soundman Jock May, special effects man Les Bowie and production designer Bernard Robinson. The ghoulish title backgrounds were drawn by cartoonist Charles Addams. *Tube.*

Maniac
(MEGASCOPE)

Rape, torch murder and insane asylum. Poor outlook.

Hollywood, Oct. 16.

Columbia Pictures release of Jimmy Sangster production, screenplay by Sangster. Stars Kerwin Mathews, Nadia Gray; features Donald Houston, Liliane Brousse. Directed by Michael Carreras. Camera, Wilkie Cooper; editor, Tom Simpson; music, Stanley Black; Asst. director, Ross MacKenzie. Reviewed at the studio, Oct. 16, '63. Running time, **87 MINS.**

Geoff Farrell .... Kerwin Mathews
Eve Beynat .... Nadia Gray
Georges Beynat .... Donald Houston
Annette Beynat .... Liliane Brousse
Inspector Etienne ...... George Pastell
Janiello .... Arnold Diamond
Salon (Gendarme) .... Norman Bird
Grace .... Justine Lord
Giles .... Jerold Wells

An incredibly confusing and unappealing melodrama, "Maniac's" market value, even as half of an exploitation package, is dubious, although title might help. The Columbia release, a product of England's ordinarily reliable Hammer Films, was written and produced by Jimmy Sangster.

First off, a teenaged girl is raped. Her father corners the culprit, hauls him off to the shed and destroys him with an oxy-acetylene torch, for which he is sent to the looney bin. (Makings of a nice "family" film, right?) In his absence, a wandering American takes up first with his daughter, then with her stepmother who, in her visits to the insane asylum, has taken a liking to her husband's guard. Still with us? The stepmother persuades the American to aid in the escape of her husband so that they will be free to wed. The fool American agrees to this. After the escape, he finds a body in the trunk of the car. He thinks it's the guard, but actually it's the husband. Pretty soon the American is on the wrong end of the oxy-acetylene torch. At this point, the plot begins to get complicated. When the dust clears, the guard is dead, the stepmother is prison-bound, the American is holding hands with the daughter.

Michael Carreras directed, although there's not much evidence of it. *Tube.*

La Derive
(The Drifting)
(FRENCH)

Paris, Oct. 22.

Productions Cinematographiques Du Languedoc production and release. With Jacqueline Vandal, Paulette Dubost, Monique Bonafous, Noelle Noblecourt, Anne-Marie Coffinet, Pierre Barouh, Jean-Loup Reynold, Jean-Francois Calve, Lucien Barjon, Nader. Written and directed by Paule Delsol. Camera, Jean Maligne; editor, Agnes Guillemot. Previewed in Paris. Running time, **84 MINS.**

Jacquie .... Jacqueline Vandal
Mother .... Paulette Dubost
Sister .... Monique Bonafous
Agathe .... Noelle Noblecourt
Claire .... Anne-Marie Coffinet
Pierre .... Pierre Barouh
Student .... Jean-Loup Reynold
Maurice .... Lucien Barjon
Jean .... Nader
Regis .... Jean-Francois Calve
Marc .... Sourine

Femme film directors have been springing up of late in the European flim industry. Now a woman here, working on her own in southern France, has come up with a penetrating look at a drifting young girl which shows insight and visual intelligence. Pic pinpoints her sentimental life plus an ability to display character without too much talk.

There is no sensationalism or peeping-tomism here, though the pic is mainly concerned with the tribulations of a pretty girl of 20 with men of various ages and types. She begins to drift when a guitarist, with whom she had run off two years ago, leaves her on a train. She had left her home in a small town for him. She gets off the train and has a brief sexual run-in with a student. Then she

hitchhikes home where an adoring mother welcomes her to the grudging antagonism of a sister, not happy with her ordinary married life.

Then the girl's further affairs are deftly etched in. There is an aging rich man with an alcoholic wife who keeps her in a big house. But she is not content and also has a local suitor. He is a simple, ordinary type who has no ambition which has her not wanting to accept him.

It all ends with her meeting a non-conformist painter and deciding to live with him even though his attitude towards women hints it will be a short-lived affair.

There is no preaching in this pic. Director Paule Delsol is content to leave all this up to the viewer. She depicts the girl's mainly inarticulate outlook in her affairs with clarity.

The feminine ability to show things in their wholeness, without trying to enforce a crusading point of view, is helpful in getting to the core of the theme. Here is a girl's way of life in the conditions she finds today. That is it.

Simple structure of the film makes it primarily an arty house item abroad, and it will need the hardsell. But it has incisiveness that could give it a boost from critics and word-of-mouth.

And, if made outside of Paris, it is technically fine with solid imagery, helped by its on-the-spot lensing and neat tally of professional and non-pro acting talents. Jacqueline Vandal has the prettiness and dramatic presence to lend the girl a sharp authenticity. Others are also well cast. Miss Delsol emerges a definite new directorial talent.

This looms as one of the most forthright pix about French youth (feminine variety) to come out of France since the New Wave movement a few years back.

A deceptively simple pic that will need careful handling. It may be worth it. *Mosk.*

A Toi De Faire Mignonne
(You Do It Cutie)
(FRENCH)
Paris, Oct. 22.

Prodis release of CICC Films Borderie-Euro International production. Stars Eddie Constantine; features Gaia Germani, Christiane Minazzoli, Elga Andersen, Philippe Lemaire, Noel Roquevert. Directed by Bernard Borderie. Screenplay, Marc-Gilbert Sauvajon, Borderie from a book by Peter Cheyney; camera, Henri Persin; editor, Christian Gaudin. At Marbeuf, Paris. Running time, 100 MINS.

Lemmy .... Eddie Constantine
Valerie .... Elga Andersen
Carletta .... Christiane Minazzoli
Geraldine .... Gaia Germani
Grant .... Philippe Lemaire
Walker .... Noel Roquevert

Eddie Constantine is again the hard drinking two-fisted FBI man who unravels a foreign mystery about a gang trying to extort money via holding a scientist with atomic secrets. He also meets plenty of available slinky girls along the way. This one has a bit more knowhow in fight stagings and some tongue-in cheek gags. But it still seems limited to lower case dualer use abroad.

Constantine, a Yank who became a star here, walks through his role with his usual charm and side

winks at the audience. Abroad it still may have the feel of a gangster pic parody, but it lacks the bright, biting decisiveness of its Yank counterparts. This one becomes a bit repetitive, not helped by its flatfooted dialog or vague scripting.

There is technical assurance plus the usual bevy of scallywags, hoods and conniving femmes. Then there are the spluttering secret service topkicks, both American and foreign, to counterpoint Constantine's unorthodox but persuasive ways of handling the situations.

In short, this should find its audiences in Europe to pay off its probable well-controlled budget, but is sans the more dynamic fillip for more demanding Yank marts on this type of comic underworld pic. *Mosk.*

Le Chemin De La Mauvaise Route
(The Way of the Wrong Road)
(FRENCH)
Paris, Oct. 15.

La Pleiade release of Sofracima production. Directed by Jean Herman. Stage by Herman; camera, Denys Clerval; editor, Nadine Trintignant; commentary, Jean-Louis Trintignant. At Studio De L'Etoile, Paris. Running time, 58 MINS.

Cinema Truth pic looks at a young delinquent couple and allows them to talk of their lives as well as interspersing their inarticulate meanderings with enacted scenes. A certain ease, sharp editing and elusive truths make this an absorbing item with supporting chances for specialized art house programs abroad because of its length.

The boy is an untutored, vain petty thief while the girl is somewhat more intelligent if socially unstable. They talk of their daily lives, stealing, love, why they do not work, war, etc., with a difficulty of expression that is revealing in its lack of premeditation.

Director Jean Herman intercuts joltingly with rock-and-roll bits, youthful gang fights, the recent Algerian War and the general dreary economic and social life around them. This counterpoints their unaffected talk. Enacting little episodes also seem to spark these two semi-outcasts.

Pic does not preach outright but does infer how these people were formed. It also does not try to say whether they will change or even if they can. Film is more a flashing glimpse of people than a treatise or social tract.

Production is technically good. Here is another in the series of authentic film looks at French society that having a vogue here currently. If they lack the form of art, they have the timeliness of authenticity that give them interest. Pix also contribute insights into new film methods and techpiques that can be absorbed by the fiction film. *Mosk.*

The Victors

Carl Foreman's three-hour job on World War II. Expert all the way. Major boxoffice.

Columbia Pictures presentation of Highroad production, produced, directed and adapted by Carl Foreman from Alexander Baron's book, "The Human Kind." Stars Romy Schneider, Melina Mercouri, Jeanne Moreau, Rosanna Schiaffino, Elke Sommer, Eli Wallach, George Hamilton, George Peppard, Albert Finney. Maurice Ronet, Vincent Edwards. Camera, Christopher Challis; editor, Alan Osbiston. Reviewed Oct. 24, 1963 at Columbia projection room, N.Y. Running time. 175 MINS.

Trower .... George Hamilton
Chase .... George Peppard
Craig .... Eli Wallach
Baker .... Vincent Edwards
Maria .... Rosanna Schiaffino
Grogan .... James Mitchum
Sikh Soldier .... Tutte Lemkow
French Lieutenant ...... Maurice Ronet
Jean-Pierre .... Joel Flateau
French Woman .... Jeanne Moreau
Regine .... Romy Schneider
Eldridge .... Michael Callan
Weaver .... Peter Fonda
Magda .... Melina Mercouri
Dennis .... Mervyn Johns
Herr Metzger .... Albert Lieven
Frau Metzger .... Marianne Deeming
Trudi .... Senta Berger
Helga .... Elke Sommer
Russian Soldier .... Albert Finney

First of all, and best of all, Carl Foreman has provided a lot of show. This is a crowded picture. Crowded with characters, incidents, change of scenery, details. Framed with a flair for panorama, a sense of our times, it has pace, shock value, point of view. The point of view is that you can hardly tell the difference in moral deterioration between victors and vanquished. Skeptical but not cynical, the film is informed by thought and redeemed by compassion. It will make a lot of money.

Having mentioned shock values these call for immediate description. There are the Dixie G.I.'s off on a "coon hunt" (their phrase) who gratuitously beat up two Negro compatriots in the war against Hitler's race hatred. The shock lies in the unsaid cowardice of a saloon full of whites who never lift a finger to protect the Negroes. Then there is the "Puppy Shoot," a contest between two battle-hardened Yanks with James Mitchum the winner. The shock lies in the gangling replacement G.I. played by Peter Fonda, a fool of a boy who tries to sleep with the squealing puppy in his overcoat amidst nerve-ragged toughs. This speaks both of the juvenility of conscripts and the brutalization of combat.

The original squad sergeant (Eli Wallach) disappears from the action about three-quarters through without explanation in the story. When his also-invalid buddy (George Peppard) hunts him out at a hospital in England he stumbles upon the ghastly truth. There is a glimpse of the sarge with his nose blown off and his face a caricature of a man. This one touch is equivalent to a thousand feet of special effects photography of bodies impaled on barbed wire and similiar stock-in-trade of war films.

Finally, and likely to create plenty of conversation, there is the shocker of a 11-year old French boy camp-follower, who wanders over to the Yanks from the Germans, a confirmed homosexual by trade. Women viewers may at first think what a darling boy, and end up shuddering at his profession. He's Joel Flateau.

Foreman tells his tale of war in

terms of vignettes, concentrating on homesickness, woman-hunger, civilian starvation, the "nice" girls who shack up with the G.I. smoothies for food, cigarettes and kicks. One of these, a pretty, no-talent fiddler in a dive, is played by Romy Schneider. Her indifference to the decent soldier (George Hamilton) and ultimate bumming around with the slicker is underplayed, but it's part of the mosaic of the decent G.I.'s own ultimate hardening. He is seen at the very end of the film after sleeping half the night with his German girl, while her gift-bribed parents look the other way. Wandering out into the Berlin rubble Hamilton accidentally encounters a tipsy Russian soldier played by Albert Finney. It is the supreme comment on the pointless slaughter incident to war's acute angles that the two men, total strangers, knife each other to death. The camera ends with a semi-longshot of their bodies in the midst of total destruction.

Geoffrey Drake's art direction rates high praise. The story is properly told in black and white photography. Color would have been too pretty for the underlying implications of monotony and mud. Foreman has incorporated a lot of newsreel footage. He has designed his narrative with great filmmaking **skill and considerable daring, recalling the early 1940s** both for nostalgia and irony. He and editor Alan Osbiston have not hesitated to jump from human tragedy to human idiocy, in order to point the connection. There is one of those U.S. theatre "Merry Christmas" lantern slides at one point and the let's-all-sing-to-the-bouncing-ball bit.

In general Foreman has had the wisdom to underplay his scenes, leave many an incident without the sequel which seems, but is not, mandatory. There may be divided opinion on some bits. The execution of the G.I. deserter in a snowy perspective is pictorially compelling (shot in Sweden) but it seems a dubious moment to feature one of Sol Kaplan's special songs. Admitting the artistic try for monumental irony, the lyrics have the unfortunate effect of drawing attention to themselves and away from the youth about to lose his life. Still, that could probably be argued either way. The Tin Pan Alley words are sufficiently dehumanizing. Which is the message of that scene.

While "The Victors" selection of varying emphases it notably original there are some trite scenes familiar from earlier war films. Melina Mercouri is the queen of the Belgian black market, proprietor of off-limit establishments, cynic and sensualist. Her affair with the G.I. Joe (Peppard) may be the one "contrived" bit of hokum in an otherwise admirably realistic accomplishment.

Foreman in his alter ego as adaptor has taken his story from an English writer, Alexander Baron, to whom all proper honor. There will be a plausible temptation to call this a director's picture, which it is. but all is made possible in the end by a good script. Which is not to deny the fine job of editing already mentioned. In such a kaleidoscopic film there is perhaps an obligation to nod to the party in charge of continuity, Joan Davis. Finally, there are the photography (Christopher Challis, Austin Demp-

ster) the sound (Buster Ambler) and the music (Kaplan) credits. All thoroughly pro.

The large cast needs carefull sifting in a film just short of three hours in running time. Vincent Edwards of the tv "Ben Casey" series comes early in the story, during the Sicilian episode. He's a good-hearted soldier who very much loves his wife back home and very much wants Rosanno Schiaffino who loves her absent husband and wants the American, too. It's a scene of considerable tenderness. But afterward the viewer sees naught of Edwards.

This Sicilian vignette, flesh crying out to flesh, is illuminated by a Sikh soldier (Tutte Lemkow) from whom the superstitious villagers flee in terror of his supposed "evil eye." The Sikh is a fine fellow, a little drunk, also homesick. He wants nothing but to hold the Italian girl's baby for a moment. Foreman may be the first director ever to cast a soldier from India in a western war film, but he missed a bet in overlooking the Brazilian division in Italy at the time. However, he has been at pains to credit and include the British, the Canadians, the French and the Russians. If the story is told from the American G.I. focus, it seems probable that our late Allies cannot object.

Nor are these G.I.'s knightly. They are dog-tired, irritable, prone to loot, sometimes undisciplined, quick to raid wine cellars. Eli Wallach is later replaced as sergeant by George Hamilton. These two men have the maximum exposure in the film. Wallach is long established as an actor, Hamilton rather newer to the screen and this seems his top performance to date. To Wallach falls one of the most human interludes. He is scouting a French villa for future company headquarters when, during the night, the bombardment renews. The widow, played with convincing delineation by Jeanne Moreau, is clearly upper class, an esthete and lover of poetry, everything the tough American is not. He is sleeping during the gunfire and awakens to find her cowering in a corner. Her sheer need for human comfort and warmth leads her into his bed, a scene which never suggests lust for a second. It is another of Foreman's shining episodes.

A number of players will enhance their careers through "The Victors". Hamilton for one. George Peppard for another. Michael Callan, as the corrupt, swaggering, smooth G.I., also makes an impression. So do two German actresses, Senta Berger (with a Russian sweetie) and Elke Sommer (with a Yank), a couple of sisters both peddling sex for food and gifts, but the one consorting with the Russians is looked down upon.

Peter Fonda is standout as the exasperatingly juvenile newcomer to the squad, a lover of dogs because he cannot relate well to humans. The bit will tug lots of good old dog-loving American hearts. Maurice Ronet has an arresting vignette as a scar-face, one-eyed French lieutenant who takes over from the G.I. squad and exterminates a pillbox full of Germans. The Yanks would have accepted their white flag surrender. The Frenchman lusts only for death of Germans.

"The Victors" is being cannily introduced by Columbia. It shows tonight (Wed.) at the San Francisco Film Festival. Later it will open on grind at the Criterion with a companion date on N.Y.'s east side. It is hard to imagine it doing other than smash business.

Land.

Trauma

Low budget indie for lower berth. Ineptly made psychological murder mystery.

Hollywood, Oct. 22.

Parade release of Joseph Cranston production. Stars John Conte, Lynn Bari, David Garner; introdues Lorrie Richards. Directed and screenplay by Robert Malcolm Young; camera, Jacques Marquette; editor, Hal Dennis; music, Buddy Collette; asst. director, Willis Oborn. Reviewed at Joe Shore's screening room, Oct. 22, '63. Running time, **93 MINS.**

Clyner	John Conte
Helen	Lynn Bari
Craig	David Garner
Luther	Warren Kemmerling
Emilyne	Lorrie Richards
Robert	Bond Blackman
Hall	William Bissell
Carla	Renee Mason
FBI Man	LeRoy Lennert
Gas Station Attendant	Robert Totten
Policeman	Alfred Chafe
Maid	Ruby Borner

The maiden effort of Artists XVI Productions, a small indie outfit, "Trauma" is said to have been brought in for $69,000. No one who views it is apt to dispute that claim. Parade release, produced by Joseph Cranston will suffice, though overlong, as a running mate with attractions aimed at audiences less inclined to grumble over mediocrity. It will get by, for example, as the supporting half of a multiple-run exploitation doubleheader.

The psychological melodrama was written and directed by Robert Malcolm Young. It is concerned with the problem of a young lady who witnesses a murder, loses her memory as a result of the traumatic incident, and comes out of her six-year spell of amnesia just as she is on the verge of becoming another victim of the murderer.

Young has written the kind of psychologically involved, introspective yarn that is more than he could handle directorially at the $69,000 plateau. Filming at that level can, indeed, be a traumatic experience. The story is fuzzy, motivations are dubious, dialog is stilted, and direction is choppy and not always sufficiently resourceful. Complicating matters is Jacques Marquette's photography which, at least on the print witnessed, is far too dark for proper visual definition. Other technical credits are generally adequate.

The acting is not too impressive, although pretty Lorrie Richards, who makes her screen bow as the amnesiac, shows promise. John Conte is rather stiff in a confusing role. Lynn Bari overemotes a bit in her brief assignment as the murderer's victim. Others of prominence are David Garner and Warren Kemmerling.

Tube.

L'Assassin Connait La Musique
(The Murderer Knows the Score) (FRENCH)

Paris, Oct. 29.

Gaumont release of Hoche, General production. Stars Maria Schell, Paul Meurisse; features Sylvie Breal, Claude Mann, Christa Lang. Directed by Pierre Chenal. Screenplay, Fred Kassak, Chenal from book by Kassak; camera, Marc Fossard; editor, Madeleine Bibollet. At Ermitage, Paris. Running time, **80 MINS.**

Agnes	Maria Schell
Lionel	Paul Meurisse
Marie-Josee	Sylvie Breal
Francis	Claude Mann
Christian	Christa Lang

Laborious would-be comedy of murder lacks the right sprightly playing, taste, wit and timing to bring it off. What remains is a fairly plodding, telegraphed affair that could have some dualer use on the Maria Schell name abroad, but which may find it hardgoing in arty spots.

Miss Schell, never noted for underplaying, here trouts out too many giggles and mannerisms that finally destroy her portrayal of a muddled divorcee. She is used by a frantic composer who needs her house in the country to finish a symphony.

Paul Meurisse also overdoes the composer role with its dandyish, sometimes sinister aspects detracting from his first accidental murder.

Director Pierre Chenal has permitted a fairly good idea to go astray. Its cynicism is too blatant, its characters too stereotyped and its pace somewhat too laggard to make its satire or parody pay off. Film appears a slim bet on its own home grounds, too. It is unfortunate because the makings of a comedy in the "Kind Hearts and Coronet" manner were there, but botched.

Mosk.

Macbeth
(TECHNICOLOR)

Kansas City, Oct. 29.

Prominent Films release of Grand Prize Films production: Sidney Kaufman, executive producer. Stars Maurice Evans and Judith Anderson; features Michael Hordern, Ian Bannen, Felix Aylmer, Malcolm Keen, Megs Jenkins, Jeremy Brett and George Rose. Produced by Phil C. Samuel, directed by George Schaefer. Technical director, Anthony Squire; camera (Technicolor), Fred A. Young; editor, Ralph Kemplen; music, Richard Addinsell, played by Sinfonia of London, conducted by Muir Mathieson. Reviewed at Rockhill Theatre, Kansas City, Oct. 20, '63. Running time, **107 MINS.**

Macbeth	Maurice Evans
Lady Macbeth	Judith Anderson
Banquo	Michael Hordern
Macduff	Ian Bannen
Doctor	Felix Aylmer
Gentlewoman	Megs Jenkins
Malcolm	Jeremy Brett
Donalbain	Barry Warren
Ross	William Hutt
Caithness	Charles Carson
Seyton	Trader Faulkner
Porter	George Rose
First Witch	Valerie Taylor
Second Witch	Anita Sharp Bolster
Third Witch	April Olrich
Angus	Brewster Mason
Menteith	Simon Lack
Fleance	Scot Finch
Bloody Sergeant	Robert Brown
First Murderer	Michael Ripper
Second Murderer	Douglas Wilmer

George Schaefer production of William Shakespeare's "Macbeth" reverses pattern by coming to the theatrical screen three years after origin for the television "Hallmark Hall of Fame." As a 107-minute treatment of the classic, it is a full version of the Shakespeare work, with but a few minor parts omitted, and thereby makes notable gains over the 90-minutes-with-time-out-for-commercials tv version. Add wide screen and Technicolor for further values.

Schaefer version headed by Maurice Evans and Judith Anderson is lusty and gory. It's just short of melodrama, successfully overcoming wordiness, and may well make this more "commercial" than ordinarily is expected of a classic.

Evans as Macbeth and Miss Anderson as Lady Macbeth are masterful as the conniving couple. Cast is excellent. Special nods go to Michael Hordern as Banquo, Ian Bannen as Macduff, George Rose as the drunken porter, and Malcolm Keen as King Duncan. Evans is called upon for everything in the acting book. No less intense is La Anderson though widescreen and color are less than flattering to her.

Costumes, mostly muted Scottish plaids and royal finery, are standout, as are the settings, former by Beatrice Dawson, with Edward Carrick credited as art director and Simpson Robinson as scenic artist. Other production angles are topflight throughout.

A special acknowledgment is made to Joyce C. Hall and Hallmark Cards. This also explains theatrical premiere of the picture in Kansas City at the Art Theatre Guild's Rockhill Theatre and much attendant local exploitation, with a personal by Evans.

Prominent Films figures it may be working as many as 25 prints throughout 1964.

Quin.

Mannheim Fest

Legacy

Mannheim, Oct. 22.

A Counterpoint (Richard Snodgrass) production. With Jessica Thomas, Dorie Zabriskie, Rick Yearry, Michael Pflueger, Mike Snodgrass. Directed and written by Richard Snodgrass. Camera and editor, Ralph Luce; music, David Campbell. At Mannheim Film Fest. Running time, **92 MINS.**

"Legacy" is the first full-length feature pic of 35-year old Richard Snodgrass, former university professor in Arizona, who reportedly has several short films to his credit. "Legacy" was shown as an official U.S. entry at this festival. Pic cost just $50,000. It took Snodgrass two and a half years to collect the money and 14 months to make the film. It's sort of a puzzle as to who would be interested in distributing this one. "Legacy" is too unconventional to appeal to average patrons and too amateurish to give it a chance with the more demanding customers. Pic looks to have it tough to get on regular programs.

Pic has an interesting general theme: Children's loneliness among adults. But both technical treatment and artistic outcome of the film are too primitive. "Legacy" has the flavor of a home production all through.

There is, however, a limited group of pix patrons (intellectuals) who give the film's topic priority if the topic is what they call important. This in fact was the case at the Mannheim festival where some intellectual reviewers lauded the film for its subject matter. (The Mannheim event is chiefly a short pic festival but the first feature pix of former short filmmakers are included on the program).

"Legacy" is composed of four episodes, all concerning juveniles.

Cast is composed of amateurs only. Several players are relatives of director Snodgrass which makes the whole thing even more amateurish and home-like production. Best that can be said about

"Legacy" is that it's a well intended filmic effort. But this isn't enough to make it impressive.

Hans.

O Neeem Jinem
(About Something Else) (CZECH)

Mannheim, Oct. 22.

Czech State film production. Stars Eva Bosakova. Directed and written by Vera Chytilova. Camera, Jan Curik. At Mannheim Film Fest. Running time, **90 MINS.**

This Czech full-length feature pic walked off with the Grand Prix at the just terminated Mannheim festival whose program includes the first full-length pix of former short film makers. Film seems to have deserved the prize. It's a highly interesting piece of new cinematic art. Pic looks okay for arty houses everywhere.

Film revolves around two episodes. One deals with the rigorous everyday training of Eva Bosakova, Czech gymnast and Olympic champion, at the time when she's about to give up her sports career. The other story revolves around a young housewife whose husband isn't very attentive to her. She eventually starts romancing with another man. The two women's problems are depicted in an interesting manner. Vera Chytilova, Czech woman director who has several shorts to her credit, employs both the methods of a feature as well as a documentary film.

There are several outstanding points about this. Foremost is the excellent camera work by Jan Curik, one of the best photographers in his country. Then there is the excellent direction and good acting. The latter especially applies to the two women. Eva Bosakova plays herself. She isn't even an actress.

Of the young film artists who recently have been coming to the fore in the Czech pix, Vera Chytilova ranks as one of the most gifted. Her initial full-length film spells promise for the future. Amazingly enough, although a considerable part of the film features sports (gymnast) sequences, it hardly ever becomes a bore even to the normally non-sport viewer.

Hans.

It's a Mad, Mad, Mad, Mad World
(CINERAMA—COLOR—ULTRA PANAVISION)

Spectacular film with some classic comedy sequences. Overdone in spots but on whole an explosive entertainment and sizzling b.o. prospect.

Hollywood, Oct. 29.

United Artists release of Stanley Kramer production. Stars Spencer Tracy, Milton Berle, Sid Caesar, Buddy Hackett, Ethel Merman, Mickey Rooney, Dick Shawn, Phil Silvers, Terry-Thomas, Jonathan Winters, Edie Adams, Dorothy Provine. Others: Jimmy Durante, Eddie "Rochester" Anderson, Jim Backus, Ben Blue, Alan Carney, Barrie Chase, William Demarest, Peter Falk, Paul Ford, Leo Gorcey, Edward Everett Horton, Buster Keaton, Don Knotts, Carl Reiner, The Three Stooges (Moe Howard, Larry Fine, Joe De Rita), Joe E. Brown, Andy Devine, Sterling Holloway, Marvin Kaplan, Charles Lane, Charles McGraw, ZaSu Pitts, Madlyn Rhue, Arnold Stang, Jesse White, Lloyd Corrigan, Selma Diamond, Stan Freberg, Louise Glenn, Ben Lessy, Bobo Lewis, Mike Mazurki, Nick Stewart, Sammee Tong, Norman Fell, Nicholas Georgiade. Directed by Kramer. Screenplay, William and Tania Rose; camera (Technicolor), Ernest Laszlo; editor, Fred Knudtson; music, Ernest Gold; asst. director, Ivan Volkman. Reviewed at the Forum, Oct. 29, '63. Running time, **190 MINS.** plus intermission.

Capt. C. G. Culpepper	Spencer Tracy
J. Russell Finch	Milton Berle
Melville Crump	Sid Caesar
Benjy Benjamin	Buddy Hackett
Mrs. Marcus	Ethel Merman
Ding Bell	Mickey Rooney
Sylvester Marcus	Dick Shawn
Otto Meyer	Phil Silvers
J. Algernon Hawthorne	Terry-Thomas
Lennie Pike	Jonathan Winters
Monica Crump	Edie Adams
Emmeline Finch	Dorothy Provine
First Cab Driver	Eddie "Rochester" Anderson
Tyler Fitzgerald	Jim Backus
Airplane Pilot	Ben Blue
Police Sergeant	Alan Carney
Mrs. Halliburton	Barrie Chase
Chief of Police	William Demarest
Second Cab Driver	Peter Falk
Col. Wilberforce	Paul Ford
Third Cab Driver	Leo Gorcey
Dinckler	Edward Everett Horton
Jimmy, the Crook	Buster Keaton
Nervous Man	Don Knotts
Tower Control	Carl Reiner
Firemen	The Three Stooges (Moe Howard, Larry Fine, Joe De Rita)
Union Official	Joe E. Brown
Sheriff Mason	Andy Devine
Fire Chief	Sterling Holloway
Irwin	Marvin Kaplan
Airport Manager	Charles Lane
Lieutenant	Charles McGraw
Switchboard Operator	ZaSu Pitts
Police Secretary	Madlyn Rhue
Ray	Arnold Stang
Radio Tower Operator	Jesse White
Mayor	Lloyd Corrigan
Culpeper's Wife (Voice)	Selma Diamond
Deputy Sheriff	Stan Freberg
Billie Sue (Voice)	Louise Glenn
George, The Steward	Ben Lessy
Pilot's Wife	Bobo Lewis
Miner	Mike Mazurki
Truck Driver	Nick Stewart
Chinese Laundryman	Sammee Tong
Detective	Norman Fell
Detective	Nicholas Georgiade
Smiler Grogan	Jimmy Durante

It's a mad, mad, mad, mad picture, and it's going to make a lot of money. The Stanley Kramer production for United Artists, lavishly filmed in Ultra Panavision and Technicolor and released in Cinerama of the more efficient, less distorted single lens variety, is a spectacular achievement in cinematic architecture, a significant addition to Hollywood film comedy and a potential boxoffice blockbuster. Being a picture of extravagant proportions, even its few flaws are king-sized, but the plusses outweigh by far the minuses.

There was method to producer-director Kramer's "Mad"ness. Springing from a cinematically fertile story and comically ripe and maneuverable screenplay by William and Tania Rose, the film is both a throwback and a milestone.

It is a throwback to the wild, wacky and wondrous time of the silent screen comedy, a kind of Keystone Kop Kaper with modern conveniences.

It is a milestone for the manner in which it has taken these primitive comedy techniques, fortified them with staggering sensations of sight and sound that represent modern filmmaking at its technically slickest, and emerged not an overstuffed anachronism, but a blend of the best of two eras—the innocent simplicity of the golden age of slapstick and the satirical "message" approach popular in these uneasy times of disenchantment, self-examination and moral reevaluation.

The plot is disarmingly simple. A group of people are given a clue by a dying man (Jimmy Durante) as to the whereabouts of a huge sum of money he has stolen and buried. Unable to come to a compromise in apportionment of the anticipated loot, each sets out for the roughly specified site of the buried cash, breaking his back to beat the others there. All are unaware that they are under secret surveillance by state police authorities, who are allowing them simply to lead the way to the money.

When eventually the greedy parties assemble and manage to unearth the loot, they are politely apprehended by an aged and disillusioned police captain (Spencer Tracy) who herds them together for a trip to jail and proceeds to abscond with the treasure. He is detected, however, in his flight, resulting in a madcap chase and a shattering, slam-bang, Harold Lloydish climax in which the suitcaseful of C-notes showers down on a mob of onlookers witnessing the precarious predicament of the principals, who are dangling enmasse from a skyscraper fire escape which has been ripped loose from its hinges by their collective weight. Ultimately they are transferred to the ladder of a fire truck which, equally unable to support their total bulk, proceeds to hurtle each member of the party through the air to an undignified landing place.

The film concludes in a hospital ward. Each thwarted fortune-hunter is in traction, each suffering from fractures of every conceivable bone in his anatomy and totally dismal disposition to match, when along comes Ethel Merman, an "old bag" mother-in-law detested by all parties present. On the floor, that most appropriate object and symbolic prop — a banana peel. Miss Merman flops head over heels, landing with a resounding thud on her derrierre. The room is instantly filled with convulsive laughter, and the picture ends on this optimistic note. Even under the more dire circumstances, the indomitable human spirit will find a way to amuse itself. For every banana peel, human nature has a laugh in readiness.

Nothing is done in moderation in this picture. All the stops are out. Nobody goes around what they can go over, under, through or into. There are a number of truly spectacular action sequences, and the stunts that have been performed seem incredible. The automobile capers are some of the most thrilling and daring on record, Mack Sennett notwithstanding. The airplane gyrations are frequently breathtaking. And it is to Kramer's great credit that he has not resorted to such obvious trickery as variable speed gimmicks. He appears to have eschewed cinematic artificiality wherever the real McCoy was safe and feasible.

Yet, as noted, the film is not without its flaws and oversights. Too often it tries to throw a wild haymaker where a simple left jab would be more apt to locate the desired target. Certain pratfalls and sequences are unnecessarily overdone to the point where they begin to grow tedious and reduce the impact of the whole. There are a few too many haymakers that don't connect and tend to minimize the force of the ones that do. It is also somewhat unfortunate that one is able to sense far in advance Tracy's devious intentions. And certain moves by the characters, such as Tracy's ultimate stupidity in enabling himself to be caught in the act of absconding after he has already proven himself to be quite a perfectionist, are terribly inconsistent, and cannot be excused simply on the grounds that this is farce. Cleverer, more adroit scriptwork was required in these areas.

An array of top-ranking comics has been rounded up by Kramer, making this one of the most unorthodox and memorable casts on screen record. The comic competition is so keen that it is impossible to single out any one participant as outstanding, but there are a number of characterizations that are dominant and exude a special, indelible flavor and personality.

Among these are Sid Caesar as an inept escape artist who gets himself and his jittery wife (Edie Adams) sealed up in the cellar of a hardware store; Phil Silvers as an opportunist who runs out of opportunities; Jonathan Winters as a powerful, but gullible, truck driver who singlehandedly batters a desert garage down to its foundations in a devastating sight gag sequence, and Terry-Thomas in his patented caricature—the outrageous personification of the Yankee notion of what the average Britisher is like.

Tracy gives another of his irresistibly natural performances, but is involved in some of the film's weaker interludes. Milton Berle is firm and persuasive as a meek, henpecked husband, surprisingly subdued in his approach, in contrast to most of the others, who make little attempt to veil their own comic identities behind the masks of characterization. Mickey Rooney and Buddy Hackett score in a runaway aircraft sequence. Dick Shawn has an overly exaggerated role to contend with, including some distorted twist business with Barrie Chase.

The three femme leads are fine: Miss Merman as a distastefully shrewish mother-in-law (though her portrayal begins to get monotonously shrill and grating after a while); Miss Adams as a nervous wife (who can't decipher a simple road map) and Dorothy Provine as Berle's holier-than-thou spouse.

Durante registers strongly as the perpetrator of all the mayhem who literally kicks the bucket to start things rolling. Solid in key support are Ben Blue, Jim Backus, Eddie "Rochester" Anderson, William Demarest, Peter Falk, Paul Ford, Mike Mazurki, Madlyn Rhue, Marvin Kaplan and Arnold Stang, latter pair in that tellingly destructive garage leveling scene with Winters.

Satisfactory in somewhat lesser

assignments are Alan Carney, Edward Everett Horton, Buster Keaton, Don Knotts, Andy Devine and Charles McGraw. Others are in the cast, some with considerable name value, have merely bits, silent reactions or voice roles to deliver. There are surprise appearances by Jack Benny and Jerry Lewis. And the stuntmen and women rate special praise for their intrepid maneuvers.

The artistic and technical work on this production is of a high order. The adroit, resourceful and often panoramically spectacular photography of Ernest Laszlo is a major contribution. So is the razzle-dazzle editing of Fred Knudtson, a masterpiece of comedy molding. Rudolph Sternad's production design has personality and authenticity. Sound by Jean Kean contains a veritable symphony of automobile disasters and packs a tremendous wallop in that delirious climactic sequence on the firetruck ladder. Ernest Gold has composed a lively and lilting score, bulk of it variations on the melody of the title theme, a catchy and meaningful tune with a set of ironical lyrics by Mack David. Titles by Saul Bass are clever and dizzying, aptly igniting the fuse for an explosive motion picture experience. *Tube.*

Palm Springs Weekend

Imitation, but good one, of Metro's "Where The Boys Are." Color, fun, action, beaucoup romance. For those who think young market.

Hollywood, Sept. 27.

Warner Bros. release of a Michael A. Hoey production. Stars Troy Donahue, Connie Stevens, Ty Hardin, Stefanie Powers, Robert Conrad, Andrew Duggan, Jack Weston, Carole Cook, Jerry Van Dyke. Directed by Norman Taurog. Screenplay by Earl Hamner Jr.; camera, Harold Lipstein; editor, Folmar Blangsted; art director, LeRoy Deane; set decorator, George James Hopkins; sound, Stanley Jones; music, Frank Perkins; asst. directors, Chuck Hansen, Stanley Goldsmith. Reviewed at Wiltern Theatre, L.A., Sept. 27, '63. Running time, **99 MINS.**

Jim Munroe .... Troy Donahue
Gail Lewis (Jane Hoover) .. Connie Stevens
Stretch Fortunel .... Ty Hardin
Bunny Dixon .... Stefanie Powers
Eric Dean .... Robert Conrad
Chief Dixon .... Andrew Duggan
Coach Campbell .... Jack Weston
Mrs. Yates .... Carole Cook
Biff Roberts .... Jerry Van Dyke
Amanda North .... Zeme North
Boom-Boom .... Bill Mumy
Cora Dixon .... Dorothy Green
Gabby .... Robert Gothie
Hap .... Greg Benedict
Fred .... Gary Kincaid
Mike .... Mark Dempsey
Dave .... Jim Shane

Similar in format and aimed at the same market as "Where The Boys Are," Warner Bros.' "Palm Springs Weekend" is a serio-comic Western version of the 1960 Metro release. The plot similarity—here, it's the Easter invasion of Palm Springs by students—makes it a natural for the teenager market.

The film exposure it provides for a lot of bright-eyed young thespians, many of whom are already familiar to tv addicts, comes off pretty well as a hymn to spring and romance but, as a social document, it's a piece of hokum. How this film will sit with the citizens of its locale should make an interesting study as "Palm Springs Weekend" makes the visitors as good clean fun-seekers while the wrecking crews are purely local.

Director Norman Taurog throws lots of activity—mostly comedy, music and instant romance—into his 99-minute epic. There's unlimited kissing and necking, most of it is just spring juices beginning to flow, and an occasional dollop of true, true love. The picture is so clean, actually, that one seamy citizen—spoiled rich lad Robert Conrad—sticks out like a searchlight at midnight. His comeuppance is clearly telegraphed but many viewers will figure that his intentions towards target Connie Stevens were more than invited. Incredibly cast as a Hollywood High School student, she puts so much minx into the role that she arouses little sympathy, making her final scene with Ty Hardin more silly than sincere.

Visitors to Palm Springs pair off with local lasses. Stefanie Powers, chick chosen by Troy Donahue, turns out to be the daughter of chief of police Andrew Duggan but this obstacle is nothing for heroic character Donahue portrays—a medical student going through college on an athletic scholarship. Ty Hardin, a Hollywood stuntman, playing goodie to Conrad's baddie for Miss Stevens' affections, is quite impressive.

Comedy, broad and plentiful, owes much to the strong second team—particularly Zeme North as the perennial plain Jane; Jerry Van Dyke, as her male counterpart; and Jack Weston and Carole Cook, who have a more glandular approach to romance than do their youthful charges. Biggest waste of talent is Mark Dempsey, one of screen's better young actors, on a nothing role as a hiccuping basketball player.

Earl Hamner Jr.'s script is laden with all the old familiar phases: detergent in the pool, bratty kid, ugly duckling into pretty duckling; switched glass business (this one's used twice), but most of them pay off in hearty laughs. Taurog's stress on action and editor Folmar Blangsted's quick cuts make for fast but occasional sloppy antics. Item—Conrad picks up Miss Stevens at a bus rest-stop. Her bags are on bus but he says they can be picked up at station. He delivers her to hotel in next scene, complete with bags, before bus arrives.

Location shooting in Palm Springs is pleasurable in Harold Lipstein's Technicolor photography, a tremendous asset to the pic, not to say a topnotch visual aid for the resort. One studio-made scene at a purported casino outside town is, by contrast, glaringly fake. An important sequence, it is kept on screen so long that the unrealistic setting is accented.

Frank Perkins' music, adequately sprightly and young-folkish, gets vocal assets from cast members Donahue, who sings Larry Kusik and Paul Evans' "Live Young" behind the credits, and Van Dyke and Hardin, who team up for "Bye Bye Blackbird." The Modern Folk Quartet, used in a casino scene, are musically impressive but ridiculous in scene as no serious poker player would put up with such caterwauling. *Tube.*

Vacances Portugaises

(Portugese Vacation)
(FRENCH)

Paris, Oct. 29.

Cocinor release of Jac Films production. With Francoise Prevost, Jean-Pierre Aumont, Michel Auclair, Catherine Deneuve, Francoise Arnoul, Daniel Gelin, Francoise Brion, Jean-Marc Bory. Directed by Pierre Kast. Screenplay, Kast, Alain Aptekman, Jacques Doniol-Valcroze, Robert Scipion; camera, Raoul Coutard; editor, Yannick Bellon. At Lord-Byron, Paris. Running time, **98 MINS.**

Francoise .... Francoise Prevost
Jean-Pierre .... Jean-Pierre Aumont
Michel .... Michel Auclair
Catherine .... Catherine Deneuve
Mathilde .... Francoise Arnoul
Daniel .... Daniel Gelin
Eleonore .... Francoise Brion
Jean-Marc .... Jean-Marc Bory
Jacques .... Jacques Doniol- Valcroze
Pierre .... Pierre Vaneck
Genevieve .... Michele Girardon
Bernard .... Bernhard Wicki
Barbara .... Barbara Laage

Elegance is striven for in this tale of assorted couples at a weekend villa, but only intermittently achieved. It depends too much on surface patter and subtle nuances about worldly couples doing and undoing their relations. Result is a fairly glib and plodding affair that is mainly for some specialized or arty situations abroad, and limited at that.

A chic Parisian couple, holed up in a Portugese chateau, has the woman inviting friends down from Paris for a weekend. This brings in an estranged couple, a pornographic editor and ex-Marxist, a scientist and his latest whining conquest, two friends and a girl playing them against each other, a noted writer and an exalted 17-year-old girl in love with him.

This is mixed into a series of scenes as each couple reaches a height or consummation, or not, and then things are shifted. But epigrams and literary-styled dialog rarely bring any of these characters to life.

The landscape is beautiful, so are some of the players. And there is some cleverness in characterization at times. But it finally bogs down into a passionless, cerebral round of ultimately futile love affairs. More depth is needed either to present it as a comedy of manners or a look at the problems of love and communication. It is technically okay with the location shooting a help. *Mosk.*

Ein Fast Anstaendiges Maedchen

(A Nearly Decent Girl)
(GERMAN-SPANISH-COLOR)

Berlin, Oct. 22.

Columbia release of Fono (Berlin) and Chamartin (Madrid) production. Stars Liselotte Pulver, Martin Held, Alberto de Mendoza. Directed by Ladislao Vajda. Screenplay, Hans Jacoby and Istvan Bekefi, after story by Bekefi and Imre Jenei; camera (Eastmancolor), Guenther Anders; editor, Antonio Ramirez. At Marmorhaus, Berlin. Running time, **92 MINS.**

Lili Steiner .... Liselotte Pulver
Steckler .... Martin Held
Carlos .... Alberto de Mendoza
Rodriguez .... Gila
Alvarez .... Manola Moran
Rosita .... Alicea Altabella

Ladislao Vajda, Hungarian-born Spanish film director, has quite a number of fine pix to his credit. But this latest, a German-Spanish coproduction, "A Nearly Decent Girl," is on the disappointing side. It lacks charm and imagination for which a rather superficial script is chiefly to blame. However, the director here must share part of the responsibility for the shortcomings. Many sequences could have stood directorial polishing. Commercially, the film's prospects apply mainly to the German-language market where the Liselotte Pulver name means the most. Otherwise, the film isn't too much of a bargain.

The thin story concerns Herr Steckler (Martin Held), general manager of a big industrial firm in Duesseldorf, Germany, who goes to Madrid on a business trip. He takes Miss Lili Steiner (Liselotte Pulver), one of the company's secretaries, along because of her mastery of the Spanish language.

The best thing about this pic is Held as the general manager. He handles his role with skill. This prototype of a virile actor is always good, even in a mediocre film. As long as he's on the screen, this is never dull.

The same can't be said of Miss Pulver and Alberto de Mendoza. The latter's performance is too pat while Miss Pulver is a bit too routine. Support is generally okay.

Pic was shot in both the German and Spanish language. The German dialog is rather frank at times. *Hans.*

A L'Aube Du Troisieme Jour

(Dawn On The Third Day)
(FRENCH-GREEK)

Paris, Oct. 29.

Dicifrance release of Films Lodice-Carayannis Film production. With Tito Vandis, Frixos, Aleka Paizi, Thanos Canellis, Marianne Kouracou, George Foundas. Directed by Claude Bernard-Aubert. Screenplay, Claude Accursi, Bernard-Aubert; camera, Jean Collomb, Dinos Katsourdis; editor, Gabriel Rongier. At Studio Logos, Paris. Running time, **100 MINS.**

Stelios .... Tito Vandis
Clopidis .... Frixos
Popi .... Aleka Paizi
Costas .... Thanos Canellis
Myrto .... Marianna Kouracou
Resistant .... George Foundas

A tale of a small isolated Greek town besieged by soldiers during some war gets a feeling for people under pressure and adequately surveys their bravery, reticence, cowardice, honor and dishonor. Without flamboyance, this makes a comment with the help of simple if telling treatment. It appears a definite language possibility abroad with chances for playoff on its theme. Arty chances are also inherent in it if skimpier.

Made by a French director in Greece, film keeps the lingo of the country intact and uses only local thesps. This keeps it from being hybrid. Director Claude Bernard-Aubert displays an insight for the people and the theme. There is perhaps too skimpy characterization to make its denouncement of war and violence, and its irony, as dynamic and shattering as it should be.

Unidentified soldiers come in to the town with one of their number dead. They claim a townsman did it and they will block their one entrance to the mainland for food and sustenance, over a bridge, until a guilty man is given up. Actually, the solider had been killed by a partisan.

So the people panic and even decide to give up a newcomer among them, though he is innocent, only to have somebody else confess.

It has fine sun-drenched lensing. The players all have a ring of authenticity. It is just that the many different types, if acceptable, rarely bring the human pitch and intensity to make it more than

a good, solid pic with commendable pacifistic overtones. For the record, original title of the pic was "Les Moutons De Poliorka" (The Sheep of Poliorka). *Mosk.*

McLintock
(PANAVISION—COLOR)

Conventional John Wayne western. B.o. outlook okay.

Hollywood, Oct. 17.

United Artists release of Michael Wayne production. Stars John Wayne, Maureen O'Hara; features Yvonne De Carlo, Patrick Wayne, Stefanie Powers, Jack Kruschen, Chill Wills. Directed by Andrew V. McLaglen. Screenplay, James Edward Grant; camera (Technicolor), William H. Clothier; editor, Otho Lovering; music, Frank De Vol; asst. director, Frank Parmenter. Reviewed at Beverly Theatre, Oct. 17, '63. Running time, 127 MINS.

McLintock	John Wayne
Katherine McLintock	Maureen O'Hara
Louise Warren	Yvonne De Carlo
Devlin Warren	Patrick Wayne
Becky McLintock	Stefanie Powers
Birnbaum	Jack Kruschen
Drago	Chill Wills
Matt Douglas Jr.	Jerry Van Dyke
Bunny Dull	Edgar Buchanan
Ben Sage	Bruce Cabot
Davey Elk	Perry Lopez
Puma	Michael Pate
Agard	Strother Martin
Matt Douglas	Gordon Jones
Governor	Robert Lowery
Youngben Sage	Ed Faulkner
Ching	H. W. Gim
Alice Warren	Aissa Wayne
Sheriff Lord	Chuck Roberson
Carter	Hal Needham
Carlos	Pedro Gonzales Jr.
Jeth	Hank Worden
Jones	Leo Gordon
Beth	Mary Petterson
Fauntleroy	John Hamilton
Loafer	Ralph Volkie
Loafer	Dan Borzage
Running Buffalo	John Stanley
Millie	Karl Noven
Camille	Mari Blanchard

Remember "The Alamo"? And the muddy free-for-all in "North to Alaska"? And the itinerant donnybrook of "The Quiet Man"? Well, "McLintock" is a kind of cinematic fricassee of leftovers from those three lusty epics, seasoned with assorted cliches of the western idiom such as the cattlemen vs. the settlers and the snooty dudes vs. the crude frontiersmen. Yet, for all of its limited inspiration and familiar trails, the Batjac production has its infectious moments and should strike a responsive chord with audiences of a more clement disposition. The United Artists release seems on safe commercial footing.

"McLintock," most of all, is a John Wayne western, and that is a category not to be underestimated since Wayne is about the last thriving exponent of a great tradition, the last active member of a select fraternity of larger-than-life western film heroes who have all gone thataway, leaving him the only one consistently at large in his natural environment—the wide open spaces.

The style of the Michael Wayne production is forked-tongue-in-cheek. Nucleus of James Edward Grant's original yarn is the marital dual between Wayne, straight-shooting, rough-and-tumble, high-living, hard-drinking cattle baron whose town has been named after him, and Maureen O'Hara, who has more reservations than a Comanche real estate agent. Offshoots of this pivotal feud are a great debate between cattlemen and homesteaders that erupt into a wild and woolly fracas in a mudbath, and some bad blood between the government and the Comanche over transfer of the latter to Fort Sill. Neither of those two issues is resolved, but the central matter of domestic tranquillity is, in the course of a cross-town chase climaxed by a public spanking.

Wayne is in his element, or home, home on the Waynge. Miss O'Hara gives her customary high-spirited performance, although it's never quite clear what she's so darned sore about. Yvonne De Carlo is attractive as Wayne's cook, Stefanie Powers likewise as his college educated daughter. Vying for the latter's affection are Patrick Wayne, who etches a likable characterization, and Jerry Van Dyke, who gives a skillfully oafish performance. Effectively type cast are Chill Wills and Edgar Buchanan, and others of prominent value are Jack Kruschen, Bruce Cabot, Perry Lopez, Michael Pate, Strother Martin, Gordon Jones, Robert Lowery, Ed Faulkner, H. W. Gim, Chuck Roberson and Mari Blanchard. John Stanley is irresistibly incoherent as an amiable Comanche with a yen for some fire water.

Andrew V. McLaglen's broad, loose direction is backed up by William H. Clothier's handsome Technicolor photography, the sturdy settings of Hal Pereira and Eddie Imazu and an adjustable score by Frank De Vol. Otho Lovering's editing is perceptive, although the Texas-sized picture could be constructively trimmed down to, say, Oklahoma size. A couple of folk ditties, one by "By" Dunham, the other by Dunham (lyrics) and De Vol (music) are incorporated to advantage. *Tube.*

The World 10 Times Over
(BRITISH)

Uneven and rather downbeat peek at an oldhat theme. Some interesting performances, but scant marquee value for U.S.

London, Nov. 5.

Warner-Pathe release of a (Michael Tnke) Cyclops Production from Associated-British. Stars Sylvia Syms, June Ritchie, Edward Judd, William Hartnell; features Sarah Lawson, Francis de Wolff, Davy Kaye. Written and directed by Wolf Rilla. Camera, Larry Pizer; editor, Jack Slade; music, Edwin Astley. At Plaza, London. Running time, 93 MINS.

Billa	Sylvia Syms
Bob	Edward Judd
Ginnie	June Ritchie
Dad	William Hartnell
Elizabeth	Sarah Lawson
Shelbourne	Francis de Wolf
Compere	Davy Kaye
Penny	Linda Marlowe
Bolton	Jack Gwillim
Brian	Kevin Brennan
Freddy	Alan White

Wolf Rilla's screenplay, which he also directed, explores in one day's fairly busy activity, the aimlessness, insecurity and heartaches of nightclub hostesses. The result is overdramatic but provides opportunities for deft thesping and occasional imaginative direction and lensing. Nightclub and location sequences in London have a brisk authenticity. The pic should be a worthwhile programmer though lacking in name value for the U.S.

Story concerns two girls, euphemistically called nightclub hostesses, who share an apartment. One (June Ritchie) is a flighty, young extrovert who is having an affair with the married son of a property tycoon. The other (Sylvia Syms) is an older girl, daughter of a country schoolmaster, who is disgusted with her job but cannot break away from it.

The slim storyline concerns the capricious way in which Miss Ritchie treats her lover on the fateful day when she tries to commit suicide by slashing her wrists. Of more interest is the visit of Miss Syms' father to London to see his daughter, his attempts to communicate with her mentally and the desperate way she humiliates him when he visits the night club and discovers the trashy way in which she makes a living.

Miss Syms, long one of Britain's most underrated screen actresses, gives an intelligent and often moving performance. Her scenes with her father (William Hartnell) are excellent. Hartnell, playing the unworldly, scholarly father, who has no contact with his daughter, also gives an observant study. The other two principals are more phonily drawn characters. It seems unlikely that the hero (Edward Judd) would put up the extreme bitchiness of Miss Ritchie for an instant, even in infatuation. Judd seems strangely uneasy in his role and Miss Ritchie, despite many firstrate moments, sometimes appears as if she is simply jumping through paper hoops.

Sarah Lawson, Francis de Wolff and Linda Marlowe cope satisfactorily with minor roles. Davy Kaye, a top nightclub entertainer here, plays a nightclub emcee with confidence.

There are too many closeups and the offbeat lensing is overdone. But at least the film is a reasonable attempt to get off the beaten track technically, if not storywise. The image of the nightclubs in this pic comes over with a depressing air of futility.

Rich.

How About Us?
(Hvad Med Os?)
(DANISH)

The beat youth vs the beat middleage is the theme of this ambitious Danish film that introduces new female star with obvious international appeal.

Copenhagen, Nov. 5.

Constantin release of Bent Christensen production. Stars Maud Berthelsen, Erno Miller, Buster Larsen, Jorn Jeppesen, Poul Hagen, Morten Grunwald, Claus Nissen. Directed by Henning Carlsen. Story and screenplay, Leif Panduro; music, Krysztof Komeda; camera, Henning Kristiansen. Running time, 95 MINS.

Shrewd businessman and artistically ambitious Bent Christensen has given controversial modern novelist Leif Panduro and daring director Henning Carlsen a free hand in their making of another grim little story about roo'less youth and concerning an age that still has firm roots in the last World War. Story brings a young bomb-banning beatnik girl extremely casually into the arms and bed of a 43-year-old coffee planter. Latter has returned to Denmark 20 years after participating in a resistance group's command killing of an informer.

Plot thus pits remembered wartime against forgetful peacetime and middleage against youth. And in neither case do the twain meet in more than a physical contact that repulses rather than relieves. Panduro, a humorist when he wrote Christensen's "The Vacuum Cleaner Gang" last year, occasionally pokes the Bourgeois in the ribs with baroque jokes. But mostly he is very grim about the whole matter.

The love affair dies rather undramatically while the returned Freedom Fighter is violently shut up by former buddies who want to make sure that he remembers to forget forever an episode they evidently never learned to justify in their own hearts either.

While the film gives realism quite a try in director Carlsen's settings or the scenes, it is peopled with cardboard characters whose excuse for being carboard must be that they are symbols of whatever Panduro finds wanting in modern man, manners and morals. The colorful photography brings the film to an international level which Panduro's and Carlsen's work fall well below.

Still, the love story has its strong moments, daring yet never cheap. In the former topflight Paris fashionmodel Maud Berthelsen, director Carlsen has not only found a face that is sure to attract worldwide attention, but he has also made the model come alive with some very sensitive acting.

Kell.

San Francisco Fest

Week-End
(DANISH)

San Francisco, Nov. 2.
Bent Christensen production. Directed by Palle Kjaerulff-Schmidt. Screenplay by Klaus Rifbjerg. Camera, George Oddner; music, Erik Moseholm. Reviewed at San Francisco Film Festival, Nov. 1, '63. Running time, **85 MINS.**

Lars .... Jens Osterholm
Tove, ... Birgit Bruel
Kjeld, Married .... Willy Rathnov
Bet. .... Elsebet Knudson
Knud, Married .... Jesper Jensen
Ilse, ... Bente Dessau
Jan, Married .... Erik Kuhnau
Birthe, Maid .... Lotte Tarp
Innkeeper .... Jorgen Beck

In a town recently treated to a front page series of articles on "wife swapping," Denmark's entry in the San Francisco Film Festival, did not come as a shock. "Week-End" sensitively succeeded, however, where the articles failed, in showing the emptiness, the joylessness, the lack of any real passion in the frantic clutching for a change-off partner.

Awarded "Best Film of 1963" in Copenhagen, banned by French and Finnish censors and withdrawn from the Cannes and Berlin Festivals, it is the frank story of a hot summer interlude by the sea. Despite the presence of their children, three married couples and a bearded bachelor — spirited, perceptive, and vigorous catalyst — — drink, dance, reach out to each other and find a repetition of familiar frustrations. "What we want," says Jens Osterholm, the bachelor," is an air raid . . . if we were forced to go through all that we might rescue someone or get killed."

The erotic by-play (heightened by a pulsating jazz score), with the usual quota of naked shots, builds to a climax of childish violence and a sense of shamed, uneasy recognition.

Klaus Rifbjerg, the iconoclastic Danish newspaperman who wrote the script, director Palle Kjaerulff-

Schmidt and producer Bent Christensen have given the festival an impressive and controversial document.

Judy.

The Courtesan
(INDIA)

A Filmkraft, Ltd. production. Features Soumitro Chatterji and Ruma Guhathakurta. Screenplay and direction by Arup Guha Thakurta. Based on a story by Bimal Mittra; music, Ali Akbar Khan. Camera, Dinen Gupta. Reviewed at Frisco Film Fest., Nov. 6, '63. Running time, **70 MINS.**

India's entry in the Frisco Film Fest is the first solo effort of Director Arup Guha Thakurta, former assistant to Satyajit Ray. It didn't rub off. Film shows none of Ray's poetic imagination, insight or technical skill.

Thakurta also wrote the screenplay for this mediocre treatment of the story of a courtesan, kidnapped as a child by a brothelkeeper, and found years later by her childhood sweetheart who then marries her. They make a new life in a distant village until her past is discovered.

Although the courtesan-wife, played with sensitivity and intelligence by the director's wife, Ruma Guhathakarta, has been a model of sweetness, helpfulness and inspiration in the village, her neighbors turn on her. It is an inexplicable rejection, for which no foundation has been laid for western comprehension in terms of character or situation.

The photography does not even do justice to the beauty of the star, daughter of a Calcutta editor and niece of one of India's best known lawyers, who has provided a graceful Indian touch to the festival.

The final straws are almost indecipherable sub-titles which turn out to be a kind of low-grade pidgin English. Surely the British could have done better than that.

Judy.

No Way Out
(FILIPINO)

San Francisco, Nov. 7.
Leon P. Lopez production. Directed by Lamberto V. Avellana. Screenplay, Rolf Bayer; music, Restie Umali. Reviewed at San Francisco Film Festival. Running time, **95 MINS.**
Major Juan de la Cruz .. Leopoldo Salcedo
Capt. Ricardo Flores .... Ronald Remy
Maria Flores .... Lalaine Bennett
Pedro .... Lou Salvader Jr.
Sgt. Cordero .... Joe Sison
Mayor Ramos .... Alfonso Carvajal
Nicolas .... Jose Vergara
Col. Matsuyama .... Kim Sung Ho
Capt. Harada .... Park Noh Shik
Lt. Iko Matsuyama .... Chol Ji Hee

Despite stilted dialogue, poor dubbing and some amateurish performances, there is something genuinely touching about "No Way Out," the Philippine entry in the San Francisco Film Festival.

A resistance drama that earnestly attacks racial stereotypes and makes a plea for love and basic human values, perhaps the very lack of sophistication—which occasionally drew laughs in the wrong places — also gives the film its moving moments. Aided, not inconsiderably, by the luminous appeal of a beautiful Korean star, Choi Ji Kee, playing a Japanese army nurse who loves a Philippine doctor she has met in a

Japanese prisoner of war camp.

The nurse's father, Col. Matsuyama, portrayed by another Korean actor, Kim Sung Ho, is in charge of a Philippine community, after the fall of Bataan and Corregidor and during the release of Philippine prisoners of war. The story centers around a Philippine rebel leader, Leopoldo Salcedo, who has escaped from Bataan and is organizing resistance against the Japanese occupation forces. The girl the rebel leader loves is kidnapped by the Japanese in order to make him give himself up. In the meantime, her brother, the doctor, returning home, is persuaded to join the rebels. The conflict that develops when the two women become hostages of the opposing forces is used to show how war twists and distorts the best of human feeling. In the end, although the nurse and her lover are killed by her father and the Japanese forces, their love has somehow triumphed and it is the father who has been destroyed.

Although the "English" voice provided for Col. Matsuyama is almost totally incomprehensible and although he is a physically gross and unattractive man, Kim Sung Ho still manages to evoke sympathy for the leader anxious to prove his Japanese leadership despite some Korean blood, the father torn between his daughter and what he thinks are his country's demands.

"No Way Out" gives the Westerner a rare glimpse of the war through Philippine eyes and its generous humanity is rewarding.

Judy.

Paula Cautiva
(ARGENTINE)

Arles Cinematografica (Hector Olivera) production. Directed by Fernando Ayala. Stars Susana Freyre, Duilio Marzio; features Lautaro Murua, Fernanda Mistral. Screenplay by Beatriz Guido and Ayala from original story by Beatriz Guido; camera, Alberto Etchebehere; sound, Jorge Vanarelli; music composed by Astor Paizzolla. Reviewed at Frisco Film Fest., Nov. 7, '62. Running time, **95 MINS.**

The major obstacle to enjoyment of this technically good, dramatically bad approach to social life and politico-business attitudes in contemporary Buenos Aires is film's uncertainty as to what it's trying to say. Although slickly made, with top-notch photography, its commercial chances in the global film market seem negligible.

Story has Duilio Marzio, former Argentine who has become U.S. citizen, returning to Buenos Aires after 15-year absence as a business consultant, for an American company on a big deal requiring approval and signature of incumbent Minister. On arrival, company's local rep fixes him up (sans explanation) with beautiful "call-girl" Susana Freyre. It follows formula of good boy meets bad girl, with usual results.

Girl is actually granddaughter of member of landed gentry, down to his last hacienda, a huge non-self-supporting ranch kept going with "fake" receptions for gullible and monied American tourists (no other nationally of tourist is ever shown) plus some support from girl, supposedly from earnings as a clerk in a fancy women's store.

Marzio, following formula, eventually proposes to girl, finds out her real calling, gives her up, but is straightened out in his moral

and political thinking when the all-important "deal" falls through as result of Minister losing office on one of those military coups that apparently occur every other Friday in Argentina. He decides to stay in Argentina, goes to girl and "The End."

Script, unfortunately, never decides whether it's a comedy or a drama. Some of the pseudo-serious scenes are frequently funny; some of the attempts at humor are heavy-handed and coarse. Subtitles are frequently guilty of bad grammar, worse spelling and odd translation. At one point a character speaks of Marzio as a "Casanova" while the subtitle shows "Don Juan." Several characters portray American tourists (so exaggerated that they destroy any intended satire).

Miss Freyre, an excellent actress with the international-type beauty that should make her a natural for leads in European or American pix, works hard to overcome the banalities of the plot. The other principals, however, including Marzio, never master their frequently ridiculous parts. Alberto Etchebehere's black and white photography of modern Buenos Aires and the ranch, "La Cautiva," is excellent but some of the shots are frequently chopped off by the poor editing. Astor Paizzolaa's score is commercial and uninspired.

Robe.

Peau De Banane
(Banana Skin)
(FRENCH—FRANSCOPE)

Paris, Nov. 5.
Omnia release of Sud Pacifique-Capitole Films production. Stars Jeanne Moreau, Jean-Paul Belmondo; features Claude Brasseur, Gert Frobe, Jean-Pierre Marielle. Directed by Marcel Ophuls. Screenplay, Claude Sautet, Daniel Boulanger, Ophuls from book by Charles Williams; camera, Jean Rabier; editor, Monique Kirsanoff. Preemed in Paris. Running time, **95 MINS.**
Cathy .... Jean Moreau
Michel .... Jean-Paul Belmondo
Charlie .... Claude Brasseur
Bordas .... Jean-Pierre Marielle
Bontemps .... Alain Cuny
Lachard .... Gert Frobe

A familiar name comes back to the screen, in this sophisticated picaresque situation comedy, via Marcel Ophuls, son of the late noted international filmmaker Max. For a first pic, Marcel displays a nice free-wheeling talent for witty comedics if it is not completely sustained throughout the lightweight pie.

Reminiscent of pre-war American films about likable confidence men and women fleecing the rich and taking pity on worthy victims, it spins a dizzying plot that manages to keep from bogging down entirely at times by the solid ease and workmanship of stars Jeanne Moreau and Jean-Paul Belmondo and the breezy direction of Ophuls.

Sometimes lacking are the brittle spark, and unflagging pacing of comedies of this type. But there is a tongue-in-cheek grace and ease that keeps this entertaining most of the way. On its star names, it looks a solid local entry and could have matching international chances if well placed and handled.

Miss Moreau is out to pluck two underhanded businessmen who ruined her father. She enlists her ex-husband into it, Belmondo, and they are off. She is not above doublecrossing her associates in the game. It winds up through taking in the brother of one of Miss

Moreau's father's ruiners and then the big man himself.

But it seems the brother was a nice chap and his money is returned as the pair go on for what looks like a light life of amiable crime. Miss Moreau is lively and

Only 10% of these films, however correctly underhanded while Belmondo's presence and timing lend themselves to this type of production. Ophuls handles it all with aplomb and style if he sometimes still cannot manage to keep this sparkling throughout.

But this shows up needed new film comedy director in the making. On the spot, free-and-easy lensing helps give this a freshness. It is technically good, with a fine supporting cast also getting into the spirit of this con-man charade. *Mosk.*

The Aimless Bullet
(KOREAN)

Kim Sung Choon production. Features Kim Chin Kyu, Choi Mu Ryong, Park Choon, Suh Kyong Hi, Suh Ae Ja, Kim Hye Jung, Lo Jae Shin, Yoon Il Bong, Moon Chung Sook, Moon Hye Ran, Yang Il Min, Lee Dae Yup, Choi Myung Su, Yoo Kae Sun, Ko Sul Bong and Park Kyong Joo. Directed by Yoo Hyun Mok. Screenplay by Lee Chong Ki; camera, Kim Hak Sung; music, Kim Sung Tae. Reviewed at Frisco Film Fest, Nov. 5, '63. Running time, 110 MINS.

Korea's entry in the Frisco Film Fest is a remarkable film in more ways than one. It's unremittingly hopeless picture of postwar, poverty-stricken Korea may come as a shock to U.S. veterans of the Korean war, but officials of the Republic of Korea are worried right now about its shock effect on their own people.

"The Aimless Bullet" was made in 1960 under great difficulties and sparse capital. It was then banned by the government because of its black picture of unemployment and because of a phrase spoken over and over by the war-crazed grandmother: "Let's get out of here!" which could be interpreted as meaning "back to our home in North Korea." (Director Yoo Hyun Mok in Frisco, insisted, through Korean government interpretors, that it was meant just as a cry to leave a miserable situation.)

Richard Dyer MacCann, U.S. State Department specialist and consultant to the National Film Production Center in Korea, "discovered" the film, persuaded the Korean government to release it in Seoul so that it could qualify as an entry in Frisco Fest.

Film is a cry against poverty, injustice and aimless existence, told through the story of one family. An elder brother (Kim Chin Kyu), caged by his conscience to work in a meaningless job; his younger brother (Choi Mu Ryong), a jobless veteran who turns to crime, and a sister (Suh Ae Ja), who becomes a prostitute.

Brilliantly detailed camera work is matched by probing sympathy and rich characterizations. While recurrent theme is the hopelessness of fighting against fate, it also suggests, not too subtly, that the source of pain in the toothache should be eliminated by the dentist as quickly as possibly. *Judy.*

The Boxer
(CZECHOSLOVAKIA)

San Francisco, Nov. 7.

Czechoslovakia Film production. Directed by Peter Solan. Screenplay, Josef Ilen, Tibor Vichta and Solan; music, William Bukovy; camera, Tibor Biath. Reviewed at San Francisco Film Festival. Running time, 120 MINS.
Jan Kopinek .... Stefan Kvietik
Kraft .... Manfred Krug
Helga .... Valentina Thielova
Venzlak .... Josef Kondrat
Willi .... Edwin Marian
Holder .... Gerhard Rachold
Gluch .... Jindrich Narenta
Stasek .... Edmund Ogrodzinski
Emil .... Janusz Bobek
Blocker .... Jan Kovacik
Magda .... Magda Godoleova

In the grim setting of a concentration camp, "The Boxer," Czechoslovakia's offbeat entry in the San Francisco Film Festival, tells of two men trying to abide by the rules of the sporting game, the keeper and his prisoner.

The Nazi commander of the camp (Manfred Krug) is a man whose heart is in boxing, a man yearning for a sparring partner, a man who goes through life "observing the rules of the game" whether they become the rules of war or the rules of a prison camp. He is a man incapable of seeing the irony in telling prisoners who have attempted to escape that they are being punished for "breaking the rules." When he spots the signs of a boxer in one of the escapers, he has him fattened up for a match and insists that it be a fair and equal one.

Stefan Kvietik plays the Czech boxer with a hungry intensity, troubled by the aspersions of his starving fellow inmates, wanting to beat his opponent and afraid to lose his own life if he does.

Under Peter Solan's direction, the fight scenes have the smell and authenticity of the real thing, ditto the concentration camp. There is one memorable scene in which the Czech boxer, regaining his strength, is overcome by the horror and sudden black smoke pouring from the gas chamber.

But this unrelieved grimness calls for a little mercy—the film needs cutting and editing to sharpen its impact, as well as shorten it. It could also use a less confused ending. *Judy.*

The Love Eterne
(FORMOSA)

Run Run Shaw production. Features Betty Loh Tih, Ivy Ling Po, Jen Chieh, Li Kun. Directed by Li Han-hsiang. Screenplay, Li Han-hsiang; camera, Ho Lan-shan; sound, Wang Yung-hua; art director, Chen Chi-jui; music, Chou Lanping. At Frisco Film Fest, Nov. 10, 1963. Running time, 133 MINS.

Exquisite beauty of the Chinese (Formosa) countryside captured in this poetic story of doomed love in Fourth Century China provided a restful interlude in the Frisco Film Fest, almost exclusively concerned with war and grim problems of contemporary life.

Chu Ying-tai, a young lady with both brains and femininity, persuades her parents to let her study, disguised as a man, at a school far from her home. She falls in love with a fellow student who, after three years of constant companionship and innumerable hints from the young lady, fails to discover the masquerade. When a matchmaker tells the "bookworm" of her love, it is too late because her parents have already betrothed her to another.

Although the film, utilizing the

musical tradition of Chinese opera, lacks commercial appeal for most Western audiences, the camerawork is superb. The depth of color through the changing seasons and the wisps of fog in the landscape have all the quality of fine Oriental art.

The screenplay, despite some repetitiousness, has humor and charm. There are Mandarin subtitles, in addition to English, for those Chinese who speak the Cantonese dialect and cannot understand spoken Mandarin. *Judy.*

Lebanon Fest

Nem Alt Meg Az Autobusz
(The Bus Did Not Stop)
(HUNGARIAN)

Beirut, Oct. 23.

Hungarofilm release of Hunnia production. With Klari Tolany, Hilda Gobbi. Directed by Janus Palashty. Screenplay, J. Csizmare; camera, M. Herczemik; editor, Sandor Borankay. At Beirut Film Fest. Running time, 65 MINS.

This Hungarian film is a fairly witty look at a group of people caught up in a police station when a whole busload is unloaded there after the theft of a watch. But if it has some clever scenes, the characters and action are mainly sterotyped and its length and treatment make this primarily a local item.

Things get complicated when a bag full of stolen loot is found on the bus. But all is worked out after all the characters have gone through some change or revealing themselves as they really are. If this pokes fun at bureaucracy, it is mainly on a cabaret revue format. It is technically good and well played. *Mosk.*

Yakilacak Kitap
(Book That Should Burn)
(TURKISH)

Beirut, Oct. 20.

Duru Film production and release. Stars Leyla Sayar, Tamer Yigit; features Ulvi Vraz, Atij Kaptan. Directed by Sureyya Duru. Screenplay, Erdogan Tunas from book by Etem Izzet Benice; camera, Ali Yaver; music, Isult Nadin. At Beirut Film Fest. Running time, 110 MINS.
Vicdan .... Leyla Sayar
Vecdet .... Tamer Yigit
Omer .... Ulvi Vraz
Friend ....Atij Kaptan

Film is a melodrama with Dickensian overtones. It is about the tribulations of an orphan girl who is raped at 12 and almost ends up marrying her own brother. But it is treated in a solid, sincere, direct manner. Film shows a budding visual flair in little known Turkish pix if this one is primarily for playoff chances in less demanding areas than in European and U.S. spots.

It is all told clearly and forthrightly and manages to make some comments on Turkish life today in seemingly moving between rural backwardness and city modernity. The little girl gets adopted by a decent aging couple. She grows up

hating men because of the raping but finally falls in love.

Director Sureyya Duru tells his tale simply and it's understandable even without subtitles, as this was shown. Characters are mainly larger than life stereotypes if the girl does have some individuality.

This is technically good with a neat, if old-fashioned, narrative style. Over 150 films are made in Turkey every year and this pic is one of the better ones. *Mosk.*

Na Bialym Szlaku
(On the White Trails)
(POLISH)

Beirut, Oct. 21.

Polski State Film release of Studio Unit production. With Leon Niemczyk, Emil Kerewicz, Ryszard Kotas, Mazmierz Talarczyk. Directed by Jaroslav Brzozowski, Andrzej Wrobel. Screenplay, Alina and Cezslaw Centkiewicz; camera, Boguslaw Lambach; editor, Lazmierz Serocki; music, Marceli Novak. At Beirut Film Fest. Running time, 75 MINS.
Sikora .... Leon Niemczyk
Weber .... Emil Karemicz
Biorn .... Ryszard Kotas
Olaf .... Kazmierz Talarczyk

Adventure pic has some good lensing in the Arctic during the last World War but not the force to bring off its ironic Pacifist yarn. Only playoff chances loom abroad on its okay action aspects.

During the last war, the Germans had some Arctic outposts as did the Free Poles. This has a Pole trying to bring in a captured German officer. The war ends, and they are given up for lost as they struggle on.

The enmity and then growing respect between the two men tries to make its statement on war's uselessness. But their scrapes and outlooks are couched in too many planted suspense interludes, and overdone dramatic treatment.

Film thus loses its bitter ironic impact but all this is viewable because of its solid feel for the landscape and the well-handled fight and trek scenes. *Mosk.*

Vacances a La Mer
(Vacation By the Sea)
(RUMANIAN-COLOR-SONGS)

Beirut, Oct. 24.

Bucaresti production and release. With I. Darie, Alexandru Monte, Alexandru Repan, Melanie Cirje. Written and directed by H. Nicolaide, Cezar Grigoriu. Camera (Sovcolor), Andre Feher; music, Gheirghie Grigoriu. At Beirut Film Fest. Running time, 75 MINS.
Stadion .... Iurie Darle
Stita .... Alexandru Monte
Florin .... Alexandru Repan
Irina .... Melanie Cirje
Anca .... Ileana Sandu
Magda .... Ana Szeses

Musical pic about a swing band which goes off to a sea resort, with the usual adventures of young boys and girls, might well have passed as an ordinary western opus if it were not for the stress on work as the real mainstay of these vacationers. There's also the handicap of the old-fashioned musical scoring of the film. It should have good results in Eastern Bloc countries on its fairly light and entertaining treatment but is too skimpy to pass for Western foreign usage.

The orch plays prewar style swing songs. They are roped into a concert at a sea resort to pay their way. Then the band gets into plenty of trouble with the organizers before all is well. The boys manage to get in some innocent romantico escapades, too.

This is generally lightweight and childish, without the zip, musical freshness and zing to make it worth trying to place alongside Yank pix of the same type. Players are engaging and color is acceptable if sometimes uneven. It's all in widescreen. *Mosk.*

Who's Minding The Store?
(COLOR)

Jerry Lewis in the kind of wild funny business that should prove irresistible to his fans and win him some new customers to boot.

Paramount release of Paul Jones production. Stars Jerry Lewis. Jill St. John; features Agnes Moorehead. John McGiver. Ray Walston, Francesca Bellini. Directed by Frank Tashlin. Screenplay, Tashlin and Harry Tugend; camera (Technicolor), Wallace Kelley; editor, John Woodcock; music, Joseph J. Lilley. Previewed at Victoria Theatre, N.Y., Nov. 14, '63. Running time. **90 MINS.**
Raymond Phiffier .... Jerry Lewis
Barbara Tuttle .... Jill St. John
Phoebe Tuttle .... Agnes Moorehead
Mr. Tuttle .... John McGiver
Mr. Quimby .... Ray Walston
Shirley .... Francesca Bellini
Mrs. Rothgraber .... Nancy Kulp
Roberts .... John Abbott
Smith .... Jerry Hausner
Lady Wrestler .... Peggy Mondo
Mattress Customer .... Mary Treen
Dowager .... Isobel Elsom
Cop .... Richard Wessel
Gourmet Manager .... Fritz Feld

Frank Tashlin and Harry Tugend have fashioned a wild screenplay, Tashlin has directed with full emphasis on the madcap nonsense and Jerry Lewis has a field day playing it all out in his uninhibited (meaning zany) style. It's fun, this "Who's Minding the Store?"

Lewis has an enviable trackrecord at the boxoffice; even his pictures which got (and deserved) a critical panning have done well. At first glance this new one would figure as one of his strongest.

But at what point does exposure become overexposure? Two hours every Saturday night with Lewis for free on television is a factor that might well be considered. Further, the present video series hasn't been successful in terms of ratings and pro appraiser comment. Show, in fact, has now been cancelled by ABC.

Paul Jones. producer, has provided a colorful production setting for Lewis' nutty antics. The filmmaker, also has gotten in an abundance of commercial display for appliances, other household items, etc., as Lewis goes to work in a department store and wrecks it department by department.

He has an especially attractive romantic vis-a-vis in Jill St. John who takes a job as elevator operator to hide the fact she's really the daughter of the store's owner. Agnes Moorehead plays the owner's domineering wife, who regards Lewis as an idiot, Frank McGiver is the owner, and Ray Walston is a dame-chasing manager. Among his prey is Francesca Bellini.

They all romp through with accent on the broad comedy and, of course, with the spotlight mainly on havoc-wreaking Lewis. Whether he's assigned to paint the top of a flagpole or demonstrate a vacuum cleaner (which, naturally, gets out of hand and runs amok around the store), Lewis puts on a show of entertaining absurdity.

This is his cup of tea, and it's no mistake that he permitted others to carry the ball, too—in directing, writing and producing.

The direction is brisk, the camera work by Wallace Kelley properly captures the sight-gag values, the editing cuts the lags to a minimum, the music by Joseph J. Lilley is nicely synchronized with the

action. And it's all dressed up in Technicolor. *Gene.*

Fun In Acapulco
(COLOR)

Lacklustre but commercially salable musical romance for the Presley buffs.

Hollywood, Nov. 8.
Paramount release of Hal Wallis production. Stars Elvis Presley; features Ursula Andress. Elsa Cardenas. Paul Lukas. Directed by Richard Thorpe. Screenplay, Allan Weiss; camera (Technicolor), Daniel L. Fapp; editor, Stanley E. Johnson; music, Joseph J. Lilley; asst. director, Michael Moore. Reviewed at Picwood Theatre, Nov. 8, '63. Running time, **100 MINS.**
Mike Windgren .... Elvis Presley
Margarita Dauphine ..... Ursula Andress
Dolores Gomez .... Elsa Cardenas
Maxmillian .... Paul Lukas
Raoul Almeido .... Larry Domasin
Moreno .... Alejandro Rey
Jose .... Robert Carricart
Janie Harkins .... Teri Hope
Mr. Harkins .... Charles Evans
Hotel Manager .... Alberto Morin
Desk Clerk .... Francisco Ortega
Bellboy .... Robert De Anda
Telegraph Clerk .... Linda Rivera
First Girl .... Darlene Tomkins
Second Girl .... Linda Rand
Musicians.. Eddie Cano, Carlos Mejia.
Leon Cardenas. Fred Aguirre
Photographer .... Tom Hernandez
Secretary .... Adele Palacios

Elvis Presley's latest appearance under the Hal Wallis-Paramount banner shapes up as a comfortable commercial attraction and should profit by the fact that it's his first release in more than six months. Presley fans won't be disappointed —he sings ten serviceable songs and wiggles a bit to boot. However, the ground covered by the plot doesn't help to increase his star stature and, for those who are not devotees, the main attraction may turn out to be the Technicolorful scenery of Acapulco.

Presley has come a long way and is deserving of better material than has been provided in this Allan Weiss screenplay in which he portrays an ex-trapeze catcher who has lost his nerve after a fatal mishap. Arriving in Acapulco, he hires on as an entertainer-life guard at a resort, in hopes the latter job may afford him the opportunity to dive off the high board and erase his fear of heights. A romantic entanglement leads to the moment of truth in which Presley, having already mastered the high board, finds himself at the famed cliff of La Quebrada at the precise moment that the featured diver (whom he has just kayoed) is ordered via loud speaker to perform his daring feat. Will Elvis take a dive—er, plunge? Well, he just happens to have his swim trunks on underneath his street clothes and his special zoomar vision catches sight of his favorite girl in the stands.

The other three-fourths of the central romantic quartet are Ursula Andress, Elsa Cardenas and Alejandro Rey, fine-looking specimens, all. Others of note in the cast are Paul Lukas as an ex-duke-turned-chef and young Larry Domasin as a business-minded urchin more or less adopted by Presley.

Richard Thorpe's direction keeps the routine story on the move, a strong asset since opportunity for developing characterization is virtually nil. Adequate production assists are fashioned by cameraman Daniel L. Fapp, editor Stanley E. Johnson, composer Joseph J. Lil-

ley and art directors Hal Pereira and Walter Tyler. Principal photography on the film, Presley's 13th and sixth for Wallis, was done in Hollywood. There are 11 songs, including the title ditty, which are pleasant within the context of the picture but don't show much promise as potential popular numbers on their own. *Tube.*

Soldier In The Rain

Offbeat service comedy-drama that doesn't quite come off. Will have to rely on cast appeal of Jackie Gleason, et al for b.o. bait.

Hollywood, Nov. 14.
Allied Artists release of Martin Jurow production. Stars Jackie Gleason, Steve McQueen; features Tuesday Weld, Tony Bill. Tom Poston, Ed Nelson. Directed by Ralph Nelson. Screenplay, Maurice Richlin, Edwards, based on novel by William Goldman; camera, Philip Lathrop; editor, Ralph Winters; music, Henry Mancini; asst. director, Austen Jewell. Reviewed at Picwood Theatre, Nov. 14, '63. Running time, **87 MINS.**
Master Sgt. Maxwell Slaughter
Jackie Gleason
Supply Sgt. Eustace Clay..Steve McQueen
Bobby Jo Pepperdine....Tuesday Weld
Pfc. Jerry Meltzer .... Tony Bill
Lt. Magee .... Tom Poston
M.P. Sgt. Priest .... Ed Nelson
M.P. Sgt. Lenahan .... Lew Gallo
Chief of Police .... Paul Hartman
Frances McCoy .... Chris Noel
Sgt. Tozzi .... Lewis Charles
1st Sgt. William Booth
Rockne Tarkington
Battalion Major .... John Hubbard
Old Man .... Sam Flint
Capt. Blekeley .... Adam West

Allied Artists will have to rely heavily on marquee merchandise to sell this novelty item because the odd and unsubstantial service comedy-drama that materializes onscreen does not figure to appeal to the taste of the average filmgoer. There is an undercurrent of charm about "Soldier In The Rain," and every once in awhile the charm surfaces, but these are only momentary rewards in a picture notoriously lacking in clarity, stability, depth and definition. The Blake Edwards production just doesn't come off.

One might classify the film a fairy tale in khaki. The screenplay by Edwards and Maurice Richlin out of a novel by William Goldman relates the bittersweet tale of two modern army buddies—a smooth operating master sergeant (Jackie Gleason) who has found a home in the service, and his hero-worshipping protege (Steve McQueen), a supply sergeant who is about to return to civvies and hopes Gleason will join him in private enterprise on the outside. After going through several adventures together, Gleason, for some mysterious reason, dies, and McQueen, for some equally mysterious reason, re-ups.

There are several sudden, and vigorous, bursts of comedy dialog, principally exchanges between Gleason, who has a complex about his bulk, and Tuesday Weld, who plays a basically sweet but dumb and ingeniously tactless 18-year-old whose idea of a compliment is to refer to him as a "fat Randolph Scott." But such mirth is only spasmodic and is snowed under by a sentimental approach that misfires and an almost perverse unwillingless to define characters or explain why such odd things are happening to them. For example, it is never clear why a pair of MP's are so hellbent on getting even with McQueen, a

friendly sort of fellow who even loves dogs. Are MP's motivated by sheer sadism? That is what one is led to believe after witnessing as brutal a fight scene as may ever have been staged on celluloid.

McQueen will not please his fans with the characterization he has created—a kind of Southern-fried boob who reminds one of Clem Kadiddlehoffer. The style of portrayal is exaggerated and unnatural, and seems unnecessary. Gleason fares better with a restrained approach, through which his natural endomorphic vitality seeps through. Miss Weld is a standout with her convincing portrait of the classic dizzy blonde as a teenager. Tony Bill scores as McQueen's screwball sidekick and Tom Poston has a couple of good scenes as a gullible lieutenant. Ed Nelson and Lew Gallo portray those inexplicably cruel MP's. Commendable supporting work is fashioned by Paul Hartman, Chris Noel, Lewis Charles, Rockne Tarkington, John Hubbard, Sam Flint and Adam West.

The screenplay's ups and downs seem to have engulfed director Ralph Nelson. He has capitalized on the scattered bright spots, but has failed to detect or delete the artificiality of McQueen's approach and appears to have been at a loss to cope with the film's fuzziness and disjointedness. Producer Martin Jurow's concoction benefits from the probing, intimate photography of Philip Lathrop and a typically expressive and obtrusive score by Henry Mancini, which is a blend of a rather plaintive, sombre theme for the dramatic interludes and a whimsical melody for the comedy passages that sounds like an afterthought to his material for "Hatari!" The film has been trimmed to a pleasantly brief running time by editor Ralph Winters, but it seems as if a lot of dramatic explanation and exposition has been snipped out in the interest of brevity. Phil Barber's sets have the proper military base look about them. *Tube.*

The Informers
(BRITISH)

Hard-hitting, violent crime thriller; intelligent performance by Nigel Patrick as a framed cop and tough, exciting climax.

London, Nov. 12.

Rank Organization release and presentation of a William McQuitty production. Stars Nigel Patrick, Margaret Whiting; features Harry Andrews, Colin Blakely, Catharine Woodville, Derren Nesbitt, Frank Finlay, Roy Kinnear. Directed by Ken Annakin. Screenplay, Alun Falconer; from 'Death of a Snout" by Dougl■ Warner; camera, Reginald Wyer; editor, Alfred Roome; music, Clifton Parker, at Leicester-square Theatre, London. Running time, **105 MINS.**

Chief Inspector Johnnoe ..	Nigel Patrick
Mary Johnnoe	Catharine Woodville
Maise	Maggie Whiting
Charles Ruskin	Colin Blakely
Bertie Hoyle	Derren Nesbitt
Leon Sale	Frank Finlay
Bestwick	Harry Andrews
Ben	Michael Coles
Jim Ruskin	John Cowley
Smythe	Allan Cuthbertson
Shorty	Roy Kinnear
Lewis	Ronald Hines
Lonergan	Peter Prowse
Hill	George Sewell
Lou Waites	Kenneth J. Warren
Lipson	Brian Wilde

Here's a tough, hard-hitting, cops-and-robbers thriller set in London's underworld which, despite the story line, situations and characters occasionally tripping themselves up, crackles along at a brisk pace and has the smell of authenticity. Police detail is taken care of expertly, with Ex-Detective Superintendent John Gosling of Scotland Yard hired as technical adviser. Locations have been carefully picked and Alex Vetchinsky's careful art work embellishes the real stuff. Thus a sharp study is made of the sinister half-world of the villains, the hideaways, streets, taverns, clubs, and poolrooms of the East End and Soho.

Douglas Warner's novel, "Death of a Snout," has been turned into a slick screenplay with dialog that is often a shade salty but stands up as the sort of yack that the characters would use in real life. The crooks' lingo is sometimes a spot puzzling, but not enough to be a problem. If this is not the way that Scotland Yard moves into action in cracking a safebreaking gang then it's the way that cinema audiences expect it to be, if they want kicks.

Central character is Chief Inspector Johnno, a dedicated cop at Scotland Yard. He has many contacts in the underworld and the snouts, or informers, feed him with many a juicy lead to solving a crime. But Johnno's chief insists that personal contact with informers should be out. From now on, scientific methods must be used. But Johnno believes he is close to cracking the gang that has been pulling off some audacious banknote robberies and is sure that one of his most wily informants can put him on the trail. So he disobeys orders.

The informer is murdered and the inspector starts to investigate. From then on it's a story of double-crossing and patient tracking down by Johnno. Johnno's teenacity is rewarded. The murdered informant's info is right enough to frighten the daylights out of the gang leader and the shadow man behind him who handles the greenbacks.

To dispose of the inspector they decide he must be framed. They use the gangster's moll to set a bribery trap and Johnno is arrested. But the dead man's brother is also on the trail. Before Johnno breaks jail, and then the gang, there is a tough free-for-all between the two gangs, making a climax that has the impact of a straight left.

Nigel Patrick, as Johnno, gives a suave, dominating performance in which, till the finale, he uses brain rather than brawn. Here is a topnotch portrayal of a thoughtful, diligent and completely dedicated policeman. Of the assorted villains, outstanding are Frank Finlay as the bossman and Derren Nesbitt, with an insidious study in oily menace, as the pimp who organizes the robberies. Roy Kinnear, Colin Blakely, John Cowley and Kenneth J. Warren also chip in with sturdy performances as underworld characters.

Harry Andrews plods through an unrewarding role as Patrick's chief and Allan Cuthbertson, as another inspector, turns in the kind of supercilious portrait which he has practically made his copyright. Only two femme performances are of any moment. Maggie Whiting, not seen nearly enough, plays the tart living a double life. In London, she is dominated by her protector, played by Nesbitt; in the suburbs she has a small son who doesn't know his mother's secret, and he plays a key figure in the climax. Miss Whiting displays some versatile emotions with sure touch. Catharine Woodville has limited opportunity as Patrick's young wife, but is appealing.

Director Ken Annakin has plunged into the melodramatics with gusto but also shrewdly has made sure that the feeling that "this could happen" is never allowed to crack. He has had a particularly smart notion in that he has used the better known names and faces as the law, and faces not so familiar to average audiences as the hunted criminals.

Main minus in his direction, or maybe it's the cutting or screenplay, is that some of the incidents become unduly intricately interlocked. In fact, in the final fight sequence, it is often difficult to remember which villain is on which side. Reginald Wyer has used his black-and-white lensing with a harsh sense of atmosphere where required.

Rich.

Mefiez-Vous Mesdames
(Be Careful Ladies)
(FRENCH—FRANSCOPE)

Paris, Nov. 12.

Gaumont release of PAC-SNEG-Zebra Film production. Stars Michele Morgan, Danielle Darrieux, Paul Meurisse, Sandra Milo. Directed by Andre Hunnebelle. Screenplay, Jean Halain, Pierre Foucaud from book by Ange Bastiani; camera, Raymond Lemoigne; editor, Jean Feyte. At Ambassade-Gaumont, Paris. Running time, **80 MINS.**

Gisele	Michele Morgan
Edwige	Danielle Darrieux
Charlie	Paul Meurisse
Landlady	Sandra Milo
Florence	Gaby Sylvia

Picaresque comedy is well plotted, but a dearth of inventive direction and frothy thesping makes it **more telegraphed than original.** It is thus a chancey export item with local possibilities better.

Paul Meurisse is usually a good sophisticated comedy actor. But here he has to bear the brunt of female homicidal plot. Even he cannot bring it off. He is abetted by the distracted support of Michele Morgan, wrong as a conniving wife, and Danielle Darrieux, too soubrettish as an aging swindler whose charm is masked in childish primping.

Meurisse is a lawyer wronged by Miss Darrieux who intends battening off women by Don Juan tactics when he gets out of jail. Answers to an ad in a paper are mainly women wanting him to do in their husbands or wanting to do him in because he poses as a millionaire. He finally marries his landlady.

Director Andre Hunnebelle has given this a slick if uninspired mounting. It lacks the pace, feeling for character and situation that could have made this familiar affair more intriguing. It is technically par. *Mosk.*

Girl In The Headlines
(BRITISH)

Crisp, competent whodunit with some sharp performances, authentic locales and red herrings.

London, Nov. 15.

British Lion-Bryanston release through BLC of a Bryanston presentation of a Viewfinder film. Stars Ian Hendry, Ronald Fraser. Features Margaret Johnston, Natasha Parry, Geiron Moore, Patrick Holt, Peter Arne, Jeremy Brett, Robert Harris, Rosalie Crutchley, Marie Burke, James Villiers. Produced by John Davis. Directed by Michael Truman. Screenplay by Vivienne Knight & Patrick Campbell, based on a novel by Laurence Payne; editor, Frederick Wilson; camera, Stanley Pavey; music, John Addison. Reviewed at Rialto Theatre, London. Running time, **93 MINS.**

Inspector Birkett	Ian Hendry
Sergeant Saunders	Ronald Fraser
Mrs. Gray	Margaret Johnston
Perlita Barker	Natasha Parry
Jordon Barker	Jeremy Brett
Herter	Keiron Moore
Hammond Barker	Peter Arne
Lindy Birkett	Jane Asher
Maude Klein	Rosalie Crutchley
William Lamonte.........	Robert Harris
Barney	Duncan Macrae
Midlred Birket	Zena Walker
David Dane	James Villiers
Inspector Blackwell........	Alan White
Superintendent	Martin Boddey
Madame Lavalle..........	Marie Burke
Walbrook	Patrick Holt
Teddy Boy	Griffith Davies
Lamotte's Secretary.....	Gabrielle Brune
Man in Club	Hught Latimer

A crisp, well made whodunit, with plenty red herrings to keep an audience guessing. Neither the screenplay nor Michael Truman's direction call for undue histrionics. Result is that the cops look, talk and behave like cops and the varied suspects, though mainly larger than life, are completely credible types.

A model is found dead in her flat, which has also been robbed. The only clues available to the police are a hidden gat, a ballpoint pen found on the floor and a cryptic entry in the girl's diary about a lunch date. Patiently and laboriously Chief Inspector Birkett (Ian Hendry) and his sidekick, Sergeant Saunders (Ronald Fraser) set out to solve the mystery and, in doing so after much frustration, they also unveil a drug ring which is the link between the various suspects. Disclosure of killer comes as little surprise, not so much from illogicality of the yarn, but because the artist concerned is clearly too big a name to be signed up for a part of seemingly comparative unimportance.

Ian Hendry and Ronald Fraser, who have most of the small element of comedy, make a good team of believable detectives. No heroics. Just patience and commonsense. Zena Walker plays Hendry's wife in credible fashion and there is a standout cameo of a conceited television idol, who is a suspect, but himself gets bumped off, superciliously played by James Villiers. Others involved in and around the murder who give sound accounts of themselves are Natasha Parry, Jeremy Brett, Kieron Moore, Peter Arne, Robert Harris, Marie Burke and Rosalie Crutchley.

Stanley Pavey's black and white photography is okay and a variety of London locales are admirably caught. Editing by Frederick Wilson is smooth and an unobtrusive musical score by John Addison is enlivened by Elizabeth Vaughan singing a song called "Casta Diva" in chirpy style. *Rich.*

I Compagni
(The Strikers)
(ITALO-FRENCH)

Rome, Nov. 5.

Paramount release of a Franco Cristadi priduction for Vides-Lux (Rome)—Mediterranee (Paris). Features Marcello

Mastroianni, Renato Salvatori, Gabriella Giorgelli, Folco Lulli, Bernard Blier, Raffaella Carra, Francois Perier, Vittorio Sanipoli, and with Annie Girardot. Directed by Mario Monicelli. Screenplay, Monicelli, Age, Scarpelli; camera, Giuseppe Rotunno; editor, Ruggero Mastroianni; music, Carlo Rustichelli. At Barberini, Rome. Running time 127 MINS.

Sinigaglia .... Marcello Mastroianni
Raoul .... Renato Salvatori
Niobe .... Annie Girardot
Adele .... Gabriella Giorgelli
Pautasso .... Folco Lulli
Martinetti .... Bernard Blier
Bianca .... Raffaella Carra
Di Meo ....'.......... Francois Perier

Finely crafted pic which tells an often serious and sober tale with enough light touches to maintain audience interest throughout. Degree of film's success will depend on how many people will overcome basic doubts about title and story content to see and enjoy the way it's been handled. Some cuts will help. The cast is a strong one for European and other arty house spectators.

Tale is about an early strike in the late 1800's by a group of north Italian factory workers who eventually rebel at long working hours and trying conditions at a plant. Their inexperience at agitation almost results in capitulation to the bosses. But they eventually make their point although they return to work, their impact has been felt, and things are likely to be different from then on.

It's the usual pattern, but director Mario Monicelli manages to lighten the tension with enough light touches, such as those which brightened his "Big Deal on Madonna Street," to give this item an offbeat flavor and considerable down-to-earth humor. Also, except for some caricatured plant toppers, he also fairly refuses to paint his strikers lilly-white, showing them to be violent, at times irresponsible, sometimes ignorant, but at all times human beings. In this sense, it is more a social than a political film.

Some viewers may be a bit disconcerted by Marcello Mastroianni's bearded makeup and unsmooth manner, but he gives this decidedly offbeat casting an interesting projection. Renato Salvatori is good as a sometime associate and Annie Girardot is fine in a small role as a goodhearted prostie. Francois Perier as a mild teacher, and Bernard Blier, as one of the leaders measure up.

Folco Lulli has the meatiest role as a hulky group boss, who dies for the cause, and makes the most of it. G:-:riella Giorgelli is appealing and shows promise as his daughter. But the large cast is full of colorful performers, who blend magnificently into the period thanks to topnotch art direction and costume design by Mario Garbuglia ρ ρ l Piero Tosi, certainly among the highlights of this pic. Pace, especially for foreign spectators who know less about (or care less for) historic details keyed to Italo feelings, could stand considerable pepping up via removal of excessive frills. Giuseppe Rotunno's camera is up to fine period feeling of whole as is Carlo Rustichelli's music. *Hawk.*

San Francisco Fest

A Pleasant Young Gentleman
(GREECE)
San Francisco, Nov. 12.

A Pericles C. Manos production. Features Ilia Livikou, Cleo Scouloudi, Alkis Yannakas and Manos Katrakis. Directed by Manolis Scouloudis. Original screenplay, Manolis Scouloudis; camera, D. I. Sakellarious C.S.C.; sound, Nikos Despotidis; art director, Xannis Stefanellis; music, Yannia Markopoulos. Reviewed at Frisco Film Fest, Nov. 11, 1963. Running time, 100 MINS.

A light-hearted, unpretentious comedy about an amiable village lad was Greece's entry at the Frisco Film Fest.

At first, everyone in the small village of Crete thought that Manuel (Alkis Yannakas) was a pious youth, the best singer in the parish a boy destined to become a bishop. At the age of 19 (according to his mother, 18 according to the program notes, 21 according to his father—somebody's arithmetic got lost in translation), he was still asking his mother where babies came from.

When he is discovered gently bussing a little girl on the cheek, and not so much later, being seduced by the innocent looking young wife of his teacher, he is sent to a toughened step-aunt widow high in the formidable mountains. She is presumably to teach him to stay away from women. But 25 years is a long time for a healthy widow. Manuel performs like a stud, tells the lady she's getting too old for that sort of thing and goes on his unsophisticated Casanova's way for more adventures while the villagers celebrate his prowess in shocked admiration and musical legend.

Since this is a Greek film, it has its moment of tragedy which, oddly, does not intrude on the merry-making spirit of the film.

Ilia Livikou who flew to Frisco for a few hours to make her shy bow at the festival is memorable as the rejected aunt, as is the famous actor Manos Katrakis as both a humorous Pan and the village poet with his magnificent voice of the classic Greek actor.

The beautiful color photography makes you understand why tourists are never the same after they visit Greece. It's the kind of film that can be enjoyed, even without bad subtitles, the whole world over. *Judy.*

Being Two Isn't Easy
(JAPAN)
San Francisco, Nov. 14.

A Daiei Motion Picture Co. production. Features Fujiko Yamamoto, Eiji Funakoshi and Hiroo Suzuki. Directed by Kon Ichikawa. Screenplay, Natto Wada from story by Michio Matsuda. Camera, Setsuo Kobayashi sound, Kimio Tobita; art director, Takashi Senda; music composed by Yasushi Akutagawa. Reviewed at Frisco Film Fest Nov. 12, 1963. Running time, 83 MINS.

Even with what is undoubtedly one of the most delectable two-year olds in all of Japan, his tribulations, joys and measles just don't have enough dramatic interest to sustain a feature length film.

What did come through in "Being Two Isn't Easy," Japan's official entry in the San Francisco Film Fest, was that it's the same the whole world over—babies are lovable and irritating: they get the sniffles, play peek-a-boo with grandma, exasperate their parents, are amazed at tv and get entangled in plastic bags.

Scriptwriter Natto Wada and her husband, Director Kon Ichikawa, have managed to catch some of the tricky business of trying to look at the world through a baby's eyes and do it, for the most part, with effective simplicity.

There is one charming scene where the baby, Hiroo Suzuki, who will undoubtedly capture the hearts of Japan and any other audience, looks up with delight at the "banana moon." And there follows a marvelous animated cartoon bit which catches the fantasy and wonder with which a child must gaze at the moon: a delicious banana to eat, a boat to sail, lovely and strange abstract shapes.

And a plump mother of an unfashionably large family points out that it's "a rockets and missiles world, but only mothers can still produce babies."

Fujiko Yamamoto and Eiji Funaskoshi are attractive as the parents in this glimpse of everyday life in Japan. *Judy.*

The Moving Finger
San Francisco, Nov. 15.

Larry Moyer Associates production. Produced, directed, edited by Larry Moyer. Features Lionel Stander, Barbara London, Art Smith, Wendy Barrie, Alan Ansara, Monroe Arnold, Barry Newman, Carol Fleming, Gary Goodrow, Otto Mjaanes, Cornelius Jones, Michael Dana. Screenplay by Moyer and Carlo Fiore. Photography, Max Glenn; music, Teddy Vann. Reviewed at Frisco Film Fest, Nov. 8, '63. Running time 100 MINS.

New York-made 'indie's original idea was to combine "Crime and Punishment" with "The Subterraneans" and "Violent Saturday." But while playing a cops 'n robber story against the ersatz bohemianism of today's Greenwich Village, the action got mired down in some weak writing, misguided direction and bad acting. Every time a flame of originality flares up it is promptly snuffed out. Pic's only hope for commercial appeal will be to follow the "pseudo-sordidness" or "slice of life" approach.

Primarily a one-man operation, "Moving Finger" includes the weaker aspects of that type of dedicated but overworked approach. Larry Moyer, who produced, directed, partially wrote and edited "Moving Finger," uses the "cinema verite" style of filming. However, in dwelling at length on the dull and dirty doings of some supposedly authentic Village types, he lets the viewer's interest get frequently sidetracked.

After a bank robbery, two of the bandits are slain but the third, wounded, manages to escape with $90,000. He finds himself in Greenwich Village and is taken in by a group of beatnik-cum-actors who "live" in the basement of the coffee house where they perform. Learning that their 'pigeon" is the one sought by the police, they decide to wait their chance to nab the money. This non-beatnik concern (they're not supposed to care

for money) is as unexplained as their failure to just muscle in and take over.

The coffee shop owner (Lionel) Stander) and his girl, Angel (Barbara London), a drunken doctor (Art Smith), and the police are other factions who separately arrive at the same idea—get the money. Angel finally cons the bandit into leaving with her. When he dies in the street, she takes the dough and takes off—to Stander, the doctor, and the police inspector. With a twist on "Treasure of the Sierra Madre," there's a non-Production Code-type ending.

Wendy Barrie is seen fleetingly as one of those weird rich women who flirt with bohemianism but can't abandon her bank accounts and bathrooms. Lionel Stander's sandpaper voice quickly becomes grating on the ear. Still working hard at being the poor man's Gregory Ratoff, he proves that, as a reader of beatnik poetry (Dan Propper's "Fable of the Final Hour") he's neither funny nor philosophical. Propper's title, incidentally, would be a better label for the pic than its present nonsensical label.

Barbara London, with all the necessary dimensions for her role except depth, is never clearly defined. Is she actually in sympathy with the wounded bandit, just a dumb brunette, or an unintentional opportunist? She moves beautifully but has little range of visual expression.

Max Glenn's photography, by intent or by lack of funds, is always underlit, a style which quickly grows monotonous. Frequently jerky movement suggests handheld cameras while some of the Washington Square shots contrast so much that *they* suggest stock footage. Occasionally an original shot indicates imaginative thinking on Glenn's part—one of the slain bandits hanging by one foot from a metal railing, and an interesting but overlong tracking shot of Angel and the bandit staggering along Bleecker Street at night during an Italian festival while the girl waits for him to die.

The beatnik scenes are, for the most part, ridiculous. They do not suggest bohemianism, but only prove that the cast is highly integrated. The "party" sequence was supposedly authentic with many Village characters playing themselves but it is doubtful that Ruth McKenney would recognize them, nor would Max Bodenheim. *Robe.*

The Enemy, the Sea
(JAPAN)
San Francisco, Nov. 12.

Ishihara International Production. Akira Nakai, producer. Features Yujiro Ishihara, Masayuki Mori, Kinuyo Tanaka, Ruriko Asoka, Hajime Hana, Gannosuke Ashinova, Shiro Osaka. Directed by Kon Ichikawa. Screenplay, Natto Wada; Camera, Yoshihiro Yamazaki; art director, Takashi Matsuyama; music composed by Yasushi Akutagawa and Tohur Takemitsu. Reviewed at Frisco Fest, Nov. 10, 1963. Running time, 100 MINS.

Although there are a few spectacular scenes of a storm at sea in "My Enemy, the Sea," one of Japan's two entries in the San Francisco Film Festival, 1963, is for the most part a disappointing account, in color, of a great sea adventure, Kenichi Horie's soli-

tary, 94-day crossing of the Pacific in his 19-foot sailboat.

It has neither the impact of a fine documentary nor the extra dimension of insight into a boy with a dream, the dream of being the first Japanese to sail alone to America.

The title is catchy, but could it have come from Horie's log? What mariner could set out on such a challenging voyage thinking of the sea only as an enemy? There is no sense here of the mystery of t. . sea or the almost mystical union between the sailor and the sea. There is only Horie, battered by the thundering waves, vomiting, shaken, coming through it all with a rather stolid "I'm glad I made the trip."

The flashbacks showing the parents' opposition to the voyage and the hostility of his few friends add nothing to the film, and in fact, distract from it. Director Kon Ichikawa, known here for his "Fires on the Plain" might have done better to concentrate solely on his hero, well portrayed by Yujiro Ishihara, and his courageous efforts to endure and reach his goal.

However, there is enough interest in Horie's trip from Osaka to San Francisco and enough excitement in the film for most sailing buffs to give it commercial possibilities here. *Judy.*

Madame Aki
(JAPANESE-TOHOSCOPE-COLOR)
Hollwood, Nov. 21.

Toho release of Ichiro Sato production. With Hisaya Morishige, Fujiko Yamamoto, Michiyo Aratama, Chieko Naniwa, Tatspya Nakadai, Hiroyuki Nagato, Mayumi Ozoro. Directed by Shiro Toyoda. Screenplay, Toshio Yasumi, from original story by Yasushi Inouye; camera, Kozo Okazaki; music, Ikuma Ran. Reviewed at Toho La Brea Theatre, Nov. 21, '63. Running time, **114 MINS.**

Japanese soap opera about the long-suffering wife of a modern business executive who has an affair with a girl who's carried a torch for him for 10 years. Although distinguished by some beautiful color photography, the Toho production is constructed on a story laced with coincidence and contrivance, and is sprinkled with overly ornate and flowery dialog. In its examination of the despair that can darken the lives of emotionally unsteady people, it does manage to hit an occasional nerve, but not often enough to be sufficiently revealing or arresting. Still, Japanese distaff audiences should gobble it up. It's a woman's picture a hanky-cranker of the first magnitude.

Toshio Yasumi's scenario, from a highly successful serialized yarn by Yasushi Inouye, follows are sad plight of an unhappily-married woman whose husband of seven years has gotten the itch and, Occidentally (cq) on purpose, has taken up with the sister of his deceased best friend. The girl lives in a world of "idealistic fantasy." She dreams of immaculate conception, foresees no fulfillment in ordinary matrimony, feels women lose their individuality in marriage. Target and upshot: a night with that bad guy of a husband during which their passion is consummated. Satisfied, the girl goes back home and the husband and wife realize they do, after all, love each other.

Fujiko Yamamoto (a Miss Japan of several years back) is fine as the wife and Michiyo Aratama fragile and sensitive as the mixed-up girl. Hisaya Morishige is convincing as the husband, and others of prominence are Tatsuya Nakadai, Chieko Naniwa, Hiroyuki Nagato and Mayumi Ozora.

Under the direction of Shiro Toyoda, cameraman Kozo Okazaki has employed some interesting visual techniques, and his color photography, as noted, is an outstanding element of the Ichiro Sato production. *Tube.*

Chair De Poule
(Gooseflesh)
(FRENCH)
Paris, Nov. 26.

Pathe release of Paris Film Inter-Europa production. Stars Robert Hossein, Georges Wilson Catherine Rouvel, Jean Sorel. Directed by Julien Duvivier. Screenplay, Rene Barjaval, Duvivier from novel by James Hadley Chase; camera, L. H. Burel; editor, Suzanne DeTroeye. At Marignan, Paris. Running time, **110 MINS.**
Daniel .... Robert Hossein
Paul .... Jean Sorel
Thomas .... Georges Wilson
Maria .... Catherine Rouvel

Vet director Julien Duvivier has listlessly concocted a sort of "Postman Always Rings Twice" affair with only a few different twists. Flat characterization, o r d i n a r y thesping and an obvious yarn relegate this mainly to local use. It does not have the fillip in pace

or suspense, for much foreign interest except for grind or play-off use on its theme and action.

A workman-turned-thief escapes from jail to hold up an out-of-the-way roadside gas station. Here he finds the aging, good natured boss with hidden money and his tarty young wife. She finds out who he is and blackmails him into opening the husband's safe. He doesn't really want to because he is really a nice guy. Back comes the husband and she supposedly accidentally kills him.

Acting also fails to give this low-life workhorse the needed snap while ordinary scripting a n d routine handling cut short the few surprise turns. Production dress is adequate. *Mosk.*

Avec Des Si
(In the Affirmative)
(FRENCH)
Paris, Nov. 19.

Films De La Pleiade release of Films 13 production. With Guy Mairesse, Julia Hugron. Written and directed by Claude Lelouch. Camera, Jean Collomb; editor, Claude Barrios. Previewed in Paris. Running .time, **80 MINS.**
Boy .... Guy Mairesse
Girl .... Julia Hugron

Some good visual ideas go astray in this pic by a young filmmaker. There is too much insistence on rapid cutting and unusual angles for their own sake. Then there is too much working in montage sequences that only intermittently have something to do with the story. Only minor arty chances for this abroad.

A sadist, who attacks little girls and women, has escaped from a prison. A man is followed in a winter drive around France, supposedly the escaped con. As he turns on the radio programs they are either shown or interpreted by rapid little sequences.

A zoom lens is also overindulged into swoop in and out incessantly. At one time it simulates the breathing of the protagonist in a snowy landscape which is effective if vague. Suspense comes with his picking up a girl hitchhiker and police tracking.

Interminable driving scenes are also somewhat overdone. Thesps pose more than act. It is photographically excellent. In short, this is a sympathetic youthful try full of excesses and somewhat stretching a good idea for a short to a full-length pic.

Director Claude Lelouch has to practice restraint and give up technique for its own sake before he can be judged as to having a possible pic future here. *Mosk.*

I MOSTRI
(The Monsters)
(ITALO-FRENCH)
Rome, Nov. 19.

Titanus-Incei release of a Mario Cecchi Gori production for Fairfilm-Incei-Montflour (Paris). Stars Vittorio Gassmann, Ugo Tognazzi; features Rik Tognazzi, Franco Castellani, Lando Buzzanca, Angela Portaluri, Marisa Merlini, Michele Mercier. Directed by Dino Risi. Story and screenplay, Age, Scarpelli, Petri, Scola Maccari; camera, Alfio Contini. At Adriano, Rome. Running time, **120 MINS.**

This item should make it three for three for producer Mario Cecchi Gori after his previous sleepers, "Sorpasso" and "Successo." It's a surefire local hit on subject matter, race and name

values of the Vittorio Gassmann—Ugo Tognazzi duo. Offshore chances are more limited, though worth consideration.

Pic is an example of the episode trend at one of its extremes: segments here, with few exceptions, are mere vignettes, 20 in all, and on vastly different subjects. Only common denominator in all is the presence of one or both of principal stars in various getups and disguises. This pokes jabs at one and all: political figures, scandal headliners, Italo manners and mores topics of more or less recent conversation.

Humor is rather caustic and free-swinging, s o m e t i m e s (sequence of blind man's exploitation; broken-down pro boxers, etc.) cruel and grotesque, fitting the film's title.

Opening sequence features Ugo Tognazzi as a Roman father giving his young son (played by his real-life son) some tips on how to short-cut one's way through everyday life by illegal devices. One sample is feigning illness and holding white handkerchief out of çar window to break through chronic Eternal City traffic jams. A few others are just silly, and could easily be done away with in two-hour pic. But on the whole, the pace is fast and amusing. Both Tognazzi and Gassmann play their meaty roles with all stops out, and there are few lags.

Technically, the pic is fancily equipped with a fine lensing job by Alfio Contini and a topical musical score of current hits supplied by RCA Italiana. *Hawk.*

La Foire Aux Cancres
(The Blockhead Fair)
(FRENCH)
Paris, Nov. 19.

CFDC release of UGC-Sirius-Raoul Ploquin production. Features Dominique Paturel, Christian Marin, Rene Lefevre, Sophie Desmarets, Jean Rochefort, Stephane Gatti. Directed by Louis Daquin. Screenplay, Pierre Tchernia, Francois Boyer, Jean Charles, Daquin, Jean Lhote, Jean Marsan from book by Jean Charles; camera, Jean Penzer; editor, Claude Nicole. At Balzac, Paris. Running time, **90 MINS.**

Teacher .... Dominique Paturel
Levasseur .... Christian Marin
Principal .... Rene Lefevre
Mother .... Sophie Desmarets
Father .... Jean Rochefort
Tutor .... Stephane Gatti

Since the surprise hit of a simple moppet pic about bucolic kid warfare "The Button War," a whole new cycle of juve pix has been springing up here. This one deals with the lovable dunce element in schools. But it is mainly a series of sketches, from good to poor, without the more leavening observation and insight into childhood to make it more than a local bet.

A group of boys intro each segment with little songs. One difficult student shows he is adept at mechanics if short on book learning when he fixes the principal's broken down car. Another shoplifts because his parents ignore him. One learns a lesson about money when he finds a bill, etc.

But each moral issue is forced and telegraphed on the episodes. Moppets range from self-conscious to easy-emoting kids while adults remain in the stereotype category. Director Louis Daquin has been content to just put these uneven bits together in a routine manner

without any visual force. Result is uneven if technically good.

Mosk.

The Prize
(PANAVISION—COLOR)

Exploitable but uneven film-ization of the Nobel Prize tale. Palatable fare for easygoing audiences.

Hollywood, Nov. 1.
Metro release of Pandro S. Berman production. Stars Paul Newman, Edward G. Robinson, Elke Sommer, Diane Baker. Directed by Mark Robson. Screenplay, Ernest Lehman, based on Irving Wallace's novel; camera (Metrocolor), William H. Daniels; editor, Adrienne Fazan; music, Jerry Goldsmith; asst. director, Hank Moonjean. Reviewed at Hollywood Paramount Theatre, Nov. 1, '63. Running time, 135 MINS.
Andrew Craig .... Paul Newman
Dr. Max Stratman Edward G. Robinson
Inger Lisa Andersen ...... Elke Sommer
Emily Stratman .... Diane Baker
Dr. Denise Marceau ....Micheline Presle
Dr. Claude Marceau...... Gerard Oury
Dr. Carlo Farelli .... Sergio Fantoni
Dr. John Garrett .... Kevin McCarthy
Count Bertil Jacobson ...Leo G. Carroll
Daranyi .... Sacha Pitoeff
Monique Souvir .... Jacqueline Beer
Hans Eckart .... John Wengraf
Ivar Cramer .... Don Dubbins
Mrs. Bergh..........Virginia Christine
Mr. Bergh .... Rudolph Anders
Saralee Garrett......... Martine Bartlett
Hilding .... Karl Swenson
Oscar .... John Qualen
Clark Wilson .... Ned Wever

This is the story about the Nobel Prize, nude swimming and Nordic morals which upset the Kingdom of Sweden when first scheduled for filming. Swedes deplored what they foresaw as a vulgarization of the serious awards given annually under the will of the inventor of dynamite. So read on—

Pandro S. Berman's screen version of the novel by Irving Wallace has the cast magnetism, glamorous production sheen and exploitable ingredients to lure the kind of easygoing audiences that will respond to its cheerier aspects and dismiss its shortcomings. Such being the case, it should make its mark at the boxoffice. However, the film is marred by inconsistency of approach and, although it has a number of juicy moments and scenes, the whole is a rather uneasy, capricious concoction of such widely divergent elements as comedy, suspense, melodrama and political topicality. Reaction will be mixed.

Stockholm during Nobel week is the setting for Wallace's smorgasbord. In Ernest Lehman's Hitchcockeyed screenplay, seven selected prizewinners convene to receive the award. The unofficial mystery of the picture is how seven such screwballs ever found time or inclination to excel in their fields of endeavor. At any rate, the man from literature (Paul Newman) senses something amiss in the behavior and physique of the man from physics (Edward G. Robinson), proceeds to snoop around for clues and ends up in a wild goose chase, with himself as the goose who almost gets cooked. It all turns out to be an elaborately devious plot by the Communists to kidnap the noted scientist and replace him at the award ceremonies with a look-alike whose favorite ism certainly isn't Americanism. Newman's sleuthing saves the day.

"The Prize" is a suspense melodrama played for laughs. Trouble is the basic comedy approach clashes with the political-topical framework of the story, so that the audience continually has to make adjustments in the attitude.

Although limited as a comic actor and confronted here with a rather difficult and unsubstantial character to portray, Newman

tackles his task with sufficient vivacity to keep an audience concerned for his welfare and amused by his antics. Robinson achieves a persuasive degree of contrast in his dual role.

For Elke Sommer, this marks her much-ballyhooed maiden appearance in a Hollywood-originated production. As an attache who gets attached to Newman, she hasn't a very scintillating role, but has the looks to make that a secondary issue, looks that stamp her a glamour doll commodity to watch in the near future. Miss Sommer has one of the leading distaff roles in Carl Foreman's "The Victors," also to be released shortly.

Diane Baker is also attractive as the niece of Robinson number one who believes that Robinson number two is her daddy, which he is not (he is a professional actor). It's a wise child that knows its own father. Micheline Presle, Gerard Oury, Sergio Fantoni and Kevin McCarthy do the best they can as those unbelievably adolescent prizewinners. Leo G. Carroll is capable as the Count who nervously presides over the ceremony. Sacha Pitoeff is deliciously sinister as the lead heavy.

Mark Robson's direction generates a lot of excitement, humor and suspense in spots, but this is offset by hokey elements, occasional exaggerations and stripping of dramatic gears as the film fluctuates between its incompatible components. The well ballyhooed nudist colony scene, incidentally, is overdone and not one of the film's stronger sequences. Exterior views of Stockholm are interesting, and the locale is carefully matched in the are direction by George W. Davis and Urie McCleary. William H. Daniels' photography is quick, observant and agile, and Adrienne Fazan's editing is especially adept at sharpening the impact of such demanding bits of business as Newman's plunge from a rooftop into a river and the heavy's ultimate death via impalement. Also aiding in this regard are the special visual effects of J. McMillan Johnson, A. Arnold Gillespie and Robert R. Hoag. Jerry Goldsmith's music satisfactorily reinforces mood and identifies character.

Tube.

Gudrun
(DANISH—COLOR)

Copenhagen, Nov. 26.
Asa release of Morten Schyberg production. Stars Laila Anderson, Jorgen Buckhoj. Written and directed by Anker. Additional dialog by Mette Budtz-Jorgensen; based on novel by Johs V. Jensen; camera (Technicolor), Henning Bendtsen; music, Ib Glindemann. Running time, 95 MINS.
Gudrun .... Laila Anderson
Manne .... Jorgen Buckhoj
Hollund ....>... Poul Reichhardt
Mr. Roscoe .... Nils Asther
Mrs. Brunn .... Birgitte Federspiel
Office Girl .... Yvonne Ingdal

Another Danish try at reaching the international market, this time with a deliberately old-fashioned, rather anti-New Wave romantic film in color and with very black and white characters. Nobel Prize winner John V. Jensen's flop of a novel about his ideal woman, broad of hip, simple of manner, sensual yet sensible and very out-or-door-ish Scandinavia, is portrayed by Laila Anderson who happens to have an interesting and Slavic rather than Scandinavian face. Miss Anderson saves this film to

make it worthwhile entry in the foreign market where otherwise only its corn has any kind of taste.

Story is about a girl who willingly and unmarriedly sleeps with the right boy while all other men around her are cast as bad. Consequently they are fought off with strong-armed, strong-legged violence by the husky Gudrun. In one fight a dramatically effective judo fight is waged between the nice boy and a stranger who happens to stroll by where Gudrun is bathing in all her stone-age woman splendor. Jogren Buckhoj really punches, but in the rest of the pic film he rather underplays his role.

Gudrun also fights off a Lesbo landlady. This does not make the film any more modern, but it still is a rather earnest production.

Occasional originality is also lavished by the camera on certain parts of Copenhagen. In a bit part, Yvonne Ingdal shows her rather funny face and displays a talent and a body that really belongs.

Kell.

Le Journal D'Un Fou
(Diary of a Madman)
(FRENCH)

Paris, Nov. 26.
Cocinor release of Marceau-Cocinor production. Stars Roger Coggio. Directed by Roger Coggio. Screenplay, Sylvie Furneau, Marcel Moussy, Coggio from story by Gogol; camera, Christian Matras; editor, Leonide Azar. At Lord Byron, Paris. Running time, 105 MINS.

Study of a psychotic's fantasies, rantings-commitment to an institution and anguish remains too much on one level to build much of a film. Its theme and treatment have it mainly an arty bet abroad, at best, but its forced thesping and literary and theatrical styles make it chancey.

Originally a Gogol short story, set in 19th Century Russia, it was done as a one-man legiter last season and has now been updated to the present, and played and directed by the actor who did it on the stage. Its double metamorphosis has made this lose edge, insight and depth.

Hallucination and reality mix from the very start. And long monologs replace the needed counterpoint between the ordinary and madness. Actor-director Roger Coggio has not been able to get the right balance to depict the man's derangement. Hence, this vacillates between some telling run-ins with regular life and his lonely imaginings and final complete madness.

Coggio lacks the flair in direction and acting to pinpoint the progression of his fantasies. The film's inability to strike a balance in style makes this turn out to be an uneven monolog. *Mosk.*

Who's Been Sleeping in My Bed?
(COLOR—PANAVISION)

Glossy production, playing out well but unamusingly ribald in spots, with Dean Martin as a TV Dr. Kildare type much sought after by young, attractive, married women. Slightly provocative comedy might get by at the boxoffice.

Paramount release of Jack Rose production. Stars Dean Martin, Elizabeth Montgomery; features Martin Balsam, Jill

St. John. Richard Conte, Macha Meril, Louis Nye, Yoko Tani. Jack Soo, Dianne Foster. Directed by Daniel Mann. Screenplay, Rose; camera (Technicolor and Panavision), Joseph Ruttenberg; editor, George Tomasini; music, George Duning. Previewed at Victoria Theatre, N.Y., Nov. 19, '63. Running time, 103 MINS.

Jason Steel	Dean Martin
Melissa Morris	Elizabeth Montgomery
Sanford Kaufman	Martin Balsam
Toby Tobler	Jill St. John
Leonard Ashley	Richard Conte
Jacqueline Edwards	Macha Meril
Harry Tobler	Louis Nye
Isami Hiroti	Yoko Tani
Yoshimi Hiroti	Jack Soo
Mona Kaufman	Dianne Foster
Tom Edwards	Elliott Reid
Charley	Johnny Silver
Dora Ashley	Elizabeth Fraser
Sam Jones	Steve Clinton
Lawyer	Daniel Ocko
Mrs. Grayson	Allison Hayes
Policeman	James O'Rear
Carol Burnett	Herself

At the outset producer Jack Rose seems to have something going for himself in "Who's Been Sleeping in My Bed?" Right away, a slick production is on view, the story basics have lots of jazzy fun potential, and Dean Martin, seemingly right for the part, plays therapist for a covey of neglected married women. But in the end it only comes off fair; some potential has been lost.

Film lends itself to provocative promotional devices centered around the screenplay angles. It's mightily suggestive to think of an actor who appears on television as a doctor, such as Kildare or Ben Casey, and then envision him as being maneuvered into moonlighting into the field of psychiatric advise (and perhaps romantic stimulation) for the glamorous dames married to his tv-business associates.

But there's the slip between cup and lip. The slip makes the difference between what might have been mischievous, zesty comedy and what is—what is being a sometimes laughable frolic that in a couple of instances is permitted to sink in its quest for sophisticated hilarity. A few of the oral cracks are juvenile trite. Disagreeable is a scene in which Martin graphically demonstrates on his analyst's couch his anxiety about a gal.

Instead of being sophisticated, the screenplay by Rose, directed by Daniel Mann, loses ground with this kind of tastelessness. This is unfortunate because a substantial part of "Who's Been Sleeping in My Bed?" plays sparkingly well. Martin is an amiable performer in light comedy and does fine with the material at hand.

Done with admirable restraint and the best kind of subtle suggestiveness is a bit in which Carol Burnett is forced into doing a nitery striptease number because she and companion Elizabeth Montgomery have been stuck with the check.

As is, the production shapes as apparently so-so boxoffice. The 103 minutes of running time add up to a few minutes to spare, a little judicious exorcism might not be out of order, and improved commercial chances could result.

Plot is one of those situation things just barely conveyed by synopsis. First there's Martin, surgeon extraordinary of the image orthicon. He has a pretty

fiance, Miss Montgomery. Her pal is Miss Burnett, a nutty secretary in a psychiartist's office.

On the loose and looking for Martin's attention are, among others, Jill St. John, Macha Meril, Yoko Tani, Dianne Foster and Elizabeth Fraser. They're all lookers. The men who prefer to forsake them for a ritualistic Wednesday night poker game include Martin Balsam, Richard Conte, Louis Nye and Jack Soo.

All behave histrionically well for the job on hand. Joseph Ruttenberg's cinematography (Technicolor-Panavision) is workmanlike, editor George Tomasini reflects competence and George Duning has contributed a good musical score. **Gene.**

Move Over, Darling
(C'SCOPE—COLOR)

Hot and cold remake of "My Favorite Wife." Good b.o. candidate, though short of blockbuster.

Hollywood, Dec. 3.

Twentieth-Fox release of Aaron Rosenberg-Martin Melcher production. Stars Doris Day, James Garner, Polly Bergen; features Chuck Connors, Thelma Ritter, Fred Clark, Don Knotts, Elliott Reid. Directed by Michael Gordon. Screenplay, Hal Kanter, Jack Sher, based on screenplay by Bella and Samuel Spewack from story by the Spewacks and Leo McCarey; camera (De Luxe), Daniel L. Fapp; editor, Robert Simpson; music, Lionel Newman; asst. director, Ad Schaumer. Reviewed at Picwood Theatre, Dec. 3, '63. Running time, 103 MINS.

Ellen Arden	Doris Day
Nicholas Arden	James Garner
Bianca Steele Arden	Polly Bergen
Stephen Burkett—"Adam"	Chuck Connors
Grace Arden	Thelma Ritter
Mr. Codd	Fred Clark
Shoe Clerk	Don Knotts
Dr. Schlick	Elliott Reid
Judge Bryson	Edgar Buchanan
Prokey	John Astin
District Attorney	Pat Harrington Jr.
Bellboy	Eddie Quillan
Desk Clerk	Max Showalter
Waiter	Alvy Moore
Jenny Arden	Pami Lee
Didi Arden	Leslie Farrell

Twentieth has a sound money-making prospect in "Move Over, Darling," a reproduction of the 1940 romantic comedy, "My Favorite Wife," which then costarred Cary Grant and Irene Dunne. The Aaron Rosenberg-Martin Melcher production is in the approximate mold of some big boxoffice blockbusters of recent years, and has as its chief marquee bait the phenomenally-popular Doris Day—a combination that holds particular promise for this upcoming holiday release.

When "Move Over, Darling" relies for the most part on the inspiration of the past, it delivers comedy that is ageless and universal in appeal. When it breaks anchor and drifts from its moornigs, the reconstructed vessel winds up in turbulent, uncharted waters and starts to flounder. In short, the comedy inspiration and restraint that distinguished the original is missing in the embellishments with which the remake is adorned. In an apparent commercially-motivated effort to satisfy the tastes of the less sophisticated by going off on occasional slapstick tangents and thus broadening the base of appeal, the new creative unit has actually succeeded in limiting the appeal of the picture by attaching heavy-handed and fundamentally irrelevant farce sequences to an intrinsically surefire premise.

Something old, something new, something borrowed, something blue is the nature of "Move Over, Darling." Its complicated history is revealed in the writing credit: screenplay by Hal Kanter and Jack Sher based on a screenplay by Bella Spewack and Samuel Spewack from a story by Bella Spewack, Samuel Spewack and Leo McCarey. And, somewhere in there, the ill-fated "Something's Got to Give."

The "old" is the basic yarn about the guy who remarries five years after his first wife is thought to have perished only to have his first wife turn up alive and kicking at the outset of his honeymoon. The "new" are the chiefly lack-lustre embellishments tagged on.

The "borrowed," to cite one example, is a telephone sequence that owes more than a little something to Shelley Berman. The "Blue" isn't of a really offensive nature, but several remarks and activities may seem to border somewhat unnecessarily on that shade for less liberal-minded audiences.

Miss Day and James Garner play it to the hilt, comically, dramatically and last, but not least (particularly in the case of the former), athletically. What is missing in their portrayals is a light touch—the ability to humorously convey with a subtle eyelash-bat or eyebrow-arch what it tends to take them a kick in the shins to accomplish. It is this element of comedy deftness that seems to have eluded scenarists Kanter and Sher, director Michael Gordon and his stars.

As a matter of fact, it has been a consistently elusive commodity in the romantic comedies of recent years, which more and more seem to have drifted into the right-uppercut or hit-him-over-the-head-with-an-umbrella school of comedy. Perhaps it is time to reevaluate, and stop underestimating modern film audiences. It is, after all, something of a paradox that as filmgoers presumably have increased in sophistication over the years, that once staple of the screen, the sophisticated comedy, has given way increasingly to the farcical approach.

Others of prominence in the cast are Polly Bergen as the sexually-obsessed second wife (it's never really much of a contest between her and Miss Day), Thelma Ritter as the understanding mother-in-law, and Chuck Connors as the male animal who shared the small island hunk of real estate alone with Miss Day for five years. Their performances are satisfactory. Good comedy efforts are contributed by Fred Clark, Don Knotts, Edgar Buchanan, John Astin and Max Showalter. Appealing moppet characterizations are etched by Pami Lee and Leslie Farrell.

Daniel L. Fapp's photography is handsome and a helpful comedy factor. There are capable producSimpSon, art directors Jack Martin Smith and Hilyard Brown and composer Lionel Newman, to cite a few. Moss Mabry's costumes are fashionable.

A title tune by Joe Lubin, Hal Kanter and Terry Melcher, sung by Miss Day over the titles, has a modern sound and beat that could make it a healthy commercial biscuit with the teenage set and, concurrently, serve as an exploitation stimulus for the picture. Lubin has also composed another ditty, "Twinkle Lullaby," the title of which tells the story. **Tube.**

Ladybug, Ladybug

Second effort of "David and Lisa" creators. Chilling but uneven study of children and adults in a nuclear crisis. Good arty prospects, but previous coin response is out of range.

Hollywood, Nov. 29.

United Artists release of Frank Perry production. No stars. Directed by Frank

Perry. Screenplay, Eleanor Perry, suggested by an article by Lois Dickert, based on an actual incident; camera, Leonard Hirschfeld; editor, Armond Lebowitz; music, Robert Cobert; asst. director, Anthony LaMarca. Reviewed at Academy Awards Theatre, Nov. 29, '63. Running time, 81 MINS.

Mrs. Maxton	Jane Connell
Mr. Calkins	William Daniels
Truck Driver	James Frawley
JoAnn's Father	Richard Hamilton
Mrs. Forbes, the Secretary	Kathryn Hays
Mrs. Hayworth	Jane Hoffman
Mother	Elena Karam
Grandmother	Judith Lowry
Mrs. Andrews	Nancy Marchand
JoAnn's Mother	Estelle Parsons
Gary	Doug Chapin
Joel	Miles Chapin
Peter	Bozo Dell
Jill	Dianne Higgins
Luke	Alan Howard
Steve	Christopher Howard
Don	David Komoroff
Brian	Donnie Melvin
Trudy	Susan Melvin
JoAnn	Linda Meyer
Harriet	Alice Playten
Sarah	Marilyn Rogers
Pattie	Jennifer Stone

From the resourceful man-and-wife creators of "David and Lisa" comes this second endeavor, a rather harrowing account of what might conceivably transpire were a falsely triggered alert of a nuclear attack to be received at a small rural school. There is much in "Ladybug, Ladybug" of value, insight and significance, and Frank and Eleanor Perry are certainly to be commended for what they have accomplished with roughly $325,000 and oodles of artistic integrity. But their film is only partially successful.

Gripping, disturbing and meaningful scenes alternate with sequences given to inexplicable lethargy or overly self-conscious artiness. And there is something radically wrong with the timing, the pace engineered by Perry, the producer-director. It is, in short, a film of strange contrasts, the whole of which is superior to some of its parts, inferior to others. As an art house attraction, the United Artists release has the timeliness and topicality (plus the Perry stamp) to do well, though it isn't likely to do anywhere near as well as "David and Lisa."

It's an ordinary day at school, according to Mrs. Perry's scenario, which was suggested by an article by Lois Dickert that was based on an actual incident. The only discord is the yellow light flashing and buzzing in the principal's office. It means "nuclear attack imminent within the hour." Since, among other things, "the news has been . . . well, not good," as news generally is, the children, as specified by Civil Defense orders, are formed into groups and dispatched home under the supervision of a teacher-per-group.

Fear begins to circulate. It begins to sift through from the adults, who are more or less able to cope with it rationally, to the children, most of whom are not emotionally equipped to deal with or even understand such circumstances. Much has been conjectured of the selfishness that might erupt with regard to bomb shelters in a time of nuclear crisis. In "Ladybug, Ladybug," this horrible prospect takes on an even more chilling tone as dramatized with children.

A cruel, officious girl who has taken charge of her parents' shelter in their absence refuses to allow a panic-stricken girl to enter. The latter hysterically races through the barren fields and finally crawls into a discarded, overturned icebox in the town dump and locks herself in. Her boy friend dashes through the fields after her. Hearing the sound of a plane, he begins burrowing, desperately seeking sanctuary from that terrifyingly tangible "boogie man" of the mid-20th-century—the bomb. In his cries of anguish at the terror of his experience rests an indictment of the kind of world he is heir to—a world for which he is not, at the moment, responsible.

The children of "Ladybug" come off quite well—as characters and actors. Not so the adults. It seems that almost everytime the camera returns to the grownups a curious lag and an aura of melodramatic artificiality arises. For example, a scene wherein the school principal's secretary, who is pregnant, is observed in the act of tidying up a deserted kindergarten classroom as she awaits her fate. It is a false and interminable sequence. Assuming from her pregnancy she has a husband, it seems more apt that she'd be busy attempting to make some sort of contact, not wandering aimlessly and tearfully around in a schoolroom. And another mystery of the picture is—whatever happened to Conelrad?, or the Emergency Broadcast System, as it is now called. No one seems to have the presence of mind to check it out.

But these are balanced to some extent by the merits, notably the scenes in the bomb shelter and those in which the children discuss such matters as death.

Acting honors, as noted, go mostly to the children, with especially telling enactments by Marilyn Rogers, Christopher Howard, Miles Chapin, Linda Meyer, Alice Playten and Donnie Melvin. Prominent in the adult department are Kathryn Hays, William Daniels, Jane Connell, Jane Hoffman, Nancy Marchand and Judith Lowry.

Much of Leonard Hirschfield's photography is quite artful—but sometimes too much so. Robert Cobert's melancholy score is conveyed via flute and string. There is a lumpiness about the editing, for which Armond Lebowitz is credited but in which director Perry no doubt played a major role. Perceptively cut individual scenes alternate with ones of an annoyingly sluggish character. *Tube*

Il Mondo di Notte No. 3
(World at Night No. 3)
(ITALIAN)
(Color)

Rome, Dec. 3.

Warner Bros. release of a Julia Film production. Directed by Gianni Proia. Commentary, Francesco Mazzie. Music Riz Ortolani (C.A.M.). At Barberini, Rome. Running time, 110 MINS.

Julia Film has another winner in its pioneering "World at Night" series with this third installment. It has all the ingredients which belted across its predessors, and maintains a position considerably above most pix of its genre which have literally invaded Italo screens in the past year. Export chances look rosy.

It's true that many will feel some of the footage is lacking in taste and discretion, that other segments are over-violent and verging on the obscene and that some of the material is repetitious. Surely, too, censor shears will be employed in various areas, depending on local susceptibilities. In Italy, though banned for those under 18, it's a wonder how much of it came through unscathed.

Combination circus sideshow, nitery strip vehicle, and travel documentary, film touches on such varied subjects as: German University duels, Fakhir sticking knives through his body, a whale hunt with small boats off Portugal, Lapland reindeer roundup, British black magic sessions, with a built-in orgy, artificial insemination, plus several strip numbers set against various action and images. Riz Ortolani (who penned "Mondo Cane" score) has come up with another lush musical track which is a major plus. Technical credits generally are very good. *Hawk.*

Vancouver Fest

Open the Door and See All the People

Vancouver, Dec. 5.

Jerome Hill production and release. Written, produced and directed by Jerome Hill. Cast: Maybelle Nash, Alec Wilder, Jeremiah Sullivan, Ellen Martin, Lester Judson, Louise Rush, John Holland, Susana De Mello, Charles Rydell, Chris Schroll, Johanna Hill, Harry Rigby, Tony Ballen, Paul Chu, Taylor Mead, Melvina Boykin, Day Tuttle, Douglas Ho, Chao Li Chi, Gwen Davies, Gene Fallon, Astride Lance, Sheilah Chang and Billy Leavitt. Photography, Gayne Rescher; music, Alec Wilder. Reviewed at Vancouver Film Festival. Running time, 91 MINS.

This new Jerome Hill comedy-fantasy, given its North American preem at the Vancouver film fest, has some whimsical moments and several sequences of airy nonsense in its 91 minutes but not enough of these to offset the vague plot line and sustain rapt interest throughout.

Film is ostensibly concerned with the differing social values and conflicting personalities of two New England families headed by 70-year old identical twin sisters, one a wealthy, superstitious and domineering hypochondriac, the other a happy-go-lucky grandmother who works as a cashier in a supermarket. Dual parts are handled expertly by Maybelle Nash, who was also in Hill's 1961 production of "The Sand Castle." Alec Wilder, who did the music for this as well as previous Hill pic, is cast as unemployed husband to the poor but happy twin sister and registers well in an ineffectual part. Background score is pleasant but not memorable. Newcomers of promise include Ellen Martin and Jeremiah Sullivan, who carry one of the two love interest sub-plots, and Susana De Mello and Charles Rydell, who manage the other.

Gayne Rescher's black and white lensing is sharp and other technical credits are competent but film meanders along too diffidently to establish itself as a major artie entry. *Shaw.*

Three Days After Immortality
(Troe Sutok Posle Bessmertiya)
(USSR)

Vancouver, Dec. 4.

Sovexport release of Dovzhenko Film Studio, Kiev, production. Directed by Vladimir Dovgan. Cast: Vladimir Zamansky, Nikolay Kriukov, Georgy Yumatov, Galina Liapina, Lilia Kalatcheva. Screenplay, Konstantin Kudiyevsky; camera, Vadim Vereshtchak; music, Yuri Shurovsky. Reviewed at Vancouver Film Festival. Black & White. Running time, 85 MINS.

Wartime heroism is theme of Russian entry in Vancouver Film Festival. Film is grandiose epic melodrama with old-fashioned visual flair that disappeared from Hollywood in the mid-thirties. Story begins on the 250th day of the bitter defense of Sebastopol by Soviet units against overwhelming German forces that resulted in official Red Army surrender of the city but resistance is continued by a small, mixed group of sailors, soldiers and civilians, including women, as they retreat stubbornly to the shores of the Black Sea. A romance that springs up between a female archeologist and seaman-leader of the group ends when he watches from the beach while she sails away to possible safety and he stays behing to meet certain death with his comrades.

Film has all the melodramatic corniness the story line suggests but simple narrative style employed by director Vladimir Dovgan conveys a certain power and glory to the hackneyed plot. Vladimir Zamansky is almost a look-alike for Dane Clark as he enacts the brooding hero-leader, and Galina Liapina is a fetching heroine with her classically-blonde beauty. Nikolay Kriukov's part as the giant who sacrifices himself to gain time for the others is played larger-than-life along traditional script lines and subsidiary love interest that ends happily is taken by Lilia Kalatcheva and Georgy Yumatov.

Music, photography and lighting are suitably keled to the epic aspect and closing scene is a blazing visual criss-cross of facial front lighting for main characters while machine gun fire and rifle shots crack and background music swells sonorously to glorious fade-out in the grand manner. Film is technically okay and sub-titles read adequately against the black and white background but subject matter and production make it a limited import prospect. *Shaw.*

Twin Sisters of Kyoto
(JAPAN-COLOR-'SCOPE)

Vancouver, Dec. 6.

Shochiku Film production and release. Produced by Ryotaro Kuwata. Directed by Noboru Nakamura. Stars Shima Iwashita (dual role), Seiji Miyaguchi, Teruo Yoshida, Tamitsu Hayakawa. Screenplay, Toshihide Gondo; camera (Eastmancolor & GrandScope), Toichiro Narushima; music, Toru Takemitsu; editor, Hisashi Sagara; atr dir., Junichi Ohzumi. Reviewed at Vancouver Film Festival. Running time, 107 MINS.

Chieco & Naeko (dual parts)	Shima Iwashita
Takichiro Sada	Seiji Miyaguchi
Ryusuke Mizuki	Teruo Yoshida
Shinichi Mizuki	Tamotsu Hayakawa

Grand prize winner of the 1963 Asian Film Festival in Seoul, "Twin Sisters of Kyoto" is a simple but dramatically effective story of Japanese traditions set in the modern day. Plot unfolds leisurely and tellingly around the only daughter of a well-to-do merchant in ancient city of Kyoto who suspects that her parents have been hiding something from her in their story of how she came to be adopted.

They have, in fact, avoided telling her that she had been abandoned as an infant in accordance with old

superstition when twin girls were born. Twins were regarded as unnatural, unlucky, as socially outcast as the illegitimate child in Western society, and to be abandoned by one's parents is something to be ashamed of but worse still is the shame of being an abandoned twin. Custom has survived longest in the venerable and charming old capital city of Kyoto and its surrounding countryside.

When the rich girl comes face to face with a young peasant girl who is her exact image the chance encounter leads to the traumatic revelation that they are indeed twin sisters and film proceeds to examine the emotional conflicts that spring up in the two girls. The poor one, now an orphan, feels a particular sense of guilt in that her sister, the rich city girl, was the adandoned one, and ultimate resolution of the girls' feelings is handled with great sensitivity by director Noboru Nakamura. Running counter is love theme with rich girl sought by a modern, educated Japanese male and the poor relation yearned after by an obi weaver's son. Film ends on telling note that girls are living in a new Japan, in which women have a freedom of equality and choice unknown in the old tradition-ridden days.

Superb acting performance by Shima Iwashita in the dual role of the two sisters highlights pic and Toichiro Narushima's stunning color photography in Shochiku GrandScope is tourist bait to the last degree.

Music score is good and technical handling of dual scenes is excellent with other credits up to standard of modern Japanese production. English sub-titles are sometimes amusing in translation but story transcends the unconscious humor. On the plus side are the sequences detailing rich pageantry of traditional Japanese festivals and compelling way in which nature blends inherently into the Japanese way of life. Pic looms as distinct art houses possibility.   *Shaw.*

America America

Greek and his dream at the turn of the century—to get to America. A soaring artistic achievement by Elia Kazan, but that artistry must be capitalized upon with plenty of sell.

Hollywood, Dec. 13.
Warner Bros. release of Elia Kazan production. Stars Stathis Giallelis. Directed and screenplay by Kazan, from his book, "America America"; camera, Haskell Wexler; editor, Dede Allen; music, Manos Hadjidakis. Reviewed at studio, Dec. 13, '63. Running time, **177 MINS.**
Stavros Topouzoglou .... Stathis Giallelis
Vartan Damadian .... Frank Wolf
Isaac Topouzoglou .... Harry Davis
Vasso Topouzoglou ..... Elena Karam
Grandmother .... Estelle Hemsley
Hohannes Gardashian ..Gregory Rozakis
Abdul .... Lou Antonio
Odysseus Topouzoglou... Salem Ludwig
Garabet .... John Marley
Vartuhi .... Joanna Frank
Aleko Sinnikoglou .... Paul Mann
Thomna Sinnikoglou ... Linda Marsh
Aratoon Kebabian ..... Robert H. Harris
Sophia Kebabian .... Katharine Balfour

In "America America," Elia Kazan has given us one of the outstanding motion picture achievements of the year, a penetrating, thorough and profoundly affecting account of the hardships endured and surmounted at the turn of the century by a young Greek lad in attempting to fulfill his cherished dream—getting to America from the old country. Since virtually all Americans have one thing in common — immigrant ancestors, most of whom emigrated here to escape some form of travail or oppression and to start a fresh new life with a clean slate—it is a film of importance, one that provides us with necessary insight into our country.

The film has flaws, but they are minor. Whatever little faults one may find with it are obliterated by one shining and distinguishing characteristic—it is honest to the core. As such, it should inspire critical acclaim and draw high praise from influential sources, two initial responses that must materialize in order to get the box-office rolling in the right direction.

That first reaction will be a critical one for the Warner Bros. release. For this is a picture that, from a crass commercial assessment, must succeed in spite of itself and must succeed on strictly artistic merits. Its cast is virtually unknown to filmgoers and its subject matter hardly calculated to entice that great easygoing "auffluent" audience generally inclined to forego films that require too much cerebral concentration and emotional participation.

Kazan's film, which he wrote, produced and directed, all brilliantly, stems from his book of the same title which evidently was inspired by tales of the experiences of his own ancestors that sifted down through the family grapevine. The picture begins with the young Greek hero witnessing and experiencing Turkish oppression of Greek and Armenian minorities, circa 1896. It follows him to Constantinople, to which he has been sent by his family with its entire accumulated fortune to pave their way. Enroute he and his fortune are soon parted by thieves. Downtrodden and impoverished, he dreams of America and slaves away to earn enough money for passage, but is driven to the depths of despair and degradation when his dearly-earned coin, too is stolen. Hardened by his misfortunes but as grimly determined as ever, he enters a new, resourceful phase of his life, one of compromise with principles, and, after several somewhat unsavory and unscrupulous affairs with women and harrowing experiences aboard a ship crossing the Atlantic, he finally arrives in the promised land —America—where, as a lowly shoeshine boy, he painstakingly earns and saves the money that will bring the other members of his large family across the sea from the old country to the land of opportunity.

Perhaps never before on the screen has man's inhumanity to man been so graphically and painfully illustrated as in the succession of misfortunes that befall Kazan's hero. Yet through it all, his indomitable spirit survives—an inspiring thing to behold. As noted, the film has its flaws. There is a vagueness about certain details and an element of confusion arises when Kazan goes somewhat arty in the latter parts of the film, but these are minor reservations.

The acting is incredibly good. In the all-important focal role of the young man with the dream, Stathis Giallelis, an unknown, makes a striking screen debut. His performance roots indelibly in the mind. In appearance something of a cross between Dirk Bogarde and the late John Hodiak, he is a major addition to the ranks of young leading men and appears to have a bright future. But, conceivably, he might never top this performance, largely because it is quite possible he may never again be blessed with such a magnificent character to portray.

The other players are just about equally superb. Virtually everyone is memorable, but perhaps the three most vividly remembered are Linda Marsh as the plain and unassuming maiden to whom the hero is treacherously betrothed, Paul Mann as her sybaritic, self-indulgent father and Lou Antonio as a thoroughly detestable crook. No less skillful are the characterizations of Harry Davis and Elena Karam as the hero's parents, Gregory Rosakis, Frank Wolff and John Marley as men who befriend him, Salem Ludwig as his uncle, Estelle Hemsley as his grandmother (she has one scene not easily forgotten), Katharine Balfour as a promiscuous wife and Robert H. Harris as her husband.

Haskell Wexler's cinematography is excellent, ranging from the most alertly intimate glimpses to great panoramic views in which the subject is a moving dot on the screen. His photographic textures and compositions are artfully designed. The long film never bogs down, and there is a minimum of dramatic confusion — a credit to the work of editor Dede Allen on a story so widespread in space and time. Gene Callahan's sets seem the very epitome of authenticity.

Manos Hadjidakis has composed a rich and flavorable score indigenous to the settings. Among the other fine contributions to Kazan's towering artistic achievement are those of costume designer Anna Hill Johnstone and sound mixer L. Robbins. *Tube.*

Eshet Ha'Gibor
(The Hero's Wife)
(ISRAELI)

Tel Aviv, Dec. 10.
Hatzvi films production and release, produced by Peter Frye and Yoseph Tzur, directed by Frye. Stars Batya Lancet. Screenplay, Batya Lancet and Yoseph Klauzner, based on story by Margot Klauzner; camera, Marco Yacovlevitz; editor, Menahem Shoval; music, Mel Keller. Running time, **90 MINS.**
Rachel .... Batya Lancet
Jerry .... Shmuel Oumani
Yoseph .... Gideon Shemer
Douby .... Baruch Klas
Rivka .... Lilly Klas

Filmed entirely on location, at the southern tip of the Sea of Galilee, this story wishes to express, in terms universal and human, the special brand of people who inhabit the Jordan River valley, a few hundred feet below sea level. The story of those people, who have come from various parts of the world to make their collective home in kibbutzim overlooking the waters upon which Jesus walked, is interwoven with a strange romance between a widow dedicated to the memory of her hero-husband, killed during Israel's War of Independence, and a Mexican male, who came to Israel to avoid his wife and child and escape responsibilities.

While the heroine, played by Batya Lancet, a warm and convincing personality with a mellow acting talent, speaks for the collective way of living, for the dedication of people who have a purpose in life and toil towards it, the Mexican, studying Hebrew in the kibbutz Ulpan (a grownups' school), is constantly being cynical, making advances at the women and, in general, trying to prove to himself that his masculine charms still work.

A muddled script, incoherent style of direction and some sincere moments of truth, are mingled in what isn't a technically perfect film, nor a mature statement of facts and emotions. Some of the comedy is lost in talk and some of the serious things said strike a comic note. Modest performances by the leading parts, some good photography and a look into a not too familiar scene of life on a kibbutz, couldn't make up for the lack of conviction in story and dialog. The music by Mel Keller (and a song composed by Barkani to lyrics by Netzer, "My Home Facing Gollan") is good, as is the mass participation of some 800 kibbutz couldn't make up for the tive settlements in the Jordan Valley area.   *Rapo.*

Sunday In New York
(COLOR)

Slight but diverting romantic romp from the legit of same name. Satisfactory b.o. prospect.

Hollywood, Dec. 17.
Metro release of Everett Freeman production. Stars Rod Taylor, Jane Fonda, Cliff Robertson; features Robert Cuip, Jo Morrow, Jim Backus, Peter Nero. Directed by Peter Tewksbury. Screenplay, Norman Krasna, from his Broadway play; camera (Metrocolor), Leo Tover; editor, Fredric Steinkamp; music, Peter Nero; asst. director, Eli Dunn. Reviewed at Stanley Warner BevHills Theatre, Dec.

11, '63. Running time, 105 MINS.
Adam .... Cliff Robertson
Eileen .... Jane Fonda
Mike .... Rod Taylor
Russ .... Robert Culp
Mona .... Jo Morrow
Drysdale .... Jim Backus
Himself .... Peter Nero

The steady succession in the past few years of sex-oriented comedies from the Broadway stage to the Hollywood screen continues with "Sunday In New York," a synthetic but engaging romp in the general tradition of such titillating trifles as "Come Blow Your Horn," "Take Her, She's Mine" and "Under The Yum Yum Tree." Actually, pound for pound, "Sunday" is a cut above the average for its lightweight class. While it won't be any world-beater at the boxoffice, the Metro release has the goods to deliver in profitable style.

Norman Krasna's screenplay, from his Broadway legiter, doesn't really get rolling until it has virtually marked time for almost an hour, but once it gets up this head of steam the entire complexion of the picture seems to change and the resultant momentum overrides the memory of the lethargic and uneventful early going. One scene brings the film to life, and to pave the way for that one scene Krasna has had to resort to a series of rather humdrum romantic contrivances. But getting there was worth the labor, because that scene is a dilly. It's the one that lumps the four leading characters together for the film's comedy payoff.

The story has to do with the sudden arrival at her brother's apartment in New York of an Albany maiden (Jane Fonda) who's fretting over that age-old puzzler —*should a girl before marriage?* By now, she has alienated herself from a well-heeled hometown beau (Robert Culp) upon whom she had matrimonial designs. Big brother (Cliff Robertson), an airline pilot, lauds the virtuous life, but when sis subsequently discovers flimsy negligee in his closet, she impulsively attempts to seduce the nearest male (Rod Taylor), a young newspaperman to whom she's grown quite attached in the course of several mutual misadventures that day. But the reluctant Taylor, respecting her virginity, demurs.

The payoff scene has Culp barging in, discovering Taylor and Miss Fonda in bathrobes, and deducing that Taylor is her brother (whom he's never met). At this critical moment, who should barge in but—natch—big brother Robertson, who's promptly introduced as Taylor's co-pilot, with resultant complications. From there on, it's all romanticomedic gravy.

Two refugees from the television theatre of operations — Everett Freeman and Peter Tewksbury— handled the reins on this venture, and guided it with impressive skill. Slick production by Freeman and nimble direction by Tewksbury make the most of Krasna's fluffy paperwork. And the entire cast is equal to the challenge. Best of the lot is Rod Taylor, a steadily rising and versatile actor who delivers a warm, flexible and appealing performance as the young journalist who

so rapidly grows fond'a Fonda. Miss Fonda, showing more becoming restraint on this outing, scores comedically and romantically as the forward-thinking lass. Robertson is convincing and chips in some highly amusing reactions as her generally befuddled pilot-brother who's implicated in a running gag (and neatly incorporated sub-plot) with girl friend Jo Morrow, who keeps hopping aboard flights to be with him, only to wind up alone in distant cities when Robertson is called off duty at the last moment. Miss Morrow is a decorative and competent addition to the cast. Culp has some fine moments as the rich suitor, and so does Jim Backus as an uncoordinated flight schedule coordinator.

Handsome Metrocolor photography by Leo Tover is a valuable assist, as are Fredric Steinkamp's tidy editing and the imaginative and persuasive art direction by George W. Davis and Edward Carfagno, notably of Robertson's masculine apartment that's so astonishingly accessible. Peter Nero, who puts in a brief appearance at the keyboard, has also contributed a breezy, modern-sounding score and is the composer of the film's two tunes. One, the bright and commercially promising title song expressively by Mel Torme, is adorned with lyrics by Carroll Coates. The other, a pleasant refrain entitled "Hello," sports words by Roland Everett. *Tube.*

La Corruzione
(Corruption)
(ITALO-FRENCH)

Rome, Dec. 10.
Arcofilm release of an Alfredo Bini production for Arco Film-S.O.P.A.C.-Burgundia Film (Paris). Stars Alain Cuny, Rosanna Schiaffino. Jacques Perrin; features Filippo Scelzo, Isa Miranda, Ennio Balbo. Directed by Mauro Bolognini. Screenplay, Fulvio Gicca, Ugo Liberatore, from story by Liberatore; camera, Leonida Barboni; music, Giovanni Fusco; editor, Nino Baragli. Previewed in Rome. Running time, 87 MINS.
Leonardo .... Alain Cuny
Stefano .... Jacques Perrin
Adriana .... Rosanna Schiaffino

Solid, well paced and constructed item in the best Italian tradition which looks headed for a good payoff on the Continent and rates definite offshore attention as well.

Tale is a topical one, capsuling as it does the world as it must currently be faced by a growing number of youths just out of school. Specifically, Stefano (Jacques Perrin) has made up his mind to become a priest. His father, a rich industrialist (Alain Cuny) whose bent is more on matter than mind, tries to steer him away. He enlists the aid of his current young girl friend, Adriana (Rosanna Schiaffino), who falls for the boy and seduces him.

Confused and horrified by his father's materialistic outlook on life, the boy tries repeatedly to escape, while his concience torments him as he feels himself inexorably giving into the lures of sex, money, and other things which have always constituted evil distractions in his mind. The windup finds him still fighting his inner battle, but obviously weakening, confronted as he is by the massive hold superficial values have on modern society.

Aside from its implications, however, the pic clicks as a psychological drama. Some of the father-son scenes are shattering in dialogue and implications, just as those between the youth and the girl are tender and moving. Taste and style are prime components, as usual, in this Mauro Bolognini directorial effort, his best in some time — perhaps since "Bell Antonio." Script is literal and performances topnotch.

Rosanna Schiaffino does her best to date as the animal-like sex symbol with a tender streak, and a most attractive one at that. Alain Cuny is properly craggy and unbending as the father. Jacques Perrin is excellent in the key role of the confused, beset youth. Isa Miranda has a short scene as his bedridden mother, but it's effective.

Production values are further pluses, both the modern settings in Milan and the yacht sequences beautifully lensed along the Italian coastline, a credit to Leonida Barboni's chiaro-scuro lensing. Music by Giovanni Fusco aids in backdropping contrasting moods. Nino Baragli's editing, except for some jumpy spots probably occasioned by last-minute cuts, is serviceable. *Hawk.*

Kings Of The Sun
(PANAVISION—COLOR)

Elaborately mounted but dramatically skimpy adventure meller. Intensely exploited spectacle aspects should lure escape-seeking audiences.

Hollywood, Dec. 4.
United Artists release of Lewis J. Rachmil production. Stars Yul Brynner, George Chakiris, Shirley Anne Field; features Richard Basehart, Brad Dexter, Barry Morse. Directed by J. Lee Thompson. Screenplay, Elliott Arnold, James R. Webb, from story by Arnold; camera (De Luxe), Joseph Macdonald; editor, William Reynolds; music, Elmer Bernstein; asst. director, Thomas Shaw. Reviewed at Goldwyn Studios, Dec. 4, '63. Running time, 108 MINS.
Black Eagle .... Yul Brynner
Balam .... George Chakiris
Ixchel .... Shirley Anne Field
Ah Min .... Richard Basehart
Ah Haleb .... Brad Dexter
Ah Zok .... Barry Morse
Isatai .... Armando Silvestre
Hunac Ceel .... Leo Gordon
Ixzubin .... Victoria Vettri
Pitz .... Rudy Solari
The Chief .... Ford Rainey
Balam .... Angel Di Steffano
The Youth .... Jose Moreno

In Lewis J. Rackmil's production of "Kings of the Sun," the Mirisch Co. and United Artists have exploitable merchandise and an acceptable avenue of escape for audiences that prefer their adventure spectacle pictorially extravagant, historically simplified and melodramatically passionate. The more discerning, demanding filmgoer will be disappointed by its synthetic, transparent approach to a potentially fascinating subject— the ancient Mayan civilization at a point of great criss. Being obviously a production of considerable expense and yet quite limited in commercial range and appeal, the boxoffice battle will not easily be won. Vivid, intensive exploitation of adventure elements and saturation booking, wherever applicable, would seem to be the logical marketing pattern.

The Elliott Arnold-James R. Webb screenplay from a story by the former is a kind of southern

western. It describes, in broad, vague, romantic strokes, the flight of the Mayan people from their homeland after crushing military defeat, their establishment of a new home, and their successful defense of it against their former conquerors thanks to the aid of a friendly resident tribe that has been willing to share the region in which the Mayans have chosen to relocate. In more intimate terms, it is the story of the young Mayan king (George Chakiris), the leader (Yul Brynner) of the not-so-savage tribe that comes to the ultimate defense of the Mayans, and a Mayan maiden (Shirley Anne Field).

Brynner easily steals the show with his sinewy authority, masculinity and cat-like grace. Chakiris is adequate, although he lacks the epic, heroic stature with which the role might have been filled. Miss Field is an attractive pivot for the romantic story. Others of importance are Richard Basehart as a high priest and advisor who gives consistently lousy advice; Brad Dexter, Barry Morse and Armando Silvestre as assorted henchmen, and Leo Gordon as a vengeful barbarian who resembles an Irish policeman.

Obviously pains have been taken to endow the production with physical authenticity. Leading assists in this regard are those of art director Alfred Ybarra and costume designer Norma Koch. Unfortunately, the same cannot be said for the dramatic area of operations. Historical and geographic exposition is vague and fuzzy and such matters as the total absence of a language barrier among these separate tribes, all of whom communicate remarkably, give the picture an aura of artificiality that cannot be rectified just by authentic props and costumes.

Direction by J. Lee Thompson has its lags and lapses, but he has mounted his spectacle handsomely and commandeered the all-important battle sequences with vigor and imagination. Joseph MacDonald's photography is dramatically composed and strikingly lighter, especially when Brynner is the subject of the lens. Brynner's body gets a big play. Often his head is chopped off in a shadow in order to focus at length on his pectoral endowments. Beefcake, as a matter of fact, disproportionately abounds. William Reynold's editing is skillful and Elmer Bernstein has composed an adventurous score for the occasion.

The picture was filmed entirely in Mexico: interiors in Mexico City and exteriors in the coastal area of Mazatlan and in Chichen Itza near Yucatan. *Tube.*

Act One

Moss Hart's own story, movingly brought to screen by Dore Schary. Memorable portrayal by Jason Robards Jr. as George S. Kaufman.

Hollwood, Dec. 12.
Warner Bros. release of Dore Schary production, with direction and screenplay by Schary, based on Moss Hart's book. Stars George Hamilton, Jason Robards Jr.; features Jack Klugman, Sam Levene, Ruth Ford, Eli Wallach. Camera, Arthur J. Ornitz; editor, Mort Fallick; music, Skitch Henderson; asst. director, Michael Hertzberg. Reviewed at the studio, Dec. 12, '63. Running time, 110 MINS.

Moss Hart .... George Hamilton
George S. Kaufman.... Jason Robards Jr.
Joe Hyman .... Jack Klugman
Richard Maxwell .... Sam Levene
Beatrice Kaufman .... Ruth Ford
Warren Stone .... Eli Wallach
Max Seigel .... Joseph Leon
Lester Sweyd .... George Segal
Mr. Hart .... Martin Wolfson
David Starr .... Sam Groom
Sam H. Harris .... Sammy Smith
Clara Baum .... Louise Larabee
Oliver Fisher .... David Doyle
Teddy Manson .... Jonathan Lippe
Archie Leach .... Bert Convy
Mrs. Hart .... Sylvie Straus
Bernie Hart .... Arno Selco
Harry the Waiter .... Allen Leaf
The Maid .... Lulu B. King

The story of the late Moss Hart as a young man on the threshold of success, so vividly chronicled by him in his autobiography of several years back, has now been brought to the screen by his early colleague Dore Shary in a film richly endowed with nostalgic, honest sentiment and inspirational values. It is these virtues that give the picture an appealing glow from within, a spark of simple humanity that transcends the specialized show biz framework in which it is encased and can trigger an emotional response from any audience.

Since this is, however, a film without a romantic nucleus, without the customary commercial concessions to filmgoers, conditioned to the boy-meets-girl formula and related cliches, the boxoffice battle may not easily be won. But the reputation and popularity of the book, the relatively unpretentious cost of the production and the artistic calibre of some of the performances could, if accompanied by sensitive handling, combine to make the Warner Bros, release an ultimate net success.

Oddly enough, "Act One," as a film, does not really spring to life until along about what might be considered its equivalent of Act 2. Just as the advents of George S. Kaufman proved to be the turning point in Hart's career, so the advent of that character, brilliantly enacted by Jason Robards Jr., is the turning point in this film. As soon as Kauf comes on the scene, the picture gains strength, clarity and momentum and roars on to its conclusion.

The story traces Hart's budding career from the point at which he has abandoned attempted heavy drama to concentrate on writing comedy to the ultimate success on Broadway of his first comedy, "Once In A Lifetime," the first of many collaborations with Kaufman. In between are illustrated Hart's many discouraging experiences, first in landing a producer for his play, later in making it tick during and after a series of tryout flops.

Considering the kind of story this is, Schary, overall, has done a remarkable job of bringing it to dramatic life on the screen. For, after all, what can be visually duller than observing two writers at work? And yet, in addition to some relatively minor directorial slipups, he is guilty of one basic error of interpretive judgment that at times threatens to derail the whole project. It is, as a matter of fact, an error commonly made by scenarists in translating from book to screen. It is the mistake of being too faithful to the original author, of translating too literally in dramatic terms his prose reflections.

Thus, recollections in the book of fervent dreams and desires, when depicted visually on the screen, come out slightly distorted and absurd. Likewise, the remembrances of a violent emotional reaction to a setback seems much too melodramatic and unreal unless it is toned down in the interpretation. Just as the imagination of a reader tends to adjust the image of the mind's eye, so as to keep matters in realistic perspective, so Schary should have adjusted Hart's understandable prose elaborations to fit the mercilessly revealing eye of the lens, which is so quick to detect dramatic artificiality.

The picture contains some memorable performances. Robards is truly marvelous as Kaufman, remarkably suggesting the late playwright not only in physical construction but in expression, mannerisms and attitude conveyed from within. It's a masterful piece of acting, a portrayal that deserves to be remembered when this year's histrionic crop is harvested and assessed for excellence. It is George Hamilton's misfortune to be pitted against such an extraordinary characterization, but this young actor, ripening with each outing, does a fine bit of work as Hart. Although overshadowed by Robards and several times victimized by the exaggerations of the scenario, Hamilton delivers a warm, compassionate, animated and appealing performance.

An outstanding supporting portrayal is fashioned by Eli Wallach as the lordly, overbearing, unreliable producer, called Warren Stone. Jack Klugman is his usual likable self as a faithful friend of Hart's, and others who make especially favorable impressions are Sam Levene, Ruth Ford, Joseph Leon, George Segal, Martin Wolfson and Sam Groom. As Archie Leach, or the young Cary Grant, Bert Convy fails to project the unique nature of that star. The other supporting players are generally satisfactory.

Photography by Arthur J. Ornitz is consistently effective in a direct, uncomplicated way, in keeping with the character of the period being depicted. Roughly the same thing might be said of Edward Carrere's production design and set decoration, accurately reproducing the physical shape of that era. Skitch Henderson's score is a vital factor in coloring and clarifying the events of the story, whenever such musical statement and embellishment is required, as it is, for example, in a series of scenes showing Hart patiently awaiting word from the thoughtless Mr. Stone. Other important assists to the production are those of editor Mort Fallick, soundman Maurice Rosenblum, costume designer Gene Coffin and makeupman Dean Newman. *Tube.*

El Dorado
(ISRAELI)

Tel Aviv, Dec. 10.

Geva Films Ltd.-Noah Films Ltd.-Mordechay Navon production and release. Stars Gila Almagor, Haim Topol. Directed by Menahem Golan. Script by Golan and Amatsia Hiouni; camera, Nissim Leon; music, Yohanan Zaray; editor, Nelly Bogor. Running time, **88 MINS.**

Margo .... Gila Almagor
Benny Sherman .... Haim Topol
Sgt. Buganov .... Yossef Yadin
Shneider .... Shay K. Ophir
Lawyer Benyamini ...... Shimon Finkel
Naomi, his daughter ....Tikva Mor
Sgt. Cohen .... Ori Levy
Wovik .... Mordechay Arnon
Kohelet .... Avner Hizkiyahu

In search of an Israeli story that might have international appeal (and be understood by foreigners), this film is based on a local play (of the same name) by playwright Igael Mossinson, adapted by Leo Filler. It tells of a released convict, trying very hard to prove his innocence as far as his latest charge has been concerned and get a fresh start, through work and studies, and the love of his lawyer's daughter.

In their unpretentious effort to secure good boxoffice returns, the producers played it safe. The picture is full of cliches, which accounts for the familiarity most viewers would feel, encountering characters and situations which seem like old friends.

Haim Topol knows that Yossef Yadin promised to prove his guilt, even though he might be innocent. His underworld accomplices use the fact that the police are out to frame him, if necessary, and induce him to participate in another caper. The fact that the lawyer, and Tel Aviv's high society are not too eager to accept him drives him to a desperate effort to prove his innocence and win his chance to rehabilitate, etc.

While a "good" police officer tries to expose the frameup, the film comes to its climax in a chase and a head-on encounter by criminals and police, with the golden-hearted prostitute (Gila Almagor) and the other girl (Tikva Mor) watching while evil is being punished and justice triumphs.

The acting is good and Miss Almagor gives a very good account of the devoted love a prostitute is capable of, including self-sacrifice when necessary. The photography is very good, especially of the old Casba area around the ancient port of Jaffa. Sound is almost adequate and the editing is smooth and professional.

It stands a good chance in Israel, but wouldn't impress foreign audiences by either the melodrama or the artistic qualities of a regular "A" picture. *Rapo.*

Aliki — My Love
(GREEK)

Hollywood Dec. 9.

Lionex Films release of Rudolph Mate-George St. George production. Stars Aliki Vouyouklaki; features Wilfrid Hyde White, Jess Conrad, Katherine Kath; with Paris Alexander, John Pardos, Roland George. Directed by Mate. Screenplay and story, St. George; camera, A. Karidis-Fuchs; music, Manos Hadjidakis. Reviewed at Beverly Canon Theatre, Dec. 9, '63. Running time, **85 MINS.**

Aliki .... Aliki Vouyouklaki
Caraway .... Wilfrid Hyde White
Barry .... Jess Conrad
Anna .... Katherine Kath
Pastrudis .... Paris Alexander
Sparks .... John Pardos
Socrates .... Roland George

Perhaps the most discouraging aspect of this import from Greece is that it was filmed directly in English with the American market in mind. The American market has rarely been so sadly underestimated. The Lionex Films release, produced by Rudolph Mate and George St. George, is too trite and puerile for acceptance in the arty sphere and too Hellenically-oriented and terrifyingly wholesome to mean anything or stimulate interest in the general Yankee market.

Written by St. George and directed by Mate, "Aliki—My Love" relates the strange tale of their heir to a hamburger sauce fortune whose estate, save for a small Greek island, vanishes when the recipe for the incomparable sauce goes to the grave with his benefactor.

The picture stars Aliki Vouyouklaki, purportedly one of the foremost young stars of Greece, in the title role. Miss V might be described as the Greek version of "Gidget" or "Tammy," or a kind of cross between Brigitte Bardot and Shirley Temple. Her acting leaves something to be desired, consisting as it does primarily of a constant Little Mary Sunshine smile, a Pollyanna disposition and occasional little sexy "accidents" such as falling into the bay and emerging from her unscheduled dip with her dress all clingy.

Wilfrid Hyde White rather unaccountably plays the crabby attorney who mellows, and Jess Conrad is the young heir. Katherine Kath does by far the best acting in the film as the cook who charms the Jekyll out of Hyde White.

Filmed on the island of Ios in Greece, the production is graced with a typical musical score by Manos Hadjidakis of "Never On Sunday" fame. *Tube.*

Living Between Two Worlds

Negro subject made for Negro audiences by Negro producers; okay for market.

Hollywood, Dec. 12.

Empire release of Horace Jackson production. Stars Maye Henderson, Hroace Jackson, Anita Poree, Mimi Dillard; features Irvin Mosley. Directed by Bobby Johnson. Screenplay, Horace Jackson; camera, Willie Sigmond; editor, Gene Evans; music, Gordon Zahler; asst. director, Ivan Dixon. Reviewed at Balboa Theatre, Dec. 11, '63. Running time, **75 MINS.**

Mom .... Maye Henderson
Bucky .... Anita Poree
Helen .... Mimi Dillard
Harvey .... Horace Jackson
Papa .... Irvin Mosley
Larry .... Kyle Johnson
Norman .... Derrick Lewis
Mrs. Peters .... Geraldine West
Orderly .... DeForest Covan
Janitor .... Lawrence LaMarr
Reverend Williamson .. Nappy Whiting

"Living Between Two Worlds," first production of a new Negro group, carries enough merit to augur a fairly promising future for the filmakers in the Negro market. Written, produced and financed by Horace Jackson, who also co-stars, this 85-minute drama of a young preacher torn between the field chosen for him at birth by his deeply religious mother, and a jazz career, shows wise use of every penny of its moderate budget and emerges as a suitable entry for its specialized market.

Evidences of amateurish treatment frequently are displayed, such as in over-direction of players in highly emotional scenes, awkward camera movement and static closeups, but the spirit of its subject is projected sincerely and tellingly.

Story motivation, sometimes a bit complex, is based upon a mother's driving desire to see her son become a minister, her only real interest in life and towering over her dislike of white people. In this role, Maye Henderson comes through in firstclass fashion and makes the part entirely believable.

Jackson, who wants to leave a field he thinks he isn't fitted for but finally is convinced it is for him, lends certain credence but isn't always up to the acting demands. Anita Poree as his devoted sister scores nicely. Mimi Dillard, with whom Jackson is in love but is afraid to marry because of his domineering mother, is in for sex appeal, showing a shapely figure in a sexy low-cleaving slip and victim of a rape by two white hoodlums, which may be exploited by distrib. Balance of cast have little to do.

Bobby Johnson, as director, goes in for moods not always pertinent to story unfoldment but generally handles his assignment in okay fashion. Camera work by Willie Sigmond is straightforward and set design by Carl Randell satisfactory. Gordon Zahler's music direction is atmospheric. *Whit.*

The Ceremony

Laurence Harvey as producer-director brings in a dreary melodrama. Dim b.o. candidate.

Hollywood, Dec. 6.

United Artists release of Laurence Harvey production, directed by and starring Harvey; features Saran Miles, Robert Walker, John Ireland. Screenplay, Ben Barzman, with additional dialog by Harvey; camera, Brian West; editor, Ralph Kemplen; music, Gerard Schurmann; assistant directors, John Quested, Pedro Vidal. Reviewed at Academy Awards Theatre, Dec. 6, '63. Running time, **106 MINS.**

Sean McKenna	Laurence Harvey
Catherine	Sarah Miles
Dominic	Robert Walker
Prison Warden	John Ireland
LeCoq	Ross Martin
Nicky	Lee Patterson
O'Brien	Jack McGowran
First Gendarme	Murray Melvin
Ramades	Carlos Casarvilla
Sanchez	Fernando Rey
Shaoush	Fernando Sanchez
Inspector	Jose Nieto
Finigan	Noel Purcell
Arab Peasant	Xan Das Bolas
Death House Guard	Barta Barray
Special Guard	Edward St. John
Gate Guard	Jose Guardiola
Police Chauffer	Jose Trinidad
2d Gendarme	Jose Manuel Martin
3rd Gendarme	Juan Olaguibel
4th Gendarme	Juan Garcia Delgado
5th Gendarme	Julio Tabuyo
6th Gendarme	James Brown
7th Gendarme	Rafael Albaicin
8th Gendarme	Ricardo Rodriquez
9th Gendarme	Manuel Pena
10th Gendarme	Carlos Chemenal
11th Gendarme	Alvaro Varela
12th Gendarme	Enrique Closas
1st Guard	Francisco Montalvo
2d Guard	Jose Riesgo
Truck Driver	Eduardo Garcia
Prison Official	Phil Posner

With "The Ceremony," actor Laurence Harvey has branched out into production and direction. If this is a representative sample of his ability in those fields, he'd better branch right back into acting—and stay put. Opaque, confusing, pretentious and dull, the United Artists release is a dim boxoffice prospect.

Ben Barzman's screenplay relates the dreary tale of a man (Harvey) about to be executed in a Tangier prison for a crime he did not commit, a murder that actually he'd tried to prevent but for which he is paying the supreme penalty as a kind of scapegoat. An elaborate escape scheme cooked up by his brother (Robert Walker) succeeds, but Harvey then discovers that little brother has been making time with his girl (Sarah Miles).

Concern is never aroused for any of the characters. The audience is thrust into the heart of the situation and never really allowed to get its bearings. It would have been wise, for example, to show the robbery during which the crime was committed for which Harvey is paying the price.

The players are all snowed under by ill-defined, unappealing roles and lock of proper direction. In addition to the three principals, none of whom comes off with any distinction whatsoever, prominent parts are essayed by John Ireland, Ross Martin, Lee Patterson, Jack McGowran, Murray Melvin and Carlos Casarvilla.

Under the dismal circumstances, the key members of the production staff have performed their tasks adequately. Among other things, "The Ceremony" is a depressingly dark film. *Tube.*

Bitter Harvest
(BRITISH-COLOR)

Another chance for Janet Munro to destroy her "Disney image" in a well-made but conventional goodtime-girl drama. Favorable b.o. prospects.

London, Dec. 10.

Rank release of an (Albert Fennell) Julian Wintle-Leslie Parkyn production. Stars Janet Munro, John Stride, Alan Badel; features Anne Cunningham, Norman Bird, Terence Alexander, Daphne Anderson, May Hallatt, Mary Merrall, Colin Gordon, Barbara Ferris, Allan Cuthbertson. Directer by Peter Graham Scott. Screenplay by Ted Willis from Patrick Hamilton's "The Street Has a Thousand Skies"; music, Laurie Johnson; editor, Russell Lloyd; camera, Ernest Steward. Reviewed at RFD Private Theatre, London. Running time **96 MINS.**

Jennie Jones	Janet Munro
Bob Williams	John Stride
Ella	Anne Cunningham
Karl Denny	Alan Badel
Mrs. Pitt	Vanda Godsell
Mr. Pitt	Norman Bird
Andy	Terence Alexander
Rex	Richard Thorp
Violet	Barbara Ferris
David Medwin	William Lucas
Nancy Medwin	Daphne Anderson
Mr. Jones	Derek Francis
Aunt Louise	Mary Merrall
Aunt Sarah	May Hallatt
Charles	Colin Gordon
Mrs. Jessup	Thora Hird
Mr. Eccles	Allan Cuthbertson

"The Day The Earth Caught Fire" and now this, "Bitter Harvest," could be a mighty help to Janet Munro in destroying the nice, fresh tomboy image built up during her sojourn with the Disney Organization. Miss Munro is a well stacked young woman, who is also hooked with the problem of a face that looks even younger than her admittedly tender years. It has taken a while for Miss Munro to pin down the opportunity of playing roles that give her more dramatic scope than the Disney roles. That she can do it is proved in "Bitter Harvest," where she plays a capricious young woman who runs the gamut of many moods.

"Harvest" is off to a flying start at the boxoffice, thereby proving that there's no friend like an old friend. For the story of the country innocent who gets caught up in the dizzy pitfalls of London nightlife is hardly likely to win an Oscar for originality. This one is taken from a Patrick Hamilton novel, but the same flimsy plot crops up in every tab paper the world over.

Surprising thing is that Ted Willis, though giving the film his usual craftsman's touch, has not come up with any surprises or twist, and director Peter Graham Scott has been no help in this matter, either. Result is a conventional yarn that leans heavily on its players, who successfully cope with some stereotyped and mushy situations, and dialog.

With their good work, and a briskness in Graham Scott's direction, pic stands up as a reasonable program topper. This bows in with a jaded Miss Munro, distinctly loaded, returning to her mews cottage late at night. Frayed nerves and unhappiness send her beserk. She smashes up the joint, rips her lavish wardrobe to pieces and tosses the gowns into the mews below. After a dangerously long, wordless sequence she collapses on the bed. Then begins the inevitable flashback. How it all happened.

Scene switches to a remote Welsh village, dismal, rainy, depressing. Miss Munro serves in her unpleasant father's village store, now becoming redundant. Miss M. longs for the chance to get away. She and her friend are picked up by a couple of city slickers in Cardiff, who feed them cheap wine and flattery. She wakes up next morning in bed, nude, and deserted by her one-night lover. Snag is that the apartment's in London, a sudden switch even for a girl who is indoctrinated with tv commercials and a desire for luxury and a chance to be a model.

Deserted, Miss Munro is befriended by a young barman who gives her his bed and tenderness with the loftiest intentions. Swiftly, too swiftly some audiences may think, she decides that London is her golden opportunity. She uses the bartender, who has fallen hopelessly for her, but lies to him, humiliates him and adapts herself to London's Dolce Vita to such an extent that soon she is installed as the mistress of an impresario and caught up in a whirl of parties. Disillusioned, she weaves her way back to her apartment one night and feeds herself a bottle of sleeping tablets. Enter police and ambulance. Jennie Jones, from remote Wales, becomes yet another victim of the dazzle and lure of the Big City bright lights. Unoriginal, but always effective final twist has the bartender, now happily walking out with a barmaid, dodging an ambulance and idly wondering who the victim might be.

Scott Graham has provided Miss Munro with two or three effective situational scenes. In Cardiff, when baby sitting, she cannot resist the luxury of taking a bath and then having to ward off the advances of the master of the house when he returns home unexpectedly. Her gauche attempt to seem at home in a flashy restaurant. Her first wondering glimpse at a backstage theatrical party and her quick absorption into the atmosphere. One or two tender moments with her bartender boy friend.

Miss Munro is given opportunities to portray innocence, gaiety, cupidity, depression, vanity, fear, cunning, tenderness, harshness, wonder and anger. All the emotions are fleeting but the star helps to mould them into a well-drawn picture of an innocent who learns quickly. One of the snags is that the time element is never made fully clear and superficially it seems that she is drawn into the web rather quicker than a girl of her sheltered background normally would be.

John Stride, a rising stage actor who is only just beginning to make his mark in pix, is solid, charming and resourceful as the infatuated bartender. Alan Badel makes a brief but telling contribution as a steely, unscrupulous theatre boss. There is also a beautifully underplayed performance by Anne Cunningham as a barmaid who has long been secretly in love with Stride.

Most of the other characters are brought in briefly to give point and body to the action. They are in such safe hands with Terence Alexander as the goodtime seducer; Barbara Ferris, Norman Bird, Allan Cuthbertson, Mary Merrall, May Hallatt, Colin Gordon, Daphne Anderson and Thora Hird. Last-named scores swiftly but heavily as a greedy landlady.

Scott has effectively brought the contrasting London locales to the screen, particularly the pub sequences. But he must realize that the gag of showing the frenzy of a wild party by flashing lights, hysterical laughter, incoherent dialog and a blurred, whirling screen to indicate tipsiness is now distinctly oldhat.

Ernest Steward's color lensing is sometimes over emphasized and more impressive than most is his capturing of the bleakness and dismal loneliness of the heroine's Welsh home background. Russell Lloyd's editing is conventionally sound while Laurie Johnson has contributed a suitably moody musical background. "Harvest" is a step in the right direction for the talented and intelligent Miss Munro, and directly points up that Stride is a young actor of presence who is worth cultivating. *Rich.*

Honolulu — Tokyo — Hong Kong
(JAPANESE—TOHOSCOPE COLOR)

Escapist fare. Very attractive young Orientals against exotic settings.

Hollywood, Dec. 9.

Toho release of Sanezumi Fujimoto-Lin Yung-Tai production. With Akira Takarada, Yu Ming, Yuzo Kayama, Yuriko Hoshi, Wang In. Directed by Yasuki Chiba. Screenplay, Zenzo Matsuyama; camera (Eastman), Rokuro Nishigaki; music, Hachiro Matsui. Reviewed at Toho La Brea Theatre, Dec. 9, '63. Running time, **102 MINS.**

Yuichi Okamoto	Akita Takarada
Wu Ai-Ling	Yu Ming
Jiro	Yuzo Kayama
Teruko	Yuriko Hoshi
Cheng Hao	Wang In

This is one for the Japanese fan mag set—a glossy romantic diversion cast with exceptionally attractive young players and set against handsome and exotic backgrounds. It is the approximate Japanese equivalent of a film that, had it been produced in Hollywood, might have had as its star array the combination of Troy Donahue-Suzanne Pleshette-Connie Stevens-Edd Byrnes or, if the target was several years more mature, Gig Young-Shirley Jones-Paula Prentiss-Jim Hutton. And that title, instead of "Honolulu-Tokyo-Hong Kong," might have

read, "Acapulco-New York-Miami Beach."

At any rate, the joint venture by Japan's Toho Co. and Hong Kong's Cathay Organization, coproduced by Sanezumi Fujimoto of the former and Lin Yung-Tai of the latter, has the production glamour and story amiability to entertain audiences, especially, in view of its lighthearted nature, as a holiday season attraction.

Written by Zenzo Matsuyama and directed with a breezy touch by Yasuki Chiba, the shallow but engaging story concerns the amour that develops between a serious-minded young Japanese businessman (Akira Takarada) and a fun-loving, high-spirited Chinese girl (Yu Ming) who lives in Honolulu and has just won a "Miss Hawaii" contest entitling her to a two-week holiday in Tokyo and Hong Kong, for which Takarada starts off as her guide and soon becomes her betrothed.

In addition to Takarada and Miss Ming, other good-looking members of the cast include Yuzo Kayama as the former's immature student-brother, Yuriko Hoshi as his girl friend, and Wang In as a fiance of 20-year's standing. Histrionically, they all have nuances to learn, but they are young and uncommonly attractive performers which should provide them with many opportunities to refine their abilities.

Filmed in Tohoscope and Eastman Color, the production contains some fairly handsome photography by Rokuro Nishigaki and a romantic score by Hachiro Matsuki. The scenario alternates among three languages—English, Japanese and Chinese — so that occasionally there are more titles on the screen than scenery. A particular annoyance for Yank audiences is the rather slurred, inarticulate English spoken by the leading players. With no sub-titles to help out, a lot of dialog gets lost in the multilingual shuffle. *Tube.*

Judex
(FRENCH)

Paris, Dec. 10.

CFF release of CFFP-Filmes production. With Channing Pollock, Francine Berge, Jean Servais, Edith Scob, Theo Sarapo, Max Montavan. Directed by Georges Franju. Screenplay, Jacques Champreux, Francis Lacassin from films by Louis Feuillade, Arthur Bernede. Camera, Jean Labussiere; editor, Gilbert Natot. At Cinematheque Franciase, Paris. Running time, **95 MINS.**

Judex	Channing Pollock
Marie	Francine Berge
Banker	Michel Vitold
Jacqueline	Edith Scob
Son	Theo Sarapo
Daisy	Sylva Koscina
Cocontin	Jacques Jouhanneau

Director Georges Franju has brought off a successful homage to the French film serials of the early, silent days in this tale of a super crook who rights wrongs and finally gives it all up for a girl. It does not chide or send up this form of pic but rather captures its essential simplicity, adventurousness and innocence that keep this entertaining in its own right.

Franju does not try to improve on the genre or update it by snap, precision and the sophistication of today's action and gangster pic methods. Its appeal comes from playing it for its all-out melodrama, coincidence and uncomplicated characters, except perhaps for the master outlaw Judex himself.

Each scene gets its real touch from its very lack of self consciousness and straining for atmosphere or technique for its own sake. Thus, the lensing is fairly harsh and ungraded, disguises are obvious and action direct. But a masked ball with people wearing bird heads, Judex' men with their black hats, capes and masks, and some clever gimmicky hideouts, video spying and chases all keep this disarmingly entertaining.

Judex goes after a nefarious banker who has sent men to prison, swindled, etc. But he does not kill him when his daughter intends to give back the ill gotten gains after the banker's supposed death. A rapacious woman burglar complicates things.

Climbs up a building's wall, trussed up figures for wrong murders, and a son recognized by his father in a death struggle are part of the histrionics of the time but do not seem garish or corny in this knowing reshaping of those long-gone silent days.

Channing Pollock, a Yank magico, has the unruffled deadpan good looks for Judex while others fit well into their black and white figures. In fact, a struggle between the black garbed female heavy and a white-clothed circus performer on a rooftop sum up the film's attitude admirably.

Franju shows that the lamented early freshness, life and zest of the first silents can be resuscitated today by a knowing assimilation and understanding of those days. Franju was one of the founders of the local French Film Museum and understands the old, early aspects of the medium.

Of course, this pic may be limited to buffs, and may need hard, specialized sell abroad because of this. But it can still be accepted with amusement by ordinary audiences since its way-out obvious plotting is still entertaining today. *Mosk.*

Three Lives of Thomasina
(COLOR)

From Walt Disney a cat story for the kids, timed nicely for the holidays.

Buena Vista release of Walt Disney production. Stars Patrick McGoohan, Susan Hampshire; features Karen Dotrice and Matthew Garber. Directed by Don Chaffey; screenplay, Robert Westerby, from the book, "Thomasina," by Paul Gallico; camera (Technicolor), Paul Beeson; editor, Gordon Stone; music, Paul Smith, conducted by Eric Rogers. At New York's Radio City Music Hall screening room Dec. 5, '63. Running time, **87 MINS.**

Andrew Mac Dhui	Patrick McGoohan
Lori MacGregor	Susan Hampshire
Mary MacDhui	Karen Dotrice
Hughie Stirling	Vincent Winter
Jamie McNab	Denis Gilmore
Rev. Angus Peddie	Laurence Naismith
Grandpa Stirling	Finlay Currie
Willie Bannock	Wilfrid Brambell
Mrs. MacKenzie	Jean Anderson
Targu	Francis De Wolff
Birnie	Jack Stewart
Constable McQuarrie	Ewan Roberts
Mr. Dobbie	Oliver Johnston
Geordie	Matthew Garber

The fanciful novel, "Thomasina," by Paul Gallico, has been put up in screen form as an alternately sentimental and parttime amusing item for children. It's a mild-mannered storybook tale, about a marmalade cat, that is set in cinematic motion.

The Walt Disney people have been laying claim of gaining proportionately more and more adults among audiences for the children-loving producer. This is not to be the case with the product at hand; it's for the matinee trade and even then there's likely to be a squirm or two.

"Three Lives of Thomasina" has been picturesquely filmed (Technicolor) in part in Inveraray, Scotland, and Black Park, Buckinghampshire, England. Interiors were done at the Pinewood Studios in London.

It is given shape just fine, technically, but it lacks excitement. Stateside moppets who prefer their entertainment along the robust lines of a World War II rerun (the military craze among youngsters outdistances outer-space concerns) may find difficulty in accepting so tender a tale as this.

The three human principals in the story taking place in a small village are Patrick McGoohan, as the local veterinarian; Karen Dotrice as his young daughter, and Susan Hampshire, an attractively grownup blonde, who lives in the forest, tends to stray animals and is regarded as a witch. Miss Dotrice's pet feline is Thomasina, who recovers from three crises, to the joy of all.

McGoohan is a handsome chap who does quite well as the kind but misunderstood vet who comes to fall in love with Miss Hampshire. As for the appealing Miss Hampshire, well, if she's a witch she can ride on our broomstick any time. Laurence Naismith is the local minister, Matthew Garber, Vincent Winter, Denis Gilmore and Finlay Currie are among the other townsfolk on view, all performing creditably. It's an all-British cast, by the way.

Director Don Chaffey gets the story told with clarity and proper attention to the colorful sets and settings. Paul Beeson's camerawork competently records the visual values and editing by Gordon Stone is to the point. Paul Smith's music has richness, as conducted by Eric Rogers, and the song, "Thomasina," by Terry Gilkyson, has enough fetching quality to go on its own. Interesting special effects make for an additional asset. *Gene.*

What A Crazy World
(BRITISH—MUSICAL)

Brash, perky musical about layabouts in London's East End. Handful of lively songs, several British "pop" favorites and combos compensate for negligible, trite storyline. Useful b.o. prospects among younger folks.

London, Dec. 3.

Warner-Pathe release of a Capricorn (Michael Carreras) production from Associated British. Stars Joe Brown, Susan Maughan, Harry H. Corbett, Marty Wilde; features Avis Bunnage, Michael Ripper, Graziana Frame, Monty Landis. Directed by Michael Carreras. Screenplay by Alan Keith, Carreras from Klein's original musical play; camera, Otto Heller; music and lyrics, Klein; editor, Max Benedict. At Rialto, London. Running time, **88 MINS.**

Alf Hitchens	Joe Brown
Marilyn	Susan Maughan
Herbie	Marty Wilde
Sam	Harry H. Corbett
Mary	Avis Bunnage
Common Man	Michael Ripper
Doris	Grazina Frame
Solly Gold	Monty Landis
Joey	Michael Goodman
Dolly	Sonny Carby
Chas	Larry Dann
Harry	Brian Cronin
Dave	Barry Bethel
Lenny	David Nott
Jervis	Alan Klein

With Freddie and the Dreamers, The Bruvvers and the Happy Wanderers

A show biz legend persists that, goodhearted as they may be, all London's East End cockneys are crummy layabouts, who toil not neither do they spin, except to lie and cop National Assistance relief. Also that they do nothing but booze, go to the dogs, play bingo and generally rough up the neighborhood. This canard has been good for plenty of themes of stage shows, especially since the establishment of the Theatre Workshop. It serves again in this perky British musical film, which is an adaptation of Alan Klein's stage musical of the same title.

Klein is a young man who hails from the environments about which he is writing. Some dramatic license is, no doubt, in order. "What a Crazy World" should attract a vigorous, if undemanding audience in Britain, because of shrewd casting aimed at the pop teenagers. In America, it is a somewhat like proposition.

Story is as trite as the gag about the slimness of a chorine's waistline. Joe Brown plays a youth in a non-understanding household. He has an urge to go places, but can't see the way. Instead he drifts around with the local young hoods. One day, he gets an inspiration. He writes a song called "What a Crazy Gang," peddles it around Tin Pan Alley and gets it published and recorded by a subterfuge. So it's fame and fortune just round the corner. But still his family wants to know when he is going to get a steady job.

On this frail pretext are hung a series of cameos of East End life and the atmosphere of the place with its independence, despair, gusty humor and vitality. This is all excellently suggested by some observant helming by Michael Carreras and the sharp, telling lensing of Otto Heller. But the story is too lacking in any element of surprise. The dialog is more boisterous than either funny or witty.

There are a handful of Klein ditties, breezily put over, one or two of which may soon be jockeying for a place among the Top 10. The music and orchestrations are rather livelier than the lyrics, most of which are predictable rhymes. The rowdy title song, a pleasing ballad, "Just You Wait and See," sung by Brown, a lark about the decline of the local Unemployment Exchange and a spirited duet called "Bruvvers" are the most memorable.

Principal reason for this unpretentious film making for ingratiating entertainment is its zestful and not too familiar cast. Brown, a slim, frail looking pop singer who wears his blond hair as though it might be a hurriedly assembled bird's nest, has a pleasantly unassuming personality and a limited, inoffensive singing voice. He contrasts usefully with his crony, Marty Wilde, who plays a cocky, arrogant lout with brash authority. Susan Maughan (as Brown's girl-

friend, who tries to give him some self respect) is no great shakes as an actress. But she is a pert miss who is forging ahead as one of the tops among the young British pop singers. Grazina Frame and Michael Goodman acquit themselves well as Brown's sister and brother.

Harry H. Corbett, from tele, plays the father with more than a touch of his tv character's mannerisms. But the screenplay gives him little alternative. Avis Bunnage repeats her stage performance as the conciliatory mum. From Monty Landis comes a little gem of a performance as an oily, opportunistic song publisher. Michael Ripper, playing the Common Man, crops up in several different characterizations very amusingly. Freddie and The Dreamers, The Bruvvers and a couple of British combos who are tops in the New Wave perhaps may sell some tabs among the younger element.

Stanley Black's musical direction and background score add to the plusses, but Max Benedict's cutting is sometimes jerky. Without setting its sights too high, "What a Crazy World" could find an appreciative public.   *Rich.*

Chateau En Suede
(Castle In Sweden)
(FRENCH-COLOR-FRANSCOPE)
Paris, Dec. 10.
Valoria Films release of Corona-Spectacles Lubroso-Euro International production. Stars Monica Vitti, Curt Jurgens, Jean-Louis Trintignant, Jean-Claude Brialy, Suzanne Flon, Francoise Hardy; features Daniel Emilfork, Sylvie. Directed by Roger Vadim. Screenplay, Vadim, Claude Choublier from play by Francoise Sagan; camera (Eastmancolor), Armand Thirard; editor, Victoria Mercanton. At Colisee, Paris. Running time, 110 MINS.
Eleonore .... Monica Vitti
Eric .... Jean-Louis Trintignant
Sebastien .... Jean-Claude Brialy
Hugo .... Curt Jurgens
Ophelie .... Francoise Hardy
Agathe .... Suzanne Flon
Gunther .... Daniel Emilfork
Grandmother .... Sylvie

This has a lot of elegant posturing, lensing and a collection of noted actors and actresses. But it lacks the right comic dash and direction to give this comedy much filmic froth.

There is the Francoise Sagan name and some suggestive undraping for possible exploitation booking abroad. But its arty chances look shaky and playoff possibilities dubious. It looms primarily as a home market item. Miss Sagan's play about an inbred Swedish family holed up in an old chateau is slim film fare at best.

Dressing in 19th Century costumes, due to the whim of its addled female proprietress, the chateau contains her aging brother and young wife, the latter's parasitic brother, an ex-wife hidden in the chateau (and unsane) and a senile grandmother. Into this, comes a cousin who springboards the action by immediately falling in love with the wife.

Then follow cannily concealed nude love scenes, the husband's attempts to kill the intruder, the apparitions of the hidden wife as a supposed ghost and the interloper's final escape.

Director Roger Vadim lacks a flair for visual comedy. And there is not enough substance to give this the dashes of the comedy on manners or the offbeat situation

---

comedy routines for which it strives.

Monica Vitti has a fragile charm and expressive face that is not up to suggesting the femme fatale while Curt Jurgens overdoes his jealous husband. Francoise Hardy, a rock singing favorite, is gauche and childish, rather than strangely tetched, as the locked-up wife. Others acquit themselves adequately.

The Eastman color is good and there is some fine outdoor Scandinavian lensing. But this little charade, which had some inventive charm on the stage, just bogs down in its elaborate screen translation.

The influence of Ingmar Bergman's philosophical comedies is apparent but without the visual flair. So all this has the look of a series of smart Vogue color photos without the cementing wit and inventiveness to make them come to life. Its best bet is for specialized handling but its general fragility, except for good lensing, will call for the hardsell.   *Mosk.*

Love With The Proper Stranger

A bachelor, a working girl and an untimely pregnancy. Uneven romantic comedy-drama reinforced with highly marketable ingredients. Despite uneven scenes, very good b.o. prospect.

Hollywood, Dec. 13.
Paramount release of Alan J. Pakula production. Stars Natalie Wood, Steve McQueen; features Edie Adams, Herschel Bernardi, Tom Bosley. Directed by Robert Mulligan. Screenplay, Arnold Schulman; camera, Milt Krasner; editor, Aaron Stell; music, Elmer Bernstein; asst. director, William McGarry. Reviewed at Westwood Village Theatre, Dec. 13, '63. Running time, 102 MINS.
Angie .... Natalie Wood
Rocky .... Steve McQueen
Barbie .... Edie Adams
Dominick .... Herschel Bernardi
Columbo .... Tom Bosley
Julio .... Harvey Lembeck
Mama .... Penny Santon
Anna .... Virginia Vincent
Guido .... Nick Alexander
Mrs. Papasano .... Augusta Ciolli
Beetie .... Anne Hegira
Elio Papasano .... Mario Badolati
The Woman .... Elena Karam
Mrs. Columbo .... Nina Varela
Gina .... Marilyn Chris
The Priest .... Wolfe Barzell

Paramount has surefire boxoffice merchandise in "Love With the Proper Stranger," an attraction marketably endowed with the hot marquee names of Natalie Wood and Steve McQueen and reinforced with an appealingly bright, optimistic slant on a fresh and provocative theme—pregnancy prior to matrimony, and how the problem is approached and solved by the male and female involved. It's a commercial strike for the team of producer Alan J. Pakula and director Robert Mulligan.

Written for the screen by Arnold Schulman, "Proper Stranger" is actually a somewhat unstable picture, fluctuating between scenes of a substantial, lifelike disposition and others where reality is suspended in favor of deliberately exaggerated hokum. For commercial purposes these elements are compatible, but artistically they are incongruous. This inconsistency of style is accompanied by an even more damaging basic inconsistency of character conception and development, but fortunately the film survives these shortcomings through its sheer breezy good nature and the animal magnetism of its two stars.

Schulman's scenario describes the curious love affair that evolves between two young New York Italians—a freedom-loving freelance musician (McQueen) and a sheltered girl (Miss Wood)—when she becomes pregnant following their one-night stand at a summer resort. In view of the kind of people they are, especially the young lady, that one-nighter seems highly unlikely—with the result that the story never seems firmly or believably rooted.

At any rate, after several misunderstandings with each other, difficulties with relatives and an abortive attempt at abortion, the two nice young people patch up their differences in a climactic scene so artificial that it gives one the impression Schulman had suddenly tired of his yarn and was determined to wrap it up as rapidly as possible.

There are some genuinely funny passages and other scenes of considerable dramatic impact in this

---

film. The more substantial portions of Schulman's script are capitalized on by director Mulligan and his cast, notably his two stars. Miss Wood plays her role with a convincing mixture of feminine sweetness and emotional turbulence. McQueen, now firmly entrenched, displays an especially keen sense of timing. Although he's probably the most unlikely Italian around (the character could and should obviously have been alerted to Irish Catholic), he is an appealing figure nevertheless.

Fine supporting work is contributed by Edie Adams as an accommodating stripper, Herschel Bernardi as Miss Wood's overly protected older brother and Tom Bosley as a jittery suitor, with other able portrayals by Harvey Lembeck, Penny Santon, Virginia Vincent, Nick Alexander, Augusta Ciolli, Anne Hegira, Mario Badolati, Elena Karam, Nina Varela, Marilyn Chris and Wolfe Barzell.

Mulligan's direction runs hot and cold, like the screenplay and the film itself. Skillful assists are fashioned by cameraman Milt Krasner, art directors Hal Pereira and Roland Anderson and composed Elmer Bernstein, whose tender score is somewhat reminiscent of his haunting one for "Mockingbird." He has also written a promising title song, for which scenarist Schulman penned the lyrics. Jack Jones sings part of it in the course of the picture. Some of the scenes seem awfully deliberate in tempo, but this appears to be more of a directorial sluggishness than a reflection on the otherwise capable editing of Aaron Stell.   *Tube.*

The Best of Cinerama
(CINERAMA—COLOR)

Interesting compilation of clips from five past Cinerama travelogs; good mass entertainment.

Hollywood, Dec. 20.
Cinerama release of sequences from past Cinerama productions; co-producers, Merian C. Cooper, Thomas Conroy; executive producer, Max E. Youngstein; editors, Lovel S. Ellis, Norman Karlin, William E. Wild; narration, Lowell Thomas. Reviewed in Cinerama screening room, Los Angeles, Calif., Dec. 20, '63. Running time, including 12-min. intermission, 153 MINS.

Cinerama is likely to have a popular feature in this well-turned-out grouping of "The Best of Cinerama." As title indicates, footage is drawn from what went before outstanding portions of company's five travelogs, starting with "This Is Cinerama," which launched the three-panel process. It will have nostalgic appeal for those who caught the forerunners, and for youngsters who never saw any of the earlier Cineramas it will strike a responsive chord.

Derived from "This Is Cinerama," "Cinerama Holiday," "Seven Wonders of the World," "Search for Paradise" and "Cinerama South Seas Adventure," no attempt is made at any definite pattern. This is out-and-out travelog. Even though film skips from country-to-country, from one part of the world to another without any particular continuity there is fascination in its unreeling.

Feature is in two parts, first of 68 minutes and second 73 minutes,

with a 12-minute intermission, which brings overall time to 153 minutes. The three-panel Cinerama propection is utilized, but sufficient strides have been made toward toning down the jumping of the panels that the seam-effect seems to be reduced to a minimum in most parts. Merian C. Cooper and Thomas Conroy are listed as producers and Max E. Youngstein, formerly a Cinerama Inc. veepee, executive producer.

Picture is probably an achievement in editing, Lovel S. Ellis as supervising editor and Norman Karlin and William E. Wild as editors copping fine credit here. Special narration was written for the overall unfoldment, with Lowell Thomas handling commentary. Expert use of orchestral and chorus backgrounding helps sustain interest which seldom lags.

Opening picks up the well-remembered roller-coaster sequence and gets feature off to a memorable start. Close attention is paid to fast movement, other rapido being caught in such sequences as bob-sledding at St. Moritz, the runaway train going up to Darjeeling in the Himalayas, acrobatic water skiing in Florida, surfboarding at Waikiki. There is much aerial photography, such as entrances to Rome and Athens, Rio de Janeiro, the Australian back-country, mountains of Africa and the memorable cross-country excursion from the Atlantic to the Pacific.

Other highlights include such sequences as La Scala Opera House in Milan, with the triumphal scene from "Aida;" gondola ride through Venice and St. Marks Square; a Papal ceremony in Rome with the late Pius XII speaking in closeup from a balcony temple dancers of Benares; the Taj Mahal; Victoria Falls; native dancing in Tahiti and Africa; men jumping from a 100-foot tower in the New Hebrides with vines bound around their ankles to catch them before they can hit the ground; high-jumping among the Watusis, in Africa.

Finale centers on sequences beginning in Cairo, thence to Mt. Sinai and the route taken by Moses when he led his people to the Promised Land. Cities of the Holy Land, Bethlehem, Nazareth, Jericho and finally Jerusalem and the Mount of Olives, scene of the Ascension, are shown in detail as a closer. *Whit.*

Winnetou (Part I)
(GERMAN-YUGOSLAV-C'SCOPE)
(Color)

Berlin, Dec. 17.
Constantin release of Rialto-Film Preben Philipsen (Berlin) production, in collaboration with Jadran-Film, Belgrade. Stars Lex Barker, Pierre Brice, Mario Adorf; features Marie Versini, Ralf Wolter, Walter Barnes, Mavid Popovic, Dunja Rajter, Chris Howland. Directed by Dr. Harald Reinl. Screenplay, Harald G. Petersson, adapted from novel of same name by Karl May; camera (Eastmancolor), Ernst Kalinke; music, Martin Boettcher; editor, Hermann Haller. Preemed in 20 West German cities. Running time, 101 MINS.
Old Shatterhand .... Lex Barker
Winnetou .... Pierre Brice
Santer .... Mario Adorf
Nscho-tschi .... Marie Versini
Sam Hawkens .... Ralf Wolter
Bill Jones .... Walter Barnes
Intschu-tschuna .... Mavid Popovic
Belle .... Dunja Rajter
British journalist .... Chris Howland

To begin with, there's something quite amusing about Karl May's "Winnetou." As "the big chieftain of the Apaches," he has become

an immortal figure with millions of Germans who read Karl May's adventure literature. But in the country where he "lived," in the good old U.S., Winnetou is unknown. Be it as it may, stateside patrons can be assured that Winnetou was and is (on the screen) a very noble, a very handsome and a very likeable Indian chief.

Rather amusing, of course, is the fact that German film producers have become western-minded and that they're able to turn out western film fare that's both exciting and non-stop fun. This applies to "Winnetou." Rialto's first big-screen, big-scale western, "Treasure of Silver Lake," became the German surprise hit of 1963. It has made a lot of coin. "Winnetou" looks to become an even bigger hit. It deserves it because it is better than "Silver Lake" in nearly every respect. What seemed unbelievable a couple of years back has become reality: That Germans can make westerns that are able to compete with bulk of the Hollywood average westerns.

Horst Wendlandt, who supervised the whole production, was well advised not to pattern the pic along a strict Hollywood pattern. The Rialto topper took care that "Winnetou" was given a substantial European touch and "a romantic German smell." This, as strange as it may sound, makes "Winnetou" something special. It's a refreshing pic. This is a film for the entire family. The conventional forms of sex, sadism and brutality are deliberately absent in this production.

With regard to the fight sequences, Wendlandt, director Reinl and the others needn't blush. Old Shatterhand, alias Lex Barker, and Winnetou (Pierre Brice) fight it out as competently as if this was made in America. Dr. Harald Reinl has staged the action scenes as if he had already made countless U.S. action pix.

In brief, the plot shows how the two principal characters, Old Shatterhand and Winnetou, first met. At first Winnetou thinks Old Shatterhand is just another of those mean palefaces who invade the territory. Then he finds out he's better than the other white men. Both have narrow escapes from death until they become brotherly friends. The inevitable evil is repped by a man named Santer. The evildoer is after the Apaches' gold.

The players obviously had much fun in Yugoslavia where the film was shot. More or less everyone comes along with a refreshing performance: Lex Barker, the most prominent American in German pix today, is right at home with his Shatterhand role. He's tall, blond, heroic, very much masculine and likeable. No doubt, this pic will bring him even more friends in Germany. Pierre Brice, a French actor, enacts Winnetou in an effective manner. Brice, a special favorite with the Teutonic bobbysox set, should climb the ladder of popularity after this.

Mario Adorf makes a typical villain. He makes him a real character. Hollywood, incidentally, already has got him via agent Paul Kohner who already has given

Horst Buchholz to the California studios. The necessary comedy is adequately supplied by Ralf Wolter and Chris Howland, an English newspaperman. Others that stand out are American Walter Barnes and Dunja Rajter, a Yugoslav belle.

The great outdoors are often breathtakingly beautiful, with the Eastmancolor lensing very good. A special word of praise must go to Martin Boettcher for his splendid musical score. Background music should go well on records and radio.

All in all, an enjoyable production which cost 4,000,000 D-Marks or $1,000,000 (remarkably high by German standards) and was more than four months in the making. "Winnetou" likely will attract young and old. The question is will "Winnetou" do as well outside Germany. One feels that it will. *Hans.*

Vidas Secas
(Barren Lives)
(BRAZILIAN)

Paris, Dec. 23.
Richers-Barreto-Trelles release and production. Written and directed by Nelson Pereira Dos Santos from the book by Graciliano Ramos. Camera, Luiz Carlos Barreto, Jose Rosa; editor. Rafael Justo. Premiered in Paris. Running time, 105 MINS.
Fabiado .... Atila Iorio
Sinha Vitoria .... Maria Ribeiro
Soldier .... Orlando Macedo
Boy .... Jofre Soares
Boss .... Os Meninas Gilvan

This sober, but not sombre, film deals with a poor migratory family in a sparsely populated, badly vegetated part of Brazil. Social protest is inherent by laying bare the life of the region, but it displays a deep insight and feeling for these people that eventually make it a statement of human adaptability and elemental outlook.

On its observation, rightness in tone and depiction of the people, it emerges as one of the most intrinsically good Brazilian films yet seen. No forced dancing and colorful folklore here, but rather a simple story of almost inarticulate people who are still interesting and arresting in their very humanity.

Director Nelson Pereira Dos Santos has taken a famous book and given it worthy film form. These people go from place to place trying to eke out a living. In the pic they take over an abandoned house and care for a rich farmer's livestock in return.

The daily chores of a man, his wife, and their children, make for an almost pastorally proficient first part. Then comes drama as a petty, spiteful policeman takes advantage of the man one day to entice him into a card game. A fight has the peasant arbitrarily arrested and beaten. He fends off becoming an outlaw or killing the policeman since he feels there is need for some lawful authority. Drought has them leaving the place and setting out again wondering if there is any place for them and whether life is so barren, ruthless and hard everywhere.

Film avoids self pity and has a series of incidents that build into a powerful mosaic of a certain type of life. It is somewhat reminiscent of Satyajit Ray's Indian pix on small town life if it may

lack those films' lyrical insight and more efficient handling of the children. It may also be familiar in the way these people are buffeted by petty officialdom, bad weather, poverty and ignorance, but it has a realistic flair and pictorial sense and solid acting to make it a moving statement rather than a tract.

Lensing is properly stark and contrasting and the acting has the right rustic flavor with a leavening of humor. It looms as a good language possibility abroad if given the right sell and specialized placement. *Mosk.*

Four For Texas
(COLOR)

Unsatisfactory western that even strong marquee names may not be able to fully bail out at the b.o.

Hollywood, Dec. 2.
Warner Bros. release of Robert Aldrich production. Stars Frank Sinatra, Dean Martin, Anita Ekberg, Ursula Andress; features Charles Bronson, Victor Buono. Directed by Aldrich. Screenplay, Teddi Sherman, Aldrich, from story by Aldrich; camera (Technicolor), Ernest Laszlo; editor, Michael Luciano; music, Nelson Riddle; asst. directors, Tom Connors, Dave Salven. Reviewed at Academy Awards Theatre, Dec. 2, '63. Running time, 124 MINS.
Zack Thomas .... Frank Sinatra
Joe Jarrett .... Dean Martin
Elya Carlson .... Anita Ekberg
Maxine Richter .... Ursula Andress
Matson .... Charles Bronson
Harvey Burden .... Victor Buono
Prince George .... Edric Connor
Angel .... Nick Dennis
Mancini .... Richard Jaeckel
Chad .... Mike Mazurki
Trowbridge .... Wesley Addy
Miss Emmaline .... Marjorie Bennett
Dobie .... Jack Elam
Maitre D' .... Fritz Feld
Ansel .... Percy Helton
Renee .... Jonathan Hole
Monk .... Jack Lambert
Beauregard .... Paul Langton
Widow .... Jesslyn Fax

Even the marquee horsepower of its star names doesn't figure to sufficiently insure "Four for Texas" against commercial misfortune. The Robert Aldrich production is a western too preoccupied with sex and romance to enthrall sagebrush-happy moppets and too unwilling to take itself seriously to sustain the attention of an adult. All things considered, it shapes up as a case of sticky wickets for the Warner Bros. release.

It is a singularly disappointing effort by Aldrich who, in addition to his producing function, directed and co-scripted with Teddi Sherman. The screenplay is a choppy and haphazard dramatization of a feud between two soldiers of fortune (Frank Sinatra and Dean Martin) who ultimately have to join forces in vanquishing the threat of their mutual enemies, a treacherous banker (Victor Buono) and an irresponsible, incredibly hapless gunslinger (Charles Bronson).

Concern for the characters is never aroused by the screenplay, and the casual manner in which it is executed by the players under Aldrich's direction only compounds the problem. Either one goes all out for the tongue-in-cheek approach or one must tackle a project such as this with serious intentions. The in-between style tends to invite disaster by alienating virtually all audience factions.

Sinatra and Martin carry on in their accustomed manner, the latter getting most of what laughs there are. The film is loaded with

distracting cleavage, thanks to the presence of Anita Ekberg and Ursula Andress. (Stacked up alongside Miss Ekberg's stupendous proportions, even Mae West might seem anemic.)

Buono, as the unappealing, dyspeptic and conniving banker and Bronson, as the gunman, make an impression. Others of note are Edric Connor, Nick Dennis, Richard Jaeckel, Mike Mazurki and Marjorie Bennett. The Three Stooges put in a brief and unnecessary appearance, and so does Arthur Godfrey, the latter unbilled. Teddy Buckner & His All-Stars are on hand for some dixieland.

Ernest Laszlo's Technicolor lenswork is adequate. William Glasgow's art direction colorful and Nelson Riddle's score atmospheric. But Michael Luciano's editing leaves something to be desired. At least one scene has been cut out that is still referred to in the dialog of a subsequent scene. The editing tends to add to the confusion. *Tube.*

Pasazerka
(Passenger)
(POLISH)

Paris, Dec. 17.

Film Polski release of Kamera production. With Aleksandra Slaska, Anna Ciepoelewska. Directed by Andrej Munk. Screenplay, Zofia Pasmysz; camera, Krzysztof Winiewicz; editor, Witold Lesewicz. Preemed in Paris. Running time **62 MINS.**

Lisa .... Aleksandra Slaska
Marta .... Anna Ciepoelewska

Polish director Andrzej Munk died last year at 36 in the midst of his fourth film. He had shot the essential scenes of his feeling about a concentration camp during the last war. Film is finished out with stills from various other scenes and a commentary. It still packs a deep human perception and a full comment on this horrendous episode.

Its length and makeup naturally limit this but it could well make up a special art house program with an unusual medium length supporting pic. This has a moving comment to make in its own right. It also appears a natural for specialized tv programming.

Pic starts with photos of Munk and explains the status of the film. Then, with stills, it shows a German woman on a ship coming back to Europe and her sudden sight of a face from out of the past. She tells her husband she had been an overseer at Aushwitz during the war, but she had actually saved one woman or tried to.

Her virsion is shown and then what really happened. It makes for one of the most balanced looks at this infamous time in human history yet filmed. There is no hysterical piling on of monstrousness but the terrible descent to controlled annihilation is there.

Film also points up how people could somehow cope with all this bestiality by accepting it as an outcome of war. It is this strange human ambivalence that gives this unfinished but powerful film its great impact. The emotional aspects of both the doomed and the executioners are also starkly blocked out.

A woman guard can cry over the death of her dog while people are being burned and slaughtered before her continuously. A German guard can smile when a little girl on her way to the gas chambre pets his dog. But he soon snaps to attention and goes on with his work of herding them along.

The leading characters are a German female guard and an inmate. The former somehow tries to assuage her later guilt, and during the camps, by helping one girl meet the man she loves and even saving her once.

Alexandra Slaska has the steely reserve and confused reactions as the guard that make her character at once ambiguous, frightening and sometimes completely clear. Anna Ciepoelewska has the right bearing and pride that can help her survive. But it is the late director Munk's unceering feeling for the complex and mixed up aspects of all the terrible things involved that help make this a stirring statement on what can happen when duty is taken as an excuse for human comportment.

Witold Lesewicz has done a knowing and comprehensive job of assembling everything as best he could. If, perhaps, some of Munk's points on the more personal plane may not be clear, his look at both the victims and guards in camps is burning and compassionate.

It shows that Poland lost one of its most gifted filmmakers in Munk's untimely death. After 20 years, this looms as the most profound look at the monstrous camps ever attempted. The film does not try to rouse hate or accuse but only to give an inkling of how human outlook can be swamped by war, indifference and vile values.

It is lensed with the right grayness and has the tone of an unhysterical summation of a recent terrible episode in human relationships. *Mosk.*

Les Tontons Flingueurs
(The Gentle Gunmen)
(FRENCH)

Paris, Dec. 17.

Gaumont release of Gaumont Ultra Film Sicilia Cinematografica Corono Film production. Stars Lino Ventura, Bernard Blier, Francis Blanche; features Jean Lefebvre, Sabine Singen, Horst Frank. Directed by Georges Lautner. Screenplay, Albert Simonin, Michel Audiard, Lautner from book by Simonin; camera, Maurice Fellous; editor, Michele David. At Balzac, Paris. Running time, **110 MINS.**

Fernand .... Lino Ventura
Raoul .... Bernard Blier
Notaire .... Francis Blanche
Brother .... Jean Lefebvre
Patricia .... Sabine Singen
German .... Horst Frank
Antoine .... Claude Rich

This is a fair gangster comedy that should have an okay career on its home grounds. But this pic vacillates between parody, farce and straight action sequences to lose the snap and uniqueness for much arty theatre possibility abroad. However, on a few successful running gags, some solid comic scenes and okay playing, this could have playoff possibilities in other climes.

An ex-gangster, who has been clean for 15 years, gets a summons from an old friend to take over his gang and the future of his daughter. The man does so when his friend dies. Follows the subduing of rival elements of the gang and marrying off the girl before he can head back to his peaceful, honest life.

Lino Ventura emulates Jean Gabin in a rough, rugged portrayal that is more surface mannerism than true emoting. Sabine Singen is too mousy and colorless as the girl in question but a strong group of character players make up the roster of hoods. A neat touch is a gang fight with silencers while the girl's fiance's father comes to claim her hand, plus a big fight in evening clothes before the wedding.

However, this has too much slang, forced dialog and uneven tempo to provide overall wit, inventiveneess and unity of tone which it now lacks. But director Georges Lautner has a brisk feel for parody that should make him okay commercially when he settles down and finds a more cohesive tone to his mounting. It is technically polished. *Mosk.*

Bebert Et L'Omnibus
(Bebert and the Train)
(FRENCH)

Paris, Dec. 23.

Warner Bros. release of La Gueville production. With Blanchette Brunoy, Pierre Mondy, Jean Richard, Michel Serrault, Jacques Higelin, Petit Gibus. Directed by Yves Robert. Screenplay, Francois Boyer; camera, Andre Bac; editor, Robert Isnardon. At Ambassade-Gaumont, Paris. Running time, **90 MINS.**

Bebert .... Petit Gibus
Tieno .... Jacques Higelin
Father .... Jean Richard
Mother .... Blanchette Brunoy
Berthoin .... Michel Serrault
Parmelin .... Pierre Mondy

Producer-direector Yves Robert struck it rich with a modest moppet bucolic warfare pic in "The Button War" two years ago. Pic was a sleeper that turned out to be a bonanza moneymaker. Now Robert wisely sticks to the same principles in his new pic which is somewhat richer in production, but is still a basically simple moppet pic.

Film should do well on its home grounds if its determined quaintness and forced bonhomie and spontaniety make it a chancey art item abroad. However its generally pleasant, and has overall entertainment values. It could be a dualer or playoff item of some worth with tv possibilities also inherent.

Story concerns a pesky but winning, curious but complaining, annoying but clever, five-year-old boy named Bebert who gets lost on a train while traveling with his big brother. Pic is about the frantic search for him. Much of the plotting is forced and there is not enough cogent observation of the little boy on his own. He is pushed into a mold of adult interpretation, even with a stream of consciousness commentary.

But director Robert has moved the story briskly to cover the essential banality and lack of story values or true child insight. There is also, sometimes, a penchant for vulgarity for its own sake rather than springing from characterization. But it all adds up to a canny commercial item that may well go the way of its big grossing predecessor, at least on European grounds. It is technically sound. *Mosk.*

White Hunter
(COLOR)

Herts-Lion International release of Signal International (George Michael) production, written, directed by and starring Michael. Features David Georgiades, June Michael, John Haddad, Carole Michael, Roger Blake, Jack Hutcheson, Emilie Georgiades. Camera (Eastmancolor), Tim Spring, John B. Kennard. Reviewed at Lytton Center, Los Angeles, Dec. 12, '63. Running time, **86 MINS.**

Although this filmed-in-Africa adventure film is self-described as a semi-documentary, the only documentary value it can truthfully claim are occasionally well-photographed views of wild beasts in their natural habitat. Pic, intended for Easter 1964 release, was screened at this time for both Academy Award and Golden Globe consideration.

No moments of sensationalism are pased up, making it a possible, by slanted advertising, potential money-maker in the action and violence market.

Evidently, Michael's purpose has been to have his own adventures (he was born in Africa and has written about it extensively) captured on film by professional cinematographers as a cinematic biography. Tim Spring and John B. Kennard have done a good job of the camerawork although beginning and ending sequences give the impression, being so amateurishly conceived, of home-movie bits attached to the more professional footage. Re-enacting his "life among the fierce denizens of the Dark Continent" (and with members of his family, friends and natives supposedly playing themselves), Michael has, probably unintentionally, created a portrait of a bloodthirsty "white hunter" with little compassion for the animals slain.

Despite the excuse that he switched, at a certain point in his life, from gun to camera, it's hard to excuse the slaughter shown in recapturing his early days. The killing done then, added to that filmed, adds up to an appalling total.

Some infrequent but fascinating shots show a pair of lions swimming a stream; two male giraffes fighting (each using his long neck for pile-driving effect as he slams his head and neck against his opponent); a baby leopard and a small baboon playing together like two puppies; and an ominous view of four lionesses stalking deer along a well-traveled highway, ignoring the humans for more defenseless prey.

To accept the film seriously as documentary one must also accept events presented as factual and without exaggeration. How, then, to rationalize an early shot showing a spear being plunged into the back of a native; animal after animal being killed before your eyes; endangering the lives of natives when, according to the script, Michael's gunbearer demonstrates his "position" by driving the white man's car straight at a group of villagers

Strange result, presumably unintended, Michael's portrayal of himself makes him a vain, self-opinionated man, with no discernible feeling for animals or many of the natives other than his spoken assurance. An evidently faked fight between a leopard and a hunter is so poorly handled that it evokes laughter rather than chills and could smartly be edited out of the film.

The sound, evidently dubbed, is excellent with only minimal use of jungle sounds. The commentary, evidently spoken by Michael, in the resonant and well-modulated voice of an experienced lecturer, is not particularly outstanding and,

in spots, even embarrassing, such as describing a rogue elephant as "a killer who moves with the speed of lightning," only to have the camera pan to a slowly-ambulating pachyderm, galumphing along with no visual sign of concern.   *Robe.*

A Stitch in Time

London, Dec. 17.

Rank Organization release of Hugh Stewart production. Stars Norman Wisdom, Edward Chapman, Jeannette Sterke, Jerry Desmonde. Directed by Robert Asher. Screenplay, Jack Davies; camera, Jack Asher; editor, Gerry Hambling; music, Philip Green. Reviewed at the Odeon, Haymarket, London. Running time, **94 MINS.**

Norman Pitkin	Norman Wisdom
Grimsdale	Edward Chapman
Janet Haskell	Jeannette Sterke
Sir Hector	Jerry Desmonde
Lady Brinkley	Jill Melford
Welsh	Glyn Houston
Matron	Hazel Hughes
Amy	Patsy Rowlands
Russell	Jeter Jones
Professor Crankshaw	Ernest Clark
Lindy	Lucy Appleby
Betty	Vera Day
Nuttall	Frank Williams
Nurse Rudkin	Jenny Morrell
Dr. Meadows	Patrick Cargill
Benson	Francis Matthews
Woman Patient	Pamela Conway
Ticehurst	Danny Green
Teddy Boy	Johnny Briggs
Dale	John Blythe

Together with turkey, plus pudding, and a steep rise in road accidents, Christmas always brings a Norman Wisdom picture. For the last 10 years, this annual event has boosted the seasonal trade, and the latest is Wisdom's best since "The Square Peg." It gains by economizing on plot, but devises a string of farcical events that put the pint-sized Wisdom through the full pratfalling routine. The thin thread linking the scenes has Wisdom as a hapless butcher's assistant causing constant commotion in a hospital, where his employer is undergoing surgery for a swallowed watch. He gets banned from the place by the hospital boss, Sir Hector (Jerry Desmonde), and the remainder of the running time is taken up by his bizarre attempts to regain entry.

The sketches follow each other thick and fast, and leave no time to brood over their naivety. Jack Davies's script is the sixth he's written for this comedian, and he knows the strength and limitations of the star. For sophisticated palates, Wisdom is mechanical, and he plays up the sentiment of the "little-man" up against authority to cloying effect.

The charm, in fact, is fabricated, and he's more of a butt than a personality.

There's an overspill of molasses in Wisdom's relationship with the orphan lassie, guaranteed to bring out hot flushes, but this stab at bringing out the human side doesn't intrude too much. Edward Chapman is fine as the principal partner-in-gags, with Jerry Desmonde providing familiar wrath and indignation as the pompous Sir Hector. Jeannette Sterke has no chance to be more than decorative as a friendly nurse, largely because Wisdom is wisely deprived of love-interest in this one. Other thesp support is functional, with Jill Melford, Patsy Rowlands, Peter Jones and Glyn Houston briefly registering types.

Hugh Stewart's production is economical, and occasionally shows it. But Robert Asher's direction is dashing, and has learned much from the speedup techniques of the Keystone Cops. Jack Asher's lensing is okay, and a jaunty musical soundtrack comes from Philip Green. In fact, it's a breezy offering for the star's addicts, who don't demand much more than that he should fall down with versatility. It's the most horizontal comedy in years.   *Otta.*